Global Road Warrior

3rd Edition

95–Country Resource for the
International Business Communicator and Traveler

WORLD TRADE PRESS ®
Professional Books for International Trade

Global Road Warrior

3rd Edition

95–Country Resource for the International Business Communicator and Traveler

MANAGING EDITOR

SIBYLLA M. PUTZI

RESEARCH & WRITING TEAM

JEFFREY E. CURRY, MBA, PH.D • CHRISTIAN HARRIS
MICHAEL TALBOT • GRETCHEN TREADWELL • MINORU KOSAKA
CAMILA RABELLO DE CARVALHO • NARGESS SAHAHMANESH • GARY FOX
GILBERT MANSERGH • JOE REIF • STEVE DONNET • LYNNE ASHDOWN
DAVID BAKER • HAMYDA ABDALA • EMILY HANSEN • IRA EISENBERG
GERALD A. FRANKEL • MAUREEN DIXON • ROBERT L. WALLACK
JUTTA JERLICH • JOYCE LYNN • PAPRIKA CLARK • NINA LU

WORLD TRADE PRESS®
Professional Books for International Trade

Global Road Warrior, 3rd Edition
ISBN 1-885073-86-0

Publisher
World Trade Press
1450 Grant Avenue, Suite 204
Novato, California 94945 USA
Tel: +1 (415) 898-1124
Fax: +1 (415) 898-1080
USA order Line: +1 (800) 833-8586
Email: orders@worldtradepress.com
www.worldtradepress.com
www.globalroadwarrior.com
www.globaltimeclock.com

Production Credits
Publication concept: Edward G. Hinkelman
Cover design: World Trade Press Edition: Ronald Blodgett and Toby Mass
Cover design: iGo Corporation Edition: Christina Nellemann, Creative Media Group, iGO Corporation
Maps: Magellan Geographix (maps.com)
Illustrations: Gary Fox
Desktop publishing: Valentina Pfeil

Disclaimer
Material for this publication has been obtained from agencies of various countries, embassies, consulates, industry and trade organizations, and from personal interviews by telephone and by correspondence. We have diligently tried to ensure the accuracy of all the information in this publication and to present as comprehensive a reference work as space would permit. The fast pace of today's business world makes the task of keeping data current and accurate an extremely difficult one. If we find errors we strive to correct them in preparing future editions. The publishers, however, take no responsibility for inaccurate or incomplete information that may have been submitted to them in the course of research for this publication. The facts published indicate the result of those inquiries and no warrantee as to their accuracy is given.

Library of Congress Cataloging-in-Publication Data

Global Road Warrior: 95-country resource for the international business
communicator and traveler / managing editor, Sibylla M. Putzi; research
and writing team, Jeffrey E. Curry ... [et al.]. -- 3rd ed.
      p. cm.
   Includes bibliographical references (p.).
   ISBN 1-885073-86-0
   1. Business travel--Handbooks, manuals, etc. I. Curry, Jeffrey E., 1953- II. Title.

 G156.5.B86 G56 2001
 910'.2'02--dc21

                                    2001017712

Table of Contents

Introduction

International Travel 7
Money 8
Visa, Passport & Customs 9
Staying Healthy 10
Traveling to a Country 12
Traveling Within a Country 13
Communications 14
Cellular Services Worldwide............. 16
Cellular Service Systems 17
The Technical Traveler 18
Travel Web-Sites 20
Business Culture 27
Emergency! 29
Time Zone Map 42
International Dialing Guide 43
Currencies of the World 57

Countries of the World

Algeria 63
Argentina 71
Australia 80
Austria 91
Bahamas 100
Bahrain 106
Belgium 115
Bermuda 125
Bolivia 131
Brazil 138
Brunei 148
Bulgaria 154
Canada 161
Chile 172
China 180
Colombia 190
Costa Rica 199
Côte d'Ivoire 206
Croatia 214
Cuba 222
Czech Republic 229
Denmark 237
Dominican Republic 244
Ecuador 251
Egypt 259
El Salvador 268
Estonia 274
Finland 282
France 291
Georgia 302
Germany 309
Greece 322
Guatemala 330
Honduras 338
Hong Kong 344
Hungary 353
Iceland 361
India 367
Indonesia 377

Iran 387
Ireland 396
Israel 403
Italy 411
Jamaica 421
Japan 428
Kenya 443
Kuwait 450
Latvia 458
Lebanon 466
Libya 473
Lithuania 481
Luxembourg 490
Macau 498
Malaysia 505
Malta 516
Mexico 524
Morocco 537
Nepal 547
Netherlands 555
New Zealand 565
Nicaragua 574
Nigeria 581
Norway 589
Oman 597
Pakistan 603
Panama 612
Paraguay 620
Peru 627
Philippines 634
Poland 643
Portugal 651
Romania 659
Russia 666
Saudi Arabia 677
Senegal 686
Singapore 692
Slovakia 700
South Africa 706
South Korea 714
Spain 721
Sri Lanka 729
Sweden 735
Switzerland 743
Taiwan 751
Thailand 759
Tunisia 767
Turkey 773
Ukraine 781
United Arab Emirates 787
United Kingdom 793
United States 809
Uruguay 837
Venezuela 843
Vietnam 850
Zimbabwe 858

ACKNOWLEDGMENTS

We owe many leaders in the international business community a debt of gratitude. Hundreds of trade and reference experts have brought this book to life. We are indebted to numerous business consultants, researchers, travel advisors, embassy and trade mission officers, attorneys, and others who answered our incessant inquiries and volunteered facts, figures, and expert opinions. It would be impossible to name them all. But, to all these many individuals, named and unnamed, we extend our thanks.

The professional talents of many researchers, authors, and editors have been combined to create the Global Road Warrior. We would like to thank Camila R. de Carvalho, Minoru Kosaka, Nargess Sahahmanesh, Nina Lu, Hamyda Abdala, Marjaneh Maroufi, David Baker, Jutta Jerlich, and Paprika Clark.

We relied heavily on the reference librarians and resources available at the libraries of the University of California at Berkeley, San Rafael Public Library, Oakland City Library, Marin County Civic Center Library, and the Marin County and University of California at Berkeley Law Lbraries. Many thanks to all of the librarians who steered us to obscure data on countries large and small.

We would also like to thank the editors at *Internet World* magazine for making sure the information on international Internet usage was as accurate as possible.

DISCLAIMER

International Travel

THE SHRINKING GLOBE

The growth of trade in the past five decades has resulted in a dramatic increase in international travel. Business travel may be expensive and time consuming, but it is also the most effective way to develop strong business relationships. First-hand experience of the countries and the people with whom you do business will give you a better understanding of a particular business culture and will also demonstrate a high level of commitment to prospective partners for a foreign market.

TRAVELING PRODUCTIVELY

The key to making a successful business trip is preparation. Good preparation will help you to focus on the purpose of your trip and maximize your productive time in a foreign country. Simply hoping for the best when you get there is a recipe for certain disaster. When preparing for a business trip it is important to establish your particular goals to ensure that your trip is a productive one. You may be in the initial stages of market research, you may want to make contact with potential distributors for your product, or you may want to return home with a signed business contract. Whatever your goals, only after they have been established can you set about planning the best way to achieve them.

GETTING IN TOUCH WITH OTHER BUSINESS WORLDS

The first step in planning your trip is thorough research. Many published sources of information exist on countries all over the world, and important information can also be gleaned from other traders familiar with the territory. This type of research will help you to focus on many important travel issues you may not have yet considered.

Time of travel is an important issue often overlooked by business travelers. National and religious holidays are different wherever you go; business travelers should try to confirm these in order to avoid arriving at inopportune times. In Saudi Arabia, for example, people practice fasting between sun up and sundown for a month before the Ramadan religious festival, making it more difficult to conduct business at this time of year. Workweeks and daily hours of operation also vary from country to country and you will need to be aware of these in order to properly structure your visit.

Getting in touch with potential foreign business contacts before you go will help you plan your schedule and will save you a lot of time upon arrival. Information on local business contacts may be available at your country's local embassy or consulate. Confirming appointments in writing before a trip will help to ensure that you get the attention you deserve upon arrival.

PACKING FOR PERSONAL TRAVEL

- Travel light.
- Quality molded suitcases last longer and are worth the money, especially if you plan to travel frequently.
- Leave room for articles purchased overseas and brought back with you. Consider packing a foldable canvas bag to handle the overflow on the way home.
- If your suitcases use keys, be sure to keep one set on your person and another in your briefcase. Bring mini locks to secure carry on baggage or day packs.
- Pack clothing that survives wrinkling.
- Bring earplugs. They'll save you from a host of foreign phonic blasts during slumber hours.
- Handiwipes will save the traveler from having to seek water sources, often not up to standard, to wipe away bacteria or grime.
- Bring a list of email or mailing addresses in case an ISP won't allow you to access these from abroad.
- Pack a medical kit that is appropriate for the destination.
- Medical Checklist:
  -Vitamins, Prescriptions
  -Birth control pills, Condoms
  -Anti-diarrhea pills, Anti-malarial pills
  -Extra eyeglasses
  -Extra contact lenses plus accessories
  -Water purification tablets
  -Medical bracelet if appropriate
- Documents to remember:
  -Passport, International health certificate
  -Visas
  -Driver's license/international driver's license
  -Travelers checks and personal checks
  -Credit cards
  -A xeroxed copy of your passport
  -Extra passport photos
  -Refund locations for travelers checks
  -Travelers check numbers
  -Birth certificate (if necessary)
  -Address book (leave photo copy at home!)
  -Letters of introduction from institutions, and business associates
  -Tickets and vouchers
  -Business cards, Business brochures

MANAGING YOUR ABSENCE

- If appropriate, give power of attorney to your attorney, accountant, business associate, or family member before you leave.
- Pay bills, both existing and those that will come due during your absence, especially telephone, utilities and payable-upon-presentation bills such as American Express and Diners Club.
- Notify police, post office, and newspaper delivery services of your absence.
- Leave your itinerary with several people in your organization and/or family.
- Leave a list of credit cards, traveler's checks, passport information, and suitcase combination lock numbers with someone accessible by telephone.

Money

Money

Foreign Exchange

The exchange rate is simply the amount of a nation's currency that can be bought at a given time for a specified amount of the currency of another country. For example, as of July 13, 2000, US$1=¥108.268, meaning that one US dollar was equal to 108.268 Japanese yen. The exchange rate is given either as a direct quote—expressed as the number of units of a foreign currency per US$(US$1=DM1.547), or as an indirect quote, expressed as the number of US$ per unit of foreign currency (DM1=US$.646), which is the reciprocal of the first quote. Because the US$ is the most commonly traded currency, international foreign exchange transactions are usually quoted directly using the US$ as the reference point.

WHEN AND WHERE TO EXCHANGE

In some lesser developed countries, as soon as you get off the plane, people may accost you to exchange your currency. Don't reach into your pocket so quickly, however. Often, these are hustlers who wish you to exchange money before you know the rate. Although private exchanges often carry a better rate of exchange, they still pose a risk. If you are new to the traveling game, it may prove more beneficial to go to the official exchange window in the airport, train station, or other point of entry until you know what you are doing.

While standing in line at the currency exchange window, do a little math in your head and decipher about how much you should get in return for your cash. Exchange windows usually post a sign with the exchange rates for buying and selling cash and traveler's checks. The "buying" columns indicate the local currency given at the window (you are "buying" it with your currency). Conversely, "selling" means when you are getting your currency back.

An important note: remain at the window and count your currency before walking away. More than one traveler has been duped by an unscrupulous exchange window clerk. If a clerk gives you a bundled stack of currency, pull it out and count it. If you feel the clerk is in error, put up an argument and don't pay attention to the line fidgeting behind you—it is your money, after all.

Preparation may prove the efficient way to expedite your initial arrival. Prepare yourself with some amount of foreign currency before departing for the country; one never knows what oddities one may encounter before ever reaching an exchange bureau.

BLACK MARKET EXCHANGES

If you are a beginning traveler, the words "black market" conjure up frightening images of shady men in dark alleys. The truth is more mundane. Some countries place their official rate of exchange unrealistically high. While this makes their economy look good on the international market, it means travelers lose money while exchanging currency. Because of this, the black market offers an intriguing alternative. You will often be approached on the street or in the airport by locals asking if you "have dollars for sale." It's just that simple.

Many travelers have moral issues with using the black market. The tangible issue, however, is legal. If caught, you can face detention in a country with a marginal legal system.

Is there a chance you could get cheated? You bet! Those new to traveling are advised to go through the usual avenues until they have mastered the rules of the game.

Traveler's Checks

Traveler's checks offer travelers an alternative to hauling around cash that can be easily stolen or lost. One can purchase traveler's checks at banks or from the American Automobile Association in the U.S. For all the positives associated with traveler's checks, however, don't forget that in some countries one may have much difficulty exchanging them. Merchants may not accept them and banks may not either. Also, those issuing traveler's checks will usually charge a fee.

Obviously, the best answer is to carry some cash with your traveler's checks. Also consider what denominations of traveler's checks you want. If traveling to several countries, you may want to consider bringing more checks in smaller denominations. If you only have larger denominations, you'll get back local currency as you spend them and then will have the added burden of constantly exchanging the currency as you move from country to country.

Credit Cards

Credit cards are accepted in cities worldwide, in most restaurants, hotels, and stores. In smaller towns, however, credit cards will be looked at with cocked eyebrows and an inquisitive expression. In addition, some smaller shops (and street vendors) obviously will not accept credit cards no matter where you are. It's good to have a little cash handy.

ATMs

Automatic Teller Machines (ATM) are quickly gaining acceptance all over the world. One can expect most modern cities to have them. "Back-country" and out-of-the-way towns are much less likely to have them, except in places like Western Europe. Keep in mind, though, that money is dispensed quickly and easily but often with a large price tag attached. Exchange rates vary dramatically. Also, maximum withdrawal amounts vary, not just with your banking institution, but with the local bank from which you want to make the withdrawl. Finally, in some countries there is no "English" option on the ATM itself.

Visa, Passport & Customs

Visas

Visa requirements vary from country to country, and it is important to obtain all the necessary documents well in advance of your trip. Also, if you expect to travel to more than one country, establish whether or not having the visa of one country will preclude you from entering another.

You may be required to produce proof of vaccination against certain diseases before entering some countries, and it may be advisable to get yourself vaccinated even when it is not required by law. In addition, it is important to ascertain whether or not any other significant health hazards exist in the country you will visit. If you have a particular medical condition, it may prove necessary to seek precautionary advice from your doctor before departing.

Be aware that many countries require that you obtain a business visa in order to conduct business. For example, a contract signed in such a country by an individual traveling on a tourist visa may not be valid.

Customs Entry

Customs entry is the regulatory process of controlling goods entering or leaving a country. It is an area international travelers dislike, and with good reason.

The customs entry process can range from relatively easy (rarely is it simple and quick) to slow and laborious, usually depending on the airport. Haneda Airport in Tokyo and Ezeiza Airport in Buenos Aires are famous for long waits.

Electronic items like cameras and laptop computers often arouse interest with customs officers. To keep the process as efficient as possible, prepare a list of such items, including serial numbers, ready for authorities to inspect and stamp. Your appearance may also serve to help or impede you. A conservative, well-groomed individual may receive a nod from a customs inspector, while an ostentatiously dressed or poorly kempt individual may not. In some countries, even a beard may keep one from clearing customs quickly.

Customs entry at most airports follow a red and green lane approach. There are two lanes: green for nothing to declare, red for dutiable items. One may usually bring personal effects into a country without duty, although exceptions exist.

Items such as alcoholic beverages, cigarettes, cigars, and foodstuffs are often limited. To carry more than the maximum amount will result in an additional fee or confiscation of the merchandise. Items such as firearms and pornography (sometimes including *Playboy* magazine) are often prohibited from entry into a country.

DUTY

Duty is the tax a traveler pays for items imported to a country. Most countries allow a minimum value of goods to be imported duty-free. For example, the U.S. imposes no duty for the first US$400 worth of goods brought in (as long the goods apply to personal use and on your person).

Product Samples

If you bring product samples on your trip, they may be subject to import duties and lengthy customs procedures. Both can be avoided by obtaining an international customs document called an ATA Carnet. Many countries already adhere to the ATA Carnet conventions, and new countries are continually being added to the system; as such, consider it important to get the most current list before traveling. For information contact the ICC (International Chamber of Commerce) in the U.S. at ICC Publishing, Inc. 156 Fifth Avenue, Suite 308, New York, NY 10010 USA, tel: (212) 206-1150, fax: (212) 633-6025; or at their Paris home office at ICC Publishing, S.A., 38, Cours Albert 1er, 75008 Paris France, tel: [33] (1) 49 53 29 23, fax: [33] (1) 49 53 29 02.

Mailing Items Home

Often, no duty is imposed for mailing items home as long as you are not mailing to yourself and the item is of low value. Your mail item will still pass through customs and stands the chance of being opened, thus, exhibit care. Also, as with anything mailed, a risk of theft exists.

One-of-a-Kind Items and Antiques

Typically, artistic items like paintings that are one of a kind are admitted duty free. The same applies if the item is an antique (over 100 years old). Otherwise, expect to pay duty.

Counterfeit Items

When traveling, peddlers often want to sell you a great imitation watch or piece of clothing for US$10. If you are caught at Customs with these copies, especially at U.S. Customs, they will be confiscated. Confiscation applies to tapes and compact discs as well as computer software.

U.S. CUSTOMS PRE-REGISTRATION

Foreign-made personal articles taken abroad are subject to duty and tax on your return unless you have proof of prior possession (i.e.: a receipt, bill of sale, an insurance policy, or a jeweler's appraisal). If you do not have proof of prior possession, items such as foreign-made watches, cameras, or tape recorders that can be identified by permanently marked serial numbers, may be taken to the Customs office nearest you or at the port of departure for registration before departing the U.S. The certificate of registration provided can expedite free entry of these items when you return.

Staying Healthy

ILLNESS

An exhausting enterprise, even the healthiest person will feel the effects of travel. The two major forms of travel sickness are air sickness and jet lag, although other illnesses are not uncommon. Imagine sitting at 30,000 feet accompanied by hundreds of others for hours on end with nothing but recycled air to breathe. Scientific studies have found many forms of bacteria (some deadly) attached to pillows and blankets, seats, and most commonly, in toilets. Wash your hands and carry a bottle of anti-bacterial lotion or soap or packs of handi-wipes to avoid contracting a nasty bug you may have to carry with you through the duration of your trip. Try not to touch public-use areas with your hands, or wash them immediately afterwards. The transfer of bacteria from hands to nose and mouth can happen as easily as rubbing your tired eyes.

Know your limitations. While some maladies are unavoidable, common sense offers the best prevention. Visiting a prostitute, overeating, or drinking all night long can lead to problems no matter what country you find yourself.

JET LAG

Jet lag isn't an illness as much as a period of adjustment. Your body operates on a natural clock based on the hours it recognizes as meant for activity, sleep, etc. Your body will feel physically and mentally disoriented during the "jet lag" period until it adjusts to the new schedule.

While there is no real way to "beat" jet lag, the best remedy is simply to allow your body a chance to adjust to the new schedule. Schedule flights to arrive in the mid afternoon, and spend that day resting. Or, upon arrival, take an hour nap, and make sure the alarm is set to wake you after the hour lest your sleep-depraved body keeps sleeping. Then remain awake until a reasonable bedtime hour. Get as much sunlight as possible. Stay away from alcohol, it will disrupt your cycles, and eat small meals high in protein. Eating a lot of starch and carbohydrates slows the body.

Dehydration while traveling also causes jet lag, particularly because high-altitude airplane air is so dry. Drink plenty of liquids, avoiding alcohol and caffeine.

Many people exhaust themselves before leaving for a trip trying to tie up all the loose ends in the office and anticipating the upcoming trip. If at all possible, try to relax before leaving and let your body prepare for the trip.

Over-the-counter remedies like Melatonin have helped many to combat jet lag and time changes by feeding the brain what it produces for rest when nightfall normally occurs.

MOTION SICKNESS

An equilibrium imbalance, often residing in the ears, can stir the stomach into an upheaval—otherwise known as motion sickness. When nauseousness occurs, uncomfortable moments ensue. Anyone may feel its effects, even those who have never experienced it before.

There are many remedies for motion sickness:

- **Medication** like Dramamine and Marezine work for most people. Consult a doctor before using any of these medicines.
- **Carbonated Drinks** add fluids and settle upset stomachs.
- **Green Olives** slow the flow of saliva in the body and settle the stomach. Green apples and dry crackers have the same effect.
- **Avoid Reading** as the eyes may cause further equilibrium imbalance as they try and focus on something when in motion.
- **Breathing Techniques** If traveling by boat, certain breathing techniques may assist the sailor from feeling green. When the boat rolls up with the wave, breathe in deeply; when it rolls down, exhale.
- **Sleep** Unfortunately, few people can sleep while traveling. Use a sleeping pill only as a last resort since it comes with side effects.

INTESTINAL ILLNESSES

Diarrhea

Diarrhea is usually caused by a bacteria or virus in your system to which your body is not accustomed.

Several medications for diarrhea exist, but most have side effects. Be sure to consult a doctor before taking any medication. Two drugs, Enterovioform and Mexaform, are available outside the U.S. to relieve diarrhea, but some medical experts consider them unsafe because they contain iodochlorhydroxyquin.

Diarrhea can become serious if the continued loss of fluids causes dehydration. If you begin suffering from diarrhea, increase your fluids intake. So called "athletic drinks" offer the best solution because they replace the sodium and potassium, as well as water.

Constipation

Constipation is easier to cure than diarrhea, although it could be just as embarrassing. It can cause headaches and irritability. There are several over-the-counter remedies available. Most tend to be taxing on the body, but they will solve the problem, usually overnight. Consult your pharmacist. Changing your diet can also help. Apples often relieve constipation as do high-fiber fruits such as figs, dates, prunes, and mangoes. Oat bran is probably the best. Add it as part of your diet.

Intestinal Gas

Although a minor problem, intestinal gas can prompt a embarrassment during a business meeting. Avoid the foods that cause it, including brussel sprouts, cabbage, spicy foods, and—bad news for brew lovers—beer. Gas also tends to expand in high altitudes, and expanding gas desires to escape.

TRAVELER'S DEPRESSION

Anyone who has traveled frequently has experienced some level of depression. Your body may feel fatigued and jet lag may take longer to wear off (if it wears off at all). Allow yourself to reschedule appointments if possible, try to get a good night's sleep, and remember that this condition is temporary.

FOOD POISONING

One of the main fears of travelers, and a valid danger, food poisoning can cause a major setback. It could, however, be avoided through careful preparation. Check the medical alerts for the country you plan to visit (your travel agent can do this for you).

Cleanliness and sanitation may not be an imperative in other countries. As such, one should practice care in choosing a place to eat. In some countries, top-end hotels may offer the only "safe" place to dine without worry. In hot and humid climates, make sure that meat has been thoroughly cooked and is served hot, especially seafood and pork. In places where water is not potable, one should avoid uncooked vegetables and fruit without thick peels. Milk and dairy products may also cause concern in countries that do not practice pasteurization. Carrying your own utensils (or chopsticks in Asia) may serve to quell woes about cutlery washed in dirty water, or not at all. If kitchen personnel has not practiced safe hygiene, one may be out of luck.

Health Information for International Travel is an annual publication from the Centers for Disease Control, and can be ordered from the U.S. Government Printing Office at, tel: [1] (202) 783-3238.

MEDICATION

Carry Your Prescription With You

If you have any pre-existing medical problems and travel abroad, be sure to carry a letter from your doctor describing your condition and information on any prescription medicines you must take. You should also have the generic names of the drugs. Leave medicines in their original, labeled containers, which should make Customs processing easier. A doctor's certificate may not suffice as authorization to bring all prescription drugs into all foreign countries. Travelers have been arrested for drug violation by carrying items considered to be prescription in their own country but as narcotics in another. If you have any doubts regarding the status of your medication, consult the embassy or consulate of the countries you will visit for precise information before departing.

Be sure to ask your doctor (and pharmacist, preferably) about any travel-related reactions that may occur from the medication. Safe medicines can develop nasty side effects when taken at 30,000 feet.

Medical Alert Bracelets

If you have allergies, reactions to certain medicines, or other unique medical problems, consider wearing a medical alert bracelet or carrying a similar warning.

International Medical Assistance

Several private organizations (such as AAA or their international counterparts) provide listings of physicians for international travelers. Membership to these organizations is generally free. Membership entitles the traveler to a number of traveler's medical aids, including a directory of physicians with their overseas' locations, telephone numbers, and doctors' fees and schedules. The physicians are generally English-speaking and provide medical assistance 24 hours a day. One such international non-profit organization is IAMAT: http://www.sentex.net/~iamat/thome.html.

IAMAT Switzerland
57 Voirets, 1212 Grand-Lancy-Geneva
(For written requests only)
IAMAT U.S.A.
417 Center Street, Lewiston, NY 14092
tel: (716) 754-4883

Other addresses of medical organizations reside in travel magazines or may be available from your travel agent. The Center for Disease Control in the U.S. provides up-to-date information on disease precautions and immunization recommendations: www.cdc.gov

In-House Physicians, a medical organization based in the U.S., provides emergency services to the meeting site or at large corporate events (i.e. Olympic Games) for corporations in the U.S. or abroad: http://www.in-housephysicians.com.

IMMUNIZATION

Most people do not remember the last time they had a vaccination, or for what it was meant. Try not to fall into this statistic. If you are heading to an area where diseases like cholera and malaria are prevalent, an over-the-counter antibiotic will not help. Prior to departure for a trip, *any* trip, update your immunization status.

Under international health regulations adopted by the World Health Organization, a country may require international certificates of vaccination against yellow fever and cholera as a condition of entry. Typhoid vaccinations are recommended for areas where there is risk of exposure. Smallpox vaccinations are rarely given. Check your health care records to insure that your measles, mumps, rubella, polio, diptheria, tetanus, and pertusis immunizations are up to date. Medication to deter malaria and other preventative measures are advisable for certain areas. Even if a country does not require immunization, it is a good idea to get immunized anyway.

Specific information about immunization requirements is available from health departments or physicians. In the U.S., it can also be obtained from the 24-hour International Travelers Hotline at the Centers for Disease Control, tel: [1] (404) 332-4559; or contact their website at: www.cdc.gov.

It is not necessary to be vaccinated against a disease you will not be exposed to, and few countries will refuse to admit you if you arrive without the necessary vaccinations. Officials will either vaccinate you, give you a medical follow-up card, or, in rare circumstances, put you in isolation for the incubation period of the disease against which you were not vaccinated. Check requirements before you depart.

If vaccinations are required, they must be recorded on approved forms. If your doctor or public health office does not have this booklet, they are often available through your government. The forms must be signed by a licensed physician or by a person designated to sign the certificate. Keep it with your passport.

HIV TESTING REQUIREMENTS

Some countries require visitors to produce certification that they are free of the human immunodeficiency virus (HIV). Most often these regulations apply to applicants for residence or work permits, but they may apply to any visitors or for some categories of temporary visitors. U.S. tests may be accepted, but you may be required to test on arrival. Check with the embassy or consulate of the countries you will visit for the latest information.

Traveling to a Country

Travel Agents

If you plan to do a lot of international travel, it is best to establish an ongoing relationship with a good travel agent. Avoid agents who specialize in tourism because they will be less attuned to your needs than will an experienced business travel agent.

Travel agents receive a commission paid by airlines and hotels (although airlines are decreasing their commissions to agents). Usually there will be no added cost to you for using their services. Agents can:
- Research and book transportation and accommodations.
- Advise on visas, immunizations, etc.
- Answer many varied questions related to overseas travel;
- Assist in locating sources of information.
- Modify your itinerary as required.

Another form of travel agency has sprung up on the internet. A plethora of on-line booking agents can now serve you at your own desk. Simply type in the website address and begin searching for the best fare. Internet giants such as Travelocity and Expedia offer air bookings directly online.

Air Transport

Air transport is the fastest and usually the least expensive means of international travel. In one day or less, you can travel to almost any major capital of the world.

For years, governments regulated the airline industry to insure safety and, often, the financial stability of airlines. Prices were the same, no matter which airline you used. Charter companies offered the only option for a reduced price. Since deregulation, a degree of chaos has reigned in the marketplace for air fares. At this time, there are dozens of fares for the same route. Since fares change so rapidly, it is difficult to give a complete report that would remain valid for any length of time. Individual airlines each have their own websites for online reservations and booking. See the Travel Websites listings.

Tip: A number of agencies have sprung up offering low-cost tickets, which actually turn out to be transfer of "mileage coupons." This is illegal. Many travelers have found themselves stranded at airports with worthless tickets.

CHARTERS

Charter airline companies do not have regularly scheduled flights. Rather, they rent out planes for very limited flights at fares without restrictions on a first-come basis. Agents often do not suggest charters because of their relative unreliability and lower commission structure.

Charter flights leave from major cities and go almost everywhere. Sometimes a charter offers the best opportunity to a major regional city such as Frankfurt or Hong Kong, where connections to other cities does not prove a problem.

Some airline companies sponsor their own package charters. Look carefully at the package offered. A low air fare may be offset by high-cost ground packages for hotel, ground transportation, etc.

Charters almost always have specific departure and return dates. Be sure you can conduct your business in the time allotted. Some include hotel accommodations and offer very attractive deals. Others include stays in several foreign capitals. Be sure to research the options and choose the one most appropriate for you.

The best procedure for finding an inexpensive charter:
- Ask your travel agent.
- Research other agents by telephone.
- Read the Sunday travel supplement of a major city paper (particularly in a port city).
- Find a travel agent in a neighborhood which has a large ethnic population of the country you plan to visit. There is a high likelihood that such agents will know of special charters to accommodate their local clientele.

WARNING

There have been occasions when airlines or companies that sell charter flights or tour packages have gone out of business with little warning, leaving stranded passengers overseas. If you hear from the media or from your travel agent that an airline is in financial difficulty, ask your agent or airline which recourse you would have if the airline ceased to operate. Some airlines may honor the tickets of a defunct airline, but they usually do so with restrictions.

11 Ways to Cut Travel Costs

1. Fly charter planes in coach class.
2. Travel off-season to save on transportation and lodging costs.
3. Stay at small hotels or pensions outside of the commercial districts of cities. Do not stay at the international hotels.
4. Try not to phone home, or use your U.S.-based calling card, or a "call-back" service.
5. When registering at hotels, show business card and request commercial rate (after asking what the regular rate is).
6. Eat where the locals eat. Don't eat American-style meals, especially breakfast. Eat only when hungry.
7. Pay for your travel using credit cards that give you bonus miles toward free flights.
8. Take public transportation whenever possible.
9. Eat and drink non-imported food and liquor.
10. Don't over-tip or double-tip. Many restaurants include a service charge in the bill.
11. Seek out discounts and bonuses offered to tourists, especially package deals.

Traveling Within a Country

Taxi

Taxi services are usually well developed in most countries and provide excellent door-to-door service within a city. Some tips:

- Be sure the meter is on and working, or settle on a price before departing.
- Ask at your hotel about appropriate tips, if any.
- Ask your travel agent beforehand about distances between airport and city, and best means of transport. Tokyo airport to downtown Tokyo, for example, can cost up to US$150.
- Have someone at the hotel write the name and address of your destination in the local language for you to show the taxi driver.

Car

Driving or renting an automobile can be an excellent alternative to public transportation in a number of instances.

Advantage of renting an automobile

- Freedom to come and go as you wish.
- You will always have a place to lock things up (get an auto with a locking trunk).
- Useful for getting to out-of-the-way places.
- Useful for transporting small amounts of goods.

Notes about renting an automobile

- Rentals require valid international or, in the U.S., state drivers license (consult with a travel agent or the national auto club of your country) and often a valid major credit card or substantial cash deposits.
- Other fees may be required for mandatory insurance.
- In some countries the safe driving condition of the rental car is your responsibility.
- Rental cars are available in most countries but for an enormously wide range of prices, usually all expensive.
- Check into insurance and liability coverage with your own insurance company or with the credit card issuer with which you are renting the car before going on your trip.

DRIVER'S LICENSE

If you intend to drive in another country, check with the embassy or consulate of the countries you will visit to learn their driver's license, road permit, and auto insurance requirements. If possible, obtain road maps before you go.

Many countries do not recognize a country-specific driver's license, but they will accept an international driver's permit, available for a slight fee at the national auto club of your country.

AUTO INSURANCE

Car rental agencies overseas usually provide auto insurance, but in some countries, the required coverage is minimal. A good rule of thumb when renting a car overseas is to purchase insurance coverage equivalent to that which you carry at home.

Bus

Buses are rarely a pleasant means of transportation while overseas. More often than not, they are crowded, dirty, run on erratic schedules, and are difficult modes of transport for someone unfamiliar with the local language.

Train

Rail transport overseas (especially in Europe) is more highly developed and relied upon than it is in the U.S. Fewer people overseas have access to automobiles and gasoline prices are significantly higher; as such, governments have made great efforts to develop this efficient form of public inter-city transportation.

For short distances, air travel often proves more trouble than it is worth—a false economy in time and expenditure. If the distances are not great, it may even take more time to get to an airport, wait, fly, and get from the airport to the destination than it does to take the train the whole distance. Furthermore, taking the train from city to city will give you time to relax and absorb what you have learned from your trip. Travel by train offers the opportunity to see the countryside and is an infinitely better environment for meeting people than traveling by air.

Some rail networks have unlimited 15-30-60-180-day use passes (e.g. Eurail Pass), which can prove helpful if you plan a heavy schedule of travel in a short period of time. While they were actually designed for the student and tourist, business people can make use of them as well.

Tip: Be sure to research local train travel rules for each country. In Spain, for example, you must present a boarding card to enter the train, even if you have a Eurail pass. Consult your travel agent for information and advice.

Communications

Telephones

European, North American, and developed countries in the Far East have telephone systems which are at least adequate. In developing countries, however, phone systems are antiquated, and the simple act of making a local call could prove nightmarishly difficult.

HOTEL TELEPHONES

Be sure to ask what the hotel surcharge will be for phone calls, and don't be surprised if they answer that it is 40 percent of the cost of the call or more (some hotels charge three times the cost of the call!).

PUBLIC TELEPHONES

One alternative to using hotel phones is to find a public phone booth. Every country has a different phone style. Instructions for use are sometimes faded, scratched off, and usually in a foreign language. Patience is a must. Hope for the weary does exist, however; European and advanced Asian phones often offer step-by-step diagram instructions on the front panel of the phone. Countries normally have two types of phones: card operated and coin or token operated.

Card Operated Phones

Most countries are moving to card phones because there is no change for thieves to steal and for phone companies to collect. It also means no more pockets-full-of-change for travelers. Cards can be purchased in hotels, newsstands, post offices, convenience stores, or cigar stores (obviously, this varies depending on the country. Some only have cards for sale at telecommunication offices). To use card phones, pick up the receiver and listen for a dial tone (remember that it may sound different than in your own home country) and insert the card. Some cards will have digital readouts telling you how much time you still have available; dial and use the phone accordingly. Phones will often indicate when your card is almost expired and will give you a chance to switch cards without breaking the call. Of course, with some phones, it's all guess work.

Coin Operated Phones

Coin-operated phones are similar to card phones in that one inserts change to talk. If calling a long-distance or international number, an operator should tell you how much money is needed and how long you can speak before inserting more money. Many countries have moved away from coin-operated phones altogether in exchange for tokens, and especially cards. One can purchase tokens in hotels and most stores, similar to cards, and use them the same as coins.

PLACING INTERNATIONAL CALLS

You won't be able to place an international call without the international access code and the country code for the country you are trying to reach. In addition, you'll also need a city/area code in most cases, and, of course, the number itself. Country codes and many city codes can all be found in the specific country chapters

in the *Global Road Warrior* and the international dialing guide which follows. You can call an operator in your home country who speaks your language and let them handle the domestic part of your call (this comes at an additional charge, which will be added to your monthly phone bill).

Travelers often use a government telephone office to make long distance and international calls because no surcharges exist. Ask your hotel clerk; they will undoubtedly know where it is. In many countries, public telephones simply do not have the capabilities to make long-distance calls with any efficiency, and PTT's (Postal, Telephone, and Telegraph offices) offer the only alternative to using hotel phones. A clerk will assign you a phone, often after you have left a returnable deposit. Time is limited.

TIPS FOR USING THE PHONE

- **Use the phone during off-peak hours.** Phone systems are similar the world round in one regard: rates change depending on when you make a call. In some countries, the difference in price is staggering.
- **Know what time it is where you are calling.** Consider the time differences from country to country. If you have no choice but to call when it is late at night at the call destination point, make sure someone knows; otherwise, you may simply get an answering machine or, even worse, someone upset about you waking them.
- **Be careful when criticizing the government.** Some people like to joke about the phones being "tapped," but in many countries it's no laughing matter. Making flip remarks could get you into a lot of trouble. Save your critiques for when you arrive safely at home.

CELLULAR TELEPHONES

Want to use your cell phone internationally? Beware that the country you are visiting may have a different cellular service standard. Thus cellular telephones from the USA will not work in Europe. Some new cell phones offer dual capability, but often at a high price.

See "Cellular Services Worldwide" on page 16 and "Cellular Service Systems" on page 17 for information.

Cell phone users have two options: rent a cell phone once they arrive in the country of destination or rent or purchase one before they leave home. We strongly recommend that you rent the phone *before* you leave home. There are many rental providers, but one that has proven to be reasonable and reliable is IMC/WorldCell.

INTERNATIONAL CELL PHONE RENTALS

IMC/World Cell
801 Roeder Road, Suite 800
Silver Spring, MD 20910
Toll free: (888) 967-5323: Fax: (301) 562-4020
E-mail worldcell@iwmcorp.com
www.worldcell.com
Under their WorldCell brand IMC rents and sells cell phones for use in more than 120 countries. One day service by courier.

Fax Machines

In the early- to mid-90s fax machines were the communication method of choice for businesses around the world. Although they have become superceded by e-mail, they are still extremely popular. In addition to phone numbers of people back home, make a list of fax numbers as well. If you don't have access to e-mail, the fax may offer you the only way to keep in touch.

Almost every hotel in even the most remote areas has a fax machine, and if not, they can tell you where to find one. They will usually charge a fee for fax services along with an additional fee for every page faxed. A minimal fee is also charged for every fax received.

E-mail

E-mail has overwhelmingly become the method of choice for most international communications. It is far cheaper than using the telephone and generally more reliable. Refer to "The Technical Traveler", which follows this section, for more information.

Postal Services

People often criticize the postal services in modern countries; but if they experienced what passes for postal service in the developing world, they would never complain again. Packages are dropped off and arrive at their destination months late, if at all. Theft is common, and postal employees often see nothing wrong with ripping open packages to see the contents. Red tape and bureaucracy can tie up delivery time almost forever, and packages could be confiscated for no reason at all if customs decides it wants to make a point.

Of course, these problems are rare in modern countries. If you are in a country like Canada, France, Germany, the U.K., the U.S., Japan, or Australia, postal services are generally efficient, and packages arrive in a reasonable amount of time.

Some ways to avoid theft with packages:

Always bring your mail to the post office itself, rather than just dropping it in a slot. This in itself could prove a chore since post offices in some countries have erratic hours of business. If an office is open, you will probably have to wait in an unending stationary line. Thieves often raid mailboxes, however; so, a little patience now will pay off later.

If you are planning on a long stay, invest in a post office box to receive mail. While this still isn't foolproof, it does guarantee that no outsiders can get their hands on it.

If you have any doubts, use a courier. In some countries, the post office simply can't be trusted. In cases like this, don't test the system, just invest in a courier service. They'll cost more, but it may prove a worthwhile investment. Some popular services like Federal Express (FedEx), United Parcel Service (UPS), DHL, and TNT offer good services internationally.

Callback Services

Callback services can potentially save international travelers a great deal of money. Here is how it works. Phone rates vary from country to country. The rates in the U.S., for example, are much less than in Brazil. A call-back user in Brazil calls a local number in Brazil that connects to a number in the US that automatically calls the Brazilian number back. Hense "call-back." The user is then charged a premium on the US rate, but much less than the Brazialian rate.

Callback services are understandably met with resistance by monopoly service providers internationally. Some governments have passed laws prohibiting callback services. Still, the U.S. Federal Communications Commission fully supports callback services, possibly because communications services in other countries are monopolies, and it is difficult for U.S. services to compete.

CALLBACK SERVICES

American International Telephonics, Inc. (U.S.) tel: [1] (949) 387-6995; fax: [1] (949)387-7995; fax toll free: 1-800-600-6151; www.aitelephone.com/callback.html.

CallNow. Communications; (U.S.) fax: [1] (212) 686-3807; email: backoffice@callnow.com; www.long-distance-phone.com.

Global Force Ltd. (U.S.); tel: [1] (609) 953-7573; toll free: 1-800-428-3888; fax: [1] (609) 953-7233; email: world@global-force.com; www.global-force.com.

GlobalTel; (U.S.)[1] (561) 999-9116; tollfree: 1-800-219-9545; fax: [1] (561) 999-0518; www.globaltel.org/.

Kallback; (U.S.) tel: [1] (206) 479-8600; toll free: 1-800-516-9992; fax: [1] (206) 479-0009; toll free in the U.S.: 1-800-516-9993; email: info@kallback.com; www.kallback.com.

Kallback Africa (South Africa); tel: [27] (11) 646-3670; fax: [27] (11) 646-5477; email: africa@kallback.co.za; www.kallback.co.za.

LCPI; (U.S.) tel: 1-800-685-0335; tel: [1] (727) 446-0420; email: service@lcpi.com; www.lcpi.com/main.html.

One World Communications;(U.S.) tel: [1] 480-491-4336; fax: [1] (480) 491-8375; email: info@owcusa.com; http://www.owcusa.com.

Telegroup Baltics; (U.K.) tel: [44] (171) 602-0705; fax: [44] (171) 602-2420; email: gredpath@telegroup.co.uk; Telegroup offers service from 70 countries; www.telegroup.lv; email: support@telegroup.lv.

World Access; email: email@worldwideplus.com; http://worldwideplus.com/longdist.

Note: Be sure to compare the prices of these and other callback services before choosing one. Prices can vary widely.

Cellular Services Worldwide

Cellular/Mobile Phone Services Worldwide

Service	Definition	System	Range
GSM	Global System Mobile Communication Utilizes satellite relay to carry digital signals.	Digital	900 mhz
AMPS	Advanced Mobile Phone Service Analog technology, still prevelant worldwide, but being phased out.	Analog	800 mhz, 900 mhz
TDMA	Time Division Multiple Access Squeezes three conversations into one cellular channel.	Digital	900 mhz
CDMA	Code Division Multiplexing Access Combines 30 khz cellular channels into a single 1.25 mhz channel to combine and recover 20-30 individual conversations at once.	Digital	900 mhz
PCS/ DCS	Personal Communications System Digital Communications System Utilizes TDMA, CDMA telephony technology to send/recieve	Digital	900 mhz, 1800 mhz
NMT	Nordic Mobile Telephony Scandanavian system popular in Eastern Europe and Russia, soon to be replaced by GSM.	Digital	450 mhz, 900 mhz
TACS/ ETACS	Total Access Control System Extended TACS AMPS with a few minor changes, operating in the 900mhz frequency band. The largest TACS networks are in the UK, but it has also been installed in many other countries around the world.	Analog	900 mhz

GSM (GLOBAL SATELLITE FOR MOBILES)
THE GLOBAL STANDARD

GSM was developed as a pan-European digital mobile telephony standard, and was placed in service in 1997. Prior to GSM technologies, cellular markets were served by incompatible analog systems (TAC, NMT, RC-2000, etc.). Today, GSM provides reliable and ubiquitous mobile telephony and data services throughout Europe and much of the world. GSM is the basis for PCS (Personal Communication Systems) worldwide, and is the technology of choice for cellular services in most of the world's emerging economies. GSM systems will be the next universal standard for mobile/cellular communications (already available in 164 countries/areas worlwide) by the year 2005.

Cellular Service Systems

Cellular/Mobile Service Systems

Region	Standard Operating System
North America	AMPS, GSM AMPS is the predominant system in North America. GSM is located in isolated regions including the US eastern seaboard, the US midwest, California, and Hawaii. Complete GSM coverage of the USA is anticipated in 2002.
South America	AMPS, GSM, NAMPS, EAMPS, TDMA AMPS is the predominant system with GSM slowly being integrated into Brazil and Chile.
Central America	AMPS AMPS is the predominant system with GSM expected to be available within 5 years.
Europe	GSM, AMPS, NMT GSM is the predominant system used.
United Kingdom	NMT, GSM NMT is the predominant system but is being slowly replaced by GSM.
Scandanavia	NMT, GSM NMT is the predominant system but is being slowly replaced by GSM.
Japan	PDC, CDMA PDC is compatible with GSM and is predominant throughout Japan.
Australia	GSM, AMPS GSM is the predominant system.
Asia	GSM, AMPS, NAMPS, TACS GSM is the predominant system.

The Technical Traveler

Before You Go

The Internet can be a great tool when preparing your trip. You can buy tickets and make reservations, often at significant discounts. You can also research the countries, the cities, and even the businesses you plan to visit, all without leaving your office (or desk). Along with the benefits come a few problems. Booking a flight with an unstable on-line source can leave you at the airport with a worthless ticket. E-tickets and hotel reservations sent by email can leave you without an official receipt.

BUYING TICKETS

We recommend buying tickets directly from the airlines' web sites or from a leading travel web site. Internet credit card theft is overblown by the media, but the danger still exists. Experts say the risk is about the same as using your credit card when ordering something by telephone.

MAKING HOTEL RESERVATIONS

Always double check by phone or fax after making reservations via email. Some companies merely offer an email option so they can "keep up with the big boys"; but, they rarely check the email. Always ask for an official receipt to be faxed to you, rather than just accepting an email reply without an official letterhead.

RESEARCHING THE TRIP

Good Luck Finding Anything

While a plethora of information exists on the World Wide Web, there is little organization. It could take an hour just to find a city code. Useful research sites lie next to frivolous home-made sites or marketing fluff. To expedite your search, try to be as specific as possible in your wording. It helps to acquire an internet address, or a 'url', before searching to avoid search engines. If you don't have an address, try specific key words that apply to your search. Merely putting in general words like "Algeria," or "city codes" will corral thousands of hits that may have nothing to do with your search.

Who Created This?

If you want the best information, it often means getting away from the library and heading to the computer for some real research. However, plenty of questionable websites exist. Always make sure the site has accurate information. Check to see who created it. Is it a reliable source? Or is it a government or corporate promotional machine? Good, useful information on the Internet is difficult to find among the marketing and propaganda.

Technology in the Country

If you are the type who can't live without a computer, you have two choices when traveling: bring along your portable, or take your chances in the country. In modern countries, computers abound. There are numerous places for you to access a computer to write a report or check your email: copy shops, hotel business centers,

cyber cafes, private offices, and the list continues. Most computers in these countries also have Internet access.

Other countries do not offer such convenient options. You may get access to a computer in just about every city in the world, but what you'll get may not be ideal: a 286 PC that's slower than a horse-drawn carriage.

Of course, bringing the laptop has its own problems. Not only is it one more thing to lug around and get through customs but also represents a target for thieves and others looking for a "wealthy" traveler (by international standards). Even if you bring a plethora of batteries, you'll need to deal with electrical adaptors for recharging; and hooking into phone lines can prove a nightmare.

Hooking Up

ELECTRICAL JACKS

Using electrical items from your own country carries a host of problems while traveling. First, the plugs will invariably be different than those at home. Adaptors are readily available from companies such as iGO Corporation (www.igo.com, see contact information on the facing page). You can usually buy one adaptor plug or a set of several if you travel to multiple countries.

Electricity also poses a problem in that the current in some countries is 220-240 volts, but in others (including the U.S.) it is 110-120 volts; so, even with plugs, electrical items won't work. iGO Corporation (and others, but iGO is more responsive) also have inexpensive electric converters. Most quality laptop computers already have voltage converters that will automatically convert anything from 110 to 240 volts to the computer's requirements. Check the label on the converters for information.

TELEPHONE JACKS

Be sure to ask at the hotel front desk whether the phone line is digital or analog before hooking onto the Internet. Unfortunately, sometimes the clerk will have no idea of what you're talking about. Worse, the hotel may have *both* analog and digital lines. Most modems will not work on digital lines, and trying to connect may destroy some older modems (new models have a sensor preventing any damage, but they still won't work on digital lines). Your best bet is to have a "Modem Saver Plus" line tester, available from iGO and others.

The second problem to solve is the type of jack. If traveling to only one country, simply find out what type of jack is used and buy an adaptor from one of the suppliers listed on the facing page or from your local travel store. Within the country, one may find jacks at travel, luggage, electronic, and some hardware stores.

Acoustic Couplers

If you think plugging your computer into a phone outlet will be impossible, or you prefer to avoid the headache, consider buying an acoustic coupler. It attaches directly to the phone receiver and requires no adaptors. Acoustic couplers are expensive (most cost around US$145), but, it may be worth the extra money.

The Connection

AMERICA ONLINE

Hooking up internationally with America OnLine is much easier thanks to the AOL Globalnet service. Before you go, type keyword *aolglobalnet*, and get a complete listing of phone numbers, connection speeds, and hourly fees.

After getting your number and arriving in the country, select "setup" on AOL's main page before signing on. Put the new number where asked, and click "ok." Then hit "sign on."

Remember that modem speeds around the world are rarely as fast as in the U.S. or Western Europe. Some connections may be extremely slow. Downloads that take minutes using 57.6Kbps modem speeds could take two hours or more. Expect slow connections and exercise patience.

COMPUSERVE

Go to the Member Services section before leaving; Compuserve offers an extensive Access Phone Numbers section there. Click on Access Phone Numbers, and Compuserve will give you two choices: one for the U.S. and Canada, another for other countries. Compuserve only features 57.6Kbps connection numbers in the U.S. In other countries, download times will be slower.

SERVICE PROVIDERS

Companies offering direct connections to the Internet (instead of going through online services) are known Independent Service Providers (I.S.P.s). I.S.P.'s exist all over the world, and almost every country has at least one connection number for travelers (many U.S. companies offer numbers in smaller countries, even though they don't have an office there). I.S.P.'s are listed in this book, under the country chapters, or you can check http://www.thelist.com, a huge database of I.S.P.'s worldwide. This list is constantly updated and offers the most up-to-date information. Once you've decided on a country, contact them for connection numbers within the country and instructions on hooking up your computer.

Be sure to look around before selecting an I.S.P. (of course, in some countries this is not an option as they may only offer one, or none at all). Ask for recommendations at a computer store in the country; but remember, that they could have a deal with the company they recommend.

Many I.S.P.'s have temporary, personal accounts for sale, but you may be able to get on for free with some fast talk. If you have impressive business cards or can pass yourself off as a computer professional, you may get a free, temporary account. Having a personal web-site virtually assures you of a free account in most under-developed or developing countries.

Web-Based Email

Perhaps the easiest way to check e-mail on the road is through a Web-based e-mail system like hotmail (http://www.hotmail.com), rocketmail (http://www.rocketmail.com), or juno (http://www.juno.com). Web-based email is free, funded by advertising on the site. Simply sign up on the site, and you will be given a user code and password for future use. The advantage to these services is checking e-mail without logging onto your home account. You can check anywhere that offers Internet connection: airports, Internet cafes, or friends' computers.

Although there have been complaints that these services were below par (not receiving or sending e-mail, or processing them with severe delays), companies have made improvements.

Some I.S.P.'s can also forward your home e-mail to this new account, although the I.S.P. may impose a slight surcharge to do so. As of July, 2000, America OnLine, Compuserve, MSN, and Prodigy do not offer email forwarding capabilities.

Computer Tips

- Have someone at home monitor your e-mail in your absence. If you are using a web e-mail service like Hotmail, they can forward important messages to you and save the letters just in case they are lost in transit.
- Attaching files to e-mail can pose a problem. Many software programs don't offer this service. Make sure to check before buying.
- Try your I.S.P. on another telephone system besides your own before leaving, if possible, to see if it still works.
- Batteries, batteries, batteries. Carry AT LEAST one extra. When using the computer, try not to do things that tax the computer's memory, as it will cause the battery to run down sooner. Turn off the 'AutoSave' function on all programs (of course, if you have trouble remembering to save, this may not be a good idea).
- Ask yourself: do you really need your laptop? It's tempting to drag it along, but if you don't need it for business meetings, it may be better to leave it at home. If your only reason for bringing your laptop is to check your e-mail, think of an alternative. You'll be better off in the long run.

ELECTRICAL AND TELEPHONE ADAPTORS

The following companies have electrical and telephone adaptors available for every socket worldwide:

THE AMERICAS

iGo Corporation
9393 Gateway Drive
Reno, NV 89511 USA
tel: (800) Dial-iGO (800-342-5446)
www.igo.com

UNITED KINGDOM/EUROPE

TeleAdapt Ltd. U.K.
The Technology Park
Colindeep Lane, London
NW9 6TA United Kingdom
tel: [44] (0) 181 233 3000
fax: [44] (0) 181 233 3132
email: teleadapt@delphi.com
Compuserve: 104047,76

AUSTRALIA/ASIA

TeleAdapt Pty. Ltd.
Locked Bag 5340
Artarmon
NSW 2064, Australia
tel: [61] (0) 2 9433 8363
fax: [61] (0) 2 9433 8369
email: 104125.577@compuserve.com
Compuserve: 10425,577

Travel Web-Sites

Travel Web-Sites

Note: All web sites were accurate as of January, 2001. If the url has changed, look up the company or site title on a search engine (http://www.yahoo.com, http://www.excite.com) for the most recent address. Capital letters within the URL should be typed as such to make sure the link is successful. World Trade Press does not endorse any of the following companies.

Airline Sites

AFRICA

African EagleAir & Safaris (Namibia—charter)
http://www.african-eagle.com.na/
Africa West Airlines
http://africawest.net
Air Afrique (Ivory Coast, western Africa)
http://www.airafrique.com
Air Austral (French airline, Renunion, Indian Ocean)
http://www.air-austral.com
Air Gabon
http://www.ana-aviation.com/airgabon.htm
Air Madagascar
http://www.air-mad.com/index.htm
Air Malawi
http://www.africaonline.co.ke/airmalawi/
Air Mauritius
http://www.airmauritius.com
Air Senegal
http://www.caboverde.com/pages/615483.htm
Air Seychelles
http://www.airseychelles.net
Air Tanzania
http://www.airtanzania.com
Air Zimbabwe
http://www.airzim.co.zw/
Alliance Air (South Africa—eastern Africa, Uganda)
http://www.africa-insites.com/uganda/alliance.htm
Bellview Airlines (Nigeria, West Africa)
http://www.bellviewairlines.com
Cameroon Air
http://www.airnautic.frcamair.htm
Congo Airlines
http://www.congoairlines.com
Daallo Airlines (South Africa)
http://www.daallo.com
Egypt Air
http://www.egyptair.com
Ethiopian Airlines
http://www.flyethiopian.com
Expedition Airways (Zimbabwe regional)
http://www.africaonline.co.zw/expedition/
Flamingo Flights (South Africa–charter)
http://www.gardenroute.co.za/t2t/ct/flamingo/index.htm
Fly Africa Adventures (Charter)
http://www.flyafrica.com
Gabon Express
http://www.gabonexpress.com

Ghana Airways
http://www.ghana-airways.com
Heyns Helicopter (South Africa—charter)
http://www.heynsheli.co.za/
Interair (South Africa—southern Africa)
http://www.travelsa.com/br/zinterai.html
Kenya Airways
http://www.kenyaairways.co.uk/
Royal Air Maroc
http://www.royalairmaroc.com
Royal Swzi Airways
http://www.tanzania-web.com/www.africanet.com/africacomnet/temp/airlines/royal2.htm
Scibe Airlift Congo
http://www.saritel.it/disdoc/dst-africa3.html
South African Airways (South Africa—intl.)
hnetttp://www.saa.co.za/
South African Express Airways (South Africa—regional)
http://www.saexpress.co.za
Speed Air Charter (South Africa)
http://www.tradepage.co.za/speedair/
TunisAir (Tunisia)
http://www.tunisair.com.tn/
Zambian Express (ZAMEX)
http://www.zamnet.zm/zamnet/zntb/zamex.html

ASIA

Air China
http://www.airchina.com
Air India (India—international)
http://www.airindia.com
Air Lanka (Sri Lanka)
http://www.airlanka.com
Air Mandalay (Myanmar)
http://www.air-mandalay.com
All Nippon Airways (Japan—international)
http://www.ana.co.jp
Asiana Airlines (Korea—international)
http://us.flyasiana.com
Bangkok Airways (Thailand—Cambodia, Laos, Singapore)
http://www.bkkair.co.th
Cathay Pacific Airways (Hong Kong—international)
http://www.cathay-usa.com
China Airlines (China—international)
http://www.china-airlines.com
China Eastern Airlines
http://www.ce-air.com/html/enindex.html
China Southern Airlines
http://www.malaysia_web.com/csn/
Dragonair (Hong Kong)
http://www.dragonair.com
Eva Air (Taiwan)
http://www.evaair.com.tw/
Garuda Indonesia (Indonesia—international)
http://www.garudausa.com

Gorkha Airlines (Nepal, air & helicopter services)
http://www.gorkhaairlines.com.np/
Indian Airlines (domestic, regional carrier)
http://indian-airlines.nic.in/
Japan Airlines (JAL) (Japan—international)
http://www.jal.co.jp (or) jal.co.jp/english/
index_e.html
Japan Air System (JAS) (Japan—international)
http://www.jas.co.jp/ (or) www.jas.co.jp/
e_jashom.htm
Jet Airways (India—domestic)
http://www.jetairways.com
Korean Air (Korea—international)
http://www.koreanair.com
Malaysia Airlines (Malaysia—international)
http://www.malaysiaairlines.com.my/
Maldivian Air Taxi (Maldives)
http://www.mataxi.com
Mandarin Air (China—domestic)
http://www.mandarin-airlines.com
Merpati Airlines (Indonesia)
http://www.merpati.co.id/
MIAT Airlines (Mongolia)
http://www.arpnet.it/~mongolia/viaggi/aereo.htm
Milne Bay Airlines (MBA) (Papua New Guinea)
http://www.mbapng.com
Necon Air (Nepal—private airline)
http://www.neconair.com
Philippine Airlines (Philippines—international)
http://www.philippineair.com
Royal Brunei (Brunei—international)
http://www.bruneiair.com
Royal Nepal Airlines (international)
http://www.royalnepal.com
Sahara Airlines (India—domestic)
http://www.saharaairline.com
Sichuan Airlines (China—domestic)
http://info.scsti.ac.cn/English/eco/air.html
Silkair (Singapore Airlines' regional carrier)
http://www.silkair.com.sg
Singapore Airlines (Singapore—international)
http://www.singaporeair.com
Skyline Airways (Nepal—domestic)
http://www.yomari.net/skyline/
Skymark Airlines (Japan)
http://www.skymark.co.jp/
Thai Airways (Thailand—international)
http://www.thaiair.com
Vietnam Airlines (domestic, international)
http://www.vietnamtourism.com/vn.airlines/
vnhome.htm

CARIBBEAN

Air Aruba (Aruba, Dutch Caribbean)
http://www.airaruba.com
Air ALM (Caribbean, Miami, Suriname, Venezuela,
Colombia)
http://www.airalm.com
Air Jamaica (Jamaica, Bahamas, Cayman, St. Lucia,
Barbados, Grenada, Bonaire, Cuba)
http://www.airjamaica.com
Bahamas Air
http://www.bahamasair.com
BWIA Airways (West Indies)
http://www.bwee.com

Cayman Airways
http://www.caymanairways.com
COPA Air (Panama)
http://www.copaair.com
Cubana (Cuba—domestic & international)
http://www.cubana.cu/
Fly BVI (Charter Service)
http://www.fly-bvi.com
Gulfstream Air (Florida, Bahamas)
http://www.gulfstreamair.com
LIAT (Caribbean—26 destinations)
http://www.liatairline.com
SVG Air (St. Vincent & Grenadines Air Taxi)
http://svgair.com

CENTRAL AMERICA

AeroMexico (Mexico, international)
http://www.aeromexico.com
COPA Airlines (Latin America)
http://www.copaair.com
Maya Island Air (Belize)
http://www.ambergriscaye.com/islandair/
Maya Airways (Belize)
http://www.mayaairways.com
Mexicana (Mexico—international)
http://www.mexicana.com
TACA (Aviateca, LACSA, NICA)
http://www.grupotaca.com/ing/index.html
Travelair (Costa Rica—domestic)
http://www.centralamerica.com/cr/tran/airindex.htm

EUROPE

Adria Airlines (Slovenia)
http://www. kabi.si/si21/aa/
AB Airlines (Barcelona, London, Nice, Shannon)
http://www.abairlines.com
Aer Lingus (Ireland—international)
http://www.aerlingus.ie/
Aerosweet Airlines (Ukraine)
http://www.aerosweet.com
Air Lithuania
http://www.airlithuania.lt/
Air Malta
http://www.airmalta.com
Air Moldova
http://www.ami.md/
Aeroflot Russia
http://www.aeroflot.com
Air Baltic (Latvia)
http://www.airbaltic.lv/
Air Europa
http://www.air-europa.com
Air France (France—international)
http://www.airfrance.fr (or) www.airfrance.com
Alitalia (Italy—international)
http://www.alitalia.it/ (Italian)
http://www.alitalia.it/eng/index.html (English)
AOM (France—international)
http://www.aom-minerve.fr/
Augsburg Airways (Germany)
http://www.augsburgair.de/en/
Austrian Airlines (Austria—international)
http://www.aua.co.at/
Azzura Air (Italy, Bergamo-Rome, Europe)
http://www.azzuraair.it/

Travel Web-Sites

Balkan-Bulgarian Airlines
http://www.balkan-air.com.pl/
Braathens Air (Norway)
http://www.braathens.no/
British Airways(England—international)
http://www.british-airways.com
British European (United Kingdom)
http://www.british-european.com/be/index.html
British Midland (London Heathrow—Europe)
http://www.iflybritishmidland.com
Cabo Verde Airlines (Cape Verde, international)
http://www.tacv.com
City Bird (Belgium-U.S. flights)
http://www.citybird.com
Condor (Germany—international)
http://www.condor.de/
Corsair (France)
http://www.pacificislands.com/airlines/corsair.html
Croatia Airlines (Croatia, Europe)
http://www.croatiaairlines.hr/
Crossair (Switzerland)
http://www.crossair.ch/
Cyprus Airways (Cyprus, Europe, Middle East)
http://www.cyprusair.com.cy/
Cyprus Turkish Airlines (Cyprus, Turkey,
Frankfurt, London)
http://www.kthy.net
Czech Airlines (CSA) (Czech—international)
http://www.csa.cz/
Easy Jet (no-frills airline, London-based)
http://www.easyjet.com
Estonian Air
http://www.estonian-air.ee/
Finnair (Finland—international)
http://www.finnair.fi
GB Airways (Britsh Airways extended network)
http://www.british-airways.com/inside/wrldwide/
partners/franchise/docs/gb.shtml
Go Fly (London-based, discount carrier)
http://www.go-fly.com
Greenlandair (domestic/intl. charter)
http://www.greenland-guide.dk/gla/default.htm
Iberia (Spain—international)
http://www.iberia.com
Icelandair (Iceland—U.S., Europe)
http://icelandair.com
**KLM Royal Dutch Airlines (Holland—
international)**
http://nederland.klm.com
Lauda Air (Germany)
http://www.LaudaAir.com
LOT Polish Airlines
http://www.lot.com
LTU International Airways (Germany—
international)
http://www.ltu.de/
Lufthansa (Germany—international)
http://www.lufthansa.com
Luxair (Luxembourg)
http://www.luxair.lu/
Malev Hungarian (Hungary—intl., mostly Europe)
http://www.malev.hu/
Maersk Air (Switzerland)
http://www.maersk-air.com

Manx Airlines (Jersey - Isle of Man)
http://www.manx-airlines.com
Martinair Holland (Holland—international)
http://www.martinair.com
MaxAir (Norway, Sweden)
http://www.maxair.com
Montenegro Airlines
http://www.montenegro-airlines.com
Olympic Airways (Greece—international)
http://www.olympicair.com
Riga Airlines (Baltics)
http://www.riga-airlines.com
Ryan Air (Ireland)
http://www.ryanair.ie/
Sabena (Belgium—international)
http://www.sabena.com
Scandianavian Airlines System (SAS)
(Scandinavia—international)
http://www.sas.se/
Skyways (Sweden)
http://www.skyways.se/start.html
Spanair (Mallorca)
http://www.spanair.com
Swissair (Switzerland—international)
http://www.swissair.com
TAP Air Portugal (Portugal— international)
http://www.tap.pt/
Tarom Romanian
http://tarom.digiro.net
TransAero (Russia)
http://www.transaero.ru/
Turkish Airlines (Turkey—international)
http://www.thy.com
www.thy.com
Ukraine International Airlines
http://www.ukraine-international.com/eng/
index.html
Uzbekistan Airways
http://www.uzbekistanairways.nl/
VLM Airlines
http://www.vlm-airlines.com
Virgin Atlantic (U.K.—international)
http://www.virgin-atlantic.com
Virgin Express (Brussels, Europe)
http://www.virgin-express.com
Wideroe Airlines (Norway)
http://www.wideroe.no/
Yugoslav Airlines
http://www.jat.com

MIDDLE EAST

Air Gulf Falcon (U.A.E.—VIP flights, charter,
cargo)
http://www.air-gulffalcon.com
El Al Israel Airlines (Israel—international)
http://www.elal.co.il
Emirates (Dubai—Europe, Africa, Asia)
http://www.ekgroup.com
Gulf Air (Bahrain, Qatar, Oman, U.A.E.)
http://www.gulfairco.com
Iran Air (Iran—Europe, Africa, Asia)
http://www.iranair.co.ir/
Kuwait Airways (Kuwait—international)
http://www.kuwait-airways.com

Middle East Airlines (Lebanon)
http://www.mea.com.lb
New Qatar Airways
http://qatarair_uae.co.ae/
Orca Air (Egypt)
http://www.orca-air.com
Pakistan International Airlines (Pakistan—international)
http://www.fly-pia.com
Royal Jordanian (Jordan—Middle East, Europe)
http://www.rja.com.jo
Royal Wings Airlines (Jordan)
http://www.royalwings.com.jo
Saudi Arabian Airlines (Saudia Arabia—international)
http://www.saudiairlines.com
Yemen Airways
http://home.earthlink.net/~yemenair/

NORTH AMERICA

Access Air (charter—based in Des Moines, IA)
http://www.accessair.com
Active Aero Group (charter management co.)
http://www.activeaero.com/two/index.html
Aerocaribe (Mexico)
http://www.aerocaribe.com
AeroLitoral (Mexico—regional carrier)
http://www.aerolitoral.com.mx
Aeromar (Mexico—private turboprop enterprise)
http://www.aeromar-air.com
AeroMexico (Mexico—international)
http://www.aeromexico.com
Air Canada (Canada—international)
http://www.aircanada.ca/
Air Jet Inc. (jet, turboprop charters—east coast)
http://www.airjetinc.com
Air Labrador (Newfoundland, Labrador)
http://www.airlabrador.com
Air North (Yukon, Northwest Territories)
http://www.airnorth.yk.net
Air Nova (Canada—regional)
http://www.airnova.ca/
Air Ontario (Canada—East Coast)
http://www.airontario.ca/
Air Trans (Atlanta, U.S.—East Coast)
http://www.airtran.com/routemap/
Alaska Airlines (western U.S., Canada, Mexico)
http://www.alaska-air.com
Aloha Airlines (Hawaii)
http://www.alohaair.com
America West Airlines (western U.S./Mexico)
http://www.americawest.com
American Airlines (U.S.—international)
http://www.AA.com
American Trans Air (U.S. domestic)
http://www.ata.com
Arctic Circle Air Service Inc. (Alaska)
http://www.arctic-circle-air.com
Atkin Air (Lincoln, CA—charter)
http://www.atkinair.com
Calm Air (Central Canada—regional)
http://www.calmair.com
Canada 3000 (Canada—domestic, Europe, Florida)
http://www.canada3000.com

Canadian Airlines Int'l (CAI)) (Canada—international)
http://www.aircanada.ca/
Cape Air (Cape Cod and Islands, Caribbean, Florida)
http://www.flycapeair.com
Colgan Air (U.S.—northeast regional)
http://www.colganair.com
Comair (Delta connection—Cincinnati, Orlando)
http://fly-comair.com/home/
CommutAir (US Air commuter, eastern U.S.)
http://www.commutair.com
Continental Airlines (U.S.—international)
http://www.continental.com
Corporate Express (Canada jet charters)
http://www.corpxair.com
Delta Airlines (U.S.—international)
http://www.delta-air.com
First Air (northern Canada)
http://www.firstair.ca/
Frontier Airlines (U.S. domestic)
http://www.flyfrontier.com
Great Lakes Airlines (Chicago/Springfield service)
http://www.greatlakesav.com/zjairlpg.htm
Greenlandair (domestic, intl. charter)
http://www.greenland-guide.dk/gla/default.htm
Hawaiian Airlines (Hawaii, U.S. **west coast, Samoa**)
http://www.hawaiianair.com
Helijet (scheduled helicopter airline service, Pacific Northwest)
http://www.helijetairways.com
Horizon Airlines (U.S./Canada west coast, Mexico)
http://www.horizonair.com
JetBlue (domestic, selected cities)
http://www.jetblue.com
Jet Express (private personal/business charter)
http://www.jetexpress.com/jetexpress.html
Kitty Hawk (cargo, freight charter)
http://www.kha.com
Legend Airlines (Dallas, L.A., Las Vegas, D.C., NYC for business executives)
http://www.legendairlines.com
Mesa Airlines (U.S., Mexico, Canada)
http://www.mesa-air.com
Mexicana (Mexico—international)
http://www.mexicana.com
Midway Air (U.S. domestic—Raleigh/Durham)
http://www.midwayair.com
Midwest Express Airlines (U.S. midwest)
http://www.midwestexpress.com
Mountain Air Express (California, Nevada)
http://mountainairexpress.com
National Airlines (Las Vegas hub, S.F.O., L.A., Chicago Midway, JFK, Newark, Philadelphia, Dallas/Ft. Worth, Miami); http://www.nationalairlines.com
New England Airlines (commuter to Block Island)
http://users.ids.net/flybi/nea/
North Vancouver Air (Canada, Vancouver region, Pacific Northwest charters)
http://www.northvanair.com
Northwest Airlines (U.S.—international)
http://www.nwa.com
Pacific Coastal (Western B.C. in Canada)
http://www.pacific-coastal.com

Travel Web-Sites

Pan Am (U.S.—Portsmouth, NH; Sanford, FL; Pittsburgh, PA; Bangor, ME; Gary, IN; Belleville, IL)
http://www.flypanam.com
Pem Air (Canada—Toronto-Pembroke, charters, freight, fire patrol services)
http://www.pemair.on.cal
Pen Air (Alaska)
http://www.penair.com
Piedmont Airlines (U.S. Air Express)
http://www.piedmont-airlines.com
Provincial Airlines (Newfoundland, Labrador)
http://www.provair.com
Regal Airways (Orlando, FL to U.S. main cities, Puerto Rico)
http://www.regalairways.com
Shuttle America (U.S.—Northeast, Mid-Atlantic)
http://www.shuttleamerica.com
Royal Air (Canada, U.K., Ireland, Spain, France)
http://www.royalair.com
Ryan International Airlines (partners with tour providers: Apple Vacations, Star Air Tours, Sunquest, Suntrips; provides executive charters)
http://www.flyryan.com
Scenic Air (Grand Canyon, Monument Valley, Bryce Canyon)
http://www.scenic.com
Sky West Airlines (Delta & United commuter affiliate—western states, Canada)
Southwest Airlines (U.S.—no-frills domestic)
http://www.iflyswa.com
Spirit Airlines (U.S. domestic)
http://www.spiritair.com
Sun Country Airlines (U.S. domestic)
http://www.suncountry.com
Tower Air (L.A., Miami, NYC, San Juan, Santo Domingo, Tel Aviv)
http://www.towerair.com
Transmeridian Airlines (U.S. charter—Americas, Europe, Caribbean)
http://www.transmeridianair.com
Trans States Airlines (regional feeder, St. Louis, JFK)
http://www.transstates.net/
TWA (U.S., Caribbean, Meixco, Europe, Africa, Middle East—hubs: St. Louis, JFK)
http://www.twa.com
United Airlines (U.S.—international)
http://www.ual.com
Vanguard Airlines (U.S.—Mid/eastern U.S.)
http://www.flyvanguard.com
WestJet (Canada—domestic)
http://www.westjet.com
Wiggins Airways (U.S.—Northeast)
http://www.wiggins-air.com
Wings of Alaska (Alaska—southeast tip)
http://www.flyingalaska.com

OCEANIA/PACIFIC RIM

Aircalin (New Caledonia)
http://www.aircalin.nc/
Air Fiji (Fiji—domestic)
http://www.airfiji.net/
Air Macau
http://www.airmacau.com.mo

Air Nauru (Australia/South Pacific)
http://www.airnauru.com.au/
Air Niugini (Papua New Guinea)
http://www.airniugini.com.pg
Air New Zealand (New Zealand—international)
http://www.airnewzealand.com/gateway.jsp
Air Pacific (Fiji, South Pacific)
http://www.airpacific.com
Air Rarotonga (Tonga—twin-engined prop-jets)
http://www.ck/edairaro.htm
Air Tahiti
http://www.airtahitinui-usa.com
Air Vanuatu
http://www.vanuatutourism.com/airvan.htm
Ansett Australia (domestic—Osaka, Hong Kong, Denpasar, Fiji)
http://www.ansett.com.au/
Flight West (Austrlalia—Queensland)
http://www.flightwest.com.au/
Freedom Air (New Zealand)
http://www.freedomair.co.nz/
Inter Island Air (American Samoa)
www.interislandair.com
Island Hoppers (Fiji helicopter service)
http://www.helicopters.com.fj/
Polynesian Airlines (New Zealand)
http://www.polynesianairlines.co.nz/
Qantas Airways (Australia—international)
http://www.qantas.com
Skywest Airlines (Australia)
http://www.skywest.com.au/
Solomon Airlines (Solomon Islands)
http://www.solomonairlines.com.au/main.htm
Spirit Airlines (Australia—no-frills carrier)
http://www.spiritairlines.com.au/
Sunflower Airlines (Fiji)
http://www.fiji.to/
Western Airlines (Australia)
http://www.avon.net.au/~westair/

SOUTH AMERICA

Aces (Colombia)
http://www.acescolombia.com
Aerocardal (Chile—executive, special services)
http://www.chilesat.net/aerocardal/
Aerolineas Argentinas (Argentina—international)
http://www.aerolineas.com.ar
Aerosur (Bolivia)
http://www.angelfire.com/on/aerosur/
Air Bolivia (LAB)
http://www.labairlines.com
Avianca (Colombia—international)
http://www.avianca.com.co/
Guyana Airways
http://www.turq.com/guyana/guyanair.html
Lan Chile (Chile—international)
http://www.lanchile.com/index2.html
Pantanal Airlines (Brazil)
http://www.pantanal-airlines.com.br/
SAETA Aireolinea Ecuador
http:/www.saeta.com.ec
Surinam Airways
http://www.slm.firm.sr/
TAM Brazilian Airlines
http://www.tam-usa.com

TAME (Ecuador)
http://www.tame.com.ec/
Transbrasil (Brazil—international)
http://www.transbrasil.com.br/
Varig (Brazil—international)
http://www.varig.com.br/english/

Hotel Sites

TOP-END

ANA Hotels International
http://www.ananet.or.jp/anahotels/e/
Conrad International Hotels
http://www.hilton.com/conradinternational/
index.html
Dusit Group Hotels & Resorts (Thailand)
http://www.dusit.com
Fairmont Hotels
http://www.fairmont.com
Four Seasons Hotels and Resorts
http://www.fourseasons.com
Hilton Hotels
http://www.hilton.com
Hyatt Hotels
http://www.hyatt.com
Inter-Continental Hotels
http://www.interconti.com
Kempinsky Hotels
http://www.kempinski.com
Leading Hotels of the World
http://www.lhw.com
Luxury Collection Hotels
http://www.luxurycollection.com
Mandarin Oriental
http://www.mandarin-oriental.com
Marriott Hotels
http://www.marriott.com
Orient Express Hotels
http://www.orient-expresshotels.com
Pan Pacific Hotels
http://www.panpac.com
Raffles Hotels
http://www.raffles.com
Ritz Carlton Hotels
http://www.ritzcarlton.com
Regent International Hotels (Asia)
http://www.regenthotels.com
Relais and Chateaux
http://www.relaischateaux.fr/
Savoy Hotel Group (England)
http://www.savoy-group.co.uk
Sheraton Hotels
http://www.sheraton.com
Sofitel Hotels
http://www.sofitel.com
St. Regis Hotels
http://www.stregis.com
Starwood Hotels and Resorts (Westin, Sheraton,
Four Points, St. Regis, Luxury Collection, W Hotels)
http://www.starwoodhotels.com
Summit Hotels (independent luxury hotels)
http://www.summithotels.com

W Hotels
http://www.whotels.com
Westin Hotels
http://www.westin.com

EXPENSIVE

Accor Hotels (Sofitel, Novotel, Mercure, Ibis, Etap
Hotel, Formule I, Motel 6, Red Roof, Coralia,
Thalassa, Atria)
http://www.accorhotel.com
Coralia Hotels
http://www.coralia.com
Crowne Plaza
http://www.crowneplaza.com
Delta Hotels (Canada, northern U.S.)
http://www.deltahotels.com
Equatorial Hotels (Asia)
http://www.equatorial.com
**Forte Hotels (Le Meridien, Posthouse London,
Travelodge)**
http://www.forte-hotels.com
Golden Tulip Worldwide
http://www.goldentulip.com
Hyatt Hotels
http://www.hyatt.com
Marriott Hotels
http://www.marriott.com
Maritim Hotels (Germany, Tenirife, Mauritius)
http://www.maritim.de
Merit Hotels (Turkey, Greece, Cyprus)
http://www.focusmm.com.au/netholding/merit/
welcome.htm
Mercure Hotels
http://www.mercure.com
Mövenpick Hotels (Germany, Czech, Switzerland,
Netherlands, Morocco, Middle East)
http://www.movenpick-hotels.com
Novotel Business Hotels
http://www.novotel.com
Omni Hotels
http://www.omnihotels.com
Prince Hotels (Japan)
http://www.princehotels.co.jp/
Radisson Hotels
http://www.radisson.com
Renaissance Hotels
http://www.renaissancehotels.com
Scandic Hotels (Scandinavia)
http://www.scandic-hotels.com/br/50/50index.html
Sol Melia Hotels (Spain, South/Latin America)
http://www.solmelia.es
Sorat Hotels (Germany)
http://www.sorat-hotels.com
Steigenberger Hotels & Resorts (Europe)
http://www.steigenberger.com
Swisshotels
http://www.swissotel.com
Thalassa International (spa hotels, France)
http://www.thalassa.com
Thistle Hotels (U.K.)
http://www.thistlehotels.com
Wyndham Hotels
http://www.wyndham.com

Travel Web-Sites

MODERATE

Accor Hotels (Sofitel, Novotel, Mercure, Ibis, Etap Hotel, Formule I, Motel 6, Red Roof, Coralia, Thalassa, Atria
http://www.accorhotel.com
Best Western Hotels
http://www.bestwestern.com
Choice Hotels (Comfort Inns/Suites, Quality Inns/ Suites, Clarion Hotels, Econo Lodges, Rodeway Inns, Sleep Inn/Suites, MainStay Suites)
http://www.choicehotels.com
Days Inn
http://www.daysinn.com
Doubletree Hotels (North America)
http://www.doubletreehotels.com
Embassy Suites
http://www.embassy-suites.com
Etap Hotels (Europe)
http://www.etaphotel.com
Fairfield Inn
http://www.marriott.com/fairfieldinn/
Formule 1 Hotels (France)
http://www.hotelformule1.com/
Four Points Hotels Sheraton (N. America/Germany)
http://www.fourpoints.com
Hampton Inns and Suites
http://www.hamptoninn-suites.com
Hilton Garden Inns
http://www.hilton.com/hiltongardeninn/index.html
Holiday Inn
http://www.basshotels.com/holiday-inn
Homewood Suites-Hilton
http://www.homewood-suites.com
Ibis Hotels
http://www.ibishotel.com
InterCity Hotels (Steigenberger, moderate hotels/ Europe)
http://www.steigenberger.com/hotels/ fs_hauptnavi.htm
Jarvis Hotels (U.K.)
http://www.jarvis.co.uk/
Motel 6 (U.S. and Ontario)
http://www.motel6.com
Novotel Business Hotels
http://www.novotel.com
Park Plaza Int'l
http://www.parkplaza.com
Prima Hotels (Israel)
http://www.intournet.co.il/prima/
Ramada Hotels
http://www.ramada.com
Red Lion Hotels
http://www.redlion.com
Red Roof Inns
http://www.redroof.com
Steigenberger Hotels & Resorts (Europe)
http://www.steigenberger.com
Travelodge
http://www.travelodge.com

Other Travel Sites

Asia Pulse (Business travel information for Asia)
http://www.buscentre.com.au/lifestyles/ business_travel/default.htm
Asian Business Watch
http://www.asianbusinesswatch.com
Centers for Disease Control
http://www.cdc.gov/
Central Europe Guide
http://www.centraleurope.com
Electronic Embassy
http://www.embassy.org/
The Embassy Page
http://www.embpage.org
Foreign Language for Travelers
http://www.travlang.com/languages/
Foreign Language Page
http://www.travlang.com/languages
International Monetary Fund
http://www.imf.org
International Translation Service
http://www.globalink.com/home.html
Passport Pal (information for traveling to Asia)
http://www.passportpal.com
Travel Warnings and Advisories (produced by the U.S. government)
http://travel.state.gov
United Nations Online
http://www.un.org/
U.S. State Department Travel Warnings
http://travel.state.gov/warnings_list.html
World Maps
http://www.maps.com
http://www.mapquest.com
World News
http://www.enews.com
World Time Information
http://www.globaltimeclock.com
World Trade Centers Association
http://www.wtca.org/

Business Culture

The Cultural Challenge

International commerce presents countless challenges to traders that they simply do not encounter in their domestic markets. Much of what makes a foreign country "foreign" and what exerts a strong influence on foreign trade is culture. While it is imperative that you know your customer, it is equally important that you know the environment in which that customer operates, i.e. the culture. From a business point of view, culture can be looked upon as a set of rules that govern the way business and personal transactions are conducted with nationals of particular nations. These rules will dictate the etiquette, traditions, values, communication, and negotiating styles of the particular culture to which they apply.

It should also be noted that culture does not necessarily refer to a whole country but rather to connected groups of people. Thus, a country may have a distinctive overall culture but within this framework many subcultures may exist. In addition, cultures are not fixed in stone–they are continually evolving and are flexible by nature. Cultures are not impervious to outside influences and younger generations, in particular, may not have the same cultural precepts as their elders.

Cultural Norms

All traders conduct business transactions in their own domestic markets in accordance with the rules and requirements of the prevailing culture; they understand what is and is not acceptable behavior. When conducting business abroad, however they are faced with a different set of rules which govern their associates' behavior, and with which they are often not familiar.

In order to be successful in global trade, businesspeople need to be aware of their own cultural influences and be sensitive to those of the nations with whom they intend to trade. They must also be sensitive to any particular biases or practices within their own culture that may lead to inappropriate judgments or assumptions about another culture; and they must try to understand that the foreign culture will also hold biases. Failure to do this can lead to serious misunderstandings that could adversely affect business relations.

Business Courtesies

Business practices vary from culture to culture and the proper protocol should be followed when operating in foreign environments–at least to the extent you can do so within the constraints of your own cultural background. Nobody expects you to behave exactly as they do; indeed it would probably be looked upon as less than sincere if you tried to become "one of them." To have some understanding of a country's cultural background, to be sensitive to the ways that your own culture may cause offense, and to adapt accordingly, should suffice. But, while there are many ways in which business practices differ, it should also be remembered that certain practices are common to all cultures—being polite and courteous, personally signing all correspondence, and responding to requests promptly will be appreciated anywhere.

Gaining Awareness

Rules of etiquette differ from culture to culture and what is acceptable in your own country may be considered rude elsewhere. As initial impressions are vital in establishing business relationships, it is important to know what is expected of you when first meeting potential business partners from another culture. Some cultures demand the use of respectful titles when addressing people while others are more informal. For example, in Japan the accepted form of greeting is the bow; subordinates bow more deeply than their superiors, and it is not common to make physical contact. In many Middle Eastern countries, however, there is much hugging, kissing, and extended hand holding upon greeting. In Middle Eastern countries, it is socially unacceptable to inquire about a colleague's wife and family, while in Mexico this practice is entirely appropriate and indeed expected. There are a host of social courtesies that accompany any relationship, and it is important to have some idea of those which might apply to the people with whom you do business.

Language

Language is central to the communication process and as such it can be a significant barrier to international trade. Being clearly understood by your business partners is of paramount importance whether you are negotiating a deal, drafting a contract or issuing instructions from your home base. While English is probably the most commonly used language in international trade, it is not spoken everywhere. Even where it is used there may be differing levels of comprehension, and different meanings may be attributed to certain words. Knowledge of the language of the market in which you are trading may be necessary in the long term; although, in general, the use of well- trained interpreters will suffice for most purposes.

When using a non-common or non-native language, remember that clear enunciation, not volume, is the key. Although it might seem laborious, speaking slowly and more clearly far outweighs the consequences of a high-speed approach that is not understood and prompts repeating, or worse, miscommunication.

Communication

Communication includes both spoken language and non-verbal expressions. Business relationships, and negotiations in particular, are highly dependent on the communication styles of the participants. While an interpreter can help with verbal expressions, success will often depend on your ability to pick up non-verbal cues,

Business Culture

and respond accordingly. Nationals of some countries tend to be very emotional, and relationships and negotiations can get volatile; others rely on very subtle body language to communicate their feelings. It is wise, and may well avoid misunderstandings, to have some idea of the general communication style of a country before you go.

Important Cultural Issues

The cultural issues you will face in your international business dealings will vary from country to country. In some, issues like punctuality and the protocol of business meetings will vary even within the country. Some countries maintain very rigid structures, and you must follow certain rules if you want any hope of success; in others, almost anything goes. There are certain aspects of business relationships where cultural issues become particularly important. Some examples include:

GREETINGS AND COURTESIES

There are a thousand different ways to greet people.

In some countries, businesspeople are very open and informal, while in others, formality is critical and you must always use a person's title when referring to them. Some countries prefer a handshake to greet people, but others shy away from any physical contact. Cultural norms also surround gift giving; some countries have extensive rules and laws defining "gift," limiting their legality, while in others lavish gifts are expected–and necessary.

BUSINESS ETHIC AND FRAMEWORK

The level of formality also changes drastically from

country to country. Some countries, like the United States and Israel, are very informal, and appointments can be made any time; in some cases one can simply walk into a business without an appointment and make a deal. In other countries, such as Switzerland and Germany, there is a much greater degree of formality. Meetings may require weeks or months of preparation with appointments made and confirmed far in advance.

DECISION MAKING

Do you expect to make a sale on your first trip to that

foreign country? In some places, this is possible; people in some countries, like Hong Kong, are more focused on deal-making than in establishing a relationship first. In others, particularly in Latin American countries, even a tentative decision will not be made until a personal relationship is established, and after consensus is reached at all levels of the hierarchy. This could, understandably, take months or even years.

WOMEN

How are women treated in the country in which you wish to do business? In many countries, both sexes are

treated equally; in many others, women simply cannot effectively conduct business with men. Is the way women are regarded in a country "simply cultural" and none of your business, or are fundamental human rights being denied? This remains a touchy subject. It could prove devastating to any business relationship to overlook or ignore this issue–or to enter a relationship unprepared.

MEETINGS

Meetings are a crucial part of doing business. In some countries, meetings are very informal, with constant in-

terruptions and a tone that may seem more like a social gathering. Others prove much more rigid, and you may need to send an agenda including a list of attendees who will be present. In some countries, punctuality is very important, and you must be on time if not somewhat early; in other places, you may be kept waiting for your host for an hour or more.

BUSINESS ATTIRE

Your attire can also have an impact on the success or failure of your foreign endeavor. Appropriate business

attire ranges from very casual as in many businesses in Israel, to extremely formal and subdued, as you will find in Japan. While it is always best to wear clothes in which you feel comfortable, your attire may need to be modified somewhat to suit a foreign environment.

In Summary

To some extent, cultural "faux pas" are unavoidable and are usually laughed off by all concerned. However, they could also lead to a total failure of business purpose and irreparable loss of profitable relationships. If you are aware of another's cultural background and have made an attempt to understand its influences, you will be better equipped to adjust your behavior and expectations without patronizing your foreign associates. When cultures collide, as they inevitably will, the damage can be greatly reduced with knowledge, understanding, and appreciation of what caused the collision.

Emergency!

Lost or Damaged Luggage

No matter what precautions are taken to avoid lost or damaged luggage, it still may happen. Making things worse, an airline's liability for lost or damaged luggage is much less than the actual value. For international flights, airlines still use the basis written at the Warsaw Convention in 1929. The limit is US$9.07 per pound of checked luggage, plus US$400 per passenger for unchecked items (paying a surcharge may increase the liability).

FOR LOST LUGGAGE

- Report the loss immediately to an airline representative, usually found at or near the baggage area.
- Describe your luggage plus any items that are unique, just in case additional identification is needed. A photo of your luggage will help, preferably with a yardstick in the photo to show the size of your luggage.
- Be prepared to insist on some help if the representative seems lax or not willing to help and ask to see a manager if you don't feel you're getting the help you need.
- Many airlines will supply money to buy items such as clothing or toiletries if the items were lost with the luggage.
- Report any luggage not returned after a few days to your insurance company.

FOR DAMAGED LUGGAGE

- Take the damaged luggage to the airline representative in the baggage area.
- Immediately point out all damage.
- Ask for a voucher to repair or replace the luggage.
- Many representatives will try to "depreciate" your luggage and tell you that they do not owe the full value of the luggage. This is a weak argument and they should vouch for the full value of the luggage after some discussion.

Being Arrested

What's that? No chance of you being arrested? Probably not, but the risk exists, particularly when dealing with new cultures. The first rule, should it happen, is not to get angry, which will only make things worse. Explain calmly that you did not mean to break the law; that may be enough. Then again, it may not.

It is important to remember that legal rights change when traveling to another country. In some countries, citizens from the U.S. and Western Europe are advised not to go to public events. Countries at war can always make a military arrest simply because they don't like the way someone looks.

If you do get arrested, here are some tips to remember:
- Do not be rude. Never show disrespect.
- Save your argument until you can deal with someone in authority.

- NEVER attempt to bribe someone. You could only strengthen the case against you. On the other hand, in some countries it is the only way to get out of trouble.
- Get legal help quickly, preferably a consular officer from your country's local embassy or a local lawyer who can resolve any misunderstandings quickly.
- If allowed to make bail, don't skip town. It's not worth the risk that you might get caught.

Auto Accidents

Your local insurance does not necessarily apply in foreign countries, so the coverage may not be as great as some hope. Even for policies that seem to apply to foreign travel, the coverage may be insufficient.

Research supplemental insurance before you go. Check with credit card companies to see what kind of insurance they offer.

Some issues and steps that should be taken when in an accident follow. Keep them handy.
- Get the names of several witnesses.
- Write information about other cars involved in the accident. Write down license numbers, as well as names, addresses, and phone numbers of others involved.
- If in a cab or bus, write down name, address, and phone number of the bus company, and identify the driver. If possible, get as much information about their insurance company as you can on the spot.
- Note the date and time of the accident, as well as the location, including cross streets.
- Write down the name and identification number of the police officer in charge.
- If someone has a camera, have them take as many photos as possible of the location, damage, injuries, and witnesses.
- Have yourself checked by a doctor as soon as possible. Excitement and shock may keep you from feeling the injury at first.
- Do not admit fault, even if you feel you were at fault.
- Remember that procedures that take place in your home country regarding an accident may not apply. Human life or possessions may carry more or less value in any given culture. Losing patience with the "illogic" may only exacerbate your problem.

The Disappearing Hotel Reservation

Two things will virtually guarantee that a hotel reservation will not disappear:
- Get written confirmation and/or locator number when the reservation is made. Agents often misspell names when making reservations, and the confirmation number may be the only way to reference the reservation.
- Review any confirmation notice the hotel sends for correct dates and length of stay. If no notice arrives, call the hotel 48 hours before arrival to verify the reservation.

Sometimes preparation is not enough. A hotel employee might mistakenly erase your reservation. Some-

Emergency!

one will call to cancel their reservation, but the employee will accidentally cancel yours. Sometimes customers will fall victim to overbooking. Whatever the reason, you are without a reservation. What do you do then?

- Stay in the lobby. Inform hotel employees that you will not leave until the problem is resolved. Don't be led into a manger's office where they can negotiate on their terms. If you raise a ruckus, it will disrupt the hotel employees from doing their job and they will have to deal with you.
- Have evidence of the reservation handy. Remind the clerk that you called from the airport.
- Ask if they still have a room available. If not, ask why not. Ask to speak to the manager of the hotel. Explain to the manager your situation. By this point, most hotels will admit their mistake (assuming you have documentation) and will get you a room in their hotel or a reservation in another hotel in the city. If the room is more expensive, ask that the manager pay the added cost.

Avoiding Crime

Violent street crime like muggings and robberies are on the rise all over the world. After people have been the victims of these types of crimes, they often realize they could have prevented the situation through better planning. Some keys points include:

- **Act and dress** Do not appear flamboyant. Avoid flashy dress and jewelry in areas that have a reputation for crime.
- **Avoid dark or empty streets** This goes without saying. If in a dimly lit area with a lot of traffic, walk quickly. If in a dimly lit area with little or no traffic, it may be a good idea to turn around and find another way to go.
- **Don't rely on maps** Street maps don't tell tourists where the dangerous areas are. Inquire of your hotel staff the places to avoid.
- **Hold onto your valuables** Always watch out for pickpockets. It would be wise to invest in a money belt to keep all valuables safe.
- **Avoid scams** If someone offers to give you something if you "follow him," don't go. Use common sense when dealing with people in other countries. The rule "if it sounds too good to be true, it probably is," applies universally.
- **If a street is crowded, it may not be safe** Pickpockets often prowl populated streets because they can run and blend in a crowd so easily.

THEFT

Pickpockets

Pickpockets range from clumsy beginners who can be easily spotted, to professionals who can steal your shoes without you knowing. Obviously, it's the latter for whom to make preparations.

The stereotype of a pickpocket is a young man dressed in black who roams the city streets. In reality, they can be anything: a group of young girls who divert your attention while one among them takes your wallet; an old man who asks questions while lifting your money, or a group of men staging a mock fight to distract you. Always be on the lookout. Some other tips:

- **Invest in a money belt.** Only fools carry their wallet in a back pocket, where it is unprotected. Fanny packs are almost as bad, letting thieves know exactly where you keep your money. If you don't want to use a money belt, put your wallet in an inside pocket with a zipper to close the pocket securely.
- **Don't put all your money in one place.** Everytime you reach in to pull out some cash, you are telling potential thieves where you keep your money.
- **Don't reach for your wallet often.** Beware of signs that read "Be Careful of Pickpockets." When travelers see the sign, they immediately reach for their wallet to make sure it's there, once again letting thieves know exactly where it is stashed.
- **Keep in your pockets only what you can afford to lose.** Remember that if it's on your person, a pickpocket exists who can take it.

Violent Crime

Luckily, crime against travelers usually is of the non-violent variety, but the potential danger still exists. Always be aware of your surroundings. If the locals tell you not to go in a part of the city, heed their advice. They know more than the author of a travel book (even this one).

No matter where you are in a new city, try not to act like a tourist. You'll be easy fodder for robbers and muggers. Also, before trying to pick up a man or woman in a bar, be careful, they may not have the best intentions.

Regional Maps

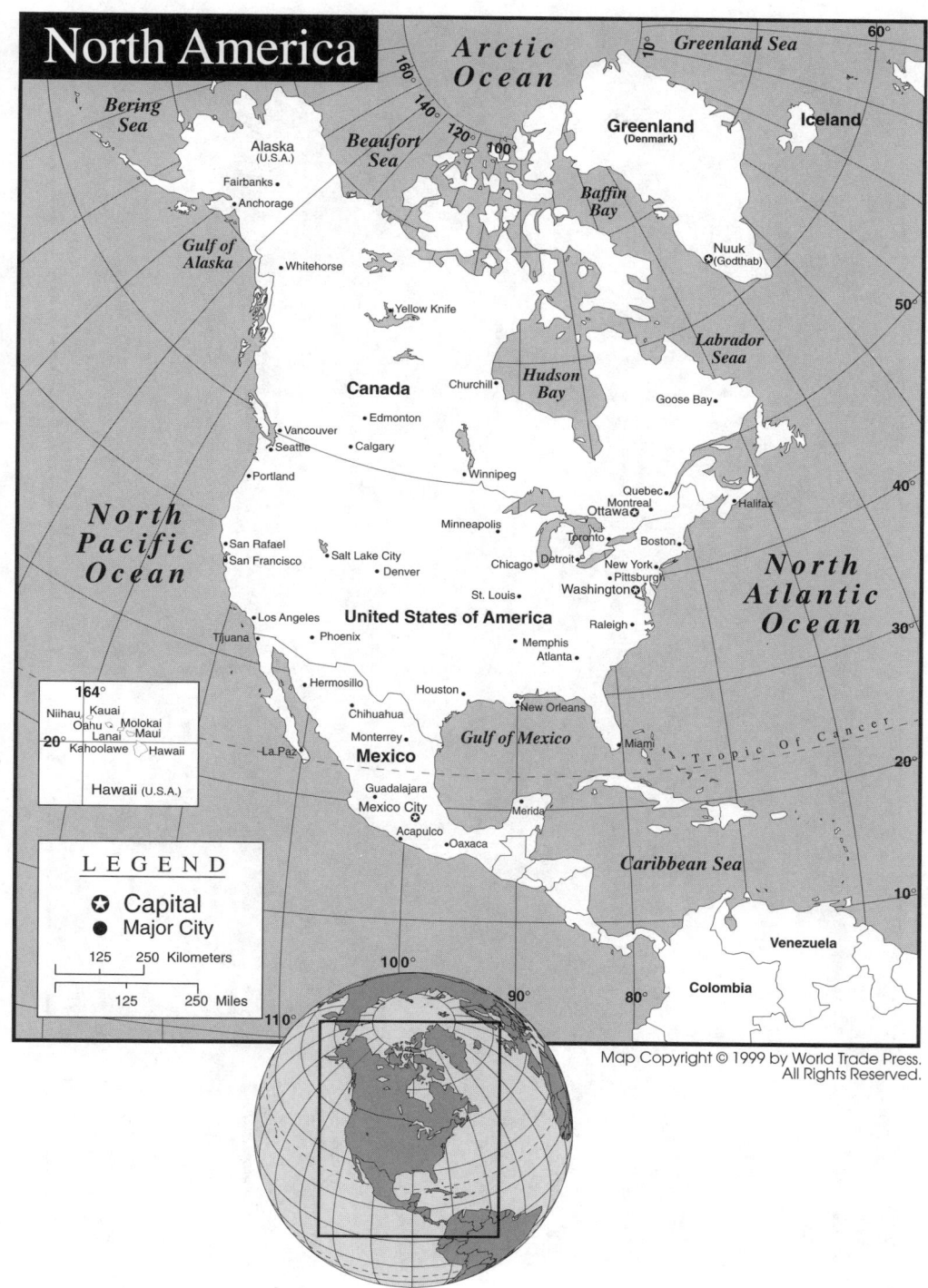

North America

Arctic Ocean

Greenland Sea

Iceland

Bering Sea

Alaska (U.S.A.)

Fairbanks

Anchorage

Beaufort Sea

Greenland (Denmark)

Baffin Bay

Gulf of Alaska

Whitehorse

Nuuk (Godthab)

Yellow Knife

Labrador Seaa

Canada

Churchill

Hudson Bay

Goose Bay

Edmonton

Vancouver

Calgary

Seattle

Portland

Winnipeg

Quebec

Montreal

Ottawa

Halifax

North Pacific Ocean

Minneapolis

Toronto

Boston

San Rafael

Salt Lake City

Chicago

Detroit

New York

San Francisco

Denver

Pittsburgh

St. Louis

Washington

North Atlantic Ocean

Los Angeles

United States of America

Raleigh

Tijuana

Phoenix

Memphis

Atlanta

Hermosillo

Houston

164°

Niihau Kauai

Oahu Molokai

20° Lanai Maui

Kahoolawe Hawaii

Hawaii (U.S.A.)

Chihuahua

New Orleans

Miami

Tropic Of Cancer

Monterrey

Gulf of Mexico

20°

La Paz

Mexico

Guadalajara

Mexico City

Merida

Acapulco

Oaxaca

Caribbean Sea

10°

LEGEND

⊛ Capital

● Major City

125   250 Kilometers

125   250 Miles

100°

90°

80°

Venezuela

Colombia

110°

60°

50°

40°

30°

Regional Maps

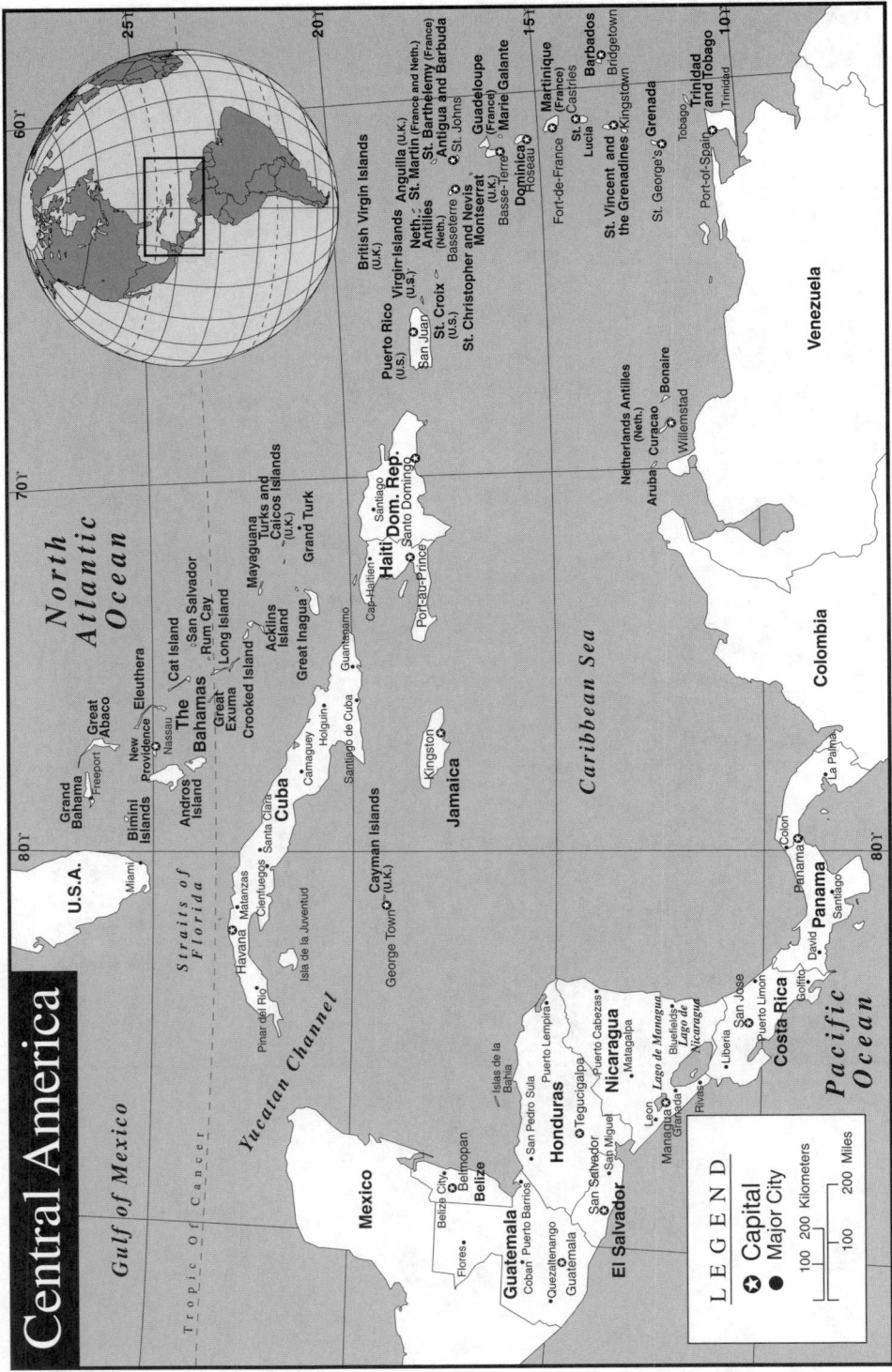

Central America

LEGEND

⊗ Capital
● Major City

100   200 Kilometers
100   200 Miles

South America

Regional Maps

Mexico

Caribbean Sea

Barranquilla
Caracas
Cucuta • San Cristobal
Ciudad Guayana
Georgetown
Paramaribo
Medellin
Venezuela
Guyana
Suriname
French Guiana (France)
Bogota
Boa Vista
Cayenne
Cali
Colombia
Mitu
Macapa

North
Atlantic
Ocean

Equator
Quito
Ecuador
Guayaquil
Iquitos
Fonte Boa
Manaus
Santarem
Belem
Sao Luis
Piura
Peru
Imperatriz
Teresina
Fortaleza
Trujillo
Rio Branco
Porto Velho
Brazil
Natal
Lima
Porto Nacional
Recife
Ica
Cusco
Bolivia
Aracaju
Salvador

South
Pacific
Ocean

Arequipa
Trinidad
Cuiaba
Brasilia
La Paz
Goiania
Cochabamba
Santa Cruz
Arica
Sucre
Belo Horizonte
Vit ria

Tropic Of Capricorn

Antofagasta
Paraguay
Rio de Janeiro
Sao Paulo
San Miguel de Tucuman
Asuncion
Curitiba
Chile
Resistencia
Florianopolis
Cordoba
Porto Alegre
Rosario
Salto
Mendoza
Uruguay
Valparaiso
Buenos Aires
Montevideo
Santiago
Argentina
Concepcion
Mar del Plata
Bahia Blanca
Valdivia
San Carlos de Bariloche
Comodoro Rivadavia

South
Atlantic
Ocean

80j 70j 60j 50j 10j 0j 10j 20j 30j 40j 50j 80j 30j 20j 10j

LEGEND

✪ Capital
● Major City

250　500 Kilometers

250　500 Miles

Falkland
Islands (U.K.)

South
Georgia
Island (U.K.)

Regional Maps

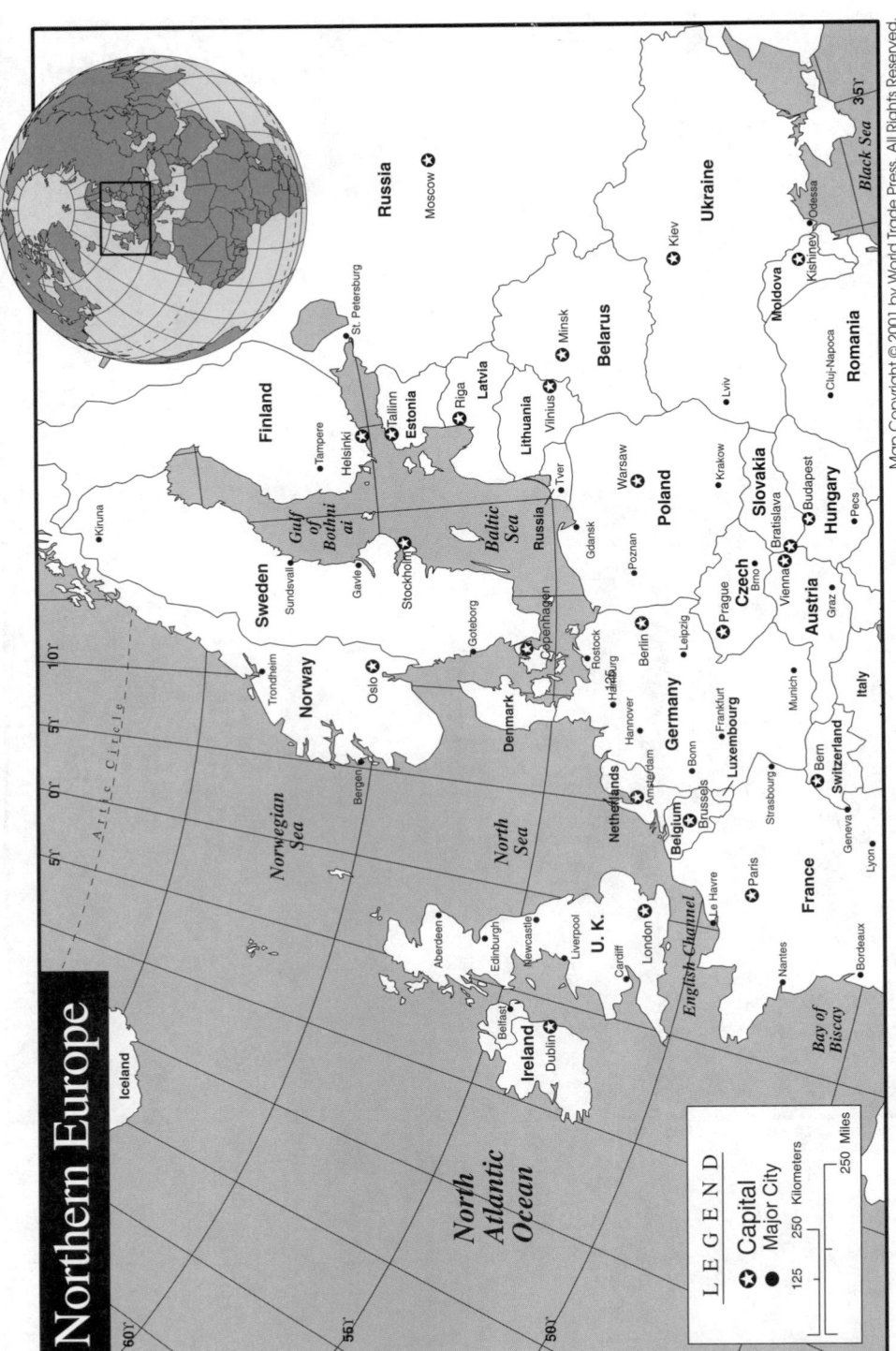

Northern Europe

LEGEND
✪ Capital
● Major City

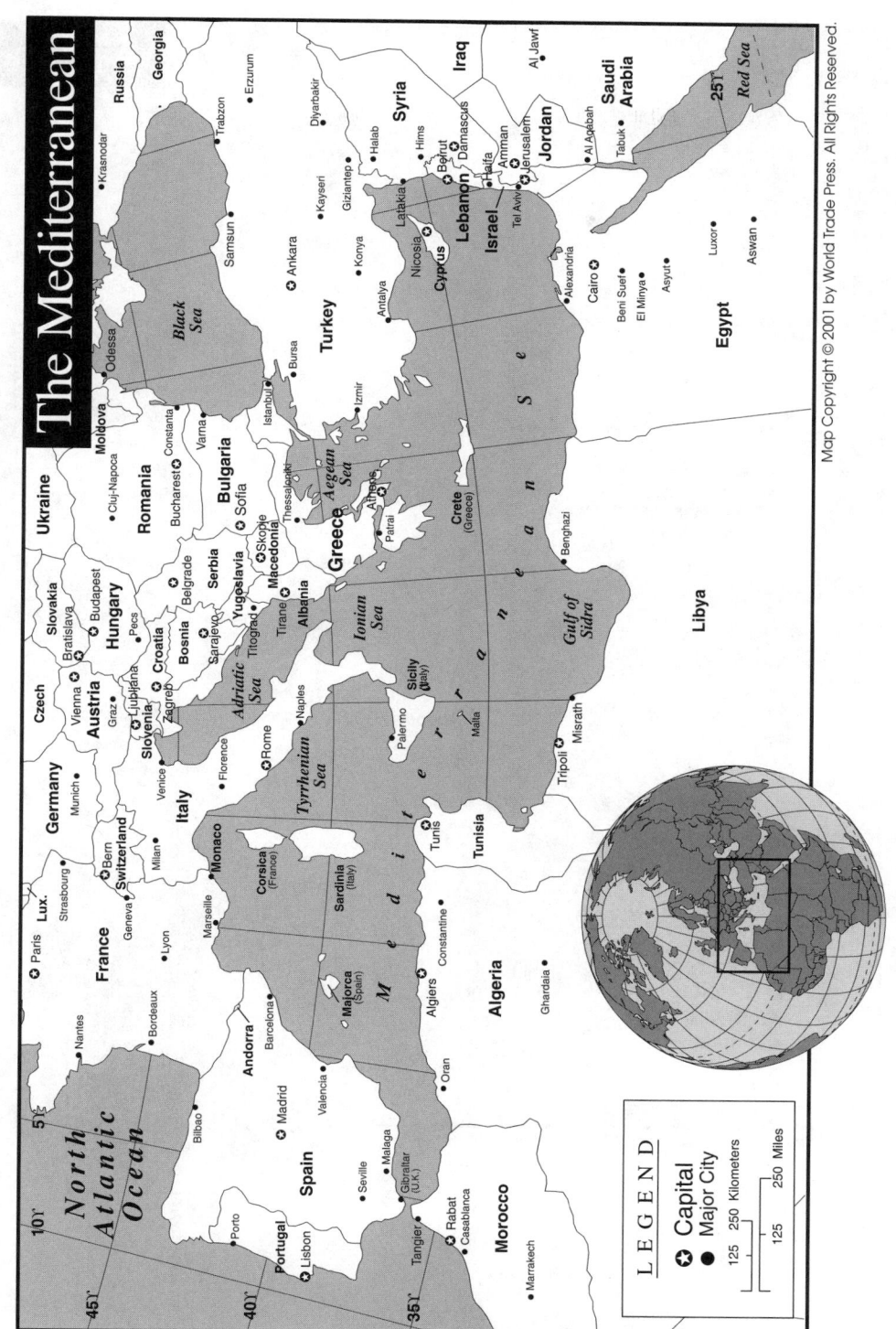

The Mediterranean

Regional Maps

Regional Maps

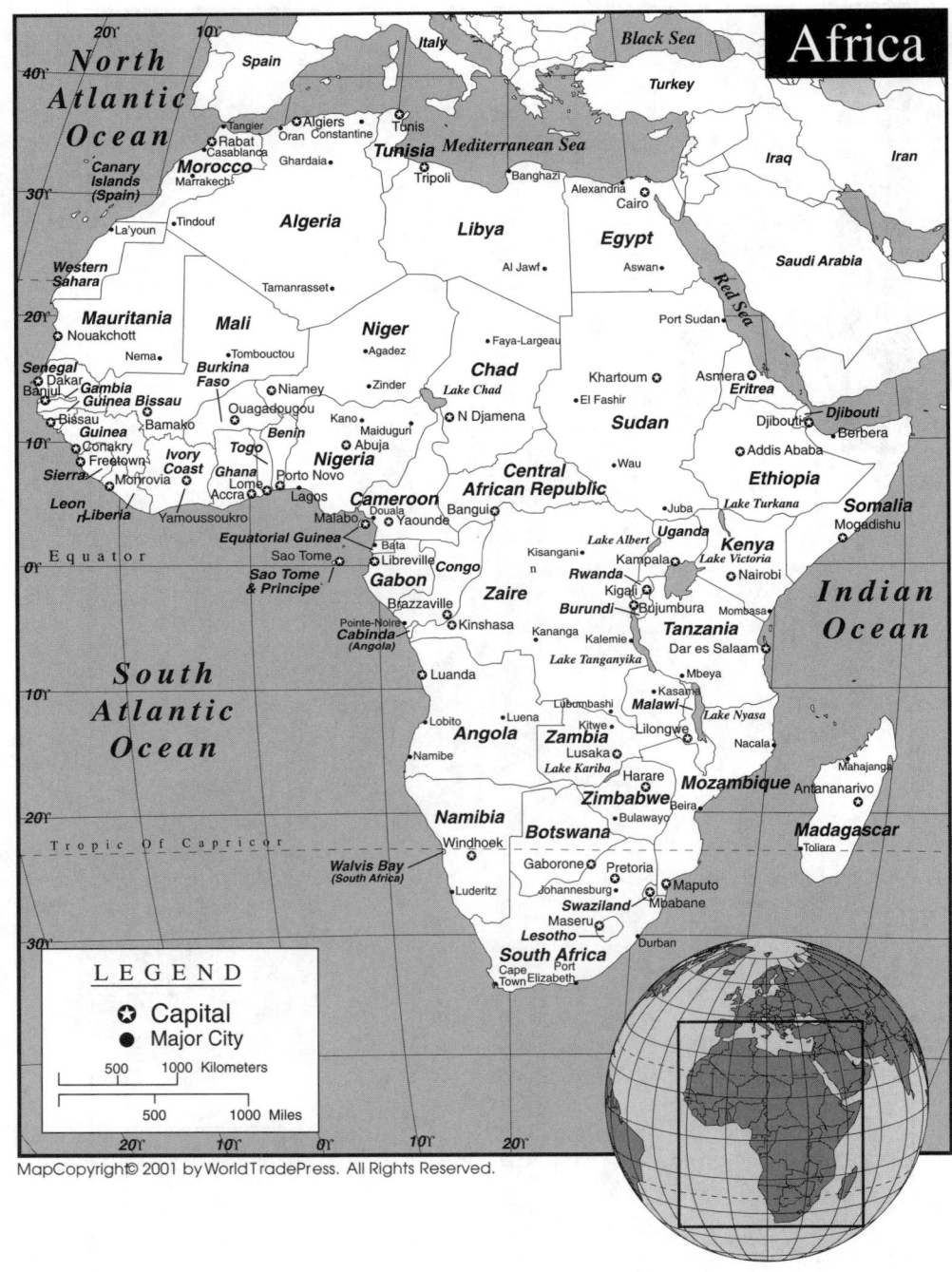

Africa

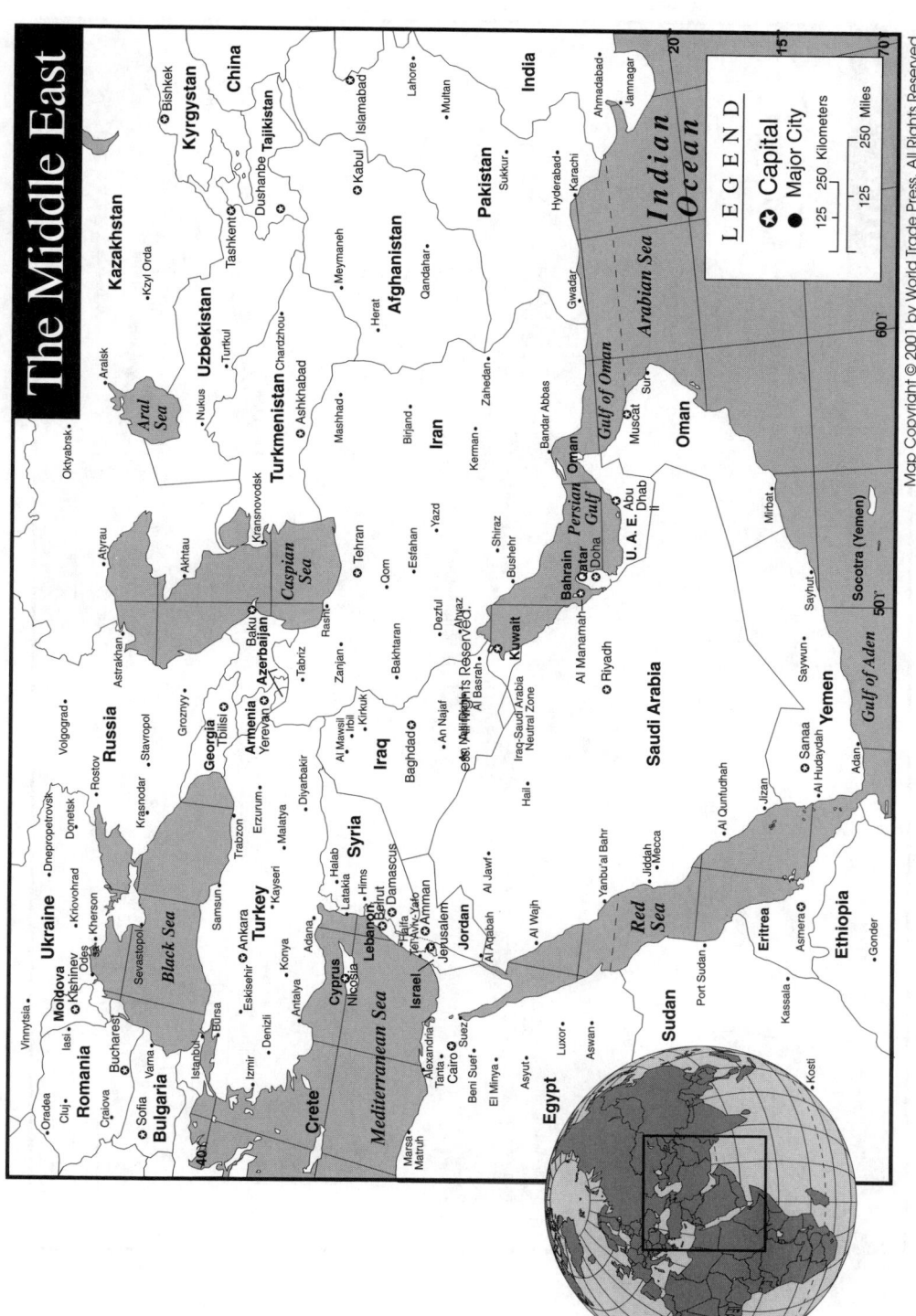

The Middle East

LEGEND
✪ Capital
● Major City

125   250 Kilometers
125   250 Miles

Regional Maps

Regional Maps

Central Asia

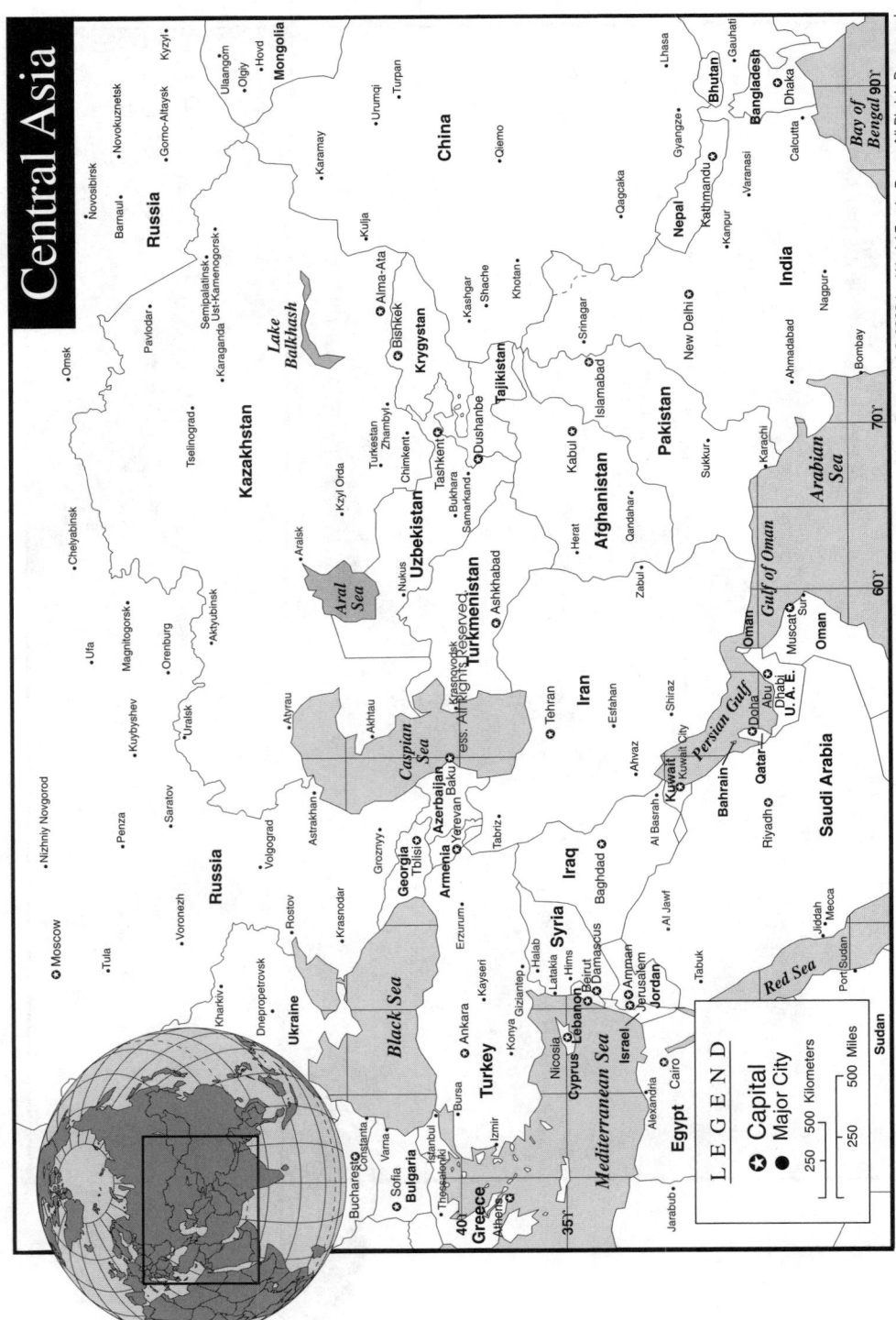

LEGEND

⊙ Capital
● Major City

250 500 Kilometers
250 500 Miles

Regional Maps

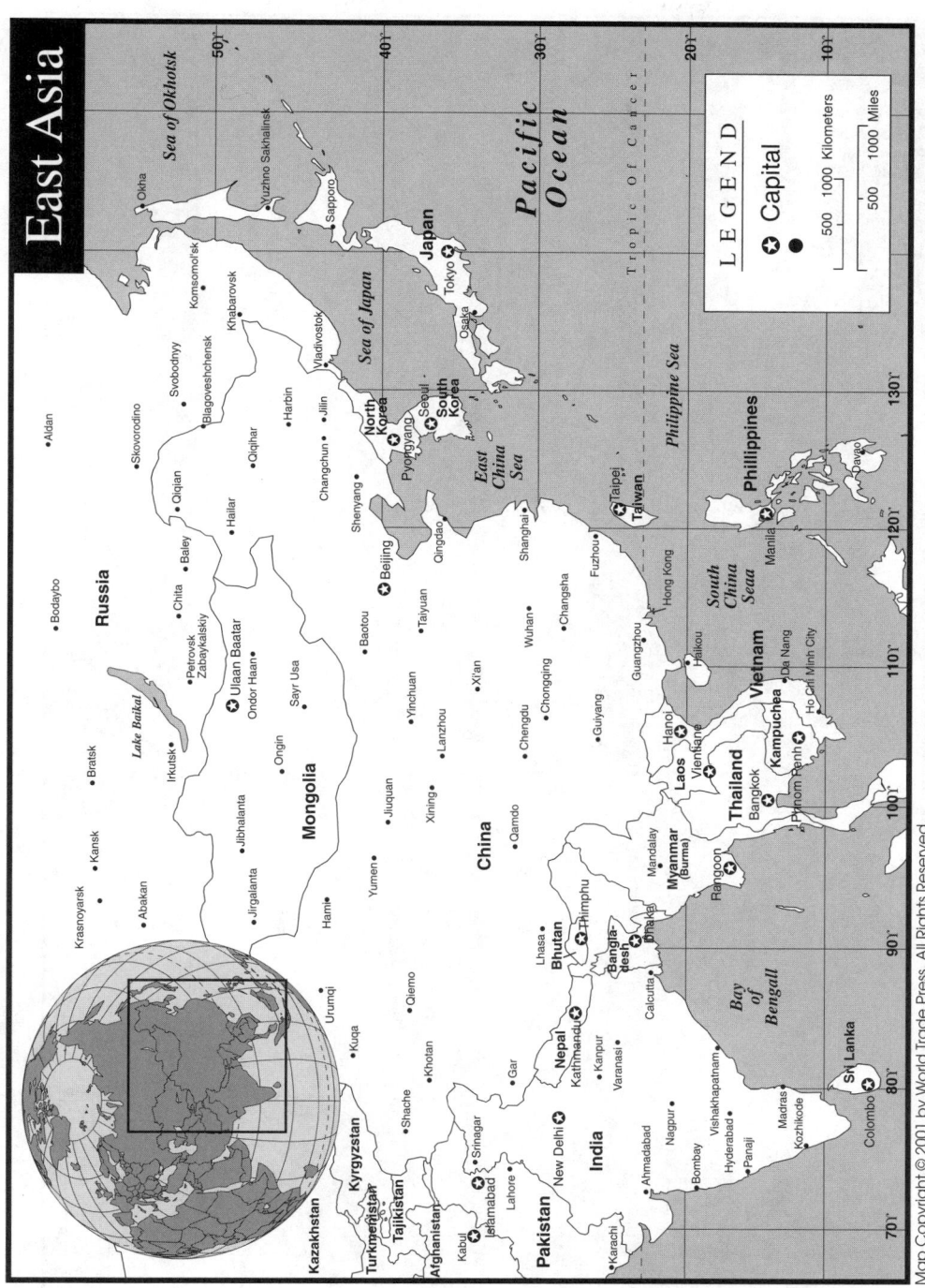

East Asia

LEGEND

⊕ Capital
●

500 1000 Kilometers
500 1000 Miles

Sea of Okhotsk

Pacific Ocean

Tropic of Cancer

Sea of Japan

Japan
Tokyo ⊕
Osaka
Sapporo
Okha
Yuzhno Sakhalinsk

Aldan
Bodaybo
Russia
Skovorodino
Svobodny
Blagoveshchensk
Khabarovsk
Komsomol'sk
Vladivostok
Harbin
Qiqihar
Jilin
Changchun

North Korea ⊕ Pyongyang
South Korea ⊕ Seoul

East China Sea

Shenyang
Beijing ⊕
Qingdao
Shanghai
Fuzhou

Philippine Sea

Krasnoyarsk
Kansk
Bratsk
Abakan
Lake Baikal
Irkutsk
Petrovsk Zabaykalskiy
Chita
Baley
Hailar
Ulaan Baatar ⊕
Ondor Haan
Sayr Usa
Ongin
Jibhalanta
Jirgalanta
Mongolia
Baotou
Taiyuan
Yinchuan
Lanzhou
Xi'an

Taipei ⊕
Taiwan

Phillippines
Manila ⊕
Davao

Urumqi
Kuqa
Hami
Yumen
Jiuquan
Xining
China
Qamdo
Chengdu
Chongqing
Guiyang
Wuhan
Changsha

Guangzhou
Hong Kong
Haikou

South China Sea

Vietnam
Hanoi
Da Nang
Ho Chi Minh City

Kazakhstan
Kyrgyzstan
Turkmenistan
Tajikistan
Afghanistan
Qiemo
Khotan
Shache
Gar
Nepal ⊕ Kathmandu
Bhutan ⊕ Thimphu
Lhasa
Kabul
Srinagar
Islamabad ⊕
Lahore
Pakistan
New Delhi ⊕
Kanpur
Varanasi
India
Ahmadabad
Bombay
Nagpur
Hyderabad
Panaji
Madras
Kozhikode
Vishakhapatnam
Calcutta
Bangla- desh ⊕ Dhaka

Bay of Bengal

Sri Lanka
Colombo ⊕

Myanmar (Burma) ⊕ Rangoon
Mandalay

Laos Vientiane
Thailand Bangkok ⊕
Kampuchea ⊕ Phnom Penh

Karachi

50°
40°
30°
20°
10°
130°
120°
110°
100°
90°
80°
70°

Regional Maps

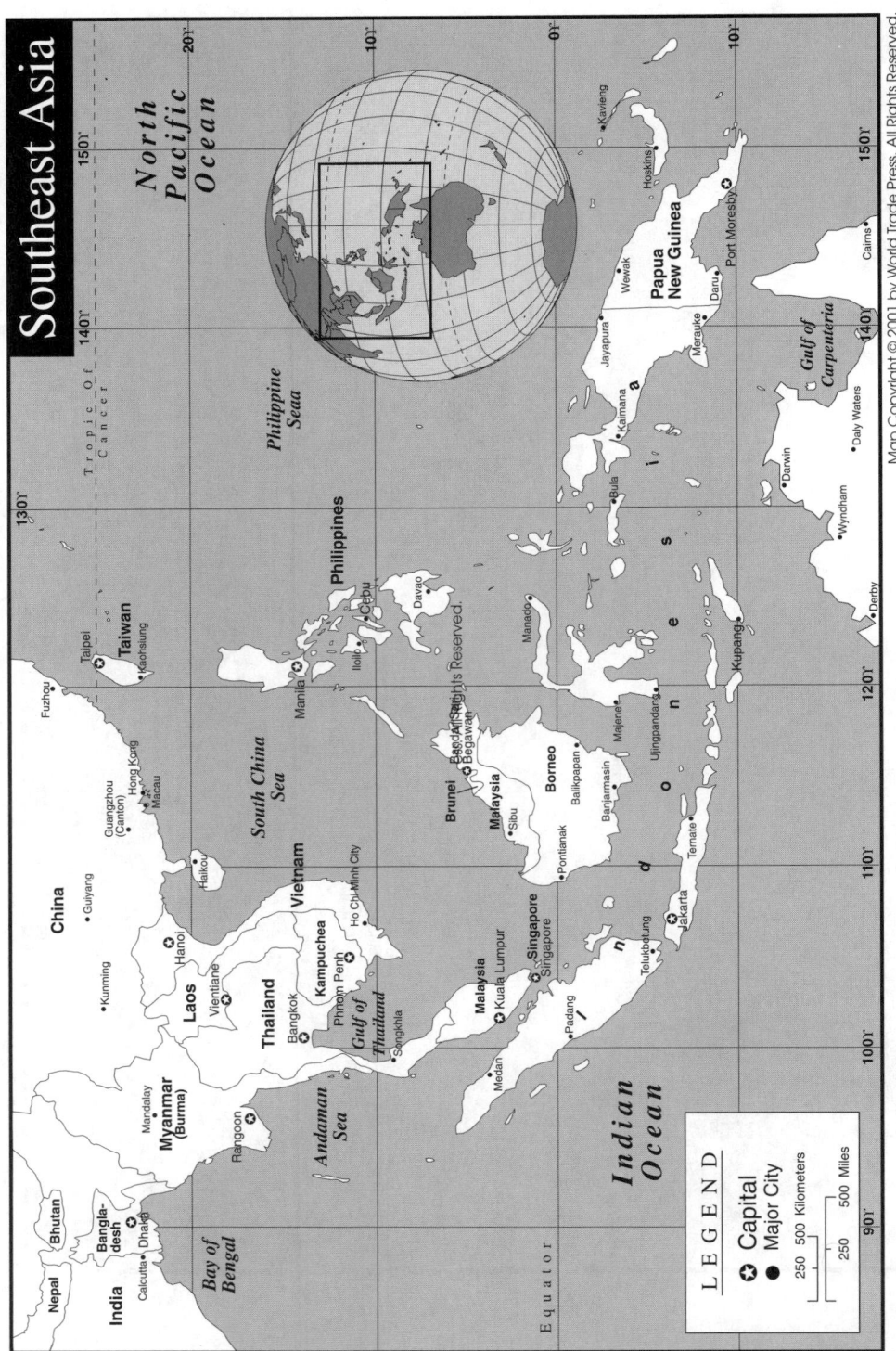

Southeast Asia

Regional Maps

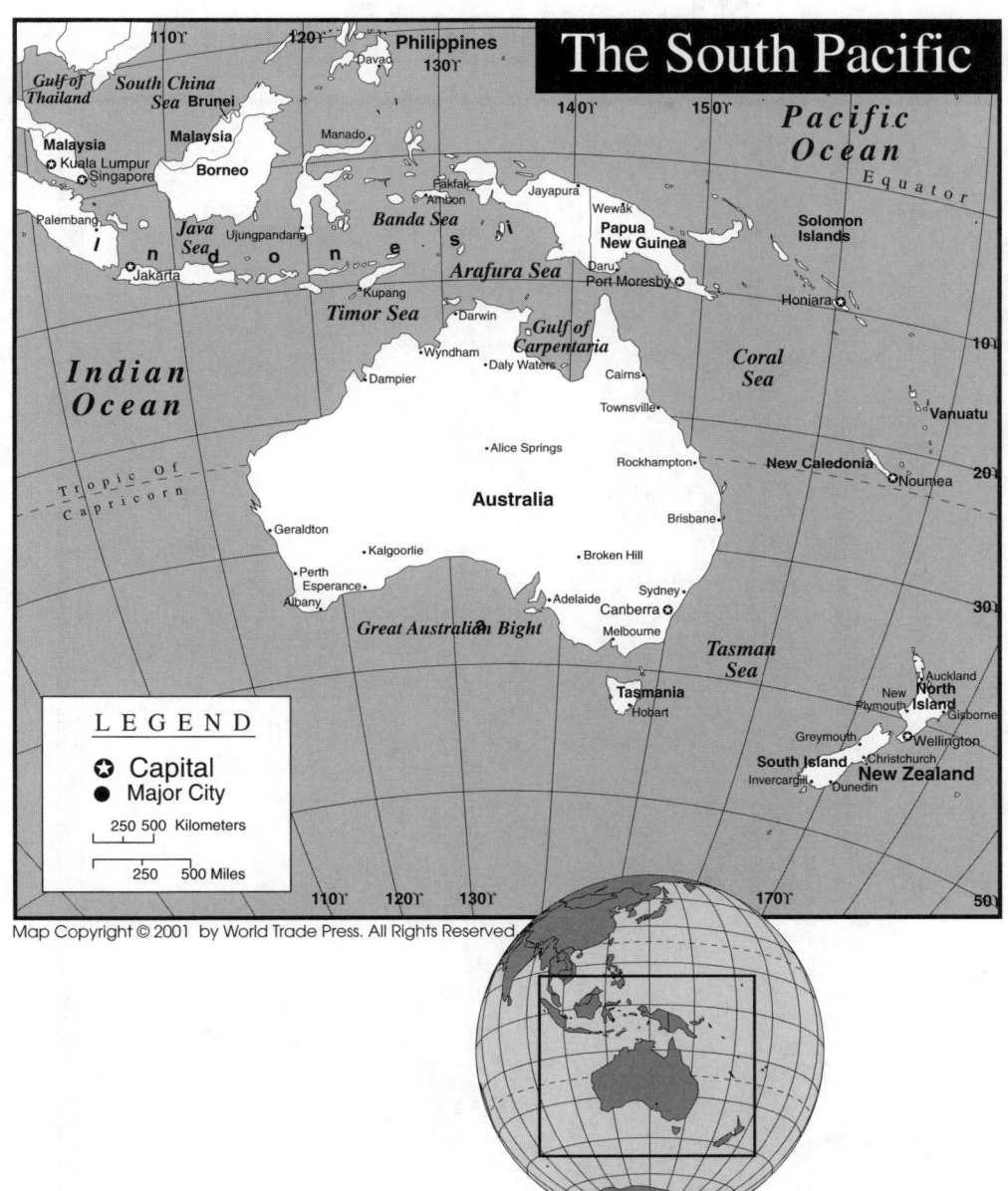

The South Pacific

Time Zone Map

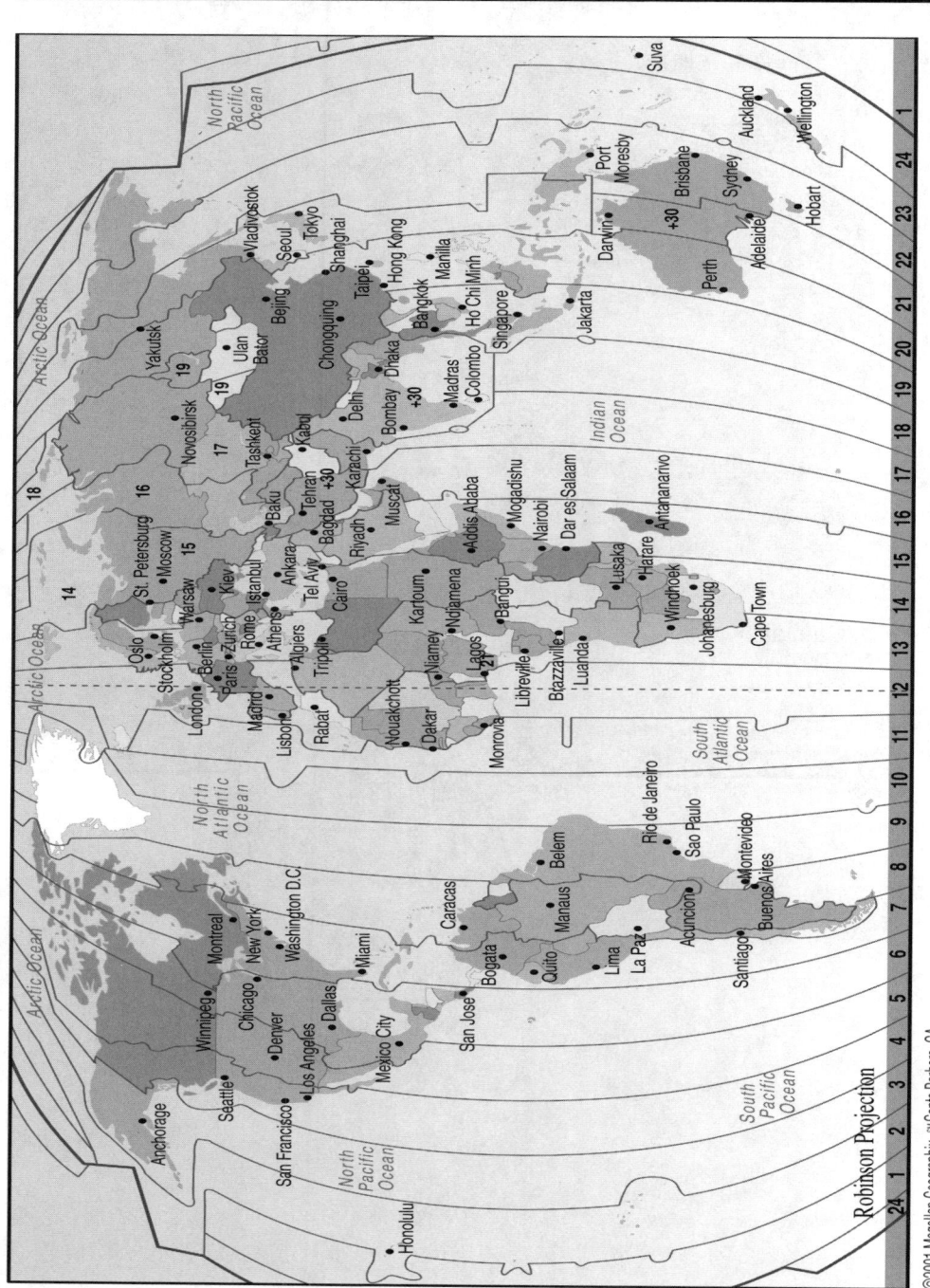

Robinson Projection

©2001 Magellan Geographix ℠ Santa Barbara, CA

International Dialing Guide

The introductory matter and table in this section provides specific information for dialing direct to over 400 cities in nearly 200 countries and territories around the world. This material has been designed to be useful for anyone, regardless of the country of origin or country of destination of their call.

Countries and territories are listed alphabetically. For each, the country dialing code, the capital city (when applicable), the city (or regional) code, and time zone information is provided. For some countries more than one city, with corresponding city codes and time zones, are listed. The capital city is indicated with a ✪.

HOW TO DIAL INTERNATIONAL CALLS

Direct dialing international calls from most countries has become quite easy in the past decade. The typical international call simply consists of dialing a series of numbers in sequence as follows:

1. The international direct dialing prefix (IDD),
2. The country code,
3. The city code, and
4. The local telephone number.

If you are calling from the United States, the IDD is 011. The IDD differs from country to country. For Brazil it is 00. Some countries do not allow direct dialing for international calls but require them to be placed through the operator. The table on the next page lists IDD prefixes for most countries that allow international direct dialing. You may need to wait for a dial tone after dialing the IDD.

The IDD is followed by the country code (shown in square brackets [ ] in the table starting on page 46), the city code or area code (if there is one) (shown in parentheses ( ) in the table starting on page 46), and the local telephone number. When city codes are not required, a * appears in place of the city code in our table.

If you are calling to other countries or territories that use the same country code as the country you are calling from, you will normally not use the international IDD prefix (the IDD prefix is sometimes called the "international access code"). For example, the United States, Canada, and many Caribbean Islands all use the country code [1], so calls made between countries within this zone will be dialed as regular long-distance calls and not as international calls.

Example: To call Chicago from London, U.K., dial:
010 + [1] + (312) + (local telephone number).
(The U.K. international access code is 010, the country code for the U.S. is [1] and the area code for Chicago is (312).)

Example: To call Sydney, Australia from Denmark, dial:
00 + [61] + (2) + (local telephone number).
(The Denmark international access code is 00, the country code for Australia is [61] and the city code for Sydney is (2).)

Example: To call New Delhi, India from Hong Kong, dial:
001 + [91] + (11) + (local telephone number).

(The Hong Kong international access code is 001, the country code for India is [91], and the city code for New Delhi is (11).

Example: To call Hong Kong from the United States, dial:
011 + [852] + (local telephone number)
(The U.S. international access code is 011, the country code for Hong Kong is [852], and there are no city codes.)

Example: To call Vancouver, British Columbia from the United States, dial:
1 + (604) + (the local number).
(The prefix 1 is used for long-distance calls within Canada, the US, and the Caribbean. (604) is the area code for British Columbia)

Example: To call any point in the Dominican Republic from the United States, dial:
1+ (809) + (local telephone number)

(The prefix 1 is used for long-distance calls within Canada, the US, and the Caribbean and (809) is the area code for the Dominican Republic.)

International Direct Dialing (IDD) Prefixes

Algeria	00*	Kuwait	00
Argentina	00	Lebanon	00
Australia	0011, (fax calls 0015)	Liberia	00
Austria	00, 900 (Vienna)	Libya	00
Bahamas	001	Liechtenstein	00
Bahrian	0	Luxembourg	00
Belgium	00	Macau	00
Bolivia	00	Madagascar	00
Brazil	00	Malawi	101
Bulgaria	00	Malaysia	00
Cameroon	00	Mexico	00
Canada	011	Monaco	00
Chile	00	Morocco	00*
China (PRC)	00	Namibia	09
Colombia	90	Netherlands	00
Congo, Democratic Rep. of (formerly Zaire)	00	Netherlands Antilles	00
Costa Rica	00	New Zealand	00
Cuba	119	Nicaragua	00
Cuba (Guantánamo Bay)	00	Niger	00
Cyprus	00	Nigeria	009
Czech Republic	00	Norway	00
Denmark	00	Pakistan	00
Dominican Republic	011	Panama	0
Ecuador	00	Peru	00
Egypt	00	Phillipines	00
El Salvador	0	Poland	0*0
Finland	00, 990, 994, 999	Portugal	00
France	00	Qatar	0
French Antilles	00	Russia	8*10
Germany	00	Saudi Arabia	00
Greece	00	Senegal	00
Guam	011	Singapore	001
Guatemala	00	Slovakia	00
Guyana	001	Somalia	19
Haiti	00	South Africa	09 or 091
Honduras	00	Spain	00
Hong Kong	001	Sri Lanka	00
Hungary	00	Sweden	00
Iceland	00	Switzerland	00
India	00	Taiwan	002
Indonesia	001, 008	Thailand	001 (except to Malaysia 007)
Iran	00	Tunisia	00
Iraq	00	Turkey	00
Ireland	00	United Arab Emirates	00
Israel	00	United Kingdom	00
Italy	00	United States of America	011
Ivory Coast	00	Venezuela	00
Jamaica	011	Vietnam	00
Japan	001	Yugoslavia	99
Korea, South	001	Zambia	00
Korea, North	00	Zimbabwe	00

* Wait for dial tone after dialing these international access codes

TIME ZONES

Time differences, that is, how many hours the given city or country is ahead or behind the four major U.S. time zones and Greenwich Mean Time, have been given in the right-hand columns in the following table. All cities in a given country or territory are in one time zone unless a †† symbol appears next to the country name. Find the city you wish to call, and the column which corresponds to the time zone you are calling from. Add or subtract the number shown to your own current time to find the time in that city.

Example: You are calling France from New York. +6 appears in the EST (Eastern Standard Time) column for France, which means France is 6 hours *ahead* of New York. Thus, when it is 9 a.m. Monday in New York, it is 3:00 p.m. Monday in France.

Example: You are calling Japan from San Francisco. +17 appears in the PST (Pacific Standard Time) column for Japan, which means Japan is 17 hours ahead of San Francisco. Thus, when it is 4:00 p.m. Monday in San Francisco, it is 9:00 a.m. Tuesday in Japan.

DAYLIGHT SAVINGS TIME

The time differences given are based on Standard Time, and may require adjustment if either you or the country you are calling is following Daylight Savings Time (DST) at the time you place the call.

Most of the United States is in DST from the first Sunday in April until the last Sunday in October. Many, but not all, countries north of the Tropic of Cancer also use DST during a similar period. DST is not used in most tropical areas. Countries in the southern hemisphere that follow a daylight savings period normally use it from mid-March through mid-October, their summertime.

The dates used for DST vary considerably from country to country and even from year to year. Also, in a few larger countries like the United States, Australia, and Brazil, some regions of the country may follow daylight savings while others do not.

If you are in DST, and the country you are calling is not, *subtract* one hour from the time shown. If you are in Standard Time, and the country you are calling is currently following DST, *add* one hour to the time shown. If you and the country you are calling are both using DST the time difference shown in the table will be correct.

Example: You are calling Japan from San Francisco in June. California follows DST in the summer, while Japan does not. The PST (Pacific Standard Time) column for Japan shows +17. Subtract one hour from this, to find that Japan is 16 hours ahead of San Francisco. Thus, when it is 4:00 p.m. Monday in San Francisco, it is 8:00 a.m. Tuesday in Japan.

FOR FURTHER INFORMATION

Listed information was current as of February 1999. City codes and dialing systems are changing rapidly as the need for more telephone numbers increases worldwide.

For codes not listed here, or for the current time anywhere in the world, call your international operator. In the United States, dial 00 for AT&T information. AT&T publishes an International Dialing Guide that is updated regularly and is free on request.

There are some resources available on the Internet. World time listed by country is at www.globaltimeclock.com. World time and dialing codes is at www.whitepages.com.au/time.shtml. Type in from where you are calling and to where you want to dial—time and code will then appear. Local Times Around the World is at http://www.hilink.com.au/times/. A list of International Dialing Codes is at http://kropla.com/dialcode.htm, and the AmeriCom Long Distance Area Decoder at http://www.xmission.com/~americom/aclookup.html will allow you to look up both U.S. and international country codes, city codes, and area codes.

International Dialing Guide

International Dialing Codes

Country	Country Code	City/Area Codes	Hours ahead or behind: EST	CST	MST	PST	GMT
Afghanistan	[93]	✪Kabul *	+9₁/₂	+10₁/₂	+11₁/₂	12₁/₂	+4₁/₂
Albania	[355]	✪Tiranë (42)	+6	+7	+8	+9	+1
Algeria	[213]	✪Algiers (2)	+6	+7	+8	+9	+1
American Samoa	[684]	✪Pago Pago *	-6	-5	-4	-3	-11
Andorra	[376]	✪Andorra la Vella *	+6	+7	+8	+9	+1
Angola	[244]	✪Luanda (2)	+6	+7	+8	+9	+1
Anguilla	[1]	✪ The Valley (264) **	+1	+2	+3	+4	-4
Antigua & Barbuda	[1]	✪St. John's (268) **	+1	+2	+3	+4	-4
Argentina††	[54]	✪Buenos Aires (11) Cordoba (351) Mendoza (361) Rosario (341)	+2	+3	+4	+5	-3
Armenia	[374]	✪Yerevan (2)	+8	+9	+10	+11	+3
Aruba	[297]	✪ Oranjestad (8)**	+1	+2	+3	+4	-4
Australia††	[61]	✪Canberra (2)	+15	+16	+17	+18	+10
		Adelaide (8)	+14₁/₂	+15₁/₂	+16₁/₂	+17₁/₂	+9₁/₂
		Brisbane (7)	+15	+16	+17	+18	+10
		Melbourne (3)	+15	+16	+17	+18	+10
		Perth (8)	+13	+14	+15	+16	+8
		Sydney (2)	+15	+16	+17	+18	+10
Austria	[43]	✪Vienna (1) Innsbruck (512) Salzburg (662)	+6	+7	+8	+9	+1
Azerbaijan	[994]	✪Baku (12)	+8	+9	+10	+11	+3
Bahamas	[1]	✪Nassau (242) **	0	+1	+2	+3	-5
Bahrain	[973]	✪Manama *	+8	+9	+10	+11	+3
Bangladesh	[880]	✪Dhaka (2) Khulna (41)	+11	+12	+13	+14	+6
Barbados	[1]	✪Bridgetown (246) **	+1	+2	+3	+4	-4
Belarus	[375]	✪Minsk (172)	+7	+8	+9	+10	+2
Belgium	[32]	✪Brussels (2) Antwerp (3) Brugge (50) Ghent (9) Liege (4)	+6	+7	+8	+9	+1
Belize	[501]	✪Belmopan (8)	-1	0	+1	+2	-6
Benin	[229]	✪Porto-Novo *	+6	+7	+8	+9	+1
Bermuda	[1]	✪Hamilton (441)**	+1	+2	+3	+4	-4
Bhutan	[975]	✪Thimphu *	+11	+12	+13	+14	+6

Country	Country Code	City/Area Codes	Hours ahead or behind: EST	CST	MST	PST	GMT
Bolivia	[591]	✪La Paz (2)	+1	+2	+3	+4	-4
		✪Sucre (64)					
		Cochabamba (42)					
		Santa Cruz (3)					
Bosnia & Herzegovina	[387]	✪Sarajevo (71)	+6	+7	+8	+9	+1
Botswana	[267]	✪Gaborone	+7	+8	+9	+10	+2
		Serowe (430)					
Brazil††	[55]	✪Brasilia (61)	+2	+3	+4	+5	-3
		Belém (91)					
		Belo Horizonte (31)					
		Curitiba (41)					
		Manaus (92)					
		Recife (81)					
		Rio de Janeiro (21)					
		Salvador (71)					
		Sao Paulo (11)					
Brunei	[673]	✪Bandar Seri Begawan (2)	+13	+14	+15	+16	+8
Bulgaria	[359]	✪Sofia (2)	+7	+8	+9	+10	+2
		Varna (52)					
Burkina Faso	[226]	✪Ouagadougou *	+5	+6	+7	+8	0
Burundi	[257]	✪Bujumbura (2)	+7	+8	+9	+10	+2
Cambodia	[855]	✪Phnom Penh (23)	+12	+13	+14	+15	+7
Cameroon	[237]	✪Yaoundé *	+6	+7	+8	+9	+1
Canada††	[1]	✪Ottawa, ON (613)	0	+1	+2	+3	-5
		Calgary, AB (403)	-2	-1	0	+1	-7
		Edmonton,AB (403)	-2	-1	0	+1	-7
		Fredericton, NB (506)	+1	+2	+3	+4	-4
		Halifax, NS (902)	+1	+2	+3	+4	-4
		London, ON (519)	0	+1	+2	+3	-5
		Montreal, PQ (514)	0	+1	+2	+3	-5
		Quebec City, PQ (418)	0	+1	+2	+3	-5
		Regina, SK (306)	-1	0	+1	+2	-6
		Saskatoon, SK (306)	-2	-1	0	+1	-7
		St. John's, NF (709)	+1 1/2	+2 1/2	+3 1/2	+4 1/2	-3 1/2
		Toronto, ON Metro (416)	0	+1	+2	+3	-5
		Toronto Vicinity (905)	0	+1	+2	+3	-5
		Vancouver, BC (604)	-3	-2	-1	0	-8
		Victoria, BC (250)	-3	-2	-1	0	-8
		Winnipeg, MB (204)	-1	0	+1	+2	-6

✪ Capital city   †† More than one time zone in this country.
* City codes not required in this country   ** This city code used for entire country or territory.
EST = US Eastern Standard Time   CST = US Central Standard Time
MST = US Mountain Standard Time   PST = US Pacific Standard Time
UTC = Universal Time Coordinated (Greenwich, England)

International Dialing Guide

International Dialing Guide

Country	Country Code	City/Area Codes	Hours ahead or behind: EST	CST	MST	PST	GMT
Cape Verde Islands	[238]	✪Praia *	+4	+5	+6	+7	-1
Cayman Islands	[1]	✪George Town (345) **	0	+1	+2	+3	-5
Central African Rep.	[236]	✪Bangui (6 digit numbers)	+6	+7	+8	+9	+1
Chad	[235]	✪N'Djamena (51)	+6	+7	+8	+9	+1
Chagos Archipelago	[246]	✪Diego Garcia (9)	+10	+11	+12	+13	+5
Chile	[56]	✪Santiago (2) Concepcion (41) Valparaiso (32)	+1	+2	+3	+4	-4
China, People's Republic	[86]	✪Beijing (10) Guangzhou (20) Harbin (451) Nanjing (25) Nanjing Fujian (596) Shanghai (21) Shenzhen (755) Tianjin (22); Wuhan (27) Xiamen (592); Xian (29)	+13	+14	+15	+16	+8
Colombia	[57]	✪Bogota (1) Barranquilla (58) Cali (2); Medellin (4)	0	+1	+2	+3	-5
Comoros	[269]	✪Moroni*	+8	+9	+10	+11	+3
Congo, Dem. Rep. of	[243]	✪Kinshasa (12)	+6	+7	+8	+9	+1
Congo	[242]	✪Brazzaville *	+6	+7	+8	+9	+1
Cook Islands	[682]	✪Avarua*	-5	-4	-3	-2	-10
Costa Rica	[506]	✪San José *	-1	0	+1	+2	-6
Côte d'Ivoire	[225]	✪Yamoussoukro *	+5	+6	+7	+8	0
Croatia	[385]	✪Zagreb (1); Split (21)	+6	+7	+8	+9	+1
Cuba	[53]	✪Havana (7)	0	+1	+2	+3	-5
Cyprus	[357]	✪Nicosia (2)	+7	+8	+9	+10	+2
Czech Republic	[420]	✪Prague (2)	+6	+7	+8	+9	+1
Denmark	[45]	✪Copenhagen *	+6	+7	+8	+9	+1
Djibouti	[253]	✪Djibouti *	+8	+9	+10	+11	+3
Dominica	[1]	✪Roseau (767) **	+1	+2	+3	+4	-4
Dominican Republic	[1]	✪Santo Domingo (809) **	+1	+2	+3	+4	-4
Ecuador	[593]	✪Quito (2) Guayaquil (4)	0	+1	+2	+3	-5
Egypt	[20]	✪Cairo (2) Alexandria (3) Al Hada (3); Port Said (66)	+7	+8	+9	+10	+2
El Salvador	[503]	✪San Salvador *	-1	0	+1	+2	-6
Equatorial Guinea	[240]	✪Malabo (9)	+6	+7	+8	+9	+1
Estonia	[372]	✪Tallinn (2)	+7	+8	+9	+10	+2

Country	Country Code	City/Area Codes	Hours ahead or behind:				
			EST	CST	MST	PST	GMT
Ethiopia	[251]	✪Addis Ababa (1)	+8	+9	+10	+11	+3
Faeroe Islands	[298]	✪Tórshavn *	+5	+6	+7	+8	0
Falkland Islands	[500]	✪Stanley* (all points 5 digits)	+1	+2	+3	+4	-4
Fiji	[679]	✪Suva *	+17	+18	+19	+20	+12
Finland	[358]	✪Helsinki (9)	+7	+8	+9	+10	+2
France	[33]	✪Paris (1)	+6	+7	+8	+9	+1
		Bordeaux (556)					
		Grenoble (476)					
		Le Havre (235)					
		Lyon (562)					
		Marseille (491)					
		Nantes (240) (251)					
		Nice (493)					
		Rouen (235)					
		Strasbourg (388)					
		Toulouse (5)					
French Antilles	[596]	Martinique*	+1	+2	+3	+4	-4
French Guiana	[594]	✪Cayenne *	+2	+3	+4	+5	-3
French Polynesia††	[689]	✪Papeete, Tahiti *	-5	-4	-3	-2	-10
Gabon	[241]	✪Libreville *	+6	+7	+8	+9	+1
Gambia	[220]	✪Banjul *	+5	+6	+7	+8	0
Georgia	[995]	✪Tbilisi (32)	+8	+9	+10	+11	+3
Germany	[49]	✪Berlin (30)	+6	+7	+8	+9	+1
		Bonn (228); Bremen (421)					
		Cologne (221)					
		Dresden (351)					
		Dusseldorf (211)					
		Essen (201)					
		Frankfurt am Main (69)					
		Frankfurt Oder (335)					
		Freiburg (761)					
		Freiburg Elb (4779)					
		Hamburg (40)					
		Hannover (511)					
		Leipzig (341)					
		Munich (89)					
		Postdam (331)					
		Stuttgart (711)					
		Würzburg (931)					
Ghana	[233]	✪Accra (21)	+5	+6	+7	+8	0

✪ Capital city   †† More than one time zone in this country.
* City codes not required in this country   ** This city code used for entire country or territory.
EST = US Eastern Standard Time   CST = US Central Standard Time
MST = US Mountain Standard Time   PST = US Pacific Standard Time
UTC = Universal Time Coordinated (Greenwich, England)

International Dialing Guide

International Dialing Guide

Country	Country Code	City/Area Codes	Hours ahead or behind:				
			EST	CST	MST	PST	GMT
Gibraltar	[350]	✪Gibraltar*	+6	+7	+8	+9	+1
Greece	[30]	✪Athens (1) Thessaloniki (31)	+7	+8	+9	+10	+2
Greenland††	[299]	✪Nuuk (Godthaab)*	+2	+3	+4	+5	-3
Grenada	[1]	✪St. George's (473) **	+1	+2	+3	+4	-4
Guadeloupe	[590]	✪Basse-Terre (81)	+1	+2	+3	+4	-4
Guam	[671]	✪Agana *	+15	+16	+17	+18	+10
Guatemala	[502]	✪Guatemala City*	-1	0	+1	+2	-6
Guinea	[224]	✪Conakry (4)	+5	+6	+7	+8	0
Guinea-Bissau	[245]	✪Bissau (all points 6 digits)	+5	+6	+7	+8	0
Guyana	[592]	✪Georgetown (2)	+2	+3	+4	+5	-3
Haiti	[509]	✪Port-au-Prince (all points 6 digits)	0	+1	+2	+3	-5
Honduras	[504]	✪Tegucigalpa (all points 7 digits)	-1	0	+2	+3	-6
Hong Kong	[852]	✪Hong Kong (2 + 7 digits) (9 + 7 digits: mobile phones)	+13	+14	+15	+16	+8
Hungary	[36]	✪Budapest (1)	+6	+7	+8	+9	+1
Iceland	[354]	✪Reykjavik (all points 7 digits)	+5	+6	+7	+8	0
India	[91]	✪New Delhi (11) Ahmadabad (79) Bangalore (80) Calcutta (33) Hyderabad (40) Jaipur (141) Madras (44) Mumbai (Bombay) (22)	$+10_{1/2}$	$+11_{1/2}$	$+12_{1/2}$	$+13_{1/2}$	$+5_{1/2}$
Indonesia††	[62]	✪Jakarta (21)	+12	+13	+14	+15	+7
		Bandung (22)	+12	+13	+14	+15	+7
		Denpasar, Bali (361)	+13	+14	+15	+16	+8
		Medan (61)	+12	+13	+14	+15	+7
		Padang (751)	+12	+13	+14	+15	+7
		Palembang (711)	+12	+13	+14	+15	+7
		Semarang (24)	+12	+13	+14	+15	+7
		Surabaya (31)	+12	+13	+14	+15	+7
		Yogyakarta (274)	+12	+13	+14	+15	+7
Iran	[98]	✪Tehran (21); Mashhad (51) Shiraz (71); Tabriz (41)	+9	+10	+11	+12	+4
Iraq	[964]	✪Baghdad (1) Basrah (40)	+8	+9	+10	+11	+3
Ireland	[353]	✪Dublin (1) Cork (21) Limerick (61); Waterford (51)	+5	+6	+7	+8	0

International Dialing Guide

Country	Country Code	City/Area Codes	Hours ahead or behind:				
			EST	CST	MST	PST	GMT
Israel	[972]	✪Jerusalem (2) Tel Aviv (3)	+7	+8	+9	+10	+2
Italy Italy has stopped using city codes. City codes are now incorporated into local numbers, including a zero (0) as a prefix.	[39]	✪Rome (06) Bologna (051) Florence (055) Milan (02) Naples (081) Turin (011) Vatican City (06) Venice (041)	+6	+7	+8	+9	+1
Ivory Coast	[225]	✪Yamoussoukro * ✪Abidjan*	+5	+6	+7	+8	0
Jamaica	[1]	✪Kingston (876) **	0	+1	+2	+3	-5
Japan	[81]	✪Tokyo (3) Fukuoka (92) Hiroshima (82) Kobe (78); Kyoto (75) Nagoya (52) Osaka (66) Sapporo (11) Yokohama (45) Cell phones (090 + 8 digits)	+14	+15	+16	+17	+9
Jordan	[962]	✪Amman (6)	+8	+9	+10	+11	+3
Kazakhstan	[7]	✪Alma-Ata (3272)	+11	+12	+13	+14	+6
Kenya	[254]	✪Nairobi (2) Mombasa (11)	+8	+9	+10	+11	+3
Korea, North	[850]	✪Pyongyang (2)	+14	+15	+16	+17	+9
Korea, South	[82]	✪Seoul (2) Cheju (64) Inchon (32) Pusan (51) Taegu (53)	+14	+15	+16	+17	+9
Kuwait	[965]	✪Kuwait *	+8	+9	+10	+11	+3
Kyrgyzstan	[996]	✪Bishkek (3312+6 digits)	+10	+11	+12	+13	+5
Laos	[856]	✪Vientiane (21) (all other points no city code)	+12	+13	+14	+15	+7
Latvia	[371]	✪Riga (2)	+7	+8	+9	+10	+2
Lebanon	[961]	✪Beirut (1)	+7	+8	+9	+10	+2
Lesotho	[266]	✪Maseru *	+7	+8	+9	+10	+2

✪ Capital city   †† More than one time zone in this country.
* City codes not required in this country   ** This city code used for entire country or territory.
EST = US Eastern Standard Time   CST = US Central Standard Time
MST = US Mountain Standard Time   PST = US Pacific Standard Time
UTC = Universal Time Coordinated (Greenwich, England)

Country	Country Code	City/Area Codes	Hours ahead or behind:				
			EST	CST	MST	PST	GMT
Liberia	[231]	✪Monrovia *	+5	+6	+7	+8	0
Libya	[218]	✪Tripoli (21)	+7	+8	+9	+10	+2
Liechtenstein	[428]	✪Vaduz*	+6	+7	+8	+9	+1
Lithuania	[370]	✪Vilnius (2)	+7	+8	+9	+10	+2
Luxembourg	[352]	✪Luxembourg *	+6	+7	+8	+9	+1
Macau	[853]	✪Macau *	+13	+14	+15	+16	+8
Macedonia	[389]	✪Skopje (91)	+6	+7	+8	+9	+1
Madagascar	[261]	✪Antananarivo (2)	+8	+9	+10	+11	+3
Malawi	[265]	✪Lilongwe * (city codes exist for other cities)	+7	+8	+9	+10	+2
Malaysia	[60]	✪Kuala Lumpur (3) Kotha Bahru (9) Melaka (6); Penang (4)	+13	+14	+15	+16	+8
Maldives	[960]	✪Malé *	+10	+11	+12	+13	+5
Mali	[223]	✪Bamako *	+5	+6	+7	+8	0
Malta	[356]	✪Valletta *	+6	+7	+8	+9	+1
Marshall Islands	[692]	✪Majuro (625) Ebeye (329)	+17	+18	+19	+20	+12
Martinique	[596]	✪Fort-De-France	+1	+2	+3	+4	-4
Mauritania	[222]	✪Nouakchott*	+5	+6	+7	+8	0
Mauritius	[230]	✪Port Louis *	+9	+10	+11	+12	+4
Mexico††	[52]	✪Mexico City (5)	-1	0	+1	+2	-6
		Acapulco (74)	-1	0	+1	+2	-6
		Cuidad Juarez (16)	-1	0	+1	+2	-6
		Durango (18)	-1	0	+1	+2	-6
		Ensenada (667)	-3	-2	-1	0	-8
		Guadalajara (3)	-1	0	+1	+2	-6
		Mazatlan (678)	-2	-1	0	+1	-7
		Mexicali (65)	-3	-2	-1	0	-8
		Monterrey (8)	-1	0	+1	+2	-6
		Nuevo Laredo (87)	-1	0	+1	+2	-6
		Tijuana (66)	-3	-2	-1	0	-8
		Veracruz (29)	-1	0	+1	+2	-6
Midway Islands	[808]		-6	-5	-4	-3	-11
Moldova	[373]	✪Kishinev (2)	+7	+8	+9	+10	+2
Monaco	[377]	✪Monaco *	+6	+7	+8	+9	+1
Mongolia	[976]	✪Ulan Bator (1)	+13	+14	+15	+16	+8
Montenegro & Serbia	[381]	✪Belgrade (11)	+6	+7	+8	+9	+1
Montserrat	[1]	✪Plymouth (664) **	+1	+2	+3	+4	-4
Morocco	[212]	✪Rabat (7 + 6 digits or 77 + 5 digits) Casablanca (2); Fez (5) Marrakech (4); Tangiers (99)	+5	+6	+7	+8	0

Country	Country Code	City/Area Codes	Hours ahead or behind:				
			EST	CST	MST	PST	GMT
Mozambique	[258]	✪Maputo (1)	+7	+8	+9	+10	+2
Myanmar (Burma)	[95]	✪ Yangon (1)	+11½	+12½	+13½	+14½	+6½
Namibia	[264]	✪Windhoek (61)	+7	+8	+9	+10	+2
Nepal	[977]	✪Kathmandu (1)	+10¾	+11¾	+12¾	+13¾	+5¾
Netherlands	[31]	✪Amsterdam (20) ✪The Hague (70) Rotterdam (10)	+6	+7	+8	+9	+1
Netherlands Antilles	[599]	✪Willemstad (9) St. Maarten (5)	+1	+2	+3	+4	-4
New Caledonia	[687]	✪Nouméa *	+16	+17	+18	+19	+11
New Zealand	[64]	✪Wellington (4) Auckland (9) Christchurch (3) Telcom Mobile Phones (25) Telecom Pager (26)	+17	+18	+19	+20	+12
Nicaragua	[505]	✪Managua (2)	-1	0	+1	+2	-6
Niger Republic	[227]	✪Niamey *	+6	+7	+8	+9	+1
Nigeria	[234]	✪Abuja (9), ✪Lagos (1) Cell Phones (90)	+6	+7	+8	+9	+1
Northern Mariana Islands	[670]	✪Saipan*	+15	+16	+17	+18	+10
Norway	[47]	✪Oslo *	+6	+7	+8	+9	+1
Oman	[968]	✪Muscat *	+9	+10	+11	+12	+4
Pakistan	[92]	✪Islamabad (51) Karachi (21); Lahore (42)	+10	+11	+12	+13	+5
Palau	[680]	✪Koror*	+14	+15	+16	+17	+9
Panama	[507]	✪Panama City*	0	+1	+2	+3	-5
Papua New Guinea	[675]	✪Port Moresby *	+15	+16	+17	+18	+10
Paraguay	[595]	✪Asuncion (21)	+1	+2	+3	+4	-4
Peru	[51]	✪Lima (1)	0	+1	+2	+3	-5
Philippines	[63]	✪Manila (2) Cebu (32), Davao (82)	+13	+14	+15	+16	+8
Poland	[48]	✪Warsaw (22) Gdansk (58); Kraków (12) Mobile Phones (0*601) and (0*602)	+6	+7	+8	+9	+1
Portugal	[351]	✪Lisbon (1) Porto (2), Faro (89)	+6	+7	+8	+9	+1

International Dialing Guide

Country	Country Code	City/Area Codes	Hours ahead or behind:				
			EST	CST	MST	PST	GMT
Puerto Rico	[1]	✪San Juan (787) **	+1	+2	+3	+4	-4
Qatar	[974]	✪Doha *	+8	+9	+10	+11	+3
Reunion Island	[262]	✪St. Denis*	+9	+10	+11	+12	+4
Romania	[40]	✪Bucharest (1)	+7	+8	+9	+10	+2
Russia††	[7]	✪Moscow (095)	+8	+9	+10	+11	+3
		Metro Moscow (096)	+8	+9	+10	+11	+3
		St. Petersburg (812)					
Rwanda	[250]	✪Kigali *	+7	+8	+9	+10	+2
St. Kitts & Nevis	[1]	✪Basseterre (869) **	+1	+2	+3	+4	-4
St. Lucia	[1]	✪Castries (758) **	+1	+2	+3	+4	-4
St. Vincents & the Grenadines	[1]	✪Kingstown (809) **	+1	+2	+3	+4	-4
San Marino	[378]	✪San Marino*	+6	+7	+8	+9	+1
São Tomé & Principe	[239]	✪São Tomé*	+5	+6	+7	+8	0
Saudi Arabia	[966]	✪Riyadh (1)	+8	+9	+10	+11	+3
		Jeddah (2)					
		Makkah (Mecca) (2)					
Senegal	[221]	✪Dakar *	+5	+6	+7	+8	0
Seychelles	[248]	✪Victoria	+9	+10	+11	+12	+4
Sierra Leone	[232]	✪Freetown (22)	+5	+6	+7	+8	0
Singapore	[65]	✪Singapore *	+13	+14	+15	+16	+8
Slovakia	[421]	✪Bratislava (7)	+6	+7	+8	+9	+1
Slovenia	[386]	✪Ljubljana (61)	+6	+7	+8	+9	+1
Solomon Islands	[677]	✪Honiara*	+16	+17	+18	+19	+11
Somalia	[252]	✪Mogadishu (1)	+8	+9	+10	+11	+3
South Africa	[27]	✪Cape Town (21)	+7	+8	+9	+10	+2
		✪Pretoria (12)					
		Bloemfontein (51), Durban (31)					
		Johannesburg (11)					
Spain City codes are now incorporated into local numbers which you dial even when in the city.	[34]	✪Madrid (91) Barcelona (93) Bilbao (94) Cordoba (957) Malaga ((95) Seville (95) Valencia (96)	+6	+7	+8	+9	+1
Sri Lanka	[94]	✪Colombo (1)	+10 1/2	+11 1/2	+12 1/2	+13 1/2	+5 1/2
Sudan	[249]	✪Khartoum (11)	+7	+8	+9	+10	+2
Suriname	[597]	✪Paramaribo*	+2	+3	+4	+5	-3
Swaziland	[268]	✪Mbabane * ✪Lobamba*	+7	+8	+9	+10	+2

Country	Country Code	City/Area Codes	Hours ahead or behind: EST	CST	MST	PST	GMT
Sweden	[46]	✪Stockholm (8) Goteberg (31); Malmö (40)	+6	+7	+8	+9	+1
Switzerland	[41]	✪Bern (31) Basel (61), Geneva (22) Lucerne (41); Zurich (1)	+6	+7	+8	+9	+1
Syria	[963]	✪Damascus (11)	+7	+8	+9	+10	+2
Taiwan All old one-digit city codes now have a prefix of 2.	[886]	✪Taipei (22) Kaohsiung (27) Taichung (24)	+13	+14	+15	+16	+8
Tajikistan	[7]	✪Dushanbe (3772)	+10	+11	+12	+13	+5
Tanzania	[255]	✪Dar es Salaam (51)	+8	+9	+10	+11	+3
Thailand	[66]	✪Bangkok (2)	+12	+13	+14	+15	+7
Togo	[228]	✪Lomé*	+5	+6	+7	+8	0
Tonga	[676]	✪Nukualofa**	-6	-5	-4	-3	-11
Trinidad & Tobago	[1]	✪Port-of-Spain (868)**	+1	+2	+3	+4	-4
Tunisia	[216]	✪Tunis (1)	+6	+7	+8	+9	+1
Turkey	[90]	✪Ankara (312) Istanbul (212), (216)	+7	+8	+9	+10	+2
Turkmenistan	[993]	✪Ashkhabad (12)	+10	+11	+12	+13	+5
Turks & Caicos Islands	[1]	✪Grand Turk (649) **	0	+1	+2	+3	-5
Tuvalu	[688]	✪Funafuti*	+17	+18	+19	+20	+12
Uganda	[256]	✪Kampala (41)	+8	+9	+10	+11	+3
Ukraine	[380]	✪Kiev (44); Odessa (048)	+7	+8	+9	+10	+2
United Arab Emirates	[971]	✪Abu Dhabi (2) Dubai (4)	+9	+10	+11	+12	+4
United Kingdom	[44]	✪London, as of April 2000: (171) becomes (020) and add '7' to begining of telephone # (181) becomes (020) and add '8' to begining of telephone # Belfast (1232) Birmingham (121) Bristol (117) Edinburgh (131) Glasgow (141) Leeds (113); Liverpool (151) Manchester (161) Sheffield (114)	+5	+6	+7	+8	0

✪ Capital city
†† More than one time zone in this country.
* City codes not required in this country
** This city code used for entire country or territory.
EST = US Eastern Standard Time   CST = US Central Standard Time
MST = US Mountain Standard Time   PST = US Pacific Standard Time
UTC = Universal Time Coordinated (Greenwich, England)

International Dialing Guide

International Dialing Guide

Country	Country Code	City/Area Codes	Hours ahead or behind:				
			EST	CST	MST	PST	GMT
United States ††	[1]	✪Washington, DC (202)	0	+1	+2	+3	-5
		Atlanta (404)	0	+1	+2	+3	-5
		Baltimore (410)	0	+1	+2	+3	-5
		Boston (617)	0	+1	+2	+3	-5
		Chicago (312) (773)	-1	0	+1	+2	-6
		Dallas (214) (972)	-1	0	+1	+2	-6
		Denver (303)	-2	-1	0	+1	-7
		Detroit (313)	0	+1	+2	+3	-5
		Honolulu (808)	-5	-4	-3	-2	-10
		Houston (713) (281)	0	0	+1	+2	-6
		Los Angeles (213), (310)	-3	-2	-1	0	-8
		Miami (305)	0	+1	+2	+3	-5
		Minneapolis (612)	-1	0	+1	+2	-6
		New York (212), (718)	0	+1	+2	+3	-5
		Philadelphia (215)	0	+1	+2	+3	-5
		Sacramento (916) (530)	-3	-2	-1	0	-8
		Salt Lake City (801)	-2	-1	0	+1	-7
		San Diego (619)	-3	-2	-1	0	-8
		San Francisco (415)	-3	-2	-1	0	-8
		San Jose (408)	-3	-2	-1	0	-8
		Seattle (206)	-3	-2	-1	0	-8
Uruguay	[598]	✪Montevideo (2)	+2	+3	+4	+5	-3
Uzbekistan	[998]	✪Tashkent (712) + 6 digits (71) + 7digits	+10	+11	+12	+13	+5
Vanuatu	[678]	✪Port Vila*	+16	+18	+19	+20	+11
Venezuela	[58]	✪Caracas (2) Maracaibo (61) Valencia (41)	+1	+2	+3	+4	-4
Vietnam	[84]	✪Hanoi (4) Ho Chi Minh City (8)	+12	+13	+14	+15	+7
Virgin Islands, British	[1]	✪Road Town (284) **	+1	+2	+3	+4	-4
Virgin Islands, U.S.	[1]	✪Charlotte Amalie* (340) St. Thomas (340)	+1	+2	+3	+4	-4
Western Samoa	[685]	✪Apia *	-6	-5	-4	-3	-11
Yemen	[967]	✪Sana'a (1)	+8	+9	+10	+11	+3
Yugoslavia	[381]	✪Belgrade (11)	+6	+7	+8	+9	+1
Zaire †† See Congo	[243]	✪Kinshasa (12)	+6	+7	+8	+9	+1
Zambia	[260]	✪Lusaka (1)	+7	+8	+9	+10	+2
Zimbabwe	[263]	✪Harare(4)	+7	+8	+9	+10	+2

Currencies of the World

The table below lists the names of the currencies and subcurrencies in use in nearly 200 countries and territories around the world. Included are the commonly used symbols for each currency. Countries are listed alphabetically. Many currencies are "soft," meaning they are either legally inconvertible, or simply undesirable because they are not very stable. The currencies most often referred to as "hard" currencies are the U.S. dollar, the Canadian dollar, the Japanese yen, the British pound sterling, the German mark, the French franc, the Swiss franc, the Italian lira, and the Dutch guilder. These currencies are easily convertible world-wide.

Up-to-date information on exchange rates, as well as on changes in the type of currency in use are available from a variety of sources. In your local area, call a major bank and ask for the foreign exchange department, or check the business section of the a major newspaper for a table of foreign exchange. Another source is Thomas Cook Currency Services; In USA tel: [1] (212) 883-0400.

The Wall Street Journal publishes the most complete table of foreign exchange rates against the dollar ("World Value of the Dollar") in its Monday edition, using Bank of America, Global Trading as its source. It also publishes a daily table of currency trading, with fewer currencies listed, and "Key Currency Cross Rates," which shows the relationships between nine hard currencies.

Other Internet sites with currency information include "Currencies of the World" at URL http://pacific.commerce.ubc.ca/trade/currencies.html; the United Nations "Operational Rates of Exchange" at URL gopher://gopher.undp.org/00/uncurr/exch_rates; "Pacific Exchange Rate Service" at www.pacific.commerce.ubc.ca/xr/; "The Currency Site" (historical tables, current rates and forecasts) at www.oanda.com/; and "Exchange Rates" (rates provided by the International Monetary Fund) at www.imf.org/external/np/tre/sdr/sdr.html..

Country	Currency	Abbreviation	Subcurrency
Afghanistan	afghani	Af	100 puls
Albania	lek	L	100 qintars (quindarka)
Algeria	dinar	DA	100 centimes
Andorra	Andorran peseta (*see* Spain) or Andorran franc (*see* France)		
Angola	new kwanza	Kz	100 lwei
Anguilla	dollar	EC$	100 cents
Antigua & Barbuda	dollar	EC$	100 cents
Argentina	peso	A$	100 centavos
Armenia	dram	(n/a)	100 luma
Australia	dollar	A$	100 cents
Austria	schilling	S	100 groschen
Azerbaijan	manat	(n/a)	100 gopik
Bahamas	dollar	B$	100 cents
Bahrain	dinar	BD	1,000 fils
Bangladesh	taka	Tk	100 paisa (sing., poisha)
Barbados	dollar	Bds$	100 cents
Belarus (Byelorussia)	ruble	BR	(n/a)
Belgium	franc	BF	100 centimes
Belize	dollar	BZ$	100 cents
Benin	franc	CFAF	100 centimes
Bermuda	dollar	Bd$	100 cents
Bhutan	ngultrum	Nu	100 chetrum
Bolivia	boliviano	Bs	100 centavos
Bosnia & Herzegovina	B.H. dinar	(n/a)	100 para
Botswana	pula	P	100 thebe

Currencies of the World

Country	Currency	Abbreviation	Subcurrency
Brazil	real	R$	100 centavos
Brunei	ringitt (or Bruneian Dollar)	B$	100 sen or cents
Bulgaria	leva	Lv	100 stotinki (sing., stotinka)
Burkina Faso	franc	CFAF	100 centimes
Burundi	franc	FBu	100 centimes
Cambodia	new riel	CR	100 sen
Cameroon	franc	CFAF	100 centimes
Canada	dollar	Can$	100 cents
Cape Verde Islands	escudo	C.V.Esc	100 centavos
Cayman Islands	dollar	CI$	100 cents
Central African Rep.	franc	CFAF	100 centimes
Chad	franc	CFAF	100 centimes
Chile	peso	Ch$	100 centavos
China, People's Rep.	yuan renminbi	Y	100 fen = 10 jiao
Colombia	peso	Col$	100 centavos
Comoros	franc	CF	100 centimes
Congo	franc	CFAF	100 centimes
Costa Rica	colon	¢	100 centimos
Côte d'Ivoire	franc	CFAF	100 centimes
Croatia	kuna	HRK	100lipas
Cuba	peso	Cu$	100 centavos
Cyprus	pound	£C	100 cents
Czech Rep.	koruna	Kc	100 haleru
Denmark	krone (pl., kroner)	Dkr	100 øre
Djibouti	franc	DF	100 centimes
Dominica	dollar	EC$	100 cents
Dominican Rep.	peso	RD$	100 centavos
Ecuador	sucre	S/	100 centavos
Egypt	pound	£E	100 piasters = 1,000 milliemes
El Salvador	colon	¢	100 centavos
Equatorial Guinea	ekwele	CFAF	100 centimes
Eritrea	nafka	Nfa	100 cents
Estonia	kroon (pl, krooni)	KR	100 senti
Ethiopia	birr	Br or E$	100 cents
European Union	European Currency Unit (ecu)		100 cents
Falkland Islands	pound	£F	100 pence (sing., penny)
Fiji	dollar	F$	100 cents
Finland	markka	mk	100 pennia (sing., penni)
France	franc	F	100 centimes
French Guiana	French franc (*See* France)		
French Polynesia	franc	CFPF	100 centimes
Gabon	franc	CFAF	100 centimes
Gambia	dalasi	D	100 butut
Georgia	lari	(n/a)	100 tetri

Country	Currency	Abbreviation	Subcurrency
Germany	deutsche mark	DM	100 pfennig
Ghana	new cedi	¢	100 psewas
Gibraltar	pound	£G	100 pence
Greece	drachma	Dr	100 lepta (sing., lepton)
Greenland	Danish krone (*See* Denmark)		
Grenada	dollar	EC$	100 cents
Guadeloupe	French franc (*See* France)		
Guam	U.S. dollar (*See* United States)		
Guatemala	quetzal	Q	100 centavos
Guinea	syli	FG	10 francs, 1 franc = 100 cent.
Guinea-Bissau	franc	CFAF	100 centimes
Guyana	dollar	G$	100 cents
Haiti	gourde	G	100 centimes
Honduras	lempira	L	100 centavos
Hong Kong	dollar	HK$	100 cents
Hungary	forint	Ft	none
Iceland	króna	IKr	100 aurar (sing., aur)
India	rupee	Rs	100 paise (sing., paisa)
Indonesia	rupiah	Rp	100 sen (not used)
Iran	rial	Rl (p., Rls)	10 rials = 1 toman
Iraq	dinar	ID	1,000 fils
Ireland	pound or punt	Ir£	100 pence (sing., penny)
Israel	new shekel	NIS	100 new agorot (sing., agora)
Italy	lira (pl., lire)	Lit or L	100 centisimi
Jamaica	dollar	J$	100 cents
Japan	yen	¥	100 sen (not used)
Jordan	dinar	JD	1,000 fils
Kazakhstan	tenge	(n/a)	100 tyyn
Kenya	shilling	KSh	100 cents
Kiribati	Australian dollar (*See* Australia)		
Korea, North	won	Wn	100 jun or chon
Korea, South	won	W	100 jeon or chon
Kuwait	dinar	KD	1,000 fils
Kyrgyzstan	som	(n/a)	(n/a)
Laos	new kip	KN	100 at
Latvia	lat	Ls	100 santims
Lebanon	pound or livre	£L	100 piastres
Lesotho	loti (pl., maloti)	L (pl., M)	100 lisente (sing., sente)
Liberia	dollar	$	100 cents
Libya	dinar	LD	1000 dirhams
Liechtenstein	Swiss franc (*See* Switzerland)		
Lithuania	litas (pl., litai)	Lit	100 centu
Luxembourg	franc	LuxF	100 centimes
Macao (Macau)	pataca	P	100 avos
Macedonia	denar	(n/a)	(n/a)
Madagascar	ariary = 5 francs	FMG	1 franc = 100 centimes
Malawi	kwacha	MK	100 tambala

Currencies of the World

Currencies of the World

Country	Currency	Abbreviation	Subcurrency
Malaysia	ringgit	RM	100 sen
Maldives	rufiyaa	Rf	100 lari
Mali	franc	CFAF	100 centimes
Malta	lira (pl., liri)	£m	100 cents
Martinique	French franc (*See* France)		
Mauritania	ouguiya	UM	5 khoums
Mauritius	rupee	MauRs	100 cents
Mexico	nuevo peso	Mex$	100 centavos
Moldova	leu (pl., lei)	(n/a)	(n/a)
Monaco	French franc (*See* France)		
Mongolia	tughrik	Tug	100 mongos
Montserrat	dollar	EC$	100 cents
Morocco	dirham	DH	100 centimes
Mozambique	metical	Mt	100 centavos
Myanmar (Burma)	kyat	K	100 pyas
Namibia	dollar	N$	100 cents
Nauru	Australian dollar (*See* Australia)		
Nepal	rupee	NRs	100 paise (sing., paisa)
Netherlands	guilder (gulden)	f.	100 cents
Netherlands Antilles	N.A. guilder	Ant.f. or NAf.	100 cents
New Zealand	dollar	NZ$	100 cents
Nicaragua	gold cordoba	C$	100 centavos
Niger	franc	CFAF	100 centimes
Nigeria	naira	dble-dashed N	100 kobo
Norway	krone (pl., kroner)	NKr	100 øre
Oman	rial	RO	1,000 baizas
Pakistan	rupee	Rs	100 paisa
Panama	balboa	B	100 centesimos
Papua New Guinea	kina	K	100 toeas
Paraguay	guarani	slashed G	100 centimos
Peru	nuevo sol	S/	100 centimos
Philippines	peso	dashed P	100 centavos
Poland	zloty	Z dashed l	100 groszy
Portugal	escudo	Esc	100 centavos
Puerto Rico	U.S. dollar (*See* United States)		
Qatar	riyal	QR	100 dirhams
Reunion Island	French franc (*See* France)		
Romania	leu (pl., lei)	L	100 bani
Russia	ruble	R	100 kopecks
Rwanda	franc	RF	100 centimes
St. Helena	pound	(n/a)	100 pence
St. Kitts and Nevis	dollar	EC$	100 cents
St. Lucia	dollar	EC$	100 cents
St. Pierre	French franc (*See* France)		
St. Vincent & Grenadines	dollar	EC$	100 cents
Samoa (American)	U.S. dollar (*See* United States)		

Country	Currency	Abbreviation	Subcurrency
San Marino	Italian lira (*See* Italy)		
São Tomé & Principe	dobra	Db	100 centimos
Saudi Arabia	riyal	SRls	100 halalat
Senegal	franc	CFAF	100 centimes
Seychelles	rupee	SR	100 cents
Sierra Leone	leone	Le	100 cents
Singapore	dollar	S$	100 cents
Slovakia	koruna	Sk	100 haliers
Slovenia	tolar	SlT	100 stotinov (stotins)
Solomon Islands	dollar	SI$	100 cents
Somalia	shilling	So. Sh.	100 cesntesimi
South Africa	rand	R	100 cents
Spain	peseta	Ptas	100 centimos
Sri Lanka	rupee	SLRs	100 cents
Sudan	pound	(n/a)	100 piasters
Suriname	guilder (gulden)	Sf. or Sur.f.	100 cents
Swaziland	lilangeni (singular) emalangeni (plural)	L (singular) E (plural)	100 cents
Sweden	krona (pl. kroner)	Sk	100 öre
Switzerland	franc	SwF	100 centimes/rappen
Syria	pound	£S	100 piasters
Taiwan	new dollar	NT$	100 cents
Tajikistan	ruble	(n/a)	(n/a)
Tanzania	shilling	TSh	100 cents
Thailand	baht	Bt or Bht	100 sastangs
Togo	franc	CFAF	100 centimes
Tonga Islands	pa'anga	T$ or PT	100 seniti
Trinidad & Tobago	dollar	TT$	100 cents
Tunisia	dinar	D	1,000 millimes
Turkey	lira	LT	100 kurus
Turkmenistan	manat	(n/a)	100 tenga
Turks & Caicos	U.S. dollar (*See* United States)		
Uganda	shilling	USh	100 cents
Ukraine	Hryvnia	UaK	100 kopiykas
United Arab Emirates	dirham	Dh	100 fils
United Kingdom	pound sterling	£	100 pence
United States	dollar	$	100 cents
Uruguay	peso uraguayo	$U	100 centesimos
Uzbekistan	som	(n/a)	100 tiyin
Venezuela	bolivar	Bs	100 centimos
Vietnam	new dong	D	100 xu or hao
Virgin Islands	U.S. dollar (*See* United States)		
Samoa	tala	WS$	100 sene
Yemen	rial	YRls	100 fils
Yugoslavia	dinar	Din	100 paras
Zambia	kwacha	ZK	100 ngwee
Zimbabwe	dollar	Z$	100 cents

Currencies of the World

Notes / Additions

Algeria

At a Glance

THE PEOPLE

Population .... 31,133,486 (July 1999 est.)
Growth Rate .... 2.1% (1999 est.)
Life Expectancy .... 69.24 years (born 1999)
Infant Mortality .... 43.82 deaths/1,000 live births

Ethnic Composition
Arabic Berber 99%
European ....less than 1%
And smaller populations of Kabyles, Chaouias, and Mzabs.

Religious Composition
Sunni Muslim... 99%
Christian and Jewish 1%

Languages Spoken
Arabic is the sole and official language, although French and Berber dialects are spoken as well.

Education and Literacy
Education in Algeria is run by the state and continues to follow the pattern laid down during the former French administration. Education is compulsory for children between 6 and 15. However, adult literacy stands at only 61.6 percent. Ten universities exist in the country.

Labor Force
Total 7,800,000
By occupation: government 29.5%, agriculture 22%, construction and public works 16.2%, industry 13.6%, commerce and services 13.5%, transportation and communication 5.2%.

THE ECONOMY
Algeria has some of the largest petroleum and natural gas reserves in the world, but the sector has never been fully exploited. While the country offers a low-cost labor force and proximity to European markets, it has been plagued by long-term political instability. Fundamentalist Islamic terrorist attacks against secular elements and foreigners have hampered development and scared off foreign investment. Tourism has been blunted as numerous foreign governments have issued advisories recommending against visiting this North African nation due to security concerns. High unemployment shows no signs of diminishing and has resulted in mass illegal immigration to E.U. nations. IMF intervention has failed to bring relief to this debt-ridden and chaotic economy.

Exports .... US$14 billion (f.o.b., 1997 est.)
Imports .... US$8.5 billion (f.o.b., 1997 est.)
Total GDP .... US$22.5 billion (1997)
GDP Per Capita .... US$4,600 (1998 est.)
Unemployment .... 30% (1998 est.)
Inflation Rate .... 9% (1998 est.)

Top Export Partners
Italy 18.8%, US 14.8%, France 11.8%, Spain 8%, Germany 7.9%.

Top Import Partners
France 29%, Spain 10.5%, Italy 8.2%, US 8%, Germany 5.6%.

Top Exports
Petroleum and natural gas 97%.

Top Imports
Capital goods, food and beverages, consumer goods.

BUSINESS WORKWEEK

Offices
Saturday to Wednesday 8a.m. to 12:30p.m. and 2p.m. to 6:00p.m.

Banks
Sunday to Thursday 8:45a.m. or 9a.m. to 3p.m. or 4p.m.

Government
Saturday to Wednesday 8a.m. to noon and 2p.m. to 5:30p.m., Thursday 8a.m. to noon.

Retail
Saturday to Thursday 9a.m. to noon, and 2p.m. to 7p.m. Many shops close at 1p.m. on Saturday (in the north, shops often close noon to 5p.m.) for a midday rest.

HOLIDAYS
New Year's ....January 1
Ramadan ends ....January 10-11*
Id al-Adha, Feast of the Sacrifice .... March 17-18
Islamic New Year ....April 8*
Ashoura April18*
Labor Day ....May 1
Mouloud, birth of Muhammad................................ June 6*
Revolutionary Readjustment ....June 19
Independence...July 5
Anniversary of the Revolution ....November 1
Leilat al-Meiraj,
Ascension of Muhammad............................. November 6*
Ramadan begins .... December 30-31*
*Note: Some dates may vary by year.

CLIMATE

Seasons
The summer months are generally warm and humid throughout Algeria, day temperatures in most areas reaching as high as 32°C (90°F) in August when the Sirocco winds blow from the south for brief periods. The period between October and May experiences rain, while the season from November to February has particularly heavy rainfall.

Regions
The coastal region has temperate climate, ranging from 13° to 24°C (55° to 75°F). The Sahara Desert on the southern part of Algeria is hot and arid, with temperatures as high as 43°C (110°F), but at night they can fall as low as 10°C (50°F). The mountain regions experience snowfall and sub-freezing temperatures.

Money & Banking

Currency
The currency of Algeria is the Dinar (DA).

Denominations
The Dinar comes in coin denominations of DA50, 20, 10, 5, 1 and 50, 20, 10, 5, and 1 centimes; also in banknotes of DA5, 10, 20, 50, 100, and 200.

Traveler's Checks and Credit Cards

Traveler's checks and currency can be exchanged at the Banque Nationale d'Algérie, Banque Extérieure d'Algerie, and the Crédit Populaire d'Algérie. Not all banks are authorized to change traveler's checks. Traveler's checks in French Francs or U.S. dollars are most recommended to avoid extra charges. Large hotels in the capital and government-run shops, as well as kiosks at the international airport, may accept traveler's checks. Cash, especially U.S. dollars, may also be exchanged, but only crisp and new notes are likely to be accepted. Cashing traveler's checks can be a difficult and a lengthy form-filling process in smaller towns, and commissions can run high.Travelers should try to change only as many dinars as they need, as reconversion is expensive.

American Express, Visa, Diner's Club, and MasterCard are accepted primarily in up-market places in main cities. Rural areas and small shops will require the use of cash. ATMs are not available in Algeria.

Travel

VISA AND PASSPORT

A valid passport is required of all visitors. A visa is also required of all, except nationals of Andorra, Argentina, Bosnia-Hercegovina, Croatia, FYROM (Former Yugoslav Republic of Macedonia), Guinea Republic, Libya, Macedonia, Malaysia, Malta, Mauritania, Senegal, Slovenia, Syria, Tunisia, Yemen, and Yugoslavia (Serbia and Montenegro), for maximum stays of three months.

Tourist, Business, and Transit visas are all issued, usually good for a maximum stay of 30 days. Period of validity varies by type of visa:

- Tourist visas are valid for approximately 30 days
- Business visas are valid for up to 90 days
- Transit visas are valid for only 48 hours.

Transit visas are not required of travelers who do not leave the airport and have confirmed tickets and documents for onward travel and continuing their journey to another country via the same or connecting flight within 24 hours.

Applications will be handled by an Algerian consulate or embassy department, with whom you may have a difficult time, depending on your location.

Business visa applications require a letter from the sponsoring company in Algeria. Usually the processing time takes only two or three days, but it can take longer. There are reports of the application process having taken up to 30 days, and the result is not necessarily the approval of your application.

Advisory

Travelers from all countries may wish to know that the U.S. Department of State advises its citizens to avoid Algeria. A state of emergency was declared in 1992 and remains in effect. Travel here is extremely dangerous due to military actions and violent crime. Foreign nationals, particularly independent business people, have been victims of arbitrary deportation and even detention.

Abduction, murder, and other types of harassment of U.S. citizens and other foreign nationals can and has come about unpredictably. The degree of terrorist activity in Algeria seems to have been declining in recent years, but assaults are still occurring in congested urban areas, on roadsides, in villages, and on public transportation. Since September of 1993, terrorist acts perpetrated against foreigners have resulted in more than 120 of their deaths.

The Department urges maximum caution, including the following measures:

- Minimize or eliminate your use of regularly scheduled flights.
- When arriving and embarking at airports, be met and escorted by prearranged, local Algerian contacts.
- If you are traveling overland, retain armed protection.

In Algiers, the capital, you should only take a room where security is provided, usually the big, internationally recognized hotels.

Everywhere in the country, nighttime travel should be avoided. Travelers are advised to check early and often on the status of things before making any travel arrangements.

RESTRICTED ENTRY

The following factors restrict entry if conditions are not met:

- You must have documentation of sufficient funds.
- No Israeli visas may be in your possession, nor Israeli exit stamps in your passport, or entry will be denied unless you have an unusual talent to talk and bribe really well
- Holders of Israeli passports are automatically denied entry
- Iranian nationals are denied entry, although they are permitted to transit across Algeria for a maximum of 48 hours.

DEPARTURE FORMALITIES

Expect an airport departure tax of AD1000, which you may pay in local currency.

The Algerian government requires all foreign visitors to exchange to local currency a minimum of AD1000 during their stay, for which one must be able to furnish documentation. The departure tax offers a nifty way to take care of the requirement—do your documented exchange as soon as you disembark so you don't forget; but, generally, you will find that American dollars go a lot further.

CUSTOMS ENTRY (PERSONAL)

Duty Free

The following items may be brought into Algeria by adult travelers without customs duty being levied:

- 200 cigarettes or 50 cigars or 250g of tobacco
- one bottle of distilled spirits (open)
- Two bottles of wine
- 150ml of perfume or 500ml of eau de cologne

Restricted

Importation or exportation of drugs, gold, and firearms is prohibited.

A temporary importation permit is required for all personal jewelry that weighs over 100g; this ensures its re-exportation.

Another alternative is to leave any articles with customs upon entry. You must declare any gold, pearls, or precious stones upon arrival.

IMMUNIZATION

You must have a yellow fever vaccination certificate if you are arriving from an infected area. If you anticipate travel in rural areas, it is highly recommended that you be vaccinated, even though it is not officially required.

TIPPING

It is fairly standard to tip in the range of ten percent.

Taxi

A ten percent tip is customary for taxi drivers.

Porters

Porters do not expect tips.

Hotels

A ten percent tip to service staff is sufficient. A service charge is sometimes included in your bill.

Restaurants

A ten percent tip is customary, assuming you are satisfied.

EMERGENCY INFORMATION

Personal Security

You are at a high level of risk the moment you set foot in Algeria, especially if you are a European or U.S. business person. In the sections of the capital where there is a significant population of Euro/American expatriates, there is generally adequate protection provided by a mix of military and other forces, including police. Still, car bombings occur, which are difficult to prevent, and fire fights between armed rebels and government security forces also take place. It is far too easy to get caught in the crossfire. In remote areas and the poorer sections of cities, protection is often not available.

Walking about can be fundamentally unhealthy. Visitors should always remain in the company of at least one known Algerian local, whether in Algiers or other cities. Some hotels provide pagers or cell phones for their patrons in order to ensure their safety.

South of Tamanrasset in Algeria, close to the Nigerian border, is an area where foreigners seem to have been heavily targeted, kidnapped, and killed, as well as assaulted and robbed.

Crime

The rate of crime overall in Algeria is somewhat high and is seemingly headed upward. Theft is the order of the day. Petty theft, home burglary, auto contents and parts, purse snatching, pickpocketing, and stick-ups on public transit are all standard fare.

It is difficult to know when to trust the police. Potentially lethal situations arise from circumstances in which armed men enter homes on the pretense that they are police, then proceed to hold the occupants at gunpoint and rob them. Sometimes it may not be a pretense.

Armed carjacking is another serious problem. Assassination of Algerians from every strata and occupational niche has taken place, and it continues at a savage pace. Untold thousands have perished.

Emergency Numbers

There is no system of national emergency telephone numbers.

HEALTH

Facilities are generally first rate in the north but less so in the south. Consider it wise to bring with you any medicines that you know will be crucial to your well-being.

Doctors and hospitals typically expect immediate cash payment, but emergency cases are handled free of charge. Medical insurance including overseas coverage, specifically medical evacuation, is essential.

According to WHO guidelines published in 1973, cholera vaccination certificates are no longer required for entry to Algeria. Cholera is still a critical risk in this country, though, and caution is essential.

Water from the tap is usually highly chlorinated, so that it may be safe, but it may also cause moderate abdominal upset. Bottled water is widely available and is advisable for the first several weeks of your stay.

The drinking water outside major towns is prone to contamination. Any used for drinking, brushing teeth, or ice should first be boiled or otherwise sterilized. Milk is unpasteurized and must be boiled. Powdered or canned milk is widely available, but be sure that it is rehydrated with purified water. Eat only well-cooked fish and meat, preferably served hot. Salads, pork, and mayonnaise can carry increased risk. Vegetables should be thoroughly cooked; peel fruit just prior to being consumed.

The risk of malaria is limited. The benign strain called vivax exists in Ihrir (Illizi Department).

Onchocerciasis (river blindness) occurs. And Bilharzia (schistosomiasis) exists, so do not swim or paddle in sluggish or stagnant fresh water. Swimming pools which are well-chlorinated and maintained should be safe.

Trypanosomiasis (sleeping sickness) is a factor for which to prepare, as are Hepatitis A, B and E. Meningococcal meningitis and Filariasis occur, especially in the dry season. Avoid tick and insect bites, which can cause viral diseases.

INTERNAL TRAVEL

Ports and airline terminals are prime terrorist targets. Come alert and prepared.

The degree of hazard in traveling overland is exceedingly high. Attacks against foreigners continue. Foolhardy behavior can easily lead to deadly consequences.

AIR

Air Algérie offers frequent services linking Algiers with the major business centers of Annaba, Constantine, and Oran. Flights originate from the domestic airport, right next door to Algiers International. All four of these cities are connected to other less prominent commercial centers and what the Algerians refer to as gateway oases, including Ghardaia, Ouargla, Amenas, and Hassi Messaoud.

When economical use of time is important, flying is the way to go in Algeria, especially when traveling from the coastal strip in the north to the far south.

Reliability of services is generally good, but expect delays in the summer when sand storms may impose.

TAXI

Taxis are metered and government licensed. They are abundant in major cities and in most smaller towns, but they are kept busy in the early evening by workers returning home. Sharing of taxis is a widespread practice here. The meter shows the correct fare, but drivers add surcharges after dark.

It is better to refrain from using unlicensed taxis, which generally prove uninsured and less safe.

AUTOMOBILE

Auto rentals can be arranged on arrival in most cities through ONAT, the government-run travel agency (see address below, under Travel Assistance). Hotels can also arrange for rentals. An International Driving Permit is required as documentation.

If you are using your own car, a *carnet de passage* is required. Cars are granted entry up to three months with no duty assessed. Insurance must also be obtained at the border. The ability to produce documentation of ownership for police scrutiny is critical. Details are available from ONAT.

The roads are reasonably well maintained, but garages are hard to find; so, make sure that your rental vehicle is in excellent repair, and carry a full complement of water and spare gasoline.

Consider it a good idea to hire and keep with you some people to provide armed protection during your travels overland. Traffic in Algeria keeps to the right-hand side.

TRAIN

Daily runs operate in the northern region of the country, linking Algiers with Oran, Béjaia, Skikda, Annaba, and Constantine. This is not a swift service, but it is fairly reliable.

To the south, there are connections once a day from
* Annaba to Tebessa via Souk Ahras
* Constantine with Touggout via Biskra (twice daily)
* Mohammadia with Bechar

Trains on these southern runs carry only second-class coaches. There are 4000km (2500 miles) of railroad right of way in Algeria.

URBAN / METRO

Municipal bus services can be found in the capital and its suburbs as well as in the coastal area. Carnets which are good for ten trips, all-day, weekly, or longer are available.

One urban transport highlight of note in Algiers: two elevators and a funicular lead visitors upward to a hill with a wonderful view of the ancient souk below in the city.

A metro is planned for the capital, but construction is yet to begin.

BUSES & TRAMS

Overland coaches connect the major cities of Algeria. It is not a mode of transportation recommended for most business travelers, but it is available and relatively economical.

Buses depart from city centers in Algiers and Oran. Obtain schedules at the depots. Services are fairly regular.

WATER TRAVEL

Ferries operated by the government call at the main coastal ports of Algiers, Annaba, Arzew, Béjaia, Djidjelli, Ghazaouet, Mostaganem, Oran, and Skikda. Check locally for schedules and ticket prices.

TRAVEL ASSISTANCE

Chambre Algérienne de Commerce et d'Industrie (CACI)
tel: (2) 574-042 or 574-444; fax: (2) 577-025
Office National Algérien du Tourisme (ONAT)
5 Boulevard Ben Boulaïd
tel: (2) 641-550, 743-376; fax: (2) 616-171
tel: (2) 605-960; fax: (2) 591-315 or 590-664
Chambre Nationale de Commerce et d'Industrie
tel: (2) 574-397; fax: (2) 577-025

Algeria

Essential Terms

English	Arabic
Yes No	Na-a'am La; mish
Good morning Hello (daytime) Hello (evening) Hello (telephone)	Al sa-lahm Al sa-lahm Ma-sa'el khair Marhaban
Good-bye	Be-kha-trahk
Please	Min-fahd-lak (M) Min-fahd-lik (F)
Thank you	Shook-rahn
Pleased to meet you	Sorirart biro'aitak
Excuse me; I'm sorry	Is-ma-leh
My name is _____	'ismii_____
I don't understand	An-na mish fahem
Do you speak English?	Hal tatakallumu l-inkliziyya?

Security Briefing

SOCIAL UNREST

Algeria is in the throes of a social revolution. In the 80's and early 90's, Algerians who were disenchanted with the great divide between the very wealthy elite and the dirt-poor masses turned to Islam as a unifying symbol of structure, safety, and equality. This led to a 1992 military take-over supported by secularists opposed to democracy. Although holding the power, the current government has many enemies. Groups opposed to the current government include secularists who favor democracy, Islamic fundamentalists who insist on a non-democratic religious state, and those who support an Islamic influenced democracy.

Algerian fundamental Islamic splinter groups are avowed terrorists who blame France, the U.S., and all other westerners for everything that is wrong with the world. They publicly announced their intent to kill all foreigners who do not leave Algeria and then made good on this threat. Over 120 foreigners have been kidnapped and murdered in Algeria in the past six years in carefully planned raids which sometimes involve dozens of attackers. Ransoms are demanded, but there is little guarantee that payments of money will keep victims unhurt or even alive. Often directed towards western business interests, aid workers are also targeted. In 1996, seven Catholic monks were decapitated by terrorists with whom they had been friendly for years.

Face-to-face attacks are increasing after years of indiscriminate bombings at airports, markets and other areas frequented by foreigners. Also on the increase are bizarre, almost ritualistic murders in which Algerian families and even entire villages are slaughtered at night by roving bands of terrorists. Thousands of Algerians from all walks of life and classes of Algerian society have been and continue to be viciously assassinated including women and children and retirees.

Most western countries advise their citizens against any "non-essential" travel to Algeria, and, if possible, to limit visits to the capital city of Algiers. Business travelers should maintain a "code-red" level of security. U.S. government employees use chartered aircraft and avoid commercial carriers because of past terrorist incidents and are restricted to embassy compounds and high-security hotels. If possible, similar precautions should be taken by "high-profile" western business travelers. You are advised to avoid taxis, buses, or other public forms of transportation from the airport to downtown Algiers. Instead, have your local Algerian hosts meet and accompany you to and from the airport. Armored cars with trained and armed drivers are suggested. Business travelers should never travel anywhere in the country unless accompanied by a known and trusted Algerian companion. Business travelers should plan to stay in the country as briefly as possible and avoid establishing patterns of behavior which increase their visibility to terrorists. The British government lists the following four hotels as meeting high security standards: the Sofitel, the El-Djazair, the International (formerly the Hilton), and the El-Aurassi.

Even if Charles Boyer could be reincarnated and personally invite you to "come with me to the Casbah," you should decline his invitation to visit Algiers' fabled market area or any of the capital city's suburbs. All meetings the business traveler attends should be limited to hotels, the city center, or fully protected workplaces—and then only by previous appointment while following "code-red" security precautions. Outside the city center, armed security protection is advisable, and visitors should be aware that even this will not guarantee their safety as the numerous murders of foreigners attests.

Communications

DIALING CODES IN ALGERIA

International country code: [213]
Selected city codes: Adrar (7), Ain Defla (3), Bejaia (5), Guerrar (9).

Dialing Algeria from Overseas

To reach Algeria from overseas, dial your country's international dialing code, then 213 (the country code for Algeria) followed by the city code and local number that you are trying to reach.

CALLING WITHIN ALGERIA

Local Calls

Due to the spotty phone system, even local calls may be difficult to place. Numerous attempts may have to be made.

Long Distance Calls

Don't expect great things since Algeria's phone system lives by an inefficient reputation.

International Calls

To dial the great beyond direct from Algeria, dial 00 (wait for second dial tone) + country code + area code + number. Post offices with connecting telephone offices (PTT) are open 24 hours in Algiers and Constantine. As always, watch for outrageous rates when calling from hotels.

PAY PHONES

Public Telephones

Well-used public telephones can be found everywhere

Algeria

in Algeria but often prove unreliable. Many calling attempts may prove necessary, making post offices or hotels better alternatives. Public phones take AD1, 5, and 10 coins.

CALL BACK

You can (potentially) save significant sums when calling in Algeria by using a call back service.

Fees for call back services vary widely, depending on the company and the type of service required. Be sure to check with these companies before leaving to compare rates.

CELLULAR PHONES

Cellular phone service is available in Algeria through Algerian PTT in an NMT 900 analog format.

Note: Your home country cell phone may not work in this country. If not, we recommend that you rent an international cell phone *before* you leave home. A major US-based cell phone rental provider is **IMC WorldCell**. For information see "International Cell Phone Rentals" on page 14.

PHONE JACK

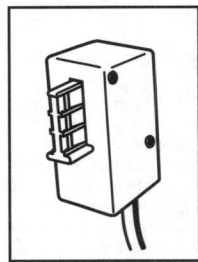

Adaptors are available through **iGo Corporation.** (See "Electrical and Telephone Adaptors" on page 19.)

FAX

Fax service is not prevalent throughout the country. Some of the more modern hotels may have fax capabilities.

POSTAL SERVICES

Postal service is slow and far from reliable. Clothing, food, and magazines are often confiscated. Airmail to North America often takes 5 to 10 days, surface mail can take between six weeks and three months. A parcels must be opened before mailing. Yellow mailboxes can be found in the cities, but it is better to drop off all mail directly at the post office.

TELEGRAM

The central post office in Algiers has telegram capabilities, but it has not proven efficient.

Business Services

BUSINESS CENTERS

International Algier Hotel; Pins Maritimes el-Mohammadia; tel: (2) 21 96 96.

Sofitel Algiers; 172 Rue Hassiba Ben Bouali; tel: (2) 68 52 10.

COURIER SERVICE

DHL; 18 ave. Franklin Roosevelt, Algiers, 16000; tel: (2) 23 00 31; Saturday to Thursday 8a.m. to 6p.m.; closed Fridays.

UPS (P.T.T.); 44 Rue Muhammad, Algiers; tel: (2) 66 33 66; fax: (2) 92 17 20.

Electrical

Current

127/220 volts, AC 50Hz.

ELECTRIC PLUG

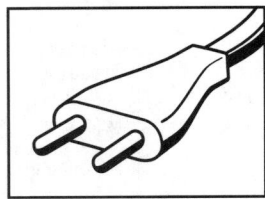

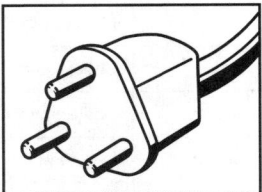

Adaptors are available through **iGo Corporation.** (See "Electrical and Telephone Adaptors" on page 19.)

Technical Support

HARDWARE/SOFTWARE VENDOR SUPPORT

Compaq/Digital; (in Switzerland) tel: [41] (22) 709-5330; fax: [41] (22) 709-5391 (Geneva); [41] (1) 801-2507; fax: [41] (1) 801-2172 (Zurich); (General U.S.) tel: (281) 518-2000; http://www.compaq.com/.

Hewlett Packard; (in Switzerland) tel: [41] (22) 780-8111; (in the U.S.) tel: [1] (408) 246-4300; http://www.hp.com/.

IBM; tel: (2) 594-877; fax: (2) 693-488; (in Germany) tel: [49] (711) 78-50; fax: [49] (711) 785-3511; (in Switzerland) tel: [41] (22) 310-0418 (French); (in the U.S.) tel: [1] (919) 517-2800; (Main Office) tel: [1] 914-765-1900; http://www.ibm.com/.

Microsoft; (in Egypt) tel: (2) 594-2445; fax: (2) 594-2194; (in Germany) tel: [49] (89) 31-760; fax: [49] (89) 3176-1000; tel: [49] (89) 3176-1199; (in Switzerland) tel: [41] (848) 858-868; fax [41] (1) 831-0869; (in the U.S.) [1] (425) 635-7222; http://www.microsoft.com/.

Internet Connection

HOW TO CONNECT

Connecting to AOL and Compuserve in Algeria is similar to using it when traveling outside your own area code. See the introductory section for detailed information on connecting to your account through a different phone number.

America Online

There are no direct access numbers for America Online in Algeria. Users will have to pay international rates to use the service.

Compuserve

There are no direct access numbers for Compuserve in Algeria. Users will have to pay international rates to use the service.

Numbers are available at *Go International*. The Compuserve Web-site also has a great deal of information, at http://www.compuserve.com.

There are no direct access numbers for Compuserve in Algeria.

Independent Service Providers

The Centre de Recherche sur l'Information Scientifique & Technique offers service to Algeria for the scientific community. Contact this organization to see if an account can be setup while you're in Algeria.

CERIST (Centre de Recherche sur l'Information Scientifique & Technique)

tel: (2132) 912-136; fax: (2132) 912-126; email: elmaouhab@ist.cerist.dz; http://www.cerist.dz/.

Business Culture

GREETINGS AND COURTESIES

An Algerian greeting is generally open and cordial. A handshake is most often followed by an embrace between men. Some businessmen still follow the French custom of kissing each other on both cheeks while embracing, while others may hold and kiss the other person's right hand. Do not let this effusive greeting lull you into a sense of well-being. Anything less friendly is considered impolite or even insulting.

Algerians address each other by title and family name. Elders are always greeted first and are often granted the honorific title of "uncle" or "aunt" even if not related. Similarly, non-related Algerian friends of the same age refer to each other as "brother" or "sister".

Arabic has replaced French as the official language. Algerian businessmen rarely speak English. Arabic/French bilingual business cards are frequently used. Although different situations call for different greetings, "Ahlan wa sahlan" (May your way be easy) or "Marhaban bikoum" (Hello to you) are common Arabic salutations.

Algerians also "talk" using gestures. Two clasped hands offer greetings at a distance. Men often slap the palm of a friend's hand to express agreement. Thanks or appreciation are demonstrated by pressing a flat right hand over your heart. To ask a guest to slow down or exhibit patience, an Algerian host joins the fingertips of his right hand and moves it up and down slightly. An extended index finger signals "beware", but Muslims never point directly at someone or something. Pointing with the left hand is an extremely crude insult and could bring business negotiations to a halt.

BUSINESS ETHIC AND FRAMEWORK

Because of the long and bitter war for independence from France, Algerians are notoriously resentful of westerners and are sometimes blatantly hostile. This attitude continues despite the fact that the government has established much more liberal trade policies and turned to western companies (big oil in particular) as sources of much needed cash. A slow and steady, low-key sales approach works best. Tact and diplomacy should always guide the business traveler since displays of impatience or emotion are considered bad manners. Glitzy, high tech presentations receive polite compliments, but basic charts and graphs continue to be the most effective promotional materials.

DECISION MAKING

The Algerian government maintains tight controls over most of the industry in the country, and business travelers will need to meet face-to-face with those in authority. Intermediaries are viewed with suspicion, and, so, regular personal visits by appointment are required.

Algerians appreciate attention, and regular correspondence, phone contact, and personal visits are important in both initiating and maintaining a strong business relationship. It is tactful to quote prices in Algerian dinars rather than in francs or dollars.

Business travelers should be constantly aware that the political situation in Algeria is volatile and almost certainly will change. There is little certainty that the government official you negotiate with will be in a position of authority for long or that even the government he represents will exist in the near future.

MEETINGS

Algerian business meetings are slow by western standards, proceeding at the pace of a camel caravan rather than a jet plane. Algerians approach business in a more relaxed atmosphere. by offering refreshments—usually coffee, tea, fruit drinks, or bottled water—and it is impolite to refuse them or to consume more than two cups. Women are routinely sent to separate rooms from the men, and is not uncommon for a female corporate vice president to be escorted to the secretarial coffee room for refreshment while a meeting proceeds.

Appointments are necessary for meetings with government officials and larger firms. Punctuality is not a major concern to most Algerian nationals, but being on time will make a good impression even if you may have to wait a while. **Tips**: Sales approach should be low-key. Be courteous, firm, and politely persistent. Signals interpreted as temper or arrogance will stifle progress. Avoid negative opinions or criticism. Quote CIF prices in Algerian dinars.

BUSINESS ENTERTAINING

Your hosts will love to join you for dinner at a hotel or restaurant, but you must be discrete in offering such an invitation ¯preferably outside the office setting. Muslims eat no pork and drink no alcohol. Algerian food has a strong French influence and features rich sauces. "Couscous", a pasta-like semolina wheat, is served often. For special occasions, it is cooked with lamb or chicken and vegetables. Also popular is "tajine" a stew made from meat and vegetables, which is named for its unusual shell-shaped cooking pot. "Chorba" soup is a broth with small pieces of meat and vermicelli. Fruit is the most common dessert, and the date-filled pastry "makrout" is a special treat.

WOMEN IN BUSINESS

The Algerian government tries to promote a positive image in the world community by occasionally appointing women to cabinet-level positions. Usually, these positions are in maternal or childhood health, education, or other "women's issues" areas that have international conferences. In reality, women are virtually invisible in Algerian business or government activities. Female business travelers should expect a very patronizing attitude or worse from Algerian businessmen. Algerian males are raised on the myth that western women come to their country seeking sexual adventures. Because of this, female business travelers without a male escort will invariably receive sexual invitations from Algerian men. If a polite "No" won't stop this behavior, make a public fuss. Algerian's detest unwanted public attention.

Many women continue to dress in chador, traditional

Muslim clothing, which covers the entire body except for the eyes. In this strongly male-dominant society, gender roles are clearly and rigidly defined. This may seem repressive to visitors with Western values, but Algerians see these attitudes as accepting different roles for which each sex is obviously suited. Recent legislation has given women more rights; however, do not expect equal treatment as you might at home.

BUSINESS ATTIRE

Men and women commonly wear Western attire in urban areas. Visitors' dress should be conservatively-cut Western clothing in all but sporting circumstances. A conservative business suit is most appropriate for both men and women. Flashy displays of wealth will not enhance your position in a country ridden with strife. One will do best to draw as little attention as possible to oneself in dress, most particularly women, who should adhere to Muslim laws of modesty by covering themselves as much as possible. Women should ensure that their dresses or skirts fall below the knee and avoid sleeveless outfits completely. Pants should never be worn by women. To wear anything less than conservative will only encourage disrepute and disparaging remarks and actions. Outside of Algiers, women may do well to don head covering.

Business Centers
Algiers
CITY VIEW

A summation for the city could read "All roads lead from Algiers" since it ties the country together and also acts as its main shipping port. Parts of Algiers are among the most beautiful in Northern Africa, with French influence contributing to a European atmosphere. The city has a rich history, beginning as a Phoenician trading post in the 1st century A.D., but the Roman City ceased after the fall of the Roman Empire. By 944, Algiers was under Arab rule, but later the city was captured by the French in 1830. World War II saw the city serving as Allied headquarters for North Africa; it has steadily grown ever since. A population of around 3 million now makes the city a busy metropolis with modern elements. The old city, known as the Casbah, is considered one of the most dangerous areas for travelers, particularly after the political and cultural upheavals of the last few years. For recreation while in Algiers, then, swimming, fishing, and sailing probably provide safer alternatives to touring around the city.

AIRPORT
Algiers Airport to City Center

Algiers Airport lies 12 miles (20 km.) from the city center. A 30-minute taxi fare to the city costs around AD400, while coaches offering a cheaper alternative leave every 30 minutes.

Airline Numbers

Air Algerie	64 57 88
Air France	64 90 10
Alitalia	64 68 50
Egyptair	63 05 05
Iberia	63 37 12
Lufthansa	64 27 36
Royal Air Maroc	63 04 58
Sabena	63 32 14
Swissair	63 33 67
Tunis Air	63 25 73

HOTELS
Top-end
El-Djazair (St. George); 24 Avenue Souidani Boudjemaa; tel: (2) 60 10 00, 59 10 00; fax: (2) 69 35 08; email: info@eldjazair-hotel.com; http://www.eldjazair-hotel.com; city center; restaurant/cafeteria; 24-hour room service; conference facilities (up to 300); secretarial service; translation; fax/photocopy facilities; hair salon; travel agency; limousine service; secure; fitness club; sauna; pool; hammam; tennis; nightclub.

Sofitel Algiers; 172 Rue Hassiba Ben Bouali; tel: (2) 685-210; fax: (2) 66 21 04; located near Hamma business center, adjacent Jardin d'Essai botanical garden; restaurant; room service; conference facilities (up to 200); business center; secretarial service; fax/photocopy facilities; non-smoking rooms available; airport shuttle; boutiques; corporate rates; sauna; health club; indoor/outdoor pools.

Expensive
International Algier Hotel; Pins Maritimes el-Mohammadia; tel: (2) 21-96 96; fax: (2) 21 06 06; located near beach and Palais des Expositions forest; restaurant; conference rooms; business center; shops; parking; health club.

El Aurassi; Boulevard Frantz Fanon; Algiers; tel: (2) 748-252; fax: (2) 632-085; 416 rooms; restaurant; conference facilities; in-room air conditioning; telephone, tv; parking; outdoor swimming pool.

Moderate
Albert; 5 Avenue Pasteur; tel: (2) 630-020.

Es Safir; 2 Rue Asselah Hocine, Algiers; tel: (2) 735-040; fax: (2) 636-376; 147 rooms; close to both the center of the city and the countryside; bar; in-room tv and telephone.

MEDICAL CARE
Clinique Centrale; 21 Ave. Claude Debussy, tel: 634617.
Clinique de la C.A.M.P.S.; Ave. Claude Debussy; tel: 656631.
Clinique des Rosiers; El Biar; tel: 781972.
Clinique des Glycines; Chemin des Glycines; tel: 605506.
Clinique des Orangers; Chemin Cheikh Bachir Brahimi, El Biar; tel: 603500.
Hôpital Central de L'arme; Birkhadem Ain Naadja; tel: (2) 56 90 15.

HEALTH CLUB
Le Fitness Club; Hotel El Djazair; 24 Avenue Souidani Boudjemaa; tel: (2) 60 10 00; for men: Sunday - Tuesday 5p.m. to 9p.m.; Wednesday, Thursday 2p.m. to 9p.m.; Friday 7a.m. to 1p.m.; for ladies: Sunday to Tuesday 2p.m. to 5p.m.; fitness room; Hammam; jacuzzi; saunas; massage.

CHAMBER OF COMMERCE
Chambre Nationale de Commerce
06, Bd Amilcar Cabral Palais Consulaire
Place Des Martyrs BP 100, Algiers
tel: (2) 574-397; fax: (2) 577-025

Argentina

Argentina

At a Glance

THE PEOPLE

Population .... 36,737,664 (July 1999 est.)
Growth Rate .... 1.29% (1999 est.)
Life Expectancy .... 74.76 years (born 1999)
Infant Mortality .... 18.41 deaths/1,000 live births (1999)

Ethnic Composition

Caucasian 85%
Mestizo, Amerindian, and other.................................. 15%

Religious Composition

Roman Catholic (nominal).. 90%
Protestant 2%
Jewish 2%
Other 6%

Languages Spoken

Spanish (official), English, Italian, German, and French

Education and Literacy

Seven years of schooling is compulsory and the adult literacy rate stands at 96.2 percent.

Labor Force

Total 14,500,000
By occupation: services 57%, industry 31%, agriculture 12%.

THE ECONOMY

Argentina has long depended on its rich agricultural land and copious natural resources. After many decades of fiscal mismanagement under military regimes, Argentina is approaching the 21st century in good, if not great, economic condition. Plagued for decades by high inflation and currency devaluations, the Menem government is considering a new means to stabilize the already improved economy. Its biggest reform under consideration is the "dollarization" of the peso wherein Argentina will actually adopt the U.S. dollar as its national currency. Unemployment still runs high and Buenos Aires is in constant conference with the IMF. Foreign investors are continuing to show interest as Argentina offers great potential if long-term stability can be achieved.

Exports .... US$26 billion (f.o.b., 1998 est.)
Imports .... US$32 billion (c.i.f., 1998 est.)
Total GDP .... US$374 billion (1998 est.)
GDP Per Capita .... US$10,300 (1998 est.)
Unemployment 12% (October1998)
Inflation Rate .... 1% (1998 est.)

Top Export Partners

Brazil, United States, Chile, E.U.

Top Import Partners

Brazil, United States, E.U.

Top Exports

Beef, wheat, corn, oilseed, manufactures, fuels.

Top Imports

Machinery and equipment, chemicals, metals, transport equipment, agricultural products.

BUSINESS WORKWEEK

Offices

Monday to Friday 8a.m. to 6 p.m.

Banks

Monday to Friday 10a.m to 3p.m. (Hours vary according to city and season.)

Government

Winter: Monday to Friday 8 a.m. to 5p.m.
Summer: 7a.m. to 4p.m.

Retail

Monday to Friday 9a.m. to 8p.m., and until 1:00p.m. on Saturdays. In the north, shops often close at noon for siesta.

HOLIDAYS

New Year's day ....January 1
Good Friday... April 10
Labor Day...May 1
Anniversary of the 1810 Revolution ....May 25
Occupation of the Islas Malvinas.......................... June 14*
Flag Day (Independence Day) ....June 22
Independence Day ....July 9
For the death of Gen. Jose
de San Martin.. August 17
Columbus Day.. October 11*
Christmas ....December 25
*Note: Some dates may vary by year.

CLIMATE

Seasons

Because Argentina lies south of the equator, the seasons are reversed from Europe, North America, and much of Asia. The best months to visit are April and May (autumn) and October and November (spring). Business goes on year-round, although December, January, and February prove the least optimal because of the Christmas season and the summer vacation schedule.

Regions

Argentina is a long, narrow country stretching from the subtropical along the northeastern border with Brazil to the subpolar region of Tierra del Fuego in the south. The western edge of the country runs along the Andes Mountains. The Central Andes include the highest mountain in South America, Aconcagua, 21,100ft. (6,960 m); but elevations gradually fall towards the south.

The Andes are high, dry, and thinly vegetated in many places. The north (Chaco) is hot and subtropical; the northeast (Misiones) is tropical and wet. The south (Patagonia) is cool, windy, and dry all year, with snow in the winter. Central areas (Pampas), with the primary business centers of Buenos Aires, Córdoba, Mendoza, and Rosario, are temperate.

Buenos Aires has a climate similar to New York City, although the winters are considerably milder and without snow, but damp and chilly. In the summer months (January and February), which are quite as hot and humid, practically everyone who can will flee the capital to nearby beach or mountains to escape the heat. Rain falls throughout the year, from 100 cm per year in Buenos Aires to less than 50 cm. in Mendoza in the foothills of the Andes

Average annual temperatures range from 24°C (75°F) to 11°C (51°F) in the capital (sea level) and Córdoba (420 m./1270 ft.), and 24°C (75°F) to 46°C (80°F) in Mendoza (820 m./2484ft.)

Argentina

Iquique
Uyuni
Villa Montes
Campo Grande
Presidente Epit cio

Bolivia

Paraguay

Antofagasta
Pedro Juan Caballero
Maring

24°

Jujuy
San Salvador de Jujuy
Rivadavia

Salta
Salta
Chaco
Formosa
Asunci n

Brazil

Curitiba

S o Francisco do Sul

Tucuman
Formosa

San Miguel de Tucum n
Santiago Del Estero
Resistencia
Misiones
Posadas

Copiap
Catamarca
Corrientes
Santo Tom
Catamarca
Santiago del Estero
Santa Fe
Corrientes
S o Borja
P rto Alegre

La Rioja
Curuz Cuati
Uruguaiana

La Serena
La Rioja
Laguna Mar Chiquita
Pelotas

San Juan
Santa Fe
Entre Ríos
Rio Grande

San Juan
C rdoba
Córdoba
Paran
Rosario

Valpara so
Mendoza
San Luis
R o Cuarto
Buenos Aires
Colonia

Santiago
San Luis
Mendoza
Jun n
Montevideo

Realic
La Plata
Uruguay

36°
Tel n
La Pampa
Santa Rosa
Buenos Aires

Concepci n
Bah a Blanca
Mar del Plata

Neuquén
Colorado
Zapala
Neuqu n
Río Negro
Negro

Atlantic

Viedma

Puerto Montt
San Carlos de Bariloche

Ocean

Esquel
Chubut
Rawson

Chubut

Comodoro Rivadavia
Colonia Las Heras
Desead
Puerto Deseado

Santa Cruz
Gobernador Gregores
Chico

48°
Puerto Santa Cruz

R o Gallegos
Stanley

Falkland Islands (U. K.)
(Las Malvinas- claimed by Argentina)

Punta Arenas
Porvenir
Tierra Del Fuego
Ushuaia

Pacific
Ocean

Chile

72°　　　　60°　　　　48°

SM Santa Barbara, CA

©2001 Magellan Geographix

Argentina
⊛ National capital
● Provincial capital
• Secondary city
⋯⋯ Railroad
── Primary road
── International border
── Province border

0　　200　　400 km
0　　　　300 mi

Money & Banking

The currency of Argentina is the Nuevo Peso (AP).

Denominations

The Nuevo Peso (AP) comes in coin denominations of AP20, 10, and 1 and 50 centavos; and banknotes of AP1, 5, 10, 20, 50, and 100.

Traveler's Checks And Credit Cards

Traveler's checks and currency can be exchanged at banks, exchange shops (*cambios*), and hotels, as well as at both Buenos Aires airports. Cash, especially U.S. dollars, commands a better exchange rate and lower fee than traveler's checks.

Cashing traveler's checks can require commissions as high as 10 percent, but can be avoided by cashing at American Express or Thomas Cook outlets. Cash is also available at automated teller machines (ATM), in larger cities. American Express, Visa, Diner's Club, and MasterCard are accepted in most up-market places in main cities. While the best exchange rate will be given for ATM and credit card transactions, retailers may add as much as a 20 percent surcharge for credit card payments. Small shops in cities and any rural transactions will require cash.

Essential Terms

English	Spanish
Yes	Sí
No	No
Good morning	Buenos Días
Hello (daytime)	Buenas Tardes
Hello (evening)	Buenas noches
Hello (telephone)	¿Hola?
Good-bye	Adiós
Please	Por Favor
Thank you	Gracias
Pleased to meet you	Encantado (a) de conocerle
Excuse me; I'm sorry	¿Perdóneme?
My name is _____	Me llamo _____
I don't understand	No entiendo
Do you speak English?	¿Habla usted inglés?

Travel

VISA AND PASSPORT

A passport that is valid for six months is required of all visitors, except nationals of Argentina, Bolivia, Brazil, Chile, Paraguay, and Uruguay who may enter with their national ID cards only.

Visas are not required for tourists from Australia, Canada, E.U. countries, the U.K., and the U.S. Other nationals must obtain visas (free) from an Argentine embassy or consulate.

Business and Transit visas are required of all visitors, except the following:

- Nationals of Andorra, Australia, Barbados, Bolivia, Brazil, Canada, Chile, Colombia, Costa Rica, Croatia, Dominican Republic, Ecuador, El Salvador, Guatemala, Haiti, Honduras, Hungary, Israel, Japan, Liechtenstein, Malta, Mexico, Monaco, New Zealand, Nicaragua, Norway, Panama, Paraguay, Peru, Poland, San Marino, Slovenia, South Africa, Switzerland, Turkey, Uruguay, U.K., U.S., Vatican City, Venezuela and Yugoslavia (Serbia and Montenegro) for stays of 90 days maximum
- Nationals of Hong Kong (British Nationals Overseas), Jamaica and Malaysia for stays of 30 days maximum
- Passengers in transit who do not leave the airport and are continuing their journey within six hours, and who are holding confirmed tickets and other documents for onward travel

Note: In spite of visa exemptions for business travelers of the countries mentioned above, it is advisable to contact the Argentinian Consulate prior to departure.

There is also a special visa with a 15-day validity, which can be issued to artists and musicians.

Tourist and Business visas are usually valid for stays up to 90 days. Extensions for an additional ninety days are possible for some nationals. The Argentinean consulate can give you more details.

If you are from a country of which a Business visa is required, your application must include your employer's letter of introduction and a letter of invitation from the contact company in Argentina, in both English and Spanish.

Allow two days for visa application processing, if you are applying in person.

DEPARTURE FORMALITIES

A US$16 departure tax exists for international flights, except those going to Montevideo (Uruguay), which will cost US$7. Domestic flights call for a US$5 departure tax. Varying rates (US$6 to 10) are charged for using the hydrofoil system to depart from Buenos Aires.

Passengers in transit are exempt.

Visitors may wish to check with their airline or travel agent, as the departure tax seems to undergo frequent changes.

CUSTOMS ENTRY (PERSONAL)

Duty-free

- Tobacco: 400 cigarettes, 50 cigars
- Alcohol: 2 liters of alcohol
- Food and others: 5 kg of foodstuffs, goods to the value of US$100 (inclusive of any duty-free items listed above)

Note: For residents returning to Argentina after a stay of less than one year in Bolivia, Brazil, Chile, Paraguay, or Uruguay:

- Tobacco: 200 cigarettes, 25 cigars
- Alcohol:1 liter of alcohol
- Food and others: 5g of foodstuffs; goods to the value of US$100 (inclusive of any duty-free items listed above)

Prohibited or Restricted

- Animals and birds from Africa or Asia (except Japan); parrots
- Fresh foodstuffs: meat, dairy products, and fruit
- Hunting guns may only be imported with a license that the traveler must procure from an Argentine Consulate before arrival. The hunter must submit personal documents, a certificate of good conduct issued by the local police of the district where the hunter lives, together with the serial number, caliber, type and brand of each gun (a maximum of two per hunter)

Argentina

Argentina

- Explosives, inflammable items
- Narcotics
- Pornographic material

Note: Gold must be declared upon arrival; it is also advisable to declare expensive consumer items as well.

IMMUNIZATION

No vaccinations are required unless arriving from an area infected with yellow fever. Tetanus vaccination and hepatitis A immunization is recommended.

TIPPING

Taxi

The tipping of metered taxicab drivers is optional. Rounding up the fare should prove sufficient as a courtesy. When unmetered taxis are used, negotiate the full fee in advance.

Porters

US$1 per bag at first-class hotels

Hotels

Hotels will add moderate service charges to your bill. Additional tips may be given to bellmen and maids.

Restaurants

Restaurants will most likely add a service charge. Otherwise, foreigners are generally expected to give a ten percent tip (*propina*).

Other

Beauty shop or barbers 5 percent; doormen 5 centavos; ushers and maitre'd, 5 percent.

EMERGENCY INFORMATION

Police and Crime

Crime continues to rise in Argentina and is the subject of national concern. The Buenos Aires streets are well lit after dark, but petty crime is widespread, especially on buses and trains. Keep a vigilant watch of your belongings. If you are a victim of crime, report it to the police. Women will find it advisable to stay in groups at night.

Avoid flashy displays of wealth; dress and behave conservatively. Foreign business visitors are often the target of thieves. Consequently, purses, laptops, and briefcases will require additional security. Do not leave valuables in cars or on tables in cafés. Keep non-essential valuables locked in hotel safes when not in use. Use credit cards and travel checks when possible to avoid carrying large sums of cash.

Carry photocopies of your passport instead of the original. Carry cash in a money belt, and use credit cards or travelers checks for most of your transactions.

Emergency Numbers

Police	101
Ambulance	107
Fire	100
Health Emergency	434-4001, 434-4104
Environmental Emergency	105
Nautical Emergency	106
Civil Defense	103

Health

There are no major health risks in Argentina. Water is potable, although locals prefer bottled mineral water. Outside main cities, it is recommended to drink only bottled water. Serious endemic diseases are scarce. Rare reports of yellow fever have come from the northeast part of the country and cases of cholera from the northern provinces. If you are traveling to rural areas between October and May, you may also be at risk for malaria.

The medical services and staff are competent in Buenos Aires; some pharmacies have English- speaking employees and are open all night. A well-stocked medical kit and travel insurance are recommended if your trip will take you outside of major urban areas for extended periods.

For more information on medical centers, including phone numbers, please see the "Business Center" section at the end of this chapter.

INTERNAL TRAVEL

AIR

Domestic travel by air is by far the most efficient way of getting around, but services are quite busy and often subject to delay.

Aerolíneas Argentinas (AR), Austral (AU) and LAPA (MJ) all offer domestic flights between Jorge Newbery (Aeroparque) and Córdoba (COR) (Pajas Blancas), as well as to other destinations throughout Argentina.

Aerolíneas offers a 30-day 'Visit Argentina Pass', with four or eight coupons for internal routes.

The primary domestic airport is Buenos Aires Aeroparque Jorge Newbury (AEP), located along the Rio de la Plata, just a few minutes distant from the major financial and commercial area. Frequent bus and taxi services are available to all parts of the city, and there is a coach connection to Ezeiza Ministro Pistarini international airport. Airport facilities include a bank/bureau de change, auto rental, and traveler information kiosk.

It is advisable to book well in advance due to the busy schedule.

TAXI

A yellow roof on a vehicle indicates a metered taxi. Cars are usually black and yellow and easy to find in cities at taxi stands; one may also hail them by standing on the street corner and waving your hand. Most cabs are metered, but make sure they start at zero when you start your journey. Cab drivers may charge extra for luggage. Radio taxis (*remises*) come without meters for a fixed fare to certain destinations. Ask about the fee before embarking.

AUTO

Cars (and motorcycles) can be rented for reasonable rates in major cities. An International Driving Permit is required; it must be stamped at the Automóvil Club Argentino's offices. Insurance is mandatory. Gasoline is expensive.

Driving in the urban areas of Argentina can be a frenetic experience. Outside the cities, many of the secondary roads have recently been upgraded, thanks to privatization programs. Tolls now exist on these and primary motorways. Rural roads, consisting of packed dirt, become impassable when it rains.

Because of the potential for crime against tourists who lose their way, rentals should only be undertaken by experienced visitors or those accompanied by a guide. Cars with drivers can also be rented for daily and weekly rates.

TRAIN

Argentina's rail network ranges over 43,000km (27,000 miles) making it among the most extensive in the world. Due to recent privatization and significant loss of subsidies for State railways, disruption has affected all long-haul services. Some suburban lines, though, have been substantially improved.

The main routes from Buenos Aires are:

- Buenos Aires–Rosario (one branch running to Tucumán and Jujuy via Córdoba, and a second to Tucumán and Jujuy via La Banda)
- Buenos Aires–Rojas, Buenos Aires–Santa Rosa
- Buenos Aires–Mar del Plata

- Buenos Aires–Las Flores–Quequén Necochea
- Buenos Aires–Bahía Blanca (where a spur provides a link to San Carlos de Bariloche)

Note: Once you have departed Buenos Aires, information is difficult to come by, so do your research in advance.

Three classes are available: air-conditioned, first class, and second class. Restaurant and sleeping cars are available for first-class travelers. Second-class passage, however, offers good value.

Discount fares: The Argempass provides visitors with unlimited first-class travel; it is only sold within Argentina through railway booking offices. Passes are available for 30, 60, or 90 days of travel. Expect a surcharge for sleeping car accommodations. The passes have to be initiated for use before 30 days elapse from the date of purchase and are valid until midnight of the last day of the term of the pass. Other group, family, and senior citizen discount passes are also available.

METRO

The metro in Buenos Aires, known as *"subte,"* is comprised of five lines, designated A to E. The fare is 50 centavos for all lines. Trains run until 1:30a.m., except Sundays when things end earlier.

If you plan to use the subway more than once, buy several tokens in advance to avoid the lines during commute hours. Maintain a high security awareness when riding the subway, especially at night.

BUSES & TRAMS

Buses (*colectivo*) run 24 hours a day in Buenos Aires but are often crowded. Expect as reckless a ride as you might in any other mode of motorized transport. Passengers pay an inexpensive flat rate.

The main bus station (Estación Terminal de Omnibus) is located at Ramos Mejía 186 in Retiro. You can call 4315-3405 or visit the second-floor office for information.

Smaller towns have their own systems, including a network of trolleybuses in Rosario, and extensive inter-city systems exist that are reliable, if not terribly comfortable.

WATER TRAVEL

There are a few river ferry services for travel to more remote towns, but only use these as a last resort. Private boats can be hired at daily and weekly rates. Buenos Aires has an efficient hydrofoil port at Darsena Norte, serving the Uruguayan cities of Montevideo and Colonia.

TRAVEL ASSISTANCE

Secretaría de Turismo de la Nación
Av. Santa Fe 883
1368 Buenos Aires, Argentina
tel: (11) 4312-5621; fax: (11) 4313-6834
websitewww.sectur.gov.ar/homepage.htm

Communications

DIALING CODES IN ARGENTINA

International country code: [54]
Selected city codes: Buenos Aires (11), Córdoba (351), Mendoza (361), Posadas (3752), Rosario (341), San Juan (364), San Rafael (3627), Santa Fe (342).

Dialing Argentina from Overseas

To reach Argentina from overseas, dial your country's international dialing code, then the country code for Argentina (54), then the city code and finally the number. If you were dialing Buenos Aires from the United States, for example, you would begin with 011, then 54, then 11 (the new city code for Buenos Aires), and finally the number of the person or business you are trying to reach.

Assistance Numbers

International direct dial access 00
Information 110
International Operator 000
International Information.................................. 4953-8000
Visitor Information (BA) ....(1) 4312-2232, 4312-6560
Visitor Information (Córdoba) ....(351) 444-027
Visitor Information (Mendoza) ....(361) 424-2800
Visitor Information (Rosario).......................(341) 424-8382

PHONE USAGE

Argentina's telephone system has been privatized and greatly improved in the past decade. City codes have recently been changed to include a preceding '2' for cities south of Buenos Aires, and a preceding '3' for those lying north of the city. Buenos Aires itself has changed its code to '11'. All local numbers now have a preceding '4'. Business hotels offer domestic telephone service that is better than using phones on the street, but charges can run high.

Many telephone exchanges and numbers are changing as Argentina upgrades the system, so wrong numbers are likely to be common for several years.

Local Calls

All local numbers have received a new prefix of 4 as Argentina goes through a telephone change. All numbers listed in this chapter have been changed accordingly. When using a phone, dial the local number, and see what happens. If you hear the word *equivocado,* you've reached a wrong number.

Long Distance Calls

Dial the area code of the region before the local number. Keep in mind that area codes in Argentina have also been changed. to include a new preceding digit. Use a zero as a prefix to the area code, for example, if you are calling to Córdoba from Buenos Aires, dial 0351 and then the local number.

International Calls

Most hotels offer international direct dial service from rooms, but the charges can run high. It is often cheaper to call collect or charge a call to a credit card.

AT&T USA Direct...............001-800- 200-1111
MCI 001-800-333-1111
Sprint 001-800-777-1111

Telephone companies also operate telephone offices from which you can make a call overseas. Calls work much as they do in Europe where an attendant gives you a number and when the booth is ready or available, your number will be called. Inside the booth you may call direct or go through an operator. Telefónica, one of Buenos Aires' two telephone companies, runs a 24-hour office on Av Corrientes 701.

PAY PHONES

Public Telephones

Public phones are readily available. Phones take tokens (*cospeles*) or cards (*tarjetas*). Different tokens apply for local and long-distance calling. One token will buy you only a couple of minutes of air time.

Telephone Cards

You can purchase cards (*tarjetas telefónicas*) at streetside kiosks, newsstands, from street vendors or even in restaurants and bars.

Coin Phone:

CELLULAR PHONES

Argentina operates mostly on an AMPS or NAMPS analog system. However, Compania de Comunicaciones Personlales del Interior also operates a TDMA digital system. Check with your operator at home to see if a partnership in Argentina exists. To call a mobile phone, one must dial 11 + 15 + 4 + local number in Buenos Aires and vicinity.

Note: Your home country cell phone may not work in this country. If not, we recommend that you rent an international cell phone *before* you leave home. A major US-based cell phone rental provider is **IMC WorldCell**. For information see "International Cell Phone Rentals" on page 14.

CALL BACK

You can (potentially) save significant sums when calling in Argentina by using a call back service. For a list of call-back services, please refer to the "Communications" section in the *Global Road Warrior* Introduction.

Fees for call back services vary widely, depending on the company and the type of service required. Be sure to check with these companies before leaving to compare rates.

PHONE JACKS

Adaptors are available through **iGo Corporation.** (See "Electrical and Telephone Adaptors" on page 19.)

FAX

Fax services are becoming more prevalent throughout the country, but the poor telephone service has made sending faxes a problem. Most hotels have fax service.

POSTAL SERVICES

Drop off all letters at post offices for best results, or at your hotel. Letters take, on average, two weeks to reach Europe and from one to two weeks to the United States. On weekdays, postal offices are open between 8a.m. and 6p.m., and on Saturdays until 1p.m. The central post office (Correo Central) is located at Sarmiento 151.

Business Services

BUSINESS CENTERS

Most top-end and expensive category hotels in Buenos Aires have business centers with computers, secretarial service, postal courier service, and fax/photocopy facilities. See individual hotel listings in "Business Centers" section to verify.

COURIER SERVICES

Buenos Aires
DHL Internacional S.A.; Moreno 963/67, Buenos Aires; tel: (11) 4347-0604/0605/0606/0607.

FedEx; Maipú 753, 1006 Buenos Aires; tel: (11) 4393-6127.

International Bonded Couriers (IMEX S.A.); Avenida Independencia 2182, Cap Fed Cp 1225; tel: (11) 4308-3555; fax: (11) 4308-3444.

UPS (Union Pak SA); Bernardo T. Irigoyen No. 974, Plata BAja, Buenos AIres; tel: (11) 4307-2174, 4307-2177; fax: (11) 4307-2182.

Cordoba
DHL Internacional S.A.; Ayacucho 95, 1st Floor office, Cordoba 5000; tel: (351) 424-5609.

SECRETARIAL SERVICE

Most top-end and expensive category hotels provide secretarial services for a fee. See individual hotel listings in "Business Centers" section.

TRANSLATION SERVICES

A Language Source ASS, Perú 428, Piso 4, BA.; tel: (11) 4342-4229.

Compagnoni-Campo;: tel/fax: (11) 4774-3875, (11) 4244-3568, CEL: (15) 4937-8721; email: mcristinacampo@impsat1.com.ar; http://www.geocities.com/SoHo/Village/6039/; legal, commercial, literary, medical translations.

Electrical

Current
220 volts AC, 50Hz

ELECTRIC PLUGS

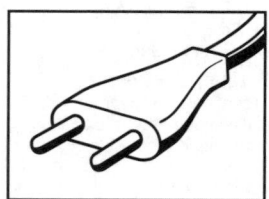

Lamp fittings are the screw type. Plug fittings in most buildings are of the 2-pin round type, although there is a push to update all plugs in the country to the 3-pin flat type, and newer buildings have those.

Adaptors are available through **iGo Corporation.** (See "Electrical and Telephone Adaptors" on page 19.)

Technical Support

HARDWARE/SOFTWARE VENDOR SUPPORT

Acer/Texas Instruments; (in the U.S.) [1] (408) 432-6200; http://www.acer.com.

Adobe; tel: (1) 4314-1212; fax: (1) 4311-5581 (All Adobe Products Except Frame Maker). tel: (1) 307-0624; fax: (1) 307-1043; (in the U.S.) tel: [1] (800) 500-7078; http://www.apple.com/.

Apple/Claris; tel: 1-314-1212;http://www.adobe.com/.

AST; (U.S. Office) tel: [1] (817) 232-9824 (International Technical Support); [1] (714) 727-4141 (Corporate Office); http://www.ast.com.

Compaq/Digital; tel: (1) 796-1616; fax: (1) 790-0535; (in the U.S.) [1] (281) 518-2000 (international technical support); fax: [1] (281) 518- 1442; http://www.compaq.com.

Corel; tel: (1) 4954-6500 (All Applications); http://www.corel.com.

Hewlett Packard; tel: [1] 4781-4061/69; (in the U.S.) tel: [1] (408) 246-4300; http://www.hp.com/.

IBM; tel: (11) 4717-4357; fax: (11) 4793-4006; (in Switzerland) tel: [41] (22) 310-0418 (in French); (in the U.S.) tel: [1] (919) 517-2800; http://www.ibm.com/.

Microsoft; tel: (1) 4316-4600; fax: (1) 4316-1922 (Client Services); (1) 316-4664 (Technical Support); (U.S. Main Office) tel: [1] (914) 765-1900;(in the U.S.) [1] (425) 635-7222; http://www.microsoft.com/.

Internet Connection

HOW TO CONNECT

Connecting to AOL and Compuserve in Argentina is similar to using it when traveling outside your own area code. See the introductory section for detailed information on connecting to your account through a different phone number.

America Online

Numbers are available at keyword: *international*. Be sure to get several local numbers before leaving. AOL's GlobalNet service charges US$12 an hour in addition to the usual charges. AOL has its GlobalNet service available at keyword: *access* (a free area).

Access: Buenos Aires (1) 345-1818; Córdoba (51) 246-654; La Plata (21) 240-856; Mar del Plata (23) 959-579; Mendoza (61) 297-411; Rosario (41) 498-853.

Compuserve

Numbers are available at *Go International*. The Compuserve Web-site also has a great deal of information, at http://www.compuserve.com.

Access: Buenos Aires (11) 4345-1818; Córdoba (351) 424-6654; La Plata (221) 424-0856; Mar Del Plata (223) 495-9579; Mendoza (261) 429-7411; Rosario (341) 449-8853.

Independent Service Providers

Many independent service providers offer discounts if you are only in town for a couple days.

Escape Internet Provider; tel: (1) 281-1444; email: info@escape.com.ar; http://www.escape.com.ar/.

ISP Canopus S.A.; tel: (1) 554-0489; fax: (1) 551-6104; email: info@canopus.com.ar; http://www.canopus.com.ar/

OneNet S.R.L.; tel: (51) 259-200; http://www.onenet.com.ar/.

SION S.A.; tel: (1) 313-2500; fax: (1) 313-0377; email: ifo@sion.com; http://www.sion.com/.

SSDNET; tel: (11) 4343-1500; email: info@ssdnet.com.ar; http://www.ssdnet.com.ar/

Tournet S.A.; tel: (1) 326-4878; fax: (1) 394-6507; email: info@tournet.com.ar; http://www.tournet.com.ar/.

VPM Internet Services; tel: [1] (800) 321-0221; tel: [1] (916) 983-9876; fax: (916) 983-4375; email: sales@vpm.com; http://www.vpm.com/.

Business Culture

GREETINGS AND COURTESIES

Argentine values emphasize the importance of personal relationships, and Argentines take time and effort to establish a personal relationship as a prerequisite to a business relationship. Individuality and candor are considered important, as are tact and diplomacy. Argentines are generally reserved and avoid calling attention to themselves. Conservative family and religious values are important guides to personal and professional behavior. Argentines also consider it a matter of pride to know the correct response, which can lead to misunderstandings when they do not in fact have a firm answer. They have a stronger work ethic than what is found in many other Latin American societies and are highly competitive. Nevertheless, they view work as a single component of life rather than the central focus.

Argentines are generally somewhat formal, although relations can involve considerable warmth and banter once a relationship has been established. The appropriate greeting consists of a firm handshake, firmness being taken as a sign of strength and confidence. Men should wait for a woman to initiate the handshake. Titles are generally used. At large gatherings, you usually introduce yourself to others, while at small and more formal gatherings, the host makes the introductions. Considerable social talk precedes any discussion of business. Be prepared to exchange business cards—yours should be in Spanish—at some point during an initial meeting. No formalities are associated with business card exchanges, however. Small gifts may be exchanged between those who are already acquainted, but wait until after the main business has been concluded to present a gift. Always bring a gift—flowers or chocolates—when invited to a home. When departing, say good-bye individually to everyone present.

DECISION MAKING

Although middle-level managers may be responsible for implementing decisions, actual decisions are almost always made at a high level of authority. Argentines will want to know your standing within the hierarchy and will wish to

Argentina

match you with someone of similar rank, although only their senior people will actually be able to approve agreements. Nevertheless, it is important to cultivate personal relationships with employees at all levels, because the quality of these relationships may strongly influence the actual decision maker even when your immediate counterpart is not the one making the decision.

WOMEN

Argentina is a traditional, male-dominated society, and women continue to occupy a secondary position in all aspects, including business. Despite this, Argentine women are generally considered to have more freedom and a greater opportunity than women in many other Latin American societies. Generally restricted to a position in the home, Argentine women nevertheless tend to be well-educated. More women are entering the workforce, albeit often in relatively low level positions, and they are becoming more responsible for monetary contributions to the family budget. Foreign businesswomen should experience few difficulties in Argentina, although they may face some rather frank questioning regarding their personal situation, as well as public comments (although these are less aggressive here than elsewhere).

MEETINGS

Meetings should be scheduled well in advance—preferably with the help of an introduction from a mutual business or social acquaintance if possible—when meeting for the first time. Meetings usually begin late, although you should generally arrive at the appointed time. Do not expect to conclude your business in a single meeting: business is a process, not an event, and time is usually not of the essence. Business may be conducted over meals or in other social situations, but this is still relatively uncommon in Argentina.

BUSINESS ATTIRE

Argentines prefer and expect conservative, formal business attire—suits for men and suits or dresses for women. Understated British style is preferred over U.S., French, or Italian. Women should wear conservative hemlines and necklines, although a sense of style is appreciated. Accessories, jewelry, and makeup should be understated and of good quality: Argentines often judge people by their dress, paying special attention to the shoes, which should be expensive and well-maintained. Attire in more rural areas and at lower levels of authority is less precise, but remains an important indication of your seriousness, status, and sense of appropriateness.

Business Centers
Buenos Aires

CITY VIEW

Buenos Aires is a sprawling, international city with a lively social scene blended into a mix of modern and colonial buildings. An efficient interstate system connects the city to other parts of the country. The only thing that may might make the roadways less efficient are the maniacal drivers that make a jaunt on the roadways an excursion of madcap lunacy.

AIRPORT

Ezeiza International Airport to City Center

Ezeiza Airport lies 20 miles (34 km.) from Buenos Aires. A half-hourly coach service, operated by Manuel Tienda León (4383-4454/8), travels downtown to all of the major

hotels for a price of about US$15 between 5:30a.m. to 10p.m. The trip takes around 45 minutes. You can find the ticket booth just outside of customs. If you seek service from the hotel to the airport, call 4314-3636. The San Martin Bus also serves the airport and downtown with buses, minibuses, and automobiles. For information and reservations, call: 4816-7676, or email: resmb@sanmartin-bus.com.ar.

A taxi counter also exists in the arrivals area. Cabs to and from the airport cost about US$35, including a freeway charge.

Airline Numbers

Aer Lingus	4312-0664
Aerolineas Argentinas	4362-5008, 4393-5122
Aeroflot	4312-5573
Aero Perú	4311-6431
Air Canada	4312-0664
Air France	4311-9863
Alitalia	4321-8421
All Nippon Airways	4314-1600
American Airlines	4312-3640
toll-free	4318-1111
Austral	4325-0505
Avianca	4394-5990
British Airways	4325-1059
Canadian Airlines	4322-3732
CATA	4775-6800
Empresa Aerea Halcon (Executive air taxi, air load, jets, helicopters)	4771-8495 / 4771-7067
Iberia	4327-2739
JAL	4393-1896
Korean Air	4311-9237
Icelandair	4325-9649
KLM	4480-9470
Ladeco	4326-9937
Lan Chile	4311-5334
Lineas Aereas Paraguayas	4393-1000
Lloyd Aereo Boliviano	4326-3595
Lufthansa	4319-0600
Pluna	4342-4420
Saeta	4393-1527
Swissair	4319-0000
TAP	4811-0984
United Airlines	4326-9111
Varig	4329-9200 or 9201
Vasp	4311-2699
Viasa	4326-5082

HOTELS

Note: Advance reservations essential throughout the year in Buenos Aires, except in January and February.

Top-end

Alvear Palace Hotel (Rélais & Chateaux); Av. Alvear 1891, Recoleta; tel: (11) 4804-4031; fax: (11) 4804-9246; email: alvear@satlink.com; city center; restaurant; conference facilities (up to 1500); business center; secretarial services; computer rentals; internet available; in-room fax/modem connections; fitness; sauna; indoor pool.

Caesar Park Buenos Aires (Westin); Posadas 1232, Recoleta; tel: (11) 4814-5150, 4819-1100; fax: (11) 4814-5160, 4819-1121; email: reservas@caesar.com.ar; business hotel in city center; 3 restaurants; conference facilities (up to 950); business center; in-room modem/fax connections; non-smoking rooms available; beauty salon; corporate rates; health/fitness; sauna; pool; access to nearby golf course.

Argentina

Claridge Hotel; Tucumán 535; tel: (11) 4314-7700; fax: (11) 4314-8022; email: reservations@claridge-hotel.com; near Calle Florida, city center; restaurant; meeting facilities (up to 600); business center; secretarial service; in-room minibar, IDD telephone, modem connection; laundry/dry-cleaning;24-hour room service; executive rooms with hair dryer, safe, butler service; limousine service; garage; health club; massage; spa; solarium; pool.

Inter-Continental; Moreno 809; tel: (11) 4340-7100; fax: (11) 4340-7199; email: buenosaires@interconti.com; restaurants; conference facilities (up to 1400); executive business center; executive services; secretarial services; in-room modem/fax connections; health/fitness center; spa; sauna; steamroom; indoor pool; whirlpool.

Sheraton & Towers; San Martin 1225, Plaza Fuerza, Retiro; tel: (11) 4318-9000; fax: (11) 4318-9346; restaurants; conference facilities (up to 5000); business center; secretarial services; in-room modem/fax connections; executive floors; 24-hour room service; shopping arcade; fitness; health club/fitness; massage; sauna; indoor/outdoor pools; tennis.

Expensive

Buenos Aires Bauen; Avenida Callao 360; tel: (11) 4370-1600; fax: (11) 4476-1305;email: bauencom@tournet.com.ar; near exhibition grounds; restaurant; conference facilities (up to 1000); secretarial services; in-room modem/fax connections; beauty salon; corporate rates; pool; sauna; (lower floors may prove noisy).

El Conquistador; Suipacha 948; tel: (11) 4805-2626; fax: (11) 4328-3252; email: conqhot@microstar.com.ar; city center; restaurant; conference facilities; secretarial service; corporate rates; fitness; sauna.

Etoile Hotel; RM Ortiz 1835, Recoleta; tel: (11) 4805-2626; fax: (11) 4805-3613; restaurant; complimentary breakfast; conference facilities (up to 180); secretarial services; fax facilities; dataports; laundry; car rental; corporate rates; health club/fitness; solarium; sauna; massage; pool; whirlpool.

Gran Hotel Colón; Carlos Pellegrini 507; tel: (11) 4320-3500; fax: (11) 4320-3516; small rooms; restaurant; conference facilities (up to 180); secretarial service; 234-hour room service; corporate rates; fitness; sauna; rooftop pool; whirlpool.

Hotel Crillon; Avenida Santa Fe 796, Retiro; tel: (11) 4310-2000; fax: (11) 4310-2020; email: hoter@movi.com.ar; near rail station, opposite Plaza St. Martin; remodeled 1995; restaurant; conference facilities (up to 300); secretarial service; in-room modem/fax connections.

Plaza San Martin Suites; Suipacha 1092; tel: (11) 4328-4740; fax: (11) 4328-9385; email: plazasm@travel.idt.net; all-suite hotel with kitchenettes; conference rooms; business center; coffee/tea makers; parking; fitness; sauna.

Moderate

Hyde Park Hotel; 572 Maipu Street; tel: (11) 4326-6076/180; fax: (11) 4322-4689; located near Florida and Lavalle pedestrian zones; restaurant; coffee shop; complimentary buffet breakfast; business center; car rental.

Continental Hotel; Av. Roque Saenz Pena 725; tel: (11) 4326-1700; fax: (11) 4322-1421; near Lavalle street mall; renovated; restaurant; conference rooms; in-room IDD telephones, minibar; 24-hour room service; business suites available; car rental; airline desk.

Lancaster; Avenida Cordoba 405; tel: (11) 4312-4061; fax: (11) 4311-3021; antique style; near exhibition grounds; restaurant; business services.

Phoenix Hotel; San Martin 780; tel: (11) 4312-4845; fax: (11) 4311-2846; in Galerís Pacifico shopping center; restaurant.

Republica; Cerrito 370; tel/fax: (11) 4382-5050; near exhibition grounds, train station; conference rooms (up to 40); secretarial service; in-room safe; hairdresser; corporate rates; massage; sauna; pool.

Savoy; Av Callao 181, Corientes; tel: (11) 4372-7788, 4370-8000; fax: (11) 4372-7066, 370-8080; http://www.savoy-hotel.com.ar/; city center; restaurant;11 meeting rooms; private offices; 24-hour room service, medical; corporate rates; fitness; pool.

Tritone; Maipu 657; tel: (11) 4325-8955; fax: (11) 4325-8969/5; city center; restaurant; conference facilities (up to 60); secretarial services; car rental; corporate rates.

Wilton Palace Hotel; Av Callao 1162, Barrio Norte; tel: 4811-1818, 4812-8024; http://www.hotelwilton.com.ar; city suburb; conference facilities (up to 120); secretarial services; in-room modem/fax connections; no-smoking rooms available; laundry/dry cleaning; parking.

MEDICAL CARE

Asociacion Israelita; 1164 Avenida Terrada; tel: (11) 4581-0070.

The British Hospital; 74 Perdiel; tel: (11) 4304-1081.

Hospital Italiano; 450 Calle Gascon; tel: (11) 4981-5010.

HEALTH CLUB

Alfa Gym; 3021 Avenida Santa Fe, Barrio Norte. Subterraneo: Aguero; tel: (11) 4826-1496.

Club de Amigos; 3885 Figuero, Alcorta Palermo; tel: (11) 4801-1213.

Health Club at the Caesar Park Hotel; 1200 Av. Posadas; tel: (11) 4814-5150.

Club Olympus; 1088 Posadas, Park Hyatt Hotel; tel: (11) 4326-1234.

Hotel Crowne Plaza Panamericano Club; Carlos Pellegrini; tel: (11) 4348-5260.

Sports and Spa Complex, Park Tower, Sheraton; San Martin 1255 at Av. del Liberator; tel: (11) 4318-9000; fax: (11) 4318-9353.

AUTO RENTAL

Note: Expect aggressive driving, tailgating and excessive speeding in Buenos Aires and throughout Argentina. Most deaths in Argentina occur from traffic accidents.

Al; Central De Alvear 678; tel: (11) 4311-1000, 4313-1515; fax: (11) 4311-7491; email: rentacar@ssdnet.com.ar.

Avis; Aeroparque Ezeiza; tel: (11) 4480-9387; Calle Cerrito 1527 (downtown), tel: (11) 4326-5542, 4326-5578, 4326-4944; fax: (11) 4326-6992.

Budget; Santa Fe 869, Av. Scalabrini Ortiz 258-1059; tel: (11) 4311-9870; fax: (11) 4311-9870.

Hertz; Aeropuerto Ezeiza; tel. 4480-0054, with offices downtown and in the provinces; main number at Pasaje Ricardo Rojas 451, tel: (11) 4312-1317, fax: (11) 4315-1809 (9a.m. to 7p.m.).

Localiza; Calle Paraguay 1122; tel: (11) 4375-1644.

National; Calle Esmeralda 1084; tel: (11) 4312-4318.

Remises Universal; chauffeured cars; Corrientes 2565, 11th Floor; tel: (11) 4951-6900.

WORLD TRADE CENTER

World Trade Center Buenos Aires, S.A.
Moreno 584-9th Floor
1091 Buenos Aires, Argentina
tel: (11) 4342-3216, 4342-3283
fax: (11) 4331-0223, 4334-3811
email: coginte@mbox.servicenet.com.ar

Australia

At a Glance

THE PEOPLE

Population .... 18,783,551 (July 1999 est.)
Growth Rate .... 0.9% (1999 est.)
Life Expectancy .... 80.14 years
(born 1999)
Infant Mortality .... 5.26 deaths/1,000 live births (1998)

Ethnic Composition

Caucasian 92%
Asian 7%
Aboriginal and other 1%

Religious Composition

Anglican..26.1%
Roman Catholic...26.0%
Protestant 24.3%
Other 33.6%

Languages Spoken

English, Vietnamese, Aboriginal languages.

Education and Literacy

Education is compulsory to age 15 in all states except Tasmania, where it is 16. Literacy rate is 99percent of the adult population.

Labor Force

Total 9,200,000
By occupation: services 73%, industry 22%, agriculture 5%.

THE ECONOMY

Australia is a highly-developed, affluent, well- educated, and industrialized country that supplies its own basic food needs while exporting large quantities of foodstuffs and mineral products. It is also one of the world's most urbanized and technologically advanced societies. It faced a sharp recession in the early 1990s, but it has fully recovered despite the problems of its neighbors in Southeast Asia. Often unsure of whether it was an Asian or a European nation, Australia has carved out its own niche in the global economy. Foreign investment that once targeted the "tigers" of the region is now looking at the thriving Australian economy. Large privatization projects, especially in telecom and airports, has made the continent-size nation the darling of the southern hemisphere.

Exports .... US$56 billion (f.o.b., 1998 est.)
Imports .... US$61 billion (f.o.b., 1998 est.)
Total GDP .... US$393.9 billion (1998 est.)
GDP Per Capita .... US$21,200 (1998 est.)
Unemployment 8.1% (1998)
Inflation Rate 1percent (1998)

Top Export Partners

Japan, South Korea, New Zealand, United States, E.U., Taiwan, Singapore, Hong Kong

Top Import Partners

United States, Japan, E.U., China, New Zealand

Top Exports

Coal, gold, meat, wool, aluminum, iron ore, wheat, machinery and transport equipment.

Top Imports

Machinery and transport equipment, computers and office machines, telecommunication equipment and parts; crude oil and petroleum products.

BUSINESS WORKWEEK

Offices

Monday to Friday 9a.m. to 5 p.m.

Banks

Monday to Thursday 9a.m. to 4p.m. (Friday 5p.m.)

Government

Monday to Friday 9a.m.to 5:30p.m.

Retail

Monday to Friday 9 a.m. to 5:30 p.m. (Thursday or Friday until 9:30p.m.), Saturday 9a.m. to 5:30p.m.

HOLIDAYS

New Year's Day..January 1
Australia Day ....January 26
Easter ....April 2-5*
Anzac Day .... April 25
Queen's Official Birthday.. June 7*
Christmas Day & Boxing Day ....December 25-26
*Note: Some dates may vary by year.

CLIMATE

Seasons

Because Australia is south of the equator, the seasons are reversed from Europe, North America, and much of Asia. Spring lasts from September to November, summer from December to February, fall from March until May, and winter from June to August. In general, the climate is very pleasant, without dramatic shifts in temperature.

Regions

There are two climatic zones: about 40 percent of Australia in the north, above the Tropic of Capricorn—Northern Territory (NT), the northern parts of Queensland (QLD), and Western Australia (WA) lie in the tropical zone. The southern remaining areas—North South Wales (NSW), Victoria (VIC), Tasmania (TAS), South Australia, and southern parts of West Australia and Queensland—are in the temperate zone.

The best months to travel in Sydney, Melbourne, and Adelaide are from the end of October to December (spring) or from February to late April (late summer and fall), when it is sunny, warm and with minimum rain. Perth and Brisbane have more sunshine and less rain than other major cities.

Average annual temperatures range from 26°C (79°F) to 9°C (49°F) in Sydney and Melbourne, with Adelaide, Brisbane, and Perth averaging highs around 30°C (86°F) and lows similar to Sydney's. Canberra has highs that average 26°C (79°F), but can get close to freezing in winter months.

Money & Banking

Currency

The currency of Australia is the Australian Dollar (A$).

Denominations

The Australian Dollar comes in coin denominations of 5, 10, 20, and 50 cents as well as A$1 and A$2. Banknotes are of A$5, A$10, A$20, A$50, and A$100 denominations.

Traveler's Checks and Credit Cards

Traveler's checks and foreign currency can be easily and efficiently exchanged at banks, foreign exchange bureaus located in the major cities, hotels, and foreign exchange kiosks at the airports. Banks offer the most variable exchange rates. Traveler's checks receive a better exchange rate than cash, or purchase Australian dollar traveler's check, which can be exchanged almost everywhere, before departure.

Credit cards are widely accepted in Australia including American Express, Visa, MasterCard, and Diners Club, as well as bank cards from the larger Australian banks. All taxis accept credit cards, and you can get cash advances from your credit card on many of the automated teller machines (ATM). Credit cards are also essential for renting a car. Long-term visitors should set up a checking account in Australia and get an ATM card. The most favorable exchange rates are given for credit card and ATM transactions.

Travel

VISA AND PASSPORT

Passports are required of all visitors, with an expiration date at least six months beyond anticipated exit date.

Visas are also required of all, except for New Zealanders with valid NZ passports, and transit passengers who do not leave the transit lounge before continuing their journey within eight hours of arriving, and who possess onward or return paperwork. Such exempt passengers must also be nationals of the following only: E.U. countries, Brunei, Canada, Fiji, Indone-

Australia *(side margin)*

sia, Japan, Kiribati, Korea (Rep. of), Liechtenstein, Malaysia, Malta, Marshall Islands, Federated States of Micronesia, Nauru, New Zealand, Norway, Papua New Guinea, Philippines, Samoa, Singapore, Solomon Islands, South Africa, Switzerland, Thailand, Tonga, Tuvalu, Vanuatu, USA, and Zimbabwe.

Travelers must also show proof of a through fare ticket and may be required to prove sufficient funds.

Electronic Travel Authority (ETA) visas are like electronic tickets, and are certainly the best way to go if you qualify: application forms are unnecessary, and a visa label is not inserted in the passport. An ETA is valid for either tourist or business trips and provides for multiple entries for stays up to three months on each occasion. ETAs are obtained from authorized travel agents and from airlines. They are also available through Australian Embassies, High Commissions, and Consulates. Travelers are forewarned that applying in person can actually be more time consuming than the aforementioned approaches. The only travelers eligible for an ETA are nationals of: E.U. countries (except Portugal), Andorra, Brunei, Canada, Iceland, Japan, Korea (Rep. of), Liechtenstein, Malaysia, Malta, Monaco, Norway, Singapore, Switzerland, Taiwan, USA. and Vatican City.

Tourist ETAs are valid for 12 months or until passport expiration, whichever comes first, and provide for multiple entries for stays up to three months on each visit.

Business ETAs are good until passport expiration.

Visitors who are ineligible for an ETA, or who are seeking a longer term of stay than an ETA provides, may apply for Tourist Visitor (Non ETA) and Business Visitor (Non ETA) visas. Both types cost about US$40.

In the case of non-ETA visas, validity depends on the type of visa, the visitor's purpose, and the term of the applicant's passport.

When issued by travel agents or airlines, ETAs are customarily processed and valid right away (if application is by telephone), or within 24 hours of the form's being received (if sent by fax or mail). If issued by an Australian government agency, processing can take three weeks or longer during peak periods.

Non-ETA visas normally take three weeks or longer during peak periods.

Working visas are also available for young (18-26 years of age) visitors who wish to be employed during their brief stay.

Note: Because Australian visa regulations change occasionally, travelers should inquire in advance. The most expedient way is to check the website of the High Commission.

website ....www.australia.org.

DEPARTURE FORMALITIES

Visitors must pay a departure tax of A$27 and will receive a tax stamp that must be attached to their ticket. The tax must be paid in Australian dollars. Travelers with multiple departures only pay the tax once. No more than A$5,000 can be exported.

CUSTOMS ENTRY (PERSONAL)

Duty-free
- Tobacco: 250 cigarettes, 250g of tobacco or cigars
- Alcohol: 1.125 liters of any alcoholic liquor
- Items for personal hygiene
- Other: goods to a value of A$400; A$200 if under 18

Prohibited or Restricted
- Non-prescribed drugs
- Weapons
- Firearms
- Certain foodstuffs and other potential sources of disease and pestilence

For more information, read the Australian Customs information, available from the Australian High Commission. Severe penalties exist for drug trafficking.

IMMUNIZATION

No proof of vaccination is required unless you have visited an area infected with yellow fever in the past two weeks, such as tropical South America or Africa. Tetanus vaccination and hepatitis A shots are recommended if travel in the "outback" is part of the itinerary.

TIPPING

Taxi
The tipping of metered taxicab drivers is optional. Rounding up the fare should prove sufficient as a courtesy.

Porters
US$1 per bag at first-class hotels only.

Hotels
Hotels will add moderate service charges to your bill. Additional tips may be given to bellmen and maids who have provided exceptional service.

Restaurants
Restaurants will most likely add a service charge. Otherwise, a 10 percent tip will prove sufficient.

Other
Other services are tipped only for special assistance.
Note: Tipping in Australia is not prevalent, although it is becoming more common in restaurants and pubs.

EMERGENCY INFORMATION

Police and Crime
Australia is relatively safe. However, the larger cities, especially Sydney, can get rough at night. Australians are heavy drinkers, so be cautious after drinking hours. Women can walk around freely, but it is advisable to travel in groups at night. The police are efficient and courteous.

Take basic precautions against petty crime. Foreign business visitors are often the target of what few thieves there are in Australia. Consequently, purses, laptops, and briefcases will require additional security. Do not leave valuables in cars or on tables in cafés. Keep non-essential valuables locked in hotel safes when not in use. Use credit cards and travel checks when possible to avoid carrying large sums of cash. Carry photocopies of your passport instead of the original. Carry cash in a money belt, and use credit cards or travelers checks for large transactions.

Emergency Numbers
This number is good throughout Australia.
Ambulance, Fire, and Police 000

Health
There are no unusual health risks in Australia. Water is potable, and meat and dairy products are safe. Food preparation hygiene standards are very high. Caution should be observed, however, if you decide to sample 'bush tucker' in the Outback—some insects and plants are extremely poisonous if not properly prepared.

Be sure to take precautions against heat and sunstroke.

Australia has well-trained doctors and dentists. Only specialized medicines (e.g., insulin) need be brought along for travel. Travel insurance is recommended if your itinerary takes you outside of the urban areas for extended periods. For more information on medical centers, including phone numbers, please see the "Business Center" section at the end of this chapter.

TAXI

Meter-operated taxis are plentiful in the cities. There is a minimum charge plus mileage. Most taxi drivers know their way around their city, and only an address or sometimes even a building name will suffice.

A nominal extra payment may be necessary for baggage and telephone bookings. Some taxis will accept credit cards.

AIR

Australians make use of aviation the same way residents of smaller countries use trains and buses. Scheduled services cover more than 150,000km (95,000 miles) over the entire continent. First- and second-class service is offered, including meals and attendant service on most routes. Recent deregulation of domestic airlines has made airline services more competitively priced.

The major domestic carriers are: Ansett Australia Airlines, Qantas Domestic, and East West, serving major resorts and cities. Also, Ansett Express, Hazelton Airlines, and Eastern Australia Airlines provide services throughout New South Wales.

Ansett WA covers Western Australia. Air North has routes across the Northern Territory. Lloyd Aviation flies throughout South Australia. Kendell Airlines is a major carrier throughout Victoria and South Australia; Sunstate Airlines operates in Victoria and Queensland. Australian Regional Airlines offers services inQueenslan. Tasmania is serviced by Airlines of Tasmania.

Most of the domestic airlines offer discounts or passes at reduced prices. Qantas Airlines will happily provide information for all domestic air carriers' special offers:

website .... www.qantas.com.au

Canberra Airport (CBR), 9km (5.5 miles) east of the city, is the domestic hub. International passengers can reach Canberra by flying to Sydney.

There are many secondary airports and smalller landing strips around the country, in all capital cities, and in territorial centers like Alice Springs, Ayers Rock, and Launceston.

AUTO

Cars, trucks, and motorcycles can be rented in major cities and smaller towns. Drivers require a international, foreign, or national driving permit, customarily valid for a period of three months. You must possess the national license in order for the international permit to be valid. Carry these documents with you when you are behind the wheel.

Due to the massive size of the country, visitors may wish to rent vehicles for intercity travel. Be prepared for adverse conditions in the outback and hectic—but courteous—driving in the cities. Credit cards and valid driving licenses are necessary for securing rentals. Age limitations vary by rental company and vehicle.

Driving on secondary roads in the Outback is challenging between November and February due to summer rainfall; many roads are dirt tracks. Road travel is easiest from April to October. Distances between towns tend to be long. All vehicles should be in excellent condition, and you are well advised to have spare water, fuel, and equipment.

Travelers should check in with local Automobile Associations prior to departurefor up-to-date status of road and climatic conditions.

TRAIN

More than 40,000km (24,850 miles) of rail crisscrosses the continent, and one track spans the country coast-to-coast: the Indian Pacific, running twice-weekly over 4350km (2704 miles) from Sydney to Perth; journey time is three days. The Indian Pacific is air-conditioned and soundproofed, offering first- and second-class sleeping cars, along with a lounge car sporting a piano, bar, and even video for first-class ticket-holders. Train cuisine, prepared in an on-board galley, is famous for its high quality.

There are other express links from provincial capitals, not all of them running daily:

- The Ghan runs between Adelaide and Alice Springs (overnight).
- The Overland joins Melbourne and Adelaide (overnight).
- The Canberra Monaro Express and the fast XPT Express make the run between Canberra and Sydney in less than five hours.
- The Sunlander and the Queenslander take six days to get between Brisbane and Cairns.
- The Prospector, one of Australia's fastest trains, links Perth and Kalgoorlie in six or seven hours.
- The Vinelander runs between Melbourne and Mildura (overnight).
- The Spirit of Capricorn connects Brisbane with Rockhampton (overnight).
- The Spirit of the Outback travels the same route as the Capricorn, but extends further to Longreach.

First- and second-class tickets can be purchased, and sleeping accommodations are available on long journeys. Scenic rail journeys abound, too. Particularly notable are the Great South Pacific Express (a train reminiscent of the Orient Express), which travels from Brisbane to Cairns, Brisbane to Sydney and Sydney to Cairns; and the Kuranda Scenic Railway, linking Cairns and Kuranda and featuring a fourteen-mile (34km) sojourn through tropical rainforest.

In general, long-distance trains have air conditioning, excellent dining facilities, and showers. Advance reservations for both seats and for sleeping berths are imperative on all long-distance trains; they can be made up to six months ahead of time. For reservations and information regarding the Ausrailpass, which provides for discounted, unlimited travel deals, contact the Australian National Travel Centre (see listing in Travel Assistance section below).

URBAN / METRO

There is no subway system distinct from the train system in any of the Australian cities.

In the State capitals you will find suburban rail networks. Sydney and Melbourne both have especially expansive systems. Trams operate in Melbourne and Adelaide.

BUSES & TRAMS

Buses and trams are the backbone of Australian urban transport systems. All major cities use these efficient and economically priced people movers.

Long-distance coaches are among the most economical ways to travel and prove extremely comfortable, featuring air conditioning, large adjustable seats, and on-board restrooms. Many even have television and videos.

Discount coach passes can be obtained for between 7 and 90 days. These include the Aussie Discoverer, the Eastern Discoverer, the Aussiepass, the Bus Australia Pass, the Down Under Pass, and more. They customarily provide unlimited travel around the entire country. It is usually significantly cheaper to buy them prior to departur, rather than waiting until you are in Australia.

Each city provides detailed maps, schedules, and fares. Visitors should take advantage of the "met" system to become familiar with a city prior to using rental cars.

Australia

WATER TRAVEL

Australia has 36,738km (22,600 miles) of coastline, countless lakes, inland waterways and estuaries, the vast majority of which can be toured by boat. There are paddle steamers you can take on the Murray River, deep-sea fishing boats that navigate the incredible Barrier Reef, and much, much more, all available for individual or charter booking.

Melbourne, Sydney, and Brisbane all have ferry and water travel systems. Sydney harbor is one of the great sights of Asia and has a water taxi service. Intercity boat service along the eastern seaboard is used primarily for cargo.

Most tour operators can arrange shipping cruises. A scheduled car-ferry service runs betweenVictoria and Tasmania.

Communications

DIALING CODES IN AUSTRALIA

International country code: [61]

Selected city codes: Adelaide (8), Brisbane (7), Canberra (2), Melbourne (3), Perth (8), Sydney (2)

Dialing Australia from Overseas

To reach Australia from overseas, dial your country's international dialing code, then the country code for Argentina (61), then the city code and finally the number. Remember that when dialing from outside the country, omit the zero preceding the area code. If you were dialing Brisbane from the United States, for example, you would begin with 011, then 61, then 7 (the city code for Brisbane), and finally the number of the person or office you are trying to reach.

Assistance Numbers

International direct dial access	00
Directory Assistance	013 (local only); 0175
Time	1194
News	1199
Translation and Interpreting	13-1450

CALLING WITHIN AUSTRALIA

Local Calls

Australia has one of the most advanced telephone systems in the world, and business travelers should have no problem making calls.

Because the country is running out of telephone and fax numbers, Australia is in the process of changing the entire dialing system so that every number in the country will be eight digits plus a two digit area code. The conversion began in 1994 and should last until 1998.

Long Distance Calls

If dialing from inside Australia, all area codes begin with a 0, which is dropped when dialing Australian numbers from outside the country. In order to achieve a uniform eight digits for its phone numbers, Melbourne has added a '9' preceding all of its numbers.

International Calls

To make a direct call overseas, dial 011 + country code + area code + number. From hotels, one may have to dial a zero or nine first to access an operator or a line. But in doing so, remember that your corporate coffers will also have to be accessed to pay off the often incredulous hotel surcharges.

International Subscriber Dialing (ISD) is available from the gold phones found in post offices, airports, and hotel lobbies. Australian telephone books list all information regarding rates, charges, and codes. Economy rates happen between 6p.m. and 8a.m., Saturday to Monday, and between 10 p.m. and 8 a.m. daily.

To reach an operator at home for collect or credit card calls:

Canada	1800-881-150
France	1800-881-330
Germany	1800-881-490
Japan	1800-881-640
U.K. BT	1800-881-440
U.K. Mercury	1800-881-417
U.S. AT&T	1800-881-011
U.S. MCI	1800-881-100
U.S. Sprint	1800-881-877

PAY PHONES

Public Telephones

Card Phone:

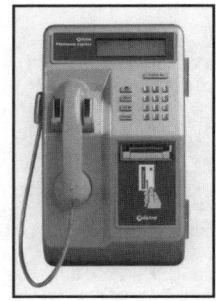

Public phones are colored red, gold, green, or blue. Red phones are for local calls only. Green, gold, and blue phones support International Direct Dialing (IDD) and Subscriber Trunk Dial (STD) services. The minimum cost of a local call is 30c.

Calling Cards

Cards are available at newsstands, supermarkets, and drugstores, and can be purchased in A$5, A$10, or A$20 increments.

Credit card phones, taking most major credit cards, are available at airports, city center locations, and most major hotels.

CELLULAR PHONES

Australia has several cellular phone providers in the digital GSM format. Optus Mobile Pty Ltd, Telstra, Vodafone Pty. Ltd all fall into the aforementioned category.

Note: Your home country cell phone may not work in this country. If not, we recommend that you rent an international cell phone *before* you leave home. A major US-based cell phone rental provider is **IMC WorldCell**. For information see "International Cell Phone Rentals" on page 14.

CALL BACK

You can (potentially) save significant sums when calling in Australia by using a call back service. For a list of call-back services, please refer to the "Communications" section in the *Global Road Warrior* Introduction.

Fees for call back services vary widely, depending on the company and the type of service required. Be sure to check with these companies before leaving to compare rates.

PHONE JACKS

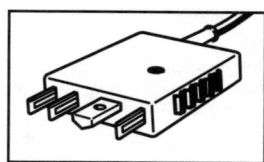

Adaptors are available through **iGo Corporation.** (See "Electrical and Telephone Adaptors" on page 19.)

FAX

Fax machines are available in most hotels and post offices, except in the outback where they may be difficult to find. The telephone system is excellent in Australia, and there should be no problem with the transmission.

POSTAL SERVICES

There are post offices in every city and even most small towns have one. Stamps are available at hotels and newsstands.

Hours of service

Monday to Friday, 9a.m. to 5p.m.

Business Services

AUDIOVISUAL RENTALS

Sydney
Haycom Staging Propriety Ltd.; Unit 20, 17-21 Bowden St.; Alexandria; tel: 9319-0466.

Melbourne
Intercity Hire; 196 Normandy Rd., South Melbourne; tel: 9646-2211.

Staging Connections; 198 Roden, W. Melbourne; tel: 9329-5899.

COMPUTER RENTALS

Sydney
The Mac Man; York St., Sydney; tel: (2) 9262-1444.

Micro Rentals Pty Ltd.; Pacific Highway, North Sydney; tel: (2) 9966-1766.

PC Hire; tel: (2) 9737-8322; toll-free: 1300-65-6858.

Tech Rental; 18 Hilly St., Mortlake; tel: (2) 9736-2066.

Melbourne
Hire Intelligence; Jersey St.; tel: 1300-65-5551.

Mac Rent; Park Street, South Melbourne; tel: (3) 9699-3999.

Microrentals; 8-12 Sandilands St., S. Melbourne; tel: (3) 9696-4189.

Southern Cross Computer Rentals; Lorimer St., Port Melbourne; tel: (3) 9676-6655.

COURIER SERVICES

City Link Messengers; Sydney, tel: (2) 9669-5533; fax: (2) 9317-5606.

Airborne Express; Unit 1/55 Kent Road, Mascot, NSW 2020; tel: (2) 9693-1566; fax: (2) 9693-2145; Melbourne: tel: (3) 9338-0911; fax: (3) 9338-3164.

Dart Couriers; Melbourne, tel: (3) 9654-6644.

DHL International; Canberra: tel: (2) 6280-6792; Adelaide, tel: (8) 8234-3111; Brisbane, tel: (7) 3845-7791; Melbourne, tel: (3) 9371-3333; Perth, tel: (8) 9277-8544.

District Messengers; Melbourne, tel: (3) 9690-2133.

FedEx; tel: (800) 021-021 (toll free in Australia only).

Sanford Couriers; Sydney, tel: (2) 9113-1521; fax: (2) 9540-2030.

UPS; 247 King St., Mascot, NSW 2020; Sydney 2020; tel: (2) 9667-1333; fax: (2) 9313-1515.

WDM International (Airborne Express); Adelaide, tel: (8) 8353-2033, fax: (8) 8235-0105; Brisbane, tel: (7) 3860-5988, fax: (7) 3860-5983; Melbourne, tel: (3) 9338-0911, fax: (3) 9338-3164; Perth, tel: (8) 9477-1333, fax: (8) 9477-1331; Sydney, tel: (2) 9693-1566, fax: (2) 9693-2145.

SECRETARIAL SERVICES

Sydney
Cullen's Secretarial; 34 Hunter St.; tel: (2) 9235-0411.

Intercity Business Center; (2) 9203-233 New South Head Rd.; Edgecliff, tel: (2) 9327-8333.

Sydney Executive Centers, 133 Alexandria St., Crows Nest; tel: (2) 9439-5488.

Melbourne
Dial-A-Secretary; 100 Albert Rd.; South Melbourne; tel: (3) 9696-2993.

Clivedon Secretarial Services; 596 St. Kilda Rd.; tel: (3) 9529-8113.

TRANSLATION SERVICES

Associated Translators and Linguists 72 Pitt St., Sydney 2000; tel: (2) 9231-3288; fax: (2) 9221-4763.

Conference Interpreters International 566 St. Kilda Rd., Melbourne; tel: 1800-339-613; fax: (3) 9521-3444.

Electrical

Current
220/240 volts AC, 50Hz.

Australia uses a flat three-pin socket, but the pins are slanted. Similar plugs can be found throughout the South Pacific.

ELECTRIC PLUG

Adaptors are available through **iGo Corporation.** (See "Electrical and Telephone Adaptors" on page 19.)

Australia

Technical Support

HARDWARE/SOFTWARE VENDOR SUPPORT

Apple/Claris; tel: (2) 9452-8000 (Sydney); (3) 9694-2200 (Melbourne); (8) 8223-6155 (Adelaide); (7) 3858-2100 (Brisbane); (6) 283-4111 (Canberra); (9) 221-2655 (Perth); http://www.apple.com.

Compaq/Digital; tel: (612) 911-1999; fax: (612) 911-9019; (General U.S.) tel: (281) 518-2000; http://www.compaq.com/.

Dell; (in the U.S.) tel: [1] (512) 338-4400; fax: [1] (512) 728-3330; http://www.dell.com/.

Hewlett Packard; tel: 3-9272-8000; (in the U.S.) tel: [1] (408) 246-4300; http://www.hp.com/.

IBM; tel: 132-426 (General Information/Toll Free in Australia); tel: (2)-9354-4000; fax: (2) 9354-7766; tel: 131-426 (Service Number); (U.S. Main Office) tel: [1] 914-765-1900; http://www.ibm.com.

Microsoft; (in Australia only) tel: 132-058; (in Switzerland) tel: [41] (848) 858-868; fax [41] (1) 831-0869; (in the U.S.) [1] (425) 635-7222; http://www.microsoft.com/.

Internet Connection

HOW TO CONNECT

Connecting to AOL and Compuserve in Australia is similar to using it when traveling outside your own area code. See the introductory section for detailed information on connecting to your account through a different phone number.

America Online

Numbers are available at keyword: *international*. Be sure to get several local numbers before leaving. AOL's GlobalNet service charges US$3.95 (US$6 in Cairns and National Access Number) an hour in addition to the usual charges. AOL has its GlobalNet service available at keyword: *access* (a free area) and download the software.

Access: Adelaide (8) 8338-2499; Brisbane (7) 3210-0180; Canberra (2) 6249-8496; Hobart (3) 6210-9000; Melbourne (3) 8623-5000; Perth (8) 9425-8000; Sydney (2) 8437-8000; Wollongong (2) 4254-1000; National Access Number (1) 9830-4148.

Compuserve

Numbers are available at keyword *Go International*. The Compuserve Web-site also has a great deal of information, at http://www.compuserve.com.

Access: Adelaide (8) 8338-2499; Brisbane (7) 3210-0180; Canberra (2) 6249-8496; Darwin (8) 8932-6610; Gold Coast (7) 5574-1580; Hobart (3) 6234-4504; Melbourne (3) 9538-0560; Newcastle (2) 4965-4412; Perth (9) 321-5233; Sydney (2) 9465-9600.

Independent Service Providers

Many independent service providers offer discounts if you are only in town for a couple days. Australia has a myriad of service providers. Below are just a few.

Access Net Australia; (Melbourne connections) tel: (3) 9686-4192; fax: (3) 9686-4189; email: info@access.net.au; http://www.access.net.au/

Access One; tel: (2) 9433-2400; corporate sales: (2) 9438-2203; fax: (2) 9437-5888; email: ozcorp@ozemail.com.au; http://www.aone.net.au/.

Braenet; tel: (2) 9550-4217; toll-free in Australia: [1] (800) 150-543; email: info@braenet.com.au; http://www.braenet.com/.

iiNet Technology; tel: (8) 9322-7770; fax: (8) 9322-6660; email: iinet@iinet.net.au; http://www.iinet.net.au/.

Integral Internet; (Sydney and Melbourne) tel: (2) 9369-2983; email: info@integral.net.au; http://www.integral.net.au/.

NetConnect Communications; tel: (3) 5332-2140; fax: (3) 5331-9909; email: info@netconnect.com.au; http://www.netconnect.com.au/.

Pegasus Networks; tel: (7) 3259-6259; fax: (7) 3255-0555; email: pegasus@pegasus.com.au; http://www.pegasus.com.au/.

Zip Internet Professionals; tel: 1300-655-577; (2) 9279-4777; fax: (2) 9247-5276; email: info@zip.com.au; http://www.zip.com.au/.

Business Culture

GREETINGS AND COURTESIES

Australians are friendly, outgoing, informal people who move to a first-name basis rather quickly. In general, let your Australian associate set the level of informality, and do not be offended if they become quite friendly immediately. The accepted greeting is smiling, making eye contact, and shaking hands. Handshakes are generally firm and brief, with a rapid, simple up-and-down motion. It is not necessary or appropriate to squeeze the other person's hand. The standard verbal greeting is "Good morning" or "Good afternoon." Avoid "G'day mate," which will be seen as patronizing. Handshakes and greetings will usually be followed by a question such as "How are you doing?" A long, detailed answer is not expected or especially wanted. After this quick, seemingly superficial exchange, the next topic will be business.

BUSINESS ETHIC AND FRAMEWORK

Originally a country of people rejected by Old World Europe (it began as a penal colony), Australia has a history and tradition of egalitarianism that can make it an easy place to do business. Australians are leery of appearing boastful or arrogant. This extends to their own accomplishments, successes, and expertise, often to the point of withholding information about themselves. This is modesty, not dishonesty. Because a person does not say they have certain experience, doesn't mean they are unqualified in a particular area. A sensitively worded direct question will get an honest answer. Similarly, Australians usually don't praise someone for a job well done. They assume everyone is doing their best. Australians value friendship, feel that being "good mates" is as important as doing business together, and consider mutually respectful relationships extremely important. They are likely to be insulted if a business relationship is deemed more important than a personal relationship. Humor is an essential part of the Australian personality. Their humor is often aimed at themselves or their country, and is often self-deprecating.

DECISION MAKING

Except for situations involving large corporations, Australians are generally results-oriented. They prefer to make quick decisions, and move fast to put their decision into action. In smaller businesses, one person could be the sole decision-maker for the entire company and might make a decision immediately. Australians are fairly conservative, however, and the decision-making process reflects this. If the proposal contains unusual or innovative terms, they will generally need time to consider it before committing to a deal.

WOMEN

Men still hold the vast majority of management positions, but Australian women are being increasingly hired for higher-level jobs. They expect to be treated seriously and with the respect to which their position entitles them. If you are dealing with a woman, do not treat her any differently than you would treat a man. Do not assume that her particular style is based on her gender. Australian companies hire people whose personalities fit the company's style. Whether a woman is friendly or more formal will not be a reflection of her gender, but her company's way of doing business. Foreign women can expect to be treated the same as men, but exactly how a woman is dealt with will depend on the person she is encountering.

MEETINGS

Meetings start on time. If you are going to be late, let your Australian associates know in advance. Australians are relaxed and informal, and will be on a first name basis very quickly. High-level executives may introduce themselves by their first name, and not do or say anything that calls attention to their rank in the company. Lower level employees can have considerable power, and authority well beyond what is usual in other countries. You might get a sense of a person's rank in the company by observing how others treat them.

BUSINESS ATTIRE

In the corporate world, conservative suits are standard. Women wear skirted suits or (not as often) suits with pants, ensembles or skirts with blouses, or dresses and jackets. Hemlines vary from just above the knee to a few inches above the ankle. Women executives tend to wear little or no makeup and simple hair styles. There is generally more latitude when dealing with smaller companies or in rural areas, where ties are not as essential or suits may not be expected. Minimal attire is a jacket and tasteful pants, shirt (understated design), and shoes. Avoid extremes in fashion, and excessive jewelry or accessories.

Business Centers
Sydney
CITY VIEW

Proud site of the 2000 Olympic Games, Sydney is also the marketing, financial, and information technology center of Australia. Located in the southeast corner of the country, it also functions as one of the world's great seaports.

AIRPORT

Kingsford Smith Airport to City Center

The airport lies 7 miles (12 km.) from the city. The international and domestic terminals are separate. An Airport Express Bus shuttles people to the central station and other downtown stops in 20- to 30-minute intervals at a welcoming rate of A$6. Regular taxi service will take passengers into town in 15 or 30 minutes at a metered fare of about A$18. An information desk is situated in the arrivals hall.

Airline Numbers

Aer Lingus	(2) 9244-2123
Air Canada, reservations	(2) 9232-5222
Air France	(2) 9244-2100, 9692-9007
Air New Zealand	(2) 13-2476
Air Lanka	(2) 9224-2234

Air Malta	(2) 9244-2011
American Airlines	(toll-free) 008-22-7151
Ansett	(toll-free) 13-1300
Ansett Express	(2) 9268-1242
Balkan Bulgarian	(2) 9244-2232
British Airways	(2) 9258-3200
Canadian Airlines	1300-65-5767
China Airlines	(2) 9244-2121
Continental	(2) 9244-2242
Country Connection Airlines	(2) 9669-5354
CSA	(2) 9247-6196
Eastern Australia Airlines	(toll-free) 13-1313
East-West	(2) 9268-1166
Garuda Indonesia	(2) 9334-9900
Gulf Air	(2) 9244-2199
Horizon Airlines	(2) 9244-2111
Jet Airways	(2) 9244-2132
KLM	(2) 9231-6988, 6333
Maersk Air	(2) 9244-2183
Malaysia Airlines	(2) 9364-3500
Malev Hungarian	(2) 9244-2131
Qantas (toll free)	13-1313
Royal Tongan	(2) 9244-2212
Sabena	(2) 9244-2135
Swissair	(2) 9231-3744, 1800-22-1339
T.A.T. European	(2) 9244-2163
Thai Airways	(2) 9251-1922
Varig	(2) 9244-2179
Vietnam Airlines	(2) 9244-2159
World Aviation Systems	(2) 9244-2111

HOTELS

Top-end

Hotel Inter-Continental; 117 Macquarie St., 2000; tel: (2) 9230-0200; fax: (2) 9240-1240; excellent location; in walking distance of business district; restaurants; business center; conference center; executive services; secretarial services; business rooms available; Club Inter-Continental floors include excellent concierge service and airport limousine transfer; fitness; massage; sauna; pool.

Sheraton On The Park; 161 Elizabeth St.; tel: (2) 9286-6000; fax: (2) 9286-6686; adjacent to Hyde Park, city center; restaurants; conference center; executive services; secretarial service; corporate rates; in-room computers; health; fitness; massage; sauna; pool; whirlpool; A$370; (Sheraton also has an airport hotel in Sydney).

The Observatory; 89-113 Kent St.; tel: (2) 9256-2222; fax: (2) 9256-2233; known for discreet service and high security; restaurant; conference rooms (up to 100); secretarial service; in-room fax machines; multiple telephones and dataports; corporate rates; fitness room; sauna; pool.

The Regent; 199 George St.; tel: (2) 9238-0000; fax: (2) 9251-2851; harborfront, overlooking opera house; restaurants; business center; conference center; secretarial service; in-room computers and fax; health; sauna; rooftop pool. (hotel under renovation until 8/99)

The Ritz-Carlton; 93 Macquarie St.; tel: (2) 9252-4600; fax: (2) 9252-4286; near Opera House and business district; restaurants; meeting and conference facilities; executive services; secretarial services; fitness; sauna; massage; pool.

Quay West Sydney; 98 Gloucester Street, the Rocks; tel: (2) 9240-6000; fax: (2) 9240-6060; city center, waterfront; restaurants; conference center; secretarial services; in-room computers; corporate rates; fitness; sauna; pool; whirlpool.

Expensive

Forum The Grace Hotel; 77 York St.; tel: (2) 9299-8777; fax: (2) 9299-8189; heart of business district; business hotel; restaurants; Business Plan benefits include dual phone lines, daily newspaper, breakfast, rooftop lounge and spa, sauna, steamroom, pool, fitness room and noon check-out; half rates in the summer months.

Furama Hotel Darling Harbor; 68 Harbour St., 2010 Darling Harbor; tel: (2) 9281-0400; fax: (2) 9281-1212; near exhibition grounds; restaurant; conference center; executive services; secretarial service; corporate rates.

Mercure Lawson; 383-389 Bulwara Rd., Ultimo; tel: (2) 9211-1499; fax: (2) 9281-3764; near airport; restaurant; conference center; corporate rates; secretarial service.

Regents Court Hotel; 18 Springfield Ave., Potts Point; tel; (2) 9358-1533; fax: (2) 9358-1833; boutique hotel; large studio rooms with kitchens; in-room dual phone lines.

Resort Hotel Macquarie; corner of Epping and Herring Rds.; tel: (2) 805-1888; toll-free: 1-800-448-8355; fax: (2) 805-0538; located in computer and light industrial district; executive office space; pool; running track; tennis; nearby golf.

Southern Cross Hotel Sydney; Elizabeth and Goulburn Sts.; tel: (2) 9282-0987; fax: (2) 9281-3287; near exhibition grounds; restaurant; conference center; secretarial service; corporate rates; health; fitness; sauna; pool.

Oakford Potts Point; 10 Wylde St., Potts Point; tel: (2) 9318-4544; fax: (2) 9357-1162; secretarial service; pool; whirlpool; golf.

Sydney Marriott; 36 College Street; tel: (2) 361-8400; fax: (2) 361-8599; city center; restaurant; conference center; executive services; secretarial services; in-room computers; fitness; sauna; pool; whirlpool.

Moderate

Capital; 111 Darlinghurst Rd., Kings Cross; tel: (2) 358-2755; city center; casino; restaurant; conference center; executive services; secretarial services; corporate rates; fitness; health; massage; sauna; pool; whirlpool.

Gazebo Court & Tower; 2 Elizabeth Bay Rd., 2011; tel: (2) 358-1999; fax: (2) 356-2951; city center; some rooms with harbor view; restaurant; conference center; secretarial service; corporate rates; sauna; pool.

The Kendall; 122 Victoria Street, Potts Point; tel: (2) 9357-3200; fax: (2) 9357-7606; city center; secretarial service.

Radisson Inn Gladesville; 165 Victoria Road, Gladesville; tel: (2) 816-3333; fax: (2) 816-2841; restaurant; conference center (up to 100); secretarial service; corporate rates; fitness; pool; whirlpool.

The Royal Garden; 431-439 Pitt St.; tel: (2) 9281-6999; fax: (2) 9281-6988; near exhibition grounds; restaurant; conference center; corporate rates; pool; whirlpool.

The Russell; 143A George St., 2000; tel: (2) 9241-3543; fax: (2) 9252-1652; central location; small, European-style hotel.

The Westbury; 221 Darlinghurst Road; tel: (2) 360-3222; fax: (2) 360-3277; restaurant; conference center; secretarial service; corporate rates; sauna; pool.

MEDICAL CARE

Debtal Emergency Service and Central Dental Laboratory; 793 George St.; tel: 9211-1011.
Royal North Shore Hospital, Pacific Highway, St. Leonards; tel: 9438-7111.
Sydney Hospital, Macquarie Street; tel: 9228-2111.
Prince of Wales Hospital, High Street, Randwick, tel: 9399-0111.
St. Vincent's Hospital, Darlinghurst Road, Darlinghurst; tel: 9339-1111.

HEALTH CLUBS

City Gym; 107 Crown St., Darlinghurst; tel: 9360-6247.
Clark Hatch Fitness Center; InterContinental Hotel, 117 Macquarie St; tel: 9251-3486.

AUTO RENTAL

Australia Wide Limousine Reservation Service; reservations, 1800-67-4142.
Avis; reservations, tel: (2) 9353-9000; fax: (2) 9353-9100.
Budget; Sydney airport, tel: (2) 9310-3101.
Dollar; Sir John Young Crs., Sydney; tel: (2) 9223-1444; North Sydney 2060, NSW, tel: (2) 9955-3970.
Hertz; reservations, tel: (3) 9698-2555; fax: (3) 9698-2295; airport, tel: (2) 9669-2444; fax: (2) 9693-5829 5a.m. to 11p.m. (chauffeur-driven cars available); William St., Corner Riley Street; tel: (2) 9360-6621; fax: (2) 9360-5145 (chauffeur-driven cars available)
Hughes Chauffeured Cars, Limousines, and Coaches; 14 Sarah St., Mascot; tel: (2) 9693-2833.

WORLD TRADE CENTER

World Trade Centre Sydney
83 Clarence Street, Level 12
Sydney, NSW 2000
Australia
tel: (2) 9350-8100; fax: (2) 9350-8199
email: giga275@hotkey.net.au
website: http://www.scoc.com.au

CONVENTION & VISITORS BUREAU

Sydney Convention & Visitors Bureau
Level 5, 80 William Street
Sydney, NSW 2011
tel: (61 2) 9331-4045; fax: (61 2) 9360-1223

Melbourne
CITY VIEW

Melbourne's population of three million makes it the country's second largest city. It is a large, industrial city, and is the country's manufacturing center.

AIRPORT

Melbourne Airport to City Center
Melbourne Airport is 14 miles (22 km.) from the city. A private bus services passengers from outside of the arrivals hall and will take you to the rail station and a few major hotels. The trip will take about 30 minutes for A$8.50. Taxis offer a 10-minute faster alternative for approximately A$25.

Airline Numbers

Aer Lingus	(3) 9920-3889
Air Calin	(3) 9920-3872
Air France	(3) 9920-3868
Air Lanka	(3) 9920-3882
Air Malta	(3) 9920-3883
Air New Zealand	(3) 9607-9896
Air Pacific	(3) 9602-6592
Alaska Airlines	(3) 9920-3702
Alitalia	(3) 9600-0511, 1300-65-3747
All Nippon Airways	(3) 9920-3879
Ansett Australia/Kendell	13-1300
Balkan Bulgarian	(3) 9920-3885
British Airways	(3) 9672-1100
Canadian Airlines	1300-65-5767
Cathay Pacific	13-1747
China Airlines	(3) 9920-3855

China Eastern..(3) 9920-3708
Continental ....(3) 9920-3858
East-West ....(39) 668-2033
Finnair ....(3) 9920-3703
Gulf Air ....(3) 9920-3886
Hawaiian Airlines...(3) 9920-3704
Jet Airlines...(3) 9920-3705
KLM .... (3) 9650-6771, 9654-5222
Korean Air ....(3) 9920-3853
Lan Chile ....(3) 9920-3881
Lot Polish...(3) 9920-3874
Malaysia Airlines ....(3) 9279-9999
Malev Hungarian ....(3) 9920-3706
Mandarin Airlines...(3) 9920-3884
Olympic Airways...(3) 9629-5022
Polynesian Airlines 1300-65-3737
Qantas 13-1313
Royal Tongan Airlines ....(3) 9920-3707
Sabena...(3) 9920-3711
Solomon ....(3) 9920-3709
South African Airways ....(3) 9920-3869
Swissair..(3) 9670-2191
Tap Air Portugal ....(3) 9920-3710
Trans World Airlines ....(3) 9920-3871
Varig Brazilian ....(3) 9920-3856
Vietnam Airlines ....(3) 9920-3857

HOTELS

Top-end

Adelphi; 187 Flinders Lane; tel: (3) 9650-7555; fax: (3) 9650-2710; ultra modern boutique hotel; glass-bottom rooftop pool.

Crown Hotel; 8 Whiteman Street, Southbank; tel: (3) 9292-6666; fax: (3) 9292-6600; located in Crown casino complex; large, newer hotel; restaurants; fitness; pool.

Le Meridien at Rialto; 495 Collins Street; tel: (3) 9620-9111; fax: (3) 9614-1219; heart of business district; restaurant; business center; conference facilities; secretarial service; corporate rates; health; fitness; massage; sauna; pool; whirlpool.

Sheraton Towers; 1 Brown Street, Southbank; tel: (3) 9696-3100; fax: (3) 9690-5889; reservations; 1-800-325-3589; restaurants; business center; in-room fax, modem connnections; fitness center; lap pool.

Sofitel; 25 Collins St.; tel: (3) 9653-0000; fax: (3) 9650-4261; reservations: 1-800-221-4542; top floors of office/shopping complex; meeting/conference facilities; in-room cable internet access.

Windsor Hotel; 103 Spring St., 3000; tel: (3) 9653-0653; toll-free in U.S.: 1-800-323-7500; fax: (3) 9650-3233; opposite Parliament House; restored rooms; award-winning restaurant; business center; conference center; secretarial service; in-room modem/fax connections; corporate rates; fitness; massage; whirlpool.

Expensive

Gordon Place Apartments; 24-32 Little Bourke Street; tel: (3) 9663-5355; fax: (3) 9663-5794; near business district, restaurants, and theaters; studios and one or two-bedroom apartments; restaurant; laundry facilities; pool; spa.

Grand Chancelor Melbourne; 131-137 Lonsdale Street; tel: (3) 9663-3161; fax: (3) 9662-3479; city center; restaurant; conference center; secretarial service; sauna; pool.

Heritage; 318-324 Flinders St.; tel: (3) 9250-1888; fax: (3) 9250-1877; opening 1988, city center; restaurant; conference center; executive services; secretarial service; in-room computers; corporate rates; fitness.

Eden on the Park; 6 Queens Road; tel: (3) 9850-2222; fax: (3) 9820-9586; city suburb; restaurant; conference rooms; secretarial service; in-room modem/fax connection; fax/photocopy facilities; corporate rates; fitness; sauna.

Melbourne Hilton on the Park; 192 Wellington Parade; tel: (3) 9419-3311; fax: (3) 9419-5630; overlooking park, 10-minute walk to business district, or free shuttle service; restaurant; conference center; secretarial service; corporate rates; fitness; sauna; pool; whirlpool.

Novotel; 270 Collins St.; tel: (3) 9650-5800; fax: (3) 9650-7100; adjacent to exhibition grounds; restaurant; conference facilities; secretarial service; corporate rates; fitness; sauna; pool; whirlpool.

Old Melbourne Hotel; tel: (3) 9329-9344 or toll-free 008/37-3005; fax: (3) 9328-4870.

Parkroyal on St. Kilda Road; 562 St. Kilda Rd, 3004; tel: (3) 9529-8888; fax: (3) 9525-1242; heart of business district; meeting area; executive desks; mobile phone rental.

Moderate

Bayview on the Park; 52 Queens Road; tel: (3) 9243-9999; fax: (3) 9243-9800; restaurant; conference facilities; secretarial service; fax/photocopy facilities; corporate rates; fitness; pool.

Crest International; 47 Barkly Street, St. Kilda; tel: (3) 9537-1788; fax: (3) 9534-0609; city suburb, near exhibition grounds; restaurant; conference rooms; secretarial service; in-room fax/modem connections; fax/photocopy facilities; corporate rates.

Elizabeth Tower Motel; 792 Elizabeth Street; tel: (3) 9347-9211; fax: (3) 9347-0396; near exhibition grounds; restaurant; conference center; secretarial service; corporate rates; pool.

Lygon Lodge Carlton; 220 Lygon Street, Carlton; tel: (3) 9663-6633; fax: (3) 9663-7297; city suburb; secretarial service; fax/photocopy facilities; corporate rates.

Magnolia Court Boutique Hotel; tel: (3) 9419-4222; fax: (3) 9416-0841.

Royal Parade Motor Inn; 441 Royal Parade, Parkville; tel: (3) 9380-9221; fax: (3) 9387-6448; near airport; restaurant; conference facilities; secretarial service; fax/photocopy facilities; corporate rates;.

Saville of South Yarra; 5/9 Commercial Road; tel: (3) 9867-2155; fax: (3) 98209726; city suburb; restaurant; conference facilities; secretarial service; fax/photocopy facilities; corporate rates.

MEDICAL CARE

Royal Melbourne Hospital; tel: (3) 9347-7000 for non-emergency illness.

the Royal Dental Hospital; Elizabeth Street at Flemington Road; tel: (3) 9341-0222.

St. Vincent's Hospital, Victoria Parade, Fitzroy; tel: (3) 9418-2211.

HEALTH CLUB

City Gym; City Baths, 420 Swanston St., Tram: Swanston Street to corner of Franklin; tel: (3) 9663-5888.

Hunts Physical; 41 Johnston St., Fitzroy. Tram: 96 to stop 13; tel: (3) 9419-3636.

Hyatt on Collins; tel: (3) 9657-1234.

AUTO RENTAL

Avis;.reservations, tel: (2) 9353-9000; fax: (2) 9353-9100; airport, tel: (3) 9338-1800; fax: (3) 9330-2870; 20-24 Franklin St., tel: (3) 9663-6366; fax: (3) 9663-2551.

Australia

Budget; 398 Elizabeth St., tel: (3) 9639-2344; airport, tel: (3) 9639-2344.

Hertz; airport, tel: (3) 9338--4044; fax: (3) 9338-4465 5a.m. to midnight; 97 Franklin St. tel: (3) 9663-6244; fax: (3) 9663-4205 (chauffeur-driven cars available both locations).

Thrifty; 390 Elizabeth St.; tel: (3) 9663-5200, offers discount rates for rentals of six days or more and for weekends.

WORLD TRADE CENTER

World Trade Centre Melbourne
WTC Post Office 286
Melbourne, Victoria 3005
tel: (3) 9235-8831; fax: (3) 9645-9844
email: lharry@mecc.aust.com
website: http://www.mecc.aust.com

Canberra

CITY VIEW

Placed strategically between Sydney and Melbourne, Australia's capital is a city of barely 300,000. Its major growth industry is tourism, and the city welcomes more than 1.25 million visitors a year.

AIRPORT

Canberra Airport to City Center

Until recently, Canberra Airport only had domestic service. There are some international flights now. The airport lies 6 miles (10 km.) from the city, with regular taxi service. The ACT minibus also provides transfers to and from the Canberra Airport. Call (2) 6280-0000 for information; or fax: (2) 6280-0990..

Airline Numbers

Air Caledonie	(2) 6257-1055
Aer Lingus	(2) 6257-1055
Air Malta	(2) 6257-1055
Air New Zealand	(2) 6213-2476
Australian Airlines	(2) 6246-1811
Ansett	(2) 6249-7715
British Airways	(2) 6257-1557
Gulf Air	(2) 6257-1055
Lloyd Air Executive Charter	(2) 6257-7780
Mandarin Airlines	(2) 6257-1055
Singapore Airlines	(2) 6247-4122
Unietd Airlines	(2) 6248-9195
Qantas	13-1313

HOTELS

Top-end

Capital Parkroyal; 1 Binara St.; tel: (2) 6247-8999; fax: (2) 6257-4903; city center, near National Convention Center; restaurants; conference facilities; business center; translation faciliites; 24-hour room service; laundry/dry cleaning; in-room cofeemaker, iron, refrigerator/minibar; car rental; parking garage; corporate rates; health club; sauna; spa; pool; nearby golf.

Hyatt Hotel Canberra; Commonwealth Ave., Yarralumla; tel: (2) 6270-1234; fax: (2) 6281-5998; city center; elegant interior; restaurants; conference facilities (up to 600); business center; secretarial service; translation faciliites; informaiton desk; car retnal; currency exchange; house doctor; laundry/dry cleaning; in-room refirgergator/minibar, cofeemaker; valet; parking garage; fitness; spa; massage; pool; whirlpool; nearby golf; fishing; bush/jungle walks; sailing; windsurfing.

Expensive

Canberra International Hotel; 242 Northbourne Avenue, Dickson; tel: (2) 6247-6966; fax: (2) 6248-7823; reservation fax: (2) 6248-8357; conference rooms; in-room kitchenettes; 24-hour room service; car rental; parking; pool.

Diplomat Boutique Hotel; Canberra Avenue and Hely Street, Griffith; tel: (2) 6295-2277; toll-free reservations 1800-35-5169; fax: (2) 6239-6432; suburb; restaurant; conference facilities; secure internal access; laundry/dry cleaning; information desk; car rental; in-room refrigerator/ minibar, cofeemaker; covered parking; itness; sauna; pool.

Oakford Kingston Gardens; 10-12 Howitt St., Kingston; tel: (2) 6239-0500; fax: (2) 6234-6342; city suburb, near airport; room service; laundry/dry cleaning; in-room refrigerator, kitchenette, cofeemaker; garage; fitness; sauna; pool; fishing; sailing.

Pavilion Hotel; Canberra Ave. and National Circuit; tel: (2) 6295-3144; fax: (2) 6295-3325; near Parliament House; restaurant; gym; spa; pool.

Moderate

Argyle Executive Apartments; CNR Currong and Boolee Streets, Reid; tel: (2) 6275-0800; fax: (2) 6275-0888; walking distance of business district; two- and three-bedroom apartments; business center; room service; laundry/dry cleaning; in-room refrigerator, kitchenette, coffeemaker, VCR; car rental; parking garage; .

Country Comfort Inn; 102 Northbourne Ave., Braddon; tel: (2) 6249-1411; toll-free: 1800-065-064; fax: (2) 6249-6878; recently renovated; restaurant; coffee shop; fax/photocopy faciliites; laundry/dry cleaning; room service; in-room refrigerator/minibar; cofeemaker; car rental; parking garage; pool; whirlpool.

Eagle Hawk Hill Resort; Federal Highway, Watson; tel: (2) 6241-6033; fax: (2) 6241-3691; restaurant; conference facilities; secretarial service; car rental; parking garage; corporate rates; fitness; sauna; pool; tennis; horse riding; bush/jungle walks.

Forrest Motor Inn; 30 National Circuit, Forrest; tel: (2) 6295-3433; toll-free reservations: 1800-35-5170; fax: (2) 6295-2119; suburb, behind Parliament House, near government offices; restaurant; conference facility.

Olims Canberra; Limestone and Ainslie Avenue, Braddon; tel: (2) 6248-5511; toll-free reservations: 1800-02-0016; fax: (2) 6247-0864; city suburb; restaurant; conference facilities (up to 280); secretarial service; in-room refrigerator/minibar; car rental; parking garage; corporate rates; nearby golf; bush/jungle walks; sailing; waterskiing.

HEALTH CLUB

Canberra Olympic Health Club; Constitution Ave.; tel: (2) 6248-6799.

Parkroyal Canberra Health & Fitness Club; Binara St.; tel: (2) 6247-8999.

YMCA of Canberra; London Cct; tel: (2) 6249-8733.

AUTO RENTAL

Avis; reservations, tel: (2) 9353-9000; fax: (2) 9353-9100; Canberra Apo, tel: (2) 6249-1601; fax: (2) 6257-4080.

Budget; Girroween St., tel: (2) 6257-1305; airport, tel: (2) 6257-1305.

Canberra Limousine; tel: 1800-641-648; fax: (2) 6239-2177.

Hertz; reservations, tel: (3) 9698-2555; fax: (3) 9698-2295; airport, tel: (2) 6249-6211; fax: (2) 6247-6260; 32 Mort Street, Braddon, tel: (2) 6257-4877; fax: (2) 6247-1327 (chauffeur-driven cars available both locations).

Austria

At a Glance

THE PEOPLE

Population .... 8,139,299 (July 1999 est.)
Growth Rate .... 0.09% (1999 est.)
Life Expectancy .... 77.48 years (born 1999)
Infant Mortality ..... 5.1 deaths/1,000 live births (1999 est.)

Ethnic Composition

German 99.4%
Croatian..0.3%
Slovene 0.2%
Other 0.1%

Religious Composition

Roman Catholic...78%
Protestant...5%
Other 17%

Languages Spoken

German.

Education and Literacy

Austria maintains an excellent and efficient education system.Currently, 99 percent of the population age 15 and over are literate.

Labor Force

Total: 3,646,000
By occupation: services 66.1%, industry 29.6%, agriculture 4.3%.

THE ECONOMY

Austria's strategic location between Central and Western Europe helps offset the limitations of its small and highly regulated economy. Its sizable reserves of raw materials, and full integration into the E.U., has allowed Austria to make steady progress. The government is taking steps to reduce the burdensome social system and the number of civil service jobs. Organized labor remains a powerful factor in Austria, with unions representing nearly two-thirds of the work force. Austria's major industries are state-run enterprises—including public utilities, banks, and the transportation network, which are now all being fully or partially privatized. Further deregulation of the telecommunications and energy sectors is expected to further boost Austria's attractiveness to foreign investment. Though tiny, Austria is positioning itself to "punch above its weight" in the E.U.

Exports .... US$62.5 billion (1998)
Imports .... US$65.8 billion (1998)
Total GDP .... US$184.5 billion (1998 est.)
GDP Per Capita .... US$22,700 (1998 est.)
Unemployment .... 7% (1999 est.)
Inflation Rate 0.9% (1998)

Top Export Partners

E.U., Eastern Europe, United States, Japan

Top Import Partners

E.U., Eastern Europe, Japan, United States

Top Exports

Machinery and equipment, iron and steel, lumber, textiles, paper products, chemicals.

Top Imports

Petroleum, foodstuffs, machinery and equipment, vehicles, chemicals, textiles and clothing, pharmaceuticals.

BUSINESS WORKWEEK

Offices

Monday to Thursday 8a.m. to 5p.m., shorter hours on Friday.

Banks

Monday to Wednesday and Friday 8a.m. to 12:30p.m. and 1:30p.m. to 3p.m. Thursday 8a.m. to 12:30p.m. and 1:30p.m. to 5:30p.m. Main branches do not close for lunch. Opening times may vary from city to city.

Government

Monday to Friday 9a.m. to 3p.m.

Retail

Monday to Friday 8a.m. to 6p.m., with large department stores keeping no lunch hour. Smaller businesses, especially outside Vienna, close for an hour or two around noon. Half-day on Saturday, except once a month, when they remain open until 5p.m.

HOLIDAYS

New Year's Day..January 1
Epiphany ....January 6
Easter Monday ....April 5*
Labor Day..May 1
Ascension Day .... May 13*
Whit Monday .... May 24*
Corpus Christi..June 3*
Assumption.. August 15
National Holiday ....October 26
All Saints' Day ....November 1
Immaculate Conception...................................December 8
Christmas Day...December 25
St. Stephens Day ....December 26

* Date may vary by year.

Note: Business vacation months are July and August. Avoid traveling to Austria on business during the two weeks before Easter and Christmas and the two weeks after Christmas.

CLIMATE

Seasons

Austrian winters are harsh and cold, with plenty of snowfall. Summers are temperate, leaning toward the cool side with occasional rainfall. If a hot day should come to pass, it may well be humid and sticky.

Regions

Tiny Austria is a very mountainous country with the western region near Switzerland providing some of the world's best ski areas. Eastern Austria, where the capital Vienna is located, is somewhat warmer although given to greater rainfall. Temperatures nationwide range from 29°C (85°F) in summer to long spells of subfreezing weather in winter.

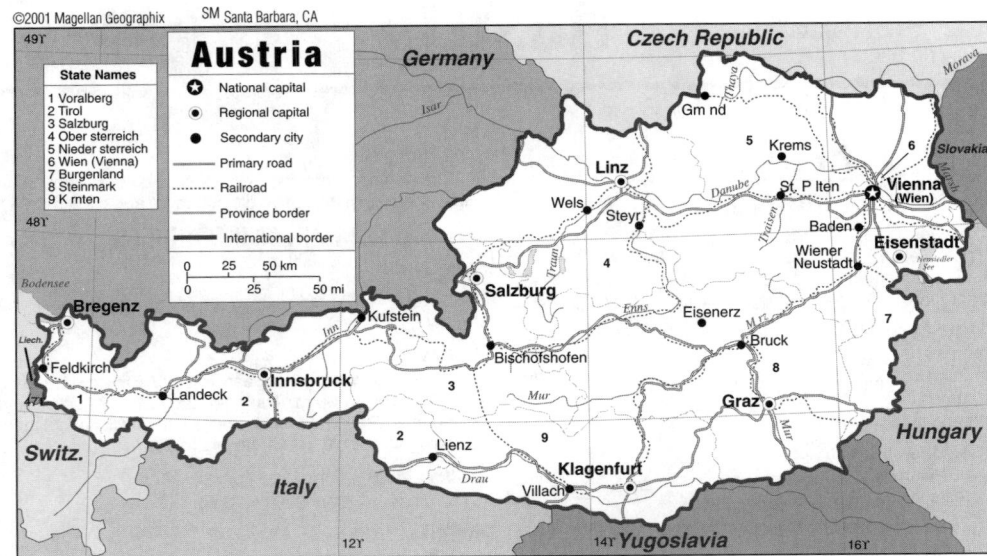

Money & Banking

Currency
The currency of Austria is the Austrian Schilling (ATS).

Denominations
The Austrian Schilling comes in coin denominations of ATS1,000, 500, 100, 50, 25, 20, 10, 5, and 1, 50, and 10 groschen; and banknotes of ATS20, ATS50, ATS100, ATS500, ATS 1,000, and ATS5,000.

Traveler's Checks and Credit Cards
Traveler's checks and foreign currency can be easily and efficiently exchanged at banks, foreign exchange bureaus located in the major cities, hotels, and foreign exchange kiosks at the airports. Banks offer the most favorable exchange rates for travel checks. Most major currencies can be exchanged at banks.

Credit cards are mostly accepted in Austria's large cities, including American Express, Visa, MasterCard, and Diners Club, as well as bank cards from the larger Austrian banks. However, credit cards have not yet found as great an acceptance in smaller shops or rural towns. You can get cash advances from your credit card on many of the automated teller machines (ATM) in the larger cities. Credit cards are also essential for renting a car. Long-term visitors should set up a checking account in Austria, and get an ATM card. The most favorable exchange rates are given for ATM and credit card transactions.

Travel

VISA AND PASSPORT
A passport that is valid for at least three months beyond anticipated exit date is required of all visitors, except for citizens of E.U. countries, Liechtenstein, Malta, Monaco, Norway, San Marino, and Switzerland who are in possession of a national ID card. Length of stay is unlimited.

Austria is a member of the Schengen group, which is a collection of nations who in March of 1995 declared themselves borderless. The others in this group include Belgium, France, Germany, Luxembourg, The Netherlands, Portugal, and Spain. Any traveler who holds a valid passport or other travel documents that are recognized by all Schengen member nations need not have a visa to travel in any of these countries. There are two caveats, however:

- If you have tickets for onward travel to a nation that does require a visa of you, it may also be required of you for entry into the Schengen nation.

- Each Schengen nation retains the right to require a visa of any nation normally exempted by the group as a whole.

Following is a list of nations normally exempt from the visa requirement (E.U. nationals are automatically exempt): Andorra, Argentina, Australia, Brazil, Brunei, Canada, Chile, Costa Rica, Cyprus, Czech Republic, Ecuador, El Salvador, Guatemala, Honduras, Hungary, Iceland, Israel, Japan, Jamaica, Liechtenstein, Malawi, Malaysia, Malta, Mexico, Monaco, New Zealand, Nicaragua, Norway, Panama, Paraguay, Poland, Republic of Korea, San Marino, Singapore, Slovak Republic, Slovenia, Switzerland, Turkey (only if a permanent resident of a Schengen country), Uruguay, U.S., Vatican City, and Venezuela.

Visa-free travel throughout the Schengen states is valid for a duration of 90 days maximum within a six-month period, commencing upon initial entry date into a Schengen country.

Of course, if this does not fit into your travel plans, you may apply for a visa anyway. The validity of your visa will be identical to that of a Schengen visitor. You may apply for either a single- or multiple-entry visa.

Travelers who are continuing their journey on the same or first possible connecting aircraft, and who are holding confirmed tickets and other travel documents, are exempt from the need for a transit visa, except for nationals of a limited list of specific countries. If you are to be only a transit passenger through Austria, you should check with the embassy or consulate to be sure about the transit visa requirement. Also be aware that transit passengers must obtain a visa from the onward destination country prior to applying for an Austrian transit visa, which is valid for five days.

Proof of sufficient funds for duration of stay, and a comprehensive medical insurance policy are also often required as part of a visa application, depending on nationality.

In-person applications are usually processed within two days. Those sent by mail can take as long as four weeks.

DEPARTURE FORMALITIES

There are no departure fees to pay when leaving Austria and no other restrictions except for the export of currency. You may not export more than ATS100,000 in currency, nor gold coins in excess of 200g per individual unless special permits have been completed prior to departure.

VAT: Prices on goods automatically include a tax of 20 percent in Austria. This tax may be reclaimed for goods exceeding ATS1,000 in value. Ask the store clerk for the relevant forms so that you can reclaim the tax upon departure or once at home.

CUSTOMS ENTRY (PERSONAL)

Duty-free

The following goods can be taken into Austria without incurring any customs duty by:

Travelers over 17 years of age arriving with duty-free goods:

* Tobacco: 200 cigarettes, 100 cigarillos, 50 cigars, or 250g tobacco
* Alcohol: 2 liters of wine, 2 liters of champagne, or fortified wine or spirits up to 22%; 1 liter of spirits
* Other: Goods of up to ATS2,500; 60ml of perfume; 1 bottle (250ml) of eau de cologne.

Travelers arriving from E.U. countries with duty-paid goods:

* Tobacco: 800 cigarettes, 400 cigarillos, 200 cigars, and 1kg of tobacco
* Alcohol: 90 liters of wine (up to 60 liters of sparkling wine), 10 liters of spirits, 20 liters of intermediate products (such as fortified wine), 110 liters of beer.

Note: Arrivals from outside Europe may bring in double the above allowances provided they have not stopped for more than 24 hours in another European country en route to Austria.

The amounts of alcohol and tobacco specified above are somewhat academic, since the import of duty-paid quantities are no longer limited between E.U. countries, technically speaking. But, if you have amounts of any items in excess of the above quantities, you may be interrogated to determine whether the goods are solely for personal use.

IMMUNIZATION

International certificates of vaccination not required unless arriving from infected areas.

TIPPING

In general, the practice of tipping is widespread, but the recipients do not expect large amounts.

Taxi

Taxi drivers usually receiveASch3-4 for a short trip, and ten percent for a longer one. Tip another ATS5 or 10 if the driver carries your bags to the curb.

Porters

Railway stations and airports maintain fixed rate charges for portering.

Hotels

Hotels will generally apply service charges to bills. Check room service bills before tipping to make sure no hotel service charge has been applied.

Restaurants

A service charge between 10 and 15 percent is usually included, but it is customary to leave an additional five percent.

Other

Beauticians, barbers: 10 percent. Cloakroom ATS7 to 15; washroom attendants ATS2 to 5; gas attendants: ATS 5; and theater ushers: ATS2 to 3.

EMERGENCY INFORMATION

Police and Crime

Crime is low and the police are friendly and efficient. However, as in every urban environment, the cities suffer from petty crime; so, take basic precautions, specially in railway stations. Foreign business visitors are often the target of what few thieves there are in Austria. Consequently, purses, laptops, and briefcases will require additional security. Do not leave valuables in cars or on tables in cafés. Keep non-essential valuables locked in hotel safes when not in use. Use credit cards and travel checks when possible to avoid carrying large sums of cash. Carry photocopies of your passport instead of the original. Carry cash in a money belt, and use credit cards or travelers checks for most of your large transactions.

Emergency Numbers

Numbers are functional nationwide.

Police... 133
Ambulance 144
Fire 122

Health

Austrian water is safe to drink; Vienna's water comes from the Styrian Alps and tastes especially pure. Food may be considered safe to eat.

The medical system in Austria is of an extremely high standard. Fees can be high; so, travelers should inquire about insurance before departure. Hotels will have access to doctors and translators that speak many languages. Visitors from Asia should be cautioned about the "heaviness" of the Austrian diet. Vegetarians will need to make special arrangements for many meals.

In eastern Austria, tick-borne encephalitis can be a hazard for those who spend any time in forested areas. Travelers can be vaccinated prior to the trip, or injections are also available from most Austrian doctors if you are infected while in country.

For more information on medical centers, including phone numbers, please see the "Business Center" section at the end of this chapter.

INTERNAL TRAVEL

AIR

Austrian Airlines and Austrian Air Services provide regularly scheduled flights between Vienna and Graz, Klagenfurt, Linz, and Salzburg.

Tyrolean Airline offers connections between Vienna and Innsbruck. Rheintalfung (WE) also has domestic flights.

There are several companies that offer charter services for both single- and twin-engined aircraft, as well as executive jets.

TAXI

Fares are set on a zone system and are metered. As such, drivers need to know the district you are going to, not only to find your destination, but to determine a fare. Look for the second and third numbers of the postal code to determine the district. A fare within the city limits might cost about ATS60, except on Sundays when fares rise. Those cabs with an illuminated 'Frei' sign indicate that they are free for hire, but you may find these difficult to find in Vienna. Main stations and larger hotels are more likely to have cabs standing by; however, if you are on a strict timeline you will do better to order in advance than to leave it to chance.

AUTO

Rental cars are widely available in major cities and rates run a full gamut. A major credit card and a valid driver's license are required for rental. Insurance is mandatory. Age limits for car rental vary by agency.

Most cities have a wealth of auto rental agencies, such as Arac, Avis, or Hertz, and auto rental is also easily arranged at airports and major railway stations. If you are a national of E.U. countries, Norway, Iceland, or Liechtenstein, then your national driver's license will enable you to drive in Austria for as long as a year. Drivers' licenses from other countries are also usually respected, but the term of validity may be shorter.

The roads in Austria are excellent. The motorist must pay tolls on all Austrian motorways, and tourists can pre-pay for either ten-day or two-month "discs." These can be obtained at major border crossings as well as at post offices.

Roadside assistance and other services are offered freely by the Austrian Motoring Association (ÖAMTC). In case of emergency breakdowns, dial 120.

TRAIN

Österreichische Bundesbahnen (ÖBB), Austrian Federal Railways, operates the train system in Austria with very efficient service. Regular intercity service links Vienna with Salzburg, Innsbruck, Graz, and Klagenfurt. There is also frequent motorrail service through the Tauern Tunnel.

Tickets for first or second class, couchette (seats that can be adjusted to bunks), or sleeper cars can be obtained from Austrian ticket offices (Reisebüro am Bahnhof) or most travel agents in the country. Also, information about local schedules and fares can be obtained by telephone at (1) 1717.

Austria offers several discount rail passes. The *Bundesnetzkarte* (National Network Pass) is sold exclusively in Austria and provides unlimited rail travel throughout the country for one month (ASch 5,900 1st class and ASch 4,300 2nd class). Another special discount pass is the *Vorteilscard*, which costs Asch1190. The Euro Domino and Euro Domino Junior passes are both valid for three, five, or ten days. Discounts are also offered for groups of six people or more.

METRO

Look for the blue 'U' signs indicating underground train. *U-Bahn*, as it is called, services most of inner Vienna. Outlying areas are serviced by the faster *S-bahn* that does not stop at all stations. S-bahn stations are marked with an 'S' sign above ground. Tickets may be purchased at machines underground or from a ticket officer if one happens to be there. These trains, like most other things in Austria, run on time.

BUSES & TRAMS

Most cities have an extensive bus and tram system that generally operates from 5:30a.m. until midnight. Almost all routes have a flat fare. Many trams service the city without a conductor. You may purchase a ticket on board (for ATS20, exact change only) or at newspaper or tobacco kiosks (Tabak-Trafik), which also sell tickets in strips of five, as well as day passes or longer-duration tourist passes.

Vienna has a comprehensive system of bus, light rail and tramway services, in addition to the metro. Most lines operate on a flat fare, and pre-purchase multiple journey tickets and passes are available. A Vienna Card, which costs ASch180, enables the visitor to travel by underground, bus, or tram for 72 hours of unlimited transit. It also entitles the holder to discounts at museums and other attractions, as well as in shops, cafés, and wine taverns. The card can be obtained at hotels or at the ticket offices of Vienna Transport.

Trams marked "*schaffnerlos*" have no conductors on board. Tickets are purchased from machines inside the carriages. They are also available in newspaper shops or from tobacconists called Trafik.

All other main towns also have bus systems, and there are tramways in Linz, Innsbruck, and Graz, as well as trolleybuses in Linz, Innsbruck, and Salzburg.

If you have pre-purchased tickets, validate them once on board in a machine usually located near the entrance or exit of the tram. Those who feel they can get away without paying face up to ATS500 in fines if they get caught by transport police patrolling the network.

WATER TRAVEL

Regularly scheduled passenger ferry services operate between mid-May and mid-September both on the Danube and on the lakes of Austria. The steamer services of the Danube are operated by DDSG Blue Danube Schiffahrt.

Tel ....(1) 588 800

Private companies also run ferries on the Danube; inquire locally, or to one of the Austrian tourist organizations.

International rail tickets are valid on Danube river boats. More information, including schedules and fares to the Slovak Republic (Bratislava), Hungary (Budapest), Yugoslavia (Belgrade), Turkey (Istanbul), and Ukraine (Yalta), is available from the *Österreichisches Werbung*.

Cruises down the Danube and out to the Black Sea can also be arranged between spring and autumn, as well as from Switzerland (Bregenz) across Lake Constance. Trip duration is between one and eight days, depending on which package you select.

TRAVEL ASSISTANCE

Austrian National Tourist Office
Margaretenstrasse 1, 1040 Vienna
tel: (1) 58-866; fax: (1) 588-6620
website: http://austria-info.at/
email: office@ains.at

Austrian Hotel Association
Hofburg, Michaelertrakt, 1010 Vienna
tel: (1) 533-0952; fax: (1) 533-7071

Vienna Hotel Reservations (Vienna Tourist Board); tel: (1) 21-114, ext. 444; fax: (1) 211-44-45; email: rooms@info.wien.at

Salzburg Information; tel; (662) 889-87-314/15/16; fax: (662) 88-987-32.

Note: Tourist kiosks exist at all arrival points in Austria. These kiosks sell excellent maps and offer accommodation information and booking services.

Essential Terms

English	German
Yes	Ja
No	Nein
Good morning	Guten Morgen
Hello (daytime)	Guten Tag
Hello (evening)	Guten Abend
Hello (telephone)	Guten Tag
Good-bye	Auf Wiedersehen
Please	Bitte
Thank you	Danke
Pleased to meet you	Angenehm
Excuse me; I'm sorry	Entschuldigung/ Verzeihung
My name is _____	Ich heiße _____
I don't understand	Ich verstehe nicht
Do you speak English?	Sprechen Sie englisch?

Communications

DIALING CODES IN AUSTRIA

International country code: [43]

Selected city codes: Bludenz (5552), Graz (316), Innsbruck (512), Kitzbuhel (5356), Klagenfurt (463), Linz (70), Salzburg (662), Vienna (1), Villach (4242), Wolfsberg (4352)

Dialing Austria from Overseas

To reach Austria from overseas, dial your country's international code, then 43 (the country code for Austria), then the city code, and finally the number. Remember that when dialing an Austrian number from outside the country, omit the zero preceeding the area code. If you were dialing Vienna from the United States, for example, you would begin with 011, then 43, then 1 (the city code for Vienna), and finally the number of the person or office you are trying to reach.

Assistance Numbers

International Information	08
Long Distance Information	09
Local Directory and Information	1611

CALLING WITHIN AUSTRIA

Local Calls

A local call takes one Austrian Schilling.

Long Distance Calls

When dialing long distance, rates become less horrendous when placed between 6p.m. and 8a.m. weekdays, or from 1p.m. Saturdays to 8a.m. Mondays. Add a zero to a city code if calling long distance within Austria.

International Calls

If calling direct, dial 00 + country code + number. You can do this from most phones with a card, or at the post of-fice where you must announce to a clerk where you are calling in order to be assigned a booth.

Off-peak rates begin at 6p.m. and last until 8a.m. daily, and throughout the weekends. You can also reach various overseas operators directly to benefit from home rates by dialing the appropriate access number:

British Telecom Direct	(22) 903-044
Canada Direct	(22) 903-013
New Zealand Direct	(22) 903-064
U.S.AT&T	(22) 903-011
U.S. MCI	(22) 903-012
U.S. Sprint	(22) 903-014

PAY PHONES

Public Telephones

Card Phone:

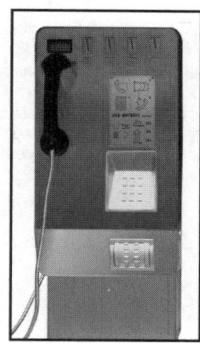

Card Phone

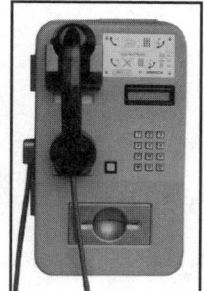

Coin Phone

Public telephones can be found most anywhere. They accept 1, 5, 10, and 20 schilling coins.
1. Insert coin
2. Pick up receiver
3. Dial
4. Press red button to speak if party answers

Calling Cards

One may purchase *Wertkartes*, as calling cards are referred to in Austria, can be purchased at post offices, train stations and some stores. They are sold in ATS50, 100, and 200 denominations. Simply insert the card and begin dialing.

CELLULAR PHONES

There are numerous cellular phone service providers in Austria. In the digital GSM 900 format Max.Mobil Telekoms and PTV Austria Mobilkom offer service for the country.

Note: Your home country cell phone may not work in this country. If not, we recommend that you rent an international cell phone *before* you leave home. A major US-based cell phone rental provider is **IMC WorldCell**. For information see "International Cell Phone Rentals" on page 14.

CALL BACK

You can (potentially) save significant sums when calling in Austria by using a call back service. For a list of callback services, please refer to the "Communications" section in the *Global Road Warrior* Introduction.

Fees for call back services vary widely, depending on the company and the type of service required. Be sure to check with these companies before leaving to compare rates.

PHONE JACK

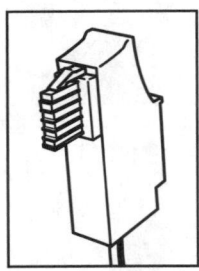

Adaptors are available through **iGo Corporation**. (See "Electrical and Telephone Adaptors" on page 19.)

FAX

Fax services are widely available, particularly in the cities. The transmission speed and results have proven excellent.

POSTAL SERVICES

Mail can be dropped off at post offices, mail boxes throughout the country, and hotels. Stamps are readily available. Airmail to North America takes on average six days. The main post office in Salzburg may be found at Residenzplatz 9, open from 7a.m. to 7p.m. Monday to Friday, and on Saturday from 8a.m. to 10a.m. In Vienna: 1. Fleischmarkt 19; Monday to Friday 8a.m. to 6p.m.

TELEGRAMS

Telegrams can be sent from anywhere in Austria, by dialing 10. They can also be sent from any post office.

Business Services

BUSINESS CENTERS

Imperial Hotels Austria; Kärntner 16, Ring 1015 Wien; tel: (1) 501 23; fax: (1) 501 10 41

Alba Hotel Accadia; Margaretenstr 53; 1050 Wien; tel: 01 / 588-500; fax: 01 / 58850-899

COURIER SERVICES

DHL; c/o **Ungarngasse**, tel: 523607

UPS; c/o **Speditionsges.m.b.H**; Am Concorde Park 1/B4, A-2320 Vienna; tel: (1) 707-8050; fax: (1) 7078-0502-600.

OFFICE RENTAL

Bürocenter Putzer; Turkenstrasse 9; tel: 317780

Trade Center; Prinz-Eugensstrasse, 16/8; tel: 5051063

TRANSLATION SERVICES

Kongresstechnik Gmbh; tel: (663) 02-6548.

Talk Training and Language; tel: (1) 586-6325.

Trade-Link; Pretulstr. 16c, A-8680 Mürzzuschlag; tel: (0676) 413-9169; fax: (0676) 341-5996; email: tradelink@netway.at.

Electrical

Current

220 volts AC, 50Hz.

ELECTRIC PLUGS

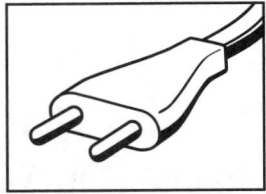

Round 2-pin plugs are the norm.
Adaptors are available through **iGo Corporation**. (See "Electrical and Telephone Adaptors" on page 19.)

Technical Support

HARDWARE/SOFTWARE VENDOR SUPPORT

Compaq/Digital; tel: (1) 878-16-0; fax: (1) 878-16-80; 01-8716-16 (CompaqCare Center); (in Switzerland) tel: [41] (22) 709-5330; fax: [41] (22) 709-5391 (Geneva); [41] (1) 801-2507; fax: [41] (1) 801-2172 (Zurich); (General U.S.) tel: (281) 518-2000; http://www.compaq.com/.

Dell; tel: 2243 34100 0; fax: 2243 34100 11(in Germany) tel: [49] (61) 039-710; (Dell- Europe) tel: [44] (134) 474-8000; (in the U.S.) tel: [1] (512) 338-4400; fax: [1] (512) 728-3330; http://www.dell.com/.

Hewlett Packard; tel: 660-6386; (in Switzerland) tel: [41] (22) 780-8111; (in the U.S.) tel: [1] (408) 246-4300; http://www.hp.com/.

IBM; tel: 660-5109; tel: (1) 17060; fax: (1) 216-0886; (in Germany) tel: [49] (711) 78-50; fax: [49] (711) 785-3511; (in Switzerland) tel: [41] (22) 310-0418 (French); (in the U.S.) tel: [1] (919) 517-2800; (U.S. Main Office) tel: [1] 914-765-1900; http://www.ibm.com/.

Microsoft; tel: (1) 610-640; fax: 6106-4200; tel: (1) 660-6520 (information); (in Germany) tel: [49] (89) 31-760; fax: [49] (89) 3176-1000; tel: [49] (89) 3176-1199; (in Switzerland) tel: [41] (848) 858-868; fax [41] (1) 831-0869; (in the U.S.) [1] (425) 635-7222; http://www.microsoft.com/.

Internet Connection
HOW TO CONNECT
Connecting to AOL and Compuserve in Austria is similar to using it when traveling outside your own area code. See the introductory section for detailed information on connecting to your account through a different phone number.

America Online
Numbers are available at keyword: *international*. Be sure to get several local numbers before leaving. AOL's GlobalNet service charges US$3.95 an hour in addition to the usual charges.AOL has its GlobalNet service available at keyword: *access* (a free area).

Access: Vienna and 50 km vicinity (71) 891-5052; National Access Number (1) 81-407.

Compuserve
Numbers are available at *Go International*. The Compuserve Web-site also has a great deal of information, at http://www.compuserve.com.

Access: Bludenz (555) 23-3882; Graz (316) 77-3950; Innsbruck (512) 57-540; Linz (732) 653-199; Salzburg (662) 4-678; Salzburg (71) 891-5161; Vienna (71) 891-5161; Vienna (1) 505-6178; Villach (42) 422-5580.

Independent Service Providers
Many independent service providers offer discounts if you are only in town for a couple days.

INS Informations und Netzwerksysteme GmbH; tel: (1) 52-184; email: office@ins.at; http://www.ins.at/.

Nacamar Data Communications GmbH; tel: (6103) 99-010; email: info@nacamar.net; http://www.nacamar.net/.

PING - Austria; tel: (1) 899-660; email: info@Austria.EU.net; http://ping.at/.

salzburg.at Internetservice; tel: (662) 4594-5412 or (662) 459-4540; fax: (662) 4594-5413; email: sales@salzburg.co.at; http://www.salzburg.co.at/.

Simon Media GmbH; tel: (316) 813-8240; fax: (316) 813-8246; email: office@sime.com; http://www.sime.com/.

Zocalo; (in the U.S.) tel: [1] (510) 540-8000; fax: [1] (510) 548-1891; email: info@zocalo.net; http://www.zocalo.net/.

KEY INTERNET SITES
University of Vienna, Institute of Applied Comuter Science and Information Systems
http://www.ifs.univie.ac.at/austria.html

Austrian Press and Information Service, Washington DC
http://www.globescope.com/web/austria/

Austrian Federal Economic Chamber, Vienna
http://www.wk.or.at/wkoehome.htm

Austrian Business Information
http://www.telecom.at/AustrianBusinessInfo/welcome.html/

Business Culture
GREETINGS AND COURTESIES
High standards of cordial formality are practiced in Austria's business society where titles and positions are very important. Forms of address are *Herr* (Mr.), *Frau* (Mrs.), and *Fraulein* (Miss), followed by professional titles, followed by professional degrees. For instance, the director of a laboratory with a doctoral degree is addressed "*Herr Direktor Dr.*" It is important to acknowledge all honorifics during first introductions. Titles of royalty (Baron, Duke, Duchess, etc.) are not used in public or business life. However, in private social settings, if a royal title is offered during introductions, it is proper to address the individual by the title—given the social circumstances. Until you are invited to use the first name, refer to both men and women over 20 as *Herr* or *Frau*, regardless of their marital status. Handshaking is a ritual in Austria. When introduced, offer a firm handshake. Men should always wait for a woman to initiate the handshake. Additionally, a younger person should wait for an older person to be the first to extend a hand. Gift giving is not a standard practice in Austrian business situations. If a gift is your favored gesture of appreciation, keep it very simple. A small token of special significance, such as an item bearing your company logo, or representing your city, country, etc. is appropriate. Gifts of substantial value are considered bad form in Austrian business practices; expensive gifts often cause the recipient discomfort while calling into question the motives of the gift-giver.

If invited to someone's home, a gift of flowers, an assortment of chocolates, or a fine cognac is a thoughtful gesture and will be well received. Though English is widely spoken in business and government, some familiarity with their official German language is appreciated by Austrians. If nothing else, it is helpful to use the German pronunciation of frequently used places and proper names.

DECISION MAKING
Because most of Austria's businesses are small, with fewer than 100 employees, you will likely be talking with the people who have decision-making authority. How rapidly decisions are rendered may depend on how thorough the foreign venturer has been in researching Austria's extensive regulatory environment.

WOMEN
Austrian women represent 50 percent of the workforce. While many women can be found in high levels of management they are rarely found as company presidents. A woman representative from a foreign company is accorded respect, and can expect to be addressed as "Mrs." regardless of whether or not she is married or uses her husband's name.

MEETINGS
Business cards are exchanged at the beginning of a meeting. Generally, Austrians embark with friendly small talk concerning background information. A first meeting may begin with conversation about the history of the company as well as Austrian history. Don't cut this discussion short by zipping to future interests. It would be appropriate to share the history of your own company with your hosts.

BUSINESS ATTIRE
In banks and law firms, dress is formal, and European tailored suits are favored. Otherwise, a charcoal gray suit, white shirt and conservative tie will never be incorrect. You may note men wearing metal clips on their shoes as a symbol of status

Austria

often associated with high rank in the corporation. Women's fashions tend to be classic and elegant. A smart tailored dress will serve, and pantsuits are usually acceptable. Bring a suitable raincoat or an umbrella for all seasons, and a proper winter coat for the chilling winter months.

Business Centers
Vienna
CITY VIEW

Vienna, or *Wien*, is a historical city with some sites dating back to the first century after Christ. Behind the history and tourist attractions, Vienna is also the cultural and business capital of Austria and a gateway to the new worlds of Eastern Europe. If no other time permits, at least take a small break to experience the austere, cultured charm of Vienna with a cup of rich Viennese coffee in one of the city's famous cafes.

AIRPORT
Vienna Airport to City Center

Vienna International Airport lies 11 miles (18 km.) east of the city. An information booth is located in the arrivals hall. There are coach, rail, and taxi services available. Trains run in intervals of 30 minutes. A special bus travels between the airport and the City Air Terminal, located under the Hilton Hotel, for a fare (payable on board) of about US$6 (ATS70). Buses also run to the South rail station and the West rail station every hour, and every 30 minutes on weekends or holidays; from there, you can catch a cab to your hotel.

Buses run in 20-minute intervals between 7:30a.m. and 11p.m. Cabs cost about six times the price of a bus for about the same travel time, 20 to 30 minutes. Cabs to and from the airport cost double since city cabs are not legally allowed to travel to the airport unless they are ordered in advance, meaning that cabs travel one way without passengers.

Executives and others preferring a more luxurious ride may also opt for limousine service, available for about the same price as a cab. Book at the ground transportation desk. Some hotels also provide shuttle service.

Airline Numbers

Aeroflot ....(1) 5121-5010
Aero Peru ....(1) 581-8925
Air Canada ....(1) 7124-6084-12
Air China...(1) 587-6533
Air Malta ....(1) 586-5909
Air Mauritius ....(1) 713-9060
Air Transbrasil ....(1) 581-8910
Airzena Georgian Airlines.......................(1) 214-7877
Alitalia .... (1) 505-7615, 505-1707
All Nippon Airways ....(1) 587-8921
American Airlines ....(1) 513-95-090
toll-free ....(1) 0660-5491
Austrian Airlines ....(1) 505-57-570, 17-890
Balkan Air ....(1) 587-5418
British Airways...(1) 7956-7567
....airport, 7007-32646
British Midland...(1) 2031-414
Canadian Airlines ....(1) 2031-414
Delta ....(1) 512-6646
El Al ....(1) 512-4561
Eva Airways..(1) 512-4501
Finnair ....(1) 587-5548

Iberia ....(1) 586-7636
Iran Air..(1) 586-5601
Japan Airlines...(1) 512-7522
JAT Yugoslav Airlines ....(1) 512-3657
KAL........................(1) 586-8101-0, cargo: (1) 7007-9747
KLM...(1) 589-924
Lauda Air.......................................(1) 514-770, 7000
LOT Polish Airlines..................................(1) 533-9810
Lufthansa..(1) 588-360, 599-11
Malev Hungarian......................................(1) 587-3318
Northwest Airlines ....(1) 51-646
Olympic Airways......................................(1) 504-4165
Pakistan International Airlines ....(1) 714-4101
Pan American..(1) 526-646
Philippine Airlines ....(1) 535-3770
Saudi Arabian Airlines ....(1) 586-9191
Singapore Airlines ....(1) 513-4656
South African Airways ....(1) 587-1585
Swissair ....(1) 587-1798, 505-5757
TAP Air Portugal......................................(1) 513-3977
Tarom-Romanian ....(1) 581-8800
Tunis Air ....(1) 581-4207
Turkish Airlines..(1) 586-2024
TWA ....(1) 587-68-680
Ukraine International Airlines ....(1) 585-1570
Uzbekistan Airways..................................(1) 581-8931
US Airways...(1) 203-1414

HOTELS
Top-end

Bristol; Kärntner Ring 1, 1015; tel: (1) 515-160; fax: (1) 515-16-550; city center; restaurant; conference facilities (up to 170); in-room modem/fax connection; secretarial service; fax/photocopy facilities; corporate rates; parking; fitness room.

Hilton Vienna; Am Stadtpark, Schottenring 11, 1030; tel: (1) 313-900; fax: (1) 3139-0160; city center; restaurants; conference center; in-room minibar, safe, hairdryer, work desk, dual-line telephones, modem connection, electronic locks; sauna; covered parking/valet or self parking; fitness.

Imperial; Kärntner Ring 17, 1015; tel: (1) 501-100; fax: (1) 501-10-410; city center; restored rooms in traditional hotel; restaurant; conference facilities (up to 200); secretarial service; fax/photocopy facilities; technical facilities; in-room minibar; corporate rates; parking garage.

Radisson SAS Palais Vienna; Weihburggasse 32, 1010; tel: (1) 515-170; fax: (1) 512-2216; city center; rooms in Biedemeier style; restaurant; secretarial service; fax/photocopy facilities; in-room modem/fax connection, minibar, trouserpress, hairdryer; non-smoking rooms available; corporate rates; parking garage; fitness room; spa; sauna; solarium.

Sacher; Philharmonikerstrasse 4, 1010; tel: (1) 514-56; fax: (1) 514-57-810; city center; restaurant; conference facility (up to 120); secretarial service; fax/photocopy facilities; parking.

Expensive

Ambassador; Neuer Markt 5, 1010; tel: (1) 514-66-0; fax: (1) 513-2999; city center; restaurant; conference center; 5-star hotel.

City Central; Taborstrasse 8, 1020; tel: (1) 21-105; fax: (1) 2110-5140; near city center; conference facility (up to 20); fax/photocopy facilities; parking.

Novotel Vienna Airport; opposite arrivals hall; tel: (1) 701-510; fax: (1) 706-2828; restaurant; 18 meeting rooms (up to 400); secretarial staff; translating/interpreting; parking.

Opernring; Opernring 11, 1010; tel: (1) 587-5518; fax: (1) 5875-518-29; conference facility (up to 20); secretarial service; fax/photocopy facilities; corporate rates; parking.

Sofitel Vienna Airport; tel: (1) 70-1510; fax: (1) 706-28-28; email: sofitel@atnet.at; connected to World Trade Center, opposite arrival hall of Vienna Airport; conference facilities (up to 600); business services; secretarial service; fax; translation; internet access; in-room hairdryer, minibar, satellite TV; parking.

Renaissance Wien; Linke Wienzeile, Ullmannstrasse 71, 1150; tel: (1) 85-040; fax: (1) 850-4100; conference-type hotel adjacent to rail station; restaurant; secretarial service; fax/photocopy facilities; in-room modem/fax connection; corporate rates; fitness room; sauna; pool.

moderate

Concordia; Schönborngasse 6, 1080; tel: (1) 401-180; fax: (1) 401-1871.

Hadrigan; Maroltingergasse 68, 1060; tel/fax: (1) 493-2062; near city center; restaurant; parking.

Ibis Wien; Mariahilfer Gürtel 22-24, 1060; tel: (1) 59-998; fax: (1) 597-9090; near exhibition grounds; restaurant; conference center; no-smoking rooms; parking.

Jäger; Hernalser Haputstrasse 187; tel: (1) 464-1310; fax: (1) 466-6208; parking; no phone in room.

Hotel Kärntnerhof; Grashofgasse 4, 1011 Vienna; tel: (1) 512-1923-0; fax: (1) 513-2228-33; email:kaerntnerhof@netway.at; city center; breakfast buffet; most rooms with bath or shower, WC, direct dial phone.

Pension Continental; Kirchengasse 1, 1070 Vienna; tel: (1) 523-2418; fax: (1) 523-2630; near Mariahilferstrasse, subway station, restaurants; buffet breakfast; parking (included in price).

Pension Wild; Langegasse 10, 1080 Wien; tel: (1) 406-5174; fax: (1) 402-2168; email: info@pension-wild.com.

Hotel Pension Andreas; Schlosslgasse 11, 1080 Wien; tel: (1) 405-3488; fax: (1) 405-3488; fax: (1) 405-3488/50; near subway stop; breakfast buffet; elevator; renovated rooms with shower, WC, phone, cable TV.

Hotel Pension Rosengarten; Underreingasse 3, 1140; tel: (1) 914-52-800; fax: (1) 9140-36-324; city suburb; no-smoking rooms; corporate rates; parking.

Hotel Post; Fleischmarkt 24, 1010 Wien; tel: (1) 51-583; fax: (1) 5158-3808; city center; breakfast buffet.

Hotel Schweizerhof; Bauernmarkt 22, 1010 Vienna; tel: (1) 433-1931; fax: (1) 533-0214; city center; breakfast buffet; rooms with bath or shower, WC, satellite TV, telephone; nearby garage.

Zur Wiener Staatsoper; Krugerstrasse 11, 1010 Vienna; tel: (1) 513-1274; fax: (1) 513-1274-15; buffet breakfast; all rooms with bath or shower, WC, satellite TV, phone; nearby garage.

mEDICAL CARE

Austrian Doctor's Board (Ärztekammer); Weihburggasse 10-12, A-1010 Vienna; tel: (1) 5150-1253; fax: (1) 515-01410.

Evangelisches Krankenhaus Wien-Währing; (Evangelical Hospital Vienna) Hans Sachs-G 10-12, 1180 Wien; tel: (1) 404-220; fax: (10 4042-2620.

Lainz - Krankenhaus der Stadt Wien; city hospital; Wolkerbergenstr. 1, 1130 Wien; tel: (1) 801-100; fax: (1) 801-10-2109.

Medical Group Fachaerzte Iugeck; Lugeck 1, A-1010 Vienna; tel: (1) 512-1818.

HEALTH CLUB

Beers Vienna Health & Dance Club; Neutorg 16, 1010 Wien; tel: (1) 535-1234; fax: (1) 5351-2345.

Donau Fitness; 1020 Wien, Taborstr. 38; tel: (1) 216-9933; fitness, life-cycles, life-step, treadmill, massage, solarium, fitness; sauna; bar.

Euro Freizeit & Fitness; Ungarg 60, 1030 Wien, tel: (1) 712-8888; Vienna Marriott Hotel, (1) 515-1866-99; Vienna Penta, Renaissance Hotel, tel: (1) 712-8888; Rennweg 79-81, 1030 Wien; tel: (1) 710-5353.

John Harris GesmbH; Nibelungeng 7, 1010 Wien; tel: (1) 587-3710.

AUTO RENTAL

Note: Drivers should note that the use of horns is prohibited within city limits. Parking is also very limited.

Avis; reservation, Weyringergasse 33, tel: 222-6558-390; fax: 222-6573-49; airport, tel: 170-0727-00; Opernring 3-5, tel: (1) 587-6241; Gudrunstrasse 179A A-1100; tel: (1) 601-870; fax: (1) 606-1278.

Budget; airport, tel: 170-072-711; fax: 170-072-711; fax: 170-073-728; Hilton Hotel, Am Stadtpark - 1030; tel: 171-46-565; fax: 171-47-238.

Europcar InterRent (National); Kärntnerring, 14; (1) 505-42-00; international reservations: tel: (1) 505-41-66; airport, tel: (1) 7007-3316.

Hertz; Kärntnerring, 17; tel: (222) 512-8677; fax: (222) 512-5034; intl. reservations, tel: (1) 713-1596; airport, tel: (222) 7007-2661; fax: (222) 7007-5395.

Mazur Limo; airport; tel: (1) 7007-64-22 or (1) 604-91-91.

Tibor Adler; chauffeured limousine; tel: (1) 216-09-90.

Rainbow Car; Biedermanngasse 29-35; tel: 802-21-30.

WORLD TRADE CENTER

World Trade Center Vienna-Airport
Vienna-Airport 1300, Austria
tel: (1) 7007-6000/1; fax: (1) 7007-6017/6027
email: wtc.vienna.airport@telecom.at

Austria

Bahamas

At a Glance

THE PEOPLE

Population .... 283,705 (July 1999 est.)
Growth Rate .... 1.36% (1999 est.)
Life Expectancy .... 74.25 years (born 1999)
Infant Mortality . 18.38 deaths/1,000 live births (1999 est.) births (1999 est.)

Ethnic Composition

Black African 85%
Caucasian 15%

Religious Composition

Baptist 32%
Anglican.. 20%
Roman Catholic... 19%
Evangelical Protestant.. 12%
Church of God 6%
Methodist... 6%
No affiliation... 3%
Other 2%

Languages Spoken

English (official), Creole

Education and Literacy

Education is under the jurisdiction of the Ministry of Education and Culture and is free in all government maintained schools. About 98 percent of the adult population is literate.

Labor Force

Total: 146,600
By occupation: services 92%, industry 3%, agriculture 5%

THE ECONOMY

The Bahamas offers a stable democratic government with an almost purely service-based economy of tourism and financial services. Industry and agriculture show no prospects of growth. Efforts to diversify the economy beyond services have met with resistance from opponents fearing potential negative effects of foreign competition. The Bahamas prospers as a "tax haven" where personal income, corporate income, capital gains, dividends, interest, royalties, estates, sales, inheritances, and payrolls are all tax-free. Real estate holdings remain taxable and foreign-owned enterprises are expected to make generous "contributions" to civic projects. The archipelago remains dependent on the ups and downs of the U.S. market which supplies the majority of its tourists. The Bahamas is also under pressure by international organizations to revise the one thing that makes this U.K. commonwealth so attractive to foreign investors: the tax code.

Exports .... US$300 million (1998)
Imports .... US1.37 billion (1998)
Total GDP .... US5.63 billion (1998 est.)
GDP Per Capita .... US$20,100 (1998 est.)
Unemployment .... 9% (1998 est.)
Inflation Rate .... 0.4 percent (1997)

Top Export Partners

United States, E.U., Norway.

Top Import Partners

United States, E.U., Iran

Top Exports

Pharmaceuticals, cement, rum, crawfish, refined petroleum products.

Top Imports

Foodstuffs, manufactured goods, crude oil, vehicles, electronics.

BUSINESS WORKWEEK

Offices

Monday to Friday 8:30 or 9a.m. to 5 or 5:30p.m.

Banks

Monday to Thursday day 9:30a.m. to 3p.m., Friday 9:30a.m. to 5p.m.

Government

Monday to Friday 9a.m. to 5:30p.m.

Retail

Most retail stores are open between 9a.m. and 5p.m. six days a week. Some maintain a five-day work week.

HOLIDAYS

New Year's Day..January 1
Good Friday...April 2*
Easter Monday ....April 5*
Whit Monday .... May 24*
Labor Day...June 4*
Independence Day ....July 10
Emancipation Day ....August 4
Discovery Day/Columbus Day..........................October 12
Christmas ....December 25-26
*Dates may vary by year.

CLIMATE

Seasons

It is generally hot and humid with light showers throughout the islands, and the temperature doesnít vary much between the four seasons. In the winter months, from November until May, the temperature hovers around 21∞C (70∞F) and in the summer months it reaches 29∞C (85∞F). The summer months can face up to 80 percent humidity.

Regions

Weather is consistent throughout this island chain.

Money & Banking

Currency

The currency of Bahamas is the Bahamian Dollar (B$).

Denominations

The Bahamian Dollar comes in coin denominations of B$25, 15, 10, 5, and 1 cents and banknotes of 50 cents, B$1, 3, 5, 10, 20, 50, and 100.

Traveler's Checks and Credit Cards

Exchange control is administered by the Central Bank. Traveler's checks and currency can be exchanged at banks, exchange shops, and hotels, as well as the airport, where commissions can run as high as 10 percent. Cash, especially

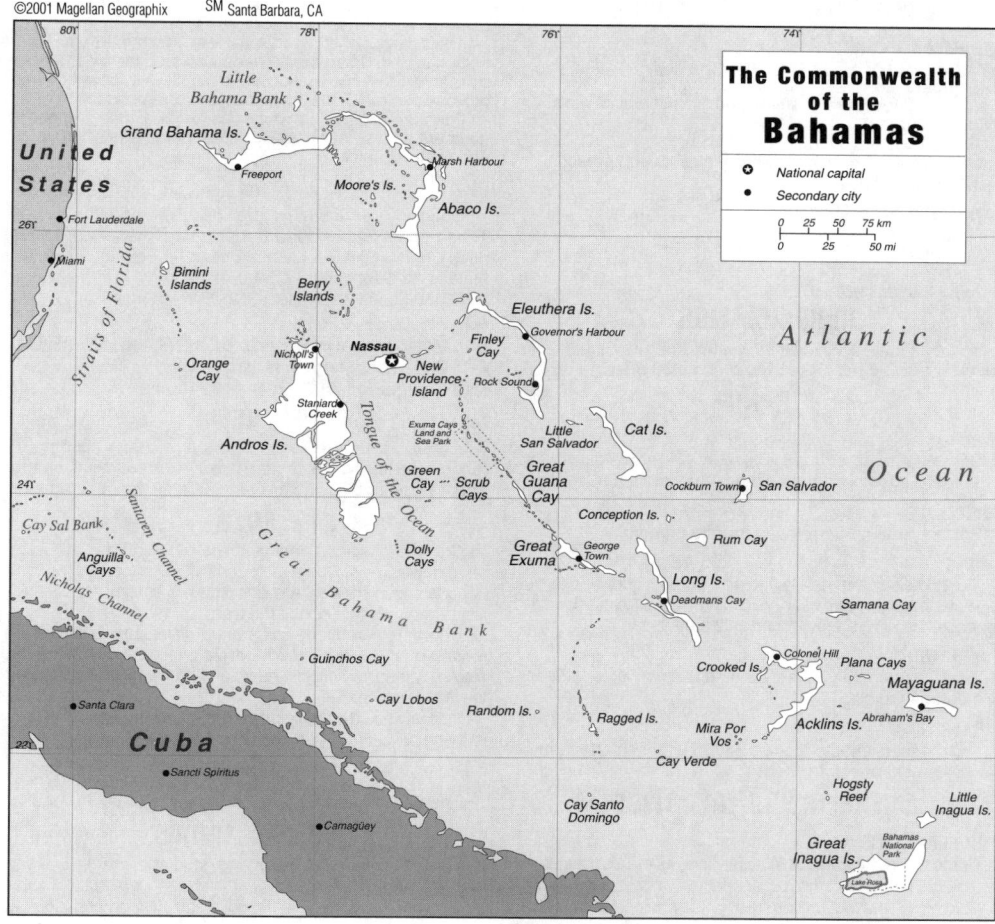

©2001 Magellan Geographix ^{SM} Santa Barbara, CA

Bahamas

U.S. dollars, commands a better exchange rate and lower fee than traveler's checks.

American Express, Visa, Diner's Club, and MasterCard are accepted in most up-market places in urban areas. Rural areas and small shops will require cash transactions. ATMs are readily available in cities for cash advances on credit cards and a limited number of ATM cards. The most favorable rates are given for credit card and ATM transactions.

Note: The Bahamian currency is not internationally accepted for exchange purposes outside of the islands. Bahamian regulations allow reconversion into foreign currency to the extent of just B$300, and only if the traveler has receipt of proof of former exchange from a foreign currency. Do not exchange your currency for more Bahamian dollars than you will need for small purchases. Use credit cards wherever possible.

Travel

VISA AND PASSPORT

Foreigners must have a valid passport, but visas are not required to enter the Bahamas for most foreigners staying less than three months. South and Central American citizens do not need visas unless staying more than two weeks.

Stays of up to eight months without a visa are permitted for nationals of Belgium, Greece, Italy, Luxembourg, The Netherlands, Iceland, Liechtenstein, Norway, San Marino, Switzerland, Turkey, the U.S., nationals of Commonwealth countries (except for nationals of Namibia and South Africa, who are allowed visa-free visits of less than 90 days, and nationals of Cameroon, Mozambique, and Pakistan who do need a visa).

All travelers must hold onward tickets, valid travel documents, and sufficient funds.

Travelers from Great Britain and Canada do not require a passport if they hold a citizenship card, a birth certificate, and photo identification. United States citizens who are not carrying a passport need a departure ticket, proof of citizenship, and photo identification for stays of up to eight months. A passport and work permit are needed for conducting business.

DEPARTURE FORMALITIES

When you leave the Bahamas by air, you will have to pay a B$15 departure tax at the airport (Freeport – B$18), payable in local currency. Transit passengers are exempt.

Non-residents of the Bahamas may take out of the country no more in Bahamian currency than B$70, although the currency has little function outside of the islands. Travelers may carry out duty-free gifts not in excess of B$600.

Bahamas

CUSTOMS ENTRY (PERSONAL)

Duty-free
- Tobacco: 200 cigarettes, 100 cigarillos, 50 cigars, or 454g of tobacco
- Alcohol: 1.136 liters of spirits and 1.136 liters of wine
- 50g of perfume
- Gifts not exceeding the value of B$100.

Note: A duty-free allowance is only available to persons over 21 years of age.

Prohibited or Restricted
- Firearms
- Weapons
- Drugs
- Radio transmitters

IMMUNIZATION

A vaccination certificate for yellow fever is required of travelers arriving from a publicized infected area.

TIPPING

Taxi
Drivers of metered taxis expect a 15 percent tip. Fees for unmetered transport should be negotiated in advance.

Porters
Porters expect B$1 per bag from foreigners.

Hotels
Most hotels automatically add a 15 percent service charge to your bill. Additional maid service tips may also be added to your hotel bill at a rate of around B$2 a day.

Restaurants
Tip 15 percent to your server unless it has already been included on the bill.

Other
Hairdressers should receive B$1 to 2; beach attendants get 15 percent of cabana bills.

EMERGENCY INFORMATION

Police and Crime
Crime in the Bahamas is relatively low, as the tourist industry is very important to the local economy. It is generally safe to walk the streets, but be careful of purse snatchers and pickpockets, especially in outdoor markets, in the city, and on the beaches. Do not leave your things unattended or your hotel doors unlocked. Avoid the Over-the-Hill area of Nassau and try not to walk alone on deserted areas of the beach at night.

Take basic precautions against petty crime. Foreign business visitors are often the target of specialized thieves. Consequently, purses, laptops, and briefcases will require additional security. Do not leave valuables in cars or on tables in cafés. Keep non-essential valuables locked in hotel safes when not in use. Carry photocopies of your passport instead of the original. Carry cash in a money belt, and use credit cards or traveler's checks for most of your transactions. Walk with your bag away from the streetside to avoid having it snatched away by thieves passing on the omnipresent motor scooters.

Visitors will find the police force to be efficient and helpful. Keeping tourists secure and happy is a Bahamian tradition.

Emergency Telephone Numbers
All services 911
For Travelers In Distress .... (242) 326-HELP

Health
The country is free from deadly tropical diseases. Tap water is considered safe, however it possesses a salty taste. Diarrhea is common for travelers who are unaccustomed to the new diet and water. The Bahamas can get extremely hot, so take necessary precautions against sun and heat stroke—drink lots of liquids and use sunblock when outdoors.

There are plenty of medical establishments with well-trained staff in urban areas. Use these facilities for emergencies only. Most medications are readily available but may prove expensive. Travel insurance is recommended.

For more information on medical centers, including phone numbers, please see the "Business Centers" section at the end of this chapter.

AIR

Domestic air travel is provided by charter services. These operations include Bahamasair Charter (UP), Pinder's Charter Service, Lucaya Beach Air Service, Taino Air, Major's Air Service and Congo Air.

Flight times from Nassau, New Providence Island:
- to Freeport is 40 minutes
- to Marsh Harbour or Treasure Cay, Abaco is 35 minutes
- to Governor's Harbour is 30 minutes
- to Georgetown on Exuma is 40 minutes.

TAXI

Metered taxis are available throughout the country, although the roads are better in some areas than others. Fares begin at B$2 and are regulated by the government.

AUTO

Car and motorbike rentals are available in the cities and some towns. Avis, Budget, Hertz, and Dollar can be found at airports and in Nassau. A national driver's license from the visitor's country is valid up to 90 days.

Drivers require credit cards and a valid driver's license for rental along with local insurance. Motorbikes and bicycles can also be rented. Motorcycle riders and passengers are required to wear crash helmets.

Visitors should be mindful that the islands are thick with tourists who have varying degrees of driving skill.

TRAIN

There is no train system available in the archipelago.

BUSES & TRAMS

The jitney bus service provides good and inexpensive service that normally runs until just after sundown in most cities and towns. A bus also services Paradise Island and stops at every hotel.

Visitors can also consider a horse-drawn carriage, which can take up to three passengers for a peaceful, dreamy ride through the roads of Nassau.

WATER TRAVEL

There is an extensive boat and airboat service among the many islands as well as liner service from the U.S. mainland. Service to other areas of the Caribbean can also be found, though most long-distance travel occurs by regular air routes.

For the more adventurous, there is passage available to the Out Islands on a mail boat that disembarks from Nassau several times weekly, delivering mail and supplies to the islands. Passengers share amenities with the crew. Make arrangements with the boat's captain at Potters Cay.

TRAVEL ASSISTANCE

Bahamas Ministry of Tourism
P.O. Box N 3701, Bay St., Nassau
tel: (242) 327-7500/04; fax: (242) 328-0945
email: e.smith@batelnet.bs

Bahamas Hotel Association
Hotel's House, Dean's Lane
Nassau
tel: (242) 322-8381; fax: (242) 326-5346

Communications

DIALING CODES IN BAHAMAS

International country code: [1]
Selected city codes: (242); this area code applies throughout the Bahamas

Dialing the Bahamas from Overseas

To reach the Bahamas, dial your country's international dialing code, the Bahamas' country code [1], the Bahamas' area code (242), and finally the number you are trying to reach. If dialing from the United States, dial 1+242+the local number.

CALLING WITHIN THE BAHAMAS

Local Calls

To make a local call from a hotel, dial 9 plus the number, but remember that you may be charged even if your call is not successfully completed.

Long Distance Calls

Check phone books or inquire for any extra codes if dialing within the Bahamas.

International Calls

The average cost of a call to the U.S. is US$1. Access numbers to foreign operators may be blocked if dialing from a hotel phone.
AT&T USA Direct ....[1] (800) 872-2881

PAY PHONES

Public Telephones

On the main islands, public phones appear much like they might in the U.S. and also allow direct dialing. On New Providence major hotels offer phones and sometimes fax services; also try the main post office on JFK Drive at Cable Beach. However, phones may be difficult to find on all the outer islands. In the Biminis, hotels and restaurants offer phones. In Andros, phones are almost nonexistent except at hotels or at the airport.

Calling Cards

If you can find them, card phones are almost always advisable over hotel phones if trying to save yourself a dent in the expense account.

CELLULAR PHONES

There are cellular phone service providers in the Bahamas. BATELCO offers AMPS-TDMA in the analog format.
Note: Your home country cell phone may not work in this country. If not, we recommend that you rent an international cell phone *before* you leave home. A major US-based cell phone rental provider is **IMC WorldCell**. For information see "International Cell Phone Rentals" on page 14.

CALL BACK

You can (potentially) save significant sums when calling in Bahamas by using a call back service. For a list of call-back services, please refer to the "Communications" section in the *Global Road Warrior* Introduction.

Fees for call back services vary widely, depending on the company and the type of service required.

PHONE JACK

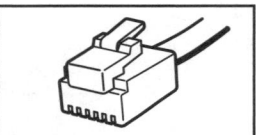

Adaptors are available through **iGo Corporation.**
(See "Electrical and Telephone Adaptors" on page 19.)

FAX

The Centralized Telephone Office on East Street in Nassau has fax services. Machines are also available at many top-end hotels, and can be rented.

POSTAL SERVICES

Packages and letters sent from the Bahamas take about seven days to reach Europe or North America. Service is generally efficient and safe.

Hours of service

Monday to Friday 9a.m. to 5p.m.

TELEGRAMS

Telegrams can be sent from most hotels, post offices, and from the Centralized Telephone Office.

Business Services

COURIER SERVICES

FedEx; tel: (242) 322-5656/1791.

TNT; tel: (242) 325-8266.

UPS; tel: (242) 322-8907.

VIP Jet Service; tel: (242) 361-6012.

SECRETARIAL SERVICES

World Trade Center Nassau; La-CariBah House 17 Collins Avenue, Nassau, N.P., Bahamas; tel: (242) 328-2250; (242) 328-5569; fax: (242) 322-8259; email: dede@grouper.batelnet.bs.

Electrical

Current

120 volts AC, 60Hz.

ELECTRIC PLUGS

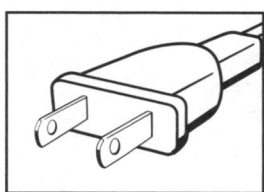

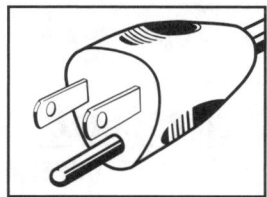

U.S. style 3-pin plugs are the norm.
Adaptors are available through **iGo Corporation.**
(See "Electrical and Telephone Adaptors" on page 19.)

Technical Support

HARDWARE/SOFTWARE VENDOR SUPPORT

Apple/Claris; (in the U.S.) tel: [1] (800) 500-7078; (in Germany) tel: [49] (1) 803-5018; (in Switzerland) tel: [41] (800) 833-310; (in the U.K.) tel: [44] (990) 127-753; http://www.apple.com/.

Compaq/Digital; (General U.S.) tel: [1] (281) 518-2000; (in Switzerland) tel: [41] (22) 709-5330; fax: [41] (22) 709-5391 (Geneva); [41] (1) 801-2507; fax: [41] (1) 801-2172 (Zurich); http://www.compaq.com/.

Hewlett Packard; (in the U.S.) tel: [1] (408) 246-4300; (in Switzerland) tel: [41] (22) 780-8111; http://www.hp.com/.

IBM; tel: 323-7350; fax: 323-8944; (U.S. Main Office) tel: [1] 914-765-1900; (in the U.S.) tel: [1] (919) 517-2800; (in Switzerland) tel: [41] (22) 310-0418 (in French) http://www.ibm.com/.

Microsoft; (in the U.S.) [1] (425) 635-7222; (in Germany) tel: [49] (89) 31-760; fax: [49] (89) 3176-1000; tel: [49] (89) 3176-1199; (in Switzerland) tel: [41] (848) 858-868; fax [41] (1) 831-0869; http://www.microsoft.com/.

Internet Connection

HOW TO CONNECT

Connecting to AOL and Compuserve in Bahamas is similar to using it when traveling outside your own area code. See the introductory section for detailed information on connecting to your account through a different phone number.

America Online

Numbers are available at keyword: *international*. Be sure to get several local numbers before leaving. AOL GlobalNet service charges US$12 an hour in addition to the usual charges. AOL has its GlobalNet service available at keyword: *access* (a free area).

Access: Nassau: 325-7004

Compuserve

Numbers are available at *Go International*. The Compuserve Web-site also has a great deal of information, at http://www.compuserve.com.

There are no direct access numbers for Compuserve in the Bahamas. Users will have to pay international rates to use the service.

Independent Service Providers

Many independent service providers offer discounts if you are only in town for a couple days. For longer stays in the country, ISP charges average

Bahama On-Line; tel: (242) 325-1000; fax: (242) (242) 325-0226; email: info@srg.com.bs; http://www.bahamas.net.bs/.

VPM Enterprises; tel: [1] (916) 983-9876; toll-free: 1-800-321-0221; fax: [1] (916) 983-4375; email: sales@vpm.com; http://www.vpm.com/.

Business Culture

GREETINGS AND COURTESIES

Bahamians are noticeably formal, but perhaps less so than in many other areas of the English-speaking Caribbean. Titles and last names are used, although Bahamians are less addicted to the use of titles than many others in Latin America and the Caribbean. Business cards (in English) are normally exchanged, but without particular formality.

DECISION MAKING

Because of the importance of consensus, few individuals have full authority to make binding decisions concerning any but the most mundane matters. Locals may assume that foreign businesspeople are fully aware of this without making it clear to them, leading to disappointments and misunderstandings.

WOMEN

Women in the Bahamas occupy a secondary status, although they often form the backbone of small-scale enterprises and are generally accorded considerable personal freedom and influence. Foreign businesswomen should experience few problems and may even be accorded special treatment by more traditional senior businessmen.

MEETINGS

Introductions are helpful but not absolutely necessary. Bahamians are often late for appointments, but foreigners are expected to be on time. Business lunch meetings are common—these are low-key events, usually limited to the people involved in the immediate discussions. Dinner meetings are uncommon, as are other outside events that combine business and social elements.

BUSINESS ATTIRE

Natural fabrics that allow skin to breathe are the way to go in a humid climate. A cotton shirt worn with a tie and lightweight trousers should serve a businessman well. Men should wear jackets when making business calls and for evening dining. Certain restaurants require more formalwear even at lunchtime. Women might wear lightweight dresses or blouses and skirts, and an evening dress for nighttime engagements. Evenings may also require some sort of light sweater or jacket to ward off any chill after a blistering day.

Business Centers
Nassau

CITY VIEW

Doing business in Nassau? Good luck. It is what most people imagine paradise to be, with sunshine and ocean everywhere. Furthermore, casinos and a lively atmosphere call even more attention to the vacation mode of operation.

AIRPORT

Nassau International Airport to City Center

The airport lies 10 miles (16 km.) from the city. There are taxi services readily available. A cab ride to downtown will cost about US$18.

Airline Numbers

Air Canada	(242) 377-8411
Abaco Air	(242) 367-2266
American Eagle	(242) 367-2231
BahamasAir	(305) 718-9115
British Airways	1-800-AIRWAYS
Congo Air	(242) 377-8329
Continental Gulfstream	(305) 871-1200
Island Express	(954) 359-0380
Pinders Charter Service	(242) 377-7008
Reliable Air Service	(242) 377-7335
Sky Unlimited	(242) 377-8993
Taino Air Service	(242) 327-5336

HOTELS

Top End

Graycliff Hotel; West Hill Street; tel: (242) 322-2796; toll free: 1-800-322-2796; fax: (242) 326-6110; historic Georgian mansion; 5-star restaurant; conference facilities (up to 20); secretarial services; fax/photocopy facilities; corporate rates; fitness room; pool; sauna.

Radisson Cable Beach & Golf Resort; Cable Beach; tel: (242) 327-6000; toll-free: 1-800-432-0221; fax: (242) 327-6987; email: radcblebch@aol.com; connected to casino; renovated; 6 restaurants; in-room minibar, safe, hair dryer, iron and ironing board, voicemail; round-trip airport transfers; fitness; pool; 18-hole golf; tennis, racquetball/squash; watersports.

Sandals Royal Bahamian Resort and Spa; Cable Beach; tel: (242) 327-6400; toll-free: 1-800-SANDALS; fax: (242) 327-6961; 6 restaurants; conference facilities (up to 450); secretarial service; fax/photocopy facilities; full-service spa; fitness room; sauna; pool; watersports.

Expensive

Best Western British Colonial Beach Resort; 1 Bay Street; tel: (242) 322-3301; fax: (242) 322-2286; restaurant; meeting and banquet facilities; private beach; pool; tennis; watersports.

Breezes Bahamas; tel: (242) 327-6153; fax: (242) 327-5155; on Cable Beach; conference facilities (up to 500); fitness room; pool; whirlpool; watersports; all-inclusive prices.

Nassau Beach Hotel; tel: (242) 327-6200; toll-free: 1-800-222-7466; fax: (242) 327-7615; on Cable Beach next to Marriott; restaurant; conference facilities; secretarial service; fax/photocopy facilities; in-room modem connections; fitness room; pool.

Wyndham Ambassador Beach; West Bay St., Cable Beach; tel: (242) 327-8231; fax: (242) 327-6727; restaurant; conference facilities; pool.

Moderate

Coral Harbor Beach House and Villas; tel:(242) 328-1036; fax: (242) 261-6514; southwest side of island; small hotel; restaurant; private beach.

Montague Beach Inn; East Shirley St. and Village Road; tel: (242) 393-0480; fax: (242) 393-6061; city suburb; restaurant; secretarial service; fax/photocopy facilities; pool; corporate rates.

PARADISE ISLAND HOTELS

Golden Palm Resort; Paradise Island; tel: 363-3311; fax: 363-3121; restaurant; secretarial service; fitness; pool; tennis; water sports; corporate rates.

Sunrise Beach Club and Villas; Casino Drive, Paradise Island; tel: 363-2234; fax: 363-2308; email: sunrise@bahamas.net.bs; restaurant; casino; conference facilities (up to 25); secretarial services; fax/photocopy facilities; pool; whirlpool; parking.

MEDICAL CARE

Doctors Hospital; (Private hospital) PO Box N03918, Shirley Street; tel: (242 322-8411.

Princess Margaret Hospital; (government hospital; PO Box N-3730, Shirley Street; tel: (242) 322-2861, 322-3117.

Stat Care Medical & Emergency Centre; PO Box N-1690, Nassau; tel: (242) 328-5596/7/8.

HEALTH CLUB

Gold's Gym Fitness and Aerobic Centre; Foot of the Paradise Island Bridge, Nassau; tel: (242) 393-6975.

AUTO RENTAL

Avis; tel: (800) 228-0668; (242) 322-4062 (national headquarters); fax: (242) 325-1076; airport, tel: (242) 352-7666; fax: (242) 352-4595; email: avis@batelnet.bs.

Budget; tel: (800) 527-0700; airport, tel: (242) 377-7405; fax: (242) 377-7489; central reservations, tel: (242) 323-7191; fax: (242) 323-7545.

Hertz; toll free tel: (800) 654-3131; (242) 377-8684 (domestic); tel: (242) 322-3646 (international); fax: (242) 327-7936 (domestic); fax: (242) 322-3110 (international).

National; tel: (800) 328-4567.

WORLD TRADE CENTER

Bahamas World Trade Center, Nassau
La-CariBah House
17 Collins Avenue
P.O. Box N-9343
Nassau, N.P., Bahamas
tel: (242) 328-2250; (242) 328-5569
fax: (242) 322-8259
email: dede@grouper.batelnet.bs

Bahrain

At a Glance

THE PEOPLE

Population 616,342 (1998)
Growth Rate 2.09% (1998)
Life Expectancy .... 74.96 years (born 1999)
Infant Mortality .... 15.54 deaths/1,000 live births (1998)

Ethnic Composition

Bahraini 63%
Asian 13%
Other Arab 10%
Iranian 8%
Other 6%

Religious Composition

Shi'a Muslim 75%
Sunni Muslim 25%

Languages Spoken

Arabic (official), English, Farsi, and Urdu

Education and Literacy

The government provides free education for all children, though less so for girls. The adult literacy rate is 85.2 percent.

Labor Force

Total: 140,000
By occupation: services 61%, industry 38%, agriculture 1% (Note: 44% of the population are not citizens.)

THE ECONOMY

Bahrain's traditional role over the centuries as a trading center has been augmented in the 20th century by the discovery of petroleum. This commodity now accounts for 60 percent of the government's income and 30 percent of the national GDP. The majority of the nation's business is devoted to services (60%) for finance, transport, and communication. The island's unique location in the Persian Gulf has made it attractive to multinationals with petroleum and off-shore banking related interests. Bahrain has a high GDP per capita but an extensive and expensive social benefits system. Unemployment is in the mid-teens and over 40 percent of the population is composed of non-nationals. The island must import most of its food, and its heavy reliance on oil and oil-related services has made it overly sensitive to commodity price swings. Fresh water resources are dwindling and oil reserves are rapidly depleting with little remedial action by the government. Any major drop in oil prices will send the economy into a rapid tailspin.

Exports .... US$4.6 billion (1996)
Imports .... US$3.7 billion (1996)
Total GDP .... US$8.2 billion (1997)
GDP Per Capita .... US$13,700 (1997)
Unemployment .... 15 percent (1996)
Inflation Rate .... 0.2 percent (1996)

Top Export Partners

India, Japan, Saudi Arabia, United States, United Arab Emirates

Top Import Partners

Saudi Arabia, United States, United Kingdom, Japan, Switzerland

Top Exports

Refined petroleum, petroleum products, aluminum.

Top Imports

Foodstuffs, machinery, consumer products, crude oil.

BUSINESS WORKWEEK

Offices

Saturday to Wednesday 7a.m. to noon, and 2:30p.m. to 5p.m., Thursday 7:30a.m. to noon.

Banks

Saturday to Wednesday 7:30a.m. to noon, Thursday 7a.m. to 11a.m.

Government

Saturday to Thursday 7a.m. to 1p.m.

Retail

Saturday to Thursday 8a.m. to 12:30p.m. and 3:30p.m. to 6:30p.m.; on Wednesdays and Thursdays stores may stay open until 9:00p.m.

Note: Bahrain is a Muslim country and businesses structure their hours and services around the required prayer breaks.

HOLIDAYS

New Year's Day .... January 1
Id al-Fitr, end of Ramadan .... January 19*
Mahurram, Islamic New Year .... April 17*
Id al-Adha, Feast of the Sacrifice .... March 28*
Ashoura .... April 26*
Mouloud, Birth of the Prophet .... June 26*
Leitat al-Meiraj, Ascension of
the Prophet .... November 6*
Ramadan begins .... December 9*
National Holiday .... December 16
*Date may vary by year.

CLIMATE

Seasons

Bahrain is hot and humid in the summer, from June to September, and has a generally mild climate in the winter, between October and May. What little rainfall there is generally occurs from December to March and averages only about 4 inches (10 cm) annually. Temperatures range from 10°C (50°F) in winter to summertime highs of 48°C (118°F).

Regions

Weather is consistent throughout this small Persian Gulf island. The highest point above sea level is the central escarpment at only 122 meters.

Money & Banking

Currency

The currency of Bahrain is the Dinar (BD).

Denominations

The Dinar comes in coin denominations of 5, 10, 25, 50, and 100 fils and banknotes of 500 fils, BD1, BD5, BD10, and BD20.

Traveler's Checks and Credit Cards

Traveler's checks and currency can be exchanged at banks, exchange shops, and hotels, as well as the airport,

Bahrain

where commissions can vary greatly. Avoid extra exchange rate charges by bringing traveler's checks denominated in U.S. dollars. Cash, especially U.S. dollars, commands a better exchange rate and lower fees than traveler's checks. There is no black market for foreign exchange.

American Express, Visa, Diner's Club, and Master-Card are accepted in larger hotels in urban areas. Smaller shops and rural areas will require local currency. ATMs are rare and only found in the capital, Manama. Credit cards and ATM transactions receive the most favorable exchange rates and lowest service charges.

Bank Locations

Citibank, N.A.; P.O. Box 548, Manama; tel: 257-124; fax: 250-510.

National Bank of Bahrain B.S.C.; P.O. Box 106, Manama; tel: 258-800; fax: 263-876

Bank of Bahrain and Kuwait B.S.C.; P.O. Box 597, Manama; tel: 253-388; fax: 275-785

Bahrain

Essential Terms

English	Arabic
Yes	Na-a'am
No	La; mish
Good morning	Al sa-lahm
Hello (daytime)	Al sa-lahm
Hello (evening)	Ma-sa'el khair
Hello (telephone)	Marhaban
Good-bye	Be-kha-trahk
Please	Min-fahd-lak (M)
	Min-fahd-lik (F)
Thank you	Shook-rahn
Pleased to meet you	Sorirart biro'aitak
Excuse me; I'm sorry	Is-ma-leh
My name is _____	'ismii____
I don't understand	An-na mish fahem
Do you speak English?	Hal tatakallumu l-inkliziyya?

Travel

VISA AND PASSPORT

A valid passport is required of all visitors to Bahrain. A visa is also required of all, except for those who are continuing onward via the next connecting flight and have confirmed tickets with appropriate travel documents, or citizens of the Gulf Cooperation Council (GCC) nations of Kuwait, Oman, Qatar, Saudi Arabia, and the United Arab Emirates. GCC nationals may stay as long as they wish. British passport holders are also exempt from the visa requirement for stays of up to 30 days.

Long-term business visas need to be arranged by the relevant company in Bahrain. The term of validity depends on your individual application and on the granting of a "non-objection certificate." Canadian and American visitors may apply for a multiple-entry visa for four-week stays; it is valid for as long as 5 years.

If you are a passport holder from a western nation (with the exception of Israel), and you possess a confirmed return or onward airline ticket, you may simply acquire a short-term visa upon arrival at Bahrain Airport or at the Bahraini customs office on the highway from Saudi Arabia. These are either a 72-hour transit visa or a 7-day tourist visa. It is also possible to extend these, once you are in-country.

Generally, though, it is preferable to obtain your visa prior to arriving in Bahrain, as complications can occur. If you are a naturalized citizen (for instance, a foreign-born American), Bahraini immigration officials will still view you as a citizen of your birth country and will not grant you a visa at the airport. If you are a woman traveling alone, you cannot be sure that the rules will apply fairly to you either. In these cases, one is advised to have your hotel arrange for the visa ahead of time, whereby the hotel acts as your sponsor. To arrange this, fax all of your passport data, your arrival and departure times, and the reason for your visit to the hotel about three weeks ahead of time. In return for acting as your sponsor, the hotel will charge a small visa fee (usually less than BD5), and you can pick up the visa at the airport or at Bahraini Customs. Be sure to confirm with the hotel a few days before arrival.

Restrictions: You will not be allowed entry to Bahrain if you have Israeli stamps in your passport. Also, if you specify that you are a writer, journalist, or editor, your visa must be sponsored by the Ministry of Information, or you will probably be denied entrance. Be aware that the government does not tolerate the practice of working in the country on a tourist visa.

DEPARTURE FORMALITIES

There is a departure tax of BD3, payable in local currency. If you prefer, you may purchase coupons in advance at airline and travel agency offices.

CUSTOMS ENTRY (PERSONAL)

Duty-free
- Tobacco: 200 cigarettes, 50 cigars, or 250g of tobacco for personal use
- Perfume: 8 oz. of perfume for personal use
- Alcohol: 1 liter of wine or spirits, 6 bottles of beer (non-Muslim passengers only)
- Personal goods
- Sales samples
- Gifts under US$667 in value

Prohibited or Restricted
- Firearms and ammunition
- Drugs
- Jewelry and all items originating in Israel may only be imported under license
- All uncut, bleached, or undrilled pearls produced outside the Gulf are under strict import regulations. Cultured pearls are illegal in any form.
- Pornographic and obscene literature and pictures
- Non-Islamic religious texts or icons

IMMUNIZATION

An international certificate of vaccination for yellow fever and cholera is required if you are arriving from infected areas within the last two weeks. Vaccination for typhoid, tetanus, and Hepatitis A are advisable. (Hepatitis B shots are recommended for long-term visitors.)

TIPPING

Taxi
Metered taxi drivers expect a 10 percent tip. Unmetered fares should be all inclusive and negotiated in advance.

Porters
Porters expect 100 fils per bag and hotel attendants expect 100 fils each.

Hotels
Hotels will add 10 to 15 percent service charge to the total bill.

Restaurants
Larger restaurants will apply service charges, although westerners are expected to add a moderate tip. When no service charge is applied, add 15 percent for full-service and round up the bill for lesser transactions.

EMERGENCY INFORMATION

Police and Crime

Due to strict Muslim laws, crime remains relatively low in Bahrain. It is generally safe to walk the streets. But use common sense and take basic precautions against petty crime as you might anywhere else. Foreign business visitors are often the target of what few thieves there are in Bahrain. Consequently, purses, laptops, and briefcases will require additional security. Do not leave valuables in cars or on tables in cafés. Keep non-essential valuables locked in hotel safes when not in use.Carry photocopies of your passport instead of the original. Carry cash in a money belt, and use credit cards or travelers checks for most of your large transactions.

The police are usually efficient and friendly. As this is an Islamic country, women are advised to dress modestly when outdoors. Respect for local social customs will help avoid harassment. Though hardly a fundamentalist nation, violators will be chastised by the locals.

Emergency Numbers

All hospitals have an emergency service and an efficient ambulance service. In Manama call:

Sulmaniya Medical Center 252761
American Mission Hospital 253 447

Health

Water in Bahrain should not be consumed since it carries risk of contamination; don't even use it for brushing your teeth, and avoid using ice cubes except at first class hotels. Raw vegetables and fruit should first be washed in a chlorine solution. Modern hotels, however, usually have their own filtration plants; consequently, eating should be safe. Ensure that meat is properly cooked and served hot. Milk may be unpasteurized. Diarrhea is common for travelers who are unaccustomed to the new diet, the water, and the heat. Take precautions against heat and sunstroke.

Bahrain has a good government-run medical service, which also serves resident foreigners. Most healthcare employees speak English and medication is readily available though it may prove pricey. Travel insurance is advisable as is an evacuation policy for long-term business visitors.

For more information on medical centers, including phone numbers, please see the "Business Centers" section at the end of this chapter.

AIR

Most of Bahrain is extremely accessible by air. Over 300 scheduled flights depart from Bahrain International Airport for other locations within the country. Check with your travel agent ahead of time, or simply enquire locally. Your hotel will probably be able to help you also.

TAXI

Metered taxis have orange and red coloring on the sides. You may hail a cab in the street, at tourist locations, or at stands outside the hotel (although these cabs may cost more). Unless the meter is working, agree on a fare before entering the cab. Fares generally start with a minimum of 800 fils. And remember that fares may go up by 50 percent between midnight and 5a.m. Cabs hailed at the airport may charge a dinar extra.

As an alternative to hailing a taxi for each individual trip, you may also hire a taxi by the hour to take you wherever you please for an unofficial price of BD5. Daily rates are also available.

Most taxi drivers are familiar with their city, but some additional directions (and a map) will probably be helpful, not to mention safer.

AUTO

Visitors may rent cars in Manama, but they require a credit card, a valid driver's license, and local insurance. Car rental is only recommended for visitor's highly experienced with Bahrain's driving customs. Cars with local drivers may be rented for daily and weekly rates.

TRAIN

There is no passenger train system in Bahrain.

METRO

No metro service exists in Bahrain.

BUSES & TRAMS

Bus routes cover most towns and villages. While it may prove slower than other modes of transport, bus travel in Bahrain is very inexpensive: 50 fils to reach any destination in Bahrain. Buses operate from 5:30 or 6:30a.m. to 9:30p.m. Check at the terminals to verify your route. Overnight travel is not recommended for visitors nor are buses advisable for travel between business meetings.

WATER TRAVEL

Travel between the main island and outlying islands works primarily by small motor boat. There is no organized passenger ferry system.Contact a local travel agent or hotel concierge for more details.

TRAVEL ASSISTANCE

Ministry of Cabinet Affairs and Information
PO Box 26613, Manama, Bahrain
tel: 211-199; fax: 210-969

Bahrain Tourism Company (BTC)
PO Box 5831, Manama, Bahrain
tel: 530-530; fax: 530-867

Security Briefing

SOCIAL UNREST

Bahrain is a long-term monarchy that has ruled without a representative Assembly since 1975. Political parties are prohibited and an Advisory Council is appointed by the Amir (emir). Several leftist and Islamic fundamentalist groups have staged occasional protests to demand the return of the Assembly and to limit the power of the Amir. The current prosperity has limited social unrest, and there is general satisfaction with the present state of affairs.

ORGANIZED CRIME

Bahrain is a major off-shore banking and shipping center in the Middle East. As such, it will attract some activity by organized crime groups, although the small size of Bahrain makes anonymity difficult. Legitimate foreign firms should have no difficulty with organized crime.

STREET CRIME

The wealth of the general population and the extensive social benefits system minimizes the development of street crime. Some vandalism of rental vehicles and harassment of western tourists has been reported during UN sponsored military activity in neighboring Arabic countries. Otherwise, street crime is very low and only basic precautions need be taken.

CULTURAL CONFLICTS

Bahrain's capital Manama is very cosmopolitan, and the country is quite liberal by Islamic Arab standards. Dress codes for women and men are more relaxed than most Gulf

Bahrain

states, though in rural areas it is best to appear more conservative in attire. Sportswear can be worn in hotel areas but shorts and sleeveless shirts should never be worn in public by either sex. Women should avoid miniskirts, tight blouses, and exposed shoulders in public. Women need only wear a head scarf if entering a mosque.

Bahrain is a strict monarchy and disparaging comments about the Amir are best left unspoken. The population is primarily Shiite Moslem and it takes a dim view of anti-Islamic statements or behavior as well. Nonbelievers can visit mosques if properly attired and suitably reverent. Alcohol is served in Bahrain but public drunkenness is unacceptable and will result in arrest.

Communications

DIALING CODES IN BAHRAIN

International country code: [973]

Dialing Bahrain from Overseas

To dial Bahrain from overseas, dial your country's international dialing code, then the country code for Bahrain (973), and finally the number you are trying to reach (there are no city codes). If you are dialing Bahrain from the United States, for example, begin with 011, then 973, and finally the number of the person or office you are trying to reach.

Assistance Numbers

International Directory (English spoken) 191
International Call Booking 151
National Directory 181
National Operator 100
Telex Information .... 19+
Telex Connection Assistance .... 10+
Telegram 131
Mobile, Pagers, & trunked mobile radio 120

CALLING WITHIN BAHRAIN

Local Calls

Due to the first-rate telephone system in Bahrain, local calls should not prove a problem. It is possible to direct dial from most anywhere. A local call costs 50 fils.

Long Distance Calls

Bahrain has no area codes to search for; simply pick up and dial the number you wish to reach.

International Calls

BATELCO (Bahrain Telephone Company) operates the sparkling telephone system in Bahrain and diligently provides the most foreign operator access numbers of any other country in the area. Furthermore, it is possible to reach the Home Country Direct access numbers from any phone:
Australia 800-061
Canada 800-100
Denmark 800-045
Hong Kong 800-852
Ireland 800-353
Japan 800-081
Malaysia 800-060
Netherlands 800-031
Philippines 800-163
Singapore 800-065
U.K. 800-044
U.S. AT&T 800-001
U.S. MCI 800-002
U.S. Sprint 800-777

If you wish to call direct and bypass the operators completely, dial 0 + country code + area code + number.

Remember, to dial direct from a card phone will cost quite a bit less than booking through a hotel operator.

PAY PHONES

Public Telephones

Phones exist for both cards and coins; if using the latter, they take 100fils coins.

Calling Cards

Cards can be purchased at the Telecommunication Centers.

CELLULAR PHONES

There are numerous cellular phone service providers in Bahrain. In the digital format, Baharain Telecommunications offers both GSM and TACS service.

Note: Your home country cell phone may not work in this country. If not, we recommend that you rent an international cell phone *before* you leave home. A major US-based cell phone rental provider is **IMC WorldCell**. For information see "International Cell Phone Rentals" on page 14.

CALL BACK

You can (potentially) save significant sums when calling in Bahrain by using a call back service. For a list of callback services, please refer to the "Communications" section in the *Global Road Warrior* Introduction.

Fees for call back services vary widely, depending on the company and the type of service required. Be sure to check with these companies before leaving to compare rates.

PHONE JACKS

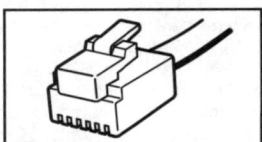

Adaptors are available through **iGo Corporation.** (See "Electrical and Telephone Adaptors" on page 19.)

FAX

Fax equipment is available at many business centers and major hotels. Dial 270-270 within the country for more information and locations.

POSTAL SERVICES

The postal system rates generally very good. Airmail takes an average of three days to reach North America. There is also an express mail service that can send letters same day to North America. You can find the Central Post Office opposite Bab Al Bahrain; the office stays open Saturday to Thursday from 7a.m. to 7:30pm.

TELEGRAM

To send a telegram, dial Batelco's telegram service: 131.

Business Services

BUSINESS CENTER

Bahrain Hilton; tel: 535-000; fax: 533-097.

COURIER SERVICES

Air Couriers; tel: 330-180.
DHL International WLL; tel: 243-1212 or 723-636.
Federal Express; tel: 530-440
TNT Express Worldwide; tel: 533-113
United Parcel Service (UPS); tel: 223-123

PRINTING/COPYING

Gulf Printing and Advertising Center; tel: 257113.
Midas Printing Co.; tel: 271357.

SECRETARIAL SERVICES

Manama Secretarial Bureau; tel: 712851.
Bahrain Business Center; Bahrain Tower; tel: 243436.

TRANSLATION SERVICES

The Translators; tel: 258283.
Polyglot Schools; P.O. Box 596, Al-Khalifa Rd.
Bahrain Business Center; Bahrain Tower; tel: 243436.

Electrical

Current

220 volts AC, 50Hz.
Lamp fittings are of both the bayonet and screw types.
Plug fittings are normally of the 13-amp pin type.

ELECTRIC PLUGS

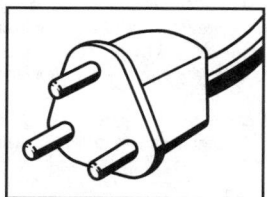

Adaptors are available through **iGo Corporation.**
(See "Electrical and Telephone Adaptors" on page 19.)

Technical Support

HARDWARE/SOFTWARE VENDOR SUPPORT

Compaq/Digital; (in the U.A.E.) tel: [971] 4-818-100; fax: [971] 4-818-313; (in Germany) tel: [49] 89-9933-0; fax: [49] 89-9933-1158; [49] 0130-6868 (CompaqCare Center/Information); [49] (0)180-5- 212111 (Technical Support); [49] (0)89-99-33-1380 (QuickLine); http://www.compaq.com.

Dell; tel: 971 452 4232; fax: 971 452 7944 (Key Information Formation Technology); (in Germany) tel: [49] (61) 039-710; (Dell- Europe) tel: [44] (134) 474-8000; (in the U.S.)

tel: [1] (512) 338-4400; fax: [1] (512) 728-3330; http://www.dell.com/.
Hewlett Packard; (in Switzerland) tel: [41] (22) 780-8111; (in the U.S.) tel: [1] (408) 246-4300; http://www.hp.com/.
IBM; tel: 210-880; fax: 210-576; (in Germany) tel: [49] (711) 78-50; fax: [49] (711) 785-3511; (in Switzerland) tel: [41] (22) 310-0418 (French); (U.S. Main Office) tel: [1] 914-765-1900; (in the U.S.) tel: [1] (919) 517-2800; http://www.ibm.com/.
Microsoft; (in the U.A.E.) tel: [971] (4) 513-888; fax: [971] (4) 527-444; (in Germany) tel: [49] (89) 31-760; fax: [49] (89) 3176-1000; tel: [49] (89) 3176-1199; (in Switzerland) tel: [41] (848) 858-868; fax [41] (1) 831-0869; (in the U.S.) [1] (425) 635-7222; http://www.microsoft.com/.
NEC; (in Israel) tel: [972] (0)9-59-3300 (UltraCare Support); (in Germany) tel: [49] (18) 0524- 1212; tel:[49] (89) 3160-1233; fax: [49] (89) 3160- 1613 (Floppy Disk and Hard Drive); tel: [49] (89) 9627-4233; fax: [49] (89) 9627-4613 (All Other Products); (in the U.S.) [1] (916) 388-0101 (Main Switchboard); http://www.nec.com/.
Toshiba; (in Germany) tel: [49] (2131) 158-319; fax: [49] (2131) 158-558; (in Switzerland) tel: [41] (1) 946-0777; fax: [41] (1) 946-0807; (in Ireland) tel: [44] (193) 282-8828; (in the U.S.) [1] (949) 583-3000 (Corporate Headquarters); http://www.toshiba.com/.

Internet Connection

HOW TO CONNECT

Connecting to AOL and Compuserve in Bahrain is similar to using it when traveling outside your own area code. See the introductory section for detailed information on connecting to your account through a different phone number.

America Online

Numbers are available at keyword: *international*. Be sure to get several local numbers before leaving. AOL has a Global-Net service available at keyword: *access* (a free area).

Unfortunately, there are no direct access numbers currently available for America Online in Bahrain. Users will have to pay international rates to use the service.

Compuserve

Numbers are available at *Go International*. The Compuserve Web-site also has a great deal of information, at http://www.compuserve.com.

There are no direct access numbers for Compuserve in Bahrain. Users will have to pay international rates to use the service.

Independent Service Providers

Independent service providers may offer discounts if you are only in town for a couple days.
Arabian.Net; tel: 296-700; fax: 296-933; email: sales@arabian.net; http://www.arabian.net/
Batelco; tel: 881-188; email: daylami@batelco.com.bh; http://www.batelco.com.bh/.
Fiberlink Communications; (in the U.S.) tel: [1] (610) 941-2050; toll-free: 1-800-546-5669; fax: [1] (610) 941-2069; email: info@fiberlinkcc.com; http://www.fiberlinkcc.com/.

Business Culture

GREETINGS & COURTESIES

The national language of Bahrain is Arabic although most business people do speak English. Farsi (Persian) is also widely spoken.

Bahrain

The standard greeting of "*salaam alaykum*" (peace be with you) is countered with a response of "*wa alaykum as-salaam*" (and peace be upon you). After this exchange there will be inquiries into health, family, travel, food intake, weather, etc. Arab men often exchange embraces and cheek kisses as well as handshakes with male counterparts. Long time acquaintances will continue to hold hands during the questions and answers.

Note: Hand holding among Arab males is common and can be uncomfortable for Western men. It is a sign of friendship, not sexual interest.

This is a male dominated society, and Bahraini men will not offer to shake a woman's hand unless the woman (usually foreign) extends her hand first. Even then, they may do so with some reluctance. Embraces are right out!

Most Bahraini businessmen have traveled overseas and are familiar with other cultures. They do, however, expect foreigners to abide by local customs while in Bahrain. Friendly greetings, rather than impersonal "just business" handshakes or polite bows, are part of those customs. A warm, firm handshake, locked eye contact, and a beaming smile are the outward signs that cover any language problem.

BUSINESS ETHIC & FRAMEWORK

Bahrain (and its capital Manama, in particular) has been a center for global trade for some time. The Bahrainis have had dealings with the majority of the world's cultures. This society, like other insular economies, depends on external trade for virtually everything. As a consequence of this level of experience and need, Bahraini business people cut honest and equitable deals.

There is little of the anti-Western sentiment in Bahrain that poisons other regional economies. Business is business, and the Bahrainis go where the trade takes them. They have an extensive financial markets infrastructure and welcome offshore banking activity from any quarter. Though Shiites by philosophy, they do not observe the tight strictures against usury (interest on loans) that limits financial dealings in fundamentalist states.

Bahrain's business people do abide by contracts, although local commercial law is very limited. A Bahraini businessman's word is his bond, and he will expect the same from foreign partners.

Note: There is limited government corruption but this will be discussed below in Politics and Graft.

DECISION MAKING

As befits business practices in a true monarchy, decision making is done at the top levels of Bahraini management. Many companies in Bahrain are family owned and the operations are managed along the family structure. Major industries (e.g., petroleum) are run directly by the royal family. In this latter case, sons are not just sons but royal princes and the CEO is the Amir.

Foreign buyers and investors should be able to gain direct and immediate access to decision makers. They should, however, make a point of asking rather than assuming that their Bahraini counterparts can make binding decisions. Visiting sellers may have to tolerate a number of "gatekeepers" before getting to see the real power echelons in a company.

Like the Kuwaitis, businessmen in Bahrain have a wealth of global experience and can tailor their business practices to their counterparts' cultures. Decisions can be made quickly or with painstaking slowness; it all depends on who is buying and who is selling.

MEETINGS

Bahrain has a very sophisticated infrastructure. Meeting facilities will generally prove very professional if not cutting edge. Bahrain is a wealthy country and they don't mind showing off that fact. Presentations will use the latest technology, and they will judge their counterparts accordingly. Telecom and computer infrastructure are not problems in Bahrain; so, visitors can "pull out all the stops" for presentations if they choose.

Initial greetings (see above) will be followed by brief introductions (in descending order of rank). When dealing with non-Arabic visitors, the normal "get to know you" chat period common to local hospitality is very brief, after which the hosts will turn directly to the agenda. While this is done to please many Western business visitors, some Asian companies will be given the more traditional pre-agenda chit chat. The Bahrainis tend to tailor their meeting style to the visitor's standards.

Note: Although English is common, Arabic translations of business cards and brochures should be considered, especially by sellers.

Corporate meetings will run on an agenda which the foreign firm should agree to in advance. The Bahrainis don't like surprises from buyers or sellers. Last-minute changes will be viewed with suspicion.

While Bahrain has a more streamlined business community than most Arabic countries, visiting sellers should not expect to cut a deal at the first meeting. The Bahrain side will want to be able to check everything out prior to signing contracts. A modicum of patience will be required.

Note: Bahraini business people are generally straightforward, but Arabic culture prevents them from discussing unpleasant topics in public. They may ask for "back channel" or one-on-one meetings after hours to work out problems. If they do, make sure that such talks do not conflict with decisions made at the general meeting. The extra meetings should be for "information only" purposes.

BUSINESS ENTERTAINING

When a Bahraini company wishes to impress a visiting firm, the entertainment can be extravagant and expense is rarely a problem. Opulent meals, overnight trips to beach resorts, or deep sea cruises on yachts can all be part of the package. The Bahrainis believe in Arabic-style hospitality and they have the wealth to lay it on very thickly.

Note: The Bahrainis have access to anything and everything; so, special dietary or medical needs should be made known in advance of arrival.

Nightlife in cosmopolitan Manama is extensive. Nightclubs, discos, and bars all serve until the wee hours. All will be placed at the disposal of guests who will never be permitted to pick up the check.

Note: It should be mentioned that this is a male-oriented society, and visiting female managers may not be invited along for any of the after-hours pub-crawling.

Business in Bahrain, though technically sophisticated, still runs based upon the personal relationship. Business entertaining is a means to gain insights into the personal side of new business associates. Visiting foreign firms, regardless of pressing schedules and jetlag, should make an effort to participate in their hosts' offerings. While being compliant guests, however, they should not be lulled into a false sense of friendship by the hosts' generosity during negotiations. Entertainment is entertainment, and business is business.

Visiting firms that wish to reciprocate local hospitality may do so, but it will not be expected while staying in Bahrain. Foreigners may find it better to wait until the Bahraini firm travels to the visitors' country. It is hard (and expensive) to match Bahraini hospitality on their own turf.

WOMEN IN BUSINESS

Women in Bahrain do lead a freer life than is most other Arabic cultures, but they are far from gaining parity with local males. Female managers are rare and women executives are nonexistent. Unless otherwise stated, it will be assumed that any foreign women in attendance at business meetings must be there in a very subordinate capacity. Once the rank of the visiting female executives has been made clear, few problems will arise with their role being accepted by the Bahrainis for general discussions. However, many local male managers will still be expecting females to "back down" should discussions become confrontational. Foreign buyers or investors can persist, but visiting sellers should immediately have male managers intercede.

BUSINESS ATTIRE

Suits, dress shirts, and ties are standard attire for men in this hot (but air conditioned) climate. Suits should always be worn for first meetings and any contact with government agencies. Less formal wear (open-neck, short-sleeve shirts and slacks) may be suitable for subsequent meetings. Visitors should make inquiries of the counterparts on this matter. Except for sports outings, shorts are not acceptable in public.

Women visitors should also adopt business suits initially. Less formal wear should be loose fitting, with dresses cut below the knee. Miniskirts and sleeveless blouses are taboo as are plunging necklines and backless tops. Head scarves are only required when visiting mosques.

Both male and female visitors should lean towards the conservative when it comes to attire. Smart tailoring and quality material are more important as the Bahrainis are discriminating dressers and quite cosmopolitan.

Business Advisory

POLITICS & GRAFT

Graft is minimal in Bahrain when compared to some other regional economies. The government (in the form of the royal family) already owns, or is partner in, most major businesses. Any problems with graft encountered by foreign firms will occur with local petty officialdom and can easily be refused.

BUSINESS FRAUD

The Bahrainis are old hands at international business as well as global finance and wish to preserve their reputation for fair dealing. Business fraud is quite rare here, although foreign firms should make known their scheduling and quality control standards early on in the business relationship. Problems can arise from differing cultural attitudes rather than outright fraud.

Business Centers
Manama

CITY VIEW

Presiding as an attractive local tourist resort, Manama acts as a beckoning oasis in the Gulf. As one of the more advanced Arab cities, Manama deftly combines a number of tourist attractions with a business center that lures the international community. The Heritage Center, located on Government Road, depicts an interesting evolution of Bahrainian falconry, pearl-diving, and boating traditions. The old town hosts the souk, which is a striking contrast to the modern skyscrapers that outline the newer part and host most of today's business in Manama. With a popula-

tion of 140,401 people, the city has embraced contemporary business practices (petroleum products are the leading industry) whist it is still common to find traditional dhows (fishing boats) builders in Manama ports and authentic goldsmiths vending their craft at the souk.

AIRPORT

Bahrain Airport to City Center

Bahrain International Airport lies 4 miles (6.5 km.) outside of Manama. Taxi services run across the causeway to the main island. Procure a list of fixed rates to designated locations from the airport. If using a cab from the airport, add one Dinar as a tip to the meter reading. You might also inquire in advance whether your hotel provides a shuttle service.

Airline Numbers

Aer Lingus 211 933
Aeroflot 292 838
Air Canada 249-242, 209 362
Air France... 213 884
Air India 223 819
Air Lanka 224 819
Air New Zealand....................................... 222 637
American Airlines 531-000
Austrian Airlines 223 336
Balkan Bulgarian Airlines 214 149
British Airways 228 333
Cathay Pacific 226 226
Cyprus Airways 209 349
Egypt Air.. 209 264
Emirates 212 008
Gulf Air 322 200
Iran Air... 210 414
Japan Airlines.. 224 917
KLM 224 234
Korean Air 212 333
Kuwait Airways 223 300
Lufthansa 210 026, 210 505
Middle East Airlines................................. 223-865
Pakistan Intl. Airlines............................... 223 808
Qantas... 213 434
Royal Jordanian 229 294
Saudia 211 550
Singapore Airlines 213 054
Sryian Air... 211 360
Turkish Airlines 211 896
TWA 223 315
Vietnam Airlines 273 001
Yemenia 214 313

HOTELS

Top-end

Bahrain Hilton; tel: 535-000; toll-free in U.S.: 1-800-774-1500; fax: 533-097; in business district; 24-hour coffee shop; business center; complimentary airport shuttle; fitness center; golf; pool; tennis; sauna; squash; parking; BD45/55.

Le Royal Meridien Bahrain; Road 112, Bldg. 40, Block 40, Block 428, Asleef District; tel: 580-000; fax: 580-333; email: meribah@batelco.com.bh; restaurant; conference center (up to 1200); secretarial service; fax/photocopy facilities; in-room modem/fax connection; fitness room; pool; sauna; whirlpool; corporate rates; BD65/75.

Sheraton Bahrain; 6 Palace Ave.; tel: 533-533; fax: 534-809; restaurant; conference facilities (up to 1500); secretarial service; fax/photocopy facilities; fitness; sauna; pool; whirlpool; corporate rates; BD60/68.

Bahrain

Expensive

Gulf; tel: 713-000; fax: 713-040; restaurant; conference facilities (up to 800); secretarial service; fax/photocopy facilities; in-room modem/fax connection; fitness; pool; sauna; whirlpool; corporate rates; BD35/40.

Fort Grande Diplomat; tel: 531-666; fax: 530-843; restaurant; conference facilities (up to 1500); secretarial service; fax/photocopy facilities; fitness room; pool; sauna; whirlpool; parking; corporate rates; BD35/40.

Ramada; Gudaibiya Avenue; tel: 742-000; fax: 742-809; restaurant; conference capacity (up to 30); secretarial service; fax/photocopy facilities; pool; parking; corporate rates; BD40/47.

Moderate

Al Jazira; Al Khalifa Road; tel: 211-810; fax: 210-726;3 km from exhibition grounds; restaurant; secretarial service; fax/photocopy facility; parking; BD21/28.

Atlas; Gudaibiya; tel: 272-212; fax: 271-736; 3 km from exhibition grounds; restaurant; secretarial service; fax/photocopy facility; parking; BD20/30.

Delmon; Road 357, Block 315; tel: 224-000; fax: 224-107; restaurant; conference facility; secretarial service; fax/photocopy facilities; fitness; pool; sauna; parking; corporate rates; 4-star hotel; BD18/20.

Claridge; Tarafa-Bin-Al-Abd-Ave, Block 320; tel: 291-888; fax: 295-808; adjacent to exhibition grounds; restaurant; secretarial service; fax/photocopy facilities; parking; corporate rates; BD28/38.

Gulf Gate Hotel; Salah Aldeen Al Youbi Avenue; tel: 210-210; fax: 213-315; restaurant; conference center (up to 250); secretarial service; fax/photocopy facilities; fitness room; pool; sauna; whirlpool; parking; BD16/20.

MEDICAL CARE

American Mission Hospital; Isa Al Kabir Ave.; tel: 253-447.
International Hospital of Bahrain; Budaiya Highway; tel: 251-666 or 591-666.
Sulmaniya Hospital; main general hospital; Sulmaniya Ave.; tel: 252-761 or 255-555; emergency services available for expatriates at a nominal fee of BD1.

AUTO RENTAL

Note: Foreign drivers, except other Gulf residents, must be in possession of an international driver's license acquired prior to arrival in Bahrain. A foreign license is not sufficient.

Avis; tel: 211-770

Bahrain Car Hiring; tel: 292-012

Budget; tel: 534-100

Euro Dollar; tel: 253-335

Europcar Interrent; tel: 342-121

Hertz; tel: 321-358

Oscar Rent; 211-682

Thrifty; tel: 801-100

Toyota Rent-a-Car; tel: 784-042

WORLD TRADE CENTER

World Trade Center Bahrain
Manama Center
Government Ave.
Manama, Bahrain, Arabian Gulf
(P.O. Box 669; Manama, Bahrain, Arabian Gulf)
tel: [973] 21-4933; fax: [973] 21-3-808

CHAMBER OF COMMERCE

Bahrain Chamber of Commerce and Industry
PO Box 5479
Manama, Bahrain
tel: 531-531; fax: 530-455

Belgium

At a Glance

THE PEOPLE

Population 10,174,922 (1998)
Growth Rate 0.09%
Life Expectancy .... 77.35 years (born 1999)
Infant Mortality .... 6.27 deaths/1,000 live births (1998)

Ethnic Composition

Flemish...55%
Walloon 33%
Mixed or other 12%

Religious Composition

Roman Catholic..75%
Protestant or other..25%

Languages Spoken

Flemish (official), French (official), German, English

Education and Literacy

Education is free and compulsory for children between the ages of 6 and 16. Literacy in the adult population is 99%.

Labor Force

Total: 4,283,000
By occupation: services 69.7%, industry 27.7%, agriculture 2.6%.

THE ECONOMY

Densely populated Belgium is one of the most highly industrialized countries in a heavily industrialized region. With few exploitable natural resources, its industrial sector has become a complex processing machine that imports raw materials and semi-finished goods and processes them for re-export. Heavily reliant on trade, Belgium's exports are equivalent to about two-thirds of its GDP; it exports twice as much per capita as Germany and five times as much as Japan. Because of its location and excellent transport infrastructure, Belgium boasts a distinct trade advantage. It also prides itself on a highly skilled, multilingual, and productive workforce. Belgium boasts the second highest household savings rate in the world (13%) just behind France and ahead of Japan. Like Japan, however, Belgium has a growing population of older people (65 years); that is expected to reach 18 percent of the population by 2010. Analysts doubt whether the generous Belgian social system can support this coming burden.

Exports .... US$120 billion (1997)
Imports .... US$115 billion (1997)
Total GDP .... US$256.3 billion (1997)
GDP Per Capita .... US$23,200 (1997)
Unemployment .... 12.75 percent (1997)
Inflation Rate .... 1.7 percent (1997)

Top Export Partners

E.U. co-members, United States, CIS nations

Top Import Partners

E.U. co-members, United States, CIS nations

Top Exports

Iron and steel, transportation equipment, tractors, diamonds, petroleum products.

Top Imports

Fuels, grains, minerals, chemicals, foodstuffs.

BUSINESS WORKWEEK

Offices
Monday to Friday 8:30a.m. to 5:30p.m.

Banks
Monday to Friday 9a.m. to 3:30p.m.

Government
Monday to Friday 9a.m. to noon and 2p.m. to 5p.m.

Retail
Monday to Saturday 9a.m. to 6p.m. or 7p.m.; department stores may stay open until 8p.m. or 9p.m.; smaller shops outside the main areas may close at noon for lunch.

HOLIDAYS

New Year's Day...January 1
Easter Monday ....April 5*
Labor Day...May 1
Ascension Day .... May 13*
Whit Monday .... May 24*
National Day...July 21
Assumption Day .... August 15
All Saints' Day ....November 1
Armistice Day ....November 11
Christmas Day...December 25
* Date may vary by year.

CLIMATE

Seasons
The climate is standard west European; maritime, temperate, and damp with mild winters and pleasant summer months. Average annual temperatures are 8°C (46°F); in January they fall to 3°C (37°F), and in July it goes up as high as 26°C (80°F).

Regions
The coastal region has more of a mild and humid climate all year round. However, the more inland you go, the more distinct the seasons become. Southeast regions have hot summers and extremely cold winters. In the highlands, rain is seldom heavy, but elsewhere rain and drizzle prevail all year round.

Money & Banking

Currency
The currency of Belgium is the Belgian Franc (BFr).

Denominations
The Belgian Franc comes in coin denominations of BFr50, 20, 5, and 1, and 50 centimes and banknotes of BFr100, BFr500, BFr1,000, BFr2,000, and BFr10,000.

Traveler's Checks and Credit Cards
Most brands of traveler's checks and major foreign currencies can be easily and efficiently exchanged at banks, foreign exchange bureaus located in the major cities, hotels, and exchange kiosks at the airports. Banks offer the most favorable exchange rate. Traveler's checks receive a better exchange rate than cash, or you can purchase the Belgian Franc traveler's check before departure, which can be exchanged almost everywhere.

Credit cards are widely accepted in Belgium including American Express, Visa, MasterCard, and Diners Club.

Belgium

You can get cash advances from your credit card from many of the automated teller machines (ATM). Credit cards are also essential for renting a car and hotel reservations. Long-term visitors should set up a checking account in Belgium and get an ATM card. The most favorable exchange rates are given for credit card and ATM transactions.

Travel

VISA AND PASSPORT

A passport, valid for a minimum three months after the anticipated exit date, is required of all visitors except citizens of E.U. countries who have a national ID card. The passport exemption is also extended to any citizen of Andorra, Liechtenstein, Malta, Monaco, San Marino and Switzerland who holds a national ID card.

Belgium is a member of the Schengen group, which is a collection of nations who in March of 1995 declared themselves borderless. The others in this group are France, Germany, Luxembourg, The Netherlands, Portugal, and Spain. Any traveler who holds a valid passport or other pertinent travel documents that are recognized by all Schengen member nations need not have a visa to travel in any of these countries. There are two caveats, however:

• If you have tickets for onward travel to a nation that does require a visa of you, it may also be required of you for entry into the Schengen nation.

• Each Schengen nation retains the right to require a visa of any national normally exempted by the group as a whole.

Following is a list of nations normally exempt from the visa requirement (E.U. nationals are automatically exempt): Andorra, Argentina, Australia, Brazil, Brunei, Canada, Chile, Costa Rica, Cyprus, Czech Republic, Ecuador, El Salvador, Guatemala, Honduras, Hungary, Iceland, Israel, Japan, Jamaica, Liechtenstein, Malawi, Malaysia, Malta, Mexico, Monaco, New Zealand, Nicaragua, Norway, Panama, Paraguay, Poland, Republic of Korea, San Marino, Singapore, Slovak Republic, Slovenia, Switzerland, Turkey (only if a permanent resident of a Schengen country), Uruguay, U.S., Vatican City, and Venezuela.

Visa-free travel throughout the Schengen states is valid for a duration of 90 days maximum within a 6-month period, commencing upon initial entry date into a Schengen country.

Of course, if this does not fit into your travel plans, you may apply for a visa anyway.

Types of visas issued are Transit and Short Stay, the latter including both tourist and business visas. Transit visas are valid for 24 hours only. Short Stay visas are good for a maximum of three months. If applying for a business visa, you must include a letter from your company stating the purpose of the visit, or from an attorney or bank manager if you are self-employed.

Allow between 24 hours and 6 weeks for processing, depending on your nationality; this applies both to postal and in-person applications. All travelers must hold onward or return tickets and sufficient funds.

DEPARTURE FORMALITIES

Generally, there are no restrictions on currency exportation or departure fees in Belgium, with two exceptions:

- If you are departing from Zaventem, expect a BFr540 departure tax.
- From Deurne, the tax is BFr280.

Usually the tax is included in the cost of your airline ticket.

CUSTOMS ENTRY (PERSONAL)

Duty Free

The following items may be brought into Belgium without customs duty being levied, if carried by adult travelers entering from non-E.U. countries, or who have purchased items duty free within the E.U.:

- 800 cigarettes, 400 cigarillos, 200 cigars, and 1kg of tobacco
- 90 liters of wine (including up to 60 liters of sparkling wine), 10 liters of distilled spirits, 20 liters of intermediate products (such as fortified wine), 110 liters of beer
- 250g of perfume

For adult travelers entering from non-EU countries:

- 200 cigarettes, 50 cigars, and 250g of tobacco
- 2 liters of still wine, 1 liter of distilled spirits, and 8 liters of Luxembourg wines (if imported via the Luxembourg border)
- 50g of perfume and 250ml of eau de toilette
- Other merchandise up to BFr2000

Note: The amounts of alcohol and tobacco specified above are somewhat academic, since the import of duty-paid quantities are no longer limited between E.U. countries, technically speaking. But, if you have amounts of any items in excess of the above quantities, you may be interrogated to determine whether the goods are solely for personal use.

Prohibited or Restricted

Unpreserved meat products are prohibited. Any other unpreserved foods must be declared. Expect strict regulations regarding the import or export of certain items, including firearms, antiquities, medications, sales samples, and business equipment.

IMMUNIZATION

Proof of smallpox, cholera, and yellow fever vaccinations is required only of travelers arriving from infected areas. Immunization against tetanus is recommended.

TIPPING

Taxi

Metered taxi fares include the tip. Unmetered fares should be inclusive and negotiated in advance.

Porters

Porters are tipped around BFr35 per bag at first-class hotels and rail depots.

Hotels

A service charge of 16 percent is included in most hotel bills. Particularly helpful staff members may be tipped moderately in addition.

Restaurants

A service charge is included in most restaurant bills. When no service charge is added, 15 percent is the standard tip. Bartenders usually appreciate it when customers buy them a drink—as will your host at better restaurants.

Other

Barbers and hairdressers should be tipped about 15 percent. Chambermaids and theater attendants are usually tipped BFr20 to 30, while washroom and service station attendants get BFr10 to 20.

EMERGENCY INFORMATION

Police and Crime

Crime, although on the increase, is not a major problem in Belgium. The police are generally efficient and courteous. However, foreign business travelers are often the preferred targets of the few thieves there are in Belgium. Consequently, purses, laptops, and briefcases will require additional security.

Brussels has the highest rate of robbery and assault in Belgium, especially in tourist areas such as the Grand Place. Pickpocketing and purse snatching must be guarded against throughout the metro system (on buses, subways, and trams), and in the three primary train stations: the North Station (Noordstation or Gare du Nord); the Central Station (Centraal Station or Gare Central), and particularly in the South Station (Zuidstation or Gare du Midi).

A few elementary precautions should protect the traveler from most problems:

- Do not leave valuables in cars or on tables in cafes.
- Keep non-essential valuables locked in hotel safes when not in use.
- Use credit cards and traveler's checks when possible to avoid carrying large sums of cash.
- Carry photocopies of your passport instead of the original.
- Carry cash in a money belt, and use credit cards or travelers checks for most of your large transactions.

Belgian law requires everyone to have official identification with them at all times, and it must be shown to any Belgian police official upon request. A passport is sufficient, and usually police are satisfied by presentation of a photocopy of the passport's identification page.

Emergency Numbers

General Emergency 112
Ambulance / Fire 100
Police... 101

Health

The climate is damp, but apart from the flu, there are no significant health risks in Belgium. The water is safe to drink, and bottled water is readily available, especially at restaurants where they prefer that you pay for water. Sanitation is of a high order, and Belgian food can be consumed without any worries beyond normal precautions one might take anywhere.

Medical service is first-rate but also expensive. Doctors and hospitals often expect immediate cash payment. It is wise to travel with medical insurance that provides for overseas coverage, including medical evacuation, although only the most extreme of medical circumstances might call for such measures.

To obtain medical assistance or referrals, call:
Central Medical Switchboard..........................(2) 648-8000
or ....(2) 479-1818

INTERNAL TRAVEL

There are many transportation options for the traveler in Belgium, and they are generally inexpensive and convenient. The number one option is usually the train; the train system in Belgium offers a vast and efficient network of rail access. Buses are profuse and auto rental is easily arranged. In the urban areas, public transport is excellent. Taxis are also abundant, but pricey. Bike rental also proves handy (you can find them at many train stations) and is popular in the northern part of the country, where the land is flat. The canals and rivers of Belgium are legendary for their tranquil beauty and can be navigated in a hired boat or enjoyed as a passenger on a specialty canal barge. Ferries abound.

AIR

Belgium has no domestic flight service. Sabena, the flagship air carrier, does provide express buses that run between the Brussels Airport and Antwerp, an important port city in Belgium. The service is free for certain categories of airline passengers with bookings on Sabena.
Sabena website......................................www.sabena.com

TAXI

Metered taxis are plentiful in the cities and the tip is included in the final meter price. Avoid unmetered taxis if possible. One can easily procure a cab in most cities at taxi stands next to every train station and many hotels. One can also phone central dispatch at any cab company to book a taxi. Outside of urban areas, it is often a little more difficult to find a cab.

Note: Most drivers know quite a bit about their city, and often only an address is enough. To be on the safe side, though, you may want a friend who is familiar with the city to write down directions.

AUTOMOBILE

Car, truck, and motorbike rentals are readily available in major cities. Chauffeur-driven cars also are available. A credit card and a valid driver's license from the visitor's country of origin are required for rental. Insurance is mandatory, and E.U. nationals are advised to acquire a Green Card, which assures that coverage will be as high as the driver's own domestic policy.

Rental vehicles can be taken into other E.U. countries, but visitors are reminded that each E.U. nation has different driving regulations. Be sure that you always have personal identification papers, driver's license, registration, and insurance papers on hand.

Belgian rules of the road are different from those in many parts of the world, and visiting motorists are advised to understand these rules thoroughly prior to driving in Belgium. Belgian drivers are famous for being aggressive, and

they expect the same from others. If you should decide to yield your right-of-way, be sure to indicate it clearly or you may cause an accident.

Maximum speed limits on Belgian highways are posted only at the borders and on roadways departing major airports. Claims of ignorance carry little weight. Speeding violations result in significant fines, and you will be expected to pay on the spot with Belgian currency. If you cannot, your vehicle may be impounded. Belgian police also routinely conduct random breath analyzer checks of drivers' blood/ alcohol levels, especially at night and on major holidays. Belgium's blood/alcohol criteria are lower than most.

A fire extinguisher, rear fog lamp, first aid box, and red warning triangle are considered to be essential equipment. The use of seat belts is compulsory, front and rear. Traffic keeps to the right-hand side.

Except for the Ardennes, major towns and cities are linked by toll-free highways. The roads in and around urban areas are normally well constructed and maintained, with extensive lighting systems, but rural thoroughfares and byways are not so liable to be lighted at night. Fog and rain often reduce visibility.

Roadside assistance and news on road conditions can be obtained in English from:
Touring Assistance.......................................(070) 344-777
This is a toll-free call within Belgium.
Belgian Police also offer updates on road conditions; tel: (02) 642-6666

For more information about driver's permits, road tax, vehicle inspection, or insurance, contact:
Belgian National Tourist Office....................212-758-8130
website...www.visitbelgium.com
Following is a list of auto rental companies at the Brussels Airport, with local phone numbers:
Avis...02-720 0944
Europcar..02-721 1178
Hertz..02-720 6044

TRAIN

A comprehensive and modern rail network runs throughout Belgium and connects to other countries via Eurocity and Intercity trains. This dense railway network has hourly trains on most lines. The main lines have even more frequent trains.

Intercity trains are the fastest, augmented by the Inter-Regional and local lines. The Belgian lines connect to all major continental European rail systems as well as to Eurostar, which provides a direct link between Brussels and London through the Channel Tunnel via super-fast trains. Five daily connections operate daily between Brussels Midi and London Waterloo. For further information and reservations, telephone:
Eurostar.. 0345 303 030
(See the segment on "Channel Crossings" in the U.K. section for more details about the Eurostar.)

Additionally, there is a high-speed train called the Thalys which runs from Brussels to Paris in only 1 hour and 25 minutes.

National Belgian Railways makes available a variety of discount fares. RUNABOUT tickets are similar to Eurail passes, allowing the visitor to travel on any and all parts of the Belgian rail system without any distance limit. They are also valid for travel to or from adjacent countries, where they may be applied to rail travel up to (or from) the border. There are two types of Runabout tickets:

• A Belgian Tourrail Pass yields five days of unlimited travel on Belgian Rail within a 17-day period. It can be purchased at railway stations.

• The Benelux Tourrail ticket provides for 5 days of rail travel within a 30-day period throughout Belgium, The

Netherlands, and Luxembourg. These tickets are also available at Belgian Railway stations.

There are also two age-oriented discount passes:

- The Go Pass, for travelers between the ages of 6 and 25, is good for 10 second-class trips. It is issued for a minimum of two passengers, or a maximum of five, and the savings are considerable. The pass is good up to six months, and can be used by people other than the ones who purchase it (so be sure you don't lose it).

- The Rail Europ Senior Card (RES) is for men over 65 or women over 60. It entitles the bearer to reductions from 30 to 50 percent as applied to the purchase of international tickets in 19 European countries.

For further information and details on any of the above, contact:

National Belgian Railways.............................02-555 2525
website ....www.visitbelgium.com/
[click on Transportation link]

Public Transport Note:

Brussels public transportation (inclusive of the next two headings) is modern and efficient. It is operated by STIB (Société des Transports Intercommunaux de Bruxelles). Metro, trams, premetro (trams that run underground for part of their route), and buses make up the system. STIB kiosks are sprinkled liberally all around the city. General hours of operation: 5:30a.m. to midnight.

URBAN / METRO

Every major town and city in Belgium has a good public transportation network. Brussels and Antwerp both have bus, tram, and metro systems. The Brussels metro and premetro system is comprised of two lines that connect the eastern and western portions of the city. Stations are recognized by a sign with a white "M" on a blue background.

Brussels and Antwerp both offer metro services with a flat-fare charge. Travelcards and multi-ride tickets are available at ticket counters. Timetables are accurate and the systems are quite efficient.

Charleroi, Ghent, and Ostend have buses and tramways, and all other cities operate at least a local bus operation. A flat-fare system is utilized, providing discounts for multi-ride tickets good for five or ten journeys. All-day tickets and multiple-mode travelcards are also available.

BUSES & TRAMS

Bus and tram services run throughout the cities, but finding an express bus service that operates between cities proves more difficult (the best bet is taking the train). A number of discount fares can be pre-purchased.

Many regional bus services exist, and they publish regional timetables, available at terminals and in many hotels.

Long-distance services also travel between towns, but expect these local lines to stop at many points along the routes. Sabena offers the closest thing to an express coach shuttle bus system (see above under Air).

In Brussels, bus stops are indicated by red and white signs. Tram stops use blue and white signs. Some stops for both are marked with the words "sur demande," which means that anyone who wishes to be a passenger can signal the vehicle to stop with a simple hand signal.

WATER TRAVEL

Belgium offers water travel internally on its rivers and canals, and its ports offer regular ferry and cruise services to the British Isles and coastal western Europe.

Ferry services operate from Ostend and Zeebrugge to English ports. P&O North Sea Ferries and Hoverspeed-Holyman are the primary operations. Information about these routes can be accessed on the following:

Ferry services website........................www.seaview.co.uk/

For information on canal travel through Bruges and Ghent, try the following website:

....www.raveneltravel.com/belgium

Another site loaded with information is:

....www.visiteurope.com/Belgium

TRAVEL ASSISTANCE

Belgian Tourist Office
61 Rue Marché-aux-Herbes
B-1000 Brussels
tel: (2) 504-0390; fax: (2) 504-0270
website: www.visitbelgium.com
[This is a highly useful website with many great links]

Tourist Information Brussels
Hôtel de Ville
Grand-Place
B-1000 Brussels
tel: (2) 513 8940; fax: (2) 514 4538

Essential Terms

English	Flemish
Yes	Ja
No	Nee
Good morning	Goeie morgen
Hello (daytime)	Goeiedag
Hello (evening)	Goeienavond
Hello (telephone)	Hallo
Good-bye	Tot ziens
Please	a.b.u. (Alstublieft)
Thank you	Dank u
Pleased to meet you	Ik zou blij zijn U te ontmoeten
Excuse me; I'm sorry	Excuseer mij; Ik verontschuldig mij
My name is _____	Mijn naam is _____
I don't understand	Ik begrijp het niet
Do you speak English?	Spreek je engels?

Communications

DIALING CODES IN BELGIUM

International country code: [32]

Selected city codes: Antwerp (3), Brussels (2), Charleroi (71), Courtrai (56), Ghent (9), Hasselt (11), La Louviere (64), Liege (4), Ostend (59) Tongeren (12), Wavre (10)

Dialing Belgium from Overseas

To dial Belgium from overseas, begin with your country's international dialing code, then Belgium's country code (32), then the city code (omitting the zero if dialing from outside the country), and finally the number. If you were dialing Antwerp from the United States, for example, you would begin with 011, then 32, then 3 (the city code for Antwerp), and finally the number of the person or office you were trying to reach.

Assistance Numbers
Operator in Brussels..1280
Domestic Operator 1307*
European Operator 1304*
International Operator 1322*
   * The '3' becomes '2' in Flemish areas, and '4' for German speakers.

CALLING WITHIN BELGIUM
Local Calls
   To complete a local call, it requires BFr10 or BFr20 at a public telephone.

Long Distance Calls
   Long distance calls are relatively easy to make, but making them from hotel rooms can prove very expensive due to surcharges. When dialing within Belgium to another city, use a zero as a prefix to the area code.

International Calls
   Direct calling is the most cost-effective way to call out of Belgium. You can do it with a high-denomination phone card. Dial 00 (then wait for dial tone or announcement) + country code + area code + number. As anywhere else, if you opt to call direct from your hotel, expect exorbitant surcharges.
Australia Direct..078-110-061
British Telecom Direct 080-010-044
Canada Direct 080-010-019
Ireland Direct...080-010-353
New Zealand Direct...080-010-064
South Africa Direct 080-010-027
U.S. AT&T 080-010-010
U.S. MCI..080-010-012
U.S. Sprint...080-010-014

PAY PHONES
Public Telephones
   Card Phone:

   Coin phones use BFr5 or BFr20 coins to operate, although not many coin phones still exist. The more prevalent alternative is the card phone, which uses the Telecard.

Calling Cards
   Telecards come in various denominations and can be purchased at PTT (post, telegram, telephonic) offices in BFr200, 600, and 1000 denominations. Telecard booths may also have lists indicating where you can buy cards.

CELLULAR PHONES
   Numerous cellular phone service providers exist in Belgium. In the digital format, Belgacom Mobile and Mo-

bistar both offer GSM service. Belgacom Mobile also offers NMT-450 service in the analog format.
   Note: Your home country cell phone may not work in this country. If not, we recommend that you rent an international cell phone *before* you leave home. A major US-based cell phone rental provider is **IMC WorldCell**. For information see "International Cell Phone Rentals" on page 14.

CALL BACK
   You can (potentially) save significant sums when calling in Belgium by using a call back service. For a list of callback services, please refer to the "Communications" section in the *Global Road Warrior* Introduction.
   Fees for call back services vary widely, depending on the company and the type of service required. Be sure to check with these companies before leaving to compare rates.

PHONE JACKS

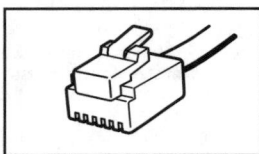

Adaptors are available through **iGo Corporation.** (See "Electrical and Telephone Adaptors" on page 19.)

FAX
Business centers in major hotels have fax machines. The service is generally very good.

POSTAL SERVICES
The postal system is generally very efficient. Letters take two days to reach other Western European destinations. Add another two days for North American service.

TELEGRAMS
Dial '905' within the country to place a telegram.

Business Services
BUSINESS CENTERS
Antwerp
Antwerp Business Center; Meir 44a, B-2000 Antwerp; tel: (3) 202-4670; fax: (3) 226-4482; email: info@abc.be; www.abc.be/.

Brussels
Contact Business Center; Rue Capouillet 9-21, 1060 Brussels; tel: (2) 536-8686.

Chateau de Spontin; 8 Chemin de Dinant 5530; Spontin; tel: (83) 69 90 55; fax: (83) 69 92 14.

Grand Hotel Oude Burg; 5 Oude Burg 8000 Brugge; tel: (50) 44 51 11; fax: (50) 44 51 00.

Meridien Hotel; Carrefour de l"Europe 3; tel: 548-4211; fax: 548-4735; email: infor@meridien.be

COURIER SERVICES

Brussels

A.E.T. Transport; Van Moerstraat 12; 1000 Brussel; tel: (2) 5120983.

FedEx; tel: (2) 752-7891.

Taxis Verts (24-hour package delivery); tel: (2) 349-4646.

UPS Express Shop Brussels; Rue de la Loi, Wetstraat 26, 1000 Brussels; tel: (2) 230-4648.

Country Offices/Toll Free Numbers

FedEx; tel: (0800) 13-555.

TNT Express; Worldwide; Brucargo; 1931 Brucargo; tel: (070) 222-122.

UPS; United Parcel Service Belgium NV; Woluwelaan 156, 1831 Diegem; tel: (800) 12-828. 6401317.

TRANSLATION SERVICES

Brussels

Accents; Square Wiser 1, Brussels; tel: (2) 230-5045; fax: (2) 230-8683.

Adintra; Omwentelingsstraat; 12/11; tel: (2) 2180145/2193301; fax: (2) 2177996.

Berlitz Translation Center; Place Stephanie 10, 1050 Brussels; tel: (2) 425-1753; fax: (2) 512-3035.

Bioc & Partners sprl-bvba; Rue Belliard, 205 box 11; Brussels; tel: (2) 230-2145; fax: (2) 231-0195.

Conference Interpreters International; Av. des Celtes, 20; Brussels; tel: (2) 734-9129; fax: (2) 734-83-025.

Dixit Interpreters and Translators; Av. des 7 Bonniers; Brussels; tel: (2) 340-9020; fax: (2) 346-1408.

Electrical

Current

220 volts AC, 50Hz.

Electrical plugs are the 2-pin round type.

ELECTRIC PLUGS

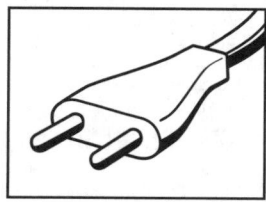

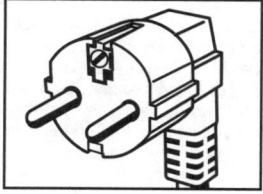

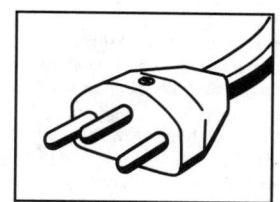

Adaptors are available through **iGo Corporation.** (See "Electrical and Telephone Adaptors" on page 19.)

Technical Support

HARDWARE/SOFTWARE VENDOR SUPPORT

Compaq/Digital; tel: (2) 716-9511; fax: (2) 725-2213; (2) 716-9696 (CompaqCare Center); (in Switzerland) tel: [41] (22) 709-5330; fax: [41] (22) 709-5391 (Geneva); [41] (1) 801-2507; fax: [41] (1) 801-2172 (Zurich); (General U.S.) tel: (281) 518-2000; http://www.compaq.com/.

Dell; tel: 02 481 91 00; fax: 02 481 92 99; (in Germany) tel: [49] (61) 039-710; (Dell- Europe) tel: [44] (134) 474-8000; (in the U.S.) tel: [1] (512) 338-4400; fax: [1] (512) 728-3330; http://www.dell.com/.

Hewlett Packard; tel: (2)-626-8806 (Dutch); tel: (0)2-626-8807 (French); (in Switzerland) tel: [41] (22) 780-8111; (in the U.S.) tel: [1] (408) 246-4300; http://www.hp.com/.

IBM; tel: (2) 225-3333; fax: (2) 225-2473; (in Switzerland) tel: [41] (22) 310-0418 (in French); (in the U.S.) tel: [1] (919) 517-2800; (U.S. Main Office) tel: [1] 914-765-1900; http://www.ibm.com/.

Microsoft; tel: (2) 730-3911; fax: (2) 726-9609; (2) 481-5252 (Information Center); (in Switzerland) tel: [41] (848) 858-868; fax [41] (1) 831-0869; (in the U.S.) [1] (425) 635-7222; http://www.microsoft.com.

Internet Connection

HOW TO CONNECT

Connecting to AOL and Compuserve in Belgium is similar to using it when traveling outside your own area code. See the introductory section for detailed information on connecting to your account through a different phone number.

America Online

Numbers are available at keyword *international*. Be sure to get several local numbers before leaving. AOL's Global-Net service charges US$6 an hour in addition to the usual charges. AOL has its GlobalNet service available at keyword *access* (a free area).

Access: Antwerp (3) 231-7615; Brugge (50) 321-404; Brussels (2) 705-2380; Charleroi (71) 306-702; Ghent (9) 234-2990; Hasselt (11) 874-255; Kortrijk (56) 256-048; Liege (4) 221-3593.

Compuserve

Numbers are available at keyword *Go International*. The Compuserve Web-site also has a great deal of information, at http://www.compuserve.com.

Access: Anvers (3) 400-1445; Brussels (2) 403-1445; Charleroi 7173-1445; Courtrai 5680-1445; Gand (9) 270-1445; Hasselt 1150-1445; Leuven 1670-1445; Liege (4) 270-1445; Mons 6525-1445; Namur 8170-1445.

Belgium

Independent Service Providers

Many independent service providers offer discounts if you are only in town for a couple days.

Belgian Internet Provider; tel: (69) 648-993; fax: (69) 648-696; email: info@bipweb.be/.; http://www.bipweb.be/

EUNet Belgium; tel: (16) 398-398; email: info@Belgium.EU.net; http://www.Belgium.EU.net/.

Euregio.Net AG; tel: (87) 561-177; fax: (87)561-122; email: info@euregio.net; http://www.euregio.net

KDD Belgium; tel: (2) 511-3116; fax: (2) 502-9158; email: mail@infoplaza.be; http://www.infoplaza.be/.

PING BELGIUM; tel: (70) 233-772; fax: (70) 233- 771; email: info@ping.be; http://www.ping.be/.

Business Culture

GREETINGS AND COURTESIES

The familiar use of first names is not the Belgium custom. Belgians who are Flemish use *Mijnheer* (Mr.), *Mevrouw* (Mrs.), or *Juffrouw* (Miss), followed by the last name only. French speaking Belgians use *Monsieur* (Mr.), *Madame* (Mrs.) and *Mademoiselle* (Miss), again followed by the last name only. First names are confined to use by family members and close friends. Belgians shake hands with everyone at the beginning and end of every meeting, and the famous Belgian handshake is quick without being too firm. As in other European countries, men should wait until a woman extends her hand in greeting. Likewise, Belgian men will wait for a woman to extend her hand to them. A polite greeting when being introduced is, "Pleased to meet you." Avoid the phrase "How do you do?" as you may be asked to be more specific. The exchange of gifts in business is not a standard Belgian practice. However, remembering someone on a special occasion is appreciated. Keep such gifts simple and practical; a gift representative of your country is acceptable. When visiting someone's home, take a small gift with you as well as flowers for your hostess, avoiding the color red if the flowers are roses. Finally, if you are the seller, it is advised you invite your colleagues to a business lunch. While business may be discussed over lunch, refrain from talking too much shop or presenting serious issues.

BUSINESS ETHIC & FRAMEWORK

Belgian business ethics are a mixture of Flemish, Dutch, German, and French cultures tempered by the nation's strong dependence on trade. Foreign companies will find that their Belgian counterparts adhere to business agreements to the letter and expect the same from partners. Quality standards for goods and services are very high, so few excuses will be accepted for the delivery of shoddy products.

Foreign firms can expect forthright dealings with Belgian companies and a good degree of transparency in negotiations. Belgians may be quick to take advantage of a counterpart's mistakes or weaknesses, but they themselves eschew deception when negotiating business. Belgians will assume that a similar attitude is being taken by the foreign delegation unless otherwise indicated.

DECISION MAKING

Belgians are tough-minded negotiators and convincing your Belgian counterpart of a deal will be difficult. It is a very traditional society and the concept of the "flat organization" is not very popular. Belgium still has an active monarchy and such hierarchical attitudes carry over into business. Decisions are made at the top, so foreign business delegations need to make sure they are dealing with decision makers rather than low-ranking gatekeepers. Belgians have a long history of international trade and are quite savvy in dealing with foreign firms. Visitors will have been heavily researched by the Belgian side and it is advisable to do the same.

Belgians are also extremely conservative when deciding on suitable business partners for joint ventures. Much depends on the nature of your business. Because Brussels is the seat of the EU government, Belgians tend to give priority to other EU members. Decisions regarding deals with non-EU partners can be slow in arriving as every detail is scrutinized to maximize advantage and minimize potential disadvantage. When looking for a quick decision, visitors should make sure they arrive with all necessary information in order. This goes for buyers as well as sellers—although the latter will receive the most scrutiny. Turnabout is fair play, and the Belgians are always willing to submit themselves to similar calls for transparency.

Note: Belgian business people are very sophisticated negotiators and remarkable linguists. The very nature of their economy has caused them to be an assertive, outward-looking society. They have quick minds but realize that time often works to their advantage when cutting deals with visiting companies. Visitors, particularly buyers, can also make use of the same ploy.

MEETINGS

When in a buying position, Belgians are extremely focused upon the business at hand. Following the exchange of greetings and business cards, they will normally proceed directly to the objectives of the business meeting. They are, however, experienced internationalists and will reverse this tendency when selling to cultures more keen on establishing a relationship prior to doing business.

Note: Keep in mind that the Belgian counterparts will have thoroughly researched a visitor's culture and business techniques in advance of negotiations.

Never be condescending in your attitude during business discussions. Displaying airs or superiority is bad form and the Belgians are well aware that their economy is tiny when put in a global perspective. They do, however, "punch above their weight" in business dealings. Even when buying, ask questions instead of giving advice, and listen carefully to answers. Belgian standards and quality are very high and foreign sellers are expected to be able to perform at the same level. By demonstrating your interest and desire to learn about their business markets, you will more successfully win their confidence in your own business practices.

It is considered bad form to remove your suit jacket in a meeting or to use first names prematurely. They are a friendly people but they grant that friendship selectively. Belgians are very sensitive to social hierarchies and their respect is difficult to regain once it has been lost by a casual or overly familiar attitude.

WOMEN IN BUSINESS

Women play a dynamic role in the work force and are found at all levels, including senior management. There are several female ministers in the government and in parliamentary positions. Foreign businesswomen should experience no difficulty in getting business done, and they should find they are treated with respect and courtesy. While there is a goodly level of feminist attitude, male and female Belgians do not see it to be in conflict with Old World manners. Women are still treated with deference in social situations and "gentlemanly" behavior abounds. Female visitors from the U.S. may find some of this behavior to be patronizing but it should be seen within the context of an older European culture.

BUSINESS ENTERTAINING

Belgians are an affable group, for the most part, and they like to mix business with pleasure, usually Epicurean in nature. Business luncheons and dinners can be lengthy and will most likely involve the consumption of Belgium's signature beers. Such meals will be relaxed and the conversation expansive. Belgians are not as formal as their German neighbors and much less reserved than their French cousins. Part of living well in Belgium means eating well, so visitors should approach these business meals with good natured gusto.

The Flemish-Walloon conflict extends even into the kitchen, and your hosts' selection of restaurants or in-house cuisine will reflect their cultural biases. Like most of Northern Europe, the emphasis will be upon meats and heavy sauces. Any special dietary needs (medical or philosophical) should be made clear by visitors in advance.

Note: Should a visiting delegation decide to reciprocate, take care in the selection of cuisine. The city of Brussels, for instance, has a dizzying array of restaurants offering local and foreign foods. Visitors may wish to avoid any local cultural conflicts by choosing something outside of the Flemish-Walloon context. Whatever venue is chosen, make sure it serves beer!

BUSINESS ATTIRE

Belgians, like many European cultures, are inclined to socially rank you by appearance alone, particularly in the French region. For men, a dark suit, a white shirt, and conservative necktie are safe. Wear lace-up shoes as opposed to loafers. Businesswomen should dress conservatively, wearing skirts and blouses. Neutral colors are preferred over bright colors and it is best to keep jewelry discreet.

Belgians are, in general, formal, and their dress reflects this. Casual attire can be seen as an indication that you are not serious, except of course in the high-tech areas where informal dress (though neat) is fast becoming a standard.

Business Centers
Brussels

CITY VIEW

Brussels, previously known as the Island of Saint-Gorick, was officially founded in 979 AD on a small island formed by two arms of the river Zenne. The town was built into a fortress, gaining importance through the centuries as a thriving city known for producing luxury goods. In the period following World War II, Brussels became a district with its own limited government, as well as being named the capital of the European Union. The popularity of the region as a governmental and institutional center has given its economy a dramatic boost. Today Brussels is known as a bustling international business center, hosting sixty foreign banks and more than 1000 business conferences per year. The city displays a fine blend of its history and culture, side-by-side with all the expected modern infrastructure. Tourists are attracted by Brussels' reputation as one of the best "beer cities" in the world, known especially for its fruit beers, and, of course, for its famous Brussels' lace, available alongside tapestries and the inimitable Belgian chocolate in outdoor markets and small shops throughout the city. This city is bilingual, with all relevant public signs printed both in French and Dutch, and English is rapidly becoming an important language because of the numerous international political organizations. In the restaurants, hotels, and cafés one should not have too many problems getting along in English. The emblem of Brussels, prominently displayed throughout the city, is a yellow iris on a blue background, a flower that grew abundantly in the bog covering the region before its development.

AIRPORT

Brussels Zaventem Airport to City Center

The airport lies eight miles (13 km.) from the city. Trains and buses run regularly to hotels from the airport, and taxis are plentiful. Trains depart every 30 minutes into town and take from 15 to 25 minutes for a fare of BFr80 (US$2.50). Cabs, meanwhile, may take about 25 to 30 minutes for a fare of BFr1,200 (US$38) but will deliver you directly to the doorstep. Look for the marked taxi stands outside of arrivals and avoid the roving cabs. Some of the more expensive hotels offer courtesy coaches. For those needing to connect to Antwerp, Sabena offers non-stop bus service from Zaventem Airport.

Airline Numbers

Aer Lingus	(2) 753-2000/1
Air Canada	(2) 513-9150
Air UK	(2) 507-7052
British Airways	(2) 548-2122/33
Delta	(2) 730-8200
KLM	(2) 507-7070
Luxair	(2) 646-3452
Sabena	(2) 723-2323
United	(2) 713-3600
Airport Information	(2) 753-2111

HOTELS

Note: Hotel rates drop considerably during the weekends, sometimes as much as 50 percent. At the end of July and most of August, weekday rates are also lowered by quite a sum.

Top-end

Hotel Astoria; 103 rue Royale; tel: (2) 227-0505; fax: (2) 217-1150; Belle Epoque style hotel; 104 rooms, 14 suites; business center with PC and Internet access; in-room modem connection, voicemail; BFr12000/25000

Hilton Brussels; 38 Boulevard de Waterloo; tel: (2) 504-1111; fax: (2) 504-2111; downtown; restaurants (incl. 24 hour); executive floor lounge; 19 meeting rooms (up to 800); in room fax/modem connection; fitness room; health club with sauna; massage; jogging area; shopping; BFr9,500/46,000.

Le Meridien; Carrefour de L'Europe 3; tel: (2) 548-4211; fax: (2) 548-4735; facing Palais de Congrès and Central Station; restaurant; business center; conference facilities (up to 200); administrative assistance; translating and conference interpreting; document binding; in-room modem connection, voicemail; small fitness center; BFr10,000/11,000.

Metropole; Place de Brouckère 31; tel: (2) 217-2300; fax: (2) 218-0220; www.metropolehotel.be; email: info@metropolehotel.be; 410 rooms; 19th Century Renaissance style; adjacent to Grand Place; restaurant; 10 meeting rooms (10 to 600); business center; secretarial service; laptops and internet available; in-room modem/fax connections; fitness; massage; sauna; whirlpool; parking; BFr9,500/35,000.

The Stanhope; 9, Rue du Commerce; tel: (20 506-9111; fax: (2) 512-1708; small, exclusive hotel with personalized service; central business district; restaurant; conference room (up to 40); secretarial service; fax/photocopy service; sauna; BFr9500/12,500.

Expensive

Amigo; Rue Amigo 1-3; tel: (2) 511-5910; fax: (2) 513-5277; tel: (2) 547-4747; fax: (2) 513-5277; Spanish Renaissance style, oldest hotel in Brussels; restaurant; 24-hour room service; meeting and conference facilities (300); banquet (200); reception (450); breakfast included; BFr6700/16,500.

Le Belson; Chausée de Louvain 805; tel: (2) 705-2030; fax: (2) 705-2043; airport shuttle service; meeting rooms; conference and banquet facilities; secretarial/fax/photocopy service; fitness; sauna; BFr 7150/7700.

Brussels Renaissance; Rue du Parnasse 19; tel: (2) 505-2929; fax: (2) 505-2555; near European Parliament; restaurants; meeting rooms (up to 360); fax/photocopying; fitness center; health club; pool; sauna; jacuzzi; parking; BFr8,000/9,000.

Europa Inter-Continental; Rue de la Loi/Westraat 107; tel: (2) 230-1333; fax: (2) 230-3628; next to European Parliament; business services; meeting, banquet and reception rooms (up to 400); fitness room; drugstore; parking; BFr8500/18,500.

Hotel President World Trade Center; boulevard Emile Jacqmain 180; tel: (2) 203-2020; fax: (2) 203-2440; adjacent to World Trade Center; restaurant; banquet and convention facilities (up to 400); 12 meeting rooms; office rental; city shuttle service; executive fitness center; sauna; massage; parking; BFr7500/10,500.

Leopold; Rue du Luxembourg 35; tel: (2) 511-1828; fax: (2) 514-1939; near exhibition grounds; restaurant; conference room (up to 30); secretarial/fax/photocopy service; sauna; parking; BFr4450/5650.

Libertel City Garden; 59 rue Joseph II; tel: 282-8282; fax: (2) 230-6437; near European Parliament; 96 rooms; 30 rooms with kitchenettes; in-room fax machines, work desk.

Novotel Off Grand Place; Rue Marche aux Herbes 120; tel: (2) 514-3333; fax: (2) 511-7723; restaurant; conference facilities (up to 25); secretarial service; fax/photocopy facilities; BFr5200.

Sheraton Brussels Hotel and Towers; Place Rogier 3; tel: (2) 224-3111; fax: (2) 218-6618; downtown; 2 restaurants; business center; 17 meeting rooms (up to 1000); indoor pool; fitness room; sauna; shops; BFr9600/10,600.

Sheraton Brussels Airport; Brussels National Airport, Zaventem; tel: (2) 725-1000; fax: (2) 725-1155; restaurant; soundproof walls; conference facilities (up to 600); secretarial/fax/photocopy service; fitness; sauna; BFr9900/10,900.

Swissôtel; Rue de Parnasse 19; tel: (2) 505-2929; fax: (2) 505-2555; 257 rooms, 41 executive rooms; across from European Parliament; restaurant; 9 conference and banquet rooms (up to 360); business center; executive rooms with fax machines, irons, ironing boards, umbrellas, and complimentary breakfast; fitness center; BFr8300/9300.

Moderate

Arctia; Rue D'Arenberg 18; tel: (2) 548-1811; fax: (2) 548-1820; city center, near railway; restaurant; conference facilities (up to 65); secretarial/fax/photocopy service; sauna; BFr3500.

Campanile; Excelsiorlaan 2, Zaventem; tel: (2) 720-9862; fax: (2) 720-9864; near airport; restaurant; conference room (up to 30); secretarial/fax/photocopy service; parking; BFr2200.

Eurocity Botanic; Rue du Brabantstraat 80; tel: (2) 223-0707; fax: (2) 223-0324; adjacent to exhibition grounds and rail station; restaurant; conference room (up to 20); secretarial/fax/photocopy service; parking; BFr2500/5,600.

Fimotel Brussels Airport; Berkenlaan 5, Diegem; tel: (2) 725-3380; fax: (2) 725-3810; conference facilities; seminar packages; parking.

Ibis; Rue du Marche aux Herbes 100; tel: (2) 514-4040; fax: (2) 514-5067; centrally located; 4 meeting rooms (up to 50); BFr 4,350/5,350.

L'Agenda; Rue de Florence 6-8; tel: (2) 539-0031; fax: (2) 539-0063; Newly renovated apartment-like rooms; currency exchange, fax, multilingual staff, room service; BFr3,300/4,100.

Mozart; Rue Marché aux Fromages 15A; tel: (2) 502-6661; fax: (2) 502-7758; between Royal Windsor and Amigo Hotels; romantic, rustic decor; BFr2500/3000.

MEDICAL CENTER

Centre Hospitalier Etterbeek-Ixelles/ Ziekenhuiscentrum Etterbeek-Elsene; Rue Jean Paquot/Jean Paquotstraat 63 1050 Brussels; 24 hours a day; tel: (2) 641-4812

Centre Hospitalier/Ziekenhuiscentrum Baron Lambert War Memorial St-Joseph/St-Jozef; Rue Baron Lambert/ Baron Lambertstraat 38, 1040 Brussels; 24 hours a day - children and adults; tel: (2) 739-8411.

Centre Hospitalier Molière Longchamp/ Molière Longchamp Ziekenhuis; Rue Marconi Marconistraat 142, 1190 Brussels; 24 hours a day; tel: (2) 348-5741.

Centre Hospitalier Universitaire Saint-Pierre/ Universitair Medisch Centrum Sint-Pieter;

Rue Haute/Hoogstraat 322, 1000 Brussels; adult emergency tel: (2) 535-4051; children emergency tel: (2) 535-4360.

Centre Hospitalier/Verplegingscentrum New Paul Brien; Rue de Foyer Schaerbeekois/ Schaarbeekse Haardstraat 36 1030 Brussels; 24 hours a day; tel: (2) 247-2225.

HEALTH CLUB

Brussels Sheraton; 3 Place Rogier; tel: (2) 219-3400.

Hilton Hotel; 38 Rue de Waterloo; tel: (2) 513-8877.

AUTO RENTAL

Alamo; airport, tel: (2) 753-2060/2061.

Avis; tel: (2) 724-0625; airport, (2) 720-0944.

Budget; airport, tel: (2) 753-2170.

Europcar; tel: (2) 721-0592.

Hertz; tel: (2) 735-4050 or (2) 702-0511; airport, (2) 720-6044.

Limousine Service; airport, (2) 721-1313; fax: (2) 721-1352; located in arrivals hall at the International First Class Limousine desk, open 6:30a.m. to 10:00p.m.

WORLD TRADE CENTER

World Trade Center Brussels
Boulevard du Roi Albert II 30
1000 Bruxelles, Belgium
tel: (2) 203-0400; fax: (2) 203-0405
email: wtc.brussels@pophost.eunet.be
website: http://brussels.wtc.be

Bermuda

Bermuda

At a Glance
THE PEOPLE

Population .... 62,472 (July 1999 est.)
Growth Rate .... 0.72% (1999 est.)
Life Expectancy .... 76.97 years (born 1999)
Infant Mortality ... 9.27 deaths/1,000 live births (1999 est.)

Ethnic Composition
Black African 61%
Caucasian 39%

Religious Composition
Anglican 28%
Roman Catholic.. 15%
African Methodist Episcopal 12%
Seventh-Day Adventist.. 6%
Methodist... 5%
Other and non-affiliated.. 34%

Languages Spoken
English (official), Portuguese

Education and Literacy
Education is free and compulsory for children between the ages of 5 and 16. The literacy rate for adults is 98 percent.

Labor Force
Total 34,633
By occupation: services 83%, industry 15%, agriculture 2%.

THE ECONOMY

Bermuda's economy and livelihood are now dependent almost entirely on the archipelago's status as a "tax haven" for international business. Its only appreciable natural resources are its great scenic beauty and its people. Though tourism has been downplayed in the last decade, it has made the most of these resources. Bermuda also stands as a leading offshore site for insurance and reinsurance corporations. Thousands of other international businesses operate in Bermuda under a variety of organizational structures. Its GDP continues to show steady growth, and its GDP per capita now ranks among the highest in the world. Bermuda is under considerable pressure from international agencies to alter its tax policies. Thus far this former British colony has resisted efforts to cut off its lifeblood by claiming that a sovereign nation has a right not to tax. It is also trying to re-establish itself as a major center for tourism.

Exports .... US$57 million (1997)
Imports .... US$617 million (1997)
Total GDP .... US$1.9 billion (1997 est.)
GDP Per Capita .... US$30,000 (1997 est.)
Unemployment .... 0.1 percent (1998)
Inflation Rate 2.1% (1997)

Top Export Partners
E.U., Brazil, Canada

Top Import Partners
United States, United Kingdom, Canada

Top Exports
Produce, re-exports of pharmaceuticals.

Top Imports
Manufactured articles, machinery and transport equipment, food and live animals, chemicals.

BUSINESS WORKWEEK

Offices
Monday to Friday 9a.m. to 5p.m.

Banks
Monday to Friday 9:30a.m. to 3p.m.

Government
Monday to Friday 9a.m. to 5p.m.

Retail
Monday to Saturday 9a.m. to 5p.m.; some shops may close earlier on Thursdays.

HOLIDAYS

New Year's Day...January 1
Good Friday...April2*
Bermuda Day ....May 24
Queen's Official Birthday......................................June 13*
Cup Match...July 23*
Somer's Day..July 24*
Labor Day... September 7*
Remembrance Day ....November 11
Christmas Day..December 25
Boxing Day...December 26
* Dates may vary by year.

CLIMATE

Seasons
The climate on the islands is influenced by the Gulf Stream, so it is generally mild and humid all year round. Rainfall is the main source of fresh water in Bermuda, and the average annual rainfall is approximately 58 inches (1,470 mm).

In the winter months, from November until May, the temperature averages around 8°C (46°F). February is the coldest month. In the summer months it reaches 32.7° (90°F) by August. The summer months can face up to 80 percent humidity, with heavier rainfall in June, July, and October.

Regions
The climate is consistent throughout the islands.

Money & Banking

Currency
The currency of Bermuda is the Bermuda Dollar (Bda$).

Denominations
The Bermuda Dollar comes in coin denominations of Bd$1 and 25, 10, 5, and 1 cents and banknotes of Bd$2, 5, 10, 20, 50, 100.
1 £ Stg. = Bd$1.63

Traveler's Checks and Credit Cards
Traveler's checks and currency can be exchanged at banks, exchange shops, and hotels. The main airport has no exchange bureau. Cash, especially U.S. dollars, commands a better exchange rate and lower fees than do traveler's checks and other currencies.

American Express, Visa, Diner's Club, and MasterCard are accepted in most up-market places in urban areas. Credit cards are necessary for car/motorbike rentals and hotel reservations. ATMs are available in Hamilton, St.

Bermuda

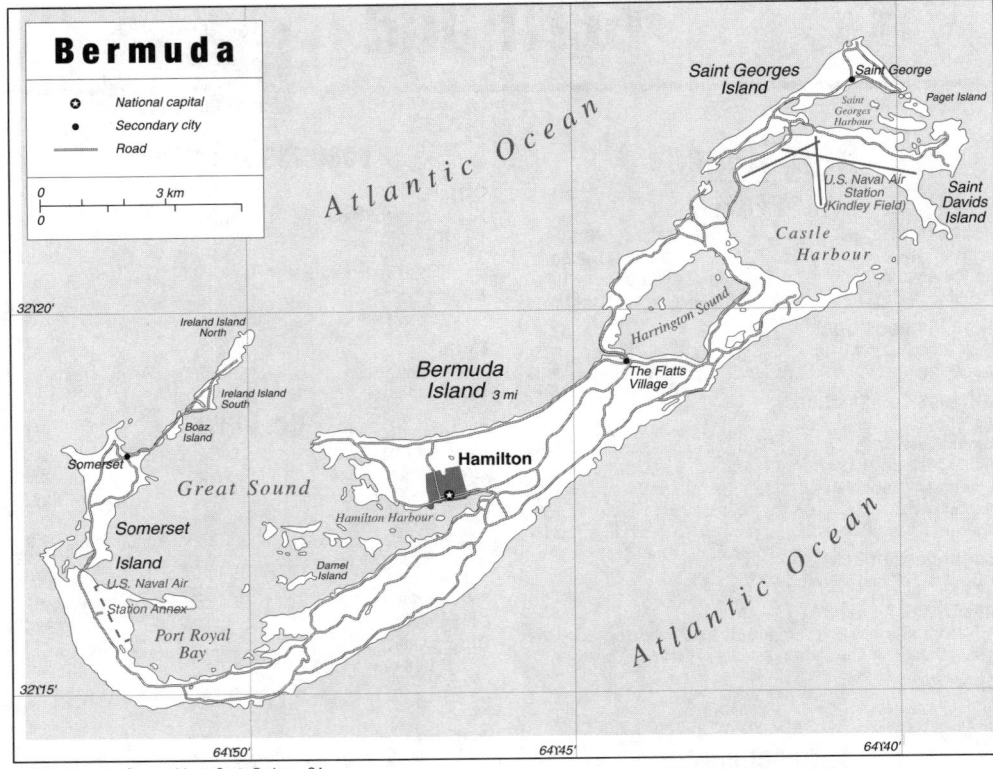

©2001 Magellan Geographix ℠ Santa Barbara, CA

George, and Somerset but are rare elsewhere. Cash is king in the countryside. Expect high prices in Bermuda due to the quantity of goods the island must import and the high number of tourists.

Travel

VISA AND PASSPORT

All visitors to Bermuda require a valid passport, except U.S. and Canadian citizens who may show some other form of identification: a birth certificate, a citizenship card, or naturalization certificate along with an official photo ID.

All travelers must be in possession of a return ticket or an onward ticket. Those traveling to another country requiring a visa must obtain one before arrival in Bermuda.

Visitors do not require a visa for stays of up to six months except for nationals of certain countries including: Albania, Algeria, Bosnia-Herzegovina, Bulgaria, Cambodia, China, Chinese residents of Hong Kong, Croatia, Cuba, Czech Republic, Haiti, Iran, Iraq, Jordan, Korea (DPR), Lebanon, Libya, Former Yugoslav Republic of Macedonia, Mongolia, Morocco, Nigeria, Pakistan, Romania, Slovak Republic, Slovenia, Sri Lanka, Syria, Tunisia, Vietnam, Yugoslavia (Serbia and Montenegro), and former Soviet republics.

For those travelers from the countries listed above, the visa allows for a length of stay of three months, initially. Extensions may be sought from Bermudian Immigration authorities. Allow four weeks for visa processing.

DEPARTURE FORMALITIES

Goods of total dollar amounts ranging from Bd$300 to 400 are permitted to be taken out of Bermuda without having to pay duty. Over that amount, a ten percent duty is applied. Keep in mind that no duty free shops exist at the airport. Items may, however, be purchased downtown and then declared at the airport. Bring all receipts for proof of purchase to avoid delays at customs. There also exists a Bd$20 departure tax; immediate transit passengers are exempt.

CUSTOMS ENTRY (PERSONAL)

Duty-free
- Tobacco: 200 cigarettes, 50 cigars, and 454g of tobacco
- Alcohol: 1.137litres (1 qt.) of spirits and wines
- US$30 gift allowance
- Up to 20 lbs. of meat and other foodstuffs brought in as passenger luggage are dutiable at the rate of 22.25% of value

Prohibited or Restricted
- Spear guns for fishing
- Firearms
- Plants, fruit, vegetables, or animals unless an import permit has been granted from the Department of Agriculture
- Non-prescribed drugs (including marijuana)

Note: All visitors should declare any prescribed drugs on arrival; regulations are strictly observed. Clearance of merchandise and sales materials for use at trade conventions must be arranged in advance with the hotel involved.

IMMUNIZATION

Visitors arriving from regions with yellow fever or cholera outbreaks require immunization certificates. It is also advisable for people with hay fever or allergies to keep medications on hand, as pollen air conditions are usually high.

Hepatitis A shots are advised, but not required.

TIPPING

Taxis

Metered taxi drivers expect a 15 percent tip from foreigners for very good service. Unmetered fares should be negotiated in advance.

Porters

Porters receive Bd$1 per bag at first class hotels and airports.

Hotels

Hotels will add service charges where applicable but chambermaids are usually tipped Bd$1 per day for the extent of the stay.

Restaurants

Restaurants usually add into the bill their desired tip rate of 15 percent; if they have not, then add it yourself. Bartenders usually receive a similar size tip.

EMERGENCY INFORMATION

Police and Crime

Crime is relatively low in Bermuda, and it is generally safe to walk the streets. Foreign business visitors are, however, often the target of thieves. Consequently, purses, laptops, and briefcases will require additional security. Do not leave valuables in cars or on tables in cafés. Keep non-essential valuables locked in hotel safes when not in use. Use credit cards and travel checks when possible to avoid carrying large sums of cash.Carry photocopies of your passport instead of the original. Use credit cards or travelers checks for most of your large transactions. Walk with your bag away from the street to avoid having it snatched away by thieves roaming about on swarms of motorbikes. To contact police for a non-emergency dial: 295-0011.

Emergency Numbers

Numbers function nationwide

Police/Fire/Ambulance 911
Air/Sea Rescue 297-1010

Health

Bermuda's warm weather and hot sun can be unforgiving; bring sun protection with you and wear it at all times regardless of your skin tone. Diarrhea is common to travelers who are unaccustomed to the new diet, the water, and the heat.

General standards of medical care in Bermuda are excellent, and most doctors are European and American trained. A fully-equipped 237-bed hospital is located near Hamilton.

As with the rest of Bermuda, prices are hefty. Travelers should definitely consider obtaining travel insurance.

Bring along any specialized medicines you may require during your stay.

For more information on medical centers, including phone numbers, please see the "Business Centers" section.

INTERNAL TRAVEL

TAXI

Many taxis are now of the mini-van variety. Most cabs are metered and fares run about Bd$4 to 5 for the first mile, and Bd$1.30 per additional mile. However, fares may vary for more than 4 passengers and if pieces of luggage are in-volved. An added 25 percent surcharge exists between midnight and 6a.m. as well as on Sundays.

Taxi drivers range from very knowledgeable to the novice. If possible, get a taxi displaying a small blue flag, driven by Department of Tourism guides. Taxis can be hired by the hour. One to four passengers should expect to pay Bd$30 for an hour and five to six persons Bd$42 per hour for a minimum of three hours.

There are horse-drawn carriages available in Hamilton.

AUTO & MOTORBIKE

An extensive network of roads run throughout the main island—but, foreign visitors are not permitted to drive automobiles in Bermuda.

Motorcycles may be rented for standard rates. Lightweight motor-assisted bicycles, called "livery cycles," are also available for rental throughout the island. Helmets and third party insurance are compulsory.

Bicycles are also widely available for rental. The Department of Tourism provides a comprehensive listing of prices and supplies.

BUSES & TRAMS

Buses are punctual, inexpensive, and very efficient. State-run buses are painted pink and blue and offer a comfortable mode of transport. Buses generally serve tourists more than they do business people. In Hamilton, the blue and pink painted poles mark bus stops. Poles painted blue on top indicate the bus will travel away from Hamilton; those painted pink on top travel in the direction of Hamilton. Outside of Hamilton one may also find bus stop poles painted black and white or green and white, or perhaps one may just find a stone shelter. Buses will not stop if they are full. Carry proper change since drivers will not make change.

Mini buses (vans) serve areas that buses do not including the Western end of the island. These run between April 1 and October 31 from 8:30a.m. to 5p.m. Passengers may flag them down anywhere and drivers will drop you where you want to go. Mini buses cost around Bd$3 per trip.

WATER TRAVEL

Bermuda's Department of Marine and Ports operates ferries for commuters as well as visitors and allows motorbikes on board for a fee. Routes exist from Hamilton to Paget, Warwick, and to Somerset and Dockyard. Ferries only travel to St. George between April and October and only on Wednesdays and Thursdays.

TRAVEL ASSISTANCE

Department of Tourism
Global House, 43 Church St.
Hamilton HM 12
tel: (441) 292-0023; fax: (441) 292-3662

Communications

DIALING CODES IN BERMUDA

International country code: [1]

Selected Area Code: (441); this area code applies throughout Bermuda.

Dialing Bermuda from Overseas

To dial Bermuda from overseas, dial your country's international dialing code, then Bermuda's country code [1], then the area code (441), and finally the number of the person you are trying to reach. From the United States, dial 1+441+the local number you wish to reach.

Bermuda

Assistance Numbers

International Operator 01
Domestic Operator 0
Local Directory 411
U.S. Directory .... 1 + area code + 555-1212

CALLING WITHIN BERMUDA

Local Calls

A local call will cost 20 cents from any pay phone and you can talk up to an hour without extra cost.

Long Distance Calls

All numbers have seven digits and will cost the same as a local call.

International Calls

To call direct to the U.S. or Canada, dial 1 + area code + number. Discounted rates occur between 7p.m. and 11p.m. and fall even lower between 11p.m. and 7a.m., except to Hawaii and Alaska. To call any other country direct, dial 011 + country code + area code + number. Calls may cost about US$2 a minute. Long-distance charges are printed in the front of telephone books.

Be warned that a hotel call could suffer a 350 percent increase in the rate! They may even charge a fee for a collect call. Thus, it proves cost effective to go in search of a pay phone, which should not be difficult in Bermuda. As a bonus, public phones also accept major credit cards. Direct access to a U.S. operator may not be available from every phone:

AT&T USA Direct 1-800-872-2881
MCI 1-800-999-9000
Sprint 1-800-623-0877

Calls may also be placed from the Cable and Wireless Office in Hamilton located at 20 Church St., opposite City Hall.

Rates are lowest between 11.pm. and 7a.m. Toll free calls to the U.S. may only be placed to car rental companies and airlines. Other toll free calls will be charged at long-distance rates.

PAY PHONES

Public Telephones

Coin Phone:

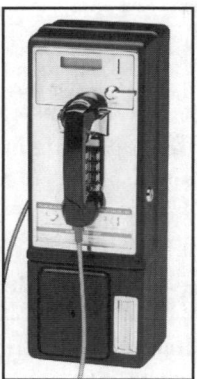

Public phones are as common as they are in the U.S. Furthermore, they look almost identical. Phones accept both phone cards and coins, and many will also take U.S. coins. Some phones also allow credit cards.

1. Deposit coins
2. Dial

Older, non-digital style phones may require a slightly different process:

1. Dial
2. Wait for party to answer
3. Insert coins

Calling Cards

Bermuda TCI Company cash cards are available at visitor centers and telephone offices.

CELLULAR PHONES

There are numerous cellular phone service providers in Bermuda. In the analog format both Bermuda Cellular and Bermuda Digital Communications Ltd offer AMPS service.

Note: Your home country cell phone may not work in this country. If not, we recommend that you rent an international cell phone *before* you leave home. A major US-based cell phone rental provider is **IMC WorldCell**. For information see "International Cell Phone Rentals" on page 14.

CALL BACK

You can (potentially) save significant sums when calling in Bermuda by using a call back service. For a list of callback services, please refer to the "Communications" section in the *Global Road Warrior* Introduction.

Fees for call back services vary widely, depending on the company and the type of service required. Be sure to check with these companies before leaving to compare rates.

PHONE JACK

Adaptors are available through **iGo Corporation.** (See "Electrical and Telephone Adaptors" on page 19.)

FAX

Many offices and business centers in major hotels have fax capabilities. Be sure to call and alert the office you are sending a fax to that you are sending a fax. One can also send faxes from the Cable and Wireless Office.

POSTAL SERVICES

Red tape abounds in the Bermudan postal service. Letters can take four to six days to reach the U.S. or the U.K., or up to two weeks to reach Canada. Stamps are only available at the post office. If possible, ask to have the letter metered. Stamps must be applied separately with glue, a sometimes messy affair.

Business Services

BUSINESS CENTERS

Marriott's Castle Harbour Resort; Tucker's Town; tel: 293-2040.

Royal Palms Hotel; Rosemont Ave.; tel: 292-1854; fax 292-1946.

COURIER SERVICES

DHL Worldwide Express; 16 Church St.; Ham. HM 11; tel: 295-3300.

FedEx; Church St. Level; Washington Mall; Ham; tel: 295-3854.

UPS; Atlantic House; 11 Par-La-Ville Rd. North, Ham. HM 11; tel: 292-6760; fax 295-0455.

Electrical

Current
110 volts AC, 60Hz.
American plugs are the standard.

ELECTRIC PLUGS

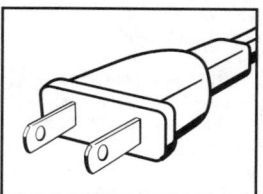

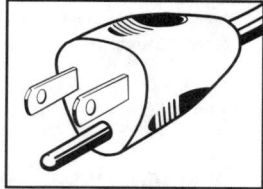

Adaptors are available through **iGo Corporation.**
(See "Electrical and Telephone Adaptors" on page 19.)

Technical Support

HARDWARE/SOFTWARE VENDOR SUPPORT

Dell; tel: 02 481 91 00; fax: 02 481 92 99; (in the U.S.) tel: [1] (512) 338-4400; fax: [1] (512) 728-3330; (in Germany) tel: [49] (61) 039-710; (Dell- Europe) tel: [44] (134) 474-8000; http://www.dell.com/.

Hewlett Packard; (in the U.S.) tel: [1] (408) 246-4300; (in Switzerland) tel: [41] (22) 780-8111; http://www.hp.com/.

IBM; tel: 295-2969; fax: 292-7813; (in the U.S.) tel: [1] (919) 517-2800; (U.S. Main Office) tel: [1] 914-765-1900; (in Switzerland) tel: [41] (22) 310-0418 (in French); http://www.ibm.com/.

Microsoft; (in the U.S.) [1] (425) 635-7222; (in Germany) tel: [49] (89) 31-760; fax: [49] (89) 3176-1000; tel: [49] (89) 3176-1199; (in Switzerland) tel: [41] (848) 858-868; fax [41] (1) 831-0869; http://www.microsoft.com/.

Internet Connection

HOW TO CONNECT

Connecting to AOL and Compuserve in Japan is similar to using it when traveling outside your own area code. See the introductory section for detailed information on connecting to your account through a different phone number.

America Online
Numbers are available at keyword *international*. Be sure to get several local numbers before leaving. AOL's Global-Net service is available at keyword *access* (a free area).

There are no direct access numbers for America Online in Bermuda. Users will have to pay international rates to use the service, so expect to pay high sums.

Compuserve
Numbers are available at keyword *Go International*. The Compuserve Web-site also has a great deal of information, at http://www.compuserve.com.

There are no direct access numbers for Compuserve in Bermuda. Users will have to pay international rates to use the service.

Independent Service Providers
Many independent service providers offer discounts if you are only in town for a couple days.

Logic Communications, Ltd.; tel: (441) 296-9600; fax: (441) 295-1149; email: info@logic.bm; http://www.log-ic.bm/.

North Rock Communications; tel: (441) 296-2700; fax: (441) 296-2701; http://www.northrock.bm/.

Business Culture

GREETINGS AND COURTESIES
Bermudians are noticeably formal, but perhaps less so than in many other areas. Titles and last names are used, although Bermudians are less addicted to the use of titles than many others in Latin America and the Caribbean. Business cards (in English) are normally exchanged, but without particular formality.

DECISION MAKING
Introductions are helpful but not absolutely necessary. Because of the importance of consensus, few individuals have full authority to make binding decisions concerning any but the most mundane matters. Locals may assume that foreign businesspeople are fully aware of this without making it clear to them, leading to disappointments and misunderstandings

MEETINGS
Bermudians often arrive late for appointments, but expect foreigners to appear on time. Business lunch meetings are common—these are low-key events, usually limited to the people involved in the immediate discussions.

WOMEN
Women often form the backbone of small-scale enterprises and are generally accorded considerable personal freedom and influence. Foreign businesswomen should experience few problems and may even be accorded special treatment by more traditional senior businessmen. There are many businesswomen from both North America and Europe operating in Bermuda in fairly high management positions.

BUSINESS ATTIRE
Despite its tropical flavor, Bermuda remains conservative and formal in attitude and dress, reflecting its British heritage. Due to the balmy weather, lightweight suits are recommended. Dining establishments often require a jacket and tie. As for Bermuda shorts, one might see them worn with kneesocks here or there; however, get to know your business associates and their manner of dress before deciding to step out in such an ensemble. Women may wear

slacks and a dressy blouse, although dresses appear more popular among natives. The cooler months may require a light jacket or sweater. And for safety sake, bring an umbrella for all seasons.

Business Centers
HAMILTON
CITY VIEW

Visitors from North America feel Hamilton, and the rest of Bermuda for that matter, is quaint and British. Brits who visit find the island Americanized. Whichever the case, most stereotypes of Bermuda ring true: sand, cottages, and sunshine wherever you look. One may find it hard to concentrate on business.

AIRPORT
Kindley Field Airport to City Center

Kindley Field lies 9.3 miles (15 km.) from Hamilton. Taxis are available; a trip to Hamilton may cost US$17. Bermuda Hosts Ltd. offer vans that provide transport to hotels. These prove a bit less costly but should be reserved in advance.

Airline Numbers
```
Air Canada .............................................(800) 776-3000
American Airlines  .................... (800) 433-7300; 293-1420
British Airways ...........................................(441) 295-4422
Continental Airlines  ................ (800) 231-0856; 293-3092
Delta ..........................................................(800) 221-1212
U.S. Air .................................... (800) 622-1015; 293-3072
Kiwi International ......................................(800) 538-5494
```

HOTELS

Note: Hotel rates are lowest from November to March.

Top-end
Elbow Beach Bermuda; 60 South Road, Paget Parish; tel: (441) 236-3535; 1-800-822-4200; fax: (441) 236-8043; 5-diamond hotel; 8 minutes from Hamilton; 5 minutes from airport; restaurants; business facilities; meeting facilities (up to 210); convention facilities (up to 110); beachside tennis; pool; health club; drug store; outdoor sports; underground caves; private beaches; US$165-$650.

Princess; Hamilton Harbor, Pitt's Bay Road, Pembroke Parish; tel: (441) 295-3000; 1-800-223-1818; fax: (441) 295-1914; near downtown, Front Street; 3 restaurants; conference and meeting rooms; business center; health club; pool; spa; putting green; tennis; access by hotel ferry to Southampton Princess golf course; US$200+.

Waterloo House (Relais et Chateux property); Hamilton Harbor, Pitts Bay Road, Pembroke Parish; tel: (441) 295-4480; 1-800-468-4100; fax: (441) 295-2585; email: waterloo@ibl.bm; 18th century manor; near downtown; meeting and business facilities; access to Coral Beach tennis club; pool; watersports; US$200+.

Expensive
Harmony Club; South Road, Paget Parish; tel: (441) 236-3500; 1-800- 225-5843; fax: (441) 236-2624; email: info@bermudahotels.com; guest house; tennis; croquet lawn; pool; saunas; beach privileges at Elbow Beach; US$110-145.

Marley Beach Cottages; South Rd., Warwick, Paget; tel: (441) 236-1143, ext. 42; fax: (441) 236-1984; email: mar@bspl.bm; kitchenettes; pool; whirlpool; US$138-249.

Palmetto Hotel & Cottages; Harrington Sound at Flatts Village, Smith's parish; tel: (441) 293-2323; fax: (441) 293-8761; restaurant; pub; beach; gardens; views; transport to golf and tennis facilities.

Rosedon; Pitts Bay Rd., Pembroke; tel: (441) 295-1640; fax: (441) 295-5904; email: info@rosedonbermuda.com; in Hamilton; historic manor; pool; US$128-256

Royal Palms Hotel; Hamilton; tel: (441) 292-1854; 1-800-678-0783; fax: (441) 292-1946; email: rpalms@ibl.bm; restored estate; in walking distance of Hamilton; business facilities; work desk; private balcony; some rooms with kitchens; US$110-180.

Surf Side Beach Club; tel: (441) 236-7100; 1-800-553-9990; fax: (441) 236-9765; 12 miles from airport; business facilities; meeting facilities (up to 15); work desk; kitchen; beach; pool; US$115-325.

Moderate
Greenbank Cottages; 17 Salt Kettle Road; tel: (441) 236-3615; fax: (441) 236-2427; email: grebank@ibl.com; ferry landing to Hamilton within walking distance; US$105-205.

Little Pomander Guest House; 16 Pomander Rd.; tel: (441) 236-7635; fax: (441) 236-8332; email: lit@bspl.bm; overlooking Hamilton Harbor; US$80-115.

Sandpiper Apartments; South Shore Rd., Warwick; tel: (441) 236-7093; fax: (441) 236-3898; kitchens; pool; whirlpool; US$78-120.

MEDICAL CARE

The King Edward VII Memorial Hospital; 7 Point Finger Road, Paget Parish; tel: 236-2345 (a fully-equipped medical facility with a 24-hour emergency room).

Note: For doctor and dentist referrals, contact the **Government Health Clinic**; 67 Victorian Street, Hamilton; tel: 236-0224.

AUTO RENTAL

Only residents are allowed cars in Bermuda, but travelers can rent mopeds and bicycles, take buses or taxis—or even walk. Moped renters should take care to lock them properly, as they are often stolen.

MOPED/SCOOTER RENTAL

Eve's Cycle Livery; Middle Road, Paget Parish; tel: 236-6247.

Oleander Cycles; Valley Rd., Paget; tel: 236-5235; Middle Road, Southampton, tel: 234-0629.

CHAMBER OF COMMERCE

Bermuda Chamber of Commerce
5 Front Street
PO Box HM 655
Hamilton HM CX
tel: (441) 295-4201; fax: (441) 292-5779

Bolivia

At a Glance

THE PEOPLE

Population .... 7,982,850 (July 1999 est.)
Growth Rate .... 1.96% (1999 est.)
Life Expectancy .... 61.43 years(born 1999)
Infant Mortality . 62.02 deaths/1,000 live births (1999 est.)

Ethnic Composition

Amerindian 55%
Mestizo 30%
Caucasian 15%

Religious Composition

Roman Catholic 95%
Protestant 5%

Languages Spoken

Spanish, Quechua, Aymara - (all official)

Education and Literacy

Adult literacy is 83.1 percent. Primary education, which lasts for eight years, is compulsory and free of charge.

Labor Force

Total: 2,500,000
By occupation (percent of GDP): services 57% industry 26%, agriculture 17%

THE ECONOMY

Bolivia is often described as having a semi-feudal economy and it is considered the least developed country in South America. The government initiated a series of reforms in the 1980s to reduce the 11,700 percent inflation down to today's tolerable level. It also agreed to privatize several larger state-owned firms. As a result, economic growth has been steadily improving. Bolivia has increased its prospects by entering into a trade association with Mexico and the Mercosur trade bloc. Continued privatization of the railroad, telecom, and energy sectors had attracted foreign interest, if not much actual investment. The major barrier to increased development remains the role of narcotics trafficking and violent crime in the Bolivian economy and society.

Exports .... US$1.1 billion (f.o.b., 1998 est.)
Imports .... US$1.7 billion (c.i.f. 1998)
Total GDP .... US$23.4 billion(1998 est.)
GDP Per Capita .... US$3,000 (1998 est.)
Unemployment .... 10 percent (1998)
Inflation Rate .... 4.4% (1998 est.)

Top Export Partners

United States, Colombia, Argentina, E.U., Peru

Top Import Partners

United States, Brazil, Japan, Chile

Top Exports

Metals, natural gas, soybeans, jewelry, wood.

Top Imports

Capital goods, chemicals, petroleum, food.

BUSINESS WORKWEEK

Offices

Monday to Friday 9 a.m. to noon and from 2:30p.m. to 6:30p.m. Some industrial concerns and companies work on Saturdays from 9a.m. to 1p.m.

Banks

Monday to Friday 9a.m. to 11:30a.m. and 2:30a.m. to 6:30p.m.

Government

Monday to Friday 9a.m. to 5p.m.

Retail

Monday to Friday 9a.m. to 12:30p.m. and 3p.m. to 7:30p.m.; Saturday 10a.m. to 3p.m.

HOLIDAYS

New Year's Day..January 1
Good Friday...April 2*
Labor day ....May 1
Corpus Christi...June 3*
Independence...August 6
All Saints' Day and Potosi ....November 18
Christmas ....December 25
    *Dates may vary by year.
Note: Individual cities also have their own holidays.

CLIMATE

Seasons

The wet season is in the summer, from December until February; in which time it can rain almost daily with only a few sunny intervals. The dry period runs from May to October. High summertime temperatures can reach 37°C (99°F) and wintertime lows in the mountains can plummet to -10°C (14 °F).

Regions

In the high Andean Plateau of the west, which also includes the capital La Paz, the climate is temperate most of the year. Here there are heavier rainfalls and a semi-tropical climate prevails, especially so in El Niño years. Towards the east, by the cities of Santa Cruz, Trinidad, and Cobija, there is a southern wind, but the climate again is tropical.

Money & Banking

Currency

The currency of Bolivia is the Boliviano (B$).

Denominations

The Boliviano (B$) comes in coin denominations of B$2 and 1 and 50, 20, 10, and 5 centavos; and banknotes of B$2, 5, 10, 20, 50, 100, and 200.

Traveler's Checks and Credit Cards

Traveler's checks and major currencies can be exchanged at banks, exchange shops, hotels, and kiosks at the airports. (British pound sterling checks are exchanged with some difficulty and sterling currency cannot be exchanged at all.) U.S. dollar-based traveler's checks are the easiest to exchange and get the best rates. The least bureaucratic processing and smallest fees can be found at American Express or Thomas Cook.

Credit cards are still not widely accepted in Bolivia, but American Express, Visa, Diner's Club, and MasterCard are accepted in a few up-market hotels, which may, however, attach a fee to the transaction. ATMs are rare even in major cities and do not function well with E.U. bank system cards. (See below for recommendations about carrying large sums of cash.)

Bolivia

SM Santa Barbara, CA

©2001 Magellan Geographix

Travel

VISA AND PASSPORT

A passport that is valid for at least six months beyond anticipated exit date is required of all visitors, except for citizens of Argentina, Paraguay, and Uruguay bearing a national identity card.

Visas are required of all visitors except for nationals of the following countries, provided they are in Bolivia as tourists only: Antigua & Barbuda, Argentina, Australia, Bahamas, Brazil, Canada, Chile, Colombia, Costa Rica, Czech Republic, Ecuador, Guatemala, Iceland, Israel, Japan, Monaco, New Zealand, Netherlands Antilles, Norway, Paraguay, Peru, Philippines, Poland, St. Lucia, St. Kitts & Nevis, St. Vincent & The Grenadines, South Africa, Switzerland, Turkey, Uruguay, U.S., and Vatican City. The usual length of stay granted is between 30 and 90 days.

Passengers in transit who do not leave the airport and are continuing their journey within t24 hours, and who are holding confirmed tickets and other documents for onward travel, are also exempt from the need for a visa.

Citizens of many countries also need to obtain special authorization from the Bolivian Ministry of Foreign Affairs prior to entry. Inquire with the embassy (or Consular section of the embassy).

All nationals who are to be in Bolivia for business purposes need a Business visa; the period of validity is 30 days. The visa application must include a company letter stating business intentions and dates of travel. Business visas expire after one month and require a local sponsor for reissuance.

Tourist visas are good for 30 or 90 days (determined by nationality) from date of entry.

Because of the enormous amount of cross-border crime, Bolivia has very strict immigration enforcement. All visitors are required to register with the immigration authorities; hotels will handle the necessary paperwork. Travelers staying at a private residence must present their passport to the Ministry of Immigration, which will eliminate any delay when leaving the country.

Allow a day or two for processing of visa applications for nationals who do not need special authorization. For those who do need prior authorization, anticipate a period between three and eight weeks before the visa is issued.

DEPARTURE FORMALITIES

An airport tax of US$20 is collected at departure, payable in local currency only. All visitors must have pre-registered with Immigration. Be prepared to show papers and requisite customs stamps upon departure.

CUSTOMS ENTRY (PERSONAL)

Duty-free

• Tobacco: 100 cigarettes, 25cigars, and 200 g.of tobacco
• Alcohol: one opened bottle of alcohol (1 liter or less)
• A reasonable quantity of perfume

Note: No customs control exists for hand luggage, so it is unnecessary to register business samples or personal items. Product samples are admitted duty-free if the intended stay is no longer than 90 days. Obtain a Determined Object Visa to avoid paying travel tax; this allows for a 30-day entry permit and may be extended if necessary.

Prohibited or Restricted

• Firearms
• Controlled drugs
• Cameras must be declared.

There are strict laws regarding the exportation of items considered to be national treasures. Pre-Columbian artifacts, particular historical paintings, authentic Spanish colonial architectural objects, some native textiles, stipulated plants, animals, and fossils—all are considered to be national treasures by the Bolivian Government. Removal from Bolivia of any such items is illegal without written permission from Bolivian government authorities. Also, any sort of fossil excavation, including the mere act of picking one up, is illegal without prior authorization in writing.

IMMUNIZATION

There are no required vaccinations, except for a yellow fever vaccination certificate if traveling from an infected country. Typhoid and yellow fever vaccinations are recommended if traveling to risk areas such as the rural districts of Beni, Chuquisaca, Cochabamba, Pando, Santa Cruz, Tarija, and certain areas of the La Paz district. Hepatitis A shots and anti-malarial medications are advised for travel to rural areas. Malaria exists in non-urban areas below 2500 meters, and resistance to chloroquine has been confirmed. Cholera is also present in some areas of the country. Travelers going from Bolivia to Brazil will need to get a yellow fever vaccination and certificate to cross the border.

TIPPING

In general, it is expected of foreigners to tip an additional ten percent on top of the service charge included in hotel and restaurant bills.

Taxi

Metered taxi drivers expect a B$1-2 tip. Unmetered fares should be negotiated in advance and include all fees.

Porters

B$4 per piece of luggage is expected at first class hotels; less is given for train station porters.

Hotels

Hotels will add a 15 percent service charge to the bill.

Restaurants

Restaurants add a 13 percent service charge to the tab.

EMERGENCY INFORMATION

Police and Crime

Crime is relatively high in Bolivia, notably in more urban areas due to high unemployment and corruption. Santa Cruz prevails as the most dangerous city in Bolivia, existing as a thoroughfare for cocaine traffic. The Chapare region between Santa Cruz and Cochabamba should be considered a high-risk area. As the government cracks down on cocoa growers under threat of U.S. sanctions, an anti-U.S. sentiment has been infused by drug lords and by radical leftists. Terrorists seek U.S. citizens as primary targets, and police may not be particularly helpful in assisting with a problem.

Street crimes such as theft from parked vehicles and pick-pocketing is widespread in La Paz, Cochabamba, and Santa Cruz. Theft of autos—late-model off-road vehicles, in particular— is on the rise. Violent assault and crimes involving weapons are infrequent; however, vehicle hijacking has become more frequent over the past year.

Beware of characters posing as police and searching your belongings, which, by law, can only be done at a police office. Bogus immigration and customs officers may also attempt to extort money from visitors for "unregistered" cameras or valuables. Demand identification and receipts for any fees 'requested'.

Take basic precautions against petty crime. Foreign business visitors are all considered to be wealthy and, therefore, likely targets of thieves. Consequently, purses, laptops, and briefcases will require additional security. Do not leave valuables in cars or on tables in cafés. Keep non-essential valuables locked in hotel safes when not in use. Use credit cards and travel checks when possible to avoid carrying large sums of cash.Carry photocopies of your passport instead of the original. Carry cash in a money belt, and use credit cards or traveler's checks for most of your transactions.

Crime in Bolivia can be very violent, and visitors have been killed over small sums of money. Resistance or belligerence will only increase the likelihood of further violence. Many business travelers from well-known corporations bring their own security. Do not take any unnecessary risks. Women should avoid traveling alone at day or night.

Emergency Numbers

Even in La Paz, police, fire, and medical personnel are best sent for by messenger. The phone system is far from efficient.

Health

Due to the high altitude in cities like La Paz, visitors should take some time to acclimatize in order to avoid symptoms such as dizziness, nausea, and shortness of breath. Eat lightly and take it easy for the first 24 hours. Those with heart conditions should use extra caution.

Risk of malaria exists throughout the year at altitudes below 2500m in rural areas. Considered relatively safe, however, are the Oruro Department, the provinces of Ingavi, Los Andes, Omasuyos, Pacajes (La Paz Dept), and Southern and Central Potosí Department. Reportedly, the predominant strain has proven resistant to chloroquine and sulfadoxine-pyrimethamine, but the disease occurs mainly in a benign vivax form. Falciparum malaria does occur in regions bordering Brazil, particularly in Guayaramerín, Riberalta, and Puerto Rico.

Never drink tap water; don't even use it for brushing your teeth, and avoid ice cubes. Refrain from eating raw vegetables and fruit unless they've been washed in a chlorine solution. Diarrhea is common for travelers who are unaccustomed to the new diet and water. Bring along a well-stocked medical kit with necessary prescription drugs. Medical personnel in Bolivia will only be useful in emergencies and even then the skills will be limited. Visitors should take out travel insurance including evacuation policies. Extreme caution should be taken in the rural areas as medical help is very limited.

For more information on medical centers, including phone numbers, please see the "Business Centers" section at the end of this chapter.

Bolivia

Bolivia

INTERNAL TRAVEL
AIR

Airlines offering domestic flights are LAB, AEROSUR, and TAM (the military airline). Due to Bolivia's mountainous topography and tropical rainforests, air travel is usually the easiest mode of transport. La Paz (El Alto), the world's highest airport, and Santa Cruz (Viru-Viru) are the primary internal airfields. There is usually a departure tax of Bs10, depending on the particular airport and destination.

TAXI

All taxis have fixed rates and sharing is common among locals. Foreigners are advised against sharing taxis with locals especially at night. Drivers expect tips from foreigners.

Taxi drivers may not be familiar with destinations. Have a friend write down extensive directions and carry maps.

AUTO

Cars and motorbikes can be rented in the major cities. These are only recommended for the experienced visitor to Bolivia.

Hertz and several local companies can be found in La Paz. An International Driving Permit is required. If you have a national license, the international permit can be obtained from the Federación Inter-Americana de Touring y Automovil. However, consider it more prudent to get the Permit before arriving in Bolivia.

One may rent cars with drivers for daily and weekly use. These rental agencies also provide additional security.

TRAIN

Bolivia has 3697km (2297 miles) of track, making up separate and unconnected systems in the western and eastern regions of the country. There is a daily through service linking La Paz and Cochabamba, and trains twice-weekly (and sometimes more frequent) on other lines.

Service tends to be a bit erratic, and schedules can change without notice. There are no sleeping-cars, but some trains do have restaurant cars.

Recently, the railways have replaced old rolling stock with new Fiat carriages from Argentina. There is a joint plan with Brazil to create a rail connection between Santa Cruz and Cochabamba.

Foreigners should increase their security awareness on the trains.

METRO

There is no subway system in any of Bolivia's cities.

BUSES & TRAMS

Some buses operate in La Paz on certain fixed routes. Look for those with colored flags signifying certain routes. Special buses (camion) also travel long distance through Bolivia. However, a hazardous and uncomfortable ride may await the adventurous. Roads outside of the cities are often impassable. This mode of transport is not advised for business travel.

WATER TRAVEL

Passenger boats operate between the numerous small islands of Lake Titicaca. Most of these depart from Copacabana.

Bolivia also has an extensive internal passenger boat system along the Amazon. This can be a risky venture, but it is often the only way to reach remote villages. Use responsible contacts to set up any travel along the Amazon. Once again, maximum security measures should be taken.

TRAVEL ASSISTANCE

Viceministerio de Turismo
Calle Mercado, Edificio Mcal. Ballivian
Piso 18, La Paz
tel: (2) 367 441; fax: (2) 374 630
email: turismo@mcei-bolivia.com
website: www.mcei-bolivia.com/Turismo
Senatur in La Paz
"Secretaria Nacional de Turismo"
Calle Mercado 1328, Casilla 1868
tel: (02) 367-463; fax: (02) 374-630

Essential Terms

English	Spanish
Yes No	Sí No
Good morning Hello (daytime) Hello (evening) Hello (telephone)	Buenos días Buenas tardes Buenas noches ¿Hola?
Good-bye	Adiós
Please	Por favor
Thank you	Gracias
Pleased to meet you	Encantado (a) de conocerle
Excuse me; I'm sorry	¿Perdóneme?
My name is _____	Me llamo _____
I don't understand	No comprendo
Do you speak English?	¿Habla usted inglés?

Communications
DIALING CODES IN BOLIVIA

International country code: [591]

Selected city codes: Copacabana (8622), La Paz (2), Santa Cruz (3), Sucre (64)

Dialing Bolivia from Overseas

To dial Bolivia from overseas, dial your country's international dialing code, then 591 (the country code for Bolivia), then the city code and finally the number. Remember that when dialing Bolivia from outside the country, omit the zero preceeding the city code. If you were dialing La Paz from the United States, for example, you would begin with 011, then 591, then 2 (the city code for La Paz), and finally the number of the person or office you are trying to reach.

Assistance Numbers

International Operator in La Paz 356-700
Operator 101
Directory Assistance.. 118

CALLING WITHIN BOLIVIA

Local Calls
Short local calls for about B.50 can be made at small street kiosks or hotels and restaurants. If you want to skip the great hunt outdoors, local calls can most easily be placed at ENTEL offices costing a couple of centavos. You can buy public phone tokens (fichas) from street vendors. Tokens vary from city to city.

Long Distance Calls
Calls outside the local area can best be placed at an EN-TEL office for inexpensive rates. Be sure to use the city code with the zero, unless calling from outside Bolivia.

International Calls
ENTEL runs the telephone operation in Bolivia, and, as such, provides telephone centers for its users (Ayacucho 267; and Edif Libertad, Calle Potosi). If you call from an EN-TEL office, a clerk will provide you with a request form to jot down the necessary information of your call (i.e. city, country, person, and number). Once you've filled out the paperwork, wait until someone calls your name when the connection has been made. Be prepared to give up your passport or a deposit as collateral. Three minutes could equal about US$8. Calls from a private hotel line could send you to the astronomical morgue, even if you attempt to reverse the charges, known in Bolivia as *por cobrar*.

Try connecting to an access number to speak to an operator in the U.S. A coin or card deposit may be necessary from a public phone.

U.S. AT&T Direct 0-800-1112
U.S. MCI 0-800-2222

PAY PHONES

Public Telephones
Card Phone:

Public phones are not an easy find in Bolivia. Finding an ENTEL office may prove a better bet.

Calling Cards
ENTEL phone cards are available at ENTEL offices or in airports. They come in denominations of B10, B20, and B50.

CELLULAR PHONES
There are numerous cellular phone service providers in Bolivia. In the analog format both ENTEL and Telefonica Celular de Bolivia offer AMPS service.

Note: Your home country cell phone may not work in this country. If not, we recommend that you rent an international cell phone *before* you leave home. A major US-based cell phone rental provider is **IMC WorldCell**. For information see "International Cell Phone Rentals" on page 14.

CALL BACK
You can (potentially) save significant sums when calling in Bolivia by using a call back service. For a list of callback services, please refer to the "Communications" section in the *Global Road Warrior* Introduction.

Fees for call back services vary widely, depending on the company and the type of service required. Be sure to check with these companies before leaving to compare rates.

PHONE JACK

Adaptors are available through **iGo Corporation.** (See "Electrical and Telephone Adaptors" on page 19.)

FAX
Faxes are available, although they be more difficult to find in rural areas.

POSTAL SERVICES
Postal service is generally efficient, although getting a post office box takes away much of the risk of theft. Airmail to Europe takes approximately three to four days. The parcel service, however, is unreliable. The main post office stands at Av. Mariscal Santa Cruz y Oruro and remains open Monday to Saturday 8a.m. to 10p.m. and Sundays from 9a.m. to noon.

Business Services

COURIER
DHL International; Ave. 14 de Septiembre 5351, Obrajes, La Paz; tel: (2) 785-522.

SHIPPING
Bolivian Intermodal Container Lines; tel: (2) 352-350 or (2) 325-726; fax: (2) 354-622; in Miami: [1] (305) 836-6960; toll-free within the U.S.: 1-800-814-4826; fax: [1] (305) 691-7614.

Rye Express Inc.; Intl. Freight Forwarders; 6964 N.W. 50th St., Miami, FL; tel: (305) 594-4206 or (305) 594-4207; fax: (305) 594-9522; email: cargo@bennrye.com.

Electrical

Current
Generally 110/220 volts AC, 50Hz. In La Paz, the currency is 110/200 volts AC, 50 Hz.

The majority of plugs are 2-pin sockets for both electrical currents, although there are some variations.

Bolivia

ELECTRIC PLUGS

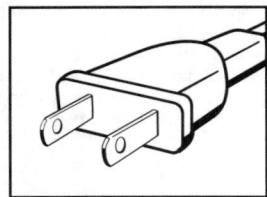

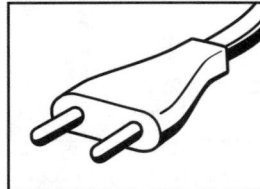

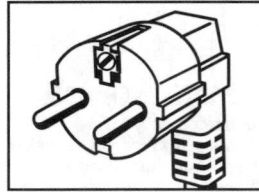

Adaptors are available through **iGo Corporation.** (See "Electrical and Telephone Adaptors" on page 19.)

Technical Support

HARDWARE/SOFTWARE VENDOR SUPPORT

Dell; (in the U.S.) tel: [1] (512) 338-4400; fax: [1] (512) 728-3330; (in Germany) tel: [49] (61) 039-710; (Dell- Europe) tel: [44] (134) 474-8000; http://www.dell.com/.

Hewlett Packard; (in the U.S.) tel: [1] (408) 246-4300; (in Argentina) tel: [54] 1-781-4061/69; (in Switzerland) tel: [41] (22) 780-8111; http://www.hp.com/.

IBM; tel: (2) 391-388; fax: (2) 361-555; fax: (2) 391-388; (U.S. Main Office) tel: [1] 914-765-1900; (in the U.S.) tel: [1] (919) 517-2800; (in Switzerland) tel: [41] (22) 310-0418 (in French); http://www.ibm.com/.

Microsoft; (Latin American HQ in U.S.) [1] (954) 489-4800; fax: [1] (954) 491-1616; (in Uruguay) tel: [598] 71-7091; (in the U.S.) [1] (425) 635-7222; (in Switzerland) tel: [41] (848) 858-868; fax [41] (1) 831-0869; http://www.microsoft.com/.

Internet Connection

HOW TO CONNECT

Connecting to AOL and Compuserve in Bolivia is similar to using it when traveling outside your own area code. See the introductory section for detailed information on connecting to your account through a different phone number.

America Online

Numbers are available at keyword *international*. Be sure to get several local numbers before leaving. AOL's Global-Net service charges US$12 an hour in addition to the usual charges. AOL has its GlobalNet service available at keyword *access* (a free area).

Access: Cochabamba (4) 257-876; La Paz: (2) 316-339; Santa Cruz (3) 322-422.

Compuserve

Numbers are available at *Go International*. The Compuserve Web-site also has a great deal of information, at http://www.compuserve.com.

Access: La Paz (2) 316-339; La Paz (Within Only) 316-551; La Paz (Within/Outside) (2) 315-876; Santa Cruz (3) 322-422.

Independent Service Providers

Many independent service providers offer discounts if you are only in town for a couple days.

BolNet; tel: (2) 316-340; email: ramiro@utama.bolnet.bo; http://www.bolnet.bo/.

CompuNet; tel: (4) 256-789; email: buzon@albatros.cnb.net; http://www.cnb.net/.

MegaLink; tel: (15) 22-149; email: admin@megalink.com; http://www.megalink.com/.

VPM Enterprises; tel: [1] (916) 983-9876; toll-free: 1-800-321-0221; fax: [1] (916) 983-4375; email: sales@vpm.com; http://www.vpm.com

Zupernet; tel: (3) 326-032; email: webmaster@zuper.net; http://www.zuper.net/

Business Culture

GREETINGS AND COURTESIES

Men and women shake hands at the beginning and end of each encounter. In smaller groups—both business and social—the host will introduce guests individually; in larger groups, you generally introduce yourself. Have business cards printed in Spanish available as a courtesy. Gifts should be modest, perhaps a token of your country or business, and only given after establishing a relationship. Do not give odd-numbered items. Other taboos include: sharp cutting objects such as letter openers, items bearing the color purple, or clothing.

DECISION MAKING

Although middle-level managers may be responsible for implementing decisions, actual decisions are almost always made at a high level of authority. While you will want to approach senior people, Bolivians will wish to match you with someone of similar business rank. It is important to cultivate personal relationships with these peers, because the quality of these relationships may strongly influence the actual decision maker, even when your immediate counterpart is not the one making the decision.

MEETINGS

Meetings should be scheduled two to three weeks in advance and reconfirmed on the meeting date. Foreigners are expected to be punctual, although locals are often late. Cafes are a popular place to do business. In this case, observe European-style etiquette and table manners. Cards are exchanged on the first business visit and modest gifts only if they have been presented to you first to avoid feelings of obligation. Bolivia's private sector business people have ample experience with U.S. and Western European business customs and practices and exhibit sophistication in that realm. A local representative is required by law for investment contracts, government agency purchases and direct sales for major products.In the case of large state-owned corporations, prepare to work with standard official red tape. Keep in mind that businesses often close for a two-hour lunch break.

WOMEN

Women in Bolivia occupy a secondary status, although they often form the backbone of small-scale enterprises and are generally afforded considerable personal freedom. Bolivian women are becoming more involved in business, and foreign businesswomen should experience few problems.

BUSINESS ATTIRE

A conservative suit will do best in a country still beset with poverty. Meetings and formal occasions require a tie. A woman can expect to wear a suit or dress. Leave flashy jewelry and expensive accessories at home, as they will not only attract unwanted attention from petty thieves but may also cause unnecessary resentment. Carry an umbrella or a raincoat from November to March.

Business Centers
La Paz

CITY VIEW

At nearly 4 km. above sea level, plants and greenery are rare in La Paz. As such, an arid, stark landscape sets the scene for the dramatic Mt. Illimani in the city's background. La Paz houses over one million residents and presides as the administrative and cultural capital of Bolivia.

AIRPORT

El Alto Airport to City Center

The airport lies 8.5 miles (14 km.) from the city center. Lloyd Aéreo Boliviano (LAB) provides a 24-hour service taking customers from the airport to the city. The trip takes approximately 20 to 30 minutes. Taxis will cost about US$8, with room for negotiation. Check with your hotel about airport transfer. Take care to watch your belongings and documents since petty theft is common at the airport.

Airline Numbers

Aerolineas Argentinas:	(2) 351711
AeroPeru	(2) 370002
Aerosur	(2) 371833
American Airlines	(2) 351360
British Airways	(2) 361332
Faucett Peruvian Airlines	(2) 325764
Iberian	(2) 358605
KLM	(2) 323965
LanChile	(2) 358377
Lloyd Aereo Boliviano	(2) 367710
Lufthansa	(2) 372170
Transportes Aereos Militares	(2) 379285
United Airlines	(2) 328397
Varig/Cruziero	(2) 314040

HOTELS

Top-end

Hacienda Villa del Sol Hotel & Spa; Puente de Aranjez no. 10, Camino Mallasa, Zona Sur; tel: (2) 740-008; fax: (2) 740-032; email: hacienda@pobox.com; 12 minutes from downtown, city outskirts; restaurant; private dining rooms; boardroom; data outlets; secretarial service; business support; pool; whirlpool; sauna; steamroom; car and driver available; US$95/115, internet promotional rate.

Hotel Plaza; Pase el Prado 1789; tel: (2) 378-311/12/13; fax: (2) 343-391; city center; restaurants; business center; spa; boutiques; email: hplaza@wara.bolnet.bo; US$110/140.

Hotel Presidente; Calle Potosí No. 920; tel: (2) 367-193; fax: (2) 354-013; restaurant; conference facilities; convention center; pool; steam and dry saunas; email: hpresi@caoba.entelnet.bo; US$116/169 (includes buffet breakfast).

Expensive

Camino Real Apart Hotel; Capitán Ravelo No. 2123; tel: (2) 314-522; fax: (2) 365-575; all rooms with kitchen; restaurant; meeting rooms; fax service; travel agency; parking; breakfast buffet included; email: caminoreal@datacom-bo.net; US$88/98.

Ritz Apart Hotel; Plaza Isabel la Catolica No. 2478; tel: (2) 433-131; fax: (2) 433-080; all suites; restaurant; secretarial service; fax; copier; 24-hour medical service; airport service; parking.

El Rey; Av. 20 de Octubre No. 1947; tel: (2) 393-016; fax: (2) 367-759; US$70/80.

Paris; Plaza Murillo esq. Bolivar; tel: (2) 319-170; fax: (2) 362-547; includes breakfast; US$70/80.

Moderate

Hotel Gloria; Calle Potosí No. 909; tel: (2) 370-010; fax: (2) 370-123; restaurants; includes breakfast; US$40/50.

Hotel Sucre Palace; Paseo el Prado No. 6136; tel: (2) 363-453; fax: (2) 390-251; includes breakfast; US$30/40.

Hotel Max Inn; Mariscal Sucre No. 1484, San Pedro; tel: (2) 374-391; fax: (2) 341-720; US$30/42.

MEDICAL CARE

Clinica Americana (English-speaking); 5809 Avenida 14 de Septiembre, Calle 9, in Obrajes (Zona Sur); tel: (2) 783-509.

Clinica Santa Maria; Av. 6 de Agosto 2487.

Unidad Sanitario Centro Piloto; tel: (2) 369-141.

AUTO RENTAL

Visitors should note that less than 5 percent of Bolivia's roads are paved, and travel outside of city regions most probably requires a 4-wheel drive vehicle. One should also note that car theft of such vehicles is high.

Hertz; General Bernardo Trigo 429; tel: (2) 325-592 or 322-654.

IMBEX Rent a Car; Avenida Montes #522; tel: (2) 379-884 or (2) 316-895; fax: (2) 379-884; cellular: 15-44376; email: imbex@khainata.com

Oscar Crespo Maurice Rent a Car; Av. Simon Bolivar 1865; tel: (2) 220-989; holidays: (2) 712-246; 24-hour tel: (2) 793-914; fax: (2) 242-608; email: ocmrent@caoba.entelnet.bo

CHAMBER OF COMMERCE

National Chamber of Commerce
Av. Mariscal Santa Cruz, No. 1392
Edificio Cámera Nacional de Comercio, piso 3
P.O. Box: 7 LP
La Paz, Bolivia
tel: (2) 378-606; fax: (2) 391-004
email: cnc@caoba.entelnet.bo

Brazil

At a Glance

THE PEOPLE

Population .... 171,853,126 (July 1999 est.)
Growth Rate .... 1.16% (1999 est.)
Life Expectancy .... 64.06 years (born 1999)
Infant Mortality . 35.37 deaths/1,000 live births (1999 est.)

Ethnic Composition

Caucasian 55%
Mulatto.. 38%
Black African 6%
Other 1%

Religious Composition

Roman Catholic.. 70%
Other and non-affiliated.. 30%

Languages Spoken

Portuguese (official), Spanish, English, French

Education and Literacy

Public education is free at all levels, and the government helps fund private schools. Literacy for the adult population is 83.5 percent.

Labor Force

Total: 65,000,000
By occupation: services 42%, industry 27%, agriculture 31%.

THE ECONOMY

Brazil has been gifted with rich mineral resources and productive agricultural land. Though the largest nation and economy in South America, it has long functioned well below its potential. Once plagued by high inflation (1,000%) its "Real Plan" of 1994 has brought the economy under control and stabilized an often erratic currency. The downturn in Asia in 1997 caused repercussions in the Brazilian stock markets from which it has not yet fully recovered. In spite of its problems, Brazil continues to attract large amounts of foreign investment intent on making inroads to the entire South American continent. There is still a great deal of concern about Brazil's ability to maintain its reserves and exchange rate should the global markets suddenly lose faith in the government's plans. Further privatization and general fiscal reforms are being watched closely as are the economies of Brazil's neighbors on whom so much depends.

Exports .... US$51 billion (f.o.b., 1998)
Imports .... US$57.6 billion (f.o.b., 1998)
Total GDP .... US$1.0352trillion (1998 est.)
GDP Per Capita .... US$6,100 (1998 est.)
Unemployment .... 8.5% (1998 est.)
Inflation Rate 2% (1998)

Top Export Partners

E.U., Latin America, United States

Top Import Partners

E.U., United States, Argentina, Japan

Top Exports

Iron ore, soybean bran, orange juice, footwear, coffee, motor vehicle parts.

Top Imports

Crude oil, capital goods, chemical products, foodstuffs, coal.

BUSINESS WORKWEEK

Offices

Monday to Friday 8:30a.m. or 9a.m. to 5:30p.m. or 6p.m.

Banks

Monday to Friday 10a.m. to 4:30p.m.

Government

Monday to Friday 9a.m. to 5p.m.

Retail

Monday to Friday 9a.m. to 6p.m., Saturday 9a.m to 12:30p.m. or 1p.m; shopping centers from 10a.m. to 10p.m.

Note: Business hours in rural areas are rarely consistent. Each locale sets its own pace in this large nation.

HOLIDAYS

Universal Confraternization Day.........................January 1
Carnival .... February 15-16*
Good Friday...April 2*
Tiradentes Day-Discovery of Brazil .... April 21
Labor Day...May 1
Corpus Christi..June 3*
Independence Day ....September 7
Our Lady Aparecida,
Patron Saint of Brazil..October 12
All Souls' Day ....November 2
Proclamation of the Republic ....November 15
Christmas ....December 25
*Date may vary by year.

CLIMATE

Seasons

The climate is varied; mostly tropical or semitropical with temperate zones. Winters (May to October) are generally mild; and in the summers (November to April) the climate is tropical all over the country. Brazil is unbearably hot from mid-December to the end of February, and the most pleasant months to visit are from April to October.

Regions

The Amazon Basin is extremely hot, and the southern plateau has a temperate temperature. Winter months in Rio de Janeiro and São Paulo are very mild to hot, while in the south of Brazil they are a bit chillier. Humidity is more extreme around the coastal towns. The northern region can suffer from frequent tropical rain from January to April, and the northeastern region has its tropical rainy season from April. Temperatures range from lows of 18°C (64°F) on the plateaus to highs of 38°C (100°F) in the interior. The average temperature is 27°C (80°F).

Money & Banking

Currency

The currency of Brazil is the Real (R$).

Denominations

The Real comes in coin denominations of R$1 and 50, 10, 5, and 1 centavos; banknotes of R$1, 5, 10, 50, 100.

Traveler's Checks and Credit Cards

Traveler's checks and most major currencies can be ex-

Brazil

States of Brazil
1 Rio Grande do Sul
2 Santa Catarina
3 Paran
4 Mato Grosso do Sul
5 S o Paulo
6 Rio de Janeiro
7 Esp rito Santo
8 Minas Gerais
9 Goi s
10 Mato Grosso
11 Rond nia
12 Acre
13 Amazonas
14 Par
15 Tocantins
16 Bahia
17 Sergipe
18 Alagoas
19 Pernambuco
20 Para ba
21 Rio Grande do Norte
22 Ceara
23 Piaui
24 Marnah o
25 Amapa
26 Rioraima

Note: Brasilia is surrounded by a federal district.

©2001 Magellan Geographix SM Santa Barbara, CA

Brazil

⊛ National capital		—— Primary road
• State capital		—— Secondary road
● Secondary city		······· Railroad
State border		International border

0   250   500   750 km
0   250   500 mi

changed at banks, exchange shops, and hotels, as well as kiosks in international airports. Banks will have the most reasonable rates and lowest service charges.

Cashing traveler's checks can be a difficult in smaller towns where commissions can run high. Weekend exchanges even in the urban areas are also difficult. Cash is best procured in the major cities before going into the rural areas. U.S. dollars are the easiest and least expensive currency to exchange.

American Express, Visa, Diner's Club, and MasterCard are accepted in most up-market places in the main cities of Brazil. Some outlets may have additional charges for credit card usuage. ATM services are widely available in urban areas. The best exchange rates are given for credit card and ATM transactions.

Visitors cannot leave the country with more money than which they arrived. Only get enough cash to last through your stay as reconversion is limited. On departure, only authorized institutions are allowed to re-convert up to US$100 into foreign exchange. The Real has little value outside of Brazil.

Travel

VISA AND PASSPORT

A passport that is valid for at least six months beyond anticipated exit date is required of all visitors, except for citizens of Argentina, Paraguay, Uruguay, and Chile who are in possession of a national identity card, and who are traveling directly from their own country to Brazil.

Visas are required of all visitors except for nationals of E.U. countries and of the following nations for tourist stays up to 90 days in duration: Andorra, Australia, Bahamas, Barbados, Bolivia, Canada, Colombia, Costa Rica, Ecuador, Iceland, Japan, Liechtenstein, Monaco, Morocco, Namibia, Norway, Peru, Trinidad & Tobago, U.K., U.S., Vatican City, and Venezuela.

Passengers in transit who do not leave the airport and are continuing their journey on a connecting flight or on the same aircraft, and who are holding confirmed tickets and other documents for onward travel, are also exempt from the need for a visa.

Brazil

Tourist visas are good for multiple entries within the 90-day period of validity. All visitors must also be in possession of onward or return tickets and sufficient funds to cover their stay.

Those traveling on business need a business visa (valid for 90 days) to engage in commerce legally and officially for purposes such as signing documents, conducting research, or executing financial transactions. The use of a tourist visa for business purposes can result in deportation. The business visa must be obtained in advance of the visit, except for U.K. nationals, who will be issued the visa on arrival, provided they fulfill all other normal tourist requirements; length of stay granted is usually a maximum of 90 days, but an extension can be obtained for a period up to six months.

Allow about a week for your visa application to be processed, in most cases.

RESTRICTED ENTRY

Travelers bearing passports issued by Central African Republic, Comoros, Korea (DPR), and Taiwan will be denied entry to Brazil, unless they are in possession of a Laissez-Passer conveyed by the Brazilian immigration authorities.

Visitors arriving from Bolivia will be given the strictest attention by customs officials due to the high level of drug traffic from that nation.

DEPARTURE FORMALITIES

The immigration permit issued to travelers upon entry to Brazil must be retained and produced when exiting. Failure to do so can result in a US$100 fine. Travelers may not take out more money than is brought into Brazil.

The airport departure tax is equivalent to US$18, payable exclusively in local currency.

CUSTOMS ENTRY (PERSONAL)

Duty-free

- Tobacco: 400 cigarettes, 250g of tobacco, or 25 cigars
- Alcohol: 2 liters of alcohol
- Up to US$500 worth of imported goods

Prohibited or Restricted

- Tourists may bring only one of each of the following items—a radio, a tape deck, a typewriter, and a camera.
- Meat and cheese products from various countries
- Other varieties of animal origin transported from Africa, Asia, Italy, Portugal and Spain.

Expect strict regulations regarding temporary import or export of items such as firearms, medications, antiquities, tropical plants, and business equipment.

IMMUNIZATION

Vaccinations and certification are not required unless arriving from areas known to be infected with yellow fever or cholera.

If intending to visit rural areas—specifically, Acre, Amazonas, Goiás, Maranhão, Mato Grosso, Mato Grosso do Sul, Pará, Rondônia, or Tocantins states and territories of Amapá and Roraim—a vaccination for yellow fever is strongly recommended, as is a weekly dose of mefloquine to ward against malaria.

Tetanus and hepatitis A shots are also advisable for those with travel plans outside of major cities.

TIPPING

Taxi

No tip is necessary for taxi drivers; but a ten percent tip for good service, or allowing drivers to keep some change, is expected from foreigners. In Rio, a 35 centavo tip per bag may be included in your fare.

Porters

Porters can expect from 50 centavos to R$1 per piece of luggage in luxury hotels. Bus and train porters receive less.

Hotels

A 10 to15 percent service charge is included in the bill, but an additional 5 percent to staff is standard.

Restaurants

Tipping 10 to 15 percent in bars and cafes is normal when service charges have not been added. There is a tendency to add the charges for Europeans and leave them off for Americans who are thought to be great tippers.

Other

Chambermaids, 50 centavos per day (in luxury hotels); valet and room service R$1; barbers & beauticians: 10 to 20 percent; washroom and shoe shine: 10 to 15 centavo.

EMERGENCY INFORMATION

Police and Crime

Crimes against visitors tend to be more common in areas surrounding hotels, bars, discotheques, nightclubs, and other similar establishments, particularly during the evening. Several Brazilian cities have formed special tourist police patrols that concentrate on such areas. (Tourists are nicknamed "filet mignon").

A high incidence of crime also takes place in buses and subway stations. Stay alert and watch your belongings. Women should avoid walking or traveling alone, particularly at night.

- Tourists in Rio de Janeiro are vulnerable to robberies and street thefts in areas close to the main beaches.
- There is a high rate of armed robbery at stoplights in all areas of Sao Paulo.
- The hotel district in Brasilia has been the site of numerous violent assaults in recent years; the relative safety of a taxi is advised when venturing out at night.

Rio de Janeiro is also notable for the huge number of street kids who survive by begging, stealing, and acting as runners for local drug dealers, and committing whatever other crimes that may put food in their mouths. The University of Sao Paulo estimates that police kill about five of these children every day. It is a pitiful scene and a potential source of crime and assault against the unwary visitor.

Be aware of your surroundings at all times. Do not resist in case of armed robbery. Surrender valuables and contact the police immediately. Thieves work in gangs and are not beyond using violence even to procure small amounts of money.

Foreign business visitors are often the target of specialized thieves. Consequently, purses, laptops, and briefcases will require additional security. Do not leave valuables in cars or on tables at cafés. Keep non-essential valuables locked in hotel safes when not in use. Use credit cards and travel checks when possible to avoid carrying large sums of cash.

All visitors should carry photocopies of their passport and immigration documents instead of the originals. Carry cash in a money belt, and use credit cards or traveler's checks for most of your transactions.

The police are either overwhelmed or part of the problem. You may even be shaken down by police in rural areas looking for bribes. Do not expect to recover stolen goods and insure accordingly. Contact your consulate in an emergency.

Emergency Numbers

Numbers function nationwide

Ambulance 192
Fire 193
Military Police 190
Civil Police... 147
Rio Tourist Police 511-5112

Health

Avoid tap water, even for brushing your teeth. Also stay away from using ice cubes except in first-class hotels. Diarrhea is common for travelers who are unaccustomed to the new diet, the water, and the humid heat. Be very careful of raw vegetables and fruit unless they've been washed in a chlorine solution. Take care to eat fresh, hot, and well-cooked seafood and meat. Milk and dairy products are pasteurized in the main cities, but should first be boiled, or avoided altogether, in rural areas.

The sun is intense, so, be careful on the beaches or even while walking in the urban areas. More deadly problems of cholera and malaria exist mainly in the Amazon Basin region and in northeastern Brazil.

Risk of exposure to malaria is constant throughout the year at altitudes below 900m in most of the country. The recommended preventative measure is a weekly dose of 250mg of mefloquine.

There are numerous other infectious diseases which can be easily contracted in the countryside. It is advisable to consult with your physician before your trip if you anticipate spending much time in rural areas.

Medical care in Brazil is adequate but expensive. Most hotels have access to multi-lingual doctors, otherwise contact your embassy or consulate. Travel insurance is advisable for all visitors. Evacuation policies are recommended for those business visitors who will be working in remote areas.

For more information on medical centers, including phone numbers, please see the "Business Centers" section at the end of this chapter.

INTERNAL TRAVEL

AIR

Brazil has one of the world's most extensive domestic air networks, providing connections between all major cities. Shuttle services run between São Paulo and Rio de Janeiro, and between Brasília and Belo Horizonte. There is also a regular service that links São Paulo directly with Brasília. Schedules and fares are listed in "Aeronautico," a monthly magazine that prints information for the country's entire domestic air network.

The Brazil Air Pass offers discounted air travel for a 21-day period. It is available for purchase only outside the country through Varig Brazilian Airlines and can be obtained in conjunction exclusively with an international carrier ticket of either Varig or British Airways. Passengers have three options:

- a pass covering all of Brazil
- a pass limited to the central and southern regions
- a pass that provides travel in the northeast part of the country

Prices range between US$290-540.
Inquiries to Varig Brazilian Airlines:
Tel .... (020) 7287-1414, 7287-3131
Fax ....(020) 7478-2199

Expect a departure tax of R$15 from both Rio de Janeiro and Sao Paulo.

TAXI

In most cities, taxis have red license plates and are fitted with meters. When unmetered, negotiate a fare before getting underway. Take care when accepting a driver's advice on where to go and where to stay. They are often paid a commission by hotels and restaurants and may not have the visitor's best interests in mind.

Two types of cabs exist in Rio, the yellow city cabs, which run about 20 percent cheaper, and the larger, air conditioned *taxi espicial*. This latter type has drivers that speak English, and the service can be ordered by phone or found outside of airports and hotels. Also, consider renting a cab and driver for a day rather than renting a car. Let the hotel recommend a driver.

AUTO

Rental cars (and motorbikes) are available in the major cities, but rates are high and the paperwork is ponderous. A credit card and valid driver's license are required. Local insurance is mandatory.

Parking in cities proves extremely difficult, and motorists are well advised to avoid the congested urban areas if possible. Driving in Brazil is "frenetic" and the traffic is horrible. Auto rental should be undertaken only by experienced visitors to Brazil. Cars with drivers can also be hired by the day and week.

TRAIN

Limited rail connections link most major towns and cities; but due to the great distances and the hot, humid climate, many travelers find these journeys to be uncomfortable. Ninety-five percent of Brazil's 22,000km (13,640 miles) of track are within 480km (300 miles) of the Atlantic coastline.

Daytime and overnight rail service, outfitted with restaurant cars and sleepers, link São Paulo and Rio de Janeiro. Connections to Buenos Aires, Santiago, Montevideo, La Paz, Santa Cruz, and Antofagasta are also available.

Due to the large size of the country, most business people use regularly scheduled air routes for inter-city travel.

URBAN / METRO

Both Rio and São Paulo have subway systems that can get you speedily across town and away from the nightmarish traffic taking place above ground. Schedules are fairly accurate and fees are low. Both lines stay open until 11p.m.

Trolleybuses run in São Paulo and in several other cities.

Fares are usually regulated with interchange between metro/ rail lines and bus routes. A feeder bus links the Rio metro with Copacabana, a popular example of this arrangement.

BUSES & TRAMS

There are extensive bus systems in all the main cities, many with air-conditioned "executivo" express coaches operating at premium fares. Local buses also run throughout Rio; however, the high incidence of crime on board does not encourage one to use them.

WATER TRAVEL

Brazil has an extensive river and ocean passenger boat service system. There are ferries that serve all ports along the Atlantic coast; boat trips are also available between the mainland and the beautiful islands of Ilha Grande, Ilhabela, and Ilha de Santa Catarina.

River transport is by far the most efficient mode of travel through the Amazon Delta. The Amazon and its tributaries offer some of the only routes to smaller villages, but travel on the river system can be dangerous, in terms of both crime and physical conditions. If your business necessitates its usage, allow trusted local business associates to set up the trip for you. Travel to the interior of Brazil intimidates Brazilians themselves, so foreigners must take care.

Brazil

TRAVEL ASSISTANCE

EMBRATUR ‹Instituto Brasileiro de Turismo (Brazilian Tourist Board)
SCN, Quadra 02
BLG 2/A, CEP 70710-500 Bras'lia, DF
tel: (61) 328-9100; Fax: (61) 328-3517
website: www.embratur.gov.br
Turisrio (State Tourism Board); Rua da Assembléia 10, 7th and 8th Floors, Rio de Janeiro; tel: (021) 531-1922.
Riotur (City Tourism Dept.); Rua da Assembléia 10, and other branches; tel: (021) 205-6447.

Essential Terms

English	Portuguese
Yes	Sim
No	Não
Good morning	Bom dia
Hello (daytime)	Boa tarde
Hello (evening)	Boa noite
Hello (telephone)	Alô
Good-bye	Adeus / Tchau
Please	Por favor
Thank you	Obrigado(a)
Pleased to meet you	Prazer em conhecê-lo (a)
Excuse me; I'm sorry	Licensa, desculpe
My name is _____	Eu me chamo_____
I don't understand	Eu não entendo
Do you speak English?	Você fala inglês?

Communications
DIALING CODES IN BRAZIL
International country code: [55]
Selected city codes: Brasilia (61), Pelotas (532), Porto Alegre (51), Rio de Janeiro (21), Salvador (71), Santos (132), São Paulo (11)

Dialing Brazil from Overseas
To dial Brazil from overseas, dial your country's international dialing code, then 55 (the country code for Brazil), then the city code and finally the number. Remember when dialing a Brazil number from outside the country, omit the zero proceeding the area code. If you were dialing Brasilia from the United States, for example, you would begin with 011, then 55, then 61 (the city code for Brasilia), and finally the number of the person or office you are trying to reach.

Assistance Numbers
International Call Information 000-333
International Operator 000-111
Local Operator (Portuguese)......................... 100
Information 102
Domestic Long Distance

Collect calls from public phones.................................. 107*
Collect calls from blue public phones.................. 000-107
AT&T in Rio de Janeiro 21-541-4944
*after dialing, ask for an international operator

CALLING WITHIN BRAZIL
One blaring complaint many visitors have in Brazil, most specifically in Rio de Janeiro, is the state of the telephone service. Not only are all telephone calls subject to a 20 percent tax., but the service often proves faulty. Needless to say, an extra dose of patience is required, and perhaps another mode of communication.

Long Distance Calls
All parts of Brazil are connected by DDD, the trunk dialing system. When calling long-distance within Brazil, first dial a zero, then the city code, found in the front of the phone directory, and the number you wish to reach.

International Calls
North America, Japan and most of Europe are linked to Brazil by a trunk dialing system (DDI). Telephone directories list the country codes. To make a direct call, dial 00 + country code + area code + phone number. Brazil has a 40 percent tax for international calls, making speech costly, but prices drop by 25 percent between 8p.m. and 5a.m. daily and all day Sunday. Brazil's national phone company, Embratel, operates Home Country Direct from private phones, hotels and the international public phones requiring a two-digit code for access: Argentina (54); Canada (14); Chile (56); France (33); Italy (39); Japan (81); Holland (31); Portugal (35); Sweden (46); U.K. (44); U.S.A. AT&T (10); MCI (12); Sprint (16); Uruguay (59).
AT&T Direct.. 000-8010
MCI Direct 000-8012
Sprint.. 000-8016

PAY PHONES
Public Telephones

Card Phones:

Instructions
1. Pick up receiver and listen for tone.
2. Insert calling card.
3. Dial number.
4. Speak into receiver.

Public Telephones
Two kinds of public phones, *orelhões*, exist: yellow for local calls, and blue for intercity (interurbana) calls. All pay telephones require a token called a *ficha*, a substitute for coins. They are available at newsstands, some major hotels, and at telephone office branches. Bear in mind that local and long-distance *fichas* exist. It is advisable to buy several to avoid getting cut off, specially if dialing long distance.

CELLULAR PHONES

Brazil's cellular service runs mostly on an AMPS analogue system, meaning GSM users are currently out of luck. A multitude of operators handle cellular services throughout Brazil.

Note: Your home country cell phone may not work in this country. If not, we recommend that you rent an international cell phone *before* you leave home. A major US-based cell phone rental provider is **IMC WorldCell**. For information see "International Cell Phone Rentals" on page 14.

CALL BACK

You can (potentially) save significant sums when calling in Brazil by using a call back service. For a list of callback services, please refer to the "Communications" section in the *Global Road Warrior* Introduction.

Fees for call back services vary widely, depending on the company and the type of service required. Be sure to check with these companies before leaving to compare rates.

PHONE JACKS

Adaptors are available through **iGo Corporation.** (See "Electrical and Telephone Adaptors" on page 19.)

FAX

Many offices and business centers in major hotels have fax capabilities, but the quality is poor compared to modern countries. Be sure to call and alert the office you wish to reach that you are sending a fax. Be sure to translate the cover letter into Portuguese. The executive reading the letter may understand your language, but the person taking it off the fax machine probably will not.

POSTAL SERVICES

Red tape abounds in the Brazilian postal service. Letters can take four to six days to reach the U.S. or the U.K., or up to two weeks to reach Canada. Stamps are only available at the post office. If possible, ask to have the letter metered. Stamps must be applied with the glue separately, which can be messy.

Business Services

COURIER SERVICES

Airborne Express (Messenger Express Rio); Rua Pedro Guedes 55, Maracana, Rio de Janeiro 20271-040; tel: (21) 568-9427; fax: (21) 263-0204; (International Bonded Couriers in Sao Paulo), Intl. Messenger Express, Rua Curitiba, 12; Tatuape, Sao Paulo, SP, 03086 100; tel: (11) 6942-9531; fax: (11) 218-5425.

DHL (MKS Transportes Especiais Ltda.); Rua Teofilo Otoni No. 15; Lojas A e B, Rio de Janeiro, FJ; tel: (21) 263-5454.

United Couriers; tel: (21) 284-1528; fax: (21) 264-8626.

UPS DO Brasil; Rua Condess DO Pinhal, 158, Sao Paulo, Brazil 04610-060; tel: (11) 241-0122 or (11) 536-9599; fax: (11) 533-2363.

PRINTING/COPYING

Document Center; Av. Olegário Maciel 511; Rio de Janeiro; tel.: 493 23 80; fax: 493 02 82.

Real Gráfica; São Paulo; tel257-4620/8033.

TRANSLATION SERVICES

Jose Carlos/ M. Maron; Rua Gustavo Sampaio, 374 / apto 102; Rio de Janeiro; telefax: (21) 275-2514 / 268-7515.

Rejane Carvalho; Av. Aquarela do Brasil; 333 BL 02 Apto 301; Rio de Janeiro; tel.: (21) 247-3577.

Electrical

Current

110 volts AC, 60Hz.
All plugs are of the 2-pin type.

ELECTRIC PLUGS

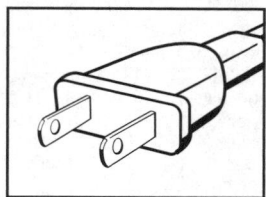

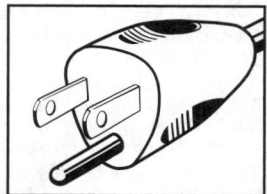

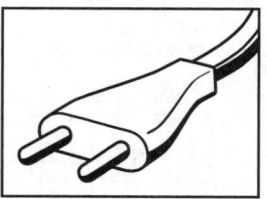

Brazil

Plug adaptors are available through **iGo Corporation.** (See "Electrical and Telephone Adaptors" on page 19.)

Technical Support

HARDWARE/SOFTWARE VENDOR SUPPORT

Acer/Texas Instruments; (in Germany) tel: [49] (4102) 488-469; fax; [49] (4102) 488-169; (in the U.S.) [1] (408) 432-6200; http://www.acer.com.

Adobe; (in Venezuela) tel: [582] 266.0176; fax: [582] 266-0757 (All Adobe Products); (in the U.S.) tel: [1] (800) 500-7078; (in Switzerland) tel: [41] (800) 833-310; http://www.adobe.com/.

Apple/Claris; tel: 11-886-8000; (in Switzerland) tel: [41] (800) 833-310; (in the U.K.) tel: [44] (990) 127-753; (in the U.S.) tel: [1] (800) 500-7078; http://www.apple.com/.

AST; (in the U.S.) tel: [1] (817) 232-9824 (International Technical Support); (in Ireland) tel: [353] (61) 492-222; (in the U.S.) tel: [1] (949) 727-4141; http://www.ast.com/.

Compaq/Digital; tel: 11-246-7866; fax: 11-524-8050; (General U.S.) tel: (281) 518-2000; (in Switzerland) tel: [41] (22) 709-5330; fax: [41] (22) 709-5391 (Geneva); tel: [41] (1) 801-2507; fax: [41] (1) 801-2172 (Zurich); http://www.compaq.com/.

Corel; tel: 011-5505-4725 (All Applications); (in the U.S.) tel: [1] (716) 871-2325 (Ask to be Forwarded to Appropriate Program); (in Germany) tel: [49] (180) 425-8210 (TS Word Perfect-32 bit); http://www.corel.com/.

Dell; (in the U.S.) tel: [1] (512) 338-4400; (in Germany) tel: [49] (61) 039-710; (Dell- Europe) tel: [44] (134) 474-8000; fax: [1] (512) 728-3330; http://www.dell.com/.

Filemaker/Claris; (in the U.S.) tel: [1] (800) 965-9090; (in Germany) tel: [49] (180) 525-8166 (Info-line); fax: [49] (180) 567-2233; tel: [49] (180) 523-6423; http://www.claris.com/.

Gateway 2000; (in the U.S.) tel: [1] (605) 232-2191; fax: [1] (605) 232-2023; (in Ireland) tel: [353] (1) 797-2000; http://www.g2k.com/.

Hewlett Packard; (in the U.S.) tel: [1] (408) 246-4300; tel: 11-709-1444; (in Switzerland) tel: [41] (22) 780-8111; http:/www.hp.com/.

IBM; tel: 0800-111-426 (toll free in Brazil); fax: 0800-133426 (toll free in Brazil); tel:11-886-3122; fax: 11-886-

3185; (U.S. Main Office) tel: [1] 914-765-1900; (in the U.S.) tel: [1] (919) 517-2800; (in Switzerland) tel: [41] (22) 310-0418 (in French); http://www.ibm.com/.

Microsoft; tel: (11) 822-5764; tel: (11) 5514-7100; fax: (11) 5514-7107/5514-7108; (11) 5506-8087 (Technical Support Phone); (11) 5506-7621 (Technical Support Fax); (in the U.S.) [1] (425) 635-7222; (in Switzerland) tel: [41] (848) 858-868; fax [41] (1) 831-0869; http://www.microsoft.com/.

NEC; tel: (11) 285-3366; tel: (11) 238-9600; fax: (11) 251-5787; (in the U.S.) [1] (916) 388-0101 (Main Switchboard); http://www.nec.com/.

Novell; tel: 000-811-638-0550 (Toll Free Technical Support); (in the U.S.) tel: [1] (408) 434-2300; fax: [1] (408) 577-5775 (Worldwide Sales Headquarters); (in Switzerland) tel: [41] (1) 308-4747; fax: [41] (1) 302-0401; http://www.novell.com/.

Quark; (in the U.S.) tel: [1] (303) 894-8899; fax: [1] (303) 894-3398 (For Products Registered in the Americas); (in Switzerland) tel: [41] (1) 808-7722; fax: [41] (1) 808-7799; http://www.quark.com/.

Toshiba; (in the U.S.) [1] (949) 583-3000 (Corporate Headquarters); (in Germany) tel: [49] (2131) 158-319; fax: [49] (2131) 158-558; (in Switzerland) tel: [41] (1) 946-0777; fax: [41] (1) 946-0807; (in Ireland) tel: [44] (193) 282-8828; http://www.toshiba.com/.

Internet Connection

HOW TO CONNECT

Connecting to AOL and Compuserve in Japan is similar to using it when traveling outside your own area code. See the introductory section for detailed information on connecting to your account through a different phone number.

America Online

Numbers are available at keyword *international*. Be sure to get several local numbers before leaving. AOL's Global-Net service charges US$12 an hour in addition to the usual charges. AOL has its GlobalNet service available at keyword *access* (a free site).

Access: Belem (91) 230-0900; Belo Horizonte (31) 271-7036; Brasilia (61) 321-0874; Campinas (19) 237-1377; Curitiba (41) 232-2120; Fortaleza (85) 264-3699; Manaus (92) 633-9198; Porto Alegre (51) 212-4999; Recife (81) 421-6262; Rio de Janeiro (21) 296-5323; Salvador (71) 358-2777; Sao Paulo (11) 5586-3200.

Compuserve

Numbers are available at *Go International*. The Compuserve Web-site also has a great deal of information, at http://www.compuserve.com.

Access: Belo Horizonte (31) 271-7036; Brasilia (61) 321-0874; Campinas (19) 237-1377; Porto Alegre (51) 212-4999; Rio de Janeiro (21) 296-5323; Sao Paulo (11) 108-1212; Sao Paulo (11) 5586-3200; Sao Paulo (11) 3824-4900.

Independent Service Providers

Many independent service providers offer discounts if you are only in town for a couple of days.

AmchamNet-Americam Chamber of Commerce for Brazil; tel: (11) 5180-3804; email: amhost@amcham.com.br/; http://www.amcham.com.br/.

Centroln; tel: (21) 542-4849; fax: (21) 295-2978; email: admin@centroin.com.br; http://www.centroin.net/.

Dialdata Systems; (São Paulo only); tel: (11) 829-4731; fax: (11) 822-4588; http://www.dialdata.com.br/.

Hipernet Telecom; tel: (11) 3741-9333; fax: 11 3741.9334; email: telecom@hipernet.com.br; http://www.hipernet.com.br/.

Horizontes Internet; tel: (31) 289-1900; fax: (31) 289-1919; email: webmaster@horizontes.com.br; http://www.horizontes.com.br/.

InfoNet Servicos Ltda.; tel: (79) 211-6277; email: webmaster@infonet.com.br; http://www.infonet.com.br/.

RioLink Internet; tel: (21) 577-8899; email: riolink@rio.com.br; http://www.rio.com.br/.

Business Culture

GREETINGS AND COURTESIES

Portuguese-speaking Brazilians are generally less formal than their Spanish-speaking Latin compatriots. Brazilians of both sexes shake hands upon meeting and when departing. Men's handshakes tend to be prolonged by most standards, especially when first introduced. Women friends touch alternate cheeks in a "kiss" (married women kiss twice, while a single woman receives a third kiss). In business, men are addressed as *Senhor* plus their surname (women as *Senhora* plus the surname). Brazilians often move rapidly to first names, often used with a title or honorific (such as *Douter—Dr.—*Fernando) for professionals. Business cards (printed in your language and Portuguese) are a necessity. Say goodbye to everyone individually when leaving.

DECISION MAKING

Although middle-level managers may be responsible for implementing decisions, actual decisions are almost always made at a high level of authority. While you should approach senior people, Brazilians will want to know your standing within the hierarchy and will wish to match you with someone of similar rank, while only their senior people will actually be able to approve agreements. Nevertheless, it is important to cultivate personal relationships with these peers, because the quality of these relationships may strongly influence the actual decision maker even when your immediate counterpart is not the one making the decision.

WOMEN

Women in Brazil occupy a secondary status in this traditionally male-dominated society, although many operate businesses and are generally accorded considerable personal freedom. Brazilian women are becoming more involved and accepted in business, and foreign businesswomen should experience few problems. Foreign female visitors should recognize that Brazilian men are easily encouraged and persistent; and that while physical contact is considered unacceptable, bold comments and exaggerated leering are commonplace. Foreign businesswomen are expected to be highly professional and not aggressive or confrontational.

MEETINGS

Contacts and introductions are important. If you do not have a mutual business acquaintance to make introductions, consult your embassy for a referral. Make appointments at least two weeks in advance. Do not try to schedule too many meetings: you are almost sure to be kept waiting for anywhere from 15 minutes to more than an hour—although you should be on time. Meetings are often interrupted and do not end abruptly. Business lunches are common, dinners less so, although business-related after-hours entertaining is highly developed.

BUSINESS ATTIRE

Brazilian standards of dress are less formal than those in other Latin American countries. Nevertheless, men should wear business suits, although they can wear a more broad range of colors and styles—for example, Italian suits in lighter weights and colors in place of the traditional dark conservative British tailoring favored elsewhere in South America. Executives usually wear three-piece suits. All ranks wear long-sleeved shirts. Foreign businesswomen should wear business suits or dresses, but more stylishness, color, makeup, and accessories are accepted and appreciated, especially in larger, coastal cities (dress is somewhat more traditional in less cosmopolitan inland locations). When invited to a home, men wear a suit, women a dress. For less formal social occasions, men wear shirts and trousers and women dresses or skirts—or pants—and blouses. Ties are seldom required for social events, although jackets may be. Jeans and sandals are for "kids," and are therefore un-businesslike. Both sexes should wear regular shoes and avoid shorts. Women in general have greater freedom in dress—although local fashions are often brash and provocative and dress that is too informal may invite unwanted attention.

Business Centers
Rio de Janeiro

CITY VIEW

Rio is a mixed blessing: one of the most beautiful landscapes in the world, crammed with seven million people and their share of waste. Despite many of the bad images Rio conjures: hillsides covered with shantytowns (called *favelas*), dirty streets, and massive poverty, business opportunities abound, and the Rio residents are among the friendliest in the world. Business tends to slow to a crawl during the Carnival.

AIRPORT

Galeão Airport to City Center

The airport lies about 12.5 miles (20 km.) northwest of the city. In the frenzy outside of arrivals, circumvent the yellow city cabs and look for the special airport taxis ("taxi especial") or the airport express buses (one of which is the Empresa Real), which shuttle passengers to all of the major hotels along the beach every 30 minutes between 5:20a.m. and 11:00p.m. If your hotel is located further away from the beach, buses will drop you at the nearest corner. The special air conditioned cabs will cost around about R$40 to Ipanema. Yellow cabs will cost about half. Traffic from the airport to the city is usually gridlocked; figure about 50 minutes to get downtown in this case.

Santos Dumont Airport

If shuttling to or from São Paulo, you will arrive at Rio's downtown airport, which lies 5 minutes from the beaches. The same transport guidelines apply as they do for Galeão Airport, except that fares will cost less, about R$24 to Ipanema.

Airline Numbers

Aerolineas Argentina	(21) 224-9242
Aero Peru	(21) 240-1622, (21) 240-0722
Air Canada	(21) 532-7200
Air France	(21) 220-2192
American Airlines	(21) 210-3126
Avianca	(21) 240-4413
British Airways	(21) 221-0922

Equatoriana ....(21) 240-1075
Iberia ....(21) 210-2415
Japan Air Lines ....(21) 221-9663
KLM ....(21) 210-1342
Lan Chile ....(21) 242-1423
Lineas Aereas Paragauyas ....(21) 220-4148
Lloyd Aero Boliviano ....(21) 220-9548
Lufthansa ....(21) 398-3855, (21) 262-0223
Pan Am ....(21) 240-2322
SAS ....(21) 210-1222
Vaisa ....(21) 224-5345

HOTELS

Top-end

Caesar Park; Avenida Vieira Souto, 460, Ipanema Beach; tel: (21) 287-3122; fax: (21) 247-7975; restaurants; conference rooms, health club, parking, pool; sauna; golf club access; R$327/455.

Inter-Continental Rio; 222 Avenida Prefeito Mendes de Morais, Sao Conrado; tel: (21) 322-2200; fax: (21) 322-5500; restaurants; business services; meeting facilities; health club; pool; sauna; tennis.

Rio Atlantica; Av. Atlântica, 2964, Copacabana; beachfront; restaurant; business center; conference rooms; multilingual staff; health club; parking; R$216/278.

Rio Palace; Avenida Atlântica, 4240, Copacabana; tel: (21) 521-3232; fax: (21) 247-1961; restaurant; business center; meeting services; gym; pool; sauna; R$216.

Sheraton Rio Hotel & Towers; Avenida Niemeyer, 121, Vidigal Beach; tel: (21) 274-1122; fax: (21) 239-5643; restaurant; business center; medical assistance; gym; pool; sauna; R$256/325.

Expensive

Copacabana Palace; Avenida Atlântica, 1702; Copacabana Beach; tel: (21) 255-7070 or 800/237-1236 in the U.S.; fax: (21) 235-7330; restaurant; pool; sauna; tennis; beach service.

Everest Rio; Rua Prudente de Morais, 1117, Ipanema Beach; tel: (21) 287-8282; fax: (21) 521-3198; restaurant; pool; sauna; tennis; beach service; business center.

Hótel Gloria; Rua do Russel, 632, Gloria; tel: (21) 205-7272; fax: (21) 245-1660; business hotel; restaurant; conference facilities; health club; golf; tennis; traditional style; R$150.

Hotel Pousada Galeão; international airport, 1st Floor, Red Sector; tel/fax: (21) 398-3852/53/54; multilingual services; fax; VIP services; R$126/132.

Rio Othon Palace; Avenida Atlântica, 3264, Copacabana; tel: 521-5522; fax: 521-6697; restaurant; business center; meeting facilities; health club; pool; US$140/168.

Moderate

Copa Sul Hotel; Av. N. Sra. de Copacabana, 1284; tel: (21) 247-7588; fax: (21) 287-7497; restaurant; multilingual services; meeting rooms; copy machine; doctor on call; airport limo; R$50/77.

Debret; Av. Atlântica, 2230, Copacabana Beach; tel: (21) 521-3332; fax: (21) 521-0899; good location; restaurant; breakfast included; US$48/55.

Grande Hotel São Francisco; Rua visconde de Inhauma, 95, Centro; tel: (21) 223-1224; fax: (21) 233-2364; city center; restaurants; convention center; multilingual services; copy machine; covered garage; R$78/87.

Novo Mundo; Praia do Flamengo, 20, Flamengo; tel: (21) 205-3355; fax: (21) 265-2364; meeting facilities.

Ouro Verde; Av. Atlántica 4240; tel: (21) 542-1887; fax: (21) 542-4597.

Vermont; Rua Visconde de Pirajá; tel: (21) 521-0057; fax: (21) 267-7046; includes self-serve breakfast buffet; US$60/70.

HEALTH CLUB

Heavy Duty Gym; Praca Arcoverde, 181 Rua Barata Ribeiro, Store I, Copacabana; tel: (21) 542-3045.

AUTO RENTAL

Note: Driving in Rio can resemble a bad day in Los Angeles. Traffic jams and very limited parking urge any potential driver to think twice before renting.

Avis; Rua 7 de Abril, 345-7 Adar 01243-000 Sao Paulo; tel: (11) 259-2188; toll-free in Brazil, tel: 0800-558-066; outside Brazil, tel: (11) 259-2188; International airport location; tel: (21) 398-3361/3357; Santos Dumont Airport, tel: (21) 262-3617/220-0171.

Hertz; International airport location; tel: (21) 398-4338; fax: 394-4337; Santos Dumont Airport, tel: (21) 240-3882; fax: (21) 262-0612; reservations, tel: (21) 240-3644 (intl.); toll-free: 0800-111-8900 (international); fax: (21) 533-0439.

Localiza; International airport location; tel: 398-5989; Santos Dumont national airport location, tel: (21) 220-5455; fax: (21) 275-1043.

WORLD TRADE CENTER

World Trade Center Rio de Janeiro
Rua da Candelaria, 9-11 andar, Centro
Rio de Janeiro, Brazil 20091-020
tel: (21) 233-8597
fax: (21) 253-3200

São Paulo

CITY VIEW

Nearly 17 million people call São Paulo home. More formal and conservative than its northern business counterpart, São Paulo stands as a cultural and educational center, and despite the pollution and crime, most people who live in São Paulo enjoy boasting about their home city.

AIRPORT

Guarulhos Airport to City Center

The airport lies 15 miles (25 km.) from the city; allow 25 5o 50 minutes to go downtown. There are regular bus and taxi services. And airport bus running every 25 minutes costs about US$6. Although Guarulhos is the main airport in São Paulo, there are two others: Viracopos and Congonhas. There is a regular bus that services the airports and transports passengers to each one.

Regular and radio taxis service Guarulhos. Purchase tickets at taxi counters in the arrival area of the airport. Regular cabs may cost you around R$25 to 40. A tourist information service, open from 9a.m. to 10p.m. can also assist.

Airline Numbers

Aerolíneas Argentinas.............................214-4233
Aeroperu..257-4866
Air Aruba 212-6864
Air Canada 258-1977
Air France...288-6577, 945-2211
Alitalia...257-1922, 945-2324
American Airlines 214-4000, 258-1244
Austral 259-6100
Austrian Airlines 257-0381
Avianca..259-8455
British Airways 259-6144

Canadian 259-9066, 945-2462
Cathay Pacific 259-0306
China Airlines 259-4066
Continental 239-1860
Ecuatoriana 259-6100
Iberia 258-5333, 945-2060
KLM 257-4011
Korean Air 283-2399
Lab Airlines..............................258-8111. 945-2425
Ladeco..257-8844
Lan Chile 259-2900. 945-2824
La Paraguayas 259-3128, 945-2404
Lufthansa....................................256-9833, 945-2220
Mexicana 255-5759
Panatanal 241-8794, 815-7733
Pluna 231-2822, 945-2130
Rio Sul 231-9164, 531-0533
SAS 259-4300
Swissair 251-4000
Taba 255-6600
Tap 259-5155, 945-2150
Tam 0800-123-100
Trans Brazil Airlines 231-1988, 945-2234
TWA 816-2578
United Airlines 253-2323, 258-0811
USAir 214-3001
Varig..534-0579, 531-0749
Vasp 220-3622, 531-0749

HOTELS

Top-end
Caesar Park Hotel Säi Paulo; Rua Augusta, 1.508; tel: (11) 253-6622; fax: (11) 288-6146; city center; restaurant; secretarial service; conference center; fitness room; sauna; parking; R$330.

Grande Hotel Ca d'Oro; Rua Augusta, 129; tel: (11) 236-4300; fax: (11) 236-4311; city center; restaurant; secretarial service; conference center; fitness center; pool; sauna; US$270.

Inter Continental São Paulo; Alameda Santos, 1.123, Jardins; tel: (11) 3179-2600; fax: (11) 3179-2619; restaurant; secretarial service; conference center; computers; fax; fitness center; R$335/365.

São Paulo Hilton; Av. Ipiranga 165; tel: (11) 256-0033; fax: (11) 257-3137; restaurant; executive services; conference center; fitness; health; pool; sauna; R$256/278.

Sheraton Mofarrej São Paulo; Al. Santos, 1.437, Jardins; tel: (11) 253-5544; fax: (11) 289-8670; restaurant; business center; conference center; health club; pool; shops; parking; heliport; R$370/395.

Expensive
Best Western São Paulo Center; Largo Sta. Efigênia, 40; tel: (11) 228-6033; fax: (11) 229-0959; restaurant; secretarial service; conference center.

Hotel Eldorado Higienópolis; Rua Marques de Itu, 836; tel: (11) 224-0666; fax: (11) 222-7194; restaurant; conference center; secretarial service; computer terminal; parking; pool; R$123/135.

Hotel Gran Corona; Rua Basilio da Gama 101; tel: (11) 259-8177; fax: (11) 257-5025; city center; restaurant; conference center; parking; R$115/130.

Novotel São Paulo Morumbi; Rua Ministro Nelson Hungria, 450; tel: (11) 844-6211; fax: (11) 844-5262; restaurant; conference center; parking; pool; R$145/174.

São Paulo Othon Palace Hotel; Rua Libero Badaro 190; tel: (11) 239-3277; fax: (11) 37-7203; restaurant; conference center; shops; parking; R$148/165.

Moderate
Augusta Palace Hotel; Rua Augusta, 467; tel: (11) 256-1277; fax: (11) 259-9637; city center; restaurant; business center; parking; pool; sauna; R$105/120.

Bristol Hotel; Rua Martins Fontes, 277; tel: (11) 258-0011; fax: (11) 231-1265; city center; R$80/90.

Horsa Excelsior São Paulo; Av. Ipiranga, 770; tel: (11) 220-0377; fax: (11) 2221-6653; restaurant; conference center; sauna; R$95.

MEDICAL CARE

Albert Einstein Hospital; 627 Avenida Albert Einstein, Morumbi, Zona Sul; tel: (11) 845-1233.

Hospital das Clínicas; 255 Avenida Doctor Enéas de Carvalho de Aguiar, Cerqueira Cesar; tel: (11) 282-2811.

Hospital São Paulo; Rua Napoleão de Barros, 715-V, Clementino; tel: (11) 549-0344.

Instant Cardiac Assistance; 44 Avenida Doctor Enéas de Carvalho de Aguiar, Cerqueira Cesar; tel: (11) 282-7766.

Samaritan Hospital; 1486 Rua Conselheiro Brotero, Higienopolis; tel: (11) 824-0022.

HEALTH CLUBS

Physis Ginasio de Condicionamento; 1336 Avenida Doutor Cardoso de Melo Vila Olympia;
tel: (11) 829-7522.

Projeto Acqua; 180 Rua Chipre, Vila Olympia; tel: (11) 829-0522.

Competition; 1080 Rua Albuquerque Lins near Avenida Anjelica Higienopolis; tel: (11) 825-1733.

AUTO RENTAL

Avis; International Airport Guarulhos; tel: (11) 945-2180; 0800-11-8066.

Budget; 328 Rua Consolação, Centro; tel: (11) 259-4122, 256-4355; fax: (11) 256-4793; airport, (11) 259-4122; local reservation center, tel: (11) 256-4355, 945-3020; fax: (11) 945-3505.

Fleet Car Rental; R. Rio Grande, 493, Vila Mariana; tel: (11) 575-2433.

Hertz; reservations, tel: (11) 214-8900 Intl.); toll-free: 0800-147-300 (domestic), 0800-11-8900 (intl.); fax: (11) 3064-5114; Rua da Consolação, 307; tel: (11) 258-8422; fax: (11) 256-2317; airport, tle: (11) 6445-2801; fax: (11) 6445-3119; chauffeur-driven cars available.

Localiza; International Airport Guarulhos; tel: (11) 945-2133; Rua da Consolação, 419, Centro, tel: 0800-31-2121.

Nacional Rent A Car; Rua Avanhandava, 40, Bela Vista; tel: (11) 256-1063.

Trevo Car; Av. Washington Luis, 7.059, Aeroporto; tel: (11) 542-2122.

WORLD TRADE CENTER

Sao Paulo World Trade Center
Av. das Nacoes Unidas, 12.551
Brooklin Novo, Sao Paulo
Brazil 04578-903
tel: (11) 3403-7100; fax: (11) 3403-7014
email: busclub@wtcclub.com.br
website: http://www.wtc.org.br

Brunei

At a Glance

THE PEOPLE

Population .... 322,982 (July 1999 est.)
Growth Rate .... 2.38% (1999 est.)
Life Expectancy .... 71.84 years (born 1999)
Infant Mortality . 22.83 deaths/1,000 live births (1999 est.)

Ethnic Composition

Malay..64%
Chinese 20%
Other 16%

Religious Composition

Muslim(official) 63%
Buddhist 14%
Christian 8%
Indigenous beliefs and non-affiliated...........................15%

Languages Spoken

Malay (official), English, Cantonese, Putungua

Education and Literacy

Education all the way through university training is free even when studying abroad. The adult literacy rate for adults is 88.2 percent.

Labor Force

Total: 144,000
By occupation: services 49%, industry 46%, agriculture 4% Note: 33% of labor force is composed foreign nationals.

THE ECONOMY

Despite certain cultural and historical similarities, Brunei stands substantially apart from neighboring Malaysia and Indonesia. Well over half of the GDP of this tiny monarchy depends on petroleum and natural gas exports. Consequently, the nation's fortunes are directly tied to international commodity prices. Low fuel prices of the late 1990s greatly reduced the coffers of this nation that has state-ownership of all major industries. Its extensive and generous social system has also been affected by this phenomenon. The government has taken some steps to reduce Brunei's dependence on oil and has even moved towards limited privatization of industry. Its tiny size and location sandwiched inside a Malaysian province keeps the monarchy in dire fear of social upheaval linked to economic downturns. Foreign investment, though interested in Brunei's natural resources, has been kept at bay by the monarchy's monopoly on large-scale business ventures.

Exports .... US$2.62 billion (f.o.b., 1996 est.)
Imports .... US$2.65 billion (c.i.f., 1996 est.)
Total GDP .... US$5.4 billion(1998 est.)
GDP Per Capita .... $17,000 (1998 est.)
Unemployment .... 4.8 percent (1994)
Inflation Rate .... 2 percent (1997)

Top Export Partners

ASEAN, Japan, South Korea, E.U., Taiwan

Top Import Partners

ASEAN, E.U., United States, Japan.

Top Exports

Crude oil, liquefied natural gas, petroleum products.

Top Imports

Machinery and transport equipment, manufactured goods, foodstuffs, chemicals.

BUSINESS WORKWEEK

Offices

Monday to Friday 8a.m. to 5p.m.; Saturday 8a.m. to noon.

Banks

Monday to Friday 9a.m. to 3p.m., Saturday 9a.m. to 11a.m.

Government

Monday to Thursday and Saturday: 7:45a.m. to 12:15p.m. and 1:30p.m. to 4:30p.m. Shorter hours during Ramadan.

Retail

Monday to Sunday 10a.m. to 10p.m.
Note: Shops and government offices outside of the capital will have hours based more upon local need and custom.

HOLIDAYS

New Year's Day..January 1
Memperingati Nuzul Al-Quran,
Anniversary of the Revelation
of the Koran.. January 7*
Hari Raya Puasa, end of Ramadan..................January 19
Chinese New Year .... February 16-18*
National Day...February23
Hari Raya Haji, Feast of the Sacrifice ....March 28*
Hizrah, Islamic New Year ....April 17*
Anniversary of the Royal
Brunei Armed Forces ....June 1
Hari Mouloud, Birth of the Prophet........................ June26*
Sultan's Birthday ....July 15
Isra Meraj, Ascension of the
Prophet Muhammad.. November 6*
Beginning of Ramadan................................. December 9*
Christmas Day...December 25
Bank's Yearly Closing ....December 31
*Dates may vary by year.

CLIMATE

Seasons

The climate is equatorial, and the temperatures range from 23° to 32°C (73-89°F) throughout the year. Humidity can run as high as 80 percent. The rainy season occurs between April and December. Rain is heaviest in November. No matter when you plan to go, bring an umbrella.

Regions

Weather throughout this tiny country is most consistent. The only variance is that the coastal region gets slightly less rainfall than the inland areas.

Brunei

Money & Banking

Currency

The currency of Brunei is the Brunei Dollar (Br$).

Denominations

The Brunei Dollar comes in coin denominations of 50, 20, 10, 5, and 1 sen, and banknotes of Br$1, 5, 10, 25, 50, 100, 500, 1,000, and 10,000.

Travelers Checks and Credit Cards

Traveler's checks and most major currencies can be exchanged at major banks, hotels, department stores, and the international airport (the best site to exchange money). Cashing checks in more rural areas may prove a little difficult, if not impossible. You can change major currencies at money-changing booths in shopping centers and foreign exchanged houses such as Thomas Cook. Keep your receipts for reconversion of currency at departure.

Note: Currency from India and Indonesia will not be accepted for exchange when entering Brunei.

Credit cards (American Express, Diner's Club, Master-Card, Visa, and JBS) are widely accepted in good hotels, restaurants, and businesses in the capital city, Bandar Seri Begawan. Rural areas will require cash for transactions. Cash and cash advances on credit cards can be obtained at ATMs in the capital.

Travel

VISA AND PASSPORT

Visitors must be in possession of a valid passport, which must hold its validity for at least six months after arrival. It is also mandatory that there be no question that the visitor is permitted by his/her own government to return to the home country subsequent to the stated date of exit from Brunei.

- U.S. citizens can stay for a maximum of ninety days without a visa.
- Visits of up to thirty days by citizens of Belgium, Denmark, France, Malaysia, New Zealand, the Netherlands, Singapore, Spain, Sweden, and the U.K. do not require a visa.
- Nationals of Canada, Indonesia, Japan, Liechtenstein, Maldives, New Zealand, Norway, Philippines, South Korea, Switzerland and Thailand do not require a visa if their stay does not exceed fourteen days.
- Australians may obtain a transit visa upon arrival in Brunei, if their stay does not exceed fourteen days.

Visa-free trips are valid only if the traveler is in possession of a return ticket. All visitors must be able to prove sufficient funds to cover their expenses for the duration of their stay in Brunei.

Only one type of visa is issued called the Short Visit Visa. The single-entry version is valid for three months. The multiple-entry visa's validity is determined by the issuing consulate.

Brunei

The business traveler must append to the visa application a letter from her/his employer which states the purpose of the visit.

You can apply for a visa at Brunei embassies overseas. If Brunei does not have an embassy or consulate in your country, try the closest British diplomatic mission.

Allow several days for visa application processing. If the consulate determines that your visa requires referral to the authorities in Brunei, then the paperwork can take as long as two months before completion.

RESTRICTED ENTRY

Nationals of Cuba, Israel, or Korea (DPR) will be denied entry to Brunei.

DEPARTURE FORMALITIES

A departure tax of Br$5 is collected for flights to Malaysia and Singapore. All other flights will be taxed Br$12. One may not export more than Br$1000 in cash notes. An unlimited amount of declared foreign currency may be carried out, so long as it does not exceed the amount imported. All flights must be reconfirmed 72 hours in advance.

CUSTOMS ENTRY (PERSONAL)

Duty-free
- Tobacco: 200 cigarettes, 250g tobacco products
- Perfume: 60ml of perfume and 250ml toilet water
- Alcohol: 2 bottles of liquor and 12 cans of beer for personal consumption only, provided declared at customs upon arrival (all non-muslim persons over 17 years of age)
- Toiletries: 60ml of perfume and 250ml eau de toilette.

Note: All alcohol must be declared upon arrival as this is an Islamic country. Failure to do so is punishable by law.

Prohibited or Restricted
- Firearms
- Non-prescribed drugs: the penalty for carrying non-prescribed drugs is death (medications must be declared)
- All pornography
- Religious icons and any text critical of Islam

IMMUNIZATION

If arriving from an infected area, yellow fever inoculations and certification are required for visitors over one year of age. Malaria, cholera, and small pox inoculations are not required. Hepatitis A shots are recommended.

TIPPING

Taxi
The tip for unmetered taxi drivers should be included as part of the fee negotiated in advance. For metered fares, just round up the total.

Porters
Br$1 per piece of luggage is expected at first-class hotels. Use this as a benchmark for porters at other venues.

Hotels
Hotels will add a service charge to the bill in most cases. Small tips can be left for especially helpful staff.

Restaurants
Restaurants add a service charge to bills, but foreigners are expected to round up the charges or leave small additional tips.

EMERGENCY INFORMATION

Police and Crime
Islam dominates life in Brunei. Therefore, penalties are extremely high for crime—as such, the crime rate remains low.

Note: Brunei prohibits the consumption of alcohol in public. Travelers caught violating the law or trafficking in illegal drugs risk arrest and imprisonment without protection afforded by their home governments.

Travelers should maintain common sense levels of precaution even though crime is minimal. Leave most of your cash, traveler's checks, jewelry, and camera in your hotel safe. Carry photocopies of your passport instead of the original. Carry cash in a money belt, and use credit cards or traveler's checks for most of your large transactions. Police are quite helpful but do not always have foreign language skills.

Note: Foreign women should avoid traveling alone at night. While this is not a fundamentalist state, women should also abide by the Islamic dress code, which requires a head covering as well as covered limbs. Women that don't comply are considered fair game for all sorts of propositions.

Health
Brunei has high sanitation standards, but do not drink the tap water; consume only bottled beverages, and avoid raw food. Stay with hot, well-cooked meat and fish. Stay away from food sold at roadside stands and stick to milder dishes. Some stomach and digestion problems may occur because of the spicy food. Dairy products should be boiled or avoided.

Malaria has been nearly eradicated, except in border areas. Cholera still exists in the countryside, and there remains some risk of tuberculosis. Tetanus and hepatitis A shots are advisable. Extended travel in the border areas will require a full range of inoculations.

Brunei has low cost, adequate medical care although there can be high fees for medicine dispensed to foreigners. Many of the staff speak English, and hospitals are well stocked. Most hotels have access to good doctors, otherwise, contact your embassy or consulate.

For more information on medical centers, including phone numbers, please see the "Business Centers" section at the end of this chapter.

INTERNAL TRAVEL

AIR
The nation of Brunei has no domestic air services.

TAXI
Taxis are available in Bandar Seri Begawan. Metered taxis are available at hotels and shopping centers.

Even though fares are normally metered, some cabs operate on a negotiated-fare basis. When using these cabs, negotiate a fare before entering. Prices for both types of cab will increase by 50 percent after 11p.m.

City Transport Service (CTS) cabs offer a much cheaper alternative to the regular taxis and are easily identified by their bright purple color. A trip to the airport costs only US$3 ($4 if ordered in advance), compared to US$30 with a regular cab. For a pickup at any major downtown hotel or a CTS pick-up point, dial their convenient hotline. CTS cabs operate between 6a.m. and 10p.m.

CTS hotline.. 343-434

AUTO
Car rentals are available in the capital city. A credit card and valid driver's license are required, as is local insurance. There are about 1800km (1080 miles) of roads in Brunei. Traffic keeps to the left, British-style.

It is more advisable to rent a car and driver for a daily or weekly rate as "self-piloting" may prove more trouble than it is worth.

It is also worth noting that in this rich nation, "real" business people never drive themselves anywhere.

Brunei

BUSES & TRAMS

There are bus stations in the town center of most major towns, including Bandar Seri Begawan. In the capital, buses operate between 6:30a.m. and 6p.m. (although many may stop around 4p.m.), and in 15- and 20-minute intervals on the main lines. Some of the latter include routes to Seria, (91km/57 miles from Bandar Seri Begawan), Kuala Belait (16km/10 miles from Seria), Tutong (48km/30 miles from Bandar Seri Begawan) and Muara (27km/17 miles from Bandar Seri Begawan).

The Central and Circle lines stop at the international airport as well as the Terrace Hotel and the Sheraton Utama Hotel. Long-distance buses to other cities leave from Bandar station.

Note: Buses are considered for use by Brunei's working classes. Foreign business people should never use them for traveling to meetings, as it is a sign of poverty.

WATER TRAVEL

Water taxis transport passengers to Kampong Ayer, Brunei's water village. Stations are located at Jalan Kianggeh and Jalan McArthur.

Ferries to points outside of Brunei depart from the new ferry terminal in Muara, which lies outside of Bandar Seri Behawan. The Straits Steamship Company offers a cargo and passenger service to Singapore.

The international ferry port in Serasa houses the ferries going to Labuan and Lawas in Malaysia. Ferries to Limbang depart from Bandar Seri Begawan (near the customs port).

Essential Terms

English	Malay
Yes	Ya
No	Tidak
Good morning	Selamat pagi
Hello (daytime)	Selamat tengahari
Hello (evening)	Selamat petang
Hello (telephone)	Helo
Good-bye	Selamat Tingall
Please	Tolong
Thank you	Terima kasih
Pleased to meet you	Seronok berjumpa denga anda
Excuse me; I'm sorry	Minta maaf
My name is _____	Nama saya
I don't understand	Sya tidak faham
Do you speak English?	Adakah anda bertutur bahasa inggeris

Communications

DIALING CODES IN BRUNEI

International country code: [673]
Selected city codes: Bandar Seri Behawan (2), Kuala Belait (3), Mumong (3), Tutong (4)

Dialing Brunei from Overseas

To dial Brunei from overseas, begin with your country's international dialing code, then 673 (the country code for Brunei), then the city code and the number you are trying to reach. If you were dialing Mumong from the United States, for example, you would begin with 011, then 673, then 2 (the city code for Mumong), and finally the number of the person or office you are trying to reach.

Assistance Numbers

Operator 0124

CALLING WITHIN BRUNEI

Local Calls

Unless calling from a private phone, where local calls are free, deposit 10 cents.

Long Distance Calls

Four area codes exist in the country of Brunei. Omit them if dialing locally.

International Calls

One may call overseas direct from hotels, from the Telekom office in the capital, from card phones, or from the airport. Dial 01 + country code + area code + number. One may also reach an access number to speak to an AT&T operator in the States. Public phones require a coin or card deposit.

AT&T Direct 800-1111

PAY PHONES

Public Telephones

Public phones take coins or cards; if using the former, deposit 10 cents for a local call. Phones accept 10 or 20 cent coins.

Calling Cards

One can purchase phone cards at Telekom offices, the international airport, post offices, or retail stores.

CELLULAR PHONES

There are numerous cellular phone service providers in Brunei. In the analog format Jabatan Telekom Brunei offers AMPS service. In the digital format JTB/Sultan offers GSM service.

Note: Your home country cell phone may not work in this country. If not, we recommend that you rent an international cell phone *before* you leave home. A major US-based cell phone rental provider is **IMC WorldCell**. For information see "International Cell Phone Rentals" on page 14.

DSTCom offices offer mobile phone rental service. They offer two systems: AMPS and GMS.

DSTCare Hotline 151

CALL BACK

You can (potentially) save significant sums when calling in Brunei by using a call back service. For a list of callback services, please refer to the "Communications" section in the *Global Road Warrior* Introduction.

Fees for call back services vary widely, depending on the company and the type of service required. Be sure to check with these companies before leaving to compare rates.

PHONE JACKS

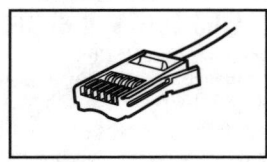

Plug adaptors are available through **iGo Corporation.** (See "Electrical and Telephone Adaptors" on page 19.)

POSTAL SERUICES

Airmail letters to Europe take two to five days, to North America seven to ten days. "Speedpost" services are also available, that are much quicker than standard postal service. Post offices remain open between 7:45a.m. to 4:30p.m. Monday to Thursday and Saturday; and from 8:00a.m. to 11:00am. and 2:00p.m. to 4:00p.m. on Friday.

Business Services

COURIER SERUICES

DHL International; SDN BHD 3, SPG 27, Bangunan PIF, Jalan Gadong, BAndar Seri Begawan, tel: (2) 444-992.

TNT Skypak; 201 2nd Floor, Jubilee Plaza; tel: (2) 221-494.

UPS - United Parcel Service; Jayapuri (B) SDN BHD, Ground floor, Block C, Unit 10, Sufi Bolkiah Bldg., Jalan Tutong, Bandar Seri Begawan; tel: (2) 242-401, 243-689; fax: (2) 238-268.

Electrical

Current
220 volts, AC, 50Hz

ELECTRIC PLUGS

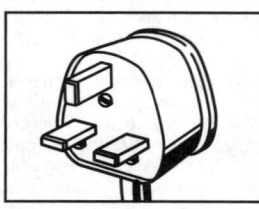

Plugs are either round or square 3-pin.

Plug adaptors are available through **iGo Corporation.** (See "Electrical and Telephone Adaptors" on page 19.)

Technical Support

HARDWARE/SOFTWARE VENDOR SUPPORT

Dell; (in Germany) tel: [49] (61) 039-710; (Dell- Europe) tel: [44] (134) 474-8000; (in the U.S.) tel: [1] (512) 338-4400; fax: [1] (512) 728-3330; http://www.dell.com/.

Hewlett Packard; (Malaysia Office) tel: [60] 03 295 2566; (in Switzerland) tel: [41] (22) 780-8111; (in the U.S.) tel: [1] (408) 246-4300; http://www.hp.com/.

IBM; tel: 324-0660; fax: 324-0662; (in Switzerland) tel: [41] (22) 310-0418 (in French); (U.S. Main Office) tel: [1] 914-765-1900; (in the U.S.) tel: [1] (919) 517-2800; http://www.ibm.com/

Microsoft; (Singapore Office) tel: [65] 337-6088; fax: [65] 337-6788; (in Switzerland) tel: [41] (848) 858-868; fax [41] (1) 831-0869; (in the U.S.) [1] (425) 635-7222; http://www.microsoft.com/.

Internet Connection

HOW TO CONNECT

Connecting to AOL and Compuserve in Brunei is similar to using it when traveling outside your own area code. See the introductory section for detailed information on connecting to your account through a different phone number.

America Online

Numbers are available at keyword: *international*. Be sure to get several local numbers before leaving. AOL has its GlobalNet service available at keyword: *access* (a free area) and download the software.

There are no direct access numbers for America Online in Brunei. Users will have to pay international rates to use the service.

Compuserve

Numbers are available at *Go International*. The Compuserve Web-site also has a great deal of information, at http://www.compuserve.com.

There are no direct access numbers for Compuserve in Brunei. Users will have to pay international rates to use the service.

Independent Service Providers

Many independent service providers offer discounts if you are only in town for a couple of days.

BruNet (JTB); tel: (2) 383-333; fax: (2) 383-888; email: noc@jtb.brunet.bn; http://www.brunet.bn/.

VIANET; (in Austria) tel: [43] 1-404-020; email: help@vianet.at; http://www.vianet.at/.

Business Culture

GREETINGS AND COURTESIES

The two largest ethnic groups are Malays (about 70 percent) and Chinese (about 18 percent). Their greetings and courtesies are often very different. Malays are generally Muslim, and their accepted greeting is the handshake, which is usually accompanied by a slight bow or nod of the head. In addition, when an older person enters a room people usually stand. Women and elderly people often don't shake hands but will offer a verbal greeting.

Brunei

DECISION MAKING

Consensus is important to Malays and they will probably require time for discussion before making a decision. These conversations will be amongst themselves, and never with outsiders present. Chinese try to avoid saying no, for fear of causing embarrassment or losing face. Rather than say no, they might say something is inconvenient or suggest an alternative.

MEETINGS

Punctuality is a sign of respect and politeness, so be on time for appointments. However, in this leisurely culture people are often late. Small talk often begins a meeting, with business addressed after people feel a certain degree of comfort with each other. Most businesspeople speak English and, as such, translators are often not required.

WOMEN

Brunei is primarily a Muslim country and women should be prepared for the restrictions this culture places on them. When meeting Malays, women will be asked personal questions about their age, marital status, and children. (These questions are asked of both men and women.) Commenting on a woman's looks might be regarded as flirting, which is taboo and might cost a woman her job. Women should dress tastefully and conservatively.

BUSINESS ATTIRE

Neat, tasteful pants, shirt, and tie (no jacket) will be appropriate attire for most business situations. If you wear a jacket and no one else does, you may remove yours once the meeting begins. The heat and humidity outside may encourage one to wear natural fabrics. Women should attire themselves conservatively to show respect for the Muslim culture.

Business Centers
Bandar Seri Begawan

CITY VIEW

Bandari Seri Begawan remains the only city of any size in Brunei. With plenty of wealth infused by the sultan, a clean, modern and expensive city has emerged, perhaps too large for the only 65,000 people who call it home.

AIRPORT

Bandar Seri Begawan Airport to City Center

The airport lies 6 miles (10 km.) from the city center. There is regular taxi service costing from US$25 to $30, although fares go up after 11p.m. If interested in less expensive cabs, head down the covered walkway toward the parking lot where the CTS taxis will take you into town for a set fare of US$3, music to the ears of those heading into an expensive city on a moderate budget.

Airline Numbers

Aer Lingus	(2) 43911
British Airways	(2) 43911/2/3
MAS	(2) 224141
Qantas	(2) 228852
Royal Brunei Airlines	(2) 242222
Singapore Airlines	(2) 227253
Thai International	(2) 242991

HOTELS

Top-end

Centrepoint Hotel; Abdul Razak Complex, Gadong 3180; restaurants; business center; convention and banquet facilities; boardrooms; sport facilities.

Sheraton Utama Hotel; Jalan Tasek; tel: (2) 244-272; fax: (2) 221-579; city center; near exhibition grounds; restaurant; no-smoking rooms; business center; conference center; secretarial service; fitness; pool; Br$245/265.

Expensive

Ang's; Jalan Tasek Lama; tel: (2) 243-554; fax: (2) 227-302; city center; 2 restaurants; a/c; phone; television; conference center; pool; Br$138/148.

Brunei Hotel Sdn Bhd; 95, Jalan Pemancha; tel: (2) 242-372; fax: (2) 226-196; coffee house; conference rooms; convention rooms; VIP room; business center; banquet rooms; interpreter; photocopier; typewriter; Br$115/180.

Jubilee Hotel; Jubilee Plaza, Jalan Kpg. Kianggeh; tel: (2) 228-070; fax: (2) 228-080; restaurant; coffee garden; offices; business center.

Riverview Hotel; Km 1, Jalan Gadong; tel: (2) 238-238; fax: (2) 237-888; restaurants; cafe; business center services; secretarial service; courier service; multilingual staff; function and banquet facilities; medical clinic; shuttle service; pool; gym; sauna; jacuzzi; Br$154/171.

Moderate

Capital; Jalan Berangan; tel: (2) 223-561; fax: (2) 228-789; city center; restaurant; coffee shop; interpreter; telex; photocopier; typewriter; Br$70/85.

Crowne Princess Hotel; L.B. 1204, km 2.5, Jalan Tutong; tel: (2) 241-128; fax: (2) 241-138; restaurant; coffee shop; business center; function room; hotel courtesy bus.

Terrace Hotel; Jalan Tasek Lama; tel: (2) 243-554; fax: (2) 227-302; restaurant; satellite television; IDD telephone; pool; Br$90/158.

MEDICAL CARE

Hart Medical Clinic; 1st Floor, 47 Jalan Sultau; tel: (2) 225--531.

Chung Medical Center; Unit G3/5 Bangunan Hj. Ahmad Laksamana; tel: (2) 240-546.

Jerudong Park Medical Center; Royal Brunei Polo Club, Jerudong Park 2021; tel: 671-433 or 671-412.

Riverview Medical Clinic; Riverview Hotel, Km 1, Jalan Gadong; tel: 238-018, ext. 8816.

AUTO RENTAL

Avis Car Rental; Brunei Airport, tel: (2) 42-4921; fax: (2) 23-1747; Sheraton Utama Hotel, tel: (2) 42-4921; fax: (2) 24-4272; headquarters, tel: (2) 42-6345; fax: (2) 42-4921.

Budget-U-Drive; Unit E17, 1st Floor, Bangunan G.P. Satu Gadong 3180; tel: (2) 445-846/47; fax: (2) 447-434; email: budget@post1.com

Maxicon Car Rental Services; 2nd Floor, Unit 3, Bangunan Hgh. Nesbah, Spg 600, 7 Km Jalan Tutong; tel: (2) 655-159/160; fax: (2) 655-156; email: maxicon@post1.com

CHAMBER OF COMMERCE

Brunei Darussalem Intl. Chamber of Commerce and Industry

P.O. Box 2246
Bandar Seri Begawan 1922
tel: (2) 236-601; fax: (2) 228-389; Telex: 2214

Bulgaria

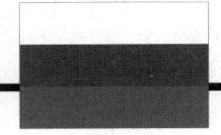

At a Glance

THE PEOPLE

Population .... 8,194,772 (July 1999 est.)
Growth Rate .... -0.52% (1999 est.)
Life Expectancy .... 72.27 years (born 1999)
Infant Mortality . 12.37 deaths/1,000 live births (1999 est.)

Ethnic Composition

Slavic..88.3%
Turk 8.5%
Romani (Gypsy) 2.6%
Other 0.6%

Religious Composition

Bulgarian Orthodox 85%
Muslim 13%
Jewish 0.8%
Roman Catholic...0.5%
Protestant..0.5%
Other and non-affiliated...0.2%

Languages Spoken

Bulgarian (official), Turkish, and Romani

Education and Literacy

Education is free of charge and compulsory to the age of 15. Adult literacy is 98 percent.

Labor Force

Total: 3,570,000
By occupation: services 41%, industry 41%, agriculture 18%

THE ECONOMY

Bulgaria is largely an industrial economy, and also one of the poorest countries in present-day eastern Europe. Once an industrial supplier for the now defunct Soviet Union, Bulgaria finds itself today with an abundance of outdated equipment and an economy unprepared to to compete in the global free markets. The government has made some efforts towards privatization, but foreign investment has not responded with much interest. An inflation rate in the hundreds of percentiles and negative GDP growth have done little to persuade the investment community that the Bulgarian economy is under control. Land reform, privatization of banks and the development of a commercial legal system are all underway. It will, however, be many years before Bulgaria can hope to see the success enjoyed by some of its neighbors to the north.

Exports .... US$4.5 billion (f.o.b., 1998)
Imports .... US$4.6 billion (f.o.b., 1998 est.)
Total GDP .... US$33.6 billion (1998 est.)
GDP Per Capita .... US$4,100 (1998 est.)
Unemployment .... 12.2% (1998 est.)
Inflation Rate .... 1% (1998 est.)

Top Export Partners

E.U., CIS, Eastern Europe, Middle East.

Top Import Partners

E.U., CIS, Eastern Europe, Middle East.

Top Exports

Machinery and equipment, agricultural and food, textiles and apparel, metals and ores, chemicals

Top Imports

Fuels, minerals, and raw materials, machinery and equipment, textiles and apparel, agricultural products, metals and ores, chemicals.

BUSINESS WORKWEEK

Offices

Monday to Friday 8:30a.m. to 5:30p.m.

Banks

Monday to Friday 9a.m. to noon and 1p.m. to 5p.m., Saturday 9 a.m. to noon

Government

Monday to Friday 8:30a.m. to 4:30p.m.

Retail

Monday to Saturday 9a.m. to 5 p.m.
Note: Many stores and government offices in rural areas close between 1p.m. to 2p.m.

HOLIDAYS

New Year's Day..January 1
National Day... March 3
Easter Monday ....April 5*
Labor Day...May 1
Education Day...May 24
Liberation Day ....September 9
Christmas ....December 24-25
*Dates may vary by year.

CLIMATE

Seasons

Climate is temperate, with warm, dry summers, and cold, wet, and snowy winters. Average temperatures in summer are 28°C (82°F) and in the winter are -6°C (25°F). The best time to visit the country is between May and October, when the weather is pleasantly spring like.

Regions

There are strong regional differences in Bulgaria. The country is dominated by mountain ranges punctuated by windswept plains and verdant valleys. The capital, Sofia (where most business is conducted), lies about 1,800 feet above sea level. The average temperature there in June is 18°C (65°F). The Black Sea coast has a mild Mediterranean weather pattern and is a favotite resort area. The winters in the mountainous areas are cold, with plenty of snow.

Money & Banking

Currency

The currency of Bulgaria is the Lev (Lv).

Denominations

The Lev (plural -leva) comes in coin denominations of Lv5, 2, and 1, and 50, 20, 10, 5, 2, and 1 stotinki (stotinki are no longer in circulation); and banknotes of Lv1, 2, 5, 10, 20, 50, 100, 200, 500, 1000, 2000, 5000, and 20,000.

Traveler's Checks and Credit Cards

Traveler's checks and major currencies can be exchanged at National Bank of Bulgaria and at the Balkan tourist office at most hotels. Keep receipts for reconverting currency on de-

Bulgaria

©2001 Magellan Geographix SM Santa Barbara, CA

parture. Cash and checks may also be exchanged at exchange shops, and at the airport (commissions are charged only on travel checks). The lev has little value outside of Bulgaria so there is no reason to export it. "Hard" currencies from the U.S. and E.U. receive optimal rates. There is no black market in Bulgarian currency, although some "street exchanges" attempt to defraud tourists.

American Express, Visa, Diner's Club, and MasterCard are accepted in most urban areas and coastal towns. ATMs can be found in Sofia and at Black Sea resorts. Cash and cash advances on ATM and credit card transactions receive the best exchange rate.

Note: Some retailers charge an additional fee for credit card use. However, it will be waived if you tell them you will not make a purchase if charged extra.

Travel
VISA AND PASSPORT

A passport that is valid for a minimum of three months beyond anticipated date of departure is required or all visitors.

Visas are required of all, except for nationals of the following three groups, for a single-entry visit up to 30 days:
- E.U. countries
- Andorra, Australia, Canada, Croatia, Czech Republic, Estonia, Hungary, Iceland, Israel, Japan, Korea (Rep. of), Liechtenstein, Lithuania, Macedonia, Malta, Monaco, New Zealand, Norway, Poland, Romania, San Marino, Slovak Republic, Slovenia, Switzerland, Tunisia, U.K., U.S., and Vatican City
- Georgia, Russian Federation, and Ukraine— nationals of these governments will be required to show possession of sufficient funds (equivalent of US$40 per day for the duration of stay) at the border or a return ticket along with a legalized invitation.

Travelers who intend to stay more than 30 days should secure a Bulgarian visa, as the fees connected with the extension of their stay in the country are much higher than the visa fees.

Types of visas:
- Single-entry, for tourism only, valid up to 30 days
- Multiple-entry, for business travelers only, available in two versions—one valid up to three months, the other valid up to six months. Applicants for this visa must include in their application a letter from their company and one from the corresponding Bulgarian business partner, which must be endorsed by the Bulgarian Chamber of Commerce. Conducting business (beyond basic research) on a tourist visa can result in immediate deportation.
- Transit visas, available in either single- or double-entry versions, valid for 24 hours per entry
- Express visas, available to nationals of E.U. countries, valid for 60 days, the term "express" derived from application processing time of less than one week

Generally, the time periods to allow for processing of visa applications are:
- 7 days for single-entry visas
- 10 days for multiple-entry visas
- instantaneous for transit visas
- between one and six days for express visas

However, be aware that processing can take up to two weeks for single- and multiple-entry applications due to mysterious bureaucratic confirmation procedures.

All visitors to Bulgaria must register with the police via their hotel or guest house within 48 hours of arrival. A US$23 entry fee is required of visitors except those from the E.U., U.S., Iceland, Switzerland, Norway, and most eastern European nations. All visitors must fill out and retain a "statistics card" for eventual presentation at departure. Keep this document with your passport.

DEPARTURE FORMALITIES

Bulgarian customs regulations are in flux. Currently, travelers who are carrying in excess of US$10,000 must state the precise amount on a customs declaration. Travelers who have entered the country with less than US$10,000, but are departing with more than that amount,

Bulgaria

must be able to document the source of these funds.

The original stamped "statistics card" (*statisticheska karta*) must be presented to immigration.

There is a US$3 airport departure fee.

CUSTOMS ENTRY (PERSONAL)

Duty-free
- 200 cigarettes or 50 cigars or 250g of tobacco
- One liter of distilled spirits and two liters of wine
- 100g of perfume
- Objects and foodstuffs intended for personal use during the stay.

The following goods must be declared:
- Objects intended for other persons
- Antiques, works of art
- Commercial samples
- Typewriters and cameras,
- Printed matter and manuscripts,
- Plants, fruits, and seeds
- Firearms and ammunition for hunting purposes;
- Currency, securities and precious stones or metals

Note: Transit passengers' luggage may be sealed by customs officers to avoid the inconvenience of a subsequent check at the departure customs.

Prohibited or Restricted
- Arms and ammunition
- Narcotics
- Pornography

Note: Bulgaria has a policy of letting "a reasonable amount" of gifts enter and exit the country untaxed. As you can imagine, this is open to interpretation by customs officials. The wealthier you appear, the greater the likelihood that you will be asked to pay fees on even simple and inexpensive articles.

IMMUNIZATION

No immunizations are necessary to gain entrance into Bulgaria unless coming from an infected area. However, immunization against poliomyelitis, typhoid, hepatitis A, and tetanus is recommended. When planning to stay for more than one month, an AIDS test may be required. Test results from other countries are not accepted; this is both a health precaution and revenue generator.

TIPPING

Taxi
Metered taxi fares are rounded up (five to ten percent is appreciated), while unmetered fares (negotiated in advance) include all fees.

Porters
Porters are not tipped.

Hotels
Hotels apply service charges directly to the bill. No other tip is necessary although many staff assume foreigners will leave some small amount.

Restaurants
Round bills up to tip at restaurants as a service charge has already been applied. Tips of ten to fifteen percent are given only in the most expensive restaurants and only by foreigners.

EMERGENCY INFORMATION

Police and Crime
Crime is on the increase, especially in Bulgaria's larger cities and more populated areas. Take basic precautions

against petty crime. Avoid flashy displays of wealth, and dress and behave conservatively. Leave most of your cash, traveler's checks, jewelry, and your camera in your hotel safe. Laptops and briefcases require constant security. Carry photocopies of your passport instead of the original. Carry cash in a money belt, and use credit cards or traveler's checks for most of your transactions.

Petty street crime is mostly directed at foreigners and others who seem to have money. Purse snatching and pickpocketing are widespread, particularly in crowded marketplaces and in shopping districts. Confidence artists ply their craft in public transportation vehicles and stations, especially buses and trains, and travelers must be skeptical about "instant friendships." They should also demand that persons contending to be officials show identification.

Incidents of baggage pilferage at Sofia Airport are commonplace. For this reason travelers should not pack items of significant value in checked luggage.

Auto theft is a frequent problem; sports utility vehicles and new European sedans are favorite targets. Almost never is a stolen vehicle recovered. Thieves also smash vehicle windows in order to steal valuables.

Official corruption is also a problem in Bulgaria and business visitors must be prepared to deal with bribery. You may also be shaken down for "special penalties" for committing unknown and non-specified acts. Demands for receipts for these fines will often cause the problem to evaporate. Such shake downs occur most often when entering and departing Bulgaria overland.

Police in cities often work with criminal gangs, so do not expect the return of stolen goods or prompt arrests. Police may even ask you to help "finance" the investigation. Insure your valuables as this may be your only hope for compensation.

Emergency Numbers
Numbers function nationwide

Police	166
Ambulance	150
Fire	160
International Calls	0123
Medical Information	155

Health
Tap water in Bulgaria is not potable; so, drink bottled water only. Don't even use tap water for brushing your teeth, and avoid ice cubes made with tap water. Avoid raw vegetables and fruit unless they've been washed in a chlorine solution. Diarrhea is common for travelers who are unaccustomed to the new diet and water. Do not eat at street stalls until your stomach has adjusted to the new environment. Even then, use caution.

Bulgarian physicians are competent and well-trained, but hospitals and clinics are not generally equipped or maintained at Western levels. Basic medical supplies can be obtained easily, but specialized treatment is often not available.

Healthcare must be paid for in cash immediately. Rates are reasonable by European standards, but medicines can be expensive. To avoid the high prices, you may wish to bring a well-stocked medical kit including all prescription medicines you may need. Medical personnel are well trained for emergencies, but, beyond that, it is best to leave the country for extended treatment. Visitors are advised to carry medical insurance and long-term business travelers should have an evacuation policy. Contact the Clinic for Foreign Citizens in Sofia at 75-361 for medical assistance.

For more information on medical centers, including phone numbers, please see the "Business Centers" section at the end of this chapter.

INTERNAL TRAVEL

AIR

Balkan-Bulgarian Airlines offers eight domestic routes linking Sofia with the coast and with major cities. The trip times to Varna and Bourgas are under one hour. Air travel is relatively cheap, only slightly more than rail travel.

TAXI

Taxis are available for cities and intercity travel. Fares are metered, except for privately owned cars.

Cab drivers at Sofia Airport will often bilk unwary travelers, and even if you can get them to run the meter, the amounts demanded in payment are often much higher.

If a cab does not run a meter, agree to a fare before going anywhere. Taxi drivers may not be familiar with their own area, let alone other cities. Be sure to have extensive directions and maps.

AUTO

Cars and motorcycles are available for rental in Sofia, easily arranged through your hotel reception desk. There are no fly-drive arrangements available through the airlines. Transactions usually occur n hard currency only—no credit cards. An International Driving Permit is mandatory, and a Green Card (insurance documentation for local policy) is compulsory also.

Vehicle rental is not advised for first-time visitors due to the chaotic road system and low security. Hired cars with drivers (or taxis) can be rented for daily and even weekly rates.

TRAIN

More than 6500km (4040 miles) of railways cross Bulgaria. Train service is efficient and links Sofia with major domestic destinations, as well as with Belgrade, Bucharest, Thessaloniki, and Istanbul.

Reservations are essential and can be made through the State Railway Office. First-class passage is recommended.
Central Railway Station 31-111

METRO

Bulgaria does not have any subway systems yet, but a metro system is under construction in Sofia.

BUSES & TRAMS

In the capital, buses run between 5a.m. and midnight, and trams and trolley services operate until 1a.m. These are the most popular means of travel throughout most Bulgarian cities, although service can prove somewhat erratic at times.

Generally, the passenger purchases a ticket for a flat fare at kiosks and newsstands and gets it validated once on board. Buses and trams are not recommended for use for transit to business meetings.

WATER TRAVEL

Regularly scheduled boats and hydrofoils operate along the Danube linking many cities, including Vidin, Lom, Kozloduj, Orjahovo, Nikopol, Svishtov, Tutrakan, and Silistra. Ferries also cross into Romania from Vidin to Calafat.

TRAVEL ASSISTANCE

Ministry of Trade and Tourism
12 Kniaz Alexander Batenberg
Sofia 1000 Bulgaria
Tourist Department
4 Lege Street, 1000 Sofia Bulgaria
tel: (2) 882 011, 981 9962-5; Fax; (2) 981 2515

Bulgarian National Tourism Promotion Office
1 St. Sophia Street, Sofia 1000 Bulgaria
Tel/fax: (2) 987 9778; email: infctr@mail.mtt.govrn.bg
Ministry of Trade and Tourism
1 Sweta Nedelja
Sofia 1000 Bulgaria
tel: (2) 8413; fax: (2) 98- 2515
Balkantourist
Boulevard Vitosha 1
Sofia 1000 Bulgaria
tel: (2) 43331; fax: 890-1014

Essential Terms

English	Bulgarian
Yes No	Da Ne
Good morning Hello (daytime) Hello (evening) Hello (telephone)	Dobro outro Dobur den Dobur vecher Zdrah vehy teh
Good-bye	Dovizhdane
Please	Molya
Thank you	Blagodarya
Pleased to meet you	Pri-ya-tno mi eh dah seh zah-poz-nah-ya z vahs
Excuse me; I'm sorry	Izvinyavaïte
My name is _____	Kahz vahm seh
I don't understand	Ne razbiram
Do you speak English?	Gho-vo-ri-teh li ahn ghliy-ski?

Communications

DIALING CODES IN BULGARIA

International country code: [359]

Selected city codes: Blagoevgrad (73), Bourgas (56), Kardjali (361), Pazardjik (34), Plovdiv (32), Smolyan (301), Razgrad (84), Sofia (2), Varna (52), Vidin (94)

Dialing Bulgaria from Overseas

To dial Bulgaria from overseas, begin with your country's international dialing code, then 359 (the country code for Bulgaria), then the city code, and finally the number. If you were dialing Sofia from the United States, for example, you would begin with 011, then 359, then 2 (the city code for Sofia), and finally the number of the person or office you were trying to reach.

Assistance Numbers

International Operator 0123
Domestic Operator 121
Information (business) 144
Information (private) 145
Telegrams 140

Bulgaria

Bulgaria

DIALING WITHIN BULGARIA

Local Calls

The telephone system is horribly antiquated in Bulgaria. Expect a long wait, even for local calls. Calls made from more secluded regions must be placed through the international operator.

Telephone service is available to most villages; however, the attempt to use it may be riddled with problems unless calling from a post office phone booth.

Long Distance Calls

To make a long distance call within Bulgaria, dial an initial zero + city code + number. Calls can be placed from any large post office and paid for upon exiting the booth at the clerk's desk.

International Calls

Direct dialing is available to more than 30 countries by dialing 00 + country code + city code + number. However, at this time, direct dial is still not available to the U.S., Canada, Latin America, and Asia. If calling any of the latter countries or continents, one must first call the operator and order the international call. The operator will then call you back when the call has been placed. Depending on the telephone traffic at the time, your wait may take a while.

All large post offices have international telephone booths, which prove far more cost effective than dialing from most hotels. Walk in and request a call, after which a booth will be assigned to you. Don't forget to pay before leaving.

To reach a U.S. operator, dial one of the convenient direct access numbers; however, these may only allow U.S. connections and may not be possible from public phones.
AT&T Direct...00-800-0010
MCI..00-800-0001
Sprint..00-800-1010

Public Telephones

Card Phone:

Public pay phones are available for coins and calling cards and can be found throughout the country.

Calling Cards

Phone cards are available from the post office for international calls.

CELLULAR PHONES

Cellular phone service is an option in Bulgaria. In the analog format Radio Telecommunication Company offers NMT-450 service. In a digital format they offer GSM service.

Note: Your home country cell phone may not work in this country. If not, we recommend that you rent an international cell phone *before* you leave home. A major US-based cell phone rental provider is **IMC WorldCell**. For information see "International Cell Phone Rentals" on page 14.

CALL BACK

You can (potentially) save significant sums when calling in Bulgaria by using a call back service. For a list of callback services, please refer to the "Communications" section in the *Global Road Warrior* Introduction.

Fees for call back services vary widely, depending on the company and the type of service required. Be sure to check with these companies before leaving to compare rates.

PHONE JACKS

Plug adaptors are available through **iGo Corporation.** (See "Electrical and Telephone Adaptors" on page 19.)

POSTAL SERVICES

The central post office in Sofia resides at 6 Gurko Street. The central office provides 24-hour telephone, telegram, and telefax services. However, the postal system is slow and not very reliable.

Business Services

COURIER SERVICES

DHL International; 10 Momina Cheshma Blvd., Druzhba 2.; tel: 79-333 (door to door service); 36 Dragan Tsankov Blvd. tel: 7146-3360.

East-European Express Ltd.; 49 Graf Ignatiev St.; tel: 883-604 or 810-330.

Han Federal Express; 7 Iskar St.; tel: 810-859; 810-843.

International Post; 11 Gurko St.; tel: 813-296 or 878-281.

In Time Courier; 12 Iskarsko Shousse Blvd.; tel: 793001-3.

Mobile Postal Services; 11 Stefanson Blvd.; tel: 383-018 or 889-443.

UPS (Bulgaria Parcel Service); 12 Iskarsko Chaussee Blvd. 1592; Sofia; tle; (2) 793-001; fax: (2) 793-740 or (2) 655-077.

TRANSLATION SERVICE

World Trade Center; 36, Dragan Tzankov Blvd, 1040 Sofia, Bulgaria; tel: (2) 9161-5052; fax: (2) 9161-3533; French, English, German.

Electrical

Current

220 volts AC, 50Hz

ELECTRIC PLUGS

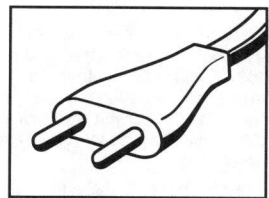

All plugs are 2-pin.

Plug adaptors are available through **iGo Corporation.** (See "Electrical and Telephone Adaptors" on page 19.)

Technical Support

HARDWARE/SOFTWARE VENDOR SUPPORT

Dell; tel: [1] (344) 748-000; fax: [1] (344) 748-008 (European Headquarter); (in Germany) tel: [49] (61) 039-710; (Dell- Europe) tel: [44] (134) 474-8000; (in the U.S.) tel: [1] (512) 338-4400; fax: [1] (512) 728-3330; http://www.dell.com/.

Hewlett Packard; (in Switzerland) tel: [41] (22) 780-8111; (in the U.S.) tel: [1] (408) 246-4300; http://www.hp.com/.

IBM; tel: (2) 973-3171; (2) 973-3186; (2) 971-2550; fax: (2) 973-3163; (in Germany) tel: [49] (711) 78-50; fax: [49] (711) 785-3511; (in Switzerland) tel: [41] (22) 310-0418 (in French); (U.S. Main Office) tel: [1] 914-765-1900; (in the U.S.) tel: [1] (919) 517-2800; http://www.ibm.com/

Microsoft; (in Germany) tel: [49] (89) 31-760; fax: [49] (89) 3176-1000; tel: [49] (89) 3176-1199; (in Switzerland) tel: [41] (848) 858-868; fax [41] (1) 831-0869; (in the U.S.) [1] (425) 635-7222; http://www.microsoft.com/.

Internet Connection

HOW TO CONNECT

Connecting to AOL and Compuserve in Bulgaria is similar to using it when traveling outside your own area code. See the introductory section for detailed information on connecting to your account through a different phone number.

America Online

Numbers are available at keyword *international*. Be sure to get several local numbers before leaving. AOL has its GlobalNet service available at keyword *access* (a free area) where you can then download the software.

Direct access numbers for America Online in Bulgaria are currently unavailable. Users will have to pay international rates to use the service.

Compuserve

Numbers are available at keyword *Go International*. The Compuserve Web-site also has a great deal of information,

at http://www.compuserve.com.

There are no direct access numbers for Compuserve in Bulgaria. Users will have to pay international rates to use the service.

Independent Service Providers

Many independent service providers offer discounts if you are only in town for a couple days.

Bulnet; tel: (2) 988-8146; fax: (2) 987-1122; email: support@bulnet.bg; http://www.bulnet.com/.

EUNet - Bulgaria; tel: (52) 259-135; tel: (52) 603-231; fax. (52) 234-540; email: Info@Bulgaria.EU.net; http://www.eunet.bg/.

Express Consult-NET; tel: (2) 624-813; info@exco.net; http://www.exco.net/.

Techno-link; tel: (2) 963-0641; fax: (2) 963-0651; email: info@techno-link.com; http://www.techno-link.com/.

Business Culture

GREETINGS AND COURTESIES

The proper greeting in Bulgaria is a hand shake for both men and women and the salutation, "Good day." Address professionals by their titles, followed by their surnames. Female friends may kiss each other's cheeks or walk arm in arm down the street. Otherwise, physical contact is not a common sight.

BUSINESS ETHIC AND FRAMEWORK

In the past, businesspeople here could only become wealthy through corruption. Corruption still exists, and honest, private businesspeople today must work hard to gain respect. The weak work ethic of the Communist era is being strengthened; careers and their accompanying skills are gaining in stature. Entrepreneurialism is on the rise. Vacant buildings and garages are being turned into shops and other small enterprises.

Office hours are usually from 9 A.M. to 6 P.M. Bulgarians like to do business on a friendly basis; business meetings are frequently held at dinner and include food and wine.

Because they're naturally hospitable, Bulgarians strive to make their foreign business associates welcome. However, it's customary for foreign businesspeople to host dinners at public restaurants for their Bulgarian associates.

DECISION MAKING

Bulgarians prefer to do business in person, not by telephone or fax, and in a social environment. In this setting, Bulgarians are reluctant to turn down a proposal outright, preferring instead to delay a decision or change the topic of discussion. Therefore, it is difficult to assess the Bulgarians' position during a meeting. Decisions are made in Bulgaria through a step-by-step process, in which no further progress is made until affirmation of the previous step. Decisions in Bulgaria are rarely final. A favorable decision could be overturned in a matter of days. Conversely, a rejection may also be turned around just as quickly. Bulgarians are wary of foreign influences and may oppose "non-Bulgarian" ideas or products. Patience in dealing with Bulgarians is often rewarded.

MEETINGS

After arranging a meeting far in advance, it's socially correct for foreign businesspeople to always arrive on time, or earlier since Bulgarians value punctuality so highly. An appointment is best scheduled in the morning or in the afternoon between 2:00 and 3:00 pm. after the lunch hour has safely passed.

Bulgarians prefer to do business in person, not by telephone or fax, and in a social environment. In this setting, Bulgarians

Bulgaria

are reluctant to turn down a proposal outright, preferring instead to delay a decision or change the topic of discussion. Therefore, it's difficult to assess the Bulgarians' position during a meeting. One may expect a significant amount of time to pass between initial contact and a reaching a satisfactory agreement. Bulgarians appreciate factual, exact, and detailed presentations.

WOMEN IN BUSINESS

Women in Bulgaria are a presence in all professions and hold a 48 percent share of the adult labor force; but seldom do they hold the higher paying jobs. However, they do receive benefits that other more developed nations may not allow their female employees; for example: a 4-month, full-paid maternity leave is standard. Bulgarian women are more flexible than their male colleagues and are generally more receptive to the proposals of foreign business associates.

BUSINESS ATTIRE

Professional men wear suits and ties, although older men prefer trousers and sweaters. A dark, conservative business suit should serve a foreign businessman well. Professional women usually wear skirts (with a blouse or sweater) and high heels to work. Women are more concerned about their public appearance than men. Winter necessitates hats, boots, gloves, scarves and heavy coats.

Clothing is expensive here; women often knit and sew for their families. For those who can afford them, European and American fashions are popular.

Business Centers
Sofia

CITY VIEW

Sofia is a tasteful city, rebuilt after World War II, but no one would confuse it with a modern metropolis. Its center is quaint with golden bricks, and horse and donkey driven carts still roam the city streets.

AIRPORT

Sofia Airport to City Center

The airport lies six miles (10 km.) from the city center. Buses run every 10 minutes during the day and every 20 minutes between 9p.m. and 12:30a.m. Coaches may be reserved ahead of time through Balkantourist. Taxis also serve the airport.

AIRLINES

Aeroflot	981-4943; 980-0067
Air Algerie	987-7325
Air France	981-7830; 980-6150
Air Ukraine	981-7830
Alitalia	808-786; 808-601
Austrian Airlines	327-061; 327-057
Armenian Airlines	540-549; 540-787
Balkan Airlines	684-148; 685-194
British Airways	684-148; 685-194
CSA	981-5408
El Al	815-289; 872-443
Hemus Air	720-754; 658-577
JAT	981-2167; 880-419
KLM	894-919
LOT	874-562; 980-3293
Lufthansa	980-4101; 980-4141
Malev	884-061; 878-607
Olympic Airlines	805-454; 807-979
Swissair	328-181; 335-012
Turkish Airlines	874-220; 883-596

HOTELS

Top-end

Castle Hotel Hrankov; Dragalevtsi Residential District, 53, Krousheva Gradina St.; tel: (2) 91-909; fax: (2) 672-945; city suburb at foot of Vitosha Mountain; restaurants; business center services; meeting hall; cell phone rental; doctor; car rental; health club; whirlpool; pool; sauna, squash, solarium, massage, and tennis for extra charge; US$225 (breakfast incl.)

Sheraton Sofia Hotel Balkan; 5, Sveta Nedelya Sq.; tel: (2) 87-6541; fax: (2) 980-6464; city center; casino; restaurants; no-smoking rooms; conference center; business center; executive services; secretarial services; beauty salon; shops; corporate rates; fitness; massage; sauna; whirlpool; US$195/310.

Vitosha;100 Anton Ivanov Blvd.; tel: (2) 6 2-4 51; fax: (2) 681-225; casino; restaurant; conference center; fitness; massage; sauna; sports ground; pool; tennis; US$165/195.

Expensive

Grand Hotel Bulgaria; 4, Tsar Osvoboditel Blvd.; tel: (2) 871-977; fax: (2) 884-177; city center; near exhibition grounds and railway; restaurant; US$90/150.

Novotel Europa; 131, Maria Louisa Blvd., tel: (2) 317-151; fax: (2) 320-011; city center; near exhibition grounds and railway; restaurant; no-smoking rooms; secretarial service; conference center; corporate rates; US$95/135.

Park Hotel Moskva; 25, Nezabravka St.; tel: (2) 71-261; fax: 656-737; city suburb; restaurant; conference center; corporate rates; US$65/90.

Rodina; 8, Tsar Boris III Blvd.; tel: (2) 91-980; fax: (2) 951-5840; city center; restaurant; conference center; secretarial service; fitness; swimming; sauna; winter sports; US$75/130.

Moderate

Deva-Spartak; 4 Arsenalska St.; tel: (2) 66-1261; fax: (2) 66-2537; city suburb; restaurant; conference center; parking.

Hemus; 31, Cherni Vruh Blvd.; tel: (2) 63-951; fax: (2) 661-318; city suburb.

Pliska; 87 Twarigradsko shosse Blvd.; tel: (2) 71-281; fax: (2) 723-952; near airport; restaurant; conference center.

Rila; 6, Tsar Kaloyan St.; tel: (2) 980-8865; fax: (2) 981-3386; city center; restaurant; conference center; secretarial service; parking; US$75/85.

MEDICAL CARE

Clinic for Foreign Citizens; Mladost 1 Housing Estate, 1 Evgeni Pavlovski St., Sofia; tel: 75-361.

Pirogov National Center of Emergency Medical Aid; 21, Totleben Blvd.; tel: 51-531.

AUTO RENTAL

Note: Car theft has become prevalent n Bulgaria; of special interest are recent sedan-type models as well as all-terrain vehicles. Drivers from outside the EU must carry an international driver's license.

Avis; Sofia airport, tel: (2) 738-023; 100 James Boucher Blvd., Hotel Vitosha 1000, tel: (2) 684-149; Hotel Sheraton, tel: (2) 888-167; Varna Intl. Airport, tel: (52) 650-832.

Eurodollar; 25, Vitosha Blvd.; tel: 875-779; fax: 981-0884.

Hertz; Blvd. Tzargradsko Shosse 73; tel: (2) 722-500; airport, tel: (2) 791-477; fax: (2) 885-729.

Canada

At a Glance
THE PEOPLE

Population .... 31,006,347 (July 1999 est.)
Growth Rate .... 1.06% (1999 est.)
Life Expectancy .... 79.37 years (born 1999)
Infant Mortality ... 5.47 deaths/1,000 live births (1999 est.)

Ethnic Composition
Caucasian 87%
Asian and other 11.5%
Amerindian 1.5%

Religious Composition
Roman Catholic.. 45%
United Church 12%
Anglican... 8%
Other and non-affiliated... 35%

Languages Spoken
English, French (both official)

Education and Literacy
For those aged 15 and over literacy is 97 percent. Primary and secondary public education is subsidized by the government and is compulsory until the age of 16.

Labor Force
Total: 15,300,000
By occupation: services 75%, industry 22%, agriculture 3%

THE ECONOMY

Canada is one of the major economies of the world and, as such, is a member of the G7. The Canadian economy is firmly entrenched in the free enterprise system, although the government has historically retained tight regulatory control over many of its major industries. The Canadian economy has experienced difficulties in the late 1990s and finds itself falling far behind its neighbor to the south (the USA) in both technology and GDP per capita. Canadian unemployment is double that of the USA and the Canadian dollar is in decline. Many Canadians are seeking employment across the border in their NAFTA co-member's economy. The government is in the process of reducing its intervention in the economy, but it is loath to give up its generous social entitlement system long considered a Canadian hallmark. High taxes needed to support the system further displace both foreign and domestic investment.

Exports .... US$210.7 billion (f.o.b., 1998)
Imports .... US$202.7 billion (f.o.b., 1998)
Total GDP .... US$688.3 billion (1998 est.)
GDP Per Capita .... US$22,400 (1998 est.)
Unemployment .... 7.8% (December 1998)

Inflation Rate 0.9% (1998)

Top Export Partners
United States, Japan, United Kingdom, Germany, South Korea, Netherlands, China.

Top Import Partners
United States, Japan, United Kingdom, Germany, France, Mexico, Taiwan, South Korea.

Top Exports
Newsprint, wood pulp, timber, crude petroleum, machinery, natural gas, aluminum, motor vehicles and parts, telecommunications equipment.

Top Imports
Crude oil, chemicals, motor vehicles and parts, durable consumer goods, electronic computers, telecommunications equipment and parts.

BUSINESS WORKWEEK

Offices
Monday to Friday 9a.m. to 5p.m. or 6p.m.

Banks
Monday to Wednesday 10a.m. to 3:30p.m., Friday 10a.m. to 4:30 p.m.

Some banks are open for longer hours and on Thursday. Automated banking machines are commonplace for after-hours banking.

Government
Monday to Friday 9a.m. to 5p.m.

Retail
Monday to Wednesday 9:30a.m. to 6p.m., Thursday to Saturday 9:30a.m. to 9p.m.

Note: Retail stores used to be closed on Sundays but since early 1992 more and more have been open seven days a week.

HOLIDAYS

New Year's Day..January 1
Good Friday..April 2*
Easter Monday ....April 5*
Canada Day ....July 1
Labor Day ....September 6*
Thanksgiving Holiday ....October 12*
Christmas Day...December 25
Boxing Day...December 26
* Dates may vary by year.
Note: Various provinces and cities have their own public holidays beyond those listed above.

CLIMATE

Seasons
Canada has four distinct seasons throughout the country, and they arrive at different times. Winter in Montreal begins in November and remains cold well into March and April. Average January temperatures are between -15° and -13°C (5 - 9°F), and average summer temperatures are about to 16 - 24°C (61 - 75°F). In Toronto, average winter months are between -1° and -8°C, and average summers are 26° and 14°C. Vancouver is mild and dry in the summer, and mild, cloudy, and wet in the winter. January temperatures are about 1° to 6°C and August is 21° to 13°C.

Regions
The vast size makes it difficult to generalize about Canada's climate. The Arctic climate of the north makes it uninhabitable, while most of the population lives within 100 miles of the U.S. border.

Canada's climate has a full range of temperatures; from sub-polar in the north to warm in the southeast and southwest.

Canada

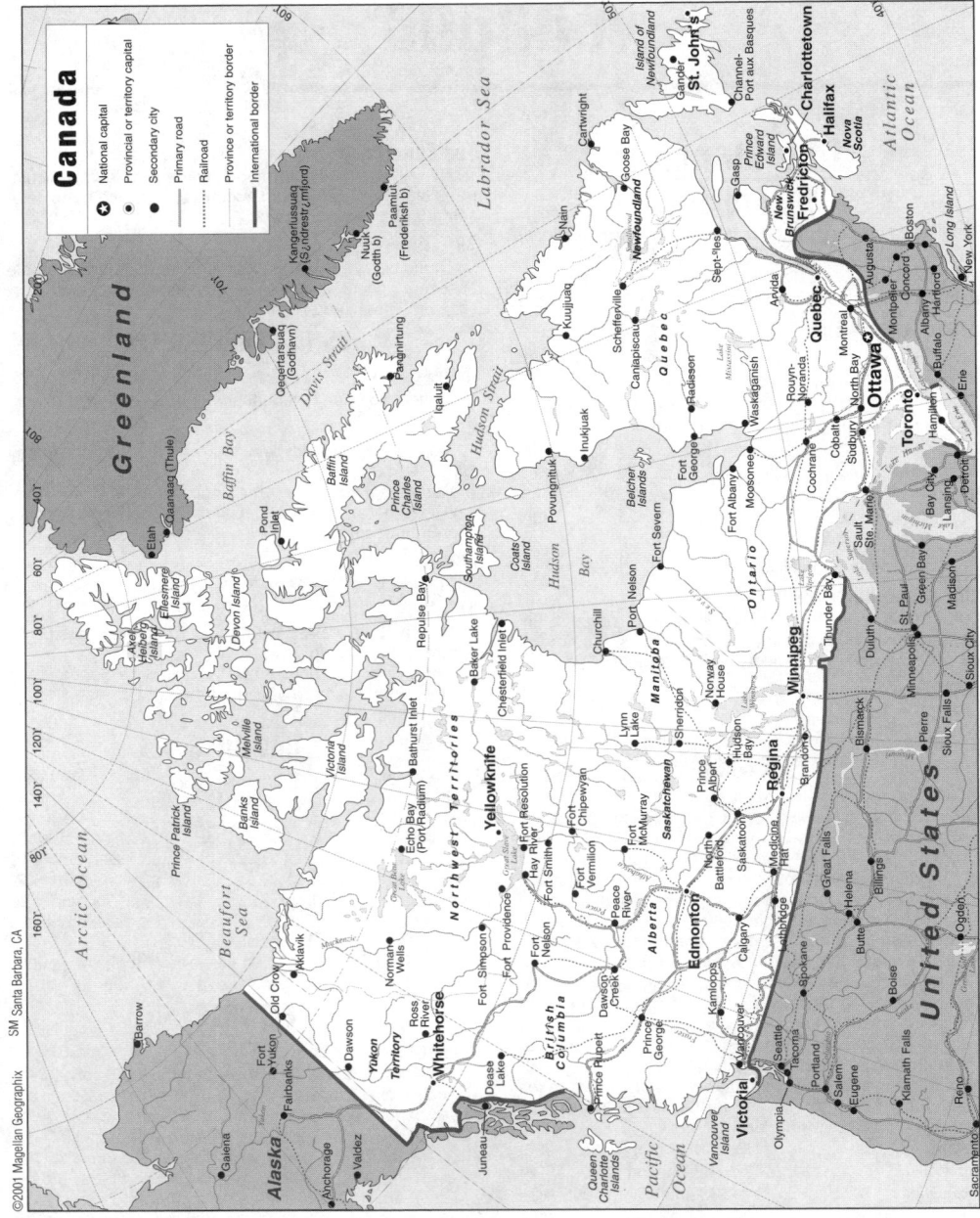

The interior usually has colder and longer winters than the coasts, with temperatures well below freezing. The Pacific coast has the warmest winters, with temperatures rarely falling below zero.

The northern territories, particularly the Yukon, have long hours of sunshine during the summer months, sometimes more than 20 hours a day. Conversely, in the winter, daylight hours are very short. Despite the long summer days, killing frosts severely hamper extensive agriculture.

Money & Banking

Currency
The currency of Canada is the Canadian Dollar (Can$).

Denominations
The Canadian Dollar comes in coin denominations of Can$1 and 50, 25, 10, 5, and 1 cents; and banknotes of Can$2, 5, 10, 20, 50, 100, 500, and 1,000.

Traveler's Checks and Credit Cards

A very efficient way to handle currency while travelling in Canada is with Canadian dollar-denominated traveler's checks. These can be purchased through Visa or American Express in many countries, and they are accepted virtually anywhere in Canada. Travelers checks in other currencies will be exchanged with a hefty commission, even in banks. Personal checks are rarely accepted at any commercial enterprise.

Visa, American Express, MasterCard, and Diner's Club are honored most everywhere. They can prove essential for identification purposes, security deposits for renting cars, booking accommodation, or purchasing tickets. They can also be used at most banks for cash advances. Automated teller machines (ATMs) are available throughout Canada. The most favorable rates for exchange are given for credit card and ATM transactions.

Essential Terms

English	French
Yes	*Oui*
No	*Non*
Good morning	*Bonjour*
Hello (daytime)	*Bonjour*
Hello (evening)	*Bonsoir*
Hello (telephone)	*Allo?*
Good-bye	*Au revoir*
Please	*S'il vous plaît*
Thank you	*Merci*
Pleased to meet you	*Enchanté*
Excuse me; I'm sorry	*Pardon*
My name is _____	*Je m'appelle* _____
I don't understand	*Je ne comprends pas*
Do you speak English?	*Parlez-vous anglais?*

Travel

VISA AND PASSPORT

A passport that is valid for one day beyond the anticipated exit date from Canada is required of all except:

- Citizens of the U.S. bearing proof of citizenship, such as a U.S. birth certificate or U.S. naturalization papers
- Nationals of Greenland who are residents thereof and entering from Greenland
- Permanent residents of the U.S. who have a U.S. alien registration card
- Citizens of France who are residents of and entering from St. Pierre & Miquelon

Visas are required of all except nationals of the following countries: Andorra, Antigua & Barbuda, Australia, Bahamas, Barbados, Botswana, Brunei, Costa Rica, Cyprus, Dominica, EU countries, Grenada, Hong Kong (SAR), Hun-

gary, Iceland, Israel (blue passports), Japan, Kiribati, Korea (Rep. of), Liechtenstein, Malaysia, Malta, Mexico, Monaco, Namibia, Nauru, New Zealand, Norway, Papua New Guinea, St. Kitts & Nevis, St. Lucia, St. Vincent & the Grenadines, Samoa, San Marino, Saudi Arabia, Singapore, Slovenia, Solomon Islands, Swaziland, Switzerland, Tuvalu, U.K., Vanuatu, Vatican City and Zimbabwe.

Note: Holders of passports certified 'British Subjects' or 'British Protected Persons' do require a visa.

There are only two types of visa: Visitor (single or multiple entry) or Transit. U.K. citizens are exempt from the need for a transit visa, although foreign nationals holding British passports may be required to have one (check with the Canadian embassy or consulate in advance).

Canadian customs officers at the point of entry are the sole arbiters of the valid length of stay for all visitors—maximum is six months. The visitor must also satisfy the customs officer that she/he has sufficient funds to cover all expenses for the duration of the stay and to cover expenses of a return trip to country of origin, as well as evidence of confirmed reservations for return travel arrangements. If the visitor desires an extension of stay, a written application must be made to the Canada Immigration Centre well in advance of the visa's expiration date. Allow six to ten days for processing of visa applications.

RESTRICTED ENTRY

The Government of Canada denies admission to travelers holding passports, identity, or travel papers issued by Bophuthatswana, Ciskei, Transkei, Venda, or the Palestine government.

DEPARTURE FORMALITIES

Vancouver levies an airport improvement fee of C$15 for international departures, and C$10 for departures to non-domestic North American locations, including Hawaii and Mexico.

Montréal (Dorval) imposes a tax of C$10 for all international departures and C$7.50 for international departures to North American destinations. Transit passengers are exempt.

CUSTOMS ENTRY (PERSONAL)

Duty-free

- Tobacco: 200 cigarettes, 50 cigars, 200g of manufactured tobacco and 400g of tobacco sticks per person over 18 years of age
- Alcohol: one bottle (1.1 liters) of distilled spirits or wine, and 24 bottles or cans (355ml) of beer or ale per person over 18 years of age (If entering Alberta, Manitoba and Québec and if you are over 19 years old and are entering British Columbia, Ontario, Prince Edward Island, Saskatchewan, Northwest Territories, Yukon, New Brunswick, Newfoundland & Labrador, and Nova Scotia)
- Gifts to the value of Can$60 per gift (not being advertising matter, tobacco or alcoholic beverages)
- A small amount of perfume for personal use only

Prohibited or Restricted

- Firearms and explosives
- Endangered species of animals and plants
- Animal products (meat, food and plant material are subject to certain restrictions and formalities.
- Dogs and domestic cats may be imported from certain rabies-free countries (including the United Kingdom and the Republic of Ireland) subject to certain restrictions and formalities (but note that rabies is present in Canada and pets will generally face quarantine on returning home). Enquire at the Canadian High Commission or Embassy for further details.

Note: There is a General Sales Tax (GST) in Canada of 7 percent on all goods and services. Visitors may reclaim this tax on accommodation and any goods purchased and taken out of the country if the amount exceeds Can$100. However, GST is not reclaimable on food, drink, tobacco, or any form of transport. To claim a rebate, a GST form must be completed, with all original receipts attached, and mailed to the address on the form.

IMMUNIZATION

A smallpox vaccination certificate is required for anyone who has been in an infected country within the previous two weeks. There are no other required vaccinations and no special precautions or serious health problems. In the Toronto area the pollen count is high and may require allergy medication. Hepatitis A and tetanus inoculations are recommended for those traveling to remote areas.

TIPPING

Taxi
Fifteen percent is considered normal.

Porters
C$1 per piece of luggage is standard.

Hotels
Room service and transport of luggage are included in bill.

Restaurants
Service charges are seldom included in bill, but taxes are included. A standard tip for wait staff and bartenders is 15 percent.

Other
Beauticians, barbers: 15 percent. Doormen and bellman: C$1.

EMERGENCY INFORMATION

Police and Crime
Crime is relatively low in Canada, but in the main cities—notably Montreal, Toronto, and Vancouver— crime does occur on a regular basis. Violent street crime is still quite rare when compared to the U.S.

Foreign business visitors are, however, often the target of thieves. Consequently, purses, laptops, and briefcases will require additional security. Do not leave valuables in cars or on tables in cafés. Keep non-essential valuables locked in hotel safes when not in use. Use credit cards and travel checks when possible. Carry photocopies of your passport instead of the original. Carry cash in a money belt, and use credit cards or traveler's checks for most of your large transactions.

Emergency Telephone Numbers
For all emergencies, one of these two numbers functions throughout the country, depending on the province:

Emergency 911
or 0

Health
Apart from flu there are no health risks in Canada. Water is safe to drink, and bottled water is readily available. Food laws are strict, and visitors can consider all foods safe. Visitors from Asia may experience some stomach disorders due to the change in diet.

Medical service is efficient and of the highest standard, and most costs are covered by health plans. You will be charged for medicines, but costs are low.

INTERNAL TRAVEL

AIR
Numerous regional airlines operate in Canada, the primary ones being:
- Atlantic Coast: Air Nova, Air Atlantic
- Western Canada: Time Air, Air BC
- Central Canada: Air Alliance, Air Ontario, West-Jet.

There are also approximately 75 airlines offering local services. Horizon Air offers 1-, 2-, and 3-week passes providing unlimited travel in Alberta, British Columbia, and six U.S. states. These passes are available through travel agents, and can only be obtained outside of Canada.

There is a departure tax for domestic flights that ranges from C$5 to C$15. What you pay depends on the airport of embarkation and on the destination.

TAXI
Taxis are plentiful in all major cities but definitely remain the most expensive mode of travel. Cabs may be reserved by telephone, or simply hailed curbside.

Fares run on a meter and do not need to be negotiated. Drivers are, for the most part, very familiar with their cities. You may want to bring directions, however, as a precaution. A few unscrupulous cab drivers may take advantage of your ignorance to increase the fares by taking "the long way".

AUTO
Car and truck rental is readily available in major cities and towns and at airports. A credit card and a valid driver's license are required for rental. Avis, Bricar, Budget, Dollar, Hertz, Thrifty, and Tilden are the major rental companies with a presence in Canada. Local insurance is mandatory. Age limits on rentals vary by agency. Driving is highly regulated in Canada, so a close inspection of driving rules is advised.

Visitors may drive on the basis of their national driver's licenses for up to three months throughout the provinces, with a few exceptions:
- In the Yukon, the permissible term is only one month
- On Prince Edward Island, it is four months
- In British Columbia, New Brunswick and Québec the law allows for six months

The Canadian Automobile Association is affiliated with most European organizations, offering full use of its facilities to affiliates' members
tel: (613) 247 0117; fax: (613) 247 0118;
website: www.caa.org

TRAIN
Train travel is very popular and a great way to see the countryside if time permits. Intercity travel is common. Purchase tickets at travel agencies or at train stations. VIA Rail Canada offers extensive routes across Canada. The regional railways are: Ontario Northland, Algoma Central, British Columbia Railway, Great Canadian Railtour Company, Québec North Shore & Labrador, Toronto Hamilton, Buffalo Railway, White Pass, and Yukon Route.

Rapid intercity trains run between Québec, Montréal, Halifax, Toronto, Windsor, and Ottawa. The fare includes a meal, drinks, and snacks.

VIA Rail operates an Eastern overnight transcontinental service linking Montréal (Québec) and Halifax (Nova Scotia).

VIA also operates a transcontinental service in the Western provinces (The Canadian) running between Toronto (Ontario) and Vancouver (British Columbia), making the trip three times weekly, transiting Winnipeg, Saskatoon, Edmonton, and Jasper. Passengers are attracted to this passage by the sensational vistas of the three colossal mountain ranges en route—the Rockies, the Selkirks, and the Coastal. The course also features the scenery of ancient glaciers, mammoth lakes, and spectacular waterfalls. All trains running between Vancouver and Toronto include sleeping cars with showers.

The transcontinental service has connections with regular services in the Atlantic provinces and in Québec City and Montréal. Long-distance train travel is extremely comfortable, replete with full restaurant amenities, air conditioning, ample reclining seats, and so forth. Alcoholic beverages, videos and films, and souvenirs are also available on board for an additional cost.

Discount rail passes:

- The Canrailpass is purchased only outside Canada; a valid passport must be presented. It provides for unlimited journeys for 12 days within a 30-day period. It is only valid on VIA Rail trains.
- The Alaska Pass grants 8-, 15-, 22- and 30-day travel periods in both Alaska and B.C., including transit on B.C. Ferries and Rail, Greyhound Lines of Canada, Alaskan Express, Norline Coaches, White Pass & Yukon Railroad, and Alaska Railroad.

Note: There are further discounts available for students and senior citizens with both of these plans.

Trains may offer the only means to reach certain remote towns and villages in winter time.

For further information on itineraries, schedules, fares, and discounts, contact VIA Rail in Canada; tel: (514) 871 600 website: www.viarail.ca

METRO

In Montreal, the Metro runs from 5:30a.m. until 1a.m. Monday through Friday and until 1:30a.m. and 2a.m. on Saturday and Sunday respectively. The system is clean and efficient with few security concerns. It also connects to 29 kilometers (18 miles) of Montreal's "Underground City" as well as to the extensive bus system. Metro tickets and transfers are good on the bus lines and vice versa.

In Toronto, the subway system has two main lines. The Bloor/Danforth line runs east to west while the Yonge/University/Spadina line covers north-south transport. Both lines operate from 5:30a.m until 2a.m., seven days a week. Tokens and tickets can be purchased at any of the 60 subway stations. A monthly "MetroPass" is also available. Visitors may acquire transit information for Toronto at: (416) 393-4636 from 7a.m. until 11:30p.m., Monday through Saturday.

BUSES & TRAMS

Canada's major cities have extensive and efficient bus and tram systems. Fares are low and inter-city lines are also available. Metropolitan buses run on a flat-fare system (standard fares, regardless of distance traveled). Riders must make fare payments with exact change. Transfers must be requested upon boarding a bus.

Traveling by long-distance coach is one of the most economic and convenient ways of getting around in Canada. All regions are well served by an expansive network of lines, the most comprehensive being the Greyhound Bus Company, which covers more than 193,000km (120,000 miles) of North America. Greyhound has a number of discount passes which can be purchased outside of North America. For more information, contact Greyhound World Travel Ltd. website: www.greyhound.com

Grayline Coaches is another company that provides transportation to major Canadian destinations.

Canada also has regional bus services, the most important of which are as follows:

- Atlantic Canada: Acadian Lines, Terra Nova Transport, SMT Eastern and CN Roadcruiser.
- Central Canada: Canada Coach Lines, Gray Coach Lines, Voyageur and Voyageur Colonial, Grey Goose Bus Lines Limited, Saskatchewan Transportation and Orleans Express.
- West Canada: Brewster Transport, Greyhound Lines of Canada and Vancouver Island Coach Lines.

Overnight bus travel may not seem the most glamorous, but for the business traveler on a tight budget, it is an excellent way to go. If you are concerned about making a certain kind of impression on a client or partner, simply take the bus to a transit point not quite as far as your ultimate destination, then switch over to one of Canada's premier railway or airline services.

WATER TRAVEL

Canada has thousands of miles worth of navigable waterways, including lakes, canals, and rivers, as well as an extensive coastline and the St. Lawrence Seaway (providing access to the Great Lakes). All of these resources have endowed Canada with one of the most advanced passenger water travel systems in the world.

Fares can be expensive in remote regions, but passenger boats are often the only means of long-distance travel in the back country. Coastal and inland ports connect with virtually any port in the Americas, Europe, or Asia.

TRAVEL ASSISTANCE

There are literally hundreds of web sites providing information about travel in Canada, as well as promotions for various trips and destinations. They are so numerous that another entire book could be dedicated just to listing them. The address below offers an excellent starting point and a source of assistance for the traveler who is already in country and acts as an agency whose first priority is to help the visitor rather than lighten his/her wallet. For advance research, references will be freely given regarding any specific province or feature the traveler wishes to investigate.

Canadian Tourism Commission
235 Queen Street, 8th Floor West
Ottawa, Ontario K1A 0H6
tel: (613) 946 1000; fax: (613) 954 3945.
email: ctc_feedback@businteractive.com
website: www.canadatourism.com

Communications

DIALING CODES IN CANADA

International country code: [1]

Selected city codes: Alberta (403), British Columbia (Vancouver area) (604), British Colombia (outside Vancouver area) (250), Manitoba (204), New Brunswick (506), Newfoundland (709), Nova Scotia (902), Ottawa (613), Toronto (metro) (416), Toronto vicinity (905), Québec (Sherbrooke) (819), Quebec (Montreal north and south shore) (450), Quebec (Quebec City) (418), Montreal (Island) (514), Saskatchewan (306), Yukon Territory (867)

Dialing Canada from Overseas

To dial Canada from overseas, begin with your country's international dialing code, then 1 (the country code for Canada), then the city code, and finally the number you are trying to reach. If dialing from the United States, simply dial [1], the Canadian area code, and the number.

Canada

Assistance Numbers

Operator 0
Domestic Information ....(area code) + 555-1212
Local Information.. 411

CALLING WITHIN CANADA

Local Calls
Simply pick up and dial to access local number. In a hotel, a local call may cost you 50 cents per call.

Long Distance Calls
Dial a long distance number with area code when calling a number outside the city you are in; between the U.S. and Canada dial 1 + area code + number.

International Calls
To make an international direct call from any phone, dial 011 + country code + area code + number. The optimum discounted rates occur between 11p.m. and 8a.m. International rates are listed in front of telephone books. Procedures are much the same as they are in the States; even the AT&T access number is the same.

AT&T Direct .... 1-800-CALL ATT

Calling card numbers can be used on any phone. Some phones also accept major credit cards. And, as always, hotel surcharges may apply, sometimes even if using your own long-distance carrier to make a call.

PAY PHONES

Public Telephones

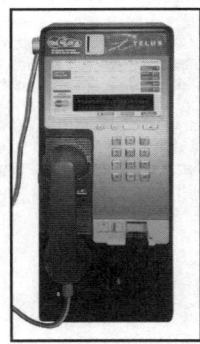

Most public telephones are coin operated, although calling card phones are becoming more popular. Coin phones cost Can$0.25 per local call.

Finding a public phone that works can be a problem in some areas: they are favorite targets of vandals, and many public phones are old and broken down. Because most Canadian pay phones accept only coins, you are advised to use a credit card or phone card for calls lasting longer than a minute if you do not want to walk around with several dollars in change weighing you down. Most public phones have instructions for using credit card.

1. Lift receiver
2. Listen for dial tone
3. Deposit coin
4. Dial

Calling Cards
Calling cards can be purchased at newsstands and hotels, although calling card phones may be difficult to come by.

CELLULAR PHONES

There are numerous cellular phone service providers in Canada, predominantly in the analog AMPS format.

Note: Your home country cell phone may not work in this country. If not, we recommend that you rent an international cell phone *before* you leave home. A major US-based cell phone rental provider is **IMC WorldCell**. For information see "International Cell Phone Rentals" on page 14.

CALL BACK

You can (potentially) save significant sums when calling in Canada by using a call back service. For a list of callback services, please refer to the "Communications" section in the *Global Road Warrior* Introduction.

Fees for call back services vary widely, depending on the company and the type of service required. Be sure to check with these companies before leaving to compare rates.

PHONE JACK

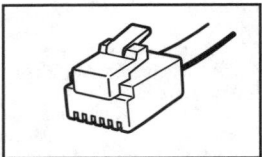

Plug adaptors are available through **iGo Corporation**. (See "Electrical and Telephone Adaptors" on page 19.)

FAX

Faxes can be found just about anywhere, and service is excellent. Prices are based on locally agreed rates.

POSTAL SERVICES

All mail to outside North America is by air only. Stamps are available just about anywhere, from hotels and newsstands to vending machines and post offices.

Hours of service
Monday to Friday 9:30a.m. to 5p.m., Saturday 9a.m. to noon.

TELEGRAMS

Telegrams must be delivered to the local Canadian Pacific or Canadian National Office and are serviced by the Canadian National Telecommunications or Canadian Pacific.

Business Services

BUSINESS CENTERS

Central Park Business Center, Vancouver, tel: (604) 435-2500.
HQ Business Centers, Vancouver, tel: (604) 443-5000.
Corporate Executive Offices, Ontario, tel: (905) 332-1320.
Execu-Center, Inc., Montreal, tel: (514) 393-1100.
Telsec Business Centers, Montreal, tel: (514) 393-8222.

For assistance in other locations, contact the Executive Suite Association at (800) 237-4741.

COURIER SERVICES

Montreal
DHL: 750 Stuart Graham, Ste. 246, Dorval; 1-800-465-4639.
FedEx: (514) 345-0130.
UPS: toll free: 1-800-263-8125 (U.S. to Canada); 1-800-742-5877 (within Canada); tel: (506) 877-4878.

Toronto

DHL: 6205 Airport Rd., Bldg. B, Ste. 400, Mississauga; (416) 244-3278.

FedEx: (416) 897-9322.

UPS: UPS; toll free: 1-800-263-8125 (U.S. to Canada); 1-800-742-5877 (within Canada); tel: (416) 736-3800.

Vancouver

DHL: 4871 Miller Rd., Unit E 109, Richmond, B.C.; (604) 278-3984.

FedEx: (604) 273-1544.

UPS; toll free: 1-800-263-8125 (U.S. to Canada); 1-800-742-5877 (within Canada); (604) 273-0014.

TRANSLATION SERVICES

Accredited Language Services (800) 755-5775.

Ad-Ex Worldwide (800) 223-7753.

AT&T Language Line Services (800) 752-0093.

Business Translation Services (800) 544-5721.

Language Lab (800) 682-3126.

Berlitz Translation/Interpretation Services:

Vancouver: (604) 685-9331

Toronto: (416) 924-7773

Ottawa: (613) 234-8686

Montreal: (514) 288-3111.

World Trade Center Montreal; 380 St. Antoine Street West, Suite 2100, Montréal, Québec, Canada H2Y 3X7; tel: (514) 849-1999; fax: (514) 849-3813; email: info@wtc-mtl.com.

Electrical

Current

110 volts AC, 60Hz

ELECTRIC PLUGS

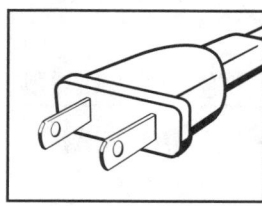

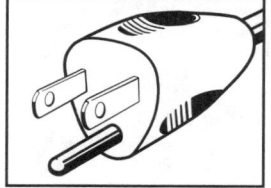

Flat 3-pin plugs are the norm in Canada.

Plug adaptors are available through **iGo Corporation.** (See "Electrical and Telephone Adaptors" on page 19.)

Technical Support

HARDWARE/SOFTWARE VENDOR SUPPORT

Apple/Claris; (in the U.S.) tel: [1] (800) 500-7078; (in Germany) tel: [49] (1) 803-5018; (in Switzerland) tel: [41] (800) 833-310; (in the U.K.) tel: [44] (990) 127-753; http://www.apple.com/.

Compaq/Digital; General U.S.) tel: (281) 518-2000; (in Switzerland) tel: [41] (22) 709-5330; fax: [41] (22) 709-5391 (Geneva); tel: [41] (1) 801-2507; fax: [41] (1) 801-2172 (Zurich); (General U.S.) tel: (281) 518-2000; http://www.compaq.com/.

Corel; (in the U.S.) tel: [1] (716) 871-2325 (Ask to be Forwarded to Appropriate Program); (in Germany) tel: [49] (180) 425-8210 (TS Word Perfect-32 bit); http://www.corel.com/.

Dell; tel: [1] (800) 387-5759 (Customer Service); [1] (800) 847-4096 (Technical Support); tel: (416) 758-2200; fax: (416) 758-2305 (Dell Canada); (in the U.S.) tel: [1] (512) 338-4400; fax: [1] (512) 728-3330; http://www.dell.com/.

Gateway 2000; (in the U.S.) tel: [1] (605) 232-2191; fax: [1] (605) 232-2023; (in Ireland) tel: [353] (1) 797-2000; http://www.g2k.com/.

Hewlett Packard; tel: (208) 323-2551; (in the U.S.) tel: [1] (408) 246-4300; http://www.hp.com/.

IBM; tel: [1] (800) 426-4968 (toll free main number); [1] (800) 565-3394 (toll free/technical assistance); (U.S. Main Office) tel: [1] 914-765-1900; [1] (506) 646-4000; (905) 316- 5000; http://www.ibm.com.

Microsoft; tel: (905) 568-0434 (in Canada, Main Office); (in the U.S.) [1] (425) 635-7222; (in Switzerland) tel: [41] (848) 858-868; fax [41] (1) 831-0869; http://www.microsoft.com/.

NEC; tel: [1] (877) 632-8324; (in the U.S.) [1] (916) 388-0101 (Main Switchboard); http://www.nec.com/.

Internet Connection

HOW TO CONNECT

Connecting to AOL and Compuserve in Canada is similar to using it when traveling outside your own area code. See the introductory section for detailed information on connecting to your account through a different phone number.

America Online

Numbers are available at keyword *international*. Be sure to get several local numbers before leaving. Go to AOL's Global-Net service available at keyword *access* (a free area) and download the software. Local numbers carry an additional hourly surcharge of US$2.95. The 800 access number is available for US$12 an hour.

Access: Calgary (403) 263-3310; Edmonton (780) 423-2222; Halifax (902) 455-2076; Hamilton (905) 529-9891; Kitchener (519) 742-8352; London (519) 433-9252; Montréal (514) 861-3555; Oshawa (905) 404-2656; Ottawa (613) 230-0589; Québec City (418) 694-7211; Regina (306) 565-0566; St. Catharines (905) 682-8845; Saskatoon (306) 652-0851; Toronto (416) 364-7288; Vancouver (604) 669-5008; Victoria (250) 995-0002; Windsor (519) 253-0708; Winnipeg (204) 946-1878.

Compuserve

Numbers are available at keyword *Go International*. The Compuserve Web-site also has a great deal of information, at http://www.compuserve.com.

Access: Calgary (403) 294-9120; Edmonton (780) 440-2744; Montreal (514) 879-5826; Toronto (416) 367-8122; Vancouver (604) 739-8194.

Canada

Sales/service: Compuserve; P.O. Box 20212; 5000 Arlington Centre Blvd.; Columbus, OH 43220; Service: (614) 5291340, (800) 8488199; Service fax: (614) 5291611. Service Hours 8a.m. to midnight (U.S. EST) weekdays, noon to 10 p.m. (U.S. EST) Saturday and Sunday.

Independent Service Providers
Many independent service providers offer discounts if you are only in town for a couple of days.

Note: There are several local ISPs and prices vary widely. Be sure to research the different ISPs in the area you plan to travel to before making a decision.

A+Net; tel: [1] (888) 301-2516; tel: (619) 558-8449; support@abac.com; http://www.apls.net/.

AT&T Canada LDS; tel: [1] (888) 288-1233; webmaster@attcanada.net; http://www.attcanada.net/.

Fiberlink Communications; tel: (610) 941-2050; (toll-free) tel: [1] (800) 546-5669; fax: (610) 941-2069; email: info@fiberlinkcc.com; http://www.fiberlinkcc.com/.

IBM Internet Connection Services; (toll-free) tel: [1] (800) 455-5056; Calgary: (403) 290-5651; Edmonton: (403) 917-4451; Montreal: (514) 846-7171; Toronto: (416) 758-5871; Vancouver: (604) 602-2401; http://www.ibm.net/.

jjj.net; tel: (914) 632-2271; fax: (914) 632-8628; email: info@jjj.com; http://www.jjj.net/.

MediaLinx Interactive; tel: (604) 320-2700; (toll-free) tel: [1] (800) 773-2121; email: customer_service@bc.sympatico.ca; http://www.sympatico.ca/.

UUNET Technologies; tel: (416) 368-6621; (toll-free) tel: [1] (800) 488-6384; email: webmaster2UUNET.cal; http://www.uu.net/.

VPM Enterprises; tel: (916) 983-9876; (toll-free) tel: [1] (800) 321-0221; fax: (916) 983-4375; email: sales@vpm.com; http: www.vpm.com/.

Business Culture
GREETINGS AND COURTESIES
Canadian customs are similar to those in the US, but Canadians are generally more formal. They do not move to a first-name basis as quickly, and are more reserved. Behavior tends to be particularly formal in Ontario and eastern Canada, and somewhat more casual in Québec and the West. However, even reserved Canadians are open, direct, and friendly. The accepted greeting is smiling, making eye contact, and shaking hands. Handshakes are generally firm and brief, with a rapid, simple up-and-down motion. It is not necessary or appropriate to squeeze the other person's hand. In general, Canadians do not welcome body contact, casual touching, or frequent gesturing. Greetings will often be followed by a question about your trip, your health, or the weather. Such questions are a form of politeness. Long, detailed answers are not expected or especially wanted. After this quick, often superficial exchange, the next topic will be business.

DECISION MAKING
Canadians have conservative natures, a respect for formality, and are visibly polite; they do not generally act in haste, but neither is excessive time taken with thinking about moving forward. Once a proposition has been laid out and all its ramifications considered, decisions are made fairly quickly. Large corporations will take longer to come to a final decision, but this is mainly due to the hierarchies and bureaucratic nature of almost any large company. In smaller businesses, where one person might be the sole authority, decisions can be made very quickly.

WOMEN
Men still hold the vast majority of management positions, but more and more women are being found at the higher levels of business. Canadian women expect to be treated seriously and with the respect to which their position entitles them. Failure to do this is considered insulting. A woman may not respond to such behavior at the moment, but she will probably express her displeasure to her colleagues later. Businesswomen are as open and direct as men, but this should not be viewed as anything more than being friendly. Treat women as you would any business associate. Foreign women should expect to be treated the same as their male counterparts, but exactly how a woman is dealt with will depend on the Canadian she is encountering. Sexual discrimination is against the law and not openly practiced, but private biases do exist. If a woman encounters discrimination, remember that this is more a reflection of that person than the company. In general, foreign women who are confident, professional, and self-assured can expect to be treated with respect and taken seriously.

MEETINGS
Meetings tend to be formal. They start on time and punctuality is expected. There will often be some polite social conversation, but business will be addressed fairly quickly. Canadians value efficiency, and once a meeting begins in earnest they like to proceed in an organized manner, wasting no time and without interruption. It is also important to always be courteous and polite. Canadians appreciate thoroughness, and will expect to be provided with all the information essential to any proposal. Not being prepared or appearing to be evasive will not be viewed positively.

BUSINESS ATTIRE
Standard attire is a business suit, especially when dealing with large companies or doing business in cities. There is generally more latitude when dealing with smaller companies, or when doing business in western Canada and rural areas. Minimal attire is a jacket and tasteful pants, shirt, and shoes. Canadian women generally favor business dresses over suits. Women should dress professionally, tastefully, and conservatively when conducting business. Avoid extremes in fashion, including excessive jewelry or accessories.

Business Centers
Montréal
CITY VIEW
Montréal is the cultural and fashion center of Canada, yet is also a major manufacturing region. An interesting mix of French culture in a North American setting makes for a unique experience.

AIRPORT
Mirabel Airport to City Center
Mirabel Airport lies 34 miles (55 km.) from the city center. There is a regular bus service for C$14.50 to downtown Montréal from outside the arrivals area, but it takes an average of 55 minutes to get there. A cab fare will cost approximately C$45 to downtown, and about C$55 to Dorval airport.

Airline Numbers
Air Canada .... (514) 393-3333, 800-361-8620
American Airlines .... (514) 397-9635
British Airways .... (514) 287-9282

toll-free .... (800) AIRWAYS
Canada Airlines International .... (514) 847-2211
toll free .... (800) 363-7530
Delta Air Lines ....(514) 337-5522
toll free .... (800) 361-1970
USAir .... (800) 428-4322

HOTELS

Top-end

Bonaventure Hilton International; 1 Place Bonaventure, H5A 1E4; tel: (514) 878-2332; fax: (514) 878-1442; located in exhibition center; restaurants; business services; pool; shops; US$160 and up.

Hôtel Inter-Continental Montreal; 360 Sant-Antoine Street West; tel: (514) 987-9900; toll-free: 1-800-361-3600; part of World Trade Center complex; underground connection to stock exchange and subway; indoor pool; sauna; fitness center; US$142 and up.

Le Centre Sheraton; 1201 Boulevard Renelevesque O, H3B 2L7; tel: (514) 878-2000; fax: (514) 878-3958; downtown; metro stop; underground city; restaurant; meeting rooms; indoor pool; sauna; whirlpool; health club.

Loews Hôtel Vogue; 1425 Rue de la Montagne, H3G 1Z3; tel: (514) 285-5555; fax: (514) 849-8903; downtown; restaurant; in-room fax machines and dual telephone lines; business center; meeting and banquet facilities (for up to 240); corporate rates; exercise room; US$240/285.

Ritz Carlton; 1228 Sherbrooke St. W.; tel: toll free: 1-800-363-0366; tel: (514) 842-4212; fax: (514) 842-3383; restaurant.

Expensive

Best Western Europa Centre-ville; 1240 rue Drummond H3G 1V7; tel: (514) 861-4089; toll-free: 1-800-361-3000; fax: (514) 861-4089; restaurant; meeting and banquet facilities; conference facilities; sauna; exercise room; indoor pool; US$70/128.

Château Royal Hôtel Suites; 1420 rue Crescent; tel: (514) 848-0999; toll free: 1-800-363-0335; fax: (514) 848-1891; restaurants; business center; meeting room; parking; US$89/102; email: reservations@chateauroyal.com.

Delta Montréal; 450 Sherbrooke St. West; tel: 286-1986; toll-free: 1-800-268-1133; fax: 284-4342; downtown, near McGill University and convention center; restaurants; business center; health club; sauna; whirlpool; squash; US$100/150.

Chateau Versailles; 1659 rue Sherbrooke O, H3H 1E3; tel: (514) 933-3611; toll-free from U.S.: 1-800-361-3664; fax: (514) 933-7102; Victorian mansions or modern rooms; restaurant; meeting facilities (up to 50); fax, laptop, and secretarial services avail.; corp rates; US$119/139.

Hôtel du Parc; 3625 du Parc Ave.; tel: (514) 288-6666; toll-free: 1-800-363-0735; fax: (514) 288-2469; restaurants; executive boardrooms; function rooms; business services; conference exhibit hall; fitness center; access to McGill athletic facilities; email: rooms@duparc.com

Hotel Radisson des Gouverneurs de Montréal; 777 rue University, H3C 3Z7; tel: (514) 879-1370; fax: (514) 879-1761; indoor pool; sauna; fitness center; US$109 and up.

Novotel Montreal; 1180 Rue de la Montagne; downtown; near Molson Center; in-room work desk and modems; dual phone lines; business center; secretarial staff; conference rooms; parking; car rental; health club; US$90/150.

Moderate

Auberge Les Passants du Sans Soucy; 171 rue St. Paul Ouest; tel: (514) 931-8841; fax: (514) 931-3233; near financial district; fax machines.

Du Fort Hotel; 1390 Rue du Fort; tel: (514) 938-8333; fax:

(514) 938-2078; tel: 1-800-565-6333; city center; restaurant; business center; parking; health club; US$75/160.

Le Nouvel Hotel; 1740 Rene-Levesque Blvd.; tel: (514) 931-8841; toll-free: 1-800-363-6063; fax: (514) 931-3233; restaurant; bar; pool.

Lord Berri; 1199 rue Berri, H2L 4C6; tel: (514) 845-9236; fax: (514) 849-9855; edge of Old Town, next to University of Quebec; nearby bus, train and subway stations; restaurant; conference rooms; multilingual staff; no-smoking rooms.

Quality Hotel Downtown; 3440, avenue du Parc, H2X 2H5; tel: (514) 845-9236; toll-free: 1-800-268-6116; fax: (514) 849-6564.

MEDICAL CARE

Cote-des-Neiges Dental Centre; 6700 rue Cote-des-Neiges, Suite 174; tel: 737-1061.

Emergency Dental Services; 800 boulevard Rene-Levesque Ouest at University; tel: 875-7971.

Jewish General Hospital; 3755 Cote Sainte-Catherine at Cote-des-Neiges; tel: 340-8222.

Poison Control Centre; tel: (800) 463-5060.

Royal Victoria Hospital; 687 Avenue Pine Ouest at University; tel: 842-1231.

St. Mary's Hospital; 3830 Avenue Lacombe at Cote-des-Neiges; tel: 345-3511.

HEALTH CLUB

Centre Sheraton; Sheraton Hotel, 1201 boulevard Rene-Levesque at Stanley; tel: (514) 878-2000.

Club Lebourgneuf Nautilus Plus; 4500 boulevard des Gradins; tel: (418) 627-3441.

Club Multitennis Québec/Nautilus Plus; 6280 boulevard Wilfrid-Hamel near Duplessy, L'Ancienne-Lorette; tel: (418) 872-0111.

Club Tennis Avantage/Nautilus Avantage; 1080 rue Bouvier near Rue Pierre Betrand; tel: (418) 627-3343.

YMCA; 1450 rue Stanley at De Maisonneuve, Metro: Peel; tel: (514) 849-8393.

YWCA; 1355 boulevard Rene-Levesque Ouest at Crescent; tel: (514) 866-9941 (Québec City, Québec).

AUTO RENTAL

Avis; 1225 rue Metcalf at Sainte-Catherine; tel: (800) 879-2847.

Budget; Central Station, 895 rue de la Gauchetiere Ouest at University; tel: (800) 268-8900 or 866-7675.

Hertz; 1475 rue Aylmer at Maisonneuve; tel: (800) 654-3001 or 842-8537.

Thrifty; 1600 rue Berri near Ontario; tel: (800) 367-2277 or 845-5954.

WORLD TRADE CENTER

World Trade Center Montréal
380 St. Antoine Street West, Suite 2100
Montréal, Québec, Canada H2Y 3X7
tel: (514) 849-1999; fax: (514) 849-3813
email: info@wtc-mtl.com
website: http://www.wtc-mtl.com/eng/index.html

Canada *(vertical side tab)*

Toronto

CITY VIEW

Toronto is a multi-ethnic city, and has the reputation of being clean and safe. The crime, graffiti, and concentrated poverty that is so apparent in other large cities is not prevalent here.

AIRPORT

Lester B. Pearson Airport to City Center

The airport lies 18 miles (28 km.) from the city center. It can take about 40 minutes to travel from the airport to downtown. Cab fares hover around C$28. There are a number of bus services, including t he Hotel Express Gray Coach that departs from the arrivals terminal every 30 minutes for C$11; The Pacific Western Co. takes passengers to major hotels downtown for C$11.45 every 20 minutes. Some hotels offer free shuttle service.

Airline Numbers

American ....(416) 283-2243
British Airways ....(416) 250-0880
Delta...(800) 843-9378
Northwest ....(800) 225-2525
United ....(800) 241-6522
USAir ....(800) 428-4322
Air Canada ....(800) 268-7240, (416) 925-2311
Canadian Airlines International ....(800) 665-1177
Air Ontario ....(416) 925-2311

HOTELS

Note: All hotels listed below are located in the city center area.

Top-end

Crowne Plaza Toronto Centre; 225 Front St. W., M5V 2X3; tel: (416) 597-1400; fax: (416) 597-8128; near exhibition grounds; restaurant; conference center; executive services; secretarial services; corporate rates; fitness; sauna; pool; whirlpool.

Delta Chelsea Inn; 33 Gerrard St. W., M5G 1Z4; tel: (416) 595-1975; fax: (585-4393; restaurant; conference center; corporate rates; secretarial service; fitness; sauna; pool.

Four Seasons; 21 Avenue Rd., M5R 2G1; tel: (416) 964-0411; fax: (416) 964-2301; near lake; restaurant; conference center; business center; secretarial service; in-room modem/fax connection, multi-line phone, voicemail; cellular phones; weekday morning complimentary limousine service to business district; health club; fitness; massage; sauna; pool; whirlpool.

King Edward; 37 King St. East; tel: (416) 863-9700; fax: (416) 367-5515; near lake; restaurant; conference center; corporate rates; secretarial service; fitness; health; sauna.

Sky Dome Hotel; 1 Blue Jays Way, M5V 1J4; tel: (416) 341-7100; fax: (416) 341-5091; near lake; restaurant; in-room computers; conference center; corporate rates; secretarial service; fitness; health; sauna; whirlpool.

Expensive

Clarion Hotel Essex Park; 300 Jarvis St., M5B 2C5; tel: (416) 977-4823; fax: (416) 977-4830; restaurant; conference center; secretarial service; corporate rates; fitness; sauna; whirlpool; pool.

Metropolitan; 108 Chestnut St.; tel: (416) 977-5000; fax: (416) 977-9513; near exhibition center and railway; restaurant; executive services; secretarial services; corporate rates; fitness; health; massage; sauna; whirlpool; pool.

Novotel Toronto Centre; 45 The Esplanade; tel: (416)

367-8900; fax: (416) 360-8285; near railway; restaurant; conference center; corporate rates; fitness; sauna; whirlpool; pool.

Sutton Place Toronto; 955 Bay St. (416) 924-9221; fax: (416) 924-1778; city center; restaurant; conference center; health; sauna; pool.

Westin Harbour Castle; 1 Harbour Square, M5J 1A6; tel: (416) 869-1600; fax: (416) 869-0573; near exhibition grounds and railway; conference center; corporate rates; executive services; secretarial services; fitness; health; sauna; whirlpool; pool; tennis.

Moderate

Best Western Roehampton; 808 Mount Pleasant Road; tel: (416) 487-5101; fax: (416) 487-5390; restaurant; conference center; pool.

Bond Place; 65 Dundes St. East; tel: (416) 362-6061; fax: (416) 360-6406; near railway; conference center; corporate rates; parking.

Comfort Downtown; 15 Charles St. East; tel: (416) 924-1222; fax: (416) 924-1369; restaurant; corporate rates.

Days Inn Toronto Downtown; 30 Carlton St.; tel: (416) 977-6655; fax: (416) 977-0502; restaurant; conference center; pool; parking.

Inn on the Lake; 1926 Lakeshore Blvd. West; tel: (416) 766-4392; fax: (416) 766-1278; near lake; restaurant; conference center; fitness; parking.

Quality Hotel Journey's End; Midtown 280 Bloor Street West, M58 1V8; tel: (416) 968-0010; fax: (416) 968-7765.

MEDICAL CARE

Metro-Central YMCA; 20 Grosvenor St. near Yonge Street Downtown; tel: (416) 975-9622
University of Toronto Athletic Center; University of Toronto, 55 Harbord St. at Spadina Avenue; tel: (416) 978-3437

AUTO RENTAL

Budget; 141 Bay St., at Front Street; tel: 364-7104.
Tilden; 930 Yonge St., near Davenport; tel: 925-4551.
Avis; Hudson Bay Centre, 80 Bloor St., E. near Park Road; tel: 964-2051.
Hertz; 128 Richmond St., E. at Jarvis; tel: 363-9022.

WORLD TRADE CENTER

World Trade Center Toronto
The Board of Trade of Metro Toronto
One Fist Canadian Place, P.O. Box 375
Toronto, Ontario M5X 1E2
tel: (416) 366-6811; fax: (416) 366-4906
email: valent@bot.com
website: http://www.bot.com

Vancouver

CITY VIEW

Despite being the center of Canada's timber and fishing industries, Vancouver is a modern, technological city that ranks with its Canadian peers in combining beauty and efficiency, but adding a splendid backdrop of Rocky Mountain wonder on one end and sparkling Pacific Ocean on the other.

AIRPORT

Vancouver Airport to City Center

Vancouver Airport lies 11 miles (15 km.) from the city center. Travel time is about 30 minutes. An Airport Express Bus travels to downtown hotels and the Pacific

Central Station for C$10 (C$17 round trip) between 6a.m. and 12:30a.m. at regular 15 to 20-minute intervals. Some hotels offer a shuttle service. Taxis and limos are also available for comparable rates (C$20), but naturally at higher cost than the bus.

Airline Numbers

American Airlines	(800) 433-7300
British Airways	(800) AIRWAYS
Delta	(604) 221-1212
Horizon Air	(800) 547-9308
United	(800) 241-6522

HOTELS

Note: All hotels listed below are located in the city center area.

Top-end

Four Seasons Hotel; 791 West Georgia St. V6C 2T4; tel: (604) 689-9333; fax: (604) 844-6744; 385 rooms; located in business district; restaurant; conference center; secretarial service; corporate rates; fitness; health; sauna; pool.

Metropolitan Hotel; 645 Howe St., V6C 2Y9; tel: (604) 687-1122; fax: (604) 643-7267; restaurant; conference center; secretarial service; corporate rates; in-room computers; fitness; massage; sauna; whirlpool; pool.

Pan Pacific Hotel; 300-999 Canada Place Way, V6C 3B5; tel: (604) 662-8111; fax: (604) 685-8690; 504 rooms; adjacent convention center and seaside; restaurant; conference center; business center; secretarial service; in-room computers, dataports, most rooms with fax machine; fitness; health; massage; sauna; pool; tennis.

Sutton Place; 845 Burrard St.; tel: (604) 682-5511; fax: (604) 682-5513; near exhibition grounds and railway; restaurant; conference center; secretarial service; corporate rates; fitness; health; massage; sauna; whirlpool; pool; tennis; golf; winter sports.

The Wedgewood; 845 Hornby St.; tel: (604) 689-7777; fax: (604) 608-5348; old-world style; restaurant; in-room computers; conference center; secretarial service; fitness; massage sauna.

Expensive

Crowne Plaza Hotel Georgia Vancouver; 801 W. Georgia St.; tel: (604) 682-5566; fax: (604) 642-5565; 313 rooms; renovated 1998; Crowne Plaza Club floor; in-room speaker phones, bathrobes, complimentary local calls.

Georgian Court; 773 Beatty St.; tel: (604) 682-5555; fax: (604) 682-8830; near seaside; restaurant; in-room computer terminals; conference center; corporate rates; fitness; sauna; whirlpool.

Fairmont Vancouver Airport; PO Box 23798, Richmond; tel: (604) 207-5200; fax: (604) 248-3219; 392 rooms; accessible from airport elevator; in-room high-speed internet access.

Hotel Vancouver; 900 West Georgia St., V6C 2WT; tel: (604) 684-3131; fax: (604) 662-1929; restaurant; parking; conference center; fitness; health; pool.

Hyatt Regency; 655 Burrard V6C 2R7; tel: (604) 683-1234; fax: (604) 689-3707; 2 blocks from Pacific Center; restaurants; business center; secretarial services; multilingual staff; meeting and exhibition facilities; health club; sauna; fitness center.

Pacific Palisades (Kimpton Group); 1277 Robson St.; tel: (604) 688-0461; fax: (604) 688-4374; renovations in progress; suites with kitchens and fax machines; fitness center; pool.

Waterfront Centre Hotel; 900 Canada Place Way; tel: (604) 691-1991; fax: (604) 691-1999; in-room data ports, cordless phones; fitness center; pool.

Westbrook; 1234 Hornby St.; tel: (604) 688-1234; fax: (604) 689-1762; near airport and seaside; restaurant; secretarial service; corporate rates; fitness; pool.

Wall Centre Garden; 1088 Burrard St.; tel: (604) 331-1000; fax: (604) 331-1001; near seaside; restaurant; in-room computers; conference center; executive services; secretarial services; corporate rates; fitness; health; massage; sauna; whirlpool; poo; sports ground; tennis; golf; winter and water sports.

Moderate

Chateau Granville; 1100 Granville St.; tel: (604) 669-7070; fax: (604) 669-4928; beachfront; restaurant; conference center; secretarial service.

Days Inn Vancouver; 921 West Pender Street, V6C 1M2; tel: (604) 681-4335; fax: (604) 681-7808; email: welcome2@daysinn-van.com; near seaside; restaurant; in-room computer terminals avail.; corporate rates; parking.

Quality Hotel Downtown; 1335 Howe St.; tel: (604) 682-0224; toll-free: 1-800-663-8474; fax: (604) 682-3546; restaurant; business services; boardrooms; data ports available; pool; fitness center access.

MEDICAL CARE

Dental Centrel, Bentall Centre; 1055 Dunsmuir St. at Burrard Street, lower mall level; tel: 669-6700.

Medicentre, Bentall Centre; 1055 Dunsmuir St. at Burrard Street, lower mall level; tel: 683-8138.

St. Paul's Hospital; 1081 Burrard St. at Davie; tel: 682-2344.

Vancouver General Hospital; 855 W. 12th Ave. between Heather and Laurel streets; tel: 875-4111.

AUTO RENTAL

Avis; tel: (604) 273-4577 or (800) 879-2847.

Budget; tel: (604) 668-7000 or (800) 268-8900.

Hertz; tel: (604) 278-4001 or (800) 263-0600.

Thrifty; tel: (604) 276-0800 or (800) 367-2277.

Tilden; tel: (604) 273-3121 or (800) 387-4747.

WORLD TRADE CENTER

World Trade Center Vancouver
999 Canada Place, Suite 400
Vancouver, British Columbia
Canada V6C 3C1
tel: (604) 681-2111; fax: (604) 681-0437
email: contactus@vancouver.boardoftrade.com
website: http://www.vancouver.boardoftrade.com

Canada

Chile

At a Glance

THE PEOPLE

Population .... 14,973,843 (July 1999 est.)
Growth Rate .... 1.23% (1999 est.)
Life Expectancy .... 75.46 years (born 1999)
Infant Mortality . 10.02 deaths/1,000 live births (1999 est.)

Ethnic Composition
Caucasian and Caucasian-Indian 95%
Amerindian 3%
Other 2%

Religious Composition
Roman Catholic... 89%
Protestant 10%
Other and non-affiliated... 1%

Languages Spoken
Spanish (official), Amerindian dialects

Education and Literacy
    State schools provide free but compulsory primary education. Adult literacy stands at 95.2 percent.

Labor Force
Total: 5,700,000
    By occupation: services 38.3%, industry 42.5%, agriculture 19.2%.

THE ECONOMY
    Chile has become one of the most efficient nations in Latin America when it comes to controlling its economy. Having fallen prey to the vagaries of capital outflows in the early 1980s, Chile revised its foreign investment model. Foreign investment must now place one-third of its funding in Chilean banks for one year prior to usage to show commitment to the economy. This has allowed the Chilean economy to grow in a controlled environment without stultifying potential. Still dependent on mineral exports, steps have been taken by the government to reposition the economy for future technology growth. Chile has also taken advantage of its membership in Mercosur as well as its close trade ties to Canada to ensure its continued importance to the Americas as well as the global economy.

Exports .... US$14.9 billion (f.o.b., 1998)
Imports .... US$17.5 billion (f.o.b., 1998)
Total GDP .... US$184.6 billion (1998 est.)
GDP Per Capita .... US$12,500 (1998 est.)
Unemployment .... 6.1 percent (1997)
Inflation Rate 4.7% (1998)

Top Export Partners
    Asia, E.U., Latin America, United States.

Top Import Partners
    Latin America, United States, E.U., Asia.

Top Exports
    Copper, other metals and minerals, wood products, fish and fishmeal, fruits.

Top Imports
    Capital goods, spare parts, raw materials, petroleum and petroleum products, foodstuffs.

BUSINESS WORKWEEK

Offices
    Monday to Friday 8:30a.m. to 12:30p.m. and 2p.m. to 6p.m.

Banks
    Monday to Friday 9a.m. to 2p.m.

Government
    Monday to Friday 8:30a.m. to 12:30p.m. and 2p.m. to 6p.m. (Rural hours may differ.)

Retail
    Monday to Friday 8a.m. to 8p.m. (includes a 3-hour break at midday), Saturday 9a.m. to 2p.m.

HOLIDAYS

New Year's Day...January 1
Good Friday and Easter Saturday........................April 2-3*
Labor Day...May 1
Battle of Iquique ....May 21
Assumption... August 15
Anniversary of 1973 Coup...........................September 11
Independence Day ....September 18
Day of the Race, Anniversary of the
Discovery of America ....October 12
All Saints' Day ....November 1
Immaculate Conception...................................December 8
Christmas Day...December 25
    *Dates may vary by year.

CLIMATE

Seasons
    The climate is "Mediterranean" in the central region and around the capital, Santiago. Chile is south of the equator so its seasons are reversed. Temperatures of around 28˚C (82˚F) in the summer (December to March), occasionally falling below zero and around 10˚C (50˚F) in the winter (June to September). Nights can get a little chilly. The rainy season is from May to August.

Regions
    The climate in Chile is quite varied due to the country's geographical location. The extreme of the desert, the high-altitude climate in the Andes, the polar conditions of the region nearest the Antarctic territory, and the moderating influences of the ocean all have great effect. The impact of El Nino has also taken a toll on general Chilean weather conditions. However, for the most part, the north is warm and dry during winter and summer, and the south remains very wet and stormy.

Money & Banking

Currency
    The currency of Chile is the Chilian Peso (Ch$).

Denominations
    The Chilian Peso comes in coin denominations of Ch$1, 5, 10, and 100 and banknotes of Ch$500, 1,000, 5,000, and 10,000.

Traveler's Checks and Credit Cards
    Traveler's checks and major currencies can be exchanged at banks, exchange shops, and hotels, as well as

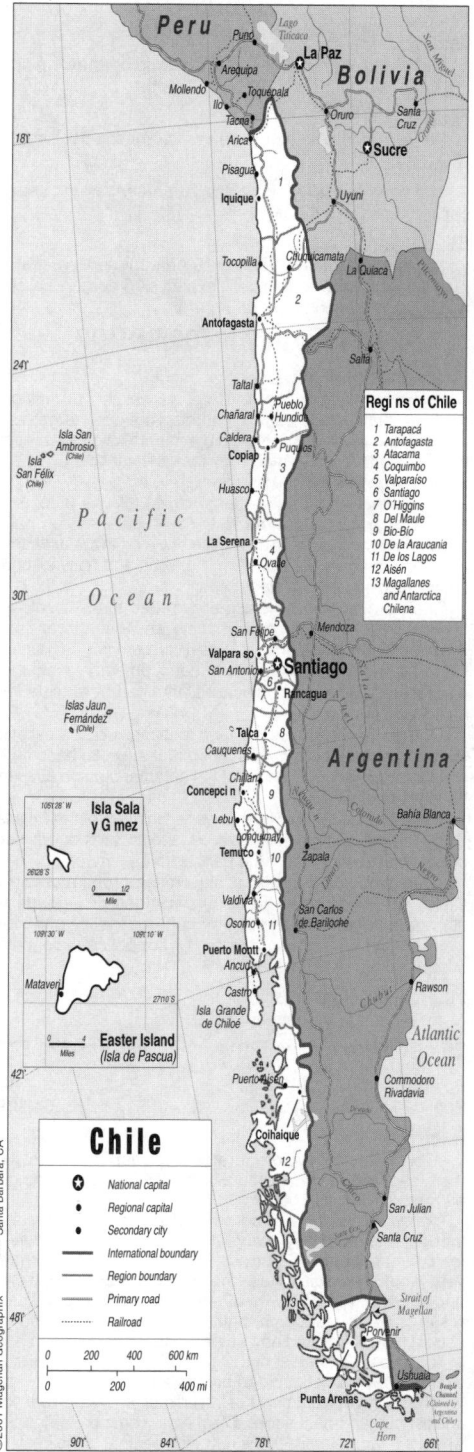

Regions of Chile

1 Tarapacá
2 Antofagasta
3 Atacama
4 Coquimbo
5 Valparaíso
6 Santiago
7 O'Higgins
8 Del Maule
9 Bío-Bío
10 De la Araucania
11 De los Lagos
12 Aisén
13 Magallanes and Antarctica Chilena

Chile

- ✪ National capital
- ● Regional capital
- ● Secondary city
- —— International boundary
- —— Region boundary
- —— Primary road
- ----- Railroad

0   200   400   600 km
0   200   400 mi

©2001 Magellan Geographix SM Santa Barbara, CA

at international airports. U.S. dollar traveler's checks may prove most cost effective in terms of extra exchange rate charges. U.S. dollars are readily exchanged although Argentine bills can be exchanged at the border. Other types of currency will be refused for exchange in rural areas and smaller towns. Carry U.S. dollars when possible.

American Express, Visa, Diner's Club, and MasterCard are accepted in most up-market places in the main cities of Chile. Cash and credit cards advances are also available at automated teller machines (ATM) in larger cities. Such cards will be of little use in the countryside where cash is king.

Exchange only enough foreign currency and travel checks during your trip to see you through a few days. For large transactions use a credit card as it has the most favorable exchange rate. Reconversion of Chilean currency at departure time is possible but purposely expensive. The Chilean peso has little value outside of being a souvenir once it crosses borders. Chileans prefer to hang on to the hard currency brought in by tourists.

Essential Terms

English	Spanish
Yes	Sí
No	No
Good morning	Buenos días
Hello (daytime)	Buenas tardes
Hello (evening)	Buenas noches
Hello (telephone)	¿Hola?
Good-bye	Adiós
Please	Por favor
Thank you	Gracias
Pleased to meet you	Encantado (a) de conocerle
Excuse me; I'm sorry	¿Perdóneme?
My name is _____	Me llamo _____
I don't understand	No comprendo
Do you speak English?	¿Habla usted inglés?

Travel

VISA AND PASSPORT

A passport is required of all visitors except:

- Nationals of Argentina, Brazil, Colombia, Paraguay, and Uruguay, provided they are not in Chile under commercial contract, as students or immigrants, and are holding a Cédula de Identitad (special identity card) for short-term visits
- Taiwanese residents of Chinese ethnicity and other nationals of Taiwan, Mexico, and Peru who are holding official travel papers issued by the Organization of American States. These documents must remain valid for at least six months beyond departure date.

Chile

Visas are not required of the following:

- Nationals of Antigua & Barbuda, Argentina, Australia, Bahamas, Barbados, Belize, Bolivia, Brazil, Canada, Colombia, Croatia, Czech Republic, Dominican Republic, Ecuador, El Salvador, EU countries, Fiji, Grenada, Guatemala, Hungary, Iceland, Israel, Jamaica, Japan, Liechtenstein, Macau, Macedonia, Malaysia, Malta, Mexico, Monaco, Morocco, New Zealand, Nicaragua, Norway, Panama, Paraguay, Poland, St. Kitts & Nevis, St. Lucia, San Marino, Slovenia, South Africa, Surinam, Switzerland, Tonga, Tunisia, Turkey, Tuvalu, U.K., Uruguay, U.S., Vatican City, Venezuela, and Yugoslavia (Serbia and Montenegro) for a maximum stay of 90 days
- Nationals of Greece and Peru for a maximum stay of 60 days
- Nationals of Costa Rica, Honduras, Indonesia, Singapore and Zimbabwe for a maximum stay of 30 days
- Passengers in transit who do not leave the airport and are continuing their journey aboard the first connecting aircraft, and who are holding confirmed tickets and other documents for onward travel, are also exempt from the need for a visa.

Note: Regulations can easily change at short notice. Check with the consulate for updated information.

Types of visa issued by the Chilean government:

- Tourist (business people usually travel on a tourist visa)
- Visitor (required of all nationals of countries that do not have diplomatic relations with the Chilean government)
- Residence (required of visitors intending to pursue employment or study, and for those who intend to make sizable business investments)

The Tourist and Visitor visas generally remain valid for 90 days, depending on nationality. The Resident visa is customarily valid for one year and renewable for a second year.

Multiple entry visas are also available; inquire at time of visa application.

Note: A processing fee, which must be paid on arrival in cash only, is levied on nationals of the U.S. (US$45), Canada (US$55), and Australia (US$30) who are visiting Chile for tourism purposes. For visa application processing, allow between one and seven days.

DEPARTURE FORMALITIES

There is a departure tax of US$18, or the peso equivalent, for destinations over 500km. For distances less than 500km, the departure tax is US$8 (or peso equivalent).

CUSTOMS ENTRY (PERSONAL)

Duty-free

- Tobacco: 400 cigarettes, 500g of tobacco, 50 cigars or 50 cigarillos
- Alcohol: 2.5 liters of alcohol (only for visitors over 18 years of age)
- Other: a reasonable quantity of perfume

Prohibited or Restricted

- Meat products, flowers, fruits and vegetables (unless permission is sought prior to traveling)
- Unregistered firearms (includes hunting rifles)

Prohibited items brought in without proper permission are liable to be confiscated at the airport.

IMMUNIZATION

International certificates of vaccination are not required unless arriving from infected areas. Cases of cholera have been reported in remote areas of Chile, however. Recommended vaccinations for travel outside of the cities: cholera, hepatitis A, polio, tetanus, and typhus. Malaria prophylaxis is also advised for trips to rural areas in hot weather.

TIPPING

Taxi

Metered taxi drivers expect a small tip or rounding up of the fare. Avoid unmetered taxis altogether.

Porters

Porters should be tipped 100 to 200 pesos per bag.

Hotels

The standard tip for hotels is 10 percent and is usually applied directly to the bill.

Restaurants

Restaurants may include a 10 percent service charge, but waiters and bartenders still expect a 10 percent cash tip (propina) in addition from foreigners.

EMERGENCY INFORMATION

Police and Crime

Crime is relatively high in Chile, especially in Santiago's markets, clubs, and bars where tourists are often targeted for robbery and theft. Women should avoid walking alone, especially at night. Chilean men may make advances if they perceive a woman's attitude as informal.

In Santiago and in other large cities, thieves prosper by working the rush hour crowds in the streets and on public transportation. One must be particularly alert in the downtown area, especially in late afternoon, at night, and on weekends, even including well-traveled areas.

Theft is also commonplace at crowded tourist locales, in subway stations, on buses and trains, and even occasionally in taxis. Wearing expensive jewelry or carrying baggage or cameras makes one a favorite target of purse snatchers and pickpockets. Bags and briefcases are lifted from restaurant chairs and outdoor cafes.

Outside Santiago, assaults and robberies occur most often in the Vina del Mar and Valparaiso areas, which become increasingly crowded at the height of summer season (December through February).

Carry photocopies of your passport instead of the original. Carry cash in a money belt, and use credit cards or traveler's checks for most of your large transactions.

Drug smuggling is still a big cross-border problem in Chile; so, never agree to carry packages or luggage for strangers. Also, keep in mind that political rallies often turn violent. Avoid becoming a victim of riot police violence by steering clear of these rallies.

Emergency Numbers

Numbers are good nationwide

Ambulance	224-4422
Fire	132
Police	133
Public Assistance	342-291

Health

Cholera exists in more rural settings and those traveling there should consider precautions. Meningoccal meningitis outbreaks may also occur.

Tap water is considered generally safe in Santiago; although, one must stay away from it in rural areas and avoid ice cubes except in first class hotels. Stay away from raw vegetables and fruit, unless they've been washed in a chlorine solution. Also, beware of raw seafood and salad, carriers of cholera, typhoid, hepatitis, and more. Meat and fish should be well cooked and served hot. Be careful with pork, as it carries the highest risk of bacteria attack and parasitic worms. Milk is best avoided altogether.

Chile can get extremely hot in summer, so take precautions against sun and heat stroke. Diarrhea is common for travelers who are unaccustomed to the new diet, water, and the heat.

All of Santiago is afflicted with a high pollution index; the skies are blanketed with a heavy smog during the winter and thick with dust in the summer. The worst pollution materializes between May and October.

Health standards have increased, and new hospitals have been built in recent years. Private hospitals offer the best facilities and service. All travelers should bring a well-stocked medical kit and any prescription drugs they may require. Travel insurance is advisable and those on extended stays in rural areas should have an evacuation policy.

INTERNAL TRAVEL

AIR

Domestic air services are provided by the Chilean airlines LAN and LADECO, and by several air taxi companies.The south of Chile relies predominantly on air links for business travel, especially. There are frequent flights to main towns during weekdays, and the schedules are fairly regular. Reservations are essential.

LAN offers one-month 'Visit Chile' passes, which cover both the northern and southern parts of the country. Passengers must purchase tickets abroad and can use them in conjunction with LAN or with other trans-oceanic air carriers for an additional surcharge. It is wise to make reservations well ahead of anticipated travel dates. Once booked, reservations can still be changed for no additional fee; but there is a small charge for each change made if it involves rerouting. Use of these passes must commence within two weeks of arrival in country.

Regular LAN flights also travel between Santiago and Easter Island, which are actually layovers en route to Tahiti. The flights go twice a week, November to February, once-weekly the rest of the year, and take five hours. Again, advance reservations are essential.

An air-taxi offers daily service throughout the summer months from Valparaíso and Santiago to the Juan Fernández Islands.

TAXI

An abundance of taxis cruise the streets in the major cities at a ratio of one for every one hundred inhabitants. They are easily distinguished by their black and yellow paint jobs and can be hailed in the streets. Standard tariffs to common destinations are displayed inside the cabs.

Most cabs have meters, but for those which do not, or for long journeys, negotiate a price beforehand. Negotiations are best handled at a taxi stand where other cabs abound, as ample supply is bound to drive the price lower. Surcharges of 50 percent apply on Sundays after 9p.m.

Hiring a cab for a day is not uncommon.

AUTO

Car and motorcycle rentals are available in major cities and at airports. A credit card and a valid driver's license are required, along with local insurance. An International or Inter-American Driving Permit may also be required, depending on the rental agency—check in advance. In addition, a sizable guarantee deposit is often compulsory.

If a rental vehicle is used, business travelers should do so only in the urban environment. A car with a hired driver is a better option for intercity travel or trips to remote areas.

The Automóvil Club de Chile will happily supply road maps (see Travel Assistance section below).

TRAIN

The state rail system runs for 8185km (5086 miles) through Chile. The primary route, beginning in Santiago in the north and terminating in the south at Puerto Montt, operates twice daily.

In Santiago, daily departures from Estación Central at Av. Bernardo O'Higgins take passengers to cities to the south. Service is good, although the geography is a limiting factor. Railway operations north of Santiago do not exist.

Out-of-country connections often use buses for part of the journey. A variety of "classes" can be procured. Reserve ahead (2-689-5401) for a seat, and think twice about your time schedule before heading to Puerto Montt by rail, as it is a journey of 20 hours!

Long-distance trains offer sleeping cars and on-board restaurant service. Business travelers may find that the trains are the only reasonable way of reaching remote areas. Overnight trips present the greatest security risks. For further details, contact the Chilean Tourist Office, SERNATUR (see Travel Assistance section below).

SUBWAY

Two metro lines (East/West and North/South) traverse the city of Santiago and provide a quick, inexpensive, and (best of all) safe means of getting from A to B. A third line is currently under construction.

Stations have clearly posted maps and schedules. The system operates on flat fares, but plans to instate distance-related fares are being considered. Purchase tickets at glass booths for either one journey or for ten trips with a book of tickets (carnet). Prices are low by any standard.

Keep in mind that the main line's East/West tickets cannot be used for the secondary North/South line. However, the reverse is acceptable.

The metro operates from 6:30a.m. to 10:30p.m. Monday through Saturday. Sunday metro service starts at 8a.m.

BUSES & TRAMS

Buses are cheap and reliable, but often crowded. Luxury buses run on longer routes going north or south—they offer toilets, air conditioning, and food service. Various companies and bus terminals offer services in specific directions. Buses within the city drive with reckless abandon and charge about 130 pesos, payable when boarding. Know your route ahead of time.

WATER TRAVEL

While there are both internal river and coastal passenger boat systems, they are known to be unreliable and infrequent; as such, they are not recommended for business travel. If it is the only transport to a remote area that you simply must reach, allow local business associates to arrange the trip. Potential for security problems is high.

TRAVEL ASSISTANCE

Servicio Nacional de Turismo (SERNATUR)
Nro. 1550 Providencia
tel: (2) 236-1420, 236-1416; fax: (2) 251-8469
email: sernatur@ctc-mundo.net
website: www.segegob.cl/sernatur
Monday to Friday: 8:30 to 6:30pm; Sat. 9a.m. to 1p.m.

Communications

DIALING CODES IN CHILE

International country code: [56]

Selected city codes: Arica (58), Concepción (41), Curico (75), La Serena (51), Los Andes (34), Punta Arenas (61), San Felipe (34), Santiago (2), Talca (71), Talcahuano (41), Valparaiso (32)

Dialing Chile from Overseas

To dial Chile from overseas, begin with your country's international dialing code, then 56 (the country code for Chile), then the city code and finally the number. If you were dialing Concepción from the United States, for example, you would begin with 011, then 56, then 41 (the city code for Concepción), and finally the number of the person or office you were trying to reach.

Assistance Numbers

Long Distance Operator .... 122 or 123
International Operator (bilingual).................................. 183

CALLING WITHIN CHILE

Local Calls

Chile provides its telephone users with a modern system. Dial the number and get connected.

Long Distance Calls

Before calling anywhere, first dial the code of the carrier you want to use: Entel (123); CTC (188); Chilesat (171); Bellsouth (181).

International Calls

To dial direct internationally from a private phone, the same applies as above. Start by dialing the carrier you wish to use (prices vary only slightly); then dial '0', followed by the country code, area code, and the number you wish to reach. Telephone centers offer another means of calling.

To bypass local operators and a number of higher rates (which can start at US$7.25 for three minutes during discount periods on Sundays and holidays and after 6p.m. weekdays), dial an access number for an operator who can help you place a call to virtually any location in the world.

AT&T 123-00*-0311
MCI (with CTC)... 188-00*-0316
Sprint 181-00*-0317
*Wait for tone before continuing.

Check with a hotel operator for AT&T access instructions and, perhaps more importantly, the impending surcharge the hotel may consequently post next to your name.

PAY PHONES

Public Telephones

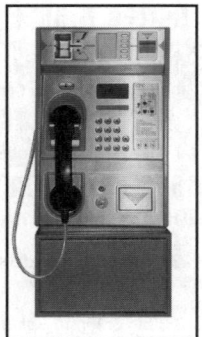

Public telephones are numerous in the cities, but it may be difficult to find operative pay phones in rural areas. Most services are provided by Compañía de Teléfonos de Chile. Two kinds of phones allow local calling.

The yellow variety requires these steps:
1. Insert a 50-peso coin
2. Dial
3. Talk - until you hear a tone indicating your three minutes are almost finished.

"intelligent", metallic phones have English instructions and allow successive calls without cutting you off, provided you don't hang up and instead push the special button to start the next call.

Calling Cards

Calling cards are available in hotels and some newsstands, although most public phones still work on coins only.

CELLULAR PHONES

There are numerous cellular phone service providers in Chile, predominantly in the analog AMPS format.

Note: Your home country cell phone may not work in this country. If not, we recommend that you rent an international cell phone *before* you leave home. A major US-based cell phone rental provider is **IMC WorldCell**. For information see "International Cell Phone Rentals" on page 14.

CALL BACK

You can (potentially) save significant sums when calling in Chile by using a call back service. For a list of callback services, please refer to the "Communications" section in the *Global Road Warrior* Introduction.

Fees for call back services vary widely, depending on the company and the type of service required. Be sure to check with these companies before leaving to compare rates.

PHONE JACK

Plug adaptors are available through **iGo Corporation.** (See "Electrical and Telephone Adaptors" on page 19.)

FAX

Faxes can only be found in major cities, and even then only in certain areas. Most hotels do not have them. If possible, check government offices.

POSTAL SERVICES

Mail service is efficient. Mail usually takes three to four days to reach North America or the U.K.

Service Times

Monday - Friday 9a.m. to 6p.m. Saturday 9a.m. to 1p.m.

TELEGRAMS

Telegrams are only available in main cities, and are serviced by Telex Chile, Transradio Chilena, and ITT Communicaciones.

Business Services

BUSINESS CENTERS

Centro de Convenciones Y Servicios San Cristobal S.A.; tel: (2) 7376669; fax: (2) 7352081.

Hotel Castellon; tel: (32) 977019; fax: (32) 977019.

COURIER SERVICES

Servicio de Correos Los conquistadores; tel: (2) 2341009; fax: (2) 2325901.

FedEx; San Camilo 190; tel: (2) 3616161; fax: (2) 3616111.

PRINTING/COPYING

Copias de Planos Ruiz Agustinas; tel: (2) 6330700; fax: (2) 6327027.

Astorga Ramirez Jose Libreria Tecnica Maipu Pje. Pinochet Lebrun; tel: (2) 5318329; fax: (2) 5318329.

TRANSLATION SERVICES

Tae Traducciones Academicas; tel: (32) 235155; fax: (32) 235155.

Chilean Language Services; tel: (2) 3349891; fax: (2) 3349891.

Electrical

Current
220 volts AC, 50Hz

ELECTRIC PLUGS

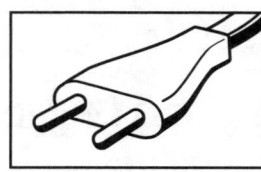

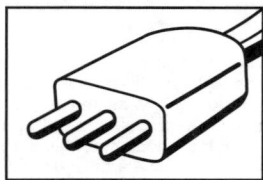

Plug adaptors are available through **iGo Corporation.** (See "Electrical and Telephone Adaptors" on page 19.)

Technical Support

HARDWARE/SOFTWARE VENDOR SUPPORT

Acer/Texas Instruments; (in the U.S.) [1] (408) 432-6200; http://www.acer.com.

Adobe; tel: (2) 236-1415; fax: (2)235-7830; (in the U.S.) tel: [1] (800) 500-7078; (in Germany) tel: [49] (1) 803-5018; (in Switzerland) tel: [41] (800) 833-310 http://www.adobe.com.

Apple/Claris; tel: 56-2-236-1415; (in the U.S.) tel: [1] (800) 500-7078; (in the U.K.) tel: [44] (990) 127-753; http://www.apple.com/. http://www.apple.com; http://www.hp.com.

AST; (in the U.S.) tel: [1] (817) 232-9824 (International Technical Support); (in Ireland) tel: [353] (61) 492-222; (in the U.S.) tel: [1] (949) 727-4141; http://www.ast.com/.

Compaq/Digital; tel: (2) 274-1911; fax: (2) 252-0540; (in the U.S.) tel: [1] (281) 518-2000 (international technical support); fax: [1] (281) 518-1442; http://www.compaq.com.

Corel; tel: 562-671-3060; (in the U.S.) tel: [1] (716) 871-2325 (Ask to be Forwarded to Appropriate Program); http://www.corel.com/.

Dell; tel: (2) 204-7100 (Asicom); (2) 686-1000 (Tandem Chile S.A.); (2) 338-7000 (Xerox Chile); (in the U.S.) tel: [1] (512) 338-4400; fax: [1] (512) 728-3330; http://www.dell.com/.

Filemaker/Claris; (in the U.S.) tel: [1] (800) 965-9090; (in Germany) tel: [49] (180) 525-8166 (Info-line); fax: [49] (180) 567-2233; tel: [49] (180) 523-6423; http://www.claris.com/.

Gateway 2000; (in the U.S.) tel: [1] (605) 232-2191; fax: [1] (605) 232-2023; (in Ireland) tel: [353] (1) 797-2000; http://www.g2k.com/.

Hewlett Packard; (Brazil Office) tel: [55] 11 709-1444; (in the U.S.) tel: [1] (408) 246-4300; http://www.hp.com/.

IBM; tel: (800) 203-037 (toll free within Chile); fax: (2) 200-6999; 800-203-300 (toll free within Chile); tel: (800) 81-426 (toll free within Chile); (U.S. Main Office) tel: [1] 914-765-1900; (in the U.S.) tel: [1] (919) 517-2800; http://www.ibm.com/.

Microsoft; (2) 330-6000; fax: (2) 218-5747; fax: (2) 218-4505; tel: (2) 330-6222; fax: (2) 204-9424; (in the U.S.) [1] (425) 635-7222; http://www.microsoft.com/.

NEC; tel: (2) 233-6767; (in the U.S.) [1] (916) 388-0101 (Main Switchboard); http://www.nec.com/.

Novell; tel: 00-02-03-683 (Toll Free Technical Support); (in the U.S.) tel: [1] (408) 434-2300; fax: [1] (408) 577-5775 (Worldwide Sales Headquarters); http://www.novell.com/.

Quark; (in the U.S.) tel: [1] (303) 894-8899; fax: [1] (303) 894-3398 (For Products Registered in the Americas); http:/ /www.quark.com/.

Toshiba; (in the U.S.) tel: [1] (714) 583-3000; http://www.toshiba.com.

Internet Connection

HOW TO CONNECT

Connecting to AOL and Compuserve in Chile is similar to using it when traveling outside your own area code. See the introductory section for detailed information on connecting to your account through a different phone number.

America Online

Numbers are available at keyword international. Be sure to get several local numbers before leaving. AOL's GlobalNet service charges US$12 an hour in addition to the usual charges and is available at keyword access (a free area).

Concepción (41) 239-514; Iquique (57) 423-619; La Serena (51) 218-721; Punta Arenas (61) 229-393; Santiago (2) 697-3081.

Compuserve

Access: Numbers are available at keyword *Go International.* The Compuserve Web-site also has a great deal of information, at http://www.compuserve.com.

Access: Concepción (41) 239-514; Iquique (57) 423-619; Punta Arenas (61) 229-400; Santiago (2) 361-0099; Santiago (2) 697-3081.

Independent Service Providers

Many independent service providers offer discounts if you are only in town for a couple days.

CTC Mundo (Spanish); tel: (2) 234-5050; email: scliente@ctcinternet.cl; http://www.ctc-mundo.net/.

ImageNet (English/Spanish); tel/fax: (954) 735-7286; email: imagenet@shadow.net; http://www.shadow.net/~imagenet/.

INTERACCESS S.A; tel: (2) 550-3000; http://www.ia.cl/.

Interarauco (Spanish); tel: (2) 208-098, (2) 249-465; tax: (2) 461-708; email: info@interarauco.com; http://www.interarauco.com/.

VPM Internet Services; tel: [1] (800) 321-0221; tel: [1] (916) 983-9876; fax: [1] (916) 983-4375; e-mail: sales@vpm.com; http://www.vpm.com/.

U.S. dollars are readily exchanged although Argentine bills can be exchanged at the border. Other types of currency will be refused for exchange in rural areas and smaller towns. Carry U.S. dollars when possible.

Chile

American Express, Visa, Diner's Club, and MasterCard are accepted in most up-market places in the main cities of Chile. Cash and credit cards advances are also available at automated teller machines (ATM) in larger cities. Such cards will be of little use in the countryside where cash is king.

Exchange only enough foreign currency and travel checks during your trip to see you through a few days. For large transactions use a credit card as it has the most favorable exchange rate. Reconversion of Chilean currency at departure time is possible but purposely expensive. The Chilean peso has little value outside of being a souvenir once it crosses borders. Chileans prefer to hang on to the hard currency brought in by tourists.

Business Culture

GREETINGS AND COURTESIES

Men shake hands with men; acquaintances also pat each other on the back or hug. Women usually do not shake hands, although more will now initiate a handshake (men should not try to shake hands with a woman unless she offers first). Men are expected to rise when women enter the room. Women may kiss female friends lightly on the right cheek. In small groups, introductions are made individually by the host, while at larger gatherings, a group "Hello" from the person being introduced suffices. Titles are not generally used, except by medical doctors. Business cards may be in English, which is commonly used by internationally oriented Chilean businesspeople (Spanish is more considerate—and practical—for smaller national firms). Write your hotel telephone number on your card to allow Chilean colleagues to reach you.

DECISION MAKING

Although middle-level managers may be responsible for implementing decisions, actual decisions are almost always made at a high level of authority. Although you should approach senior people, Chileans will want to know your standing within the hierarchy and will wish to match you with someone of similar rank. Nevertheless, it is important to cultivate personal relationships with these peers, because the quality of these relationships may strongly influence the actual decisionmaker even when your immediate counterpart is not the one making the decision.

WOMEN

Women in Chile generally occupy a somewhat secondary status in this traditionally male-dominated society, although many operate businesses and are generally accorded considerable personal freedom. Many Chilean women reach high levels of professional attainment, and foreign businesswomen should experience few problems, although some may feel more comfortable if they are escorted when in public to avoid possible difficulties. Nevertheless, foreign businesswomen are expected to be highly professional, appropriate, and not aggressive or confrontational.

MEETINGS

Contacts and introductions are important. If you do not have a mutual business acquaintance to make an introduction, consult your embassy for a referral. Appointments should be made at least two weeks in advance, and reconfirmed. Chileans are generally punctual, although either you or your Chilean counterpart may be acceptably late by about 15 minutes. Meetings are also expected to end on time, although not abruptly. Initial meetings are spent largely on introductory and social matters—you must be prepared to discuss yourself and your company to establish your bona fides—and several meetings are usually required to complete an agreement. Eye contact and good posture are necessary and lapses may be noted unfavorably. The atmosphere is usually informally relaxed but correct. Business lunches are common and are restricted to the parties discussing the business at hand. Dinners are likely to be more social, and spouses may be included if the primary purpose is social. Chileans are also generally more likely to invite foreign associates to their homes than are many other South Americans.

BUSINESS ATTIRE

Chileans, who are fairly fashion conscious, expect both men and women to dress conservatively and elegantly in dark suits of good quality. Remember that climate varies widely by latitude and altitude. Dark suits and dresses are appropriate for most social occasions, such as dinner, while a dark suit and a cocktail dress constitute appropriate formalwear. Flashy attire, jewelry, makeup, and accessories are inappropriate. Note that Chileans wear only real jewelry and look down on costume jewelry.

Business Centers
Santiago

CITY VIEW

Santiago seems like an immense city, but the downtown area is actually small and easy to get around in. The city is prone to traffic jams and pollution has been a problem in recent years clouding the spectacular surrounding views of the Andes mountains. To make up for it, beaches, ski slopes, vineyards and countryside are all within a day trip's reach.

AIRPORT

Comodoro Arturo Merino Benitez Airport to City Center

The airport lies 10 miles (16 km.) from the city center and travel time is about 30 minutes. Coach service is available between the airport and some top-end hotels, and runs every 30 minutes between 6a.m. and midnight. Regular bus service is available for about US$1.50 and a taxi will cost around US$20. Express buses for US$1.75 depart every half hour from the arrivals terminal between 6:30a.m. and 9p.m. and deliver passengers to the Moneda Street bus terminal, where a taxi ride is then only a short hop to a hotel.

Airline Numbers

Aer Lingus	(2) 231-8626
Aeroflot	(2) 632-4092
Aerolíneas Argentinas	(2) 394-121
Aero Perú	(2) 274-3434
Air Canada	(2) 337-0000
Air France	(2) 698-2421
Alitalia	(2) 698-3336
A.L.T.A.	(2) 334-5872; 600-301-6000
American	(2) 699-3905
Avant	(2) 335-3077
Avianca	(2) 695-4105
British Airways	(2) 232-9560/ 7859
Canadian Pacific	(2) 393-058
Ecuatoriana	(2) 696-4251
Iberia	(2) 698-1716
KLM	(2) 233-0991
Ladeco	(2) 601-9445, (2) 251-7204
LAN-Chile	(2) 601-9165, (2) 232-8712

LASSA ....(2) 273-4354
Lineas Aereas Paraguayas (LAP) .... (2) 671-4404
Lufthansa ....(2) 696-1072
Lloyd Aereo Boliviano (LAB) .... (2) 671-2334
National .... (2) 639-5666; (2) 632-8040
SAS ....(2) 391-105
Swissair ....(2) 337-014
Transportes Aereos
Robinson Crusoe...(2) 531-3772
Varig..(2) 395-261
Viasa ....(2) 698-2401

HOTELS

Top End

Hotel Carrera; Teatinos 180; tel: (2) 698-2011; fax: (2) 672-1083; city center; restaurant; conference center; corporate rates; executive services; secretarial services; fitness; health; massage; sauna; pool; whirlpool; racquetball; US$240.

Plaza San Francisco Kempinski; Avda. Libertador Bdo. O'Higgins 816; tel: (2) 639-3832; fax: (2) 639-7826; city center; no-smoking rooms; restaurant; conference center; executive services; secretarial services; in-room computers; fitness; health; massage; sauna; pool; whirlpool; US$220/240.

Sheraton San Cristobal; Avda. Santa Maria 1742; tel: (2) 233-5000; fax: (2) 234-1732; restaurant; business center; corporate rates; fitness; health; sauna; pool; tennis; US$195/215.

Radisson Royal Santiago; Vitacura 2610; tel: (2) 2036-000; fax: (2) 203-6001; city center; conference center; secretarial services; in-room computers; corporate rates; fitness; health; massage; sauna; pool; whirlpool; US$230/240.

Expensive

Acacias De Vitacura; El Manantial 1781; tel: (2) 211-8601; fax: (2) 212-7858; city suburb; conference center; in-room computers; secretarial services; free parking; corporate rates; pool; US$85/128.

Bonaparte; Av. Ricardo Lyon 1229; tel: (2) 223-8554; fax: (2) 204-8907; restaurant, lounge; French-chateau style; free parking; pool; 4 stars; US$90/125.

Holiday Inn Crowne Plaza; Av. Libertador Bdo. O'Higgins 136; tel: (2) 381-042; fax: (2) 336-015; US$125/139.

Parlamento; Avenida Santa Maria 281; tel: (2) 735-2401; fax; (20 777-1784; city center; restaurant; computer terminals; conference center; corporate rates; fitness; pool; sauna; tennis; a four star experience at US$90/100.

Moderate

Gran Palace; Huerfanos 1178 Piso 10; tel: (2) 671-2551; fax (2) 695-1095; city center; near railway station; conference center; corporate rates; sauna; US$37/43.

Manquehue; Esteban Dell'Orto 6615, Las Condes; tel: (2) 212-8862; fax: (2) 220-9729; city center; restaurant; meeting rooms; free parking; fitness; pool; 4 stars; US$65/95.

Metropoli; Doctor Sotero Del Rio 465-476; tel: (2) 672-3987; fax: (2) 695-2196; city center; near railway; restaurant; meeting room; no-smoking rooms; corporate rates; US$40/50.

Presidente; Avenida Eliodoro Yañez 867; tel: (2) 235-8015; fax: (2) 235-9148; city center; near exhibition grounds; restaurant; free parking; 4 stars; US$88/99.

Rothenburg Best Western; Avenida Las Condes 13343, Las Condes; tel/fax: (2) 215-1535; suburb; restaurant; conference center; corporate rates; fitness; sauna; pool; 4 stars; US$65/92.

Tupahue; San Antonio 477; tel: (2) 638-3810; fax: (2) 639-5240; email: tupahue@chilnet.cl; restaurant; meeting room; pool; free parking; 4 stars; US$55.

MEDICAL CARE

Hospital Clinico Universidad de Chile; Santos Dumont 999 Clasificador 5, correo 7; tel: 678-8000; emergency: 678-8165; fax: 777-8759.

Hospital de Carabineros; Av. Simon Bolivar 2200; tel: 225-6333; fax: 253-5315.

Note: Your hotel staff are often the best resource in an emergency.

CAR RENTAL

Avis; tel: 1230-020-2530 (intl. reservations - ask for Net 521); (2) 601-9966; Locations: Airport; Sheraton Hotel, Av. Santa Maria 1742; Crowne Plaza Hotel, Alameda 136.

Dollar; Intl Airport, tel; (2) 601-8606; fax: (2) 228-0943; Malaga 115, Office 913, Las Condes, tel: (2) 245-6175; fax: (2) 228-0943.

Hertz; Av. Costanera 1469, tel: (2) 235-1022; fax: (2) 264-1013; Intl airport, tel: (2) 601-0477; Natl airport, tel: (2) 601-9262; Hyatt Regency Hotel, tel: (2) 245-5936.

LYS; Miraflores #541; tel: (2) 633-7600; fax: (2) 639-9332; email: lys@chilepac.net; http://lemuy.chilepac.net/lys/.

Star; tel: (2) 277-3469; fax: (20 277-0327; email: jorgefau@entelchile.net; will deliver to your hotel.

United; Padre Mariano #430; tel: (2) 236-1483; fax: (2) 236-1476.

WORLD TRADE CENTER

World Trade Center Santiago
Av. Nueva Tajamar 481, Suite 101
Las Condes
Santiago - Chile
tel: (2) 339-7000; fax: (2) 339-7001
email: wtcsn@ctc_mundo.net
website: http://www.wtcsantiago.cl

China

At a Glance
THE PEOPLE

Population .... 1,246,871,951 (July 1999 est.)
Growth Rate .... 0.77% (1999 est.)
Life Expectancy .... 69.92 years (born 1999)
Infant Mortality . 43.31 deaths/1,000 live births (1999 est.)

Ethnic Composition

Han..91.9%
Zhuang, Uygur, Hui, Yi, Tibetan,
Miao, Manchu, Mongol, Buyi,
Korean, and other nationalities....................................8.1%

Religious Composition

Confucian, Tao, and Buddhist philosophy.................. 96%
Muslim 3%
Christian 1%

Languages Spoken

Mandarin (Putonghua - official), Cantonese, Fukien, Hakka, plus many local and tribal dialects.

Education and Literacy

Literacy for those over the age of 15 is 81.5 percent.

Labor Force

Total: 623,900,000
By occupation: services 13%, industry 33%, agriculture 54%

THE ECONOMY

The most difficult part of assessing the economy of China is the fact that the Beijing government closely guards its commercial statistics. The few numbers that are released are considered by analysts to be grossly inaccurate. This does not bode well for a nation once thought to be the most promising economy in the world. All positive prognosis was dashed during the financial crisis that struck Asia in 199. Reliant on other Asian economies for investment, China found itself adrift as its neighbors tried to salvage their own crumbling finances. It was also revealed during this crisis that very few foreign investments in China were actually profitable. Inefficient and unprofitable state-owned companies still dominate the Chinese economy and official corruption remains rampant. China's non-convertible currency, the renmibi, continues to be artificially propped up domestically making this giant nation totally dependent on foreign currency reserves. Although having made inroads towards becoming a modern economy, China's technology is borrowed by and large and its labor force remains primarily agricultural. As over 100 million displaced farm workers roam the country in search of the wealth found only in China's coastal cities, the politicians in Beijing fear the potential for upheaval. Worse yet, China's "official" GDP growth rate is insufficient to service the debts already incurred by the business sector. The "real" problem may be considerably worse.

Exports .... US$183.8 billion (f.o.b., 1998)
Imports .... US$140.17 billion (c.i.f., 1998)
Total GDP .... US$4.42 trillion (1998 est.)
GDP Per Capita .... US$3,600 (1998 est.)
Unemployment officially 3% in urban areas; probably 8%-10% data from rural areas N/A (1998 est.)
Inflation Rate .... -0.8% (1998 est.)

Top Export Partners

Hong Kong, Japan, United States, South Korea, E.U., Singapore.

Top Import Partners

Japan, United States, Taiwan, South Korea, Hong Kong, E.U., Russia.

Top Exports

Clothing, miscellaneous consumer goods, fabrics, footwear, mineral fuels, plastic toys, electrical machinery

Top Imports

Plastics, fabrics, telecommunications equipment, electrical machinery and switchgear, cotton, yarn

BUSINESS WORKWEEK

Offices

Monday to Friday 8a.m. to noon and 2p.m. to 5p.m., Saturday 8a.m. to noon.

Banks

Monday to Friday 8a.m. to noon and 2p.m. to 5p.m., Saturday 8a.m. to noon.

Government

Monday to Friday 8a.m. to noon and 2p.m. to 5p.m., Saturday 8a.m. to noon.

Retail

Monday to Saturday 8a.m. to 6p.m. (some stay open later). Most stores are open seven days a week.

Note: All China runs on Beijing time. In a country as large as this, 7a.m. in western Qinghai Province, it's pitch black year round.

HOLIDAYS

Solar New Year ....January 1
Lunar New Year .... February 15-18*
International Women's Day .... March 8
Labor Day..May 1
Army Day... August 1
Teachers' Day ....September 9
National Days .... October 1-2
*Dates may vary by year.

CLIMATE

Seasons

China has the full range of seasons due to its geographical location and vast size.

Regions

The region around Beijing has hot, wet summers, very cold, dry, and sunny winters, and mild springs. The January average daily temperature ranges from -23˚ to 11˚C (-9˚ to 51˚F). In July the range is from 16˚ to 40˚C (61˚ to 103˚F).

Winters in Shanghai and the Yangtse River valley are short, wetter, and warmer than Beijing. In the south humidity can border on the tropical while western China has vast desert ranges and dry, dusty weather. The far north near Mongolia and the Korean peninsula can have prolonged sub-freezing weather in winter and windblown but mild summers.

China

China
- ✪ National capital
- ◉ Province capital
- • City
- —— Province border
- —— Road
- ···· Railroad
- ▬▬ International border

0　　　500 km
0　　　500 mi

Money & Banking

Currency

The currency of China is the Renmibi Yuan, and is abbreviated as RMB.

Denominations

The Renmibi comes in coin denominations of RMB1, and 5, 2, and 1 fen and 5 and 1 chiao/jiao; and banknotes of RMB1, 2, 5, 10, 50, 100, and 1, 2, and 5 chiao / jiao.

Note: China's currency is not traded on the international markets and, therefore, considered to have no value outside of the nation's borders.

Traveler's Checks and Credit Cards

You can exchange major currencies and traveler's checks at branches of the Bank of China, at the airport kiosks, and Friendship Stores. Keep all your transaction receipts because you will be asked for them if you decide to reconvert your RMB before departure. RMB's are useless outside of China except as souvenirs and the reconversion rate is highly unfavorable. Only convert currency in small amounts.

American Express, Visa, and MasterCard are widely accepted in large cities, and the Bank of China will give cash advances on them, but only for a large service charge. ATMs can be found in urban areas although the exchange rate is less favorable than found in regular bank exchanges. Transactions in rural areas will require RMBs and visitors should never pay for goods or services with foreign currency. Such transactions are illegal.

Travel

VISA AND PASSPORT

A passport is required of all visitors and must have a term of validity of at least six months for any single entry which is within three months of the visa's date of issue; a minimum of nine months of passport validity must remain in order for either double or multiple entries to be permitted within six months of the date of the visa's issue.

Visas are required of all visitors.

Although it is now permissible for individuals to arrange their own itineraries, the vast majority of trips are put together by CITS (China International Travel Service), the official travel agency of China. Communications with CITS are customarily managed by a tour operator who offers several package tours, one of which is selected by the visitor. Funds for payment of

China

accommodations and other tour costs must then be deposited with CITS via a home (Chinese) bank. Documentation of deposit of funds must be shown to CITS officials upon arrival. Be prepared to show a copy of your itinerary indicating arrival and departure dates.

A Tourist visa is required to enter the country and may be issued to an individual who is either a tour group member or an independent traveler. A Transit visa is required to leave the country. Both are available at any Chinese embassy or consulate. Anyone arriving without a visa will be fined RMB2,000 at the point of entry and may not be allowed to enter the country. Visa validity is usually three months from the date of issue, but it depends on the terms specified in the package tour, or on the arrangements an individual has been able to negotiate.

A Transit visa is required for any stopover, even if travelers do not intend to leave the plane. The period of validity for Transit visas is generally ten days. Travelers in transit may also be required to produce their visa for the subsequent destination or a valid airline ticket for onward travel.

The terms of Business visas are not uniform rather are determined by Chinese immigration officials after scrutinizing the visa application. The Business visa application must have appended to it an official Chinese governmental department invitation or a state-approved company invitation indicating length of stay. Conducting business on a regular tourist visa will result in deportation at the very least.

Foreigners traveling in China are required to carry their visa with them at all times. Allow between three and five days for processing of visa applications made in person; postal applications generally take between two and three weeks after they are received by the appropriate authorities.

Certain areas of China are restricted to foreigners; any travel to Tibet must be approved prior to arrival. One can make travel arrangements for visiting Tibet prior to arriving in China. Once in China, it is necessary to join a group for travel in Tibet. This can be carried out by most Chinese travel agencies, who will acquire necessary permits and handle collection of fees. Individual travelers are required to have a special permit and must obtain permission to visit Tibet from one of the groups listed in the Travel Assistance section below. Further information is also available from the Chinese Embassy or from a Chinese consulate.

Throughout China, authorities commonly confiscate passports and impose exit bans against persons involved in commercial disputes. It is a good idea to memorize the telephone number of your consulate, which may make inquiries with local authorities on your behalf.

RESTRICTED ENTRY

Persons attempting to enter China who are in possession of a quantity of religious materials judged as being in excess of what is appropriate for personal use are sometimes detained and fined.

Individuals considered to be conducting themselves in what Chinese officials look upon as immoral or inappropriate behavior may be detained and expelled.

DEPARTURE FORMALITIES

An airport departure tax of RMB90 will be collected. It is advisable to reconfirm your departing airline reservations at 72-, 48- and 24-hour intervals prior to leaving, as the Chinese have a habit of selling off the seats of tourists that do not reconfirm. Should they do this, you will not be reimbursed.

Visitors will have been asked to declare all valuables and monies upon entry. A document showing this declaration must be presented at departure (Chinese authorities want to make sure you leave with less money than you had when you arrived).

CUSTOMS ENTRY (PERSONAL)

Duty-free

- Tobacco: 400 cigarettes (600 cigarettes for stays of over six months)
- Alcohol: 2 liters of alcoholic beverages
- Other: a reasonable amount of perfume for personal use

Prohibited or Restricted

- Arms and ammunition
- Radio transmitters
- Unregistered professional filming equipment
- Anti-government literature or material
- Chinese authorities have been known to seize documents, letters, and literature, which they determine is pornographic, political, or meant for religious proselytism. Magazines with photographs of even the merest risque quality and considered ordinary in Western countries might be viewed as pornography by Chinese officials. Books, films, tapes, compact disks, and records may be seized in order to determine whether they violate Chinese prohibitions.

IMMUNIZATION

Cholera and yellow fever vaccinations are required if arriving from any infected area within five to six days. Vaccinations for Hepatitis A, typhoid, tetanus, and influenza are suggested for all travelers, as is a polio booster and a tuberculosis skin test. If planning to reside long-term, a locally administered HIV test is required of all foreigners.

TIPPING

Tipping is officially prohibited. However, the changing nature of the country has brought about changes in expectations and customs.

Taxi

Metered taxi fares are usually rounded up by a few RMB. Avoid unmetered taxis altogether.

Porters

Porters receive RMB10 per bag.

Hotels

Hotels will apply service charges to all bills.

Restaurants

Restaurants will apply service charges, but foreigners are expected to leave a few RMB for the waitstaff.

EMERGENCY INFORMATION

Police and Crime

China was generally among the safest countries in the world; however, crime is on the rise in recent years. Beware of your belongings in major cities, especially in crowded areas—restaurants, bars, hotel lobbies, and tourist sites included. The police are often part of the problem, although punishment for crime is severe. Police think nothing of asking foreigners for fees to investigate a complaint or crime.

Take basic precautions as you might anywhere else. Foreign business visitors are assumed to be wealthy and are often the target of thieves. Consequently, purses, laptops, and briefcases will require additional security. Do not leave valuables in cars or on tables in cafés. Keep non-essential valuables locked in hotel safes when not in use. Use credit cards and travel checks when possible to avoid carrying large sums of cash.

Do not expect the police to investigate reports of theft. When making a report on stolen goods, get a copy to present to customs officials at departure time lest they think you sold the items.

Penalties in China can be draconian. Foreigners caught violating even minor laws may be subject to expulsion or imprisonment. Drug offense penalties include the death penalty.

Emergency Numbers

Numbers function nationwide although rural areas have very few telephones.

Police... 110
Foreigners' section 553102
Fire 119
First Aid 120
Information 116

Health

China still has very basic health problems and in many cases primitive sanitation. Never drink tap water; don't even use it for brushing your teeth, and avoid ice cubes. Don't eat raw vegetables and fruit unless they've been washed in a chlorine solution. Most canned food is contaminated with lead. Diarrhea is common for travelers who are unaccustomed to the new diet and water.

In winter, the dry air causes sinus problems, skin dryness, and problems for contact lens wearers. Bring along a well-stocked medical kit and any prescription drugs you will require.

Medical care even in major cities is inadequate by modern standards (see life expectancy statistics for China) and should be used only for emergency services. Competent, highly trained doctors and nurses can be found in major metropolitan areas, but many of them cannot speak any foreign languages. Hospital facilities are spartan, and the medical technology is not state of the art.

Visitors should carry medical insurance with an emergency evacuation policy. Major urban hotels have doctors on call or access to English-speaking doctors, but most curative measures rely on holistic and herbal methods.

INTERNAL TRAVEL

AIR

Most long-distance domestic journeys are by air. The Civil Aviation Administration of China (CAAC) provides routes linking Beijing with more than eighty other cities.

Tickets are normally purchased by guides, the price having been included in tour charges. Independent travelers can get bookings through a local Chinese International Travel Service (CITS) agent, who will charge a small commission, or at special booking offices.

You should purchase tickets well in advance, especially if you plan to travel during May, September, or October. There are numerous connections from Beijing/Guangzhou (Peking/Canton) to Hong Kong, as well as to other cities.

The departure tax is currently RMBY50.

TAXI

In Beijing, taxis are plentiful; however they have a reputation for manipulating the fare. Stand in line at a taxi stand or the hail one from the hotel lobby. Have a stash of small bills for payment I in case the driver claims he has no change. Also be sure that the meter starts after you get into the cab and not before. The government sets all cab fares according to vehicle size. Do not pay more than what is on the meter, unless a highway toll exists. Drivers speak little besides Chinese, so carry directions and a map with you. Many drivers are not familiar—or pretend not to be—with their own city. Major hotels will arrange for "professional" taxi service, which can help alleviate many problems.

AUTO

Rental vehicles are available in urban areas, but they are not recommended for foreigners as Chinese traffic laws are vague. Hired cars with local drivers can be procured at daily and weekly rates.

TRAIN

There is an extensive network of railroads crisscrossing the country. They are the primary means of transportation for both people and goods. The main routes connect Beijing to Guangzhou, Shanghai, Chengdu, Harbin, and Urumqi.

There are four levels of service: hard seat and soft seat for short trips, and first- and second-class sleepers for overnight trips. First class is very cheap by international standards and relatively comfortable; be sure to reserve seats in advance.

Trains are widely used by business people for inter-city travel. Trains are also the only means to reach more remote villages. They are also a great way to gain insights into your Chinese counterparts.

Note: Foreigners pay higher prices than locals for train tickets. Attempts to circumvent this system can result in severe punishment.

METRO

Beijing has an extensive subway system that runs from 5a.m. until 11p.m. This system gets heavy usage during peak business hours and signs are only in Chinese. English-speaking foreigners can get scheduling and fare information from the information booths located at most stations.

There is also a subway line in Guangzhou, the capital of Guangdong Province in China's south, and limited metro services in Tianjin.

China also inherited a very modern subway system in Hong Kong.

BUSES & TRAMS

There are reasonably priced bus and tram services but primarily in the cities. Some limited inter-city routes also exist. Guides accompanying every visitor or group do their best to ensure that travel on these systems is as trouble-free as possible—but prepare yourself for a confusing maze of routes and schedules as well as packed-sardine conditions; these are not recommended for business use.

WATER TRAVEL

China has an extensive river and coastal port passenger boat travel system. It is rarely used by business people, foreign or domestic, except when it is the only way to reach remote areas.

All of China's major rivers are serviced by river ferries. Coastal ferries run between Dalian, Qingdao (Tsingtao), Tianjin (Tientsin), and Shanghai. Regularly scheduled ferry services link mainland China with Hong Kong. Shanghai and Hong Kong also have cruise liner connections to many ports around the world.

Foreigners should allow trusted local contacts to set up any water travel itineraries.

TRAVEL ASSISTANCE

China International Travel Service (CITS)
Head Office; 103 Fuxingmennei Avenue
Beijing, 100800
tel: (10) 66 01 11 22, 66 01 20 55
fax: (10) 66 01 20 13

China National Tourism Administration (CNTA)
Department of Marketing and Promotion
9A Jianguomennei Avenue; Beijing 100740
tel: (10) 65 20 11 14, (10) 65 12 29 05
fax: (10) 65 12 28 51
website: www.cnta.com

China

China

Tibet Tourism Administration
Yuanlin Road
Lhasa, Tibet 850001
tel: (891) 633 5472; fax: (891) 683 4632

Tibetan Tourism Office
Room 3423 Poly Plaza
14 Dongzhimenanjie
Beijing
tel: (10) 65 00 11 88 (ext 3423), 65 93 65 38
fax: (10) 65 91 82 58, 65 93 65 38

Essential Terms

English	Mandarin
Yes No	How-duh boo-shing
Good morning Hello (daytime) Hello (evening) Hello (telephone)	Dzow ahn Nin how Wahn ahn Ne hao
Good-bye	Dzy jen
Please	Ching
Thank you	Sheh-sheh
Pleased to meet you	Hun gow-slingnung ren-shi nin
Excuse me; I'm sorry	Dway boo chee, bow-chen
My name is _____	War jow_____
I don't understand	Wo boo ming-bai
Do you speak English?	Nee hway shwaw ying-yu mah?

Communications
DIALING CODES IN CHINA

International country code: [86]

Selected city codes: Beijing (10), Fuzhou (591), Guangzhou (Canton) (20), Kunshan (520), Lanzhou (931), Huhhot (Inner Mongolia) (471), Shanghai (21), Shenyang (24), Tianjin (22), Xiamen (592), Xian (29)

Dialing China from Overseas

To dial China from overseas, dial your country's international dialing code, then 86 (the country code for China), then the city code, and finally the number. If you were dialing Beijing from the United States, for example, you would begin with 011, then 86, then 10 (the city code for Beijing), and finally the number of the person or office you were trying to reach.

Assistance Numbers

Information 116
Local information 114
General information .... (10) 5130828

CALLING WITHIN CHINA
Local Calls

The Chinese have not yet fully discovered the benefits of telephones, but they're trying. Many are paying up to RMB 5,000 (about US$575) for private lines, others tote around cellular phones that are even more expensive. Telephone companies hold auctions for numbers; the number 8 is a favorite because the Chinese word for eight, *ba*, is similar to *fa*, part of the verb meaning "to become wealthy."

Long Distance Calls

When calling long distance within China, dial the '0' before the area code. There is no need to dial the area code when calling within that area. When calling China from a foreign country, omit the '0' before the area code.

International Calls

Because of the antiquated phone systems, it is often easier to make international calls than local ones.

PAY PHONES
Public Telephones

Card Phone:

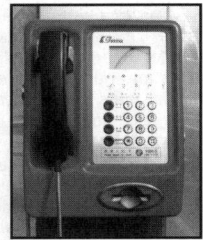

There are few public telephones on Chinese city streets. It normally takes repeated efforts to make a successful local call, and clarity is poor. Callers often must shout to make themselves heard. And because the call will be automatically be disconnected after 20 seconds of silence, if you're put on hold you must keep shouting, singing, whistling, or humming to yourself. Luckily, all calls are free.

CELLULAR PHONES

China has a great many cellular phone providers offering both digital and analog services. If you have a cellular phone, inquire with your phone provider as to whether or not a roaming agreement can be set up with one of the many chinese cellular service companies.

Note: Your home country cell phone may not work in this country. If not, we recommend that you rent an international cell phone *before* you leave home. A major US-based cell phone rental provider is **IMC WorldCell**. For information see "International Cell Phone Rentals" on page 14.

CALL BACK

You can (potentially) save significant sums when calling in China by using a call back service. For a list of callback services, please refer to the "Communications" section in the *Global Road Warrior* Introduction.

Fees for call back services vary widely, depending on the company and the type of service required. Be sure to check with these companies before leaving to compare rates.

PHONE JACK

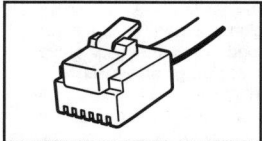

Plug adaptors are available through **iGo Corporation.** (See "Electrical and Telephone Adaptors" on page 19.)

FAX

Faxes can be hard to come by. Some top-end hotels may have faxes but only with incoming services. Rates are expensive.

POSTAL SERVICES

Letters to Europe take approximately one week and to North America take about 10 days. All incoming mail should say "the People's Republic of China."

Business Services

BUSINESS CENTERS

The hotels on the list that follows have business services, from complete to rudimentary.

Beijing Asia, Beijing, Beijing Airport, Beijing Exhibition Center, Beijing Hotel Palace Tower, Beijing International, Capital, Chang Fu Gong (New Otani), China World, Dong Fang, Gloria Plaza, Grace, Grand, Great Wall Sheraton, Holiday Inn Crowne Plaza, Holiday Inn Downtown, Holiday Inhn Lido, Hua Bei, Jianguo, Jinglun (Hotel Beijing-Toronto), Jing Guang New World, Jinlang, Kempinski, Kunlun, Novotel Song He, Olympic, Palace, Peace, Sara, Shangri-La, Swissotel Beijing, Taiwan, Traders, Xin Da Du, Xizhimen, Yanshan, Yue Xiu, Zhaolung.

Also try the China World Trade Center at 1 Jianguomenwai Dajie; tel: (10) 5052277.

Guangzhou Bai Yun, Central, China, Dong Fang, Equatorial, Garden, GITIC Plaza, Holiday Inn City Center, Holiday Inn Riverside, Landmark, Novotel Guangzhou, Ocean, Parkview Square, Ramada Pearl, Vitory, White Swan.

The Central Hotel also has office space rentals.

Shanghai City, Cypress, Equatorial, Garden, Holiday Inn Yin Xing, Jinjiang, Jinjiang Tower, Jing An Guest House, Nikko Longbai, Novotel Shanghai Yuan Lin, Ocean, Park, Peace, Portman Shangri-La, Regal Shanghai, Shanghai Hilton International, Shanghai International Airport, Shanghai JC Mandarin, Sheraton Hua Ting, Westin Taiping Yang, Xijiao Guest House, Yangtze New World.

TRANSLATION SERVICES

Business centers are the best source of translators.

COURIER SERVICES

Beijing

FedEx; c/o **Beijing Air Cargo Transportation Service Center**, Inside Chao Yang Gymnasiums, Tuan Jie Hu Liu Litun Xi Kou, Chao Yan Qu, Beijing 100026; tel: (10) 5011017; fax: (10) 5011015.

TNT; c/o **Beijing TNT Skyupak-Sinotrans Ltd.**, 14 Shu Guang Xi Li, Chao Yan Qu, Beijing 100028; tel: (10) 4677877 (pickups), 4672517 (customer service); fax: (10) 4677894.

UPS; c/o **Beijing Sinotrans Ltd.**, 25 Xibinhe Road, an Dingmen Wai; tel: (10) 4225670; fax: (10) 4226694.

Guangzhou

FedEx; c/o **Guangzhou China National Foreign Trade Corporation**, 20th Fl., 53 Hua Le Road, Guangzhou 510060; tel: (20) 3805669; fax: (20) 3805674.

TNT; c/o **Guangzhou Sinotrans Guangdong**, Airfreight Department, 1131 Guang Yuan Road Central, Guangzhou; tel: (20) 668092, 6680957/9; fax: (20) 6680950.

UPS; c/o **Guangzhou Sinotrans Ltd.**, Airfreight Department, 1131 Guang Yuan Road Central; tel: (20) 6680964; fax: (20) 2485760.

Shanghai

FedEx; c/o **Shanghai Qian Tang Company**, Room 460, Shanghai Center Building, 1376 Nanjing Xi Lu, Shanghai 200040; tel: (21) 2798040; fax: (21) 2798042.

TNT; c/o **Shanghai TNT Skypak-Sinotrans Ltd.**, Shanghai Branch, Number 3 Lane, 211 Xin Hua Road, Shanghai 200052; tel: (21) 2400819; fax: (21) 2400883.

Electrical

Current

220/240 volts AC, 50Hz

ELECTRIC PLUGS

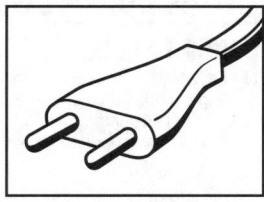

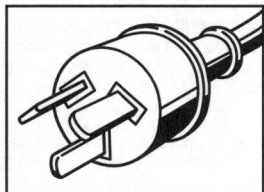

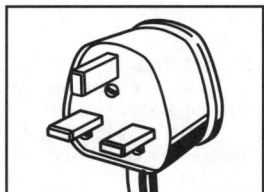

Flat three prong plugs are the norm. Hotels often will have adaptors available for a fee.

Plug adaptors are available through **iGo Corporation.** (See "Electrical and Telephone Adaptors" on page 19.)

China

Technical Support
HARDWARE/SOFTWARE VENDOR SUPPORT

Dell; tel: (604) 810-4977 (for Dell China listing); fax: (604) 810-4273; (Dell- Europe) tel: [44] (134) 474-8000; (in the U.S.) tel: [1] (512) 338-4400; fax: [1] (512) 728-3330; http://www.dell.com/.

Filemaker/Claris; (in Germany) tel: [49] (180) 525-8166 (Info-line); fax: [49] (180) 567-2233; tel: [49] (180) 523-6423; (in the U.S.) tel: [1] (800) 965-9090; http://www.claris.com/.

Hewlett Packard; (fax) tel: 10 6505 3888; (in Switzerland) tel: [41] (22) 780-8111; (in the U.S.) tel: [1] (408) 246-4300; http://www.hp.com/.

IBM; tel: (10) 643-76677; fax: (10) 643-62870; (in Switzerland) tel: [41] (22) 310-0418 (in French); (U.S. Main Office) tel: [1] 914-765-1900; (in the U.S.) tel: [1] (919) 517-2800; http://www.ibm.com/.

Microsoft; tel: (10) 6261-7711; fax: (10) 6253-6630; (in Switzerland) tel: [41] (848) 858-868; fax [41] (1) 831-0869; (in the U.S.) [1] (425) 635-7222; http://www.microsoft.com/.

NEC; (in Hong Kong) tel: [852] 795-2111 (UltraCare Support); (in the U.S.) [1] (916) 388-0101 (Main Switchboard); http://www.nec.com/.

Toshiba; (in Germany) tel: [49] (2131) 158-319; fax: [49] (2131) 158-558; (in Switzerland) tel: [41] (1) 946-0777; fax: [41] (1) 946-0807; (in Ireland) tel: [44] (193) 282-8828; (in the U.S.) [1] (949) 583-3000 (Corporate Headquarters); http://www.toshiba.com/.

Internet Connection
HOW TO CONNECT

Connecting to AOL and Compuserve in China is similar to using it when traveling outside your own area code. See the introductory section for detailed information on connecting to your account through a different phone number.

America Online

Numbers are available at keyword *international*. Be sure to get several local numbers before leaving. Go to keyword *access* (a free area) and download the software.

Direct access numbers for America Online in China are unavailable. Users will have to pay international rates to use the service.

Compuserve

Numbers are available at keyword *Go International*. The Compuserve Web-site also has a great deal of information, at http://www.compuserve.com.

There are no direct access numbers for Compuserve in China. Users will have to pay international rates to use the service.

Independent Service Providers

Many independent service providers offer discounts if you are only in town for a couple of days.

China Vision; tel: (571) 713-1869; fax: (571) 791-0973; e-mail: ChinaV@China-Vision.com; http://www.china-vision.com/.

Chuanglian Communication and Network Co., Ltd.; tel: (800) 810-8500; tel:(800) 810-0220; email: info@hichina.com; http://www.hichina.com/.

East Telecom Co.ltd Beijing; tel: (10) 8207-6688; support@public.east.cn.net; http://www.east.net.cn/.

Resources Link Network Ltd.; tel: (852) 2850 8979; info@resolink.com; http://www.deltamac.com/.

VIANET; tel: [43] 1-404-020; fax: [43] 1-404-0240; e-mail: info@vianet.at; http://www.vianet.at/.

Business Culture
GREETINGS AND COURTESIES

Handshaking is the accepted greeting. Chinese usually shake hands very lightly instead of taking the hand firmly and forcefully pumping it, and in China a handshake may last as long as 10 seconds. Upon meeting someone, Chinese lower their eyes slightly as a sign of respect. Staring into the eyes of a Chinese might make them uncomfortable. Face—being respected by one's peers—is very important to the Chinese. They are enormously sensitive to maintaining face in everything they do. Saying or doing anything that causes someone to lose face can instantly destroy a relationship and any business that might result from it. Never insult or openly criticize someone in front of others. Don't make fun of a Chinese, even if only as a joke. Do not treat someone as a person of lowly rank if their position in the company is high. A person's face is also their company's face. The relationship you develop with a person represents your relationship with his entire company. Gifts are important, expressing friendship and symbolizing hopes for success. But expensive gifts can cause personal embarrassment and political or social awkwardness. For wrapped gifts, gold or red are appropriate colors. White and black are colors of mourning.

DECISION MAKING

Written contracts are secondary in China to personal commitments between associates. Some executives prefer to sign a principal agreement and let their subordinates work out the details at a later time. Chinese usually feel that single contracts are just one component of a larger relationship.

WOMEN

Officially, women are given many of the same rights as men in China. There are still many disciminatory practices taking place, however, and recent legislative changes may lead to women losing ground. Women are usually the first to be laid off from economically hurting businesses, and few business leaders are women. Foreign businesswomen should not experience any discrimination. Women in China for business should act and dress in a formal manner.

MEETINGS

Meetings are considered very formal in China. It is a good idea to send a list of your representatives before the meeting, and to include their rank in your company. You should also request a similar list. You will be led into a room in which the Chinese are already present. Your team leader should enter first. Teams sit across a table, leaders opposite each other and others seated in descending order of importance. Small talk will come first. Business is addressed once people feel comfortable with each other. The head of the host team will deliver a short welcome speech, then turn the floor over to the visitors. Your senior team member should speak for your company; avoid conflicting statements from other team members. When talking, your spokesman should address the senior Chinese representative. Chinese prefer to hear a proposal as a broad overview, and then respond to specific issues or questions point by point. Business cards are a common opening to business meetings, and are more impressive if one side is translated into Chinese characters.

BUSINESS ATTIRE

Dress styles are changing quickly in today's China. The uniform-like Mao jacket is being replaced by Western-style suits and, sometimes, ties. Foreigners should dress formally. Women should avoid low necklines and hemlines that rise above the knee. Jewelry will be noticed; modest gold jewelry and a quality watch will count in your favor. However, avoid overly expensive jewelry or showy ornaments.

Business Centers
Beijing

CITY VIEW

Beijing is located at the northwestern corner of the North China Plain, just inside the Great Wall, which cuts through the municipal area and approaches to within 60km or the city center. The latest census reports that 10.8 million people call it home, with over seven million living within the city proper. It is a sprawling city that seems to stretch forever, yet lacks many of the appearances of a modern city in the late twentieth century. There are few skyscrapers, and it is actually a conservative city, not a great center of industrial production nor in the forefront of commercial innovation.

AIRPORT

Beijing/Peking Airport to City Center

The airport lies 18.5 miles (30 km.) from the city center. Travel time is 45 minutes by bus, or 30 minutes by taxi (which would be substantially more expensive). Hotels often offer complimentary pick-up services if located nearby; others offer pick up service for a fee.

Airline Numbers

Aeroflot Soviet Airlines ....(10) 500-2412
Air France.. (10) 505-1818
Alitalia.. (10) 500-2233 ext 139
All Nippon Airways ....(10) 512-5551
Asiana Airlines ....(10) 500-2233 ext 139
British Airways .... (10) 512-4070-5, 512-4080
CAAC .... (10) 558861
Canadian Airlines ....(10) 500-1956
Cathay Pacific ....(10) 500-3339
Dragonair ....(10) 505-4343
Finnair .... (10) 512-7180
Iran Air ....(10) 512-4940
Japan Airlines ....(10) 500-2221
JAT Yugoslave Airlines .... (10) 500-3388 Ext. 426
LOT Polish Airlines ....(10) 500-2233
Lufthansa... (10) 512-3535
Mongolian Airlines (MIAT) ....(10) 501-4544
Northwest Airlines ....(10) 500-4529
Pakistan International...................................(10) 532-3274
Philippines Airlines ....(10) 532-3992
Qantas... (10) 500-2481
Romanian Air Transport ....(10) 532-3552
Scandinavian Airlines (SAS) .... (10) 512-0575
Singapore Airlines .... (10) 504-4138
Swissair ....(10) 512-3555
Thai International .... (10) 512-3881
United Airlines ....(10) 512-8888

HOTELS

Top End

China World Hotel; 1 Jianguomenwai Ave., Da Bei Yan; tel: 6505-2266; fax: 6505-3165; part of World Trade Center; ultra modern, 3 restaurants; coffee shop, pool, health center, business center, shopping, bowling, indoor tennis; squash courts; golf simulators; medical clinic; US$240/370.

Great Wall Sheraton; 10 North Donghuan Rd.; NE Beijing, Chooyang District; tel: (10) 500-5566; fax: 6500-1938; located in the embassy district; modern; 5 restaurants; coffee shop; gym; pool; tennis; shops; karaoke; US$170/250.

Guangdong Regency; 2 Wang Fujing Ave.; tel: 513-6666; 2 blocks from the Forbidden City; new; non-smoking rooms; 4 restaurants; business center; shops; bank; fitness room; pool; game room; US$140/190.

Kunlun Hotel; No. 2 Xin Yuan Nan Lu, Chaoyang District; tel: 6500-3388; fax: 6506-1158; 20 minutes from downtown; 10 restaurants; coffee shops; conference/banquet facilities; business center; shopping center; health club; helipad; US$130/310.

Palace Hotel; 9 Goldfish Lane, Wangfujin; tel: 6512-8899; fax: 6512-9050; 3 blocks east of Tiananmen Square; 6 restaurants; coffee house; 24-hour business center; gymnasium; pool; solarium; luxury shops; Rolls Royce pick-up service from airport; US$260/340.

Expensive

Beijing Hilton; 1 Dongfang Lu, Dongsanhuan Beilu, Chaoyang District; tel: 6466-2288; fax: 6465-3052; standard Hilton amenities; restaurants; health club.

Holiday Inn Downtown Beijing; 98 Bei Li Shi Lu, Xi Cheng Qu; tel: 6833-8822; fax: 6834-0696.

Holiday Inn Lido; Jichang Road and Jiang Tai Road; tel:6437-6688; fax:6436-7652; near airport in large commercial complex; restaurants; supermarket; deli; gym; pool; drugstore.

New Otani Chang Fu Gong; 26 Jian Guo Men Wai Street; tel: 6512-5555; fax: (10) 6513-9810.

Novotel Beijing Wangfujin; 88 Dengshikou, Dongcheng District; tel: 513-8822; just off China's most famous shopping street; restaurant; coffee shop; health center; karaoke; excellent value; US$140.

Moderate

Beijing Hotel; 33 East Chang'An Ave.; tel: 6513-7766; fax: 6513-7307; modern in traditional Chinese style; 7 restaurants; coffee shop; shopping arcade; business center; airline ticket office; billiard room; karaoke; traditional Chinese medicinal clinic; US$110.

Hua Du Hotel; 8 Xin Yuan South Rd., Chao Yang District; tel: 500-1166; 2 restaurants; small supermarket; beauty salon; karaoke; US$68/88.

Jianguo Hotel;5 Jianguomenwai Dajie; tel: (10) 6500-2233; fax: (10) 6500-2871; restaurants; spacious rooms.

Movenpick; Xiao Tianzhu Village; tel: (10) 6456-5588; near airport; health club; pool; European atmosphere.

Tianten Hotel; 1 Tiyunguan Rd., Chongwen District, SE; tel: 711-2277; near Temple of Heaven and National gymnasium; 10 restaurants; business center; airline ticket office; shopping; health room; sauna; billiards; US$60/125.

MEDICAL CARE

Asia Emergency Assistance Ltd. (AEA); 14 Liangmahe South Road, 1/F; tel: 6462-9112/9100; fax: 6462-9111.

Beijing Union Medical College Hospital; 1 Dong Shai Fuyuan Hutong; tel: (10) 512-7733, ext. 217 for emergencies.

Beijing Union Medical College Hospital; Dongdan Bei Dajie; tel: (10) 529-6114, 529-5286, 529-5296 or 529-5822.

Friendship Hospital, Foreigners' Section; tel: (10) 338-671, ext. 441.

International SOS Assistance (SOS); Kunlun Hotel, Office Ste. 433, 2 Xin Yuan Nan Lu; 6500-3419; fax: 6501-6048.

MEDEX Assistance Corp.; Regus OFfice 19, Beijing Lufthansa Center; No. 50 Liangmaqiao Rd.; tel: 6465-1264; fax: 6465-1267; email: medexasst@aol.com.

HEALTH CLUB

International Club (only tennis or Dancing); 21 Jianguomenwai Dajie, Chaoyang; tel: (10) 6532-2188.

AUTO RENTAL

Blue Sky (Lantian) Car Rental Co.; tel: (10) 205-5888, 205-6888, 201-8888.

Capital Car Co.; tel: (10) 513-8893 or 852-3664

CITS; tel: (10) 601-1122 ext. 2081, 601-4146.

WORLD TRADE CENTER

World Trade Center Beijing
Jia No. 1 North Street Qingnianhu
Andingmenwai, Dongcheng
Beijing, 100011 P.R.C.
tel: (10) 6427-7428; fax: (10) 6427-7425
email: wtcbj@public.bta.net.cn
website: http://ccpitbj.asiansources.com

Guangzhou

CITY VIEW

Formerly known as Canton, Guangzhou is the cultural center of southeast China. It is internationally known as a seaport, and has a strong affinity with neighbor Hong Kong.

AIRPORT

Baiyun Airport to City Center

The airport lies 4 miles (7 km.) from the city. It typically takes about 20 minutes to travel to downtown Guangzhou from Baiyun Airport, whether by bus or taxi.

Construction is underway for a new international airport, set for completion in 1998 or 1999. Because Baiyun is the busiest airport in China, the new international gateway is particularly important to the country.

Airline Numbers
CAAC

Domestic	(20) 666-2969
International	(20) 666-1803
Singapore Airlines	(20) 335-8886
Malaysian Airline System	(20) 335-8828

HOTELS

Top End

Furama Hotel Guangzhou; 316 Changdi Lu; tel: 8186-3288; fax: 8186-3388; email: fhg@furama-hotels.com; restaurants; coffee house; business center; secretarial services; multi-function center.

Shangri-La; 78 Beishan Rd. tel: 797-7951; fax; 707-3545/799-6637; 5 restaurants; deli; complimentary airport shuttle for selected domestic flights; meeting and conference facilities; gym; jacuzzi; jogging trails; tennis; sauna; massage; bicycling.

White Swan; No. 1 South St., Shamian Island; tel: 8188-6968; fax: 8186-1188; US$200/350.

Expensive

China Hotel; Liu Hua Lu; tel: 8666-6888; fax: 8677-7014; US$98/134.

Dong Fang;120 Liu Hua Rd.; tel: 666-9900; fax: 666-2775.

Garden; 368 Huanshi Dong Lu; tel: 333-8989; fax: 335-0467; US$92/290.

Gitic Plaza Hotel; 339 Huanshi Dong Rd.; tel: 8331-1888; fax: 8331-1666; US$98/220.

Gitic Riverside; 298 Yan Jiang Zhong Rd.; tel: 8383-9888; fax: 8381-4448; US$60/150.

Holiday Inn City Centre Guangzhou; 28 Guangming Lu; tel: 8775-3126; fax: 8775-3126; US$130/225.

Novotel Guanzhou Jing Nan; tel: (21) 418-888; fax: (21) 429-645.

MEDICAL CARE

The first People's Hospital of Guangzhou; tel: 8642.

Guangzhou No. 1 Hospital; tel: (21) 333-090.

The First hospital of Guangzhou Medical College; tel: (21) 70-371.

First People's Municipal Hospital; 602 Renmin Bei Lu; tel: (21) 333-3090.

Second People's Municipal Hospital; 63 Xinfeng Lu, Emergency Ward; tel: (21) 881-5321.

Zhongshan Hospital; 107 Yanjiang 1 Lu; tel: (21) 888-2012.

Chinese Medicine Hospital; 16 Zhuji Lu; emergency tel: (21) 888-6111.

Foreign Guest Medical Clinic; Dongfang Hotel, 120 Liuhua Lu; tel: (21) 666-9900; emergency services only after 9:30pm.

HEALTH CLUB

The China Hotel; Liuhua Lu; tel: (21) 666-6888.

Dongfang Hotel; 120 Ciu Ha Road; tel: (21) 666-2946.

Guangdong International; 339 Huanshi Lu; tel: (21) 331-1888.

Holiday Inn City Center; Huanshi Dong, 28 Guangming Road; tel: (21) 776-6999.

Ramada Pearl; 9 Mingyue 1 Lu; tel: (21) 777-2988.

White Swan; Shamian Island; tel: (21) 888-6968.

AUTO RENTAL

Driving is not recommended because traffic is unsafe. Apart from traffic, a businessperson driving his or her own car would be considered a loss of face, as not even local businesspeople drive themselves. Cars with drivers are available at major hotels.

WORLD TRADE CLUB

World Trade Club Guangzhou (AF)
No. 809, 8/F, South Tower
No. 371-375 Huan Shi Dong Rd.
Guangzhou, P.R.C. 510095
tel: (20) 778-7768; fax: (20) 776-9011
(No services)

Shanghai

CITY VIEW

Shanghai is being reborn with new buildings and roads going in all directions. While the overpopulation (13.5 million) that has threatened the city seems a thing of the past, it remains to be seen if the changes are permanent or not. A much more vibrant city than its counterpart, Beijing, it has also become the financial and commercial center point of the country.

AIRPORT

Hangqiao Airport to City Center

The airport lies nine miles (15 km) west of Shanghai. Buses and taxis are available at the airport. Figure about 30 to 40 minutes to travel downtown for a cost of US$9 to $11 in a cab. Major hotels have desks in the airport where you can order a shuttle. A metro link connecting the airport and city is under construction, and should be completed around 2005.

Airline Numbers

Air France ....(21) 255-8866
Alitalia.. (21) 255-3957
Canadian Airlines International ....(21) 258-2582
Cathay Pacific ....(21) 433-6435
Dragon Air ....(21) 433-6435
Japan Airlines ....(21) 433-3000
Korean Airlines ....(21) 258-8450
Northwest Airlines .... (21) 279-8100
Singapore Airlines ....(21) 279-8000
United Airlines ....(21) 255-3333

HOTELS

Top End

Garden Hotel Shanghai; 58 Maoming Nan Lu; tel: 6415-1111; fax: 6472-8877; city center; modern/traditional blend; spacious rooms; restaurants; business center; indoor pool; gym; tennis; US$220/320.

Hilton International; 250 Hua Shan Rd., 1000-40; tel: (21) 6248-0000; fax: (21) 6248-3868; www.hilton.com; non-smoking floors; restaurants; meeting facilities; 24-hour business center; fitness center; whirlpool; sauna; squash; lounge. US$185/220.

Portman Shangri-La; 1376 Nanjing Xi Lu; tel: 6279-8888; fax: 6279-8887; state-of-the-art hotel in Shanghai Center Complex; restaurants; 24-hour business center; travel agency; airline office; health club; indoor golf machine; tennis/squash courts; pools; US$185/295.

Shanghai JC Mandarin; 1225 Nan Jing Xi Lu; tel: 6279-1888; fax: 6279-2314; on Shanghai's most famous shopping street; 7 restaurants; business center; medical clinic; fitness center; indoor pool; tennis and squash; US$240/280; 25% discount through asia-hotels.com.

Sheraton Hua Ting; 1200 Cao Xi Bei Lu; tel: 6439-1000; fax: 6439-1000; near Hongqjao development zone; non-smoking rooms; japanese rooms; restaurants; 24-hour business center; health club; fitness center; tennis; indoor pool; bowling; shopping; free airport shuttle; subway outside entrance; US$180/200.

Sofitel Hyland; 5095 Nan Jing Rd., East; tel: 6351-5888; fax: 6351-7625; riverfront on shopping street; 3 restaurants; business center; fitness area; US$185/220.

Westin Shanghai; 5 Zun Yi Nan Rd.; tel: 6275-8888; fax: 6275-5420; near airport, in Hongqiao Development Zone; 5 restaurants; business center; hot tubs; pool; tennis; gym; nearby 18-hole golf; US$175/280.

Expensive

City Hotel Shanghai; 5-7 Shan Xi Rd., Lu Wan District; tel: 6255-1133; fax: 6255-0211; walking distance to Shanghai exhibition center; 3 restaurants; free buffet breakfast; coffee shop; business center; internet hookup; function rooms; hotel doctor; karaoke; US$105/235.

Holiday Inn Crowne Plaza; 400 Pan Yu Rd.; tel: 6282-2014; near consulate district; business center; secretarial services; gym; tennis; sauna; steambath; pool; $US136/280; 35% discount through asia-hotels.com.

Jing An Hotel; 370 Huashan Rd.; tel: 6248-1888; fax: 6248-2657; heart of business district; Spanish style; large gardens; restaurants; function rooms; business center; conference center; fitness; recreation center; 40% discount through asia-hotels.com.

Novotel Shanghai Yuan Lin; 201 Baise Rd., tel: 6470-1688; fax: 6470-0008; next to Shanghai Botanical Garden; restaurants; multi-purpose function rooms; business center; rooftop swimming pool; tennis; shuttle service to downtown; karaoke; 50% discount through asia-hotels.com.

Moderate

Cypress Hotel; No. 2419 Hong Qiao Rd.; tel: 6268-8868; fax: 6268-1878; near airport and Hong Quio Development Zone; luxury residential district; 3 restaurants; business center; 4 banquet rooms; meeting rooms; indoor pool; bowling alley; squash/tennis courts; sauna; shopping center; US$85/150; 40% discount through Asia-hotels.com.

Shanghai Jianguo; 439 Cao Xi Rd. (North); tel: 437-5926; fax: 433-4959; US$80/150.

Shanghai Mansions; 20 Beusuzhou Rd.; tel: 324-6260; fax: 326-9778; near Bund district; US$80/90.

Shanghai YMCA; 123 Xi Zang Rd. (South); tel: 6326-1040; fax: 6320-1957; restaurants; 24-hour cafe; banquet halls; shopping; gym; beauty salon; massage; karaoke; US$85/150.

MEDICAL CARE

Huashan Hospital; 12 Wulumuqi Zhong Lu; tel: (21) 431-1600.

Huadong Hospital; 221 Yanan Xi Lu, 2nd floor; tel: (21) 6248-3180 ext. 310.

Huashan Hospital; 12 Wulumuqi Zhong Lu, 18th floor; tel: (21) 6248-9999 ext. 1900.

Shanghai People's Hospital No. 1; 190 Bei Suzhou Lu; tel: (21) 6324-0010.

Shanghai No. 9 People's Hospital; 639 Zhizaoju Lu; tel: (21) 6377-4831 (SB).

HEALTH CLUB

New Town Club; 35 Loushanguan Lu, Hongqiao; tel: (21) 6275-7888.

Shanghai Hilton International Hotel; 250 Huashan Lu, Jingan; tel: (21) 6248-0000.

Shanghai Portman Shangri-la Hotel; Portman Shangri-la Hotel, seventh floor, 1376 Nanjing Xi Lu, Jingan; tel: (21) 6279-8888.

AUTO RENTAL

Many large hotels offer chauffeured car rentals. The most reliable car rental company for self-drive vehicles is: **Shanghai Dazhong Hertz Rental Company**; 98 Guohuo Lu; tel: 6318-5666.

WORLD TRADE CENTER

World Trade Center Shanghai
5/F Jinling Mansion
No. 28 Jinling Road (W)
Shanghai, PRC 200021
tel: (21) 6387-8173; fax: (21) 6387-4966
email: wtc-sh@online.sh.cn
website: http://www.ccpit-shanghai.com

Colombia

At a Glance

THE PEOPLE

Population .... 39,309,422 (July 1999 est.)
Growth Rate .... 1.85% (1999 est.)
Life Expectancy .... 70.48 years (born 1999)
Infant Mortality ... 24.3 deaths/1,000 live births (1999 est.)

Ethnic Composition

Mestizo 58%
Caucasian 20%
Mulatto..14%
Black African 4%
Amerindian-black mix 3%
Amerindian 1%

Religious Composition

Roman Catholic..95%
Other and non-affiliated..5%

Languages Spoken

Spanish (official), numerous tribal languages

Education and Literacy

School is compulsory for nine years in cities and for five years in rural areas. Literacy nationwide is 91.3 percent.

Labor Force

Total: 16,800,000
By occupation: services 46%, industry 24%, agriculture 30%

THE ECONOMY

Colombia has opened its economy to greater international trade, investment, and competition but its fortunes are still a function of its close neighbors' economies. The Colombian government has pursued more prudent fiscal, exchange rate, and monetary policies, as well as instituted major changes in the areas of finance and labor law. However, Colombia continues to be plagued by the debilitating influence exercised by illegal drug trade and anti-government guerilla-related violence. Government attempts to control inflation have been undercut by the influx of foreign cash related to the drug trade. The economy has a high rate of official unemployment and exports are stagnating due to recessions in many bordering economies and in Japan. Foreign investment has remained uninterested in approaching Colombia's chaotic environment.

Exports .... US$11.3 billion (f.o.b., 1998 est.)
Imports .... US$14.4 billion (f.o.b., 1998 est.)
Total GDP ....US$254.7 billion (1998 est.)
GDP Per Capita .... US$6,600 (1998 est.)
Unemployment .... 15.7% (1998 est.)
Inflation Rat(1998 est.) .... 16.7% (1998 est.)

Top Export Partners

United States, E.U., Japan, Venezuela.

Top Import Partners

United States, E.U., Brazil, Venezuela, Japan.

Top Exports

Petroleum, coffee, coal, bananas, fresh cut flowers. (Note: Considerable money has been brought into the Colombian economy via the illegal production and export of cocaine.)

Top Imports

Industrial equipment, transportation equipment, consumer goods, chemicals, paper products.

BUSINESS WORKWEEK

Offices

Monday to Friday 8a.m. to noon and 2p.m. to 5:30 or 6 p.m. Some offices and most international firms have adopted a continuous workday from 8a.m. to 5pm.

Note: Firms in the warmer towns such as Cali tend to start at 7a.m. and finish earlier.

Banks

Monday to Friday 9a.m. to 3p.m.

Note: On the last Friday of the month, banks only stay open until noon.

Government

Monday to Friday 8a.m. to 12:30p.m. and 2p.m. to 5:30p.m. Note: Offices are generally open to the public only in the afternoon.

Retail

Monday to Saturday 9a.m. to 12:30p.m. and 2:30p.m. to 7p.m.

Note: Some stores are open for a few hours on Sundays. Hours in rural areas may differ significantly

HOLIDAYS

New Year's Day...January 1
Epiphany ....January 11*
St. Joseph's Day ....March 22*
Maundy Thursday...April 1*
Good Friday..April 2*
Labor Day..May 1
Ascension Day .... May 17*
Corpus Christi..June 7*
Saints Peter and Paul...July 5*
Independence...July 20
Battle of Boyaca .... August 7
Assumption...August 16*
Discovery of America .... October 18*
All Saints' Day .... November 1*
Independence of Cartagena......................... November 15*
Immaculate Conception..................................December 8
Christmas Day..December 25

*Date may vary by year.

CLIMATE

Seasons

The climate in Columbia, depending on altitude, varies considerably from place to place. There is little seasonal variation in temperature, but December, January, and February are the driest months. The dry season is called "verano" and the wet season is referred to as "winter" (_invierno_).

Regions

Weather wise, Columbia can be divided into two areas. The coastal front and the Eastern Plains get extremely hot and damp. Meanwhile, the central inland region, including Bogota, remains cool for the most part. An intermediate climate exists in the rest of the country. Rain falls heaviest in the west coast of the country.

Bogotà has temperatures of around 20°C (68°F) in the

Central Departments

1 Risaralda
2 Caldas
3 Cundinamarca
4 Quind o
5 Tolima
6 Districto Especial

Colombia

✪	National capital
●	Department capital
•	Secondary city
⊠	Airport
⚓	Port
▬	International border
⋯	Province border
—	Road
⋯	Railroad

0	100	200 km
0	100 mi	

summer, and falls to 8˚C (46˚F) in the winter. Barranquilla, in the north, stays around 32˚C (91˚F) in the summer, and 24˚C (75˚F) in the winter.

Money & Banking

Currency

The currency of Colombia is the Colombian Peso (Col$).

Denominations

The Colombian Peso (Col$) comes in coin denominations of Col$5, 10, 20, 50, 100, 200, and 500, and banknotes of Col$500, 1,000, 2,000, 5,000, and 10,000.

Traveler's Checks and Credit Cards

Not all banks will exchange traveler's checks and currency; this can even vary by branches of the same bank. Exchange shops (cambios), first class hotels, and kiosks at international airports also do exchange but rates are less favorable. The exchange of U.S. dollars provides the most favorable rates for foreigners. Avoid black marketeers at all costs.

Cashing traveler's checks and exchanging currency will require the use of passport identification. Some banks even require a photocopy as part of the paperwork. The whole process can be difficult and lengthy, especially in smaller towns where commissions may also run high.

American Express, Visa, Diner's Club, and MasterCard are accepted in most large hotels and retail outlets in the main cities. ATMs can only be found in major cities but even then they are still rare. In rural areas, transactions will be cash only.

Essential Terms

English	Spanish
Yes	Sí
No	No
Good morning	Buenos días
Hello (daytime)	Buenas tardes
Hello (evening)	Buenas noches
Hello (telephone)	¿Hola?
Good-bye	Adiós
Please	Por favor
Thank you	Gracias
Pleased to meet you	Encantado (a) de conocerle
Excuse me; I'm sorry	¿Perdóneme?
My name is _____	Me llamo _____
I don't understand	No comprendo
Do you speak English?	¿Habla usted inglés?

Travel

VISA AND PASSPORT

A passport that is valid for six months or more beyond date of entry is required of all. Sizable fines are levied when passports are not stamped upon arrival, and if stays of more than 90 days are not approved by the Colombian Immigration Agency (Departamento Administrativo de Seguridad, Jefatura de Extranjeria, "DAS Extranjeria").

Visas are not required of those who are traveling for tourism purposes for stays up to 90 days, except nationals from the following countries, who must have a visa regardless of the purpose of their visit: Afghanistan, Algeria, Angola, Benin, Botswana, Burkina Faso, Burundi, Cameroon, Cape Verde, Central African Republic, Chad, China (PR), Comoros, Congo (Dem. Rep. of), Congo (Rep. of), Cuba, Czech Republic, Djibouti, Dominican Republic, Egypt, Equatorial Guinea, Eritrea, Ethiopia, Gabon, Gambia, Ghana, Guinea, Guinea-Bissau, Haiti, Hong Kong, India, Iran, Iraq, Ivory Coast, Jordan, Kenya, Korea (DPR), Lebanon, Lesotho, Liberia, Libya, Madagascar, Malawi, Mali, Mauritania, Mauritius, Morocco, Mozambique, Namibia, Nicaragua, Niger, Nigeria, Pakistan, Rwanda, São Tomé e Príncipe, Senegal, Seychelles, Sierra Leone, Slovak Republic, Somalia, South Africa, Sri Lanka, Sudan, Swaziland, Syria, Tanzania, Togo, Tunisia, Uganda, Vietnam, Taiwan, Yemen, Zambia, and Zimbabwe.

Upon arrival, all visitors must be able to document possession of sufficient funds to cover expenses during their stay. The amount required is generally about US$20 per day.

Types of visas issued: Tourist, Business, Temporary Worker, Technical Assistant, Journalist, Religious, and Student.

Tourist visas are valid for three months from date of entry. The term of validity of all other visas depends on the purpose of the visit, as stated in the visa application. All types except business visa are for single-entry only.

Business visas, which can be single- or multiple-entry, are valid for up to three years and are renewable. A business visa application must include an invitation from a Colombian sponsor company or a government agency.

Possession of an onward ticket is usually requested when arriving in Colombia by air, but it is not commonly requested at land crossings. However, be aware that when exiting Colombia by land or air, you must be able to show an exit stamp in your passport from the DAS. It is advisable to get the stamp while you are in a major city (or upon arrival at the airport), since it may prove difficult to find a DAS office in smaller towns. Thirty-day extensions of your stay can also be granted at any DAS office. Allow between ten and fifteen days for processing of visa applications.

DEPARTURE FORMALITIES

Travelers leaving from El Dorado International Airport will pay a US$23 departure tax for international flights and US$18 for domestic flights, usually included in the price of the airline ticket. If you have stayed longer than 60 days, the international departure tax is doubled. Passengers who are transiting within 24 hours are exempted from paying the tax.

CUSTOMS ENTRY (PERSONAL)

Duty-free

- Tobacco: 200 cigarettes, 50 cigars, and 500g of tobacco
- Alcohol: 2 bottles of wine or spirits
- Other: a reasonable quantity of perfume
- Emeralds and articles made of gold or platinum need a receipt from the place of purchase which must be presented to customs on departure
- Personal electronic or camera equipment

Prohibited or Restricted

- Firearms or explosives
- Controlled drugs
- Vegetables, plants or plant material
- Meat and food products of animal origin.

IMMUNIZATION

A certified yellow fever vaccination is required for entry to Colombia for visitors arriving from infected areas. Vaccination for yellow fever is advised for travelers who intend to visit the following endemic areas: the foothills of the Cordillera Oriental (both eastern and western), from the Ecuadorian frontier to the border with Venezuela, the Magdalena River middle valley, Urabá, the Sierra Nevada foothills, Amazonia, and the eastern plains (Orinoquia).

Cases of cholera have also been reported. Vaccinations recommended are: cholera, hepatitis A, malaria, polio, tetanus, typhoid, and yellow fever.

TIPPING

Taxi

Tipping is not customary, but it is always appreciated.

Porters

Porters at hotels and airports expect about 100 pesos per piece of luggage.

Hotels

A 10- to 15-percent service charge is usually included in the bill. Other moderate tips may be left for particularly helpful staff.

Restaurants

A 10- to 15 -percent service charge is often included in the tab. Otherwise, tip this same percentage to waiters and bartenders.

Other

Chambermaids: Col$200 per day. Barbers, beauticians: 10 to 15 percent. Doorpersons, attendants, and small services: Col$200. Bogotá's shoeshine boys depend on their tips for survival, and expect about 300-500 pesos.

EMERGENCY INFORMATION

Police and Crime

Colombia is one of the most dangerous countries in the world. Crime goes well beyond petty theft, and violence is common. Based on the Colombian government's own statistics, the murder rate of 77.5 per 100,000 inhabitants is almost 900 percent that of the U.S. Narcotics and rebel guerrilla violence account for much of this, but common criminals commit an estimated 75 percent of reported murders.

Theft of hand-carried bags and travel documents is common, particularly at airports, and especially at El Dorado Airport in Bogota. Taking irregular taxis, which are often distinguishable by a driver with a companion and non-standard markings, is unsafe. Getting into a cab that is already conveying one or more persons is not a good idea. Travel by bus can also be dangerous. Extortion and kidnappings, particularly on rural buses, are not uncommon. Bars and nightclubs are often scenes of violence.

Drugging of tourists occurs often and is most commonly done with the drug Scopolamine (*burundanga*). It can incapacitate its victim within a few seconds. It may be administered as liquid, spray, dust, or smoke. Drinks, cigarettes, even chewing gum may be considered dangerous if offered by strangers in public places or transport. The most frequent drugging incidents take place in bars and nightclubs, and may also occur in buses and cabs. Concentrate on your belongings and your surroundings, and do not get distracted in crowded areas.

Take basic, common-sense precautions when out and about, and try to blend in with the populace. Do not walk about alone and preferably go with a Colombian native. Avoid flashy displays of wealth, and dress and behave conservatively. Leave most of your cash, traveler's checks, jewelry, and your camera in your hotel safe. Many South Americans carry "mugging" money with them, in case of such an event, and stash the rest of their necessary cash in a sock or a shoe.

Carry photocopies of your passport instead of the original. Use credit cards or traveler's checks for most of your transactions. Walk with your bag under your arm and away from the street to avoid having it snatched or cut away.

Never exchange money in the street or carry a package for a stranger. Punishment for crime especially drug trafficking and possession is severe.

One common scam has a local who is posing as a policeman approach an obvious foreign visitor, saying he needs to "check" the visitors's currency for the possible presence of counterfeit U.S. dollars. The person hands over the money, is given a receipt, and then the "policeman" disappears.

One of the most terrifying realities is the existence of "Sicarios," Medellin's teenage assassins. Police say that there are about 2,000 of these pre-pubescent killers on the streets of Medellin. Typically, they are hired by the Medellin cartel, other drug dealers, even businessmen, and police to slay their rivals. Independent sources contend that there are between 5,000 and 7,000 young people living in the city who have been hired to commit murder at least once.

Terrorist and guerilla groups often target foreign executives, specially American, for kidnappings and bombings. High-level executives should take necessary security precautions. If planning to travel within Colombia, check with your embassy for current travel warnings. There is no such thing as too much security in Colombia. As a note, hundreds of visitors have come and gone to the country unharmed. The basic recommendation dictates that you do not travel alone at night, or without the attendance of a Colombian native that you trust, and that you keep your wits about you during the day.

Emergency Numbers

Emergency medical service	277-6666
All services, urban areas	112
All services, rural areas	01
Tourist assistance	669-200

Health

The high altitude of Bogota may cause some dizziness or other symptoms of altitude sickness upon arrival. Take it easy the first day, and stay away from alcohol and heavy meals until your body has had a chance to adjust.

Avoid tap water; bottled water is inexpensive. Drink only those cartons of milk and juices sold in supermarkets that are marked with expiration dates. Stay away from raw produce. Eat well-cooked food while it is still hot. A threat of cholera and dysentery exists in rural areas, but visitors who take proper precautions regarding diet are generally not at risk.

If you are a casualty of Scopolamine attack, be sure to seek medical assistance as soon as possible. Scopolamine is usually blended with other narcotics; it can induce brain damage.

Most doctors and specialists have been trained overseas and speak English. Unfortunately, poor nursing lets the medical care system down, so it should be utilized for emergency treatment only. Medicines are in short supply. Carry a well-stocked medical kit with all the prescription drugs you require. Bring documentation for prescription drugs and syringes.

As is true with general security, health awareness in this country must be at maximum at all times. Most good hotels have an in-house doctor or access to one. Otherwise, contact your embassy or consulate. Both doctors and hospitals will often demand immediate cash payment. A travel insurance package for health services, including an evacuation policy, should be acquired by all travelers.

For more information on medical centers, including phone numbers, please see the "Business Centers" section at the end of this chapter.

INTERNAL TRAVEL

AIR

The internal air network is excellent, linking all major cities and including the Caribbean coastal area. Domestically, Colombia is served by Avianca, Aces, SAM, Intercontinental, Satena, and Aires airlines. The larger cities have daily connections, and the smaller ones have less frequent service, sometimes just once a week. Avianca and American Airlines offer regular flights to Bogota from Cali and Barranquilla. San Andrés is a standard stopover point for Avianca, Lacsa and Sahsa airlines.

Flights originate from most major Colombian cities providing connections between the mainland and San Andrés and Providencia islands.

Local helicopter flights are also available from many locations. Inquire locally for more information. Your hotel is a good source of information.

One cautionary note: Many ground-tracking and radar stations are sabotaged by drug smugglers and rebels in order to protect illicit drug shipments. Over a thousand people have perished in Colombian air incidents since 1986. As with most things in this country, safety cannot be assumed.

TAXI

Taxis are plentiful, but use only well-marked cabs. Do not share or get into a taxi carrying another person unknown to you, even when the driver tells you that your companion is for protection. Take only metered taxis, if possible.

Cabs cost about US$5 from the airport—30 percent more at night. A taxi in town will cost about US$1 per mile. Passengers should always insist that the meters are used, or agree on a price before leaving. Some cabs do not have meters; these are not recommended.

At hotels, you can either order by phone, or find standing by outside the taxis that have green and cream paint jobs. The green and creams prove more costly than the others but are safer and cleaner.

Stay on high-security alert when using taxis, as some work hand in hand with criminal gangs. One of the more popular taxi scams involves the driver feigning a mechanical breakdown. He then requests the assistance of the passenger to get out and help push the cab to a "jump-start," separating the passenger from his luggage. The driver then starts the car and drives away.

Businesspeople may do best to order cabs for city travel through their hotel concierge. Women travelers should not ride alone at night.

AUTO

Cars and motorbikes can be rented in urban locations, but they are only recommended for experienced visitors to Colombia. Avis, Hertz, Budget and National have rental offices in major cities and at airports. An International Driving Permit is required.

Road travel can be hazardous throughout Colombia and is particularly dangerous in the countryside due to guerrilla activity. Nevertheless, carjackings have also occurred on city streets.

Traffic laws and signal lights are frequently ignored, especially late at night and during early morning hours. Speed limits are generally non-existent. Pedestrians are almost never given the right of way.

Automobile travel after dark is dangerous because of poor illumination, unmarked roadwork, potholes, stalled vehicles, wandering livestock, and motorists driving without using their headlights.

Cars with responsible drivers and security teams can be hired for daily and weekly usage. It may be best to let your hotel concierge or local business associate set up this type of transportation.

TRAIN

Rail services, for the most part, carry only freight. Air travel remains the quickest and most comfortable way to get around the country for intercity travel.

URBAN

Bogotá has an extensive bus, trolleybus, and minibus system, as well as a funicular railway. The network operates on a flat-fare basis. If you are feeling good about security, you may want to try one of the shared taxis (buseta), which are inexpensive and will stop on demand. There is a supplementary charge for airport and out-of-town destinations.

Most cities have fairly comprehensive bus and "*buseta*" systems. VELOTAX minibuses are efficient, but most other buses suffer frequent breakdowns. Generally, it is not recommended that business people use the bus systems if other modes of transit are available.

BUSES & TRAMS

The long distances between major urban areas means that most travelers prefer air travel. However, modern, air-conditioned coaches connect most major cities. Police stops may occur along the way, though, and the potential for a bandit or guerrilla attack is never remote.

Buses run on fairly precise schedules and do not wait to reach passenger capacity before embarking as is the case in many other South American countries.

Reportedly, the best coach lines are Flota Magdalena, Expresso Boliviano, and Expresso Palmita. About 42 separate companies run modern buses and minibuses between towns and cities along the coast.

WATER TRAVEL

Colombia has 3,000 km of ocean coastline (Atlantic and Pacific), as well as an extensive river transport system along the Amazon and Choco rivers. The Magdalena, though, is the main river artery for commerce in Colombia. Some cargo boats will take passengers, but this is not a fast way to travel.

A ferry service links the mainland with the San Andrés and Providencia islands, embarking from the Mulle de Pegasos. This trip is long (three days) but cheap. Contact the Maritima San Andrés office for information regarding other maritime connections to San Andrés.

Security risks are high for foreign passengers; water transport should only be used for reaching otherwise unapproachable regions.

TRAVEL ASSISTANCE

Ministerio de Desarollo Economico
Carrera 13, No 28-01
Pisos 5-9
Santa Fe de Bogotá, DC
tel: (1) 320 0077, 287 4865; fax: (1) 287 6025

Corporacion Nacional de Turismo
Apdo Aereo 8400
Calle 28, No 13A-15
16º-18º
Santa Fe de Bogotá, DC
tel: (1) 283 9466; fax: (1) 284 3818

Communications

DIALING CODES IN COLOMBIA

International country code: [57]

Selected city codes: Armenia (67), Barranquilla (58), Bogotá (1), Bucaramanga (76), Cali (2), Cartegena (5), Cartago (656), Cucuta (75), Ibague (82), Manizales (68), Medellin (4), Neiva (88), Palmira (22), Pereira (63), Santa Marta (54)

Dialing Colombia from Overseas

To call a Colombian number from overseas, begin with your country's international dialing code, then 57 (the country code for Colombia), then the city code and finally the number. If you were dialing Bogotá from the United States, for example, you would begin with 011, then 57, then 1 (the city code for Bogotá), and finally the number of the person or office you are trying to reach.

Assistance Numbers

Long Distance Operator 09
Directory Assistance 114
AT&T Bogota 297-3282

CALLING WITHIN COLOMBIA

Local Calls

Calls to smaller areas can be difficult and often must be made through an international operator.

Long Distance Calls

Calling within Colombia has been enhanced by automated systems connecting larger towns. If a private phone is not accessible, an intercity call must be placed at a TELECOM office or a long-distance telephone booth. Dial 9 + area code + number.

International Calls

Long distance phones can be found at TELECOM offices, airports, or bus stations. To call direct, dial 90 + country code + area code + number; but expect to pay a possible deposit of US$18 to US$36. The surest and cheapest way of calling out of the country is dialing a home-country direct service, which can also help place calls to other countries. Calling from a public telephone requires a coin or a telephone card to get a dial tone. If calling from a hotel phone, check with the hotel operator for access instructions and, perhaps more importantly, surcharge information to save yourself a trip to the shock ward.

Canada Direct 980-19-0057
U.K. Direct 980-44-0057
U.S. AT&T Direct 980-11-0010
U.S. MCI 980-16-0001

PAY PHONES

Public Telephones

Pay phones can be found in major cities, but many are not in service. Most hotels have phones that are operational, although there may be a slight charge.

Calling Cards

Phone cards are the best value (for the effort of calling) as they allow direct dialing.

CELLULAR PHONES

There are numerous analog phone service providers in Colombia. Celumovil, Cocelco, Comcel S.A., Celcaribe, Occel S.A., all offer AMPS-TDMA analog service.

Note: Your home country cell phone may not work in this country. If not, we recommend that you rent an international cell phone *before* you leave home. A major US-based cell phone rental provider is **IMC WorldCell**. For information see "International Cell Phone Rentals" on page 14.

CALL BACK

You can (potentially) save significant sums when calling in Colombia by using a call back service. For a list of call-back services, please refer to the "Communications" section in the *Global Road Warrior* Introduction.

Fees for call back services vary widely, depending on the company and the type of service required. Be sure to check with these companies before leaving to compare rates.

PHONE JACKS

Plug adaptors are available through **iGo Corporation.** (See "Electrical and Telephone Adaptors" on page 19.)

FAX

Fax services are only available at top-end hotels, and the service is not cheap.

POSTAL SERVICES

Send all letters by airmail, it is much more reliable than surface mail. Most people in Colombia have post office boxes to avoid theft. If you are planning for a long stay, try to get one.

TELEGRAM

Facilities are available at top-end hotels in Bogotá or through national ENDT telecommunications offices. Telex service also exist at major hotels throughout the country.

Business Services

COURIER SERVICES

Airborne Express De Colombia; Av. Eldorado No 84A-55, Le-30A, Sanfafe De Bogota; tel: (1) 263-0298; fax: (1) 410-2975.

DHL; Carrera 13 No. 75-74, Bogota; tel: (1) 321-7012; Import/Export, Trans 93 No. 62-70, INterior 17 Alamos, Santafe de Bogota, D.C.; tel: (1) 434-3061.

International Courier Service; tel: (1) 236-6696

Intertrade Courier International; Carrera 39 No. 24-22, Bogotá; tel: (1) 244-0309; fax: (1) 269-3794.

Sky Courier International; tel: (1) 236-3122.

UPS (T.G. Express); Parque Industrial San Cayetono, Calle #50 #79-94 Interior #10, Bogota; tel: (1) 415-5613; fax: (1) 415-4116.

SECRETARIAL SERVICES

Acción Bogotá; Carrera 11 No. No. 69-43; tel: (1) 217-6030.

Manos de Bogotá; Calle 46 No. 15-09; tel: (1) 232-4540.

A-Servil; Carrera 13 No. 58-83, office 404; tel: (1) 211-5922.

Colombia

TRANSLATION SERVICES

Berlitz; Calle 83 No. 19-24; tel: (1) 236-0040.
Alyev; Carrera 10 No. 16-67, office 611; tel: (1) 284-8539.

Electrical

Current

110/120 volts AC, 50/60Hz are the most common, although 150-volt supplies may be found.

ELECTRIC PLUGS

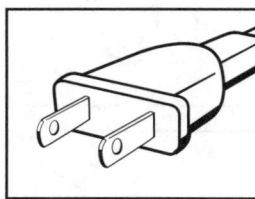

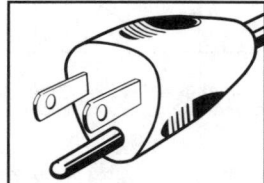

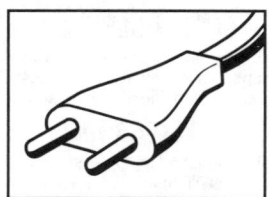

American style 2-pin plugs are the most common.
Plug adaptors are available through **iGo Corporation.**
(See "Electrical and Telephone Adaptors" on page 19.)

Technical Support

HARDWARE/SOFTWARE VENDOR SUPPORT

Apple/Claris; tel: 1-312-1371; (in the U.K.) tel: [44] (990) 127-753; (in the U.S.) tel: [1] (800) 500-7078; http://www.apple.com/.

Compaq/Digital; tel: 1-312-0145; fax: 1-312-0164; (General U.S.) tel: (281) 518-2000; http://www.compaq.com/.

Corel; tel: 1-2150-411 (All Applications); (in the U.S.) tel: [1] (716) 871-2325 (Ask to be Forwarded to Appropriate Program); http://www.corel.com/.

Dell; tel: (1) 616-6066 (ComWare Colombia); [57] (1) 616-8488 (Informatica Ltda); (1) 667-7333 (Cali) City code is unknown, but city name is Cali. (Sisa Colombia); (1) 295-9111 (Xerox Colombia); (in the U.S.) tel: [1] (512) 338-4400; fax: [1] (512) 728-3330; http://www.dell.com/.

Filemaker/Claris; (in Germany) tel: [49] (180) 525-8166

(Info-line); fax: [49] (180) 567-2233; tel: [49] (180) 523-6423; (in the U.S.) tel: [1] (800) 965-9090; http://www.claris.com/.

Gateway 2000; (in the U.S.) tel: [1] (605) 232-2191; fax: [1] (605) 232-2023; (in Ireland) tel: [353] (1) 797-2000; http://www.g2k.com/.

Hewlett Packard; (Brazil Office) tel: (55) 11-7090-1444; (in the U.S.) tel: [1] (408) 246-4300; http://www.hp.com/.

IBM; tel: (1) 623-0111; (9) 8001-7555 (toll free within Colombia); fax: (1) 257-9839; (in Switzerland) tel: [41] (22) 310-0418 (in French); (U.S. Main Office) tel: [1] 914-765-1900; (in the U.S.) tel: [1] (919) 517-2800; http://www.ibm.com/.

Microsoft; tel: (1) 317-3838; fax: (1) 317-3494; (in Medellin) tel: (4) 312-3434; fax: (4) 322-3450; tel: (2) 664-000; fax: (2) 664-5530; (in the U.S.) [1] (425) 635-7222; http://www.microsoft.com/.

NEC; (in the U.S.) [1] (916) 388-0101 (Main Switchboard); http://www.nec.com/.

Novell; tel: 980-120-962 (Toll Free Technical Support); (in Switzerland) tel: [41] (1) 308-4747; fax: [41] (1) 302-0401; (in the U.S.) tel: [1] (408) 434-2300; fax: [1] (408) 577-5775 (Worldwide Sales Headquarters); http://www.novell.com/.

Quark; (in the U.S.) tel: [1] (303) 894-8899; fax: [1] (303) 894-3398 (For Products Registered in the Americas); (in Switzerland) tel: [41] (1) 808-7722; fax: [41] (1) 808-7799; http://www.quark.com/.

Toshiba; (in the U.S.) [1] (949) 583-3000 (Corporate Headquarters); (in Switzerland) tel: [41] (1) 946-0777; fax: [41] (1) 946-0807; (in Ireland) tel: [44] (193) 282-8828; http://www.toshiba.com/.

Internet Connection

HOW TO CONNECT

Connecting to AOL and Compuserve in Colombia is similar to using it when traveling outside your own area code. See the introductory section for detailed information on connecting to your account through a different phone number.

America Online

Numbers are available at keyword: *international*. Be sure to get several local numbers before leaving. AOL's GlobalNet service charges US$6 an hour in addition to the usual charges. Go to keyword: *access* (a free area) and download the software.

Access: Barranquilla (5) 356-8010; Bogota (1) 622-4111; Cali (2) 885-8377; Medellin (4) 513-9393.

Compuserve

Numbers are available at *Go International*. The Compuserve Web-site also has a great deal of information, at http://www.compuserve.com.

Access: Bogota (1) 410-8953; Bogota (1) 410-3986; Bogota (1) 410-3987; Bogota (1) 410-8492; Bogota (1) 410-3988; Bogota (1) 622-4111; Bogota (1) 347-0600; Cali 2660-3900; Medellin (4) 513-9393.

Independent Service Providers

Many independent service providers offer discounts if you are only in town for a couple of days.

Andinet On Line S.A.; tel: (1) 622-6556; fax: (1) 218-7480; email: ventas@andinet.com; http://www.andinet.com/.

CC-Net Digital Services; tel: (1) 622-5880; tel: (1) 622-5860; tel: (1) 622-5862; fax: (1) 622-5883; email: www.mng@cc-net.net; http://www.cc-net.net/.

ColombiaNET; tel: (2) 330-5723; fax: (2) 331-8298; http://www.colombianet.net/.

Latino Net (Spanish); tel: (1) 232-8419/ 232-8375; fax: (1) 232-8584; email: latino@olga.latino.net.co; http://www.latino.net.co/.

VPM Internet Services; tel: [1] (800) 321-0221; tel: [1] (916) 983-9876; fax: [1] (916) 983-4375; email: sales@vpm.com; http://www.vpm.com/.

Business Culture

GREETINGS AND COURTESIES

Men shake hands with each other and with women; women grasp each others' forearms. Men and women friends may kiss each other on the cheek, and men may hug. If meeting lower level workers, shake hands with those closest to you when you are introduced and upon leaving. Business cards in Spanish are not considered necessary, although always be sure that your card contains your title. Status distinctions are very important in Colombia, and people will want to know yours immediately. When presenting a business card, hold it by the end between the index and middle fingers so the print faces the recipient and no print is obscured. At social gatherings, you will be introduced individually by the host or hostess; when leaving, say goodbye individually to anyone to whom you have been introduced.

DECISION MAKING

Actual decisions are almost always made at a high level of authority. Although Colombians will want to know your standing within the hierarchy and will wish to match you with someone of similar rank, always try to approach the most senior person. Not only are senior people likely to be more internationally oriented, but they will also be able to play host while assessing you in order to pair you with the correct Colombian counterpart. It is important to cultivate personal relationships with both superiors and peers, because the quality of these relationships may strongly influence the actual decision maker.

WOMEN

Women in Colombia generally occupy a somewhat secondary status in this traditionally male-dominated society, although many operate businesses and are generally accorded considerable personal freedom. Colombian women are becoming more common and accepted in business, and foreign businesswomen should experience few problems. Nevertheless, in Colombia foreign businesswomen are expected to be highly professional, appropriate, and not aggressive or confrontational. They should also avoid any behavior that might be construed as flirtatious, as Colombians can engage in extremely macho behavior. Women should take taxis and go out escorted at night.

MEETINGS

Introductions are very important. If you do not have a mutual business acquaintance to make an introduction, consult your embassy for a referral. Many foreign businesspeople find it highly useful to have a local contact to serve as a go-between and to handle local arrangements. Make appointments at least one week in advance. Be punctual for appointments, but do not expect Colombians to be on time (although punctuality is becoming more valued in larger cities and internationally oriented firms). Expect to be offered coffee at the beginning of every meeting; always accept graciously, even if you only take a sip. Never attempt to plunge directly into a discussion of business—social topics must always be addressed first to establish the necessary personal connection. In fact, social preliminaries may consume several meetings before business matters can be broached—always allow more time for business in Colombia than you would elsewhere, even in South America. Because the midday meal remains largely a family occasion when many businesspeople return home, business lunches generally have not caught on in Colombia. Dinners with colleagues are more common, but these are essentially social occasions.

BUSINESS ATTIRE

Colombians judge people by their appearance and by how well they are dressed—dress impeccably to make a favorable impression. Men's hair should be short and conservatively cut. Men should wear a dark conservatively cut suit and tie; women should wear a dark suit or an elegant business-like dress. Climate varies by altitude, but men should always wear a jacket regardless; if it is hot, they will probably be invited to remove it, but let your Colombian colleague suggest it. A suit or a dress are the appropriate attire for a social occasion, such as a dinner invitation.

Business Centers
Bogotá

CITY VIEW

Bogotá is an interesting combination of modern skyscrapers and beautiful churches coupled with shantytowns and poverty. Traffic jams are common, and pollution is becoming more a way of life.

AIRPORT

El Dorado Airport to City Center

The airport is located 7.5 miles (12 km.) from the city center. Buses (called "Consuls") to Bogotá leave every 30 minutes. It takes about 20 minutes to travel between the airport and Bogotá.

Note: Beware of theft and petty crime in the airport.

Airline Numbers

Air Canada	(1) 210-4428, 310-3226
Aires	(1) 257-3000
Alitalia	(1) 285-7305, 287-1375
American Airlines	(1) 285-1111
Avianca	(1) 295-4611, 243-1613
British Airways	(1) 218-0200
Satena	(1) 286-2701
SAM	(1) 286-8402

HOTELS

Top End

Bogotá Hilton; Carrera 7 No. 21-16; tel: (1) 285-6020; standard Hilton amenities and service.

Casa Medina; Carrera 7 No. 69A-22; tel: (1) 217-0288; fax: (1) 249-3170; email: casamedina@relaischateaux.fr; restaurant; business center (fax, copying, PC's, cell phone rental); secretarial and translation services; meeting rooms, Dr. on call; massage; taxi transport; airport pickup with notification; this hotel is considered a national monument; US$182/271. To reserve from the U.S. call: (212) 682-9254.

Charleston; Carrera 13, 85-46; in walking distance of commercial district; restaurant; secretarial and translating services; fax and copier; Dr. on call; sauna; gym; free parking; private car and driver for hire; airport pickup with advance notification; US$182/271. To reserve from the U.S. call: (212) 682-9254.

Hotel Bogotá Royal; Calle 100 No. 8-A-01; tel: (1) 218-

9911; fax: 218-3362; downtown financial district in World Trade Center complex; business information center; translation and secretarial services; temporary offices; meeting rooms; US$220/350.

Expensive

Embassy Suites; Calle 70, No. 6-22; tel: (1) 317-1338; in the U.S.: 1-800-EMBASSY; downtown 2.5 miles; restaurant; meeting facilities; VIP services; fax; modem lines; gym.

Hotel Bacata; Calle 19 No. 5-20; tel: (1) 283-8300; fax: (1) 281-7249; email: hbacata@colomsat.net.co; restaurant; convention and banquet facilities; Col$120.000/164.000.

Hotel Bogotá Plaza; Calle 100 No. 18-A-30; tel: (1) 286-1111; fax: 02-184-050; email: travelweb@hotelbook.com; restaurant; business center; conference facilities; meeting and banquet facilities; doctors on call; golf; health club; fitness center; car rental; US$139/150.

Hotel de Ville; Calle 100, No. 13-55; res: (1) 611-8064; fax: (1) 611-1791; email: h.ville@colomsat.net.co; restaurant; business information services, photo copiers, typewriters, fax, laser equipment; computer, cell phones and modems available; bilingual secretarial services; translators and interpreters; car and limo rental; Col$80.000/112.000 for internet users.

Hotel Maria Isabel Bogota; Ave. 33 (Calle 11), No. 15-05; tel: 288-0399; fax: 288-6563; reservas@mariaisabel.com; restaurant; meeting rooms; convention center; banquet hall; airport pick up; US$62/147.

Hotel Melía Santa Fe; Av. Pepe Sierra (Calle 116); tel: 612-8791; fax: 616-8804; 20 minutes from city center; restaurant, breakfast buffet; meeting hall; executive services; parking; US$134.

Tequendama Intercontinental; Carrera 10, 26-21; tel: 286-1111; fax: 282-2860; email: bogota@interconti.com; located in international center; 3 restaurants; business center and services; health club; putting green; tour office; car rental; tour office; US$135/225.

Moderate

Hostal Linden; Calle 36 No. 14-39 Interior 5; tel: (1) 287-4239; fax: (1) 232-8205; small hotel; personal care; airport transport; US$50.

Hostería de la Candelaria; Calle 9, No: 3-11; tel: (1) 342-1727; fax: (1) 282-3420; small and personal.

MEDICAL CARE

Hospital Santa Fé; Cra. 7 Pepe Siera

Clinica del Country; Cra. 15 No. 84-13, tel: (1) 257-0901/257-3100; private hospital.

Clinica de Marly; Calle 50 No. 9-57; tel: (1) 287-1020.

Clinica de Maternidad David Restrepo; Calle 61 No. 9-68; tel: (1) 255-5055.

Hospital San Ignacio; Cra. 7-A No. 40-62; tel: (1) 285-0020.

AUTO RENTAL

Travelers should reconcile the dangers of crime in Colombia before deciding to rent a car; be certain to take out some insurance and park in guarded lots if available.

Avis; national reservations, tel: 610-4810; fax: 218-9766; intl. reservations, tel: 980-12-0028; airport, tel: 266-2147; fax: 218-9766; Avenida 15, No. 101-45, tel: 610-4455/610-4810; fax: 218-9766.

Budget; Avenida 15 No. 107-08; tel: 612-5040; 213-6383.

Hertz; domestic reservations, tel: (1) 268-8956; intl. reservations, tel: (1) 215-3500; airport, tel: 413-9302; Hotel Tequendama, tel: 284-1080; Hotel La Fontana Diag 127 NO #21A-10, tel: 274-9490; chauffeur-driven cars available.

National; Calle 100 No. 14-46; tel: 612-5635.

WORLD TRADE CENTER

World Trade Center Bogota
Calle 100 #8A - 49. Torre B. Mezzanine
Bogota, Colombia, S.A.
tel: (1) 218-3206
fax: (1) 611-3712
website: http://www.wtcbogota.com
email: wortrade@colomsat.net.co

Costa Rica

At a Glance

THE PEOPLE

Population .... 3,674,490 (July 1999 est.)
Growth Rate .... 1.89% (1999 est.)
Life Expectancy .... 76.04 years (born 1999)
Infant Mortality . 12.89 deaths/1,000 live births (1999 est.)

Ethnic Composition

Caucasian (including Mestizo) 96%
Black African 2%
Amerindian 1%
Chinese 1%

Religious Composition

Roman Catholic.. 95%
Other and non-affiliated.. 5%

Languages Spoken

Spanish (official), English

Education and Literacy

Primary and secondary education is free. The adult literacy rates stands at 94.8 percent

Labor Force

Total: 868,300
By occupation: services 37.9%, industry 35.1%, agriculture 27%

THE ECONOMY

Costa Rica has, like many of its Latin American neighbors, become dependent on tourism and the export of farm commodities. Following an economic crisis in the 1980s, Costa Rica has aimed for macroeconomic stability through diversification of its exports and privatization. Both efforts have been largely disappointing. Although having been chosen as a site for an Intel microchip plant, Costa Rica has had little luck in attracting other investment in technology or industry. Most foreign investment, especially by the all-important mid-sized companies, has been put off by the high taxes needed to maintain the Costa Rican social services program. This tiny nation, with a foot in both the Caribbean and the Pacific, has had continual problems with keeping its population happy while remaining true to economic directives from the IMF. Torn between potential political problems or a cut off of international funding, the government is treading lightly while awaiting a general upswing in its Latin American neighbors' economies.

Exports .... US$3.9 billion (f.o.b., 1998)
Imports .... US$4.5 billion (c.i.f., 1998)
Total GDP .... US$24 billion(1998 est.)
GDP Per Capita .... US$6,700 (1998 est.)
Unemployment   5.6% (1998 est.) [much underemployment]
Inflation Rate .... 12% (1998 est.)

Top Export Partners

United States, EU, Guatemala, El Salvador

Top Import Partners

United States, Japan, Mexico, Guatemala, Venezuela, E.U.

Top Exports

Coffee, bananas, textiles, sugar.

Top Imports

Raw materials, consumer goods, capital equipment, oil.

BUSINESS WORKWEEK

Offices

Monday to Friday 8a.m. to 12p.m. and 2p.m. to 6p.m., Saturday 8 a.m. to 11 a.m.

Banks

Monday to Friday 9a.m. to 3p.m.

Government

Monday to Friday 7:30a.m. to 4p.m.

Retail

Monday to Saturday 8a.m to noon and 2p.m. to 6p.m.
Note: Midday closing times may be longer in rural areas and also apply to government offices.

HOLIDAYS

New Year's Day..January 1
Feast of St. Joseph .... March 19
Maundy Thursday...April 1*
Good Friday..April 2*
Anniversary of the Battle of Rivas .... April 11
Labor Day...May 1
Corpus Christi.. June 3*
St. Peter and St. Paul..June 29
Anniversary of the Annexation of
Guanacaste Province ....July 25
Our Lady of the Angels.. August 2
Assumption... August 15
Independence Day ....September 15
Columbus Day...October 12
Abolition of the Armed Forces Day.................December 1
Immaculate Conception....................................December 8
Christmas Day...December 25
(San Jose only) ....December 28-31
*Date may vary by year.

CLIMATE

Seasons

The climate is mild in the central highlands and tropical and subtropical in coastal areas. There are only two seasons in Costa Rica: May to November is the wet season, and December to April the dry season.

Regions

There are three distinct climatic zones: the coastal and northern plain has somewhat continuous rain on the Atlantic watershed, and temperatures of approximately 25° to 38° C (77 to 100°F); the central valleys and plateaus also have regular rain from April to November with temperatures of 15° to 25°C (59° to 77°F); and the more mountainous areas are less rainy, more windy, and colder in temperature.

Money & Banking

Currency

The currency of Costa Rica is the Costa Rican Colon (C).

Costa Rica

Denominations

The Costa Rican Colon comes in coin denominations of C20, 10, and 5, and 50 and 25 centimos; and banknotes of C50, 100, 500,1,000, and 5,000.

Traveler's Checks and Credit Cards

Traveler's checks, in U.S. dollar denominations only, can be exchanged at banks, exchange shops, hotels, and international airports at tourist exchange rates, which can severely differ from place to place. There will also be a commission charge for the exchange. Larger banks may offer the best exchange rates, but not all may accept your particular brand of traveler's check. Cashing traveler's checks can be difficult in smaller towns where commissions can be very high. Avoid black marketers at all cost as they

may slip you counterfeit cash. Consult your bank about current exchange rates before departure.

Cash, especially U.S. dollars, can be exchanged without a charge. Try to take only crisp and new notes as wrinkled and soiled notes are likely to be refused. In rural areas they will only exchange small denomination currency.

In the capital, San Josè, American Express, Visa, Diner's Club, and MasterCard are accepted in most up-market hotels and restaurants. Some banks in the capital offer cash advances on credit cards, but make sure you bring your passport. Outside of the city, credit cards will be of little use. ATMs are rare in Costa Rica, and the few that exist do not function well with foreign banks.

Essential Terms

English	Spanish
Yes	Sí
No	No
Good morning	Buenos días
Hello (daytime)	Buenas tardes
Hello (evening)	Buenas noches
Hello (telephone)	¿Hola?
Good-bye	Adiós
Please	Por favor
Thank you	Gracias
Pleased to meet you	Encantado (a) de conocerle
Excuse me; I'm sorry	¿Perdóneme?
My name is _____	Me llamo _____
I don't understand	No comprendo
Do you speak English?	¿Habla usted inglés?

Travel

VISA AND PASSPORT

A passport that is valid for a minimum of six months beyond the date of entry is required of all, except Canadian and U.S. citizens who have proof of identity, such as a certified birth certificate or official I.D. with a photograph. Tourist Cards can be issued to these visitors at any Costa Rican consulate, or at the office of any airline that services Costa Rica which can be found at the international airports of Amsterdam, Aruba, Barranquilla, Caracas, Curaçao, Panama, or Port of Spain. Expect a cost of approximately US$2.

Visas are required of all visitors except for nationals of:

- Argentina, Austria, Belgium, Brazil, Canada, Denmark, Finland, Germany, Hong Kong, Hungary, Israel, Italy, Japan, Korea (Rep. of), Liechtenstein, Luxembourg, Netherlands, Norway, Panama, Paraguay, Poland, Portugal, Romania, Spain, Sweden, Switzerland, Uruguay, U.S., and the U.K. (including all its dependencies except subjects of Bermuda and the Cayman Islands, whose maximum allowable stay is thirty days) for a stay up to 90 days
- Antigua & Barbuda, Australia, Bahamas, Bahrain, Barbados, Belize, Bolivia, Bulgaria, Chile, Colombia, Czech Republic, Dominica, France, French Overseas Possessions, Grenada, Guatemala, Guyana, Honduras, Iceland, Ireland, Jamaica, Kenya, Kuwait, Mexico, Monaco, New Zealand, Oman, Philippines, Qatar, Russian Federation, St. Kitts & Nevis, St. Lucia, St. Vincent & The Grenadines, San Marino, Saudi Arabia, Singapore, Slovak Republic, South Africa, Suriname, Taiwan, Trinidad & Tobago, UAE, Vatican City and Venezuela for a maximum stay of 30 days
- Any country who is a passenger in transit, and who does not leave the airport, continuing onward within 48 hours,

and holding confirmed tickets and other documents for onward travel— except citizens of China (PR), who must have a transit visa issued by the Immigration Department in San José.

The categories of visa issued are Tourist and Business. All visitors requiring a visa must also hold documents necessary for travel and entry to the next destination.

Visas are valid for 30 or 90 days. The Immigration Department in San Jose can expedite renewal or extension of visas, with varying periods of validity.

Some visitors may have to pay a deposit upon entry, depending on nationality or other factors.

The amount of time for processing of visa applications is between one day and two weeks, depending on the nationality of the applicant. Additionally, some visas require the special authorization of the Immigration Department.

RESTRICTED ENTRY

Due to a fear of drug trafficking and general crime, entry is often prohibited to males with long hair and beards, those poorly dressed, Gypsies, Amerindian people from neighboring countries, or anyone who is determined by customs officers to lack sufficient funds.

DEPARTURE FORMALITIES

Every visitor whose stay exceeds 48 hours is required to pay a US$37 tax upon departure from the international airport.

In spite of what other border officials may tell you, there is no tax for exiting by land or sea. Visitors may export no more than the equivalent of US$50 in local currency.

CUSTOMS ENTRY (PERSONAL)

Duty-free
- Tobacco: 500 cigarettes
- Alcohol: three liters of alcoholic beverage
- Other: a reasonable quantity of perfume for personal use

Prohibited or Restricted
- Firearms
- Controlled drugs

IMMUNIZATION

No inoculations are required, unless you are arriving from a known infected area. Long-term visitors may be required to take an AIDS test. Vaccinations which are advised even for visits to urban areas include: cholera, hepatitis A, malaria, and typhoid.

TIPPING

Taxi
Tippings for metered taxi drivers is optional and usually involves rounding up the fare.

Porters
Porters in first class hotels receive 100 to 200 centimos per bag.

Hotels
A service charge between 10 and 15 percent is typically included in the bill, along with a 3 percent tourism tax, as required by law.

Restaurants
A service charge between 10 and 15 percent is typically added to the tab; if not, leave a similar amount for the waitstaff.

Other
Barbers, beauticians: 10 percent. Small services: 100 to 200 centimos.

EMERGENCY INFORMATION

Police and Crime

Crime is low in both cities and rural areas. However, the recent influx of refugees and subsequent unemployment have increased the rate of petty theft, muggings, and carjackings, which occur with frequency in downtown San Jose, at the airport, at beaches, national parks, other tourist attractions, and even on tourist buses.

Take basic precautions against petty crime. Avoid flashy displays of wealth, and dress and behave conservatively. Leave most of your cash, traveler's checks, jewelry, and your camera in your hotel safe. Try to park in paid lots and do not leave any valuables in your car. Business travelers are often targets of thieves; so, laptops and briefcases require extra care.

Carry photocopies of your passport instead of the original; the police may ask to see these. Carry cash in a money belt, and use credit cards or traveler's checks for most of your transactions. Walk with your bag away from the street to avoid having it snatched away by passing thieves on motorbikes. Due to regional drug trafficking, never carry a stranger's baggage or packages.

The police are generally helpful and friendly if treated with respect. But local law enforcement personnel have limited capabilities, particularly in rural areas.

Costa Rica depends upon tourists and it makes every attempt to guarantee their safety.

Emergency Telephone Numbers

Police.. 104
Fire 103
Ambulance .... 225/1436 or 228/2187

Health

Tap water should be avoided though most hotels have a filter system, otherwise, boil the water for 10 to 15 minutes. Some bottled water is unsafe for consumption, so ask the hotel clerks for recommended brands. Wash all fresh fruits and vegetables in a chlorine solution. Avoid uncooked seafood and meats as they may carry cholera.

An outbreak of Dengue Fever has recently swept Central America. Thus far in Costa Rica, the outbreak is concentrated in Puntarenas, near popular tourist areas. Unfortunately, a vaccine has yet to be discovered. In affected areas, take precautions against the fever-carrying mosquitoes by covering up with clothing and by using repellent.

Common diseases include diarrhea, amoebic and bacillary dysentery, intestinal diseases, and AIDS. The air quality in the capital is poor; compounded with the often damp weather it can lead to the common cold or bronchial problems.

Medical care is reasonable, and the costs are low. However, these facilities should be used for emergencies only. Travelers should carry medical insurance as well as an evacuation policy if they anticipate an extended stay.

INTERNAL TRAVEL

AIR

SANSA, which is a national airline, offers services linking San José with provincial cities and towns. A bus takes passengers from the airline's offices in San José to the airport. Several smaller airlines also provide domestic flights.

Reservations for internal air travel must be made from within Costa Rica only, so it is not possible to book passage in advance of your visit.

TAXI

In San José, taxis are plentiful and inexpensive. Most are colored red, except for those colored orange, which serve the Juan Santamaria Airport. Usually, one gets a cab simply by hailing it in the streets. Your hotel may also be willing to get one for you by telephone, but it really is not necessary.

Travelers should be mindful to select taxis that have working locks, door handles, and functioning meters (called "*marias*"), and decline any driver's invitation to ride in the front seat—there have been a number of kidnappings of foreigners under such circumstances in recent years.

Fares should be negotiated in advance for unmetered cabs and for those where the driver says the "*maria*" is out of order.

AUTO

Rental cars and motorbikes can be found in the capital but are not recommended for first-time visitors. Major auto rental agencies have offices in San Jose. An International Driving Permit or valid driver's license from the visitor's country of origin is required.

Hired cars with drivers can be rented on a daily and weekly basis and are probably a better alternative for the business traveler in particular.

TRAIN

Two passenger rail lines transport people between San José and Limón and between San José and Puntarenas on the Pacific route. Trains originate from two different stations in San José. They are efficient, although they can be crowded; and reservations should be made in advance.

METRO

There are no subway systems in Costa Rica's cities.

BUSES & TRAMS

Buses service most of the cities, but they can be incredibly crowded. Inter-city bus lines are also available but not dependable. Neither system is recommended for use by business travelers. Contact the Department of Tourism for details.

WATER TRAVEL

Despite having coastlines on two oceans and many rivers, almost nothing in the way of water transit stands available to the visitor who simply wants to get from one point to another. There are many expedition-type trips that can be arranged on Costa Rica's rivers, and the beaches are legendary for swimming and surfing, but transportation is best found in other venues.

TRAVEL ASSISTANCE

The Department of Tourism within Costa Rica should be able to answer any questions regarding travel with the country, although finding someone who can speak English may prove difficult.

Instituto Costarricense de Turismo
(Costa Rica Tourist Board)
Edificio Genaro Valverde
Calles 5 y 7, Avenida 4
1000 San José
tel: 223 1733; fax: 223 5452, 255 4997
website: www.tourism-costarica.com
Cámara Nacional de Turismo (CANATUR)
Apartado 828
1000 San José
tel: 234 6222; fax: 253 8102
email: canatour@tourism.co.cr
Costa Rican Tourist Board
tel: 222 1090; (in the U.S.): 1-800-327-7033

Communications

DIALING CODES IN COSTA RICA

International country code: [506]

Dialing Costa Rica from Overseas

To call a Costa Rican number from overseas, begin with your country's international dialing code, then 506 (the country code for Costa Rica), and finally the number you are trying to reach. There are no city codes in Costa Rica.

Assistance Numbers

International Operator 116
International Information/Directory 124
North America Operator 09-1
Domestic Collect Calls 110
Local Information/Directory 113

CALLING WITHIN COSTA RICA

Local Calls

All numbers have seven digits in Costa Rica. Stores or hotels may allow a local call on their phones.

Long Distance Calls

No area codes apply in this country. Simply dial the seven-digit number.

International Calls

To make an international direct call, dial 00 + country code + area code + number. To the U.S., calls cost about US$2 to $3 a minute. To Europe rates may skyrocket. Discounted rates apply between 10p.m. and 7a.m. daily, and on weekends. Hotel phones are by far the most costly to use if they offer international access. USA Direct phones exist at the airport or high-end hotels.

British Telecom 167
Canada Telecom 161
U.S. AT&T 114
U.S. MCI 162
U.S. Sprint 163

Public phones require coin or card deposit before dialing a direct access number.

AT&T Direct 0-800-0-114-114

PAY PHONES

Public Telephones

Card Phone:

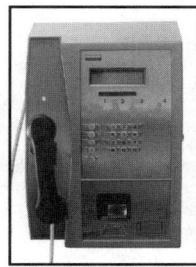

Phones exist virtually everywhere but often accompanied by long lines of people or non-functioning parts. Phones accept 5-, 10- and 20-centimos coins.

1. Lift receiver
2. Wait for dial tone
3. Insert coin
4. Dial
5. Coin will drop

6. Begin talking
7. When you hear a beep, either say your farewell or drop in more coins.

Calling Cards

Phone cards are just beginning their journey in Costa Rica. Coin-operated phones still dominate.

CELLULAR PHONES

Costa Rica has cellular service in the analog format. AMPS service is provided by Instituto Costarricense de Electrodad (ICE).

Note: Your home country cell phone may not work in this country. If not, we recommend that you rent an international cell phone *before* you leave home. A major US-based cell phone rental provider is **IMC WorldCell**. For information see "International Cell Phone Rentals" on page 14.

CALL BACK

You can (potentially) save significant sums when calling in Costa Rica by using a call back service. For a list of call-back services, please refer to the "Communications" section in the *Global Road Warrior* Introduction.

Fees for call back services vary widely, depending on the company and the type of service required. Be sure to check with these companies before leaving to compare rates.

PHONE JACK

Plug adaptors are available through **iGo Corporation.** (See "Electrical and Telephone Adaptors" on page 19.)

FAX

Fax services are widely available. Radiografica offers fax and international telex services. Call 23-1609 to send or receive faxes. To see if you have received a fax, call them at 87-0513 or 87-0511. You can also include the number of your hotel with the fax, and Radiografica will notify you immediately.

POSTAL SERVICES

Mail boxes abound, but do not use them. Instead, take mail directly to the post office to avoid theft. Most mail is sent to post office boxes. Air mail takes about five days to reach the U.S., Canada, or Western Europe. Costa Rica also offers an express service, which isn't overnight but is faster than regular delivery.

Business Services

COURIER SERVICES

Airborne Express/Intl. Bonded Couriers; Lacsa Courier, Paseo Colon, Calles 30 Y 32, Casa 3092, San Jose; tel: 221-0111; fax: 221-3111.

DHL International; Paeo Colon, Calle 34 Edifico Elizabeth, 1er Piso; tel: 257-2785.

UPS; Union Pak de Costa Rica, S.A.); Avenida, 3, Calle 30 Y 32, San Jose; tel: 257-7447; fax: 257-5343.

TRANSLATIONS

Naranjo Translation Service; tel/fax: 450-0365; Mark Mellin.

Costa Rica

Electrical

Current
110/220 volts, 60Hz

ELECTRIC PLUGS

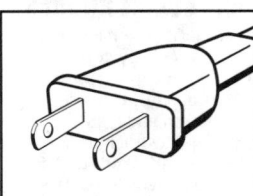

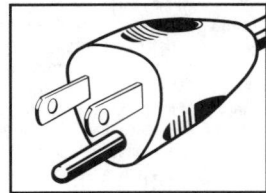

Plug adaptors are available through **iGo Corporation.** (See "Electrical and Telephone Adaptors" on page 19.)

Technical Support

HARDWARE/SOFTWARE VENDOR SUPPORT

Compaq/Digital; (General U.S.) tel: (281) 518-2000; (in Switzerland) tel: [41] (22) 709-5330; fax: [41] (22) 709-5391 (Geneva); tel: [41] (1) 801-2507; fax: [41] (1) 801-2172 (Zurich); http://www.compaq.com/.

Corel; (in the U.S.) tel: [1] (716) 871-2325 (Ask to be Forwarded to Appropriate Program); (in the U.S.) tel: [1] (613) 728-3733 (Customer Service); fax: [1] 613- 761-9176; http://www.corel.com.

Dell; tel: [506] 297-1111 (Componentes El Orbe); [507] 220-1033 (Xerox de Costa Rica); [507] 279-1836 (Integracom de Centroamérica); (in the U.S.) tel: [1] (512) 338-4400; fax: [1] (512) 728-3330; http://www.dell.com/.

Hewlett Packard; (Venezuela Office) tel: [58] 2 239 5664; (in the U.S.) tel: [1] (408) 246-4300; http://www.hp.com/.

IBM; (in Colombia) tel: [57] (1) 623-0111; fax: [57] (1) 257-9839; (U.S. Main Office) tel: [1] 914-765-1900; (in the U.S.) tel: [1] (919) 517-2800; (in Switzerland) tel: [41] (22) 310-0418 (in French); http://www.ibm.com/.

Microsoft; tel: 280-5100; fax: 280-5070; (in the U.S.) [1] (425) 635-7222; (in Switzerland) tel: [41] (848) 858-868; fax [41] (1) 831-0869; http://www.microsoft.com/.

Internet Connection

HOW TO CONNECT

Connecting to AOL and Compuserve in Costa Rica is similar to using it when traveling outside your own area code. See the introductory section for detailed information on connecting to your account through a different phone number.

America Online

Numbers are available at keyword: *international.* Be sure to get several local numbers before leaving. AOL's GlobalNet service charges US$12 an hour in addition to the usual charges. Go to keyword: *access* (a free area) and download the software.

Access: San Jose 287-0800.

Compuserve

Numbers are available at *Go International.* The Compuserve Web-site also has a great deal of information, at http://www.compuserve.com.

Access: San Jose 287-0800.

Independent Service Providers

Many independent service providers offer discounts if you are only in town for a couple of days.

Pointe Communications; tel: [1] (281) 486-8337; email: sales@pointecom.net; http://www.pointecom.net/.

Business Culture

GREETINGS AND COURTESIES

Men and women customarily shake hands on meeting and when departing; some women pat each others' left arms. Titles are abundant and important, with people usually being addressed by their title and last name. Business cards in both your language and Spanish are useful, although not indispensable, and translations into Spanish of any literature are appreciated as a courtesy.

DECISION MAKING

Somewhat untraditional when compared to other Latin American countries, Costa Ricans do not necessarily make decisions from the top. They may prefer a group consensus before deciding how to proceed. A personal relationship must be established before any agreement can be reached.

MEETINGS

If you do not have a mutual business acquaintance to make an introduction, consult your embassy for a referral. Prior appointments are necessary—make them two weeks in advance. Be punctual—Costa Ricans generally will not keep you waiting, except perhaps when paying bills. Expect considerable discussion of nonbusiness topics. Business entertaining takes place in the evenings and may include spouses.

WOMEN

Although women in Costa Rica generally occupy a somewhat secondary status in this traditionally male-dominated society, they are becoming more common and more accepted in business in general, and foreign businesswomen should experience few problems. Although women can feel comfortable traveling alone, they should nonetheless take care to behave and dress conservatively.

BUSINESS ATTIRE

More formal in style than other Latin American countries, businessmen will do well to wear a dark, conservative suit and should expect to wear a jacket during a meeting. Foreign businesswomen might wear dark-colored, conservatively cut, and tailored suits or dresses. Cotton and silk fabrics will wear better in the warmer climates along the coast. The wet season (May to September) requires a lightweight raincoat or umbrella and perhaps a wrap for the cool air following the showers.

Costa Rica

Business Centers
San José

CITY VIEW

Expect to spend some time in San José, no matter where in the country you plan to travel. As the transportation hub of the country, everything eventually passes through the city. San José is also one of the most "North American" of the Latin American capitals, with shopping malls and fast food outlets everywhere.

AIRPORT

Juan Santamaria Airport to City Center

The airport is located 11 miles (18 km.) from the city center. Buses and coaches are available, although they do not run between midnight and 6a.m. If choosing to use a taxi, decide on a price before departing as drivers often don't use meters. A trip into the city takes approximately 30 minutes and should cost from US$9 to US$11. A shared ride (colectivo) will cost US$2.

Airline Numbers

Sansa	21-94-14, 33-03-97
Aeronaves	32-14-13
Aeronaves de Costa Rica	32-14-13, 32-11-76
American Airlines	22-56-55
Aviateca	55-49-49
British Airways	56-46-29, 56-52-64
LACSA	31-00-33
Travelair	220-3054

HOTELS

Top-end

Barceló San José Palacio; Robledal de La Urucca; tel: 220-2034; fax: 220-2036; email: palacio@sol.cacsa.co.cr; restaurant; casino; conference room; jacuzzi; gym; tennis; car rental; shuttle service; travel agency; pool. US$130/135.

Cariari; airport highway, 20 minutes north of San José; tel: 39-00-22; fax: 39-28-03; golf; tennis; pools; horses; bus service.

Sheraton Herradura; airport highway; tel: 39-00-33; fax: 39-22-92; health club; tennis; golf; spa.

Expensive

Balmoral; C. 7 y 9, Ave. Central; tel: 222-5022; fax: 221-7826; email: info@balmoral.co.cr; restaurant; casino; conference rooms; car rental; travel agency; US$65/76.

Best Western Irazú; tel: 232-4811; fax: 232-4549; email: bestwestern@irazu.co.cr; restaurant; casino; conference room; jacuzzi; gym; tennis; travel agency; car rental; shuttle service; pool; US$65/69.

Gran Hotel Costa Rica; C. 1 y 3, Ave. 2; tel: 221-4000; fax: 22103501; email: gran@centralamerica.com; restaurant; casino; conference room; car rental; US$50/62.

Hotel President; C. 7 y 9, Ave. Central; tel: 222-3022; fax: 221-1205; restaurant; conference room; car rental; US$60/70.

Sol Inn Torremolinos; C. 40, Ave. 5 Bis; tel: 22-52-66; fax: 55-31-67; email: torremolinos@centralamerica.com; restaurant; conference room; jacuzzi; gym; travel agency; pool; US$45/55.

Moderate

Bougainvillea; 10 minutes north of San José; tel: 33-66-22; fax: 22-52-11; pool; jacuzzi; garden; 10-minute walk from downtown; US$48/58.

Hotel Ambassador; C. 26 y 28, Paseo Colón; tel: 221-8155; fax: 255-3396; email: infor@hotelambassador.co.cr; restaurant; pool; includes continental breakfast; US$50.

Hotel Ejecutivo Napoléon; between 5th and 40th St., Paseo Colón; tel: 258-0772; fax: 222-9487; email: napoleon@sol.racsa.co.cr; restaurant; travel agency; car rental; pool; US$40/45.

Hotel Europa; C. Central, Ave. 5; tel: 222-1222; fax: 221-3976; email: europa@sol.racsa.co.cr; restaurant; bar; conference room; car rental; shuttle service; pool; US$37.

Hotel Mansión Blanca; Paseo de Los Estudiantes; tel: 222-0423; fax: 222-0423; shuttle service; private baths; air conditioned; US$25/30.

MEDICAL CARE

Calderon Guardia; Ave. 9, Calle 17; tel: 22-41-33.

Clinica Americana; Calle Central/1, Ave. 14; tel: 22-10-10.

Clinica Biblica; Calle Cantral/1, Ave. 14; tel: 221-3922; emergency: 257-0466.

HEALTH CLUB

Cariari Country Club; off the airport hwy, west of San José; 18-hole golf course, tennis, equestrian, exercise room.

Corobicí Hotel; northeast corner of La Sabana Park, health club; tel: 32-81-22.

Costa Rica Country Club; Escazú; 9-hole golf course, tennis, swimming pool.

Costa Rica Tennis Club; La Sabana; tennis; swimming pool; steam baths.

Indoor Club; Curridabat, east San José; tennis, swimming, racquetball, squash.

AUTO RENTAL

Adobe; Centro Comercial Plaza Aventura; tel: 221-5425; fax: 221-9286; email: adobecar@sol.racsa.co.cr

Avis; national reservations, tel: 293-2222; intl. reservations, 0800-011-0092; airport, 442-1321; Hotel Cariari, tel: 239-0022; Hotel Corobici, tel: 232-9922; Hotel Camino Real, tel: 228-3029/228-3025; In U.S., tel. (800) 331-1212.

Budget; reservations: Calle 30, Paseo Colón San José; tel: 233-3284; fax: 554-966; airport, tel: (4) 41-444; fax: (4) 41-444; email: budget@sol.racsa.co.cr; In U.S., tel: (800) 527-0700.

Hertz; domestic reservations, tel: 221-1818; intl. reservations, tel: 233-1447; airport, tel: 221-1818; fax: 233-7254; Calle 38 Paseo Colón; tel: 223-5959; email: hertzcr@sol.racsa.co.cr; In U.S., tel: (800) 654-3001.

National; South side from Mazda, next to Bantec Building La Uruca; tel: 290-8787; fax: 290-0431; email: national@natcar.com; In U.S., tel: (800) CAR-EURO.

WORLD TRADE CENTER

World Trade Center of San Jose, Costa Rica, S.A.
c/o Royal Hotels International Inc.
1001 South Bayshore Drive, Suite 2210
Miami, FL 33131
tel: [1] (305) 377-0304
fax: [1] (305) 577-3347

Côte d'Ivoire

At a Glance

THE PEOPLE

Population .... 15,818,068 (July 1999 est.)
Growth Rate .... 2.35% (1999 est.)
Life Expectancy .... 46.05 years (born 1999)
Infant Mortality . 94.17 deaths/1,000 live births (1999 est.)

Ethnic Composition

Black African (including 3m foreigners)....................... 98%
Non-Africans.. 2%

Religious Composition

Muslim 60%
Animist and indigenous 28%
Christian 12%

Languages Spoken

French (official), Baoule, Dioula, and 58 other native dialects.

Education and Literacy

Primary education is six years long but not compulsory. Only about 40.1 percent of the population over age 15 is literate.

Labor Force

Total: 5,700,000
By occupation (as a GDP%): services 49%, industry 20, agriculture 31%. Note: Over 80% of the population works in agriculture.

THE ECONOMY

The economy of Côte d'Ivoire—or the Ivory Coast—has a major agricultural component and is, thus, highly sensitive to fluctuations in international commodity prices, weather, and crop conditions. Attempts by the government to encourage diversification have had few positive results. Literacy is quite low and the population's life expectancy is one of the lowest in the world. Foreign investors have also been thwarted by the lack of infrastructure, poor banking environment, and the widespread cronyism that props up many of this nation's businesses. Discovery of extensive off-shore oil and gas has given Côte d'Ivoire a glimmer of hope. However, the austerity demands placed upon the economy by international lenders is forcing the government to choose between immediate gratification or an unguaranteed future.

Exports .... US$4.3 billion (f.o.b., 1998)
Imports .... US$2.5 billion (f.o.b., 1998)
Total GDP .... US$24.2 billion (1998 est.)
GDP Per Capita .... US$1,680 (1998 est.)
Unemployment .... 14 percent (1996)
Inflation Rate .... 6% (1998 est.)

Top Export Partners

E.U., Burkina Faso, Mali, United States

Top Import Partners

E.U., Nigeria, United States, Ghana

Top Exports

Cocoa, coffee, tropical woods, petroleum, cotton, bananas, pineapples, palm oil, cotton, fish.

Top Imports

Food, consumer goods, capital goods, fuel, transport equipment.

BUSINESS WORKWEEK

Offices

Monday to Friday 9a.m. to 1p.m. and 2p.m. to 5:30p.m.

Banks

Monday to Friday 8a.m. to 11:30a.m. and 2:30p.m. to 4:30p.m.

Government

Monday to Friday 8a.m. to noon and 2:30p.m. to 6p.m.

Retail

Monday to Friday 8a.m. to noon and 2:30p.m. to 6:30p.m., Saturday 8a.m. to noon and 2:30p.m. to 5:30p.m.
Note: Midday break periods tend to be longer in hotter weather. Rural areas may have erratic schedules based on weather, seasons, and local custom.

HOLIDAYS

New Year's ....January 1
Id al-Fitr, end of Ramadan.............................January 19*
Id al-Adha, Feast of the Sacrifice .... March 28*
Good Friday..April 2*
Easter Monday ....April 5*
Labor Day ....May 1
Ascension Day .... May 13*
Whit Monday .... May 24*
National Day.. August 7
Assumption .... August 15
All Saints' Day ....November 1
Felix Houphouet-Boigny
Remembrance Day ....December 7
Christmas ....December 25
*Exact dates may vary.

CLIMATE

Seasons

The country is typically dry between December and April and rainy from May to July. There is another short, dry period between August and September. October and November are rainy once again.

Regions

The country generally sees the same hot, humid climate, although the conditions are more extreme in the north. This is an equatorial region, so, travelers can expect considerable heat year round. Temperatures can reach as high as 43°C (109°F) but average around 29°C (84°F). Coastal weather can be slightly cooler.

Money & Banking

Currency

The currency of the Côte d'Ivoire is the CFA Franc (CFA).

Denominations

The CFA Franc (CFA) comes in coin denominations of CFA 250, 100, 50, 25, 10, 5, and 1; and banknotes of CFA 500, 1,000, 2,500, 5,000, and 10,000.

Traveler's Checks and Credit Cards

Banks will exchange traveler's checks, however, you may have to shop around to find the one that handles your brand of check. Larger hotels, restaurants, and a few urban retailers accept traveler's checks. Carrying French franc or

Côte d'Ivoire

U.S. dollar-denominated traveler's can help reduce commission charges.

American Express and Mastercard/Access are accepted in many establishments in the biggest city, Abidjan. The most favorable exchange rates are given for credit card transactions. There are no ATMs in Côte d'Ivoire, and very few banks (SGBCI) in Abidjan will give cash advances on credit cards. Rural areas will only accept cash.

Travel

VISA AND PASSPORT

A passport that is valid for at least six months beyond anticipated exit date is required of all visitors, except for nationals of Benin, Burkina Faso, Mali, Mauritania, Niger, Senegal, and Togo who are in possession of a national identity card.

Visas are required of all visitors except for:

- Citizens of other nations that are members of the Economic Community of West African States (ECOWAS), for visits up to three months

- Nationals of Andorra, Chad, Ghana, Monaco, Morocco, Seychelles, Tunisia and Vatican City, for visits up to three months
- Passengers in transit who do not leave the airport and are continuing their journey within 12 hours on either the same or first available connecting flight, and who are holding confirmed tickets and other documents for onward travel

For tourist visa applications, documentation of a hotel booking or a letter of invitation from an Ivory Coast resident must be appended. Business visa applicants must include official letters from companies in both their home country and in the Ivory Coast which substantiate the reason(s) for the visit.

Citizens of the following countries must obtain a pre-authorization—in addition to the visa—from the Ivory Coast Ministry of Security: Afghanistan, Albania, Algeria, Angola, Bangladesh, Bolivia, Cambodia, Chile, China (PR), Colombia, Cuba, Egypt, Iraq, Iran, Indonesia, Jordan, Korea (DPR), Laos, Lebanon, Libya, Myanmar, Nicaragua, Pakistan, Philippines, Singapore, Sudan, Sri Lanka, Syria, Thailand, Vietnam, and Yemen.

Tourist and business visas are both valid for three months. Allow two working days for processing of applications which are submitted in person.

DEPARTURE FORMALITIES

Exportation of Ivorian currency is strictly prohibited. Dollars may be exported only with permission from an authorized Ivorian bank.

There is a departure tax of CFAfr3000 applicable for African destinations and CFAfr5000 for all other destinations. If traveling within the country, get a seat reconfirmation stamped onto your ticket since airlines consistently overbook.

CUSTOMS ENTRY (PERSONAL)

Duty-free

- Tobacco: 200 cigarettes, 25 cigars, 100cigarillos,or 250g of tobacco
- Alcohol: one bottle of wine, and one bottle of distilled spirits
- 0.5 liter of toilet water, 0.25 liter of perfume
- Other: one video camera, one still-photo camera, one portable typewriter, one pair of binoculars, one tape recorder
- **Note**: You must be able to prove with a receipt that these items are at least 6 months old

Prohibited or Restricted

- Sporting guns may only be imported under license.
- Limits are placed on a variable list of personal effects so contact the Consulate prior to departure

IMMUNIZATION

An international health certificate showing current yellow fever immunizations is required. Precautions against cholera are essential in this high- risk country. In addition, advance malaria treatment (even in urban centers) as well as inoculation against typhoid, tetanus, hepatitis A, and diphtheria are strongly advised. **Note**: Resistance to the chlorinique malaria treatment has been reported.

TIPPING

Taxi

In unmetered taxis, fares are negotiated with all fees included. For metered taxis, just round up the fare.

Porters

Porters at hotels and depots receive CFA200 per bag.

Hotels

Hotels will include a service charge in all bills when applicable.

Restaurants

Restaurants usually include a service charge. If they do not, tip 10 to 15 percent.

EMERGENCY INFORMATION

Police and Crime

A coup d'etat began on December 23, 1999, and the Ivory Coast is now experiencing political uncertainty, which will continue until restoration of democracy. The political situation is fluid, but the temporary government seems to have the security situation fairly well in hand. Life has mostly returned to normal. Nonetheless, violent demonstrations have occurred in the past and could recur without warning. Renewed military action is still a possibility.

Crime has now reached the critical level in the Ivory Coast. Bandits armed with sophisticated weapons attack and steal cars in Abidjan. Even native bus drivers fear bandit gangs who may strike on long-distance journeys (especially in the central western region of the country); thus, drivers may delay a trip until a convoy of buses has been assembled. Contact your embassy before embarking on a trip to other regions of the country for security updates. The Liberian border region remains unsettled due to civil war.

It is wise to travel only by hired car at night. Always stay in groups on the city streets, both day or night. Avoid the Treichvill, Adjame, Abobo, and the Plateau business districts after dark. Pedestrians should beware of danger at the DeGaulle and Houphouet-Boigny bridges, which cross the lagoon in Abidjan, even in the daytime. When faced with resistance, armed criminals have used violence.

More than 6,000 convicts were able to escape from the prison in Abidjan during the coup, increasing the threat of crime in an area where it is already extremely high. The Liberia/Ivory Coast border region is also unstable and potentially dangerous. Travelers to the region and to other remote parts of the country may be faced with roadblocks, vehicle searches, and armed military personnel.

Petty theft exists, especially in crowded areas, so take precautions. Avoid flashy displays of wealth, and dress and behave conservatively. Leave most of your cash, traveler's checks, jewelry, and your camera in your hotel safe. Carry photocopies of your passport instead of the original. Carry cash in a money belt, and use credit cards or traveler's checks for most of your transactions.

Women should avoid traveling alone at night. Business travelers are all assumed to be wealthy, so it is advised to hire a private security service for lengthy stays. Police have good intentions but are overwhelmed by the amount of crime (although some officers are even working with criminal gangs). Carry insurance for all articles of value.

Business travelers need to be aware of the potential for fraud inherent in Nigerian scam operations, which target foreigners and threaten both financial disaster and physical harm. Persons considering business deals in the Ivory Coast that involve investment in Nigeria—particularly with the Central Bank of Nigeria or the Nigerian National Petroleum Company—are urged to consult with their respective Departments of Commerce or Departments of State prior to extending any information or financial commitments—or even traveling to the Ivory Coast.

Emergency Numbers

Ambulance / Fire 180

Health

Do not drink tap water or use ice cubes; bottled water is safe and available. Wash all vegetables in a chlorine solution, peel fruits, and avoid uncooked food. Drink only powdered or tinned milk and avoid other dairy products since they are most likely unpasteurized.

Malaria, leprosy, tuberculosis, smallpox, tetanus, typhoid, polio, and yellow fever are among the tropical diseases of the Ivory Coast, and the number of reported AIDS cases is rising. Heat and the dry climate cause skin infections. Iron all laundry to discourage skin parasites.

Hepatitis A & B, meningitis, river blindness, and sleeping sickness pose danger as well when travelling in the bush country.

Medical care is substandard and medicines are in short supply. Carry a well-stocked medical kit with all the prescription drugs you require. A travel insurance package including an evacuation policy should be acquired by all business travelers. As is true with general security, health awareness in this country must be at maximum at all times.

INTERNAL TRAVEL
AIR

Air Ivoire offers domestic flights several times per week from Abidjan to San Pédro, Korhogo, and Man. All the airports are linked to city centers by bus and taxi. The airport tax is CFAfr800 on domestic flights.

Passengers should be aware that, in general, airline travel within West Africa is customarily overbaked, schedules are limited and may change without notice, and that airline service quality varies considerably. It is advisable to get your seat reconfirmation stamped right onto the ticket. Also, have extra funds for food and lodging in case you encounter unexpected delays, and be sure to arrive at the airport a minimum of two hours prior to scheduled departure time.

TAXI

Abidjan's taxi system is two-tiered: those colored red are more expensive, and they will take you anywhere in the city. Your hotel can phone the taxi company to arrange for the cab to meet you.

The second tier of taxis is zone-based; cabs are all painted in different colors, which correspond to the different zones of the city. These cabs are simply hailed streetside. A quick observation of the locals' style should give you basis for knowing how to attract the driver's attention. Taxis of one zone will not cross into another, and they are all shared cabs. Passengers are dropped off via the most convenient route for the driver. These cabs are much cheaper than the red ones, although some suggest that you never should share a cab with a stranger(s).

Most cities have taxis, and most of them have a meter, but you may have to insist in order for the driver to turn it on. Also, beware of imposters driving unmarked cars; only go with cars that have a clearly marked 'taxi' sign.

AUTO

Car rental in the Ivory Coast can be expensive and is not necessarily recommended for first-time business visitors. Rental cars are most easily found in Abidjan and other major cities and at the airport. Insurance is mandatory for the driver as is an International Driving Permit.

The country's roadway system is an exception in Africa in that most of it is in quite good condition. But night driving is hazardous due to poor lighting and to vehicles which often drive without headlights. Gas stations are fairly frequent.

Bribes, direct and indirect, are somewhat commonplace on the part of police and other security officials, particularly at checkpoints along the highway and in the vicinity of Abidjan's Port Bouet Airport.

TRAIN

The Ivory Coast has passenger services that are typically efficient and comfortable. The Abidjan–Niger railway is perhaps the most modern in Africa. It operates fast domestic trains several times daily, linking Abidjan with Bouaké and Ferkessédougou.

A daily Express train runs between Abidjan and Ouagadougou in Upper Volta, and there is a Rapide that costs approximately a third less and provides another connection between Abidjan and Bouaké once a day, stopping at several smaller stations along the way.

The Abidjan–Niger railway is also especially useful for traveling to and from neighboring Burkina Faso and Liberia.

Reservations are required, and prices vary by season and holiday.

BUSES & TRAMS

Small buses service the cities and are, for the most, part comfortable and efficient. Larger buses ("bush taxis") exist for longer journeys. City buses are efficient for the most part, but inter-city lines can experience delays. Business travelers should avoid these buses unless no other means of transport can be found.

Travelers can also find large, modern luxury-class coaches for the longer journeys. These are actually cheaper and far more comfortable than the "bush taxis" so prevalent in other African countries. They service more secondary destinations than the train does and more economically.

Bush taxis cover the entire country, leaving throughout the day with no fixed schedules. Some of these are Peugeot sedans, most of them are minibuses.

WATER TRAVEL

The port city of Abidjan has both a local ferry service and cruise passenger lines to other African ports. There is no extensive river transport system for passengers.

TRAVEL ASSISTANCE

Office Ivoirien du Tourisme et de l'Hôtellerie
01 BP 8538, 2nd Floor, EECI Building
Place de la République, Abidjan 01
tel: 2020-6500; fax: 2022-5624

Security Briefing
SOCIAL UNREST

Cote d'Ivoire has been in a state of unrest since December of 1999, when the government was overthrown in a military coup—the second in a dozen years. The new regime appears to be in control, but violent demonstrations erupt without warning and the country remains in danger of civil war.

An influx of illegal immigrants from neighboring countries has further destabilized the nation. Several hundred thousand impoverished refugees from Liberia and Sierra Leone have found their way to Cote d'Ivoire in recent years. Most live in and around Abidjan, and efforts to evict or repatriate them have sometimes been met with violence.

ORGANIZED CRIME

Cote D'Ivoire is a transshipment point for Asian heroin and Latin America cocaine destined for the U.S. and Europe. Substantial quantities of Marijuana are also grown here, but most of it is consumed domestically.

STREET CRIME

Over 6,000 convicts escaped from the penitentiary in Abidjan during the 1999 coup d'etat, vastly increasing an already critical crime problem in the nation's unofficial capital. Pickpocketing and "grab and run" crimes are common in crowded areas, and carjackings, home invasions, and armed robberies of businesses are mounting. Foreigners are frequently targeted, and criminals are usually armed and resort to violence when faced with resistance.

Côte d'Ivoire

It is particularly dangerous to visit the Treichville, Adjame, Abobo, and Plateau districts of Abidjan after dark. The De-Gaulle and Houphouet-Boigny bridges crossing the lagoons are likewise dangerous for pedestrians, even in the daytime. Many hotels, restaurants, nightclubs, and supermarkets provide security guards to protect clients and their vehicles. However, foreigners are cautioned not to wear expensive jewelry, carry valuable documents or large amounts of cash, or walk the streets after dark.

Essential Terms

English	French
Yes	Oui
No	Non
Good morning	Bonjour
Hello (daytime)	Bonjour
Hello (evening)	Bonsoir
Hello (telephone)	Allo?
Good-bye	Au revoir
Please	S'il vous plaît
Thank you	Merci
Pleased to meet you	Enchanté
Excuse me; I'm sorry	Pardon
My name is _____	Je m'appelle _____
I don't understand	Je ne comprends pas
Do you speak English?	Vous parlez anglais?

Communications
DIALING CODES IN THE CÔTE D'IVOIRE

International country code: [225]

Dialing the Côte d'Ivoire from Overseas

To call a Côte d'Ivoire number from overseas, begin with your country's international dialing code, then 225 (the country code for the Côte d'Ivoire), and finally the number. There are no city codes in Cote D'Ivoire.

Assistance Numbers

Post office/
Telecommunications 2034-6000

CALLING WITHIN THE CÔTE D'IVOIRE

Local Calls

Decent service accompanies any local calling. Please note that telephone numbers have recently changed in this country. Previously, numbers had six digits; they will now have eight. An elaborate conversion system was put in place by Cote d'Ivoire Telecom.

Long Distance Calls

As of January 2000, telephone numbers in the Ivory Coast now have eight digits. The following directory was put in place by Cote d'Ivoire Telecom to help callers navigate the system of old 6-digit numbers into the new 8-digit format. (**Note:** numbers listed in the Global Road Warrior have already been changed to the new format)

- All numbers beginning with: **20 - 21 - 22 - 29 - 31 - 32 - 33 - 34 - 37- 38** are now preceded by: **20**. (example: 20 22 12 34)
- All numbers beginning with: **23 - 24 - 25 - 26 - 27 - 28 - 30 - 35 - 36- 56 - 58 - 75** are now preceded by: **21**. (example: 21 36 12 34)
- All numbers beginning with : **40 - 41 - 42 - 43 - 44 - 47 - 48 - 52** are now preceded by: **22** (example: 22 43 12 34)
- All numbers beginning with: **45 - 46 - 50 - 51 - 53 - 54 - 55 - 57** are now preceded by: **23** (example: 23 57 12 34)
- All numbers beginning with: **39 - 49 - 59** are now preceded by: **24** (example: 24 59 12 34)
- All numbers beginning with: **62 - 64 - 68** are now preceded by: **30** (example: 30 64 12 34)
- All numbers beginning with: **63 - 65 - 66 - 97** are now preceded by: **31** (example: 31 63 12 34)
- All numbers beginning with : **76 - 77 - 78 - 84** are now preceded by:: **32** (example: 32 77 12 34)
- All numbers beginning with: **70 - 79** are now preceded by: **33** (example: 33 70 12 34)
- All numbers beginning with: **71 - 72 - 78 - 84** are now preceded by: **34** (example : 34 72 12 34)
- All numbers beginning with: **91** are now preceded by: **35** (example : 35 91 12 34)
- All numbers beginning with: **86** are now preceded by: **36** (example: 36 86 12 34)

International Calls

The post office or the Hotel Ivoire provide international access in public booths. Three-minute minimums accompany the huge rates. Reduced rates occur between 7p.m. and 7a.m.; to North America it may cost about US$10 when compared to the regular rate of US$15. In theory, if dialing yourself, the direct call method means dialing 00 + country code + area code + number.

U.S. AT&T Direct 00-111-11
U.S. MCI 1001
BT Direct 00-111-44

PAY PHONES

Public Telephones

Card Phone:

Although they exist, most public phones don't work.

Calling Cards

The post office sells telephone cards for the card phones; however, be advised that some don't work. Cards are also available for international calls costing from US$3 to $25.

CELLULAR PHONES

Cellular phone service is available in the Cote D'Ivoire, predominantly in a digital format. Comstar, Loteny Telecom, Societe Ivoirenne de Mobiles all provide GSM service in this country.

- **Comstar**: all numbers beginning with: 01 - 02 - 03 are now preceded by: 03 (example: 03 02 12 34).
- **Loteny Telecom (Télécel)**: all numbers beginning with 04 - 05 - 06 - 60 - 73 - 74 - 87 - 88 - 89 - 92 - 94 - 95 - 96 - 99 are now preceded by: 05 (example: 05 74 12 34).
- **SIM (Ivoris)**: all numbers beginning with: 07 - 08 - 09 - 61 - 67 - 69 - 80 - 81 - 82 - 83 - 85 - 90 - 93 - 98 are now preceded by: 07 (example: 07 81 12 34).

Note: Your home country cell phone may not work in this country. If not, we recommend that you rent an international cell phone *before* you leave home. A major US-based cell phone rental provider is **IMC WorldCell**. For information see "International Cell Phone Rentals" on page 14.

CALL BACK

You can (potentially) save significant sums when calling in Cote d' Ivoire by using a call back service.

Fees for call back services vary widely, depending on the company and the type of service required. Be sure to check with these companies before leaving to compare rates.

PHONE JACK

Plug adaptors are available through **iGo Corporation**. (See "Electrical and Telephone Adaptors" on page 19.)

FAX

Do not assume that every major hotel or office will have a fax. They are available, but not yet widespread.

POSTAL SERVICES

Mail is efficient, taking about five days to reach the U.S. or Western Europe. Try to send mail in the Côte d'Ivoire to a post office box rather than a street address.

Hours of service
Monday to Friday 7:30a.m. to noon and 2:30p.m. to 6p.m.

Business Services

BUSINESS CENTERS

Golf Inter-Continental; Boulevard Lagunaire, La Riviera; tel: 2243-1044; fax: 2243-0544; email: abidjan@interconti.com.

Ivoire Inter-Continental; Boulevard de la Corniche; tel: 2244-1045; fax: 2244-0050; email: ivoire@interconti.com.

Sofitel Abidjan; Avenue Delafosse Prolongee 01Abidjan 01; tel: 2022-1122/00; fax: 2021-2028.

COURIER SERVICES

DHL International Cote d'Ivoire; Blvd. Giscard D'Estaing - Zone 4, BP 4869, Abidjan 01; tel: 2022-0522.

UPS Cote D'Ivoire; Immeuble Nanan, Yamousso Escalier I Appt. 141, Abidjan; tel: 2125-9740; fax: 2125-9740.

Electrical

Current
220/230 volts AC, 50Hz

ELECTRIC PLUGS

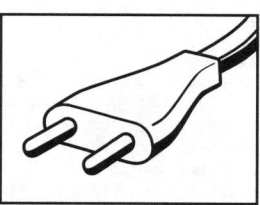

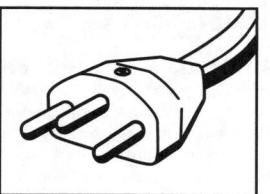

Round 2-pin plugs are standard.
Plug adaptors are available through **iGo Corporation**. (See "Electrical and Telephone Adaptors" on page 19.)

Technical Support

HARDWARE/SOFTWARE VENDOR SUPPORT

Dell; tel: 21-25-40-80/25-34-30; fax: 21-24-98-99; (in Germany) tel: [49] (61) 039-710; (Dell- Europe) tel: [44] (134) 474-8000; (in the U.S.) tel: [1] (512) 338-4400; fax: [1] (512) 728-3330; http://www.dell.com/.

Hewlett Packard; (in Switzerland) tel: [41] (22) 780-8111; (in the U.S.) tel: [1] (408) 246-4300; http://www.hp.com/.

IBM; tel: 20-325-207; fax: 20-328-351; (in Switzerland) tel: [41] (22) 310-0418 (in French); (U.S. Main Office) tel: [1] 914-765-1900; (in the U.S.) tel: [1] (919) 517-2800; http://www.ibm.com/.

Microsoft: (In Morocco) tel: [212] (2) 958-888; fax: [212] (2) 958-585; (in Switzerland) tel: [41] (848) 858-868; fax [41] (1) 831-0869; (in the U.S.) [1] (425) 635-7222; http://www.microsoft.com/.

Internet Connection

HOW TO CONNECT

Connecting to AOL and Compuserve in the Côte d'Ivoire is similar to using it when traveling outside your own area code. See the introductory section for detailed information on connecting to your account through a different phone number.

America Online
Numbers are available at keyword *international*. Be sure to get several local numbers before leaving. AOL's Global-Net service is available at keyword *access* (a free area) where you can download the software. Users will have to pay an additional US$24 an hour to use the service.

Access: Abidjan 20-328-855

Compuserve
Numbers are available at keyword *Go International*. The

Côte d'Ivoire

Compuserve Web-site also has a great deal of information, at http://www.compuserve.com.

Access: Abidjan 20-328-855.

Independent Service Providers

Many independent service providers offer discounts if you are only in town for a couple of days.

Africa Online; tel: 20-219-000; fax: 20-219-001; email: info@AfricaOnline.co.ci; http://www.africaonline.co.ci/.

Africom; tel: 20-217-071; fax: 20-217-072; email: 75740.535@compuserve.com; email: mayega@africom.com; http://www.africom.com/.

Orstom; tel: 21-243-779; fax: 21-246-504; email: morliere@abidjan.orstom.ci; email: brou@abidjan.orstom.fr; email: postmaster@abidjan.orstom.ci; http://abidjan.orstom.fr/.

Business Culture

GREETINGS AND COURTESIES

Firm handshakes, the exchange of business cards, and most other standard western business courtesies are observed here. However, Ivorians tend to be more formal and a bit more assertive than most other Africans, and indeed, many U.S. and European business people. When being introduced, wait for the locals to extend their hands in greeting before shaking hands, and make sure to use proper names and titles. Allow your hosts to talk about themselves and their company before explaining your business or launching into a sales pitch. It is considered quite good form to inquire about another's family, but never initiate, or allow yourself to be drawn into, a discussion of politics.

BUSINESS ETHIC AND FRAMEWORK

Yamoussoukro, the birthplace of the late dictator, Felix Houphouet-Boigny, has been the nation's official capital since 1983. However, the seat of government and the actual center of economic and political power in the country is Abidjan.

Foreign investment accounts for about 40 percent of the country's total capital resources, and France—which provides about 25 percent of the total capital flowing to Ivorian enterprises, and up to 60 percent of all foreign investment—is overwhelmingly the most important player in the nation's economy.

Cote d'Ivoire's central location and reliable connections with neighboring countries makes it a preferred platform from which to conduct West African operations. The nation boasts two active seaports—including the Port of Abidjan, which is the most modern in West Africa—and is linked by an excellent network of more than 8,000 miles of paved roads. Regular air service is available to and from Europe as well as destinations within the region, and rail service is being upgraded.

Cote d'Ivoire's telecommunications infrastructure is well developed by African standards and includes cellular telephone service, Internet access, and a public data communications network; but, it operates well below capacity. The domestic telephone system consists of open-wire lines and microwave radio relays. International calls are transmitted via two INTELSAT satellite stations (1 Atlantic Ocean and 1 Indian Ocean) and two coaxial submarine cables.

The city of Abidjan is one of the most sophisticated and cosmopolitan in the region, with modern real estate developments available for commercial, industrial, retail, and residential use. Its schools are good by regional standards and include an excellent international academy based on a U.S. curriculum and several excellent French-based institutions.

However, the recent military coup has rendered life in Abidjan quite dangerous and jeopardized progress toward privatizing the economy, expanding public and private investment, and institutionalizing democracy and the rule of law in Cote d'Ivoire.

DECISION MAKING

As is generally true throughout West Africa, success in business in Cote d'Ivoire depends largely on personal contacts and well-placed political connections. Organizations here, be they public or private, tend to be more bureaucratic than in the West, and decision-making power is usually concentrated at the top. Be patient but persistent, and cultivate your contacts.

MEETINGS

Business meetings in Cote D'Ivoire seldom begin or end on time but, otherwise, are conducted much they way one might expect in Europe or the United States, albeit a bit more formally. Fluency in French is essential, as most Ivorians will not speak English even if they are able.

Business cards or "Cartes De Visite" are widely used here, and catalogs, marketing, and advertising materials prepared in French are essential. Titles and degrees are frequently used here, especially by expatriates and those who have been schooled abroad. Foreign business representatives should do likewise and include their title, translated in French, on their correspondence and business cards.

WOMEN IN BUSINESS

Females are nearly as evident in corporate offices here as they are throughout most of the modern capitalist world, although few have yet made it to the top. Women seeking to do business here are treated respectfully, but with a double standard. Dress modestly, behave professionally, and wear a wedding band even if you are not married.

BUSINESS ENTERTAINING

It is customary here for visiting representatives of foreign corporations to be entertained by local hosts. Abidjan offers a selection of good restaurants and bars, and credit cards are generally accepted. The major hotels also provide meeting rooms and a sophisticated level of communications and presentation support.

BUSINESS ATTIRE

The business dress code for Ivorians is similar to that observed in the U.S. and Europe, with certain concessions made to the tropical climate. Tropical weight suits are standard for men, sans tie except when calling on senior executives and government officials. More casual attire—slacks and short-sleeved shirts—is appropriate for entertaining clients and other more social occasions. Women wear sleeveless cotton dresses or lightweight skirts and blouses to the office or when making business calls. Stockings, gloves, and hats are thankfully never worn here. On the other hand, feminine evening attire is often very high fashion (this is a Francophone community, after all), although men may be decidedly more casual. It is wise to check the dress requirements before attending an important meeting or social function.

Business Advisory

POLITICS AND GRAFT

Demands for bribes from police other security officers are commonplace, especially at highway checkpoints and near Abidjan's Port Bouet Airport. Corruption is also rampant among government ministers and bureaucrats, and cronyism dominates the business culture of Cote d'Ivoire, where French multinationals control most of the country's foreign trade and Lebanese expatriates monopolize domestic commerce.

BUSINESS FRAUD

Foreigners, including Europeans and Americans, are the favored victims of Nigerian scam operators, and the consequences are often financial loss and physical harm. Foreigners contemplating business deals in Cote d'Ivoire with individuals promoting investment in Nigeria, especially the Central Bank of Nigeria or the Nigerian National Petroleum Company, are strongly urged to check with their national embassy and to seek the advice of a reputable attorney before making financial commitments. Cote d'Ivoire's legal system is a mix of Napoleonic civil law and indigenous custom; the courts are weak, and victims of fraud have little hope of recourse.

Business Centers
Abidjan
CITY VIEW

Abidjan lies on the southern edge of the Ivory Coast along the Ebrie Lagoon. The geography is unique in that the lagoon is separated from the Gulf of Guinea and the Atlantic by the Vridi Plage sandbar. Light industry in the city is aimed at export markets with a large portion of workers involved with coffee production. Just a small seaside village in 1898, the city is now populated by approximately 3 million people and is comprised of six districts. Treichville may be the most interesting for visitors, for it is the site of the city's largest market and nightclub area. Business will most likely be conducted in the more reknowned commercial district, Le Plateau. This is also home to the National Museum displaying a splendid array of Ivorian Art. Tourists will also enjoy a walk in the Parc du Banco rain forest reserve on the northwestern edge of town. Be wary walking everywhere in Abidjan, though, for it is a typical large city ridden with typical large crime incidence.

AIRPORT

Port Bouet Airport to City Center

Port Bouet Airport lies 10 miles (16 km.) from downtown Abidjan. Expect a somewhat crazed environment in and outside the terminal, with hustlers rustling up all kinds of business, even inside Customs. A bus runs every 10 minutes, and taxis are available for the 25-minute trip into town. If not wanting to deal with the taxi circus outside, consider becoming a guest of the Hotel Ivoire and board their shuttle bus. Hail a taxi from there.

Airline Numbers

Air Afrique	2020-3000
Air France	2021-9093
Air Guinée	2032-6064
Air Inter Ivoire	2127-8465
Air Ivoire	2020-6666
Air Transivoire	2127-8415
American Airlines	2022-1315
Cameroon Airlines	2021-1919
Cathay Pacific	2022-6243
Egyptair	2032-5719
Ethiopian Airlines	2021-5538
Ghana Airways	2032-2783
MEA - Middle East Airlines	2022-6282
Nigeria Airways	2022-3565
RAM - Royal Air Maroc	2021-2038
SAA - South African Airways	2021-8250
Sabena	2021-2936
Swissair	2021-5572
TAP - Air Portugal	2021-1755

HOTELS

High-end

Hotel Le Marly; Boulevard de Marseille, Biétry, Abidjan; 33 rooms; located 10 minutes from the center of town and 5 minutes from the airport; restaurant; bar; in room tv, telephone, air conditioning; swimming pool; lagoon setting.

Ivoire Inter-Continental; Boulevard de la Corniche; tel: 2244-1045; fax: 2244-0050; email: ivoire@interconti.com; 750 rooms; 5 miles from city center; 5 restaurants; 14 function rooms; reception, classroom and banquet facilities; business center; secretarial service; in-room a/c, cable tv, telephone; airport pickup (fee); parking; health club; sauna; pool; tennis; golf.

Sofitel Abidjan; Avenue Delafosse Prolongee 01 Abidjan 01; tel: 2022-1122/00; fax: 2021-2028; 214 rooms; city center; restaurant; bar; conference facilities; business center services; secretarial services; 5 meeting rooms for up to 150; dataport; in-room ac; 24-hour rooms service; tennis; pool; water sports; shopping; CFA75,200/80,000.

Expensive

Grand Hotel; 17 Rue Monigny; tel: 2033-5424; telex: 23807; traditional style; 10km from airport; airport service; restaurant; meeting room for up to 40.

Novotel Abidjan; 10 Avenue Du General-De-Gaulle, Abidjan 01; tel: 2021-2323; fax: 2033-2636; 137 rooms; in center of the city; conference facilities; business center; parking; swimming pool.

Tiama; Avenue de la Republique, Abidjan; tel: 2022-6463; fax: 2021-4017; 145 rooms.

Moderate

Ibis Abidjan Marcory; Boulevard Valery Giscard, D'Estaing, Abidjan 15; tel: 2124-9255; fax: 2135-8910; 133 rooms; located in a suburb near the airport; restaurant; bar; conference facilities (up to 30); business center; in room air conditioning; parking; swimming pool.

Ibis Abidjan Plateau; Boulevard Roume 7, Abidjan 04; tel: 2021-0157; fax: 2021-7875; 190 rooms; in a suburb near the coast; restaurant; bar; conference facilities (up to 80); business center; in room air conditioning; parking.

MEDICAL CARE

Hopital de Port Bouet; tel: 2127-8500.

Polyclinique Internationale Ste Anne Marie; tel: 2244-5132; fax: 2244-6860.

AUTO RENTAL

Due to the high incidence of traffic accidents, especially at night due to poorly lit roads and other vehicles as well as highway checkpointsby the police or security requesting bribes we highly recommend against renting an auto.

Côte d'Ivoire

Croatia

At a Glance

THE PEOPLE

Population 4,671,584 (1998)
Growth Rate 0.13% (1998)
Life Expectancy ....73.75 years (born 1998)
Infant Mortality.................... 8 deaths / 1,000 births (1998)

Ethnic Composition

Croat...78%
Serb...12%
Hungarian...0.5%
Slovenian..0.5%
Other 9%

Religious Composition

Catholic 76.5%
Orthodox...11.1%
Muslim 1.2%
Protestant 0.4%
Other 10.8%

Languages Spoken

Serbo-Croatian (official), Italian, Hungarian, Czech, German.

Education and Literacy

The population over the age of 15 has a literacy rate of 97 percent.

Labor Force

Total: 1,440,000
By occupation: industry 31.1%, agriculture 4.3%, services 64.6%.

THE ECONOMY

As a former republic within Yugoslavia, Croatia was one of the most productive economies of the region. Since independence Croatia has, unfortunately, had to combat its legacy of inefficient communist-era central planning along with the extensive damage wrought to its infrastructure during its internal wars. Its former "cash cows' of shipbuilding, island-resort tourism, and oil production have also been greatly limited by the ongoing strife in neighboring Serbia and Albania. Very little foreign investment has been attracted to this potentially lucrative Adriatic-port nation although much was promised once internal conflicts ceased. While the government has made some overdue macroeconomic changes it has yet to shed itself of the massive numbers of state-owned businesses. Privatization and financial system reforms are seen as keys to Croatia economic future regardless of other Balkan conflicts.

Exports ....US$4.3 billion (1997)
Imports ....US$9.1 billion (1997)
Total Trade ....US$13.4 billion (1997)
GDP Per Capita...US$4,500 (1997)
Unemployment 15.9% (1998)
Inflation Rate 3.7% (1997)

Top Export Partners

E.U., Slovenia, Czech Republic.

Top Import Partners

E.U., Slovenia.

Top Exports

Machinery, chemicals, foodstuffs, live animals, raw materials, petroleum, beverages, tobacco.

Top Imports

Machinery components, foodstuffs, farm animals, raw materials, refined fuel, lubricants.

BUSINESS WORKWEEK

Offices

Monday to Friday 8a.m. to 7p.m,. with a one-hour break at 1p.m.

Banks

Monday to Friday 7:30a.m. to 7p.m.; Saturday 8a.m. to noon.

Government

Monday to Friday 8a.m. to 6p.m. Offices in rural areas may keep less regular hours.

Retail

Monday to Friday 8a.m. to 7 or 8p.m., with a one- hour break at 1p.m.; Saturday 8a.m. to 2 or 3p.m.

HOLIDAYS

New Year's Day...January 1
Easter Sunday..April 4*
Easter Monday ....April 5*
Labor Day...May 1
Statehood Day..May 30
Date of Antifascist Struggle ....June 22
All Saint's Day ....November 1
Christmas ....December 25-26
*Date may vary by year.

Money & Banking

Currency

The currency of Croatia is the Kuna (KN). KN1 = 100 lipas

Denominations

The Kuna (KN) comes in coin denominations of 1, 5, 10, and 50 lipas and bill denominations of a KN5, 10, 20, 50, 100, 500 (REVIEW at EDIT)

Traveler's Checks and Credit Cards

Banks in Croatia have lengthy daily hours and will exchange traveler's checks and foreign currency at a one percent commission. Other exchange kiosks at airports and city centers will charge similar fees. No black market currency trade exists in Croatia at this time. The Kuna may be exchanged back into hard currency but only at banks and only with a receipt of previous conversion. Prepare to show passport identification at all exchange offices. Exchange rates are moderate. Soiled or worn currency will be nearly impossible to exchange. U.S. dollars and German marks are the most desirable foreign currencies.

Major venues, retailers, and hotels on the mainland readily accept American Express, Visa, Mastercard and Diners Club. Most banks allow cash advances on credit / bank cards but only Splitska Banca accepts the Visa card for such purposes. ATM machines are numerous in cities but rural areas and outlying island communities are not

connected to the system. Credit card, bank card, and ATM transactions receive the best exchange rates.

American Express: Atlas Travel, Trg Zrinjskoga 17 (tel: 46-13-586).

Diner's Club; Praska ulica 5; tel: 480-2222.

Eurocard; Samoborska 145, Zagrebacka banka d.d.d; tel: 378-9555.

Visa; Splitska banka, Vlaska 26; trle: 481-4106; Zrinjevac 16, tel: 428-177.

CLIMATE

Seasons

This beautiful Mediterranean climate is similar to Italy's east coast and Greece's northern reaches. Winters are mild with lows of 12°C (54°F) and Croatia has hot, dry summers 33°C (94°F). The rainy season runs from mid-November until early March.

Regions

Croatia has a wide variance of regional geography from coastal plains to mountains to over 1,100 islands. Mountain regions are colder and more humid while the islands have a hot Mediterranean climate not unlike Greece's archipelago. Coastal Dubrovnik in the Dalmatia region has long been a European vacation spot with moderate sunny climes. The nation's crescent shape puts its central Slavonia region deep into the Balkan ranges where the capital, Zagreb, enjoys moderately colder and wetter weather.

Travel

VISA AND PASSPORT

All visitors require valid passports. Visitors from Australia, the U.S., Canada, New Zealand, and the U.K. do not require visas for internal travel lasting less than 90 days. All other foreigners need visas, which can be obtained prior to departure at no charge from Croatian consulates and embassies. All visitors must register in each city or region upon arrival. Business and multiple entry visas can be obtained in advance for travellers with an invitation from a Croatian government agency or local company.

Note: Travel to any Balkan country should be preceded by checking with your foreign office or Department of State. Useful websites are: http://www.fco.gov.uk.travel in the U.K., and http://travel.state.gov in the U.S.

DEPARTURE FORMALITIES

There is no limit on the export or import of registered foreign currency. Export or import of up to KN2,000 in Croatian money is permitted. The airport departure tax is the equivalent of KN37. Departure taxes do not exist for other forms of cross- border travel.

CUSTOMS ENTRY (PERSONAL)

Duty-free

- Tobacco: 400 cigarettes, 50 cigars, and 250g of tobacco
- Alcohol: 1 liter of spirits and 2 liters of wine
- Other: 50ml of perfume and 250ml eau de toilette

Prohibited
- Weapons
- Controlled drugs
- Anti-government material

IMMUNIZATION

An international health certificate and yellow fever vaccinations are required of visitors from infected areas. Hepatitis A prophylaxis and tetanus immunization are recommended as is basic travel insurance. Business people on extended stays should consider evacuation insurance.

TIPPING

Taxi
Round up fares the nearest KN amount although a larger tip will be expected from Western visitors.

Porters
No tip is required.

Hotels
Service charges where applicable will be added to the bill.

Restaurants
Most restaurants will add a service charge to the bill. As is the case with taxis, foreigners from the West are expected to tip beyond the service charge, but not significantly. Whatever the case, give all monies directly to the server and do not leave cash on the table.

EMERGENCY INFORMATION

Police and Crime
Croatia is not to far beyond martial law. It has a highly trained and disciplined police force that works with the military to keep crime to an absolute minimum in the cities; this also applies to the countryside to a great degree. Foreign visitors will have few if any problems if they take basic precautions.

Foreign business visitors are, however, often the target of what few thieves exist in Croatia. Consequently, purses, laptops and briefcases will require additional security. Do not leave valuables in cars or on tables in cafés. Keep non-essential valuables locked in hotel safes when not in use. Use credit cards and travel checks when possible to avoid carrying large sums of cash.

The only major security problem resides in the countryside where several areas have not been fully de-mined since the recent conflicts. Do not journey to the rural areas without adequate guidance. The main police station is located at: Petrinliska 30; tel: 456-311; the station has an office for visa matters.

Emergency Numbers
Useful throughout the country:

Police	92
Fire brigade	93
Ambulance	94
City Emergency Center	985
Anti-Terrorist Activity Department	985
Road Assistance	987

Health
Medical care in Croatia is neither free nor expensive. Bring along specialized medicines (e.g., insulin) as supplies may be limited. Doctors are, for the most part, well trained but suffer from poor facilities. Travel insurance is recommended.

Use bottled water although major hotels have potable tap water. Read the general travel health tips at the beginning of this book as most apply to this region.

For more information on medical centers, including phone numbers, please see the "Business Centers" section at the end of this chapter.

TAXI

Taxis are only available in the cities. Rates are reasonable and the service is generally fraud-free. Expect fares to rise by 20 percent Sundays, holidays, and between 10p.m. and 5a.m. Baggage stored in the trunk will cost extra.

Radio Taxi 970

Ask for a driver that speaks your language.

AUTO

Rental cars can be found in urban areas but visitors should purchase ample insurance. Visitors bringing in their own cars should have a green card and driver's license. The major rental agencies are present in main cities and an international drivers license is preferred. Drivers must be over 21 years of age. Hired cars with drivers are recommended for first-time visitors. Long-term business visitors should hire a car with a driver for the duration of their visit. If involved in an accident, be sure to take the car registration number, driver's license number, name, address, and phone number of the other party. Report the accident immediately to the nearest police station. One can also call the Hrvat Ski Auto Klub who will direct you to the nearest service center, tel: (1) 415-800, 412-412.

BUS

The bus service in Croatia is extensive and efficient for both inter- and intra-city travel. Daily Inter-city buses service Frankfurt, Munich, Stuttgart, Trieste, and Vienna. Twice-weekly buses travel to Berlin and Zurich. Prices are moderate for inter-city travel and cheap for just getting around town. One may purchase tickets either in advance for long trips or from conductors for short hops. Buses will more likely leave early than late, so schedule yourself accordingly.

Central Bus Station, Marin Drzic Avenue; take Tram 6 from the City Center; tel: 060-340-340.

Domestic Bookings	(1) 615-7986
Intl. Bookings	(1) 615-7983
Croatiabus	(1) 213-200, 235-857

TRAIN

Trains prove cheaper than the bus system and are often more comfortable for long distance travel, especially overnight. One may reserve first- and second-class seating in advance for inter-city transport, but local trains are restricted to second class only. Special "executive" trains between major cities must be reserved in advance and only offer first-class accommodations for business travelers. Daily service to Budapest, Geneva, Graz, Paris, Venice, and Vienna exists.

Mai Rail Station, KIng Tomislav Square 12.

Zagreb Main Railway	(1) 272-244 or 272-245
Arrivals/Departure Information	9830
Croatia Express Travel Agency	431-900
Croatian Railway	(1) 451-111

TRAVEL ASSISTANCE

Tourist Information 0800-200-200

Croatian National Tourist Office
Ilica 1a, 10000 Zagreb
tel: (1) 456-455; fax: (1) 428-674
website: http://www.htz.hr/
email: info@htz.hr

Zagreb Tourist Board and
Kaptol 5, 10000 Zagreb
tel: (1) 481-4051, 481-4052, 481-4054; fax: (1) 481-4056
website: www.zagreb-touristinfo.hr
email: info@zagreb-touristinfo.hr

Zagreb Convention Bureau
Kaptol 5, 10000 Zagreb
tel: (1) 481-4343; fax: (1) 481-4949

website: http://www.zagreb-convention.hr
email: zagreb.convention@ccb.hr
Zagreb Airport Hotel Reservation Desk
tel: (1) 456-2262

Essential Terms

English	Croatian
Yes No	*Da* *Ne*
Good morning Hello (daytime) Hello (evening) Hello (telephone)	*Dobro jutro!* *Zdravo* *Dobro vece* *Zdravo*
Good-bye	*Zdravo*
Please	*Molim*
Thank you	*Hvala*
Pleased to meet you	*Drago mi je*
Excuse me; I'm sorry	*Oprostite; Pardon, Izvinite*
My name is _____	*Zovem se_*
I don't understand	*Ja ne razumjem*
Do you speak English?	*Govorite li englaski?*

Communications
DIALING CODES IN CROATIA

International country code: [385]
Selected city codes: Dubrovnik (20), Rijeka (51), Osijek (34) Split (21), Zagreb (1).

Dialing Croatia from Overseas
To dial Croatia from overseas, dial your country's international dialing code, then 385 (the country code for Croatia), then the city code, and finally the number you wish to reach. If you were dialing Zagreb from the United States, for example, you would begin with 011, then 385, then 1 (the city code for Zagreb), and finally the number of the person or office you were trying to reach.

Assistance Numbers
Directory Assistance 988
International Operator 901
International Directory Assistance.............................. 989
Current Time 95
Telegrams 96

CALLING WITHIN CROATIA

Local Calls
Local calls can be made from any phone, public or private.

Long Distance Calls
One may place long distance phone calls from both pay telephones and private lines. City/area codes are necessary for calling outside of the region in which you find yourself.

International Calls
The international direct dialing code for Macedonia is '99'. You would then dial the country code + city/area code + the number that you are trying to reach. Check with your long distance provider about a calling card before leaving your country of origin.
AT&T 080-0220-111
MCI...080-022-0112
U.S. Sprint..080-022-0113
Those searching for cheaper rates than hotels normally offer, may place calls from telephone centers located in main post offices, located at Jurisiceva 13 and Branimirova 4, adjacent main rail station.

PAY PHONES

Public Telephones
Card Phone:

Public pay phones are fairly common and exist in bus and train terminals, hotel lobbies, drugstores, and restaurants throughout the country. As usual, hotel room calls will most likely cost much more than public phones. Public phones work on a card or token system. Some phones have a flag with a button on them that, when pushed, will provide the user with English instructions. Other than that, one may use the public telephone office at main post offices to place long distance or international calls.

Calling Cards
Public phones work on a token or calling card- based system. Phone cards, available in most newspaper and tobacco kiosks and post offices throughout the country, can be purchased in 50-, 100-, 200-, and 500-unit increments.

CELLULAR PHONES

Croatian Telecom and VIP Net provide GSM digital service. Croatian Telecom also offers NMT analogue service.

Note: Your home country cell phone may not work in this country. If not, we recommend that you rent an international cell phone *before* you leave home. A major US-based cell phone rental provider is **IMC WorldCell**. For information see "International Cell Phone Rentals" on page 14.

CALL BACK

You can (potentially) save significant sums when calling in Croatia by using one of the call back services listed below. Fees for call back services vary widely, depending on the company and the type of service required. Be sure to check with these companies before leaving to compare rates.

For a list of callback services, please refer to the "Communications" section in the *Global Road Warrior* Introduction.

Croatia

PHONE JACKS

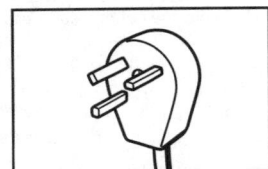

Plug adaptors are available through **iGo Corporation.** (See "Electrical and Telephone Adaptors" on page 19.)

FAX

Fax machines may be found in post offices and major hotels. Check with your hotel about usage.

POSTAL SERVICES

The postal service is reliable. Mail can be sent to Poste Restante at various post offices in the country. Or, if you are a member, send mail care of American Express in Zagreb. Your hotel may also provide useful postal service information. The main post office in Ljubljana is located at: Jurisceva 13. To find the exact rate for postage, call 981.

Hours of service

Jurisiceva 13; daily 7a.m. to 8p.m.; Sardes 7a.m. to 8p.m., Sundays/holidays 8a.m.to 2p.m.

Branimirova 4; 24 hours, Monday to Saturday.

Zagreb Airport; daily, 7a.m.to 9p.m.

Central Bus Station; 24 hours.

Other post offices:

Monday to Friday 7a.m. to 8p.m., Saturday until 2p.m. Larger post offices may remain open until 10p.m.

TELEGRAMS

For telegram service, dial '96'. You can also contact the nearest post office for telegram information. Your hotel may also provide you with information.

Business Services

BUSINESS CENTER

Esplanade Hotel; Mihanoviceva 1; tel: (1) 456-6666; fax: (1) 457-7907.

Holiday Hotel; Ljubljanska Avenija B.B.; tel: (1) 157-999; fax: (1) 156-857

Inter-Continental Zagreb; Krsnjavoga 1; tel: (1) 455-3411; fax: (1) 483-6005.

Sheraton Zagreb; Kneza Borne 2; tel: (1) 455-3535.

COURIER SERVICE

Airborne Express (RGW Express Airfreight GmbH); Postfach 75 04 33, 60534 Frankfurt/Main, Germany; tel: [49] (6969) 80-080; fax: [49] (6969) 800-840; Freight Service: Cargo Partner, Ivana Sibla 15, 10020 Zagreb; tel: (1) 660-1493, fax: (1) 660-1495.

DHL International (Zagreb), D.O.O.; Planinska bb, Zagreb 10000; tel: (1) 239-4110.

Federal Express (Ivan Air d.o.o.); tel: (1) 725-772.

TNT Express Worldwide; Kraljice Katarine 18, 10410 Velika Gorica; tel: (1) 722-977 PABX; fax: (1) 723-032.

UPS Croatia (Intereuropa Sajam Ltd.); Av. Dubrovnik 15,

10020 Zagreb; bookings and enquires (1) 655-1301; fax: (1) 652-0338.

SECRETARIAL SERVICE

World Trade Center Zagreb; Avenija Dubrovnik 15; 10 020 Zagreb; tel: (1) 650-3232; fax: (1) 652-7260; http://www.zv.hr; email: ngelincic@zv.hr.

TRANSLATION SERVICE

World Trade Center Zagreb; Avenija Dubrovnik 15; 10 020 Zagreb; tel: (1) 650-3232; fax: (1) 652-7260; http://www.zv.hr; email: ngelincic@zv.hr.

Electrical

220 volts AC, 50Hz.

ELECTRIC PLUGS

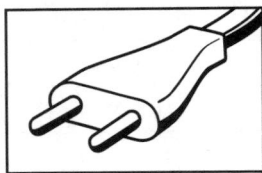

Plug adaptors are available through **iGo Corporation.** (See "Electrical and Telephone Adaptors" on page 19.)

Technical Support

HARDWARE/SOFTWARE VENDOR SUPPORT

Apple/Claris; tel: (1) 332-2666; fax: (1) 332-2667; (In Germany) tel: [49] (1) 803-5018; (In Switzerland) tel: [41] (800) 833-310; (in the U.K.) tel: [44] (990) 127-753; (in the U.S.) tel: [1] (800) 500-7078; http://www.apple.com/.

Compaq/Digital; (in Switzerland) tel: [41] (22) 709-5330; fax: [41] (22) 709-5391 (Geneva); [41] (1) 801-2507; fax: [41] (1) 801-2172 (Zurich); (General U.S.) tel: (281) 518-2000; http://www.compaq.com/.

Dell; tel: (1) 365-0666; fax: (1) 365-0677; (Distributor); (in Germany) tel: [49] (61) 039-710; (Dell- Europe) tel: [44] (134) 474-8000; (in the U.S.) tel: [1] (512) 338-4400; fax: [1] (512) 728-3330; http://www.dell.com/.

IBM; tel: (1) 612-4500; fax: (1) 611-1119; (in Germany) tel: [49] (69) 6654-9003; (in Switzerland) tel: [41] (22) 310-0418 (in French); http://www.ibm.com/.

Microsoft; tel: (1) 480-2500; fax: (1) 484-3688; (in Germany) tel: [49] (89) 31-760; fax: [49] (89) 3176-1000; tel: [49] (89) 3176-1199; (In Switzerland) tel: [41] (848) 858-868; fax [41] (1) 831-0869; (in the U.S.) [1] (425) 635-7222; http://www.microsoft.com/.

Internet Connection

HOW TO CONNECT

Connecting to AOL and Compuserve in Croatia is similar to using it when traveling outside your own area code. See the introductory section for detailed information on connecting to your account through a different phone number.

America Online

Numbers are available at keyword *international*. Be sure to get several local numbers before leaving. AOL has a new GlobalNet service that charges US$6 an hour in addition to the usual charges. Go to keyword *access* (a free area) and download the software.

Access: Dubrovnik (20) 413-710, Rijeka (51) 227-664, Split (21) 355-410, Zagreb (16) 117-055.

Compuserve

Numbers are available at *Go International*. If you are using CompuServe 2000, use GO PHONES within CompuServe 2000 to search for access numbers. The Compuserve Web-site also has a great deal of information, at http://www.compuserve.com/.

Access: Zagreb (1) 611-7055, Dubrovnik (2) 041-3710, Split (2) 135-5410, Rieka (5) 122-7664

Independent Service Providers

Many independent service providers offer discounts if you are only in town for a couple of days.

CARNet; Croatian Academic and Research Network; tel: (1) 616-5656; http://www.CARNet.hr/.

HiNet; tel:(1) 481-5800; http://www.hinet.hr/.

Iskon d.o.o.; tel: (1) 617-7155; http://www.iskon.hr/.

VPM Internet Services; tel: 1-800-321-0221; http://www.vpm.com/.

Business Culture

BALKAN NOTES

Centuries of war and the subsequent re-drawing of borders in the Balkan states have resulted in many mis-matches between geo-political boundaries and ethnic as well as religious boundaries. Business culture is often related to the customs and culture of the ethnicity and religion of your business associates, rather than to their nationality. The practice of a strong and conservative patriarchy is inextricably linked to eastern Orthodox Christianity as well as to Islam. For a foreign businesswoman, this may present complications. It is important for men and women to discern in advance the ethnicity and religion of the people in a Balkan state with whom you hope to conduct business

BACKGROUND

Newly independent from Yugoslavia in 1991, Croatia is populated mostly by ethnic Croats, a Slavic people who are predominantly Catholic. A minority eastern Orthodox ethnic Serb population exists, but their numbers have dropped during the 1990's from 12 percent to approximately 5 percent. In addition, a small Slavic Muslim minority exists. Although oriented to the West, Croatia is still struggling to recover from war.

GREETINGS AND COURTESIES

People greet each other with a handshake in Croatia. A man waits for a woman to extend her hand first. The family name is preceded by *Gospodine* (Mr.), *Gospodjo* (Mrs.), or *Gospodjice* (Miss). Address professionals by their title, followed by their surname. The younger person greets first. First names are used only among friends and relatives, who may greet each other with an embrace and by lightly kissing each cheek. The most common greetings include: *Dobra jutro* (Good morning), *Dobra dan* (Good day), *Dobra jutro* (Good evening. Common ways to say hello are, *Zdravo* (Be healthy), or *Bok* (Hi). To say goodbye, say, *Zbogom* (With God), or *Do videnja* (Until we meet again).

BUSINESS ETHIC AND FRAMEWORK

Croats are optimistic, hospitable, and proud of their newly-won independence. Taking pride in their historical ties to the West, the country hopes to establish a democratic society with rights for all citizens. Croatia suffered much damage to its infrastructure and housing stock during war in the early 1990's. An outcome of this is a high cost of borrowing, a shortage of working capital, and a resulting failure to pay suppliers on time or at all. Therefore, foreign businessmen are advised to obtain a confirmed letter of credit as a basis to conduct business with a new local partner.

The principal language of Croatia is Serbo-Croatian, a Slavic language identical to that spoken in Serbia. Croat businessmen usually also speak German, English, and Italian, as well as other Slavic languages. "Business Centers" are available at some major hotels in Zagreb for secretarial, communication, and translation services.

Like other members of the former Yugoslav federation, Croatia had a "self-management" economic system where most management decisions at companies were based on market principles. As a result, Croat business managers are familiar with market economy philosophy and customs.

DECISION MAKING

Management style is authoritative, and little delegation of authority exists in companies. As a result, decisions are usually made only by the top decision-maker in a company, or another clearly-designated decision-maker. Use caution, since business in Croatia is not always transparent. Do not consider negotiations completed or even progressing well until confirmed so by the key decision-maker. Decisions are rarely made during the first contact.

MEETINGS

Make appointments in advance, and re-confirm before the meeting. A letter of introduction is helpful. Punctuality is important, and business meetings generally proceed according to schedule. It is standard procedure to distribute business cards, as well as any other printed literature you may have. Business gift-giving is not expected, but a pen or like item with your company's logo would be an appreciated gesture. The conduct of business is somewhat relaxed and informal in Croatia, and building strong personal relationships is important. Socializing after your meeting, perhaps for lunch, can help solidify business relationships.

BUSINESS ENTERTAINING

Croats prove very sociable and hospitable, and you can expect to be included in a business lunch or invited to a home for a meal. People take turns paying restaurant checks; the bill is never split. Lunch is the main meal of the day, with a light supper later in the evening. If invited to a home, suggested gifts for your hosts include a bottle of wine, sweets, or an odd number (even numbers are associated with funerals) of flowers. Avoid roses, which carry a romantic connotation. It is impolite not to accept refreshments. Croats dining etiquette follows continental style, with the fork in the left hand and the knife remaining in the right. Hands are kept above the table. Mealtime conversation is lively, but it is best to avoid sensitive political subjects.

WOMEN

Although gender relations in neighboring Serbia are based on a strong patriarchy, Slovene and Croat societies are to a large extent Catholic and more westernized, with women enjoying more egalitarian treatment. Croat wives participate fully in family decision-making. Many work outside the home, leaving children at daycare centers or with grandparents. Their pay lags behind men, however, and they are not well-represented in management positions.

Customarily, women do not go alone to bars, or even to some cafes, which tend to resemble all-male clubs. As a foreign businesswomen, you may feel more comfortable dining alone at your hotel, rather than enduring stares in restaurants.

BUSINESS ATTIRE

Croats follow European fashions, but are less formal than some European cities. Appearances and a well-groomed look are important. Urban Croat businessmen wear suits and ties for special occasions, and for some business or professional events, but more casual clothes in the conduct of everyday life. Woman customarily wear dresses in the workplace. Other appropriate choices for women are skirts and blouses, and slacks.

Business Advisory

POLITICS & GRAFT

Croatia is another new republic formed out of the often violent breakup of the former Yugoslavia. Croatia's government was recognized by the 1995 Dayton agreement that established the nation's borders. In theory, it has a parliamentary democracy, but in practice it is not far removed from the single-party dominance of its Socialist past. Croatia is propped up to some degree by international agency funding, although its economy is far more stable than most in the Balkans. It is still heavily burdened with bureaucrats, so, foreign firms can expect some requests for outright bribes and "special fees" from civil servants and inspection officials. Overall, however, prospective business people should not consider Croatia a very corrupt place to do business. Most graft will be rather petty in nature and will most likely occur in rural areas.

BUSINESS FRAUD

Not much interest presently exists in privately funded business projects in Croatia since many global firms see the entire region as unstable. Most investment comes from international agencies, though Croatia is relatively wealthy compared to neighbors Albania, Bosnia-Herzegovina, and Serbia-Montenegro. Business fraud in Croatia, like graft, is minimal, but few major projects outside of infrastructure are being funded. Once foreign private investors decide to enter the Croatian market en masse and privatization of state-owned companies begins, there may be greater reason for concern. Foreign firms working in Croatia should take the following basic precautions:

- Move investment into the country in small increments based on satisfactory performance by the local partner.

- Keep working capital offshore and out of local banks until it is needed.

- Make sure your company does a good "due diligence" investigation before signing any contracts.

- Assure that you have your own contacts in the local government as well as keeping your own embassy involved.

Business Centers
Zagreb

The city of Zagreb is the political, administrative, and cultural hub of the country. With a population of over 1 million, the city continues to grow from its medieval roots into a modern, bustling capital, while still retaining the flavor of its history in its architecture. The business district lies between the rail station and the Old Town.

AIRPORT

Pleso Airport to City Center

Taxis await passengers just outside of the International Arrivals exit. Expect to pay about US$18 to $20 for the trip into town. If arriving at night after 10p.m., expect to pay about 20 percent more than the meter reads. The same applies to Sundays and holidays. Buses make the trip into town in about 20 to 25 minutes and deliver and pick up passengers at the Central Bus Station on Marin Drzic Avenue. Buses from the airport run between 6:30a.m. and 8p.m. hourly, or after flight arrivals. Buses to the airport operate according to flight schedules between 4a.m. and 9p.m. on an hourly basis.

Numbers

Airport	456-2222
Flight Information	626-5222
Customs	456-2145
Police	456-2381, 456-2437
VIP Lounge Reservation	456-2113, 456-2200
Business Lounge	456-2651, 456-2653
Tourist Information	456-2262

Airline Numbers

Adria Airlines	(1) 481-0011, 481-0016
Aeroflot	(1) 421-602, 421-825, 456-2258
Air Bosnia	(1) 456-2672
Air France	(1) 455-8355, 456-2591
Austrian Airlines	(1) 420-255, 456-2257, 456-2360
Avioimpex	(1) 482-9441, 456-2457
British Airways	(1) 455-3336, 456-2506
Croatia Airlines	(1) 481-9638, 427-752, 456-2017
	434-355, fax: 433-324, airport, 456-2479
Ésa	(1) 434-355, 456-2479
KLM	(1) 457-3133
LOT	(1) 437-525
Lufthansa	(1) 483-6182, 456-2237
Malaysian Airlines	(1) 481-0777, 456-2701
SAS	(1) 426-030
Swissair	(1) 420-255, 456-2257, 456-2360

HOTELS

Top-End

Esplanade; Mihanoviceva 1; tel: (1) 456-6666; fax: (1) 457-7907; http://lhw.com/zagreb/esplanade.html; email: hotel-esplanade@tel.hr; 214 rooms; 9 suites; city center; adjacent to train station; restaurants; piano bar; conference facilities (up to 400); business center; secretarial service; garage; car rental; corporate rates.; nightclub.

Inter-Continental Zagreb; Krsnjavoga 1; tel: (1) 455-3411; fax: (1) 483-6005, 444-431; email: zagreb@interconti.com; 414 rooms; 40 suites; 2 presidential suites; city center; restaurants; conference facilities (up to 1000); business center; secretarial service; in-room satellite tv, radio, minibar, telephone, hair drier; garage; car rental; beauty salon; shops; fitness; solarium; indoor pool.

Croatia

Expensive

Holiday; Ljubljanska Avenija B.B.; tel: (1) 157-999; fax: (1) 156-857; 290 rooms; located in western suburb; casino; restaurants; conference facilities (up to 300); business center; rooms for disabled; car rental; parking; fitness; disco.

Palace; Strossmayerov trg 10; tel: (1) 481-4611, 275-611; fax: (1) 481-1358, 275-870; 125 rooms; 3 suites; 5 minutes walk from city center; casino; restaurant; Venetian coffee shop; meeting facilities; in-room minibar, a/c, satellite tv; parking; elevator; shops; corporate rates.

Tomislavov dom; Sljemenska cesta bb; tel: 455-5833; fax: 455-5834; located on Medvednica Mountain peak in forest; Zagreb views; 64 rooms; 2 suites; dining room.

Moderate

Astoria; Petrinjska Ulica 71; tel: (1) 484-1222; fax: (1) 484-1212;125 rooms; city center, near main railway; Chinese restaurant; breakfast served; meeting facilities.

Babylon; Sveta Nedjelja-Novaki; Betonska 5; tel: 337-1500; fax: 337-1044; west entrance of Zagreb; 28 rooms; restaurants; in-room shower, toilet, telephone, minibar, satellite tv.

Central; Branimirova 3; tel: (1) 484-1122; fax: (1) 484-1304; located in business district; casino; restaurant, buffet, coffee shop; elevator.

Dom obrtnika Hunjka; Sljeme bb; tel: 485-0397; fax: 461-4355; located in countryside; 23 rooms with bathroom or shower/toilet.

Dubrovnik; Gajeva 1; tel: (1) 455-5155; fax: (1) 424-451; email: dubrovnik@hotel-dubrovnik.tel.hr; 262 rooms; 7 suites; city center, near Ban Jelacia Square; restaurant; meeting facilities; rooms with shower/toilet; phone, satellite tv.

Hotel "I"; Remetinecka cesta 106; tel: 614-2115; fax: 654-2115; located at Azagreb West entrance; 219 rooms; restaurant; in-room satellite tv.

International; Miramarska 24; tel: 610-8800; fax: 615-9459; located in business district; restaurant; casino.

Laguna; Kranjceviceva 29; tel: (1) 382-0222; fax: (1) 382-0035; 340 rooms, 5 suites; 4 tram stops from city center; restaurant; conference facilities; in-room phone, minibar, satellite tv; some rooms with bath or shower/toilet; parking; fitness; sauna.

Park; Ivanjicgradska 52; tel: (1) 233-3422; fax: (1) 220-820; 5 km from city center; parking.

MEDICAL CARE

Croatian Medical Board; for information of private practitioners, Subiceva 9.

Health Care Centre Novi Zagreb; Avenija V. Holjevca 22; tel: 652-8755; dental care center.

Health Care Centre Centar; Runjaninova 4; tel: 484-3666.

Emergency Centar; Draskovi´ca 19; tel: 460-0911; open 24 hours.

University Hospital KBC Salata; Salata 2; tel: 455-2333.

24-hour Pharmacies

Note: 24-hour pharmacies may only dispense medicines on a physician's prescription or case history presentation after 8p.m. Normal pharmacy hours: 7a.m. to 8p.m. Monday to Friday, Saturday 7a.m. to 3p.m.

Centralna Ljekarna; Trg bana Josipa Jelacica 3; tel: 481-6198.

Ljekarna at Ilica 301; tel: 375-0321.

Ljekarna at Drizanska 4; tel: 299-2350.

LJekarna at Avenija V. Holjevca 22; tel: 652-5425.

Ljekarna at Ozaljska 1; tel: 397-586.

HEALTH CLUB

Aerobic Center-Fitness, Alplan Sport d.o.o.; Av. Dubrovnik 14, Zagrebaãki velesajam - paviljon 6; tel: (1) 655-0502; body building, aerobics, yoga, solarium, massage, and more.

Hippodrome Zagreb; Radoslava Cimermana 5 or X. juzna obala 5; tel: 652-8520; riding.

Mladost Sports Park; Jarunska cesta 5; tel: 365-8555; Olympic sized pools; tennis; basketball; volleyball; handball; football; field hockey grounds; volleyball sports hall nearby.

Recreational Sports Centre Jarun; Jarun bb; tel: 383-2827; southwest part of the city; regatta course; rowing and kayaking clubs; yachting, waterskiing/surfing/diving clubs; triathalon; beach volleyball; boccie alleys; baseball./softball clubs; anglers' society; football; basketball; mini golf; table tennis; cycle paths; par course; paddleboating; canoeing; fishing.

AUTO RENTAL

Note: Seat belts are mandatory for front seat.

Avis; tel: (1) 456-2285; airport, tel: (1) 626-5840 8a.m. to 8p.m.; Inter-Continental Hotel, tel: (1) 483-6006 8a.m. to midnight; Ul Republike Austrije 5, tel: (1) 447-228 Monday to Friday 8a.m. to midnight.

Budget; Sheraton Hotel, Kneza Borne, 2; tel: (1) 455-4936.

Europcar; airport, tel/fax: (1) 655-4003; Atlantis Travel Agency, tel: (1) 434-444; fax: (1) 434-474.

Hertz; tel: (1) 484-7222; fax: (1) 484-6005; airport, tel/fax: (1) 484-6777; 8a.m. to 8p.m.; chauffeur-driven and ski-equipped vehicles available.

INA/ITR; tel: (1) 456-2073 or 456-2074.

Niva; tel: (1) 456-2263 or 456-2553.

VIP Car; Mihanoviceva, 1; tel: 457-2148.

WORLD TRADE CENTER

World Trade Center Zagreb
Avenija Dubrovnik 15; 10 020 Zagreb
tel: (1) 650-3232; fax: (1) 652-7260
website: http://www.zv.hr
email: ngelincic@zv.hr
Services: Trade Education Services; Group Trade Missions; Trade Fair and Mart; World Trade Center Club; International Trade Library; Translating Services; Publications; Meeting Facilities; Secretarial Services; Hotel; Trade Information Services; Temporary Offices.

Cuba

At a Glance

THE PEOPLE

Population .... 11,096,395 (July 1999 est.)
Growth Rate .... 0.4% (1999 est.)
Life Expectancy .... 75.78 years (born 1999)
Infant Mortality ... 7.81 deaths/1,000 live births (1999 est.)

Ethnic Composition

Mulatto 51%
Caucasian 37%
Black African 11%
Chinese 1%

Religious Composition

Roman Catholic...85%
Other and non-affiliated...15%

Languages Spoken

Spanish

Education and Literacy

Elementary education is compulsory for five years. The literacy rate for the adult population is 95.7 percent.

Labor Force

Total 4,500,000
By occupation: services 58%, industry 22%, agriculture 20%.

THE ECONOMY

Cuba is one of the last nations to maintain a communist-style economy. As such, the government has tight control of every aspect of commerce and all production is centrally planned. Long dependence on subsidies from the former Soviet Union and a continuing embargo by the United States has left Cuba to enter the 21st century as very poor nation. Never very prosperous under Castro's rule, the GDP has dropped by 35 percent since 1989. The government has taken some steps to allow market economics into the agricultural sector, but it is far too little to revive this economy. As of late, there has been an attempt to promote tourism, but results have been less than stellar since the U.S. (just 90 miles away) still bans its citizens from free travel to Cuba. Unlike its communist brethren, Cuba has not had a change of leadership since its revolution. Analysts see little hope of change until the "old guard" passes into the history books and communist doctrine can be pushed aside.

Exports .... US$1.4 billion (f.o.b., 1998 est.)
Imports .... US$3 billion (c.i.f., 1998 est.)
Total GDP .... US$17.3 billion (1998 est.)
GDP Per Capita .... US$1,560 (1998 est.)
Unemployment .... 6.8% (1997 est.)
Inflation Rate .... N/A

Top Export Partners

Russia, E.U., Canada

Top Import Partners

E.U., Russia, Mexico

Top Exports

Sugar, nickel, tobacco, shellfish, medical products, citrus, coffee.

Top Imports

Petroleum, food, fuel, machinery, chemicals.

BUSINESS WORKWEEK

Offices

Monday to Friday 8:30a.m. to 12:30p.m. and 1:30p.m. to 5:30p.m.

Banks

Monday to Friday 9a.m. to 5p.m.

Government

Monday to Friday 8:30a.m. to noon and 1:30p.m. to 5p.m.

Retail

Monday to Friday 8:30a.m. to noon and 1:30p.m. to 5p.m. with slightly shorter hours on weekends. Until recently, it was customary to be closed on Sundays, but more retail stores are staying open on Sundays now.

HOLIDAYS

Liberation Day ....January 1
Labor Day..May 1
Anniversary of the 1953 Revolution ....July 25-27
Wars of Independence Day...............................October 10
Note: Since 1959 religious or ethnic holidays have not been recognized but many are still celebrated.

CLIMATE

Seasons

The climate is mostly tropical or semitropical with temperate zones, moderated by trade winds; droughts are also common. Dry season occur from November to April, and rainy seasons from May to October. Average temperatures range from 21˚C (70˚F) to 27˚C (77˚F). High temperatures can reach 40˚C (104˚F) in summer.

Regions

The eastern coast can be hit by hurricanes from August through October. All coastal areas tend to be hot and humid. Mountain areas can get the most rain during the rainy season.

Money & Banking

Currency

The currency of Cuba is the Cuban Peso (Cu$).

Denominations

The Cuban Peso comes in coin denominations of 40, 20, 5, 2, and 1 centavos; and banknotes of Cub$1,3, 5, 10, 20, and 50.

Traveler's Checks and Credit Cards

Traveler's checks can be exchanged at banks, exchange shops, hotels, and international airports. Cash, especially U.S. dollars, can also be exchanged at tourist exchange rates, but try to take only, crisp and new notes; wrinkled and soiled notes are likely to be refused. Smaller-denomination bills will get you further than large notes for which many locals have no change.

Cashing traveler's checks can be difficult and lengthy, especially in smaller towns where commissions can run high. Although the U.S. dollar is a favorite currency, U.S.-issued traveler's checks will not be accepted, nor will be American Express checks.

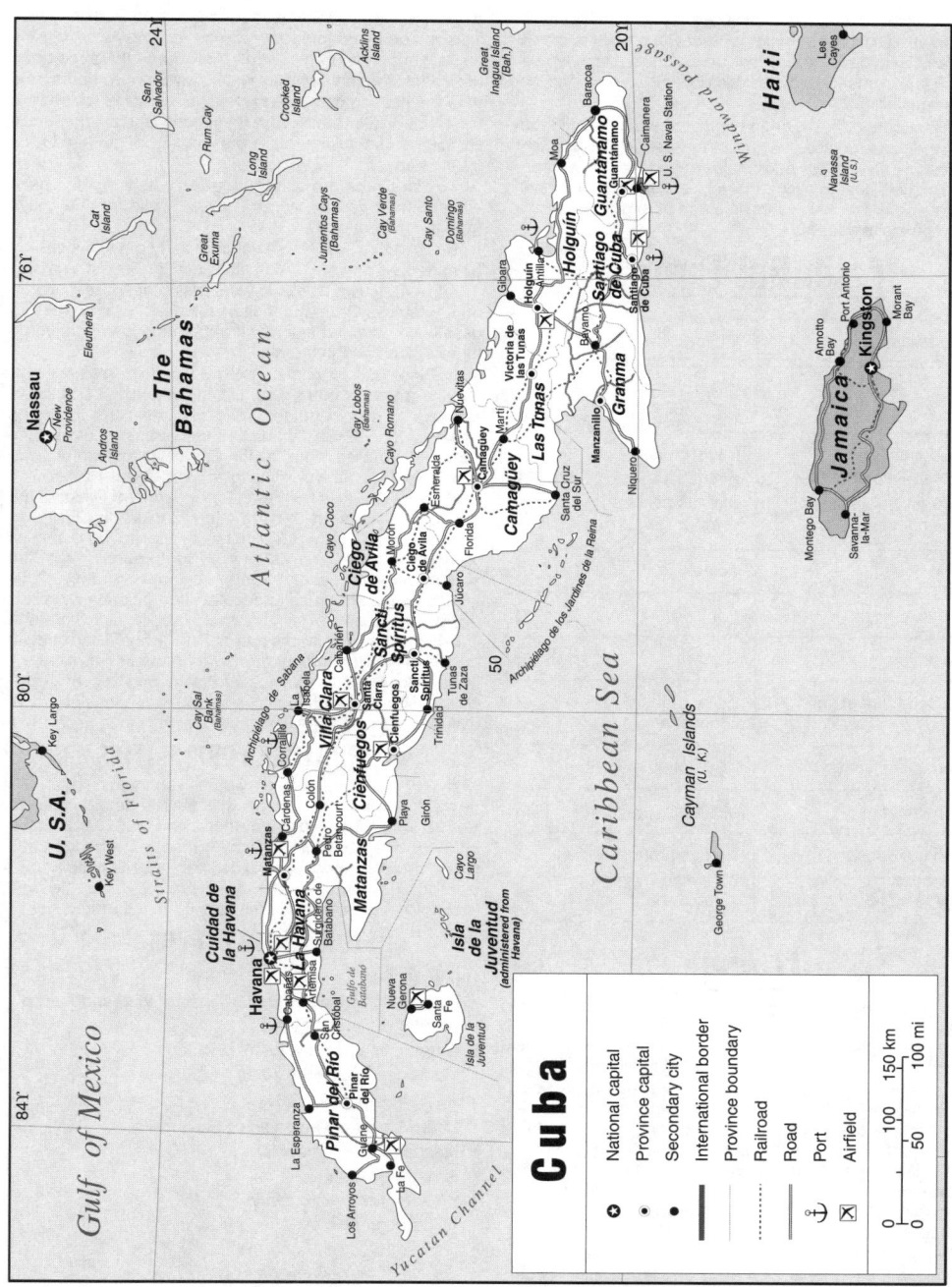

Cuba

Cuba

Cuba

- National capital
- Province capital
- Secondary city
- International border
- Province boundary
- Railroad
- Road
- Port
- Airfield

0	50	100	150 km
0		50	100 mi

©2001 Magellan Geographix ℠ Santa Barbara, CA

Visa, Diner's Club, and MasterCard are accepted in most up-market places in the main cities of Cuba, unless drawn from a U.S. account. Cards will be charged at tourist exchange rates. American Express and Optima cards will not be accepted at all.

Visitors cannot re-exchange currency when leaving the country without receipts, so keep all evidence of exchange of currency. Visitors will find a reluctance to reconvert currency; so, it is best to exchange your original cash in small amounts on a day-to-day basis so as not to get stuck with Cuban pesos at departure time.

Essential Terms

English	Spanish
Yes	Sí
No	No
Good morning	Buenos días
Hello (daytime)	Buenas tardes
Hello (evening)	Buenas noches
Hello (telephone)	¿Hola?
Good-bye	Adiós
Please	Por favor
Thank you	Gracias
Pleased to meet you	Encantado (a) de conocerle
Excuse me; I'm sorry	¿Perdóneme?
My name is _____	Me llamo _____
I don't understand	No comprendo
Do you speak English?	¿Habla usted inglés?

Travel

VISA AND PASSPORT

A passport that is valid for six months minimum beyond the anticipated length of stay is required of all visitors.

A visa is required of all except for visitors in possession of a Tourist Card. This special document is available through prescribed tour operators, airlines, and travel agents, who are licensed by the Cuban government to issue the Tourist Card, which is valid for a single trip only of thirty days maximum duration. Once in Cuba, a visitor may extend the stay by applying at the Immigration Office.

Business travelers need a visa regardless of nationality. Exceptions are made for journalists and for visitors whose purpose for being in Cuba is to attend a conference or to further academic studies.

A Visitor's Card is required of any person wishing to reside with family or friends in Cuba for a limited time.

All travelers must report in person to the Immigration Office for registration immediately upon arrival during normal business hours. If your stay is to exceed ninety

days in length, you will be required to have an exit permit. This will be given to you when you register.

Passengers in transit who do not leave the airport and are continuing their journey within seventy-two hours, and who are holding confirmed tickets, documents for onward travel, and sufficient funds for length of stay (generally US$50 per day minimum), are exempt from the need for a transit visa.

Tourist Cards are to be used before six months have elapsed from date of issue. They are valid for thirty days from the date of entry.

Business visas are also valid for thirty days, but can be extended, as can the period of validity for Tourist Cards.

Allow up to two weeks for processing of applications for both Business visas and Visitors Cards. Tourist Cards can usually be obtained in a day if application is in person, up to a week if through the mail.

Note for U.S. travelers: The U.S. does not maintain diplomatic relations with Cuba. U.S. travelers will find themselves in a sort of nether world of regulations regarding travel to Cuba. Officially, the U.S. government does not "license" any transactions relating to either tourism or business for U.S. citizens wishing to visit Cuba. However, it does seem that the U.S. Treasury Department (which is the agency in charge of these matters) looks the other way these days, as many U.S. citizens encounter no problems visiting Cuba, as long as they do so through one of the aforementioned travel agents or tour operators. This should be construed as anecdotal information only, not as advice. If you are a U.S. citizen wishing to visit Cuba and you would like to know the letter of the law, you can contact the Treasury Department directly for more information.

Note for Cuban expatriates: Persons originally of Cuban citizenship who are now nationals of different countries are required to carry a Cuban passport if they left Cuba since 1970.

DEPARTURE FORMALITIES

If your stay exceeds ninety days, you must have an exit permit for departure. Officials will collect a departure tax of US$20 from Havana and Varadero, and US$10 from other airports. Keep receipts whenever money is changed officially.; this will allow pesos to be changed back into foreign currency. The reconversion rate is not very favorable, so it is best to have spent your pesos before departure.

CUSTOMS ENTRY (PERSONAL)

Duty-free
- Tobacco: 200 cigarettes, 50cigars, or 250g of tobacco
- Alcohol: 3 liters of spirits
- Other: gifts up to a value of US$50
- Medicines: maximum 10 kg

Prohibited or Restricted
- Natural fruits or vegetables
- Meat and dairy products
- Anti-government material
- Weapons and ammunition
- All pornographic material
- Controlled drugs
- Jewelry (non-personal use)
- Video cassettes and household appliances

IMMUNIZATION

Travelers coming from or going through infected areas must have certificates of vaccination against cholera and yellow fever. Tetanus and hepatitis A inoculations are advised.

Cuba

TIPPING

Taxi

Taxis are not generally tipped beyond rounding up the fare. Drivers assume foreigners will add a small tip, especially if the driver has acted as "tour guide" during the trip. When using an unmetered taxi, negotiate the fare in advance.

Porters

Porters at first class hotels and depots receive US$1 per bag.

Hotels

Service charges will usually be applied to the bill. Otherwise, concierge: US$5 for special arrangements; maids: US$1 per night's stay.

Restaurants

When a service charge has not been applied to the bill, ten percent is customary.

EMERGENCY INFORMATION

Police and Crime

Crime in Cuba is relatively low compared to other countries in the region, but it is on the rise. Take basic precautions and stay alert in central Havana and in the old section of the city for hustlers and tricksters. Avoid flashy displays of wealth, and dress and behave conservatively. Leave most of your cash, traveler's checks, jewelry, and your camera in your hotel safe. Carry photocopies of your passport instead of the original. Carry cash in a money belt, and use credit cards or travelers checks for most of your large transactions.

Business travelers are assumed to be wealthy, so, extra care should be taken with laptops and briefcases.

Do not expect the police to recover stolen articles. Carry insurance for anything you cannot afford to lose. Also take care to check your hotel and restaurant bills thoroughly. The practice of "padding" checks for confused foreigners is quite common.

Emergency Numbers

Numbers function nationwide

Police... 116
Fire 115
All services 26811

Health

General health has improved since the 1959 revolution. Malaria, diphtheria, poliomyelitis, tuberculosis, and tetanus have been almost eradicated. There has been a decline in health standards, however, since the Soviets cut off their subsidies to Cuba in 1991.

Use bottled water. Never drink tap water or even use it for brushing your teeth. Do not use ice cubes except in first-class establishments. Avoid raw vegetables and fruit unless they've been washed in a chlorine solution. Diarrhea is common for travelers; so, come prepared with medication. Avoid eating at street stalls until you acclimate to the Cuban weather and diet.

Cuban medical services are well distributed in both urban and rural area. Once considered to have some of the best medical care and doctors in the world, Cuba now struggles to maintain health standards. Medicines are in short supply and facilities are poorly maintained. Stock your personal medical kit with any prescription drugs you require and bring basic items as well. Cuban doctors are competent but have few resources to work with nowadays. Consequently, they should be used for emergency services only. All travelers should have medical insurance and long-term business travelers may wish to purchase evacuation policies. Most good hotels have access to multi-lingual doctors; otherwise, contact your embassy or consulate.

For more information on medical centers, including phone numbers, please see the "Business Centers" section at the end of this chapter.

INTERNAL TRAVEL

AIR

Cubana Air operates regularly scheduled services linking most main towns.

Advance reservations are essential, as the number of flights is limited.

TAXI

Taxis are available but hard to come by, expensive, and very old. Look for taxis marked "dollar tourist taxi" since those marked "peso taxis" are only available to citizens of Cuba. Cabs can be ordered through the hotel. Most new taxis have meters which start at US$1. Be sure to negotiate a price before leaving if your cab has no meter.

AUTO

Cars can be rented in Havana, but it is an expensive procedure. Bicycles are easily available for rental.

Hired cars with drivers are probably a better bet for short-term business visitors. Keep in mind, however, that this service is government controlled and that the drivers are essentially government employees. Do not discuss sensitive or confidential information in front of them. Also note that auto rental is a "cash and carry" proposition.

TRAIN

The main railway route is between Havana and Santiago de Cuba, running twice daily. Some of the trains on the route are outfitted with air conditioning and also offer refreshments. There are also some through trains between Havana and other towns.

Whether the Cuban passenger train service is suitable for business use is a judgement that the individual traveler will have to make.

BUSES & TRAMS

Buses, minibuses and shared taxis are plentiful in Havana, and operate on a low flat fare basis. The buses are frequent, often crowded, somewhat lacking in comfort and a little threadbare.

WATER TRAVEL

As a Caribbean island, Cuba has an extensive coastal water travel system. It is, however, heavily controlled by the government for security reasons. Business travelers can arrange boat transport to numerous cities on the island. The costs are reasonable, but the travel is slow. It is best to use boat transport only when no other means is available.

TRAVEL ASSISTANCE

Infotour Main Office
General travel information and hotel availability; Palacio del Turismo, Obispo 252, Habana Vieja; tel: 61-1544.

Havanatur
Calle 2, No. 7 e/1 y 3
Miramar, Municpo Play
Havana
tel: 33-2273.

Ministerio de Turismo
Calle 19, No 710
Entre Paseo y A
Vedado, Havana
tel: (7) 330 545; fax: (7) 334 086
email: promo@mintur.mit.cma.net

Empresa de Turismo Internacional (Cubatur)
Calle 23, F157
Entre Noveda y Calzada
El Vedado,Havana
tel: (7) 244 155
fax: (7) 243 526, 243 530

National Tourist Office; Cuban Tourist Board
Avercida Malecon y Calle G, Vaedado, Habana 4;
tel: (7) 32-0571; Telex: 511238.

Communications
DIALING CODES IN CUBA

International country code: [53]
Selected city codes: Havana (7), Santiago de Cuba Santia (226)

Dialing Cuba from Overseas
To call a Cuban number from overseas, dial your country's international dialing code, then 53 (the country code for Cuba), then the city code, and finally the number you are trying to reach.

Assistance Numbers
International Operator (U.S.) 119
Information (daytime) 113
Information (night) 60-7110

CALLING WITHIN CUBA

Local Calls
Local calls are best made from the hotel.

Long Distance Calls
To call within Cuba, dial area code + number. If not from the hotel, domestic calls can be placed from telecommunication centers (centro telefonico) in Havana or Varadero.

International Calls
The best bet for direct dialing is from a hotel where the operator will have the available codes: 88 + country code + area code + number. Hotels will implement a surcharge of up to 20 percent on the already high overseas rates. Collect calls are not allowed unless you are dialing from a private home.

International calls can also be placed from the telecommunications centers that offer two types of phones (domestic and international); however, these do not allow credit card or collect calling. Calls may cost from US$2 to $2.50 a minute.

You may reach an AT&T operator from Guantanamo Bay only.
AT&T Direct 935

PAY PHONES

Public Telephones
Public phones are available, but many don't take phone cards.

Calling Cards
Phone cards are available for public phones, or from the hotel desk for the hotel's own card phones.

CELLULAR PHONES
Cellular service in Cuba is limited, but does exist. Cubacel provides AMPS analog service for the island.

Note: Your home country cell phone may not work in this country. If not, we recommend that you rent an international cell phone *before* you leave home. A major US-based cell phone rental provider is **IMC WorldCell**. For information see "International Cell Phone Rentals" on page 14.

CALL BACK
You can (potentially) save significant sums when calling in Cuba by using a call back service. For a list of callback services, please refer to the "Communications" section in the *Global Road Warrior* Introduction.

Fees for call back services vary widely, depending on the company and the type of service required. Be sure to check with these companies

PHONE JACKS

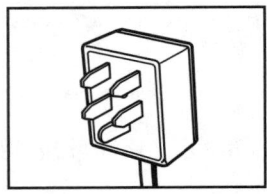

Plug adaptors are available through **iGo Corporation.** (See "Electrical and Telephone Adaptors" on page 19.)

FAX
Fax machines are very difficult to find in Cuba. Some top-end hotels may have them.

POSTAL SERVICES
Letters to North America can take two weeks, and to Europe packages have taken several weeks to arrive. Send all mail from Cuba by air mail. You can acquire stamps from your hotel or from Havana's main post office.

TELEGRAMS
Telegram services are the most popular form of communication in Cuba, considering the poor telephone and postal services. Telegrams can be sent from all post offices in Havana and RCA offices in major hotels.

Business Services
COURIER SERVICE

UTISA S.A./DHL; Avenida 1ra y 42, Miramar Playa, Diudad de la Habana; tel: (7) 24-1876.

OFFICE RENTAL

World Trade Center; Calle 21 No. 661, Plaza, P.O. Box 4237, Havana; tel: (7) 31-1160; fax: (7) 33-3042; email: correo@camara.com.cu; website: http:// www.camaracuba.com.

SECRETARIAL SERVICES

World Trade Center; Calle 21 No. 661, Plaza, P.O. Box 4237, Havana; tel: (7) 31-1160; fax: (7) 33-3042; email: correo@camara.com.cu; website: http:// www.camaracuba.com.

TRANSLATION SERVICES

World Trade Center; Calle 21 No. 661, Plaza, P.O. Box 4237, Havana; tel: (7) 31-1160; fax: (7) 33-3042; email: correo@camara.com.cu; website: http://www.camaracuba.com.

Electrical

Current
110/120 volts AC, 60Hz

ELECTRIC PLUGS

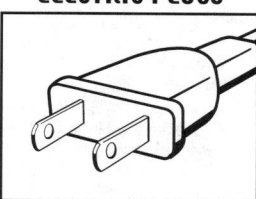

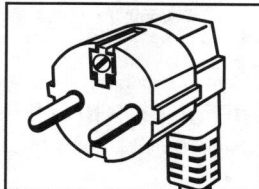

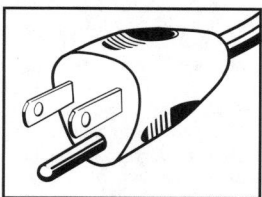

American style 2-pin plugs are the most popular, although some top-end hotels may use round 2-pin plugs.

Plug adaptors are available through **iGo Corporation.** (See "Electrical and Telephone Adaptors" on page 19.)

Technical Support

HARDWARE/SOFTWARE VENDOR SUPPORT

Compaq/Digital; (General U.S.) tel: (281) 518-2000; (in Switzerland) tel: [41] (22) 709-5330; fax: [41] (22) 709-5391 (Geneva); tel: [41] (1) 801-2507; fax: [41] (1) 801-2172 (Zurich); http://www.compaq.com/.

Dell; (in the U.S.) tel: [1] (512) 338-4400; fax: [1] (512) 728-3330; (in Germany) tel: [49] (61) 039-710; (Dell- Europe) tel: [44] (134) 474-8000; http://www.dell.com/.

IBM; (in Colombia) tel: [57] (1) 623-0111; fax: [57] (1) 257-9839; (U.S. Main Office) tel: [1] (914) 765-1900; fax: [1] (914) 288-1147; (in the U.S.) tel: [1] (919) 517-2800; (in Switzerland) tel: [41] (22) 310-0418 (in French); http://www.ibm.com/.

Microsoft; (In Costa Rica) tel: [506] tel: 280-5100; fax: [506] 280-5070; (in the U.S.) [1] (425) 635-7222; (in Switzerland) tel: [41] (848) 858-868; fax [41] (1) 831-0869; http://www.microsoft.com.

NEC; (in the U.S.) [1] (916) 388-0101 (Main Switchboard); (in Germany) tel: [49] (18) 0524- 1212; tel:[49] (89) 3160-1233; fax: [49] (89) 3160- 1613 (Floppy Disk and Hard Drive); tel: [49] (89) 9627-4233; fax: [49] (89) 9627-4613 (All Other Products); http://www.nec.com/.

Internet Connection

HOW TO CONNECT

Connecting to AOL and Compuserve in Cuba is similar to using it when traveling outside your own area code. See the introductory section for detailed information on connecting to your account through a different phone number.

America Online
Numbers are available at keyword *international*. Be sure to get several local numbers before leaving.

There are no direct access numbers for America OnLine in Cuba. Users will have to pay international rates to use the service.

Compuserve
Numbers are available at keyword *Go International*. The Compuserve Web-site also has a great deal of information, at http://www.compuserve.com.

There are no direct access numbers for Compuserve in Cuba. Users will have to pay international rates to use the service.

Independent Service Providers
Many independent service providers offer discounts if you are only in town for a couple of days.

Fiberlink Communications Corp.; [1] (714) 788-2904 (although based in the United States, Fiberlink has Cuban connection numbers).

VPM Enterprises; tel: [1] (916) 983-9876; toll free in the U.S.: 1-800-321-0221; fax: [1] (916) 983-4375; email: sales@vpm.com; website: http://www.vpm.com/.

Business Culture

GREETINGS AND COURTESIES

Men usually shake hands with women and each other, although women seldom shake hands with other women. Titles are commonly used, especially "Doctor" and "Professor." Business cards printed in both Spanish and English are the norm, although most businesspeople do speak English. Cubans love to entertain, and will not hesitate to invite visiting business associates to a meal at their home or in a restaurant.

DECISION MAKING

Foreign businesspeople are expected to be on time, but Cubans can be more relaxed about scheduling. It is best to have a prior appointment, but many Cuban businesspeople will accept a cold call. Authority is narrowly concentrated and actual decisions are almost always made at a high level—more often than not at a government agency. However, cultivate your Cuban business relationships; they will be invaluable in cutting through the bureaucracy and getting a deal accomplished.

WOMEN

Women are well-educated and respected in the business environment, although most managerial positions are still held by men. Foreign businesswomen should experience few problems in business, generally experiencing greater acceptance than do local women. Women may dress as they please; trousers are acceptable, though shorts are not.

Cuba

BUSINESS ATTIRE

Tropical weight (the very lightest due to the extreme heat) suits or sports coats and trousers are expected of men for business dealings.

Business Centers
Havana

CITY VIEW

Although not touched very much by the wars and revolutions, the city and many of its structures are still run down and in need of repair, much like the former Soviet Union. However, it remains a cultural center and carries whispers of history in its cracks and its myriad of 1950's cars roving the streets. Clubs and cinemas and a few new resorts now endow the city with a modern cultural twist along the edges.

AIRPORT

International José Martí Airport to City Center

The airport lies 11 miles (18 km.) from downtown Havana. Bus and taxi services are available 24 hours a day. A taxi ride into Havana will cost approximately US$15, and into Varadero about US$10.

Airline Numbers

Air Canada	(7) 7-49-11
Air Cubana	(7) 33-4949
Aerocaribbean	(7) 33-4543
Aeroflot	(7) 33-3200
Aerolíneas Argentinas	(7) 33-3730
AOM French Airlines	(7) 33-3997
Condor	(7) 33-3524
Iberia	(7) 33-5041
Lasca	(7) 33-3114
Ladeco	(7) 33-3252
LTU International Airlines	(7) 33-3254
Martinair	(7) 33-4364
Mexicana de Avioacón	(7) 33-3531
TAAG	(7) 33-3527
Viasa	(7) 33-3228

HOTELS

Top-end

Château Miramar; Ave. 1ra. between 60 and 70, Miramar; Cuidad del la Habana; tel: (7) 33-0225; fax: (7) 33-0224; smaller hotel; convenient for business travelers; personal service.

Meliá Cohiba; Ave. Paseo between 1A and 3A, Vedado; tel: (7) 33-36-36; fax: (7) 33-13-33; 11 meeting rooms and banquet halls; rooms standard with satellite t.v., telephone, minibar.

Hotel Nacional; Calle O, Esq 21, Vedado; tel: (7) 33-35-64/67, fax: (7) 33-50-54, 33-31-09; business oriented; cafeteria; medical services; shops; snack bar; pools; tennis; restaurants; ballroom for 200; meeting rooms; business services.

Victoria; Calle 19 at M; tel: (7) 33-35-10; fax: (7) 33-3109; business oriented; social room; pool; shops; car rental; currency exchange; restaurant.

Expensive

Inglaterra; tel: (7) 33 85 93, telex 51-2222; fax: (7) 33-82-54; restaurant; cafeteria; grill; shops; colonial style.

Plaza Hotel; Ignacio Agramonte #267, exq. Neptuno, Habana Vieja; tel: (7) 33-8583; fax: (7) 33-8591/92; snack bar, solarium; shops; rental cars.

Comodoro; Ave. 3ra. Esq A, Calle 62, Miramar, Cuidad de la Habana; tel: (7) 33-2011; fax: (7) 33-2368; business oriented; medical services; 3 restaurants; cafeteria; pools; rental car; laundry; superior service.

Copacabana; Ave. Pimera #4404, entre Calle 44 y 46, Playa, La Habana; reservations: (7) 33-0238; tel: (7) 33-1037 and 33-1263; fax: (7) 33-28-46; new; full service; water sports; 2 restaurants; beach resort; views.

Neptuno; Av. 3 at 70th; tel: (7) 29-08-81; fax: (7) 33-23-43; west of city; seaside location.

Habana Libre; Calle L e/23 y 25, Vedado, Ciudad de la Habana; tel: (7) 33-4011; fax: (7) 33-3141; largest hotel in Havana; former Hilton; centrally located.

Hotel Atlantico; Ave. Terrazas, Santa Maria del Mar, Habana del Este, Ciudad de la Habana; tel: (6) 33-5502/0523; fax: (6) 80-2646; reservations: (6) 33-0238; 3 conference rooms; video rooms; grill; rental car; medical; restaurant; cafeteria.

Hotel Sevilla; Trocadero #55 entre Prada y Zuleta, Habana Vieja; tel: (7) 33-8560; fax: (7) 33-8582; traditional hotel; renovated; pool; fitness room; sauna.

Presidente; Calzada and G; tel: (7) 32-75-21; fax: (7) 33-37-53; pool, gardens; restaurants; 1930's style.

MEDICAL CENTERS

Hospital Cira Garcia; Calle 30, Esq. 4, Miramar, Havana; tel: 33-2516.

Hospital Hermanos Almeijeiras; central Havana, San Lazaro and Belascoaía; tel: 70-7721.

AUTO RENTAL

Note: Also consider hiring a car and driver as an alternative to rentals.

If planning to rent a car, be sure to reserve well in advance due to car shortages, especially during high season.

Havanautos; José Martí Airport; Terminal 1, tel: 45-21-75; Terminal 2, tel: 54-24-13; Miramar, Complejo Ibero Star Tritón-Neptuno, tel: 33-29-21; Vedado Hotel, tel: 33-3484.

Cubanacán; José Martí Airport, Terminal 2 (no phone); Miramar, Hotel Comodoro; tel: 33-1706 or 22-5551, ext. 181.

Infotour; Palacio del Tourismo, Calle Obispo, Havana; tel: 61-1544.

WORLD TRADE CENTER

Chamber of Commerce of the Republic of Cuba-Havana WTC
Calle 21 No. 661, Plaza
P.O. Box 4237
Havana, Cuba
tel: (7) 30-4436
fax: (7) 33-3042
email: correo@camara.com.cu
website: http://www.camaracuba.com

Czech Republic

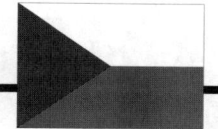

At a Glance

THE PEOPLE

Population .... 10,280,513 (July 1999 est.)
Growth Rate .... -0.01% (1999 est.)
Life Expectancy .... 74.35 years (born 1999)
Infant Mortality ... 6.67 deaths/1,000 live births (1999 est.)
deaths/1,000 live births (1999 es

Ethnic Composition

Czech 94.4%
Slovak.. 3%
Other 2.6%

Religious Composition

Roman Catholic.. 39.2%
Protestant 4.6%
Orthodox... 3%
Other and non-affiliated... 13.4%
Declared atheist 39.8%

Languages Spoken

Czech (official), Slovak

Education and Literacy

Education is free through the university level. The adult literacy rate is 99 percent.

Labor Force

Total: 5,124,000
By occupation: services 50.9%, industry 42.2%, agriculture 6.9%

THE ECONOMY

The Czech Republic was one of the many eastern European countries that had been a satellite of the U.S.S.R. communist regime. Once free of this influence the Czechs cast off socialism and went hammer and tongs into the free markets. They also cast off their former brethren in Slovakia in the process; GDP growth was double-digit and foreign investment flowed in freely. The initial success of the new Czech economy served as an example to other emerging economies for most of the 1990s. An economic downturn in 1997 brought growth to a halt, however, and the government soon found itself backing an austerity program. Foreign investment still finds the Czech economy attractive and the republic's recent admission to NATO is seen as a preface to eventual E.U. membership. GDP began to grow at a respectable rate (2.7 percent) in 1998 and better conditions are predicted for 1999 and the early 21st century.

Exports .... US$23.8 billion (f.o.b., 1998)
Imports .... US$26.8 billion (f.o.b., 1998)
Total GDP .... US$116.7 billion (1998 est.)
GDP Per Capita .... US$11,300 (1998 est.)
Unemployment .... 7% (1998 est.)
Inflation Rate 10.7% (1998)

Top Export Partners

E.U., Central Europe (CEFTA), the CIS countries

Top Import Partners

E.U., Central Europe (CEFTA), the CIS countries

Top Exports

Manufactured goods, machinery and transport equipment, chemicals, raw materials

Top Imports

Machinery and transport equipment, manufactured goods, chemicals, raw materials and fuel oil

BUSINESS WORKWEEK

Offices

Monday to Friday 8a.m. or 9a.m. to 5:00p.m.

Banks

Monday to Friday 8a.m. to 3:30 or 4:30p.m.

Government

Monday to Friday 9a.m. to 5:00p.m.

Retail

Monday to Friday 9a.m. to 6p.m.
Saturday 9a.m. to noon (Food stores open between 6 and 7a.m. and close between 6 and 7p.m. Some department stores stay open until 8p.m.)
Note: Many small shops, offices, and those government services in rural areas often close for an hour at noon.

HOLIDAYS

New Year's Day...January 1
Easter Monday ....April 5*
Labor Day..May1
Day of the Apostles St. Cyril and
St. Methodius ....July 5
Anniversary of the Martyrdom of Jan Hus ....July 6
Independence Day ....October 28
Christmas ....December 24-25
St. Stephen's Day...December 26
* Date may vary by year

CLIMATE

Seasons

The Czech Republic has a temperate climate with four distinct seasons. The republic has cold winters with heavy snows and mild summers with frequent thunderstorms. In July temperatures are about 21°C (70°F), but in January lows average about -1°C (30°F).

Regions

The western region enjoys a moderate climate, with overcast winters and cool summers. The east of the country has a more Mediterranean climate, with mild, wet winters and warm summers. The eastern, northern, and southern hills experience the most snow during the winter months.

Money & Banking

Currency

The currency of the Czech Republic is the Czech Koruna (Kc).

Denominations

The Czech Koruna comes in coin denominations of Kc50, 20, 10, 5, 2, and 1, and 50, 20 and 10 halers; and banknotes of Kc20, 50, 100, 200, 500, 1,000, and 5,000.

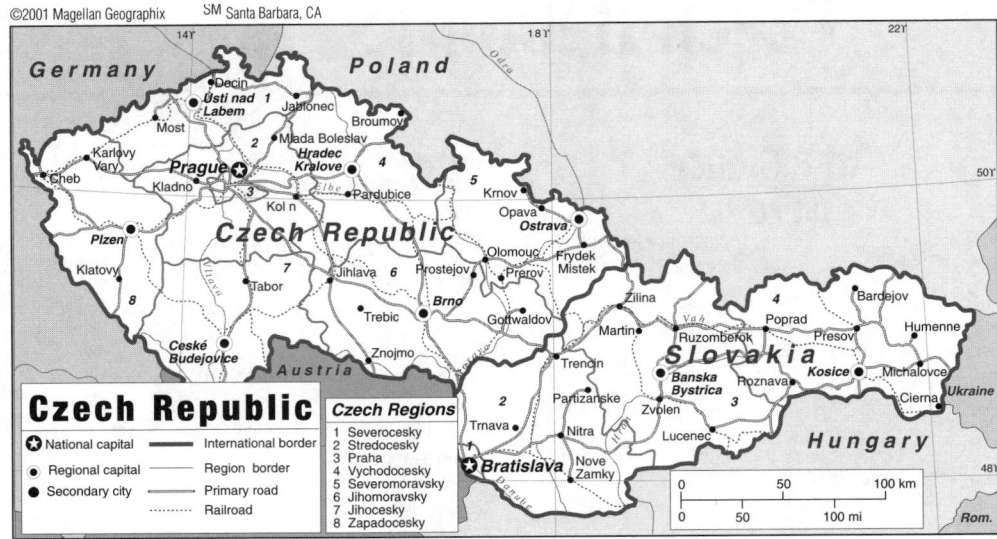

©2001 Magellan Geographix ᴿᴹ Santa Barbara, CA

Czech Republic

⊗ National capital	──── International border
● Regional capital	──── Region border
● Secondary city	──── Primary road
	········· Railroad

Czech Regions
1 Severocesky
2 Stredocesky
3 Praha
4 Vychodocesky
5 Severomoravsky
6 Jihomoravsky
7 Jihocesky
8 Zapadocesky

Traveler's Checks and Credit Cards

Traveler's checks and most major currencies can be exchanged at banks, exchange kiosks, and main hotels in Prague, as well as at international airports. There is no black market in currency now that the Koruna is fully convertible. Service fees are lowest at banks and their exchange rates are more favorable.

American Express, Visa, Diner's Club, and MasterCard are accepted in most up-market places in Prague and most other Czech cities. Cash advance on credit cards can also be obtained at main banks in the capital. ATMs (*bankomat*) are widely available and, along with credit cards, receive the most favorable rates of exchange. Wise visitors make most large purchases with their credit cards in the Czech Republic.

Visitors cannot reconvert currency when leaving the country unless they have receipts for the original conversion, so keep all evidence of exchange; this is another good reason to use credit cards. Only very rural areas will require cash for every purchase.

Travel
VISA AND PASSPORT

A passport that is valid for eight months minimum at the date of visa application, and for at least two months after the expiration date of the visa, is required of all except for citizens of Germany, who may enter if in possession of a national ID card.

Visas are required of all except nationals of the following countries:

- U.K. (except those holding passports with the notation '"British Overseas Citizen," of whom a visa is required), Canada, and Slovak Republic for stays of six months maximum
- Other E.U. countries for stays of three months maximum
- Andorra, Argentina, Bulgaria, Chile, Croatia, Cuba, Cyprus, Estonia, Hungary, Iceland, Israel, Japan, Korea (Rep. of), Latvia, Lithuania, Malaysia, Malta, Mexico, Monaco, New Zealand, Norway, Poland, San Marino, Singapore, Slovenia, Switzerland, Uruguay, U.S., and Vatican City for stays ranging between one and three months
- Belarus, Kazakhstan, Kyrgyzstan, Moldova, Romania, Russian Federation, Turkmenistan and Ukraine for stays of varying length, depending on individual circumstances. Travelers from these countries should contact a Czech embassy prior to traveling for details.

Any visitor who does not need a visa may, nonetheless, be required to substantiate that they are have at least US$25 per day for the duration of their stay.

Business visitors will need a suitable visa, which requires an invitation from a Czech company or government official. Only basic business research can be conducted on a tourist visa.

Single-entry and Multiple-entry visas are valid for three or six months, respectively, from the date of issue. Usually, Single-entry visas qualify for an extension.

Transit and Double-transit visas are also issued; these are valid for 48 hours per entry.

All travelers must have onward tickets, valid travel documents, and sufficient funds. Registration in each town is no longer enforced, but the law is still on the books. Consider it best to check with your hotel operator about this procedure. Carry copies of your visa and passport to leave at hotel offices.

Generally, only one working day is required for visa application processing.

DEPARTURE FORMALITIES

Airport departure taxes are included in the ticket price.
Note: The export of antiques is prohibited.

CUSTOMS ENTRY (PERSONAL)

The following items may be brought into the Czech Republic without incurring customs duty taxes:

- Tobacco: 200 cigarettes or 100 cigarillos or 50 cigars or 250g tobacco
- Alcohol: 1 liter of spirits and 2 liters of wine (only half the above mentioned quantities for stays of 2 days or less)
- Other: 500ml of perfume or 250ml eau de toilette
- Gifts up to Kc3000
  Note: All items of value, such as cameras and tents,

must be declared at Customs on entry to enable export clearance on departure. The export of antiques is prohibited. Firearms can be imported if accompanied by a Firearms Permit issued by a Czech diplomatic mission abroad. In this case up to 1000 shot cartridges and 50 bullets can be imported free of duty.

Prohibited or Restricted
• All forms of pornographic literature

IMMUNIZATION
No immunizations are necessary for visitors from any country unless arriving from an infected area. Tetanus and hepatitis A inoculations are advised for those traveling to rural areas or on extended stays.

TIPPING
Taxi
Rounding up the fare by Kc10 or adding a 10 percent tip for good service is standard.

Porters
Porters at first-class hotels and transport depots receive Kco.50 (50 halers) per bag.

Hotels
Hotels add service charges to the bill where applicable, and no additional tip is necessary.

Restaurants
When service charges are not applied, a 10 percent tip is standard. It is also common to buy your bartender or host a drink, especially if you have been engaging them in conversation.

EMERGENCY INFORMATION
Police and Crime
Crime is on the increase in the Czech Republic, especially in more urban settings. Foreign business travelers are often assumed to be carrying lots of valuables. Take basic precautions. Avoid flashy displays of wealth, and dress and behave conservatively. Leave most of your cash, traveler's checks, jewelry, and your camera in your hotel safe. Carry photocopies of your passport instead of the original. Carry cash in a money belt, and use credit cards or traveler's checks for most of your transactions. Laptops and briefcases will require additional security. Do not leave valuables in cars or on tables in cafés. While Czech crime is nowhere near as big a problem as it is in western European cities, business people should still take special precautions at night in urban areas.

Emergency Numbers
Numbers function nationwide although operators have limited language skills.
General emergency 158
Medical emergency 155
Fire 150
Towing service 154

Health
Never drink tap water or use it for brushing your teeth, and avoid ice cubes except in outlets where you can be assured of potability. Even most Czechs use bottled water if only to avoid the chlorinated flavor of local tap water.

Most dining establishments abide by good health standards, but street stalls should be avoided. Don't eat raw vegetables and fruit unless they've been washed in a chlorine solution. Diarrhea is common for travelers who are unaccustomed to the new diet and water so bring proper medication.

There is a national Health Service that runs the medical system, but it is far from free—even for locals. Only emergency service is provided free to foreigners. A good travel insurance plan is advisable. Czech doctors are skilled, but their facilities are not good by western standards. Some long-term visitors may consider an evacuation policy in the event of serious illness. Most good hotels have access to multi-lingual doctors; otherwise, contact your embassy or consulate.

INTERNAL TRAVEL
AIR
Czech Airlines (CSA) provides an extensive domestic air service. There are regular flights between Prague and Ostrava, Brno, Karlovy Vary, as well as routes linking these destinations with one another. For more information:
website .... www.csa.cz/en/

TAXI
Radio-taxis provide a way to avoid "black" taxis that overcharge or pull various other stunts. Cabs should be visibly marked with an identification number and the name of the company. Inside the car, check the full price list. Some may include such oddities as a "foreign language fee". Be sure to negotiate a price and ask for a metered-printed receipt before going anywhere. Cabbies have been known to drive away with passenger luggage if not satisfied with the price at ride's end.

Within the city, or from the airport, the driver should set the meter at one. The number two setting should only be used at night, when fares double. Drivers may overcharge by setting the meter at a higher level, leaving it off all together, or by "getting lost. "

Drivers may not know (or pretend not to know) their way around, so be sure to carry directions and maps. First-time visitors should allow their hotel concierge to arrange taxi trips.
Prague Taxi Services:
AAA Taxi 6104-3399
Microlux 35-03-20
Profi 6104-5555

AUTO
Cars and motorbikes are readily available for rental in most large towns and cities through Hertz, Avis, Eurodollar, and other companies. A credit card and a valid driver's license is required (no international license needed). Local insurance is mandatory. Age limits vary by rental agency.

Highways run from Prague to Plzen, and from Podebrady to Bratislava (Slovak Republic) via Brno. Users of the Czech roadways must purchase a vignette (season ticket) costing about Kc800 for each year. A ten-day vignette is also available for a lower price.

Driving is quite orderly except in Prague, where auto use by foreigners is not advisable. Hired cars with drivers can be procured at reasonable rates and are the standard among foreign executives making short-term visits to Czech cities.

Note: Foreign tourists driving themselves are often the target of law enforcement officers hoping to exploit the many obscure rules of Czech driving. Speed limits change often and there are numerous "special equipment" requirements. Beware.

TRAIN
Much of the country is accessible by rail, as are many international destinations. A wide variety of classes can be reserved, and overnight travel to other countries is easily scheduled. Trains are a standard form of business travel; the rail lines are comfortable and efficient, and prices are quite reasonable.

Czech Republic

Train travel is a great way to meet Czech business travelers and to see a lot of the country in the process. Do make reservations in advance.

Note: 'Os' indicates slow train, 'Ex' means express, and 'R' means fast train. Czech rail lines connect to most major European systems.

Railway information .... 2422-4200.

METRO

Three different subway lines provide the quickest method to navigate Prague. Look for signs with a white 'M' that indicate a station. Trains run between 5a.m. and midnight, at two- to ten-minute intervals and operate on a flat fare basis. The metro is a much more advisable form of travel in Prague than driving a rented auto.

BUSES & TRAMS

Inter-city buses cover the areas of the country not accessible by rail. The bus system is comfortable and efficient. Local buses operate at about 1Kc per kilometer. Luggage may cost up to 6Kc to travel with you. Most cities also have a local bus system in the absence of trams.

Trams pick up where the metro leaves off, and they travel the city streets on the surface rather than beneath it. There are 21 different tram lines in Prague that reach every corner of the city. Tickets are purchased in advance at tobacconist shops or in any shop with a sign posted that reads, "*Predprodej Jizdenek*".

Trolleybuses, tramways, and municipal buses also operate in Brno, Ostrava, Plzen, and numerous other towns. Most services run from 4:30p.m. to midnight. All the cities run on flat-fare systems, and pre-purchased passes can be purchased. Tickets are punched in a machine upon entering the tram or bus. A separate ticket is needed for changing routes; expect a fine for riding without a ticket.

Blue logos on bus and tram stops indicate all-night service.

WATER TRAVEL

Navigable waterways exist in the country. The main river ports can be found in Prague, Ústí nad Labem, and Decín.

TRAVEL ASSISTANCE

For reservations and help with internal travel, contact:
Czech Tourist Authority
Vinohradská 46, PO Box 32
12041 Prague 2, Czech Republic
tel: (2) 24 25 79 59; fax: (2) 24 24 75 16
website: www.czech.cz

Essential Terms

English	Czech
Yes No	Ano Ne
Good morning Hello (daytime) Hello (evening) Hello (telephone)	Dobré ráno Dobré odpoledne Dobry vecer Dobry den
Good-bye	Na shledanou
Please	Prosím
Thank you	Dekuji
Pleased to meet you	Tesi mne ze vas poznavam
Excuse me; I'm sorry	Prominte
My name is _____	Jmenuji se ____
I don't understand	Nepozumim
Do you speak English?	Mluvite anglicky?

Communications

DIALING CODES IN THE CZECH REPUBLIC

International country code: [420]

Selected city codes: Breclav (627), Brno (5), Ceske Budejovice (38), Havirov (6994), Ostrava (69), Pilsen (19), Prague (2). Be sure to dial zero when dialing a number from within the Czech Republic.

Dialing Czech Republic from Overseas

To reach the Czech Republic from overseas, dial your country's international dialing code, then 420 (the country code for the Czech Republic), then the city code, and finally the number. If you were dialing Prague from the United States, for example, you would begin with 011, then 420, then 2 (the city code for Prague), and finally the number of the person or office you are trying to reach.

Assistance Numbers

International Information.. 0149
Domestic Information 02-121
Prague Information.. 02-120
Telephone Usage Information 0139

CALLING WITHIN THE CZECH REPUBLIC

Local Calls

Local call can be expensive from hotels. If possible, make calls from phone booths on the street, which cost Kc3 per call.

Long Distance Calls

For calls within the country and outside your city, dial the city code preceded by a zero similar to most European cities (for example, 02 for Prague). Then proceed to dial the number you are trying to reach.

International Calls

Place an international call by dialing 00 + country code + area code + number. Calls assisted by an operator will cost roughly US$2 a minute to Australia, Canada, Japan, and the U.S. International calls can be placed most conveniently from main post offices since Czech Telecom has not yet provided ample connection to international lines from regular phones, often prompting numerous attempts to dial internationally.

AT&T Direct...00-42-000-101
MCI...00-42-00-001
Sprint...00-420-87-187
Bell Canada...00-420-00-151

Public phones require a coin or card deposit first.

PAY PHONES

Public Telephones
Card Phones:

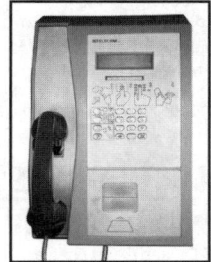

Public telephones are in booths, including kiosks for international calls. The basic rate is 3Kc.

Calling Cards
Most pay phones use calling cards, which can be purchased at newsstands, airports, rail stations, metro stations, large department stores and hotels in denominations of 50, 100, and 150.

CELLULAR PHONES

Both analog and digital service are options for cellular phone users in the Czech Republic. Radio Mobil and Eurotel Prague offer GSM digital service. Eurotel also offers NMT-450 analog service.

Note: Your home country cell phone may not work in this country. If not, we recommend that you rent an international cell phone *before* you leave home. A major US-based cell phone rental provider is **IMC WorldCell**. For information see "International Cell Phone Rentals" on page 14.

CALL BACK

You can (potentially) save significant sums when calling in Czech Republic by using a call back service. For a list of callback services, please refer to the "Communications" section in the *Global Road Warrior* Introduction.

Fees for call back services vary widely, depending on the company and the type of service required. Be sure to check with these companies before leaving to compare rates.

PHONE JACKS

Plug adaptors are available through **iGo Corporation.** (See "Electrical and Telephone Adaptors" on page 19.)

FAX

Fax service is abundant, primarily because of the problems with the mail service. Most hotels and offices have them. They are also beginning to appear in private shops.

POSTAL SERVICES

Mail service is relatively inexpensive but rarely efficient. Mail to and from North America takes about 10 days. There are separate windows for many services in post offices, make sure you're in the right one.

Business Services

BUSINESS CENTERS

ABF, A.S.; tel: (2) 20513302, 20511110-13.
Prague Hilton Atrium; tel: (2) 24841111.
Incheba; tel: (2) 24195404, 24195261.

COURIER SERVICES

Airborne Express Freight (CR S.R.O.); Areal ZPA Jinonice, Radlicka 117, CZ-158 00 Praha 5; tel: (2) 569-4232; fax: (2) 569-4277.
DHL Czech Republic: Bezecka 1, Praha 6, 16900; tel: (2) 2051-1133.
EPS (Express Parcel System/Airborne Express); Na Cihadle 4, Praha 6; tel: (2) 2431-3751; fax: (2) 2431-2829.
Messenger; Na Cihadle 51, 160 00 Prague 6; tel: (2) 311-6398.
RSE; Severozapadni 8/285; 140 00 Prague 4; tel: (2) 761-728; fax: (2) 763-249.

UPS (Czech Parcel Service); Komunardu 39, 170 00 Praha 7, Prague; tel: (2) 6671-2458, 6671-2442; fax: (2) 6671-2133.

PRINTING/COPYING

AA Nonstop; tel: (2) 421-6009.
Copy General, S.R.O.; tel: (2) 410-2227, 2310, (2) 423-0020.

TRANSLATION SERVICES

Media Market ILS S.R.O.; (2) 2317669, 2319877.

Abram,S.R.O.; tel: (2) 232-2068,7983,6117.

Agentura Jas, S.R.O.; tel: (2) 263-358, 2422-8341.

Electrical

Current

220 volts AC, 50Hz, although some parts of Prague use 110 volts.

ELECTRIC PLUGS

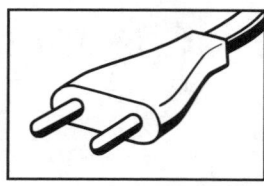

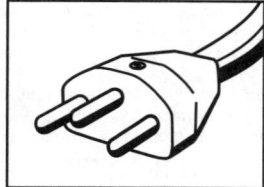

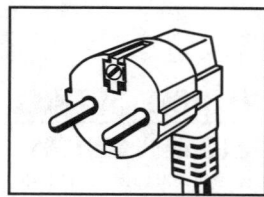

Hotels use standard international 2-pin European plugs, and lamp fittings are screw-type.

Plug adaptors are available through **iGo Corporation**. (See "Electrical and Telephone Adaptors" on page 19.)

Technical Support

HARDWARE/SOFTWARE VENDOR SUPPORT

Apple/Claris; tel: 2-611-42-424; (in Germany) tel: [49] (1) 803-5018; (in Switzerland) tel: [41] (800) 833-310; (in the U.K.) tel: [44] (990) 127-753; (in the U.S.) tel: [1] (800) 500-7078; http://www.apple.com/.

AST; (in the U.S.) tel: [1] (817) 232-9824 (International Technical Support); (in Ireland) tel: [353] (61) 492-222; (in the U.S.) tel: [1] (949) 727-4141; http://www.ast.com/.

Compaq/Digital; (in Switzerland) tel: [41] (22) 709-5330; fax: [41] (22) 709-5391 (Geneva); tel: [41] (1) 801-2507; fax: [41] (1) 801-2172 (Zurich); (General U.S.) tel: (281) 518-2000; http://www.compaq.com/.

Dell; (in Germany) tel: [49] (61) 039-710; (Dell- Europe) tel: [44] (134) 474-8000; (in the U.S.) tel: [1] (512) 338-4400; fax: [1] (512) 728-3330; http://www.dell.com/.

Filemaker/Claris; (in Germany) tel: [49] (180) 525-8166 (Info-line); fax: [49] (180) 567-2233; tel: [49] (180) 523-6423; (in the U.S.) tel: [1] (800) 965-9090; http://www.claris.com/.

Hewlett Packard; tel: (2) 471 7321;(in Switzerland) tel: [41] (22) 780-8111; (in the U.S.) tel: [1] (408) 246-4300; http://www.hp.com/.

IBM; tel: (2) 671-06111; fax: (2) 671-06041; (in Germany) tel: [49] (711) 78-50; fax: [49] (711) 785-3511; (in Switzerland) tel: [41] (22) 310-0418 (in French); (U.S. Main Office) tel: [1] 914-765-1900; (in the U.S.) tel: [1] (919) 517-2800; http://www.ibm.com/.

Microsoft; tel: (2) 6119-7111; fax: (2) 6119-7100; (2) 2150-3222; tel: (2) 2150-3222 (Technical Support); (in Germany) tel: [49] (89) 31-760; fax: [49] (89) 3176-1000; tel: [49] (89) 3176-1199; (in Switzerland) tel: [41] (848) 858-868; fax [41] (1) 831-0869; (in the U.S.) [1] (425) 635-7222; http://www.microsoft.com/.

NEC; (in Germany) tel: [49] (18) 0524- 1212; tel:[49] (89) 3160-1233; fax: [49] (89) 3160- 1613 (Floppy Disk and Hard Drive); tel: [49] (89) 9627-4233; fax: [49] (89) 9627-4613 (All Other Products); (in the U.S.) [1] (916) 388-0101 (Main Switchboard); http://www.nec.com/.

Toshiba; (in Germany) tel: [49] (2131) 158-319; fax: [49] (2131) 158-558; (in Switzerland) tel: [41] (1) 946-0777; fax: [41] (1) 946-0807; (in Ireland) tel: [44] (193) 282-8828; (in the U.S.) [1] (949) 583-3000 (Corporate Headquarters); http://www.toshiba.com/.

Internet Connection

HOW TO CONNECT

Connecting to AOL and Compuserve in the Czech Republic is similar to using it when traveling outside your own area code. See the introductory section for detailed information on connecting to your account through a different phone number.

America Online

Numbers are available at keyword *international*. Be sure to get several local numbers before leaving. AOL's GlobalNet service charges US$6 an hour in addition to the usual charges. Go to keyword *access* (a free area) and download the software.

Access: Brno (5) 4124- 8090; Ceske Budejovice (38) 635-8291; Hradec Kralove (49) 612-093; Liberec (48) 510-9416; Olomouc (68) 524-3656; Ostrava (69) 212-563; Plzen (19) 745-6995; Prague (2) 2481-5281; Ruzyne Prague Airport (2) 2011-3739; Zlin (67) 721-9831.

Compuserve

Numbers are available at keyword *Go International*. The Compuserve Web-site also has a great deal of information, at http://www.compuserve.com.

Access: Prague (2) 2481-5281; Ruzyne Prague Airport (2) 2011-3739.

Independent Service Providers

Many independent service providers offer discounts if you are only in town for a couple of days.

INICIA, s.r.o.; tel: (2) 2030-4050; email: info@ini.cz; http://www.ini.cz/.

Luko Czech-Net; tel: (2) 2038-5111; fax: (2) 2038-5112; email: info@czech.net; http://www.czech.net/.

Video Online; tel: (2) 2184-4333; fax: (2) 2184-4335; email: info@vol.cz; http://www.vol.cz/.

zlin.net; tel: (67) 761-9111; fax: (67) 32-673; email: zlin.net@zln.cz; http://www.zln.cz/index.html.CP1250.

Czech Republic

Business Culture

GREETINGS AND COURTESIES

Czechs typically greet foreigners warmly. Shake hands with everyone you first meet in the Czech Republic, even children. It is customary to shake hands again on your departure. However, a man usually waits for women and older people to extend their hands first. Czechs also commonly greet others with "How do you do?" It is polite to use titles when greeting Czechs.

DECISION MAKING

Many Czechs have adopted the German propensity for slow, methodical decision making. Patience is essential. Foreign businesspeople should be prepared to make several trips to the country before any decision is finalized. As business regulations are in a state of flux, it's important to hire a local business lawyer; don't depend on your Czech associates or joint-partner for legal clarifications. Czech contact with foreigners was restricted until fairly recently, so it may take some time to establish a close business relationship. A price-conscious people, Czechs will require generous credit terms.

MEETINGS

Prior appointments are mandatory, but long-range ones may not be necessary in this new business climate. Two to three weeks should suffice. Czech businesspeople are punctual and they expect foreign associates to be, also. English and German are commonly used as the languages of commerce; however, many old enough to be in positions of power will not have studied English, so expect to hire a translator. And it's a good idea to have instruction manuals and the like translated into Czech. Presentations should be detailed and thorough. Proposals should be competitive.

Business cards will be exchanged. If your company has been in existence for a while, note its founding date on your card, along with any university degree above a bachelor's level you've earned. (Education is highly respected.)

Expect to engage in casual conversation before conducting business; it's acceptable to ask about your counterpart's family. Strong, pre-sweetened Turkish coffee may be served. "Power" breakfasts are rare, but business lunches are increasingly popular, with business being discussed before or after the meal, but not during it. Insist on paying only if the meeting was your idea.

WOMEN

Because they are viewed as a novelty, foreign women often have more success in business than Czech women. Women make tremendous contributions to the Czech economy, composing more than 47 percent of the Czech Republic's labor force, although most of their jobs are entry level. There is a significant inequity in wages, favoring men.

BUSINESS ATTIRE

Czechs generally follow conservative patterns of dress. Conservative suits (dark, with ties and white shirts) are usually worn by businessmen. Women's business attire consists of dark skirts and dresses. It is best to be discreet as expensive dress is still not possible for many. However, because life under the Communist regime was restrictive, some Czech businesspeople celebrate their newly found freedom by wearing trendy European fashions. Note that Czechs dress up for cultural events; to not do so is frowned upon.

Business Centers
Prague

CITY VIEW

Prague was one of the first cities of eastern Europe to become a tourist attraction. Now firmly entrenched as a foreigner's mecca, prices follow suit. But for the expense, one has the privilege of viewing a historical gem in Prague, some of its buildings over 900 years old. The center is a small area filled with ancient structures. Farther out lie the shops and cafes. Prague is also the home of tremendous nightlife, with theaters and nightclubs seemingly everywhere.

AIRPORT

Ruzyne Airport to City Center

The airport lies 11 miles (18 km.) from Prague, and about 30 minutes away. There are bus, coach, and taxi services available. Czech Airlines provides a shuttle service to the major hotels between 7:30a.m. and 9:30p.m. for a fee of Kc60 (US$2.30). A cab will cost roughly Kc450 to 550 (US$18 to $22). If traveling by day, be sure the meter is set at 1 rather than 2 (the nighttime setting), or your fare will cost double.

Airline Numbers

Aeroflot	232-33-33
Air Algerie	2422-9110
Air Canada	231-2675
Air France	2422-7164
Air India	2421-2474
Alitalia	2481-0079
Austrian Airlines	231-18-72
Balkan Bulgarian Airways	26-90-82
British Airways	232-90-20
Centennial Airlines	36-63-27
CSA	2010-4111
Delta	2423-2258
El Al	2421-7349
Finnair	2421-1986
KLM	2422-8678
LOT	231-75-24
Lufthansa	2481-1007
Malev	2481-2671
SAS	2421-4749
Sabena	2011-4323
Swissair	2481-2111
Varig	52-75-75

HOTELS

Top-end

Diplomat; Evropska 15, Prague 6; tel: (2) 2439-4111; fax: (2) 2439-4215; near airport; restaurant; business service center; secretarial service; conference rooms; fitness center; sauna; pool.

Grand Hotel Bohemia; tel: (2) 2480-4111; fax: (2) 232-9545; elegant meeting facilities; efficient staff; city center.

Hotel Savoy; Keplerova ul. 6; Prague 1; tel: (2) 2430-2430; fax: (2) 2430-2128; located on castle hill; conference rooms (up to 35); business center; fitness room.

Inter-Continental Praha; Namesti Curieovych 43-5; tel: (2) 2488-1111; fax: (2) 2481-1216; city center; restaurant; conference facilities; secretarial service; corporate rates; fitness; sauna; pool; whirlpool.

Palace; Panska 12, Prague 1; tel: (2) 2409-3111; fax: (2)

Czech Republic

2422-1240; city center; restaurant; conference facility (up to 50); secretarial service; corporate rates; sauna; US$280.

Renaissance Prague; V Celnici 7; tel: (2) 2182-2100; fax: (2) 2182-2200; city center; restaurant; conference facilities (up to 240); secretarial service; corporate rates; fitness; sauna; pool; US$230.

Expensive

Best Western Hotel Bila Labut; Biskupska 9; tel: (2) 2439-4111; fax: (2) 232-2905; email: cchotels@login.cz; city center; restaurant; secretarial service; corporate rates; fitness; massage; sauna; whirlpool; CZ2500.

City Hotel Morán; tel: (2) 2491-5208; fax: (2) 297533.

Harmony; Na Porici 31; tel: (2) 232-0016; fax: (2) 231-0009; city center; restaurants; corporate rates.

Kampa; Vsehrdova 16, Prague 1; tel: (2) 2451-0409; fax: (2) 2451-0377.

Mövenpick Prague; Mozartova 26/1; tel: (2) 5715-1111; fax: (2) 5715-3131; city suburb; restaurant; conference facilities (up to 350); secretarial service; corporate rates.

Pension U Raka; Cerninska 10, 118 00 Prague 1; tel: (2) 351453, (2) 2051-1100; fax: (2) 353074 or (2) 2051-0511; rustic decor; helpful staff.

Prague Hilton-Atrium; Pobrezni 1, Prague 8; tel: (2) 2484-1111; www.hilton.com; business service center; conference hall (up to 1,350); meeting rooms; press centers; banquet rooms; secretarial service; corporate rates; fitness; sauna; pool.

Praha Hotel; Susicka 20, Prague 6; tel: (2) 2434-1111; near airport; business center; secretarial service; conference facilities (up to 108); corporate rates; tennis and volleyball courts; sauna.

President; Namesti Curieovych 100; tel: (2) 231-4812; fax: (2) 231-8247; near exhibition grounds; casino; restaurant; conference facilities; secretarial service; corporate rates; sauna.

U Páva; U luzickeho seminare 106, Mala Strana; tel: (2) 2451-0922; fax: (2) 53-33-79.

Moderate

Apollo; Kubisova 22, Liben; tel: (2) 688-0628; fax: (2) 688-4570; city suburb; restaurant; conference center; corporate rates.

Axa; Na Porici 40; tel: (2) 2481-2580; fax: (2) 2481-2067; city center; restaurant; corporate rates; fitness; massage; sauna; pool; CZ1800

Hotel Central; Rybna ulice 8; 11000 Prague 1; tel: (2) 2481-2734; fax: (2) 232-8404; quiet street; city center; English service.

Hotel Hlavkova Kolej; Jenstejnska 1, Prague 2; tel: (2) 29-21-39/29-58-23); 24-hour reception desk; shared baths.

Hotel Sax; Jansky Vrsek 3, Prague 1; tel: (2) 53-84-22; fax: (2) 53-84-98; quiet area; helpful staff; private baths; breakfast included; business clientele.

Interhotel Parkhotel; Veletrzni 20, Prague 7; tel: (2) 380-7111; adjacent to exhibition grounds; restaurant; conference rooms (up to 200); secretarial service; corporate rates.

Mepro; tel: (2) 549167; fax: (2) 561-8587.

Opera; tel: (2) 231-5609; fax: (2) 231-1477.

Pension Louda; Kubisova 10; (2) 688-1491; fax: (2) 688-1488; family-run guesthouse; city suburb; 20 minutes by tram to city center.

MEDICAL CARE

Hospital na Bulovce; Budinova 2, Prague 8; tel: 822-425 (English Speaker).

Hospital Strahov; Jezdecka, Prague 6; tel: 354-441.

HEALTH CLUB

Aerobic Club Monika; 7 Maiselova, Josefov; tel: 232-48-68.

Body and Fitness Club Korinek; 7 Bolzanova, Nove Mesto; tel: 26-06-79.

Bohemia Club; 2 Slovenska, weight room and gym equipment.

Club Hotel; Praha Pruhonice in Pruhonice; tel: 643-6501.

FIT Club Classic; 38 Vinohradska, Vinohrady; tel: 25-8483.

Hotel Atrium; 1 Pobrezni; tel: 2484-1111.

Hotel AXA; 40 Na Porici, Metro: Namesti Republiky; tel: (2) 232-9359; fax: (2) 232-2172.

Hotel Forum; 1 Kongresova, Vysehrad; tel: 61-19-1326.

International Hotel; Namesti Curieovych, Josefov; tel: 231-1812

Panorama Hotel; 7 Milevska; tel: 6116-1111.

Plavecky Stadion; 74 Podolska, 20 minutes south of the city in Podoli; tel: 43-9152.

Sportakcent; 30 Jungmannova, Nove Mesto; tel: 236-8023.

AUTO RENTAL

Alamo Dvorak; Vystaviste, Praha 7; tel/fax: 37-01-76; airport, tel/fax: 2011-3554.

Avis Rent-A-Car; Klimentska 46, tel: (2) 2185-1225; at Prague Airport, tel: 316-6739, fax: (2) 185-1225; Headquarters: E. Krasnohorske 9/134; tel: (2) 2185-1225; fax: (2) 2185-1229.

Budget; reservations, 49 Stresovicha, tel: 2061-0095; fax: (2) 2061-0094; at Prague Airport, tel: 316-5214; at Hotel Intercontinental, Curies Square 5, tel/fax: 231-9595.

Czech Auto Rent; 5 Uruguayska; tel: 25-0552; at Prague Airport, tel: 334-4554.

Europcar; 26 Parizska; tel: 24-81-05-15; fax: 24-81-00-39; at Prague Airport, tel: 316-78-49.

Hertz; 28 Karlovo Namesti, Prague 2; tel: 290-122; fax: 297-836, 292-147; at Prague Airport, tel: 312-0717; at Hotel Diplomat, 15 Evropska, tel: 2439-4174.

Kompas Tourism, 17 Narodni Trida, tel: 232-1916.

WORLD TRADE CENTER

World Trade Center Prague
Economic Chamber of the Czech Republic
Argentinsnska 38
CZ-170 05 Prague
Czech Republic
tel: (2) 6679-4111; fax: (2) 6671-0805

Denmark

Denmark

At a Glance
THE PEOPLE

Population .... 5,356,845 (July 1999 est.)
Growth Rate .... 0.38% (1999 est.)
Life Expectancy .... 76.51 years (born 1999)
Infant Mortality ... 5.11 deaths/1,000 live births (1999 est.)

Ethnic Composition
Scandinavian..91%
Eskimo, Faroese, German 9%

Religious Composition
Evangelical Lutheran...91%
Protestant and Roman Catholic 2%
Other 7%

Languages Spoken
Danish (official), English, Faroese, Greenlandic, German.

Education and Literacy
Schooling is compulsory for nine years and tuition is free through the university level. Adult literacy is 99 percent.

Labor Force
Total: 2,895,950
By occupation: services 70%, industry 25%, agriculture 5%

THE ECONOMY
Denmark's economy features highly productive agriculture and state-of-the-art industry. It also exhibits an extensive government social welfare system and a heavy dependence on export trade. Denmark's government is committed to reducing its unemployment rate and downsizing its social service programs to affordable levels. For all of its problems, Denmark has weathered the worldwide slump of the early 1990s primarily because of its reasonably well-diversified economy and low-but-dependably-steady economic growth. Denmark exports approximately 25 percent more than it imports, and its recent current account surplus remains strong. Limitations on wage increases and low inflation are contributing to improved export competitiveness. Denmark is still outside of full E.U./euro integration but it is expected, like Sweden, to soon get on board. This will go a long way towards keeping this tiny nation central to trade in northern Europe.

Exports .... US$48.8 billion (f.o.b., 1998)
Imports .... US$46.1 billion (f.o.b., 1998)
Total GDP .... US$124.4 billion (1998 est.)
GDP Per Capita .... US$23,300 (1998 est.)
Unemployment .... 6.5% (1998 est.)
Inflation Rate .... 1.8% (1998 est.)

Top Export Partners
E.U., United States.

Top Import Partners
E.U., Norway, United States, Japan

Top Exports
Machinery and instruments, meat and meat products, fuels, dairy products, ships, fish, chemicals

Top Imports
Semi-refined petroleum, machinery and equipment, chemicals, foodstuffs, textiles, paper

BUSINESS WORKWEEK
Offices
Monday to Thursday 8:30a.m. to 5:30p.m., Friday 8:30a.m. to 7p.m.
Note: Some offices advance the working schedule during summer.

Banks
Monday to Friday 9:30a.m. to 4p.m.

Government
Monday to Friday 9:30a.m. to noon and 1:30p.m. to 4p.m.

Retail
Monday to Friday 9 a.m. to 5:30 p.m., Saturday 9a.m. to noon.
Note: Some large retailers and department stores keep longer evening hours.

HOLIDAYS
New Year's Day...January 1
Easter..April 1 - 5*
General Prayer Day..April 30*
Ascension Day .... May 13*
Whit Monday .... May 24*
Constitution Day ....June 5
Christmas ....December 25 - 26
*Dates may vary by year.

CLIMATE
Seasons
The climate is temperate with damp, cold winters and pleasant summer months. Rain falls frequently throughout the year. The average temperature in February is 0°C (32°F), and the warmest temperatures are found during July at about 21°C (70°F).

Regions
As a peninsula and a group of islands jutting out into both the North and Baltic seas, Denmark gets its share of cold winds and wet weather. Composed of a great deal of low lying land, flooding is a continual threat in parts of Jutland and Lolland. Denmark's highest point is only 173 meters so there is little to keep weather patterns from moving quickly across this small country.

Money & Banking
Currency
The currency of Denmark is the Danish Krone (DKr).

Denominations
The Danish Krone (DKr) comes in coin denominations of DKr20, 10, 5, 2, and 1 and 50 and 25 ore; and banknotes of DKr50, 100, 500, and 1,000.
1 £ Stg. = DKr11.26

Traveler's Checks and Credit Cards
Traveler's checks and most foreign currencies can be easily and efficiently exchanged at banks, foreign exchange bureaus located in the major cities, hotels, and foreign exchange kiosks at the airports. Banks offer the most variable exchange rates. Outside office

Denmark

©2001 Magellan Geographix ^{SM} Santa Barbara, CA

hours, there are exchange offices available at the Central Railway Station and at some bank locations in Copenhagen.

Credit cards are widely accepted in Denmark including American Express, Visa, MasterCard, and Diner's Club, as well as bank cards from the larger Danish banks.

You can get cash advances from your credit card on many of the automated teller machines (ATM). Credit cards are also essential for renting a car. Long-term visitors should set up a checking account in Denmark, and get an ATM card. Credit card and ATM receive the most favorable exchange rates.

Travel

VISA AND PASSPORT

A passport that is valid for at least two months beyond the last day of the visit to Denmark is required of all except nationals of:

- Finland, Iceland, Norway, and Sweden who are holding identification papers, such as a driver's license or ID card, as long as travel is entirely within Scandinavia
- Other E.U. countries who have a national ID card, for tourist visits up to three months maximum
- For nationals of the U.S., passports need to be valid for duration of stay only.

Visas are required of all except the following nationals, for stays up to three months maximum: Andorra, Argentina,

Australia, Bermuda (provided holding a British Dependent Territories passport), Brazil, Brunei, Canada, Chile, Costa Rica, Cyprus, Czech Republic, Ecuador, El Salvador, Estonia, Guatemala, Honduras, Hungary, Iceland, Israel, Jamaica, Japan, Korea (Rep. of), Latvia, Liechtenstein, Lithuania, Malaysia, Malta, Mexico, Monaco, New Zealand, Nicaragua, Norway, Panama, Paraguay, Poland, San Marino, Singapore, Slovak Republic, Slovenia, Switzerland, Uruguay, U.K., U.S., Vatican City, and Venezuela.

Passengers in transit who do not leave the airport and are continuing their journey aboard the first connecting aircraft, and who are holding confirmed tickets and other documents for onward travel, are also exempt from the need for a visa.

Citizens of the following nations must have a visa, despite the possibility they may be transiting via the same aircraft: Afghanistan, Bangladesh, Congo (Dem. Rep.), Eritrea, Ethiopia, Ghana, Iran, Iraq, Nigeria, Pakistan, Somalia, and Sri Lanka.

All travelers must have onward tickets, valid travel documents, and sufficient funds.

The types of visa issued are: Tourist, Business, Transit, and Airport Transit. Tourist and Business visas are generally valid for a period of six months from the date of their issue for stays up to three months maximum. Transit visas are good for 24 hours.

For business visa applications, a confirmation written by the business associate in Denmark must be provided; either a fax or a letter should be conveyed directly to the visa department of a Danish embassy.

Allow between six and eight weeks for visa application processing, except for U.K. nationals, who may receive one the same day as that of application.

DEPARTURE FORMALITIES

No more than DKr40,000 per person may be taken out of Denmark. There are no other restrictions for departure from Denmark. Airlines tickets usually include the airport departure taxes.

CUSTOMS ENTRY (PERSONAL)

Duty-free

Non-Danish residents arriving from an E.U. country with duty-paid goods purchased in an E.U. country:

- Alcohol: 1.5 liters of spirits or 3 liters of sparkling wine (under 22%), 90 liters of table wine and 12 liters of beer
- Tobacco: 300 cigarettes, 150 cigarillos, 75 cigars, or 400g of tobacco
- There is no limit to any other personal commodities, including beer.
- Residents of non-E.U. countries entering from outside the E.U. (excluding Greenland) with merchandise purchased in non-E.U. countries:
- Alcohol: 1 liter of spirits or 2 liters of sparkling wine (maximum 22 percent), 2 liters of table wine
- Tobacco: 200 cigarettes, 100 cigarillos, 50 cigars, or 250g of tobacco
- Food: 500g of coffee or 200g of coffee-extracts, 100g of tea or 40g of tea-extracts
- Perfume: 50g of perfume, 250ml of eau de toilette
- Other articles: value up to DKr1350 (DKr750 if items were purchased on an airline or ferry)

Note: Only those aged 17 or over are allowed to import alcohol or tobacco products. Coffee extract products' import is limited to those aged 15 or over. It is not legal to bring fresh foods into the country unless vacuum packed.

Although since June 30, 1999 there has been no legal limit on the quantities of duty-free alcohol and tobacco that travelers may carry into most of the E.U. countries (for personal use exclusively), Denmark, Finland, and Sweden will continue enforcing limits until 2004.

IMMUNIZATION

No inoculations are required for entry. International Certificates of Vaccination not required unless arriving from an infected area.

TIPPING

Taxi

It is not necessary to tip taxi drivers, though most riders round up the fare.

Porters

Porters at first-class hotels and transport depots receive Dkr5 per bag.

Hotels

Hotels add a 15 percent service charge to all bills.

Restaurants

Restaurants usually add a 15 percent service charge to the tab. It is customary to offer to buy your bartender or host a drink in the absence of an applied service charge.

EMERGENCY INFORMATION

Police and Crime

Denmark is one of the safest countries in the world and quite avant garde. The people are honest and law abiding, but take general precautions in the larger cities, especially Copenhagen, where petty crime exists.

Foreign business visitors are often the target of thieves. Consequently, purses, laptops, and briefcases will require additional security. Do not leave valuables in cars or on tables in cafés. Keep non-essential valuables locked in hotel safes when not in use. Use credit cards and travel checks when possible to avoid carrying large sums of cash.

While the Danes love their beer, drunk driving is severely punished, so be discreet. Fines and jail sentences apply to foreigners and locals alike. The police force is helpful and efficient. They are also accommodating to law-abiding travelers.

Emergency Numbers

General emergency .... 112 (no coins required)

Health

Living and traveling in Denmark pose no serious health risks for most westerners. Visitors from southern Asia or other warm climates may find the weather problematic.

Cleanliness is a Danish passion. As food laws are strict, the food and tap water are safe. The diet is rather heavy, especially for Asian visitors. Allow yourself time to acclimate before indulging in Danish delicacies.

The medical establishment is of a very high standard, and its services are often free to foreign travelers. Many pharmacies are open 24 hours a day.

INTERNAL TRAVEL

AIR

Scheduled domestic air services are excellent and radiate outward from Copenhagen (Kastrup). Other airports linked by domestic airline connections include Rønne, Billund, Esbjerg, Karup, Skrydstrup, Sønderborg, Thisted, Ålborg, and Århus.

Due to the relatively small size of Denmark and the abundance of airfields, domestic flights usually take less than 30 minutes in duration. Generally, limousines are available for transit to the traveler's intended destination at most airports.

Discounts are available for domestic airline tickets bought inside Denmark; inquire locally. Discounts for family, children, and students are also available.

TAXI

Except in Copenhagen, taxis can be difficult to find. Visitors can reserve a taxi, if needed. Drivers are, for the most part, quite honest and accommodating.

AUTO

Auto rental is readily available to motorists over age 20 in larger towns and cities. Reservations can easily be made through airlines or travel agents. A credit card and valid driver's license, as well as proof of insurance, are needed. Nationals of E.U. countries are advised to acquire a Green Card, which raises the level of insurance that comes with the rental vehicle to that of the motorist's own personal policy. Driving in Denmark is very civilized and safe, but visitors need to study the rule book.

Hired cars with drivers can be procured at reasonable daily and weekly rates.

Note: As mentioned earlier, drunk driving laws are strict, and visitors should not tempt fate in this beer-drinking country.

Denmark

Denmark

TRAIN

The railway system in Denmark is extensive. Main cities on every island of this nation are linked by the rail network: Copenhagen, Odense, Esbjerg, Horsens, Randers, Herning, and Ålborg.

Danish State Railways (DSB) runs many express trains named Lyntogs, providing long-haul, non-stop travel. Newspapers, magazines, and snack food are available on these trains, as are pay phones. The IC3 is a new kind of intercity train, even faster and more direct than the Lyntogs. Seats must be reserved in advance.

One may also easily schedule overnight international travel from Denmark, which serves as an acceptable and widespread type of business travel throughout the Continent.

METRO

Copenhagen has an efficient and comfortable subway system (S trains) that serves most of the city, day and night. It has recently opened a line that serves the airport, making access to the city both easy and inexpensive. Schedules, maps, and fares are clearly marked at all stations. Additional information can be acquired from attendants on the platforms.

BUSES & TRAMS

Copenhagen has an extensive city bus system (no trams) that is both efficient and reasonably priced. An inter-city bus system exists in Denmark, but it is rarely used by business travelers. Smaller cities have their own local bus systems, but they are not recommended for business travel.

WATER TRAVEL

This nation of peninsulas and islands has an elaborate water taxi and ferry system for both local and international travel. Frequent ferry sailings from Kalundborg to Århus, Ebeltoft to Sjællands Odde and Rønne to Copenhagen are quite convenient.

Costs are low compared to air fares, and travel is comfortable if somewhat slower. The larger ferries have restaurants and cafeterias, and many have TV, cinema, and video lounges, as well as shops, sleeping rooms, and recreation areas for children. Local car ferries connect most of the islands to Denmark's road network. International cruise lines also call at Copenhagen's harbor for those looking to make global connections.

TRAVEL ASSISTANCE

Danmark's Turistråd (Danish Tourist Board)
Vesterbrogade 6 D
DK-1606 Copenhagen V, Denmark
tel: 33 11 14 15; fax: 33 93 14 16
email: dt@dt.dk
website: www.dt.dk; www.visitdenmark.com

Wonderful Copenhagen Convention and Visitors Bureau
Gammel Kongevej 1
DK-1610 Copenhagen V, Denmark
tel: 33 25 74 00; fax: 33 25 74 10
email: woco@woco.dk
website: www.woco.dk

Hotel Accommodations
National Hotel Association ....(31) 35-60-88

Essential Terms

English	Danish
Yes	Ja
No	Nej
Good morning	Godmorgen
Hello (daytime)	Goddag
Hello (evening)	Godaften
Hello (telephone)	Hei
Good-bye	Farvel
Please	Vaer så venlig
Thank you	Tak
Pleased to meet you	Det var morsomt
Excuse me; I'm sorry	Undskyld
My name is _____	Mit navn _____
I don't understand	Jeg forstår ikke
Do you speak English?	Snakker de engelsk

Communications
DIALING CODES IN DENMARK
International country code: [45]

Dialing Denmark from Overseas
To reach Denmark from overseas, dial your country's international dialing code, then 45 (the country code for Denmark), and finally the number. There are no city codes.

Assistance Numbers
International Operator 113
International Directory 115
International Rate Information 141
National Information Service 118

CALLING WITHIN DENMARK
Local Calls
The general rule is 1 Krone = 1 Minute. A beep indicates that your time is running short, in which case either prepare for disconnection, or drop in another Krone.

Long Distance Calls
Eight digits are required for all parts of the country. Happily, there are no city codes for which to search.

International Calls
To call direct internationally, dial 009 + country code + number. To call Greenland or the Faroe Islands, dial 009 + 3-digit code + number. The 3-digit code for Greenland is 299; the Faroe Islands use 298.

Discounts apply after 10 p.m. Telephone centers in post offices and train stations offer better rates than hotels, which apply the usual massive surcharges. And keep in mind there is a DKr35 surcharge for any operator-assisted calls.

To benefit from the same rates you might get at home, and to get assistance with credit card calls or collect calls, dial one of the following access numbers:

Australia 80-01-00-61
Canada Direct 80-01-00-11
U.K. BT..80-01-04-44
U.K. MCL...80-01-00-14
U.S. AT&T Direct.................................80-01-00-10
U.S. MCI..80-01-00-22
U.S. Sprint..80-01-08-77

PAY PHONES

Public Telephones

Danish phones accept DKr1 and 5 coins.
1. Lift receiver
2. Dial number (with area code)
3. Wait for an answer
4. Deposit coins

You can make another call on the same coins if your time has not yet expired.

Calling Cards

Telecom shops and kiosks sell cards in denominations of DKr20, 50, and 100.

Card Phone:

CELLULAR PHONES

Dansk Mobiltelefon and TeleDanmark Mobil both offer digital service to Denmark. TeleDanmark Mobil also offers analog service of various kinds.

Note: Your home country cell phone may not work in this country. If not, we recommend that you rent an international cell phone *before* you leave home. A major US-based cell phone rental provider is **IMC WorldCell**. For information see "International Cell Phone Rentals" on page 14.

CALL BACK

You can (potentially) save significant sums when calling in Denmark by using a call back service. For a list of call-back services, please refer to the "Communications" section in the *Global Road Warrior* Introduction.

Fees for call back services vary widely, depending on the company and the type of service required. Be sure to check with these companies before leaving to compare rates.

PHONE JACKS

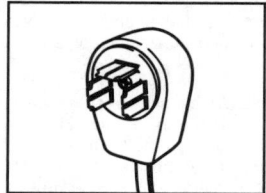

Plug adaptors are available through **iGo Corporation.** (See "Electrical and Telephone Adaptors" on page 19.)

FAX

Faxes are widely available and very reliable.

POSTAL SERVICES

Mail service is efficient. Mail boxes are painted red.

Hours of service

Monday-Friday 9a.m. to 5:30p.m.
Saturday 9a.m. to noon.

TELEGRAMS

Telegrams can be sent by phone, by dialing 122.

Business Services

BUSINESS CENTERS

DSB Restauranter and Kiosker A/S; tel: 86 13 14 1; fax: 86 19 32 60

COURIER SERVICES

Airborne Express Denmark A/S; Amager Landevej 149, 2770 Kastrup/Copenhagen, tel: (32) 52-5440; fax; (32) 52-3140.

Concorde Couriers; tel: (32) 52-5252.

DHL Worldwide Express A/S; Jydekrogen 14, Valiensbaek 2625; tel: 7013-1131; airport, Nordic Operation, Smedekaervej 33, Kastrup 2770, tel: (32) 52-7021.

TNT; c/o **Post and Telegraf V Aesener**; tel: (33) 93-2410.

UPS Denmark A/S; Naverland 7, 2600 Glostrup, Copenhagen; tel: 4323-8888; toll-free in Denmark, tel: 167-822-054; fax: 4323-8800.

TRANSLATION SERVICES

Alpha Lingua Kobenhaun; tel: (33) 146626
Hopstock Sprachendienst Virum; tel: 45-857050
Iff Berlitz - Koben; tel: (33) 113333

Electrical

Current

220 volts AC, 50Hz

ELECTRIC PLUGS

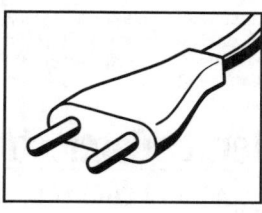

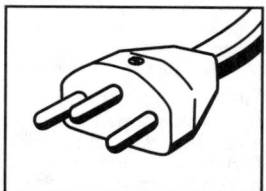

Denmark

Plug adaptors are available through **iGo Corporation.** (See "Electrical and Telephone Adaptors" on page 19.)

Technical Support

HARDWARE/SOFTWARE VENDOR SUPPORT

Dell; tel: 4517-0100; fax: 4517-0117(in Germany) tel: [49] (61) 039-710; (Dell- Europe) tel: [44] (134) 474-8000; (in the U.S.) tel: [1] (512) 338-4400; fax: [1] (512) 728-3330; http://www.dell.com/.

Gateway 2000; (in Ireland) tel: [353] (1) 797-2000; (in the U.S.) tel: [1] (605) 232-2191; fax: [1] (605) 232-2023; http://www.g2k.com/.

Hewlett Packard; tel: (0) 39 294099; (in Switzerland) tel: [41] (22) 780-8111; (in the U.S.) tel: [1] (408) 246-4300; http://www.hp.com/.

IBM; tel: 233-000; tel: 8739-6000; tel: 9933-7800; tel: 8739-6000; (in Germany) tel: [49] (711) 78-50; fax: [49] (711) 785-3511; (in Switzerland) tel: [41] (22) 310-0418 (in French); (U.S. Main Office) tel: [1] 914-765-1900; (in the U.S.) tel: [1] (919) 517-2800; http://www.ibm.com/.

Microsoft; tel: (44) 890-111; fax: (44) 685-510; (44) 890-111 (technical support); (in Germany) tel: [49] (89) 31-760; fax: [49] (89) 3176-1000; tel: [49] (89) 3176-1199; (in Switzerland) tel: [41] (848) 858-868; fax [41] (1) 831-0869; (in the U.S.) [1] (425) 635-7222; http://www.microsoft.com/.

NEC; tel: 8030-1005 (UltraCare Support); (in Germany) tel: [49] (18) 0524- 1212; tel:[49] (89) 3160-1233; fax: [49] (89) 3160-1613 (Floppy Disk and Hard Drive); tel: [49] (89) 9627-4233; fax: [49] (89) 9627-4613 (All Other Products); (in the U.S.) [1] (916) 388-0101 (Main Switchboard); http://www.nec.com/.

Quark; (in Switzerland) tel: [41] (1) 808-7722; fax: [41] (1) 808-7799; (in the U.S.) tel: [1] (303) 894-8899; fax: [1] (303) 894-3398 (For Products Registered in the Americas); http://www.quark.com/.

Toshiba; (in Germany) tel: [49] (2131) 158-319; fax: [49] (2131) 158-558; (in Switzerland) tel: [41] (1) 946-0777; fax: [41] (1) 946-0807; (in Ireland) tel: [44] (193) 282-8828; (in the U.S.) [1] (949) 583-3000 (Corporate Headquarters); http://www.toshiba.com/.

Internet Connection

HOW TO CONNECT

Connecting to AOL and Compuserve in Denmark is similar to using it when traveling outside your own area code. See the introductory section for detailed information on connecting to your account through a different phone number.

America Online

Numbers are available at keyword *international.* Be sure to get several local numbers before leaving. AOL's GlobalNet service charges US$6 an hour in addition to the usual charges. Go to keyword *access* (a free area) and download the software.

Access: Aarhus 8624-9071; Copenhagen 3644-2246.

Compuserve

Numbers are available at keyword *Go International.* The Compuserve Web-site also has a great deal of information, at http://www.compuserve.com.

Access: Copenhagen 3644-5464.

Independent Service Providers

Many independent service providers offer discounts if you are only in town for a couple of days.

BusinessNet Danmark A/S; tel: 7020-7720; fax: 7020-7721; email: salg@businessnet.dk; http://www.businessnet.dk/.

Tele Danmark Internet; tel: 8678-3300; fax: 8678-3800; http://www.inet.tele.dk/.

UNI-C; tel: 3587-8899; fax: 3587-8890; email: sektornet@uni-c.dk; http://www.uni-c.dk/.

WebPartner ApS; tel: 3543-8248; fax: 3543-8249; email: info@webpartner.dk; http://www.webpartner.dk/.

Business Culture

GREETINGS AND COURTESIES

Handshakes are the formal greeting between Danes and with foreign businesspeople. Handshakes are usually firm and brief, and are done upon each meeting and when leaving. Although businesspeople will often deal on a first name basis with those they know, family names and titles are always used for initial introductions. Gifts are rarely exchanged in business, and are not expected as part of the business relationship. If invited into a home, a bouquet of flowers will always be appreciated. Presenting business cards upon introduction is most important. Listing a street address instead of a P.O. box lends credibility and builds confidence in your company.

DECISION MAKING

Decisions in Danish firms are normally made by the ranking officer present. Each division has authority to make decisions and capitalize on opportunities that may present themselves. The size of the deal usually has a lot to do with who makes the final decision; larger deals are usually decided upon by senior members. There usually isn't a lot of haggling; Danes prefer well organized and factually informative presentations that are efficient and to the point.

WOMEN

Women are highly accepted and respected in business; they generally receive equal pay and hold high positions within Danish firms. Working mothers are given flexible work hours so they can maintain both career and family. Danish women expect to be treated seriously and with the respect to which their position entitles them. Failure to do this is considered insulting. Businesswomen are as open and direct as men, but this should not be viewed as anything more than being friendly. Foreign women should expect to be treated the same as their male counterparts. It is usually acceptable to shake hands with a woman when being introduced in a business environment.

MEETINGS

Meetings should be scheduled in advance and you should be prompt for appointments. When you arrive for a meeting and are greeted by the receptionist or secretary you should present your business card and wait until being escorted to the meeting room. Advise your Danish counterparts in advance of who will be attending from your firm and do not bring anyone unannounced. The Danes do not like a lot of paperwork or memos exchanged either during or following a meeting. They prefer to sit down together, and discuss issues and keep everyone informed with short meetings. Documenting all stages of a negotiation is not required or advised.

BUSINESS ATTIRE

Proper attire is very important to Danish businesspeople. Suits and ties are always worn; a double breasted jacket or a vested suit is considered proper business attire. Wearing colorful suspenders or bow ties is considered silly or trivial. Women usually wear dresses or skirts and blouses, but the dress code for women is a bit informal. It is, however, always conservative. Men may consider packing a tuxedo because senior businessmen stage more black-tie dinners than in many other countries. Be sure to prepare for the cold climate which prevails most of the year.

Business Centers
Copenhagen
CITY VIEW

Copenhagen is a bustling metropolis with over 1.5 million people, but it has a more small-town, bohemian feel. Few towers shoot up into the sky, most of the buildings don't even reach six stories high. However, the city captures the Scandic avant-garde flavor in its smoke-filled cafes and modern-dressed individuals; it also offers the mystical treasure hunter such gems as the Little Mermaid from Hans Christian Anderson.

AIRPORT

Kastrup Airport to City Center

The airport lies 6 miles (10 km.) from the city. Travel time is approximately 30 minutes. Coaches leave the airport every 10 minutes and buses every 15 minutes from 6a.m. to 11:30p.m. The subway now also links to the airport, perhaps offering the cheapest and most efficient way to get into town.

HOTELS

Top-end

D'Angleterre; Kongens Nytorv 34; tel: (33) 12-00-95; fax: (33) 12-11-18. Over DKr1,100; swimming pool, nightclub, royalty and rock stars.

Palace Hotel; Radhuspladsen 57; tel: (33) 14-40-50; fax: (33) 14-52-79; conference facilities for up to 80; located on Radhuspladsen near Tivoli.

Plaza; Bernstorffsgade 4; tel: (33) 14-92-62; fax: (33) 93-93-62; Library bar nominated by Forbes as one of five best bars in the world.

SAS Royal Hotel; Hammerichsgade 1; tel: (33) 42-60-60; fax: (33) 42-61-00; business services; convention facilities; fitness center; downtown.

SAS Scandinavia; Amager Boulevard 70; tel: (33) 11-24-23; fax: (31) 57-01-93.

Expensive

Gentofte Hotel; Gentoftegade 29; tel: (39) 68-09-11; fax: (39) 68-06-11; 8 meeting rooms; golf course; 8km from downtown; bus line stop; inexpensive single rooms including breakfast.

Grand Hotel; Vesterbrogade 9; tel: (31) 31-36-00; fax: (31) 31-33-50; downtown near Central Railway Station; meeting rooms for up to 100; fitness center nearby.

Imperial Hotel; Vester Farimagsgade 9; tel: (33) 12-80-00; fax: (33) 93-80-31; centrally located; meeting room for up to 100; bar and restaurant.

Kong Frederik; Vester Volgade 25-27; tel: (33) 12-59-02; fax: (33) 93-59-01.

Neptun; tel: (33) 13-89-00; fax: (33) 14-12-50.

Nyhavn 71; Nyhavn 71; tel: (33) 11-85-85; fax: (33) 93-15-85; near historic harbor; two 10-person meeting rooms.

Phoenix Copenhagen; Bredgade 37; tel: (33) 95-95-00; fax: (33) 33-98-33; former housing of aristocracy; conference facilities for up to 100; business services.

Sheraton; Vester Sogade 6; tel: (33) 14-35-35; fax: (33) 32-12-23.

Moderate

Ascot; Studiestraede 61; tel: (33) 12-60-00; fax: (33) 14-60-40; downtown; DKr 670 to 800.

Copenhagen Admiral; Toldbodgader 24-28; tel: (33) 11-82-82; fax: (33) 32-55-42.

Hotel Christian IV; tel: Dronningens Tvaergade 45; tel: (33) 32-10-44; fax: (33) 32-07-06; near Relenborg Palace; quiet area; no meeting rooms.

Radisson SAS Globetrotter; Engvej 171; tel: (31) 55-14-33; fax: (31) 55-81-46; convention facilities for up to 600; business service center; pool, fitness room; near airport.

Triton; Helgolandsgade 7-11; tel: (31) (31) 32-66; fax: (31) (31) 69-70.

AUTO RENTAL

Note: When parking in the city, use parking discs, which can be found at gas stations, post offices, tourist offices, banks, and some police stations. They allow up to three hours of parking on city streets. The disc's hand should point to the quarter hour following time of arrival.

Any questions regarding parking discs or car travel in general should be directed to the **Danish Motoring Organisation**; tel: 43 93 09 00.

Avis; 1 Kampmandsgade (downtown), tel: (33) 15-2299, fax: (33) 32-7455; airport, tel: (32) 51-2299, fax: (32) 51-3051.

Europcar/InterRent; 17 Gyldenlovsgade (downtown); tel: (33) 11-62-00; airport, tel: 32-50-30-90.

Hertz; reservations, tel: (33) 32-3332, fax: (33) 32-7405; downtown; tel: (33) 12-77-00; airport intl. terminal, tel: (32) 50-9300, fax: (32) 52-2216; domestic terminal, tel: (32) 50-3040; fax: (32) 500-006; Ved Vesterport 3, tel: (33) 12-7700; fax: (33) 15-4955.

WORLD TRADE CENTER

World Trade Center Copenhagen
Bygstubben 13-2950
Vedbaek, Denmark
tel: (3) 917-9800
fax: (3) 120-5521

Dominican Republic

Dominican Republic

At a Glance

THE PEOPLE

Population .... 8,129,734 (July 1999 est.)
Growth Rate .... 1.62(1999 est.)
Life Expectancy .... 69.73 years (born 1999)
Infant Mortality . 42.52 deaths/1,000 live births (1999 est.)

Ethnic Composition
Caucasian 16%
Black African 11%
Mulatto.. 73%

Religious Composition
Roman Catholic... 95%
Other 5%

Languages Spoken
Spanish

Education and Literacy
Literacy for the population aged 15 and over stands at 82.1 percent.

Labor Force
Total: 2,600,000
By occupation: services 63%, industry 22%, agriculture 15%

THE ECONOMY

The Dominican Republic is potentially one of the larger markets in Latin America. Following the economic turmoil of the 1990s, when the GDP fell by 5 percent and inflation doubled, the Dominican Republic implemented a series of governmental reforms. It eliminated many price controls and subsidy programs in an attempt to stabilize its economy and put it on a free market basis. As a result, the GDP increased 3 percent and inflation dropped to single-digit rates. However, increased government spending led to the renewed inflationary pressures seen today. It also caused the consumer price index to jump and exchange rates to drop. Today's economy has stabilized but at an unacceptable level. Unemployment is still a major problem and the Dominican Republic has been slow to resolve the question of its foreign debt obligations. Doubts remain among the global investment community about the government's ability to properly oversee this struggling economy.

Exports .... US$997 million (1997 est.)
Imports .... US$3.6 billion (1998)
Total GDP .... US$39.8 billion (1998 est.)
GDP Per Capita .... US$5,000 (1998 est.)
Unemployment .... 16% (1997 est.)
Inflation Rate .... 6% (1998 est.)

Top Export Partners
United States, E.U., Canada, Japan, Puerto Rico.

Top Import Partners
United States, E.U., Venezuela, Dutch Antilles, Mexico, Japan.

Top Exports
Ferro-nickel, sugar, gold, coffee, cocoa.

Top Imports
Foodstuffs, petroleum, cotton and fabrics, chemicals and pharmaceuticals.

BUSINESS WORKWEEK

Offices
Monday to Friday 7:30a.m. to noon and 1:30p.m. to 5p.m.

Banks
Monday to Friday 8a.m. to 5p.m.

Government
Monday to Friday 7:30a.m. to 2:30p.m.

Retail
Monday to Friday 8a.m. to noon and 2p.m. to 6p.m., Saturday 8a.m. to noon.
Note: In rural areas government services and business offices may take extended midday breaks but remain open later in the day.

HOLIDAYS

New Year's Day..January 1
Epiphany ....January 6
Our Lady of Altagracia.......................................January 21
Duarte..January 26
Independence... February 27
Good Friday..April 2*
Pan-American Day .... April 14
Labor Day..May 1
Foundation of Sociedad la Trinitaria.......................July 16
Restoration Day .... August 16
Our Lady of Mercedes................................September 24
Columbus Day..October 12
United Nations Day ....October 24
All Saints' Day ....November 1
Christmas Day...December 25
*Dates may vary by year.

CLIMATE

Seasons
The climate in the Dominican Republic is tropical, and the temperatures can rise as high as 37°C (98°F) in the summer months, between June and October, with high humidity. The dry season is between November and April when the temperatures hover around 30°C (85°F), with cooler nights. Hurricane season occurs between June to November.

Regions
The Dominican Republic shares a Caribbean island with its neighbor Haiti. The republic is comprised of rugged mountain areas, convoluted coastlines, and verdant valleys. Temperatures are highest in the valleys and lowest in the mountain regions. Other than that, the nation has virtually the same humid tropical weather throughout.

Money & Banking

Currency
The currency of Dominican Republic is the Dominican Republic Peso (RD$).

Denominations
The Dominican Republic Peso (RD$) comes in coin denominations of RD$1 and 50, 25, 10, 5 and 1 centavos; and banknotes of RD$1, 5, 10, 20, 50, 100, 500, and 1,000.

Dominican Republic

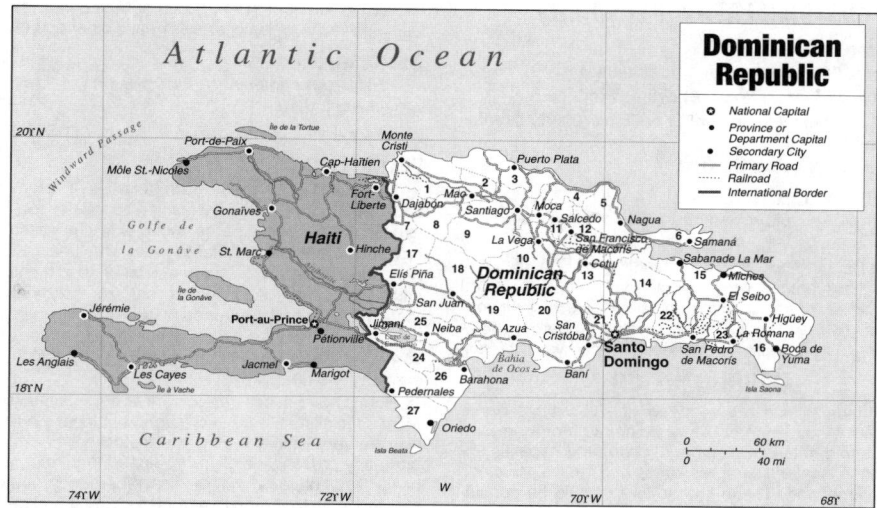

©2001 Magellan Geographix ℠ Santa Barbara, CA

Traveler's Checks and Credit Cards

Traveler's checks can be exchanged at banks, exchange shops, hotels, and international airports at tourist exchange rates. State-run banks may offer the best exchange rates and no transaction fees. Rates can change quickly in the Dominican Republic, so the timing of your exchanges is important. Avoid black marketeers at all cost. Cashing traveler's checks can be a difficult and lengthy form filling process, especially in smaller towns.

Major currencies, especially U.S. dollars, can be exchanged without a charge at banks and hotels. Try to take only crisp and new notes, as wrinkled and soiled notes are likely to be refused. Keep all of your receipts if you are planning reconversion at departure.

Major credit cards such as American Express, Visa, Diner's Club, and MasterCard are easily accepted in good hotels and restaurants in urban areas. Usage in the countryside is very limited. Some banks in the capital offer cash advances on credit cards, but make sure you bring your passport for identification. ATMs are rare, even in the capital, and they are not compatible with many European banking systems.

Travel

VISA AND PASSPORT

A passport that is valid at least six months beyond the date of departure is required of all visitors except nationals of:

- Canada and U.S. who are holding suitable ID— birth certificate, driver's license, or other appropriate documentation.
- Germany, if holding a National Identity Card.

Note: These nationals must also have Tourist Cards, obtainable on arrival.

Tourist Cards are given to visitors of the Dominican Republic, valid for stays up to 90 days. They can be obtained on arrival for US$10, though this tends to be a somewhat lengthy process. It is advisable to apply for them in advance of your visit. Extensions are also possible.

Citizens of the following nations are eligible for Tourist Cards:

- Albania, Andorra, Antigua & Barbuda, Argentina, Aruba, Australia, Bahamas, Barbados, Brazil, Bulgaria, Canada, Chile, Curaçao, Czech Republic, French Overseas

Territories, Hawaii, Hungary, Iceland, Israel, Jamaica, Japan Korea (Rep. of), Liechtenstein, Mexico, Monaco, Norway, Paraguay, Peru, Poland, Puerto Rico, Romania, Russian Federation, St. Lucia, St. Vincent & the Grenadines, San Marino, Suriname, Switzerland, Trinidad & Tobago, Turks and Caicos Islands, Uruguay, U.K., U.S., U.S. Virgin Islands, Venezuela, and Yugoslavia (Serbia and Montenegro)

- Expatriates residing permanently in Canada, Denmark, France, Germany, Greece, Ireland, Italy, The Netherlands, Portugal, Spain, U.K., and the U.S.

Applications for a passport may be made at the airport in the Dominican Republic, as well as at any of its embassies or consulates.

Visas are required of all except those holding a Tourist card.

Note: In addition to a visa, nationals of China (PR) must have an authorization issued by the Director of the Migration / Immigration Department.

Types of visa issued: Tourist (single-entry) and Business (single- or multiple-entry). Tourist visas have a term of validity of 60 days. Single-entry Business visas have a 60-day term of validity. Multiple-entry Business visas have a term of validity up to a year.

Allow just a few days for processing of Tourist Cards. On the other hand, it takes between six and eight weeks for processing of applications for Business and Tourist visas, which must be forwarded to authorities in the Dominican Republic, unless solicited by cable (expense paid by applicant).

DEPARTURE FORMALITIES

Visitors departing at Las Americas International Airport will have to pay a departure tax of US$10. Black market transactions are illegal for exchange of pesos to hard currency of your country. No more than US$10,000 or its equivalent in another currency may be taken out of the Dominican Republic at the time of departure. Tourist cards must be presented to immigration officials at departure.

Dominican Republic

CUSTOMS ENTRY (PERSONAL)

Duty-free

- Tobacco: 200 cigarettes or 1 box cigars
- Alcohol: two liters of alcohol beverage (opened)
- Other: a reasonable amount of perfume (opened), cameras, and film
- Gifts up to a value of US$100

Prohibited or Restricted

- All animal, agricultural, and horticultural products
- Drugs

Note: Bringing goods into the Dominican Republic may entail a long procedure at Customs. Certain imported goods officially exonerated may still be delayed, to the consternation of many a business traveler. Apparent impatience on your part will only cause further delays and fees.

IMMUNIZATION

No immunizations are required unless visitors arrive from areas of known infection or epidemic. For long-term stays, typhoid, tetanus, diphtheria, polio, and hepatitis immunizations, malaria suppressants, and rabies vaccines are recommended. These precautions should be considered mandatory for work in rural areas.

TIPPING

Taxi

Metered taxi drivers are usually tipped ten percent. Unmetered fares should be negotiated in advance and include all costs.

Porters

Porters at first class hotels and transport depots receive RD$5 per bag.

Hotels

Hotels will apply service charges, usually about ten percent, directly to the bill. Chambermaids should be tipped RD$15 per day.

Restaurants

While a ten percent service charge is included in most restaurant bills, it is customary to tip an additional 10 to 15 percent if service is exceptional. One may buy a drink for a bartender in lieu of a tip.

EMERGENCY INFORMATION

Police and Crime

The countryside is not dangerous, but street crime prevails in the cities. Santo Domingo is a large city with much poverty, so take basic precautions against petty crime, especially at night. Special care should be taken in certain areas such as the Simon Bolivar sector of the capital and the backstreets of Los Charamicos in Sosua. Avoid flashy displays of wealth, and dress and behave conservatively. Leave most of your cash, traveler's checks, jewelry, and your camera in your hotel safe. Hustlers may offer their services as guides in the downtown areas of Santo Domingo and in the Zona Coloniale. It will take several refusals before they give up their pursuit.

Carry photocopies of your passport instead of the original. Carry cash in a money belt, and use credit cards or traveler's checks for most of your transactions. Walk with your bag away from the street to avoid having it snatched away by passing thieves on motorcycle. Avoid contact with the drug trade and never carry a stranger's baggage.

The Dominican Republic tends to suppress political dissent quite harshly. Stay clear of social unrest and avoid political discussions unless applicable to your business dealings.

The police force is often part of the crime problem, so do not expect the return of stolen goods or thorough investigations. Carry insurance for laptops, jewelry, and other valuables.

Emergency Numbers

Police, fire, and ambulance (nationwide) 911
Alternative number,
for all services 711/809 472 7111

Health

Never drink tap water—don't even use it for brushing your teeth. Drink bottled water or boil water for 10 to 15 minutes before use. Use ice cubes only when assured they have been made from potable water. Don't eat raw vegetables and fruit unless they've been washed in a chlorine solution. Be careful when eating out, eat only well-cooked meat; make sure the seafood is fresh and the milk pasteurized. Avoid street food stalls until fully acclimated. This nation has tropical heat and humidity, so watch out for sunburn and heat stroke.

Hotels have access to doctors and medical assistance. Most specialists are trained abroad but local medical facilities are very limited. Carry a well-stocked medical kit and bring any prescription drugs you need to take on a regular basis. If you have a major medical emergency, you are best advised to go to Puerto Rico (U.S.). Carry travel medical insurance and add an evacuation policy if you plan a long-term stay.

INTERNAL TRAVEL

AIR

Bávaro Sun Flight and Dorado Air offer limited services between Santo Domingo, Santiago, Samaná, Punta Cana, and Puerto Plata. Planes can also be chartered. For further information, contact the airlines upon arrival in the Dominican Republic.

TAXI

Taxis operate in most cities, but driving is undisciplined. Always determine or negotiate a price beforehand when using unmetered cabs. Carry explicit directions and maps for your destination. In rural areas, private citizens often volunteer to act as taxi drivers; this can be risky, but it is often the only means available.

AUTO

Visitors can rent cars and motorbikes in Santo Domingo; Hertz and Avis have offices there, and so do some local companies. The minimum age for approved auto rental is 25. A credit card and valid driver's license are required along with local insurance.

Driving in the Dominican Republic proves quite chaotic, even though there are not many cars. In old Santo Domingo, for instance, streets are narrow, and blind corners abound; so, exercise great care, as Dominican drivers customarily use their horns instead of their brakes. Only experienced visitors should consider driving themselves around.

A decent system of roads exists, including the Sanchez Highway, which runs westward between Santo Domingo and Elias Pina along the Haitian frontier; the Mella Highway running eastward from Santo Domingo to Higuey; and the Duarte Highway extending north and west between Santo Domingo and Santiago, and onward to Monte Cristi, which sits on the northwest coast.

Many roads in the Dominican Republic are not all weather; so, four-wheel-drive vehicles are recommended. Checkpoints close to military installations are common, though no serious problems have been reported (those near the border with Haiti are the most liable to be sensitive).

TRAIN

There are few rail lines in the Dominican Republic, but none have a passenger service suitable for regular business travel. Like rural taxi service, slow (often late) trains are sometimes the only means to reach remote areas.

METRO

There is no metro system in the Dominican Republic.

BUSES & TRAMS

Bus service exists between major cities. Buses are large and comfortable, but schedules are not always observed.

Caribe Tours...687-3171
Metro Tours 566-6590

In downtown Santo Domingo, buses operate along major streets but without fixed stops. Just flag one down and tell the driver where you need to go. Minibus services also stand at your disposal. Local service in rural areas runs on erratic schedules, if at all.

About 7,000 share-taxis (*Carro de Conchos*) roam the streets in Santo Domingo, providing 24-hour service; these stop on demand. Fares are more than what you would pay for bus or minibus transit.

Horse-drawn carriages can be hired in most cities, a delightful way to tour around a town's parks and plazas.

WATER TRAVEL

As an island nation, the Dominican Republic has both a domestic and an international water travel system. Local boat routes should only be used for business in remote areas. International cruise boats dock in Santo Domingo. Your hotel and local travel agents serve as the best sources of information and assistance with reservations.

TRAVEL ASSISTANCE

Secretaría de Estado de Turismo (Ministry of Tourism)
Avenida México Esq.
30 de Marzo, Edificio D
Santo Domingo, Dominican Republic
Postal address: Apdo 497, Santo Domingo
tel: 221 4660
fax: 682 3806
Email: sectur@codetel.net.do
website: www.dominicana.com.do
**Consejo de Promoción Turistica
(Tourism Promotion Council)**
 Avenida Mexico 66
Santo Domingo, Dominican Republic
tel: 685 9054
fax: 685 6752
email: cpt@codetel.net.do
website: www.domrep-hotels.com.do
   Note: Also incorporates the National Hotel and Restaurant Association

Essential Terms

English	Spanish
Yes	Sí
No	No
Good morning	Buenos días
Hello (daytime)	Buenas tardes
Hello (evening)	Buenas noches
Hello (telephone)	¿Hola?
Good-bye	Adiós
Please	Por favor
Thank you	Gracias
Pleased to meet you	Encantado (a) de conocerle
Excuse me; I'm sorry	¿Perdóneme?
My name is _____	Me llamo _____
I don't understand	No comprendo
Do you speak English?	¿Habla usted inglés?

Communications

DIALING CODES IN DOMINICAN REPUBLIC

International country code: [809]

Dialing the Dominican Republic from Overseas

To dial the Dominican Republic from overseas, dial your country's international dialing code, then 809 (the country code for the Dominican Republic), and finally the number. There are no city codes.

Assistance Numbers

Bilingual Operator... 0
Directory Information 1411

CALLING WITHIN THE DOMINICAN REPUBLIC

CODETEL operates one of the most advanced telephone systems in Latin America and most services are available.

Local Calls

It will cost 25 centavos to make a local call from a pay phone.

Long Distance Calls

To dial long distance within the Dominican Republic, head for a Codetel office to smooth the way for a clean call. Simply walk into a booth, dial 1 and provide the number you are dialing to get connected. Pay upon exiting.

International Calls

It is recommended to do the same as above when dialing international, otherwise it may take some time to determine the international dialing code procedure, which is

Dominican Republic

Dominican Republic

listed as 1-800-751-2701. Collect calls may be placed from hotels or through the AT&T access number; if dialing from a pay phone, first deposit a coin.

AT&T Direct...1-800-872-2881
MCI access..1-800-888-8000

Direct dial long distance service is also available and other long distance companies offer competitive rates.

PAY PHONES

Public Telephones
There are a number of telephones in the cities, although finding one that works may take some searching. Most pay phones are coin operated.

Calling Cards
Calling cards can be purchased at hotels and newsstands.

CELLULAR PHONES
Cellular phone service is an option in the Dominican Republic, but most companies are using an analog format. BOATPHONE, TRICOM, All Americas Cable & Radio, and CODETEL all offer AMPS analog cellular service.

Note: Your home country cell phone may not work in this country. If not, we recommend that you rent an international cell phone *before* you leave home. A major US-based cell phone rental provider is **IMC WorldCell**. For information see "International Cell Phone Rentals" on page 14.

CALL BACK
You can (potentially) save significant sums when calling in Dominican Republic by using a call back service. For a list of callback services, please refer to the "Communications" section in the *Global Road Warrior* Introduction.

Fees for call back services vary widely, depending on the company and the type of service required. Be sure to check with these companies before leaving to compare rates.

PHONE JACK

Plug adaptors are available through **iGo Corporation**. (See "Electrical and Telephone Adaptors" on page 19.)

FAX
Fax machines are available at hotels and numerous telecommunications centers. Check with your hotel for the closest telecommunications center if they do not have one.

POSTAL SERVICES
Mail service is slow and unreliable, often taking more than 10 days to reach Western Europe. Many businesses use a courier service, that can deliver the next day.

TELEGRAMS
Large hotels can send telegrams, as well as the RCA Global Communications Inc. and the ITT-America Cables and Radio Inc., both in Santo Domingo.

Business Services

COURIER SERVICES
AGSAP; tel: 687-1117/688-7829.

Airborne Express (Intl. Bonded Couriers); Mustafa Kemal, Ataturk #38, Santo Domingo; tel: 542-5265; fax: 563-0814; in Santiago, Ave. Las Carreras #62, Apro. 1-B, Santiago de Los Caballeros, tel: 247-3507; fax: 247-3508.

DHL Dominicana SA; Av. Sarasota 26, Santo Domingo; tel: 534-5888.

FedEx Santo Domingo, tel: 565-3636; Santiago office, tel: 583-4713/4093

UPS; c/o **Dominican Parcel Service S.A.**; Calle Jose Amado Soler Esquina, Ave. Abraham Lincoln, Edificio Progressus, Santo Domingo; tel: 563-5639; fax: 565-9561, 541-9143.

TRANSLATION SERVICES
Garcia Luis H.; tel: 567-7004/530-9428

Electrical

Current
110 volts AC, 60Hz.

Continental 2-pin plugs are the norm. Be advised that constant power outages occur, so prepare to go for hours without electricity. Larger hotels have back-up generators, but you may do well do bring a flashlight nonetheless.

ELECTRIC PLUGS

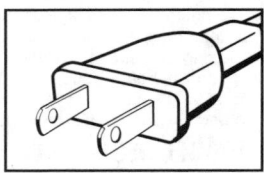

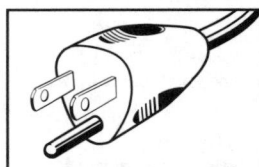

Plug adaptors are available through **iGo Corporation**. (See "Electrical and Telephone Adaptors" on page 19.)

Technical Support

HARDWARE/SOFTWARE VENDOR SUPPORT

Acer/Texas Instruments; (in the U.S.) [1] (408) 432-6200; (in Germany) tel: [49] (4102) 488-469; fax; [49] (4102) 488-169; http://www.acer.com/.

Adobe; (in the U.S.) tel: [1] (800) 500-7078; (in Germany) tel: [49] (1) 803-5018; (in Switzerland) tel: [41] (800) 833-310; http://www.adobe.com/.

Apple/Claris; (in Miami) [1] (305) 265-4939; (in the U.S.) tel: [1] (800) 500-7078; (in the U.K.) tel: [44] (990) 127-753; http://www.apple.com.

AST; (in the U.S.) tel: [1] (817) 232-9824 (International Technical Support); (in Ireland) tel: [353] (61) 492-222; (in the U.S.) tel: [1] (949) 727-4141; http://www.ast.com/.

Compaq/Digital; (Houston Office, U.S.) tel: [1] (713) 370-0670; fax: [1] (713) 514-1740; (General U.S.) tel: (281) 518-2000; (in Switzerland) tel: [41] (22) 709-5330; fax: [41]

(22) 709-5391 (Geneva); http://www.compaq.com/.

Corel; (in the U.S.) tel: [1] (613) 728-3733 (Customer Service); fax: [1] 613-761-9176; (in the U.S.) tel: [1] (716) 871-2325 (Ask to be Forwarded to Appropriate Program); http://www.corel.com/.

Dell; tel: [1] (809) 567-8231 (Xerox Dominicana); (in the U.S.) tel: [1] (512) 338-4400; fax: [1] (512) 728-3330; http://www.dell.com/.

Filemaker/Claris; (in the U.S.) tel: [1] (800) 965-9090; (in Germany) tel: [49] (180) 525-8166 (Info-line); fax: [49] (180) 567-2233; tel: [49] (180) 523-6423; http://www.claris.com/.

Gateway 2000; (in the U.S.) tel: [1] (605) 232-2191; fax: [1] (605) 232-2023; (in Ireland) tel: [353] (1) 797-2000; http://www.g2k.com/.

Hewlett Packard; (in the U.S.) tel: [1] (408) 246-4300; (U.S. Office) tel: [1] 208-323-2551 for Printer, Plotter, Fax, Scanner; tel: [1] (208) 344-4131 for HP DeskJet 680C and DeskWriter 680C Printers; tel: [1] (970) 635-1000 for HP Vectra PC, NetServer, Mass Storage; tel: [1] 208-323-4663 for HP Pavilion; tel: [1] 970-346-8682 for HP OmniBook Notebook PC; tel: [1] 208-376-3686 for PhotoSmart PC Photography System; http://www.hp.com.

IBM; (in Jamaica) tel: (876) 926-3200; fax: (876) 926-3225; (U.S. Office, Information) tel: [1] 914-765-1900; fax: [1] 914-288-1147; (in Switzerland) tel: [41] (22) 310-0418 (in French); http://www.ibm.com/.

Microsoft; (In Costa Rica) [506] 298-2000; (in the U.S.) [1] (425) 635-7222; tel: [1] 506-293-5860; (in Switzerland) tel: [41] (848) 858-868; fax [41] (1) 831-0869; http://www.microsoft.com/.

NEC; (in the U.S.) [1] (916) 388-0101 (Main Switchboard); (in Germany) tel: [49] (18) 0524- 1212; tel:[49] (89) 3160-1233; fax: [49] (89) 3160- 1613 (Floppy Disk and Hard Drive); tel: [49] (89) 9627-4233; fax: [49] (89) 9627-4613 (All Other Products); http://www.nec.com/.

Novell; (in the U.S.) tel: [1] (408) 434-2300; fax: [1] (408) 577-5775 (Worldwide Sales Headquarters); tel: 800-638-9273; (in the U.S.) [1] 801-429-5588 (English Technical Support); [1] 801-429-3693 (Spanish Technical Support); [1] 801-429-3694 (Portuguese Technical Support); http://www.novell.com.

Quark; (in the U.S.) tel: [1] (303) 894-8899; fax: [1] (303) 894-3398 (For Products Registered in the Americas); (in Switzerland) tel: [41] (1) 808-7722; fax: [41] (1) 808-7799; http://www.quark.com/.

Toshiba; (in the U.S.) [1] (949) 583-3000 (Corporate Headquarters); (in Germany) tel: [49] (2131) 158-319; fax: [49] (2131) 158-558; (in Switzerland) tel: [41] (1) 946-0777; fax: [41] (1) 946-0807; (in Ireland) tel: [44] (193) 282-8828; http://www.toshiba.com/.

Internet Connection
HOW TO CONNECT

Connecting to AOL and Compuserve in the Dominican Republic is similar to using it when traveling outside your own area code. See the introductory section for detailed information on connecting to your account through a different phone number.

America Online

Numbers are available at keyword *international*. Be sure to get several local numbers before leaving. AOL's Global-Net service charges US$12 an hour in addition to the usual charges. Go to keyword *access* (a free area) and download the software.

Access: Santo Domingo 533-9181.

Compuserve

Numbers are available at keyword *Go International*. The Compuserve Web-site also has a great deal of information, at http://www.compuserve.com.

Access: Santo Domingo 533-9181.

Independent Service Providers

Many independent service providers offer discounts if you are only in town for a couple days.

Codetel; tel: 685-3133; tel: 1-200-1279; ayuda@codetel.net.do; http://www.codetel.net.do/.

Fiberlink; tel: (800-LINK-NOW); tel: (215) 793-6500; fax: (215) 793-6565; sales@fiberlinkcc.com; www.fiberlinkcc.com.

ICE Networks; tel: (787) 764-1234; fax: (787) 764-1661; email: webmaster@icepr.com; http://www.icepr.com.

Opus Neworx; tel: (809) 625-5949 or (868) 628-1950; fax: (868) 628-1969; email: sysop@opus.co.tt.; http://www.opus-networx.com/

Business Culture
GREETINGS AND COURTESIES

Handshakes are common for both men and women, both when meeting and upon departing. Friends may embrace, and women friends may hold each other by the shoulders and kiss. Business cards should be printed in Spanish, although most businesspeople speak English. At social events, the host will usually make individual introductions.

DECISION MAKING

Actual decisions are almost always made at a high level of authority. Although you should approach senior people, Dominicanos will wish to match you with someone of similar rank. It is important to cultivate personal relationships with these peers, because the quality of these relationships may strongly influence the actual decisionmaker.

WOMEN

Although women in the Dominican Republic generally occupy a somewhat secondary status in this traditionally male-dominated society, many operate businesses and may be accorded considerable personal freedom. Dominican women are becoming more common and more accepted in business in general, but businesswomen may experience more difficulty than men in doing business.

MEETINGS

Make appointments for meetings well in advance, but reconfirm shortly beforehand. Dominicanos are not punctual, although you should be. Business lunches are relatively common, but only as a means to further the development of the social bond. Although English is spoken, communication in Spanish may be preferred.

BUSINESS ATTIRE

A conservative business suit will do best in the Dominican Republic. Light weight materials better combat the humid weather. Cocktail buffets and evening dinner engagements require more formal attire since dining carries somewhat of an artistic grace in the Caribbean. Conservative elegance is the order of the night.

Dominican Republic

Dominican Republic

Business Centers
Santo Domingo
CITY VIEW

Discovered by the Colombus brothers in 1498, Santo Domingo has grown into a tourist-haven. With sand, surf, and sun everywhere, it may require much energy to get any work done.

AIRPORT

Internacional de las Americas Airport to City Center

The airport lies 18 miles (30 km.) from the city, and travel time is about 45 minutes. There is regular bus service from 7a.m. to 5:30p.m., and taxis are always available at a standard price of DR$200 to the city center.

Airline Numbers

Santo Domingo

Air Canada	(809) 541-5151
American Airlines	(809) 542-5151
Dominicana Airlines	(809) 724-7100
Island Air	(809) 949-0241

United States numbers

Air Aruba	(800) 882-7822
Air Jamaica	(800) 523-5585
ALM	(800) 327-7230
American Airlines	(800) 433-7300
British West Indian Airlines	(800) 538-2942
Cayman Airways	(800) 422-9626
Continental	(800) 231-0856
Delta	(800) 323-2323
Mexicana	(800) 531-7921
Northwest Airlines	(800) 447-4747
TWA	(800) 892-4141
United	(800) 538-2929
USAir	(800) 428-4322

International Carriers

Air Canada	(800) 776-3000
Air France	(800) 237-2747
British Airways	(800) 247-9297
Iberia	(800) 772-4642
KLM	(800) 777-5553
Lufthansa	(800) 645-3880

HOTELS

Top-end

Grand Hotel Lina & Casino; tel: 563-5000; fax: 686-5521.

Jaragua Renaissance Resort; 367 George Washington Ave.; tel: 221-2222; fax: 686-0528; city center; restaurant; casino; conference facilities (up to 1200); secretarial service; corporate rates; fitness; sauna; pool; whirlpool; US$150.

Santo Domingo; Avenida Independencia; tel: 221-1511; fax: 535-4050; city center; restaurant; conference facilities; secretarial service; sauna; pool; US$118.

Santo Domingo Sheraton Hotel and Casino; George Washington Ave. 365; tel: 221-6666; fax: 687-8150; city center; restaurant; casino; conference facilities (up to 750); secretarial service; in-room modem/fax connection; corporate rates; fitness; sauna; pool; US$125.

Quinto Centenario Inter-Continental; Ave. George Washington 218; tel: 221-0000; fax: 221-2020; city center; restaurant; conference facilities (up to 1500); secretarial service; corporate rates; pool; whirlpool; US$160.

Expensive

El Embajador; Avenida Sarasota 65; tel: 221-2131; fax: 532-5306; city center; restaurant; conference center; secretarial service; corporate rates; health; sauna; pool; tennis; water sports; US$85.

Plaza Naco; Avenida Tiradentes; tel: 541-6226; fax: 541-7251; city center; restaurant; conference facilities; secretarial service; fitness; pool; US$85.

Moderate

Hispaniola Hotel & Casino; Avenida Independencia and Abraham Lincoln; tel: 221-7111; fax: 535-4050; restaurant; pool; tennis; US$70.

Continental Hotel; Avenida Maximo Gomez 16; tel: 689-1151; fax: 687-8397; restaurant; conference facilities (up to 125); secretarial service; corporate rates; pool; US$55.

Napolitano; Avenida George Washington 101; tel: 687-1131; fax: 687-6814; city center; restaurant; corporate rates; pool; US$60.

Palacio Nicolas de Ovando; Calle Las Damas 53; tel: 687-3101; fax: 688-5170; city center; restaurant; conference center; pool; US$50.

MEDICAL CARE

Centro Medico UCE; Avenida Maximo Gomez; tel: 682-0171.

Centro Otorrinolaringologia y Especialidades; Avenida 27 de febrero; tel: 682-0151.

Clinica Abreu; Avenida Independencia; tel: 688-4411.

Clinica Dr. Abel Gonzalez; Avenida independencia; tel: 682-6001/08.

AUTO RENTAL

Undisciplined driving on roads that range from excellent to poor demand defensive driving on the part of the visitor. Night travel on inter-city highways and in rural areas is discouraged due to excessive speeding and vehicles being driven with malfunctioning headlights.

Avis; national reservations, tel: 533-9295; international reservations: 800-228-0668; Ave. Abraham Lincoln Esqu. Sarasota, PO Box 176-9, tel: 535-7191; fax: 535-1747; airport, tel: 549-0468/0469.

Budget; tel: 800-437-9440 or (809) 567-0175; downtown: 567-0173; airport: 549-0351; fax: 549-0346; Ave. JFK Esq-Lope de Vega, tel: 567-0175; fax: 567-0177.

Dollar; tel: 685-1519

Hertz; Mercantil Santo Domingo, Ave. Independencia 454, tel: 221-5333; fax: 221-8927; Las Americas International Airport, tel: 549-0454; fax: 221-8927.

Honda Rent A Car; tel: 567-1015/6.

National; tel: 800-227-7368; 562-1444/542-0162.

Thrifty; tel: 685-9191.

WORLD TRADE CENTER

World Trade Center Santo Domingo

Winston Churchill Ave., Torre BHD, 4th Floor
PO Box 95-2
Santo Domingo, Dominican Republic
tel: [1] (809) 544-2222
fax: [1] (809) 544-0502
email: amcham@codetel.net.do
website: http://www.amcham.org.do

Ecuador

At a Glance

THE PEOPLE

Population .... 12,562,496 (July 1999 est.)
Growth Rate .... 1.78% (1999 est.)
Life Expectancy .... 72.16 years (born 1999)
Infant Mortality . 30.69 deaths/1,000 live births (1999 est.)

Ethnic Composition

Mestizo (Amerindian and Caucasian) 55%
Amerindian 25%
Caucasian 10%
Black African 10%

Religious Composition

Roman Catholic.. 95%
Other and non-affiliated... 5%

Languages Spoken

Spanish (official), local Amerindian dialects

Education and Literacy

Education is compulsory for ages 6 through 14 but compliance is low in rural areas. Nationwide adult literacy is 90.1 percent.

Labor Force

Total: 4,200,000
By occupation: services 53%, industry 18%, agriculture 29%.

THE ECONOMY

Ecuador has a very large agricultural component to its economy as well as significant oil exports. Consequently, this tiny South American nation is highly subject to fluctuations in world commodity prices. Even its service sector is heavily tied to the commodity portion of the economy. Downturns in oil prices during the 1990s were compounded by damage caused by El Nino in three of Ecuador's other main exports: banana crops, coffee beans, and ocean shrimp. The government has been unsuccessful in turning the economy away from reliance on these troubled exports. (Currently, the U.S. has taken Ecuador's behalf in trying to pry open the E.U. to South American bananas.) Unable to keep its commitments to the WTO, Ecuador has also made itself unattractive to foreign investment. Most were already concerned about the nation's lack of stable political leadership. Though oil prices have risen in the latter part of 1999, Ecuador's government has continued to misstep when trying to revitalize this stagnant economy.

Exports .... US$3.4 billion (f.o.b., 1997)
Imports .... US$2.9 billion (c.i.f., 1997)
Total GDP .... US$58.7 billion (1998 est.)
GDP Per Capita .... US$4,800 (1998 est.)
Unemployment   12% with broad underemployment (1998 est.)
Inflation Rate .... 43% (1998 est.)

Top Export Partners

United States, Latin America, E.U., Asia.

Top Import Partners

United States, E.U., Latin America, Asia.

Top Exports

Petroleum, bananas, shrimp, coffee, cocoa.

Top Imports

Transport equipment, consumer goods, vehicles, machinery, chemicals.

BUSINESS WORKWEEK

Offices

Monday to Friday 8a.m. to 1p.m. and 2p.m. to 6:30p.m.; Saturdays 8:30a.m. to 2p.m.

Banks

Monday to Friday 9a.m. to 1:30p.m.

Note: Most banks offer "after-hours" service to the public from 2:30p.m. to 6p.m. Monday to Friday, and from 9:30a.m. to 2p.m. on Saturdays.

Government

Monday to Friday 8:30a.m. to 12:30p.m. and 1:30p.m. to 4p.m.

Retail

Monday to Friday 9a.m. to 1p.m. and 3p.m. to 7p.m.; Saturdays 10a.m. to noon or 2p.m.

Note: Rural hours for all business and government services are more attuned to local custom than to a fixed schedule.

HOLIDAYS

New Year's Day...January 1
Epiphany ....January 6
Carnival .... February 15-16*
Holy Thursday ....April 1*
Good Friday...April 2*
Easter Saturday...April 3*
Labor Day..May 1
Battle of Pichincha...May 24
Birth of Simon Bolivar..July 24
Independence of Quito .... August 10
Independence of Guayaquil ....October 9
All Saints' Day ....November 1
All Souls' Day ....November 2
Independence of Cuenca ....November 3
Founding of Quito (Quito only) ....December 6
Christmas Day...December 25

*Date may vary by year.

CLIMATE

Seasons

The climate varies by altitude rather than seasons. The driest seasons are June to October, but the sun shines all year round. Tropical rains are also quite common even during the "dry" season. Temperature extremes run from 15˚C (59˚F) to 38˚C (100˚F) over the entire country.

Regions

As the name of the country implies, Ecuador has an equatorial climate. The Amazon jungle has a hot, humid climate, while the Galàpagos Islands are rather cooler. Guayaquil and the coastal plain (Costa), also have a hot, humid climate, influenced by the marine currents in the Pacific Ocean. The weather is temperate in Quito and the highlands, and the average temperature all year round there is approximately 13˚C (55˚F). The best time to visit is between December and April.

Ecuador

Money & Banking

Currency

The currency of Ecuador is the Sucre (Su).

Denominations

The Sucre comes in coin denominations of Su50, 20, 10, 5, and 1 and banknotes of Su100, 500, 1,000, 5,000, and 10,000.

Traveler's Checks and Credit Cards

Traveler's checks, in U.S. dollar denominations preferably, can be exchanged at banks, exchange kiosks, hotels, and international airports. Larger banks may offer the best exchange rates. Rates of commission hover between one and four percent. Keep all receipts (of any exchanges) if you plan to reconvert currency at departure. This is very important if you are exchanging large amounts that might draw government attention.

Most major currencies, especially U.S. dollars, can be exchanged without a charge. Try to take only crisp and new notes; wrinkled and soiled notes are likely to be refused. Business visitors should avoid all forms of black marketeer exchanges even though their rate is significantly better than the government "official" rate.

Major credit cards like American Express, Visa, Diner's Club, and MasterCard are easily accepted in good hotels, large restaurants, and some major retail outlets in Quito and Guayaquil. Most banks in the capital offer cash advances on credit cards, but make sure you bring your passport. identification. (Additionally, an American Express office is located in Avenida Amazonas, Quito.) The most favorable exchange rates are given for credit card transactions. ATMs can be found in the capital but service is not dependable.

Essential Terms

English	Spanish
Yes No	Sí No
Good morning Hello (daytime) Hello (evening) Hello (telephone)	Buenos días Buenas tardes Buenas noches ¿Hola?
Good-bye	Adiós
Please	Por favor
Thank you	Gracias
Pleased to meet you	Encantado (a) de conocerle
Excuse me; I'm sorry	¿Perdóneme?
My name is _____	Me llamo _____
I don't understand	No comprendo
Do you speak English?	¿Habla usted inglés?

Travel

VISA AND PASSPORT

Passports that are valid for a minimum of six months are required of all visitors except Colombian nationals, who can enter using a national identity card. Passports (or copies with entry stamps) must be carried at all times. Foreigners are subject to arrest if caught without a passport. Stays of 90 days or less necessitate a return or onward travel ticket upon entry to Ecuador.

A visa is required only of nationals of Algeria, Bangladesh, China (PR), Costa Rica, Cuba, Guatemala, Honduras, India, Iran, Iraq, Jordan, Korea (DPR), Korea (Rep. of), Lebanon, Libya, Nigeria, Pakistan, holders of a Palestinian Authority passport, Sri Lanka, Sudan, Syria, Taiwan, Tunisia, Vietnam, Yemen and members of the Sikh religion of any nationality. This list may change with little notice, so visitors are advised to check with any Ecuadorian consulate immediately prior to planning their trip.

Travelers from the countries listed above must also have a visa even while in transit, unless resuming their journey out of Ecuador by the first available connecting flight, or the same one, within 48 hours; and providing they are holding confirmed onward travel tickets and do not leave the airport.

Anyone wishing to stay in Ecuador beyond a three-month period must also apply for a visa. the maximum allowable stay is six months.

Those with visas must register with the Ministry of Government and the Director General of Migration in Ecuador within 30 days of their entry.

Types of visas issued: Tourist, Business, Transit, Student, and Cultural Exchange (free of charge).

Tourist, Business, and Transit visas are valid for six months maximum. Student visas remain valid up to a year (renewable). Cultural Exchange visas are also valid up to a year.

Business visas require an invitation from an Ecuadorian sponsor or government agency. Do not attempt to conduct business transactions while using a tourist visa.

Note: It is not legal to study if the visitor only has a Tourist visa.

Applications must be conducted in person (appointments are necessary), with the visa usually being issued the same day.

DEPARTURE FORMALITIES

A US$25 airport departure tax is payable in U.S. funds. Twelve percent of the ticket price is payable as a tax for domestic flights.

CUSTOMS ENTRY (PERSONAL)

Duty-free
- Tobacco: 300 cigarettes, 50 cigars, or 200g of tobacco
- Alcohol: 1 liter of alcohol
- Other: a "reasonable" amount of perfume, gifts and personal effects (This is open to broad interpretation by customs officials.)

Prohibited or Restricted
Prior permission is required for the import of:
- Firearms and ammunition
- Narcotics
- Fresh or dry meat and meat products
- Plants and vegetables

IMMUNIZATION

Preventive measures against cholera, hepatitis, typhoid, polio, and rabies are recommended, especially for travel outside of urban areas. Malaria and dengue fever are reported on the Pacific coast and provinces along the eastern border. Plague and Paragomiasis (oriental lung fluke) have been reported in limited areas. Rabies and hepatitis (A & B) are widespread in Ecuador. One can consider risk of Yellow Fever to exist everywhere except urban centers. A certificate of vaccination may be necessary to facilitate your departure from Ecuador.

TIPPING

Taxi
Tipping is not necessary for taxi drivers. But if satisfied with the service, rounding up the fare is recommended.

Porters
Porters at depots generally receive 50 centavos per piece; hotel porters receive about slightly more.

Hotels
A 15 percent service charge is generally included in the hotel bill.

Restaurants
A ten percent service charge is often included in the restaurant tab. If service is exceptional, another ten percent can be added. It is customary to buy your bartender a drink in place of a tip.

Other

Barbers and beauticians generally receive ten percent. Specialized guides should be tipped a minimum of $10 to $15 per day, per person. One-day guides for outdoor activities can be tipped about 15 percent of the trip cost.

EMERGENCY INFORMATION

Police and Crime

There are high levels of street crime in city areas, especially Quito, where pickpocketing, armed robbery, and muggings are common. Avoid travel to the northern province of Sucumbios, and areas of Carchi Province adjacent to the Colombian border where crime, extortion, and kidnapping of foreigners occur with regularity. Colombia-based organized crime, drug traffickers, and armed insurgents pose a threat in other areas bordering Colombia. And one should not approach the Peruvian border anywhere except at official checkpoints. Maritime safety standards are low, so be careful when traveling to the islands off the coast of Ecuador.

Guayaquil has undergone a dramatic increase in the incidence of kidnappings for ransom, frequently in conjunction with carjackings. Travelers must be alert to their surroundings, especially in the well-known restaurant district called Urdesa.

The President of Ecuador has exercised his authority to impose states of emergency in parts of the country on several occasions, most often in response to soaring crime rates. Under states of emergency, military forces carry out joint patrols with police, with curfews often imposed. Expanded search authority is granted to the enforcers under these circumstances, and roadblocks are often put in place to verify vehicle registration and personal identification. Foreign citizens should have identification with them at all times, especially proof of citizenship. During the greater part of 1999, Guayas Province—including Guayaquil—has been under this status.

Take basic precautions against petty crime, especially in tourist areas (the colonial center of Quito, in public parks, the Las Penas neighborhood, and the El Malecon waterfront promenade in Guayaquil). Foreign business visitors are all considered to be rich and are often the target of thieves. Consequently, purses, laptops, and briefcases will require additional security. Do not leave valuables in cars or on tables in cafés. Keep non-essential valuables locked in hotel safes when not in use. Use credit cards and travel checks when possible to avoid carrying large sums of cash. Avoid all suspicion of any connection to the drug trade, and never carry a stranger's baggage.

The holding of foreign business people for ransom is a reality in Ecuador's border regions. Many corporate travelers bring their own armed security when traveling to areas near Colombia and Peru. Women travelers in all sections of Ecuador should avoid going out alone at night and should have a high security awareness even when riding in a cab.

Police officers in rural areas are often part of the crime problem. Some may attempt to "shakedown" visitors or solicit bribes. Demands for receipts usually puts an end to such requests. All visitors should consider their stance on bribery in advance of travel to border areas. Police, both rural and urban, cannot be depended upon to investigate crimes or return stolen property. Anything which you cannot afford to lose should be insured.

Emergency Numbers

Police	101
Fire	102
Ambulance (Quito)	131
Hospital	241-540
US Embassy Quito	(2) 562-890/561-749
US Consulate Guayaquil	323-570/327-893

Health

Tap water in Ecuador should be viewed as potentially contaminated. Do not drink tap water or use it for brushing teeth or as ice cubes. Bottled water is safe and readily available. Otherwise, boil water for 10 to 15 minutes before use, or apply purifiers. Wash all vegetables in a chlorine solution, and eat only those fruits that can be peeled without contamination. Eat only well-cooked food while it is still hot. Pork, salad, and mayonnaise pose increased risk. Powdered or tinned milk is advisable, but only when mixed with safe water. Avoid dairy products, raw seafood, rare meat, and roadside stands and street vendors.

Malaria, TB, tetanus, typhoid, muscular neuritis, yellow fever, and hepatitis are endemic here; take precautions before departure. Heat and the dry climate cause skin infections and encourage the spread of skin parasites. Also be aware that the high altitude in Quito may come with some temporary discomfort. Shortness of breath, fitful sleep, dizziness, headaches, energy loss and prolonged respiratory infections are all signs of altitude-related illness.

Medical treatment outside of the major cities is very limited. Ecuador's medical facilities should be used for emergencies only. Travel insurance with a medical evacuation policy is highly advised for all business travelers. Bring along a well-stocked medical kit with any prescription drugs that may be required.

INTERNAL TRAVEL

AIR

Flying is the most often used means of transit for intercity travel. The national airlines SAETA, SAN, and TAME offer frequent services between Quito and Guayaquil and between other destinations around the country. Several smaller airlines provide connections between the coast and the eastern part of Ecuador. Airports for these secondary destinations include Cuenca, Manta, Esmeraldas, Lago Agrio, and Coca.

There is a 12 percent departure tax included in the ticket price.

The Galapagos Islands are served by daily flights at 1p.m. from both Quito and Guayaquil on national airlines. Non-Ecuadorians are charged more for tickets on the route (US$40 is the current additional fee for visiting a national park). The primary airports of the Galapágos are Baltra and Caráquez.

TAXI

Taxis are widely available, especially in larger towns and cities, but reserve in advance. Ask at the hotel for information. Fares are cheap, but negotiate beforehand. Cabs are metered in Quito, rarely elsewhere. Be sure that the cab has a number on the car door, as reports of thieves masquerading as drivers in unmarked yellow cars have surfaced. Hailing a cab from the street is deemed safe during the daytime only.

AUTO

Automobile rentals are available in urban areas. Avis, Budget, National, and Hertz all have offices in Ecuador. An International Driving Permit is not required.

Many bridges and roads sustained heavy damage during the 1997-1998 weather conditions brought about by El Nino. Most of them have not been substantially repaired, resulting in frequent delays and detours. Road work is being done at a fast pace, but the effect of earthquakes and flooding on so much of Ecuador's transportation network (mostly in the south) have taken a heavy toll.

It is probably just as well that the foreign traveler not also attempt to be a motorist in Ecuador, at least so for any but the most experienced business travelers to the country. Security risks are formidable outside of the cities, and rental cars are of little use in urban areas. It is better to hire a car with a local driver for a daily or weekly rate. Let your hotel concierge or local business contacts arrange this service.

TRAIN

Rail service has been severely limited since 1983, when floods devastated the country. The earthquake of 1987 did even more damage to the rail system. Limited sections are in operation, including Riobamba to Quito and Alausí to Guayaquil. These passenger lines should be used only as a last resort. As picturesque as these rail lines are, this service is not really suitable or punctual enough for business travel.

METRO

There is no metro system in any of Ecuador's cities.

BUSES & TRAMS

Although bus travel has greatly improved, frequent traffic accidents involving buses do not encourage this mode of travel. It can also prove dangerous due to the high rate of crime. Overcrowding and sketchy road conditions can make for a long trip. It is, however, sometimes the only way to reach remote villages without hiring a private car. Purchase tickets well in advance if traveling long distance.

Quito and Guayaquil operate local bus and minibus services at flat fares. While convenient for getting across town, they are not very suitable for attending business meetings. "Serious" business people in Ecuador arrive at meetings by hired taxi or privately chauffeured car.

WATER TRAVEL

Ecuador has international passenger service calling at its Pacific ports as well as a river system serving the Amazon basin. But the rocky coastline means that coast hopping is an inefficient and dangerous way for the visitor to travel. Several navigable rivers do flow eastward into the Amazon River basin, but the region is often off-limits to visitors because of a border dispute with Peru. Use of the river system can also have high security risks.

If river trips are deemed necessary, allow trusted local business associates to arrange the itinerary and hire the boat service.

Not many passenger services exist from the mainland to the Galapágos Islands. However, once a traveler manages passage there, perhaps via air, they can expect to find tourist boats, hired yachts, and local mail steamers are available for travel between islands.

TRAVEL ASSISTANCE

Ministerio de Turismo
Avenida Eloy Alfaro 32300 y Carlos Tobar
Quito, Ecuador
Tel; (2) 225 101, 507 555, 507 570
Fax; (2) 507 565, 507 564
email: linfo@ecua.net.ec
website: wwwpub4.ecua.net.ec/mintur

Corporación de Comercio Exterior, Industrializacion, Pesca y Turismo Subsecretaría de Turismo
Avenida Eloy Alfaro N32-300 y Carlos Tobar
Quito, Ecuador
tel: (2) 507 562, 507 560, 228 303
fax: (2) 507 565, 229 330
email: ecuainfo@interactive.net.ec

Camara Provincial de Turismos (CAPTUR)
Avenida 6 de Diciembre 1424 y Carrión
Quito, Ecuador
tel: (2) 224 074, 509 860; fax: (2) 507 682

Asociación Ecuatoriana de Agencias de Viajes y Turismo (ASECUT)
Casilla 9421
Edificio Banco del Pacifico
5º Piso Avenida
Amazonas 720 y Veintimilla
Quito, Ecuador
tel: (2) 503 669; fax: (2) 285 872

Hotel Accommodations
Association Hotelera del Ecuador .... (2) 453-942

Communications

DIALING CODES IN ECUADOR

International country code: [593]

Selected city codes: Ambato (3), Cayambe (2), Cuenca (7), Esmeraldas (6), Guayaquil (4), Ibarra (6), Loja (7), Machachi (2), Portoviejo, Quevedo (5), Quito(2), Salinas (4), Santo Domingo (2), Tulcan (6)

Dialing Ecuador from Overseas

To dial Ecuador from overseas, dial your country's international dialing code, then 593 (the country code for Ecuador), then the city code and finally the number. If you were dialing Guayaquil from the United States, for example, you would begin with 011, then 593, then 4 (the city code for Guayaquil), and finally the number of the person or office you were trying to reach.

Assistance Numbers
International Operator 116
Long Distance Operator 105
Local Operator/Directory 104
AT&T in Quito 566-995

CALLING WITHIN ECUADOR

Local Calls

A local call can be made from stores with a *telefono* sign in the window if no private phone is available. Other than that, head for an EMETEL office to place a call or a fax between 8a.m. to 9:30p.m. A local call costs S1,500.

Long Distance Calls

Calling within Ecuador may be safest when placed in an EMETEL office. However, lines are often overloaded making for a frustrating experience.

International Calls

To bypass certain language difficulties, dial an overseas operator.
Argentina 999-161
Brazil 999-177
Chile 999-179/166/168
France 999-180
Spain 999-176
Switzerland... 999-160
U.K. 999-178
U.S. AT&T 999-119
U.S. MCI.. 999-170
U.S. Sprint... 999-171
Venezuela 999-173

Keep in mind that these access numbers may not be available from every phone.

Ecuador's EMETEL offices also allow direct or collect calls, but no call backs. Collect calls are limited to a few countries only. Be aware that hotels may include a 20 percent surcharge on already high rates.

Ecuador

PAY PHONES

Public Telephones

Most pay phones are card operated. Be aware that even if no one is on the other line, the call may be charged.

Calling Cards

Cards (tarjetas) can be purchased at hotels and news stands for local and long distance calls. They do not work for international calls.

CELLULAR PHONES

Analog cellular service is provided by Conecel S.A.

Note: Your home country cell phone may not work in this country. If not, we recommend that you rent an international cell phone *before* you leave home. A major US-based cell phone rental provider is **IMC WorldCell**. For information see "International Cell Phone Rentals" on page 14.

CALL BACK

You can (potentially) save significant sums when calling in Ecuador by using a call back service. For a list of call-back services, please refer to the "Communications" section in the *Global Road Warrior* Introduction.

Fees for call back services vary widely, depending on the company and the type of service required. Be sure to check with these companies before leaving to compare rates.

PHONE JACK

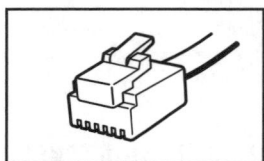

Plug adaptors are available through **iGo Corporation**. (See "Electrical and Telephone Adaptors" on page 19.)

FAX

Faxes are available at most hotels,or at the EMETEL office.

POSTAL SERVICES

Mail service is unreliable. Certify all air mail and be sure to mark it 'Por Avion'. Letters and postcards to the U.S. will take between seven to ten days; to Europe, it will take ten days to two weeks. Post offices outside the major cities are often unfamiliar with rates and will quote the wrong prices. One may have to bribe a postman if expecting packages from abroad. Post offices in Quito are generally open between 7:30a.m. and 7p.m. Monday to Friday, and Saturdays between 8a.m. and 1p.m. or 2p.m.

TELEGRAMS

Telegrams can be sent from many hotels until 10p.m., as well as the chief telegraph office in most cities.

Business Services

COURIER SERVICES

Guayaquil

Airborne Express (Intl. Bonded Couriers).; Repan SA; Avenidas de las Americas, 300 Metros Norte de Aduana, en Zona de Cargo; tel: (4) 690-444; fax: (4) 690-452.

DHL International del Ecuador, S.A.; 8va. Oeste #100 y Av. San Jorge, Guayaquil; tel: (4) 282-469.

Quito

Airborne Express (Intl. Bonded Couriers); Rio coca y Ernandina Esquuina, Quito; terl: (2) 456-830; fax: (4) 290-280.

DHL International del Ecuador, S.A., Eloy Alfaro y de los juncos, Lote 113-A, Quito; tel: (2) 485-100.

UPS; Iñaquitory Naciones Unidas, Oficina 203, Quito; tel: (2) 460-469, 460-608; fax: (2) 443-637.

Electrical

Current

120 volts AC, 60Hz

ELECTRIC PLUGS

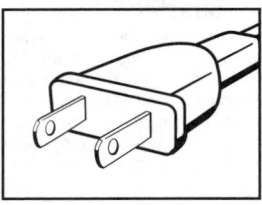

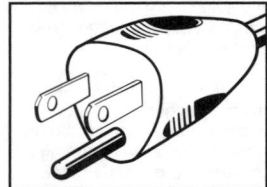

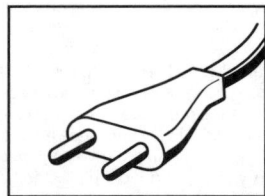

Plug adaptors are available through **iGo Corporation**. (See "Electrical and Telephone Adaptors" on page 19.)

Technical Support

HARDWARE/SOFTWARE VENDOR SUPPORT

Compaq/Digital; (Houston Office, U.S.) tel: [1] (713) 370-0670; fax: [1] (713) 514-1740; (in the U.S.) tel: [1] (281) 518-2000 (General U.S.); fax: [1] (281) 518-1442; http://www.compaq.com.

Dell; tel: (2) 506-831 (Comlasa del Ecuador); (2) 441-856 (ComWare Ecuador); (2) 430-993 (Xerox Ecuador); (in the U.S.) tel: [1] (512) 338-4400; fax: [1] (512) 728-3330; http://www.dell.com/.

Hewlett Packard; (Venezuela Office) tel: (58) 2 239 5664; (in the U.S.) tel: [1] (408) 246-4300; http://www.hp.com/.

IBM; tel: (2) 565-100; fax: (2) 565-145; (in the U.S.) tel: [1] (919) 517-2800; (U.S. Main Office) tel: [1] 914-765-1900; http://www.ibm.com/.

Microsoft; tel: [506] 298-2000; (in the U.S.) [1] (425) 635-7222; (in Switzerland) tel: [41] (848) 858-868; fax [41] (1) 831-0869; http://www.microsoft.com/.

NEC; (in the U.S.) [1] (916) 388-0101 (Main Switchboard); (in Germany) tel: [49] (18) 0524- 1212; tel:[49] (89) 3160-1233; fax: [49] (89) 3160- 1613 (Floppy Disk and Hard Drive); tel: [49] (89) 9627-4233; fax: [49] (89) 9627-4613 (All Other Products); http://www.nec.com/.

Toshiba; (in the U.S.) [1] (949) 583-3000 (Corporate Headquarters); (in Germany) tel: [49] (2131) 158-319; fax: [49] (2131) 158-558; (in Switzerland) tel: [41] (1) 946-0777; fax: [41] (1) 946-0807; (in Ireland) tel: [44] (193) 282-8828; http://www.toshiba.com/.

Internet Connection
HOW TO CONNECT

Connecting to AOL and Compuserve in Ecuador is similar to using it when traveling outside your own area code. See the introductory section for detailed information on connecting to your account through a different phone number.

America Online

Numbers are available at keyword *international*. Be sure to get several local numbers before leaving. AOL's Global-Net service charges US$12 an hour in addition to the usual charges. Go to keyword *access* (a free area) and download the software.

Access: Guayaquil (4) 511-000; Manta (5) 629-142; Quito (2) 505-000.

Compuserve

Numbers are available at keyword *Go International*. The Compuserve Web-site also has a great deal of information, at http://www.compuserve.com.

Access: Guayaquil (4) 511-000; Quito (2) 505-000.

Independent Service Providers

Many independent service providers offer discounts if you are only in town for a couple of days.

Ecuador On-Line; tel: (2) 461-159; fax: (2) 461-158; http://www.eolnet.net/.

Hoy.Net; tel: (229) 545-546; fax: (5932) 506-820; email: ventas@hoy.net; http://www.hoy.net/.

INTERCOM - Nodo Ecuanex; tel: (2) 553-553; email: admin@ecuanex.net.ec; http://www.ecuanex.apc.org/.

VPM Internet Service; tel: [1] (800) 321-0221; tel: [1] (916) 983-9876; fax: [1] (916) 983-4375; email: sales@vpm.com; http://www.vpm

Business Culture
GREETINGS AND COURTESIES

Handshakes are standard for both men and women when meeting and departing, although handshakes become less common at subsequent meetings. Male friends hug and female friends kiss. Titles are important indicators of status and are used extensively (along with last names). The host will usually introduce each guest individually to others.

DECISION MAKING

Decisions are almost always made at a high level of authority. It is important to cultivate personal relationships with Ecuadorean employees, because these relationships may strongly influence decisions in the long run.

MEETINGS

Prior appointments are necessary for meetings, espe-cially with larger firms. Meetings take place in offices or restaurants. Be punctual, although your Ecuadorean counterpart may be as much as 20 minutes late. Business is generally conducted in Spanish; the business elite often speak English. A low-key, non-pressure sales pitch is appreciated in Ecuador. Approach negotiations in a firm yet courteous, confident and good natured manner. Avoid topics of economic or political nature.

WOMEN

Although women in Ecuador generally occupy a somewhat secondary status, many operate businesses and are generally accorded considerable personal freedom. Foreign businesswomen should experience few problems, but they are expected to be highly professional. Do not appear flirtatious or available; a friendly but somewhat aloof manner will suit any business occasion.

BUSINESS ATTIRE

Ecuadorians appreciate sharp dressers. Dark, conservative businesswear is suitable for any business occasion. The humid weather may dictate a lighter weight fabric. A jacket or suit coat may not be necessary depending on the advice of your Ecuadorian associate. Women may attire themselves in conservative dresses. The same clothing can be worn to an evening event, in hotel dining rooms and nicer restaurants.

Business Centers
Guayaquil
CITY VIEW

Until recently Guayaquil was a small city, but business has entered in a big way. It is one of South America's fastest growing cities and Quito's commercial rival.

AIRPORT
Simon Bolivar Airport to City Center

The airport lies 3 miles (5 km.) from the city. There is regular bus and taxi service. Taxis cost about US$5 to downtown and buses charge $3 if more than 10 passengers board.

HOTELS
Top-end

Continental; Chile y 10 De Agosto; tel: 329-270; fax: 325-454; near airport; conference center; secretarial services; corporate rates.

Grand Guayaquil; Boyaca y 10 De Agosto; tel: (4)-329-690; fax: (4) 327-251; located in city center; conference center; executive business center; secretarial services; translations; courier services; corporate rates.

Hilton Colon Guayaquil; Ave. Francisco de Orellana; tel: (4) 689-000; fax: (4) 689-149; www.hilton.com; conference rooms, business center; data ports; airport shuttle; ballrooms.

Swissotel (Oro Verde); 9 De Octubre Y Garcia Moreno; tel: (4) 327-999; fax: (4) 329-350; near airport and city center; conference center; secretarial services; corporate rates; fitness center.

Uni Hotel; Clemente BAllen 406; tel: (4) 327-100 (for reservations in the US, call (800) 223-5652); fax: (4) 328-352; near airport and city center; secretarial services; conference center; corporate rates.

Expensive

Boulevard; Avenida 9 De Octubre 432; tel: (4) 566-700; fax: (4) 560-076; city center; conference center; secretarial services; corporate rates.

Moderate

Palace; Chile 214 y Luque; tel: 4-321-080; fax: (4) 322-887.

Rizzo; Calle Clemente Ballen 319 Y Chile; tel: (4) 325-210.

Samarina; 9 De Octubre Y Malecon, La Libertad; tel: (4) 785-167; fax: (4) 786-423.

MEDICAL CARE

Clinica Kennedy; tel: 396-963.

AUTO RENTAL

Avis; airport, tel: 339-9268; fax: 298-6272; El Salvador Hotel, tel: 224-2710; Hotel Camino Real, tel: 223-9103; fax: 298-6272; Hotel Presidente, tel: 243-4444, ext. 185; fax: 298-6272; 12 Calle 2-73, Zona 9; tel: 331-2750; fax: 332-1263; (800) 221-1084 (in the U.S.).

Bugdet; reservations, (2) 545-761; fax: (2) 562-705; airport, tel: (4) 288-510; Ave. of the Americas #900, tel: (4) 284-559; fax: (4) 283-656; in front of Oro Verde Hotel, tel: (4) 329-898, 328-571; fax: (4) 326-949; (800) 527-0700 (in the U.S.).

Hertz; domestic tel: (4) 327-895; intl. tel.: (4) 310-818, intl. fax: (4) 313-491; airport (ORo Rent a Car) tel: (4) 293-011; fax: (4) 293-012; Hotel Oro Verde (Oro Rent a Car), tel: (4) 327-895; fax: (4) 329-350; (800) 654-3131 (in the U.S.).

WORLD TRADE CENTER

World Trade Center Guayaquil
Circunvalacion Sur
206 Y Unica
Urdesa Central
tel: (4) 299-180; fax: (4) 299-840
email: xcortes@telconet.net

Quito

CITY VIEW

Quito is the capital of Ecuador and many feel it is the loveliest city in South America. Modern construction has been limited in the last 20 years, giving the city an antiquated feeling that is disappearing from other cities in the region.

AIRPORT

Take care not to let valuables out of your sight even at the request of customs officials, or you may not see them again.

Mariscal Sucre Airport to City Center

Quito's airport lies five miles (8k.m.) from the city center. Taxis should cost around US$3 to US$5 from the airport to the new town (25 to 30 minutes). Prices go up at night. Buses run every 20 minutes between 6a.m. and 11p.m. and cost US$3 if more than 10 passengers are on board (30 to 40 minutes).

AIRLINES

Aeroflot	(2) 524-356
Air France	(2) 523-596
Alitalia	(2) 509-061
American Air	(2) 561-144
Aeroperu	(2) 561-699
Argentinas	(2) 551-524
Avianca	(2) 508-843
British Airways	(2) 540-000
Ecuatoriana	(2) 434-646
Iberia	(2) 540-456
Icelandair	(2) 561-820
Korean Air	(2) 543-505
KLM	(2) 455-562
Ladeco	(2) 522-590
Lufthansa	(2) 541-300
Saeta Internc.	(2) 542-148
TAME	(2) 524-023
Varig	(2) 563-316
Viasa	(2) 543-257

HOTELS

Top End

Alameda Real; Roca 653 Amazonas; tel: (2) 562-345; fax: (2) 565-759; city center; conference center; secretarial services; fitness center; corporate rates.

Crowne Plaza; Av. De Los Shyris 1757 y NN.UU; tel: (2) 445-306; fax: (2) 251-958; downtown; banquet and meeting facilities; exercise room.

Quito; Avenida Gonzalez Suarez 2500; tel: (2) 544-600; fax: (2) 567-284; city center; conference center; executive services; secretarial services; corporate rates.

Expensive

Republica; Avenue Republica and Azuay; tel: (2) 436-553; fax: (2) 437-667; city suburb; in-room computer terminals available; conference center; corporate rates.

Sebastian; Almagro 822 y Cordero; tel: (2) 222-400; fax: (2) 222-500; city center; conference center; secretarial service; fitness center.

Tambo Real; Avenidas 12 De Octubre y Patria; tel: (2) 563-820; fax: (2) 554-964; city center; conference center; executive service; secretarial service.

Moderate

Alejandro; Avenida 10 De Agosto 3976; tel: (2) 439-974; fax: (2) 439-948; near airport; conference center; corporate rates.

Chalet Suisse; Reina Victoria & Calama, P.O. Box 17078703; tel: (2) 562-700; fax: (2) 563-966; telex: (2) 2766 Chusi Ed; email: hosuisse@impsat.net.ec; secretarial service; fax; internet.

Floresta; Isabel La Catolica 1015; tel: (2) 225-376; fax: (2) 500-422; near airport and city center; in-room computer terminals available; conference space; secretarial service; corporate rates.

Gd'oro; Santa Rosa 436 y Armero; tel: (2) 543-033; fax: (2) 565-725; near airport and city center; conference space; corporate rates.

Real Audiencia; Bolivar 220 y Guayaquil; tel: (2) 512-711; fax: (20 580-213; city center; secretarial service; corporate rates.

MEDICAL CARE

Clinica Americana; tel: 234-471.

Voz Andes Hospital; tel: 241-540.

WORLD TRADE CENTER

World Trade Center Quito
Av. 12 de Octubre 1830 y Cordero
Tower B - Floor One
Quito-Ecuador, 17-12-964
tel: (2) 229-226; 229-227; 229-233
fax: (2) 229-234
email: wtcuio1@wtcuio.org.ec
website: http://www.wtca.org/wtc/guito.html

Egypt

At a Glance

THE PEOPLE

Population .... 67,273,906 (July 1999 est.)
Growth Rate .... 1.82% (1999 est.)
Life Expectancy .... 62.39 years (born 1999)
Infant Mortality . 67.46 deaths/1,000 live births (1999 est.)

Ethnic Composition
Hamitics (Egyptian, Bedouin, Berber) 99%
Nubian and other... 1%

Religious Composition
Sunni Muslim.. 94%
Coptic Christian and other... 6%

Languages Spoken
Arabic (official), English, French

Education and Literacy
Education is compulsory for ages 6 to 12. Adult literacy remains low at 51.4 percent.

Labor Force
Total: 17,400,000
By occupation: services 38%; industry 22%, agriculture 40%

THE ECONOMY

Modern Egypt was confronted in the early 1990s with external debt, declining growth, severe payment imbalances, double-digit inflation, and shrinking foreign reserves. The government responded with a comprehensive economic reform program supported by the IMF. The program freed interest and exchange rates and sharply reduced the budget deficit while reining in growth of the money supply. The government also developed a framework for public-sector reform and privatization. It liberalized trade and investment policies as well, moving toward a more decentralized, market-oriented economy. The result has been relative improvement in overall economic stability. Foreign investment has recently moved into Egypt in the form of stock market purchases. But all is not so positive. Tourism, a main component of Egypt's service sector, has been negatively impacted by terrorist attacks on visitors. Added to this is the rising tide of unemployment and population growth. Egypt's low literacy rate will sadly keep this ancient nation from benefiting from the global expansion into technological businesses.

Exports .... US$5.5 billion (f.o.b., FY97/98 est.)
Imports .... US$16.7 billion (c.i.f., FY97/98 est.)
Total GDP .... US$188 billion (1998 est.)
GDP Per Capita .... US$2,850 (1998 est.)
Unemployment .... 10% (1998 est.)
Inflation Rate 3.6% (1998)

Top Export Partners
E.U., United States, Japan

Top Import Partners
United States, E.U., Japan

Top Exports
Crude oil and petroleum products, cotton yarn, raw cotton, textiles, metal products, chemicals.

Top Imports
Machinery and equipment, foods, fertilizers, wood products, consumer goods, capital goods.

BUSINESS WORKWEEK

Offices
Sunday to Thursday 8:30a.m. to 4:00p.m.
Sunday to Thursday 9:00a.m. to 5:00p.m. (multinational companies)

Banks
Monday to Thursday 8:30a.m. to 2:00p.m., Sunday 10a.m. to noon.

Government
Sunday to Thursday 8a.m. to 3p.m.

Retail
Winter: Monday to Saturday 10a.m. to 9p.m.
Summer: Monday to Saturday 10a.m. to 10p.m.
Note: Some retail shops may close between 2p.m. and 4p.m., and on Friday afternoons. During Ramadan most businesses and government offices close at 1p.m.

HOLIDAYS

New Year's Day...January 1
Id al-Fitr, end of Ramadan............................January 19*
Id al-Adha, Feast of the Sacrifice .... March 28*
Coptic Easter Monday...April 12*
Islamic New Year ....April 17*
Evacuation Day..June 18
Mouloud, Birth of Mohamed .... June 26*
Revolution Day..July 23
Armed Forced Day ....October 6
Popular Resistance Day....................................October 24
Leilat al-Meiraj .... November 6*
Victory Day.. December 23*
*Date may vary by year.

CLIMATE

Seasons
Egypt's summers are dry and hot with temperatures reaching as high as 38˚C (100˚F). Winters are more moderate with approximate temperatures of 10˚C (50˚F). Evenings can be chilly. In the spring, hot, dusty winds blow from the deserts.

Regions
The desert areas have virtually no rain year round, whereas the region around the Nile River experiences a fair amount of rain and flooding. The desert plateau can be quite inhospitable with extreme heat and sand storms.

Money & Banking

Currency
The currency of Egypt is the Egyptian Pound (£E).

Denominations
The Egyptian Pound (£E) comes in coin denominations of 5, 10, 20, 25, and 50 piasters and banknotes of 25, 50 piasters and £E1, 5, 10, 20, 50, and 100.

Traveler's Checks and Credit Cards
There are no restrictions on changing currency in Egypt, but you must receive a receipt for all transactions for departure customs purposes. Traveler's checks and most currency can be exchanged at banks, exchange shops, and some larger hotels in the capital. The international airport

Egypt

Delta area Governorates	
1	Al Iskandariyah
2	Kafr ash Shaykh
3	Ad Daqahliyah
4	Dumyat
5	Bur Sa'id
6	Al Isma'iliyah
7	Ash Sharqiyah
8	Al Gharbiyah
9	Al Minufiyah
10	Al Qalyubiyah
11	Al Qahirah

SM Santa Barbara, CA

©2001 Magellan Geographix

may accept traveler's checks but charges can be very high. Not all banks are authorized to change all types of traveler's checks. There are also Thomas Cook and American Express offices in Cairo and some outlying cities. It is best and most economic to do the majority of exchanges in Cairo. (The black market for currency is almost extinct in Egypt and should be avoided by visitors anyway.)

American Express, Visa, Diner's Club, Eurocards, JCB cards, and MasterCard are accepted in larger outlets and hotels in main cities. Bank Misr and the national Bank of Egypt give cash advances on credit cards. These banks also have ATM services scattered throughout Egypt's cities. The most favorable exchange rates are given for credit card and ATM transactions. In the rural areas, only Egyptian currency will be accepted for transactions.

Essential Terms

English	Arabic
Yes No	Na-a'am La
Good morning Hello (daytime) Hello (evening) Hello (telephone)	Sabah el kher Ma-sa'el khair Ma-sa'el khair Salam 'alekum
Good-bye	Ma'as salama
Please	Min-fahd-lak (M) Min-fahd-lik (F)
Thank you	Shook-rahn
Pleased to meet you	Tasharrafna
Excuse me; I'm sorry	Is-ma-leh
My name is _____	'ismi_____
I don't understand	An-na mish fahem
Do you speak English?	enta bititkallim inglizi?

Travel

VISA AND PASSPORT

A passport that is valid for six months minimum beyond the anticipated exit date is required of all visitors.

A visa is required of all except nationals of the following countries:

- Kuwait, for stays of six months maximum
- Bahrain, Guinea, Libya, Oman, Qatar, Saudi Arabia, Syria, and United Arab Emirates, for stays of 90 days maximum
- Jordan (if bearing a five-year passport), for stays of 30 days maximum
- Any country if the visitor is a cruise ship passenger entering Egypt through any port, for a stay of three days maximum

There are only two types of visa issued: Tourist and Business (Single- and Multiple-entry). Business visas and multiple entry visas are issued after presentation of documents verifying the business and necessity of multiple entry.

Visitors arriving overland and by sea, or those who have previously experienced difficulty with their visa status in Egypt, must obtain a visa prior to arrival. Persons arriving from Israel should have their visa stamp put on a separate piece of paper.

Citizens of Australia, Canada, New Zealand, the U.K., and the U.S. are usually permitted simply to obtain visas when they arrive at Cairo International Airport, provided they have passports that are valid for at least six months. However, it is advisable to check with the airline they are using to ensure that they are permitted, upon embarkation for Egypt, to board the airliner without a visa. It may be pref-

erable to obtain a visa in advance, if possible. Visas of this type are valid for 30 days and can be renewed.

The terms of validity of visas vary, but they are generally good for six months, commencing with the date the visa is issued, for stays of three months maximum.

All visitors, except those from Canada, E.U. countries, and the U.S. must register with local authorities (at hotel, local police station, or the central passport office) within seven days of arrival. Many hotels will expedite this process for their guests.

Allow seven days for processing of visa applications.

DEPARTURE FORMALITIES

A maximum of £E100 may be exported out of Egypt at any time. Larger amounts require advance government permission. There is an airport departure tax of £E 21, payable in local currency.

CUSTOMS ENTRY (PERSONAL)

Duty-free
- Tobacco: 200 cigarettes, 25 cigars or 200g of tobacco
- Alcohol: one liter of alcoholic beverage
- Other: a reasonable amount of perfume and one liter of eau de cologne; gifts up to the value of £E500

Prohibited or Restricted
- Drugs
- Firearms
- Cotton
- Pornography

Note: All cash, credit cards, travelers checks, and gold in excess of £E500 is to be declared upon arrival. You may also be required to declare expensive electronic equipment, such as cameras, video cameras, or computers, to ensure that they will travel out with you upon departure.

Egyptian customs officers are likely to enforce strict regulations regarding temporary import or export of articles like computer peripherals, modems, and printers, for which payment of customs fees is valid. Commercial samples and merchandise must have an import/export license that is issued by the Egyptian Ministry of Trade and Supply prior to travel and are to be declared on arrival.

IMMUNIZATION

There are no vaccinations required for entry into Egypt unless you are arriving from an area infected with yellow fever or cholera (Egypt considers most of Africa and Asia infected areas). Travelers arriving without proper health records may be quarantined. Evidence of an AIDS test is required for anyone staying more than 30 days. Anti-malaria pills are recommended from June to October even for urban travel. Hepatitis A and tetanus inoculations are also advised for all travel in Egypt.

TIPPING

Locally known as "*baksheesh*," tipping adds a vital supplement to the low wages earned by Egyptians. Do not tip professionals, businessmen, or others who might consider themselves your equals. Bear in mind, however, that requests for tips from persons who have performed no service may be politely refused.

Taxi
Taxi drivers are generally tipped between 10 and 15 percent of the fare.

Porters
Porters are generally tipped between 50 piasters and £E1 per piece. Services as small as opening a door may also require a small supplement.

Egypt

Hotels
A 12 percent service charge is generally included with the bill, but an additional five percent is customary. Chambermaids should receive £E1 per day.

Restaurants
A 12 percent service charge is generally added to the tab at tourist restaurants and nightspots, but an additional five percent is customary.

Other
Barbers and beauticians: ten percent. Small services: 30 piasters.

EMERGENCY INFORMATION

Police and Crime
Although few incidents of violent crime occur, Egypt's larger cities, especially Cairo, are ideal places for pickpockets, so take basic precautions. Foreign business visitors are often the target of thieves. Consequently, purses, laptops, and briefcases will require additional security. Do not leave valuables in cars or on tables in cafés. Keep non-essential valuables locked in hotel safes when not in use. Use credit cards and travel checks when possible to avoid carrying large sums of cash.

Women can face verbal or sexual harassment if traveling alone, so dress conservatively, avoid eye contact, do not go topless on the beaches, and do not wander through the bazaars alone. Many women in Egypt still choose to wear a veil, some say to mitigate physical or verbal advances.

Although the police are renowned for corruption in Cairo, they are efficient in performing their duties. However, most investigations of non-violent crime are cursory. Foreigners are assumed to be rich and their losses easily replaced. Carry insurance for expensive items you cannot afford to have stolen.

Stepped-up security measures have been the result of terrorist attacks that have victimized tourists as recently as 1996 and 1997. Most attacks, however, have occurred outside of the Cairo area. One should remain aware that off-road travel also poses risks with the presence of leftover mines. Travel anywhere outside of the cities should be done in the company of trusted locals.

Emergency Numbers
Numbers function nationwide.

Police (emergency)	122
Tourist Police	126
Ambulance	123

Health
Do not drink tap water or use ice cubes. Use bottled water only. Wash all vegetables in a chlorine solution, peel fruits, and avoid uncooked food. Drink only pasteurized milk.

Hepatitis, fungal infections, bilharzia, typhoid, various fevers, and in some areas, malaria and rabies are prevalent. Obtain appropriate inoculations prior to arrival. AIDS is also a risk from both sexual contact and poor hospital sanitation. During March, the desert wind coats the cities with Sahara dust. Along with the intense heat and the dry climate, this can cause skin infections and respiratory problems.

Avoid bathing in the Nile or walking barefoot in the wet mud as this can encourage skin parasites that may result in neural infections. Use protection when in the sun and take precautions against heatstroke.

The medical system is adequate for minor illnesses and basic emergencies. Larger hotels have access to multi-lingual doctors. They are well trained, but Egyptian medical facilities are sub-standard. Bring a well-stocked medical kit with extra amounts of any special medicines you require. Travel medical insurance is a must for all visitors, and an evacuation policy should be procured for long-term residents.

INTERNAL TRAVEL

AIR
Egypt Air provides daily flights between Cairo, Alexandria, Luxor, Aswan, Abu Simbel, New Valley, and Hurghada. For information about schedules, contact local Egypt Air offices.

Air Sinai offers services along the following routes: Cairo to Tel Aviv; Cairo to El Arish; Cairo to St. Catherine and Eilat (seventy-five minutes); and Cairo to Ras El Nakab, Luxor, and Sharm el-Sheikh.

TAXI
The easily identifiable black and white taxis (black and orange in Alexandria) are operated by independent drivers and, as such, may operate by their own rules. It is not uncommon to pick up other passengers heading in the same direction. Meters seldom work, so prepare to bargain for a price before departure. (Bargaining is the Egyptian national sport.)

Taxis are, for the most part, inexpensive and efficient. Typical fares range from £E3 to £E5 from downtown to the airport; to the pyramids from £E10 to £E15; and to Mohandiseen £E3 to £E5. Taxis stationed outside of your hotel will charge huge fares; so, head out to the streets to hail a cab if you are on a budget. Taxis can also be hired for the day. Inter-city taxis (*servees* or *bijous*) ply regular routes between Egypt's main towns and urban areas.

AUTO
Visitors may procure rental cars in Cairo and Alexandria through Avis, Hertz, Budget, and local companies. A credit card and a valid driver's license are required along with proof of local insurance. For temporary import of a visitor's own vehicle, a Carnet de Passage or a deposit is required. Vehicles (including motorcycles) are legally required to carry a red hazard triangle and a fire extinguisher. Age limitations vary by agency.

Along with the Nile Valley and Delta, which have an extensive network of roadways, there are high-quality roads along the African Red Sea and Mediterranean coasts. The road that loops through the oases of the Western Desert between Asyut and Giza is now also fully paved.

Driving in the cities is chaotic at best and is advisable only for the highly experienced visitor. Rural areas are much more amenable but should only be traveled with proper guidance from locals. Getting lost in the desert can quickly lead to injury or death.

For the less adventurous and the novice business visitor, cars with drivers can be hired for daily and weekly rates.

TRAIN
The Egyptian State Railway operates an intercity rail network that covers the country, offering the best train travel in the region. This comprehensive rail network offers a high level of service and is routed along an east–west line between Sallom, close by the Libyan border, to Alexandria and Cairo, and running along the Nile to both Luxor and Aswan. Links to Port Said and Suez are also in service. Trains run frequently from Cairo to Alexandria, and several luxury air-conditioned daytime and nighttime trains featuring sleeping and restaurant cars run from Cairo to Luxor and Aswan. Make reservations a week prior to ensure space on the overnight train, either through a travel agency or through:

Compagnie Internationale des Wagons Lits
Egypte, 9 Sharia Menes, Heliopolis
tel: (2) 414 5801

Many local Egyptian business people transit between cities by train, and it gives visitors some useful insights and maybe even some contacts.

Egypt

METRO

Operated by the government and built by the French, the metro offers a calmly clean experience in travel—especially when compared to what goes on in the streets above; this is also the only subway in Africa. Scheduled expansion for a subway line running to the Pyramids is underway. Fares range from 25p to 50p. Trains operate from 6a.m. to midnight with reasonable punctuality. Bear in mind that the first car of each train is reserved for women.

BUSES & TRAMS

In Cairo, look for the red and white buses originating from Midan Tahrir or the blue and white buses or microbuses in Tahrir Square. They cost from 25p to 50p. Expect to have a local adventure and lots of crowding. Most buses wait at city terminals to fill up, so delays may occur. Schedules prove to be elusive at best.

A national bus system also runs along the coastal road and through the Nile Valley. Primary routes pass between Cairo and St. Catherine, Sharm el-Sheikh, Dahab, Ras Sudr, El-Tour, Taba and Rafah; from Suez to El-Tour and Sharm el-Sheikh; and from Sharm el-Sheikh to Taba, Neweiba, El-Tour, Dahab, and St. Catherine.

Long-distance buses operated by private bus companies originate at Al Azhar Station (45 Al Azhar) and Ramsis Station in Ramsis Square. Alexandria and other cities operate similar systems. None is recommended for regular business use.

Cairo and Alexandria both operate tram systems. They are quite punctual but, like the buses, extremely crowded. These trams can be used for quick cross-town travel, but they are not advisable for use when attending important meetings.

WATER TRAVEL

Egypt has a Nile river passenger boat system as well as access to the many ports of the Mediterranean through Alexandria and Port Said. Red Sea access through the Suez Canal is also open to passenger travel. The Suez and Alexandria/Said routes are common for use by business travelers working in the Middle East.

A steamer service links Hurghada with Sharm el-Sheikh in Sinai. Additionally, two new ferries run a daily service (expect a travel time of between five and six hours). Traditional Nile sailboats (*feluccas*) are available for hire by the hour for beautiful, relaxed sailing along the river. Nile cruises also sail between Luxor and Aswan. These cruise lines can be readily booked through travel agents. The Nile river passenger system is used primarily for access to smaller southern towns.

TRAVEL ASSISTANCE

Ministry of Tourism
Misr Travel Tower, Abassia Square
Cairo, Egypt
tel: (2) 284 1707; 282 8439; fax: (2) 285 9551
website: www.touregypt.net

Hotel Accommodations
Egyptian Hotel Association
Tel (2) 712-134

Communications

DIALING CODES IN EGYPT

International country code: [20]
Selected city codes: Alexandria (3), Aswan (97), Asyut (88), Benha (13), Cairo (2), Damanhour City (45), El Mahal-lah (El Kubra) (43), El Mansoura (50), Luxor (95), Port Said (66), Shebin El Kom (48), Sohag (93), Tanta (40)

Dialing Egypt from Overseas

To dial Egypt from overseas, dial your country's international dialing code, then 20 (the country code for Egypt), then the city code, and finally the number. If you were dialing Alexandria from the United States, for example, you would begin with 011, then 20, then 3 (the city code for Alexandria), and finally the number of the person or office you are trying to reach.

Assistance Numbers

Directory 10
Phone Information 140

CALLING WITHIN EGYPT

Local Calls

Calls can be placed anywhere in the country: hotels, telephone offices, shops, and cigarette kiosks. Beware of long lines at times.

Long Distance Calls

Dial zero preceding an area code when dialing long distance within Egypt. You may call from telephone offices, businesses, hotels or homes. Calling long distance from coin phones is not possible in Egypt's chaotic world of operation.

International Calls

Overseas calls may only be made from hotels or telephone offices (open 24 hours or from 7a.m. to 10p.m. daily). At the telephone office, make a deposit before going into a booth and calling. Expect waiting; but if you'd prefer not to do it in the public realm, you can also prepay and then receive the call at another number. Cairo telephone offices are open a convenient 24 hours.

To circumvent the madness of confusion, you might try dialing for a collect call through a foreign operator:
AT&T (Cairo) 510-0200
MCI 335-5770

Dial (02) preceding the access numbers if outside of Cairo. If connected to a number by one of these operators, you will still have to pay for the call as if you were calling Cairo. Large, luxury hotels may even have special direct call phone booths to the U.K., Canada and Japan.
AT&T USA Direct .... (2) 510 2000

PAY PHONES

Public Telephones
:

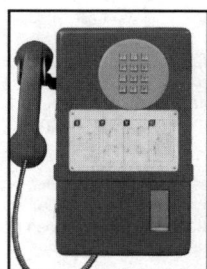

Phones are located in some hotels, cigarette kiosks, train stations, telephone offices, airports and public buildings. Press the red button on the telephone when the party you are dialing answers, or you'll be promptly disconnected. Telephone offices will charge a three-minute minimum.

Egypt

Calling Cards

Phone cards are available at telephone offices for the bright orange telephones. You can use them to call both long distance and international.

CELLULAR PHONES

Arab Republic of Egypt Natl Telecom. Org. offers both analog and digital cellular service.

Note: Your home country cell phone may not work in this country. If not, we recommend that you rent an international cell phone *before* you leave home. A major US-based cell phone rental provider is **IMC WorldCell**. For information see "International Cell Phone Rentals" on page 14.

CALL BACK

You can (potentially) save significant sums when calling in Egypt by using a call back service. For a list of callback services, please refer to the "Communications" section in the *Global Road Warrior* Introduction.

Fees for call back services vary widely, depending on the company and the type of service required. Be sure to check with these companies before leaving to compare rates.

PHONE JACKS

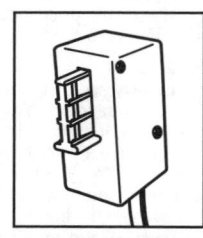

Plug adaptors are available through **iGo Corporation**. (See "Electrical and Telephone Adaptors" on page 19.)

FAX

Faxes are more prevalent than ever, but the poor telephone service makes them unreliable. They are often found in major hotels but may not be in government offices or private businesses.

POSTAL SERVICES

Mail services are loaded with red tape. Packages coming into Egypt are often stifled with huge fees. Export licenses may be required for packages leaving Egypt. Many travelers have said letters mailed from major hotels reach their destination much faster than those from post offices. Most post offic-

es are often extremely crowded. Red mailboxes handle regular Egyptian mail; the blue boxes service overseas airmail letters; and the green dispense express mail within Cairo. Allow 5 days for European mail and 8 to 10 days for mail to America. Many businesses use courier services.

Hours of service

Central Post Office: 24 hours
Others: Saturday to Thursday 8:30a.m. to 3p.m.

Business Services

COURIER SERVICES

DHL; 20 Gamal el Din Abdul Mahasen, Garden City, tel: (2) 355-7301; 34 Abdel Khalek Sarwat, tel: (2) 393-5322; 35 Ismail Ramzi, Heliopolis, tel: (2) 246-3571; Maadi Office, 43, St. nr 6, Maadi, tel: (2) 375-8900.

Federal Express; 1079 Corniche el Nil, Garden City, tel: (2) 355-0427; 24 Syria Mohandeseen, tel: (2) 349-0986; Golf, Maadi, tel: (2) 350-7172

SOS Sky International; 45 Shehab, Mohandeseen; tel: (2) 346-0028/346-2503

TNT Skypac International Express; 33 Dokki, Dokki; tel: (2) 348-8204/348-7228.

World Courier Egypt; 17 Qasr el Nil; tel: (2) 777-678/741-313.

SECRETARIAL SERVICE

World Trade Center Cairo; 1191 Corniche El Nil B2007, Cairo, Egypt; tel: (2) 578-8054; fax: (2) 774-233; email: bkasseb@intouch.com.

TRANSLATION SERVICE

World Trade Center Cairo; 1191 Corniche El Nil B2007, Cairo, Egypt; tel: (2) 578-8054\056; fax: (2) 774-233; email: bkasseb@intouch.com; English, Arabic, French translations.

Electrical

Current

Most areas use 220 volts AC, 50Hz (240-volt appliances also work on this current), but some smaller towns still rely on 110-380 volts AC.

ELECTRIC PLUGS

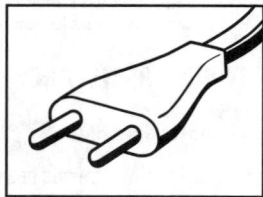

Plug adaptors are available through **iGo Corporation**. (See "Electrical and Telephone Adaptors" on page 19.)

Technical Support

HARDWARE/SOFTWARE VENDOR SUPPORT

Acer/Texas Instruments; (in Germany) tel: [49] (4102) 488-469; fax; [49] (4102) 488-169; (in the U.S.) [1] (408) 432-6200; http://www.acer.com/.

Apple/Claris; tel: (2) 346-1710; (2) 346-0674; (2) 346-1379;(in Germany) tel: [49] (1) 803-5018; (in Switzerland) tel: [41] (800) 833-310; (in the U.K.) tel: [44] (990) 127-753; (in the U.S.) tel: [1] (800) 500-7078; http://www.apple.com/.

AST; (in the U.S.) tel: [1] (817) 232-9824 (International Technical Support); (in Ireland) tel: [353] (61) 492-222; (in the U.S.) tel: [1] (949) 727-4141; http://www.ast.com/.

Compaq/Digital; (in Switzerland) tel: [41] (22) 709-5330; fax: [41] (22) 709-5391 (Geneva); tel: [41] (1) 801-2507; fax: [41] (1) 801-2172 (Zurich); (General U.S.) tel: (281) 518-2000; http://www.compaq.com/.

Corel; (in the U.A.E.) [971] 4-523-526 (All Applications); (in Germany) tel: [49] (180) 425-8210 (TS Word Perfect-32 bit); (in the U.S.) tel: [1] (716) 871-2325 (Ask to be Forwarded to Appropriate Program); http://www.corel.com/.

Dell; tel: [20] (2) 360-2234; fax: [20] (2) 361-4576 (Computek & Electronics House); (in Germany) tel: [49] (61) 039-710; (Dell- Europe) tel: [44] (134) 474-8000; (in the U.S.) tel: [1] (512) 338-4400; fax: [1] (512) 728-3330; http://www.dell.com/.

Filemaker/Claris; (in Germany) tel: [49] (180) 525-8166 (Info-line); fax: [49] (180) 567-2233; tel: [49] (180) 523-6423; (in the U.S.) tel: [1] (800) 965-9090; http://www.claris.com/.

Gateway 2000; (in the U.S.) tel: [1] (605) 232-2191; fax: [1] (605) 232-2023; (in Ireland) tel: [353] (1) 797-2000; http://www.g2k.com/.

Hewlett Packard; (in Switzerland) tel: [41] (22) 780-8111; (in the U.S.) tel: [1] (408) 246-4300; http://www.hp.com/.

IBM; tel: (2) 349-2533; fax: (2) 360-1227; (in Germany) tel: [49] (711) 78-50; fax: [49] (711) 785-3511; (in Switzerland) tel: [41] (22) 310-0418 (in French); (in the U.S.) tel: [1] (919) 517-2800; (U.S. Main Office) tel: [1] 914-765-1900; http://www.ibm.com/.

Microsoft; (In Saudi Arabia) tel: [966] (1) 488-1165; fax: [966] (1) 488-1576; (in Switzerland) tel: [41] (848) 858-868; fax [41] (1) 831-0869; (in the U.S.) [1] (425) 635-7222; http://www.microsoft.com/.

NEC; (in Israel) tel: [972] (09) 59-3300 (UltraCare Support); (in the U.S.) [1] (916) 388-0101 (Main Switchboard); http://www.nec.com/.

Toshiba; (in Germany) tel: [49] (2131) 158-319; fax: [49] (2131) 158-558; (in Switzerland) tel: [41] (1) 946-0777; fax: [41] (1) 946-0807; (in Ireland) tel: [44] (193) 282-8828; (in the U.S.) [1] (949) 583-3000 (Corporate Headquarters); http://www.toshiba.com/.

Internet Connection
HOW TO CONNECT

Connecting to AOL and Compuserve in Egypt is similar to using it when traveling outside your own area code. See the introductory section for detailed information on connecting to your account through a different phone number.

America Online

Numbers are available at keyword *international.* Be sure to get several local numbers before leaving. AOL's Global-Net service charges US$6 an hour in addition to the usual charges. Go to keyword *access* (a free area) and download the software.

Access: Alexandria (3) 484-3175; Cairo (2) 456-0100; Hurghada (65) 445-044; Luxor (95) 379-800; Sharm El Sheikh (62) 661-636.

Compuserve

Numbers are available at key word *go international.* The

Compuserve Web-site also has a great deal of information, at http://www.compuserve.com.

Access: Alexandria (3) 484-3175; Cairo (2) 456-0100; Hurghada (65) 445-044.

Independent Service Providers

Many independent service providers offer discounts if you are only in town for a couple of days.

Access Internet Services; tel: (2) 305-7007; fax: (2) 345-0170; email: info@access.com.eg; http://access.com.eg/.

AlexComm; tel: (3) 484-8200; tel: (3) 484-8300; email: sales@alexcomm.net; http://www.alexcomm.net/.

ETS Net; tel: (2) 301-5905; tel: (2) 301-5950; fax: (2) 345-5035; email: info@etsnet.com.eg; http://www.etsnet.com.eg/.

Internet Egypt; tel: (2) 356-2882; fax: (2) 354-9611; email: info@internetegypt.com; http://www.internetegypt.com/.

SHAHD FOR COMMUNICATION & ELECTRONICS; tel: (2) 414-2781; tel: (2) 414-2782; fax: 291-7281; email: info@shahd.com; http://shahd.com/.

Business Culture
GREETINGS AND COURTESIES

Businesspeople in Egypt are generally friendly and open. They will usually greet people with a firm handshake. Always wait for a woman to extend her hand before shaking; if no hand is offered, simply smile and nod. Social status is very important in Egypt. Family and social connections are also important, perhaps even more so than personal accomplishments. Expect several invitations to have coffee and meals, to the point where you may feel crowded and overwhelmed. Titles are used often; wait to use first names until you are invited.

BUSINESS ETHIC AND FRAMEWORK

An ancient culture based on nomadic heritage makes for a different mood of business than what Westerners may be accustomed to. Changes in contract terms, conditions, or royalties can only be expected in a culture and economy on the move. Acquainting oneself with the culture may assist in the business process coupled with a large dose of patience and flexibility. Finding a good Egyptian agent or local representative may serve quite helpful in a decidedly bureaucratic business environment. Respecting the Muslim traditions should be considered obligatory.

DECISION MAKING

Businesspeople in Egypt won't usually say "no," but if your question doesn't get an answer you should take it as a negative response. "Yes" also means different things in Egypt; Arabs may say "yes" even when they mean something less. Remain flexible and patient at all costs. In a culture that respects age and experience, one may do best to send one's top experienced executive to establish an effective partnership.

WOMEN

Egypt is one of the most progressive countries in the Arab world regarding women's rights. Women are very active at all levels of society. Drastic revisions have been made in marriage and divorce laws. An Egyptian woman can sue for divorce if her husband takes a second wife without her permission. Foreign businesswomen should have no problems in Egypt. Men should take care not to speak with an unknown Egyptian woman since it violates etiquette.

Egypt

MEETINGS

Always make appointments; cold calls are not appreciated. Although you should always be on time for meetings, your Egyptian counterparts will probably be late. Time is not as fixed and segmented as in the West. Meetings will usually go much later than planned; Egyptians enjoy socializing. Thus, when entering a business setting, show a personable side by chatting about non-related topics instead of just getting straight down to business. Telephone calls, visitors and constant offerings of tea may interrupt any meeting.

BUSINESS ATTIRE

Conservative business suits are the order of the day. Light weight fabrics prove helpful in the stifling summer months. Women should take care to cover themselves appropriately; dresses or skirts should, at the minimum, cover the knees, and blouses and dresses should cover as much of the arm as possible so as not to offend the very traditional Egyptians. The less seen, the better heard.

Business Centers
Alexandria

CITY VIEW

Alexandria, also known as Maydan Altahir, is probably better known for its past than its present. In its prime, the city was a center for philosophy and the arts. It is a modern city with many of the problems and concerns of other cities.

AIRPORT

Airport to City Center

The airport lies 4 miles (7 km.) from the city. There is regular bus service to downtown Alexandria and Cairo. There is also a limousine service and taxi service available.

HOTELS

Top-end

Helnan Palestine; Montazah Palace; tel: (3) 547-3500/4033; fax: (3) 540-1331; email: helnan@ritsec2.com.eg; city suburb; rates: US$110/138

Hotel Mercure Romance; 303 Tareek El Gueish, Saba Pacha; tel: (3) 588-0911; fax: (3) 587-0526; city suburb; restaurant; conference facilities (up to 250); secretarial service; corporate rates.

Montazah Sheraton Hotel; Corniche Road, El Montazah; tel: (3) 548-0550; fax: (3) 5401331; rates: US$117/145; located on the beach; conference facilities (up to 700); secretarial service; in-room modem/fax connections; corporate rates; pool; US$135.

Ramada Renaissance; 544 El Geish Ave., Sidi Bishr; tel: (3) 549-0935/548-3977; fax: (3) 431-1690; city suburb, near airport; conference center; secretarial service; corporate rates; US$82/102.

Expensive

Aida Beach Hotel; 77 km., Alex. - Matrouh Rd.; tel: (3) 990-851; fax: (3) 990-867; rates: US$55/69

Hotel Delta; 14 Champollion St., Mazarita; tel: (3) 482-5542/9053/5188; email: hoteldelta@hotmail.com; city center; restaurant; conference center; secretarial service; corporate rates; US$52/64

Hotel Sofitel Alexandria Cecil Hotel; 26 July St., Saad Zaghloul Square; tel: (3) 483-7173; fax: (3) 483-6401; city center; casino; conference facilities (up to 150); secretarial service; corporate rates; fitness; sauna; US$65/75.

Landmark; 163 Salam Aref Street, San Stefano; tel: (3) 587-7851; fax: (3) 588-0515; city center; restaurant; conference facilities; pool; US$60/80.

Plaza Hotel; 394 El Gueish St., Zizinic; tel: (3) 587-8714; fax: (3) 587-5399; rates: US$70/80

Windsor Hotel; 17 El Shohada St., Raml Station; tel: (3) 808-700/123; fax: (3) 809-090; rates: US$36/46

Moderate

Agami Palace; Al Bittash Beach, El Agami; tel: (3) 430-0386; fax: (3) 430-9364; restaurant; pool; rates: US$19/27

New Swiss Cottage; 346 El Gueish St., Gleem; tel: (3) 587-5830; fax: (3) 587-0455; rates: US$20/25

San Giovanni; 205 Saad Zaghloul St., Raml Station; tel: (3) 547-3585/546-7775; fax: (3) 546-4408; restaurant; rates: US$36/48

AUTO RENTAL

Avis; Cecil Hotel, tel: 2483-7173; fax: 280-7463.

WORLD TRADE CENTER

Al Dawilyah Commercial Center

Fahed Al Salem Street - 3rd Floor, Office No. P. O. Box 22, Safat 13001, Kuwait
tel: [965].240-4275
fax: [965].252-8011

Cairo

CITY VIEW

Cairo was the capital and cultural center of Egypt 1,000 years ago, and it remains the center of life in the country. Cairo's population hovers around 20 million people living in or around the city, with at least 5 million living in squalor and slums. There are several different regions of the city, including Islamic Cairo with its old-style architecture, and Giza with its pyramids.

AIRPORT

Cairo International Airport to City Center

The airport lies 14 miles (22.5 km.) from the city, in Heliopolis. There are coach services leaving the airport every few minutes, and taxis are readily available. Travel time could be as short as 30 minutes, but expect a much longer commute during rush hour.

Airline Numbers

Airline	Number
Air Canada	(2) 575-8939
Air France	(2) 574-3516/479/624
Air India	(2) 393-4864/73/75
Air Sinai	(2) 760948
Alitalia	(2) 574-3488
Austrian Airlines	(2) 574-2755
Brazilian Airways	(2) 391-1397
British Airways	(2) 578-0743/6
Bulgarian Airlines	(2) 393-1211
Cathay Pacific	(2) 302-9627/8
Czechoslovak Airlines	(2) 393-0416
Delta	(2) 341-9409
EgyptAir	(2) 392-0999/575-0600
El-Al Israel Airlines	(2) 341-1620
Emirates	(2) 340-1087
Ethiopian Airlines	(2) 574-0603
Finnair	(2) 776-895
Garuda Indonesia Airways	(2) 340-1948
Malev	(2) 753111
Japan Airlines	(2) 574-0695

Kenya Airways.. (2) 576-2494
KLM .... (2) 574-8004/6
Korean Airlines ....(2) 574-9360
Lufthansa ....(2) 339-8339
Olympic Airways ....(2) 393-1279
Qantas..(2) 749-900
SAS ....(2) 575-3955
Saudia ....(2) 574-7575/8
Singapore Airlines ....(2) 575-0276
Sabena ....(2) 751-194
Sudan Airways ....(2) 574-7145
Turkish Airlines ....(2) 758-939
TWA ....(2) 574-9904
United Airlines ....(2) 391-1950

HOTELS

Top-end

Cairo Meridien; Corniche El Nil Roda Island, Garden City; tel: (2) 362-1717; fax: (2) 362-1927; city center; restaurant; conference facilities (up to 500); secretarial service; corporate rates; pool; US$145.

Cairo Nile Hilton; Tahrir Square; tel: (2) 578-0444/578-0666; fax: (2) 578-0475; email: rhilton@ritsec2.com.eg; city center; conference facilities (up to 1000); secretarial service; pool.

Four Seasons Cairo; at The First Residence 35 Giza Street, P.O. Box 663-12612; Al Orman, Giza 12311, Cairo; tel: (2) 573-1212; fax: (2) 568-1616; admin. fax: (2) 569-7580; 273 rooms and suites; restaurant; bar and grill; library bar; meet rooms; 24-hour business center; cellular phone; secretarial service; translation service; in-room minibar, two telephones, video/laserdisc avail., ironing board, iron, safe, hairdryer, coffee servce, cable network, computer/fax avail., dataport, internet connect, multi-line hone, voicemail, speakerphone; 24-hour room service; laundry/dry cleaning; non-smoking rooms; express check-in/out; newsstand; gift shop; sundries; parking; hair salon; health club; spa; massage; pool; whirlpool.

Marriott Cairo; Saraya El Gezira St., Zamalek; tel: (2) 340-8888; fax: (2) 341-1752; email: marriott@ritsec3.com.eg; city center; restaurant; sauna; pool; US$115.

Mena House Oberoi; Pyramid Road; tel: (2) 383-3222/383-3444; fax: (2) 383-7777; restaurant; conference facilities (up to 1500); pool; US$110.

Ramses Hilton; 1115 Corniche El Nil; tel: (2) 574-4400/575-8000; fax: (2) 575-7152; email: rhilton@ritsec2.com.eg.

Sheraton Hotel and Towers; Galaa Square; tel: (2) 336-9800; fax: (2) 336-4601; casino; conference facilities (up to 500); in-room modem/fax connections; fitness; sauna; pool; US$150.

Semiramis Intercontinental Hotel; Corniche El Nil St., Garden City; tel: (2) 355-7171; fax: (2) 356-3020; email: cairo@interconti.com; city center; restaurant; conference facilities (up to 2000); fitness; sauna; pool; US$95.

Swissotel Cairo El Salam; Abdel Hamid Badawi Street, Heliopolis; tel: (2) 297-4000; fax: (2) 297-6037; city suburb; restaurant; casino; conference facilities (up to 400); secretarial service; corporate rates; fitness; sauna; pool; whirlpool; US$135.

Expensive

Atlas Zamalek; 20 Gameat El Dowal, El Arabia Street, Dokki; tel: (2) 346-4175; fax: (2) 347-6958; US$70.

Flamenco Hotel; 2 El Gezirah El Wosta St., Zamalek; tel: (2) 340-0815; fax: (2) 340-0819; email: flamencohtl@rite.com; near city center; restaurant;

conference center (up to 2000); secretarial service; fitness; sauna; whirlpool; US$60.

Helnan Shepheard Hotel; Corniche el Nil, Garden City; tel: (2) 355-3800; fax: (2) 355-7284; email: helnan@ritsec2.com.eg; city center; US$80.

Maadi; Maadi Entrance, Maadi; tel: (2) 350-5050; fax: (2) 351-8710; email: maadi@link.com.eg

Novotel Cairo Airport; at the airport, Heliopolis; tel: (2) 291-8520; fax: (2) 291-4794; restaurant; conference facilities; secretarial service; fitness; sauna; pool; US$100.

Safir Cairo; El Missaha Square, Dokki, Giza; P.O. Box 138 Orman, Giza; tel: (2) 348-2424; fax: (2) 342-1202; email: safir@ritsec2.com.eg

Moderate

Bel Air Cairo; Mokkatam Hill; tel: (2) 506-0911; fax: (2) 506-2816; US$52.

Cairo Khan; 12, 26th July St.; tel: (20 392-2015; fax: (2) 390-6799; city center; restaurant; conference room (up to 60); corporate rates; US$40.

MEDICAL CARE

Al Salam Hospital; 3 Syria, Mohandeseen; tel: (2) 346-7062/3

Anglo-American Hospital Zohoreya; next to the Cairo Tower, Zamalek; tel: (2) 341-8630

As Salam International Hospital; Corniche el Nil, Maadi; tel: (2) 363-8050, 363-4196, 363-8424, 363-8764

Ain Shams University Hospital; Al Khalefa El Maamoun St. Abbasseya; tel: (2) 260-5806, contact: Dr. Hala Salman

Arab Contractors Hospital Autostrade; Nasr City; tel: (2) 828-907, 832-543, 838-642, 833-501

Italian Hospital; Abbassia; tel: (2) 821-433

Nile Badrawi Hospital; Corniche el Nil, Maadi; tel: (2) 363-8688, 363-8167/8

AUTO RENTAL

Avis; airport, tel: (2) 483-7173; fax: (2) 291-4277; Meridien Hotel, tel: (2) 362-1717; fax: (2) 989-400; NIle Hilton Hotel, tel: (2) 578-0321; fax: (2) 766-432; Meridien Heliopolis, tel: (2) 290-5055; fax: (2) 290-1819.

Budget; reservations, tel: (2) 340-0070; fax: (2) 341-3790; airport, tel: (2) 443-775; Marriott Hotel, tel: (2) 340-8888.

CRC; 66 El Orouba St., Heliopolis, Cairo; tel: (2) 417-8768/9; fax: (2) 417-8765

Eurocar Interrent Egypt; Max Bldg., Lebanon St., Mohandessin, Cairo; tel: (2) 303-5630; fax: (2) 303-6123/575-9554.

Hertz; airport, tel: (2) 265-2430; Ramsis Hilton, tel: (2) 574-4400; Forte Grand Pyramids Hotel, tel: (2) 383-0383; Sonestta Cairo, tel: (2) 262-8111; Semiramis Inter-Continental Hotel, tel: (2) 354-3239; chauffeur-driven cars available.

Limousine Misr; Misr Travel Tower, Abbassia Sq., 13th Floor; tel: (2) 285-6721; airport: (2) 418-9675/418-9676; fax: (2) 285-6124

WORLD TRADE CENTER

World Trade Center Cairo
1191 Corniche El Nil
B2007
Cairo, Egypt
tel: (2) 578-8054; fax: (2) 774-233
email: bkasseb@intouch.com

El Salvador

At a Glance

THE PEOPLE

Population .... 5,839,079 (July 1999 est.)
Growth Rate .... 1.53% (1999 est.)
Life Expectancy .... 70.02 years (born 1999)
Infant Mortality . 28.38 deaths/1,000 live births (1999 est.)

Ethnic Composition

Mestizo 94%
Amerindian 5%
Caucasian 1%

Religious Composition

Roman Catholic.. 75%
Other 25%

Languages Spoken

Spanish, Nahua dialect, English

Education and Literacy

Education is compulsory for the first nine years. Nation-wide adult literacy is 71.5 percent.

Labor Force

Total: 2,200,000
By occupation: services 45%, industry 15%, agriculture 40%

THE ECONOMY

The economy of El Salvador continues to reap benefits from sound economic programs and its commitment to a free economy. Conservative fiscal policies have driven inflation down to 2 percent (from 10 percent in 1996), while unemployment remains stable if not low. Overall economic reforms include the elimination of price controls and tariff barriers and the removal of government-sanctioned monopolies in coffee, sugar, and cotton exports. The government has also formulated a plan to privatize the banking system. Still largely dependent on agriculture, El Salvador is prone to slumps in world commodity prices. Its trade deficit is sizeable but is somewhat offset by external aid and hard currency sent home by its many emigres. Continued privatization has attracted limited foreign investment especially in telecommunications and coffee production. As El Salvador improves itself for entry into the 21st century, the global markets are adopting a wait-and-see policy towards this tiny nation's economy.

Exports .... US$1.96 billion (1997)
Imports .... US$3.5 billion (1997)
Total GDP .... US$17.5 billion (1998 est.)
GDP Per Capita .... US$3,000 (1998 est.)
Unemployment .... 7.7 percent (1997)
Inflation Rate 2.6% (1998)

Top Export Partners

United States, Guatemala, E.U., Costa Rica, Honduras.

Top Import Partners

United States, Guatemala, Mexico, Panama, Venezuela, Japan.

Top Exports

Coffee, sugarcane, shrimp, textiles, chemicals.

Top Imports

Raw materials, fuel, consumer goods, capital goods.

BUSINESS WORKWEEK

Offices

Monday to Friday 8a.m. to noon and 2:30p.m. to 6p.m.

Banks

Monday to Friday 9a.m. to 1p.m. and 1:45p.m. to 5p.m. All banks are closed June from 29 to 30 and December 3 to 31 for balancing.

Government

Monday to Friday 7:30a.m. to 3:30p.m.

Retail

Monday to Friday 8a.m. to noon and 2:30p.m. to 6p.m. Saturday 8a.m. to 2p.m. (Retailers in urban areas tend to keep later evening hours.)

Note: In rural areas the opening hours and midday break for businesses and government offices are scheduled by local custom based on the seasonal needs of the agricultural community.

HOLIDAYS

New Year's Day..January 1
Easter..April 2-5*
Labor Day...May 1
Corpus Christ ....June 3*
San Salvador Festiva ....August 4-6
Independence Day ....September 15
Discovery of America ....October 12
All Souls' Day ....November 2
First Call of Independence ....November 5
Christmas ....December 24-25
*Date may vary by year.

CLIMATE

Seasons

El Salvador has two main seasons: the dry season (from November to April) and the wet season (from May to November). In general, the climate is warm with temperatures ranging from approximately 32°C (90°F) in the summer and 18°C (64°F) in the winter.

Regions

Temperatures vary with altitude rather than season. Some inland areas are dry all year round, while the coastal region receives the most rain. The capital's climate is moderate with an average temperature of 22°C (72°F).

Money & Banking

Currency

The currency of El Salvador is the Salvadorian Colon (C).

Denominations

The Salvadorian Colon (C) comes in coin denominations of C1, as well as 100, 50, 25, 10, 5, and centavos; and banknotes of C5, 10, 25, 50, and 100.

Traveler's Checks and Credit Cards

Traveler's checks, in U.S. dollar denominations only, can be exchanged at banks, exchange shops, hotels, and international airports at tourist exchange rates, which can severely differ from place to place. Expect a commission charge for the exchange. Larger banks may offer the best exchange rates,

El Salvador

El Salvador
- ⊛ National capital
- ⊙ Department capital
- ● City
- ☒ Airfield
- ↓ Port
- ▬▬ International border
- ┈┈ Department border
- ══ Road
- ┉┉ Railroad

0 10 20 30 40 km
0 10 20 30 mi

Department Names
1 Ahuachapan
2 Santa Ana
3 Sonsonate
4 La Libertad
5 Chalatenango
6 San Salvadore
7 Cuscatlán
8 La Paz
9 San Vicente
10 Cabañas
11 Usulután
12 San Miguel
13 Morazán
14 La Unión

SM Santa Barbara, CA
©2001 Magellan Geographix

but not all may accept your particular brand of traveler's check. Cashing traveler's checks can be difficult in smaller towns where commissions may run very high. Avoid black marketers at all cost as they may slip you counterfeit cash. Consult your bank about current exchange rates before departure.

Cash, especially U.S. dollars, can be exchanged without a charge. Try to take only crisp and new notes as wrinkled and soiled notes are likely to be refused. In rural areas they will only exchange small denomination currency. Salvadoran Colónes are not accepted in Guatemala or Honduras, so reconvert your currency before traveling to these neighboring countries.

In the capital, San Salvador, American Express, Visa, Diner's Club, and MasterCard are accepted in most up-market hotels and restaurants. Some banks in the capital offer cash advances on credit cards, but make sure you bring your passport. Outside of the city, credit cards will be of little use. ATMs are rare in El Salvador and the few that exist do not function well with foreign banks.

Travel

VISA AND PASSPORT

A Salvadorian Tourist Card and a passport that is valid for a minimum of six months beyond the day of departure are both required of all visitors. Tourist cards are issued to travelers by Salvadorian consulates, major airlines servicing El Salvador, and at the El Salvador International Airport upon arrival. Tourist cards cost US$10, unless issued by your airline, and are valid for one entry, for a 90-day stay. Retain this document with your other travel papers.

A visa is required of all, except nationals of Argentina, Austria, Belgium, Chile, Colombia, Costa Rica, Denmark, Finland, France, Germany, Guatemala, Honduras, Iceland, Ireland, Israel, Italy, Japan, Korea (Rep. of), Liechtenstein, Luxembourg, Netherlands, Nicaragua, Norway, Panama, Paraguay, Spain, Sweden, Switzerland, Uruguay, the U.K., and the U.S.

Passengers in transit who do not leave the airport and are continuing their journey aboard the first connecting aircraft, and who are holding confirmed tickets and other documents for onward travel, are also exempt from visa requirements.

Business visa applications must have an invitation from a Salvadorian company or government agency appended, along with a photo of the visitor. Both Business and Tourist visas are renewable through the immigration office in El Salvador.

Allow 48 hours as the usual processing time for visa applications. Two weeks is more plausible if there are any complications or special authorizations needed.

Note: Nationals of China, Cuba, Egypt, Jordan, Iraq, Iran, Korea (Dem. Rep. of), Libya, Palestinian Authority, Syrian Arab Republic, and Sudan must have a special authorization from the immigration offices in El Salvador, so processing time can be as long as three weeks.

DEPARTURE FORMALITIES

There is an airport departure tax of US$24.65 (which includes a US$2.65 Immigration Tax). Expect searches through luggage and belongings. Tourist cards must be presented at departure to immigration officials.

El Salvador

CUSTOMS ENTRY (PERSONAL)

Duty-free

- Tobacco: 200 cigarettes or 50 cigars
- Alcohol: 2 liters of alcoholic beverage
- Other: gifts not exceeding the value of US$500; no more than 6 units of perfume

  Note: Restrictions now exist for the import and export of plants, animals, fruits, and vegetables. Inquire at the consulate or embassy for the latest regulations.

Restricted

- Unlicensed firearms
- Controlled drugs

IMMUNIZATION

An international certificate of vaccination is not required unless arriving from an infected area. Recommended vaccinations include malaria, cholera, Hepatitis A, typhoid, and rabies. All childhood immunizations should be current.

TIPPING

Taxi

No tip is necessary, unless hiring a cab for a whole day. Most riders simply round up the fare.

Porters

Porters at first-class hotels and transport depots are usually tipped C5 per bag.

Hotels

When a service charge has not been applied to the bill, a 10 percent tip for staff is customary.

Restaurants

A 10 percent tip in restaurants and nightclubs is customary.

EMERGENCY INFORMATION

Police and Crime

A civil war lasting 12 years has left behind its mark of violence and a devaluation of human life. Crime on all levels exists throughout the country. Carjackings and armed assault are especially frequent on roads outside the capital. Travel in the evening and early-morning hours is strongly discouraged. Criminals become violent quickly and those victims unwilling to surrender belongings or who put up an argument. face violence and even death.

Criminals have been known to follow travelers from the airport to private residences or secluded stretches of road where robberies and assaults are committed. The road to the airport should be avoided after dark. Travelers with conspicuous amounts of baggage, late-model cars, and foreign license plates are particularly vulnerable to crime. Foreigners should also stay away from the eastern part of San Salvador after sunset.

Foreign business visitors are often the special target of thieves. Consequently, purses, laptops, and briefcases will require additional security. Business travelers from high-profile companies may wish to consider bringing along security personnel for travel in rural areas.

Do not leave valuables in cars or on tables in cafés. Keep non-essential valuables locked in hotel safes when not in use. Use credit cards and travel checks when possible to avoid carrying large sums of cash. The drug trade operates in El Salvador, so, never carry a stranger's baggage.

Women should either travel in groups or take an authorized taxi. The urban police are friendly and generally helpful. However, in rural areas they can also be part of the crime problem.

Emergency Numbers

Ambulance ....(226) 51-11
General emergency... 121 or 123
Civilian Police ....(298) 18-49, 18-56
National Police ....(271) 44-22

Health

Health standards have improved considerably. However, the water is rarely potable, so use bottled water even for brushing your teeth. Stay away from raw vegetables and fruit unless they've been washed in a chlorine solution or have thick peelable skins. Since milk is unpasteurized, one should also avoid dairy products. Diarrhea is common for travelers who are unaccustomed to the new diet and the heat. Take proper precautions and bring along medication.

El Salvador can get extremely hot, so take precautions against sun and heat stroke, drink lots of liquids, and use sunblock whenever outdoors.

Rabies also poses a problem in El Salvador. Bats and dogs mainly transmit the disease. If bitten by any kind of animal, seek immediate medical attention. A rabies vaccine exists for those at high risk of exposure in rural areas.

The Ministry of Public Health and Social Welfare coordinates the medical establishment. Facilities are not of a high standard but are adequate for emergency use. Hotels have access to multi-lingual doctors and medical assistants. Bring extra quantities of any special medicines you require. Travel insurance is advised as is an evacuation policy for travelers in remote areas.

For more information on medical centers, including phone numbers, please see the "Business Centers" section at the end of this chapter.

INTERNAL TRAVEL

AIR

Domestic flights are available between San Salvador and San Miguel, La Unión, and Usulután. Domestic airlines fly out of Ilopango Airport, 13km (8mi) east of San Salvador. These are all short flights, of course, and tend to be expensive.

TAXI

Most private taxis are not metered, so negotiate a price beforehand. Taxis can also be hired by the day. If you need a cab on the spur of the moment, it can be hailed curbside. Large hotels often provide their own taxi service. If possible, use one of these taxis, as they tend to be much more knowledgeable about the city. Keep a map handy.

AUTO

Car rental is available in San Salvador. It is only recommended for experienced visitors. A credit card, valid driver's license, and local insurance are required.

Car hijackings are frequent, especially in the cities, and motorists are advised to limit travel to daytime only, and with doors locked. New cars, particularly those with foreign plates, are prime targets. More dangerous still are the driving habits of the locals and the unpredictable state of repairs in Salvadorian streets.

For the business traveler especially, hired cars with drivers are advised. They can be procured on a daily or weekly basis, and your hotel can arrange this service for you.

TRAIN

More than 600km (372 miles) of railroad track link San Salvador with Acajutla, Cutuco, San Jerónimo, and Angiuatu. Rail lines also connect the major cities within El Salvador, but the services are somewhat erratic and the amenities not overly comfortable. These services are advised only for access to remote villages where auto travel may not be feasible.

BUSES & TRAMS

Buses are the primary mode of motorized travel for the average El Salvadorian. Local and inter-city lines are vast, but they are neither punctual nor comfortable. These are, like the trains, a poor substitute for auto travel. Business people should use them only as a final option.

WATER TRAVEL

El Salvador has limited passenger boat service. Neither ocean-going nor river services are often used by business travelers unless accessing remote areas.

TRAVEL ASSISTANCE

Corporacion Salvadoreña de Turismoa

CORSATUR (Salvadorian Tourism Corporation)
Bvd del Hipodromo 508, Col. San Benito
San Salvador, El Salvador
tel: 243 7835-7; fax: 243 0427
email: corsatur@salnet.net
website: www.elsalvadorturismo.gob.sv

Carretera a Santa Tecla

CASATUR (Salvadorian Chamber of Tourism)
Centrao Comercial Feria Rosa, Local 107-B
San Salvador, El Salvador
Tel/fax: 243 2458
email: camara.turismo@salnet.net

Instituto Salvadoreño de Turismo

ISTU (Salvadorian Institute of Tourism)
619 Calle Rubén Darío
San Salvador, El Salvador
tel: 222 8000, 222 0960; fax: 222 1208

Essential Terms

English	Spanish
Yes	Sí
No	No
Good morning	Buenos días
Hello (daytime)	Buenas tardes
Hello (evening)	Buenas noches
Hello (telephone)	¿Hola?
Good-bye	Adiós
Please	Por favor
Thank you	Gracias
Pleased to meet you	Encantado (a) de conocerle
Excuse me; I'm sorry	¿Perdóneme?
My name is ____	Me llamo ____
I don't understand	No comprendo
Do you speak English?	¿Habla usted inglés?

Communications

DIALING CODES IN EL SALVADOR

International country code: [503]

Dialing El Salvador from Overseas

To dial El Salvador from overseas, dial your country's international dialing code, then 503 (the country code for El Salvador), and finally the number. There are no city codes.

Assistance Numbers

International Operator 119

CALLING WITHIN EL SALVADOR

Telephoning still has a long way to go in El Salvador. Since it is very difficult to acquire new phone lines for business and homes, cellular phones have become popular for businesspeople.

Long Distance Calls

Calling long distance within El Salvador is not expensive. It costs about ten cents for three minutes.

International Calls

Antel runs the telephonic operation in El Salvador and has offices throughout the country from which one can try placing a call. Calling out of El Salvador means dialing 0 + country code + area code + number. Check with the hotel or Antel office for proper calling procedure. All three major phone companies in the U.S. have operator service to connect you from El Salvador.

AT&T access 800-1785
MCI access.. 800-1767

AT&T Direct requires local coin payment through the call duration.

CELLULAR PHONES

Telemovil El Salvador presently provides analog cellular service for El Salvador. Other companies may be in existence, providing service in both digital and analog formats.

Note: Your home country cell phone may not work in this country. If not, we recommend that you rent an international cell phone *before* you leave home. A major US-based cell phone rental provider is **IMC WorldCell**. For information see "International Cell Phone Rentals" on page 14.

CALL BACK

You can (potentially) save significant sums when calling in El Salvador by using a call back service. For a list of call-back services, please refer to the "Communications" section in the *Global Road Warrior* Introduction.

Fees for call back services vary widely, depending on the company and the type of service required. Be sure to check with these companies before leaving to compare rates.

PHONE JACKS/ADAPTORS

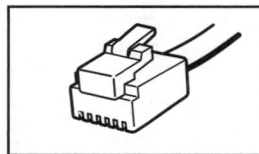

Plug adaptors are available through **iGo Corporation.** (See "Electrical and Telephone Adaptors" on page 19.)

POSTAL SERVICES

Mail service is adequate, but it is recommended to use courier services, which are also available.

Business Services

BUSINESS CENTER

Camino Real Inter-Continental; Boulevard Los Heroes y Avenida Los Sisimiles; tel: 279-3888.

Hotel El Salvador; 89 Avenida Norte y 11 Calle Poniente, Col. Escalon; tel: 298-5444.

Hotel Presidente; Final Avenida La Revolucion, Col. San Benito; tel: 279-4444.

San Salvador Marriott; Avenida de La Revolucion; tel: 243-4444.

Best Western Siesta Hotel; Blvd Los Proceres 200 Mts Oriente; tel: 243-0377.

Terraza Hotel; 85 Avenida Sur y Calle Padres Aguilar; tel: 263-0044.

COURIER SERVICES

Airborne Express; Primera Calle Poniente Y, 63 Ave. Norte, Edif. Comercial, Colonia Escalon, A-M Local 15-A, Primer Nivel, San Salvador; tel: 260-5950; fax: 260-6067.

DHL de El Salvador S.A. de C.V.; 47 Av. Norte #104, San Salvador, C.A.; tel: 260-7722; http://www.dhl.com.sv/; Monday to Friday 8a.m. to 7p.m., Saturday 8a.m. to 2p.m.

Federal Express; Urgente Express, Avenida el Espino No. 68, Urb. Madre Selva, Antiguo Camino a Cuscatlan, La Libertad, Frente al Hotel Plaza San Martín; tel: 243-7244; fax: 243-7005; Monday to Friday 8a.m. to 6p.m.

UPS/Courier International, S.A.; Calle El Progreso No. 3139, Colonia Roma, San Salvador; tel: 245-0400; fax: 223-5268.

Electrical

Current

110 volts AC, 60Hz

ELECTRIC PLUGS

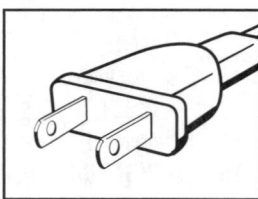

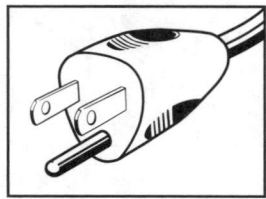

Plug adaptors are available through **iGo Corporation.** (See "Electrical and Telephone Adaptors" on page 19.)

Technical Support

VENDOR SUPPORT

Dell; tel: [503] 788-000 (Xerox de El Salvador); [503] 224-2809 (Siprose); (in the U.S.) tel: [1] (512) 338-4400; fax: [1] (512) 728-3330; http://www.dell.com/.

Hewlett Packard; (Venezuela Office) tel: [58] 2 239 5664; (in the U.S.) tel: [1] (408) 246-4300; http://www.hp.com/.

IBM; (in Colombia) tel: [57] (1) 623-0111; fax: [57] (1) 257-9839; (in the U.S.) tel: [1] (919) 517-2800; (U.S. Main Office) tel: [1] 914-765-1900; http://www.ibm.com/.

Microsoft; (In Costa Rica) tel: [506] 298-2020; tel: [506] 298-2000; (in the U.S.) [1] (425) 635-7222; http://www.microsoft.com/.

Internet Connection

HOW TO CONNECT

Connecting to AOL and Compuserve in El Salvador is similar to using it when traveling outside your own area code. See the introductory section for detailed information on connecting to your account through a different phone number.

America Online

Numbers are available at keyword *international*. Be sure to get several local numbers before leaving. AOL's GlobalNet service charges US$12 an hour in addition to the usual charges. Go to keyword *access* (a free area) and download the software.

Access: San Salvador 260-3434.

Compuserve

Numbers are available at keyword *Go international*. The Compuserve Web-site also has a great deal of information, at http://www.compuserve.com.

There are no direct access numbers for Compuserve in El Salvador. Users will have to pay international rates to use the service.

Independent Service Providers

Many independent service providers offer discounts if you are only in town for a couple of days.

InterSal, S.A. de C.V.; tel: [503] 263-4967; fax: [503] 263-5022; email: delvalle@SAdeCV.com; also in New Jersey: [1] (201) 974-1757; fax: [1] (201) 974-1757; email: info@SAdeCV.com; http://www.SAdeCV.com/delvalle/.

Interglobal Internet Services; tel: 273-5027; fax: 273-8632; email: interglobal@baham.com; http:/www.fbaham.com/interglobal.

Fiberlink Communications Corp.; tel: [1] (714) 788-2904; email: info@fiberlinkcc.com; http://www.fiberlinkcc.com/.

Pointe Communications; tel: [1] (281) 486-8337; email: sales@pointecom.net; http://www.pointecom.net/.

Business Culture

GREETINGS AND COURTESIES

Handshakes are common among both men and women when meeting and upon departing, although some people will limit greetings to a nod. Male friends may hug, and women friends may kiss briefly and lightly on the cheek. Titles are commonly used—with last names—and only very close friends use first names or surnames without a title. If from the U.S., avoid referring to yourself as American since Salvadorans also consider themselves as such. Salvadorans highly regard the use of formal etiquette. Prepare to engage in courtesies with a very respectful manner. Spanish business cards provide a valuable courtesy, and small gifts bearing the logo of your company will also serve well.

BUSINESS ETHIC AND FRAMEWORK

Establishing local contacts will help considerably in paving the way for a smoother ride. Bureaucratic and cultural difficulties, including delays and interruptions, might best be handled by a local who better understands their precepts. Salvadorans place emphasis on their social and personal relations and, as such, will conduct business on a similar platform. Engaging in pressure tactics to rush a decision or business relationship will not impress and might instead serve to break off sound opportunities. Establishing trust through personal friendships will gain the most credibility.

MEETINGS

Prior appointments are necessary for meetings; it is suggested to make them two weeks in advance. Since Salvadorans base much of their business on personal relationships, one should prepare to spend considerable time with social pleasantries. A more relaxed attitude in the Salvadoran culture also dictates patience on the part of visiting entrepreneurs, who undoubtedly often run on a more hasty time schedule. Set aside plenty of time to conduct business. Business lunches are quite popular since most businesses break for a two-hour lunch. Although foreigners are expected to be on time to a business meeting (though not necessarily for social occasions), Salvadorans often arrive late.

DECISION MAKING

A personal relationship is considered a prerequisite to a business relationship and must be established before any agreements can be reached. Salvadorans will want to know your standing within the hierarchy and will wish to match you with someone of similar rank, although only their senior people will actually be able to approve agreements. Nevertheless, it is important to cultivate personal relationships with these peers, because the quality of these relationships may strongly influence the actual decisionmaker even when your counterpart is not the one making the decision.

WOMEN

Salvadoran women are becoming more common and more accepted in business in general, and foreign businesswomen should experience few problems. Nevertheless, foreign businesswomen are expected to be highly professional and appropriate, without displaying aggressive or confrontational behavior. Women may generally go on the streets and dine alone, but may feel more comfortable if escorted.

BUSINESS ATTIRE

Although not considered a first-world country, Salvadorans nevertheless exhibit a sense of fashion. Dark, conservative business suits are considered appropriate attire for men. Lightweight fabrics of cotton or linen may better combat the heat. Conservative and stylish business suits or elegant dresses—with stockings and heels—are worn by women. A business suit or a dress will also serve appropriately if you are invited to a meal or other social occasion. Casualwear will not suffice for after-business events.

Business Centers
San Salvador

CITY VIEW

San Salvador is a city with problems. Earthquakes have ravaged the country throughout history, and older buildings (which would have dated as far back as 17th century) are gone. Unemployment stands over 50 percent. Pollution is a serious problem, and traffic jams are an everyday occurrence. With a population of close to 500,000 people, the city does offer a modern infrastructure and hotel accommodations can be quite comfortable. The city is located in the center of the country, and the surrounding area is very beautiful. One day excursions are an excellent way to see the countryside and even witness active volcanoes. Inside the city, a visit to the Museo Nacional Davíd J Guzmán will uncover an interesting assortment of El Salvador archeology.

AIRPORT

Comalapa International Airport to City Center

The airport lies 38 miles (60 km.) from the city and involves a 45-minute drive in a rental car or taxi ride. Tourist information remains open between 8a.m. and 5:30p.m. A coach service between the airport and San Salvador is available from 6a.m. to 7p.m. Taxis are also available.

Airline Numbers

Aerolineas Argentinas 224-3936
American Airlines 298-0777/ 0666
Continental Airlines 223-8968, 239-9501
COPA (Panama) 223-2042, 271-2333
LACSA (Costa Rica) 298-1322
Mexicana 271-5936, 271-5950
TACA International Airlines 222-244, 224-0044
VARIG (Brazil) 226-0840, 225-8526

HOTELS

Top End
Camino Real Inter-Continental; Boulevard Los Heroes y Avenida Los Sisimiles; tel: 279-3888; hotline: 223-3610; in the U.S./Canada: 1-800-7CAMINO; fax: 223-5660; located in commercial area; 3 restaurants; meeting rooms; conference facilities; business center; in-room voicemail and modem lines; corporate rates; fitness; sauna; pool.

Hotel Presidente; Final Avenida La Revolucion, Col. San Benito; tel: 279-4444; fax: 223-4912; located in the Zona Rosa; 3 restaurants; conference rooms; business center; free airport transfers; beauty salon; shops; health club; fitness; sauna; pool.

Expensive
Best Western Siesta; Blvd Los Proceres 200 Mts Oriente; tel: 243-0377; fax: 243-3732; telex: 002 0104; restaurant; conference facilities; business center; disabled facilities; security; parking; pool; tennis.

Casa Austria Guest House; 2 locations: Santa Elena (new part of town near US Embassy) and Colonia Escalón (well serviced residential area); tel: 278-3581, 278-3610, 278-3401; fax: (503) 278-3105; five guest houses with four rooms each; business center with internet access; in-room telephone, tv.

Hotel Escalon Plaza; 89 Ave.Norte #141, Col. Escalón; tel: 263-7480; fax: 264-1580; located in a well-serviced commercial area; restaurant; bar; business center; in-room air conditioning, cable tv, telephone; room service; parking.

Terraza; 85 Avenida Sur y Calle Padres Aguilar; tel: 263-0044; fax: 263-3223; city suburb; restaurant; conference facilities; business center; secretarial service; fax/ photocopy facilities; parking; corporate rates; fitness; pool.

HEALTH CARE

Note: Your hotel staff may recommend a European or U.S.-trained doctor in San Salvador.

Hospital de Diagnostico; Urbanizacion la Esperanza, Segunda Diagonal #429; tel: 226-5111.

Hospital de la Mujer; Colonia Escalon, Calle Juan Jose Canas y 81 Av. Sur; tel: 279-1440.

El Salvador

Estonia

At a Glance
THE PEOPLE

Population 1,421,335 (1998)
Growth Rate .... -0.99% (1999)
Life Expectancy .... 62.5 years (born 1999)
Infant Mortality .... 13.98 deaths/1,000 live births (1998)

Ethnic Composition
Estonian 64.2%
Russian 28.7%
Ukrainian 2.7%
Byelorussian.. 1.5%
Finn 1%
Other 1.9%

Religious Composition
Evangelical Lutheran..................................... 40%
Russian Orthodox.. 25%
Estonian Orthodox... 25%
Other and non-affiliated.................................. 10%

Languages Spoken
Estonian (official), Ukrainian, Russian

Education and Literacy
Education is compulsory for 12 years. Adult literacy stands at 100 percent.

Labor Force
Total: 785,000
By occupation: services 38%, industry 42%, agriculture 20%

THE ECONOMY

Historically, Estonia enjoyed greater success, prosperity, and industrialization than did many other regions under Soviet domination. Since 1992, following the collapse of the U.S.S.R., Estonia has pursued a market economy. It has freed most prices and encouraged privatization. Its success at attracting foreign investment brought it to the forefront of Europe's emerging markets. As such, it was the only Baltic state not required to have a transition period prior to its implementation of a free trade agreement with the E.U. The government of Estonia has successfully positioned the country as the gateway between East and West. It continues to aggressively pursue trade reform and economic integration to attract foreign businesses and joint ventures. However, it does have some pressing problems. Its growing current account deficit (inflows versus outflows) and double-digit inflation require immediate action. The government, though recognizing the problem, is loath to tamper with the low unemployment that is keeping the population at work and away from political rallies.

Exports .... US$2 billion (1996)
Imports .... US$3.2 billion (1996)
Total GDP .... US$9.34 billion (1997)
GDP Per Capita .... US$6,450 (1997)
Unemployment .... 3.6 percent (1997)
Inflation Rate .... 11.2 percent (1997)

Top Export Partners
E.U., Russia, Latvia.

Top Import Partners
E.U., Russia.

Top Exports
Textiles, food products, machinery and equipment, metals.

Top Imports
Machinery and equipment, foodstuffs, minerals, textiles, metals.

BUSINESS WORKWEEK

Offices
Monday to Friday 8:30a.m. to 5:30p.m.

Banks
Monday to Friday 9:30a.m. to 5:30p.m. (Some banks have Saturday hours until noon.)

Government
Monday to Friday 9a.m. to noon, 1p.m. to 5p.m.

Retail
Monday to Friday 8 a.m. to 5:30p.m. Saturday 8a.m. to 4p.m. (Many large retailers in urban areas keep evening hours as late as 9p.m.)

HOLIDAYS

New Year's Day...January 1
Independence Day ....February 24
Good Friday...April 2*
Labor Day..May 1
Victory Day, Battle of Vonnu 1919 ....June 23
Midsummer Day ....June 24
Christmas ....December 25-26
*Dates may vary by year.

CLIMATE

Seasons
Estonia has a maritime climate with wet but mild winters and cool—but even wetter—summers. Temperatures range from average lows of 5˚C (41˚F) to average highs of 15˚C (59˚F).

Regions
The proximity of the Baltic Sea influences the climate with heavy rainfall in inland regions and less on the coastal plain. The plains are given to high winds. Rainfall is heaviest in the summer and lightest during the winter months.

Money & Banking

Currency
The currency of Estonia is the Kroon (EEK).

Denominations
The Estonian Kroon (EEK) comes in coin denominations of EEK1, as well as 50, 20, 10, 5, and 1 senti; and banknotes of EEK1, 2, 5, 10, 25, 100, and 500.

Travellers Checks
Traveler's checks and most currency can be exchanged at banks, exchange shops, main hotels in Tallinn, and international airports. Cashing traveler's checks can be a difficult and a lengthy form-filling process, especially in smaller towns where commissions can run high. Exchanging cash, especially U.S. and E.U. currencies, proves much easier (fewer forms) and the rates are better.

American Express, Visa, Diner's Club, Eurocard, and MasterCard are accepted in most up-market places in ur-

Estonia

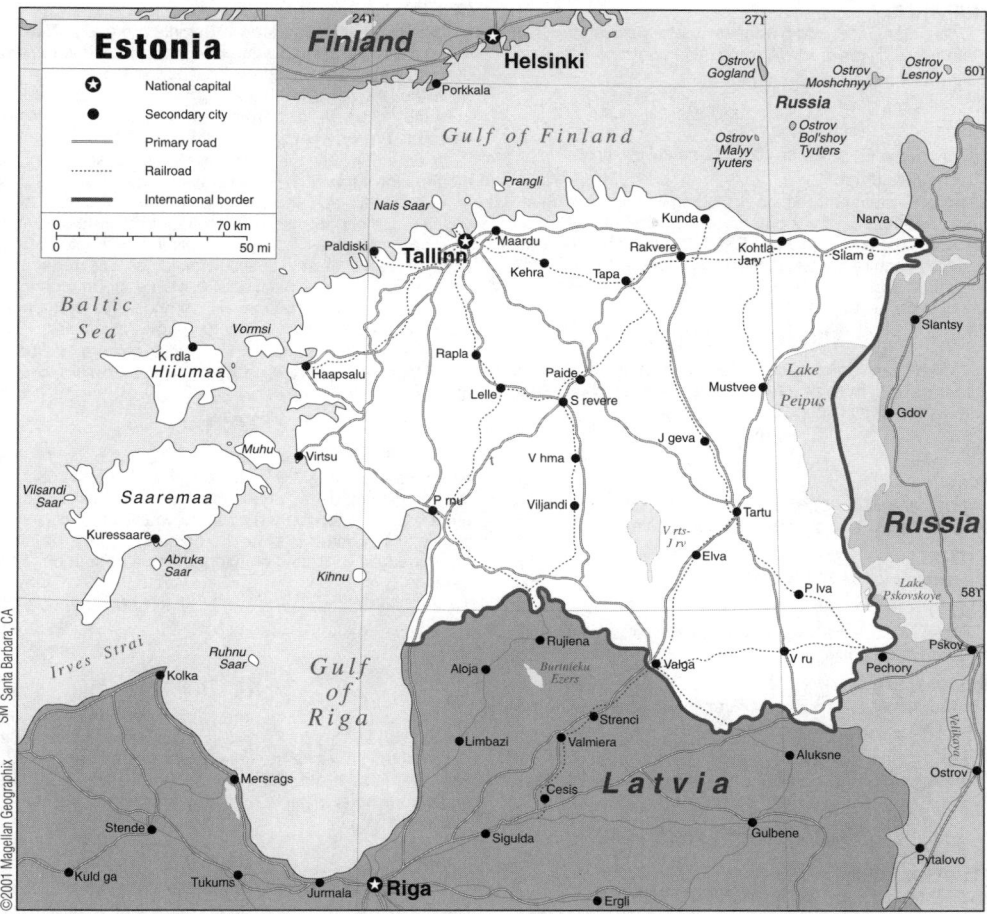

ban areas. Cash advances on credit cards can also be obtained at main banks in the capital. ATMs are not that common except in Tallinn. They are not compatible with every banking system—so, check the signage before use. Credit card and ATM transactions receive the most favorable exchange rates.

Visitors cannot reconvert currency when leaving the country without receipts. Keep all evidence of currency exchanges.

Travel
VISA AND PASSPORT

Travelers to Estonia will need a valid passport. All visitors (excluding citizens of the E.U. nations, Poland, Czech Republic, Slovakia, and Hungary) also require visas, which are available from Estonian embassies or at the border. A visa to Latvia or Lithuania will also be accepted for entry into Estonia. It is advisable to get visas in advance of travel to Estonia to prevent time consuming border delays. Visas cost EEK140 but U.S. citizens can receive visas for free. Business visas require an invitation from a government agency or a local company. An AIDS test will be required for long-term visitors.

Registration with local police within 24 hours of arrival is not mandatory in cities like Tallinn or Tartu, but it is advisable to register if traveling along the Gulf of Finland and Russian borders. Customs declaration forms may be required on arrival.

DEPARTURE FORMALITIES

An airport departure fee is required but varies by destination point. Some airlines will include the fee in the ticket price. There is no charge for departure by land or sea.

CUSTOMS ENTRY (PERSONAL)
Duty-free
- Tobacco: 200 cigarettes or 25 cigars or 250g tobacco
- Alcohol: 1 liter of spirits, 1 liter of wine, 10 liters of beer. (These alcohol limits relate to those aged 21 years and over. For those between 18 - 21: 2 liters of wine, not exceeding 21% vol)
- Manufactured articles of total value not exceeding EEK 5000
- Foodstuffs of total quantity not exceeding 10kg; coffee, tea, spices and seeds may not exceed 3kg.

Estonia

Prohibited

- Uncut diamonds, scrap and waste of precious metals or other metals covered with precious metals
- Firearms or silencers
- Military badges
- Biomedical preparations
- Out of date Estonian currency or postal stamps
- Controlled drugs

   Note: Certain other items, including live animals, medicines, and hunting weapons require special permits. Currency in excess or equal to EEK80,000 must be declared. You may acquire more customs information at the following number in Estonia: 6318-607. An English-language website also exists: http://www.customs.ee/

IMMUNIZATION

An international certificate of vaccination is not required unless arriving from an infected area. Tetanus and Hepatitis A inoculation is suggested.

TIPPING

Taxi

For metered fares, 10 to 15 percent tip is customary. Unmetered fares should be negotiated in advance.

Porters

Porters receive EEK5 per bag.

Hotels

Hotels include service charges on the bill, but small tips are always appreciated.

Restaurants

Most restaurants will apply service charges to the bill; otherwise, 15 percent is a standard.

Other

Beauticians and barbers: 10 percent. Small services: five to 10 percent.

EMERGENCY INFORMATION

Police and Crime

Crime occurs with regular frequency in Estonia in the form of muggings, pickpocketing, and car theft. Favorite targets include foreigners and small groups leaving bars at night. Credit card fraud has also found its niche in the ways of criminal activity. Take precautions with your credit card numbers and report any suspect transactions to your credit card company immediately.

As in any other country, take basic precautions against petty crime. Avoid flashy displays of wealth, and dress and behave conservatively. Leave most of your cash, traveler's checks, jewelry, and your camera in your hotel safe. Carry photocopies of your passport instead of the original. Carry cash in a money belt, and use credit cards or traveler's checks for most of your transactions. Laptops, briefcases, and technical equipment require increased security.

Women should avoid traveling alone. All visitors should be skeptical of easily acquired companions. Foreigners have been known to fall prey to druggings and robbery on passenger trains and even in restaurants. Stay aware of your surroundings.

Emergency Numbers

Ambulance	003
Police	002
Fire	001
Emergency	112
Estonian-Finnish Medical Center	238-376
Baltic Medical Partners	6311-222

Health

Overall, health standards in Estonia are good. Diarrhea is common for travelers who are unaccustomed to the new diet and water, and, in extreme cases, could ruin your business trip. As such, bottled water is highly recommended over tap water. Visitors from Asia may find the Estonian diet quite heavy. Allow yourself time to acclimate.

In emergencies, the medical system is adequate. Although highly trained medical professionals exist, hospitals and clinics still lack equipment and resources. As such, a serious medical condition may call for treatment outside of Estonia. Hotels have access to multi-lingual doctors. Bring extra amounts of any special medicines you require. In case you need some basics, at least one 24-hour pharmacy exists in most towns. Travel insurance is recommended including an evacuation policy for long-term visitors.

For more information on medical centers, including phone numbers, please see the "Business Centers" section at the end of this chapter.

TAXI

Government taxis are colored light green or light yellow and have fixed prices. Private taxis must have the name of the company and their phone number on the taxi. Although meters exist, one would do best to watch them closely. If possible, negotiate a price beforehand. "Marshrut-taxis" are minbuses operating on fixed routes that seat up to ten persons.

Tulika Takso	6552-552, 603-044
Esra	6410-440
VIP	6399-399

AUTO

Car rental and chauffeured car service can be found in the capital. Driving in Estonia is relatively civil but it does pose security risks for the uninitiated. A hired car with a local driver is advisable for most foreign business travelers. Allow your hotel or local business contacts to set up this service for you.

TRAIN

Estonia's rail service is underdeveloped, but service exists in the Tallinn metropolitan area as well as to destinations outside of Estonia. Traveling from Tallinn to Tartu takes approximately 3.5 hours.

Tallinn Rail Station; Toompuiestee 35; EE0090 Tallinn; tel: 6156-851; fax: 6156-192

METRO

There is no metro service outside of the normal train service in Tallinn.

BUSES & TRAMS

Buses are inexpensive and remain one of the best ways to travel around the city. Express buses also link Estonia's cities together; they are, however, not normally used by visiting business people.

The tram system in Tallinn reaches every part of the city. Though crowded at peak periods, it is a quick way to get across town. Taxis and hired cars should be used for attending important meetings.

WATER TRAVEL

Ferry services link Scandinavia with Estonia. Boats arrive at *Reisisadam*, or in the case of the smaller hydrofoils, at Linnahall Speedboat Harbor. Taxis will sprint you into downtown for about Eek25. Buses also service the ports. International cruise ship travel also serves Tallinn port.

TRAVEL ASSISTANCE

Tallinn Tourist Information Center
Raekoja plats 10, Tallinn EE0001
tel: 6313-940; fax: 6313-943
email: info@tallinn.turism.ee

Estonian Tourist Board
Pikk 71;
tel: 641-1420; fax: 641-1432;
email: info@turism.ee

Essential Terms

English	Estonian
Yes No	Jaa Ei
Good morning Hello (daytime) Hello (evening) Hello (telephone)	Tere hommikust Päevast Headõhtut Tere
Good-bye	Head aega
Please	Palun
Thank you	Tänan
Pleased to meet you	Va-gah ryym-sahf
Excuse me; I'm sorry	Vabandage
My name is _____	Minu nimi on____
I don't understand	Ma ei saa aru
Do you speak English?	Kas te räägite inglise keelt?

Communications

DIALING CODES IN ESTONIA

International country code: [372]
Selected city codes: Rakvere (32), Tallinn (2), Tartu (7)

Dialing Estonia from Overseas

Three different telephone systems operate in Estonia—all with different codes. To reach a digital number (recognizable by seven digits beginning with 6) dial your international access code + the local number (no city codes necessary). The mobile system requires your international access code + 372 + 5 + local number. To dial an analogue number (any six-digit local number), dial your country's international dialing code + 372 + the city code (without the initial 2), and finally the local number. If you were dialing Tallinn from the United States, for example, you would begin with 011, then 372, then 2 (the city code for Tallinn), and finally the number of the person or office you were trying to reach.

If calling from Russia, use 014 instead of 372 as the country code.

Assistance Numbers

Information 07

Ekspress Hotline (for English help) 631 32 22
Operator 115
Collect Calls 116
Information 8-1188, 8-1184
Infotelefon (also in English)...............................626-1111*
*call between 8a.m. and 10p.m.; closed Sunday.

CALLING WITHIN ESTONIA

Local Calls

If you find a phone that still takes coins, simply pick up and dial, it may just be free. If not, deposit 20 senti if the phone even works at all. Local calls simply require straightforward dialing of the number, thankfully no other codes apply. To call a mobile phone number from an analogue phone, dial 8 + (wait for a tone) + number.

Long Distance Calls

As the analogue phone system rapidly changes over to digital, expect changes in phone numbers. The old analogue numbers have six digits (five in smaller towns). Digital numbers begin with a 6 followed by six digits.

To make an intercity call, dial 8 (wait for tone on an analogue phone) + area code + number.

International Calls

To call direct, dial 8 + 00 + country code + area code + number. You'll have to wait for a tone after the initial "8" from an analogue number. From a cell phone, there is no preceding "8" necessary. Simply dial 00 + country code + number.

To the U.S., the rate is about Eek24. You can order a call from a post office operator, which will cost about one third less than from a public phone. If calling from a hotel phone, expect mega-Mir rates. To bypass the rate race and get a decent shot at a more reasonable deal, dial:
AT&T Direct..8-00-8001-001

AT&T allows you to place calls to most countries in the world.

PAY PHONES

Public Telephones

There are three types of public phones: the archaic Soviet analogue phones, the new cellular system, and a new digital system. In Tallinn, expect digital card phones. One can also place calls from telephone offices; in Tallinn the office is located at Narva 1; tel: 640-2666. Opening hours go from 8a.m. to 7p.m. weekdays, and 9a.m. to 4p.m. on Saturdays. To order a call at any time, call 116.

Calling Cards

Card phones are the way to go for digital access. You can get a card in Eek30, 50, or 100 denominations at hotels, post offices, or kiosks.

Card Phone:

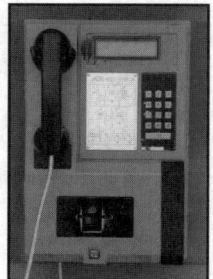

CELLULAR PHONES

Eesti Mobiil Telefon and Radiolinja Estonia AS both provide digital GSM service in Estonia. Eesti Mobiil Telefon also provides analog service in the NMT-450 format.

Note: Your home country cell phone may not work in this country. If not, we recommend that you rent an international cell phone *before* you leave home. A major US-based cell phone rental provider is **IMC WorldCell**. For information see "International Cell Phone Rentals" on page 14.

CALL BACK

You can (potentially) save significant sums when calling in Estonia by using one of the call back services listed below. Fees for call back services vary widely, depending on the company and the type of service required. Be sure to check with these companies before leaving to compare rates.

PHONE JACKS

Plug adaptors are available through **iGo Corporation.** (See "Electrical and Telephone Adaptors" on page 19.)

FAX

Fax machines are available at most business offices and hotels, as well as central post offices. Window #19 handles faxes at the central post office in Tallinn (see postal services for opening hours). The central telephone office (Narva 1) also sends faxes. Prices start at Eek4 within Estonia. To Europe, a fax may cost about Eek20 for the first page; add Eek10 to Asia and America, and another Eek10 to Australia. Telex services are also available where fax machines are found.

POSTAL SERVICES

Mail to Western Europe takes about six days. Mail to North America can take up to two weeks. Incoming mail could take considerably longer. To speed things along, address mail in the local language or at least the familiar format (country, city with index number, street, house number, and then name). Major hotels have postal facilities for posting mail and buying stamps. Mailboxes are rare.

The main post office in Tallinn is located at Narva 1. Open Monday to Friday: 8a.m. to 7p.m. Saturday 9a.m. to 5p.m.

Business Services

BUSINESS CENTERS

ESKO Koolitus; Vana-Posti 7; tel: 631-3073; fax: 631-3075; conference and training center

Olümpia Hotel Business Center; Liivalai 33; tel: 631-5835; fax: 631-5675; conference rooms; computers, audiovisual equipment.

Sakala Centre; Rävala 12; tel: 44-4942; fax: 646-6019; event center; meeting rooms; five large halls; translation systems; catering service.

Viru Hotel; Viru väljak; tel: 630-1370; fax: 630-1303; conference center; computers; internet.

COURIER SERVICES

Airborne Express; Express service: RGW Express; Postfach 750433, 60534 Frankfurt/Main, Germany; tel: (69) 698-0080; fax: (69) 6980-0840.

DHL International Eesti AS; 5 Joe St., Tallinn EE0001; tel: (2) 319-385.

Express Mail Service; Central Post Office, Narva 1; Window #1: 7:30a.m. to 8p.m., Saturday 9a.m. to 4p.m.; Window #8: 8a.m. to 7p.m., Saturday 9a.m. to 5p.m.; branch office: Toompuiestee 33a, Monday to Friday: 8a.m. to 5p.m.; For pick-up call: 631-3921.

FedEx; Linter + Co.; tel: (2) 625-8727.

TNT Worldwide Eesti AS; Lennujaama 2; tel: 640-1470; fax: 640-1473; Monday to Friday 9a.m. to 5p.m.; email: tnt@online.ee

UPS Estonia; Nafta Street 1, 0001 Tallinn; tel: (2) 423-369; fax: (2) 466-179.

PHOTOCOPYING

Canon; Pärnu 32; tel: 44-1333; 9a.m. to 7p.m. weekdays; Saturday 11a.m. to 5p.m.

Jajaa; Pärnu 32; tel: 441-333.

Kumalo; Müürivahe 30; tel: 44-6539; 9a.m. to 6p.m. weekdays; Saturday 9a.m. to 4p.m.

Xerox; Narva 18; tel: 43-8374; 9a.m. to 6p.m. weekdays; Saturday 11a.m. to 3p.m.

TRANSLATION

Estonian Holidays; Viru Hotel, Viru väljak 4; tel: 6301-940.

Estonian Legal Translation Center; Tõnismägi 8; tel: 6316-136.

Online Tõlkebüroo; Pärnu 20a; tel/fax: 6313-191.

P.S. Äri Tõlkebüroo; Narva 7-604; tel: 43-3611; fax: 43-3611.

Electrical

Current
220 volts AC, 50Hz
European style 2-pin plugs are the norm.

ELECTRIC PLUGS

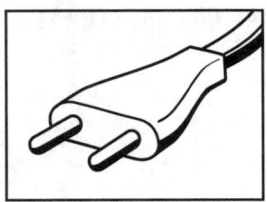

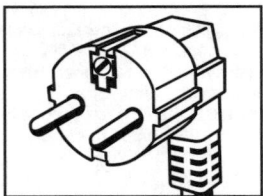

Plug adaptors are available through **iGo Corporation.** (See "Electrical and Telephone Adaptors" on page 19.)

Technical Support
HARDWARE/SOFTWARE VENDOR SUPPORT

Apple/Claris; (in Germany) tel: [49] (1) 803-5018; (in Switzerland) tel: [41] (800) 833-310; (in the U.K.) tel: [44] (990) 127-753; (in the U.S.) tel: [1] (800) 500-7078; http://www.apple.com/.

Compaq/Digital; (in Switzerland) tel: [41] (22) 709-5330; fax: [41] (22) 709-5391 (Geneva); tel: [41] (1) 801-2507; fax: [41] (1) 801-2172 (Zurich); (General U.S.) tel: (281) 518-2000; http://www.compaq.com/.

Dell; (in Germany) tel: [49] (61) 039-710; (Dell- Europe) tel: [44] (134) 474-8000; (in the U.S.) tel: [1] (512) 338-4400; fax: [1] (512) 728-3330; http://www.dell.com/.

Gateway 2000; (in the U.S.) tel: [1] (605) 232-2191; fax: [1] (605) 232-2023; (in Ireland) tel: [353] (1) 797-2000; http://www.g2k.com/.

Hewlett Packard; (in Switzerland) tel: [41] (22) 780-8111; (in the U.S.) tel: [1] (408) 246-4300; http://www.hp.com/.

IBM; tel: 611-2500; fax: 611-2401; (in Germany) tel: [49] (711) 78-50; fax: [49] (711) 785-3511; (in Switzerland) tel: [41] (22) 310-0418 (French); (in the U.S.) tel: [1] (919) 517-2800; (U.S. Main Office) tel: [1] 914-765-1900; http://www.ibm.com/.

Microsoft; tel: 650-4999; (in Germany) tel: [49] (89) 31-760; fax: [49] (89) 3176-1000; tel: [49] (89) 3176-1199; (in Switzerland) tel: [41] (848) 858-868; fax [41] (1) 831-0869; (in the U.S.) [1] (425) 635-7222; http://www.microsoft.com/.

NEC; (in Germany) tel: [49] (18) 0524- 1212; tel:[49] (89) 3160-1233; fax: [49] (89) 3160- 1613 (Floppy Disk and Hard Drive); tel: [49] (89) 9627-4233; fax: [49] (89) 9627-4613 (All Other Products); (in the U.S.) [1] (916) 388-0101 (Main Switchboard); http://www.nec.com/.

Toshiba; (in Germany) tel: [49] (2131) 158-319; fax: [49] (2131) 158-558; (in Switzerland) tel: [41] (1) 946-0777; fax: [41] (1) 946-0807; (in Ireland) tel: [44] (193) 282-8828; (in the U.S.) [1] (949) 583-3000 (Corporate Headquarters); http://www.toshiba.com/.

Internet Connection
HOW TO CONNECT

Connecting to AOL and Compuserve in Estonia is similar to using it when traveling outside your own area code. See the introductory section for detailed information on connecting to your account through a different phone number.

America Online
Numbers are available at keyword *international*. Be sure to get several local numbers before leaving. AOL's GlobalNet service charges US$6 an hour in addition to the usual charges. Go to keyword *access* (a free area) and download the software.
Access: Tallinn (6) 410-730.

Compuserve
Numbers are available at *Go International*. The Compuserve Web-site also has a great deal of information, at http://www.compuserve.com. Technical support is available by calling Germany: [49] 1805-25-81-46.
Access: Tallinn (6) 410-730.

Independent Service Providers
Many independent service providers offer discounts if you are only in town for a couple days.
Anet; tel: 641-0012; fax: 331-2514; email: info@anet.ee; http://www.anet.ee/.

ASE Computers; tel: 627-2172; fax: 627-2171; email: ase@ase.ee; http://www.ase.ee/.

EUnet/Data Telecom; tel: 626-6299; fax: 626-6292; email: dt@data.ee; http://www.unet.ee/.

Teleport; tel: 628-5600; fax: 641-0001; email: ifo@teleport.eehttp://www.teleport.ee/.

Business Culture
GREETINGS & COURTESIES

Estonians are a warm, effusive people. Business greetings involve long hand shakes, wordy welcomes, and extensive, though friendly, eye contact. In many ways, the Estonians have found a middle ground between the bear hugs of the Russian greeting and the coolness of the Teutonic handshake. Smiles abound in this country and small gifts are often exchanged among business people. Initially, keep your gifts discreet and business oriented. More personal gifts can be given as the relationship grows. Be careful not to outspend or outshine your Estonian host with the quality of your gift as Estonians do not like to be reminded of their rank in the world economies.

BUSINESS ETHIC & FRAMEWORK

Estonia is caught between aspiring to become an established E.U. member and a desire to take advantage of all the loopholes and shortcuts offered to a emerging market. Local business people understand the long-term benefits of making honest deals with foreign investors and traders. Estonians also recognize that their population is a long way from being able to afford the high prices and tight regulation of the developed West.

Business visitors will find that Estonians are very willing to abide by contracts with foreign firms and deliver the specified quality. Corruption is nowhere near the levels of neighboring Russia. However, those same visitors will find the streets flooded with counterfeit goods and smuggled commodities. This dichotomy, in Estonian minds at least, serves both the long-term economic needs of major domestic businesses while servicing the short-term desires of the population. It should also be noted that many of Estonia's E.U. neighbors flock to its shores to enjoy this special take on market economics and ethics.

DECISION MAKING

Estonian business, like most of developing Europe, is largely hierarchical. Virtually every decision will require approval from the highest echelons. Consequently, it is best to start as close to the top as possible when seeking to negotiate a business deal. Don't be surprised if you are referred back down the chain of command as the main benefit of the Estonian system is that it protects top managers from being involved until all details have been worked out. Middle management serves as both filter and buffer. A foreign firm's ability to circumvent this often tedious system is based entirely upon whether they are in a buying or selling position. Buyer will start at the top while sellers will have to satisfy themselves at a point no higher than the middle. (For speed of decisions, see "Meetings")

MEETINGS

Estonian business people are an educated, if not experienced, group. The demise of close to a half century of communist rule has left many Estonian companies headed by either elders with little knowledge of modern business standards or novice managers with more enthusiasm than acumen. Whatever the case, Estonian business people are generally eager to please and impress foreigners.

Meetings will most often start with a welcoming speech by the highest level Estonian manager present. Visitors should respond in kind. Elder Estonians are unlikely to speak any other foreign language than Russian, though younger managers will often speak English. Visitors should assume they will need to employ a translator and it is best if they procure their own.

A single meeting will rarely be sufficient to secure a deal—buying or selling. The wheels of Estonian business turn slowly but nowhere near as slowly as those of Asian counterparts. Visitors should keep in mind that the legal system in Estonia is nascent, at best, in the area of contract law. Take the time made available by the slowness of Estonian decisionmaking to assess your counterparts as the "relationship" may be all that binds the contract.

BUSINESS ENTERTAINING

Eating and drinking are an important part of the social aspect of business meetings, and Estonians like to play host. The food can be heavy and alcohol consumption during business hours is common (but not to excess as in some Russian quarters). Like many nations with little contract law, Estonians prefer to do business with people they like (and trust), as such, much conversation at the dining table will be social rather than business oriented. The Estonians are a friendly, gregarious people, and they treat social reserve in visitors with distrust or as a form of snobbery. Visitors should loosen up and enjoy the hospitality as it is very sincere.

Note: Visitors on extended stays in Estonia should attempt to reciprocate this hospitality. Seek the advice of local hoteliers, restaurateurs, or even translators to determine menus and venues. In no way, however, should visitors seek to outdo their Estonian counterparts; they are already well aware of their limited budgets and facilities.

WOMEN IN BUSINESS

It is unlikely that foreign female managers will meet female counterparts in Estonia. The Estonian women—in most, but not all cases—will be acting in the role of secretaries and assistants. Female visitors should not be surprised if it assumed that they perform the same role in the visiting delegation. To avoid mistakes, rumpled feelings, and the need for embarrassing corrections, foreign companies should make known the gender and rank of their delegation members in advance of arrival. When a female manager heads the visiting delegation, all subordinates should defer to her at all times.

Another annoying habit of Estonian men (in fact most eastern European men) is the use of gratuitous sexual remarks in the presence of women. While they may considerate such comments witty and somehow complimentary, foreign women may find it crude and demeaning. The extent to which a visitor should challenge this behavior is really a function of whether the visitor is buying or selling. As is true elsewhere in the world, sellers must be more tolerant than buyers.

BUSINESS ATTIRE

Estonian business is fairly formal in attitude, and the climate makes the wearing of business suits tolerable. Men adopt the standard dark suit, white shirt, and necktie. Quality shoes, once an impossible commodity to get during Soviet times, are now standard. In fact, visitors may find that Estonians will make an extra effort to examine a foreigner's footwear as a barometer of success. Both men and women visitors should be well shod.

As mentioned above under "Security Briefing", Estonian women may dress in a more sexually provocative manner than Western counterparts. Local styles often cross the line into garishness. Foreign female managers can avoid unwanted comments and attention by maintaining a conservative business dress standard.

Note: Both male and female visitors should avoid displays of wealth in the form of jewelry or overtly expensive garments. Such things only serve to cause resentment or feelings of inferiority by Estonian counterparts, neither of which are the basis for a solid business relationship.

Business Advisory

POLITICS & GRAFT

The Estonian government is doing its level best to keep its population happy while attending to the economic measures necessary for it join the E.U. These two goals often diverge and do so most pointedly when it comes to controlling the levels of black marketeering. However, foreign firms will find little pressure to become involved in graft, especially as compared to Estonia's Russian and Belarussian neighbors.

BUSINESS FRAUD

As is the case with graft, the Estonian effort to become a contributing member of the E.U. has encouraged its business people to stay on the "up and up" with foreign firms. Fraud is minimal, and most contract disputes derive from a difference in quality standards rather than outright attempts at fraud. Estonia currently enjoys an above average reputation for conducting honest business with foreigners, and it knows the importance of maintaining that reputation.

Business Centers
Tallinn

CITY VIEW

Tallinn is a small city, a population hovering around 415,000, but has become a growing Eastern European business center. With electronics and computer companies providing the city some economic boost, a draft plan for the city emphasizing further development. Bordered in the north by the Baltic Sea and in the south by Lake Ülemiste, Tallinn also serves as an important port city, which remains ice free almost year round. Points of interest include the Old Town, recently added to Unesco's World Heritage List. As such, much of Tallinn's cultural and historical intrigue centers around it. A myriad of music festivals, choral concerts, and art events provide further spark to the city. With theaters, exhibition halls, and museums to further keep the visitor busy, it's no wonder that tourism employs 10 percent of the population.

AIRPORT

Tallinn Airport to City Center

The airport lies 2.5 miles (4 km.) from the city. Bus #2 collects passengers outside of the arrivals hall every 20 minutes. The end of the line is located a few hundred meters from the Viru Hotel downtown. The fare costs Eek7 and tickets may be purchased on board. For those visiting for the first time, or those seeking convenience, hail a taxi to deliver you in front of the door you seek. Average travel time is 20 minutes.

Airline Numbers

Aeroflot	638-8887
Air Baltic	631-2240
	Airport: 638-8887
Avies (taxi flights)	638-8022

Estonian Air 6401 101, 6401 160
.... charter flights: 42-7451
ELK Airways 638-8887
.... charter flights: 42-7451
Finnair 6311 455, 6388 353
LOT Polish Airlines... 646-6051
.... Airport: 638-8950
Lufthansa 638-8077
.... Airport: 638-8940
SAS 631-2240, 631-2241
.... Airport: 638-8553

HOTELS

Top-end

Olümpia; Liivalaia 33; tel:6315-315, res.; tel: 6315-333, front desk; fax: 6315-675; 405 rooms; 2 restaurants; 3 bars; breakfast buffet; standard and business class floors; business center; conference facilities; secretarial service; fax/photocopy facilities; internet available; in-room radio, satellite tv, minibar, desk; courier service; laundry/drycleaning; doctor facilities; bank; hairdresser; flowers; books; car rental; travel agency; newspaper stand; souvenir shop; corporate rates; 26th-floor weight room; glass-wall saunas; pool; Eek1600/1900/2200.

Palace; Vabaduse väljak 3; tel: 6407-300; fax: 6407-299; email: palace@finest.ee; http://www.finest.ee; bordering old city; small-scale luxury hotel; 2 restaurants; conference room (up to 10); business services; modem outlets; in-room satellite tv, bathroom; sauna; Eek2200/2800.

Park Consul Schlossle (a Golden Tulip Hotel); Pühavaimu 13/15; tel: 6997-700; fax: 6997-777; email: pctallinn@consul-hotels.com; located in Old Town; historic, English-style estates; 23 exquisite, restored rooms; personal service; US$200+.

Viru Hotel; Viru väljak 4; tel: 630-1311, info.; tel: (6) 301-311, booking fax: (6) 301-303; http://www.viru.ee; email: reservation@viru.estpak.ee; centrally located; casino; restaurants; cafe; standard and business class rooms; upper rooms with view of Old Town; conference facilities (up to 250); corporate rates; saunas; whirlpool; nigthclub; Eek1300/1600/1900.

Expensive

Central; Narva 7c; tel: 6339-800; fax: 6339-900; city center, neighborhood location; reknowned Italian restaurant; 2 bars; breakfast buffet; conference facilities (up to 200); no-smoking rooms, allergy rooms; room service; laundry/drycleaning service; ironing service; news stand; hairddresser; car retnal; travel agency; parking; massage; US$65/75.

Pirita; Regati 1; tel: 639-8600; fax: 639-8821; suburb, near exhibition grounds; casino; restaurant; breakfast buffet; business-class rooms available; conference facilities; corporate rates; weight rooms; saunas; pool; shopping mall;Eek760/980/1190.

Rataskaevu; Rataskaevu 7; tel: 441-939; fax: 443-688; located in central old town; art-nouveau decor; singles/doubles/deluxe doubles/suites; restaurant; corporate rates; Eek 970/1500.

St. Barbara; Roosikrantsi 2a; tel: 631-3991; fax: 631-3992; bordering old city; Palace Hotel sister hotel; cellar German restaurant; clean rooms; singles/doubles/luxury suites; Eek 1152/1344/1520.

Moderate

Burmani Willa; Kadaka 62; tel/fax: 53-2085; restored 1920's bungalow; conference rooms; transportation, interpreters provided upon request; Eek700.

Dzingel; Männiku 89; tel; 610-5201; fax: 585-411; suburb; restaurant; breakfast, sauna included in price; modern rooms; Eek370/490/650.

Metropol; 8B Mere Blvd., 10111 Tallinn; tel: (6) 674-500.

Hotel Stroomi; Randla 11; tel: 6304-200; fax: 6304 500; email: stroomi@netexpress.ee; full-service hotel; restaurant; renovated rooms; non-smoking rooms available; Eek230/550/850.

MEDICAL CARE

Baltic-American Medical and Surgical Clinic; Antakalnio 124, *Vilnius, Lithuania*; tel: [370-2} 74-2020; excellent healthcare service in case of emergency.

Baltic Medical Partners; (for dental care) Tartu mnt. 32; tel: 6311-222.

DKN Medical Center; 103 Parnu; tel: 557-908; fax: 557-508.

ESMED; private clinic; Ehitajate 137; tel: 6579-118.

Estonian-Finnish Medical Center; private clinic; Regati pst. 1, Pirita Hotel; tel: 6398-585.

Tallinn Central Hospital; Ravi 18; tel: 620-7010.

HEALTH CLUBS

Balance Club; Harju 6; tel: 6310-510; located in the old city, featuring aerobics, sauna, weightroom, and whirlpool.

TOP Fitness Club; in the Piriti Hotel; Regati pst. 1; tel: 6396-707; aerobics; pool; sauna; Turkish bath; weight rooms.

AUTO RENTAL

Note: Expect haphazard driving. A Green Card insurance is required of all drivers. By law, all vehicles must drive with their lights on 24 hours a day.

Avis; tel: (6) 388-222; fax: (6) 388-220; www.avis.ee; Headquarters office: Lilvalaia 33, tel: 631-5932, 631-5931; Lennujaama Tee 2, tel: 638-8221; 638-8222; fax: 638-8220; Hotel Olympia; tel: 631-5930, fax: 631-5931.

Balti Autoliising; tel: (6) 638-8148; fax: (6) 388-142.

Baltlink; Viru Hotel; tel: 421-003; fax: 450-893

Palace Hotel; tel: 444-761.

Budget; tel: (6) 638-8599; fax: (6) 388-599; www.budget-rentacar.com.

Eurodollar; downtown tel: 630-1526; fax: 630-1562; airport: 638-8071.

Europcar; Magdaleena 3C; tel: 650-2561; fax: 650-2560; airport: 638-8031.

Hertz; tel: (6) 388-923; fax: (6) 388-953; www.hertz.com; GSM (24h helpline): (6) 501-7911.

WORLD TRADE CENTER

World Trade Center Tallinn
RET Development Group Ltd.
8 Ahtri Street
Tallinn EE0001
tel: (2) 626-1020; fax: (2) 626-1019
email: signe@wtc.ee
website: http://www.wtc.ee/

CHAMBER OF COMMERCE

Estonian Chamber of Commerce and Industry
Toom-Kooli 17
Tallinn, EE0001
tel: 646-0244; fax: 646-0245
email: koda@koda.ee

Finland

At a Glance

THE PEOPLE

Population .... 5,158,372 (July 1999 est.)
Growth Rate .... 0.15% (1999 est.)
Life Expectancy .... 77.32 years (born 1999)
Infant Mortality ..... 3.8 deaths/1,000 live births (1999 est.)

Ethnic Composition

Finn 93%
Swedish 6%
Lapp 0.11%
Other 0.89%

Religious Composition

Evangelical Lutheran 89%
Non-affiliated 9%
Greek Orthodox 1%
Other 1%

Languages Spoken

Finnish (official), English (spoken by most every citizen and used as the language of commerce),Swedish, Lapp, Russian

Education and Literacy

Education is compulsory for nine years. Adult literacy is 100 percent.

Labor Force

Total: 2,533,000
By occupation: services 70.5%, industry 20.9%, agriculture 8.6%

THE ECONOMY

Finland's economy has put its per capita GDP on par with EU powerhouses like the UK and Germany. Though sporting a large agriculture sector, Finland is dominated by services. Its telecom and finance businesses are world-class and it has the highest rate of Internet connectivity in the world. An early member of the EU, and nowadays one of the main proponents of the euro, Finland has been instrumental in bringing the globe's attention to both Scandinavia and eastern Europe. But all is not perfect in this vibrant economy. A generous social system has not only burdened the nation with high taxes but it perpetuates a level of unemployment (14.6 percent) that is large even by European standards. Finland is also heavily dependent on the export of raw materials. This makes its revenues too easily impacted by global commodity fluctuations. Its other growing problem is the potential for economic implosion by its close neighbor and trading partner, Russia.

Exports .... US$43 billion (f.o.b., 1998)
Imports .... US$30.7 billion (f.o.b., 1998)
Total GDP .... US$103.6 billion (1998 est.)
GDP Per Capita .... US$20,100 (1998 est.)
Unemployment ....12% (1998 est.)
Inflation Rate .... 1.5% (1998 est.)

Top Export Partners

E.U., United States, Japan, Russia, CIS

Top Import Partners

E.U., United States, Japan, Russia, CIS

Top Exports

Paper and pulp, machinery, chemicals, metals, timber.

Top Imports

Foodstuffs, petroleum and petroleum products, chemicals, transport equipment, iron and steel, machinery, textile yarn and fabrics, fodder grains.

BUSINESS WORKWEEK

Offices

Monday to Friday 8a.m. to 4:40p.m.

Banks

Monday to Friday 9:15a.m. to 6:15p.m.

Government

Winter: Monday to Friday 8a.m. to 4:15p.m.
Summer: Monday to Friday 8a.m. to 3:15p.m.

Retail

Shops: Monday to Friday 9a.m to 6p.m.; Saturday 9a.m. to 2p.m.

Large department stores: Monday to Friday 9a.m. to 8p.m.; Saturday until 6p.m.

Note: Business hours are greatly affected by the lengthy periods of darkness in more northern regions of the country as well as by local custom.

HOLIDAYS

New Year's Day ....January 1
Epiphany ....January 6
Good Friday ....April 2*
Easter Monday ....April 5*
May Day .... April 30-May 1
Ascension Day .... May 13*
Whitsun .... May 23*
Midsummer Day ....June 25-26*
All Saints' Day .... November 1*
Independence Day ....December 6
Christmas ....December 24-26
*Date may vary by year.

CLIMATE

Seasons

The winters are long and severe from January to April; but, generally, Finland's temperature remains relatively low for its high altitude. Summers are short, but generally warm, with average temperatures of 16˚C (61˚F), and temperatures sometimes reaching 25˚C (77˚F). Since the summer season is so short, most Finns take holiday time during those months. As such, business travel should be avoided during the summer.

Regions

The south receives the least amount of snow which begins in December and remains for 100 days. Inland areas and Lapland in the far north can have snow for as long as 200 days. Helsinki's temperature can drop to -15˚C (5˚F), and on rare occasions fall to -30˚C (-22˚F).

Money & Banking

Currency

The currency of Finland is the Markka (F Mk).

Finland

Finland

⊛ National capital
◉ Provincial capital
● Secondary city
.... Primary road
---------- Railroad
—— Province border
══ International border

Province (lääni) Name
1 Lappi
2 Oulu
3 Vaasa
4 Keski Suomi
5 Kuopio
6 Pohjois-Karjala
7 Turku Ja Pori
8 Häme
9 Mikkeli
10 Kymi
11 Uusimaa
12 Ahvenanmaa

SM Santa Barbara, CA

©2001 Magellan Geographix

Denominations

The Markka comes in coin denominations of FMk10, 5, as well as 1, and 50 and 10 pennia; and banknotes of FMk10, 20, 50, 100, 500, and 1,000.

Traveler's Checks and Credit Cards

Traveler's checks and foreign currency can be easily and efficiently exchanged at banks, foreign exchange bureaus, hotels, and foreign exchange kiosks at the airports. Banks offer the most variable exchange rates.

Traveler's checks receive a better exchange rate than cash, or you can purchase Finnish currency traveler's check before departure, which can be exchanged almost everywhere.

Credit cards are widely accepted in Finland including American Express, Visa, MasterCard, Eurocard, and Diners Club, as well as bank cards from the larger Finnish banks.

You can get cash advances from your credit card on many of the automated teller machines (ATM). Credit cards are also essential for renting a car or hotel rooms. Long-term visitors should set up a checking account inflaming, and get an ATM card. Credit card and ATM transactions receive the most favorable exchange rates. Transactions on check and credit card can be conducted in Euros if so requested.

Essential Terms

English	Finnish
Yes	Kyllä
No	Ei
Good morning	Hyvää huomentá
Hello (daytime)	Päivää
Hello (evening)	Hyvää iltaa
Hello (telephone)	Hei
Good-bye	Hyvästi
Please	Olkaa hyvä
Thank you	Kiitos
Pleased to meet you	On hauska tavata teidät
Excuse me; I'm sorry	Anteeksi
My name is _____	Nimeni on _____
I don't understand	En ymmärrä
Do you speak English?	Puhutteko englantia?

Travel

VISA AND PASSPORT

A passport that is valid for a minimum of three months beyond your anticipated exit date is required of all visitors, except for citizens of the following countries, who must also hold a national ID card:

- EU countries (except the U.K., Greece, and Ireland), and the French Overseas Departments of Guadeloupe, Martinique, and Réunion.
- Norway, Iceland, Liechtenstein, San Marino, and Switzerland

Visas are required of all, except for nationals of the following countries, whose maximum stay of three months without a visa begins the moment the traveler enters any Scandinavian country:

- Andorra, Argentina, Australia, Bahamas, Barbados, Bermuda, Bolivia, Botswana, Brazil, Canada, Chile, Costa Rica, Cyprus, Czech Republic, Ecuador, El Salvador, Estonia, Grenada, Guatemala, Honduras, Hungary, Israel, Jamaica, Japan, Korea (Rep. of), Latvia, Lesotho, Lithuania, Malawi, Malaysia, Malta, Mexico, Monaco, Namibia, New Zealand, Nicaragua, Panama, Paraguay, Poland, Seychelles, St. Vincent & the Grenadines, Singapore, Slovak Republic, Slovenia, Swaziland, Trinidad & Tobago, U.K., Uruguay, U.S., and Vatican City.
- Nations listed above as having passport exemptions
- Passengers in transit who do not leave the airport and are continuing their journey within 24 hours, and who are holding confirmed tickets and other documents for onward travel, are also exempt from the need for a visa.

Visas are necessary for stays beyond three months and for legal employment in Finland during one's stay, except in the case of nationals of Norway, Denmark, Sweden, and Iceland.

Transit visas are valid up to five days. There are single-entry and double-entry visas, valid a maximum 90 days. Multiple-entry visas are valid up to a year. Visa extensions are generally fairly easy to obtain.

Allow several days for visa application processing, or several weeks if your application is referred to the Finnish Ministry of the Interior.

E.U. nationals may live and be legally employed in Finland up to three months with no need of visas or permits. For periods beyond three months, E.U. nationals may simply obtain a residence permit (no work permit is required) at the local police station. Customarily, this is valid for five years.

DEPARTURE FORMALITIES

A foreigner may take out of Finland no more than US$1500 in equivalent Finnish funds without government approval. No other restrictions for departure exist. Airport departure fees are included in the price of tickets.

CUSTOMS ENTRY (PERSONAL)

Duty-free

The following goods may be brought into Finland from **non-E.U. countries** without incurring customs duty:

- 200 cigarettes, or 50 cigars, or 250g of tobacco
- Two liters of mild alcoholic drink or sparkling wines (less than 22% by volume)
- One liter of strong alcoholic drink (more than 22% by volume).
- 50gm of perfume, 250ml eau de toilette

The following goods may be brought into Finland from **E.U. countries** without incurring customs duty:

- 300 cigarettes, or 150 cigarillos, or 75 cigars, or 400g of tobacco
- 15 liters of beer and five liters of wine and three liters of mild alcoholic drink or sparkling wines (less than 22% by volume), or one liter of strong alcoholic drink (more than 22% by volume)
- Non-commercial goods to a value of Fmk1100
- 50g perfume and 250ml eau de toilette

The amounts of alcohol and tobacco specified above are strictly academic at most E.U. borders, since the import of duty-paid quantities are no longer limited between most E.U. countries. Denmark, Finland, and Sweden, however, will continue to impose limits until 2004.

Prohibited or Restricted

- The importation of drinks containing more than 60 percent alcohol by volume
- Home wine and beer manufacturing kits
- Whale meat
- The import and export of food, plants, medicines, narcotics and dangerous drugs, chemicals, firearms and ammunition, explosives, nuclear and radioactive substances, pornography, and works of art are subject to certain restrictions and formalities.

Note: In general, dogs and cats may be imported, provided they are accompanied by a certificate issued by a competent veterinary surgeon to the effect that 30 days prior to entry, and within the previous year, they have been vaccinated against rabies. The certificate must be in Finnish, Swedish, English, or German. Dogs and cats from rabies-free countries (Sweden, Norway, Iceland, U.K., Ireland, Australia, and New Zealand) do not require a certificate if imported direct. Contact the Finnish Tourist Board for further details.

IMMUNIZATION

There are no inoculation requirements for entry to Finland, unless you are arriving from an infected area. Tetanus and Hepatitis A inoculations are recommended for extended travel in rural areas. Campers and trekkers are advised to take precautions which may prevent tick bites, and to consider immunization to prevent tick-borne encephalitis from developing.

TIPPING

Taxi

Taxi drivers do not expect tips but they will add FMk4 to all fares after 6p.m.

Porters

Tip hotel porters FMk 3 to 5 per bag.

Hotels

The bill in hotels always includes a 15 percent service charge.

Restaurants

The bill in restaurants and clubs includes a 15 service charge. However, many Finns also leave the extra change, if there is any, as a tip.

Other

Cloakroom attendants receive between Fmk 3 and 5; reception clerks get FMk 5 to 10 for extra service. Ushers and barbers are usually not tipped.

EMERGENCY INFORMATION

Police and Crime

Crime remains relatively low in Finland. However, take basic precautions against petty crime. Foreign business visitors are, however, often the target of what few thieves there are in Finland. Consequently, purses, laptops, and briefcases will require additional security. Do not leave valuables in cars or on tables in cafés. Keep non-essential valuables locked in hotel safes when not in use. Use credit cards and travel checks when possible to avoid carrying large sums of cash.

Emergency Numbers

Numbers function nationwide.

Police / Fire emergency.. 112
Medical emergency 008
Dental emergency 736-1666
Ambulance 006
Police (non-emergency) 10022

Health

Traveling in Finland carries no serious health risk. Food laws are strict, food is safe, and tap water is potable. Visitors from Asia may find the Finnish diet quite heavy. All visitors should give themselves time to acclimate to the weather and different day/night patterns.

The local authorities are responsible for the medical establishment, which is of an extremely high standard, and its services are often free to foreign travelers. Public hospitals do not accept U.S. insurance nor foreign credit cards. However, most private hospitals do accept credit card payment. Some pharmacies stay open 24 hours a day.

Your hotel will have access to more information, otherwise call the emergency hospital for foreigners at the Helsinki University Central Hospital at tel: 4711. For 24-hour health care information call: (9)0-10-023.

For more information on medical centers, including phone numbers, please see the "Business Centers" section at the end of this chapter.

INTERNAL TRAVEL
AIR

Finnair offers a comprehensive network of domestic air services. Daily flights connect 20 cities, venturing north as far as Ivalo on the 67th parallel. There are 23 domestic airfields in Finland. A number of discount airfare bargains are available, including the Nordic Air Pass, which permits the traveler to pre-purchase from 4 to 10 discounted flight coupons.

TAXI

Taxis all have yellow "Taksi" signs, which are lighted when the taxi is vacant. Taxis can be found at taksi stands, or they can be hailed from the street. All fares should be metered or negotiated before leaving. Fares are reasonable by European standards, and drivers are well informed as well as honest. Fares rise at night (10p.m. to 6a.m.), Saturdays (4p.m. to midnight), and all day Sundays.

AUTO

Car rental is available in Helsinki as well as other larger towns. A valid driver's license and credit card are required. Local insurance requirements vary by the renter's country of origin. Most rental agencies require that the renter be at least 21 years of age.

Driving in Finland is quite civilized, although visitors should review the rule book prior to leaving the rental agency. Detailed maps are also available. About 77,000km (47,000 miles) of roadway exists in Finland.

The primary roads are generally always passable, well surfaced, and well maintained. The Finns frown upon horn blowing. In many areas, warnings of deer, elk, and reindeer crossings are posted. Visitors may obtain more information about driving in Finland at the following location:

Autoliitto
(Automobile and Touring Club of Finland)
Hämeentie 105A, 00101 Helsinki
Telephone: (9) 774 761; fax: (9) 77 47 64 44

Bicycles can be rented in most towns and are especially recommended during the summer.

TRAIN

There lies 6000km (3700 miles) of railway in Finland, with the most modern of rolling stock. A number of rail services span the country, including a train that travels at 140 mph. Travel by rail is inexpensive and efficient and is a common way for business travelers to reach the northern regions in winter time. Main rail connections also offer car-sleeper trains. One can make reservations beforehand, although there are usually seats available.

Reservations are necessary for 'EP' express trains. All tickets remain valid for a month. Discount fares are available in a number of packages, including the Finnrail Pass, which gives the traveler unlimited transit for a period of three, five, or ten days within a one-month period, first- or second-class.

Trains also connect to passenger boat services.

For further information, you may contact:

Finnish Railways
Vilhonkatu 13, 001 Helsinki
tel: (9) 707 3519; fax: (9) 707 4290
website: www.vr.fi

URBAN / METRO

Helsinki has a single east-west Metro line that operates from 6a.m. until 11:20p.m. Each ticket is good for one hour of usage and the line connects with numerous bus and tram routes. It offers a convenient and efficient way for quick crosstown travel.

An efficient and integrated transit system exists in Helsinki, encompassing metro, bus, and tramway services, ferry services to the Suomenlinna Islands, and suburban rail lines. A zonal flat-fare system applies to all modes (including ferries), with no transfer fee between services. Tickets for multiple trips and an assortment of discount passes can be purchased in advance.

Tram No. 3 goes by the majority of the primary tourist attractions, and the city even provides a brochure in English (free) for anyone who wishes to make the trip.

The Helsinki Card is valid for periods of one, two, or three days. It provides for no-ticket travel on public transport, and for free entrance to over 50 museums as well as other spots of interest in the city. The card is accompanied by a guidebook, which has particulars about the museums and other discounts. You can inquire with the Tourist Board (see "Travel Assistance" section, following) for costs and further details.

BUSES & TRAMS

Buses are the best way to travel through Finland, with more than 300 buses linking Helsinki with the most remote parts of the country. Intercity buses prove inexpensive and efficient. Bus stations all have shops and restaurants. Baggage that is left at one bus station will be forwarded to its destination, even if bus transfers or different bus companies might be involved. Tickets can be purchased through the Finnish Tourist Board.

Helsinki operates a local bus and tram service that serves every corner of the city. These are commonly used for daily business travel, and visitors will find them to be clean and efficient. Most all connect with the main metro route.

WATER TRAVEL

The port of Helsinki provides both European and domestic ferry travel. It is a common point of embarkation for Russia through St. Petersburg. International cruise lines also use Helsinki as a port for transoceanic travel.

Lake steamers and motor vessels ply the inland waterways, offering a wide range of routes and distances. Popular routes include the 'Poet's Way' linking Tampere and Virratthe, the 'Silver Line' connecting Hämeenlinna and Tampere, and the routes of the Saimaa Lake. Regular services also run on Lake Inari and Lake Päijänne, and on Lake Pielinen, the latter also serviced by car ferry. Meals and refreshments are available on lake steamers as are overnight accommodations.

TRAVEL ASSISTANCE

Helsinki City Tourist Office
Phojoisesplanadi 19, FIN-00100 Helsinki
tel: (9)0-169-3757; fax: 169-3839
Finnish Hotel Association; (9) 176 455
Finnish Hotel Council; (9) 632 488
Finnish Tourist Board; (9) 403 011
Matkailun Edistämiskeskus
(Finnish Tourist Board)
Töölönkatu 11, P.O. Box 625
Helsinki, Finland 00101
tel: (9) 417 6911
fax: (9) 41 76 93 99
Tourist Information
Eteläesplanadi 4
Helsinki, Finland 00131
tel: (9) 41 76 93 00, 41 76 92 11
Fax; (9) 41 76 93 01
email: mek@mek.fi
website: www.mek.fi

Communications

DIALING CODES IN FINLAND

International country code: [358]
Selected city codes: Helsinki (9), Espoo-Esbo (9), Pori (2), Tammerfors (3), Turku (2), Uleaborg (8), Vaasa (6), Vanda-Vantaa (9)

Dialing Finland from Overseas

To dial Finland from overseas, dial your international dialing code, then 358 (the country code for Finland), then the city code and finally the number. If you were dialing Helsinki from the United States, for example, you would begin with 011, then 358, then 9 (the city code for Helsinki), and finally the number of the person or office you were trying to reach.

Assistance Numbers

International Information... 92020
International Operator 92022
Calls to the CIS 92027
International Tariff Information 9800-8353
Long-distance Operator & Directory........................ 92015
Helsinki/Domestic Information...................................... 118
News in English.. 10040

CALLING WITHIN FINLAND

Local Calls

Local calling does not entail dialing the city code or any extra codes.

Long Distance Calls

When calling within Finland, add a zero preceding the city code, which should be omitted when calling from abroad. For example, if calling from Tampere to Helsinki, dial 09 + local number.

International Calls

To dial an international number directly, dial 990 + country code + area code + number. Collect calls or credit card calls may be made by using a country direct number:
Canada...(9) 800-100-11
U.K. BT..(9) 800-104-40
U.K. MCL...(9) 800-102-89
U.S. AT&T...(9) 800-100-10
U.S. MCI..(9) 800-102-80

PAY PHONES

Public Telephones

Public telephones require Fmk1 or Fmk5 coins or a telephone card, which may be purchased at kiosks. Calls may also be placed from post and telephone offices. In this case, one may pay the attendant after the call has been made.

Card Phone:

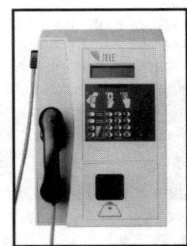

Finland

CELLULAR PHONES

Telecom Finland offers both analog and digital cellular service in numerous formats. Alands Mobiltelefon and Radiolinja Oy offer cellular service in a GSM digital format.

Note: Your home country cell phone may not work in this country. If not, we recommend that you rent an international cell phone *before* you leave home. A major US-based cell phone rental provider is **IMC WorldCell**. For information see "International Cell Phone Rentals" on page 14.

To dial a cell phone number within Finland, first dial a '0'.

CALL BACK

You can (potentially) save significant sums when calling in Finland by using a call back service. For a list of callback services, please refer to the "Communications" section in the *Global Road Warrior* Introduction.

Fees for call back services vary widely, depending on the company and the type of service required. Be sure to check with these companies before leaving to compare rates.

PHONE JACKS

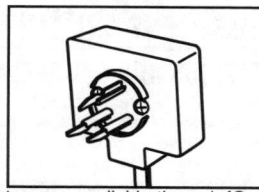

Plug adaptors are available through **iGo Corporation**. (See "Electrical and Telephone Adaptors" on page 19.)

FAX

Fax machines are widely available and used often. Their service is generally very good.

POSTAL SERVICES

Stamps can be purchased at many locations, including hotels and newsstands. Mail boxes are yellow, and are often bolted to a wall.

Hours of service

Monday-Friday 9a.m. to 5p.m.

TELEGRAMS

Telegrams are available through post offices or most hotels.

Business Services

BUSINESS CENTERS

Helsinki Airport Congress, Congress Center; Middle Terminal, Helsinki-Vantaa Airport; tel: (9) 818-3620; telefax: (9) 818-3629.

Regus Business Centre; World Trade Center, Aleksanterinkatu 17, 00100 Helsinki; tel: (9) 696-9166; telefax: (9) 6969-2666.

COURIER SERVICES

Airborne Express (ASG Air & Sea Oy); Pl 1, FI-01531 Vantaa; tel: (9) 584-294.

Cargo Express; Metsäläntie 2-4, P.O. Box 9, 00621 Helsinki; tel: 105-2050; telefax: 205-203-105.

DHL International; Valimotie 7, 01510 Vantaa; tel: (9) 777-991; telefax: 105-203-105.

Federal Express; Fritz Companies Finland Oy, Vanha Porvoontie 229, FIN-01380 Vantaa; tel: (0) 8009-0092; fax: (9) 172-9380.

TNT Suomi Oy; Tullimiehentie 2; P.O. Box 210, 01531 Vantaa; tel: (9) 476-266; telefax: (9) 4762-6716.

UPS; Valimotie 22, 01510 Vantaa; tel: (800) 877-877; (9) 613-2477; telefax: (9) 870-2267.

COPYING/PRINTING SERVICES

Gummerus Kirjapaino Oy; Etelä-Esplanadi 22 A, 00130 Helsinki; tel: (9) 684-4430; fax: (9) 684-44330; email: printing@gummerus.fi; http://www.gummerus.fi.

Hansaprint Oy; Pieni Roobertinkatu 11; tel: (9) 601-502; telefax: (9) 601-203.

Helprint Oy; Pursimiehenkatu 26; tel: (9) 622-0640; telefax: (9) 175-360.

Miktor Painotalo; Mekaanikonkatu 19; tel: (9) 755-2020; telefax: (9) 755-7651.

Multiprint; Yrjönkau 12; tel: (9) 642-032; telefax: (9) 643-203.

TRANSLATION SERVICES

Finnish Association of Translators and Interpreters; Museokatu 9 B 23; tel: (9) 445-927; fax: (9) 445-937; email: sktl@megabaud.fi.

Katkov Alla Tui; tel: (51) 379-4454.

World Trade Center; Regus Business Center, tel: (9) 6969-166; Swedish, Finnish, English, German, French, Spanish, and more.

Electrical

Current

220 volts AC, 50Hz

ELECTRIC PLUGS

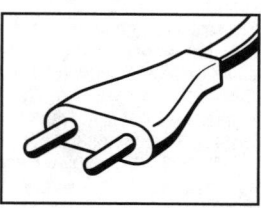

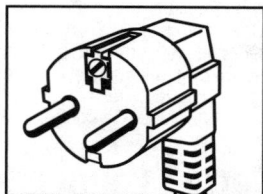

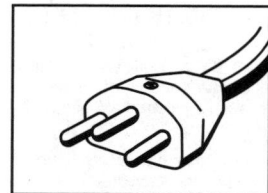

Plug adaptors are available through **iGo Corporation**. (See "Electrical and Telephone Adaptors" on page 19.)

Technical Support

HARDWARE/SOFTWARE VENDOR SUPPORT

Acer/Texas Instruments; (in Germany) tel: [49] (4102) 488-469; fax; [49] (4102) 488-169; (in the U.S.) [1] (408) 432-6200; http://www.acer.com/.

Apple/Claris; tel: 0800-118-083 (Apple Assistance); (in Germany) tel: [49] (1) 803-5018; (in Switzerland) tel: [41] (800) 833-310; (in the U.K.) tel: [44] (990) 127-753; (in the U.S.) tel: [1] (800) 500-7078; http://www.apple.com/.

AST; (in the U.S.) tel: [1] (817) 232-9824 (International Technical Support); (in Ireland) tel: [353] (61) 492-222; (in the U.S.) tel: [1] (949) 727-4141; http://www.ast.com/.

Compaq; tel: (9) 615-599; fax: (9) 6155-9898; 9800-206-720 (CompaqCare Center); (9) 6155-9870 (QuickLine); (in Switzerland) tel: [41] (22) 709-5330; fax: [41] (22) 709-5391 (Geneva); tel: [41] (1) 801-2507; fax: [41] (1) 801-2172 (Zurich); (General U.S.) tel: (281) 518-2000; http://www.compaq.com/.

Dell; tel: (9) 613-4613; fax: (9) 613-46500; (in Germany) tel: [49] (61) 039-710; (Dell- Europe) tel: [44] (134) 474-8000; (in the U.S.) tel: [1] (512) 338-4400; fax: [1] (512) 728-3330; http://www.dell.com/.

Gateway 2000; (in the U.S.) tel: [1] (605) 232-2191; fax: [1] (605) 232-2023; (in Ireland) tel: [353] (1) 797-2000; http://www.g2k.com/.

Filemaker/Claris; (in Germany) tel: [49] (180) 525-8166 (Info-line); fax: [49] (180) 567-2233; tel: [49] (180) 523-6423; (in the U.S.) tel: [1] (800) 965-9090; http://www.claris.com/.

Hewlett Packard; tel: (9) 203 47288; (in Switzerland) tel: [41] (22) 780-8111; (in the U.S.) tel: [1] (408) 246-4300; http://www.hp.com/.

IBM; tel: 9800-42680; fax: 9800-426-426; fax: (9) 459-6902; (in Switzerland) tel: [41] (22) 310-0418 (in French); (in the U.S.) tel: [1] (919) 517-2800; (U.S. Main Office) tel: [1] 914-765-1900; http://www.ibm.com/.

Microsoft; tel: (9) 525-502-500; tel: (9) 525-502-5026; (in Switzerland) tel: [41] (848) 858-868; fax [41] (1) 831-0869; (in the U.S.) [1] (425) 635-7222; http://www.microsoft.com/.

Quark; tel: (9) 20-314-580; (in Switzerland) tel: [41] (1) 808-7722; fax: [41] (1) 808-7799; (in the U.S.) tel: [1] (303) 894-8899; fax: [1] (303) 894-3398 (For Products Registered in the Americas); http://www.quark.com/.

Toshiba; (in Germany) tel: [49] (2131) 158-319; fax: [49] (2131) 158-558; (in Switzerland) tel: [41] (1) 946-0777; fax: [41] (1) 946-0807; (in Ireland) tel: [44] (193) 282-8828; (in the U.S.) [1] (949) 583-3000 (Corporate Headquarters); http://www.toshiba.com/.

Internet Connection

HOW TO CONNECT

Connecting to AOL and Compuserve in Finland is similar to using it when traveling outside your own area code. See the introductory section for detailed information on connecting to your account through a different phone number.

America Online

Numbers are available at keyword *international*. Be sure to get several local numbers before leaving. AOL's GlobalNet service charges US$6 an hour in addition to the usual charges. Go to keyword *access* (a free area) and download the software.

Access: Helsinki (9) 680-2933

Compuserve

Numbers are available at *Go international*. The Compuserve Web-site also has a great deal of information, at http://www.compuserve.com.

Access: Helsinki (9) 686-240.

Independent Service Providers

Many independent service providers offer discounts if you are only in town for a couple of days.

ClariNET Oy; tel: (9) 549-1549; email: asiakaspalvelu@clarinet.fi; http://www.clarinet.fi/.

Clinet Oy; tel/fax: (9) 4354-2272; fax: (9) 455-5276; email: clinet@clinet.fi; http://www.clinet.fi/.

EUnet Finland Oy; tel: (9) 478-4800; fax: (9) 478-4808; email: wanted@eunet.fi; http://www.eunet.fi/.

NetSonic Oy; tel: (9) 3509-7650; fax: (9) 455-4434; email: netsonic@netsonic.fi; http://www.netsonic.fi/.

Planet Media Oy; tel: (500) 752-752; fax: (05) 217-187; email: help@planet.fi; http://www.planet.fi/. netsonic@netsonic.fi

Business Culture

GREETINGS AND COURTESIES

Mr., Mrs., and Miss are rarely used in Finland. Upon first meeting a businessperson of high rank, speak the person's first name and last name followed by their title or position. From then on, address the person by title alone. Greet persons without senior position by first and last names; from then on, first name alone. The standard greeting is a handshake followed by "hello" or "good day." If invited to a dinner, wait for the host to assign you a seat and keep conversation light. Do not partake of a drink or meal until the host has first begun or it has been proposed to do so. Polite etiquette dictates that one only use hands for eating bread. Pizza, french fried potatoes, or anything else should be approached with fork and knife. Expect the host, which could be yourself, to pay for the entire meal, since it is uncommon to split the cost. When ready, ask for the bill. If invited to a home, a visitor normally brings a gift of flowers.

An invitation to a sauna carries high esteem in Finland and involves certain honorable etiquette, including reserved behavior. For those wondering about its importance, a trip to a sauna corresponds to a round of corporate golf, and can well be looked upon as the national pastime of Finland.

MEETINGS

Punctuality firmly entrenched in the ways of the reliable Finns, a foreign businessperson is expected to exhibit similar on-time regularity; this applies to both business and social realms. Finns are normally quite reserved and conservative; as such, avoid personal questions or further physical contact beyond a handshake. Keep presentations low-key. Since loyalty and reliability serve as the key business qualities for a Finn, well-developed personal contact establishing trust over a period of time will serve your meetings well.

DECISION MAKING

Finns like to get right down to business. Promptly after the meeting, a letter outlining what was discussed should be sent to reduce the possibility of misunderstanding. Decisions are rendered by ranking personnel depending on the size of the deal. Well organized, straight-forward, and factually informed presentations are most likely to speed business relationships.

WOMEN

Almost all women work outside the home and can be found in all levels of the business world, including top management, top levels of government including prime minis-ter, in education, and within the Finnish Interpol. If a woman decides to have children, she can receive an 11-month ma-ternity leave and a monthly allowance for each child until the child reaches the age of 17. Since women enjoy such acceptance and support from the Finnish system, there is little need to push ahead for feminist recognition. Foreign businesswomen should therefore experience few, if any, difficulties conducting business in Finland.

BUSINESS ATTIRE

Finns emulate European fashion trends. In banking and financial circles, dark suits, white shirts and a tie are stan-dard. Other industries might don less formal attire. In the summer, sports jackets, trousers, a tie, or short sleeve shirts and no tie. Women dress in relatively informal dress-es or skirt and blouse combinations. Many restaurants and evening social functions require a jacket. The cold winter conditions mandate a heavy overcoat and hat, the latter to be politely taken off upon entering a room. Raincoats, um-brellas, and a sweater are suggested for all seasons.

Business Centers
Helsinki

Despite the wind and rain, Helsinki is one of the most enjoyable places in all of Europe to visit. The city looks much the same as it did a century ago - there are no large high rises despite the rather large population count of 891,000. The location of the city on a lush peninsula along the south coast of Finland adds to its quaint Scandinavian atmosphere. There is plenty to do around the city. The Ate-neum Art Gallery and the National Museum display an ex-cellent assortment of Finnish art. Helsinki is particularly pleasant in the summertime, when a ferry ride to nearby Suomenlinna Island will be time well spent.

AIRPORT

Helsinki-Vantaa Airport to City Center

The airport lies 12 miles (19km) from downtown Helsinki. Contingent on traffic, it takes an average of 25 to 40 minutes to travel from the airport to the city center by cab. Airport taxis will transport a few passengers to their varying destinations at approximately US$12 (Fmk60) per person. Regular taxi fares range from US$25 to $32 (Fmk110 to 140).

Finnair operates an excellent bus service to the Finnair City Air Terminal at the main rail station downtown and also the Inter-Continental Hotel. Buses depart from just outside the terminal. Fares cost a pleasant Fmk 22 (about US$4.75) and buses run between 5:45a.m. and 1a.m. in 20-minute intervals during the day, and in 30-minute inter-vals otherwise.

Airline Numbers

Aeroflot	(9) 659-655
Air Baltic	(9) 228-021
Air France	(9) 625-862
American Airlines (toll free)	(9) 800-14620
Austrian Airlines	(9) 171-311
Balkan Bulgarian	(9) 647-752
British Airways	(9) 650-677
Czech Airlines	(9) 622-3577
El Al	(9) 6150-7440
Estonian Air	(9) 6151-3900
Finnair	(9) 81-881
Interflight Ltd Oy (business flights)	(9) 8700-230
Japan Airlines	(9) 7001-7400
Jetflite (business flights)	(9) 822-766

KLM Royal Dutch Airlines (Airport)	870-1747
LOT	(9) 660-400
Malaev Hungarian	(9) 622-0922
Lufthansa	(9) 348-110
Qantas Airways	(9) 447-522
Sabena	(9) 175-300
SAS	(9) 228-021
Singapore Airlines	(9) 680-2770
Swissair	(9) 175-300
TAP-Air	(9) 6150-7550
Thai	(9) 133-840
United Airlines	(9) 6226-2211
Varig	(9) 613-2815

HOTELS

Top End

Cumulus Seurahuone; 12 Kaivokatu, Helsinki; 118 rooms; located across the street from the railway station in the heart of Helsinki; restaurant; bar; conference facilities; in-room cable tv, safe, mini bar, hair dryer; sauna.

Radisson SAS Helsinki; Runeberginkatu 2; tel: (9) 69-580; fax: (9) 431-0995; 3 restaurants; business center; 12 conference rooms with advanced electronic services; gym; sauna; pool; Fmk 1120/1220.

Hesperia Helsinki; Mannerheimintie 50; tel: (9) 69-580; fax: (9) 431-0995; city center; restaurants; conference facilities; secretarial service; corporate rates; underground parking; fitness; sauna; solarium; golf simulator; pool; Fmk1150/1430.

Strand Inter-Continental; John Stenbergin Ranta 4; tel: (9) 39-351; fax: (9) 393-5255; restaurant; conference facilities; secretarial service; in-room modem/fax connections; corporate rates; fitness; sauna; pool; Fmk1130/1280.

Expensive

Hotel Anna; Annankatu 1; tel: (9) 616-621; fax: (9) 602-664; email: info@hotelanna.com; 61 rooms; located in the center of Helsinki; breakfast service; conference facilities (up to 12); in-room data port, tv, telephone, radio, mini bar, hair dryer; sauna.

Arctica Kalastajatorppa; Kalastajatorpantie 1; tel: (9) 45-811; fax: (9) 458-1668; city center; restaurant; conference facilities; secretarial service; fitness; sauna; pool; Fmk 890/990.

Best Western Seaside; Ruholahdenranta 3; tel: (9) 69-360; fax: (9) 693-2123; city center; overlooking harbor; restaurants; buffet breakfast; business center; meeting and banquet facilities; underground parking; saunas.

Hotel Kamp; Pohjoisesplanadi 29; tel: (9) 576-111; fax: (9) 576-1122; 179 rooms; historical hotel; 2 restaurants; conference facilities; business center; in-room cable tv, movies, safe; parking; fitness center; massage.

Ramada Presidentti; Eteläinen Rautatiekatu 4; tel: (9) 6911; fax: (9) 694-7886; city center, near rail station; restaurant; casino; conference facilities (up to 400); corporate rates; sauna; pool.

Rivoli Jardin Hotel; Kasarmikatu 40; tel: (9) 681-500; fax: (9) 656-988;55 rooms; located in Helsinki's business and shopping center; courtyard breakfast; bar; in-room air conditioning, cable tv, mini bar; parking; sauna.

Sokos Hotel Vaakuna; Asema-aukio 2; tel: (9) 131-181; fax: 1311-8234; 4-star hotel next to railway station and city air terminal; restaurants; sauna; Fmk655/840.

Inter-Continental Helsinki; Mannerheimintie 46-48; tel: (9) 799-755; fax: (9) 4055-3255; city center; restaurant; conference facilities; secretarial service; in-room modem/fax connections; corporate rates; fitness; sauna; pool; Fmk 690.

Finland

moderate

Aurora; Hesinginkatu 50; tel: (9) 717-400; fax: (9) 714-240; city suburb; restaurant; conference facilities; secretarial service; fitness; sauna; pool; Fmk380/460.

Hotel Cumulu Merihotellli; John Stenbeckin ranta 6; tel: (9) 69-121; fax: (9) 691-2214; Fmk450/580.

Park Hotel Käpylä; Pohjolankatu 38; tel: (9) 799-755; fax: (9) 792-781; email: parkhotel@park.pp.fi; located in historical section, suburb; restaurant; conference facilities; secretarial service; in-room modem/fax connections; corporate rates; sauna; pool.

Rantasipi Airport Hotel; Fobert Huberintie 4; tel: (9) 87-051; fax: (9) 822-846; Fkm410/770.

Sokos Hotel Helsinki; Yliopistonkatu 8; tel: (9) 131-401; fax: (9) 176-014; quiet location near city center; restaurants; sauna.

mEDICAL CARE

Helsinki University Central Hospital; tel: 4711; for 24-hour emergency hospital treatment for foreigners: Toolo Hospital, Topeliuksenkatu 5; tel: (9) 0-471.

Hospital Mehilainen; Pohjoinen, Hesperiankatu 17, FIN-00260, Helsinki; tel: (9) 431-4221; fax: (9) 431-4218.

HEALTH CLUBS

Esport Center (tennis / squash / badminton); Koivumankkaantie 3, 02260 ESPOO; tel: (9) 502-4700; fax: (9) 422-006.

Keskustan Piukat Paikat; Salomonkatu 17 C, 2nd floor (women); Runeberginkatu 3, street level (men); tel: (9) 5860-3410; fax: (9) 6932-8011; http://www.piukkis.com.

Makelanrinne Swimming Center; Mäkelänrinteen Uintikeskus, Mäkelänkatu 49; (9) 3484-8800; (9) 3484-8809.

AUTO RENTAL

Avis; airport, 982-2833; fax: 982-1380; Pohjoinen Rautatiekatu 17, 100; tel: 944-511; fax: 944-9933.

Budget; central reservations, tel: (9) 859-8333; fax: (9) 685-3350; airport, tel: 9870-1606, fax: 9870-1604; Malminkatu 24; tel: 9685-3311; fax: 9685-3350.

Europcar; reservations, tel: (9) 493-973; telefax: (9) 497-376; airport, (9) 7515-5700; Hotel Hesperia, (9) 4780-2220.

Hertz; reservations, tel: 800-112-233; fax: (9) 1667-1444; email: hertz@hertz.fi; airport, tel: (9) 1667-1300; fax: (9) 167-1382; downtown, Mannerheiminte 44, tel: (9) 1667-1200; fax: (9) 1667-1390,449-285. Chauffeur-driven cars available.

Lacara International Rent a Car; Hämeentie 12, 00530 Helsinki; tel: (9) 719-062; fax: (9) 736-105; http://www.lacarac.com.

Limousine Service; reservations, tel: (9) 292-2211; fax: (9) 288-551.

Scandia Rent; Jousenkaari 12, Espoo; tel; (9) 464-181; fax: (9) 464-339.

Transvell Oy; Ormuspellontie 5; tel: (9) 351-3300; fax: (9) 351-3510.

WORLD TRADE CENTER

World Trade Center Helsinki
Aleksanterinkatu 17
P.O. Box 800
00101 Helsinki
tel: (9) 6969-2020; fax: (9) 6969-2027
email: sirpa.rissa-anttilainen@wtc.fi
website: http://www.wtc.fi

Trade Information Services
tel: (9) 6969-2121; fax: (9) 6969-2122
email: anne.leinovaara@wtc.fi

FAIR AND CONGRESS SERVICE

The Finnish Fair Corporation - FINNEXPO
Suomen Messut
Helsinki Fair Centre
Rautatieläisenkatu 3, P.O. Box 21
00521 Helsinki
tel: (9) 15-091; fax: (9) 142-358

CHAMBER OF COMMERCE

Central Chamber of Commerce
Fabianinkatu 14, P.O. Box 1000
00101 Helsinki
tel: (9) 650-133; fax: (9) 650-303

Helsinki Chamber of Commerce
Kalevankatu 12
00100 Helsinki
tel: (9) 644-601

France

At a Glance

THE PEOPLE

Population .... 58,978,172 (July 1999 est.)
Growth Rate .... 0.27% (1999 est.)
Life Expectancy .... 78.63 years (born 1999)
Infant Mortality ... 5.62 deaths/1,000 live births (1999 est.)

Ethnic Composition

Celtic Caucasian 90%
Teutonic / Slavic European 5%
North African and other 5%

Religious Composition

Roman Catholic.. 90%
Protestant.. 2%
Jewish 1%
Muslim 1%
Other and non-affiliated.. 6%

Languages Spoken

French (official), various regional dialects

Education and Literacy

Education is compulsory between the ages of 6 and 16. The adult literacy rate is 99 percent.

Labor Force

Total: 25,500,000
By occupation: services 69%, industry 26%, agriculture 5%

THE ECONOMY

France is one of the most successful economies in the E.U. It has a highly diversified industrial sector, a growing high-tech component, and an agricultural sector that gives the nation true self-sufficiency in foodstuffs. For all of this success, France still has some burdens that concern both its own government as well as those of the E.U. France's still largely socialist oriented government provides a generous social welfare system with public spending standing at about 55 percent of GDP. The state owns and protects many major industries and the agriculture sector is virtually impervious to foreign competition by means of tariffs. Unemployment remains high and the government hopes to generate new job openings by reducing the length of the work week to 35 hours. Foreign investment has been put off by the plan as well as by France's other stringent employment and social benefit laws. As all this occurs, France is experiencing a "brain drain" as its highly trained technical people seek other economies with kinder attitudes towards entrepreneurship. French strength in the E.U. has caused its fellow members, especially the U.K. and Germany, to ask Paris to get its own affairs in order before throwing its weight about in Brussels.

Exports .... US$289 billion (f.o.b., 1998)
Imports .... US$255 billion (f.o.b., 1998)
Total GDP .... US$1.32 trillion (1998 est.)
GDP Per Capita .... US$22,600 (1998 est.)
Unemployment 11.5% (1998)
Inflation Rate 0.7% (1998)

Top Export Partners

E.U., United Sates, Japan, Russia

Top Import Partners

E.U., United Sates, Japan, Russia

Top Exports

Machinery and transportation equipment, chemicals, foodstuffs, agricultural products, iron and steel products, textiles and clothing

Top Imports

Crude oil, machinery and equipment, agricultural products, chemicals, iron and steel products

BUSINESS WORKWEEK

Offices

Monday to Friday 8a.m. or 9a.m. to 12:30p.m. and 2p.m. to 6p.m.

Note: Overtime in France has been virtually abolished. Even management personnel are not permitted to work "after hours." The government has gone as far as patrolling company parking lots after normal working hours. Even laptop computers are checked to make sure no one is taking work home with them.

Banks

Monday to Friday 9a.m. to 4:30p.m; in certain areas they may close between 12p.m. and 2p.m.; some banks close on Mondays, certain others remain open on Saturday. The day preceding a bank holiday, banks close at noon.

Government

Monday to Friday 9a.m. to noon and 2p.m. to 6p.m.

Retail

Retail outlets vary widely, but common hours are Monday to Friday 10a.m. to 9p.m., slightly shorter hours on the weekend. Most stores close on Sundays, and some even on Monday.

HOLIDAYS

New Year's Day..January 1
Easter Monday ....April 5*
Labor Day...May 1
Liberation Day ....May 8
Ascension Day .... May 13*
Whit Monday ....June 1*
National Day, Fall of the Bastille ....July 14
Assumption...August 15
All Saints' Day ....November 1
Armistice Day ....November 11
Christmas Day..December 25
  *Date may vary by year.

CLIMATE

Seasons

The climate is west European—maritime, temperate, and damp, with mild winters and pleasant summer months, although a very hot day may bring some humidity and stickiness. Owing to the size of the country and the varying altitude, temperatures vary widely from area to area. Avoid business travel from mid-July to mid-September when many French people go on holiday. It is sometimes said that Paris is populated only by tourists in August—many foreign vacationers find this to be an added attraction.

France

©2001 Magellan Geographix SM Santa Barbara, CA

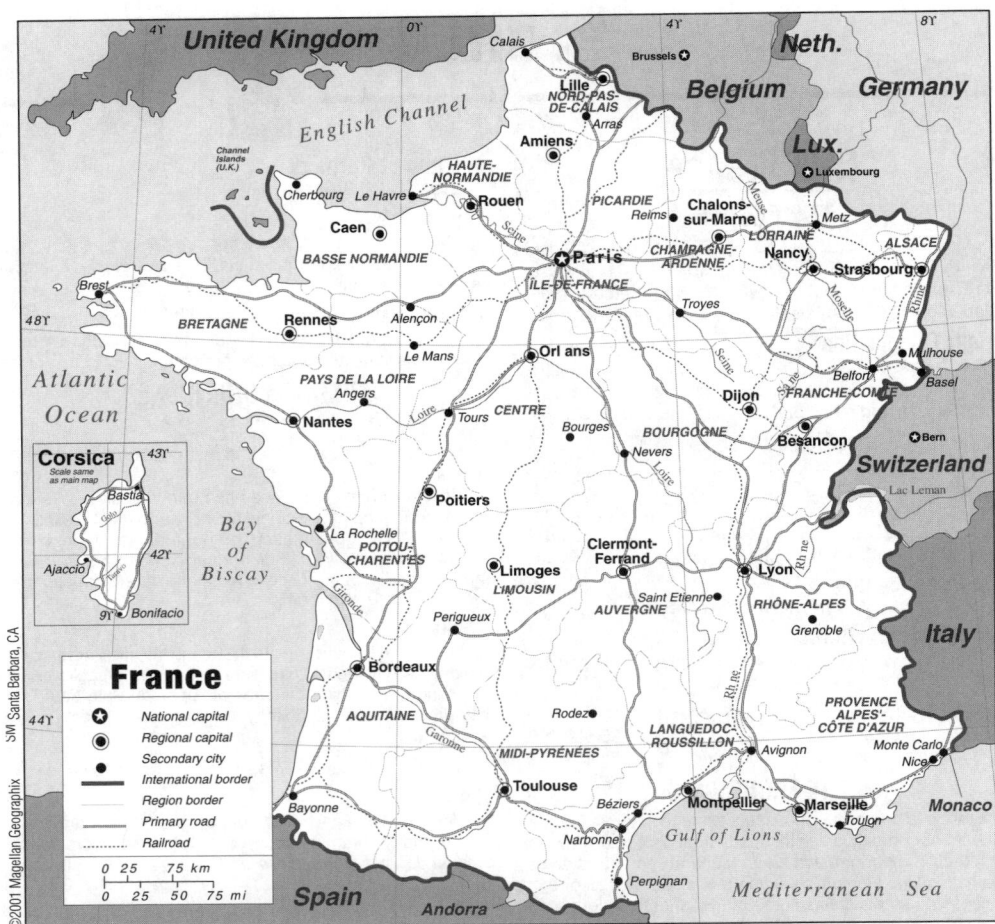

Regions

The northwest has a moderate climate, small temperature changes, and much rainfall. Inland, the weather becomes more seasonal with hot summers and cold winters. The eastern coastal region has more of a Mediterranean climate and it is mild in the winters and hot and dry during the summer months. In the east of the country, the weather is prone to thunderstorms and rainfall in the summers.

In Paris, average temperatures are 3°C (37°F) in January, and 18°C (64°F) in July. In Bordeaux, the temperatures hover around 5°C (41°F) in January, and 20°C (68°F) in July.

Money & Banking

Currency

The currency of France is the French Franc (FFr).

Denominations

The French Franc (FFr) comes in coin denominations of FFr10, 5, 2, and 1 and 50, 20, 10, and 5 centimes; and banknotes of FFr10, 20, 50, 100, 200, and 500.

Traveler's Checks and Credit Cards

Most brands of traveler's checks and foreign currency can be easily and efficiently exchanged at banks, foreign exchange bureaus located in the major cities, hotels, and foreign exchange kiosks at the airports; of these, banks offer better exchange rates. Traveler's checks receive a more favorable exchange rate than cash. French stores will not accept any substitute for francs when using cash for transactions.

Credit cards are widely accepted in France including American Express, Visa, MasterCard, Eurocard, JCB, and Diners Club.

You can get cash advances from your credit card on many of the automated teller machines (ATM). Credit cards are also essential for renting a car. Long-term visitors should set up a checking account in France and get an ATM card. Credit Card and ATM transactions receive the optimal exchange rate. Transactions on check and credit card can be conducted in euros if so requested.

Essential Terms

English	French
Yes	Oui
No	Non
Good morning	Bonjour
Hello (daytime)	Bonjour
Hello (evening)	Bonsoir
Hello (telephone)	Allo?
Good-bye	Au revoir
Please	S'il vous plaît
Thank you	Merci
Pleased to meet you	Enchanté
Excuse me; I'm sorry	Pardon
My name is _____	Je m'appelle _____
I don't understand	Je ne comprends pas
Do you speak English?	Parlez-vous anglais?

Travel

VISA AND PASSPORT

A passport that is valid for a minimum of three months beyond anticipated exit date is required of all visitors, except for citizens of other E.U. countries, and of Andorra, Liechtenstein, Monaco, San Marino and Switzerland, provided they are holding current national identification cards.

France is a member of the Schengen group, which is a collection of nations who in March of 1995 declared themselves borderless. The others in this group are Belgium, Germany, Luxembourg, The Netherlands, Portugal, and Spain. Any traveler who holds a valid passport or other travel documents that are recognized by all Schengen member nations need not have a visa to travel in any of these countries. There are two caveats, however:

- If you have tickets for onward travel to a nation that does require a visa of you, it may also be required of you for entry into the Schengen nation.
- Each Schengen nation retains the right to require a visa of any national normally exempted by the group as a whole.

Following is a list of nations normally exempt from the visa requirement (E.U. nationals are automatically exempt): Andorra, Argentina, Australia, Brazil, Brunei, Canada, Chile, Costa Rica, Cyprus, Czech Republic, Ecuador, El Salvador, Guatemala, Honduras, Hungary, Iceland, Israel, Japan, Jamaica, Liechtenstein, Malawi, Malaysia, Malta, Mexico, Monaco, New Zealand, Nicaragua, Norway, Panama, Paraguay, Poland, Republic of Korea, San Marino, Singapore, Slovak Republic, Slovenia, Switzerland, Turkey (only if a permanent resident of a Schengen country), Uruguay, U.S., Vatican City, and Venezuela.

Passengers in transit who do not leave the airport and are continuing their journey aboard the first-connecting aircraft, and who are holding confirmed tickets and other documents for onward travel, are also exempt from the need for a visa.

Note: Your are always required to carry a transit visa in France if you are from one of several particular countries. Contact the French embassy or consulate to be sure that your country is not one of them.

Visa-free travel throughout the Schengen states is valid for a duration of 90 days maximum within a 6-month period, commencing upon initial entry date into a Schengen country.

So-called short-stay visas are available in 30-, 60-, or 90-day versions. Both single and multiple entry types can be obtained, valid for a maximum 90 days per entry. Transit visas are available in single and multiple entry versions, also, and are valid for five days; the day of arrival counts as the first day of validity period. Visa extensions are not granted; a new application is necessary each time.

If you are unable to travel on a Schengen basis, or require a visa for some other reason(s), then your visa application will take between one and three days for processing for most nationals. However, nationals of certain Middle Eastern, Eastern European, and other assorted countries may need a minimum of 28 days for application processing. Again, check with the embassy or consulate to find out if your country of origin is one of these.

DEPARTURE FORMALITIES

Personal effects in luggage are normally not subject to customs duties nor the 18.6 percent VAT. There are no restrictions on bringing in or taking out French or foreign currency, but amounts exceeding FFr50,000 or the equivalent must be declared. A value added tax (VAT) is added to the price of many goods in France; however, travelers may often receive a refund at customs or thereafter if they've filled in the proper paperwork. Ask for these forms when you make the purchase. Airport departure fees are included in the price of most airline tickets.

CUSTOMS ENTRY (PERSONAL)

Duty-free

Passengers over 17 years of age entering from countries outside the E.U. or passengers over 17 years of age entering from an E.U. country with duty-free goods:

- Tobacco: 200 cigarettes, 50 cigars, 100 cigarillos or 250g of tobacco
- Alcohol: 1 liter of spirits or 2 liters of alcoholic beverage up to 22 percent; 2 liters of wine
- Other: 50g of perfume and 250ml of eau de toilette; other goods not exceeding the value of FFr300 (FFr150 per person under 15 years of age)

Passengers over 17 years of age entering from an E.U. country with duty-paid goods:

- Tobacco: 800 cigarettes, 200 cigars, or 1kg of tobacco
- Alcohol: 90 liters of wine, including up to 60 liters of sparkling wine; 10 liters of spirits; 20 liters of intermediate products; 110 liters of beer
- Perfume: 75g of perfume and 375ml of eau de toilette
- Other: other goods to the value of FFr4200 (FFr1100 per person for those under 15 years of age)

Prohibited or Restricted

- Gold objects (except personal jewelry below 500g in weight)
- Controlled drugs
- Firearms and explosives

Note: The amounts of alcohol and tobacco specified above are somewhat academic, since the import of duty-paid quantities is no longer limited between E.U. countries, technically speaking. But, if you have amounts of any items in excess of the above quantities, you may be interrogated to determine whether the goods are solely for personal use.

IMMUNIZATION

No immunization certificates are required unless arriving from regions with known infections or recent epidemics. Check with a French consulate prior to travel. Tetanus and hepatitis A inoculations are recommended for those visitors anticipating extended travel in the rural areas of France.

TIPPING

Taxi

Taxi drivers charge per passenger and per piece of luggage. Moderate tips can be given for exceptional service—which is rare.

Porters

Porters at first-class hotels and transport depots receive FFr5 per piece of luggage.

Hotel

A service charge of approximately 12 to 15 percent is normally included in the bill.

Restaurants

A standard service charge of 15 percent is usually included in the tab. Review all restaurant bills carefully before paying.

Customarily, the restaurant patron leaves small change along with the amount of the tab. Leave more if the service has been exceptional. In more rural areas, where the service charge may not be applied, 15 percent is a standard tip.

EMERGENCY INFORMATION

Police and Crime

France is a relatively safe country. However, the larger cities of Paris, Nice, Lyons, and Marseille can get rough at night. In Paris one should keep special watch in the Bastille area, Montparnasse, Rue du Faubourg-Montmartre, and Pigalle. One should always remain attentive in the subways and in train stations where pickpockets prowl. Do not get distracted by gypsy children who operate in tourist areas.

Foreign business visitors are often the target of thieves. Consequently, purses, laptops, and briefcases will require additional security. Do not leave valuables in cars or on tables in cafés. Keep non-essential valuables locked in hotel safes when not in use. Use credit cards and travel checks when possible to avoid carrying large sums of cash. It is best to hold a bag in front of you when walking in crowded places. Stay aware of your surroundings as neighborhoods in French cities change from respectable to problematic in just a few blocks.

At night, women are advised to travel in groups, or to take an authorized taxi. The police are efficient and courteous. However, they have limited language skills beyond French and a smattering of English. Their patience with demanding foreigners can be limited, too.

Emergency Numbers

Numbers function nationwide.

Police	17
Fire department	18
Ambulance	15

Health

Tap water is safe to drink, but bottled water is preferred in France, as tap water comes full of minerals. Apart from normal digestive problems caused by change in diet, there are no extraordinary diseases in France. The damp weath-

er may cause sinus trouble, colds, and flu. Visitors from Asia may find the French diet to be on the heavy side, especially in rural areas. Urban areas provide a wide variety of cuisines. Allow time for acclimation.

The medical service equals any Western standards. France has an abundance of skilled doctors, but they are likely to charge more if they speak English. There is also a national health service, for which foreigners may be eligible in emergency matters.

For more information on medical centers, including phone numbers, please see the "Business Centers" section at the end of this chapter.

INTERNAL TRAVEL

AIR

Air France is the major domestic air carrier, with domestic routes that link Paris (from Charles de Gaulle and Orly airports) with 45 other cities and towns. Independent airlines, such as AOM and Air Liberté, operate extensive domestic services.

For schedule and fare information, try the internet for:

Air France .... www.airfrance.com
French Government
Tourist Office .... www.tourisme.gouv.fr

TAXI

Rates for city fares are shown inside the taxis. An additional supplement exists for some trips, including to and from race tracks and airports; luggage costs an extra FFr6 per piece. Some taxis generally linger around hotels; most stand by at taxi ranks in major intersections of urban areas. Arrangements can also be made by telephone. Fares start at Ffr13. In rural areas, taxi service is limited, and companies must be contacted by telephone

There is a company, with a presence in most major towns of France, called Eurotaxi, providing multilingual drivers.

AUTO

Rental cars are widely available throughout France. A valid driver's license and credit card are required along with proof of local insurance. Age requirements vary by rental agency.

There are more than 28,500km (17,700 miles) of national roads (routes nationales), which bear the prefix 'N.' Regular motorways have the prefix 'A'. Minor roads (designated in yellow on Michelin road maps) are the charge of départements rather than the Government and are classified 'D' roads.

It is advisable to avoid cross-country motor travel altogether between roughly July 25 and August 10 and from August 25 to about September 10. These are the two peaks of holiday travel in France, clogging the roads for miles (kilometers).

Driving in the countryside of France is one of the great experiences of Europe. However, driving in urban areas, especially Paris, is rarely worth the headaches and cursing. A better bet is to use the taxi and public transport systems.

TRAIN

French Railways (SNCF) oversees a nationwide network interconnecting most of France by rail. More than one-third of the tracks have been electrified. The TGV (Train à Grande Vitesse) runs from Paris to Brittany and southwest France, and between Paris and Lyons, and is considered the fastest train in the world, running at over 186 mph (300 kph). Trains are a widely used mode of intercity business travel throughout the E.U.—and they are a great way to meet European counterparts.

Efficient train services link most of France and other parts of Europe. This includes the "Chunnel" service under the English Channel to London.

The Chunnel, a marvel of modern engineering, is the huge undersea tunnel that provides a direct land link between Paris and London via rail. It is also a combination road and rail connection between Calais (France) and Folkestone (U.K.).

EUROSTAR: The passenger-only rail connection of the Chunnel is Eurostar, a high-speed train operated by the railways of France, U.K., and Belgium. It runs between London (Waterloo station) and Paris (Gare du Nord), with a trip time of three hours. Currently, there are 12 daily departures to London. The Eurostar also runs between Paris Disneyland and London. Eurostar trains offer standard-class and first-class passage, a full buffet and bar, and a staff that is both highly trained and multi-lingual. More information is readily accessible on the website:
Eurostar.. www.eurostar.com

Cars, trucks, motorcycles, or bicycles can be transported on Le Shuttle, which runs between Folkestone (U.K.) and Calais (France). Vehicles are transported through the tunnel on one-deck or two-deck shuttles, determined by height. A provision also exists for coaches, minibuses, caravans, and camper vans. Passengers generally ride in their vehicles. If you need to transport heavy goods, you will be conveyed on a special shuttle that has separate passenger coaches for drivers. The trip takes about 35 minutes between station destinations, or about one hour from roadway to roadway. Trains operate daily all year, two to five per hour, determined by the season and the hour. You can book a reservation in advance through Eurotunnel Customer Service, or just show up and take your chances (pretty safe) on getting a slot.

Rail service within France is possibly the most sophisticated, modern, and efficient in the Western world. First- and second-class overnight couchettes are available between most major cities, as well as full-service sleeper car service. Trains have bars, buffets, and food service to your seat.

A number of service levels exist, but tickets should be reserved in advance. The foreign visitor can expect a wide range of special tickets available to him/her, and most of them must be purchased prior to travel. More information can be obtained on the internet:
SNCF website .... www.sncf.fr

Also, one may call a special English language hotline available by telephone:
SNCF Hotline .... [33] (8) 3635 3539

METRO

Paris has what is widely regarded as the world's foremost urban transport network. Le Métro was built in 1900 for the Paris Exhibition. Constantly updated and expanded since then, the density of the métro network in the central portion of the city means it is the perfect way to get around in Paris. Navigating the system is deceptively easy: to reach the station (Correspondance) of your destination, look for the Correspondances sign—the name of the line's terminus—on the platform. Then simply follow the appropriate signs toward that terminus until the train reaches your stop along the way on that same line. Maps can be found inside the trains and on station platforms. Regardless of the journey's length or the number of changes, a single flat-fare ticket is all that is required, excepting the suburban section of certain lines. A carnet of ten tickets is much more convenient and a substantial savings over buying singly each time. First trains of the day depart at about 5a.m., last trains at approximately 12:30a.m.

See Bus/Tram (following) for information about passes which can also be used on the Métro.

BUS / TRAM

Local: All the major towns in France have excellent, comprehensive bus systems. France's urban systems are heavily subsidized by the national government, and prices are low. The service is clean and efficient, reaching every corner of each city served. One can expect to find schedules and maps posted at well-marked stops.

In Paris, buses use the same tickets as the métro, but bus lines are sliced into fare sections. One ticket can cover one or two fare stages, and two tickets will cover two or more stages. The first bus service of the day commences at 6a.m., and the last runs at 9p.m., except for certain lines that run until 12:30a.m. Schedules are posted in bus shelters and at bus stops. In the suburbs, fares and tickets are standardized with private operators.

Intercity: Intercity bus travel serves smaller towns, with the bulk of intercity travel being done by train or car. Long-distance bus lines include Europabus and Eurolines. Syndicat National des Entreprises de Tourisme (SNET) is a third source, acting as a coordinator for numerous smaller coach lines. Local services beyond towns and cities are known as being generally adequate. Timetables and other information is only available locally.

Rail: A vast network of conventional suburban rail services is operated by French Railways (SNCF). On the outskirts of Paris, these systems have a fare structure and ticketing mechanism integrated with Paris' other systems of public transport.

The RER (fast suburban services) runs three primary routes from Paris to suburbs and outlying towns. Line A: St Germain-en-Laye to Boissy-St-Leger or Marne-la-Vallée; Line B: Remy-les-Chevreuses to Roissy via Châtelet-les-Halles and the Gare du Nord; Line C: Gare d'Orléans-Austerlitz to Versailles. The lines are segmented into fare stages which vary with distances, except inside the metropolitan zone, which uses the same flat-fare system as the métro.

Passes: A Paris Visite pass provides for between three and five consecutive days of unlimited transit on most types of public transport.

A *Carte Orange Hebdomadaire* (most popular among Parisians) provides for unlimited travel, for a period up to a week, on most types of public transport.

Billets de Tourisme are 2-, 3-, 4-, or 7-day passes that entitle travelers to any amount of transit for the term of the pass on all Paris métro and bus lines (métro and RER/RATP first-class). (Not included are minibuses, special bus services, and RER/SNCF lines). These passes are available in Paris from 50 métro stations, all seven main-line railway stations, and certain banks, as well as from:
RATP Tourist Office
54 quai de la Rapée
tel: (1) 44 68 2020.

Carte Orange passes are valid for one calendar month of unlimited journeys, within a given radius, on Paris buses, RER and métro, suburban (SNCF) railways, and certain suburban buses (RATP). The pass is available at any Paris or suburban métro or railway station, Paris bus station, or specially licensed shop. A passport-size photo is required.

WATER TRAVEL

There are almost 9000km (5600 miles) of navigable waterways in France. The country has an elaborate river travel system and numerous Atlantic and Mediterranean ports for international cruise travel. There is also a passenger/ auto ferry system to the U.K. as well as to many continental European ports. This ferry system is commonly used by business people and, like the trains, is a great way to make contacts during a very relaxed trip. Reservations are recommended.

Boats can also be chartered, with crews or without, from the smallest of cabin cruisers up to large converted barges (péniches), accommodating up to 24 passengers and a crew of eight. Hotel boats (converted barges with restaurant and accommodations) can also be found in some areas, spanning a wide range of price and comfort. For more information, contact the regional or national tourist board.

Cruising the canals of France is a wonderful way to see the country. These waterways offer a spectacular variety of scenery and a way to visit many historic villages, towns, and other sites not normally traveled by tourists. Prime areas for canal travel are Alsace, Burgundy, Camargue, Charente, Franche-Comté, Maine-Anjou, Midi, and Sancerrois. For more information about canal cruises, try this website: www.franceway.com/rives_df/boat.htm

State-run auto ferries called 'BACs' provide connections between the mainland and the larger islands off the Atlantic coast. They also make the crossing regularly of the mouth of the Gironde. The Société Nationale Maritime Corse-Mediterranée (SNCM) operates roll-on/roll-off ferries and passenger ferries to the island of Corsica. The boats cross from Marseilles and Nice to Ajaccio, Propriano and Bastia on Corsica.

For more information, you can contact SNCM directly: tel: (4) 9156-3200; fax: (4) 9156-3636

TRAVEL ASSISTANCE

Direction du Tourisme
(French Government Tourist Office)
2 rue Linois
75740 Paris, Cedex 15, France
Tel .... (1) 4437 3600
Fax .... (1) 4437 3636
website .... www.tourisme.gouv.fr
Maison de la France
(Tourist Information Agency)
20 avenue de l'Opéra
75001 Paris, France
Tel .... (1) 4296 7000
Fax .... (1) 4296 7071
email .... admin@france.com
website .... www.franceguide.com

Communications
DIALING CODES IN FRANCE
International country code: [33]

Selected city codes: Aix-en-Provence (4), Bordeaux (5), Cannes (4), Cherbourg (2), Grenoble (4), Lourdes (5), Lyon (4), Marseille (4), Monaco (4), Nice (4), Paris (1), Rouen (2), Toulouse (2), Tours (2)

Dialing France from Overseas
To dial France from overseas, dial your country's international dialing code, then 33 (the country code for France), then the city code, and finally the number. If you were dialing Paris from the United States, for example, you would begin with 011, then 33, then 1 (the city code for Paris), and finally the number of the person or office you are trying to reach.

Assistance Numbers
Local Telephone Directory Assistance 12
Operator 13
Time (in Paris) 4033-8400h

CALLING WITHIN FRANCE
Telephone services in France are among the best in Western Europe.

Long Distance Calls
Hotels add a surcharge to calls made from rooms. Calling with a phone card is usually cheaper. Long distance calls within France require a preceding zero in front of the city code.

International Calls
International calls from France prove least costly between 10:30p.m. and 8a.m. Monday to Friday, and 2p.m. to 8a.m. Saturday and Sunday.

To place a direct international call, dial 00 + your country code + city code + number. And remember, calls placed from hotel rooms might cost your pocketbook a few extra large holes.

You can also go to a post office to make long-distance or international calls.

PAY PHONES
Public Telephones
Most public phones use cards only.

Calling Cards
Cards, *télécartes*, can be purchased at post offices, railway ticket counters, news stands, tobacconists, and hotels. Cards come in 50 and 120 units, for 40Ffr and 96Ffr respectively.

CELL PHONES
Itinéris, SFR (Societé Francaise du Radiotéléphone), and Bouygues Telecom provide GSM service in France.

Note: Your home country cell phone may not work in this country. If not, we recommend that you rent an international cell phone *before* you leave home. A major US-based cell phone rental provider is **IMC WorldCell**. For information see "International Cell Phone Rentals" on page 14.

When dialing a cell phone in France one must dial certain preceding prefixes:
Itineris 607, 608
SFR 603, 609, 610, 611, 612, 613, 614, 615, 616

CALL BACK
You can (potentially) save significant sums when calling in France by using a call back service. For a list of callback services, please refer to the "Communications" section in the *Global Road Warrior* Introduction.

Fees for call back services vary widely, depending on the company and the type of service required. Be sure to check with these companies before leaving to compare rates.

PHONE JACKS

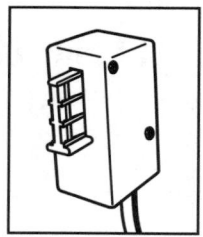

Plug adaptors are available through **iGo Corporation.** (See "Electrical and Telephone Adaptors" on page 19.)

FAX

Fax machines are located at all post offices and most hotels.

POSTAL SERVICES

The mail service is generally very good, although international items are subject to a customs inspection.

Hours of service
Monday from Friday 8a.m. to 7p.m.
Saturday from 8a.m. to noon.

Rates
Stamps can be purchased at most hotels, as well as post offices, newsstands, and book stores.

Business Services

AUDIOVISUAL RENTALS

Paris
Inter Congress; 16 rue Armand-Carrel; tel: (1) 4200-7001.
Reels on Wheels; 7 rue Decrés; tel: (1) 4542-5866.

Lyon
VISEA; 32 rue Childebert; tel: (4) 7837-4069.
Espace Pierre Cardin; tel: (1) 4266 -1730; fax: (1) 4266-1781.
Hotel de Saint Germain; tel: (1) 4548-9164; fax (1) 4548-4622.
Hyatt Regency Paris - Madeleine; 24 blvd. Malesherbes; tel: (1) 5527-1234; fax: 5527-1235
Sheraton Prince de Galles; 33 ave. George V; 24-hour business center; tel: (1) 5323-7777; fax: (1) 5323-7878.

OFFICE SPACE OR RENTAL

Executive Relocations; tel: (1) 4755-6029; fax: (1) 47-55-60-86; contact: July Braham; email: judy@executive-france.com

EBSC; located 15 minutes outside of Paris; secretarial/administrative service; answering machine service; postbox; email; domiciliation; offices; meeting space; 78639 Morainvilliers; tel: (1) 39-75-30-82; fax: (1) 3975-2279; email: ebsc33@ebsc.com

GBC; fully-equipped offices by the month or year; tel: (1) 4694-7575; fax: (1) 4694-7576; email: gbc-offices.com.

Buroservices; World Trade Center Paris
Palais Des Congrés, 2 Place de la Porte Maillot
BP 18, 75853 Paris Cedex 17; tel: (1) 4068-1425; fax: (1) 4068-1421.

COMPUTER RENTALS

Paris
Computerloc; 43 rue du Chemin-Vert, Boulogne; tel: (1) 4609-1550.
Locamicro; 3 rue St. Felicité; tel: (1) 4532-8001.

Lyon
R.A.I.L.; 72 rue Tronchet; tel: (4) 7893-0827.

COURIER SERVICES

Airborne Express; BP 10359, 95706 Roissy CDG; tel: (1) 4864-5430.
CRIE; tel: (1) 4293-1111.
DHL International; Z1. Paris Nord II, 241 Rue de la Belle Etoile, BP 50252; tel: (1) 4817-6600.
FedEx: 125 Av Luis Roche; Guennevilliers; tel: (1) 4085-3800.
UPS (France) S.A.; 87 Ave. de L'Aerodrome BP 39, 94310 Orly; tel: (1) 400-2880.

SECRETARIAL SERVICES

Paris
Dernis; 23 av de Wagram; tel: (1) 4622-9898.
Erom; 84 rue de Richelieu; tel: (1) 4296-5063.
Interim Nation; 63 blvd Haussmann; tel: (1) 4265-6126.

Lyon
Secrétariat Relais; 87 av Roger-Salengro; (4) 69120.
Vaulx-en-Velin; tel: (4) 7826-5776.
Secrétariat Service 2000; 23 cours Aristide-Briand; 69300 Caluir; tel: (4) 7808-0620.

TRANSLATION SERVICES

3 I Paris; tel: (1) 4033-0681.
AABI; tel: (1) 4059-8026.
World Trade Center Paris
Palais Des Congrés, 2 Place de la Porte Maillot
BP 18, 75853 Paris Cedex 17; tel: (1) 4068-1425; fax: (1) 4068-1421.

Electrical

Current
220 volts AC, 50Hz. Some older hotels may still use 110 volts.

2-pin plugs are the norm.

ELECTRIC PLUGS

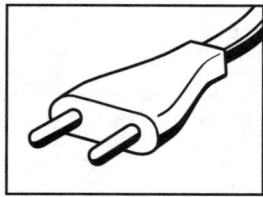

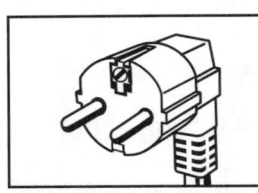

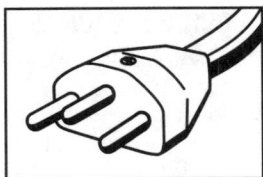

Plug adaptors are available through **iGo Corporation**. (See "Electrical and Telephone Adaptors" on page 19.)

Technical Support

HARDWARE/SOFTWARE VENDOR SUPPORT

Apple/Claris; 1-69-29-29-29 (Apple Assistance Center); (in Switzerland) tel: [41] (800) 833-310; (in the U.K.) tel: [44] (990) 127-753; (in the U.S.) tel: [1] (800) 500-7078; http://www.apple.com/.

Compaq/Digital; tel: (1) 4133-4100; fax: (1) 4133-4400; (1) 4133-4455 (CompaqCare Center); (1) 6986-7396 (QuickLine); Minitel 3616 (FaxPaq); (in Switzerland) tel: [41] (22) 709-5330; fax: [41] (22) 709-5391 (Geneva); tel: [41] (1) 801-2507; fax: [41] (1) 801-2172 (Zurich); (General U.S.) tel: (281) 518-2000; http://www.compaq.com/.

Dell; (in Germany) tel: [49] (61) 039-710; (Dell- Europe) tel: [44] (134) 474-8000; (in the U.S.) tel: [1] (512) 338-4400; fax: [1] (512) 728-3330; http://www.dell.com/.

Gateway 2000; (in the U.S.) tel: [1] (605) 232-2191; fax: [1] (605) 232-2023; (in Ireland) tel: [353] (1) 797-2000; http://www.g2k.com/.

Hewlett Packard; tel: 143 623 434; (in Switzerland) tel: [41] (22) 780-8111; (in the U.S.) tel: [1] (408) 246-4300; http://www.hp.com/.

IBM; tel: (0801) 631-213; tel: (238) 557-750; (in Switzerland) tel: [41] (22) 310-0418 (in French); (in the U.S.) tel: [1] (919) 517-2800; (U.S. Main Office) tel: [1] 914-765-1900; http://www.ibm.com/.

Microsoft; tel: (1) 6986-4646; fax: (1) 6446-0660; tel: (1) 6986-1020 (Technical Support Phone); fax: (1) 6928-0028 (Technical Support Fax); (in Switzerland) tel: [41] (848) 858-868; fax [41] (1) 831-0869; (in the U.S.) [1] (425) 635-7222; http://www.microsoft.com/.

NEC; tel: (0)1 6987-4123 (UltraCare Support); (in the U.S.) [1] (916) 388-0101 (Main Switchboard); http://www.nec.com/.

Novell; (in Germany) tel: [49] (211) 563-2777 (System support); tel: [49] (6196) 904-477; fax: [49] (211) 563-2772; (in Switzerland) tel: [41] (1) 308-4747; fax: [41] (1) 302-0401; (in the U.S.) tel: [1] (408) 434-2300; fax: [1] (408) 577-5775 (Worldwide Sales Headquarters); http://www.novell.com/.

Toshiba; (in Germany) tel: [49] (2131) 158-319; fax: [49] (2131) 158-558; (in Switzerland) tel: [41] (1) 946-0777; fax:

[41] (1) 946-0807; (in Ireland) tel: [44] (193) 282-8828; (in the U.S.) [1] (949) 583-3000 (Corporate Headquarters); http://www.toshiba.com/.

Internet Connection

HOW TO CONNECT

Connecting to AOL and Compuserve in France is similar to using it when traveling outside your own area code. See the introductory section for detailed information on connecting to your account through a different phone number.

America Online

Numbers are available at keyword *international*. Be sure to get several local numbers before leaving. AOL's Global-Net service charges US$3.95 an hour in addition to the usual charges. Go to keyword *access* (a free area) and download the software.

Access: National Access Number 083-606-1310; this number is available anywhere on the French mainland (as well as Corsica) at local call rates. Paris - GSM (Cell) Access Only 014-064-1670.

Compuserve

Numbers are available at *Go International*. The Compuserve Web-site also has a great deal of information, at http://www.compuserve.com.

Access: Monaco (49) 215-0203; National (8) 3606-1319; Paris (1)4102-0304; Paris (1) 4188-0840.

Independent Service Providers

Many independent service providers offer discounts if you are only in town for a couple of days.

Altranet; tel: (4) 6868-5858; fax: 46868-5859; http://www.altranet.fr/.

CalvaCom; tel: (1) 3463-1919; fax: (1) 3463-1948; email: scom1@calva.net; http://www.calvacom.fr/.

France-Teaser; tel: (1) 4750-6248; fax: (1) 4750-6293; email: sales@teaser.fr; http://www.teaser.fr/.

FranceNet; tel: (1) 4392-1234; fax: (1) 4392-1445; email: info@francenet.fr; http://www.francenet.fr

InterNeXT; tel: (1) 4515-1450; fax: (1) 4515-1454; email: Info@InterNeXT.fr; http://www.internext.fr/.

IBM Internet Connection Services; tel: (1) 8045-5056; http://www.ibm.net/.

RECIF; tel: (1) 4740-8888; fax: (6) 0841-2225; email: dprillot@recif.fr; http://www.recif.fr/.

Business Culture

GREETINGS AND COURTESIES

As well as demonstrating high levels of pride in their culture, heritage, and country, the French take a special pride in their language. It is a boon to the foreign businessperson to speak fluent French. However, an apology for not being familiar with their language will smooth the path to a relationship with your French associates. The customary greeting includes *Monsieur* (Mr.), *Madame* (Mrs.), or *Mademoiselle* (Miss) followed by the last name. Do not use first names unless invited to do so. Appropriate titles such as Doctor and Professor should be honored. Common salutations are *"Bonjour"* (Hello), and *"Comment allez-vous?"* (How are you?). Always use the *vous* form, not the *tu* form, in addressing business colleagues.

The French tend to exercise formality; they are very private people who adhere to tradition and revere a bit of ceremony. Shake hands with everyone during introductions and again when taking leave. Normally, one waits for the woman to extend her hand. However, in large groups where several introductions are going on, it is not a fall from grace should a man first extend his hand to a woman. The French handshake entails a light grip with one shake; avoid arm-pumping firmness or backslapping.

Though the exchange of business gifts is not a general practice, gifts that appeal to the intellect or aesthetics are well received. Avoid gifts with large, prominent stamps of your company name. While an invitation into a French colleague's home is rare, the visitor who wants to demonstrate French "etiquette" will appreciate the following: send flowers in advance (avoid chrysanthemums and roses), bring chocolates or a gift to the hostess, and send a thank you note the very next day.

DECISION MAKING

Patience is required in France. There is a hierarchy in place often involving a cumbersome bureaucracy, and few managing executives are inclined to cross boundaries or speed up the process. Extensive labor laws and a complex system of social benefits and protections encourage French caution and impede the decision-making process. Additionally, the French have an inordinate amount of interest in details and foreign venturors should come prepared to linger over details with their French colleagues.

WOMEN

French women have yet to realize their numbers in the higher levels of corporate management where age-old patriarchal customs still reign. However, women's presence is substantial in traditional occupations, from secretarial to mid-management work. Additionally, they are highly regarded for their entrepreneurial achievements as well as their contributions in academics, education, and the arts.

MEETINGS

As in many European countries, punctuality is very important for business (although for the French, not necessarily for social engagements). The French tend to be very diplomatic, reserved, sober, and discreet. A foreign representative should present a program in a formal, logical, comprehensive, and intelligent; manner; and, speakers should prepare to field detailed questions. Find out in advance whether French is the only language of the firm. Never assume that your French colleagues or counterparts will speak English or another language.

One should also remain aware that dining and leisure represent an important portion of French culture; workaholics do not gain any points here. A two to three-hour lunch over a three-course meal, wine, and coffee may well prove an excellent grounds to accomplish some business. If doing so, one should wait for the host to initiate business discussion, which may well not happen until dessert. Until then, the French enjoy cultured and intelligent conversation, often comprised of a debate or opinionated discussion.

Do not broach the subject of money (considered uncultured), and avoid personal questions of your host. Take care not to speak with raised tone, an abhorrent stereotype of many foreigners in France. Observe high etiquette, eating delicately with fork and knife even those foods you may handle by hand at home. Never speak with a full mouth, use a tissue when sneezing or sniffling, and discreetly blow your nose. To hail a waiter, simply say "garçon". If hosting a luncheon or dinner, be certain to choose a good restaurant since the French know their food well.

BUSINESS ATTIRE

In one of Europe's fashion meccas, one might find it surprising that business dress remains conservative: dark suits and ties. Jackets stay on in offices. Sports jackets and ties are not uncommon in the South. Women also dress conservatively in suits, or classic coordinates of subdued colors. French women do not wear slacks in the business arena; business suits are considered the norm; this also applies for a lunch or dinner appointment.

Business Centers
Paris

CITY VIEW

Paris may be one of the most popular cities for tourism in the world, but it is also an active metropolis for many facets of business ranging anywhere from banking to fashion. Cultural aspects of the city embrace centuries of history while hip cafes pop up every day gaining their own "nouveau" recognition. When scheduling business appointments keep in mind that it is best to avoid Le Louvre or the Eiffel Tower during weekends and holidays. A Saturday morning meeting, if possible in liue of a Thursday afternoon, will be much more pleasurable time to sightsee. There is so much to do and see in Paris, it is often best to plan an agenda according to individual taste once already in the city. There are dozens of tourist guides and entertainment brochures circulating for free all over town. One guidebook alone cannot capture the romance and intrigue of grand Paris!

AIRPORT

Charles de Gaulle Airport to City Center

The airport lies 14.5 miles (23 km.) from the city. Offering the most efficient means to get downtown on schedule, trains run between the airport and downtown every 15 minutes. Catch a shuttle bus from Terminal 1 to the RER station, which runs from Terminal 2. Once aboard the RER B line, expect a 30-minute ride for a fare of Ffre35 (about US$7). The RER stops at Gare du Nord, Chatelet, St. Michel, Luxembourg, Port Royal, and Denfert-Rochereau stations.

Air France buses going from the airport to the Porte-Maillot Metro station, the Palais de Congres, and the Place Charles de Gaulle Etoile depart in 20-minute intervals for a fare of Ffr55. Expect at least a 40-minute ride, and more if traffic is congested. For those transferring to Orly Airport, a shuttle bus departs in 20-minute intervals for a fare of Ffr60 (about US$12). Prepare to snooze as the trip will take from an hour to an hour and a half.

Taxis cost about Ffr250 during daytime hours and take from 45 minutes to an hour to central Paris. Fares rise after 8p.m.

Orly Airport to City Center

If arriving at Orly, you can catch the free shuttle bus to get to the RER rail station where you will hop aboard the C2 express train to the central stations in Paris (Gare d'Austerlitz, St. Michel, Invalides). The fare will run about Ffr30. Trains leave in 15-minute intervals and the trip downtown will take approximately 25 minutes.

The Air France buses leave in 15-minute intervals until 11p.m. and take about 30 minutes to an hour to reach the Air France City Terminal near Les Invalides metro station in central Paris. The fare costs a budget pleasing Ffr32.

A shuttle bus serving Charles de Gaulle Airport departs

France

in 20-minute intervals for a fare of Ffr60. Expect an hour to an hour and a half ride.

As can be expected, cabs offer the more expensive way to get to central Paris. A fare might cost between Ffr145 and 165. Expect a 20- to 30-minute ride, unless your cab gets caught in traffic— in this case, it's anyone's guess.

Airline Numbers

Aeroflot	(1) 422-5438
Air Afrique	(1) 4421-3232
Air Algérie	(1) 4703-7400
Air Canada	(1) 4450-2020
Air France	
information	(1) 4408-2424
reservations	(1) 4408-2222
offices	(1) 4299-2364, 4325-7395
Air Guadelupe	(1) 4266-9060
Air India	(1) 4266-9060
Air Inter	(1) 4723-5958, 4555-0772
Air Liberté	(1) 4028-4331
Air Littoral	(1) 4735-7071
Air Martinique	(1) 4256-2100
Air UK	(1) 4927-9801
Alitalia	(1) 4494-4400
All Nippon Airways	(1) 4431-4431
American Airlines	(1) 6932-7307
(toll free)	(1) 0523-0035
Austrian Airlines	(1) 4266-3466
Bangkok Airways	(1) 4289-5545
Bangladesh Biman	(1) 4289-1147
British Airways	(1) 4778-1414
British Midland	(1) 4742-3062
Canadian Airlines	(1) 4953-0707
China Airlines	(1) 4225-6360
Continental	(1) 4299-0909
toll free	(1) 0525-3181
Corsair	(1) 4979-4979, 4273-1064
CSA	(1) 4742-1811
EgyptAir	(1) 4494-8500
El-Al	(1) 4742-4129
Garuda Indonesian	(1) 4495-1550
Iberia	(1) 4047-8090
Japan Air Lines	(1) 4435-5500
KLM	(1) 4456-1900, 4465-1818
LOT Polish Airlines	(1) 4742-0560
Lufthansa	(1) 4265-3735
MAS	(1) 4742-2600
Malev	(1) 4261-5790
MEA	(1) 4266-9393
Northwest Airlines	(1) 4266-9000
Philippine Airlines	(1) 4296-0140
Qantas	(1) 4494-5200
Royal Air Maroc	(1) 4494-1310
Royal Jordanian	(1) 4261-5745
Royal Nepal	(1) 4046-9521
Sabena	(1) 4494-1919/13
SAS	(1) 4742-0614
Singapore Airlines	(1) 4553-9090
South African Airways	(1) 4927-0550
Swissair	(1) 4581-1101
TAP (Air Portugal)	(1) 4486-8950
TAT	(1) 4261-8210, 4279-0505
Thai	(1) 4420-7080
Tower Air	(1) 4451-5656
Tunis Air	(1) 4212-3131
TWA	(1) 4069-7000
United	(1) 4742-2514/44
UTA	(1) 4017-4646, 4017-4444

Top-end

Hotel De Crillon; 10 place de la Concorde; tel: (1) 4471-1500; fax: (1) 4471-1502; 43 suites; opulent restored palace with rooms designed by Sonia Rykiel; restaurants; tea salon; meeting facilities; secretarial service; in-room mini bar; 24 hour room service; fitness center; Ffr2600/3550.

Grand Hotel Inter-Continental; 2 rue Scribe; tel: (1) 4007-3232; fax: (1) 4266-1251; Paris' biggest luxury hotel; 3 restaurants; no-smoking rooms; conference facilities; business services; parking; health club; Ffr1700/2100.

Hyatt Regency Paris - Madeleine; 24 blvd. Malesherbes; tel: (1) 5527-1234; fax: (1) 5527-1235; business-boutique hotel; restaurant; business center; in-room data ports, dual-line phones; voice mail; meeting area; gym; FFr2400.

Le Bristol; 112 rue de Faubourg St-Honoré, 8th arr.; tel: (1) 5343-4300; fax: (1) 5343-4326; elegant, discreet hotel; individually decorated rooms; restaurant; in-room data ports and dual-line phones; computers and fax available upon request; business center; conference facilities; fitness center; adjacent to beauty spa center; sauna; pool; Ffr2500/3700.

Le Parc; 55-57 ave. Raymond-Poincare; tel: (1) 4405-6666; fax: (1) 4405-6600; A Westin Demeure hotel near Eiffel Tower; English-style; top-class restaurant; conference facilities (up to 500); business area; in-room data ports, dual-phone lines; fitness room; Ffr2200.

Ritz; 15 Place Vendôme, 1 arr.; tel: (1) 4260-3830; fax: (1) 4260-2371; exclusive, intimate hotel; restaurant; conference facilities; business services; secretarial service; corporate rates; health club/spa; sauna; pool; beauty salon; Ffr2600/3500.

Royal Monceau; 37 ave. Hoche; tel: (1) 4299-8800; fax: (1) 4299-8990; grand palace hotel; restaurants; rooms with data port available; fitness/spa facilities; pool; Ffr2250/2450.

Sheraton Prince de Galles; 33 ave. George V; tel: (1) 5323-7777; fax: (1) 5323-7878; restaurant; 24-hour business center; conference facilities; corporate rates; fitness; Ffr2495.

Sofitel Paris Arc de Triomphe; 14 rue Beaujon; tel: (1) 5389-5050; in the U.S. 1-800-SOFITEL; fax: (1) 5389-5051; 135 rooms; business hotel near Champs Elysées; restaurant; conference facilities (up to 80); secretarial service; in-room dual telephone lines; data port; voice mail; corporate rates; Ffr2250.

Expensive

Acacias St-Germain; tel: (1) 4548-9738; fax: (1) 4544-6357; 41 rooms; located in the heart of the Left Bank within walking distance to Montparnasse, Notre Dame and St. Germain des Pres; breakfast room; in-room cable tv, mini bar, hair dryer; 24-hour room service.

Edouard VII; 39 Avenue de l'Opera; tel: (1) 4261-5690; fax:(1) 4261-4773; 80 rooms; restaurant; conference facilities; secretarial service; in-room cable tv, mini bar, safe, direct dial telephone; corporate rates; Ffr950/1400.

Hotel Montalembert; 3 rue de Montalembert, Left Bank; tel: (1) 4549-6868; fax: (1) 4549-6949; 51 rooms; located just off blvd. St. Germain; modern design; restaurant; in-room mini bar; room service; Ffr1695.

Hotel Square; 3 rue de Boulainvilliers; tel: (1) 4414-9190; fax: (1) 4414-9199; modern rooms; personal phone and fax numbers; dual-line telephones; boardroom; art gallery; nearby health club privileges for Ffr100; Ffr1350/1700.

Hotel Vernet; 25 rue Vernet; tel: (1) 4431-9800; fax: (1) 4431-8569; smaller, sister hotel to Royal Monceau; near exhibition grounds; restaurant; meeting room; secretarial service; corporate rates; sauna; pool; whirlpool; shared fitness facilities with Royal Monceau; Ffr1700.

St. James Paris; 4 Place du Chancelier Adenauer; tel: (1) 4405-8181; fax: (1) 4405-8182; château-hotel; restaurant; bar-library; meeting rooms; conference facilities; secretarial service; corporate rates; health club; jacuzzi; Ffr1500/1800.

Terrass; 12 rue Joseph-de-Maistre, arr. 18; tel: (1)4606-7285; fax: (1) 4252-2911; 101 rooms; restaurant; meeting facilities; in-room data port, mini bar; corporate rates; car rental; Ffr880/1020.

Moderate

Arley Tour Eiffel; 34 Rue Viala, arr. 15; tel: (1) 4058-1166; fax: (1) 4577-5742; email: Arleytroueiffel@adi.fr; renovated rooms; conference facilities; secretarial service; corporate rates.

Brittanique; 20 Avenue Victoria, 1 arr.; tel: (1) 4233-7459; fax: (1) 4233-8265; email: mailbox@hotel-britannique.fr; 40 rooms; British-style hotel; in-room modem/fax connection, mini bar; internet available; Ffr762.

De Sevigne; 6 rue de Belloy, arr. 16; tel: (1) 4720-8890; fax: (1) 4070-9873; in a residential area close to the Arc de Triomphe, the Champs-Elysees and the Eiffel Tower; restaurant; bar; meeting space; secretarial service; in-room cable tv, telephone, mini bar; corporate rates.

Gaillon Opera (Best Western); 9 rue Gaillon, arr. 2; tel: (1) 4742-4774; fax: (1) 4742-0123; secretarial service; corporate rates; Ffr500/600.

Hôtel Passy Eiffel; 10 rue de Passy, 16 arr.; email: hameau.passy@wanadoo.fr; tel: (1) 4525-5566; fax: (1) 4288-8988; renovated, traditional hotel; business services; in-room direct dial, mini bar, cable tv; Ffr 620/750.

Les Jardins d'Eiffel; 8 rue Amelie, arr. 7; tel: (1) 4705-4621; fax: (1) 4555-2808; 4-star hotel; meeting facilities; in-room modem/fax connection; corporate rates; sauna; Ffr560/660.

Parc Montsouris; tel: (1) 4589-0972; fax: (1) 4580-9272; 4, rue du Parc Montsouris; 35 rooms; charming and quiet hotel along Montsouris park; in-room cable tv, direct dial telephones.

Relais du Louvre; 19 rue des Prêtres St.-Germain l'Auxerrois; tel: (1) 4041-9642; fax: (1) 4041-9644; in-room cable tv, direct dial telephone, mini bar; Ffr850.

Timhotel Elysees Cambaleres; 16 rue Cambaceres, arr. 8; tel: (1) 4265-7140; fax: (1) 4924-9148; 34 rooms; secretarial service; business center; corporate rates; Ffr800/900.

Timhotel Invalides; 35 boulevard de Latour-Maubourg; tel: (1) 4556-1078; fax: (1) 4705-6508; intimate hotel; conference center; secretarial service; corporate rates; sauna; Ffr650.

Timhotel Montmartre; 11 Rue Ravignan; tel: (1) 4255-7479; fax: (1) 4255-7101; 60 rooms; located in city center.

World Trade Center

Special arrangements/discounts are available at the following hotels through the World Trade Center:

Home Plazza Bastille
Close to Bastille Square

Hotel Saint James & Albany ****
Close to Le Louvre

Hotel La Villa Maillot ****
Close to the WTC

Hotel Concorde Group:
Concorde La Fayette ****
Same complex than WTC and Palais des Congres

Ambassador ****

Center of Paris - right bank

Lutetia ****
Center of Paris - left bank

Saint-Lazare ****
Center of Paris - right bank

Louvre ****
In front of Le Louvre

Flats for rent (1 week and more) are also available.

MEDICAL CARE

CHNO des Quinze Vingts (hospital); 28 rue de Charenton, 75571 Paris cedex 12; tel: (1) 4002-1520; fax: (1) 4628-6066.

Hôpital Franco-Britannique de Paris; 48 Rue de Villiers, Levallois-Perret; tel: (1) 4639-2222.

Hôpital Américain de Paris; 63 Boulevard Victor-Hugo, Neuilly; tel: (1) 4641-2525.

HEALTH CLUB

Centre de Danse du Marais; 41 Rue du Temple; Metro: Hotel-de-Ville; tel: (1) 4277-5819.

Club Quartier Latin; 19 Rue de Pontoise, 5th arr; Metro: Maubert-Mutualite; tel: (1) 4354-8245.

Green Club; 242 Rue de Charenton 12th arr.; Metro: Dugommier; tel: (1) 4342-1970.

AUTO RENTAL

Avis; reservations office, tel: (1) 4610-6060; fax: (1) 4621-6560; Charles de Gaulle Airport, tel: (1) 4862-3434 or (1) 4862-5959; fax: (1) 4862-3292; Orly Airport, tel: (1) 4975-4491; fax: (1) 4975-4502; most major train stations have Avis outlets.

Budget; Charles de Gaulle Airport, tel: (1) 4862-7047; fax: (1) 4862-7047; Orly Airport, South Terminal, tel: (1) 4975-5601, fax: (1) 4975--5538.

Budget; Charles de Gaulle Airport, tel/fax: (1) 4862-7047; Orly Airport, tel: (1) 4975-5601; fax: (1) 4975-5538; Gare de Lyon, tel: (1) 4344-1001; fax: (1) 434508411.

Didier Martin Service (for chauffeured limousine); tel: (1) 4554-7107 or (1) 4557-8732.

Europcar; tel: (1) 3043-8282.

Hertz; reservations: tel: (1) 3938-3838; fax: (1) 3938-3513; Charles de Gaulle airport, tel: (1) 4862-2900; fax: 4862-5856; Orly airport, tel: 4687-1044; fax: 4975-8454; most major trains stations also have Hertz outlets in Paris; chauffeur-driven cars available.

Eurodollar; tel: (1) 4346-1150.

WORLD TRADE CENTER

World Trade Center Paris
Palais Des Congrés
2 Place de la Porte Maillot
BP 18
75853 Paris Cedex 17
tel: (1) 4068-1425; fax: (1) 4068-1421
email: wtcparis@ccip.fr
http://www.ccip.fr

CHAMBER OF COMMERCE

Chambre de Commerce de Paris
27 avenue de Friedland
75382 Paris, Cedex 08
tel: (1) 4289-7000; fax: (1) 4289-7286

Georgia

Georgia

At a Glance

THE PEOPLE

Population .... 5,066,499 (July 1999 est.)
Growth Rate .... -0.74% (1999 est.)
Life Expectancy .... 64.63 years (born 1999)
Infant Mortality . 52.01 deaths/1,000 live births (1999 est.)

Ethnic Composition

Georgian...70.1%
Armenian...8.1%
Russian 6.3%
Other 15.5%

Religious Composition

Christian Orthodox 75%
Muslim 11%
Armenian Apostolic 8%
Other and non-affiliated...6%

Languages Spoken

Georgian (official), Russian, Armenian, Azeri

Education and Literacy

Education is compulsory for 12 years. Adult literacy stands at 99 percent.

THE ECONOMY

Since the demise of the USSR, Georgia has found independence from Russian surpervision to be both politically and economically problematic. Intermittent internal political violence has blunted the efforts of the government to get control of the economy. This unstable political environment has caused a once thriving tourist trade to wither as well as stunting the nation's exports of minerals and foodstuffs. Georgia is almost totally reliant on chaotic Russia for its energy needs and most of its trade is with other CIS economies. Although working with the IMF on a recovery program, Georgia is placing most of its hope in the development of an international transportation corridor and the Caspian pipeline. Both of these projects are slated to pass through Georgian and CIS territory. It is hoped that these projects will bring the foreign investment which has been slow to materialize. For all of its titular independence, Georgia still finds itself tied to the fates of Russia and other CIS nations. With high unemployment and a severe trade deficit, Georgia is desperately searching for ways to make its well educated population productive.

Exports .... US$230 million (f.o.b., 1997 est.))
Imports .... US$931 million (c.i.f., 1997 est.)
Total GDP .... US$11.2 billion (1998est.)
GDP Per Capita .... US$2,200 (1998 est.)
Unemployment .... 16 percent (1997)
Inflation Rate 10.5% (1998est.)

Top Export Partners

Russia, Turkey, Armenia, Azerbaijan, Bulgaria

Top Import Partners

Russia, Turkey, Azerbaijan

Top Exports

Citrus fruits, tea, wine, other agricultural products, machinery and parts, ferrous and nonferrous metals, textiles, chemicals, fuel re-export

Top Imports

Fuel, grain and other foods, machinery and parts, transport equipment

BUSINESS WORKWEEK

Offices

Monday to Friday 9a.m. to 6p.m.

Banks

Monday to Friday 10a.m. to 7p.m., with an extended break during the day that varies by locality. Some banks close early on Friday and are open Saturday.

Government

Monday to Friday 9a.m. to 3p.m.

Retail

Monday to Friday 9a.m. to 7p.m. Saturday 9a.m. until 2p.m.

HOLIDAYS

Christmas ....January 6
Easter ....April 9-12*
Independence Day ....May 26
New Year...December 31
* Date may vary by year.

CLIMATE

Seasons

Located on the shores of the Black sea, Georgia has all four seasons with cold wet winters and hot summers. Its delightful springs and sunny summers made it a well-known beach resort destination for the old Soviet states.

Regions

Rainfall is common in the west year round, and snow falls heavily during the winter in the mountain regions. Tbilisi, which lies in a valley and partially on the slopes of high hills, experiences drafty winters with temperatures ranging to a low of 5˚C (41˚F). Summers at the coast are hot and dry with temperatures averaging 31˚C (88˚F).

Money & Banking

Currency

The currency of Georgia is the lari (GL).

Denominations

The Georgian lari (GL) comes in banknote denominations of GL1, 5, 10, 20, 50, 100, 500, 1000.

Travel

VISA AND PASSPORT

A passport that is valid for a minimum of six months from the date of visa application is required of all visitors.
A visa is required of all except:
* Citizens of CIS (except Tajikistan nationals, of whom a visa is required)
* Nationals of Poland and Bulgaria
* Travelers with valid multiple-entry visas for Armenia or Azerbaijan
Visas, though, need not be acquired prior to arrival.

Georgia

Georgia

- Republic capital
- Autonomous republic center
- Autonomous oblast center
- City
- International border
- Province boundary
- Railroad
- Primary road

0   25   50   75 km

0   50 mi

©2001 Magellan Geographix   SM Santa Barbara, CA

Travelers who enter the country through the Tbilisi airport will be given a temporary stamp from passport control, along with instructions on obtaining a visa from the Consular Division of the Ministry of Foreign Affairs. Customarily, the visas are granted before five days elapse. If you would prefer to get your visa in advance from a Georgian embassy or consulate, then that option is also open to you.

Types of visas issued:

- Tourist - single entry only, terms of two weeks, one month, or three months
- Business - multiple entry, terms of six months or one year
- Transit, authorizing stopovers for a maximum of three days.

Tourist visas have a validity of three months beyond the date of issuance for stays of a maximum of three months. Business visas have a validity of one year from the date of issue for stays of a maximum of three months per entry. Transit visas are valid for three days only; transit passengers must also hold valid documentation of onward or return travel arrangements.

Nationals of countries in which Georgian diplomatic representation is nonexistent may procure visas for US$20 upon arrival at the Tbilisi international airport; this is a 24-hour service provided by the Visa Branch of the Consular Department of the Ministry of Foreign Affairs. The service

is appropriate only for visits of 14 days maximum. Whenever possible in these cases, the Consular Department of the Ministry of Foreign Affairs should be informed by the inviting party prior to the traveler's planned visit.

Business visa applications must include a letter of request, originating with the applicant's employer, which explains both the purpose of the visit and the position of the applicant in the organization.

Applications are to be made no less than three working days and no more than three months before the anticipated date of departure. Usually, visa application processing takes only a day for Tourist applications made in person, or three to four days from the date of receipt for postal applications. Business visa applications take a bit longer—allow ten days from the day of application initiation.

Note: Georgia is a sovereign nation, one of the Newly Independent States (NIS). Therefore, the embassies and consulates of the Russian Federation (CIS) no longer issue tourist visas that are valid for Georgia.

DEPARTURE FORMALITIES

Airport departure fees of US$10 are included in most airfares. Customs forms must be presented by all visitors at time of departure.

CUSTOMS ENTRY (PERSONAL)

Duty-free

- Tobacco: 200 cigarettes or 250g of tobacco products
- Alcohol: three liters of wine or ten liters of beer
- Other: a reasonable quantity of perfume for personal use; gifts up to a value of GL100, with weight not exceeding 10 kg

Note: On entering the country, tourists must complete a customs declaration form that must be retained until departure. This allows for the import of articles intended for personal use, including currency and valuables (such as jewelry, cameras, computers, etc.), that must be registered on the declaration form. Customs inspections can be long and detailed especially during periods of political turmoil.

Prohibited or Restricted

- Military weapons and ammunition
- Narcotics and pschotropic drugs
- Pornography
- Loose pearls
- Anything to be carried in for another person or business

If you have questions regarding items that may be imported, an information sheet is available on request from Intourist.

Prohibited Exports:

Lottery tickets, State loan certificates, antiques and works of art (unless authorization has been ordained by the Ministry of Culture), saiga horns, Siberian stag, punctuate and red deer antlers (unless acquired on organized, sanctioned hunting trips), and punctuate deer skins.

IMMUNIZATION

An International Certificate of Vaccination is not required unless you are arriving from an infected area. Tetanus and hepatitis A shots are advised for those on extended visits.

TIPPING

Taxi

A 10 to 15 percent tip is customary for metered taxi rides. Unmetered rides should include all costs in the negotiated fee.

Porters

Porters in transport depots and first-class hotels receive GL1 per bag.

Hotels

Tips are usually not necessary in Georgian hotels, as all service charges are applied to the bill.

Restaurants

A 15 percent tip is customary when service charges have not been applied to the bill.

Other

Beauticians and barbers, 10 percent. Small services, 5 to 10 percent.

EMERGENCY INFORMATION

Police and Crime

Violent crime is increasing throughout Georgia. Anonymous, sporadic gunfire, quite often celebratory, is actually a serious hazard to contemplate before venturing out from one's lodgings, especially at night.

Personal Security: The Gali region of Georgia has seen terrorist activities due to conflict with Abkhazia. South Ossetia and the northern mountain areas along the border with Russian Chechnya and Dagestan also fall into the category of troublesome areas to avoid. Overland travel, in general, involves risk of robbery and hijackings. A recent increase of terrorist activity in separatist-controlled Abkhazia has resulted in outbreaks of renewed fighting; these skirmishes include attacks against international observers. Land mines are another threat to travelers there. So-called Abkhaz 'border officials' may demand that travelers purchase a 'visa' from the so-called 'Ministry of Foreign Affairs of Abkhazia.'

Crime: High-tech crime is present. Hotel rooms, telephones, and meeting rooms may be 'bugged.' For this reason, visiting foreign operations may wish to set up their own accommodations. Business people should plan to take security precautions. Many corporate executives bring their own armed and highly trained security personnel; this should be cleared in advance with Georgian officials.

Some corruption exists within the local and central governments. Business travelers may also find that their deals with local companies involve the bribing of public officials. Police in rural areas and at borders are often prone to "shaking down" travelers. Requests for receipts usually puts a stop to this activity.

Take basic precautions against petty crime, especially on the Tbilisi Metro at night. Foreign business visitors are often the target of thieves. Consequently, purses, laptops and briefcases will require additional security. Do not leave valuables in cars or on tables in cafés. Keep non-essential valuables locked in hotel safes when not in use. Use credit cards and travel checks when possible to avoid carrying large sums of cash. Do not expect much sympathy from local police in the event of non-violent robbery. They assume all visitors are rich and will not really miss lost goods.

Emergency Numbers

Fire	01
Police	02
Ambulance	03

Health

Medical care is limited in Georgia, despite the presence of well-trained doctors and nurses. Medicines are in short supply; carry a well-stocked medical kit with all the prescription drugs you require, as well as disposable needles and pain killers (check first to be sure that what you plan to bring can be legally imported). A travel insurance package including an evacuation policy should be acquired by all business travelers.

Do not drink tap water or use ice cubes; bottled water is safe and available. Wash all vegetables in a chlorine solution, peel fruits, and avoid uncooked food. Drink only powdered or tinned milk and avoid other dairy products since they are most likely unpasteurized.

Asian visitors may find the Georgian diet heavy, and westerners may be unaccustomed to breakfasts that include large quantities of vegetables. Give yourself some time to acclimate before diving into Georgian cuisine. Stay away from street stalls.

INTERNAL TRAVEL

AIR

Domestic flights are available linking Tbilisi's Central Airport with Kutaisi, Senaki, and Butami. Orbi Georgian Airlines (NQ) and Air Georgia (DA) are the major air carriers, and small planes are also available for charter. Close to the mountains, you may find helicopters for charter also at a fairly high rate. For more information, you may wish to contact Orbi Georgian Airlines at the Georgian Embassy in Paris: tel: [33] (1) 4502-1157; fax: [33] (1) 4502-1601

Georgia

TAXI

Taxis are found only in urban areas. They can be hailed on the street, but be sure to negotiate the fare before the cab leaves the curb. For reasons of personal security, it is not advisable to get into a cab which is already occupied by another party, in spite of the fact that many locals share cabs frequently.They are predominantly privately owned cars, usually driven by their entrepreneurial owners. One can also find registered taxis in designated areas. Few taxis are metered, so you must negotiate a price before commencing your trip. Generally, the rates for foreigners are unreasonably high, so be prepared to haggle about that each time.

While it may surprise you that private citizens offer their service for transport, in small towns this is the taxi service method—so, be prepared to negotiate firmly but in good humor, and keep your security awareness at full alert.

AUTO

Car rental agencies can be found in Tbilisi. Makes and models are limited, and few are dependable. Required documentation includes an International Driving Permit.

Outside of Tbilisi, roads are in generally poor condition and have neither shoulder markings nor center lines. Nighttime driving proves especially hazardous, and there are reports of robberies and carjackings committed against foreign tourists, though it is not the norm. Do not pull over for anyone other than the police or military. Inter-city roads are usually two-lane affairs; motorists attempting to pass slower vehicles may encounter high-speed oncoming traffic.

Motorists should also be aware that gasoline is hard to come by, especially outside of urban areas. In this land of shortages, the locals have developed the purchase and caching of fuel into a fine art, so supply can be limited at times. It is advisable to carry extra fuel cans and to gas up before leaving a known source behind and heading off for parts unknown.

Traffic in the cities tends toward chaotic. A better idea than driving oneself is to hire a car and driver by the day or week, at least for your first visit. The going daily rate is about US$20 per day for both the driver and the vehicle, plus gasoline. Your hotel or a local business contact can suggest a reputable company.

TRAIN

Georgia has close to 1600km (987 miles) of railway. But lines are slow, being single-track, and rolling stock is outdated. The Government has reinstated order and procedure on the Transcaucasian Railway, which had experienced armed attacks on trains, chronic fuel shortages, sabotage of bridges and track, and the armed struggle in Abkhazia. From this chaos, remarkably, has emerged an essentially sound rail infrastructure.

The main line of the Transcaucasian Railway joins two major railway branches, from Yerevan (Armenia) and from Baku (Azerbaijan). The main line extends onward toward Russia along the coast of the Black Sea. Rail travel in both the west and the north is difficult due to the conflict in Abkhazia. Rail travel in other parts of the country is possible, but services are sporadic to many destinations.

Nevertheless, trains are the best way to travel throughout the country, in spite of some risk of robbery. Tickets are available in train stations and from some travel agents outside the country. The two classes of train are distinguished primarily by the comfort of the seats. Purchase tickets in advance for the best seats. When traveling overnight, be sure to lock your cabin door, and make certain it is secured from inside by anchoring it in a closed position with strong cord or wire. Dining cars on Georgian trains can be nightmarish, so bring along some food if you have a sensitive stomach.

Reservations are necessary for all trains. For more details, contact the nearest Georgian consulate or embassy, or a travel agent, or write directly to:
Georgian Railways
Tsaritsa Tamara 15
380012 Tbilisi, Georgia

METRO

The city offers a small underground metro, buses, and trolleybuses. The metro is a three-line system that runs from 6a.m. until 11p.m. The service is efficient for daily business use, and it connects with bus/tram lines to reach every corner of the city.

BUS / TRAM

Public transportation in Tbilisi is reasonably priced and reliable. Most other urban centers in Georgia also have extensive bus and tram systems. Few locals own cars. While the fares are low, so is the level of maintenance, and reliability is not high. Do not depend on these for business travel

Most inter-city travel is done by train, but bus lines run from inland cities to the coast during summer months. The buses are fairly reliable, but not too comfortable. Routes link most major towns in the country and run regularly between Tbilisi and regional centers within the country, as well as to Turkey, Russia, Armenia, and Azerbaijan.

WATER TRAVEL

Georgia's Black Sea ports offer ferry service to other Georgian coastal towns as well as to foreign nations bordering the sea. Schedules are punctual and prices moderate. Comfort levels vary greatly from company to company. The international ferry lines on the Black Sea are regularly used by regional business people, and the ferries can offer a great way to make contacts. Trips tend toward leisurely, and first-class overnight accommodations can be reserved.

TRAVEL ASSISTANCE

State Department of Tourism of Georgia
80 Chavchavadze Avenue
380062 Tbilisi, Georgia
tel: (32) 226 125; fax: (32) 294 052

Essential Terms

English	Russian
Yes No	Da Nyet
Good morning Hello (daytime) Hello (evening) Hello (telephone)	Dobroye utro Dobriy dyeni Dobriy vyechyer Zdrahstvooyt eh
Good-bye	Dosvidaniya
Please	Pozhalusta
Thank you	Spasibo
Pleased to meet you	Och een pree ahtnah
Excuse me; I'm sorry	Izvinitye
My name is _____	Ma ah / Fahmeelee ah _____
I don't understand	Ya nye ponimayu
Do you speak English?	Vi gahvahreet eh pah ah ngleeyskee

Communications

DIALING CODES IN GEORGIA

International country code: [995]
Selected city codes: Suhumi (881), Tbilisi (883)

Dialing Georgia from Overseas

To dial Georgia from overseas, dial Georgia's international dialing, then 995 (the country code for Georgia), then the city code and finally the number. If you were dialing Tbilisi from the United States, for example, you would begin with 011, then 995, then 32 (the city code for Tbilisi), and finally the number of the person or office you are trying to reach.

CALLING WITHIN GEORGIA

Local Calls

Calling may either require a coin or a token.

Long Distance Calls

If calling outside the hotel, head for a "mezhdugorodny" phone at a post office or airport. If this sounds complicated, it probably is since calling in general may be a confusing wreck of rust falling off the old Iron Curtain. The general guideline for the old Russian system is dialing 8 (wait for dial tone) + city code + number. Getting connected may prove a headache. If a number is not available by dialing direct, an operator may be able to connect you. However, this too may feel like going to war without a weapon thanks to unhelpful operators or failed connections.

International Calls

Ask about the number for a direct international call at your hotel or at the post office. There may be a wait of 24 hours or more to order a call, since it still may yet be routed through Moscow or elsewhere on the changing, disjointed system. For those on the customer list, thank your lucky stars that AT&T has made a connection to Georgia allowing possible access to smooth connections and more reasonable rates.
AT&T USA Direct ....8 * 0288
*Wait for a dial tone after dialing the initial eight.

PAY PHONES

Public Telephones

Public phones in Georgia are a maze of confusion. Some take coins, others take tokens. Some work, others don't.

CELLULAR PHONES

MegaCom Ltd. operates an AMPS analogue system (same as North America) and Diur La-Ole handles a GSM digital system in Georgia.

Note: Your home country cell phone may not work in this country. If not, we recommend that you rent an international cell phone *before* you leave home. A major US-based cell phone rental provider is **IMC WorldCell**. For information see "International Cell Phone Rentals" on page 14.

CALL BACK

You can (potentially) save significant sums when calling in Georgia by using a call back service. For a list of callback services, please refer to the "Communications" section in the *Global Road Warrior* Introduction.

Fees for call back services vary widely, depending on the company and the type of service required. Be sure to check with these companies before leaving to compare rates.

PHONE JACKS

Plug adaptors are available through **iGo Corporation**. (See "Electrical and Telephone Adaptors" on page 19.)

FAX

Faxes are becoming more popular, although they can still only be found in urban areas. Georgia's antiquated telephone system often delays faxes, but still far outpaces regular mail service.

POSTAL SERVICES

There have been a number of complaints regarding Georgian postal delivery. Some packages take months to deliver, if they are delivered at all. Letters could take an equally long time to reach their destination.

Business Services

COMPUTERS

Alta Computer; accessories, computers; software; D. Agmashenebeli 172; tel: (32) 941-750; fax: (32) 941-759; mobile tel: 8 w 7740-3890; email: alta@access.sanet.ge; http://www.alta.com.ge

United Global Technologies (Compaq Computers; engineering group); 17a Chavchauadza Ave.; tel: (32) 220-505; fax: (32) 220-206.

COURIER SERUICE

DHL Worldwide Express; 105, Tseretile Ave., Tbilisi 380019; tel: 344-826.

Federal Express; operated through Argotourtel; tel: 999-042.

TNT; ICS Ltd., 3V Anjaparidze Street, 380079 Tbilisi; tel: 250-328; fax: 250-329.

UPS; Nlkovan, Vazisubani 10-32, Tbilisi 380052; tel: 3278-9239.

Electrical

CURRENT

220 volts AC, 50Hz.

ELECTRIC PLUGS

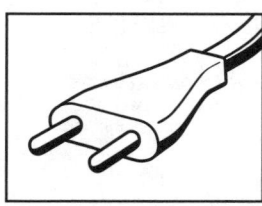

Plug adaptors are available through **iGo Corporation**. (See "Electrical and Telephone Adaptors" on page 19.)
Note: Bring a flashlight to combat frequent power outages.

Technical Support

HARDWARE/SOFTWARE VENDOR SUPPORT

Acer/Texas Instruments; (in Germany) tel: [49] (4102) 488-469; fax; [49] (4102) 488-169; (in the U.S.) tel: [1] (408) 432-6200; http://www.acer.com/.

Adobe; (in Germany) tel: [49] (1) 803-5018; (in Switzerland) tel: [41] (800) 833-310; (in the U.S.) tel: [1] (800) 500-7078; (in the U.S.) tel: [1] (716) 633-3600; http://www.adobe.com/.

Apple/Claris; (in Germany) tel: [49] (1) 803-5018; (in Switzerland) tel: [41] (800) 833-310; (in the U.K.) tel: [44] (990) 127-753; (in the U.S.) tel: [1] (800) 500-7078; http://www.apple.com/.

AST; (in the U.S.) tel: [1] (817) 232-9824 (International Technical Support); (in Ireland) tel: [353] (61) 492-222; (in the U.S.) tel: [1] (949) 727-4141; http://www.ast.com/.

Compaq/Digital; (in Switzerland) tel: [41] (22) 709-5330; fax: [41] (22) 709-5391 (Geneva); tel: [41] (1) 801-2507; fax: [41] (1) 801-2172 (Zurich); (General U.S.) tel: (281) 518-2000; http://www.compaq.com/.

Corel; (in Germany) tel: [49] (180) 425-8210 (TS Word Perfect-32 bit); (in the U.S.) tel: [1] (716) 871-2325 (Ask to be Forwarded to Appropriate Program); http://www.corel.com/.

Dell; (in Germany) tel: [49] (61) 039-710; (Dell- Europe) tel: [44] (134) 474-8000; (in the U.S.) tel: [1] (512) 338-4400; fax: [1] (512) 728-3330; http://www.dell.com/.

Filemaker/Claris; (in Germany) tel: [49] (180) 525-8166 (Info-line); fax: [49] (180) 567-2233; tel: [49] (180) 523-6423; (in the U.S.) tel: [1] (800) 965-9090; http://www.claris.com/.

Gateway 2000; (in the U.S.) tel: [1] (605) 232-2191; fax: [1] (605) 232-2023; (in Ireland) tel: [353] (1) 797-2000; http://www.g2k.com/.

Hewlett Packard; (in Switzerland) tel: [41] (22) 780-8111; (in the U.S.) tel: [1] (408) 246-4300; http://www.hp.com/.

IBM; (in Russia) [7] (095) 940-2000; fax: [7] (095) 940-2070; (in Germany) tel: [49] (711) 78-50; fax: [49] (711) 785-3511; (in Switzerland) tel: [41] (22) 310-0418 (in French); (in the U.S.) tel: [1] (919) 517-2800; (U.S. Main Office) tel: [1] 914-765-1900; http://www.ibm.com/.

Microsoft; (in Germany) tel: [49] (89) 31-760; fax: [49] (89) 3176-1000; tel: [49] (89) 3176-1199; (in Switzerland) tel: [41] (848) 858-868; fax [41] (1) 831-0869; (in the U.S.) [1] (425) 635-7222; http://www.microsoft.com/.

NEC; (in Germany) tel: [49] (18) 0524- 1212; tel:[49] (89) 3160-1233; fax: [49] (89) 3160- 1613 (Floppy Disk and Hard Drive); tel: [49] (89) 9627-4233; fax: [49] (89) 9627-4613 (All Other Products); (in the U.S.) [1] (916) 388-0101 (Main Switchboard); http://www.nec.com/.

Toshiba; (in Germany) tel: [49] (2131) 158-319; fax: [49] (2131) 158-558; (in Switzerland) tel: [41] (1) 946-0777; fax: [41] (1) 946-0807; (in Ireland) tel: [44] (193) 282-8828; (in the U.S.) [1] (949) 583-3000 (Corporate Headquarters); http://www.toshiba.com/.

Internet Connection

HOW TO CONNECT

Connecting to AOL and Compuserve in Georgia is similar to using it when traveling outside your own area code. See the introductory section for detailed information on connecting to your account through a different phone number.

America Online

Numbers are available at keyword *international*. Be sure to get several local numbers before leaving. Go to keyword *access* (a free area) and download the software.

There are no direct access numbers for America Online in Georgia. Users will have to pay international rates to use the service.

Compuserve

Numbers are available at *Go International*. The Compuserve Web-site also has a great deal of information, at http://www.compuserve.com.

There are no direct access numbers for Compuserve in Georgia. Users will have to pay international rates to use the service.

Independent Service Providers

Independent service providers may offer discounts if you are only in town for a couple of days.

BasriNet; tel; (222) 76-829; fax: (222) 76-839; http://www.basri.net/.

ICN (Information Caucasus Network); tel: (32) 936-013; tel: (32) 935-580; email: webmaster@caucasus.net; http://www.caucasus.net/.

MultiMedia Centre; tel: (32) 335-904; fax: (32) 987-618; email: contact@mmc.net.ge; http://www.mmc.net.ge/.

SA Net; tel: (32) 987-414; fax: (32) 001-367; email: postmaster@sanet.ge; http://www.sanet.ge/.

Georgia

Business Culture

GREETINGS AND COURTESIES

Georgians are hospitable and welcoming toward foreign businesspeople. They consider it an honor and a pleasure to entertain foreign guests. An invitation to a Georgian home is an invitation to feast, and your host will be offended if you do not partake generously. Georgian hosts propose endless rounds of toasts at dinner, usually with the local wines. In business settings, greet others with a handshake when entering and leaving a room. Although Georgians demonstrate informality, begin by addressing a man with "*batoni*" and the name with which he introduces himself, and a woman by "*kalbatoni*" and her introduced name. First name greetings are common between friends and relatives, and often with colleagues; however, one should wait until a higher ranking elder suggests that you do so.

DECISION MAKING

Georgians are benefiting from a modern economy, but are new to capitalist business procedures. Corruption poses the most serious roadblock to business dealings in Georgia, with government bureaucracy firmly entrenched from the days of the Iron Curtain. Organized crime elements appear with regularity in the new Republic, as do officials seeking bribes. Personal contacts offer the best method of pushing decisions through. However, in general, Georgian businesspeople have difficulty with the decision-making process. They have a reputation for saying "yes" to everything and continuing to do as they please.

MEETINGS

Arrange business meetings in Georgia far in advance. It may take weeks or even months to arrange visas and travel details. It is important to arrive on time and to bring business cards.

WOMEN

Women are treated traditionally in Georgia, and professional women must work hard to prove themselves before they are treated equally. Despite the difficulties, women hold a wide variety of positions in government and business. In addition to their careers, most Georgian working women also have full responsibility for their homes and children.

BUSINESS ATTIRE

Business attire remains conservative and dress leans toward European. A suit and tie should be worn for all meetings. Traditional sentiments encourage women to wear conservative clothing, accessories, and hairstyles as well. Avoid excessive jewelry, it won't bring you any additional sales and may attract thieves.

Business Centers

CITY VIEW

A city whose name means "hot", has garnered its title from its sulfuric springs. Tbilisi has retained its ancient look despite the fires and wars that have ravaged the city. Almost 1.5 million people call Tbilisi home: Georgians, Armenians, Russians, Azerbaijanians, Kurds, and several other cultures inhabit the city limits. There are several cultural attractions that are noteworthy in Tbilisi, including the Narikhala Fortress and a 5th-century Sioni Cathedral Church.

AIRPORT

Airport to City Center

Tbilisi International Airport (TBS) is situated 11 miles (18km) from the center of town. There are both taxis and buses available for transport into town, which should take approximately 20 minutes.

Airline Numbers

Alack...959-189
Air Georgia/ORBI 988-500, 294-053
Business Club Orioni...............................997-031
Lidia...985-945
Trans Air Globe 235-481

Currently, flights to Tbilisi operate from Amsterdam, Bonn, Frankfurt, Istanbul, Köln (Cologne), Moscow, Paris, and Prague.

HOTELS

Top-end
Sheraton Metechi Palace Hotel; Telavi Street 20; tel: (32) 958-220; fax: (32) 001-127, ext. 132; restaurant; business services; meeting rooms; fitness; pool.

Expensive
Abkhaziya Hotel; tel: (32) 73-697.

Intourist Hotel; 11/1 Ninoshvili Street; tel: (32) 93-808.

Hotel Kolkhi; 31 Shanidze Str.; tel: 226-679; fax: 234-093; 24 rooms; in the Vera district; restaurant; bar; business center; in-room tv, telephone.

Iveria Hotel; tel: (32) 930-488.

Lux Guest House; 47 Nutsubidze Street; tel: 939-162; breakfast and dinner included with accommodations.

Sakartvelo Hotel; tel: (32) 24-001.

Villa Berika; 9 Dtsotsenidze Str, 3 Micro Region, Plato Nuttsubidze; tel/fax: (32) 93-35-62; restaurant.

Moderate
Hotel Medea; 40 Mitskevichi Str.; tel: (32) 370-125; fax: (32) 941-243; rooms with bath; satellite antenna; telephone/fax services; breakfast included; US$120.

Hotel Tamuna; Kandelaki Street 23; tel: (32) 233-432; fax: (32) 969-777; email: moambe@geocities.com; rooms with bath; restaurant/bar; satellite antenna; independent generator; telephone/fax services; conference hall; gift shop; pool.

AUTO RENTAL
Avis; L.L.C. Madohavagi, 1 Rustaveli Avenue; tel: 923-594.

Hertz; Tbilisi Airport; tel: 995-003; fax: 995-122. Tbilisi Downtown; Sheraton Hotel, 20 Telavi Street; tel: 995-003; fax: 995-122.

MEDICAL CARE

City Hospital No. 2; Constitution Street, 2, Tbilisi 380025; tel: 954-423.

State Medical University; Kazbegi Street, 19, Tbilisi 380009; tel: 951-227; fax: 290-492.

HEALTH CLUBS

Laguna Vere; water sports complex; 34 Kostava Side-str., Sanapiro, Tbilisi; tel: 998-231; fax: 998-960.

CHAMBER OF COMMERCE

Georgian Chamber of Commerce and Industry
11 Chavchavadze Ave.,
380079 Tbilisi

Germany

At a Glance

THE PEOPLE

Population .... 82,087,361 (July 1999 est.)
Growth Rate 0.01% (1999)
Life Expectancy .... 77.17 years (1999 est.)
Infant Mortality ... 5.14 deaths/1,000 live births (1999 est.)

Ethnic Composition

German 91.5%
Turkish..2.4%
Italians 0.7%
Greeks 0.4%
Poles 0.4%
Other .... 4.6% (made up mostly of
people fleeing the war in the former Yugoslavia)

Religious Composition

Protestant..38%
Roman Catholic...34%
Muslim 1.7%
Unaffiliated or other...26.3%

Languages Spoken

German (official); English is widely understood.

Education and Literacy

Education is compulsory for 10 years and the literacy rate stands at 99 percent of adults.

Labor Force

Total ....8.2 million (1998)
By occupation: industry 33.7%, agriculture 2.7%, services 63.6% (1998).

THE ECONOMY

Germany accounts for roughly 25 percent of the E.U.'s total GDP. With one of the world's highest standards of living, Germany's refined infrastructure, skilled (but expensive) workforce, financial stability, and geographical location put it both physically and economically at the crossroads of Western and Central Europe. Germany has experienced continued problems with weak domestic consumption and rising unemployment. A near confiscatory domestic tax system, restrictive work rules, high social system costs, strong unions, and tight government regulation have driven away foreign investment as well as homegrown entrepreneurs. Many German industrial mainstays are opening new plants overseas rather than on home soil where they could have generated German jobs. Added to these problems has been the reabsorption of the former East Germany at a price tag of US$100 billion per year. Nationwide unemployment hovers around 10 percent with pockets in the East racking up figures nearing the 20 percent mark. The German government has made moves in recent months to reduce its contribution to theE.U.in hopes of spreading some largesse at home. Germany's current domestic boom has been driven by a weak Euro which is underpinned by the Deutschemark. Like several otherE.U.members, Germany is facing a major growth in the number of citizens over the age of 65 and retired (21%). The impact on the social system is expected to reach potentially catastrophic levels in 2010.

Exports .... $510 billion (f.o.b., 1998 est.)
Imports .... $426 billion (f.o.b., 1998 est.)
Total .... US$936 billion (1998 est.)
GDP Per Capita .... $22,100 (1998 est.)
Unemployment .... 10.6% (1998 est.)
Inflation Rate 1.8% (1997)

Top Export Partners

E.U. 55.5% (France 10.7%, U.K. 8.5%, Italy 7.4%, Netherlands 7.0%, Belgium-Luxembourg 5.8%), U.S. 8.6%, Japan 2.3% (1997 est.)

Top Import Partners

E.U. 54.3% (France 10.5%, Netherlands 8.5%, Italy 7.8%, U.K. 7.0%, Belgium-Luxembourg 6.2%), U.S. 7.7%, Japan 4.9% (1997) .

Top Exports

Machinery 31%, vehicles 17%, chemicals 13%, metals and manufactures, foodstuffs, textiles (1997) .

Top Imports

Machinery 22%, vehicles 10%, chemicals 9%, foodstuffs 8%, textiles, metals (1997).

BUSINESS WORKWEEK

Offices

Monday to Friday 8a.m. to 4p.m.
Many businesses close early on Fridays (see note below).

Banks

Monday to Friday 8:30a.m. to 1p.m. and 2:30p.m. to 4p.m.
In large cities banks remain open throughout the day.

Government

Monday to Friday 8:30a.m. to 12:30p.m. and 2p.m. to 5p.m.

Retail

Monday to Friday 8a.m. to 7p.m. (Saturday until 4p.m.). Smaller shops in non-touristed areas may close for a couple of hours around noon.
Note: Most shops, many banks and some offices are open slightly longer on "long Thursday" and may permit employees to leave early on Friday to offset the time.

HOLIDAYS

New Year's Day..January 1
Good Friday..April 2*
Easter Monday ....April 5*
Labor Day...May 1
Ascension Day .... May 13*
Whit Monday .... May 24*
Christmas...December 25-26
*Date may vary by year.

CLIMATE

Seasons

The climate is temperate, with mild summers of around 29°C (85°F). The winters are generally cold (sub-freezing is common), wet, and damp with high rainfall and moderate snow. Heavy snows are reserved for Alpine regions.

Regions

Germany has a very diverse geography with mountains, plains, and rich valleys as well as North Sea and Baltic coastlines. The south is generally more mountainous and colder,

Germany *(sidebar)*

with large amounts of snowfall in the winter. The southwest is far milder and sunnier. The northwest lowlands receive the chilly but acceptable North Sea winds while the eastern sector remains moderate.

Money & Banking

Currency

The currency of Germany is the Deutsche Mark (DM).

Denominations

The Deutsche Mark comes in coin denominations of DM5, 2, and 1, and 50, 10, 5, 2, 1 pfennigs; and banknotes of DM10, 20, 50, 100, 200, 500, 1,000.

Traveler's Checks and Credit Cards

Most brands of traveler's checks and foreign currency can be easily and efficiently exchanged at banks, foreign exchange bureaus located in the major cities, hotels, and foreign exchange kiosks at the airports. Banks offer the most variable exchange rates. Traveler's checks receive a better exchange rate than cash, or you can purchase German traveler's checks before departure.

Credit cards widely accepted in Germany include American Express, Visa, MasterCard, and Diners Club. Travelers can get cash advances from credit cards on many of the automated teller machines (ATM). The best exchange rates are given for credit card and ATM transactions.

Note: Some transactions may appear on credit card and bank statements in Euro denominations rather than Deutsche marks. The Euro does not yet exist as a physical currency but theE.U.countries transact business in Euro units.

Essential Terms

English	German
Yes	Ja
No	Nein
Good morning	Guten Morgen
Hello (daytime)	Guten Tag
Hello (evening)	Guten Abend
Hello (telephone)	Guten Tag
Good-bye	Auf Wiedersehen
Please	Bitte
Thank you	Danke
Pleased to meet you	Angenehm
Excuse me; I'm sorry	Entschuldigung/ Verzeihung
My name is _____	Ich heisse _____
I don't understand	Ich verstehe nicht
Do you speak English?	Sprechen Sie Englisch?

Travel
VISA AND PASSPORT

A passport is required of all visitors, except for those bearing national ID cards from the following countries: Austria, Belgium, Denmark, France, Germany, Greece, Iceland, Ireland, Italy, Liechtenstein, Luxembourg, Malta, Monaco, The Netherlands, Portugal, San Marino, Spain, and Switzerland.

Germany is a member of the Schengen group, which is a collection of nations who in March of 1995 declared themselves borderless. The others in this group are France, Belgium, Luxembourg, The Netherlands, Portugal, and Spain. Any traveler who holds a valid passport or other travel documents that are recognized by all Schengen member nations need not have a visa to travel in any of these countries. There are two caveats, however:

- If you have tickets for onward travel to a nation that does require a visa of you, it may also be required of you for entry into the Schengen nation.
- Each Schengen nation retains the right to require a visa of any nation normally exempted by the group as a whole.

Following is a list of nations normally exempt from the visa requirement in Germany, most of which derive this status from the Schengen agreement (E.U. nationals are automatically exempt): Andorra, Argentina, Australia, Bolivia, Brazil, Brunei, Canada, Chile, Colombia, Costa Rica, Croatia, Cyprus, Czech Republic, Ecuador, El Salvador, Guatemala, Honduras, Hungary, Iceland, Israel, Jamaica, Japan, Kenya, Liechtenstein, Malawi, Malaysia, Panama, Malta, Mexico, Monaco, New Zealand, Nicaragua, Norway, Panama, Paraguay, Poland, Republic of Korea, San Marino, Singapore, Slovak Republic, Slovenia, Switzerland, Turkey (only if a permanent resident of a Schengen country), Uruguay, U.S., Vatican City, and Venezuela.

Visa-free travel throughout the Schengen states is valid for a duration of 90 days maximum within a six month period, commencing upon initial entry date into a Schengen country. Of course, if this does not fit into your travel plans, you may apply for a visa anyway.

Two types of visa are issued: Transit and Short Stay. The latter applies to either tourism or business purposes, normally authorizing stays up to 90 days, and may be used within a 12-month period.

Transit visas are good for 5 days, including the day of arrival in Germany. Travelers who are continuing their journey on the same or first possible connecting aircraft, and who are holding confirmed tickets and other travel documents, are exempt from carrying a transit visa, except for nationals of: Afghanistan, Angola, Bangladesh, Bulgaria, Congo (Dem. Rep.), Ethiopia, Gambia, Ghana, India, Iran, Iraq, Jordan, Lebanon, Nigeria, Pakistan, Romania, Somalia, Sri Lanka, Sudan, Syria and Turkey. These travelers must have a transit visa with them at all times.

It is not mandatory to be in possession of a return ticket when you arrive, but it is a good idea if possible. Otherwise, be prepared to prove sufficient funds for the duration of your visit.

If you are applying for a business visa, you will need to include a letter from your employer, or from a certified accountant, bank manager, or attorney if you are self-employed.

If you are not exempt from the visa requirement, allow up to eight weeks for processing.

DEPARTURE FORMALITIES

Any amount of German or foreign currency may be brought into or taken out of the country without formality. Airport departure taxes are included in airline ticket costs. No other restrictions apply.

CUSTOMS ENTRY (PERSONAL)

Duty Free

The following items may be brought into Germany without customs duty being levied if visitors are arriving from an E.U.country with goods purchased tax free:
- 200 cigarettes or 100 cigarillos or 50 cigars or 250g of tobacco
- 1 liter of distilled spirits having an alcohol content in excess of twenty-two percent, or two liters of liqueurs or spirits having an alcohol content less than twenty-two percent, or two liters of sparkling wine or liqueur
- 2 liters of other wine of any sort
- 50g of perfume or 250ml of eau de toilette
- 500g of coffee, or 200g of coffee extracts
- personal effects to a maximum value of DM350

The following items may be brought into Germany without customs duty being levied if visitors are entering from an E.U. country (except Denmark) with tax-paid goods:
- 800 cigarettes and 400 cigarillos and 200 cigars and 1kg of tobacco
- 90 liters of wine (including a maximum 60 liters of sparkling wine)
- 10 liters of distilled spirits or liqueur having an alcohol content in excess of twenty-two percent
- 20 liters of intermediate products (for example, fortified wine)

Germany

- 110 liters of beer.
- 50g of perfume or 250ml of eau de toilette
- Personal goods up to a maximum of DM350, including foodstuffs, but excluding gold and gold alloys, which must be declared
- Fresh meat up to a maximum of two pounds

The amounts of alcohol and tobacco specified above are somewhat academic, since the import of duty-paid quantities are no longer limited betweenE.U.countries, technically speaking. But, if you have amounts of any items in excess of the above quantities, you may be interrogated to determine whether the goods are solely for personal use.

Note: If you are purchasing valuable articles in Germany, you can apply for a refund of the VAT (value added tax) by obtaining the required documents where purchases are made. Submit the documents when departing Germany.

IMMUNIZATION

Immunizations are not necessary for visitors unless they are arriving from an area infected with yellow fever or other communicable diseases.

TIPPING

Tipping is not customary in Germany. Service charges are usually included in the tab (Bedienung). Some mild form of tipping is inherent in the common practice of rounding up charges to the nearest whole DM.

Taxi

Taxi drivers are tipped by rounding up the fare.

Porters

Porters at depots receive DM1 per bag.

Hotels

Hotels apply service charges directly to the bill, usually in the range of 10 to 15 percent.

Restaurants

Most restaurants include service charges in the tab. The customer usually rounds up to the nearest whole number and the difference is given to the server. Servers are usually well paid, but they will happily accept additional gratuities.

If no service charge is included, a 15 percent tip is standard.

Note: Visitors should note that German restaurants may offer pretzels or other forms of bread appetizers on the table prior to the meal; these are charged to your bill by the piece eaten.

EMERGENCY INFORMATION

Police and Crime

Germany is a relatively safe country, but as with all large industrial countries, exercise caution in urban areas—especially East Berlin, which is known for its increasing crime rate. Train stations and their environs also offer their share of shady characters lurking about, especially in the nighttime hours. However, most street crimes do not involve personal assault, consisting primarily of pickpocketing or theft of unattended items. A few elementary precautions should protect the traveler from most problems:

- Do not leave valuables in cars or on tables in cafés.
- Keep non-essential valuables locked in hotel safes when not in use.
- Use credit cards and traveler's checks when possible to avoid carrying large sums of cash.
- Carry photocopies of your passport instead of the original.
- Carry cash in a money belt, and use credit cards or travelers checks for most of your large transactions.

At night, women are advised to travel in groups or to take a taxi. The police are very efficient and courteous, and have good foreign language skills.

Emergency Numbers

Ambulance / General emergency 112
Police 110
Fire 115

HEALTH

Apart from the common flu, there are no significant health risks in Germany. The water is safe to drink, and bottled water is readily available, especially at restaurants where they prefer that you pay for water. Milk is pasteurized. Sanitation is of a high order and German food can be consumed without any worries beyond normal precautions.

The German National Health Service is among the best in the world, and its services are often free to foreign travelers. Nevertheless, it is recommended that visitors have their own private insurance for treatment by specialists outside the national system, which can prove expensive. (Private doctors and hospitals often expect immediate cash payment.) Such insurance should provide for overseas coverage, specifically. It should also include medical evacuation, although only the most extreme of medical circumstances might call for such measures.

Some hospitals (*Krankenhaus*) and pharmacies (*Apotheke*) are open 24 hours a day. Drug stores (*Drogerie*) in Germany do not sell medical supplies, but rather cosmetic items such as lotions and detergents.

Pharmacists remain open from 9a.m. to 6p.m. Monday through Friday, and 9a.m. to noon on Saturday. All pharmacists can provide the addresses of services available outside normal opening hours.

INTERNAL TRAVEL

AIR

Domestic air travel is widely available, but unless one is in a real rush, the German train system can usually convey the traveler almost as quickly. Lufthansa is the main domestic air carrier. Deutsche BA and Eurowings also provide regular services between major cities. A host of regional airlines or air taxi services also have routes between smaller urban centers.

Most airports in the west offer daily services to Leipzig as well as weekly flights to Dresden on a number of airlines. Domestic air links are operated daily from Berlin, Bremen, Cologne/Bonn, Düsseldorf, Frankfurt-am-Main, Hamburg, Hannover, Munich, Nuremberg, Stuttgart and Westerland/Sylt (summer only).

Frankfurt/M (Frankfurt-am-Main) is the hub of domestic air operations. From there, all airports in Germany lie within an average of 50 minutes flight time. Even remote destinations, such as Helgoland, Sylt, and some other Friesian Islands, can be reached via the smaller airlines, although some services are seasonal.

TAXI

Taxis are available in all towns and cities. Be aware that prices change depending on the time of day, and that surcharges exist for waiting and for extra or particularly bulky luggage. In Munich, one has a much better chance of securing a cab at a taxi stand rather than hailing it in the streets. Taxis are all metered and travel receipts are available.

AUTOMOBILE

The roads in Germany are generally first-rate. Driving provides a good way to tour the country. Parking, though, can prove problematic in many of the smaller towns. The Autobahns are a dream-come-true for the enthusiastic motorist, but they can also offer a terrifying experience for the less brave of heart due to their high-speed nature. The code on the Autobahn calls for vehicles to stay in the right lanes unless they are passing. Indeed, if a driver stays in the left lane with no one in sight for miles, a light-flashing Mercedes may appear right behind out of nowhere. Headlight flashing indicates, "Move—quickly!" With little room for error at such high speeds, drivers need to pay attention and concentrate. Drivers in Germany are quick and decisive, they expect the same from others. Driver error is the main cause of traffic accidents for foreign visitors. Large-scale accidents on the Autobahn with 45 to 50 cars involved are not all that uncommon.

Note: Pedestrians should be mindful of the fact that it is illegal to cross the road when a pedestrian crossing light is red, regardless of whether oncoming traffic exists. On-the-spot fines are common.

Auto rentals are available in most towns and one can find rental desks at over 160 railway stations through a collaborative program between German Railways and Hertz, Avis, Europcar, and Sixt/Budget. In the larger urban areas, chauffeur-driven cars can be booked. When arranged beforehand, cars can also be reserved at airports and hotels. A number of airlines, including Lufthansa, have "fly-drive" packages. Contact the National Tourist Office for details (see local listings for addresses and phone numbers below in "Travel Assistance").

Foreign travelers may use their own cars in Germany up to a year, as long as they have a driver's license from their own country or International Driving Permit and automobile registration papers. Insurance is required by law. E.U. nationals who take their own cars should also obtain a so-called Green Card, which raises the minimum auto insurance coverage to match the levels provided by their own domestic policies.

In western Germany, speed limits are fairly high; this part of the country is crisscrossed by a thoroughly modern network of roadways (Autobahnen) ranging over 10,500km (6563 miles). Speed limits in eastern Germany tend to be a bit lower due to road conditions that do not quite equal those of the West. As a whole, the system extends over 487,000km (303,000 miles) of roads; the entire country is accessible to motorists. Use of this system is free at present, but introduction of a toll is under consideration.

Traffic signs are international, and traffic keeps to the right-hand side of the road. Roadside assistance, including a helicopter service, is provided by the ADAC (German automobile association). Emergency telephones are located along the roadways. If you use these telephones, ask the operator specifically for road service assistance (*Strassenwachthilfe*).

Following are the phone numbers of several auto rental agencies in Germany:

Avis.. (0180) 555 77
Hertz ....(0180) 533-3535
Interrent.. (0180) 522 11 22
Sixt/Budget ....(0180) 5252525

TRAIN

Rail services in the western part of Germany rank among the most advanced in the world. The rail services in the eastern part of Germany are of lower standards, but an effort is under way to improve them. The eastern and western train systems have now been fully merged, although fares in the east still appear cheaper.

Train travel in Germany (and Europe) offers an ideal way to mix business and pleasure. It is also a common way for business people to travel between cities. First-class facilities are available for overnight and day trips.

A basic description of the rail system in Germany follows. The range of fare alternatives, routes, facilities, timetables, and passes is immense; regard it as a good start for understanding the essential—along with suggestions on how to acquire more details.

Virtually every town has rail access, and usually the main station (*Hauptbahnhof*) is situated directly downtown in every city for convenient access. German trains offer efficient, comfortable, and punctual service.

The comprehensive **InterCity, or IC** network (300 trains every day), links the major cities hourly and enables prompt transfers between trains. Over 50 cities, including Berlin, Leipzig, Erfurt and Dresden, are served.

High speed **ICE (Inter City Express)** trains— traveling at 280kph (175mph)—offer conveyance between most of Germany's major cities in far less travel time than regular express or regional trains. Currently operating hourly on selected connections only, this service is constantly expanding. It is somewhat more expensive than the other lines, but most passengers feel it is well worth it.

The **InterRegio** system provides connections between regional centers every two hours in western Germany, and every two to four hours in eastern Germany. Comprised of 26 lines, these longer-distance trains are supplemented by the commuter networks in the larger cities.

EC (EuroCity) trains offer the fastest service between major cities beyond Germany's borders throughout Europe.

Departure and arrival times of all lines are coordinated, so that it is convenient for passengers to make the transfers they need.

Connections with Berlin in the IC/EC/ICE network (which currently has 8 primary axis) are increasing continually. Several InterCity connections, including one ICE, run every 1 to 2 hours.

The InterRegio trains have buffet cars providing light refreshments and drinks and some seating. InterCity and EuroCity trains are equipped with a restaurant car with 48 seats and offering a full menu and beverages throughout the journey. Many of the sleeping cars have showers, with air-conditioning on most long-distance overnight trains. Attendants serve refreshments in the sleeping cars. Beds must be booked in advance, and some trains have couchettes (seats that fold down into long beds or bunks) only.

In addition to those amenities, the newer InterCity Express trains include both buffet cars and restaurant carriages. "At-your-seat" service is provided for first-class passengers. A service car offers conference space, calling card telephones, and a fully appointed office (copy machine, fax, etc.).

Again, advance booking is necessary for all of the long-distance trains, as early in your travel planning process as possible. These are highly popular trains.

German Rail Passes are available at travel agencies and allow for unlimited travel in specific time frames (additional surcharges are levied on certain lines, such as the ICE trains).

There is a plethora of other fares and passes available. Details on current prices and sites to obtain them are available from German Rail or the Tourist Office. Check the following website for timetables and further information:

German Rail website ....www.bahn.de/

URBAN / METRO

Major cities in Germany offer subway (U-Bahn) service to most every part of town and connect passengers quickly to their destinations. Well-marked stations and maps allow for easy accessibility, with trains passing through stations in quick intervals. The U-bahn transports people underground within the city limits. Look for the white signs with a large "U" indicating an underground stop. The faster S-bahn (*Schnellbahn*, meaning express train) covers the outlying areas of cities and most often connects airports to city centers.

In many towns, multi-ride tickets are available at discounted rates, and daily travel tickets for unlimited transit are available. In larger cities, one may gain admission to the transport system with tickets purchased from sophisticated vending machines prior to boarding. Fares are reasonable and rates are clearly indicated. A wide range of relevant maps and leaflets stands available to travelers at kiosks located close to these machines.

Often, no conductor appears on the underground trains, but random inspections are continual, and passengers not holding valid tickets are fined immediately.

In Berlin, the Berliner Verkehrs-Betriebe, referred to popularly as the BVG (Berlin Public Transport), oversees a wide-ranging network of buses, underground, and S-Bahn. Regional services provided by Deutsche Reichsbahn, lines R1-14, complement the BVG. The underground lines 1 and 9 run a 24-hour service throughout the weekend, commencing on Friday night.

BUSES & TRAMS

Buses and trams serve small towns and villages, and are much more prevalent in towns without railway stations. Local buses and trams in urban areas service specific routes and operate on precise timetables. Very few long distance services exist; those that do are usually hired by tour groups. Purchase tickets in advance from well-marked vending machines and validate the tickets on board.

WATER TRAVEL

Germany has an extensive river and ocean port system. Both systems have passenger lines with access to local and international terminals. Though not commonly used by business travelers, these water travel systems can fill in the gaps of an itinerary that focuses on smaller towns.

Eastern Berlin's White Fleet provides 30 scheduled ferry services and short trips around the city. It also offers routes that include the Saale and Elbe rivers, several lakes, and ports of call in the Mecklenburger Lake District. The ferries of the BVG provide further egress among Berlin's many districts.

Regularly scheduled boat services are conducted on most inland waterways and lakes, as well as along the coast. One can find ferry and short-hop passage on the Danube, Main, Moselle, Rhine, Neckar and the Weser, as well as on Ammer See, Chiemsee, Königssee and Lake Constance.

In addition to these scheduled services, pleasure cruises are available on virtually all navigable waters. The KD German Rhine Line operates on the Rhine, Main, and Moselle rivers. There are 19 ships that run daily from April to late October. Cruises with live entertainment on board can be arranged, as well as excursions between The Netherlands and Switzerland, and along the Moselle. In conjunction with the White Fleet out of Dresden, the KD also operates cruises on the Elbe River between Dresden and Hamburg.

Ferries also connect Germany to the Russian Federation, Latvia and Lithuania.

Check locally with any of the companies mentioned above for more details, or with the offices of pertinent agencies listed below in the "Travel Assistance" section. Your hotel will usually have brochures and contact numbers for these ship lines, and others.

TRAVEL ASSISTANCE

Deutsche Zentrale für Tourismus e.V. (DZT)
[German National Tourist Office]
Beethovenstrasse 69, 60325 Frankfurt/M
tel: (69) 974 640 or 75720; fax: (69) 751 903.
Berlin ....30-262 -6031
Hamburg..40-300-51-249

Munich................................. 89 212-3970; fax: 89 293 582
website ....www.germany-tourism.de

LOCAL TOURIST INFORMATION
Bavarian Tourist Board/Oktoberfest and more
tel: 89-21 23 97 30; fax: 89-29 35 82
email: tourismus@bayern.btl.de
Berlin Tourismus
tel: 30/25 00 25; fax: 30/25 00 24 24
website: www.berlin.de

Communications
DIALING CODES IN GERMANY
International country code: [49]

Selected city codes: Bad Homburg (6172), Berlin (30), Bonn (228), Bremen (421), Chemnitz (371), Cologne (Köln) (221), Cottbus (355), Dresden (351), Düsseldorf (211), Erfurt (361), Essen (201), Frankfurt am Main (west) (69), Frankfurt Oder (east) (335), Gera (365), Halle (345), Hamburg (40), Hannover (511), Heidelberg (6221), Koblenz (261), Leipzig (341), Magdeburg (391), Mannheim (621), Munich (89), Neubrandenburg (395), Nürnberg/Nuremberg (911), Potsdam (331), Rostock (381), Saal (38223), Schwerin Meckenburg (385), Stuttgart (711), Wiesbaden (611).

DIALING GERMANY FROM OVERSEAS

To dial Germany from overseas, begin with your country's international dialing code, then 49 (the country code for Germany), then the city code, and finally the number. Omit the zero preceding city codes if dialing Germany from overseas. If you were dialing Berlin from the United States, for example, you would begin with 011, then 49, then 30 (the city code for Berlin), and finally the number of the person or office you are trying to reach.

ASSISTANCE NUMBERS IN GERMANY

Operator .... 03 or 010
International Operator 0010
International Directory 00118
Domestic Directory .... (0) 1188
E.U. Information 001188

CALLING WITHIN GERMANY

Local Calls
From a public booth a local call will cost DM0.30 (30 Pfennig). Calling involves a straightforward coin deposit and dial of the local number.

Long Distance Calls
Area codes exist for each locality in Germany. Use the preceding (0) if dialing from outside the region you are trying to reach, unless calling from outside the country when the zero is omitted.

International Calls
International calls can be placed from public booths labeled *Inlands und Auslandsgespräche,* meaning domestic and international calls. Those booths sporting a picture of a bell indicate they can also receive calls. If you don't have a phone card, you may have to carry a large sack of DM5 coins, as overseas calls prove costly (four minutes to the U.S. will cost about 15DM).

Otherwise, it may just be easier to head for a post office, located in every town or district, and ask to place a call at the long distance counter (*Ferngespräch*). The clerk will then direct you to a booth where you may dial. Pay at the counter after the call has been completed. Hotels, as anywhere else, will charge a fortune for the privilege of using their phones. To connect to a home operator, you must pay for the local connection.

Australia Direct 0130-80-00-61
Canada Direct 0130-00-14
Ireland Direct 0130-80-03-53
New Zealand Direct 0130-80-00-64
South Africa Direct 0130-80-00-27
U.K. (BT) 0130-80-00-44
U.S. AT&T Direct 0130-00-10
U.S. MCI 0130-00-12
U.S. Sprint 0130-00-13

PHONE JACKS/ADAPTORS

Most new German buildings and homes take the following phone jacks:

PHONE JACKS

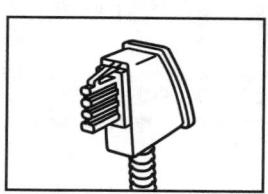

Plug adaptors are available through **iGo Corporation.** (See "Electrical and Telephone Adaptors" on page 19.)

CELLULAR PHONES

A few companies offer cellular service on the GSM digital network, mostly in the standard 900MHz range, except for one DCS system run by E-Plus, a digital system which operates on an 1,800MHz frequency. T-Mobil also operates a C-450 analogue system.

Note: Your home country cell phone may not work in this country. If not, we recommend that you rent an international cell phone *before* you leave home. A major US-based cell phone rental provider is **IMC WorldCell**. For information see "International Cell Phone Rentals" on page 14.

CALL BACK

You can (potentially) save significant sums when calling in Germany by using one of the call back services listed below. Fees for call back services vary widely, depending on the company and the type of service required. Be sure to check with these companies before leaving to compare rates.

For a list of callback services, please refer to the "Communications" section in the *Global Road Warrior* Introduction.

FAX

Faxes are available in all hotels and most offices. The service is excellent.

POSTAL SERVICES

Postal service is very good. Expect no additional charge when sending airmail within Western Europe.

Hours of service

Monday to Friday 8a.m. to 6p.m.
Saturday 8a.m. to 1p.m.

TELEGRAMS

Telegrams can be sent during offices hours from any post office. Also check with your hotel to find out if they offer telegram service.

PAY PHONES

Public Telephones

A number of coin- and card-operated public phones are available, including several new card phones in Eastern Germany. Card telephones ar e the most efficient and cheapest way to place all types of calls.

Most card operated telephones have instructions for use written on them in French, English, and Italian.

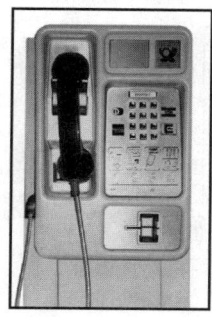

Germany

Calling Cards

Calling cards can be purchased in hotels, newsstands, and post offices. These telephones provide an efficient way to place telephone calls, both nationally and internationally.

Business Services

BUSINESS CENTERS

Berlin
Regus Business Centre GmbH; Unter den Linden 21, 10117 Berlin; tel: (30) 2092-4000; fax: (30) 2092-4000; email: berlin.lindencorso@regus.de.

Hamburg
HQ Hamburg; Sachsenfeld 2/4, Hansa Carree Bldg., 20097 Hamburg; tel: (40) 2350-5562; fax: (40) 2350-5566.

Frankfurt
Executive Office Center Frankfurt; Haus Hohenzollern, Düsseldorfer Str. 1-7, D-60329 Frankfurt am Main; tel: (69) 271-360; fax: (69) 2713-6200; email: service@eocf.de.

COURIER SERVICES

Berlin
Airborne Express; Atege- Airfreight Div., Quitzowstr. 11-17, 10559 Berlin; tel: (30) 397-3970.
Federal Express; tel: (30) 334-1051.
TNT; tel: (30) 823-5011.
United Parcel Service Berlin; Industriestraße 4-9, 12099 Berlin; tel: (0800) 882-6630.
United Parcel Service Berlin; Lengederstraße 17-19, 13407 Berlin; tel: (0800) 882-6630
United Parcel Service Berlin; Industriestraße 1, 15366 Dahlwitz-Hoppegarten; tel: (0800) 882- 6630.

Dusseldorf
Federal Express; tel: (211) 658-980.
TNT; tel: (211) 250-0513.
UPS Express Shop Düsseldorf; Berliner Allee 48, 40212 Düsseldorf; tel: (211) 836-640.

Frankfurt
DHL; tel: (69) 669-040.
Federal Express; tel: (69) 230-492.
TNT; tel: (69) 230-492.
UPS Express Shop Frankfurt; Gallusanlage 2-4, 60329 Frankfurt; tel: (069) 242-9260.

Hamburg
Courier Express; tel: (40) 677-0011.
Der Kurier; tel: (40) 291919.

DHL; tel: (40) 553-6011.
Federal Express; (40) 511-0041.
UPS Express Shop Hamburg; Georgsplatz 1, 20099 Hamburg; tel: (40) 325- 6870.

Munich
City Car; tel: (89) 555-444.
Centro Car; tel: (89) 770-077.
TNT; (89) 310-3301.
UPS Express Shop Munich; Brienner Straße 59, 80333 Munich; tel: (089) 549- 0720

Country Offices/Toll Free Numbers
DHL (country office); DHL WORLDWIDE EXPRESS GmbH; Monzastraße 2, D-63225 Langen; tel: 06103-76-560; fax 06103-765-6111
Federal Express; tel: 0130-7573.
UPS; tel: 0130-826630.

SECRETARIAL SERVICE

Berlin
Aktiver Buroservice; Mommsenstrasse 28, in Charlottenburg; tel: (30) 323-7588.
Aniger; Mommsenstrasse 19, in Charlottenburg; tel: (30) 323-8099.

Frankfurt
World Trade Center; tel: (335) 557-3000; fax: (335) 557-3003; email: info@wtcbb.de
website; http://www.wtcbb.de

TRANSLATION SERVICES

Berlin
AIIC Helen Ferguson; Forster Str. 51, 10999 Berlin; tel: (030) 618-4918.
International Association of Conference Center Interpreters, tel: (30) 392-6567.
Intertext; Greifswalder Strasse 5, in Prenzlauer Berg; tel: (30) 4210-1804.
I-Punkt; Schöngerrstrasse 35, 12621 Berlin; tel: (30) 563-9106; fax: (30) 563-9107.
Kern Sprachdienste; in Mitte; tel: (30) 2045-0903.
Profi Ubersetzungsdienst; Tauentzienstrasse 15, in Charlottenburg; tel: (30) 210-0080.
Thomas Unger Interface GmbH; conference interpreters; technical translators; tel: 0800-885-000; outside of Germany, tel: [49] 30-885-0000-0.
Trans-tech; Carstenn str. 43B; tel: (30) 817-3840; fax: (30) 817-7832.

Frankfurt
Büro Theilhaber; tel: (69) 635-5566.
World Trade Center; tel: (335) 557-3000; fax: (335) 557-3003; email: info@wtcbb.de
website; http://www.wtcbb.de; English, Polish, French, Russian, Swedish, Danish, Norwegian, German, Arabian (also with interpreters).

Hamburg
Alster-Sekretariat; tel: (40) 456475.
Technical Translation Service; tel: (40) 409409.

Munich
Eckert Übersetzungservice; tel: (89) 8566-3326; fax: (89) 8566-3327.
SD Translation Service; tel: (89) 290-15158.

CONVENTION ASSISTANCE

German Convention Bureau (GCB)

Münchener Str. 48, D-60329 Frankfurt/Main; tel: (69) 242-9300; fax: (69) 2429-3026; email: info@gcb.de

COMMERCIAL INFORMATION

Deutscher Industrie- und Handelstag (Association of German Chambers of Industry and Commerce); 148 Adenauerallee, 53113 Bonn; tel: (228) 1040; fax: (228) 104-158; website: http://www.ihk.de/diht

Federal Trade Information Office

tel: [49] (221) 205-7347; fax: [49] (221) 205-7212

Electrical

CURRENT

220 volts AC, 50Hz

ELECTRIC PLUGS

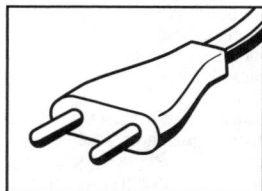

Plug adaptors are available through **iGo Corporation.** (See "Electrical and Telephone Adaptors" on page 19.)

Technical Support

HARDWARE/SOFTWARE VENDOR SUPPORT

Apple/Claris; tel: [49] (1) 803-5018; (in Switzerland) tel: [41] (800) 833-310; (in the U.K.) tel: [44] (990) 127-753; (in the U.S.) tel: [1] (800) 500-7078; http://www.apple.com/.

Compaq/Digital; tel: (89) 9933-0; fax: (89) 933-1158; tel: (130) 6868 (CompaqCare Center/Information); (0180) 521-2111 (Technical Support) tel: (89) 9933-1380 (QuickLine); (in Switzerland) tel: [41] (22) 709-5330; fax: [41] (22) 709-5391 (Geneva); tel: [41] (1) 801-2507; fax: [41] (1) 801-2172 (Zurich); (General U.S.) tel: (281) 518-2000; http://www.compaq.com/.

Corel; tel: (180) 425-8210 (TS Word Perfect-32 bit); (in the U.S.) tel: [1] (716) 871-2325 (Ask to be Forwarded to Appropriate Program); http://www.corel.com/.

Dell; tel: (61) 039-710; (Dell- Europe) tel: [44] (134) 474-8000; (in the U.S.) tel: [1] (512) 338-4400; fax: [1] (512) 728-3330; http://www.dell.com/.

Filemaker/Claris; tel: (180) 525-8166 (Info-line); fax: (180) 567-2233; tel: [49] (180) 523-6423; (in the U.S.) tel: [1] (800) 965-9090; http://www.claris.com/.

Gateway 2000; (in Ireland) tel: [353] (1) 797-2000; (in the U.S.) tel: [1] (605) 232-2191; fax: [1] (605) 232-2023; http://www.gateway2000.com/.

Hewlett Packard; tel: (0180) 5258-143; (in Switzerland) tel: [41] (22) 780-8111; (in the U.S.) tel: [1] (408) 246-4300; http://www.hp.com/.

IBM; (in Switzerland) tel: [41] (22) 310-0418 (in French); (in the U.S.) tel: [1] (919) 517-2800; (U.S. Main Office) tel: [1] 914-765-1900; http://www.ibm.com/

Microsoft; tel: (89) 31-760; fax: (89) 3176-1000; tel: (89) 3176-1199; tel: (89) 3176-1199 (information); (in Switzerland) tel: [41] (848) 858-868; fax [41] (1) 831-0869; (in the U.S.) [1] (425) 635-7222; http://www.microsoft.com/.

Toshiba; tel: (2131) 158-319; fax: (2131) 158-558; (in Switzerland) tel: [41] (1) 946-0777; fax: [41] (1) 946-0807; (in Ireland) tel: [44] (193) 282-8828; (in the U.S.) [1] (949) 583-3000 (Corporate Headquarters); http://www.toshiba.com/.

Internet Connection

HOW TO CONNECT

Connecting to AOL and Compuserve in Germany is similar to using it when traveling outside your own area code. See the introductory section for detailed information on connecting to your account through a different phone number.

America Online

Numbers are available at keyword *international*. Be sure to get several local numbers before leaving. AOL's Global-Net service charges US$3.95 an hour in addition to the usual charges. Go to keyword *access* (a free area) and download the software.

Access: National Access Number 01914; GSM (Cell) Access Number (0171) 41-914; GSM (Cell) Access Number 22144.

Compuserve

Numbers are available at *Go International*. The Compuserve Web-site also has a great deal of information, at http://www.compuserve.com.

Access: All cities 01910; Berlin (30) 691-000; Berlin (30) 690-820; Cologne (221) 240-6202; Dortmund (231) 446-1032; Dresden (351) 880-0000; Düsseldorf (211) 479-2424; Frankfurt (69) 7399-8611; Freiburg (761) 207-4724; Hamburg (40) 691-3666; Hannover (511) 724-2909; Karlsruhe (721) 859-818; Köln (221) 240-6202; Mannheim (621) 156-9000; Munich (89) 6655-9393; Nuremberg (911) 519-1500; Stuttgart (711) 226-1699; Tuebingen (707) 175-0424.

Independent Service Providers

Many independent service providers offer discounts if you are only in town for a couple of days.

AXIS information systems GmbH; tel: (9131) 691-350; fax: (9131) 691-349; email: info@axis.de; http://www.axis.de/.

Cable & Wireless ECRC GmbH; tel: (89) 926-990; fax: (89) 9269-9170; email: info@ecrc.de; http://www.ecrc.de/.

Ebner & Martin Informationssysteme GmbH; tel: (2131) 527-3930; fax: (2131) 5273-9387; email: info@arkaden.net; http://www.arkaden.net/

Interactive Networx GmbH; tel: (1801) 123-123; fax: (30) 2543-1289; email: info@snafu.de; http://www.inx.de/.

NCC GmbH; tel: (621) 126-050; fax: (621) 126-0533; email: info@ncc-mannheim.net; http://www.mannheim-netz.de/.

NetUSE Kommunikationstechnolog; tel: (431) 3864-

Germany

3500; fax: (431) 3864-3599; Info@NetUSE.DE; http://www.netuse.de/(in German).

SpaceNet GmbH; tel: (89) 323-560; fax: (89) 3235-6299; email: presse@Space.Net; http://www.space.net/ (in German).

Business Culture

GREETINGS AND COURTESIES

High standards of formality are the norm in German companies where titles and position are very important. Use professional titles, followed by professional degrees. For instance, the male director of a laboratory with a doctoral degree is addressed as "Herr Direktor Doktor..." even in social conversation. (Germans holding doctoral degrees and professorships have the titles made part of their legal name and must be addressed as such.)

Normally, you will be introduced to persons of high rank by a junior member. If many introductions are taking place, you need only shake hands with the senior colleague. A very firm handshake and direct eye contact leave a good impression. When meeting a German couple, shake hands with the wife first. All adult women are addressed as "Frau" as the word "Fräulein" for unmarried women has fallen into disfavor.

Though English is widely spoken in the west, German is the language of business when on German turf. Do not assume English will be spoken, as this assumption offends Germans. They are not quite as sensitive as the French, but Germans are concerned that so few people worldwide are learning German. Ask, prior to meetings, if English is acceptable, and prepare accordingly, bringing a translator if necessary. East Germans may also speak Polish or Russian.

Gift-giving is not a standard business practice. In fact, the exchange of business gifts is subject to German laws. A small gift representing your country or company is allowable (less than US $60), and all goods given or exchanged must be marked by your company name and logo.

The Germans are avid greeting card senders and conscientious correspondents. Remembering someone's birthday or a special occasion in the form of a card is greatly appreciated. In business as well as social situations, always be punctual. Germans gauge a good amount of your character on punctuality and adherence to schedules.

Note: In Germany, a person's office is considered personal space. A visitor must knock on the door ("open-door policies" do not exist) and wait to be invited in by the occupant. If you do not get a response to the knock, it does not mean the office is unoccupied; it may only mean that the occupant has no desire to interrupt what they are doing to speak with anyone. Low-level bureaucrats use this ploy to an annoying extent.

BUSINESS ETHIC & FRAMEWORK

By European standards, Germany has efficient methods for transacting business. They are very attentive to details and honest in their dealings. Unions have a great deal of input into corporate decisions, so work rules are very stringent.

Contracts are adhered to very strictly. Germany has rules for every aspect of life and there is usually an accompanying form to fill out. Visitors from more flexible business cultures will find this burdensome, but it does bring a certain order to the many layers of management found in German companies.

Germans take their leisure time very seriously, and, unlike Americans, do not define themselves by their occupations. Management personnel work eight-hour days and weekend work is uncommon. Sunday is sacrosanct in this Christian nation, but inroads are being made to have Sunday shopping.

Germans have some of the longest vacation periods in the world and they use every day of them. (Even entry-level people can receive 5 weeks of paid vacation.) For the most part, when German managers are on vacation they are incommunicado. August and September are prime months for vacations with long ski holidays thrown in during winter. Germans do work hard and play hard but the hierarchical nature of their management teams often makes it difficult to get information when key personnel are on holiday.

DECISION MAKING

Within German corporations, many departments will make a decision by consensus. Decisions involving new projects or large amounts of money must be made by a top-level management board. Hierarchy rules the process. Individuals do not make independent decisions but can make strong recommendations.

Germans don't like to be pushed for a decision, and too much pressure can jeopardize success. While it is a developed economy, German business does not move at the breakneck pace of the Americans or the British. When buying, the Germans deliberate and discuss every detail. Patience will be required. When selling, the Germans like to pour on the technical data—for which they have tremendous regard—and they expect the buyer to absorb it with equal relish. Decisions in Germany are never made at the "big picture" level.

Note: There are normally at least two signatures appended to German contract agreements. Take care to note precisely who can authorize or decide upon specific matters. Some German executives have binding power, while some have authority to commit the firm in specific areas only.

MEETINGS

German business people are courteous but few will find them overly social during meetings. They are precise, direct, and to-the-point—so, few pleasantries will precede the business at hand. After greetings and rather stiff handshakes, cards will be exchanged. Business cards should note company name, job title, academic degrees, and all relevant contact information. If visiting in Germany, have the cards translated in advance as this will greatly impress the language-conscious Germans.

Do not sit until the German host invites you to do so. If selling, be thoroughly prepared with facts and information regarding your product, business, and industry. Be well informed about competitors in your field. It is guaranteed your German counterparts will be highly knowledgeable and will use their own information to question you. The Germans love statistics and technical data and will expect to be quizzed when they are in a selling mode.

Beverages will be offered but no alcohol is consumed at German office meetings. Meetings are run on a strict agenda, which may even include a pre-set time for ending the meeting. Each attendee will receive a copy of the agenda in advance, if possible, as the Germans do not like surprises or impromptu presentations. As a rule, the Germans like to prepare thoroughly for meetings and are not very good at thinking on their feet. Foreign buyers may use this attribute to their advantage by straying from the agenda to "flat foot" their counterparts. Visiting sellers will just have to get with the program.

Note: The Germans are a highly educated and intelligent people but their education and social system is bent towards rote memorization and closely controlled order. Meetings in Germany are designed to proceed in a linear path with a predictable outcome. Visitors (especially buyers) can decide if this pre-programmed method serves their own interests or not.

WOMEN IN BUSINESS

Over 40 percent of the German work force is female, but the percentage is much lower in the top echelons of corporate management. Women fare much better in legislative posts. German women in management operate with much the same matter-of-fact, competent manner in business as their male counterparts. However, while scrupulously polite to foreign businesswomen, German men usually do not take them as seriously as they do male counterparts. However, a conscientious, well-prepared presentation will receive the attention and respect it deserves, especially if it is technically oriented.

BUSINESS ENTERTAINING

For all of their stiffness in the business setting, the Germans do like to loosen up and socialize outside of the office. Business luncheons will often include wine or beer but overindulgence is frowned upon at all times. Food in Germany is quite heavy and vegetarians may find themselves at a loss. Asian visitors, especially, will find the portions unwieldy and the predominance of meat and potatoes staggering. The Germans are proud of their cuisine and each region has a specialty. Visitors wishing to ingratiate themselves should pay high compliments to the food preparation.Those visitors with dietary requirements should make them known in advance.

Major cities in Germany have many restaurant cuisines available for choice if visitors wish to reciprocate their German host's hospitality. Germans are a well-traveled lot and are usually willing to experiment with new foods.

The Germans tend to eat a big midday meal and a lighter meal in early evening, so business dinners are not that common. More likely at night, business associates will get together for some marathon beer tasting and socializing. Teetotalers will have a long night and visiting drinkers should pace themselves. Germans pride themselves in both their beer and the ability to consume it without showing the effects to any great degree. After a few beers are downed, discussions can go anywhere. The Germans are well informed and have an opinion about everything. Visitors should note that while the Germans are highly critical of other societies, they are very defensive about their own. Visiting sellers should be particularly careful to avoid any criticism of Germany, past or present. Only Germans can criticize Germany.

Note: Like many continental European societies, the smoking of cigarettes is still popular. Most restaurants and all bars are smoke filled. Smoking in the office is common, especially in eastern Germany. Social situations will most always involve some members of the group smoking. Visitors that are really annoyed should be discreet in their criticisms — especially sellers.

BUSINESS ATTIRE

For men, a conservative dark or gray suit, white shirt, and subdued tie serve best. Bowties are common in corporate offices but must be hand tied to pass muster. For women in management, well-tailored suits and dresses are standard. Visitors may find that German women dress a little less conservatively for the office than British or American counterparts. This is neither a provocation nor invitation for comment. It is simply an accepted style choice.

Although Germans take pride in smart and fashionable appearance, they also tend to embrace natural elements. Some of the more high-tech German companies have adopted the American "corporate casual" look, but neatness still rules in this environment.

Note: Keep jewelry to a minimum and make sure it is top quality. Leave the cheap watch at home. The same goes for pens. Writing instruments have a cult-like following in Germany, so bring along a good pen for business meetings. It will be noticed and noted.

Business Centers
Berlin

CITY VIEW

Once again the cultural and official political capital of Germany, many say that Berlin never really lost its title, even during Germany's divided days. An already large and diverse city has now become even grander with the re-addition of its eastern half; majestically designed buildings that have been renovated and reconstructed, surrounded by wide avenues signifying past pomp and ceremony have restored the facade of Berlin to much of its former glory. However, the question still remains how well the internal framework will formulate itself as old-age East meets the modern West. The initial excitement of reunification long worn off, Berlin faces continued construction frenzy with a national government that relocated from Bonn in 1999 coupled with perilous financial and political hazards in trying to get its eastern side up to speed. To compensate for the added draw of visitors eager to see the revitalized Berlin, new hotels have sprung up and old ones have been magnificently renovated. But, never only concentrating on business, Berlin also offers a myriad of cultural, historical, and natural sights along with a very diverse population. A city of many lakes and splendid parks, the capital of Germany gives visitors and inhabitants something of everything. As the Berliner saying goes, "Berlin tut gut." (Berlin does a person well). Except for the harrowing traffic that has arisen with the now twice-as-large capital, the city's residents can well be proud of their historical and international gem.

AIRPORT

Tegel Airport to City Center

Located 5 miles (k.m.) northwest from Berlin's center, one can catch a 20- to 25-minute cab ride for about DM25 to the center of town. Otherwise, bus #109 circles between the arrivals terminal and downtown (along Kurfürstendamm to the Berlin Zoo train station) in 10 to 15-minute intervals. The fare will cost a budget-welcoming DM3.80 for the 30-minute ride. The bus travels along Kurfürstendamm to Bahnhof Zoo rail station. From there, travelers can catch the subway (U-bahn) to other destinations.

Airline Numbers

Lufthansa	(30) 887588
Air Canada	(30) 8825879
American Airlines	(130) 4114
British Airways (toll free)	(130) 3636
TWA	(30) 882-7096
United Airlines	(30) 6616

HOTELS

Top End

Bristol Hotel Kempinski; Kurfürstendamm 27, Berlin 10719; tel: (30) 884-340; fax: (30) 883-6075; 315 rooms; 44 suites; city center; restaurants; conference rooms; business center; in-room cable tv, minibar, data ports; laundry/dry cleaning; car rental; valet, room service; security; currency exchange; shopping arcade; beauty salon; newsstand; parking; corporate rates; fitness center; spa; solarium, steam room; massage; indoor pool; DM 330/390.

Germany

Germany

Grand Hyatt Berlin; Marlene-Dietrich-Platz 2, Potsdamerplatz, D-10785; tel: (30) 2553-1234; fax: (30) 2553-1235; 340 rooms; opened 1998; restaurants; 9 function rooms (up to 850); communications center with secretarial service; fax machine on request; dataport; internet; voicemail; in-room safe; garage; Regency Club floor; rooftop fitness club; steam bath; sauna; solarium; massage; beauty center; indoor pool; whirlpool; terrace.

Inter-Continental Berlin; Budapester Strasse 2, Tiergarten, 10787; tel: (30) 26-020; fax: (30) 2602-2600; email: berlin@interconti.com; 443 rooms, 67 suites; 132 non-smoking rooms; city center, near Kurfurstendamm; restaurants; business center; conference center, 31 function rooms; secretarial service; in-room satellite tv, movies, video, 2-line telephones, voicemail, modem connection, minibar, safe, trouser press; business rooms with fax machine, pc/printer, mobile phone, internet and email access; laundry/valet service; 24-hour front desk/ room service; concierge; beauty salon; shops; sauna; pool; jacuzzi; beauty spa; shops; flower shop; garage; valet parking; bike rental; fitness club; pool; DM345/395.

Expensive

Berlin Hilton; Mohrenstrasse 30, D-10117; tel: (30 202-30; fax: (30) 2023-4269; toll-free in U.S.: 1-800-774-1500; 500 rooms; located on Platz der Akademie; constructed in 1991; restaurants, taverns, bars; conference center (up to 500) with modem connection, ISDN lines; executive services; secretarial service; translation service; rental offices; some rooms with kitchenette and balcony; non-smoking rooms; 24-hour room service; laundry/ironing service; hairdresser; corporate rates; fitness; massage; sauna; solarium; pool; whirlpool; squash; bowling alley; disco; DM 310/350.

Park Consul; Alt-Moabit 86a, Tiergarten; tel: (30) 390-780; fax: (30) 3907-8900; email: pcberlin@consul-hotels.com; business facilities; high-security locks; in-room shower/wc, hairdryer, minibar, ISDN lines, radio, cable tv; nearby fitness center.

Steigenberger Berlin - an SRS Hotel; Los-Angeles-Platz 1, Berlin, D-10789; tel: (30) 2127-0; email: SteigenbergerBerlin@compuserve.com; near Kurfurstendamm; restaurant; bierstube; meeting facilities; secretarial service; translation service; in-room cable tv, in-house movies, IDD telephone, minibar, a/c, hairdryer, modem connection, safe deposit box; Executive Club; ironing, and shoeshine on arrival; 24-hour front desk; barber/beauty services; laundry/dry cleaning; room service; valet parking; sauna; massage; indoor pool.

Moderate

Arco Hotel; Geisbergstrasse 30, 10777 Berlin; tel: (30) 235-1480; fax: (30) 2147-5178; email: arco-hotel@t-online.de; web: http://www.arco-hotel.deturn-of-the-century hotel; most rooms with bathroom; in-room satellite tv, safe, telephone; parking; garden.

Berlin Excelsior Hotel; Hardenbergstrasse 14, D-10623 Berlin tel: (30) 31550; fax: (30) 3155-1002; located in financial district; 320 rooms, junior suites, and penthouse suite; restaurant; meeting facilities (up to 120); in-room bathrooms, a/c, minibar, cable tv, safe, hair dryer.

Berlin Mark Hotel (Golden Tulip Hotels); Meinekestraße 18-19, 10719 Berlin; tel: (30) 880-020; fax: (30) 8800-2804; 231 rooms; restaurant; complimentary breakfast; in-room cable tv, minibar; 14 rooms remodeled for business with fax connections and work space.

Econtel; Sömmeringstrasse 24-26, Charlottenburg, D-10589; tel: (30) 846-810; fax: (30) 3468-1163; 205 rooms; located between Tegel Airport and city center; restaurant; bar; breakfast buffet; in-room shower/WC, color tv, telephone, safe; no-smoking rooms available; conference

center; corporate rates.

Hotel Alt-Tempelhof; Luise-Henriette-Strasse 4, Tempelhof; tel: (30) 75-6850; fax: (30) 7568-5100; 53 rooms; 2 conference rooms (up to 25); in-room fax/modem connection, bathroom, direct dial phone, cable tv, hairdryer, minibar, fruit basket; garage parking (DM20).

Scanhotel Castor; Fuggerstr 8 / Ecke Kalckreuthstr, D-10777 Berlin; tel: (30) 213-030; fax: (30) 2130-3160; 78 rooms; buffet breakfast; bar; small meeting room; in-room bathroom, telephone, cable tv, radio, minibar, hairdryer, direct dial phone; non-smoking rooms.

MEDICAL CARE

Elizabeth Hospital; Lützowstr. 24; tel: 25061.
Charité-Krankenhaus; Schumannstrasse 20-21, Berlin;(30) 28-020.

HEALTH CLUB

Bad am Spreewaldplatz; Wiener Strasse 59, Kreuzberg, Berlin; tel: (30) 612-7057.

Dörbrandt; Kurfürstendamm 182-183; tel: (30) 882-6301.

Fit Fun; Uhlandstr. 194; tel: (30) 312-5982.

Nautilus Fitness Center; Brabanterstr. 18; (30) tel: 822-9175.

Sport- und Erholungszentrum (SEZ); Landsberger Allee 77, Friedrichshain, Berlin; tel: (30) 421- 820.

Sportscenter Gerstenberger; 19-21 Koernerstrasse; tel: (30) 261-29-37.

Vitality Pool & Fitness Club; Inter-Continental Hotel, Budapester Strasse 2, Tiergarten, D-10787; whirlpool, saunas, fitness equipment and solarium.

CHAMBER OF COMMERCE

Berlin Chamber of Commerce
Fasanenstrasse 85
D-10623 Berlin
tel: (30) 315-100; fax: (30) 315-103
email: service@berlin.ihk.de

WORLD TRADE CENTER

World Trade Center Berlin
c/o Philipp Holzmann AG
Heerstrabe 16
14052 Berlin, Germany
tel: (30) 300-620; fax: (30) 3006-2148

Frankfurt

CITY VIEW

Lying in the geographical center of Western Germany, Frankfurt stands as a vast industrial city and transportation hub. Frankfurt airport is one of the busiest in the world. Although not much for the aesthetic eye to rave about, much of Germany's business takes place in Frankfurt, which also plays host to many international conventions, for which its massive exposition grounds were built. A fairly temperate climate helps enhance the industrial city.

AIRPORT

Frankfurt-Main Airport to City Center

The airport lies seven miles (12 km.) from the city center. Downstairs, inside Terminal 1, passengers can catch an S-bahn to the *Hauptbahnhof* (main train station) in the center of town. The trip will cost about DM5.50 for a 10-minute ride. You may purchase a ticket from the machines or at a ticket window. Intercity and ICE trains also stop at

Frankfurt airport for passengers going to other parts of Germany. If you prefer door-to-door service, catch a cab outside the arrivals area for a fare of about DM40. The voyage into town can last anywhere from 20 to 40 minutes depending on traffic.

Airline Numbers

Lufthansa	(69) 230621
Air Canada	(69) 250131
American Airlines	
Frankfurt	(69) 230591
toll free	(130) 4114
British Airways	
Frankfurt	(69) 250121
toll free	(130) 3636
Continental Airlines	(69) 757475
Delta Airlines	(69) 664-1212
Northwest	(69) 666-6611
TWA	(69) 770601
United Airlines	(69) 605020
USAir	
Frankfurt	(69) 670-8041
toll free	(130) 3375

HOTELS

Top End

Frankfurt Marriott Hotel; Hamburger Allee 2, D-60486 Frankfurt; tel: (69) 79-550; fax: (69) 7955-2432; opposite exhibition grounds; restaurant; 62 business rooms; 10 meeting rooms; secretarial service; business services; in-room data ports, voicemail; sauna; massage; solarium; whirlpool.

Hessischer Hof; Friedreich-Ebert-Anlage 40; tel: (69) 75-400; fax; (69) 754-0924; near exhibition grounds; restaurant; conference facilities; secretarial service; in-room modem/fax connection; corporate rates; fitness room.

Inter-Continental Frankfurt; Wilhelm-Leuschner-Strasse 43; tel: (69) 26-050; fax: (69) 252-467; email: frankfurt@interconti.com; ask for special rates; restaurant; business center; internet access; executive room; secure parking; conference facilities; secretarial service; in-room modem/fax connections; corporate rates; fitness; sauna; pool; whirlpool.

Kempinsky Hotel; Bunsstrasse 459; tel: 6102-5050; fax: 6102-505-445; located in park; restaurant; business center; 19 conference/banquet rooms; complimentary limousine transfer to airport; no-smoking rooms; fitness; sauna; massage; indoor/outdoor pools;

Sheraton Arabella Grand; Konrad-Adenauer; Strasse 7; tel: (69) 29-810; fax: (69) 298-1810; http://www.sheraton.com; restaurant; conference facilities; secretarial service; corporate rates; fitness; sauna; pool; whirlpool.

Steigenberger Frankfurter Hof; Am Kaiserplatz; tel: (650) 372-1700; located in Frankfurt Center/financial district; restaurants; meeting and banquet rooms; business center; barber/beauty salons; fitness center/gym.

Expensive

Am Zoo; Alfred-Brehm-Platz 6, D-601316 Frankfurt; tel: (69) 49-07-71; fax: (69) 43-98-68.

Arabella Congress Hotel; Lyoner Str. 44-48; tel: (69) 66-330; fax: (69) 663-3666; conference/banquet rooms; sauna; pool; tennis.

Astron Frankfurt Airport; Mörfelderstrasse 113; email: Fra-airport@astron-hotels.de; restaurant; meeting facilities; internet available; in-room modem/fax

connection; corporate rates; fitness; sauna.

Astron Hotel - Die Villa; Emil-Sulzbach-Strasse 14-16; tel: (69) 979-9070; fax: (69) 9799-0711; email: fra-city@astron-hotels.de; adjacent exhibition grounds; breakfast room; parking.

Continental; Baselerstrasse 56, D-60329, Frankfurt; tel: (69) 23-03-41; fax: (69) 23-29-14.

Holiday Inn Frankfurt-Main-Taunus; Am Main-Taunus-Zentrum 1; tel: (6196) 76-30; fax: (6196) 72-996; 15 minutes from exhibition grounds; 3 restaurants; beer garden; seminar, banquet, meeting rooms (up to 350); business rooms available with in-room modem/fax connections; business center services for meetings; gift shop.

Lindner Congress Hotel; Bolongarostrasse 90; tel: (69) 330-0200; fax: (69) 3300-2999; restaurant; bistro; banquet and conference rooms; voicemail; in-room modem/fax connection; internet access; wellness center; sauna; solarium;

Mercure Frankfurt; Voltastrasse 29; tel: (69) 79-260; fax: (69) 7926-1606; near exhibition grounds; restaurant; conference facilities; secretarial service; corporate rates; fitness; sauna; whirlpool.

Novotel Frankfurt-City West; Lise-Meitner-Strasse 2; tel: (69) 79-3030; fax: (69) 7930-3930; city center; near exhibition grounds; restaurant; 13 meeting rooms; secretarial staff; translation/interpreting; videoconferencing; sauna; solarium; whirlpool.

Mozart; Parkstrasse 17, D-60322 Frankfurt; tel: (69) 55-08-31; fax: (69) 596-45-59.

Moderate

Best Western National; Baselerstrasse 50, D-60329 Frankfurt; tel: (69) 27-39-40; fax: (69) 23-44-60; 100 meters to railway; restaurant; conference facilities; secretarial service.

Corona Hotel; Hamburger Allee 48, D-60486 Frankfurt; tel: (69) 77-90-77; fax: (69) 70-86-39.

Florentina; Westendstrasse 23, D-60325 Frankfurt; tel: (69) 74-60-44; fax: (69) 74-79-24.

Palmenhot; Bockenheimer Landstrasse 89-91; tel: (69) 753-0060; fax: (69) 7530-0666; restaurant; secretarial service; in-room modem/fax connections; corporate rates.

Ramada Hotelgarni Nordwest Zentrum; Walter-Möller-Platz; tel: (69) 580-930; fax: (69) 582-447; meeting room; secretarial service; in-room modem/fax connection; corporate rates; fitness; sauna; pool; whirlpool.

Schwille; Grosse Bockenhelmerstrasse 50, D-60313 Frankfurt; tel: (69) 92-01-00; fax: (69) 920-10-999.

MEDICAL CARE

Holy Spirit Hospital; Langestr. 4-6; tel: 21961.

Red Cross Hospital; Eschenheimer Anlage 1-5; tel: 40330.

Sachsenhausen Hospital; Schifferstr. 10; tel: 60591.

WORLD TRADE CENTER

World Trade Center Frankfurt (Oder) GmbH
Im Technologiepark 1
15236 Frankfurt (Oder)
tel: (335) 557-3000; fax: (335) 557-3003
email: info@wtcbb.de
website: http://www.wtcbb.de

Germany

Greece

Greece

At a Glance

THE PEOPLE

Population .... 10,707,135 (July 1999 est.)
Growth Rate .... 0.41% (1999 est.)
Life Expectancy .... 78.43 years (born 1999)
Infant Mortality ... 7.13 deaths/1,000 live births (1999 est.)

Ethnic Composition

Greek..98%
Other 2%

Religious Composition

Greek Orthodox...97%
Muslim 1.3%
Other 0.7%

Languages Spoken

Greek (official), English, French

Education and Literacy

Education is compulsory for nine years. The current literacy rate is 95 percent nationwide.

Labor Force

Total: 4,210,000
By occupation: services 52%, agriculture 23%, industry 25%

THE ECONOMY

Greece is one of the poorer members of the E.U. and it has yet been able to accept the euro as its currency. Most of the ancient nation's foreign currency inflows come from tourism along with aid from other E.U. members. The government controls more than 50 public enterprises, including the most prominent social insurance funds and nearly three-quarters of the banking industry. A change in accounting methodology during 1994 yielded a 20 percent "increase" in GDP, but this artificial increase has had little real impact. To its credit, Greece has made great strides in infrastructure development, particularly in transportation and communications. The government has adopted strict monetary controls and a frugal fiscal policy to help stem inflation. These measure were not popular but were deemed necessary if Greece was to attain full EU membership (and euro acceptance) by 2001. Foreign investment has been eager to gain footholds in Greece, but most are awaiting the results of the governmental austerity and privatization programs.

Exports .... US$12.4 billion (f.o.b., 1998)
Imports .... US$27.7 billion (c.i.f., 1998)
Total GDP .... US$143 billion (1998 est.)
GDP Per Capita .... US$13,400 (1998 est.)
Unemployment .... 10 percent (1998 est.)
Inflation Rate .... 3.9% (1998 est.)

Top Export Partners

E.U., United States

Top Import Partners

E.U., United States

Top Exports

Manufactured goods, foodstuffs, fuels

Top Imports

Technology, consumer goods, foodstuffs, fuels

BUSINESS WORKWEEK

Offices

Monday to Friday 8a.m. to 1:30p.m. and 4:30p.m. to 7:30p.m., Saturday 8a.m. to 1:30p.m.

Banks

Monday to Thursday 8a.m. to 2p.m., Friday until 1p.m. Many banks stay open afternoons and evenings during tourist season to handle currency exchange.

Government

Monday to Friday 7:30a.m. to 3p.m. (May to September); 8a.m. to 3:30p.m. (October to May)

Retail

Tuesday, Southward, Friday 8:30a.m. to 1:30p.m. and 5:30p.m. to 8:30p.m.; Monday, Wednesday, Saturday 8:30a.m. to 2:30p.m.

Note: Midday breaks vary in length and start time based on local custom and seasonal needs. Many shops have evening hours all week.

HOLIDAYS

New Year's Day..January 1
Epiphany ....January 6
Clean Monday ....February 22*
Independence Day .... March 25
Greek Orthodox Easter ....April 9-12*
Labor Day..May 1
Whit Monday .... May 31*
Assumption..August 15
Ochi Day, 1940 Greek
defiance of Italy ....October 28
Christmas ....December 25-26

*Date may vary by year.

CLIMATE

Seasons

The Mediterranean climate in Greece is pleasant and sunny most of the year. The rainy season is from November to March. In general, winters are mild and wet; summers are hot and dry.

Regions

Warm weather prevails in the south with summertime temperatures in Athens rising above 38˚C (100˚F) in August and September. The north of the country is colder but still mild in the winter, and the islands have moderate winters and extremely hot summers. Nationwide, winter temperature averages 10˚C (50˚F).

Money & Banking

Currency

The currency of Greece is the Drachma (Dr).

Denominations

The Drachma comes in coin denominations of Dr100, 50, 20, 10, 5, 2, and 1 and banknotes of Dr100, 500, 1,000, 5,000, and 10,000.

Traveler's Checks and Credit Cards

Traveler's checks and currency, preferably in U.S. dollars or sterling, can be exchanged at all banks, exchange shops, post offices, hotels, and international airports. The

Greece

Region Names			
1	vros	27	Kefallin a
2	Rodh pi	28	Z kinthos
3	X nthi	29	Fthi tis
4	Dr ma	30	Evritan a
5	S rrai	31	Aitol a Kai
6	Kilk s		Akarnania
7	P lla	32	Fok s
8	Fl rina	33	Voiot a
9	Kastor a	34	vvoia
10	Greven	35	Attik
11	Koz ni	36	Argol s
12	Imath a	37	Korinth a
13	Thessalon ki	38	Akha a
14	Kav la	39	Il a
15	Khalkidhik	40	Messin a
16	Pier a	41	Arkadh a
17	Io nnina	42	Lakon a
18	Thesprot a	43	Khani
19	Pr veza	44	Reth mni
20	rta	45	Ir klion
21	L risa	46	Las thi
22	Tr kala	47	
23	Kardh tsa	48	S mos
24	Magnis a	49	Kikl dhes
25	K rkira	50	Kh os
26	Levk s	51	L svos

lowest commission fees are found at banks. There is no black market in drachma exchange. Keep all receipts of exchange for reconversion at departure.

American Express, Visa, Diner's Club, Eurocard, JCB, and MasterCard are accepted in selected places in more urban Greece. Most businesses still deal with cash. ATMs can be found in major urban areas for use in getting cash or cash advances on credit cards. ATMs will not be found in small towns. The best exchange rates are given for credit card and ATM transactions.

Travel

VISA AND PASSPORT

Travelers must be in possession of a passport that is valid for at least six months beyond their anticipated exit date. Exempted from this requirement are E.U. nationals who have a national ID card and sufficient funds to cover the length of their stay, and nationals of Switzerland and Monaco who also have national ID cards.

Greece is a member of the Schengen group, which is a collection of European nations who in March of 1995 de-clared themselves borderless. Any traveler who holds a valid passport or other travel documents that are recognized by all Schengen member nations need not have a visa to travel in any of these countries. There are two caveats, however:

- If you have tickets for onward travel to a nation that does require a visa of you, it may also be required of you for entry into the Schengen nation.

- Each Schengen nation retains the right to require a visa of any national normally exempted by the group as a whole.

If you are from one of the following countries, then you need not apply for a visa (E.U. nationals are automatically exempt):

- Nationals of Andorra, Argentina, Australia, Bolivia, Canada, Chile, Croatia, Cyprus, Czech Republic, Ecuador, Honduras, Hungary, Iceland, Israel, Japan, Korea (Rep. of), Latvia, Liechtenstein, Lithuania, Malaysia, Malta, Mexico, Monaco, New Zealand, Nicaragua, Norway, Panama, Paraguay, Poland, St. Kitts & Nevis, San Marino, Singapore, Slovak Republic, South Africa, Switzerland, U.K., U.S., and Vatican City for stays of a maximum of three months

- Nationals of Uruguay, Brazil, and El Salvador for maximum stays of two months
- Singapore nationals for a period of two weeks maximum
- Passengers in transit who do not leave the airport and are continuing their journey within forty-eight hours, and who are holding confirmed tickets and other documents for onward travel, are also exempt from the need for a visa, except for nationals of Angola, Bangladesh, Congo (Rep. of), Eritrea, Ethiopia, Ghana, India, Iran, Iraq, Nigeria, Pakistan, Somalia, Sri Lanka, Sudan, Syria and Turkey. If you are a citizen of any of these countries, you must always have a visa with you, even if you are just transiting via the same aircraft.

If you apply, you will be issued one of two different Schengen-standardized visas:

- Short Stay (Tourist and Business) - single and multiple entry. This visa is good for up to three months per entry, and valid if used within six months of issuance.
- Transit (and Airport Transit) - single and double entry. This is good for five days per entry.

Visas cannot be extended, and must be applied for anew each time. Allow about five days for processing of application. Business applicants must append a letter of reference from their employer.

DEPARTURE FORMALITIES

All travelers must declare any amount exceeding the equivalent of US$1,000 upon departure. Antiquities taken out of Greece without appropriate authorization from the Archaeological Service in Athens can result in prosecution, fines, and a possible jail sentence. Permission must be granted well in advance of departure.

There is an airport departure tax of Dr6,000 included in the price of the airline ticket.

CUSTOMS ENTRY (PERSONAL)

Duty-free

The particulars of this information may be changed by the Government at any time. You may wish to check with Greek customs officials just before you travel for latest updates.

Passengers from EU countries with duty-paid goods:

- Tobacco: 400 cigarettes or 1400 cigarillos or 200 cigars, or 1kg of tobacco
- Alcohol: 90 liters of wine (including up to 60 liters of sparkling wine); 10 liters of spirits; 20 liters of intermediate products (i.e. fortified wine); 110 liters of beer.

Note: Although there are no legal limits imposed on importing duty-paid tobacco and alcoholic products between E.U. countries, customs officials may question travelers if they exceed the above amounts and may ask them to prove that the goods are for personal use only.

Passengers from other countries, or from EU countries with goods bought duty-free:

- Tobacco: 200 cigarettes or 50 cigars or 100 cigarillos or 250g of tobacco
- Alcohol: 1 liter of alcoholic beverage over 22% or 2 liters of wine
- Perfume: 50g of perfume and 250ml of eau de cologne
- Food: 500g of coffee or 200g of coffee extract; 100g of tea or 40g of tea extract
- Other: gifts up to a total value of Dr25,000

Note: The tobacco and alcoholic allowances listed above are not available to passengers under the age of 18.

Prohibited or Restricted

- Plants with soil
- One windsurfboard per person may be imported/exported duty-free, if registered in the passport on arrival.

- The export of antiquities is prohibited without the express permission of the Archaeological Service in Athens. Those who ignore this will be prosecuted.

IMMUNIZATION

No inoculations are required for entry to Greece unless visitors are arriving within six days of leaving areas infected with yellow fever.

TIPPING

Taxi

A tip is not expected but rounding up the bill is appreciated.

Porters

Porters: 150 drachma per piece of luggage.

Hotels

A service charge is included in most hotel bills. In its absence, 10 percent is the standard tip.

Restaurants

A 15 service charge is included in most restaurant and nightclub bills.

Other

Barbers, beauticians: 10 percent. Stewards: 400 drachma per day.

EMERGENCY INFORMATION

Police and Crime

Though Greece has the lowest crime rate in Western Europe, take basic precautions against petty crime. Most of the crimes committed against tourists are by other visitors. Foreign business visitors are often the target of thieves. Consequently, purses, laptops, and briefcases will require additional security. Do not leave valuables in cars or on tables in cafés. Keep non-essential valuables locked in hotel safes when not in use. Avoid flashy displays of wealth, and dress and behave conservatively. Use credit cards and travel checks when possible to avoid carrying large sums of cash. Walk with your bag away from the street to avoid having it snatched away by thieves passing by on motorbikes. **Note**: Greece is a very "male-oriented society", so, women business travelers should dress modestly and try not to travel alone, especially in the evening.

Emergency Numbers

Police	100
Tourist Police	171
All-Night Weekend Pharmacy	107
Doctors on Duty	105
Emergency Red Cross Ambulance	150
Emergency IKA Ambulance	646-7811
Fire	199
Emergency Hospitals/Clinics	106
Red Cross Blood Bank	821-9391
Road Assistance (car breakdown)	104
Road Assistance (express service)	154

Health

There are no serious health risks in Greece. Tap water is safe, but do not drink well water: Bottled water is widely available. Try to avoid uncooked meat and sea food. Sanitation is of a reasonable standard, but carry disinfectants in more rural areas and on the islands. Air pollution is high in Athens, which can lead to respiratory problems. Guard against heat stroke and sunburn during summer months even while working in the cities.

Medical care is adequate and a visit to a general practitioner may indeed cost you nothing. Medicines at pharmacies are inexpensive by European standards. Your hotel will have access to a list of reputable doctors. Carry a well-stocked medical kit if you are planning extensive work in the islands or rural areas. Travel insurance is also recommended for work in these areas.

For more information on medical centers, including phone numbers, please see the "Business Centers" section at the end of this chapter.

INTERNAL TRAVEL

AIR

Olympic Airways offers domestic service connecting a vast assemblage of cities and islands for roughly three times the standard ferry rate. At the international airport, Olympic has a terminal of its own and for domestic purposes is known as Athens West. Many flights are offered, with the following cities as main hubs: Athens, Rhodes, Chios, Heraklion, Karpathos, Kefaloniá, Kos, Mykonos, and Thessalonika.

TAXI

You can either hail a cab on the streets or reserve one by telephoning a local taxi company, incurring a small surcharge for the service. Fares are very reasonable, although there is an extra charge to travel to and from the airport or train/bus station. Make certain that the meter is running from the moment the ride begins. Check to see if the number '1' registers in one of the four corners of the face of the meter, which signifies the base fare. Fares carry an additional charge between 12a.m. and 5a.m., and also for trips to out-of-district locations, when you will then see the number '2'. Drivers also charge extra for each piece of luggage. Have directions written on paper and carry maps until you are oriented. Taxis run on a "per-share" basis, so the driver may pick up additional passengers.

AUTO

Greece's road network is good, overall, covering about 116,150km (72,174 miles), mostly paved. Auto rentals are available in all major Greek cities, with all the world's auto rental agencies at your service. This can be an expensive proposition, though, especially after figuring in the mandatory insurance. A credit card and valid driver's license are also required.

E.U. nationals may bring a car, motorcycle, caravan, boat, or trailer into Greece for a term of six months, easily extended to 15 months.

Roadside assistance for motorists is available from the ELPA (Greek/Hellenic National Tourism Organization), 2-4 Messogion Street, 115 27 Athens. tel: (1) 778 6642; fax: (1) 779 1619.

There are competent mechanics in most towns, and gasoline is easily found.

Driving in Greek cities is "intense", and it is not advisable for novice visitors. Urban public transport proves more than adequate for business use. In rural areas, rental cars may be a necessity (though still expensive). Most rental agencies have a minimum age of 23 for drivers.

TRAIN

Daily service exists to all major cities and ports. The two primary railway stations, both in Athens, are Peloponnissos (with trains to the Peloponnese) and Larissa (with trains to northern Greece, Evia and Europe). You can get tickets and train information from the Hellenic Railways Organization (OSE), 1 Karolou Street, 104 37 Athens, or at 6 Sina Street, Athens. tel: (1) 529-7865; fax: 524-4156. Recorded rail information is accessible at: tel: (1) 145-147.

Heading north, regular daily trains run from Athens to Thessaloniki, Thebes, Livadia, Paleofarsala, Larissa, Plati,

Edessa, Florina, Seres, Drama, Komotini, Halkida, and Alexandroupolis (connections from Thessaloniki and Larissa). Going south, regular daily trains run from Athens to Corinth, Kiato, Xylokastra, Diakofto, Patras, Mycenae, Olympia, Argos, Tripoli, Megalopolis, and Kalamata.

Tour cards give travelers unlimited travel for 10, 20, or 30 days. Prices depend on the number of passengers in the package trip. These passes can be bought in advance outside of Greece (ask your travel agent for information). Eurail passes can also be used on the Greek train system.

Trains can be crowded during summer months, so get advance bookings. Various classes are available for overnight trips.

METRO

The Attiko Metro in Athens also goes by the name "Ilektrikos", Greek for electrical, to differentiate between this system and the diesel trains operated by the Greek National Railways company, OSE. It is brand new, with modern, gleaming stations featuring exhibits of the many archaeologic findings unearthed during excavation. It is an excellent way to get about, inexpensive (250 drachma), and with frequent trains running from 5a.m to midnight.

The traveler purchases a ticket at the point of embarkation and then validates it in the machines at the station before boarding. Tickets apply for one trip only and cannot be used as fare on other modes of Athens' public transport (for example, buses and trolley buses).

The Attiko Metro operates three lines at this time:

- The Blue Line, from Syntagma to Ethniki Amyna
- The Red Line, from Syntagma to Sepolia
- The Green Line, from Pireaus to Kifissia
  Some stations to note:
- Pireaus: the station is on the waterfront in the central port, making it a vital link for those wishing to take a ferry.
- Neo Faliro: across the way from the Peace and Friendship stadium.
- Monastiraki: the Athenian flea market, near the Plaka.
- Omonia: one of two main squares, lying at the center of Athens.
- Irini: serving the Olympic stadium.
- Kifissia: a northern suburb of great beauty, whose name means "There, where it is windy."

BUS / TRAM

Bus service in Greece is extensive, linking Athens with all major towns in Attica, the Peloponnese, and northern Greece. Fares are cheap. On the islands, service varies with demand, and the traveler should check timetables carefully. On some islands, mechanized transport is not permitted, so islanders use donkeys, carts, and boats to get around.

The Greek/Hellenic Railways Organization Ltd. (OSE) provides bus routes to northern Greece from Athens, departing from the terminus at Karolou Street; and to the Peloponnese, embarking from the station at Sina Street.

Terminal A (100 Kifissou Street) and Terminal B (260 Liossion Street) are the two mainline bus terminals in Athens. Enquire at one of these stations for information on buses from Athens to the provinces.

The Greek long-distance coach services of KTEL offer an extensive network of transport around the country.

Urban buses also run throughout Athens itself and in most major towns. In general, the systems are efficient and reliable. Be sure to have exact change for your fare.

Twenty trolley bus routes run throughout Athens and Pireaus, operated by the state-run ILPAP. Purchase a ticket at a kiosk or from a specially licensed shop (usually a to-

Greece

bacconist or newsstand) before boarding, then validate it in the machines that are on board. Board the trolley wherever you see the yellow ILPAP sign. Service is good.

You can obtain information by telephoning ILPAP at: tel: (01) 362-1794 or (01) 362-2631.

WATER TRAVEL

It is both inexpensive and easy to journey around the Greek islands on boats. Most boats and ferries departing for the outer islands leave the mainland from Pireaus, with the highest frequency of sailings during the summer. Travelers may purchase tickets at travel agencies, ticket agencies in the train station, or directly at the boats. However, in the summer season, it is best to reserve in advance with a travel agent. The Greek/Hellenic National Tourist Organization is a source of information on fares and schedules (see 'Travel Assistance').

Athens has two main ports:

- Piraeus - Port Authority; tel: (01) 451-1311
- Rafina - Port Authority; tel: (02) 942-2300

Three classes of tickets—First Class, Second Class and Tourist Class—are available, offering various levels of comfort. Passengers can book couchette cabins for longer voyages or to avoid excess sun. Restaurant facilities exist on most ships. Once in the islands, water taxis provide inter-island travel.

Hydrofoils from the mainland are also available for business people in a hurry. They are twice as fast but cost twice as much. It is advisable to reserve in advance during peak periods, as seats are not always available. Also be aware that high winds or inclement weather will cause the local port authority to cancel service. The hydrofoils also do not serve as many islands as the regular boat service. For more information regarding hydrofoil schedules and fares, contact Flying Dolphins: tel: (1) 922-7772; Fax 923-2101.

TRAVEL ASSISTANCE

Ellinikos Oragnismos Tourismou (EOT)
(Tourist Organization of Greece)
P.O. Box 1017; Odos Amerikis 2, 105 64 Athens, Greece
tel: (1) 322 3111/19; fax: (1) 322 4148
email: <infoxenios@areianet.gr>
website: www.areianet.gr/infoxenios/GNTO
ELPA
(Greek/Hellenic National Tourism Organization)
2-4 Messogion Street; 115 27 Athens
tel: (1) 778-6642; fax: (1) 779-1619

Communications

DIALING CODES IN GREECE

International country code: [30]
Selected city codes: Argos (751), Athens (1), Corfu (Kerkyra) (661), Corinth (741), Iraklion (Kritis) (81), Kavala (51), Larissa (41), Patrai (61), Piraeus Pireefs (1), Rodos (241), Salonica (Thessaloniki) (31), Tripolis (71), Volos (421), Zagora (426)

Dialing Greece from Overseas

To dial Greece from overseas, dial your country's international dialing code, then 30 (the country code for Greece), then the city code and finally the number. If you were dialing Athens from the United States, for example, you would begin with 011, then 30, then 1 (the city code for Athens), and finally the number of the person or office you are trying to reach.

Assistance Numbers

International Operator & Directory 161
International Directory from Athens 162
Domestic Operator 151
Long Distance Directory 132
Local Directory 131

CALLING WITHIN GREECE

Local Calls

A call within the city will cost one unit of your phone card.

Long Distance Calls

Calling long distance within Greece is simplified through use of a phone card since rates vary from place to place. Rates drop between 9p.m. and 5a.m.

International Calls

OTE operates a modern telephone service in Greece with offices open from 7a.m. to 10p.m., or to midnight in larger towns. OTE offices allow you to make direct international calls from a metered booth. The main offices in Athens are located at Patission St. and also on Stadiou St. A clerk will direct you to a booth and you can pay after the call is completed. Dialing from a public phone will cost one unit of your phone card. Dial 00 + country code + area code + number. To access an operator in the U.S. from a public phone requires deposit of a coin. AT&T will also connect you with other countries when dialing from Greece.

AT&T Direct 00-800-1311
MCI 00-800-1211

PAY PHONES

Public Telephones

If you are unable to comprehend the Greek telephone booth procedure, try relieving your headache by pressing 'i', located on the top of the panel, for English instructions.

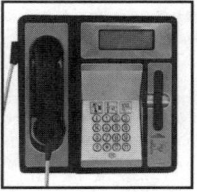

1. Lift receiver
2. Wait for tone
3. Insert Phone Card
4. Dial number

Calling Cards

Phone cards for 100, 500 or 1000 units can be purchased at corner stores or tourist shops.

CALL BACK

You can (potentially) save significant sums when calling in Greece by using a call back service. For a list of callback services, please refer to the "Communications" section in the *Global Road Warrior* Introduction.

Fees for call back services vary widely, depending on the company and the type of service required. Be sure to check with these companies before leaving to compare rates.

CELLULAR PHONES

Greece operates on the GSM network, which means North American cellular phones will not work because they use a different standard. Panafon and STET offer GSM service in Greece.

Note: Your home country cell phone may not work in this country. If not, we recommend that you rent an international cell phone *before* you leave home. A major US-based cell phone rental provider is **IMC WorldCell**. For information see "International Cell Phone Rentals" on page 14.

PHONE JACKS

Plug adaptors are available through **iGo Corporation.** (See "Electrical and Telephone Adaptors" on page 19.)

POSTAL SERVICES

Postal service is inefficient, and is quickly being replaced by fax machines as the best way to send messages. Mail boxes are bright yellow. Any letter or package being sent out of Greece must be taken, unopened, to a post office for inspection. The main post office in Athens on 100 Eolou St., and a branch office in Syntagma Square stay open on Sundays from 9a.m. to 1p.m. and 2p.m respectively.

Hours of service

Monday-Saturday 7:30a.m. to 7:30p.m.
Sunday 9a.m. to 2p.m.

Essential Terms

English	Greek
Yes	Ne
No	Óchi
Good morning	Kaliméra
Hello (daytime)	Kalispéra
Hello (evening)	Kalispéra
Hello (telephone)	Ya su
Good-bye	Chérete
Please	Parakaló
Thank you	Efcharistó
Pleased to meet you	Hero poli ya tin gnori mi a
Excuse me; I'm sorry	Me sinchoríte
My name is ____	Me le ne ____
I don't understand	Den katalavéno
Do you speak English?	Mi la te anglika?

Business Services

COURIER SERVICES

Aces Couriers; 8 Dioharous str. 115 28; tel: (1) 725-7770; fax: (1) 724-9370.

Air Courier Services; 3 Livadias str.; tel: (1) 284-3531; fax: (1) 284-6931.

DHL International Hellas DPE; Alimou 44 & Roma 17, Alimos, 17455 Athens; Monday to Friday 8a.m. to 7p.m., Saturday 9a.m. to 4p.m., tel: (1) 989-0000; Athens Express Center, Filellinon 28 & Peta 1, Syntagma; tel: (1) 323-9481; Monday to Friday 9a.m to 7p.m., Saturday 9a.m. to 2p.m.

Federal Express (Speedex Courier); tel: (1) 994-3200; export/import services.

Kanga Services Couriers S.A.; 3 Makrinitsas str.; tel: (1) 646-6400; fax: (1) 646-0714; email: kanga@ath.fortnet.gr

TNT Skypak; 32 El. Venizelou and Char. Trikoupi Strs., Glyfada; tel: (1) 960-2800; fax: (1) 960-2342.

UPS Greece (Head Office); 98a Alimou Str., Argiroupoli, 16452; tel: (1) 996-6840; Thessaloniki, tel: (31) 424-420.

Electrical

Current

220 volts, 50Hz

ELECTRIC PLUGS

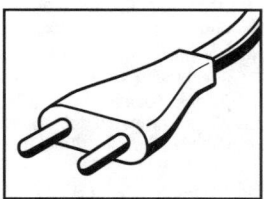

Plug adaptors are available through **iGo Corporation.** (See "Electrical and Telephone Adaptors" on page 19.)

Technical Support

HARDWARE/SOFTWARE VENDOR SUPPORT

Hewlett Packard; tel: 1 689 64 11; (in Switzerland) tel: [41] (22) 780-8111; (in the U.S.) tel: [1] (408) 246-4300; http://www.hp.com/.

IBM; tel: (1) 688-1220; fax: (1) 680-1300; (in Germany) tel: [49] (711) 78-50; fax: [49] (711) 785-3511; (in Switzerland) tel: [41] (22) 310-0418 (in French); http://www.ibm.com/.

Microsoft; tel: (1) 680-6775 through (1) 680-6779; fax: (1) 6806 780; tel: (1) 924-7030; fax: (1) 921-5363 (technical support); (in Switzerland) tel: [41] (848) 858-868; fax [41] (1) 831-0869; (in the U.S.) [1] (425) 635-7222; http://www.microsoft.com/.

Internet Connection

HOW TO CONNECT

Connecting to AOL and Compuserve in Greece is similar to using it when traveling outside your own area code. See the introductory section for detailed information on connecting to your account through a different phone number.

America Online

Numbers are available at keyword *international*. Be sure to get local numbers before leaving. AOL's GlobalNet service charges US$6 an hour in addition to the usual charges. Go to keyword *access* (a free area) and download the software.

Access: Athens (1) 964-7707; Heraklion (81) 324-495; Ioannina (651) 66-801; Kavala (51) 227-545; Corfu Kerkyra Island (661) 36-445; Patras (61) 270-074; Rhodes (241) 39-875; Thessaloniki (31) 242-043.

Compuserve

Numbers are available at *Go International*. The Compuserve Web-site also has a great deal of information, at http://www.compuserve.com.

Access: Athens (1) 964-7707; Corfu (66) 136-445; Heraklion (81) 324-495; Ioannina (65) 166-801; Kavala (51) 227-545; Patras (61) 270-074; Rhodes (241) 39-875; Thessaloniki (31) 242-043.

Independent Service Providers

Many independent service providers offer discounts if you are only in town for a couple of days.

AstroNet; tel: (241) 35-835; fax: (241) 36-798; email: webmaster@astronet.gr; http://www.astronet.gr/.

CompuLink Network S.A.; tel: (1) 924-9761; fax: (1) 924-9290; email: info@compulink.gr; http://www.compulink.gr/.

FORTHnet SA (Hellenic Telecommunications and Telematic Applications Company); tel: (1) 729-5100; tel: 8139-1200; fax: 8139-1207; pr@forthnet.gr; http://www.forthnet.gr/.

HellasNet; tel; (1) 899-3000; fax: (1) 899-2006; email: webmaster@netor.gr; http://www.hellasnet.gr/.

IBM Internet Connection Services; tel: (1) 688-1220; fax: (1) 680-1300; toll-free in the U.S.: tel: [1] (800) 455-5056; email: ibm_direct@gr.ibm.com; http://www.ibm.net/ (click on Global Services).

Business Culture

GREETINGS AND COURTESIES

In general, Greeks shake hands firmly, usually making direct eye contact, both on meeting and departing. Slapping a friend's arm at shoulder level is common among men. An embrace and kiss is customary among family and friends. Politely ask about your colleague's health and family before going on to business. Use titles whenever applicable; Greeks are proud of their professional standing. Formality is soon dispensed with, however, and Greeks may ask you to use their first name. Pretentiousness isn't appreciated and smiling too much may cause your Greek hosts to become suspicious of your sincerity.

If invited into a Greek home, consider it an honor and dress appropriately. Small gifts are appropriate as are flowers for the hostess; however, take care in selecting appropriate gifts since a Greek is wary of a bribe. Praise your host's children and, with parental approval, give them a small gift. Favorite topics of conversation for Greeks include sports (especially the Olympics), food, wine, and Greece's contributions to history. Avoid speaking about Cyprus, Turkey, and other aspects of international politics which have affected Greece.

MEETINGS

Prior appointments are not always necessary unless visiting a factory or government office, but phoning ahead is appreciated. Reconfirm any appointments by phone a day in advance. If you are going to be late, a phone call is appreciated. Although Greeks often arrive tardy, they appreciate your efforts to be there on time. Come prepared with plenty of business cards to hand out at the start of your meeting. Avoid making appointments on Wednesday afternoons; many businesses are closed. Also keep in mind to avoid business visits in July and August and the weeks prior to and following Easter and Christmas.

Meetings may take place in an office, but also in hotel lobbies and cafes. Socializing is a vital part of Greek culture, even in business. As such, prepare to meet in person rather than over the phone. Greeks value personal contact, which may take place even after a meeting: at dinner, in a tavern, or a nightclub. Patience and courtesy will develop the trust vital to Greek business transactions; trying to hurry a meeting along may be considered rude. Also prepare for a number of interruptions during meetings. Introduce written documents as the very last item.

DECISION MAKING

Greeks tend to exhibit verbal and physical expressiveness; if your host becomes quiet and withdrawn, something is probably wrong. Come prepared for leisurely discussions over strong coffee and *ouzo*, the national liqueur; refusing such an invitation is considered an insult. Greeks love to haggle in all aspects of business and expect the same in return. However, good bargaining takes time. Patience is a prerequisite to reaching an agreement; imposing deadlines will greatly displease your Greek counterparts, and losing one's temper will serve no purpose at all.

WOMEN

Women gained prominence and rights in the 1980s, but machismo is still alive and well in this region of the world. Women hold many jobs, but usually low-level positions. Women should take care to behave conservatively; fun-loving or chatty behavior may invoke advances other than business. Frequent smiling may also cause a Greek to assume you are flirting.

BUSINESS ATTIRE

Wear a conservative suit for most of the year. Winters can be chilly. Bring a raincoat and umbrella, especially if you are staying in northern Greece. Women wear dresses more often than their Western counterparts; however, whatever a woman decides to wear, keep it conservative to help garner more respect. Women should bring woolen clothing and a heavy coat if they plan on staying in the winter. In the spring and autumn, take a raincoat. White and light-colored suits are not often worn.

Business Centers
Athens

CITY VIEW

It is difficult to love Athens. The *nefros* (smog) clogs the skies and historical monuments (such as the Acropolis) stand next to sloppily-built apartment high rises. The pollution problem, however, is being targeted by a new 2.8 million dollar subway system to be completed in time for 2004 Olympics. As far as sightseeing goes, a visit to the outstanding Acropolis will leave an impression, pollution in the air or not. If time allows, a trip to outlying islands may prove to hold more of idyllic Greece than the country's capital.

AIRPORT

Hellinkon Airport to City Center

The airport lies 6 miles (10 km.) from the city center. If possible, travel very light or with baggage marked with an easy-to-identify ribbon or tie to circumvent the hazards of the masses at the baggage carousels. Regular bus and coach services, for fares of about Dr250, will take you into town in 20- to 30-minute intervals between 6a.m. and midnight. From midnight to 6a.m. buses leave hourly. Olympic Airways buses depart every 30 minutes from the West Terminal.

Taxis should cost around Dr2100 for a 20- to 30-minute ride (longer if arriving during rush hour) into town; baggage will cost extra and fares will double between midnight and 6a.m. If traveling during daytime hours, make sure the meter is turned on and that the number "1" (basic fare) is showing in one of the corners of the meter; a "2" indicates double fare.

Note: A new Athens International Airport will open in March 2001.

Airline Numbers

Air Afrique...(1) 331-1048
Air Canada ....(1) 322-3206
Air France ....(1) 323-8507
Air India ....(1) 360-3584
Air Lanka ....(1) 324-9098
Air Malta ....(1) 957-0390
Air New Zealand..(1) 323-9000
Alitalia..(1) 995-9200
American Airlines ....(1) 323-6768
Austrian Airlines ....(1) 960-1240
Avianca..(1) 360-2001
Balkan-Bulgarian Air.......................................(1) 363-4675
Biman-Airlines of Bangladesh ....(1) 322-7750
Britannia Airways..(1) 323-3562
British ....(1) 325-0601
Cathay Pacific ....(1) 324-0233
Continental Airways.......................................(1) 323-7853
Cyprus Airways ....(1) 324-6965
Delta Airlines ....(1) 323-5242
Egyptian Airways..(1) 323-8907
Emirates ....(1) 330-4023
Ethiopian Airways...(1) 322-4551
Gulf Air ....(1) 322-9544
Icelandair...(1) 924-2646
Japan Airlines ....(1) 325-2075
KLM ....(1) 322-2208
Lauda Air ....(1) 322-4618
Libyan Airways ....(1) 324-4816
Lufthansa...(1) 771-6002
Luxair...(1) 923-9002
Olympic Airways
domestic ....(1) 929-2235
international ....(1) 929-2555
Sabena..(1) 960-0021
Singapore Airlines ....(1) 323-9111
South African Airways ....(1) 361-6305
Swissair..(1) 323-7581
Syrian Air...(1) 323-8711
TAP Air Portugal...(1) 325-1711
Turkish Airlines ....(1) 322-1035
United Airlines ....(1) 924-2645

HOTELS

Top-end

Astir Palace Vouliagmeni Hotel; 166 71 Vouliagmeni; consists of three luxury hotels located close to the airport; 2 restaurants; bar; conference facilities (up to 500); in-room air conditioning, mini bar, hair dryer, cable tv, telephone; 24 hour room service; swimming pool; water sports.

Athens Ledra Marriott; 115 Syngrou Avenue; tel: (1) 934-7711; fax: (1) 935-8603; city suburb; restaurant; conference facilities; secretarial service; fax/photocopy facilities; corporate rates; pool; whirlpool.

Divani Apollon Palace Hotel; 10 Agiou Nicolaou Llious Str., Vouliagmeni; tel: (1) 891-1100; fax: (1) 965-8010;286 rooms; located at the sea resort of Kavouri; business center; in-room balconies, air conditioning; shops; indoor and outdoor swimming pools; sauna.

Divani Caravel; 2 Vassileos Alexandrou; tel: (1) 725-3725; fax: (1) 725-3770; restaurant; secretarial service; conference facilities; fax/photocopy facilities; corporate rates; in-room safe; fitness; sauna; pool.

Hilton Athens; 46 Vassilissis Sofias Avenue; tel: (1) 725-0201; fax: (1) 725-3110; restaurant; business center; conference facilities; secretarial service; fax/photocopy facilities; corporate rates; sauna; pool.

Expensive

Andromeda; 22 Timoleontos Vassou Street; tel: (1) 643-7302; fax: (1) 646-6361; restaurant; conference facilities; secretarial service; fax/photocopy facilities; corporate rates.

Herodion; 4 Rovertou Galli St.; tel: (1) 923-6832/36; fax: (1) 923-5851; restaurant; meeting facilities; in-room electric socket and safe; corporate rates.

Novotel Mirayia Athens; 4-6 Mihail Voda; tel: (1) 825-0422/30; fax: (1) 883-7816; restaurant; conference facilities (up to 600); secretarial service; corporate rates; gift shop; pool.

Zafolia; 87-89 Alexandras Avenue; tel: (1) 644-9002/9012; fax: (1) 644-2042; restaurant; roof garden; convention facilities; fax/photocopy facilities; pool.

Moderate

Amalia; 5 Amalias Str.; located in the heart of the city, opposite the Greek parliament building and by Syntagma Square; restaurant; bar; conference facilities; in-room air conditioning, cable tv, mini bar.

Hotel Plaka; Kapnikareas 7; tel: (1) 322-2096; fax: (1) 322-2412; conference facilities; secretarial service; fax/photocopy facilities; corporate rates.

Hotel Plaza; 78 Aharnon & 1 Katrivanou; tel: (1) 822-5111/8; central location; restaurant; roof garden.

MEDICAL CARE

Hygeia Hospital; Kifisias Avenue& Erythou, Stavrou 4, GR-15123 Amarousion, Athens; tel: (1) 682-7940; fax: (1)-684-5089.

Sotira General Hospital (University of Athens); 152, Messogion Avenue - GR-115 27 Athens; tel: (1) 771-9975; fax: 777-8838; e-mail: gpp@hol.gr.

AUTO RENTAL

Avis; reservations: 46-48 Queen Amalias Ave., tel: (1) 322-4951, fax: (1) 322-0216; Intl. Airport, tel: (1) 322-4951, fax: (1) 995-3440; Domestic Terminal, tel: (1) (1) 322-4951; Hilton Hotel, 46 Queen Sophias Ave., (1) 725-0301; http://www.avis.com/reserve-a-car or http://www.avis.com/business_rate_plans/; Corfu, tel: 0661-24-404; Crete Airport, tel: 081-229-402.

Hertz; reservations, (1) 994-2850, fax: (1) 993-8856; Intl. Airport, tel: (1) 961-3625; telex: 226316; Domestic Airport, tel: (1) 981-3701; Hotel Inter-Continental, tel: 921-8360; Ledra Marriott Hotel, tel: 934-7711; http://www.hertz.com; chauffeur-driven cars available.

Greece

Guatemala

At a Glance

THE PEOPLE

Population .... 12,335,580 (July 1999 est.)
Growth Rate .... 2.68% (1999 est.)
Life Expectancy .... 66.45 years (born 1999)
Infant Mortality . 46.15 deaths/1,000 live births (1999 est.)

Ethnic Composition
Mestizo 56%
Amerindian 44%

Religious Composition
Roman Catholic... 90%
Protestant 5%
Mayan and other 5%

Languages Spoken
Spanish (official), various Amerindian dialects

Education and Literacy
Education is compulsory for only six years. The literacy rate is at 55.6 percent nationwide.

Labor Force
Total: 3,320,000
By occupation: services 14%, industry 28%, agriculture 58%

THE ECONOMY

Though agriculture accounts for only 25 percent of the GDP, Guatemala is by and large an agrarian economy with over half of its people employed in farming. Having ended 36 years of civil strife in 1996 this tiny nation has been seeking stability in the hopes of future growth. Unfortunately, Guatemala is very far behind the development curve when compared to other emerging markets. Energy generation is scarce and the obsolete telecommunications system remains state-owned. Calls for privatization have not been met with much enthusiasm by the beleaguered government. Poor transportation infrastructure has kept the nation from being taken seriously as a member (or potential member) of regional trade pacts. The Guatemalan workforce is generally poorly trained and the low literacy rate precludes any technological development for decades. Foreign investment has been understandably slow to materialize. The Guatemalan government finds itself having arrived too late at the global development table and with far too little.

Exports .... US$2.9 billion (1997)
Imports .... US$3.3 billion (1997)
Total GDP .... US$45.7 billion (1998 est.)
GDP Per Capita .... US$3,800 (1998 est.)
Unemployment .... 5.2 percent (1997)
Inflation Rate 6.4% (1998)

Top Export Partners
United States, El Salvador, Costa Rica, E.U., Honduras

Top Import Partners
United States, Mexico, Venezuela, Japan, E.U.

Top Exports
Coffee, sugar, bananas, cardamon, beef

Top Imports
Fuel and petroleum products, machinery, grain, fertilizers, motor vehicles

BUSINESS WORKWEEK

Offices
Monday to Friday 8a.m. to 6p.m.; Saturday 8a.m. to 12p.m.

Banks
Monday to Friday 9a.m. to 3p.m. (with many variations by individual banks, some staying open as late as 7p.m.); Saturday 9a.m. to 12:30p.m.

Government
Monday to Friday 8 a.m. to 4:30p.m. or 9a.m. to 3:30p.m.

Retail
Monday to Saturday 9:30a.m. to 7:30p.m.; large retailers may also stay open on Sundays.

Note: In rural areas a midday break that may last up to 2 hours is taken according to weather conditions and local custom.

HOLIDAYS

New Year's Day..January 1
Epiphany ....January 6
Easter..April 2-5*
Labor Day...May 1
Anniversary of the Revolution ....June 30
Assumption, Guatemala City only .... August 15
Independence Day ....September 15
Columbus Day..October 12
Revolution Day...October 20
All Saints' Day ....November 1
Christmas ....December 24-25
New Year's Eve...December 31
   *Date may vary by year.

CLIMATE

Seasons
The climate varies with altitude rather than season. It is generally temperate in the highlands and semitropical on the coastal plain. The coastal lowlands are hot and humid. In the highlands, days and nights are slightly cooler. The two main seasons are rainy and dry. The rainy season lasts from May to October. Prepare for dusty conditions during the dry season.

Regions
The Caribbean and Pacific coastal plains are hot year round with temperatures rising to 38°C (100°F) in the summer months. January temperatures in Guatemala are approximately 30°C (86°F), and as low as 7°C (45°F) during the evening. The warmest months are March, April, and May with the average temperature in the capital reaching 34°C (93°F), but it can turn chilly by comparison at night.

In Quezaltenango, the cold months have temperatures of around 24°C (75°F) during the day, but will fall to below zero at night; during the summer months the temperature rises to 33°C (92°F), again with cooler nights. The Caribbean coast is wet all year around.

NOTES: Departmentos that are not labeled have the same name as their Capitals.

Guatemala asserts historical claims to Belize and shows it as a Departmento on its official government maps.

Guatemala	
✪	National capital
⊙	Departmento capital
●	Secondary city
━━	International border
───	Departmento border
───	Primary road
········	Railroad

0   70 km
0   50 mi

Money & Banking

Currency

The currency of Guatemala is the quetzal (Q).

Denominations

The quetzal comes in coin denominations of 25, 10, 5, and 1 centavos; and banknotes of 50 centavos, and Q1, 5, 10, 20, 50, and 100.

Traveler's Checks and Credit Cards

Traveler's checks can be exchanged at banks, exchange shops, hotels, and international airports at tourist exchange rates, with various rates of exchange. Larger banks may offer the best exchange rates. There is both a black market and a government-tolerated grey market in currency exchange. The latter will be found at border crossings where no official bank is present and the former should be avoided all together.

U.S. dollars are the best foreign currency to bring to Guatemala as any other currency can involve bureaucratic hassles during exchange. Locals will also accept U.S. currency for regular transactions at, or near, the regular exchange rate. Expect to barter at tourist shops and markets. However, do not expect the same at Guatemalan Indian markets where merchants will rarely barter down even 10 percent.

Major credit cards like American Express, Visa, Diner's Club, and MasterCard are accepted in good hotels and restaurants at the same exchange rate as cash. Some banks in the capital offer cash advances on credit cards, but make sure you bring you passport. ATMs are rare even in the capital. If traveling outside of Guatemala City or major towns, it is recommended that you carry cash.

Essential Terms

English	Spanish
Yes	Sí
No	No
Good morning	Buenos días
Hello (daytime)	Buenas tardes
Hello (evening)	Buenas noches
Hello (telephone)	¿Hola?
Good-bye	Adiós
Please	Por Favor
Thank you	Gracias
Pleased to meet you	Encantado (a) de conocerle
Excuse me; I'm sorry	¿Perdóneme?
My name is ____	Me llamo ____
I don't understand	No comprendo
Do you speak English?	¿Habla usted inglés?

Travel

VISA AND PASSPORT

A passport that is valid for three months beyond the period of the visitor's stay is required of all. Visas are required of all except the following (for tourism visits of one month maximum):

- nationals of Andorra, Argentina, Australia,Belize, Brazil, Canada, Chile, Costa Rica, El Salvador, Honduras, Israel, Japan, Liechtenstein, Mexico, Monaco, New Zealand, Nicaragua, Norway, Panama, Paraguay, San Marino, Switzerland, Taiwan, U.K., Uruguay, U.S., Vatican City, and Venezuela
- nationals of Bahrain, Czech Republic, Iceland, Kuwait, Philippines, Poland, Saudi Arabia, Slovenia and South Africa, provided they are entering by air and obtain a Tourist Card at the airport
- Passengers in transit who do not leave the airport and are continuing their journey aboard the first connecting aircraft within 24 hours, and who are holding confirmed tickets and other documents for onward travel

Note: Nationals of Andorra, Argentina, Austria, Belgium, Chile, Denmark, Finland, Germany, Israel, Italy, Japan, Liechtenstein, Luxembourg, Monaco, The Netherlands, Norway, Sweden, Switzerland and Uruguay can extend their stays up to three months through a written agreement.

An Exit Permit (cost: Q2.50) is also required of all, except:

- Visitors who are holding a Tourist Card
- Visitors declared exempt from the visa requirement by the immigration authorities
- Visitors staying less than 30 days

Visas are required for longer stays or if a traveler has an official or diplomatic passport.

Types of visa issued:

- Visitor/Tourist, single and multiple entry. This visa is good for up to three months per entry, and valid if used within 30 days of issuance.
- Business, multiple-entry. This visa is good for up to six months per entry, and valid if used within 30 days of issuance. Business visa applicants must also append a letter from their employer detailing the type of business and the company's relative standing, as well as the planned activities of the applicant.

You need allow only a day from the receipt of the application until the issue of the visa, in most cases.

Restricted Entry:

Entry and transit are refused to deportees of other countries unless they are nationals of Guatemala. There is a long list of nationalities—mostly in Africa, Asia, the Middle East, and Eastern Europe—for whom special authorization must be granted by the Department of Immigration before they are granted a visa. Check with the Guatemalan embassy or consulate to ascertain whether your country is currently on this list. If it is, then you will be required to make your application in person, and the whole process will take between four and five weeks.

DEPARTURE FORMALITIES

If staying in Guatemala for more than 30 days, an exit permit is required for a fee of Q2.50 by all travelers except those holding a tourist card. A departure tax of US$20 applies to all international flights.

CUSTOMS ENTRY (PERSONAL)

Duty-free

- Tobacco: 80 cigarettes or 99 grams of tobacco
- Alcohol: 1.5 liters (2 bottles) of alcohol
- Perfume: 2 bottles of perfume

Prohibited or Restricted

- Unregistered firearms
- Controlled drugs
- Foreign and local currency import and export is limited to the equivalent of US$5000 without government permits.

IMMUNIZATION

No immunizations are necessary unless you are coming from an area infected with Yellow Fever, in which case you will need an International Certificate of Vaccination. Be advised that cholera is found in Guatemala, so precautions are suggested. Malaria prophylaxis as well as tetanus and hepatitis inoculations are advised for those traveling in the rural areas.

TIPPING

Taxi

Tipping is not necessary as the fare is negotiated beforehand, and all fees are included in the charge. However, if you wish to do so, 5 to 10 percent will be appreciated.

Porters

Porters receive Q5 per bag at first-class hotels and transport depots.

Hotels

Hotels will apply service charges directly to the bill.

Restaurants

In restaurants, 15 percent is considered standard unless the service charge is applied to the bill.

EMERGENCY INFORMATION

Police and Crime

Guatemala is renowned for petty theft and common crime, although, since 1992, the military has stepped in to provide additional support to the police. Airport theft is common. Avoid riding in unauthorized taxis, and always carry your passport / visa (or copies) in case police in Guatemala request it of you.

The outskirts of the cities are dangerous at night. However, recent incidents involving shootings, kidnappings, rapes, and violent assaults have also occurred during daylight hours. Be especially careful in Guatemala City. Intercity travel after sunset anywhere in Guatemala is extremely dangerous. Armed bandits roam the highways and persons in private vehicles as well as buses have been robbed, abducted, and murdered. Lock doors at all times. Punishment for crimes (especially drug trafficking) is severe.

Politics can become violent quite quickly in Guatemala, so avoid protest rallies or intense political discussions. Travelers driving in over the border of Guatemala should leave themselves plenty of time for border crossing formalities so that they may arrive at a major town before dark.

Take basic precautions. Avoid flashy displays of wealth, and dress and behave conservatively. Leave most of your cash, traveler's checks, jewelry, and your camera in your hotel safe. Carry cash in a money belt, and use credit cards or traveler's checks for most of your transactions. Carry copies of your passport and visa. Walk with your bag away from the street to avoid having it snatched away by passing thieves. Never exchange money in the street or carry a package for a stranger.

Police in rural and border areas often play part in the crime problem. Demands for bribes are not uncommon. Do not expect prompt or comprehensive investigations of nonviolent robberies. Carry insurance for anything you cannot afford to replace.

Emergency Numbers

Numbers function nationwide.
Police.. 120
Ambulance 128
Fire 123

Health

Cholera, Hepatitis A, malaria, diarrhea, amoebic and bacillary dysentery, paratyphoid, and typhoid fever are endemic. Tuberculosis is common, especially within the Indian population.

Use caution when eating in Guatemala. Hotel dining is the best recommendation until you acclimate. Do not drink tap water, don't even use it for brushing teeth; try also to keep your mouth closed in the shower to keep from swallowing water; also avoid ice cubes; bottled water is safe and available. Wash all vegetables in a chlorine solution, peel fruits, and avoid uncooked food. Use caution with lettuce, tomatoes, thin-skinned vegetables, and berries. Drink only pasteurized milk.

Pollution in Guatemala City ranks as terrible. It may increase symptoms of asthma, hay fever, and other allergies. Visitors may also suffer from a lack of energy since the city lies 5,000 feet above sea level. Do not exert yourself until you have acclimated. Take care to guard yourself against overexposure to heat and sun. And keep yourself hydrated with plenty of fluids as the high altitude will increase respiration and decrease body fluid.

Medical care is of a high standard in Guatemala City, and many local doctors are trained overseas and have multi-lingual abilities. Outside the city, however, shortages of basic medicines and equipment exists. Carry a well-stocked medical kit with any prescription drug you may need on a regular basis. Travel insurance is advised and an evacuation policy should be procured by those working in remote rural areas.

For more information on medical centers, including phone numbers, please see the "Business Centers" section.

TAXI

Taxi cars can be reserved by phone, but rarely on the street. Hotels will have taxis available. A flat rate applies for short or long-distance travel within cities. The option of hiring a driver by the hour also exists. Always bring written directions and maps as drivers may not be familiar with city streets.

AUTO

Due to the poor condition of Guatemalan roads as well as numerous security issues, auto rental by visitors is not advised. Hired cars with drivers are suggested.

TRAIN

There is very limited passenger train travel in Guatemala. A regular line runs to Mexico and an infrequent line serves the Guatemala City–Puerto Barrios route. The station is located at 10 Avenida in Zone 1 of Guatemala City.

METRO

There is no metro system in Guatemala.

BUSES & TRAMS

Regular city uses prove inexpensive but crowded. They are not known for their efficiency and, worse, encounter frequent accidents due to human error or equipment failure. Also, pickpockets and robbers frequently rob foreigners on the public buses. Another set of more expensive buses (*preferecial*) offer more comfortable conditions, but not necessarily more secure. After 10:30p.m., jitneys service urban customers until buses resume at 4a.m. None of these forms of public transport is recommended for business travelers.

WATER TRAVEL

Guatemala has no extensive river passenger boat system. Both the Caribbean and Pacific coastal ports provide international cruise line harbors as well as very limited coastal ferry-type service. Only the cruise line services provide sufficient security for business travel.

TRAVEL ASSISTANCE

Guatemala Tourist Commission; 7a Ave. 1-17, Zona 4, Centro Civico; tel: (2) 331-1333/47; fax: (2) 331-8893; email: inguat@guate.net; website: http://www.travel-guatemala.org.gt

Communications

DIALING CODES IN GUATEMALA

International country code: [502]
Selected city codes: Guatemala City (2), All other cities (9)

Dialing Guatemala from Overseas

To dial Guatemala from overseas, begin with your country's international dialing code, then 502 (the country code for Guatemala), then the city code, and finally the number. If you were dialing Guatemala City from the United States, for example, you would begin with 011, then 502, then 2 (the city code for Guatemala City), and finally the number of the person or office you were trying to reach.

Assistance Numbers

International Operator (English) 98
Local International Operator.. 171
Long Distance Operator 91
Operator 196
Guatemalan Operator (Spanish) 121
Information (Spanish) 124

CALLING WITHIN GUATEMALA

Local Calls

All numbers should now have seven digits.

Long Distance Calls

There are no area codes with which to contend in Guatemala.

International Calls

Guatel runs the telephone system here, providing telecommunications offices in all towns for domestic and international calls. Once you announce your call along with pertinent information to the operator, wait for the clerk to announce your name and direct you to a booth. Pay upon exiting and expect large sums, sometimes up to US$25 for three minutes. However, hotels may plunge the dagger even further, with a possible 400 percent surcharge! Furthermore, the hotel operator may block efforts to reach the access number of one of the other long distance companies. An international operator may assist more readily; but if not, you can attempt to call your phone company directly. If all else fails, go to a pay phone. To call direct, dial 00 + country code + area code + number. Rates fall between 7p.m. and 7a.m. daily.

AT&T Direct phones exist at the airport and the Guatel office in Guatemala City. At other phones dial:

Canada... 198
Italy.. 193
Spain 191
U.S. AT&T 190
U.S. MCI... 189
U.S. Sprint 195

AT&T reminds callers that public phones require local coin payment through the call duration.

PAY PHONES

Public Telephones

Known as *telefono monedero*, public phones are few and far between, even in main towns. Those that do exist accept 10, 15, or 25-centavo coins. As unbelievable as it may sound, in this instance, due to a lack of better alternatives, calling from a hotel is recommended even with a 400 percent surcharge. Collect calls are possible from some public phones in the major towns, but only to Central America, Mexico, and the U.S.

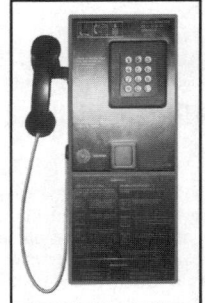

CELLULAR PHONES

Cellular users should be advised that Guatemala service runs on a NAMPS (narrowband analogue) system and operates in the 800MHz band. Comnicaciones Celulares operates a cellular service in this country.

Note: Your home country cell phone may not work in this country. If not, we recommend that you rent an international cell phone *before* you leave home. A major US-based cell phone rental provider is **IMC WorldCell**. For information see "International Cell Phone Rentals" on page 14.

CALL BACK

You can (potentially) save significant sums when calling in Guatemala by using a call back service. For a list of callback services, please refer to the "Communications" section in the *Global Road Warrior* Introduction.

Fees for call back services vary widely, depending on the company and the type of service required. Be sure to check with these companies before leaving to compare rates.

PHONE JACK

Plug adaptors are available through **iGo Corporation**. (See "Electrical and Telephone Adaptors" on page 19.)

FAX

Faxes are prevalent, but the phone system still does not support them and they can be unreliable. It is best to call ahead and tell the person that you are sending a fax.

POSTAL SERVICES

Postal service is efficient for Latin America. Packages and letters generally take about a week to make it to Western Europe or the U.S. There is also an express service that is not overnight delivery but does guarantee a relatively quick service. The post office in Guatemala City is located on the corner of 7th Ave. and 12 Calle in Zone 1 of the city.

TELEGRAMS

Telegrams can be sent from most post offices. They can be sent express at double the normal rate. The telegraph office in Guatemala City is located on the corner 7th Ave. and 12 Calle opposite the post office.

Business Services
COURIER SERVICES

Airpak; 7 Avenida A 4-30, Zona 9; tel: 334-4327; fax: 331-0454.

Cargo Express UPS; 2 Calle 6-40, Zona 9; tel: 334-3794, 331-6707.

DHL; 7 Avenida 2-42, Zona 9; tel: 332-3023; fax: 331-1612.

International Bonded Courier de Guatemala; 4 Avenida 3-39, Zona 9; tel: 332-6633, 334-5938; fax: 331-6352.

Jet Express International Courier; 4 Avenida 12-46, Zona 9; tel: 334-3834, 331-1903; fax: 331-0209.

Sky Courier International; Avenida La Reforma 8-60, Zona 9, Edificio Galerias Reforma, Local 214; tel: 331-0805, 331-9021; fax: 331-9002.

Electrical

Current

   120 volts AC, 60 Hz

ELECTRIC PLUGS

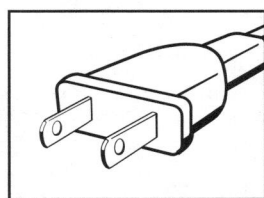

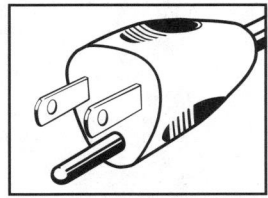

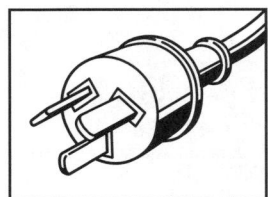

   Most plugs are American 2-pin, but be prepared for no electricity in some rural areas.

   Plug adaptors are available through **iGo Corporation.** (See "Electrical and Telephone Adaptors" on page 19.)

Technical Support
HARDWARE/SOFTWARE VENDOR SUPPORT

Dell; tel: [502] (2) 943-039 (Commercial Lemar S.A.); [502] (2) 234-4811 (Xerox Guatemala); [502] (2) 332-0472 (Sistemas Integrados S.A);(in the U.S.) tel: [1] (512) 338-4400; fax: [1] (512) 728-3330; http://www.dell.com/.

Hewlett Packard; (Venezuela Office) tel: [58] 2 239 5664;(in the U.S.) tel: [1] (408) 246-4300; http://www.hp.com/.

IBM; (in Colombia) tel: [57] (1) 623-0111; fax: [57] (1) 257-9839; (in the U.S.) tel: [1] (919) 517-2800; (U.S. Main Office) tel: [1] 914-765-1900; http://www.ibm.com/.

Microsoft; (in Costa Rica) tel: [506] 298-2020 (Technical Support); [506] 298-2000; (in the U.S.) [1] (425) 635-7222; http://www.microsoft.com/.

Internet Connection
HOW TO CONNECT

   Connecting to AOL and Compuserve in Guatemala is similar to using it when traveling outside your own area code. See the introductory section for detailed information on connecting to your account through a different phone number.

America Online

   Numbers are available at keyword: *international*. Be sure to get several local numbers before leaving. AOL's GlobalNet service charges US$12 an hour in addition to the usual charges. Go to keyword: *access* (a free area) and download the software.

Access: Guatemala City (2) 300-931.

Compuserve

   Numbers are available at *Go International*. The Compuserve Web-site also has a great deal of information, at http://www.compuserve.com.

Access: Guatemala City 230-0931.

Independent Service Providers

   Many independent service providers offer discounts if you are only in town for a couple of days.

Comtech; tel: 336-4320; tel: 335-5855, ext. 407; email: ayuda@comtech.net.gt; http://pronet.net.gt/.

Corporación de Telecommunicaciones S.A.; tel: 331-5818; email: info@c.net.gt; http://www.corpotelsa.com/;

TikalNet; tel: 362-0457; tel: 362-0487; fax: 362-9661; email: ventas@tikal.net.gt; http://www.tikal.net.gt

Business Culture
GREETINGS AND COURTESIES

   Handshakes are the common greeting among both men and women; these are gentle—almost limp—and somewhat prolonged. Women may pat each other's right forearm or shoulder instead of shaking hands. Male friends often hug and may kiss on the cheek; female friends may also exchange a light hug and lightly kiss each other on the cheek. Keep in mind that Guatemalans have less need for space around them than does the average American. Guatemalans stand closer to each other. While speaking, maintain eye contact and give an occasional smile as Guatemalans are a warm people who enjoy people contact. However, where city people may enjoy talking to or meeting strangers and lending assistance, country dwellers tend toward the shy side. Gift-giving or an invitation to a meal are common social pleasantries in Guatemala as are social outings with business associates. Business and social time often overlap as individuals are esteemed as more important than schedules.

MEETINGS

   Appointments should be made two weeks in advance. Punctuality is generally admired by Guatemalans, but strict adherence to it is not observed. Since personal relationships

Guatemala

are so highly regarded, take care not to jump right into business. Inquiring about family and spouses is appreciated and almost expected, often beyond what North Americans or Europeans may find normal. Business cards in Spanish are a courtesy rather than a necessity (although other materials should be translated). Come prepared with most materials written in Spanish (business cards, pamphlets, etc.), and that concentrate on educational and technical content rather than sales-oriented pitches.

DECISION MAKING

Actual decisions are almost always made at a high level of authority. Guatemalans will want to know your standing within the hierarchy and will wish to match you with someone of similar rank. Personal contacts and relationships carry great value with businesspeople in Guatemala. As such, one should establish such a relationship even before business has begun. Do not be surprised to encounter easy accessibility to key people in the decision making hierarchy since personal relationships are so valued. However, one must also take care to offer the same personal availability for contact in order to establish a trusting relationship with a Guatemalan.

WOMEN

Although women in Guatemala generally occupy a somewhat secondary status in this traditionally male-dominated society, many operate businesses and may be accorded considerable personal freedom. In general, foreign businesswomen should experience few problems; and may even find business relationships with Guatemalan males to be a superior experience to that of a male colleague at home. However, in the off-hours of business, women may find the opposite to be true and may face unwanted attention. Women should take care not to behave aggressively, but rather with graciousness. Women can generally walk the streets and dine alone, but may feel more comfortable if escorted.

BUSINESS ATTIRE

A conservative business suit will serve best in Guatemala as business tends toward formal. Guatemalans appreciate well-dressed individuals and exhibit great care with their appearance, even in after-hours settings. Take care to avoid dressing too casually. Women should dress conservatively in order to avoid unwanted advances. Women generally prefer skirts to slacks. Knees and thighs are considered sexual; as such, women should take care to wear skirts that fall below the knee. Tank or low-cut, clingy tops and sleeveless shirts are absolutely discouraged since modesty is a virtue. Guatemala City can become cool at night, thus, a jacket or sweater is recommended for evening wear. Consider a collapsible umbrella or a poncho for the frequent afternoon rainshowers, especially in September.

Business Centers
Guatemala City

CITY VIEW

Even so its large size, Guatemala City is not visited by many foreign tourists. It is better known as a transportation hub and administrative capital than for its aesthetics. A city of over 2 million inhabitants, Guatemala City is a convergence of 5-star hotels, excellent restaurants, universities, malls, a plethora of cars, and many thousands of people living in slums. Hundreds arrive daily from the highlands to seek employment in the capital where unemployment is already high. The discrepancy between rich and poor is quite notable if visitors care to take a look around outside the business center. An efficient transportation system transports thousands daily throughout the city. Coffee should keep sleepy visitors awake as it is the city's main export. For those who have perked up, they can visit one of many sights including the Museum of Archaeology and Ethnology, the central market, and the Olympic City. Noteworthy regional towns for a day trip include Chinautla, specializing in handmade pottery, and San Pedro and San Juan Sacatepéquez both of Indian historical significance.

AIRPORT

La Aurora Airport to City Center

The airport lies 4 miles (7 km.) from the city. Taxis are available but be sure they are well-marked as such and that a registration number exists on the left and right doors. Expect about a 20 minute ride into the city for a fare of about Q40. A bus going into the city leaves in 30-minute intervals; however, expect the travel time to be double that of a taxi.

Airline Numbers

Aerolineas Argentinas	331-1276, 331-1539
Air France	331-9524, 331-9691
Alitalia	331-1276, 331-1539
American Airlines	334-7379, 334-7379
Aviateca	336-4181, 332-0302
British Airways	334-5981/4
Continental Airlines	331-2051, 335-3338
COPA	331-6813, 331-8443, airport: 331-8790
Delta	331-6836, 331-6840
El Al	331-9507, 334-3314
Iberia	334-3816/7
Japan Airlines	331-8597, 331-8531
KLM	337-0222/4
Korean Air	333-5755/6
LACSA	332-3907, 331-0906
Ladeco Chilean	334-6238, 334-6246
LAN Chile	331-2070, 331-2077
Lineas Areas Paraguayas	334-0937
Lufthansa	337-0113/16, 337-0333
Mexicana	333-6001, 333-6011
SAHSA	335-2958, 335-2671, airport: 331-6660
SAM/Avianca	331-6311, airport: 334-7903
South African Airways	351-3071
TACA	332-2360, 331-9172, airport: 332-0394
United Airlines	airport: 332-1995, 332-1977
Varig	331-1952/55

HOTELS

Top-end

Hyatt Regency Guatemala; Complejo Tikal Futura, Calzada Roosevelt 22-43, Zona 11; tel: 440-1234; website: www.hyatt.com; part of the Tikal Futura business complex; 205 rooms; suites; Presidential suite; restaurant; bar; in-room a/c, hairdryer, satellite tv, minibar, safe, IDD phone, voicemail; Regency Club floors; airport limousine; florist; valet parking; travel agency; car rental; photo service; shopping mall; entertainment center; beauty salon/barber; currency exchange; doctor; childcare; fitness; massage; sauna; health bar; indoor pool; 3 whirlpools; 10 cinemas; bowling.

Quinta Real Guatemala (a Summit Hotel); Prolongacion Blvd Los Proceres, Km9, Zona 15; tel: 365-5050; fax: 365-5051; 129 rooms; residential area, located in hills above city; all-suite hotel; restaurant; bar; conference facilities; business center; secretarial service; in-room a/c, minibar, radio, direct dial phone, tv, smoke alarms, sound proof windows, robe, safe; some rooms with fax; 24-hour room

Guatemala

service, hairdryer; laundry; valet services; concierge; porter/bellhop; doctor; pharmacy; disabled facilities; boutiques; newsstand; gym; pool; gardens.

Westin Camino Real; 14 Calle y Avenida Reforma, Zona 10; email: caminor@guate.net; tel: 333-4633; toll free: 800-228-3000; fax: 337-4313; 404 rooms; 3 restaurants; cafe; bar; 15 conference rooms (up to 1200); business center; guest office with PC computer terminals, printer, photocopier, fax; in-room data port, minibar, cable tv, electronic locks, smoke detectors, sprinklers, safe; non-smoking rooms available; executive club floor; handicapped floors; shopping center; airline office; travel agency; health club; fitness; sauna; steam bath; massage; 2 pools; jacuzzi; tennis; disco.

Expensive

Crowne Plaza Las Americas; Avenue of the Americas 9-08, Zona 13; tel: 339-0676; fax: 339-0690; 194 rooms; restaurant; bar; conference rooms; secretarial service; fax/photocopy facilities; in-room modem/fax connection; corporate rates; fitness; sauna; pool.

Clarion Suites; 14 Calle 3-08, Zona 10; tel: 363-3333; toll-free: 1-800-CLARION; fax: 363-3303; all-suite hotel; restaurant; kitchenettes available; conference room (up to 30); airport transfer; fitness; sauna; pool; $100-150.

Cortijo Reforma (a Golden Tulip Hotel); Avenida Reforma 2-18, Zona 9; tel: 332-0712; toll-free: 1-800-333-1212; fax: 331-8876; 150 rooms; located in business district; restaurant; bar; coffee shop; conference rooms; secretarial service; fax/photocopy facilities; laundry service; valet services; hairdresser; airport transportation; parking; corporate rates; fitness; sauna; pool; $85-135.

Melia Guatemala; Duda Las Americas 9-08; tel: (2) 390-0676; fax: 339-0690; 194 rooms; outside city center; 2 restaurants; bar; conference facilities; business center; in-room a/c, hairdryer, minibar, radio, razor socket, safe, satellite tv, smoke alarm, sprinkler system, direct dial phone, temperature control; 24-hour room service; laundry; disabled facilities; beauty salon; boutiques; car rental; security; valet services; concierge; parking; fitness; spa; pool.

Princess Reforma; 13 Calle 7-65, Zona 9; tel: 334-4545; fax: 334-4546; email: princgua@guate.net; 110 rooms; boutique hotel, renovated 1996; restaurant; 8 conference rooms (up to 300); secretarial service; fax/photocopy facilities; in-room modem/fax connection, 2-line phone, work desk, hairdryer, safe; non-smoking rooms available; gift shop; car rental; luggage storage; corporate rates; fitness; sauna; pool; spa; $89-223.

Radisson Suites Villa Magna; 1a. Avenida 12-46, Zona 10; tel: 332-9797; toll-free: 1-800-777-7800; 1-2 room suites with kitchenettes; restaurant; conference facilities (up to 300); secretarial service; fax/photocopy facilities; in-room safes; corporate rates; fitness; sauna; pool; tennis.

Ramada Conquistador; Via 5, 4-68, Zona 4; tel: 331-2222; toll-free: 1-800-468-3571; fax: 334-7245; 159 rooms; restaurant; conference rooms (up to 750); secretarial service; fax/photocopy facilities; in-room safes; corporate rates; pool; $55-250.

Moderate

Guatemala Fiesta; 1A Avenida 13-22, Zona 10; tel: 332-5555; fax: 368-2366; restaurant; conference rooms; fitness; pool.

Ritz Continental; 6A Avenida "A" 10/13, Zona 1; tel: 238-1671; fax: 238-1527; 202 rooms; restaurant; bar; 16 conference rooms (up to 400); business center; in-room modem/fax connections, a/c, cable tv, executive desk; room service; laundry cleaning service; corporate rates; fitness; solarium; pool; nightclub; $55-132.

Stofella; 2A Avenida 12-28, Zona 10; tel: 334-6191; fax: 331-0823; email: stofella@quetzalnet.com; continental breakfast included; business area; secretarial service; fax/computer rental; security vaults; electronic keys.

MEDICAL CARE

Centro Médico; 6a Avenida 3-47, Zona 10; tel: 332-3555.

Hospital Herrera Llerandi; 6a Avenida 8-71, Zone 10; tel: 334-5959.

Hospital Los Arcos; 6a. avenida 20-88, zona 10; tel: 368-0130.

Note: Top-end hotels also have in-house doctors.

AUTO RENTAL

Note: Maniacal drivers characterize much of Guatemala's roadways. Also take care not to driver after sundown as the streets become even more hazardous with a high incidence of carjackings.

Avis; national reservations, 331-2750; intl. reservations, tel: 999-1395; 12 calle 2-73, Zona 9; tel: 331-2750 or 331-2734, fax: 332-1263; airport, tel: 331-0017; fax: 332-4596; Hotel Camino Real, tel: 336-6875, fax: 336-6875.

Budget; Avenida La Reforma, Zona 9; tel: 334-8352/3, 334-3865, 334-2571. 332-5691, fax: 331-2807; airport, tel: 331-0273; fax: 331-2807.

Dollar; Avenida La Reforma 6-14, Zona 9; tel: 334-1538, 334-1541, 334-8285/7; airport, tel: 331-7185; at the Hotel Ritz, tel: 238-1929 or 232-3446.

Guatemala Rentautos; 19 Calle 16-91, Zona 12; tel: 473-1330.

Hertz; reservations, tel: (2) 33-2242, fax: (2) 31-7924; intl. reservations, tel: (2) 332-4025; fax: (2) 31-9220; 7a avenida 14-76, Zona 9; tel: 334-2540/1 or 332-2242 or 334-7421; airport, 331-1711.

Limosinas de Guatemala; 7a. calle 15-75, Zona 16; Colonia La Montaña; tel: 332-6677/8; fax: 332-6678.

National; 14 calle 1-42, Zona 10; tel: 368-3057, 368-0175, 337-1767; airport, tel: 331-8365, 331-8218.

Thrifty Car Rental; Ave. La Reforma y 11 Calle Esquina, Zona 9; tel: 332-1130 or 332-1220 or 331-6131; airport, 332-1230.

WORLD TRADE CENTER

World Trade Center Guatemala City
c/o Royal Hotels International Inc.
Brickell Bay Tower
1001 Brickell Bay Drive, Suite #2210
Miami, FL 33131
tel: [1] (305) 377-0304; fax: [1] (305) 577-3347

CHAMBER OF COMMERCE

Cámara de Comercio de Guatemala
10a Calle 3-80, Zona 1, Guatemala City
tel: 238-2681/5; fax: 251-4197
email: camcomgu@guate.net

CONVENTION BUREAU

Guatemala Visitor and Convention Bureau
Diagonal 6, 10-65, Zona 10, Of. 402
Guatemala City
tel: 332-7952/6; fax: 332-7958
email: fundesa@guate.net

Honduras

At a Glance
THE PEOPLE

Population .... 5,997,327 (July 1999 est.)
Growth Rate .... 2.24% (1999 est.)
Life Expectancy .... 64.68 years (born 1999)
Infant Mortality .. 40.84 deaths/1,000 live births (1999 est.)

Ethnic Composition

Mestizo 90%
Amerindian 7%
Black African 2%
Caucasian 1%

Religious Composition

Roman Catholic.. 97%
Protestant and non-affiliated 3%

Languages Spoken

Spanish (official), Amerindian dialects

Education and Literacy

Six years of education is compulsory. The literacy rate is 72.7 percent of those citizens15 years and older.

Labor Force

Total: 1,300,000
By occupation: services 20%, industry 18%, agriculture 62%.

THE ECONOMY

Honduras is one of the poorest countries in the western hemisphere. Its problems range from heavy public debt to in-adequate health, education, and energy infrastructure. The government pushed ahead with bank and finance reform in the mid-1990s with some good effects. Privatization efforts in state-run businesses like telecommunications and lumber have found little interest in the global investment community. Underemployment (estimated at 30 percent) and a high infla-tion rate have placed additional drags on development. While global investors see the potential for utilizing inexpensive la-bor, it is keeping a hands-off attitude toward Honduras until the government gets a better grip on economic problems. Honduran political leaders can now only tighten the fiscal belt to paint a picture of reasonable stability and wait to see what few investment funds come their way.

Exports .... US$1.3 billion (1996)
Imports .... US$1.8 billion (1996)
Total GDP .... US$14.4 billion (1998 est.)
GDP Per Capita .... US$2,400 (1998 est.)
Unemployment .... 6.3 percent (1997)
Inflation Rate .... 14.5% (1998 est.)

Top Export Partners

United States, E.U., Japan

Top Import Partners

United States, Guatemala, Japan, Mexico, El Salvador

Top Exports

Bananas, coffee, shrimp, lobster, minerals, meat, lumber

Top Imports

Machinery and transport equipment, industrial raw ma-terials, chemical products, manufactured goods, fuel and crude oil, foodstuffs

BUSINESS WORKWEEK
Offices

Monday to Friday 9a.m. to noon and 2p.m. to 6p.m, Sat-urday 8a.m. to noon.

Banks

Monday to Friday 9a.m. to 3p.m.

Government

Monday to Friday 7:30a.m. to 3:30p.m.

Retail

Monday to Friday 9a.m. to noon and 2p.m. to 6p.m., Sat-urday 8a.m. to 5p.m.
Note: In rural areas, the midday break may last longer and evening hours may be extended by local custom.

HOLIDAYS

New Year's Day...January 1
Easter...April 2-5*
Labor Day...May 1
Independence Day ....September 15
Discovery Day ....October 12
Army Day...October 21
Christmas ....December 25
*Date may vary by year.

CLIMATE
Seasons

Honduras is hot and humid almost year round. Tempera-tures vary by altitude rather than season. The average high temperature nationwide is 32˚C (90˚F) and the average low is 20˚C (68˚F). Temperatures are coolest in mountain areas.

Regions

The Caribbean coast can experience a lot of rain, the heaviest being from September to February. In Tegucigalpa, the capital, the climate remains more temperate and the dry season takes place from December to May. The capital can get chilly between December and January when the temper-ature in the city hovers around 23˚C (73˚F).

Money & Banking
Currency

The currency of Honduras is the lempira (L).

Denominations

The lempira (L) comes in coin denominations of 50, 20, 10, 5, 2, and 1 centavos; and banknotes of L1, 2, 5, 10, 20, 50, and 100.

Traveler's Checks and Credit Cards

Visitors to Honduras are advised to take traveler's checks denominated in U.S. dollars.Traveler's checks, can be exchanged at banks, exchange shops, hotels, and inter-national airports at tourist exchange rates, with various rates of exchange. Larger banks may offer the best ex-change rates. Black marketers only offer slightly better rates and they should be avoided. Banks in rural areas rarely deal with travel checks so bring cash.

Only U.S. dollars can be exchanged with any degree of ease in Honduras. Other currencies, even from bordering economies, will generate a bureaucratic nightmare. U.S. dollars receive a better rate than traveler's checks.

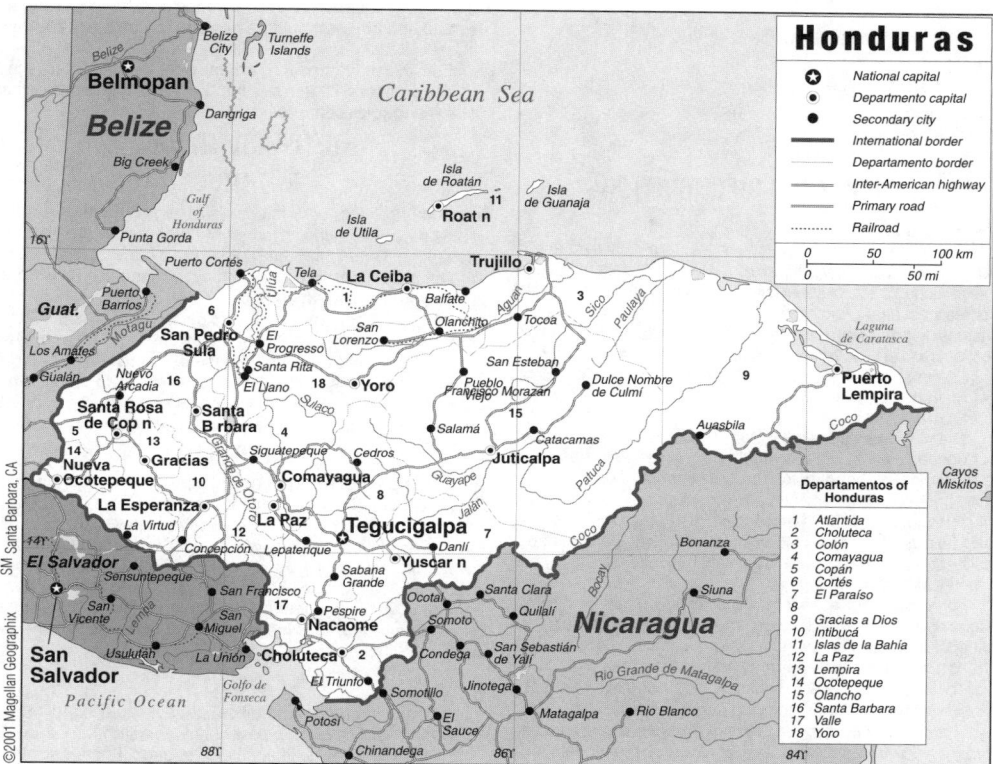

Honduras

✪	National capital
⊙	Departamento capital
●	Secondary city
——	International border
——	Departamento border
——	Inter-American highway
......	Primary road
....	Railroad

0   50   100 km
0   50 mi

Departamentos of Honduras

1 Atlántida
2 Choluteca
3 Colón
4 Comayagua
5 Copán
6 Cortés
7 El Paraíso
8
9 Gracias a Dios
10 Intibucá
11 Islas de la Bahía
12 La Paz
13 Lempira
14 Ocotepeque
15 Olancho
16 Santa Barbara
17 Valle
18 Yoro

©2001 Magellan Geographix   SM Santa Barbara, CA

Visa and MasterCard are easily accepted in good hotels and restaurants but not always at the same exchange rate as cash. Other credit cards will not be accepted. Some banks in the capital and Credomatic offices offer cash advances on credit cards but make sure you bring your passport. ATMs are rare even in the capital.

Travel

VISA AND PASSPORT

Visitors to Honduras need a passport valid for six months beyond the arrival date. No visas are required for people who are nationals of Argentina, Australia, Canada, Chile, Costa Rica, El Salvador, Guatemala, Iceland, Japan, Liechtenstein, Malta, Monaco, New Zealand, Nicaragua, Norway, Panama, Poland, Puerto Rico, San Marino, Switzerland, U.K., Uruguay, U.S., and Vatican City, if their stay does not exceed 30 days. A 60-day extension can be granted once inside the country. Citizens of all other countries must obtain a Tourist Card, which can be acquired at Honduran consulates or embassies for only US$2 to $3.

Travelers must show proof of a return ticket upon arrival. Business and multiple entry visas require an invitation from a Honduran company or government agency. If you are planning to stay in Honduras longer than 90 days, you need to obtain an exit permit from immigration.

Allow one or two working days for processing of your application, unless authorization from the Ministry of Foreign Affairs is necessary, in which case matters can take as long as three weeks to a month to resolve themselves.

DEPARTURE FORMALITIES

There are no departure formalities for Honduras or any exit taxes at land borders. Airport departure fees of US$25 are included in ticket prices.

CUSTOMS ENTRY (PERSONAL)

Duty-free
- Tobacco: 200 cigarettes, 100 cigars, or 454g of tobacco
- Alcohol: 2 liters of alcoholic beverage
- Other: a reasonable amount of perfume for personal use; gifts up to a total value of US$1,000

Prohibited or Restricted
- Unregistered firearms
- Controlled drugs

IMMUNIZATION

No immunizations are required for entry to Honduras unless you are arriving from an infected area. Dysentery and stomach parasites are common and malaria is endemic in coastal regions. Prophylaxis against these should be taken and mosquito nets brought along for a good night's sleep. It is advisable to inoculate against typhoid, tetanus, and hepatitis A.

TIPPING

Taxi
Rounding up the metered fare is standard. Negotiate unmeterd fares in advance.

Honduras

Porters
Porters are customarily not tipped.

Hotels
Hotels will add service charges directly to the bill.

Restaurants
Restaurants will normally add a service charge. Otherwise, 15 percent is standard.

EMERGENCY INFORMATION

Police and Crime
Crime is on the upswing and ranges from petty theft to carjackings, rape, and murder. Travelers should take serious security precautions. Watch for street crime and theft in urban and coastal recreational areas. Profit-driven kidnappings are also becoming increasingly frequent. Criminals are more apt to engage in physical violation of their victims than used to be the case.

Criminals in San Pedro Sula, Tela, Trujillo, and Tegucigalpa have shown a real inclination to target foreign visitors in particular.

The road from San Pedro Sula Airport has become cause for concern due to highway robberies, believed to be armed bandits preying on tourists. The Department of Olancho (the road between Limones and La Union) is also considered dangerous due to high incidences of car and busjackings, rapes, and killings. Do not to walk on isolated beaches alone, especially at night. Women should exhibit special care due to a high incidence of rape.

Foreign business visitors are often the target of thieves. Consequently, purses, laptops, and briefcases will require additional security. Do not leave valuables in cars or on tables in cafés. Keep non-essential valuables locked in hotel safes when not in use. Use credit cards and travel checks when possible to avoid carrying large sums of cash.

The police force is in the process of converting to a civilian organization from military. Lack of resources, materials, and manpower make them inefficient at crime control. In rural areas, they may even be part of the problem.

There is some corruption within the local and central governments. Business travelers may also find that their deals with local companies involve the bribing of public officials. Besides making the personal decision of whether or not to participate in such dealings, check on your legal position in your own country. Some nations now have stiff penalties for their business people who bribe officials overseas.

Emergency Numbers
Numbers function nationwide.

Police 199
Ambulance (Red Cross) 37-8654
Paramedics 39-9999
Hospital 32-2322
Fire 198

Health
Honduras can get extremely hot, so take precautions against sun and heat stroke, drink lots of liquids, and use sun block whenever outdoors. Never drink tap water—don't even use it for brushing your teeth—and avoid ice cubes. Avoid eating raw vegetables and fruit unless they've been washed in a chlorine solution. Eat only in recommended restaurants or hotels. Local cuisines can be spicy, so allow yourself time to acclimate. Diarrhea is common for travelers who are unaccustomed to the new diet and the heat. Take proper precautions and bring along medication.

The central government coordinates the medical establishment. Facilities are not of a high standard but adequate for emergency use. Hotels have access to multi-lingual doctors and medical assistants. Medicines are in short supply. Carry a well-stocked medical kit with all the prescription drugs you require. A travel insurance package including an evacuation policy should be acquired by all business travelers.

For more information on medical centers, including phone numbers, please see the "Business Centers" section at the end of this chapter.

INTERNAL TRAVEL

AIR
Local airlines, with Isleña Airlines and Líneas Aéreas Nacionales being the primary operations, offer daily services linking Tegucigalpa and other major towns. Isleña also provides services to Utila, the most economical Bay Island (along the Caribbean coast).

The main airports are Tegucigalpa, Dr. Ramón Villeda Morales Airport, 17km (11 miles) from the middle of San Pedro Sula, and La Ceiba's airfield. There are also more than 30 smaller airfields that can handle both commercial aviation and light aircraft. A hospital and airport tax of 2.5 percent is included in the air fare for domestic flights.

TAXI
Fares are not metered and should be negotiated before departing for your destination. In most towns, however, there is a basic flat rate in effect. You may want to begin your negotiations by letting the driver know you are aware of the flat rate. Many drivers will pick up extra passengers along the way. One can also rent a cab by the hour or even by the day. Make sure you have good directions or a map before departing as drivers are not always well informed—or pretend as much.

AUTO
Rental cars (and motorbikes) are available in most Honduran cities. They are expensive by any standard. A credit card and valid driving license are required. Local insurance may be required. While main highways are well paved, most Honduran roads are sub-standard. Unless you are on an extended visit, rental cars are not a good idea for business travelers. Driving alone in rural areas also presents a security risk. Hired cars with drivers (or taxis) are sufficient for most needs.

TRAIN
Trains are strictly a last resort to be used only for reaching certain remote areas. The trains are slow, primitive, and quite cheap. Services are not reliable, so check to see if things are actually running just before you are set to embark.

There are three railways in the north coast region, used mainly for hauling cargo between banana plantations. Passenger train services in the north run only between San Pedro, Puerto Cortés, and Tela.

A single passenger line runs in the southern part of Honduras on an erratic schedule. Make all inquiries and bookings locally.

METRO
There is no metro system in Honduras.

BUSES & TRAMS
Numerous bus line serve locals in Honduran cities as well as providing inter-city service. Local buses usually run from 5a.m. until 9p.m. and prices are cheap. Conditions may prove crowded and uncomfortable during peak hours. Intercity lines usually run from 6a.m. with a last bus in the afternoon so that the final destination is reached before dark to avoid crime problems. Intercity fares are cheap but business travelers may find them too uncomfortable to forego a hired car service.

Honduras

WATER TRAVEL

Ferries sail out of ports on the Caribbean, Atlantic, and Pacific coastlines. Several times weekly, there are crossings from Puerto Cortés and La Ceiba to the Bay Islands. For necessary details, contact the local port authorities. Most business people use the reasonably priced commuter air services for these same routes to save time.

TRAVEL ASSISTANCE

Instituto Hondureño de Turismo

PO Box 3261

Edificio Europa, 5to Piso

Colonia San Carlos, Avenida Ramon Cruz,

Tegucigalpa, Honduras

tel: 222 2124 or (1 800) 222 8687 (toll free; within Honduras only); tel/fax: 222 6621

email: ihturism@hondutel.hn

website: www.hondurasinfo.hn

Essential Terms

English	Spanish
Yes	Sí
No	No
Good morning	Buenos días
Hello (daytime)	Buenas tardes
Hello (evening)	Buenas noches
Hello (telephone)	¿Hola?
Good-bye	Adiós
Please	Por favor
Thank you	Gracias
Pleased to meet you	Encantado (a) de conocerle
Excuse me; I'm sorry	¿Perdóneme?
My name is _____	Me llamo _____
I don't understand	No comprendo
Do you speak English?	¿Habla usted inglés?

Communications

DIALING CODES IN HONDURAS

International country code: [504]

Honduras has changed all of its telephone numbers from 6 digits to seven. You can access a conversion table at http://www.7digitos.hn/tabla.gif

Dialing Honduras from Overseas

To dial Honduras from overseas, dial your country's international dialing code, then 504 (the country code for Honduras), and finally the number. There are no city codes.

CALLING WITHIN HONDURAS

Local Calls

Direct dial only exists in Tegucigalpa and San Pedro Sula.

Long Distance Calls

Calls within Honduras can be placed from hotels or public phones. Hondutel's telephone offices provide another alternative.

International Calls

Hondutel operates the international telephone service in Honduras and provides telecommunications centers in all towns, their service also including collect calls. Direct dial international is only available in Tegucigalpa, San Pedro Sula, La Ceiba, the Bay Islands, and a few other select places. To place a direct call, dial 00 + country code + area code + number.

Look for AT&T Direct phones at the airport in Toncontin or at Hondutel offices. Otherwise, try accessing AT&T or MCI for collect or calling-card calls by dialing the following numbers:

U.S. AT&T	123
U.S. MCI	122

Access is not available from every phone.

PAY PHONES

Public Telephones

Coin phones accept 10-centavo coins. Remember, however, that the rest of the country outside of Tegucigalpa and San Pedro Sula does not have direct dial capability.

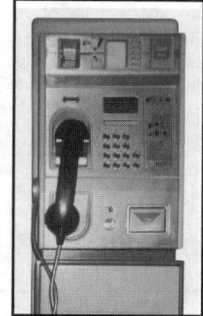

CELLULAR PHONES

If intending to use cellular communications, bear in mind that Honduras operates on an AMPS analog standard, the same as the U.S.; Inversiones Rocafuerte S.A. operates the system.

Note: Your home country cell phone may not work in this country. If not, we recommend that you rent an international cell phone *before* you leave home. A major US-based cell phone rental provider is **IMC WorldCell**. For information see "International Cell Phone Rentals" on page 14.

CALL BACK

You can (potentially) save significant sums when calling in Honduras by using a call back service. For a list of callback services, please refer to the "Communications" section in the *Global Road Warrior* Introduction.

Fees for call back services vary widely, depending on the company and the type of service required. Be sure to check with these companies before leaving to compare rates.

Honduras

PHONE JACK

Plug adaptors are available through **iGo Corporation.** (See "Electrical and Telephone Adaptors" on page 19.)

FAX

Some top-end hotels offer slow services.

POSTAL SERVICES

Airmail will take between 7 to 10 days.

Hours of service

Monday to SaturdBusiness Services

COURIER SERVICES

Airborne Express (Consolidaciones y Carga de Honduras); 10 Calle, 11 Avenida S.O. No. 75, Barrio Paz Barahona, San Pedro Sula; tel: 502-111; fax: 509-871.

DHL de Honduras; tel: 239-4882; Colonia Palmira, Ave. Republica of Chile; Frente Oficina Principal Banexpo, Tegucigalpa, M.D.C., tel: 220-1805.

Federal Express (Gutierrez Cargo); tel: 239-0340; fax: 238-5051.

UPS (Courier International, S.A.); Hotel Maya, Edif. Panamericano Local 4, 3RA Calle 2DA Avenida, N.O. Barrio Guamilito, San Pedro Sula; tel: 578-805; fax: 578-921.

Electrical

Current

110/220 volts AC, 60Hz.

ELECTRIC PLUGS

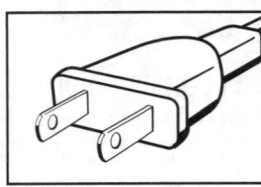

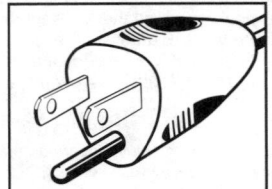

Plug adaptors are available through **iGo Corporation.** (See "Electrical and Telephone Adaptors" on page 19.)

Internet Connection

HOW TO CONNECT

Connecting to AOL and Compuserve in Honduras is similar to using it when traveling outside your own area code. See the introductory section for detailed information on connecting to your account through a different phone number.

America Online

Numbers are available at keyword *international*. Be sure to get several local numbers before leaving. Go to keyword *access* (a free area) and download the software.

There are no direct access numbers for America Online in Honduras. Users will have to pay international rates to use the service.

Compuserve

Numbers are available at *Go International*. The Compuserve Web-site also has a great deal of information, at http://www.compuserve.com. There are no direct access numbers for Compuserve in Honduras. Users will have to pay international rates to use the service.

Independent Service Providers

Many independent service providers offer discounts if you are only in town for a couple of days.

Compunet S. de R.L.; tel/fax: 232-8480; email: info@compunet.hn; http://www.compunet.hn/.

HONDUDATA; tel: 221-4014; fax: 236-9471; http://www.hondudata.hn/.

Hon.net; email: comtek@hon.net; http://www.comtek.hn.net.

Optinet; tel: 235-6754; http://www.optinet.hn/.

Psinet S. de R.L.; tel: 443-4137; tel: 443-0371; email: ventas@psinet.hn; http://www.psinet.hn/.

Business Culture

GREETINGS AND COURTESIES

Handshakes are the common greeting among both men and women; handshakes are gentle—almost limp—and somewhat prolonged, except among Hondurans already involved in and familiar with international business standards. Titles are important, and foreign visitors should call their business counterparts by their title and last name unless requested to do otherwise.

MEETINGS

Appointments are necessary and should be made two weeks in advance. Allow plenty of time in this Latin American country, where time runs slower than it might at home. Punctuality and a hurried manner are not emphasized in this culture, and so, one must come prepared to wait. Bring materials written or translated into Spanish; although many businesspeople and government officials may speak some English, it will nonetheless make a good impression and also assist those who do not have extensive command of the English language, for example, engineers and technicians. Be sure to concentrate on socializing and avoid getting straight down to business as it will emphasize that you also place importance on establishing personal contact, very much valued in Honduras.

DECISION MAKING

It is important to first establish a personal relationship, possibly through several meetings, before a business deal can be concluded. It is important to cultivate relationships with Honduran peers because the quality of these relationships may strongly influence the actual decisionmaker even when your immediate counterpart is not the one making the decision. Negotiations will most likely take longer than they might in the U.S., thus, time should be set aside to accommodate such deliberations.

WOMEN

Although women generally occupy a secondary status in heavily male-dominated and *macho*-influenced Honduras, many operate businesses and may be accorded considerable personal freedom. Foreign businesswomen are expected to be highly professional, appropriate, and not aggressive or confrontational. Women may generally go on the streets and dine alone, but may feel more comfortable if escorted.

BUSINESS ATTIRE

In general, Latin Americans follow meticulous grooming habits. As such, one should never appear in too casual an attire, even after hours. A conservative business suit will do well for both men and women. Keep in mind the more humid climate and stick to natural fabrics, if possible. Nights can get cool, so bring suitable covering. A collapsible umbrella is also suggested for frequent afternoon showers most specially in the rainy season: mid-May to mid-September.

Business Centers
Tegucigalpa

CITY VIEW

Tegucigalpa, christened "silver hill" by the Spaniards who first discovered it as a mining town in 1578, is bustling with over 897,000 people. A mountainous city with pleasant climate, it is actually less expensive to stay across the Río Choluteca in Comayagüela (the old capital). However, expect more dangerous conditions for the trade off, and do not travel in the old capital after dark. Hondurans call Tegucigalpa "Tegus," which proves much easier to pronounce. The patron saint of Tegucigalpa himself is honored in the Historical center's Cathedral. "La zona viva" is the modern commercial section, which is the best bet for dining and shopping.

AIRPORT

Toncontin Airport to City Center

Tegucigalpa's Toncontin Airport (TGU) is 4 miles (7km) southeast of the center of town. Taxis and buses are available to the city, along with a few rental car agencies. Some of the nice hotels will also provide transportation, but call ahead. There is also a restaurant, bar, and post office in the terminal.

Airline Numbers

Aeroservicios 33-1296
American Airlines 232-1347, 232-1414
American Airlines .... airport: 233-9680/85
Aviateca 31-2469
Caribbean Air 233-1906
Continental Airlines 233-7889, 233-7835
Iberia 231-5223, 231-5247
Isleña Airlines 233-1130, 239-3084/85
LACSA/TACA 233-9797, 234-1675

HOTELS

Note: Be sure to have advance reservations before traveling to Honduras during the high season.

Top-end

Camino Real Inter Continental; Avenida Roble, PO Box 2122; tel: 231-1300; fax: 231-1400; 157 rooms; in business district.

Honduras Maya; Avenida Republica de Chile, Colonia Palmira; tel: 232-3191; fax: 232-7629; restaurant; conference facilities; corporate rates; pool; US$110/125.

Plaza San Martin; Frente Plaza San Martin, Colonia Palmira; tel: 237-2928; fax: 231-1366; city center; restaurant; corporate rates; fitness; US$90/110.

Expensive

Alameda; Boulevard Suyapa; tel: 232-6874; fax: 232-6932; 75 rooms; US$54.

Aparthotel Guijarros; tel: 235-6852, 235-8764; fax: 235-8767; all-suites and apartments; complimentary airport transfer; cafeteria; fax/photocopy facilities; secretarial/ translation service; in-room modem connection; on-site security; sauna; pool.

Hotel Portal del Angel; new boutique hotel; complimentary breakfast; meeting room; laptop computers available; fax/photocopy facilities; secretarial service; fitness room; on-site security;

La Ronda; 6a Calle Avenida Jerez; tel: 237-8151; fax: 237-1454; city center; restaurant; conference facilities (up to 300); secretarial service; fax/photocopy facilities; corporate rates; US$45/65.

Leslie's Bed and Breakfast Place; Colonia Palmira San Martin #452; tel: 239-0641; fax: 232-1687; breakfast cafe (included); fax services; in-room data port, cable tv; fitness center; US$59/69.

Moderate

Istmania; 5 Ave. entre 7 y 8, Calle no. 1438; tel: 237-1639; fax: 237-1446; city center; restaurant; conference room (up to 30); corporate rates; US$30/35.

MEDICAL CARE

Centro Dental D`Anzo; Centro Comercial Centro America, Segundo Nivel, Local 24-B; tel: 239-3328.

Los Lomas Medical Center; Edificio Plaza Colprosumah, Boulevard Juan Pablo II; tel: 39-3417; fax: 39-3424.

AUTO RENTAL

Avis; http://www.avis.com; tel: 553-0088, 552-2872, 552-0088.

Budget; airport, tel: 336-927; Blvd. Comunidad Economica, Europea Comayaguela D.C.; tel: 335-171, fax: 335-170, 335-161.

Hertz; http://www.hertz.com; Villa Real Main Downtown; tel: 239-0772; fax: 232-0870; there is also a Hertz desk at the airport.

WORLD TRADE CENTER

World Trade Center Tegucigalpa
c/o Royal Hotels International, Inc.
1001 South Bayshore Drive, Suite 2210
Miami, FL 33131
tel: [1] (305) 377-0304; fax: [1] (305) 577-3347

CHAMBER OF COMMERCE

Federación de Cámeras de Comercio e Industrias de Honduras (FEDECAMARA)
Edificio Castañito 2er Nivel
6a Avenida Colonia Los Castaños, Tegucigalpa
tel: 232-6083; fax: 232-1870

Cámara de Comercio e Industrias de Tegucigalpa
Bulevar de Centroamérica, Apdo 3444
Tegucigalpa
tel: 232-8110; fax: 231-2049

Hong Kong

At a Glance
THE PEOPLE
Population .... 6,847,125 (July 1999 est.)
Growth Rate .... 1.9% (1999 est.)
Life Expectancy ....78.81years (born 1999)
Infant Mortality ...... 5.2 deaths/1,000 live births (1999 est.)

Ethnic Composition
Chinese 95%
Other 5%

Religious Composition
Buddhist philosophy and local religions 90%
Christian 10%

Languages Spoken
Cantonese, Mandarin (official), English.

Education and Literacy
Full-time education in compulsory between the ages of 6 and 15. Adult literacy is 92.2 percent.

Labor Force
Total: 3,251,000
By occupation: services 62%, industry 32.5%, agriculture 5.5%.

THE ECONOMY
Hong Kong was reabsorbed by China in 1997. Since then it has experienced its first recession since its 30-year rise to wealth. Caught between an Asian currency crisis and a shift to new reign, Hong Kong has seen retail sales slump and tourism plummet. It also saw sky-high property prices fall and the loss of property tax revenue that had previously kept the government's coffers filled. The "special administrative region" has highly developed business, communications, and transportation infrastructures and one of the best ports in East Asia. Port facilities are currently beyond capacity, however, and improvements will not be ready for several years. Rivals Singapore and Taiwan stand ready to fill in the gap and Hong Kong's status as a "free port" is tenuous. As Hong Kong approaches the next century it finds itself with rising inflation and something it had never experienced before: growing unemployment.
Exports ...... US$188.08 billion (includes re-exports, 1997)
Imports .... US$208.63 billion (c.i.f., 1997)
Total GDP .... US$168.1 billion (1998 est.)
GDP Per Capita .... US$25,100 (1998 est.)
Unemployment ....5.5% (1998 est.)
Inflation Rate ....2.9% (1998 est.)

Top Export Partners
United States, Japan, EU, Singapore

Top Import Partners
Japan, Taiwan, United States, Singapore, South Korea

Top Exports
Clothing, textiles, yarn and fabric, footwear, electrical appliances, watches and clocks, toys.

Top Imports
Foodstuffs, transport equipment, raw materials, semi-manufactures, petroleum, fuels

BUSINESS WORKWEEK
Offices
Monday to Friday 9a.m. to 1p.m. and 2p.m. to 5p.m., Saturday 9a.m. to 1p.m.

Banks
Monday to Friday 10a.m. to 4:30p.m., Saturday 9a.m. to 12:30p.m.

Government
Monday to Friday 9a.m. to 1p.m. and 2p.m. to 5p.m., Saturdays 9a.m. to 1p.m.

Retail
Monday to Saturday 10a.m. to 6p.m.
Many large retailers are open until 9p.m.

HOLIDAYS
Solar New Year ....January 1
Lunar New Year .... February 15-18*
Day after Ching Ming..April 6*
Easter..April 2-5*
Tuen Ng, Dragon Boat Festival .... June 9*
Hong Kong's reversion to
Motherland and Inauguration of SAR ....July 1
Victory Day for War of
Resistance against Japan ....August 9*
Christmas ....December 25-26
*Date may vary by year.

CLIMATE
Seasons
The weather in the summer is tropical—hot, humid, and rainy. Winter weather comes with plenty of cloudy, windy, and "chilly" spells with a seemingly never ending drizzle also covers the city. The average January weather ranges from 8° to 23°C (47° to 74°F). The winds stop suddenly in March, and Hong Kong enjoys a pleasant spring, complete with April showers and mild temperatures.

Regions
Big, crashing thunderstorms arrive towards the end of May, and in June the temperature begins rising, reaching the average high of 34°C (94°F) from July through September. Typhoon (hurricane) season begins in July and lasts through October. November settles down and offers the traveler the best time of the year to visit Hong Kong.

Money & Banking
Currency
The currency of Hong Kong is the Hong Kong Dollar (HK$).

Denominations
The Hong Kong Dollar comes in HK$10, 5, 2, and 1, and coin demominations of 50, 20, and 10 cents; and banknotes of HK$20, 50, 100, HK$500, 1,000.

Traveler's Checks and Credit Cards
Hong Kong's position as Asia's leading financial center means that it's very easy to change money; have money wired or transferred to you. Traveler's checks can be cashed at banks, hotels and exchange kiosks throughout the city.

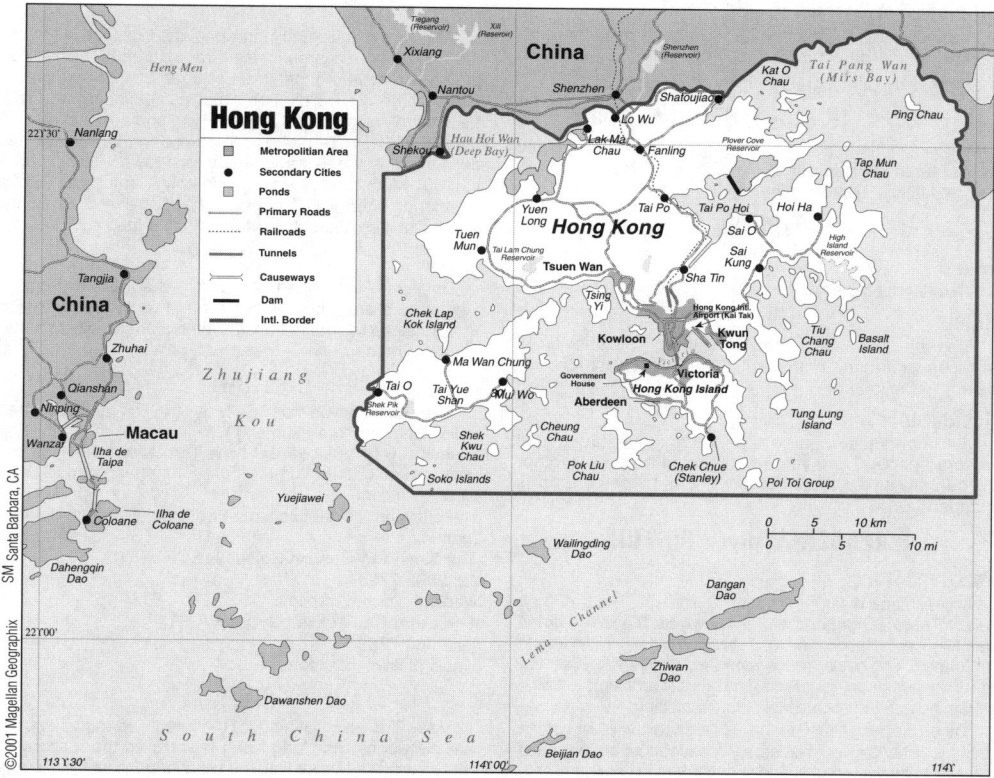

In Hong Kong almost any foreign currency may be bought and sold on the open market. Commissions can run as high as 5 percent at the airport. Hotels give you the poorest rate, banks are somewhere in the middle, and foreign exchange houses such as Thomas Cook will offer the most favorable exchange rates.

The Hong Kong dollar is pegged to the U.S. dollar, so many shops accept payments with U.S. dollars or other major currencies for large purchases, although you probably won't get the official exchange rate.

Major credit cards are accepted almost everywhere except very small shops and street vendors. ATMs abound for cash advances on credit cards or simple withdrawals.

Travel

VISA AND PASSPORT

A passport is required for entry to Hong Kong, which must be valid at least one month beyond your intended stay (for some nationalities, six months). The visa policy is fairly liberal: British citizens are allowed a 12-month stay without a visa; U.S. citizens are allowed a one-month stay; most others are allowed a three-month stay. For nationals of certain countries, stays of only one month or 14 days are permitted, depending on nationality. Those wishing to stay longer than the visa-free period allotted for their nationality must apply for a visa before traveling to Hong Kong.

It is required by law to have a return ticket when entering Hong Kong. Carry a letter of intent when traveling on business. To obtain a work visa, submit a letter of employment

and a visa application to Hong Kong Immigration. The process generally takes eight weeks to complete. The Immigration Office may be contacted for country-specific visa information:

Hong Kong Immigration Department
Immigration Tower
7 Gloucester Road, Wanchai
tel: 2824-6111; fax: 2877-7711
email: enquiry@immd.gcn.gov.hk
Web: www.info.gov.hk./immd/english/welcome

DEPARTURE FORMALITIES

No requirements other than a ticket to another destination are needed for departure. Departure fees of HK$50 are usually included in airfares.

CUSTOMS ENTRY (PERSONAL)

Duty-free
- Tobacco: 200 cigarettes, 50 cigars, or 250g of tobacco
- Alcohol: 1 liter bottle of wine or spirits
- Other: 60ml perfume

Note: (a) If arriving from Macau, duty-free imports for Macau residents are limited to half the above cigarette, cigar, and tobacco allowance. (b) Aircraft crew and passengers in direct transit via Hong Kong are limited to 20 cigarettes or 57g of pipe tobacco. (c) The import of live animals is strictly controlled. (d) Firearms must be declared upon entry and handed into custody until departure. (e) Non-prescribed drugs may not be brought in without a doctor's certificate of use.

Hong Kong

Prohibited or Restricted
- Firearms must be declared and handed over for safe-keeping until departure
- Mammalian pets are quarantined for 8 months

IMMUNIZATION
No vaccinations are required unless traveling recently from an area infected with cholera or yellow fever. Tetanus and hepatitis A are recommended.

TIPPING

Taxi
Taxi drivers expect a 10 percent gratuity.

Hotels
Tips are now expected in Hong Kong hotels for small services, preferably 10 percent. Other service charges will be applied to the bill.

Restaurants
A 10 percent surcharge is added to the restaurant bill for large parties, and you are expected to leave another 10 percent at the table. Otherwise, a 15 percent tip is standard.

EMERGENCY INFORMATION

Police and Crime
Unlike many Western cities of similar size, Hong Kong is relatively safe. Organized gangs known as Triads run drugs, gambling, prostitution, and loan sharking but have little impact on tourists. The heavy police presence makes it unlikely that you'll encounter any problems. The biggest problems are pick-pocketing and the occasional purse snatching.

Take basic precautions. Avoid flashy displays of wealth, dress and behave conservatively. Leave most of your cash, traveler's checks, jewelry, and your camera in your hotel safe. Carry photocopies of your passport instead of the original. Carry cash in a money belt, and use credit cards or traveler's checks for most of your transactions.

Though once a corruption-free enclave, there are reports of corruption with the arrival of mainland Chinese officials. Business travelers may find that their deals with local companies involve the bribing of public officials. Besides making the personal decision of whether or not to participate in such dealings, check on your legal position in your own country. Some nations now have stiff penalties for their business people who bribe officials overseas.

Hong Kong police are polite, efficient, and honest. Any problems or crimes reported to them will be dealt with promptly.

Emergency Numbers
Police, Fire and Ambulance 999
Royal Hong Kong Police (emergency) 527-7177

Health
Hong Kong's tap water is safe to drink, but most locals boil it anyway. Food from street vendors is also safe for the most part. During summer, beware of heat related problems.

Most personal care products can be found in Hong Kong, but they are often very expensive. Bring a sufficient supply of your prescription medications.

Most major hotels have a house doctor. Hong Kong also has several hospitals that were started by the British government and some excellent private hospitals as well.

For more information on medical centers, including phone numbers, please see the "Business Centers" section at the end of this chapter.

TAXI
Taxis are plentiful in Hong Kong and Kowloon, although there is an extra charge for the Cross Harbour Tunnel. You may hail a cab from the street or go to a hotel taxi queue. Meters start at HK$15. For better navigational purposes, taxis traveling in Hong Kong and Kowloon are colored red; taxis in the New Territories are green; and Lantau Islands taxis are blue. An average fare around town will cost about HK$60. Most drivers speak primarily Cantonese with a smattering of English. If possible, have all directions on paper in Chinese characters. If not, bring a map.

AUTO
Driving in Hong Kong varies from chaotic to traffic jam. Rental cars are available but are not really advisable for visitors since the mass transit systems are so efficient and cabs are numerous.

TRAIN
The Kowloon-Canton Railway (KCR) runs between Hung Hom and the mainland China border; the Light Rail Transit (LRT) services the New Territories. Services are also available to the airport. Fares are cheap and the service is efficient.

Following are telephone numbers to call for further information:
The Kowloon-Canton Railway (KCR)
tel: 2602-7799
website: www.kcrc.com/
The Light Rail Transit System (LRT)
tel: 2468-7788
website: www.kcrc.com/

METRO
Mass Transit Railway (MTR) offers three routes in Central, Kowloon, and Hong Kong Island's northern shore as well as a cross-harbor link. It is more expensive than a ferry but much faster and far and away surpasses a cab in peak traffic hours. Fares range from HK$4 to HK$12.50.

For visitors, an MTR Tourist Ticket is available allowing visitors to buy tickets worth HK$50 or HK$200. They are much more convenient than buying a ticket for each trip.

Following is a contact for more information:
The Mass Transit Railway (MTR)
tel: 2881-8888
website: www.mtrcorp.com/

BUSES & TRAMS
Buses and minibuses service all areas. Buses all display their destinations (in both Chinese and English) on the top panels above the windshield. Bring exact change for fares ranging from HK$1.20 to HK$34.20. Consult a tourist kiosk or the Hong Kong Tourist Association for maps and schedules.

Minibuses offer less structured service, and passengers may disembark wherever they please. Look for the red stripe along the outside of the bus. Conversely, maxicabs, recognizable by their green stripe, run on certain routes only and have set prices. Expect to pay between HK$4 and HK$15.

Tramways are the oldest form of mass transport in Hong Kong, operating continuously since 1904, and still one of the cheapest and most scenic ways to get around. For the flat fare of just HK$2 you can traverse some of Hong Kong's most colorful districts.

The Peak Tram is a quick way to Victoria Peak, Hong Kong's highest point. It makes the 373-meter climb in eight minutes, providing you with incredible views of the island and harbor. It runs from 7a.m. until midnight every day, and there is a free shuttle on an open-top double decker bus running from 10a.m. to 9p.m. between the tram's Terminus Station and the Star Ferry Pier in Central.

Following are contact numbers for more information:

First Bus 2136-8888
Kowloon Motor Bus 2745-4466
Citybus 2873-0818
Hong Kong Tramways Ltd. 2548-7102
Peak Tramways..................................... 2849-7654
Hong Kong Transport Bureau 2189-2189

WATER TRAVEL

Hong Kong means "fragrant harbor" in Chinese, and water travel is the soul of the city. The famous Star Ferry regularly runs between Kowloon and Hong Kong Island (Wanchai or Central) from 6:30a.m. to 11:30p.m. The trip takes about 10 minutes and affords one with outstanding views. Businesspeople and tourists alike transit the waterways lending the trip a mixed, eclectic mood while surrounded with enchanting scenery. Upper deck (first-class) travel will cost HK$2.20.

The major outlying Islands such as Lantau, Lamma, Cheung Chau, and Peng Chau are served by larger ferries. These embark from the Island Pier, located close to the Star Ferry Pier. Fares are lower on weekdays. On public holidays, Saturday afternoons, and Sundays the fares almost double for non-residents of the Islands.

Check the Hong Kong Tourist Association kiosks for schedules. Hydrofoil ferries to Macau run on regular schedules and are common for business travel. Most major international cruise lines also dock in Hong Kong.

Following are contact numbers for the three main ferry companies:

Star Ferry Co.. 2366-2576
Hong Kong & Yaumatei Ferry Co., Ltd. 2542-3081
Polly Ferry Co., Ltd. (Hydrofoils) 2711-1630

TRAVEL ASSISTANCE

Hong Kong Tourist Association
9-11th Floor, Citicorp Centre
18 Whitfield Road
North Point, Hong Kong
tel: 2807 6543
or 2508 1234 (recorded tourist information)
fax: 2806 0303
email: info@hkta.org

Hotel Accommodations

Hotels are plentiful throughout Hong Kong. After the crush of persons seeking accommodation in late 1996 and early 1997 before the Chinese took rule, things have settled down, and the colony is now witnessing a severe drop in occupancy rate, meaning much friendlier prices.

Essential Terms

English	Cantonese
Yes	Hoe-geh
No	Ng-tak
Good morning	Jou-sran
Hello (daytime)	Lay gay hoemah
Hello (evening)	Joe-tao
Hello (telephone)	Wai!
Good-bye	bye-bye
Please	ng goy
Thank you	Daw jyeh (for a gift)
	Ng goy (for service)
Pleased to meet you	Hoe goe-hing nung gow geen dow lay
Excuse me; I'm sorry	Dui ng joo
My name is _____	Ngaw gaw meng gyoo _____
I don't understand	Ngoh M ming
Do you speak English?	Jeong taai-taai sik gong

Communications

DIALING CODES IN HONG KONG

International country code: [852]

Dialing Hong Kong from Overseas

To dial Hong Kong from overseas, dial your country's international dialing code, then 852 (the country code for Hong Kong), and finally the number. There are no city codes.

Assistance Numbers

International Direct Dial Assistance............................. 001
International Calling Assistance 013
Operator-assisted International calls........................... 010
Local Directory Service 1081
Information Services Department.................... 2842-8777
International Information Service...................... 2739-1818
Local Directory Assistance (English)...................... 1081
Police Hotline (non-emergency) 2527-7177

CALLING WITHIN HONG KONG

Local Calls

Local calls can be easily made, although calls from a hotel usually come with a hefty surcharge, even for local calls. Hong Kong's telephone system if fully digitalized.

International Calls

Business centers and hotels offer direct dialing for international calls, but with high extra charges. As an alternative, you can use a Phonecard or MCI World Phone service, tel: 800-96-1121. MCI allows country-to-country calls.

Hong Kong

Hong Kong

PAY PHONES
Public Telephones

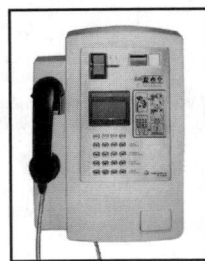

There aren't many pay phones in the street. However, look for them in hotel lobbies, post offices, ferry terminals, Hong Kong Telecom offices, offices of Cable & Wireless, and the airport.

It is perfectly acceptable to walk into a shop and ask to use the phone to make a local call. Shopkeepers usually have their phones right on the counter in plain view from the street; after all, if they can lure you into their store with a free phone call, you might just buy something.

Calling Cards

Phonecards can be purchased in denominations of HK$40, HK100, or HK250 in shops or at hotels. Without a Phonecard, you will need a pocketful of H$5 unless the call remains brief.

CALL BACK

You can (potentially) save significant sums when calling in Hong Kong by using a call back service. For a list of call-back services, please refer to the "Communications" section in the *Global Road Warrior* Introduction.

Fees for call back services vary widely, depending on the company and the type of service required. Be sure to check with these companies before leaving to compare rates.

CELLULAR PHONES

As the city of technological and economic wonder, Hong Kong boasts many cellular phone systems ranging from digital to analogue. Communications Services International offers GSM and TACS service. Hutchinson Telecom adds CDMA to the list; SmarTone handles GSM; and Pacific Link offers both TDMA and ETACS service. Many top-end hotels rent cell phones, and if not, will point you in the right direction.

Note: Your home country cell phone may not work in this country. If not, we recommend that you rent an international cell phone *before* you leave home. A major US-based cell phone rental provider is **IMC WorldCell**. For information see "International Cell Phone Rentals" on page 14.

PHONE JACKS

Plug adaptors are available through **iGo Corporation.** (See "Electrical and Telephone Adaptors" on page 19.)

FAX

Hong Kong has one of the most advanced fax and telecommunication services in Asia.

POSTAL SERVICES

Postal services are widely available, and letters take three to five days to reach Western Europe or North America.

Hours of service

Monday to Friday 8a.m. to 6p.m., Saturday 8a.m. to 2p.m.

Business Services
BUSINESS CENTERS

All major hotels have these centers, gathering under one roof secretarial and translation services, computer, fax, and telex capabilities, business card printing services, and a host of others. Some hotel center fees can border on the unconscionable, so you may want to check out business centers outside the hotels. These centers will not only rent you a private desk for HK$3,500 (about US$453) per month and up, but provide you with a private address, answering and forwarding services, and lawyers and accountants to help you register your company.

Asia Business Centre 3rd Floor, The Centremark, 287-299 Queen's Road, Central; tel: 5448773; fax: 8540203.

Central Executive Business Centre 11/F Central Building, Pedder Street, Central; 8417888.

China Traders Centre Regal Airport Hotel; offices and conference rooms by the hour, day, week, or month.

COURIER SERVICES

Airborne Express; Airborne Freight Corp., Unit B, G/F Phase 1, Mtl Warehouse Bldg., Berth One Kwai Chung; tel: 2786-3223; fax: 2796-3881.

DHL Intl. (Hong Kong) Ltd.; DHL House, 13 Mok Cheong St., Tokwawan, Kowloon; tel: 2764-4888.

FedEx; Shop 127B, 1/F, Shopping Arcade, New Mandarin Plaza, Tsim Sha Tsui East, Kowloon; tel: 366-889.

TNT; 6th Floor, Chung Nam Centre, 414 Kwun Tong Road, Kwun Tong, Kowloon; tel: 389-5279; fax: 343-2714.

UPS; Suite 602 North Tower, World Finance Center, Harbour City, Tsim Sha Tsui, Kowloon; tel: 735-3535; fax: 738-5073.

TRANSLATION SERVICES

A-Tech Translation Services 1504 Kelly Communications Centre, 570 Nathan Road, Tsim Sha Tsui, Kowloon; tel: 3881662; fax: 3854522.

Chang Jiang Translanguage Centre 3/F Wai Hing Communications Building, 17 Wing Ho Street, Hong Kong; tel: 8153145; fax: 8541620.

China Communication Translation Services 1/F, 129 Queen's Road, Central; tel: 5418585; fax: 8540549.

International Information Service Ltd. 10-3 Wing On Plaza, 62 Mody Road, Tsim Sha Tsui, Kowloon; tel: 7391818; fax: 7213692.

Electrical

Current
200 volts AC, 50Hz.

ELECTRIC PLUGS

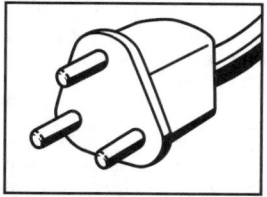

Plug adaptors are available through **iGo Corporation.** (See "Electrical and Telephone Adaptors" on page 19.)

Technical Support

HARDWARE/SOFTWARE VENDOR SUPPORT

Acer/Texas Instruments; (in Germany) tel: [49] (4102) 488-469; fax; [49] (4102) 488-169; (in the U.S.) [1] (408) 432-6200; http://www.acer.com/.

Adobe; tel: 2608-3645; fax: 2601-6936 (Adobe Frame Products); tel: 2811-4228; fax: 2811-2263 (All Adobe Products except Frame); (in Switzerland) tel: [41] (800) 833-310; (in the U.S.) tel: [1] (800) 500-7078; (in the U.S.) tel: [1] (716) 633-3600; http://www.adobe.com/.

Apple/Claris; tel: 2506-8888; (in Switzerland) tel: [41] (800) 833-310; (in the U.K.) tel: [44] (990) 127-753; (in the U.S.) tel: [1] (800) 500-7078; http://www.apple.com/.

AST; (in the U.S.) tel: [1] (817) 232-9824 (International Technical Support); (in Ireland) tel: [353] (61) 492-222; (in the U.S.) tel: [1] (949) 727-4141; http://www.ast.com/.

Compaq/Digital; tel: 2868-1382; fax: 2524-9533; (in Switzerland) tel: [41] (22) 709-5330; fax: [41] (22) 709-5391 (Geneva); tel: [41] (1) 801-2507; fax: [41] (1) 801-2172 (Zurich); (General U.S.) tel: (281) 518-2000; http://www.compaq.com/.

Corel; tel: 8100-3729 (All Applications); (in the U.S.) tel: [1] (716) 871-2325 (Ask to be Forwarded to Appropriate Program); http://www.corel.com/.

Dell; tel: 2508-0500; fax: 2887-2040;(Dell- Europe) tel: [44] (134) 474-8000; (in the U.S.) tel: [1] (512) 338-4400; fax: [1] (512) 728-3330; http://www.dell.com/.

Filemaker/Claris; (in Germany) tel: [49] (180) 525-8166 (Info-line); fax: [49] (180) 567-2233; tel: [49] (180) 523-6423; (in the U.S.) tel: [1] (800) 965-9090; http://www.claris.com/.

Gateway 2000; (in the U.S.) tel: [1] (605) 232-2191; fax: [1] (605) 232-2023; (in Ireland) tel: [353] (1) 797-2000; http://www.g2k.com/.

Hewlett Packard; tel: (800) 96 7729; (in Switzerland) tel: [41] (22) 780-8111; (in the U.S.) tel: [1] (408) 246-4300; http://www.hp.com/.

IBM; tel: 2825-6222; fax: 2810-0210; (in Switzerland) tel: [41] (22) 310-0418 (French); (in the U.S.) tel: [1] (919) 517-2800; (U.S. Main Office) tel: [1] 914-765-1900; http://www.ibm.com/

Microsoft; tel: 2804-4222; fax: 2560-2217; 2804-4222 (AnswerPoint/Microsoft Technical Support); 2535-9293 (AnswerPoint/Microsoft Technical Support Faxback Service); 2804-4277 (Microsoft Club Member Hotline); (in Switzerland) tel: [41] (848) 858-868; fax [41] (1) 831-0869; (in the U.S.) [1] (425) 635-7222; http://www.microsoft.com/.

NEC; tel: 795-2111 (UltraCare Support); (in the U.S.) [1] (916) 388-0101 (Main Switchboard); http://www.nec.com/.

Novell; (in Australia) tel: [61] 2-925-3000 (Asia Pacific Support Center); (in Japan) [81] 3-5481-1161; (in Switzerland) tel: [41] (1) 308-4747; fax: [41] (1) 302-0401; (in the U.S.) tel: [1] (408) 434-2300; fax: [1] (408) 577-5775 (Worldwide Sales Headquarters); http://www.novell.com/.

Quark; (Singapore Office) tel: [65] 467-6675; (in the U.S.) tel: [1] (303) 894-8899; fax: [1] (303) 894-3398 (For Products Registered in the Americas); http://www.quark.com/.

Toshiba; (in the U.S.) [1] (949) 583-3000 (Corporate Headquarters); (in Germany) tel: [49] (2131) 158-319; fax: [49] (2131) 158-558; (in Switzerland) tel: [41] (1) 946-0777; fax: [41] (1) 946-0807; (in Ireland) tel: [44] (193) 282-8828; http://www.toshiba.com/.

Internet Connection

HOW TO CONNECT

Connecting to AOL and Compuserve is similar to using it when traveling outside your own area code. See the introductory section for detailed information on connecting to your account through a different phone number.

Hong Kong Telecom has linkups to the International Database Access Service (IDAS); Dialcom electronic mail and data base access system; Infonet, the single-source, worldwide data communications and information network; and International High-Speed Document Transfer Service. For information, call either of the two 24-hour offices (listed in the phone book).

America Online
Numbers are available at keyword *international*. Be sure to get several local numbers before leaving. AOL's GlobalNet service charges US$6 an hour in addition to the usual charges. Go to keyword *access* (a free area) and download the software.

Access: Hong Kong 2519-9040.

Compuserve
Numbers are available at Go International. The Compuserve website also has a great deal of information, at http://www.compuserve.com.

Access: Hong Kong 3002-3333.

Independent Service Providers

Many independent service providers offer discounts if you are only in town for a couple of days.

HK Supernet Ltd; tel: 2335-3600; fax: 2719-8469; email: info@pacific.net.hk; http://www.hk.super.net/.

HKNet Co Ltd; tel: 2110-2288; fax: 2110-0088; http://www.hknet.com/.

i-Wave Limited (EXA Net); tel: 2370-2800; fax: 2370-2807; email: info@exa.net; http://www.i-wave.net/.

LinkAGE Online Ltd.; tel: 2331-8123; fax: 2795-1262; email: info@hk.linkage.net; http://www.hk.linkage.net/.

Netfront Internet Services; tel: 2517-1209; fax: 2548-0448; email: support@netfront.net; http://www.netfront.net/.

VIANET; (in Austria, providing service in Hong Kong); [43] 1-404-020; http://www.vianet.at

Vision Online; tel: 2311-8855; fax: 2311-8881; email: info@vol.net; http://www.vol.net/.

Business Culture
GREETINGS AND COURTESIES

A handshake is the accepted greeting. Chinese usually shake hands very lightly instead of taking the hand firmly and forcefully pumping it, and in Hong Kong a handshake may last as long as 10 seconds. Upon meeting someone, Chinese lower their eyes slightly as a sign of respect. Staring into the eyes of a Chinese might make them uncomfortable. The concept of face is also important in Hong Kong, and foreigners should be aware of this factor in all aspects of their Hong Kong business dealings. Saying or doing anything that causes someone to lose face can instantly destroy a relationship, perhaps forever.

DECISION MAKING

Hong Kong Chinese try to avoid a direct negative response, for fear of causing embarrassment or losing face. Instead of directly saying no, they are likely to say something is inconvenient or is under consideration. They might also say, "Yes, but it will be difficult," which is often their way of saying no. If there is bad news, they might convey it through an intermediary or hint at it rather than saying it directly. After a deal has been negotiated, some executives prefer to sign a short general agreement and allow others to work out the details. Avoid this if possible, as it can lead to misunderstandings and result in strained relationships.

WOMEN

Women are treated better than in many other business arenas but are still not regarded as equal to men. Most executives are men, with women being relegated to the role of secretary. Chinese women with high social standing can achieve higher positions. Most travel agents, public relations executives, and sales staff are women. Women traveling to Hong Kong will find little if any open discrimination; however, they should behave professionally and dress formally. A self-confident, poised woman might accomplish more, and do it faster, than a male colleague because Chinese may feel that if she has been chosen to represent her company, she must be someone with great ability.

MEETINGS

Before a meeting, it is customary to provide as much detail as possible about the issues under discussion. Also include a list of your representatives who will attend the meeting, with the team leader's name first. Others should be listed in order of seniority or importance at the meeting. Your team will be led into a room in which the Hong Kong team is already present. Your team leader should enter first. Teams sit across a table, leaders opposite each other and others seated in descending order of importance. Small talk will come first. Business is addressed after people feel comfortable with each other. The head of the host group will deliver a short welcome speech, then turn the floor over to the visitors. Your senior team member should speak for your company; always avoid conflicting statements from other team members. When speaking, your spokesman should address the Hong Kong senior representative. Hong Kong Chinese prefer to hear a proposal as a broad overview; they will then respond to specific issues or questions point by point.

BUSINESS ATTIRE

Business attire is Western in style and relatively formal. Summers are extremely hot and humid; lightweight clothing is more comfortable, but it should remain formal. Winters can be chilly, but extremely heavy clothing is not needed. In monsoon season, raincoats and umbrellas should be kept handy.

Business Centers
Hong Kong
CITY VIEW

Hong Kong, the quintessential city of commerce, lies sprawling for miles, but etched into an amazing scenic backdrop of hills and water. A gleaming symbol of capitalism, it now stands at the edge of balancing the Western world it has come to charm, and an age-old Chinese world that has come to re-own it. There are several districts that encompass Hong Kong. The Central District is located on Hong Kong Island and is a focal point of international business. The Hong Kong Bank presents a visible landmark here, extending 180 meters high into the horizon. Ferries, existing since the 1880s, run from the island to the Kowloon district where there are many hotels. Hong Kong fashion can be found mostly in the area in and around Landmark Centre. To escape from the hustle and bustle inside the city take a tram up to Victoria Peak, the highest point on Hong Kong Island.

AIRPORT
Chek Lap Kok Airport to City Center

Another step toward ushering out an old era, Kai Tak Airport along with its incredibly thrilling landing views has now closed with the opening of the long-awaited Chek Lap Kok airport, Hong Kong's single largest construction project ever. Complete with restaurants, fast-food chains, air-mail center, V.I.P. rooms, and even a prayer room, Chek Lap Kok is state of the art. Placed on the island of Lantau, west of Hong Kong Island, the airport lacks its predecessor's location appeal' however, an efficient transportation system was designed to make the trip into town as painless as possible. Figure about 40 minutes to Kowloon.

Taxis are conveniently located in front of the main terminal and color coded according to destination: red for Hong Kong Island and Kowloon, blue for Lantau Island, and green for the New Territories. Fares range from HK$320 to HK$350. The transportation center just in front of the terminal building houses the Airport Express, limousines, shuttle buses, and coaches all in designated bays for easier access. Major hotels also provide shuttle or limousine service that pick up or drop off at the transportation center. Hotel airport representatives are standing by should you have forgotten to reserve in advance.

The MTR link provides another method of travel into town for roughly HK$100/150. Trains will depart every 8 minutes and take about 25 minutes into town.

Airline Numbers

Air Canada	2522-1993
Air France	2524-8210
Air India	2522-1176
Air Lanka	2529-9708
Air Mauritius	2523-1114
Air New Zealand	2524-9041
Air Niugini	2524-2151
Alitalia	2543-6998
All Nippon Airways	2848-4111
Ansett Australia	2862-8111
Asiana Airlines	2523-3531
British Airways	2523-3031
Canadian Airlines	2868-3123
Cathay Pacific	2747-1888
China Airlines	2843-9800
CSA	2868-3231
East Asia Airlines	2859-3111
Far East Hydrofoil	2859-3111
Garuda Indonesia	2840-0000
Gulf Air	2882-2823
Dragonair	2590-1328, 2868-6788
Japan Airlines	2847-4600
KLM Royal Dutch Airlines	2808-2118
Korean Air	2733-7111
Lauda Air	2525-5221
Lufthansa	2868-2313
Malaysian Airlines	2521-8181
Northwest Airlines	2524-9261
Philippine Airlines	2366-2371
Qantas Airways	2842-1450
Scandinavian Airlines	2865-1370
Singapore Airlines	2520-2233
Swissair	2821-8211
Thai Airways	2525-7051
United Airlines	2810-4888
Varig Brazilian Airlines	2511-1828
Virgin Atlantic Airways	2532-3030

HOTELS

Note: With a plethora of hotels, many stand far below occupancy. Rates may, therefore, vary significantly, and many hotels will offer their rooms for less than list price.

Top-end

Conrad International; Pacific Place, 88 Queensway; tel: 2521-3838; fax: 2521-3888; restaurant; spacious rooms; 24-hour business center; notebook and cell phone rental; in-room internet access; executive floors with in-room fax machines, private check-in, butler service, complimentary breakfast, and private meeting room; health club; pool; whirlpool; HK$2,950/3,150.

Excelsior; 281 Gloucester Road, Causeway Bay; tel: 2894-8888; fax: 2895-6459; 3 restaurants; business center; conference facilities (up to 350); secretarial service; corporate rates; executive floors; health club; gym; indoor tennis; HK$2,400.

Grand Hyatt; 1 Harbour Road, Wanchai; tel: 2588-1234; toll-free: 1-800-400-3319; fax: 2802-0677; email: concierge@hyatt.com; adjacent Convention and Exhibition Center; 8 restaurants; business center and services; Regency Club rooms with separate business facilities; in-

room safe; airport limousine; taxi shuttle service to Central and Pacific Place; pool; tennis; driving range; putting green; jogging track; HK$3,200/3,450.

Harbour Plaza; 20 Tak Fung Street, Hung Hom, Kowloon; tel: 2621-3188; fax: 2621-3311; email: hp-book@harbour-plaza; 416 rooms; 6 restaurants; bar; conference facilities; business center; 2 executive floors; 24 hour room service; parking; fitness; roof-top pool; whirlpool; sauna.

Hong Kong Renaissance; 8 Peking Road, Tsim-Sha-Tsui, Kowloon; tel: 2375-1133; fax: 2375-6611; email: renhotel@hk.linkage.net; restaurant; conference facilities (up to 550); secretarial service; fax/photocopy facilities; corporate rates; fitness; sauna; pool; whirlpool; HK$2050/2200.

Hyatt Regency; 67 Nathan Road, Tsim-sha-Tsui, Kowloon; tel: 2311-1234; toll-free: 1-800-233-1234; email: general@hyattregency.com.hk; fax: 2739-8701; restaurants; business center; internet/email access; meeting/banquet facilities; modem lines; business rooms; Regency Club lounge; in-house nurse; airport limousine; in-room safe; privileges at nearby fitness center; HK$2150.

Island Shangri-La; Pacific Place, Supreme Court Road, Hong Kong Island; tel: 2877-3838; fax: 2521-8742; http: www.shangri-la.com; 6 restaurants; business center; limousine and car rental; medical clinic; library; meeting/conference facilities; in-room fax machines, fax/data connections, safes; health club; solarium; massage; gym; sauna; steambath; jacuzzi; flexiology; HK$2450/2700.

J.W. Marriott; One Pacific Place, 88 Queensway; tel: 2841-3000; toll-free: 1-800-228-9290; fax: 2845-0737; http://www.marriott.com/marriott/HKGDT; 4 restaurants; business center; secretarial service; meeting rooms; voicemail, dual phone lines; data ports; in-room safe; health club; massage; solarium; sauna; pool; whirlpool.

Kowloon Shangri-La; 64 Mody Road, Tsim Sha Tsui East, Kowloon; tel: 2721-2111; fax: 2723-8686; 725 rooms; 5 restaurants; bar; conference facilities; in-room data port, cable tv, safe, direct dial; room service; parking; fitness center; swimming pool.

Mandarin Oriental; 5 Connaught Road, Central; tel: 2522-0111; fax: 2810-6190; near Star Ferry terminal, heart of business district; personalized service; large rooms; restaurants; business center; banquet and meeting rooms (up to 300); in-room safes; fitness; pool; HK$3,000.

New World Harbour View; 1 Harbour Road, Wanchai, Hong Kong Island; tel: 2802-8888; fax: 2802-8833; email: nwhv@hkstar.com; on top of Hong Kong convention and exhibition center; restaurant; conference facilities; business center; secretarial service; internet; in-room modem/fax connection; corporate rates; fitness; sauna; pool; whirlpool; HK$2700.

The Peninsula; Salisbury Road, Kowloon; tel: 2366-6251; fax: 2722-4170; world-famous hotel; detailed and personal service; restaurants and rooftop restaurant; business center; butler service; chauffeur-driven Rolls Royces available; two-line phones; in-room fax machines and modem connection; V.I.P. rooms; meeting and banquet facilities; heli-pad; fitness; spa; indoor pool; HK$2,900.

The Regent; 18 Salisbury Road; tel: 2366-6251; fax: 2739-4546; known as one of Hong Kong's best business hotels, located on waterfront; restaurants; conference/meeting facilities; 24-hour business services; business center; secretarial/translation services; cell-phone rental; in-room safes, dual phone lines, voice mail, fax/computer connections, fitness; sauna; pool; whirlpool; HK$2200/3900.

Ritz-Carlton; 3 Connaught Road, Central; tel: 2877-6666; fax: 2877-6778; restaurants; data ports; fax machines

Hong Kong

Hong Kong

available on request; meeting facilities; secretarial service; corporate rates; Ritz-Carlton Club floors; fitness; sauna; pool; whirlpool; HK$2,850.

Sheraton Hong Kong Hotel and Towers; 20 Nathan Road, Tsim-Sha-Tsui, Kowloon; tel: 2369-1111; fax: 2739-8707; 4 restaurants; bar; conference facilities; business center; ballroom; in-room video, safe; room service; parking; fitness center; swimming pool; sauna.

Expensive

Century; 238 Jaffe Road, Wanchai, Hong Kong Island; tel: 2598-8888; fax: 2598-8866; restaurant; conference facilities; secretarial service; fax/photocopy facilities; corporate rates; in-room safe; pool; HK$1600/1800.

Grand Plaza; 2 Kornhill Road, Quarry Bay, Hong Kong Island; tel: 2886-0011; fax: 2886-1738; restaurant; conference facilities (up to 80); secretarial service; fax/photocopy facilities; fitness; sauna; pool; whirlpool; HK$1250.

Grand Tower; 627-641 Nathan Road, Mong Kok, Kowloon; tel: 2789-0011; fax: 2789-0945; restaurant; conference facilities; secretarial service; fax/photocopy facilities; corporate rates; HK$1050.

Kowloon Hotel; 19-21 Nathan Road, Kowloon; tel: 2369-8698; fax: 2739-9811; sister hotel to the Peninsula with signing privileges; restaurants; in-room printer/fax; computer/tv; in-room safe; meeting rooms; secretarial service; fax/photocopy facilities; corporate rates; HK$1,500.

Luk Kwok; 72 Gloucester Road, Wanchai, Hong Kong Island; tel: 2866-2166; fax: 2866-2622; restaurant; conference facilities; secretarial service; fax/photocopy facilities; in-room safe; HK$1400.

Miramar; 130 Nathan Road, Tsim-Sha-Tsui, Kowloon; tel: 2368-1111; fax: 2369-1788; restaurant; conference facilities; secretarial service; fax/photocopy facilities; corporate rates; in-room safe; fitness; sauna; pool; HK$1300.

Omni Prince; Harbour City, Canton Road, Tsim-Sha-Tsui, Kowloon; tel: 2736-1888; fax: 2736-0066; restaurants; conference facilities; secretarial service; fax/photocopy facilities; pool; HK$1600.

Royal Garden; 69 Mody Road, Tsim-Sha-Tsui, Kowloon; tel: 2721-5215; fax: 2369-9976; restaurant; conference facilities; business center; gift shop; fitness center; sauna; swimming pool; tennis court.

The Kimberly; 28 Kimberley Road, Tsim-Sha-Tsui, Kowloon; tel: 2723-3888; fax: 2723-1318; restaurant; conference facilities; secretarial service; fax/photocopy facilities; in-room modem/fax connection; corporate rates; fitness; sauna; HK$1350.

Royal Pacific; 33 Canton Road, China Hong Kong City, Tsim-Sha-Tsui, Kowloon; tel: 2736-1188; fax: 2736-1212; restaurant; business center; secretarial service; conference facilities; internet available; in-room modem/fax connection and safe; corporate rates; fitness; sauna; whirlpool; HK$1900.

Wharney; 57-73 Lockhart Road, Wanchai, Hong Kong Island; tel: 2861-1000; fax: 2865-6023; restaurant; conference facilities; in-room safe; fitness; sauna; pool; HK$1350.

Moderate

Concourse; 20-46 Lai Chi Kok Road, Mong Kok, Kowloon; tel: 2397-6683; fax: 2381-3768; restaurant; conference facilities (up to 200); secretarial service; fax/photocopy facilities.

Eaton; 380 Nathan Road, Yau Ma Tei, Kowloon; tel: 2782-1818; fax: 2782-5563; restaurant; conference facilities (up

to 160); secretarial service; fax/photocopy facilities; corporate rates.

Guangdong; 18 Prat Avenue, Tsim-Sha-Tsui, Kowloon; tel: 2739-3311; fax: 2721-1137; restaurant; conference facilities; secretarial service; fax/photocopy facilities; corporate rates; HK$1100.

Prudential; 222 Nathan Road, Tsim-Sha-Tsui, Kowloon; tel: 2311-8222; fax: 2367-6537; conference facilities; secretarial service; fax/photocopy facilities; corporate rates; in-room safe; pool; HK$1000.

Regal Riverside; Tai Chung Ku Road, Shatin, New Territories; tel: 2649-7878; fax: 2637-4748; suburb; restaurant; conference facilities; secretarial service; fax/photocopy facilities; corporate rates; fitness; sauna; pool.

The Salisbury - YMCA of Hong Kong; 41 Salisbury Road, Tsim-Sha-Tsui, Kowloon; harborfront, a YMCA like no other; restaurant; conference facilities; secretarial service; in-room safe; fitness; sauna; pool; whirlpool; HK$880/1030.

Wesley; 22 Hennessy Road, Wanchai, Hong Kong Island; tel: 2866-6688; fax: 2866-6633; 251 rooms; restaurant; conference facilities; in-room mini bar; parking; corporate rates.

MEDICAL CARE

Hong Kong Adventist Hospital; 40 Stubbs Road, Hong Kong Island; tel: 2574-6211.

The International Association for Medical Assistance to Travelers; 417 Center St., Lewiston, NY 14092; tel: (716) 754-4883.

Queen Elizabeth Hospital; Wylie Road, Kowloon; tel: 2710-2111.

Queen Mary Hospital; Pokfulam Road; tel: 2855-3111.

HEALTH CLUB

The Gym; 18th floor Melbourne Plaza, 33 Queens Road, Central.

Tom Turk Health Clubs; Bond Centre, West Wing, 13th floor, 89 Queensway, Hong Kong Island; tel: 2521-4541; Albion Plaza, 2-6 Granville Road, Tsimshatsui, Kowloon; tel: 2368-8293.

AUTO RENTAL

Avis (Far East Rent A Car Limited); Ground Floor, Bright Star Mansion, 93 Leighton Road, Causeway Bay; tel: 2890-6988; fax: 2895-3686.

DCH Rent-a-Car; 20 Kai Cheung Road, Kowloon Bay; tel: 2768-2277.

WORLD TRADE CENTER

World Trade Centre Hong Kong
8/F Asia Pacific Centre
8 Wyndham Street
Central, Hong Kong
P. R. C.
tel: 2894-8083; fax: 2577-9708

CONVENTION AND EXHIBITION CENTERS

Cosmopolitan Business and Convention Centre; 28/F, 38 Russell Street, Causeway Bay; tel: 2106-1888; fax: 2106-1333; http://www.business.centres.com

Hong Kong Convention and Exhibition Centre; 1 Expo Drive, Wan Chai; tel: 2582-8888; fax: 2582-8828; email: hkcec@hkstar.com

Hungary

At a Glance
THE PEOPLE

Population .... 10,186,372 (July 1999 est.)
Growth Rate .... -0.2% (1999 est.)
Life Expectancy .... 71.18 years (born 1999)
Infant Mortality ... 9.46 deaths/1,000 live births (1999 est.)

Ethnic Composition
Hungarian.. 90%
Gypsy 4%
Other 6%

Religious Composition
Roman Catholic..67.5%
Calvinist..20%
Lutheran 5%
Other and non-affiliated..7.5%

Languages Spoken
Hungarian (official), German

Education and Literacy
Education is compulsory until age 16. Literacy is 99 percent nationwide.

Labor Force
Total: 4,500,000
By occupation: services 65%, industry 26.7%, agriculture 8.3%.

THE ECONOMY
Hungary has survived its "stabilization program" of 1995 and greatly improved its macroeconomic position. Its admission to NATO in 1999 was seen as a prelude to eventual full membership in the E.U. early next century. The country's well-educated workforce has adapted well to changes in the economic environment, despite rising unemployment levels and inexperienced management. Economic growth has been slow but is expected to gain momentum in the next few years unless it is derailed by renewed inflation. Although Hungary has an acceptable road network and an extensive railway system, its limited air facilities and poor telecommunications system are in dire need of upgrading; this serves to limit economic growth in the short term. Foreign investment has been pouring in since 1998 and Hungary's international bond rating has been given good grades. Current concerns are the nearby regional conflicts in the Balkans and ongoing governmental privatization plans.

Exports .... US$20.7 billion (f.o.b., 1998)
Imports .... US$22.9 billion (f.o.b., 1998)
Total GDP .... US$75.4 billion (1998 est.)
GDP Per Capita .... US$7,400 (1998 est.)
Unemployment 10.8% (1997)
Inflation Rate .... 14% (1998 est.)

Top Export Partners
E.U., Poland, Czech Republic, Russia

Top Import Partners
E.U., Poland, Czech Republic, USA

Top Exports
Consumer goods, foodstuffs, agricultural products, machinery and equipment, fuels and electricity.

Top Imports
Raw materials, consumer goods, machinery and equipment, fuels and electricity, agricultural products.

BUSINESS WORKWEEK

Offices
Monday to Friday 8a.m. to 4:30p.m.

Banks
Monday to Friday 9 or 10a.m. to 4p.m. (1p.m. on Friday)

Government
Monday to Friday 9a.m. to 3:30p.m., Saturday 9a.m. to noon.

Retail
Food stores: Monday to Friday 7a.m. to 7p.m., Saturday 7a.m. to 2 p.m.; Department stores: Monday to Wednesday and Friday 10a.m. to 6p.m.; Thursdays until 8p.m.; Saturday 9a.m. to 1p.m.

HOLIDAYS
New Year's Day..January 1
Anniversary of 1848 uprising
against Austrian rule... March 15
Easter Monday ....April 5*
Labor Day...May 1
Constitution Day .... August 20
Day of the Proclamation of the
Republic ....October 23
Christmas ....December 25
Boxing Day..December 26
*Date may vary by year.

CLIMATE

Seasons
The climate is temperate, with four distinct seasons. Hungary has dry summers and cold, snowy winters. In the winter, minimum temperature falls to about -14˚C (7˚F). The average summer temperature hovers around 36˚C (97˚F), with the hottest months being July and August. By October the winter begins to set in and brings on the cold.

Regions
The west experiences more rainfall than the east, with maximum rainfall in the winter and draughts occurring during the summer. The Great Plain is given to heavy winds and cooler weather. Budapest has a temperate climate most of the year.

Money & Banking

Currency
The currency of Hungary is the Hungarian Forint (Ft).

Denominations
The Hungarian Forint comes in coin denominations of Ft200, 100, 50, 20, 10, 5, 2, and 1, and 50, 20, and 10 fillér coins. Bills are denominated in Ft200, 500, 1000, 5000, 10000.

Traveler's Checks and Credit Cards
Traveler's checks, Eurocheques, and most foreign currency can be exchanged at banks and travel agencies

Hungary

Hungary

National capital
County capital
Secondary city
International border
Primary road
Railroad
County border

Austria
Slovakia
Ukraine
Romania
Croatia
Yugoslavia

Mosonmagyar v r
Sopron
Gy r
Tatab nya
K szeg
P pa
Szombathely
Ajka
Veszpr m
Zalaegerszeg
Bogl rlelle
Nagykanizsa
Kaposvar
Szeksz rd
Kom
Baja
P cs

Danube
Esztergom
Budapest
Érd
V rpalota
Duna jv ros
Kecskem t
Kiskunf legyh za
Kiskunhalas
Szeged
Mak

Balassagyarmat Salg tarj n Miskolc
Eger
Gy ngy s
Hajd boszorm ny
J szber ny
P sp klad ny
Szolnok
Nagk r s
Mezot r
Szentes
Orosh za
Gyula
H dmezov s rhely

S toralja jhely
Kazincbarcika
Leninv ros
Ny regyh za
Debrecen
T r kszentmikl
B k scsaba
M t szalka

Counties of Hungary
1 Gy r-Moson Sopron
2 Kom rom-Esztergom
3 Budapest
4 Pest
5 N gr d
6 Heves
7 Borsod-Aba j-Zempl n
8
9 Hajd Bihar
10 J sz-Nagykun Szolnok
11 B k s
12 Csongr d
13 B cs-Kiskun
14 Fej r
15 Veszpr m
16 Vas
17 Zala
18 Somogy
19 Tolna
20 Baranya

0 25 50 km
0 25 50 mi

©2001 Magellan Geographix SM Santa Barbara, CA

throughout Hungary. (The national OTP Bank does not charge commission fees.) Post offices only cash Euro-cheques.

American Express, Visa, Diner's Club, and MasterCard are accepted in most up-market places in Budapest and other large cities. Cash advance on credit cards can also be obtained at main banks in the capital and at numerous ATMs throughout the country. Holders of Eurocheck cards can get personal checks cashed at all banks and in many hotels and restaurants.

Visitors cannot re-exchange currency when leaving the country without receipts, so keep all evidence of currency exchanges, ATM transactions, and check cashing.

Budapest Card

The Budapest Card gives you unlimited travel on public transport, free admission to several museums, and discounts on sightseeing tours, restaurants, and other attractions. One can usually purchase the card at most hotels, metro stations, museums, and tourist information offices. At a cost of approximately Ft2600, the card is a great deal and could save you a lot of money.

Travel

VISA AND PASSPORT

A passport that is valid for six months beyond the intended exit date is required of all, except for nationals of Austria, Belgium, France, Germany, Liechtenstein, Luxembourg, Slovenia, Spain and Switzerland who are holding a national ID card.

Visas are required of all except:

* Nationals of U.K., for a visit of six months maximum
* Nationals of Argentina, Australia, Belarus, Bosnia and Herzegovina, Canada, Bulgaria, Chile, Croatia, Cyprus, Czech Republic, Estonia, EU countries, Former Yugoslav Republic of Macedonia, Iceland, Israel, Japan, Korea (Rep. of), Latvia, Liechtenstein, Lithuania, Malaysia,

Mexico, Moldova, Monaco, Norway, Panama, Poland, Romania, Seychelles, Slovak Republic, Slovenia, Switzerland, Ukraine, Uruguay, U.S., and Yugoslavia, for a visit of 90 days maximum
* Nationals of Costa Rica, Cuba, Ecuador, Malta, Nicaragua, San Marino and South Africa for a visit of 30 days maximum
* Nationals of Singapore for a visit of 14 days maximum
  Types of visa issued:
* Tourist / Business, single- or double-entry. Valid for a 30-day stay per entry, must be used within six months of the issue date.
* Tourist / Business, multiple entry. Valid for six months from the issue date.
* Transit (or Airport Transit), single, double, or multiple. Valid for a 48-hour stay per use, must be used within six months from issue date.
  Prices of visa vary according to type.
  Carry two additional passport photographs for unexpected document requirements. Those visitors staying more than 30 days must register with the local police within 48 hours (possible through the hotel), unless staying in a private residence. Visas must be acquired in advance and will not be issued at point of entry.

All passengers must hold onward tickets, valid travel documents, and sufficient funds. Travelers are required to declare any foreign funds in their possession upon entry to facilitate re-export of the funds upon departure.

Allow several weeks for processing of visa applications, in most cases. However, some nationals such as those from New Zealand, Australia, and several other countries—mostly in Central and South America—are eligible to receive their visas through a much shortened procedure, sometimes on the same day, for an extra fee of about US$20.

DEPARTURE FORMALITIES

There is no departure tax for visitors leaving from Ferihegy Airport in Budapest or by overland routes.

Hungary

CUSTOMS ENTRY (PERSONAL)

Duty-free
- Tobacco: 500 cigarettes, 100 cigars, or 500g of tobacco
- Alcohol: one liter of distilled spirits, one liter of wine, and five liters of beer
- Other: 250g of perfume; gifts to the value of Ft270,000

Prohibited or Restricted
- Local currency is limited to Ft300,000 for import and Ft200,000 for export, which must be declared. Foreign currency for export is limited to the amount declared on import. An unlimited amount may be imported, provided it has been declared upon arrival.
- Special permits are required to export many items, such as food, medicine, tools, textiles, art work, and items of precious metal. Stamps and protected works of art cannot be exported. For more information call: (1) 175-7533 or (1) 116-0170, extension 460.

IMMUNIZATION

There are no inoculations necessary to gain admittance into Hungary, however, tetanus and hepatitis A shots are recommended.

TIPPING

Taxi
For metered fares, 10 to 15 percent is standard.

Porters
Porters receive Ft100 per piece of luggage.

Hotels
Hotels will apply service charges to the bill but Ft100 is adequate for incidental services.

Restaurants
A 10 to 15 percent tip is standard, and is paid directly to the staff member. Do not leave it on the table. It is customary to buy your bartender or restaurant host a drink if you have been engaging them in conversation.

EMERGENCY INFORMATION

Police and Crime
Hungary is one of the safer countries in Europe. The people are honest and law abiding, and it is rare to see a police officer in the streets. Still, in a city that now attracts thousands of tourists, petty crime is on the rise. Street crime, only occasionally involving violence, occurs most often at night near major hotels and restaurants and on public transportation. Passport theft has become a frequent problem, especially when riding public transportation.

Foreign business visitors are often the special target of thieves. Consequently, purses, laptops, and briefcases will require additional security. Do not leave valuables in cars or on tables in cafés. Keep non-essential valuables locked in hotel safes when not in use. Use credit cards and travel checks when possible to avoid carrying large sums of cash.

Hungarian police are very helpful and quite efficient. Report all problems or crimes immediately. But be wary of anyone looking like a policeman who asks you for any travel documents, I.D.s, credit cards, etc., since thieves have been known to impersonate officers in order to steal from tourists. If a policeman approaches you, ask to see their badge and I.D. card, which should have a photo, hologram, and official rank.

Emergency Numbers
Numbers function nationwide.

Police...107
Ambulance 104
Fire 105

Health

Bottled water is preferred in Hungary, although tap water is relatively safe. However, if prone to stomach upset, bottled water is recommended, at least for the initial first few weeks. Apart from normal digestive problems caused by change in diet, there are no extraordinary diseases here. Visitors from Asia may find the Hungarian diet to be somewhat heavy and with a higher fat content than that to which they are accustomed. Larger cities have a variety of cuisines available, of course, which will allow time to acclimate. Hotel chefs are also accommodating when it comes to special preparations.

The medical service is of a high standard. Hungary has an abundance of skilled doctors, but they are likely to charge more if they speak English. Fees are reasonable. Emergency transport and first aid are free to visitors. It is advisable to bring any prescription drugs that will be used regularly.

If you find yourself in need of emergency dental attention, call: 330-189. Pharmacists are generally open from 8a.m. to 5p.m., although there is round-the-clock emergency service in every district.

For more information on medical centers, including phone numbers, please see the "Business Centers" section at the end of this chapter.

INTERNAL TRAVEL

Domestic transportation in Hungary is efficient, extensive, and reasonably priced.

AIR

There are currently no regularly scheduled domestic flights, but several routes are in the planning stages.

TAXI

Taxis are numerous in the cities, but it is much more economical to use the bus or tram systems. Check to make sure the meter is running while en route; if not, the passenger has no obligation to pay. Assuming you are charged the correct fare, it will be quite reasonable. Be sure to write all directions on paper and to carry maps. Many drivers may not speak English.

AUTO

Rental cars can be found at Ferihegy Airport or at Budapest, Express, Volán tourist offices, and at major hotels. Many local car rental agencies are sprinkled around the country, but rates generally run high. Necessary documentation: A pink format E.U. license is accepted, but an International Driving Permit may be required if a green license is held. For most other nationals, a valid license from your country is acceptable along with a major credit card. The minimum age is to rent in Hungary is 21.

Motorists can count on good roads, easily available fuel, and all-night gas stations. Eight arterial roads span the country, all (except the M8) beginning from central Budapest. Budapest and eastern Hungary are linked by the M3. The M1, running between Györ and Vienna, and the M7 hugging Lake Balaton are the two main highways out of Budapest.

Generally, the road system is good. Expect some roads to have tolls. Rental cars are recommended only for travelers who are planning to do business outside urban areas, although driving in Hungary is usually orderly and civilized. If you do rent, make sure you observe each town's "pay and display" parking regulations.

Roadside assistance is provided by:
The Hungarian Automobile Club
Rómer Flóris utca 4/A, H-1024 Budapest
tel: (1) 212-2938, or

For 24-hour emergency service tel. (1) 212-2821.
email: mak@mail.datanet.hu
website: www.autoklub.hu

TRAIN

Train services are extensive and most lines are efficient. Facilities are sometimes less than first rate, but all major cities are connected by this effective system.Tickets can be purchased 60 days in advance for domestic travel.

Three international trains also operate daily, linking Vienna, Salzburg, Zurich, Basel, and Dresden. A variety of classes are available, and train travel is quite common for business people. In all cases, reservations are advised.

Travel agents in many countries sell the Hungarian Flexipass, which allows unlimited first-class rail travel within Hungary for either 5 days in a 15-day period, or 10 days in a 30-month period.

All train services are handled by MAV, the Hungarian rail operator: tel: (1) 322-0660; fax: (1) 342-8342

METRO

Three underground lines connect Buda and Pest. Stations are identifiable by the large 'M' sign.Trains run frequently, if somewhat noisily, between 4:30a.m. and 11:10p.m.

Single tickets may be used for any of three lines for not more than three stops within 30 minutes of purchase. Be sure to validate the ticket at the station entrance lest you get caught in a surprise control check. Schedules and fares are posted in every station.

BUSES & TRAMS

Urban: Buses service most of the cities. If the route is busy, express buses will shuttle passengers without stopping. Look for the red numbering. Super express buses also exist, which do not stop between terminals. These are recognizable by the letter 'E' following the usual red express number on the bus. In all cases, validate your ticket after you board.

Trams and trolleys offer another mode of transport in the main cities. Fares are comparable to local buses, and you must validate tickets in the punch machines on board.

In Budapest, there is also a Pioneers' Railway (Hüvösvölgy–Széchenyi Hill), a cogwheel railway (Városmajor–Széchenyi Hill), a funicular, and a chairlift.

Intercity: Budapest is linked with major provincial towns by Volán, which runs yellow-and-red buses to the smaller, more remote cities and villages. Between neighboring cities and towns, Volán runs yellow buses. You can purchase tickets at Volán long-distance bus terminals throughout the country. A season ticket also stands at one's disposal. This intercity bus system is used by many as an alternative to train travel. Fares are cheaper, but overnight travel can prove uncomfortable.

Passes: Single-trip tickets costing Ft60 apply for tram, metro, trolley, local trains, and buses, but only remain valid for one route. Day passes are available for Ft500; these apply for any of the public transportation modes in Budapest. A three-day pass costs Ft1200.

WATER TRAVEL

Though landlocked, Hungary has an elaborate passenger boat system along the Danube and Lake Balaton. Regular services operate from the Spring until late Autumn.

On Lake Balaton, ferries between Tihanyrév and Szántódrév operate daily throughout the summer every 40 minutes, from 6:20a.m. until midnight. During the rest of the year, hours of operation are from 6:30a.m. to 7:30p.m.

Ferries appropriate for cars and buses operate hourly on the Danube, between Párkány (Sturovo) and Esztergom.

Services are offered year-round (except when the Danube is frozen) from 8a.m. until 6p.m daily.

The Budapest Travel Company (BKV) and MAHART also run ferries through the Roman Embankment (Római Part) and the city center. For more details, contact:

MAHART
Belgrád Rakpart
1056 Budapest
tel: (1) 318 1704 or 318 1586 or 266 4198
fax: (1) 318 7740; email: mahart-tours@aux.net

Hydrofoil and ferry services to Vienna and other European and Hungarian cities are available from late spring to mid-autumn.

TRAVEL ASSISTANCE

Hungarian Tourist Board (Tourinform)
Sütö-u. 2, H-1052 Budapest
tel: (1) 317 9800; fax: (1) 317 9656
email: tourinform@mail.hungarytourism.hu
website: www.hungarytourism.hu

Hungarian National Tourist Office (HNTO)
Margit Körút 85, 1024 Budapest
tel: (1) 355 1133; fax: (1) 375 3819
email: htbudapest@hungarytourism.hu

Ministry of Economic Affairs (Tourism Field)
Vigadó u 6, 1051 Budapest
tel: (1) 302 2355
fax: (1) 332 9750
email: webmaster@gm.hu; website: www.gm.hu

Essential Terms

English	Hungarian
Yes	Igen
No	Nem
Good morning	Jóreggelt
Hello (daytime)	Jó napot
Hello (evening)	Jóestét
Hello (telephone)	Jó napot kivanok
Good-bye	Viszontlatasra
Please	Kérem
Thank you	Köszönöm
Pleased to meet you	Örülök, hogy megismerhetem
Excuse me; I'm sorry	Bocsanat
My name is ____	A nevem ____
I don't understand	Nem értem
Do you speak English?	Bezsél angolul?

Communications

DIALING CODES IN HUNGARY

International country code: [36]

Selected city codes: Abasar (37), Balatonaliga (84), Budapest (1), Debrecan (52), Dorgicse (80), Fertoboz (99), Gyongyos (37), Gyor (96), Kaposvar (82), Kazincbarcika (48), Komlo (72), Miskolc (46), Nagykanizsa (93), Papa (89), Pecsvarad (72), Rem (36), Szekesfehervar (22), Szolnok (56), Varpalota (80), Veszprem (88)

Note: ITD in Hungary has recently changed the initial digit of all numbers beginning with "1" in Budapest to "3". Thus, if a number were previously 123-4567, one should now dial: 323-4567. The area code remains unchanged.

Dialing Hungary from Overseas

To dial Hungary from overseas, dial your country's international dialing code, then 36 (the country code for Hungary), then the city code and finally the number. If you were dialing Budapest from the United States, for example, you would begin with 011, then 36, then 1 (the city code for Budapest), and finally the number of the person or office you were trying to reach.

Assistance Numbers

International Operator 09
International Directory (English) 267-5555
Domestic Operator 01
Directory Information 117-0170
Directory Information in Budapest 117-2200
English-speaking Information 267-7111
Rural Directory 267-3333

Also try the English language phone book available in most hotels or sold in English-language bookstores.

CALLING WITHIN HUNGARY

The former state-owned telecommunications firm MAT-AV is now managed by a US/German consortium, which intends to greatly upgrade the archaic system, including installation of 600,00 new phone lines.

Local Calls

A three-minute local call will cost about 10Ft. Seven-digit numbers apply for Budapest and six-digit numbers elsewhere.

Note: ITD in Hungary has recently changed the initial digit of "1" in Budapest phone numbers to "3". Thus, if a number were previously 123-4567, one should now dial: 323-4567.

Long Distance Calls

All long distance codes have two digits, except Budapest. Calling between 6p.m. and 7a.m. will afford the cheapest rates. If experiencing difficulty, as the modernizing process may change many of the numbers and codes in Hungary, ask for assistance.

International Calls

If using a public phone, look for the red variety or the new blue phones possessing digital display. These phones can be found at post offices, on the street, or inside the metro stations. Calling from any hotel phone will most likely set your budget back at much greater percentages than using an outside phone. Budapest's phone office also allows international direct calls, but with a three-minute minimum to the U.S. To reach a home operator, try one of the following numbers:

Australia Direct .... 00 80-61+11
Canada Direct 00 80-00-12-11
Ireland Direct 00 80-00-35-31
New Zealand Direct 00 80-00-64-11
U.K. (BT) 00 80-04-40-11
U.K. (Mercury) 00 80-00-44-12
U.S. AT&T 00 80-00-11-11
U.S. MCI 00 80-00-14-11
U.S. Sprint 00 80-00-18-77

*Wait for a dial tone after the initial 00.

PAY PHONES

Public Telephones

There are various colored phones to watch for when attempting to make a call. Red phones allow international and domestic calls. Yellow phones allow domestic calls only, and gray card phones exist almost everywhere nowadays. Phones that still take coins accept 10Ft and 20Ft coins. Those phones with a black and white arrow and the word *Visszahivhato* printed on them, indicate a number for callback purposes. Post offices also have telephones. Those that are open 24 hours are located near the western and eastern train stations in Budapest. Otherwise, regular post office hours are between 8a.m. and 6p.m. weekdays, and 8a.m. to 2p.m. on weekends.

Calling Cards

There are some public phones that use cards, particularly in the cities. Cards can be purchased in newsstands and hotels.

CELLULAR PHONES

Hungary's cellular system is primarily digital. Westel 900 and Pannon GSM operate the two GSM systems.

One analogue system operated by Westel Radiotelefon does exist; however, it operates in the 450 MHz range, designed by Nokia and Eriksson for rugged terrain in the Nordic countries.

Note: Your home country cell phone may not work in this country. If not, we recommend that you rent an international cell phone *before* you leave home. A major US-based cell phone rental provider is **IMC WorldCell**. For information see "International Cell Phone Rentals" on page 14.

CALL BACK

You can (potentially) save significant sums when calling in Hungary by using a call back service. For a list of callback services, please refer to the "Communications" section in the *Global Road Warrior* Introduction.

Fees for call back services vary widely, depending on the company and the type of service required. Be sure to check with these companies before leaving to compare rates.

PHONE JACKS

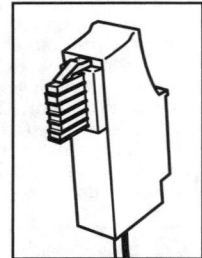

Plug adaptors are available through **iGo Corporation.** (See "Electrical and Telephone Adaptors" on page 19.)

POSTAL SERVICES

For detailed information on postal services dial 117-2200 within Hungary. Postal services are generally efficient, by Eastern European standards. Stamps are available in hotels, newsstands, and tobacco shops.

Hours of service

Monday to Friday 9a.m. to 10p.m.
Saturday 9a.m. to 3p.m.
Main post offices in Budapest are open 24 hours a day.

Business Services

BUSINESS CENTER

Budapest Marriott; V. Apáczai Csere János utca 4; tel: 266-7000.

Hilton Hotel; Hess András ter 1-3; tel: 214-3000; fax: 156-0285.

Hotel Gloria; Blathy Otto Str. 22, H-1089; tel: (1) 210-4120; fax: (1) 210-4129.

COURIER SERVICES

Airborne Express (RGW Express Kft); Ferihegy 1, Airport Cargo I Building 23, Budapest 1185; tel: (1) 296-5500; fax: (1) 296-6639.

DHL Hungary; East-West Trade Center, Rakoczi ut 1-3, Budapest 1088; tel: 266-7777; Monday to Friday 8a.m. to 6p.m.; Saturday 8a.m. to 2p.m.

Federal Express Hungary (Royal Express Forwarding); tel: (1) 216-3606.

UPS Hungary Ltd.; Bookings and Enquiries, tel: (1) 262-0000; Kozuna St. 4, H-1108 Budapest.

Electrical

Current

220 volts AC, 50Hz

ELECTRIC PLUGS

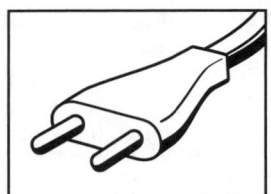

Plug adaptors are available through **iGo Corporation.** (See "Electrical and Telephone Adaptors" on page 19.)

Technical Support

HARDWARE/SOFTWARE VENDOR SUPPORT

Compaq/Digital; (in Switzerland) tel: [41] (22) 709-5330; fax: [41] (22) 709-5391 (Geneva); tel: [41] (1) 801-2507; fax: [41] (1) 801-2172 (Zurich); (General U.S.) tel: (281) 518-2000; http://www.compaq.com/.

Dell; (in Germany) tel: [49] (61) 039-710; (Dell- Europe) tel: [44] (134) 474-8000; (in the U.S.) tel: [1] (512) 338-4400; fax: [1] (512) 728-3330; http://www.dell.com/.

IBM; tel: 1-372-1111; fax: 1-372-1199; (in Switzerland) tel: [41] (22) 310-0418 (in French); (in the U.S.) tel: [1] (919) 517-2800; (U.S. Main Office) tel: [1] 914-765-1900; http://www.ibm.com/

Microsoft; tel: (1) 437-2800; fax: (1) 437-2899; tel: (1) 267-4636 (technical support); (in Switzerland) tel: [41] (848) 858-868; fax [41] (1) 831-0869; (in the U.S.) [1] (425) 635-7222; http://www.microsoft.com/.

Toshiba; (in Germany) tel: [49] (2131) 158-319; fax: [49] (2131) 158-558; (in Switzerland) tel: [41] (1) 946-0777; fax: [41] (1) 946-0807; (in Ireland) tel: [44] (193) 282-8828; (in the U.S.) [1] (949) 583-3000 (Corporate Headquarters); http://www.toshiba.com/.

Internet Connection

HOW TO CONNECT

Connecting to AOL and Compuserve in Hungary is similar to using it when traveling outside your own area code. See the introductory section for detailed information on connecting to your account through a different phone number.

America Online

Numbers are available at keyword *international*. Be sure to get several local numbers before leaving. AOL's GlobalNet service charges US$6 an hour in addition to the usual charges. Go to keyword *access* (a free area) and download the software.

Access: Budapest (1) 429-8235; Gyor (96) 318-644.

Compuserve

Numbers are available at *Go International*. The Compuserve Web-site also has a great deal of information, at http://www.compuserve.com.

Access: Budapest (1) 291-9999.

Independent Service Providers

Many independent service providers offer discounts if you are only in town for a couple days.

Euroweb International; tel; (1) 224-4111; fax: (1) 224-4100; email: info@euroweb.hu; http://www.euroweb.hu/.

MATAV Rt.; tel: 458-0410 or 458-0050; fax: 3458-0405; http://www.matav.hu/.

SPRYNET; (a U.S. company offering service in Hungary); tel: [1] (425) 957-8000; toll-free in the U.S.: 1-800-777-9638; fax: [1] (425) 957-6000;

Telnet Hungary; tel: (1) 359-3142; http://www.telnet.hu; email: info@telnet.hu

Business Culture

GREETINGS AND COURTESIES

The customary greeting in Hungary is a handshake, and a man waits for a woman to extend her hand first. When greeting a Hungarian, use the person's proper title along with the surname. Bring a good supply of business cards to Hungary. They should be printed in your language as well as in Hungarian. Businesspeople are accustomed to having letters and accounts translated into Hungarian. Hand out your business cards at business as well as social meetings. A polite gesture in Hungary is to bring a gift to your hosts. Because Hungarians typically begin work early in the morning, evening visits usually end before 11p.m.

Meals (dinner, in particular) are for socializing, not discussing business. They usually take place in restaurants (homes are often too small) and last a long time, accompanied by musicians or entertainers. Hungarians eat continental style, with the fork remaining in the left hand at all times. Good conversation topics revolve around food, wine, horses, history, and Hungary itself.

Hungarians like their "personal space" and usually stand about two feet apart when conversing.

DECISION MAKING

Make all the essential arrangements weeks ahead of time, especially for governmental meetings. Hungarians are greatly legalistic in their approach to negotiations. They will want to review the terms of an agreement many times, seeking clarification of each item and asking numerous questions. Despite an atmosphere of openness, most businessmen in positions of power came of age under the closed thinking of Communism. They tend to think more associately and subjectively than abstractly.

Hungarians are legalistic in their approach to negotiations. They prefer to review the terms of an agreement many times, seeking clarification of each item and asking numerous questions. The decision-making process is long and complicated, especially when the government is involved. Patience is essential. Still, the country's new entrepreneurs may prefer to quicken the pace on smaller projects.

In either case, a lot of socializing will precede the signing of deals. Some important decisions are made by individuals, others by group consensus. Price remains a major factor in all negotiations. Terms and conditions on credit are high priorities.

Consider hosting a cocktail party in a prestigious hotel after your deal has been finalized. Once a decision is made, it will usually remain in place.

MEETINGS

Request essential meetings weeks ahead of time, in writing (English is acceptable), especially when dealing with governmental agencies. Don't set up trips between July and August or from mid-December to mid-January, as these are holiday/vacation periods. Numerous trade organizations exist. Initial contacts for buy/sell agreements can be established through Commerce and Trade officials. It is very helpful to establish a rapport with a Hungarian representative prior to your initial visit to help you to establish contacts. Chose with care, as your clients will expect you to maintain this allegiance.

Punctuality is expected. Business cards will be exchanged. Come prepared with card printed in Hungarian. Presentations should be precise and thorough. If you don't speak Hungarian or German with some fluency, an interpreter will be needed; these are available through travel agents.

Hungarians have a strong work ethic. Many have had to take on extra part-time jobs to keep up with the rising cost of living, and they expect foreigners to approach their business with the same no-nonsense can-do zeal. Maintain a reserved disposition.

WOMEN IN BUSINESS

Although women are found in a wide variety of business and government positions, they must usually still prove themselves capable to their male counterparts before being accepted as equals. Nonetheless, foreign businesswomen should experience few difficulties and will generally be accorded respect.

The term *asszony* is sometimes used for foreign married women of distinction, following their name, as in Eleanor Roosevelt *asszony*.

BUSINESS ATTIRE

The Hungarians are a stylish people. However, in the business world, dark, conservative attire works best -- suits and ties for men, suits or conservative dresses for women. For more formal evening events, tuxedos and gowns may be appropriate. (Budapest's climate is temperate, with seasons of almost equal length.)

Horseback riding is extremely popular here, and foreigners may be invited to participate. Bring suitable clothing.

Business Centers
Budapest

CITY VIEW

Budapest is one of the most beautiful cities in Europe, as well as one of the easiest to understand. It is the financial, political, and cultural center of the country. This international city offers travelers everything from high-end shops and the famous Esceri flea market to theater, ballet, opera, and disco dancing.

AIRPORT

Budapest Ferihegy Airport to City Center

The airport lies 10 miles (16 km.) from the city. Figure approximately 30 minutes in travel time. A regular bus services any address in Budapest for a fare of Ft1,200 (US$5). Taxis are also available, but for heftier fares of about Ft4300 (US$17.50).

Airport..(1) 296-9696

Airline Numbers

Aerflot.. (1) 3180-5955
Air Canada .... (1) 317-9109

British Airways ....(1) 318-3299
CSA .... (1) 318-3175, 318-3045
Delta ....(1) 318-7922
Lauda ....(1) 317-9299
Lufthansa ....(1) 296-6506
Lufthansa Cargo........................(1) 296-5111, 5222, 5333
LOT ....(1) 317-2444
SAS ....(1) 318-5377
Swissair ....(1) 317-2500

HOTELS

Top-end

Atrium Hyatt Hotel; Roosevelt Ter. 2; tel: (1) 266-1234; fax: 266-9101; email: atriumhyatt@pannoniahotels.com; city center, a short walk from the Castle District.; 3 restaurants serving international and Hungarian cuisine; casino; conference facilities; secretarial service; fax/photocopy facilities; in-room safe; in-room color TV, hairdryer, minibar, radio, telephone; currency exchange; corporate rates; fitness; sauna; pool.

Budapest Marriott; V. Apáczai Csere János utca 4; tel: 266-7000; all rooms with view of the Danube; 3 restaurants; coffee shop; conference facilities; business center; secretarial service; car/airline desk; in-ram color TV, hairdryers, minibar, radio, phone; health club; sauna; indoor pool; squash.

Kempinsky Hotel Corvinus Budapest; Erzsébet Ter 7-8; tel: (1) 266-1000; fax: (1) 266-2000; email: hotel@kempinsky.hungary.net; most exclusive hotel in Budapest, catering to the rich and famous; restaurant; 2 bars; coffee shop; conference facilities; secretarial service; in-room modem/fax connection, safe, color TV, hairdryer, minibar, radio, telephone; currency exchange; corporate rates; sauna; pool; fitness center.

Expensive

Béke Radisson SAS; Teréz Korút 43; tel: 332-3300; modern hotel, recently renovated; near public transportation; popular with Americans; offering old-world charm with modern amenities; restaurant; coffee shop; conference facilities; in-room color TV, hairdryer, minibar, radio, safe, phone; currency exchange; sauna; massage; pool.

Budapenta; Krisztine Körút 41; tel: (1) 155-6333; near rail terminal; Castle Hill views.

Danubius Thermal Helia; Karpat Utca 62/64; tel: (1) 270-3277; fax: (1) 270-2262; email: danubius@hungary.net; 2 restaurants; conference facilities; secretarial service; fax/photocopy facilities; in-room color TV, hairdryer, minibar, radio, phone; currency exchange; corporate rates; fitness; massage; sauna; pool; whirlpool/spa; golf; tennis.

Gellért; Gellert Ter 1; tel: (1) 385-2200; fax: (1) 366-6631; http://www.hungary.net/danubius/gellert.html; popular Karoly Gundel restaurant; conference facilities; secretarial service; fax/photocopy facilities; wide variety of rooms; in-rom color TV, hairdryer, minibar, radio, phone; sauna; pool; famous spa/thermal bath complex.

Forum; Apáczai Csere János U. 12-14; tel: (1) 317-8088; fax: (1) 317-9808; located on the Danube; restaurant; conference facilities; secretarial service; fax/photocopy facilities; in-room safe; corporate rates; fitness; sauna; pool.

Hotel Gloria; Blathy Otto Str. 22, H-1089; tel: (1) 210-4120; fax: (1) 210-4129; email: gloria@hotelgloria.com/; located near exhibition grounds; restaurant; conference facilities; business center; secretarial service; internet available; corporate rates; sauna.

Mercure Buda; Krisztina Körút 41-43; tel: (1) 356-6333; fax: (1) 355-6964; email:

mercurebuda@pannoniahotels.hu; geared towards business travelers; located near rail station; two restaurants; 2 bars; coffee shop; conference facilities; secretarial service; in-room color TV, hairdryer, minibar, radio, phone; currency exchange; souvenir shop; corporate rates; massage; sauna; pool; nightclub.

Novotel Budapest Centrum; Alkotás Utca 63-67, 1123; tel: (1) 209-1990; fax: (1) 466-5636; email: novotel@pannoniahotels.hu; early 80's hotel; greared towards business travelers; connected to Budapest Convention Center; 3 restaurants including the Bowling Brasserie where you can actually bowl, 2 bars; conference facilities; in-room modem/fax connection; laptops and internet available; in-room color TV, minibar, radio, phone; currency exchange; shops; corporate rates; massage; fitness; sauna; pool.

Moderate

Astoria; V. Kossuth Lajos utca 19; tel: (1) 317-3411; old-fashioned hotel, centrally located.

Erzsébet; v. Károlyi Mihály utca 11-15; tel; 338-2111; located in central Pest; modern hotel. **Taverna**; V. Váci utca 20; tel: 338-2533; centrally located on Pest's main shopping street.

Victoria; Bem Rakpart 11, 1011; tel: (1) 457-8080; fax: (1) 457-8088; email: victoria@victoria.hu; internet available; corporate rates; sauna.

MEDICAL CARE

Central State Hospital; XII, Kutvolgyi ut 4; tel: (1) 155-1122.

HEALTH CLUB

Andi Studio; 29 Hold Utca; tel: (1) 111-07-40.

Budapest Marriott; V. Apáczai Csere János utca 4; tel: 266-7000

AUTO RENTAL

Note: You'll save time and money if you rent a car through a travel agent before you arrive. Be sure to find out about various charges that could be added, including insurance and deposits. Most rental cars have standard shift, and air conditioning is not always available. It's also a good idea to check for any obvious body damage on the car and make sure to an employee notes it on your contract. Also give the tires a once over and don't accept any vehicle that looks like it might be unsafe.

Avis; reservations, tel: (1) 118-4240; fax: (1) 118-4158; airport, tel: (1) 296-6421; fax: (1) 296-9696.

Budget; reservations, tel/fax: 214-0420; airport, tel/fax: (1) 296-8197 or 269-8481; Hotel Mercure Buda, tel/fax: (1) 214-0420.

Europcar; Krisztina krt. 41-43, tel: 156-6333.

Fötaxi/Inter-rent; Vaskapu utca 16; tel: 215-4466.

Hertz; reservations, 431-0999; fax: 431-0998; airport, Terminal 1, tel: 296-7171; fax: 431-0998; Terminal 2, tel: 296-6988; fax: 431-0998; Budapest Marriott Hotel, tel: 266-4361; chauffeur-driven cars available.

WORLD TRADE CENTER

World Trade Center Budapest
Kecskemeti utca 14
Budapest, Hungary H-1053
tel: (1) 338-2416; fax: (1) 318-3731
website: http://www.dbassoc.hu
email: jvasvari@dbassoc.hu

Iceland

At a Glance
THE PEOPLE

Population .... 272,512 (July 1999 est.)
Growth Rate .... 0.57% (1999 est.)
Life Expectancy .... 78.96 years (born 1999)
Infant Mortality ... 5.22 deaths/1,000 live births (1999 est.)

Ethnic Composition
Caucasian (Celtic & Nordic) 100%

Religious Composition
Evangelical Lutheran... 96%
Other Christian 3%
Animist and non-affiliated 1%

Languages Spoken
Icelandic

Education and Literacy
Literacy stands at 100% nationwide.

Labor Force
Total: 131,000
By occupation: services 70%, industry 24.9%, agriculture 5.1%

THE ECONOMY
Iceland follows the Scandinavian economic model based in capitalist ownership coupled with extensive social welfare systems. Unemployment is kept low with a large government jobs sector and income is distributed more by mandate than market forces. The fishing industry has historically dominated the country's export economy, and Iceland produces very few other items for trading purposes. Like all economies reliant on commodity prices, Iceland is attempting to diversify without upsetting long standing social and cultural orders. The government has put forth large privatization programs aimed at attracting foreign investment. Some of its other goals include reducing the budget and current account deficits, limiting foreign borrowing, and containing inflation. Iceland has remained outside of the E.U. (as has trading neighbor Norway) in an effort to retain its control over historic fishing rights and its generous social welfare system. As the euro-zone nations become stronger, Iceland will have to choose between titular economic independence and financial viability.

Exports .... US$1.9 billion (f.o.b., 1998)
Imports .... US$2.4 billion (f.o.b., 1998)
Total GDP .... US$6.06 billion (1998 est.)
GDP Per Capita .... US$22,400 (1998 est.)
Unemployment .... 3% (1998 est.)
Inflation Rate 1.7% (1998)

Top Export Partners
E.U., United States, Japan

Top Import Partners
E.U., Norway, United States

Top Exports
Fish and fish products, animal products, aluminum, ferro-silicon, diatomite.

Top Imports
Machinery and transportation equipment, petroleum products, foodstuffs, textiles.

BUSINESS WORKWEEK
Offices
Monday to Friday 9a.m. to 5p.m.
Monday to Friday 8a.m. to 4 p.m.- June, July, August

Banks
Monday to Friday 9a.m. to 4p.m.

Government
Monday to Friday 9a.m. to 5p.m.

Retail
Monday to Thursday 9a.m. to 6p.m., Friday 10a.m. to 10p.m.; Saturday 10a.m. to 4p.m. or earlier. Some supermarkets are always open. Many shops are closed on Saturdays during June, July and August

Note: Icelandic business seems to slow down in the autumn and winter as virtual 24-darkness occurs.

HOLIDAYS
New Year's Day...January 1
Maundy Thursday..April 1*
Good Friday...April 2*
Easter Monday ....April 5*
Ascension Day .... May 13*
Whit Monday .... May 24*
National Day...June 17
Bank Holiday ....August 2*
Christmas ....December 24-26
*Date may vary by year.

CLIMATE
Seasons
Despite the country's northerly geographical location, Iceland has a more moderate climate than expected. The warmth from the gulf stream and underground steam from volcanic action affects the general climate on the island.

The seasons can really be defined as light and dark. Winters are very long and most severe from January to April. Two to three months of continuous daylight exist in the summer, while the winters from November through January have only two to three hours of daylight.

Regions
The south has a lot of rainfall throughout the year. Reykjavik only gets about three sunny days per year. Northern Iceland is sunnier and more temperate. Summers are short, but generally warm, with average temperatures in Reykjavik about 11˚C (52˚F), in July and -1˚C (30˚F) in January.

Money & Banking
Currency
The currency of Iceland is the Iceland Krona (IKr).

Denominations
The Iceland Krona comes in coin denominations of IKr100, 50, 10, 5, and 1, and banknotes of IKr100, 500, 1,000, 5,000.

Traveler's Checks and Credit Cards
Traveler's checks (especially those denominated in British pounds, Deutschmarks, and U.S. dollars) and foreign currency can be easily and efficiently exchanged at banks,

Iceland

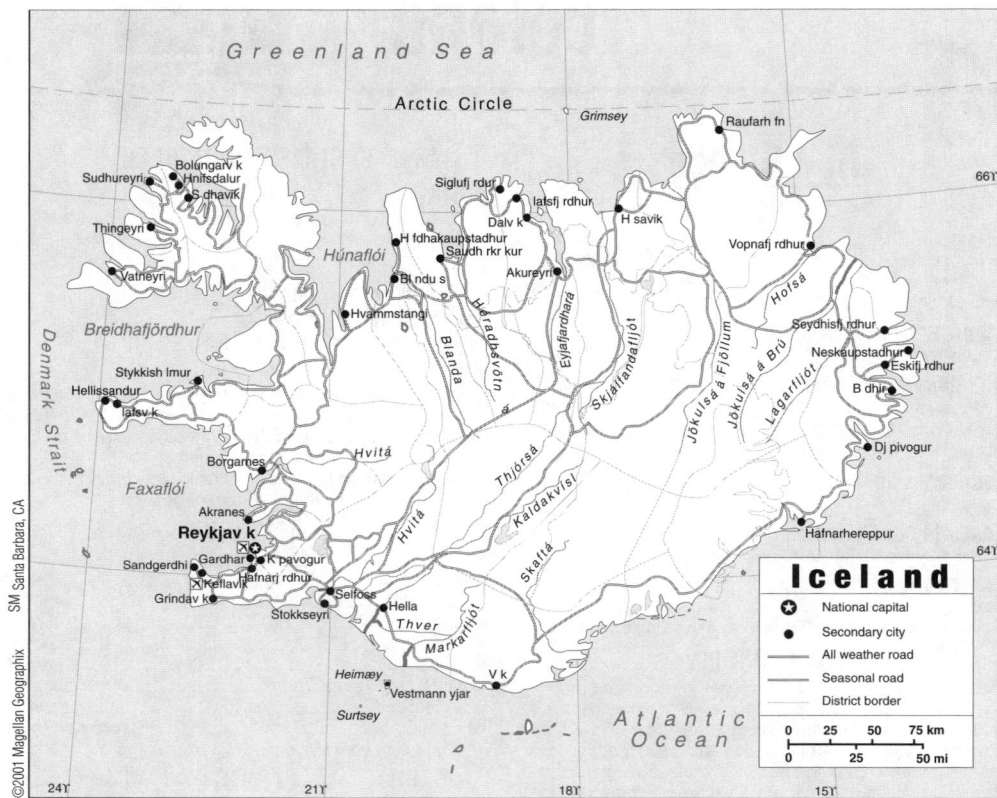

foreign exchange bureaus, hotels, and foreign exchange kiosks at the airports. Banks offer the most variable exchange rates. Eurocheques are only cashed at 75 percent of face value and should not be used in Iceland.

Traveler's checks receive a better exchange rate than cash, or you can purchase Icelandic currency traveler's checks before departure, which can be exchanged almost everywhere. Try to exchange your money back before leaving the country.

Credit cards are accepted everywhere, and Icelanders use cards for even small purchases. American Express, Visa, MasterCard, Eurocard, and Diners Club, as well as bank cards from the larger Icelandic banks can all be considered easy to use in this country. Visa, however is the most popular, with MasterCard a close second. American Express and Discover cards aren't used as widely but are accepted in some places, especially the capital.

You can get cash advances from your credit card on many of the automated teller machines (ATM). ATMs are only found at bank locations. Credit cards are also essential for renting a car. Long term visitors should set up a checking account in Iceland and get an ATM card.

Travel
VISA AND PASSPORT

A passport that is valid for three months minimum beyond intended exit date is required of all nationalities except: Austria, Belgium, France, Germany, Italy, Liechtenstein, Luxembourg, the Netherlands, Switzerland, Finland, Norway, Denmark, and Sweden, provided the traveler from these countries is bearing a national identity card.

For stays of 90 days or less, no visa is required of nationals of Andorra, Antigua & Barbuda, Australia Bahamas, Brazil, Brunei, Canada, Chile, Cyprus, Czech Republic, Dominica, Estonia, EU countries, Grenada, Guyana, Hungary, Israel, Japan, Kiribati, Korea (Rep. of), Latvia, Liechtenstein, Lithuania, Malaysia, Malta, Mexico, Monaco, New Zealand, Norway, Poland, St. Lucia, St. Vincent & the Grenadines, San Marino, Seychelles, Singapore, Slovak Republic, Slovenia, Solomon Islands, Switzerland, Tuvalu, U.K., Uruguay, U.S., Vanuatu, and Vatican City.

All other visitors must have made visa arrangements in advance of travel.

There is only one type of visa, the Entry visa, which comes in either a Business or Tourist flavor, valid for 90 days.

An additional 90-day extension is available from immigration once a visitor is in Iceland. The time period for a traveler's stay begins when entering any Scandinavian territory.

Allow about five days for visa application processing from the time the consulate or embassy receives your forms.

DEPARTURE FORMALITIES

A departure tax of Ikr1250 will be collected when leaving from the Keflavik airport. To avoid delays, pay the exit tax at the time you reserve your airline ticket. Certain VAT may be refunded at departure. Secure forms when making purchases.

CUSTOMS ENTRY (PERSONAL)

Duty-free
- Tobacco: 200 cigarettes or 250g of tobacco products
- Alcohol: 1 liter of spirits or 1 liter of wine (under 21 percent proof) or 6 liters of beer (8 liters of Icelandic beer) Visitor must be over 20 years of age.
- Other: up to US$100 worth of gifts may be brought into Iceland duty free; all currency must be declared upon arrival
  Note: All fishing equipment must be disinfected, and a certificate of disinfection issued by an official veterinary authority should be presented on arrival.

Prohibited or Restricted
- Drugs
- Firearms
- Uncooked meat
- Unregistered radios and telephones
- All fishing equipment must be disinfected and certified

IMMUNIZATION
No vaccinations are required unless you are arriving from an infected area.

TIPPING
In general, tipping is not necessary and is considered to be an insult. However, it is acceptable to tip your guide or driver after a long tour.

Taxi
Rounding up the fare is sufficient.

Porters
Porters are not usually tipped.

Hotels
Hotels apply service charges directly to the bill.

Restaurants
Most restaurants will apply service charges to the bill. It is customary to buy your bartender or host a drink if you have been engaging them in conversation.

EMERGENCY INFORMATION

Police and Crime
Crime is relatively low in Iceland, and most of the population is concentrated in a small area of the country. However, in more urban settings, take basic precautions. Downtown Reykjavik can get a bit rowdy on weekend nights.

Foreign business visitors can be the special target of thieves. Consequently, purses, laptops, and briefcases will require additional security. Do not leave valuables in cars or on tables in cafés. Keep non-essential valuables locked in hotel safes when not in use. Use credit cards and traveler's checks when possible to avoid carrying large sums of cash.

Police in Iceland are very helpful and efficient. Report all serious problems and crimes immediately.

Emergency Numbers
General information (nationwide) 112

Health
Living and traveling in Iceland pose no serious health risks. The only problematic illnesses are common cold and flu. Food laws are strict, so food is safe as is tap water. The Icelandic diet may take some time to get used to, so give yourself time to acclimate.

The medical establishment is of a very high standard and its services are often free to foreign travelers. Pharmacies sometimes remain open 24 hours a day. Good hotels will have access to multi-lingual doctors.

For more information on medical centers, including phone numbers, please see the "Business Centers" section at the end of this chapter.

INTERNAL TRAVEL

AIR
Íslandsflug and Air Iceland offer domestic services to 12 airports, ten of which are primary destinations that connect with regional carriers in the eastern, western, and northern parts of the country.

Icelandair also offers a variety of special air packages for the internal traveler, including Air Rover, Fly As You Please, and Air/Bus Rover.

There is a departure tax of Ikr165 for all domestic flights as well as for flights to the Faroe Islands and to Greenland.

TAXI
Taxis are available from all hotels and airports. A typical trip within town will cost about US$7 to US$9. Fares go up weekends and evenings. Smoking inside of a cab is not permitted unless you have received permission from your driver.

Drivers are typically knowledgeable of their cities, but written directions can be helpful.

B.S.R. Taxi 561-0000/551-1720
Borgarbílar 552-4400
Hreyfill 588-5522

AUTO
Travelers may rent cars in Iceland in most major towns or they may ferry them over from the European mainland. Rentals require a credit card and valid license along with current insurance. It is advisable to have an International Driving Permit, even though it is not required legally. A driver must be over 20 years old in order to be able to rent an automobile.

Rentals are expensive, costing about IKr3500 plus a 24.5 percent tax. Cars brought from the mainland must receive an inspection in Iceland. Motorists are advised that gasoline in Iceland is among the world's most expensive.

There are 12,000km (7500 miles) of roads, most of which are gravel rather than paved. Icelandic law requires vehicles to drive with headlights on at all times; do not attempt to operate a vehicle if you have been drinking. The blood-alcohol limit is 0.5 and penalties are heavy. Winter driving is hazardous. Many roads outside the capital are not paved, nor well marked.

There is a useful brochure, 'The Art of Driving on Icelandic Roads,' available from the Icelandic Tourist Board (see 'Travel Assistance' section for contact information).

TRAIN
No railway service exists in Iceland.

METRO
There is no subway system in Iceland.

BUSES & TRAMS
Bus services are efficient and connect the entire country during the summer. There is limited service in the winter. Buses within the capital operate on twenty different routes. Pay upon boarding with exact change or with discount tickets, available at the City Hall Information Desk or from the driver. A variety of multi-use passes are available.

Bus information 551-2700

WATER TRAVEL
Ferry service between Reykjavik and many smaller cities is available. There are both passenger and passenger-auto ferry routes, such as the regular service that runs be-

Iceland

tween Reykjavík and Akranes. International cruise lines also serve Reykjavik port. For more information, call: 551-6050. In Akranes you may dial: 431-2275.

TRAVEL ASSISTANCE

Icelandic Tourist Board
Laekjargata 3, 101 Reykjavik
tel: 535-5500
fax: 535-5501
email: info@icetourist.is
website: www.icetourist.is

Essential Terms

English	Icelandic
Yes No	Já Nei
Good morning Hello (daytime) Hello (evening) Hello (telephone)	Góan dag Goan dag Gott kvöld Halló
Good-bye	Bless
Please	Gjöru svovel
Thank you	Takk fyrir
Pleased to meet you	Kondu sæll
Excuse me; I'm sorry	Fyrirge fou
My name is _____	Ég heiti ___
I don't understand	Ég skil ekki
Do you speak English?	Talar pu ensku?

Communications

DIALING CODES IN ICELAND

International country code: [354]

Dialing Iceland from Overseas

To dial Iceland from overseas, dial your country's international dialing code, then 354 (the country code for Iceland), and finally the number. If dialing Reykjavik, the city code (1) is also necessary.

Assistance Numbers

International Operator 09
International Directory 08
Long-Distance Operator 02
National Directory 03

CALLING WITHIN ICELAND

Local Calls

A local call will cost you an IKr10 coin.

Long Distance Calls

All numbers in Iceland now have 7 digits, eliminating the hassle of determining regional codes.

International Calls

You can call direct from most phones by dialing 00 + country code + area code + number. It might be best to go ahead and purchase a 100-unit phone card at the post office for the procedure.

You can also reach an overseas operator directly for collect or calling-card calls. If calling from a pay phone, deposit a coin or card first.

British Telecom Direct .... 999-044 (deposit 5kr)
Canada Direct 999-010
U.S. AT&T 800-9001
U.S. MCI... 800-9002

PAY PHONES

Public Telephones

Usually located somewhere indoors, public phones can be found in post offices, hotels, and transportation hubs. Phones require deposits of IKr5, 10, or 50.
1. Lift receiver
2. Deposit coin
3. Dial

The main telephone office in Reykjavik is located in Austurvöll Square.

Calling Cards

Post offices sell phone cards, which are recommended in the larger denomination if you are making a direct international call on a public phone.

CELLULAR PHONES

As most of the rest of Europe, Iceland's cellular operations run on a GSM digital system, operated here by Post og Simamalastofnunin and Landssimi Islands hf. If you have a GSM phone, check with your service provider at home to see if a partnership in Iceland exists.

An analogue NMT450 system also exists. Run by Post og Simamalastofnunin, the NMT450 was specially developed by Nokia and Ericsson for the harsh terrain in Scandinavia.

Note: Your home country cell phone may not work in this country. If not, we recommend that you rent an international cell phone *before* you leave home. A major US-based cell phone rental provider is **IMC WorldCell**. For information see "International Cell Phone Rentals" on page 14.

CALL BACK

You can (potentially) save significant sums when calling in Iceland by using a call back service. For a list of callback services, please refer to the "Communications" section in the *Global Road Warrior* Introduction.

Fees for call back services vary widely, depending on the company and the type of service required. Be sure to check with these companies before leaving to compare rates.

PHONE JACK

Plug adaptors are available through **iGo Corporation.** (See "Electrical and Telephone Adaptors" on page 19.)

FAX/MODEM

Public fax facilities are available at hotels. No tax impulsing exists in Iceland, thus a filter is not necessary for modem connection. The telephone system runs on an RJ-11 cable, the same as in North America, as well as 22UK. Check with your hotel front desk before plugging in to ascertain whether modem hookup is available.

POSTAL SERVICES

The postal service is very efficient. Mail to Western Europe takes two to three days, and mail to North America takes three to five days.

Hours of service

Monday to Friday 8:30a.m. to 4:30p.m.

TELEGRAMS

Telegrams can be sent from most hotels, and from the Telegraph Office in Reykjavik.

Business Services

COURIER SERVICES

Airborne Express; Flutningsmidlunin Jonar, Skutuvogi 1E, 104 Reykjavik; tel: 535-8050; fax: 535-8058.

DHL; Faxafen 9, Reykjavik 108; tel: 535-1122; Monday to Friday 8a.m. to 6p.m.

Federal Express; Flutningsmid Lunin Jonar; tel: 535-8000.

TNT Express Worldwide; Sudurlandsbraut 26, Reykjavik, IS-108; tel: 550-7300; fax: 550-7309; telex: 2183 POSEXT IS.

UPS (Zimsen Forwarding); Hedinsgata 1-3, Reykjavik 105; tel: 588-0170; fax: 588-0180

Electrical

Current

220 volts AC, 50Hz.

ELECTRICAL SOCKET

Most fittings are 2-pin. Lamp fittings are typically screw-type.

ELECTRIC PLUGS

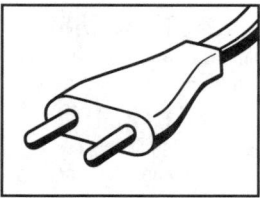

Plug adaptors are available through **iGo Corporation**. (See "Electrical and Telephone Adaptors" on page 19.)

Technical Support

HARDWARE/SOFTWARE VENDOR SUPPORT

Compaq/Digital; (Norwegian Office) tel: [47] 2207-2000; fax: [47] 2207- 2001; [47] 2207-2020 (CompaqCare Center); [47] 2207-2022 (QuickLine); (General U.S.) tel: (281) 518-2000; http://www.compaq.com/.

Dell; (Dell- Europe) tel: [44] (134) 474-8000; (in Germany) tel: [49] (61) 039-710; (in the U.S.) tel: [1] (512) 338-4400; fax: [1] (512) 728-3330; http://www.dell.com/.

Filemaker/Claris; (in Germany) tel: [49] (180) 525-8166 (Info-line); fax: [49] (180) 567-2233; tel: [49] (180) 523-6423; (in the U.S.) tel: [1] (800) 965-9090; http://www.claris.com/.

Hewlett Packard; (Norway Office) tel: [47] (0)22 116299; (in Switzerland) tel: [41] (22) 780-8111; (in the U.S.) tel: [1] (408) 246-4300; http://www.hp.com/.

IBM; tel: 569-7700; (in Switzerland) tel: [41] (22) 310-0418 (in French); (in the U.S.) tel: [1] (919) 517-2800; (U.S. Main Office) tel: [1] 914-765-1900; http://www.ibm.com/.

Microsoft; (In Denmark) tel: [45] (44) 890-111; fax: [45] (44) 685-510; (in Switzerland) tel: [41] (848) 858-868; fax [41] (1) 831-0869; (in the U.S.) tel: [1] (425) 635-7222; http://www.microsoft.com/.

NEC; (in Norway) tel: [47] 22-768-68500 (UltraCare Support); (in the U.S.) [1] (916) 388-0101 (Main Switchboard); http://www.nec.com/.

Toshiba; (in Germany) tel: [49] (2131) 158-319; fax: [49] (2131) 158-558; (in Switzerland) tel: [41] (1) 946-0777; fax: [41] (1) 946-0807; (in Ireland) tel: [44] (193) 282-8828; (in the U.S.) [1] (949) 583-3000 (Corporate Headquarters); http://www.toshiba.com/.

Internet Connection

HOW TO CONNECT

Connecting to AOL and Compuserve in Iceland is similar to using it when traveling outside your own area code. See the introductory section for detailed information on connecting to your account through a different phone number.

America Online

Numbers are available at keyword *international*. Be sure to get several local numbers before leaving. AOL's Global-Net service charges US$6 an hour in addition to the usual charges. Go to keyword *access* (a free area) and download the software.

Access: Reykjavik 551-1666.

Compuserve

Numbers are available at *Go International*. The Compuserve Web-site also has a great deal of information, at http://www.compuserve.com.

Access: Rejkjavik (354) 551-1666.

Independent Service Providers

Many independent service providers offer discounts if you are only in town for a couple of days.

EUnet - Iceland; tel: 525-4950; fax: 561-561 0999 0999; email: intis@isnet.is; http://www.isnet.is/

Centrum; tel: 575-7070; fax: 511-7070; email: skima@skima.is; http://www.centrum.is

Snerpa; tel: 456-5470; fax: 456-5072; email: snerpa@snerpa.is; http://www.snerpa.is/.

Business Culture

GREETINGS AND COURTESIES

In Iceland, only first names are used while Mr. and Mrs. are deemed honorific titles to address someone of rank, such as the nation's president or bishop. You are welcome to introduce yourself using Mr. *(Herra)*, Mrs. *(Fru)* and Miss *(Froken)*, and Icelanders will honor that courtesy title, for they enjoy making foreigners feel comfortable. When being introduced to either men or women, a handshake and a pleasant greeting is the standard greeting. Gifts that represent your company or country are considered thoughtful. Things are very expensive in Iceland and even the smallest gift is well received. You will never insult an Icelander with a bottle of Scotch or a fine liquor.

MEETINGS

Prior appointments need not take place to gain a visit with an Icelandic business person; however, one should take care to plan ahead during the summer season: May to September, when many people travel overseas. Business meetings are not formal; however, your Icelandic colleagues appreciate getting straight down to business. Icelanders are friendly and receptive during meetings and exercise reserve when making presentations. They will appreciate your preparedness. Because Icelandic corporations are small, you'll likely be in the company of an authorized decision maker.

WOMEN

The fact that Iceland has had the first woman president in the world tells the visitor much about women's contribution to the Icelandic business culture. Women are included in practically every aspect of commerce in the country and have, for centuries, worked alongside the men to develop their land and business communities.

BUSINESS ATTIRE

Icelanders are fashion conscious and casual attire will never mean jeans. Dark suits are worn in banking circles; jackets and ties are the business norm. Women should dress conservatively in light woolens of natural colors, avoiding too much make-up. And if the word 'Iceland' has not already put up a red arctic flag, remember to dress very warmly in the winter months.

Business Centers
Reykjavik

CITY VIEW

A relatively small city with plenty of European charm, Reykjavik is quickly becoming one of the most popular places to visit in Europe. With plumes of steam rising from the surrounding thermal springs, it is no wonder the city was named Reykjavik, meaning Bay of Smokes. Avant-garde and Scandic, surrounded by mountains and fresh, clean air, visitors will arrive in Iceland's gateway city pleasantly warmed to find much else besides ice.

AIRPORT

Keflavik Airport to City Center

The airport lies 28 miles (45 km.) from the city. Travel time is approximately 45 minutes. There is regular bus and coach service; airport buses leave the Scandic Hotel Lofteisir for the airport two hours and fifteen minutes before departure times. Taxi and limousine services are also readily available.

Airline Numbers

Icelandair	569-0100
International Reservations	505-0100
Domestic	505-0200
Ticket Office	505-0300
Islandsflug	561-6060
Leiguflug	562-8011

HOTELS

Top-end

Hotel Saga; Hagatorg; tel: 552-9900; fax:562-3980; near university grounds; 2 restaurants including rooftop grill; conference/banquet facilities; secretarial service; fax/photocopy facilities; corporate rates; non-smoking rooms available; fitness; sauna; solarium; beauty salon.

Expensive

Esja; Suurlandsbraut 2; tel: 505-0950; fax: 505-0955; restaurant; conference facilities; pool.

Grand Reykjavik; Sigtun 38; tel: 568-9000; fax: 568-0675; located adjacent to exhibition grounds; restaurant; conference facilities; corporate rates.

Hotel Borg; Posthusstraeti 11; tel: 551-1440; fax: 551-1420; restaurant; conference facilities; secretarial service; fax/photocopy facilities; US$100/125.

Hotel Holt; Bergstadastreti 37; tel: 552-5700; fax: 562-3025; restaurant; meeting facilities.

Hotel Leifur Eiriksson; tel: 562-0800; fax: 562-0804.

Island; Armula 9; tel: 568-7111; fax: 568-9957; restaurant; conference facilities.

Scandic Hotel Loftleisir; Reykjavikurflugvöllur; tel: 552-2322; fax: 505-0905; restaurant; conference facilities; fitness; sauna; pool.

Smarar Guest House; tel: 551-6522

Moderate

City Hotel; Ranargata 4 A; tel: 551-8650; fax: 552-9040.

Lind; Rauararstigur 18; tel: 562-3350; fax: 562-3351; restaurant; conference facilities.

Reykjavik; Rauararstigur 37; tel; 562-6250; fax; (1) 562-6350; restaurant; corporate rates.

MEDICAL CARE

Borgarspitaliann City Hospital; tel: 569-6600.

Reykavik Health Centers; tel: 552-2400.

AUTO RENTAL

Atlas; Dalshraun 9; tel: 565-0660; fax: 565-3801.

Avis; Sigtún 5; tel; 562-4433; fax: 562-3590.

Bonus Car Rental; Kleppsvegur 150; tel: 568-8700; fax: 568-8370.

Budget; Ármúli 1; tel: (1) 880-880; fax: (1) 881-881.

Hertz; airport, tel: (1) 505-0600; fax: (1) 505-0650.

CHAMBER OF COMMERCE

Verzlunarrád Islands
Hús verslunarinnar, Kringlan 7
103 Reykjavik
tel: 588-6666; fax: 568-6564
email: mottaka@chamber.is
website: http://www.chamber.is

Reykjavik Business Development Office
Adalstraeti 6, 101 Reykjavik
tel: 563-2250; fax: 563-2249
email: info@rvk.is

India

At a Glance

THE PEOPLE

Population .... 1,000,848,550 (July 1999 est.)
Growth Rate .... 1.68% (1999 est.)
Life Expectancy .... 63.4 years (born 1999)
Infant Mortality . 60.81 deaths/1,000 live births (1999 est.)

Ethnic Composition

Indo-Aryan...72%
Dravidian 25%
Mongoloid and other..3%

Religious Composition

Hindu 80%
Muslim 14%
Christian 2.4%
Sikh 2%
Buddhist and other 1.6%

Languages Spoken

Hindi (official/national language for 30% of population), Bangali (official), Telugu (official), Marathi (official), Tamil (official), Urdu (official), Gujarati (official), Malayalam (official), Kannada (official), Oriya (official), Punjabi (official), Assamese (official), Kashmiri (official), Sindhi (official), Sanskrit (official), English is used for national, political, and commercial communication.

Education and Literacy

Education is free, but not compulsory, for the first eight years. Literacy nationwide is only 52 percent.

Labor Force

Total: 370,000,000
    By occupation: services 18%, industry 15%, agriculture 67%

THE ECONOMY

India has a massive population set to be the world's largest early in the 21st century. Two-thirds of its people are engaged in agriculture which accounts for 30 percent of GDP. India has a thriving high-tech sector and, it turns out, more engineers every year than any other nation. Sadly, its industrial base, formerly dependent on exporting to the now defunct USSR, has yet to recover from the nation's socialist past. Foreign capital, once rebuffed in the 1980s, has begun to return, lured by liberalized trade policies. The energy, transportation, financial services, and telecommunications sectors are specifically targeted for development. The Indian economy is also gifted with something that few emerging markets can claim: a 300 million strong middle class. Only occasional instances of nationalism and anti-foreign bias have blemished what is otherwise a promising economic picture.

Exports .... US$32.17 billion (f.o.b., 1998)
Imports .... US$41.34 billion (c.i.f., 1998)
Total GDP .... US$1.689 trillion (1998 est.)
GDP Per Capita .... US$1,720 (1998 est.)
Inflation Rate .... 14% (1998 est.)

Top Export Partners

United States, Japan, E.U., Hong Kong.

Top Import Partners

United States, E.U., Saudi Arabia, Japan.

Top Exports

Clothing, gems and jewelry, engineering goods, chemicals, leather manufactures, cotton yarn, fabric.

Top Imports

Crude oil and petroleum products, machinery, gems, fertilizer, chemicals.

BUSINESS WORKWEEK

Offices

Monday to Friday 9:30a.m. to 5p.m.; Saturday 9:30a.m. to 1p.m.

Banks

Monday to Friday 10a.m. to 2p.m.; every second Saturday 10a.m. to 12:30p.m.

Government

Monday to Saturday 10a.m. to 5p.m. (closed very second Saturday)

Retail

Monday to Saturday 9a.m. to 7p.m.

HOLIDAYS

New Year's Day..January 1
Republic day..January 26
Feast of Sacrifice.. January 28*
Good Friday...April 2*
Ram Navami and Mahabir Jayanti .... March/April
Buddha Purnima..May 14*
Muharram, Islamic New Year .... May 17*
Birth of the Prophet .... June 26*
Janmashtami .... August
Independence Day .... August 15
Dussehra, Diwali and Guru
Nanak Jayanti.......................................October/November
Mahatma Gandhi's Birthday ....October 2
Christmas ....December 25-26
    *Dates may vary by year.

CLIMATE

Seasons

India's climate is extremely diverse. Parts of the Ladakh region in Kashmir are among the coldest inhabited places on earth. The Himalaya Mountain ranges are also very cold (and remain mostly uninhabited).

Monsoon winds bring rain and replenish the rivers, lakes, and aquifers, thereby sustaining the agriculture. The main south-west monsoon brings rain between May and September (with Bombay and the west coast receiving rains in late May, and Delhi nearly a month later). The north-east monsoon brings rain to the southern state of Tamil Nadu.

Delhi sees its most comfortable climate between October and March; May and June offer biting heat; and July to September sticky, humid air.

Regions

Temperatures in the northern plains and western deserts can reach 49°C (120°F) between May and June, though their ground temperatures can be as low as -18°C (0°F) winter. The lower peninsular India enjoys a moderate climate, though it can get hot and humid between March and June.

India

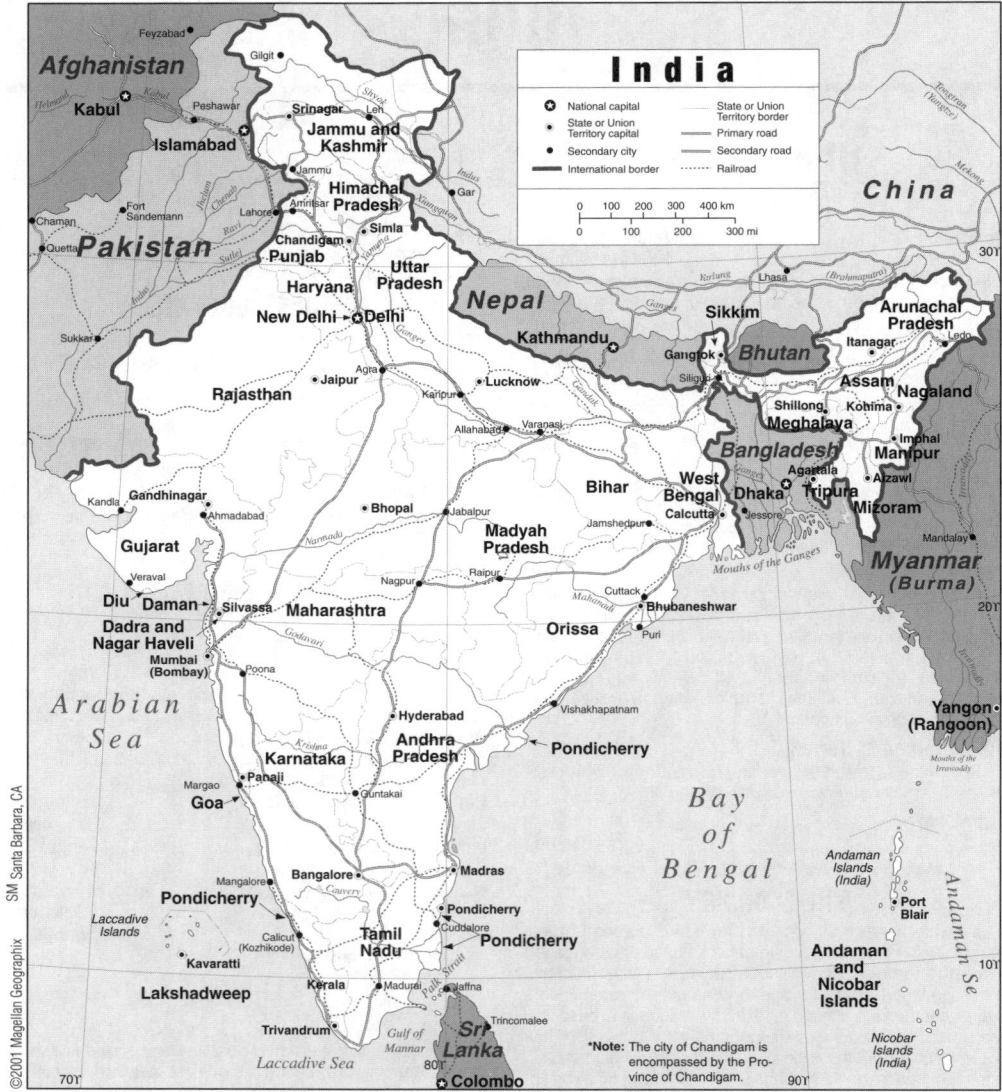

Money & Banking

Currency

The currency of India is the Rupee (Re, plural Rs).

Denominations

Rupee (Rs) comes in coin denominations of Rs5, 2, 1, and 50, 25, 20, 10, and 5 paise; and banknotes of Rs1, 2, 5, 20, 50, 100, and 500.

Traveler's Checks and Credit Cards

Traveler's checks can be changed at large banks throughout India. However, there is no guarantee that every bank will take your brand of check or currency. Some prefer only certain traveler's checks in certain currencies and it may take a few stops before you get one that will ex-change your particular check or currency. You might save yourself extra hassle by traveling with both American Express and Thomas Cook checks in British sterling as well U.S. dollars. With currency, it is also best to bring in dollars and pounds for exchange. Fees for all types of exchange vary by agency. It is best to exchange a fairly large amount at one time to avoid frequent headaches. Keep all ex-change receipts (encashments) if you plan to reconvert at departure.

Note: Black market exchange is both illegal and of little real value to visitors.

Visa, Mastercard, American Express, Diner's Club, and Japanese Credit Bureau cards are accepted at large out-lets and hotels throughout India. Cash advances are avail-able at state banks. American Express permits the purchase of dollar and pound denominated traveler's checks if covered by a personal check for the same amount. The American Express office in Delhi is located at: Block A, Connaught Place (closed on Sundays).

Note: Wire transfers of money in India are very difficult, so bring credit cards or plenty of traveler's checks.

Essential Terms

English	Hindi
Yes No	Han Nahin or na
Good morning Hello (daytime) Hello (evening) Hello (telephone)	Namaste Namaste Namaste Namaste
Good bye	Namaste
Please	Krip ya
Thank you	Sukria
Pleased to meet you	Ahp ko mil keh koo-sheeh'wee
Excuse me; I'm sorry	Ma-ahf
My name is _____	Meraa naam ___ hai
I don't understand	Mai nahi samajhaa
Do you speak English?	Kyaa aap angrejii bolate hain?

Travel

VISA AND PASSPORT

A passport that is valid for a minimum of six months beyond expected exit date is required of all visitors.

A visa is also required of all, except:

- Nationals of Nepal and Bhutan for a stay up to three months
- Nationals of the Maldives for a stay or stays totaling 90 days maximum in a six-month period
- Passengers in transit who do not leave the airport and are continuing their journey within 72 hours, and who are holding confirmed tickets and other documents for onward travel (there are special restrictions for transit passengers from Pakistan and Bangladesh -- check with the Indian consulate)

Types of visa issued are:

- Tourist - term of six months, and valid if used within six months of issuance
- Business - term of three months, six months, one year, or two years, and valid if used within two years of issuance
- Transit - ordinarily good for 72 hours, but can be extended to 15 days by Immigration officials
- Long Term - term up to five years, commencing with issuance

A Business visa application must include a letter from the applicant's employer stating business intentions and dates of travel, as well as an invitation extended by a company in India.

Allow a week or two for processing of visa applications submitted in person; postal submissions will generally take between four and six weeks.

RESTRICTED ENTRY

Entry is denied to Afghanistan nationals if there is evidence of boarding or transit in Pakistan on their ticket or passport.

The following states require special permits or government authorization in order for foreign visitors to be permitted to visit: Arunachul Pradesh, Andaman & Nicobar Islands, Lakshadweep Islands, Manipur, Mizoram, Nagaland, Sikkim. Authorization is obtained fairly easily in most cases simply by indicating intent in the Indian visa application.

DEPARTURE FORMALITIES

A departure tax of RS150 is levied at all airports (with the exception of Mumbai) for flights to Afghanistan, Bangladesh, Bhutan, Maldives, Myanmar, Nepal, Pakistan and Sri Lanka. For all other destinations, the departure tax is RS500. There is no departure tax for land or sea exits. It is strictly prohibited to export any amount of Indian currency.

CUSTOMS ENTRY (PERSONAL)

Duty Free
- Tobacco: 200 Cigarettes or 50 cigars or 250g of tobacco
- Alcohol: 1 liter of alcoholic beverage
- Perfume: 250ml eau de toilette
- Camera: 1 still camera/1 movie camera
- Gifts in value of up to Rs750 (Rs6000 for Indian nationals)
- Visitors from Nepal cannot bring in any goods duty-free

Prohibited or Restricted
- Addictive drugs
- Weapons
- Explosives
- Plants
- Ivory
- Animal fats
- Gold and silver bullion; coins not in current use
- Foreign currency exceeding US$10,000 in value (including traveler's checks) must be declared to customs on arrival. Importing Indian currency is prohibited.

IMMUNIZATION

Travelers must provide evidence of yellow fever immunization if they arrive from a country affected by Yellow Fever (such as tropical Africa or South America). The World Health Organization considers cholera endemic in India, and a vaccination may be required if traveling on to other countries. Malaria also poses a threat in most regions, including Delhi and Bombay. Tetanus and hepatitis inoculations are advisable for urban travel.

TIPPING

Taxi
Drivers are tipped 10 percent of the fare as are guides, when service is not already included.

Porters
Porters are tipped 5 to 10 rupees per bag.

Hotels

Hotels usually apply service charge directly to the bill. Otherwise, 10 to 15 percent is standard.

Restaurants

When service charges are not already applied, 10 percent is the standard tip.

EMERGENCY INFORMATION

Police and Crime

Apart from New Delhi, other main urban areas (such as Bombay, Calcutta, Madras, and Bangalore) are generally safe for travellers. However, take precautions against petty theft and pickpockets.

Delhi has been the site of numerous political bombings in public places and aboard public transportation. Avoid demonstrations, large crowds (which may prove somewhat difficult in India), or other forms of civil unrest. Periods following elections also pose risks when political demonstrations and episodes of violence often erupt.

The Kashmir Valley and the cities of Jammu and Srinagar are considered very dangerous due to continuing strife between Pakistan and India. Terrorist activities, including kidnapping and murder, are frequent. Travel to those areas is strongly discouraged.

Travel in the northeast states requires caution due to sporadic violence by ethnic insurgent groups. Extra security personnel have been deployed to the region, however, visitors are encouraged not to travel outside major cities at night.

To blend in better with the scenery on the streets, avoid flashy displays of wealth, and dress and behave conservatively. Leave most of your cash, traveler's checks, jewelry, and your camera in your hotel safe. Carry photocopies of your passport instead of the original. Carry cash in a money belt, and use credit cards or travelers checks for most of your transactions. Pickpocketing is rampant in urban areas.

Women should dress modestly to avoid harassment and should try not to travel alone. On public transportation, women should sit in the family or women's sections.

Check with your embassy for travel warnings if planning to travel outside of the main cities.

Emergency Numbers

Numbers function nationwide

Police	100
Ambulance	102
International Calls	186

Health

Avoid tap water, as over 80 percent of diseases in India are related to contaminated water. Use bottled water only, even for brushing teeth (boil water for 20 minutes or use purification systems if bottled water is unavailable). Wash vegetables and fruit in potable water before eating. Stay away from poorly cooked meats. Indian spices are often used to cover the taste of spoiled food, so avoid street stalls for dining. Indian food can be "hot" and difficult to digest for those not used to heavy spices. Give your stomach time to acclimate before diving headlong into Indian cuisine.

Malaria is endemic, and there are high incidents of hepatitis (A,B, &C) and typhoid. Polio also exists. Other disease include yellow and dengue fever, and the dust can cause allergies. The sun and heat can literally kill. Take medication and inoculations before departure. Resistance to chloroquine (administered for malaria) has been confirmed.

Hospitals are inexpensive but only good for emergencies. Doctors are well trained but they are limited by the sub-standard facilities. In case of serious illness and operation, you are best advised to leave the country.

Carry a well stocked medical kit with any and all prescription drugs that you require on a regular basis. Travel insurance with an evacuation policy is recommended. India is still given to plague-level epidemics, so, check with health officials immediately prior to travel.

For more information on medical centers, including phone numbers, please see the "Business Centers" section at the end of this chapter.

INTERNAL TRAVEL

AIR

Indian Airlines (IC) is the main domestic carrier. Their network links more than 70 cities via four international airports and 115 other airfields. IC also offers regular service to the adjacent countries of Bangladesh, Pakistan, Nepal, Sri Lanka, Singapore, Afghanistan, Thailand, and the Maldives.

Air India, the international carrier, also operates internally along the Mumbai (Bombay)-Delhi, Mumbai-Calcutta, Delhi-Calcutta and Mumbai-Chennai (Madras) routes.

Other domestic airlines include Archana Airways, Gujerat Airways, Jagson Airways, Jet Airways, Sahara Airways and Alliance Air, a division of Indian Airlines. Deregulation has improved service dramatically, and increased the number of smaller operators. Sahara and Jet are probably the most stable of the new competitors.

TAXI

Taxis are available in all cities and towns. Insist that the meters be used. Fares change from time to time and meters are not always updated. It may be difficult to determine the right fare, but drivers should have a list of fares for inspection.

If the meter does not run (as is the case about two-thirds of the time) or the driver refuses to turn it on, negotiate a fare before boarding. Prepaid taxi booths are cropping up here and there (at airports and often at main rail stations) and significantly reduce the risk of pressured haggling. Written directions for all drivers will serve you well, since many do not speak English, or may not know where your destination is located. Carry a map.

Note: When in need of a quick mode of transport for a short jaunt, and a cab cannot be found, consider hailing a rickshaw. Be sure to negotiate a fare *before* getting on board. Generally, it will cost half as much as a conventional taxi. Rickshaws should not be used for attending important business meetings.

AUTO

While rental cars are available in urban areas, driving in India is so chaotic as to make car rental inadvisable. One alternative is to rent a "tourist car," which is like an unmetered taxi, air-conditioned and chauffeur-driven. These are available at a rate slightly more than a regular taxi, and are licensed by the Government of India Tourist Office. Ordinary taxis may also be rented for the day. Generally, a day rate for either type of transit will specify a limited amount of mileage, and the client will be responsible for the per diem expenses of the driver.

TRAIN

India's train system is the largest in Asia. Express services connect all the major cities, and most of the rest of the country is served by local lines. There are also buses that link up with the trains in order to serve portions of the country that are not part of the rail system. Always take into account that you will probably need extra time when traveling by rail, since trains usually seem to run notably late.

Business travel by train is widespread, often the only means to reach remote areas safely. It may be frustrating and uncomfortable at times, but the train is an essential part of the travel experience in India.

Seven classes of passenger accommodations exist on Indian trains, which can be confusing. Contact a travel agent in your country for help reserving train passes. Many are available outside of India. Also, as a foreign national you can often take advantage of the tourist quota allotment when booking tickets, which makes it easier to reserve a seat.

A special Indrail Pass is available, which is a non-transferable ticket enabling the visitor to take any train—with no restrictions—during the period of the pass validity. Foreign nationals, as well as Indians residing abroad who hold a valid passport, may purchase the Indrail Pass with foreign currency only.

Some stations now accept credit card payment, which is appealing when considering the long lines at the other ticket counters. Reservations are always recommended.

METRO

There is a metro in Calcutta, completed in 1995, that runs along the busy north-south axis of the city from Dum-Dum (near the airport) to Tollygunj, traversing a total length of 16.45km (10 miles). There are seventeen stations at intervals of about one km. Trip time end-to-end is 33 minutes; trains come every ten minutes. Hours of operation are 8:30a.m. to 9:20p.m. Monday through Saturday; on Sundays, service is from 2:30p.m. to 9:20p.m. The fare structure is based on distance zones, and varies from Rs3 to Rs7. It is the first (and only) underground metro in India.

BUSES & TRAMS

Bus services connect all of the country, including the mountainous regions that offer no train service. However, bear in mind that traveling by roadway in India can be a grueling experience reserved for the adventurous or those with some extra time to spare.

The quality of bus service varies greatly from one state to the next, but the main routes often have a range of choices in terms of comfort level: ordinary, express, semi-luxe, deluxe, deluxe air-con, and even deluxe sleeper. There are both government and privately run operations, the latter usually faster and more comfortable (and more expensive).

Generally speaking, travel by bus is not so pleasant, featuring cramped conditions and a slow pace. However, it is the only means of traveling to Kashmir, and the best way to go from Uttar Pradesh to Nepal. Buses are also faster than the trains in northern Bihar and in most of Rajasthan.

One important footnote: reckless driving is unfortunately common, and fatal accidents involving dozens of people are not as rare as one would wish. Buses are not recommended for business travel, except in the most extreme circumstances.

Local transport also includes:
• Three-wheeled auto-rickshaws
• Cycle-rickshaws, which are generally no longer found in main cities, but still are a vital part of the transit options in small towns and villages
• Tongas (horse-drawn carriages)

WATER TRAVEL

India has a ferry system linking Calcutta, Chennai, and Vishakapatnamto with the Andaman Islands (Port Blair), and running between Cochin / Calicut and the Lakshadweep Islands. Services are seasonal, and are usually do not operate during the monsoon. There is also regular hydrofoil service between Goa and Mumbai (Bombay).

River travel is not recommended for business purposes, as it presents too many security risks.

TRAVEL ASSISTANCE

Ministry of Tourism
Transport Bhavan
1 Parliament Street, New Delhi 110 001
tel: (11) 371 8379
fax: (11) 371 0518
email: info@tourisminindia.com
website: www.tourisminindia.com
Government of India Tourist Office (GITO)
88 Janpath, New Delhi 110 001
tel: (11) 332-0342, 332-0005, 332-0008, 332-0266
Tel/fax: (11) 332-0109
India Tourism Development Corp., Ltd. (ITDC)
L1 Conaught Place, New Delhi 111 001
tel: (11) 332-0331 or 332-2336
fax: (11) 332-0331

Communications

DIALING CODES IN INDIA

International country code: [91]
Selected city codes: Ahmedabad (79), Amritsar (183), Bangalore (80), Bar (293842), Baroda (265), Bhopal (755), Bombay/Mumbai (22), Calcutta (33), Chandigarh (172), Delhi (11), Hyderabad (40), Jaipur (141), Jullundur (181), Kanpur (512), Madras (44),Mumbai (Bombay) (22), Poo (1785), Poona (212), Surat (261)

Dialing India from Overseas

To dial India from overseas, dial your country's international dialing code, then 91 (the country code for India), then the city code and finally the number. If you were dialing Bombay from the United States, for example, you would begin with 011, then 91, then 22 (the city code for Bombay), and finally the number of the person or office you are trying to reach.

Assistance Numbers

International Operator 186
Domestic Long Distance Operator 183
Domestic Operator 180
Local Information.. 197

CALLING WITHIN INDIA

As in many cases when traveling to India, observe patience when using the telephones. Poor service is expected. Local service is provided mostly by open wire and obsolete electromechanical and manual switchboard systems. Digital systems have slowly been introduced over the last 10 years.

Local Calls

A local call will cost Re1 or Rs5 depending where you call. If connection is immediate, you can feel elated. Otherwise, dig in for a long wait.

Long Distance Calls

Add a zero in front of an area code + number. Long distance calls usually prove an expensive matter. You can call through the hotel, certain public phones or private call boxes, which are really shops with signs reading PCO/STD/ISD. You may dial on your own at a call box and digital readouts on the phones indicate how much you owe the shopkeeper. Rates fall by 50 percent after 6p.m. and by 75 percent after 9p.m.

International Calls

The International Subscriber Dialing System allows one to dial direct without an operator in on the act. Simply dial

India

00 + country code + area code + number. Hotels may add a mega charge to your phone-home experience. Always inquire first.

One can alternatively call from ISD/STD offices or at a crowded post office if you feel like experiencing life among the people. Digital readouts on the ISD/STD private call boxes allow for easy payment after the call has been completed. But make sure to double check receipt information, such as number and time called, if dialing from a telephone office. One never knows what kind of additions the local spirits may conjure up on the bill.

Note: Reports have also surfaced that telephone charge cards and credit cards used in the private STD/ISD offices have later seen massive charges on their accounts with fraudulent calls.

Home Country Direct allows the caller to speak to an operator at home to place collect or credit card calls.

Australia 000-6117
Canada.. 000-167
Germany.. 000-4917
Italy 000-3917
Japan.. 000-8117
Netherlands 000-3117
New Zealand 000-6417
Singapore 000-6517
Spain 000-3417
Taiwan.. 000-88617
Thailand.. 000-6617
U.K. 000-4417
U.S. AT&T 000-117

However, as in other countries, accessing the access number may prove an arduous task. Public phones may not allow the calls. And if hotels don't block the calls, they may charge an exorbitant amount to connect you. Always ask first.

PAY PHONES

Public Telephones

Phoning from a public phone will only add to your study of randomness while in India. If available, you may get through immediately. But then again, you may not.

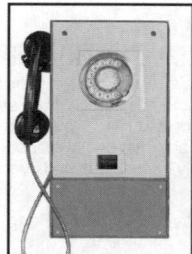

Calling Cards

Telephone cards may be purchased at telephone offices, but don't expect them to work everywhere.

CELLULAR PHONES

India operates solely on the GSM digital system A plethora of operators offer service.

Note: Your home country cell phone may not work in this country. If not, we recommend that you rent an international cell phone *before* you leave home. A major US-based cell phone rental provider is **IMC WorldCell**. For information see "International Cell Phone Rentals" on page 14.

CALL BACK

You can (potentially) save significant sums when calling in India by using a call back service. For a list of callback services, please refer to the "Communications" section in the *Global Road Warrior* Introduction.

Fees for call back services vary widely, depending on the company and the type of service required. Be sure to check with these companies before leaving to compare rates.

PHONE JACKS

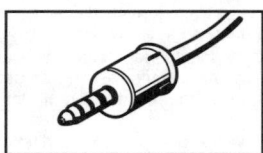

Plug adaptors are available through **iGo Corporation**. (See "Electrical and Telephone Adaptors" on page 19.)

FAX

Fax services are only readily available in hotels. However, one may have some difficulty sending them because of the poor phone system.

POSTAL SERVICES

Postal service is generally efficient, but there some additional duties may crop up for packages sent to other countries. Stamps are available at hotels. A small canister of glue may prove helpful as Indian stamps and envelopes do not have glue. If sending from outside your hotel, make sure that the seller cancels the postage in your presence, lest it get taken off and resold after your visit.

Note: The city of Bombay is now officially known as Mumbai. It has been reported that all mail using the name Bombay has been returned unopened.

TELEGRAMS

Most hotels offer 24-hour telegram service.

Business Services

COURIER SERVICES

Airborne Express (Continental Carriers); Roy Apartments, G/F1, Opp. Sahar Aircargo Complex, saltar, Andheri East, Bombay (Mumbai) 400099; tel: (22) 836-2134; fax: (22) 261-6801.

DHL India; tel: (22) 850-5151 or (22) 850-5050.

Bombay: Airfreight House, Lok Bharati Complex, Marol Maroshi Rd., Andhei (East), Bombay (Mumbai) 400059; tel: (22) 850-2039; Monday to Saturday 9:30a.m. to 5:30p.m.

Calcutta: Azimganj House, Ground Floor, 7 Camac Street, Calcutta 700017; tel: (33) 242-6914; Monday to Friday 9a.m. to 8:30p.m.; Saturday 9a.m. to 5:30p.m.

Federal Express; tel: (22) 570-0801;

Delhi: (11) 628-5911;

Bombay: (22) 570-0801;

Bangalore: (80) 559-5933;

Chennai (Madras); (44) 823-7707;

Other cities, contact Blue Dart: (22) 422-1588.

TNT Express Worldwide (India); 1F Maurya Centre, 48 Gariahat Rd., Calcutta 700 019; tel: (33) 464-4340/88, (33) 464-4963/64/65/66/67; fax: (33) 466-0056.

New Delhi: E-4 Defense Colony; New Delhi 110 024; tel:

(11) 461-6969, 461-0565/66/67/68; fax: (11) 461-0980.
UPS India (Elbee Services Ltd.), Elbee Services Ltd., Jal Building, Plot No. 177, Nehru Road, Vile Parle (east), Bombay (Mumbai) 400093; tel: (22) 822-5971; fax: (22) 611-6727.

Electrical

Current
220 volts AC, 50Hz

ELECTRIC PLUGS

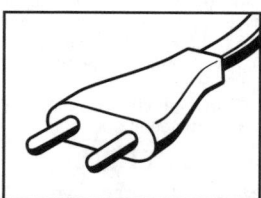

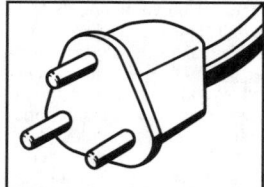

2- and 3-pin plugs are the norm.
Plug adaptors are available through **iGo Corporation.** (See "Electrical and Telephone Adaptors" on page 19.)

Technical Support

HARDWARE/SOFTWARE VENDOR SUPPORT

Acer/Texas Instruments; (in Germany) tel: [49] (4102) 488-469; fax; [49] (4102) 488-169; (in the U.S.) [1] (408) 432-6200; http://www.acer.com/.

Adobe; tel: (2) 636-8450; fax: 2-636-8534; (in Germany) tel: [49] (1) 803-5018; (in Switzerland) tel: [41] (800) 833-310; (in the U.S.) tel: [1] (800) 500-7078; (in the U.S.) tel: [1] (716) 633-3600; http://www.adobe.com/.

Apple; 80-228-1234 (Bangalor); 11-436-3030, x 101 (New Delhi); (in Switzerland) tel: [41] (800) 833-310; (in the U.K.) tel: [44] (990) 127-753; (in the U.S.) tel: [1] (800) 500-7078; http://www.apple.com/.

AST; (in the U.S.) tel: [1] (817) 232-9824 (International Technical Support); (in Ireland) tel: [353] (61) 492-222; (in the U.S.) tel: [1] (949) 727-4141; http://www.ast.com/.

Compaq/Digital; tel: 80-559-6023/6024; fax: 80-559-6025; (in Switzerland) tel: [41] (22) 709-5330; fax: [41] (22) 709-5391 (Geneva); tel: [41] (1) 801-2507; fax: [41] (1) 801-2172 (Zurich); (General U.S.) tel: (281) 518-2000; http://www.compaq.com/.

Corel; tel: 11-335-1948 (All Applications); (in Germany) tel: [49] (180) 425-8210 (TS Word Perfect-32 bit); (in the U.S.) tel: [1] (716) 871-2325 (Ask to be Forwarded to Appropriate Program); http://www.corel.com/.

Dell; tel: (80) 5545126; fax: (80) 5545738 (Bangalore); (22) 4973336 (Mumbai); (Dell- Europe) tel: [44] (134) 474-8000; (in the U.S.) tel: [1] (512) 338-4400; fax: [1] (512) 728-3330; http://www.dell.com/.

Filemaker/Claris; (in Germany) tel: [49] (180) 525-8166 (Info-line); fax: [49] (180) 567-2233; tel: [49] (180) 523-6423; (in the U.S.) tel: [1] (800) 965-9090; http://www.claris.com/.

Gateway 2000; (in the U.S.) tel: [1] (605) 232-2191; fax: [1] (605) 232-2023; (in Ireland) tel: [353] (1) 797-2000; http://www.g2k.com/.

Hewlett Packard; tel: 11 682 6035; (in Switzerland) tel: [41] (22) 780-8111; (in the U.S.) tel: [1] (408) 246-4300; http://www.hp.com/.

IBM; tel: (80) 526-7117; fax: (80) 527-7991; (in Switzerland) tel: [41] (22) 310-0418 (in French); (in the U.S.) tel: [1] (919) 517-2800; (U.S. Main Office) tel: [1] 914-765-1900; http://www.ibm.com/.

Microsoft; tel: (80) 559-5733; fax: (80) 559-7133; tel: (11) 646-0694; tel: (11) 646-0767; fax: (11) 647-4714; (in Switzerland) tel: [41] (848) 858-868; fax [41] (1) 831-0869; (in the U.S.) [1] (425) 635-7222; http://www.microsoft.com/.

NEC; (in Germany) tel: [49] (18) 0524- 1212; tel:[49] (89) 3160-1233; fax: [49] (89) 3160- 1613 (Floppy Disk and Hard Drive); tel: [49] (89) 9627-4233; fax: [49] (89) 9627-4613 (All Other Products); (in the U.S.) [1] (916) 388-0101 (Main Switchboard); http://www.nec.com/.

Novell; (in Australia) tel: [61] 2-925-3000 (Asia Pacific/Far East Support Center); (in Switzerland) tel: [41] (1) 308-4747; fax: [41] (1) 302-0401; (in the U.S.) tel: [1] (408) 434-2300; fax: [1] (408) 577-5775 (Worldwide Sales Headquarters); http://www.novell.com/.

Quark; (Singapore Office) tel: [65] 467-6675; (in the U.S.) tel: [1] (303) 894-8899; fax: [1] (303) 894-3398 (For Products Registered in the Americas); http://www.quark.com/.

Toshiba; (in Germany) tel: [49] (2131) 158-319; fax: [49] (2131) 158-558; (in Switzerland) tel: [41] (1) 946-0777; fax: [41] (1) 946-0807; (in Ireland) tel: [44] (193) 282-8828; (in the U.S.) [1] (949) 583-3000 (Corporate Headquarters); http://www.toshiba.com/.

Internet Connection

HOW TO CONNECT

Connecting to AOL and Compuserve in India is similar to using it when traveling outside your own area code. See the introductory section for detailed information on connecting to your account through a different phone number.

America Online

Numbers are available at keyword *international*. Be sure to get several local numbers before leaving. AOL has a new GlobalNet service available at keyword *access* (a free area) and download the software.

There are currently no AOL access numbers in India, and no plans to install any in the near future.

Compuserve

Numbers are available at *Go International*. The Compuserve Web-site also has a great deal of information, at http://www.compuserve.com.

There are no direct access numbers for Compuserve in Bahrain. Users will have to pay international rates to use the service.

Independent Service Providers

Many independent service providers offer discounts if you are only in town for a couple of days.

Calport Technologies; tel: (33) 475-5884; fax: (33) 476-3021; email: niel@cal.indiax.com; http://www.indiax.com/cal/.

IndianNet; tel/fax: (617) 7833443; email: proxyma@indian.net; http://www.indian.net/.

K M R Online; tel: 434-2716; tel: 434-2393; fax: 434-2393; email: sales@kmronline.net; http://www.kmronline.net/.

National Centre for Software Technology; tel: (22) 620-1606; fax: (22) 621-0139; email: ramani@SAATHI.NCST.ERNET.IN; http://www.ncst.ernet.in/

Southern Online Services; tel: (40) 241-999; fax: (40) 241-444; email: info@sol.net.in; http://www.sol.net.in/.

VSNL; tel: (22) 262-4020; fax: (22) 262-4027; telex: (11) 84229; email: helpdesk@giasbm01.vsnl.net.in; http://www.vsnl.net.in/.

Business Culture
GREETINGS AND COURTESIES

Indians greet each other (and say good-bye) with the *namaste*, which is formed by pressing the palms together (fingers up) below the chin and nodding the head. When greeting superiors or to show respect, a slight bow is added. When meeting foreigners, Indian men will shake hands. Indian men do not generally shake hands with or otherwise touch women (as a gesture of respect for a woman's dignity and privacy). Indian women who are educated or familiar with international customs may offer their hands to foreigners as a courtesy. When meeting a woman, a man should wait for her to initiate a handshake. If she does not, smile and nod slightly. When in public, men should not initiate a conversation with an Indian woman who is alone. Indians value titles; if someone has a title, use it when greeting them. The suffix *"ji"* after a last name is a general term of respect. Indians generally ask permission before leaving other people. Showing respect for others (especially those who are older) is very important. In a group, greet the eldest person first.

DECISION MAKING

Decisions are made slowly. Indians require time to discuss every aspect of a deal, and then usually take more time before giving a final answer. Be patient and plan other activities while waiting. Impatience is viewed as rude, and high-pressure attempts to get things done faster will be resisted and resented. Decisions are made at the top of the hierarchy, so whenever possible cultivate and maintain good relationships with the highest-ranking executives.

WOMEN

India is a male-dominated society. Foreign businesswomen should experience few problems but, in general, women are not accorded the same level of respect as men. Indians who have had more exposure to international dealings will be more used to dealing with women; older men will usually be more traditional and less open. Behaving in a professional, confident, and poised manner will help overcome some of this resistance. Women should be particularly aware of any behavior that might be considered flirtatious. Women who wish to entertain a male associate should do so during the day (business lunches are more popular than dinners anyway). An Indian man will probably offer to pay the bill, but will not push the point if you politely insist on paying. Women should be prepared for personal questions about their age, marital status, and whether they have children. (These are common topics of conversation and are asked of both men and women.)

MEETINGS

Indians value punctuality in others, but will often be late themselves. Also, traffic is extremely heavy in Indian cities and sometimes prevents people from getting to an appointment at all. This can require rescheduling, so if possible build a few extra days into your travel plans. Indian executives generally prefer to meet in the late morning or early afternoon. Schedule appointments well in advance (30 days ahead is suggested) and reconfirm appointments when you arrive in India. Most meetings will begin with pleasant small talk over a cup of tea and perhaps food. Do not refuse any food or drink offered. Always accept; if you do not like it, leave it in front of you. Indians usually entertain in private clubs.

BUSINESS ATTIRE

Business clothing is casual but neat. Standard attire for men is pants and short-sleeved shirts; however, a jacket should be worn to initial meetings or when seeing government officials. For more formal meetings (and during the cooler season) a lightweight suit will suffice. Do not wear leather clothing or any accessories made from animals. If you are traveling to New Delhi in northern India during the winter months, bring warmer clothes. During the monsoon season, bring a few extra changes in clothing and an umbrella and large plastic bags if you intend on keeping your things somewhat dry. The damp weather does not allow things to dry properly. A handkerchief or cloth may prove helpful to dry off any wet spots where you must sit.

Women should wear casual dresses or pant ensembles. It is acceptable for foreign women to wear the traditional sari (Indian women in particular admire foreigners who do so), but wear a sari only if you feel comfortable in one. Women should always dress conservatively. Do not wear skirts that rise above the knee, and never wear a sleeveless dress or blouse. Men should not wear Indian caps (they are generally worn by villagers and lower-class people).

Business Centers
Calcutta
CITY VIEW

Calcutta's image as a filthy, poverty-stricken city, is largely unfair and overblown. It has problems, to be sure, but it is also one of the most fascinating cities on Earth. Many Himalayan states in the northeast have recently been opened by the government, giving travelers even more to see.

India

AIRPORT

Calcutta Airport to City Center

The airport lies 11 miles (17 km.) from the city. Travel time is approximately 45 minutes (although it could be much longer with traffic). Regular (if that is possible) bus service exists outside the terminal, but the destinations may appear quite unclear. A 24-hour bus travels to major hotels and the Indian Airlines city office in 10-minute intervals between 5:30a.m. and 10p.m. Estimate 40 minutes to an hour in travel time. Taxis are available; and to avoid starting off on the wrong foot, it is suggested to head for the prepaid taxi service counter, which closes after 10p.m.

Airline Numbers

Aeroflot .... (33) 22-1415, 242-9831
Air France .... (33) 29-0011
Air India .... (33) 242-2356
Bangladesh Biman .... (33) 29-3709, 29-2832
British Airways .... (33) 29-3453
Burma (Myanmar) Airways .... (33) 572611
Cathay Pacific/KLM .... (33) 403-2112
Damana Airways .... (33) 475-5660
East West Airlines .... (33) 29-0667
Indian Airlines .... (33) 26-3390
JAL .... (33) 24-8370
KLM .... (33) 247-4593
Lufthansa... (33) 29-9365
ModiLuft .... (33) 29-6256, 29-8437
Qantas .... (33) 47-0718
Royal Nepal Airlines .... (33) 29-3949
Sahara India Airlines .... (33) 247-2795
Singapore Airlines .... (33) 29-9293, 29-1525
Swissair .... (33) 47-4643
Thai International... (33) 29-9846

HOTELS

Top-end

Oberoi Grand; 15 Jawaharlal Nehru Road; tel: (33) 249-2323; fax: (33) 249-1217; http://lhw.com/calcutta/oberoigrand.html; email: arai@oberoi-cal.com; located in commercial center; 4 deluxe restaurants; tea lounge; 2 bars; disco; conference facilities; 24-hour business center; secretarial services; ballroom; electronic key cards; 24-hour room service; laundry/dry cleaning; car rental; pharmacy; shops; hair salon; health club; fitness; pool.

Taj Bengal; 34-B Belvedere Road, Alipore; tel: (33) 248-3939; fax: (33) 248-1766; residential district near city center; 4 deluxe restaurants; 2 bars; tea lounge; conference facilities (up to 600); secretarial services; in-room minibar, cable TV, hairdryer; 24-hour room service; laundry/dry cleaning; disabled facilities; hair salon; pharmacy; shops; parking; fitness; pool; tennis; golf; disco/nightclub.

Expensive

Best Western Kenilworth; 1-2 Little Russel Street; tel: (33) 242-8394; fax: (33) 242-5136; downtown; restaurant; 24-hour coffee shop; complimentary American breakfast; conference facilities; secretarial service; fax/photocopy facilities; 24-hour room service; laundry; car rental; currency exchange; health club.

Hotel Airport Ashok; Calcutta Airport, Gate 1; tel: (33) 552-9111, 511-9111; fax: (33) 552-9137, 511-9137; 16 Km from downtown; 4 restaurants; tea lounge; 2 bars; sound-proofed rooms; secretarial services; laundry/dry cleaning; hair salon; pharmacy; shops; car rental; pool.

Hotel Hindustan International; 235/1 A.J.C. Bose Road; tel: (33) 247-2394/2395/2396; fax: (33) 247-2824; 1 Km from downtown; restaurant; conference facilities; secretarial service; fax/photocopy facilities; in-room modem/fax connection; 24-hour room service; laundry/dry cleaning; hair salon; car rental. currency exchange; shops; corporate rates; fitness; sauna; pool; whirlpool.

Park Hotel; 17 Park Street; tel: (33) 249-7336, 249-7342; fax: (33) 249-7343, 249-8027; downtown boutique hotel; 4 deluxe restaurants; 2 bars; tea lounge; conference/banquet facilities; 24-hour secretarial services; laundry/dry cleaning; luxury floor suites; hair salon; car rental; pharmacy; shops; fitness; pool; disco.

Moderate

Hotel Ruttdeen; 21B Dr UN Brahmachari Street; tel: (33) 247-5240, 402-878; fax: (33) 247-5240; 1 Km from downtown; restaurant; bars; conference rooms; car rental.

Lytton Hotel; 14 Sudder Street; tel: (33) 249-1872, 249-1873, 249-1875; restaurant.

Quality Inn; 12 Jawaharlal Nehru Road; tel: (33) 243-0301; fax: (33) 248-6650; restaurant; conference facilities.

AUTO RENTAL

Hertz; 10A Ho Chi Minh Sarani, tel: (33) 242-3561; fax: (33) 242-5136; Hotel New Kenilworth, 1 & 2 Little Russel St., tel: (33) 242-8394.

WORLD TRADE CENTER

World Trade Center Calcutta
24-B Park Street
Calcutta 700 016, India
tel: (33).249-7603; fax: (33).229-2665
email: wtccal@cal.vsnl.net.in
website: http://www.dclgroup.com

CHAMBER OF COMMERCE

Indian Chamber of Commerce
India Exchange, 4 India Exchange Place
Calcutta 700 001
tel: (33) 220-8393; fax: (33) 201-0289

Delhi

CITY VIEW

Although New Delhi is only the third largest city in India, it stands as the business capital and in many ways also represents the most international side of India. It is a strange combination of "Old" Delhi, with its mosques and Muslim monuments, and "New" Delhi, with gleaming government buildings and clean streets.

AIRPORT

Indira Gandhi International Airport to City Center

The airport lies 10 miles (16 km.) from the city. Although a 24-hour coach and bus service might exist, taxis offer the best available option. Be sure to go to a prepay counter to pay your fare, lest you fall prey to moneysharks in the form of cab drivers. A prepaid fare might range from Rs100 to Rs200. Figure about 45 minutes to get into the center of town. Hotels, such as the Sheraton, in the southern end of town will require half the time.

Airline Numbers

Aeroflot.. (11) 331-2916
Air Canada .... (11) 372-0015
Air France .... (11) 331-0407
Air India .... (11) 331-1225
Air Lanka .... (11) 332-4789
Air New Zealand .... (11) 371-3366

Alitalia .... (11) 331-1019
British Airways .... (11) 332-7428
Gulf Air .... (11) 332-2018
Iran Air .... (11) 60-4397
Iraqi Airways .... (11) 331-8632
Japan Airlines .... (11) 332-3409
KLM .... (11) 331-5841
LOT Polish Airlines .... (11) 332-4308
Lufthansa .... (11) 332-3206
PIA .... (11) 331-6121
Royal Nepal Airlines .... (11) 332-0817
Syrian Arab Airlines .... (11) 34-3218
Thai International .... (11) 332-3608

HOTELS

Note: Occupancy is usually full due to companies often lodging their employees in hotels rather than apartments; be sure to reserve far in advance of your intended stay.

Top-end

Ashoka; 50-B Chanakyapuri; tel: (11) 60-0121; fax: (11) 687-3216; adjacent Nehru Park.

Hyatt Regency; Bhikaiji Cama Place, Ring Road; tel: (11) 688-1234; fax: (11) 688-6833; located in a suburb; 3 restaurants; Regency Club; business facilities; conference facilities; fitness; sauna; pool.

Le Meridien; Windsor Place, Janpath; tel: (11) 371-0101; fax: (11) 371-4545; city center; restaurants; meeting room; secretarial service; fax/photocopy facilities; corporate rates; in-room safe; fitness; sauna; pool; tennis.

Maurya Sheraton & Towers; Sardar Patel Marg, Diplomatic Enclave; tel: (11) 301-0101; fax: (11) 301-0908; located in southern Delhi; 3 restaurants; all standard Sheraton amenities.

New Delhi Hilton; Barakhama Avenue, Connaught Place; tel: (11) 332-0101; fax: (11) 332-5335; city center; city views; 7 restaurants; business room floors; conference facilities; library; secretarial service; fax/photocopy facilities; fitness; sauna; pool.

The Oberoi; Dr. Zakir HussainMarg.; tel: (11) 436-3030; fax: (11) 436-0758; near exhibition grounds; restaurant; conference facilities; secretarial service; fax/photocopy facilities; corporate rates; fitness; sauna; pool; whirlpool; adjacent to and arrangements with the Delhi Golf Club.

The Taj Mahal; Number One Mansingh Road; tel: (11) 301-6162; fax: (11) 301-7299; city center; 4 restaurants; 24-hour coffee shop; conference facilities; fitness; pool.

Taj Palace Inter-Continental; 2 Sardar Patel Marg, Diplomatic Enclave; tel: (11) 301-0404; fax: (11) 301-1252; restaurant; conference facilities; secretarial service; fax/photocopy facilities; sauna; pool.

Expensive

Claridges; 12 Aurangzeb Road; tel: (11) 301-0211; fax: (11) 301-0625; 5-star hotel; restaurant; conference facilities; secretarial service; fax/photocopy facilities; corporate rates; fitness; sauna; pool; whirlpool.

Imperial Janpath; tel: 332-5332; fax: 332-4542.

Moderate

The Centaur Delhi Airport; Gurgaon Road; tel: (11) 545-2223; fax: (11) 545-2256.

Siddarth; 3 Rajendra Place; tel: (11) 571-2501; fax: (11) 578-1016; 5-star hotel; restaurant; conference facilities; secretarial service; fax/photocopy facilities; sauna; pool.

Best Western Surya; Friends Colony; tel: (11) 683-5070; fax: (11) 683-7758; 5-star hotel; restaurant; conference facilities; secretarial service; fax/photocopy facilities; fitness; pool.

Park Hotel; 15 Parliament Street; tel: (11) 373-2477; fax: (11) 373-2025; 5-star hotel.

Hotel Samrat; Chanakyapuri; tel: (11) 603030; fax: (11) 688-7047; 5-star hotel.

Qutab; Sheheed Jeet Singh Marg; tel; (11) 660-060; fax: (11) 696-0828; 5-star hotel, located in a suburb; restaurant; conference facilities; corporate rates; fitness; pool.

AUTO RENTAL

Note: Due to the horrendous traffic conditions, driving one's own car should not be considered. Hiring a chauffeur-driven car from one of the following agencies presents a far better option for a price of about Rs600 for a day.

Budget; reservations, tel: (11) 331-8600; fax: (11) 379-182; G-3 Arunachal Bldg., 19 Barakhamba Rd., tel 371-5658; fax: 330-202.

Hertz; Ansal Chamber 1 GF-29, 3 Bhikaji Cama Place; tel: (11) 619-7188; Hotel Hans Plaza, Barakhamba Road, tel: (11) 331-8517; fax: (@2) 492-1171; chauffeur-driven cars available.

SITA Travel; F-12 Connaught Place; tel: (11) 31 6-514.

WORLD TRADE CENTER

Delhi-Gurdaon World Trade Center
c/o Energetic Construction Private Limited
C-8/1A, Vasant Vihar
New Delhi - 110 057
tel: (11) 614-3282, (11) 614-3284
fax: (11) 614-1759
email: ecplwtc@del3.vsnl.net.in
website: http://www.wtcindia.com

CHAMBERS OF COMMERCE

Associated Chambers of Commerce and Industry of India (ASSOCHAM)
2nd Floor, Allahabad Bank Building
17 Parliament Street, New Delhi 110 001
tel: (11) 336-0704
fax: (11) 373-5917

Federation of Indian Chambers of Commerce (FICCI)
Federation House, Tansen Marg
New Delhi 110 001
tel: (11) 331-9251
fax: 330-0714

Indonesia

At a Glance

THE PEOPLE

Population .... 216,108,345 (July 1999 est.)
Growth Rate .... 1.46% (1999 est.)
Life Expectancy .... 62.92 years (born 1999)
Infant Mortality .... 57.3 deaths/1,000 live births (1999 est.)

Ethnic Composition

Javanese (Mountain Malays) 45%
Sundanese 14%
Madurese 7.5%
Coastal Malays 7.5%
Chinese 5%
Other 21%

Religious Composition

Muslim 88%
Protestant 5%
Roman Catholic 3%
Hindu, Buddhist and other 4%

Languages Spoken

Bahasa Indonesia (official), English, Dutch, Javanese, local dialects

Labor Force

Total: 67,000,000
By occupation: services 38%, industry 18%, agriculture 44%

THE ECONOMY

Formerly a totally agrarian society, Indonesia has moved its economy decidedly towards technology and services within the last thirty years. Considered to be one of Asia's mini-dragon economies, Indonesia set a course in the 1970s and '80s towards full modernization. Its dreams were dashed in 1997 with the financial crisis that swept through much of the southeast Asian region. Corrupt banking procedures and rampant cronyism were exposed to global public view and the long-standing president, Suharto, was driven from office. Ensuing financial reforms were mild at best and foreign investment continued to flow out. The next few years will be very tough for this expansive archipelago as it is estimated that over half of its 200 million-plus population has been returned to the pre-developmental poverty of the 1960s. Growing unemployment and inflation are eating away at what little progress has been made in financial reform. All the while, foreign investment is maintaining a wait-and-see attitude. Like many of its neighbors, Indonesia's future is tied directly to the success (or failure) of Japan.

Exports .... US$49 billion (f.o.b., 1998 est.)
Imports .... US$24 billion (f.o.b., 1998 est.)
Total GDP .... US$602 billion (1998 est.)
GDP Per Capita .... US$2,830 (1998 est.)
Unemployment .... 15%-20% (1998 est.)
Inflation Rate .... 77% (1998 est.)

Top Export Partners

Japan, United States, Singapore, South Korea, Taiwan, China

Top Import Partners

Japan, United States, South Korea, E.U., Singapore, Australia, Taiwan

Top Exports

Textiles, garments, wood products, electronics, footwear

Top Imports

Manufactures, raw materials, foodstuffs, fuels

BUSINESS WORKWEEK

Offices

Monday to Friday 8a.m. to 4p.m. or 5p.m.

Banks

Monday to Saturday 8a.m. to 3p.m.

Government

Monday to Thursday 8a.m. to 3p.m., Friday 8a.m. to 11:30a.m.

Retail

Monday to Friday 9a.m. to 9p.m. (slightly shorter hours on the weekends)

Note: Office and retail hours in rural areas are more attuned to local custom and seasonal needs. In all areas, allowances must be made for Islamic prayer periods during working hours.

HOLIDAYS

New Year's Day .... January 1
Id al-Fitr, end of Ramadan .... January 19*
Id al-Adha, Feast of the Sacrifice .... March 28*
Good Friday .... April 2*
Muharram, Islamic New Year .... April 17*
Vesak Day .... May 30*
Mouloud, Prophet
Muhammad's Birthday .... June 26*
Indonesian National Day .... August 17
Ascension of the Prophet
Muhammad .... November 6*
Christmas Day .... December 25
*Date may vary by year.

CLIMATE

Seasons

Indonesia is located right on the equator and stretches thousands of miles east to west. Weather is hot and humid almost year round, and it really only has two seasons: wet and wetter. From June through to November it is "dry" with temperatures averaging approximately 28˚C (82˚F). From November to June it is "wet", with heavy rainfall and typhoons. Temperatures can exceed 40˚C (104˚F).

Regions

Indonesia stretches along the equator with no real regional climate differences.

Indonesia

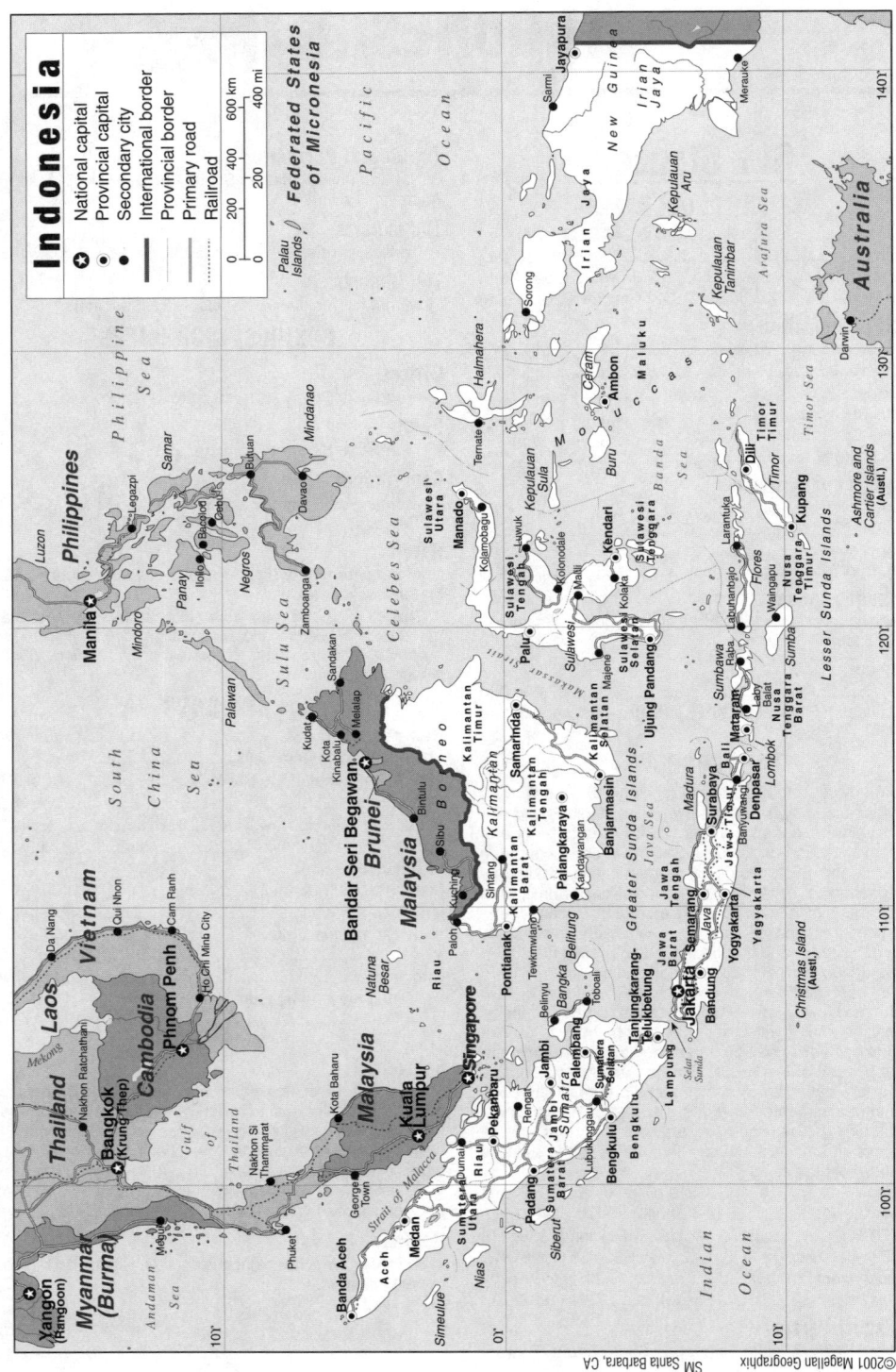

Indonesia

- ⊗ National capital
- ⊙ Provincial capital
- ● Secondary city
- — International border
- — Provincial border
- ··· Railroad

| 0 | 200 | 400 | 600 km |
| 0 | 200 | 400 mi |

Money & Banking

Currency
The currency of Indonesia is the Rupiah (Rp).

Denominations
The Rupiah (Rp) comes in coin denominations of Rp500, 100, 50, and 25, and banknotes of Rp100, 500, 1,000, 5,000, 10,000, 20,000, and 50,000.

Traveler's Checks and Credit Cards
Traveler's checks and currency are best exchanged at foreign banks such as Bank of America, Chase Manhattan, and a number of European and Japanese banks. Larger banks offer the best exchange rates and Indonesian banks the worst. Due to the nation's ongoing currency problems there is a thriving black market but it is best avoided.

Cash, especially U.S. dollars, can also be exchanged at reasonable rates at larger hotels and exchange kiosks in urban areas.

Note: Wrinkled and soiled notes are likely to be refused.

Carry small change at all times, as many cabbies and shops do not change larger bills.

Larger establishments in Jakarta and Bali accept major credit cards. American Express, Visa, Diner's Club, MasterCard, and Japanese Credit Bureau cards can receive cash advances at banks and selected ATMs in Jakarta. Rural areas—which is most of Indonesia—will only accept cash for transactions. Keep all receipts from every exchange if you plan on reconverting at departure.

Note: The rupiah has little value outside of Indonesia beyond souvenir purposes. The reconversion rate is not very favorable, so do not exchange more currency or checks than you need for the extent of your visit.

Essential Terms

English	Indonesian
Yes	*Ya*
No	*Tidak*
Good morning	*Selamat pagi*
Hello (daytime)	*Selamat siang*
Hello (evening)	*Selamat sore*
Hello (telephone)	*Halo*
Good-bye	*Sampai Jumpa*
Please	*Tolong*
Thank you	*Terima kasih*
Pleased to meet you	*Saya sangat gembira bertemu anda*
Excuse me; I'm sorry	*Permisi*
My name is _____	*Nama saya_____*
I don't understand	*Saya tidak mengerti*
Do you speak English?	*Apakah andabisa bichara*

Travel

VISA AND PASSPORT
A passport that is valid for a minimum of six months beyond date of entry is required of all visitors.

A visa is required of all, except for tourism visits of 60 days (which can be extended) for the following:

* Nationals of Argentina, Australia, Brazil, Brunei, Canada, Chile, Egypt, EU countries (except Portugal), Hungary, Iceland, Japan, Korea (Rep. of), Kuwait, Liechtenstein, Malaysia, Maldives, Malta, Mexico, Monaco, Morocco, New Zealand, Norway, Philippines, Saudi Arabia, Singapore, Switzerland, Thailand, Turkey, U.K., United Arab Emirates, U.S., Venezuela and Yugoslavia (Serbia and Montenegro)

* Passengers in transit who do not leave the airport and are continuing their journey within eight hours, and who are holding confirmed tickets and other documents for onward travel

Journalists and business visitors must have both a visa and special permission, regardless of nationality.

Note: Severe fines and even prison sentences are imposed if a visitor exceeds the visa-free stay of 60 days.

Types of visa issued are:

* Tourist - single entry only. This visa is good for up to four weeks, and valid if used within three months of issuance.

* Business/Social - single and multiple entry. This visa requires approval by the Immigration Office. The term 'Social' means that the visitor intends to stay with friends or family while in Indonesia. The single-entry version is good for up to five weeks, valid if used within three months of issuance. The multiple-entry visa is for Business only (not Social), and is good for 60 days per stay, and valid for up to one year.

* Transit - single entry only. This visa is good for 14 days per entry, and valid for 90 days.

All visitors must be able to substantiate sufficient funds, at a minimum of US$2,000 cash or travelers checks. Credit cards may not be used as substantiation.

Allow two days for visa applications made in person, or one week after receipt of postal applications. Applications which necessitate referral to Immigration in Indonesia may take as long as two months to process.

Note 1: Those travelers wishing to enter Aceh or Irian Jaya must acquire a special permit, issued by the Indonesian Immigration Office and the State Police Headquarters in Jakarta. Upon arrival in either state, visitors are required to report to the office of the local police.

Note 2: East Timor is not part of Indonesia any longer. Currently, the U.N. is acting as the administrative authority. Contact the nearest U.N. office for information regarding travel there.

Restricted Entry:
* Nationals of Israel and Portugal must obtain approval and a special permit from Immigration in order to be admitted.

* Nationals of China (PR) and CIS must have approval from Immigration prior to entry. Nationals of China (PR) must also have sponsorship in Indonesia, and are required to travel in groups of five people minimum.

* All visa applicants from Afghanistan, Algeria, Bangladesh, Cameroon, Congo (Rep. of), CIS, Ethiopia, Ghana, India, Iraq, Iran, Nigeria, Pakistan, Somalia, Sri Lanka, Tanzania, Uganda, and Yemen must have special approval from Indonesian Immigration.

DEPARTURE FORMALITIES

There is a departure tax of Rs50,000 for international flights. Currency exchange can be accomplished at most airports with proper exchange receipts.

CUSTOMS ENTRY (PERSONAL)

Duty-free

For a one-week stay:

- Tobacco: 200 cigarettes, 50 cigars or 100g of tobacco
- Alcohol: less than 2 liters of alcohol (opened)
- Other: a reasonable quantity of perfume; gifts up to the value of US$100

For a 2-week stay:

- Tobacco: 400 cigarettes, 100 cigars, or 200g of tobacco
- Other: a reasonable quantity of perfume; gifts up to the value of US$100

For a stay of more than two weeks:

- Tobacco: 600 cigarettes, 150 cigars, or 300g of tobacco
- Other: a reasonable quantity of perfume; gifts up to the value of US$100

Prohibited or Restricted

- Cameras and jewelry must be declared on arrival.
- It is prohibited to import weapons, ammunition, non-prescribed drugs, fresh fruit, television sets, cordless telephones or other electronic equipment, Chinese publications, medicines, and pornography.

IMMUNIZATION

No immunizations are required for entry to Indonesia unless coming from an area infected with Yellow Fever; in this case, an International Certificate of Vaccination is required. Malaria prophylaxis as well as tetanus and hepatitis A inoculations are recommended especially for rural travel.

TIPPING

Note: Customarily, small change is almost never dispensed, so visitors should carry their own supply for tipping purposes.

Taxi

Taxi drivers usually receive 15 percent of the metered amount.

Porters

Porters receive R2000 per piece of luggage.

Hotels

Hotels usually apply a 10 percent service charge directly to the bill.

Restaurants

Restaurants usually apply service charges to the bill. If not, then a 10 percent tip is customary.

EMERGENCY INFORMATION

Police and Crime

Since the political and economic situation in Indonesia remains shaky, visitors are encouraged to avoid crowds and disturbances and to exercise caution. Riots still take place in various places, including the islands of Java, Sumatra, and Bali. It is suggested that you register with your embassy upon arrival for the duration of your visit. Chinese nationals may find that they are the particular target of political violence.

The provinces of Aceh, West Kalimantan, Irian Jaya, and East Timor have been the sites of unrest even prior to the current political unrest. Travelers to these regions should stay in larger towns. If intending to travel to Irian Jaya, a special permit is required. Contact the Indonesian consulate or embassy in your area for details.

High levels of street crime exist in urban areas, so take basic precautions. Incidents involving theft, or even murder, in taxi cabs have been known. Exercise prudence when choosing a cab, or allow your hotel to set up regular transport for you. Otherwise, stick to taxis lined up in front of hotels.

As Indonesians become poorer, the tourists seem richer. Foreign business visitors are often the target of thieves. Consequently, purses, laptops, and briefcases will require additional security. Do not leave valuables in cars or on tables in cafés. Keep non-essential valuables locked in hotel safes when not in use. Use credit cards and travel checks when possible to avoid carrying large sums of cash.

Women may face a degree of sexual harassment when out alone, especially after dark. This is a Muslim country, so dress with modesty to avoid confrontations. Bali is predominantly Hindu, however, foreign women are nevertheless encouraged to don more conservative clothing.

The police are quite efficient in urban areas, but may be part of the crime problem in rural precincts. Some corruption exists within the local and central governments. Business travelers may also find that their deals with local companies involve the bribing of public officials. Besides making the personal decision of whether or not to participate in such dealings, check on your legal position in your own country. Some nations now have stiff penalties for their business people who bribe officials when overseas.

Emergency Numbers

Numbers function nationwide.

Police.. 110
Fire 113
Ambulance 118

Health

Never use tap water except in first-class hotels. Bottled water is safe and readily available. Otherwise, boil water for 10 to 15 minutes. Wash all vegetables in a chlorine solution, peel fruits, and avoid uncooked food. Drink only pasteurized milk products.

The heat and humidity may cause skin infections and encourage skin parasites, so come prepared. Malaria exists throughout Indonesia except in the main tourist areas of Bali and Java. Air pollution in Jakarta is a major problem for those with respiratory disorders.

The medical system is sub-standard and getting worse. You are advised to go to Singapore for serious medical needs. Carry along a well-stocked medical kit when traveling in rural areas. Bring extra amounts of any medication you require. Hotels will have access to a list of multilingual doctors. Travel insurance with an evacuation policy is recommended.

For more information on medical centers, including phone numbers, please see the "Business Center" section at the end of this chapter.

INTERNAL TRAVEL

AIR

Indonesia has an excellent domestic air system linking Jakarta with most major towns. Flights originating in Jakarta leave from Terminal 1 at the Soekarno Hatta International Airport. Domestic airlines include: Bouraq Indonesia Airlines (BO), Garuda Indonesia (GA), Merpati Nusantara Airlines (MZ) and Sempati Air (SG). There is a departure tax of Rp11,000.

Discount fares for domestic flights are offered via the Asean Air Pass, which is available in a variety of types that give access to different combinations of cities. The pass must be purchased outside Indonesia and can be acquired at Garuda Indonesia offices in Europe, Australia, Japan, and the U.S. For more information, contact Garuda Indonesia at: tel: (020) 7486-3011; fax: (020) 224-3971

TAXI

Taxis are widely available in most major cities and in some of the smaller towns. Taxis with meters are only found in large cities and tourist areas. Taxis can be distinguished by their yellow number plates, common to all Indonesian public transport vehicles.

In smaller towns, bicycle taxis are prevalent. However, because of reports of robbery and even murder in Jakarta cabs, one is advised to call a taxi company directly or to employ one from a hotel taxi line. Do not go with an unlicensed car. Make sure no other passengers already occupy the cab, and insist that the driver use the meter, if there is one. Taxis can be hired by the day.

Bemos are either motorized tricycles for two, or, on smaller islands, old vans that travel the smaller roads and pick up passengers along the street. Since the bemos are privately operated, any passenger is a candidate for financial profit, but a foreigner much more so. Be sure to negotiate a fare before entering. Various other forms of pedicabs, rickshaws, and motorized transport also exist but are not regularly used by foreign business travelers.

Note: When using taxis, always write directions on paper in case your driver does not understand your native tongue or does not know where your intended destination might be. Carry a map.

AUTO

Rental cars can be found in most urban areas but they can be very expensive. A credit card and valid license (sometimes an International Driving Permit) are required.

Traffic in urban areas is congested and chaotic. In parts of Jakarta, you cannot drive on certain streets unless at least three people are in the car. Traffic delays occur regularly and prove lengthy. Outside of the cities, signage is minimal.

Roughly half of Indonesia's roadway network is paved. Java has the best roads, and Bali and Sumatra both have decent networks also. The road systems are poor on the other islands but are improving with the increase in tourism. Tolls remain in effect on some of the major urban roads.

Chauffeur-driven automobiles are also widely available and may offer the best option for most travelers. Rental cars are not advisable for first-time visitors.

TRAIN

Rail services link cities on the island of Java and offer relative comfort in the first class accommodations. The Bima Express, which offers restaurant and sleeping cars and some air conditioning, runs between Jakarta and Surabaya and offers first class service only. Rail services are also available on Sumatra between Belawan, Medan, and Tanjong Bala/Rantu Prapet (usually several trains daily), as well as between Panjang and Palembang (usually three trains daily). There are three service levels, ranked by price—first-class service is available only for express services. Trains are a common form of business travel for locals. All train travel must be booked in advance.

Note: Schedules in Indonesia contain a lot of "jam karet" ("rubber time"). Don't expect anything to leave or arrive according to a posted schedule.

METRO

There is no metro service in any of Indonesia's cities.

BUSES & TRAMS

Intercity: Bus lines are extensive on all of the islands and to all of the cities. Travel can prove very slow, and because of the jam karet ("rubber time") reality, no complex journeys involving two or more transfers should be attempted in a single day. A trip to Bali from Jakarta can take two days.

Buses are not very efficient, although they are inexpensive. Fares are approximately equivalent to third-class train tickets. One positive aspect is that many buses on the intercity routes have air conditioning.

Urban: Local city buses most often prove too crowded to recommend. Jakarta is the only city that has a standard bus service of sufficient size to be considered as a viable option by a business traveler. Double-decker buses bustle along the streets there.

WATER TRAVEL

Indonesia offers two main types of passenger boat travel between its many islands. The first is a basic ferry service (*prahu*) that can run the gamut from motorized to wooden sailing ships. The second is a set of seven modern German-manufactured vessels of the Pelini line (state-owned) that offer four classes of service to all of the islands. These can be used for overnight trips as well short jaunts. Information about all passenger boat travel is available from travel agencies or directly from the local "syanbandar" or harbormaster. International cruise lines also serve the Jakarta and Bali areas.

For further information, contact the Indonesia Tourism Promotion Board (see following section for telephone and address).

TRAVEL ASSISTANCE

Directorate-General of Tourism
16/19 Jalan Medan Merdeka Barat
P.O. Box 1409, Jalan Medan Merdeka Barat
Jakarta 10110, Indonesia
tel: (21) 383-823 or 383-8221 or 383-8234
fax: (21) 386-7589 or 386-0828
email: nusa@indobiz.com
website: www.tourismindonesia.com
Indonesia Tourism Promotion Board
9th Floor, Bank Pacific Building
8J1 Jend Sudirman
Jakarta 10220, Indonesia
tel: (21) 570-4879 or 570-4917
fax: (21) 570-4855
email: nusa@indobiz.com
website: www.tourismindonesia.com

Communications

DIALING CODES IN INDONESIA

International country code: [62]
Selected city codes: Bandung (22), Cirebon (231), Denpasar (Bali) (361), Jakarta (21), Madiun (351), Malang (341), Medan (61), Padang (751), Palembang (711), Sekurang (778), Semarang (24), Solo (271), Surabaya (31), Tanjungkarang (721), Yogyakarta (274)

Dialing Indonesia from Overseas

To dial Indonesia from overseas, dial your country's international dialing code, then 62 (the country code for Indonesia), then the city code, and finally the number. If you were dialing Jakarta from the United States, for example, you would begin with 011, then 62, then 21 (the city code for Jakarta), and finally the number of the person or office you are trying to reach.

Assistance Numbers

Operator 101
International calls 104/194
Directory assistance (Jakarta)....................................... 104
Directory assistance (elsewhere) 106
International Information... 102
Domestic Long-distance operator: 100

CALLING WITHIN INDONESIA

Local Calls

Telecom offices are often open 24 hours. The best service can be found in private telecommunication offices, which can be found throughout the country. These offices, such as Warpostal, Warparpostes, or Wartel, are open 7:30a.m. to midnight, although some are increasingly open 24 hours.

Long Distance Calls

Long distance calls can be made from any telecom office or hotels. Beware, hotels often tack on a high surcharge with long distance calls.

PAY PHONES

Public Telephones

Card Phone:

Public pay telephones are rare, but are available in hotels and post offices. Most phones require cards.

Calling Cards

Cards can be purchased at hotels and many retail stores.

CELLULAR PHONES

Indonesia operates on several different cellular systems including, AMPS (PT Telekomindo Prima Bhakti, PT Komselindo), NAMPS (PT Metro Seluler Nusantara), and NMT-470 (PT Mobile Selular Indonesia) analog, as well as GSM digital (PT Telkomsel, PT Excelcomindo, PT Satelindo).

Note: Your home country cell phone may not work in this country. If not, we recommend that you rent an international cell phone *before* you leave home. A major US-based cell phone rental provider is **IMC WorldCell**. For information see "International Cell Phone Rentals" on page 14.

CALL BACK

You can (potentially) save significant sums when calling in Indonesia by using a call back service. For a list of call-back services, please refer to the "Communications" section in the *Global Road Warrior* Introduction.

Fees for call back services vary widely, depending on the company and the type of service required. Be sure to check with these companies before leaving to compare rates.

PHONE JACKS

Many of the newer buildings have phone jacks similar to those found in the United States:

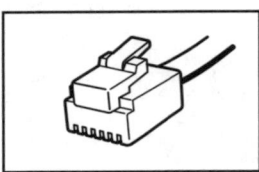

But some older buildings still feature the following phone jack:

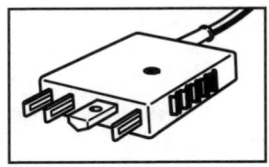

Plug adaptors are available through **iGo Corporation.** (See "Electrical and Telephone Adaptors" on page 19.)

FAX

Faxes are available in hotels. The shortage of good phone lines has limited the popularity.

POSTAL SERVICES

The postal service is good in the cities and generally poor in rural areas. All international packages must be inspected before sending. You can not insure parcels.

TELEGRAMS

Telegrams can be sent from telegraphic offices. In Jakarta, offices are open 24 hours a day, but outside the city services are less efficient.

Business Services

COURIER SERVICES

Airborne Express; Airborne Bldg., Jl. Wijayai No. 2A, Jakarta Selatan 12170; tel: (21) 723-3364; fax: (21) 723-3368.

Birotika Semesta PT; Jalan HR Rasuna Said Setiabudi Bldg.; Jakarta; tel: (21) 517-989.

City Link Indo PT; Jalan Thamrin Wisata Hotel; Jakarta; tel: 333-432.

DHL (P.T. Birotika Semesta/DHL); Mustika Centre, 7th Floor, JL. Gatot Subroto Kav. 74-75, Jakarta 12870; tel: (21) 830-6688.

Inter Pacific Citra PT; Jalan Pang-lima Polim Raya 15; Jakarta; tel: 735-613.

UPS (Pt. Cardig Air); Halim Perdanakusuma Airport, Jakarta 13610; tel: (21) 800-9339; fax: (21) 809-1954.

SECRETARIAL SERVICES

Asian & Pacific Coconut Community; Wisma Bakrie; Jalan H.R. Rasuna Said Kav. B-1; tel: (21) 510-073.

Manggala Business Center; Manggala Wanabakti, Jalan Jend; Gatot Subroto Ged; tel: (21) 570-0279.

OFFICE RENTAL

Benchmark Serviced Offices; 2nd Floor, The Ascott Jakarta, The Golden Triangle, No 2 Jalan Kebon Kacang Raya, Jakarta 10230; tel (62 21) 315 3243; fax (62 21) 391 3717, email: benchmrk@rad.net.id.

TRANSLATION SERVICES

Most hotels have business centers with translation services. In addition:

Commercial Advisory Foundation; Jalan Probolinggo 5; Jakarta; tel: (21) 344-485.

Henry Suryopranoto SH Assocs.; Jalan hayam Wuruk, Harco Bldg. D34-35; Jakarta; tel: 656-021.

Electrical

Current

110 volts AC, 50Hz. Some areas (including Jakarta) have 220 volts AC, 50Hz.

ELECTRIC PLUGS

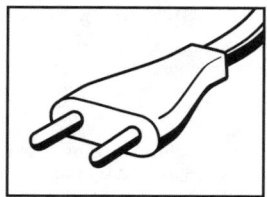

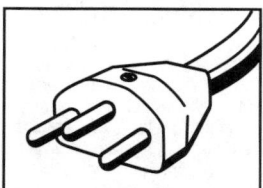

Most plugs are of the flat 2-pin variety.

Plug adaptors are available through **iGo Corporation**. (See "Electrical and Telephone Adaptors" on page 19.)

Technical Support

HARDWARE/SOFTWARE VENDOR SUPPORT

Acer/Texas Instruments; (in Germany) tel: [49] (4102) 488-469; fax; [49] (4102) 488-169; (in the U.S.) [1] (408) 432-6200; http://www.acer.com/.

Adobe; (Singapore Office) tel: [65] 276-9990 (Adobe Frame and UNIX); fax: [65] 276-9991; [65] 276-9198 (All Adobe Products except Frame Products); [65] 274-3877; (in the U.S.) tel: [1] (800) 500-7078; (in the U.S.) tel: [1] (716) 633-3600; http://www.adobe.com/.

Apple/Claris; tel: (21) 380-1780; (in Switzerland) tel: [41] (800) 833-310; (in the U.K.) tel: [44] (990) 127-753; (in the U.S.) tel: [1] (800) 500-7078; http://www.apple.com/.

AST; (in the U.S.) tel: [1] (817) 232-9824 (International Technical Support); (in Ireland) tel: [353] (61) 492-222; (in the U.S.) tel: [1] (949) 727-4141; http://www.ast.com/.

Compaq/Digital; (Singapore Office) tel: [65] 750-4328; fax: [65] 750-7385; (in Switzerland) tel: [41] (22) 709-5330; fax: [41] (22) 709-5391 (Geneva); tel: [41] (1) 801-2507; fax: [41] (1) 801-2172 (Zurich); (General U.S.) tel: (281) 518-2000; http://www.compaq.com/.

Corel; (in Germany) tel: [49] (180) 425-8210 (TS Word Perfect-32 bit); (in the U.S.) tel: [1] (716) 871-2325 (Ask to be Forwarded to Appropriate Program); http://www.corel.com/.

Dell; tel: [1] (604) 810-4977 (for Dell listings in Indonesia); fax: [1] 604-810-4273; (Dell- Europe) tel: [44] (134) 474-8000; (in the U.S.) tel: [1] (512) 338-4400; fax: [1] (512) 728-3330; http://www.dell.com/.

Filemaker/Claris; (in Germany) tel: [49] (180) 525-8166 (Info-line); fax: [49] (180) 567-2233; tel: [49] (180) 523-6423; (in the U.S.) tel: [1] (800) 965-9090; http://www.claris.com/.

Gateway 2000; (in the U.S.) tel: [1] (605) 232-2191; fax: [1] (605) 232-2023; (in Ireland) tel: [353] (1) 797-2000; http://www.g2k.com/.

Hewlett Packard; tel: 21 350 3408;(in Switzerland) tel: [41] (22) 780-8111; (in the U.S.) tel: [1] (408) 246-4300; http://www.hp.com/.

IBM; tel: 21-251-2922 (general information); fax: 21-251-2933; tel: 21-252-1222 (product information); fax: 21-252-1233; (in Switzerland) tel: [41] (22) 310-0418 (in French); (in the U.S.) tel: [1] (919) 517-2800; (U.S. Main Office) tel: [1] 914-765-1900; http://www.ibm.com/.

Microsoft; tel: (21) 570-4254 (Technical Support); fax: (21) 520-8122; (in Switzerland) tel: [41] (848) 858-868; fax [41] (1) 831-0869; (in the U.S.) [1] (425) 635-7222; http://www.microsoft.com/.

NEC; (in Australia) tel: [61] 008-027-260 (UltraCare Support); (in the U.S.) [1] (916) 388-0101 (Main Switchboard); http://www.nec.com/.

Novell; (in Australia) tel: [61] 2-925-3000 (Asia Pacific Support Center); (in Switzerland) tel: [41] (1) 308-4747; fax: [41] (1) 302-0401; (in the U.S.) tel: [1] (408) 434-2300; fax: [1] (408) 577-5775 (Worldwide Sales Headquarters); http:/ /www.novell.com/.

Quark; (Singapore Office) tel: [65] 467-6675; (in the U.S.) tel: [1] (303) 894-8899; fax: [1] (303) 894-3398 (For Products Registered in the Americas); http://www.quark.com/.

Toshiba; (in Germany) tel: [49] (2131) 158-319; fax: [49] (2131) 158-558; (in Switzerland) tel: [41] (1) 946-0777; fax: [41] (1) 946-0807; (in Ireland) tel: [44] (193) 282-8828; (in the U.S.) tel: [1] (949) 583-3000 (Corporate Headquarters); http://www.toshiba.com/.

Internet Connection

HOW TO CONNECT

Connecting to AOL and Compuserve in Indonesia is similar to using it when traveling outside your own area code. See the introductory section for detailed information on connecting to your account through a different phone number.

America Online

Numbers are available at keyword *international*. Be sure to get several local numbers before leaving. AOL's Global-Net service charges US$6 an hour in addition to the usual charges. Go to keyword *access* (a free area) and download the software.

Access: Denpasar Bali (361) 289-652; Jakarta (21) 386-4550; Jakarta Airport (21) 550-2925; Surabaya (31) 545-5952.

Compuserve

Numbers are available at *Go International*. The Compuserve Web-site also has a great deal of information, at http://www.compuserve.com.

Access: Denpasar Bali (36) 128-9652; Jakarta (21) 386-4550; Jakarta (21) 527-1000; Jakarta Airport (21) 550-2925; Surabaya (31) 545-5952.

Independent Service Providers

Many independent service providers offer discounts if you are only in town for a couple days.

INDOSATnet; tel: (21) 386-9416; tel: (21) 386-9862; fax: (21) 352-0520; email: sales@indosat.net; http://www.indosat.net.id/.

MitraNet; tel: (31) 5012-05051; fax: (31) 501-2049; email: info@mitra.net.id; http://www.mitra.net.id/.

Pacific Internet; tel: (21) 3190-0162; fax: 3190-0169; http://www.pacific.net.id/.

PT Transmedia Media Indonesia; tel: (21) 526-8777; fax; 526-8789; http://www.access.net.id/.

Radnet; tel: (21) 252-6363; fax: (21) 252-4777; http://www.rad.net.id/.

VIANET; (in Austria offering connection services in Indonesia); tel: [43] (1) 404-020; http://www.vianet.at.

Business Culture
GREETINGS AND COURTESIES

It is important to show respect for status, position, and age. Indonesians are quiet, discrete, and polite almost to the point of shyness. They neither disagree in public nor express anger in public. The accepted greeting (for both meeting and saying good-bye) is the handshake, which is gentle. First introductions are usually accompanied by a slight bow of the head. At subsequent meetings, the handshake is omitted and a simple nod or slight bow is standard. When greeting older people, the bow takes on more significance. Titles are important. If a person has a title, it should be used in greetings as well as general conversation. A man may shake a woman's hand, but this should be the only public physical contact between men and women. If invited to a meal, do not begin eating until your host has invited you to do so. Gifts are appreciated if invited to a home. And as an extra note of caution: avoid eating or passing anything with the left hand (the left hand is traditionally used for cleanup when toilet paper is not at hand, and therefore remains taboo in social settings).

DECISION MAKING

Decisions are made slowly. Indonesians avoid saying no, and might instead say *belum* ("not yet"). Because harmony is so highly valued, an Indonesian will go to great lengths to avoid disagreeing for fear of disappointing someone. He or she might also agree with something simply to be polite, agree to do something that cannot be done, or may not admit to mistakes. Consensus decision making with respect for authority, including one's elders, means business deals are often slow to take shape. Impatience will be viewed as rude, and high-pressure attempts to speed up the process will be resisted and resented. Engaging a local partner who is politically connected in the realms of your particular branch of business proves extremely helpful. Remember that personal relationships are the basis for business.

WOMEN

Women hold positions of responsibility in Indonesian businesses, and foreign women are accepted and respected. The family is important, and women should be prepared for personal questions about their age, marital status, and whether they have children. (These are common topics of conversation and are asked of both men and women.) Women should be very careful about their handbags on the street (purse-snatchers often use motorcycles). Foreign businesswomen will probably not face discrimination, but they may encounter some conservative thinking from businesspeople in Indonesia. Women who take male associates to a business dinner should arrange payment beforehand (with the restaurant maitre d'), or the man might insist on paying for the meal. In Java, women who invite a man to a business dinner should include his wife in the invitation.

MEETINGS

A simple rule for business in Indonesia is to be patient and be prepared. Indonesians value punctuality in others, but will often be late themselves. The expression 'rubber time' (*jam karet*) definitely applies to the Indonesian mode of life. Expect meetings to start late, and do not express impatience regarding this state of culture. If you are late to an appointment, traffic will be readily accepted as a reason (and, in Jakarta at least, will probably be the truth). Business does not supersede individual relationships, and meetings can easily be interrupted by personal matters; do not show annoyance when interruptions occur. At group meetings, never publicly criticize anyone or anything. All criticism is given in private. Getting around Jakarta proves difficult and all meetings tend to last longer than expected. As such, do not schedule too many appointments for one day (ideally, no more than three or four), and leave adequate time between meetings so your schedule will not progressively become later as the day unfolds.

BUSINESS ATTIRE

The climate is tropical. There is a dry season (June to September) and a wet season (December to March), but regardless when arriving, one can expect hot and humid weather. A lightweight jacket and tie are required when calling on government officials, and suits are standard for most business situations. Outside Jakarta, business is conducted less formally, especially with smaller companies. A jacket is not always required in such situations, but men should at least wear a shirt and tie. Women should dress tastefully and conservatively. Fashionable short skirts are accepted in Jakarta and other large cities, but women should never wear a sleeveless dress or blouse to show respect for the Muslim culture. Except at beaches and sports facilities, shorts should not be worn by men or women.

Business Centers
Jakarta
CITY VIEW

Jakarta is the center of government, commerce and industry and has an extensive communications network. A city of contrasts, modern skyscrapers and poverty-stricken hovels, traditions and current trends try to successfully co-exist. Rich in history and ethnic diversity, Jakarta lives up to the national motto: Unity in Diversity.

AIRPORT

Soekarno Hatta Airport to City Center

The airport lies 12 miles (20 km) from the city. Figure approximately one to two hours in travel time, depending on traffic (afternoon and evening traffic being the worst). Air-conditioned coaches run every 30 minutes to five different terminals in the city from 6:30a.m. to 11p.m. for a price of about Rp3,500. An information desk is located in the arrivals hall.

Taxis are available 24 hours a day for around Rp25,000. Silver Bird cabs offer the most expensive mode of travel; and Blue Bird the most economical. And before going into shock over an inflated meter bill at trip's end, remember that an airport surcharge and toll road fees will add to the metered fare. Inquire of the total price before entering the cab. A shuttle bus also services Halim Perdana Kusuma Airport in Jakarta.

Airline Numbers

Aer Lingus	(21) 521-1500
Air Canada	(21) 588-185
Air China	(21) 520-6467
Air India	(21) 385-8845
Air Lanka	(21) 521-2340
Air New Zealand	(21) 391-5501
All Nippon Airways	(21) 835-6214
Alitalia	(21) 571-998
American Airlines	(21) 231-1132
Ansett Australia	(21) 391-5508
Asiana Airlines	(21) 326-885, 333-363
British Airways	(21) 570-3742, 521-1500
British Midland	(21) 632-9065
Canadian Airlines International	(21) 323-730
Cathay Pacific	(21) 380-6660, 515-1747
China Airlines	(21) 251-0788
China Southern Airlines	(21) 520-2980
Continental Micronesia	(21) 334-417
Czechoslovak Airlines	(21) 315-0383
Delta Airlines	(21) 521-2340
Egypt Air	(21) 654-0670
Emirates Airlines	(21) 574-2436
EVA Airways	(21) 520-6456, 520-5828
Finnair	(21) 570-1666
Garuda Indonesian Airways	
	(21) 334-4525, 310-0568, 231-1801
Gulf Air	(21) 577-0789
Japan Airlines	(21) 572-3211
KLM	(21) 252-6730
Kuwait Airways	(21) 550-1037
Lufthansa	(21) 570-2005
Malaysian Airlines	(21) 522-9682
Northwest Airlines	(21) 520-3152
Pakistan International	(21) 633-3203
Philippine Airlines	(21) 526-7786
Qantas	(21) 230-0277
Royal Brunei	(21) 521-1842
Royal Jordanian	(21) 244-1915
Saudi Arabian Airlines	(21) 835-6201
Scandinavian Airlines System	(21) 252-4081
Sempati Air	(21) 801-1612
Singapore Airlines	(21) 520-6899
South African Airways	(21) 570-1666
Swissair	(21) 384-0625
Thai Airways International	(21) 314-0607
Trans World Airlines	(21) 835-6214

United Airlines	(21) 570-7520
US Airways	(21) 632-9066
UTA French Airlines	(21) 550-1474
Varig Brazilian Airlines	(21) 835-6214

HOTELS

Top-end

Aryaduta Jakarta; Jalan Prapatan 44/48; tel: (21) 386-1234; fax: (21) 380-9990; city center; restaurant; conference facilities; secretarial service; corporate rates; in-room safe; fitness; sauna; pool; US$180+.

Borobodour Inter-Continental; Jalan Lapangan Banteng Selatan; tel: (21) 380-5555; fax: (21) 380-9595; located in the city center; recently renovated; rooms, suites, and apartments; restaurant; conference facilities; secretarial service; business center; fitness; pool; US$180+.

Grand Hyatt; Jalan MH Thamrin Kav 28-30, Friendship Circle; tel: (21) 390-1234; fax: (21) 390-6426; adjacent Plaza Indonesia Shopping Mall; restaurants; 24-hour business center with offices; Regency-Club rooms with fax machines and data ports; fitness; pool; US$200+.

Jakarta Hilton; Jl. Jend Gatot Subroto; tel: (21) 570-3600; fax: (21) 573-3089; large congress center; standard Hilton amenities; US$135-235.

Jakarta Mandarin Oriental; Jalan MH Tharin; tel: (21) 314-1307; fax: (21) 314-8680; renovated; restaurants; 24-hour cafe; 24-hour business center; Club rooms; health club; pool; US$180-200.

Le Meridien; Jalan Jenderal Sudirman Kav 18-20; tel: (21) 251-3131; fax: (21) 571-1633; near exhibition grounds; restaurant; conference facilities; secretarial service; in-room modem/fax connection, safe; corporate rates; fitness; sauna; pool; US$190.

The Regent; Jalan HR Rasuna Said; tel: (21) 252-3456; fax:(21) 252-4480; opened 1996; 5 restaurants; spacious rooms, balconies; butler service; business center; conference facilities; in-room modem/fax connection, 3 telephone lines, fax machine on request; club floor; 24-hour Regent Club; health club; fitness; sauna; pool; US$195+.

Sari Pan Pacific; Jalan M.H. Thamrin; tel: (21) 323-707; fax: (21) 323-650; located in business and diplomatic area; 2 restaurants; business floors; business center; conference facilities; secretarial service; in-room modem/fax connection; corporate rates; fitness; pool; US$160-230.

Shangri-La; Jalan Sudirman Kav 1, Bni City Complex; tel: (21) 570-7440; fax: (21) 570-3530; tallest hotel in Indonesia; restaurants; business center; in-room modem/fax connection, voicemail, 3 phone lines, work desk, safe; Horizon Club rooms; corporate rates; fitness; sauna; pool; US$210-300.

Expensive

Atlet Century Park; Jalan Pintu Satu, Senayan; tel; (21) 571-2041; fax: (21) 571-2191; email: hacp@rad.net.id; restaurant; conference facilities; secretarial service; business floors; in-room modem/fax connection; fitness; sauna; pool; US$115/140.

Jayakarta Tower; Jalan Hayam Wuruk 126; tel: (21) 625-1233; fax: (21) 629-5000; city center; restaurant; conference facilities; secretarial service; fax/photocopy facilities; sauna.

Omni Batavia Hotel; Jl. Kali Besar Brt 46; tel: 690-4118; fax: 690-4092; business center; business floor; fitness club; US$120/150.

Sahid Jaya Hotel; Jalan Sudirman; tel: (21) 570-4444; fax: (21) 573-3168; renovated deluxe hotel; praiseworthy service; restaurant; business center; conference facilities;

Indonesia

Indonesia

secretarial service; in-room modem/fax connection, safe; corporate rates; fitness; sauna; pool; US$116/170.

Moderate

Equatorial Jakarta; Jalan Fachrudin No. 3; tel: (21) 230-3636; fax: (21) 230-0880; city center; restaurant; meeting facilities; secretarial service; fax/photocopy facilities; corporate rates; sauna; pool; whirlpool; US$90.

Ibis Kemayoran; 79-81 Jalan Bungur Besar Raya; tel: (21) 421-0111; fax: (21) 421-1458; near exhibition grounds; conference facilities; secretarial service; fax/photocopy facilities; corporate rates; fitness; sauna; pool; US$90.

MEDICAL CARE

Catholic Hospital; St. Vincentius a Laulo, Surabaya/Java; tel: (21) 7562.

Central Hospital; Jalan Dipenogoro 71, Jakarta; tel: (21) 330-808, (21) 333-085.

Doctors-on-Call; tel: (21) 683-444, (21) 681-444 (English-speaking doctors who make house calls).

Pertamina Hospital; Keayoran; tel: (21) 787-215.

St. Carolus Hospital; Jalan Selemba Raya 41; tel: (21) 390-4441, (21) 390-4442.

Sumber Waras Hospital; Jalan Kiai Tapa, Grogol; tel: (21) 568-2022, (21) 560-5793.

Rumah Sakit Pondok Indah Hospital, Jalan Metro Duta Kav. UE; tel: (21) 767-525, (21) 768-347.

AUTO RENTAL

Avis; Jalan Diponegoro 25; tel: (21) 314-2900; fax: (21) 33-1845; Sukarno-Hatta Airport, arrivals hall, tel: (21) 550-6096.

Bara Bentala Indonesia PT; Jl. Kb Jeruk Raya 126; tel: (21) 536-2222.

Hertz; toll-free in country, tel: 001-800-65-7788; Kanindo Plaza 4th Floor, JL. Jend atot, Subroto, Dav 23; tel: (21) 252-3333; fax: (21) 525-8093, Monday to Friday 8:30a.m. to 5p.m., Saturday 8:30a.m. to 12:30p.m.; chauffeur-driven cars available.

Martha Limousine Service; Jl. Jambu 33; tel: (21) 314-3567.

PT Blue Bird; Jalan HOS, Cokroaminoto No. 107; tel: (21) 325-607, (21) 333-461, (21) 333-485.

VIP Car Rental; Jl Raya Wolter Monginsidi 125; tel: (21) 720-5559.

WORLD TRADE CENTER

World Trade Center Jakarta
World Trade Center Building, 2nd Floor
Jalan Jendral Sudirman Kav. 29-31 L.2
Jakarta, 12920, Indonesia
tel: (21) 521-1125; fax: (21) 252-2135
email: wtcjk@cbn.net.id
website: http://www.wtcjk.or.id

CHAMBER OF COMMERCE

Kamar Dagang dan Industri Indonesia (KADIN)
3rd-5th Floors, Chandra Building
Jalan MH Thamrin 20, Jakarta 10350
tel: (21) 324-000; fax: (21) 315-0241

CONVENTION ASSISTANCE

Deputy Director, Directorate-General of Tourism
16/19 Jalan Medan Merdeka-Barat
Jakarta 10110
tel: (21) 386-0934; fax: (21) 386-0828

Notes

Iran

At a Glance
THE PEOPLE

Population 68,959,931 (1998)
Growth Rate 2.04% (1998)
Life Expectancy .... 68.25 years (born 1999)
Infant Mortality .... 48.95 deaths/1,000 live births (1998)

Ethnic Composition
Persian 51%
Azerbaijani 24%
Gilaki and Mazandarani 8%
Kurd 7%
Other 10%

Religious Composition
Shi'a Muslim 89%
Sunni Muslim 10%
Other and non-affiliated 1%

Languages Spoken
Persian (farsi - official), Turkish, Kurdish, Arabic.

Education and Literacy
Education is cost-free (but not compulsory) at all levels from elementary school through university. Nationwide literacy is 72.1 percent.

Labor Force
Total: 15,400,000
By occupation: services 46%, industry 21%, agriculture 33%

THE ECONOMY
Iran's economy has been shaped by the Islamic philosophy and socialist leanings of its government. All large industries are owned by the state and the financing of new enterprises is limited by the nation's poor access to international financing. Exports are dominated by petroleum which has made the economy vulnerable to swings in commodity prices. Despite the free market rhetoric of the President Khatami few advances have been made to dismantle the state-owned enterprises, especially since the rise in oil prices. Unemployment is well above 25 percent and inflation hovers in the double digits. Iran has recently made overtures to the U.S. government to settle old disputes in the hopes of gaining access to global financing to help diversify the economy. However, Iran's proximity to Iraq and the presence of large numbers of Islamic fundamentalists in the Assembly have given investors reason to pause.

Exports .... US$19 billion (1997)
Imports .... US$15.6 billion (1997)
Total GDP .... US$371.2 billion (1997)
GDP Per Capita .... US$5,500 (1997)
Unemployment .... 30 percent (1998)
Inflation Rate .... 23 percent (1997)

Top Export Partners
Japan, E.U.

Top Import Partners
E.U., Japan, United Arab Emirates, Russia

Top Exports
Petroleum, carpets, fruits, nuts, hides, iron, steel

Top Imports
Machinery, military supplies, metal works, foodstuffs, pharmaceuticals, technical services, refined oil products

BUSINESS WORKWEEK

Offices
Weekdays and Saturday 8:30a.m. to 1p.m. and 3p.m. to 7p.m. Closed Fridays.

Banks
Saturday to Wednesday 8:30a.m. to 4p.m., Thursday 8:30a.m. to noon. Closed Fridays.

Government
Saturday to Wednesday 8a.m. to 2p.m.

Retail
Saturday to Wednesday 8:30a.m. to 9p.m. Limited hours during the Ramadan month.

HOLIDAYS
Id al-Fitr, end of Ramadan .... January 19*
National Holiday, Fall of the Shah .... February 11
Oil Nationalization Day .... March 20
Now Ruz, the Iranian New Year .... March 21-24
Id al-Adha, Feast of the Sacrifice .... March 28*
Islamic Republic Day .... April 1
Revolution Day .... April 2
Ashoura .... April 26*
Mouloud, Birth of Muhammad .... June 26*
Martyrdom of Imam Ali .... July 14
Leilat al-Meiraj, Ascension of
Muhammed .... November 6*
*Dates may vary by year.

CLIMATE

Seasons
Partly due to its altitude, Iran experiences great extremes of climate. Most parts of the country face bitter cold winters and suffocating hot summers. Spring and autumn offer the finest times to visit Iran.

Regions
The far north and west of the country experience regular rainfall and are the coldest parts of Iran. Winters are harshest on the Azerbaijan border; between December and January, temperatures there can fall as low as -20°C (4°F) and the snow will remain until early spring. In the central north, the region around the Caspian Sea is humid, damp, and rainy. Central Iran is hot in the summer and gets worse as you go south. Further south towards the Persian Gulf, winter is less severe, but summers are dry and extremely hot (35°C / 95°F).

The four seasons are very apparent in Tehran, and the climate changes dramatically from northern to southern parts of the city. In the summer, you only have to drive a few miles up town to escape the dry, polluted heat of the south.

Money & Banking

Currency
The currency of Iran is the Iranian Rial (IR).

Denominations
The Iranian Rial (IR) comes in coin denominations of

Iran

©2001 Magellan Geographix   SM Santa Barbara, CA

Iran

- ✪ National capital
- ◉ Province capital
- • Secondary city
- Interntional border
- Province border
- Primary road
- Railroad

0   100   200 km
0   150 mi

IR250, 100, 50, 20, 10, 5; and banknotes of IR100, 200, 500, 1,000, 2,000, 5,000, 10,000.

Traveler's Checks and Credit Cards

The official currency is the rial, although it is referred to as "toman" (a unit of ten Rials), so be careful when converting money not to get the two confused. Some banks do offer currency exchange, and you need your passport with you when changing money. Most of the top hotels have banking facilities, which will deal with currency exchange. The Iranian rial is pegged to the U.S. dollar, which remains the easiest currency to exchange or denominated travel check to cash.

Changing cash or traveler's checks in any major convertible currency can be done in Tehran, Shiraz, and Isfahan. In smaller towns go to Bank Melli Iran; otherwise, changing cash, or traveler's checks in particular, will prove difficult. There are also a number of Bureaux de Change offering a free market rate (black market), but the receipts may not be valid. Receipts will be needed for reconversion at departure. Currency exchange machines do not exist.

Foreigners may open an account in Iran, but this will involve detailed paper work. A few foreign banks are represented in Tehran, but they mainly deal with government officials. It is also possible to transfer money from abroad into a large bank in Iran, but the process may take a long time.

Mastercard and Eurocard are the most widely accepted cards in urban areas but only at major outlets. In rural areas only cash will be accepted for transactions.

State banks will give cash advances on credit cards, but, like many things in Iran, the process is tedious. ATMs are not to be found in Iran in any great numbers or necessarily in working condition. There is one located at the Bank Sepah.

Bank Locations

Bank Markazi Joumhouri Islami Iran (Central Bank); Ferdowsi Avenue P.O.Box 1136-58551, Tehran.

Agricultural Cooperative Bank of Iran (a.k.a. Bank Taavon Keshavarzi Iran); No. 129 Patrice Lumumba Street, Jalal-Al-Ahmad Expressway, P.O. Box, 14155/6395, Tehran.

Bank Mellat; Park Shahr, Varzesh Avenue, P.O. Box 11365/5964, Tehran.

Essential Terms

English	Persian
Yes	Bale
No	Na
Good morning	Salam
Hello (daytime)	Salam
Hello (evening)	Salam
Hello (telephone)	Alo
Good-bye	Khoda hafez
Please	Khahesh mikonam
Thank you	Tashakkor mikonam
Pleased to meet you	Ra mo'arrefi konam
Excuse me; I'm sorry	Bebakhshid
My name is _____	Esme man_____ast
I don't understand	Man nemifahmam
Do you speak English?	Englisee sohbat meekoneed?

Travel

VISA AND PASSPORT

A passport—valid for at least six months beyond the anticipated visit—and a visa are required of most visitors. Possession of a return travel ticket is also required. Nationals from Bosnia-Herzegovina, Saudi Arabia, and Turkey are not required to have a visa if the intended stay does not exceed six months. Transit passengers re-embarking within 24 hours are also exempt, provided they are holding onward or return verification and are not leaving the airport.

Obtaining visas can prove tricky unless you hail from Slovenia, Macedonia, Japan, Turkey, or Singapore. The costs are relatively high, and regulations are confusing and can change with little or no warning. For tourist visas, a number of forms must be filled out and then sent to the Ministry of Tourism in advance of travel. These forms can take months to return or may never come back at all.

Business visa applications must be accompanied by a letter of invitation from the sponsoring company in Iran; this will in turn be submitted to the Iranian Ministry of Foreign Affairs for authorization. Multiple entry business visas may also be procured, if the Iranian authorities find the invitation acceptable.

Visitors must procure all visas in advance. Allow at least a four-week lead time, with the exception of Pilgrimage visas, which may take only two weeks. However, once inside Iran, it is comparatively easy to get an extension directly from the Ministry of Foreign Affairs in Tehran on any type of visa.

Business, Tourist, and Pilgrimage visas remain valid for stays of up to one month, and must be used within 3 months from date of authorization. Transit visas are valid for 5 days.

Note: Nationals of Israel will not be allowed entry under any circumstances. Women who are determined to be dressed immodestly will also be refused entry.

A Note to Americans

The U.S. does not have diplomatic relations with Iran. American citizens of Iranian origin, who are considered to be Iranian citizens, have been detained and harassed by Iranian authorities.

DEPARTURE FORMALITIES

There is a tax of IR1500, payable by foreigners, on all international flight departures. The tax is not included in the price of the ticket and must be paid in cash at the airport.

Foreigners may not take the following items out of the country: antiques, works of art, historic manuscripts, valuable coins, or gems.

Wrought gold of up to 150g in weight without gems, and up to 3kg of wrought silverware without gems may be exported.

Note: Customs officials will list certain high-value objects which may be in your possession upon arrival. These items must not be sold and have to be presented to Customs on departure. If you intend to visit Iran again using the same passport, be sure that these listed items are canceled by Customs officials when you leave Iran.

CUSTOMS ENTRY (PERSONAL)

Duty-free
- Tobacco: 200 cigarettes or equivalent in tobacco products
- Other: a reasonable quantity of perfume for personal use; gifts on which the import duty/tax does not exceed IR11,150

Note: Cameras, electronics, and currency should be declared upon arrival.

Prohibited or Restricted
- Alcoholic beverages
- Narcotics
- Guns and ammunition
- Aerial photo cameras
- Other: Transmitter/ receiver apparatus, cassettes, videos, fashion magazines, pornography

IMMUNIZATION

Vaccinations for malaria, typhoid, polio, yellow fever, cholera, hepatitis A, tetanus, tuberculosis, and dysentery are recommended, though not required.

TIPPING

Taxi
Taxi drivers usually receive 10 percent of the metered amount. Negotiate unmetered fares in advance.

Porters
Porters receive IR1000 per piece of luggage.

Hotels
Hotels usually apply a 10 percent service charge directly to the bill.

Restaurants
Restaurants usually apply service charges to the bill; if not, then a 10 percent tip is customary.

EMERGENCY INFORMATION

Police and Crime
Since 1978, the Islamic Sharia Law rules have been applied, and punishments for crimes are severe. Anyone can be

Iran

arrested for anything that goes against the Islamic rule, including the possession of alcohol or blaspheming. Once arrested, you will be provided with a translator, but officials may detain you without trial for some time. Crime on the streets, however, remains very low, and travelers should feel quite safe walking about. It is wise to avoid all political discussions.

Take basic precautions against petty crime. Avoid flashy displays of wealth, dress and behave conservatively. Leave most of your cash, traveler's checks, jewelry, and your camera in your hotel safe. Carry photocopies of your passport instead of the original, and if the hotel requires to keep your passport, supply them with a photocopy. Carry cash in a money belt, and use credit cards for most of your transactions. Guard against theft on public transport.

Women, especially, should abide by Islamic rules. Dress very modestly, in loose-fitting clothes that cover from head to ankle and wrist. Do not smoke or drink alcohol in public. In rural areas you may be required to wear a head scarf. Women should be accompanied by other females or another foreign male when in public to avoid harassment. **Note**: Many Iranian men assume western women have virtually no morals. Prepare for rude comments.

The police have a better reputation in Iran than in other countries in the region, although corruption still exists. Police work alongside the revolutionary guards, who are responsible for protecting Islamic rule. Both groups have little patience with visitors unwilling to abide by local custom.

Emergency Numbers
Numbers function nationwide:
Air raid and rocket attack
emergency assistance 198
Ambulance 123
Fire 125
General emergencies 123
Police 110
Traffic accidents 197

Health
Malaria, yellow fever, typhoid, tuberculosis, cholera, polio, hepatitis, and rabies are endemic in more rural areas. Take care against exposure to the intense sun and heat in summer.

Tap water is generally safe, but bottled water is widely available and recommended. Wash all vegetables, peel fruits, and try to avoid uncooked food. Carry a Swiss Army Knife to peel fruit. Most milk sold in stores is pasteurized, however, take care to verify this at purchase. Food in restaurants is safe to consume, but it is wise to eat it hot and cooked. Avoid Iranian sausages, which have been known to cause stomach cramps. Carry pills or other remedies for stomach upset.

In the summer, air pollution poses a major health hazard in Tehran's inner city, leading to headaches and stomach pains. The heat may also cause weakness. One might carry a small folding umbrella of light color to ward off the sun's stinging rays during the summer months. Health care is adequate. Although most specialists left the country after the revolution, there remains an abundance of Western-trained doctors. Most hospitals are state run, but sub-standard. Plenty of private hospitals exist in Tehran; but, for major illnesses one is advised to leave the country.

Carry a well-stocked medical kit even for urban visits. It is also advisable to carry a water bottle that you can refill with bottled mineral water when on the road. Prepare for squat toilets anywhere outside the realm of your hotel. Although they are clean, they do not provide toilet paper. Carry tissue if you prefer not to use the water spritzers. Travel insurance with an evacuation policy is a must for long-term business visitors.

AIR
The considerable size of Iran can mean that internal flights may offer the most practical means of transport for you. Domestic flights are offered by both Iran Air and Aseman Air between Tehran, Tabriz, Esfahan, Shiraz, Mashhad, Ahwaz, Kish, Zahedan, and other major urban areas.

TAXI
Taxis are readily available in all cities. Orange and blue taxis are urban and will carry more than one customer at a time. They prove much less expensive than private or hotel-taxis (RI4,000 to 7,000 per hour). Remember to negotiate prices beforehand. Write all directions and translate them in detail. Make sure to carry a local map.

AUTO
Due to security risks, rental cars are not recommended for visitors; besides, the expense is prohibitive. Hired cars with drivers can be reserved on a daily and weekly basis. Let your hotel or local contacts refer an agency. In any case, wild driving and chaotic traffic can be expected.

TRAIN
The rail system in Iran is relatively new and limited in scope; it is operated by the Iranian Islamic Republic Railways. Various service levels exist including sleeper cars. Reservations are required.
Iranian Republic Railways .... (21) 555-120

METRO
There is a modern metro system that serves the city of Tehran. A ride outside of the city will cost 700 Rials, and a ride within town will cost 300 Rials.
Iranian Metro 874-0163/4/5/6

BUSES & TRAMS
Iran's cities are filled with buses and mini-buses, none of which can be recommended for business travel. Security risks are high, and service is bleak.

WATER TRAVEL
Iran has international passenger boat and ferry service on the Caspian Sea, the Gulf of Oman, and the Persian Gulf. The latter two areas have enormous security risks for foreign travelers and should be avoided. Iran does not have extensive internal passenger boat travel.

TRAVEL ASSISTANCE
Esfahan .... (31) 21-555
Tehran .... (21) 892-2125
Tehran's Tourist Information Office is located at: 11 Dameshq St., Vali-e Asr Ave. Another information kiosk is located at: Bayhaghey Park-O-Ride.

Borj Travel Agency; tel: 205-6616; fax: 205-6632; email: borj@apadana.com; airline rep., visas, hotel reservations, domestic/intl. tours, express train insurance.

Security Briefing
SOCIAL UNREST
Iran is a "theocratic republic", and the state religion is Islam. Any protest against the government is considered anti-Islam and, therefore, illegal. Most demonstrations that take place in Iranian streets are state-organized protests against foreign government or are support rallies for other Islamic nations. Westerners (universally designated as "infidels") should keep off the streets during these demonstrations as violent attacks are common.

Protest against the Iranian government by the population have taken place recently but nowhere near on the scale of the student protests that brought the fundamentalists to power in 1979. The police keep a close watch on social unrest and quash anything that is even slightly threatening. Visitors are warned to keep their political opinions to themselves.

ORGANIZED CRIME

Iran has an extensive black market in currency exchange. Visitors on business should avoid this as it can become a pretext for arrest or expulsion. Technically, prostitution, drug trafficking, and gambling (organized crime favorites) are illegal (anti-Islamic) and can be punishable by death. However, Iran does grow poppies for opium production, and it is a major transshipment point for heroin. Foreign firms should, however, have no interference from organized crime.

STREET CRIME

Islamic law (sharia), which governs Iran, posts some extreme penalties for crime (amputation, stoning, etc.). Consequently, street crime is very minimal. These draconian measures coupled with Persian hospitality make Iran's streets very safe day or night and also very clean and free of beggars and peddlers. Of course, the temptation to steal from rich foreigners is still present and basic precautions should be taken.

CULTURAL CONFLICTS

The potential for cultural conflicts is very high in Iran. The Iranians observe a strict dress code and even men need to keep their arms and legs covered. Women must only reveal the face, hands, and feet. Rather than the rebuke one might receive for a dress code violation in another Islamic country, in Iran you may be arrested. Other sensitive areas include public shows of affection between sexes, consumption, or possession of alcohol and the wearing of non-Islamic religious symbols. Any disparaging remark (it doesn't take much) regarding, Allah, Mohammed, or Islam is grounds for arrest and incarceration.

Many Iranians hold deep-seated resentments of Western governments. There is little point in discussing the merits of this resentment as local opinions are unlikely to change. Visitors showing support for the U.S., the U.K., or the United Nations may find themselves under verbal attack or worse. Western governments are viewed by some Iranians not just as political entities but as a instruments of a system bent on cultural imperialism. Visitors should avoid being dragged into discussions regarding the relative merits of their home culture. Most opinions in Iran on this topic are immutable.

Communications

DIALING CODES IN IRAN

International country code: [98]

Selected city codes: Ahwaz (61), Arak (861), Isfahan or Esfahan (31), Ghazvin (281), Ghome (251), Hamadan (81), Karadj (261), Kerman (341), Mashhad (51), Rezaiyeh (441), Shiraz (71), Tabriz (41), Tehran (21)

Dialing Iran from Overseas

To dial Iran from overseas, dial your country's international dialing code, then 98 (the country code for Iran), then the city code, and finally the number. If you were dialing Isfahan from the United States, for example, you would begin with 011, then 98, then 31 (the city code for Isfahan), and finally the number of the person or office you are trying to reach.

CALLING WITHIN IRAN

Local Calls

A local call will be free from a hotel or the airport. Otherwise, try and find one of the yellow phones, which exist for local calls only. Calling locally from a shop is also possible for RI 20.

Long Distance Calls

Special long-distance phones can be found at airports, main bus stations, and telegraph offices in Tehran, where you can book the call with a wait. Naturally, guests can also place calls from a hotel, but with an added surcharge. On the scale of headaches, prepare for an extra-strength Tylenol when trying to call from outside Tehran. In general, one must go through an operator to get connected to a long-distance destination.

International Calls

Telephoning from Iran is no simple task. Overseas calls are best placed from Tehran or a main telephone or telegraph office outside of Tehran. Bookings may take hours or even days, and even then there may be an added wait to get connected. From hotels, a possible 100 percent added commission will make waiting time even more excruciating. As an added quirk, calls have been known to be monitored by curious listeners.

PAY PHONES

Public Telephones

The telephone nightmare continues in the public telephone system that offers phones that are often out of order or not functioning well. Yellow phones only deal with local calls. A local call will require a 50-Rial coin.

Calling Cards

The telephone system in Iran is advancing. Presently, most public telephones operate on a coin-based system. You may be able to find card phones in Tehran.

CALL BACK

You can (potentially) save significant sums when calling in Iran by using a call back service. For a list of callback services, please refer to the "Communications" section in the *Global Road Warrior* Introduction.

Fees for call back services vary widely, depending on the company and the type of service required. Be sure to check with these companies before leaving to compare rates.

CELLULAR PHONES

The Telecom Company of Iran operates a GSM digital system for cellular users.

Note: Your home country cell phone may not work in this country. If not, we recommend that you rent an international cell phone *before* you leave home. A major US-based cell phone rental provider is **IMC WorldCell**. For information see "International Cell Phone Rentals" on page 14.

PHONE JACKS

Iran

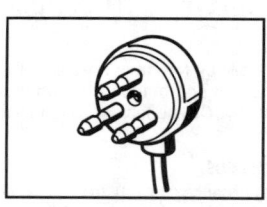

Plug adaptors are available through **iGo Corporation.** (See "Electrical and Telephone Adaptors" on page 19.)

FAX

Faxing has become more established in the inter-city service realm. Top-end hotels will also have fax service.

POSTAL SERVICES

Post boxes are yellow. Airmail to Europe and North American can take two weeks, and incoming mail can take much longer. Stamps can be purchased at some cigarette shops and hotels. The main post office in Tehran is located at Shariati Street.

Hours of service

Saturday to Thursday 7:30a.m. to 2p.m. Some major post offices stay open until 7p.m.

TELEGRAMS

Telegrams can be sent from the entral Telegraph Office in major cities.

Business Services

COURIER SERVICES

DHL Intl. Tehran; No. 353 Dr. Beheshti Ave. before Valiasr, Tehran 15116; tel: (21) 871-9170.

TNT Skypak International; 2nd Floor, No: 153; Felestin Ave., Tehran; tel: (21) 646-3143, 646-5588; fax: (21) 640-0105.

INTERPRETERS

Interpreters may be found through the Tourist Information Offices.

Tehran Tourist Information Office; 11 Dameshq St., Vali-e Asr Ave.

Electrical

CURRENT

220 volts AC, 50Hz.

ELECTRIC PLUG

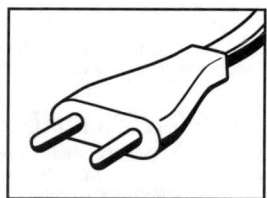

Plug adaptors are available through **iGo Corporation.** (See "Electrical and Telephone Adaptors" on page 19.)

Technical Support

HARDWARE/SOFTWARE VENDOR SUPPORT

Compaq/Digital; (in the U.A.E.) tel: [971] 4-818-100; fax: [971] 4-818-313; (in Switzerland) tel: [41] (22) 709-5330; fax: [41] (22) 709-5391 (Geneva); tel: [41] (1) 801-2507; fax: [41] (1) 801-2172 (Zurich); (General U.S.) tel: (281) 518-2000; http://www.compaq.com/.

Corel; (in the U.A.E.) tel: [971] 4-523-526 (All Applications); (in Germany) tel: [49] (180) 425-8210 (TS Word Perfect-32 bit); (in the U.S.) tel: [1] (716) 871-2325 (Ask to be Forwarded to Appropriate Program); http://www.corel.com/.

Dell; (in the U.A.E.) tel: [971] 452-4232; fax: [971] 452-7944 (Key Information Technology - Mr. Selwyn de Souza); (Dell-Europe) tel: [44] (134) 474-8000; (in the U.S.) tel: [1] (512) 338-4400; fax: [1] (512) 728-3330; http://www.dell.com/.

Hewlett Packard; (in Switzerland) tel: [41] (22) 780-8111; (in the U.S.) tel: [1] (408) 246-4300; http://www.hp.com/.

IBM; (U.A.E. Offices) tel: [971] (4) 321-321; fax: [971] (4) 321-322; (in Germany) tel: [49] (711) 78-50; fax: [49] (711) 785-3511; (in Switzerland) tel: [41] (22) 310-0418 (in French); (in the U.S.) tel: [1] (919) 517-2800; (U.S. Main Office) tel: [1] 914-765-1900; http://www.ibm.com/.

Microsoft; (in Saudi Arabia) tel: (966) (1) 488-1165; fax: (966) (1) 488-1576; (in Switzerland) tel: [41] (848) 858-868; fax [41] (1) 831-0869; (in the U.S.) [1] (425) 635-7222; http://www.microsoft.com/.

NEC; (in Israel) tel: [972] (0)9-59-3300 (UltraCare Support); (in the U.S.) [1] (916) 388-0101 (Main Switchboard); http://www.nec.com/.

Novell; (in Germany) tel: [49] (211) 563-2777 (System support); tel: [49] (6196) 904-477; fax: [49] (211) 563-2772; (in Switzerland) tel: [41] (1) 308-4747; fax: [41] (1) 302-0401; (in the U.S.) tel: [1] (408) 434-2300; fax: [1] (408) 577-5775 (Worldwide Sales Headquarters); http://www.novell.com/.

Quark; (in Switzerland) tel: [41] (1) 808-7722; fax: [41] (1) 808-7799; (in the U.S.) tel: [1] (303) 894-8899; fax: [1] (303)

894-3398 (For Products Registered in the Americas); http://www.quark.com/.

Toshiba; (in Germany) tel: [49] (2131) 158-319; fax: [49] (2131) 158-558; (in Switzerland) tel: [41] (1) 946-0777; fax: [41] (1) 946-0807; (in Ireland) tel: [44] (193) 282-8828; (in the U.S.) [1] (949) 583-3000 (Corporate Headquarters); http://www.toshiba.com/.

Internet Connection
HOW TO CONNECT

Connecting to AOL and Compuserve in Iran is similar to using it when traveling outside your own area code. See the introductory section for detailed information on connecting to your account through a different phone number.

America Online

Numbers are available at keyword *international*. Be sure to get several local numbers before leaving. Go to keyword *access* (a free area) and download the software.

There are no direct access numbers for America Online in Iran. Users will have to pay international rates to use the service.

Compuserve

Numbers are available at *Go International*. The Compuserve Web-site also has a great deal of information, at http://www.compuserve.com.

There are no direct access numbers for Compuserve in Iran. Users will have to pay international rates to use the service.

Independent Service Providers

Many independent service providers offer discounts if you are only in town for a couple of days.

IPM; tel: (21) 254-3860; fax: (21) 256-4003; email: ipminfo@vax.ipm.ac.ir

MZ3 Communications; tel: (21) 227-3240; tel: (21) 225-6410; fax: (21) 227-3952; email: kmostofi@mz3.com; http://www.mz3.com/.

VPM Enterprises; (U.S. company) tel: [1] (916) 983-9876; toll-free in the U.S.: 1-800-321-0221; fax: [1] (916) 983-4375; email: sales@vpm.com; http://www.vpm.com/

Business Culture
GREETINGS & COURTESIES

The national language of Iran is Farsi (Persian), though Arabic and several other minority tongues are spoken. English is common among university people and the business community.

The hospitality common to the Middle East is magnified tenfold in Iran. Greetings involve lengthy inquiries about every aspect of the visitor's personal life and family. Visitors are expected to show similar interests in their hosts. The standard salutation is *salam* (peace) with a reply of *salam aleikom* (peace be with you), and, in this respect, is very similar to the Arabic. For male visitors, handshakes are offered to foreigners and new acquaintances, while embraces are offered to friends. Foreign women should offer their hand but should never expect an embrace from male Iranians. Iranian women present during greetings may not be introduced at all or even offer to introduce themselves.

All visitors are treated as *mehmun* (guests) and the host will feel obliged to take care of everything for his guests. Foreigners (even from the West) are treated with a deference that is unmatched anywhere in the world. Virtual strangers will offer tourists free meals, transportation, or

rooms for the night.

Note: Some visitors treat the solicitous behavior of the Iranians with suspicion rather than gratitude. In reality, Iranian kindness is a custom of hospitality handed down over centuries of living in a hostile environment.

BUSINESS ETHIC AND FRAMEWORK

Iranian business people fall into two main categories: those that see the beneficial potential of international business, and those that view foreign business people with suspicion, even disgust. The former recognize the value of equitable and honest deals. They will carry out contracts as specified with the hopes of engendering future contracts or investment.

The latter, more distrustful group may look for any opportunity to take advantage of the foreign firm in the belief that they themselves are being dealt with in a similar fashion. Some may even believe that they are "owed" the right to interpret the contract to their sole benefit. Foreign firms should take pains to determine which category their new Iranian partners fit.

Islamic law has very specific strictures against "usury", which is interpreted as meaning the charging of interest (of any size) on loans. This adds a new twist to international finance as creditors are considered sinners. Bank or private loans are unacceptable and would-be creditors must now become equity partners in a deal with all of the inherent risk. Foreign firms may have to readjust their thinking regarding finance to work effectively with Iranian firms.

DECISION MAKING

The family lies at the center of Iranian life, and many companies are run along lines of kinship. All decisions are made at the top, either by a single person or by a small council. Visiting firms should make sure they are dealing with authority figures before entering negotiations.

Iran has been off the global business scene for many years outside of sporadic oil sales. As it re-enters normal economic relations, it will be feeling its way slowly. Foreign companies should expect Iranian business decisions (buying or selling) to be made slowly. They will want to deliberate and assure themselves that they are getting the best possible deal. Some of this reluctance comes from past dealings with oil conglomerates, and the remainder stems from a lack of self-confidence caused by a decade of economic isolation.

MEETINGS

Foreigners should come prepared to spend a good deal of time in social intercourse with their Iranian counterparts at the first meeting. Lots of handshaking, card exchanges, elaborate introductions, and non-business conversation will fill up the early part of the agenda. Hospitality will rule the Iranian hosts' schedule, and every effort will be made to make the visitors comfortable before talks begin. Food, drink, room temperature, and seating arrangements will all be tailored to the visitors' liking.

Once talks begin, visitors can expect very cordial but disciplined negotiating from the Iranian side. They are neither novices nor experts at global business, but they can drive a hard bargain. Brinkmanship and ultimatums are standard ploys as are side meetings and back-channel discussions. The Iranians use their traditional hospitality to lull visitors into a sense of security and well being. Keep your wits about you, and focus on the business at hand—not the social aspects. Don't expect any quick deals: the Iranians like to deliberate at length before the final decision is made.

Hierarchies are rigidly observed in Iran, and only counterparts of equal rank should address each other. To this end, visiting firms should make sure their business cards accurately reflect their position in the delegation.

Note: Although most Iranian business people will speak English, all visitors (especially sellers) should make the effort to have all of their materials translated into Farsi.

WOMEN IN BUSINESS

Women have no role in business in Iran and foreign firms that include female managers in their delegations may have problems. Women's opinions are of little value here and Iranian men will ignore such input when offered. Iranian businessmen will show little respect for foreign men that are subordinate to visiting female executives. Some fundamentalist firms may object to even having women in the room.

Foreign buyers and investors can risk defying this cultural bias if they choose but visiting sellers are best advised to reconsider the inclusion of female executives in their delegations. Iran is in the process of change but its views on women are unlikely to alter any time soon.

BUSINESS ENTERTAINING

Part of Iranian hospitality is the desire to entertain. The Iranians love to show off their cuisine and their meals can go on for hours. Dinners may even include interludes of live entertainment. Visitors should arrive with big appetites and a willingness to try every dish. **Note**: Any dietary restriction, either philosophical or medical, should be made known to the hosts in advance. To be unable to amply provide for a guest is a major sin for an Iranian.

There is not much nightlife in Iran, and the bar scene ceased to exist in 1979. After-business-hours entertainment is quite limited, though visitors may be invited to a private home. This invitation is a great honor and should not be declined except under the most dire circumstances.

Note: Alcohol is not served in Iran, nor is it permitted for import by foreigners. During Ramadan, Moslems fast until sunset every day and then have a very limited meal. Business entertainment will be curtailed during this period.

BUSINESS ATTIRE

Male visitors should dress in dark suits and white shirts for initial meetings and for meetings with government agencies. No ties! Subsequent meetings may not require suit jackets, but men should keep their arms covered. Shorts or short-sleeve shirts are not advisable.

Visiting females must observe a strict dress code and never expose any skin beyond face, hands, and feet. Loose dresses should reach mid-calf at the minimum. While the chador is not required, a long robe or coat (the ankle length roupush) is recommended and should be worn at all times in public. A head scarf of muted tone and no pattern must be worn in public. Women can expect major and immediate problems should they violate the dress standards in public. Make-up should be absolutely unnoticeable. These standards apply to all females over the age of seven.

Business Advisory

POLITICS & GRAFT

There are supposedly no political parties in Iran, and only one group, the Islamic Revolution, controls power. It is still a very destitute country with poorly paid bureaucrats; so, foreign firms should expect some graft when working on major projects. Graft in Iran, however, is nowhere on the scale it was during the time of the Shah. The graft nowadays may even be written directly into the licensing fees for the project. Refusal to comply with the bribery system will

most likely bring the project to a screeching halt.

Foreign firms should make this ethical decision before considering projects in Iran. They should also determine their legal responsibilities in their home countries regarding bribery overseas.

BUSINESS FRAUD

As mentioned earlier, some companies in Iran wish to foster good global business relations and will comply with all aspects of a contract or joint-venture agreement. Other Iranian firms only wish to punish the presumed past sins of evil foreign conglomerates by defrauding them of investment money and inventories; only a good due-diligence background check will determine to which philosophy your new Iranian partner adheres.

Business Centers
Tehran
CITY VIEW

Tehran is a relatively new city compared to some of the ancient lines traceable in other Iranian cities, but visitors will still find rich history embedded in attractions such as the Golestan Palace. This "Rose Garden" palace was home to the reigning Qajars (Agha Mohammad KhAne Qajar procalimed Tehran his capital in 1785) and now modestly showcases objects illustrating various aspects of Iranian heritage. With a population now rising to approximately 6,760,000, Tehran is a modern city with expansive and somewhat confusing grid-like boulevards lined with all of the most modern amenities of a western metropolis. Oil, oil, and more oil brought wealth into Iran beginning in the early 1960's. While growth through oil deposits led to an exploding economy, the war with Iraq during the 1990's suppressed much of Iran's ability to thrive at its highest potential through this resource. The government is now attempting to alleviate some of the dependence on the oil industry and emphasizes agriculture and light industry at higher levels. The U.S. economic embargo has made these endeavors difficult, but the city of Tehran has managed to grasp advanced levels of technology and hold its own

AIRPORT

Mehrabad Airport to City Center

The airport lies 7 miles (11 km.) from the city. Tehran United Bus Company runs buses to the airport for a typical fare of Rl10; expect about a 45-minute ride to the city. If one prefers a trip that takes 15 minutes less, taxis are also available for fares that cost around Rl10,000.

Airport.. 199, 91028., 9111

Airline Numbers

Aeroflot	(21) 884-8480, 880-8672
Air France	(21) 670-4111 to 17, 670-2093/4/5
Air India	(21) 873-5956, 873-9762
Alitalia	(21) 871-3801, 871-1512, 871-1889
Austrian Airlines	(21) 874-5311/2/3/4, 873-2488
Balkan Airlines	(21) 8779-444 to 50
British Airways	(21) 204-4552
Emirates	(21) 879-6786 to 92
Gulf Air	(21) 225-3284/85/86/87, 225-3275
Iran Air	(21) 880-0313, 882-6532
JAL	(21) 880-8217/18/19
KLM	(21) 204-4757
Kuwait Airways	(21) 880-8802
	880-8763, 880-8661, 880-8352
Lufthansa	(21) 872-3482/83/84/85/86/87
Pakistan Intl. Airline	(21) 880-8253/4/5

Swissair ....(21) 874-8332/3/4/5
Syrian Airlines ....(21) 889-5584/5
Turkish Airlines..(21) 874-8452

HOTELS

A central hotel reservations center for Iran now exists. Visit or call the following locations:

No. 103, Fatemi Square, Fatemi bldg., Tehran; tel: (21) 886-2320/21; fax: (21) 656-892

Airport Office: tel: (21) 9102-3863.

Note: Unwed couples will not be allowed to share a room. Also, prepare for the fact that even top-end hotels have lost somewhat of their lustre due to things having stood still on the economic front for so long. Although they are clean, hotels are generally somewhat in need of renovation.

Top-end

Azadi Grand (former Hyatt Hotel); Chamran Highway, Evin Cross Road; tel: (21) 207-3021 to 3029; fax: (21) 207-3038, 207-3061;412 rooms, 48 suites; near Alborz mountains, 20 to 30 minutes from city; restaurant; lounge; conference facilities (up to 1000); business center; 24-hour service; barber; book shop; craft shop; shopping center; health club; fitness; dry and steam sauna; indoor pool; ping pong; US$150-200.

Esteghlal (formerly Hilton); Chamran Expressway and Valie-Asr Ave.; tel: (21) 204-0011/12/13/14/15; fax: (21) 204-7041; email: Est.Hotel@www.dci.co.ir; http://www.Esteghlalhotel.com; 495 rooms, 47 suites; rooms; near exhibition grounds, residential neighborhood on hill 20 to 30 minutes from city; restaurant; 24-hour coffee shop; conference facilities; secretarial service; fax/photocopy facilities; communication services; in-room satellite tv; 24-hour room service; hairdresser; gift shop; luggage storage; medical care; parking; fitness; sauna; massage; pool; tennis; US$120+.

Homa Hotel Tehran (former Sheraton Hotel); No. 51, Shaheed Khoddami Street, Vali-e-Asr Avenue, Tehran 19946; tel: (-21) 8773021-38; central reservations for Homa Hotel Group: 877-6796 & 879-6597; fax: (21) 879-7179; central reservations fax: (21) 879-9302; 140 rooms, 28 suites; 4 royal suites; located in residential neighborhood on hill 20 to 30 minutes from city.

Laleh International Hotel (former Inter-Continental); Dr Fatemi Avenue, PO Box 14155-1771; tel: (21) 65-5021-9/656-021-9; fax: (21) 655-517/655-588; residential neighborhood on hill 20 to 30 minutes from city; restaurants; coffee shop; 24-hour communication services; banking; barber shop; 24-hour room service; laundry; sauna; pool.

Expensive

Enghelab; 50 Taleghani Avenue, Ex. Takhte Jamshid; tel: (21) 646-6285, 641-9311; fax: (21) 646-6285; email: add:eng-hotel@www.dci.co.ir; 248 single rooms, 199 double rooms, 25 suites; city center; rooftop restaurant; conference facilities; fax facilities; central video and satellite systems; no-smoking rooms; in-room minibar, a/c, bath, tv, video facilities; 24-hour room service; laundry; barber; medical clinic; shop; parking; sauna; pool. US$59-76.

Ferdowsi Grand Hotel; 24, Foroughi St., Ferdowsi Ave.,; tel: (2) 671-9991/2/3; fax: (21) 671-1449; 7 single rooms, 55 doubles, 4 suites.

Howeyzeh; crossing of O. Nejat-ol-Lahi St., Taleghani Ave.; tel: (21) 880-4344 to 58; fax: (21) 890-4823; 9 single rooms, 196 doubles; coffee shop; conference hall; in-room telephone, tv, a/c; library; prayer room; taxi service.

Tehran Grand; Vali-e-Asr and Motahari Avenue; tel: (21) 872-1656/57/58/59/60; fax: (21) 871-3857; fax: (21) 623-857; 84 double rooms, 14 suites; near city center; restaurant; conference facilities; central video system; in-room a/c, bathroom; prayer room; library; shop; taxi service.

Moderate

Evin; Evin & Chamran Expressway; tel: (21) 207-8606; fax: (21) 209-0425; 52 double rooms; 5 suites; near airport; restaurant; parking; pool.

Jahan; 523, Taleghani Cross Rd., Vali-e-Asr. Ave.; tel: (21) 640-2958, 640-2914, 640-0442; fax: (21) 646-3033; 6 singles rooms, 48 doubles, 6 suites.

Hotel Mashad; Ave. Taleghani Dr. Mofatteh St. No. 190; tel: 882-5145/5146/5147, 838-113, 838-114; fax: 882-2681; French-style decor; 20 single rooms, 145 double rooms, 15 suites; parking.

Omid; East Nosrat St., 16th Azar Ave., Keshavarz Blvd.; tel: (21) 641-4564, 641-8679, 641-8623; fax: (21) 641-9986; 2 single rooms, 14 double rooms, 7 suites; restaurant; coffee shop; central video; laundry; elevator.

Raamtin Residence Hotel; 1081 Valiasr Ave., south of Saai Park; tel: (21) 872-2786/7/8, 871-637, 871-7856; fax: (21) 871-8593; apartments and suites; located in north Tehran; restaurant; conference facilities; in-room bathroom, kitchen facilities, color tv, direct dial phone, a/c; table tennis.

Roodaki; Arfa St., Hafez Ave.; tel: (21) 670-6955/6; fax: (21) 670-6320; 48 suites.

Tehran Kowsar; Vali E-Asr, Khosro Khavar Avenue; tel: (21) 898-371; fax: (21) 889-1615; restaurant; conference facilities; in-room safe; corporate rates; fitness; sauna; pool; whirlpool; US$50.

HEALTH CARE

Iamat Center; Physicians' Building, 7th fl., Keshvarz Blvd., Teheran; tel: (21) 655-128.

AUTO RENTAL

Elahieh; (21) 200-2233.

Novin; (21) 205-2883.

Omid; (21) 220-1277.

Pirooz; (21) 254-9632.

Saman; (21) 207-3368.

Sepehr; (21) 821-4129.

Velenjak; (21) 240-1356.

WORLD TRADE CENTER

Real Estate Investment Group Co.
Al Dawliyah Commercial Center
Fahed Al Salem St, 3rd Floor
PO Box 22, Safat 13001
KUWAIT
tel: [965] 240-4275; fax: [965] 252-8011

CHAMBER OF COMMERCE

Export Promotion Center
PO Box 1148, Vali-e-Asr Avenue
Dr Chamran Crossing, Tehran
tel: (21) 21911; fax: (21) 204-2858

Ireland

At a Glance

THE PEOPLE

Population .... 3,632,944 (July 1999 est.)
Growth Rate .... 0.38% (1999 est.)
Life Expectancy .... 76.39 years (born 1999)
Infant Mortality ... 5.94 deaths/1,000 live births (1999 est.)

Ethnic Composition
Celtic Caucasian 99%
Other 1%

Religious Composition
Roman Catholic.. 93%
Anglican... 3%
Other and non-affiliated.. 4%

Languages Spoken
Irish Gaelic (official), English

Education and Literacy
Education is compulsory for nine years. Adult literacy is 98 percent nationwide.

Labor Force
Total: 1,370,000
By occupation: services 62.1%, industry 22.9%, agriculture 15%

THE ECONOMY
Ireland's economy has converted itself over the last twenty years from being based in agriculture into a high-tech and service oriented powerhouse. Only ten years ago Ireland was considered the "sick man" of Europe, but after extensive E.U. investment this little island is referred to as the "Emerald Dragon." It sports the highest GDP growth rate in Europe (8 percent) and it attracts foreign investment in high-end, value-added technologies. Its highly educated workforce is tapped by some of the largest corporations in the world. Though for well over a century Ireland suffered a massive immigration of its impoverished citizens, nowadays some of the hottest job prospects in Europe can be found in Dublin's industrial parks. But all is not perfect in the Emerald Isle. Double-digit unemployment is still a problem for many of its rural citizens. Ireland is also under pressure from its fellow E.U. members to alter its very attractive tax regimen that has been so instrumental in a luring foreign investment.

Exports .... US$60.9 billion (f.o.b, 1998)
Imports .... US$43.7 billion (c.i.f., 1998)
Total GDP .... US$67.1 billion (1998 est.)
GDP Per Capita .... US$18,600 (1998 est.)
Unemployment .... 7.7% (1998 est.)
Inflation Rate 2.4% (1998)

Top Export Partners
E.U., United States

Top Import Partners
E.U., United States

Top Exports
Chemicals, data processing equipment, industrial machinery, live animals, animal products

Top Imports
Food, animal feed, data processing equipment, petroleum and petroleum products, machinery, textiles, clothing.

BUSINESS WORKWEEK

Offices
Monday to Friday 9a.m. to 5:30p.m.

Banks
Monday to Friday 10a.m. to 4p.m.; Thursday until 5p.m. in Dublin.

Government
Monday to Friday 9a.m. to 5p.m.

Retail
Monday to Friday 9a.m. to 8p.m., slightly shorter hours on weekends.
Note: Business hours in rural western Ireland are more attuned to local custom and seasonal needs.

HOLIDAYS

New Year's Day...January 1
St. Patrick's Day .... March 17
Good Friday...April 2*
Easter Monday ....April 5*
May Day Holiday ....May 3*
June Bank Holiday ....June 7*
August Bank Holiday ....August 2*
October Bank Holiday .... October 25*
Christmas ....December 25
St. Stephen's Day..December 26
*Dates may vary by year.

CLIMATE

Seasons
Weather in Ireland has been characterized as wet and overcast year round. The four seasons can be distinguished to some degree on the eastern seaboard. While it does receive a lot of rainfall (that's how Ireland stays so green), overall it has a temperate maritime climate. Temperatures nationwide run from average lows of 7°C (45°F) to average highs of 21°C (70°F).

Regions
As a north Atlantic island nation, Ireland receives more than its share of rough weather. The west coast takes the brunt of the wind and rain but its southwest area receives enough warmth from the Gulf Stream to sprout palm trees. Central Ireland's river districts are temperate by comparison to the coasts, and the eastern part of the tiny nation receives the chilly winds of the Irish sea.

Money & Banking

Currency
The currency of Ireland is the Irish Punt (Ir£).

Denominations
The Irish Punt (Ir£) comes in coin denominations of Ir£1, as well as 50, 20, 10, 5, 2, and 1 pence and banknotes of Ir£ 5, Ir 10, 20, and 50.

Ireland

Traveler's Checks and Credit Cards

Traveler's checks (especially those denominated in British pounds, Deutschmarks and U.S. dollars) and most foreign currency can be easily and efficiently exchanged at banks, foreign exchange bureaus, hotels, and foreign exchange kiosks at the airports. Banks offer the most favorable exchange rates. Eurocheques can also be cashed.

Traveler's checks receive a better exchange rate than cash, or you can purchase Irish currency denominated traveler's checks before departure, which can be exchanged almost everywhere in the country.

Credit cards are widely accepted in Ireland including American Express, Visa, MasterCard, Eurocard, and Diners Club, as well as bank cards from the larger Irish banks.

You can get cash advances from your credit card on many of the automated teller machines (ATM). ATMs can be found even in small Irish villages. The best exchange rates are given for credit card and ATM transactions involving foreign banks. Transactions on check and credit card can be conducted in Euros if so requested.

Travel

VISA AND PASSPORT

Foreigners must have a valid passport, except nationals of the E.U. and Switzerland, who may hold a national identity card instead. Visas are not required for nationals of most countries for stays under 90 days, but foreigners may be asked to show return or onward tickets.

DEPARTURE FORMALITIES

You can take up to Ir£100 in Irish currency out of the country. Airport departure fees are included in the airline fare.

CUSTOMS ENTRY (PERSONAL)

Duty-free

Goods obtained duty- and tax-free in the E.U.:

- Tobacco: 800 cigarettes, 400 cigarillos, or 200 cigars, or 1kg of tobacco
- Alcohol: 10 liters of spirits (more than 22 percent proof), plus 20 liters of alcoholic drinks under 22 percent proof (e.g. fortified wine); up to 25 liters of wine; not more than 50 liters of beer

Note: Although there are now no legal limits imposed on importing duty-paid tobacco and alcoholic products from one E.U. country to another, travelers may be questioned at customs if they exceed the above amounts and may be asked to prove that the goods are for personal use only.

Goods obtained duty- and/or tax-free in the E.U., or duty- and tax-free on a ship or aircraft, or goods obtained outside the E.U.:

- Tobacco: 200 cigarettes or 100 cigarillos or 50 cigars or 250g of smoking tobacco
- Alcohol: 1liter of spirits (more than 22% proof) or 2 liters of other alcoholic beverages, including sparkling or fortified wine, plus 2 liters of table wine
- Other: 50g of perfume and 250ml of eau de toilette; goods to the value of 142Ir£ (73Ir£ for passengers under 15 years old)

Note: Tobacco and alcoholic beverages are only available to passengers over 17 years of age.

IMMUNIZATION

Visitors do not need vaccination certificates unless arriving from areas of known infection or epidemic. Tetanus inoculation is recommended for travel to rural areas of Ireland.

TIPPING

Taxi

Taxi drivers generally receive 10 percent of the fare total as a tip.

Porters

For porters, 50 pence per bag is standard.

Hotels

A service charge is often included in a hotel bill; tip extra only for extraordinary service.

Restaurants

A service charge of 10 to 15 percent is often included in a restaurant bill. In its absence, a 15 percent tip is standard. It is customary to buy your bartender a drink, especially if you have been engaged in conversation. But tipping is not customary in pubs unless you have table service.

EMERGENCY INFORMATION

Police and Crime

The Republic of Ireland is a relatively safe country, and little of Northern Ireland's political violence spills over the border. However, Dublin, like all large cities, is suffering from increasing crime rates. Avoid dimly lit streets at night, and know your destination before departure. Women can walk around freely, but it is advisable to travel in groups at night. The police are efficient and courteous.

Foreign business visitors are often the target of thieves. Consequently, purses, laptops, and briefcases will require additional security. Do not leave valuables in cars or on tables in cafés. Keep non-essential valuables locked in hotel safes when not in use. Use credit cards and travel checks when possible to avoid carrying large sums of cash.

Take care when leaving a city pub at night as this can pose security risks.

Emergency Numbers

Numbers function nationwide.

Police, Fire, Ambulance 999
Operator 10

Health

There are no serious health risks and the only problematic illness is the common flu. Ireland has strict food laws, thus, making food safe for consumption and tap water potable.

Note: The Irish diet can pose problems for visitors from cultures with lighter cuisines, such as Asian countries. Irish cities have an eclectic mix of restaurants to give you time to adjust before you dive headlong into an Irish breakfast.

Ireland has a private and national health service. Social insurance tax is a requirement for resident foreigners and will cover medical charges. under the nation's health service.

INTERNAL TRAVEL

AIR

Aer Lingus and several other carriers offer domestic air services throughout Ireland. Aer Aran serves the Aran Islands (out of Galway). In addition to Galway, other domestic airports include Sligo, Carrickfinn (CFN) in Co Donegal, and Kerry (Farranfore) (KIR) in Co Kerry. Bus and taxi services into nearby cities is usually available, but some taxis must be booked in advance to assure ground transport. Enquire locally.

TAXI

Taxis are easily available in most cities, and the fare is generally reasonable. Cabs that cruise are not easily found, though; you need to head for the nearest taxi stand at a rail or bus station, or at a hotel. Most Irish cabbies know their cities well, but written directions are always a good idea, especially if you have any difficulty with the language or accent here.

AUTO

Car rental is available in most Irish cities and at all airports. It can be a good idea to rent a car here if you need to travel to smaller towns, as some regions are not well served by public transport. A credit card, a valid license, and local insurance is required. Irish rental cars cannot be ferried out of the country.

Driving in Ireland is quite civilized, although you will be driving on the left hand side. Roads are generally well maintained, and signage is excellent. Major roadways have good lighting systems for night driving. One note: Each town has its own "pay and park" system.

Ireland

TRAIN

Rail services in Ireland are operated by Iarnród Eireann (Irish Rail). Express trains run between all the major cities, even to Northern Ireland, and offer a comfortable alternative to domestic air service. There are two classes of trains, with higher class trains offering buffet and restaurant cars. DART is a fast new suburban rail service, linking Howth and Bray around Dublin Bay, including a connection to Dun Laoghaire, the ferry port which lies at the bottom cusp of the bay.

A number of discount passes are available, called Explorer tickets, offering a variety of rail-only and rail/bus combined travel. These generally apply for a specified period of time for unlimited travel within Ireland, and some include Northern Ireland. The Eurail pass system is also valid.

Travel by train is good, but there is less of it than one might wish. Expect expensive rail fares, with significant gaps in the routes. Frequency of services also is less than fully realized. Reservations are advisable. For further information, tap into the Irish Rail website: http://www.irishrail.ie/

METRO

The only city in Ireland with anything close to a subway system is Dublin. The Dublin Area Rapid Transit (DART) travels mostly above ground while servicing the city and its many surrounding suburbs. The service operates every 15 minutes, and every five minutes during peak travel periods. Hours of operation are 7a.m. until midnight, Monday through Saturday, and from 9:30a.m. until 11p.m. on Sunday. Stations are well marked and the fares are inexpensive. DART also connects with the Dublin bus system.

BUSES & TRAMS

Bus Éireann provides bus service throughout Ireland, with a nationwide system of vehicles and routes that connects all the major urban areas as well as many towns and villages. Service to more remote areas, however, is generally infrequent.

Irish cities also have extensive local bus and/or streetcar service. Fares are low, but many times buses are overcrowded and behind schedule. Nevertheless, they are a common form of travel for business commuters.

For schedules and information, log onto the Bus Éireann website at: www.buseireann.ie.

WATER TRAVEL

Ferries shuttle passengers and cars to and from France between Rosslare and Cork in Ireland and LeHavre and Cherbourg in France. Overland links are also available through the U.K. to France. Ferries to Wales and England take about four hours. Many ferry companies are now providing high-speed services and cutting-edge craft on many of the Irish sea routes.

For information on routes and fares, contact:

Brittany Ferries
www.brittany-ferries.com
Irish Ferries
www.irishferries.com
P&O Irish Sea
www.poirishsea.com
Stena Line
www.stenaline.com
Swansea-Cork Ferries
www.swansea-cork.ie

There is also a river passenger boat system, but it is rarely used nowadays for business travel.

TRAVEL ASSISTANCE

Bord Fáilte Eireann
Baggot Street Bridge
Dublin 2, Ireland
tel: (1) 602 4000
fax: (1) 602 4100
emaill: fdowney@irishtouristboard.ie
website: www.ireland.travel.ie

Communications

DIALING CODES IN IRELAND

International country code: [353]

Selected city codes: Arklow (402), Cork(21), Dingle (66), Donegal (77), Drogheda (41), Dublin (1), Dundalk (42), Ennis (65),Galway (91), Kildare (45), Killarney (64), Limerick (61),Sligo (71), Tipperary (62), Tralee (66), Tullamore (506),Waterford (51), Wexford (53).

Dialing Ireland from Overseas

To dial Ireland, dial your country's international dialing code, then 353 (the country code for Ireland), then the city code and finally the number. If you were dialing Cork from the United States, for example, you would begin with 011, then 353, then 21 (the city code for Cork), and finally the number of the person or office you were trying to reach.

Assistance Numbers

Irish Operator 10
Northern Ireland International Directory 153
Northern Ireland Operator 100

CALLING WITHIN IRELAND

Since 1992, some Dublin phone numbers changed; numbers that began with a 2 or 4 are now prefixed with 8, and those that began with a 95 or 98 are prefixed with a 2.

Local Calls

A 3-minute local call costs 20p.

Long Distance Calls

If calling long distance within Ireland, include the city prefix. To call northern Ireland, dial 08 and then the Northern Ireland code including the zero.

International Calls

To place a direct call, you can use any phone and dial direct. Remember you cannot reach an international operator from a card phone.

AT&T USA Direct 1-800-550-000
MCI..1-800-551-001
Sprint..1-800-552-001

PAY PHONES

Public Telephones

Telecom Eireann offers an advanced digital public phone system in place throughout the country. A succession of beeps indicates the telephone needs more change. A/B phones require you to press the A button to speak. If no one answers, press the B button and your change should be returned.

Ireland

Calling Cards

British Telecom card phones have become almost standard. Relieve the coin hassle by purchasing a card in 10-, 20-, 50- or 100-unit denominations. But remember that you cannot access an international operator at a card phone. Mercury operates another telephone system in Northern Ireland with its own phone cards and telephones.

CELLULAR PHONES

Eircell operates a GSM digital system and a TACS analogue system (operating in the 900 MHz range) for mobile phone users in Ireland.

Note: Your home country cell phone may not work in this country. If not, we recommend that you rent an international cell phone *before* you leave home. A major US-based cell phone rental provider is **IMC WorldCell**. For information see "International Cell Phone Rentals" on page 14..

CALL BACK

You can (potentially) save significant sums when calling in Ireland by using a call back service. For a list of callback services, please refer to the "Communications" section in the *Global Road Warrior* Introduction.

Fees for call back services vary widely, depending on the company and the type of service required. Be sure to check with these companies before leaving to compare rates.

PHONE JACKS

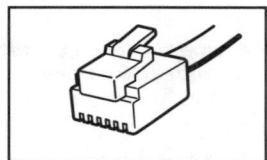

Plug adaptors are available through **iGo Corporation.** (See "Electrical and Telephone Adaptors" on page 19.)

FAX/MODEM

Fax services are efficient. They can be found at most hotels and business offices. About 70 percent of the telephones in Ireland are now digital; so, computer users beware if you own an analogue modem. IBM's Modem Saver might prove a necessary tool to avoid a burnout.

POSTAL SERVICES

Ireland generally has good postal service. Mail arrives in Western Europe within a couple of days and in North American in no more than one week. Mail boxes are painted green. The main post office in Dublin lies on O'Connell Street.

Hours of service

Monday to Friday 9a.m. to 5:30p.m. or 6p.m. Saturday 9a.m. to 1p.m.

Business Services
BUSINESS CENTERS

Abbey Executive Business Services; 45 Lower O'Connell Street, Dublin 1; tel: (1) 731-700.

Abbey House Services Offices; 15/17 Upper Abbey Street, Dublin 1; tel: (1) 724-911.

Ballsbridge Business Bureau; 44 Northumberland Road, Dublin 4; tel: (1) 688-244.

Carmichael House; 60 Lower Baggot Street, Dublin 2; tel: (1) 762-240.

COURIER SERVICES

Airborne Express (City Air Express); Until 93, Newtown Industrial Estate, Coolock, Dublin 17.

DHL; Customer Service, tel: 1800-725-725; Dublin: (1) 844-4111; Shannon: (61) 472-655; Waterford: (51) 357-470; Cork: (21) 312-311; Athlone: (902) 72-346.

Federal Express; tel: 1800-535-800.

UPS; tel: 1800-575-757; Unit 134, Slaney Close, Dublin Industrial Estate, Glasnevin, Dublin 11.

Electrical
Current

220 volts AC, 50 Hz

ELECTRIC PLUGS

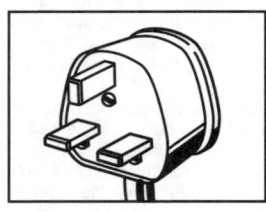

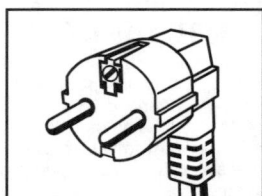

Plug adaptors are available through **iGo Corporation.** (See "Electrical and Telephone Adaptors" on page 19.)

Technical Support
HARDWARE/SOFTWARE VENDOR SUPPORT

Compaq/Digital; (U.K. Office) tel: (44) 1-81-332-3000; fax: (44) 1-81-332-3409; (44) 1-81-332-3888 (CompaqCare Center); (44) 1-81-332-9499 (QuickLine); (44) 1-81-332-3550 (FaxPaq); (General U.S.) tel: (281) 518-2000; http://www.compaq.com/.

Ireland

Corel; tel: 01-708-2600 (Corel Corporation); (in the U.S.) tel: [1] (716) 871-2325 (Ask to be Forwarded to Appropriate Program); http://www.corel.com/.

Dell; tel: (1) 286-0500; fax: (1) 286-2020; (Dell- Europe) tel: [44] (134) 474-8000; (in the U.S.) tel: [1] (512) 338-4400; fax: [1] (512) 728-3330; http://www.dell.com/.

Hewlett Packard; tel: (0) 1662 5525; (in Switzerland) tel: [41] (22) 780-8111; (in the U.S.) tel: [1] (408) 246-4300; http://www.hp.com/.

IBM; tel: 1-660-3744; fax: 1-850-205-205 (toll free within Ireland); fax: 1-850-401-601; (in the U.S.) tel: [1] (919) 517-2800; (U.S. Main Office) tel: [1] 914-765-1900; http://www.ibm.com/.

Microsoft; tel: 706-5353; (in Switzerland) tel: [41] (848) 858-868; fax [41] (1) 831-0869; (in the U.S.) [1] (425) 635-7222; http://www.microsoft.com/.

NEC; tel: 01-838-1216 (Ultracare Support); (in the U.S.) [1] (916) 388-0101 (Main Switchboard); http://www.nec.com/.

Novell; (in Germany) tel: [49] (211) 563-2777 (System support); tel: [49] (6196) 904-477; fax: [49] (211) 563-2772; (in Switzerland) tel: [41] (1) 308-4747; fax: [41] (1) 302-0401; (in the U.S.) tel: [1] (408) 434-2300; fax: [1] (408) 577-5775 (Worldwide Sales Headquarters); http://www.novell.com/.

Toshiba; (in Germany) tel: [49] (2131) 158-319; fax: [49] (2131) 158-558; (in Switzerland) tel: [41] (1) 946-0777; fax: [41] (1) 946-0807; (in Ireland) tel: [44] (193) 282-8828; (in the U.S.) [1] (949) 583-3000 (Corporate Headquarters); http://www.toshiba.com/.

Internet Connection

HOW TO CONNECT

Connecting to AOL and Compuserve in Ireland is similar to using it when traveling outside your own area code. See the introductory section for detailed information on connecting to your account through a different phone number.

America Online

Numbers are available at keyword *international*. Be sure to get several local numbers before leaving. AOL's Global-Net service charges US$6 an hour in addition to the usual charges. Go to keyword *access* (a free area) and download the software.

Access: Cork (21) 278-273; Dublin (1) 613-7000; Shannon (61) 474-503.

Compuserve

Numbers are available at *Go International*. The Compuserve Web-site also has a great deal of information, at http://www.compuserve.com.

Access: Cork (21) 278-273; Dublin (1) 406-0100; Shannon (61) 474-503.

Independent Service Providers

Many independent service providers offer discounts if you are only in town for a couple of days.

ANU Internet Services; tel: 982-8300; fax: 982-8593; email: info@anu.net; http://www.anu.ie/.

Esat Net; tel: (1) 216-6300; fax: (1) 216-6399; email: info@esat.net; http://www.esat.net/.

Indigo; tel: (1850) 730-073; fax: (1) 701-0394; email: info@indigo.ie; http://www.indigo.ie/.

Ireland On-Line; tel: (1) 604-6800; fax: (1) 604 6888; email: sales@iol.ie; http://www.iol.ie/.

Business Culture
GREETINGS AND COURTESIES

Ireland standards of business and etiquette are less formal than most European countries, and the Irish have a reputation for friendliness and sociability. While the country is bilingual—English and Gaelic—English is the language of business. Proper greetings include the forms Mr., Mrs., or Miss before you are invited to use first names, an invitation the Irish quickly extend. A handshake and a few words such as "How do you do" or "Pleased to meet you" are common greetings. A handshake following meetings is considered good manners. In all cases, men should wait for a woman to extend her hand first.

MEETINGS

Schedule a meeting at least 2 or 3 weeks prior to arrival. While punctuality is always good practice, the Irish tend to be on the late side when keeping appointments. Cards may be exchanged before the meeting begins or after formal introductions have taken place. Spend some time in the initial meeting stages developing rapport with your Irish counterparts before launching into highly technical or serious presentations. Conversation is a gifted trait for the Irish. A trip to a local pub on invitation from the Irish host may serve to build more personal bonds, considered important in Irish culture.

DECISION MAKING

A very democratic system of hierarchy exists within the corporate or work environment. Joint consultation between management and employees is an important activity towards the rendering of decisions. This interactive process between management and employees is highly meaningful to Irish workers and it serves foreign ventures to respect the process. While senior management gets involved in the majority of decisions, lower levels are consulted and heard from before final decisions are made. Once a deal has been struck, it is important to maintain on-time deliveries.

WOMEN

Women in Ireland are definitely part of the working fabric of business. Many with university degrees, they hold various positions within companies. Although traces of male machismo may exist in random places as they might anywhere else, foreign businesswomen should experience few problems in Ireland.

BUSINESS ATTIRE

Business attire should remain informal and comfortable. However, suits are always worn to an initial business meeting. Women should wear suits or wool blazers with a skirt. Men and women alike are advised to remember their raincoats and umbrellas and should be prepared for cool weather.

Business Centers
Dublin
CITY VIEW

Known for its beautiful Georgian architecture and extensive literary history, Dublin is a welcoming city for any traveler. Situated on the River Liffey, it is filled with friendly people and numerous pubs where you can enjoy Dublin's own Guiness Stout. For great food and conversation be sure to visit the Temple Bar section of town.

AIRPORT

Dublin Airport to City Center

The airport lies 7 miles (11 km.) from the city. Buses leave every 10 minutes for Dublin, and coaches leave every 30 minutes for a fare of about Ir£2.50. Expect a 30-minute trip. For a more private ride with door-to-door service, hail a taxi outside of arrivals for a rate of about Ir£8.50; however, keep in mind t hat the trip into town takes about the same time as it does the coach.

Airline Numbers

Aer Lingus .... (1) 844-4747
American Airlines .... (1) 602-0550
Delta .... (1) 844-4170, 676-8080
Ryanair ....(1) 844-4411
British Midland ....(1) 842-2011

HOTELS

Top-End

Berkeley Court; Landsdowne Road, Ballsbridge; tel: (1) 660-1711; fax: (1) 661-7238; five-star hotel located in Dublin's most prestigious district; favored by dignitaries and celebrities; restaurant; conference facilities; secretarial service; in-room modem/fax connection; photocopy facilities; corporate rates; fitness; sauna; pool, several leisure and outdoor activities nearby.

The Davenport; Merrion Square; tel: (1) 607-3500; fax: (1) 661-5663; elegant luxury hotel; centrally located next to Trinity College; restaurant; bar; conference facilities; secretarial service; in-room modem/fax connection, safe; corporate rates; fitness; sauna; pool.

The Fitzwilliam; St. Stephen's Green, Dublin 2; tel: (1) 478-7000; fax: (1) 478-7878; new hotel (7/98); centrally located near Grafton Street shops; known for impeccable service; gourmet restaurant; brasserie; garden views; 3 conference rooms; in-room fax machines and ISDN lines, CD player.

The Shelbourne; 27 Stephen's Green; tel: (1) 676-6471; fax: (1) 661-6006; famous Georgian hotel favored by royalty since 1824; restaurant; conference facilities; fax/photocopy facilities; secretarial service; in-room modem/fax connection; Shelbourne Club, Dublin's premier fitness club, on premises.

Expensive

Forte Posthouse; Dublin Airport; tel: (1) 808-0500; fax: (1) 844-6002; four-star hotel; traditional Irish food, European and Chinese meals; bar with live music on weekends; conference facilities; secretarial service; 24-hour courtesy coach to airport.

The Morgan; 10 Fleet Street, Temple Bar; tel: (1) 679-3939; fax: 679-3946; www.themorgan.com; new boutique hotel in trendy Temple Bar district; meals and alcohol available; conference facilities; in-room Internet/ISDN lines, fax/modem access and voicemail; gym.

Moderate

Central Hotel; 1-5 Exchequer Street; (1) 679-7302; fax: (1) 679-7303; www.centralhotel.ie; three-star hotel in city center; restaurant; licensed to sell wine; conference facilities; secretarial service; fax/photocopy facilities; corporate rates.

North Star; Amiens Street 1; tel: (1) 836-3136; fax: (1) 836-3561; www.regencyhotels.com; located in the city center near the financial district and Temple Bar; completely upgraded in 1999; restaurant; licensed to sell wine; conference facilities; secretarial service; corporate rates; gym; leisure complex on premises.

AUTO RENTAL

Avis; reservations, tel: (21) 281-111; fax: (21) 281-122; Dublin airport, tel: (1) 605-7500; fax: (1) 605-7565; 1Hanover St. East, tel: (1) 6057500, (1) 605-7520; Cork Airport, tel: (21) 965-045; fax: (1) 314-185; http://www.avis.com.

Budget; reservations, tel: (90) 324-668, (90) 324-678; fax: (90) 324-759; Dublin airport, tel: (1) 844-5150, (1) 844-4150; fax: (1) 844-5919; Dublin ferry port, tel: (1) 837-9611, fax: (1) 837-9802; Cork airport, tel: (21) 314-000; fax: (21) 343-448.

Malone Car Rental; 26 Lombard St., Dublin 2; tel: (1) 670-7888; fax: (1) 670-7844.

Hertz; reservations, tel: (1) 676-7476; fax: (1) 668-1961; telex: 33207; Dublin airport, tel: (1) 844-5466, fax: (1) 844-4371, telex: 80124, 6a.m. to 11p.m.; 149 Upper Leeson St., tel: 01 (1) 660-2255, fax: (1) 668-1961; Cork airport, tel: (21) 965-849; fax: (21) 310-617, telex: 80124 8a.m. to 11p.m.; http://www.hertz.com; chauffeur-driven cars available.

Value Car Rental; tel: (1) 842-8072; fax: (1) 842-8539; http://www.value-car-rental.com/

WORLD TRADE CENTER

World Trade Center Dublin
Treasury Holdings Ltd.
1st Floor, 25 Herbert Place
Dublin 2, Ireland
tel: (1) 676-5300; fax: (1) 676-5399

CHAMBER OF COMMERCE

Chambers of Commerce of Ireland
22 Merrion Square, Dublin 2
tel: (1) 661-2888; fax: (1) 661-2811
email: chambers@ciol.ie

Israel

At a Glance

THE PEOPLE

Population .... 5,749,760 (July 1999 est.)
Growth Rate .... 1.81% (1999 est.)
Life Expectancy .... 78.61 years (born 1999)
Infant Mortality ... 7.78 deaths/1,000 live births (1999 est.)

Ethnic Composition

Judaic.. 82%
Arab and other.. 18%

Religious Composition

Judaism.. 82%
Muslim.. 14%
Christian 2%
Druze and other.. 2%

Languages Spoken

Hebrew (official), Arabic (official), English

Education and Literacy

Education is state-funded and compulsory for 11 years. Adult literacy is 95% nationwide.

Labor Force

Total: 2,300,000
By occupation: services 69.7%, industry 27.7%, agriculture 2.6%

THE ECONOMY

Israel's overall economy relies heavily on government participation. As the island of Judaism is a tumultuous Arabic sea, Israel is dependent on the import of oil, military equipment, grains, and the majority of its raw materials. The government has incurred a massive foreign debt in its effort to prop up the general economy and its besieged political structure. Israel has targeted high-technology development and commodities in its effort to earn foreign currency. As a result, technology, cut diamonds, and produce have become the nation's leading exports. Its large service sector has been unable to find a solid international customer base. Israel's recurring current account deficits are countered by transfer payments from the overseas Jewish community and substantial foreign loans. Foreign investment has been reluctant to tap into Israel's highly educated workforce due to the continued political instability in the region. This reluctance has combined with the generous social service system to cause chronic unemployment and underemployment while GDP grows at a rate more applicable to an agrarian society. Israel's latest economic battle has been to absorb a new wave of immigration from eastern Europe that has arrived with skills but little in the way of capital.

Exports .... US$22.1 billion (f.o.b., 1998)
Imports .... US$26.1 billion (f.o.b., 1998)
Total GDP .... US$101.9 billion(1998 est.)
GDP Per Capita .... US$18,100 (1998 est.)
Unemployment .... 8.7% (1998 est.)
Inflation Rate .... 5.4% (1998 est.)

Top Export Partners

United States, E.U., Japan

Top Import Partners

E.U., United States, Japan

Top Exports

Machinery and equipment, cut diamonds, chemicals, textiles and apparel, agricultural products, metals.

Top Imports

Military equipment, capital goods, rough diamonds, oil, consumer goods.

BUSINESS WORKWEEK

Offices

Sunday to Thursday 8a.m. to 4p.m., Friday 8a.m. to 1p.m.

Banks

Sunday to Thursday 8:30a.m. to 12:30p.m. and 2:30p.m. to 6:30p.m.

Government

Sunday to Thursday 7:30a.m. to 4p.m.

Retail

Sunday to Thursday 9a.m. to 8p.m., Friday 10p.m. to 3 p.m.

HOLIDAYS

Passover (public holidays on first and
last days of festival)..April 1-7*
Independence Day ....April 21*
Shavuot .... May 21*
Rosh Hashanah..................................... September 11-12*
Yom Kippur...October 10
Succot .... September 25 - October 1*
* Dates may vary by year.
Note: Islamic and Christian holidays are observed by the respective local communities. None are legal holidays.

CLIMATE

Seasons

The climate ranges from temperate to sub tropical, with plenty of sunshine. There are two distinct seasons: a mild, rainy winter from November through March, and a warm season from April until mid-October.

Regions

Regional conditions vary greatly. The coast can be hot and humid, while the hill regions have dry summers and moderately cold winters. The Negev has year-round semi-desert conditions. Average temperatures range from 5°C (41°F) in Jerusalem in the winter to over 40°C (95°F) in Eilat in midsummer.

Money & Banking

Currency

The currency of Israel is the New Israel Shekel (NIS).

Denominations

The New Israel Shekel (NIS) comes in coin denominations of NIS5, and 1, and 50, 10, and 5 agorot; and banknotes of NIS10, 50, 100, and 200.

Traveler's Checks and Credit Cards

Traveler's checks are accepted throughout Israel. Besides banks, most of the top hotels have facilities which will deal with currency exchange. The U.S. dollar and the Brit-

Israel

Israel

- ⊛ National capital
- ⊙ District capital
- ● Secondary city
- ▬ International boundary
- District boundary
- Divided highway
- Primary road
- Railroad
- ● Oil pipeline
- ▤ Oil storage
- ↓ Primary port
- ⊠ Airfield
- ⁚⁚ Historical area
- Built-up area

| 0 | 10 | 20 | 30 | 40 km |
| 0 | 10 | | 20 | 30 mi |

©2001 Magellan Geographix   SM Santa Barbara, CA

ish pound are the easiest currencies to exchange. Checks denominated in those currencies are also the easiest to cash. Currencies from Arabic nations other than Egypt or Jordan will not be accepted.

Exchanging cash or cashing traveler's checks is best done in the large cities although it can be done with some difficulty in smaller towns. Keep all the exchange receipts as they will be needed for reconversion at departure.

Mastercard, Visa, American Express, and Eurocard are the most widely accepted cards in urban areas but only at major outlets. In rural areas cash is best used for transactions.

Banks in Jerusalem and Tel Aviv will give cash advances on credit cards. Major cities are also well supplied with ATMs. The best exchange rates are given for credit card and ATM transactions.

Travel

VISA AND PASSPORT

Foreigners must have a passport valid for a minimum six months beyond intended arrival date, an onward or return ticket, and proof of sufficient funds. A three-month visa will be issued to most foreigners, without charge, upon arrival. Citizens of the U.S., U.K., Canada, Australia, New Zealand, Japan, and the E.U. countries are not required to have visas for stays up to 90 days. Nationals of British dependent territories do need a pre-authorized visa. There is a long list of additional countries whose nationals do not need visas— check with the closest embassy or consulate about it.

Persons intending to visit an Arab country (not including Egypt or Jordan) following a visit to Israel should arrange it so that their passport does not contain an Israeli visa or stamp. Otherwise, entry may be denied at your destination.

Special border crossings to Jordan, including the Arava Checkpoint north of Eliat and the Jordan River Crossing, are allowed. However, those wishing to cross should have prearranged visas through an authorized travel agent. Check with your embassy or the Israeli Tourist Office for the latest information. Entry requirements are subject to rapid change due to political changes in East Jerusalem and the Gaza Strip, West Bank, Golan Heights, and neighboring Lebanon.

DEPARTURE FORMALITIES

Up to US$100 in Israeli currency may be exchanged upon departure without proof of foreign exchange transaction, but keep all exchange receipts anyway. Airport departure fees are usually included in the price of the airfare.

CUSTOMS ENTRY (PERSONAL)

Duty-free
- Tobacco: 250 cigarettes or 250g of tobacco products
- Alcohol: 1 liter of spirits; 2 liters of wine
- Other: 250ml of eau de cologne or perfume; gifts up to the value of US$125

Note: Animals, flowers, plants, and seeds may not be imported without prior permission. Fresh meat may not be imported.

Prohibited or Restricted
Israel maintains prohibitions on most agricultural products. Any and all items that might threaten national security or the very general "public morals" are prohibited.

Note: Israel is in a perpetual state of wartime security awareness. Airline security is especially tight. However, you can expect prolonged searches or questioning at any point of entry or departure. Delays may result when bringing in any form of electronics equipment. Even toiletries are subject to scrutiny and may be confiscated for security reasons (most specifically at border crossing with Jordan). Foreign nationals with Arab surnames may experience close scrutiny.

IMMUNIZATION

Foreigners do not currently need vaccination certificates to enter Israel unless arriving from areas of known infection or epidemic. Tetanus and hepatitis A inoculations are recommended for those visitors expecting travel outside of the cities.

TIPPING

Taxi
Taxi drivers do not expect a tip but are happy to get one. Most riders just round up the fare.

Porters
Porters receive NIS2 per piece of luggage.

Hotels
Hotels will apply a 15 percent service charge directly to the bill, as required by law.

Restaurants
Restaurants are also required by law to collect a service charge of 15 percent. If the service charge is not included on the tab (as it often is not if the diners are from the U.S.), add 15 percent.

EMERGENCY INFORMATION

Police and Crime
Apart from political upheaval with terrorist activities, street crime is relatively low in Israel. The most recent terrorist actions have taken place in highly frequented shopping and pedestrian areas and on public buses in an attempt to ruin the lucrative tourist trade. Visitors should avoid the West Bank and Gaza regions unless visiting tourist destinations by daylight. Travel after dark is not recommended in any region. Visitors to Jerusalem should take care to respect Orthodox traditions and to dress modestly. Avoid the old city at night, unless in the Jewish quarter, and remain cautious at religious sites on holy days, Fridays, and Saturdays.

Take basic precautions against petty crime. Avoid flashy displays of wealth, dress and behave conservatively. Leave most of your cash, traveler's checks, jewelry and camera in your hotel safe. Carry photocopies of your passport instead of the original. Carry cash in a money belt, and use credit cards or traveler's checks for most transactions.

Foreign women should be aware that Islamic traditions are observed in the more Arab-populated regions of Israel. Dress modestly, do not smoke in public, and remain conservative in behavior.

Emergency Numbers
The following numbers apply to Tel Aviv only:

Police... 100
Ambulance 101
Fire 102

Health
Traveling in Israel poses no serious health risks beyond those of heat and sun. The sun is strong and the climate hot, so use protection. Digestive problems pose the only problematic illness some visitors might experience due to Israeli cuisine. However, food laws are extremely strict, and agriculture is strictly managed. Tap water is potable, and a good selection of mineral bottled water is available.

Israel has a private and national health service, and both are of an extremely high standard. Most doctors speak English and medical costs prove reasonable. Travel insurance is advisable for long-term visitors.

Israel

Israel

For more information on medical centers, including phone numbers, please see the "Business Centers" section at the end of this chapter.

INTERNAL TRAVEL

AIR

Israir (ISR) and Arkia/Israel Inland Airways (IZ) both operate extensive services linking Tel Aviv with Jerusalem, Haifa, Rosh Pina, and Eilat. The country is so small, though, that air transit is rarely necessary.

TAXI

Private taxis and Sheruts (shared taxis), which offer less expensive means of transport, are available. Taxis operate 24 hours a day, even on holidays. By law, Israel requires its taxi drivers to use a meter, so be sure your driver turns on the meter when your journey begins. Two separate tariff rates exist: Tariff 1 between 5:30a.m. and 9p.m., and the higher Tariff 2 between 9p.m. and 6a.m. A passenger may request a receipt at journey's end.

AUTO

Rental vehicles are available in Tel Aviv and Jerusalem—a credit card, valid driver's license, and local insurance are required. Rental cars and fuel can be quite expensive, but there is an excellent system of roadways linking all towns in Israel.

It should be noted that security checkpoint officers throughout Israel spend a lot of time inspecting rental vehicles. Hiring a car with a local driver may offer a more expedient means of travel for short-term visitors.

TRAIN

Israel Railways operates a small but efficient network, providing regular services between Tel Aviv and Herzliya, Netanya, Hadera, Haifa, Akko (Acre), and Nahariya, and a daily train connecting Tel Aviv and Jerusalem, which runs along a beautiful scenic route. While the rail services do link the major cities, they do not reach into rural areas.

All services stop on religious holidays and between sunset Friday and sunset Saturday (the Shabbat). Train travel does pose some security risks during periods of political stress.

Rail Information ....(3) 693-7515

METRO

Israel has no metro system.

BUSES & TRAMS

Dan and *EGGED* companies offer efficient and inexpensive bus service within Israel offering both local and intercity routes. With a few exceptions, service is suspended between sunset Friday and sunset Saturday (the *Shabbat*). Please note that bus bombings are common in Israel as they present a terrorist with an easy and potentially bloody target. Business travelers should use these only as a last resort for reaching remote villages.

New Tel Aviv Bus Terminal ....(3) 638-4040
EGGED Company ....(3) 537-5555

WATER TRAVEL

Israeli ports are serviced by Mediterranean cruise services as well as by ferry services to points in North Africa and Europe. Ferries also cross the Sea of Galilee (Lake Kinneret) between Ein Gev kibbutz and Tiberias, and coastal ferries port-hop along the Israeli shoreline.

Like all travel to and from Israel, the passenger boat and ferry systems are subject to tight security controls.

TRAVEL ASSISTANCE

Ministry of Tourism
P.O. Box 1018
King George Street 24
Jerusalem, Israel
tel: (2) 675-4811; fax: (2) 625-3407
website: www.infotour.co.il

Essential Terms

English	Hebrew
Yes	Ken
No	Lo
Good morning	Boker tov
Hello (daytime)	Boker tov
Hello (evening)	Erev tov
Hello (telephone)	Shalom
Good-bye	Shalom
Please	Beh va ka sha
Thank you	Todah
Pleased to meet you	Naim meod
Excuse me; I'm sorry	Sli ha
My name is _____	Shmee_____
I don't understand	Lo meh veen
Do you speak English?	Ata medaber anglit

Communications

DIALING CODES IN ISRAEL

International country code: [972]
Selected city codes: Beer Sheva (7), Dimona (7), Haifa (4), Jerusalem (2), Nazareth (6), Tel Aviv (3), Ramat Gan (3), Rehovot (8), Tiberias (6), Tsefat (6).

Dialing Israel from Overseas

To dial Israel from overseas, dial your country's international dialing code, then 972 (the country code for Israel), then the city code and finally the number. If you were dialing Haifa from the United States, for example, you would begin with 011, then 972, then 4 (the city code for Haifa), and finally the number of the person or office you are trying to reach.

Assistance Numbers

Information 144
International Operator 188
Telegrams 171

PHONE USAGE

Local Calls

Local calls require either shekels or a phone card at public telephones. Telephones using cards are the cheaper alternative.

Long Distance Calls

Be sure to dial the city code you wish to reach when dialing long distance within Israel, but remember to omit the initial zero in the code when doing so.

International Calls

Israel's telephone company, Bezek, may charge more than if you try to reach an access number for your home country. Major calling cards may be used. AT&T's service can also link you to another country.

AT&T USA Direct 177-100-2727

If you call direct, dial 00 + country code + area code + number. Economy rates are available between 1a.m. and 8a.m., followed by discounted Saturday and Sunday rates. A 10-unit phone card will generally only buy you a few, short minutes to the U.S. on a direct call. You can make collect calls from any public telephone with only one Telecard unit. As alternatives, the central post office in Jerusalem, or Bezek's public telephone centers found in major cities, offer more economical rates than hotel phones.

PAY PHONES

Public Telephones

All telephone directories are in Hebrew, but a special English-language version exists for tourists.

Calling Cards

Kiosks, newsstands, bookshops, post offices, or hotels sell telecards, which prove cheaper than the coin method. Denominations of 10, 20 and 50-units can be purchased.

CELLULAR PHONES

Cellcom Israel Ltd. offers cellular phone service in a TDMA digital system, and an AMPS analog format. Motorola Pelephone Cellular Communications Ltd. offers NAMPS analog service. You can rent cell phones at Ben Gurion Airport or at your hotel. It's illegal to talk and drive; so if you rent a car, be sure to ask the rental agent for a hands-free set.

Note: Your home country cell phone may not work in this country. If not, we recommend that you rent an international cell phone *before* you leave home. A major US-based cell phone rental provider is **IMC WorldCell**. For information see "International Cell Phone Rentals" on page 14.

Mobile phones, pagers, and premium services need a prefix before dialing the number:

Cellcom	51, 52
Orange	54, 55
Pagers	58
Paltel	59
Pelephone	50, 51
Premium Services	56, 57

CALL BACK

You can (potentially) save significant sums when calling in Israel by using a call back service. For a list of callback services, please refer to the "Communications" section in the *Global Road Warrior* Introduction.

Fees for call back services vary widely, depending on the company and the type of service required. Be sure to check with these companies before leaving to compare rates.

PHONE JACKS

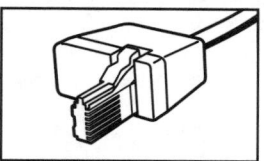

Some older buildings in Israel may use the following phone jack:

Plug adaptors are available through **iGo Corporation.** (See "Electrical and Telephone Adaptors" on page 19.)

FAX

Fax machines have replaced telegrams and telexes as the major way of sending transmissions. All of the larger hotels have fax machines, and service is generally very good.

POSTAL SERVICES

Mail can be very slow, for both domestic and international packages. Post offices are affixed with a white deer on a blue shield. Mail boxes are painted red. You may also send telegrams from post offices.

Hours of service

Main offices: 8:30a.m. to 6p.m.; Branch offices: Sunday to Thursday 8:30a.m. to 12:30p.m. and 2:30p.m. to 5:30p.m., Friday 8a.m. to noon.

Business Services

BUSINESS CENTER

Dan Hotel Tel Aviv; 99 Hayarkon Street; tel: (3) 520-2525; fax: (3) 524-9755

Hilton Hotel Tel Aviv; Hayarkon Street, Independence Park; tel: (3) 520-2222; fax: (3) 527-2711.

COURIER SERVICE

Airborne Exp[ress (Atid Intl. Transport); 29 Lilienblum Sreet, Tel Aviv; tel: (3) 519-7814; fax: (3) 510-7616.

DHL Tel Aviv (Shigur Express Ltd. T/A); 5 Hapardes Street, Azur 58001; tel: (3) 557-3552.

Federal Express; (3) 577-7777.

UPS; 21 Bar-Kochva St., Bnei Brak 51260; tel: (3) 577-0101; fax: (3) 618-4048.

Israel

SECRETARIAL SERVICE

Executive Business Center; 99 Hayarkon, Tel Aviv.
Gova-Office Services & Systems Ltd.; 10 Dizengoff, Tel Aviv.

TRANSLATION SERVICES

Jerusalem

Israel Translators Association; PO Box 9082,
Jerusalem; tel: (2) 643-7927.

Tel Aviv

Interlingua; 17 Bograshov, Tel Aviv; tel: (3) 528-1385; fax:
(3) 525-1173.

Electrical

CURRENT

220 volts AC, 50Hz.

ELECTRIC PLUGS

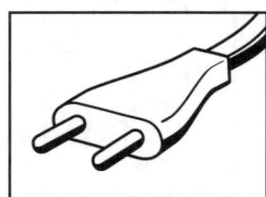

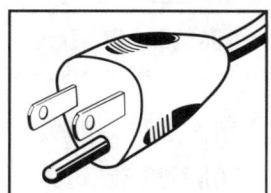

Plug adaptors are available through **iGo Corporation**.
(See "Electrical and Telephone Adaptors" on page 19.)

Technical Support

HARDWARE/SOFTWARE

VENDOR SUPPORT

Corel; (02) 6793-723 (All Applications); (in Germany) tel:
[49] (180) 425-8210 (TS Word Perfect-32 bit); (in the U.S.)
tel: [1] (716) 871-2325 (Ask to be Forwarded to Appropriate
Program); http://www.corel.com/.

Dell; tel: (3) 559-9868 (Unitech Technologies R.S. Ltd. in
Holon/Mr. Roy Mussafi); fax: (3) 559-0166; (Dell- Europe)
tel: [44] (134) 474-8000; (in the U.S.) tel: [1] (512) 338-
4400; fax: [1] (512) 728-3330; http://www.dell.com/.

Filemaker/Claris; (in Germany) tel: [49] (180) 525-8166
(Info-line); fax: [49] (180) 567-2233; tel: [49] (180) 523-
6423; (in the U.S.) tel: [1] (800) 965-9090; http://
www.claris.com/.

Hewlett Packard; (in Switzerland) tel: [41] (22) 780-8111;
(in the U.S.) tel: [1] (408) 246-4300; http://www.hp.com/.

IBM; tel: 3-697-8500; 177-022-3888 (toll free within Israel);
fax: 3- 695-9985; (in Switzerland) tel: [41] (22) 310-0418 (in
French); (in the U.S.) tel: [1] (919) 517-2800; (U.S. Main
Office) tel: [1] 914-765-1900; http://www.ibm.com/.

Microsoft; tel: (9) 952-5353; fax: (9) 952-5333; (in
Switzerland) tel: [41] (848) 858-868; fax [41] (1) 831-0869;
(in the U.S.) [1] (425) 635-7222; http://www.microsoft.com/.

Novell; (in Germany) tel: [49] (211) 563-2777 (System
support); tel: [49] (6196) 904-477; fax: [49] (211) 563-2772; (in
Switzerland) tel: [41] (1) 308-4747; fax: [41] (1) 302-0401; (in
the U.S.) tel: [1] (408) 434-2300; fax: [1] (408) 577-5775
(Worldwide Sales Headquarters); http://www.novell.com/.

Toshiba; (in Germany) tel: [49] (2131) 158-319; fax: [49]
(2131) 158-558; (in Switzerland) tel: [41] (1) 946-0777; fax:
[41] (1) 946-0807; (in Ireland) tel: [44] (193) 282-8828; (in
the U.S.) [1] (949) 583-3000 (Corporate Headquarters);
http://www.toshiba.com/.

Internet Connection

HOW TO CONNECT

Connecting to AOL and Compuserve in Israel is similar to
using it when traveling outside your own area code. See the
introductory section for detailed information on connecting to
your account through a different phone number.

America Online

Numbers are available at keyword *international*. Be sure
to get several local numbers before leaving. AOL's Global-
Net service charges US$6 an hour in addition to the usual
charges. Go to keyword *access* (a free area) and download
the software.

Access: Tel Aviv (3) 972-1922

Compuserve

Numbers are available at *Go International*. The Compuserve Web-site also has a great deal of information, at
http://www.compuserve.com.

Access: Haifa (4) 862-9160; Jerusalem (2) 673-8917; Raanana
(9) 771-2034; Tel Aviv (3) 639-3332; Tel Aviv (3) 639-3308.

Independent Service Providers

Many independent service providers offer discounts if
you are only in town for a couple of days.

ACTCOM - ACTive COMmunication Ltd.; tel: (4) 867-
6115; fax: (4) 867-6088; email: info@actcom.co.il; http://
www.actcom.co.il/?264,63/.

IsraCom; tel: (6) 626-5260; fax: (6) 626-5260; http://
www.isracom.net.il/.

GezerNet; tel: (8) 927-0648; tel: (50) 546-229; fax: (8) 927-
0736; http://www.gezernet.co.il/.

NetVision; tel: (4) 856-0560; email: info@NetVision.net.il;
http://www.new.netvision.net.il/.

Business Culture

GREETINGS AND COURTESIES

A warm handshake is the customary greeting, and good friends will sometimes accompany the handshake with a friendly pat on the back or shoulder. In general, Israelis do not embrace or hug upon greeting. Israelis stand quite close to one another when speaking, and they will often touch each other lightly on the arm as they talk. Many Israelis retain their reserve while in public, though many others are very expressive with their hands and bodies. Israel is so full of settlers from various backgrounds and countries that nearly anything goes—you will see all types of greetings and behaviors on the streets of any Israeli city. All are acceptable; it is one of the easiest countries in the world in which to be a stranger. A variety of languages are heard, and Israelis are accustomed to making do with hand gestures and other pantomimes to make themselves understood—and to understand others.

DECISION MAKING

Like much else in Israel, decision making is loose and flexible. In general there is little emphasis on status, rank, or title. Most managers and executives are accessible, and often have authority to make decisions on the spot. Business success will probably take time, and patience is a must. Every bureaucrat seems to have the power to change, amend, and even ignore rules and regulations which would otherwise seem to be spelled out quite clearly.

WOMEN

Women are well represented and highly visible in the workforce and in government, many of them holding positions of significant authority. They serve in the military, where their role is being continuously expanded, and overall discrimination seems to be less evident than in many other countries where they supposedly enjoy equality. Foreign businesswomen should experience few difficulties conducting business as Israelis are quite accustomed to dealing with women. Israeli society remains, however, male-dominated; the Hebrew word for 'woman' is exactly the same as the word for 'wife'.

MEETINGS

There are no hard and fast rules, although foreign businesspeople should generally make prior appointments for meetings, and should make every attempt to be on time. Be aware, however, that the frenzied and harried pace of business will sometimes require that your appointments run late, or that other distractions will dictate the actual time of appointments. In general, business discussions proceed slowly, often interrupted by coffee and small talk; and it is unwise to attempt to speed this process along. However, meetings do not drag on needlessly—and almost never over long lunches. Instead, they are conducted at the place of business, in a frank and straightforward manner. Terms and potential problems are openly discussed before reaching agreement. Despite the otherwise fast pace of business, most Israelis do not like to conduct meetings by telephone, preferring instead a face to face meeting. They will be well prepared and ready to do business, and foreign businesspeople should also be well prepared and knowledgeable about the discussions.

BUSINESS ATTIRE

Israeli business attire tends toward the informal, although Israelis are very fashion conscious and always try to wear what is in style. Use your best judgment. Formal attire is almost never required. Many Israeli businessmen wear slacks and open-collared shirts to the office, but business suits are becoming more common. Women generally wear conservative suits or dresses. Remember that most of the year the weather remains somewhat humid and warm, except in the winter months between December and March. In synagogues, women should wear long sleeves and skirts or dresses that cover the knees, and men should wear a head covering.

Business Centers
Tel Aviv

CITY VIEW

Tel Aviv is Israel's business capital, as well as its fashion and media capital. A huge, modern city, Tel Aviv attracts the cosmopolitan set of Israel and offers an exciting flair. Packed with culture as well as beaches, the city evokes comparisons with Rio de Janeiro as it offers a bit of everything, including multi-ethnicity. However, its age-old setting surrounded with tradition and history, might make Tel Aviv that much more interesting.

AIRPORT

Ben Gurion International Airport to City Center

The airport lies 12 miles (20 km.) from the city. A coach (#475) operated by Egged leaves every 15 to 20 minutes for Tel Aviv's central bus station, where a taxi can then be hailed. The bus fare costs approximately NIS6 and runs between 4a.m. and midnight. An alternative in the form of United Tours shuttle bus #222 departs hourly for the El Al City Terminal (in Tel Aviv's central rail station) as well as to the major hotels along the seaside for a fare of NIS10. An El Al bus will also take El Al's arriving passengers to the airport terminal in Tel Aviv. Buses take between 30 minutes to an hour to get to their various destinations.

Passengers can find a taxi stand outside the terminal, which offers set fares of about NIS50 and will help locate the proper taxi to your destination. One can expect a 30- to 40-minute ride. *Sheruts*, or shared taxis, offer a cheaper alternative for longer distance jaunts to Haifa or Jerusalem, for example. Each passenger pays his/her own fixed rate, depending on exact destination.

Airline Numbers

Aer Lingus	(3) 525-3444
Aerolineas Argentinas	(3) 652-253
Air Canada	(3) 510-0579, 527-3781
Air France	(3) 664-4333
Air New Zealand	(3) 527-9255
Air Sinai	(3) 510-4281
Alitalia	(3) 544-9922
American Airlines	(3) 510-4322
Arkia	(2) 541-2222, 692-222
Austrian Airlines	(3) 653-535
British Airways	(3) 510-1581
Cathay Pacific	(3) 523-0414
Czech Airlines	(3) 523-8825
Delta Airlines	(3) 290-972
Eastern Airlines	(3) 234-147
El Al	(3) 514-1222
Iberian Airlines	(3) 290-976
KLM	(3) 527-2722
Lufthansa	(3) 510-1621
Olympic	(3) 294-381
Qantas	(3) 652-163

Israel

SAA .... (3) 510-2828
Sabena ....(3) 654-411
SAS ....(3) 510-1177
Swissair ....(3) 510-2626
Tarom Rumanian Airlines............................... (3) 662-030
Tower Air ....(3) 659-421
Turkish Air .... (3) 652-333
United Airlines ....(3) 544-9555
Varig.. (3) 650-567

HOTELS

Top-end

Carlton; 10 Eliezer Peri St.; tel: (3) 520-1818; fax: (3) 527-1043; seaside location; restaurant; conference/banquet facilities; videoconference capability; executive club; business packages; secretarial service; in-room modem/fax connection; 24-hour room service; laundry/dry cleaning; valet; medical facilities; corporate rates; sauna; pool.

Dan Panorama; Charles Clore Park; tel: (3) 519-0190; fax: (3) 517-1777; email: danhtls@danhotels.co.il; city center location; restaurants; conference facilities (up to 2500); secretarial service; corporate rates; free shuttle service; health club/fitness; massage; sauna; pool; whirlpool; sea sports.

Dan Tel Aviv; 99 Hayarkon Street; tel: (3) 520-2525; fax: (3) 524-9755; near city center; restaurant; conference facilities (up to 500); secretarial service; in-room modem/fax connection; executive business center; business lounge; corporate rates; fitness; sauna; pools; whirlpool; US$206+.

Hilton Tel Aviv; Hayarkon Street, Independence Park; tel: (3) 520-2222; fax: (3) 527-2711; Telex: 33-556; seaside location; 5 restaurants; business center; meeting/banquet facilities (up to 2000); in-room modem/fax lines; Sabbath elevator; on-call doctor; fitness; pool; tennis; boating; US$220+.

Ramada Continental; 121 Hayarkon Street; tel: (3) 527-2626; fax: (3) 521-5588; seaside location; restaurant; conference facilities; secretarial service; in-room modem/fax connection; corporate rates; fitness; sauna; pool; whirlpool.

Expensive

Alexander All Suites; 3 Habakook Street; tel: (3) 546-2222; fax: (3) 546-9346; email: alexanho@netvision.net.il; near exhibition grounds; restaurant; meeting facilities; secretarial service; in-room safe; fitness; sauna; pool.

Kfar Maccabiah Hotel; Ramat-Gan; tel: (3) 671-5715; fax: (3) 574-4678; adjacent to park and sports and country club complex; restaurants; coffee bar; cafeteria; congress center; US$124+.

Marina; 167 Hayarkon Street; tel: (3) 521-1777; fax: (3) 521-1770; seaside location; conference facilities; secretarial service; in-room safe; corporate rates; pool; US$115+.

Moriah Plaza; 155 Hayarkon Street; tel: (3) 527-1515; fax: (3) 527-1065; city center; restaurant; conference facilities; secretarial service; pool; US$120+.

Yamit Park Plaza; tel: (3) 671-5715; fax: (3) 574-4678; located on seaside promenade and city center; Planet Hollywood restaurant; buffet breakfast; business services; banquet facilities; pool; jacuzzi; US$125+.

Moderate

City; 9 Mapo Street; tel: (3) 524-6253; fax: (3) 546-7687; city center; conference facilities; secretarial service; in-room modem/fax connection; US$75+.

Metropolitan; 11-15 Trumpeldor Street; tel: (3) 519-2727; fax: (3) 517-2626; 4-star hotel; city center; restaurant; conference facilities; secretarial service; in-room modem/fax connection; corporate rates; pool; US$92+.

Top Hotel; 36 Ben Yehuda Street; tel: (3) 517-0941; fax: (3) 546-7687; city center; meeting facilities; secretarial service; in-room modem/fax connection.

MEDICAL CARE

Refer to the "Jerusalem Post" newspaper for after-hours pharmacies and emergency medical facilities.

HEALTH CLUB

California Health Club; 10 Shitrit Hadar Yossef, Tel Aviv.

City Gym; 36 Harakevet, Tel Aviv.

Nelson Michal; 10 Ben Yehuda, Tel Aviv.

Olympus; 1 Alexander Yanai, Tel Aviv.

AUTO RENTAL

Note: Cars traveling in less frequented tourist areas are at risk. Vehicles have been damaged, rental cars being popular targets. Roads in Gaza and the West Bank are of poor quality.

Autorent; 42 Haatzmaut Road.; tel: (3) 632-3660.

Avis; reservations, tel: (3) 272-346; fax: (3) 271-752; 12 Hamasger in Tel Aviv, tel: (3) 636-0000; fax: (3) 687-1169; Tel Aviv airport, tel: (3) 977-3208, (3) 971-2315, 113 Hayarkon St., (3) 527-1752, (3) 527-2314; Jerusalem: 22 King David St., (2) 6249-0014; fax: (2) 624-3552.

Budget; reservations, tel: (3) 562-3111; fax: (3) 561-1549; Hayarkon Str. 99 - Dan Tlv Hotel, tel: (3) 524-5233, fax: (3) 524-5234; Tel Aviv airport, (3) 971-1504, fax: (3) 971-1522; Jerusalem: 8 King David Street; (2) 248-991, fax: (2) 625-9456.

Europcar; 126 Hayarkon; tel: (3) 527-3434.

Hertz; reservations, (3) 684-1000; fax: (3) 561-3239; Tel Aviv airport, tel: (3) 977-2444; Tel Aviv Hilton Hotel, tel: (3) 523-8588; Dan Panorama Hotel, tel: (3) 517-3554; Atarim Station, tel: (3) 522-3322; Jerusalem: 18 King David Street, tel: (2) 231-351; Hyatt Hotel Jerusalem, tel: (2) 8115-069.

Sun Tours Rent a Car; 125 Hayarkon; tel: (3) 523-7017.

WORLD TRADE CENTER

World Trade Center Israel, Tel-Aviv
Industry House
29 Hamered Street
Tel-Aviv, 61500 Israel
tel: (3) 519-8815; fax: (3) 519-8770
email: trade@industry.org.il
website: http://www.industry.org.il

CHAMBER OF COMMERCE

Chamber of Commerce, Tel Aviv
84 Hahashmona'im
Tel Aviv

Italy

At a Glance

THE PEOPLE

Population .... 56,735,130 (July 1999 est.)
Growth Rate .... -0.08% (1999 est.)
Life Expectancy ....78.51 years (born 1999)
Infant Mortality ..... 6.3 deaths/1,000 live births (1999 est.)

Ethnic Composition

Caucasian (southern European) 99%
Other 1%

Religious Composition

Roman Catholic.. 98%
Other and non-affiliated.. 2%

Languages Spoken

Italian (official), German, French, Slovene

Education and Literacy

Education is state-funded and compulsory between the ages of 6 and 14. The adult literacy rate is 97 percent.

Labor Force

Total: 22,851,000
By occupation: services 61%, industry 32%, agriculture 7%

THE ECONOMY

Italy is one of the "trillion dollar" economies of Europe and a member of the G7 economic powers. Its economy is rooted in free enterprise but with substantial government intervention. Lacking in many natural resources, Italy imports the bulk of its energy and raw materials. Its largely industrial north continues to outpace the agrarian south where unemployment often reaches 20 percent. Italy's membership in the E.U. has been of great benefit to the nation by forcing the central government to achieve relative economic stability. With full use of the Euro coming in 2002, Italy will finally have a currency that will function effectively in international markets. The most pressing challenges facing Rome are the modernization of the nation's communication and transportation infrastructures along with a restructuring of labor practices. All three areas must be corrected if Italy is to remain globally competitive and near the top of the international economic listings.

Exports .... US$243 billion (f.o.b., 1998)
Imports .... US$202 billion (f.o.b., 1998)
Total GDP .... US$1.181 trillion (1998 est.)
GDP Per Capita .... US$20,800 (1998 est.)
Unemployment .... 12.5% (1998 est.)
Inflation Rate .... 1.8% (1998 est.)

Top Export Partners

E.U., United States, OPEC nations

Top Import Partners

E.U., OPEC nations, United States

Top Exports

Metals, textiles and clothing, production machinery, motor vehicles, transportation equipment, chemicals.

Top Imports

Industrial machinery, electric power, chemicals, transport equipment, petroleum, fuel, metals, food, agricultural products.

BUSINESS WORKWEEK

Offices

Monday to Friday 8:30a.m. to 12:30p.m. and 3:30p.m. to 7:30p.m. Some Italian firms have just a two-hour lunch break.

Banks

Monday to Friday 8:30a.m. to 1:30p.m. and from 3p.m. to 4:30p.m.

Government

Monday to Friday 8:30a.m. to 1:30p.m. and from 2:30p.m. to 3:30p.m.

Retail

Monday to Friday 10a.m. to 6p.m., slightly shorter hours over the weekend. Large department stores and retailers may stay open later in urban areas.

Note: Most businesses that do not cater to the tourist trade close down in August for vacation.

HOLIDAYS

New Year's Day...January 1
Epiphany ....January 6
Easter Monday ....April 5*
Liberation Day .... April 25
Labor Day...May 1
Assumption... August 15
All Saints' Day ....November 1
National Unity Day..November 5
Immaculate Conception....................................December 8
Christmas Day..December 25
St. Stephen's Day...December 26
*Date may vary by year.

CLIMATE

Seasons

When people speak of a Mediterranean climate, they have Italy in mind. Mild, rainy winters and hot, dry summers are the standard. Average temperatures range from between 11° and 19°C (52° - 66°F) in the winter. Summers can get as hot as 32°C (90°F). The rain usually begins at the end of October. May, June, September, and October are the best months for travel.

Regions

The region of Foggia experiences the lowest rainfall (average of 18 inches). The summer brings hot winds from the south known as *La Bora*, which affects the Adriatic's currents and sometimes cause Venice to flood. Sirocco winds, originating from Africa's Sahara Desert, bring dust along with the heat.

In winter, the Venetian canals have been known to freeze solid, and the Naples gardens have suffered from frost as well. During Rome's summer it gets humid and muggy, as do the semitropical western regions along the Liguria Sea.

Cold northern winters are expected, but Sardinia and Sicily can also get snow. Calabria, at the tip of "the boot," gets enough snow in the winter to maintain a ski resort.

Italy

Italy

Regions of Italy	
1	Valle D'Aosta
2	Piemonte
3	Lombardia
4	Trentino-Alto Adige
5	Veneto
6	Friuli-V
7	Liguria
8	Emilia-Romagna
9	Toscana
10	Umbria
11	Marche
12	Lazio
13	Abruzzi
14	Molise
15	Campania
16	Puglia
17	Basilicata
18	Calabria
19	Sicilia
20	Sardegna

*Provinces have the same name as their capitals.

SM Santa Barbara, CA

©2001 Magellan Geographix

Money & Banking

Currency

The currency of Italy is the Italian Lira (Lit).

Denominations

The Lira (Lit) comes in coins of Lit1,000, 500, 200, 100, 50, 20; and banknotes of Lit1,000, 2,000, 5,000, 10,000, 20,000, Lit50,000, and 100,000.

Traveler's Checks and Credit Cards

It is quite easy to exchange traveler's checks and major foreign currency at banks, hotels, foreign exchange bureaus, hotels, and foreign exchange kiosks at the airports. Banks offer the most favorable exchange rates. Traveler's checks may receive a better exchange rate than cash.

American Express, Visa, MasterCard, Eurocard, and Diners Club are widely accepted. You can get cash advances from your credit card on many of the automated teller machines (ATM). Long term business visitors should set up a local checking account, and get an ATM card. The most favorable exchange rates will given for credit card and ATM transactions. Transactions on check and credit card can be conducted in Euros if so requested. Keep all exchange receipts for reconversion at departure.

Foreign Exchange Offices:

American Express (Rome); Piazza di Spagna 38; tel: (06) 72-782.

American Express (Milan); Via Brera 3.

Thomas Cook (Rome); Via Barberini 21; tel: (06) 482-8082.

Essential Terms

English	Italian
Yes No	Sí No
Good morning Hello (daytime) Hello (evening) Hello (telephone)	Buon giorno Buona sera Buona notte Ciao
Good-bye	Arrivederci
Please	Per favore/per piacere
Thank you	Grazie
Pleased to meet you	Piacere. Lieto di conoscerti
Excuse me; I'm sorry	Mi scusi
My name is _____	Mi chiamo_____
I don't understand	Non capisco
Do you speak English?	Parla inglese?

Travel

VISA AND PASSPORT

A passport that is valid for a minimum six months beyond expected entry date is required of all visitors except for nationals of Austria, Belgium, France, Germany, Liechtenstein, Luxembourg, Malta, Monaco, Netherlands, Portugal, San Marino, Spain, and Switzerland, all of whom may enter with only a national ID card.

Italy is a member of the Schengen group, which is a collection of nations who in March of 1995 declared themselves borderless. The others in this group are Belgium, France, Germany, Luxembourg, The Netherlands, Portugal, and Spain. Any traveler who holds a valid passport or other travel documents that are recognized by all Schengen member nations need not have a visa to travel in any of these countries. There are two caveats, however:

• If you have tickets for onward travel to a nation that does require a visa of you, it may also be required of you for entry into the Schengen nation.

•

• Each Schengen nation retains the right to require a visa of any national normally exempted by the group as a whole.

Following is a list of nations normally exempt from the visa requirement (E.U. nationals are automatically exempt): Andorra, Argentina, Australia, Brazil, Brunei, Canada, Chile, Costa Rica, Cyprus, Czech Republic, Ecuador, El Salvador, Guatemala, Honduras, Hungary, Iceland, Israel, Japan, Jamaica, Liechtenstein, Malawi, Malaysia, Malta, Mexico, Monaco, New Zealand, Nicaragua, Norway, Panama, Paraguay, Poland, Republic of Korea, San Marino, Singapore, Slovak Republic, Slovenia, Switzerland, Turkey (only if a permanent resident of a Schengen country), Uruguay, U.S., Vatican City, and Venezuela.

Passengers in transit who do not leave the airport and who continue their journey aboard the first connecting aircraft within 48 hours, and who are holding confirmed tickets and other documents for onward travel, are also exempt from the need for a visa. However, if you are a national of one of the following countries, you must have a visa with you at all times: Afghanistan, Bangladesh, Congo (Dem. Rep.), Eritrea, Ethiopia, Ghana, India, Iran, Iraq, Nigeria, Pakistan, Senegal, Somalia, and Sri Lanka.

Visa-free travel throughout the Schengen states is valid for a duration of 90 days maximum within a 6-month period, commencing upon initial entry date into a Schengen country. All visitors are required to register with Italian police within three days of entering the country; most hotels will perform this service for you.

DEPARTURE FORMALITIES

You must declare in advance if you plan to export the equivalent of Lit20million (US$15,540) by filling out a V2 declaration form. Airport departure fees are included in the airfare.

CUSTOMS ENTRY (PERSONAL)

Duty-free

Passengers over 17 years of age arriving from E.U. countries with duty-paid goods:

Tobacco: 800 cigarettes and 400 cigarillos or 200 cigars and 1kg of tobacco

Alcohol: 90 liters of wine (including up to 60 liters of sparkling wine); 10 liters of spirits; 20 liters of intermediate products (such as fortified wine); 110 liters of beer

Other: goods up to a value of Lit500,000

Passengers over 17 year of age from other countries, or from EU countries with goods bought duty free:

• Tobacco: 200 cigarettes or 100 cigarillos or 50 cigars or 250g of tobacco

• Liquor; 750ml of spirits (over 22% proof), or 2 liters of fortified or sparkling wine

• Other: 60g of perfume and 250ml of eau de toilette; 500g of coffee or 200g of coffee extract; 100g of tea or 40g of tea extract

Note: Although there are now no legal limits imposed on importing duty-paid tobacco and alcoholic products from one E.U. country to another, travelers may be questioned at customs if they exceed the above amounts and may be asked to prove that the goods are for personal use only.

IMMUNIZATION

Foreigners do not need proof of vaccination unless arriving from a region of known infection or epidemic. Tetanus and hepatitis A inoculations are advised for extended stays in rural areas of Italy.

TIPPING

Taxi

Expect to tip the taxi driver 500 lire or 15 percent of the fare, whichever is more.

Porters

Porters usually receive 2000 lire per piece of luggage.

Hotels

Service charges are applied directly to the hotel bill. However, you could consider leaving the maid 1,500 lire per day per visit at the end of your stay.

Restaurants

All restaurants include a cover charge per person (pane e coperto) and often a 12 percent service charge as well. For excellent service in restaurants, tip the waiter an additional 5 percent. If a wine steward is involved, tip 10 percent of the cost of the wine.

EMERGENCY INFORMATION

Police and Crime

Italy as a whole is a relatively safe country, but be careful in its more urban areas. Rome, especially, is suffering from increasing crime.

Foreign business visitors are often the special target of thieves. Consequently, purses, laptops, and briefcases will require additional security. Do not leave valuables in cars or on tables in cafés. Keep non-essential valuables locked in hotel safes when not in use. Use credit cards and travel checks when possible to avoid carrying large sums of cash.

Walk with your bag or briefcase away from the street to avoid having it snatched away by thieves passing on the ubiquitous motorbikes. Be aware that groups of children may act as distractions while others (*scippatori*—the snatchers) steal goods from bags and pockets. Gypsy children often wave cardboard or paper signs in front of unwary tourists while their cohorts cleverly clean pockets during the melee. Be extra careful on public transportation, airports, and train stations. Avoid dimly lit streets at night and know your destination before departure.

Women can walk around freely, but they are advised to travel in groups at night and to avoid talking to strangers. Italian men may prove a bit more aggressive in speech and physical contact. It is best to ignore advances, and if things begin to get out of hand, protest loudly. Police are quite helpful in such situations.

Visiting business people should note that criminal activity in "legitimate" business still exists, but to a much lesser degree than 20 years ago. Make sure you know with whom you are dealing before transacting business or signing contracts.

Emergency Numbers

Numbers function nationwide.

Police.. 112
Ambulance 113
Fire 115

Health

Traveling in Italy poses no serious health risk, and the only problematic illness is sinus problems due to the heavy pollution in cities. Tap water is potable. Food is safe and excellent to eat. Allow yourself time to acclimate before fully indulging. The sun proves strong in the summer and the climate hot, so use protection.

Italy has a national health service, but the private sector provides better medical help. There are no medical charges for expatriates with adequate insurance. Most doctors are multi-lingual, and medical costs are reasonable.

Health spas can be found throughout the country, some dating from the Roman era. For more information on medical centers, including phone numbers, please see the "Business Centers" section at the end of this chapter.

INTERNAL TRAVEL

AIR

All major cities are served by domestic carriers, including Alitalia (AZ), and there are over 30 domestic airports. However, internal air travel is expensive in Italy, and Italiana generally favor the trains and buses for domestic transit. For details regarding schedules and fares, contact the airlines directly, or ENIT, the Italian State Tourist Office (see "Travel Assistance" section following for address and phone).

TAXI

Services are available both within and between all cities. Cabs can only be contracted at taxi stands, often located beside major hotels, or by telephone. If you have to phone for a cab, the meter starts as soon as the driver gets the call, and not when he actually picks you up. Charges are displayed on a rate card posted in the cab. Fares should be metered or a price decided upon before leaving.

In the case of Venice, cabs (gondolas) float on water and are known as water taxis; these do not have meters; as such, negotiate a fare before leaving the dock. Expect about L20,000 for even a short distance. Fares rise after 10p.m.

Write and translate all directions for drivers (or gondoliers) onto paper, as drivers may not know exactly where your destination is located. Carry a map.

AUTO

Car rental is available in most of Italy's cities. It can prove very expensive (US$350 per week for a compact car) through the major car rental firms. Generally, small local firms will rent cars at a better rate, but only locally. There are numerous discount-rate fly/drive deals available in Italy, some of which must be arranged in advance while the traveler is still outside the country. A credit card and valid driver's license is required for rental, as is insurance.

Italy has an excellent network of roadways and major highways, some of which assess tolls. Fuel can be expensive, particularly in the countryside, and many stations are closed between noon and 3p.m. Roadside assistance is available from the Auto Club of Italy (ACI) simply by dialing 116 at the nearest telephone booth.

Driving in rural areas remains fairly civilized, but urban driving—especially in Rome—can be terrifying. It is not recommended for any but the most experienced visitors. (Visitors may also rent motorbikes, but with the same provisos as rental cars.) One can expect to find most of the same major auto rental agencies in Italy as in the rest of the E.U.

TRAIN

Rail service links all portions of the country, except the islands, which are connected to the mainland with ferries. Do not expect trains to run nearly as punctual as in other parts of Europe; however, it still beats road travel. Both state and private companies provide services that are cheap, simple, and efficient.

Intercity and Eurocity trains offer the quickest mode of rail transport because they serve only the major stops. These lines connect with the major European cities and they are commonly used for overnight business travel.

Many different classes of travel are available. For most services, prices are decided based upon distance. Special fares also exist that offer unlimited service for one price for a limited time:

- Italy Railcard passes offer unlimited travel throughout the entire system of the Italian State Railways. Bearers are entitled to passage on any Eurocity or Intercity train, and on the 'Eurostar Italia', for periods of 8, 15, 21, or 30 days.
- The Italy Flexcard offers the same type of arrangement, with a validity of 4, 8, or 12 days travel within a one-month period.
- The Kilometric Card gives discounts based on the number of people traveling as a group and the total distance traveled.

For more information, contact:

Italian State Railways (FS); www.fs-on-line.com

METRO

Rome and Milan both offer extensive subway services that enable one to get across town faster than on any other transport during rush hours.

In Rome, there are two lines:

- Metropolitana A, from Via Ottaviano by way of Termini station to Via Anagnina, and also linking up with the new Ottaviano-San Pietro route
- Metropolitana B, running between Termini Station, by way of Exhibition City (Via Laurentina), and then onward to Rebibbia.

Passengers may purchase both daily and monthly passes. In Rome, ATAC Service at Piazza del Cinquecento sells tickets for all the different modes of public transport. The Rome Metro stops running at 11:30p.m.

In Milan, the metro runs until midnight. Tickets in Milan will cost about L1500 and can be purchased at the Metro stations as well as at bars and tobacconists. Both metro systems are highly recommended for daily commuting.

BUS/TRAM

Intercity: Good services provide connections between all towns and cities. The buses are swift and dependable and reach the more remote destinations not accessed by the trains.

Urban/Local: An extensive network of local buses exists, including services on Sicily and Sardinia. Buses generally provide connections with rail services in remote areas.

In Rome, bus service is extensive, and the lines' itineraries are designed to complement both the metro and the tram services in the city. The fare structure is also integrated among the various modes. The traveler can buy a weekly pass or a flat-fare ticket from a station or roadside machine.

For specific routes, bus fares are usually purchased in booklets of five or multiples thereof and are inserted into a validation mechanism when the traveler boards the bus. Further information can be obtained at the ATAC booth outside the Termini station.

Rome, Milan, Naples, and Turin also have tram operations. Rome's is a 28km (17mi) system with eight routes. Trolleybuses also operate in several other towns.

WATER TRAVEL

Numerous automobile and passenger ferries run throughout the year between Italian ports, the principals being Venice, Genoa, La Spezia, Civitavecchia, Naples, Messina, Cagliari, Bari, Pescara, Ancona, Trieste, Palermo, Catania, Livorno, and Brindisi.

Both hydrofoil and regular boat services make the runs between the mainland and Italy's islands of Capri, Elba, Giglio, Sardinia, Sicily, and the Aeolian Islands.

In Venice, one has almost no choice but to take some sort of water transport if one plans to go to the city center. Waterbuses (vaporetti and motoscafi) and water taxis are available. The waterbuses stop by the docks every few minutes. Bus #1 travels between Piazza San Marco and Piazzale Roma with 13 intermediate stops. Unlimited day or week passes are available from ticket booths on the boat platforms if you plan to use the boats often. Otherwise, a single ticket will cost about L4,500 for most routes.

Italy's many port towns also serve both Mediterranean and Atlantic cruise ship lines.

TRAVEL ASSISTANCE

Ente Nazionale Italiano per il Turismo (ENIT)
Via Marghera 2, 00185 Rome
tel: (6) 49-711; fax: (6) 446-3379
email: sedecentrale.enit@interbusiness.it
website: www.enit.it

Communications

DIALING CODES IN ITALY

International country code: [39]

Selected city codes: Brindisi (0831), Capri (081), Como (031), Florence (055), Genoa (010), Milan (02), Naples (081), Padova (049), Palermo (091), Pisa (050), Rome (06), Turin (011), Venice (041), Verona (045), Vatican City (06).

Dialing Italy from Overseas

The city codes in Italy recently changed to include a preceding zero even when dialing from abroad. To dial Italy from overseas, dial your country's international dialing code, then 39 (the country code for Italy), then the city code preceded by a zero, and finally the number. If you were dialing Florence from the United States, for example, you would begin with 011, then 39, plus 055 (the city code for Florence), and finally the number of the person or office you were trying to reach.

CALLING WITHIN ITALY

Local Calls

Calls within a city must also include a preceding zero in the area code of that city in which you find yourself. For example, if you are in Rome, you must now dial 06 (Rome's area code) + the local number.

Long Distance within Italy

Long distance dialing between cities in Italy remains unchanged. Dial 0 + area code + number.

International Calls

Direct international calls can be made from public phones using phonecards. Dial 00 to get out of Italy, then the respective country and area codes, and the number.

A 24-hour Telecom office in Milan is located at Galleria V. Emanuele II. Calls may also be placed from the Stazione Centrale between 8a.m. and 9:30p.m.

PAY PHONES

Public Telephones

The majority of pay phones accept Lit100 and Lit200 and *gettoni*, tokens that are available at tobacco shops and newsstands.

Calling Cards

Cards are available at post offices, hotels, and some newsstands.

CELLULAR PHONES

Telecom Italia Mobile offers 3 different systems in the cellular realm, including GSM, RTMS-450, and ETACS. Omnitel-Pronto Italia also offers GSM cellular service to Italy.

Note: Your home country cell phone may not work in this country. If not, we recommend that you rent an international cell phone *before* you leave home. A major US-based cell phone rental provider is **IMC WorldCell**. For information see "International Cell Phone Rentals" on page 14.

CALL BACK

You can (potentially) save significant sums when calling in Italy by using a call back service. For a list of callback services, please refer to the "Communications" section in the *Global Road Warrior* Introduction.

Fees for call back services vary widely, depending on the company and the type of service required. Be sure to check with these companies before leaving to compare rates.

PHONE JACKS

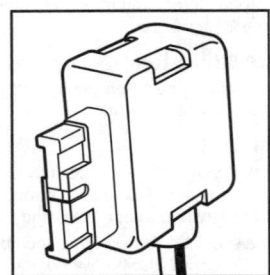

Plug adaptors are available through **iGo Corporation.** (See "Electrical and Telephone Adaptors" on page 19.)

FAX

Most hotels have fax machines and the service is generally good. Italian businesses do not like to receive faxes, however, and they should only be used for international communication.

POSTAL SERVICES

Mail service is very poor, taking five days to reach destinations and Italy, and up to three weeks to reach North America. Many people use the Vatican City post office, which is generally much more efficient.

Hours of service

Monday to Friday 8a.m. to 2p.m., Saturday 8a.m. to 1p.m.

Vatican City: Monday to Friday 8:30a.m. to 7p.m. (closed Wednesdays), Saturday 8:30a.m. to 6p.m.

Milan; via Cordusio 4, off Piazza Cordusio; Monday to Friday 8a.m. to 8p.m.; Saturday 8a.m. to 2p.m.

TELEGRAMS

Telegrams can be sent from post offices. They can be expensive.

Business Services

COURIER SERVICES

Airborne Express Italia S.R.L.;

• Milan: c/o s.e.a. - Palazzina Spedizionieri, Aeroporto Malpensa, 21010 Varese; tel: (2) 4009-9775

Rome: Via Ivo Oliveti n. 3, 00054 Fiumicino; tel: (6) 6502-9149.

DHL International S.R.L.; Viale Milanofiori, Palazzo U3 Strada 5, Rozzano (MI) 20089; tel: 167-345-345 (toll free) or 02-57571;

Opening hours: Mon-Fri 08:30-18:30; Sat-Sun Closed; Holidays Closed.

• DHL Florence: Via Buozzi 5 Fizzonasco (MI) 20090; Opening hours; Mon-Fri 07:30-19:30; Sat-Sun Closed; Holidays Closed

• DHL Rome; Via Carlo Botta 41; Roma (Labicana) 00184; Opening hours: Mon-Fri 08:30-18:30; Sat-Sun Closed; Holidays Closed

• DHL Verona; Via Mezzacampagna, 56 Verona; 37061; Opening hours: Mon-Fri 08:30-19:00; Sat 08:30-11:45; Sun Closed; Holidays Closed

Federal Express; 167-833-040.

UPS Italia; Via G. Fantoli, 15/2, Milan; tel: (02) 50791; fax: (02) 5540-0180.

• Milan: (070) 22-079.

• Florence and Venice: (079) 269-750.

• Rome: (0931) 757-358/9.

OFFICE SERVICE

Omtra srl.; 13, v. Pesaro, Milan; tel: (2) 664-2951; fax: (2) 6642-9549.

Regus Business Centre srl; 21, Monte de Pieta, Milano; tel: (2) 863-371; fax: (2) 8633-7400.

TRANSLATION SERVICES

CRL-Cooperativa Romana Lingue; Via Laurentina 567; tel: (06) 5920459; fax: (06) 5917916.

Translation Agency S.A.S.; conference interpreting for business meetings and trips; personnel for trade shows and fairs in Italy and abroad; Via Repubblica, 21, 56040 Casaloldo (MN), Italy; fax: (376) 748-165; email: translag@mail.wrnet.it

Electrical

Current
220 volts AC, 50Hz.

ELECTRIC PLUGS

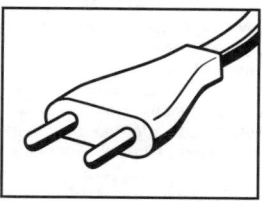

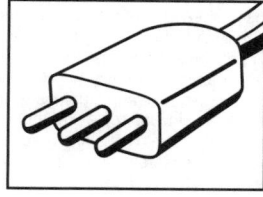

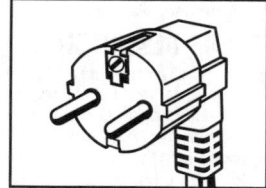

Plug adaptors are available through **iGo Corporation.** (See "Electrical and Telephone Adaptors" on page 19.)

Technical Support

HARDWARE/SOFTWARE VENDOR SUPPORT

Apple/Claris; tel: (02) 2732-6292/3/4/5/6 (Apple Assistance); (in Switzerland) tel: [41] (800) 833-310; (in the U.K.) tel: [44] (990) 127-753; (in the U.S.) tel: [1] (800) 500-7078; http://www.apple.com/.

AST; (in the U.S.) tel: [1] (817) 232-9824 (International Technical Support); (in Ireland) tel: [353] (61) 492-222; (in the U.S.) tel: [1] (949) 727-4141; http://www.ast.com/.

Compaq/Digital; tel: (02) 5759-01; fax: (02) 824-2015; (01) 67825012; (in Switzerland) tel: [41] (22) 709-5330; fax: [41] (22) 709-5391 (Geneva); tel: [41] (1) 801-2507; fax: [41] (1) 801-2172 (Zurich); (General U.S.) tel: (281) 518-2000; http://www.compaq.com/.

Corel; tel: (02) 452-812-08 (WordPerfect Business Applications); (in Germany) tel: [49] (180) 425-8210 (TS Word Perfect-32 bit); (in the U.S.) tel: [1] (716) 871-2325 (Ask to be Forwarded to Appropriate Program); http://www.corel.com/.

Dell; (in Germany) tel: [49] (61) 039-710; (Dell- Europe) tel: [44] (134) 474-8000; (in the U.S.) tel: [1] (512) 338-4400; fax: [1] (512) 728-3330; http://www.dell.com/.

Filemaker/Claris; (in Germany) tel: [49] (180) 525-8166 (Info-line); fax: [49] (180) 567-2233; tel: [49] (180) 523-

6423; (in the U.S.) tel: [1] (800) 965-9090; http://www.claris.com/.

Gateway 2000; (in Ireland) tel: [353] (1) 797-2000; (in the U.S.) tel: [1] (605) 232-2191; fax: [1] (605) 232-2023; http:/ /www.g2k.com/.

Hewlett Packard; tel: (02) 264 10350; (in Switzerland) tel: [41] (22) 780-8111; (in the U.S.) tel: [1] (408) 246-4300; http://www.hp.com/.

IBM; tel: (06) 00-7666; tel: 1670-16338 (toll free within Italy) fax: (06) 00-7151; fax: (06) 00-7152; fax: (06) 600-7153; (in Switzerland) tel: [41] (22) 310-0418 (in French); (in the U.S.) tel: [1] (919) 517-2800; (U.S. Main Office) tel: [1] 914-765-1900; http://www.ibm.com/.

Microsoft; tel: (02) 703-921; fax: (02) 7039-2020; (02) 7039-8398 (Technical Support); (in Switzerland) tel: [41] (848) 858-868; fax [41] (1) 831-0869; (in the U.S.) [1] (425) 635-7222; http://www.microsoft.com/.

NEC; tel: 1-678-20062 (UltraCare Support); (in the U.S.) [1] (916) 388-0101 (Main Switchboard); http://www.nec.com/.

Novell; (in Germany) tel: [49] (211) 563-2777 (System support); tel: [49] (6196) 904-477; fax: [49] (211) 563-2772; (in Switzerland) tel: [41] (1) 308-4747; fax: [41] (1) 302-0401; (in the U.S.) tel: [1] (408) 434-2300; fax: [1] (408) 577-5775 (Worldwide Sales Headquarters); http://www.novell.com/.

Quark; (in Switzerland) tel: [41] (1) 808-7722; fax: [41] (1) 808-7799; (in the U.S.) tel: [1] (303) 894-8899; fax: [1] (303) 894-3398 (For Products Registered in the Americas); http://www.quark.com/.

Toshiba; (in Germany) tel: [49] (2131) 158-319; fax: [49] (2131) 158-558; (in Switzerland) tel: [41] (1) 946-0777; fax: [41] (1) 946-0807; (in Ireland) tel: [44] (193) 282-8828; (in the U.S.) [1] (949) 583-3000 (Corporate Headquarters); http://www.toshiba.com/.

Internet Connection

HOW TO CONNECT

Connecting to AOL and Compuserve in Italy is similar to using it when traveling outside your own area code. See the introductory section for detailed information on connecting to your account through a different phone number.

America Online
Numbers are available at keyword *international*. Be sure to get several local numbers before leaving. AOL's Global-Net service charges US$6 an hour in addition to the usual charges. Go to keyword *access* (a free area) and download the software.

Numbers
Ancona (071) 280-4597; Bari (080) 531-6139; Bergamo (035) 231-786; Bologna (051) 647-2048; Bolzano (0471) 981-783; Brescia (030) 242-0587; Catania (095) 532-557; Florence (055) 501-5540; Genoa (010) 588-162; Gorizia (048) 147-4034; Milan (02) 869-0561; Naples (081) 780-9138; Olbia (0789) 67-613; Padua (049) 807-6801; Palermo (091) 335-841; Parma (0521) 238-460; Perugia (075) 500-2357; Rimini (0541) 53-031; Rome (06) 6519-8504; Trieste (040) 938-0051; Turin (011) 533-554; Udine (0432) 295-260; Venice (041) 534-0331; Verona (045) 800-2387.

Compuserve
Numbers are available at *Go International*. The Compuserve Web-site also has a great deal of information, at http://www.compuserve.com.

Numbers
Access: Ancona (071) 280-4597; Bari (080) 531-6139;

Bergamo (035) 231-786; Bolzano (0471) 981-783; Brescia (030) 242-0587; Catania (095) 532-557; Florence (055) 501-5540; Genoa (010) 588-162; Milan (02) 2247-9532; Naples (081) 780-9138; Olbia (0789) 67-613; Padua (049) 807-6801; Parma (0521) 238-460; Rimini (0541) 53-031; Rome (06) 5195-7347; Venice (041) 534-0331, Verona (045) 800-2387.

Independent Service Providers

Many independent service providers offer discounts if you are only in town for a couple of days.

Numbers

ALINET Italia; tel: (51) 656-3611; fax: (51) 239-245; http://www.alinet.it/.

Cassiopea Network; tel: (51) 253-551; email: sysop@cassiopea.it; http://www.cassiopea.it/.

FASTnet S.R.L.; tel: (71) 290-0444 or 218-1250; fax: (71) 291-311; email: info@fastnet.it; http://www.fastnet.it/.

I.NET S.p.A.; tel: (2) 409-061; fax: (2) 4090-6262; in Rome, tel: (6) 399-541; fax: (6) 3995-4242; email: info@inet.it; http://www.inet.it/.

In.Ternet; tel: (552) 383-023; fax: (552) 303-849; http://www.ittc.it/.

Pro.Net S.R.L.; tel: (6) 664-0385; fax: (6) 664-0384; email: info@pngroup.net; http://www.pngroup.net/.

Tizeta Informatica; tel: (51) 346-346; fax: (51) 345-070; email: info@izeta.it; http://www.tizeta.it/.

WaveNet; tel: (0) 313-3640; fax: (0) 4313-3640; email: info@wavenet.it; http://www.wavenet.it/.

Business Culture

GREETINGS AND COURTESIES

Italians usually greet each other with a handshake, an elbow grasp and *ciao* (hello or good-bye). Male friends also embrace and pat backs. Persons of the same gender often walk arm in arm in public. Good friends often greet each other with kisses on both cheeks. Invitations to meet family are a mark of special favor, not extended until the third or fourth visit, and should always be accepted. All university graduates have a title and expect to be addressed as *dottore* (liberal arts), *avvocato* (law), *ingengnere* (technical field), or *professore* (academics and most medical doctors). Exchange cards only in business situations when introduced; hand a card to everyone present. To show respect, look at a card after receiving one. Have one side of your card printed in Italian. and include your title. Titles should appear on business cards. When invited into a home, bringing a gift is not expected, although the host will accept chocolates or flowers. If you are bringing flowers, take an odd number and avoid chrysanthemums (which are used to decorate graves). Also avoid red flowers that signify secrecy and passion, and yellow flowers, symbolizing jealousy.

DECISION MAKING

The decisionmaker can be hard to find, partly because she or he may not be part of the organizational structure. Most organizations base their power in one person, usually a man, who builds alliances on personal relationships. Power structures here, like those in much of the world, are multi-layered; but in Italy, the most important layers are those farthest from the public eye and are usually centered on an autocratic ruler. Negotiations should be conducted between executives of equivalent rank; though middle-level employees usually begin business relationships. Important decisions are usually not decided upon in meetings because participants may feel forced to agree in order to get along. Arguments are often a test of strength, and visitors who are not prepared for this style can easily get off track. Interruptions are frequent and haggling is common. Italians may display great disappointment when desired concessions are not made; they can readily become loud and emotional.

WOMEN

Women have always been the supreme authority at home. Although they have made recent significant inroads in business, much of the country is still run by men. For a woman to openly contradict her husband in front of strangers is the paramount insult. However, Italian women possess their own healthy degree of confidence in those business realms in which they do operate.

MEETINGS

Schedule meetings late in the morning and not too close after lunch. Written agendas are made and distributed, but few take them seriously. Allow extra meeting time; up to 20 minutes late is still considered on time, and stopping a meeting that is longer than anticipated may be viewed as rude. It is suggested that one prepare trade catalogs or business literature in Italian. Italian businesspeople prefer presentations that are informal but polished, with facts and graphs whenever relevant. They also like presenters who seem confident in themselves and their product. Business hours are usually from 9am to 1pm and 3 to 7pm. It is best to make appointments for business and governmental visits.

BUSINESS ATTIRE

Italians dress as well as they can at all times, and are proud of their position as world-class fashion-setters. Demand is often for trendy apparel, with a distinctive "American" look and a high content of natural fiber. Wear medium weight clothing with a light topcoat or raincoat in winter and light business clothing for summer. Conservative business suits are best for meetings. Dark glasses are usually removed when entering a building.

Business Centers
Rome

CITY VIEW

Rome has an image of a city that time forgot, with its colosseum and museums. In reality, the historical center is small, and most of the city has become modern and high-tech. Despite the fact that the city is teeming with people and tourists, the Italian flavor of the city yet remains.

AIRPORT

Leonardo da Vinci Airport to City Center

The airport lies 22 miles (35 km.) from the city. There are regular bus services and taxis available. If seeking a cab, bypass the taxi scouts and head for a taxi stand outside the terminal. Stick to the white and yellow cabs, which are licensed. Negotiate a fare before departing if the meter is not running. The usual fare runs around Lit60,000, which should include baggage. Expect about 45 minutes to an hour to get into town.

COTRAL buses operate to Magliana and Lepanto underground stations, and also provides a night service to Roma Tiburtina running between 1:15a.m. and 5a.m. Bus tickets cost between Lit4,500 and 7,000.

Trains also run to the airport and will take passengers directly to Rome's main rail station (Termini Station) in 30 minutes time between 7:38a.m. to 10:08p.m. on an hourly basis. Fares cost Lit15,000. Trains also run to Tiburtina Station in eastern Rome with stops in between; fares cost Lit11,400.

Airline Numbers

Aer Lingus Reservations ....(06) 481-8518
Air Canada ....(06) 422-2146
Air France...(06) 488-55-63
Air New Zealand.......................................(06) 488-07-61
Alitalia .... (06) 6-56-31
American ....(06) 474-1240
British Airways 47-99-91
Cathay Pacific ....(06) 487-01-50
Delta Airlines ....(06) 4773
Qantas..(06) 48-64-51
Singapore ....(06) 481-89-43
TWA ....(06) 67-641

HOTELS

Top-end

Eden; Via Ludovisi 49; tel: 478-121; fax: 482-1584; elegant, luxurious landmark hotel renovated in 1994; stunning views; a favorite of Hemingway, Ingrid Bergman, Fellini and other famous names; rooftop restaurant; conference facilities (up to 110); in-room safe, modem connection, VCR and CD player; heated towel racks; corporate rates; fitness; US$280-400.

Excelsior; Via V. Veneto 125; tel: 47081; fax: 482-6205; luxurious hotel host to royalty and Hollywood stars; restaurant; bar; conference facilities (up to 1000); translation, secretarial services; fax/photocopying facilities; cellular phone rental; medical services, limousine service; hair salon.

Holiday Inn Crowne Plaza Rome Minerva; Plazza Della Nunerva 69; tel: 6994-1888; fax: 679-4165; reservations: 1-800-780360; e-mail: minerva@pronet.it; centrally located; fully renovated; extremely comfortable with beautiful stained-glass lobby ceiling; restaurant; 6 conference facilities; secretarial services; fax/photocopying facilities; ISDN/modem lines; 24-hour room service; corporate rates; fitness; US$250-350.

Le Grand; Via Vittorio Emanuele Orlando 3; tel: 4709; fax: 474-7307; centrally located; a favorite with dignitaries and celebrities, rich in history; newly renovated; conference facilities; business center; translation services; modem connections; fax/photocopying facilities; non-smoking rooms available; medical services; hair salon; limousine service; US$282-1,168.

Majestic; Via Veneto 50; tel: 486841; fax: 488-0984; 19th century elegance with modern amenities and spacious rooms; restaurant; cafe; conference facilities (up to 150); secretarial services; fax/photocopying facilities; in-room safe; corporate rates; US$250-350.

Expensive

Ariston; Via Filippo Turati 16; tel 446- 5399; fax: 446-5396; email: hotelariston@hotelariston.it; conference facilities (up to 100); business center; secretarial services; fax/photocopying facilities; internet access; corporate rates; US$200-270.

D'Inghilterra; Via Bocca Di Leone 14; tel: 69981; fax: 6992-2243; near the Spanish Steps; elegant and cozy with past guests including Lizst, Mendelssohn, Mark Twain, and Hemingway; restaurant; bar; meeting facilities (up to 20); secretarial services; fax/photocopying facilities; US$180-240.

Forum; Via Tor de Conti 25; tel: 679-2446; fax: 678-6479; e-mail: forum@venere.it; elegant, exclusive hotel in the Ancient city; roof garden restaurant overlooking the Roman ruins; American bar; conference facilities; (up to 100)

corporate rates; breakfast included;US$140-200.

Giulio Cesare; Via degli Scipioni 287; tel: 321-0751; fax: 321-1736; email: giulioce@uni.net; conference facilities (up to 40); secretarial services; fax/photocopying facilities; internet access; in-room modem connection, safe; corporate rates; US$200-250.

Moderate

Alpi; tel: 444 1235; fax: 444 1257; secretarial services; fax/photocopying facilities; US$100-140.

American Palace Eur; Via Laurentina 554; tel: 541971; fax: 591-1740; restaurant; conference facilities; secretarial services; fax/photocopying facilities; corporate rates; US$110-160.

Canada; tel: 445 7770; fax: 445 0749; centrally located; elegant furnishings in a friendly atmosphere; meeting rooms; in-room safe; fax/photocopying facilities; buffet breakfast included; US$100-127.

Clodio; Via di Santa Lucia 10; tel: 372-1122; fax: 3735-0745; conference facilities (up to 70); fax/ photocopying facilities; corporate rates; US$110-150.

Delle Muse; VIa T. Salvini 18; tel: 06-808-8333; fax: 06-808-5749; located in quiet and elegant area of Parioli; recently renovated; restaurant; conference capacity (up to 40); fax/photocopying facilities; Internet access; corporate rates; US$63-160.

Grand Ritz; VIa D. Chelini 41; tel: 06-808-3751; fax: 06-8081394; located near Piazza Euclide in elegant Parioli district; very modern, first-class hotel; conference facilities (up to 500); secretarial services; fax/photocopying facilities; in-room modem connection; US$117-219.

Hermitage; Via Eugenio Vayna 12; tel: 686-4231; fax: 687-6976; conference facilities; corporate rates; US$110-180.

Internazionale; Via Sistina 79; tel: 678 4686: fax: 678 4764; corporate rates; US$110-150.

Mondial; Via Torino 127; tel: 474-6451; fax: 481-5832; conference facilities (up to 25); secretarial services; fax/photocopying facilities; in-room modem connection; corporate rates; US$110-150.

Princess; tel: 664931; fax: 664 9384; e-mail: info@hotelprincess.com; 2 restaurants; bar; conference facility (up to 300); gift shops; corporate rates; 2 pools; US$120-150.

Santa Costanza; Viale XXI Aprile 4; tel: 446-7230; fax: 446-9142; conference facilities (up to 50); in-room modem connection; corporate rates; US$110-150.

Tre Api; tel: 678 3500; fax: 678 8478; secretarial services; fax/photocopying facilities; corporate rates; US$80-120.

MEDICAL CARE

Santo Sprito; Lungotevere, Sassia 1; tel: (06) 68-351; emergency: (06) 462-371.

HEALTH CLUBS

American Workout; 5 Via G. Amendola; tel: (06) 474-62-99.

Largo Somalia; tel: (06) 86-21-24-11.

Navona Health Center; 39 Via dei Banchi Nuovi; tel: (06) 689-61-04.

Roman Sport Center; 33 Via del Galoppatoio; tel: (06) 320-16-67 and 60.

AUTO RENTAL

Avis; Ciampino airport, 40; tel/fax: (06) 7934-0195; 38A Via Sardegna; tel: (06) 4282-4728, fax: (06) 4201-0282; 1231 Via Tiburtina, tel: (06) 413 0812; fax: (6) 4199 4262; Stazione Termini, 185, tel: (06) 481-4373; fax: (06) 4890-4820.

Budget; Ciampino Airport, tel; (06) 7934-0368; fax: (06) 7934-0368; Fiumicino Airport, tel: (06) 6501-0678; fax: (06) 6595-6664; Termini Railway Station, tel: (06) 488-0049.

Europcar; 7 Via Lombardia; tel: (06) 487-12-74 or 482-57-01.

Hertz; Fiumicino airport, (06) 6501-1553; fax: (06) 652-9119; Roma Ciampino Airport, tel: (06) 7934-0616; fax: (06) 7934-0095; Hilton Hotel, Via Cadlolo, 101, tel: (06) 534-3758; fax: (06) 3534-8922. (chauffeur-driven cars available).

Maggiore; 8a Via Po and 225 Via Tor Cervara; tel: (06) 229-15-30 or toll-free: 16-78/67-067.

Thrifty; 60 Via Boncompagni; tel: (06) 482-09-66.

WORLD TRADE CENTER

World Trade Center Rome
Via Giuseppe Celani
31 00152 Roma
tel: (06) 5820-2351; fax: (06) 537-1084

Milan

CITY VIEW

Standing in the north as Italy's business and finance capital, Milan also acts as a manufacturing and transportation hub. Famous as well for its fashion industry, Milan represents Italy's modern side.

AIRPORT

Linate Airport to City Center
The airport lies 6 miles (10 km.) from the city. There is regular bus and coach service, and taxis are available. A 20 to 40-minute taxi ride into town will run between Lit24,000 and 28,000.

From 6a.m. to 11p.m. it is also possible to take a SEAV bus bound for central station (Stazione Centrale). Buses depart every 20 to 30 minutes for a Lit3,000 to Lit5,000 fare. City bus #73 also travels to Piazza San Babila until midnight. The number for airport information follows: (02) 7485-2200.

Airline Numbers

Aer Lingus Reservations	(02) 760-00080
Air Canada	(02) 2952-3943
Alitalia	(02) 26-8-51/2/3, or (02) 62-811
American	(02) 2900-4919, 167-865-027
British Airways	(02) 809-041
Qantas	(02) 865-0168

HOTELS

Top-end
Brunelleschi; Via Baraccchini 12; tel: 8843; fax: 804924; restaurant; conference facilities (up to 40); secretarial services; fax/photocopying facilities; US$220-250.

Four Seasons Hotel; Via Gesù 8, tel: 77088; fax: 77085000; restaurants; business center; US$340-440.

Grand Duomo; Via San Raffaele 1; tel: 8833; fax: 864-62027; restaurants; in-room safe; conference facilities (up to 100); secretarial services; fax/ photocopying facilities; corporate rates; US$240-340.

Principe di Savoia; Piazza della Repubblica 17; tel: 62301; fax: 659-5838; restaurant; conference facilities (up to 40); secretarial services; fax/ photocopying facilities; US$220-250.

Expensive
Executive; Via Don Luigi Sturzo 45; tel: 6294; fax: 653240; restaurant; conference facilities (up to 800); secretarial

services; fax/photocopying facilities; safe in room; corporate rates; US$150-180.

Galles; Via Ozanam1; tel: 204841; fax: 204-8422; restaurant; safe, modem connection in room; conference facilities (up to 200); secretarial services; fax, photocopying facilities; corporate rates; US$150-200.

Madison; Via Gasparotto 8; tel: 6707-4150; fax: 6707-5059; safe in room; conference facilities (up to 110); secretarial services; fax/photocopying facilities; corporate rates; US$150-240.

Raffaello; Vlale Certosa 108; tel: 327-0146; fax: 327-0440; conference facilities (up to 180); corporate rates; US$150-200.

Moderate

D'Este; Viale Bligny 23; tel: 5832-1001; fax: 5832-1136; conference facilities (up to 90); corporate rates; US$120-180.

Leonardo Da Vinci; Vla Senigallia 6; tel: 64071; fax: 6407-4839; restaurant; conference facilities (up to 1200); secretarial services; fax/ photocopying facilities; US$110-150.

San Carlo; Via N. Torriani 28; tel: 669-2937; fax: 670-3116; restaurant; conference facilities (up to 40); secretarial services; fax/photocopying facilities; in-room safe; corporate rates; US$100-140.

MEDICAL CARE

The Fatebenefratelli Hospital; 23 Corso Porta Nuova; tel: (02) 636-31-16 or (02) 63-631.

Ospedale Maggiore Policlinico; 35 via Francesco Sforza; tel: (02) 550-31 or (02) 551-1655.

Note: A 24-hour pharmacy is located in the Stazione Centrale.

HEALTH CLUB

American Contourella; 1/A Piazza della Repubblica, Repubblica; tel: [39] (02) 655-27-28.

Club Conti; 15 Corso Como, Near Stazione Garibaldi; tel: [39] (02) 657-02-94.

Forum Sports Center; Via D. Vittorio, Assago; tel: [39] (02) 48-85-7.

Skorpion Club; 24/26 Corso Vittorio Emanuele Center; tel: [39] (02) 78-14-24 or 79-60-98.

Sport Italia; 9 Via Piranesi; tel: [39] (02) 738-24-37.

AUTO RENTAL

Avis; airport, tel: (02) 715-123, fax: (02) 7000-3932; Piazza Diaz 6; tel: (02) 890-10645; fax: (02) 863-494.

Budget; airport, tel: (02) 717-210; fax: (02) 7386-6473; Main Railway Station, tel: (02) 669-0934, fax: (02) 669-0934.

Europcar; Piazza Armando Diaz 6; tel: (02) 720-22460.

Hertz; Linate Airport, tel: (02) 7029-0297, fax: (02) 738-8465; Via Gonzaga 5, Piazza Missori, tel: (02) 7200-4567; fax: (02) 7200-4567; Milan railway station Galleria, Delle Carrozze, tel: (02) 669-0061, fax: (02) 6698-6929.

WORLD TRADE CENTER

World Trade Center Italy S.R.L., Milan
World Trade Center Milano
Via Tamburini 13
20123 Milano, Italy
tel: (02) 463-260; fax: (02) 485-6161

Jamaica

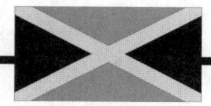

At a Glance

THE PEOPLE

Population .... 2,652,443 (July 1999 est.)
Growth Rate .... 0.64% (1999 est.)
Life Expectancy .... 75.62 years (born 1999)
Infant Mortality . 13.93 deaths/1,000 live births (1999 est.)

Ethnic Composition

Black African 90.4%
Mulatto 7.3%
East Indian 1.3%
Caucasian 0.2%
Other 0.8%

Religious Composition

Protestant 55.9%
Roman Catholic 5%
Animist and non-affiliated 39.1%

Languages Spoken

English, Creole.

Education and Literacy

Nationwide literacy above the age of fifteen is 85 percent.

Labor Force

Total: 1,140,00
By occupation: services 41%, industry 19%, agriculture 40%

THE ECONOMY

Jamaica's economy is based on the commodities of bauxite, sugar, and tourism. It is particularly vulnerable to world commodity price fluctuations and the vagaries of the weather. Jamaican labor is generally available at a low cost, but there is a shortage of skilled labor. This latter problem requires local companies to look abroad for technical and managerial personnel. When the low skill levels are combined with the island's sub-standard infrastructure, it is easy to see why foreign investment has stayed clear of all but the tourism sector. Double-digit inflation and widespread unemployment add to the government's economic problems.

Exports .... US$1.7 billion (1997)
Imports .... US$2.8 billion (1997)
Total GDP .... US$8.8 billion (1998 est.)
GDP Per Capita .... US$3,300 (1998 est.)
Unemployment .... 16.5% (1997 est.)
Inflation Rate .... 9.9% (1998 est.)

Top Export Partners

United States, E.U., Canada, Norway, France

Top Import Partners

United States, Mexico, Japan, E.U., Venezuela

Top Exports

Alumina, bauxite, sugar, bananas, rum

Top Imports

Machinery and transport equipment, construction materials, fuel, food, chemicals

BUSINESS WORKWEEK

Offices

Monday to Friday 9a.m. to 5p.m.

Banks

Monday to Thursday 9a.m. to 2p.m., Friday 9a.m. to 5p.m. A few banks open on Saturdays.

Government

Monday to Friday 8a.m. to 4:30p.m.

Retail

Monday to Friday 9a.m. to 7p.m. Some shops may close on Wednesday or Thursday. Large urban retailers may have extended evening hours.

Note: There is half-day closing of the downtown Kingston retail shops on Wednesdays and uptown stores on Thursdays.

HOLIDAYS

New Year's Day .... January 1
Ash Wednesday .... February 17*
Good Friday .... April 2*
Easter Monday .... April 5*
National Labor Day .... May 23
Independence Day .... August 6*
National Heroes Day .... October 18*
Christmas .... December 25-26
*Dates may vary by year.

CLIMATE

Seasons

Jamaica is hot and tropical year round. Rain is likely to fall all year round, but the rainiest months are May and October.

Regions

Weather is consistent throughout the island, though it can be slightly cooler in the mountains.

Money & Banking

Currency

The currency of Jamaica is the Jamaican Dollar (J$).

Denominations

The Jamaican Dollar comes in coin denominations of J$1, as well as 50, 25, 20, 10, 5, and 1 cents; and banknotes of J$1, 2, 5, 10, 20, 50, 100, and 500.

Traveler's Checks and Credit Cards

Only U.S. dollar denominated traveler's checks can be exchanged at banks, exchange shops, hotels, and international airports. Exchange rates can severely differ from place to place, and some outlets charge service fees. Banks offer the best rate of exchange. Hotels will usually offer 2 to 5 percent below the bank rate. Avoid black marketers at all cost. Consult your bank about current exchange rates before departure.

Major currencies can be exchanged without a charge at banks, hotels, and exchange kiosks. In rural areas exchanges may be difficult. Try to carry small bills as many establishments may not have change for larger notes.

American Express, Visa, Diner's Club, and MasterCard are accepted in most larger hotels and restaurants in the

Jamaica

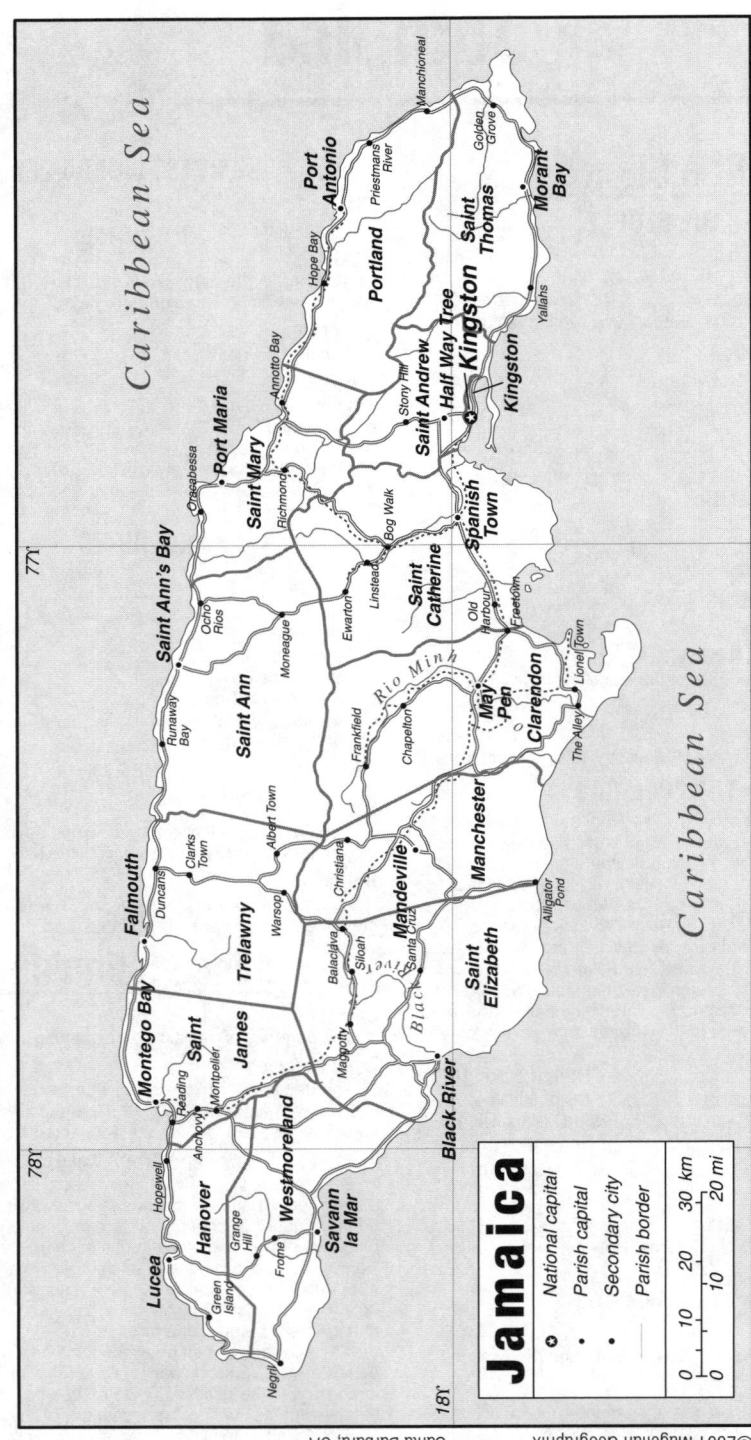

Caribbean Sea

Caribbean Sea

Manchioneal

Golden Grove

Morant Bay

Port Antonio

Priestmans River

Saint Thomas

Yallahs

Portland

Hope Bay

Kingston

Kingston

Annotto Bay

Saint Andrew

Half Way Tree

Stony Hill

Port Maria

Saint Mary

Oracabessa

Richmond

Bog Walk

Spanish Town

Saint Catherine

Linstead

Ewarton

Old Harbour

Freetown

Saint Ann's Bay

Ocho Rios

Moneague

Rio Minh

Lionel Town

Runaway Bay

Saint Ann

Frankfield

Chapelton

May Pen

Clarendon

The Alley

Albert Town

Clarks Town

Christiana

Mandeville

Manchester

Alligator Pond

Falmouth

Duncans

Warsop

Balaclava

Siloah

Santa Cruz

Rivers

Saint Elizabeth

Trelawny

Black River

Montego Bay

Saint James

Magpotty

Reading

Montpelier

Anchovy

Westmoreland

Savanna la Mar

Hanover

Lucea

Hopewell

Green Island

Frome

Grange Hill

Negril

77°

78°

18°

Jamaica

⊕ National capital

• Parish capital

• Secondary city

— Parish border

0	10	20		30 km
0		10	20	20 mi

capital, Kingston. Some banks in the capital offer cash advances on credit cards, but make sure you bring your passport. for identification. The capital is also well stocked with ATMs. In most other areas of the island, credit card usage and ATMs are rare.

American Express Offices:

Grace Kennedy Limited; 19-20 Knutsford Blvd., Kingston 5; tel: (876 929-6290.

Allied Insurance Brokers; 2 Market Street, Montego Bay; tel: (876) 952-9470.

Grace Tours Ltd.; 1-3 Evelyn St., Ocho Rios; tel: (876) 974-8812.

Travel

VISA AND PASSPORT

Foreigners must have a valid passport that will not expire during the term of their stay. U.S. and Canadian citizens may enter with only a valid national ID if entering from their nation of origin. However, if entering from another country, they must carry a passport. The majority of foreign visitors do not need a visa if staying less than 90 days, and many of the nationalities who do may obtain one on arrival. But foreigners from some countries, including Argentina, Brazil, Chile, Costa Rica, Ecuador, and Japan, will need visas for stays exceeding 30 days. Nationals of Venezuela will need a visa if staying beyond 14 days. All visitors must be able to verify proof of sufficient funds and possession of onward or return travel arrangements.

Types of visa issued: Entry and Transit, terms of stay and validity determined by immigration, depending on details in the application and nationality. If you are making a business visit, a Work Permit is mandatory. Your nearest Jamaican consulate or embassy can help you expedite the process.

Allow two days or so for applications made in person, add the time of send and return delivery to postal applications. Cases that are referred to immigration in Kingston can take much longer.

DEPARTURE FORMALITIES

All passengers, except those in transit, must pay a departure tax of J$1,000 (approx. US$30) in cash when exiting by air. Only items manufactured in Jamaica may be carried out duty free.

CUSTOMS ENTRY (PERSONAL)

Duty-free

- Tobacco: 200 cigarettes or 50 cigars or 250g tobacco
- Alcohol: 2 liters of spirits (excluding rum); 2 liters of wine
- Other: gifts to the value of J$150 during each 6-month period; 340ml of eau de toilette; 150g of perfume
- Amounts exceeding J$150,000/US$10,000 (or its equivalent in any other foreign currency) must be declared at Jamaican Customs.

Prohibited or Restricted

- Explosives and firearms
- Dangerous drugs (including marijuana)
- Meat, flowers, fresh fruit, rum, vegetables (unless canned), coffee in any form and honey cannot be brought into Jamaica
- Cats and dogs are also prohibited unless arriving directly from the U.K. and having been born and bred there. Owners must have a certificate from the Ministry of Agriculture, Fisheries and Food (Hook Rise, Tolworth, Surbiton, Surrey) and a permit for their import from the Ministry of Agriculture, Hope Gardens, Kingston 6.

Note: All trade samples need an import license, obtainable from the trade board:

Trade Board
107 Constant Spring Road
Kingston, Jamaica
tel: 969-0478; fax: 925-6513

IMMUNIZATION

Foreigners arriving from areas of known infection or epidemic must have vaccination certificates for yellow fever and cholera. Polio, hepatitis, and typhoid inoculations are recommended.

TIPPING

Taxi

Taxi drivers receive the equivalent of 10 percent of the fare.

Porters

Porters receive J$15 per piece of luggage.

Hotels

Tip 10 percent at hotels when service charges have not been applied to the bill. Chambermaids get J$30 per day for the duration of the stay.

Restaurants

Tip 10 to 15 percent in restaurants and bars unless service is already included in your bill. Check your bills carefully.

EMERGENCY INFORMATION

Police and Crime

Crime prevails in the cities and larger towns where poverty is endemic. Gang violence and drug- related crime occur in neighborhoods west of downtown Kingston up to the very edges of the central downtown area. Curfews have often been imposed in these areas. If you are robbed, do not resist; several victims have met with violence and even death after resisting robbery attempts.

Caution should be exercised when traveling to and from Kingston Airport via Mountain View Avenue and Windward Toad, and most certainly after dark. Visitors should not walk outside after dark or at any time in neighborhoods known for high crime rates. Major resorts feature higher security measures since they are self contained. Crowded buses are also a common stage for crime.

Foreign business visitors often offer a target to thieves, as it is assumed that all tourists are wealthy. Consequently, purses, laptops, and briefcases will require additional security. Do not leave valuables in cars or on tables in cafés. Keep non-essential valuables locked in hotel safes when not in use. Use credit cards and travel checks when possible to avoid carrying large sums of cash.

Police in urban areas are generally helpful, but in rural areas the police may be part of the crime problem. Carry insurance for goods that you cannot afford to lose.

There is some corruption within the various local governments. Business travelers may also find that their deals with local companies involve the bribing of public officials. Besides making the personal decision of whether or not to participate in such dealings, check on your legal position in your own country. Some nations now have stiff penalties for their business people who bribe officials overseas.

Emergency Numbers

Numbers function nationwide.

Ambulance 110
Air-sea rescue 119

Health

Although the tap water may be chlorinated, bottled water is available and might be recommended to avoid upset stomach. When eating out, make sure the seafood is fresh and meats are well cooked. Jamaica has a tropical climate, so watch out for sunburn and heat stroke. Otherwise, no major health risks exist on the island.

There are public hospitals in each parish and comprehensive medical emergency services in Kingston and Montego Bay. If you find yourself in a remote part of the country, ambulance service for critical patients can be provided by the Jamaica Defense Force's helicopter corps.

Hospital facilities are good for most emergencies. However, if you have a major medical problem, you are best advised to seek care in the nearby U.S. Carry travel insurance with an evacuation clause if you plan an extended stay.

For more information on medical centers, including phone numbers, please see the "Business Centers" section at the end of this chapter.

INTERNAL TRAVEL

AIR

Air Jamaica Express (previously Trans Jamaica Airlines) provides services between Kingston, Montego Bay, Port Antonio, Mandeville, Ocho Rios, and Negril. It is a quick way to travel and may be worth the money if you are traveling on business. Frequent daily flights operate throughout the winter season, and shuttle flights connect the two primary airports. For more information, log on to the following website: http://airjamaica.com/express.html

TAXI

Be sure to take only licensed taxis—those with red and white "PP" license plates. Check on standard fares since pre-determined rates exist. However, not all fares are metered. Negotiate such fares in advance. Be sure to write extensive directions on paper for the driver, and carry a map.

AUTO

Both international and local operators rent autos and motorcycles in Jamaica's major cities. You will find them at airports and hotels. A credit card, local insurance, and a valid driver's license are required. A general consumption tax of 15 percent is levied on auto rental transactions.

Driving takes place on the left hand side of the road. Road conditions range between excellent and terrible, and the attitude of other drivers can often seem to hover somewhere between insanity and suicide. Urban driving is chaotic, but if you have a fender-bender, stay calm and do not be drawn into a brawl with an emotional, irritated Jamaican driver.

About one-third of Jamaica's roads are paved. Rural roads are fairly calm. Visitors should never drive in rural areas at night, though, due to security risks. Poorly marked roadblocks (such as those that local residents often deploy as a combination political billboard and street theatre piece) and big street dance events are major road hazards throughout Jamaica—another good reason to stay off the roads at night.

Bike: You can rent a bicycle in a town of any size in Jamaica. Carry lots of spare parts—especially tires— if you are bringing your own bike.

BUSES & TRAMS

Private buses and minibuses handle most urban transport. Do not expect straightforward scheduling practices or punctuality. Fares for tourists are higher than for locals, and there is little hope in arguing the point with the driver. Buses often operate full to overflowing. Still, it is a cheap way to travel and a wonderful way to get to know a few people.

Buses are, however, rarely used for regular business travel at the management level. Managers and executives use hired cars or taxis.

WATER TRAVEL

Kingston port is serviced by many international passenger cruise lines. Jamaica also has a ferry service running between the many smaller port cities. In addition, a number of companies offer yacht tours along the coastline. Contact the Jamaica Tourist Board (see listing in next section, 'Travel Assistance').

TRAVEL ASSISTANCE

Jamaica Tourist Board (JTB)
64 Knutsford Boulevard, Kingston 5, Jamaica
tel: 929-9200; fax: 929-9375
email: jamaicatrv@aol.com
website: www.jamaicatravel.com
Jamaica Hotel and Tourist Association
2 Ardenne Road, Kingston, Jamaica
tel: (876) 926-3635/ 3
fax: (876) 929-1054

Communications

DIALING CODES IN JAMAICA

International country code: [1]
Area code: (876); this code is used for the entire country.

Dialing Jamaica from Overseas

To dial Jamaica from overseas, dial your country's international dialing code, then 1 (the country code), 876 (the are code for Jamaica), and finally the number. There are no city codes.

Assistance Numbers

International Operator 980-0000
International Assistance 113
Directory 114
Long-Distance Directory.. 112

CALLING WITHIN JAMAICA

Local Calls

In all of Jamaica there are seven digits to dial within the same area code.

Long Distance Calls

To dial long distance within Jamaica, dial 0 + the seven-digit local number.

International Calls

Prepare for high rates from the company called Telecommunications of Jamaica (TOJ). Direct dialing appears to be the most effective way of getting through to an international number without joining the Jamaican circus. Even then it is interesting:
1. Dial 113
2. Wait for tone
3. Press the # button
4. Wait for tone
5. Dial number

AT&T Direct phone booths exist in key locations and it may also be possible to connect from room phones at top-end hotels. Some operators will maintain that you cannot connect to the access numbers or keep you from trying. If you follow through with your objective from a hotel room, try dialing one of the following numbers:
Canada Direct 0-800-222-0016
U.K. 0-800-364-5263
U.S. AT&T 0-800-872-2881

U.S. MCI..0-800-674-7000
U.S. Sprint..0-800-877-8000
From a card phone the process changes:
Canada Direct .... #4
U.K. .... #5
U.S. AT&T .... #1
U.S. MCI... #2
To make a collect call from a digital phone:
1. Dial 113
2. Wait for tone
3. Press # button
4. Wait for tone
5. Press 0 for operator
The rule of thumb in Jamaica is never give or show your calling card to anyone except hotel or overseas operators. The phone scamming industry is huge.

PAY PHONES

Public Telephones

Public phones can be found in the streets, but there may be long lines to use them. They also exist in small hotels or in major towns at TOJ offices, which are open Monday to Friday, from 8a.m. to 4p.m.; and on Saturday until noon.
1. Lift receiver
2. Wait for a clicking tone
3. Dial
4. Wait for connection
5. Deposit coins

Calling Cards

Jamaica TelCo card phones are now more ubiquitous than coin phones. Cards can be purchased at retail stores, banks, and hotels in J$20, 100, 200 and 500 denominations.
1. Lift receiver
2. Insert phone card
3. Dial 113
4. Listen for tone
5. Press # button
6. Dial number
7. Wait for connection
8. Press the Talk button

CELLULAR PHONES

Telecom Jamaica operates the cellular system in Jamaica and uses an AMPS analogue system, same as the U.S. Unfortunately, GSM users are out of luck.

Note: Your home country cell phone may not work in this country. If not, we recommend that you rent an international cell phone *before* you leave home. A major US-based cell phone rental provider is **IMC WorldCell**. For information see "International Cell Phone Rentals" on page 14.

CALL BACK

You can (potentially) save significant sums when calling in Jamaica by using a call back service. For a list of call-back services, please refer to the "Communications" section in the *Global Road Warrior* Introduction.

Fees for call back services vary widely, depending on the company and the type of service required. Be sure to check with these companies before leaving to compare rates.

PHONE JACKS

Plug adaptors are available through **iGo Corporation.** (See "Electrical and Telephone Adaptors" on page 19.)

FAX

Fax machines are widely used, but the service depends on the telephone connection.

POSTAL SERVICES

Letters to North America can take weeks, if they ever arrive. Long-term residents have found that using a courier service is much more efficient. The service will receive the mail for them in Miami, then forward it to a private messenger on the island who will deliver the mail within a day or two.

Hours of service

Monday to Thursday 9a.m. to 5p.m., Friday 9a.m. to 4p.m., Saturday 9a.m. to 1p.m.

TELEGRAMS

Facilities for sending telegraphs are widely available.

Business Services

COURIER SERVICES

Airborne Express (International Bonded Couriers); 7 Trafalgar Road, KIngston 5; tel: 927-6011; fax: 978-4875.

DHL; 60 Knutsford Blvd., Kingston 5; tel: 929-2554.

FedEx; 75 Knutsford Blvd., Kings0ton 5; tel: 926-1456; 960-9192.

Guardsman Armoured Courier Services Ltd.; 4 Emmaville Cres., KIngston CSO; tel: 928-5387, 928-1798.

UPS (Mail Box International); Shop 12, New Kingston Shopping Center, 30 Dominica Drive, Kingston; tel: 968-8288; fax: 968-8464.

OFFICE RENTAL

The Business District Ltd.; 40 Duke St., Kingston; tel: 967-2399.

SECRETARIAL SERVICES

Hamilton Knight Associates, Ltd.; 3A Paisley Ave.; Kingston; tel: 929-4632.

Personnel Services, Ltd.; 1 St. Lucia Ave.; Kingston; tel: 926-7893, 926-8991.

Placement & Business Services Ltd.; 35 C Spring Rd., Kingston 10; tel: 926-8359, 929-1769.

Professional Typing and Secretarial Services; Shop 2, 2 King St.; tel: 967-2241.

Temps, Ltd.; 13 Duke St.; Kingston; tel: 922-0580.

TRANSLATION SERVICES

Hamilton Knight Associates Ltd.; 3A Paisley Ave.; Kingston; tel: 929-4632.

Jamaica

Electrical

Current

110 volts AC, 50Hz, although some hotels offer 220 volts AC, 50Hz.

ELECTRIC PLUGS

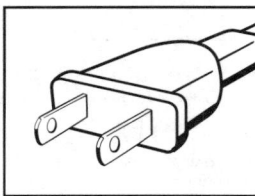

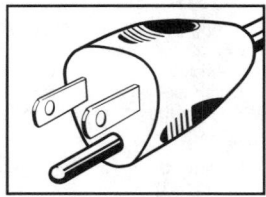

American 2-pin sockets are the standard, although many hotels offer 3-pin single phase sockets as well.

Plug adaptors are available through **iGo Corporation.** (See "Electrical and Telephone Adaptors" on page 19.)

Technical Support

Apple/Claris; (in Miami) [1] (305) 265-4939; (in the U.S.) tel: [1] (800) 500-7078; (in the U.K.) tel: [44] (990) 127-753; http://www.apple.com/.

Compaq/Digital; (Houston Office, U.S.) tel: [1] (713) 370-0670; fax: [1] (713) 514-1740; (in the U.S.) tel: [1] (281) 518-2000 (international technical support); fax: [1] (281) 518-1442; http://www.compaq.com.

Dell; (U.S. Office) tel: [1] 512-338-4400; fax: [1] 512-728-3330; (Dell- Europe) tel: [44] (134) 474-8000; http://www.dell.com/.

Filemaker/Claris; (in the U.S.) tel: [1] (800) 965-9090; (in Germany) tel: [49] (180) 525-8166 (Info-line); fax: [49] (180) 567-2233; tel: [49] (180) 523-6423; http://www.claris.com/.

Hewlett Packard; (in the U.S.) tel: [1] (408) 246-4300; (in Switzerland) tel: [41] (22) 780-8111; http://www.hp.com/.

IBM; tel: 926-3200; fax: 926-3225 (IBM World Trade Corp.); fax: 926- 3225; (in the U.S.) tel: [1] (919) 517-2800; (U.S. Main Office) tel: [1] 914-765-1900; (in Switzerland) tel: [41] (22) 310-0418 (in French); http://www.ibm.com/.

Microsoft; (In Costa Rica) tel: [506] 298-2020 (technical support); tel: [506] 298-2000; (in the U.S.) [1] (425) 635-7222; (in Switzerland) tel: [41] (848) 858-868; fax [41] (1) 831-0869; http://www.microsoft.com/.

Toshiba; (in the U.S.) [1] (949) 583-3000 (Corporate Headquarters); (in Germany) tel: [49] (2131) 158-319; fax: [49] (2131) 158-558; (in Switzerland) tel: [41] (1) 946-0777; fax: [41] (1) 946-0807; (in Ireland) tel: [44] (193) 282-8828; http://www.toshiba.com/.

Internet Connection

HOW TO CONNECT

Connecting to AOL and Compuserve in Jamaica is similar to using it when traveling outside your own area code. See the introductory section for detailed information on connecting to your account through a different phone number.

America Online

Numbers are available at keyword *international*. Be sure to get several local numbers before leaving. Go to keyword *access* (a free area) and download the software.

There are no direct access numbers for America Online in Jamaica. Users will have to pay international rates to use the service.

Compuserve

Numbers are available at *Go International*. The Compuserve Web-site also has a great deal of information, at http://www.compuserve.com.

There are no direct access numbers for Compuserve in Jamaica. Users will have to pay international rates to use the service.

Independent Service Providers

Many independent service providers offer discounts if you are only in town for a couple of days.

Colis Internet Service; tel: 754-3377; tel: 754-3383; fax: 968-2748; email: compuworks@colis.com; http://www.colis.com/.

KasNet Online Communications Ltd.; tel: 927-8838; fax: 978-0680; email: info@kasnet.com; http://www.kasnet.com/profile.htm/.

Business Culture

GREETINGS AND COURTESIES

Men usually shake hands with women and each other, although women seldom shake hands with other women. Titles are commonly used, especially "Doctor" and "Professor." Business cards printed in English are expected. The host will usually make introductions. Jamaicans like to entertain and are likely to invite foreign businesspeople to their homes for a meal or other event. A small gift is expected and it is appropriate to bring flowers or a bottle of wine.

DECISION MAKING

Foreign businesspeople are expected to be on time, but Jamaicans can be more relaxed about schedules. Authority is narrowly concentrated and actual decisions are almost always made at a high level. Foreigners should cultivate peer relationships, because the quality of these relationships may strongly influence the actual decision maker even when your immediate counterpart is not the one making the decision.

WOMEN

Although women in Jamaica generally occupy a somewhat secondary status in this traditional, male-dominated society, many operate businesses and are accorded considerable personal freedom. In general, foreign businesswomen should have few problems in business, generally experiencing greater acceptance than do local women. Note that women may be verbally harassed on the street; they can ignore such behavior, but may feel more comfortable if they are escorted or use taxis.

BUSINESS ATTIRE

Tropical weight suits or sports coats and trousers are expected of men for business dealings. Foreign business-women should wear conservative suits or dresses, but may generally dispense with stockings. Styles are somewhat less fashionable and daring than those worn elsewhere. However, an evening outing may require a man to wear a sport coat, and a woman a skirt and blouse. Bring an umbrella for the frequent showers.

Business Centers
Kingston

CITY VIEW

Kingston scares many visitors, sometimes for good reason. There are places awash in squalor, and places you simply do not go to if you value your life. Despite that, it is an active business center with a great deal of culture, and lest anyone forget, an attractive climate for sun worshipers.

AIRPORT

Norman Manley International Airport to City Center

The airport lies 11 miles (17.5 km) from the city. There are regular bus and coach services.

Airline Numbers

Air Jamaica	(876) 922-4661
	1-800-523-5585
Air Jamaica Express	923-8680
	1-800-523-5585
Air Canada	(416) 925-2311
	1-800-776-3000
ALM	(305) 477-0955
	1-800-327-7230
American Airlines	(876) 924-8305/9
	1-800-433-7300
American Trans Air	1-800-225-2995
British Airways	(876) 929-9020
	1-800-247-9297
British West Indies Airways	(876) 929-3770
	1-800-327-7401
Caribbean Airlines	(876) 960-2100/3, 924-8425
Cayman Airways	(876) 926-1762/4, 926-7778/9
	1-800-422-9626
Condor	1-800-542-6975
Copa	(305) 477-7333
	1-800-359-2672
Cubana	978-3406/3410
Continental Airlines	(876) 924-8271, 924-8272
LTU	1-800-888-0200
Northwest Airlines	
Montego Bay	(876) 952-4033
	1-800-225-2525
Trans World Airlines (TWA)	
Montego Bay	(876) 952-3124
	1-800-892-4141
USAir	
Montego Bay	(876) 952-3124
	1-800-428-4322

HOTELS

Le Meridien Jamaica Pegasus; 81 Knutsford Boulevard; tel: 926-3690; fax: 929-5855; e-mail: jmpegasus@cwjamaica.com; centrally located in financial & business district; six restaurants; bar; conference facilities (up to 1000); secretarial services; audio visual equipment; fax, photocopying/fax facilities; in-room safe and modem connection; corporate rates; fitness room; pool; tennis; hair salon; shops; 24-hour room service; US$140+.

Wyndham Kingston; 77 Knutsford Boulevard; tel: 926-5430; fax: 929-7439; restaurants; conference facilities; secretarial services; fax/ photocopying facilities; corporate rates; fitness room; US$200+.

Expensive

Terra Nova; 17 Waterloo Road; tel: 926-2211; fax: 929-4933; restaurants; conference facilities (up to 150); secretarial services; fax/photocopying facilities; in-room safe and modem connection; corporate rates; US$120-150.

Morgan's Harbour Hotel, Beach Club, and Yacht; Port Royal; tel: 967-8040; fax: 967-8073; restaurants; conference facilities (up to 90); secretarial services; fax, photocopying facilities; in-room safe and modem connection; corporate rates; US$125+.

Moderate

Four Seasons; 18 Ruthven Road; tel: 929-7655; fax: 929-5964; restaurant; conference facilities (up to 100); secretarial services; fax/photocopying facilities; in-room safe and modem connection; corporate rates; fitness room; US$80+.

Sutton Place; 11 Ruthven Road; tel: 926-1207; fax: 926-8443; restaurant; conference facilities (up to 500); in-room safe; US$80+.

MEDICAL CARE

The **International Association for Medical Assistance to Travelers** provides references to specialists in all areas of medicine. The IAMAT Center in Kingston is the F.I.S.H. Clinic at 19 Gordon Town Road; tel: 927-1106 or 927-1021.

University Hospital at the University of the West Indies campus in Mona, East Kingston; tel: 927-6621.

AUTO RENTAL

Note: Persons renting cars should remain alert due to haphazard driving conditions that range from superb to terrible. Potholes and stray animals make night driving hazardous. Robbery of persons involved in "accidents" is also not unknown.

Avis; 3 Oxford Road; tel: 926-1560; in the U.S.; tel: (800) 331-1212; fax: 926-9406.

Budget; Norman Manley International Airport; tel: 938-2189; in the U.S.; tel: (800) 527-0700.

Hertz Car Rental; Norman Manley International Airport; tel: 924-8028; in the U.S.; tel: (800) 654-3131.

Island Car Rentals; airport, 924-8075, 924-8389; 17 Antigua Avenue; KIngston; tel: 1-800-892-4581; tel: (876) 926-5991.

National; tel: 1-800-227-3876.

CHAMBER OF COMMERCE

Jamaica Chamber of Commerce
7 East Parade, Kingston
tel: 922-0150; fax: 924-9056

Japan

At a Glance

THE PEOPLE

Population .... 126,182,077 (July 1999 est.)
Growth Rate .... 0.2% (1999 est.)
Life Expectancy .... 80.11 years (born 1999)
Infant Mortality ... 4.07 deaths/1,000 live births (1999 est.)

Ethnic Composition

Japanese..99.4%
Other 0.6%

Religious Composition

Shinto and Buddhist..84%
Christian 0.7%
Other and non-affiliated..15.3%

Languages Spoken

Japanese

Education and Literacy

Literacy for those age 15 and over is 99 percent.

Labor Force

Total: 67,230,000
By occupation: services 61%, industry 33%, agriculture 6%

THE ECONOMY

Throughout the 1970s and '80s Japan was hailed as the most dynamic economy in the world. It was vaunted as the vanguard of the impending dominance by the Asian economies. Its businesses were heavily controlled (and often financed) by the governments's Ministry of International Trade and Industry in what analysts saw as a "socialist free market" economy. Japanese companies seemed poised to unseat the American behemoth in the competition for the title of top economic power. Unfortunately by the early 1990s all the flaws in the "Japanese model" became exposed and Japan tumbled into malaise. Its GDP growth rate has shrunk to below 1 percent and its companies have sustained years of losses and even bankruptcies. Japanese workers once thought to have "lifetime employment" find themselves without jobs or prospects. Long dependent on importing most of its raw materials and fuel, Japan has been further crippled by the decline in the value of its currency against the U.S. dollar. The government's attempts to stimulate the economy through public works projects has combined with declining tax revenues to give Japan the largest budget deficit (as a percent of GDP) among the industrialized economies. Japan enters the 21st century not having led Asia to the top, but rather into a sustained decline.

Exports .... US$440 billion (f.o.b, 1998)
Imports .... US$319 billion (c.i.f., 1998)
Total GDP .... US$2.903 trillion (1998 est.)
GDP Per Capita .... US$23,100 (1998 est.)
Unemployment .... 4.4% (November 1998)
Inflation Rate .... 0.9% (1998 est.)

Top Export Partners

ASEAN nations, United States, E.U., China

Top Import Partners

ASEAN nations, United States, E.U., China

Top Exports

Machinery, motor vehicles, consumer electronics

Top Imports

Manufactures, foodstuffs, raw materials, fossil fuels

BUSINESS WORKWEEK

Offices

Monday to Friday, 9a.m. to 5p.m., and Saturday from 9a.m. to noon.

Banks

Monday to Friday, 9a.m. to 3p.m., closed Saturday.

Government

Monday to Friday, 9a.m. to 5p.m., closed Saturday. (Local government offices are open the first and third Saturdays of the month until noon.)

Retail

Shops stay open from 10a.m. to 6 or 7p.m. Most shops are open on weekends but closed one day during the week.

HOLIDAYS

New Year's Day...January 1
Coming of Age Day ....January 15
National Foundation Day.................................February 11
Vernal Equinox Day...March 20*
Greenery Day ....April 29
Constitution Day ....May 3
Declared Official Holiday ....May 4
Children's Day ....May 5
Respect for the Aged Day ....September 15
Autumnal Equinox Day...............................September 22*
Sports Day..October 10
Labor Thanksgiving Day...............................November 23
Emperor's Birthday.......................................December 23
  * Dates may vary by year.
  Note: In addition to the above public holidays, many Japanese companies and government offices traditionally close for several days during the New Year's holiday season (December 28 to January 3). Although it depends on the company, many close during "Golden Week" (April 29 to May 5) and the traditional "O-Bon" (Festival of Souls) period for several days in mid-August (usually about August 12 to 15).

CLIMATE

Seasons

Summers are humid and warm—the standard East Asia monsoon season. Rains fall heavily during June. The typical Tokyo July high temperature hits 31°C (88°F) and torrid spells reach 35°C (95°F)—about the same as New York City or Budapest. Japan lies in the track of Pacific summer typhoons (the Asian term for hurricane), so heed the warnings you hear. Spring and fall are justifiably celebrated for beautiful weather—warm days, cool nights, fresh breezes, and cherry blossoms.

Regions

Thanks to cold out of Siberia, Tokyo's January temperatures are about the same as those in London or Washington, D.C. Shikoku and Kyushu winters are more mild, while Hokkaido and northern Honshu have severe winters with heavy

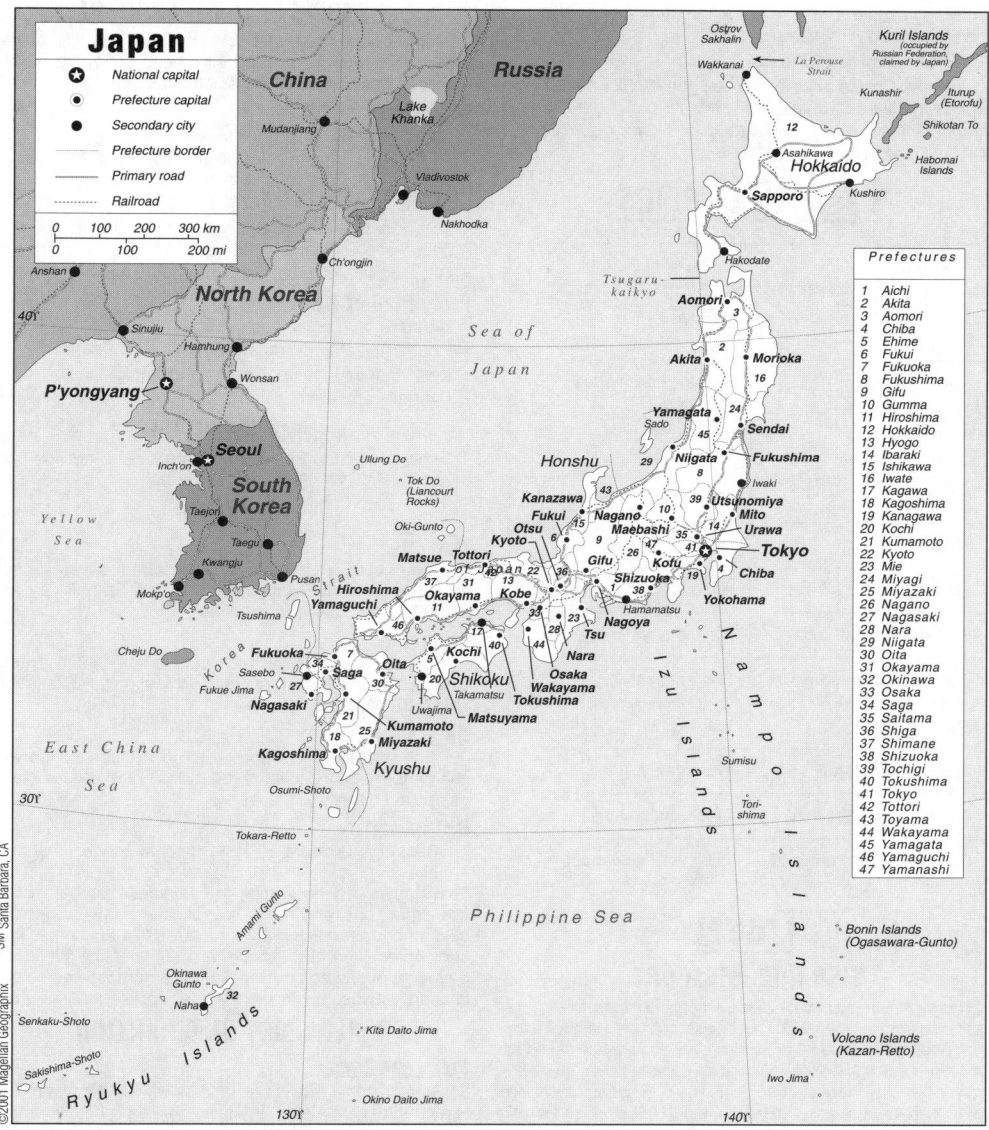

Japan

✪	National capital
◉	Prefecture capital
●	Secondary city
───	Prefecture border
───	Primary road
·····	Railroad

0	100	200 300 km
0	100	200 mi

Prefectures

1	Aichi
2	Akita
3	Aomori
4	Chiba
5	Ehime
6	Fukui
7	Fukuoka
8	Fukushima
9	Gifu
10	Gumma
11	Hiroshima
12	Hokkaido
13	Hyogo
14	Ibaraki
15	Ishikawa
16	Iwate
17	Kagawa
18	Kagoshima
19	Kanagawa
20	Kochi
21	Kumamoto
22	Kyoto
23	Mie
24	Miyagi
25	Miyazaki
26	Nagano
27	Nagasaki
28	Nara
29	Niigata
30	Oita
31	Okayama
32	Okinawa
33	Osaka
34	Saga
35	Saitama
36	Shiga
37	Shimane
38	Shizuoka
39	Tochigi
40	Tokushima
41	Tokyo
42	Tottori
43	Toyama
44	Wakayama
45	Yamagata
46	Yamaguchi
47	Yamanashi

SM Santa Barbara, CA

©2001 Magellan Geographix

snows. Japan's climate is generally temperate but it has extremes from the sub-arctic of Hokkaido to the subtropical of Okinawa. The further south you go the warmer each season becomes.

Money & Banking

Currency

The currency of Japan is the yen (¥).

Denominations

The yen (¥) comes in coin denominations of ¥1, 5, 10, 50, 100, and 500; and banknotes of ¥1000, 5000, and 10000.

Traveler's Checks and Credit Cards

It is illegal in Japan to use any currency other than yen. Only special foreign exchange banks, major hotels, and exchange shops will cash traveler's checks or exchange currency. The Japanese are very sensitive about the value of their currency internationally. Any attempts by foreigners to use anything but yen will be taken as an insult. Keep all receipts of exchange for reconversion. There is no black market for yen in Japan and there is a single rate of exchange. Be aware that currency exchange is a time consuming process in Japan.

American Express, Visa, MasterCard, and Diners Club are widely accepted. You can get cash advances from your credit card on many of the automated teller machines

(ATM). The most favorable exchange rates will be given for credit card and ATM transactions.

American Express Offices:

Yurakucho Chiyod Aqu; Tokyo; tel: [85] (3) 321-40280. Open Monday - Saturday, 9:30a.m. to 6 p.m.

American Express Traveler's Service; 1-8-17 Umada Kitaku; Osaka City; [81] (6) 3414-102.

Essential Terms

English	Japanese
Yes	Hai
No	Iie
Good morning	Ohayo-gozaimasu
Hello (daytime)	Konichiwa
Hello (evening)	Konbanwa
Hello (telephone)	Moshi-moshi
Good-bye	Sayonara
Please	Dozo
Thank you	Arigato
Pleased to meet you	Hajimemashite
Excuse me; I'm sorry	Sumimasen
My name is ____	Watashi wa ____ desu
I don't understand	Wakarimasen
Do you speak English?	Eigo o hanashimasu ka?
Can we meet tomorrow?	Ashita oai deki masu ka?

Travel

VISA AND PASSPORT

Foreigners must have a valid passport, but most foreigners visiting Japan for tourism or business don't need visas if their stay does not exceed 90 days. However, you may be asked to show proof of sufficient funds and an onward ticket out of Japan. If you stay more than 90 days, you can get an extension for tourism or business, but you'll need to get an Alien Registration Card and carry it with you at all times.

Check with the nearest Japanese embassy or consulate to determine if your country is on a list of those requiring visas. Generally, visa applications are processed in three to seven days if presented in person. If referral to Tokyo is necessary, it can then take up to a month for things to be resolved.

DEPARTURE FORMALITIES

You can take up to ¥5 million in Japanese currency or any amount of foreign cash out of the country without special permission.

If you leave Japan through Narita Airport, you will have to pay a ¥2,000 "Passenger Facility Service Charge." There is a departure tax of ¥945 from Fukuoka Airport, ¥2040 at New Tokyo International Airport, and ¥2650 at Kansai Airport. There are no fees for land or sea departures.

CUSTOMS ENTRY (PERSONAL)

Compared to most East Asian nations, Japan is relaxed about what foreigners bring into the country. You must, however, declare unaccompanied luggage.

Duty-free

- Personal effects you don't plan to sell
- ATA carnet items: professional equipment, commercial samples, and advertising material you don't plan to sell
- Alcohol: three bottles (0.760 liters) each
- Tobacco: 50 cigars or 200 cigarettes, or 250 grams of tobacco or combination total
- Gifts, souvenirs, other: up to ¥200,000 worth

Prohibited or Restricted

- Narcotics and other illegal drugs
- Counterfeit or imitation money
- Items that infringe upon copyrights and patents
- Firearms and ammunition

IMMUNIZATION

Proof of vaccination is needed only when arriving from an area of known infection or epidemic.

TIPPING

Taxi

Taxi drivers are not tipped. If you hire a driver, it's normal to tip him ¥500 (about US$4.50) for a half day and ¥1,000 (about US$9) for a full day.

Porters

Porters are paid a fee—in airports, ¥200 (about US$1.80) per bag, and in railroad stations, ¥300 (about US$2.70) per bag.

Hotels

Full-service hotels add a 10 to 15 percent service charge to the bill. Economy "business hotel" has all charges applied directly to the bill.

Restaurants

Restaurants add a 10 to 15 percent service charge to the bill.

Note: As a general rule, the Japanese neither ask for nor expect tips, and rarely accept them without considerable embarrassment. If a visitor would like to express special appreciation of a service, a small financial gift should be made; imprinted envelopes for this purpose can be purchased. Enclose paper money only, not coins.

EMERGENCY INFORMATION

Police and Crime

Japan's crime rate is one of the lowest in the world. This is a country where even the few homeless politely remove their shoes when sleeping on a newspaper or park bench. However, with a severe recession and a changing Japanese picture of fortune, crime may become more prevalent. Obviously, due to sheer size, Tokyo and Osaka pose more risk than do other cities. Even so, crime remains amazingly low. Police officers are available at kiosks on most major streets, but many speak only Japanese.

To be on the safe side, take basic precautions. Leave most of your cash, traveler's checks, jewelry, and your camera in your hotel safe. Since most of Japan still operates on a cash system and crime is low, it isn't strange to carry around large amounts of cash. However, to avoid hassle if you happen to fall victim to a random crime, use credit cards or traveler's checks for most of your transactions.

Foreign businessmen rarely come into contact with the "yakuza" or Japanese mafia. The yakuza do, however, become involved in many legitimate businesses in Japan. Make sure you know the backgrounds of the companies you are dealing with before signing any contracts.

Emergency Numbers

The following numbers are good throughout Japan. The dispatcher may not speak English.

Police.. 110
Fire or Ambulance 119
Police (General Information in English)................. 3501-0110

Public phones have a red emergency button that you press before placing the call. In this case, the phone does not require a coin deposit.

Health

Japan is possibly one of the healthiest nations in the world. Public health standards are high and the tap water is safe to drink. Whatever you need to handle a headache, stomach upset, cold, or allergy, remedies are readily available as are a whole range of personal care products in local department stores or neighborhood pharmacies.

Japan's medical care is of the highest standard, and most specialists also speak English. Hotels have access to multi-lingual doctors.

For more information on medical centers, including phone numbers, please see the "Business Centers" section at the end of this chapter.

Japan Helpline... 0120-461-997.

INTERNAL TRAVEL

AIR

All Nippon Airways, Japan Airlines (JAL), Japan Air System, as well as a number of other airlines, provide a comprehensive network of air travel extending throughout Japan and its islands. Haneda (HND) is Tokyo's domestic airport. A monorail train relays the traveler from Hamamatsu-cho in Tokyo to Haneda.

Primary air routes are Tokyo–Osaka, Tokyo–Sapporo, Tokyo–Fukuoka, and Tokyo–Naha. You can buy tickets directly from machines at the domestic departure counter at Tokyo International and Osaka International. You may also telephone the airline directly, of course, or book through an agent.

You can always go by rail and ferry to one of the small islands, but flying is not much more expensive and certainly quicker. Inquire about discounts—there are some surprising ones, based on things like number of people traveling together or the combined age of married passengers.

websites to check for more information:
Airline info:
www.jp-tour.com/english-site/flijap.html
Japan Airlines (JAL):
www.jal.co.jp/
All Nippon Airways:
www.svc.ana.co.jp/eng
Japan Air System:
www.jas.co.jp/E_JASHOM.htm

TAXI

Taxis offer the most convenient (and most expensive) way for foreigners to get around in Japan's cities. Generally, the cabs are immaculate, the seats often covered in protective vinyl, with drivers who wear white gloves, keep a small vase with flowers inside the car, and actually try to be polite and efficient. Of course, this may be somewhat shocking at first, but visitors will adjust easily.

Fares rise by 30 percent after 11p.m. You can hail a cab, or call ahead to a taxi stand, which will cost an additional ¥500 to 600. Licensed cabs in Japan have green license plates. Lights in the windshield indicate if a taxi is available; a green or blue light means free, and red signals occupied. Your fare will read on the meter; bargaining is not practiced. Also, bear in mind that the rear left door opens automatically when you get in and out of the cab. In some cases, cab drivers may avoid foreigners due to potential communication problems.

Have your destination written down in Japanese characters, and if going someplace uncommon—for example, a company office or a friend's house—bring a map with the destination pinpointed and perhaps a nearby landmark by which to navigate. Hotels will provide you with such a map, if you ask. Street addresses often aren't consecutive, very few streets have names, and even when they do, the name isn't part of the address.

AUTO

Rental car agencies can be found in urban areas and at airports. Prices are comparable to European rentals as is the price of fuel. An International Driving Permit is necessary, and visitors must purchase ample insurance.

The roads in Japan are excellent. Driving in the cities can be unnerving, and finding a parking place is sometimes nearly impossible. Parking garages do exist, but at a premium cost. Outside of major metropolitan areas, though, it is remarkably civil with other motorists who are cautious and thoughtful. There are many expressways linking the cities of Japan. Signage presents a major problem for foreign motorists who do not read Japanese.

Hired cars with drivers are recommended for first-time visitors.

Motorcycle: Motorcycling can offer an excellent way of traveling around in Japan. Small 50cc 'step-thrus' are easy to rent—and you do not need a license to drive one.

TRAIN

Almost no region exists in Japan that you cannot access by train. Japanese trains are clean, comfortable, on time, and frequent—at peak hours, Tokyo commuter trains pass through the stations every 1.5 minutes. Its world-renowned *shinkansen* (bullet trains) hurtle through the countryside at 260k.p.h. (162 m.p.h.); prices follow suit.

Japan rail travel offers varying levels of cost and service: super express (shinkansen), limited express, express, berth, and reserved seat. The shinkansen is only slightly cheaper than flying, but still more convenient because train terminals are usually located in city centers.

Purchase your tickets from a vending machine, which has a map posted above it showing destination stations and the corresponding fare. Maps, however, might prove difficult to read if they are in Japanese only; you may be better off just finding the right train and buying the lowest fare possible, then paying the difference when you disembark.

Generally, station names are displayed in both Japanese and Roman alphabets. Also, the station signs indicate which was the previous station, and which will be the next.

Discount fares are available for intercity travel. A Japan Rail Pass is the most inexpensive method to travel around Japan. It gives you one, two, or three weeks of unlimited first-class or coach travel on JR lines and associated bus and ferry lines at rates ranging from ¥27,800 to ¥78,000 (about US$249 to US$698). Travel on the Narita Express Airport train is included in the JR Pass.

No matter which train you take, be aware that assorted surcharges crop up; for example, rail pass holders have to pay a sleeper charge of more than ¥5,000 (about US$45) on the shinkansen, even though no sleeper cars on the shinkansen exist.

Japan

Bullet train 107
JR Trains Tokyo Station ....(3) 3231-1880

METRO

Major cities have subways as fast and efficient as the trains. A place where all Japanese politeness falls aside, there is no shame in pushing and shoving your way onto a train if a crowd forms. In many cases, however, orderly lines form behind platform indicators where the train door will stop. Subway routes are color coded, and maps exist in most stations. In Tokyo and Osaka, stops are written in Japanese characters as well as the Roman alphabet, and often a voice announces the stop, first in Japanese, then in English. There are dozens of stops and many interconnections with JR lines that travel longer distances.

Fares: Fares start at ¥140 (about US$1.25). A prepaid card to purchase JR train tickets from any ticket vending machine at any JR station is available in the form of the JR Orange Card.

The prepaid IO card allows one to pass through automatic ticket gates in central Tokyo without hassling to buy individual tickets each time. These cards and the JR Orange Card are available at ticket offices, JR Reservations ticket offices at JR stations, or from special vending machines.

For a price of ¥1,460, one may purchase a one-day ticket for unlimited travel on JR trains, subways, and buses.
Tokyo Subways ....(3) 3834-5577
Subway Information (Tokyo) ....(3) 3837-7111

Tokyo's large public transport complex consists of tramways, buses, two underground metro systems, and six railways. There is an integrated flat fare in effect for the bus, underground, and tram services operated by the Tokyo Transportation Bureau. The Eidan underground, a larger seven-line network, operates on a separate fare system.

BUSES & TRAMS

In the large urban areas, with their highly developed metro and rail systems, bus and tram services are minor adjuncts to the public transit picture as a whole. In some cities such as Kyoto, though, buses comprise the primary means of public transit. In smaller cities, buses serve principally as a link to the next train station.

Intercity: Japan has extensive local and intercity bus systems that connect with rail and metro lines. The intercity buses are slower than most trains, but they are also significantly cheaper. For overnight travel, a reclining bus seat may be more comfortable than many train accommodations, and less fussy. Overnight buses ply all the major routes between cities ranging in size from Tokyo all the way to tiny rural villages. Buses are safe and clean but not smoke free, so bring a tolerance for second-hand smoke.

Urban: If you are taking the green city buses in Tokyo, the fare always remains the same, regardless of distance traveled. Enter the bus through the front door, and pay your fare to the driver. On other bus services, passengers board at the rear, taking a ticket with a number on it. Upon leaving the bus, pay the driver an amount corresponding to the number printed on your ticket, which is displayed on a board next to the driver.

One difficulty for foreigners in using the bus system is the fact that almost all signage is in Japanese only. Figuring out how to navigate the system may prove confusing, especially in Tokyo. Get help from an experienced colleague the first time or two, and get your hotel to give you directions also.

Log on to this website for information about Japan Rail's express bus network:
JR Kanto @ www.jrbuskanto.co.jp/

WATER TRAVEL

Ferries to the southern island of Shikoku and Kobe exist directly from Kansai Airport. A shuttle bus outside of the arrivals hall will whisk passengers to the terminal every 10 minutes. Jetfoil ferries depart in frequent intervals. Ask at the airport information counters for timetables and tickets. Ferries also depart from Tokyo, Osaka, and Kobe ports. In this case, however, be sure to procure information in advance since signs are only written in Japanese.

TRAVEL ASSISTANCE

The Japan National Tourist Organization (JNTO) is as solicitous of the traveler as you might expect in such a hospitable society. Its offices worldwide provide literature and information, and its employees can answer questions or steer you in the right direction. The JNTO is acutely aware of how expensive it is to travel in Japan, and so it publishes Economical Travel in Japan, a free source of budget-saving information. JNTO has 16 overseas offices and three in Japan.

Japan National Tourist Organization (JNTO)
Overseas Promotion Department
2-10-1 Yuraku-cho, Chiyoda-ku
Tokyo 100-0006, Japan
tel: (3) 3216-1902
fax: (3) 3216-1846
website: http://www.jnto.go.jp
Tourist information toll-free (within Japan):
Western Japan ....(120) 44-4800
Eastern Japan .... (120) 22-2800
Tokyo...(3) 3503-4400
Kyoto ....(75) 371-5649
(For these local numbers, the charge is ¥10 for every three minutes.)
Tourist Information Centre
B1F, Tokyo International Forum
3-5-1 Marunouchi, Chiyoda-ku
Tokyo 100-0005, Japan
tel: (3) 3201-3331; fax: (3) 3201-3347
Kyoto office
tel: (75) 371-5649

Communications

DIALING CODES IN JAPAN

International country code: [81]
Selected city codes: Chiba (43), Fuchu (Tokyo) (423), Hiroshima (82), Kawasaki (Kanagawa) (44), Kobe (78), Kyoto (75), Nagasaki (958), Nagoya (52), Naha (Okinawa) (98), Osaka (6), Sapporo (11), Sasebo (956), Tachikawa (Tokyo) (425), Tokyo (3), Yokohama (45), Yokosuka (Kanagawa) (468)

Dialing Japan from Overseas

To dial Japan from overseas, dial your country's international dialing code, then 81 (the country code for Japan), then the city code, and finally the number. If you were dialing Tokyo from the United States, for example, you would begin with 011, then 81, then 3 (the city code for Tokyo), and finally the number of the person or office you were trying to reach.

Assistance Numbers

International Phone Communications Services
(Kokusai Denshin Denwa Co.) 0057
International Operator 0051
Japan Helpline..(120) 461-997
Information Corner (Multilingual).................(45) 671-7209
Japan Hotline ....(3) 3586-0110

Japan

CALLING WITHIN JAPAN

Telephone service in Japan is first-rate and you can call virtually anywhere from nearly any location.

Local Calls

NTT (Nippon Telephone and Telegraph) handles domestic and local calls. Simply pick up the receiver and dial. Public phones require a ¥10 coin or a phone card. If after a time short beeping noises occur, your conversation will soon end. If you wish to continue talking, insert another coin or card.

Long Distance Calls

When you call long-distance within Japan, include the 0 with the area code. When calling Japan from overseas, omit the 0. Long distance calls are 40 percent cheaper between 11p.m. and 8a.m.; international rates vary according to carrier.

International Calls

Japan has three international call carriers: Kokusai Denshin Denwa (KDD), International Telecom Japan (ITJ) and International Digital Communications (IDC). This makes a difference when you try to direct dial internationally because each has its own international access number. Japan's country code is 81.

To direct dial internationally, dial the international access number—it depends on the carrier—then the country code, then the area code (if there is one), and the phone number. For example, to call World Trade Press direct on a KDD phone, dial 001 (KDD's access code), then 1 (U.S. country code), followed by 415 (San Francisco's city code), plus the local number: 898-1124. The cheapest time to call internationally from Japan is between 11p.m. and 5a.m. Before calling from your hotel room, check to see how vast the hotel surcharges are; then consider using a pay phone.

PAY PHONES

Public Telephones

Public telephones are everywhere, color-coded in a wide variety of colors and service offerings.

1. Lift receiver and listen for a dial tone.
2. Insert coin or telephone card.
3. If using a telephone card, a screen will tell you how much money is left on the card.
4. Dial number and wait for ring; a solid tone indicates the phone on the other end is ringing; short, succinctly repeated tones indicate the line is busy.
5. Instructions are included in Japanese for using the phone.
6. Pushing this button will automatically ring an operator for emergency situations.

Calling Cards

Calling cards won't save you any money, but they are very convenient and they can be purchased in stores, souvenir stands, hotels, and vending machines; a ¥1,000 card buys 105 3-minute calls. The green-and-gold phones take as many cards as you can feed them.

CELLULAR PHONES

Japan offers a multitude of choices for the cellular phone user. Both analog and digital networks exist.

Cell phone numbers require a prefix for dialing:

Cell Phones .... 090 + 8-digit number
PHS phones .... 0770 + 8-digit number

Note: Your home country cell phone may not work in this country. If not, we recommend that you rent an international cell phone *before* you leave home. A major US-based cell phone rental provider is **IMC WorldCell**. For information see "International Cell Phone Rentals" on page 14.

CALL BACK

You can (potentially) save significant sums when calling in Japan by using a call back service. For a list of callback services, please refer to the "Communications" section in the *Global Road Warrior* Introduction.

Fees for call back services vary widely, depending on the company and the type of service required. Be sure to check with these companies before leaving to compare rates.

PHONE JACKS

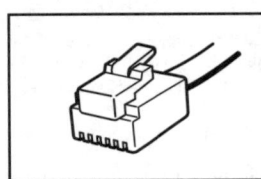

Plug adaptors are available through **iGo Corporation**. (See "Electrical and Telephone Adaptors" on page 19.)

FAX

Fax machines are everywhere—in almost every hotel, most businesses, many homes, even in 24-hour convenience stores. Most hotels also have telexes. Your hotel can refer you to a business center or a KDD office from which you can send faxes, telegrams, and telexes. Major post offices can also send telegrams.

POSTAL SERVICES

A bright red 'T' with a line above it marks Japanese post offices, while mailboxes are a brilliant orange-red. As with most other services in Japan, one can expect efficient and dependable service. A letter takes about five days to get to the U.S. The easiest way to mail a letter or package is from your hotel's front desk. The weight for a parcel cannot exceed 20kg. International Business Mail (EMS) service is available at post offices handling international mail. International money orders are also available at main post offices.

Hours of service

International postal branches remain open from 8a.m. until 7 or 8p.m. Monday to Friday, and also for a time on Saturdays.

Rates

Postcards to anywhere in the world cost ¥70, and aerograms cost ¥80. Letters up to 10 grams cost ¥80 to Asia; ¥100 to Oceania, the Middle East, and North and Central America; and ¥120 to Europe, Africa, and South America.

TELEGRAMS

Hotels cannot send telegrams, but they can refer you to a business center where you can send one. Major post offices can also send telegrams.

Domestic 115
Overseas ....(3) 3344-5151

Business Services

BUSINESS CENTERS

Many first-class hotels have business centers providing secretarial and delivery services, computers, fax machines, and telephones.

Tokyo Akasaka Prince, ANA Hotel Tokyo, Capitol Tokyu, Century Hyatt, Dai-Ichi Hotel Annex, Ginza Tokyu, Hilton, Imperial, Mitsui Urban Hotel Ginza, New Otani, New Takanawa Prince, Okura, Pacific Meridien, Palace, Seiyo Ginza, Tokyo Renaissance Ginza Tobu.

Nagoya Castle, Fitness, Nagoya Hilton, International Hotel Nagoya, Kanko.

Osaka ANA Sheraton, Hilton International, Nankai South Tower, Toyo.

COURIER SERVICES

Airborne Express (Tokyo); 6-46 Kohnan, 4-chome, Minato-ku, tokyo 108; tel: (3) 5461-8411.

Airborne Express (Osaka); 10-47 Nanko Higashi, 4-chome, Suminoe-ku, Osaka 559; tel: (6) 225-2115.

DHL Worldwide Express; 37-8 Higashi-Shinagawa, 1-chome, Shinagawa-ku, Tokyo 140; tel: (3) 5479-2580.

FedEx (Tokyo); 3-10, Tatsumi, Koto-ku 135; tel: (toll-free) (12) 003-200.

FedEx (Osaka) 3-6, Honden 3-chome, Nishi-ku 550; tel: (6) 584-6565

TNT (Tokyo); Number 7 Koike Building, 4th Floor, 3-6 Minami-Shinagawa 2-chome, Shinagawa-ku 140; tel: (3) 3740-4300 fax: (3) 3740-4306.

TNT (Nagoya) 1-515, Tokugawa, Higashi-ku 461; tel: (52) 937-4831 fax: (52) 937-4796 Tlx: 2425506 TNTTYO J.

TNT (Osaka) 2-6-2, Hotarugaike-Nishimachi, Toyonaka 560; tel: (6) 843-7562 fax: (6) 843-5043 Tlx: 2425506 TNTTYO J.

UPS (Chiba) Unistar Air Cargo (UPS Yamato Co., Ltd.), 717-74, Futamata, Ichikawa City; tel: (473) 27-1040 fax: (473) 28-3120.

OFFICE RENTAL

Business Center Chuo Co., Ltd.; 2-9-7 Kajicho, Chiyoda-ku, Tokyo; tel: (3) 3252-7311.

Century 21 SKY Realty Inc.; Yatsuka Bldg. 1F, 1-3-8 Higashi Azabu, Minato-ku, Tokyo; tel: (3) 3585-0021; email: c21sky@beehive.twics.com.

KDD Business Quarters; KDD Otemachi Bldg. 21F, 1-8-1 Otemachi, Chiyoda-ku, Tokyo; tel: (3) 3243-9180; http://www1.kcom.ne.jp/kbq/index/; email: kbq@ma.kcom.ne.jp.

Tokyo Executive Center, Inc.; Madre Matsuda Bldg., 4-13 Kioicho, Chiyoda-ku, Tokyo; tel: (3) 3239-8800.

PRINTING/COPYING

You'll need business cards as soon as you land. If you haven't already had them made, your first-class hotel can usually arrange to have them printed within a couple of days. They should have at least your name and company name in Japanese on the reverse—a translation of your address isn't necessary. Here are three of the many printers in Tokyo who print business cards:

Aoyama Printing Company Tokyo Printing Service, 10-2, Kita Aoyama 3-chome, Minato-ku 107; tel: (3) 3406-3884 fax: (3) 3406-6695.

Preseez, Inc. 1-25-20, Shirogane, Minato-ku 108; tel: (3) 3444-9742 fax: (3) 5423-7010.

Press Man Basement 1, Tokyo Kotsu Kaikan Building, 2-10-1 Yurakucho, Chiyoda-ku; tel: (3) 3211-7916 fax: (3) 3211-7937.

Kinko's Taisei Yaesu Bldg. 2-8-8; Yaesu; Tokyo, 104J; tel: (13) 278-3911; fax: (13) 278-3922.

In Osaka

In Osaka a business card service exists directly at Kansai Airport on the 4th Floor.

SECRETARIAL SERVICES

ABA Secretarial Services; 13-8 Ichiban-cho, Chiyoda-ku, Tokyo; tel: (3) 3221-1331.

Access Business Associates; Ichiban-cho KK bldg., 13-8 Ichiban-cho, Chiyoda-ku, Tokyo; tel: (3) 3221-1011.

Akasaka Prince Hotel Tower Executive Service Center; 1-2 Kioicho, Chiyoda-ku, Tokyo; tel: (3) 3262-5165.

Office Japan Co., Std.; 3-1-3 Takaban, Meguro-ku, Tokyo; tel: (3) 3792-6666.

TRANSLATION SERVICES

Business Associates, Inc. 1-2-9, Shinjuku, Shinjuku-ku; Tokyo; tel: (3) 3225-1931 fax: (3) 3225-1930/1933.

Idea Institute, Inc. 1-19-15, Ebisu, Sibuya-ku; Tokyo; tel: (3) 3446-8660 fax: 3446-3134.

Japan Translation Center Ltd. 1-21, Kanda Nishiki-cho, Chiyoda-ku; Tokyo; tel: (3) 3291-0655 fax: (3) 3294-0657.

Guide-Interpreters

Japan has about 1,200 licensed guide-interpreters. You can hire one through the **Japan Guide Association**, Shin Kokusai Building, 3-4-1, Marunouchi, Chiyoda-ku, Tokyo; tel: (3) 3213-2706.

Electrical

Current

100volts AC, 60Hz.

ELECTRICAL SOCKET

Be aware that Japan's wattage is lower than most countries that have similar sockets; as such, sensitive equipment may need to be adjusted or, if possible, used with batteries. See below for electrical plug schematic.

ELECTRIC PLUGS

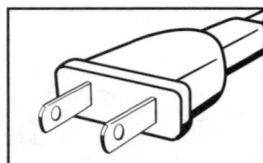

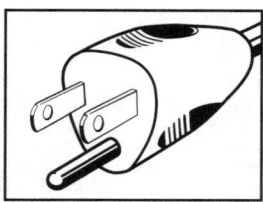

Plug adaptors are available through **iGo Corporation.** (See "Electrical and Telephone Adaptors" on page 19.)

Technical Support

HARDWARE/SOFTWARE VENDOR SUPPORT

Acer/Texas Instruments; (in Germany) tel: [49] (4102) 488-469; fax; [49] (4102) 488-169; (in the U.S.) [1] (408) 432-6200; http://www.acer.com/.

Adobe; tel: (3) 5423-8184; fax: (3) 5423-8209 (Technical Support Center for Macintosh, Windows and UNIX products); tel: (3) 5250-2141; fax: (3) 5250-2149 (Adobe Framemaker); http://www.adobe.com.

Apple/Claris; tel: 3-5717-7500; 3-5717-7700; (in Switzerland) tel: [41] (800) 833-310; (in the U.K.) tel: [44] (990) 127-753; (in the U.S.) tel: [1] (800) 500-7078; http://www.apple.com/.

AST; (in the U.S.) tel: [1] (817) 232-9824 (International Technical Support); (in Ireland) tel: [353] (61) 492-222; (in the U.S.) tel: [1] (949) 727-4141; http://www.ast.com/.

Compaq/Digital; tel: (3) 5402-5700; fax: (3) 5402-5974; (General U.S.) tel: (281) 518-2000; http://www.compaq.com/.

Corel; tel: (3) 5645-8379 (All Applications); (in the U.S.) tel: [1] (716) 871-2325 (Ask to be Forwarded to Appropriate Program); http://www.corel.com/.

Dell; tel: (604) 810-4977 (for Dell listings in Japan); fax: (604) 810- 4273; (in the U.S.) tel: [1] (512) 338-4400; fax: [1] (512) 728-3330; http://www.dell.com/.

Filemaker/Claris; (in Germany) tel: [49] (180) 525-8166 (Info-line); fax: [49] (180) 567-2233; tel: [49] (180) 523-6423; (in the U.S.) tel: [1] (800) 965-9090; http://www.claris.com/.

Gateway 2000; (in the U.S.) tel: [1] (605) 232-2191; fax: [1] (605) 232-2023; (in Ireland) tel: [353] (1) 797-2000; http://www.g2k.com/.

Hewlett Packard; tel: 3 3335 8333; (in Switzerland) tel: [41] (22) 780-8111; (in the U.S.) tel: [1] (408) 246-4300; http://www.hp.com/.

IBM; tel: 3-3586-1111; 0120-04-1992; fax: 44-200-8600; (in Switzerland) tel: [41] (22) 310-0418 (in French); (in the U.S.) tel: [1] (919) 517-2800; (U.S. Main Office) tel: [1] 914-765-1900; http://www.ibm.com/.

Microsoft; tel: (3) 5354-4500 (Technical Support); (in Tokyo) tel: (3) 5454-2300; (in Osaka) (6) 6245-6995; (in Switzerland) tel: [41] (848) 858-868; fax [41] (1) 831-0869; (in the U.S.) [1] (425) 635-7222; http://www.microsoft.com/.

NEC; tel: (3) 3255-9539 (UltraCare Support); (in the U.S.) [1] (916) 388-0101 (Main Switchboard); http://www.nec.com/.

Novell; tel: (3) 5481-1161 (Technical Support Center); (in the U.S.) tel: [1] (408) 434-2300; fax: [1] (408) 577-5775 (Worldwide Sales Headquarters); http://www.novell.com/.

Quark; tel: 3-3499-9009 (Tokyo); 43-297-3511 (Makuhari); (in the U.S.) tel: [1] (303) 894-8899; fax: [1] (303) 894-3398 (For Products Registered in the Americas); http://www.quark.com/.

Internet Connection
HOW TO CONNECT

Connecting to AOL and Compuserve in Japan is similar to using it when traveling outside your own area code. See the introductory section for detailed information on connecting to your account through a different phone number.

America Online

Numbers are available at keyword *international*. Be sure to get several local numbers before leaving. AOL's GlobalNet service charges US$3.95 an hour in addition to the usual charges. Go to keyword *access* (a free area) and download the software.

Access: Chiba (043) 420-1851; Chiba (043) 420-2010; DDI National Number (0077) 2286-3939; Fukuoka (92) 624-2188; Hiroshima (082) 503-0318; Kanazawa (076) 292-8880; Kawasaki (044) 329-5570; Kawasaki (044) 329-1070; Kita-Kyushu (093) 752-2510; Kobe (078) 435-0350; Kyoto (075) 803-3150; Kyoto (075) 813-3221; Nagano (026) 238-0202; Nagoya (052) 339-0030; Nara (0743) 682-900; Niigata (025) 282-1013; Niigata (025) 282-4373; Nishinomiya (0798) 372-861; Nishinomiya (0798) 376-160; Osaka (06) 6535-7091;Osaka (06) 6578-7230; Sapporo (011) 700-2531; Sapporo (011) 708-8030; Sendai (022) 717-9133; Shizuoka (054) 621-0666; Tokorozawa (042) 920-3426; Tokyo (03) 3570-5051; Tokyo (03) 3599-1801; Tokyo (03) 3599-4011; Tokyo (03) 3599-7011; Tokyo (03) 3599-7040; Yokohama (045) 590-1727; Yokohama (045) 590-2321.

Compuserve

Numbers are available at *Go International*. The Compuserve Web-site also has a great deal of information, at http://www.compuserve.com.

Access: Nationwide (070) 670-488-888; Tokyo (03) 3523-5002.

Independent Service Providers

Many independent service providers offer discounts if you are only in town for a couple of days. For longer stays in the country, ISP charges average ¥3,000 for a hook up and ¥1,000 a month (for two hours of service). Be sure to call your ISP and get any special instructions before leaving. They may be able to suggest a service in Japan.

ASAHI Net; tel: (3) 3569-3522 (English); fax: (3) 3569-3501; email: eap-net@asahi-net.or.jp; http://www.asahi-net.or.jp/.

Cable and Wireless Japan; tel: (3) 5470-2100; fax: (3) 5470-8530; email: info@majic.ne.jp; http://www.majic.co.jp/.

Global OnLine Japan; tel: (3) 5334-1700; tel: (3) 5334-1720 (Sales); (3) 5334-1770 (Corporate sales); fax: (3) 5334-1711; email: sales@gol.com; http://www.gol.com/.

Janis II Online Information Service; tel: (3) 3255-8880; fax: (3) 3255-8857; email: pperkins@mail.asianet.net; http://www.asianet.net/.

SANYei interNET Inc; tel: 78-325-5777 (ask for English assistance); fax: 78-321-0999; email: english-support@sanynet.ad.jp; http://www.sanynet.ne.jp/.

Tokyo Internet Corporation; tel: (3) 3341-6301; fax: (3) 3341-6305; http://www.tokyonet.ad.jp/.

Typhoon Inc.; tel: (3) 3759-1261; fax: (3) 3759-1262; email: info@typhoon.co.jp; http://www.typhoon.co.jp/.

Japan

Japan

Telephone Usage

The high telephone rates can become an issue. Users are charged ¥10 (about US$0.90) for three minutes of local calls. Many users wait until late at night to use the Internet, taking advantage of lower calling rates.

KEY INTERNET SITES

Japan Information Resource Center
http://futures.wharton.upenn.edu/~hernb108/jp.html.

Japanese Sources of Information
http://pclsp2.kuicr.kyoto-u.ac.jp/4.html.

JETRO (Japan External Trade Organization)
http://www.jetro.go.jp/index.html.

Keidanren (Japan Federation of Economic Orgs.)
http://www.keidanren.or.jp.

Business Culture

GREETINGS AND COURTESIES

Although the accepted form of salutation between Japanese is the bow, most Japanese with international experience will not expect a bow from a foreigner. If the situation is unclear, wait for the Japanese either to offer a hand or to bow, and reciprocate accordingly. Always address a person with the honorific title *san* following the last name. Do not use it when referring to yourself, however. First names are not used. Business cards are always presented upon first meeting as are gifts, but they are generally not opened in front of the giver. Do not give items in units of four; the word four, or *shi* in Japanese, also means death. Also avoid giving sharp items such as knives, scissors, or letter openers since superstition labels these as improper. If a situation calls for removing your shoes, place them facing outward, or the Japanese host may do it for you so you can easily step into them when leaving. Offices and residences often provide slippers for indoor walking and extra toilet slippers in the toilet area. Always remove any kind of footwear, besides socks, when entering a tatami (woven bamboo mat) room.

The concept of face remains basic to Confucian etiquette. Face is self-respect, status in the eyes of others. Losing face is abhorrent, having it or gaining it is prized. Open criticism and the disrespect for authority and elders cause loss of face in any relationship, personal or business. As such, the word 'no' often implies a personal affront. The Japanese use "maybe" or "not sure" to soften the tone if the situation does not call for a 'yes' answer.

DECISION MAKING

In many companies, ideas are often initiated by lower level employees and then passed on via formal and informal channels to higher-ranking managers for review. Middle-level managers are usually the prime source for decisions on company policy. Their importance means that foreign businesspeople must work to establish close relations with many different company employees. They cannot simply meet the top management and assume a solid relationship has been formed.

Furthermore, one must not underestimate the importance of harmony and consensus in the Japanese realm. As such, one must take much time into account for the necessary discussions between parties to transpire, formal and informal. Japanese often use the social realm to discuss and sway opinion to their side. If face saving for an individual is somehow involved, expect even more delays. Patience in Japan is an elementary virtue. To lose one's temper or press for a decision will most likely cause your counterparts to withdraw or use it against you. Novice negotiators might find the Japanese patiently biding time, expecting a foreigner to cave in with pressures of timelines and impatient business methods.

WOMEN

Although women have recently become more accepted in business, traditional notions of male supremacy persist in most business circles. Women earn only about 60 percent as much as their male counterparts, and very few women hold senior management positions. In these days of recession and company downsizing, women are often the first on the cutting block. While women of exceptional skill or talent may achieve some success in business, they are usually relegated to subservient positions, such as secretaries. They are described by some as "flowers", decorations to enhance atmosphere. This gender inequality carries over into family life, where women are primarily responsible for the family budget and the education and careers of family members but shoulder the blame for family failures. Foreign women will receive respect, however, not as much as their male counterparts.

MEETINGS

Any business meeting, especially one with a larger company, needs to be scheduled weeks in advance. Before the meeting, you should mail or fax a detailed document outlining the matter to be discussed or the agenda. The Japanese do not like surprises. Your first meeting may take place with young managers, which is not necessarily a bad sign as junior executives usually initiate business relationships. When you enter a Japanese building for a meeting, the members of your delegation should remove their coats immediately on entry and put them back on only when they leave. Once the meeting has begun, prepare for often long presentations; it is imperative to show alert and conscious attention, even if your mind has long drifted into the twilight zone. Protracted silence from the Japanese does not necessarily mean they are negative to ideas. Instead, Japanese mentality suggests it is not prudent to commit to an idea in the first round; time must pass to reflect on the matter, and proper reflection entails silence.

Take care to speak slowly with clear enunciation, primarily for understanding, but also because rushing indicates impatience, a trait expected of foreigners and often used by the more patient Japanese to procure advantage.

CONTRACTS

Once something is in the contract, the Japanese will follow it to the letter. But woe unto anyone who leaves something out of a contract, assuming that it is understood. It may be standard practice where you come from, but you can't count on it being standard practice in Japan.

BUSINESS CARDS

Holding and exchanging business cards in Japan is standard operating procedure. Japanese love them. Come prepared to collect and offer many. Business cards are normally exchanged during the first meeting. Correct etiquette dictates that you carefully read the card that has been given to you, and with a polite bow exchange your own, which has hopefully been printed in English and Japanese. Since it serves as an honorable symbol, one should take care not to write on someone's card--at least not in their presence.

BUSINESS ATTIRE

Japanese attire is often conservative and formal. British style is favored over American and definitely over Italian. Dark suits of fine tailoring and expensive but understated accessories are recommended for both men and women. Women should wear conservative necklines, sleeves, and makeup.

Skirts, blouses, and suit jackets worn with stockings, even in the most humid of days, are almost uniform for Japanese women. Very often, companies will provide their employees with uniforms or outfits that carry the company mark outside the perimeters of the office and to promote uniformity.

There are two exceptions to the formality. If you find yourself in a small-scale business such as fashion, jewelry, or arts and crafts, your contacts would expect you to dress more casually and freely. If you work in a local concern, you may be expected to dress like your fellow workers.

To weather a Tokyo or Osaka winter, you need to dress as warmly as you would in Britain or the Maryland-Virginia area of the United States. For Hokkaido and northern Honshu, bundle up on a Swedish scale; for Shikoku and Kyushu, think southeastern United States (but definitely not Florida, which is more like Okinawa).

DINING

There's much more to Japanese food than you see in restaurants in foreign countries. Look for *okonomiyaki*, a kind of pancake or omelet that diners prepare themselves at the table; *tempura*, deep-fried prawns, fish, or vegetables; *sushi*, raw fish and vinegared rice, often wrapped in seaweed and sometimes with a surprise dose of *wasabi* (horseradish) lurking inside; *sashimi*, raw fish eaten with soy sauce; *tonkatsu*, a deep-fried pork cutlet; *shabu-shabu*, slices of tender beef that you hold with chopsticks, swirl in boiling water, then dip in a sauce; *yakitori*, skewered, grilled beef and chicken kabobs with a sweet glaze, and *shojin ryori*, Zen Buddhist vegetarian cuisine.

Eating your way through Japan can be expensive, although reasonable and cheap eateries exist. You can find cheap food in street stalls throughout the country as well as in traditional style noodle and ramen restaurants. Yakitori restaurants can be spotted by paper lanterns usually strung over the front entrance. These are casual, local eateries where the orders are spoken right to the cook behind the counter. Many restaurants have plastic food displays in the windows to which foreigners may point if they cannot navigate the menu. And take advantage of the fact that most restaurants serve lunch for less than half the price of dinner for the same food. Keep in mind, too, that some of the best restaurants are in major hotels.

Proper etiquette mandates cleaning your hands with the washcloth provided before eating. Hold your chopsticks as far to the back end as possible for polite dining. Never wave them about, play with them, or use them as conversation aids. When you have finished, place them flat across the top of the bowl or plate, or on the chopstick holder; never leave them sticking upright in leftover food or rice. If unsure about etiquette, just wait and observe how the Japanese handle it.

A note of caution: Japanese of both sexes are heavy-duty drinkers. Face falls by the wayside; all is forgiven if you embark upon something ridiculous when drunk. Japanese are happy imbibers, too. A business traveler is already under enough stress, however, so it's best to resist the nightly invitations to overindulge in sake and beer. Drunken revelry may also be a ploy for the Japanese to gain the upper hand in business when the foreigner is too tired to make any headway.

Business Centers
Tokyo
CITY VIEW

Tokyo is the national, business, financial, and cultural capital of Japan. It is home to more than 11 million people as well as Japan's largest banks and Asia's top stock market, the Tokyo Securities and Stock Exchange. For a city of such size, Tokyo remains amazingly clean. However, the rows of uniform buildings and humidity-attacked apartment blocks on the outskirts may leave much for the eye to desire. This applies to most Japanese cities. To compensate for it, however, a traditional Japanese interior holds an austere sense of calm and beauty accompanied by exquisite packaging and presentation.

AIRPORT
Narita Airport to City Center

New Tokyo International Airport at Narita is a business traveler's nightmare. It is 41 traffic-choked miles (66 km.) from the city center. Considering its passenger volume, Narita seems small, chaotically busy, and grindingly slow in customs. However, the always service-oriented Japanese will assist you in recovering from the nightmare at an information counter in the arrivals hall. Next-day luggage delivery service also exists for about ¥2,000 if you have excess baggage that you prefer not to carry from the airport to your hotel.

Narita Airport ....(476) 32-2800

Shuttle Bus The Airport Limousine Bus takes 90 minutes to hours to reach various hotels in central Tokyo and charges from ¥2,800 to ¥3,500 (about US$24 to $30). Service also goes to Yokohama. Purchase your tickets at the Airport Limousine counter located outside of customs. Other hotels also have service. Ask at the desk outside of arrivals.

Taxi Tokyo Taxi ....(3) 3648-0300

A taxi may well cost you ¥20,000 by the time you get to your destination in downtown Tokyo. All unlimited expense accounts aside, it may still take hours to reach your destination, depending on traffic.

Train The Narita Express Train departs from the basement of both domestic and international terminals for Tokyo Station. It will deliver you into downtown Tokyo for a more pleasant fare of about ¥3,000 in just under an hour. Trains also go to Shinjuku station or to Yokohama. Costs go up if you prefer to travel in the first class green car, or in your own compartment. Trains leave in 30-minute intervals between 7:30a.m. and 9:30p.m. The Narita Express requires advance reservations. You will find information counters at Narita Airport and on the lower level of Tokyo Station (Marunouchi side). Pick up a timetable and schedule brochure at an information counter.

The Airport Narita rapid train takes a bit longer to the same destinations as the Narita Express, but costs about half the price if you have time on your hands.

Another express train, Keisei Skyliner, departs for Keisei Ueno Station between 6a.m. and 10p.m. in 30 to 40-minute intervals. Expect an hour ride for a fare of ¥1800. The Limited Express train takes an extra 15 minutes at a cost of ¥1,000. Trains stop at Nippori Station where travelers can connect to JR trains.

Other Japan Rail (JR) trains depart from the basement levels every 45 minutes between 7a.m. and 9p.m. JR trains travel a bit slower and stop more frequently. It takes about one and a half hours for a cost of ¥1400 (US$12).

Hotel Shuttle Buses Hotels near Narita Airport most likely offer free shuttle services. Be sure to inquire when booking.

Haneda Airport Transfers Those unfortunate souls who must still continue on to another domestic destination after an arduous overseas flight can catch the Airport Limousine Bus that specifically services the route between Narita and Haneda. Expect a ¥3,000 fare and an hour to 90 minutes for the trip.

Haneda Airport to City Center

Haneda Airport lies much closer to town, with much easier

and cheaper access to the city center. Taiwan-based China Airlines is the only international carrier serving Haneda.
Haneda Airport ....(3) 3747-8010
If you don't have to do business in Tokyo, another strategy is to fly into Osaka, Nagoya, or Fukuoka instead of the usual convoluted method of flying into Tokyo, taking a train to Haneda and then catching a domestic connecting flight to any of those cities.

Monorail The monorail offers the best way from Haneda to the Hamamatsu-cho Train Station. The ride takes 15 minutes and costs ¥300 (about US$2.70)—considering the horrible taxi alternative, it is one of the best bargains in Japan. From there you can take a taxi.

Taxi Tokyo Taxi ....(3) 3648-0300
Fares cost around ¥6,000 in Yen and 45 minutes to an hour in time.

Bus The comfortable Airport Bus provides steady service from Haneda to many Tokyo hotels. Head for the Airport Limousine counter for information and to purchase tickets.

Airline Numbers
Aer Lingus .... (3) 5275-1666
Aerolineas Argentinas ....(3) 3433-1195
Aeroflot ....(3) 3434-9671
Air Canada ....(3) 3586-3891
Air China ....(3) 5251-0711
Air France res. (3) 3475-1511, cargo: 3475-2275,
....ticketing 3475-2355
Air India .... res. (3) 3214-1981, cargo: 3215-3144
....ticketing 3214-7639
Air Lanka ....(3) 3573-4261
Air Mauritius ....(3) 3543-6241
Air New Zealand...................................(3) 3287-1641
Alaska Airlines.....................................(3) 3407-8386
Alitalia...(3) 3580-2242
All Nippon Airways .... (3) 3272-1212, 3552-6311
.................domestic res. 0120-029-222; intl. 0120-029333
American Airlines .... (3) 3214-2111, 0120-000860
Ansett Australia ....(3) 5210-0791
Asiana Airways.....................................(3) 3582-6600
Austrian Airlines ....(3) 3597-6100
Avianca...(3) 3593-7603
Balkan Bulgarian ....(3) 5276-4091
Bangladesh Bimna ....(3) 3593-8811
British Airways ....(3) 3593-8811
Canadian Airlines International ....(3) 3281-7426
Cargolux..(3) 5689-7470
Cathay Pacific ....(3) 3504-1531
China Airlines ....(3) 3436-1661
China Eastern Airlines..........................(3) 3506-1166
Continental Airlines ....(3) 5464-5050
Continental Micronesia...........................(3) 3508-6411
CSA Czech Airlines ....(3) 3409-7414
Delta Airlines ....(3) 5275-7000
Dragon Air Hong Kong ....(3) 3506-8361
Egypt Air...(3) 3288-0022
El Al Israel Airlines ....(3) 3288-0022
Ethiopian Airlines.................................(3) 3281-1990
EVA Airways Corp.................................(3) 3546-2100
Finnair .... (3) 3222-6801
Garuda Indonesian Airlines ....(3) 3593-1181
GSA Japan Inc. ....(3) 5472-0330
Hawaiian Air ....(3) 3214-4774
Iberia Airlines................ (3) 3578-3555, cargo: 3578-3570
Iran Air..(3) 3586-2101
Japan Airlines .... (3) 3456-2111, 0120-255931
Japan Air System ....(3) 3438-1155
Japan Asia Airways ....(3) 3455-7511

KLM ....(3) 3216-0771
Korean Air .... (3) 5443-3311
Kuwait Airways ....(3) 3597-0625
LOT Polish Airlines...............................(3) 3437-5741
Lufthansa..(3) 3580-2111
Malaysia Airlines ....(3) 3503-5961
Mexicana ....(3) 5401-2239
Norhwest Airlines ....(3) 3533-6000
Pakistan International ....(3) 3216-6511
Philippine Airlines ....(3) 3580-1579
Olympic Airways ....(3) 3201-0611
Qantas...................... res. (3) 3593-7000, sales 5401-7700
Royal Nepal...(3) 3574-8410
Sabena.. (3) 3585-6151
SAS ....(3) 3503-8101
Saudi Arabian Airlines ....(3) 3591-9081
Singapore Airlines ....(3) 3213-3431
South African Airways ....(3) 3470-1901
Swissair ....(3) 3212-1016
Thai Airways ....(3) 3503-3311
Trans World Airlines ....(3) 3212-1477
Turkish Airlines.....................................(3) 5251-1551
United Airlines ....(3) 3817-4411
Varig Brazilian Airlines ....(3) 3211-6751
Virgin Atlantic Airways ....(3) 3499-8811

TOKYO HOTELS

Top-end
Four Seasons at Chinzan-So; 2-10-8 Sekiguchi, Bunkyo-ku; tel: (3) 3943-2222; fax: (3) 3943-2300; set in Chinzan-so gardens; restaurants; conference facilities (up to 1,000); secretarial service; in-room modem/fax connections; complimentary shuttle bus to subway; complimentary limousine service to Tokyo Station; corporate rates; fitness; sauna; pool;

Hotel Okura; 10-4 Toranomon 2-chome, Minato-ku; tel: (3) 3582-0111; fax: (3) 3582-3707; near business districts; popular for dignitaries; restaurant; business center; executive services; secretarial service; meeting lounge; conference room; in-room fax machines and modem lines; computer terminals; no-smoking rooms; handicapped access; corporate rates; fitness; health; massage; sauna; pool; whirlpool; Japanese garden.

Imperial Hotel; 1-1-1 Uchisaiwaicho Chiyoda-ku; tel: (3) 3504-1111, toll-free (800) 223-6800 in US and Canada fax: (3) 3581-9146; http://www.imperialhotel.co.jp; 6 restaurants; conference/banquet facilities (up to 3,000); executive service center with computers, secretarial service, translation service, periodical library, media interview room; music room; in-room fax machines, 3 telephones, modem connection, private email address, internet access; safe, hair dryers, toiletries; non-smoking rooms available; corporate rates; saunas; pool.

Park Hyatt Tokyo; 3-7-1-2 Nishi-Shinjuku; tel: (3) 5322-1234; fax: (3) 5322-1288; new; top floors of high rise; private ambiance; modernist residence-style rooms with office; restaurant; business center; library; conference and banquet rooms; 24-hour video conferencing capabilities; secretarial service; in-room dual phone lines, voice mail; modem port; fax machines; health club, fitness center; indoor pool; library.

Seiyo Ginza; 1-11-2 Ginza Chuo-ku; tel: (3) 3535-1111; fax: (3) 3535-1110; intimate hotel; individually -decorated rooms; restaurant; conference facilities; secretarial service; in-room modem/fax connection; corporate rates; limousine service.

Tokyo Hilton; 6-6-2 Nishi-Shinjuku, 6-chome; tel: (3) 3344-5111, U.S. toll-free: (800) HILTONS; fax: (3) 3342-6094; http://www.hilton.com/; city center; restaurants; conference facilities (up to 1300); secretarial service; computers available; in-room modem/fax connections; 24-hour room service; complimentary transport to Shinjuku Station; parking; corporate rates; fitness; sauna; pools; tennis.

Westin Tokyo; 1-4-1 Mita, Meguro-ku (in Yebisu Garden Place); tel: (3) 5423-7000; fax: (3) 5423-7600; large neoclassical rooms; restaurant; conference facilities; secretarial service; in-room modem/fax connection; corporate rates; shops; fitness; sauna; whirlpool; pool; large landscaped gardens.

Expensive

Dai-Ichi Hotel Annex; 1-5-2 Uchisaiwai-cho, Chiyoda ku; tel: (3) 3503-5611 fax: (3) 3503-5777.

Ginza Tokyu; 15-9 Ginza, 5-chome, Chuo-ku; tel: (3) 3541-2411; fax: (3) 3541-6520; restaurant; conference facilities; secretarial service; corporate rates; sauna.

Holiday Inn Crowne Plaza Metropolitan; 1-6-1 Nishi-Ikebukuro, Toshima-ku; tel: (3) 3980-111; fax: (3) 3980-5600; restaurant; business center; conference facilities; secretarial service; in-room modem/fax connection; corporate rates; sauna; pool.

New Takanawa Prince; 3-13-1 Takanawa, Minato-ku; tel: (3) 3442-1111; fax: (3) 3444-1234; city suburb, adjacent to the Takanawa Prince; gardens; meeting rooms.

Palace; 1-1-1 Marunouchi, Chiyoda-ku; tel: (3) 3211-5211 fax: (3) 3211-6987; adjacent to Imperial Palace with views; restaurant; conference facilities (up to 500); secretarial service; corporate rates; Imperial garden.

Shinjuku Washington Hotel; 3-3-15 Nishi-Shinjuku, Shinjuku-ku; tel: (3) 3343-3111; fax: (3) 3342-2575; business hotel; restaurant.

Tokyo Renaissance Ginza Tobu; 14-10 Ginza, 6-chome, Chuo-ku; el: (3) 3546-0111, toll-free (800) 228-2828 in US fax: (3) 3546-8990; restaurant; conference facilities (400); secretarial service.

Moderate

Fairmont Hotel; 2-1-17 Kudan Minami, chiyoda-ku; tel: (3) 3262-1151 fax: (3) 3264-2476.

Ginza Capital; 3-1-5 Tsukiji, Chuo-ku; tel: (3) 3543-8211; fax: (3) 3543-7839.

Hotel East 21 Tokyo; 6-3-3 Toyo, Koto-ku; tel: (3) 5683-5683; fax: (3) 5683-5775; restaurants; no-smoking rooms available; business center; banquet halls; ball room; PC terminal rental; health club; gym/sauna/bath/pool/jacuzzi.

Hotel Sunroute Tokyo; 2-3-1 Yoyogi, Shibuya-ku; tel: (3) 3375-3211; fax: (3) 3379-3040; restaurant.

New Otani Inn; 1-6-2, Shinagawa-ku, Osaki; tel: (3) 3779-9111; fax: (3) 3779-9181; city center; ¥11,000/21,000.

The President Hotel; 2-2-3 Minami-Aoyama, Minato-ku; tel: (3) 3497-0111; fax: (3) 3401-4816; restaurant.

Airport Hotels
Narita Airport Vicinity

Radisson Hotel Narita Airport; 650-35 Nanaei, Tomisato-machi, Chiba; tel: (4) 7693-1234; fax: (4) 7693-4834; new, modern resort hotel; restaurants; pool; frequent airport shuttle service; pool; ¥21,000/30,000.

Hotel Nikko Narita; 500 Tokko, Narita; tel: (4) 7632-0032; fax: (4) 7632-3993; restaurant; meeting facilities (200); pool; ¥12,000+.

Narita Winds Hotel; tel: (4) 7633-1111; fax: (4) 7633-1108; restaurants; banquet and meeting rooms; soundproof rooms; regular airport shuttle service; ¥10,000/21,000.

Narita Airport Resthouse; Narita Airport; tel: (4) 7632-1212; fax: (4) 7632-1209; ¥10,000/13,000.

Haneda Airport

Haneda Tokyu; 8-6 Haneda-Kuko, 2-chome; tel: (3) 3747-0311; fax: (3) 3747-0366; at airport; restaurant; conference facilities (up to 200); pool; ¥18,500/26,800.

Yokohama

Royal Park Hotel Nikko; 1-1-1 Minato Mirai, Nishi-ku, Yokohama; tel: (45) 221-1111; fax: (45) 224-5153; top floors of Landmark Tower; outstanding views; conference facilities; fitness; pool; ¥25,000+.

Yokohama Grand Inter-Continental; 1-1-1 Minato Mirai, Nishi-ku, Yokohama; tel: 45-223-2222; fax: 45-221-0650; adjacent Yokohama Convention Center; restaurants; meeting facilities; health club; fitness; massage; sauna; indoor pool; jacuzzi; ¥26,500.

TOKYO MEDICAL CARE

International Clinic; 1-5-9, Azabudai, Roppongi, Minato-ku; tel: (3) 3582-2646, (3) 3583-7831 (very near Clark Hatch Fitness Center).

Ishikawa Clinic; Azabu Sakurada Heights 2F, 3-2-7 Nishi Azabu, Minato-ku; tel: (3) 3401-6340.

Japan Red Cross Medical Center (Nihon Sekijuji-sha Iryo Center); tel: (3) 3400-1311.

King's Clinic tel: (3) 3409-0764.

Seibo International Catholic Hospital; (Seibo Byoin); 2-5-1, Naka Ochiai, Shinjuku-ku; tel: (3) 3951-1111.

St. Luke's International Hospital (Seiroka Byoin); 10-1, Akashi-cho, Chuo-ku; tel: (3) 3541-5151 (member American Hospital Association).

Tokyo Medical and Surgical Clinic; 32 Mori building, 3-4-30, Shiba-Koen, Minato-ku; tel: (3) 3436-3028.

Yamauchi Dental Clinic; Shiroganedai Gloria Heights 1F, 3-16-10, Shiroganedai, Minato-ku; tel: (3) 3441-6377 (member American Dental Association).

TOKYO HEALTH CLUBS

Note: Certain top- class hotels also have health clubs that outside customers may be able to use for a fee.

Clark Hatch Fitness Center, Azabu Towers, 2-1-3, Azabudai, Minato-ku, Tokyo; tel: (3) 3584-4092.

Club on the Park; Park Hyatt Tokyo, 3-7-1-2 Nishi-Shinjuku, Shinjuku-ku; tel: (3) 5322-1234; fax: (3) 5322-1288; on 47th floor of hotel; 6:30a.m. to 9:30p.m.; ¥4,000 spa entrance fee, free to hotel guests.

Do Sports Plaza Shinjuku; Shinjuku Sumitomo Bldg., 2-6-1 Nishi Shinjuku, Shinjuku-du; tel: (3) 3344-1971.

Gold Health Gym; 1-4-7 Shimo Meguro, Meguro-ku; tel: (3) 3490-9329.

Nautilus Clubs;

Aoyama: Dame Aoyama 7F, 2-27-25 Minami Aoyama, Minato-ku; tel: (3) 3423-070;

Ikebukuro: Sumitomo Ikebukuro Ekimae Bldg. 3F, 1-10-1 Higashi Ikebukuro, Toshima-ku, http://www.sumitomo-rd.com/nautilus/, tel: (3) 3982-4640;

Shibuya: No. 3 Saito Bldg. 7F, 34-5 Udagawacho, Shibuya-ku, tel: (3) 3780-5551;

Shinjuku: Tokyo MInami Shinjuku Bldg. 2F, 2-7-8 Yoyogi, Shibuya-ku.

TOKYO AUTO RENTAL

Traffic snarls, Japanese road signs, driving on the left hand side, narrow roads, high-cost tolls (US$100 on the Shikoku-Honshu bridge), and huge parking costs all serve to promote other options of transportation in Tokyo, Osaka, and most large cities in Japan. Because the public network is so highly developed, there are very few places where one cannot go without a car.

Alamo; Toppan Yaesu Bldg., 2-2-7 Yaesu, Chuo-ku; tel: (3) 3276-8140.

Avis; MYK Bldg., 13-19 Ginza, 3-chome, Chuo-ku; tel: (3) -5550-1016, 5550-1011; fax: (3) 5550-1012; http://www.avis.com.

Budget; 1-29-6 Nihombashi Kakigaracho, Chuo-ku; tel: 0120-150801.

Hertz Asia Pacific; Shibakoen Ridge Bldg. 2F, 1-8-21 Shiba Koen, Manato-ku; tel: (3) 5401-7651; http://www.hertz.com; tel: (3) 3772-8200; 5403-7171; toll-free international: 0120-489-882; fax: (3) 5401-7656.

Nissan Rent A Car; 3-2-10 Shirokanedai, Minato-ku; tel: (3) 5424-4123.

WORLD TRADE CENTER

World Trade Center Tokyo
37th Fl., World Trade Center Building
4-1, Hammamatsu-cho 2-chome, Minato-ku
Tokyo 105-6137
tel: (3) 3435-5651/7; fax: (3) 3436-4368
email: wtcto@mx3.mesh.ne.jp

CHAMBER OF COMMERCE

Tokyo Chamber of Commerce and Industry
3-2-2 Marunouchi
Chiyoda-ku, Tokyo
tel: (3) 3283-7500

Japan Chamber of Commerce and Industry
3-2-2 Marunouchi
Chiyoda-ku, Tokyo
tel: (3) 3283-7984

Fukuoka

CITY VIEW

Fukuoka is the commercial and cultural center of the island of Kyushu, with 1.2 million inhabitants. Although smaller when compared to cities such as Tokyo and Osaka, it acts as a major travel hub for the country.

AIRPORT

Fukuoka Airport to City Center
Fukuoka Airport lies a mere 10 km (6 miles) from the city center. You can enter Japan through Fukuoka and catch a domestic flight to Tokyo's Haneda Airport, thus avoiding the congestion of Tokyo's Narita Airport.

Taxi A taxi to downtown Fukuoka will cost about ¥1,500 (about US$13.50).
Subway The fastest and cheapest way to town is the new subway line—it runs every three to eight minutes, takes five to six minutes to arrive at Tenjin Station in the city center, and costs only ¥220 (about US$2).

FUKUOKA HOTELS

Top-end
Hotel Il Palazzo; tel: (92) 716-3333 fax: (92) 724-3330.
New Otani Hakata; 1-1-2, Watanabe Dori, Chuo-ku; tel: (92) 714-1111 fax: (92) 715-5658.
Expensive
ANA Hotel Hakata; 3-3 Hakata-Ekimae, 3-chome, Hakata-ku; tel: (92) 471-7111 fax: (92) 472-7707; opposite central

rail station; restaurant; meeting rooms; health club; pool; shops.

Fukuoka Yamanoue; tel: (92) 771-2131 fax: (92) 771-8888.
Nishitetsu Grand; 6-60 Daimyo 2-chome; tel: (92) 771-7171; fax: (92) 715-5658.
Umino Nakamichi; 18-25 Saitozaka, Higashi-ku; tel: (92) 603-2525; fax: (92) 603-2828; city suburb.
Moderate
Centraza Hakata; 4-23 Hakata-Eki Chuogai, Hakata-ku; tel: (92) 461-0111; fax: (92) 461-0171.
Clio Court; tel: (92) 472-1111 fax: (92) 474-3222.
Hakata Miyako; 2-1-1 Hakata-eki Higashi, Hakata-ku; tel: (92) 441-3111 fax: (92) 481-1306; restaurant; meeting rooms.
Hokke Club Fukuoka-Ten; 3-1-90 Sumiyoshi Hakata-ku; tel: (92) 271-3171; fax: (92) 272-2095.

FUKUOKA HEALTH CARE

Fukuoka University Hospital; 7-45-1 Nanakuma, Jonan-ku; tel: (92) 741-8452.
Hirashima Women's Clinic; Solon Akasaka Bldg. 1-9-33 Daimyo, Chuo-ku; tel: (92) 733-1877.
Kanenokuma Hospital; 212-19 Kanenokuma, Oaza, Hakata-ku; tel: (2) 504-0055.

FUKUOKA HEALTH CLUBS

American Gym; 2-12-5 Daimyo, Huo-ku; http://www.bekkoame.or.jp/~life.g/americangym/index.htm; tel: (92) 761-8058.
Cube Sports Club Hakata; 2-7-16 Sumiyoshi, Hakata-ku; tel: (92) 271-3313.
L B Gym; 1-16-7-@F Kashiiekimae, Hiiashi-ku; tel: (92) 681-8011.

FUKUOKA AUTO RENTAL

Eki Rent-A-Car; NIhon Shokudo Shin Hakata Bldg. 9F, 5-11 Hakataeki chuogai, Hakata-ku; tel: (92) 441-0880.
Hertz; 1-17-13 Nakajima, Kokurakita-ku, Kitakyushu City; tel: (93) 533-0820.
Mazda Rent-A-Lease Co.; 5-11 Hakataeki Chuogai, Hakata-ku; tel: (92) 471-7551.
Nissan Rent-A-Car; 2-11-25 Asano, Kourakita-ku, Kitakyushu City; tel: (3) 521-0397.
Toyota Rent-A-Car; 3-2 Tenyamachi, Hakata-ku; tel: 0120-489446.

CHAMBER OF COMMERCE

Fukuoka Chamber of Commerce and Industry
2-9-28 Haktaekimae, Hakata-ku
Fukuoka City, Fukuoka Prefecture
tel: (92) 441-1111
Kitakyushu Chamber of Commerce and Industry
Shokou Boueki Kaikan 7F, 1-35 Furusenbamachi
Kokurakita-ku
Kitakyushu City, Fukuoka Prefecture
tel: (93) 541-0181

OTHER ASSISTANCE

Fukuoka City Tourist Information
tel: (92) 431-3003
Fukuoka Convention and Visitors Bureau
tel: (92) 733-5050

Nagoya

CITY VIEW

More than 2.2 million people live within Nagoya's 126.5 square mile area. It is a prosperous industrial center, but with few sites of interest to visitors.

AIRPORT

Komaki Airport to City Center

Flights from Komaki Airport can take you to Tokyo's Haneda Airport in the amount of time you'd be standing in customs at Narita Airport. Nagoya Komaki International Airport is 18 km (11 miles) north of the city.

Shuttle Bus The shuttle bus leaves every 10 to 15 minutes and takes you to city center in about 40 minutes for ¥700 (about US$6.25).

Taxi A taxi ride to city center will cost up to ¥5,000 (about US$45), depending on traffic conditions.

NAGOYA HOTELS

Top-end

Nagoya Hilton; 1-3-3 Sakae, Naka-ku; tel: (52) 212-1111 fax: (52) 212-1225; restaurants; conference facilities.

Nagoya Tokyu; 6-8 Sakae 4-chome, Naka ku; tel: (52) 251-2411; fax: (52) 251-2422; restaurant; conference facilities; in-room modem/fax connections; corporate rates; fitness; sauna; pool.

Westin Nagoya Castle; 3-19 Hinokuchi-cho, Nishi ku; tel: (52) 521-2121 fax: (52) 531-3313; city suburb.

Expensive

International Hotel Nagoya; 3-23-3 Nishiki, Naka-ku; tel: (52) 961-3111 fax: (52) 962-5937; restaurant; conference facilities.

Nagoya Kanko; 1-19-30 Nishiki, Naka-ku; tel: (52) 231-7711; fax: (52) 231-7719; restaurant; conference facilities.

Nagoya Miyako; 4-9-10 Meieki, Nakamura-ku; tel: (52) 571-3211 fax: (52) 571-3242.

Moderate

Castle Plaza; 4-3-25 Meieki, Nakamura-ku; tel: (52) 582-2121 fax: (52) 582-8666; restaurant; conference facilities.

Fitness Hotel; tel: (52) 562-0330 fax: (52) 562-0331.

NAGOYA MEDICAL CARE

Iryohojin Nagoya Toei Clinic; 2-11-25 Sakae, Naka-ku; tel: (52) 201-1111.

Katsumata Hospital; 1-32-22 Shin Sakae, Naka-ku; tel: (52) 241-0408.

Nagoya University Hospital; 65 Tsurumaicho, Showa-ku; tel: (52) 741-2111.

NAGOYA HEALTH CLUB

The Creston Club; Parco West Wing 7F, 3-29-1 Sakae, Naka-ku; tel: (52) 264-8511.

Fitness Club How's Sakae; 3-27-18 Sakae, Naka-ku; tel: (52) 261-3541.

Nagoya City Sports Shinko Jigyo Dan, Inae Sports Center; 1-48-19 Shin Sakae, Naka-ku; tel: (52) 251-7531.

OTHER ASSISTANCE

Nagoya Congress Center
1-1 Atsuta-nishimachi, Atsuta ku
tel: (52) 683-7711; fax: (52) 683-7777
website: http://www.u-net.city.nagoya.jp/ncc_e/index.html

Osaka

CITY VIEW

Osaka is a powerful economic and political center. In search of space for its economic engine and 8.5 million people, it is literally growing into the sea, with a number of artificial islands to support a new airport and trade fair site.

Bear in mind that Osaka is gritty and industrial—even more so than Tokyo. If you can, stay in relatively serene Kyoto and take the 20-minute bullet-train ride to Osaka to do business.

KANSAI INTERNATIONAL AIRPORT

Still very new, Kansai International Airport has replaced Itami as the main international hub in the city. Built on a man-made strip of land 30 miles northeast of Osaka, Kansai is Japan's first 24-hour airport and very user-friendly. Information counters that help travelers book rooms, find appropriate transportation, and locate information exist on each side of the arrivals lobby area

All types of transportation are available:

Taxis will whisk passengers to central Osaka for an ominous ¥18,000 (about US$160).

Bus A more heartening alternative exists in the airport bus (¥1700), which will take you to the main rail station in Osaka where you can transfer to a taxi, subway, or trains heading for all destinations. Bus services to Kyoto and Kobe cost about ¥1800.

Train Trains depart from the basement of Kansai. The fastest option (45 minutes) exists in the LImited Express train known as "Haruka" for a cost of ¥2930. However, you must make advance reservations. The alternative "Kanku Kaisoku" costs a bit less (¥1140) but takes 45 minutes longer; no reservations necessary. Trains that service Kobe and Kyoto depart in 30-minute intervals and take about an hour and a half for a price of ¥1800. These run until 10:30p.m.

Ferry Hydrofoil services to Kobe, Kyushu and Shikoku zip away from Kansai's ferry port at frequent intervals. The port lies 5 minutes by shuttle bus from the main airport terminal. Inquire at the airport information counters for information.

ITAMI AIRPORT

Itami Airport to City Center

Osaka Itami International Airportl lies 16 km. (10 miles) northwest of the city, and an easy half-hour ride by bus, train or taxi to city center.

Shuttle Bus The shuttle bus to Osaka Railway Station leaves every 15 minutes and costs ¥340 (about US$3).

Taxi A taxi to the station will cost about ¥5,000 (about US$45).

OSAKA HOTELS

Top-End

ANA-Sheraton Hotel; 3-1 Dojimahama, 1-chome, Kita-ku, 530; tel: (6) 347-1112; fax: (6) 348-9208; restaurant; conference facilities; business center; secretarial service; corporate rates; health club; fitness; sauna; pool; boutiques; executive floor with meeting and video rooms and secured entrance.

Imperial Hotel; 8-50 Tenmabashi 1-chome; Kita- ku, 530; tel: (6) 377-2100; fax: (6) 377-3622; near water; restaurants; banquet halls; meeting rooms; complimentary shuttle to Osaka Station; multi-floor fitness club; driving ranges; pool.

New Otani Osaka; 1-4-1 Shiromi, Chuo-ku; tel: (6) 941-1111 fax: (6) 941-9769; near Osaka Castle; conference rooms; deluxe rooms available; business center with free computer usage.

Japan

Osaka Hilton International; 1-8-8 Umeda Kita- ku; tel: (6) 347-7111fax: (6) 347-7001; opposite Osaka Station; opulent decor; spacious interiors; in-room modem line; banquet halls, meeting rooms; executive floor rooms includes complimentary breakfast and cocktails, personalized concierge service, separate registration.

Ritz Carlton Osaka; 2-2-25 Umeda, Kita-ku, 530; tel: (6) 343-7000; fax: 343-7001; new hotel located in the business district; large rooms; executive floors; fitness center; indoor pool.

Royal; 5-3-68 Nakanoshima, Kita-ku; tel: (6) 448-1121 fax: (6) 448-4414; restaurants; conference center (up to 2,000); business center; complimentary shuttle to Osaka Station; fitness room; sauna; pool.

Expensive

Hotel New Hankyu and Annex; 1-35 Shibata, Kita-ku; tel: (6) 372-5101; fax: (6) 374-6885; near Osaka Station; restaurant; conference facilities; fitness club; rooms in the New Annex are a bit larger.

Hotel Nikko Kansai Airport; 1 Senshu-Kuko Kita; tel: (0724) 55-1111; fax: (0724) 55-1155; direct connection to Kansai passenger terminal; 6 restaurants; spacious, soundproof rooms.

Osaka Grand; 2-3-18 Nakanoshima, Kita-ku; tel: (6) 202-1212 fax: (6) 227-5054; restaurants; conference rooms; business center.

Osaka Tokyu; 7-20 Chaya-machi, Kita-ku; tel: (6) 373-2411 fax: (6) 376-0343; restaurant; conference facilities; meeting rooms; corporate rates; pool; shops.

Radisson Miyako Hotel; 1-55 Uehonmachi 6-chome, Tennoji-ku; tel: (6) 773-1111; fax: (6) 773-3322; 13 restaurants; conference facilities; fax/photocopy facilities; secretarial service; basement train stop; shuttle service to Kansai Airport; health club; sauna; pool.

Nankai South Tower; 1-60 Namba, 5-chome, Chuo-ku; tel: (6) 646-1111; fax: (6) 648-0331; 12 restaurants; conference facilities; secretarial service; in-room modem/fax connection; fax/photocopy facilities; fitness; sauna; whirlpool.

Osaka Dai-Ichi; 1-9-20 Umeda, Kita-ku; tel: (6) 341-4411; fax: (6) 341-4930; cylindric tower building; business-class hotel; restaurants; banquet halls; meeting rooms; limousine bus to Itami Airport.

Moderate

International Hotel Osaka; 2-33 Hummachibashi Chuo-ku; tel: (6) 941-2661; fax: (6) 941-5362; near business district; restaurant; banquet halls; meeting rooms.

Moriguchi Prince; Kawahara cho, 1 Moriguchi-shi; tel: (6) 994-1111; fax: (6) 994-1100; restaurant; pool.

Osaka International Community Center Hotel; tel: (6) 773-8181 fax: (6) 773-0777.

Shin Osaka Sen-I City; 2-2-17 NIshi Miyahara; tel: (6) 394-3331; fax: (6) 394-3335; restaurant; conference facilities.

Tennoji Miyako; 10-48 Hiden-in-Cho, Tennoji-Ku; tel: (6) 779-1501 fax: (6) 779-8800; restaurant; meeting rooms.

OSAKA MEDICAL CARE

Osaka University Hospital; 1-50, Fukushima, 1-chome, Fukushima; tel: (6) 451-0051 (emergency patients by ambulance only)

Sumitomo Hospital; 2-2, Nakanoshima, 5-chome, Kita-ku; tel: (6) 443-1261.

Tane General Hospital; 1-2-31, Sakaigawa, Nishi-ku; tel: (6) 581-1071.

Yodogawa Christian Hospital; 9-26, Awaji, 2-chome, Higashi Yodogawa-ku; tel: (6) 322-2250.

OSAKA HEALTH CLUB

Life Sports KTV Tenroku; 1-2-25 Nagar Nishi, Kita-ku; tel: (6) 6352-8820.

Osaka YMCA; 1-5-6 Tosabori, Nishi-ku; tel: (6) 6441-0895.

United Sport Club XAX Umeda; tel: (6) 6347-7051.

OSAKA AUTO RENTAL

Avis; reservations office, (3) 555-1016; fax: (3) 555--1012.

Hertz; (7) 2469-0561.

Nippon Rent-A-Car; 1-4-10 Sonezaishinchi, Kita-ku, Osaka; (6) 6344-0919.

Nissan Rent-A-Car; 5-6-10 Toyosaki, Kita-ku, Osaka; tel: (6) 6371-4123.

Toyota Rent & Lease Osaka Co.; 1-20-19 Simanouchi, Chuo-ku, Osaka; tel: (6) 6241-6070.

WORLD TRADE CENTER

World Trade Center Osaka
Osaka WTC Building
50th Floor, Mail Box #2
1-14-16 Nanko-kita, Suminoe-ku
Osaka 559-0034
tel: (6) 6615-7000; fax: (6) 6616-4130
website: http://www.wtco.osakawtc.or.jp
email: wtcok@wtco.osakawtc.or.jp

CHAMBER OF COMMERCE

Osaka Chambers of Commerce and Industry
2-8 Honmachibashi, Chuo-ku
Osaka City
tel: (6) 6944-6200

Kenya

Kenya

At a Glance
THE PEOPLE
Population .... 28,808,658 (July 1999 est.)
Growth Rate .... 1.59% (1999 est.)
Life Expectancy .... 47.02 years (born 1999)
Infant Mortality . 59.07 deaths/1,000 live births (1999 est.)

Ethnic Composition
Black African 99%
Asian, Arab, Caucasian 1%

Religious Composition
Protestant 38%
Roman Catholic 28%
Indigenous beliefs 26%
Muslim 6%
Other and non-affiliated 2%

Languages Spoken
English (official), Swahili (official), numerous tribal dialects

Education and Literacy
The government finances eight years of primary school. Literacy stands at 78.1 percent of the adult population.

Labor Force
Total: 8,7800,000
By occupation: services 15%, industry, 10%, agriculture 75%

THE ECONOMY
Kenya's workforce is primarily agrarian although farming only contributes 27 percent of GDP. Always deemed to have great potential, Kenya has repeatedly stumbled on its road to in-dustrialization. The nation's many years of socialism did not help matters. However, its current policy framework has begun to emphasize the role of a free market. The economy has turned to market-based pricing incentives in place of long-standing price controls. A liberalized investment code and a new foreign exchange system have also been put in place. While the government has made some progress in removing impediments to the development of a free market, reform re-mains far from complete. Privatization has been slow as foreign investors are leery of the unstable political situation. Still in pro-cess are major government programs to control population growth, curb corruption, and reduce the size of the civil service.
Exports .... US$2 billion (f.o.b., 1998)
Imports .... US$3.05 billion (f.o.b., 1998)
Total GDP .... US$43.9 billion (1998 est.)
GDP Per Capita .... US$$1,550 (1998 est.)
Unemployment .... 50% (1998 est.)
Inflation Rate 2.5% (1998)

Top Export Partners
Uganda, E.U., Tanzania, United States

Top Import Partners
E.U., United Arab Emirates, Japan, United States

Top Exports
Tea, coffee, petroleum products

Top Imports
Machinery and transportation equipment, petroleum and petroleum products, iron and steel, raw materials, foodstuffs, consumer goods.

BUSINESS WORKWEEK
Offices
Monday to Friday 8a.m. to 1p.m. and 2p.m. to 5p.m.

Banks
Monday to Friday 9a.m. to 3p.m. (Also open on the first and last Saturdays of month from 9a.m. to 11a.m.)

Government
Monday to Friday 8a.m. to 1p.m. and 2p.m. to 5p.m.

Retail
Monday to Friday 10a.m. to 8p.m., slightly shorter hours on Saturday and Sunday.
Note: Business hours in rural areas are attuned to local custom and seasonal needs.

HOLIDAYS
New Year's ....January 1
Id al-Fitr, end of Ramadan ....February 19*
Id al-Adha, Feast of the Sacrifice .... March 28*
Easter ....April 2-5*
Labor Day ....May 1
Madaraka Day, Anniversary of
Self-Government ....June 1
Independence Day ....December 12
Christmas ....December 25-26
*Dates may vary by year.

CLIMATE
Seasons
Kenya is located directly upon the equator and has two main seasons: the "long rains" from March to May and the "short rains" from October through November. Otherwise, it has a very temperate climate year round.

Regions
The coastal areas have a tropical climate, with regular monsoon winds. The lowlands are hot and dry, while the high-lands are more temperate. Average temperatures range from lows of 10˚C (50˚F) to highs of 28˚C (˚82F).

Money & Banking
Currency
The currency of Kenya is the Kenyan Shilling (KSh).

Denominations
The Kenyan Shilling (KSh) comes in coin denominations of KSh10, 5 and 1, and 50, 10, and 5 cents; and banknotes of KSh10, 20, 50, 100, 200, 500, and 1,000.

Traveler's Checks and Credit Cards
Travelers' checks and major foreign currencies can be exchanged for Kenyan Shillings at banks and exchange bureaus. Fees rarely exceed 1 percent.
Visa and MasterCard are accepted at larger hotels and a few retailers in Nairobi. Only cash will be accepted in rural areas. You can get cash advances from your Visa card only at a Barclay's Bank. ATMs are virtually non-existent. Keep all exchange receipts for reconversion at departure.

Kenya

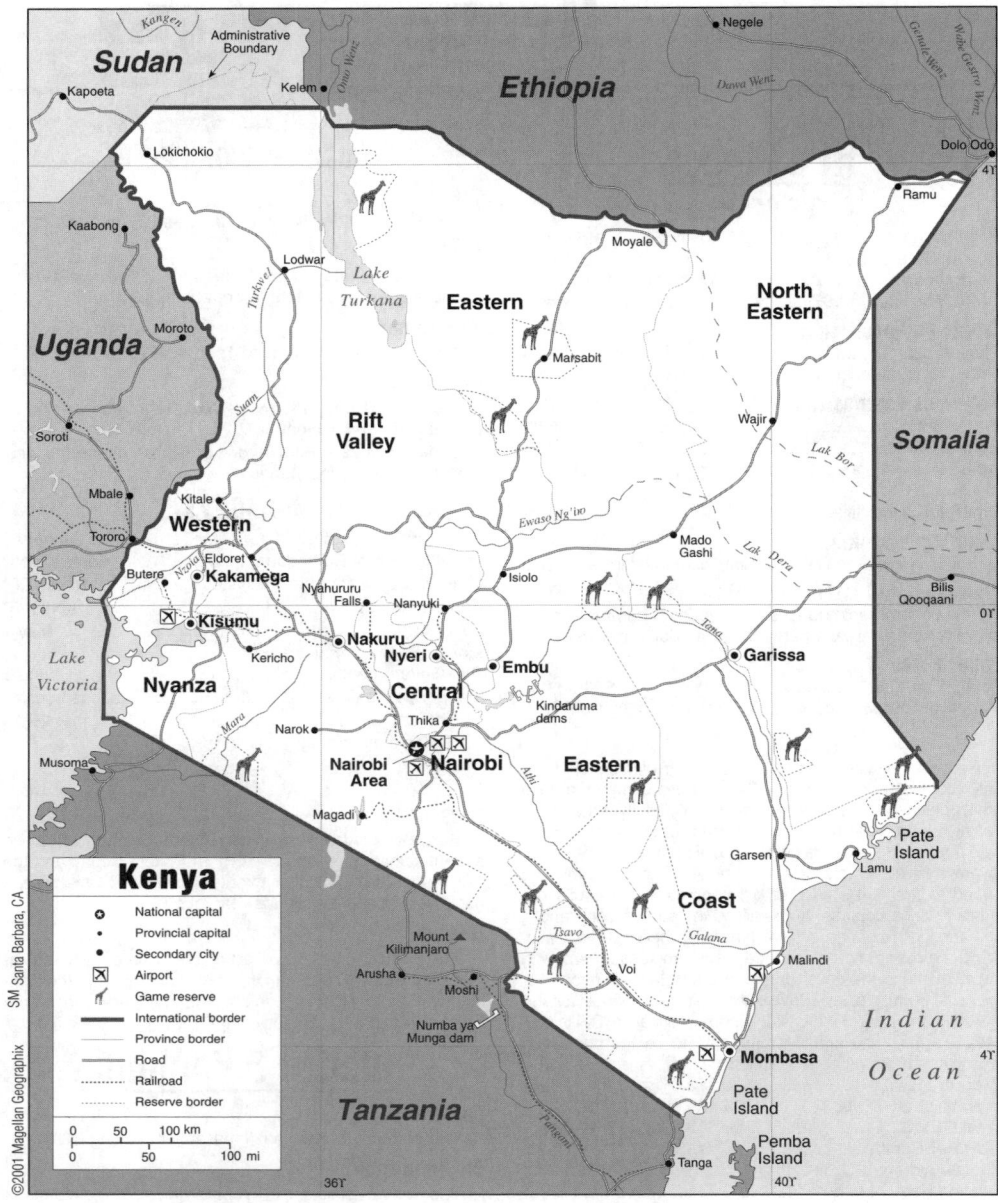

Travel

VISA AND PASSPORT

A passport that is valid for three months beyond the date of entry is required of all visitors. Visas are required of all business travelers of any nationality.

A visitor's pass must be obtained by all visitors upon arrival, regardless of visa status. It is issued at the port of entry upon substantiation of adequate funds for the stay and an onward ticket. Visitors' passes are valid for three months and are renewable for up to one year.

For tourism purposes only, nationals of the following countries are exempt from the need for visas:

- Australia, Austria, Belgium, Canada, France, Germany, Italy, Japan, Luxembourg, The Netherlands, New Zealand, South Africa, Spain, Switzerland, U.K., and U.S. for a maximum period of 30 days
- Denmark, Eritrea, Ethiopia, Finland, Ireland, Norway, San Marino, Sweden, Turkey, and Uruguay for stays of three months maximum
- Most U.K. Commonwealth countries and colonies for stays of three months maximum

- Passengers in transit who do not leave the airport and are continuing their journey aboard the identical or first-connecting aircraft, and who are holding confirmed tickets and other documents for onward travel, are also exempted from the need for a visa.

  Types of visa issued:

- Single entry—good for stays up to three months, and valid if used within three months of issuance

- Multiple entry—good for terms of either one or two years. This is the visa for business travelers, and the application for it must include an invitation or statement of business from a local company or government agency.

- Transit—good for 72 hours

  Extensions and renewals are issued by Immigration in Nyayo House, Uhuru Highway, Nairobi; or at either the Mombasa or Kisumu offices.

  Normally, allow a day or so for processing of applications made in person at an embassy or consulate, or approximately five days for postal applications.

DEPARTURE FORMALITIES

An airport tax of US$20, or the equivalent in freely convertible hard currency, including Kenya Shillings, will be charged at departure. Land or water departures are not taxed. The export of local currency is prohibited.

CUSTOMS ENTRY (PERSONAL)

Duty-free

The following goods may be imported into Kenya by passengers over 16 years of age without incurring customs duty:

- Tobacco: 200 cigarettes, 50 cigars, or 225g of tobacco
- Alcohol: 1 bottle of spirits or wine
- Perfume: 1 pint of perfume

Prohibited or Restricted

Note: Firearms and ammunition require a police permit. Gold, diamonds, and wildlife skins or game trophies not from the authorized Kenyan government department are prohibited.

IMMUNIZATION

An international health certificate showing current yellow fever immunizations is required of travelers arriving from other sub-Saharan African countries with known infections. Precautions against cholera are also essential in Kenya. In addition, advance malaria treatment (even in urban centers) as well as inoculation against typhoid, tetanus, hepatitis A & B, and diphtheria are strongly advised.

Note: Resistance to the chlorinique malaria treatment has been reported.

TIPPING

Taxi

Taxi drivers generally receive a 10 percent tip.

Porters

Porters receive a fee of KSh50 per bag.

Hotels

Unless a service charge is already added, it is customary to include a10 percent tip to hotel bills.

Restaurants

Most restaurants include a service charge of 10 percent on restaurant bills.

EMERGENCY INFORMATION

Police and Crime

Kenyan cities suffer from increasing crime. Be especial-

ly careful in the vicinity of cheap hotels in Nairobi, where robberies may take place. Armed robbery and carjackings are common. Reports have also been made of thieves snatching objects from open vehicle windows while cars are stopped at stoplights or in heavy traffic. Thieves and con artists have been known to impersonate hotel employees, police officers, or government officials.

Foreign business visitors are assumed to be wealthy and are often the target of thieves. Consequently, purses, laptops, and briefcases will require additional security. Do not leave valuables in cars or on tables in cafés. Keep non-essential valuables locked in hotel safes when not in use. Use credit cards and travel checks when possible to avoid carrying large sums of cash.

The Kenyan postal system is not entirely reliable, and monetary instruments such as credit cards and checks are often stolen. The safest way of sending envelopes and packages has proven to be the use of international couriers. Insurance coverage should be in place for anything of value.

Highway banditry is common in much of North Eastern province, the Eastern Province, and the northern part of Rift Valley province. Incidents also occur on the Nairobi-Mombasa Road. Visitors are advised not to drive after dark, nor to walk alone or at night in public parks, along footpaths or beaches, and in poorly lit areas.

Women are advised to travel in groups at night. The police are generally courteous but not very efficient in dealing with reports of crime. In rural areas the police are prone to shaking down foreigners for "special fees" to supplement the low wages. Carry insurance for your valuables, because once they are stolen, do not expect to see them again.

Note: Some corruption exists within the local and central governments. Business travelers may also find that their deals with local companies involve the bribing of public officials. Besides making the personal decision of whether or not to participate in such dealings, check on your legal position in your own country. Some nations now have stiff penalties for their business people who bribe officials overseas.

Emergency Numbers

Hospital (Nairobi)..45-301
All services ....336-886 / 501-280

Health

Do not drink tap water or use ice cubes; bottled water is safe and available. Wash all vegetables in a chlorine solution, peel fruits, and avoid uncooked food. Drink only powdered or tinned milk and avoid other dairy products since they are most likely unpasteurized.

Malaria, leprosy, tuberculosis, smallpox, tetanus, typhoid, polio, and yellow fever are among the tropical diseases that are found in Kenya, and the number of reported AIDS cases is rising. Hepatitis A & B, meningitis, river blindness, and sleeping sickness pose danger as well when traveling in the bush country. Dysenteries and various diarrheal diseases are widespread. Avoid the bites of mosquitoes, sand flies, and tsetse flies, and protect against hookworm by wearing shoes at all times.

Nairobi and Mombasa both have good medical facilities. Generally, though, medical care is substandard and pharmaceuticals are in short supply, although there is fairly good emergency medical service and dental care. Carry a well-stocked medical kit with all the prescription drugs you require, and also include in it a stock of sterilized syringe needles and drip needles for emergencies.

A travel insurance package including an evacuation policy should be acquired by all business travelers. As is true with general security, health awareness in this country must be at maximum at all times.

Kenya

INTERNAL TRAVEL
AIR

Kenya is well traveled by air, a safe and relatively economical means of spanning the country's large size quickly. Primary domestic carriers are Air Kenya Aviation, Kenya Airways, and Equator Airlines.

Mombasa, Nairobi, Kisumu, Nanyuki, Malindi, Lamu, Amboseli, Masai Mara, Nyeri, and Samburu are all interconnected and well serviced with a network of over 250 airfields, some of which are limited in terms of size, services or upkeep. It is advisable to check locally and book early, as many of these flights are popular.

TAXI

Taxis are cheap and abundant in Mombasa, Nairobi, and other cities, but many are decrepit.

The matatu, an African-style shared taxi, is usually a minibus or pick-up truck, carrying as many as seven passengers at a time. It provides a cheap and colorful service in many cities, as well as outlying routes between towns.

There are also many London-style black cabs in operation in major towns. In these, fares are normally metered. In the others, and in the many matatus that thread the streets of Kenyan cities, fares are customarily negotiated prior to departure. It is not advised to share a cab with strangers.

Cabs can be rented by the day as well.

AUTO

Visitors may find automobiles for rent in Nairobi, Mombasa, Malindi, and any coastal resort area or other large city. With a major credit card and a valid license from your country of origin, you can either rent as self-drive or pay a little extra for a driver. Be advised that some of the cars are not in good repair; you may want to audition your driver, also. Rental proves affordable in cities, and bodes especially well for the business traveler, but in outlying areas car rental can be prohibitively expensive.

Roads in Kenya are generally in good repair. If traveling to rural areas, be sure to rent a four-wheel-drive vehicle.

TRAIN

Kenya's train services are among the best in Africa. They are comfortable, although sometimes less than efficient. Kenya Railways offers service twice daily between Nairobi and Mombasa, one an overnight journey. Sleeping compartments and dining car are available. First class offers the finest service, with 2-berth compartments. Second class is comfortable but basic. Third class (which should be avoided) is a bit too basic for many traveler's tastes.

Trains also run between Nairobi and Mombasa to Kisumu, Malaba, Nanyuki, Eldoret, Voi, Taveta, and Kitale. Kenyan trains are popular, despite the slow deterioration of the rolling stock and tracks. The trains are usually on schedule and are considered safer than buses or matatus.

METRO

Kenya has no metro services.

BUSES & TRAMS

Kenya has numerous intercity and local bus lines. All parts of the country are interconnected, with Nairobi as the hub. Buses are frequent and cheaper than trains, but they come along with a somewhat frenetic driving style that can prove unnerving. They are also uncomfortable and tend to be just too crowded for long trips. Local buses and matatu mini-buses are not recommended for business travelers.

WATER TRAVEL

Kenya is served by international cruise lines through the port of Mombasa as well as an Indian Ocean coastal ferry system.

On Lake Victoria, Ugandan, and Tanzanian ports can be reached from ferries out of the Kenyan harbor at Kisumu, sailing to Kendu Bay, Homa Bay, and Asembo Bay. These ferry systems serve local needs but are rarely used by foreign business travelers due to slow speed.

TRAVEL ASSISTANCE

Ministry of Tourism & Wildlife
Italia House, P.O. Box 54666, Nairobi
tel: (2) 331-030, fax: (2) 217-604
Kenya Tourist Board
P.O. Box 30630, Nairobi,
tel: (2) 604-245/6, 600-804, 500-488
fax: (2) 501-096
email: ktb@Form-net.com
or info@kenyatourism.org
website: www.kenyatourism.org
Kenya Tourist Development Corporation
P.O. Box 42013
Utaliib House, Uhuru Highway, Nairobi
tel: (2) 330-820; fax: (2) 227-815

Essential Terms

English	Swahili
Yes	Ndiyo
No	Hapana
Good morning	Habari ya asubuhi
Hello (daytime)	Habari ya alasiri
Hello (evening)	Habari za jioni
Hello (telephone)	Jambo
Good-bye	Kwaheri
Please	Tafadhali
Thank you	Asante
Pleased to meet you	Nimefurahi sana kukutana na wewe
Excuse me; I'm sorry	Samahani
My name is _____	Jina langu ni _____
I don't understand	Sielewi
Do you speak English?	Unasema kingereza?

Communications

DIALING CODES IN KENYA

International country code: [254]

Selected city codes: Anmer (2845), Bamburi (11), Embakasi (2), Gigiri (2), Kabete (2), Karen (2882),Kiambu (154), Kiikuyu (154), Kisumu (35) Langata (2), Mombasa (11), Nairobi (2), Nakuru (37),Shanzu (11), Thika (151), Uthiru (2)

Dialing Kenya from Overseas

To dial Kenya from overseas, dial your country's international dialing code, then 254 (the country code for Kenya), then the city code and finally the number. If you were dialing Mombasa from the United States, for example, you would begin with 011, then 254, then 11 (the city code for Mombasa), and finally the number of the person or office you were trying to reach.

Assistance Numbers

International Operator 0196
International Information... 0191
Operator 900
Directory Assistance.. 991

CALLING WITHIN KENYA

Local Calls

Calling around town in Kenya costs KSh3.

Long Distance Calls

You can call long distance from a public phone or the post office. You may have to wait for the operator and then again for the call to be placed. Tanzania and Uganda are both considered long distance, not international.

International Calls

Make a direct call from a private home or a hotel room by dialing 001 + country code + area code + number. But beware of massive surcharges ranging anywhere from 25 to 100 percent. The International call office at the Kenyatta Conference Center, which is open until 6p.m., offers the quietest surroundings when placing an overseas call. You can also call from a post office and pre pay for a station-to-station call, which costs approximately US$4.50 a minute. Card phones are another option.

PAY PHONES

Public Telephones

There may be lines to use phones. It will cost KSh3 to make a local call from pay phones, which accept KSh1 and 5 coins.
1. Lift receiver
2. Insert money
3. Wait five beeps
4. Dial
5. Coins drop when call has been answered

Calling Cards

Post offices sell phone cards in KSh200, 400 or 1000 denominations. A KSh200 card will buy you three minutes to North America. Cards can be purchased at the Nairobi Extelcoms office, open from 8 a.m. to midnight, or at the Kenyatta Conference Center.

CELLULAR PHONES

Kenya Posts & Telecoms Company offers ETACS analog service for mobile users. Siemens Communications Limited has an outlet in Nairobi. Call (2) 723-717 or fax: (2) 726-128.

Note: Your home country cell phone may not work in this country. If not, we recommend that you rent an international cell phone *before* you leave home. A major US-based cell phone rental provider is **IMC WorldCell**. For information see "International Cell Phone Rentals" on page 14.

CALL BACK

You can (potentially) save significant sums when calling in Kenya by using a call back service. For a list of callback services, please refer to the "Communications" section in the *Global Road Warrior* Introduction.

Fees for call back services vary widely, depending on the company and the type of service required. Be sure to check with these companies before leaving to compare rates.

PHONE JACKS

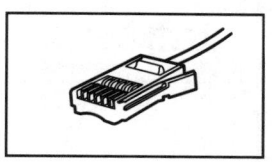

Plug adaptors are available through **iGo Corporation.** (See "Electrical and Telephone Adaptors" on page 19.)

FAX

Fax machines have become increasingly popular in Kenya. There is at least one at every major hotel and also at the Nairobi General Post Office or the Kenyatta International Conference Center. Service is adequate.

POSTAL SERVICES

The main post office in Nairobi is open 24 hours. Mailboxes are located throughout the city and rural areas, painted red. Stamps are available at most hotels. However, the Kenyan mail system has been known to be unreliable; monetary instruments are frequently stolen.

Postal Hours: Monday to Friday 8a.m. to 5p.m.; Saturday 8a.m. to 1p.m.

TELEGRAMS

Telegrams are still easy to make, not to mention inexpensive. They can be sent from most post and telegraph offices and hotels as well as from private telephones.

Business Services

BUSINESS CENTERS

Kenyatta International Conference Center; tel: (2) 332-383; fax: (2) 252-779.

Nairobi Hilton; Mama Ngina St.; tel: 334-000l; fax: 339-462.

COURIER SERVICES

DHL; Longonot Place, Kijabe St., P.O. Box 67577, Nairobi;

Kenya

tel: (2) 225-855; Hours: Monday to Friday 8a.m. to 9p.m., Saturday/Sunday/Holidays 8:30a.m. to 4p.m.

Federal Express; East AFrica Cargo, tel: (2) 240-113.

UPS Kenya; Nolfolk towers Harry Thuku Rd., Apartment D61, PO Box 46586, Nairobi; tel: (2) 252-200; fax: (2) 241-182.

Electrical

Current
220/240 AC, 50Hz.

ELECTRIC PLUGS

Plug adaptors are available through **iGo Corporation.** (See "Electrical and Telephone Adaptors" on page 19.)

Technical Support

HARDWARE/SOFTWARE VENDOR SUPPORT

Compaq/Digital; (in Switzerland) tel: [41] (22) 709-5330; fax: [41] (22) 709-5391 (Geneva); tel: [41] (1) 801-2507; fax: [41] (1) 801-2172 (Zurich); (General U.S.) tel: (281) 518-2000; http://www.compaq.com/.

Corel; (in Germany) tel: [49] (180) 425-8210 (TS Word Perfect-32 bit); (in the U.S.) tel: [1] (716) 871-2325 (Ask to be Forwarded to Appropriate Program); http://www.corel.com/.

Dell; tel: (2) 441893; fax: (2) 440235 (Ramtek International KENYA LTD); (Dell- Europe) tel: [44] (134) 474-8000; (in the U.S.) tel: [1] (512) 338-4400; fax: [1] (512) 728-3330; http://www.dell.com/.

IBM; tel: (2) 446-910; tel: (2) 447-884/5; fax: (2) 447-012; (in Switzerland) tel: [41] (22) 310-0418 (in French); (in the U.S.) tel: [1] (919) 517-2800; (U.S. Main Office) tel: [1] 914-765-1900; http://www.ibm.com/.

Microsoft; (in South Africa) [27] (11) 445-0145; fax: [27] (11) 445-0045/6 (customer service); (in Germany) tel: [49] (89) 31-760; fax: [49] (89) 3176-1000; tel: [49] (89) 3176-1199; (in Switzerland) tel: [41] (848) 858-868; fax [41] (1) 831-0869; (in the U.S.) [1] (425) 635-7222; http://www.microsoft.com/.

NEC; (in Germany) tel: [49] (18) 0524- 1212; tel:[49] (89) 3160-1233; fax: [49] (89) 3160- 1613 (Floppy Disk and Hard Drive); tel: [49] (89) 9627-4233; fax: [49] (89) 9627-4613 (All Other Products); (in the U.S.) [1] (916) 388-0101 (Main Switchboard); http://www.nec.com/.

Toshiba; (in Germany) tel: [49] (2131) 158-319; fax: [49] (2131) 158-558; (in Switzerland) tel: [41] (1) 946-0777; fax: [41] (1) 946-0807; (in Ireland) tel: [44] (193) 282-8828; (in the U.S.) [1] (949) 583-3000 (Corporate Headquarters); http://www.toshiba.com/.

Internet Connection

HOW TO CONNECT

Connecting to AOL and Compuserve in Kenya is similar to using it when traveling outside your own area code. See the introductory section for detailed information on connecting to your account through a different phone number.

America Online

Numbers are available at keyword *international*. Be sure to get several local numbers before leaving. AOL's Global-Net service charges US$6 an hour in addition to the usual charges. Go to keyword *access* (a free area) and download the software.

Access: Mombasa (11) 222-040; Nairobi (2) 240-333.

Compuserve

Numbers are available at *Go International*. The Compuserve Web-site also has a great deal of information, at http://www.compuserve.com.

There are no direct access numbers for Compuserve in Kenya. Users will have to pay international rates to use the service.

Independent Service Providers

Many independent service providers offer discounts if you are only in town for a couple of days.

Fiberlink Communications Corp.; tel: [1] (714) 788-2904; http://www.fiberlinkcc.com/ (although a United States company, fiberlink offers access numbers for Kenya).

Inter-Connect Ltd; tel: (2) 711-140; fax: (2) 718-418; info@iconnect.co.ke; http://www.iconnect.co.ke/.

NairobiNet Online; tel: (2) 217-406; fax: (2) 243-512; email: info@nbnet.co.ke; http://www.nbnet.co.ke.

Business Culture

GREETINGS AND COURTESIES

Shaking hands is the customary greeting in Kenya, and there are many different types of shakes for different relationships. For example, a long, extended clasp for well-known acquaintances and a brief, standard handshake for someone you've just met. When greeting a person of elder status, grasp your right wrist with your left hand while shaking hands. Kenyans tend to be conservative and formal in business situations. Titles, such as Doctor and Professor, should always be used when applicable. Expect to know someone a while before using their first name. Initial greeting periods in Kenya are always marked by a rather lengthy period of basic questions about your family, country, etc. Politics is an acceptable area of conversation in Kenya, but subjects such as sex and local rituals are considered taboo. Women do not look men in the eye upon greeting.

DECISION MAKING

As in most highly bureaucratic systems, decisions in Kenya business almost invariably come from the few people at the top of a particular company or organization. Further, expect progress in your business venture to come very slowly and only after extensive personal interaction between you and your contacts, as Kenyans like to feel they truly know you before reaching any agreements. Don't try to rush any business decision, or you may destroy the entire relationship.

WOMEN

Businesswomen in Kenya are still relatively rare. A foreign woman sent to do business in Kenya should dress very conservatively, conduct herself with the utmost tact and seriousness, and preferably be accompanied by her spouse.

BUSINESS ATTIRE

Kenyan businessmen dress in the British fashion. A two- or three-piece suit is standard in Nairobi. In the coastal regions, however, a more casual style is acceptable, including wearing open-necked shirts and shorts to meetings. When dining at a restaurant, a jacket and tie is standard. Women should wear dresses or skirts. The wearing of traditional Kenyan clothes by a foreigner is appreciated, provided they are worn correctly.

Business Centers
Nairobi

CITY VIEW

Nairobi can be a great example of modern African life, with rustic homes lying next to skyscrapers. It is a relatively small town, and you can get just about everywhere by walking. It is also far from a safe area, particularly at night when the police seem to disappear. The natives call it "Nairobbery," and with good reason.

AIRPORT

Jomo Kenyatta International Airport to City Center

The airports lies 8 miles (13 km.). The airport has a 24-hour bank. Buses run every 30 minutes, and taxis are available in front of the terminal. The Mercedes taxis with the government Kenya seal on the side offer fixed government fares of about KSh700. Otherwise, prepare to bargain. Expect 30 minutes in travel time.

Airline Numbers

Aeroflot	(2) 220-746
Air Canada	(2) 218-776/7
Air France	(2) 217-512
Air India	(2) 334-788
Alitalia	(2) 224-362
British Airways	(2) 334-362
EgyptAir	(2) 227-887
Japan Airlines	(2) 220-591
Kenya Airways	(2) 229-271, 823-000, 823-456
Qantas Airways	(2) 213-221
Sabena	(2) 241-212, 243-269
Saudi Arabian Airlines	(2) 230-337
South African Airways	(2) 229-663
Swissair	(2) 331-012

HOTELS

Top-end

Grand Regency; Uhuru Highway/ Loita Street; tel: 211-199; fax: 217-120; restaurants; conference facilities; secretarial services; fax/photocopying facilities; in-room safe, modem connection; corporate rates; fitness room; sauna; pool; whirlpool; US$130-180.

Intercontinental Nairobi; City Hall Way; tel: 210-171; fax: 210-675; adjacent to exhibition grounds; restaurants; casino; conference facilities (up to 400); secretarial facilities; fax/photocopying facilities; in-room safe; pool; whirlpool; US$160-200.

Nairobi Hilton; Mama Ngina St.; tel: 334-000l; fax: 339-462; 4 restaurants; business center; in-room electronic safe; corporate rates; fitness room; health club; sauna; massage; pool; nearby golfing privileges; US$125+.

Expensive

New Stanley; Kimathi Street/Kenyatta Avenue; tel: 333-233; fax: 229-388; email: 6204836@eln.attmail.com; restaurant; conference facilities (up to 300); secretarial services; fax, photocopying facilities; in-room safe; fitness room; sauna; pool; whirlpool; US$110-130.

Safari Park; Thika Road; tel: (2) 802-493; fax: (2) 802-477; located in a suburb; casino; conference facilities; corporate rates; fitness; sauna; pool; whirlpool.

Moderate

Marble Arch; Lagos Road; tel:240-940; fax: 245-724; near exhibition grounds; restaurant; conference facilities (up to 100); secretarial services; fax/photocopying facilities; in-room modem connection; corporate rates; US$60-80.

Sixeighty; Kenyatta Ave; tel: 332-680; fax: 218-314; restaurant; conference facilities (up to 50); secretarial services; fax/photocopying facilities; in-room safe; corporate rates; US$60+.

The Landmark; Chiromo Road; tel: (2) 862-300; fax: (2) 802-322; located in suburb; restaurant; conference facilities; secretarial service; corporate rates; pool.

MEDICAL CARE

Achelis; Scientific and Hospital Division Centenary House, Westlands, off Ring Road; tel: (2) 449-284/5/6; fax: (2) 449-287.

Medivac; tel: (2) 561-643 or 564-412; fax: (2) 562-695.

Nairobi Hospital; Argwings-Kodhek Road; tel: (2) 2140.

AUTO RENTAL

Note: Excessive speed, unpredictable local driving habits, and the lack of basic safety equipment on many vehicles are daily hazards on Kenyan roads. Travel outside major cities at night should be avoided.

Avis; at College House, University Way, Nairobi

tel: 2542 334 31; fax: 2542 215 421.

Hertz; /UTC at Fedha Towers, Standard Street, Nairobi; tel: 2542-214 456; fax: 2542-216 871.

Market Car Hire; P.O. Box 49713, Nairobi; tel: (2) 225-797 or 335-735; fax: (2) 339-779; email: market@form-net.com

Suntrek Car Hire; P.O. Box 48146, Nairobi; tel: (2) 225-679 or 335-741; fax: (2) 334-965; email: suntrek@form-net.com

WORLD TRADE CENTER

World Trade Center Nairobi
PO Box 4002
Ruwi, Muscat
Sultanate of Oman
tel: [96] (8) 795-929; fax: [96] (8) 795-974

CHAMBER OF COMMERCE

Kenya National Chamber of Commerce
PO Box 47024, Ufanisi House
Hailé Sélassie Avenue, Nairobi
el: (2) 334-413; fax: (2) 340-664

Kuwait

At a Glance

THE PEOPLE

Population 1,913,285 (1998)
Growth Rate 4.1% (1998)
Life Expectancy .... 74.76 years (born 1999)
Infant Mortality .... 10.74 deaths/1,000 live births (1998)

Ethnic Composition

Arab... 80%
South Asian 9%
Persian 4%
Other 7%

Religious Composition

Muslim.. 85%
Christian, Hindu, Parsi, and other 15%

Languages Spoken

Arabic (official), English

Education and Literacy

The government provides free education through post-secondary. Literacy nationwide is only 78.6 percent.

Labor Force

Total: 1,000,000
By occupation: services 80%, industry 15%, agriculture 5%

THE ECONOMY

The Kuwaiti economy is based in oil production and related industries. Since the Iraqi occupation and the Persian Gulf War in 1990-91, Kuwait has expended large sums to rebuild its infrastructure. The non-oil economy has been sluggish, due in large part to the changing demographics after the war. Kuwait's population has dropped by more than 20 percent from pre-war levels. Further, many of the Palestinians who previously lived in Kuwait with their families were expelled following the war and have been replaced by single guest workers. These new immigrants tend to send more of their earnings home rather than spend them in the local economy. Currently, over 68 percent of the adult population of Kuwait is made up of foreign nationals. Despite the continuation of a substantial trade surplus, reconstruction expenditures have significantly reduced Kuwaiti assets and are forcing a reassessment of the existing economic system. The generous social benefits program run by the state has added to the burden as oil revenues have declined. Government moves towards privatization have been thwarted by the royal family's reluctance to give up its control. Consequently, foreign investment has been rebuffed and Kuwait's continues to grow at a mere 1 percent per annum.

Exports .... US$14.7 billion (1997)
Imports .... US$7.7 billion (1997)
Total GDP .... US$46.3 billion (1997)
GDP Per Capita .... US$22,300 (1997)
Unemployment .... 1.8 percent (1997)
Inflation Rate .... 3.2 percent (1997)

Top Export Partners

Japan, India, United States, Singapore, E.U.

Top Import Partners

United States, E.U., Japan

Top Exports

Oil, fertilizers

Top Imports

Food, construction materials, vehicles and parts, clothing

BUSINESS WORKWEEK

Offices

Saturday to Thursday 8a.m. to 5p.m.

Banks

Saturday to Thursday 8a.m. to noon. Commercial area bank branches offer extended opening hours Saturday, Monday, and Wednesday from 4:30p.m. to 6p.m.

Government

Saturday to Thursday 8a.m. to 2p.m.

Retail

Winter hours: Saturday to Thursday 8a.m. to 1p.m. and 4p.m. to 10p.m.
Summer hours: Saturday to Thursday 8a.m. to 1p.m. and 3p.m. to 6p.m.

HOLIDAYS

New Year's Day..January 1
Id al-Fitr, end of Ramadan..............................January 19*
Kuwaiti National Day ....February 25
Id al-Adha, Feast of the Sacrifice ....March 28*
Islamic New Year ....April 17*
Birth of the Prophet ....June 26*
Ascension of the Prophet .... November 6*
Ramadan Begins .... December 9*
    *Dates may vary by year.

CLIMATE

Seasons

The summer months are dry and hot, and winters are short and cool. Levels of humidity are low. June and July can bring sandstorms, and the winter may bring some rainfall. January temperatures hover around 15°C (59°F), April temperatures around 21°C (70°F), and the summer temperatures can peak at 45°C (113°F).

Regions

There are few, if any, regional climatic differences in Kuwait.

Money & Banking

Currency

The currency of Kuwait is the Kuwaiti Dinar (KD).

Denominations

The Kuwaiti Dinar (KD) comes in coin denominations of KD100, 50, 20, 10, 5, and 1 fils; and banknotes of 250fils and 500 fils, and KD1, 5, 10, and 20.

Traveler's Checks and Credit Cards

Traveler's checks and currency can be exchanged at banks, exchange shops, hotels, and international airports at tourist exchange rates. Larger banks offer the best exchange rates. Keep all receipts for reconversion at departure.

Kuwait

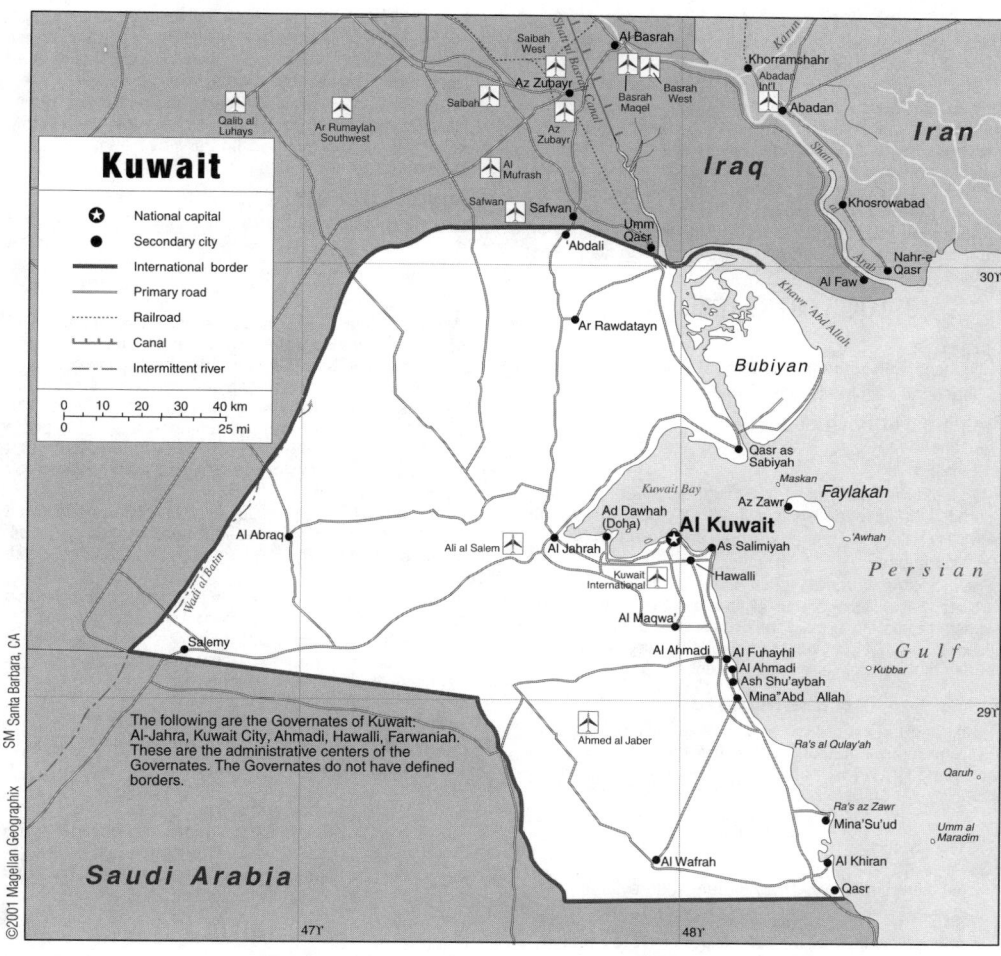

Kuwait

- ✪ National capital
- ● Secondary city
- ▬▬ International border
- ▬▬ Primary road
- ········· Railroad
- ⊢⊢⊢⊢ Canal
- – · – · Intermittent river

0 10 20 30 40 km
0   25 mi

The following are the Governates of Kuwait: Al-Jahra, Kuwait City, Ahmadi, Hawalli, Farwaniah. These are the administrative centers of the Governates. The Governates do not have defined borders.

©2001 Magellan Geographix   SM Santa Barbara, CA

Major credit cards like American Express, Visa, Diner's Club, and MasterCard are widely accepted throughout Kuwait, but smaller restaurants and *souks* (markets) may ask for cash. Cash advances on credit cards can be secured from ATMs located throughout the country. The most favorable exchange rates are given for ATM and credit card transactions.

Bank Locations

Al-Ahli Bank; P.O.Box 1387, Safat,13014; tel: 240-0900; fax: 242-4557.

Bank of Bahrain and Kuwait; P.O. Box 24396 Safat,13104; tel: 241-7140; fax: 244-0937.

Bank of Kuwait & the Middle East; P.O.Box 71 Safat, 13001; tel: 965-245-9771; fax: 965-246-1430.

Burgan Bank; P.O.Box 5389 Safat, 13054; tel: 243-9000; fax: 246-2516.

Commercial Bank of Kuwait; P.O.Box 2861 Safat, 13029; tel: 241-1001; fax: 245-0150

Industrial Bank of Kuwait; P.O.Box 3146 Safat, 13032; tel: 245-7661; fax: 246-2057.

Kuwait Finance House; P.O.Box 24989 Safat, 13110; tel: 244-5050; fax: 240-9414.

Kuwait Real Estate Bank; P.O. Box 22822 Safat, 13089; tel: 245-8177; fax: 246-2516.

National Bank of Kuwait; P.O.Box 95 Safat, 13001; tel: 242-2011; fax: 245-9032.

The Gulf Bank; P.O.Box 3200 Safat, 13032; tel: 244-9501; fax: 244-5212

Travel

VISA AND PASSPORT

Passports (valid for six months beyond departure date) and visas are required of all foreigners traveling to Kuwait, except nationals of Bahrain, Oman, Qatar, and United Arab Emirates for stays of up to three months. Saudi Arabian citizens are welcome for unlimited stays with no visa necessary.

Transit visas are not necessary as long as passengers have onward tickets and remain at the airport the entire interval between connecting flights.

For all others, visas must be acquired prior to entry. In addition, all travelers must hold onward tickets, valid travel documents, and sufficient funds.

There are Business, Visitor's, Work, and Transit visas. Kuwait does not issue tourist visas; in lieu, large hotels can sponsor Visitor's visas for individuals.

Business travelers normally get a one-year multiple-entry visa. Business visa applications must be accompanied by letters of guarantee from the foreign company, and visitors must be sponsored by a Kuwaiti company.

Note: Admission is prohibited to holders of Israeli passports.

DEPARTURE FORMALITIES

An airport tax of KD2 (about US$7) must be paid upon departure. Transit passengers are exempt. No taxes exist for land or sea departures.

CUSTOMS ENTRY (PERSONAL)

Duty-free
• Tobacco: 500 cigarettes or 907g of tobacco
• Reasonable amounts of personal effects

Prohibited or Restricted
• Alcohol of any kind
• Narcotics
• Unsealed milk products, salty fish, unsealed olives and pickles, food made abroad, fresh vegetables, shellfish and its products, fresh figs, and mineral water, pork
• Pornography
• Items manufactured in Israel

Note: Expect stringent penalties for attempting to smuggle restricted items. Dogs, cats, and birds require a veterinary certificate. Firearms and explosives required a special import license. Contact the Ministry of the Interior for further details.

IMMUNIZATION

No vaccinations are necessary unless visitors are arriving from an area infected with yellow fever. Cholera, tetanus, hepatitis, and typhoid vaccinations are advised for travel in rural areas.

TIPPING

Taxi
Taxi drivers are tipped only for long journeys.

Porters
Porters typically receive 250 fils per piece of luggage.

Hotels
All service charges are applied directly to the bill.

Restaurants
A 10 percent tip is customary unless service charges have been applied to the bill.

EMERGENCY INFORMATION

Police and Crime
Crime is relatively low in Kuwait, but take basic precautions. Foreign business visitors are often the target of what few thieves there are in Kuwait. Consequently, purses, laptops, and briefcases will require additional security. Do not leave valuables in cars or on tables in cafés. Keep non-essential valuables locked in hotel safes when not in use. Use credit cards and travel checks when possible to avoid carrying large sums of cash.

Women should not walk alone and should abide by local dress codes. Unfortunately, foreign women —especially Europeans—can expect some degree of verbal harassment from Arab men.

There is some corruption within the local and central governments. Business travelers may also find that their deals with local companies involve the bribing of public officials. Be-

sides making the personal decision of whether or not to participate in such dealings, check on your legal position in your own country. Some nations now have stiff penalties for their business people who bribe officials overseas.

Note: The border area between Iraq and Kuwait is considered extremely hazardous. Foreigners unwittingly crossing this poorly marked border have been detained and even imprisoned in Iraq.

Emergency Numbers
Ambulance 431-1759, 431-1769
Fire 241-8714
Police...199

Health
Although water in Kuwait City may be chlorinated, it advisable to use bottled water to avoid stomach upset. When eating out, make sure the seafood is fresh. Use only pasteurized milk. The sun is strong in the desert, and is especially severe between June and August. In Kuwait City, special ambulances stand at attention to attend to people who collapse due to the heat. Watch out for sunburn and heat stroke. Drink plenty of liquids if your work requires you to be outdoors.

Bring all prescription medicines that will be needed on a regualr basis. For work in desert rural areas, carry a well-stocked medical kit. The dust in the desert areas may also cause bronchitis.

Hotels have access to multi-lingual doctors and medical assistants. Most specialists are trained abroad and speak English. If you have a major medical problem, you are advised to leave the country. Travel insurance and evacuation policies are strongly recommended for long-term visitors.

AIR

There are no regularly scheduled domestic air services serving Kuwait internally.

TAXI

Taxis have a red license plate and are available to be hired by the day. All fares should be negotiated before departing. Most taxis are reserved in advance. All directions should be written down in translation. Carry a map.

AUTO

Auto rental is available in Kuwait City, but rentals are quite expensive by U.S. or European standards. A credit card, local insurance, and a valid driver's license are required. Hired cars with local drivers are also available for daily or weekly rates. Visitors are cautioned not to drive into desert areas without proper guidance.

Note: Women in Kuwait are now permitted to drive.

BUSES & TRAMS

There are both local and intercity bus routes in Kuwait. They are, however, used almost exclusively by poor guest workers.

Note: Management-level business people in Kuwait travel only by taxi, hired car, or chauffeured private vehicle.

WATER TRAVEL

International cruise lines serve Kuwait through the port at Kuwait City. There is a very limited coastal ferry service, and it is not recommended for business travelers.

TRAVEL ASSISTANCE

Ministry of Information
PO Box 193, 13002 Safat, As-Sour St.
tel: 243-6644; fax: 242-9758

Essential Terms

English	Arabic
Yes No	Na-a'am La; mish
Good morning Hello (daytime) Hello (evening) Hello (telephone)	Al sa-lahm Al sa-lahm Ma-sa'el khair Marhaban
Good-bye	Be-kha-trahk
Please	Min-fahd-lak (M) Min-fahd-lik (F)
Thank you	Shook-rahn
Pleased to meet you	Sorirart biro'aitak
Excuse me; I'm sorry	Is-ma-leh
My name is _____	'ismii____
I don't understand	An-na mish fahem
Do you speak English?	Hal tatakallumu l-inkliziyya?

Security Briefing

SOCIAL UNREST

The high GDP per capita of Kuwait has always kept social unrest to a minimum. Since the Gulf War, there has been movement towards a more democratic government and away from royal rule of the emir. Currently about 60 percent of the legislature is composed of delegates considered in "opposition" to the royal family. Six of sixteen cabinet posts are held by similar opponents, though none in strategic positions. The emir still has a very strong power base in Kuwait. Democracy is a touchy subject in this country and not one that should be discussed by foreigners without forethought. A word to the wise: Most business of any size in Kuwait has connections to the emir or his family.

ORGANIZED CRIME

For all intents and purposes, organized crime does not exist in Kuwait.

STREET CRIME

Kuwaiti cities are extremely safe. This is a very wealthy country with a generous social system; so, there is very little reason to resort to crime. This does not mean that common sense precautions should not be taken, especially in more rural areas.

CULTURAL CONFLICTS

Only about 33 percent of the population of Kuwait is Kuwaiti; the balance are guest workers from many countries. Consequently, a wide variety of cultures are tolerated (although Palestinians were expelled during the Gulf War for their pro-Iraqi sentiments).

Kuwait is a fairly secular Moslem nation, but foreigners should maintain conservative dress standards. Women's dresses should be cut below the knee and bare shoulders or backs must be avoided. Foreigners may even visit mosques if appropriately attired.

Communications

DIALING CODES IN KUWAIT

International country code: [965]

Dialing Kuwait from Overseas

To dial Kuwait from overseas, dial your country's international dialing code, then 965 (the country code for Kuwait), and finally the number. There are no city codes.

Assistance Numbers

International Operator 021
International Directory 022
Operator 118
Local Directory 101

CALLING WITHIN KUWAIT

Local Calls

Kuwait's smooth-running system makes calling easy anywhere you dial. All numbers have seven digits.

Long Distance Calls

Kuwait has no area codes and, as such, no hassles.

International Calls

To call overseas direct, dial 00 + country code + area code + number. Keep in mind that booking a call through an operator is much more costly than dialing direct from a card phone. Unfortunately for the rest of the traveling world, direct access to a foreign operator is only available to the United States as of yet. Americans may kiss the ground and begin dialing:
AT&T USA Direct 800-288
MCI 800-624

PAY PHONES

Public Telephones

Kuwait has made phoning a pleasure when compared with others in the region. The telephone system is fast and efficient. Public phones take 50 and 100fils coins.

Calling Cards

There are two styles of card phones in post offices and telecommunication offices, which also happen to sell the cards for their use. Cards come in KD5 or 10 denominations.

CELLULAR PHONES

Kuwait Mobile Telephone Systems Company operates an ETACS and GSM digital system for those intending to use cellular phones.

Note: Your home country cell phone may not work in this country. If not, we recommend that you rent an international cell phone *before* you leave home. A major US-based cell phone rental provider is **IMC WorldCell**. For information see "International Cell Phone Rentals" on page 14.

CALL BACK

You can (potentially) save significant sums when calling in Kuwait by using a call back service. For a list of callback services, please refer to the "Communications" section in the *Global Road Warrior* Introduction.

Fees for call back services vary widely, depending on the company and the type of service required. Be sure to check with these companies before leaving to compare rates.

Kuwait

PHONE JACKS

Plug adaptors are available through **iGo Corporation.** (See "Electrical and Telephone Adaptors" on page 19.)

FAX

Fax services have largely been restored following the Iraqi invasion in 1991. Faxes are available at most hotels, and service is good.

POSTAL SERVICES

It is best to avoid surface mail within the country, it can move at a snail's pace. Airmail to Europe and the U.S. can take up to 10 days. Post office boxes should be used instead of mailboxes. The Ministry of Post and Telegraph Offices are located at Abdullah Al Salem Square from Saturday to Wednesday 7a.m. to 2p.m., and Thursday from 7a.m. to noon.

Hours of Service

Saturday to Wednesday 7a.m. to 2p.m., Thursday 7a.m. to noon.

TELEGRAMS

Telegrams are available at the Ministry of Post and Telegraph Services but must be handed to the post office.

Business Services

BUSINESS CENTERS

Kuwait Plaza; Fahd Af Salem Street; tel: 243-6686; fax: 241-2198.

Le Meridien Kuwait; Al-Hilali Street, Safat; tel: 245-5550; fax: 243-8391

COURIER SERVICES

Airborne Express (Aramex Internaitonal Courier); Al-Gaz Tower 9th Floor, Sharq, Kuwait; PO Box 23985, Safat 13100; tel: 241-6990.

DHL; DHLA International Trans Co. W.L.L.; Old TV Center,

Arabian Gulf St., Dasman, PO Box 26523, Safat 13126; tel: 244-2375; Saturday to Friday 24 hours.

Federal Express; tel: 564-0677; Saturday to Thursday 8a.m. to 8p.m.; Customer Automation Help Desk: 09714-821-066.

UPS Kuwait; PO Box 20637, Safat 13067; tel: 434-4822; fax: 434-4622.

Electrical

Current

240 volts AC, 50Hz.

ELECTRIC PLUGS

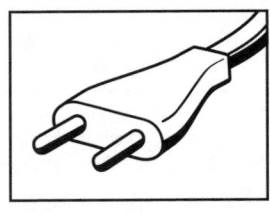

Plug adaptors are available through **iGo Corporation.** (See "Electrical and Telephone Adaptors" on page 19.)

Technical Support

HARDWARE/SOFTWARE VENDOR SUPPORT

Acer/Texas Instruments; (in Germany) tel: [49] (4102) 488-469; fax; [49] (4102) 488-169; (in the U.S.) [1] (408) 432-6200; http://www.acer.com/.

Adobe; (in the U.A.E.) tel: (971) 4-219787; fax: (971) 4-210724; (in Switzerland) tel: [41] (800) 833-310; (in the U.S.) tel: [1] (800) 500-7078; (in the U.S.) tel: [1] (716) 633-3600; http://www.adobe.com/.

Apple/Claris; (in the U.A.E.) tel: [971] 4-233-438; (in Switzerland) tel: [41] (800) 833-310; (in the U.K.) tel: [44] (990) 127-753; (in the U.S.) tel: [1] (800) 500-7078; http://www.apple.com/.

AST; (in the U.S.) tel: [1] (817) 232-9824 (International Technical Support); (in Ireland) tel: [353] (61) 492-222; (in the U.S.) tel: [1] (949) 727-4141; http://www.ast.com/.

Compaq/Digital; (U.A.E. Office) tel: [971] 4-818-100; fax:

[971] 4-818-313; (in Switzerland) tel: [41] (22) 709-5330; fax: [41] (22) 709-5391 (Geneva); tel: [41] (1) 801-2507; fax: [41] (1) 801-2172 (Zurich); (General U.S.) tel: (281) 518-2000; http://www.compaq.com/.

Corel; (in the U.A.E.) tel: [971] 4-523-526; (in the U.S.) tel: [1] (716) 871-2325 (Ask to be Forwarded to Appropriate Program); http://www.corel.com/.

Dell; tel: 2414140; fax: 2425592 (Al Alamiah); (Dell-Europe) tel: [44] (134) 474-8000; (in the U.S.) tel: [1] (512) 338-4400; fax: [1] (512) 728-3330; http://www.dell.com/.

Filemaker/Claris; (in Germany) tel: [49] (180) 525-8166 (Info-line); fax: [49] (180) 567-2233; tel: [49] (180) 523-6423; (in the U.S.) tel: [1] (800) 965-9090; http://www.claris.com/.

Gateway 2000; (in the U.S.) tel: [1] (605) 232-2191; fax: [1] (605) 232-2023; (in Ireland) tel: [353] (1) 797-2000; http://www.g2k.com/.

Hewlett Packard; (in Switzerland) tel: [41] (22) 780-8111; (in the U.S.) tel: [1] (408) 246-4300; http://www.hp.com/.

IBM; tel: 243-9900; fax: 242-4577; (in Switzerland) tel: [41] (22) 310-0418 (in French); (in the U.S.) tel: [1] (919) 517-2800; (U.S. Main Office) tel: [1] 914-765-1900; http://www.ibm.com/

Microsoft; (U.A.E. Office) tel: [971] 4-513-888; fax: [971] 4-527-444; (in Switzerland) tel: [41] (848) 858-868; fax [41] (1) 831-0869; (in the U.S.) [1] (425) 635-7222; http://www.microsoft.com/.

NEC; (in Israel) tel: [972] (0)9-59-3300 (UltraCare Support); (in the U.S.) tel: [1] (916) 388-0101 (Main Switchboard); http://www.nec.com/.

Novell; (in Germany) tel: [49] (211) 563-2777 (System support); tel: [49] (6196) 904-477; fax: [49] (211) 563-2772; (in Switzerland) tel: [41] (1) 308-4747; fax: [41] (1) 302-0401; (in the U.S.) tel: [1] (408) 434-2300; fax: [1] (408) 577-5775 (Worldwide Sales Headquarters); http://www.novell.com/.

Quark; (in Switzerland) tel: [41] (1) 808-7722; fax: [41] (1) 808-7799; (in the U.S.) tel: [1] (303) 894-8899; fax: [1] (303) 894-3398 (For Products Registered in the Americas); http:/ /www.quark.com/.

Toshiba; (in Germany) tel: [49] (2131) 158-319; fax: [49] (2131) 158-558; (in Switzerland) tel: [41] (1) 946-0777; fax: [41] (1) 946-0807; (in Ireland) tel: [44] (193) 282-8828; (in the U.S.) [1] (949) 583-3000 (Corporate Headquarters); http://www.toshiba.com/.

Internet Connection

HOW TO CONNECT

Connecting to AOL and Compuserve in Kuwait is similar to using it when traveling outside your own area code. See the introductory section for detailed information on connecting to your account through a different phone number.

America Online

Numbers are available at keyword *international*. Be sure to get several local numbers before leaving. Go to keyword *access* (a free area) and download the software.

There are no direct access numbers for America Online in Kuwait. Users will have to pay international rates to use the service.

Compuserve

Numbers are available at *Go International*. The Compuserve Web-site also has a great deal of information, at http://www.compuserve.com.

There are no direct access numbers for Compuserve in Kuwait. Users will have to pay international rates to use the service.

Independent Service Providers

Many independent service providers offer discounts if you are only in town for a couple days.

Gulfnet Kuwait; tel: (2) 426-728; fax: (2) 413-523; email: info@kuwait.net; http://www.kuwait.net/.

KEMS Gulfnet International; tel: 244-3800; fax: 244-3807; sales@kems.net; http://www.kems.net/.

Business Culture

GREETINGS & COURTESIES

The standard greeting of "*salaam alaykum*" (peace be with you) is met with a response of "*wa alaykum as-salaam*" (and peace be upon you). After this brief exchange, inquiries into health, family, travel, food intake, weather, etc. will ensue amid much handshaking. Arab men often exchange embraces and cheek kisses as well as handshakes. Long-time acquaintances will continue to hold hands during the many questions and answers. **Note**: Hand holding among Arab males is common and can be uncomfortable for Western men. It is a sign of friendship, not sexual interest.

This is a male-dominated society, and Kuwaiti men will not offer to shake a woman's hand unless the woman (usually foreign) extends her hand first. Even then, they may do so with some reluctance. Often, local men will not even introduce the females who are accompanying them. If the women are not introduced, foreigners should not presume to introduce themselves. This is considered to be a major faux pas. Most Kuwaiti women will, however, introduce themselves.

Arabic culture demand high levels of hospitality and part of this is an enthusiastic and heartfelt greeting. They will expect the same in return. A warm, firm handshake, locked eye contact, and a beaming smile are the outward signs that cover any language problem. Most Kuwaiti businessmen have traveled overseas and are familiar with other cultures. They do, however, expect foreigners to abide by local customs while in Kuwait. Friendly greetings, rather than impersonal "just business" handshakes or polite bows, are part of those customs.

BUSINESS ETHIC & FRAMEWORK

Kuwaitis are experienced international businessmen, and they have been part of global trade since the 1930s. They have a reputation for cutting honest, equitable deals and standing by them. Kuwaitis expect the same from foreign partners.

Kuwait has a sophisticated financial sector and lots of money to back it up. This is not an emerging market, and woe to anyone who thinks they can pull a "fast one" on a Kuwaiti firm. Treat them as equals or pay the price. They have done business all over the world and they are familiar with every negotiating style practiced. The best way to approach them is with an informed mind and an honest heart. Save the tricks and condescension for somewhere else.

DECISION MAKING

This is a very hierarchical society, and many Kuwaiti companies are structured around family units. Even when they are not family run, decisions still come from the top. The concepts of horizontal management and dispersed authority have not reached Kuwaiti management circles.

However, Kuwaiti decision making is somewhat speedier than in other Middle Eastern countries because local managers are more adept at international business. Their hierarchies are more akin to Japanese companies where decisions can be reached by quick consensus when the situation calls for it.

Companies in Kuwait have access to all of the latest technology and information gathering systems available. Many are fluent in English. Information does still tend to flow from the bottom up. Foreign sellers will find that decisions in regard to their proposals are slower in coming than those received by foreign buyers or investors.

Note: Kuwaitis are capable of putting together any form of financing needed for a project because they are not strict observers of the Islamic strictures against interest payments (usury). Combined with their adherence to contracts, it makes doing business in Kuwait very attractive.

MEETINGS

Kuwait's long-term involvement with international trade has given them a breadth of business experience unmatched in the Middle East. While they do observe the Islamic requirements of good hospitality, Kuwaitis also like to focus on the business at hand. Initial greetings will be followed by brief introductions (in descending order of rank). When dealing with non-Arabic visitors, the normal "get to know you" chat period is very brief, after which the hosts will turn directly to the agenda. While this is done to please many Western business visitors, some Asian companies will be given the more traditional pre-agenda chit chat. The Kuwaitis tend to tailor their meeting style to the visitor's standards.

Note: Although English is common, Arabic translations of business cards and brochures should be considered, especially by sellers.

Meeting facilities will generally be very professional, if not cutting edge. Kuwait is a wealthy country and Kuwaitis don't mind letting visitors know that fact. Presentations will use the latest technology, and they will judge their counterparts accordingly. (Don't show up to do a sales presentation with a flip chart and a felt-tip pen!) Telecom and computer infrastructure are not problems in Kuwait.

Corporate meetings will run on an agenda which the foreign firm should agree to in advance. The Kuwaitis don't like surprises from buyers or sellers. Last-minute changes will be viewed with suspicion.

While Kuwait has a more streamlined business community than most Arabic countries, don't expect to cut a deal at the first meeting. The Kuwait side will want to be able to check everything out prior to signing contracts. A modicum of patience will be required.

Note: Kuwaiti business people are generally straight forward, but Arabic culture prevents them from discussing unpleasant topics in public. They may ask for "back channel" or one-on-one meetings after hours to work out problems. If they do, make sure that it is clearly stated that the issues discussed will not bind the topics of the general meeting. The extra meetings are for "information only" purposes.

WOMEN IN BUSINESS

Women are very rare at the Kuwaiti executive level and mid-level management is the highest they usually reach—and never with male subordinates. Their experience has made Kuwaiti companies at ease with the concept of foreign women in key business roles, however. Visiting firms should make the presence of female executives in their delegations known well in advance of arrival. Otherwise, Kuwaiti businessmen will assume the women are only secretaries or assistants. Once the proper role is known there should not be any other major problems. Do be aware that Kuwaiti men will expect women to back down in any confrontation so sellers beware!

Note: As the nightlife in Kuwait is rather tame, visiting females may even be invited along for after business get-togethers.

BUSINESS ENTERTAINING

This is a very wealthy country, and business entertaining can be lavish. Kuwaiti companies spend heavily to impress smaller foreign companies and to let big foreign corporations know that Kuwait is a major player on the global stage.

Elaborate meals, golf outings, and touring excursions can all be part of business entertaining. It will all be done in a first-class manner. If the visitors are in a buying or investing mode, they can also expect some gifts.

Note: It is hard to outspend the Kuwaitis when it comes to business entertaining and reciprocate only if your budget permits you to reasonably match your hosts' largesse; otherwise, just sit back and enjoy the treatment.

BUSINESS ATTIRE

Kuwait is a hot, dry country, but air conditioning abounds in buildings and autos alike. Business suits are worn by most Kuwaiti managers, though some may opt for traditional Arab garb, including the headdress.

Male and female visitors should wear conservative, well-made, tailored suits. Cheap just does not fly in Kuwait; this applies for leisure clothing as well. Kuwaitis have very sophisticated taste in clothing, and they judge accordingly.

Note: Women in Kuwait do have greater discretion in clothing than in most Islamic countries, but even leisure wear should expose very little flesh. Err on the side of conservatism.

Business Advisory
POLITICS & GRAFT

Kuwait's wealth gives it the ability to pay its public servants well. Foreign firms should not experience many problems with graft.

BUSINESS FRAUD

Fraud is rare in Kuwait. They have a thriving financial services sector that cannot afford such a reputation. Contracts in all sectors are abided by, for the most part. Any delivery schedule or quality control problems will be the result of cultural differences and not an intent to defraud.

Business Centers
City View
KUWAIT CITY

Kuwait is a modern city, particularly when compared to the cities of neighboring countries. Built on harsh desert ground, Kuwait City is home to two million residents who live in blissful decadence thanks to the country's oil-based wealth. In 1991, the city began to rebuild the large portion of structures that had been destroyed during the Iraqi invasion. Unfortunately, most of the cultural treasures formerly found in the National Museum were either looted or destroyed. The Tareq Rajab Museum holds a private collection of Islamic art that now attracts more tourists as a result of the National Museum's demise. Ascending the Kuwait Towers is also an agreeable segment on the sightseeing agenda, for these modern 600-foot landmarks offer an observation deck, shops, and restaurant in hand with an imaginative glimpse of what once spread before the lands below.

AIRPORT

Kuwait Airport to City Center

The airport lies 10 miles (16 km.) from the airport. There are regular bus services, and taxis are available for about KD5. Look for the red and orange cars. All five-star hotels provide car service to and from the airport.

Airline Numbers

Aer Lingus	241-9814
Aeroflot	240-4838
Air China	243-8568
Air France	242-0504
Air India	243-8158
Air Lanka	242-4444
Alitalia	241-4403, ext. 103 or 104
Biman Bangladesh	244-1041
British Airways	242-5635
EgyptAir	242 1603
Emirates	243-8690
Gulf Air	245-0180
Indian Airlines	245-6700
KLM	242-5747
Kuwait Airways	243-3388
Lufthansa	242-2493
MEA	242-3070
Olympic	242-0002
PIA	242-1043
Qatar Airways	245-8888
Saudia	242-6310
Tarom	244-1041
Turkish Airlines	245-3820

HOTELS

Top-end

Holiday Inn Crowne Plaza Kuwait; Airport Street; Farwaniya; tel: 474-2000; fax: 473-2020; city suburb; restaurants; in-room safe; conference facilities (up to 500); secretarial services; fax/photocopying facilities; corporate rates; fitness room; sauna; pool; whirlpool; US$80-220.

Kuwait Sheraton; Fahd Al Salem Street, Safat; tel: 242-2055; fax: 244-8032; 5 restaurants; in-room safe, modem connection, fax machine, clothes press; conference facilities (up to 1000); secretarial services; health club; sauna; pool; squash; golf simulator; US$180+.

Le Meridien Kuwait; Al-Hilali Street, Safat; tel: 245-5550; fax: 243-8391; renovated; restaurants; business center; conference facilities (up to 180); secretarial services; fitness room; sauna; pool; US$180+.

Radisson SAS Kuwait; Al Bida Beach, Safat; tel: 575-6000; fax: 575-0155; located on beach, city suburb; restaurant; conference facilities; secretarial service; fax/photocopy facilities; in-room modem/fax connection; corporate rates; fitness; sauna; pool.

Safir International Kuwait, Bneid al-Gar; Safat; tel: 253-3000; fax: 252-3681; located on Corniche, city center; 3 restaurants, conference facilities (up to 800); secretarial services; fax/photocopying services; corporate rates; fitness room; sauna; pools; billiards; bowling; US$210-220.

Expensive

Carlton Tower; Al-Shuhada'd Street; tel: 245-2740; fax: 240-1624; 4-star hotel; city suburb; conference facilities (up to 250) secretarial services; fax/photocopying facilities; in-room safe and modem connection; corporate rates; US$120-160.

Kuwait Plaza; Fahd Af Salem Street; tel: 243-6686; fax: 241-2198; 5-star hotel; restaurants; conference facilities (up to 500); business center; secretarial services; fax/photocopying facilities; internet; corporate rates; US$130-150.

Moderate

Oasis Hotel Kuwait; P.O. Box 26855; tel: 246-5489; fax: 246-5490; 500 meters from ocean; breakfast included in price; restaurants; pool.

MEDICAL CARE

Ahmadi Hospital; tel: 398-5153.

Dar Al-Shifa Hospital; Safat; tel: 242-3157.

Mowasat Hospital; Salmiya; tel: 571-1533.

Al Adan Hospital; Sabahia; tel: 394-0600.

Hadi Hospital; Safat; tel: 531-2555.

Mubarak Al-Kabeer Hospital; tel: 531-2700.

Amiri Hospital; Sharq; tel: 245-1442.

International Clinic; Salmiya; tel: 574-5111.

Al Rashid Hospital; Salmiya; tel: 562-4000.

HEALTH CLUB

Kuwait Sheraton; Fahd Al Salem Street, Safat; tel: 242-2055; fax: 244-8032.

AUTO RENTAL

Avis; headquarters, tel: 246-5082, 245-3828; fax: 245-3829; Holiday Inn Hotel, tel: 474-2000; fax: 245-3829; HIlton Hotel, tel: 253-3000; fax: 245-3829.

Budget; central reservations, tel: 481-0709, 481-0844; fax: 481-0879; airport, tel: 471-9273; Shuwaikh Industrial Area, Pepsi Cola Street, tel: 481-0879.

Hertz; airport, 431-9326; fax: 431-9246, 24 hours, 7 days; Al Marzouk Sons Company, Safat 13072, tel: 484-8034; fax: 484-8035.

WORLD TRADE CENTER

World Trade Center Kuwait
Al Dawliyah Commercial Center
Fahed Al Salem Street, 3rd Fl., Office #1
PO Box 22
Safat 13001, Kuwait
tel: 240-4275; fax: 252-8011

CHAMBER OF COMMERCE

Kuwait Chamber of Commerce and Industry
PO Box 775, Chamber's Building
Ali as-Salem Street, 13008 Safat
tel: 246-3600; fax: 246-4110

Kuwait

Latvia

At a Glance

THE PEOPLE

Population 2,385,396 (1998)
Growth Rate .... -1.41% (1998)
Life Expectancy .... 67.11 years (born 1999)
Infant Mortality .... 17.44 deaths/1,000 live births (1998)

Ethnic Composition

Latvian..51.8%
Russian...33.8%
Other Slavic..14.4%

Religious Composition

Lutheran 55%
Roman Catholic...24%
Russian Orthodox..20%
Other and non-affiliated...1%

Languages Spoken

Lettish (official), Lithuanian, Russian

Education and Literacy

Education is compulsory until age 16 years of age. Adult literacy is 100 percent nationwide.

Labor Force

Total: 1,400,000
By occupation: services 43%, industry 41%, agriculture 16%

THE ECONOMY

Latvia's eastern Baltic location has always made it an important center for east-west commercial trading. After leaving the USSR in 1991, Latvia posted some of the highest GDP growth rates in Europe. The government passed its first balanced budget in 1997 and GDP growth still remains above 6 percent. This tiny maritime nation attracts considerable foreign investment looking to tap into the high education levels of the local population and developed infrastructure; but, all is not perfect in this Baltic republic. Latvia still relies heavily on its former Soviet bloc neighbors for much of its energy needs and other resources. Consequently, Latvia runs huge trade and current account deficits (20 percent and 10 percent respectively). Unfortunately, as most of these CIS economies are themselves struggling, they cannot offer much in the way of markets for Latvian goods. The government in Riga is still hopeful of joining the WTO, but its E.U. membership seems a long way off. Though hardly a basket case, Latvia may soon qualify for "sick man" status.

Exports .... US$1.4 billion (1997)
Imports .... US$2.3 billion (1997)
Total GDP .... US$10.4 billion (1997)
GDP Per Capita .... US$4,260 (1997)
Unemployment .... 7 percent (1997)
Inflation Rate .... 7.4 percent (1997)

Top Export Partners

CIS nations, E.U.

Top Import Partners

CIS nations, E.U.

Top Exports

Machinery and equipment, timber, textiles, foodstuffs

Top Imports

Fuels, machinery and equipment, chemicals

BUSINESS WORKWEEK

Offices

Monday to Friday 9a.m. to 6p.m.

Banks

Monday to Friday 10a.m. to 2p.m., 3p.m. to 8p.m.

Government

Monday to Friday 10a.m. to 3p.m.

Retail

Monday to Friday 10a.m. to 7p.m., Saturday and Sunday 10a.m. to 4p.m.
Note: Some department stores keep later hours. Rural shops schedule based on local custom and seasonal needs.

HOLIDAYS

New Year's Day..January 1
Good Friday..April 2*
Labor Day..May 1
Midsummer festival .... June 23-24
National Day, proclamation of the
Republic ....November 18
Christmas ....December 25-26
New Year's Eve...December 31
*Date may vary by year.

CLIMATE

Seasons

The climate in Latvia is temperate with four distinct seasons. Weather in Latvia can be described as ranging between the maritime and continental. The average winter temperature is 6°C (43°F), and the average temperate in July hovers around 17°C (63°F).

Regions

Eastern Latvia has warm, mild summers but very harsh winters. The west and northwest along the Baltic coast can experience long periods of blustery and wet weather.

Money & Banking

Currency

The currency of Latvia is the Latvian Lat (Ls).

Denominations

The Latvian Lat comes in coin denominations of Ls2 and 1, as well as 50, 20, 10, 5, and 1 santims; and banknotes of Ls5, 10, 20, 50, 100, and 500.

Traveler's Checks and Credit Cards

Traveler's checks were first legalized for use by foreigners in 1992 in the Baltic states. Checks can be exchanged at banks, exchange shops, and hotels, as well as international airports with various rates of exchange. Larger banks offer the best exchange rates. Consult your bank about current exchange rates before departure. Keep all receipts for reconversion. Exchanges can be time consuming; so, convert large amounts and keep the balance of cash in your hotel safe.

Latvia

Travel

VISA AND PASSPORT

Cash can also be exchanged at the same outlets as traveler's checks. Small-denomination German DM and U.S. dollars appear to be most easily changed and have the highest value.

Major credit cards such as American Express, Visa, Diner's Club, and MasterCard are accepted in most up-market places in the main cities, but smaller restaurants and shops may ask for cash. Only a few banks in the capital offer cash advances on credit cards, but make sure you bring along your passport for identification. ATMs are nowhere to be found, so bring cash or traveler's checks.

American Express Office

Latvia Tours, Kalku iela 8; tel: 7213-652; (check issuance and replacement only, no cashing).

All travelers to Latvia will need a valid passport and most also need a visa (not including British passport holders, or nationals of the Czech Republic, Republic of Ireland, Lithuania, Poland, the Slovak Republic, USA, and Vatican City). Business and tourist visas are available from a Latvian embassy. A visa to Estonia or Lithuania will also be accepted for entry into Latvia. It is possible to obtain a visa from Riga Airport upon arrival, but these visas are only valid for 10 days.

Business and multiple-entry require an invitation from a local company or government agency. Attempting to transact business other than basic commercial research on a tourist visa can result in deportation. Any contracts signed while on a tourist visa can be declared invalid.

DEPARTURE FORMALITIES

There are no departure taxes for visitors leaving Latvia from Riga Airport. If you are intending to export an item that is older than 1945 in manufacture, it requires an export permit from the Ministry of Culture (Valdemara 11, tel: 7225-770), and may be subject to VAT. There are no taxes for departures by land or sea.

CUSTOMS ENTRY (PERSONAL)

Duty-free
- Tobacco: 200 cigarettes, 20 cigars, or 200g tobacco
- Alcohol: 1 liter of alcoholic beverages
- Other: Ls15 (max) of food; Ls300 (max) of new duty free goods; Ls225 (max) of other new goods

Prohibited or Restricted
- Narcotics
- Guns and ammunition (without a police import permit)
- Pornography

Note: All animals need an international veterinarian passport. It is advisable to declare expensive items such as jewelry and furs.

Customs Information 7323-858

IMMUNIZATION

No international certificates of vaccination are required unless you are arriving from an area of known infection or epidemic.

TIPPING

Taxi
Taxi drivers usually receive 10 percent of the metered amount. Unmetered fares should be negotiated in advance.

Porters
Porters receive Ls1 per piece of luggage.

Hotels
Hotels usually apply a 10 percent service charge directly to the bill.

Restaurants
Restaurants usually apply service charges to the bill. If not, then a 10 percent tip is customary.

EMERGENCY INFORMATION

Police and Crime
Crime is on the increase in Latvia, especially in more urban areas. Take basic precautions against petty crime, especially in crowds, aboard public transportation, and in parks. Remain alert to your surroundings when exchanging money outside of the hotel. Pickpockets often lurk nearby. Foreign cars are also frequent targets of theft. Outside of the city center unlit streets are common and should be avoided.

Foreign business visitors are often the special target of thieves. Consequently, purses, laptops, and briefcases will require additional security. Do not leave valuables in cars or on tables in cafés. Keep non-essential valuables locked in hotel safes when not in use. Use credit cards and travel checks when possible to avoid carrying large sums of cash.

Police are, for the most part, very helpful to foreigners. However, most foreign business people are assumed to be wealthy and, by Latvian standards, overly demanding. When reporting a crime, remain courteous. You should in no way imply that local police are not professional or concerned.

Emergency Numbers
Numbers function nationwide.

Ambulance 03
Fire 01
Police.. 02
Police 24-hour emergency 7219-310

Health
Bottled water should be used, although major hotels in Latvia have potable tap water. Read the general travel health tips at the beginning of this book as most apply to this region. Vegetables and fruit may be considered safe to eat, but take care not to drink unpasteurized milk. Diarrhea is common for travelers who are unaccustomed to the new diet and water. The Latvian diet is "heavy" and Asian visitors may need some time to adjust. Hotel chefs are usually accommodating to visitors with special dietary needs.

Medical personnel are well trained, but Latvian facilities are sub-standard. Local hospitals should be used only for the early stages of emergency treatment. Carry a well-stocked medical kit and bring all prescription medicines you require. Travel insurance is recommended along with a evacuation policy.

For more information on medical centers, including phone numbers, please see the "Business Centers" section at the end of this chapter.

TAXI

A gas shortage has caused taxi prices to skyrocket. Taxis are efficient but very expensive. Flag an orange and black state-owned taxi from the street for a metered fare if you are interested in saving money. Otherwise, private cabs are also on the prowl, but their fares must be negotiated in advance. Have directions written down and translated. Always bring along a city map.

Taxi Service.. 070 or 077

AUTO

Auto rental is available in Riga, but the expense and low quality of the vehicles makes the transaction hard to recommend. If you do decide to rent, make sure the vehicle has theft insurance as rental cars are often targeted. **Note**: Urban travel can be done more easily by taxi, and intercity travel is best left to the train system.

TRAIN

Train services cover the country. They are inexpensive and efficient for regular use. Trains also run to other international cities such as Berlin, St. Petersburg, Sofia, and Moscow. Trains are a common form of overnight and intercity business travel in all of the Baltic states. All trains should be reserved in advance. First-, second-, and third-class travel is available.

Telephone train information.. 007
Central Train Station 232-134
Advance Bookings... 233-397

METRO

No subway system exists in Latvia.

BUSES & TRAMS

Buses, mini-buses, and trams are the most efficient way to get around Latvian cities. They reach every corner of the city and are commonly used by local business people. Tokens can be purchased at hotels and newsstands, or on board. The main bus station, from which inter-city buses depart, lies in the proximity of the Central Market. Trams sell 14 santim tickets aboard the cars or you can purchase tickets at newsstands or kiosks.

Intercity bus lines also compete with the train system. While comfortable for short trips, overnight travel—especially to other Baltic countries—is not very pleasant. All intercity bus tickets should be purchased at least a day in advance.

WATER TRAVEL

Two Latvian tour companies in Jurmala operate ferries that service Swedish and German ports a couple of times a week. International cruise lines also serve the Latvian port at Jurmala.

Ferry Information 7329-882
Transline Baltic Tours... 7329-514
Baltic Tour 7329-903

TRAVEL ASSISTANCE

Riga Tourist Information Bureau; Skarnu iela 22; tel: 7221-731; fax: 7227-680.

National Tourist Board of Latvia; Pils laukums 4, Riga LV-1050; tel: 722-9945; fax: 722-9945.

Essential Terms

English	Latvian
Yes	Ja
No	Ne
Good morning	Labrit
Hello (daytime)	Labdien
Hello (evening)	Labakar
Hello (telephone)	
Good-bye	Sveiki / Ardievu
Please	Ludzu
Thank you	Paldies
Pleased to meet you	Ka ri ju su vards?
Excuse me; I'm sorry	Atvainojiet
My name is _____	Mani sauc____
I don't understand	Es nesaprotu
Do you speak English?	Vai jus runajat

Security Briefing

SOCIAL UNREST

Latvia currently experiences little social unrest. But this is not to say that there are no sensitive subjects and discussions to avoid. Latvia still has a minority Russian population and a few indigenous citizens that yearn for the days of the Soviet empire. These sentiments are greatly subdued, but every tremor from Russia reverberates through Latvia. The fewer opinions expressed by visitors on this matter, the better.

ORGANIZED CRIME

While there are certainly elements of both local and Russian mafiya present in Latvia, they are not dominant forces. Organized crime in Latvia has nowhere near the level of penetration into "legitimate" business that exists in neighboring Russia or Belarus. Foreign business visitors to Latvia will not experience any problems or requests for special "contracts" normally associated with business in Latvia's eastern neighbors.

STREET CRIME

Latvia has a very low level of street crime and only in rare instances does it involve foreign visitors. Only basic precautions against pickpockets and luggage pilferers need be taken. When visiting rural areas, avoid walking the streets at night as lighting is minimal and awfully tempting for thieves.

CULTURAL CONFLICTS

Latvia is a very tolerant nation, for the most part, and it reserves its cultural biases for its former Russian over-seers. About the only conflict that could emerge would be if foreign visitors made the ignorant assumption that Latvia was still under Russian/Soviet control or was better off when it was.

Communications

DIALING CODES IN LATVIA

International country code: [371]
Selected city codes: Daugavpils (54), Liepaia (34), Riga (2).

Dialing Latvia from Overseas

To dial Latvia from overseas, dial your country's international dialing code, then 371 (the country code for Latvia), then the city code and finally the number. If you were dialing Riga from the United States, for example, you would begin with 011, then 371, and then number of the person or office you were trying to reach. Many numbers have been updated to include seven digits.

Assistance Numbers

International Operator 8-194, 287-344
International Urgent Calls.. 8-15
Intercity Connections.. 282-222
Intercity Long Distance.. 8-12
Analogue Telephone Operator 1-115
Directory Enquiries.. 09

CALLING WITHIN LATVIA

Local Calls

You have three minutes to get your point across if dialing locally from a pay phone.

Long Distance Calls

Go to the post office if you intend to place a long distance call within Latvia. Dial the area code and number. Six-digit numbers indicate that the number you are calling is an old Soviet-style analogue phone. In this case, if dialing from a digital phone: dial 2 (wait for the tone) + six-digit number.

If you've commandeered one of the dinosaur analogue phones and are trying to reach a digital number, dial 1 (wait for the tone) + number.

International Calls

To place an international call, you can go to the post office or to satellite telephones located in hotels. Sample rates include a possible US$4 per minute to the U.S. Dial 00 + country code + area code + number. It could take from 10 minutes to an hour to place a call. Outside of Riga, it could take even longer since you have to book through a local operator who will have to go through Riga and check availability in order to place the call. You'll probably have to take a seat, if not a bed, as the procedure could take anywhere from hours to days.

Try to access a U.S. operator for more fortune in placing a call overseas. Wait for a dial tone when dialing the initial eight.
U.S. AT&T (outside Riga)...............................8-27007-007
U.S. AT&T (within Riga) 7007-007

Latvia

Latvia

PAY PHONES

Public Telephones
Card Phone:

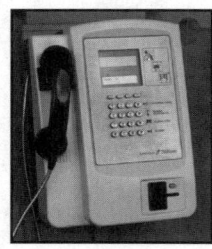

Colorful public phones stick out in the crowd of gray. Many use tokens (*zhetons*).
1. Insert token
2. Dial
3. Wait for an answer
4. Coin will slip down

Calling Cards
Post offices, kiosks and shops sell phone cards (*telekartes*), in 1-, 5-, and 10 Lati denominations.

CELLULAR PHONES
Latvia Mobile Telephone Company (Labvijas Mobilais Telefons) operates a GSM digital system as well as an NMT-450 analogue system, which operates at 450MHz. BalTel offers GSM service to Latvia as well.

Note: Your home country cell phone may not work in this country. If not, we recommend that you rent an international cell phone *before* you leave home. A major US-based cell phone rental provider is **IMC WorldCell**. For information see "International Cell Phone Rentals" on page 14. Cellular service/rentals also available froma: **Labvijas Mobilais Telefons**; tel: 777-3111

CALL BACK
You can (potentially) save significant sums when calling in Latvia by using a call back service. For a list of callback services, please refer to the "Communications" section in the *Global Road Warrior* Introduction.

Fees for call back services vary widely, depending on the company and the type of service required. Be sure to check with these companies before leaving to compare rates.

PHONE JACKS

Plug adaptors are available through **iGo Corporation**. (See "Electrical and Telephone Adaptors" on page 19.)

FAX
Facilities are available at the **Main Post Office**, Brivibas 19, tel: (2) 224-155.

POSTAL SERVICES
Airmail has improved over the past few years, but it is still grossly inefficient. Airmail could take two weeks to arrive in the U.S., and incoming mail could take much longer. The main post office remains open 24 hours a day and is located at Brivibas 19.

TELEGRAMS
Most hotels have services. To send a telegram from a public phone, dial '06'.

Electrical

Current
220 volts 50Hz.

ELECTRIC PLUGS

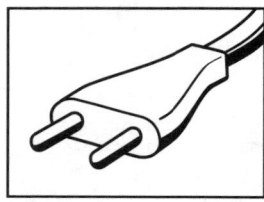

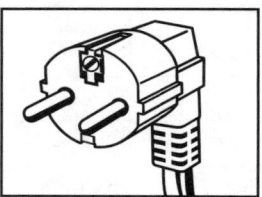

Plug adaptors are available through **iGo Corporation**. (See "Electrical and Telephone Adaptors" on page 19.)

Business Services

BUSINESS CENTERS
Man-Tess Hotel; Teatra 6; tel: 216-056; fax: 821-249.

COPYING SERVICE
Formula Kopiju Centrs; Skolas 2; tel 7240-210.

COURIER SERVICES
Airborne Express; Express Service: RGW Express Airfreight; GmbH, Cargo City Sued/Geb. 638, 60549 Frankfurt, Germany; tel: [49] (69) 698-0080; fax: [49] (69) 6980-0840.

Freight Service: Airborne Freight; c/o ASF Air Sra Oy, Pl 1, FI-01531 Vantaa, Finland; tel: (9) 584-294; fax: (9) 5842-7310.

DHL International (Latvia) SIA; 55, Brivibas St., Riga LV1050; tel: (2) 701-3292.

DHL International (Latvia) SIA; Dzintaru 22, Ventspils 3602; tel: (2) 366-5406.

DHL International (Latvia) SIA; Diku 10, Liepaja 3401; 348-0212.

EMS; Brivibas 19, Post Office 51; tel: 7018-738.

Federal Express (Baltic Express SVC); tel: (2) 326-067.

TNT Worldwide; Rezeknes 1; tel: 7138-432.

UPS Latvia; 13.Janvara iela 33, LV-1050 Riga, tel: (2) 722-2247, 721-2185; fax: (2) 721-1509;　e-mail: ekllps@ups.apollo.lv.

Additional UPS offices in Latvia:

Talsu iela 31, LV-3602 Ventspils; tel: 366-5161; fax: 366-4286; e-mail: ups@rdven.lvnet.lv.

Gimnazijas iela 16, LV-5403 Daugavpils; tel/fax: 542-1180; e-mail: ups@dpu.lv.

Kungu iela 21a, LV-3400, Liepaja; tel: 342-4414.

Jelgava; tel: 305-5213.

Valmiera; tel: 422-5320.

Salacgriva; tel: 404-1760

Kuldiga; 332-2721

SECRETARIAL SERVICES

World Trade Center; tel: 732-2242; fax: (7) 783-0035; website: http://www.wtcr.bkc.lv; email: mail@wtc-riga.lv

TRANSLATION/INTERPRETING

Letonis; Caka 114; tel: 274-747.

Lingva Serviss; Gleznotaju 5; tel: 7228-993.

World Trade Center; tel: 732-2242; fax: (7) 783-0035; website: http://www.wtcr.bkc.lv; email: mail@wtc-riga.lv.

Technical Support
HARDWARE/SOFTWARE VENDOR SUPPORT

Compaq/Digital; (in Switzerland) tel: [41] (22) 709-5330; fax: [41] (22) 709-5391 (Geneva); tel: [41] (1) 801-2507; fax: [41] (1) 801-2172 (Zurich); (General U.S.) tel: (281) 518-2000; http://www.compaq.com/.

Dell; (in Germany) tel: [49] (61) 039-710; (Dell- Europe) tel: [44] (134) 474-8000; (in the U.S.) tel: [1] (512) 338-4400; fax: [1] (512) 728-3330; http://www.dell.com/.

Hewlett Packard; (in Switzerland) tel: [41] (22) 780-8111; (in the U.S.) tel: [1] (408) 246-4300; http://www.hp.com/.

IBM; tel: 707-0300; fax: 707-0399; (in Germany) tel: [49] (711) 78-50; fax: [49] (711) 785-3511; (in Switzerland) tel: [41] (22) 310-0418 (in French); (in the U.S.) tel: [1] (919) 517-2800; (U.S. Main Office) tel: [1] 914-765-1900; http://www.ibm.com/

Microsoft; (in Germany) tel: [49] (89) 31-760; fax: [49] (89) 3176-1000; tel: [49] (89) 3176-1199; (in Switzerland) tel: [41] (848) 858-868; fax [41] (1) 831-0869; (in the U.S.) [1] (425) 635-7222; http://www.microsoft.com/.

NEC; (in Germany) tel: [49] (18) 0524- 1212; tel:[49] (89) 3160-1233; fax: [49] (89) 3160- 1613 (Floppy Disk and Hard Drive); tel: [49] (89) 9627-4233; fax: [49] (89) 9627-4613 (All Other Products); (in the U.S.) [1] (916) 388-0101 (Main Switchboard); http://www.nec.com/.

Toshiba; (in Germany) tel: [49] (2131) 158-319; fax: [49] (2131) 158-558; (in Switzerland) tel: [41] (1) 946-0777; fax: [41] (1) 946-0807; (in Ireland) tel: [44] (193) 282-8828; (in the U.S.) [1] (949) 583-3000 (Corporate Headquarters); http://www.toshiba.com/.

Internet Connection
HOW TO CONNECT

Connecting to AOL and Compuserve in Latvia is similar to using it when traveling outside your own area code. See the introductory section for detailed information on connecting to your account through a different phone number.

America Online

Numbers are available at keyword *international*. Be sure to get several local numbers before leaving. AOL's Global-Net service charges US$6 an hour in addition to the usual charges. Go to keyword *access* (a free area) and download the software.

Access: Riga 724-2457.

Compuserve

Numbers are available at *Go International*. The Compuserve Web-site also has a great deal of information, at http://www.compuserve.com.

Access: Riga (72) 42-457.

Independent Service Providers

Many independent service providers offer discounts if you are only in town for a couple of days.

EUNet - Latvia; tel: (7) 721-0909; fax: (7) 732-6513; email: info@EUnet.lv; http://www.EUnet.lv/.

VR Parks; tel: (7) 204-110; fax: (7) 204-093; email: parks@parks.lv; http://www.parks.lv/.

Business Culture
GREETINGS & COURTESIES

Latvians are an outward looking and friendly people. Business greetings involve long hand shakes and friendly eye contact. In many ways, the Latvians, like the Estonians, have found a middle ground between the bear hugs of the Russian greeting and the coolness of the Teutonic handshake. Small gifts are often exchanged among business people early in the relationship. Initially, keep your gifts discreet and business oriented. More personal gifts can be given as the relationship grows. Be careful not to outspend or outshine your Latvian hosts and be aware that much socializing will precede any talk of business. The Latvians like to do business with friends not just acquaintances.

BUSINESS ETHIC & FRAMEWORK

Latvia is trying to make itself as attractive as possible to both foreign investors and to the E.U. membership committee. While they will do their level best to fulfill contracts with and duties to foreign firms, Latvians may also have less seemly domestic dealings. Hardly as corrupt as its neighbors Russia or Belarus, some under-the-table activity does exist in Latvia. Such activity usually occurs in deals that do not affect foreign interests. The Latvian government wishes to maintain a reputation for honest dealing in its international economic affairs as it eyes potential E.U. membership.

DECISION MAKING

Like many other cultures with long histories of subjugation, Latvia still revels in hierarchy. This trait is passed through to the decision making process for business where "top down" is an apt description. Power is concentrated in the upper echelons and information tends to flow unidirectionally (up).

Foreign business people may wish to start as far up the local ladder as possible in Latvia as there are no decision makers at lower levels. If you are in a buying position, you can start at the top. Sellers coming to Latvia may find that they will have to endure many interviews with "gatekeepers" before reaching a real decision maker.

MEETINGS

Latvian business people are not an experienced group when it comes to business meetings. Latvian business people are, however, generally eager to please and impress foreigners. Like many of their Baltic neighbors, Latvi-

Latvia

an companies are headed by either elders with little knowledge of modern business standards or novice managers with more enthusiasm than business savvy.

Meetings will most often start with a welcoming speech by the highest level Latvian manager present. Visitors should respond in kind. Elder Estonians are unlikely to speak any other second language than Russian, though younger managers will often speak English. Visitors should assume they will need to employ a translator and it is best if they procure their own.

A single meeting will rarely be sufficient to secure a deal—buying or selling. The wheels of Baltic business turn slowly and visitors should be suspicious of any quick deals. Keep in mind that the legal system in Latvia is new to the area of contract law. Take the time made available by the slowness of Latvian decision making to assess your counterparts as the "personal relationship" may be all that binds the contract.

WOMEN IN BUSINESS

It is unlikely that foreign female managers will meet many female counterparts in Latvia. For the most part, women will be acting in the role of secretaries and assistants when attending meetings. It will be assumed that female visitors will be performing the same role in the visiting delegation. To avoid causing problems, foreign companies should make known the gender and rank of their delegation members in advance of arrival. When a female manager heads the visiting delegation, all subordinates should defer to her at all times. While there are few women in top positions, Latvian managers are perfectly willing to accept them in visiting delegations.

Latvian male managers do, however, maintain the Baltic European habit of making gratuitous sexual remarks in the presence of women. While the local males may consider such comments witty and somehow complimentary, foreign women may find it crude and demeaning. Note: The extent to which a visitor should challenge this behavior is really a function of whether the visitor is buying or selling. As is true elsewhere in the world, sellers must be more tolerant than buyers.

BUSINESS ENTERTAINING

Latvians like to mix business with pleasure and they are keen socializers. Business entertaining provides an opportunity for them to display Latvian hospitality as well as to size up there foreign counterparts. Alcohol consumption is a big part of socializing in this part of the world and teetotalers (especially males) may be viewed with suspicion. Don't overdo it, but make an effort to participate.

Visitors from Asian cultures may find the food exceedingly heavy and unappealing. However, what is offered should be tried as the offense caused by not doing so is similar to that caused in Asian societies when foreigners decline the local fare.

Latvian hosts like to offer the best their budgets will allow, and their hospitality is genuine. Only under the most pressing circumstances should an offer of dinner or a social outing be declined. Remember, the personal relationship can make or break a deal in Latvia.

Note: Visitors on extended stays in Latvia should attempt to reciprocate the local hospitality. Seek the advice of local hoteliers, restaurateurs or even translators to determine menus and venues. In no way, however, should visitors seek to outdo their Latvian counterparts. Rather than impress, you will only offend.

BUSINESS ATTIRE

Baltic region business is fairly formal in attitude and the climate makes the wearing of business suits tolerable. Men adopt the standard dark suit, white shirt, and necktie. Quality shoes, once an impossible commodity to get during Soviet times, are now standard. In fact, visitors ay find that locals will make an extra effort to examine a foreigner's footwear as a barometer of success. Both men and women visitors should be well shod.

As mentioned above under Security Briefing, Latvian women may dress in a more sexually provocative manner than their foreign counterparts. Local styles often cross the line into garishness. Foreign female managers can avoid unwanted comments and attention by maintaining a conservative business dress standard.

Note: Both male and female visitors should avoid displays of wealth in the form of jewelry or overtly expensive garments. Such things only serve to cause resentment or feelings of inferiority by Latvian counterparts, neither of which are the basis for a solid business relationship.

Business Advisory
POLITICS & GRAFT

Like its other Baltic neighbors, Latvia is making a genuine effort to avoid getting a reputation for shady dealings and political bribery. The government makes no more demands of foreign firms than most E.U. governments. Taxation and commercial laws are, however, in the early stages of development, so, foreigners can expect the legal landscape to change. They should not, however, experience the retroactive taxation and ownership changes that plague Chinese and Russian business sectors. Only on the rarest occasion will a foreign firm be approach with a request for bribes or "special fees" for their project.

BUSINESS FRAUD

Just as the politicians are trying to keep Latvia on the "straight and narrow", so, too, is the private business community in its dealings with foreign firms. Outright fraud or theft is quite rare when dealing with foreign contracts, although the domestic commerce does have its less legal side. Foreign companies may have problems with their Latvian counterparts in regards to product quality or timely contract fulfillment, but the problems will not be intentional. Latvian companies are making a transition into the modern global economy but they still lack many of the skills and logistic systems necessary to meet international standards. Your patience and assistance will be rewarded.

Business Centers
Riga
CITY VIEW

Riga is centrally located in the Republic of Latvia, with a warm water port on the Baltic Sea that has been the envy of its larger neighbors for centuries. Since regaining independence from the former USSR in 1990, it has attracted tourist attention with its pastoral landscape, scenic coastline, 28 museums, 7 professional theatres, concert halls, and a zoo. The city is known as the educational center of Latvia, housing more than 160,000 students at 220 schools and 23 higher education establishments. The rich history and culture of the area are chronicled in such outstanding historical sites such as Riga Castle, dating to at least 1209, various gothic structures of the Old Town, and the Monument of Liberty created by Latvian sculptor Karlis Zale. The famed Dome Cathedral boasts a pipe organ that was the world's largest at the time of its construction in 1884, with

6718 pipes. The economic climate of Riga has always centered itself around ocean trade, beginning with the original settlement by Liv merchants and fishermen of the area surrounding the Riga river, the key artery for trade with foreign visitors. Due to its ideal location as the crossroads between neighboring Russia, Scandinavia, and Eastern and Western Europe, the harbor at Riga has served for centuries as a crucial source of income and spur for development. Currently boasting a population of more than 900,000, Riga is gearing up for its 800th anniversary in 2001 and finding its identity as a center for industry based on local resources.

AIRPORT

Spilva Airport to City Center

The airport lies approximately 5 miles (8 km) southwest of Riga. The bus stop for Bus No. 22 running to city center is located outside the airport arrivals exit and across the small parking lot. Buses run every half hour, and cost LLS0.18, while taxis will run LLS2 with an additional LLS0.40 for baggage. Taxis must be ordered at the counter in the arrival hall at, tel: (2) 720-7509. The airport currency exchange office is open from 6a.m. to 10p.m.

Riga International Airport, Airport Riga, LV-1053 Riga, Latvia; tel. (2) 720-7135; fax (2) 721-1767.

Airline Numbers

Aeroflot.. (2) 207-472, 278-774.
Air Baltic ....(2) 720-7777; fax: 722-4282
.... airport; tel:(2) 720-7777; fax: (2) 720-7505.
British Airways..(2) 720-7136.
CSA ....(2) 720-7136
Finnair ....(2) 720-7136
Israeli Air ....(2) 223-591
LOT Polish Airlines............. (2) 242-870; fax: (7) 242-869.
Lufthansa.. res., (7) 207-183
.... Via Riga Travel Agency, (7) 285-901
.... airport, (7) 207-009
SAS ....(2) 720-7136

HOTELS

Top-end

Radisson SAS Daugava; 24 Kugu Street; tel: 706-111, Riga; fax: 706-1100; restaurant; conference facilities (up to 500); secretarial services; fax/ photocopying facilities; in-room modem connection; corporate rates; fitness room; pool; US$150-200.

Hotel de Rome; Kalku 28; tel: 882-0050, 708-7600; fax: 882-0059, 708-7606; restaurant; conference facilities (up to 70); fax/photocopying facilities; in-room safe, modem connection; corporate rates; fitness room; US$180.

Man-Tess; Teatra 6, Riga; tel: 721-6056; tel: 721-0225; fax: 782-1249; 18th Century building; quiet getaway; restaurant; business center; US$120-170.

Metropole; Aspazijas bulvaris 36/38, Riga; tel: 722-5411; fax: 721-6140;e-mail: metropole@brovi.lv; restaurant; bar; conference facilities (up to 40); minibar; corporate rates; US$160-180.

Eurolink; Aspazijas bulvaris 22; tel: 722-0531; fax: 721-6300; e-mail: eurolink@brovi.lv; restaurant; 2 conference facilities; (up to 40); cable t.v.; minibar; sauna; corporate rates; US$140 up.

Park Hotel Ridzene; Reimersa 1, Riga; tel: 732-4433; fax: 728-2100; email: Park_Hotel@ridzene.lv; in-room climate control, satellite TV; trouser press, minibar, hairdryer, safe, internet connection.

Expensive

Riga; Aspazijas bulevari 22; tel: 721-6285; tel: 721-6109; fax:

722-9828; restaurant; conference facilities (up to150); secretarial services; fax/photocopying facilities; in-room satellite TV, refrigerator; corporate rates; fitness; US$160-180.

Moderate

Hotel Latvija; Elizabetes 55; tel:722-2211; tel: 721-1755; fax: 728-3595; tel: 782-0240;

e-mail: admin@latvija.hotel.lv; restaurant; conference facilities (up to 100); secretarial services; fax/photocopying facilities; in-room modem connection; corporate rates; sauna; jacuzzi; US$90-110.

Hotel "Victoria"; A. Caka 55; tel: 701-4111; fax: 701-4140; fax: 731-0629; restaurant; corporate rates; US$60.

MEDICAL CARE

A&S Health Care; (Private Dental Clinic); Lacplesa 60.

ARS Clinic; Skolas 5; 24-hour English service, tel: 201-001.

City Clinical Hospital No. 1; Bruninieku iela 8.

Emergency Dental Service; at Stabu iela 9; tel: 274-546.

Gailezers Hospital No. 7; Hipokrata iela 2; tel: 536-466; head of emergency, tel: 536-703.

HEALTH CLUBS

A + S; Lacplesa 60; tel: 7289-567.

Davids; Valdemara 23a; tel: 7224-148.

Radisson SAS Daugava Hotel; 24 Kugu Street; tel: 706-1111.

AUTO RENTAL

Note: The blood alcohol limit in Latvia is zero; and road checks are frequent. Drivers are aggressive.

Avis; Riga International Airport; tel: (2) 720-7353; Hours: Sun - Sat 9:00a.m.- 8:30p.m; Downtown Office, Aspazijas Bulv 32, Riga, LV-1050, tel: (7) 225-876; Hours: Sun 10a.m. to 5p.m., Mon. to Fri. 9a.m. to 6p.m., Sat. 10a.m to 5p.m.

Eurodollar; airport, tel: 720-7710.

Europcar; Riga International Airport; tel: (7) 222-637; fax: (7) 820-360; Downtown Office: 10 Basteja Boulevard, LV-1050 Riga; tel: (7) 222-637; fax: (7) 820-360.

Hertz; Riga Airport; tel: (7) 207-980; fax: (7) 207-981; email: mail@hertz.apollo.lv; hours: Mon to Fri 10:30 a.m. to 2:30 p.m. and 3: 30p.m. to 8: 30 p.m.; Sat. to Sun. 11a.m. to 8:30p.m. Hertz will also arrange for after-hours pick up.

WORLD TRADE CENTER

World Trade Center Riga
2 Elizabetes Street
Riga LV-1340, Latvia
tel: (7) 322-242; fax: (7) 830-035
website: http://www.wtcr.bkc.lv
email: mail@wtc-riga.lv

CHAMBER OF COMMERCE

Latvian Chamber of Commerce
Brivibas 21, Riga LV-1849
tel: 7225-595; fax: 7820-092
email: chamber@sun.lcc.org.lv

Latvia International Commerce Center
Tirgonu iela 8, Riga
tel: 7221-278; fax: 7820-374

Lebanon (sidebar)

Lebanon

At a Glance
THE PEOPLE
Population .... 3,562,699 (July 1999 est.)
Growth Rate .... 1.61 percent (1999 est.)
Life Expectancy .... 70.93 years (born 1999)
Infant Mortality . 30.53 deaths/1,000 live births (1999 est.)

Ethnic Composition
Arab..95%
Armenian 4%
Other 1%

Religious Composition
Islam...70%
Christian 29%
Other and non-affiliated...1%

Languages Spoken
Arabic (official), French, Armenian, English

Education and Literacy
Education is compulsory for five years. The adult literacy rate is 86.4 percent.

Labor Force
Total: 1,000,000
By occupation: services 62%, industry 31%, and agriculture 7% (does not include 1 million foreign workers)

THE ECONOMY
Lebanon is still trying to recover from the devastation of the 1975-91 civil war. In 1993 the government launched the "Recovery 2000" program which set up a financially robust banking system and laid groundwork for the Lebanese stock market. It has slowly pushed the economy towards industrialization. On again, off again armed conflicts with Israeli neighbors has made progress slow. The war-ravished infrastructure is still in dire need of repair and modernization. Direct foreign investment has been deterred by the local political problems, so the nation has had to finance its recovery through debt rather than equity investment. Rampant unemployment and high inflation are taking both an economic and political toll. Lebanon, whose capital Beirut was once considered the Paris of the Middle East, finds itself with the will —but few of the means — to return to its former economic glory.

Exports .... US$711 million (f.o.b., 1997)
Imports .... US$7.5 billion (c.i.f., 1997)
Total GDP .... US$15.8 billion (1998 est.)
GDP Per Capita .... US$4,500 (1998 est.)
Unemployment .... 18 percent (1997)
Inflation Rate .... 5 percent (1998 est.)

Top Export Partners
Saudi Arabia, Kuwait, Switzerland, United Arab Emirates, Syria, Jordan, United States

Top Import Partners
E.U., United States, Turkey

Top Exports
Paper and paper products, food stuffs, textiles and textile products, jewelry, metals and metal products, electrical equipment and products, chemical products, transport vehicles

Top Imports
Machinery and transport equipment, foodstuffs, consumer goods, chemicals, textiles, metals, fuels

BUSINESS WORKWEEK
Offices
Monday to Friday 8:30a.m. to 1:30p.m., 3p.m. to 6p.m.

Banks
Monday to Friday 8a.m. to noon, 2p.m. to 4p.m.; Saturday 8a.m. to 1p.m.

Government
Monday to Saturday (November through May) 8a.m. to 2p.m., and until 1:30p.m. (June through October)

Retail
Monday to Saturday 8a.m. to 7p.m. Shorter hours on weekends.
Note: All businesses make scheduling allowances for Islamic prayer periods.

HOLIDAYS
New Year's Day...January 1
Id al-Fitr, end of Ramadan..............................January 19*
Feast of St. Maron..February 9
Arab League Anniversary...................................March 22
Id al-Adha, Feast of the Sacrifice ....March 28*
Easter, Western Church..April 5*
Greek Orthodox Easter ....April 9-12*
Islamic New Year ....April 17*
Ashoura..April 26*
Ascension Day, Western Church ....May 13*
Mouloud, Birth of Muhammad ....June 26*
Assumption...August 15
All Saints' Day ....November 1
Leilat al-Meiraj, Ascension of
Muhammad .... November 6*
Independence Day ....November 22
Christmas Day..December 25
*Date may vary by year.

CLIMATE
Seasons
The climate is typically Mediterranean, warm and humid, with few seasonal extremes. Winters are mild and wet, summers are hot and dry. Temperatures rarely exceed 30˚C (85˚F) in the summer.

Regions
There are few regional differences, but it is generally cooler in the mountain areas with some snow in the winter. Hot and dry is the most common weather report.

Money & Banking
Currency
The currency of Lebanon is the Lebanese pound L£. Its principal subdivision is 100 piasters. It comes in bill denominations of L£1, 5, 10, 20, 50, 100, 500, 1000, 5000, and 10000.

Traveler's Checks and Credit Cards
Travelers checks and currency denominated in British

Lebanon

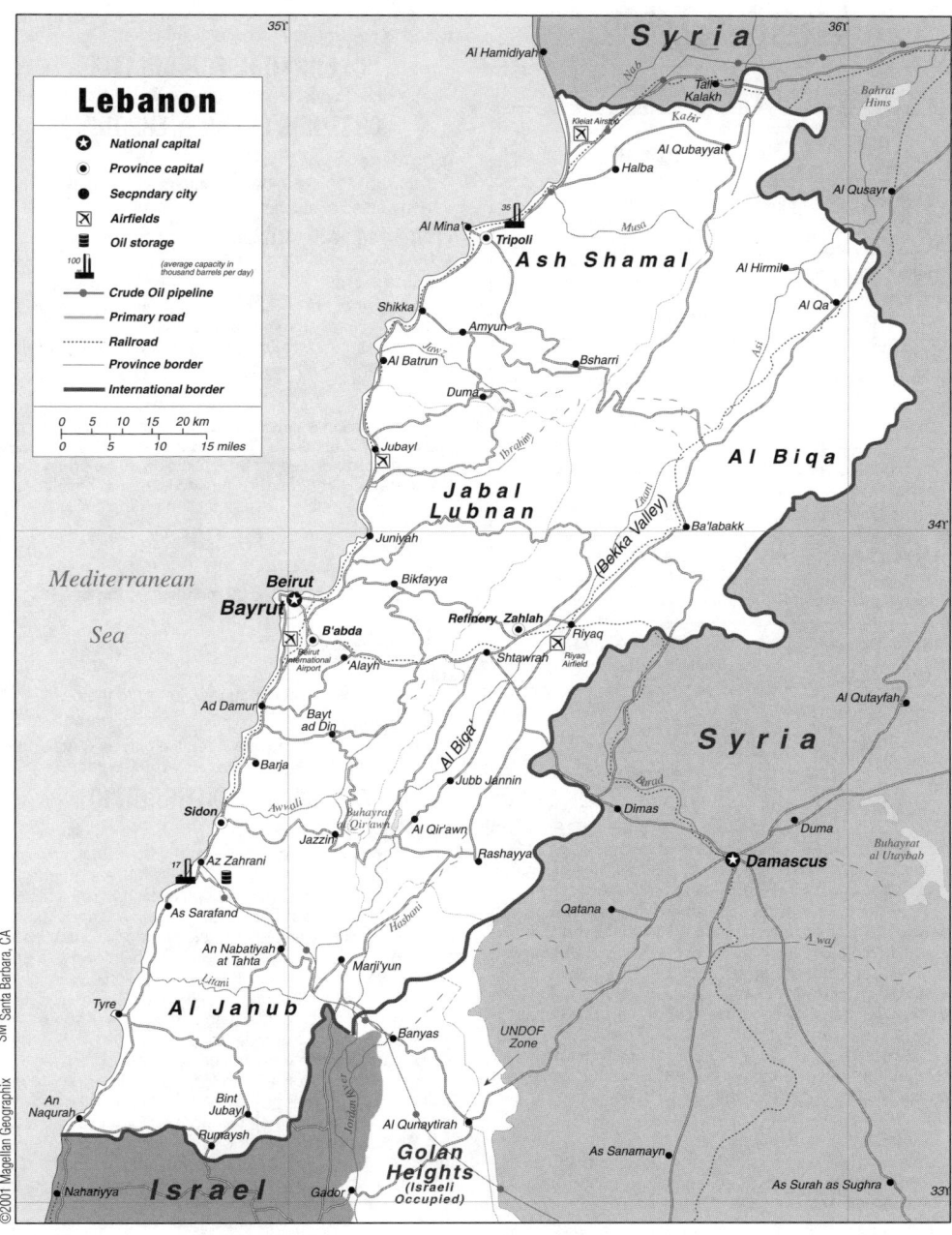

pounds or U.S. dollars are most easily exchanged and often the only currency accepted at banks. Hotels and international airports also exchange money at tourist exchange rates with various rates of exchange. Larger banks offer the best exchange rates, but avoid black marketers at all cost. Consult your bank about current exchange rates before departure. Keep all receipts for reconversion. at departure.

Major credit cards like American Express, Visa, Diner's Club, and MasterCard are accepted in up-market places in the main cities, but smaller restaurants and *souks* (markets) will most likely ask for cash. Some banks in the capital offer cash advances on credit cards, but make sure you bring you passport for identification. ATMs are rare and only available at banking locations. ATMs have very limited access to international banking services.

Lebanon

Essential Terms

English	Arabic
Yes	Na-a'am
No	La; mish
Good morning	Al sa-lahm
Hello (daytime)	Al sa-lahm
Hello (evening)	Ma-sa'el khair
Hello (telephone)	Marhaban
Good-bye	Be-kha-trahk
Please	Min-fahd-lak (M) Min-fahd-lik (F)
Thank you	Shook-rahn
Pleased to meet you	Sorirart biro'aitak
Excuse me; I'm sorry	Is-ma-leh
My name is ____	'ismii____
I don't understand	An-na mish fahem
Do you speak English?	Hal tatakallumu l-inkliziyya?

Travel

VISA AND PASSPORT

Passports are required for travel to Lebanon, except for nationals of Syria who may travel with a valid national ID. Passports must be valid for at least three months beyond the estimated duration of stay. Nationals of Arab League countries must have passports valid for more than a year beyond date of entry.

Visas, for travel of either a business or tourist nature, are required for all foreigners (except nationals of the Gulf Cooperation Council) and may be obtained from a Lebanese consulate or embassy in advance of arrival. Nationals of Australia, Austria, Belgium, Canada, Denmark, Finland, France, Germany, Greece, Holland, Ireland, Italy, Japan, Luxembourg, Norway, Portugal, South Korea, Spain, Sweden, Switzerland, U.K., and the U.S. may now acquire their visas at a border entrance or airport. However, since visa regulations are subject to change on short notice, always check with an embassy.

Types of visa issued:
* Visitor and Business - single or multiple entry. This visa is good for stays up to three months per entry, and must be used within six months of issuance.
* Transit - single entry. This visa is available upon entry.

Business visas require an invitation and sponsorship by a Lebanese company or government agency.

Allow a day or so for processing of your visa application, if made in person at a Lebanese embassy or consulate. For postal applications, figure several days plus postal delivery time.

Restricted Entry

The government of Lebanon refuses entry and transit to holders of Israeli passports and to holders of passports containing a visa for Israel. Nationals of India may be required to present a return or onward ticket.

DEPARTURE FORMALITIES

There is no longer any departure tax levied on foreign travel.

CUSTOMS ENTRY (PERSONAL)

Duty-free
* Tobacco: 200 cigarettes, 20 cigars, or 200g of tobacco
* Two bottles of alcohol.

Prohibited or Restricted
* Narcotics or addictive drugs
* Pornography
* No export of antiques is permitted without previously arranged approval from customs authorities.

Note: A valid import licence is required for any arms or ammunition.

IMMUNIZATION

Immunization is recommended for such diseases as typhoid and tuberculosis. Tetanus and Hepatitis A inoculations are also advised for travel outside of the urban areas. Certification is required for those visitors arriving from areas of known Yellow Fever infection or epidemic.

TIPPING

Taxi
Taxi drivers are tipped by rounding up the fare.

Porters
Porters receive L£500 per piece of luggage.

Hotels
Hotels apply service charges directly to the bill.

Restaurants
Most restaurants include a service charge. When not included it is customary to leave a tip of 10 percent.

EMERGENCY INFORMATION

Police and Crime
Lebanon's crime rate, mainly in Beirut, is on the increase. Take basic precautions against petty crime. Avoid flashy displays of wealth, and dress and behave conservatively. Leave most of your cash, traveler's checks, jewelry, and your camera in your hotel safe. Carry photocopies of your passport instead of the original. Carry cash in a money belt, and use credit cards or traveler's checks for most transactions.

Women can walk around freely, but they are advised to travel in groups to avoid harassment. They should also abide by local dress standards.

Political violence is not uncommon. Visitors should exercise extreme caution and avoid the southern suburbs of Beirut, the Biqa' Valley, and southern Lebanon, where Syrian military forces, Israeli military forces, the South Lebanon Army, and Hizballah vie to control parts of Lebanese territory. Civilians in these areas continue to suffer artillery and aerial attacks, bombings, and abductions. The Government of Lebanon does not have effective control in certain areas of the country. Foreigners traveling to Lebanon are encouraged to register at their embassy in Beirut.

Emergency Numbers
Emergency police	16
Police	386 440 425
Fire	310-105
Ambulance	386 675

Health
Lebanon is a relatively healthy and hygienic country.

Lebanon

The primary health hazards for the visitor are associated with the heat; take measures to avoid dehydration, whose initial symptoms can be subtle. Do not drink tap water or use ice cubes; bottled water is safe and available.

Milk is usually pasteurized, and other dairy products are also safe for consumption. Local seafood, poultry, meat, vegetables, and fruit are considered safe to eat. Wash all vegetables in a chlorine solution, peel fruits, and avoid uncooked food. Dysenteries and various diarrheal diseases are widespread, especially for travelers who are unaccustomed to the heat and diet.

Lebanese hospitals are well-equipped and modern. Doctors are highly qualified—reportedly among the finest in the world—and all speak either French or English. Most hospitals are private, and they require proof of your ability to make full payment before treatment is provided, even in emergency cases. A travel insurance package including an evacuation policy should be acquired by all business travelers. The two top hospitals in Lebanon are the Hôtel Dieu in Achrafieh, Beirut and the American University/AUB Hospital in Hamra, Beirut.

In spite of excellent services and skills, medicines and pharmacological equipment are scarce, so come prepared. Carry a well-stocked medical kit with all the prescription drugs you require, and also include in it a stock of sterilized syringe needles and drip needles for emergencies. Be sure to check with Lebanese customs officials in advance for clearance of import of any prescription drugs or medical equipment you intend to carry with you.

INTERNAL TRAVEL
AIR

There is no domestic air service in Lebanon. It is a tiny country, and can be traversed end-to-end in three hours by automobile.

TAXI

Most taxis have an official fare and are recognizable by their red license plates. However, many 'pirate taxis' are also cruising for fares. They are more costly than service taxis, and look the same, so be sure to inquire before you get into the cab.

The less expensive taxis, known as service taxis, are usually shared. These operate on set routes, and passengers may get off where they please. If your particular destination is not on the fixed route, you will have to transfer to another service taxi.

If you prefer to head straight to your destination without any intermediate stops, you can elect to pay the driver for the other empty seats and have your own private taxi. Keep in mind that prices double after 10p.m. Long-distance routes are also negotiable, even as far as Jordan and Syria.

AUTO

Automobiles are available for rental in Beirut primarily, but also in other main towns. An International Driving Permit and Green Card insurance are required. Rates are fairly high, and the roads are infamous for their poor condition.

Lebanese drivers are skilled, aggressive, and unpredictable. Urban streets are clogged, and sidewalks are often blocked by parked cars, forcing pedestrians out onto the roadways. Traffic jams are common. Speed limits, police, and traffic signals are openly ignored, and lanes are usually unmarked. Because public transit is limited, roads are congested. The prime times for traffic bottlenecks are 7:30am-9:30am and 4:30pm-7:00pm. If you like driving in Mexico City or Rome, you will like Beirut.

It is best to rent a four-wheel drive, even if you intend to stay within urban confines. Due to the high security risks, automobile rental is not recommended for any but the most experienced travelers to Lebanon. Hired cars with local drivers are a more secure means of transport. Allow your hotel or local business contacts to set up this service for you.
Thrifty Car Rental; Beirut: www.thrifty.com.lb/

TRAIN

There is no passenger train system in Lebanon.

METRO

Lebanon's cities do not have metro service.

BUSES & TRAMS

Intercity buses operate between Beirut and other main towns. Fares are low, but service is unreliable, and timetables essentially non-existent. Many hotels also provide complementary bus services for their clientele.

Within urban areas, bus services operate in all the major cities, but rides are not comfortable or efficient. Bus bombings have occurred, and rival political groups often disrupt regular routes. These are not recommended for business travelers.

WATER TRAVEL

International cruise lines with connections to Mediterranean cities service the port at Beirut. There is also a limited domestic passenger boat service for Lebanon's coastal cities.

TRAVEL ASSISTANCE

Ministry of Tourism
550 Central Bank Street, Beirut
P.O. Box 11-5344
tel: (1) 340-940-4; fax: (1) 340-945
email: mot@Lebanon-Tourism.gov.lb
website: www.lebanon-tourism.gov.lb

Communications
DIALING CODES IN LEBANON

International country code: [961]
Selected city codes: Beirut (1), Tripoli (6), Zahle (8).

Dialing Lebanon from Overseas

To dial Lebanon from overseas, dial your country's international dialing code, then 961 (the country code for Lebanon), then the city code and finally the number. If you were dialing Beirut from the United States, for example, you would begin with 011, then 961, then 1 (the city code for Beirut), and finally the number of the person or office you are trying to reach.

CALLING WITHIN LEBANON

Local Calls

If not from a hotel, local calls can be placed from shops or the government-run telephone office in Beirut.

Long Distance Calls

Calling within Lebanon is now quite straightforward. Long-distance calls are as easy as local calls.

International Calls

The general rule is that hotel phones are expensive, but at least in working order. To place a direct overseas call means dialing 00 + country code + area code + number. Satellite phone offices have cheaper rates (US$2 to $4 per minute). The government-run telephone office in Beirut also allows international calls, charging approximately US$2 to $3 per minute. No collect calls are allowed from Lebanon, unless you happen to be blessed with a connection through AT&T.

AT&T Direct (Beirut) 426-801
AT&T Direct (outside Beirut) 01-426-801

CELLULAR PHONES

Libancel SAL and FTML operate GSM digital systems for cellular users in Lebanon. Analogue users are in luck as well if they have a phone operating on an AMPS system (same as U.S.). The analogue system is operated in Lebanon by Spacetel.

Note: Your home country cell phone may not work in this country. If not, we recommend that you rent an international cell phone *before* you leave home. A major US-based cell phone rental provider is **IMC WorldCell**. For information see "International Cell Phone Rentals" on page 14.

CALL BACK

You can (potentially) save significant sums when calling in Lebanon by using a call back service. For a list of call-back services, please refer to the "Communications" section in the *Global Road Warrior* Introduction.

Fees for call back services vary widely, depending on the company and the type of service required. Be sure to check with these companies before leaving to compare rates.

PHONE JACKS

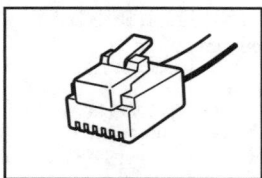

Plug adaptors are available through **iGo Corporation.** (See "Electrical and Telephone Adaptors" on page 19.)

FAX

Fax services are available at stationery shops and most hotels.

POSTAL SERVICES

Service to Europe takes about four days, service to North America takes about seven. Mail sent to Lebanon could take much longer to arrive.

Business Services

AUDIO VISUAL EQUIPMENT

Eltek; Jdeidet El Meten, Beirut; tel: (1) 249-666, 249-777; fax: (1) 265-618; http://www.elekpro.com, or http://www.eltek.com.lb; sound equipment and accessories, video equipment and accessories.

COURIER SERVICES

Airborne Express (Aramex Intl. Courier); PO Box 55606, Beirut; tel: (1) 484-036.

DHL (SNAS Lebanon); tel: (1) 390-900; Park Building, Ground Floor; Sami El Solh Avenue, PO Box 166/439, Beirut; 24 hours, Monday to Sunday.

Federal Express (Falcon Express); tel: (1) 345-385.

UPS Lebanon; 16-5001 Achrafieh, Sassine Square, Le Doyen Building; tel: (1) 218-575.

Electrical

Current

110/220 volts AC, 50Hz. Lebanon's electrical system often suffers from fluctuation and blackouts.

ELECTRIC PLUGS

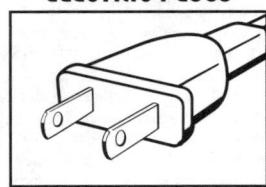

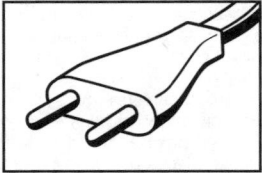

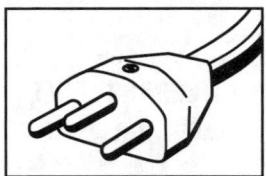

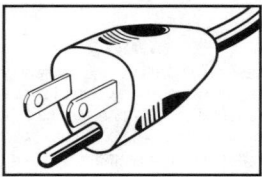

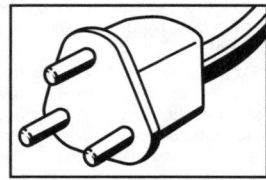

Plug adaptors are available through **iGo Corporation.** (See "Electrical and Telephone Adaptors" on page 19.)

Technical Support

HARDWARE/SOFTWARE VENDOR SUPPORT

Acer/Texas Instruments; (in Germany) tel: [49] (4102) 488-469; fax; [49] (4102) 488-169; (in the U.S.) [1] (408) 432-6200; http://www.acer.com/.

Adobe; (in Germany) tel: [49] (1) 803-5018; (in Switzerland) tel: [41] (800) 833-310; (in the U.S.) tel: [1] (800) 500-7078; (in the U.S.) tel: [1] (716) 633-3600; http://www.adobe.com/.

Apple/Claris; (in the U.A.E.) tel: [971] 4-513-888; fax: [971] 4-527-444; (in Switzerland) tel: [41] (800) 833-310; (in the U.K.) tel: [44] (990) 127-753; (in the U.S.) tel: [1] (800) 500-7078; http://www.apple.com/.

AST; (in the U.S.) tel: [1] (817) 232-9824 (International Technical Support); (in Ireland) tel: [353] (61) 492-222; (in the U.S.) tel: [1] (949) 727-4141; http://www.ast.com/.

Compaq/Digital; (UAE Office) tel: (971) 4-818-100; fax: (971) 4-818-313; (in Switzerland) tel: [41] (22) 709-5330; fax: [41] (22) 709-5391 (Geneva); tel: [41] (1) 801-2507; fax: [41] (1) 801-2172 (Zurich); (General U.S.) tel: (281) 518-2000; http://www.compaq.com/.

Corel; (in the U.A.E.) tel: [971] 4 523-526 (All Applications); (in the U.S.) tel: [1] (716) 871-2325 (Ask to be Forwarded to Appropriate Program); http://www.corel.com/.

Dell; tel: (1) 40-1880 (S.E.T.S. S.A.L.); (Dell- Europe) tel: [44] (134) 474-8000; (in the U.S.) tel: [1] (512) 338-4400; fax: [1] (512) 728-3330; http://www.dell.com/.

Filemaker/Claris; (in Germany) tel: [49] (180) 525-8166 (Info-line); fax: [49] (180) 567-2233; tel: [49] (180) 523-6423; (in the U.S.) tel: [1] (800) 965-9090; http://www.claris.com/.

Gateway 2000; (in the U.S.) tel: [1] (605) 232-2191; fax: [1] (605) 232-2023; (in Ireland) tel: [353] (1) 797-2000; http://www.g2k.com/.

Hewlett Packard; (in Switzerland) tel: [41] (22) 780-8111; (in the U.S.) tel: [1] (408) 246-4300; http://www.hp.com/.

IBM; (1) 562-444; fax: (1)563-444; (in Switzerland) tel: [41] (22) 310-0418 (in French); (in the U.S.) tel: [1] (919) 517-2800; (U.S. Main Office) tel: [1] 914-765-1900; http://www.ibm.com/.

Microsoft; (Turkish Office) tel: [90] 212-2585998; fax: [90] 212 2585954; (in Switzerland) tel: [41] (848) 858-868; fax [41] (1) 831-0869; (in the U.S.) [1] (425) 635-7222; http://www.microsoft.com/.

NEC; (in Israel) tel: [972] (0)9-59-3300 (UltraCare Support); (in the U.S.) [1] (916) 388-0101 (Main Switchboard); http://www.nec.com/.

Novell; (in Germany) tel: [49] (211) 563-2777 (System support); tel: [49] (6196) 904-477; fax: [49] (211) 563-2772; (in Switzerland) tel: [41] (1) 308-4747; fax: [41] (1) 302-0401; (in the U.S.) tel: [1] (408) 434-2300; fax: [1] (408) 577-5775 (Worldwide Sales Headquarters); http://www.novell.com/.

Quark; (in Switzerland) tel: [41] (1) 808-7722; fax: [41] (1) 808-7799; (in the U.S.) tel: [1] (303) 894-8899; fax: [1] (303) 894-3398 (For Products Registered in the Americas); http://www.quark.com/.

Toshiba; (in Germany) tel: [49] (2131) 158-319; fax: [49] (2131) 158-558; (in Switzerland) tel: [41] (1) 946-0777; fax: [41] (1) 946-0807; (in Ireland) tel: [44] (193) 282-8828; (in the U.S.) [1] (949) 583-3000 (Corporate Headquarters); http://www.toshiba.com/.

Internet Connection

HOW TO CONNECT

Connecting to AOL and Compuserve in Lebanon is similar to using it when traveling outside your own area code. See the introductory section for detailed information on connecting to your account through a different phone number.

America Online

Numbers are available at keyword *international*. Be sure to get several local numbers before leaving. AOL's GlobalNet service charges US$24 an hour in addition to the usual charges.

Go to keyword *access* (a free area) and download the software.

Access: Beirut (1) 655-955; Jal El Dib (1) 405-932; Jal El Dib (1) 406-187.

Compuserve

Numbers are available at *Go International*. The Compuserve Web-site also has a great deal of information, at http://www.compuserve.com.

Access: Beirut (1) 655-955; Jal El Dib (4) 405-932; Jal El Dib (4) 406-187.

Independent Service Providers

Independent service providers may offer discounts if you are only in town for a couple days.

Fiberlink Communications; (a U.S. company) tel: [1] (215) 793-6500; fax: [1] (215) 793-6565; email: info@fiberlinkcc.com; http://www.fibernlinkcc.com/.

Intracom; tel: (1) 792-340; email: sales@intracom.net.lb; http://www.intracom.net.lb/main/.

Business Culture

GREETINGS AND COURTESIES

Greetings are important, and will often be accompanied by questions about one's health or family. The standard greeting is the handshake, which is acceptable when meeting both men and women. A man should wait for a woman to initiate a handshake, however. If she doesn't, he should smile and nod slightly. Titles are important; if a person has one, be sure to use it. Personal space is less than in many other cultures, so don't be surprised if Lebanese associates stand close.

MEETINGS

Arrive on time, but expect your Lebanese associates to be late. Personal relationships receive more importance than schedules. Thus, expect small talk to precede any business meeting.

DECISION MAKING

People's feelings are often taken into account, and an individual's needs can influence how a decision is made or what it will be. Lebanese do not like to directly criticize something. Instead, they might hint they'd like to see changes, or suggest an alternative that leaves room for compromise. Decisions are made slowly. If you push for faster action or impose a deadline, you could do more harm than good. Ultimately, your personal relationship with your Lebanese colleagues will be crucial to how things go.

WOMEN

Women (especially Christians) can be found in many aspects of business. Middle Eastern culture puts many restrictions on women, but foreign women will generally be accepted and treated with respect in business. Being professional, poised, and self-confident will help. Do not make prolonged, direct eye contact with Lebanese men.

BUSINESS ATTIRE

Standard attire is a conservative suit. Lightweight fabrics might prove more comfortable in the summer months. Women should wear tasteful, conservative clothing. The climate in Lebanon is generally warm, if not downright hot in the summer. Rains come in the winter and travelers should come prepared with an umbrella.

Lebanon

Business Centers
Beirut
CITY VIEW

Beirut is beginning to move away from the battle-weary city of the past two decades, but scars remain much to the regret of many who once traveled to Lebanon for its beauty. However, its citizens remain vibrant and warm. Beirut's plan to rebuild its infrastructure has made the streets busy and traffic often nightmarish. Many areas of the city are not safe to travel, even during daylight hours.

AIRPORT

Beirut International Airport to City Center
The airport lies 10 miles (16 km.) from the city center. A taxi trip into town will take about 20 minutes and will cost approximately £L25,000. Minibuses run every 30 minutes for about £L300, and regular buses travel to city center for about £L500 between 7a.m. and 7p.m.

HOTELS

Top-end
Al Bustan; Beit-Mery (30 min from city center); tel: 425-2589; fax: 970-4002; city suburb; 2 restaurants; business center; conference facilities (up to 450); secretarial services; fax/photocopying facilities; corporate rates; fitness center; sauna; pool; whirlpool; US$195.

Beirut Marriott Hotel; Jnah (2 miles from airport); tel: (1) 824-494/5; fax: (1) 824-489; 5 restaurants; business center; fitness club; rooftop pool; US$155+.

Bristol; Rue Madame Curie; tel: (1) 351-400; fax: (1) 351-409; restaurant; conference facilities (up to 600); secretarial services; fax, photocopying facilities; in-room modem/fax connection, safe; business floors; corporate rates; fitness room; US$175-200.

Inter-Continentale Vendome; Ain el-Mreysseh; tel:(1) 369280; fax:(1) 369169; boutique hotel; personalized service; rooms with seaside views; restaurant; business center; US$230+.

Summerland; Jnah; tel: (1) 313030; fax: (1) 863163; restaurant; conference facility (up to 1200); secretarial services; fax/photocopying facilities; in-room modem/fax connection; fitness room; sauna; pool; whirlpool; US$185-200.

Expensive
Alexandre; Rue Adib Ishak Achirafieh; tel: (1) 324-347; fax: (1) 203-940; restaurant; conference facilities (up to 500); secretarial services; fax, photocopying facilities; corporate rates; fitness room; US$90-110.

Beau Rivage; Ramlet El-Baida; tel: (1) 864-330; fax:(1) 819-836; restaurant; conference facilities (up to 200); secretarial services; fax, photocopying facilities; in-room modem/fax connection; corporate rates; fitness room; sauna; pool; whirlpool; US$130-155.

Beirut Commodore; Commodore Street; tel: (1) 350-400; fax:(1) 345-8067; 3 restaurants; business center; club floor; conference facilities (up to 500); secretarial services; fax/photocopying facilities; in-room modem/fax connection; corporate rates; pool; US$145+.

Cavalier; Abdel Baki Street, Hamra; tel: (1) 353-001; fax:(1) 347-681; restaurant; meeting facilities (up to 30); secretarial services; fax/photocopy facility; in-room modem/fax connection; US$105-153.

La Cigale; Zalka Highway, Zalka; tel: (1) 893-441; fax:(1) 898-773; located in suburb; restaurant; conference facilities (up to 200); secretarial services; fax/photocopying facilities; in-room safe, modem/fax connection; corporate rates; US$110+.

Le Gabriel; Independence Avenue; tel: 203-700; fax: 320-094; 2 restaurants; business center; pool; steambath; US$120+.

Holiday Tower; Dbayeh 507 Center, Dbayeh Highway; tel: (1) 520-190; fax:(1) 413-334; restaurant; conference facilities (up to 400) secretarial services; fax/photocopying facilities; in-room safe, modem/fax connection; corporate rates; fitness room; US$110-120.

Moderate
Royal Garden; Rue de Lyon, Hamra; tel: (1) 350-010; fax: (1) 353-241; restaurant; meeting facilities; secretarial service; fax/photocopy facilities; in-room modem/fax connection; corporate rates; pool; US$65+.

AUTO RENTAL

Avis; tel: (1) 398-850 or 398-851; http://www.avis.com.

Budget; central reservations, tel: (1) 833-032; fax: (1) 833-027.

Hertz; reservations, tel: (1) 427-283; fax: (1) 427-285; Beirut Airport, tel: (1) 423-244; fax: (1) 427-285; Sami El Solh Street, Ministry of Industry Petroleum Bldg./70-118 Antelias, tel: (1) 423-244; fax: (1) 427-285.

WORLD TRADE CENTER

World Trade Center Beirut
Brickell Bay Tower
1001 Brickell Bay Drive, Suite #2210
Miami, FL 33131 USA
tel: [1] (305) 377-0304; fax: [1] (305) 577-3347

CHAMBER OF COMMERCE

Beirut Chamber of Commerce and Industry
PO Box 11-1801, Sanayeh, Beirut
tel: (1) 353-390; fax: (1) 602-374
website: http://www.2.ccib.org.lb

Libya

At a Glance

THE PEOPLE

Population .... 5,115,450 (July 2000 est.)
Growth Rate .... 2.42% (2000 est.)
Life Expectancy .... 75.45 years
Infant Mortality . 30.08 deaths/1,000 live births (2000 est.)

Ethnic Composition

Berber and Arab 97%
Some Greeks, Maltese, Italians, Egyptians, Pakistanis,
Turks, Indians, and Tunisians 3%

Religious Composition

Sunni Muslim 97%

Languages Spoken

Arabic, Italian, and English are spoken in most large urban areas.

Education and Literacy

The government has invested heavily in education, funding free schooling at all levels. Seven years are compulsory. Adult literacy of males is 87.9 percent; of females, 63 percent.

Labor Force

Total: 1,200,000
280,000 are resident foreign workers.
By occupation: services and government 54%, industry 29%, agriculture 17%.

THE ECONOMY

The economy of Libya is based mainly upon the oil sector, which makes up almost all export earnings and about one-quarter of the GDP. Oil revenues coupled with a low population give Libya one of the highest per capita GDP's in all of Africa. Inefficient resource use and import restrictions have led to shortages of some daily basic staples including foodstuffs. The climate and poor soils severely inhibit farm output, and Libya imports about 75 percent of its national food requirements. The non-oil manufacturing and construction sectors account for about 20 percent of the GDP and have expanded from processing mostly agricultural products to include the production of steel, petrochemicals, iron, and aluminum. The increase in oil prices in 1999 boosted export revenues and played a role in spurring on Libya's economy. Since the U.N. lifted its embargo on Libya, the country has been courting foreign investment. There has been some interest from international investors.
Exports .... US$6.6 billion (f.o.b., 1998 est.)
Imports .... US$7 billion (f.o.b., 1998 est.)
Total Trade .... US$13.6 billion (f.o.b. 1995)
GDP Per Capita .... US$$7,900 (1999 est.)
Unemployment .... 30% (1998 est.)
Inflation Rate .... 18% (1999 est.)

Top Export Partners

Italy 40%, Germany 17%, Spain 12%, France 4%, Sudan 4%, U.K. 3%.

Top Import Partners

Italy 23%, Germany 12%, UK 9%, France 7%, Tunisia 5%, Belgium 4%.

Top Exports

Crude oil, refined petroleum products, natural gas.

Top Imports

Machinery, transport equipment, food, manufactured goods.

BUSINESS WORKWEEK

Offices

Monday to Friday 9a.m. to 5p.m., Saturday 9a.m. to noon.

Banks

In winter, Saturday to Wednesday 8a.m. to noon; with extra hours from 4p.m. to 5p.m. on Saturday and Wednesday during the summer.

Government

Monday to Friday 10a.m. to 5p.m.

Retail

Monday to Friday 10a.m. to 7p.m., slightly shorter hours on the weekend.

HOLIDAYS

Id al-Fitr, end of Ramadan .... January 9*
Id al-Adha, Feast of the Sacrifice .... March 18*
Evacuation Day .... March 28
Islamic New Year .... April 8*
Ashoura .... April 17*
Evacuation Day .... June 11
Mouloud, Birth of Muhammad .... June 16*
Egyptian Revolution Day .... July 23
Revolution Day .... September 1
Italian Evacuation Day .... October 7
Leilat al-Meiraj
(Ascension of the Prophet) .... October 27
Id al-Fitr (End of Ramadan) .... December 3
   *Date may vary by year.

CLIMATE

Seasons

The climate varies according to region, from Mediterranean to extreme desert temperatures. The winter is cool with irregular rainfall.

Regions

Mediterranean along the coast; dry with extreme heat in the interior, with hot and dry winds in the spring and fall.

Average temperatures in the main cities are 16°C in the winter months, and around 30°C in the summers. In the deserts, temperatures will rise to 40°C during the day and fall to bellow zero at night.

Money & Banking

Currency

The currency of Libya is the Libyan Dinar (LD).

Denominations

The Libyan Dinar comes in coin denominations of 100, 50, 20, 10, 5, and 1 dirhams; and banknotes of 250 and 500 dirhams, and LD1, 5, and 10.

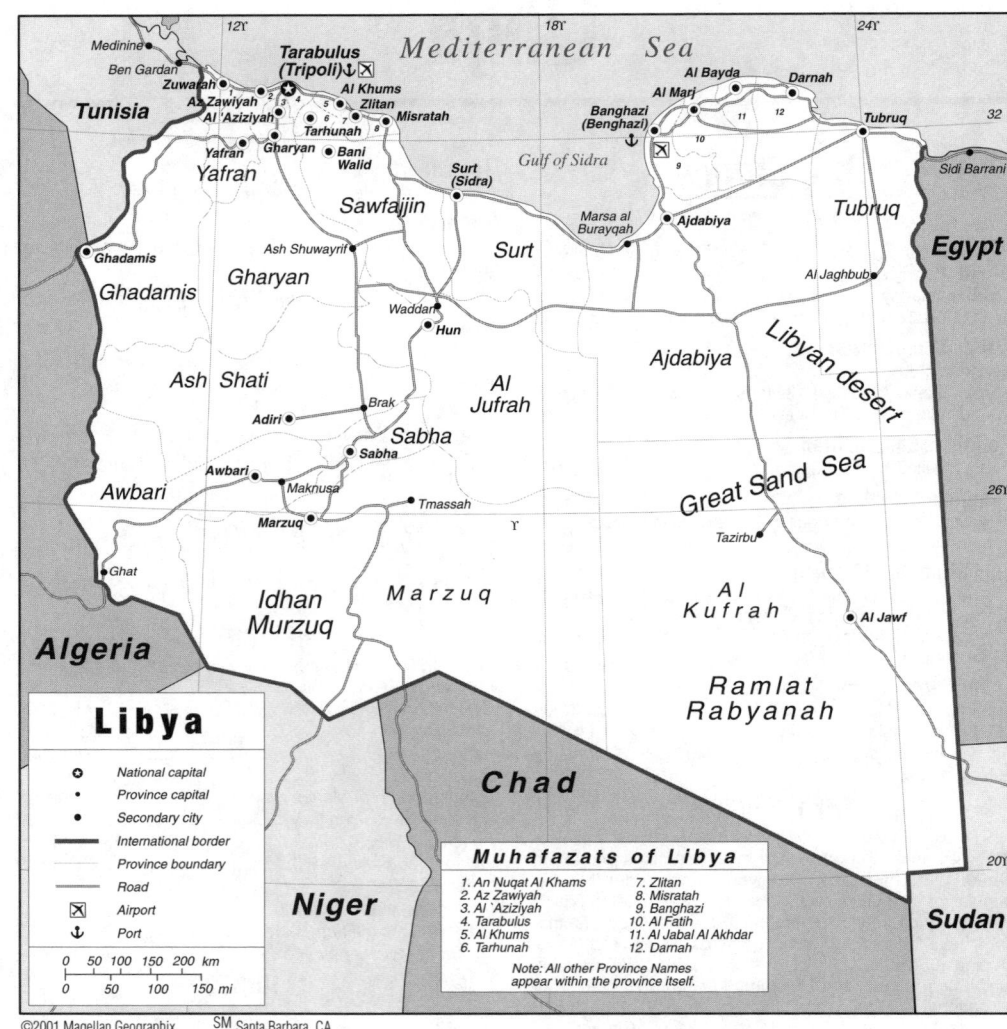

Traveler's checks

Travelers can exchange currency at banks, exchange shops, hotels, international airports, Tripoli's souq al-Attara, and the taxi station at tourist exchange rates with various rates of exchange. Larger banks may offer the best exchange rates. Consult your bank about current exchange rates before departure. Try to take only crisp and new notes, wrinkled and soiled notes are likely to be refused.

Officially it is forbidden to bring U.S. dollars into Libya. However, the U.S. dollar continues to be one of the most popular currencies to exchange; many of the hotels charge in U.S. dollars. Keep all bank exchange receipts for customs checks upon departure, as officials will compare your remaining dollars with the receipts and your currency declaration upon arrival. As such, one might expect to be found out if one has participated in the black market with the money declared at customs; also, undercover police operate all around to further discourage black market activity.

Credit cards may not be easily accepted, except perhaps in some up-market places in the main cities, but smaller restaurants and *souks* (markets) will most likely ask for cash. Some banks in the capital offer cash advances on credit cards, but make sure you bring you passport.

For reasons of the embargo, traveler's checks may be refused.

Bank Locations

Arab Banking Corporation; P.O. Box 3578, Tripoli; tel: (21) 335-0227; tel: 335-0220; fax: (21) 335-0229

Central Bank of Libya; P.O. Box 1103, Tripoli; tel: 213-3591.

Essential Terms

English	Arabic
Yes	Na-a'am
No	La; mish
Good morning	Al sa-lahm
Hello (daytime)	Al sa-lahm
Hello (evening)	Ma-sa'el khair
Hello (telephone)	Marhaban
Good-bye	Be-kha-trahk
Please	Min-fahd-lak (M)
	Min-fahd-lik (F)
Thank you	Shook-rahn
Pleased to meet you	Sorirart biro'aitak
Excuse me; I'm sorry	Is-ma-leh
My name is _____	'ismii____
I don't understand	An-na mish fahem
Do you speak English?	Hal tatakallumu l-inkliziyya?

Travel

VISA AND PASSPORT

A passport which is valid for at least six months and a visa are both required for travel to Libya. Citizens of all Arab League countries are exempt if holding valid I.D. cards. Also exempt are transit passengers who are continuing their journey by the same or first-connecting aircraft within 24 hours, are in possession of return or onward documentation, and do not leave the airport.

Both tourist and business visas remain valid for 90 days. An official invitation from a company official will best enable the business traveler to procure a visa, as the Libyan company will help handle visa requirements. All travelers must be in possession of at least US$500, or the equivalent thereof, to gain entry into Libya.

It is necessary to register with the police when arriving at your destination (cost of LD5). This can often be accomplished through the hotel for an additional small fee. Visas may be difficult to obtain and may require an invitation from an official agency or business. Visa applications may have to be filled out in Arabic before they are submitted to the embassy with a fee.

Questions may be directed to a Libyan consulate, or to the Permanent Mission of the Socialist People's Libyan Arab Jamahiriya to the U.N. at (212) 752-5775.

Note: Israeli citizens, or those persons carrying an Israeli stamp in their passport, will not be admitted to Libya.

Note for U.S. Travelers

At press time, U.S. passports were not valid for travel to, in, or through Libya without a special validation from the U.S. State Department. In addition, the U.S. Treasury Department prohibits all financial and commercial or travel-related transactions by U.S. citizens, resident aliens, anyone physically located in the U.S., except those specifically licensed by the U.S. Treasury Department. Current U.N. Security Council sanctions against Libya include an air and selective export embargo and an assets freeze, making it difficult for nationals of many other countries to enter or leave Libya or to receive funds when in Libya.

Currently, the four categories of persons eligible for consideration for passport validation are: (a) professional reporters (b) American Red Cross (c) Humanitarian Considerations (d) National Interest. Requests for special validation must be accompanied by supporting documentation according to the category under which validation is sought, and may be forwarded in writing to the following address:

Deputy Assistant Secretary for Passport Services; U.S. Department of State; 1111 19th St., NW, Ste. 260; Washington, D.C.20522-1705; Attn: Office of Passport Policy and Advisory Services; tel: (202) 955-0231, 955-0232; fax: (202) 955-0230.

DEPARTURE FORMALITIES

You must buy an exit stamp upon arrival, and notifying the police upon arrival is also necessary. Otherwise, departure will be delayed regardless of your flight time if officials think that malpractice, rather than ignorance, is the cause of violating this law. **Note**: Keep a copy of the forms given since they officials will request them upon departure.

There is a departure tax of LYD3, payable in local currency.

CUSTOMS ENTRY (PERSONAL)

Duty-free
- Tobacco: 200 cigarettes, 250g of tobacco or 25 cigars
- Other: a reasonable amount of perfume
- Cameras and currency must be declared upon arrival

Prohibited or Restricted
- All alcohol
- The import of obscene literature
- Pork, pork products, and any kind of food
- All goods made in Israel or manufactured by companies that do business with Israel are prohibited

*For a full list of prohibited items contact the nearest Libyan diplomatic representative. Dogs and cats need two veterinary health certificates and a rabies inoculation card.

IMMUNIZATION

Although malaria has been eradicated in Libya, inoculation is advisable against other endemic diseases such as typhoid, tuberculosis, infectious hepatitis, as well as yellow fever. Antirabies protection is advised for walkers and cyclists.

TIPPING

Tipping is not widespread in Libya and is only expected by those giving personalized service.

Taxi
Taxi drivers appreciate a tip, although it is not necessary.

Porters
Porters generally receive half a Dinar per heavy bag.

Hotels
Hotels generally receive a 10 percent tip.

Restaurants
A 10 to 20 percent service charge is usually included in the bill.

EMERGENCY INFORMATION

Police and Crime

Crime in Libya is relatively low. It is generally safe to walk the streets, but take basic precautions against petty crime. Avoid flashy displays of wealth, and dress and behave conservatively. Leave most of your cash, traveler's checks, jewelry, and your camera in your hotel safe. Carry photocopies of your passport instead of the original. Carry cash in a money belt, and use credit cards or traveler's checks for most transactions.

Never carry a stranger's baggage. There is some corruption in the police and armed forces, but they are generally efficient. Women should not travel alone, and must expect to face a certain amount of harassment and definite segregation. In many cases, they will not be admitted to a hotel without a male escort. Islamic rule dictates that women should not be addressed, and, as such, they will face an often stony silence.

Emergency Numbers

For emergencies, please consult your embassy in Libya.

Health

Although tap water may be chlorinated in the main city, it is suggested that one stick with bottled water for drinking. Outside the main cities, one can expect contaminated water. As such, only drink bottled water, even for brushing your teeth, and avoid ice cubes. Don't eat raw vegetables and fruit unless they've been washed in a chlorine solution. Stay away from milk as it is most likely unpasteurized; this also applies to ice cream and dairy products. Diarrhea is common for travelers who are unaccustomed to the new diet and water. The dust and smog may cause bronchitis. Endemic diseases include typhoid, dysenteries, venereal diseases and infectious hepatitis, A and E.

Medical services are adequate and many of the doctors and physicians are trained abroad; however, lack of supplies due to embargoes disable much of their effectiveness. For more serious medical care you are advised to leave the country.

AIR

Until recently, internal flights in Libya were not recommended due to the continuing embargo affecting the upkeep and maintenance of aircraft and the availability of spare parts. With the reopening of the international airport, though, domestic routes are now on the increase.

Jamahiriya Libyan Arab Airlines (LN) offers swift and frequent internal flights between Tripoli, Benghazi, Sebha, Al Bayda, Mersa Brega, Tobruk, Misurata, Ghadamès, and Al Khufrah. There is also an hourly LN shuttle between Tripoli and Benghazi.

Embargo

Because there is a UN embargo on Libya, it is impossible to fly into Tripoli, which used to be Libya's most vital connection to the world. The only remaining direct connections are the ferries, running between Tripoli and three other countries' ports. The most frequent boats run to and from Valeta on Malta, which is poorly run and has greatly varying fares depending on where you buy your ticket (Libya is easily the most expensive at US$200 for one way). Somewhat sporadic connections also exist to Morocco (Casablanca) and to Egypt (Alexandria), sometimes once a week, other times less. Purchasing the ticket in Morocco or Egypt is again the most reasonable. At Libyan prices, you can expect to spend US$300 one way. The ferry to Morocco takes four days, to Egypt about two days.

TAXI

Private and collective taxis are available in cities. Collective taxis take numerous passengers to a specific destination and prove most ubiquitous. Fares should be agreed upon before departing since meter usage is rare.

AUTO

Cars are available for rent. Due to the embargo, however, do not expect to find the major international car rental companies in Libya. A driver's license from your home country is required for a three-month period.

METRO

No metro system exists in Libya.

BUSES & TRAM

The Libya International Bus Company runs full-service air conditioned buses to Alexandria, Cairo, Damascus, and Benghazi. Travelers heading toward the Egyptian border may also catch a minibus that travels between Benghazi and Tobruq. Urban bus service, however, proves haphazard and crowded.

WATER TRAVEL

Ferries operate between Valetta in Malta and Libya for rather large sums and low standards. One is urged to purchase tickets on the Malta side, as in Libya it may well cost US$200 for a one-way fare.

Two alternate routes exist to Libya from Alexandria in Egypt and Casablanca in Morocco. However, trips take from 2 to 4 days respectively. Again, think about purchasing tickets from the gateway cities outside of Libya for more friendly fares.

TRAVEL ASSISTANCE

General Board of Tourism; PO Box 71981, Tripoli, Libya.

AZAR Travel & Tourism Services Company; Jamal Abdulnaser Street, Main Coastal Road, Zuara, Libya; European Agent Mobile Phone: [49] (177) 288-6866; fax: [49] (721) 961-4795.

Security Briefing

SOCIAL UNREST

Col. Muammar al-Qadhafi runs a tight ship of state (although he has no official government title) and there are no political parties. Libya describes its form of government as a Jamahiriya (State of the Masses) and rule is maintained through a vast series of small local councils. This brand of socialism does not allow for dissent, so, incidents of social unrest are few. There are some nationalist Arab underground movements, but they are very weak and rarely surface.

Street demonstrations do occur but are organized by the government to show support for Qadhafi or other anti-Western governments. Visitors should avoid these demonstrations as they often erupt into violent disorder.

ORGANIZED CRIME

Libya has supported international terrorist groups in the past, some of which have financed their own operations through drug trafficking and gun running. There have also been smuggling rings that sprouted up around the UN embargo begun in 1992 (now in suspension). Organized crime in the traditional sense does not exist in this Islamic socialist state where People's Councils control every aspect of daily life.

Libya

STREET CRIME

Street crime is minimal in Libya where a generous social system, tight policing, and an oil-fed prosperity preclude the need and opportunity to steal. Basic precautions should still be taken especially at beach resorts and tourist areas.

CULTURAL CONFLICTS

Libya is an Islamic state, though not fundamentalist. It does observe a conservative dress code for men and women (see Advice below). Pork and alcohol are illegal as is the wearing of non-Islamic religious symbols. Socializing between men and women that are not spouses or blood relatives cannot take place in public without bringing rebuke. Women cannot travel (or even walk through a town) alone. Women are not permitted to assert themselves in the presence of men and some men will not even speak to women in public.

While Qadhafi is often a subject of ridicule internationally, any derisive comments made in public (or sometimes even in private) about him while in Libya can result in arrest. The same holds true for any anti-Islamic statements.

Communications

DIALING CODES IN LIBYA

International country code: [218]

Selected city codes: Agelat (282), Benghazi (61), Benina (63), Derna (81), Gharian (41), Misuratha (51), Sabratha (24), Sebha (71), Taigura (26), Tripoli (2133), Tripoli Airport (22), Zawai (23), Zuara (25).

Dialing Libya from Overseas

To dial Libya from overseas, dial your country's international dialing code, then 218 (the country code for Libya), then the city code, and finally the number. If you were dialing Benghazi from the United States, for example, you would begin with 011, then 218, then 61 (the city code for Benghazi), and finally the number of the person or office you were trying to reach.

CALLING WITHIN LIBYA

Local Calls

Local calls can be placed from any phone in Tripole or Benghazi directly. Calls outside of this area may require an operator's assistance. In some areas, local calling may not be possible.

Long Distance Calls

The cities of Tripoli and Benghazi are linked telephonically, but, other than that, long-distance calling still has a way to go in terms of development. Use area codes when dialing to another city.

International Calls

International calling may use up a certain amount of patience since there are a restricted number of lines available. Incoming calls prove a simpler process if you are able to arrange for the party you want to reach to call you. Other than that, PTT (Post, Telephone and Telegraph) offices offer the most convenience, the word 'convenient' being totally relative. Offices are located in most towns. Direct calling entails dialing 00 + country code + area code + number.

PAY PHONES

Public Telephones

PTT (Post, Telephone and Telegraph) offers telephones for public use.

Calling Cards

Cards can be purchased at the Telecommunication Centers.

CELLULAR PHONES

Libya operates its cellular service on a GSM digital system.

Note: Your home country cell phone may not work in this country. If not, we recommend that you rent an international cell phone *before* you leave home. A major US-based cell phone rental provider is **IMC WorldCell**. For information see "International Cell Phone Rentals" on page 14.

CALL BACK

For a list of callback services, please refer to the "Communications" section in the *Global Road Warrior* Introduction.

PHONE JACK

Plug adaptors are available through **iGo Corporation**. (See "Electrical and Telephone Adaptors" on page 19.)

FAX

Luxury hotels and post and telecommunication offices have fax services. However, the shortage of telephone lines may affect service. Late night automatic fax facilities in private offices offer the best bet.

POSTAL SERVICES

Libya has a fair postal system. However, due to the air embargo, letters and packets may take triple as long to reach their destination since they must go by overland routing. Furthermore, mail is subject to censorship. Facilities are available in the main cities.

TELEGRAMS

Telegrams can be sent from the Central Telegraph Office in major cities.

Business Services

COURIER SERVICE

DHL - Mahri Worldwide Express Air Freight; Ahmed Swaihly St., Mahri House, PO Box 12499, Tripoli-SPLAJ; tel: (21) 444-3782; Saturday to Thursday 8a.m. to 5p.m.

TNT - ADM Express via TNT EW CAI; tel: (21) 77-864, refer CAI, tel: (21) 70-326, refer CAI; fax: (21) 77-864, refer CAI; telex: 23533 SKYPK-UN (CAI).

Electrical

Current

150/220 volts AC, 50Hz.

ELECTRIC PLUGS

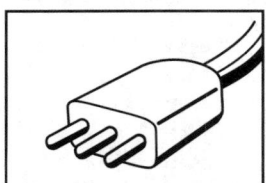

Plug adaptors are available through **iGo Corporation.** (See "Electrical and Telephone Adaptors" on page 19.)

Technical Support

HARDWARE/SOFTWARE VENDOR SUPPORT

Compaq/Digital; (U.AE. Office) tel: [971] 4-818-100; fax: [971] 4-818-313; (in Switzerland) tel: [41] (22) 709-5330; fax: [41] (22) 709-5391 (Geneva); tel: [41] (1) 801-2507; fax: [41] (1) 801-2172 (Zurich); (General U.S.) tel: (281) 518-2000; http://www.compaq.com/.

Corel; (in the U.A.E.) tel: [971] 4-523-526 (All Applications); (in Germany) tel: [49] (180) 425-8210 (TS Word Perfect-32 bit); (in the U.S.) tel: [1] (716) 871-2325 (Ask to be Forwarded to Appropriate Program); http://www.corel.com/.

Dell; (in Egypt) tel: [20] 2-360-2234 (Electronics House in Cairo/Mr. Jamal El Bidweihy); fax: [20] 2-361-4576; (in Germany) tel: [49] (61) 039-710; (Dell- Europe) tel: [44] (134) 474-8000; (in the U.S.) tel: [1] (512) 338-4400; fax: [1] (512) 728-3330; http://www.dell.com/.

Filemaker/Claris; (in Germany) tel: [49] (180) 525-8166 (Info-line); fax: [49] (180) 567-2233; tel: [49] (180) 523-6423; (in the U.S.) tel: [1] (800) 965-9090; http://www.claris.com/.

Gateway 2000; (in the U.S.) tel: [1] (605) 232-2191; fax: [1] (605) 232-2023; (in Ireland) tel: [353] (1) 797-2000; http://www.g2k.com/.

Hewlett Packard; (in Switzerland) tel: [41] (22) 780-8111; (in the U.S.) tel: [1] (408) 246-4300; http://www.hp.com/.

IBM; (Egypt Office) tel: [20] 2-349-2533; fax: [20] 2-360-1227; (in Switzerland) tel: [41] (22) 310-0418 (in French); (in the U.S.) tel: [1] (919) 517-2800; http://www.ibm.com/.

Microsoft; (U.A.E. Office) tel: [971] 4-513-888; fax: [971] 4-527-444(in Switzerland) tel: [41] (848) 858-868; fax [41] (1) 831-0869; (in the U.S.) tel: [1] (425) 635-7222; http://www.microsoft.com/.

Novell; (in Germany) tel: [49] (211) 563-2777 (System support); tel: [49] (6196) 904-477; fax: [49] (211) 563-2772; (in Switzerland) tel: [41] (1) 308-4747; fax: [41] (1) 302-0401; (in the U.S.) tel: [1] (408) 434-2300; fax: [1] (408) 577-5775 (Worldwide Sales Headquarters); http://www.novell.com/.

Quark; (in Switzerland) tel: [41] (1) 808-7722; fax: [41] (1) 808-7799; (in the U.S.) tel: [1] (303) 894-8899; fax: [1] (303) 894-3398 (For Products Registered in the Americas); http://www.quark.com/.

Toshiba; (in Germany) tel: [49] (2131) 158-319; fax: [49] (2131) 158-558; (in Switzerland) tel: [41] (1) 946-0777; fax: [41] (1) 946-0807; (in Ireland) tel: [44] (193) 282-8828; (in the U.S.) [1] (949) 583-3000 (Corporate Headquarters); http://www.toshiba.com/.

Internet Connection

HOW TO CONNECT

Connecting to AOL and Compuserve in Libya is similar to using it when traveling outside your own area code. See the introductory section for detailed information on connecting to your account through a different phone number.

America Online

Numbers are available at keyword *international*. Be sure to get several local numbers before leaving. Go to keyword *access* (a free area) and download the software.

There are no direct access numbers for America Online in Libya. Users will have to pay international rates to use the service.

Compuserve

Numbers are available at *Go International*. The Compuserve Web-site also has a great deal of information, at http://www.compuserve.com.

There are no direct access numbers for Compuserve in Libya. Users will have to pay international rates to use the service.

Independent Service Providers

Many independent service providers offer discounts if you are only in town for a couple of days.

Libya Telecom & Technology; tel: (21) 335-0831; fax: (21) 335-0832; email: support@lttnet.com; http:www.lttnet.com/.

VPM Enterprises; tel: [1] (800) 321-0221; http://www.vpm.com (although a United States company, VPM offers access numbers in Libya).

Internet Cafes

Tripoli

Alhaithem for Computers; Alarousi mosque-Hi alandalus, Tripoli; tel: (21) 477-9514; email: al_haithem@lttnet.net; Monday through Friday, 9:30a.m. to 2a.m.; LD2.5 per hour of use.

Atlantic; Zarka El Yamama 2 Second Floor, Tripoli; tel: (21) 483-4252; fax: (21) 483-1861; email: Surf_Atlantic@hotmail.com; Monday through Friday, 9a.m. to 1a.m.; LD4 per hour of use.

Atlas Internet Cafe; Abou-Nawas-Girgarish; tel/fax: (21) 483-1355; email: atlascenter@hotmail.com.

Regatta Village Cyber Cafe; Regatta Village Ghergarish, Tripoli; tel: (21) 483-2301/7, ext: 2461; fax: (21) 483-2300; email: regatta_tripoli@hotmail.com; http://www.regatta.homepage.com/; LD3 per hour of use.

Sendibad Internet Cafe; Hai Demashq. Alhadba, Tripoli; tel/fax: (21) 360-5063; email: sendibad@hotmail.com; LD3.50 per hour of use.

Business Culture

GREETINGS & COURTESIES

The national language of Libya is Arabic, though some older people speak Italian and easterners may speak Egyptian. Most business people speak passable English.

Very little business has been conducted with the outside world by Libya since 1992; so, it is difficult to say exactly how visiting business people might be treated. The following are just general facts regarding Arabic cultures.

The standard "*salaam alaykum*" (peace be with you) is met with a response of "*wa alaykum as-salaam*" (and peace be upon you). After this brief exchange, inquiries into health, family, travel, food intake, weather, etc. will ensue amid much handshaking. Arab men often exchange embraces as well as handshakes. Good friends will continue to hold hands during the many questions and answers.

Libyan men will not offer to shake a woman's hand unless the woman (usually foreign) extends her hand first. Even then, Libyan men may ignore the gesture. Some Libyan men will not even speak to women in public.

Often, local men will not introduce the females who are accompanying them. The women are left to stand behind and wait patiently. **Note**: If the women are not introduced, visitors should not presume to introduce themselves as this is considered to be improper.

BUSINESS ETHIC & FRAMEWORK

Libyan ethics, business related and otherwise, have mystified the developed world for several decades. Libya does have a socialist economy, and it is very suspect of free markets and capitalism. Almost all major businesses are state-owned, and the risk of expropriation of foreign-owned assets is high.

Foreign firms can expect to have their operations either partnered with a government agency or with a "private partner" handpicked by the government. Every locality has a People's Council that can veto any project within its purview. These councils will have to be dealt with along with central government agencies. Though Libyan leaders understand the need to attract foreign investment, socialist and Islamic politics make it difficult for them to accept input from the developed economies.

Note: Some, but not all, Libyans believe in the strict adherence to Islamic teachings forbidding usury (the taking of interest on loans). This belief will not necessarily scuttle any project, but it will require some imaginative financial arrangements. In such cases, lenders that would normally have been creditors (e.g., banks) must be made full-risk equity partners in the project.

DECISION MAKING

Two attributes will drive the Libyan decision-making process. Firstly, Arabic cultures tend to be very hierarchical, and power is held closely near the top. Either a single person (e.g., Qadhafi) or a small group (e.g., People's Councils) will make all decisions. Foreign firms must make sure they are negotiating with the right people before commencing discussions.

Secondly, Libya's recent isolation has made them very suspect of the outside world. They even distrust their fellow Arabs let alone Western and Asian business people. This distrust will put a drag on the decision-making process as information will be examined time and again to make sure there are no loopholes or mistakes. The Libyan fear of being tricked by wily business people from the developed economies hangs heavy in the air. Foreigners should never try to rush the Libyans or give them the impression that something important is being withheld.

MEETINGS

Libyans, like most Arab cultures, have a strong regard for hospitality. Their meeting facilities may be somewhat out of date, but they are amiable hosts. After an initial greeting, they will want to chat with their guests for some time on non-business topics; this is not just cordiality but a sincere desire to get to know their counterparts. Visitors are advised to do the same because business in Libya is based more upon personal relationships than contracts. Local commercial law is thin on the ground and what little there is does not favor foreigners. Trust is everything in such an environment.

During this early chatting phase, business cards will be exchanged and job titles noted. Although Libyan business people do speak English, visitors will impress their hosts if the business cards and other materials have been translated into Arabic in advance.

Seating will be based upon rank, and counterparts usually sit opposite each other. In this hierarchical society, only equals address each other. There are no free-for-all discussions. Drinks (tea or coffee) and light foods will be served during the meeting. Any medical requirements (e.g., caffeine or sugar allergies) should be made known in advance of arrival.

Note: Libyan telecom infrastructure and meeting facilities may not be able to handle cutting-edge presentation technology. Call ahead to find out what technology they can and cannot support.

The meeting proper will proceed according to an agenda that should be approved by both sides. Any surprises will be viewed by the Libyans as tricks and not last-minute ideas. The meetings will move slowly as the Libyans review details and reach consensus. (When the Libyan side is buying the process is even slower.) Visitors should never expect to cut deals at the first meeting. Remember, rushing the Libyans will only make them suspect your motives.

Arabic negotiators have a tendency to ask for side meetings to discuss "sensitive" (read: bad news) topics. Visitors should grant this request with the proviso that these back-channel talks are not binding.

Warning: Contracts signed in Libya will be in Arabic and should be independently translated by the foreign firm before signing. If translators are used during negotiations, visitors should procure their own to prevent conflicts of interest.

WOMEN IN BUSINESS

Women fill few managerial roles in Libya and they never supervise male employees. Visiting female managers and women executives may find it difficult to get Libyan men to take their roles seriously. The rank and gender of the visiting delegates should be made known in advance of arrival. Female executives should be deferred to by their staff at all times to reinforce their status.

As mentioned earlier, some Libyan males refuse to speak to women that are not relatives. Visiting buyers or investors should not have any problems overcoming this silent treatment. Visiting sellers, however, should seriously consider the pros and cons of including women in their delegations.

BUSINESS ENTERTAINING

While Libya does have a certain level of wealth, visitors should not expect lavish business dinners. Food will be simple but plentiful. It may be served in a dining room setup in a desert tent (a Qadhafi favorite) to lend an authentic atmosphere to the occasion. Alcohol is not served as it is illegal. **Note**: Libyan food may not appeal to everyone but all dishes should be tried; not to do so insults the host. Special dietary needs should be made known well in advance of arrival.

Nightlife in Libya is minimal, so, there is not an after-hours bar or disco scene. Long talks over coffee may be the most that can be expected. If invited to a Libyan home, accept the invitation as it is a great honor; to decline is a grave insult.

BUSINESS ATTIRE

Men should wear dark suits, white shirts, and conservative ties for initial meetings and any contact with Libyan government agencies. This can be a hot climate, but not every facility is air conditioned, so, lightweight materials are the best choice. Subsequent meetings may demand less formal attire (e.g., golf shirts and slacks), but visitors should take their cues from the Libyans. Locals may adopt native robes but this is not necessarily a signal of informality. Err on the side of formality.

Foreign women should adopt similarly conservative styles. Avoid short skirts (dresses should be cut below the knee) and never wear any kind of tight or revealing styles. For less formal attire, stay the conservative course. No shorts or miniskirts, and keep shoulders and backs covered. Halters and tubetops are not acceptable in Libya. To be fully inconspicuous, adopt the ankle length, loose-fitting robe of the local women. Some rural locales may require women to wear head scarves at all times in public.

Note: For some dinner parties, the Libyan hosts may ask both male and female visitors to wear native dress. To comply is a sign of mutual respect, and the robes are surprisingly comfortable and cool during hot spells.

Business Advisory

POLITICS & GRAFT

The government owns most major businesses already, so, there is little need for graft. Foreign firms can expect a government component to be part of any sizable trade deal or joint venture.

BUSINESS FRAUD

Libya has been off the global business scene for some time and will need a little more time to get up to speed on international standards. Libyan firms are, for the most part, honest brokers; but, misunderstandings regarding delivery dates, production schedules, and quality control can arise. Foreign firms should make the required standards evident early in the relationship. Follow-up should be thorough and implemented over an extended period. Never assume.

Note: Some Libyans still view businesses from certain economies as "the enemy." The temptation to defraud a wealthy, global conglomerate may be powerful; so, foreign firms should be wary. While it may be good to trust your Libyan partner, it is better to verify.

Business Centers
Tripoli

CITY VIEW

Economically, the city of Tripoli has thrived since the early 1970's when the country's export oil earnings began to sky rocket. On the western side of the northern border of the Mediterranean Sea, Tripoli is Libya's largest city with 990,700 inhabitants. Originally coined Oea, the "queen of the sea", the city was one of the three trading centers set up by the Phoenicians in approximately 900 B.C. Along with many monuments depicting tales of Libyan history, the city possesses lush greenery with olive trees, palms, grapevines, and orange groves. The Al-Saraya al-Hamra Castle is particularly intriguing, illustrating the quarters and former lifestyles of Libya's past royalty.

AIRPORT

Tripoli International Airport to City Center

The airport lies 21 miles (35 km.) from the city center. Regular bus and taxi service exists to the main hotels and into town. However, since an international air embargo with Libya exists, travelers will not be able to fly into Tripoli. The closest gateway cities into which to fly are Tunis or Cairo.

Airline Numbers

Aeroflot	(21) 444-1527
AirMalta	(21) 444-6896
Alitalia	(21) 335-0018
British Airways	(21) 335-1277
Libyan Arab Airlines	(21) 36-021
Swissair	(21) 335-0052
Turkish Airlines	(21) 335-1252

HOTELS

Top End

Al-Mahari; Sharah al-Fatah; tel: (21) 333-4090/1; tlx: 22090; located in east Tripoli, on beachfront; 3 restaurants; coffee shop; in-room tv, direct telephone, radio and air conditioning; sauna; pool; US$165.

Bab Albagar; tel: (21) 335-0676; 2 restaurants; air conditioning; satellite tv; pool.

Grand Hotel Al-Kabir; Alfath Street; tel: (21) 444-5940, 444-5950; fax: (21) 44-5959; beach front near Green Square, city center; 2 restaurants; coffee shops; conference facilities (up to 300); in-room tv, direct dial phone, radio, air conditioning; car rental; steambath; sauna; pool; beach; US$165.

Expensive

Al-Kabir Hotel; Sharah Ell Fatah, PO Box 275, Tripoli; tel: (21) 45-940; in central Tripoli overlooking the harbor and the corniche; 350 rooms; 2 restaurants; bar; conference facilities up to 300; in room tv, refrigerator, air conditioning; steambath; pool; beach access; cinema.

Corinthia Tripoli Hotel; (Sales office in U.K. for details) tel: [44] (0) 208-943-4194; fax: [44] (0) 208-977-8410; http://www.corinthia.com/; email: london@corinthia.com; 250 rooms; 2 restaurants; coffee shop; business center; conference center; air conditioned; parking; fitness center; sauna; 2 pools.

Hotel Ozo; Benghazi lake; 240 rooms; restaurant; coffee shop; in-room tv, telephone.

Moderate

Beach Annex; tel: (21) 77-865; fax: (21) 77-866; located near the city center; 101 rooms; restaurant.

Hotel Quoze Eltek; Misurata; tel: (51) 614-633/617-4614.

AUTO RENTAL

Grand Hotel Al-Kabir; Alfath Street; tel: (21) 444-5940, 444-5950; fax: (21) 44-5959.

Wesaam Touring Services Co.; PO Box 12983, Tripoli; tel: (21) 361-4291.

WORLD TRADE CENTER

World Trade Center Tripoli
Al Fatah Tower - 18th Floor
186 - 188 - 189 Suites
Tripoli, Libya

Lithuania

At a Glance

THE PEOPLE

Population .... 3,620,756 (July 2000 est.)
Growth Rate .... -0.29% (2000 est.)
Life Expectancy .... 69.09 years (2000 est.)
Infant Mortality . 14.67 deaths/1,000 live births (2000 est.)

Ethnic Composition

Lithuanian...80.6%
Russian 8.7%
Polish 7%
Byelorussian..1.6%
Other 2.1%

Religious Composition

Primarily Roman Catholic; others include: Lutheran, Russian Orthodox, Protestant, evangelical Christian Baptist, Islam, Judaism.

Languages Spoken

Lithuanian is the official language. Polish and Russian are widely spoken as well.

Education and Literacy

Education is compulsory and free for all children between the ages of 6 and 16 years old. There are four major universities. The adult literacy rate is extremely high: 98 percent. Lithuanian is the most common language, although classes are also taught in Polish, Russian, and Yiddish.

Labor Force

Total 1,800,000
By occupation: industry 30%, agriculture 20%, services 50%.

THE ECONOMY

Because of a poor response to the August 1998 Russian financial crisis and ill-planned macroeconomic policies, Lithuania faced an economic and financial crisis in 1999. Preliminary figures indicate 10 percent unemployment (the highest level since independence in 1991), 3 percent negative GDP growth, and a budget deficit estimated at between 8 and 9 percent of the GDP. In November 1999, Prime Minister Kubilius took control of the government and the economy with a commitment to fiscal restraint, economic stabilization, and accelerated reforms. The conservative 2000 budget is based on a 2 percent GDP growth forecast, 3 percent inflation, and a 2.8 percent budget deficit. Lithuania was asked in December 1999 to begin E.U. accession talks in 2000. Lithuania still faces economic challenges in the form of privatization of the large state-owned utilities, especially in the energy sector, and reducing the high current account deficit.

Exports .... US$3.3 billion (f.o.b. 1999)
Imports .... US$4.5 billion (f.o.b. 1999)
Total Trade .... US$7.8 billion (f.o.b. 1999)
GDP Per Capita .... US$4,800 (1999 est.)
Unemployment 10% (1999)
Inflation Rate .... 0.3% (1999 est.)

Top Export Partners

Russia 17.4%, Germany 15.8%, Latvia 12.7%, Denmark 5.9%, Belarus 5.2%.

Top Import Partners

Russia 20.4%, Germany 16.5%, Denmark 3.8%, Belarus 2.2%, Latvia 2%.

Top Exports

Machinery and equipment 19%, mineral products 19%, textiles and clothing 19%, chemicals 10%, foodstuffs.

Top Imports

Machinery and equipment 30%, mineral products 16%, chemicals 9%, textiles and clothing 9%, foodstuffs.

BUSINESS WORKWEEK

Offices

Monday to Friday 9a.m. to 6p.m.; offices may close for lunch between 1p.m. and 2p.m.

Banks

Monday to Thursday 9a.m. to 3p.m. Banks may close earlier with little or no warning.

Government

Monday to Thursday 10a.m. to 4p.m.

Retail

Monday to Friday 10a.m. to 8p.m. Slightly shorter hours on the weekends.

HOLIDAYS

New Year's Day..January 1
Independence Day ....February 16
Day of the Restoration of the
Lithuanian State .... March 11
Easter Monday ....April 24*
Anniversary of the Coronation
of Grand Duke Mindaugas of Lithuania....................July 6
All Saints' Day ....November 1
Christmas ....December 25-26
*Date may vary by year.

CLIMATE

Seasons

The climate in Lithuania is temperate with four distinct and equal-in-length seasons, ranging between the maritime and continental. The average winter temperature is 6.1°C (43°F), and the average temperate in July is around 17.1°C (63°F).

Regions

There are few regional differences in Lithuania.

Money & Banking

Currency

The currency of Lithuania is the litas (litai, pl.).

Denominations

The litas comes in coin denominations of 5, 2, and 1 Litas and 50, 20, 10 cents; and banknotes of 1, 2, 5, 10, 20, 50, and 100 litas.

Traveler's checks

Traveler's checks were legalized for foreigners in 1992 in the Baltic states; however, they are still not as popular as in Western Europe. Travelers may exchange them at banks, exchange shops, hotels, and international airports at tourist ex-

Lithuania

change rates, with various rates of exchange. Larger banks may offer the best exchange rates but avoid black marketers at all cost. Consult your bank about current exchange rates before departure. Keep all receipts for reconversion.

Cash can also be exchanged, and is the most popular form of payment; but try to take only crisp and new notes, wrinkled and soiled notes are likely to be refused.

Credit cards are now accepted regularly in the Baltic states. Take care not to lose your credit card as most transactions are not authorized prior to purchase. Smaller restaurants and shops may ask for cash.

American Express

The most easily accepted card in the Baltic states is the American Express.

American Express; Seimyniskiu 18, tel: (2) 724-156, fax (2) 721-815; 8a.m. to 5p.m., Fri. 8a.m. to 4p.m.

24-hour currency exchanges

Gedimino 7; Gelezinkelio 6; Savanoriu 15a.

Bank Locations

Hermis Bank; Jogailos 9a/1, tel. (+370-2) 22 47 57, fax (+370-2) 22 44 77; 8a.m. to 4p.m., Fri. 8a.m. to 3p.m.; Antakalnio 40, tel: (2) 709-154, 8a.m. to 6:30p.m., Fri. 8a.m. to 5:30p.m.; Gedimino 26, tel: (2) 617-963, 8:00 - 16:00, Fri. 8a.m. to 3p.m.; Saltoniskiu 29, tel: (2) 790-084; 8a.m. to 6p.m., Fri. 8a.m. to 5p.m.; Verkiu 29, tel. (2) 722-901, 8a.m. to 4p.m., Fri. 8a.m. to 3p.m.; Vokieciu 9, tel: (2) 627-869, 8a.m. to 4p.m., Fri. 8a.m. to 3p.m.

Lietuvos Taupomasis Bankas; Pamenkalnio 13, Riga, tel: (2) 230-811; fax: (2) 230-800, email: info@ltb.tdd.lt.

Essential Terms

English	Lithuanian
Yes No	Taip Ne
Good morning Hello (daytime) Hello (evening) Hello (telephone)	Labas rytas Laba diena Labas vakaras Alio
Good-bye	Viso gero
Please	Prasom
Thank you	Aciu
Pleased to meet you	Malonu jus matyti
Excuse me; I'm sorry	Atsiprasau
My name is _____	Mano vardas yra __
I don't understand	As nesuprantu
Do you speak English?	Ar jus kalbate

Travel

VISA AND PASSPORT

Visitors to Lithuania need a valid passport and visa. Tourist or business visas are not required for stays of 90 days or less for the following nationalities: Australia, Bulgaria, Canada, Cyprus, Czech Republic, Denmark, Estonia, Hungary, Iceland, Ireland, Italy, Japan, Latvia, Liechtenstein, Malta, Norway, Poland, Slovak Republic, Slovenia, Sweden, Switzerland, UK, USA, Vatican City, and Venezuela. Nationals of South Korea do not need a visa, unless visiting for more than 15 days.

Nationals of certain other countries, including Belgium, Finland, France, Germany, Greece, Israel, Luxembourg, Monaco, the Netherlands, New Zealand, Portugal, San Marino, South Africa, and Spain, do not require a separate visa for Lithuania if they already hold a valid Estonian or Latvian visa.

Visitors planning to travel on to Russia, even in transit, will require a Russian visa.

DEPARTURE FORMALITIES

Visitors leaving from Vilnius Airport are not subject to any departure taxes. Antiques live under special consideration in Lithuania. If planning to take an antique out of the country, ask the shop in advance of your purchase to provide an export license; otherwise, refer questions to the Committee for Cultural Heritage, located at Snipiskiu 3; tel: 724-005

CUSTOMS ENTRY (PERSONAL)

Duty-free
- Tobacco: 200 cigarettes, 50 cigars, or 250g tobacco
- Alcohol: 1 liter of spirits or 3 liters of wine and champagne
- Perfume: a reasonable amount

Prohibited or Restricted
- Explosives
- Addictive drugs (there may be an exception for medical reasons)

The Lithuanian Customs Department is located at Jaksto 1/25, tel: 226-415.

IMMUNIZATION

No international certificates of vaccination are required unless you are arriving from an infected area.

TIPPING

Taxi
Fares include a tip.

Porters
Porters generally receive US$.50 per bag.

Hotels
No tip is expected in hotels; service is included in the price.

Restaurants
It is customary to leave a 10 to 15 percent tip.

EMERGENCY INFORMATION

Police and Crime
Crime is on the increase in Lithuania, especially in more urban areas. Take basic precautions against petty crime. Avoid flashy displays of wealth, and dress and behave conservatively. Leave most of your cash, traveler's checks, jewelry, and your camera in your hotel safe. Carry photocopies of your passport instead of the original. Carry cash in a money belt, and use credit cards or traveler's checks for most transactions. Walk with your bag away from the street to avoid having it snatched away by motorcycle thieves. Never carry a stranger's baggage.

Emergency Numbers
Ambulance	03
Fire	01
Police	02
Psychology Hotline	(2) 613-380
Alcoholics Anonymous	(2) 615-488

Health
Avoid tap water and stick to bottled water to avoid stomach upset. Diarrhea is common for travelers who are unaccustomed to the new diet and water. Take care when eating outside the main cities as hygiene remains subpar. Freshwater fish pose some risk of tapeworm.

Although the standard of health care is improving now, medical services should only be used for emergencies. Medicines and pharmacological equipment are not quite equal to Western standards, so come prepared.

TAXI
Taxis (taksi) display green illuminated signs and can be hailed in the street, but with more ease at taxi ranks. Watch that the meter is turned on and running according to the time of day; night rates being more expensive. Private taxis can be ordered from hotels and display checkered signs. Fares run at Lit1 to 1.5 per kilometer. Ekspress taxis, the same cabs that service the airport, are considered the most honest and reliable. Minicabs offer a mid-range compromise between bus and cab. They run on specific routes and will pick up and drop off anywhere along the way.

Vilniaus taksi	228-888
Ekspres Taksi	251-111
Lanria	617-961

Lithuania

AUTO

Driving in Lithuania is somewhat maniac. Wear a seatbelt, and be sure not to have a drop of alcohol on your breath. The legal alcohol limit is zero, and penalties are stiff. Winter roads prove specially hazardous as they are rarely plowed. Lighting is often poor and streets poorly marked. Roads in Lithuania range from two- to six-lane highways connecting major cities, to small dirt roads traversing the countryside. Motorists should navigate carefully as street lanes are not always clearly marked. Drivers must remain alert to slow-moving horse carts or trucks traveling at night without taillights or reflectors. Dark-clothed pedestrians walking along unlit roads or darting across dimly lit streets or highways pose a risk to unsuspecting drivers. Driving with caution is urged at all times. To drive in Lithuania you must have held a valid drivers license from your country of residence for at least two years. An international driving permit is required for licenses written in a non-roman alphabet.

TRAIN

Train services cover much of the country and prove efficient. Trains also service Riga, Moscow, Kaliningrad, Minsk, St. Petersburg, and Warsaw. Train connections also take the traveler to Berlin, Budapest, Prague, and Sofia. The central rail station in Vilnius finds itself at Gelezinkelio 16. Purchase tickets to the left of the main building. Windows 3 and 4 sell tickets to Western Europe. Keep in mind that agents will no longer sell tickets 5 minutes before a scheduled departure. For information, call (2) 630-088 or 630-086. For reservations, call (2) 626-947, at least a day in advance of travel. The office remains open Monday to Saturday between 8a.m. and 8p.m., and Sundays from 8a.m. to 5p.m.

Service Levels

Coupe; compartment of 4 beds with door

Platzkart; compartment of 4 beds without door

Obshchi; 2 benches for eight passengers

BUS/TROLLEY

Comfortable, long-distance luxury buses run by Eurolines Baltic International, take travelers from Lithuania to many European cities. Buses depart from the main bus station at Sodu 22 in Vilnius.; tel: 251-377 or email: eurolines@post.5ci.lt; for all other buses, information, (2) 262-482, intl. (2) 3350277; booking, 262-977.

For a trip within Lithuania, buses may prove faster than the train. Call (22) 262-977 for domestic information.

For rides within town, one can purchase tickets at kiosks for Lit0.60 and join the masses. Purchased on board, tickets will cost Lit0.75. Public transportation runs between 6a.m. and 1a.m. Bus and trolley tickets are not interchangeable.

WATER TRAVEL

A passenger ferry travels between Kiel, in Germany, and Klaipeda. Other services to Ahus and Stockholm in Sweden, and Fredericija in Denmark are mainly cargo. However, tickets to Ahus and Stockholm are available from Krantas Shipping at the Klaipeda Hotel, tel: (6) 365-444; fax: (6) 365-443.

Klaipeda International Ferry Terminal: Perkelos 10 in Klaipeda; tel: (6) 255-255; fax: (6) 256-060.

Ferries also travel between Tallinn in Estonia and Helsinki (21/2 hours) and Stockholm (overnight).

DFDS Baltic Line .... 496-400; fax: 496-480
email: dfds.balticlinie@dlaipeda.omnitel.net

Estline in Estonia ....[372] (6) 316-636

Estin Linjat.. [372] (6) 318-606.

Eurolines Baltic Intl. 251-377
email: eurolines@post.5ci.lt.

TRAVEL ASSISTANCE

Hotel Accommodations

HotelsBaltics.com; Refer to this site for internet reservations in Lithuania.

Lithuanian Hotel Association; Ukmerges St. 20, 2005 Vilnius; tel: (2) 726-560; fax(2) 726-191.

National Association of Hotels and Restaurants; Gedimino pr. 46, 2001 Vilnius; tel: (2) 621-606; fax: (2) 227-432.

General Tourism

Lithuanian State Department of Tourism; Vilniaus 4/35 2600 Vilnius; tel: (2) 622-610; fax: (2) 226-819; email: tb@tourism.lt

Lithuanian Tourism Association; Ukmerges St. 20, 2005 Vilnius; tel/fax: (2) 726-191.

Vilnius Tourist Information Centre; Pilies 42, Vilnius; tel/fax: (2) 620-762; email: turizm.info@vilnius.sav.lt.

Security Briefing

SOCIAL UNREST

Visitors to Lithuania will not experience much in the way of visible social unrest. Beneath the surface there is disgruntlement in the minority communities. Once repressed by their Soviet rulers, the Lithuanians were quick to show the few Russians and Ukrainians that remained after independence a taste of their own medicine. Flare ups are few and far between, but, as is true in the rest of the Baltics, any instability in Russia brings about almost immediate concerns in Lithuania. The return of the Soviet empire is a frightening specter for Lithuanians but a pipedream of the Slavic minorities. Foreigners will have little success in asking either side of the discussion to take a new perspective. Opinions are low key, but they are resolute.

CULTURAL CONFLICTS

Lithuanians, like most people that have suffered repression, keep most of their vitriol reserved for their former repressors. Foreigners, in general, are quite welcome—those wanting to spend hard currency are especially welcome. Only those visitors that deride Lithuanian culture or lump it in with Russia will have a "conflict", which may prove memorable. Lithuania retained its culture and language over many centuries of attack and against heavy odds; disrespect will not be taken lightly. **Note:** The little chunk of Russia (Kaliningrad) sandwiched in between Lithuania and Poland is still a sore point for Lithuania (as well as Poland).

Communications

DIALING CODES IN LITHUANIA

International country code: [370]

Selected city codes: Druskininkai (33), Ignalina (29), Kaunas (7), Kaisiadorys (56), Klaipeda (6), Marijampole (43), Mazeikiai (93), Moletai (30), Palanga (36), Panevezys (54), Plunge (18), Rokiskis (78), Siauliai (21), Silute (41), Trakai (38), Utena (39), Vilnius (2), Zarasai (70)

Dialing Lithuania from Overseas

To dial Lithuania from overseas, dial your country's international dialing code, then 370 (the country code for Lithuania), then the city code, and finally the number. If you were dialing Vilnius from the United States, for example, you would begin with 011, then 370, then 2 (the city code for Vilnius), and finally the number of the person or office you were trying to reach.

Assistance Numbers

International Operator 07

Directory Information (Kaunas) 22-222
Directory Information (Vilnius) 622-222
Telegram Booking 8-199
Infotelefonas (information service) 2704-000
Infotelefonas Commercial Directory 222-181

CALLING WITHIN LITHUANIA

Local Calls
Calling locally is mostly free in Lithuania.

Long Distance Calls
Dial 8 (wait for tone) + 2 + area code + number to call long distance within Lithuania.

Estonia, Latvia Calls
To place a call to Estonia, dial 8 + 10 + 372 + local number. Analogue numbers have 6 digits with a city code of 22. Digital numbers will have 7 digits with an initial '6'.

Latvian calls may be dialed as 8 + 10 + 371 + city code without the '2' + local number. If you cannot get through with this dialing method, try 8 + 013 + city code for a six-digit number. Seven-digit numbers will not require a city code.

International Calls
To make a direct phone call, dial 8 (wait for tone) + 10 + country code + area code + number. You can dial direct from a hotel, post office, or main train stations with card phones. If you prefer, a phone call can also be booked through an operator at the central phone and telegraph office, located at Vilniaus 33, Monday to Friday 8a.m. to 10:30p.m., weekends 8a.m. to 10p.m. Direct dialing, however, is only available to certain cities. A call to North America or Australia will cost about Lit7.32 per minute; to Europe, Lit5.80 per minute, and to South America or Asia, about Lit10 per minute. Thirty percent discounts apply between 10p.m. and 6a.m. Except from a public phone, you can reach an American operator for assistance in placing a call by dialing:

AT&T .... (8) 196
Sprint .... (8) 197

(Wait for a tone after the initial "8.")

PAY PHONES

Public Telephones
Card Phone:

Card phones are most ubiquitous in central Vilnius and may also be used for international calls. Some ancient Soviet-style phones still exist in smaller towns. As in Russia, a local call might still be free, or the search for a token begins. Otherwise, phones take 15 kopeck coins or tokens (*zetonas*), which can be purchased at a post office.

Calling Cards
News kiosks and post offices sell phone cards for the newer phones that exist in hotels, airports, train stations, and main post offices. Phone cards cost from Lit4 to Lit30.

CELLULAR PHONES/PAGERS
Lithuania offers GSM digital or NMT analogue cellular services. To place a call to a cell phone from within Lithua-

nia, dial 8 (wait for tone) + operator code + number. For example, with an Omnitel phone, you would dial 8 + 298 (the code for Omnitel) + number. Omit the initial 8-2 from the codes if dialing a cellular phone from outside the country.

Comliet 8-290
Omnitel 8-298
Bite 8-299

Note: Your home country cell phone may not work in this country. If not, we recommend that you rent an international cell phone *before* you leave home. A major US-based cell phone rental provider is **IMC WorldCell**. For information see "International Cell Phone Rentals" on page 14. Other rental sources:

Bit GSM; store: Gedimino 39; tel: (2) 224-206; office: (2) 231-300.

Comliet; Architektu 146; tel: (2) 292-929.

Hertz; Ukmerges 2; tel: (2) 726-940; fax: (2) 726-970; email: hertz@auste.elnet.lt

Nelte; (pagers) Vytenio 9-25; tel: (2) 232-334; fax: (2) 232-287; email: nelte@aiva.lt

Omnitel; (pagers and cell phones) Jaksto 24; tel: (2) 623-851, or T. Sevcenkos 25; tel: (2) 232-929.

CALL BACK
You can (potentially) save significant sums when calling in Lithuania by using one of the call back services listed below. Fees for call back services vary widely, depending on the company and the type of service required. Be sure to check with these companies before leaving to compare rates.

For a list of callback services, please refer to the "Communications" section in the *Global Road Warrior* Introduction.

PHONE JACK

Plug adaptors are available through **iGo Corporation**. (See "Electrical and Telephone Adaptors" on page 19.)

FAX
Fax machines are available at most hotels, as well as the **Foreign Tourists Service Bureau**; tel: (2) 356- 074, or also at the **Telegraph Center**, open 24 hours, and located at Universiteto 14/2; tel: (2) 626-649; fax: (2) 223-451.

POSTAL SERVICES
Postal services are efficient, particularly compared to other Eastern European countries. An airmail letter will cost Lit1.20. The central post office in Vilnius is located at:

Gedimino pr. 7, Vilnius; tel: (2) 616- 759.

Opening hours
Monday to Friday 8a.m. to 8p.m., weekends 11a.m. to 7p.m.

TELEGRAMS
Telegrams can still be sent from most hotels and post offices. The central post office has a telegram office. For telegram booking, call: 8-199.

Lithuania

Business Services

COURIER SERVICES

Airborne Express; Express Service: RGW Express Airfreight GmbH; Postfach 75 04 33, 60534 Frankfurt/Main, Germany; tel: [49] (69) 698-0080; fax: [49] (69) 6980-0840.

Freight Service: ASG Lithuania Ltd.; Kirtimu 47b Lt-2028, Vilnius; tel: (2) 64-0537; fax: (2) 64-1237.

DHL International Lietuva; Dariaus Ir Gireno Str 40, Vilnius 2600; tel: (2) 267-722; Donelaicio 46, Kaunas 3000; tel: (7) 223-129; Vilties Str 1, Klaipeda 5800; tel: (6) 340-247.

Express Mail Service; Vokieciu 7; tel: 618-024; Monday to Friday 7:30a.m. to 4:30p.m., closed between noon and 1p.m.

Federal Express; Elf 91; tel: (2) 630-397.

Serciciul de Comunicatii Postale Speciale;

MD-2068, str.Alecu Russo, 2, Kishinev; tel: (2) 444-195.

TNT Express Worldwide; Rinktines 26; tel: 732-528; Monday to Thursday 8a.m. to 5p.m., Friday until 4p.m.

UPS; Vasario 16-osios 2a; tel: 226-111; Monday to Friday 8a.m. to 7p.m.

COPYING SERVICES

Orgtechniniu Paslaugu Centras; Pamenkalnio 26; tel: (2) 227-906; Monday to Friday 9a.m. to 6p.m.

Projektservisas; Gostauto 8; tel: (2) 617-674; Monday to Friday 8:30a.m. to 5:30p.m.

Spalvoto Kopijavimo Centras; Saltiniu 3a; tel: (2) 631-082; Monday to Friday 9a.m. to 6p.m.

Zurnalistas; Gedimino 21; tel: (2) 620-931; Monday to Friday 9a.m. to 7p.m.; Saturday 11a.m. to 5p.m.

TRANSLATIONS/INTERPRETING

Litinterp; Bernardinu 7/2; tel: (2) 223-850; fax: (2) 223-559; email: litinterp@post.omnitel.net

Magistrai; Gedimino 56/1; tel/fax: (2) 619-891; email: magistrai@auste.elnet.lt

Naujasis Zodis; Basanaviciaus 23; tel: 650-110.

Parvate; Lvovo 9; tel/fax: (2) 722-191; email: parvat3e@post.5ci.lt.

Skelbk; Pamenkalnio 26; tel: (2) 222-132.

Vertimai; Sv. Ignoto 6; tel: 613-808.

Electrical

Current

120/220 AC, 50Hz.

ELECTRIC PLUGS

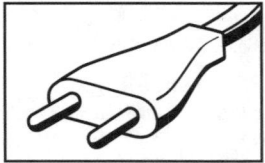

Plug adaptors are available through **iGo Corporation.** (See "Electrical and Telephone Adaptors" on page 19.)

Technical Support

HARDWARE/SOFTWARE VENDOR SUPPORT

Dell; (in Germany) tel: [49] (61) 039-710; (Dell- Europe) tel: [44] (134) 474-8000; (in the U.S.) tel: [1] (512) 338-4400; fax: [1] (512) 728-3330; http://www.dell.com/.

Filemaker/Claris; (in Germany) tel: [49] (180) 525-8166 (Info-line); fax: [49] (180) 567-2233; tel: [49] (180) 523-6423; (in the U.S.) tel: [1] (800) 965-9090; http://www.claris.com/.

Hewlett Packard; (Russian Office) tel: (7) 095 923 50 01; (in Switzerland) tel: [41] (22) 780-8111; (in the U.S.) tel: [1] (408) 246-4300; http://www.hp.com/.

IBM; tel: (2) 221-103; fax: (2) 222-173; (in Germany) tel: [49] (711) 78-50; fax: [49] (711) 785-3511; (in Switzerland) tel: [41] (22) 310-0418 (in French); (in the U.S.) tel: [1] (919) 517-2800; http://www.ibm.com/.

Microsoft; (Russian Office) [7] (501) 967-8585; fax: [7] (501) 967-8500; (in Germany) tel: [49] (89) 31-760; fax: [49] (89) 3176-1000; tel: [49] (89) 3176-1199; (in Switzerland) tel: [41] (848) 858-868; fax [41] (1) 831-0869; (in the U.S.) [1] (425) 635-7222; http://www.microsoft.com/.

NEC; (in Germany) tel: [49] (18) 0524- 1212; tel:[49] (89) 3160-1233; fax: [49] (89) 3160- 1613 (Floppy Disk and Hard Drive); tel: [49] (89) 9627-4233; fax: [49] (89) 9627-4613 (All Other Products); (in the U.S.) [1] (916) 388-0101 (Main Switchboard); http://www.nec.com/.

Toshiba; (in Germany) tel: [49] (2131) 158-319; fax: [49] (2131) 158-558; (in Switzerland) tel: [41] (1) 946-0777; fax: [41] (1) 946-0807; (in Ireland) tel: [44] (193) 282-8828; (in the U.S.) [1] (949) 583-3000 (Corporate Headquarters); http://www.toshiba.com/.

Internet Connection

HOW TO CONNECT

Connecting to AOL and Compuserve in Lithuania is similar to using it when traveling outside your own area code. See the introductory section for detailed information on connecting to your account through a different phone number.

America Online

Numbers are available at keyword *international.* Be sure to get several local numbers before leaving. AOL's GlobalNet service charges US$6 an hour in addition to the usual charges. Go to keyword *access* (a free area) and download the software.

Access: Kaunas (7) 311-340, Vilnius (2) 251-707, Vilnius (2) 734-115.

Compuserve

Numbers are available at *Go International.* The Compuserve Web-site also has a great deal of information, at http://www.compuserve.com.

There are no direct access numbers for Compuserve in Lithuania. Users will have to pay international rates to use the service.

Many independent service providers offer discounts if you are only in town for a couple of days.

EUnet Lithuania; tel: (2) 791-213; fax: 226-267; email: info@eunet.lt; http://www.eunet.lt/.

Interneka; tel: (7) 311-270; tel: (7) 313-031; email: info@interneka.lt; http://www.interneka.lt/; (Lithuanian only).

Omnitel; tel: (2) 232-929; fax: (2) 231-313; http://www.omnitel.net/; (Lithuanian only).

Taide; tel: (47) 3306-6750 ; fax: (47) 3306-6760; email: info@taide.net; http://www.taide.net/; (Norwegian company, in English).

Internet Cafes
Kaunas
Cafe Internet; Vilniaus Street 26 LT3000, Kaunas; tel: (7)) 225-364; email: mezer@takas.lt; http://www.cafenet.ot.lt/.
Vilnius

Angare; Jasinskio 14, Vilnius; (2) 251-729; fax: (2) 251-730; email: public@lithill.lt

Grazina; Sevcenkos 29-22, Vilnius; (2) 724-893; fax: (2) 725-089; Monday through Saturday, 9a.m. to 5p.m.

Internet Cafe; Ukmerges 41 Vilnius; tel: (2) 724-893; fax: (2) 725-089; email: vpk.info@taide.lt; Monday through Saturday, 9a.m. to 5p.m.

Business Culture
GREETINGS & COURTESIES

For all of its past filled with conflict and foreign invasion, Lithuania has a friendly population. Its desire to join the E.U. makes business visitors particularly welcome. Initial greetings will involve long handshakes and friendly smiles. Embraces will accompany this greeting after a longer-term association has been established. Small gifts may be exchanged (even flowers) when new guests arrive. Small talk will involve discussion of travel and family which serves the purpose of getting to know business associates before attending to business. Visitors will always receive great deference in Lithuania, and visitors from the west (especially the U.S.) may find the level of courtesy a bit much. It is sincere, however, and it should be accepted gracefully.

BUSINESS ETHIC & FRAMEWORK

Like its Baltic neighbors, Lithuania presents a separate set of business ethics to foreign firms than it does for purely domestic operations. The desire to become an E.U. member has required that foreign firms be dealt with in an honest and forthright manner comparable to most economies of Northern Europe. On the domestic front, however, visitors may find counterfeit goods and smuggled commodities in good supply. This dichotomy derives from the Lithuanian government's need to placate both western business requirements and the demands of the domestic population for a bit of the "good life" today. Foreigners will find that Lithuanian companies are willing and able to abide by contract terms and service agreements. Problems are rarely caused intentionally and mostly center around differing views of quality.

DECISION MAKING

Hierarchies are prevalent in Lithuanian business and decisions are made at the top. Foreign business visitors in a buying or investing mode should demand to deal only with the highest echelons; anything less is a waste of time. Visitors arriving to make sales in Lithuania may have to content themselves with having to meet with several layers of lower management before gaining access to the real decision-makers. Even when dealing with the highest levels, both buying and selling decisions by Lithuanian management take much longer than in developed economies. A fear of being taken advantage of by Western counterparts causes the delay and is a holdover from the Soviet era.

MEETINGS

Lithuanian managers tend to fall into two large categories: either they are relatively young and enthusiastic about the new market economics, or they are elders still in place from the Soviet era. Neither will have the advantage of modern business training, although it is more likely in the former than the latter. Meetings will be formal affairs and Lithuanians will make an effort to show their best face. Formal introductions (in declining order of rank) and an exchange of formal greetings will open initial meetings. Attendees will be seated opposite their ranking counterpart; so, it is important that visiting delegations make their job titles clear in advance of arrival. Lithuanians rarely wish to get directly into business discussions; as such, visitors can expect a lot of chitchat before serious discussions begin. Lithuanians like to make deals with people they know well, so, don't expect to sign a contract after just one meeting. Great deference is shown to the hierarchy, and junior members of visiting delegations should never address ranking members of the Lithuanian group directly. Equals deal with equals only.

Most Lithuanian companies will offer small gifts after the initial meeting and visitors should be prepared to reciprocate with business related tokens. Keep the gifts discreet and make no attempt to flaunt the wealth of your firm as it will only insult your hosts.

Each meeting will be concluded with a rather formal sounding recap of the day's topics and a toast to future dealings is quite common. Lithuanian hosts will often make an offer of an evening's socializing at this time. Decline only if absolutely necessary since these social relationships are more binding than the scant Lithuanian contract law.

WOMEN IN BUSINESS

Women managers are few and far between in Lithuania but the local male managers are not adverse to working with foreign female counterparts. Unless openly stated otherwise, however, it will be assumed that women in attendance at business meetings are there in the capacity of secretary or executive assistant. Visiting delegations should make the gender and rank of their managers clear in advance of arrival. Remember that names are not always a gender indicator so the addition of Mr., Mrs. or Ms. will assist in this area. Trade delegations often use pictures accompanied by a short CV to clarify the issues of rank and gender.

Female visitors, regardless of their managerial ranking, may find that male counterparts are not beyond making sexual comments in both social and business situations. This cultural nuance may be offensive to some but rebukes should be as diplomatic as possible since these comments are a standard in local life. Of course, visitors in a selling mode must be more tolerant than those who have arrived to buy or invest.

BUSINESS ENTERTAINING

A recent past of subjugation and poverty has not repressed the Lithuanian desire to "eat, drink and be merry."

Lithuania

They are a very gregarious culture and they like to show their guests a good (sometimes exhausting) time. Lavish dinners (by Baltic standards) with heavy food and lots of alcohol are a common form of business entertainment. Visitors with dietary restrictions should make their needs known in advance to avoid embarrassing the hosts. Visitors from Asia may find the food unappealing in appearance and content. However, just as Asian cultures expect visitors to try their cuisine, Asians visiting Lithuania should act accordingly.

Business visitors to Lithuania on extended stays should attempt to reciprocate their hosts' hospitality. Seek the advice of local restaurateurs and hoteliers but make no effort to outshine the Lithuanian counterparts.

Besides business dining, Lithuanians enjoy theater evenings and country outing; these may serve as useful alternatives when planning a social get-together. Once again, seek local advice (e.g., a hotel concierge) when making such plans.

BUSINESS ATTIRE

Lithuanian business is fairly formal in attitude and the climate makes the wearing of business suits tolerable. Men adopt the standard dark suit, white shirt, and necktie. Quality shoes, once an impossible commodity to get during Soviet times, are now standard. Both men and women visitors should be well shod as it is an indicator of wealth.

Lithuanian women may dress in a more sexually provocative manner than Western counterparts. Local styles can often seem unsuitable for business and more suitable for the cocktail lounge. Foreign female managers can avoid unwanted comments and attention by maintaining a conservative business dress standard.

Note: Both male and female visitors should avoid showy displays of wealth in the form of jewelry or overtly expensive garments. Such things only serve to cause resentment by less privileged Lithuanian counterparts.

Business Advisory

POLITICS & GRAFT

Lithuania has very little problem with graft or political favor seeking when it comes to dealing with foreign firms. Its desire to keep a reputation for fair dealing and reasonable government oversight of business is part of its strategy for gaining acceptance to the E.U. Foreign firms only need to be concerned with the fact that commercial law and taxation systems are still in the formative stages in Lithuania. Laws and taxes will change but the government resists the concept of retroactive regulation or confiscatory tax regimes.

BUSINESS FRAUD

In keeping with Lithuania's desire to enter the E.U., business fraud is minimal (especially when compared to neighboring Russia) and foreign firms will have few problems. Contract and trade disputes are usually based in differing concepts regarding the quality of goods and services rather than intentional fraud.

Business Centers
Vilnius

CITY VIEW

According to legend, Vilnius was founded after a Lithuanian Duke dreamt of an iron wolf howling with the sound of 100. After consulting a dream interpreter, the Duke built a city surrounded by a wall that would represent the wolf and stand strong as the 100 he heard howling in his dream. Now home to one of the largest Old Towns in Europe, Vilnius is a sight to behold, balanced serenely by the hand of nature and the architectural hands of its builders. The Old Town is noted for being part of the World Heritage list due to the illustrious army of Gothic, Renaissance, Baroque, and Classical architecture. Famous cathedrals worthwhile visiting include Cathedral Square, the focal point of the city. Known as the Jerusalem of Europe in the 19th Century for its large Jewish heritage, this capital city today houses a diverse population of approximately 600,000. The city's main industrial concentration lies in metal, ship building, light machinery, paper, and chemical products.

AIRPORT

Vilnius Airport to City Center

The airport is located approximately 3.5 miles (5 km) from city center, or old town Vilnius. There are two buses running from the airport with tickets available for purchase from the driver for LTL0.75 Bus No. 1 goes to the railway station, while No. 2 runs to the northern suburbs through Lukisku square and Gedimino, the main street in Vilnius' city center. Taxis from the airport will cost around LTL10. To avoid being overcharged for taxis, refer to a sign listing prices at the taxi stand. Airport currency exchange operates 24 hours in the arrival hall.

Vilnius International Airport, Rodûnios kelias str. 10a, Vilnius LT-2038, Lithuania; tel: (2) 262-135.

Airline Numbers

Aeroflot	(2) 260-357
Air Baltic	(2) 236-000; fax: (2) 233-139.
Air Lithuania	(2) 229-706, (2) 541-400
Austrian Airlines	airport, (2) 226-063.
British Airways	airport, (2) 262-167.
Estonian Air	airport, (2) 739-022
Finnair	(2) 619-339
Lithuanian Airlines	(2) 630-116
LOT	Hotel Skrydis-Vilnius Airport, (2) 739-020
	email: lotvno@lot.com.
Lufthansa	res. (2) 262-222, 636-049
	(2)223-147
	airport, (2) 636-049
SAS	airport, (2) 395-500

HOTELS

Top End

Radisson SAS Astorija Hotel; Didzioji 35/2; tel: (2) 220-110; fax: (2) 221-762; email: VNOZH@dbs.lt; located in central Old Town; restaurant; breakfast buffet; business rooms available; business services; minibar; wheelchair accessible; non-smoking rooms; Lit400-720.

Stikliai; Gaono 7; tel: (2) 627-971; fax: (2) 223-870; email: stikliai@mail.tipas.lt; located in Old Town; atrium restaurant; soundproofed rooms; secure parking; car and limousine rental; fitness room; sauna; pool; Lit580-720.

Expensive

Business Guest House; Saltoniskiu 44; tel: (2) 753-761; fax: (2) 722-298; email: bgh@tdd.lt; small, modern hotel; fax/photocopy facilities; laundry service; secure parking; sauna; pool.

Centrum; Vytenio 9/25; tel: (2) 232-770; fax: (2) 232-760; email: Centrum@post.omnitel.net; opened 1995; located in Centrum Business Center, near Old Town; restaurant; cafe; conference facilities; fax/photocopy facilities; singles with shower or bath; airport transfers; sauna; pool; Lit200-480.

City Park Hotel; Stuokos-Guceviciaus 3; tel: (2) 615-123; tel: (2) 223-515; fax: (2) 617-745; email: citypark@is.lt.; opposite Cathedral Square; cellar-bar restaurant; luxury rooms available with desks; Lit360-500.

Grybas House; Ausros vartu 3a; tel: (2) 619-695; tel: 221-854; fax: (2) 222-416; email: grybashouse@taide.lt; located in Old Town; small guesthouse hotel, 7 rooms; filtered water; heated bathroom floors; car service available; Lit320+.

Ida Basar; Subaciaus 3; tel/fax: (2) 622-909.; located in Old Town; 4 modern, luxury apartments; meeting facility; fax facilities; kitchenettes; fireplace; in-room satellite TV, mini-bar; trouser press; hairdryer available; Lit380+.

Neringa; Gedimino 23; tel: (2) 610-512; fax: (2) 614-160; email: neringa@tdd.lt; located on main street city center; top floors renovated; restaurant; conference facilities; computer and fax service; car rental office; Lit340-480.

Sarunas; Raitininku; 4; tel: (2) 723-666; fax: (2) 724-355; email: sarunas@tdd.lt; large rooms, apartments available; restaurant; conference facilities; in-room minibar; room service; secure parking; car rental; fitness; Lit 380-460.

V & G Hotel Club; Pilies 10; tel: (2) 312-206; fax: (2) 312-207; email: info@hotelclub.lt; cordless phone; in-room safe, satellite television, mini bar; Lit 750-800.

Moderate

AB Lietuvos Telekomas Sveciu Namai; Vivulskio 13a; tel: (2) 790-588; fax: 790-521; near Old Town; 10 rooms; small, new hotel for business travelers; english speaking receptionists; Lit 150-225.

Draugyste; Ciurlionio 84; tel: (2) 236-711; tel: 236-603; fax: (2) 263-101; email: hotel.draugyste@post.omnitel.net; large hotel located adjacent to Vingis park; renovated rooms available; all rooms with bath; restaurant; conference facilities; secretarial service; fax/photocopy facilities; hotel safe; in-room electric socket; room service; corporate rates; sauna; massage; Lit190-270.

Hotel Alexander; Juodasis Kelias 80; tel: (2) 220-832; fax: (2) 220-810; suburb; guest house, mansion; all rooms with satellite TV; shared baths; secured parking; gym; saunas; pools; fishing ponds; tennis; gardens; Lit340.

Karolina; Sausio 13- osios 2; tel: (2) 453-939; fax: (2) 269-341; email: hotel@karolina.lt; located in a suburb; renovated rooms available; restaurant; 3 conference rooms; secretarial services; fax/photocopy facilities; fitness; sauna; pool; tennis; Lit280-320.

Lietuva; Ukmerges 20; tel: (2) 726-092; fax: (2) 722-130; email: lietuva@aiva.lt; large hotel, Soviet style; business rooms available; business facilities; secure parking; car rental; doctor; dentist; barber; Lit180-600.

Naujasis Vilnius; Ukmerges 14; tel: (2) 726-756; fax: (2) 723-161; email: hotelnv@is.lt; business hotel; renovated rooms; fax/photocopy facilities; car rental desk; secure parking; Lit340-400.

Sanvita; Seimyniskiu 21; tel: (2) 723-428; tel: 722-090; fax: (2) 750-036; small hotel, 8 rooms; large, renovated rooms with desks; cafe; in room TV; Lit296-311.

Skrydis; Rodunes kelias 8; tel: (2) 262-223 or 739-362; fax: (2) 306-498; near airport; 50 rooms with varying amenities.

Zalias Tiltas; Gedimino Pr. 12; tel: (2) 615-460; fax: (2) 221-716.

MEDICAL CARE

Baltic-American Medical and Surgical Clinic; 124 Antakalnio St., Vilnius University Antakalnis Hospital; tel: (2) 746-134, (2) 742-020, (2) 742-590; (English spoken).

Denticja (Dental Care); Grybo 32/10, Antakalnis; tel; 709-124; high-standard of care.

Gedimino Vaistine Pharmacy; Gedimino 27; tel: (2) 610-135; 24-hour line: (2) 624-930.

Lithuanian AIDS Center; Kairukscio 2; tel: (2) 720-465.

OB & GYN Out-Patient Care; Jasinskio 17; tel: 791-312; email: kravcenka@post.omnitel.net

Rega (Optician); Pilies 32; tel: (2) 620-073; and Antakalnio 57; tel: (2) 749-208. Monday to Saturday.

Trauma Department, St. Jacob Hospital; 10 Lukiskiu Square; tel: (2) 624-483.

AUTO RENTAL

A & A Litinterp; Bernardinu 7-2; tel: (2) 223-850; fax: (2) 223-559; email: litinterp@post.omnitel.net; cars. minibuses, chauffeur-driven vehicles.

Avis; Vilnius Airport, Rodunios Kelias Street 2, Vilnius, 2038; tel: (2) 306-820; Hours: Sun. to Sat. 8a.m. to 7p.m. Downtown Office; Hotel Najasis Vilnius, Dariaus Ir Gireno 32 A, Vilnius, 2039; tel: (2) 306-820; Hours: Sun. to Sat. 8a.m. to 6p.m.

Balticar; tel: (2) 460-998; fax: (2) 758-924.

Europcar; Vilnius Airport, Roduneskelias, 2038 Vilnius; tel: (2) 263-442; fax: (2) 220-439; Downtown Office: Vilnius - L., Stuokos-Guceviciaus 9-1; 2001 Vilnius; tel: (2) 220-207; fax(2) 220-439.

Hertz; Vilnius Airport: Rodunes Kelias 2, Vilnius; tel: (2) 260-394; fax: (2) 726-970; hours: Monday-Friday 9a.m. - 5p.m., Sa-Su 10a.m.-3p.m.; tel: (2) 26 03 94; Vilnius Downtown Office: Kalvariju 14, Vilnius; tel: (2) 726-940; fax: (2) 726-970; hours: Mon. to Fri. 8a.m. to 6p.m., Sat. until 4p.m., closed Sundays; chauffeur-driven cars available.

Limousine Rental; tel: (2) 721-642.

Rimas; tel/fax: 776-213.

HEALTH CLUBS

Lietuvos Vaidu ir Jaunimo Centras; Ukmerges 25; tel: 725-657; aerobics; weight room; sauna; pool.

Nautilus Sporto Lubas; Savanoriu 22; tel: 637-974; weight room; aerobics.

Vandens SportRumai Vilnius; Aerporto 13; tel; 269-041; 50-meter pool.

Villon Hotel Fitness Center; Vilnius-Riga Highway (A2), in the Villon Hotel; weight room; pool; jacuzzi; aerobics.

WORLD TRADE CENTER

World Trade Center Vilnius
18, V. Kudirkos Str.
2600 Vilnius
Lithuania
tel: (2) 222-630; fax: (2) 222-621
email: wtcvilnius@post.omnitel.net

CHAMBER OF COMMERCE

Association of Lithuanian Chambers of Commerce and Industry
V. Kudirkos Str. 18 - 2600 VILNIUS
tel: (2) 222-617; fax: (2) 222-621.

Vilnius Chamber of Commerce
Algirdo 31
tel: (2) 235-450/550; fax: (2) 661-542.

Lithuania

Luxembourg

Luxembourg *(left margin)*

At a Glance

THE PEOPLE

Population .... 437,389 (July 2000 est.)
Growth Rate .... 1.27% (2000 est.)
Life Expectancy .... 77.13 years
Infant Mortality ... 4.83 deaths/1,000 live births (1999 est.)

Ethnic Composition

Celtic (with French and German blend), Portuguese, Italian, and European (guest and worker residents.)

Religious Composition

Roman Catholic..97%
Protestant and Jewish...3%

Languages Spoken

Luxembourgian is the predominant language, followed by German, French, and English.

Education and Literacy

Adult literacy is 100 percent, and school attendance is compulsory between ages 6 and 15.

Labor Force

Total: 236,400
By occupation: services 83.2%, industry 14.3%, agriculture 2.5% (1998 est.).

THE ECONOMY

Luxembourg's prosperous economy features moderate growth, low inflation, and negligible unemployment. The industrial sector of Luxembourg has grown more diversified, branching off into high-tech industries and shedding some of its reliance on the dominant steel industry. During the past decade, growth in the financial services sector has more than compensated for the decline in steel. Services, especially banking, account for an ever-growing portion of the economy. As a member of the E.U., Luxembourg can participate in the advantages of the open European market. Agriculture remains a small but stable sector and is based on highly productive, family-owned farms.

Exports .... US$7.5 billion (f.o.b., 1998)
Imports .... US$9.6 billion (c.i.f., 1998)
Total GDP .... $17.1 billion (1998 est.)
GDP Per Capita .... US$34,200 (1999 est.)
Unemployment .... 2.7% (1999 est.)

Inflation Rate 1.1% (1999)

Top Export Partners

Germany 33%, France 20%, Belgium 12%, U.K. 6%, U.S. 5%, Netherlands 4%.

Top Import Partners

Belgium 36%, Germany 27%, France 12%, Netherlands 5%, U.S. 4%.

Top Exports

Finished steel products, chemicals, rubber products, glass, aluminum, other industrial products.

Top Imports

Minerals, metals, foodstuffs, quality consumer goods.

BUSINESS WORKWEEK

Offices

Monday to Friday 8:30a.m. to noon and from 2p.m. to 6p.m.

Banks

Monday to Friday 9a.m. to noon, 1:30p.m. to 4:30p.m., until 5p.m. on Thursdays; but banks could vary greatly.

Government

Monday to Friday 9a.m. to 2:30p.m.

Retail

Monday 2p.m. to 6p.m.; Tuesday to Saturday 9a.m. to noon and 2p.m. to 6p.m.

HOLIDAYS

New Year's Day...January 1
Carnival .... March 6
Good Friday... April 21
Easter Monday ....April 24*
May Day ....May 1
Ascension Day ....June 1*
Whit Monday ....June 12*
National Day...June 23
Assumption...August 15
Luxembourg City Kermesse
(City of Luxembourg only ....September 1
All Saints' Day ....November 1
Christmas ....December 25
St. Stephen's Day...December 26
   *Date may vary by year.

CLIMATE

Seasons

The climate is cool, temperate, and rainy. May and June are hot and sunny, December and March are the colder months with a lot of snow.

Winters are wet, but above freezing, and summer temperatures go as high as 75°F. It rains generously all year round.

Regions

Luxembourg has little regional differences.

Money & Banking

Currency

The currency of Luxembourg is the Luxembourg Franc (LFr).

Denominations

The Luxembourg Franc comes in coin denominations of LFr50, 20, 5, and 1, and 50 centimes; and banknotes of LFr100, 500, 1,000, 2,000, 5,000.

Traveler's checks

Traveler's checks and foreign currency can be easily and efficiently exchanged at banks, foreign exchange bureaus located in the major cities, hotels, and foreign exchange kiosks at the airports. Banks offer the most variable exchange rates. Traveler's checks receive a better exchange rate than cash, or you can purchase Luxembourg currency traveler's checks before departure, which can be exchanged almost everywhere.

Luxembourg

All major credit cards are widely accepted in Luxembourg and you can get cash advances from your credit card on many of the automated teller machines. Long-term visitors should set up a checking account in Luxembourg and get an ATM card.

Belgian Francs are also widely accepted throughout the country and hold equivalent value with the Luxembourg Franc.

American Express

Amex Holdings, Inc., Ave De La Porte Neuve 34, Luxembourg 2227, Luxembourg; tel: 35241891

VAT (Value Added Tax)

Goods purchased for export may receive a sales tax refund of 12 percent. Inquire about a refund form at the shop where you are purchasing your goods. If the shopkeeper has properly filled out the form, a customs officer will then stamp the paperwork when you exit Luxembourg, and a refund will be forthcoming.

Luxembourg

Essential Terms

English	French
Yes	Oui
No	Non
Good morning	Bonjour
Hello (daytime)	Bonjour
Hello (evening)	Bonsoir
Hello (telephone)	Allo?
Good-bye	Au revoir
Please	S'il vous plaît
Thank you	Merci
Pleased to meet you	Enchanté
Excuse me; I'm sorry	Pardon
My name is _____	Je m'appelle _____
I don't understand	Je ne comprends pas
Do you speak English?	Parlez-vous anglais?

Essential Terms

English	German
Yes	Ja
No	Nein
Good morning	Guten Morgen
Hello (daytime)	Guten Tag
Hello (evening)	Guten Abend
Hello (telephone)	Guten Tag
Good-bye	Auf Wiedersehen
Please	Bitte
Thank you	Danke
Pleased to meet you	Angenehm
Excuse me; I'm sorry	Entschuldigung/ Verzeihung
My name is _____	Ich heiße _____
I don't understand	Ich verstehe nicht
Do you speak English?	Sprechen Sie Englisch?

Travel

VISA AND PASSPORT

A passport that is valid for at least three months beyond anticipated length of stay is required of all visitors except:

• citizens of E.U. countries holding a national ID card

• citizens of Andorra, Liechtenstein, Malta, Monaco, San Marino and Switzerland who possess a national ID card

Luxembourg is a member of the Schengen group, which is a collection of nations who in March of 1995 declared themselves borderless. The others in this group are Belgium, Germany, France, The Netherlands, Portugal, and Spain. Any traveler who holds a valid passport or other travel documents that are recognized by all Schengen member nations need not have a visa to travel in any of these countries. There are two caveats, however:

• If you have tickets for onward travel to a nation that does require a visa of you, it may also be required of you for entry into the Schengen nation.

• Each Schengen nation retains the right to require a visa of any national normally exempted by the group as a whole.

Following is a list of nations normally exempt from the visa requirement (E.U. nationals are automatically exempt): Andorra, Argentina, Australia, Brazil, Brunei, Canada, Chile, Costa Rica, Cyprus, Czech Republic, Ecuador, El Salvador, Guatemala, Honduras, Hungary, Iceland, Israel, Japan, Jamaica, Liechtenstein, Malawi, Malaysia, Malta, Mexico, Monaco, New Zealand, Nicaragua, Norway, Panama, Paraguay, Poland, Republic of Korea, San Marino, Singapore, Slovak Republic, Slovenia, Switzerland, Turkey (only if a permanent resident of a Schengen country), Uruguay, U.S., Vatican City, and Venezuela.

Passengers in transit who do not leave the airport and are continuing their journey aboard the first connecting aircraft within 72 hours, and who are holding confirmed tickets and other documents for onward travel, are also exempt from the need for a visa (except nationals of Afghanistan, Angola, Bangladesh, Democratic Republic of Congo, Eritrea, Ethiopia, Ghana, India, Iran, Iraq, Lebanon, Nigeria, Pakistan, Somalia, Sri Lanka, Syria and Turkey—these travelers must always have a transit visa).

Visa-free travel throughout the Schengen states is valid for a duration of 90 days maximum within a six-month period, commencing upon initial entry date into a Schengen country.

Of course, if this does not fit into your travel plans, you may apply for a visa anyway. If you apply, you will be issued one of two different Schengen-standardized visas:

• Short Stay (Tourist and Business)—single and multiple entry. This visa is good for up to three months per entry, and valid if used within six months of issuance.

• Transit (and Airport Transit)—single and double entry. This is good for five days per entry.

Substantiation of the visitor's purpose, such as an official letter of invitation or a confirmed hotel booking, must be provided, as well as proof of sufficient funds. Visa extensions are not available. A new application must be initiated each time.

Allow between two days and three weeks for application approval, varying according to the applicant's nationality and purpose of visit.

DEPARTURE FORMALITIES

A departure tax of US$10 is levied.

CUSTOMS ENTRY (PERSONAL)
Duty-free
Travelers arriving from EU countries:
- Tobacco: 800 cigarettes, 400 cigarillos, 200 cigars, or 1000g of tobacco
- Alcohol: 90 liters of wine inclusive of 60 liters of sparkling wine, 10 liters of spirits, and 20 liters under 22 percent vol, 110 liters of bee

Note: Alcohol and tobacco products are only available to passengers of 17 years of age or over.

Travelers arriving from other European countries and from outside Europe:
- Tobacco: 200 cigarettes, 50 cigars, 100 cigarillos, or 250g of tobacco
- Alcohol: 1 liter of spirits over 22 percent or 4 liters of wine
- Other: 50g of perfume and 250ml of toilet water, other goods to the value of LFr 2600

The amounts of alcohol and tobacco specified above are somewhat academic, since the import of duty-paid quantities is no longer limited between E.U. countries, technically speaking. But, if you have amounts of any items in excess of the above quantities, you may be interrogated to determine whether the goods are solely for personal use.

IMMUNIZATION
No vaccinations are required unless you are arriving from an infected area.

TIPPING
Taxi
Taxi drivers expect a 10 to 15 percent gratuity.

Porters
Porters generally receive LFr20 per bag.

Hotels
A 10 to 15 percent service charge is generally added to the bill; if in doubt, ask.

Restaurants
A 10 to 15 percent service charge is generally added to the tab. However, it is customary to round up the bill anyway.

EMERGENCY INFORMATION
Police and Crime
Luxembourg is a safe country, although the more urban areas can get rough at night. Take the normal basic precautions against petty crime. Avoid flashy displays of wealth, and dress and behave conservatively. Leave most of your cash, traveler's checks, jewelry, and your camera in your hotel safe. Carry photocopies of your passport instead of the original. Carry cash in a money belt, and use credit cards or traveler's checks for most transactions.

Never carry a stranger's baggage. Women can walk around freely, but they are advised to travel in groups at night as they might be in any other city. The police are efficient and courteous.

Emergency Numbers
Medical emergency 012
Ambulance/ Fire 112
Police.. 113

Health
Bottled water is preferred in Luxembourg, but tap water is safe to drink. Apart from normal digestive problems caused by change in diet, there are no extraordinary diseases here. The damp weather may cause sinus trouble, colds, and flu.

The medical service is of a high standard. Luxembourg has an abundance of skilled doctors who speak English; comprehensive social services cover most medical costs, and foreigners may be eligible.

INTERNAL TRAVEL
AIR
The only major airport is the Luxembourg International Airport (called Findel), located approximately six kilometers outside the capital, Luxembourg City. There are no regularly scheduled domestic flights. Due to the small size of the country, buses, trains, and automobiles are the primary means of travel.

TAXI
Taxis are abundant, and they are all metered. A minimum charge is standard, and a ten percent surcharge is levied between the hours of 10p.m. and 6a.m. On Sundays, fares increase by 25 percent. Taxis may be engaged either at a taxi stand or by telephone, but may not be hailed curbside. A tip in the range of 10 to 15 percent is customary.

AUTO
Most major auto rental agencies are represented; look for them at the airport or in offices in the cities and through hotels. Rental rates are high, but fuel is relatively inexpensive, among the cheapest in all of western Europe. To drive in Luxembourg, you must have held a valid drivers license from your country of residence for a period of at least one year. An international driving permit is required for licenses written in a non-roman alphabet.

Luxembourg has a modern, well-maintained system of highways and secondary roads. In mountainous areas, winding roads and cyclists sometimes slow traffic, and roads can prove congested during rush hour in the Luxembourg City environs. Visitors should drive defensively in high volume commuter and tourist traffic, or during winter fog and ice. Seatbelts are mandatory and horns may only be used for emergency situations. It is required of all motorists to carry Luxfr600 for payment of fines, which are assessed on the spot. Fines for driving while intoxicated are high.

For roadside assistance and further information, contact Automobile Club du Grand-Duché de Luxembourg, 54 route de Longwy, Bertrange, Luxembourg-Helfenterbruck; tel: 450 0451; website: http://www.acl.lu).

TRAIN
Luxembourg's train services rank among the most efficient in Europe, but not nearly as extensive as those in the other Benelux nations. Chemins de Fer Luxembourgeois (CFL) is the name of the national railway, and it is fully networked with the bus system. Recently, the CFL has initiated a regular schedule system called "horaire cadencé", which provides for a minimum of one train per hour at the same time each hour at every station. Almost every railway station has luggage storage facilities.

Reduced fare packages are available for weekend travel and holiday return. In addition, the Benelux Tourrail pass offers discounts all year long on rail travel in Luxembourg, Belgium, and the Netherlands, conferring unlimited travel for any five-day period within a 30-day term. Both CFL rail and CRL buses are covered by this pass. The Öko Pass (Luxfr160) is a one-day ticket for unlimited travel on all forms of public transport. The Luxembourg Card (Luxfr350 for one day) also offers unlimited travel on all forms of public transport for one to three days and includes free entrance to 34 tourist attractions.

For more detailed information, contact CFL (tel: 4990-4990 or 4990-5572; web site: http://www.cfl.lu/

Luxembourg

Luxembourg

METRO

Luxembourg has no metro / underground transit system.

BUS

Bus services in Luxembourg-Ville are efficient. One-trip, flat-fare tickets cost LFr40 for short hops around the city (not more than 10km) and may be used for one hour only. Ticket booklets consisting of 5 tickets cost LFr640. These tickets remain valid on the entire public transit network and may also be used for transit between buses and trains. Passengers may also purchase a one-day ticket for LFr160. Particular timetables are posted at their respective stops. One may purchase complete time schedules at stations or book shops. Long-distance buses also operate within Luxembourg.

TRAMS

There are no tram services at this time. However, a new Railway-Tram service that will operate on the CFL national railway lines is in the planning stage and will provide service to the suburbs and within the confines of Luxembourg City itself.

WATER TRAVEL

The Alzette River is the main waterway in the country, but there is no particular water travel of any consequence for the business traveler. Inquire locally, either in riverfront cities or through your hotel, to determine if there may be a private charter available which could be of interest to you.

TRAVEL ASSISTANCE

Office National du Tourisme (ONT)
1 rue du Fort Thüngen
(Postal address: BP 1001)
L-1010 Luxembourg-Ville, Luxembourg.
tel: 428-282; fax: 4282-8238
email: info@ont.lu
website: http://www.ont.lu
City Tourist Office Luxembourg
Place d'Armes
L-1136 Luxembourg-Ville, Luxembourg
tel: 222-809; fax: 467 070
email: touristinfo@luxembourg-city.lu
website: http://www.luxembourg-city.lu (or)
http://www.lcto.lu

Communications

DIALING CODES IN LUXEMBOURG

International country code: [352]

Dialing Luxembourg from Overseas

To dial Luxembourg from overseas, dial your country's international dialing code, then 352 (the country code for Luxembourg), and finally the number. There are no city codes.

Assistance Numbers

International Operator 0010
International Directory 016
Domestic Directory 017

CALLING WITHIN LUXEMBOURG

Local Calls

You can spend unlimited time chatting on a local call inside the city for Lfr5.

Long Distance Calls

Outside of the city or town in which you find yourself, a call will cost Lfr 5 for the first three minutes. There are no area codes to contend with thanks to the size of this country.

International Calls

To call direct from Luxembourg, dial 00 + country code + area code + number. If you prefer to pay later, or much less than from a hotel phone, head to a post office telephone center, ask to make a call, and pay the clerk upon exiting your assigned booth without any added surcharges. For help with collect or calling-card calls to the U.S., dial a convenient access number.
AT&T USA Direct Access 0-800-0111
MCI 0-800-0112

PAY PHONES

Public Telephones
Card Phone:

Public telephones are everywhere, color-coded in a wide variety of colors and service offerings. International phones have a yellow sign showing a telephone dial with a receiver in the middle.

Calling Cards

Cards are available at hotels and newsstands.

CELLULAR PHONES

Enterprise des P&T Luxembourg operates a GSM digital system in Luxembourg as well as an NMT-450 network. If you own a compatible phone, check with your operator at home to see if a roaming agreement in Luxembourg exists.

Note: Your home country cell phone may not work in this country. If not, we recommend that you rent an international cell phone *before* you leave home. A major US-based cell phone rental provider is **IMC WorldCell**. For information see "International Cell Phone Rentals" on page 14.

CALL BACK

You can (potentially) save significant sums when calling in Luxembourg by using one of the call back services listed below. Fees for call back services vary widely, depending on the company and the type of service required. Be sure to check with these companies before leaving to compare rates.

For a list of callback services, please refer to the "Communications" section in the Global Road Warrior Introduction.

PHONE JACKS

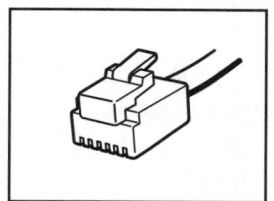

Plug adaptors are available through **iGo Corporation.** (See "Electrical and Telephone Adaptors" on page 19.)

FAX

Fax services are widespread. One can telefax from the downtown Luxembourg post office between 7a.m. and 7p.m.

POSTAL SERVICES

Mail service to the rest of Europe takes two to three days, four to ten to reach North America. The main office downtown is located at 25, rue Aldringen, tel: 49-911.

Hours of service

Monday to Friday 7a.m. to 7p.m., but will not accept packages after 5p.m.; branch post offices are usually open until 5p.m.

Business Services

COURIER SERVICES

DHL Luxembourg; 1, rue de l'Etang, Z.A.E Weihergewann, Contern, 5326; tel: 350-909; Monday to Friday 8a.m. to 8p.m.

Federal Express; tel: 0800-355-55(toll free), or [32] (2) 752-7392; Freight Hotline: [32] (2) 752-7392; 8:30a.m. to 6p.m.

TNT Express Worldwide; Zone Industrielle Sandweiler - Hall 5, L-5280 Sandweiler; tel: 357-394; fax: 357-397.

TRANSLATION/INTERPRETING

ITOC; translations, interpreting, business services, consulting; tel: 422-288-1; fax: 422-288-50; email: itoc@hermesnet.com

World Trade Center; the World Trade Center offers translation services for members, as well as other business services; tel: 408-654; fax: 408-608; email: rorelux@pt.lu

Electrical

Current

220 volts AC, 50Hz.

ELECTRICAL SOCKET

European 2-pin plugs are the norm.

ELECTRIC PLUGS

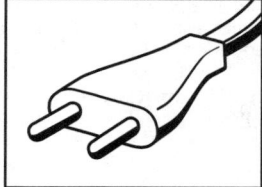

Plug adaptors are available through **iGo Corporation.** (See "Electrical and Telephone Adaptors" on page 19.)

Technical Support

HARDWARE/SOFTWARE VENDOR SUPPORT

Compaq/Digital; (in Switzerland) tel: [41] (22) 709-5330; fax: [41] (22) 709-5391 (Geneva); tel: [41] (1) 801-2507; fax: [41] (1) 801-2172 (Zurich); (General U.S.) tel: (281) 518-2000; http://www.compaq.com/.

Dell; (in Germany) tel: [49] (61) 039-710; (Dell- Europe) tel: [44] (134) 474-8000; (in the U.S.) tel: [1] (512) 338-4400; fax: [1] (512) 728-3330; http://www.dell.com/.

IBM; tel: (2) 225-3333; fax: (2) 225-2473; (in Germany) tel: [49] (711) 78-50; fax: [49] (711) 785-3511; (in Switzerland) tel: [41] (22) 310-0418 (in French); (in the U.S.) tel: [1] (919) 517-2800; http://www.ibm.com/.

Microsoft; (in Belgium) tel: [32] (02) 730-3911; fax: [32] (02) 726-9609; (in Germany) tel: [49] (89) 31-760; fax: [49] (89) 3176-1000; tel: [49] (89) 3176-1199; (in Switzerland) tel: [41] (848) 858-868; fax [41] (1) 831-0869; (in the U.S.) [1] (425) 635-7222; http://www.microsoft.com/.

NEC; (in Germany) tel: [49] (18) 0524- 1212; tel:[49] (89) 3160-1233; fax: [49] (89) 3160- 1613 (Floppy Disk and Hard Drive); tel: [49] (89) 9627-4233; fax: [49] (89) 9627-4613 (All Other Products); (in the U.S.) [1] (916) 388-0101 (Main Switchboard); http://www.nec.com/.

Toshiba; (in Germany) tel: [49] (2131) 158-319; fax: [49] (2131) 158-558; (in Switzerland) tel: [41] (1) 946-0777; fax: [41] (1) 946-0807; (in Ireland) tel: [44] (193) 282-8828; (in the U.S.) [1] (949) 583-3000 (Corporate Headquarters); http://www.toshiba.com/.

Internet Connection

HOW TO CONNECT

Connecting to AOL and Compuserve in Luxembourg is similar to using it when traveling outside your own area code. See the introductory section for detailed information on connecting to your account through a different phone number.

America Online

Numbers are available at keyword *international.* Be sure to get several local numbers before leaving. AOL's GlobalNet service charges US$6 an hour in addition to the usual charges. Go to keyword *access* (a free area) and download the software.

Access: Luxembourg: 341-501

Compuserve

Numbers are available at *Go International.* The Compuserve Web-site also has a great deal of information, at http://www.compuserve.com.

Access: Luxembourg (352) 349-933

Independent Service Providers

Many independent service providers offer discounts if you are only in town for a couple of days.

Global Media Systems; tel: 482-811; fax: 482-811/0; email: info@gms.lu; http://www.gms.lu/.

Spectrum Technology; tel: 2512-3211; fax: 2512-3311; email: conseil@hermesnet.com; http://www.hermesnet.com/. (in French only).

RESTENA; tel: 424-409; fax: 422-473; email: admin@restena.lu; http://www.restena.lu/.

Internet Cafes

Chiggeri; 15, rue du Nord Luxembourg 2229, Luxembourg; tel: 229-936; fax: 228-135; email: chiggeri@pt.lu; http://www.chiggeri.lu/english/main.htm/; rate: LFr100 per1/2 hour of use.

Business Culture

GREETINGS AND COURTESIES

Formality and standards of etiquette are well-etched into Luxembourg's business and social communities. While most of its executives speak three languages—French, German, and Luxembourgish—French is the language of commerce. Forms of address will vary depending on whom you meet. The German form is Herr (Mr.), Frau (Mrs. or Ms.), and Fraulein (Miss), followed by the person's title or surname. French forms are Monsieur (Mr.), Madame (Mrs. or Ms.), and Mademoiselle (Miss), also followed by the title or surname.

DECISION MAKING

One should make appointments prior to any meeting. Avoid holiday periods, including July and August. Phone in advance if you're running late since punctuality is prioritized. Businesspeople fluent in the language of their audience will be well respected. A relationship with Luxembourg business requires a sincere interest in the country, the people, and the desire to improve working conditions. Reply promptly to requests for information, price quotes, deliveries, and terms.

WOMEN

While most women prefer raising families to working outside the home, many women have integrated into the workforce. Typically, women are found in traditional positions as secretaries, legal assistants, and translators. Foreign businesswomen shouldn't face discrimination, however, as most businesspeople are well accustomed to dealing with women in high, managerial positions.

BUSINESS ATTIRE

Three-piece dark suits are appropriate; as are shirts and ties of somber tones. Women should always wear sweaters, wool skirts, or business suits—never pants—when conducting business. Dress is generally more formal than in North America when dining out.

Business Centers
Luxembourg City

CITY VIEW

Walking might afford the best way to view this amazingly picturesque capital with its myriad of historical sights and architectural delights set in natural surroundings. But lest the mystique of romanticism fool anyone, Luxembourg also houses a wealth of power, seating the E.C. Council of Ministers deciding the economic future of the European Community, and also being home to the highest per capita income in Europe.

AIRPORT

Findel Airport to City Center

The airport lies 4.5 miles (7 km.) from the city. There are regular bus and taxi services available. A taxi ride into town will cost about LFr600. For a less expensive alternative, Luxair runs a bus service in 30-minute intervals between 6a.m. and 10:45p.m. to the Luxembourg Air Terminal at the rail station. The fare costs about LFr140 for a 20-minute ride into town.

Airline Numbers

British Airways	348-347
Icelandair	40-27-27-27
Luxair	436-161
Sabena	212-12

HOTELS

Top-end

Inter-Continental Luxembourg; 12, Rue Jean Engling; tel: 43-781; fax: 436-095; email: luxembourg@interconti.com; 337 rooms; located in suburb, 5 minutes from downtown; 2 restaurants; bar; snack bar; 14 function rooms (up to 400); fax/photocopy facilities; secretarial services; in-room tv, movies, minibar; 24-hour room service; laundry; valet; free airport shuttle; free parking; corporate rates; fitness; sauna; massage; solarium; indoor pool; LFr6700/7700.

Le Royal; 12, Boulevard Royal, L-2449; tel: 241-6161; fax: 225-948; email: sm@hotelroyal.lu; restaurant; conference facilities (up to 650); secretarial service; business center; in-room a/c, 2-line phone, 24-hour Reuters Stock Exchange reports, CNN, Japan satellite tv, modem/fax connection; 24-hour room service; non-smoking rooms available; boutiques, hairdresser; free airport shuttle; underground garage; fitness; sauna; solarium, indoor pool; whirlpool; LFr9200/10,200.

Sofitel Hotel Luxembourg; European Centre, BP 512, L-2015; tel: 437-761; fax: 439-195; 104 rooms; city center; opened 1993; restaurant; coffee shop; cocktail lounge; conference facilities; 24-hour room service; laundry service; disabled facilities; valet services; florist; parking; sauna; solarium; indoor pool.

Expensive

Best Western International; 32, Place de la Gare; tel: 485-911; fax: 493-227; email: info@hotelinter.lu; 49 rooms; opposite Air Terminal downtown; French restaurant; complimentary breakfast; 2 conference rooms (up to 50); business lounge; 5 meeting rooms; in-room modem/fax connection, minibar, hairdryer, satellite tv, safe; laundry/valet service; non-smoking rooms; LFr3800/4900.

Gand Cravat; 29, Boulevard F.-D. Roosevelt; tel: 221-975; fax: 226-711; email: contact@hotelcravat.lu; 58 rooms (6 single, 52 doubles); located near rail station; 2 restaurants; bar; conference facilities (up to 100); in-room minibar, satellite/cable tv, video, voicemail, fax machine, analog dataport, desk; room service (7a.m. to 11p.m.); laundry/dry cleaning/ironing service; butler/valet service; 24-hour check in/out; concierge; corporate rates; LFr3900/4700.

Golden Tulip Hotel Central Molitar; Avenue De La Liberte 28; tel: 489-911; fax: 483-382; email: molitor@pt.lu; 36 rooms; business district; restaurant; lounge; conference facilities (up to 35); business center with internet access, fax/email service; in-room hairdryer, safe, smoke detectors, coffee/tea making facilities; room service; some rooms with trouser press; laundry; car rental; parking; small pets allowed.

Hotel City; Coin ave Liberté et bd Strasbourg, L - 2561; tel: 291-122; fax: 291-1133; 35 individually decorated rooms, renovated 1993; corner of shopping boulevards; adjacent railway/bus station and business center; breakfast room; bar; meeting room (up to 100); in-room bathroom, satellite tv, hairdyrer, minibar, direct dial phone, safe; room service; laundry; parking; elevator; nearby sauna, pool.

Hotel Grunewald; 10 -14 route d'Echternach, 1453 Dommeldange; tel: 436-062; fax: 420-646; 25 rooms; outside city center, 4km.; restaurant; bar; meeting rooms; in-room bathroom, minibar, safe, radio, hairdryer, cable tv, direct dial phone; room service; elevator; parking; LFr3900+.

Hotel Marco Polo; 27, rue du Fort Neipperg, L-2230; tel: 406-4141; fax: 404-884;www.marco-polo.lu/inf-an.htm; email: mail@marco-polo.lu; 300 meters from railway station; in-room shower/WC, hairdryer, direct-dial phone, satellite tv, minibar, safe; garage; LFr3950+.

Parc Belair; 109, Avenue du X Septembre; tel: 442-323; fax: 444-484; email: belair@hpb.lu; 52 rooms (39 double rooms, 13 suites); 2 km. from city center; 3 restaurants; bar; conference facilities (up to 120); business center; in-room minibar, satellite/cable tv, video, modem/fax connection, safe; room service; laundry/dry cleaning/ironing service; 24-hour check in/out; corporate rates; fitness; whirlpool; LFr4200/4700.

Parc Luxembourg; 120, Route d'Echternach, L-1453; tel: 435-643; fax: 436-903; located in suburb; restaurant; conference facilities; corporate rates; fitness; sauna; pool; whirlpool; LFr3600/4700.

President Hotel; 32 Place De Gare, L-1024; tel: 486-161; fax: 486-180; 35 rooms; located in business district; restaurant; bar; conference facilities; business center; in-room a/c, minibar, tv, direct dial phone, dataport (some rooms), movies, refrigerator (some rooms), safe, direct dial phone, bathroom, shower or whirlpool, radio butler; room service; room service (limited); laundry service; currency exchange; doctor on call; beauty salon; florist; car rental; airport transfer; parking; pool; whirlpool.

Sheraton Aerogolf; Route de Treves, Findel; tel: 340-571; fax: 340-217; http://www.sheraton.com; email: sheraton_aerogulf@ittsheraton.com; 148 rooms and suites; located 300 meters from airport; 2 restaurants; 5 meeting rooms (up to 180); secretarial service; fax/photocopy facilities; in-room modem/fax connection; 24-hour room service; 36 non-smoking rooms; free airport shuttle between 6a.m. and 11p.m.; scheduled city shuttle service; free parking; 18-hole golf club opposite hotel; BFr6300/6800.

TOP Inn Side Residence Hotel; 1 Rue Enri M. Schnadt, 1015; tel: 490-006/1; fax: 490-680; 158 rooms; located in suburbs; restaurant; bar; conference facilities; in-room a/c, minibar, direct dial phone, cable tv, CNN, movies, smoke alarms; limited-hour room service; laundry service; porter/bell hop; parking; small pets allowed; health club.

Moderate

Campanile; 22, Rte de Treves, L-2633; tel: 349-595; fax: 349-495; 108 rooms; suburbs; restaurant; meeting facilities; in-room phone, tv; non-smoking rooms; pets.

Empire; 34, Place de la Gare; tel: 485-252; fax: 491-937; 35 rooms; restaurant; in-room phone, tv; pets; corporate rates; LFr1800/3400.

Hotel Francais; 14, Pl. d'Armes, L-1136; tel: 474-54; fax:

464-274; 21 rooms; restaurant; meeting facilities; in-room phone, tv; pets.

Ibis; Route de Treves, Findel; tel: 438-801; fax: 438-802; email: H0974@accor-hotels.com; near airport; restaurant; corporate rates; LFr2600/3700.

Nobilis (a SNR Hotel); 47, Avenue de la Gare, L-1611; tel: 49 4-9 71; fax: 40 3-1 01; 47 rooms; renovated 1993; 5 minutes from rail station; restaurant; bar; conference facilities (up to 50); business center; in-room bath/shower combination, hairdryer, tv, a/c; laundry/dry cleaning; elevator; physically disabled facilities; concierge; currency exchange; free parking; corporate rates; LFr3300/3600.

Parc-Belle-Vue Hotel; 5, avenue Marie-Thérèse, L-2132; tel: 456-141; fax: 456-141/222; email: bellevue@hpb.lu; 58 rooms with 4 suites; 0.5 km. from city center; conference facilities; business center; 24-hours check-n/out; in-room satellite/cable tv; laundry/dry cleaning/ironing service.

Relais Mercure Luxembourg Centre; 30 rue Joseph Junck, L-1839; tel: 492-496; fax: 492-109; email: H1458@accor-hotels.com; 67 rooms; renovated 1995; 200 meters from train station; snack bar; continental buffet; 24-hour front desk; pets allowed; elevator; safe box; in-room bathroom, minibar, cable tv, movies, smoke detector, desk, physically disabled equipped; elevator; laundry; garage; car rental;

HEALTH CLUB

Mondorf-les-Bains Cure and Thermal Spa Resort; (Cure center; sports and leisure club; hotel) Domaine Thermal Mondorf-les-Bains; PO Box 52, L-5601 Mondorf-les-Bains; tel: 661-212-1; Tourist Office: Sydicat d'Initiative Mondorf-les-Bains, 26-28 avenue des Bains; L-5612 Mondorf-les-Bains; tel: 67-575; **Mondorf Le Club**; bodybuilding, climbing wall; tennis; squash; thermal springs; indoor/outdoor pools; wave-bath.

AUTO RENTAL

Avis; Findel Airport, Luxembourg, 1110; tel: 435-171; 2, place de la Gare, Ancien Batiment Grande Vitesse; tel: 489-595.

Budget; 300, route de Longwy; tel: 441-938.

Continental; 8, route de Treves, Senningen; tel: 348-571.

Eurodollar; 191, route de Lngwy; tel: 440-861.

Europcar; Findel, Luxembourg Airport; tel: 434-588; fax: 405-882; Luxembourg City, 84 Rte De Thionville; tel: 404-228; fax: 405-882.

Hertz; Findel Airport; tel: 434-645; fax: 435-029.

InterRent; 84, route de Thionville; tel: 404-228.

WORLD TRADE CENTER

World Trade Center Luxembourg
6-10, Place de la Gare, 4th Floor
L-1616 Luxembourg
tel: 408-654; fax: 408-608
email: rorelux@pt.lu

CHAMBER OF COMMERCE

Chamber of Commerce
7 rue Alcide de Gasperi
1615 Luxembourg
tel: 423-9391; fax: 438-326

Macau

At a Glance

Population .... 445,594 (July 2000 est.)
Growth Rate .... 1.83% (2000 est.)
Life Expectancy .... 81.6 years
Infant Mortality ... 4.49 deaths/1,000 live births (2000 est.)

Ethnic Composition
Chinese 95%
Portuguese 3%
Other 2%

Religious Composition
Buddhist 50%
None/Other 35%
Roman Catholic 15%

Languages Spoken
Portuguese is the official language, however, Chinese (Cantonese) is used most frequently; Cantonese is the language of commerce. English is also spoken in most tourist areas.

Education and Literacy
Macau has one university, which closely mirrors Macau's economic expansion pursuits in its educational offerings, most specially business administration and engineering. Most of the students come from Hong Kong. Portuguese, Chinese, and English influence through the years has offered Macau a unique educational environment. Adult literacy stands at 90 percent (around 93% of males and 86% of females are literate).

Labor Force
Total: 281,117
By occupation: industry 31%, restaurants and hotels 28%, other services 41%.

THE ECONOMY

Macau's economy can be seen as limited in its scope. It is based largely on tourism. A major draw and a substantial source of tourist revenue is gambling. In industry, the textiles and fireworks manufacturing prove the most significant. There has been an effort to branch out and diversify the industry of this tiny nation. Small industries like toys, artificial flowers, and electronics have popped up in recent years. The dominant tourist sector has accounted for roughly 25 percent of Macau's GDP, this is not including gambling, which probably represents over 40 percent of GDP. The clothing industry has provided about three-fourths of all export earnings. Macau is reliant upon China for most of its fresh water, food, and energy imports. Macau receives most of its raw materials and capital goods from Japan and Hong Kong. Throughout 1998 and 1999, Macau's economy was weak. The country reverted to Chinese administration on December 20, 1999.

Exports .... US$1.7 billion (f.o.b., 1999)
Imports .... US$1.5 billion (c.i.f., 1999)
Total Trade .... US$3.2 billion
GDP Per Capita .... US$17,500 (1998 est.)
Unemployment 6.9% (1999)
Inflation Rate .... -3% (1999 est.)

Top Export Partners
U.S. 48%, E.U. 31%, Hong Kong 8%, China 7%.

Top Import Partners
China 33%, Hong Kong 24%, E.U. 11%, Taiwan 10%, Japan 8%.

Top Exports
Textiles, clothing, toys, electronics, cement, footwear, machinery.

Top Imports
Raw materials, foodstuffs, capital goods, lubricants, fuel.

BUSINESS WORKWEEK

Offices
Monday to Friday 9:a.m. to 5:30p.m.

Banks
Monday to Friday 9:30a.m. to 4p.m., Saturday 9:30a.m. to noon.

Government
Monday to Friday 10a.m. to 3p.m.

Retail
Monday to Friday 10a.m. to 8p.m., slightly shorter hours on weekends.

HOLIDAYS

New Year..January 1
Chinese Lunar New Year .... February 5-8*
Ching Ming Festival...April 5*
Easter ....April 21-24*
Anniversary of Portuguese Revolution .... April 25
Labor Day...May 1
Dragon Boat Festival... May 30*
Camoes/Day of Portugal ....June 10
St. John the Baptist, Patron
Saint of Macau ....June 24
National Day of the People's
Republic of China ....October 1
Portuguese Republic Day....................................October 5
Chung Yeung, Festival of
Ancestors .... October 6*
All Souls' Day .... November 2*
Restoration of Portuguese
Independence, 1640.......................................December 1
Immaculate Conception...................................December 8
Winter Solistice..December 22
Christmas ....December 24-25
*Date may vary by year.

Unofficial Holidays
The Chinese residents of Macau observe Buddhist holidays that vary with the lunar calendar.

CLIMATE

Seasons
The climate is subtropical but generally cooler than its neighboring region due to the sea breeze, with temperatures averaging around 22°C (72°F) in the summer months. Temperatures in the winter occasionally drop below 10°C. From spring to summer is very wet and humid. October to December are the most pleasant times to visit the area.

Regions
There are few regional differences.

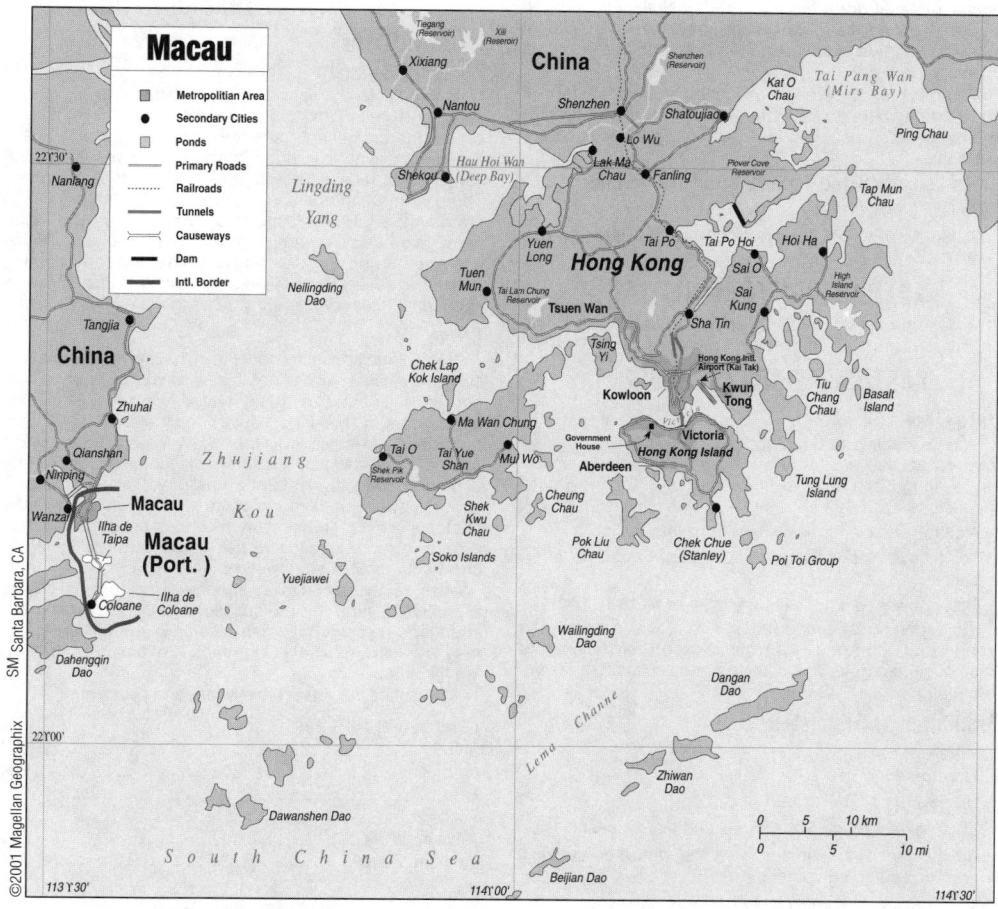

Money & Banking

Currency

The currency of Macau is the Pataca (P).

Denominations

The Pataca comes in coin denominations of P5, and 1, and 50, 20, and 10 avos; and banknotes of P10, 20, 50, 100, 500, and 1,000.

Traveler's checks

Traveler's checks and currency can be exchanged at banks, exchange shops, and hotels, as well as international airports, at tourist exchange rates, with various rates of exchange. Larger banks may offer the best exchange rates, but avoid black marketers at all cost. Consult your bank about current exchange rates before departure. Keep all receipts for reconversion.

Cash can also be exchanged, but try to take only crisp and new notes, wrinkled and soiled notes are likely to be refused.

Major credit cards, American Express, Visa, Diner's Club, and MasterCard, are easily accepted in most up-market places in the main cities, but smaller restaurants and shops may ask for cash. Some banks in the capital offer cash advances on credit cards, but make sure you bring you passport.

Some banks in the capital offer cash advances on credit cards, but make sure you bring your passport.

Travel

VISA AND PASSPORT

Macau was made a Special Administrative Region of China, effective December 20, 1999. The policy is that of "one country, two systems": Macau maintains its own economic, political, and social systems under an agreement that has a term of 50 years. Both Chinese and Portuguese continue to be the official languages.

All visitors are required to have a valid passport, regardless of nationality. A visa is not necessary for nationals of Australia, Austria, Brazil, Canada, EEC Countries, Finland, India, Japan, Malaysia, Mexico, New Zealand, Norway, Philippines, Singapore, Sweden, Switzerland, South Africa, South Korea, Thailand, and the United States for visits of less than 20 days.

Residents of Hong Kong may enter with a Hong Kong Identity Card or a Hong Kong Permanent Identity Card for stays of up to 90 days. Those carrying a Hong Kong reentry permit may stay up to 20 days.

For most other nationals, visas may be procured upon

arrival in Macau for a fee of MOP100. Nationals of countries that do not have diplomatic relations with Portugal must obtain visas in advance from Portuguese consulates overseas.

There is only one type of visa, and it is valid for stays of up to 20 days. It can be extended for one month, free of charge, by applying to the immigration office once you are in Macau.

- Individual: MOP100 (or MOP50 for children under 12)
- Family: MOP200
- Group: MOP50 per person for officially affiliated groups of 10 or more individuals.

DEPARTURE FORMALITIES

A departure tax of MOP130 (HK$25) per person is levied on all visitors, payable in local currency.

CUSTOMS ENTRY (PERSONAL)

Duty-free

A reasonable amount of tobacco, alcohol, and perfume for personal use. No export duties apply. But those returning to Hong Kong must comply with Hong Kong customs' regulations. Duty-free allowances are as follows:

- Alcohol: one liter of spirits and one liter of wine
- Tobacco: 200 cigarettes, or 50 cigars, or 250 gr. of tobacco
- Other goods with a maximum value of MOP 10,000

No export duties are levied, but, as travel is usually via Hong Kong, the Hong Kong import/export regulations are to be observed (refer to the Hong Kong section for relevant information).

Prohibited or Restricted

- Drugs
- Firearms
- Narcotics
- Endangered species of animals and plants, pesticides
- A 5 percent duty is imposed on the import of electrical appliances and equipment.

IMMUNIZATION

No inoculations are required, unless you are arriving from an area infected with cholera, or if cholera has been detected in either Hong Kong or Macau. Check for latest information.

TIPPING

Taxi

A tip of about ten percent beyond the metered fare is customary. If you are in a cab without a meter, the fare you negotiate in advance should be inclusive of any tip.

Porters

Usually, a tip in the range of about MOP 50 per bag is sufficient; conveyance of baggage under difficult circumstances or inordinately long distances calls for a greater amount, of course.

Hotels

Usually, a service charge of ten percent is added to the bill. You may want to tip individually to certain staff, or add a gratuity directly to the bill.

Restaurants

A service charge of ten percent is generally added to the tab, but a modest additional tip is customary.

EMERGENCY INFORMATION

Police and Crime

Personal Security

Violence stemming from organized crime has increased recently in Macau and has the potential for being a security concern to the general public. Police claim the violence is linked exclusively to gang wars, mostly over shrinking gambling profits, reduced due to regional economic downturn. There were 37 murders in Macau between January 1 and December 20, 1999. Police, public officials, or gang members have been the targets of most of the violence, which has generally occurred around casinos in the early morning hours. It is advisable for visitors to travel in groups, and only in the daytime or during early evening hours.

Crime

Petty crime sometimes occurs in the tourist areas, especially the vicinities of casinos. There have also been a number of incidents of gang-related violence, including bombings and shootings, usually near casinos.

Visitors are advised to take basic precautions against petty crime. Avoid flashy displays of wealth, and dress and behave conservatively. Leave most of your cash, traveler's checks, jewelry, and your camera in your hotel safe. Carry photocopies of your passport instead of the original. Carry cash in a money belt, and use credit cards or traveler's checks for most of your transactions.

Walk with your bag away from the street to avoid having it snatched away by motorcycle thieves. Never carry a stranger's baggage. Women can walk around freely, but they are advised to travel in groups to avoid harassment in the night hours.

The police are relatively efficient and courteous.

Emergency Numbers

S.O.S.	999
Ambulance	999
Fire	999
Police	999
Judiciary Police	919
Maritime Police	559-944

Health

There are no chronic endemic diseases, and tap water is considered safe to drink. However, diarrhea is common for travelers who are unaccustomed to the new diet and water, so bottled water is probably a good idea, especially if a visitor is not staying long. Wash all vegetables in a chlorine solution, peel fruits, and avoid uncooked food. Drink only powdered or tinned milk and avoid other dairy products since they are most likely unpasteurized. Most fare served in restaurants is perfectly healthful.

Should you become ill or injured, there is the option of traveling to Hong Kong, only a short hydrofoil or helicopter ride away. However, medical services in Macau are excellent, and many of the doctors and physicians have been trained abroad. There are two hospitals in Macau (including one with a new wing of operating rooms, and surgical and medical clinics), as well as other private clinics and health centers, and hotel doctors in top-end hotels.

A travel insurance package that includes an evacuation policy should be acquired by all business travelers.

INTERNAL TRAVEL

AIR

A little over half the flights that service Macau's Airport fly to destinations in China, including Air Macau's daily flights to Beijing and Shanghai. Cities outside of China include Bangkok, Pyongyang, Singapore, Taipei, Kuala Lumpur, Manila, and Lisbon. Otherwise, visitors first fly to Hong Kong and travel to Macau via ferry or helicopter.

There is a website for Macau's own airline, Air Macau: www.airmacau.com

TAXI

Most of the taxis in Macau are black with a cream colored top. Radio taxis are yellow (tel: 519 519). Fares start at MOP9 for the initial 1500 meters, with MOP1 for every 220 meters following. Expect surcharges of P$5 and P$10 for trips from Macau to Taipa and Coloane respectively, but not for the reverse trip.

Rickshaws and pedicabs are also available for hire; the Hotel Lisboa and the ferry terminal are the two primary pickup locations. Chauffeur-driven limousines can also be easily procured. Negotiate fares prior to departure. Write all directions on paper for your driver.

AUTO

Rental cars are available at hotels or at the ferry terminal. To drive in Macau, travelers must have held a valid drivers license from their country of residence for at least two years. Although not required, an international driving permit is recommended for translation purposes and should be presented in addition to a valid driver's license from your country of residence. Renters must register their driver's license with the local traffic authorities.

Traffic in Macau moves on the left. Roads are usually congested throughout the day. There are two bridges: one is a span to Taipa Island, and the other a new bridge sustaining a four-lane highway that runs between the international airport and the border with China at Zhuhai.

BUS

Bus services, which are efficient and inexpensive, operate throughout the city. Buses run between 7a.m. and midnight. Fares cost P$2 within the city. Buses 3, 3A, 10, 12, 23, 28C, and 32 also service the piers. Fares to Taipa and Coloane Village cost P$2.50 and P$3.30 respectively.

WATER TRAVEL

Jetfoil, turbocats, foilcats, and express service ferries operate in 15- to 30-minute intervals and take about 55 minutes to cross the waters between Hong Kong and Macau. Ferries depart from the Macau Outer Harbour Maritime Terminal. Fares range from MOP$182 for first-class night service on the jetfoil to MOP$119 for standard class on the Catamaran. The jetfoil offers the fastest crossing in 55 minutes, while the Turbo Cat makes the crossing in one hour; for the Catamaran, add 10 minutes. Boat tickets are also available at the airport arrivals hall. See the "Business Centers" section for further information and telephone numbers.

TRAVEL ASSISTANCE

**Direcção dos Serviços de Turismo
(Macau Government Tourist Office)**
Largo do Senado 9, Edificio Ritz, Macau
tel: 315 566 or 340 390 (tourist hotline)
fax: 510 104.
email: mgto@macautourism.gov.mo
website: http://macautourism.gov.mo

Central Office of the Government of Macau SAR
Alameda Dr Carlos D'Assumpção, Nape, Macau
tel: 797 8111; fax: 725 468 or 797 8117
website: http://www.macau.gov.mo

Essential Terms

English	Cantonese
Yes	*Hoe-geh*
No	*Ng-tak*
Good morning	*Jou-sran*
Hello (daytime)	*Lay gay hoemah?*
Hello (evening)	*Joe-tao*
Hello (telephone)	*Wai!*
Good-bye	*bye-bye*
Please	*ng goy*
Thank you	*Daw jyeh (for a gift)*
	Ng goy (for service)
Pleased to meet you	*Hoe goe-hing nung gow geen dow lay*
Excuse me; I'm sorry	*Dui ng joo*
My name is _____	*Ngaw gaw meng gyoo _____*
I don't understand	*Ngoh M ming*
Do you speak English?	*Jeong taai-taai sik gong*

Communications

DIALING CODES IN MACAU
International country code: [853]

Dialing Macau from Overseas
To dial Macau from overseas, dial your country's international dialing code, then 853 (the country code for Macau), and finally the number. There are no city codes.

Assistance Numbers
International Directory 101
English/Chinese Directory 181
Portuguese Directory.. 185

CALLING WITHIN MACAU

Local Calls
Local calls are free from private phones, shops, and restaurants. An advanced digital telecommunications system ensures hassle-free calling.

Long Distance Calls
No long distance codes exist on the island of Macau. Simply dial the number you wish to reach. To Hong Kong, dial 01 + number.

International Calls
To make a direct international call, dial 00 + country code + area code + number, except to Hong Kong, which requires one to dial 01 + number. If not from the hotel, you can make an international call from the telephone office connected to the main post office at Leal Senado (8a.m. to midnight, Monday to Saturday; 9a.m. to midnight on Sundays); or the telephone office on Avenida do Dr Rodrigo

Macau

Rodrigues (9a.m. to 8p.m. Monday to Saturday). Make a deposit with the clerk who will dial for you.

To reach an operator in the U.S., dial:

AT&T 0800-111
MCI 0800-131

PAY PHONES

Public Telephones

A little difficult to find on the spot, some public phones are located in hotel lobbies or near the main post office. P1 will buy you five minutes of air time.

Calling Cards

Some telephones take cards, which can be purchased in denominations of P50, 100 and 200 at the telephone center in the main post office.

CELLULAR PHONES

Compania de Telecom Macau offers a GSM digital service and a TACS analogue system.

Note: Your home country cell phone may not work in this country. If not, we recommend that you rent an international cell phone *before* you leave home. A major US-based cell phone rental provider is **IMC WorldCell**. For information see "International Cell Phone Rentals" on page 14.

CALL BACK

You can (potentially) save significant sums when calling in Macau by using one of the call back services listed below. Fees for call back services vary widely, depending on the company and the type of service required. Be sure to check with these companies before leaving to compare rates.

For a list of callback services, please refer to the "Communications" section in the Global Road Warrior Introduction.

PHONE JACKS

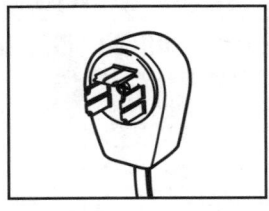

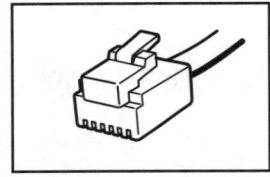

Plug adaptors are available through **iGo Corporation**. (See "Electrical and Telephone Adaptors" on page 19.)

FAX

Major hotels have fax facilities.

POSTAL SERVICES

Expect about five to seven days for airmail to Europe and North America. Mail service is efficient.

TELEGRAMS

Telegrams can be sent from hotels and telecommunications offices.

Business Services

COURIER SERVICES

DHL Transportes Lda., tel: 372-828; 14-16 Beco do raia Grande, Edif. Hoi Tin R/C; Monday to Friday 9a.m. to 6:30p.m., Saturday 9a.m. to 1p.m.

Federal Express; tel: 703-333; Av. De Amizade R/C, Loja "N", EDF Chong Yu; Monday to Friday 9a.m. to 6p.m., Saturday 9a.m. to 5p.m.

TNT Macau; tel: 2331-2663, 2331-4600; fax: 2331-2266, 2331-3191; telex: 3811 TNT Hong Kong.

UPS Hong Kong; Ste. 602-610 North Tower, World Finance Center, Harbour City, Tsimshatsui, Kowloon; tel: (852) 2735-3535; fax: 2738-5071.

Electrical

Current

220 volts AC, although some older buildings may still use 110 volts AC, 50Hz

ELECTRIC PLUGS

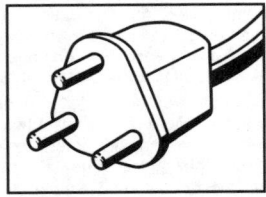

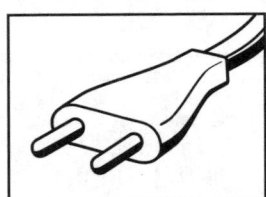

Plug adaptors are available through **iGo Corporation**. (See "Electrical and Telephone Adaptors" on page 19.)

Technical Support

HARDWARE/SOFTWARE VENDOR SUPPORT

Apple/Claris; (in Australia) tel: [61] (2) 9452-8000; (in Hong Kong) tel: [852] (1) 2506-8888; (in Switzerland) tel: [41] (800) 833-310; (in the U.K.) tel: [44] (990) 127-753; (in the U.S.) tel: [1] (408) 996-1010 (Corporate Headquarters); http://www.apple.com/.

Compaq/Digital; (Hong Kong Office) tel: (01) 2868-1382; fax: (01) 2524-9533; (in Switzerland) tel: [41] (22) 709-5330; fax: [41] (22) 709-5391 (Geneva); tel: [41] (1) 801-2507; fax: [41] (1) 801-2172 (Zurich); (General U.S.) tel: (281) 518-2000; http://www.compaq.com/.

Dell; tel: (604) 810-4948; (in Germany) tel: [49] (61) 039-710; (Dell- Europe) tel: [44] (134) 474-8000; (in the U.S.) tel: [1] (512) 338-4400; fax: [1] (512) 728-3330; http://www.dell.com/.

IBM; tel: 786-687; fax: 782-136; (in Hong Kong) tel: (852) 2825-6222; fax: (852) 2810-0210; (in Switzerland) tel: [41] (848) 858-868; fax [41] (1) 831-0869; (in the U.S.) [1] (425) 635-7222; http://www.microsoft.com/.

Microsoft; (in the Philippines) tel: [63] (2) 811-0062; fax: [63] (2) 811-0458; (in Switzerland) tel: [41] (848) 858-868; fax [41] (1) 831-0869; (in the U.S.) [1] (425) 635-7222; http://www.microsoft.com/.

NEC; (in Hong Kong) tel: (1) 795-2111 (UltraCare Support); (in the U.S.) [1] (916) 388-0101 (Main Switchboard); http://www.nec.com/.

Internet Connection
HOW TO CONNECT

Connecting to AOL and Compuserve in Macau is similar to using it when traveling outside your own area code. See the introductory section for detailed information on connecting to your account through a different phone number.

America Online

Numbers are available at keyword *international.* Be sure to get several local numbers before leaving. AOL's Global-Net service charges US$6 an hour in addition to the usual charges. Go to keyword *access* (a free area) and download the software.

Access: Macau 861-441

Compuserve

Numbers are available at *Go International.* The Compuserve Web-site also has a great deal of information, at http://www.compuserve.com.

Access: Macau 861-441

Independent Service Providers

Many independent service providers offer discounts if you are only in town for a couple days.

Companhia de Telecomunicacoes de Macau;

tel (Hotline): 1000; e-mail: mktg@macau.ctm.net

Fiberlink Communications; (a U.S. company offering service in Macau) tel: [1] (610) 941-2050; toll free in the U.S.: 1-800-546-5669; fax: [1] (610) 941-2069; email: info@fiberlinkcc.com; http://www.fiberlinkcc.com/.

Internet Cafes

Internet cafes may not be an option in Macau. Check with your hotel to see if there is an establishment that offers Internet service to the public.

Business Culture
GREETINGS AND COURTESIES

Macau's population is about 95 percent Chinese. Handshaking is the accepted greeting. Chinese usually shake hands very lightly. Upon meeting someone, they will lower their eyes slightly as a sign of respect. Staring into the eyes of a Chinese might make an individual uncomfortable. Face, a measure of one's dignity, remains a crucial element in Chinese culture. Saying or doing anything that causes someone to lose face can instantly destroy a relationship. Never insult or openly criticize someone in front of others. Do not treat someone as a person of lowly rank if their position in the company is high. A person's face reflects the company's face. The relationship you develop with an individual represents your relationship with his or her entire company.

DECISION MAKING

Chinese try to avoid saying no, for fear of causing embarrassment or losing face. Instead of directly saying no, it is more common to say something is inconvenient or under consideration. If bad news stands on the horizon, a Chinese might well convey it through an intermediary or hint at it rather than state it directly. One would be well advised to practice the same in order to save face.

WOMEN

Women will probably not find open discrimination; however they should behave professionally and dress formally. A self-confident, poised woman could achieve a great deal because Chinese may feel that if she has been chosen to represent her company, she is someone with great ability.

MEETINGS

Meetings will begin with small talk. Business is addressed only after people feel comfortable with each other. One person, preferably your group's senior member, should be designated as your spokesperson, and this person should lead discussions throughout the negotiation process. Ensure that other team members do not openly contradict the designated spokesperson. If there is debate to be had, do it when your hosts are not present.

Remember, also, that business cards are essential. Treat cards with respect; do not simply pocket them or cast them casually aside. Take care to look at the card and offer thanks. Never write on a card. Consider the way you treat a business card as another important means to show respect to an individual.

BUSINESS ATTIRE

The cultural call for respectable image along with aspirations of success call for proper attire. Business attire is Western in style and relatively formal. Maintaining a polished and manicured look will help to garner respect. Bring an umbrella for the summer monsoon months.

Business Centers
CITY VIEW

Since December 1999, the People's Republic of China has had sovereignty over Macau. Formerly a territory of Portugal, Macau was once one of the most important commercial centers in the Orient and an essential port for routes to Europe, China, and Japan. Its quaint, cobblestone streets are filled with intriguing points of historical interest.

Macau is made up of a small, narrow peninsula and includes the islands of Taipa and Coloane, which are connected by bridge and causeway. The country name comes from the Chinces A-mangao, or "Bay of A-ma". Most of the population is Chinese and lives in the city, with Cantonese and Portuguese representing the official languages. English is also widely used.

Tourism and gambling are the main industries and the city is very popular with travelers who ferry over from Hong Kong. As a free port, trade is still vital and the mainland supplies the majority of food and consumer goods to the country. Natural resources include fish, and agriculture includes rice, vegetables, some cattle, buffalo, pigs and poultry. Among Macau's exports are toys, fireworks, incense, and electronics. Gold smuggling also flourishes. Macau is part of the World Trade Organization.

AIRPORT

Macau International Airport to City Center

Taxis and buses are available at Macau's Airport. Taxis will cost about MOP40.00. The AP1 Airport Bus takes passengers into central Macau, to major hotels, the Macau Ferry Terminal, and finally the Macau/China border crossing. Expect to pay MOP6.00. Buses depart every 15 minutes from the airport. One can purchase boat tickets for Hong Kong in the airport arrivals hall.

HELICOPTER

Operating between the Macau Maritime Terminal and Hong Kong's main sea terminal in Shun Tak Center (above MTR's Sheung Wan station on Hong Kong Island), helicopters fly in 30-minute intervals between 9:30a.m. and 6p.m. and in one-hour intervals between 6p.m. and 10p.m. on a daily basis. The cost of the 20-minute trip starts at P$1,202 from Macau (P$1,206 from Hong Kong) for weekday flights plus an added P$100 for weekends and holidays. Book helicopter reservations in advance.

FERRY

Jetfoil, turbocats, foilcats, and express service ferries operate in 15 to 30-minute intervals and take about 55 minutes to cross the waters. Ferries depart from two points in Hong Kong: Shun Tak Center on Hong Kong Island, or the China Ferry Terminal adjacent to Harbour City on Kowloon Island (for Jumbocats and hover ferries). Jetfoils run 24 hours a day. Tickets cost between P137 and P254, depending on class of travel and time of day. Passengers are advised to arrive 30 minutes prior to departure to complete immigration procedures and any baggage check-in formalities. Many high-speed ferries and jetfoils only allow carry-on luggage on board. Other luggage will have to be checked in at the terminal for a fee or handled by a luggage service.

From Macau, ferries depart from the Macau Outer Harbour Maritime Terminal. Fares range from MOP$182 for first class night service on the jetfoil to MOP$119 for standard class on the Catamaran. The jetfoil offers the fastest crossing in 55 minutes, while the Turbo Cat makes the crossing in one hour; for the Catamaran, add 10 minutes. Boat tickets are also available at the airport arrivals hall.

Transportation Numbers

East Asia Helicopter ....(853) 790-7040
....in Hong Kong: (852) 2859-3359
Jetfoil Pier.. 572-983
Far East Hydrofoil Co. ....(853) 790-7039
....in Hong Kong: (852) 2859-6596
CTS-Parkview Turbo Cat ....(853) 726-789
....in Hong Kong: (852) 2921-6688
Hong Kong & Yaumati Ferry Co...............(852) 2516-9581
Hong Kong Hi-Speed Ferries ....(852) 2815-3043
Kowloon HK Ferries Catamaran...................(853) 726-301
....in Hong Kong: (852) 2516-2325
Central HK Ferries Catamaran.....................(853) 726-301

HOTELS

Top End

Bela Vista; 8-10 Rua Comendador Kou Ho Neng; tel: (853) 965-333; fax: (853) 965-588; suites; small, very exclusive, century-old hotel; restaurant with verandah; bar; conference room (12); transportation service; P$1,700+.

Hyatt Regency Macau; 2 Estrada Almirante Marques Espartero, Taipa Island; tel: (853) 83-1234; fax: (853) 83-0195; e-mail: hyatt@macau.ctm.net; 326 rooms; resort setting; 2 restaurants; cafe; bar; deli; poolside restaurant; business center; 11 function rooms; fax facilities; business equipment available; 24-hour. room service; laundry; doctor on call; hair salon; florist; shops; gym; aerobics; spas; sauna; massage; solarium; pool; whirlpool; tennis; squash; basketball; bike rental.P$990+.

Mandarin Oriental; 956-1110 Avenida de Amizade, Outer Harbour; tel: (853) 567-888; fax: (853) 594-589; e-mail: mandarin@macau.ctm.net; 435 rooms; near ferry terminal; 5 restaurants; bar; cafe; snack shop; casino; 7 function rooms (up to 240); business center; secretarial services; computers; Internet access; translation; in-room safe; in-room fax machines on request; 24-hour. room service; express laundry; medical clinic; hair salon; florist; shops; car rental; parking; limousine and shuttle service; gym; health center; sauna; pool; whirlpool; tennis; squash; P$1,080+.

New Century; Estrada Alimirante Marques Esparteiro; tel: (853) 831-111; fax: (853) 832-222; restaurants; meeting/banquet facilities; business center; shuttle service to ferry and casinos; fitness; sauna; massage; pool; tennis; squash; P$1,050+.

Expensive

Pousada de Sao Tiago; Fortaleza de S. Tiago da Barra, Avenida da Republica; tel: (853) 378-111; fax: (853) 853-552-170; 24 rooms; located in residential area; originally a fortress built in the early 17th century by the Portuguese; overlooks Macau Harbor; European style; restaurants; conference room (up to 24); pool; terrace; P$1,118+.

Pousada Ritz; Rua Boa Vista; tel: (853) 339-955; fax: (853) 317-826; 3 restaurants; conference facilities (up to 200); gym; sauna; indoor pool; whirlpool; P$1,180+.

Moderate

Grandeur; Rua de Pequim; tel: (853) 781-233; fax: (853) 781-211; e-mail: grandeur@macau.ctm.net; 338 rooms; downtown; 3 restaurants including revolving rooftop restaurant; karaoke bar; coffee shop; business center; banquet facilities; hair salon; limousine service; non-smoking rooms available; gym; sauna; steam room; indoor pool; P$800-900.

Nam Yue; Avendida Do Dr. Rodrigo Rodrigues, Edf. Centro International; tel: (853) 726-288; fax: (853) 726-726; 288 rooms; Chinese restaurant; bar; coffee shop; business center; conference facilities; non-smoking rooms available; transportation service; laundry; hair salon; parking; fitness; sauna/spa; pool; nightclub. P$680+.

New World Emperor; Rua de Xangai; tel: 781-888; fax: 782-287; 395 rooms; located in new city center development; remodeled in 1998; restaurant; bar; coffee shop; conference facilities; fax/photocopy facilities; secretarial/translation services available; 24-hour. room service; laundry; limousine service; shuttle service; parking; sauna; P$780+.

AUTO RENTAL

Avis; Mandarin Oriental Hotel, Shopping Arcade/Car Park; tel: 336-789; fax: 314-112; Maritime Terminal/Pier, First Floor 1022, Avenida Da Amizade, Macau, 4305; tel: 726-571.

Happy Rent a Car; No. 64, Istmo Ferreira do Amaral, G/F Macau; tel: 439-393; fax: 439-696; Hotel New Century, tel: 831-212; Macau Ferry Terminal, tel: 726-868; fax: 726-888.

WORLD TRADE CENTER

World Trade Center Macau SARL
Avenida da Amizade, No. 918
Edificio World Trade Center, 17th Floor
tel: 727666; fax: 727633
email: wtcmc@macau.ctm.net
http://www.wtc.macau.com

Malaysia

At a Glance

THE PEOPLE

Population .... 21,793,293 (July 2000 est.)
Growth Rate .... 2.01% (2000 est.)
Life Expectancy .... 70.83 years
Infant Mortality . 20.96 deaths/1,000 live births (2000 est.)

Ethnic Composition

Malay and other indigenous 58%
Chinese 26%
Indian.. 7%
Others.. 9%

Religious Composition

Peninsular Malaysia
Muslim (Malays), Buddhist (Chinese), Hindu (Indians);
Saba
Muslim 38%
Christian 17%
Other 45%
Sarawak
Tribal religion... 35%
Buddhist and Confucianist.. 24%
Muslim.. 20%
Christian 16%
Other 5%

Languages Spoken

Peninsular Malaysia: Malay, English, Chinese dialects, Tamil.
Sabah: English, Malay, numerous tribal dialects, Chinese (Mandarin and Hakka dialects predominate)
Sarawak: English, Malay, Mandarin, numerous tribal languages.

Education and Literacy

Religious and secular schools train students. Compulsory education lasts nine years. Overall adult literacy is 83.5 percent. Adult literacy is over 80 percent in Peninsular Malaysia and dips down to 60 percent in Sabah and Sarawak. Along gender lines there is quite a disparity. In the adult population 89.1 percent of males are literate, as opposed to 78.1 percent of females.

Labor Force

Total: 9,300,000
By occupation: manufacturing 27%, agriculture, forestry, and fisheries 16%, local trade and tourism 17%, services 15%, government 10%, construction 9%.

THE ECONOMY

Malaysia's GDP grew 5 percent, spurred on by a dynamic export sector. The export sector itself grew over 10 percent. The country has made a remarkable economic comeback in 1999 from its worst recession since its independence in 1957. The significant export surplus allowed the country to build up its financial reserves to $31 billion by the end of 1999. Malaysia's economic stability, in which both unemployment and inflation stand at 3 percent or less, has made it possible for the government's relaxation of most of the capital controls that had been implemented in 1998. These controls were an effort to counter the effects of the Asian financial crisis. Malaysia is expected to contin-

ue this positive trend in 2000, predicting GDP growth of 5 percent to 6 percent. While Malaysia's immediate economic situation is positive, the long-term prospects are questionable. The government's lack of reforms in the corporate sector could hinder prolonged growth.

Exports .... US$83.5 billion (1999 est.)
Imports .... US$61.5 billion (1999 est.)
Total Trade .... US$145 billion (1999 est.)
GDP Per Capita .... US$10,700 (1999 est.)
Unemployment .... 3% (1999 est.)
Inflation Rate 2.8% (1999)

Top Export Partners

U.S. 23%, Singapore 16%, Japan 11%, Hong Kong 5%, Netherlands 5%, Taiwan 5%, Thailand 3%.

Top Import Partners

Japan 21%, U.S. 18%, Singapore 14%, Taiwan 5%, South Korea 5%, Thailand 4%, China 3%.

Top Exports

Electronic equipment, petroleum and liquefied natural gas, chemicals, palm oil, wood and wood products, rubber, textiles.

Top Imports

Machinery and equipment, chemicals, food, fuel and lubricants.

BUSINESS WORKWEEK

Offices

Monday to Friday 8:30a.m. to 5:30p.m, Saturday 8:30a.m. to 1p.m.
*There is a gradual move toward a five-day week of 40 working hours.

Banks

Monday to Friday 9:30a.m. to 4p.m., Saturday 9:30a.m. to noon.

Government

Monday to Friday 8a.m. to 4:15p.m., Saturday 8a.m. to 12:30p.m.

Retail

Monday to Friday 10a.m. to 10p.m. for larger stores and department stores, slightly shorter hours on the weekend; 9:30a.m. to 7p.m. others.

HOLIDAYS

New Year's Day....................................January 1
(Except in Johor, Keday, Kelantan, Perlis and Terengganu.)
Hari Raya Puasa
(end of Ramadan) ....January 8-10*
Chinese New Year .... February 5-7*
Hari Raya Haji, Feast
of the Sacrifice...March 16-18*
Maal Hijrah ....April 6*
Labor Day...May 1
Vesak Day... May 18*
Official Birthday of HM the
Yang di-Pertuan Agong...June 3
Mouloud, Prophet Muhammad's
Birthday June15*

Malaysia

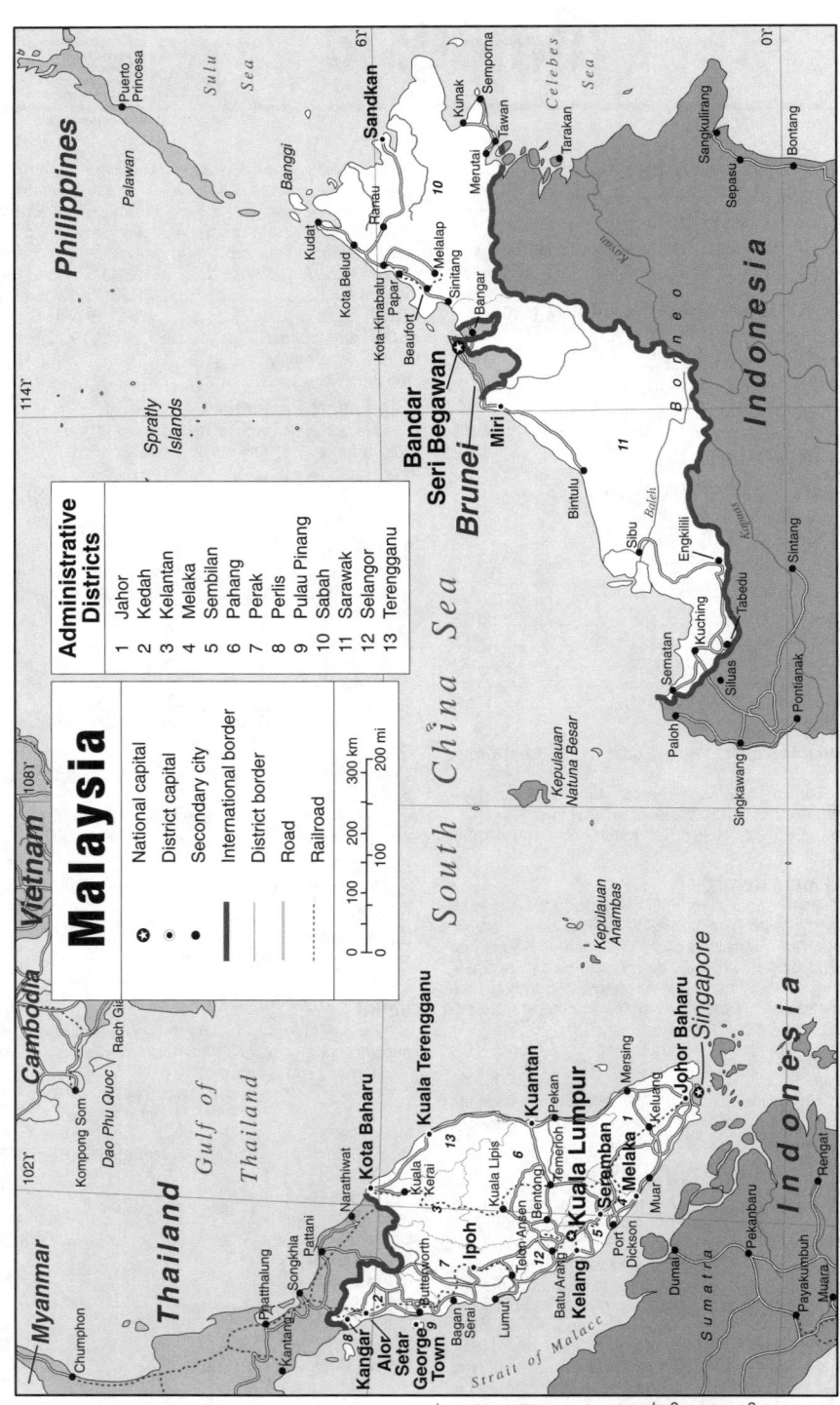

Administrative Districts

1 Jahor
2 Kedah
3 Kelantan
4 Melaka
5 Sembilan
6 Pahang
7 Perak
8 Perlis
9 Pulau Pinang
10 Sabah
11 Sarawak
12 Selangor
13 Terengganu

Malaysia

- ✪ National capital
- • District capital
- • Secondary city
- —— International border
- —— District border
- —— Road
- ⋯⋯ Railroad

0 100 200 300 km
0 100 200 mi

National Day...August 31
Deepavali ....October 26*
Christmas Day...December 25
Hari Raya Puasa
(End of Ramadan)................................... December 29-31
*Date may vary by year.

CLIMATE

Seasons
Malaysia is generally warm and humid all year round, with temperatures ranging from 70˚F to 90˚F.

Regions
The hill resorts are generally cooler. There are two monsoon seasons on the coastal areas—June to September in the southwest and October to March in the northeast. The monsoon brings heavy rain in both coastal areas.

Money & Banking

Currency
The currency of Malaysia is the ringgit (RM).

Denominations
The ringgit comes in coin denominations of RM1, and 100, 50, 20, 10, 5, and 1 sen; and banknotes of RM1, 5, 10, 20, 50, 100, 500, and 1,000.

Traveler's checks
Traveler's checks can be exchanged for Malaysian ringgit at any bank, authorized exchange sho, hotel, and international airport at tourist exchange rates with various rates of exchange. Larger banks may offer the best exchange rates, but avoid black marketers at all cost. Consult your bank about current exchange rates before departure. Keep all receipts for reconversion.

Cash can also be exchanged but try to take only crisp and new notes, wrinkled and soiled notes are likely to be refused.

Major credit cards, American Express, Visa, Diner's Club, and MasterCard, are easily accepted in most up-market places in the main cities, but smaller restaurants and shops may ask for cash. Some banks in the capital offer cash advances on credit cards but make sure you bring your passport.

Travel

VISA AND PASSPORT
Travelers to Malaysia need a passport that is valid for at least six months at date of entry, but visas are not required for visits of up to three months for most countries, except nationals of Bangladesh, Bhutan, China (PR), Cuba, India, North Korea, Myanmar, Nepal, Nigeria, Pakistan, Sri Lanka, Taiwan, and Vietnam. "Visa relaxation" is usually granted for nationals of those countries named (except Nigeria) for purposes of transiting Malaysia for under 72 hours, so long as the traveler is carrying confirmed onward airline tickets to a third country, which must be verified before arriving. Check with the nearest Malaysian consulate to verify visa status.

Business visitors are issued passes upon arrival for attending business meetings and conducting business negotiations in Malaysia. Those visitors who plan to engage in any kind of work (consulting or overseeing of installations) must apply for a business or professional pass prior to arrival in Malaysia.

Visas issued are for Social or Business status, both single- and multiple-entry. The Malaysian High Commission determines length of stay, depending mainly on the nationality of the applicant.

Allow about two working days for visa application processing, if applying in person. Proof of sufficient funds and an onward or return ticket are routinely required.

RESTRICTED ENTRY
Citizens of Israel and Yugoslavia (Montenegro and Serbia), nationals of the British Dependent Territories, foreign women who are six months or more pregnant (except in transit), and those with a slovenly appearance that bespeaks neglect will be denied entry. Taiwanese passports are not recognized as valid, unless they are supplemented with a travel document and an entry visa (inquire of the Malaysian High Commission for details).

DEPARTURE FORMALITIES
Visitors leaving from Kuala Lumpur International Airport will have to pay departure tax of RM40 for international flights, and RM20 if traveling to Brunei, Indonesia, Philippines, or Thailand from airports outside of Kuala Lumpur. Domestic flights carry a departure tax of RM5.

CUSTOMS ENTRY (PERSONAL)

Duty-free
- Tobacco: 200 cigarettes, 50 cigars, or 225g of tobacco
- Alcohol: 1 liter of spirits, wine, or malt liquor
- Other: perfumes in opened bottles to the value of RM200; gifts and souvenirs not exceeding a total value of RM200; 100 matches

Prohibited or Restricted
Visitors must declare valuables and may have to pay a deposit. It is prohibited to import any goods from Israel. Nonprescribed drugs, weapons, pornography and any cloth bearing the imprint or reproduction of any verses of The Koran are prohibited. Drug-smuggling carries the death penalty.

IMMUNIZATION
No vaccination certificates are required of visitors to Malaysia unless they are arriving from a country infected with cholera or yellow fever; including Central America and Central Africa. Entering without a valid certificate brings a quarantine period of up to six days.

A certificate of cholera vaccination is not required for entry into Malaysia, but it could be required if a traveler is going on to a country infected with cholera. Risk of malaria exists only in some isolated inland areas. Coastal and urban areas are safe, with the exception of Sabah, where the risk is year-round, mainly in the malignant falciparum form. This strain is reportedly thoroughly resistant to chloroquine and highly resistant to sulfadoxine / pyrimethamine.

TIPPING
A government tax of five percent, and a service charge of 10 percent, are customarily included in bills.

Taxi
Tipping taxi drivers is optional.

Porters
Porters typically get tipped RM1 per piece.

Hotels
A tip modestly in excess of the included 10 percent service charge is customary.

Restaurants
A 10 to 15 percent service charge is often included in restaurant tabs. If not, a 10 percent tip in restaurants and nightspots is customary.

Note: Leave the bargaining to road side stalls and small shops, as larger stores and department stores have fixed prices.

EMERGENCY INFORMATION

Police and Crime

Violent crime, especially against foreigners, is uncommon in Malaysia. However, foreign visitors will encounter the usual potential for petty crime, such as automobile break-ins, burglaries, pickpocketing, and purse snatchings. These latter are called "snatch-thefts," in which the perpetrators are in cars or on motorcycles, snagging purses, cell phones, laptops, and so forth from unsuspecting pedestrians, then speeding off. Occasionally pedestrians are injured or knocked to the ground in the course of the crime's commission.

Pickpocketing is common in crowded public places, and credit card fraud is a growing crime problem. Take the same precautions you would take in your own country.

A few elementary precautions should protect the traveler from most problems:

- Do not leave valuables in cars or on tables in cafés.
- Keep non-essential valuables locked in hotel safes when not in use.
- Use credit cards and traveler's checks when possible to avoid carrying large sums of cash.
- Carry photocopies of your passport instead of the original.
- Carry cash in a money belt, and use credit cards or travelers checks for most of your large transactions.

Walk with your bag away from the street to avoid having it snatched away by motorcycle thieves. Never carry a stranger's baggage.

Women are safe to walk the streets, but to avoid harassment, they are advised to travel in groups at night. The police are friendly and helpful.

Penalties run extremely high in Malaysia for drug trafficking, and the 1983 Dangerous Drug Act has made the death penalty mandatory for possession of more than 15 grams of heroin.

Emergency Numbers

For anywhere in Malaysia, call:
Police, Ambulance and Fire brigade 999
Police in Kuala Lumpur 292-4444

Health

Kuala Lumpur has high sanitation standards, but do not drink tap water or eat raw food in more rural areas. Stay away from food sold at roadside stands, and generally stick to milder dishes. Some stomach and digestion problems may be caused by the spicy food.

Diarrhea is common for travelers who are unaccustomed to the new diet and water, so bottled water is probably a good idea, especially if a visitor is not staying long. Wash all vegetables in a chlorine solution, peel fruits, and avoid uncooked food. Drink only powdered or tinned milk and avoid other dairy products since they are most likely unpasteurized. Most fare served in restaurants and hotels is perfectly healthful.

Medical services are adequate and reasonably priced, and many of the staff speak English. Pharmacies are scarce, but hospitals carry necessary drugs.

For more information on medical centers, including phone numbers, please see the "Business Centers" section at the end of this chapter.

INTERNAL TRAVEL

Note: Internal travel can be extremely difficult during major festivals, unless bookings have been made long in advance. The main holidays are Hari Raya Pusa, the Chinese New Year, and Hari Raya Haji.

Note: Kuala Lumpur's public transport system is infamous—rush-hour transit in the city is to be avoided at any cost.

AIR

The Malaysian Airline System (MAS), which includes both Malaysia Airlines and Pelangi Air, is the primary domestic carrier, crisscrossing Peninsular Malaysia and East Malaysia, including both Sarawak and Sabah, and also flying to Brunei.

Kuala Lumpur Subang (KUL), lying 22 km (14 miles) west of the city, is the primary domestic airport. Others are being developed, and there are many small airstrips in use.

It is less costly to fly to East Malaysia from Johor Bahru than from Kuala Lumpur (also known as KL). Flying in East Malaysia is really the quickest way to travel within the eastern region. During school holidays, flights are often fully booked, and delays due to weather are common.

There is a Malaysian departure tax for domestic flights of RM5.

TAXI

Taxis are one of the more efficient ways to get around town. One may find cabs at taxi stands, through a radio-paging system, or cruising the streets. Shared taxis are also common. Taxis are metered, but some drivers charge more than the metered rate during peak hours, or when it is raining, or when the passenger's destination involves driving through a heavily congested area. A 50-percent increase in price occurs from midnight to 6a.m. An extra RM1 is charged for taxis ordered by phone. Pre-purchased taxi coupons are available at the Kuala Lumpur railway station and the airport. Otherwise, the meter flag falls at about RM1.50 for the first kilometer, and an additional 10 sen for each 200 meters traveled. Long-distance cabs are also available for inter-city travel at about twice the rate of a rental car; business travelers may consider this a good option. Rickshaws have virtually disappeared in KL, but they remain a veritable mode of transport in more outland areas.

AUTO

Most major car rental companies are located at the airport. Technically, an International Driving Permit is required, but for most nationals a driver's license from their own country is sufficient, as long as it is endorsed by the Registrar of Motor Vehicles in Malaysia.

Most roads are well-marked and in fairly good condition. Because traffic in Malaysia moves on the left, pedestrians must make a point of looking purposefully in all directions when crossing roads. Motorcyclists beat the traffic jams by weaving briskly around vehicles and pedestrians. Afternoon and morning rush-hours are intense, but traffic slows down substantially when it rains.

Bottlenecks are common in Kuala Lumpur. Like many urban areas, development of the road system has not kept up with the proliferation of motorized vehicles. Multi-laned highways often merge into narrow two-lane roads in the center of a town and cause added congestion. Many narrow and winding streets were built a century ago and are not designed to handle motorized traffic.

In the Peninsular states, most roads are paved, and roadsigns giving directions are clear and well-positioned. Malaysia's north-south highway system is paved and very well maintained. This four-lane highway stretches from Singapore to the Thai border, spanning 890km (553 miles) from Bukit Kayu Hitam (on the Kedah-Thailand border) to Johor Bahru. The west coast of Malaysia also has a well-developed system of paved roads between major cities. These two-lane highways are usually congested; drive defensively as serious accidents occur often on these two-lane roads.

TRAIN

The Malayan Railway services connect much of the country and connect it to other countries like Singapore. Deluxe or First Class (with upholstered seats), Eksekutif or Second Class (with padded leather seats), and Ekonomi or Third Class (with cushioned plastic seats) are offered, but space should be reserved in advance. The daytime 'Express Rakyat' zips passengers between Singapore and Butterworth, continuing onward to Thailand. The commuter service, named KTM Komuter, runs between Kuala Lumpur and Seremban (south), Port Klang (west), and Rawang (north). Two of Malaysia's seaports, Padang Besar and Penang on the west coast, are served by passenger lines. Sarawak has no rail services.

The express trains are fully modern, and many offer buffet cars and sleeping berths; some are also air-conditioned. East Malaysia has only one railway line, running along the coastline from Kota Kinabalu (Sabah), and then heading inland up through a mountainous jungle valley to a small town called Tenom.

Malayan rail passes are offered for 10- or 30-days, but do not apply to express service, and must be purchased in advance. For rail information, contact the rail station in Kuala Lumpur at the following number, tel: 274-7434.

SUBWAY/METRO

Kuala Lumpur's light rail transit (LRT) system is now in its first phase of operation. Look for the LRT logo to find the stations; timetables are posted inside.

BUS

Conventional buses, 'Bas Mini' fixed-route minibuses, taxis, and pedi-cabs (trishaws) that are government-licensed, form the backbone of the KL public transit system. While urban bus fares vary, 'Bas Mini' have flat fare rates. They are especially used for shorter journeys and are usually crowded.

In terms of overland buses, Peninsula Malaysia's bus system is fast, economical, and extensive. It is generally regarded as the best way to get around (although the long-distance taxis are much more luxurious and comfortable). Sabah also has top-notch roads, and minibuses are easily found along the main routes. Buses travel the major trunk road in Sarawak, but hardly anywhere else in that part of Malaysia.

WATER TRAVEL

The main ports of Malaysia include Georgetown on Penang Island and Port Kelang for Kuala Lumpur. Coastal ferries offer frequent sailings between Butterworth and Penang, and regularly-scheduled passenger service exists between Port Kelang and both Sabah and Sarawak. Boats are also easily chartered, and river taxis and buses are plentiful.

No boat services are available between Peninsula and East Malaysia, but fast boats for hire frequent the rivers of both Sarawak and Sabah. Indeed, small rivercraft are often the most practical mode of transit in East Malaysia, even within the towns, and they provide the only means of reaching the more removed settlements (unless you have access to helicopters).

TRAVEL ASSISTANCE

Tourism Malaysia
17th Floor, Menara Dato' Onn
Putra World Trade Centre
45 Jalan Tun Ismail
50480 Kuala Lumpur Malaysia
tel: (3) 293-5188; fax: (3) 293-5884 or 0207.
email: tourism@tourism.gov.my.
website: http://www.tourism.gov.my

Hotel Accommodations

Malaysian Association of Hotels.................... (3) 242-0516
Tourism Information .... (3) 293-5188

Essential Terms

English	Malay
Yes	Ya
No	Tidak
Good morning	Selamat pagi
Hello (daytime)	Selamat tengahari
Hello (evening)	Selamat petang
Hello (telephone)	Helo
Good-bye	Selamat Tinggal
Please	Tolong
Thank you	Terima kasih
Pleased to meet you	Seronok berjumpa dengan anda
Excuse me; I'm sorry	Minta maaf
My name is _____	Nama saya
I don't understand	Saya tidak faham
Do you speak English?	Adakah anda bertutur bahasa inggeris

Communications

DIALING CODES IN MALAYSIA

International country code: [60]

Selected state codes: Johore (State) (7), Kelantan (State) (9), Melaka (State) (6), Negeri Sembilan (State) (6), Penang (State) (4), Perak (State) (4), Perlis (State) (4), Sabah (State) (8), Sarawak (State) (8), Selangor (State) (3), Terengganu (State) (9).

Selected city codes: Alor Star (4), Baranang (3), Bintulu (86), Broga (3), Cheras (3), Dengkil (3), Depala Batas (4), Ipoh (5), Johor Bahru (7), Kanjang (3), Kedah (4), Kepala Batas (4), Kota Bharu (9), Kota Kinabalu (88), Kuala Lumpur (3), Kuantan (9), Kuching (82), Labuan (87), Machang (97), Maran (97), Miri (8), Muar (6), Pahang (9), Port Dickson (6), Semenyih (3), Seremban (6), Sibu (84), Sintok (4), Sri Aman (83), Sungei Besi (3), Sungei Renggam (3).

Dialing Malaysia from Overseas

To dial Malaysia from overseas, dial your country's international dialing code, then 60 (the country code for Malaysia), then the city code and finally the number. If you were dialing Ipoh from the United States, for example, you would begin with 011, then 60, then 5 (the city code for Ipoh), and finally the number of the person or office you are trying to reach.

Assistance Numbers

International Operator 108
Directory Assistance.. 103
General Inquiries 102
Outstation 101

CALLING WITHIN MALAYSIA

Local Calls

Unlimited local chatting time can be had by simply dialing the local number after depositing 10 sen in a public telephone.

Long Distance Calls

Placing long distance calls within Malaysia requires one to dial the city code with a preceding zero followed by the number which you wish to reach.

International Calls

International calls from Malaysia may be placed from card phones (Kadfons), which are located throughout Malaysia. Telekom offices provide collect call opportunities. Hotel operators can assist in the procedure of calling direct, but usually will charge much higher rates. Bypass the outrage by dialing Home Country Direct:

British Telecom.. 800-0044
Canada Direct 800-0017
New Zealand Telecom 60-700-6401
Telecom Australia... 800-0061
Telecom South Africa 800-0027
U.S. AT&T 1-800-80-0011
U.S. MCI...1-800-80-0012
U.S. Sprint 800-0016

Calls may require local payment throughout the duration of the call.

PAY PHONES

Public Telephones

Public phones using cards and coins are available throughout the country. Coin phones cost 10 sen.

Press *2 and English instructions will magically appear on a screen.

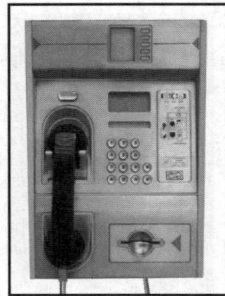

Calling Cards

Pre-paid phone cards may be purchased at the airport, telephone offices, convenience stores, or service stations. There are two types of cards, Kadfon and Unicard, and these cards can only be used at their respective phones. If a card runs out of time while in the midst of your call, press * and you may insert a new one without losing the connection.

CELLULAR PHONES

Malaysia boasts a multitude of cellular systems, both analogue and digital. Among them, a three different GSM networks, operated by Celcom, Binariang, and Telekom Malaysia. Other systems include an AMPS analogue, as well as ETACS, NMT-470, and DCS1800.

CALL BACK

You can (potentially) save significant sums when calling in Malaysia by using one of the call back services listed below.

Fees for call back services vary widely, depending on the company and the type of service required. Be sure to check with these companies before leaving to compare rates.

For a list of callback services, please refer to the "Communications" section in the *Global Road Warrior* Introduction.

PHONE JACK

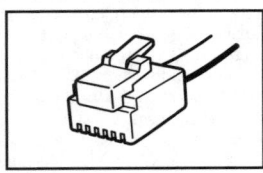

Plug adaptors are available through **iGo Corporation.** (See "Electrical and Telephone Adaptors" on page 19.)

FAX

Faxes are available at all Kedai Telekom and Telegraph offices, and at the Central Telecoms Building, tel: (3) 232-9492.

POSTAL SERVICES

Mail usually runs well.

Hours of service

Monday to Saturday 8a.m. to 5p.m.

Rates

Airmail letters cost about U.S.30 cents to Britain and U.S.40 cents to the U.S. for 10 grams or less.

TELEGRAMS

Telegrams can be sent from major hotels or any telegram office.

Business Services

AUDIOVISUAL RENTALS

Tan & Co.; 326 Jln. Tuanku Abdul Rahman; tel: (3) 298-0293.

Vu-Graph; 4 Jln. Radin Anum 2; Bandar Baru; Sri Petaling; tel: (3) 958-4911.

COURIER SERVICES

Airborne Express; Lot1-Block C, Mas Cargo Bldg. Complex, Jalan Garuda, Bayan Lepas, 11900 Penang, West Malaysia; tel: 626-4916; fax: 626-4667.

DHL; DHL Worldwide Express Sdn Bhd, Lot 14 Jalan 51/A/223, Petaling Jaya, Slangor Darul Ehsan 46100; tel: (3) 757-1188.

Federal Express; Federal Express Services (M) Sdn Bhd, Ground Floor, Wisma CSA, Jalan Bersatu 13/4, Petaling Jaya, 46200; tel: (3) 758-4688.

Nationwide Express; tel: (3) 792-8566.

O A S Airfreight Systems; (M) Sdn Bhd 765-1 Jln Sultan Azlan Shah Blepas, Penang tel: (4) 643-1460.

Overseas Courier Service; tel: (3) 243-4222.

TNT Skypak; tel: (3) 755-7744.

UPS; No. 11 Jalan Tandang Wisma Ali Bawal 46050 Petaling Jaya Selangor Darul; Ehsan; tel: (3) 794-1233; Penang office: 759-1 Jalan Sultan Azlan Shah Taman Kota Nibong 11900 Bayan Lepas Penang; tel: (4) 643-3530.

CONVENTION FACILITIES

Carcosa Seri Negara (Landmarks Hotels); Taman Tasik Perdana, 50480 KL; tel: (3) 282-1888; fax: (3) 282-7888; http://www.carcosa.com.my/; email: carcosa@mol.net.my; traditional colonial mansion; restaurant; bar; function room (up to 200); boardrooms; theater; drawing room; lawn and gardens (up to 600).

PRINTING/COPYING

Stenoprint; tel: (3) 248-7989.

Tricomas Marketing Sdn. Bnd.; tel: (3) 719-0061.

Sally Printing Services; tel: (3) 441-4829.

SECRETARIAL SERVICES

Ansacom; Lot 138, first floor; Wisma HLA; Jln. Raja Chulan; tel: (3) 242-8780.

Mascaya Business Center; tel: (3) 243-4357.

TeleSecretarial Service Center; tel: (3) 274-7533.

Unique Commercial Services; 100 Jln. Pudu Lama; tel: (3) 238-2706.

Worldwide Business Services; tel: (3) 274-9219.

TRANSLATION SERVICES

Art Wing Promotion; tel: (3) 985-5663.

Ho Translation Service; tel: (3) 238-1528.

O&M Management Consultants; tel: (3) 232-9988.

Worldwide Business Services; tel: (3) 274-7533.

Electrical

CURRENT

220 volts AC, 50Hz.

ELECTRIC PLUG

Plug adaptors are available through **iGo Corporation**. (See "Electrical and Telephone Adaptors" on page 19.)

Technical Support

HARDWARE/SOFTWARE VENDOR SUPPORT

Adobe; tel: [1] (800) 808-821; fax: [63] (2) 636-8534; (in Switzerland) tel: [41] (800) 833-310; (in the U.S.) tel: [1] (800) 500-7078; http://www.adobe.com/.

Apple/Claris; (in Australia) tel: [61] (2) 9452-8000; (in Switzerland) tel: [41] (800) 833-310; (in the U.K.) tel: [44]

(990) 127-753; (in the U.S.) tel: [1] (408) 996-1010; http://www.apple.com/.

AST; (in the U.S.) tel: [1] (817) 232-9824 (International Technical Support); (in Ireland) tel: [353] (61) 492-222; (in the U.S.) tel: [1] (949) 727-4141; http://www.ast.com/.

Compaq/Digital; (in Switzerland) tel: [41] (22) 709-5330; fax: [41] (22) 709-5391 (Geneva); tel: [41] (1) 801-2507; fax: [41] (1) 801-2172 (Zurich); (General U.S.) tel: (281) 518-2000; http://www.compaq.com/.

Dell; tel: (3) 201-8481; fax: (3) 201-8482; (Dell- Europe) tel: [44] (134) 474-8000; (in the U.S.) tel: [1] (512) 338-4400; fax: [1] (512) 728-3330; http://www.dell.com/.

Gateway 2000; (in the U.S.) tel: [1] (605) 232-2191; fax: [1] (605) 232-2023; (in Ireland) tel: [353] (1) 797-2000; http://www.g2k.com/.

Hewlett Packard; tel: 03 295 2566; (in Switzerland) tel: [41] (22) 780-8111; (in the U.S.) tel: [1] (408) 246-4300; http://www.hp.com/.

IBM; tel: (3) 717-7788; fax: (3) 717-2188; (in Switzerland) tel: [41] (22) 310-0418 (in French); (in the U.S.) tel: [1] (919) 517-2800; http://www.ibm.com/.

Microsoft; tel: (3) 793-9595; fax: (3) 295-2065; (in Switzerland) tel: [41] (848) 858-868; fax [41] (1) 831-0869; (in the U.S.) [1] (425) 635-7222; http://www.microsoft.com/.

NEC; tel: (3) 758-7788; fax: (3) 757-7566 (NEC Sales, Head office in Malaysia); tel: (3) 238-7788; fax: (3) 232-3322; (in the U.S.) [1] (916) 388-0101 (Main Switchboard); http://www.nec.com/.

Novell; (in Australia) tel: [61] 2-925-3000 (Asia Pacific Support Center); (in Switzerland) tel: [41] (1) 308-4747; fax: [41] (1) 302-0401; (in the U.S.) tel: [1] (408) 434-2300; fax: [1] (408) 577-5775 (Worldwide Sales Headquarters); http://www.novell.com/.

Quark; (Singapore Office) tel: [65] 467-6675; (in the U.S.) tel: [1] (303) 894-8899; fax: [1] (303) 894-3398 (For Products Registered in the Americas); http://www.quark.com/.

Internet Connection

HOW TO CONNECT

Connecting to AOL and Compuserve in Malaysia is similar to using it when traveling outside your own area code. See the introductory section for detailed information on connecting to your account through a different phone number.

America Online

Numbers are available at keyword *international*. Be sure to get several local numbers before leaving. AOL has a new GlobalNet service that charges US$6 an hour in addition to the usual charges. Go to keyword *access* (a free area) and download the software.

Access: Johor Baru (7) 223-0953; Kota Kinabalu (88) 256-079; Kuala Lumpur (3) 468-7000; Kuala Lumpur (3) 634-5407; Kuantan (9) 552-1000; Kuching (82) 230-757; Penang (4) 264-5188

Compuserve

Numbers are available at *Go International*. The Compuserve Web-site also has a great deal of information, at http://www.compuserve.com.

Access: Johor Bahru (7) 222-9849; Kota Kinabalu (88) 256-079; Kuala Lumpur (3) 2055-4870; Kuching (82) 230-757; Penang (4) 633-6000.

Independent Service Providers

Many independent service providers offer discounts if you are only in town for a couple of days.

Malaysia

Malaysia Online (Applied Information Management Services Sdn Bhd); tel: (3) 201-4988; fax: (3) 201-8948; email: support@aims.com.my; http://www.mol.net.my/.

MIMOS Berhad; tel: (3) 8996-5000; fax: (3) 8996-1898; email: noc@jaring-my; http://www.jaring.my/jaring/.

Plexus Online; tel: (3) 202-8800; fax: (3) 202-8899; email: info@plexus.net; http://www.plexus.net/.

TMnet/Telekom Malaysia; tel: (3) 704-1515; fax: (3).707-4591; email: custcare@tm.net.my; http://www.tm.net.my/.

Internet Cafes

HYPERJAYA Internet and Cafe; 2F (8, 9, 10) Komplex City Plaza, Menara MPKS II, Alor Setar, Kedah 05000 Malaysia; tel: (4) 733-3133; email: wmssb@tm.net.my; Sunday through Friday 11a.m. to 9p.m.

Harmoni Pujangga Cyber Cafe; 1st Floor, Kamsis Rahim Kajai, Universiti Kebangsaan Malaysia, Bangi, Selangor Darul Ehsan, Malaysia; tel/fax: (3) 824-1117; email: hpujangga@waumail.com; Monday through Sunday 10 a.m. to 4 a.m.

HyperNet Zone Internet Cafe; 32 1st Flr Lorong Usahaniaga 1, Taman Usahaniaga, 14000 Bukit Mertajam, Penang, Malaysia; tel: (4) 537-9457; email: hypernetzone@asia.com; Monday through Sunday 11a.m. to 1a.m.; RM3 per hour.

Layar Internet Cyber Cafe; 10-U, Jalan Cenderawasih, Larkin jaya,80530 Johor Bahru; tel: (7) 331-1920; fax: (7) 331-4546; email: Layar@pd.jaring.my; http://Layar.cjb.net; Monday through Sunday 24 hours a day; RM 5 per hour.

Business Culture
GREETINGS AND COURTESIES

Malaysia is home to Malays, Chinese, and Indians, and Malaysian behavior is shaped largely by their specific cultural background. Among Malays, the accepted greeting is a handshake, which is usually accompanied by a slight bow or nod of the head, especially when greeting someone older. In addition, when an older person enters a room, people usually stand. Women and elderly people often don't shake hands but will offer a verbal greeting. Chinese lower their eyes slightly as a sign of respect upon meeting someone. Chinese usually shake hands very lightly, and a handshake may last as long as ten seconds. Face, a measure of one's dignity, is crucial to Chinese. Saying or doing anything that causes someone to lose face can instantly destroy a relationship. Indians are the third largest ethnic group in Malaysia.

DECISION MAKING

Consensus is important to Malays, and they will probably require time for discussion before making a decision. These conversations will be amongst themselves, and never with outsiders present. Decisions will therefore rarely be made quickly. It is best not to press for a response. Chinese try to avoid saying no, for fear of causing embarrassment. Rather than say no, they might say something is inconvenient or suggest an alternative. They may also tell you what they think you want to hear, as a way of being polite.

WOMEN

Women hold positions of leadership in Malaysian businesses, and foreign women can expect to be accepted and respected. The family is important, and women should be prepared for personal questions about their age, marital status, and whether they have children. (These questions are asked of both men and women.) Any compliments a man pays a Malay woman should concern her work, not her looks. Commenting on a woman's looks might be regarded as flirting, which is taboo and might cost a woman her job. Most public physical contact between men and women is taboo. When foreign women deal with Malay men, they should behave formally, avoid touching men (even foreign men), and keep a proper distance. Do not make prolonged eye contact with Malaysian men, as this will probably be looked upon as flirtatious.

MEETINGS

Punctuality is a sign of respect and politeness, so be on time for appointments. Malays consider people more important than schedules, however, and they are often late for appointments. Asians are more at ease as a group than as individuals. Nevertheless, they prefer to work with one individual from a company for the duration of the relationship. Designate one person, preferably your group's senior member, as your spokesperson. Avoid conflicting statements from other team members in the presence of your Malaysian associates. Your team leader should enter the room first. Group leaders sit opposite each other, with others in descending order of importance. Small talk will usually come first; all business is addressed as people feel comfortable with each other.

BUSINESS ATTIRE

Malaysia is hot and humid all year, so wear natural fibers that breathe (cotton, linen); you will be more comfortable. Neat, tasteful pants, shirt, and tie (no jacket) will be appropriate for most business situations. If you wear a jacket and no one else does, you may remove yours once the meeting begins. Women should always dress tastefully and conservatively. A skirt and blouse or shirt and trousers are usually appropriate. Hemlines should never be above the knee, and women should avoid wearing a sleeveless dress or blouse. Both men and women should avoid bright or loud colors. Yellow is the color of royalty; don't wear yellow to a formal event or while visiting the palace.

Business Centers
Kuala Lumpur
CITY VIEW

Meaning "Muddy Confluence", Kuala Lumpur presents a delightful architectural blend of modern, Moorish, and Chinese influences. Founded in 1857 by Chinese tin miners, the city has enjoyed rapid growth since 1880. The commercial area showcases the world's tallest buildings, the Petronas Twin Towers, completed in 1996. Other parts of the city feature quaint Chinese wooden shop houses with surrounding mixed residential areas made up of modern bungalows and brick flats. A mix of Asia and India, Kuala Lumpur boasts a bit of flavor from each, including exotic blends of food, a smattering of fancy mosques and colorful Muslim saris, and a well-streamlined business climate.

Industry comprises of soap and food factories, iron foundries, and engineering works all in the suburb of Sungai Besi. Tin and rubber smelting, engineering workshops, sawmills, and cement manufacturing is also part of the area's industry.

Made up of over one and a half million people, the city is filled with bustling streets and a cosmopolitan aura. It is an impressive gathering place for travelers and business people from around the world.

AIRPORT

Kuala Lumpur International Airport to City Center

Replacing Subang Airport, the new airport lies 46 miles from Kuala Lumpur in Sepang. Travel time will take approximately one hour. Due to a scheduled but non-existent rail link, travelers must opt for other forms of transportation. A cab may be hailed for about RM80. Express buses also depart for various destinations including Kuala Lumpur, Nilai, Subang, and Shah Alam between 5a.m. and 11p.m. daily. Purchase tickets at express coach counters in the arrival concourse. An airport/taxi limousine service also exists on a 24-hour basis. Head for specified counters at the arrival concourse. Depending which level of service you desire, Premier Service or Budget Service, you will get a limousine or taxi respectively.

Airline Numbers

Aeroflot	(3) 261-3331
Air Canada	(3) 242-4311
Air France	(3) 232-6952
Air India	(3) 242-0166
Air Lanka	(3) 746-4500
Air New Zealand	(3) 242-5577, 746-5772
Alitalia	(3) 238-0366
All Nippon Airways (ANA)	(3) 244-1331
Ansett Australia	(3) 201-9211
Asiana	(3) 244-2900/2815
Balkan Bulgarian	(3) 241-9245
British Airways	(3) 232-5797
Canadian Air	(3) 242-5533
Cargolux	(3) 746-1249
Cathay Pacific	(3) 238-3377, 746-3550
China Airlines	(3) 223-8144
Continental Micronesia	(3) 242-4311
Dragonair	(082) 233-322, (082) 238-059
Emirates	(3) 232-5288
Eva Airways	(3) 261-7500
Garuda Indonesia	(3) 746-2627
Green Air	(3) 262-2981
Gulf Air	(3) 241-2676
Iran Air	(3) 261-0411
JAL	(3) 261-1722
KLM	(3) 242-7011
Korean Airlines	(3) 242-8311
Kuwait Airlines	(3) 746-2329
Lauda Air	(3) 248-8033
Lufthansa	(3) 261-4666
Malaysian	(3) 230-8844, 261-0555, 746-3000
Northwest Airlines	(3) 261-9501
Pakistan Intl.	(3) 242-5444
Philippine Airlines	(3) 242-9040
Qantas	(3) 238-9133, 746-2580
Royal Brunei	(3) 230-7166
Saudi Arabian Airlines	(3) 201-0088
Sempati Air	(3) 263-1612
Singapore Airlines	(3) 298-7033, 292-3122
Swissair	(3) 291-3254
Thai	(3) 293-7100, 201-1913, 201-2900
United Airlines	(3) 261-1433
Vietnam Airlines	(3) 241-2416
Virgin Airlines	(3) 243-0321

HOTELS

Top-end

The Crown Princess; City Square Center, Jalan Tun Razak, 40450 KL; tel: (3) 262-5522; fax: (3) 262-4492; http://www.crownprincess.com.my/; 576 rooms and suites; restaurant; coffee house; conference facilities, 7 function rooms; ballroom (up to 700); business center; secretarial service; in-room a/c, IDD phone, color tv, movies, CNN, minibar, safe; ladies' floor with lounge, complimentary breakfast, personalized butler service; 24-hour room service; laundry service; health center; gym; sauna; massage; aerobics; pool; whirlpool; gardens; RM390+.

Istana; 73 Jalan Raja Chulan; tel: (3) 241-9988; fax: (3) 244-0111; 516 rooms; located in city center's "Golden Triangle"; 4 restaurants; conference facilities (2500); business center; secretarial service; conference room; ballroom; in-room modem/fax connection, safe; corporate rates; 24-hour room service; hair salon; limousine service; parking; fitness; sauna; pool; whirlpool; tennis; squash; entertainment center; RM480+.

J.W. Marriott Hotel; 183 Jalan Bukit Bintang; tel: (3) 2715-9000; fax: (3) 2715-7000; http://www.marriottHotels.com/KULDT/; located downtown in the Golden Triangle; 514 rooms, 32 suites; 2 restaurants; cafe; 20 meeting rooms; conference/banquet facilities; business center; secretarial service; in-room work desk, 2-line phone, voicemail, cable tv, newspaper (M-F), minibar, coffeemaker, a/c, dataport, safe; 24-hour room service; laundry; hair salon; executive floors; newsstand; shop; limousine service; parking; fitness; sauna/spa; pool; whirlpool; tennis; golf; jogging track.

Mandarin Oriental; Kuala Lumpur City Centre, 50088 KL; tel: (3) 380-8888; fax: (3) 380-8833/380-6228; http://www.mandarin-oriental.com/kualalumpur/; email: reserve-mokul@mohg.com; city center, adjacent Petronas Twin Towers; 643 rooms and suites; executive apartments; Club Floors; restaurants; cafe; bar; ballroom (up to 2400); 2 conference rooms; 12 meeting rooms (up to 200); boardroom; secretarial service; 3 workstations with computers/internet; in-room dataports, dual telephone lines, voicemail, IDD, coffee/tea making facilities, minibar, hairdryer, daily paper, fresh fruits, safe, movies; 24-hour room service; personalized butler service available; limousine service; gym; massage; sauna; steam rooms; spa treatments; pool; jacuzzi; tennis; squash; aerobics; exercize programming; US$158+.

Nikko Hotel Kuala Lumpur; 165 Jalan Ampang, 50450 KL; tel: (3) 261-1111; toll free in Malaysia: 1-800-883-292; fax: (3) 261-1122; toll-free fax in Malaysia: 1-800-883-290; http://www.hotelnikko.com.my/; email: reservation@hotlenikko.com.my; 470 rooms, 14 suites; restaurants; coffee house; pub; ballroom (up to 1000); 5 function rooms (up to 40 each); business center; secretarial service; in-room a/c, IDD phone, movies, tea making, minibar, hairdryer, safe; 24-hour room service; 24-hour laundry/valet; non-smoking floor; rooms for handicapped; parking; health club; gym; unisex spa with massage, sauna; jacuzzi; pool; RM500+.

The Pan Pacific; Jalan Putra; tel: (3) 4042-5555; fax: (3) 4041-7236; http://www.panpac.com/malaysia/kuala_lumpur/hotels/hotel.html; email: bc@ppkl.po.my; 550 rooms and suites; restaurants; bar; conference facilities (up to 350); ballroom (up to 500); business center; secretarial service; Internet connection; in-room a/c, safe, hairdryer, minibar, IDD phone, color tv, movies, CNN, coffee/tea maker, iron/ironing board; 24-hour room service; laundry/valet; Pan Pacific floors with butler service; hair salon; shops; currency exchange; car rental; limousine rental; corporate rates; fitness; spa; massage; sauna; pool; whirlpool; tennis; RM480+.

Parkroyal Kuala Lumpur; Jala Sultan Ismail, 50250 KL; tel: (3) 242-5588; fax: (3) 241-5524; http://www.kl-hotels.com/parkroyal/; 336 rooms and suites; restaurant;

Malaysia

12 function rooms; ballroom (up to 500); business center; in-room CNN news, movies, a/c, ISD/IDD phone, minibar, safe, desk, bathrobes, iron/ironing board, coffee/tea making facilities, kimono; 24-hour room service; laundry/valet; personal butler; shopping arcade; luggage storage; limousine service; parking; health center; saunas; steam baths, massage; pool; tennis; air-conditioned squash courts; RM190+.

Renaissance Kuala Lumpur Hotel; GPO Box 13357; tel: (65) 235-2490; fax: (65) 235-7620; http://www.renaissancehotels.com/KULRN/; 399 rooms; located in heart of the financial district; elegant decor; 6 restaurants; cafe; 2 bars; conference facilities (up to 1200);convention center; secretarial service; business center; in-room a/c, modem/fax connection, hairdryer, IDD phone, color tv, movies, coffee/tea maker; safe; laundry/dry cleaning; doctor on call; hair salon; florist; shops; travel desk; car rental; limousine service; parking; corporate rates; 24-hour fitness; sauna; steambath, massage; Olympic-size pool; whirlpool; tennis; RM300+.

New World Renaissance Kuala Lumpur; Jalan Sulan Ismail and Jalam Ampang; tel: (3) 263-6888; fax: (3) 263-1888; http://www.renaissancehotels.com/KULNW/; 521 rooms; executive floor rooms, Presidential suite; 4 restaurants, bars; cigar divan; 24-hour dining; ballroom (up to 2800); 17 function rooms (up to 130 each); 24-hour business center; secretarial service; in-room safe, minibar, coffee, dataports, 3 telephones, voicemail; room service; laundry/valet; non-smoking rooms; beauty parlor; parking; 24-hour gym; sauna; Olympic-size pool; whirlpool.

Shangri-La; 11 Jalan Sultan Ismail; tel: (3) 232-2388; fax: (3) 230-1514; e-mail: slkl@shangri-la.com; 720 rooms; one of the country's most elegant hotels, located in business and shopping district; 3 restaurants; coffee shop; bar; pub; cigar boutique; conference facilities (up to 2,000); secretarial service; fax/photocopy facilities; in-room safe; 24-hour. room service; laundry; clinic; hair salon; florist; shopping arcade; postal service; parking; limousine; fitness; sauna; pool; whirlpool.

Expensive

Equatorial; Jalan Sultan Ismail; tel: (3) 2161-7777; fax: (3) 2161-9020; http://www.equatorial.com/kul/; email: reservations@kul.equatorial.com; 300 rooms; 5-star hotel, city center; restaurants; conference facilities (up to 20); business center; secretarial service; in-room modem/fax connection, a/c, movies, tv with CNN, CNBC, NHK, Sports channel; IDD phone, hairdryer, minibar, safe; Club Floor with library, complimentary breakfast, concierge, secretarial service; non-smoking rooms; room service; laundry; shopping arcade; tour desk; beauty salon/barber; currency exchange; limousine; parking; corporate rates; fitness; spa; sauna; pool; RM180+.

The Federal; 35 Jalan Bukit Bintang; tel: (3) 248-9166; fax: (3) 243-8381; 404 rooms; located in business and shopping districts; newly refurbished; restaurants; meeting/banquet facilities; business center; in-room a/c, hairdryer, minibar, safe; florist; shopping arcade; limousine service; pool; bowling; gardens.

Forum Fairlane; Jalan Walter Grenier; tel: (3) 8996-8000; fax: (3) 8996-8001; located in the Golden Triangle; restaurants; coffee shop; bar; 6 function rooms (up to 200) conference/banquet facilities; business center; in-room fax machines and modem, hairdryer, tea making facilities, safe; room service; laundry/valet services; hotel doctor; limousine service; valet parking; fitness; steambath; massage; indoor pool; whirlpool; aerobics; RM310+.

Grand Continental; Jalan Belia/Raja Laut; tel; (3) 293-

9333; fax: (3) 294-8429; restaurants; banquet/conference facilities; business center; barber/beauty salon; limousine service; shopping; doctor; sauna/spa; pool.

Grand Olympic; Jalan Hang Jebat, 50150 KL; tel: (3) 238-7888; fax: (3) 238-1488; restaurant; coffee house; karaoke lounge; business center; in-room hairdryer, IDD phone, tv, movies, safe box; room service; laundry service; currency exchange; drugstore; limousine service; RM145+.

Melia Kuala Lumpur; 16 Jalan Imbi; tel: (3) 242-8333; fax: (3) 242-6623; 300 rooms; Chinese & Spanish restaurants; piano lounge; daily buffet breakfast; business center; meeting/banquet facilities (up to 400); hotel doctor; in-room a/c, safe; 24-hour room service; limousine service; shops; parking; health center; pool; disco.

MiCasa Hotel Apartments; 368B, Jalan Tun Razak, 50400 KL; tel: (3) 2161-8833; fax: (3) 2161-1186; http://www.micasahotel.com; email: micasa@po.jaring.my; complimentary buffet breakfast; meeting/function rooms; business center; internet access; room service; daily housekeeping; 24-hour reception; 24-hour security/maintenance; laundry/dry cleaning service; shuttle to selected offices; hair salon; store; grocery service; in-house doctor/dentist; limousine service; free parking; gym; pool; children's pool; whirlpool; tennis; children's playroom; RM340+.

Pacific Regency Hotel and Apartments; 8 Lorong P. Ramlee, 50250 KL; tel: (3) 201-1592; fax: (3) 201-4715; 153 units, studios, 1- and 2-bedroom; restaurants; karaoke lounge; meeting room; in-room tv, kitchen, rice cooker, water heater; room service; laundry; babysitting; minimart; limousine service; parking; fitness; disco; RM270+.

Park Plaza International Hotel (formerly Radisson); 138 Jalan Ampang; tel: (3) 466-8866; fax: (3) 466-9966; 278 rooms; located in business district; restaurants; cafe; bar; business center; 5 meeting rooms; banquet hall (up to 400); business center; in-room dataport, voicemail, IDD phone, minibar, a/c, CNN, satellite tv, movie channel, coffee/tea making facilities, bathrobe, hairdryer, safe; rooms for disabled; laundry; Plaza Club floor with Sky Lounge privileges, data ports; non-smoking rooms; barber/beauty salon; currency exchange; hotel doctor; limousine service available; parking; fitness; sauna; indoor pool; whirlpool.

Quality Hotel; Jalan Raja Laut, PO Box 11586, 50750 KL; tel: (3) 293-9233; fax: (3) 293-9634; 250 rooms, 13 suites; restaurant; coffee house, bar; banquet facilities (up to 250); meeting room; business center; secretarial service; in-room hairdryer, a/c, tv, movies, IDD phone, minibar, coffee/tea making facility, safe; room service; concierge; drugstore; florist; shuttle service; parking; gym; sauna; pool; jacuzzi; squash court; game room; darts; snooker; Karaoke room; RM310+.

Moderate

Furama Hotel; SDN. BHD.(27795-M), Kompleks Selangor, Jalan Sultan, 50000 KL; tel: (3) 230-1777; fax: (3) 230-2110; email: furamakl@tm.net.my; www.furama.com.my; coffee house; conference room; in-room magnetic key card, a/c, tv, video, minibar; room service; parking; health center; RM98+.

Katari Pudu; 38, Jalan Pudu; tel: (3) 201-7777; fax: (3) 201-7911/2; www.katari.com.my; 100 rooms; located near Chinatown; restaurant; conference rooms; secretarial service; fax/photocopy facilities; in-room a/c, tv, IDD phone; room service; laundry service; 24-hour reception; corporate rates; RM138.

Hotel Midah; Jalan Kampung Attap, KL; tel: (30 273-9999; fax: (3) 273-9199; restaurant; bar; meeting room; seminar room; conference facilities; business center; in-room a/c, keycard, cable tv, IDD phone, minibar, tea maker, hairdryer; laundry; tour desk; minibar; limousine service; RM180+.

Hotel Nova; Sdn. Bhd., 16-22 Jalan Alor,

50200 Kuala Lumpur; tel: (3) 243-1818; fax:(3) 242-9985; http://www.novahtl.com; email: cemal@novahtl.com; 154 rooms; coffee shop; in-room a/c, color tv, IDD dialing, tea/coffeemaker, key card; laundry service; 24-hour security; tour service; free parking; RM98+.

Mandarin Hotel; 2-8 jalan Sultan, 50000 KL; tel: (3) 230-3000; fax: (3) 230-4363; restaurant; coffee house; room service; travel service; hair salon; health center; RM173+.

The Plaza Hotel; Jalan Raja Laut; tel: (3) 235-2498; fax: (3) 235-1416; 235-7620; 160 rooms; located on Jalan Raja laut in the central downtown district; 2 restaurants; cafe; bar; conference/banquet facilities; business center; secretarial service; in-room safe; 24-hour room service; laundry/dry cleaning; doctor on call; shop; parking; health club; sauna; steam bath; pool; FM140+.

Stanford Hotel; 449, Jalan Tuanku, Abdul Rahman, 50100 KL; tel: (3) 291-9833; fax: (3) 293-6482; coffee house; seminar room; business center; in-room cable tv, video, IDD phone, minibar; shopping arcade; limousine service; RM150.

Vistana Hotel; 9 Jalan Lumut, off Jalan Ipoh, 50400 KL; tel: (3) 442-8000; fax: (3) 441-1400; 4-star business hotel, near World Trade Center and The Mall; restaurants; seminar room; business center; in-room radio, minibar, hairdryer, refrigerator, a/c, IDD phone, movies, cable tv, coffee/tea making; health center; RM120.

Wenworth Hotel; Jalan Yew, 55100 KL; tel: (3) 983-3888; fax: (3) 982-8088; 265 rooms and suites; restaurant; cafe; lounge; seminar room; business center; in-room tv, desk. a/c, IDD phone, safe, coffee/tea maker; shopping arcade; limousine service; health center; pool; RM180+.

MEDICAL CARE

Damai Service Hospital; Lot 241-243, Jalan Ipoh, 51200 KL; tel: (3) 443-4900; fax: (3) 443-5399.

Gleneagles Intan Medical Centre; No. 282-286 Jalan Ampang, 50450 KL; tel: (3) 457-1300; emergency: (3) 455-2718; fax: (3) 457-2933; on embassy row.

Malaysian Medical Association; tel: (3) 441-8972; fax: (3) 441-8187; http://www.mma.org.my; email: mma@tm.net.my

National Heart Institute; Lot 24, Seksyen 24, Jalan Tun Razak, 50400 KL; tel: (3) 298-1333; emergency: (3) 298-2918; fax: (3) 298-2824; 10-minutes from Nikko Hotel.

Sentosa Medical Centre; Lot 626, Seksyen 47, NO. 36 Jalan Chemor, 50400 KL; tel: (3) 443-7166; fax: (3) 443-7761.

Tawakal Specialist Centre; 202A Jalan Pahang, 53000 KL; tel: (3) 423-3599; emergency room: (3) 423-0733; fax: (3) 422-8063; 15 minutes from Legend Hotel and Mall.

HEALTH CLUB

Alpha Dimension; Menara Genesis; tel: (3) 241-3882.

Clark Hatch Fitness; Kuala Lumpur Hilton Hotel; tel: (3) 241-3537.

Klang Executive Club; Kompleks Barkeley, Klang; tel: (3) 342-7623.

Mandarin Oriental Vitality Club; Mandarin Oriental Hotel, Kuala Lumpur City Centre, 50088 KL; tel: (3) 380-8888; gym, pool; jacuzzi; tennis; squash; physical assessment, personalized exercise programming, aerobics; whirlpool; massage; saunas; steam rooms; spa treatments.

Poliklinik Central Fitness Centre; 115 Jln Gombak; tel: (3) 422-7896.

Regent Health Club; The Regent Hotel, 160, Jalan Bukit Bintang, 55100 KL; tel: (3) 241-8000; gym with Cybex weight training machines, saunas, steambaths, massage, whirlpools, air conditioned squash court, locker facilities, safe boxes; 6a.m. to 10p.m. daily.

Taiwei Executive Recreation Centre; Plaza Hotel; tel: (3) 292-1409.

AUTO RENTAL

Avis; 40 Jalan Sultan Ismail, Kuala Lumpur, 50250; tel: (3) 242-3500; Sebang Intl Airport, Counter B-16, Arrival level, main terminal, Sebang, Kuala Lumpur; tel: (3) 8776-4540.

Ace Car Rental; 28A, Jalan SS15/4B, 47500 Subang Jaya, Selangor d. Ehsan; tel: (3) 731-7625; fax: (3) 731-7626.

Budget; 29 Jalan Yap Kwan Seng; tel: (3) 262-5116; fax: (3) 264-9362.

Hertz; Kuala Lumpar Intl Airport; Lot 16, Car Park D; tel: (3) 8787-4572; fax: (3) 8787-4573; Kompleks Antarabangsa, Lot 2 Ground Floor, Jalan Sultan Ismail; tel: (3) 248-6433; tel: (3) 242-1014/242-4891.

National; Shop 9, Ground Floor, President House; Jalan Sultan Ismail; tel: (3) 248-0522; fax: (3) 248-2823.

Thrifty; LPPKN Building, Holiday Inn City Centre Annex, 12-B Jalan Raja Laut; tel: (3) 293-2388; Basement, Bangunan Yee Seng, 15 Jalan Raja Chulan; tel: (3) 230-2591; fax: (3) 238-8578.

WORLD TRADE CENTER

Putra World Trade Center
41 Jalan Tun Ismail
Level 3, Convention Complex
50480, Kuala Lumpur
tel: (3) 449-3169; fax: (3) 449-3160
email: wtckl@pwtc.com.my
website: http://www.pwtc.com.my/pwtc

CHAMBER OF COMMERCE

National Chamber of Commerce and Industry
37 Jalan Kia Peng
50450 Kuala Lumpur
tel: (3) 254-2677; fax: (3) 255-4946

Malta

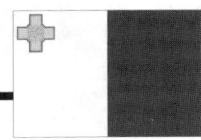

At a Glance

THE PEOPLE

Population .... 391,670 (July 2000 est.)
Growth Rate .... 0.74% (2000 est.)
Life Expectancy 77.94
Infant Mortality ... 5.94 deaths/1,000 live births (2000 est.)

Ethnic Composition

Maltese (descendants of ancient Carthaginians and Phoenicians, with strong elements of Italian and other Mediterranean stock)

Religious Composition

Roman Catholic... 91%
Other 9%

Languages Spoken

Both Maltese and English are official languages. Italian is also widely spoken.

Education and Literacy

Compulsory, free primary education lasts between ages 6 and 16. At the junior high school level a student may choose to follow a Junior Lyceum course for further studies, or an Area Secondaries course for technical studies. Adult literacy is 88 percent. There is no difference in literacy percentages along gender lines.

Labor Force

Total: 143,700

By occupation: industry 24%, services 71%, agriculture 5%.

THE ECONOMY

Malta's major resources are a productive labor force, limestone, and a favorable geographic location. Malta is externally dependent upon other nations for food production, about 80 percent of its food needs are met by foreign suppliers. Malta also has limited freshwater supplies and no domestic energy sources. The economy is dependent on foreign trade, manufacturing (especially electronics and textiles), and tourism. In 1999, over 1 million tourists visited the island. Malta is politically divided over the question of whether or not to become a part of the E.U. Malta's sizable budget deficit remains a key concern for the country's future ability to maintain a competitive place in a global economy.

Exports .... US$1.8 billion (f.o.b., 1998)
Imports .... US$2.7 billion (f.o.b., 1998)
Total Trade .... US$4.5 billion (f.o.b., 1998)
GDP Per Capita .... US$13,800 (1999 est.)
Unemployment .... 5.5% (September 1999)
Inflation Rate .... 1.8% (1999 est.)

Top Export Partners

France 20.7%, US 18.1%, Germany 12.6%, UK 7.7%, Italy 4.8%.

Top Import Partners

Italy 19.3%, France 17.8%, UK 12.4%, Germany 10.5%, US 8.9%.

Top Exports

Machinery and transport equipment, manufactured goods.

Top Imports

Machinery and transport equipment, manufactured goods; food, drink, and tobacco.

BUSINESS WORKWEEK

Businesses in Malta operate on winter and summer schedules. Summer is officially designated as June 16 to September 30. Winter officially takes place from October 1 to June 15.

Offices

Summer: Monday to Friday 8a.m. to 1p.m.

Winter: Monday to Friday 9a.m. to 1p.m. and 2:30p.m. to 6p.m.

Banks

Summer: Monday to Friday 8:30a.m.to 12:30p.m., extended hours on Fridays between 2:30p.m. and 4p.m.; Saturday 8a.m. to 11:30a.m.

Winter: Monday to Friday 8:30a.m. to noon., plus extended hours between 2:30p.m. and 4p.m. on Tuesday and Friday; Saturday 8:30a.m. to noon.

Government

Summer: 7:30a.m. to 1:30p.m.

Winter: 7:45a.m. to 12:30p.m. and 1:15p.m. to 5:15p.m.

Retail

Monday to Friday 9a.m. to 7p.m., with a three-hour lunch break; until 10p.m. in touristed areas, slightly shorter hours on Saturdays. An open-air market in Valletta takes place on Sunday mornings.

HOLIDAYS

New Year's Day..January 1
St. Paul's Shipwreck.. February 10
St. Joseph Day .... March 19
Freedom Day... March 31
Good Friday...April 21*
St. Joseph the Worker..May 1
Sette Giugno-Memorial of 1919 Riot .... June 7*
St. Peter and St. Paul ....June 29
Assumption.. August 15
Our Lady of Victories.....................................September 8
Independence Day ....September 21
Immaculate Conception..................................December 8
Christmas Day...December 25

*Date may vary by year.

CLIMATE

Seasons

The climate is generally warm, rain falls for a very short period, and there is no snow, fog, or wind. November to April are the winter months with temperature of around 14˚C, and May to October are the summer months with temperatures averaging 32˚C. The hottest months are from mid-July to mid-September, but the evenings are always cool, accompanied by sea breeze. There is some rain from October to January.

Regions

There are few regional differences.

Malta

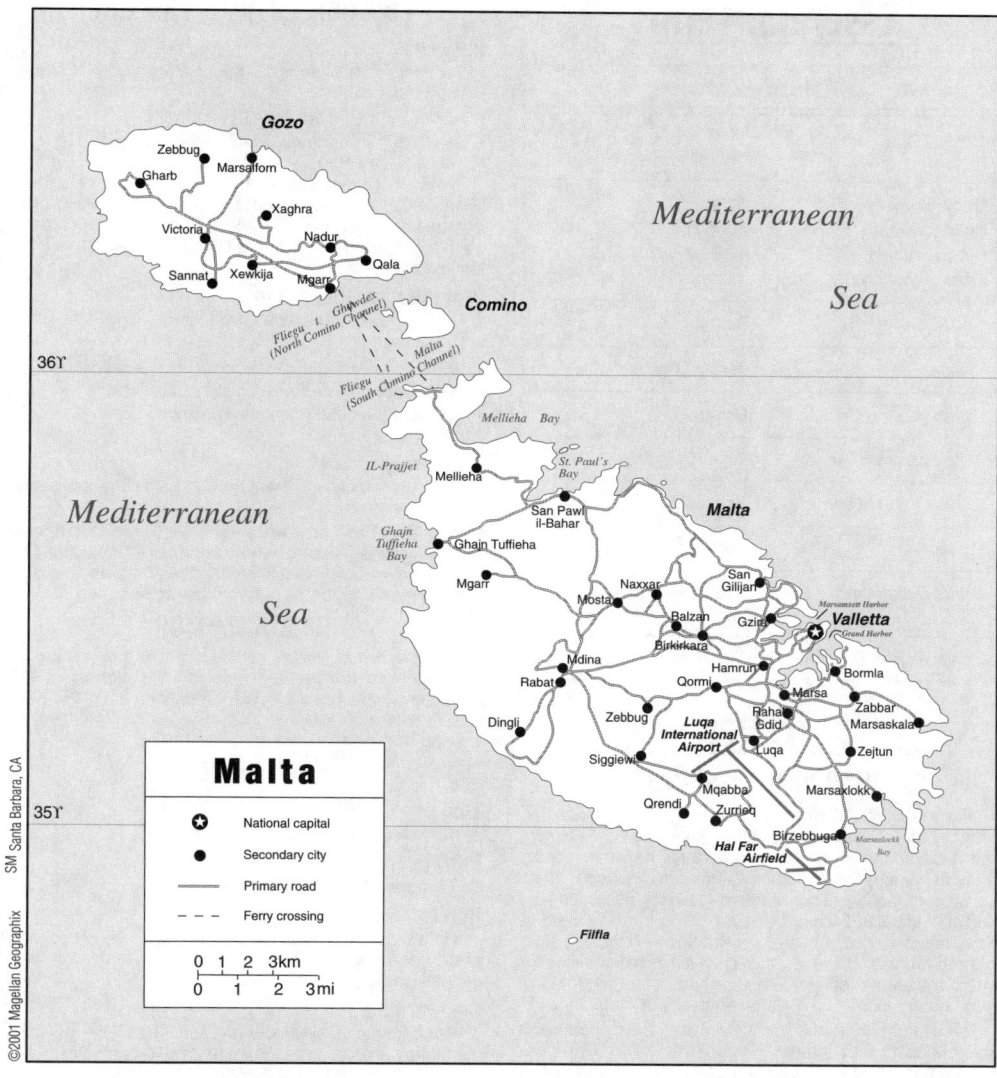

Money & Banking

Currency

The currency of Malta is the Maltese Lira (LM).

Denominations

The Maltese Lira comes in coin denominations of LM1, and 50, 25, 10, 5, 2, and 1 cents, and 5, 3, and 2 mils; and banknotes of LM2, LM5, LM10, and LM20.

Traveler's checks

Traveler's checks and currency can be exchanged at banks, exchange shops and hotels at tourist exchange rates, with various rates of exchange. One may exchange currency at the airport on a 24-hour basis; however, keep in mind that on Saturdays one may not exchange more than LM100. Larger banks may offer the best exchange rates, but avoid black marketers at all cost. Consult your bank about current exchange rates before departure. Keep all receipts for reconversion.

Cash can also be exchanged but try to take only crisp and new notes, wrinkled and soiled notes are likely to be refused.

Major credit cards, American Express, Visa, Diner's Club, and MasterCard, are easily accepted in most up-market places in the main cities, but smaller restaurants and shops may ask for cash. Some banks in the capital offer cash advances on credit cards but make sure you bring your passport. Some banks in the capital offer cash advances on credit cards, but make sure you bring you passport.

Essential Terms

English	Maltese
Yes	Iva
No	Le
Good morning	Bongu
Hello (daytime)	Bongu
Hello (evening)	Il-lejl-it-tajjeb
Hello (telephone)	Allo!
Good-bye	Sahha
Please	Jekk joghgbok
Thank you	Grazzi
Pleased to meet you	Ghandi pjacir
Excuse me; I'm sorry	Skuzani
My name is ____	Jisimni____
I don't understand	Yi ddispyachini ma nifimsh
Do you speak English?	Titkellem bl-ingliz?

Travel

VISA AND PASSPORT

Nationals of Austria, Belgium, France, Germany, Greece, Italy, Luxembourg, Netherlands, Portugal, Spain, and Switzerland need only show their national identity cards at immigration. All other visitors are required to have a passport. Visas are not required for many countries—including Australia, Britain, Canada, European Union members, Japan, Korea, and the United States—for a stay of up to three months. However, there is a list of nationalities for whom a visa is required. For information on the status of your country, contact a Maltese embassy or consulate.

Passengers in transit who do not leave the airport and are continuing their journey within 24 hours, and who are holding confirmed tickets and other documents for onward travel, are also exempt from the need for a visa.

Only single-entry and transit visas are issued prior to arrival in Malta. The single-entry visa is valid for one month; the transit visa is good for 24 hours only. For extension or renewal, the visitor can apply to the Embassy or High Commission. Visitors who take day trips out of Malta for periods of 24 hours or less do not need to acquire another entry visa when they return to the island.

Multiple-entry visas valid for one year can be issued in Malta by the Immigration Police.

Allow about ten working days for processing of visa applications made in person at a consulate or embassy.

DEPARTURE FORMALITIES

Not more than LM25 in local currency may be exported from Malta. Non-residents may take out with them the balance of unspent foreign currencies they brought into Malta.

CUSTOMS ENTRY (PERSONAL)

Duty-free
- Tobacco: 200 cigarettes, 50 cigars, 100 cigarillos, or 250g tobacco
- Alcohol: 1 liter of spirits or1 liter of wine
- Other: 10ml perfume; 125ml eau de toilette; gifts up to the value of LM50

Note: It is advisable to declare any larger or unusual items of electrical equipment brought into the island (such as video cameras, portable televisions or video recorders), as this will prevent duty being levied on these items when leaving the country.

Prohibited or Restricted
- Firearms and ammunition, explosives
- Pornography
- Wireless transmitting apparatus (i.e. CB radios, cordless telephones, walkie-talkies, etc.)
- No more than LM50 in local currency
- Counterfeit goods
- Unlicensed drugs
- Particular plants and meat products which require an import license
- Pets must have prior approval of the Director of Agriculture and Fisheries for entry into Malta Dogs and Cats must have rabies vaccinations at least 20 days and not more than six months before they are imported

IMMUNIZATION

A certificate of yellow fever vaccination is required of travelers who are arriving from infected areas. Despite WHO guidelines issued in 1973, Maltese Immigration may also require a cholera vaccination certificate from travelers arriving from endemic areas.

TIPPING

Taxi
Tip taxi drivers 10 percent of the fare.

Porters
Tip porters 25 cents per bag.

Hotels
Hotels customarily include a tip in the bill, between 10 and 15 percent. Hotel maids gratuities run at the rate of 50 cents a week.

Restaurants
Restaurants usually include a tip in the bill; in any case, customary amount is between 10 and 15 percent.

Other
Hairdressers, 10 percent; cloakroom attendants, 25 cents.

EMERGENCY INFORMATION

Police and Crime
A low rate of violent crime helps promote Malta as a destination. One must, however, be aware that break-ins and car theft do occur with increasing regularity. A few elementary precautions should protect the traveler from most problems:
- Do not leave valuables in cars or on tables in cafés.
- Keep non-essential valuables locked in hotel safes when not in use.
- Use credit cards and traveler's checks when possible to avoid carrying large sums of cash.
- Carry photocopies of your passport instead of the original.
- Carry cash in a money belt, and use credit cards or travelers checks for most of your large transactions.

- Walk with your bag away from the street to avoid having it snatched away by motorcycle thieves.
- Never carry a stranger's baggage.
- Women should avoid traveling alone at night

Caution is advised around the nightclubs in the Paceville area, as intemperate drinking and minimal crowd control can combine to precipitate brawling.

Emergency Numbers

Police.. 191
Ambulance 196
Fire 199

Health

Avoid tap water as it may cause stomach upset even so it is chlorinated. Diarrhea is common for travelers who are unaccustomed to the new diet and water.

Medical services are adequate and many of the doctors and physicians have been trained abroad and speak English and Italian.

However, for more serious medical care you are advised to leave the country. A travel insurance package that includes an evacuation policy should be acquired by all business travelers. Medical evacuation is expensive, and payment of costs must be borne by the visitor.

Medicines and pharmacological equipment are scarce, so come prepared. Pharmacies are open throughout the week and on a rotating basis on Sundays; schedules are posted in the newspaper. Sunday opening times are as follows: 9a.m. to 12:30p.m. in Malta, and 7:30a.m. to 11a.m. in Gozo.

INTERNAL TRAVEL

AIR

A helicopter service operates year round, flying between Malta International Airport and Xewkija Heliport on Gozo eight times per day. The flight takes only ten to fifteen minutes and can be a speedy option to the ferry service. During low season, expect to pay about LM12 for a one-way fare, and LM16 for a same-day roundtrip flight.

TAXI

The government controls all meter fares. Taxis are white with red license plates. Drivers are knowledgeable of the towns, but carry written directions just to be sure. The taxis are safe but expensive.

AUTO

To rent a car and drive in Malta, you must have a valid drivers license from your country of residence. Renters are responsible for and must pay all traffic fines before leaving Malta. Both Avis and Hertz have desks at the airport, and both local and major agencies can be found on the main island. You can rent bicycles and motorcycles, too.

Traffic drives on the left side, and seat belts are not mandatory. Roads flood easily and are often narrow, winding, and congested, with poor visibility around curves. Also keep in mind that parking is hard to find in Valletta. If you should have an accident, call the police immediately at 191. The police in Foriana, Valetta must endorse driver's licenses for those renting vehicles.

TRAIN

There are no train services in Malta.

SUBWAY

No subway or metro exists in Malta.

BUS

The main bus station lies in Valletta with buses connecting all parts of Malta. Fares cost between 11 and 16 cents. Regular and reliable services operate between Valletta, Sa Maison, Luqa, and Victoria (Gozo) to all towns. Buses are the principal mode of public transit, but they are old, fairly uncomfortable, and ill-equipped to protect the passenger from summer's heat.

WATER TRAVEL

Car ferry service operates between Cirkewwa in Malta and Mgarr on Gozo, with about 14 crossings a day between 6a.m. and 10:30p.m. In April and May, one night crossing is added. And between June and October, the company further adds extra night crossings. Expect a 20-minute ride for an adult fare of LM1.50; if driving, LM5.00 per car.

Hovermarine service shuttles passengers in 35 minutes from Sliema or Sa Maison to Gozo on a daily basis, excluding Sundays, between July and September.

Gozo Channel Company...................243-964, 580-435/6
in Gozo 556-114, 556-743

HELICOPTER

For those preferring air service, helicopters fly between Malta International Airport and Xewkija Heliport on Gozo seven times daily. During low season, expect to pay about LM12 for a one-way fare and LM16 for a same-day roundtrip flight.

TRAVEL ASSISTANCE

National Tourism Organization
280 Republic Street, Valletta CMR 02
tel: 224-444/5; fax: 224-401
email: info@visitmalta.com
website: http://www.visitmalta.com
Tourist Information Office
1, City Arcades, Valletta
tel: 237-747

Communications

DIALING CODES IN MALTA

International country code: [356]
City/Area codes: Malta does not require city or area codes when dialing numbers within the country. All numbers are six digit numbers.

Dialing Malta from Overseas

To dial Malta from overseas, dial your country's international dialing code, then 356 (the country code for Malta), and finally the number. There are no city codes.

Assistance Numbers

International Operator 194
Local Directory 190
Time 195
Star Services 150

CALLING WITHIN MALTA

Local Calls

If your hotel doesn't offer local call service, try going into a bar or shop to make a local call.

Long Distance Calls

All numbers in Malta have six digits without area codes. It will cost 10 to 20 cents to call anywhere in the islands.

International Calls

To make a direct call international, dial 00 + country code + area code + number. Telemalta offices offer international dialing if you prefer rates that don't shoot through your hotel ceiling. You could also try one of the international public phone boxes if you happen to spot one. Discount rates apply between 9p.m. and 8a.m. daily and all day Sunday. To reach an operator in the U.S., dial:

AT&T USA DIrect 0800-890-110

PAY PHONES

Public Telephones
Malta's new digital phone system has greatly decreased the annoyance of the previous dinosaur relic. Card phones are blue, and coin phones yellow. Phone booths have instructions in both Maltese and English. One may also place calls from a Maltacom branch: South Street in Valletta, Bisazza Street and the Plaza Shopping Center in Sliema, the Malta International Airport, Qawra, and St. Paul's Bay.

Calling Cards
Prepaid Telecards come in LM5 and LM2.50 denominations. Purchase cards at Maltacom offices, post offices, Mid-Med banks, newsstands, and other establishments with the Telecard sign.

CELLULAR PHONES
Malta has an ETACS analogue cellular system operated by Telecell Ltd., which also rents phones and even delivers them to your hotel during office hours. A one to seven-day rental will cost LM5.75 per day. Airtime costs approximately LM0.14 per unit. Contact Telecell at: 482-820 or fax: 446-166.

Note: Your home country cell phone may not work in this country. If not, we recommend that you rent an international cell phone *before* you leave home. A major US-based cell phone rental provider is **IMC WorldCell**. For information see "International Cell Phone Rentals" on page 14.

CALL BACK
You can (potentially) save significant sums when calling in Malta by using one of the call back services listed below. Fees for call back services vary widely, depending on the company and the type of service required. Be sure to check with these companies before leaving to compare rates.

For a list of callback services, please refer to the "Communications" section in the Global Road Warrior Introduction.

PHONE JACKS

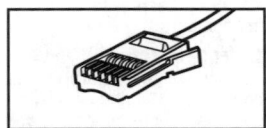

Plug adaptors are available through **iGo Corporation.** (See "Electrical and Telephone Adaptors" on page 19.)

FAX
Services are available in most hotels and offices. Maltacom branches also offer fax services. Offices are located on South Street and Bisazza Street in Valletta, and in the Plaza Shopping Center in Sliema. Malta International Airport also has a Maltacom office. Opening hours occur between 8a.m. and 10:30p.m., except at the South Street Branch (Monday to Saturday business hours only).

POSTAL SERVICES
The service is efficient and inexpensive. One may purchase stamps at most hotels. The main post office is located at Auberge d'Italie on Merchants Street in Valletta. An airport post office with a telex booth also exists, open between 7a.m. to 7p.m.

Opening Hours
Monday to Saturday 7:30a.m. to 6p.m. both winter and summer.

TELEGRAMS
Telegrams can be sent from Telemalta Corporation, St. George's Road, St. Julians or from the branch telegraph office on South Street in Valletta. Some top-end hotels also can provide telegram services.

Business Services
COURIER SERVICE

Airborne Express; Maltafast C/O Wings Couriers, 22 St. Anne Street, Floriana, Vlt 16, Malta; tel: 241-616; fax: 226-480.

DHL; DHL Building, Trq G. Vassalio, Luqa; tel: 800-148; Monday to Friday 8a.m. to 7p.m., Saturday 8a.m. to 3p.m.

Federal Express; Airsped Express Ltd., tel: 693-715.

TNT Skypak; Cassar & Cooper Ltd., Air Cargo House, Luqa Bypass, Luqa; tel: 666-999; fax: 678-000.

UPS; Airswift Courier Ltd., 14, Zurrieq Road, Luqa, Malta LQAO4; tel: 697-756, tel: 809-283; fax: 809-282.

Electrical
Current
240 volts AC, 50Hz.

ELECTRIC PLUG

Plug adaptors are available through **iGo Corporation.** (See "Electrical and Telephone Adaptors" on page 19.)

Technical Support
HARDWARE/SOFTWARE VENDOR SUPPORT

Acer/Texas Instruments; (in Germany) tel: [49] (4102) 488-469; fax; [49] (4102) 488-169; (in the U.S.) [1] (408) 432-6200; http://www.acer.com/.

Adobe; tel: 239-200; fax: 248-603 (BDS Ltd); (in Germany) tel: [49] (1) 803-5018; (in Switzerland) tel: [41] (800) 833-310; (in the U.S.) tel: [1] (800) 500-7078; http://www.adobe.com/.

Apple/Claris; (in Germany) tel: [49] (1) 803-5018; (in Switzerland) tel: [41] (800) 833-310; (in the U.K.) tel: [44] (990) 127-753; (in the U.S.) tel: [1] (408) 996-1010 (Corporate Headquarters); http://www.apple.com/.

AST; (in the U.S.) tel: [1] (817) 232-9824 (International Technical Support); (in Ireland) tel: [353] (61) 492-222; (in the U.S.) tel: [1] (949) 727-4141; http://www.ast.com/.

Compaq/Digital; (in Switzerland) tel: [41] (22) 709-5330; fax: [41] (22) 709-5391 (Geneva); tel: [41] (1) 801-2507;

fax: [41] (1) 801-2172 (Zurich); (General U.S.) tel: (281) 518-2000; http://www.compaq.com/.

Corel; (in Germany) tel: [49] (180) 425-8210 (TS Word Perfect-32 bit); (in the U.S.) tel: [1] (716) 871-2325 (Ask to be Forwarded to Appropriate Program); http://www.corel.com/.

Dell; tel: [365] 241720; fax: [356] 241726 (Intercomp LTD); (in Germany) tel: [49] (61) 039-710; (Dell- Europe) tel: [44] (134) 474-8000; (in the U.S.) tel: [1] (512) 338-4400; fax: [1] (512) 728-3330; http://www.dell.com/.

Filemaker/Claris; (in Germany) tel: [49] (180) 525-8166 (Info-line); tel: [49] (180) 567-2233; tel: [49] (180) 523-6423; (in the U.S.) tel: [1] (800) 965-9090; http://www.claris.com/.

Gateway 2000; (in Ireland) tel: [353] (1) 797-2000; (in the U.S.) tel: [1] (605) 232-2191; fax: [1] (605) 232-2023; http://www.g2k.com/.

Hewlett Packard; (Italian Office) tel: [39] (2) 264 10350; (in Switzerland) tel: [41] (22) 780-8111; (in the U.S.) tel: [1] (408) 246-4300; http://www.hp.com/.

IBM; fax: 235-145; telex: 1278 OJAMED; (in Switzerland) tel: [41] (22) 310-0418 (in French); (in the U.S.) tel: [1] (919) 517-2800; http://www.ibm.com/.

Microsoft; (Italian Office) tel: [39] (2) 703-921; fax: [39] (2) 7039-2020; [39] (2) 70-300-703; (Fax-on-Demand Service); [39] (2) 70-398-398 (Technical Support); (in Switzerland) tel: [41] (848) 858-868; fax [41] (1) 831-0869; (in the U.S.) [1] (425) 635-7222; http://www.microsoft.com/.

NEC; (in Italy) tel: [39] 1-678-20062 (UltraCare Support); (in the U.S.) [1] (916) 388-0101 (Main Switchboard); http://www.nec.com/.

Novell; (in Germany) tel: [49] 211-5632-744 (European Support Center); (in Switzerland) tel: [41] (1) 308-4747; fax: [41] (1) 302-0401; (in the U.S.) tel: [1] (408) 434-2300; fax: [1] (408) 577-5775 (Worldwide Sales Headquarters); http://www.novell.com/.

Quark; (in Switzerland) tel: [41] (1) 808-7722; fax: [41] (1) 808-7799; (in the U.S.) tel: [1] (303) 894-8899; fax: [1] (303) 894-3398 (For Products Registered in the Americas); http://www.quark.com/.

Toshiba; (in Germany) tel: [49] (2131) 158-319; fax: [49] (2131) 158-558; (in Switzerland) tel: [41] (1) 946-0777; fax: [41] (1) 946-0807; (in Ireland) tel: [44] (193) 282-8828; (in the U.S.) [1] (949) 583-3000 (Corporate Headquarters); http://www.toshiba.com/.

Internet Connection
HOW TO CONNECT

Connecting to AOL and Compuserve in Malta is similar to using it when traveling outside your own area code. See the introductory section for detailed information on connecting to your account through a different phone number.

America Online

Numbers are available at keyword *international*. Be sure to get several local numbers before leaving. AOL's Global-Net service charges US$6 an hour in addition to the usual charges. Go to keyword *access* (a free area) and download the software.

Access: Valletta 241-005.

Compuserve

Numbers are available at *Go International*. The Compuserve Web-site also has a great deal of information, at http://www.compuserve.com.

Access: Valetta 241-005.

Independent Service Providers

Many independent service providers offer discounts if you are only in town for a couple of days.

FastNet; tel: 333-364; fax: 333-366; email: sales@fastnet.net.mt; http://www.fastnet.net.mt/.

Kemmunet; tel: 489-002; fax: 492-744; email: info@kemmunet.net.mt; http://www.kemmunet.net.mt/.

LinkNET; tel: 486-199; fax: 485-039; email: info@mail.link.net.mt; http://www.link.net.mt/.

MaltaNET; tel: 489-600; fax: 489-603; email: info@maltanet.net; http://www.maltanet.net/.

Internet Cafes
Sliema

Waves Internet Cafe' & Bar; 139/140 Tower Road, Sliema SLM 08 Malta; tel: 342-242; email: info@wavesinternet.com; http://www.wavesinternet.com; Monday through Sunday, 12p.m. to sometime in the morning.;

Valletta

YMCA Internet Cafe; 178 Merchant Street, Valletta; tel: 240-680; email: ymca@waldonet.net.mt; http://www.ymcavalletta.org/; Monday through Saturday, 10a.m. to 10p.m.

Business Culture
GREETINGS AND COURTESIES

Despite their well-deserved reputation for friendliness and a helpful disposition, the Maltese are often reserved with first-time visitors. When this is the case, take the first approach. Even a phrase or two in their complex language will be greatly appreciated. Close male friends will hug briefly. Nearly everyone in Maltese business deals in the English language.

MEETINGS

Malta has been called a rock combining history and romance, lying halfway between Europe and Africa and therefore subject to cultural ambivalence. Maltese generally have a relaxed attitude toward business protocol, but the longer-established firms tend to retain some of the reserve and conservatism for which British culture is noted. The only thing foreign businesspeople can expect is variety; there is no one sure method for dealing with Maltese businesses. Punctuality is always appreciated, however.

BUSINESS ATTIRE

Light clothing is adequate in summer as the weather can become quite warm. Layering is appropriate in winter for cooler temperatures similar to other parts of southern Europe. Dress conservatively for business meetings and official occasions. If spending some relaxation time on the beach, women should kindly refrain from topless bathing as it is not suitable in Malta.

Business Centers
Valletta
CITY VIEW

Named after Jean Parisot de la Valette, leader of the order of Hospitalers, Valletta became the capital on Malta in 1570. Situated near Mt. Sceberras with two harbors, the city eventually became a strategic naval and military base under British rule. During WWII, the harbor withstood endless bombings, and it was here where the Italian fleet surrendered in 1943.

Malta

Valletta is filled with fascinating architecture dating from the 1500s, including St. John's Co-Cathedral, the Palace of the Grand Masters, and the Castile and Leon Auberge. The city is also the focal point for many of Malta's cultural institutions, with the Maneol Theatre, one of Europe's oldest, still in operation.

With tourism the main industry, the city is also the center of a large transit trade and local island trade. Valletta's population is 9,263.

AIRPORT

Malta International Airport to City Center

The airport lies in Luqa, five miles (eight km.) from the city. A taxi booth stands outside of the Welcomer' Hall where passengers pay a fixed rate (set by region) before boarding a cab. Staff will hand passengers a voucher to present to the taxi driver. Bus No. 8 runs between the airport and Valletta on a regular basis. Look for the bus stop outside of the Check-in Hall. Car rental companies are located inside of the Welcomers' Hall. Phone the following number to get connected to a car rental agency: 249-600. Or look up an agency in the auto rental listings below and call direct. A car park exists adjacent to the main terminal building on the lower passageway. The first 10 minutes of parking are free, 1 hour costs 40c. A 24-hour foreign exchange bureau is located through the Baggage claim area or from the Welcomers' Hall. Restaurants, cafeterias, and even a McDonald's Drive-thru are located at the airport for the visitor's dining pleasure.

Airport Authorities

Police	6399
Airport Security	6999
Airport Security Manager	6317
MIA Security	6012
Customs	6119
Immigration	6416
Malta Intl. Airport	249-600, fax: 249-563

Airline Numbers

Air Canada	356-3358, 338-8980
Air Malta	662-211, groups: 2299-9401
Air Malta in Valletta	240-686/7/8
	email: valletta@airmalta.com
Air Malta Helicopter Services	677-291, 2299-9138
CSA	356-333407, 333408

SEA TRAVEL

Malta - Catania, Sicily; a weekly service shuttles passengers operates between April and May, twice a week from June until July, and 4 times a week during high summer. The eight hour crossing will cost approximately LM18, during low season, and LM25 if crossing with a car. **Gozo Channel Company** ......243-964, 580-435/6 in Gozo 556-114, 556-743

Licata/Catania/Poazallo - Malta; daily passenger-only catamaran service exists between June and September, and three times a week during the rest of the year with *Virtu Ferries*. Expect about a three-hour journey for a fare of LM34 roundtrip.

Malta - Syracuse/Catania/Reggio Calabria; *Terrenia* car ferries cross from Malta to Italy three times a week. A trip to Catania will cost about LM21 one way for passengers, and LM31 for cars; to Reggio Calabria about LM23.

Malta - Naples; *Tirrenia* also offers weekly ferry service from Naples.

Malta - Libya; service between Libya and Malta exists on a daily basis. One may also sail from Catania in Italy to either Tripoli or Benghazi.

HOTELS

Top-end

The Bay Point Radisson SAS; St. George's Bay, St. Julians; tel: 374-894; fax: 374-895; 256 rooms; http://www.islandhotels.com/; email: info@radisson.com.mt; 242 rooms; restaurants; bars; lounges; conference/banquet facilities (up to 1200); business center; secretarial service; in-room cable tv, direct-dial phone, trouser press, hairdryer, safe, minibar; 24-hour room service; health center; sauna; massage; pool; diving center.

Corinthia Palace Hotel; De Paul Ave, St. Anton; tel: 440-301/9; fax: 465-713; http://www.corinthia.com/palace/; email: palace@corinthis.com; 155 rooms and suites; located at center of island, adjacent to Presidential Palace; restaurants; bar; conference/banquet facilities (up to 500); 2 boardrooms; business center; secretarial service; press room; in-room a/c, cable tv, radio, direct-dial phone, minibar, trouser press, hairdryer, safe, balcony; 24-hour room service; health center; gym; pool; tennis/squash; watersports; nearby 18-hole golf.

Le Meridien Phoenicia; The Mall, Floriana - Valetta; tel: 225-241; fax: 235-254; email: info@phoenicia.com.mt; 1920's-style hotel located in Floriana with views of the harbor; restaurants; bar; conference facilities (up to 300); secretarial service; boardroom; fax/photocopy facilities; in-room a/c, cable tv, radio, IDD phone, dataport, minibar, trouser press, hairdryer, electronic safe; 24-hour room service; valet; 24-hour laundry; corporate rates; fitness; 7 acres of gardens; pool; whirlpool; beach transport in summer.

Westin Dragonara Resort; Dragonara Rd., St. Julians; tel: 381-000; fax: 378-877; http://www.westinmalta.com/; email: westindrag@kemmunet.net.mt; 313 rooms and suites; 3 restaurants; 2 snack bars; 2 bars; 2 lounges; casino; 15 meeting rooms; conference and business center; 2 executive levels; non-smoking floors; handicapped floors; office rooms; all rooms with view; health/fitness center; 2 pools (indoor and outdoor); water sports; dive school; tennis; nearby golf.

Expensive

Bernard Hotel; St. Augustine Road, St. George's Bay, St. Julians; tel: 373-900; fax: 314-726; http://www.digigate.net/alpine/bernard.htm; email: hotelbernard@hotelbernard.com.mt; 84 rooms, 3 suites; restaurants; bar; lounge; meeting room (up to 50); board room (up to 12); business center; in-room direct-dial phone, satellite tv, radio, a/c; rooftop pool.

Best Western Les Lapins; Ta' Xbiex Yacht Marina, Ta' Xbiex; tel: 342-551; fax: 343-902; email: info@les-lapins.com; http://www.bestwestern.com; 191 rooms, 20 suites; located between Valletta and Sliema; 2 restaurants; bar; meeting space (up to 250); in-room a/c; 2 pools.

Diplomat (Howard Johnson); 173 Tower Road, Sliema; tel: 345-361/6; fax: 345-351; email: diplomat@vol.net.mt; restaurants; coffee shop; bar and rooftop bar; conference facilities (up to 150); secretarial services; office equipment; in-room blackout curtains, hairdryer, trouser press, a/c, heating, direct-dial hone, satellite tv, minibar, safe; 24-hour room service; laundry/dry cleaning.

Fortina Hotel; Tigne Seafront, Sliema; tel: 343-380 or 343-300-89; fax: 339-388; email: info@hotelfortina.com; reservations@hotelfortina.com; 220 rooms; waterfront hotel; 3 restaurants; meals included; deluxe rooms with fax machines; in-room safe box, a/c, heating, radio, tv, direct-dial phone, minibar; gym; Thalasso therapy spa; 3 indoor pools; 4 outdoor pools; jacuzzis.

Malta

Victoria Hotel; George Borg Olivier St., Sliema SLM 12; tel: 334-711; fax: 334-771; http://www.victoriahotel.com; email: victoria@victoriahotel.com; 120 rooms and suites; boutique hotel; restaurant; rooftop terrace; bar; conference/banquet facilities (up to 200); business center with mobile phones; secretarial service; in-room a/c, heating, satellite tv, radio, minibar, direct-dial phone; executive rooms with dataport; room service; dry-cleaning services; gift/newsstand; medical services; information room; car rental; underground parking; pool; whirlpool.

Moderate
Castille Hotel; Castille Square, Valletta; tel: 243-677 or 243-678; fax: 243-678; 38 rooms; 1585 mansion, located near New Quay Ferry; renovated 1988; rooftop restaurant; meetings (up to 20); in-room a/c, bath, phone, tv; elevator; parking; roof garden.

Day's Inn; 76 Cathedral Street, Sliema SLM 06; tel: 339-118; fax: 310-033; email: daysinn@nextgen.net.mt; 100 rooms; restaurant; bar; cafe; in-room a/c, tv; meeting facilities; elevator; facilities for disabled; pool.

Imperial Hotel; 1 Rudolph St., Sliema SLM 06; tel: 344-787; fax: 336-471; 95 rooms; restaurant; bar; cafe; lounge; conference facilities; in-room a/c, tv; elevator; facilities for disabled; pool.

Midas Hotel; 45, Tigne Street, Sliema SLM 11; tel: 335-895; fax: 344-556; http://www.tourist.vol.net.mt/Midas/; 50 rooms, most with harbor views; roof-top restaurant; bar; lounge; meeting/conference facilities (up to 60); secretarial service; in-room a/c, heating, fans, direct-dial phone; elevators; currency exchange; games room; sun terraces.

Hotel Milano Due; The Strand, Gzira GZR03 (Sliema); tel: 345-040/1/2/3/4; fax: 345-045; email: milano2@digigate.net; 108 rooms; located near promenade; rooftop restaurant; pizzeria; diabetic/vegetarian menus; fax facilities; 24-hour front desk; in-room bathroom, a/c, direct-dial phone, radio, tv, hairdryer, safe, minibar; laundry service; currency exchange; 2 elevators; doctor on call; 24-hour security; porter service; free parking.

Osborne; 50, South Street, Valletta; tel: 243-656/7; fax: 232-120. 51 rooms, 1 suite; restaurant; breakfast buffet; lounge; bar; conference room; in-room color tv, direct-dial phone, a/c, hairdryer; 2 elevators; roof jacuzzi, decks.

Patricia Hotel; Guze Howard Street, Sliema SLM09; tel: 336-285/6/7;fax: 342-866; http://www.clthotels.com.mt/; email: lino@clthotels.com.mt; 47 rooms; restaurant; lounge; bar; in-room bath; direct-dial phone, radio, safe, satellite tv, a/c; roof sun deck.

Plevna Hotel; 2 Thornton Street, Sliema SLM 11; tel: 331-031; fax: 336-496; email: roosendaal@waldonet.net.mt; http://www.roosendaal.com.mt/plevna.htm; 100 rooms; complimentary buffet breakfast; restaurant; bar; lounges; conference room; in-room direct-dial phone, tea/coffee making facilities, a/c, satellite tv, safe; room service; laundry; ironing room; 24-hour reception; currency exchange; private beach club; pool; rooftop sun terrace; watersports.

Sliema Chalet; 117 Tower Road, Sliema SLM 16; tel: 335-575, 335-576; fax: 333-249; http://www.vol.net.mt/com/chalet/; email: sliemachalet@vol.net.mt; restaurant and pizzeria; meeting room; fax facilities; in-room a/c, heating, fans, satellite tv, direct-dial phone, radio, safe; seaview rooms with balcony; facilities for disabled; pool; sunbathing terrace.

Windsor Hotel; Windsor Terrace, Sliema SLM 10; tel: 346-053; fax: 334-301; http://www.tourist.vol.net.mt/The_Windsor/; email: windsorhotel@link.net.mt; 50 meters from Promenade; restaurant; piano bar; in-room a/c,

bathroom, hairdryer, heating, balcony, satellite tv, radio, direct-dial phone, minibar; elevator; gym; roof-top pool.

MEDICAL CARE
The Dental Association of Malta; Federation of Professional Bodies, Medisle Village, St. Andrews. tel: 338-851.

Gozo General Hospital/Ta'Ibrag Hospital; located on Gozo; tel: 561-600, 562-700.

Medical Association of Malta; Alamein Road, Pembroke STJ 07; tel: 378-851; fax: 376-540.

Mt. Carmel Hospital; located in Attard; tel: 415-183/4/5; psychiatric hospital.

St. Luke's Hospital; tel: 241-251, 247-860; general and teaching hospital.

Sir Paul Boffa Hospital; located in Floriana; tel: 224-491, 224-581 (cancer/skin/convalesence/fever).

HEALTH CLUB
Athenaeum; Corinthia Palace Hotel, De Paul Ave, St. Anton; tel: 440-301/9; fax: 465-713; gym; indoor Hydrotherapy pools; outdoor swimming pool; jacuzzi; mud baths; Finnish therapy saunas; oxygen therapy; Reiki relaxation techniques; Feedback therapy; massage; gardens; beauty salon.

AUTO RENTAL
Avis; airport, tel: 6999-6077; 5 Sacred Heart of Jesus Street, Qawra-Bugibba, Bugibba; tel: 246-640; tel: 225-986.

Alamo; airport, tel: 6999-6067.

Budget; airport, tel: 6999-6068.

Europcar; International Airport; tel: 6999-6507; fax: 373-673; Sliema - Alpine Travel; tel: 335-249; fax: 337-421.

Hertz; reservations, tel: 314-637, fax: 333-153; Telex: 1255; Monday to Friday 8:30a.m. to 12:30p.m., Saturday-Sunday 8:30a.m. to 12:30p.m.; airport, tel: 6999-6078.

National; airport, tel: 6999-6069.

Sixt; airport, tel: 6999-6460.

Thrifty; airport, tel: 6999-6344.

CHAMBER OF COMMERCE
Malta Chamber of Commerce
Exchange Buildings, Republic Street
Valletta VLT 05
tel: 233-873/247-233; fax: 245-223
email: admin@chamber-commerce.org.mt.
website: chamber-commerce.org.mt

CONVENTION BUREAU
Malta National Tourist Office, Conference Division
280 Republic Street, Valletta, CMR 02
tel: 234-448; fax: 220-401
email: ntom.info@tourism.org.mt

Mediterranean Conference Center
Dar Il-Mediteranean, Valletta - Malta
tel: 241-454; 243-840; fax: 245-900
Telex: 1304 - VALMTG
website: http://www.visitmalta.com/CIT/MCC/

Mexico

At a Glance

THE PEOPLE

Population .... 100,349,766 (July 2000 est.)
Growth Rate .... 1.53% (2000 est.)
Life Expectancy .... 71.49 years
Infant Mortality . 26.19 deaths/1,000 live births (2000 est.)

Ethnic Composition

Indian-Spanish (Mestizo).. 60%
Amerindian 30%
Caucasian 9%
Other 1%

Religious Composition

Nominal Roman Catholic.. 89%
Protestant 6%

Languages Spoken

Spanish, Mayan dialects, Nahuatal and other indigenous languages.

Education and Literacy

Education spending rose dramatically, from 2.6 percent of GDP in 1988 to 4 percent in 1994. School enrollments at all levels have risen accordingly. Schooling is free and compulsory between ages 6 and 18. Adult literacy stood at 89.6% in 1995. Along gender lines literacy is as follows: 91.8 percent of all adult males are literate as opposed to 87.4 percent of adult females.

Labor Force

Total: 38,600,000
By occupation: agriculture 24%, industry 21%, services 55%.

THE ECONOMY

Mexico's free market economy is a patchwork quilt of modern and out-of-date industry. Privatization has increased over the past 18 years. The number of state-owned enterprises in Mexico has fallen from more than 1,000 in the early 1980's to less than 200 in 1999. The Zedillo administration is privatizing and expanding competition in sea ports, railroads, natural gas distribution, telecommunications, electricity, and airports. Increased employment, higher wages, and private consumption became the leading drivers of Mexico's recent economic growth. Mexico still needs to overcome many structural problems, such as the disparity in income distribution. The top 20 percent of income earners account for 55 percent of all income. Since the implementation of NAFTA in 1994, trade with the U.S. and Canada has nearly doubled. In a move to avoid a homogenous portfolio of trade partners, Mexico is pursuing additional trade agreements with many Latin America countries. The Zedillo administration has also signed a free trade deal with the E.U. The government is pursuing conservative economic policies in 2000, but projects an economic growth rate of 4.5 percent. A strong U.S. economy and high international oil prices account for much of this growth.

Exports .... US$136.8 billion (f.o.b., 1999)
Imports .... US$142.1 billion (f.o.b., 1999)
Total GDP .... US$865.5 billion (1999 est.)
GDP Per Capita .... US$8,500 (1999 est.)
Unemployment .... 2.5%, plus underemployment (1998)
Inflation Rate .... 15% (1999 est.)

Top Export Partners

U.S. 89.3%, Canada 1.7%, Spain 0.6%, Japan 0.5%, Venezuela 0.3%, Chile 0.3%, Brazil 0.3%.

Top Import Partners

U.S. 74.8%, Germany 3.8%, Japan 3.5%, Canada 1.9%, South Korea 2%, Italy 1.3%, France 1%.

Top Exports

Manufactured goods, oil and oil products, silver, coffee, cotton.

Top Imports

Metal-working machines, steel mill products, agricultural machinery, electrical equipment, car parts for assembly, repair parts for motor vehicles, aircraft, and aircraft parts.

BUSINESS WORKWEEK

Offices

Monday to Friday 9a.m. to 6p.m. There is a one to two hour break for lunch.

Banks

Monday to Friday 9a.m. to 1:30p.m., and limited transactions from 4p.m. to 6p.m.

Government

Monday to Friday 9a.m. to 1p.m.

Retail

Monday to Friday 9a.m. to 9p.m., shorter hours on the weekend.

HOLIDAYS

New Year's Day..January 1
Three Kings Day...January 6
Constitution Day..February 5
Birthday of Benito Juárez .... March 21
Holy Thursday ....April 20
Good Friday..April 21
Easter Monday ....April 24*
Labor Day..May 1
Cinco de Mayo ....May 5
Mother's Day ....May 10
Presidential Address to the Nation ....September 1
Independence Day ....September 16
Discovery of America ....October 12
All Saints' Day ....November 1
Day of the Dead ....November 2
Anniversary of the Revolution ....November 20
Our Lady of Guadaloupe ....December 12
Christmas ....December 25-26
New Year's Eve..December 31
*Date may vary by year.

CLIMATE

Seasons

Nearly half of Mexico is classified by an arid climate, including the northern high desert and mountains. Much of the central plateau and mountains, about 23 percent of the country, has a temperature climate accompanied by moderate rainfall. The remainder of the country is classified as warm, humid or semi-tropical, including most of the Gulf coastal plain, the Isthmus and Tehuantepec, and the

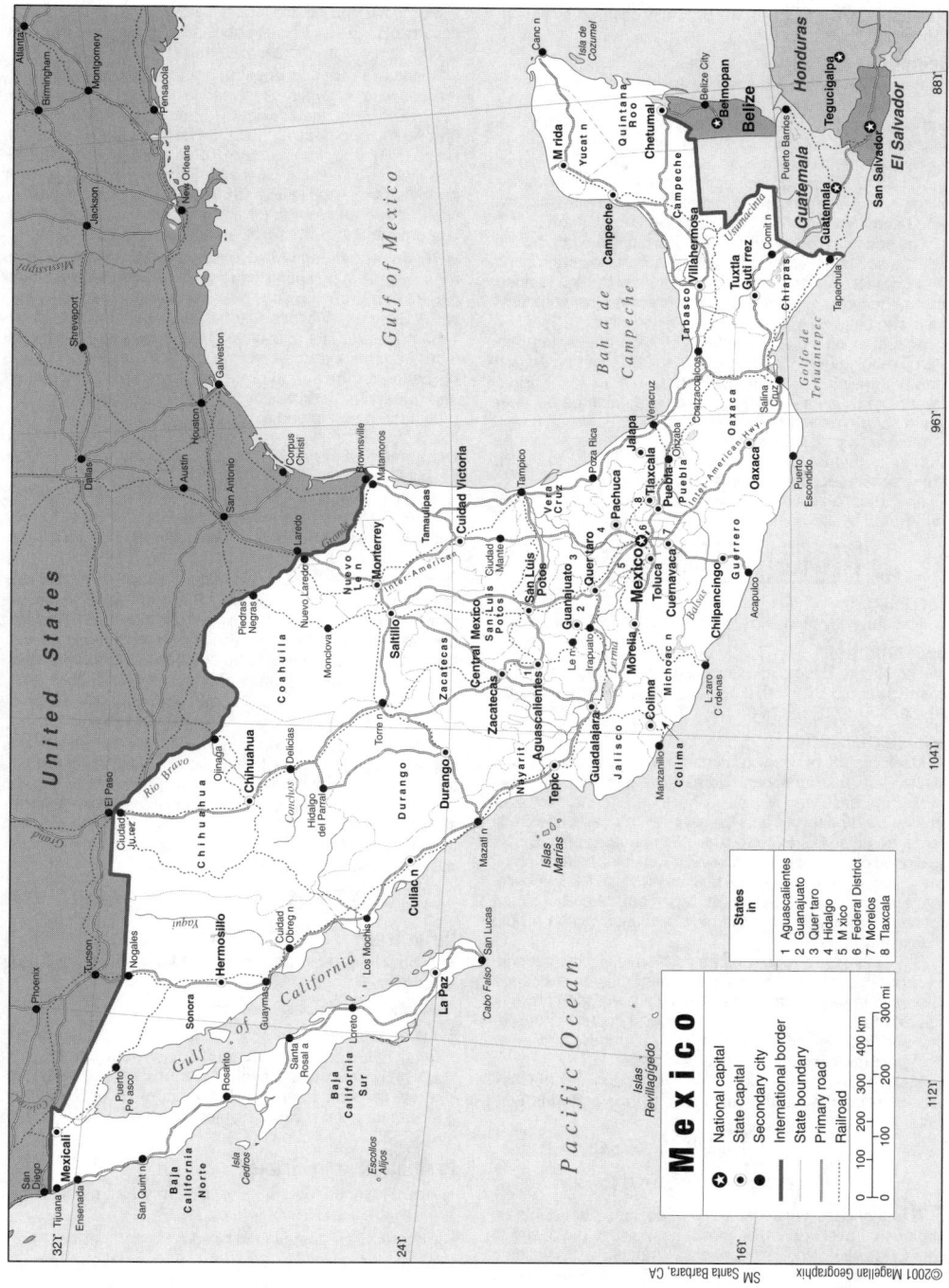

Mexico

Mexico

States in
1 Aguascalientes
2 Guanajuato
3 Querétaro
4 Hidalgo
5 México
6 Federal District
7 Morelos
8 Tlaxcala

★ National capital
• State capital
● Secondary city
— International border
— State boundary
— Primary road
‥‥ Railroad

| 0 | 100 | 200 | 300 | 400 km |
| 0 | 100 | 200 | 300 mi |

Mexico

Yucatan Peninsula, which are generally covered by savannah or rain forest.

Regions

Mexico is a vast country with very distinct regional climates with micro climates within them to match the varied terrains and altitudes. The northern half of the county, including the states of Sonora, Chihuahua, Nuevo Leon, Coaahuila, Durango, Sinaloa, parts of Zacatecas, San Luis Potosi, Tamaulipas, and Baja California, has the aridity and temperature extremes of the southwestern U.S. Monterrey has temperatures that range from blistering heat to freezing nights in January.

The southern half of the country lies within the tropics, but only the southeast and southwest coasts and low-lying parts of the interior have tropical climates (marked by high temperatures, humidity, and rainfall); nevertheless, the southeast coast can be hit by "Arctic Express" winter winds.

Acapulco, on the southwest coast, has January temperatures ranging from 22° to 31°C (72° to 88°F) and an August temperature ranging from 25° to 33°C (77° to 91°F). Even the tropical altitude of the central plateau creates year round spring-like temperatures.

Mexico City, at 2,240 meters (7,250 feet) elevation, has a January temperature range of 5° to 21°C (41° to 70°F). Rainy season occurs from late May to September.

The Pacific coast has generally warm temperatures moderated by the ocean and sometimes fog.

Money & Banking

Currency

The currency of Mexico is the Nuevo Peso (Mex$).

Denominations

The Nuevo Peso comes in coin denominations of 10, 5, 2, and 1, and 50, 20, 10, 5 centavos; and banknotes of 10, 20, 50, 100, 200, and 500.

Traveler's checks

Major brands of travelers's checks and credit cards (Visa, MasterCard, and American Express) are generally accepted in Mexico, especially in cities and tourist areas. However small shops and restaurants usually take only cash, and credit cards are unfamiliar to merchants off the beaten path. Banks give good exchange rates on traveler's checks, better than on cash, but money exchange houses do just the opposite, charging commissions of up to 5 percent. Mexican airport counters and banks offer the best exchange rates on both checks and cash.

U.S. dollars are widely accepted, especially in major cities, border towns, and resort areas, although the exchange rate used in retail purchases is usually lower than the official rate for more formal exchanges. But some remote areas are actually unfamiliar with U.S. currency, and other foreign currencies are generally not used.

Mexico has many automated teller machines (ATMs); especially in urban and tourist areas (Cirrus and Plus).

Travel

VISA AND PASSPORT

A tourist card, which is provided by flight attendants on airplanes, travel agents, or consulates, is required of all visitors to Mexico. Proof of citizenship is necessary to validate the card. Canadian, Japanese, and U.S. citizens need only the tourist card for entry (original birth certificate and photo ID can be used for proof of citizenship). Other nationals need both a passport and a visa. Contact your nearest Mexican Consulate to check the policy for your country since regulations are complex.

For those holding the Tourist Card or other visa-replacing documents, no visa (tourist or business) is required for a stay of up to three to six months, depending on nationality.

Visas are required of all others. In addition, citizens of the following nations are required to obtain special prior authorization from the Mexican Ministry of the Interior: Afghanistan, Bangladesh, Bosnia-Herzegovina, Cambodia, China (PR), Iraq, Iran, Jordan, Korea (DPR), Lebanon, Libya, Nigeria, Pakistan, Sri Lanka, Syria, Taiwan, Turkey, and Vietnam. Application processing usually takes between three and four weeks. Inquire at a Mexican consulate or embassy.

If you are entering Mexico for the purpose of installing, repairing, or maintaining equipment; visiting factories and plants; or performing your profession, you must have a visa. A Business Visitor's Card is also required of all business travelers. The application for the card must include a letter from the visitor's employer, which assumes financial obligation for the period of the applicant's visit and names appropriate Mexican business contacts or sponsoring company(ies). If you intend to stay beyond 30 days, you must also acquire a multiple-entry card and a letter from the local Department of Trade & Industry confirming that the sponsoring Mexican company is a member in good standing.

Allow two working days for processing of visa applications made in person; by mail, allow about a week. Do not apply until your anticipated travel date is less than three months hence.

Note: No summary account of the exceedingly complex Mexican regulations regarding Passports and Visas will likely be fully adequate. Check with the Mexican Consulate prior to traveling. Non-compliance with regulations will certainly cause the traveler to be fined and returned (at carrier's expense) to the country of origin.

DEPARTURE FORMALITIES

Upon departure, tourist cards must be returned. Missing cards can cause lengthy delays and hassles. Expect a departure tax of US$13.37 at the airport, but it is usually included in the price of your ticket. Archaeological artifacts are not permitted to leave Mexico. Visitors driving their own vehicles into Mexico and flying to another country must leave their car in customs bond at the Mexico City Airport.

CUSTOMS ENTRY (PERSONAL)

Duty-free

- Tobacco: 400 cigarettes, or 50 cigars, or 250g of pipe tobacco

- Alcohol: 3 liters of wine or spirits

- Other: a reasonable amount of perfume or eau de toilette; 1 stills camera, 1 portable film or video camera, and up to 12 unexposed rolls of film or video cassettes for each camera; a reasonable amount of personal and electrical goods; various objects with the value of up to US$300 or equivalent

Prohibited or Restricted

- Any uncanned food, pork or pork products, plants, fruits, vegetables and their products

- Firearms and ammunition need an import permit*

- All pets require a veterinary certificate. Dogs and cats need a rabies vaccination certificate. Birds need an import permit. Archaeological relics may not be exported

*Entering Mexico with any type of firearm or ammunition without prior written authorization from Mexican authorities carries a penalty of up to 5 years in prison.

Mexico

IMMUNIZATION

No proof of vaccination is required unless travelers are arriving from areas afflicted with cholera or yellow fever. For travelers arriving directly from the U.S., there is no vaccination requirement to enter Mexico. Immunizations against diphtheria, typhoid, polio, tetanus, and hepatitis A are advisable, however.

TIPPING

Taxi
Taxi drivers are tipped 10 to 15 percent.

Porters
Porters, bellboys, maids, and room service waiters should be tipped a small amount (US$1 per bag or day).

Hotels
Most hotels do not append a surcharge for gratuity, so it is appropriate to tip staff that has not been regularly tipped through the course of your stay. The range is 15 percent for good service, 20 percent for excellence.

Restaurants
Some restaurants add a 15 percent service charge to bills. Those that do not should be tipped that amount for ordinary good service, 20 percent for excellent service.

EMERGENCY INFORMATION

Police and Crime
Crime continues to pose a serious problem in Mexico, especially in Mexico City. Robbery, muggings, attacks, and sexual assaults in taxis have become more frequent and violent (see taxi section). Crimes against women are also increasing. Walking alone at night is not considered safe, nor is driving, especially after 1a.m. Visitors should lock doors and windows if traveling by car. Use private parking lots when parking. Never take a stranger into the car, with a special warning against prostitutes, who have been known to assault clients. The most frequently reported crimes involve taxi robberies, armed robbery, pickpocketing and purse snatching. The area behind the U.S. Embassy and the Zona Rosa are frequent sites of street crime. Exercise care if using an ATM card or machine. Try to make transactions during daylight hours, preferably inside commercial establishments.

Use caution if frequenting nightclubs or bars as some establishments may contaminate or drug drinks. Unaccompanied patrons are the most frequent victims (this applies to most crimes).

Stay on well-frequented streets and beaches and avoid off-the-path ruins or trails. The U.S. Embassy also warns that travelers to Chiapas should exercise extreme caution as an armed rebel presence still exists in more remote mountainous areas. An increasing resentment against foreigners by some segments of the local population induce cases of extreme hostility and assaults. Avoid demonstrations and other activities that may be deemed political by Mexican authorities. Contact your embassy before traveling to the Chiapas region for further security information. Military roadblocks may be encountered when traveling (especially in Chiapas, Guerrero, Oaxaca, and Puebla states), and tourists should prepare to show identification and have vehicles searched. The area of Ciudad Juarez has become the focal point for narcotics smuggling in recent years. Avoid disreputable bars and nightclubs and exercise caution when visiting the entertainment district to the west of Avenida Juarez.

In general, avoid any kind of display of wealth; dress and behave very conservatively. Leave most of your cash and traveler's checks in your hotel safe, and jewelry or other accessories should be left home altogether. Carry photocopies of your passport instead of the original. Carry cash in a money belt, and use credit cards or traveler's checks for most transactions. Walk with your bag away from the street to avoid having it snatched away by motorcycle thieves. Never carry a stranger's baggage.

While some Mexican police officers are friendly, helpful and competent, they are generally of little help in emergency situations; in such cases, contact your consulate.

Emergency Numbers
All services 08
(Police, Fire, Ambulance: nationwide)

Mexico City:
Police.. 06
All other services 08

Guadalajara:
State Police ....(3) 617-5838
Highway Patrol ....(3) 612-7194
Tourist Office (days only) ....(3) 614-0606 x11

If an emergency arises, call the Mexican Ministry of Tourism's 24-hour hotline: tel: (5) 250-0123

The hotline can provide both immediate assistance and general, non-emergency information and referrals as well.

Health
Never drink tap water; don't even use it for brushing your teeth, and avoid ice cubes or risk contracting 'Montezuma's Revenge', a nasty rendition of food poisoning. Avoid raw vegetables and fruit unless they've been washed in a chlorine solution, or with boiled or bottled water, and peel them yourself. Diarrhea is common for travelers who are unaccustomed to the new diet and water. Be sure to drink plenty of liquid to avoid dehydration. The high altitude in Mexico City and Guadalajara may cause temporary shortness of breath, headache, fatigue, and nausea. The dust and smog may cause bronchitis. Air pollution in Mexico City and Guadalajara is especially severe from December to May. If you get a cold or the flu, you can fend off bronchitis by getting out of the city to a place with fresh air and a relaxing pace; one of the many beach or mountain resorts will do just fine. If you can't get away, don't hang around the streets too much, always travel in air conditioned taxis and buses, and avoid cigarette smoke. Treatment includes steam inhalation and hot drinks to loosen phlegm, plus a balanced and varied diet with plenty of liquids. If yours is a severe case of bacterial bronchitis—marked by greenish phlegm—you may need to see a doctor for antibiotics. Viral bronchitis produces a clear phlegm. No medicine directly combats viral infections; you can take medicines for the symptoms, but the only treatment is rest, liquids, good nutrition, and the avoidance of irritants.

Most of Mexico is extremely hot, so take precautions against sun and heat stroke, drink lots of liquids, and use sunblock when outdoors.

Generally, Mexico has good medical care, but try and stay with big-city doctors and hospitals. Your consulate and major hotels can refer you to a good practitioner.

Bring your own prescription medicines, vitamins, women's sanitary products, deodorant, shaving lotion, and the like. The kinds of products you're used to are in short supply and very expensive, if they're available at all. Make sure your prescription medicines are properly labeled and that you don't have excessive amounts, or you could run into trouble at the border, both upon entering and leaving Mexico.

Mexico

INTERNAL TRAVEL
AIR

Aeroméxico and Mexicana provide an extensive network of regularly scheduled daily flights between major commercial centers. To fly between Mexico City and Monterrey, for instance, takes about 75 minutes; Mexico City to Guadalajara is 55 minutes. The flights are economical and, for the business traveler who wishes to avoid long, uncomfortable train or bus rides, are the preferred mode of transit. Smaller start-up airlines have taken over many of the domestic routes that the larger airlines have let go, but be wary of their reliability.

A number of Mexico's smaller airports have the capacity to accommodate large planes and serve as destinations and points of embarkation for some international flights. Charter aircraft are also widely available.

TAXI

Essentially, three different categories of taxis can be found in Mexico City:

* For metered cabs, look for the yellow and white taxis (normally Volkswagens), or orange taxis (Sitio, the radio cabs). These usually charge slightly more.
* Turismo taxis, which have English-speaking drivers, customarily stand outside main hotels. These are not metered, so fares are negotiated before starting the journey.
* Peseros are green and white cabs that are share-taxis running along fixed routes, with fares that are based on the distance traveled.

Travelers who arrive at Mexico City's Benito Juarez International Airport are advised to take airport taxis only—yellow, with an airport insignia painted on the door—after paying the set fare at a special booth inside the terminal.

Taxis prove the most convenient way to get around the city, but because of the traffic jams, it may be better to walk any short distances. Furthermore, due to robbery, beatings, and sexual assaults on passengers, the U.S. State Department warns its citizens to avoid taking any taxi not summoned by telephone or on their behalf by a responsible individual or contracted in advance at the airport. These radio taxis are known as "sitio". It is advisable to use these most of the time; in Mexico City, avoid taking taxis parked outside the Bellas Artes theater, in front of nightclubs, restaurants, or cruising the city.

When calling in for a sitio radio cab, be sure to request a license plate number and the name of the driver. Radio cabs can be called at the following telephone numbers:

* **Within Mexico:** (5) 271-9146, (5) 271-9058, (5) 272-6125
* **Within Mexico City:** (5) 516-6020, (5) 566-0077

If you are taking a metered cab, ask if the meter is operational before leaving by asking, *"¿Funciona el taxímetro?"* If there is no meter, bargain for a price before departure. If you don't speak Spanish, ask a hotel bellhop to negotiate a price and relay it to you. An average fare around downtown will cost between 5 and 203 pesos.

Directions

Don't plan on simply being able to give the driver the address of your destination. The Mexican system confuses even the taxi drivers. Instead, give him the name of the hotel, building, or the name of a place and landmark that lies in proximity.

AUTO

Driving in Mexico is primarily for the truly adventurous. In many areas of the country, driving takes on the characteristics of a frontier trek. In Mexico City, the world's largest and most polluted urban center, it can be a nightmare. The only exception

to the general rule dictating that outsiders refrain from driving in Mexico involves the towns near the U.S. border. Travelers can also generally include Monterrey as a reasonable place for them to drive, because the city has new four-lane toll roads connecting it to Nuevo Laredo and Reynosa, making it a straightforward three-hour drive from the border. The distances are short enough, the roads in good enough repair, the law enforcement and services availability good enough—and the alternatives poor enough—to make driving to these bustling industrial and commercial centers a reasonable proposition.

If you drive your own car into Mexico, you need Mexican auto insurance, which you can buy at crossings on either side of the border for about US$10 to US$20 a day. If you get into an accident and don't have Mexican insurance, you will probably end up in jail while the authorities decide what to do about you; under Mexico's Napoleonic Code legal system, you are basically guilty until proven innocent.

If you are driving your car from the U.S. into Mexico and expect to travel outside the border zone or free trade zone (including the Baja California Peninsula and the Sonora Free Trade Zone), you will need to obtain a permit for temporary importation of the car. The permit is valid for periods of up to six months and is good for multiple crossings during that time. Be certain to carry the permit with you at all times, but do not leave it in the car, since you will need it if the car is stolen or damaged. If you are stopped and are unable to present valid documents, the car can be confiscated immediately.

U.S. car rental companies have varying restrictions on their cars being taken into Mexico from the U.S. Or you can rent a car at exorbitant rates from the Mexican branches of U.S.-based auto rental firms, in which case you can expect to pay upwards of US$80 a day (US$400 per week) for a Volkswagen Beetle, including insurance. Neither your personal auto insurance nor your credit card car rental insurance coverage will be in force in Mexico. Carefully check your rental car—it is common to get one with bald tires, dents, scratches, and missing parts. In addition to the safety issues these conditions suggest, you can be charged for them upon return unless you have noted them in writing before signing the contract and accepting the vehicle.

Never park illegally in Mexico: the police will either confiscate your license plates—which means a trip to the police station to pay a fine—or confiscate the car should the license plates be welded to the car. Always obey the speed limits in the cities and towns to avoid a "fine" that seems to be payable directly to the police officer. Use only premium fuel: sin at the Pemex stations. It is only 87 octane, but it is the highest grade available in Mexico. Do not park cars on the street, especially at night. After 1a.m. the streets become more dangerous. If involved in an accident, many local drivers prefer to disappear into the traffic mass than deal with police, who will likely arrive seeking bribes or prisoners.

If you run into road trouble—have a breakdown or an accident, run out of fuel, need a tow, or seek protection from criminals—the Green Angels can come to your aid. The Mexican Tourism Administration operates the Angeles Verdes, a radio-dispatched fleet of 250 trucks with bilingual drivers who patrol certain sections of highway from 8a.m. to 8p.m. Roadside phones to call them exist within their patrol areas. Their services are free, and they sell parts and fuel at cost. (They do appreciate tips.)

Angeles Verdes (24 hours, toll free)................. 250-4817

TRAIN

Train travel in Mexico is not an option for business purposes, and when cost is factored in, it does not compete with the deluxe buses. In general, Mexico's state-run train system is for those with lots of time, personal padding, and patience. Plan

Mexico

on bringing your own food, water, and toilet paper as well. Under these conditions, even a short haul like the 12-hour trip from Mexico City to Guadalajara can seem endless. One exception does exist in *El Regiomontaño*, which runs between Nuevo Laredo and Mexico with stops in Monterrey, Saltillo, and San Luis Potosi. The sleeper fare costs about US$90.

For more information, call the Mexican National Railways, tel: (5) 547-1084.

SUBWAY

The metro systems in Mexico City and Guadalajara are well planned. Businesspeople may want to consider using them, especially given the congested nature of surface traffic. A metro also exists in Monterrey, but it is only a single track running east-west, serving the suburbs and residential areas.

Approximately five million people crowd onto the metro daily, making for hot and cramped conditions; luggage is not allowed. The metro is very safe, but beware of pickpockets (the crowds make their job easier). Carry valuables on the front of your person. A ride will cost about 40 centavos (US$0.12).

Mexico City's metro stations are clean and well lit, and the trains are modern and quiet. Guadalajara's metro system is not as clean and efficient, but it travels to all the important places for a pleasing price.

BUS

Government-owned buses are a good way to get around town, as long as you avoid rush hours and the routes used by tourists. Fares cost only a few centavos; but again, beware of pickpockets. Privately owned microbuses are less likely to harbor pickpockets. They also run along major streets; hold out your hand when the one you want comes by; each has a route sign on the windshield. Tell the driver where you want to get off—shout "baja" (for "down")—or push the button near the door. The fares begin at about US$0.20. Guadalajara also has an excellent bus system that provides comprehensive service throughout the city. Monterrey's system is not as easy to use, and a taxi is a better choice there. Taxis are also the best way to get around Tijuana.

If traveling long distance, use only first-class buses (*de lujo* or *ejecutivo* or *plus*) that travel on "toll" roads. Travel only in daylight hours. These modern buses have reclining seats, video monitors, toilets, and stewards serving snacks and beverages. Buses make stops for meals along the way, but pack your own lunch should the restaurant possibly not appeal to you. Also, note that smoking is permitted, meaning that the air on board is often thick and cloudy. Air conditioners, if they are working at all, are often turned to glacier setting; as such, bring a sweater or endure the icebox conditions. Reserve your seat a day in advance for these buses. They tend to keep their schedules, somewhat of a miracle in Mexico; so, be on time.

For more information, you can call directly to Central de Autobuses, tel: (5) 533-2047.

WATER TRAVEL

Auto and passenger ferries link Baja California and the Mexican mainland. The steamers sail between La Paz (Baja) and Mazatlán daily, and three or four times per week between La Paz and Topolobampo. Also served is the Guaymas and Santa Rosalia (Baja) link across the Gulf of California. You can take a ferry twice a week between Puerto Vallarta and Cabo San Lucas, at the southern tip of Baja.

Ferries also link the mainland with Cozumel and Isla Mujeres in the Caribbean.

TRAVEL ASSISTANCE

SECTUR (Secretaria de Turismo)
Presidente Mazaryck 172, Colonia Polanco
11570 México DF, Mexico
tel: (5) 254 8920; fax: (5) 254 0942
website: http://www.mexico-travel.com
FONATUR
(Fondo Nacional de Fomento al Turismo)
22nd Floor, Insurgentes Sur 800
Colonia del Valle, 03100 México DF, Mexico
tel: (5) 687 2697 or (250) 0123 0153 (travel hotline)
fax: (5) 687 5052
website: http://www.fonatur.gob.mx
Consejo de Promocion Turistica de Mexico
Mariano Escobedo 550, 8th Floor
11580 México DF, Mexico
tel: (5) 255 5026 or 255 0830; fax: (5) 203 1087
email: cptmex@infosel.net.mx
Mexico City Tourist Information, 24-hour ....
(call collect by dialing 91 first) ....(5) 250-0123
Tourist Legal Advice, 24 hour..
..............(5) 625-8618, 250-0151, (5) 250-8419, 250-8601
Mexico City Consumer Protection
....(5) 761-3811/3801
Mexican National Railways..........................(5) 547-1084
Central de Autobuses ....(5) 533-2047
Taxis, Mexico City ....(5) 516-6020, 566-0077
Angeles Verdes (Green Angels Emergency Road Service) 24-hour toll free.. 250-4817

Essential Terms

English	Spanish
Yes No	Sí No
Good morning Hello (daytime) Hello (evening) Hello (telephone)	Buenos días Buenas tardes Buenas noches ¿Sí, diga? ¿Mande?
Good-bye	Adiós
Please	Por favor
Thank you	Gracias
Pleased to meet you	Encantado (a) de conocerle
Excuse me; I'm sorry	Lo siento
My name is _____	Me llamo _____
I don't understand	No comprendo
Do you speak English?	¿Habla usted inglés?

Communications

DIALING CODES IN MEXICO

International country code: [52]

Selected city codes: Acapulco (74), Apizaco (241), Cancun (98), Celaya (461), Chihuahua (14), Ciudad Juarez (16), Cuernavaca (73), Culiacan (67), Guadalajara (3), Hermosillo (62), Juchita (971), Merida (99), Mexico City (5), Monterrey (8), Playa del Carmen (987), Puebla (22), Puerto Vallarta (322), San Luis Potosi (48), Tampico (12), Tijuana (66), Torreon (17), Veracruz (29).

Dialing Mexico from Overseas

To dial Mexico from overseas, dial your country's international dialing code, then 52 (the country code for Mexico), then the city code and finally the number. If you were dialing Acapulco from the United States, for example, you would begin with 011, then 52, then 748 (the city code for Acapulco), and finally the number of the person or office you are trying to reach.

Assistance Numbers

International Operator (English Speaking) 090
Long-distance Operator 020
Local Directory Assistance 040
Long-distance Directory Assistance 01
Mexico long-distance station-to-station 91
Mexico long-distance person-to-person 92

DIALING WITHIN MEXICO

Local Calls

Mexico's attempts to join the modern, technological world are hampered by an antiquated phone system. There aren't enough lines; switching equipment is archaic and overworked; connections are often scratchy; the number of digits in phone numbers varies from city to city; and public phones are more out of order than not. Because public phones are often broken, calling from your hotel room or lobby will prove more efficient, if more expensive. Shops with the telephone logo in the window and telephone company offices also allow public calls.

Long Distance Calls

Call long distance within Mexico on Ladatel phones, which are located in *caseta de larga distancia*, hotels, airports, railway and bus stations, and on major streets. Instructions are in Spanish, English, and French. Dial 91 + area code + number to make a long-distance domestic call. Call expenses are reduced after 5p.m. on weekdays and all day on weekends.

International Calls

International calls are especially expensive, particularly if using the Mexican phone system. A 30-minute operator-assisted call to the U.S. from Mexico City could cost US$100 when you include hotel surcharges. AT&T and MCI offer off-peak, long distance discounts, and the local telephone book has details on other long distance discounts. It's also less expensive to call collect or to use your phone card. Another solution is the **AT&T Message Service**, which allows you to leave a message up to one minute long for anyone with access to a phone anywhere in the world.

AT&T USA Direct 95 (800) 462-4240
MCI 95 (800) 674-7000

If for some reason this does not work, dial direct from Ladatel phones by pressing 95 (or 96 for person-to-person or collect calls) to reach the U.S. and Canada; you do not need to press 1 for the country code. Press 98 (or 99 for person-to-person or collect calls) to reach other countries; then dial the country code, area code, and local phone number.

PAY PHONES

Public Telephones

Because public phones are so often broken, it is much easier—although also more expensive—to make local calls from your hotel room or lobby. You can also use phones in telephone company offices and in certain shops (usually those with a telephone symbol in the window or on a sign).

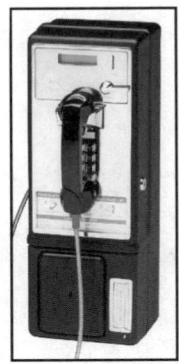

CALL BACK

For a list of callback services, please refer to the "Communications" section in the *Global Road Warrior* Introduction.

PHONE JACK

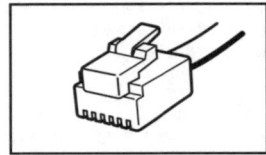

Plug adaptors are available through **iGo Corporation.** (See "Electrical and Telephone Adaptors" on page 19.)

CELLULAR PHONES

A multitude of companies operate cellular systems in Mexico, most all use the AMPS analogue system.

Note: Your home country cell phone may not work in this country. If not, we recommend that you rent an international cell phone *before* you leave home. A major US-based cell phone rental provider is **IMC WorldCell**. For information see "International Cell Phone Rentals" on page 14.

FAX

Fax machines are widely available in hotels and major post offices, but they are not as advanced as those in the U.S. In addition, Mexico's phone system is not as advanced as first-world countries, which could cause delays.

POSTAL SERVICES

Mexico's mail service is notorious for delays and poor service. Whenever possible avoid surface mail and use couriers or fax service instead. If going by post, send everything airmail, which delivers a package to the U.S. in six days and to Europe within two weeks. The express service, known as *Entrega Inmediata*, takes from 2 to 3 days. Another service, Mex-Post, is also very reliable. The red tape for all incoming packages is thick.

Hours of service

Monday to Friday 8a.m. to 10p.m., Saturday 8a.m. to 8p.m., Sunday 9a.m. to 4p.m.

TELEGRAMS

Telegrams can be sent from almost anywhere. In small towns, it may be the best way to send a message internationally. Many hotels have telefax services. Telegrams may be given to Telegrafo Nacionales. In Mexico City, the main office resides at Balderas y Colón, Mexico 1 DF.

Business Services

COMPUTER RENTAL

Consultores en Informática y Computación; M. Avila Camacho 156; tel: 282-5777.

Computers Rentals Init, S.A. de C.V.; Felix Parra 114, Sn. José Insurgentes; tel: 615-1540 con 12 líneas; support: 660-0102, 680-0098.

Compu-Renta, S.A. de C.V.; Av. Circunvalación 117, Col. Atlántida Coyoacán; tel; 689-1804, 686-6222.

Comunicaciones y Satélites, S.A.; Prieto 621; tel: 523-3348, 536-0895.

Xsistemas, S.A. de C.V.; Peten 477-B, Col. Narvarte; tel: 605-1068, 605-4251.

COURIER SERVICES

Airborne Express; C/O Pegaso Express S.A. De C.V., Lago Wetter No 147, Col Pensil, Mexico City 11470; tel: (5) 203-6811; fax: (5) 531-8503.

Airborne Express; C/O Pegaso Express S.A. De C.V., Lopez Cotilla No 1904-A, Col Ladron De Guevara, Guadalajara, Jal 44160; tel: (3) 630-3896; fax: (3) 615-2242.

CRC Mensajería nacional e internacional (Mexico City); Av. Tlahúac 1577 condominio 21, Fracc. Marasoles; tel: 840-3435; fax: 840-3435.

DHL (Mexico City); Paseo da Reforma 76, Col. Juárez, 06600, tel: (5) 546-5302, 227-0299; fax: (5) 546-5939, 592-6463.

DHL (Guadalajara); Lázaro Cárdenas 1299, Fracc. Industrial Alamo, 44900, tel: (3) 670-1885, fax: (3) 670-2141.

DHL (Monterrey); Carretera Miguel Alemán Valdez No. 205, Col. Lindavista, 67130 Guadalupe, tel: (8).

Federal Express (Mexico City); Insurgentes Sur 899, Col. Nápoles 03810 Mexico, D.F.; tel: 228-8103; fax: 228-8170.

Federal Express (Mexico City); Francisco Sarabia 17, Peñón de los Baños, 15520, Mexico, D.F.; tel: (5) 785-6144; fax: (5) 785-1569.

Federal Express (Monterrey); Calle B No. 506, Parque Industrial Almacentro, 66600 Apodaca, N.L.; tel: [1] (800) 900-1100; tel: (83) 69-3659; fax: (83) 69-3654.

Mexpost (Mexico City); Netzahualcóyotl 109, Col. Centro; tel: 709-9606; fax: 709-9606.

UPS (Mexico City); Almacen Fiscalizado No. 21, Aduana Aeropuerto International, Benito Juarez, Mexico City, Mexico 15520 C.P., tel: (5) 228-7900, fax: (5) 228-7981.

UPS (Guadalajara); Río Obi 1781, Col. Alamo Industrial, 44910; tel: (3) 657-9201; fax: (3) 635-7981.

UPS (Monterrey); Frandisco Rocha, number 480, Col. Jardin de San Jeronimo, Monterrey, Nuevo Leon 66640, Mexico; tel: (83) 339-358, fax: (83) 339-389.

SECRETARIAL SERVICE

Alto Nivel Secretarial y Administrativo S.A.; Boulevard Miguel Avila Camacho 1994-102; tel: 398-3011/7650.

Manpower S.A.; Miguel Laurent 15; tel: (5) 559-9702, 559-5161, 559-5480, 575-3764.

Secretariás Temporales S.A.; Rio Danubio 69; tel: (5) 514-7844.

Servicios Secretariales Ejecutivos A.P.; Baja California 245-404; tel: (5) 584-7865.

TRANSLATION/INTERPRETING

Alarsa, S.A.; Río Pánuco 150, Col. Cuauhtémoc; tel: 525-6575/208-9437; fax: 208-1146.

Berlitz de México, S.A. de C.V.; Ejercito Nacional 503 PB, Col. Polanco; tel: 531-4653/531-4353; fax: 255-3817.

Centro Integral de Traducción e Interpretación; (CITI); Av. Chapultepec 471-302, Col Juárez; tel: 286-9192/286-8832.

Lanser de México; Durango 247, Piso 4, 06700; tel: (5) 208-5735, 514-0605.

Linguamundo; Skytel: 227-7979 clave: 527-9786; tel/fax: 533-3051; email: 103503.2555@compuserve.com

Guzmán Dibella y Asociados, S.C.; Hacienda Huaracha 139, Col. Bosques de Echegaray, Naucalpan, Edo. de México; tel; 560-0932/363-2939; fax: 560-0932.

Recursos Técnicos Para Conferencias, S.C.; Eugenia 13-602, Col Nápoles; tel: 543-5011/543-3517; fax: 543-3262.

Sittco; Melchor Ocampo 193, Desp. A, Plaza Galerias; Tel/fax: (5) 260-0676.

Traducciones Willy de Winter; Horacio 528-404, Col. Polanco; tel: 545-5764/254-7446/203-2585; fax: 531-0348; Compuserve: 74174,172

TransComp, S.A. de C.V.; Calz. Vallejo s/n esq. poniente 122, Col. Vallejo; tel: 567-9909; fax: 567-9856; email: tra@mpsnet.com.mx

Electrical

Current

110 volts, 60Hz

ELECTRIC PLUGS

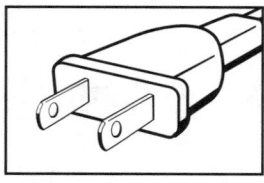

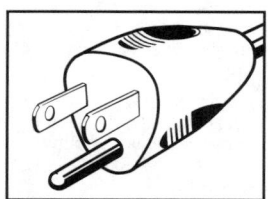

Plug adaptors are available through **iGo Corporation.** (See "Electrical and Telephone Adaptors" on page 19.)

Mexico

Technical Support
HARDWARE/SOFTWARE VENDOR SUPPORT

Acer/Texas Instruments; (in the U.S.) [1] (408) 432-6200; (in Germany) tel: [49] (4102) 488-469; fax; [49] (4102) 488-169; http://www.acer.com/.

Adobe; tel: (2) 535-8262; fax: (2) 535-8426; (in Switzerland) tel: [41] (800) 833-310; (in the U.S.) tel: [1] (800) 500-7078; http://www.adobe.com/.

Apple/Claris; (Canada Support) tel: [1] (905) 513-5803; (in the U.S.) tel: [1] (408) 996-1010(Corporate Headquarters); (in the U.K.) tel: [44] (990) 127-753; http://www.apple.com/.

Compaq/Digital; tel: (5) 229-7900; fax: (5) 229-7930; (General U.S.) tel: (281) 518-2000; http://www.compaq.com/.

Corel; tel: 0[1] (800) 024-2673 (All Applications); (in the U.S.) tel: [1] (716) 871-2325 (Ask to be Forwarded to Appropriate Program); http://www.corel.com/.

Dell; tel: [52] (5) 228-7(800) 250-7111; fax: [52] (5) 228-7840/228-6842/228-6843; (in the U.S.) tel: [1] (512) 338-4400; fax: [1] (512) 728-3330; (Dell- Europe) tel: [44] (134) 474-8000; http://www.dell.com/.

Hewlett Packard; in D.F. tel: 326 46 00; in Guadalajara - tel: 669 95 00; in Monterey: 378 42 40; (in the U.S.) tel: [1] (408) 246-4300; http://www.hp.com/.

IBM; tel: (01-800) 003-2500 (toll free within D.F.); tel: 70-59-60; (in the U.S.) tel: [1] (919) 517-2800; http://www.ibm.com/.

Microsoft; tel: (5) 265-3399 (Applications and Operating Systems); tel: (5) 265-3380 (Client Services); (5) 261-2199 (Fast Tips); (in the U.S.) [1] (425) 635-7222; http://www.microsoft.com/.

NEC; tel: 5-669-0422 (UltraCare Support); (in the U.S.) [1] (916) 388-0101 (Main Switchboard); http://www.nec.com/.

Novell; tel: 95-800-638-9273 (Toll Free Technical Support - dial AT&T access number first, if available); (in the U.S.) tel: [1] (408) 434-2300; fax: [1] (408) 577-5775 (Worldwide Sales Headquarters); http://www.novell.com/.

Quark; (in the U.S.) tel: [1] (303) 894-8899; fax: [1] (303) 894-3398 (For Products Registered in the Americas); http://www.quark.com/.

Toshiba; (in the U.S.) [1] (949) 583-3000 (Corporate Headquarters); (in Germany) tel: [49] (2131) 158-319; fax: [49] (2131) 158-558; (in Switzerland) tel: [41] (1) 946-0777; fax: [41] (1) 946-0807; (in Ireland) tel: [44] (193) 282-8828; http://www.toshiba.com/.

Internet Connection
HOW TO CONNECT

Connecting to AOL and Compuserve in Mexico is similar to using it when traveling outside your own area code. See the introductory section for detailed information on connecting to your account through a different phone number.

America Online

Numbers are available at keyword *international*. Be sure to get several local numbers before leaving. AOL's Global-Net service charges US$3.95 an hour in addition to the usual charges. Go to keyword *access* (a free area) and download the software.

Access: Guadalajara (3) 818-0201; Hermosillo (62) 185-226; Mexico City (1) 943-2265; Mexico City (5) 442-3442; Mexico City (5) 448-8400; Monterrey (8)122-9999.

Compuserve

Numbers are available at *Go International*. The Compuserve Web-site also has a great deal of information, at http://www.compuserve.com.

Access: Ciudad Juarez (16) 160-928; Cuernavaca (73) 225-002; Guadalajara (3) 134-1000; Leon (47) 735-710; Mexico City (5) 262-0000; Mexico City (5) 262-4500; Monterrey (8) 369-4880; Monterrey (8) 155--4000; Nationwide (1) (800)926-6000; Puebla (22) 119-200; Veracruz (29) 225-800.

Independent Service Providers

Many independent service providers offer discounts if you are only in town for a couple of days.

CIATEQ; tel: (4) 211-2600; fax: (4) 216-9963; email: webmaster@ags.ciateq.mx; http://www.ags.ciateq.mx/.

CMACT.SA; tel: (8) 378-0636; http://www.cmact.com/.

DataNet, S.A. de C.V. (PSI Net International); tel: (5)118-4577; tel: (5) 118-4868; fax: (5) 739-1676; email: sales@data.net.mx; http://www.data.net.mx; (Spanish; serving Mexico City).

Terra Guadalajara; tel: (3) 818-6000; fax: (3) 818-6615email: cobranza@vianet.com.mx; http://www.terra.com.mx/; (serving Guadalajara, Spanish).

Terra México, D.F.; tel: (5) 241-1500; fax: (5) 241-5158; email: aclientesmex@infosel.net.mx; http://www.terra.com.mx/; (Spanish).

MPSNet; tel: (5) 639-6075; Monterrey (3) 359-3303, email: wramirez@mpsnet.com.mx; Guadalajara (3) 813-0099, email: whs@mpsnet.com.mx; Acapulco (74) 86-8182/8184, email: info@acanet.com.mx (Spanish).

Networks Mexico; tel: (5) 523-0826; email: info@netmex.com; http://www.netmex.com/; (serving Guadalajara and Mexico City, Spanish).

SPIN-Internet; tel: (5) 687-0666; fax: (5) 687-8166; http://www.spin.com.mx/; (serving Mexico City, Spanish).

Internet Cafes
Acapulco

Acanet Internet Cafe; 1632 Costera Miguel Alleman, Gran Plaza, Acapulco; tel: (7) 486-8182; tel: (7) 486-8184; fax: (7) 486-9186; email: acanet@acanet.com.mx; http://www.myfreeoffice.com/internetcoffe.

D Byte Internet Coffe; Hidalgo #20 Local 4 Centro c.p. 39300, Acapulco; tel: (7) 483-2755; fax: (7) 483-2755; email: dbyte@prodigy.net.mx; Monday through Saturday, 11a.m. to 8p.m.; 30 Pesos per hour of Internet use.

Chihuahua

Cybercafe Canaco; Av. Cuauhtemoc 1800 3th floor Chihuahua, Chihuahua; tel: (14)16-00-00; fax: (14)151-928; email: cfn@infosel.net.mx; Monday through Friday, 9a.m. to 2p.m., Saturday 9a.m. to 1p.m.; 20 Pesos per hour of Internet use.

Ciudad Juarez

Web & Play C@fe; 33 Av. Ejercito Nal. 7624 Cd. Juarez Chihuahua; tel: (16) 176-773; email: web-play@web-play.com; email: web-play@web-play.com; http://www.web-play.com/.

Guadalajara

eCoffee - Internet & Café (MR); La Gran Plaza, Local K-12 Av. Vallarta # 3959 Colonia Don Bosco Vallarta, Guadalajara; tel: (3) 123-1551; fax: (3) 123-1552; email: ecoffee@usa.net; http://www.ecoffee.com.mx/; Monday through Saturday 10a.m. to 9p.m., Sunday 12p.m. to 8p.m.; 30 Pesos per hour of Internet use.

Hackers; Pedro Moreno 863-A Centro, Guadalajara; tel: (3) 826-6762; fax: (3) 826-6762; email:

hackers@megared.net.mx; http://www.geocities.com/hackersgdl/hackersgdl.html/; Monday through Saturday, 10a.m. to 12p.m.; 20 Pesos per hour of Internet use.

INTERNETPURO.COM; Centro Magno Av. Vallarta, 2425 Primer Nivel (in the mall), Guadalajara; tel: (3) 630-2210; fax: (3) 630-2660; email: info@internetpuro.com; Monday through Sunday, 9a.m. to 1:30a.m.; 0.50 Pesos per minute of Internet use.

Mexico City Area

Axon Cyber Cafe; International Airport (Mexico City) Sala E (Gate E), Local No. 27 PB.; tel: (5) 786-9399; fax: (5) 786-9372; email: aeropuerto@axon.com.mx; http://www.axon-cybercafe.com/; Monday through Sunday, 9a.m. to 9p.m.; 1 Peso per minute.

Bar Internet EL REY; Dr. Claudio Bernard 149 Col. Doctores, 06720 Mexico City (Near the Balderas subway stop); tel: (5) 761-3973; fax: 5) 761-3973; email: elrey@only.at; Monday through Saturday 11a.m. to 9p.m.; 20 pesos per hour.

Cyberspace Cafe; Mazatlan 148, Condesa Mexico City; tel: 211-6877; email: corp@mpsnet.com.mx; Monday through Saturday, 10a.m. to 11p.m.; 30 Pesos per one half of an hour.

El Claustro; Calle 4 No. 48 Int. 1, COL. San Pedro de los Pinos, C.P. 11870 Mexico D.F.; tel: (5) 643-1208; fax: (5) 271-6580; email: lcpp@hotmail.com; Monday through Saturday, 9a.m. to 9p.m.; 20 Pesos per hour of Internet use.

Escape Ciber Cafe; Av de la Paz 23 San Angel Mexico D.F. Mexico; tel: (5) 550-7611; fax: (5) 550-7852; email: jenader@elsitio.com; Sunday through Thursday, 9a.m. to 11p.m., Friday and Saturday 9a.m. to 2a.m.; rates vary from US$2.50 to US$4 per hour of Internet use.

Javachat Cafe Internet; Genova 44-K Zona Rosa Mexico City; tel: (5) 525-6853; fax: (5) 514-6856; email: javachat@yahoo.com; http://members.tripod.com/~javachatcafe; Monday through Saturday, 10a.m. to 10p.m.; US$3.60 per hour of Internet use.

Kodkod Cafe Internet; Cumbres de Maltrata, 373 Esquina Monte Alban Colonia Narvarte, Mexico City; tel: (5) 696-9661; fax: (5) 696-9661; email: kodkod@starmedia.com; Monday through Saturday, 9a.m. to 11p.m.; US$2 per hour of Internet use.

Monterrey

CyberPress; Plaza Monyor Local 24 Centro Comercial HEB Hda Los Morales Felix Galvan y Plaza Las Americas; tel: (8) 135-8202; email: cyber_press@email.com; Monday through Saturday, 7a.m. to 10p.m.; 20 Pesos per hour of Internet use.

INFOSKY; Ave. del Estado # 215-A Col. Tecnológico a una cuadra y media del Tecnológico de Monterrey (ITESM); (8) 387-7287; tel: (8) 318-9774; fax: (8) 318-9774; email: infosky@infosel.net.mx; http://paginas.infosel.com/infosky/; Monday through Friday, 9a.m. to 11p.m., Saturday 9a.m. to 9p.m.; 25 Pesos per hour of Internet use.

ZCAFE; 1000 Batallon de San Patricio, Local 2408 Garza Garcia, Monterrey; tel: (8) 368-4838; fax: (8) 368-4855; Monday through Friday, 9a.m. to 8p.m.; 50 Pesos per hour of Internet and computer use.

Business Culture

GREETINGS AND COURTESIES

It is the norm to shake hands when introduced to someone of the same sex. A man being introduced to a woman will bow slightly, and shake hands only if the woman initiates this interaction. Foreign men should do the same when meeting Mexican women. It is polite to greet (and say good-bye to) every member of a group individually. Direct eye contact between equals can go on for some time. Avoiding eye contact might be interpreted as a sign that a person is hiding something or is not to be trusted. Introductions are, in general, quite formal and the following mood similar until more confidence has been established. An air of reserve will most likely be better received than an informal, back-slapping how do you do.

DECISION MAKING

Mexicans are extremely polite, to the point of avoiding an awkward truth by telling someone what they want to hear instead. They will rarely say something can't be done, and also may agree to do something that is in fact not possible. They have great respect for authority. Power resides in the hands of the few (or one) at the top of the company hierarchy. The head of a company has the final word, and it is not often questioned by employees. Mid-level managers do not make decisions, and are trained to not disturb the status quo. Keep in mind that a confrontational or pushy method will not serve business well. One might instead lose respect and garner one an uneducated appearance.

WOMEN

Latin cultures are known for their male chauvinism and women should be prepared to deal with this. It's very rare for women to hold top management positions in Mexican companies, and a woman simply may not be given the same respect as a man, or be taken as seriously. To counter this, women should be well-poised, behave in a completely professional manner, and dress conservatively. Complementing women is part of Mexican culture, but in some situations such remarks might also be a way to judge a woman's availability. A quick acknowledgment will suffice if the remark is polite. Remaining coolly professional will usually discourage unwanted attention. However, women should be aware that a bruised male ego could destroy a business relationship. Business breakfasts, lunches, and dinners are common, but women traveling alone should not arrange a dinner with a man. Lunches should take place in the woman's hotel restaurant so the check can be put on the room bill. If it is presented at the table, a man will not allow a woman to pay. After business hours, women should have an escort if they go out at night. In general, women should not go to a bar alone.

MEETINGS

Be prepared for meetings to take longer than anticipated, and to be frequently interrupted by phone calls and people. Showing annoyance at such interruptions will be considered impolite. Mexicans sometimes schedule several meetings at the same time, assuming some appointments will not be kept. They also set meetings for times when they know they will not be available, or at strange hours. The best time to schedule an appointment is between 10a.m. and 1p.m., or 4p.m. and 6p.m. The people you meet with will probably not have the power to enter into an agreement, so determine which of them will be reporting to company superiors. Negotiation meetings will usually take place in a hotel, conference center, or other comfortable surroundings. Subordinates will arrive first; an executive with higher status will arrive later. Prepare initially for relaxed small talk and pleasantries. Getting right to business will be viewed as rude and perhaps suspicious. When the time is right, the senior Mexican representative will give a welcoming speech and turn the meeting over to the visitors. After your position has been stated, the Mexican team leader will answer, item by item, suggesting any changes.

Mexico

Business travelers should keep in mind the horrendous traffic problems in Mexico City and leave themselves ample time to get from point to point, with extra allowances during the May to September rainy seasons, which make the easy-to-flood streets even more problematic.

BUSINESS ATTIRE

Your attire will be viewed as a sign of your respect for your associates, and your attitude toward the business in general. In urban areas, especially Mexico City, suits and European fashions are preferred for men. Don't remove your jacket or loosen your tie unless your host makes this suggestion. Women should wear conservative dresses or suits. Jewelry, makeup, and heels are standard, but this is a matter of personal taste. In smaller towns and rural areas, suits or expensive clothing are viewed as showing off.

Business Centers
Guadalajara
CITY VIEW

With a population of about six million, Guadalajara is the most important financial and commercial center in the country outside of Mexico City. In fact, some might call it a mini Mexico City, smog factor included. It is an interesting combination of agricultural center and industrial hub, and also a major player in Mexico's electronics industry, boasting its largest export sector.

Founded in 1531, the city became a hub for Indian slave hunting in the 16th century. In 1810, Miquel Hidalgo y Costilla led an independence movement which abolished slavery in all of Mexico. Several of the city's churches date from the colonial period, and the governor's palace, dating from 1743, is one of the best examples of Spanish architecture in the country.

Industry has remained strong since 1940 and consists mainly of corn, textiles, shoes, chemicals, building materials, tobacco products, and soft drinks.

Growth has been steady for this city, sometimes known as the most Mexican of Mexican cities. In spite of its size, it is still considered the place where one can enjoy a slower pace and more traditional atmosphere. Lovely parks, squares, and the old-world style of the colonial heart of the city make Guadalajara a place where tourists can truly experience the rich culture and traditions of Mexico.

AIRPORT

Miguel Hidalgo International Airport to City Center

The airport lies 12 miles (19 km.) from the city center. Minibuses take travelers from the airport to their hotels. Taxis and limousines are also available.

Monterrey
CITY VIEW

Monterrey is the third largest center in Mexico, and the capital of the northern state of Nuevo León. It is an industrial center that lies only 150 miles from the U.S. border, yet the city is also known for its institutions of higher learning. It is partly surrounded by mountains and on the floodplain of the eastward-flowing Rio Santa Catarina.

It wasn't until around 1930 that the city began to flourish, when the Inter-American Highway was built. Prior to that, its distance from Mexico City and lack of metals caused the

area to remain insignificant. Originally discovered in 1579, Monterrey remained unnoticed until the late 19th century. With the opening of the Laredo, Texas railway in 1882 came smelting and industrial enterprises.

Monterrey has hundreds of light industries including beer, cigarettes, pottery, glass, and textiles. Several universities also grace the area, including: Monterrey Institute of Technology and Higher Education, Nuevo Leon University, Labastida University, Regiomonane University, and the University of Monterrey.

Since 1775, the city has steadily grown from a population of 258 to its current count of 1,702,000.

AIRPORT

Mariano Escobedo International Airport to City Center

The airport lies 14 miles (22 km.) from the city center. Aueropuerto Transportaciones runs minibuses taking travelers from the airport to their hotels

Airline Numbers

Aeroméxico	(8) 40-87-60, 40-87-66 to -69
American Airlines	(8) 340-30-31
Mexicana	(8) 45-30-77
Continental Airlines	(8) 43-70-01, 44-70-25

Mexico City
CITY VIEW

Mexico City is the country's political, financial, commercial, industrial, and cultural center, and the home of nearly 20 million people—making it one of the world's largest cities. It sprawls seemingly forever, yet possesses a surprisingly advanced infrastructure. However, shantytowns ring the high-tech center and an eternal shroud of smog hovers above the city and its approximate three million cars.

As one of the oldest cities in the Western Hemisphere, it has also stood as a focal point of Latin American history since the 16th century. Surrounded by mountains and built on the ruins of Tenochtitlan, the ancient Aztec capital, it sits on what was once a lake bed. The city itself is rich in culture, with everything from elegant colonial mansions to magnificent, ancient pyramids.

Industry includes construction and the manufacturing of chemicals, plastics, cement, yarns and textiles, and tourism. Mexico's stock exchange and financial institutions are also headquartered here.

Visitors will find an exciting, vibrant city still struggling with the effects of expansion and growth.

AIRPORT

Benito Juárez International Airport to City Center

The airport lies 3.75 miles (6 km.) from the city. Subways run to and from the airport, but luggage larger than a shoulder bag is not allowed on the trains. If your hotel does not provide a shuttle service, a taxi is probably the best way to get to and from the airport. Use only the regulated airport taxis, which are recognizable by their yellow color with an airport symbol on the door. Head for the taxi counter in the arrivals area to prepay a set fare. Expect to pay between US$10 and $15 for a 30-minute ride downtown. The reverse trip will cost a bit more.

Airline Numbers

Aeromar	(5) 207-66-66
Aeroméxico	(5) 207-60-93
Aerovias de México	(5) 203-75-43
Aerovias Oaxaqueñas	(5) 510-01-62

Air France .... (5) 566-00-66
Air Panama .... (5) 566-68-60, 566-75-57
Alitalia .... (5) 533-12-40 to -43
American Airlines .... (5) 209-14-00
Aviación de Chiapas .... (5) 762-01-99
Avianca .... (5) 535-02-27
British Airways .... (5) 511-73-79
Continental Airlines .... (5) 203-11-48
Delta Airlines .... (5) 202-16-08
Iberia .... (5) 592-29-88
Icelandair .... (5) 511-84-61
Japan Air Lines.................................. (5) 533-55-15 to -19
KLM Royal Dutch Airlines .... (5) 202-44-44
LACSA Lineas Aereas
Lufthansa .... (5) 202-88-66
Mexicana .... (5)660-44-44
SAS Scandinavian Airlines .... (5) 202-85-33
Swissair .... (5) 533-63-63
TAN-SAHSA Lineas Aereas
United Airlines .... (5) 531-83-44, (5) 531-45-28

HOTELS

Note: Hotel rates are often negotiable.

Top-end

Camino Real (Leading Hotels of the World); Mariano Escobedo 700, Polanco; tel: (5) 203-2121; fax: (5) 250-6897 or (5) 250-6723; http://www.caminoreal.com/mexico/ ; 709 rooms and suites; located in business district on 8 acres; only resort hotel in the city, gardens and patios; 10 restaurants, including city's best French restaurant, Fouquet's of Paris; bar; conference facilities (up to 1500); business center; secretarial service; in-room a/c, minibar, satellite tv, direct-dial phone, modem/fax connection, safe; 24-hour room service; concierge; beauty salon/barber; corporate rates; health club; fitness; sauna; pool; tennis; 8.5 acres of gardens; US$212.

J.W. Marriott Hotel Mexico City; Andres Bello 29, 11560; tel: (5) 282-8888; fax: (5) 282-8807; http://marriotthotels.com/ MEXJW/; 299 rooms, 12 suites; Polanco district; executive floor; restaurant; bar; 9 meeting rooms; business center; secretarial service; in-room a/c, dual-line pone, voicemail, dataports, satellite tv, movies, newspaper, minibar, hairdryer, bathrobe, safe; 24-hour room service; laundry valet; concierge; some rooms with kitchen; hair salon/barber; gift shop; newsstand; car rental; complimentary parking; health club; solarium; sauna; pool; whirlpool.

Hotel Marquis Reforma; Paseo de la Reforma, colonia Cuauhtémoc, 06500; tel: (5) 211-3600; fax: (5) 211-5561; http://www.hotelmarquisrfma.com.mx/; email: marquis@ri.redint.com; 84 suites, 124 art deco rooms; near financial center; business hotel; La Jolla restaurant; bar; corporate lounge; business services; meeting facilities (up to 600); corporate center; in-room cable tv, minibar, fax machine, personal computer; room service; laundry/valet; beauty salon/ barber; disabled access; fitness; sauna; jacuzzi.

Presidente Inter-Continental México; Campos Eliseios 218, Polanco, 11560; tel: (5) 327-7700; fax: (5) 327-7730; email: mexicocity@interconti.com; 659 rooms and suites; 1999 and 2000 renovations to many rooms; located in business district; 6 restaurants (including Maxim's de Paris); tea room, bar; lounge; 13 function rooms; business center with Internet access, audio/ visual equipment; conference facilities (up to 1500); translation services; 9 Club floors; in-room data ports, dual-line phone, minibar, cable tv, hairdryer, radio, temperature control; 24-hour room service; laundry/dry cleaning; medical facilities; florist; hair salon; shops; airline desk; car rental; parking; gym.

Expensive

Fiesta Americana Reforma; 80 Paseo de la Reforma Ave., 06600; tel: (5) 705-1515; fax: (5) 705-1313; 610 rooms; located in cultural and financial district; restaurants; bars; convention facilities; business center; in-room a/c, smoke detectors, bath, phone, radio, satellite tv, minibar, hairdryer, purified water; 24-hour room service; non-smoking rooms; facilities for disabled; elevator; concierge; medical service; currency exchange; free parking; fitness; nightclub.

Plaza Lancaster; Roberto Fulton 2, Sor Juana Ines de la Cruz, Tlalnepantla, Edo. de Mexico, C.P. 54000; northern Mexico City; tel: (5) 228-9500; fax: (5) 228-9528; http:// lancaster.com.mx; info@lancaster.com.mx; located in suburb; 117 rooms; 3 restaurants; conference facilities (up to 1200); secretarial service; fax/photocopy facilities; in-room a/c, heating, satellite tv, minibar, safe; 24-hour room service; laundry/dry cleaning; valet; 30 executive floor rooms with computer/fax facilities; currency exchange; tobacco shop; boutique; travel agency; car rental; valet parking; fitness; sauna; steambath; whirlpool; tennis; nightclub.

Radisson Paraiso Mexico City; Cuspide 53, Col. Parques de Pedegral, 14020, southern Mexico City; tel: (5) 606-4211; fax: (5) 606-4006; 229 rooms, 7 suites; located in suburb; restaurant; bar; 5 meeting rooms; business center; secretarial service; translation service; in-room direct-dial phones, a/c, minibar, safe, satellite tv; 24-hour room service; laundry/valet; non-smoking rooms available; physically disabled services; elevator; medical services; currency exchange; beauty parlor; car rental; travel agency; corporate rates; fitness.

San Marino Suites; 107 Rio Tiber St., Cuouhtemoc, Mexico City DF 06500; tel: (5) 525-4886; fax: (5) 511-7800; 74 rooms; restaurant; coffee shop; delicatessen; bar; conference facilities; business center; secretarial service; in-room a/c, cable tv, direct-dial phone, key card, kitchenette, refrigerator, radio; room service; laundry service; security; non-smoking rooms; newspaper; 24-hour front desk; concierge; private garage; valet parking; fitness center.

Sevilla Palace; Avenida Paseo de la Reforma 105; tel: (5) 566-8877; fax: (5) 535-3842 or (5) 703-1521; restaurants; bar; conference facilities; business center; secretarial service; in-room modem/fax connection, tv, safe; concierge; tour desk; corporate rates; fitness; massage, pool; whirlpool.

Moderate

Best Western Hotel de Cortés; Av. Hidalgo 85, 06300; tel: (5) 518-2181; fax: (5) 512-1863; 1660 hotel; 29 rooms; located in historical center; restaurant; meeting space (up to 30); in-room tv, minibar; laundry/valet service; non-smoking rooms; 24-hour front desk.

Best Western Hotel Ritz; Avenida Francisco I Madero 30, Col. Centro; tel: (5) 518-1340; fax: (5) 513-3466; 140 rooms; restaurant; bar; conference facilities (60); secretarial service; fax/photocopy facilities; in-room color satellite tv, minibar; corporate rates.

Best Western Majestic; Madero 73, Zocalo Plaza; tel: (5) 521-8600; fax: (5) 512-6282; 85 rooms; historical building; rooftop restaurant; bar; meeting rooms; travel agency; disabled access.

Calinda Geneve Quality Inn; Londres 130, La Zona Rosa; tel: (5) 211-0071; fax: (5) 208-7422; 311 rooms; meeting facilities; some rooms with a/c.

Century Hotel Zona Rosa; 142 rooms, all non-smoking; conference facilities (up to 100); secretarial service; in-room a/c, bathrooms, balconies, minibar, cable tv, minibar, hairdryer, modem connection, phone; 24-hour room service; laundry/valet; concierge; disabled access;

Mexico

currency exchange; safe boxes; security; tour desk; doctor on call; car rental; elevators; pool.

Casa Blanca Hotel; Lafragua No. 7, 06030; near city center; conference facilities; in-room a/c, cable tv, direct-dial phone, fresh purified water; laundry service; guest laundromat; disabled access; beauty salon; car rental; indoor parking; pool.

Del Angel; Rio Lerma 154, Col. Cuauauhtemoc, 06500; tel: (5) 533-1032; fax: (5) 533-1027; 100 rooms; near city center, business district; restaurant; bar; coffee shop; conference facilities (up to 150); secretarial service; fax/photocopy facilities; in-room a/c, cable tv, movies, minibar; room service; laundry; shoe shine service; valet; elevators; tour desk; concierge; doctor on call; luggage hold; corporate rates.

Doral; Avenida Sullivan 9, Col. San Rafael, 06470; tel: (5) 592-2866; fax: (5) 592-2762; 164 rooms; restaurant; lounge; conference facilities; secretarial service; fax/photocopy facilities; in-room safe; corporate rates; free parking.

Gran Hotel de la Ciudad de Mexico; 16 de Septiembre No. 82, Col. Centro, México, D.F., 06000; tel: (5) 510-4949, 510-4041 to 49; fax: (5) 512-2085; reservations: 512-9275; toll-free for Mexico: 91-800-462-4240; 124 rooms and suites; located in historical center, Zocalo; restaurant; cafeteria; bar; conference facilities; business center; in-room a/c, satellite tv, minibar; room service; laundry/valet; medical care; beauty salon/barber; travel agency; car rental; covered parking.

Maria Cristina; Rio Lerma 31, DF 06500; tel: (5) 566-9688. 703-1787; fax: (5) 566-9194; 136 rooms, 14 suites; located in Zona Rosa; colonial style; bar; in-room cable tv; garden

Mexico City Days Inn; Rio Lerma #237, Col. Cuahutemoc, DF 06500; tel: (5) 211-0109; toll free: 800-DAYS-INN; fax: (5) 208-2014; renovated 1999; one block from Reforma Blvd. and Chapultepec; restaurant; cafe; coffee shop; bar; meeting facilities (up to 200); in-room cable tv; room service; disabled access; gift/tobacco shop; travel agency; indoor parking; tennis.

Regente Hotel; Paris 9, Mexico City, CP 06030; 138 rooms; located near avenues Reforma and Insurgentes; restaurant; bar; conference facilities; secretarial service; in-room a/c, purified water, phone, cable tv; room service; guest laundromat; laundry service; doctor on call; porter; car rental.

Residencia Polanco; Newton 272; tel: (5) 203-9145; fax: (5) 203-9144; apartments with kitchenettes; some with balcony; rooftop bar.

Royal Plaza; Parroquia 1056 Colonia Santa Cruz Atoyac, 03310; tel: (5) 605-8943; fax: (5) 688-2229; 132 rooms; located in business district; restaurant; bar; conference facilities; in-room a/c, cable tv, smoke alarms; 24-hour room service; laundry/cleaning; newsstand; parking; nightclub.

Segovia Regency; Av. Chapultepec No. 328 roma, Mexico D.F. 06700; tel: (5) 208-8634; fax: (5) 525-0391; 10 minutes from business district, near Zona Rosa; restaurant; bar; conference facilities (up to 45); in-room phone, color tv, a/c, drinking water, safe, radio; room service; travel agency; parking.

MEDICAL CARE

The International Association for Medical Assistance to Travelers (IAMAT) provides referrals for specialists in all areas of medicine. The **IAMAT Center** in Mexico City is located at 745 Paseo de las Palmas, tel: 520-3132, 520-3119, 540-1282 or 540-2484.

American British Cowdray Hospital; Calle Sur 136-201; tel: (5) 277-5000; for emergencies: (5) 516-8077, 515-8359.
Hospital Angeles del Pedregal; Camino de Santa Teresa 1055, Col. Héroes de Padierna; tel: 652-1188.
Mexican Red Cross; tel: (5) 557-5757 or 393-1111.

HEALTH CLUB

Camino Real Health Club; Camino Real Hotel, 700 Mariano Escobedo, Colonia Anzures; Metro: Chapultepec; tel: [52] (5) 203-2121; fax: [52] (5) 83-1730.

Centro Aerobico Casa Nova Gym; Plaza Cuapa, 610 Avenida Acoxpa, Colonia Residencial Villa Coata; Metro: Tasquena; tel: [52] (5) 594-4736.

Ego's Gym; 46A Tlaxcala between Monterrey and Medellin, Colonia Roma, near La Zona Rosa; Metro: Chilpancingo or Centro Medico; tel: [52] (5) 564-1905; aerobics, karate, weights, Nautilus, steam baths; Monday to Friday 7a.m. to 10p.m., weekends 9a.m. to 2p.m.

Hotel Aristos Health Club; 276 Paseo de la Reforma, Colonia Juarez; Metro: Insurgentes;
tel: [52] (5) 211-0112; fax: [52] (5) 514-4473.

Los Cedros Fitness Center; Presidente Inter-Continental Hotel, Campos Eliseios 218, Polanco, 11560; tel: (5) 327-7700.

Sevilla Palace Health Club; Sevilla Palace Hotel, 105 Paseo de la Reforma, Colonia Tabacalera;
Metro: Hidalgo or Revolucion; tel: [52] (5) 566-8877.

AUTO RENTAL

Avis; Mexico City Intl Airport; tel: (5) 762-3688; reservations; tel: (5) 588-8888; at the airport, tel: 762-3688; 308 Reforma, tel: 533-1336; national long distance: 91-800-70-777; emergency: (5) 91-800-70-634.

Budget; reservations, tel: (5) 566-6800; at the airport, tel: 784-3011, 784-3118; domestic long-distance reservations, tel: 91-800-70-017.

Hertz; Mexico Airport-International Gate; tel: (5) 784-7628; fax: (5) 785-6841; Versalles No. 6; tel: (5) 592-8343; fax: (5) 566-0458; Camino Real Hotel, Mariano Escobedo 700; (5) 203-2121; fax: (5) 566-0458.

National; reservations, tel: (5) 575-2279; at the airport, tel: 762-8426, 785-9788; long-distance reservations, tel: (5) 91-800-00-395; Hotel Crown Plaza, tel: 128-5000; Hotel Four Seasons, tel: 230-1818.

WORLD TRADE CENTER

World Trade Center Mexico City
Montecito 38
Col. Napoles
C.P. 03810 Mexico, D.F.
tel: (5) 682-8200; fax: (5) 682-7779
email: wtcmx@wtcmexico.com.mx
Web: http://www.wtcmexico.com
Temporary offices, secretarial/translation services; meeting facilities.

Morocco

At a Glance

THE PEOPLE

Population 29,661,636 (1999)
Growth Rate 1.84% (1999)
Life Expectancy .... 68.87 years
Infant Mortality .... 50.96 deaths/1,000 live births (1999)

Ethnic Composition

Arab-Berber...99.1%
Other 0.7%
Jewish 0.2%

Religious Composition

Muslim...98.7%
Christian 1.1%
Jewish 0.2%

Languages Spoken

Arabic is the official language of the country, several Berber dialects, and French, which is often the language of business and government.

Education and Literacy

Education now surpasses national defense as the largest item in the government's budget. Schooling is free and compulsory through primary school. Females leave school younger than males. The overall adult literacy of Morocco is 43.7 percent. About 56.6 percent of males are literate compared to only 31 percent of females. Most university students benefit from government stipends.

Labor Force

Total: 11,000,000
By occupation: agriculture 50%, services 35%, industry 15%.

THE ECONOMY

The primary economic concerns of Morocco are controlling government spending, freeing up restrictions on private activity and foreign trade, and attaining a form of sustainable economic growth. With the support of the IMF, the World Bank, and the Paris Club of creditors, Morocco has worked towards this goal. A program of economic reform has been implemented; the dirham is now fully convertible for current account transactions, and the government is privatizing various enterprises. Agriculture, a significant part of the Morrocan economy, has been hampered by drought, contributing to an economic slowdown in 1999. The increased levels of precipitation in 2000 have led Morocco to predict a growth of around 6 percent. Morocco still faces the problems of freeing up restrictions on the economy for trade with the E.U., paying down the external debt, and attracting foreign investment. Improving education is a must for increased job prospects for Moroccans of tomorrow.

Exports .... US$7 billion (f.o.b. 1997)
Imports .... US$10 billion (c.i.f. 1997)
Total Trade .... US$16.6 billion (1996)
GDP Per Capita .... US$3,200 (1998)
Unemployment .... 19 percent (1998)
Inflation Rate .... 2-3 percent (1998)

Top Export Partners

France 27%, Spain 11%, India 7%, Japan 6%, Italy 5%.

Top Import Partners

France 22%, Spain 10%, U.S. 7%, Germany 6%, Italy 6%.

Top Exports

Phosphates and fertilizers, food and beverages, minerals.

Top Imports

Semiprocessed goods, machinery and equipment, food and beverages, consumer goods, fuel.

BUSINESS WORKWEEK

Offices

Monday to Friday 8:30a.m. to 6p.m. During Ramadan, offices are typically open 9a.m. to 2p.m.

Banks

Monday to Friday 9:30a.m. to 1p.m.

Government

Monday to Friday 9a.m. to 4p.m. Many government offices are open for shorter hours during Ramadan.

Retail

Monday to Friday 9:30a.m. to 1p.m. and 3p.m. to 7:30p.m., with slightly shorter hours on the weekends and during Ramadan. Many shops close on Fridays. In Tangier, shops may open an hour earlier.

HOLIDAYS

New Year's Day...January 1
Id al-Fitr, End of Ramadan ....January 6-7*
Independence Manifesto Day...........................January 11
Festival of the Throne, Anniversary
of King Hassan's accession .... March 3
Id al-Adha, Feast
of the Sacrifice..March 14-15*
Islamic New Year ....April 3*
Labor Day..May 1
National Day..May 23
Mouloud, Birthday of the Prophet...................June 13-14*
Oued ed-Dahab Day, Anniversary
of 1979 Annexation .... August 14
Anniversary of the King's
and People Revolution ....August 20*
Anniversary of the Green March ....November 6
Independence Day ....November 18
Id al-Fitr .... December 31*
    *Date may vary by year.
    Note: Avoid major holidays for business travel, most specifically Ramadan and Moloud, the Prophet's birthday.

CLIMATE

Seasons

The climate is temperate with humidity above 70 percent throughout most of the year, although cooler nights come in the winter. The winter months, between October and April, hold plenty of rain.

Regions

A Mediterranean climate exists in the coastal region. Temperatures in the summer hover around 27°C (81°F) and in the winter they fall to approximately 8°C (46°F). The southern re-

Morocco

Province names are the same as their capitals.

SM Santa Barbara, CA

©2001 Magellan Geographix

gion remains hot and dry year round. The mountain region is cooler in the summer, and gets much snow in the winter. The desert areas have temperatures of 44°C (111°F) in the summer daytime to 3°C (37°F) in the winter.

Money & Banking

Currency
The currency of Morocco is the Moroccan Dirham (DH).

Denominations
The Moroccan Dirham comes in coin denominations of DH5 and 1, and 50, 20, 10 and 5 centimes and banknotes of DH10, 50, 100, and 200.

Traveler's checks
Traveler's checks can be exchanged at only authorized banks, the BMCE (Banque Marocaine du Commerce Extérieur), exchange shops, hotels, and international airports. Shops may also exchange checks if you purchase something. The rates of exchange vary, larger banks may offer the best exchange rates, but avoid black marketers at all cost. Consult your bank about current exchange rates before departure. Keep all receipts for reconversion.

Cash can also be exchanged, but try to take only crisp and new notes, wrinkled and soiled notes are likely to be refused.

Major credit cards, American Express, Visa, Diner's Club, and MasterCard, are easily accepted in most up-market places in the main cities, but smaller restaurants and *souks* (markets) may ask for cash. Some banks in the capital offer cash advances on credit cards, but make sure you bring your passport.

Travel

VISA AND PASSPORT
Foreigners visiting Morocco need a passport, which must remain valid for 6 months beyond the date of entry into Morocco. For some nationalities, groups of three whose trip was planned by a travel agent may enter with no more than an identity card.

Visas are not required from nationals of Australia, Canada, E.U. countries, Japan, U.K., U.S., Andorra, Argentina, Bahrain, Brazil, Chile, Congo (Rep. of), Ivory Coast, Guinea, Hungary, Iceland, Indonesia, Japan, Korea (Rep. of),

Kuwait, Libya, Liechtenstein, Mali, Malta, Mexico, Monaco, New Zealand, Niger, Norway, Oman, Peru, Philippines, Puerto Rico, Qatar, Romania, Saudi Arabia, Senegal, Singapore, Switzerland, Tunisia, Turkey, United Arab Emirates, or Venezuela for visits of up to three months. Other nationalities should check with the nearest Moroccan consulate for information regarding visa regulations.

Passengers in transit who do not leave the airport and are continuing their journey aboard the first-connecting aircraft, and who are holding confirmed tickets and other documents for onward travel, are also exempt from the need for a visa (except for citizens of Algeria, who are always required to hold a transit visa).

Nationals of Algeria, Angola, Benin, Burundi, Ethiopia, Guinea-Bissau, Iraq, Iran, Jordan, Lebanon, Madagascar, Malawi, Mozambique, Rwanda, Sudan, Syria, Togo, and Zimbabwe must obtain prior approval to enter Morocco from Immigration authorities in Rabat; generally, this takes about six weeks.

The types of visa issued are:

- Single entry—This visa is good for up to three months, and valid if used within six months of issuance.
- Double entry—This visa is good for up to three months, unlimited entries, and valid if used within six months of issuance.
- Transit—single entry. This is good for one day.

All visitors are eligible for extended stay beyond three months, provided that one fills out the application at a police station within two weeks of arrival. Nationals of France and Spain may remain in Morocco indefinitely, simply by reporting their intent within the first three months within the country.

If you have been to Morocco before, then a completed and documented visa application will only take two to three days to process. However, first-time visitors are advised that processing their visa application can take three weeks or longer, since it is normally sent to Rabat for official clearance.

All currency or traveler's checks must be declared upon entry.

DEPARTURE FORMALITIES

It is illegal to export Moroccan dirhams. However, half the Moroccan currency purchased may be re-exchanged for foreign currency upon production of bank vouchers. If your stay did not exceed 48 hours, all of the Moroccan currency purchased may be re-exchanged.

RESTRICTED ENTRY

Those holding Israeli passports will be denied entry as will any travelers deemed by authorities to have a "scruffy" appearance.

Travel in the Western Sahara is restricted. Would-be visitors to that area can acquire information as to required procedures from the Moroccan Embassy.

CUSTOMS ENTRY (PERSONAL)

Duty-free

- Tobacco: 200 cigarettes, 50 cigars, or 250g of tobacco
- Alcohol: 1 liter of spirits and 1 liter of wine
- Other: 50g of perfume

Prohibited or Restricted

- Those wishing to bring in sporting guns and corresponding ammunition must obtain a special permit from the Moroccan police, which is granted if the traveler is holding an official permit from the country of origin.

IMMUNIZATION

If you anticipate entering Morocco from an area where cholera is prevalent, you should be vaccinated prior to travel and carry your certificate with you. If you intend to travel to sub-Saharan Africa, you must be inoculated against yellow fever. It is advisable, even with the low level of risk that exists in Morocco, that all travelers be vaccinated for cholera, tetanus, and typhoid.

TIPPING

Taxi

Taxi drivers should not be tipped, except for those that pick you up at the airport.

Porters

Porters, guides, parking lot attendants, and the like may perform unsolicited services to obtain a tip; for some it is a way to make a living. One may tip between DH3 and 5 for small services. Porters usually get DH3 to 5 per bag. Tip movie theater ushers 50 centimes and hotel maids DH5 per week.

Restaurants

Restaurant waiters in Morocco generally expect to be tipped. Tips vary from 10 percent in more expensive restaurants to a few dirhams in cafes, depending on the amount of the bill.

EMERGENCY INFORMATION

Police and Crime

Generally, crime in Morocco is relatively low. It is usually safe to walk the streets, but this is a country in which a little more vigilance than normal is necessary. A few elementary precautions should protect the traveler from most problems:

- Do not leave valuables in cars or on tables in cafés.
- Keep non-essential valuables locked in hotel safes when not in use.
- Use credit cards and traveler's checks when possible to avoid carrying large sums of cash.
- Carry photocopies of your passport instead of the original.
- Carry cash in a money belt, and use credit cards or travelers checks for most of your large transactions.
- Walk with your bag away from the street to avoid having it snatched away by motorcycle thieves.
- Never carry a stranger's baggage.
- Women should avoid traveling alone at night

The crime rate in Moroccan urban areas is high. The unwary visitor is an easy mark for those looking to take advantage. Foreign visitors have been targeted for crimes and scams of all types, robberies, assaults, muggings, thefts, purse snatching, and pick-pocketing. The parks, beaches, and medina/market areas are the sites most exposed to petty crime. Falsifying credit card bills and shipping inferior carpets instead of the actually purchased rugs are two of the most prevalent complaints from foreign visitors.

Be especially vigilant if using ATM machines, and expect aggressive panhandling by persons who would just as soon rob you. Another typical scam is for the locals to "befriend" foreigners and then ply them with drugged food, drinks, or cigarettes, taking advantage of their altered state to steal money, sexually harass, or worse.

The classic "guide" scam is another common ploy; legitimate guides can be arranged through travel agencies or hotels. If you choose to drive, beware of the old bump-and-rob routine, wherein another driver taps your car with his, then proceeds to rob you when you emerge to inspect the damages. Taxis and trains are generally crime free and may be a preferable way to get around in cities.

Women not in the company of men may experience verbal abuse. It is not advisable to respond in any way, as subsequent physical attack by the big-mouth is not uncommon.

Travel in the countryside has its dangers, too. With a legacy of armed civil clashes, thousands of unexploded land mines remain in the Western Sahara and in neighboring Mauritania and have occasionally detonated, causing injuries and death.

Hashish is common but illegal; possessing it may lead to arrest. Mosques are off limits to non-Muslims. When outdoors, women should dress modestly to avoid sexual harassment. In case of crime, report to the police, who are generally helpful.

Emergency Numbers

Medical emergencies 15
Police... 19

Health

There have been cases of rabies, hepatitis, eye infection, stomach ailments, venereal diseases and AIDS. The climate also encourages asthma, arthritis, and sinus ailments.

Do not drink water from *wadis* or itinerant water sellers, who are prone to sell you tap water. A number of excellent bottled waters exist: Sidi Ali, Sidi Harazem, and Imouzzer (still waters), and Oulmes (sparkling) are all sourced from natural springs.

Wash all vegetables in a chlorine solution, peel fruits, and avoid uncooked food. Try to eat at more expensive restaurants until your digestive system adjusts to the spicy food. Drink only pasteurized milk. Observe local papers for announcements of any health warnings or epidemics. For those traveling to the southern desert, beware that billharzia worms live in the streams and oases. Avoid drinking the water or walking barefoot there. Giardia bacteria live in mountain streams.

Medical care is adequate, and many of the doctors speak English. For minor problems, go to the pharmacies—they are well trained to deal with emergencies.

Competent medical care is available, especially in Casablanca and Rabat, although not every facility meets first-rate quality standards; specialized treatment may be unavailable. For non-emergency matters, one is well off, particularly in major urban areas, although the staff will most likely be unable to speak English beyond a rudimentary level.

Those planning to travel in remote areas are advised to bring along a medical kit, as well as a Moroccan phone card, in case of emergency. Rapid ambulance service usually is not available. A travel insurance package that includes an evacuation policy should be acquired by all business travelers. Medical evacuation is expensive, and payment of costs must be borne by the visitor.

INTERNAL TRAVEL

AIR

If time is a real constraint, then a domestic flight may be worth the rather expensive fare. Royal Air Maroc (AT) offers regularly scheduled flights from Casablanca to Agadir, Al Hoceima, Dakhla, Fès, Marrakech, Ouarzazate, Oujda, Rabat, Tangier, and Tetouan.

A new, smaller domestic carrier, called Regional Airlines, adds access to secondary airfields in more remote areas, as well as being an additional resource for reaching some of the same destinations serviced by AT. Inquire locally either in Casablanca or in the southern city of Laayoune, or through your travel agent.

To contact Royal Air Maroc for more details, you may wish to use the internet.

website: http://www.royalairmaroc.com.

TAXI

There are two types of taxi in Morocco: petit or grand. The "Petite Taxis" are very cheap and have a distinctive, bright color that is different in each town—blue in Rabat, red in Casablanca, and so forth. They are smaller cars (maximum three passengers) and are usually metered. They can and do take on additional passengers who are going in the same direction en route. Petit taxis only drive within the confines of the town and cannot transport you beyond the city limits to the airport, for instance.

Grand taxis are larger cars (usually Mercedes) that carry groups of people (or individuals) for longer distances, normally between cities. You will negotiate a fare prior to leaving, and be aware that drivers may choose to pick up other passengers along the way. Grand taxis usually have fixed prices for set destinations.

AUTO

Roads, particularly in the northern and northwest regions, are highway class. Major car rental companies are represented in Casablanca, Tangier, and Agadir. Rental rates are generally expensive, but deals can be made with smaller local companies. Foreign driver's licenses are accepted as are International Driving Permits. Third Party insurance is a requirement. For Europeans, a Green Card is also necessary. Local agents can arrange appropriate insurance coverage.

The primary Moroccan roads, particularly those traversing parts north and northwest, fulfill the category of all-weather highway. The cities of Tangier, Rabat, Fez, and Casablanca are connected via modern freeways, and two-lane highways link major cities. More to the interior, in the region lying south of the High Atlas Mountains, road travel can be difficult, especially in winter.

Keyword for driving on city streets: congestion. Traffic signals often do not function and are difficult to see. Secondary rural roads are narrow and often poorly paved. Scooters, pedestrians, and animal-drawn carts of all sizes and shapes frequent all roads, including the freeways. Driving at night is not advisable.

Be forewarned that Moroccan police officers often stop drivers for inspection, both within the city limits and on highways, and customs roadblocks are seemingly everywhere. Have your papers in order.

Fuel is cheap, and available virtually everywhere. Traffic moves on the right-hand side of the road. Overall, it is a manageable undertaking to drive in Morocco, but it is challenging and requires much attention.

TRAIN

Morocco's Office National des Chemins de Fer (ONCF) operates a thoroughly modern rail system that connects most of the primary centers of business and trade. The trains are comfortable and fast, with restaurant and bar cars; sleeping cars are available on many of the overnight runs.

The system proves inexpensive and offers excellent service. First class is the recommended way to travel, if only to garner a better chance of acquiring a seat.

A useful route travels from Fès to Rabat and Casablanca, running five times daily with an added two overnight trains. The line from Casablanca to Marrakech offers two daytime trains with one overnight (without sleepers). Also, Monday through Friday, a train runs every half-hour from Kenitra to Rabat. A sleeper service is provided between Marrakech and Tangier.

Both first- and second-class seats should be reserved in advance. The European Inter-Rail pass is good in Morocco, and a discount on a ferry ticket may be available with the same pass, depending on port and ferry company.

For information, you may wish to contact the railway office directly:

Office National des Chemins de Fer
(ONCF)
Boite Postale 1029, Rue Abderrahman
El Ghafiqui Agdal, MA-Rabat
tel: (7) 774-747, 772-385; fax: (7) 774-480.
website: http://www.oncf.org.ma/

SUBWAY

No metro system exists in Morocco.

BUS

Urban

Extensive bus services exist in Casablanca and in many other main towns. Advance tickets are sold, and the fare is very cheap.

Inter-City:

The major towns are linked by an extensive system of coach services. The two largest lines are CTM (servicing the entire country) and SATAS, linking Casablanca, Agadir, and the region south of Agadir. Coaches with air-conditioning are available on several different lines.

One can expect frequent and regular connections, but buses can get crowded. The wise traveler will purchase tickets in advance and will arrive well before scheduled departure to be sure of having a seat. Ticket prices are quite low. A tip to the guard is customary for loading luggage. The driving is sometimes a bit breathtaking.

For further information, you may wish to contact:

CTM
23 Rue Leon l'Africain
MA-Casablanca

tel: (2) 312 061 or 312-061; fax: (2) 317-579

WATER TRAVEL

Regular ferries (car and passenger) shuttle between southern Spain and Tangier. Car ferry service exists between Algeciras in Spain to Ceuta, Almeria to Melilla, and Malaga to Melilla. Car ferries as well as hydrofoils operate between Algeciras and Tangier, Gibraltar, and Tangier; a hydrofoil service also runs between Tarifa and Tangier.

COMANAY .... (2) 303-012, 302-006
Gibmar/Med Travel .... (9) 935-872/7
COMARIT Ferry .... (2) 293-329, 293-381
Ferry Maroc (Casablanca) .... (2) 246-299
Ferry Maroc (Tangier) .... (9) 931-681
Transmediterreana .... (9) 941-101, 935-307
Compagnie Limadet-Ferry .... (9) 933-633/9

TRAVEL ASSISTANCE

Office National Marocain de Tourisme
Angle 31 rue Oued Fès et avenue Abtal, Agdal
Rabat, Morocco
tel: (7) 681 531 or 681 532
fax: (7) 777 437
email: visitemorocco@mbox.azure.net
website: http://www.tourism-in-morocco.com

Hotel Accommodations

Fédération Nationale de
l'Industrie Hôtelière .... (2) 319 083

The following telephone numbers for **city tourism offices** can provide information before or after your arrival in Morocco. All numbers should be preceded by (212) when calling from outside Morocco.

Casablanca. tel: (02) 271 177; Fax (02) 205 929
Agadir. tel: (08) 846 377; fax: (08) 846 377
Laayoune. tel: (08) 891 694; fax: (08) 891 695
Marrakech. tel: (04) 436 239; fax: (04) 436 057
Rabat. tel: (07) 730 562; fax: (07) 727 917
Fez. tel: (05) 623 460; fax: (05) 624 370

Essential Terms

English	Arabic
Yes No	Na-a'am Wakha
Good morning Hello (daytime) Hello (evening) Hello (telephone)	Sabah al-kher Ma-sa'el kher Ma-sa'el kher Al sa-lahm 'alaykum
Good-bye	Ma'as-salaama
Please	'Afak(M) 'Afik(F)
Thank you	Shukran
Pleased to meet you	Sorirart biro'aitak
Excuse me; I'm sorry	Is-ma-leh
My name is _____	Ismee___
I don't understand	Ma fhemtesh
Do you speak English?	Tatakallem ingleezee?

Communications

DIALING CODES IN MOROCCO

International country code: [212]

Selected city codes: Agadir (88), Beni-Mellal (348), Berrechid (2), Casablanca (2), El Jadida (334), Fés (5), Kenitra (73), Marrakech (4), Meknes (55), Mohammedia (332), Nador (660), Oujda (668), Rabat (7), Tangiers (99), Tetouan (996)

Dialing Morocco from Overseas

To dial Morocco from overseas, dial your country's international dialing code, then 212 (the country code for Morocco), then the city code and finally the number. If you were dialing Casablanca from the United States, for example, you would begin with 011, then 212, then 2 (the city code for Casablanca), and finally the number of the person or office you were trying to reach.

Assistance Numbers

International Information 12
Direct Dial International 00
Directory Assistance 16
Telegrams 14

CALLING WITHIN MOROCCO

Local Calls

You can make a local call from any phone box, but don't expect great clarity on the lines. You can pay for better connections through hotels. However, hotels may charge Drh5 for a local call that normally goes for DH1.50 on another phone.

Long Distance Calls

Area codes exist in eight zones in Morocco, which should be listed inside the booth. Use them when trying to reach a number outside of the zone in which you find yourself.

International Calls

To make a direct call, dial 00 (wait for dialing tone) + country code + area code + number. Calls are charged in three-minute increments. Thus, if you talk for four minutes, you'll be charged for six. Furthermore, it may take several tries to get through without hearing a busy signal, a recording, or flat-out silence. At the post office, the operator will arrange the call for you. If you prefer even smoother service, try connecting to an AT&T operator in the U.S.:

AT&T U.S. Direct...002-11-0011
MCI Direct 002-11-0012

On Saturday afternoons and evenings, and all day Sundays and holidays, long-distance calls are 40 percent less expensive. You'll also save on calls made after 10 p.m. during the week.

PAY PHONES

Public Telephones

Coin and card phones make up the public system and can also be found at the main post office (PTT). You can also try to make local calls from restaurant and shop telephones. Coin phones accept 10, 20 and 50 centimes as well as DH1 coins. You'll have to deposit a minimum of DH1.50 for any call for 12 local minutes.

Instructions
1. Insert coin or card
2. Dial

Calling Cards

You can usually buy Telecartes, or telephone cards, at newspaper stands, various kiosks, the PTT, or the teleboutiques. It's not a good idea to purchase these cards from street vendors, since you'll be charged more for less calling time.

Cellular phones

Office National des Postes et Telecom offers GSM digital service as well as an NMT-450 analogue service, designed for the harsh terrain, to cellular users. Cell phones are very popular and considered a status symbol, so usage in public places is very common. Visitors can usually rent cell phones at all major hotels.

Note: Your home country cell phone may not work in this country. If not, we recommend that you rent an international cell phone *before* you leave home. A major US-based cell phone rental provider is **IMC WorldCell**. For information see "International Cell Phone Rentals" on page 14.

CALL BACK

You can (potentially) save significant sums when calling in Morocco by using one of the call back services listed below. Fees for call back services vary widely, depending on the company and the type of service required. Be sure to check with these companies before leaving to compare rates.

For a list of callback services, please refer to the "Communications" section in the *Global Road Warrior* Introduction.

PHONE JACKS

Plug adaptors are available through **iGo Corporation**. (See "Electrical and Telephone Adaptors" on page 19.)

FAX

Fax machines are available in business centers of major hotels, teleboutiques, kiosks and the PTT in major cities. Costs range from DH50 to DH100 per page.

POSTAL SERVICES

It is best to avoid Morocco's postal system whenever possible since it can prove slow and unreliable. All packages and registered letters must also be inspected by the post office before being sent. Poste Rapide, offered through the local post office, provides a good alternative. Also, consider courier service, which is popular—or fax or e-mail.

TELEGRAMS

Telegram facilities are available at most post offices.

Business Services

BUSINESS CENTERS

El Kandara Hotel; 44 Boulevard d'Anfa; tel: (2) 262-937; fax: (2) 220-617; translation, photocopies, telex, fax, internet access, safe rental, car rental, meeting rooms.

COURIER SERVICE

Airborne Express; Trans Africa Top Express, Quartier Des Hopotaux, Casablanca; tel: (2) 278-117; fax: (2) 271-025.

Federal Express; World Express is the FedEx service contractor in Morocco, tel: (2) 542-133; tel: (2) 542-134.

UPS; 210, boulevard Zerktouni, Casablanca, Morocco; tel: (2) 483-636.

TRANSLATION/INTERPRETING

Casablanca

Business Translation Service; tel: (2) 267-288; fax: (2) 267-386 (conference interpreting).

G.I.P. (Groupement d'"Interprétes Professionels); tel: (2) 256-558; fax: (2) 252-612 (Arabic, English, German, Spanish, French).

Intranet; tel: (2) 200-727; (English, Arabic, Spanish, French).

Maghreb Traduction; tel: (2) 312-793; fax: (2) 312-793.

Electrical

CURRENT

220 volts AC, 50Hz.

ELECTRICAL SOCKET

European style 2-pin plugs are the norm.

ELECTRIC PLUGS

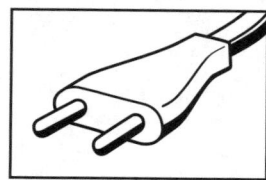

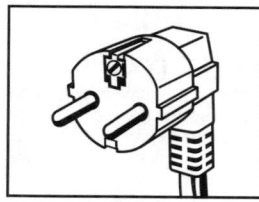

Plug adaptors are available through **iGo Corporation**. (See "Electrical and Telephone Adaptors" on page 19.)

Technical Support

HARDWARE/SOFTWARE VENDOR SUPPORT

Acer/Texas Instruments; (in Germany) tel: [49] (4102) 488-469; fax; [49] (4102) 488-169; (in the U.S.) [1] (408) 432-6200; http://www.acer.com/.

Adobe; (in Spain) tel: [34] (3) 423-6767; fax: [34] (3) 426-0825; (in Germany) tel: [49] (1) 803-5018; (in Switzerland) tel: [41] (800) 833-310; (in the U.S.) tel: [1] (800) 500-7078; http://www.adobe.com/.

Apple/Claris; (in Italy) tel: [39] (2) 2732-6292/3; (in Switzerland) tel: [41] (800) 833-310; (in the U.K.) tel: [44] (990) 127-753; (in the U.S.) tel: [1] (408) 996-1010 (Corporate Headquarters); http://www.apple.com/.

AST; (in the U.S.) tel: [1] (817) 232-9824 (International Technical Support); (in Ireland) tel: [353] (61) 492-222; (in the U.S.) tel: [1] (949) 727-4141; http://www.ast.com/.

Compaq/Digital; (in Switzerland) tel: [41] (22) 709-5330; fax: [41] (22) 709-5391 (Geneva); tel: [41] (1) 801-2507; fax: [41] (1) 801-2172 (Zurich); (General U.S.) tel: (281) 518-2000; http://www.compaq.com/.

Dell; tel: [212] (2) 980633/980165; fax: [212] (2) 982219 (Computronic); (in Germany) tel: [49] (61) 039-710; (Dell-Europe) tel: [44] (134) 474-8000; (in the U.S.) tel: [1] (512) 338-4400; fax: [1] (512) 728-3330; http://www.dell.com/.

Filemaker/Claris; (in Germany) tel: [49] (180) 525-8166 (Info-line); fax: [49] (180) 567-2233; tel: [49] (180) 523-6423; (in the U.S.) tel: [1] (800) 965-9090; http://www.claris.com/.

Gateway 2000; (in the U.S.) tel: [1] (605) 232-2191; fax: [1] (605) 232-2023; (in Ireland) tel: [353] (1) 797-2000; http://www.g2k.com/.

Hewlett Packard; (in Switzerland) tel: [41] (22) 780-8111; (in the U.S.) tel: [1] (408) 246-4300; http://www.hp.com/.

IBM; tel: (2) 221-421; fax: (2) 294-0661; (in Switzerland) tel: [41] (22) 310-0418 (in French); (in the U.S.) tel: [1] (919) 517-2800; http://www.ibm.com/.

Microsoft; tel: 295-8080; fax: 295-8585; (in Germany) tel: [49] (89) 31-760; fax: [49] (89) 3176-1000; tel: [49] (89) 3176-1199; (in Switzerland) tel: [41] (848) 858-868; fax [41] (1) 831-0869; (in the U.S.) [1] (425) 635-7222; http://www.microsoft.com/.

NEC; (in Germany) tel: [49] (18) 0524- 1212; tel:[49] (89) 3160-1233; fax: [49] (89) 3160- 1613 (Floppy Disk and Hard Drive); tel: [49] (89) 9627-4233; fax: [49] (89) 9627-4613 (All Other Products); (in the U.S.) [1] (916) 388-0101 (Main Switchboard); http://www.nec.com/.

Novell; (in Germany) tel: [49] (211) 563-2777 (System support); tel: [49] (6196) 904-477; fax: [49] (211) 563-2772; (in Switzerland) tel: [41] (1) 308-4747; fax: [41] (1) 302-0401; (in the U.S.) tel: [1] (408) 434-2300; fax: [1] (408) 577-5775 (Worldwide Sales Headquarters); http://www.novell.com/.

Quark; (in Switzerland) tel: [41] (1) 808-7722; fax: [41] (1) 808-7799; (in the U.S.) tel: [1] (303) 894-8899; fax: [1] (303) 894-3398 (For Products Registered in the Americas); http:/ /www.quark.com/.

Toshiba; (in Germany) tel: [49] (2131) 158-319; fax: [49] (2131) 158-558; (in Switzerland) tel: [41] (1) 946-0777; fax: [41] (1) 946-0807; (in Ireland) tel: [44] (193) 282-8828; (in the U.S.) [1] (949) 583-3000 (Corporate Headquarters); http://www.toshiba.com/.

Internet Connection

HOW TO CONNECT

Connecting to AOL and Compuserve in Morocco is similar to using it when traveling outside your own area code. See the introductory section for detailed information on connecting to your account through a different phone number.

America Online

Numbers are available at keyword *international*. Be sure

to get several local numbers before leaving. Go to keyword *access* (a free area) and download the software.

There are currently no access numbers available in Morocco.

Compuserve

Numbers are available at *Go International*. The Compuserve Web-site also has a great deal of information, at http://www.compuserve.com.

There are no direct access numbers for Compuserve in Morocco. Users will have to pay international rates to use the service.

Independent Service Providers

Many independent service providers offer discounts if you are only in town for a couple of days.

AIM - Autoroutes de l'Information & Multimedia; tel: (2) 395-364/65; fax: (2) 395-421; email: aim@aim.net.ma; http://www.aim.net.ma/.

Casanet; tel: (2) 994-114; fax: (2) 994-113; email: sa@menara.net.ma; http://www.casanet.net.ma/.

Itissalat Al-Maghrib (Maroc Telecom); tel: 0800-0800; email: staff@onpt.net.ma; http://www.iam.net.ma/.

L&L Technologies; tel: (2) 397-794; tel: (2) 397-694; fax: (2) 397-714; email: chemssy@techno.net.ma; http://www.techno.net.ma/.

Internet Cafes
Casablanca

EGC Multimedia; 84 bd grande ceinture hay mohammadi Casablanca; tel: (2) 624-028; email: egc@iam.net.ma; Monday through Friday, 9a.m. to 11p.m.; 10 Dirham per hour of Internet use.

Tangier

Nem Net Café; 39, rue Imam Layti, Tangier; tel: (9) 939-084; email: nem-net@iam.net.ma; Monday through Friday 9a.m. to 12a.m.; US$1 per hour of Internet use.

Business Culture
GREETINGS AND COURTESIES

Arabic is the preferred language here, though French is also widely spoken. English is gaining in popularity, but the first two languages lend a certain formality to Moroccan greetings and local businesspeople prefer to use them. International sophisticates of both genders brush cheeks or kiss; close friends may exchange several kisses on both cheeks. Most rural Moroccans will shake hands (always the right, or both). Greetings usually include asking about each other's health and that of their families. If in doubt, follow French manners, which are the most common.

WOMEN

A woman's place in the world of Islam depends almost solely on the dictates of her husband at home; in public, she is all but hidden in robes. The traditional veil has largely disappeared in the cities, though some rural women maintain the custom. These restrictions are less prevalent in Morocco. In urban areas women usually receive more education than their rural counterparts, and may work outside the home.

MEETINGS

Meetings tend to be slow-paced, beginning with lengthy amenities and only gradually approaching the stated purpose. Any urgency is regarded as indicating uncertainty and therefore identifies an undesirable partner. Those familiar with the game will find chess a reasonable comparison, with one exception: the chess player only cares for

winning, while Moroccans will be content with coming out slightly ahead of their visitor.

TRADITIONAL DINING

If invited to a home, or to a traditional Moroccan meal, certain rituals are observed. As in Asian countries, meal presentation carries important weight. As one enters the room, one begins by shaking hands with the first person on the right and continuing around from right to left, being careful not to begin with the mistress of the house. Persons then seat themselves on a divan, organizing pillows around and behind them for comfort. Before the meal, a special washing basin is brought to the table over which one holds his hands as water is poured over them. Dry hands with the towel provided. The host, usually seated opposite the guest of honor, may begin the meal by saying *Bismillah*, meaning Praise be to God, after or before taking a bite at the start of the meal. However, the rest of the meal he spends attending personally to his guests. It is courtesy to try a little of each dish by helping oneself from the platters with thumb and first three fingers. Once the meal has been consumed, one will once again wash hands over the basin. The traditional mint tea will follow most every meal.

BUSINESS ATTIRE

Morocco's business attire is more relaxed than many Muslim countries, especially in the cities. Conservative Western business dress is becoming more common. Women should take care to attire themselves very modestly, not only to respect the Muslim culture, but also to avoid harassment. Consider long-sleeved blouses and skirts that fall below the knee, or long, flowing pants. Men may wear shorts, but only in beach or poolside settings. Covering the head to limit water loss is always a good idea in this climate.

Business Centers
Rabat
CITY VIEW

Rabat's culture is a combination of European and Muslim, with mosques sitting next to cafes and theaters. A sense of tradition pervades an ancient imperial city. As the city of gardens, Rabat is filled with trees and flowers to lend some peace to the otherwise hectic pace of city life.

AIRPORT

Salé Airport to City Center

The airport lies 6 miles (10 km.) from the city. Travel time is approximately 15 minutes. Regular taxi service exists.

Airline Numbers

Air RAM .... (7)311-122, 314-141, 361-620
.... airport, 364-184
Air France.. (7) 707-066

HOTELS

Top End

La Tour Hassan Meridien; 26 Rue Chellah; tel: (7) 704-201; fax: (7) 731-866; 139 rooms; 32 luxury rooms; 21 suites; city center; traditional Moorish style; restaurant; bar; conference rooms; business center; in-room a/c, direct dial phone, satellite tv, safe, minibar, hairdryer; 24-hour room service; hair salon; newsstand; shops; parking; fitness; Hammam; solarium; pool; jacuzzi; night club.

Rabat Hilton; PO Box 450, Souissi; tel: (7) 675-656; fax: (7) 671-492; http://www.hilton.com/hotels/RBAHITW/index.html;

269 rooms; 27 suites; located in shopping, business district with views of the gardens, Eucalyptus forests and Atlantic Ocean; restaurants; bar; cafe; meeting/conference facilities; business center; in-room a/c, cable tv, bidet, balcony, hairdryer, bathrobe, minibar, work desk; kitchenettes available in suites; 24-hour room service; doctor on call; airline desk; car rental; transportation services; parking; computers and software available; fitness; indoor/outdoor pools; jogging track; near Dar Es-Salam golf course, free golf shuttle service; gardens; tennis.

Safir Rabat; Place Sidi Makhlouf; tel: (7) 734-747; fax: (7) 722-155; http://www.hotelsafir-rabat.com; email: sales@hotelsafir-rabat.com; 189 rooms; 8 suites; 5 minutes from city center; 2 restaurants; coffee shop; conference facilities (up to 300); business center; secretarial service; fax/photocopy facilities; 24-hour room service; laundry; non-smoking rooms available; shop; bank; airline desk; newsstand; tobacconist; car rental; hairdresser; corporate rates garage; airport transfer; fitness; sauna; pool; nearby tennis, beach.

Expensive

Le Soundouss; 10 Place Talha; tel: (7) 675-959/19/29; fax: (7) 675-868; email: soundouss@mtds.com; city center; 2 restaurants; tea salon; piano bar; business center; conference facilities (up to 100); in-room a/c, minibar, dual telephone lines, voicemail, interenet/fax connection, safe, international tv; 24-hour room service; non-smoking rooms; medical service.

Moderate

Hotel Balima; Avenue Mohammed V; tel: (7) 708-625; fax: (7) 707-450; city center; restaurant; secretarial services; fax/photocopy facilities; in-room safe; corporate rates.

Ibis Moussafir; near Agdal station, 5km. from airport.

Rabat-Chellah; 2 Rue d'Ifni; tel: (7) 760-209; fax: (7) 762-365; 120 rooms; city center; restaurant; bistro; patio bar; conference facilities; in-room a/c, bathroom, direct dial phone, satellite tv.

MEDICAL CARE

Hopital Avicenne; BP 1326, Rabat R.P.; tel: (7) 674-000, 671-549, 674-888; telefax: (7) 673-232.

AUTO RENTAL

Avis; Sale Airport; tel: 776-7503; 7 Rue Abou Faris El Marini; tel: 776-7503.

Hertz; Airport, Rabat; tel: 770-9227, telex: 21884; 467 Bd. Mohamed V, tel: 770-9227, tel: 67-366.

Europcar; Rabat-Sale Airport; tel: (7) 24-141; fax: (7) 310-230; Rabat - 25 Bis, Rue Patrice Lumumba; tel: (7) 24-141; fax: (7) 310-230.

CHAMBER OF COMMERCE

La Fédération des Chambres de Commerce et d'Industrie du Maroc
6 rue d"Erfoud, Rabat-Agdal
tel: (7) 767-078; fax: (7) 767-076

COMMERCIAL ASSISTANCE

Office of Industrial Development (ODI)
10 Rue Ghandi, PO Box 211
Rabat, Morocco
tel: (7) 708-460; fax: (7) 707-695; Telex: 36053

WORLD TRADE CENTER

Ghazi Al Saqabi Group of Co`s
Al dawliyah Commercial Center

Fahed Al Salem Street, 3rd Fl.,Office No.1
P.O. Box 182, Safat 13002, Kuwait
tel: (5) 240-4275; fax: (5) 252-8011

Casablanca
CITY VIEW

Forget about Hollywood's images; the real Casablanca is a modern, industrial city housing more than half of Morocco's factories with a population of over 3 million. As the largest city in the country, it stands at the center of Morocco's financial and economic activity. For those still wondering, the movie Casablanca was filmed entirely in Hollywood studios.

AIRPORT
Casablanca Airport to City Center

The airport lies 19 miles (30 km.) from the city. Travel time is about 35 minutes.

Airline Numbers

Aeroflot	(2) 206410
Air France	(2) 294040
Alitalia	(2) 314181
British Airways/ GB Airways	(2) 307629
KLM	(2) 203222
Lufthansa	(2) 312371

HOTELS

Top End

Le Royal Mansour Meridien; 27 Avenue de l'Armee Royale; tel: (2) 313-011; fax: (2) 312-583; www.lemeridien-hotels.com; 182 rooms and suites; city center; renovated; restaurants; conference facilities (up to 700); business center; secretarial/translation service; in-room a/c, minibar, movies, safe; laundry; limousine service; airport shuttle available; butler service; hairdresser; barber; shops; florist; bank; parking; fitness; sauna; turkish bath; solarium; massage.

Hyatt Regency Casablanca; Place Mohammed V; tel: (2) 261-234; fax: (2) 220-180; http://casablanca.hyatt.com/casab/; email: mkt_sls@hyatt.co.ma; city center overlooking Old City; 5 restaurants; conference facilities (up to 700); business center; secretarial service; in-room minibar, hairdryer, climate control, satellite tv, bathrobes, direct dial phone, voicemail, dataport, safe; 24-hour room service; laundry/valet service; express check in; hairdresser; florist; video security; bank; medical office; parking; airport representative; corporate rates; florist; shops; medical center; fitness; sauna; Turkish bath; massage; pool; whirlpool; squash; nearby golf and beach.

Sheraton Casablanca; 100 Avenue des F.A.R.; tel: (2) 317-878; fax: (2) 315-136; www.sheraton.com/; 306 rooms; 32 suites; 4 restaurants; 2 lounges; conference facilities (up to 450); secretarial service; fax/photocopy facilities; in-room direct dial phone, voicemail, dataport, work desk, satellite tv, a/c, hairdryer; safe; 24-hour room service; non-smoking rooms; parking; gift shop; beauty salon; car rental; corporate rates; health club; gym; sauna; solarium; massage; pool; whirlpool; disco; squash.

Expensive

Crowne Plaza Hotel Casablanca; Rond Point Hassan II; tel: (2) 488-033; fax: (2) 229-3035; www.basshotels.com/crowneplaza?_franchisee=CASMO; 180 rooms; 22 suites; restaurant; coffee shop; bar; conference facilities (up to 150); secretarial service; fax/photocopy facilities; in-room modem/fax connection, minibar, direct dial phone, satellite

Morocco

tv, a/c, safe; corporate rates; free parking; fitness; sauna; hammam; pool.

Hotel Riad Salam; Boulevard de la Corniche; tel: (2) 391-313; fax: (2) 391-345; http://www.riadsalam.co.ma/information.htm; 197 rooms; located in suburb facing Atlantic Ocean; 3 restaurants; conference facilities (up to 600); secretarial service; fax/photocopy facilities; in-room tv, video, minibar, direct dial phone, a/c, satellite tv, hairdryer, balcony, coffee maker; 24-hour room service; laundry; porter; airline desk; shops; parking; corporate rates; fitness; solarium; Thalassotherapy; sauna; massage; 2 pools (ocean and fresh water); beach; 5 tennis courts; squash; bowling; minigolf; nightclub.

Safir Casablanca; 160 Avenue des Far, Casablanca, Morocco 20000; tel: (2) 311-212; fax: (2) 316-514; http://www.safir-morocco.com/; 294 rooms; city center; restaurant; coffee shop; bar; conference facilities (up to 600); meeting rooms (up to 70); business center; secretarial service; in-room a/c, movies, safe, smoke alarms, sound proof windows; some rooms with coffee/tea maker, minibar, newspaper, satellite tv, direct dial phone, temperature control, bathrobe, minibar; 24-hour room service; laundry; newsstand; valet service; beauty salon; barber; car rental; boutique; doctor; florist; parking; fitness club; sauna; pool.

Moderate

El Kandara; 44 Boulevard d'Anfa; tel: (2) 262-937; fax: (2) 220-617; 213 rooms; 10 suites; hotel located near exhibition grounds; restaurant; coffee shop; snack bar; conference facilities (up to 100); secretarial service; business center; in-room a/c, bathrooms, direct dial phone, satellite tv, radio, minibar, safe; 24-hour room service; beauty parlor; boutiques; car rental; parking; corporate rates; sauna; pool; nightclub.

Idou Anfa; 85 Boulevard d'Anfa; tel: (2) 200-235, 200-136; fax: (2) 200-029; http://www.idouanfa.com/f.html; email: info@idouanfa.com; 208 rooms; 12 suites; city center, restored 1996; restaurant; coffee shop; bar; conference facilities (up to 350); secretarial service; business center (email: bizcenter@idouanfa.com); in-room a/c, bathrooms, satellite tv, direct dial phone; 24-hour room service; 2 non-smoking floors; beauty parlor; shops; parking; corporate rates; sauna; solarium; massage; pool; nightclub.

Toubkal; 9 Rue Sidi Belyout, 2100 Morocco; tel: (2) 311-414; fax: (2) 312-287; 70 rooms; adjacent Old City; restaurant; conference facilities; secretarial service; fax/photocopy facilities; in-room a/c, minibar, color tv, direct dial pone; luxury suites available; parking; corporate rates.

Kenzi Basma; 30 Avenue Moulay Hassan1, Casablanca, Morocco 20000; tel: (2) 23-323; 99 rooms; 15 suites; 3-star hotel in business district; piano bar; in-room a/c, phone, minibar, satellite tv, bathroom; pool; nightclub.

MEDICAL CARE

Ambulance services:

Aero Multi Services Atlas; 6, rue Hajeb; tel: (2) 332-464; fax: (2) 332-037.

Maroc Assistance International; 216, Bd. Med V; tel: (2) 303-030, 303-031.

Medecins d'Urgences; 2, rue Assanaoubar; tel: (2) 443-207, 443-333.

AUTO RENTAL

Avis; Mohammed V Airport; tel: 233-9072; 19 Ave Des Far; tel: 231-2424.

Carrentals Maroc; tel: (2) 263-827; http://www.maroc.net/carrentals; email: carrentals@maroc.net.

Europcar; Casablanca Airport, tel: (2) 339-161; Complexe des Habous, 44 Ave. des F.A.R., tel: 313-737.

Hertz; Mohamed V Airport, Casablanca; tel: 233-9181; Casablanca Agence, 25 Rue De Foucauld, Casablanca; tel: 484-710; fax: 294-403.

WORLD TRADE CENTER

World Trade Center

Real Estate Investment Group Co.
Fahed Al Salem Street
Al Dawliyan Commercial Center, 3rd Floor, Office No. 1,
PO Box 22
Safat 13001, Kuwait
tel: (2) 445-774, 445-775; fax: (2) 445-776
No services are offered at this time.

CHAMBER OF COMMERCE

Chambre de Commerce et d'Industrie de Casablanca
Boite Postale 423
98, Boulevard Mohamed V, Casablanca;
tel: (2) 264-327, 264-371; fax: (2) 248-436

COMMERCIAL ASSISTANCE

Moroccan Center for Export Promotion
23 Boulevard Drardot
Casablanca, Morocco
tel: (2) 302-210; fax: (2) 301-793; Telex: 27847

Nepal

At a Glance

THE PEOPLE

Population .... 24,702,119 (July 2000 est.)
Growth Rate .... 2.34% (2000 est.)
Life Expectancy .... 57.84 years
Infant Mortality . 75.93 deaths/1,000 live births (2000 est.)

Ethnic Composition

Newars, Indians, Tibetans, Gurungs, Magars, Tamangs, Bhotias, Rais, Limbus, Sherpas.

Religious Composition

Hindu 90%
Buddhist 5%
Muslim 3%
Other 2%

Languages Spoken

Nepali, plus 20 other languages divided into numerous dialects. Educated Nepalese can speak some English.

Education and Literacy

A free countrywide primary education system is under development. Five years of schooling are compulsory. Literacy is estimated at 40.9 percent for males; 14 percent for females.

Labor Force

Total: 10,000,000
By occupation: agriculture 81%, services 16%, industry 3%.

THE ECONOMY

Nepal is one of the poorest countries in the world. It lacks industrial development and natural resources to draw foreign investment. Agriculture is the mainstay of the economy, providing a subsistence living for over 80 percent of the population. Agriculture accounts for over 40 percent of Nepal's GDP. Industrial activity centers around the processing of agricultural produce. Production of textiles and carpets has expanded in recent years and accounts for about 80 percent of foreign exchange earnings. Agricultural production maintains a growth rate close to 2 percent higher than the population growth rate. Since 1991, Nepal's government has been instituting economic reforms, such as reducing business licenses and registration requirements in order to simplify investment procedures. The government has also been cutting expenditures by reducing subsidies, privatizing state industries, and laying off civil servants. Of late, political instability and five different governments over the past few years has hampered the country's ability to implement key economic reforms. Nepal has considerable scope for accelerating economic growth by utilizing its potential in tourism and hydropower. These two areas are the most promising prospects for foreign investment. Foreign interest in trade or investment in other areas is low and will remain so because of the small size of the economy, its lack of technological advancement, and its remote geographic location. The international community's role of funding more than half of Nepal's development budget and more than 28 percent of total budgetary expenditures will, in all probability, continue as a major aspect of this nation's growth.

Exports .... US$485 million (f.o.b., 1998)
Imports .... US$1.2 billion (f.o.b., 1998)
Total Trade .... US$1.685 billion (1998)
GDP Per Capita .... US$1,100 (1999 est.)
Unemployment .... N/A%; substantial underemployment
Inflation Rate .... 11.8% (FY98/99 est.)

Top Export Partners

India 33%, US 26%, Germany 25%.

Top Import Partners

India 31%, China/Hong Kong 16%, Singapore 14%.

Top Exports

Carpets, clothing, leather goods, jute goods, grain.

Top Imports

Gold, machinery and equipment, petroleum products, fertilizer.

BUSINESS WORKWEEK

Offices

Monday to Friday 9a.m. to 5p.m.

Banks

Sunday to Thursday 10a.m. to 2:30p.m., Friday 10a.m. to noon.

Government

Monday to Friday 9a.m. to 5p.m.

Retail

Sunday to Friday 10a.m. to 7p.m. Many businesses are closed or work shorter hours on Fridays. Business hours are also shortened during the winter.

HOLIDAYS

National Unity Day...January 11
Martyrs' Day ....January 29
Rashtriya Prajatantra Divas-
National Democracy Day...............................February 19*
Maha Shivaratri - in honour of
Lord Shiva .... March 4*
Napalese Women's Day .... March 8
Holi Festival, Ram Nawami
(Birthday of Lord Ram) ....March 19-20*
Navabarsha- New Year's Day ....April 4*
Baishakh Purnima, Birthday of
Lord Buddha...May 18*
Indra Jatra—Festival of Rain God........................August *
Rakshya Bandhan (Janai Purnima)....................August 15
Krishna Asthami
(Birthday of Lord Krishna) ....September
Dasain, Durga Puja
Festival...September/October*
Deepawali, Festival of
Lights..October 26-29*
Queen Aishworya's Bithday ....November 7
Constitution Day...November 8
King Birendra's Birthday ....December 29
    *Date may vary by year.
    Note: The government of Nepal announces the exact dates of holidays at the beginning of each Nepali year (April).

CLIMATE

Seasons

The climate ranges from subtropical in the south to cool summers and severe winters in the northern mountains. Monsoons from the Indian Ocean bring lot of rainfall in the sub-Himalayan region from June to September.

Nepal

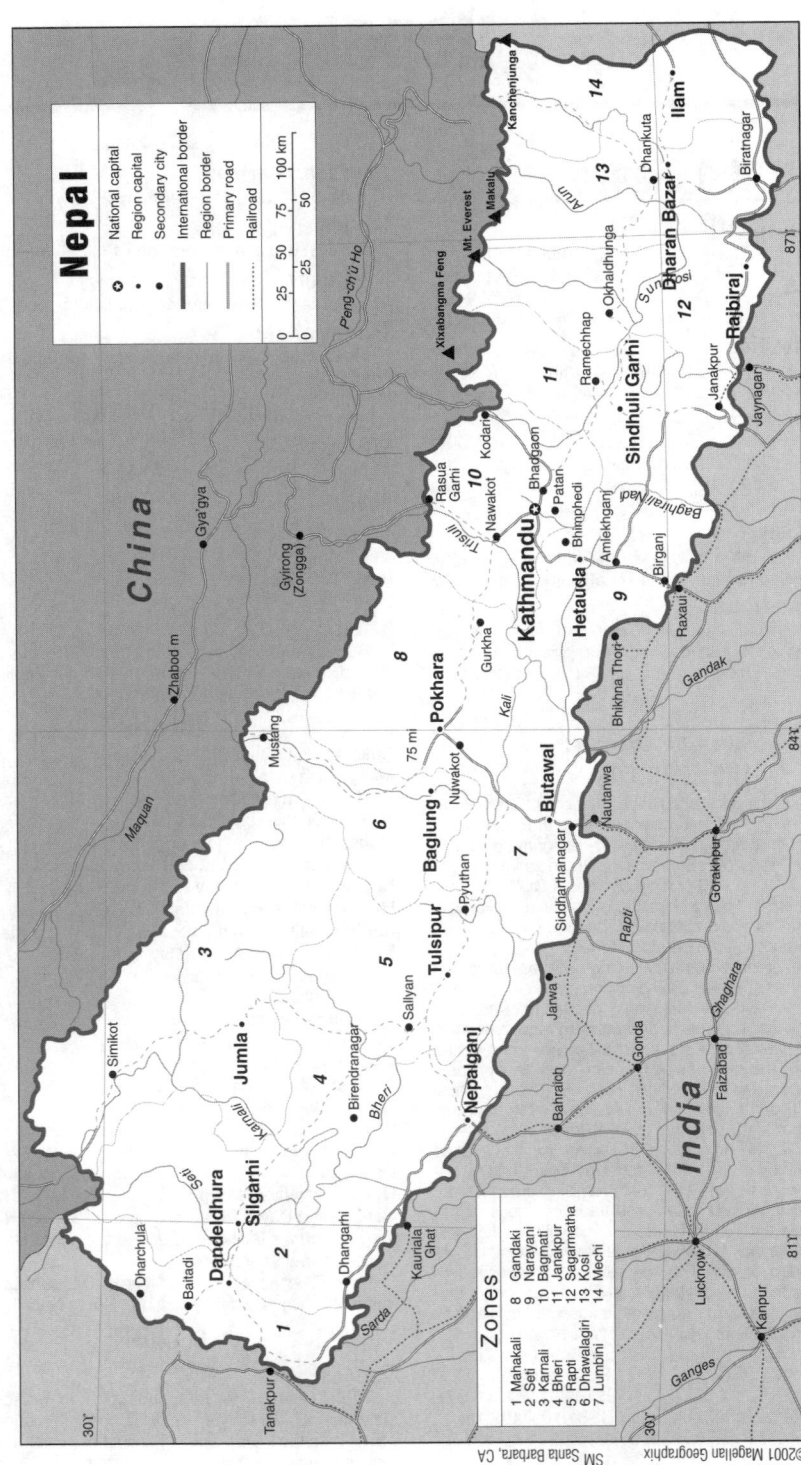

Nepal

- ✪ National capital
- • Region capital
- · Secondary city
- —— International border
- —— Region border
- ····· Primary road
- ···· Railroad

0 25 50 75 100 km
0 25 50 75

Zones

1	Mahakali	8	Gandaki
2	Seti	9	Narayani
3	Karnali	10	Bagmati
4	Bheri	11	Janakpur
5	Rapti	12	Sagarmatha
6	Dhawalagiri	13	Kosi
7	Lumbini	14	Mechi

Regions

Higher altitudes have mild temperatures, while lower grounds experience extremes of temperature.

Money & Banking

CURRENCY

The currency of Nepal is the Nepalese Rupee (NR).

Denominations

The Nepalese Rupee comes in coin denominations of NR1 and 5, and 25, 10, and 5 paisa; and banknotes of 1, 2, 5, 10, 20, 50, 100, 500, and 1,000.

Traveler's checks

Traveler's checks and currency can be exchanged at banks, exchange shops, hotels, and international airports at tourist exchange rates with various rates of exchange. Larger banks may offer the best exchange rates, but avoid black marketers at all cost. Consult your bank about current exchange rates before departure. Keep all receipts for reconversion. Keep in mind, however, that only 15 percent of the currency exchanged may be reconverted into U.S. dollars at the time of departure.

Cash can also be exchanged, but try to take only crisp and new notes, wrinkled and soiled notes are likely to be refused.

Major credit cards, American Express, Visa, and MasterCard are easily accepted in most up-market places in the main cities, but smaller restaurants and shops may ask for cash. Some banks in the capital offer cash advances on credit cards, but make sure you bring your passport.

American Express; c/o Yeti Travels Pvt. Ltd., GPO Box 76, Durbar Marg, Kathmandu; tel: 223-596.

Visa and Mastercard; service center, Durbar Marg at Alpine Travel Service, tel: 225-020, 225-362.

The service offices are open between 8a.m. and 8p.m. Sunday to Friday, and between 10a.m. to 4p.m. on Saturdays and holidays.

Travel

VISA AND PASSPORT

Foreigners must have a passport and visa to visit Nepal. (Nationals of India do not require a visa). Visas good for 60 days are issued at ports of entry upon arrival.

The only type of visa normally issued is the Tourist visa: single, double, and multiple re-entry. Business may be conducted on a tourist visa. The term of visitation is usually 60 days, and it remains valid if used within six months of issuance. The fee for a visa varies with the number of entries and duration of stay requested, if beyond the normal 60 days. Apply for extensions in Nepal at the Department of Immigration, Kathmandu (tel: 494-273 or 494-337), or at the Immigration Office in Pokhara. Maximum permissible stay in Nepal is 120 days in a calendar year. Apply for extensions once you are in the country at the Department of Immigration in Kathmandu or at the Immigration Office in Pokhara.

Passengers in transit who do not leave the airport and are continuing their journey aboard the first-connecting aircraft, and who are holding confirmed tickets and other documents for onward travel, are exempt from the need for a visa.

If intending to travel into Tibet from Nepal by an overland route, contact your embassy before doing so for immigration information.

DEPARTURE FORMALITIES

Expect an airport departure tax of NR700 ($US8) to most international destinations. If flying domestically, expect to pay about NR50.

Penalties for overstaying may include fines and imprisonment. Export of local currency is prohibited.

CUSTOMS ENTRY (PERSONAL)

Duty-free
- Tobacco: 200 cigarettes or 50 cigars
- Alcohol: 1.15 liters of distilled spirits or 12 cans of beer
- Film: camera, 15 rolls; video, 12 rolls
- Perfume: a reasonable amount of perfume

All baggage must be declared upon arrival and departure. There are limits on the importation of certain goods including cameras (1), movie or video camera (1), ordinary camera (1), tape recorder (1), and electronic goods. Objects of archaeological or historical interest may not be exported; and certain antique articles must be referred to the Department of Archaeology before export. Cats and dogs need veterinary and rabies vaccination certificates.

Immigration Office 412-337, 418-573
Department of Archaeology....................213-701, 213-702
Customs Office......................................470-110, 472-266
The Department of Immigration issues trekking permits. One is advised to use registered trekking agencies since these use licensed tourist guides.

Prohibited
- Narcotics, arms, and ammunition

IMMUNIZATION

Travelers arriving from areas afflicted with yellow fever are required to have a vaccination certificate. Cholera inoculation is not mandatory, but a good idea. Travelers on working assignments in the health care field or those that will be in close contact with the locals (i.e., teachers, missionaries, and peace corps workers) are advised to get a vaccination against Hepatitis B.

TIPPING

Tipping in Nepal averages around 10 percent for services in tourist hotels and restaurants. Tip taxi drivers if they have proved extra helpful. Outside the sphere of services for foreign visitors, tipping is not customary and can be cause for some personal discomfort for the intended recipient. Tip only when appropriate.

EMERGENCY INFORMATION

Police and Crime

Superstition is strong among the locals, and outsiders are generally regarded as potential polluters of Nepal's heritage. The rate of violent personal crime in Kathmandu is low, relative to cities of comparable size elsewhere. But petty crime is commonplace, as in most places in the world frequented by foreign visitors these days.

A few elementary precautions should protect the traveler from most problems:
- Do not leave valuables in cars or on tables in cafés.
- Keep non-essential valuables locked in hotel safes when not in use.
- Use credit cards and traveler's checks when possible to avoid carrying large sums of cash.
- Carry cash in a money belt, and use credit cards or travelers checks for most of your large transactions.
- Walk with your bag away from the street to avoid having it snatched away by motorcycle thieves.

- Never carry a stranger's baggage.
- Women should avoid traveling alone at night

A rural Maoist insurgency leading to the deaths of over 1,400 people has been going on since February of 1996. The violence usually targets Nepalese government personnel and facilities, but foreign visitors have been robbed by armed Maoists. Exercise extreme caution and discretion at all times, especially in the following districts: Jajarkot, Kalikot, Rolpa, Rukum, Salyan, and Sindhuli districts, those most afflicted with the insurgency; Dolakha, Gorkha, Kabhre Palanchok, Dang, Dolpa, Pyuthan, Ramechaap, Sindupalchok, and Surkhet districts are also to be avoided or visited only in the daytime. Local assistance is advisable. Check with your embassy upon arrival for the latest updates about the security situation. Public demonstrations and strikes may also occur, during which time businesses will close and transportation may be disrupted.

Emergency Numbers

Fire .... (1) 221-177
Police... 100
Police, Bhrikutimandap...................................(1) 226-998
Tourist Police (Babar Mahal)..................................211-293
Ambulance (Bhimsenthan)............................ (1) 211-959
Ambulance (Bishal Bazar)................................(1) 211-121
Red Cross Ambulance Service ....(1) 228-094
Himalayan Rescue Dog Squad 290-800

Health

Do not drink tap water or use ice cubes; bottled water is safe and available. Wash all vegetables in a chlorine solution, peel fruits, and avoid uncooked food. Drink only powdered or tinned milk and avoid other dairy products since they are most likely unpasteurized. Only eat meat and fish that have been well-cooked, and preferably served hot. Mayonnaise, pork, and salad often bear increased risk of intestinal problems.

Altitude sickness is also common for those traveling to higher altitudes for trekking. Headaches, shortness of breath, or nausea are common symptoms. Take a few days to acclimatize before embarking on any major excursion.

Medical care is very limited in Nepal. Patan Hospital, located in Lagankhel, is the most practical hospital for visitor care. Generally, English is spoken in most Nepalese medical facilities, and major hotels have doctors on staff. For serious illness or emergency, you are advised to leave the country, usually to Singapore, Bangkok, or New Delhi. Medicines and pharmacological equipment are scarce, so come prepared. Carry a well-stocked medical kit with all the prescription drugs you require, and also include in it a stock of sterilized syringe needles and drip needles for emergencies. However, if in need, pharmacies along New Road in Kathmandu sell Western medicines at reasonable prices.

A travel insurance package that includes an evacuation policy should be acquired by all business travelers.

INTERNAL TRAVEL

AIR

Royal Nepal Airlines offers an extensive schedule of domestic flights to more than 30 destinations in the interior of Nepal, with Kathmandu as the central hub. A number of other airlines provide regular services, as well as charter, to popular destinations: Buddha Airlines, Cosmic Air, Gorkha Airlines, Lumbini Airways, Manakamana Airways, Necon Air, and Yeti Airways.

The flights are fairly expensive and often canceled or delayed due to inclement weather. It is a good idea to book a flight one week prior at least, and keep reconfirming your reservation, as names have a way of slipping off the passenger manifests due to overbooking.

The domestic airline terminal in Kathmandu is somewhat shoddy and often filled with frenzied passengers waiting for delayed flights. Foreign travelers must make payments in foreign hard currency only. Nepalese and Indian passengers may pay in rupees.

Helicopters are also available for charter from the Royal Nepal Airlines Corporation.

Make inquiries through your travel agent, as the Nepalese domestic airlines are not too established on the internet (the Royal Nepal Airlines website— http://www.royalnepal.com— does not include information on domestic flights).

TAXI

Taxis and auto-rickshaws are easy to find in Kathmandu, provided it is before sundown. Metered three-wheel scooters called Tempos offer fares slightly less than taxis. Negotiate fares beforehand if riding in a private taxi or rickshaw.

Metered taxis have black license plates with white letters. The initial fares for metered cabs start at NR7 and go up by NR2 every couple hundred meters. At night the fares go up 50 percent. The slightly more upscale Kathmandu Yellow Cabs that travel in Kathmandu, Patan, and suburbs may also be found on the streets between 7a.m. and 9p.m.
Kathmandu Yellow Cab.................................... tel: 420-987
Night Taxi Service .... tel: 224-374

AUTO

Driver's license information is not applicable for renting a car in Nepal since all rental cars must be chauffeur driven. Roads are generally in poor condition and driving habits are no better. During the June to September monsoons, mountain and hill roads are especially treacherous and often impassable due to mud slides. Prepare for congested and chaotic traffic conditions in the Kathmandu Valley. Many motorists are neither certified nor trained to drive; coupled with poorly maintained vehicles and unmarked sidewalks and crossings, the rate for traffic related deaths is high.

Visitors can rent bicycles and motorcycles from hotels or bike shops. Motorcyclists must have a driver's license.

TRAIN

Light gauge railways in Nepal run limited service. The Nepal Janakpur-Jayanager Railways (NJJR) is one such operation, a passenger and freight service in eastern Terai. In general, though, travel by train is not an option in Nepal.

BUS

Buses offer the primary form of transportation, especially for inter-city travel. They prove extremely inexpensive, but also uncomfortable and slow. They are to be found on virtually every road in Nepal, paved and unpaved, and some of them run specifically for tourists. The latter are somewhat more expensive, but it is advisable to stick to these buses, unless you enjoy livestock and poultry as companions. One is advised to travel during the daytime only, due to highway and vehicular safety considerations.

City bus lines service the greater Kathmandu area, including the neighboring cities of Bhaktapur and Patan. City buses originate at the City Bus Park on the eastern side of Tundikhel parade grounds.

Trolleybuses run frequently along the 11km. (7-mile) Kathmandu–Bhaktapur road. They originate at Tripureshwor, near the Dashrath Stadium. Private minibuses link the trolleybus route with nearby villages. On the buses and trolleybuses of the Transport Corporation of Nepal, a four-zone fare system is in effect. Conductors issue color-coded tickets, which represent transit for the appropriate zones.

Long-distance public buses depart from Gongabu Bus Park on Ring Road in Kathmandu. The higher-end tourist bus-

Nepal

es leave from Thamel in the vicinity of the Karmachari San-chaya Kosh Building.

TRAVEL ASSISTANCE

Nepal Tourism Board
Bhrikuti Mandap, Kathmandu, Nepal
tel: (1) 256-909 or 256-229
fax: (1) 256-910
email: info@ntb.wlink.com.np (or)
ntb@mos.com.np
website: http://www.welcomenepal.com
Ministry of Tourism
Tripureshnawar, Kathmandu, Nepal
tel: (1) 211-286; fax: (1) 227-758
Hotel Association of Nepal
tel: (1) 412-705 or 424-914
fax: (1) 424-914

Essential Terms

English	Nepali
Yes	Ā
No	Ahā
Good morning	Namaste
Hello (daytime)	Namaste
Hello (evening)	Namaste
Hello (telephone)	Namaste
Good-bye	Namaste
Please	Kripayaa
Thank you	Dhanyabaad
Excuse me; I'm sorry	Hajur
My name is _____	Mero naam___ho
I don't understand	Maile bujhina
Do you speak English?	Tapaai agreji bolna saknuhunchha?

Communications

DIALING CODES IN NEPAL

International country code: [977]
Selected city codes: Bhaktapur (1), Dhangadi (91), Gorkha (64), Kathmandu (1), Nepalgunj (81)

Dialing Nepal from Overseas

To dial from overseas, dial your country's international dialing code, then 977 (the country code for Nepal), then the city code and finally the number. If you were dialing Kathmandu from the United States, for example, you would begin with 011, then 977, then 1 (the city code for Kathmandu), and finally the number of the person or office you are trying to reach.

Assistance Numbers

International...186
Domestic Long Distance 180
Directory 197

CALLING WITHIN NEPAL

Local Calls

Calls from a hotel room are usually free. Otherwise they will cost Rs2.

Long Distance Calls

To call long distance within Nepal, use the area code preceded by a zero. A call may cost between Rs15 and NR50 a minute.

International Calls

Telecommunication centers that are privately owned offer all manner of telecommunication services, including email services. Telephone-only outposts can be found by looking for the ISD/STD/IDD signs. International direct dialing is available only to Kathmandu. Direct calls may cost anywhere from NR180 to NR200 per minute from Kathmandu and more elsewhere in Nepal. Direct dial is available to 47 countries by dialing the country code + area code + number. If your country is not amongst the 47, then dial 186 to place a call with the operator. The Nepal Telecommunication Corporation office near the stadium also offers telephone and telex services.

Collect calling is only available to the U.K., Canada, and Japan. If you can't call collect, have your party phone back. Charges at the phone centers will reflect the duration of your chat at about NR10 per minute, no matter which way you choose to call.

PAY PHONES

Public Telephones

There are no public phones to be found in Nepal, except at the airport or city shops.

INTERNATIONAL CALLS

The International Telephone Office in Kathmandu is open Sunday to Friday, 10a.m. to 5p.m,. but international calls can be difficult to make. IDD is available in Kathmandu only at hotels and private telephone offices. All other calls go directly to the operator.

CELLULAR PHONES

Note: Your home country cell phone may not work in this country. If not, we recommend that you rent an international cell phone *before* you leave home. A major US-based cell phone rental provider is **IMC WorldCell**. For information see "International Cell Phone Rentals" on page 14.

CALL BACK

You can (potentially) save significant sums when calling in Nepal by using one of the call back services listed below. Fees for call back services vary widely, depending on the company and the type of service required. Be sure to check with these companies before leaving to compare rates.

For a list of callback services, please refer to the "Communications" section in the Global Road Warrior Introduction.

PHONE JACK

Plug adaptors are available through **iGo Corporation.** (See "Electrical and Telephone Adaptors" on page 19.)

FAX

Travel agencies and a few hotels have fax capabilities. The service is poor due to the antiquated phone system. A fax service booth also exists at the airport as well as the Nepal Telecommunication Corporation office.

POSTAL SERVICES

Do not send valuables through the postal service, it is unreliable at best. Be sure letters are hand-cancelled at the main post office (near the Dharahara Tower). Air, surface, and express mail service are available. Some hotels also have postal services available.

Hours of service

Sunday to Friday 10a.m. to 5p.m., until 4p.m. during the winter; Friday 10a.m. to 3p.m.

TELEGRAMS

The Central Telegraph Office in Kathmandu has a 24-hour international telephone and telegram service.

Business Services

BUSINESS CENTER

Note: Many hotels have a business center at the disposal of their guests. Please see hotel listings to ascertain which hotels have them.

Megha Malhar Convention Center; adjacent Soatee Crowne Plaza Hotel; meetings (up to 650); boardroom; multi-function room; conference support; public address system, sound and lights, audio-visual aids; translation units.

Yak & Yeti Hotel; Durbar Marg; tel: (1) 413-999; 2 Pentium II Deskpower 5000 and 2 Pentium III Deskpro computers, laptop computers, digital color scanners, color printers, cell phones, fax machine, laser printers, typing, translation, secretarial service, photocopying, email, 64Kbps internet line, courier service.

COURIER SERVICE

Airborne Express; Intertours Nepal, Gpo Box 3896, Pratap Bhavan, Kantipath Kathmandu; tel: (1) 115-619; fax: (1) 225-324.

Federal Express; Nepal Travel Agency, tel: (1) 413-188.

TNT Express Worldwide; Swift Air Cargo Service, Kantipath; tel: (1) 474-508, 474-594; fax: (1) 474-508, 225-524.

UPS; Nepal Air Courier Express (P) Ltd., Putali Sadak, Ramshah Path, P.O. Box 4417, Kathmandu, Nepal; tel: (1) 225-854; fax: (1) 225-915.

Technical Support

HARDWARE/SOFTWARE VENDOR SUPPORT

Hewlett Packard; (India Office) tel: [91] 11 682 6035; (in Switzerland) tel: [41] (22) 780-8111; (in the U.S.) tel: [1] (408) 246-4300; http://www.hp.com/.

Microsoft; (India Office) tel: [91] (11) 646-0694 or [91] (11) 646-0767; fax: [91] (11) 647-4714; (in Switzerland) tel: [41] (848) 858-868; fax [41] (1) 831-0869; (in the U.S.) [1] (425) 635-7222; http://www.microsoft.com/.

Electrical

Current

220 volts AC, 50Hz. There are frequent power outages. European 2-pin plugs are the norm, although there are many variations depending on how old the building is.

ELECTRICAL PLUG

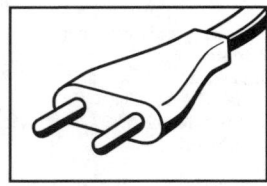

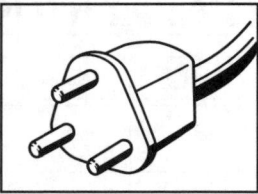

Plug adaptors are available through **iGo Corporation**. (See "Electrical and Telephone Adaptors" on page 19.)

Internet Connection

HOW TO CONNECT

Connecting to AOL and Compuserve in Nepal is similar to using it when traveling outside your own area code. See the introductory section for detailed information on connecting to your account through a different phone number.

America Online

Numbers are available at keyword *international*. Be sure to get several local numbers before leaving. AOL service in Kathmandu costs US$12 an hour in addition to usual charges. Go to keyword *access* (a free area) and download the software.
Kathmandu (1) 241-025

Compuserve

Numbers are available at *Go International*. The Compuserve Web-site also has a great deal of information, at http://www.compuserve.com.
Access: Kathmandu (1) 241-025.

Independent Service Providers

Many independent service providers offer discounts if you are only in town for a couple of days.

Capital Online Pvt. Ltd.; tel: (1) 240-864; email: info@col.com.np; http://www.col.com.np/.

Everest Net Pvt. Ltd.; tel: (1) 546-010; fax: (1) 539-431; email: info@enet.com.np; http://www.enet.com.np /.

Himalayan Online Service Pvt. Ltd.; tel: (1) 220-848; tel: 244-952; info@hons.com.np; http://www.hons.com.np/.

Internet Cafes
Kathmandu
Dharana Cyberspace; GPO BOX NO. 8975, EPC-1069 Boudhanath, Kathmandu-6 Nepal; tel: (1) 495-777; tel: (1) 480-177; fax: (1) 494-178; email: dharana@wlink.com.np; http://www.geocities.com/dcyberspace/; Monday through Friday, ... 6:30a.m. to 9:30p.m.

EasyLink Cyber Cafe; P.O.Box: 5273 Bhagawatisthan, Thamel Kathmandu; tel: (1) 429-562; tel: (1) 411-346; fax: (1) 425-933; email: easylink@visitnepal.com; http://www.visitnepal.com/easylink/.

Rabi's Cyber Cafe; Thamel, Bhagawatisthan P.O.Box # 8975 EPC 5117, Kathmandu; tel: (1) 419-177; fax: (1) 422-264; email: rabi@hons.com.np; http://www.geocities.co.jp/SilkRoad-Ocean/3964/; Monday through Friday, 8a.m. to 8p.m.

Business Culture

GREETINGS AND COURTESIES

The traditional greeting is the *namaste*, formed by placing the palms together in front of the chin or chest and saying *namaste*. Nepalese do not usually shake hands, but some men might shake hands with foreigners. Nepalese generally ask permission before leaving someone. Titles are important. If a person has a title be sure to use it. One should also remain aware that if gifts are given, they should not be opened in the presence of guests. It is considered impolite.

MEETINGS

Appointments are necessary. Punctuality is important, and being on time will be viewed as an indication of your seriousness about your business. Many government officials will initially meet at a restaurant for a business dinner, but after one or two meetings many extend an invitation to their home. This is generally a sign that things are going well. Nepali is the main business language; however, many business people speak English as well as Hindi.

DECISION MAKING

Decisions are made slowly. Consider confidence building a major necessity that must precede any business negotiations. Foreign business people should expect to spend time getting to know their prospective partners. Impatience will be viewed as rude, and high-pressure attempts to get things done faster will be resisted and resented. Asian culture highly values relationships and harmony.

BUSINESS ATTIRE

Men can consider slacks and a short-sleeved shirt appropriate business attire. A jacket should be worn to first meetings or when seeing government officials. Avoid leather or any accessories made from animals. Women should wear casual dresses or pantsuits, but take care to avoid wearing a sleeveless dress or blouse. April to September is warm. The months between November and February can prove quite cold. The monsoon season occurs from mid-June to mid-September; be sure to bring a rain coat or an umbrella if visiting during this time.

Business Centers
Kathmandu

CITY VIEW

Kathmandu is trying to pull away from the shantytowns and poverty that still exist on the city's outskirts. The city proper is a conglomeration of historical temples and shopping areas. With large hotel chains starting to move into the city, Kathmandu hopes to draw in a new type of clientele beyond the usual backpacker contingent.

AIRPORT

Tribhuvan Airport to City Center

The airport lies 4 miles (6.5 km.) from the city. A coach meets all flights and takes passengers to the city. Metered taxi and limousine services are also available. A fixed-rate taxi service run by the Airport Queue Taxi Service Management Committee is also available; one may find the taxi counter in the arrivals hall near the exit.

Airline Numbers

Aeroflot ....(1) 212-397, 227-399
Air Canada .... (1) 224-854, 212-080, 222-838
Air France.......................................(1) 223-541, 223-339
Air India ....(1) 415-637, 416-721
Air Lanka .... (1) 223-502, 223-162, 212-831
Alitalia ....(1) 222-339, 220-215
American West...................................225-275, 220-155
Bangladesh Biman .... (1) 222-544, 416-582
British Airways ....(1) 222-266, 226-611
Burma Airways ....(1) 224-839
Cathay Pacific ....(1) 24-944, 248-947
CAAC ....(1) 411-302
China Airlines ....(1) 412-778
China Southwest Airlines .... (1) 411-725, 411-726
Dragon Air .... (1) 223-162, 227-229, 231-890
Druke Air .... (1) 225-166, 227-229
Eva Airways...(1) 414-318
Everest Air ....(1) 224-188, 228-392
Indian Airlines .... (1) 223-053, 413-053, 419-649
Japan Airlines...............................(1) 222-839, 224-854
KLM...(1) 224-895, 224-896
Korean Air ....(1) 212-080, 216-080
Lufthansa ....(1) 223-052
Nepal Airways ....(1) 410-786, 418-494
Northwest Airlines ....(1) 410-089, 418-389
Pakistan International Airlines .... (1) 223-102
Qantas..(1) 220-245, 221-774
Royal Brunei....................................(1) 410-208, 417-710
Royal Nepal Airlines ....(1) 214-640, 220-757
SAS ....(1) 524-232, 524-732
Saudi Arabian Airlines ....(1) 222-787. 227-387
Singapore Airlines .... (1) 223-233, 220-759
Swiss Air..(1) 222-452
Thai International............................. (1) 224-917, 223-565

Helicopter Service

Asian Airlines (Helicopter ....(1) 410-086, 416-116
Asian Helicopter ....(1) 415-506
Himalayan Helicopters ....(1) 225-150

HOTELS

Top-end

The Everest; New Baneswor; tel: (1) 488-100, 488-099, 220-288; fax: 490-288, 488-130, 226-088; email: everest@vishnu.ccsl.com.np; 162 rooms; located near airport; restaurants; coffee shop; bar; conference facilities (up to 200); secretarial service; business center; in-room a/c, color tv, heating, phone, minibar; 24-hour room service; laundry service; elevator; beauty parlor; barber; shopping arcade; corporate rates; fitness; pool; garden; US$130+.

Yak&Yeti; Durbar Marg; tel: (1) 413-999; fax: (1) 227-782; http://www.yakandyeti.com; city center; restaurant; pastry shop; casino; business center; conference facilities (up to 350); executive secretarial service; fax/photocopy facilities; word processing; reference library; in-room IDD telephone, minibar, cable tv, a/c; 24-hour room service; laundry/valet service; non-smoking rooms available; currency exchange; doctor on call; florist; shopping arcade; postal service; corporate rates; fitness; 2 pools; US$175+.

Expensive

Bluestar; Thamel; tel: (1) 4130632, 418-733, 228-833, 226-100; fax: (1) 417-133, 226-820; email: hotel@bluestar.mos.com.np; 100 rooms, 5 apartments; restaurant; conference facilities (up to 800); business center; secretarial service; fax/photocopy facilities; in-room phone, satellite tv, socket; 24-hour room service; laundry/ valet; department store; 24-hour security; currency exchange; hair/beauty salon; doctor on call; complimentary airport transfer; secure parking; health center; indoor pool; squash; US$92/110.

Royal Singi Hotel; PO Box 13168, Lal Durbar; tel: (1) 424-190, 424-191; fax: (1) 424-189, 425-802; email: hotel@rsingi.wlink.com.np; 85 rooms, 4 suites; city center; 3 restaurants; bar; business center; meeting room (up to 50); in-room IDD phone, tv, minibar; 24-hour room service; laundry; foreign exchange; travel desk; beauty parlor; doctor on call; health club with Oriental therapy; US$99+.

Sherpa; Durbar Marg; tel: (1) 227-000; fax: (1) 222-026; http://www.info-nepal.com/members/sherpa; email: sherpa@mos.com.np; 96 rooms; restaurants; bar; banquet room; conference facilities (up to 100); business center; secretarial service; in-room phone, minibar, color tv; 24-hour room service; elevator; doctor on call; travel desk; shopping arcade; corporate rates; health club; sauna; steambath; pool; rooftop terrace; US$105+.

Moderate

Hotel Ambassador; PO Box 2769, Lazimpat; tel: (1) 413-632, 418-733; fax: (1) 417-133; email: kghouse@wlink.com.np; near Royal Palace; business center; secretarial service; airport shuttle; house doctor on call; electrical and solar heating; gift shop; parking; garden; US$35+.

Marco Polo Business Hotel; PO Box 2769, Kamaladi; tel: (1) 415-432, 416-432; fax: 418-832, 418-479; email: kgh@thamel.mos.com.np; secretarial service; personal computers; fax/telex/photocopy facilities; shopping arcade; house doctor on call.

Summit Hotel; Kopundol Height; tel: (1) 521-810, 524-694; fax: (1) 523-737; email: summit@wlink.com.np; located in suburb; restaurant; conference facilities; business center; secretarial service; fax/photocopy facilities; Internet available; in-room phone, satellite tv, electric socket; room service; parking; corporate rates; pool; gardens.

MEDICAL CARE

CIWEC Clinic; Durbar Marg; tel: 228-531.

HealthNet Nepal; Institute of Medicine, Health Learning Materials Center, PO Box 2533, Maharajgunj, Kathmandu; tel: (1) 412-202; fax: (1) 413-795.

Nepal International Clinic; Hitti Durbar; tel: 419-713, 412-842.

HEALTH CLUB

Clark Hatch Fitness Center; Radisson Hotel, Ward No. 2, Lazimpat; tel: 419-358; gym with Life fitness machines; steam and sauna bath; jacuzzis; aerobics; massage; pool; changing rooms.

Hotel Shahanshah International Sports Centre; P.O. Box 6535, Dhapasi, Kathmandu; Head Office: Jawalakhel, Ekantakuna, Patan, NEPAL.; tel: (1) 522-665, 524-029; fax: (1) 524-029; ladies' and men's gyms; ladies' and men's saunas; ladies' and men's jacuzzis; ladies' and men's steam baths; aerobics; squash; bowling; indoor tennis court; indoor and outdoor pools; restaurants; bar; executive club bar; children's amusement park.

CHAMBER OF COMMERCE

Chamber of Commerce of Nepal
Teku (Behind Teku Hospital
Kathmandu, Nepal P.O.Box: 269.
tel: 230-407, 233-196, 233-302; fax: 1-227-322

Federation of Nepalese Chambers of Commerce & Industry
Shahid Sukra Milan Marg, Teku.
P.O. Box 269, Kathmandu
tel: 230-407, 233-302; fax: 227-322

Notes

Netherlands

At a Glance

THE PEOPLE

Population .... 15,892,237 (July 2000 est.)
Growth Rate .... 0.57% (2000 est.)
Life Expectancy .... 78.28 years
Infant Mortality ... 4.42 deaths/1,000 live births (2000 est.)

Ethnic Composition
Dutch 96%
Moroccans, Turks, and other.. 4%

Religious Composition
Unaffiliated 36%
Roman Catholic... 34%
Protestant.. 25%
Muslim 3%
Other 2%

Languages Spoken
Dutch is the official language of the Netherlands. English, French, German, and Frisian are spoken in varying degrees.

Education and Literacy
The government allocates 17 percent of its national budget to education. The government funds eight universities and five professional institutes. Ten years of schooling are compulsory. Literacy is 99%.

Labor Force
Total: 6,600,000
By occupation: services 75%, manufacturing and construction 23%, agriculture 2%.

THE ECONOMY
Since the early 1980's, the government of the Netherlands has been withdrawing its hand in the economy. Industrial activity is predominantly in chemicals, petroleum refining, food processing, and machinery. A highly efficient agricultural sector provides large surpluses for the food-processing industry and for exports. The Dutch are one of the top three nations worldwide in the value of their agricultural exports. The Netherlands was ahead of the curve in successfully addressing the issue of public finances and stagnating job growth before many of its European partners. This has helped to cushion the economy from a slowdown in the euro area. In 1998, the Netherlands experienced a 3.8 percent GDP growth, followed in 1999 by a slightly lower GDP growth of 3.4 percent. The outlook is positive for 2000. The GDP should continue to grow, but will unlikely surpass last year's level. The nation will also end the year with a small budget surplus.

Exports .... US$169 billion (f.o.b., 1998)
Imports .... US$152 billion (f.o.b., 1998)
Total Trade .... US$321 billion (1998)
GDP Per Capita .... US$23,100 (1999 est.)
Unemployment 3.5% (1999)
Inflation Rate .... 2.2% (1999 est.)

Top Export Partners
E.U. 78% (Germany 27%, Belgium-Luxembourg 13%, France 11%, U.K. 10%, Italy 6%), Central and Eastern Europe, U.S.

Top Import Partners
E.U. 61% (Germany 20%, Belgium-Luxembourg 11%, U.K. 10%, France 7%), U.S. 9%, Central and Eastern Europe.

Top Exports
Machinery and equipment, chemicals, fuels; foodstuffs.

Top Imports
Machinery and transport equipment, chemicals, fuels; foodstuffs, clothing.

BUSINESS WORKWEEK

Offices
Monday to Friday 8:30p.m. to 5:30p.m.

Banks
Monday to Friday 9a.m. to 4p.m., main branches until 5p.m.; Thursday evenings 4:30p.m. to 7p.m.

Government
Monday to Friday 8:30a.m. to 4p.m.

Retail
Store hours are generally from 9a.m. to 6p.m. weekdays, with one late evening per week, 9a.m. to 5p.m. on Saturday and closed on Sunday.

HOLIDAYS

New Year's Day...January 1
Good Friday...April 21*
Easter Monday ....April 24*
Queen's Day... April 30
National Liberation Day ....May 5
Ascension Day .... June 1*
Whit Monday .... June 12*
Christmas ....December 25-26
*Date may vary by year.

CLIMATE

Seasons
The Netherlands, for the most part is damp, foggy, temperate, mildly tropical, with little variation. Its weather rarely dips below freezing or rises above 80˚F. In recent years, however, the extremes have become more extreme, and the seasons are more distinct. Rain is common throughout the year.

Regions
Coastal regions can experience more Mediterranean climates, the midlands are more foggy and rainy.

Money & Banking

Currency
The currency of Netherlands is the Guilder (NLG).

Denominations
The Guilder comes in con denominations of NLG5, 2.5 and 1, and 25, 10 and 5 cents; and banknotes of NLG10, NLG25, NLG50, NLG100, NLG250, and NLG1,000.

Traveler's checks
Traveler's checks and foreign currency can be easily and efficiently exchanged at banks, foreign exchange bureaus located in the major cities, hotels, and foreign exchange kiosks at the airports and main rail stations. Banks offer the most variable exchange rates. Traveler's checks receive a better exchange rate than cash, or you can purchase Dutch Guilder Travelers checks before departure, which can be exchanged almost everywhere.

Credit cards, American Express, Visa, MasterCard, and Diner's Club, are widely accepted in the Netherlands, and you can get cash advances from your credit card on many of the automated teller machines (ATM).

Personal checks may be difficult to exchange, so, long-term visitors should set up a checking account in the Netherlands and get an ATM card.

A value-added tax (VAT) of 17.5 percent is included in sales prices. However, if your purchase price exceeds NLG300, and the store in which you purchased your goods participates in the VAT refund program, ask the clerk to complete a Tax-Free Check. Take this check, with the receipt and the item(s) purchased to the Tax-Free office at Schiphol Airport to receive the refund. The office will charge a 30 percent commission for the procedure.

Travel
VISA AND PASSPORT

A passport that is valid for a minimum of three months beyond the anticipated end of the visit is required of all except:

- Travelers holding a national ID card from any of the E.U. countries, Andorra, Iceland, Liechtenstein, Malta, Monaco, San Marino, or Switzerland
- Nationals of Cyprus who possess a Government of Cyprus Certificate of Identity
- Travelers who possess a Certificate of Identity from Hong Kong

It is a good idea to carry a return ticket, although it is not obligatory. You may also be required to provide substantiation of sufficient funds to cover expenses for the length of your anticipated stay.

The Netherlands is a member of the Schengen group, which is a collection of nations who in March of 1995 declared themselves borderless. The others in this group are Belgium, Germany, Luxembourg, France, Portugal, and Spain. Any traveler who holds a valid passport or other travel documents that are recognized by all Schengen member nations need not have a visa to travel in any of these countries. There are two caveats, however:

- If you have tickets for onward travel to a nation that does require a visa of you, it may also be required of you for entry into the Schengen nation.
- Each Schengen nation retains the right to require a visa of any national normally exempted by the group as a whole.

Following is a list of nations normally exempt from the visa requirement (E.U. nationals are automatically exempt): Andorra, Argentina, Australia, Brazil, Brunei, Canada, Chile, Costa Rica, Cyprus, Czech Republic, Ecuador, El Salvador, Guatemala, Honduras, Hungary, Iceland, Israel, Japan, Jamaica, Liechtenstein, Malawi, Malaysia, Malta, Mexico, Monaco, New Zealand, Nicaragua, Norway, Panama, Paraguay, Poland, Republic of Korea, San Marino, Singapore, Slovak Republic, Slovenia, Switzerland, Turkey (only if a permanent resident of a Schengen country), Uruguay, U.S., Vatican City, and Venezuela.

Passengers in transit who do not leave the airport and are continuing their journey aboard the first-connecting aircraft, and who are holding confirmed tickets and other documents for onward travel, are also exempt from the need for a visa. But there are exceptions to this exemption, and nationals of some countries who are traveling through the Netherlands must always carry a transit visa, even if not exiting the airport. Check transit regulations regarding your country with an embassy or consulate prior to traveling.

Visa-free travel throughout the Schengen states is valid for a duration of 90 days maximum within a six-month period, commencing upon initial entry date into a Schengen country.

Your nationality or your travel plans may preclude your using the Schengen option, so you may need to apply for a visa anyway. If you apply, you will be issued one of two different Schengen-standardized visas:

- Short Stay (Tourist and Business)—single and multiple entry. This visa is good for up to three months per entry, and valid if used within six months of issuance.
- Transit (and Airport Transit)—single and double entry. This is good for five days per entry.

Expect visa application processing to be completed within 24 hours (if application is made in person), but be aware that the process can take as long as six weeks for nationals of certain countries.

DEPARTURE FORMALITIES

All flower bulbs to be sent or taken out of the country must be inspected by the Plant Disease Service. Dutch flower-bulb dealers will know all the legal provisions and can arrange for shipment. Proof must be shown for taking large quantities of items out of the Netherlands; they must be for personal use only. There are no other departure formalities.

CUSTOMS ENTRY (PERSONAL)

Duty-free

Travelers arriving from E.U. countries with duty-paid goods:

- Tobacco: 800 cigarettes, 400 cigarillos, 200 cigars, 1kg tobacco

- Alcohol: 90 liters of wine including up to 60 liters of sparkling wine; 10 liters of spirits and 20 liters of fortified wine and 110 liters of beer

These allowances are only for travelers aged 17 years and above.

Travelers from non-E.U. European countries or bought duty free within the E.U.:

- Tobacco: 200 cigarettes, 50 cigars, 100 cigarillos, or 250g of tobacco
- Alcohol: 1 liter of alcoholic beverages stronger than 22· proof or 2 liters less than 22· proof or 2 liters of fortified wine; 2 liters of wine; 8 liters of non-sparkling Luxembourg wine
- Other: 50g of perfume and 250ml of eau de toilette; other goods to the value of NLG380

Although there are now no legal limits imposed on importing duty-paid tobacco and alcoholic products from one EU country to another, travelers may be questioned at customs if they exceed the above amounts and may be asked to prove that the goods are for personal use only.

Travelers originating from outside Europe:

- Tobacco: 400 cigarettes, 100 cigars, 500g tobacco
- Alcohol: wine, spirits and perfume same as for non-E.U. European countries
- Other: other goods to the value of NLG125

Enquiries concerning current import regulations should be made to the Royal Netherlands Embassy in the country of departure or to the national Chamber of Commerce.

Prohibited or Restricted

Cats and dogs imported into the Netherlands from any countries other than Belgium or Luxembourg require a health certificate and a rabies certificate. The importation of psittacine birds (parrots or parrot-like birds) is limited to two per family, and a health certificate is required for each bird. The importation of monkeys is prohibited. For more information, contact the Agricultural Department at the Royal Netherlands Embassy.

The importation of firearms and ammunition requires a license.

IMMUNIZATION

No vaccinations are required for entry to the Netherlands unless one has been infected within two weeks prior to arrival.

TIPPING

Taxi

Taxi drivers are often tipped 10 percent.

Porters

Porters and doormen are customarily tipped between G1 and G2.

Hotels

Hotels include a 15 percent service charge in their bill; however, if service is deemed attentive, an additional tip is appreciated. G1 to 2 is standard for doormen and other service staff.

Restaurants:

A 15-percent service charge is included in all restaurant bills, but most patrons round up a smaller bill to the nearest guilder. A larger bill is rounded up to the nearest five.

Other

Service charges are included in most published prices of cafes, nightspots, beauty salons, and tour companies. However, an added tip is always appreciated.

Netherlands

EMERGENCY INFORMATION

Police and Crime

The Netherlands remains relatively safe, but theft is common in the larger cities. A few elementary precautions should protect the traveler from most problems:

- Do not leave valuables in cars or on tables in cafés.
- Keep non-essential valuables locked in hotel safes when not in use.
- Use credit cards and traveler's checks when possible to avoid carrying large sums of cash.
- Carry photocopies of your passport instead of the original.
- Carry cash in a money belt, and use credit cards or travelers checks for most of your large transactions.
- Walk with your bag away from the street to avoid having it snatched away by motorcycle thieves.
- Never carry a stranger's baggage.

Prostitution is legal in the Netherlands and mainly concentrated in the picturesque area by Amsterdam's canals. Don't be surprised if you catch a real-life scantily-clad figure sitting in a window boasting her wares.

In general, women can walk around freely, but they're advised to travel in groups at night.

In Amsterdam, three types of areas in particular are risky:

- The red-light district, the Central Train Station, restaurants, and public transportation, particularly Trams One, Two, and Five running between the Museum district and the Central Station
- The train line from Schiphol Airport to Amsterdam Central Station is thick with thieves who work in pairs, one to distract the victim and the other to steal the temporarily unguarded laptop, briefcase, or purse
- Automobiles—watch for theft, especially the clearly marked rental cars of foreign visitors

Police are generally friendly, helpful, and effective.

Emergency Numbers

Emergency (Police, Fire, Ambulance)	112
Ambulance (Amsterdam)	0611
Ambulance (The Hague)	322-2111
Ambulance (Rotterdam)	414-1414

Health

Tap water is safe to drink. There are no extraordinary diseases here and community health standards are extremely high. Most doctors speak English and German and sometimes even French. However, AIDS poses a big problem, as do other venereal diseases.

The Dutch have an excellent medical service, an abundance of skilled doctors who speak English, and comprehensive social services (which cover all E.U. countries). Pharmacies have all the necessary drugs, and dental work is good. Apotheek is the Dutch word for pharmacy. Schedules of other pharmacies on duty are posted on store windows. One can call the following number for pharmacy schedule information and emergency doctor and dentist referral:

Pharmacy Assistance ....(20) 694-8709

INTERNAL TRAVEL

AIR

Several airlines fly passengers domestically. KLM Cityhopper (WA) flies between Eindhoven and Amsterdam. Transavia Airlines (HV) runs regularly scheduled flights. Martinair Holland (MP) offers cargo, charter, and passenger services. KLM or the Netherlands Board of Tourism can provide further information.

TAXI

Taxis are recognized by their bright "taxi" sign on the roof. One can find taxi booths at most train stations and airports. It is difficult to hail taxis from the street corner; most must be reserved in advance, or entered from a taxi stand. One may order a taxi from taxicentrale, tel: (20) 677-7777. Several prominent taxi ranks are found at Rembrandtplein, Central Station, and Leidseplein.

Fares are metered and language does not often prove a problem. Expect to pay about NGL10 to 15 for a trip within the downtown area in Amsterdam. Although not required, passengers normally tip 10 percent.

AUTO

If your stay in Amsterdam does not absolutely require a car, it is advisable to avoid renting due to difficult parking and harrowing roads. However, the rest of the Netherlands offers an outstanding road network. Tolls are collected at certain tunnels and bridges. Driving is on the right side and rush hours occur between 7a.m. and 9a.m., and 5p.m. to 7p.m.; avoid driving during these peak times.

Although special bicycle lanes exist, drivers should take special care to be mindful of cyclists, who are seemingly everywhere in the Netherlands. Lanes also exist in the middle of many two-way city streets that are reserved for trams, buses, and taxis.

One can expect to find the major car rental companies represented at hotels and at the airport. Driving requires a license from your home country. One is advised to have a Green Card for insurance, or risk only the minimum legal coverage of one's own insurance policy at home. Most gas stations accept credit cards.

The road system is excellent, and fuel is usually plentiful. The ANWB (Royal Dutch Touring Club) is the motorist association in The Netherlands, Postbus 93200, 2509 XB The Hague (tel: (70) 314-1420).

TRAIN

The rail service is highly efficient and connects all cities. Like most other European countries, the Netherlands offers the higher speed, mostly express Eurocity service (EC), Intercity service (IC), and regular express and local services. Both local and Intercity trains run half hourly, at least on all major routes. Bus timetables are integrated with rail schedules, and a uniform fare structure is in effect throughout the country.

Rail Rover passes allow passengers unlimited travel for one, three, five, or seven days, for one price. The Netherlands also has Public Transport Link Rovers that work in conjunction with rail rover passes and offer unlimited bus and tram service within the country.

One can acquire schedule information and tickets at the GVB tickets office across from the Central Rail Station. Or, contact the Dutch Railway (NV Nederlandse Spoorwegen), which is state-owned and oversees all rail operations in the country. website: http://www.ns.nl.

SUBWAY

Within The Netherlands' cities, public transport is highly developed. Tickets, called *strippenkaart*, are uniform throughout the country. The strippenkaart is a strip of 15 tickets, which are accepted everywhere as payment for transit in standard zones. One may purchase a strippenkaart at the GVB offices, railway stations, post offices, and certain tourist offices. The strippenkaart tickets are also accepted on the metro, buses, trams, trains, and even canal boats. All cities also offer single- and multiple-day tickets for use on any part of their transit system.

In Amsterdam, an efficient two-line metro system covers mostly southeastern suburbs to the center of the city and offers some relief from the congested streets. The metro runs from 6a.m. to midnight Monday through Friday, starting at 6:30a.m Saturdays and 7:30a.m. Sundays. Multiple, pre-paid tickets as well as maps are available at the GVB office opposite Central Station. One may validate tickets at stamping machines on the platforms. Rotterdam also has a subway system, marked by the letter 'M'.

BUS / TRAM

Bus services are excellent for short trips within a city and also after midnight when the subway and trams no longer operate. The bus infrastructure in the Netherlands is extensive, and long-distance coaches operate between the cities, but fares generally run about the same as rail travel, the preferable mode of transport in this well-networked country.

Fares are based on zones. Be sure to validate your tickets or day cards at the stamping machines near the front of buses and the rear of trams.

Trams are a mainstay of the Netherlands' civic transport systems. Amsterdam has 17 tram lines, providing a reliable, fast, frequent service and making it the best way to get around the capital. Trams keep the same hours as the metro, mostly embarking from Centraal Station: numbers 1 and 2 ply the main canal routes, 19 is a line to Museumplein and Concertgebouw, and 9 or 14 will take you to the Muziektheater and Waterlooplein market. A visitor-oriented Circle Tram (#20) now operates throughout central Amsterdam, providing an overview of major attractions and hotels, and functioning as a shuttle.

The city of Rotterdam has excellent tram and bus services, operating on a zonal system in conjunction with the two-line underground network. Schedules and tickets are available at the Central Station.

The Hague also has tram and bus services. Inquire at the Central Station, Koningin Julianaplein.

WATER TRAVEL

In Amsterdam, Canal Buses embark every 25 to 45 minutes, plying the waters between Central Station and Rijksmuseum. Watertaxis operate from 9a.m. to 1a.m., Monday through Sunday, and can transport 8 to 25 passengers. Visitors can also rent pedalos (also called canal bikes) and small boats to navigate the canals themselves.

Ferry service is available to the Wadden Islands, over the Ijsselmeer (formerly the Zuyder Sea) and Schelde Estuary. A service also crosses the Waddenzee to link the Frisian Islands. Boat Tours runs outings from Amsterdam, Rotterdam, Arnhem, Utrecht, Groningen, Giethoorn, Maastricht, and Delft. StenaLine provides a daily service for freight, trailers, and private cars.

TRAVEL ASSISTANCE

Nederlands Bureau voor Toerisme
PO Box 458
2260 MG Leidschendam, The Netherlands
tel: (70) 370 5705; fax: (70) 320 1654
email: info@nbt.nl
website: http://www.holland.com
GVB Central Office
[public transportation]
Prins Hendrikkade 108-114
Amsterdam, The Netherlands
website: http://www.apti.is.nl/index.html
Amsterdam Tourist Information
VVV, Stationsplein 10, opposite Central Station
tel: (06) 3403-4066.
Public Transport Information
tel: 0900-9292, calls are charged per minute
website: http://www.ovr.nl/

National Reservations Center
[hotel accommodations]
tel: (70) 419-5544
email: info@hotelres.n
website: http://www.hotelres.nl

Essential Terms

English	Dutch
Yes	Ja
No	Nee
Good morning	Goedemorgen
Hello (daytime)	Goedemiddag
Hello (evening)	Goedenavond
Hello (telephone)	Dag / Hallo
Good-bye	Dag
Please	Alstublieft
Thank you	Dank u
Pleased to meet you	Aangenaam
Excuse me; I'm sorry	Pardon
My name is _____	Ik heet____
I don't understand	Ik begrijp het niet
Do you speak English?	Spreek je engels?

Communications

DIALING CODES IN THE NETHERLANDS

International country code: [31]

Selected city codes: Amsterdam (20), Arnmem (26), Deventer (570), Eindhoven (40), Groningen (50), The Hague (70), Haarlem (23), Heemstede (23), Hillegersberg (10), Hilversum (35), Hoensbroek (45), Hoogkerk (50), Hoogvliet (10), Loosduinen (70), Maastricht (043), Nijmegen (24), Oud Zuilen (30), Rotterdam (10), Utrecht (30).

Dialing Netherlands from Overseas

To dial the Netherlands from overseas, dial your country's international dialing code, then 31 (the country code for the Netherlands), then the city code and finally the number. If you were dialing Amsterdam from the United States, for example, you would begin with 011, then 31, then 20 (the city code for Amsterdam), and finally the number of the person or office you were trying to reach.

Assistance Numbers

International Operator	0900-8418
International Directory	0900-0412
Directory Assistance	0900-8008
Transportation information	0900-9292

0900 numbers cost from NLG0.20 per minute to 1.05.

CALLING WITHIN THE NETHERLANDS

Local Calls

The less expensive rate occurs Monday to Friday 6p.m. to 8a.m. and throughout the weekends.

Long Distance

To place a long-distance call within the Netherlands, include an initial zero before the city code.

International

To make a direct international call dial 00 + country code + area code + number. Rates fall between 6p.m. and 8a.m. on weeknights, and throughout the weekend. Calls may be placed from phone booths, post offices, and hotels, although the latter will prove the most costly route. A Call Direct service where one can reach a home operator and reverse charges or call collect exists for certain countries. Dial 0800-022 + the 4-digit code applying to your country. See the Amsterdam Yellow Pages for a code listing.

AT&T U.S. Direct...0800-022-9111
MCI Direct 0800-022-9122

PAY PHONES

Public Telephones

Public telephone booths accept 25 cents, NLG1 and NLG2.5 coins, and cards. For coin phones the following instructions apply:

1. Lift receiver
2. Insert money
3. Dial

Unused coins will be returned.

One may also place telephone calls from the Telehouse, Raadhuisstraat 46-50 in Amsterdam, behind Dam Square; or also from the Teletalk Center on Leidestraat 101.

Calling Cards

Cards are available at post offices, rail stations, and any shop with a *PTT-Telephone Card* poster in the window.

CELLULAR PHONES

Royal Dutch Post & Telecom and *LIbertel* operate GSM digital systems for cellular users. Royal Dutch P & T also operates an NMT-450, as well as an NMT-900 system for analogue customers.

Note: Your home country cell phone may not work in this country. If not, we recommend that you rent an international cell phone *before* you leave home. A major US-based cell phone rental provider is **IMC WorldCell**. For information see "International Cell Phone Rentals" on page 14.

CALL BACK

For a list of callback services, please refer to the "Communications" section in the *Global Road Warrior* Introduction.

PHONE JACK

Plug adaptors are available through **iGo Corporation.** (See "Electrical and Telephone Adaptors" on page 19.)

FAX

Fax machines are widely available and service is good.

POSTAL SERVICES

Mail boxes are red and posted throughout the cities and rural areas. The mail system is very efficient. The main post offices are located at:

Amsterdam; Oosterdokskade 3-5 and Singel 250.

The Hague; Prinsestraat

Rotterdam; Coolsingel and Delftseplein.

Hours of service

Monday-Thursday 9a.m. to 5p.m.
Friday 8:30a.m. to 8p.m.
Note: Main post offices have extended hours.

Business Services

AUDIOVISUAL RENTALS

Amsterdam

Ruad Audiovisueel Centrum; Kiuperbergweg 33; tel: (20) 697-8191.

The Hague

Computersverhuur; Regentesseln 9; tel: (70) 356-3252.

Rotterdam

A&V Center; Admiraliteitskade 85; tel: (10) 414-8888.

COURIER SERVICES

Airborne Express; Airborne Express (Netherlands) Bv, Capronilaan 33-35, 1119 Np Schiphol-Rijk; tel: (20) 655-8080; fax: (20) 655-8022.

DHL; tel: 0800-0552 or (20) 655-5555; Kruisweg 601, PO Box 508, Hoofddorp, 2132 NA; hours: Monday to Friday 8:30a.m. to 6p.m., Saturdays until 4p.m., Sundays 10a.m. to 4p.m.

Federal Express; tel: (0800) 022-2333; tel: (20) 500-5699.

TNT; tel: 0800-1234.

UPS; tel: 0800-099-1300; Deccaweg 16, 1042 AD Amsterdam.

The Hague

DHL; tel: 0800-0552.

Federal Express; tel: (0800) 022-2333; tel: (20) 500-5699.

TNT; tel: 0800-1234.

UPS; tel: 0800-099-1300.

Rotterdam

DHL; tel: 0-800-0552.

Federal Express; tel: (0800) 022-2333; tel: (20) 500-5699.

TNT; tel: 0800-1234.

UPS; tel: 0800-099-1300.

SECRETARIAL SERVICES

Amsterdam
Keser Uitzendburo; Vijzelstraat 7; tel: (20) 622-0241.

The Hague
ASB; Spuistraat 72; tel: (70) 346-9446.

Rotterdam
ASB; Westblaak 19; tel: (10) 411-5530.

Electrical

Current
220 volts AC, 50Hz.

ELECTRIC PLUGS

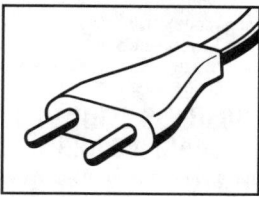

Plug adaptors are available through **iGo Corporation**. (See "Electrical and Telephone Adaptors" on page 19.)

Technical Support

HARDWARE/SOFTWARE VENDOR SUPPORT

Apple/Claris; tel: (6) 022-1517 (Apple Assistance); (in Switzerland) tel: [41] (800) 833-310; (in the U.K.) tel: [44] (990) 127-753; (in the U.S.) tel: [1] (408) 996-1010 (Corporate Headquarters); http://www.apple.com/.

AST; (in the U.S.) tel: [1] (817) 232-9824 (International Technical Support); (in Ireland) tel: [353] (61) 492-222; (in the U.S.) tel: [1] (949) 727-4141; http://www.ast.com/.

Compaq/Digital; tel: 1820-65888; fax: 1820-37349; 82065805 (CompaqCare Center); 820-72366 (QuickLine); (in Switzerland) tel: [41] (22) 709-5330; fax: [41] (22) 709-5391 (Geneva); tel: [41] (1) 801-2507; fax: [41] (1) 801-2172 (Zurich); (General U.S.) tel: (281) 518-2000; http://www.compaq.com/.

Corel; tel: 020-581-3766 (WordPerfect Business Applications); 020- 683-6050 (Corel WordPerfect); (in Germany) tel: [49] (180) 425-8210 (TS Word Perfect-32 bit); (in the U.S.) tel: [1] (716) 871-2325 (Ask to be Forwarded to Appropriate Program); http://www.corel.com/.

Dell; tel: 020 581 8818; fax: 020 681 2751; (Dell- Europe) tel: [44] (134) 474-8000; (in the U.S.) tel: [1] (512) 338-4400; fax: [1] (512) 728-3330; http://www.dell.com/.

Filemaker/Claris; (in Germany) tel: [49] (180) 525-8166

(Info-line); fax: [49] (180) 567-2233; tel: [49] (180) 523-6423; (in the U.S.) tel: [1] (800) 965-9090; http://www.claris.com/.

Gateway 2000; (in Ireland) tel: [353] (1) 797-2000; (in the U.S.) tel: [1] (605) 232-2191; fax: [1] (605) 232-2023; http://www.g2k.com/.

Hewlett Packard; tel: (0)20 606 8751; (in Switzerland) tel: [41] (22) 780-8111; (in the U.S.) tel: [1] (408) 246-4300; http://www.hp.com/.

IBM; tel: (20) 513-5151; fax: (20) 513-6807; (in Switzerland) tel: [41] (22) 310-0418 (in French); (in the U.S.) tel: [1] (919) 517-2800; http://www.ibm.com/.

Microsoft; tel: (20) 500-1005 (Customer Service); tel: (20) 500-1005 (Dutch Speaking); tel: (20) 500-1053 (English Speaking); (in Switzerland) tel: [41] (848) 858-868; fax [41] (1) 831-0869; (in the U.S.) [1] (425) 635-7222; http://www.microsoft.com/.

NEC; tel: (0)30-283-2888 (UltraCare Support); (in the U.S.) [1] (916) 388-0101 (Main Switchboard); http://www.nec.com/.

Novell; (in Germany) tel: [49] (211) 563-2777 (System support); tel: [49] (6196) 904-477; fax: [49] (211) 563-2772; (in Switzerland) tel: [41] (1) 308-4747; fax: [41] (1) 302-0401; (in the U.S.) tel: [1] (408) 434-2300; fax: [1] (408) 577-5775 (Worldwide Sales Headquarters); http://www.novell.com/.

Quark; tel: 318-69-3300; (in Switzerland) tel: [41] (1) 808-7722; fax: [41] (1) 808-7799; (in the U.S.) tel: [1] (303) 894-8899; fax: [1] (303) 894-3398 (For Products Registered in the Americas); http://www.quark.com/.

Toshiba; (in Germany) tel: [49] (2131) 158-319; fax: [49] (2131) 158-558; (in Switzerland) tel: [41] (1) 946-0777; fax: [41] (1) 946-0807; (in Ireland) tel: [44] (193) 282-8828; (in the U.S.) [1] (949) 583-3000 (Corporate Headquarters); http://www.toshiba.com/.

Internet Connection

HOW TO CONNECT

Connecting to AOL and Compuserve in the Netherlands is similar to using it when traveling outside your own area code. See the introductory section for detailed information on connecting to your account through a different phone number.

America Online
Numbers are available at keyword *international*. Be sure to get several local numbers before leaving. AOL's Global-Net service charges US$6 an hour in addition to the usual charges. Go to keyword *access* (a free area) and download the software.

Numbers are available at *Go International*. The Compuserve Web-site also has a great deal of information, at http://www.compuserve.com.

Amsterdam (20) 682-6015; Eindhoven (40) 257-0102; Groningen (50) 311-1464; Rotterdam (10) 437-1255; The Hague (70) 388-9699.

Compuserve
Access: Amersfoort (33) 711-0510; Amsterdam (20) 711-0510; Apeldoorn (55) 711-0510; Arnhem (26) 711-0510; Breda (76) 711-0510; Den Helder (223) 711-510; Eindhoven (40) 711-0510; Groningen (50) 711-0510; Rotterdam (10) 711-0510; Sliedrecht (184) 711-510; Zwolle (38) 711-0510.

Independent Service Providers
Many independent service providers offer discounts if you are only in town for a couple of days.

Netherlands

Netherlands

Business Internet Trends; tel: (8) 648-688; fax: (8) 643-334; http://www.bit.nl; email: info@bit.nl/.

EuroNet Internet; tel: (20) 535-5555; fax: (20) 535-5400; email: info@euronet.nl; http://www.euro.net/.

InTouch; tel: (20) 675-2060; fax: (20) 675-8429; email: info@intouch.nl; http://www.intouch.nl/.

Netland Internet Services; tel: (20) 562-8282; fax: (20) 562-8281; email: info@netland.nl; http://www.netland.nl/.

UUNET; tel: (20) 495-2727; tel: (20) 495-2828; fax: (20) 495-2737; support@NL.net; http://www.nl.net/.

INTERNET CAFES

To check email or get internet access if you have none available to you where you stay, visit one of the following cafes. Hourly charges usually apply.

Amsterdam

Cafe Internet; Korte Nieuwendijk 30, Old Center; tel: 620-0902; http://cybercafe.euronet.nl/; email: visitor1@cafe.euronet.nl; open until 1a.m.

Cybernetlounge; van Woustraat 82 1073 LP, Amsterdam; tel: (20) 777-5060; fax: (20) 777-5061; email: info@cybernetlounge.com; http://www.cybernetlounge.com/; Monday through Friday, 10a.m. to 12p.m.; 0.18 Guilder per minute of Internet use.

easyEverything; Reguliersbreestraat 22, Amsterdam; email: mike.v@easyeverything.com; http://www.easyeverything.com/; Open seven days a week, 24 hours a day.

In De Waag; Nieuwmarkt, Old Center; http://www.waag.org

La Bastille Internet Cafe; Lijnbaansgracht 246 1017rk, Amsterdam; tel: (20) 623-5604; fax: (20) 620-6809; email: info@labastille.nl; http://www.labastille.nl/; Monday through Friday 10a.m. to 12a.m.; 0.17 Guilder per minute of Internet use.

The Internet Cafe; Martelaarsgracht 11 Amsterdam Noord Holland 1012 TN Netherlands; tel: (20) 627-1052; email: info@internetcafe.nl; http://www.internetcafe.nl/; Monday through Saturday, 9a.m. to 1am.

MySter 2000; Lijnbaansgracht 92, Jordaan; tel: 620-2970; http://www.euro.net/sala/myster; email: myster@net.info.nl; open until 5p.m.; Thursdays until 8p.m.

Eindhoven

CyberQuest; Het Internetcafé in Laser Quest Eindhoven Oude Stadsgracht 15, Eindhoven; tel: 40-2443131; email: cyberqst@iaehv.nl; http://www.iae.nl/users/cyberqst/; Monday through Sunday, 1p.m. to 1a.m.

Trafalgar Pub; Trafalgar Pub Dommelstraat 21, Eindhoven; tel: (40) 244-8820; email: trafalgar@iaehv.nl; http://www.dse.nl/trafalgar/.

Rotterdam

JoHo Cybercafe; Goudsesingel 47a, 3031 ED, Rotterdam; tel: (10) 2409077; email: rotterdam@joho.nl; http://www.joho.nl/; Monday through Saturday, 10a.m. to 6p.m.; 10 Guilders per hour of Internet service.

The CAT@Zine Internet Corner; Virgin Megastore, The Mall, Rotterdam Passage 1, 3011 AG Rotterdam; tel: (10) 411-1752; email: tim@catazine.net; http://www.catazine.net; Monday through Saturday, 11a.m. to 6p.m.

QuakePub; Zevenkampsering 305 3068 Hg Rotterdam; tel: (10) 286-9168; fax: (10) 420-6939; email: Info@quakepub.nl; http://www.quakepub.nl/; Monday through Saturday, 4p.m. to 12a.m.; 8.80 Guilders per hour of Internet use.

Business Culture

GREETINGS AND COURTESIES

The Dutch are quite formal, and expect the same from visitors. First names are not used in either business or social settings. The acceptable form of address, *Deheer* (Mr.) and *Mevrouw* (Mrs. or Miss), along with a firm handshake with both men and women is proper. Eye contact is extremely important. When being introduced, use only your last name prefaced by Mr., Mrs., Miss, Dr., etc. The Dutch are disciplined, conservative, polite, and attentive to the smallest detail. Punctuality is essential, and a sense of decorum will serve you well. In business dealings, gifts are only exchanged after a relationship has been well established or a successful transaction completed. Avoid logo trinkets; quality counts and a well-thought-out gift will go much further with your Dutch counterparts than a cheap present with your company's logo. Gifts from your own country, or native to your area of the world, are favorably received. If visiting your colleague's home, which is not common, a bottle of fine wine is always appreciated.

BUSINESS ETHIC AND FRAMEWORK

English is the language of business in the Netherlands. The Dutch are a very hard working people, deserving of the familiar saying, "In Rotterdam, shirts are sold with the sleeves rolled up!" Additionally, they are known to "size you up" by how you are introduced into their business community. An introduction from a large banking concern, investment house, or accounting firm will easily gain you access to the top-ranking officer of many Dutch businesses. Should you initiate your own letter of introduction, clearly state your intentions, current credentials, and annual report or background material on the senior management of your company. Conducting business over lunch is not unusual. Business dinners are uncommon, however. If you do find yourself at dinner with your colleague, use the time to develop your relationship; avoid business discussions, and absolutely do not discuss money during the meal.

DECISION MAKING

In the Netherlands the corporate hierarchy often includes a chief executive of the firm and several managing directors who are each responsible for separate departments or divisions in the corporation. The process for making decisions will be very analytical and will require enough time for your Dutch colleagues to consider all aspects of the deal and its consequences. Depending both on the amount of money and business involved in a transaction, a managing director usually has authority to render decisions without consent from the board.

WOMEN

Women still face opposition in achieving senior management positions, and women in the work force must constantly overcome resistance from their male Dutch counterparts. While many of Netherlands' women do choose to work, most feel their duties in life are to family and home. Women traveling to the Netherlands may encounter questions regarding their marital status and their career choices. Respond with humor and patience; be brief in your explanations and get on to business.

MEETINGS

Formality is essential when doing business in the Netherlands. After being led to the meeting room, your host will direct you to your seat. Business cards are exchanged with everyone at the beginning of meetings and your card should include your title, professional degrees, and the founding date of your company. The meeting will begin with few preliminaries as the Dutch like to get down to business straightaway. Be organized and specific, factual, and to the point. It is advisable to provide an outline of your proposal so that your Dutch colleagues can identify discussion points. Visual aids representing statistical data (graphs, charts, etc.) are considered valuable tools. Make certain these peripherals are relevant. Show-biz techniques and high-pressure sales tactics may bring the meeting to a premature close. Be careful when making promises; oral agreements and statements of intent can be legally binding. Follow up your meeting with a letter outlining the points discussed and future expectations.

BUSINESS ATTIRE

Dress conservatively in dark suits of natural fiber, reflecting good quality. Ties should be somber to avoid drawing special attention. The idea is to blend into the Netherlands' business community, not stand out in it. Women should also dress in subdued colors; suits and dresses are appropriate. Bring a jacket or sweater for unpredictable and often cool weather. An umbrella would also serve helpful for frequent rainy days.

Business Centers
Amsterdam

CITY VIEW

Amsterdam is one of the world's great cities, a combination of wealth and small-town sensibilities. It has the image of a "liberal" town, but the businesspeople are just as interested in making money as they would be anywhere else.

AIRPORT

Amsterdam Airport to City Center

The airport lies 9 miles (15 km.) from the city. A KLM Airport Shuttle runs every 30 minutes from 6:30a.m. to 8p.m. and stops at selected hotels. Expect to pay NLG17.50 for a one way fare. Purchase tickets in the arrivals hall at the transport desk or directly from the driver.

Trains run directly from the airport to Amsterdam Central Station, every 15 minutes, and to other points (the convention center) and cities, including Rotterdam and the Hague. Trains run 24 hours a day, in 30-minute intervals between 6a.m. and midnight, and every hour otherwise. Fares cost NLG5.50 for the 20-minute one-way trip downtown.

For those requiring door-to-door service, taxis await you outside the arrivals hall. A fare into downtown Amsterdam will cost about NLG65. The ride takes approximately 30 minutes. However, if you hit evening or morning rush hours, it may take longer. Taxis will also take passengers as far as the Hague and also Rotterdam.

Airline Numbers

Airport flight information	06-9292
Aer Lingus	
Reservations	(20) 623-8620
Ticket Sales	(20) 601-0065
Aeroflot	(20) 627-05-61
Air Canada	(20) 604-1489, 601-5363
Air France	(20 446-88-00
Air India	(20) 624-81-09
Air UK	(20) 601-06-33
Alitalia	(20) 577-7420, 577-7444
British Airways	(20) 565-00-66

British Midland Airways	(20) 662-22-11
Cathay Pacific	(20) 653-52-25
China Airlines	(20) 646-10-01
Delta	(20) 661-00-51
El-Al	(20) 664-01-01
Garuda Indonesia	(20) 627-2626
Icelandair	(20) 627-01-36
JAL	(20 675-98-79
KLM	(20) 474-77-47
Lufthansa	(20) 668-58-51
Malaysian Airlines	(20) 626-24-20
Northwest Airlines	(20) 627-71-41
Philippine Airlines	(20) 646-43-46
Qantas	(20) 638-80-81
Singapore Airlines	(20) 646-60-66
South African Airways	(20) 568-54-44
Thai Airways	(20) 622-18-77
United Airlines	(20) 662-32-36

HOTELS

Note: Occupancy is very tight from April to June and from September to November, especially in the top-end and expensive brackets. Be sure to book well in advance if planning to travel during these times.

Top-end

Amstel Inter-Continental Hotel; Professor Tulpplein 1; tel: (20) 622-6060; fax: (20) 622-5808; city center; restaurant; conference facilities; secretarial service; in-room fax machine, dual telephone lines, voicemail, videorecorder, CD player; fitness; sauna; pool.

Amsterdam Hilton Schiphol Airport; Herbergierstraat 1; tel: (20) 603-4567; fax: (20) 648-0917.

Amsterdam Marriott; Stadhouderskade 19-21; tel: (20) 607-5555; fax: (20) 607-5511; located on Leidseplein, city center; restaurant; conference facilities; business floor; fitness; sauna.

Golden Tulip Barbizon Palace; Prins Hendrikkade 59-72; tel: (20) 556-4564; fax: (20) 624-3353; opposite central rail station; 19 separate houses; restaurant; conference facilities (up to 550); business center; secretarial service; internet; in-room modem/fax connection; corporate rates; secure parking; fitness; sauna.

Grand Hotel Krasnapolsky; Dam 9; tel: (20) 554-9111; fax: (20 531-1778; http://www.drasnapolsky.nl; near exhibition grounds; 7 restaurants; conference facilities (up to 1600); business center; secretarial service; events agency; in-room modem/fax connection, safe; secured garage; private boat dock; beauty center.

Hotel de l'Europe; Nieuwe Doelenstraat 2-8; tel: (20) 623-4836; fax: (20) 624-2962; email: hotel@leurope.nl; city center; restaurant; conference facilities (up to 90); business center; secretarial service; in-room modem/fax connection, safe, dual telephones, voicemail; corporate rates; fitness; sauna; pool.

Pulitzer (ITT Sheraton); Prinsengracht 315-331; tel: (20) 523-5235; fax: (20) 627-6753; renovated 17th and 18th century houses along canal; 2 restaurants; conference facilities; in-room safe; non-smoking floors.

Expensive

Ambassade; Herengracht 341; tel: (20) 626-2333; fax: (20) 624-5321; historic center; renovated 17th and 18th Century houses; dual telephone lines; in-room desk and safe; Dutch breakfast.

Hotel Estherea; Singel 305; tel: (20) 624-5146; fax: (20) 623-9001; email: estherea@xs4all.nl; located on canal in city center in 17th century buildings; family-run

Netherlands

establishment; in-room bathroom, telephone, tv, safe, minibar, hairdryer; friendly service.

Jan Luyken Hotel & Residence; Jan Luykenstraat 58; tel: (20) 573-0730; fax: (20) 676-3841; breakfast restaurant; conference facilities; in-room safe.

Jolly Hotel Carlton; Vijzelstraat 4; tel: (20) 624-1929; fax: (20) 626-6183; city center, overlooking floating flower market; renovated; photocopy/fax facilities.

Le Meridien Apollo; Apollolaan 2, 1077; tel: (20) 673-5922; fax: (20) 570-5744; email: info@meridien.nl; http://www.meridien.nl/; city center; restaurant; conference facilities.

Mercure Amsterdam Airport; Oude Haagseweb 20; tel: (20) 617-9005; fax: (20) 615-9027.

Novotel Amsterdam; Europaboulevard 10; tel: (20) 541-1123; fax: (20) 646-2823.

Park Hotel; Stadhouderskade 25; tel: (20) 671-7474; fax: (20) 664-9455; city center; restaurant; conference facilities (up to 150); secretarial service; fax/photocopy facilities; in-room safe; corporate rates.

Moderate

Amstel Botel; Oosterdokskade 2-4; tel: (20) 626-4247; fax: (20) 639-1952; near rail station.

Amsterdam Prinsengracht; Prinsengracht 1015; tel: (20) 623-8926; fax: (20) 623-8926; city center; breakfast restaurant; garden.

Hotel Aalborg; Sarphatiepark 106-108; tel:(20) 679-9057; fax: (20) 676-6560; located in old Amsterdam, south; breakfast restaurant.

Hotel Casa 400; James Wattstraat 75; tel: (20) 665-1171; fax: (20) 663-0379; near Amstel rail station; restaurant; conference facilities; **Note**: hotel closed in winter.

Hotel Heemskerk; Jan Willem Brouwerstraat 25; tel: (20) 679-4980; fax: (20) 671-0726; near World Trade Center and RAI; city center; breakfast restaurant.

Hotel Toren; Keizersgracht 164; tel: (20) 622-6352; fax: (20) 626-9705; http://www.toren.nl; breakfast restaurant; conference facilities; in-room safe.

Ibis Amsterdam Airport; Ibis Amsterdam Airport, Schipholweb 181; tel: (20) 502-5100; fax: (20) 657-0199.

Rembrandt Residence Hotel; Herengracht 255; tel: (20) 622-1727; fax: (20) 625-0630; 17th century houses; breakfast restaurant; conference facilities.

MEDICAL CARE

Academisch Medisch Centrum; Meibergdreef 9; tel: 566-9111.

Onze Lieve Vrouwe Gasthuis; 179 Le Oosterparkstraat; tel: 599-91-11.

Vrije Universiteit Medical Center; 1117 De Boelelaan; tel: 584-91-11.

HEALTH CLUB

The Garden Gym; 158 Jodenbreestraat; Metro: Waterlooplein. Tram: 9, 14; tel: [31] (20) 626-87-72.

Splash Fitness Club; Ramada Renaissance Hotel, 1 Kattengat; tel: [31] (20) 627-10-44.

Sporting Club Leidseplein; 18 Korte Leidsedwarsstraat; Tram: 1, 2, 5, 6, 7, 10, 11; tel: [31] (20) 620-66-31.

AUTO RENTAL

Avis; Amsterdam Schiphol Airport, Aankomstpassage 5, Amsterdam, 1118 AA; tel: (20) 655-6050; Klokkenbergweg 15, Amsterdam, 1101 AK; tel: (20) 430-9511; Nassaukade 380, Amsterdam, 1054 AD; tel: (20) 683-6061.

Europcar; Luchthaven Schiphol - aankomstpassage 10, arrival hall plaza, Amsterdam; tel: (20) 316-4190; fax:(20) 604-1439; Overtoom 197, Amsterdam; tel: (20) 683-2123; fax: (20) 616-4257.

Hertz; Schiphol Airport, Box 75584 Schiphol Centrum, Amsterdam; tel: (20) 601-5416; fax: 601-0798; Overtoom 333, Amsterdam; tel: (20) 612-2441; fax: (20) 612-5464; Engelsesteeg 4, Amsterdam; tel: (20) 623-6123; fax: (20) 626-2395.

WORLD TRADE CENTER

World Trade Center Amsterdam
Strawinskylaan 1
1077 XW Amsterdam
The Netherlands
tel: (20) 575-9111; fax: (20) 662-7255
email: WTCA@buvoha.com
Services include: meeting facilities, club, hotel, temporary offices, secretarial services, translation services, videoconferencing.

World Trade Center Amsterdam Airport
Schiphol Boulevard 105
1118 BG Schiphol Airport
The Netherlands
tel: (20) 446-6333; fax: (20) 653-5042

CHAMBER OF COMMERCE

Amsterdam Chamber of Commerce and Industry
Euro-Info Center, PO Box 2852
1000 CW Amsterdam
tel: (20) 523-6705; fax: (20 523-6732

The Hague Chamber of Commerce and Industry
PO Box 29718, Konigskade 30
2502 LS The Hague
tel: (70) 328-7100; fax: (70) 324-0684
website: http://www.denhaag.kzk.nl
email: info@denhaag.kzk.nl

CONVENTION BUREAU

The Netherlands Convention Bureau
Amstelkijk 166
1079 LH Amsterdam
tel: (20) 646-2580; fax: (20) 644-5935
website: http://www.nicongress.nl
email: ncb@xs4all.nl

New Zealand

At a Glance

Population .... 3,819,762 (July 2000 est.)
Growth Rate .... 1.17% (2000 est.)
Life Expectancy .... 77.82 years
Infant Mortality ... 6.39 deaths/1,000 live births (2000 est.)

Ethnic Composition
New Zealand European..74.5%
Maori 9.7%
Asian and Other 7.4%
Pacific Islander..3.8%

Religious Composition
Unspecified or none 33%
Anglican...24%
Presbyterian 18%
Roman Catholic..15%
Methodist...5%
Baptist 2%
Other Protestant...3%

Languages Spoken
English (official), Maori.

Education and Literacy
Ten years of schooling are compulsory. Literacy is 99 percent.

Labor Force
Total: 1,860,000
By occupation: services 65%, industry 25%, agriculture 10%.

THE ECONOMY

Since the 1980's, the government of New Zealand has been instituting major economic restructuring, moving toward a more industrialized, free market economy, away from its history as an agrarian economy dependent on concessionary British market access. New Zealand seems to recognize the necessity of this in order to compete globally. This dynamic growth has boosted real incomes, increased the technological capabilities of industry, and contained inflationary pressures. New Zealand boasts one of the lowest rates of inflation in the industrial world. Per capita GDP has steadily increased rivaling that of the big west European economies. A key vulnerability of New Zealand is its dependence on trade. Its growth is intertwined with the economic performance of the U.S., Europe, and Asia.

Exports .... US$12.2 billion (f.o.b., 1998 est.)
Imports .... US$11.2 billion (f.o.b., 1998 est.)
Total Trade .... US$23.4 billion (1998 est.)
GDP Per Capita .... US$17,400 (1999 est.)
Unemployment .... 7% (1999 est.)
Inflation Rate .... 1.3% (1999 est.)

Top Export Partners
Australia 21%, Japan 13%, U.S. 13%, U.K. 6%.

Top Import Partners
Australia 22%, U.S. 20%, Japan 11%, U.K. 5%.

Top Exports
Dairy products, meat, fish, wool, forestry products, manufactures.

Top Imports
Machinery and equipment, vehicles and aircraft, petroleum, consumer goods, plastics.

BUSINESS WORKWEEK

Offices
Monday to Friday 8:30a.m. to 5p.m.

Banks
Monday to Friday 9a.m. to 4:30p.m.

Government
Monday to Friday 8:30a.m. to 5p.m.

Retail
Monday to Friday 9a.m. to 5:30p.m., Thursdays and Fridays until 9p.m.; Saturday 9a.m. to 12:30p.m. Some shops may be open on Sundays.

HOLIDAYS

New Year's Day.. January 1-2
Waitangi Day, Anniversary of
1840 Treaty ....February 6
Good Friday...April 21*
Easter...April 24*
ANZAC Day, Anniversary of
1915 Landing at Gallipoli.. April 25
Queen's Official Birthday..June 5*
Labor Day..October 23*
Christmas Day...December 25
Boxing Day .... December 27*
*Date may vary by year.

CLIMATE

Seasons
Because New Zealand is south of the equator, the seasons are reversed from Europe, North America, and much of Asia: spring lasts from September to November, summer from December to February, fall from March until May, and winter from June to August. In general, the climate is very pleasant, without dramatic shifts in temperature.

The climate is temperate on the island, with approximately 2,000 hours of sunshine a year, and there is hardly any temperature difference between the seasons. The summer temperature hovers around 30°C, and it seldom falls bellow zero in the winter. But do expect windy conditions.

Regions
Temperature variations occur more on the South island than on the North island, where temperature differences are 8 to 10°C.

Money & Banking

Currency
The currency of New Zealand is the New Zealand Dollar (NZ$).

Denominations
The New Zealand Dollar comes in coin denominations of NZ$2 and 1 and 50, 20, 10 and 5 cents; and banknotes of NZ$5, 10, 20, 50, and 100.

New Zealand

Traveler's checks

Traveler's checks and foreign currency can be easily and efficiently exchanged at banks, foreign exchange bureaus located in the major cities, hotels, and foreign exchange kiosks at the airports. Banks offer the most variable exchange rates. Traveler's checks receive a better exchange rate than cash, or you can purchase New Zealand dollar traveler's check before departure, which can be exchanged almost everywhere.

Credit cards, American Express, Visa, MasterCard, and Diners Club are widely accepted in the New Zealand, and you can get cash advances from you credit card on many of the automated teller machines (ATM).

Long-term visitors should set up a checking account in New Zealand and get an ATM card.

Travel

VISA AND PASSPORT

A passport that is valid for at least three months beyond date of departure is required of all visitors. In addition, all visitors must have sufficient funds to cover the duration of their stay.

Visas are not required by the nationals of the following countries for stays up to three months: Andorra, Argentina, Australia, Bahrain, Brazil, Brunei, Canada, Chile, Czech Republic, all E.U. countries, Hong Kong (Special Administrative Region or British Nationals Overseas passports), Hungary, Iceland, Indonesia, Israel, Japan, Kiribati, Korea (Rep. of), Kuwait, Liechtenstein, Malaysia, Malta, Monaco, Nauru, New Zealand Associated Territories, Norway, Oman, Qatar, San Marino, Saudi Arabia, Singapore, Slovenia, South Africa, Switzerland, Thailand, Tuvalu, United Arab Emirates, Uruguay, U.S., Vatican City, and Zimbabwe; U.K. nationals are eligible for visa-free stays up to six months (providing they hold a full 10-year passport and onward or return tickets).

Passengers in transit who do not leave the airport and are continuing their journey aboard the first-connecting aircraft, and who are holding confirmed tickets and other documents for onward travel, are also exempt from the need for a visa. But there are exceptions to this exemption, and nationals of some countries who are traveling through New Zealand must always carry a transit visa, even if not exiting the airport. Check transit regulations regarding your country with the New Zealand Immigration Service prior to traveling.

Types of visa issued, and usual length of time required to process the application are as follows:

- Visitor: 7 days
- Business: 14 days
- Transit: 7 days
- Work: 14 days
- Student: 7 days

All visas are single-entry, unless special arrangements are made. The maximum permissible stay is usually 9 months within an 18-month period. For those entering without a visa, the maximum three-month stay may be extended once the visitor is in the country—contact the New Zealand Immigration Service.

DEPARTURE FORMALITIES

All visitors are required to pay a departure tax of NZ$20.

CUSTOMS ENTRY (PERSONAL)

Duty-free
- Tobacco: 200 cigarettes, 50 cigars, 250g tobacco, or a mixture thereof up to 250g
- Alcohol: 4.5 liters of wine or beer; 1.125 liters or 40 ounces spirits or liqueurs
  Other: a reasonable amount of perfume for personal use; goods to a total value of NZ$700

Prohibited or Restricted
The import of any of the following items is prohibited:

- Firearms or other weapons (a special permit may be procured from the New Zealand police to allow import)
- Ivory in any form
- Tortoise or turtle shell jewelry and ornaments
- Medicines using musk, rhinoceros or tiger derivatives
- Carvings or anything made from whalebone or bone from any other marine animals
- Cat skins or coats

- Certain drugs, such as diuretics, depressants, stimulants, heart drugs, tranquilizers, or sleeping pills, unless documented by a doctor's written prescription
The New Zealand government publishes a full list of personal items allowed for import without incurring duty, such as jewelry and photographic or sporting equipment. Visitors are advised not to take fruit or plant material with them.

IMMUNIZATION

No vaccinations are required for entry to New Zealand unless one has been infected within two weeks prior to arrival.

TIPPING

Tipping is not necessary in New Zealand as a GST (goods and service tax) is added to all bills. Many visitors tip anyway, usually in the range of 10 to 15 percent.

EMERGENCY INFORMATION

Police and Crime
New Zealand is a relatively safe country, though the larger cities can get rough at night. A few elementary precautions should protect the traveler from most problems:

- Do not leave valuables in cars or on tables in cafés.
- Keep non-essential valuables locked in hotel safes when not in use.
- Use credit cards and traveler's checks when possible to avoid carrying large sums of cash.
- Carry photocopies of your passport instead of the original.
- Carry cash in a money belt, and use credit cards or travelers checks for most of your large transactions.
- Never carry a stranger's baggage.
- Women should avoid traveling alone at night
The most typical crime is theft from hostels, cars, and camper vans. Violent crime directed at tourists is unusual.

Emergency Numbers
Ambulance, Fire, and Police 111

Health
Expect no unusual health risks here. The water is potable, and meat and dairy products are safe. Visitors should take precautions against heat and sunstroke.

No dangerous wild animals or snakes live in New Zealand. Annoying sandflies are unfortunately abundant in Fiordland, but they can be kept at bay with insect repellent. The sole poisonous creature is the rare katipo spider.

New Zealand has well-trained doctors and dentists and an efficient and inexpensive medical service. Medical facilities, public and private, are high quality, and many hotels have doctors on call. Telephone numbers for hospitals and doctors can be found in the front of local telephone directories. If visitors need pharmaceutical supplies or drugs outside customary shopping hours, they can consult the listing 'Urgent Pharmacies' in the local directory.

INTERNAL TRAVEL

AIR

Even though New Zealand is relatively small and pretty easy to navigate, it can make sense to fly, especially for the business traveler. A number of discounts make flying economical. The entire country is accessible by air.

The two major domestic airlines are Ansett New Zealand and Air New Zealand. The latter also has partial ownership of several smaller airlines (Eagle Air, Mt. Cook Airline, and Air Nelson) that group together as Air New Zealand Link. This set-up provides comprehensive coverage of the country, providing access to dozens of smaller airports around the islands, and further enhanced by the fact that Qantas New Zealand, Mt. Cook, and Air New Zealand all fly between the major airports.

TAXI

New Zealand has a plethora of taxi services. Cabs are generally late-model sedans that can carry four or five passengers, and station wagons can also be reserved from some companies. There is no standard taxicab color or signage, lighted or otherwise. Taxis may be hailed on the street, engaged at taxi stands, or reserved by telephone, email, or even internet. Taxis are metered, and though a tip is not necessarily expected, many passengers tip in the 10-percent range.

Special services and vehicles are also available. The maxi taxi, for instance, is a minibus that can carry up to ten people, and the charges are metered per vehicle regardless of how many are riding. Also look for cabs that accommodate business travelers (called Executive/Business); these come equipped with mobile telephones, fax machines, and drivers attuned to the special needs of the business passenger.

A great internet resource for more information about taxis and other types of hired vehicles is The New Zealand Taxi Federation & Limousine and Shuttle Association:

website: http://www.taxinet.org.nz/

AUTO

Local and international auto rental companies are represented at airports and hotels in most cities. If traveling to both islands of New Zealand, keep in mind that many rental agencies will not allow their cars to travel inter-island. It will most likely prove cheaper to fly anyway.

Driver's licenses from a visitor's country of origin are sufficient documentation for car rental for nationals of some 52 countries, including all E.U. nations, Australia, Canada, U.S., South Africa, Switzerland, and Norway. The minimum age for driving a rental car is 21.

Driving conditions in general are good all over New Zealand. The roads are well maintained and well signposted, and journeys are short between major destinations.

Traffic drives on the left and always yields to cross-traffic coming from the right-hand side. Except at crosswalks, pedestrians must accommodate themselves to the vehicular presence on roadways rather than having the right-of-way.

For more information, contact:

The New Zealand Automobile Association

tel: (9) 377 4660; fax: (9) 309 4563
website: http://www.aa.co.nz

TRAIN

Tranz Rail Ltd. provides a reliable railway service over 4000km (2485 miles) of track. Express trains and routes oriented toward commute or business travel are few, but train travel is pretty fast. Many or most of the routes feature panoramic views of natural splendor. The rolling stock is comfortable and modern, and fares are sometimes less than bus fare along the same routes.

Express service exists between Auckland and Wellington, Totorua, Tauranga; also between Wellington and Napier, as well as between Christchurch and Invercargill, Picton, and Greymouth. Some trains have dining cars, but overnight services offer no sleeping cars.

A three-in-one pass called Travelpass New Zealand incorporates train, ferry, and coach services for unlimited travel on TranzScenic trains, Interislander ferry services, and InterCity coaches. The traveler can choose amongst a number of terms, varying between five days and about eight weeks. Other discount passes are available. All passenger rail service is one-class only. Contact: **Tranz Rail**

Reservations

tel: (4) 498 3303; fax: (4) 498 3090
website: http://www.tranzlink.co.nz

SUBWAY

No subway service exists in New Zealand, which may be just as well, lest travelers miss any of the picturesque outdoor scenery.

BUS / TRAM

Regional bus networks provide extensive scheduled services that reach most parts of the country. InterCity serves both islands; Newmans operates on the North Island; and Mt. Cook Landline covers the South Island. Buses on main routes are frequent (once daily at least), reliable, and usually clean and modern—but they can also prove slow and expensive. Reservations are advised.

In the cities and main towns, one can expect generally good local bus services. In Wellington, a trolley system also exists. Both Wellington and Auckland have zonal fares featuring day passes and pre-purchase tickets.

The shuttle bus offers another alternative that is smaller, cheaper and more genial than the big buses. Many of the shuttle buses are meant to accommodate foreign visitors, in particular, and offer extra features that may prove valuable to the business traveler.

Contacts:

InterCity Coachlines
website: http://www.intercitycoach.co.nz

Newmans Coachlines
website: http://www.newmanscoach.co.nz

Tourism New Zealand
(see address in Travel Assistance section)

WATER TRAVEL

Ferry service operates between Wellington on the North Island and Picton on the South Island. Ferries cross Cook Strait three times a day on weekends and four on weekdays, carrying vehicles and passengers. The three-hour trip can get a bit rough, depending on the weather. One should definitely book ahead in the summer months, but prepare for last-minute cancellations if the weather is intemperate.

Buses connect the ferry terminal with the Wellington and Picton train stations and depart 35 minutes prior to each sailing; buses also meet all ferries. Contact Tranz Rail reservations (see 'Train' above) to book passage.

A fast inter-island ferry called TOPCAT makes the crossing between Wellington and Picton in 1 hour and 40 minutes, carrying 580 passengers and 240 vehicles; it operates year round.

TOPCAT website: http://topcatferry.co.nz

TRAVEL ASSISTANCE

Tourism New Zealand

Fletcher Challenge House
89 The Terrace, Wellington, New Zealand
tel: (4) 472 8860. fax: (4) 478 1736
email:enquiries@nztb.govt.nz
website: http://www.nztb.govt.nz

Hotel Accommodations

Motel Association of New Zealand.....................(4) 385-8011
Hotel Association of New Zealand ....(4) 385-1369

Tourist Information

Auckland Visitor Center..................................(9) 366-6888

Communications

DIALING CODES IN NEW ZEALAND

International country code: [64]

Selected city codes: Auckland (9), Bell South Mobile Phones (GSM) (21), Christchurch (3), Dunedin (3), Hamilton (7), Hastings (6), Invercargill (3), Napier (6), Nelson (3), New Plymouth (6), New Zealand External Territories (24), North Island (Central and Eastern) (7), North Island (North) (9), North Island (West) (6), Palmerston North (6), Rotorua (7), South Island (3), Tauranga (7), Telecom Mobile Phones (AMPS/DAMPS) (25), Timaru (3), Wanganui (6), Wellington (4), Whangarei (9).

Dialing New Zealand from Overseas

To dial New Zealand from overseas, dial your country's international dialing code, then 64 (the country code for New Zealand), then the city code and finally the number. If you were dialing Auckland from the United States, for example, you would begin with 011, then 64, then 9 (the city code for Aukland), and finally the number of the person or office you were trying to reach.

Assistance Numbers

International Operator 0172
Domestic Operator 010
Domestic Directory 018

CALLING WITHIN NEW ZEALAND

Local Calls

It will cost 20 cents for a local call.

Long Distance Calls

Area codes run under the name of STD codes in New Zealand. The general rule is to use the area code even if you find yourself in the same area code but at fair distance from the site you are calling. The front of the telephone book lists all codes. Dial 03 for all South Island calls.

International Calls

Make a direct international call by dialing 00 + country code + area code + number from many phones. Discount rates vary from country to country. To the U.S. and Canada, rates fall between 10p.m. and 8a.m. Monday to Saturday, and all day Sunday. All country codes, charges and instructions are listed in the front of New Zealand telephone books. But, as always, inquire in advance about extra surcharges that your hotel will only too gladly tack onto your bill.

Connect to an operator in your home country for collect or credit card calls through a Home Country Direct number.

Australia 000-961
Canada 000-919
U.K. 000-944
U.S. AT&T 000-911
U.S. MCI.. 000-912
U.S. Sprint.. 000-999

PAY PHONES

Public Telephones

Most public phones now operate with cards. Old phones that take coins, however, still exist here and there and in remote areas. Coin phones allow one to practice alphabetical prowess by pressing "A" if the party answers, and "B" for a refund if they don't.
1. Insert money
2. Dial
3. Press "A" if party answers
   (or) Press "B" for a refund if no one answers

To operate a card phone:
1. Lift receiver
2. Insert card
3. Dial

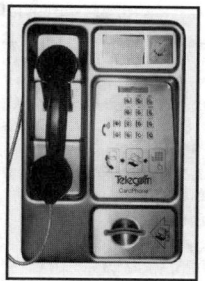

Calling Cards

Shops, visitor information centers, newsstands, and service stations with the green Phonecard symbol sell phone cards in NZ$5, 10, 20 and 50 denominations.

CELLULAR PHONES

GSM digital service is provided by Bell South New Zealand and Telecom Australia. Analogue users can get service through Telecommobile Communications. Check with your provider at home to see if a partnership in New Zealand exists.

CALL BACK

You can (potentially) save significant sums when calling in New Zealand by using one of the call back services listed below. Fees for call back services vary widely, depending on the company and the type of service required.

Note: Your home country cell phone may not work in this country. If not, we recommend that you rent an international cell phone *before* you leave home. A major US-based cell phone rental provider is **IMC WorldCell**. For information see "International Cell Phone Rentals" on page 14.

For a list of callback services, please refer to the "Communications" section in the *Global Road Warrior* Introduction.

PHONE JACKS

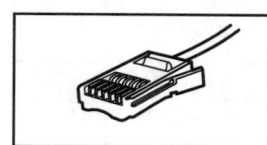

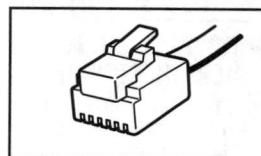

Plug adaptors are available through **iGo Corporation.** (See "Electrical and Telephone Adaptors" on page 19.)

POSTAL SERVICES

Postal service is excellent.

Hours of service

Monday-Thursday 9a.m. to 5p.m.
Friday 9a.m. to 8p.m.

Business Services
COURIER SERVICES

Airborne Express; P.O. Box 73-034, Auckland International Airport; tel: (6) 356-2829; fax: (6) 356-5545.

Airborne Express; 565 Wairakei Road, Christchuch; tel: (3) 358-7580; fax: (3) 358-0720.

DHL; toll free in New Zealand, tel: 0800-800-020; tel: (9) 636-5000; 49 Mahunga Dr., Mangere, Auckland; Monday to Friday 7a.m. to 8p.m., Saturday, 8:30a.m. to 3p.m., Sunday 9a.m. to noon; Christchurch, tel: (3) 358-0747.

Federal Express; toll free in New Zealand, tel: 0800-733-339; tel: (9) 256-8300.

Roadrunner Couriers; tel: (9) 897-111.

TNT Express Worldwide; 6 Doncaster St., Mangere, Auckland; tel: (9) 255-0500; fax: (9) 255-0501; 105 Brisbane St., PO Box 3864, Christchurch, tel: (3) 366-7344; Pick-Up Hotline, tel:366-3692; fax: (3) 365-0640.

UPS; Centre Tom Pearce & Geoffrey Roberts Road, Auckland International Airport, Auckland; tel: (9) 275-4006; fax: (9) 275-4343.

TRANSLATION SERVICES

Auckland Language Center; 97 Shortland St.; second floor; Auckland; tel: (9) 303-1962.

UniService Translation Center; University of Auckland; tel: (9) 302-3378.

Electrical

Current
230 volts AC, 50 Hz.

ELECTRICAL PLUG

Plug adaptors are available through **iGo Corporation**. (See "Electrical and Telephone Adaptors" on page 19.)

Technical Support
HARDWARE/SOFTWARE VENDOR SUPPORT

Apple/Claris; (in Australia) tel: [61] (2) 9452-8000; (in the U.K.) tel: [44] (990) 127-753; (in the U.S.) tel: [1] (408) 996-1010 (Corporate Headquarters); http://www.apple.com/.

Compaq/Digital; tel: (9) 307-3969; fax: (9) 309-9198; (General U.S.) tel: (281) 518-2000; http://www.compaq.com/.

Dell; tel: (9) 309-5335; fax: (9) 309-5909; (Dell- Europe) tel: [44] (134) 474-8000; (in the U.S.) tel: [1] (512) 338-4400; fax: [1] (512) 728-3330; http://www.dell.com/.

Hewlett Packard; tel: 09 356 6640; (in Switzerland) tel: [41] (22) 780-8111; (in the U.S.) tel: [1] (408) 246-4300; http://www.hp.com/.

IBM; tel: (4) 576-5999; fax: (4) 576-5529; tel: 0800-801-800 (toll free within New Zealand); tel: 0800-733-222; (in Switzerland) tel: [41] (22) 310-0418 (in French); (in the U.S.) tel: [1] (919) 517-2800; http://www.ibm.com/.

Microsoft tel: (9) 358-5800; fax: (9) 358-3726; tel: (9) 357-5575 (Technical Support); fax: (9) 357-50516 (Technical Support); (in Switzerland) tel: [41] (848) 858-868; fax [41] (1) 831-0869; (in the U.S.) [1] (425) 635-7222; http://www.microsoft.com/.

Internet Connection
HOW TO CONNECT

Connecting to AOL and Compuserve in New Zealand is similar to using it when traveling outside your own area code. See the introductory section for detailed information on connecting to your account through a different phone number.

America Online
Numbers are available at keyword *international*. Be sure to get several local numbers before leaving. AOL's Global-Net service charges US$6 an hour in addition to the usual charges. Go to keyword *access* (a free area) and download the software.

Access: Auckland (9) 379-2810; Auckland (9) 359-0707; Christchurch (3) 358-0514; Christchurch (3) 377-7608; Dunedin (3) 477-7001; Hamilton (7) 838-0007; Hamilton (7) 839-7901; Napier (6) 835-0854; Wellington (4) 499-8312; Wellington (4) 802-5900.

Compuserve
Numbers are available at Go International. The Compuserve Web-site also has a great deal of information, at http://www.compuserve.com.

Access: Auckland (9) 357-6642; Christchurch (3) 338-9387; Dunedin (3) 471-7510; Hamilton (7) 838-9966; Wellington (4) 473-7949.

Independent Service Providers
Many independent service providers offer discounts if you are only in town for a couple of days.

Asia Online Internet Company of New Zealand; toll free in New Zealand, tel: 0800-843-638; (Auckland) tel: (9) 363-0800; fax: (9) 363-0801; (Wellington) tel: (4) 495-2960; fax: (4) 499-9573; email: help@nz.asiaonline.net; http://www.iconz.co.nz/.

CLEAR Net; toll free in New Zealand, tel:0800-888-800; tel: (508) 888-800 (Residential); tel: (508) 555-500 (Business); email: question@clear.co.nz; http://www.clear.net.nz/.

Earthlight Communications, Ltd.; tel: (3) 479-0303; fax: (3) 477-5463; email: ecl@earthlight.co.nz; http://www.earthlight.co.nz/.

Lynx Internet, Ltd.; tel: (3) 379-0568; fax: (3) 365-4852; info@lynx.co.nz; http://www.lynx.co.nz/.

Internet Company of New Zealand; toll free in New Zealand, tel: 0800-843-638; (Auckland) tel: (9) 358-1186; fax: (9) 300-3122; (Wellington) tel: (4) 495-2960; fax: (4) 499-9573; email: help@iconz.co.nz; http://www.iconz.co.nz/.

Voyager New Zealand Ltd.; toll free in New Zealand, tel: 0800-869-243; email: consumer.enquiries@voyager.co.nz; http://home.voyager.co.nz/.

INTERNET CAFES

Auckland

ACB CyberLink; 9 Fort Street, Ground Floor of Auckland Central Backpackers, Auckland; tel: (9) 358-4877; (9) 358-4872; email: backpackers@acb.co.nz; http://www.acb.co.nz/; Monday through Sunday, 24 hours a day; 5 New Zealand dollars per hour of Internet use.

Citinet Cybercafe; 22 Kitchener St., Auckland; tel: (9) 377-3674; email: gma@citinet.co.nz; http://www.citinet.co.nz/; Monday through Saturday, 10a.m. to 10p.m.; 1 New Zealand dollar per 5 minutes of Internet use.

Click City; 674 Dominion Road Balmoral, Auckland; tel: 9-623-5001; fax: 9-623-4003; email: click@ihug.co.nz; http://www.click.co.nz/; Monday through Friday, 9a.m. to 11p.m.

Christchurch

Cyber Pass Internet Cafe; 27 Chancery Lane City, Christchurch; tel: (3) 365-9000; cybcafe@ihug.co.nz; http://www.cyberpass.co.nz/; Monday through Friday, 9a.m. to 9p.m., Saturday and Sunday, 11a.m. to 6p.m.; 6 New Zealand dollars per hour.

Cyber Cafe Christchurch; Shop 1,2,3 Gloucester Arcade 127 Gloucester Street, Christchurch; tel: (3) 365-5183; fax: (3) 365-9037; email: info@cybercafe-chch.co.nz; http://www.cybercafe-chch.co.nz/; Monday through Sunday, 8a.m. to 10p.m.; 5 New Zealand dollars per hour of Internet use.

Wellington

PhoneNet at the Barber's; 173 Cuba Street, Wellington; tel: (4) 382-8030; fax: (4) 382-8029; email: phonenet@xtra.co.nz; http://phonenet.virtualave.net/; Monday through Sunday, 10 a.m. to 10 p.m.; 8 New Zealand dollars per hour of use.

Business Culture

GREETINGS AND COURTESIES

New Zealanders are generally friendly, outgoing, social people, and they promote a hospitable, friendly atmosphere. After people get to know each other, behavior becomes more casual, even as far as first name basis; but follow the lead of your host or associate before moving to a more relaxed attitude. They appreciate people who are open, direct, honest, and have a sense of humor. Talking loudly, being physically demonstrative, and any other behavior that calls attention to oneself is frowned upon. The accepted greeting (both for meeting someone and saying good-bye) is smiling, making eye contact, and shaking hands. Handshakes are generally firm and brief, with a rapid, simple up-and-down motion. It is not necessary or appropriate to shake especially hard or squeeze the other person's hand. When meeting a woman, wait for her to extend her hand. If she doesn't, smile and nod slightly.

BUSINESS ETHIC AND FRAMEWORK

New Zealanders are practical, hard-working people, and pride themselves on their traditional ability to make something out of nothing. Fundamentally conservative and thrifty, they do not like to see anything go to waste or be casually discarded. It has been said that a New Zealander can fix an entire machine with a piece of wire. New Zealanders tend to trust others, until they are given a reason not to. Once this happens, it can be extremely difficult, and sometimes impossible, to regain that broken trust. Two of the quickest ways to lose trust are acting dishonestly and showing bad faith in your business dealings.

DECISION MAKING

New Zealanders tend to be very honest and direct. Their inherent thriftiness sometimes becomes evident in an avoidance of unnecessary expenses (such as overseas phone calls or faxes) or unneeded progress reports. It can also delay a final decision or slow down negotiations. If you need a response to a question or issue by a specific time, make this clear to your associates—but do so politely, and never aggressively. If they understand you really do need an answer by a certain time they will do their best to respond. However, this urgency must be real. If you impose a deadline as a negotiating tactic, you will risk being viewed as dishonest, faith will be broken, and you could permanently damage—or destroy—a business relationship.

WOMEN

Women are found in all levels of business, including management positions, and expect to be treated seriously and with the respect to which their position entitles them. In New Zealand, a certain formality is the norm all the time, and if you are dealing with a woman be sure not to treat her any differently than you would treat a man in the same position. Also, do not assume that the way she responds to you is based on her gender. New Zealand businesswomen are as open and direct as the men; if a woman is friendly, do not attach special importance to this. Treat women as business associates instead of as women. Foreign women can expect to be treated the same as men, but exactly how a woman is treated will depend on the person she is encountering. Women who are professional and self-assured can expect to be treated with respect and taken seriously.

MEETINGS

Meetings should be set up in advance, especially when dealing with government officials. Punctuality is important. You might even consider arriving at a meeting or appointment a little early. Before business, there will usually be pleasant small talk, which will probably be about the culture, sports, and sights of New Zealand. If you make a presentation to a New Zealand company, it should be detailed and complete. Agreements and proposals should state everything clearly, and all terms and conditions should be explained in detail.

BUSINESS ATTIRE

Standard attire is a conservative suit (especially when meeting with government officials). Women should wear tasteful, conservative clothing appropriate for business.

Business Centers
Auckland

CITY VIEW

Probably the first thing noticed in Auckland is the harbor. New Zealand is almost entirely surrounded by water, and boats are everywhere. It is a relatively small city (with a population of a little more than one million people), but is one of the region's main business centers.

AIRPORT

Mangere Airport to City Center

The airport lies 14 miles (22.5 km.) from the city. An information desk is located in the international arrivals hall. An Airbus departs from the airport for the Downtown Airline Terminal in 20-minute intervals, between 6:20a.m. and 10p.m. The NZ$12 ride takes about 30 minutes. The Airbus also stops at the rail station, and any other bus stop requested. Purchase tickets from the driver. For information about the Airbus service, call (9) 275-7685. Shared shuttle buses leave from the west side of the international terminal. Taxis also make the trek downtown in approximately 30 minutes at a cost of around NZ$40.

Airline Numbers

Aer Lingus	(9) 379-4455
Aerolineas Argentinas	(9) 379-3675
Air Canada	(9) 379-3371
Air New Zealand	(9) 357-3000
Air Pacific	(9) 379-2404
American Airlines	(9) 309-9159
Ansett New Zealand	(9) 302-2146
British Airways	(9) 367-7500
Canadian Airlines International	(9) 309-0735
Cathay Pacific	(9) 379-0861
Continental Airlines	(9) 379-5680
Delta Airlines	(9) 379-3370
Garuda Indonesia	(9) 366-1855
Japan Airlines	(9) 379-9906
Mt. Cook Airlines	(9) 309-5395
Polynesian Airlines	(9) 309-5396
Qantas	(9) 379-0306, toll free (800) 808-767
Singapore Airlines	(9) 379-3209
TWA	(9) 373-4826
United Airlines	(9) 379-3800

Local Airlines

Great Barrier Airlines	(9) 275-9120
Gulf Island Air	(9) 372-7428

HOTELS

Top-end
Hyatt Regency Auckland; Corner Waterloo Quadrant and Princes Street; tel: (9) 366-1234; fax: (9) 303-2932; city center; 2 restaurants; conference facilities (up to 400); business center; secretarial service; laundry/dry cleaning; theater; library; car rental; in-room a/c, tv, minibar, refrigerator, phone, iron, coffeemaker; parking garage; drug store; florist; shopping arcade; health club; tennis; water sports; nightclub.

The Pan Pacific; Mayoral Drive, Wellesley; tel: (9) 366-3000; fax: (9) 366-0121; restaurant; coffee shop; conference facilities (up to 600); house doctor; valet/laundry service; parking garage; in-room tv, minibar, refrigerator, phone, coffee maker; sauna.

Parkroyal; corner Customs and Queen Streets; tel: (9) 377-8920; fax: (9) 307-3739; city center; ocean views; restaurant; conference facilities; business center; room service; in-room a/c, tv, minibar, refrigerator, phone, iron, coffee maker; house doctor; dry cleaning; valet; parking; health club; gym.

Sheraton Auckland; 83 Symonds Street; tel: (9) 379-5132; fax: (9) 377-9367; restaurant; conference facilities; secretarial service; fax/photocopy facilities; 24-hour room service; beauty salon; car rental; laundry; house doctor; in-room a/c, tv, minibar, refrigerator, phone, coffee maker; shopping arcade; corporate rates; fitness; sauna; indoor pool; bicycle hire; disco.

Expensive
Auckland Airport Travelodge; KIrkbride and Ascor Roads, mangere; tel: (9) 275-1059; fax: (9) 275-7884; 2 restaurants; conference facilities; business center; in-room balcony/lanai, tv, minibar, refrigerator, phone, coffee maker; laundry/; dry cleaning; car rental; parking garage; airport transfers; gym; pool; jacuzzi; tennis; gardens.

Centra; 128 Albert Street; tel: (9) 302-1111; fax: (9) 302-3111; city center; restaurant; conference facilities; business center; in-room tv, minibar, refrigerator, phone, iron, coffee maker; parking garage; laundry; car rental.

Novotel Auckland; 8 Customs Street East; tel: (9) 377-8920; fax: (9) 307-3739.

Quality Anzac Avenue; 150 Anzac Avenue; tel: 99) 379-8509; fax: (9) 379-8582; city; restaurant; conference rooms; room service; in-room a/c, tv, minibar, refrigerator, radio, phone, coffee maker; laundry; parking garage; car rental; handicap facilities; sauna.

Quality Logan Park; 187 Campbell Road, Greenlane; tel: (9) 634-1269; fax: (9) 636-8115; near exhibition grounds, restaurant; conference facilities (up to 300); secretarial service; fax/photocopy facilities; corporate rates; pool; whirlpool.

Waipuna Hotel and Conference Center; 58 Waipuna Road, Mt. Wellington; tel: (9) 527-3114; fax: (9) 527-1937; located in suburb; restaurant; conference facilities; secretarial service; fax/photocopy facilities; corporate rates; fitness; pool.

Moderate
Eden Park Motor Inn; 697 New North Road, Mt. Albert; tel: (9) 846-0086; fax: (9) 849-4024; city center; restaurant; conference facilities; fitness; pool.

Best Western International Motel; 87 Greenlane Road, Remuera; tel: (9) 520-0074; fax: (9) 520-0072; near exhibition grounds; restaurant; laundry; in-room tv, refrigerator, phone, kitchenette, coffee maker; car rental; pool; jacuzzi.

Park Towers; 3 Scotia Place; tel: (9) 309-2800; fax: (9) 302-1964; city center; restaurant; conference facilities; secretarial service; fax/photocopy facilities; corporate rates.

Portage Peninsula Motor; Elm Street;, Avondale; tel: (9) 828-1179; fax: (9) 828-3496; near airport, conference facilities; secretarial service; fax/photocopy facilities; corporate rates; sauna; pool.

Ranfurly Evergreen Lodge; 285 Manukau Road, Epsom 3; tel: (9) 638-9059; fax: (9) 630-8374.

Whitaker Lodge; 21 Whitaker Place; tel: (9) 377-3623; fax: (9) 377-3621.

MEDICAL CARE

Adventist Hospital; 188 St. Heliers Bay Rd., St. Heliers, Auckland; tel: (9) 575-2100.

Order of St. John's Ambulance; Offers health and dental information and assistance daily 24 hours; tel: 579-90999.

HEALTH CLUB

Don Oliver's Fitness Centre; 2 Rankin Ave., New Lynn; tel: (9) 826-0204; fax: (9) 818-9815

Tepid Baths; 102 Customs St.; tel: (9) 379-4794.

AUTO RENTAL

Avis; Auckland Airport, main terminal; tel: (9) 275-7239; Auckland Downtown, 17 - 19 Nelson Street, (North Island); tel: (9) 379-2650; (There are over 40 branches throughout the country and at all major airports.

Budget; airport, tel: (9) 256-8451.

Hertz; toll free in New Zealand, tel: 0800-654-321; airport; tel: (9) 256-8690 (Airport delivery service).

Letz Rent A Car; airport; tel: 275-6890.

Maui Rentals; Richard Pearse Drive, Mangere; tel: 275-3013.

WORLD TRADE CENTER

World Trade Center Auckland
135 Albert Street, 20th Floor
P.O. Box 105-225
Auckland, New Zealand
tel: (9) 820-5000; fax: (9) 820-7100

CHAMBER OF COMMERCE

Auckland Chamber of Commerce
100, Mayoral Drive, Auckland;
tel: (9) 309-6100; fax (9) 309-0081.

CONVENTION BUREAU

New Zealand Convention Association
PO Box 33-1202
Suite, 3, Level 1, 15 Huron Street
Takapuna, Auckland
tel: (9) 486-4128; fax: (9) 486-4126
website: http://www.conventionsnz.co.na
email: admin@nzconventions.co.nz

Christchurch

CITY VIEW

Christchurch is one of the largest cities in New Zealand's South Island. It is a small city and concedes most of New Zealand's business to Auckland.

AIRPORT

Christchurch Airport to City Center

The airport lies six miles (10 km.) from the city. Buses run every 30 minutes from 6:30a.m. to 10p.m. Pacific Tourways runs a shuttle service to the major hotels in town. Taxis are available 24 hours a day but will implement a service charge after 10p.m. Expect the taxi ride into town to take about 15 minutes; buses will take double the time.

HOTELS

Top-end

Christchurch Parkroyal; KIlmore and Durham Streets; tel: (3) 365-7799; fax: (3) 365-0082; city center; 2 restaurants; conference facilities; business center; translation/interpreting; dry cleaning/laundry; valet; house doctor; 24-hour room service; in-room a/c, tv, minibar, refrigerator, phone, iron, coffee maker; boutique; drug store; shopping arcade; handicap facilities; parking garage; fitness; sauna; tennis.

The George; 50 Park Terrace; tel: (3) 379-4560; fax: (3) 366-6747; email: info@the george.com; luxury boutique hotel; city center; 2 restaurants; conference facilities (up to 160); laundry; car rental; in-room a/c, tv, minibar, refrigerator, IDD phone, coffee maker, movies; parking; gym; tennis; nearby golf.

Expensive

Centra Christchurch; Cashel and High Streets; tel: (3) 365-8888; fax: (3) 365-8822; restaurant; conference facilities; fitness.

Camelot on the Square; 66 Cathedral Square; tel: (3) 377-5757; fax: (3) 377-5777; restaurant; meeting facilities; secretarial service; fax/photocopy facilities; in-room modem/fax connection, safe; corporate rates.

Hotel Grand Chancellor; 161 Cashel St.; tel: (3) 379-2999; toll free in New Zealand, tel: 0800-275-337; fax: (3) 379-0999; email: res@grandc.co.nz; convention facilities; business center; doctor on call; in-room refrigerators; non-smoking rooms available.

The Chateau on the Park; 189 Deans Avenue; tel: (3) 348-8999; fax: (3) 348-8990; restaurant; conference facilities (up to 300); secretarial service; fax/photocopy facilities; corporate rates; pool.

Noahs Christchurch; Worcester Street and Oxford Terrace; tel: (3) 379-4700; fax: (3) 379-5357; near city center; restaurant; conference facilities.

Moderate

The Garden; 108 Marshland Road; tel: (3) 385-3132; fax: (3) 385-3132; suburb; restaurant; conference facilities (up to 150); secretarial service; fax/photocopy facilities; corporate rates; pool; whirlpool.

Christchurch Airport Plaza; Memorial Avenue; tel: (3) 358-3139; fax; (3) 358-3029; near airport; restaurant; conference facilities; corporate rates.

Pacific Park Christchurch; 263 Bealey Avenue; tel: (3) 379-8660; toll free in New Zealand, tel: 0800-228-228; fax: (3) 366-9973; near exhibition grounds; restaurant; meeting facilities; secretarial service; fax/photocopy facilities; courtesy coach to city; corporate rates; whirlpool.

Russley; 73 Roydvale Avenue; tel: (3) 358-8289; fax: (3) 358-3953; located near airport; restaurant; conference facilities; secretarial service; fax/photocopy facilities; fitness; sauna; pool.

RESTAURANTS

Bardellis $$; Italian; 98 Cashel Mall; tel: (3) 353-0001Espresso 124 Char-grilled Steak, Lamb, and Seafood etc. $$124 Oxford Terr.; tel: (3) 365-0547.

Lone Star Cafe $$; quarterback-size steaks, chickens, ribs, and burgers, and french fries; 26 Manchester St.; tel: (3) 365-7086.

50 on Park Restaurant and Bar $$$; Pacific Rim Cuisine; The George Hotel, 50 Park Terrace; tel: (3) 379-4560.

Pescatore $$$; seafood; The George Hotel, 50 Park Terrace; tel: (3) 379-4560.

HEALTH CARE

Bethseda Hospital; 235 Harewood Rd. Bishopdale, Christchurch; tel: (3) 359-6292.

AUTO RENTAL

Avis; Christchurch International Airport, Harewood, Terminal Building; tel: (3) 358-9661; Downtown Christchurch, 26 Lichfield Street; tel: 3-379-6133.

Hertz; Christchurch International Airport; tel: (3) 358-6730; fax: (3) 342-5694; Christchurch Downtown, 44-46 Lichfield Street; tel: (3) 366-0549; fax: (3) 379-9850.

CHAMBER OF COMMERCE

Canterbury Employers Chamber of Commerce
tel: (3) 366-5096; fax: (3) 379-5454
website: http://www.cecc.org.nz

Canterbury Development Council
tel: (3) 379-5575; fax: (3) 379-5554
website: http://www.cdc.org.nz

Nicaragua

At a Glance

THE PEOPLE

Population .... 4,812,569 (July 2000 est.)
Growth Rate .... 2.2% (2000 est.)
Life Expectancy .... 68.74 years
Infant Mortality . 34.79 deaths/1,000 live births (2000 est.)

Ethnic Composition

Mestizo (mixed Amerindian and white) 69%
Caucasian 17%
Black (Jamaican origin) 9%
Amerindian 5%

Religious Composition

Roman Catholic 95%
Protestant 5%

Languages Spoken

Spanish (official), English, Amerindian, indigenous languages.

Education and Literacy

While schooling is free and compulsory between the ages of 6 and 13, the completion rate of primary school is only 20 percent. Adult literacy is 65.7 percent.64.6 percent of adult males are literate while 66.6 percent of females are literate.

Labor Force

Total: 1,700,000
By occupation: services 43%, agriculture 42%, industry 15%.

THE ECONOMY

Currently, Nicaragua is one of poorest countries in the Western Hemisphere, with low per capita income, and huge external debt. This is due in part to poor government decisions made over the past decade. Both overall GDP and GDP per capita have fallen significantly from their early 1980s levels. The government has, however, recently attempted to reform the economy, primarily by stabilizing the currency and implementing basic structural adjustment measures. These reforms have been successful to some extent, but there has been very little economic growth. Unemployment still exceeds 50 percent in some areas, and the country still has a chronic gap in its balance of payments. The IMF, however, approved a debt relief plan under the Highly Indebted Poor Countries Initiative. And a property accord was implemented to resolve ongoing disputes about property confiscated by the Sandanistas during the war. A free trade agreement with Mexico has already bolstered agricultural exports and may help inject some well-needed money for growth. In 1999 Nicaragua's GDP grew 6.3 percent, inflation remained at about 12 percent, and unemployment dropped. The outlook for growth in 2000 is uncertain at best.

Exports .... US$573 million (f.o.b., 1998 est.)
Imports .... US$1.5 billion (c.i.f., 1999 est.)
Total Trade .... US$2.308 billion (1998 est.)
GDP Per Capita .... US$2,650 (1999 est.)
Unemployment .... 10.5% (1999 est.)
Inflation Rate .... 12% (1999 est.)

Top Export Partners

U.S. 35%, Germany 13%, El Salvador 10%, Spain 4%, Costa Rica 4%, France 2%.

Top Import Partners

U.S. 31%, Costa Rica 11%, Guatemala 8%, Venezuela 6%, El Salvador 5%, Mexico 4%.

Top Exports

Coffee, shrimp and lobster, cotton, tobacco, beef, sugar, bananas, gold.

Top Imports

Machinery and equipment, raw materials, petroleum products, consumer goods.

BUSINESS WORKWEEK

Offices

Monday to Friday 8:30a.m. to noon, 2:30p.m. to 5:30p.m., Saturday 8:30a.m. to 11:30a.m.

Banks

Monday to Friday 8:30a.m. to 4:30p.m., Saturday 8:30a.m. to 11:30a.m.

Government

Monday to Friday 8:30a.m. to noon, 2:30p.m. to 4:30p.m.

Retail

Monday to Friday 9a.m. to 6p.m., shorter hours on the weekend (actual hours vary).

HOLIDAYS

New Year's Day .... January 1
Holy Wednesday .... April 19
Maundy Thursday .... April 20*
Good Friday .... April 21*
Labor Day .... May 1
Liberation Day .... July 19
Managua local holiday .... August 10
Battle of San Jacinto .... September 14
Independence Day .... September 15
All Souls' Day .... November 2
Immaculate Conception Day .... December 8
Christmas .... December 25
*Date may vary by year.

CLIMATE

Seasons

Nicaragua's climate is, on the whole, tropical with some regional differences. Humidity is high, with average annual temperatures of 80˚F. The rainy season occurs from June to November.

Regions

It is generally much cooler in the northern highlands. The coastal region along the Caribbean is usually always hot and damp with rain a possibility year round.

Money & Banking

Currency

The currency of Nicaragua is the Nicaraguan Gold Cordoba (C$).

Nicaragua

Denominations

The Nicaraguan Gold Cordoba comes in banknotes of 50, 25, 10, and 5 centavos, and C$1, 5, 10, 20, 50, and 100.

Traveler's checks

Traveler's checks and currency can be exchanged at banks, exchange shops, hotels, and international airports at tourist exchange rates. Larger banks may offer the best exchange rates, but avoid black marketers at all cost. Consult your bank about current exchange rates before departure. Keep all receipts for reconversion.

Most currencies can also be exchanged, but try to take only crisp and new notes. Wrinkled and soiled notes are likely to be refused.

Major credit cards, American Express, Visa, Diner's Club, and MasterCard are accepted in most up-market places, in the cities. However, do not rely on credit cards or even traveler's checks since many places still do not accept them. Some banks in the capital offer cash advances on credit cards, but make sure you bring your passport.

Travel

VISA AND PASSPORT

A passport valid for six months beyond the expected departure date, a return ticket, and adequate funds for the duration of the stay are required for entry to Nicaragua.

Tourist cards are issued when visitors enter Nicaragua. They are valid for 30 to 90 days for most, depending on nationality, and can be extended by applying to the Office of Immigration. Failure to obtain an extension results in delayed departure and payment of a fine.

Visas are required for nationals of these countries only: Afghanistan, Albania, China (PR), Cuba, Bosnia and Herzegovina, Colombia, Haiti, India, Iran, Iraq, Jordan, Korea (Rep. of), Lebanon, Libya, Nepal, Pakistan, Somalia, Sri Lanka, Vietnam, and Yugoslavia (Serbia and Montenegro).

A visitor may conduct business in Nicaragua with a Tourist Card, as long as a letter from the visitor's client or employer in the country is appended to it.

Types of visa issued are Business and Tourist, both initially valid for a month beyond date of issue; you may get extensions in Managua at Immigration.

As a relatively small percentage of travelers through Nicaragua need a visa, the process is not streamlined. Allow four to six weeks for application processing; special authorization is required from the Nicaraguan Ministry of Foreign Affairs.

DEPARTURE FORMALITIES

A departure fee of US$20 exists in Nicaragua.

CUSTOMS ENTRY (PERSONAL)

Duty-free

- Tobacco: 200 cigarettes or 500g tobacco
- Alcohol: 3 liters of spirits or wine
- Other: 1 large bottle or three small bottles of perfume or eau de cologne

Prohibited or Restricted

- Canned or uncanned meats, leather, and dairy products
- Firearms not covered by the regulations governing the importation of firearms for sporting purposes
- Medicines without prescription documentation
- Military uniforms
- Cats and dogs require veterinary and rabies vaccination certificates, and an import permit

   Note: Archaeological items, artefacts of historic or monetary value, and gold are prohibited exports.

IMMUNIZATION

Typhoid, polio, diphtheria, and cholera vaccinations are recommended for all travelers. A yellow fever vaccination certificate is required by all travelers arriving from infected areas. The risk of malaria continues year round in 119 municipalities; in the remaining 26 municipalities, within the departments of Masaya, Madriz, and Carazo, risk of transmission is negligible. Rabies is also present.

TIPPING

Taxi

No tip for taxi drivers.

Porters

US$.50 per bag for porters.

Hotels

Customary tips are 10 percent of the bill for hotels. Maids, U.S.$0.50; Porters, U.S. $1 per bag.

Restaurants

One is not expected to tip at restaurants since the bill usually includes a 15 percent tax for service. However, since wages are small, a 10 percent tip is very much appreciated.

EMERGENCY INFORMATION

Police and Crime

Violent crime is on the increase in Managua. Carjackings, robberies, and violent assaults occur with more frequency, particularly in poorer neighborhoods. Take basic precautions against petty crime. Try to blend in with the locals. Leave valuables in the hotel safe and avoid wearing expensive jewelry or carrying camera equipment. Be aware of your surroundings at all times.

Motorists are advised to drive with doors locked and windows closed. Robberies often occur on crowded buses and in open markets, especially in the "Mercado Oriental" market. In case of armed robbery, surrender your valuables and contact the police immediately. Armed criminal activity still occurs in remote areas of the northern/central departments of Nueva Segovia, Madriz, Jinotega, Matagalpa, Estili, and Boaco.

Travel to these areas is, thus, strongly discouraged. Avoid travel on major highways past daylight hours. Land mines in certain rural areas in the north make off road driving a serious liability. Road travel after dark is hazardous in all areas of the country. If involved in an accident, do not move the car or you may be held legally liable for the accident. Law requires that a driver be taken into custody in any injury accident. The detention lasts until a judicial decision is reached; this could last weeks or even months. To bypass the wait, the injured party may sign a waiver, usually as the result of a cash settlement, relieving the driver of further liability.

Carry photocopies of your passport instead of the original. Carry cash in a money belt, and use credit cards or traveler's checks if possible.

Be aware that firecrackers are a popular form of entertainment lest you freeze in shock thinking that gunfights are being started by children.

Women should avoid traveling alone at night. While some Nicaraguan police officers are friendly and helpful in an emergency, you are best advised to contact your consulate.

Emergency Numbers

Police 118
Fire 265-0162
Ambulance (Red Cross) 265-1761

Health

General health has improved in recent years. Nevertheless, do not drink tap water or use ice cubes; bottled water is safe and available. Wash all vegetables in a chlorine solution, peel fruits, and avoid uncooked food. Drink only powdered or tinned milk and avoid other dairy products since they are most likely unpasteurized. Only eat meat and fish that have been well cooked, and preferably served hot. Mayonnaise, pork, and salad often increase the risk of intestinal problems.

Ordinary medical services are adequate, and many of the doctors and nurses have been trained abroad. For major or emergency services, though, medical care is generally substandard, and pharmaceuticals are in short supply. Carry a well-stocked medical kit with all the prescription drugs you require, and also include in it a stock of sterilized syringe needles and drip needles for emergencies.

A travel insurance package that includes an evacuation policy should be acquired by all business travelers.

INTERNAL TRAVEL

AIR

There are three airlines that operate domestically, flying mainly between Managua and both Bluefields and Puerto Cabezas. Nica Airlines is the primary carrier.

The air service in Nicaragua is not highly developed. Many or most of the airstrips have little in the way of safety equipment or boarding security. And yet, hundreds of passengers fly every day on domestic flights. Over the past three years, despite some political unrest, there have been only two hijackings, both commuter flights.

Inquire at the airport in Managua, through your travel agent, or at your hotel, for further information about domestic flights.

TAXI

Taxis are available at the airport or in Managua only. Agree on fares before leaving, since cabs have no meters. If sharing a cab with others, establish whether riders are sharing the fare or whether each rider must pay it separately.

AUTO

Traffic in Nicaragua drives on the right. Driving may prove the quickest way to get around since public transportation is slow and crowded. However, roads are in deplorable condition with potholes, obstacles, and insufficient lighting. Night driving is not recommended when crime is high and obstacles harder to navigate. Stay on main roads to reduce the risk of encountering unexploded land mines and armed robbery. One can rent a car from the airport or at higher-end hotels. To rent a car and drive in Nicaragua, you simply need a valid driver's license from your country of residence.

BUS

Reserve seats whenever possible as buses are always crowded. Public buses are slow, hot, and also crowded. They are also notorious for petty theft and, as such, not recommended. If you do happen to get on a bus, take care not to nod off while in transit; keep your eyes wide open to watch your belongings.

WATER TRAVEL

Twice-weekly ferry service goes to the Corn Islands from Bluefields. Lake Nicaragua also offers boat service from Granada to San Carlos, with intermediate stops at San Jorge and Ometepe. Schedules are variable; hydrofoil service is planned.

TRAVEL ASSISTANCE

INTUR
Nicaraguan Institute of Tourism
Hotel Intercontinental
1 cuadra al Oeste y 1 cuadra al Sur
Managua, Nicaragua
tel: 222 2962 or 222 3333; fax: 222 6610
email: promocion@intur.gob.ni
website: http://www.intur.gob.ni

Essential Terms

English	Spanish
Yes	Si
No	No
Good morning	Buenos dias
Hello (daytime)	Buenos tardes
Hello (evening)	Buenos Noches
Hello (telephone)	¿Hola?
Good-bye	Addios
Please	Por Favor
Thank you	Gracias
Pleased to meet you	Enchanted (a) de concealer
Excuse me; I'm sorry	¿Perdoname?
My name is _____	Me llama _____
I don't understand	No comprendo
Do you speak English?	¿Habla usted Inglés?

Communications

DIALING CODES IN NICARAGUA

International country code: [505]

Selected city codes: Boaco (54), Chinandega (3410, Diriamba (4222), Esteli (71), Granada (55), Leon (311), Managua (2), Masatepe (44), Masaya (52), Nandaime (4522), Rivas (46), San Juan Del Sur (4682), San Marcos (43), Tipitapa (53).

Dialing Nicaragua from Overseas

To dial Nicaragua from overseas, dial your country's international dialing code, then 505 (the country code for Nicaragua), then the city code, and finally the number. If you were dialing Leon from the United States, for example, you would begin with 011, then 505, then 311 (the city code for Leon), and finally the number of the person or office you were trying to reach.

Assistance Numbers

International Operator 116
Domestic Operator 110
Information 112

CALLING WITHIN NICARAGUA

Local Calls

Dialing local should be quite straightforward.

Long Distance Calls

Domestic calls are possible from any phone.

International Calls

Place a call at any Telcor office between 7a.m. and 10p.m.; but expect waiting unless you are an earlybird. When you do get to the counter, announce your call and the length of time you plan to speak. A call to the U.S. costs about US$10 for three minutes. To Europe it will cost slightly more, about US$11.50 for three minutes. To make a direct call, dial 164 (in Managua; 02-164 in other locations) + the country code + area code + number. To reach a U.S. operator to place a call to any country, dial one of the following access numbers:

AT&T 174
MCI (Outside of Managua, dial 02 first) 166
Sprint 171

These access numbers are not available from public phones.

PAY PHONES

Public Telephones

Pay phones allow both domestic and international calls.

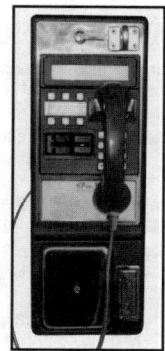

Nicaragua

Calling Cards

The calling card was introduced to Nicaragua in 1994.

CELLULAR PHONES

NicaCell and *Teleglobo* both operate AMPS analogue systems for cellular users in Nicaragua.

Note: Your home country cell phone may not work in this country. If not, we recommend that you rent an international cell phone *before* you leave home. A major US-based cell phone rental provider is **IMC WorldCell**. For information see "International Cell Phone Rentals" on page 14.

CALL BACK

You can (potentially) save significant sums when calling in Nicaragua by using one of the call back services listed below. Fees for call back services vary widely, depending on the company and the type of service required.

For a list of callback services, please refer to the "Communications" section in the Global Road Warrior Introduction.

PHONE JACK

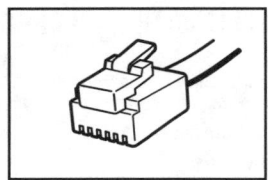

Plug adaptors are available through **iGo Corporation**. (See "Electrical and Telephone Adaptors" on page 19.)

FAX

Fax services are not widely available.

POSTAL SERVICES

Airmail to the U.S. takes about one week, to Europe service takes about two weeks. One is strongly urged not to send valuables.

Hours of service

Monday to Saturday 9a.m. to 5:30p.m.

TELEGRAMS

Telegram facilities are available at major hotels in Managua.

Business Services

COURIER SERVICE

Airborne Express; International Bonded Couriers, Hotel Camino Real, Km. 9.5 Carretera Norte, Managua; tel: 263-1411; fax: 263-1380.

DHL; Av. Bolivar Casa 802, Managua; tel: (2) 284-081; fax: 284-081; Monday to Friday 8a.m. to 6p.m.; Saturday 8a.m. to noon; closed Sundays.

Federal Express (Passus Velox, S.A.); tel: 266-6494, tel: 266-2988; fax: 266-6493.

TNT (NICAPOST); Frente Residencial Los Mircedes; KM 9 1/2 C. Norte, Apdo 2441, Managua; tel: (2) 222-824, 222-418; fax: (2) 222-882, 632-217.

UPS; IML Air Couriers Nicaragua, Plaza España, Edificio Málaga Módulo A3-B, Managua, Nicaragua; tel: (2) 664-289; fax: (2) 664-505.

Electrical

Current

110 volts AC, 60Hz.

ELECTRIC PLUGS

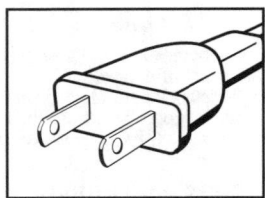

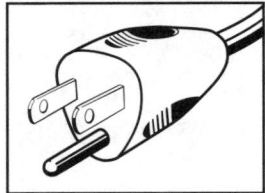

Plug adaptors are available through **iGo Corporation**. (See "Electrical and Telephone Adaptors" on page 19.)

Technical Support

HARDWARE/SOFTWARE VENDOR SUPPORT

Apple/Claris; tel: 278-3030; fax: 278 0041 (vendor support); (in Miami) [1] (305) 265-4939; (in the U.K.) tel: [44] (990) 127-753; (Corporate U.S. Headquarters) [1] (408) 996-1010; http://www.apple.com/.

AST; (in the U.S.) tel: [1] (817) 232-9824 (International Technical Support); (in Ireland) tel: [353] (61) 492-222; (in the U.S.) tel: [1] (949) 727-4141; http://www.ast.com/.

Compaq/Digital; (Houston Office, U.S.) tel: [1] (713) 370-0670; fax: [1] (713) 514-1740; (in the U.S.) tel: [1] (281) 518-2000 (international technical support); fax: [1] (281) 518-1442; http://www.compaq.com.

Dell; tel: 00[1] (800) 220-1006 (Toll Free Call); (in the U.S.) tel: [1] (512) 338-4400; fax: [1] (512) 728-3330; (Dell-Europe) tel: [44] (134) 474-8000; http://www.dell.com/.

Hewlett Packard; (Venezuela Office) tel: [58] 2 239 5664;(in the U.S.) tel: [1] (408) 246-4300; http://www.hp.com/.

IBM; (in Colombia) tel: [57] (1) 623-0111; fax: [57] (1) 257-9839; (in the U.S.) tel: [1] (919) 517-2800; http://www.ibm.com/.

Microsoft; tel: [506] 298-2020 (Technical Support); tel: [506] 298-2000 (Customer Service); (in the U.S.) [1] (425) 635-7222; http://www.microsoft.com/.

Toshiba; (in the U.S.) [1] (949) 583-3000 (Corporate Headquarters); (in Switzerland) tel: [41] (1) 946-0777; fax: [41] (1) 946-0807; (in Ireland) tel: [44] (193) 282-8828; (in the U.S.) [1] (949) 583-3000 (Corporate Headquarters); http://www.toshiba.com/.

Internet Connection

HOW TO CONNECT

Connecting to AOL and Compuserve in Nicaragua is similar to using it when traveling outside your own area code. See the introductory section for detailed information on connecting to your account through a different phone number.

America Online

Numbers are available at keyword *international*. Be sure to get several local numbers before leaving. AOL's GlobalNet service charges US$12 an hour in addition to the usual charges. Go to keyword *access* (a free area) and download the software.

Access: Managua (2) 669-786.

Compuserve

Numbers are available at *Go International*. The Compuserve Web-site also has a great deal of information, at http://www.compuserve.com.

Access: Managua (2) 669-786.

Independent Service Providers

Many independent service providers offer discounts if you are only in town for a couple of days.

IBW Internet Gateway Nicaragua; tel: 278-6328 fax 278-6370; http://www.ibw.com.ni/.

NicaNet; tel: 278-5528; fax: 278-6898; email: webmaster@nicanet.com.ni; http://www.nicanet.com.ni/

Internet Cafes

Granada

Inter C@fe; Del Teatro Karawala 1C. al Lago, Frente al Hotel Colonial, Granada; tel: 552-7284; Monday through Saturday, 9a.m to 10p.m; US$3.50 per hour of use.

Managua

Cyber-Café; De la Vicky 1 cuadra al oeste, 2 cuadras al sur., Managua; tel: 278-8526; email: cyber_cafe@mixmail.com; http://www.cybercafe.com.ni/; Monday through Saturday, 8 a.m. to 10 p.m.

San Juan Del Sur

Casa Internacional Joxi; Hotel JOXI, San Juan Del Sur; tel: (4) 58-2483; fax: (4) 582-348; email: casajoxi@tmx.com.ni; http://www.tmx.com.ni/turismo/casajoxi/; Monday through Saturday, 7a.m. to 10p.m.; US$7.50 per hour of use.

Business Culture

GREETINGS AND COURTESIES

Handshakes are appropriate for both men and women. Male friends may hug and female friends may hug each other briefly and brush their cheeks while making a kissing motion. Considerable deference is usually shown to the elderly. Baseball is very popular in Nicaragua and will prove a popular subject of discussion. Politics and the economic crisis are also popular discussion topics.

BUSINESS ETHIC AND FRAMEWORK

Respect and personal dignity lie at the core of Nicaraguan business and social culture. Although Nicaraguans are generally informal, their business and social culture is based on correct, often strongly hierarchical, but personal relationships. To Nicaraguans, work is far from the most important part of life, but it is an increasingly important sphere, and they do adhere to the forms and protocols that govern it.

MEETINGS

Appointments are necessary and should be made at least two weeks in advance. Generally speaking, one should expect an hour or more delay for formal meetings and events as Nicaraguans operate in a less punctual fashion and go by 'Hora Nica'. Business deals may require several meetings and repeated trips to the country. Siestas are common after the midday meal.

DECISION MAKING

Despite recent experience with communal forms of decision making, actual decisions are nevertheless almost always made at a high level of authority. It is important to cultivate personal relationships with all peers, however, because the quality of these relationships may strongly influence the actual decision maker even when your immediate counterpart is not the one making the decision.

WOMEN

Although women generally occupy a secondary status in heavily male-dominated and *macho*-influenced Nicaragua, many operate businesses and may be accorded considerable personal freedom. Nicaraguan women are becoming more common and more accepted in business in general, although their presence remains rare in the upper levels of business. In general, foreign businesswomen should experience few problems.

BUSINESS ATTIRE

Businessmen are expected to wear suits, but standards are generally informal and businessmen often dispense with jackets and ties. In general, it is somewhat inappropriate to dress too elegantly in Nicaragua. Avoid flashy attire, accessories, jewelry, or makeup.

Business Centers

Managua

CITY VIEW

Managua is an odd-looking city. An earthquake in 1972 ravaged the town and destroyed the city center. It has since gone undeveloped, unless you count the shantytowns that spring up every now and again.

AIRPORT

Augusto Cesar Sandino Airport to City Center

The airport lies 5.5 miles (9 km.) from the city. There is regular bus service and taxis are available. The taxi ride into downtown will take about 20 minutes for a cost of approximately US$15.

Airline Numbers

Aeroflot	(2) 660-565
Aerosegovia	(2) 787-162
Air France	(2) 662-612
American Airlines	(2) 663-900
Atlantic Airlines	(2) 223-037
Aviateca	(2) 663-136
Continental Airlines	(2) 782-834
Copa Airlines	(2) 675-438
Grupo Taca	(2) 663-136
Iberia	(2) 664-440
Interamerican Airlines	(2) 770-582
Japan Airlines	(2) 663-588
KLM	(2) 668-053
LTU	(2) 667-332
La Costena	(2) 631-228
Mayan World Airlines	(2) 703-851
Mexicana	(2) 663-588
Varig Air France	(2) 662-612

HOTELS

Top-end

Camino Real; Carretera Norte KM 9 1/2; tel: (2) 631-381; reservations, 631-410; fax: (2) 631-380, (2) 631-6909; http://www.caminoreal.com.ni; email: cic@caminoreal.com.ni; near airport; restaurant; conference facilities (up to 2000); business center; secretarial service; fax/photocopy facilities; in-room modem/.fax connection, IDD phone, cable tv; room service; cellular phone rental; car rental; barber shop/beauty salon; parking; airport shuttle; corporate rates.

Inter-Continental; Octava Calle Sur Oeste 101; tel: (2) 283-530; fax:(2) 285-208; email: managua@interconti.com; city center; restaurants; casino; business center; function rooms (up to 200); secretarial service; business room options with mobile phones, fax machines, PC with printer, Internet access; in-room tv, IDD telephone, minibar; laundry/valet service; 24-hour room service; airport shuttle service; parking; health club; fitness; massage; sauna; pool.

Las Mercedes; Carretera Norte KM 11; tel: (2) 631-011; fax: (2) 631-082; email: mercedes@ns.tmx.com.ni; near airport; restaurant; conference facilities (up to 1,000); secretarial service; fax/photocopy facilities; corporate rates.

Expensive/Moderate

Barcel O Playa Montelimar; Carreter De Masachapa Km 65, Municipio De San Rafael Del Su On The Beach, Managua; 202 rooms; located on the beach; restaurant; bar; business center; conference facilities; in room air conditioning, cable tv, minibar, balcony, hair dryer; 24 hour room service; fitness center.

Estrella; Semaforos de la Rubenia 26 al Norte; tel: (2) 897-010; fax: (2) 897-104; email: hestrella@ibw.com.ni; restaurant; bar; conference facilities; business center; in-room air conditioning, tv, telephone; room service; parking; swimming pool.

Hotel Best Western Las Mercedes; Km.11 Carretera Norte, Frente al Aeropuerto Internacional; (2) 631-011; fax: (2) 631-083; e-mail: lm@munditel.com.ni.

Hotel Casa Real (B&B); Rotonda Darío 2c. Oeste, 2c. Sur, 1/2c. Este; tel: (2) 783-838; fax: (2) 678-240; e-mail: casareal@ibw.com.ni; in room mini bar, air conditioning, tv, internet, fax, hair dryer.

Hotel Cesar; Km 8 1/2 Carretera Sur; tel: 265-2728; fax: 265-2888; http://www.HotelCesar.com; email: info@HotelCesar.com; restaurant; bar; in-room air conditioning, tv, fax/internet connection; outdoor gardens; pool; garden; US$59/65.

Hotel Europeo Managua (B&B); Canal 2, 75 mts. Oeste; tel: (2) 682-130; email: europeo@ibw.com.ni; located near the new downtown Managua; bungalows and single and double rooms; restaurant; business center; in-room air conditioning, cable tv, telephone, private bath, hot water.

Hotel Ticomo; Carretera Sur KM 8 1/2; tel: (2) 650-210; fax: (2) 651-529; email: thorton@ibw.com.ni; restaurant; conference facilities; pool; tennis.

La Posadita De Bolonia (B&B); Canal 2, 3c. Norte, 75 mts. Sur; tel: (2) 662081; fax: (2) 686-692; email: ntour@nicanet.com.ni; 8 private rooms in boarding house.

Mansion Teodolinda; tel: (2) 281-050; fax: (2) 224-908; email: hotel@teodolinda.com.ni; located in the heart of Managua; restaurant; conference room; fax facilities; kitchenette; in-room refrigerator, desk; room service; parking; swimming pool.

Princess Managua; KM 4.5 Carretera A masaya, Managua; tel: (2) 705-045; fax: (2) 702-574; email: princess@munditel.com.ni 104 rooms; in room cable tv, desk, telephone.

HEALTH CARE

Bautista Hospital; tel: 497-333, 497-118.
Berta Calderon Hospital; tel: 601-787, 601-303.
Clinica de Asma y Alergia; Reparto Serrano #12, Managua; 92) 278-1169.

Hospital Bautista de Nicaragua; P.O. Box 709, Managua; tel: (2) 249-7327; fax: (2) 249-7326; email: direchb@ibw.com.ni.
Montoya Medical Center; tel: 281-054.
Radiology Institute; tel: 662-740, 666-005.

HEALTH CLUB

Hotel Inter-Contiental; 101 Octavia Calle S.O.; tel: (2) 283-530; health club, pool; fitness instruction, beauty salon, massage, sauna, changing room, showers.

AUTO RENTAL

Avis; A.C. Sandino Airport; (2) 650-1112; Hotel Camino Real, KM 9 Carr, North; tel: (2) 631-381 ext 243; Pista Juan Pablo II, Edif. Automotriz; tel: (2) 651-163.

Hertz; Augusto Cesar Sandino Airport, tel: (2) 668-400, tel: (2) 31-237; fax: (2) 668-400; telex: 1390; Intercontinental Hotel, Avenida Bolivar, Lomas De Tiscapa; tel: (2) 623-531, tel:(2) 623-539, ext. 1; fax: (2) 668-400; telex: 1390.

Popular Rent- A-Car (operated by Hertz); Km 4 - Caretera Sur; tel: (2) 668-400.

WORLD TRADE CENTER

World Trade Center of Nicaragua
Brickell Bay Tower
1001 Brickell Bay Drive, Suite # 2210
Miami, Florida 33131, USA
tel: (305) 377-0304
fax: (305) 577-3347

CHAMBER OF COMMERCE

Camera de Comercio de Nicaragua
Pista Ruben Dario, ENEL Central 500 Mts. al Sur
Managua, Nicaragua, Aptdo. Postal 2720; tel: (505) 267-3099, (505) 267-3633
fax: (505) 267-3098.

Centro de Informacion Comercial
Apartado 2142, Km 6, Darretera a Masaya
Managua
tel: (2) 783-075
fax: (2) 783-087
email: cei@ibw.com.ni

Nigeria

At a Glance

Population .... 123,337,822 (July 2000 est.)
Growth Rate .... 2.67% (2000 est.)
Life Expectancy .... 51.56 years
Infant Mortality . 74.18 deaths/1,000 live births (2000 est.)

Ethnic Composition

There are 250 ethnic groups in Nigeria, the largest ones are: Hausa and Fulani 29%, Yoruba 21%, Igbo (Ibo) 18%, Ijaw 10%, Kanuri 4%, Ibibio 3.5%, Tiv 2.5%.

Religious Composition

Muslim 50%
Christian 40%
Indigenous beliefs 10%

Languages Spoken

English (official), Hausa-Fulani, Yoruba, Ibo, Fulani.

Education and Literacy

Six years of primary education are compulsory. Education in the southern states is more advanced than in the northern states. The overall literacy of the country is 57.1 percent. Literacy of males is 67.3 percent; of females, 47.3 percent.

Labor Force

Total: 42,844,000
By occupation: agriculture 54%, industry 6%, services 40%.

THE ECONOMY

The Nigerian economy is based primarily on oil. Plagued by political instability, corruption and violence, Nigeria has lacked a stable economic program, wallowing in a period of turmoil. The country is now undergoing a substantial economic reform under the new civilian administration. Nigeria's former military dictators failed to diversify the country's economy, relying so heavily on the oil sector. The oil industry provides 20 percent of GDP, 95 percent of foreign exchange earnings, and about 65 percent of budgetary revenues. The agricultural sector has not been able to keep up with rapid population growth. Nigeria, a once large exporter of food, must now import food. In 2000, Nigeria is likely to receive a debt-restructuring deal with the Paris club as well as a $1 billion loan from the IMF, both dependent on whether or not economic reforms are instituted. Increased foreign investment combined with high international oil prices should push growth over 5 percent in 2000-01.

Exports .... US$13.1 billion (f.o.b., 1999)
Imports .... US$10 billion (f.o.b., 1999)
Total Trade .... US$23.1 billion (1999)
GDP Per Capita .... US$970 (1999 est.)
Unemployment 28% (1994)
Inflation Rate .... 12.5%(1999 est.)

Top Export Partners

U.S. 35%, Spain 11%, India 9%, France 6%, Italy.

Top Import Partners

U.K. 13%, U.S. 12%, Germany 10%, France 9%, Netherlands.

Top Exports

Petroleum and petroleum products 95%, cocoa, rubber.

Top Imports

Machinery, chemicals, transportation equipment, manufactured goods, food and animals.

BUSINESS WORKWEEK

Offices

Monday to Friday 8a.m. to 12:30p.m., 2p.m. to 4:30p.m.; Saturday 8a.m. to 12:30p.m.

Banks

Monday to Friday 8a.m. to 4p.m.; a few banks now also offer services on Saturdays.

Government

Monday to Friday 8a.m. to 3:30p.m.

Retail

Monday to Friday 8a.m. to 5p.m., Saturday 8a.m. to 4:30p.m.

HOLIDAYS

New Year's Day..January 1
Id-al Fitr, end of Ramadan.........................January 10-12*
Id al-Kabir, Feast of the Sacrifice ....March 18*
Good Friday..April 21*
Easter Monday ....April 24*
Worker's Day...May 1
Mouloud, Birth of the Prophet............................June 16*
National Day...October 1
Christmas ....December 25
Boxing Day...Dec. 26
Id-al-Fitir .... December 30-31*
*Date may vary by year.

CLIMATE

Seasons

The Nigerian climate is generally tropical and wet, with well defined wet and dry seasons. Nights are cool and temperatures will drop from 43˚C (109˚F) in the January daytime hours to 4˚C (39˚F) in the evening. The rainy season lasts from April to October. Harmattan winds blows across from the Sahara Desert during the dry season.

Regions

The climate in the north is dry, and in the south it is hot and humid all year round with average temperatures of 29˚C (84˚F). Rain is less frequent in the north.

Money & Banking

Currency

The unit in Nigeria is the naira, typically written N. N1 = 100 Kobo. In May, 1992, 1, 5, 10, and 25 Kobo coins and 50k and N1 notes were withdrawn from circulation.

Foreign Exchange

Importing or exporting more than N20 is prohibited. All visitors must exchange the equivalent of US$100 into local currency upon arrival. There is no limit to the foreign currency imported, but it must be declared on arrival; export is limited to the amount declared. Regulations are subject to change with little warning.

Traveler's checks

Traveler's checks can be exchanged at banks, ex-

change shops, hotels, and international airports at tourist exchange rates. Larger banks may offer the best exchange rates, but avoid black marketers at all cost; a severe penalty exists if you are caught; they can be found hanging around airports. Consult your bank about current exchange rates before departure. Keep all receipts for reconversion. One may not export in excess of N100 in notes.

Major credit cards: American Express, Visa, Diner's Club, and MasterCard are accepted in up-market places in Lagos. However, it is recommended that one arrive with US$100 dollar bills that are more readily exchangeable to procure a friendlier exchange rate. The import of foreign currency is unlimited; however, export is limited to the amount you declared upon arrival. Some banks in the capital offer cash advances on credit cards, but make sure you bring your passport. One can transfer money via Western Union at the First Bank of Nigeria or via MoneyGram through United Bank of Africa. However, do not expect the high-speed turnaround time that you might get at home.

Travel
VISA AND PASSPORT

A passport valid for a minimum of six months beyond the expected departure date, a return ticket, and a mandatory yellow fever vaccination certificate are required for entry to Nigeria.

Visas are required of all except nationals of Benin, Burkina Faso, Cameroon, Cape Verde, Chad, The Gambia, Ghana, Guinea, Guinea-Bissau, Ivory Coast, Liberia, Mali, Mauritania, Morocco, Niger, Senegal, Sierra Leone, and Togo for stays of up to 90 days.

Passengers in transit who do not leave the airport and are continuing their journey aboard the first-connecting aircraft, and who are holding confirmed tickets and other documents for onward travel, are also exempt from the need for a visa. But there are exceptions to this exemption, and nationals of some countries who are traveling through Nigeria must always carry a transit visa, even if not exiting the airport. Check transit regulations regarding your country with a Nigerian embassy or consulate prior to traveling. Types of visa issued are:

- Tourist—single, double, and multiple entry, good for up to three months
- Business—single and multiple entry, valid for up to three months
- Transit—valid for 48 hours

Apply for a tourist or business visa at the nearest Nigerian embassy. To obtain a business visa, you must present a letter from your Nigerian business contact. Apply well in advance of travel dates. A business visa allows a maximum stay of 90 days. Any attempt to enter Nigeria without a valid visa is considered an illegal activity. Airport visas are not available.

Allow for two days of visa application processing time if done in person, or seven (working) days if done through the mails.

Dash is the general term used in Nigeria for gift, favor, tip, or bribe. Dash is usually paid in advance to expedite a lengthy customs process, however, it is greatly discouraged. It has been noted of late that bribery at the airport has been curtailed.

Note: Do not surrender your passport or baggage to anyone except uniformed customs or immigration personnel.

DEPARTURE FORMALITIES

You cannot depart Nigeria legally unless you can prove that you entered legally—you do that by providing your stamped entry visa.

Both a passport and a visa are mandatory for entry. The visa must be obtained prior to arrival. If anybody promises you entry into the country without a visa, it is indicative of intent to defraud by exploiting your inadvertent illegal presence once you are already in the country under false pretenses, threatening bodily harm and extortion.

Exporting more than N50 of Nigerian currency is illegal. A departure tax of US$35 for international flights, or N100 for domestic flights, is charged. Transit passengers are exempt.

CUSTOMS ENTRY (PERSONAL)

Duty-free
- Tobacco: 200 cigarettes or 50g cigars or 200g of tobacco
- Alcohol: 1 liter of distilled spirits and one liter of wine
- Perfume: 60g of perfume
- Gifts not exceeding the value of N300, excluding photographic equipment, electronics, jewelry, and luxury goods

Prohibited or restricted
Prohibited items include:
- Addictive drugs
- Pornography
- Sparkling wine and champagne, soft drinks, and beer
- Vegetables, fruits, eggs, and cereals, whether preserved or fresh
- Precious metals, including jewelry
- Mosquito nets and textile fabrics

Attempts to circumvent these restrictions result in heavy fines and imprisonment.

Antiquities may only be purchased from the Director of Antiquities or an accredited agent. Be sure to acquire a clearance permit before arriving at customs upon departure.

IMMUNIZATION

Yellow fever and cholera vaccinations are required with a filled-out vaccination certificate. Anti-malarial medication is recommended. Other immunizations are required only if you are coming from an infected area.

A visitor's risk of getting yellow fever is greatest in Kaduna and Lagos states.

TIPPING

Taxi
The fare negotiated before the trip begins is inclusive.

Porters
Tip about N50 per piece.

Hotels
A 10 percent gratuity is customary if a service charge has not been included in the bill. In many cases, it may be more effectual to tip the individuals directly.

Restaurants
Ten to fifteen percent is customary in most restaurants.

EMERGENCY INFORMATION

Police and Crime
Crime in Nigeria is high. One is advised never to travel alone and to let someone you trust know where you are located at all times. Be wary of violent crime in Lagos and the southern half of the country, as well as the oil-producing states in the southeast, and Kaduna State. The border area near Lake Chad in the northeast has also reported problems. Armed muggings, assaults burglary, carjackings, and extortion are widespread. Never carry all your cash with you. In case of robbery, it is imperative that one have extra cash available to bail oneself out. Armed robbery at night is a serious problem. Unauthorized checkpoints manned by bandits are prevalent. More secure areas include Victoria Island and Ikoyi (where several expatriates live). Be sure to register with your embassy upon arrival and to maintain a current registration. However, do not rely on the embassy for any legal help. Police roadblocks are common. However, due to the crackdown on bribery, one may do better not to offer money directly but to pass it to your driver who may then discreetly pass it on to the one collecting. Police, however, are slow to help in an emergency.

Ethnic tensions run high and riots are common. Attempts to introduce the Islamic legal code, Sharia, in the northern part of the country may result in further unrest and disturbances. Avoid public gatherings and riots at all costs. Carry a digital shortwave radio and tune into the BBC to keep informed and alerted of ethnic and religious crisis.

Take basic precautions. Avoid flashy displays of wealth, and dress and behave conservatively. Leave most of your cash, traveler's checks, jewelry and your camera in your hotel safe, if not at home. Carry photocopies of your passport instead of the original. Carry cash in a money belt, and use credit cards or traveler's checks for most transactions. Walk with your bag away from the street to avoid having it snatched away by motorcycle thieves. Never carry a stranger's baggage.

When outdoors, women should dress modestly to avoid sexual harassment. In case of crime, report to the police, they are generally helpful. In case of political uprising, curfews are imposed that may last more than a week. Persons caught out in the streets are subject to arrest during these times.

Emergency Numbers
Eko Hospital ....(01) 631-520
St. Nicholas Hospital ....260-0072/73/74/75 to 79

Health
Malaria, cholera, hepatitis, stomach ailments, meningitis, venereal diseases and AIDS are all present in Nigeria. Malaria in Nigeria has proven resistant to chloroquine. Larium (mefloquine) is the prescribed prophylactic of choice against malaria here. However, if you plan on staying in the country beyond a few weeks, one is urged to consider the side effects of long-term usage, including retinal damage or chronic liver damage. Some may also exhibit toxic reac-

Nigeria

tions, even with short-term usage. Also bear in mind that if one is taking mefloquine, it disqualifies you from receiving Halfan, the most effective treatment for malaria. Both combined depress the heart rate to dangerous levels. The malarial mosquito is most active between 2a.m. and daylight. Mosquito nets are the most effective method to combat mosquito attack while you are sleeping. Just make sure the net has no holes before dozing off. If an insect should land on you, do not slap it but rather flick it away as it may secrete an acid that will cause a wound. Plenty of insects exist in Nigeria that can cause some infection, including one that lays its eggs in wet laundry, which then produce maggots that get into the skin. Thus, one should take care that linens and clothes have been ironed.

AIDS also poses a big problem in the country. If receiving any sort of medical injection, be sure that it is a disposable needle from a sterile packet.

One should also take a course of vaccine against typhoid before arriving in the country.

Never drink tap water or use ice cubes; bottled water is available, but check to make sure the seal on the bottle has not been broken. A common scam involves simply refilling the bottle from the tap, even in hotels and restaurants. Purification tablets can also be used. If you should suffer from serious diarrhea, which carries the danger of being cholera, UNICEF salts mixed with spring water provide the best treatment. Cholera can kill within a few hours. Thus, it is wise to travel with a few packets of the salts to remedy the threat.

Wash all vegetables in a chlorine solution (1 teaspoon bleach per one gallon of spring water), peel fruits, and avoid uncooked food. Be sure cooked food is served hot. Drink only pasteurized milk. Try to eat milder foods until your digestive system adjusts to the local spices.

Venomous snakes and scorpions also exist; take care when walking outdoors; and check shoes and clothes before donning them.

For major medical help, you are advised to leave the country. Embassies may offer some assistance for an emergency airlift. Take enough medication to last through your trip as it is either scarce or counterfeit in Nigeria. Carry a written medical note if your medication is anything more than aspirin or generic medicine. Private care may offer high standards.

INTERNAL TRAVEL
AIR

Domestic air travel is deemed unsafe by many, owing to poor maintenance of the airplanes and the bad condition of equipment at the airports.

Nigeria Airways (WT) flies between Lagos, Port Harcourt, Benin City, Enugu, Calabar, Kano, Kaduna, Jos, Yola, Sokoto, and Maiduguri. You can make charter arrangements in Lagos with Pan-African Airlines, Aero Contractors, or Delta Air Charter. Book all domestic flights well ahead of time, and for a date perhaps earlier than you need, to allow for the considerable delay that is typical here with internal air services. Fuel shortages sometimes disrupt domestic air travel also.

Facilities are primitive, and maintenance is questionable. Internal flights do not depart from Murtala Mohammed Airport, rather from an older airport that is 10km away.

Regardless of airline, boarding is always a hectic scramble for seating, and most flights are routinely overbooked. For the business traveler especially, a more viable alternative could be the private airlines, which, for fairly reasonable fares, are usually more reliable and efficient than Nigerian Airways. Inquire through your travel agent, or check with your hotel in Nigeria.

TAXI

Taxis are not allowed to collect people at the airport, so travelers will have to use a "hired car." Tourist Tours, or travel advisers, stationed around the arrival area will guide you to a hire-car parking area. Rides to downtown hotels average US$15, but the price can be haggled down. One is advised to have someone meet you at the airport upon arrival to avoid the scammers waiting for you at the there.

In Lagos, regular taxis are yellow; agree on prices before departure. Public transport, including taxis, is not recommended due to the high incidence of armed crime.

AUTO

In general, it is recommended that one hire a chauffeur-driven vehicle. A driver will prove in invaluable in assisting the traveler—and in relation to car rental rates, costs almost nothing.

Rental cars cost an average of US$150 per week with unlimited mileage, all taxes and insurance included, for the least expensive vehicle. A moderate sized vehicle costs US$375 per week. Gas is not included. Insurance costs are covered by the rental fee, but inquire about this and be sure to read the rental contract. One is advised to rent cars from hotels. Roads are in disrepair, however, and the accident rate among the highest in the world. Road rules are seldom followed and many cars lack proper lighting. One may also have problems getting fuel when shortages occur. Road travel has also become increasingly hazardous due to illegitimate checkpoints manned by armed personnel, including police and soldiers. Avoid night driving at all costs. Flooding during the rainy season between May to October makes roads more dangerous.

In order to rent a car, or drive a car in Nigeria, you must have held a valid drivers license from your country of residence for at least one year. An international driving permit is required for all licenses written in a non-roman alphabet.

TRAIN

Although slower than buses, trains are less expensive. Daily service runs between Lagos and Kano, and Port Harcourt to Maidugur. These two lines connect Kaduna and Kafanchan. A branch line runs from Zaria to Kaura Namoda and Gusau.

A daily service operates on both main routes. Travelers can book sleeping cars in advance. Three classes of travel are offered, and air-conditioning and restaurant cars are part of the rolling stock on some trains.

SUBWAY

No subway or metro system exists in Nigeria.

BUS

Buses in downtown Lagos and Abuja are crowded; public transportation throughout Nigeria is dangerous and should be avoided. Furthermore, traffic congestion is a common occurrence.

On the other hand, traveling between cities by bus (in the shape of Ford transit vans) is far safer than going by bush taxi, and fairly comfortable. All the main cities are linked by bus lines, and there are many private companies. In most cities, all the bus offices tend to locate in the same part of town.

WATER TRAVEL

Ferry service is available on the Benue and Niger rivers as well as on the south coast. A ferry service also sails to Lagos Island. Inquire locally to determine schedules and fares.

TRAVEL ASSISTANCE

Federal Ministry of Tourism and Culture
Old Secretariat, Garki, Abuja, Nigeria
tel: (9) 234-2770; fax: (9) 234-1351
Nigerian Tourist Board
PO Box 2944
Trade Fair Complex, Badagry Expressway
Lagos, Nigeria
tel: (1) 618-665

Communications

DIALING CODES IN NIGERIA

International country code: [234]
Selected city codes: Abuja (9), Badagry (1); Enugu (42), Jos (73), Kaduna (62), Kano (64), Lagos (1), Ibaden (22), Ogbomosho (38), Port Harcourt (84), Wari (53).

Dialing Nigeria From Overseas

*To call to Nigeria from overseas, begin with your country's international dialing code, followed by Nigeria's country code (234), the local city code and finally the number.

Assistance Numbers

Foreign Operator 191
There is no directory assistance available.

CALLING WITHIN NIGERIA

Long Distance Calls

Use the city codes when dialing long distance within Nigeria.

International Calls

Nigeria Telecom (NITEL) runs the telephone operation in Nigeria. Service is spotty. Direct dialing is available from Lagos, Kaduna, Abuja, Port Harcourt, Ibadan, Kano, and many other cities. Dial 009 + country code + area code + number. NITEL offices provide decent service for just such calls; but it costs about quadruple what it does if you were calling Nigeria from overseas. The average cost of a call might run US$10 to $15 for a three-minute call to the U.S., U.K., or Australia. Business centers seem to offer better options with private telephone service. Pay upon completing the call. However, the best and simplest option may be to have the party from overseas try and call you.

Specially-marked AT&T phones for direct access to an operator in the States can be found in telephone calling centers.

PAY PHONES

Public Telephones

NITEL has installed more card phones for public use, and the general report is that they actually work. Airports, hotels, and some government offices have public card phones.

Calling Cards

NITEL sells telephone cards, however, they may be hard to come by since they are only available at NITEL offices.

CELLULAR PHONES

International Wireless Inc./Comstar and *EMIS Nigeria* provide GSM service for cellular users in Nigeria. Recently, *DSC Communications Corporation* contracted to provide AMPS analogue service in Lagos and will be linked to Nitel, the local telephone service provider.

Note: Your home country cell phone may not work in this country. If not, we recommend that you rent an international cell phone *before* you leave home. A major US-based cell phone rental provider is **IMC WorldCell**. For information see "International Cell Phone Rentals" on page 14. Call Back

You can (potentially) save significant sums when calling in Nigeria by using one of the call back services listed below. Fees for call back services vary widely, depending on the company and the type of service required. Be sure to check with these companies before leaving to compare rates.

For a list of callback services, please refer to the "Communications" section in the *Global Road Warrior* Introduction.

PHONE JACKS

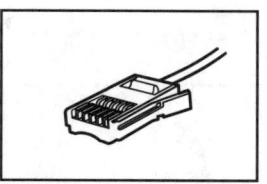

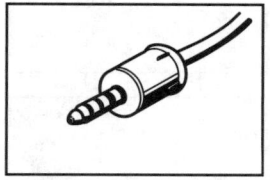

Plug adaptors are available through **iGo Corporation.** (See "Electrical and Telephone Adaptors" on page 19.)

FAX

Faxes may be received and sent at major hotels and businesses. Fax machines are few and far between, although most hotels that serve foreign clientele have them.

POST OFFICE

Postal services are available at post offices and many of the major hotels. Airmail to North America often takes five to seven days. However, mail is unreliable. A courier service may prove far more effective.

TELEGRAMS

Some top-end hotels have services.

Business Services

COURIER SERVICE

Airborne Express; 23 Adeyemo Alakija Street, Victoria Island, Lagos; tel: (1) 619-809.

DHL; tel: (1) 452-7086; DHL House, Isolo Expressway, New Airport Rd. Junction, Isolo, Lagos; Monday to Friday 8a.m. to 9p.m.; Saturday/Sunday 9a.m. to 6p.m.

Der Kurier Nigeria Limited; 56, Muritala Mohammed International Airport Road; Lagos; tel: (1) 497-5589; fax: (1) 493-2483.

Federal Express Nigeria; represented by Red Star Express, 1 International Airport Road, Lagos; tel: (1) 452-8621, 452-8623.

TNT Nigeria; TransNationwide Express PLC, Plot 2-82, Gbagada Express Way, Gbagada, PMB 21672 Ikeja, Lagos; tel: (1) 825-980; fax: (1) 822-831.

Transportation Solutions Inc.; 430 West Merrick Rd., Ste. 22, Valley Stream, New York 11580; tel: 561-5700; toll free in the U.S. 1-800-606-8529; door-to-door delivery in Nigeria; 2 - 3 day shipments; freight consolidator; global collection; special services.

UPS Nigeria; Plot 16, Oworonshoki Expressway, Gbagada Industrial Estate, PO Box 2780, Ikeja, Lago; tel: (1) 824-212, 824-222; fax: (1) 262-1419.

World Courier; 12 Mobolaji Bank Anthony way, Ikeja, Lagos; tel: (1) 496-6891.

Electrical

Current
230 volts, 50Hz.

ELECTRIC PLUGS

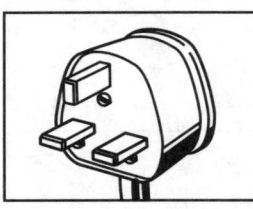

Adapters are hard to find, and most visitors have found it is best to bring a generous supply. The common plugs are three-prong, square-pin attachment plug and the three-prong, flat-blade type. Plug adaptors are available through **iGo Corporation**. (See "Electrical and Telephone Adaptors" on page 19.)

Technical Support

HARDWARE/SOFTWARE VENDOR SUPPORT

Dell; (in Germany) tel: [49] (61) 039-710; (Dell- Europe) tel: [44] (134) 474-8000; (in the U.S.) tel: [1] (512) 338-4400; fax: [1] (512) 728-3330; http://www.dell.com/.

Gateway 2000; (in Ireland) tel: [353] (1) 797-2000; (in the U.S.) tel: [1] (605) 232-2191; fax: [1] (605) 232-2023; http://www.g2k.com/.

IBM; tel: (1) 263-6288; tel: (1) 263-6078; (in Germany) tel: [49] (711) 78-50; fax: [49] (711) 785-3511; (in Switzerland) tel: [41] (22) 310-0418 (in French); (in the U.S.) tel: [1] (919) 517-2800; http://www.ibm.com/.

Microsoft; (in Saudi Arabia) tel: [966] (1) 488-1165; fax: [966] (1) 474-0576; (in Germany) tel: [49] (89) 31-760; fax: [49] (89) 3176-1000; tel: [49] (89) 3176-1199; (in Switzerland) tel: [41] (848) 858-868; fax [41] (1) 831-0869; (in the U.S.) [1] (425) 635-7222; http://www.microsoft.com/.

NEC; (in Germany) tel: [49] (18) 0524- 1212; tel:[49] (89) 3160-1233; fax: [49] (89) 3160- 1613 (Floppy Disk and Hard Drive); tel: [49] (89) 9627-4233; fax: [49] (89) 9627-4613 (All Other Products); (in the U.S.) [1] (916) 388-0101 (Main Switchboard); http://www.nec.com/.

Novell; (in Germany) tel: [49] (211) 563-2777 (System support); tel: [49] (6196) 904-477; fax: [49] (211) 563-2772; (in Switzerland) tel: [41] (1) 308-4747; fax: [41] (1) 302-0401; (in the U.S.) tel: [1] (408) 434-2300; fax: [1] (408) 577-5775 (Worldwide Sales Headquarters); http://www.novell.com/.

Quark; (in Switzerland) tel: [41] (1) 808-7722; fax: [41] (1) 808-7799; (in the U.S.) tel: [1] (303) 894-8899; fax: [1] (303) 894-3398 (For Products Registered in the Americas); http:/www.quark.com/.

Toshiba; (in Germany) tel: [49] (2131) 158-319; fax: [49] (2131) 158-558; (in Switzerland) tel: [41] (1) 946-0777; fax: [41] (1) 946-0807; (in Ireland) tel: [44] (193) 282-8828; (in the U.S.) [1] (949) 583-3000 (Corporate Headquarters); http://www.toshiba.com/.

Internet Connection

HOW TO CONNECT

America Online
Connecting to AOL and Compuserve in Nigeria is similar to using it when traveling outside your own area code. See the introductory section for detailed information on connecting to your account through a different phone number. AOL's GlobalNet provides service for an added US$6 an hour in addition to the usual charges.

Access: Kano (64) 648-183; Lagos (1) 264-7778; Port Harcourt (84) 236-492.

Compuserve
Numbers are available at *Go International*. The Compuserve Web-site also has a great deal of information for travelers, at http://www.compuserve.com.

Access: Kano (64) 648-183; Lagos (1) 264-7778.

Independent Service Providers
Cyberspace Ltd.; tel: (1) 262-4288; fax: (1) 262-4287; email: info@cyberspace.net.ng; http://www.cyberspace.net.ng/.

Hyperia; tel: (1) 320-1234; tel: (1) 262-6976; email: info@hyperia.com; http://www.hyperia.com/.

LinkServe Nigeria Ltd.; tel: (1) 262-3900; tel: (1) 262-3133; fax: (1) 262-3906; email: chima@linkserve.com.ng; http://www.linkserve.net/.

NigeriaNet; tel: (1) 493-2401/2; fax: (1) 493-2193; email: info@nigerianet.com; http://www.nigerianet.com/.

Internet Cafes
Lagos
CyberVille Ilupeju; 2b, Oba Adetona Street, Ilupeju Estate, Lagos; tel: (1) 497-7484; fax: (1) 497-7484; email: info@ngcyberville.com; http://www.ngcyberville.com/; Monday through Saturday, 8a.m. to 8p.m.; N12 per minute of use.

Hyperia Internet Cafe; Sunaina Plaza 23, Adeola Odeku Victoria Island Lagos; tel: (1) 262-2287; fax: (1) 320-1200; email: cs@hyperia.com; http://www.hyperiacafe.co/; Monday through Friday, 9a.m. to 9p.m., Saturday and Sunday 10a.m. to 8p.m.

Tab Systems & Services; First Floor, 50, Olowu Street, Lagos; tel: (1) 493-8646; fax: (1) 497-7894; email: tabsystems@micro.com.ng; http://tabsystems.freeservers.com/; Monday through Friday, 9a.m. to 8p.m., Saturday and Sunday, 9a.m. to 7p.m.; N10 per minute of use.

Turner Technologies NG; 148 Obafemi Awolowo way Ikeja (Near airport), Lagos; tel: (1) 493-6167; email: info@gettouch.com; N15 per minute of use.

Business Culture

GREETINGS AND COURTESIES

A simple handshake is the common greeting in Nigeria. Men who are close friends, however, often do not shake hands. Women often hug other women friends. Titles such as doctor, chief, and director should always be used when applicable.

MEETINGS

Standards of punctuality are relatively high in Nigeria. Foreigners are expected to be prompt, and meetings usually start on time. "Formally informal" might best describe the standard procedure for meetings. A lengthy period of greetings and personal conversation always precedes any actual talk of business. To show haste during this formality would be very insulting.

The first meeting as a whole will be somewhat formal, conducted in the office. Once the all-important personal rapport is achieved, however, subsequent—and more substantive—meetings will be conducted over long lunches at restaurants, as well as at your Nigerian counterpart's home.

Because the phone system is unreliable, the vast majority of business takes place face to face. Make an appointment in person (be prepared to wait hours just for an appointment). On the day of the meeting, be sure to arrive on time (and continue to wait). If you plan to see a number of people in a short amount of time, bring an ample supply of business cards. Visit each office and leave a letter—on letterhead—describing your business. Then return the next day and visit the office again. Many offices will see you on the spot

DECISION MAKING

Of all African nations, Nigeria is the most populous as well as the most culturally diverse. Over 250 ethnic groups, each with its own language, comprise the extraordinary cultural tapestry that is Nigeria. However, the three largest of these groups, the Ibo in the east, the Yoruba in the west, and the Housa-Fulani in the north, basically dominate both the country and its business community, thus simplifying an otherwise overly complex situation. Entrenched bureaucracy and governmental red tape, unfortunately, remain the basic characteristics of Nigeria's business culture. Nigerians are accustomed to this system, and move easily through it, so follow their lead and do not try to impose different standards in an effort to more quickly get things done.

When attempting to reach an important decision with a Nigerian firm, it is imperative that you deal with the top people in the company. To rely on lower-level people is to risk serious delays and complications. A good inside contact is invaluable in getting through to the necessary decision makers. Further, once you've gained an inside connection to the decision making echelon in a Nigerian firm, you may rest assured that the company will deal with the formidable and imposing governmental regulations affecting all foreign business transactions.

COMMERCIAL FRAUD

Due to the large presence of business fraud, one is urged to contact the Embassies or Department of Commerce in your country before departing for Nigeria or making any sort of financial commitments. Tap into the 419 Coalition website, sponsored by a company that has been a target of numerous scamming attempts in Nigeria and wishes to help others in awareness. Business scams rule the day and come in hundreds of forms, including very sophisticated schemes involving government. Scams generally involve phony offers of either outright money transfers or lucrative sales or contracts with promises of large commissions or up-front payments. Alleged deals frequently invoke the authority of one or more ministries or offices of the Nigerian government and may even cite by name the support of a NIgerian government official. it seems almost too simplistic to state that any unsolicited proposal should be very carefully examined. The foreign embassies can offer little help with a deal or money gone astray, which happens all too frequently.

WOMEN

Women in most of the regions of Nigeria maintain a significant degree of prestigious and powerful positions in the business community. A foreign businesswoman can thus expect to be well-received, though a restrained and unaggressive demeanor is recommended.

BUSINESS ATTIRE

Nigerians tend to be very fashion conscious and those in the business community are always well-dressed. There is, however, no "dress code," except for formal business events. For important business meetings, however, men should wear a suit and tie, women a dress. Cottons and linens are most recommended to combat the humidity and heat. Bring an umbrella during rainy season. A sweater may prove necessary if going north or even in the evenings at times.

Business Centers
Lagos

CITY VIEW

As the most populated city in Nigeria, Lagos stands as the industrial and commercial hub of the country. To quell the massive urbanization, the government has moved its official capital to Abuja. But Lagos, with a population of over 4 million, remains the focal point for Nigerian business. Manufacturing in the city revolves mostly around machinery, motor vehicles, electronic equipment, chemicals, beer, processed food, and textiles. Lagos is also the best bet for culture in Nigeria, as the site of the National Library of Nigeria, the National Museum, and the National Theater. On the Bight of Benin (part of the Atlantic Ocean) in the southwestern part of the country, Lagos was originally an old Yoruba town, which later grew as a Portuguese seaport and trade center (it was designated Lagos after the Portuguese city of the same name). Slave trade was a major activity up until 1861 when it was annexed by Great Britain.

AIRPORT

Murtala Muhammed Airport to City Center

The airport lies 21 miles (30 km.) from the city. Taxi services are available, and some hotels have their own vehicles for free service to and from the airport. Police are cracking down on the slick operators canvassing the airport in search of a buck. Persons without a ticket are not allowed entrance into the airport. However, it is stressed that one have someone to meet upon arrival. Be mindful of criminals posing as cab drivers or other such transport operators.

Airline Numbers

Aeroflot	(1) 263-7223
Air Afrique	(1) 616-405, 616-467, 616-391
Air France	(1) 262-1392
Air Gabon	(1) 262-1456, 263-7104
Air India	(1) 263-5418

Nigeria

Alitalia .... (1) 261-1559
Bellview Airlines .... (1) 614-342
British Airways .... (1) 262-1225
Cameroun Airlines .... (1) 261-4993, 774-5729
Egypt Air .... (1) 261-9233
Ethiopian Airlines .... (1) 263-7658, 263-2690
Ghana Airways .... (1) 269-2658
KLM .... (1) 261-9336, 200-8000
Lufthansa .... (1) 266-4883, 266-4430
Nigeria Airways .... (1) 497-0872, 263-3055
.... fax: (1) 264-459
SwissAir .... (1) 263-678, 263-893
.... fax: (1) 261-8480

HOTEL

Top End

Le Meridien Eko Hotel & Casino; Kuramo Waters, Victoria Island; tel: (1) 615-000, 619-845; fax: (1) 615-205, 615-243; business hotel near seaside; renovated 1991; restaurants; casino; conference facilities (up to 850); business center; secretarial service; in-room a/c, minibar, tv, phone; 24-hour room service; non-smoking rooms; shops; disabled facilities; parking; corporate rates; fitness; health; massage; sauna; pool; beach; tennis, volleyball courts; golf.

Excelsior Hotel; 3-15 Ede Street, Pmb 1167, Agapa, Lagos; tel: (1) 803-680/81; located in suburb; restaurant; casino; meeting/banquet rooms; non-smoking rooms; air conditioning; wheelchair access; parking.

Federal Palace Hotel Suites; Ahmadu Bello Way, Victoria Island, Lagos; tel: (1) 262-3116, 261-3303; fax: (1) 262-3912, 261-9009; renovated in 1989; restaurant; conference facilities, banquet hall; air conditioning; parking; sauna; pool; tennis.

Sheraton Lagos Hotel and Towers, 30 Mobolaji Bank Anthony Way, Ikeja, tel: (1) 497-8660/9, telex: 27202, fax: (1) 497-0321/2; 4 restaurants; conference facilities (up to 350); business center; secretarial service; airline desk; executive services; 41 towers rooms and suites; 24-hour room service; non-smoking rooms; bakery; corporate rates; parking; pool; lighted tennis; jogging track; nightclub.

Expensive

B Jays; 24, Samuel Manuwa Str., Samuel Manuwa Str., of Ozumba Mbadiwe, Victoria Island, Lagos; tel: (1) 261-2391, 262-2902, 262-3706; fax: (1) 262-2903.

Baywatch Guest House; 25, Oju Olobun Close, Victoria Island; tel: (1) 262-2215; fax: (1) 262-2903; restaurant.

Bristol; 8 Martins St.; tel: (1) 266-1204; 83 rooms; located in city center; restaurant; bar; in-room air conditioning, telephone, tv; parking; car hire.

Federal Palace Hotel; 26 Ahmadu Bello Way, Ikoyi; tel: (1) 261-0464.

Festac '77; Mile 2 Badagry Expressway; tel: (1) 880-210; fax: (1) 880-839; 528 rooms; near beach and airport; suites; swimming pool; tennis.

Ikoyi; KIngsway Road; Ikoyi Island; tel: (1) 603-200; fax: (1) 685-833; 296 rooms; located in affluent and prestigious Ikoyi Island; restaurant; bar; conference facilities; in-room air conditioning, telephone, tv; swimming pool.

Lagos Airport; Ikeja Village; tel; (1) 490-1000; fax: (1) 493-7573; near airport; restaurant; casino; conference facilities; secretarial service; executive services; computer terminal; in-room safe; hair dresser; health; massage; pool; tennis.

Logistic Guest House; Plot 836, Adetokunbo Ademola, Victoria Island; tel: (1) 261-9736; fax: (1) 262-2136.

New World Hotel; Allen Avenue@ Toyin Street

Victoria Lodge; 5A Olugin Agbage Street, Victoria Island; tel: (1) 262-0885; fax: (1) 262-2136.

AUTO RENTAL

Avis; Eko Hotels, Ademola Adetokunbo, Victoria Island; tel: (2) 6246-0019 x6261; Holt Leasing, 24 Creek Rd, Apapa; tel: 587-1531; fax: (1) 587-7931.

Intra; tel: (1) 634884.

Mandilas Travel (Hertz); tel: (1) 663514.

Nigerian Rent-a-Car (Avis); tel: (1) 846336.

Safedrive; tel: (1) 844615.

HEALTH CARE

Abebe Clinic; 87 Awolowo Road, Ikoyi, Lagos; tel: (1) 269-0080.

General Hospital; 1 Broad street, Lagos; tel: (1) 630-500.

Kings Hospital; 19 Keffi street, Ikoyi, Lagos; tel: (1) 680-096.

Mount Pleasant Medical; 65 Ojuelagba road, Surulere, Lagos; tel: (1) 584-8550.

St. Francois Medical Centre; 22 Keffi St, South-West Ikoyi, Lagos; tel: (1) 269-2305; fax: (1) 774-2818.

HEALTH CLUBS

Sheraton Lagos Hotel and Towers, 30 Mobolaji Bank Anthony Way, Ikeja, tel: (1) 497-8660/9, telex: 27202, fax: (1) 497-0321.

WORLD TRADE CENTER

World Trade Center of Nigeria
Western House, 8th Floor
8/10 Broad Street, P.O. Box 4466
Lagos, Nigeria
tel: (1) 263-5376; fax: (1) 264-7279

CHAMBER OF COMMERCE

Nigerian Association of Chambers of Commerce, Industries, Mines & Agriculture
Private Mail Bag 12816
15a Ikorodu Road; Maryland, Ikeja, Lagos
tel: (1) 496-4727, 496-4737
fax: (1) 496-4737

Lagos Chamber of Commerce & Industry
Commerce House (1st Floor)
1, Idowu Taylor Street
Victoria Island
tel: (1) 261-3911, 261-3917
fax: (1) 261-0573

Norway

At a Glance

Population .... 4,481,162 (July 2000 est.)
Growth Rate .... 0.5% (2000 est.)
Life Expectancy .... 78.65 years
Infant Mortality ... 3.98 deaths/1,000 live births (2000 est.)

Ethnic Composition
Germanic (Nordic, Alpine, Baltic), Sami.

Religious Composition
Evangelical Lutheran...86%
Unknown 10%
Protestant and Roman Catholic 3%
Other 1%

Languages Spoken
Standard Norwegian (Bokmal) and New Norwegian (Nynorsk) are the official languages. There is also small Sami speaking population which is split into nine different dialects, but the Sami also speak Norwegian.

Education and Literacy
Education is free through the university level and is compulsory from ages 7 to 16. Literacy is around 100 percent.

Labor Force
Total: ....2.7 million
By occupation: services 74%, industry 22%, agriculture, forestry, and fishing 4%.

THE ECONOMY

Norway's economy is a prosperous one. The economic character is a balance between a free market economy and government intervention. The government oversees certain areas of the economy by subsidizing agriculture and fishing, as well as other industry in areas with sparse resources. The valuable petroleum sector is also controlled by the government. The only country that exports more oil than Norway is Saudi Arabia. Almost half of the country's GDP is spent on the public sector, the welfare system accounting for a large portion of this expenditure. Norway has a great many natural resources such as petroleum, hydropower, fish, lumber, and minerals. Its identity in the global economy is based on the export of these raw materials. Of these raw materials, Norway, as one would guess, is most dependent upon the price of oil as the cornerstone of its raw material exports. Norway imports more than half its food. In 1994, Norway decided to stay out of the E.U. In 1999, growth was quite low at less than 1 percent. This can be attributed to weak investment in the oil industry. Growth should increase in 2000, maybe to as high as 2.7 percent.

Exports .... US$47.3 billion (f.o.b., 1999 est.)
Imports .... US$38.6 billion (f.o.b., 1999 est.)
Total Trade .... US$85.9 billion (1999 est.)
GDP Per Capita .... US$25,100 (1999 est.)
Unemployment .... 2.9% (1999 est.)
Inflation Rate .... 2.8% (1999 est.)

Top Export Partners
E.U. 77% (U.K. 17%, Germany 12%, Netherlands 10%, Sweden 10%, France 8%), U.S. 7%.

Top Import Partners
E.U. 69% (Sweden 15%, Germany 14%, U.K. 10%, Denmark 7%), U.S. 7%, Japan 4%.

Top Exports
Petroleum and petroleum products 55%, machinery and equipment, metals, chemicals, ships, fish (1997).

Top Imports
Machinery and equipment, chemicals, metals, foodstuffs.

BUSINESS WORKWEEK

Offices
Monday to Friday 8a.m. to 4p.m. Most businesses, in particular banks and government office, will close at 3p.m. in the summertime.

Banks
Winter: Monday to Friday 8:15a.m. to 3:30p.m.
Summer: Monday to Friday 8:15a.m. to 3p.m., until 5p.m. on Thursdays. (see above)

Government
Monday to Friday 9a.m. to 4:30p.m. (see above)

Retail
Monday to Friday 9a.m. to 5 or 6p.m., on Thursdays stores stay open later in Oslo; weekends 9a.m. to 1 or 3p.m.

HOLIDAYS

New Year's Day..January 1
Maundy Thursday..April 20*
Good Friday...April 21*
Easter Monday ....April 24*
May Day ....May 1
Whit Monday .... May 12*
Constitution Day...May 17
Ascension Day .... June 1*
Christmas Day...December 25
Boxing Day..December 26
*Date may vary by year.

CLIMATE

Seasons
Temperature and weather in Norway is quite variable depending on the time of year and particular area. Snow may last for several months a year, but winters and summers are generally mild in the southern parts. Above the Arctic Circle, the sun shines day and night for some of the summer and doesn't appear at all for part of the winter.

Regions
Rain is more abundant on the west coast. Inland tends to have colder winters and warmer summers than the coast.

Money & Banking

Currency
The currency of Norway is the Norwegian Krone (NKr).

Denominations
Norwegian Krone comes in coin denominations of NKr20, 10, 5 and 1 and 50 and 50 öre; and banknotes of NKr50, 100, 200, 500, and 1,000.

Traveler's checks
Traveler's checks and foreign currency can be easily and efficiently exchanged at banks, foreign exchange bu-

Norway

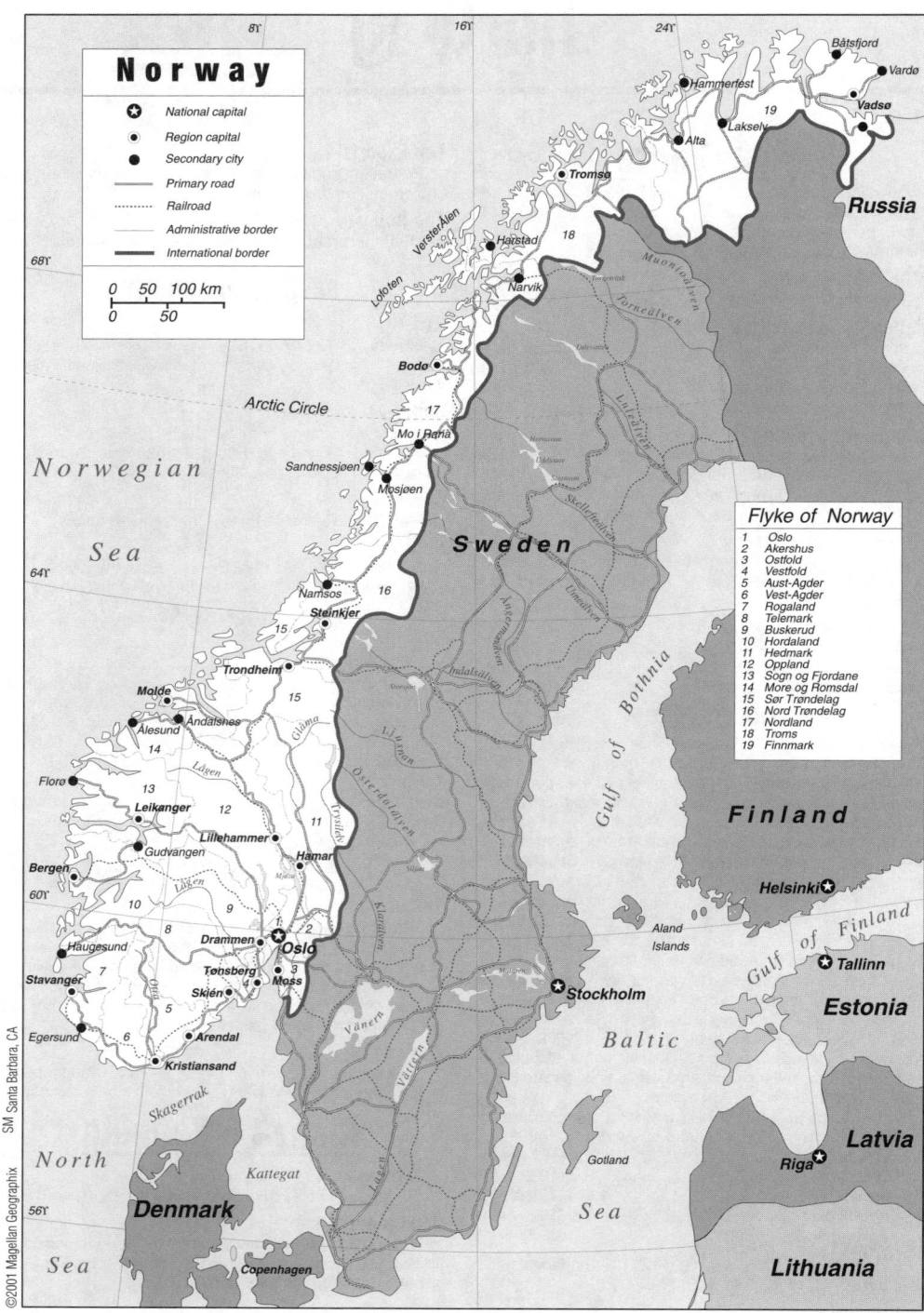

Norway

- ✪ National capital
- ◉ Region capital
- ● Secondary city
- —— Primary road
- ········ Railroad
- —— Administrative border
- ▬▬ International border

0   50   100 km

Flyke of Norway

1 Oslo
2 Akershus
3 Ostfold
4 Vestfold
5 Aust-Agder
6 Vest-Agder
7 Rogaland
8 Telemark
9 Buskerud
10 Hordaland
11 Hedmark
12 Oppland
13 Sogn og Fjordane
14 More og Romsdal
15 Sør Trøndelag
16 Nord Trøndelag
17 Nordland
18 Troms
19 Finnmark

Russia

Båtsfjord
Vardø
Hammerfest
Vadsø
Lakselv
Alta
Tromsø
Harstad
Vesterålen
Narvik
Lofoten
Bodø
Arctic Circle
Mo i Rana
Sandnessjøen
Mosjøen

Norwegian

Sea

Sweden

Namsos
Steinkjer
Trondheim

Molde
Åndalsnes
Ålesund

Florø
Leikanger
Lillehammer
Gudvangen
Hamar
Bergen
Haugesund
Drammen
Oslo
Stavanger
Tønsberg
Moss
Skién
Arendal
Egersund
Kristiansand

Finland

Helsinki

Gulf of Bothnia

Stockholm

Åland
Islands

Gulf of Finland

Tallinn
Estonia

Baltic

Gotland

Riga
Latvia

Skagerrak

North

Denmark

Kattegat

Sea

Lithuania

Copenhagen

Sea

SM Santa Barbara, CA

©2001 Magellan Geographix

Norway

reaus located in the major cities, hotels, and foreign exchange kiosks at the airports. Banks offer the most variable exchange rates. Traveler's checks receive a better exchange rate than cash, or you can purchase and Norway 's currency traveler's check before departure, which can be exchanged almost everywhere. Besides banks, one may exchange currency at the airport, rail stations, and major hotels. The Central Rail Station currency exchange office in Oslo is open Monday to Saturday 8a.m. to 7:30p.m. and Sundays 12p.m. to 6p.m.; during the summer between 8a.m. and 11p.m. daily.

Credit cards, American Express, Visa, MasterCard, and Diners Club are widely accepted in Norway, and you can get cash advances from you credit card on many of the automated teller machines (ATM).

Credit cards are also essential for renting a car. Long-term visitors should set up a checking account in Norway, and get an ATM card.

Essential Terms

English	Norwegian
Yes No	Ja Nei
Good morning Hello (daytime) Hello (evening) Hello (telephone)	God morgen God dag God kveld / aften God dag
Good-bye	Ha det, på gjensyn
Please	Vaer sa snill
Thank you	Takk
Pleased to meet you	Hyggelig å treffe deg
Excuse me; I'm sorry	Unnskyld
My name is _____	Jeg heter_____
I don't understand	Jeg forstår ikke
Do you speak English?	Snakker du engelsk?

Travel

VISA AND PASSPORT

A passport that is valid for a minimum of three months beyond anticipated exit date is required for most nationals, but some are excepted. Nationals of Iceland, Liechtenstein, and Switzerland may enter with a national ID card instead of a passport. E.U. nationals may travel with a valid national ID card if they are coming for touristic purposes only.

Nationals of most countries do not need to obtain a visa. Nationals of Bulgaria, China (PR), Egypt, Kuwait, Pakistan, Philippines, Russian Federation, and Turkey do require a visa.

There is only one type of visa issued, called an Entry visa. It is valid for 90 days within any six-month period. You can obtain an extension or renewal by applying at a Norwegian embassy. No application fee is charged if you are a citizen of a country named in the previous paragraph.

For any stay that will exceed 90 days, you must receive authorization from Norwegian authorities. The 90-day period begins when you enter any Nordic area, including Sweden, Norway, Finland, Denmark, and Iceland.

Allow one or two business days for processing of visa applications for most nationals. For some, though, the process can take between three and eight weeks. Check with the embassy or consulate to get a sense of your particular situation and to determine if you are even required to have a visa.

DEPARTURE FORMALITIES

There are no departure fees leaving Norway. Export of any currency is limited to NKr25,000.

CUSTOMS ENTRY (PERSONAL)

Duty-free
Residents of European countries:
- Tobacco: 200 cigarettes or 250g of tobacco products and 200 leaves of cigarette paper (arrivals over 16 years of age only)
- Alcohol: 1 liter of spirits and 1 liter of wine or 2 liters of wine and 2 liters of beer (arrivals over 20 years of age only)
- Other: goods to the value of NKr1200
Residents of non-European countries:
- Tobacco: 400 cigarettes or 500g of tobacco products and 200 leaves of cigarette paper (arrivals over 16 years of age only)
- Alcohol:1 liter of spirits and 1 liter of wine or 2 liters of wine and 2 liters of beer (arrivals over 20 years of age only)
- Other: goods to the value of NKr1200

Prohibited or Restricted
- Spirits over 60 percent volume (120· proof) and wine over 22 percent volume
- Certain foodstuffs (including eggs, potatoes, meat, meat products, dairy products and poultry)
- Mammals, birds, exotic animals
- Narcotics, medicines, and poisons
- Firearms, ammunitions, explosives

IMMUNIZATION

There are no requirements for travelers unless you are arriving from an infected area.

TIPPING

Taxi
No tip is expected, although 5 to 10 percent is appreciated.

Porters
Porters: NKr5 to 10 per piece.

Hotels
A service charge of between 10 and 15 percent is included in most hotel bills.

Restaurants
A gratuity of 10 to 15 percent is usually included in the tab. Good waiters expect up to five percent additional tip.

Other
Barbers, beauticians: 5 to 10 percent.

EMERGENCY INFORMATION

Police and Crime

Norway has a low crime rate. In some parts of Oslo and surrounding areas, you can become the target of a purse-snatcher or pickpocket if you appear to be affluent. A recent scam is for criminals to target diners in hotels, especially buffets, stealing briefcases, purses, laptops and other such items left unattended at the table. Violent crime is almost nonexistent, though, and thieves and burglars almost never carry weapons.

A few elementary precautions should protect the traveler from most problems:

* Do not leave valuables in cars or on tables in cafés.
* Keep non-essential valuables locked in hotel safes when not in use.
* Use credit cards and traveler's checks when possible to avoid carrying large sums of cash.
* Carry photocopies of your passport instead of the original.
* Carry cash in a money belt, and use credit cards or travelers checks for most of your large transactions.
* Never carry a stranger's baggage.
The police are extremely efficient and courteous.

Emergency Numbers

Ambulance 113
Police... 112
Fire 110

Health

Tap water is safe to drink. Apart from normal digestive problems caused by changes in diet, there are no extraordinary diseases here. Colds and flu are a problem due to the cold and damp weather; take extra vitamins to compensate for the lack of sunlight. Because Norwegians are heavy consumers of alcohol, the laws are very strict about drinking and driving.

The medical services are of a high standard, with an abundance of skilled doctors who speak English. Comprehensive social services cover most medical costs, regardless of citizenship. Doctors speak English and/or German. One may find pharmacy (*Apotek*) schedules listed in newspapers or posted in the windows of other pharmacies.

INTERNAL TRAVEL

AIR

Norway's primary domestic airlines—Widerøe Norsk Air, SAS, SAFE, and Braathens—service a network of approximately 50 airports in western Norway's fjord country and along the coast. Distances are long in Norway, so air travel is worth considering. The traveler can also charter an airplane at most airports.

For more information, contact Widerøe Flyveselskap A/S, Torpveien 128, 3233 Sandsfjord. tel: 8100-1200; fax: 3348-2691.

TAXI

Most cab fares are metered with fares starting at around NKr24. Expect to pay a few kroners more at night and on weekends when a 15 percent surcharge goes into effect. Taxis may be engaged at a taxi stand, on the street (so long as you are not standing within 100 meters of a taxi stand), or booked by telephone. Drivers usually speak English.

AUTO

Major auto rental companies have agents at airports and in the cities, but rates are high. An international driving permit or national driving license is required. Traffic drives on the right and seatbelts are mandatory, as are running headlights, even during the day. Parking, especially in cities and towns, is difficult. Gas stations are abundant, although tourists may only use credit cards in many of them. Motorists encounter road tolls also, costing anywhere from NKr5 to NKr50.

With Norway's mountainous geography, roads tend to be narrow and twisting. The northerly latitude causes road conditions to be unpredictable, depending on the time of year and current weather conditions. Many roads are closed altogether from late fall until late spring, due to snowfall.

Drivers should be aware that posted speed limits are substantially lower than those in other European countries. Penalties for drunk driving are severe, and police controls occur frequently in the evening and at night. Foreigners are not exempt.

For emergency road service and further information, contact the Norwegian Automobile Association.

Norwegian Automobile Association (NAF)
P.O. Box 494 Sentrum
0105 Oslo, Norway
tel: 2234 1400; fax: 2234 1420
email: nafmaster@publicis.no

website: http://www.naf.no

TRAIN

An excellent train system services Norway's vast expanse, as well as the territories of Sweden and Finland. If traveling north, one can catch some glimpses of Norway's famous fjords and spectacular scenery.

The main routes are:

* Oslo–Trondheim (Dovre Line)
* Trondheim–Bodø (Nordland Railway)
* Oslo–Bergen (Bergen Railway)
* Oslo–Stavanger (Sorland Railway).

There are also connections to Halden (Malmö) and to Charlottenburg (Stockholm) along routes to Sweden. The Oslo-Bergen line is especially popular and requires reservations well in advance.

Passengers must make advance reservations for passage on express trains. Some services offer buffet/restaurant service, and sleeping cars (private or communal) that may even include feather blankets! Heavy luggage may be sent ahead of time.

Scanrail passes are available for 21 days of unlimited rail travel within Denmark, Norway, Sweden, and Finland. Passes also cover some ferry routes, and 50 percent off the fare of others.

For more detailed information, contact NSB (Norwegian State Railways). tel: 8150 0888; fax: 6127 9097; website: http://www.nsb.no

SUBWAY

Consisting of eight lines, Oslo's underground system makes for a pleasant journey through town. Stations are recognizable by the 'T' sign. A single-fare ticket will start at about NKr18. Fares should be purchased in advance and self-cancelled in machines on board.

Transport Passes

An Oslo Card will not only afford you access to public transportation, but to various museums and attractions as well. A one-day pass will cost NKr130.

BUS /TRAM

Buses and trams service Oslo efficiently and punctually. Pay the driver on board.

Norway also has a comprehensive long-distance bus network, with links between every major city and to more remote areas.

Norway

Principal routes are:
- Bø (in Telemark) to Haugesund (8 hours)
- Ålesund–Molde–Kristiansund to Trondheim (8 hours)
- Fauske to Kirkenes (4 days), with connections to the northern Bø line

The Inter-Nordic line operates between Trondheim and Stockholm. Extensive regional services are also provided, a number of which are owned and operated by companies that have interests in ferry lines. For route information and seat reservations, contact NOR-WAY Bussekspress AS. tel: (81) 544 444; fax: (23) 002 449; email: ruteinformasjon@nor-way.com; website: http://www.nor-way.no.

WATER TRAVEL

Bergen and the northern coastal towns are linked by steamers, which offer views of the islands and fjords. Obviously not meant for business travel, water travel is meant for travelers with time and a penchant for sightseeing. As with other forms of transport in Norway, service is punctual. Schedules vary by season.

TRAVEL ASSISTANCE

Tourist Information
Norwegian Tourist Board (Norges Turistrad)
Drammensveien 40, P.O. Box 2893 Solli
NO-0230 Oslo, Norway
tel: 2292-5200; fax: 2256-0505
email: norway@ntr.no
website: http://www.ntr.no (or)
www.visitnorway.com
Oslo Promotion
Oslo Visitors and Convention Bureau
Grev Wedels plass 4
NO - 0151 Oslo
tel: 2310-6200; fax: 2310-6201
website: www.oslopro.no
Tourist Information Office; Vestbaneplassen 1. Oslo; tel: 2283-0050.

Communications

DIALING CODES IN NORWAY
International country code: [47]
City codes: There are no city codes for any area of Norway. All phone numbers are eight digits.

Dialing Norway from Overseas
To dial Norway from overseas, dial your country's international dialing code, then 47 (the country code for Norway), and the number. All telephone numbers in Oslo have changed to eight digits and begin with 22 or 23.

Assistance Numbers
International Operator	00
International Information (English)	181
Domestic Operator	117
Domestic or Scandinavian Information	180

CALLING WITHIN NORWAY

Local Calls
Dial all digits when placing a call anywhere in Norway. Local calls cost NKr2 or NKr3 from public and hotel phones.

Long Distance Calls
Check a phone directory for English instructions. Calling within Norway should be quite straightforward. Be sure to have plenty of NKr5 or 10 coins when calling with change.

International Calls
You can attempt direct dialing from most any telephone. Dial 095 + country code + number. The cheapest rates are available between 5p.m. and 8a.m. Remember to inquire first about hotel rates to avoid suffering from shock. If you prefer, speak with an overseas operator and he or she will assist you with credit card or collect calls, perhaps even to other countries:
Australia Direct	800-199-61
British Telecom	800-190-44
Canada Direct	800-191-11
Ireland Direct	800-193-53
South Africa Direct	800-199-27
U.S. AT&T Direct	800-190-11
U.S. MCI	800-199-12

The main telephone offices (telegrafkontor) are usually located in city centers. In Oslo the office is located at: Kongensgate 21; Monday to Friday 8:30a.m. to 9p.m., weekends 10a.m. to 5p.m.

PAY PHONES

Public Telephones
Coin Phone:

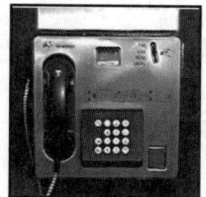

Phones can be found everywhere in Norway. Use NKr1, 5, or 10 coins. The minimum deposit is 2 Krone.
To use a push-button phone:
1. Lift receiver
2. Wait for dial tone
3. Insert coins
4. Dial number

A screen on the phone will indicate how much credit you have left. Short beeps during your conversation indicate your time is almost finished.

Calling Cards
Norway has new, green pay phones using special cards available at kiosks.

CELLULAR PHONES
Telenor Mobil A/S and *Netcom GSM A/S* provide digital users with a GSM system in Norway. For analogue users, *Telenor Mobil* also provides NMT-450 and NMT-900 systems. The Nordic Mobile Telephone (NMT) system is designed for the rougher Scandinavian terrain and operates on a different frequency than do analogues in the United States.
Note: Your home country cell phone may not work in this country. If not, we recommend that you rent an international cell phone *before* you leave home. A major US-based cell phone rental provider is **IMC WorldCell**. For information see "International Cell Phone Rentals" on page 14.

CALL BACK
You can (potentially) save significant sums when calling in Norway by using one of the call back services listed below. Fees for callback services vary widely, depending on the company and the type of service required. Be sure to check with these companies before leaving to compare rates.
For a list of callback services, please refer to the "Communications" section in the *Global Road Warrior* Introduction.

Norway

PHONE JACKS

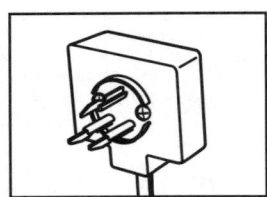

Plug adaptors are available through **iGo Corporation.** (See "Electrical and Telephone Adaptors" on page 19.)

FAX

Fax machines are widely available, in post offices and most hotels.

POSTAL SERVICES

The postal service is generally very good. Mail within Europe will take about 2 to 4 days. Purchase stamps at kiosks or hotel desks if you cannot find a post office. The main post office in Oslo is located at Dronningensgate 15.

Hours of service
Main Post Office:
Monday to Friday 9a.m. to 8p.m.
Saturday 9a.m. to 3p.m.

Local Post Offices
Monday- Friday 8a.m. or 8:30a.m. to 4p.m. or 4:30p.m.
Saturday 9a.m. to 1p.m.

Business Services

BUSINESS CENTERS/SERVICES

Regus Business Centre Oslo AS; C J Hambros pl 2 C; tel: 2299-6000.

Siemens Business Services A/S; PO Box 120 Veitvet, Ostre Aker Vei 90, Oslo; tel: 2263-2000; fax: 2263-2008.

COMPUTER RENTALS

MacRent; Thomas Heftyes gate 52; tel: (2) 443030.

COURIER SERVICES

Airborne Express; Intersped As, Postboks 324 Okern, 0511 Oslo; tel: 2265-6550; fax: 2265-8825.

DHL; PO Box Pb. 203, Alnabru 0614 Oslo; tel: 8100-1345; fax: 2264-6693.

Express Bud AS; Verkseier Furulunds v 49; tel: 2290-5757.

Euro City Transport; Stansev. 2, Postboks 170 Kalbakken; tel: 2333-8100.

Federal Express (Universal FDX AS);
Oslo Aircargo Center, Edvard Griegs veg 2060 Gardermoen, Norway; tel: 6394-0300; fax: 6394-0390.

UPS; UPS of Norway Inc., Stromsveien 344, 1081 Oslo; tel: (800) 33-470; fax: 2232-3420.

TRANSLATION SERVICES

Noricom; Kjøpmannsgata 11; PO Box 341, Sentrum, 7001 Trondheim; tel: (47) 7350-2300; fax: (47) 7350-2530; email: anthun.spraaktjenester@noricom.no.

Electrical

Current
220 volts AC, 50Hz.

ELECTRIC PLUGS

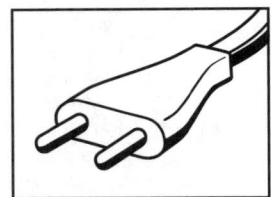

Plug adaptors are available through **iGo Corporation.** (See "Electrical and Telephone Adaptors" on page 19.)

Technical Support

HARDWARE/SOFTWARE VENDOR SUPPORT

Apple/Claris; tel: (800) 11-006; (in Switzerland) tel: [41] (800) 833-310; (in the U.K.) tel: [44] (990) 127-753; (in the U.S.) tel: [1] (408) 996-1010 (Corporate Headquarters); http://www.apple.com/.

Compaq/Digital; tel: 2207-2000; fax: 2207-2001; 2207-2020 (CompaqCare Center); 2207-2022 (QuickLine); (in Switzerland) tel: [41] (22) 709-5330; fax: [41] (22) 709-5391 (Geneva); tel: [41] (1) 801-2507; fax: [41] (1) 801-2172 (Zurich); (General U.S.) tel: (281) 518-2000; http://www.compaq.com/.

Dell; tel: [47] 67116800; fax: [47] 67116865; (Dell- Europe) tel: [44] (134) 474-8000; (in the U.S.) tel: [1] (512) 338-4400; fax: [1] (512) 728-3330; http://www.dell.com/.

Hewlett Packard; tel: (0) 22 116299; (in Switzerland) tel: [41] (22) 780-8111; (in the U.S.) tel: [1] (408) 246-4300; http://www.hp.com/.

IBM; tel: 6699-8000 (toll free within Norway); fax: 6699-9333; (in Switzerland) tel: [41] (22) 310-0418 (in French); (in the U.S.) tel: [1] (919) 517-2800; http://www.ibm.com/.

Microsoft; tel: (22) 22-550; fax: (22) 95-0664; (22) 22-580 (Microsoft Sales Support); (in Switzerland) tel: [41] (848) 858-868; fax [41] (1) 831-0869; (in the U.S.) [1] (425) 635-7222; http://www.microsoft.com/.

Internet Connection

HOW TO CONNECT

Connecting to AOL and Compuserve in Norway is similar to using it when traveling outside your own area code. See the introductory section for detailed information on connecting to your account through a different phone number.

America Online

Numbers are available at keyword *international*. Be sure to get several local numbers before leaving. AOL's GlobalNet service charges US$6 an hour in addition to the usual charges. Go to keyword *access* (a free area) and download the software.

Access: All Parts of Norway 2241-8710; Trondheim 7350-3800.

Compuserve

Numbers are available at *Go International*. The Compuserve Web-site also has a great deal of information, at http://www.compuserve.com.

Access: Bergen 5522-7105; Oslo 2318-4444; Stavanger 5169-9914.

Independent Service Providers

Many independent service providers offer discounts if you are only in town for a couple of days.

Bergen Nett og Media AS; tel: 5592-6700; fax: 5592-6701; email: drift@bgnett.no; http://www.bgnett.no/; (Norwegian only).

MultiNet AS; tel: 7387-4410; fax: 7387-4411; email: info@multinet.no; http://www.multinet.no/.

Nextra AS; tel: 2277-1900; fax: 2277-1910; email: firmapost@nextra.no; http://www.nextel.no/; (Norwegian only).

Telia Internett AS; tel: 2201-2950; http://internett.telia.no/.

INTERNET CAFES

Oslo

Akers Mic Nettcafe; Akersgata 39 Oslo; tel: 2241-2190; email: underworld105@hotmail.com; Monday through Saturday, 12p.m. to 8p.m.; NKr40 per hour of use.

Studenten; Karl Johansgate 45, Oslo; tel: 2242-5680; email: studenten@studenten-cafe.no; http://www.studenten-cafe.no/; Monday through Saturday, 12p.m. to 8p.m.; NKr40 per hour of use.

Underworld - Internet Cafe & Bar; Akersgata 39, Oslo; tel: 2233-3898; email: underworld105@hotmail.com; Monday through Friday, 11a.m. to 7p.m, Saturday 11a.m. to 6p.m; free computer use.

Business Culture

GREETINGS AND COURTESIES

Be prepared for a tight grip when shaking hands with your Norwegian associates, both men and women. Upon initially meeting, use titles followed by the family name. In most cases, you'll quickly be asked to use first names, perhaps even nick-names, as formal address is not the custom in either the business or social communities. Titles are seldom used, but be attentive to how Norwegian co-workers address one another and follow the lead. Be sure to stand when being introduced.

BUSINESS ETHIC AND FRAMEWORK

The business environment is both reserved and relaxed, and while Norwegians are pleasant to do business with, they keep business and personal relationships separate. If sending a letter of self-introduction, provide plenty of background information regarding your firm, and clearly state your purpose and intentions. In Norway, punctuality counts in establishing confidence and trust, so be on time.

DECISION MAKING

Due to an informal and direct business climate, one may expect easy access to top management without the typical front office formalities and hoopla. Decisions are made by consensus; they take time and require patience. It is advised that foreign ventures highlight the national advantages to Norway in their propositions for business relations. Be aware that punctuality and strict adherence to payment and delivery date contracts are key elements in Norwegian business.

MEETINGS

Meetings should be scheduled in advance, and take care to arrive on time. One can rest assured that your audience has done its homework on your firm, products, competitors, etc. Your presentation should be straightforward and sufficiently backed with essential points, supporting data, and pertinent substance regarding your proposition. Norwegians have a knack of getting straight to the point in an economy that relies almost completely on buying and selling, thus prompting a desire to keep developing new business relationships.

WOMEN

Norwegian women are found working in every aspect of the business community, holding high positions in government agencies and other organizations. A few women top executives are also present in shipping, rail transport, and banking. Women in business can expect to be treated with respect, and as in most of the rest of forward-thinking Scandinavia, they are not openly discriminated against.

BUSINESS ATTIRE

Conservative, casual dress is customary. Light–weight attire is appropriate in summer months. Business suits are more commonly seen in winter months. In many offices, however, men wear sweaters instead of jackets and ties. Women also dress informally, in dresses or coordinated outfits. However, fashion trends are present in the streets and a nordic avant garde fashion prevails. Take necessary woolens and wraps for the frigid winter months.

Business Centers
Oslo

CITY VIEW

Oslo is historically renowned as a quiet and small capital. In recent years the city has come into its own, offering cultural, culinary, and visual delight without losing its quaint and traditional flair. Most of the city can be reached by walking from the city center, which is unusually pedestrian friendly. The natural surroundings allow Oslo some welcome reprieve from the usual big-city, concrete-jungle syndrome.

Harald III of Norway founded Oslo at the beginning of the twentieth century, but the settlement was actually already well inhabited as a royal viking residence prior to Harald's claim. A Viking Museum exists in the city today depicting much of Norway's rich and noble past. Oslo was destroyed by a fire in 1624 but rebuilt rather meticulously through endeavors subsequently put forth by King Christian IV of Denmark and Norway.

The nautical tactics initiated by the vikings live on in Oslo today, but shipping has recently been surpassed by advanced technology industries. Telecommunications, biotechnology, information technology, petroleum and offshore exploration, and engineering businesses now employ the majority of Oslo's 480,000 residents.

AIRPORT

Gardermoen Airport to City Center

With the closure of Fornebu Airport in late 1998, Gardermoen Airport provides Oslo with a more up to date facility for air travel in and out of Norway. Unfortunately, the 33 kilometer distance from Oslo's center prompts higher transport prices. Expect to pay about NKr650 or more for a taxi into town. A more budget-friendly alternative exists in buses that take passengers to the Airport Bus Terminal, located behind the main train station in Oslo, which stands a short distance from hotels and pedestrian center. The 50-minute ride will cost NKr60.

Oslo Airport 8155-0250

Airline Numbers

American Airlines 8001-0120
Austrian Airlines 8100-0125
Braathens ASA.................................... 8152-0000
Delta Airlines TMS.............................. 2293-6630
Icelandair.. 2203-4050
Iran Air.. 2283-7460
Lufthansa.. 8100-3300
Malaysia Airlines 2291-0730
SAS 2217-0020
SAFE 6712-2070

HOTELS

Top-end

The Continental; Stortingsg. 24/26; tel: 2282-4000; Theatercafe; restaurant; conference facilities; secretarial service; fax/photocopy facilities; Internet; in-room modem/fax connection; in-room fax machine upon request; corporate rates.

The Grand; Karl Johansgate 31; tel: 2321-2000; fax: 2342-1225; traditional abode of Nobel winners; city center; restaurant; conference center (up to 310); redecorated rooms; secretarial service; fax/photocopy facilities; in-room modem/fax connection; dual phone lines; in-room safe; fitness; spa; sauna; pool.

Radisson SAS Plaza; Sonja Henie Plass 3; tel: 2205-8000; fax: 2205- 8010; adjacent to Central Rail Station; restaurants; Sky bar; conference hotel (up to 1,100); secretarial service; fax/photocopy facilities; SAS check-in; business rooms available; in-room safe; corporate rates; sauna; rooftop pool.

Radisson SAS Scandinavia; Holbergsgate 30; tel: 2329-3000; fax: 113-017; near Royal Palace; SAS check-in; airport shuttle; health; fitness; solarium; pool.

Royal Christiania; tel: 2310-8000; fax: 2310-8080; near rail station; restaurant; bar; conference facilities (up to 450); corporate rates; in-room tv, telephone, hairdryer; fitness; swimming pool; sauna.

Expensive

Ambassadeur (Best Western); Camilla Collettsvel 15; tel: 2327-2300; email: post@hotelambassadeur.no; located in diplomatic section; themed rooms; restaurant; conference facilities; secretarial service; sauna; pool.

First Hotel Bastion; Skippergt. 7, PO Box 27 Sentrum; tel: 2247-7700; fax: 2233-1180; bar; conference facilities; business center; sauna; whirlpool.

Frogner House; Skovveien 8; tel: 2255-3782; fax: 2256-0500; city center; meeting facilities (up to 10); secretarial service; fax/photocopy facilities; hotel safe; corporate rates.

Gabelshus; Gabels Gate 16; tel: 2327-6500; fax: 2327-6560; restaurant; conference facilities (up to 150); secretarial service; fax/photocopy facilities; corporate rates.

Moderate

Bondeheimen; Rosenkrantzgt 8; tel: (2) 42-95-30; fax: (2) 41-94-37; city center; meeting facilities (up to 25); corporate rates; sauna.

Clarion Hotel Royal Christiania; Biskop Gunnerusgate 3; tel: 2310-8000; fax: 2310-8080; restaurant; bar; conference facilities; business center; in-room data port, air conditioning, cable tv, minibar; room service; parking; fitness; swimming pool; tennis.

Helfsfyr; Stromsvn 108; tel: (2) 265-7000; fax: (2) 645-252.

Hotel Foenix, Dronningens Gate 19; tel: 2242-5957; fax: 2233-1210; email: info@foenix.com; 64 rooms; located in downtown Oslo, approximately a 3 minute walk from the Central train and bus stations; restaurant; in-room tv, private bath.

Hotel Stefan; Rosenkratzgate 1; tel: 2331-5500; fax: 2333-7022; email: stefan@rainbow-hotels.no; central location; restaurant; conference facilities; business center; in-room telephone, data port, air conditioning, cable tv, mini bar; fitness.

MEDICAL CARE

City Medical Center; tel: 2217-0950.

Emergency Medical Service; tel: 2211-7777.

Jernbanetorvets Apotek—24-hour Pharmacy; Jernbanetorget 4B; tel: 2241-2482; fax: 2236-3410.

The National Hospital University of Oslo; Pilestredet 32; tel: 2886-7010; fax: 2286-7580.

Oslo Kommunale Tannlegavakt: Toyen Senter - Dental services; Kolstadgata 18; tel: 2267-3000.

HEALTH CLUB

Better Bodies Gym; Bergensv. 2 A; tel: 2216-3848.

Galaxy Sport & Fitness Club; Veitvetv. 8; tel: 2216-1156.

High Energy; 10 Osterhausgaten; tel: 2236-0600.

Friskoteket A/S; 9A Bogstadveien; tel: 2246-0090.

the SAS Scandinavia; 30 Holbergsgate; tel: 2211-3000.

Yogasenteret; Bogstadv. 11; tel: 2259-1975.

AUTO RENTAL

Avis; Munkedamsveien 27, Oslo; tel: 2323-9200.

Budget Rent a Car; at Fornebu Airport; tel: 6753-7924; downtown at the Oslo Spektrum; tel: 2217-1050.

Europcar; Gardermoen - Airport, Arrival Hall; tel: 6481-0560; fax: 6481-0561; Oslo- Haakon VII Gate 9; tel: 2283-1242; fax: 2283-1243.

Hertz; Fornebu Airport; tel: 6758-3100;

SAS Scandinavia Hotel 30, Holbergsgate; tel: 2221-0000; fax: 2211-0093; Volvo Isberg, Oekernveien 115; tel: 2265-6610; fax: 2265-3550.

WORLD TRADE CENTER

World Trade Center Oslo
Pilestredet 17; 0164 Oslo Norway
tel: 2220-9808; fax: 2236-1920

CHAMBER OF COMMERCE

Oslo Chamber of Commerce
Drammensveien, 30 - 0255 OSLO 2;
tel: 2255-7400; fax: 2253-8853

Norwegian Trade Council
Drammensveien 40; 0243 Oslo Norway
tel: 2292-6300; fax: 2292-6400
website: http://www.index.no

Oman

Oman

At a Glance

THE PEOPLE

Population .... 2,533,389 (July 2000 est.)
Growth Rate .... 3.46% (2000 est.)
Life Expectancy .... 71.78 years
Infant Mortality . 23.28 deaths/1,000 live births (2000 est.)

Ethnic Composition

Arab, Baluchi, South Asian (Indian, Pakistani, Sri Lankan, Bangladeshi), African.

Religious Composition

Ibadhi Muslim 75%
Also: Sunni Muslim, Shi'a Muslim, Hindu

Languages Spoken

Arabic (official), English, Baluchi, Urdu, and Indian dialects.

Education and Literacy

Since 1970, the government has made education a high priority in order to enhance the domestic workforce. In 1986, Oman's first university opened. Students are awarded yearly government scholarships for study abroad. Literacy is approaching 80 percent.

Labor force

Total: 850,000
By occupation: NA.

THE ECONOMY

Oman's economic strength lies in its oil industry. In 1999, its economic position improved significantly, due mainly to the mid-year increase in oil prices. The government is proceeding with the development of commercial law to draw foreign investment, the privatization of its utilities, and increasing budgetary outlays. Oman continues to liberalize its markets in an effort to gain access into to the World Trade Organization (WTO). Its financial situation in 2000 looks up with the increase in oil prices.

Exports .... US$7.2 billion (f.o.b., 1999 est.)
Imports .... US$5.4 billion (f.o.b., 1999 est.)
Total Trade .... US$12.6 billion (1999 est.)
GDP Per Capita .... US$8,000 (1999 est.)
Unemployment .... NA%
Inflation Rate .... -0.07% (1999 est.)

Top Export Partners

Japan 21%, China 16%, Thailand 16%, South Korea 12%, U.S. 3%.

Top Import Partners

U.A.E. 23% (largely reexports), Japan 16%, U.K. 13%, U.S. 7.5%, Germany 5%.

Top Exports

Petroleum, reexports, fish, metals, textiles.

Top Imports

Machinery, transportation equipment, manufactured goods, food, livestock, lubricants.

BUSINESS WORKWEEK

Offices

Saturday to Wednesday 8a.m. to 1p.m. and 4p.m. to 7p.m. Thursday 8a.m. to 1p.m. These hours are slightly reduced during the Holy Month of Fasting, Ramadan.

Banks

Saturday to Wednesday 8a.m. to noon. Thursday 8a.m. to 11:30a.m.

Government

Saturday to Wednesday 7:30a.m. to 2:30p.m. During Ramadan, offices open and close one hour later than usual.

Retail

Saturday to Thursday 8a.m. to noon or 1p.m., 4p.m. to 8p.m. Some retail outlets are also open Thursday for slightly shorter hours. Most are closed on Friday. Souks are open Sunday to Thursday 8a.m. to 11a.m. and 4p.m. to 7p.m.

HOLIDAYS

Id al-Fitr, End of Ramadan .... January 8*
Id al-Adha, Feast of the Sacrifice .... March 18*
Muharram, Islamic New Year................................. April 7*
Mouloud, Birth of the Prophet............................. June 16*
Leilat al-Mairaj, Ascension
of the Prophet.. October 27*
National Day... November 18
Birthday of the Sultan .... November 19
Ramadan begins .... November 30*
Id al-Fitr, End of Ramadan .... December 31*
   *Exact date may vary.

CLIMATE

Seasons

Hot and humid along the coast, hot and dry in the interior, summer monsoon in the far north. Oman experiences extremely hot and humid summers and mild winters. December to March the climate hovers around 10°c to 30°C (50°-87°F), but then it gets exceedingly hot with summer temperatures rising to as high as 48°C (118°F), with humidity of 100 percent on the coast. Unless you are a true heat lover, winters are the best time to visit.

Regions

A few regional climate differences exist in Oman, although it tends to remain hotter in the desert area and inland than in coastal regions.

Money & Banking

Currency

The currency of Oman is the Omani Rial (OR).

Denominations

The Omani Rial comes in con denominations of 500, 250, 200, 100, 50, 25, 10 and 5 baiza; and banknotes of 100, 200, 250 and 500 baiza, and RO1, 5, 10, 20 and 50.

Traveler's checks

Traveler's checks and currency can be exchanged at banks, exchange shops, hotels, and international airports at tourist exchange rates. Larger banks may offer the best exchange rates, but avoid black marketers at all cost. Consult your bank about current exchange rates before departure. Keep all receipts for reconversion. Banks do not cash personal checks.

Most currencies can also be exchanged, but try to take only crisp and new notes, wrinkled and soiled notes are likely to be refused.

Oman

Major credit cards, American Express, Visa, Diner's Club, and MasterCard, are easily accepted in most up-market places in the cities, but smaller restaurants and *souks* (markets) may ask for cash. Some banks in the capital offer cash advances on credit cards, but make sure you bring your passport.

Travel

VISA AND PASSPORT

All visitors must have a passport (valid for at least 3 months from the time of entry) and a business or tourist visa. A visitor may obtain a Business visa (but not a Tourist visa) that provides for multiple entries and maximum individual visits of six months. For the business traveler, validity of the visa can be as long as two years, depending on nationality and other criteria. The longest-term tourist visa is three months, single or multiple entry.

The first step in being issued a visa is to get a No Objection Certificate (NOC) from the Royal Oman Police Immigration Department. This official document states that there is no objection from any quarter of your entering the country (NOC's are not required for U.S. citizens and some others—check with the Oman embassy as to the status of your

country). Note that women traveling unaccompanied seem to encounter no obstacles procuring an NOC.

The NOC may be issued at an embassy, or one's hotel can make the necessary arrangements in advance. Send a copy of the first page of your passport and four passport photos, along with your itinerary specifying date and time of arrival in particular, and a contact telephone number where you may be notified when your NOC is ready. Allow about ten days for this service, for which you will be charged a small fee; you will also be expected to stay in the hotel for at least three nights.

When you receive your NOC's number, a fax or telex will go to your airline from Omani Immigration with the number of your NOC and authorization to permit you to board a flight to Muscat. Without this number, you would not be permitted to board the aircraft. When you reach the Muscat airport, you must proceed to an NOC window, where an officer will give you a form that you then take to the agent at passport control, who will give you your visa.

Allow approximately one week for processing of your NOC application, if made in person at an embassy or consulate—two to three weeks is typical for postal applications. Having your hotel or company sponsor handle the NOC advance is clearly the best way to handle it.

Entry into the country is strictly controlled. Unless specifically designated on a visa or NOC, one may not enter the country by road. Officials will frequently search baggage and may confiscate video tapes to determine if they are pornographic. Anyone attempting entry without prior permission will be deported on the next exiting flight.

Restricted Entry

Any journalist planning to work in the country must apply to the Ministry of Information. Palestinian-born people will probably encounter difficulties obtaining an NOC. Travelers bearing Israeli passports will be refused transit or entry.

DEPARTURE FORMALITIES

An airport departure tax of OR3 is charged to all international travelers. One may not export antique Omani daggers *(Khanjars)*, meaning those over 50 years old.

CUSTOMS ENTRY (PERSONAL)

Duty-free

- Perfume: 227ml perfume and eau de cologne
- A reasonable amount of tobacco products for personal use only
- Non-Muslims may bring in one litre of alcoholic beverage

Prohibited or Restricted

- Alcohol
- Narcotics
- Fresh foods
- Firearms (including toys and replicas)
- Pornographic films/literature

Note: Videos are subject to censorship. All animals need an import license; dogs and cats from rabies infected areas will be quarantined for six months.

IMMUNIZATION

Vaccinations against yellow fever are required of anyone arriving from an infected area. Anti malaria precautions are strongly recommended. Typhoid, gamma globulin, tetanus, and polio shots are also recommended.

Pet owners must submit a rabies vaccination record and a health certificate. Importing any pet requires a permit from the Ministry of Agriculture and Fisheries/Department of Animal Health before travel. Pets may be subjected to a six-month quarantine, which may not be required if the pet comes from a rabies-free area.

TIPPING

The practice did not used to be expected in general, but it has become more popular and fairly widespread now. Ten percent is a reliable amount.

Taxi

Ten percent is customary.

Porters

Tip bag handlers and facilitators 200 baizas per piece.

Hotels

Ten percent gratuity is usually included in the final bill, but it generally does not go to service personnel. Tip individually for best effect.

Restaurants

As with hotels.

Other

Barbers, beauticians: 5 to 10 percent. Small services: 100 baizas.

EMERGENCY INFORMATION

Police and Crime

Crime is low in Oman, but take basic precautions — especially in crowded tourist areas, where pickpockets are common. A few elementary precautions should protect the traveler from most problems:

- Do not leave valuables in cars or on tables in cafés.
- Keep non-essential valuables locked in hotel safes.
- Use credit cards and traveler's checks when possible to avoid carrying large sums of cash.
- Carry photocopies of your passport instead of the original.
- Carry cash in a money belt, and use credit cards or travelers checks for most of your large transactions.
- Never carry a stranger's baggage.
- Women should avoid traveling alone at night

In case of crime, report to the police, who are generally helpful and efficient. Women are advised to dress modestly to avoid verbal abuse.

Emergency Numbers

All services 999

Health

Outside Muscat, do not drink tap water or use ice cubes; bottled water is safe and available. Wash all vegetables in a chlorine solution, peel fruits, and avoid uncooked food. Drink only powdered or tinned milk and avoid other dairy products since they are most likely unpasteurized. Only eat meat and fish that have been well-cooked and preferably served hot. Mayonnaise, pork, and salad often bear increased risk of intestinal problems. Avoid food from street vendors, but virtually all restaurant fare is perfectly healthy.

Oman's public health service is extensive (and free for Omani nationals). There are about 86 health centers, 65 preventive health centers, and 46 hospitals. Quality of care is excellent, with many doctors and nurses who have been educated in the West. Costs are high for foreign patients.

A travel insurance package that includes an evacuation policy should be acquired by all business travelers. Medical evacuation is expensive, and payment of costs must be borne by the visitor.

INTERNAL TRAVEL

AIR

Oman Air (WY) provides domestic operations, flying between Salalah and Seeb airports in approximately 90 minutes, as well as scheduled flights to Khasab, Sur, and Dibba and Massirah Island. Inquire through your hotel or travel agent.

TAXI

Taxis are typically very expensive. Prices should be decided before leaving. The network of microbus/taxis and service taxis is extensive. These shared vehicles may also be engaged for only one passenger.

AUTO

Rental cars are available from Avis and Budget, with offices in hotels throughout Oman. Rates are high. Visitors must have a driver's license or International Driving Permit to show in order to obtain a local license from the police. It remains valid for 90 days only, but a new one may be procured. Severe penalties are levied for drinking while intoxicated.

Much has been accomplished with Oman's infrastructure in terms of asphalt roads. Isolated communities have now been connected to main centers, and mountain roads have been constructed. Primary routes run north to south. With the network of roads in the country completed, attention is now turning to improving local road networks.

Oman

BUS

ONAT (Oman National Transport Company) offers service to the major provincial towns. Service is comfortable but can be slow. Reservations are only accepted for express luxury bus service to Salalah. Expect a long haul of 12 hours. A twice-daily service also travels to Dubai and takes about six hours. The main bus center is located in Ruwi, Muscat where you can find bus timetables.

WATER TRAVEL

Salalah acts as Oman's major seaport and lies about 600km. south of Muscat.

TRAVEL ASSISTANCE

Directorate General of Tourism
P.O. Box 550
Postal Code 113, Muscat, Sultanate of Oman
tel: 796 527; fax: 794 213 or 794 239
email: tourism@mocioman.org
website: http://www.mocioman.org

Essential Terms

English	Arabic
Yes	Na-a'am
No	La; mish
Good morning	Al sa-lahm
Hello (daytime)	Al sa-lahm
Hello (evening)	Ma-sa'el khair
Hello (telephone)	Marhaban
Good-bye	Be-kha-trahk
Please	Min-fahd-lak (M)
	Min-fahd-lik (F)
Thank you	Shook-rahn
Pleased to meet you	Sorirart biro'aitak
Excuse me; I'm sorry	Is-ma-leh
My name is _____	Ismii____
I don't understand	An-na mish fahem
Do you speak English?	Hal tatakallumu l-inkliziyya?

Communications

DIALING CODES IN OMAN

International country code: [968]

City codes: There are no city codes for any area of Oman. All phone numbers are six digits.

Dialing Oman from Overseas

To dial Oman from overseas, dial your country's international dialing code, then 968 (the country code for Oman), and finally the number. There are no city codes.

Assistance Numbers
International Operator 195
Directory Assistance (English) 198
Operator 190

CALLING WITHIN OMAN

Local Calls
Yet another smooth-running telephone system in the Arab Peninsula makes local dialing quite straightforward and painless. All numbers have six digits.

Long Distance Calls
No area codes exist in Oman; simply pick up and dial the number you wish to reach.

International Calls
Dialing home direct is no problem even at a card phone. Dial 00 + country code + area code + number. You can also call from a telephone office.

PAY PHONES

Public Telephones
Card Phone:

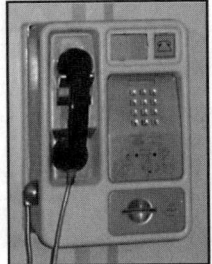

Calling Cards
Most phones are of the card variety. Phone cards can be purchased at central telephone offices.

CELLULAR PHONES
General Telecom Organization operates an analogue NMT-450 system as well as a GSM system for digital users.

Note: Your home country cell phone may not work in this country. If not, we recommend that you rent an international cell phone *before* you leave home. A major US-based cell phone rental provider is **IMC WorldCell**. For information see "International Cell Phone Rentals" on page 14.

PHONE JACKS

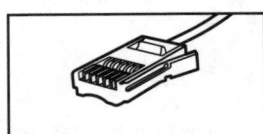

Plug adaptors are available through **iGo Corporation.** (See "Electrical and Telephone Adaptors" on page 19.)

FAX

Fax machines are proliferate in Oman, largely replacing the postal service as the main means of business communications.

POSTAL SERVICES

Mail service within the capital is good, but not as reliable as anywhere else. There is no home delivery. Airmail to Europe or North America can take up to three weeks.

Business Services

BUSINESS CENTER

Note: Many hotels have business centers for guests that include secretarial services, PC and printers, translations, photocopying, communications, boardrooms.

COURIER SERVICE

DHL; Rumaila 106, Sultan Qaboos St., Wattayah, PO Box 833, Ruwi 112; tel: 563-599; Saturday to Thursday 7a.m. to 10p.m., Friday 9a.m. to 6p.m., Holidays 9a.m. to 6p.m.

Federal Express; Oman Express, tel: 773-3311; fax: 773-5554.

UPS; Travel and Allied Services LLC, Eihab Bldg., Muttrah High Street, P.O. Box 889, 113 Muttrah, Muscat; tel: 796-989; fax: 793-849.

TRANSLATION SERVICES

Buzalma Trading; 424 PC 118; tel: 566-430.

Polyglot Institute; tel: 707-475.

Electrical

CURRENT

240 volts AC, 50Hz.

ELECTRIC PLUGS

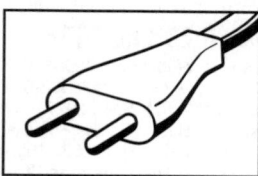

Plug adaptors are available through **iGo Corporation**. (See "Electrical and Telephone Adaptors" on page 19.)

Internet Connection

HOW TO CONNECT

Connecting to AOL and Compuserve in Oman is similar to using it when traveling outside your own area code. See the introductory section for detailed information on connecting to your account through a different phone number.

America Online

Numbers are available at keyword international. Be sure to get several local numbers before leaving. Go to keyword access (a free area) and download the software. The connection charge will cost you US$6 an hour in addition to the usual charges.

Access: Muscat 706-844.

Compuserve

Numbers are available at *Go International*. The Compuserve Web-site also has a great deal of information, at http://www.compuserve.com.

Access: Muscat 706-844.

Independent Service Providers

Many independent service providers offer discounts if you are only in town for a couple of days.

Fiberlink Communications Corp.; tel: [1] (714) 788-2904 (although a United States company, Fiberlink has access numbers for Oman Internet users); http://www.fiberlinkcc.com/.

Oman Internet; tel: 1313 (toll-free in Oman); tel: 696-844; fax: fax 691-338; fax: 631-600; email: mohammed@gto.net.om; http://www.gto.net.om/.

Business Culture

GREETINGS AND COURTESIES

English is the primary business language, although Arabic is the official language of the country. Omanis hold titles in high regard. Always use professional titles like doctor or professor. If you are a Ph.D., be sure to have it printed on your business card; it may help sway your Omani counterparts. Until recently, Omanis weren't allowed higher education; consequently, in many cases, an Omani will respect a degree more than an individual's competence.

BUSINESS ETHIC AND FRAMEWORK

One of the most modern of the Gulf countries, Oman is considered more tolerant of Western culture than are many other Arab countries. Omanis are very honest in their business dealings, and expect foreigners to be the same. Personal relationships dictate business transactions.

MEETINGS AND DECISION MAKING

Generally one decisionmaker exists in a company. Always make prior appointments for business meetings, and foreigners should arrive on time. However, one may encounter others to have an appointment at the same time. Expect continuous interruptions by family, friends, and business associates, as well as by frequent telephone calls and servings of coffee, tea, or another beverage, which one should not decline to uphold politeness. Omanis place great importance on polite gestures and do not respond well to overly frank words. Once the business discussion has begun, however, it will proceed in a relatively straightforward manner, unless it occurs during prayer time, when a host may halt proceedings to pray.

Oman

WOMEN

Women have more freedoms in Oman than most other Middle Eastern countries. Many Omani women are educated and hold management positions in companies. Many foreign women who are doctors work in Oman. They can order at restaurants and drink alcohol. Foreign businesswomen are generally treated with respect and are not discriminated against, but they should remember to act professionally at all times. There may be some resistance to a woman being sent to close some deals.

BUSINESS ATTIRE

Western style business attire is more commonly found in Oman than in neighboring countries. A suit and tie will serve as appropriate business attire and will also double for formal occasions. To respect the culture, a woman should don conservative clothing, making sure to cover arms and legs lest it distract from her business intentions and detract from the level of respect she is shown. Lightweight materials are advisable for all clothing throughout the year.

Business Centers
Muscat

CITY VIEW

As a former stopover port for sea traders traveling between Arabia and India, Muscat presides as the economic, political, and social center of the country. Still retaining an authentic Arab feel by abstaining from high-rise development and Western influence, Muscat sets the stage for Old World Arabian charm while at the same time offering updated amenities and infrastructure.

AIRPORT

Seeb International Airport to City Center

The airport lies 25 miles (40 km.) from the city. Taxis and buses to the city are readily available. The 20-minute cab ride into town will cost about US$25.

Airline Numbers

Aer Lingus	677-718
Air Canada	566-046
Air India	708-639
American Airlines	708-635
British Airways	702-244
EgyptAir	796-134
Gulf Air	703-555
KLM	566-737
Lufthansa	708-986
Oman Aviation	707-222
Swissair	701-813, 703-303

HOTELS

Top-end

Al-Bustan Palace Inter-Continental; Mutrah; tel: 799-666; fax: 791-269; email: albustan@interconti.com; 247 rooms and suites; located between Muscat and Ruwi; beachfront; 4 restaurants with supper club and beach pavilion; bar; lounge; conference facilities (up to 1500); business centers and services; voicemail; in-room satellite tv, video, 2 direct-dial phones, voicemail, internet/email, bathrobes, minibar, safe, fruits, mineral water; 24-hour room service; laundry/valet; business room with fax, photocopier, pc/printer, VCR, mobile phone, secretarial services; non-smoking rooms; beauty salon/barber; airline desk; shops; car rental; valet parking; free parking; health club with sauna; pool; whirlpool; tennis; squash; beach; watersports.

Grand Hyatt Muscat; Shatti Al Qurm, 133 Muscat; tel: 602-888; fax: 605-282; http://muscat.hyatt.com/; email: hyattmct@omantel.net.om; 280 rooms and suites; restaurants; tea lounge; bar; conference facilities (up to 600); Hyatt Business Center; secretarial service; in-room fax connection, safe, a/c, IDD phone with voicemail, satellite tv, minibar, hairdryer; 24-hour room service; Regency Club floors with complimentary breakfast, two board rooms, private terrace; car rental; bank; fitness center/gym; sauna; steam bath; massage; pool; whirlpool; waterfalls; tennis; squash; watersports; beach access; nightclub.

Expensive

Qurum International; Qurum; tel: 571-700; fax: 571-414; near seaside; conference center; business center; secretarial service; computer terminal; in-room safe; car rental; 24-hour on-call doctor service; downtown shuttle service; no-smoking rooms; gift and book shop; fitness; health; sauna; pool; whirlpool.

Ruwi Novotel; PO Box 2195, Ruwi, Muscat; tel: 704-244; fax: 704-248; http://www.bestlodging.com/sites/17541/index.shtml; 105 rooms; city center; restaurant; conference facilities (up to 210); secretarial service; translation/interpreting service; videoconferencing; fax/photocopy facilities; in-room a/c, direct dial phone, satellite tv, minibar; elevator; safe box; airport transportation; corporate rates; pool; private beach club; nightclub; OR32+.

Moderate

Beach; Muscat; tel: 696-601; fax: 696-609; 46 rooms (including 7 apartments); located in a suburb near the coast with easy access to the highway; restaurant; conference facilities; secretarial service; in-room minibar, air conditioning, cable tv, telephone, hairdryer; 24 hour room service; parking; fitness center; swimming pool.

Mayan; Medinat Qaboos, Bowsher; tel: 592-900; fax: 592-979; suburb; restaurant; conference facilities (up to 250); executive services; secretarial services; no-smoking rooms; corporate rates; pool.

Mina; Ruwi; tel: 711-828; fax: 714-981; 28 rooms; located in the center of town close to the airport; restaurant; in-room air conditioning, tv, telephone; corporate rates.

MEDICAL CARE

Al Khoula Hospital; Wattayah; tel: 560-455.
Harab Dental Surgery; Qurum; tel: 563-814.
Muscat Pharmacy; Muttrah Suq., tel: 712-782; Ruwi, High Street, tel: 702-542; Al Bustan Palace Hotel, tel: 799-666; Medinat Qaboos Shopping Center, tel: 602-135. **Note**: Pharmacies usually stay open between 8a.m. and 1p.m. and 4p.m. to 9p.m.; on a rotating basis, certain pharmacies are also open 24 hours. Check the newspaper for weekly listings.

HEALTH CLUB

Fontana Health Club; Radisson Hotel, Al Kuleiah Street, Muscat 133; tel: 687-777; fully-equipped gym, massage, sauna, steam rooms.

Pakistan

At a Glance

THE PEOPLE

Population .... 141,553,775 (July 2000 est.)
Growth Rate .... 2.17% (2000 est.)
Life Expectancy .... 61.07 years
Infant Mortality . 82.49 deaths/1,000 live births (2000 est.)

Ethnic Composition

Punjabi, Sindhi, Pathan, Baloch, Muhajir (i.e. Urdu-speaking immigrants from India and their descendents).

Religious Composition

Muslim (Sunni 77%, Shi'a 20%) 97%
Christian, Hindu, and other.. 3%

Languages Spoken

Punjabi 48%
Sindhi 12%
Siraiki (Punjabi variant) 10%
Pashtu 8%
Urdu (official)... 8%
English (official of Pakistani elite and most government ministries, Burushaski, and other 8%
Balochi... 3%
Hindko... 2%
Brahui.. 1%

Education and Literacy

Relatively little funding is devoted to education programs. Overall adult literacy is at around 37.8 percent. for males it is 50percent and for females 24.4 percent.

Labor Force

Total: 38,600,000
By occupation: agriculture 44%, industry 17%, services 39%.

THE ECONOMY

Pakistan is a country of both economic and political turmoil. It is a poor and heavily populated country, suffering from a a costly ongoing struggle with India and a lack of foreign investment. Pakistan's economic future continues to be hampered by its weak foreign exchange position, notably its continued reliance on international creditors for hard currency inflows. Presently the country faces $32 billion in external debt. Foreign loans and grants provide approximately one quarter of all government revenue, but debt service obligations total nearly half of the government's expenditure. The IMF has remained silent on future disbursements from its $1.56 billion bailout package initiated in 1999. Other international financial institutions are sizing up the Musharraf administration's ability and resolve to implement necessary fiscal reforms. Pakistan has made privatization the primary factor in the country's economic revival but may have a problem attracting new foreign investors without a good word from the World Bank. Musharraf's far-reaching economic agenda includes steps to privatize public sector assets, widen the tax net, and improve its balance of trade position. The Bank has withheld its approval pending resolution of the pricing dispute between the government and independent power producers.

Exports .... US$8.4 billion (f.o.b., 1999)
Imports .... US$9.8 billion (f.o.b., 1999)
Total Trade .... US$18.2 billion (1999)

GDP Per Capita .... US$2,000 (1999 est.)
Unemployment .... 7% (97/98 est.)
Inflation Rate .... 6% (1999 est.)

Top Export Partners

U.S. 22%, Hong Kong 7%, U.K. 7%, Germany 7%, U.A.E. 5%.

Top Import Partners

U.S. 8%, Japan 8%, Malaysia 7%, Saudi Arabia 7%, U.A.E. 7%.

Top Exports

Cotton, fabrics, and yarn, rice, other agricultural products.

Top Imports

Machinery, petroleum, petroleum products, chemicals, transportation equipment, edible oils, grains, pulses, flour.

BUSINESS WORKWEEK

Offices

Sunday to Thursday 9a.m. to 4p.m.

Banks

Monday to Saturday 9a.m. to 1:30p.m., Friday 9a.m. to noon.

Government

Sunday to Thursday 8:30a.m. to 2p.m.

Retail

Saturday to Thursday 9a.m. to 7p.m.

HOLIDAYS

Id al-Fitr, end of Ramadan.............................. January 10*
Id al-Adha, Feast of the Sacrifice .... March 18*
Pakistan Day, Proclamation of
Republic in 1956.. March 23
Ashoura...April 17-18*
Good Friday..April 21*
Easter Monday ....April 24*
Muharram, Islamic New Year................................April 28*
Labor Day..May 1
Eid-i-Milad-un-Nabi, Birth
of the Prophet.. June 16*
Independence Day .... August 14
Defense of Pakistan Day...............................September 6
Anniversary of Death of
Quaid-i-Azam ....September 11
Allama Iqbal day..November 9
Birthday of Quaid-i-Azam/
Christmas ....December 25
Bank Holiday, End of Ramadan ....December 31
*The dates for these holidays are based on a lunar calendar and may vary from the date listed.

CLIMATE

Seasons

Pakistan is a hot country, with temperatures capable of rising to 51°C (124°F). Earthquakes are common. Rainfall is generally low, but from July to September the monsoon can bring rain storms with a fall in temperature and an increase in humidity. The best time to visit Pakistan is between September and March when temperatures remain moderate between

Pakistan

Pakistan		
⊙	National capital	
•	Provincial capital	
•	Secondary city	
⊠	Airport	
	International border	
	Province border	
	Road	
	Railroad	
	Trail	

0	100	200	300 km
0		100	200 mi

*Note:
The City of Islamabad is encompassed by the Province called Islamabad Captial Territory. Federally Administered Tribal Areas is designated a territory. The Pakistani-administered portion of the disputed Jammu and Kashmir region includes Azad Kashmir and the Northern Areas.

SM Santa Barbara, CA

©2001 Magellan Geographix

60°F and 70°F (15 to 27°C). If visiting the northern region of the country, one will find it best between May and September; otherwise, expect cold temperatures.

Regions

Indus Valley can suffer from the hottest weather. Along the Indus River flooding can occur. The highlands have cooler weather. From November through to March, temperatures in the north will fall to -1°C (30°F).

Money & Banking

Currency

The currency of Pakistan is the Pakistan Rupee (Re, singular; PRs, plural).

Denominations

The Pakistan Rupee comes in coin denominations of PRe1, and 50, 25, 10 and 5 paisa; and banknotes of PRe1, 5, 10, 50, 100, 500, and 1,000.

Traveler's checks

Traveler's checks and currency can be exchanged at banks,

exchange shops, and hotels, as well as international airports, at tourist exchange rates. Larger banks may offer the best exchange rates but avoid black marketers at all cost. Consult your bank about current exchange rates before departure. Keep all receipts for reconversion. Banks do not cash personal checks.

Most currencies can also be exchanged, but try to take only crisp and new notes; wrinkled and soiled notes are likely to be refused. Travel with small bills and coins, as shops and restaurants often do not have change and will likely not accept traveler's checks.

Major credit cards are accepted in most up-market places in the cities, (American Express being most common), but smaller restaurants and *souks* (markets) may ask for cash. Some banks in the capital offer cash advances on credit cards, but make sure you bring your passport.

Essential Terms

Although there are local variations, the predominant business language of Pakistan is English.

Travel

VISA AND PASSPORT

A valid passport (valid for six months beyond the intended length of stay) and a Pakistani visa are required for entry to Pakistan. Visas are not available at airports in Pakistan and must be obtained before arrival. Visas are available at any embassy or consulate of Pakistan. To qualify for a visa, you must submit a completed application, a valid passport and photo, and documentation for return or further travel plans. For business travelers, a company in Pakistan must append a letter inviting the foreign national to conduct business with them.

You may apply for a single entry, double entry, or multiple entry visa. It is valid if used within six months of issue date. The multiple entry visa is good for six journeys maximum in a year, commencing the date of your first entry, and any one stay may not exceed three months.

Note: Visa requirements can change with scant notice. It is best to inquire at an embassy or consulate of Pakistan as early as possible prior to travel to allow for extra time potentially required by new visitation regulations.

Restricted Entry

Nationals of Israel will be refused entry into the country as will nationals of Afghanistan who have previously traveled through India. Taiwanese passport holders must register with police in Pakistan within 24 hours of their arrival.

DEPARTURE FORMALITIES

International airport departure taxes are levied at several rates, depending on your class of travel: PRs400 for economy class, PRs600 for business or club class, PRs800 for first class. Domestic flights impose a PRs40 tax. There is an additional PRs700 Foreign Travel Tax levied on tickets issued in Pakistan. Transit passengers are exempt from all departure taxes.

Note: One may not export antiques.

CUSTOMS ENTRY (PERSONAL)

Duty-free

- Tobacco: 200 cigarettes, 50 cigars, or 500g tobacco
- 250ml of perfume and eau de toilette (opened)
- Other: 1 still and/or movie camera and 10 rolls of film.
- Personal computer with accessories that do not exceed 50,000 rupees in value, carried by business people who require it for their work.
- Gifts with a maximum value of PRs2000

Prohibited or Restricted

- Alcohol
- Matches
- Plants
- Fruit and vegetables
- Local currency in excess of PRs100

If a visitor imports alcohol by mistake or with the intention of taking it out of Pakistan, it will be held by customs and returned upon departure.

Precious stones and jewelry can be exported up to a value of PRs10,000 (Rs5000 for nationals of Afghanistan, the Gulf States, Iran, and Nepal) and carpets to the value of PRs25,000, if accompanied by an export permit. All items are subject to proof of having been purchased in foreign currency. The export of antiques is prohibited. Clear purchases with museum officials in Karachi or Lahore, if unsure about their exportation.

IMMUNIZATION

Travelers arriving within five days of leaving or transiting areas infected with cholera and/or yellow fever must have vaccination certificates. Immunizations against polio, typhoid, and meningitis are advisable, as well as prophylactic antimalarial drugs. Malaria is present throughout Pakistan below 2000 meters altitude.

TIPPING

Taxi

Taxi drivers are customarily tipped about 10 percent.

Porters

Porters, bellboys, maids, and room service waiters should be tipped a small amount (PRs10 per bag or day).

Hotels

Some hotels append a surcharge for gratuity, but it is often appropriate to tip staff that has not been regularly tipped through the course of your stay. The range is 10 percent for good service, 15 percent for excellence.

Restaurants

Some restaurants add a 10 percent service charge to bills. Those that do not should be tipped that amount for ordinary good service, 15 percent for excellent service.

EMERGENCY INFORMATION

Police and Crime

Crime is relatively high in Pakistan, having increased since the end of the Afghan War. The U.S. Department of State warns its citizens against all travel to Pakistan, having ordered the departure of all non-emergency official personnel. Americans should be advised that once official personnel have left the country, both the Embassy and the Consulates will only provide minimal consular services. If traveling to Pakistan, be sure to get an update of the security situation from your government before departing for the country. Major religious holidays prompt the increase in violent crime.

Karachi and Lahore, in particular, experience high crime levels. Violent crime has increased including carjackings, armed robbery, and house invasions. An underpaid and undermanned police force exacerbates the situation. Visitors are advised to avoid travel after dark. Use hotel shuttles over taxis, which are subject to police harassment. Be especially careful in valleys and mountain areas, where armed bandits have been known to rob people passing through. Kidnappings for money and political murders have also occurred in recent years along with a growing heroin trade. The Northwest Frontier Province, designated as tribal area, proves hazardous as clashes between tribes occur as does smuggling. A permit is required from the Home and Tribal Affairs Department to enter the area, and an armed guard may be assigned.

The Punjab Province has experienced a dramatic increase in sectarian violence and foreigners are not immune. Avoid public transportation and crowded areas.

Karachi and Hyderabad have seen outbreaks of ethnic and sectarian violence with random bombings, shootings, and mass demonstrations. Curfews have resulted. Overland travel is discouraged, and the Government of Pakistan recommends travelers to limit their movement to Karachi. If travel to the interior of Sindh Province is necessary, the government asks visitors to register with police well in advance so that security arrangements can be made.

Petty crime also poses a threat throughout the country. Avoid flashy displays of wealth, and dress and behave conservatively. Leave most of your cash, traveler's checks, jewelry, and your camera in your hotel safe. Carry photocopies of your passport instead of the original. Carry cash in a money belt, and use credit cards or traveler's checks for most transactions.

Walk with your bag away from the street to avoid having it snatched away by motorcycle thieves. Never carry a stranger's baggage. The police are efficient. Women are advised to dress very modestly when outdoors; women may also expect to receive a certain amount of verbal harassment from men in Pakistan.

Emergency Numbers

Islamabad Police	23333
Islamabad Fire	27222
Karachi Police	222-222, 224-400
Karachi Fire Brigade	74891

Health

Do not drink tap water or use ice cubes; bottled water is safe and available. Wash all vegetables in a chlorine solution, peel fruits, and avoid uncooked food. Drink only powdered or tinned milk and avoid other dairy products since they are most likely unpasteurized. Only eat meat and fish that have been well cooked, and preferably served hot. Mayonnaise, pork, and salad often bear increased risk of intestinal problems.

Cholera, diarrhea, leprosy, meningitis, paratyphoid, and typhoid fever exist. Malaria, hepatitis, amoebic and bacillary dysentary, and intestinal infection are common. Elephantiasis (filariasis) and Bilharzia (schistosomiasis) are endemic, but not widespread. Observe the usual precautions for poor sanitation conditions. Dust from farmyards can cause breathing problems, increase allergies, and lead to eye infections.

Ordinary medical services are adequate, and many of the doctors and nurses have been trained abroad. For major or emergency services, though, medical care is generally substandard, and pharmaceuticals are in short supply. Carry a well-stocked medical kit with all the prescription drugs you require; include in your kit a stock of sterilized syringe needles and drip needles for emergencies.

Military hospitals, usually open to locals and foreigners, often offer the best facilities. Expect to pay a small fee. A travel insurance package that includes an evacuation policy should be acquired by all business travelers. Medical evacuation is expensive, and payment of costs must be borne by the visitor.

INTERNAL TRAVEL
AIR

The domestic air travel hub is the Islamabad/Rawalpindi International Airport, five miles outside Islamabad, a 20-minute taxi ride. State-owned Pakistan International Airlines (PIA), and smaller independents Aero Asia and Shaheen, provide vi-

tal connections to 35 domestic destinations. Many daily flights link Karachi, Lahore, Rawalpindi, and other business centers.

Air travel is the fastest and most efficient way to travel, and it can also be somewhat thrilling, as aging turboprops bump and skim their way around towering mountains, often flying below their peaks. Pilot skills and extra maintenance on account of harsh conditions are important. Before landing, one may hear the following announcement, "Ladies and Gentlemen, Inshallah (God willing), we will be shortly landing."

Security is tight in the terminals. Expect a bodily search, and your luggage to be X-rayed, metal detected, tagged, stamped, and punched. Flights are often overbooked, but seats can usually be acquired by sweet-talking (or, naturally, bribing) a porter or other agent. A departure tax of PRs40 is levied for internal flights. For more information, you may wish to contact:

Pakistan International Airlines
website: http://www.fly-pia.com

TAXI

In the cities, taxis are yellow; auto-rickshaws also operate in most locations. You can hail cabs in the street, and some taxi ranks do exist, although taxis are most easily found around hotels. They are inexpensive and probably the most efficient mode of urban travel in Pakistan. It is best to hire taxis for round trips, as they can be difficult to find if you are not in a hotel district. It may also prove difficult to find a taxi after dark, since during Ramadan taxis are not allowed to operate after sundown. Airport arrivals should check with their hotel to see if an airport shuttle exists since cabs are often subject to police harassment, especially at night.

Fares must be negotiated, and if you have more than one driver bidding, you can get a good deal. Traditionally, though, foreign visitors are initially proposed a rate that is two or three times what a local would pay, so be prepared for some serious bottom-line dealing every time you take a cab. You will soon get an accurate feeling for what fare amounts should be after a couple of trips. Start the bidding a bit below your final number just to keep your driver's dignity intact.

AUTO

Auto rental is available in major cities, and at Rawalpindi, Karachi, and Lahore airports. Most hotels are also able to book cars for their guests. You must have an International Driving Permit, or a valid driver's license from your own country.

Traffic keeps to the left-hand side in Pakistan. The highway network that connects major cities is maintained fairly well, but roads are crowded, and drivers are aggressive and not particularly well trained. Many vehicles, especially large trucks and buses, are in poor shape. Secondary roads, including many major highways, suffer from a lack of maintenance and often have numerous potholes, sharp drop-offs, and barriers lacking signposts. Driving without an experienced local driver or guide is not recommended.

For assistance determining and even booking in advance for auto rental, either with a driver or self-drive, you may wish to contact the following website: http://tours.hypermart.net/car.htm.

TRAIN

Pakistan has an extensive rail network, owing to the past colonial presence of Great Britain. Modern, however, it is not. Sixty percent of the track and 30 percent of the rolling stock is supposed to have been scrapped by now, but instead is in service every day. Dacoits (armed bandits) have held up express trains on the run between the port in Karachi and Lahore. Nevertheless, it is a vital transport link for Pakistan, and a great way to see some parts of the country, although there are no railway lines into the mountains. It is also sometimes the only practical way to reach certain locations.

The rail link between Karachi in the south and Peshawar in the North-West Frontier Province spans the country, connecting most main population and business centers. Running from Karachi to Lahore, Rawalpindi and Peshawar, the route features several daylight and overnight trains. The majority of other routes have numerous daily trains.

Travelers should book reservations in advance for overnight service and long-distance journeys. Business travelers should choose the AirCon class if available, or first class if not. Do not consider economy or second-class passage, unless you are a seasoned traveler who is not squeamish about much. Even first class can be crowded and hot. Soap and towels, bedding, and toilet paper can be obtained from the reservations office for AirCon or first class, but is not otherwise supplied.

Discounts of 25 percent are available to individual travelers. For more information, inquire locally at Pakistan Railways offices. You may wish to visit their website, although much of it is under construction at this time: http://www.pakrailway.gov.pk/.

METRO

There is no subway system in Pakistan.

BUS / TRAM

Long-distance "Flying Coach" buses and regional buses go just about anywhere, but are somewhat slow. Regularly scheduled services link towns and villages throughout the country. There is hourly service of the Lahore–Rawalpindi–Peshawar circuit, for instance.

Always reserve a seat beforehand and, if traveling any distance, opt for an air conditioned coach. Bus stations are generally located in the center of most towns, and your hotel can assist in booking passage. Many of the routes travel along narrow, winding roads with lethal sheer embankments. The invocation of "Inshallah" will most probably be heard on occasion from your driver, as the buses maneuver along the sometimes treacherous mountain roads.

On the urban front, there are extensive bus services operating in Karachi, Lahore, and other large towns, as well as minibuses. The buses are easily identifiable, as they are brightly and profusely decorated. Safety is not assured, and local buses are usually crowded, sometimes packed.

For brief amusement— not for serious transit —the three-wheeled motorized rickshaws and two-horse-drawn tonga carriages are a cheap and enjoyable diversion. Large Westerners will not fit in a rickshaw. Jeeps, pick-ups, wagons, and vans are also popular forms of road transport.

WATER TRAVEL

The Indus River is a vital commercial byway for Pakistan, but not for movement of passengers. There really is no efficient means of personal transport either up the river or along the coastline, other than what you may be able to arrange locally on an irregular basis. Large quantities of freight are shipped from Karachi's main port to the north and to Punjab.

TRAVEL ASSISTANCE

Pakistan Tourism Development Corporation (PTDC)
House No 170, Street 36
F-10/1 Islamabad, Pakistan
tel: (51) 294 550 or 294 189; fax: (51) 294 540
email: ptdc@isb.comsats.net.pk
Or: tourism@isb.comsats.net.pk
website: http://www.tourism.gov.pk
Travel & Culture Services Pakistan
website: http://tours.hypermart.net/

Communications
DIALING CODES IN PAKISTAN
International country code: [92]
    Selected city codes: Abbotabad (5921), Bahawalpur (621), Faisalabad (41), Ghourghushi (5799), Gujranwala (431), Hyderabad (221), Islamabad (51), Karachi (21), Lahore (42), Multan (61), Okara (442), Peshawar (91), Quetta (81), Sahiwal (441), Sarhodha (451), Sialkot (432), Sukkur (71).

Dialing Pakistan from Overseas
To dial Pakistan from overseas, dial your country's international dialing code, then 92 (the country code for Pakistan), then the city code, and finally the number. If you were dialing Islamabad from the United States, for example, you would begin with 011, then 92, then 51 (the city code for Islamabad), and finally the number of the person or office you were trying to reach.

Assistance Numbers
International Operator 0102
Operator 17

CALLING WITHIN PAKISTAN
Long Distance Calls
One may dial direct to many cities in Pakistan. However, if you find yourself outside Islamabad, it could take a while since all calls are routed through the capital city. Domestic service has been described as erratic.

International Calls
To call international direct from Pakistan, dial 00 + country code + area code + number. A public call office (PCO) provides international access. In large cities PCOs stay open 24 hours. These offices are often located near post offices; but expect long waits, specially if located outside of Islamabad through which all calls must be routed first. Calls to North America may cost about R150 for the first three minutes and PRs50 for each additional minute. One can also place a call from a hotel, but surcharges will apply, often at mind boggling rates.
U.S. AT&T Direct... 00-800-01001
MCI Direct 00-800-12001

PAY PHONES
Public Telephones
There are no public pay phones in Pakistan.

CELLULAR PHONES
Cellular phone service for international calls is considered more reliable than on a standard phone in Pakistan. Three cellular companies operate digital and analogue systems in Pakistan. *Paktel* and *Pakcom* operate AMPS analogue systems, and *Pakistan Mobile Communications* runs a GSM system.
Note: Your home country cell phone may not work in this country. If not, we recommend that you rent an international cell phone *before* you leave home. A major US-based cell phone rental provider is **IMC WorldCell**. For information see "International Cell Phone Rentals" on page 14.

CALL BACK
You can (potentially) save significant sums when calling in Pakistan by using one of the call back services listed below. Fees for call back services vary widely, depending on the company and the type of service required. Be sure to check with these companies before leaving to compare rates.
For a list of callback services, please refer to the "Communications" section in the *Global Road Warrior* Introduction.

Pakistan

PHONE JACK

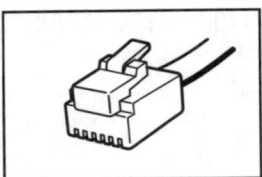

Plug adaptors are available through **iGo Corporation.** (See "Electrical and Telephone Adaptors" on page 19.)

FAX

Fax machines are scarce and can be expensive. Check with your hotel to see if they have one. Otherwise head for the Pakistan Telephone and Telegraph department.

POSTAL SERVICES

Mail service is generally inefficient. Use a courier service instead.

Hours of service

General post-offices in main cities are open 24 hours a day. All mail should be insured, and valuables should not be sent.

Rates

Postal rate is 45 paisa for 10 grams or less.

TELEGRAMS

There are services in top end hotels and some post offices.

Business Services

COURIER SERVICE

Karachi

Airborne Express; Aramex International Courier, Worldwide House, C-17, Korangi Road, Dha, Phase-Ii, Ext, Karachi-75500; tel: (21) 544-696; fax: (21) 588-0606.

DHL: 8 Banglor Town, Co-operative Housing Society, Sharah-e-Faisal, Karachi; tel: (21) 454-2470 up to 79, (21) 454-2480 up to 89.

Federal Express; Gerry's International, Karachi; tel: (111) 711-111.

TNT Express Worldwide Pakistan; Ground Floor, Rukhsana Building, Shaheed - E - Millat Rd.; tel: (21) 454-3037; fax; (21) 454-5900, 453-4266.

UPS; ACB Forwarding Systems (PVT) Ltd., 7 Amber Castle P.E.C.H.S. Block-6 Shahra-E-Fascal, Karachi, 75400; tel: (21) 1113-23232, tel: (21) 454-0710; fax: (21) 454-8500, fax: (21) 453-6454.

Lahore

DHL: 165 P Gulberg II; tel: (42) 575-7010, 575-7020, 7030, 7040, 7050.

Note: expect 2 t o 3 days delay for customs clearance.

Electrical

Current

220 volts AC, 50Hz.

ELECTRICAL SOCKET

Round 2- or 3-pin sockets are the norm.

ELECTRIC PLUGS

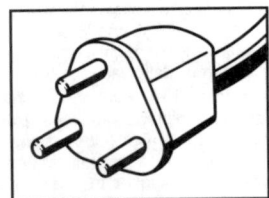

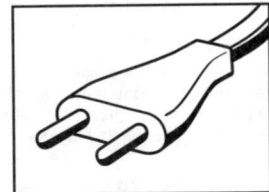

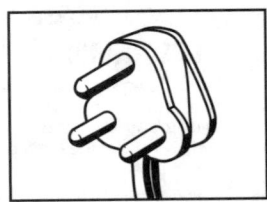

Plug adaptors are available through **iGo Corporation.** (See "Electrical and Telephone Adaptors" on page 19.)

Expect sudden power outages or voltage fluctuations in Pakistan. As such, one should ensure that sensitive equipment is fitted properly with voltage regulators. A flashlight may also prove helpful in the dark.

Technical Support

HARDWARE/SOFTWARE VENDOR SUPPORT

Compaq/Digital; (UAE Office) tel: [971] 4-818-100; fax: [971] 4-818-313; (in Switzerland) tel: [41] (22) 709-5330; fax: [41] (22) 709-5391 (Geneva); tel: [41] (1) 801-2507; fax: [41] (1) 801-2172 (Zurich); (General U.S.) tel: (281) 518-2000; http://www.compaq.com/.

Dell; (in the U.A.E.) tel: [971] 452-4232 (Key Information Technology in Dubai/Mr. Selwyn de Souza); fax: [971] 452-7944; (in Germany) tel: [49] (61) 039-710; (Dell- Europe) tel: [44] (134) 474-8000; (in the U.S.) tel: [1] (512) 338-4400; fax: [1] (512) 728-3330; http://www.dell.com/.

Hewlett Packard; (in Switzerland) tel: [41] (22) 780-8111; (in the U.S.) tel: [1] (408) 246-4300; http://www.hp.com/.

IBM; tel: (21) 566-1760; fax: (21) 568-2411; (in Germany) tel: [49] (711) 78-50; fax: [49] (711) 785-3511; (in Switzerland) tel: [41] (22) 310-0418 (in French); (in the U.S.) tel: [1] (919) 517-2800; http://www.ibm.com/.

Microsoft; (in Saudi Arabia) tel: [966] (1) 488-1165; fax: [966] (1) 488-1576; (in Switzerland) tel: [41] (848) 858-868; fax [41] (1) 831-0869; (in the U.S.) [1] (425) 635-7222; http://www.microsoft.com/.

NEC; (in Israel) tel: [972] 09-59-3300 (UltraCare Support); (in the U.S.) [1] (916) 388-0101 (Main Switchboard); http://www.nec.com/.

Internet Connection
HOW TO CONNECT

Connecting to AOL and Compuserve in Pakistan is similar to using it when traveling outside your own area code. See the introductory section for detailed information on connecting to your account through a different phone number.

America Online

Numbers are available at keyword *international*. Be sure to get several local numbers before leaving. AOL's Global-Net service charges US$12 an hour in addition to the usual charges. Go to keyword *access* (a free area) and download the software.

At this time there are no internal AOL numbers for Pakistan. An international dial-up solution will have to be found.

Compuserve

Numbers are available at *Go International*. The Compuserve Web-site also has a great deal of information, at http://www.compuserve.com.

At this time there are no internal Compuserve numbers for Pakistan. An international dial-up solution will have to be found.

Independent Service Providers

Many independent service providers offer discounts if you are only in town for a couple of days.

Brain.Net; tel: (42) 111-222-888; fax: (42) 783-2039 (this listing is in Lahore, but they offer service in eleven other cities in Pakistan); email: info@brain.com.pk; http://www.brain.net.pk/.

COMSATS; tel: (51) 920-6605/7; fax: (51) 922-4800; email: info@comsats.net.pk; http://www.comsats.net.pk/.

Cyber Internet Services; tel: (21) 111-445-566; fax: (21) 568-6745; email: info@cyber.net.pk; http://www.cyber.net.pk/.

Nexlinx; tel: (42) 571-4911; tel: (42) 111-432-432; fax: (42) 575-8041; fax: (42) 575-9092; email: info@nexlinx.net.pk; http://www.nexlinx.net.pk/.

Supernet; tel: (51) 272-860; fax: (51) 272-862; http://www.super.net.pk/.

Zoooom Net; tel: (42) 111-966-666; fax: (42) 586-9660; email: info@zoooom.net; http://www.zoooom.net/.

Internet Cafes
Islamabad

Airnet Internet Cafe; Empire centre, Jinnah Super, F-7 Markaz, Islambad; tel: 265-0130; email: m.afzalkhan@usa.net; Sunday through Saturday, 10a.m. to 2a.m.; PRe40 per hour of use.

Browser Internet Cafe; Suite# 11, Block# 12-C main jinnah super market, Islamabad; tel: (51) 265-0137; email: browserpk@yahoo.com; Sunday through Saturday, 24 hours a day; PRe35 per hour of use.

Karachi

ACN Cyber Cafe; 26-a, nachs, off: Tariq road, Karachi; tel: (21) 452-3265; fax: (21) 452-3264; email: cafe@acn.com.pk; http://www.acn.com.pk/; Sunday through Friday, 9a.m. to 9p.m.; PRe50 per hour of use.

Cyber Valley; Shop # 3,Latif Plaza, Opposite Disco Bakery, Block-6, Gulshan-e-Iqbal, Karachi; tel: (21) 474-301, tel: (21) 496-9972/3; email: info@cybervalley.com.pk; http://www.cybervalley.com.pk/; Sunday through Saturday, 10a.m. to 12a.m.; US$0.50+ per hour of use.

Kafiee's Internet Cafe; R-4 Block 20, Al-Noor, F.B.Area, Karachi; tel/fax: (21) 636-0207; email: kafiee@hotmail.com; http://www.geocities.com/kafiee/;

Sunday through Saturday, 24 hours a day. PRe40 per hour of use.

Planet Earth Cyber Cafe; 7, Byjhs Block 7/8 AMIR Khurso Road, Karachi; tel: (21) 453-0556; fax: (21) 453-0557; email: cri786@cyber.net.pk; http://www.planetearth.net.pk/; Sunday through Saturday, 10a.m. to 10 p.m.; PRe50 per hour of use.

Lahore

Cyber C@fe; 140-Bank Square Market Model Town Lahore; tel/fax: (42) 583-8861; email: cybercafe@www.com; http://tahirs.virtualave.net/cyber.html; Sunday through Saturday, 11 a.m. to 11p.m.; PRe40 per hour of use.

Hotline; Asif Plaza Link Road Model Town, Lahore; tel: (42) 516-9059; email: hotline_hccs@hotmail.com; http://hccs.cjb.net/; Sunday through Saturday, 8:00 a.m. to 2:00 a.m.

Java Point Internet Cafe; Nishtar Road Multan, Lahore; tel: (61) 547-097, tel: (61) 542-320; fax: (61) 581-187; email: javapoint_internetcafe@yahoo.com; PRe50 per hour of use.

Planet Internet; 57 Bank Square Market Model Town, Lahore; tel: (42) 856-561; email: planet@nexlinx.net.pk; http://planet.homepad.com/; Sunday through Saturday, 10:30a.m. to 10:30p.m.

Peshawar

AST Net Cafe; Basement, Gul Haji Plaza, University Road, Peshawar; tel: 43-031, tel: 844-550; email: ast_netcafe@yahoo.com; Sunday through Saturday, 9a.m. to 10p.m.; PRe35 per hour of use.

Global Net; 9,10 Basement Orakzai Plaza Town Chowk University Road, Peshawar; tel: 844-182; email: globenet@psh.paknet.com.pk; http://www.globalnetcafe.homestead.com/; Sunday through Saturday, 7a.m. to 11p.m.; PRe40 per hour of use.

Rawalpindi

SysPro NetCafe; CB 789 Main Street No 10 Basement Enjoyland Games Center Qaziabad Near Marir Hassan Rawalpindi; tel: (51) 556-3133, tel: (51) 558-5076; fax: (51) 556-7520; email: webmasters@syspro.itgo.com; http://www.syspro.itgo.com/; Sunday through Saturday, 10a.m. to 1:45a.m.; PRe30 per hour of use.

Business Culture
GREETINGS AND COURTESIES

Pakistanis are a friendly, hospitable people who respect their elders. A handshake is the standard greeting, and should be gentle. Many Pakistanis will extend their wrist rather than their hand. A man should not initiate a handshake with a woman or touch a woman in public. Foreign women may offer a handshake when meeting a Pakistani man, unless there are indications that this will be offensive. Pakistanis should be addressed with their title if they have one. If invited to a home, the host will appreciate a small gift or a souvenir from your country. Some Muslim men practice a form of marriage or family life where women may not associate with men outside of the family; in this case, one may not inquire about her if visiting his home, nor invite her to an outside social function. Appropriate gifts for a host include flowers or foreign chocolates. Small electronic products are also appreciated as a business gift. Avoid discussing politics or religion since the topic can get volatile specially when it relates to India.

BUSINESS ETHIC AND FRAMEWORK

Pakistan is a devoutly Muslim country. The family is the most important social unit, and Pakistanis tend to be loyal to their specific ethnic groups rather than to the country as a whole. Pakistanis work hard, but will often put family or kinship considerations above business. Fate is also an important element of Pakistani culture (particularly in rural areas). They truly believe that once people do the best they can, the outcome is in the hands of God.

MEETINGS AND DECISION MAKING

Appointments are necessary. You will very likely be dealing with the Pakistani government or one of its many companies. In this male-oriented society, a man will be the primary representative for your company or business. Pakistanis are not especially concerned about time, but they expect foreigners (Westerners in particular) to arrive punctually. Schedule meetings later in the morning rather than earlier. Pakistanis like to socialize before conducting business, so expect meetings to begin with pleasant small talk. You will probably be offered something to drink; always accept, or you might insult your associate; the same rings true if you are invited to a meal. Decisions are made slowly; be patient.

WOMEN

Pakistan is a male-dominated society and women are not accorded the same respect as men. Foreign women should always act professional, confident, and poised. Still, they may not receive the same respect as a male colleague. Women should prepare for questions about their age, marital status, and whether they have children (such questions are asked of both men and women). Women should not go out alone at night; at a bazaar, they should go in a group or accompanied by a man.

BUSINESS ATTIRE

A conservative business suit and tie will I do well for important business meetings. In the summer months, one can do away with the jacket, except for government meetings. Women should wear business suits, preferably slacks. With respect to the culture, women should take care to wear very conservative clothing, preferably loose-fitting and covering as much skin as possible; if not, a woman risks more than the usual exposure to unsolicited comments and harassment.

Business Centers
Lahore
CITY VIEW

As Pakistan's cultural center, Lahore is the country's most visited city; however, it hasn't yet been overrun by tourists or refugees. It still retains some of its exotic charm, with tombs and mosques at seemingly every corner (including one of the largest in the world), gardens and parks interspersed, and crowded streets filled with cultural sights and sounds.

AIRPORT

Lahore International Airport to City Center

The airport lies 8 miles (12 km.) from the city. Buses run from sunup to sundown in 10-minute intervals, and taxis are available. Expect a 20-minute trip to downtown.

Airline Numbers

Air Canada	(42) 305-229
Air France	(42) 214-422
British Airways	(42) 301-575
Gulf Air	(42) 302-111
Indian Airlines	(42) 211-249
JAL	(42) 304-265
KLM	(42) 312-789
Lufthansa	(42) 61-011
Northwest Orient	(42) 417-231
Philippine Airlines	(42) 302-662
PIA	
Flight inquiries	(42) 370-061
Reservations	(42) 306-415
Singapore Airlines	(42) 303-269
Saudia	(42) 305-413
Swissair	(42) 62-007
Thai Airways	(42) 305-943
THY Turkish Airlines	(42) 303-503

HOTELS

Top-end

Avari Lahore; 87 Shahrah E.; tel: (42) 631-0646, 637-5805; tel: 636-5365; fax: (42) 636-5367, 636-8694; http://www.avari.com/lahore.htm/; email: lahore@avari.com; city center; restaurants; conference facilities (up to 600); business center; executive deluxe suites; in-room fax, satellite tv, voicemail, minibar, safe; 24-hour room service; laundry/dry cleaning; complimentary airport shuttle; 24-hour doctor on-call; beauty salon; car rental; airline desk; health club; gym; massage; steam bath; jogging track; badminton; volleyball; horse riding.

Pearl Continental Lahore; Shahrah-e-Quaid-e-Azam; tel: (42) 636-0210; fax: (42) 362-760; http://www.pchotels.com/pcl-home.htm/; email: pclhr@pchotels.com; opposite Governor House; 5 restaurants; business center; secretarial service; 24 hour room service; business suites; electronic in-room safe; mini bar; alarm; radio; satellite TV; hair dryers; international direct dialing; in-house doctor; pharmacy; car rental desk; money changer; travel desk; florist; bookstore; jewelry shop; parking; health club; gym; sauna; massage; pool; tennis.

Moderate

Best Western Shalimar Hotel; 36 Liberty Market, Gulberg III, Lahore; tel: (42) 575-8811; fax: (42) 571-2800; email: bwslp@brain.net.pk; 82 rooms; restaurant; recently renovated; meeting rooms; business center; fax service; secretarial service; television; in room refrigerator; 24-hour room service; Concierge; pool.

Hilltop Hotel; Dr. Mahmood Hussain Rd.; tel: (21) 453-2441/4; fax: (21) 454-6891; email: hilltoppk@yahoo.com; http://www.paks.net/hilltop; near Tariq Rd. shopping center; restaurant; fax/Internet service; 24 hour room service; complimentary airport shuttle; cable TV; air conditioned; mini refrigerator in rooms; extra power generator; car rental; safe deposit locker; foreign currency exchange.

Holiday Inn Lahore; 25-26 Egerton Road; tel: (42) 631-0077; fax: (42) 631-4515; email: holiday@brain.net.pk; suites available; air conditioned; mini bar; safe; radio; iron; coffee maker; room service; beauty salon; gift shop; parking; pool; whirlpool.

Karachi
CITY VIEW

Pakistan's bustling business center, Karachi, is a sprawling city where ancient bazaars and mosques sit side by side with new hotels and office buildings. A plethora of action takes place in the city streets, filled with restaurants, shops, and commerce.

Pakistan

AIRPORT

Quaid-i-Azam International Airport to City Center

The airport lies 10 miles (15 km.) from the city. Coaches run according to arrivals. A bus departs every 30 minutes. Taxis are also available. A trip into downtown normally takes about 25 minutes.

Airline Numbers

Aeroflot	(21) 520-211
Air Canada	(21) 566-1712/3/4
Air China	(21) 435-570
Air France	(21) 520-131
Air Lanka	(21) 528-286
Alia Royal Jordanian	(21) 512-027
Alitalia	(21) 511-098
Biman	(21) 510-069
British Airways	(21) 516-067
Cathay Pacific	(21) 520-683
CSA	(21) 568-0008
Egypt Air	(21) 513-233
Emirates	(21) 519-611
Gulf Air	(21) 525-237
Indian Airlines	(21) 522-034
Iran Air	(21) 515-001
JAL	(21) 515-001, 510-162
JAT	(21) 516-388
KLM	(21) 516-273
Korean Air	(21) 529-898
Kuwait Airways	(21) 510-603
LOT	(21) 520-589
Lufthansa	(21) 515-416
Philippine Airlines	(21) 516-537
PIA	(21) 511-061
Royal Nepal Airlines	(21) 515-061
Sabena	(21) 219-331
Saudia	(21) 513-122
Singapore Airlines	(21) 521-618
Swissair	(21) 512-069
Tarom	(21) 437-290
Thai Airways	(21) 511-513
THY Turkish Airlines	(21) 523-249

HOTELS

Top-end

Avari Towers Karachi Renaissance; Fatima Jinnah Road 242-243; tel: (21) 566-0100; fax: (21) 568-0310; email: towers@avari.com; city center; restaurants; conference facilities (up too1000); business center with internet service; executive deluxe suites, non-smoking rooms; in-room fax, voicemail; satellite TV; minibar; in room safe; car rental; airline desk; 24 hour room service; doctor on-call; airport shuttle; laundry/dry cleaning; health club; fitness; massage; sauna; steam bath; pool; jacuzzi; tennis; golf; scuba diving.

Karachi Marriott Hotel; 9 Abdullah Haroon Rd.; tel: (21) 568-0981; fax: (21) 568-1610; adjacent to U.S. Consulate; 5 minutes to business district; restaurants; 24-hour coffee shop; conference facilities; business center; complimentary airport shuttle; executive club floors; non-smoking rooms; car rental desk; gift shop; health club; sauna; pool; tennis; squash.

Karachi Sheraton Hotel; Club Road; tel: (21) 521-021; city center; restaurant; conference facilities (up to 1500); secretarial service; fax/photocopy facilities; in-room modem/fax connection; corporate rates; fitness; sauna; pool; whirlpool.

Expensive

Beach Luxury Hotel; M.T. Khan Road; tel: (21) 551-1031; fax: (21) 561-1625, 561-0673; email: beach@avari.com; 150 rooms; waterfront location; restaurant; conference facilities; (up to 3000); business services; internet/email services; executive suites; in-room satellite tv; doctor on call; gift/souvenir shop; safe deposit boxes; currency exchange; laundry/dry cleaning; car rental; game room; parking; pool.

Holiday Inn Crowne Plaza Karachi; 25-26 Egerton Rd.; tel: (21) 566-0611; fax: (21) 568-3146; 411 rooms; restaurant; coffee shop; meeting facility; satellite TV: air conditioning; non-smoking rooms; in-room IDD phone; minibar; pool.

Moderate

Metropole Hotel; tel: (21) 512-051.

Karachi Sarawan; Raja Ghazanfar Ali Road, Saddar; 130 rooms; restaurant; coffee shop; bar; photocopier; radio; phone; game room; parking.

Karachi Sky Towers; Raja Ghazanfar Ali road, Saddar; tel: (21) 567-5211/12/13/14/15; fax: 512-331; http://www.pakmall.com/skytowers/; 24 hour room service; TV; mini bar; international direct dialing; laundry service; doctor on call.

Midway House Hotel; Stargate Road, Karachi Airport; tel: (21) 480-371; (21) 457-1815; 280 rooms; near airport; restaurant; coffee shop; bar; business center; conference facilities; radio; air conditioning; room service; parking/garage; pool; tennis.

MEDICAL CARE

Aga Khan Hospital; Stadium Rd.; tel: (21) 420-051.

Imam Clinic and General Hospital; ST-5 Block - 1 North Nazimabad, Karachi; tel: (21) 662-5111; fax: (21) 662-61111.

Karachi Adventist Hospital; 91 Depot Lines, M.A. Jinnah Rd.; tel: (21) 721-8021/24; 721-8086/89; fax; (21) 722-7010.

AUTO RENTAL

Avis; Lahore Airport, tel: (42) 631-4630; Avari Hotel Lahore (chauffeur-driven only), 87 Shahrah E Quaid I Azam; tel: (42) 636-5366; Holiday Inn Lahore (chauffeur-driven only), 25-26 Egerton Road; tel: (42) 631-0077; Karachi Centre, 13 Services Mess, Mereweather Road; tel: (21) 567-3269 (chauffeur-driven cars available); Karachi Airport, tel: (21) 454-0670/71.

WORLD TRADE CENTER

World Trade Center Karachi
10 Khayaban-E-Roomi
Block-5, KDA Scheme No. 5
Clifton, 75600, Karachi, Pakistan
tel: (21) 586-3826; fax: (21) 587-1863

CHAMBER OF COMMERCE

Overseas Investors' Chamber of Commerce
PO Box 4833, Talpur Road, Karachi
tel: (21) 241-0814; fax: (21) 242-7315
email: zaheer@oicci.khi.sanpk.undp.org

Chamber of Commerce and Industry
Aiwan-e-Tijarat Road; Karachi-74000
tel: (21) 241-2414, 241-0587; fax: (21) 241-6095
email: kcc@PakistanBiz.com

Panama

At a Glance

THE PEOPLE

Population .... 2,808,268 (July 2000 est.)
Growth Rate .... 1.34% (2000 est.)
Life Expectancy .... 75.47 years
Infant Mortality ... 20.8 deaths/1,000 live births (2000 est.)

Ethnic Composition

Mestizo (mixed Indian and
European ancestry) 70%
Amerindian and mixed (West Indian) 14%
White 10%
Indian.. 6%

Religious Composition

Roman Catholic... 85%
Protestant 15%

Languages Spoken

Spanish (official), and English are widely spoken. Many Panamanians are bilingual

Education and Literacy

Education is free and compulsory for children aged seven through 15. Fees may be charged for higher education. Nearly 91 percent of the population can read and write.

Labor Force

Total: 1,044,000
By occupation: agriculture 18%, industry 18%, services 64%

THE ECONOMY

Panama's service-based economy, with an emphasis on tourism, banking, and commerce, is largely attributable to its prime geographic location. The construction industry in Panama has grown, spurred on by the passing over of the Panama Canal and various U.S. military installations. Though export demand is likely to remain flat in some key markets (particularly the Andean countries), GDP growth in Panama in 2000 will still be around 3.5 percent. Certain reform initiatives from the previous administration, including the privatization of public utilities, remain uncompleted. President Moscoso is unlikely to overturn any previous reforms, and her populist approach to government make it unlikely that any new initiatives will be undertaken any time soon. The government has failed to come up with a cohesive economic policy or framework. The only significant step it has taken by year end 1999 has been an increase in agricultural tariffs.

Exports .... US$4.7 billion (f.o.b., 1999 est.)
Imports .... US$6.4 billion (f.o.b., 1999 est.)
Total Trade .... US$11.1 billion (1999 est.)
GDP Per Capita .... US$7,600 (1999 est.)
Unemployment 13.1% (1997)
Inflation Rate .... 1.5% (1999 est.)

Top Export Partners

U.S. 40%, Sweden, Costa Rica, Spain, Benelux, Honduras.

Top Import Partners

U.S. 40%, Central America and Caribbean, Japan.

Top Exports

Bananas 43%, shrimp 11%, clothing 5%, sugar 4%, coffee 2%.

Top Imports

Capital goods 21%, crude oil 11%, foodstuffs 9%, consumer goods, chemicals.

BUSINESS WORKWEEK

Offices

Monday to Friday 8a.m. to noon, 2p.m. to 5p.m. or 6p.m.; Saturday 9a.m. to noon.

Banks

Monday to Friday 8a.m. to 1:30p.m.

Government

Office hours for government offices vary, and it is advisable to check prior to visiting any government office, however, many are open Monday to Friday 8:30a.m. to 4:30p.m.

Retail

Monday to Saturday 9a.m. to 6p.m. Retail hours vary, but they are slightly shorter on the weekends. Many businesses are closed Sunday.

HOLIDAYS

New Year's Day...January 1
National Martyrs' Day ....January 9
Carnival ....March 7*
Good Friday..April 21*
Labor Day..May 1
Foundation of Panama City............................August 15*
Revolution Day ....October 11
All Souls' Day ....November 2
Independence from Colombia ....November 3
Independence Day (Colón only).................. November 10*
Independence from Spain ....November 28
Immaculate Conception,
Mother's Day ....December 8
Christmas ....December 25
*Date may vary by year.

CLIMATE

Seasons

Days are hot, nights much cooler; temperatures range from 32˚C (90˚F) daytime and fall to 21C (70˚F) in the evening practically all year round. Humidity is always high at about 80 percent. The rainy season takes place between October and November, and the best months to visit are mid-December and late March.

Regions

Temperatures vary according to geography. The climate is less tropical on higher elevations. In mountain areas the average annual temperature ranges from 10˚C to 19˚C (50-66˚F) at various mountain elevations.

Panama

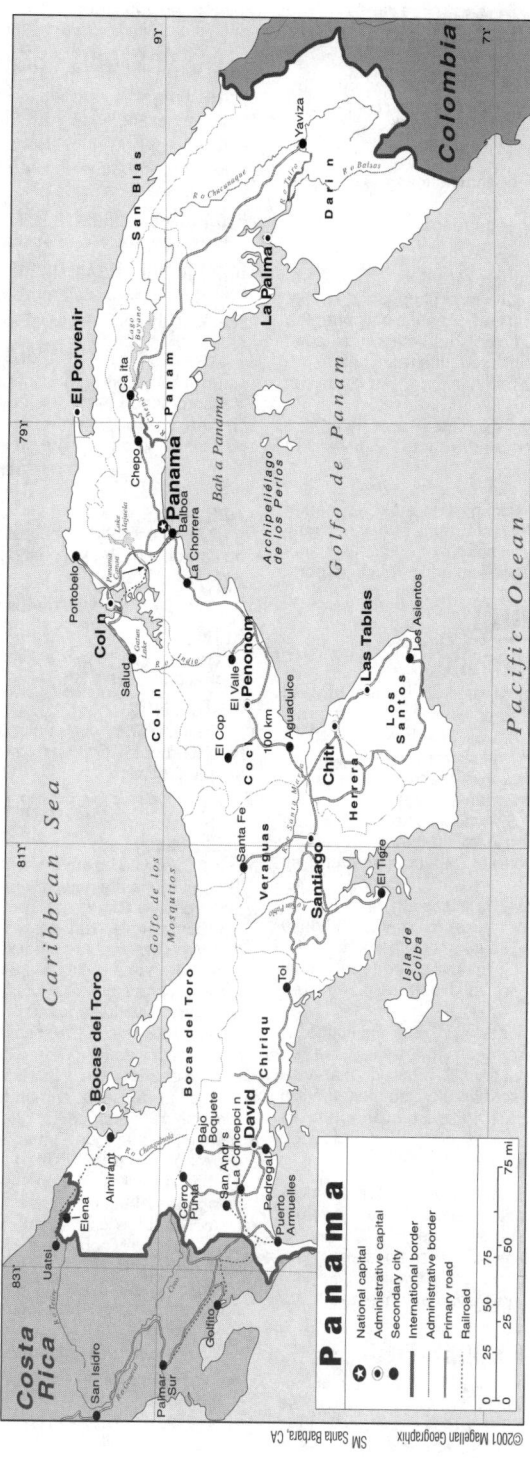

Panama

Money & Banking

Currency

The currency of Panama is the Balboa (B), however, the Balboa exists in coin form only since the official paper currency is the U.S. dollar.

Denominations

The Balboa comes in coin denominations of B100 and 1, and 50, 25, 10, 5 and 1 centesimos.

*There is no Panamanian paper currency.

Travelers checks

Travelers checks and currency, mostly in U.S. dollars, can be exchanged at banks, exchange shops, and hotels, as well as international airports. Larger banks may offer the best exchange rates but avoid black marketers at all cost. Consult your bank about current exchange rates before departure. Keep all receipts for reconversion. Banks do not cash personal checks.

Most currencies can also be exchanged, but try to take only crisp and new notes, wrinkled and soiled notes are likely to be refused.

Major credit cards, American Express, Visa, Diner's Club, MasterCard are easily accepted in most up-market places in the cities, but smaller restaurants and shops may ask for cash. Some banks in the capital offer cash advances on credit cards, but make sure you bring your passport.

Travel

VISA AND PASSPORT

A passport that is valid for at least six months beyond anticipated exit date is required of all visitors to Panama. Panamanian law mandates that all travelers must either procure a Tourist Card from their airline when entering Panama, or acquire a visa at a Panamanian consulate or embassy prior to traveling to Panama. There is a long list of countries, including the U.S., whose citizens need not obtain a visa, and another long list of countries whose citizens must. Check with the nearest Panamanian embassy or consulate.

For those whose nationality qualifies them, a Tourist Card can be issued (instead of a visa) for stays of 30 days maximum (90 days extension is customarily granted, at the Immigration authorities' discretion). The same terms apply to visas, and both documents are valid for three months beyond date of issue.

Allow a day or two for processing of visa application if applying in person; the process can take as long as ten days or more, depending on nationality. Panamanian visa regulations may change with scant notice, so travelers are advised to check with the nearest Panamanian embassy before embarking.

Restricted Entry

Immigration regulations are inflexibly enforced. Non-cooperation with them will result in forcible return to your country of origin, at the expense of the carrier.

Many of those requiring visas also need special authorization from the Panamanian Immigration authorities prior to entry. Again, check with the Panamanian embassy or consulate for clarification.

DEPARTURE FORMALITIES

Any traveler with a visa is required to obtain an exit permit if they have been in the country more than 30 days. The Treasury Ministry provides a Paz y Salvo form, which the visitor passes along to Immigration, where officials attach the form to your passport and issue an exit stamp valid for one week. All travelers must pay an exit tax of US$20.

CUSTOMS ENTRY (PERSONAL)

Duty-free
- Tobacco: 500 cigarettes, 50 cigars, or 500g tobacco
- Alcohol: 3 bottles of alcohol
- Perfume: perfume and eau de cologne in opened bottles for personal use

Prohibited or Restricted
- Fruit, vegetable, and animal products

Immigration Department
Director General de Imigracion

Apartado 1870, Balboa 5; tel: 227-1077; fax: 227-1227.

IMMUNIZATION

For protection against hepatitis, a gamma gobulin shot is recommended. It is also advisable to get vaccinations for cholera, typhoid, tetanus, diphtheria, yellow fever, and polio if traveling outside the main city.

TIPPING

Taxi
Drivers do not expect tips. Any intended gratuity should be figured in with the pre-trip negotiated fare.

Porters
50 - 75 centesimos per piece.

Hotels
Generally, a 10 percent service charge is figured into the overall tab.

Restaurants
If a restaurant does not include a service charge, tip 10 to 15 percent —or 20 percent in a fine restaurant with outstanding service.

EMERGENCY INFORMATION

Police and Crime
Until now, Panama has been moderately dangerous. Though moderate now, the growing crime level in the Colon and Panama City areas is serious. Police checkpoints are now commonplace on weekends. The high-crime spots in the Panama City area are Chorillo, Ancon, Curundu, Vera Cruz Beach, Panama Viejo, and the Madden Dam overlook. The types of crimes are characteristic of most major metropolitan areas in the world, ranging from rape to petty theft, muggings, armed robberies, purse-snatchings, and "quick-naps" at ATM street machines (involving a brief kidnapping and robbery of ATM user after cash withdrawal).

The incidence of crimes involving unlawful weapons is climbing as is the number of arrests for illegal weapons possession, countrywide. Armed violence in urban settings is increasing at an alarming rate.

Airport theft is common, and the traveler should decline riding in unauthorized taxis or sharing one with a stranger. Demonstrations occasionally occur with anti-U.S. sentiment and are typically nonviolent. However, one is advised to avoid such demonstrations.

Take basic precautions against crime, especially at night. A few elementary precautions should protect the traveler from most problems:
- Do not leave valuables in cars or on tables in cafés.
- Keep non-essential valuables locked in hotel safes when not in use.
- Use credit cards and traveler's checks when possible to avoid carrying large sums of cash.

- Carry photocopies of your passport instead of the original.
- Carry cash in a money belt, and use credit cards or travelers checks for most of your large transactions.
- Walk with your bag away from the street to avoid having it snatched away by motorcycle thieves.
- Never carry a stranger's baggage.
- Women should avoid traveling alone at night

Never exchange money in the street or carry a package for a stranger. The police are generally helpful. Punishment for crime (especially drug trafficking) is severe.

Emergency Numbers

Police 62-6963
Fire 103
Ambulance (Hospital Santo Tomas) 25-1436

Health

Water in the two main cities, Panama City and Colón, is safe to drink. In more rural settings, this is often not the case. Also, diarrhea is common for travelers who are unaccustomed to the new diet and water, so bottled water is probably a good idea, especially if a visitor is not staying long. Wash all vegetables in a chlorine solution, peel fruits, and avoid uncooked food. Drink only powdered or tinned milk and avoid other dairy products since they are most likely unpasteurized. Most fare served in restaurants is perfectly healthful.

Malaria and yellow fever are more common in rural areas, but hepatitis and tuberculosis are a major threat everywhere (especially in poorer areas).

Panama is extremely hot, so take precautions against sun and heat stroke, drink lots of liquids, and use sunblock when outdoors.

The medical system is adequate in larger cities; medical staff can usually speak English. Costs are as high as in North America, but private medical services are reliable and modern. Panama guarantees health care facilities for both nationals and foreign visitors who may need them. Nevertheless, a travel insurance package that includes an evacuation policy should be acquired by all business travelers. Medical evacuation is expensive, and payment of costs must be borne by the visitor.

TAXI

Taxis in Panama are abundant. You can recognize them easily due to their bright, distinctive paint jobs. They also have a number painted on them, which you may use to register any complaints (or compliments). Taxis may be hailed in the street, engaged at a taxi stand, or reserved by telephone. Many people share cabs, called a *colectivo*; there is a small surcharge for each additional passenger.

Fares are determined by zones in Panama City, rather than meters. Drivers must have a zone chart with them at all times. In the event that a passenger does not feel the charges are correct, he/she may request that the zone chart is consulted. Because most cabs are not metered, you should settle the fare before embarking, which is a good time to ask the driver to show you the zone charges. The fares for traveling within city boundaries are quite reasonable, generally ranging between US$1 and US$2, which makes this good transportation for the business traveler.

AUTO

The major car rental companies are represented in Panama City and in David, both at the airport and downtown: Hertz, Budget, Thrifty, and Dollar all have offices in these cities, and elsewhere. Either a driver's license from the traveler's country of origin or an International Driving Permit are acceptable documentation.

Panama City is linked to Colon by the Trans-Ishman

Highway and to Costa Rica by the Pan-American Highway. From April through December, though, the rainy season renders many roads unusable, especially outside urban areas.

Traffic conditions can be tricky. Many vehicles are not well maintained, including buses and taxis, so, driving can be hazardous. Effective use of brakes and signaling by Panamanian drivers are often both notoriously absent. Add to these factors dense traffic, poor or non-existent signs or traffic signals, neglected street repairs, and many uninsured motorists (insurance is not mandatory in Panama), and you have a situation that should give pause to many travelers considering self-drive auto rental.

TRAIN

Passenger service is no longer offered by the Ferrocarril de Panamá, which is currently operating freight trains only between Panama City and Colon. The national rail service is being sold off as a victim of NAFTA.

BUS / TRAM

A bus system services all accessible areas of the country. Embarkation from Panama City to any of the major cities in the interior, such as El Valle, Colon, David, or Aton, requires going to the new Gran Terminal de Albrook, located near the downtown area. Buses leave throughout the day at hourly intervals or less, depending on destination. It is not a rapid form of transportation, but it is fairly comfortable and dependable.

The traveler can take an overnight bus from Panama City to Bocas del Toro, Chiriqui Grande, and Changuinola. This service is offered by Union de Buses Panamericanos (tel: 229-6333), whose office is situated on Via Fernandez de Cordoba, next to a restaurant called Felicidad. The buses are air-conditioned and full service.

Urban buses are easily recognized, painted in bright, colorful schemes. Most are the "school bus" variety, with seating that is sometimes lacking in comfort and no air-conditioning, but they service almost every part of the city. Passengers pay a flat fare at the turnstile when boarding.

SUBWAY

No subway service exists in Panama.

WATER TRAVEL

Boats are the primary means of transport in many regions of Panama, particularly between Bocas del Toro and San Blas archipelagos. Also, Kuna Indian merchant ships carry both passengers and cargo between Puerto Obaldía and Colón along the San Blas coast. Inquire locally to arrange passage.

Of course, the Panama Canal is the major shipping route for freight and passengers. For ferry service, contact Crucero Express:

tel: 264-5564 or 226-3326; fax: 264-3453.

TRAVEL ASSISTANCE

Director General de Imigracion
Apartado 1870
Balboa 5, Republic of Panamá
tel: 227-1077; fax: 227-1227
IPAT (Institute of Tourism)
Instituto Panameño de Turismo
Apartado 4421, Centro de Convenciones ATLAPA
Vía Israel, Panamá 5, Republic of Panamá
tel: 226-7000 or 226-3167 or 226-4614
fax: 226-3483
website: http://www.ipat.gob.pa

Essential Terms

English	Spanish
Yes	Sí
No	No
Good morning	Buenos días
Hello (daytime)	Buenas tardes
Hello (evening)	Buenas noches
Hello (telephone)	¿Hola?
Good-bye	Adiós
Please	Por favor
Thank you	Gracias
Pleased to meet you	Encantado (a) de conocerle
Excuse me; I'm sorry	¿Perdóneme?
My name is _____	Me llamo _____
I don't understand	No comprendo
Do you speak English?	¿Habla usted inglés?

Communications

DIALING CODES IN PANAMA

International country code: [507]

Dialing Panama from Overseas

To dial Panama from overseas, dial your country's international dialing code, then 507 (the country code for Panama), and finally the number. There are no city codes.

Assistance Numbers

Directory 102

CALLING WITHIN PANAMA

Local Calls

Dialing local should prove fairly straightforward.

Long Distance Calls

No extra digits exist for long-distance calls in Panama to the joy of those who dislike the search for codes.

International Calls

For an international direct call, dial 00 + country code + area code + number from any phone. Discounted rates apply between 10p.m. and 7a.m. daily. An operator assisted call will cost twice the sum of a direct call. To make a collect or credit card call to the U.S., dial one of the access numbers. Public phones will require a deposit for the procedure.

AT&T 109
Sprint 115
MCI 108
to reach MCI from a
military base 2810-108

PAY PHONES

Public Telephones

The Panamanian phone system ranks well compared with many of its neighbors. Telephones exist all around for public use.

CELLULAR PHONES

BellSouth Corporation de Panama operates an analogue AMPS system in the country.

Note: Your home country cell phone may not work in this country. If not, we recommend that you rent an international cell phone *before* you leave home. A major US-based cell phone rental provider is **IMC WorldCell**. For information see "International Cell Phone Rentals" on page 14.

CALL BACK

You can (potentially) save significant sums when calling in Panama by using one of the call back services listed below. Fees for call back services vary widely, depending on the company and the type of service required. Be sure to check with these companies before leaving to compare rates.

For a list of callback services, please refer to the "Communications" section in the Global Road Warrior Introduction.

PHONE JACK

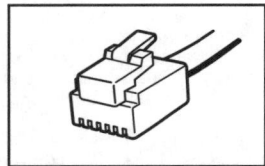

Plug adaptors are available through **iGo Corporation**. (See "Electrical and Telephone Adaptors" on page 19.)

FAX

Fax machines are widespread, and service is generally good. Most commonly they are found in hotels and hotels.

POSTAL SERVICES

Mail to North America takes up to one week. Airmail to Europe takes about 5 to 10 days. Incoming mail could take considerably longer. It is best not to send anything valuable.

Hours of service

Monday to Friday 6:30a.m. to 5:45p.m., Saturday 7a.m. to 5p.m.

TELEGRAMS

Most post offices and top-end hotels have telegram services.

Business Services

COURIER SERVICES

Challenge Air Express; tel: 226-7161.

DHL; Calle 50 No. 82; Nuevo Campo Alegre; tel: 263-8818; fax: 269-6440.

Federal Express Panama; tel: 236-7811, toll-free800-1122; Monday to Friday 8:30a.m. to 5:30p.m., Saturday 9a.m. to 1p.m.

TransExpress; tel: 225-5189.

UPS Panama; Union Park of Panama S.A., Edf. Torre Swiss Bank, Planta Baja, Calle 53E, Nueva Urban, Obarrio; tel: 269-9222; fax: 269-9250.

Panama

OFFICE RENTAL

Executive Office Center; tel: 263-7555.

SECRETARIAL SERVICES

Servicio Profesionales Empresariales; Urb. Marbella; tel: 264-9034.

TRANSLATION SERVICES

Trasecsa; Avenida Cuba y Calle 34, 34-20; Panama; tel: 225-1354.

Electrical

Current

120 volts AC, 60Hz.

ELECTRIC PLUGS

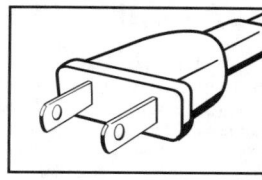

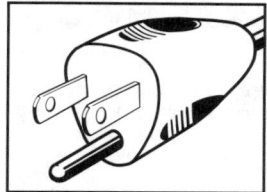

Plug adaptors are available through **iGo Corporation.** (See "Electrical and Telephone Adaptors" on page 19.)

Technical Support

Acer/Texas Instruments; (in Germany) tel: [49] (4102) 488-469; fax; [49] (4102) 488-169; (in the U.S.) [1] (408) 432-6200; http://www.acer.com/.

Adobe; (in the U.S.) tel: [1] (305) 593-5900; fax: [1] (714) 633-3600;(in the U.S.) tel: (716) 633-3600; or tel: (305) 591-6800; fax: (305) 599-7000; (in Switzerland) tel: [41] (800) 833-310; http://www.adobe.com/.

Apple/Claris; (in Miami) [1] (305) 265-4939; (in the U.K.) tel: [44] (990) 127-753; (in the U.S.) tel: [1] (408) 996-1010 (Corporate Headquarters); http://www.apple.com/.

AST; (in the U.S.) tel: [1] (817) 232-9824 (International Technical Support); (in Ireland) tel: [353] (61) 492-222; (in the U.S.) tel: [1] (949) 727-4141; http://www.ast.com/.

Compaq/Digital; (Houston Office, U.S.) tel: [1] (713) 370-0670; fax: [1] (713) 514-1740; (in the U.S.) tel: [1] (281) 518-2000 (international technical support); fax: [1] (281) 518-1442; http://www.compaq.com.

Corel; (in the U.S.) tel: [1] (613) 728-3733 (Customer Service); fax: [1] 613- 761-9176; http://www.corel.com.

Digital; (in the U.S.) tel; [1] (508) 952-3777 x5034 (Customer Relations); fax: [1] (603) 884-1036; e-mail: wwibs@MKO.mts.doc.com; http://www.digital.com.

Dell; tel: 008-0[1] (800) 507-0962; (Latin America Division) [1] 512- 728-4397; (U.S. Office) tel: [1] 512-338-4400; fax: [1] 512-728- 3330.

Filemaker/Claris; (in Germany) tel: [49] (180) 525-8166 (Info-line); fax: [49] (180) 567-2233; tel:´[49] (180) 523-6423; (in the U.S.) tel: [1] (800) 965-9090; http:// www.claris.com/.

Gateway 2000; (U.S. Office) tel: [1] (605) 232-2191 (International Technical Support); http://gw2k.com.

Hewlett Packard; (Venezuela Office) tel: [58] 2 239 5664; (in the U.S.) tel: [1] (303) 894-8899; fax: [1] (303) 894-3398 (For Products Registered in the Americas); http:// www.quark.com/.

IBM; (in Colombia) tel: [57] (1) 623-0111; fax: [57] (1) 257-9839; (in the U.S.) tel: [1] (919) 517-2800; (in Switzerland) tel: [41] (22) 310-0418 (in French); http://www.ibm.com/.

Microsoft; (in Costa Rica) tel: [506] 298-2020; tel: [506] 298-2000; (in the U.S.) [1] (425) 635-7222; http:// www.microsoft.com/.

Novell; 00[1] (800) 638-9273 (Toll Free Technical Support - dial AT&T access number first, if available, wait for prompt, and then dial the toll free number); (in the U.S.) tel: [1] (408) 434-2300; fax: [1] (408) 577-5775 (Worldwide Sales Headquarters); (in Switzerland) tel: [41] (1) 308-4747; fax: [41] (1) 302-0401; http://www.novell.com/.

Quark; (U.S. Office) tel: [1] (303) 894-8888; (in the U.S.) tel: [1] (303) 894-8899; fax: [1] (303) 894-3398 (For Products Registered in the Americas); http:// www.quark.com/.

Toshiba; (in the U.S.) [1] (949) 583-3000 (Corporate Headquarters); (in Germany) tel: [49] (2131) 158-319; fax: [49] (2131) 158-558; (in Switzerland) tel: [41] (1) 946-0777; fax: [41] (1) 946-0807; (in Ireland) tel: [44] (193) 282-8828; http://www.toshiba.com/.

Internet Connection

HOW TO CONNECT

Connecting to AOL and Compuserve in Panama is similar to using it when traveling outside your own area code. See the introductory section for detailed information on connecting to your account through a different phone number.

America Online

Numbers are available at keyword *international*. Be sure to get several local numbers before leaving. AOL's Global-Net service charges US$6 and US$12 an hour in addition to the usual charges. Go to keyword *access* (a free area) and download the software.

Access: Panama City 210-6400; Panama City 210-6500; Panama City 263-1611 (this number costs US$12).

Compuserve

Numbers are available at *Go International*. The Compuserve Web-site also has a great deal of information, at http://www.compuserve.com.

There are no direct access numbers for Compuserve in Panama. Users will have to pay international rates to use the service.

Independent Service Providers

Many independent service providers offer discounts if you are only in town for a couple of days.

Únete de Panamá; tel: 263-8727; email: info@unete.com.pa; http://www.panaweb.com/.

Sinfonet (PSINet); tel: 206-3000; tel: 265-6000; info@sinfo.net; http://www.sinfo.net/.

Internet Cafes
Panama City

Cyber @ljan; Edificio Campo Alegre 1er Piso oficina 1-A Vía España, in frot of the Hotel Continental and the Champs Sports; tel/fax: 264-9864; email: aljan@hotmail.com; Monday to Saturday, 9a.m. to 9p.m.; US$2 per hour of use.

CyberCentro Panamá, Internet@Cafe; Sun Tower Mall, Ricardo J. Alfaro AVE. First Floor #32, Panama City; tel: 236-3290; fax: 236-5033; email: ccp@mail.ccp.pty.com; http://www.ccp.pty.com/; Monday to Saturday, 10a.m. to 10p.m., Sunday 12p.m. to 8p.m.; US$4 per hour of use.

Internet Cafe @ Panama; San Francisco 76th Street, 1 Plaza Caesar Panama City; tel: 270-1053; email: escorcia@intercafe.com; http://www.inter-cafe.com/; Tuesday through Sunday 11:30 a.m. to 11:30 p.m.; US$1.50 per 30minutes of use.

Internet y Copias; Via Espana, Carrasquil la.edificio Villa Espana, frente a la entrada de La Ulacit; tel: 224-3462; fax: 221-1916; email: internetycopias@hotmail.com; http://www.geocities.com/Eureka/Gold/3759/; Monday to Saturday, 9a.m. to 10p.m.; US$1.50 per hour of use.

Business Culture
GREETINGS AND COURTESIES

Handshakes are appropriate among businesspeople, both men and women—when arriving and leaving—although casual acquaintances generally nod when meeting while good friends hug. Panamanian women may embrace lightly or brush cheeks in a kiss; they seldom shake hands with each other, although they may do so in a business situation. Panamanians find titles important: *Señor* (MIster) and *Señora* (Ms.) general titles; *Licenciado* (university degreed); *Ingeniero* (male engineer), and *Doctor* (lawyer, or someone with an advanced degree). Entertaining for business normally occurs over dinner rather than during lunch, since many still take a noon break, or *siesta*.

BUSINESS ETHIC AND FRAMEWORK

Panamanians are generally considered relaxed, easygoing, and informal by Latin American standards, although they nevertheless have a regard for formal dignity and hierarchical and class distinctions. Although they have become more accustomed to North American business norms, their values continue to emphasize the importance of personal relationships, and they still take time and effort to establish a personal relationship before a business relationship.

MEETINGS AND DECISION MAKING

Prior appointments are necessary and should generally be made two weeks in advance. Panamanians generally consider punctuality unimportant, however, they do appreciate it. Most meetings are held informally. Authority is rather narrowly concentrated and actual decisions are almost always made at a high level. Cultivate relationships at all levels, however, because the quality of these relationships may strongly influence the actual decision maker even when your immediate counterpart is not the one making the decision.

WOMEN

Although women generally occupy a secondary status in heavily male-dominated and *macho*-influenced Panama, they are accorded considerable personal freedom and many operate businesses. Foreign businesswomen should experience few problems. Although women may generally go out on the streets and dine alone, most will feel more comfortable if escorted.

BUSINESS ATTIRE

Due to the tropical climate, one is well advised to stick to lightweight, natural fabrics such as linen and cotton. Men should wear suit and tie, although your Panamanian host will likely relieve you of your misery by suggesting you remove your coat. Women will do well with lightweight dresses and suits.

Business Centers
Panama City
CITY VIEW

Panama City is a thriving city with areas that harken back 100 years with an Old Spanish influence. However. American influence has not escaped the city as visible in the Banking District, with its gleaming skyscrapers and other monuments to industry. As the only city in the world with a rainforest within the city limits, a business survey also ranked Panama City as one of the top three cities in which to live.

AIRPORT

Tocumen Airport to City Center

The airport lies 17 miles (27 km.) from the city. Taxi service is available and cab sharing is common.

Airline Numbers

Aeroperlas	263-5363, 223-5300, 269-4555
Aerotaxi	264-8644, 264-2950
Alas Chiricanas	64-6448
American Airlines	269-6022
Ansa	26-7891, 26-6898
Chitreana de Aviacón	226-3069
Continental Airlines	264-4124
Panama Air International	227-2371
Parsa	226-3803, 226-3883
Transparsa	226-0842, 226-0932

HOTELS

Top-end

El Panama; Via España 111; tel: 269-5000; fax: 223-6080; http://www.elpanama.com/; email: reservas@elpanama.com; city center; casino; restaurants; conference facilities with AV equipment; secretarial service; fax/photocopy facilities; in-room modem/fax connection; Internet service; non-smoking rooms available; safe; cable TV; radio; hair dryer; voice mail; mini bar; translation service; laundry service; corporate rates; fitness; sauna; pool; whirlpool.

Miramar Inter-Continental Panama; Miramar Plaza, Balboa Ave.; tel: 214-1000; fax: 223-4891; email: panama@interconti.com; near beach; 2 restaurants; bars; 6 function rooms (up to 600); business center; 5 Club Intercontinental floors, 2 Business Room floors; voice mail; in-room safe; Concierge; car rental; limousine service; boutiques; garage parking; fitness center; sauna; pool.

Radisson Royal Panama Hotel; Calle 53 Este Marbella; tel: 265-3636; fax: 265-3550; email: - Radisson@Sinfonet.net; 112 rooms; adjacent to World

Trade Center; 2 restaurants; bar; meeting rooms (up to 120); business center with fax service; modem connection; TV with cable; coffee makers; in-room safe; mini bar; cellular phone rental; 24-hour room service; doctor on call; fitness; sauna; Turkish bath; pool; whirlpool.

Expensive

Golden Tulip Costa del Sol; Via España & Federico Boyd Ave.; tel: 206-3333; fax: 206-3336; http://www.costadelsol-pma.com/panama/costadelsol.htm/; email: costasol@sinfo.net; 242 suites; all-suite hotel; kitchenettes; two telephones in room; dataport; air conditioned; mini bar; satellite TV; international direct dialing service; restaurant; conference room; business center; secretarial service; beauty parlor; Internet; limousine/car rental; parking; washer/dryers; gym; sauna; massage; pool; tennis.

Riande Continental Airport; Interamericana Eldorado 6-999; tel: 220-3333; fax: 220-5017; near airport; restaurant; conference facilities (up to 300); corporate rates; fitness; pool.

Panama Marriott; Calle 52 y Ricardo Arias - Area Bancaria; tel: 210-9100; fax: 210-9110; restaurant; bar; room service; air conditioning; mini bar; babysitting service; hairdryer; data ports on telephone; voice mail; speaker phone; Concierge; laundry service; car rental; fitness room; sauna; pool; whirlpool.

Riande Continental; Via España; tel: 263-9999; fax: 269-4559; restaurant; bar; conference facilities; air conditioned; international direct dialing; cable TV; Concierge; safe deposit box; sauna; pool.

Riande Granada; Calle Eusebio A. Morales; tel: 263-7477; fax: 263-7197; near city center; casino; conference facilities (up to 150); fitness; pool.

Moderate

Best Western Hotel Suites Central Park; Via Espana 67; tel: 223-9630; city center; restaurant; bar; non-smoking rooms; radio alarm clock; computers available; cable TV; mini bar; room service; fitness center; pool; jacuzzi; tennis squash courts.

Gran Hotel Soloy; Calle 30 & Avenida Peru; tel: 227-1133; fax: 227-0884; email: soloy@sinfo.net; 200 rooms; city center; restaurant; 2 bars; casino; conference facility; in room safe; mini bar; cable TV; Concierge; 24 hour room service; laundry service; boutiques and shops; parking; 2 pools; disco.

Executive Hotel; Calle 52 Y Aquilino de la Guardia; tel: 264-3333; fax: 269-1944; 24 hour restaurant/cafe with music; bar; cable TV; room service; parking pool.

Roma; Avenida Justo Arosemena, Calle 33; tel: 227-3844; fax: 227-3711; email: hroma@pananet.com; 150 rooms; restaurant; meeting facilities (up to 300); fax/photocopy facilities; cable TV; 24 hour room service; laundry service; safety deposit boxes; car rental facilities; pool.

MEDICAL CARE

Centro Medico Bella Vista; Av. Peru and Calle 39; tel: 27-4022.

Centro Medico Paitilla; Av. Balboa and CL. 52, Paitilla; tel: 63-6060, 69-4643.

Hospital Del Nino (Children's Hospital); CL. 34 1-81, La Exposicion, Hospital Sto. Tomas; tel: 25-1546.

Hospital Santa Fe; Via Simon Bolivir y Av. Frangipani; tel: 27-4733.

Hospital Santo Tomas; Av. Balboa, La Exposicion; tel: 27-4122.

HEALTH CLUB

Caesar Park Athletic Club; Via Israel & 77th Street, El Dorado; tel: 226-407; fitness; aerobics; spa, saunas; pool; tennis.

Coronado Club Suites Resort; Apartado 4381, Panama 5; tel: 255-4444; fax: 255-4380; golf.

El Club de Montana; Apartado 6-1996, El Dorado; tel: 230-1969; fax: 230-1557; tennis.

AUTO RENTAL

Avis; CL 55 2, El Cangrejo; tel: 264-0722; Tocumen Intl Airport; tel: 238-4037; Marco A Gelabert Airport, Albrook Field, Avenida Cansield, Edificio 870; tel: 232-7202.

Dollar; toll-free: 001-800-111-0005; Airport, tel: 238-4033; fax; 238-4032; 50th Street Rental Office, Panama City, tel: 226-8100; fax: 226-8191; Tumba Muerto Rental, Richardo J. Alfaro Ave., tel: 236-8013; fax: 236-7906.

Hertz; Tocumen Airport; tel: 238-4106; Calle 55, Panama City; tel: 263-6910; Ceasar Park Hotel, Via Israel Y Calle 77, Panama City; tel: 226-4077.

International; CL. 55, El Cnagrejo; tel:2 64-4540; at the airport, tel: 238-4044.

WORLD TRADE CENTER

World Trade Center Panama
53rd St. Marbella
P.O. Box 0832-0064
Panama City, Panama
tel: (7) 265-7866
fax: (7) 269-6126
email: wtcpn@wtcpn.com
http://www.wtcpn.com

CHAMBER OF COMMERCE

Camera de Comercio Industrias y Agricultura de Panama
Apartado Postal 225
tel: 775-4851, 774-6227
fax: 775-4577;
email: camchi@chiriqui.com.

Paraguay

At a Glance

THE PEOPLE

Population .... 5,585,828 (July 2000 est.)
Growth Rate .... 2.64% (2000 est.)
Life Expectancy .... 73.68 years
Infant Mortality . 30.81 deaths/1,000 live births (2000 est.)

Ethnic Composition
Mestizo (mixed Spanish and Amerindian)................... 95%
White and Amerindian... 5%

Religious Composition
Roman Catholic.. 90%
There are also several Mennonite and other Protestant denominations.

Languages Spoken
Spanish is the official language of business and government. Guarani is a dialect spoken in certain rural communities.

Education and Literacy
Paraguay maintains a well developed educational system, with the result that its literacy rate is high by South American standards. Literacy stands at 92.1 percent. Among adult males literacy is around 95.5 percent, while adult female literacy is slightly lower at 90.6 percent.

Labor Force
Total 1,700,000
By occupation: agriculture 45%.

THE ECONOMY

Because of the importance and influence of the large informal sector of Paraguay's economy, an accurate economic measure is difficult to obtain. The informal sector is comprised of the re-export of consumer goods to surrounding countries as well as the activities of thousands of small businesses and urban street merchants. A large percentage of the population is agrarian, often on a subsistence basis. From 1995 to 1997, Paraguay's formal economy grew by an average of about 3 percent annually, but the GDP declined slightly in 1998 and 1999. On a per capita basis, real income has not moved, listlessly hovering at 1980 levels. Many have attributed Paraguay's poor economic performance to corruption, lack of progress on structural reform, and deficient infrastructure. In 2000. growth should recover, may be to as much as 2 percent.

Exports .... US$3.1 billion (f.o.b., 1999 est.)
Imports .... US$3.2 billion (f.o.b., 1999 est.)
Total Trade .... US$6.3 billion (1999 est.)
GDP Per Capita .... US$3,650 (1999 est.)
Unemployment .... 12% (1998 est.)
Inflation Rate 5% (1999)

Top Export Partners
Brazil, Argentina, E.U.

Top Import Partners
Brazil 34%, U.S., Argentina, Uruguay, E.U., Hong Kong.

Top Exports
Soybeans, feed, cotton, meat, edible oils.

Top Imports
Road vehicles, consumer goods, tobacco, petroleum products, electrical machinery.

BUSINESS WORKWEEK

Offices
Monday to Friday 8a.m. to noon and 3p.m. to 5:30p.m. or 7p.m., Saturday 8a.m. to noon.

Banks
Monday to Friday 8:45a.m. to 4p.m., but the public is received only up to 12:15p.m.

Government
Monday to Friday 9a.m. to 4p.m.

Retail
Monday to Friday 10a.m. to 7p.m., with a two or three hour break in the day, usually between noon and 3p.m., Saturday 7:30 a.m. to 1p.m.

BUSINESS WORKWEEK

Offices
Monday to Friday 8a.m. to noon and 3p.m. to 5:30p.m. or 7p.m., Saturday 8a.m. to noon.

Banks
Monday to Friday 8:45a.m. to 4p.m., but the public is received only up to 12:15p.m.

Government
Monday to Friday 9a.m. to 4p.m.

Retail
Monday to Friday 10a.m. to 7p.m., with a two or three hour break in the day, usually between noon and 3p.m., Saturday 7:30 a.m. to 1p.m.

HOLIDAYS

New Year's Day..January 1
San Blás, Patron Saint of Paraguay................. February 3
Heroes' Day... March 1
Maundy Thursday...April 20*
Good Friday...April 21*
Labor Day...May 1
Independence Day Celebrations .... May 14-15
Ascension Day .... May 21*
Corpus Christi... June 11*
Peace of Chaco..June 12
Founding of Asunción... August 15
Battle of Boquerón, Anniversary
of the Discovery of America ....September 29
All Saints' day..November 1
Immaculate Conception...................................December 8
Christmas ....December 25
*Date may vary by year.

CLIMATE

Seasons
Paraguay's climate is warm, humid, and sub tropical. Being south of the equator, seasons are reversed, with winters from June to September. Temperatures range from 34˚C (93˚F) in January, to 14˚C (60˚F) in June. The rainy season occurs from October to April, with heaviest rainfall occurring between December and March. The best time to visit the country is from May to September, when the temperature hovers around 24˚C (75˚F).

Paraguay

Departments of Paraguay	
1	Alto Paraguay
2	Alto Paran
3	Amambay
4	Boquer n
5	Caaguaz
6	Caazap
7	Canindey
8	Central
9	Chaco
10	Concepci n
11	Cordillera
12	Guair
13	Itap a
14	Misiones
15	eembuc
16	Nueva Asunci n
17	Paraguar
18	Presidente Hayes
19	San Pedro

Paraguay

◎	National capital
•	Department capital
•	Secondary city
▬	International border
―	Department border
―	Primary road
⋯	Railroad

0   100   150 km
0   50   100 mi

©2001 Magellan Geographix
SM Santa Barbara, CA

Regions

Rainfall is heaviest around the northeast, near the Brazilian frontier. Otherwise there are few regional differences.

Money & Banking

Currency

The currency of Paraguay is the Guarani (G).

Denominations

The Guarani comes in coin denominations of G100, 50, 10, 5, and 1 and banknotes of G500, 1,000, 5,000, 10,000, and 50,000.

Traveler's checks

Traveler's checks and currency, mostly in U.S. dollars, can be exchanged at banks, exchange shops, upscale hotels, and international airports at tourist exchange rates. Larger banks may offer the best exchange rates but avoid black marketers at all cost. Consult your bank about current exchange rates before departure. Keep all receipts for reconversion. Banks do not cash personal checks.

Most currencies can also be exchanged, but try to take only crisp and new notes, wrinkled and soiled notes are likely to be refused.

Major credit cards, American Express, Visa, Diner's Club, and MasterCard, are accepted in most up-market places in Asunción, but smaller restaurants and shops may ask for cash. Some banks in the capital offer cash advances on credit cards, but make sure you bring your passport. ATM machines most likely will not accept foreign credit cards.

Paraguay

Essential Terms

English	Spanish
Yes No	Sí No
Good morning Hello (daytime) Hello (evening) Hello (telephone)	Buenos días Buenas tardes Buenas noches ¿Hola?
Good-bye	Adiós
Please	Por favor
Thank you	Gracias
Pleased to meet you	Encantado (a) de conocerle
Excuse me; I'm sorry	¿Perdóneme?
My name is _____	Me llamo _____
I don't understand	No comprendo
Do you speak English?	¿Habla usted inglés?

Travel

VISA AND PASSPORT

A passport that is valid for six months beyond the anticipated exit date is required of all, except citizens of Argentina, Bolivia, Brazil, Chile and Uruguay who have valid ID cards and are traveling directly from their own countries to Paraguay as tourists. You will need your passport for cashing traveler's checks, at military and police checkpoints, and for checking into hotels. If you are staying in one place for any length of time, you should carry a photocopy of the passport; stash the original in a safe place, such as a safe deposit at your hotel. Be sure that you receive an entry stamp when arriving, so that you might exit without having to pay additional fees.

Visas are also required of all, except for the following visitors, as long as they are entering as tourists and plan stays of 90 days maximum:

- Citizens of E.U. countries (with the exception of Ireland)
- Nationals of Argentina, Australia, Bolivia, Brazil, Canada, Chile, Colombia, Costa Rica, Ecuador, Guatemala, Israel, Japan, Malaysia, Norway, Peru, South Africa, Switzerland, Uruguay, U.S., and Venezuela
- Transit passengers who are continuing their journey within six hours on the first (or same) connecting aircraft, provided they are holding return or onward documentation and do not leave the airport.

Tourist and Business visas are issued, either single or multiple entry, and valid if used within three months, with a term of three months. Included in the visa application must be a certificate of good health from a doctor, and a certificate of good conduct from one's local police department. Business visa requirements also include a cover letter from an employer naming the visitor's business contact in Paraguay.

Allow two working days for visa applications made in person. It takes about a week, in addition to delivery time, for postal applications.

DEPARTURE FORMALITIES

Personal effects such as alcohol and tobacco are allowed to be taken out of Paraguay in limited quantities. Customs officials process papers and check cars sporadically at overland crossings. Paraguay levies a departure tax of US$18 for international flights.

CUSTOMS ENTRY (PERSONAL)

Duty-free

The following items may be imported into Paraguay without incurring customs duty:

- Tobacco: a reasonable quantity of tobacco
- Alcoholic beverages
- Perfume: a reasonable quantity for personal use

IMMUNIZATION

Travelers arriving from or traveling to an endemic or infected area must have a yellow fever vaccination certificate. Preventive measures against cholera are recommended. Malaria is reported in some areas.

TIPPING

Taxi

Usually, taxi drivers are not tipped.

Porters

G2,000 per bag is appropriate.

Hotels

A service charge of 10 to 15 percent is usually included in the bill. If not, then you may wish to add that amount to the total— it is expected.

Restaurants

Normally a gratuity of 10 to 15 percent is figured into the tab. It is appropriate to add that amount if it has not already been included.

EMERGENCY INFORMATION

Police and Crime

Crime is on the increase in Paraguay. Cities experience a prevalence of pickpocketing and mugging, particularly during evening hours around hotels and airports. Do not pack valuables in your checked baggage. Take basic precautions. Try to blend in with the locals. Leave valuables at the hotel safe and avoid wearing expensive jewelry or carrying camera equipment. Be aware of your surroundings at all times. Do not resist in case of armed robbery; instead, surrender valuables and contact the police immediately.

Carry several photocopies of your passport instead of the original. Carry cash in a money belt, and use credit cards or traveler's checks for most transactions. Walk with your bag away from the street to avoid having it snatched away by motorcycle thieves. Never carry a stranger's baggage.

Women should avoid traveling alone at night. While some police officers are friendly and helpful, you are best advised to contact your consulate in the event of an emergency.

Emergency Numbers

All services	00
Asuncion Hospital de Clinicas	80-982

Health

General health has improved since the 1959 revolution. Malaria, diphtheria, poliomyelitis, tuberculosis, and tetanus have been almost completely eradicated.

Never drink tap water in greater Paraguay, even for brushing your teeth; and avoid ice cubes. Although water in Asuncion is chlorinated, it may yet cause stomach upset. Don't eat raw vegetables and fruit unless they've been washed in a chlorine solution. Milk is not pasteurized; thus, one should avoid ice cream and dairy products that have been made with unboiled milk. If using powdered milk, make sure the water used with it has been properly sterilized. Diarrhea is common for travelers who are unaccustomed to the new diet and water. The dust and smog may cause bronchitis.

Hospitals and medical facilities are generally concentrated in the cities, and about 60 percent of the population has access to healthcare facilities. For more complicated medical problems, you are best advised to leave the country.

INTERNAL TRAVEL

AIR

Domestic operations are managed by the three major airlines of Paraguay: Transportes Aéreos del Mercosur (TAM), Aerolineas Paraguayas (ARPA), and Lineas Aereas Paraguayas (LAPSA). Flights linking Asunción with Concepción, Ciudad del Este, and Encarnación are available, though often delayed or canceled due to inclement weather. There are also flights to some destinations farther north in Paraguay and to some points in the Chaco. Inquire locally or through your travel agent for more information.

TAXI

Taxis are abundant in Asunción and in other major cities and towns. Usually, they are metered, but a surcharge is often levied at night. You can hail cabs on the street; they are also found clustered in the hotel districts.

AUTO

Automobiles can be rented at the airport in Asunción (Hertz and National) or through local agencies for tourists in major cities and towns. You must have a valid driver's license from your country of residence or an international driving permit. Driving in Paraguay is somewhat hazardous; traffic regulations are routinely ignored and most roads (about 90 percent) are unpaved and clogged with obstructions such as animals, ox carts, vehicles without headlights, and unpredictable pedestrians. Of the roads that are paved, most are of rough cobblestone. There are two primary roadways paved with asphalt and adequately maintained that run from Asunción: one to Ciudad del Este close to the Brazilian border, and one to Encarnación and Argentina. Motorists are advised to use extreme caution as hazard signage is usually nonexistent.

TRAIN

Ancient wood-burning trains ply the rails in Paraguay, operated by Ferrocarril Presidente Carlos Antonio Lopez (FCPCAL). Virtual museum pieces, they are remarkably inexpensive, but also remarkably slow. A weekly service links Asunción with Encarnación (431km / 268 miles), and a weekly service connecting San Salvador and Abay. A link also travels between Asunción and Areguá, along Lago Ypacaraí. Rail travel is not the best alternative for the business traveler, as services tend to be unreliable and entire routes may be eliminated for months on end. Inquire locally for more information.

BUS / TRAM

Long-distance buses run frequently to destinations throughout the country. Compared to the train or to auto rental, buses usually prove to be the cheapest and most efficient mode of transportation. Express connections exist between major urban centers.

Within Asunción, there are bus and mini-bus services operated by private companies. Passengers pay the conductor upon boarding; the fare is based on a two-zone system. There are also two government-operated tramways in the city. Several other of the larger cities also have bus systems. None of these is recommended for the business traveler.

SUBWAY

No subway system exists in Paraguay.

WATER TRAVEL

Paraguay is a landlocked country, but river cruises to major tourist attractions are available, as well as throughout the Chaco. No regular commuter or ferry service exists. For details regarding cruises, contact the Secretaría Nacional de Turismo (see Travel Assistance, following).

TRAVEL HELP

Hotel Accommodations
Travelers are advised to talk to a reputable travel agent before making reservations in Paraguay, for up-to-date information.
Secretaría Nacional de Turismo
Palma 468, casi 14 de Mayo
Asunción, Paraguay
tel: (21) 441 530 or 441 620; fax: (21) 491 230
email: ditur@infonet.com.py

Communications

DIALING CODES IN PARAGUAY

International country code: [595]
Selected city codes: Asunción (21), Ayolas (72), Capiata (28), Concepcion (31), Coronel Bogado (74), Coronel Oviedo (521), Encarnacion (71), Hernandarias (63), Ita (24), Pedro J Caballero (36), Pilar (86), San Antonio (27), San Ignacio (82), Stroessner: Ciudad Pte. (61), Villarrica (541), Villeta (25).

Dialing Paraguay from Overseas

To dial Paraguay from overseas, dial your country's international dialing code, then 505 (the country code for Paraguay), then the city code and finally the number. If you were dialing Asunción, for example, you would begin with 011, then 595, then 21 (the city code for Asunción), and finally the number of the person or office you were trying to reach.

Assistance Numbers

International operator 0010
Local operator 010
Information 12
ANTELCO 44-001

CALLING WITHIN PARAGUAY

Local Calls
Public phones take tokens (fichas), not coins. A local, three minute call will cost about 10 cents.

Long Distance Calls
Since it is not possible to make long distance calls from public phones in Paraguay, telephone offices and some roadside service stations offer this capability. Area codes are in effect throughout the country. Dial '0' prior to the area code when calling long distance within the country.

International Calls
To make a direct international call, dial 002 + country code + area code + number. Rates to the U.S. run at about

US$2.85 per minute during regular hours and US$2.53 during off-peak hours. Antelco, the national telephone conglomerate, operates an office on the corner of 14 de Mayo and General Diaz in Asunción, which provides direct service to connect with home operators in Argentina, Australia, Brazil, Germany, Japan, Uruguay, and the U.S. These operators will assist in collect and credit card calls, which prove less costly than local payment.

AT&T Direct...008-1-800
MCI..008-11-800
Sprint..008-12-800

PAY PHONES

Public Telephones

Tokens (*fichas*) to use public phones may be purchased at post offices, bars, and tobacco kiosks, which may be far easier to locate than the actual telephones themselves. If you do happen to find a phone:

1. Pick up receiver
2. Wait for tone
3. Insert token into slot
4. Dial number

If the tone is busy, hang up phone and token will be returned.

Note: Keep in mind that if you use a public phone, keep conversations short since the phone may be in demand by others who do not have use of a phone at home.

CELLULAR PHONES

Antelco and *Telefonica Celular del Paraguay* operate AMPS analogue systems for cellular users in Paraguay.

Note: Your home country cell phone may not work in this country. If not, we recommend that you rent an international cell phone *before* you leave home. A major US-based cell phone rental provider is **IMC WorldCell**. For information see "International Cell Phone Rentals" on page 14.

* **Note**: Some hotels also rent phones.

CALL BACK

You can (potentially) save significant sums when calling in Paraguay by using one of the call back services listed below. Fees for call back services vary widely, depending on the company and the type of service required. Be sure to check with these companies before leaving to compare rates.

For a list of callback services, please refer to the "Communications" section in the *Global Road Warrior* Introduction.

PHONE JACK

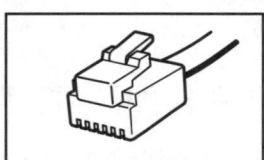

Plug adaptors are available through **iGo Corporation.** (See "Electrical and Telephone Adaptors" on page 19.)

FAX

Only a few top end hotels have fax services.

POSTAL SERVICES

Airmail to Europe takes five to seven days. Airmail to North America takes about five days. Incoming mail can take much longer. Do not send valuables in Paraguay. The General Post Office is located at Alberdi and El Paraguayo Independiente.

Hours of Service

Monday to Friday 7:30a.m. to noon, 2:30p.m. to 7:30p.m., Saturday 8a.m. to 1p.m.

TELEGRAMS

Telegrams can be sent from most hotels.

Business Services

COURIER SERVICE

Airborne Express; Eagle Express Courier, Ibanez Del Campo 730, Asuncion; tel: (21) 450-887; fax: (21) 490-585.

Consolidate Air Courier; Pdte. Franco e/Ayolas, 1er Piso, Ofc 12; tel: (21) 493-011, 442-623; fax: (21) 442-623.

DHL; Espana 676 c/Boqueron y Rosa Pena; tel: (21) 211-035; Monday to Friday 8a.m. to 7p.m., Saturday 9a.m. to noon.

Express Mail Service; Benjamin Contant 402 y Alberdi; tel: (21) 446-307, 498-112/6; fax: 445-913; airport, tel: 206-195/6.

Federal Express; Asuncion Express Courier, Sargento Insfran esq. Primer Prtesidente; tel: (21) 297-475; fax: (21) 291-358.

Sky Courier; O'Leary 515, 2 Piso Edif. Itá Ybaté; tel: (21) 443-785, 444-178; fax: (21) 443-671.

TNT; Intertrade Courier Intl., Mariscal Lopez 196, Calle Constitucion; tel: (21) 214-781, 214-782; fax: (21) 214-780.

UPS; Air Systems International, O'Leary 409-10, 1er Piso, Oficina 125 Asunción; tel: (21) 491-463; fax: (21) 445-111.

COMPUTER SERVICE

Capitolio S.R.L.; Dr. Insfrán 2345 - Ofic. 11; tel: 494-714; email: info@capitolio.com.py; Proxima, Acer, Microsoft, Novell; software, computer service, scanners, access, cable, Internet/intranet.

ITEC; Cerro corá 2275c, Vice Pdte. Sánchez; tel: 226-405; email: itec@infonet.com.py; Service, technical support.

SISTECO Paraguay, S.R.L.; Bral. Genes c/San Rafael, Galeria Colonial; email: sisteco@mmail.com.py; computers and accessories.

Tecnoplan; Mayor Fleitas 207 esq. Eligio Ayala; Telefax: 222-511, 214-413; email: tecplan@mail.pla.net.py; service and installation.

TRANSLATION/INTERPRETING

Beachy Jonathan W. Llc; tel/fax: 294-355; email: jonathan@ui28.una.py.; English and Spanish.

Clebsch Madelaire Alfredo Traducciones; Simón Bolivar 980e/EE. UU. y Parapiti; tel/fax: 444-328 cc: 135; English, German, Spanish.

Melgarejo Gloria, Llc; Diaz de Solis 1032; tel: 481-467; French, English, Spanish.

Recalde M.A. Elida De, DRA.; O'Leary 1084, telefax: 441-497; English, Portuguese, Spanish.

Electrical

Current

220 volts AC, 50Hz

ELECTRIC PLUGS

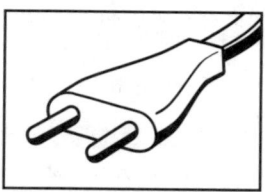

Plug adaptors are available through **iGo Corporation**. (See "Electrical and Telephone Adaptors" on page 19.)

Technical Support
HARDWARE/SOFTWARE VENDOR SUPPORT

Compaq/Digital; (Argentina Office) tel: (54) 1-796-1616; fax: (54) 1-790- 0535; (in the U.S.) tel: [1] (281) 518-2000 (international technical support); fax: [1] (281) 518-1442; http://www.compaq.com.

Dell; (Latin America Division) tel: [1] 512-728-4397; (Main Office) tel: [1] 512-338-4400; fax: [1] 512-728-3330; http://www.dell.com.

Hewlett Packard; (Brazil Office) tel: [55] 11 709 1444; (in the U.S.) tel: [1] (408) 246-4300; http://www.hp.com/.

IBM; tel: (21) 442-811; fax: (21) 418-7278; (in the U.S.) tel: [1] (919) 517-2800; http://www.ibm.com/.

Microsoft; (Uruguay Office) tel: [598] (2) 774-934; fax: [598] (2) 774-935; (in the U.S.) [1] (425) 635-7222; http://www.microsoft.com/.

Internet Connection
HOW TO CONNECT

Connecting to AOL and Compuserve in Paraguay is similar to using it when traveling outside your own area code. See the introductory section for detailed information on connecting to your account through a different phone number.

America Online
Numbers are available at keyword *international*. Be sure to get several local numbers before leaving. Go to keyword *access* (a free area) and download the software.

There are no direct access numbers for America Online in Paraguay. Users will have to pay international rates to use the service.

Compuserve
Numbers are available at *Go International*. The Compuserve Web-site also has a great deal of information, at http://www.compuserve.com.

There are no direct access numbers for Compuserve in Paraguay. Users will have to pay international rates to use the service.

Independent Service Providers
Many independent service providers offer discounts if you are only in town for a couple days.

Infonet; tel: (21) 440-970; tel: (21) 440-104; fax (21) 440-270; email: webmaster@conexión.com.py; http://www.infonet.com.py/.

Internet Highway; tel: (21) 662-609; email: info@highway.com.py; http://www.highway.com.py/.

Planet; tel: (21) 440-840; fax: (21) 440-840; email: admin@pla.net.py; http://www.pla.net.py/.

UNINET; tel: 498-817/818/820/788; email: negocios@uninet.com.py; http://www.uninet.com.py/.

Business Culture
GREETINGS AND COURTESIES

Handshakes are customary among both men and women both when arriving and leaving, although there is a range of variations including nods to other men and slight bows to women. Male friends may hug; female friends may kiss each other's cheek. Business cards in Spanish are considered important, and it is a courtesy to translate other materials as well. In general, visiting business people should have a command of Spanish since only few Paraguayan business people speak English well. Use *Señor* followed by the title of office when speaking with government officials, i.e., *Señor Minstro*, *Señor Administrador General*, etc. Use titles for high government officials as follows: *Excelentisimo Senor Ministro* for Ministers of State, and *Su Senoría* for Subsecretaries of State. Use *Doctor* before a surname for graduates in medicine, economics, and law. At social events be sure to shake hands and say good-bye to everyone individually. Paraguayans normally arrive up to 30 minutes late for social engagements.

BUSINESS ETHIC AND FRAMEWORK

Paraguayans are punctiliously courteous and genuinely friendly. Respect and personal dignity lie at the core of Paraguayan business and social culture, both of which are based on correct, often strongly hierarchical, but personal relationships. To Paraguayans, work is far from the most important part of life, but they do adhere strictly to the forms that govern this nevertheless important sphere. They will not hesitate, however, to break a business appointment to help out a friend or family member, and foreigners should not be irritated by this type of disruption in plans.

MEETINGS AND DECISION MAKING

Prior appointments are very important, and should be made two to four weeks in advance. Paraguayans are generally informal about appointment times. Authority is rather narrowly concentrated and actual decisions are almost always made at a high level. Cultivate all relationships, however. They may strongly influence the actual decision maker even when your immediate counterpart is not the one making the decision.

WOMEN

Paraguayan women are becoming more common and more accepted in business in general, although their presence remains rare in the upper levels of business. In general, foreign businesswomen should experience few problems; some even consider it an advantage that Paraguayans dislike contradicting or offending women and may defer to them.

BUSINESS ATTIRE

Lightweight suits and ties will serve a man well for business in this tropical climate. A dinner jacket is recommended for evening events. Women should wear a conservative two-piece suit or similar attire, preferably in lightweight cotton or linen to combat the heat during the warmer months from December to March. However, one should prepare for sudden changes in temperature during the months before and after peak summer. An overcoat and woolens are recommended during the winter months. A compact umbrella will serve well for rain showers throughout the year.

Paraguay

Business Centers
Asunción

CITY VIEW

An urban explosion and a lack of zoning has turned Asunción into a rambling mess of a city, with buildings sprawled out across its expanse. However, high rises have been contained in the city's business center. The Río Paraguay, above whose east bank the capital stands, lends the city a breath of natural touch. More than a few of Paraguay's best offerings do not lie far from Asunción.

AIRPORT

Silvio Pettirossi Airport to City Center

The airport is 10 miles (16 km.) from the city. Buses and taxis are available. Travel time to the city is about 20 minutes; a bus ride may take from 50 to 60 minutes.

Airline Numbers

Aerolíneas Argentinas	(21) 49-10-12
Aéroperú	(21) 49-31-22
Air France	(21) 49-87-68
Alitalia	(21) 66-04-35
American Airlines	(21) 44-33-30
Iberia	(21) 49-33-51
LATN	(21) 21-22-77
Líneas Aéreas del Cobre	(21) 44-70-28
Líneas Aéreas Paraguayas	(21) 49-10-46
Lloyd Aéreo Boliviano	(21) 49-47-15
Lufthansa	(21) 44-79-64
PLUNA	(21) 49-01-28
Varig	(21) 49-74-51

HOTELS

Top-end

Excelsior; Chile 980; tel: (21) 495-632; fax: (21) 496-748; 140 rooms; city center; casino; restaurants; bar; business center; secretarial service; conference facilities (up to 800); in-room safe; mini bar; international direct dialing; cable TV; data port in room; hair dryer; 24 hour room service; baby sitting service; doctor on call; beauty salon; barber; mall complex; Concierge; parking; sauna; corporate rates; fitness center; pool; golf; tennis; disco.

Hotel Resort & Casino, Yacht Y Golf Club Paraguayo; Avenue Del Yacht 1; tel: (21) 906-117; fax: (21) 906-120; http://www.hotelyacht.com.py/ingles/index.html; suburb; located near beach; bar; casino; restaurant; conference facilities; business center; in-room phone; 24 hour room service; shops; car and limousine rental; parking; fitness; pool; 18-hole golf; squash; watersports; hockey; soccer; horseback riding; disco.

Expensive

Cecilia; Estados Unidos 341; tel: (21) 210-365; fax: (21) 497-111; e-mail: cecilhotel@uninet.com.py; city center; restaurant; conference facilities; in-room phone (international direct dialing); cable TV; air conditioned; some rooms with fax machine in the room; fitness; pool.

Chaco; Caballero 285; tel: (21) 492-066; fax: (21) 444-223; e-mail: chacotel@infonet.com.py; 72 rooms; city center, 300m from rail station; restaurant; bar; meeting facilities (up to 50); secretarial service; fax/photocopy facilities; in-room modem/fax connection; cable TV; air conditioned; corporate rates; parking; pool.

Gran Hotel De Paraguay; tel: (21) 200-051; historic building located in suburb; 5 minutes from city center;

restaurant; meeting facilities; in-room phone; air conditioned; parking; pool; tennis.

Hotel Guaraní; Oliva Y Independencia National; tel: (21) 491-131/9; fax: (21) 443-638; 168 rooms; city center; casino; restaurant; conference facilities (up to 350): in-room phone; air conditioned; parking; fitness; sauna; pool; jogging track.

Itá Enramada; Cacique Lambare and Ribera Del Rio Paraguay; tel: (21) 333-041/6; fax: (21) 905-717; email: ita@mmail.com.py; suburb; casino; restaurants; meeting facilities (up to 300); air conditioned; 24-hour room service; sauna; Turkish bath; pool; tennis.

Mandu Ara; Calle Mexico 554 C/Azara; tel: (21) 490-223; fax: (21) 490-224; standard rooms and suites with kitchenettes available; bar; conference rooms; business center with Internet access; mini bar; air conditioned; TV; car rental; health club; pool; tennis.

Moderate

Plaza; Eligio Ayalas Y Paraguari; tel: (21) 444-772; fax: (21) 448-834; near airport; in-room phone; room service.

Presidente; Azara C/ Ind Nacional; tel: (21) 494-931/2; fax: (21) 444-057; near city center; restaurant; in-room phone.

Hotel Westfalenhaus; Stgo. 1 M Benitez 1577c/Stma. Trinidad; tel: (21) 292-374; fax: (21) 291-241; email: westfalenhaus@pla.net.py; business center with mobile phone rental and Internet service; apartments with a/c, living rooms; cable tv; international direct dialing; bathroom; kitchenette; pool; massage.

Zaphir Hotel; Estrella 995, Casilla Postal 3234; tel: (21) 490-025, 440-339, 490-713; fax: (21) 490-72169; restaurant; snack bar; international direct dialing; cable TV; air conditioned.

MEDICAL CARE

Centro Medico Bautista; Avenida Republica Argentina, corner of Andrés Campos Cervera; Emergency tel: 607-944; central telephone, tel: 600-171.

Cruz Roja Paraguaya; (Red Cross); tel: 204-900.

IPS - Hospital Central; tel: 290-136, 290-137/138/139.

Hospital de Clínicas; corner of Avenida Dr J Montero and Lagarenza; tel: 80-982/983/984.

Hospital Nacional; tel: 024-450/451/452/453/454.

Lacimet (Laboratorio Central e Instituto de Medicina Tropical); tel: 292-653/654.

AUTO RENTAL

Hertz; Airport; tel: 206-195; Av. España 2499 esq. Sta. Rosa; tel: (21) 605-086.

Localiza; tel: (21) 446-233; Airport, tel: (61) 504-770.

National; tel: (21) 492-157, 491-379; fax: (21) 445-890; Yesgros 501, tel: 491-379.

WORLD TRADE CENTER

World Trade Center Asuncion
1001 Brickell Bay Drive, Suite #2210
Miami, Florida 33131
tel: [1] (305) 377-0304; fax: [1] (305) 577-3347

CHAMBER OF COMMERCE

Camara y Bolsa de Comercio
Estrella 540, Asunción
tel: (21) 442-135/136; fax: (21) 442-135.

Peru

At a Glance

THE PEOPLE

Population ....27,012,899 (July 2000 est.)
Growth Rate ....1.75% (2000 est.)
Life Expectancy .... 70.01 years
Infant Mortality..... 40.6 deaths/1,000 live births (2000 est.)

Ethnic Composition

Amerindian 45%
Mestizo (mixed Amerindian and white) 37%
Caucasian 15%
Black, Japanese, Chinese, other.................................. 3%

Religious Composition

Roman Catholic.. 90%
Other 10%

Languages Spoken

Spanish is primarily used by the media, the government, and businesses, but Quechua and Aymara are also widely spoken by Indians in the Andean highlands.

Education and Literacy

Education is nominally free and compulsory; an estimated 88.7 percent of the urban population can read and write compared with 30 percent of the population living in the isolated mountainous areas. There is a national university in almost every major city but only a fraction of applicants are accepted each year.

Labor Force

Total: 7,600,000
By occupation: agriculture, mining and quarrying, manufacturing, construction, transport, services.

THE ECONOMY

Peru's implementation of far reaching privatization completed post 1990 in the mining, electricity, and telecommunications industries, has given the economy a more market oriented character. Growth was strong in 1994 to 1997 largely due to strong foreign investment and the cooperation between the Fujimori government and the IMF and World Bank. During this time, inflation was also brought under control. In 1998, the financial crisis in Asia, the impact of El Nino on agriculture, and unstable Brazilian markets eroded some of Peru's growth. 1999 was not much of an improvement for Peru, with the lasting effects of El Nino and the Asian financial crisis still being felt. In June 1999, the government of Peru did manage to complete negotiations for an Extended Fund Facility with the IMF, although it subsequently had to renegotiate the targets. The recovery of Peru's fishing industry and improved commodity prices should help drive GDP growth above the 5 percent in 2000.

Exports .... US$5.9 billion (f.o.b., 1999 est.)
Imports .... US$8.4 billion (c.i.f., 1999 est.)
Total Trade ....US$14.3 billion (1999 est.)
GDP Per Capita...............................US$4,400 (1999 est.)
Unemployment ....7.7% (1997) Underemployment issues.
Inflation Rate ....5.5% (1999 est.)

Top Export Partners

U.S. 25%, China 8%, Japan 7%, Switzerland, Germany, U.K., Brazil.

Top Import Partners

U.S. 19%, Colombia 6%, Venezuela 5%, Chile 4%, Brazil 4%.

Top Exports

Fish and fish products, copper, zinc, gold, crude petroleum and byproducts, lead, coffee, sugar, cotton.

Top Imports

Machinery, transport equipment, foodstuffs, petroleum, iron and steel, chemicals, pharmaceuticals.

BUSINESS WORKWEEK

Offices

Monday to Friday 8:30a.m. to 5p.m. Certain shops and businesses take a 3-hour siesta and open between 11a.m. and 1p.m. and 4p.m. to 8p.m. Some businesses also work on Saturday mornings.

Banks

Monday to Friday (January through March) 8:30a.m. to 12:30a.m.; Monday to Friday (April through December) 9:15a.m. to 3:30p.m.

Government

Monday to Friday 8:30a.m. to 5p.m.

Retail

Monday to Friday 10:30a.m. to 7:30p.m. Slightly shorter hours on the weekend. Some stores may close between 1p.m. and 4p.m.

HOLIDAYS

New Year's Day...January 1
Maundy Thursday...April 20*
Good Friday...April 21*
Labour Day...May 1
Day of the Peasant...June 24*
St. Peter and St. Paul...June 29
Independence...July 28-29
St. Rose of Lima.. August 30
Battle of Angamos ....October 8
All Saints' Day ....November 1
Immaculate Conception..................................December 8
Christmas ....December 25

*Date may vary by year.

Travel to Peru between January and March should be avoided since most Peruvians take their vacation at this time. Also try and avoid Easter and Christmas for business travel.

CLIMATE

Seasons

Peru's climate is warm, humid, and sub-tropical.There is little rainfall along the coast, although the winter is foggy, and cool. Winters (May to October) are generally mild. During the summers (November to April) the climate is tropical all over the country. Peru is unbearably hot from mid-December to the end of February, and the most pleasant months to visit are from April to October. Temperature range from 34°C (93°F) in the summer, to 14°C (60°F) in the winter.

Regions

In Lima the temperature is moderate year round.

Peru

Money & Banking

Currency

The currency of Peru is the Nuevo Sol (S/).

Denominations

The Nuevo Sol comes in coin denominations of S/5, 2 and 1, and 50, 20, 10, and 5 centimos; and banknotes of S/ 10, S/20, S/50 and S/100.

Traveler's checks

Traveler's checks and currency, but mostly in U.S. dollars, can be exchanged at banks, exchange shops, hotels, and international airport, at tourist exchange rates. Larger banks may offer the best exchange rates, but avoid black marketers at all cost. Consult your bank about current exchange rates before departure. Keep all receipts for reconversion. Banks do not cash personal checks.

Peru

Most currencies can be exchanged but try to take only crisp and new notes, wrinkled and soiled notes are likely to be refused.

Visa is the most used credit card in Peru. but most credit cards, American Express, Visa, Diner's Club, and MasterCard, are easily accepted in good hotels, shops, and car rental places, but smaller restaurants and shops may ask for cash. Some banks in the capital offer cash advances on credit cards, but make sure you bring you passport.

Essential Terms

English	Spanish
Yes No	Sí No
Good morning Hello (daytime) Hello (evening) Hello (telephone)	Buenos días Buenas tardes Buenas noches ¿Hola?
Good-bye	Adiós
Please	Por favor
Thank you	Gracias
Pleased to meet you	Encantado (a) de conocerle
Excuse me; I'm sorry	¿Perdóneme?
My name is _____	Me llamo _____
I don't understand	No comprendo
Do you speak English?	¿Habla usted inglés?

Travel

VISA AND PASSPORT

Foreigners must have a passport, valid for 6 months beyond the intended length of stay, and onward tickets. A visa is not necessary for tourist visits up to 90 days. Business travelers who will not be reimbursed in Peru for their services, may travel into the country on a tourist visa. Business visitors who will be receiving pay in country require a business visa and a a prepared tax declaration is necessary from the Dirección General de Constribuciones. Contact a consulate or embassy before departure to check for any requirements or regulations that may have changed.

DEPARTURE FORMALITIES

The tourist card you have filled in on arrival will be required for departing. Visitors on business visas must have certification from the Ministry of Economy and Finance that Peruvian income taxes were paid. An airport departure tax of US$25 is charged.

CUSTOMS ENTRY (PERSONAL)

Duty-free
- Tobacco: 400 cigarettes, 50 cigars, or 250g of tobacco
- Alcohol: 3 bottles not exceeding 2.5 liters
- Perfume: a reasonable amount of perfume for personal use

IMMUNIZATION

Consult a physician on the advisability of gamma globulin shots against hepatitis, and malaria suppressants for certain areas of Peru. An international certificate of vaccination is required for Yellow Fever if arriving from an infected area.

TIPPING

Taxi
Taxi drivers do not expect tips; hired drivers should be tipped at your discretion, but car watchers get about US$0.10.

Porters
Railway porters get about US$0.15 per bag, airport porters US$0.50 to US$1 depending on the number of bags.

Hotels
A government tax of 28 percent already exists on hotel bills.

Restaurants
Restaurants: tip 5 percent if the 15 percent service charge was added, or 15 percent if it was not.

Other
Hairdressers and coatcheck attendants should only be tipped in very expensive establishments.

EMERGENCY INFORMATION

Police and Crime
Peru is considered dangerous, and terrorism is not uncommon. In Lima, muggings have been known to take place in broad daylight. Airport theft is common; avoid riding in unauthorized taxis or sharing one with a stranger. Stick to well-known tourist routes, and travel in groups when possible. Keep valuables in a hotel safe, wear a money belt, and avoid flashy jewelry (if you do wear a watch, wear a plastic one). Carjackings have also become common. Certain areas of Peru are especially dangerous. Check with your consulate for current security information before undertaking any travel in rural Peru. Shining Path (*Sendero Luminoso*) guerillas continue to operate in the provinces of Junin, Huanuco, San Martin, and Ayacucho. The U.S. Embassy has designated certain areas as "restricted" for its personnel. The Peruvian government has designated its own "emergency zones" around the country, which also includes most of metropolitan Lima. Police and military personnel in these emergency zones are given extraordinary powers to detain and hold people.

An agreement signed in October of 1998 meant to end the border conflict between Peru and Ecuador. Crossing or approaching the Peru-Ecuador border anywhere except at official checkpoints is considered extremely dangerous. A demilitarized zone is in effect until the border demarcation process has been completed.

Dress and behave conservatively. Leave most of your cash, traveler's checks, and your camera in your hotel safe. Carry photocopies of your passport instead of the original. Carry cash in a money belt, and use credit cards or traveler's checks for most transactions. Walk with your bag away from the street to avoid having it snatched away by motorcycle thieves. Never carry a stranger's baggage or exchange money in the street. Women should avoid traveling alone at night. The police are generally helpful and efficient, and punishment for crime (especially drug trafficking) is severe.

Emergency Numbers
Emergency/police...4-33-3333
Terrorism/Hijacking 4-33-3833
Tourist Police (Lima) 225-8698, 225-8699
.... fax: 476-7708

Peru

Assist Hotline

For complaints regarding poor service, lost property, or unfair charges, call:

INDEPCOPI.............................tel: (1) 224-7888, 224-8600

.... Toll-Free: 0-800-42579

Health

Tap water is unsafe to drink; boil water or use the bottled kind. Wash all vegetables in a chlorine solution, peel fruits, and avoid uncooked food. Eat food while it is still hot. Try to eat at more expensive restaurants until your digestive system adjusts to the local spices. Drink only pasteurized milk.

A cholera epidemic started in Peru in 1991 and spread around Latin America. Yellow fever, hepatitis, and tuberculosis are major threats everywhere, especially in poorer rural areas.

Peru is extremely hot, so take precautions against sun and heat stroke, drink lots of liquids, and use sunblock when outdoors.

High-altitude destinations such as Cusco and Lake Titicaca pose threat of altitude sickness for travelers who are unaccustomed to the thin air. Malaria exists in the eastern jungle areas of Peru.

The medical system is adequate in larger cities, and medical staff can usually speak English, but use them for emergencies only.

TAXI

Taxis cannot be hailed from the street. They are stationed at hotels and airports. Fares are not metered and should be negotiated before departing. If you are only going for a short distance, a tip is not expected.

AUTO

Drivers should not travel alone on rural roads. Be sure to carry spare tires, parts, and fuel in remote areas where great distances exist between service areas. Highway accidents involving buses and trucks are very frequent due to poor maintenance, excessive speed, and dangerous driving habits. A valid driver's license fromyour country of residence is required for auto rental. If renting for a period over 3 months in duration, the renter is required to get an international driver's license.

BUS

Buses are the major means of transportation in the cities. Service can be slow but is generally comfortable. Avoid traveling the highways by bus as accidents are frequent due to poor maintenance and reckless driving.

TRAIN

Rail service is sporadic. Some lines are closed during the winter, other areas are not accessible by train. Service can be disrupted by landslide damage.

WATER TRAVEL

A ferry runs from Pucallpa to Iquitos, the journey taking about five days. Ferry service is also available from Iquia to the borders of Colombia and Brazil, a journey of two to three days.

TRAVEL HELP

Hotel Accommodations

Asosiación de Hoteles,
Restaurantes y Afines .... (14) 468 773

Communications

DIALING CODES IN PERU

International country code: [51]

Selected city codes: Arequipa (54), Ayacucho (6491), Cajamarca (44), Callao (1), Chiclayo (74), Chimbote (44), Cusco (84), Huancavelica (6495), Huancayo (64), Ica (34), Iquitos (94), Lima (1), Puerto Maldonado (84), Paita (74), Piura (74), Pucallpa (64), Tacna (54), Talara (74), Trujillo (44), Yurimaguas (94)

Dialing Peru from Overseas

To dial Peru from overseas, dial your international dialing code, then 51 (the country code for Peru), then the city code and finally the number. If you were dialing Arequipa, for example, you would begin with 011, then 51, then 94 (the city code for Arequipa), and finally the number of the person or office you are trying to reach.

Assistance Numbers

International Operator 108
Operator 100
Directory 103

CALLING WITHIN PERU

Local Calls

Lima phone numbers now all have seven digits. All other areas should have six digits. Local calls can be placed at hotels, public phones, corner shops, and restaurants.

Long Distance Calls

Use area codes when dialing long distance within Peru. Dial a preceding zero in all cases. Thus, dial 0 + 1 + local number when making a call to Lima from anywhere else in the country.

International Calls

In Lima, the telephone offices may be crowded. So either get to a public phone or call from a hotel. To call direct, dial 00 + country code + area code + number. Expect surcharges from hotels, which you may want to enquire about before making a call.

Mid to large-size towns have Telefonica offices run by Telefonica del Peru, the privatized version of the former ENTEL. To make a call from a telephone office, announce the number you want to reach and the clerk will assign you a booth. Pay upon exiting. Rates diminish after 9p.m. daily, and on Sundays.

To reach a U.S. operator, dial:

AT&T 171
MCI.. 170

However, accessing these numbers may not be possible from every phone.

PAY PHONES

Public Telephones

Peruvian public phones traditionally take tokens (rins or fichas), but the archaic system is on its way out as coins and cards take over Peru.

Calling Cards

Known as *tarjetas telefonicas*, phone cards have begun their surge in Peru with the charm of offering the least expensive way to call home. An S/30 card will buy 4.5 minutes of chatting time at the cost of about US$13. Phone cards are available for purchase at corner shops or on the streets in the center of town.

CELLULAR PHONES

Telefonica del Peru and *Tele2000* operate AMPS-TDMA analogue systems for cellular users in Peru.

Note: Your home country cell phone may not work in this country. If not, we recommend that you rent an international cell phone *before* you leave home. A major US-based cell phone rental provider is **IMC WorldCell**. For information see "International Cell Phone Rentals" on page 14. Phones are also available for rent from *Telefonica del Peru*, at certain top-end hotels, and at the following location: **RentaCel**; 3190 Av. Javier Prado Este; tel: (1) 955-5520.

CALL BACK

You can (potentially) save significant sums when calling in Peru by using one of the call back services listed below. Fees for call back services vary widely, depending on the company and the type of service required. Be sure to check with these companies before leaving to compare rates.

For a list of callback services, please refer to the "Communications" section in the *Global Road Warrior* Introduction.

PHONE JACK

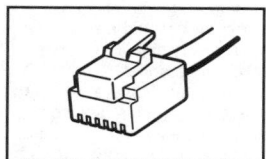

Plug adaptors are available through **iGo Corporation**. (See "Electrical and Telephone Adaptors" on page 19.)

FAX

Fax machines have become popular in the last few years, and now can be found in most hotels, at Telefonica del Peru offices, and small public booths.

POSTAL SERVICES

Postal service is unreliable, at best. There is an express mail service that also is unreliable.

Hours of service

Monday to Saturday 8a.m. to 6p.m., Sunday 8a.m. to noon.

TELEGRAMS

Services are available at most hotels in Lima.

Business Services

COURIER SERVICE

Airborne Express; International Bonded Couriers, Calle Lord Cochrane #324, Miraflores 18, Lima; tel: (1) 221-2616; fax: (1) 422-0323.

DHL; Haedo 105, c/Independencia nacional, Asuncion; tel: (1) 496-683; Monday to Friday 8a.m. to 7p.m., Saturday 9a.m. to noon.

Federal Express; Scharff International Courier; tel: (1) 575-1884; fax: (1) 575-1889.

International Bonded Couriers; 324 Lord Chocrane; tel: (1) 221-2616; fax: (1) 422-0323.

UPS Peru; Union Pak del Peru, S.A.., Ave. del Ejercito 2107 San Isidro-27, Lima; tel: (1) 264-0105; fax: (1) 264-6340.

TRANSLATION SERVICE

Berlitz Centers del Peru; 236 Av. Santa Cruz; tel: (1) 440-7681; fax: (1) 441-7225.

Centro de Traducciones Tecnicas; Av. Los Insurgentes M2 K LT 1; tel: 275-2200; fax: 275-2203.

Servicios Profesionales y Administrativos; 552 Las Begonias - Of. 17; tel: (1) 441-2913; fax: (1) 442-7429.

Electrical

Current

220 volts AC, 60Hz.

ELECTRIC PLUGS

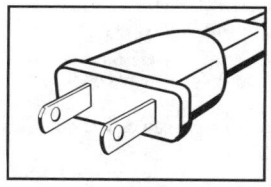

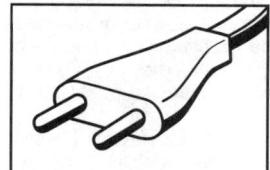

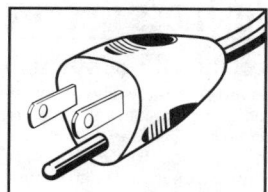

Plug adaptors are available through **iGo Corporation**. (See "Electrical and Telephone Adaptors" on page 19.)

Technical Support

HARDWARE/SOFTWARE VENDOR SUPPORT

Dell; tel: (14) 42-0111; (U.S. Office) tel: [1] 512-338-4400; fax: [1] 512-728-3330; http://www.dell.com.

Hewlett Packard; (Brazil Office) [55] 11 709 1444; (in the U.S.) tel: [1] (408) 246-4300; http://www.hp.com/.

IBM; tel: (1) 349-0040; tel: (1) 349-0050; fax: 349-0235; (in the U.S.) tel: [1] (919) 517-2800; http://www.ibm.com/.

Microsoft; (in the U.S.) tel: [1] (425) 936-8661 (Customer Services); tel: [1] (214) 714-9100 (Technical Support for Latin America); (in the U.S.) [1] (425) 635-7222; http://www.microsoft.com/.

Internet Connection

HOW TO CONNECT

Connecting to AOL and Compuserve in Peru is similar to using it when traveling outside your own area code. See the introductory section for detailed information on connecting to your account through a different phone number.

America Online

Numbers are available at keyword *international*. Be sure to get several local numbers before leaving. AOL has a new GlobalNet service that charges US$6 an hour in addition to the usual charges. Go to keyword *access* (a free area) and download the software.

Access: Lima (1) 421-1560, Lima (1) 211-0500.

Compuserve

Numbers are available at *Go International*. The Compuserve Web-site also has a great deal of information, at http://www.compuserve.com.

Access: Lima (1) 421-1560.

Independent Service Providers

Many independent service providers offer discounts if you are only in town for a couple of days.

Electro Data S.A.; tel: (1) 476-1208; tel: 224-7784; fax: (1) 476-6780; email: webmaster@electrodata.com.pe; http://www.electrodata.com.pe/.

InterAxis S.A.; tel: (1) 241-2832; fax: (1) 242-1596; email: produccion@iaxis.com.pe; http://www.iaxis.com.pe.

La Red S.A.; tel: (54) 286-700; fax: (54) 281-333; email: info@LaRed.net.pe; http://www.LaRed.net.pe/.

Red Cientifica Peruana (RCP); tel: (1) 421-1343; fax: (1) 421-8086; email: gcomercial@rcp.net.pe; http://ekeko.rcp.net.pe/ .

TCI S.A.; tel: (1) 421-3222; fax: (1) 421-8950; email: ventas@tci.net.pe; http://www.tci.net.pe/.

Business Culture

GREETINGS AND COURTESIES

Handshakes are customary among both men and women, both when arriving and leaving. Male friends may hug and female friends may kiss each other's cheek; men may also lightly kiss the cheek of women friends. Note that friends of the same sex may walk arm in arm. Titles are important, and business associates are addressed by their title and surname until they request otherwise; *Doctor* is commonly used as a title of respect for lawyers and those with an advanced degree. *Licenciado* applies to a man with a university degree, and *Ingeniero* for an engineer. Business cards in Spanish are expected, and it is a courtesy to translate other materials as well. At social events be sure to shake hands and say good-bye to everyone individually.

BUSINESS ETHIC AND FRAMEWORK

Peruvians are among the most formal and reserved of all South Americans. To Peruvians, work is far from the most important part of life, but they do adhere strictly to the forms that govern this nevertheless important sphere. Appropriateness is critical, and Peruvians value diplomacy, tactfulness, and sensitivity as much as they dislike overt aggressiveness and bluntness. Consider speaking Spanish as an almost prerequisite in establishing respectful contact as Lima remains mostly monolingual.

DECISION MAKING

Peruvians generally work in a structured environment, and the lines of authority are clearly drawn. Authority is rather narrowly concentrated and actual decisions are almost always made at a high level. Cultivate all employee relationships, because their quality may strongly influence the actual decision maker even when your immediate counterpart is not the one making the decision.

WOMEN

Many women operate businesses, especially small-scale businesses, have considerable personal freedom, and are becoming more common and accepted in general; but their presence remains rare in the top levels of large companies. In general, foreign businesswomen may experience problems gaining acceptance in conservative Peru; some traditional Peruvian businessmen have refused to do business with foreign businesswomen and have considered the assignment of a woman as an insult by the sponsoring firm. Nevertheless, foreign businesswomen are making some progress, but must be careful to be highly professional, appropriate, and neither aggressive nor confrontational. Although women may generally go on the streets and dine alone, many will feel more comfortable if escorted.

MEETINGS

Contacts and introductions are extremely important. If you do not have a mutual business acquaintance to introduce you, consult your embassy for a referral. Prior appointments are important, should be made two to four weeks in advance, and should be reconfirmed in Spanish by fax or writing. It is very difficult to see most Peruvians on short notice without a personal introduction. Peruvians are seldom punctual, although you are expected to be on time. Avoid scheduling appointments between noon and 3p.m., as it is often lunch or siesta time. Because business relationships are founded on personal relationships, several meetings and more than one trip may be required to conclude an agreement. Business entertaining is fairly common, and the business lunch is rapidly becoming an institution; however, a business dinner usually remains a much more social occasion. Business is seldom discussed directly at business lunches and almost never at dinners. During negotiations, only those directly involved are invited out, although following completion of a deal, a more general celebratory invitation may be issued.

BUSINESS ATTIRE

Foreign businessmen are expected to wear light- to medium-weight, dark, conservative suits—depending on the season. (Heavier weight fabric is needed in the Andes.) Foreign businesswomen should wear dresses or skirts and blouses, with or without jackets. Formal wear is seldom needed, although it may be for government or top-level private affairs, in which case a tuxedo or cocktail dress is needed. A suit or a dress would be appropriate for social occasions, such as an invitation to dinner (parties are slightly more formal than dinners). For less formal social occasions, conservative resort-type attire is suitable, although jeans may also be worn by both sexes. Neither men nor women should wear shorts, and women should avoid anything revealing. Do not wear Indian clothing; you can lose face or even offend some people. Visitors are advised not to dress too well outside of business situations because this can provoke hostility and attract thieves. Flashy or excessive attire, accessories, or jewelry, and excessive makeup should be avoided.

Business Centers
Lima
CITY VIEW

Despite its location next to the sea, Lima is often hot, polluted, and its large population contributes to a noisy downtown. Violent street crime in downtown Lima has also become a problem due to high unemployment and a widening gap between rich and poor. Shantytowns ring the city and roads remain potholed and unkempt. The upper class neighborhoods of San Isidro and Miraflores, the new cultural and commercial center of Lima, offer the visitor somewhat safer haunts around which to wander.

AIRPORT

Jorge Chávez International Airport to City Center

The airport lies 10 miles (16 km.) from the city center. There are regular bus and coach services, and taxs are available. Use only taxis at the official taxi stand in front of the terminal. These cabs charge a flat fee of about US$20 for the 30-minute ride into town. Unofficial taxis bear stickers in the front windshield and offer cheaper rates, but negotiating is necessary. A shuttle bus operated by Transhotel takes passengers to the major hotels in LIma for a fare of about US$10 to $12, or less, depending on the number of passengers.

Airline Numbers

Aereolineas Argentinas	(1) 444-0810, 241-3327
AeroPerú	(1) 241-0606, 368-0420
Aero Condor	(1) 4425663, 422-0461
AeroMexico	(1) 444-4441
Air France	(1) 444-9285
All Nippon Airways (ANA)	(1) 444-444'
Americana	(1) 4478216, 447-8662
American Airlines	(1) 442-8595
Avianca	(1) 221-7530
British Airways	(1) 422-6600
Canadian Airlines	(1) 444-4441
Cathay Pacific	(1) 444-4441
Continental	(1) 221-4340, 221-6987
El Al	(1) 447-9785
Expreso Aéreo	(1) 444-9978
Faucett Peru	(1) 575-1811
Iberia	(1) 421-4616
Japan Airlines	(1) 221-7501
LACSA	(1) 446-0033
Lan Chile	(1) 446-6958, 241-5522
Lufthansa	(1) 442-4455
Qantas	(1) 221-3039
Saeta Airlines	(1) 422-1710
Trans World Airlines	(1) 221-3205
United	(1) 421-3334
Varig	(1) 4424031, 442-4361

HOTELS

Top-end

Hotel Las Américas; Av. Benavides 415, Miraflores; tel: (1) 444-7272 and 241-2820; fax: Hosts and Reservations (1) 444-1137; fax: (1) 445-2733; http://www.hoteleslasamericas.com/ingles/setp001.htm; email: Postmaster@americas.com.pe or email: amerihtl@chavin.rcp.net.perestaurants; business center; conference facilities; secretarial service; in-room modem/fax connection; air conditioned; in room cable TV; radio; hair dryer; mini bar; work suites available; pool.

Miraflores César's Hotel; Esq La Paz y Diez Canseco Casilla; tel: (1) 444-1212; fax: (1) 444-4440; restaurants; 2 bars; conference facilities (up to 270); secretarial service; fax/photocopy facilities; car rental; non-smoking rooms; air conditioned; in room TV; radio; international direct dial; 24-hour room service; corporate rates; parking; fitness; sauna; pool.

Sheraton Lima; Paseo de la Republica 170; tel: (1) 315-5000; fax: (1) 315-5015; 438 rooms; city center; casino; 3 restaurants; bars; conference facilities (up to 1,000); secretarial service; fax/photocopy facilities; full business center; 24 hour room service; beauty salon; gift shop; travel agency; car rental; parking; corporate rates; sauna; fitness; tennis; nearby golf.

Expensive

Libertador; Los Eucaliptos 550, San Isidro; tel: 421-6666; tel: (1) 421-6680; fax: (1) 423-011; city center; rooftop restaurant; conference facilities (up to 150); secretarial service; fax/photocopy facilities; in-room safe; air conditioned; corporate rates; fitness; sauna; whirlpool.

MarÌa Angola Miraflores; Avenida La Paz, MIraflores; tel: (1) 444-1280; fax: (1) 446-2860; restaurant; conference facilities (up to 80); secretarial service; in-room modem/fax connection; fax/photocopy facilities; air conditioned; in room safe; parking; corporate rates; sauna; pool.

Miraflores Plaza Park Hotel; Av. Malecón de la Reserva 1035; tel: (1) 242-3000; fax: (1) 242-3393; email: mirapph@ibm.net; http://www.mira-park.com; European-style hotel; restaurants; conference rooms; business center; pc/internet access; cell phone and beeper rental; dual-line telephones; voicemail; dataport; gift shop; doctor; sauna; pool; squash.

Moderate

Britania; Avinguda San Borja Sur 653; tel: (1) 224-2006; fax: (1) 476-8030; city center; restaurant; meeting facilities (up to 40); air conditioning; corporate rates.

Crillon; Ave. Nicolas De Pierola 58; tel: (1) 428-3290; fax: (1) 432-5920; central location; 3 restaurants; bar; coffee shop; conference facilities (up to 3,000); air conditioning; in room TV; nearby golf and tennis.

Hostal Miramar Ischia; Malecón Cisneros 1244, Miraflores; tel: (1) 446-6969; fax: (1) 445-0851; email: miramarisch@perutravel.org; ocean views; air conditioning; meals cooked by owners.

Hostal Señorial; José González 567, Miraflores; tel: (1) 444-5755; tel: (1) 445-7306; fax: (1) 445-9724; family-run hotel; garden.

Limatambo; Avenida Aramburu 1025, San Isidro; tel: (1) 441-9615; fax: (1) 440-9584; 4-star hotel; suburb; restaurant; conference facilities; fax facilities; in-room safe; air conditioning; cable TV; parking.

MEDICAL CARE

Note: Most local health care providers do not accept foreign health care coverage and require cash payment for services. Private facilities in Lima may accept major credit cards.

Clinica Anglo-Americana; Cdra. 3 CA. Alfredo. Salazar, San Isidro; tel: (1) 221-3656; fax: (1) 442-8274.

Centro Medico Las Palmeras De San Isidro; 1475 Av. Javier Prado Oeste; tel: (1) 442-5879; fax; (1) 422-8721.

Centro Medico Moderno; 1631 Av. Nicolas de Pierola - 201; tel: 428-1813.

Centro Medico San Pedro Norte; 237 Jr. 12 De Julio; tel: 533-3318.

Centro Quiropractico Americano; 411 Gral. Borgoño, tel: (1) 445-8710.

Philippines

At a Glance

THE PEOPLE

Population ....81,159,644 (July 2000 est.)
Growth Rate ....2.07% (2000 est.)
Life Expectancy .... 67.48 years
Infant Mortality ... 29.52 deaths/1,000 live births (2000 est.)

Ethnic Composition

Christian Malay...91.5%
Muslim Malay 4%
Chinese 1.5%
Other 3%

Religious Composition

Roman Catholic..83%
Protestant...9%
Muslim 5%
Buddhist and Other 3%

Languages Spoken

Filipino (based on Tagalog) and English are the official languages.

Education and Literacy

The Philippines have one of the highest literacy rates in East Asia and Pacific Area. About 95 percent of the population 10 years of age and older are literate, despite the multiplicity of languages.

Labor Force

Total: .... 32 million
By occupation: agriculture 39.8%, government and social services 19.4%, services 17.7%, manufacturing 9.8%, construction 5.8%, other 7.5%.

THE ECONOMY

The economy of the Philipines is comprised largely of light industry and agriculture. In 1998 the Philippine economy deteriorated, largely as a result of the Asian financial crisis and poor weather conditions. Economic growth dropped from around 5% in 1997 to around -0.5% in 1998. In 1999 the growth rate recovered, rising to 2.9%. The government has promised to continue its economic reforms of improving infrastructure, overhauling the tax system to bolster government revenues, and moving toward further deregulation and privatization of the economy, in order to help the Philippines keep up with the development in the newly industrialized countries of East Asia.

Exports ....US$34.8 billion (f.o.b., 1999 est.)
Imports ....US$30.7 billion (f.o.b., 1999 est.)
Total Trade ....US$65.5 billion (1999 est.)
GDP Per Capita................................US$3,600 (1999 est.)
Unemployment ....9.6% (October 1998)
Inflation Rate 6.8% (1999)

Top Export Partners

U.S. 34%, E.U. 20%, Japan 14%, Netherlands 8%, Singapore 6%, U.K. 6%, Hong Kong 4%.

Top Import Partners

U.S. 22%, Japan 20%, South Korea 8%, Singapore 6%, Taiwan 5%, Hong Kong 4%.

Top Exports

Electronic equipment, machinery and transport equipment, garments, coconut products.

Top Imports

Raw materials and intermediate goods, capital goods, consumer goods.

BUSINESS WORKWEEK

Offices

Monday to Friday 8a.m. to 5p.m.; offices may close for lunch between noon and 2p.m.; Saturday 8a.m. to noon.

Banks

Monday to Friday 9a.m. to 3p.m.

Government

Monday to Friday 8a.m. to 5p.m., or 9a.m. to 6p.m.

Retail

Monday to Sunday 9a.m. to 7p.m. Some retail outlets work shorter hours on Saturday and Sunday.

HOLIDAYS

New Year's Day..January 1
Bataan Day... April 9
Maundy Thursday...April 20*
Good Friday..April 21*
Labor Day...May 1
Independence Day ....June 12
National Heroes' Day .... August 27
Barangay Day..September 11
National Thanksgiving Day.........................September 21
All Saints' Day ....November 1
Bonifacio Day ....November 30
Christmas ....December 25
Rizal Day...December 30
Last Day of the Year..December 31
*Date may vary by year.

CLIMATE

Seasons

The Philippines can be divided into four main island groups: Luzon in the north (the largest island and the site of Manila), a central group of islands called Visas; the southernmost island, Mindanao; and the southwestern province of Palawan, consisting of more than 1,700 islands.

Typically hot and humid all year-round throughout the region, the Philippine islands do have a dry and a wet season.

The best months to visit and conduct business are from December to May. These months offer cooler and drier conditions.

Regions

In the northern part of the country that includes Manila, the wet season occurs from June to October. Heavy rains, or monsoons, may fall and flooding may occur during these times. December to May temperatures in Manila range from 21° to 31°C (70°-88°F), the hottest temperatures are in April and May when daylight temperatures may rise as high as 35°C. The southern regions have similar ranges of temperatures, but rainfall is distributed more evenly throughout the year. In the highlands, temperatures are often 5° to 10°C (9°-18°F) cooler than Manila.

Philippines

Regions

1 Batanes
2 Cagayan
3 Ilocos Norte
4 Ilocos Sur
5 Abra
6 Kalinga-Apayao
7 Mountain
8 La Union
9 Benguet
10 Ifugao
11 Isabela
12 Nueva Vizcaya
13 Quirino
14 Pangasinan
15 Nueva Ecija
16 Aurora
17 Quezon
18 Zambales
19 Tarlac
20 Bataan
21 Pampanga
22 Bulacan
23 Rizal
24 Cavite
25 Laguna
26 Batangas
27 Camirines Norte
28 Camirines Sur
29 Catanduanes
30 Mindoro Occidental
31 Mindoro Oriental
32 Marinduque
33 Albay
34 Sorsogon
35 Romblon
36 Masbate
37 Northern Samar
38 Samar
39 Eastern Samar
40 Aklan
41 Capiz
42 Antique
43 Iloilo
44 Negros Occidental
45 Negros Oriental
46 Siquijor
47 Cebu
48 Leyte
49 Southern Leyte
50 Bohol
51 Camiguin
52 Surigao del Norte
53 Surigao del Sur
54 Zamboaga del Norte
55 Zamboaga del Sur
56 Misamis Occidental
57 Misamis Oriental
58 Agusan del Norte
59 Agusan del Sur
60 Lanao del Norte
61 Lanao del Sur
62 Burkidnon
63 North Cotabato
64 Maguindanao
65 Sultan Kudarat
66 South Cotabato
67 Davao
68 Davao del Sur
69 Basilian
70 Davao Oriental
71 Sulu
72 Tawi Tawi
73 Palawan

Philippines

- National capital
- Regional capital
- Secondary cities
- Regional boundary
- Railroad
- Primary road
- International border

0	50	100	150	
0	50	100	150 mi	

Money & Banking

Currency
The currency of Philippines is the Philippine Peso (P).

Denominations
The Philippine Peso comes in coin denominations of P1 and 50, 25, 10, 5 and 1 centavos; and banknotes of P2, 5, 10, 20, 50, 100, 500, and 1,000.

Traveler's checks
Traveler's checks and currency can be exchanged at banks, hotels, department stores, and the banking counter in the Ninoy Aquino International Airport (NAIA) in Manila. Banks in Manila offer the best rate of exchange. Licensed money changers in Manila also offer competitive exchange rates. In the provinces the exchange rates are lower, sometimes by as much as 20 percent, than at banks in the capital. In the provinces many banks will only exchange traveler's checks of up to US$100 or less. Transactions require passports and all receipts must be kept for reconversions. Hotels and larger department stores will accept traveler's checks as payment.

Cash is often easier to exchange than traveler's checks, commanding a better rate. Only clean new bills are accepted. Cash is also widely available from automated teller machines (ATMs) particularly in Manila, and long-staying visitors may wish to consider opening a bank account there.

Credit cards are widely accepted in hotels, restaurants, and businesses in the Philippines, especially in urban areas. A traveler can obtain cash using a credit card from selected banks.

American Express travelers may obtain a cash advance or purchase traveler's checks from the company office in Manila using a personal check.

Travel

VISA AND PASSPORT
A passport valid for 6 months beyond the length of stay and an onward ticket are required for entry to the Philippines. A visa is not required for stays up to 21 days. Citizens of countries that do not have diplomatic relations with the Philippines will need a visa. Other kinds of visas exist for business people if they intend to work in the Philippines or investors investing above US$75,000.

DEPARTURE FORMALITIES
A departure tax of P500 will be collected from all travelers departing on an international flight. Domestic travelers can expect to pay P50. Antiques carried out of the Philippines must be accompanied by a certificate from the National Museum. Non-residents of the Philippines may carry up to P500, or US$3,000 in foreign currency, out of the country

CUSTOMS ENTRY (PERSONAL)

Duty-free
• Tobacco: 400 cigarettes, 50 cigars, or 250g tobacco
• Alcohol: 2 liters of alcoholic beverage
• Other: a reasonable amount of clothing, jewelry and perfume for personal use

Prohibited or Restricted
• Firearms and explosives
• Pornographic material, seditious or subversive material
• Narcotics and other internationally prohibited drugs (unless accompanied by a medical prescription)
Note: Non-residents of the Philippines may carry up to P500 in foreign currency into the country, and must declare amounts over US$3,000.

IMMUNIZATION
International certificates of vaccination are required if you are arriving from an area infected with cholera, smallpox, or yellow fever. An international certificate of vaccine for yellow fever is required if you are transiting or arriving from infected area within 5 days. Cases of cholera have been reported in the Philippines. Vaccinations for cholera, malaria, polio, tetanus, and typhoid are recommended. Travelers remaining in the Philippines longer than 6 months require a valid AIDS clearance certificate.

TIPPING

Taxi
Taxi: 10 percent.

Porters
Porters: 10 centavos per piece.

Hotels and Restaurants
Hotels, restaurants: 10 percent. Doorman:10 centavos.

EMERGENCY INFORMATION

Police and Crime
Poverty and crime work hand in hand in the Philippines, and both are common. Be especially careful when traveling in valley and mountain areas, where guerrillas have been known to kidnap for money and political reasons. Some parts of Mindanao and Negros Island as well as Quezon Province and the Cordillera and Bicol regions of Luzon remain areas of security concern. In Mindanao, crime and insurgent activity may make travel hazardous to and within the provinces of Tawi-Tawi, Maguindanao, Lanao Del Sur, Lanao Del Norte, Sulu, Basilan, Zamboanga del Sur, Zamboanga del Norte, North and South Cotabato, and Sultan Kudarat. Carrying a gun is not uncommon in the Philippines.

Manila police are efficient and friendly. But take basic precautions against pickpockets and jewelry snatchers, especially in crowded tourist areas. Petty theft is high throughout the country. Lower quality nightclubs may also pose the threat of drugging and robbery. Exercise caution when approached by strangers. Never accept food or drink from a stranger.

Avoid flashy displays of wealth, and dress and behave conservatively. Leave most of your cash, traveler's checks, jewelry, and your camera in your hotel safe. Carry photocopies of your passport instead of the original. Carry cash in a money belt, and use credit cards or traveler's checks for most transactions. Walk with your bag away from the street to avoid having it snatched away by motorcycle thieves. Never carry a stranger's baggage.

Emergency Numbers
Police and Fire	757
24-hour Tourist Police	116
Police (Manila)	599-011
Police (Makati)	816-0495
Fire (Makati)	816-2553
Fire (Manila)	581-176
Ambulance	503-011
24-Hour Pharmacy (Makati)	881-957

Health
Do not drink tap water or use ice cubes outside of international standard hotels and top end restaurants n Manila; bottled water is available. Wash all vegetables in a chlorine solution, peel fruits, and avoid uncooked food. Drink only pasteurized milk. Rats, fleas and mosquitoes are a health hazard. AIDS is a growing problem.

Medical care is of a reasonable standard in Manila, but

virtually nonexistent in more rural settings. Many of the doctors have been trained overseas and speak English.

For more information on medical centers, including phone numbers, please see the "Business Centers" section at the end of this chapter.

TAXI

Plenty of the more expensive hotel taxis exist offering a clean, safe, and sure ride, and a flat rate. Order one at your hotel, which should also have a taxi rate chart at your disposal. Otherwise, ask in advance about the fare. Cabs may also be hired by the hour. Outside of hotels, a taxi may be hard to find. Avoid non-metered cabs. If a driver tells you his meter is broken, exit the cab and find a new one. Air conditioned cabs will charge slightly more, P3.50 to start as opposed to P2.50 for a regular taxi. Drivers will also add and additional fee to the final fare (from P7.50 for regular cabs to P12.50 for air conditioned cabs) Carry small bills as drivers may not have change.

AUTO

Driving habits in the Philippines are haphazard. Roads are crowded and in rural areas often shared by water buffalo and other slower moving entities. Avoid travel off of main highways and paved roads, specially at night. In the monsoon season, flashfloods frequently occur causing road delays. To rent a car and drive in the Philippines you must produce a valid drivers license from your country of residence. An international driving permit is required for all licenses written in a non-roman alphabet.

BUS

Buses should be avoided. They are slow and crowded. Buses travel on most major routes in downtown Manila except Roxas Boulevard. Air conditioned buses charge about P6 for a short ride. Know your destination and tell the driver who will then charge you accordingly and issue a receipt. Converted army jeeps called *jeepneys* travel city and rural roads and may be flagged down for an extra inexpensive and quick jaunt. Pay the driver after getting on board. The word '*para*' indicates to the driver that you want to stop.

TRAIN

Trains are best for travelers who are not in a hurry. Long range train travel is not really an option, only the railway line from Manila to Naga remains in operation, and offers a long, slow ride of 12 hours.

SUBWAY

The **Metro Rail**, also called the **Light Rail Transit** (LRT) maintains a 9 mile (5.5 km.) route running parallel to Roxas Boulevard. During rush hours the Metro is jammed and no large objects will be allowed on board. Procure a tourist map to view the routes.

WATER TRAVEL

Ferry offers a viable way to travel from one major island port to another. First-class service is provided by local shipping companies. Contact one of these shipping lines for further details.

TRAVEL ASSISTANCE

Department of Tourism; T.M. Kalaw Street, Rizal Park; Metro Manila; PO Box 3451; tel: (2) 599-031.

Hotel and Restaurant Association; Regina Building, Trasierra cor. Aguirre Sts., Legaspit Vlg., Makati, Metro Manila; tel: (2) 815-4659; 815-4661; fax: (2) 810-3821.

Essential Terms

English	Tagalog
Yes No	Oo or Opo (polite) Hindi or Hindipo (polite)
Good morning Hello (daytime) Hello (evening) Hello (telephone)	Magandang umaga Magandang hapon Gudnait/Magandang gabi Halo
Good-bye	Paalam na po (person departing) Adyos po (person left behind)
Please	Paki lang
Thank you	Salamat sa i yo
Pleased to meet you	Nagagalak akong makilala kayo
Excuse me; I'm sorry	Ipagpaumanhin mo/ Ikinalulungkot ko
My name is _____	Ang pangalan ko ay __
I don't understand	Hind konaiintindihan
Do you speak English?	Nagsasalita ka ba ng ingles?

Communications

DIALING CODES IN THE PHILIPPINES

International country code: [63]

Selected city codes: Angeles (455), Bacolod (34), Baguio City (74), Bantagas (43), Cacayan de Oro (8822), Caloocan (2), Cavite (46), Cebu City (32), Cotabato (64), Dagupan (75), Davao (82), General Santos (83), Iligan City (63), Iloilo City (33), Laguna (448), Lipia (43), Lucena (42), Manila (2), Masbate (56), Naga City (5421), Ozamis City (88), Pampanga (Evantelco) (455), Pasay (2), Puerto Princesa (48), Quuezon City (2), Sanfernando - La Union (72), San Pablo (93), Subic Bay (47), Tacloban (53), Tarlac City (452), Zamboanga (62).

Dialing the Philippines from Overseas

To dial the Philippines from overseas, dial 011, then 63 (the country code for the Philippines), then the city code, and finally the number. If you were dialing Manila, for example, you would begin with 011, then 63, then 2 (the city code for Manila), and finally the number of the person or office you are trying to reach.

Assistance Numbers

Emergency	166
Tourist Assistance	(2) 501-660, 501-728
Directory assistance	114
Direct dialing assistance	112

Philippines

Operator-assisted domestic calls 109
Operator-assisted international 108

CALLING WITHIN THE PHILIPPINES

Local Calls

Calling locally may be more difficult than placing an international call, if that is conceivable. Expect bad connections, busy signals or disconnections if you are fortunate enough to have found a phone that works at all. A local call from a hotel will cost about P14.

Long Distance Calls

Calling long distance within the Philippines may prove no different than a local call in terms of connections and wait times. To make a long distance call, dial 0 + area code + number; you'll feel like you've won the lottery if connected successfully.

International Calls

To make a direct call overseas, dial 00 + country code + area code + number. Keep in mind that operator-assisted calls may run 30 percent more than dialing direct. The Philippine Long Distance Telephone Company (PLDT) office also provides international access if you prefer not to dial from the hotel, which most likely will implement the usual outrageous surcharge. If possible, try connecting directly to an overseas operator for calling card, collect, or credit card calls. If dialing from a public phone, you will have to insert a coin or card first.

AT&T USA Direct 105-11
Canada Direct 105-12
MCI 105-14
Sprint 105-16
U.K. Direct 105-44

PAY PHONES

Public Telephones

Local calls cost 75 centavos on a red public phone and are unlimited, but don't expect great service. In fact, don't even expect good service. If you're lucky, your message will barely get through. The newer silver phones will cost P2 for a local call. Most pay phones on the streets are not operational, but hotels and post offices also have pay phones that usually work. Most use coins as calling cards are just beginning their introductory period in the country.

Calling Cards

PLDT phone cards (Fonkards) may be purchased for the card phones available.

CELLULAR PHONES

Note: Your home country cell phone may not work in this country. If not, we recommend that you rent an international cell phone *before* you leave home. A major US-based cell phone rental provider is **IMC WorldCell**. For information see "International Cell Phone Rentals" on page 14.

CALL BACK

You can (potentially) save significant sums when calling in Philippines by using one of the call back services listed below. Fees for call back services vary widely, depending on the company and the type of service required.

For a list of callback services, please refer to the "Communications" section in the *Global Road Warrior* Introduction.

PHONE JACK

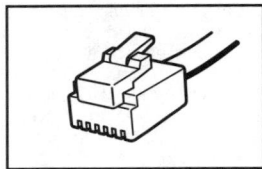

Plug adaptors are available through **iGo Corporation.** (See "Electrical and Telephone Adaptors" on page 19.)

FAX

Fax machines are widespread, but the poor telephone system can delay some faxes. Most hotels have fax services, although the charge can be expensive. A one page fax to Europe costs P350 (US$14).

POSTAL SERVICES

Service is adequate, although airmail should be used when possible. Many hotel concierges carry stamps. Airmail takes about one week to reach Europe and North America. Letters are likely to be processed faster if they are dropped off at the mail distribution center near the domestic airport in Manila.

Hours of service

Monday to Friday 9a.m. to 5p.m.

Rates

Postal rates within the Philippines are P2 (US$0.08) per 20 grams for regular three week delivery. One week delivery will cost P3 (US$0.12), while overnight delivery is P16 (US$0.62). Letters to the U.S. and Europe will cost P9.

Business Services

BUSINESS CENTERS

Mandarin Oriental Hotel; Makati Avenue; tel: (2) 816-3601.

Peninsula Manila Hotel; Corner of Ayala & Makati Avenues; tel: (2) 812-3456; 24-hour business center.

Philippine Convention and Visitors Corporation, 4th Floor, Suites 10-17, Legasi Towers, 300 Roxas Boulevare, Metro Manila

PO Box EA-459; tel: (2) 575-031.

The Manila Hotel; One Rizal Park; tel: (2) 527-0011

Shangri-La Makati Hotel; Makati Avenue, Makati; tel: (2) 816-6801; 24-hour business center.

Sofitel Grand Boulevard Hotel; 1990 Roxas Boulevard; tel: (2) 526-8588.

COMPUTER RENTAL

Hotels with business centers offer computers for use and rental, often even for non-guests. See business centers listings for locations.

COURIER SERVICES

You must allow two to three business days for most courier shipments between the Philippines and international destinations. The transit time for Federal Express packages may improve once the company has set up its transit center at the former Subic Bay Naval Base.

Irasan St, San Dionisio, Paranaque, Metro Manila; tel: (2) 820-2920; fax: (2) 820-2917.

DHL; Pair-Pags Center, Ninoy Aquino Airport; tel: (2) 551-5632; fax: (2) 832-3401; World Center Building, Floor 6, 330 Sen Gil Puyat Avenue, Makati City, Manila; Monday to Friday 8a.m. to 60.m., Saturday 8a.m. to 2p.m.; holidays 8a.m. to 1p.m.

Federal Express; 288 Escolta Twin Towers, Escolata, Manila; tel: 241-5450; tel: (2) 552-5353; fax: 552-5352.

TNT; Manila; tel: (2) 817-2871.

UPS; Metro Manila Office, 888 Delbros Avenue Barrio Sto. Nino, Paranaque, Metro Manila; tel: (2) 551-5640, tel: (2) 512-1355, tel: (2) 512-1350.

PRINTING/COPYING

Printing/copying centers are difficult to find, but most business centers can do basic copying/printing services.

SECRETARIAL SERVICES

Secretarial services are usually available at most hotel business centers.

TRANSLATION SERVICES

Executive Centerpoint 106 Legaspi Street, Legaspi Village; tel: (2) 815-9872.

Westin Philippine Plaza CCP Complex, Roxas Boulevard; tel: (2) 832-0701.

EuroComm 814 Masikap Extension; tel: (2) 922-3961, fax: (2) 922-3861.

Electrical

Current
110/220 volts AC, 60Hz.

ELECTRIC PLUGS

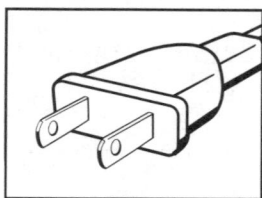

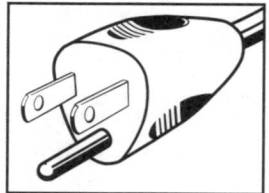

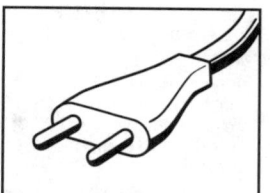

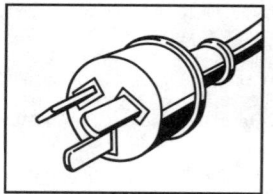

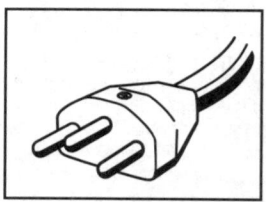

Plug adaptors are available through **iGo Corporation.** (See "Electrical and Telephone Adaptors" on page 19.)

Frequent power outages occur throughout the islands. Bring a flashlight in case of sudden darkness.

Technical Support
HARDWARE/SOFTWARE VENDOR SUPPORT

Compaq/Digital; (Singapore Office) tel: (65) 750-4328; fax: (65) 750-7385; (General U.S.) tel: (281) 518-2000; http://www.compaq.com/.

Corel; (in Hong Kong) tel: [852] 8100-3729 (All Applications); (in the U.S.) tel: [1] (716) 871-2325 (Ask to be Forwarded to Appropriate Program); http://www.corel.com/.

Dell; tel: (604) 810-4988 (Sales); (604) 810-4977 (Technical Support); (in the U.S.) tel: [1] (512) 338-4400; fax: [1] (512) 728-3330; http://www.dell.com/.

Hewlett Packard; tel: 65 272 5300; (in the U.S.) tel: [1] (408) 246-4300; http://www.hp.com/.

IBM; tel: 819-2000 (General Information); tel: 819-2426 (Product Support); fax: 818-6520; (in Switzerland) tel: [41] (22) 310-0418 (in French); (in the U.S.) tel: [1] (919) 517-2800; http://www.ibm.com/.

Microsoft; tel: (2) 811-0062; tel: (2) 892-2295; tel: (2) 892-2495; fax: (2) 813-2493; (in Switzerland) tel: [41] (848) 858-868; fax [41] (1) 831-0869; (in the U.S.) [1] (425) 635-7222; http://www.microsoft.com/.

Toshiba; (in Germany) tel: [49] (2131) 158-319; fax: [49] (2131) 158-558; (in Switzerland) tel: [41] (1) 946-0777; fax: [41] (1) 946-0807; (in Ireland) tel: [44] (193) 282-8828; (in the U.S.) [1] (949) 583-3000 (Corporate Headquarters); http://www.toshiba.com/.

Internet Connection
HOW TO CONNECT

Connecting to AOL and Compuserve in the Philippines is similar to using it when traveling outside your own area code. See the introductory section for detailed information on connecting to your account through a different phone number.

America Online

Numbers are available at keyword international. Be sure to get several local numbers before leaving. AOL has a new GlobalNet service that charges US$6 an hour in addition to the usual charges. Go to keyword access (a free area) and download the software.

Access: Baguio (74) 443-2180; Cebu (32) 255-1902; Cebu (32) 253-0561; Davao (82) 222-4191; Davao (82) 297-7480; Iliolo (33) 509-2222; Manila (2) 843-4977; Manila (2) 859-8111; National (except for Manila) (2) 180-0188-87626.

Compuserve

Numbers are available at *Go International*. The Compuserve Web-site also has a great deal of information, at http://www.compuserve.com.

Access: Manila (2) 843-0702, (2) 843-4977.

Independent Service Providers

Many independent service providers offer discounts if you are only in town for a couple of days.

Broline; tel: (2) 893-7771; fax: (2) 893-7795; email: info@broline.com; http://www.broline.com/.

Compass Internet; tel: (2) 636-5091/92; fax: (2) 636-5092; email: sales@compass.com.ph; http://www.compass.com.ph.

Mosaic Communications, Inc.; tel: (32) 253-0013; (32) 253-2196; fax: (32) 253-2019; email: e-mail: info@cebu.mozcom.com; http://www.cebu.mozcom.com.

Philippines Online; tel: 411-4652; tel: 411-4566; email: sales@philonline.com; http://www.philonline.com/.

Sky Internet, Inc.; tel: 411-2000; email: corpsales@skyinet.net; http://www.skyinet.net.

Yahoo Computer Services; tel: (2) 751-4170; fax: (2) 751-4171; http://www.ycs.com.ph/.

Internet Cafes
Cebu City

Cyberminds Internet; #3-4 Doña Josefa Arcade, Gen. Maxelom Ave.,Cebu City; tel/fax: (32) 233-4755; email: wtchatower@techemail.com; Seven days a week, 24 hours a day; P25 per hour of use.

Cyberscape Internet Café; J Y Square Lahug Cebu City, F C Quad Mandaue City and Osmeña Bldg. Pelaez Street, Cebu City; tel:(32) 233-4481; fax: (32) 345-0594; email: Cyberscape@eudoramail.com; http://cyberscape.cjb.net; Seven days a week, 24 hours a day; P20 per hour of use.

EarthwebCafe; Ayala Center Cebu Business Park Stall 286 - A Level II, Cebu City; tel: (32) 233-3461; email: webmaster@earthwebcafe.com; http://www.earthwebcafe.com/; Monday through Sunday, 8a.m. to 2a.m.;

Real Site Internet Cafe; Gen. Maxilom Ave. Cebu; tel/fax: (32) 233-3947; email: realsite@mozcom.com; http://realsite.mozcom.com/; Monday through Sunday, 9a.m. to 3a.m.; P20 per hour of use.

Manila

Cyberw@y Cafe; 156 N. Domingo Street, San Juan, Metro Manila; tel/fax: (2) 744-3851; emai: cyberwaycafe@fcmail.com; http://w3.to/cyberwaycafe/; Monday through Sunday, 9:30a.m. to 9:30p.m.

Hot Bits Cafe and Internet Diners; 1199 Masangkay St., Tondo Manila; tel: (2) 252-6334; email: info@hotbitscafe.com; http://www.hotbitscafe.com/; Monday through Sunday, 7a.m. to 9p.m.; US$1.30 per hour of use.

Netopia; 155 SMRC bldg. B. Gonzales St., cor Katipunan Ave. Quezon City, Metro Manila; tel: (2) 434-2189; email: info@netopia.ph; http://www.netopia.ph/; Monday through Sunday, 9a.m. to 9p.m.; P50 per hour of use.

Spaceworld Internet Cafe; 1711 M. Adriatico Street Malate, Manila; tel: (2) 525-5151; fax: (2) 303-6509; email: worx@i-manila.com.ph; Monday through Sunday, 9a.m. to 2a.m.; P60-90 per hour of use.

Business Culture
GREETINGS AND COURTESIES

Filipinos greet each other by establishing direct eye contact, raising their eyebrows slightly, and letting them fall as eye contact is made. This will usually include a friendly smile and, between men, a casual handshake. A man should not initiate a handshake with a woman; wait for her to hold out her hand. Handshakes are not firm; they are light and don't last long. Filipinos should be addressed as Mr., Ms., or Dr., or with another title if they have one. It is important to defer to people of rank, status, age, and seniority. Be formal when first meeting someone whose position entitles them to respect. This includes older members of an associate's family or kinship group. Government officials are particularly sensitive to being treated with respectful formality.

Hiya Filipinos are extremely sensitive about individual public image and self-esteem. Their culture combines the Asian idea of face (personal dignity and respect by one's peers) with the Spanish idea of love-of-self (amor propio). The result is an easily-offended sense of dignity, and Filipinos are careful that their words, actions, or thoughts are never insulting. Social behavior is determined by the Philippine concept of *hiya* (translated literally as shame). To be publicly ridiculed or criticized, or to not live up to expectations, results in *hiya* and a loss of self-esteem.

BUSINESS ETHIC AND FRAMEWORK

Filipinos believe in family loyalty, reverence for religious beliefs, respect for one's self-image, social harmony, and avoiding direct confrontation or conflict. The family is the major social, and often business, unit. It extends to distant relatives, and may include godparents, sponsors, or old friends. Personal favors, granted and owed, are also extremely important. When one is done a favor, it is expected to be returned "with interest," and on request. The dynamic of owed favors ties Philippine groups together, and people will avoid being in the debt of someone from a rival group. In the Philippine business world, someone who has a large accumulation of unreturned favors can be extremely effective in getting results.

DECISION MAKING

The well-being of the group, harmony, and consensus

are extremely important, and decisions take time. Usually, the person who makes a final decision will not be at the meeting at which the proposal is laid out. Having things go smoothly is more important than articulating personal opinions, and telling "inconvenient" truths or being "too honest" must be avoided for fear of making others uncomfortable. "Yes" has a variety of meanings: it can mean "yes," "maybe," or even "highly unlikely."

WOMEN

In the Philippines, women have long been treated more equally than in other Asian countries. The ideal Filipina is modest, shy, self-effacing, and loyal. Aggressive women who interact freely with men are not admired by women in this culture. Women are not essentially viewed as inferior, and hold positions of authority in business, politics, government, and law, with more visibility and power than in many other Asian nations. Foreigners should be aware that Philippine culture is conservative, especially when it comes to public interactions between men and women.

MEETINGS

Meetings should be set up far in advance (ideally by a third party who knows you and the Filipinos who will attend), and should be confirmed when you reach the Philippines. When a meeting is set, a common question is, "Is that Filipino time or Western time?" Filipino time will generally mean the meeting will start half-an-hour to an hour late. Even in the best of circumstances, traffic (particularly bad in Manila) and weather (sudden tropical cloudbursts) often make the most punctual people late.

BUSINESS ATTIRE

Filipinos dress well for business and judge others by their clothes. Dress neatly, carefully, tastefully, and wear quality clothing. The weather will probably be warm, but men should wear a jacket and tie. Follow the lead of your host in removing the jacket once a meeting has begun. Women should wear a business suit or matching ensemble, preferably with stockings. Filipinas are quite fashion-conscious, and this is a culture where foreign women who are similarly inclined can indulge themselves. But avoid extremes in clothing or jewelry. Off-hours tip: do not wear shorts on the street, and avoid sandals (or you will be labeled a "hippie").

Business Centers
Manila

CITY VIEW

Over half the Philippine industry is in Manila, a huge city with sprawling suburbs that seem to go forever. The city proper is not large, but you won't think so flying into Ninoy Aquino Airport.

AIRPORT

Ninoy Aquino Airport to City Center

The airport lies 4.5 miles (7 km.) from downtown Manila. Buses and taxis are available, and some top-end hotels have a shuttle, or even limousine service, that will take travelers to and from the airport for a fee. The trip into town takes about 30 minutes by taxi and 45 minutes by buses that leave every 20 minutes. Nissan offers an Airport Coupon Taxi Service at Gates 1 and 2 in the arrival lobby. Rates are fixed according to destination. Pay the taxi attendant on duty at the Nissan Coupon Taxi counters, open between 5:30a.m. and the last flight of the day. To contact the Ninoy Aquino Airport, call: (2) 832-2938.

Airline Numbers

Aeroflot Soviet Airlines	(2) 86-7756
Aerolift	(2) 817-2361, 817-2369
Air Canada	(2) 810-4461, 844-9221
Air France	(2) 815-6970
Air India	(2) 815-1280, 815-2441
Air Nauru	(2) 818-3580
Air Nuigini	(2) 810-1846, 8190-2206
Air Philippine	(2) 843-7011
Alitalia	(2) 850-265, 812-3351
American Airlines	(2) 817-8645, 810-3228
Bourag Airlines	(2) 833-2902
British Airways	(2) 817-0361, 815-6556
Canadian Airlines International	(2) 8102-6565
Canadian Pacific Airways	(2) 815-9401
Cathay Pacific	(2) 815-9417
China Airlines	(2) 59-0086
Continental Air Micronesia	(2) 818-8701
Eastern Airlines	(2) 87-2971
Egyptair	(2) 815-8476
Enurates Aurkubes	(2) 816-0809, 816-0744
Finnair	(2) 818-2601, 818-2621
Garuda Indonesian Airlines	(2) 86-2458, 86-2205
Gulf Air	(2) 817-6909
Japan Airlines	(2) 812-1591, 810-9352
KLM Royal Dutch Airlines	(2) 8154790
Korean Air	(2) 815-8911, 815-9261
Kuwait Airways	(2) 817-2778
Lufthansa German Airlines	(2) 810-5018, 810-4596
Malaysian Airlines	(2) 57-5761
Northwest Airlines	(2) 819-7341
Pacific Airways	(2) 8322731-32, 8332390-91
Pakistan International Airways	(2) 818-0502
Philippine Airlines	(2) 818-0111, 831-6541
Qantas Airways	(2) 815-9491, 815-9431
Royal Brunei Airlines	(2) 8171631-34
Royal Jordanian Airlines	(2) 818-5901
Sabena Belgian Airlines	(2) 50-8636
Saudi Arabian Airlines	(2) 818-7866
Scandinavian Airlines System	(2) 810-5050
Singapore Airlines	(2) 810-4951, 810-4960
Thai Airways International	(2) 81-58421
United Airlines	(2) 81-85421

HOTELS

Top End

Mandarin Oriental; Makati Avenue; tel: (2) 750-8888; fax: (2) 817-2472; http://www.mandarin-oriental.com/; email: reserve-momnl@mohg.com; 448 rooms; restaurants; conference facilities; business center with cellular phone rental; in-room modem/fax connection, dual-line telephones; International direct dial facility; voice mail; cable TV; 24-hour room service; medical/dental service; laundry & valet service; airport transfers; lobby shop; barber shop; beauty salon; flower shop; babysitting service; fitness; sauna; massage; pool.

Peninsula Manila; Corner of Ayala & Makati Avenues; tel: (2) 812-3456; fax: (2) 815-3402; 500 rooms; restaurant; 24-hour business center ; conference facilities (up to 800); secretarial service; fax/photocopy facilities; in-room safe; mini-bar; hairdryer; Internet access; satellite TV; radio; coffee and tea maker; fax; 24 hour room service; shops; business plan available with limousine airport transfer; secure parking; fitness; sauna; pool; whirlpool.

Shangri-La Edsa Plaza; 1 Garden Way, Ortigas Center; tel: (2) 633-8888; fax: (2) 631-1067; city center; restaurants; conference facilities; secretarial service; fax/photocopy

Philippines

facilities; in-room modem/fax connection; safe; air conditioning; TV; IDD telephone; minibar; tea making facilities; corporate rates; parking; fitness; sauna; pool; whirlpool.

Shangri-La Makati; Makati Avenue, Makati; tel: (2) 816-6801; fax: (2) 818-4089; located in central business district; 6 restaurants; 24-hour business center; ballroom (up to 2,000), banquet facilities (up to 1,000); two Club floors; 6 non-smoking floors; spa; pool.

The Manila; One Rizal Park; tel: (2) 527-0011; fax: (2) 527-0077; city center, restaurants; conference facilities (up to 1,000); 24-hour business center; secretarial service; fax/photocopy facilities; in-room safe; corporate rates; parking; fitness; sauna; pool; whirlpool.

Westin Philippine Plaza; CCP Complex, Roxas Boulevard; tel: (2) 832-0701; fax: (2) 832-3485; resort hotel nearest convention and trade center; 5 restaurants; conference/banquet facilities; parking; fitness; pool; garden.

Expensive

Hyatt Regency Manila; 2702 Roxas Boulevard, Pasay City; tel: (2) 833-1234; fax: (2) 833-5913; located near convention center; smaller, personal hotel; colonial style; restaurant; conference facilities; fax/photocopy facilities; in-room fax, answering machine, safe; parking; sauna; pool.

Inter-Continental Manila; 1 Ayala Avenue, Makati; tel: (2) 815-9711; fax: (2) 817-1330; restaurant; conference facilities (up to 800); secretarial service; fax/photocopy facilities; business rooms available with work desk, fax, copier, scanner, dataports, and laptops; fitness; pool.

Nikko Manila Garden; Ayala Center, Makati; tel: (2) 810-4101; fax: (2) 817-1862; near airport; restaurant; conference facilities; secretarial service; fax/photocopy facilities; corporate rates; fitness; sauna; pool.

Philippine Village Airport; Nayong Pilipino Complex, Naia Road, Pasay City; tel: (2) 833-8080; fax: (2) 833-8248; located in suburb near airport; conference facilities (up to 2,000); secretarial service; fax/photocopy facilities; corporate rates; parking; fitness; pool.

Sofitel Grand Boulevard; 1990 Roxas Boulevard; tel: (2) 526-8588; fax: (2) 526-0111; city center; casino; restaurant; conference facilities (up to 300); business center; secretarial service; fax/photocopy facilities; in-room modem/fax connection, safe; corporate rates; parking; pool.

Moderate

Ambassador; 2021 A. Mabini Street, Malata; tel: (2) 506-011; fax: (2) 521-5557; near railway station; restaurant; conference facilities (up to 250); secretarial service; fax/photocopy facilities; corporate rates; parking; pool.

Aurelio; Roxas Boulevard and Padre Faura Street, Ermita; tel: (2) 509-061; fax: (2) 586-702; restaurant; conference facilities.

Las Palmas Manila; 1616 A. Mabini Street, Malate; tel: (2) 506-661; fax: (2) 522-1699; city center; restaurant; conference facilities; secretarial service; fax/photocopy facilities; pool.

Rembrandt; 26 Thomas Morato, Quezon City; tel; (2) 924-9904; fax: (2) 924-4947; near exhibition grounds; restaurant; conference facilities (up to 450); secretarial service; fax/photocopy facilities; corporate rates; fitness; sauna; pool; whirlpool.

Royal Palm Manila; 1227 A. Mabini Street Cor. Padre Faura Street, Ermita; email: royal@iconn.com.ph; city center; restaurant; conference facilities (up to 300); business center; secretarial service; fax/photocopy facilities; in-room modem/fax connection; Internet available; hotel safe; secure parking.

MEDICAL CARE

Boie Pharmacy; Makati; tel: 881-957; 24-hour pharmacy.
Medical Center Manila; 112 General Luna St.; tel: 591-661.
Makati Medical Center; 2 Amorsolo St. at De la Rosa Street; tel: 815-9911 or 815-9944; private hospital; dental care also.
Manila Doctors' Hospital; 667 U.N. Ave., Ermita; tel: 503-011.
Mercury Drug (pharmacy); 777 J.P. Rizal St., Makati; tel: (2) 871-444; also 483 Padre Faura St., Ermita; tel: 585-495.
University Drug; (24-hour pharmacy) tel: 593-857.

HEALTH CLUB

Mandarin Oriental Manila; Makati Avenue; tel: (2) 816-3601.
Manila Peninsula Hotel; Corner of Ayala & Makati Avenues; tel: (2) 819-3456.
The Manila Hotel; One Rizal Park; tel: (2) 470-011.
Reed Fitness Center - Century Park Sheraton Hotel, Pablo Ocampo Sr. Street, Malate; tel: (2) 522-1011.
Westin Philippine Plaza; CCP Complex, Roxas Boulevard; tel: (2) 832-0701.

AUTO RENTAL

Avis; Holiday Inn Manila Pavillion, Un Ave (Cnr M Orosa St), Ermita; tel: (2) 525-2206 LOCAL 2339; Manila Pavilion Hotel, Roxas Boulevard between Padre Faura and Santa Monica streets.; tel: (2) 844-8498; Ninoy Aquino Intl Airport, Mia Rd, Pasay; tel: (2) 832-2088.
Hertz; China Banking Corporation Building, Paseo de Roxas, Makati; tel: (2) 831-9827, tel: 832-5325.
Sunshine Limousine Service; tel: (2) 506-601, 832-5322.

WORLD TRADE CENTER

World Trade Center Metro Manila
WTCMM Complex, Financial Center Area
Roxas Blvd. along Sen. Gil Puyat Avenue, Ext.
Pasay City, Philippines 1300
tel: (2) 551-5151; fax: (2) 551-5208

CHAMBER OF COMMERCE

Manila Chamber of Commerce
410 Shurdot Building, Intramuros, Manila
tel: (2) 498-321

Philippine Chamber of Commerce
ODC International Plaza
7th Floor, 219 Salcedo St., Legaspi Village, Makati, Metro Manila
tel: (2) 817-6981

CONVENTION BUREAU

Philippine Convention and Visitors Bureau
4th Floor, Suites 10-17, Legasi Towers
300 Roxas Boulevare, Metro Manila,
PO Box EA-459;
tel: (2) 575-03

Poland

At a Glance

THE PEOPLE

Population ....38,646,023 (July 2000 est.)
Growth Rate ....-0.04 percent (2000 est.)
Life Expectancy .... 73.19 years
Infant Mortality ..... 9.61 deaths/1,000 live births (2000 est.)

Ethnic Composition

Poles 97.6%
German 1.3%
Ukranian 0.6%
Byelorussian 0.5%

Religious Composition

Roman Catholic..95%
Eastern Orthodox, Protestant, other.............................5%

Languages Spoken

Polish is the official language, but English, French, German, and Russian are also understood to varying degrees.

Education and Literacy

Virtually the entire population, about 99%, is literate. All primary and secondary education is free.

Labor Force

Total 17,700,000
By occupation: industry and construction 29.9%, agriculture 26%, trade, and services 44.1%.

THE ECONOMY

Poland is touted by many as the quintessential success story of a transition from the state owned to the privately owned. This transition in the post soviet era can be seen in the privatization of state-owned small and medium sized companies, and the introduction of liberal law on establishing new companies, marking the rapid development of a private sector now responsible for close to two thirds of all economic activity. In contrast, Poland's agricultural sector remains impaired by structural problems, inefficient small farms, lack of investment, and surplus labor. The overarching desires to become a part of the E.U., improving Poland's worsening current account deficit and firming up Poland's monetary policy, now focused on inflation targeting dictate most of Poland's economic policy. The government continues to keep the budget deficit in check at around 2% of GDP. Institutional reforms continued in pensions, health care, and public administration throughout 1999, but resulted in underestimated or unforseen fiscal pressures. Restructuring and privatization of the coal and steel industries has begun, but is far from completion. Growth in 2000 at its current rate of progress should top that of 1999.

Exports ....US$27.8 billion (f.o.b., 1999)
Imports ....US$40.8 billion (f.o.b., 1999)
Total Trade ....US$68.6 billion (f.o.b. 1999)
GDP Per Capita................................. US$7,200 (1999 est.)
Unemployment ....11% (1999 est.)
Inflation Rate ....8.4% (1999 est.)

Top Export Partners

Germany 36%, Italy 5.8%, Russia 5.6%, Netherlands 4.7%, France 4.6%, Ukraine 3.8%, U.K. 3.8%.

Top Import Partners

Germany 25.8%, Italy 9.4%, France 6.5%, Russia 5.1%, UK 4.9%, US 3.8%, Netherlands 3.8%.

Top Exports

Manufactured goods and chemicals 57%, machinery and equipment 21%, food and live animals 12%, mineral fuels 7%.

Top Imports

Manufactured goods and chemicals 43%, machinery and equipment 36%, mineral fuels 9%, food and live animals 8%.

BUSINESS WORKWEEK

Office

Monday to Friday 8a.m. to 4p.m.

Banks

Monday to Friday 8a.m. to 6p.m.; in larger cities, Saturday 9a.m. to 1p.m.

Government

Monday to Friday 8a.m. to 6p.m.

Retail

Monday to Friday 10a.m. to 7p.m.; department stores 9a.m. to 8p.m., slightly shorter hours on the weekend.

HOLIDAYS

New Year's Day..January 1
Easter Monday ....April 24*
Labor Day...May 1
Proclamation of 1791 Constitution ....May 3
Victory Day..May 9
Corpus Christi.. June 22*
Assumption..August 15
All Saints' Day ....November 1
Independence Day ....November 11
Christmas ....December 25-26
*Date may vary by year.

CLIMATE

Seasons

The seasons exist, with bitter cold winters, with heavy snow storms; and hot summers, with frequent thunderstorms. In July the temperatures are about 21°C (70°F), January they are about -1°C (30°F).

Regions

The western region enjoy a moderate, maritime climate, with overcast winters and cool summers. Inland experiences the most snow during the winter months.

Money & Banking

Currency

The currency of Poland is the Zloty (PLN).

Denominations

The Zloty comes in coin denominations of PLN5, 2 and 1 and 50, 20, 10, 5, 2 and 1 groszy; and banknotes of PLN10, 20, 50, 100, and 200. (The old notes, valid until the end of 1997, are in denominations of PLN2,000,000, 1,000,000, 500, 000, 100,000, 5000, 2000, 1000, 500, 200, and 100.)

Poland

* A province has the same name as its capital except where noted.

Poland

- ✪ National capital
- ◉ Regional capital
- ● Secondary city
- —— Primary road
- ······ Railroad
- —— Province border
- ▬▬ International border

| 0 | 50 | 100 |
0 50 100 mi

©2001 Magellan Geographix
SM Santa Barbara, CA

Traveler's checks

Traveler's checks and currency can be exchanged at banks, exchange shops, hotels, and international airports, at tourist exchange rates, with various rates of exchange, larger banks may offer the best exchange rates, but avoid black marketers at all cost. Consult your bank about current exchange rates before departure. Keep all receipts for re-conversion.

Most currencies can also be exchanged, but try to take only crisp and new notes, wrinkled and soiled notes are likely to be refused.

American Express, Visa, Diner's Club, and MasterCard are easily accepted in up-market places in the cities, but smaller restaurants and shops may ask for cash. Some banks in the capital offer cash advances on credit cards, but make sure you bring your passport.

Travel

VISA AND PASSPORT

Foreigners must have a valid passport. Nationals of many countries including the EU, United States, and the U.K., do not require a visa for stays not exceeding 90 days (6 months for U.K. citizens). Nationals from other countries such as Australia, Canada, and Japan do require a visa. Check with the nearest Polish embassy or consulate for visa information.

DEPARTURE FORMALITIES

A customs declaration form, stamped by Polish officials upon entering Poland, must be retained by the traveler and presented upon departure.

CUSTOMS ENTRY (PERSONAL)

Duty-free

- Tobacco: 250 cigarettes, 50 cigars, or 250g tobacco
- Alcohol: 1 liters of alcoholic beverage
- Other: gifts up to value of US$100

Note: (a) Fur, leather and gold articles are subject to customs duty. (b) The export of antiques, works of art and certain other items from Poland is prohibited. (c) A customs declaration must be presented at the border. (d) Firearms and narcotics are prohibited. (e) Duty-free shops are located at border crossing points. Payment for purchases can be made either in foreign or local currency, traveler's checks or credit cards.

Essential Terms

English	Polish
Yes	Tak
No	Nie
Good morning	Dzien dobry
Hello (daytime)	Dzien dobry
Hello (evening)	Dobry wieczor
Hello (telephone)	Czesc
Good-bye	Do widzenia
Please	Prosze
Thank you	Dziekuje
Pleased to meet you	Milo mi pana /pania poznac
Excuse me; I'm sorry	Przepraszam
My name is _____	Mam na imie
I don't understand	Nie rozumiem
Do you speak English?	Czy pan pani mowi po angielsku?

IMMUNIZATION

No vaccinations are required for travel to Poland unless you are arriving from an infected area.

TIPPING

Taxi

Tip taxi drivers about 10 percent.

Restaurants

Restaurants include a service charge of 10 to 15 percent, but diners usually round off the bill for the waiter and add another 10 percent if entertainment was provided.

EMERGENCY INFORMATION

Police and Crime

Petty and violent crime are on the increase in Poland, especially in urban areas like Warsaw and in railway stations. Car theft is common, specially if a car is newer. Carjackings also occur with frequency. Take care on public transport and watch your belongings specially when a distraction or commotion around you suddenly occurs.

Take basic precautions. Avoid flashy displays of wealth, and dress and behave conservatively. Leave most of your cash, traveler's checks, jewelry, and your camera in your hotel safe. Carry photocopies of your passport instead of the original. Carry cash in a money belt, and use credit cards or traveler's checks for most transactions. Walk with your bag away from the street to avoid having it snatched away by motorcycle thieves. Never carry a stranger's baggage.

Women are advised to not travel alone at night. The police force has lessened in size and diminished in efficiency in recent years.

Emergency Numbers

Ambulance	999 or 628-24-24
Medical	31-86-69
Police	997
Roadway assistance	981

Health

Although chlorinated, avoid tap water as it may cause stomach upset early on in your stay; bottled water is widely available. Bring along necessary toiletries, they may be hard to come by in Poland.

Low humidity and air pollution (especially in Krakow) may cause respiratory and allergy problems. Flu and common colds are common, as is gastroenteritis in the summer.

Medical care is of a reasonable standard in Krakow and Warsaw but not in more rural settings. Medical care is socialized but expensive for foreigners. Bring extra eyeglasses, prescription drugs, and other necessities.

For more information on medical centers, including phone numbers, please see the "Business Centers" section at the end of this chapter.

TAXI

Taxis are available in all cities, either in the streets, at taxi stands, or by phone. Radio taxis are most recommended. Buying a discount card from the driver ensures a 10 percent discount, as well as a card with the company's phone number to show when needing to order a cab by phone. Hotel taxis charge about double but prove reliable. If you opt to hail a cab from the streets, be sure that the taxi has advertising marked on the outside and a rate sheet glued to the window. One is advised to avoid cabs around Warsaw central rail station. Head across the street and order one at the Marriott Hotel instead. Cabs in the Old Town of Warsaw are also questionable, as are those waiting around squares and traffic circles.

A surcharge exists from 11p.m. to 5a.m., as well as for any trips outside of the city. The driver may ask to be paid in hard currency. Carry small notes since they also may not have change on hand. Round up the fare to tip.

Radio Taxis

Express Taxi	9663
Halo-Taxi	9626
Partner Taxi	9669
Radio Taxi	633-3333
Super Taxi	9622
Tele-Taxi	9627

AUTO

As with most parts of Europe, cars must come equipped with emergency tools such as a hazard triangle. Seat belts are mandatory and traffic drives on the right. Night driving is hazardous due to poor lighting and vehicles or tractors that have no lights on at all. Motorists should be aware that trams have the right of way. Accidents due to drunk driving are very common even though the legal blood alcohol limit is almost zero percent. In order to rent a car, or drive a cat in Poland, you must have held a valid drivers license from your country of residence for at least one year. An International driving permit is required along with your license. Persons driving their own cars should carry their car registration cards and a vlaid Green Card insurance, along with their national driver's license.

Polski Zwiazek Motorway (PZM)	981

Pulawska 28, 02-513, Warsaw; tel: (22) 496-904; fax: (22) 496-915.

Poland

BUS/TROLLEY

Buses offer the best way to get around the cities. They are usually efficient and comfortable; but expect crowds during rush hour coupled with slower service. There is a flat fee, and pre-purchased tickets are available from street kiosks and new stands. A sign with "Bilety MZK" indicates tickets are sold at that location. Validate tickets in machines on board buses and trolleys. For those staying in town for about a week, 7-day tourist tickets are available.

TRAIN

All areas of Poland are accessible by train services run by Polish State Railway (PKP). International service is available to Western Europe through Connections to Berlin, Moscow, Paris, Vienna, Budapest, and Prague exist. EuroCity, InterCity, and Express trains require prior reservations. Keep watch over your possessions when traveling by train.

SUBWAY

An 11-station subway system exists in Warsaw.

WATER TRAVEL

Ferry transit to and from Denmark, Finland, and Sweden is available through Pol Ferries. Contact either Pol Ferries or the Polish National Tourist Office in Warsaw for ferry information. Travelers can purchase tickets from travel agents.
Pol Ferries; ul. Chalubinskiego 7, 00-613, Warsaw; tel: (22) 830-0930; fax: (22) 830-0071.

TRAVEL ASSISTANCE

Warsaw Information Center
Zamkowy Square 1/13, 00-262 Warsaw
tel: (22) 635-1881; fax: (22) 831-0464

Communications

DIALING CODES IN POLAND

International country code: [48]
    Selected city codes: Bialystok (85), Bydgoszcz (52), Bytom (32), Czestochowa (34), Gdansk (58), Gdynia (58), Gliwice (32), Katowice (32), Krakow (12), Lodz (55), Lublin (81), Olsztyn (89), Poznan (61), Radom (48), Rzeszow (17), Szczecin (Stettin) (91), Sopot (58), Sosnowiec (32), Torun (56), Warsaw (22), Zabrze (32).

Dialing Poland from Overseas

To dial Poland from overseas, dial your country's international dialing code, then 48 (the country code for Poland), then the city code and finally the number. If you were dialing Krakow from the United States, for example, you would begin with 011, then 48, then 12 (the city code for Krakow), and finally the number of the person or office you were trying to reach.

Assistance Numbers

International Operator
(English speaking) 901
International Code Information 930
Domestic Operator 900
Long Distance Information 912
Local Information 913

CALLING WITHIN POLAND

Local Calls

Calling locally will cost you an 'A' token (50gr) for three minutes. If you plan on talking longer, be sure to stock up on tokens to feed the box or you will be unromantically disconnected. If using a telephone card, one minute will cost one unit.

Long Distance Calls

Use a 'C' token for any long distance calling. A zero must precede any area code within the country. Wait for a second dial tone after dialing 0, then proceed with the number. If the place you are dialing has no direct access, try to dial 900.

International Calls

Connect to an English-speaking operator at AT&T or MCI first. Connecting to these overseas operators is not possible from public phones. Either pay to get the connection through your hotel, or go to a main post office where a clerk directs you to a booth and collects payment afterward; another alternative is a card phone.
AT&T .... 0 * 0-800-111-1111
MCI .... 0 * 0-800-111-2122
    * Wait for a second dial tone after the initial 0
To call direct, dial 00 + country code + area code + number. Expect to pay about US$8 to US$12 for calls to the U.S. or Europe at the post office. Reduced rates apply on long-distance calls placed between 4p.m. and 6a.m.

PAY PHONES

Public Telephones

Phones are not nearly as readily available here as in other parts of Europe, and they are often out of order as well. There are three kinds of telephones: gray dial phones (for local calls only), newer yellow push button phones, and the newest blue phones, which are most effective. A and C tokens can be purchased at the post office. But prepare to lose them even if you aren't connected. Try not to insert the tokens until you've been connected.

1. Place token in slide slot
2. Lift receiver
3. Dial
4. Insert coins when connected (some phones accept the token first)

Calling Cards

Post offices and news kiosks sell 50, and 100-unit cards. You can find card phones in better hotels, post offices, and, recently, more readily in the streets and news stands.

CELLULAR PHONES

Polska Telefonia Cyfrowa and *Polkomtel* operate GSM digital systems for cellular phone users in Poland. An NMT-450 analogue service is also available from *Centertel*.
    Note: Your home country cell phone may not work in this country. If not, we recommend that you rent an international cell phone *before* you leave home. A major US-based cell phone rental provider is **IMC WorldCell**. For information see "International Cell Phone Rentals" on page 14.

CALL BACK

You can (potentially) save significant sums when calling in Poland by using one of the call back services listed below. Fees for call back services vary widely, depending on the company and the type of service required. Be sure to check with these companies before leaving to compare rates.

For a list of callback services, please refer to the "Communications" section in the *Global Road Warrior* Introduction.

PHONE JACK

Plug adaptors are available through **iGo Corporation.** (See "Electrical and Telephone Adaptors" on page 19.)

FAX

Except for large hotels, fax machines may be difficult to find in Poland. They may also be found in post offices.

POSTAL SERVICES

International mail is unreliable and often accompanied by red tape. Only send packages if you must. Mailboxes are painted green for local mail, blue airmail, and red for all classes.

Hours of service

Monday to Friday 8a.m. to 6p.m.

TELEGRAMS

Telegram services are available at post offices and most hotels.

Business Services

BUSINESS CENTER

Bristol Hotel; Krakowskie Przedmiescie 42/44; tel: (22) 625-2525.

Sheraton Warsaw; Ul Prisa 2; tel: (22) 657-6100; 24 hour business center.

COURIER SERVICE

Airborne Express; Messenger Service Stolica S.C., C/O Airborne Express, Warsaw Airport, Ul. Wirazowa 35, Room 220, 02-158 Warszawa; tel: (22) 606-6802; fax: (22) 606-6802.

Federal Express Poland; Messenger Service Stolica; tel: (22) 868-0257. For customs clearance information, call Universal Express, tel: (22) 606-6511.

TNT Express Worldwide; No 1 Swirki i Wigury Street, 02-143 Warsaw; tel: (22) 650-4348, 650-2841; fax: (22) 650-2841, 650-4095.

UPS Poland; Polish Parcel Service Polkurier Ltd., 17 Stycznia str. 47, 02-146 Warsaw; tel: (22) 650-4545; fax: (22) 650-1661.

TRANSLATION SERVICES

Adwich; Ireneusz; Czerniakowska 36/18; Warsaw; tel: (22) 400-539.

Intertext; Bagatela 10/25; Warsaw; tel: (22) 21-718; fax: (22) 219-718.

Kot; Jozef, Krymska 2/44; Warsaw; tel: (22) 421-536

Lang Help; Aleje Jerozolimskie 23/34; Warsaw; tel: (22) 214-434

Wojczakowski; Zbigniew; Klaudny 18/152; tel: (22) 338-370

Electrical

Current

220 volts AC, 50Hz.

ELECTRIC PLUGS

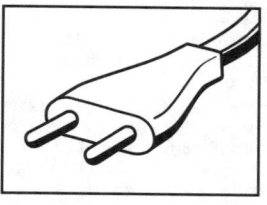

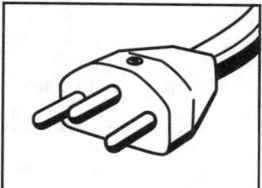

Plug adaptors are available through **iGo Corporation.** (See "Electrical and Telephone Adaptors" on page 19.)

Technical Support

HARDWARE/SOFTWARE VENDOR SUPPORT

AST; (in the U.S.) tel: [1] (817) 232-9824 (International Technical Support); (in Ireland) tel: [353] (61) 492-222; (in the U.S.) tel: [1] (949) 727-4141; http://www.ast.com/.

Compaq/Digital; (in Switzerland) tel: [41] (22) 709-5330; fax: [41] (22) 709-5391 (Geneva); tel: [41] (1) 801-2507; fax: [41] (1) 801-2172 (Zurich); (General U.S.) tel: (281) 518-2000; http://www.compaq.com/.

Corel; tel: 71-728-141 x289 (All Applications); (in Germany) tel: [49] (180) 425-8210 (TS Word Perfect-32 bit); (in the U.S.) tel: [1] (716) 871-2325 (Ask to be Forwarded to Appropriate Program); http://www.corel.com/.

Dell; (in Germany) tel: [49] (61) 039-710; (Dell- Europe) tel: [44] (134) 474-8000; (in the U.S.) tel: [1] (512) 338-4400; fax: [1] (512) 728-3330; http://www.dell.com/.

Filemaker/Claris; (in Germany) tel: [49] (180) 525-8166

(Info-line); fax: [49] (180) 567-2233; tel: [49] (180) 523-6423; (in the U.S.) tel: [1] (800) 965-9090; http://www.claris.com/.

Gateway 2000; (in the U.S.) tel: [1] (605) 232-2191; fax: [1] (605) 232-2023; (in Ireland) tel: [353] (1) 797-2000; http://www.g2k.com/.

Hewlett Packard; tel: 22 37 50 65; (in Switzerland) tel: [41] (22) 780-8111; (in the U.S.) tel: [1] (408) 246-4300; http://www.hp.com/.

IBM; tel: (22) 878-6777; fax: (22) 878-6888; (in Germany) tel: [49] (711) 78-50; fax: [49] (711) 785-3511; (in Switzerland) tel: [41] (22) 310-0418 (in French); (in the U.S.) tel: [1] (919) 517-2800; http://www.ibm.com/.

Microsoft; tel: (22) 661-5400; fax: (22) 661-5434; (22) 865-9966 (Technical Support); (22) 865-9933 (Information Service); (in Switzerland) tel: [41] (848) 858-868; fax [41] (1) 831-0869; (in the U.S.) [1] (425) 635-7222; http://www.microsoft.com/.

NEC; (in Germany) tel: [49] (18) 0524- 1212; tel:[49] (89) 3160-1233; fax: [49] (89) 3160- 1613 (Floppy Disk and Hard Drive); tel: [49] (89) 9627-4233; fax: [49] (89) 9627-4613 (All Other Products); (in the U.S.) [1] (916) 388-0101 (Main Switchboard); http://www.nec.com/.

Novell; (in Germany) tel: [49] (211) 563-2777 (System support); tel: [49] (6196) 904-477; fax: [49] (211) 563-2772; (in Switzerland) tel: [41] (1) 308-4747; fax: [41] (1) 302-0401; (in the U.S.) tel: [1] (408) 434-2300; fax: [1] (408) 577-5775 (Worldwide Sales Headquarters); http://www.novell.com/.

Quark; (in France) tel: [33] (1) 4084-7220; (in Germany) tel: [49] (7141) 455-255; (in the U.S.) tel: [1] (303) 894-8899; fax: [1] (303) 894-3398 (For Products Registered in the Americas); http://www.quark.com/.

Toshiba; (in Germany) tel: [49] (2131) 158-319; fax: [49] (2131) 158-558; (in Switzerland) tel: [41] (1) 946-0777; fax: [41] (1) 946-0807; (in Ireland) tel: [44] (193) 282-8828; (in the U.S.) [1] (949) 583-3000 (Corporate Headquarters); http://www.toshiba.com/.

Internet Connection
HOW TO CONNECT

Connecting to AOL and Compuserve in Poland is similar to using it when traveling outside your own area code. See the introductory section for detailed information on connecting to your account through a different phone number.

America Online

Numbers are available at keyword *international*. Be sure to get several local numbers before leaving. AOL has a new GlobalNet service that charges US$6 an hour in addition to the usual charges. Go to keyword *access* (a free area) and download the software.

Access: Gdansk (58) 769-0400; Katowice (32) 205-4441; Krakow (12) 429-3113; Lodz (42) 639-8020; Poznan (61) 856-0405; Szczecin (91) 480-6000; Warsaw (22) 521-0300, Warsaw (22) 521-0700; Wroclaw (71) 343-9090.

Compuserve

Numbers are available at *Go International*. The Compuserve Web-site also has a great deal of information, at http://www.compuserve.com.

At this time there are no internal Compuserve numbers for Poland. You will have to find an international dial-up solution

Independent Service Providers

Many independent service providers offer discounts if you are only in town for a couple of days.

Infonet; tel: (71) 320-2489; fax: (71) 321-7446; infonet@infonet.wroc.pl; http://www.infonet.wroc.pl/(Polish only).

Internet Technologies Polska; tel: (22) 534-8000; fax: (22) 534-8001; email: info@ipartners.pl; http://www.it.pl/; (Polish only).

PDi sp. z o.o.; tel: (42) 630-2194; email: sales@pdi.net; http://www.pdi.net/.

PerytNET Ltd; tel: (22) 851-4223; fax: (22) 675-6737; email: info@perytnet.pl; http://www.perytnet.pl/; (Polish and English versions).

Polska OnLine; tel: (22) 868-0808; fax: (22) 846-6271; email: info@pol.pl; http://www.pol.pl/; (Polish only).

Internet Cafes
Krakow

Cafe Internet; Aleja Slowackiego 29, Krakow; tel: (12) 339-144; email: cafe@kompit.com.pl; http://www.kompit.com.pl/.

O CyberCafe; Klub 'U Louisa' Rynek Główny 13, Krakow; tel: (12) 421-8092; email: cafe@raptor.bci.krakow.pl; http:/ /www.bci.krakow.pl/cafe.

Witamy w Cybercafe; 10.5 Rynek G3ówny 13, Krakow, BCI i Klub u Louisa; tel: (12) 218-092; email: cafe@bci.krakow.pl.

Warsaw

Casablanca Internet Cafe; Krakowskie Przedmiescie 4/6, 00-333, Warsaw; tel: (22) 828-1447; fax: (22) 826-6786; email: casemail@casablanca.com.pl; http://www.casablanca.com.pl/; Monday thorugh Thursday 9a.m to 1a.m., Friday and Saturday, 9a.m. to 2a.m., Sunday 10a.m. to 12p.m.; PLN12 per hour of use.

Cyber Cafe; 12 Nowogrodzka Street, Warsaw; tel: (22) 622-6611; email: olasme@ornak.waw.pdi.net; http://www.pdi.net/cybercafe/index.html/; Monday through Saturday, 10a.m. to 9p.m.; US$0.50 per hour of use.

Multimedia Room; 62 Wspolna st. room 164, Warsaw; tel: (22) 627-1641/42; fax: (22) 622-2560; email: media@ddc.daewoo.com.pl; Monday through Friday, 10am. to 8pm.; PLN5 per hour of use.

Planet 808 Internet Club; 2 Krolewska St., Warsaw; tel/ fax: (22) 828-9107; email: info@planeta808.ii.pl; http://www.planet808.ii.pl/; Monday through Saturday, 10a.m. to 12a.m.; PLN5 to PLN8 per hour of use.

Business Culture
GREETINGS AND COURTESIES

It is the custom in Poland to shake hands upon meeting, and on departure. Be wary of shaking hands over a threshold, for Poles consider that bad luck. Business cards, in both your language and Polish, are exchanged with all participants in meetings. It is also invaluable to obtain letters of introduction. In both business and formal settings, use a person's professional title and surname; first names are used only after a close relationship has been established. An invitation into a Polish home is rare, and an honor. Guests normally bring flowers to the host, in an odd number and never red roses. Toasting (usually done over hard liquor rather than wine or beer) is customary at both informal and formal dinners and guests are welcome to reciprocate. It is rude in Poland to begin eating before everyone has been served.

BUSINESS ETHIC AND FRAMEWORK

The main reason for any Polish success in business is the

Poles' geniality that turns businesspeople into friends. Poles are willing to assist on any level, while attempting to acquire management skills and gain experience in international business. Although traditional ineffective methods are bowing to more progressive methods of doing business, patience is still essential with Polish businesspeople. The human connection is an important component of business relations in Poland; Polish businesspeople insist on trust and confidence in their prospective partners before they sign any agreement. Foreign businesspeople should be willing to take the time and effort necessary to build a good relationship with their Polish associates, for only then will they be amenable to discussing business. Courtesy demands that foreign businesspeople make contact with the highest levels of Polish organizations; if possible, with the person actually in charge. Poles see it as an insult to do otherwise.

DECISION MAKING

The Polish spirit is composed of self reliance and individualism. In addition, most Poles are blunt; if they don't like the way negotiations are proceeding, they will not hesitate to tell a foreign visitor what they think. Poles have survived war, loss of territory, and submission to outside governments. They enter the decision-making process fearless. The details of an agreement are important to Poles; every point must be spelled out and explained. Decisions by committee continue to be a deeply rooted tradition that prolongs conclusion of all agreements. Once a decision has been made, it is easily overturned. Poles will make a decision only when they feel right about a deal— and no sooner.

WOMEN

An old-world mentality toward working women continues to fill the workplace in Poland. Although women in Poland are architects, factory managers, and high-level bureaucrats, and are represented in almost every other profession in the workforce, male chauvinism is still alive. Polish women do have equal access to higher education, however. The credibility of professional women has been given a boost by Poland's Prime Minister Suchock, and this indicates that their presence in high levels of business and government will increase. Members of the younger generations are more willing to accept women in positions of power.

MEETINGS

Prior appointments are necessary for doing business in Poland. Any communication to plan meetings with Polish business partners should be done by fax or telex; those methods are more reliable than the undependable Polish mail system. A further impediment is the telephone system in Poland, which also remains inefficient. Foreign businesspeople should expect confusion with meetings to be the norm. Appointments are sometimes suspended or canceled without notice; the wrong people may even arrive. It is important to leave early for meetings, since Polish transportation is notoriously slow. Presentations in Poland should be thoroughly prepared. Poles are aggressive and encourage competition in their business dealings. In Poland, no agreement is final until signed and even then agreements can easily fall apart due to changed circumstances or a decrease in the level of trust.

BUSINESS ATTIRE

Appropriate business dress in Poland consists of dark business suits of a conservative cut; understated dresses for women are acceptable. Conservative business attire is suitable for both formal and informal Polish functions. Women, especially, should dress conservatively, a suit or dress. While always neatly attired, Poles are not especially fashion conscious, although that may change as the economy progresses. Poles usually attire themselves more formally when visiting or entertaining. Bundle up in the winter with woolens as the winters turn very cold. An umbrella may prove handy throughout the year.

Business Centers
Warsaw
CITY VIEW

Warsaw is a very new-looking city, which may come as a surprise until you consider most of the city was destroyed during World War II. It is one of Eastern Europe's business centers, and is busy upgrading to shore up business. Improvements to the city are well underway, including fresh storefronts, infrastructure, and a flourishing restaurant scene. The city's old town has been rebuilt to provide medieval charm for those wishing to experience a piece of the city's long history.

AIRPORT

Okecie Airport to City Center

The airport lies 6 miles (10 km.) from the city center. Regular bus services depart in 30-minute intervals. One will recognize the Airport City Bus by its yellow color with a list of destinations printed on the side. Avoid the cab sharks awaiting you outside of customs and head for a telephone in the departure hall to order a radio cab (see taxi section for numbers), which will take about 10 minutes to arrive. If taking a cab, be sure to negotiate a fare before departing. Figure on about 30 minutes to reach Warsaw's center by bus, and 25 minutes by taxi.

Airline Numbers

Air France	(22) 628-12-81
Alitalia	(22) 26-28-01
American Airlines	(22) 625-30-02
Bulgarian Airlines	(22) 62-112-78
British Airways	(22) 628-94-31, 628-3991
CSA	(22) 26-38-02
Finnair	(22) 26-87-64
Lufthansa	(22) 630-25-55
Sabena	(22) 628-60-61

HOTELS

Top-end

Le Royal Meridien Bristol; Krakowskie Przedmiescie 42/44; tel: (22) 625-2525; fax: (22) 625-2577; http://www.bristol.polhotels.com/; email: romwo222@pol.pl; 206 rooms; located at edge of Old Town; renovated in 1992; 3 restaurants; conference facilities (up to 100); business center; secretarial service; fax/photocopy facilities; laundry and dry cleaning service; 24 hour room service; babysitting service; car service; news-stand; other shops - "Guerlain", "Cartier"; corporate rates; health club; sauna; pool.

Holiday Inn Warsaw; 48/54 Zlota Street; tel: (22) 697-3999 ; fax: (22) 697-3899; http://www.basshotels.com/holiday-inn/?_franchisee=WRSPL; email: holiday@orbis.pl; 336 rooms; adjacent to exhibition grounds; near railway; restaurant; conference facilities (up to 220); secretarial service; fax/photocopy facilities; radio; alarm clock; air conditioning; satellite TV; dataport on phone; direct dial phone; safe; coffee / tea maker; hairdryer; iron; mini bar; phone in the bathroom; corporate rates; parking; fitness; sauna; whirlpool.

Sheraton Warsaw; Ul Prisa 2; tel: (22) 657-6100; fax: (22) 657-6200; http://www.sheraton.com/ property.taf?prop=201; 352 rooms; new hotel; located near embassies; 4 restaurants; cafe; 2 bars; 24-hour business center with Internet capability; in-room modem/fax connection; safe; dual phone lines; voicemail; satellite TV; beauty salon; florist; gift shops; office suites available; 140 non-smoking rooms; Concierge; butler service for Tower floor with rooms with fax/copier/printer; car rental; airport shuttle; health club; 2 pools.

Warsaw Marriott; Aleje Jerozolimskie 65-79; tel: (22) 630-6306; fax: (22) 830-0311; http://marriotthotels.com/ marriott/WAWPL/; 523 rooms; city center; near railway; renovated rooms; restaurant; bars; casino; conference facilities (up to 1,000); secretarial service; fax/photocopy facilities; in-room modem; satellite TV ; in-room safe; fax connection; 24-hour room service; hair salon/barber; newsstand; rental car desk; shoe shine station; corporate rates; health club; sauna; whirlpool.

Expensive

Jan III Sobieski; Plac Artura Zawiszy 1; tel: (22) 579-1000; fax: (22) 659-8828; fax: (22) 658-1366; http:// www.sobieski.com.pl/; 418 rooms; city center; restaurant; 2 bars; conference facilities (up to 250); secretarial service; fax/photocopy facilities; in-room modem/fax connection; hairdresser; safe deposit box; laundry; covered parking; corporate rates; fitness.

Mercure; Aleja Jana Pawla II, 22; tel: (22) 620-0201; fax: (22) 620-8779; 252 rooms; city center; near railway; 2 restaurant; cafe; conference facilities (up to 300); secretarial service; fax/photocopy facilities; in-room safe; satellite TV; radio; direct-dial telephone; minibar; air-conditioning; airport shuttle service; corporate rates; parking; fitness; sauna; pool.

Victoria Inter-Continental; Krolewska II; tel: (22) 657-8011; fax: (22) 657-8057; email: warsaw@interconti.com; 360 rooms; city center, near exhibition grounds; restaurant; bar; casino; conference facilities (up to 450); secretarial service; fax/photocopy facilities; air conditioning, direct dial phones; shops; airline desk; car rental; corporate rates; parking; fitness; sauna; pool.

Moderate

Europejski; Krakowskie Przedmiescie 13; tel: (22) 826-5051; fax: (22) 826-1111; email: europej@orbis.pl; 237 rooms; city center; restaurant; conference (350); satellite TV; radio; direct-dial telephone; minibar; room service; hairdresser; coffee shop; news stand; dry-cleaning/ pressing service; art gallery; corporate rates.

Felix; Ulica Omulewska 24; tel: (22) 100-691; fax: (22) 130-255; http://www.felix.com.pl/; email: info@felix.com.pl; near airport; restaurant; meeting facilities (up to 40); secretarial service; fax/photocopy facilities; hairdresser; corporate rates; parking; fitness; sauna.

Grand; Ulica Krucza 28; tel: (22) 629-4051; fax: (22) 621-9724; 214 rooms; email: wagrand@orbis.pl; restaurant; casino; conference facilities (up to 100); business center with fax, photocopier, and computer; in room trouser press; in room hair dryer; hair dresser; newsstand; gift shop; corporate rates;fitness; sauna; pool.

Novotel; Ulica 1 Go Sierpnia 1; tel: (22) 846-4051; fax: (22) 846-3686; email: nwarszaw@orbis.pl; suburb, near airport; restaurant; bar; conference facilities (up to 300); satellite TV ; radio; direct-dial phone; room service; non-smoking rooms; news stand; corporate rates; parking; pool.

Solec; Ulica Zagorna 1; tel: (22) 625-4400; fax: (22) 625-

4424; 157 rooms; restaurant; bar; meeting rooms (up to 150 people); fax; telex; photocopier; satellite TV; direct-dial phone; hairdresser; flower shop; news stand; parking.

Vera; Ulica Bitwywarszawskiej 1920R 16; tel: (22) 227-421; fax: (22) 236-256; suburb, near airport, railway and exhibition grounds; restaurant; conference facilities (up to 150); satellite TV; radio; direct-dial telephone; room service; refrigerators (in 30 rooms); non-smoking rooms; parking; corporate rates.

MEDICAL CARE

Emergency Medical Servicel; tel: 628-2424.

Technodent; Sliska 10; tel: 203-548.

Wojciech Ejchman; Iberyjska 6/84; tel: 426-646.

HEALTH CLUB

Hotel Bristol Health Club; Krakowskie Przedmiescie 42/44; tel: (22) 625-2525.

Sheraton Warsaw; Ul Prisa 2; tel: (22) 657-6100.

AUTO RENTAL

Avis; Warsaw Intl Airport, Arrival Hall - Terminal 1; tel: (22) 650-4872; Warsaw Marriot Hotel, Al. Jerozolimskie 65/79; tel: (22) 630-7316.

Budget; 17 Stycznia 32, tel: (22) 846-7310; fax: (22) 846-5986; airport, tel: (22) 650-4062; Marriott Hotel, tel: (22) 630-7280; fax: (22) 630-6946.

ECU; 65/79 Jerozolimskie Ave., tel: (22) 630-5292 8a.m. to 8p.m.; tel: (22) 723-8686, 723-9263 24 hours; limousine service available

Eurodollar; tel/fax: (22) 650-1483, 650-1484; toll free: 0-800-200-39.

Europcar; Warsaw Airport, tel: (22) 650-2564; fax: 650-2563; 6 Moliera St.; tel: (22) 827-9984; fax: 827-9985; Krakow airport, tel: (12) 856-444; Krakow, 2 Szlak Street; tel: (12) 633-7773; fax: (12) 632-7362.

Hertz; International Airport, Warsaw; tel: (22) 650-2896; fax: (22) 650-3490; Parking House, Nowogrodzka 27; tel: (22) 621-1360; fax: (22) 629-3875; Hotel Victoria, 11 Krolewska Street; tel: (22) 827-4185.

Intercar; 24 Powazkowska St.; tel: (22) 388-724; fax: 388-723; cellular: 0-601-22-4845/46/47.

Orbis; tel: (22) 293-875, 274-185.

WORLD TRADE CENTER

World Trade Center Warsaw
The Palace of Culture & Scient
1 Plac Defilad (PKiN)
Warsaw 00-901, Poland
tel: (22) 656-7711; fax: (22) 656-7133

CHAMBER OF COMMERCE

Polish Chamber of Commerce
PO Box 361
ul. Trebacka 4, 00074 Warsaw
tel: (22) 826-0143; fax: (22) 827-9478
email: mailbox@kig.pl.

Portugal

At a Glance

THE PEOPLE

Population ....10,048,232 (July 2000 est.)
Growth Rate ....0.18% (2000 est.)
Life Expectancy .... 75.75 years
Infant Mortality ..... 6.05 deaths/1,000 live births (2000 est.)

Ethnic Composition

Homogeneous Mediterranean stock in mainland, Azores, Madeira Islands; citizens of African descent who immigrated to mainland during decolonization number less than 100,000.

Religious Composition

Roman Catholic.. 94%
Protestant denominations, other 6%

Languages Spoken

Portuguese.

Education and Literacy

Education has been compulsory since 1911. An estimated 87+ percent of the population age 15 and over can read and write.

Labor Force

Total: 4,750,000
By occupation: services 60%, industry 30%, agriculture 10%.

THE ECONOMY

Portugal is a growing, sturdy capitalist economy. Its per capita GDP (an estiamted $151.4 billion) is two-thirds that of the four big West European economies. Throughout 1998, Portugal enjoyed significant and stable economic growth, while its interest rates dropped and unemployment remained low. In 1998 the country became a member of the European Monetary Union (EMU). On January 1st of 1999, Portugal was one of 11 European countries to introduce the euro. The country continues to run a trade deficit and a balance of payments deficit. The government is working to institute a modernized capital plant and increase the country's competitiveness in the increase integration into world markets. Growth remains stable in 2000, as the continued economic integration of Europe rolls along. One area that Portugal must improve upon to remain a viable part of the growing world market is its education system, particularly in the high-tech arena.

Exports ....US$25 billion (f.o.b., 1998)
Imports ....US$34.9 billion (f.o.b., 1998)
Total Trade ....US$59.9 billion (1998)
GDP Per Capita............................. US$15,300 (1999 est.)
Unemployment ....4.6% (1999 est.)
Inflation Rate ....2.4% (1999 est.)

Top Export Partners

E.U. 82% (Germany 20%, Spain 16%, France 14%, U.K. 12% Netherlands 5%, Benelux 5%, Italy), U.S. 5%.

Top Import Partners

E.U. 77% (Spain 24%, Germany 15%, France 11%, Italy 8%, U.K. 7%, Netherlands 5%), U.S., Japan.

Top Exports

Clothing and footwear, machinery, cork and paper products, hides and skins.

Top Imports

Machinery and transport equipment, agricultural products, chemicals, petroleum, textiles.

BUSINESS WORKWEEK

Offices

Monday to Friday 9a.m. to 1p.m. and 2p.m. or 3p.m. to 6p.m. or 7p.m.

Banks

Monday to Friday 8:30a.m. to 3p.m.; in Lisbon, some banks may stay open between 6p.m. and 11p.m.

Government

Monday to Friday 9a.m. to noon and 2p.m. to 5p.m.; check hours of a particular department before visiting.

Retail

Monday to Friday 9a.m. to 1p.m. and 3p.m. to 7p.m., Saturday 9a.m. to 1p.m.

In addition, there are growing numbers of shopping centers (centros comercials) in urban areas that remain open at lunch time and have more flexible hours on weekday evenings and weekends.

HOLIDAYS

New Year's Day...January 1
Carnival Day...March 7*
Easter..April 21-23
Liberty Day .... April 25
Labor Day...May 1
Portugal Day...June 10
Corpus Christi .... June 22*
St. John the Baptist .... June 24*
Assumption...August 15
Proclamation of the Republic ....October 5
All Saints' Day ....November 1
Restoration of Independence ....December 1
Immaculate Conception...................................December 8
Christmas ....December 25

*Date may vary by year.

Note: Business travelers will do best to avoid July and August for travel to Portugal as most business people take a holiday during this time.

CLIMATE

Seasons

The climate in Portugal is temperate, mainly dry and hot in the summer, not too cold in the winter.

Regions

The mainland has extremes of climate, particularly true of central Portugal where there are cold, sharp winters and very hot summers. Climate in mainland Portugal is varied; the eastern and southeastern coastal area is Mediterranean in climate with long hot summers and short winters. The north and west is temperate with much colder winters.

Portugal

Money & Banking

Currency
The currency of Portugal is the Escudo (Esc).

Denominations
The Escudo comes in coin denominations of Esc200,100 50, 20, 10, 5, 2.5, 1 and 50 centavos; and banknotes of Esc500, 1,000, 2,000, 5,000, and 10,000.

Traveler's checks
Traveler's checks and foreign currency can be easily and efficiently exchanged at banks, foreign exchange bureaus located in the major cities, hotels, and foreign exchange kiosks at the airports. Banks offer the most variable exchange rates. Traveler's checks receive a better exchange rate than cash. The exchange counter at the airport in Lisbon is open 24 hours. Santa Apolónia Railway station has an exchange counter open until 10p.m.

American Express, Visa, MasterCard, and Diners Club, are widely accepted in Portugal. You can get cash advances from your credit card on many of the automized teller machines (ATM), which also show transactions in English. Long term visitors should set up a checking account in Portugal, and get an ATM card.

Essential Terms

English	Portuguese
Yes No	Sim Não
Good morning Hello (daytime) Hello (evening) Hello (telephone)	Bom dia Boa tarde Boa noite Ola
Good-bye	Adeus
Please	Faz favor
Thank you	Obrigado(a)
Pleased to meet you	Prazer em conhecê-lo(a)
Excuse me; I'm sorry	Desculpe / Sinto muito
My name is ____	Chamo me ____
I don't understand	Não compreendo
Do you speak English?	Fala inglês?

Travel

VISA AND PASSPORT

Foreigners must have a passport valid for 90 days beyond the intended length of stay. European nationals may carry a national identity card instead. A visa is not required by many countries (including Australia, Canada, EU, Japan, New Zealand, U.K., U.S.) for stays up to 60 days.

DEPARTURE FORMALITIES

A traveler can leave Portugal with the same amount of foreign currency that was brought in. There are no other departure formalities.

CUSTOMS ENTRY (PERSONAL)

Duty-free

The following goods may be imported into Portugal by visitors over 17 years of age from non-E.U. countries without incurring customs duty or government tax:

- Tobacco: 200 cigarettes, 100 cigarillos, or 50 cigars or 250g of tobacco
- Alcohol:1 liter of spirits over 22 percent or 2 liters of spirits up to 22 percent; 2 liters of wine
- Other: 50g of perfume and 250ml of eau de toilette; 500g of coffee or 200g of coffee extract; 100g of tea or 40g of tea extract; further goods up to Esc7500

Visitors over 17 years of age from E.U. countries may import goods in the following quantities without incurring customs duty or government tax:

- Tobacco: 200 cigarettes, 100 cigarillos, 50 cigars, or 250g of tobacco

- Alcohol: 1 liter of spirits over 22 percent, or 2 liters of spirits up to 22 percent; 2 liters of wine
- Other: 50g of perfume and 250ml of eau de toilette; 500g of coffee or 200g of coffee extract; 100g of tea or 40g of tea extract; further goods up to Esc60,000

Visitors over 17 years of age arriving from E.U. countries with duty-paid goods:

- Tobacco: 800 cigarettes, 400 cigarillos, 200 cigars, or 1kg of tobacco
- Alcohol: 90 liters of wine (including up to 60 liters of sparkling wine); 110 liters of beer

Note: Although there are now no legal limits imposed on importing duty-paid tobacco and alcoholic products from one E.U. country to another, travelers may be questioned at customs if they exceed the above amounts and may be asked to prove that the goods are for personal use only.

IMMUNIZATION

No inoculations are required unless you are arriving from an infected area, but a typhoid shot and polio booster are recommended.

TIPPING

Tipping to all service people in Portugal is very appreciated and somewhat expected.

Taxi

Taxi drivers get 10 percent.

Hotels

Room service waiters: 5 to 10 percent of the bill.

Restaurants

Restaurants will add a service charge and tax, but extra tipping is customary: Five percent is appropriate for lower-end restaurants, and 10 percent for the waiter, and something for special service from the maître d', captain, and busboy in higher end restaurants.

EMERGENCY INFORMATION

Police and Crime

Portugal is a relatively safe country, but theft is common in larger cities and pickpockets are prevalent. Lisbon suffers increasingly from car theft. Be extra careful on public transportation, in underground car parks, airports, and street fairs and do not leave valuables in cars or on tables in cafes.

Avoid flashy displays of wealth, and dress and behave conservatively. Leave most of your cash, traveler's checks, jewelry, and your camera in your hotel safe. Carry photocopies of your passport instead of the original. Carry cash in a money belt, and use credit cards or traveler's checks for most transactions. Walk with your bag away from the street to avoid having it snatched away by motorcycle thieves. Never carry a stranger's baggage.

Women are advised to travel in groups at night and to take taxis after midnight. The police are efficient and courteous, and most speak some English.

Emergency Numbers

Emergency	112
Police (Lisbon)	726-8022
Fire (LIsbon)	342-2222
Ambulance (Lisbon)	301-7777
AIDS Helpline	759-9943
Accidental Poisoning Information	795-0143
Pregnancy Helpline	395-2143
Drug Abuse Information	726-7766

Health

Tap water is safe to drink, but most people prefer bottled mineral water. Community health standards are high, and

Portugal

there are no extraordinary diseases in the Portugal. Some beaches on the Estoril Coast (close to Lisbon) are polluted.

Digestive problems may occur for people unaccustomed to the cuisine. Wash all vegetables in a chlorine solution, peel fruits, and avoid uncooked food. Drink only pasteurized milk.

The Portuguese medical service is adequate, if a little overcrowded; however, for more serious medical care, try the private hospitals. Pharmacies in Lisbon have all the necessary drugs, but come prepared. Pharmacies are usually open Monday to Friday 9a.m. to 1p.m. and 3p.m. to 7p.m.; Saturday 9a.m. to 1p.m. One or more pharmacists stay open otherwise on a rotating basis. Check with the hotel front desk.

For more information on medical centers, including phone numbers, please see the "Business Centers" section at the end of this chapter.

TAXI

Look for the black and green or beige cars in Lisbon if you wish to find a taxi. Taxis are metered and charge based on distance. An extra charge of about Esc300 may be levied on baggage. One may wave them down on the streets or go to a taxi stand. Smaller towns have taxis that are distinguishable by the letter 'A' marked on the car. Negotiate fares in such cases as the cars are not metered. Taxis offer a reliable way to get around, but keep an eye on the meter when the amount that you owe is stated by the driver since the it may not match the meter.

AUTO

Portugal has one of the highest rates of automobile accidents and fatalities in all of Europe. Road travel can be hazardous due to poor illumination on narrow, rough roads, potholes, confusing road signs, poorly marked road works, vehicles without working lights, slow-moving road repair, and agricultural machinery. Other problems you may encounter are vehicles moving at excessive speeds, unpredictable driving habits of the locals, and reckless motorcyclists. Fines for traffic violations are steep and in many cases have to be paid on the spot.

TRAIN

Other parts of the country may be reached by train. First and second class cars are available for the rail traveler. Unlimited rail travel within Portugal is also made possible with *Bilhetes Turisticos* (tourist tickets) for 7, 14, or 21 days. International trains depart from Santa Apolónia Station.

Rail Information ....(1) 888-4025

SUBWAY

Lisbon offers a modern subway that has operated since 1959. Tickets cost Esc70 and remain valid for one hour. One may also purchase 10-ticket booklets.

WATER TRAVEL

Travel by way of boat is possible from all ports along the coast, as well as from all major river ports. Contact a shipping line in one of these ports for more information.

Communications

DIALING CODES IN PORTUGAL

International country code: [351]

Selected city codes: Portugal has incorporated all city codes into the local numbers. The new codes are as follows: Land-line phones and faxes (2), Toll-free (8), Internet Dial-up numbers (6).

Dialing Portugal from Overseas

To dial Portugal from overseas, dial your country's international code, then 351 (the country code for Portugal), then the city code, and finally the number. If you were dialing Llsbon, for example, you would begin with 011, then 351, then 1 (the city code for Lisbon), and finally the number of the person or office you were trying to reach.

Assistance Numbers

International Operator 098
European Operator (Algeria, Morocco) 099
Domestic Operator 090
Directory 118
Time 15
Alarm Service 161

CALLING WITHIN PORTUGAL

Local Calls

Go ahead and dial the local number and see what happens. The Portuguese phone system is notoriously dubious.

Long Distance Calls

When calling within Portugal, keep the zero preceding a city code and then follow by dialing the local number.

International Calls

You can call direct from modern phone boxes or post offices by dialing 00 + country code + area code + number. Private phones are less costly than public phones except in hotels where, to some consternation, you will start seeing double. Bars also offer telephones, however the rates may vary depending on the management. Off-peak rates happen between 10p.m. and 8a.m. daily, the lowest after midnight and also on weekends. You can also reach an overseas operator by dialing the appropriate access number; but, unfortunately, not all phones offer this capability.

Australia Direct 05017-6110
British Telecom.. 0505-0044
Canada Direct 05017-1226
Ireland Direct 0505-0353
U.S. AT&T Direct... 0800800128
U.S. MCI... 05017-1234
U.S. Sprint... 05017-1877

PAY PHONES

Public Telephones

Card Phone:

Portuguese phones use 5, 10, 20, 50, and 100 escudos coins.
1. Lift receiver
2. Insert coins in slot
3. Listen for dial tone
4. Dial
5. Coins will drop if connection is made

A tone will warn you when time is running short. If you lose hair trying to make a call, you won't be the first, thanks to the often unreliable phone system.

Portugal

Calling Cards

Specially marked card phones (*crediphones*) exist to take away the hassle of change. Post offices, Telecom offices, and tobacco stores sell phone cards. One should note that there are two types of phone cards. The Telecom card operates best in Lisbon and Porto. The Crediphone is prevalent in other cities.

CELLULAR PHONES

Telecel and *Telecom Moveis Nacionais* operate GSM systems for digital users in Portugal.

Note: Your home country cell phone may not work in this country. If not, we recommend that you rent an international cell phone *before* you leave home. A major US-based cell phone rental provider is **IMC WorldCell**. For information see "International Cell Phone Rentals" on page 14. GSM phones are available for rent at the airport in Lisbon for a 3-day minimum.

The international dialing code for mobile phones in Portugal is '268'.

CALL BACK

You can (potentially) save significant sums when calling in Portugal by using one of the call back services listed below. Fees for call back services vary widely, depending on the company and the type of service required. Be sure to check with these companies before leaving to compare rates.

For a list of callback services, please refer to the "Communications" section in the Global Road Warrior Introduction.

PHONE JACKS

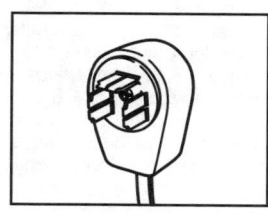

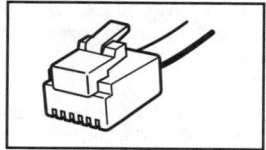

Plug adaptors are available through **iGo Corporation**. (See "Electrical and Telephone Adaptors" on page 19.)

FAX

All major hotels have fax machines, and service is generally adequate.

POSTAL SERVICES

Postal service is generally good. Airmail to the U.S. takes two to four days.

Hours of service

Central post offices: Monday to Friday 8 a.m. to 9p.m.; main post offices are often open on Saturdays as well from 9a.m. to 6p.m.

TELEGRAMS

Most hotels have telegram facilities. A public office, open Monday to Friday between 9a.m. and 6p.m., exists at Praca D Luis 30-1.

Business Services

BUSINESS CENTER

Belem Cultural Center; Praço do Imperio, 1400 Lisbon; tel: (1) 301-0606, 362-1476; fax: (1) 361-2500; meeting facilities and high-tech equipment.

Lisboa Business Center; Rua Alexandre Herculano, No. 5; tel: (1) 317-5800; fax: (1) 357-5658; email: cenese@mail.telepac.pt; 45 furnished offices, secretarial service; translations, messenger service, meeting room (up to 16), parking, 24 hrs., Monday to Saturday.

Meridien Park Atlantic Hotel; Rua Castilho 149; tel: (1) 383-0900.

Ritz Inter-Continental Hotel; Rua Rodrigo da Fonseca 88; tel: (1) 383-2020.

COMPUTER RENTAL

Intess; Rua S. Juliao 62; Lisbon; tel: (1) 87-9947.

COURIER SERVICES

Airborne Express; Edificio Sagres, R/C Sala "E", Quinta Da Francelha-Prior Velho, 2685 Sacavem; tel: (1) 941-0264; fax: (1) 940-0723.

DHL; tel: (1) 80-8520.

Federal Express; tel: (0800) 244-144.

TNT Express Worldwide; Rua C, Edificio 77, Aeroporto de Lisboa; tel: (1) 854-5050, Customer Service; tel: (1) 854-5000, General; fax: (1) 840-3080.

UPS; Quinta Do Figo Maduro, 1 Rua Particular S/N, 2685 Sacavem; free phone tel: 0800-20-5020.

PRINTING/COPYING

Arco Iris; Arco Iris Shopping Mall, Ave. Julio dinis 6A; Lisbon; tel: (1) 76-1850.

Soctip; Rua Dona Estefania 195A; Lisbon; tel: (1) 54-3280.

SECRETARIAL SERVICES

Streamline Services; Rua Iracy Doyle 9, 3 Esq.; 2750 Cascais; tel: (1) 483-0149; fax: (1) 486-1409.

Hospedeiras de Portugal; Rua borges Carneiro 63-3D; 1200, Lisbon; tel: (1) 60-4353.

Lisboa Business Center; Rua Alexandre Herculano, No. 5; tel: (1) 317-5800; fax: (1) 357-5658; email: cenese@mail.telepac.pt; 45 furnished offices, secretarial service; translations, messenger service, meeting room (up to 16), parking, 24 hrs., Monday to Saturday.

Intess; Rua S. Juliao 62; tel: (1) 87-9947.

TRANSLATION SERVICES

Centro Europeu de Linguas; Ave. Padre Manuel da Nóbrega 3A; tel: (1) 80-8282.

CI - Congresso E Informatica, lda; Rua Cidade de Cadiz, 14- 3 Dto. A; tel: (1) 776-2697; fax: (1) 726-9851; email: cijcr@mail.telepac.pt; Portuguese/Spanish/English/French/Italian.

GUIA Traducções e Representações Lda; tel: (1) 486-2358; fax: (1) 486-2389; email: guiatrad@mail.telepac.pt.

Triplicado (Relocation Service); Av. 25 Abril, Lote 83, Vila Fria; tel: (1) 421-0932; fax: (1) 421-0933; email: info@triplicado.com.

Traduções Técnicas - José Casquilho; tel:(1) 259-5284; fax: (1) 259-5284; email: jctraduz@esoterica.pt.

Electrical

Current
220 volts AC, 50 Hz.

ELECTRIC PLUGS

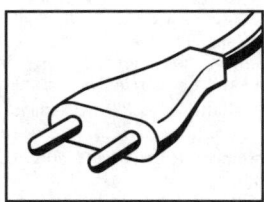

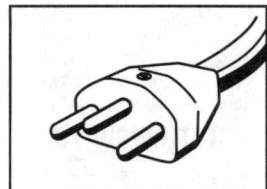

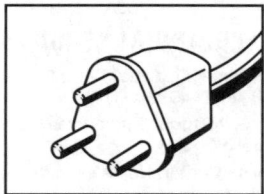

Plug adaptors are available through **iGo Corporation**. (See "Electrical and Telephone Adaptors" on page 19.)

Technical Support

HARDWARE/SOFTWARE VENDOR SUPPORT

Dell; (in Germany) tel: [49] (61) 039-710; (Dell- Europe) tel: [44] (134) 474-8000; (in the U.S.) tel: [1] (512) 338-4400; fax: [1] (512) 728-3330; http://www.dell.com/.

Hewlett Packard; tel: (0) 144 17 199; (in Switzerland) tel: [41] (22) 780-8111; (in the U.S.) tel: [1] (408) 246-4300; http://www.hp.com/.

IBM; tel: (1) 791-5168; fax: (1) 791-5055; (in Switzerland) tel: [41] (22) 310-0418 (in French); (in the U.S.) tel: [1] (919) 517-2800; http://www.ibm.com/.

Microsoft; tel: (1) 440-9200; fax: (1) 441-2101; (1) 440-9280/1/2/3 (Standard Technical Support); fax: (1) 441-

1655; (in Switzerland) tel: [41] (848) 858-868; fax [41] (1) 831-0869; (in the U.S.) [1] (425) 635-7222; http://www.microsoft.com/.

NEC; tel: 01-388-9107 (UltraCare Support); (in the U.S.) [1] (916) 388-0101 (Main Switchboard); http://www.nec.com/.

Internet Connection

HOW TO CONNECT

Connecting to AOL and Compuserve in Portugal is similar to using it when traveling outside your own area code. See the introductory section for detailed information on connecting to your account through a different phone number.

America Online
Numbers are available at keyword *international*. Be sure to get several local numbers before leaving. AOL's Global-Net service charges US$6 an hour in addition to the usual charges. Go to keyword *access* (a free area) and download the software.
Access: Faro (6) 289-817-034; Funchal (6) 291-223-398; Lisbon (6) 1417-2935; Lisbon (6) 213-540-477; Lisbon (6) 213-522-081; Porto (6) 226-002-946.

Compuserve
Numbers are available at *Go International*. The Compuserve Web-site also has a great deal of information, at http://www.compuserve.com.
Access: Faro (6) 289-817-034; Funchal (6) 291- 223-398; Lisbon (6) 214-172-935; Porto (6) 22 6-002-946.

Independent Service Providers
Many independent service providers offer discounts if you are only in town for a couple of days.
DIRAC; tel: 21 312-9732; fax: 21 312-9701; email: info@dirac.pt; http://www.dirac.pt/; (English and Portugese).
Fleximédia; tel: 244-829-933; fax: 244-829-932; email: info@fleximedia.pt; http://www.fleximedia.pt/.
Teleweb, S.A.; tel: 213-105-000; fax: 213-105-904; email: info@teleweb.pt; http://www.teleweb.pt/.
VIA NET.WORKS; tel: 213-199-200; fax: 213-199-201; email:info@via-net-works.pt; http://www.via-net-works.pt/.

Internet Cafes
Lisbon
Cyber.bica; Duques Bragança Street, 7 Lisbon; tel/fax: 1322-5004; email: cyberbica@cyberbica.com; http://www.cyberbica.com/; Monday through Saturday, 12p.m. to 2a.m.; Esc600 per hour of use.
PostNet - Braamcamp; Rua Braamcamp No.9 Loja A c/v 1250-048 Lisbon; tel: 21-351-1050; fax: 21-351-1051; email: infolis02@postnet.pt ; http://www.postnet.pt/; Monday through Sunday, 8a.m. to 8p.m.; Esc150 per hour of use.

Business Culture

GREETINGS AND COURTESIES
Most men greet by enthusiastically hugging and slapping each other's backs. Women who know each other well greet with a kiss on both cheeks. A firm handshake with eye contact is an important custom when first meeting and departing. Business cards are essential in Portuguese business; make sure you always have them available in both English and Portuguese. Use titles with the last name until invited to do otherwise; first names are usually only used among close friends. Titles include *Senhor, Senhora, Senhorita, Doutor* (for anyone with a university degree), and *Engenheiro* or *Arquitecto* for

those in the appropriate technical fields. Most Portuguese are very reserved; you will not see the extensive gestures their Spanish neighbors favor. Even in the more outgoing areas, it takes time to establish friendships. Portuguese also respect manners; a simple "please" or "thank you" will go a long way to establishing a relationship. Although English is widely used and spoken, especially in urban areas and tourist spots, try to communicate in Portuguese. Learning even a few words and phrases is greatly appreciated. When talking to Portuguese, avoid conversations about politics and the government. It is also impolite to appear too inquisitive in your conversations. Some popular topics of conversation are family, pleasing aspects of Portugal, sports, and personal interests.

BUSINESS ETHIC AND FRAMEWORK

The Portuguese businessperson is usually conservative and formal, and at the same time courteous and gracious. Business style is restrained but not formal and Portuguese businesses prefer careful preparation and clear terms. Individualism is important, but emphasis in terms of respect and deference is usually placed on age, seniority, educational background, and financial standing. The contract has always been honored and respected in law and by a centuries-old tradition of keeping international agreements.

MEETINGS AND DECISION MAKING

Avoid making appointments between noon and 3p.m.; all offices are closed. Prior appointments are essential, especially for government visits. You should arrive to meetings on time, even though the host will usually take a casual approach to being timely. It is best to take a conservative approach to meetings, and be sure to check all dates and times accordingly. Business rarely takes place during dinner. Don't be surprised if meetings run late; people and relationships are thought of as more important here than ending a discussion prematurely. Before going to the first meeting, try to find someone who supports your position within the Portuguese company who can lobby for you. Face-to-face meetings are more popular than those over the telephone. Meetings usually begin with casual, friendly conversation and are often held in old, intimate coffee houses. Business discussions often take place during long lunches. Portuguese businesspeople prefer to consider a proposal carefully before accepting anything. Opinions will usually come quicker than decisions.

WOMEN

Women working outside the home, at least in urban areas, are becoming more common. Female business managers are most common in the cities; rural areas still cling to conservative ideas. Throughout the country, however, the emphasis still remains on women as homemakers with absolute authority in domestic matters. As Portugal emerges into a democracy, women are slowly acquiring positions of power. They still hold many entry-level jobs in businesses, though even this is a step up from a few years ago. Men still remain dominant in much of the culture, though foreign businesswomen should be treated with respect. Street theft can be a problem, and women should be sure to hold handbags tightly, especially in the urban areas.

BUSINESS ATTIRE

Dress in a conservative suit with a topcoat or raincoat during the winter. Lisbon's streets are mostly cobblestone; bring sturdy, comfortable shoes. Men wear suits to work, though sport jackets are gaining popularity. Because of the usually pleasant temperatures, cotton summerwear will prove the most comfortable. Laundering services are ex-

pensive compared with other Western European countries. Appropriate dress is highly recommended when visiting official buildings or restaurants. It is considered unacceptable to walk around the streets in shorts or bikini tops. Theft is a problem, particularly in Lisbon, and businesspeople should be advised not to appear too much like a tourist.

Business Centers
Lisbon
CITY VIEW

Although once one of the most important ports in centuries past catapulting the city to be one the wealthiest in Europe, Lisbon today is probably one of the smallest and most unpretentious capitals in Western Europe. Set on and around hills next to the sea, Lisbon still retains some of its cobblestoned streets, some Moorish influence, as well as a blend of people from all over the world.

AIRPORT

Portela de Sacavem Airport to City Center

The airport lies 4.5 miles (7 km.) from the city. A regular Aerobus service delivers passengers to downtown Lisbon at Restauradores Square in 20-minute intervals between 7a.m. and 9p.m. Passengers may purchase tickets from the driver. Taxis from the airport cost between Esc1500 to 2000 (more after 10p.m.) for a 20-minute ride into town, about double if traffic exists. Make sure the meter is running before departing. Local buses #45 and #83 serve the budget traveler and also stop at Restauradores Square.

Airport Flight Information 841-6990

Airline Numbers

Air France	(1) 790-02-02
Alitalia	(1) 353-61-41
Air New Zealand	(1) 316-1617
British Airways	(1) 346-61-41
Toll free	0500-1251
Delta	(1) 353-76-10
Iberia	(1) 355-81-19
KLM	(1) 847-63-54
Lufthansa	(1) 357-38-52
Portugalia	(1) 842-55-59
Sabena	(1) 346-55-72
SAS	(1) 347-30-61
SATA Air Açores	(1) 353-95-11
Swissair	(1) 347-11-11
TAAG Air Angola	(1) 357-58-99
TAP Air Portugal	(1) 841-6990
Toll free	0808-21-31-41
TWA	(1) 314-71-41
Varig	(1) 353-91-53
Toll free	0500-1234

HOTELS

Top-end

Lisboa Sheraton Hotel and Towers; Rua Latino Coelho 1; tel: 213-120-000; fax: 21 213-547-164; 381 rooms; near city center; restaurants; in-room safe; direct dial telephones; some rooms with fax/modem connection (called "smart rooms", desigend for the business traveler); air conditioning; parking; corporate rates; health club; pool.

Meridien Park Atlantic; Rua Castilho 149; tel: 21-381-8700; fax: 21-389-0505; email: reservas.lisboa@lemeridien.pt; opposite Parque Eduardo VI, adjacent to Ritz Inter-Continental; 330 rooms;

restaurant; conference facilities (up to 550); business center, secretarial service; fax/photocopy facilities; Internet; in-room modem/fax connection; in-room safe; 24 hour room service; satellite TV; Beauty parlour; news stand; jewelry; handicraft shop; antiques; secure parking; non-smoking floors; sauna; massage.

Ritz Inter-Continental; Rua Rodrigo da Fonseca 88; tel: 2169-2020; fax: 2169-1783; 265 rooms; city center; restaurant; bar; conference facilities (up to 600); business center, executive rooms with in-room modem/fax connection; air conditioning; in room safe; 24-hr room service; non-smoking rooms available; shops; hairdresser; parking; gym; sauna; solarium; pool; jacuzzi; golf.

Expensive

Altis (Best Western); Rua Castilho 11; tel: 21-310-6000; fax: 21-310-6060; city center; 303 rooms; restaurant; bar; 15 conference facilities (up to 3,000); secretarial service; fax/photocopy facilities; sound proof rooms; air conditioning; satellite TV; radio; direct access telephone; safe; minibar; parking; health club; sauna; solarium; pool.

Albergaria Senhora do Monte; Calcada Do Monte; tel: 218-866-002 /3 /4 /5; fax: 21-887-7783; 28 rooms; city center; bar; rooms service; in-room safe; satellite TV; direct dial phones; air conditioning; corporate rates; currency excahnge; babysitting service.

Fénix; Praca Marques de Pombal 8; tel: 213-862-121; fax: 213-862-127; fax: 213-860-131; email: h.fenix@ip.pt; 123 rooms; city center; restaurant; bar; conference facilities (up to 120); in-room safe; air conditioning; direct dialing phones; satellite TV; minibar; tobacconist; other shops; corporate rates; baby sitting service; health centre; tennis; pools.

Melia Confort Lisboa; Avda. Duque de Louie 41; tel: 21-351-0480; fax: 21-353-1865; central location in business area; suites hotel; restaurant; bar; coffee shop; conference facilities; in-room safe; room service; doctor on call; laundry service; boutique; shops; car rental desk; parking; fitness center; sauna; pool; jacuzzi; solarium.

Mundial; R.D. Duarte 4; tel: 1-884-2000; fax: 1-884-2110; http://www.hotel-mundial.pt/; email: mundial.hot@mail.telepac.pt; city center; recently renovated; 300 meters from Rossio Square; restaurant; bar; meeting rooms (up to 130); in-room safe; air conditioning; satellite TV; minibar; parking.

Principe Real; Rua da Alegria 53; tel: 21-346-0116; fax: 21-342-2104; 24 rooms; center of the city; restaurant; bar; secretarial services; air-conditioning/heating; direct dial phone; in room safe; satellite TV; radio; 24 hour room service; dry cleaning service; tea served in room daily; Concierge; valet/laundry service; babysitting service.

Radisson SAS Hotel Lisboa; Av. Marechal Craveiro Lopes, 390; tel: 217-599-639; fax: 217-586-949; 221 rooms; near airport/subway; oversized rooms; business rooms available; conference facilities; no-smoking rooms available; satellite TV, video channels; minibar; trouser press; electronic safe; complimentary shuttle; parking; shops; health club; sauna; jacuzzi.

York House; Rua das Janelas Verdes 32; tel: 21-396-2435; fax: 21-397-2793; 34 rooms; quaint inn, with differing rooms, "all shapes and sizes"; located in convent near embassies; dining hall; bar; courtyard.

Moderate

Britania; Rua Rodrigues Sampaia 17; tel: 21-315-5016; fax: 21-315-5021; 30 rooms; city center; bar; air-conditioning; in room mini-bar; in room safe; satellite TV; direct dial phones; in room modem outlets; hairdryers; laundry service; parking.

Best Western Eduardo VII; Avenida Fontes P. Melo 5; tel: 213-568-822/00; fax: 213-568-833; http://www.hoteleduardovii.pt/; email: sales@hoteleduardovii.pt; 140 rooms; city center, near metro; rooftop restaurant; conference facilities (up to 200); secretarial service; fax/photocopy facilities; in-room safe; satellite TV; radio; direct dial telephone; minibar; sound proof windows; secure parking; corporate rates.

Executive Inn Hotel; Av. Conde Valbom, 56-62; tel: 21-795-1157, tel: 795-1159; fax: 21-795-11 66; 72 rooms; new quarters of Lisbon; restaurant; satellite TV and video; radio; minibar; direct dial telephone; wake up call system; safe deposit; air conditioning; car service; room service; parking.

Miraparque; Avenida Sidonio Pais 12; tel: 21-352 4286; fax: 21-357-8920; email: miraparque@esoterica.pt; 100rooms; city center, overlooking Eduardo VII Park; near subway; renovated rooms; restaurant; bar; meeting room (up to 20); in-room safe; air-conditioning; mini-bar; satelite TV; room service.

MEDICAL CARE

British Hospital; Rua Saraiva de Carvalho 49, tel: 60-2020.

Hospital Santa Maria; University teaching hospital; tel: (1) 797-5171; fax: (1) 797-8821; email: hsm.cm@mail.telepac.pt.

International Health Center; tel: (1) 484-5317.

HEALTH CLUB

Centro Comercial das Amoreires; Avenida Duarte Pacheco; tel: 69-29-07.

Estoril Sol Health Club; Estoril Sol Hotel, Parque Palmela, Cascais; tel: 28-23-31.

Health Club Soleil is located at several hotels:

Sheraton Hotel; 1 Rua Latino Coelho; tel: 55-33-55; **Meridien Hotel**; 149 Rua Castilho; tel: 69-23-80.

AUTO RENTAL

Avis; Lisbon Da Portela Airport; tel: (1) 843-5550; Av Praia Da Vitoria 12 C, Lisbon; tel: (1) 356-1177; Saint Apolonia Rail Station, Estacao, Caminho De Ferro, De Santa Apolonia, Lisbon; tel: (1) 881-0469.

Budget; Rua Dra. Iracy Doyle, 6a; tel: (1) 482-1291; fax: (1) 462-1291; email: budget@portugal-info.com.

Europcar; Portella Airport, tel: (1) 840-1176; fax: (1) 847-3180; Santa Apolonica Rail Station, tel: (1) 886-1573; fax: 886-1573; LIsbon de Aguiar, Av. Antonio Augusto Aguiar 24C/D; tel: (1) 353-5115; fax: (1) 353-6757.

Hertz; Portela Airport, Lisbon; tel: (1) 849-0831; fax: (1) 840-1496; Av Republica, Av da Republica 64A.; tel:(1) 793-3647; fax: (1) 793-3128; Lisbon Downtown, Rua Castilho 72; tel: (1) 381-2430; fax: (1) 387-4164; Visconde Seabra, Rua Visconde Seabra 10; tel: (1) 797-0458; fax: (1) 797-0371.

WORLD TRADE CENTER

World Trade Center Lisbon
Av. do Brasil, 1-9
1700 Lisbon, Portugal
tel: (1) 792-3700; fax: (1) 792-3701
email: wtc@telepac.pt

CHAMBER OF COMMERCE

Cámara de Comércio e Indústria Portuguesa
Rua das Portas de Santo Antão 89;
tel: (1) 322-4050; fax: (1) 322-4051.

Romania

At a Glance

THE PEOPLE

Population ....22,411,121 (July 2000 est.)
Growth Rate ....-0.21% (2000 est.)
Life Expectancy .... 69.93 years
Infant Mortality ... 19.84 deaths/1,000 live births (2000 est.)

Ethnic Composition

Romanian 89.1%
Hungarian 8.9%
German 0.4%
Ukrainian, Serb, Croat, Russian, Turk,
and Gypsy 1.6%

Religious Composition

Romanian Orthodox Church.. 70%
Unaffiliated 18%
Roman Catholic (3% Uniate)... 6%
Protestant 6%

Languages Spoken

Romanian, Hungarian, and German are all widely spoken throughout Romania.

Education and Literacy

Almost 97 percent of the population can read and write. Education is compulsory for four years in rural areas, and seven years in the cities. Admission to an advanced institution depends on a variety of factors, including the student's social background.

Labor Force

Total 9,600,000
By occupation: agriculture agriculture 36.5%, industry 34.4%, services 29.1%.

THE ECONOMY

When the Soviet Union fell Romania found itself in the position of a cog without a machine. Its industrial position was out of date and ill suited to the needs of the country. In 1997, Romania began on macroeconomic revamping and a restructuring program, but reform has been a difficult and slow going process. Restructuring in Romania included far reaching financial and agricultural reforms and the liquidation of energy-intensive industries. In 1999 Romania's economy shrank for a third straight year. This time by an estimated 4.8%. In August of 1999 Romania reached an agreement with the IMF for a loan of US$547 million, but release of the second tranche was postponed in October of the same year, due to unresolved private sector lending requirements and differences between the IMF and Romania over budgetary spending. Bucharest avoided defaulting on mid-year debt payments, but in doing so, the government had to draw significantly upon reserves. By the end of 1999 these reserves were replenished to an estimated $1.5 billion. The government's priorities have changed. They now include: shoring up fiscal policy, obtaining further IMF lending, accelerating privatization through private sector incentive, and the restructuring of unprofitable Romanian companies. In late 1999 Romania was invited by the E.U. to begin the process of enterance into its ranks.

Exports ....US$8.4 billion (f.o.b., 1999 est.)
Imports ....US$9.6 billion (f.o.b., 1999 est.)

Total Trade ....US$18 billion (1999 est.)
GDP Per Capita...............................US$3,900 (1999 est.)
Unemployment ....11 % (1999 est.)
Inflation Rate ....44 % (1999 est.)

Top Export Partners

Italy 22%, Germany 19.6%, France 5.9%, US 3.8%.

Top Import Partners

Germany 17.5%, Italy 17.4%, France 6.9%, US 4.2%.

Top Exports

Textiles and footwear 33.4%, metals and metal products 19.1%, machinery and equipment 9.5%, minerals and fuels 6.1%.

Top Imports

Machinery and equipment 23%, fuels and minerals 14.2%, chemicals 8.7%, textiles and footwear 17.1%.

BUSINESS WORKWEEK

Offices

Monday to Friday 7a.m. to 3:30p.m., Saturday 7a.m. to 12:30p.m.

Banks

Monday to Friday 9a.m. to noon, 1p.m. to 3p.m., Saturday 9a.m. to 12:30p.m.

Government

Monday to Friday 9a.m. to 2:30p.m., Saturday 9a.m. to noon.

Retail

Monday to Saturday 6a.m. to 9p.m., Sunday 6a.m. to noon.

HOLIDAYS

New Year.. January 1-2
Good Friday..April 28*
Easter Monday .... May 1*
International Labor Day .... May 1-2
National Day...December 1
Christmas ....December 25

*Date may vary by year.

Note: Business travelers should try and avoid traveling to Romania during the month of August when many Romanians go on holiday.

CLIMATE

Seasons

The climate is temperate with hot and sunny summers, and cold and cloudy winters. In July average temperatures are about 24˚C (75˚F) and in January around 0˚C (32˚F). her are northern cold winds in the winter, and westerly winds from the Atlantic in the summer.

Regions

Temperature decreases in higher altitudes, in the northwest, and around the southeast, near the Black Sea. Rain is heaviest in the west of Romania.

Romania

SM Santa Barbara, CA
©2001 Magellan Geographix

Money & Banking

Currency

The currency of Romania is the Leu (pl. Lei).

Denominations

The Leu comes in coin denominations of 100, 50, 20 and 10, 5, and 3, and banknotes of 500, 1,000, 5,000, and 10,000.

Traveler's checks

Traveler's checks can be exchanged at banks, exchange shops, and hotels, as well as international airports, at tourist exchange rates. With various rates of exchange, larger banks may offer the best exchange rates, but avoid black marketers at all cost. Consult your bank about current exchange rates before departure. Keep all receipts for reconversion.

Most currencies can also be exchanged, but try to take only crisp and new notes, wrinkled and soiled notes are likely to be refused.

American Express, Visa, Diner's Club, MasterCard are accepted in up-market places, but smaller restaurants and shops in more rural areas may ask for cash. Some banks in the capital offer cash advances on credit cards, but make sure you bring your passport.

Travel

VISA AND PASSPORT

Foreigners must have a valid passport and visa. Nationals of Bulgaria, CIS, Croatia, Czech Republic, Hungary, Poland, Slovak Republic, Slovenia, Yugoslavia, United States, Cyprus, San Marino, Mexico and Turkey do not require a visa for stays of 30 days, some longer. Tourist and business visas are available. Visas can be obtained in advance from the Romanian Embassy in the traveler's country of residence or at the airport in Bucharest. Visas may also be obtained at border crossings, but the cost is slightly higher. Certain nationalities require an official notarized invitation from a company or an individual in Romania in order to procure a visa at all. The process will take minimum 30 days. Check with the nearest Romanian consulate or embassy for the latest information regarding requirements for entering the country, as they are subject to change.

DEPARTURE FORMALITIES

Foreigners must have an exit form (*talon de iesire*—a small white paper obtained on entering the country and placed inside the passport) to leave Romania. No more than 5,000 Romanian lei may be exported. Up to US$50,000 cash may be exported, so long as it was declared on entry. Customs regulations prohibit the export of some items. Tourists should save all receipts for presentation to customs authorities.

CUSTOMS ENTRY (PERSONAL)

Duty-free
- Tobacco: 200 cigarettes or 200g of tobacco
- Alcohol: 1 liter of spirits; 4 liters of wine or beer
- Other: gifts up to a value of 1000 Euro

Prohibited or Restricted
- Ammunition and explosives
- Narcotics
- Pornographic material
- Uncanned meats, animal and dairy products
- Radioactive substances

Note: Certain goods such as art, electrical items, foreign currency over 1,000 Euro in value, and jewelry must be declared upon entry into Romania. Keep all endorsed customs declarations to show when exiting the country.

IMMUNIZATION

Only visitors arriving from infected areas need vaccination certificates, but it is suggested that polio and hepatitis vaccinations be current.

TIPPING

Tipping is generally about 10 percent in Romania. U.S. dollars are readily accepted for tips.

Taxi

Taxi: 5 to 10 percent is customary, depending on distance.

Hotels

Hotels and restaurants generally expect 5 percent; porters receive about 50 lei per bag.

Restaurants

Waiters receive 5 to 10 percent.

Other

Hairdressers and barbers 5 to 10 percent.

EMERGENCY INFORMATION

Police and Crime

Theft is common in larger cities and pickpockets are prevalent. Bucharest suffers increasingly from car theft. Take extra care on public transportation, in underground car parks, train stations, parks, and in airports; and do not leave valuables in cars. Only travel in marked taxis. The police advise foreign tourists to ask for an identity card if stopped by a supposed policeman or man of the law. Money exchange schemes targeting travelers have become increasingly common, including scams involving individuals posing as plainclothes policemen. Also, take care on overnight trains, where a number of thefts and assaults have occurred, including thefts from passengers in closed compartments. Although not sources of crime per se, one should avoid stray dogs, which roam the streets of Bucharest in numbers.

Avoid flashy displays of wealth, and dress and behave conservatively. Leave most of your cash, traveler's checks, jewelry, and your camera in your hotel safe. Carry photocopies of your passport instead of the original. Carry cash in a money belt, and use credit cards or traveler's checks for most transactions. Walk with your bag away from the street to avoid having it snatched away by motorcycle thieves. Never carry a stranger's baggage.

Women are advised to travel in groups at night or to take taxis after midnight. Policing is adequate.

Emergency Numbers

Police	955
Ambulance	961
Emergency Hospital	962
Special Ambulance (pregnant women, or those with small children)	969
Fire	981
Automobile Assistance (Bucharest)	927
Outside Bucharest	area code + 12345

Health

Although tap water is chlorinated, one is advised to stick with bottled water, at least for the first few days of your stay.

Digestive problems may occur for people unaccustomed to the cuisine.

Romania has poor medical service, and also suffers from overcrowding.Although doctors may be competent, basic medical supplies and medicines are scarce, so come prepared. For more serious medical care, go to nearby Germany, Austria, or Greece.

TAXI

Use marked taxis only. All taxis are metered. Cabs can be found in the streets, standing in front of hotels, or phoned in from hotels. If a cab is not metered, negotiate a fare before leaving. Expect to pay no more than Lei50,000 for a trip across town.

7 ABC	942
Cobalcescu	945
Cris Taxi	946
Galati	953
Pacific Motors Taxi OK	312-5114
Titan	953

AUTO

Roadways in Bucharest are in decent condition. However, do not expect the same on secondary roads, which are often poorly lit, narrow, and in disrepair. Persons renting a car must have a valid passport, international insurance policy (green card in Europe), and an international driving permit. Avoid travel at night since roads are generally poorly lit and in poor repair. Drivers should note that the alcohol limit is strictly enforced, but that seatbelts are not mandatory.

Bucharest Road Assistance	927
Other parts of the country	12345

TRAIN

All train services run efficiently and are inexpensive. Just about any part of the country is accessible by train as are other major European capitals. All trains offer first- and second-class compartments. The train system offers four classes of service all indicated by a color code: yellow for the quickest Inter-City trains, green for express service, red for accelerated, and blue for local.

SUBWAY

A metro also exists in Bucharest. As is the case for any bus or trolley, purchase tickets for the metro from hotels or booths on the streets that are painted yellow. Tickets should be validated once on board. The metro operates between 5:30a.m. and 11p.m.

BUS

Buses are crowded and do not run on schedule, but otherwise offer an inexpensive way to go. Purchase tickets at kiosks near bus stops, at tobacco stands, or from a conductor. Long-distance buses service most of the country; but do no expect highly comfortable conditions.

TROLLEYS

Streetcars are another way to get around town in Bucharest. Tickets are available on board or at tobacconists. Beware of pickpockets, however, on the often crowded systems.

WATER TRAVEL

Traveling by boat to other countries is possible in Romania. The primary international port in the country is in Constanta, a port of call for many cruise ships. Ferry service runs on the Danube, from Orsova to Bulgaria. Ferry service is also available on the European riverway from Rotterdam to Constanta by way of the Romanian Danube Canal and the Black Sea. River cruises are also available. Contact the shipping lines, or a Romanian Tourism Promotion office for more information.

TRAVEL ASSISTANCE

Romanian National Tourist Office; http://www.rezq.com/ont/.

Romanian Tourism Promotion Office; http://www.turism.ro/.

Romania

Essential Terms

English	Romanian
Yes	Da
No	Nu
Good morning	Buna dimineata
Hello (daytime)	Buna ziua
Hello (evening)	Buna seara
Hello (telephone)	Buna ziua
Good-bye	La revedere
Please	Ma rog
Thank you	Multumesc
Pleased to meet you	Sint incintat sa va cunosc
Excuse me; I'm sorry	Scuzati-ma
My name is _____	Numele meu este__
I don't understand	Eu (nu) inteleg
Do you speak English?	Vorbiti engleza?

Communications

DIALING CODES IN ROMANIA

International country code: [40]

Selected city codes: Arad (572), Bacau (34), Brasov (68), Bucuresti (Bucharest) (1), Cluj-Napoca (64), Constanta (41), Connex (Mobile Phones) (92 or 93), Craiova (51), Galati (36), Iasi (32), Oradea (59), Dialog (Mobile Phones) (94 or 95), Pitesti (48), Ploiesti (44), Satu-Mare (61), Sibiu (69), Telemobil (98), Timisoara (561), Tirgu Mures (65).

Dialing Romania from Overseas

To dial Romania from overseas, dial your country's international dialing code, then 40 (the country code for Romania), then the city code, and finally the number. If you were dialing Bucharest from the United States, for example, you would begin with 011, then 40, then 1 (the city code for Bucharest), and finally the number of the person or office you were trying to reach.

Assistance Numbers

Information	area code + 11515
Local Time	958
International Calls	971
Domestic Calls	991

CALLING WITHIN ROMANIA

Local Calls

Local calls should only entail straightforward dialing, unless, of course, the phone does not operate properly.

Long Distance Calls

Dialing long distance in Romania means first dialing a zero, then area code + number.

International Calls

Prepare for bad connections if you do happen to connect at all. Try to start with U.S. access numbers to reach an American operator. Public phones may require a coin or card deposit.

AT&T	01-800-4288
MCI	01-800-1800

If attempting to call direct, dial 00 + country code + area code + number. You can call from telephone centers by ordering your call with the clerk. He or she will ask for a deposit depending on where you are calling. Then wait for your city, country, and phone booth number to be announced and proceed to your indicated booth. As always, expect tremendous surcharges if attempting to dial from your hotel.

PAY PHONES

Public Telephones

Card Phone:

You can use 20-, 50-, and 100-lei coins to use the non-orange public telephones; the orange telephones take cards only.

Calling Cards

Telephone cards are available at post offices, selected hotels, and street kiosks.

CELLULAR PHONES

MOBIL ROM and *MOBIFON* operate GSM digital systems for cellular users in Romania. *Telefonica Romania* operates an analogue NMT-450 system as well.

Prefixes when dialing cellular networks apply:

Connex (MoviFon)	092
Dialog (MobilRom)	094
Telemobil	0186

Note: Your home country cell phone may not work in this country. If not, we recommend that you rent an international cell phone *before* you leave home. A major US-based cell phone rental provider is **IMC WorldCell**. For information see "International Cell Phone Rentals" on page 14.

CALL BACK

You can (potentially) save significant sums when calling in Romania by using one of the call back services listed below. Fees for call back services vary widely, depending on the company and the type of service required.

For a list of callback services, please refer to the "Communications" section in the Global Road Warrior Introduction.

PHONE JACK

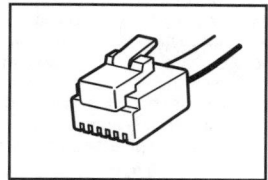

Plug adaptors are available through **iGo Corporation.** (See "Electrical and Telephone Adaptors" on page 19.)

FAX

Fax machines may be difficult to come by, and the service is generally slow because of the poor telephone system.

POSTAL SERVICES

The mail service is unreliable. Ask at your hotel for a courier service instead. The main post office is located at 10, Matei Millo St. in the same vicinity as the telephone company.

Hours of Service

Monday to Friday 7:30a.m. to 7:30p.m.

TELEGRAMS

Telegrams are probably the most inexpensive form of international communication in Romania. They can be sent from post offices or most hotels.

Business Services

BUSINESS CENTER

Athenee Palace Hilton; 1-3 Episcopiei Street; tel: (1) 315-1212

Inter-Continental; 4 Nicolae Balcescu Boulevard; tel: (1) 310-2020.

World Trade Center; 2 Expozitei Blvd., Sector 1 tel: (1) 222-0362; fax: (1) 222-4870; website: http://www.wtcb.ro; email: wtcb@wtcb.ro;

Services: office rental; secretarial service; translations; telephone/fax service; convention center; trade missions.

COURIER SERVICE

Federal Express (International Romexpress); tel: (1) 211-1580.

TNT Express Worldwide (Romcargo); SOS, Bucharesti-Pioiesti, KM 16.5; Otopeni Airport; tel: (1) 231-1921, 231-1996; fax: (1) 231-1945.

UPS Romania; Romtrans SA, Calea 13 Septembrie nr. 81-83, Block 77ab, Bucharest 7000; tel: (1) 410-0604; fax: 410-9910.

Electrical

Current

220 volts AC, 50Hz.

ELECTRIC PLUGS

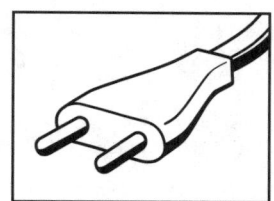

Plug adaptors are available through **iGo Corporation.** (See "Electrical and Telephone Adaptors" on page 19.)

Technical Support
HARDWARE/SOFTWARE VENDOR SUPPORT

Apple/Claris; tel: 1-212-1047; (in the U.K.) tel: [44] (990) 127-753; (in the U.S.) tel: [1] (408) 996-1010 (Corporate Headquarters); http://www.apple.com/.

Compaq/Digital; (in Switzerland) tel: [41] (22) 709-5330; fax: [41] (22) 709-5391 (Geneva); tel: [41] (1) 801-2507; fax: [41] (1) 801-2172 (Zurich); (General U.S.) tel: (281) 518-2000; http://www.compaq.com/.

Dell; (in Germany) tel: [49] (61) 039-710; (Dell- Europe) tel: [44] (134) 474-8000; (in the U.S.) tel: [1] (512) 338-4400; fax: [1] (512) 728-3330; http://www.dell.com/.

Filemaker/Claris; (in Germany) tel: [49] (180) 525-8166 (Info-line); fax: [49] (180) 567-2233; tel: [49] (180) 523-6423; (in the U.S.) tel: [1] (800) 965-9090; http://www.claris.com/.

Hewlett Packard; (in Switzerland) tel: [41] (22) 780-8111; (in the U.S.) tel: [1] (408) 246-4300; http://www.hp.com/.

IBM; tel: (1) 224-1544; fax: (1) 224-3922; (in Germany) tel: [49] (711) 78-50; fax: [49] (711) 785-3511; (in Switzerland) tel: [41] (22) 310-0418 (in French); (in the U.S.) tel: [1] (919) 517-2800; http://www.ibm.com/.

Microsoft; tel: (1) 222-9016; fax: (1) 222-9012; tel: (1) 312-0948 (Technical Support); (in Germany) tel: [49] (89) 31-760; fax: [49] (89) 3176-1000; tel: [49] (89) 3176-1199; (in Switzerland) tel: [41] (848) 858-868; fax [41] (1) 831-0869; (in the U.S.) [1] (425) 635-7222; http://www.microsoft.com/.

Internet Connection
HOW TO CONNECT

Connecting to AOL and Compuserve in Romania is similar to using it when traveling outside your own area code. See the introductory section for detailed information on connecting to your account through a different phone number.

America Online

Numbers are available at keyword *international*. Be sure to get several local numbers before leaving. AOL's Global-

Net service charges US$6 an hour in addition to the usual charges. Go to keyword *access* (a free area) and download the software.

Access: Bacau (34) 110-733; Brasov (68) 472-102; Bucharest (1) 303-8123; Cluj.-Napora (64) 191-894; Constanta (41) 691-502; Timisoara (56) 221-002.

Compuserve

Numbers are available at *Go International*. The Compuserve Web-site also has a great deal of information, at http://www.compuserve.com.

There are no direct access numbers in Romania. Users will have to pay international rates to use the service.

Independent Service Providers

Many independent service providers offer discounts if you are only in town for a couple of days.

CCTC- cluj; Computer Communication & Training Center; tel: (1) 212-5430/1; fax: (1) 312-7053; email: info@buc.osf.ro; http://www.soroscj.ro/.

ITCNet; tel: (1) 232-2770, tel: (1) 232-1432; fax: (1) 230-7845, fax: (1) 232-0468; email: office@itcnet.ro; http://www.itcnet.ro/.

Logic TELECOM S.A.; tel: (1) 321-3635; fax: (1) 321-3730; email: salesforce@logicnet.ro; http://www.logicnet.ro/; (English and Romanian).

PC-Net Data Network; tel: (1) 330-3523; tel: (1) 330-3524; email: sales@pcnet.ro; http://www.pcnet.ro/.

Business Culture

GREETINGS AND COURTESIES

Use formal forms of address in Romania, *Domnul* for "Sir" and *Doamna* for "Madam" until it is indicated by your host to switch to a first-name basis. Use titles for professionals or older Romanians, *Doctor Iliescu* for Doctor, *Engineer Donescu* for engineers. Romanians consider entertaining guests to be an honor, but it is rare for foreign guests to be invited into a Romanian home. It is customary to bring gifts to business associates in Romania, perhaps inexpensive pens or lighters imprinted with your company's logo. When dining, several toasts are exchanged and guests are expected to contribute. *Noroc* means "cheers" in Romanian. Romanian hosts will likely want you to stay for dinner as long as possible. Don't be in a rush to leave. However, in many cases one may not be invited out to dinner until a deal is closing due to budget constraints. Flowers prove an appropriate gift for most social occasions. Be sure flowers are offered in odd numbers; an even-numbered count applies to dour occasions only.

BUSINESS ETHIC AND FRAMEWORK

Doing business in Romania can be a frustrating experience, but patience may pay off. Bitter toward Communists, Romanians have eagerly embraced the free market system, and display a new excitement in their business dealings, especially when compared to previous years when strong new businesses were rare. However, red tape still accompanies most transactions, and corruption may well prove a problem as well. A lack of legal specialists to interpret changing laws also makes closing a deal difficult at times.

MEETINGS AND DECISION MAKING

Meetings in Romania should be held on a one-to-one basis. Write in advance to garner an appointment. Romanians appreciate a letter written in English. But consider an interpreter for the actual meeting depending on the level of English that your business counterparts exhibit. Come prepared to give a business card to every person attending a meeting. Academic titles lend respect to your position in a Romanian's eyes.

Romanians are often distrustful, even of their own people. Foreign businesspeople are often told what the Romanian thinks they want to hear rather than the facts as they exist. Prepare for a lengthy meeting. Business presentations should be filled with facts and figures and organized to speed the decision-making process. Commonly, no one wants to carry responsibility, and decisions are passed from office to office with the plea, "It's not my problem."

WOMEN

Women in Romania are treated with extreme respect and courtesy. Romania maintains traditional attitudes toward women, and women attempting to work as professionals have to work hard to prove themselves in order to be treated equally. Romanian women are very common in the workplace under the new economy due to financial need. Foreign women may run into resistance in conducting business with Romanian males, but a firm, professional attitude should hold sway.

BUSINESS ATTIRE

Conservative suits will serve both men and women well in a country still recovering from economic woes. Avoid flashy clothes, including designer threads, and excessive jewelry, which may cause envy and attract unnecessary attention. The style is normally casual, albeit neat and polished, unless it concerns an evening event, such as restaurant dining and theater, in which case more formal attire is appropriate.

Business Centers
Bucharest

CITY VIEW

Bucharest combines buildings dedicated to business with tourist attractions and historical sights.

AIRPORT

Otopeni Airport to City Center

The airport lies 10 miles (16 km.) from the city center. A coach service runs 24 hours every 60 minutes. Travel time is about 35 minutes. Taxis also service the airport and entrepreneurs will descend upon the new arrivals. One should not pay more than about US$20. Agree on a fare before departing. The airport coach costs about L600. The InterContinental Hotel also provides a shuttle service for its guests for a price of US$20. Otherwise, tour operators can supply transfers at competitive rates. Check with your travel agent about arrangements.

Airline Numbers

TAROM
Romanian Air Transport 615-2747, 615-0499

HOTELS

Top-end

Athenee Palace Hilton; 1-3 Episcopiei Street; tel: (1) 303-3777; fax: (1) 315-2121; http://www.hilton.com/hotels/BUHHITW/; email: sales.bucharest@hilton.com; 272 rooms; city center; restaurants; conference facilities; business center; in-room mode/fax connection; no-smoking rooms available; hair salon; health club; pool.

Crowne Plaza; 1 Poligrafiei Street, Bucharest; tel: tel: (1) 224-0034; fax: (1) 224-1126; email: cplazza@fx.ro; 164 rooms;

near the international airport; 2 restaurants, a bar, swimming pool bar, and a cafe; business center; conference facility (200 people); 2 direct dial telephones per room; coffee maker; air conditioned; television; laundry facilities; parking garage; fitness center; indoor swimming pool.

Inter-Continental; 4 Nicolae Balcescu Boulevard; tel: (1) 310-2020; fax: (1) 312-0486; email: bucharest@interconti.com; 390 rooms and 13 Suites; renovated; city center; restaurant; bar; conference facilities (up to 600); business center; no-smoking rooms; barber/beauty shop; newsstand; airline desk; Car rental; airport shuttle; Concierge; parking; fitness; spa; solarium; sauna; pool; nightclub/disco.

Majestic; 11, Academiei Street, Sector 1; tel: (1) 311-3212, 312-1967; fax: (1) 310-2799, 310-2380; email: majestic@rotravel.com; 74 rooms; city center; restaurant; 24-hour room service; meeting room; business center with Internet connection, computers; non-smoking and disabled rooms; in-room tv, minibar; direct dial telephones with message service; safe; beauty salon; fitness; sauna; massage.

Sofitel; 2 Expozitiei Boulevard; reservations tel: (1) 224-3000; fax: (1) 224-2536; http://www.sofitel.com/; email: sofitel@sofitel.ro; 202 rooms; new hotel, adjacent World Trade Center, city center; 2 restaurants; bar; conference facilities; fax/photocopy facilities; non-smoking floors; fitness; sauna; nearby health club access.

Expensive

Bucuresti; 63-81 Victoriei Avenue; tel: (1) 312-7070; fax: (1) 312-0927;446 rooms; city center; restaurant; conference facilities (up to 500); business center; air conditioning; direct dial telephone; satellite TV; minibar; 24 hour room service; parking; corporate rates; fitness; sauna; pool.

Lebada; Boulevard Biruintei Nr. 3, Sector 2; tel: (1) 255-3000, 255-3010; fax: (1) 255-0041; 30 rooms; located in suburb (10Km from downtown); refurbished palace in park; restaurant; bar; conference facilities (up to 80); telex and fax service; safeboxes; Concierge; beauty parlor; sauna; massage; pool; tennis.

Lido; B-dul Magheru 5-7 Sector 1, 70161, Bucarest; tel: (1) 314-7248; fax: (1) 312-1414; 119 rooms; restaurant; conference facility; bar; television; air conditioned rooms; laundry facilities; various shops; parking; fitness center; pool.

Moderate

Ambassador; B-dul Magheru Nr. 40; tel: (1) 615-9080; fax: (1) 312-1239; 70 rooms, 10 suites; conference center; restaurant (seats 400); telephone; radio; television; fitness center; pool.

Boulevard; 21 B-dul Regina Elisabeta; tel: (1) 315-3300; fax: (1) 312-3923; 89 rooms; restored hotel; central location; restaurant; conference facilities (up to 50); TV; telephone.

Caro; Str. Barbu Vacarescu 164A, Bucharest; tel/fax: (1) 242-1108; email: caro@itcnet.ro; 52 rooms; coference facilities; in room data-ports; air conditioning; direct dial telephones.

Continental; 56 Calea Victoriei; tel: (1) 638-5022; fax: (1) 312-0134; near financial district and former Royal Palace; conference facilities (up to 80); car rental; shuttle/taxi service available; buffet breakfast included; tel: (1) 6145348; fax: (1) 3120134.

Dorobanti (Howard Johnson); Calea Dorobanti 1-7; tel: (1) 211-5450; fax: (1) 211-5484; email: doro@rotravel.com; 298 rooms; city center; restaurant; conference facilities (up to 500); secretarial service; fax/photocopy facilities; corporate rates; parking.

Helvetia; Charles de Gaulle Square; tel: (1) 223-0556; fax:

(1) 223-0567; http://helvetia.netvision.net.il/; email: helvetia@ines.ro; 30 rooms; restaurant; fax/email facilities; satellite TV; direct dialing telephones; room service; limousine service; parking.

MEDICAL CARE

Balsam Drug Store; Cal Victoriei 147; tel: 650-2170.

Carol Davila Clinical Hospital; Cal Grivitei 4; tel: 650-7096, 650-7147, 650-7297, 650- 7544, 650- 7647.

Emergency Clinical Hospital; Cal Floreasca 8; tel: (1) 615-8139, 679-4080, 679-4310, 679-4412.

Gheorghe Marinescu Clinical Hospital; Sos Berceni, tel: 682-6220, 682-7775, 683-2130.

Municipal Clinical Hospital; Spl Independentei 169; tel: 637-2190, 637-2900, 638-6005.

SRL Drugstore; Cal Victoriei 14; tel: 613-7766.

Titan Clinical Hospital; Bd Muncii 49; tel: 643-3265, 644-0020; 644-0040.

HEALTH CLUB

Athenee Palace Hilton; 1-3 Episcopiei Street; tel: (1) 315-1212.

Le Club and Health Center; World Trade Center, 2 Expozitei Blvd., Sector 1; tennis, squash, indoor pool, bar, billiards room, gym, sauna, Hammam, jacuzzi, restaurant; tel: (1) 311-0045.

AUTO RENTAL

Avis; Bucharest Otopeni Airport; (1) 230-0054; Hotel Hilton Bucharest, 1-3 Episcopiei Street; tel: (1) 315-1212; Hotel Intercontinental, Bucharest; tel: (1) 614-0400; Hotel Minerva, Bucharest; tel: (1) 312-2738.

Dacia; tel: (1) 650-7076, 211-0410; airport, tel: (1) 212-0040.

Eurodollar; Take Ionescu 27; tel: (1) 650-2595, 659-6629.

Europcar; Bucharest Otopeni Airport; tel: (1) 312-7078; fax: (1) 633-7501; Bucharest Hotel, Calea Vlictoriei 68-82; tel: (1) 614-2889; (1) 224-3523; Intercontinental Hotel, Boulevard Balcescu, Bucharest; tel: (1) 613-7040; fax: (1) 224-3523.

Hertz; Bucharest Airport, Otopeni Airport, Bucharest; tel: (1) 230-3259; fax: (1) 230-3257; Reservation Number; tel: (1) 337-3934.

WORLD TRADE CENTER

World Trade Center Bucharest
2 Expozitei Blvd., Sector 1
Bucharest, 78 334 Romania
tel: (1) 222-0362; fax: (1) 222-4870
website: http://www.wtcb.ro
email: wtcb@wtcb.ro
Services: office rental; secretarial service; translations; telephone/fax service; convention center; trade missions; health club.

World Trade Center Bucharest-Victoria
170, Stirbei Voda Street
B1. 10G, ET.2, AP. 6
Bucharest, Romania
tel: (1) 311-0045; fax: (1) 311-0781

CHAMBER OF COMMERCE

Chamber of Commerce of Romania
22, Nicolae Balcescu Blvd.
79502, Sector 1, Bucharest
tel: (1) 615-4703; fax: (1) 312-2091

Russia

At a Glance

THE PEOPLE

Population 146,393,569 (1999)
Growth Rate ....-0.33% (1999 est.)
Life Expectancy .... 65.12 years
Infant Mortality........ 23 deaths/1,000 live births (1999 est.)

Ethnic Composition

Russian 81.5%
Tatar.. 3.8%
Ukrainian 3%
Chuvash 1.2%
Bashkir 0.9%
Byelorussian 0.8%
Moldavian 0.7%
Other 8.1%

Religious Composition

Russian Orthodox, Muslim, Jewish, Buddhist, Catholic, Protestant, other.

Languages Spoken

Russian (official); more than 140 other languages and dialects.

Education and Literacy

Russia has a literacy rate of 98 percent. Education is mostly state funded and compulsory for 10 years. State-funded stipends are available for higher education.

Labor Force

Total: 66,000,000

THE ECONOMY

Russia suffered drastic changes in its attempt to reform its centrally planned socialist economy. By taking the steps of dissolving both its political and economic structure simultaneously, the country has been plunged into governmental and commercial chaos. Widespread corruption, cronyism, and the rise of a brutal criminal class that involves over 70 percent of the nation's businesses have caused a severe pull-back in foreign investments of all types. Massive currency devaluations and the lack of a bonafide legal structure have dashed all hopes of the Russian economy becoming a major force in global commerce.

Exports ....US$71.8 billion (1998est.)
Imports ....US$58.5 billion (1998 est.)
Total Trade ....US$130.3 billion(1998 est.)
GDP Per Capita.................................. US$4,000 (1998 est.)
Unemployment ....11.5% (1998 est.)
Inflation Rate ....84% (1998 est.)

Top Export Partners

Ukraine, Germany, U.S., Belarus, other Western and less developed countries.

Top Import Partners

Europe, North America, Japan, Third World countries.

Top Exports

Petroleum and petroleum products, natural gas, wood and wood products, metals, chemicals, and a wide variety of civilian and military manufactures.

Top Imports

Machinery and equipment, consumer goods, medicines, meat, grain, sugar, semifinished metal products.

BUSINESS WORKWEEK

Offices

Monday to Friday 9a.m. to 6p.m.

Banks

Monday to Friday 9:30a.m. to 5:30p.m.

Government

Monday to Friday 9a.m. to 6p.m.

Retail

Monday to Saturday 9a.m. to 5p.m., smaller shops closing for an hour during lunch time; many shops are now also open on Sundays and 24-hour shops are becoming more common.

HOLIDAYS

New Year.. January 1-2
Orthodox Christmas ....January 7
Defenders of the Fatherland Day ....February 23
International Women's Day .... March 8
Day of the Unity of the Peoples.............................. April 2
Orthodox Easter ....April 12*
Spring and Labor Day .... May 1-2
Victory Day ....May 9
Independence Day ....June 12
National Flag Day..August 22
Revolution Day ....November 7
New Year's Eve..December 31
    *Date may vary by year.

Unofficial Holidays

By custom, the Monday preceding a public holiday on a Tuesday is taken as an additional public holiday, in which case the preceding Saturday is the working day.

CLIMATE

Seasons

Russia's summers, in general, are mild, with an average temperature of 22°C (71°F) in Moscow, and the winter months are generally bitterly cold and dry with an average temperature of -9°C (15°F).

Regions

Russia spans from northeastern Europe to eastern Central Asia, so the climate varies widely from place to place, from the arctic climate of Siberia to the mild temperatures of the south.

Money & Banking

Currency

The currency of Russia is the Ruble (R).

Denominations

The Ruble comes in coin denominations of R100, 50, 20, 10, 5 and 1 and banknotes of R100, 200, 500, 1,000, 5,000, 10,000, 50,000, 100,000. Ruble bills issued before 1993 have been declared invalid.

Traveler's Checks and Credit Cards

Most major credit cards are accepted at hard currency

Russia

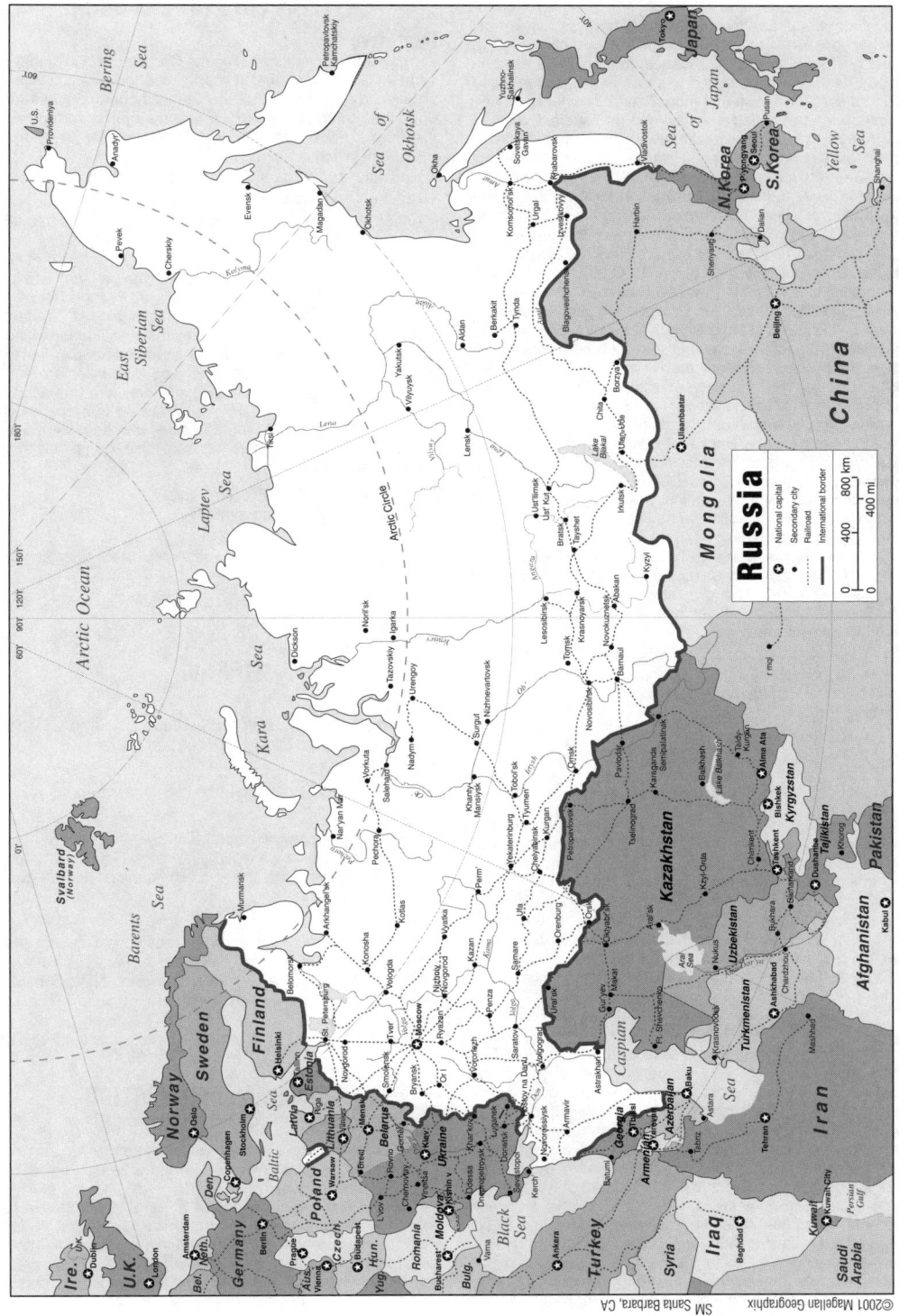

Russia

shops, restaurants, and stores in major Russian cities. However, there are few processing facilities, and most transactions are not authorized prior to purchase; so in case of loss of credit card, cancel immediately. Keep in mind that you may be asked to show your passport when using a card for a cash advance. Traveler's checks can be exchanged at specified cashiers in larger hotels. Expect to pay service charges, sometimes as much as 5 percent, when exchanging currency. Transactions should be recorded on the currency declaration form issued upon your arrival in Russia. Keep all transaction receipts in case of any problems encountered when leaving the country.

One is urged to avoid changing money on the street due to tricks and ruses used to snare extra dollars. Take care that you do not accept rubles issued before 1993 as they are invalid. Counterfeit U.S. bills have invaded Russia, most specifically US$20 and US$100 bills. As such, bills are often carefully inspected. It is useful to bring along a good supply of small denomination U.S. dollars to use in stores; even taxi drivers will often prefer foreign currency payments. Take crisp, new bills as old or soiled bills are often not accepted. Other currencies will prove more difficult to use in Russia.

Many shops, restaurants, and smaller hotels do not accept traveler's checks. Banks will often cash checks for dollars, but be sure to have well-known checks such as American Express, Thomas Cook, or VISA. Have your passport ready for identification. Also prepare for the instance that some establishments list prices in dollars, but may only accept rubles.

American Express has had a presence in Moscow for a long time. Its traveler's checks and credit cards are still more widely accepted than others. You may cash American Express checks at their offices. Hotel bills may be paid with Mastercard and Visa.

Amex Moscow ....(95) 254-4305
Amex St. Petersburg ....(812) 315-7487

Western Union also has agents in Moscow and St. Petersburg for money transfers.

Travel

VISA AND PASSPORT

Foreigners traveling to Russia need a valid passport (valid for 3 months beyond the intended departure date) and a Russian visa, which must be obtained prior to arriving in Russia. Visitors also need to register through their hotel or sponsor if the visit will exceed three days. Visitors staying with a friend must to a local visa registration office to register. Exit dates stamped on the visa must be strictly observed. Business visas require an official invitation from a Russian host organization. Do not attempt to do business when using a tourist visa

DEPARTURE FORMALITIES

All foreigners need an exit visa to depart Russia. For short stays, the exit visa is issued with the entry visa; for longer stays it must be obtained by the sponsor after the traveler's arrival. The customs declaration form that was received upon entering the country must be retained to show when you exit the country. Russia's changing customs laws are inconsistently enforced. Any item worth more than 300,000 Rubles is subject to a 600 percent duty. Items of historical or cultural value may be exported only with written approval of the Ministry of Culture and payment of 100 percent duty. Caviar must be accompanied by a receipt from a store licensed to sell to foreigners. Electrical appliances, carpets, precious metals and furs are also prohibited for export. Rubles cannot be exported from Russia.

CUSTOMS ENTRY (PERSONAL)

Duty-free

Duty-free regulations within the Commonwealth of Independent States are liable to change at short notice. Travelers are advised to contact the Embassy or Consulate for up-to-date information. Goods that may be imported into the Russia Federation by persons over 16 years of age without incurring customs duty:

- Tobacco: 1000 cigars or cigarillos, or 1000g of tobacco.
- Alcohol: 1.5 liters of spirits, two liters of still wine.
- Other: a reasonable quantity of perfume for personal use, gifts up to a value of US$1000.

Note: On entering the country, tourists must complete a customs declaration form that must be retained until departure. Customs allows the import of articles intended for personal use, including currency and valuables. Cameras, jewelry, computers, and musical instruments should all be declared. Be sure to have the form stamped upon arrival to avoid difficulties in taking currency and valuables back out. Customs inspection can be long and detailed. It is advisable when shopping to ask for a certificate from the shop that states that goods have been paid for in hard currency. Presentation of such certificates should speed up customs formalities.

Prohibited or Restricted

- Military weapons and ammunition
- Narcotics
- Photographs and printed matter directed against the CIS/Russia
- Loose pearls
- Fruits and vegetables
- Live animals

TIPPING

Taxi

If a meter is used, simply round up the fare to tip. Taxi drivers typically get tipped 10 to 15 percent.

Porters

Porters typically get tipped 50 kopeks per bag.

Hotels

There is no tipping for hotel employees except porters who one can satisfy with US$1 per bag. Hotels will often add a 5 to 15 percent service charge as well as a 20 percent VAT tax.

Restaurants

In the past, wait staff and other restaurant employees typically did not get tipped; however nowadays, staff increasingly expects a tip of 10 to 15 percent, dependent on service. Service is spotty and minimal.

Other

Barbers and beauticians typically get tipped 5 to 10 percent.

EMERGENCY INFORMATION

Police and Crime

Violent and petty crime, as well as gang warfare, are on the increase here, especially in urban areas. A series of skinhead attacks occurred in 1998 against persons of African and Asian origin prompting a warning for travelers. Russia is also renowned for its growing and powerful mafia. Political tension and terrorist activity continues in and around Chechnya and the adjacent republics of Dagestan and Ingushetia. Travelers are urged to avoid those areas.

Although Moscow still ranks lower in crime than most

U.S. cities, take basic precautions against petty crime. Theft remains the most prevalent form of crime in Moscow. Hotel rooms and train compartments count as frequent targets. If traveling on an overnight train, take precautions to jam your door to keep crime out. Watch your belongings when in crowded public places and subways. Private cabs also pose a certain risk for assault. Most tour companies offer "transfer service" to and from airports and rail stations. These can be expensive but secure if you are a first-time visitor.

Avoid flashy displays of wealth, as jewelry theft is high; dress and behave conservatively, although most likely you will still be "spotted" as foreign, often just by the way you walk and behave. Carry cash in a money belt, and use credit cards or traveler's checks when possible. Limit the amount of information that you provide if using local services of banking, security, and medical treatment. Reports have surfaced regarding financial and credit information slipping into mafia hands and used for extortion purposes.

Women must never travel alone at night, and they should use only authorized taxis. Carry a can of mace or other such spray in case of any problems. The police force has lessened in size and diminished in efficiency in recent years, and policemen speak poor English. Never carry a stranger's baggage; however be sure to carry identification at all times.

Emergency Numbers

Ambulance .... 03 (no coins needed)
Fire .... 01 (no coins needed)
Police.. 02 (no coins needed)
Pharmacy Information 927-0561
(information on available medications at 40 Moscow pharmacies)

Health

Avoid drinking tap water; bottled water is widely available. Wash all vegetables, peel fruits, and avoid uncooked food. Drink only pasteurized milk. Bring along necessary toiletries, as they may be hard to come by in Russia.

Air pollution (especially high in Moscow and St. Petersburg) may cause respiratory problems and affect people with allergies. Flu and colds are common due to cold winter months.

Medical care standards fall well below Western standards. Bring along prescription drugs and other necessities, as medicines are scarce. Medical care is free and widely available throughout Russia, however, if entering quality facilities in major cities, expect to make cash payments. One is advised to carry insurance as well as extra evacuation insurance in case of medical emergency since Russian fees to evacuate from some regions could run as high as US$50,000!

For more information on medical centers, including phone numbers, please see the "Business Centers" section at the end of this chapter.

IMMUNIZATION

Make sure all your immunization shots are up to date.

TAXI

Three types of taxis exist: official, private taxis, and private cars. Official taxis are recognizable by a "T" and checkered emblems on the doors. As do the private taxis, official cabs will also have a small green light in the windshield. Private taxis offer the most comfort and reliability. For a Russian, a cab hailed for the hour might cost from US$8 to $10; however, it will take some negotiating in Russian to procure a similar price. Walking away from a cab after saying the price is too high may give you some leverage in negotiating. Another cab will soon come along if the first one doesn't work out. Before entering a cab, agree on the destination, price, and approximate travel time.

In Moscow and St. Petersburg, the best way to hail a taxi is to stand on the side of the street with your hand out. Do not be surprised if a cash-hungry private driver stops for you and bargains for a ride. However, due to crime, avoid unmarked cabs or even taxis that already have a rider inside. Note that in some smaller cities and parts of larger ones, private citizen drivers may be the only service available.

To order a cab, one is officially required to give two hours notice; however, they will often arrive within a few minutes. If a driver appears to be taking a roundabout way, it may often be due to one-way streets, roadblocks, and construction.

Moscow
Moskovskoe taksi 238-1001
Private Cabs/Limousines
Krasnaya gorka 381-2746, 454-6291
Taxi Service.. 203-0247, 248-2665
Hertz-Interavto.. 277-4032

St. Petersburg,
TOR... 265-1333.
Taksi na zakaz 294-1552;
Taksi Park N1 .... 312-3297, 314-5168.

Private Cabs/Limousines
Svit 356-9329

Directions
Most taxi drivers are familiar with their city, but can only speak Russian. If possible, have someone you trust write directions that you can give to the driver.

TRAIN

Russia is known for its train system, among the most comfortable in Europe. The major hassle is buying tickets. Foreigners must buy them in the station from special "foreigner windows," although the clerks generally only speak Russian. As such, it is suggested that one purchase tickets from a hotel tourist desk or through Intourist. Overseas offices of Intourist will also make advance reservations for pick-up at your departure point.

In St. Petersburg, one may purchase tickets for all routes at Central Railway Booking, nab. Kanala Briboedova 24, tel: 162-3344. International trains leave from Varshavskiy Station, metro stop Baltiyskaya. Trains to Moscow leave from Moskovskiy Station, metro stop Ploshchad Vosstaniya.

Moscow–St. Petersburg
The Red Arrow trains travel between Moscow and St. Petersburg. The overnight train with sleeping compartments offers a pleasant way to rest and experience something of Russia while in transit. An attendant will wake you just before arriving at your destination—unless you have accidentally left the radio on, in which case you will be awakened at 6a.m. with a blaring national anthem. If one has purchased the train ticket with rubles, the attendant will collect a surcharge for the use of sheets and towels. Note that train compartments are not segregated. One should also be advised that overnight trains experience occasional incidents of crime and theft. Try not to travel alone and keep doors and belongings secured.

Dining cars keep irregular hours and shut down without notice. However, each passenger car comes equipped with a coal-fired samovar for making hot water for tea and coffee. Bring instant soups and bread if your trip is a lengthy one. Trans-Siberian routes have stop-overs at various stations to allow passengers to disembark for supplies.

SUBWAY

The Moscow subway is very efficient and offered state-of-the-art service even before the iron curtain came down.

Russia

Expect crowds and station signs written in Cryllic script. Thus, it is advisable to study your destination in Cryllic before getting underway.

The efficient St. Petersburg 4-line subway operates between 5:30a.m. and 12:30a.m. Purchase the 1500-ruble tokens at any of the 55 subway stations. Tokens are valid for one trip including any changes.

BUS/TRAM

Buses are quickly replacing trains as the major system of transportation in Russia. Many come equipped with toilets and refrigerators.

Daily express buses also travel between Helsinki, Finland and Russia. Contact Sovavto Express Bus, tel: 298-1352, or at Hotel Astoria, Pulkovskaya, and Grand Europe in St. Petersburg.

Trams can be quite cheap but decrepit, especially in St. Petersburg. Drivers are unreliable and have been known to abandon their trams at meal times. Use them only if there is no alternative.

TRAVEL ASSISTANCE

Intourist; 13/1 Milyutinsky Per., 101000 Moscow; tel: (095) 923-92-8575; fax: (095) 234-3778; http://www.intourist.ru/Eng/s_bureau.htm; email: info@intourist.ru.

Essential Terms

English	Russian
Yes	Da
No	Nyet
Good morning	Dobroye utro
Hello (daytime)	Dobriy dyen'
Hello (evening)	Dobriy vyechyer
Hello (telephone)	Zdrahstvooyt eh
Good-bye	Dosvidaniya
Please	Pozhalusta
Thank you	Spasibo
Pleased to meet you	Ocheen preeahtnah
Excuse me; I'm sorry	Izvinitye
My name is _____	Menyâ zavoôt_____
I don't understand	ya nye ponimayu
Do you speak English?	Vi gahvahreeteh pah ahngleeyskee

Communications

DIALING CODES IN RUSSIA

International country code: [7]

Selected city codes: Moscow (095), St. Petersburg (812), Minsk (0172)

Dialing Russia from Overseas

To dial Russia from overseas, dial your country's international dialing code, then 7 (the country code for Russia), then the city code, and finally the number. If you were dialing Moscow, for example, you would begin with 011, then 7, then 095 (the city code for Moscow), and finally the number of the person or office you were trying to reach.

Assistance Numbers

Inter-city directory... 07
Operator 09
Time 08
City Payphone Directory................................... 059
St. Petersburg Address Directory.................... 061
International Calls.. 8-194
Interntational Communications.............. 247-1787

CALLING WITHIN RUSSIA

Local Calls

Dial "8" before the town number needed, except in Moscow where the number should be "2." Some hotel phones do not have dials. Pick them up, ask the operator for *go-rod* (Russian for outside), and wait for a dial tone.

Long Distance Calls

Long distance or international calls can be made from your hotel, or you can go to a long-distance telephone office (you will be asked to pay in advance there). Calls may be limited, and the poor telephone system can be a hindrance.

International Calls

You can find international telephones at state-run telephone offices where cards can be purchased for the procedure. From Moscow and St. Petersburg, dial 8 (wait for dial tone) + 10 + country code + area code + number. Or, pay in advance at a designated kiosk in the office and either dial yourself or get connected by the operator. In this case, you must wait for your call and booth to be announced.

Some hotels have satellite telephone booths to place calls, others require you to book the call through hotel reception if no direct dial is available from your room. As always, expect sky-high surcharges to grace your bill, anywhere from US$5 to US$25 per minute!

British Telecom.....................................8-10-800-497-7266
Canada Direct 8-10-800-497-7233
U.S. AT&T (Moscow)... 755-5042
U.S. AT&T (St. Petersburg)................................ 325-5042
U.S. AT&T (Vladivostok) 425-008
U.S. AT&T (all other areas) 8-095-755-5042
U.S. Sprint...(95) 155-6133
U.S. MCI...8-10-800-497-7222

*For those numbers beginning with '8', you must wait for a dial tone after the initial "8."

PAY PHONES

Public Telephones

A three-minute limit exists for phone usage if a line of people is waiting to use the telephone; but no extra charge is imposed for exceeding the three-minute limit. Pay phones require tokens, which may be purchased at kiosks, newsstands, and in selected stores.

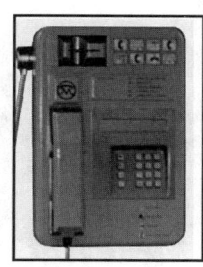

Calling Cards

AT&T offers direct service to Russia, although it can be expensive: US$3 per minute plus a US$2.50 service charge. You can also use a Russian or Baltic card to call home just long enough to say "call me."

CELLULAR PHONES

A plethora of cellular service providers exist in Russia. Between them, most types of systems are offered including: NMT-450, AMPS, and D-AMPS for analogue users, and GSM, TDMA, CDMA for digital. Delta Telecom in St. Petersburg (tel: 314-6126) and Russian Telecom offer GSM systems. St. Petersburg Telecom (tel: 315-4105) offers a NAMPS system. Europeans can usually use their own phones in Russia but should prepare for high fees.

Note: Your home country cell phone may not work in this country. If not, we recommend that you rent an international cell phone *before* you leave home. A major US-based cell phone rental provider is **IMC WorldCell**. For information see "International Cell Phone Rentals" on page 14.

Other Cellular Service Providers/Rental

BeeLine; Lesnoryadskiy per., 18; tel/fax: 747-9971; 9a.m. to 9p.m. daily; English spoken; service provider; general info: 755-0055; http://www.beeline.ru.

MTK; Mal. Dmitrovka ul, 5; tel: 974-2555; fax: 974-2550; Nokia official distributor; sale and service of BeeLine cell phone.

TeleFun; Vernadskogo prosp., 59; tel/fax: 431-6910, 432-0803; Kadashevskaya nab., 22, tel/fax: 929-9267; Monday to Sat. 10a.m. to 6p.m.; sale and rental of cellular phone.

Shercomservice; Sheremetevo-2 Airport; tel: 956-4680; cellular phone rental; English spoken; 24-hours; Metro: Rechnoy Vokzal.

CALL BACK

Phone rates from Russia are much higher than those of many other countries. You can (potentially) save significant sums by using one of the call back services listed below. Fees for call back services vary widely, depending on the company and the type of service required. Be sure to check with these companies before leaving to compare rates.

For a list of callback services, please refer to the "Communications" section in the *Global Road Warrior* Introduction.

PHONE JACK

Plug adaptors are available through **iGo Corporation.** (See "Electrical and Telephone Adaptors" on page 19.)

FAX

Fax machines are very popular in Russia, something of a status symbol. They can be found at most hotels.

POSTAL SERVICES

Public mailboxes are difficult to find on the streets of Russia. Most hotels have mail drop off services, which are generally adequate.

St. Petersburg

The main post office is located at Pochtamtckaya ul., 9; tel: 312-8302.

Business Services

BUSINESS CENTER

Note: Many top-end or expensive category hotels have business centers. See hotel listings in Business Centers section at the end of the chapter.

Moscow

Biznes-tsentr v gostinitse "Metropol"; Teatralnyy pr-d, 1, in the Metropol Hotel; tel: 927-6941; fax; 927-6930; M - F 8a.m. to 10p.m. weekends 8a.m. to 8p.m.; English, German, French; courier services available.

Artel Biznes i Telekommunikatsii; Novyy Arbat ul., 2nd floor; tel: 955-2323, 291-3374; email: telecom@artel.ru; 9a.m. to 8p.m. daily; English spoken; offices, cellular phone rental, fax, photocopying, telephone, lamination, book binding.

Biznes tsentr na Krasnoy Ploshchadi; Red Square, 2nd Floor; tel: 921-0911; fax: 921-4609; email: bcint@dol.ru; M - Sat. 8a.m. to 8 p.m., Sun. 8a.m. to 6p.m.; telephones, cell phone, pagers, computers, photocopying, translations, express mail.

Moskovskiy biznes tsentr; MIra prosp., 72; tel/fax: 258-5320; M - F 9a.m. to 6p.m.; English spoken; office rental, business services, sports, restaurants, supermarket.

Radisson Slavyanskaya Hotel; Berezhkovskaya Nabereznaya 2; tel: (095) 941-8427; fax: (095) 240-6915.

St. Petersburg

American Business Center; Nevskiy prosp., 25; tel: 326-2560, 326-2570; M - F 9a.m. to 6p.m.; office space, translators, library, equipment, conference hall.

Business-Center; Nevskiy pr., 85 (moskovskiy Station); tel: 277-2514.

Congress Business Center; Galerny proezd, 3; tel: 352-0869.

St. Petersburg Trade and Commercial Chamber; Chaykovskogo u., 46-48; tel: 279-0383.

World Trade Center; Tambovskaya ul., 12; tel: 112-9272.

COURIER SERVICES

Moscow

DHL; Main office: Samotechnyy 3-iy per., 11/2; tel: 956-1001; fax: 974-2106; email: track@DHL.com; internet: www.DHL.com; M -F 9a.m. to 8p.m.

FedEx; 1st Floor, World Trade Center, 12 Kransnopresnenskaya Nab., 3rd Entrance, Moscow, tel: (95) 234-2585 or (95) 234-9943; fax: 234-9945Daily 8a.m. to 8p.m.

Inservis Kurer; Bol., Afanasevskiy per., 17, tel: 203-0281, 203-0119; M - F 9a.m. to 6p.m.; English, German, French;

Moscow courier service; mail delivery in Russia, CIS, and overseas; customs service.

Sitiekxpress; Petrovka ul., 27; tel: 200-6569; tel/fax: 200-6749; M - F 8a.m. to 8p.m.; English spoken; Moscow and St. Petersburg courier services.

TNT Express Worldwide; Baltiyskiy 3-iy per., 3; tel: 931-9640; tel: 937-3222; fax: 931-9644; M - F 9a.m. to 6p.m., Sat. 10a.m. to 2p.m.; English spoken; courier, express, international express; Denezhnyy per., 1; tel: 201-2585; M - F 9a.m. to 7p.m., Saturday 10a.m. to 2p.m.

UPS; Head Office: Bol. Tishinskiy per., 8, bl. 2; tel: 961-2211, 254-4015; M - F 9a.m. to 7p.m.; English, German, French; http://www.ups.com; courier, air cargo, customs clearing; Intl. Trade Center, Krasnopresnenskaya nab., 12; M - Th. 9a.m. to 6p.m., Fri. 9a.m. to 5p.m.; English spoken;

St. Petersburg

DHL; Griboedova kan. nab., 5, kom. 325, tel: 311-2649; Nevskiy prosp., 57, tel: 325-6100, M -F 9a.m. to 6p.m.; Izmaylovskiy pr. 4, in the Hotel Hevskij Palace; tel: 326-6400.

FedEx; u. Mayakovskaya 2; tel: (812) 273-2139; M - F 9a.m. to 5:30p.m., Sat. 9a.m. to 2p.m.

Garantpost JV Courier Service; Liteyney prospekt 50; tel: (812) 312-2693.

TNT; Nab. Reki Moiki, 58, liter A, 190000 St. Petersburg; tel: (812) 118-3330 ; fax: 118-3495; Shturmanskaya Str. 12., St. Petersburg; tel: (812) 327-8705; fax: (812) 327-8704.

Pony Express; Razezzhaya ul., 5; tel: 113-3465; M - F 9a.m. to 6p.m.

UPS; 51 Shpalernaya Str., 193015 St-Petersburg; tel: (812) 327-8540; fax: (812) 327-8197.

SECRETARIAL SERVICE

Note: Some top-end or expensive category hotels offer translation or interpreting services. See hotel listings in Business Centers section at the end of the chapter.

Moscow

Biznes-tsentr v gostinitse "Metropol"; Teatralnyy pr-d, 1; tel: 927-6941; fax: 927-6930; M - F 8a.m. to 10p.m.; English, German, French.

Prestizh; Babegorodskiy 1-yy per., 5; tel: 238-9943; M - F 9a.m. to 7p.m.; English.

TRANSLATION/INTERPRETING

Note: Some top-end or expensive category hotels offer translation or interpreting services.

Moscow

Aspira; Karpanov a per., 3, Moscow; tel/fax: (95) 205-7084; http://www.4unet.ru/~aspira/. email: aspira@4unet.ru; M - F 10a.m. to 7p.m.

Atlas Language Services; Prosp. Vernadskogo 29, office 805; tel: (95) 131-4522; fax: 138-2350; email: atlas@atl.ru; M - F 9a.m. to 7p.m.; over 50 languages.

Dialekt; Novozavodskaya ul., 27; tel: 145-8956, 145-9845; M- F 10a.m. to 4p.m.; oral and written translations in all languages.

Poliglot; Chayanova ul., 18, 2nd floor; tel: 251-9647, 250-1501; M - Sat. 10a.m. to 10p.m.; editing and written translating.

Sluzhba federalnykh novostey; (Federal News Service); Obolenskiy per., 10, 2nd floor; tel: 245-5800; email: fednews@fednews.ru; information and transcription services for press conferences.

St. Petersburg

ASMATEP+FT; tel: (812) 594-2659; fax: (812) 594-2659; http://www.navigator.spb.ru/ft/; email: ft@ft.spb.su.

Assotsiatsiya gidov-perevodhikov i tur-menedzherov; Serpukhovskaya ul., 30; tel: (812) 112-7699; Association of Guides and Interpreters.

Central Translations Bureau (Znanije), Ltd.; 3 par. Antonenko, St. Petersburg; 35 languages; tel: (812) 315-7477; fax: (812) 319-9103; email: gurumast@telecom.lek.ru.

Electrical

Current

Mostly 220V and usually alternating current. One is advised to carry a small pocket flashlight as many stairwells and entranceways may be dark.

ELECTRIC PLUGS

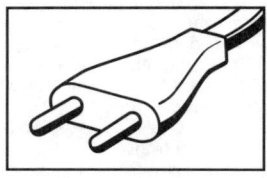

Plug adaptors are available through **iGo Corporation**. (See "Electrical and Telephone Adaptors" on page 19.)

Technical Support

HARDWARE/SOFTWARE VENDOR SUPPORT

Compaq/Digital; tel: (95) 967-3138; fax: (95) 967-1701; (in Poland) [48] (22) 640-0111; fax: [48] (22) 640-0001; (in Switzerland) tel: [41] (22) 709-5330; fax: [41] (22) 709-5391 (Geneva); [41] (1) 801-2507; fax: [41] (1) 801-2172 (Zurich); (General U.S.) tel: (281) 518-2000; http://www.compaq.com/.

Hewlett Packard; (in Switzerland) tel: [41] (22) 780-8111; (in the U.S.) tel: [1] (408) 246-4300; http://www.hp.com/.

IBM; tel: (95) 940-2000; fax: [95] 940-2070; (in Germany) tel: [49] (711) 78-50; fax: [49] (711) 785-3511; (in Switzerland) tel: [41] (22) 310-0418 (French); (in the U.S.) tel: [1] (919) 517-2800; (Main Office) tel: [1] 914-765-1900; http://www.ibm.com/.

Microsoft; tel: [7] (095) 916-7171; fax: [7] (095) 916-7112; (in Germany) tel: [49] (89) 31-760; fax: [49] (89) 3176-1000; tel: [49] (89) 3176-1199; (in Switzerland) tel: [41] (848) 858-868; fax [41] (1) 831-0869; (in the U.S.) [1] (425) 635-7222; http://www.microsoft.com/.

Toshiba; (in Germany) tel: [49] (2131) 158-319; fax: [49] (2131) 158-558; (in Switzerland) tel: [41] (1) 946-0777; fax:

[41] (1) 946-0807; (in Ireland) tel: [44] (193) 282-8828; (in the U.S.) [1] (949) 583-3000 (Corporate Headquarters); http://www.toshiba.com/.

Internet Connection

HOW TO CONNECT

Connecting to AOL and Compuserve in Russia is similar to using it when traveling outside your own area code. See the introductory section for detailed information on connecting to your account through a different phone number.

America Online

At this time, AOL has no local access numbers in Russia.

At press time, America Online had no local access numbers in Russia. Check their list of current access numbers at http://intlaccess.web.aol.com/ to see if any numbers have been activated or to locate numbers in neighboring countries.

Compuserve

Numbers are available at *Go International.* If you are using CompuServe 2000, use GO PHONES within CompuServe 2000 to search for access numbers. The Compuserve Website also has a great deal of information for travelers at http://www.compuserve.com/.

At press time, Compuserve had no local access numbers. Check their list of current access numbers to see if any numbers have been activated or to locate numbers in neighboring countries.

Independent Service Providers

Many independent service providers offer discounts if you are only in town for a couple of days.

Cityline Ltd., tel: (95) 232-0289; fax: (95) 248-7848; info@cityline.ru; http://www.cityline.ru/.

Corbina Telecom; tel: (95) 728-4000; http://www.corbina.net; (English and Russian).

Cronyx Plus Ltd. / RiNet; tel. (95) 238-3922, 232-1738; fax: (95) 238-3922; admin@rinet.ru; http://www.rinet.ru/ ; (English and Russian).

GlasNet; tel: (95) 785-1100; fax: (95) 785-1096; support@glasnet.ru; http://www.glasnet.ru/; (English and Russian).

Metrocom; tel: (812) 118-3122; fax: (812) 118-3123; sales@metrocom.ru; http://www.metrocom.ru/; (English and Russian).

Nevalink; tel: (812) 113-4712; tel: 310-5628; tel: 310-9951; fax: (812) 110-5764; info@nevalink.ru; http://www.nevalink.ru/; (English and Russian).

PeterLink; tel: (812) 113-5722; tel: 310-0327; tel: 310-0337; fax: (812) 310-0105; info@peterlink.ru; http://www.peterlink.ru/; (English and Russian).

PTT-Teleport Moscow; (95) 946-9383; webmaster@ptt.ru; http://www.ptt.ru/.

Golden Telecom; tel: (95) 787-1000; fax: (95) 787-1010; email: info@goldentelecom.ru ; http://www.goldentelecom.ru/; (English and Russian).

Business Culture

GREETINGS AND COURTESIES

Russians like to shake hands and give their name when meeting with visitors for the first time. While conversing with Russians, it is proper to maintain direct eye contact. Looking away is considered rude. Russians give a high priority to addressing others using correct titles. Failure to use a title is impolite and Russians find it offensive. To deter-

mine associates' correct titles, refer to their business cards. Business cards should be printed in both your language and in Russian. Offering your card with both hands serves as an introduction in Russia; present cards to everyone in a meeting. Appropriate gifts for Russians include fine books, chocolates, desk accessories, tokens from your country, or an item with your company logo. Other gifts that are appreciated are items that are currently unavailable in Russia. Heavy drinking is ingrained in the Russian style of doing business; sweets and cookies are also often offered at business meetings.

BUSINESS ETHIC AND FRAMEWORK

Russians have a work ethic that drives them to persevere with an agenda until completion once discussions have begun. Even though privately owned businesses are increasing, most businesses in Russia are still government owned. That means miles of red tape and endless waiting along with a fair amount of corruption. It takes an abundance of patience, as well as flexibility, to do business in Russia. The increase in development of private enterprise demonstrates that Russian business people are hardworking, disciplined, and quick learners. The stimulus of a free market is erasing the former work ethic of struggling to meet deadlines after months of inactivity. Russians prefer to have a brief social conversation before beginning any meeting.

MEETINGS

Russian hospitality is recognized worldwide. This hospitality extends to business meetings. Russian hosts often take foreign guests out on the town. Dinner, floor shows, and lots of drinking are all part of Russian business entertainment. But setting up a meeting in Russia can be a daunting task. Because of a scarcity of secretaries, it is impossible to leave messages and difficult to arrange meetings in Russia. It is advisable to confirm a meeting several times before the appointment; having written confirmation is also a good idea. Appointments in Russia often go awry. It is common for meetings to get postponed or canceled without notice. Incredibly, the wrong people will sometimes arrive for your meetings. It may be necessary to employ an interpreter for a meeting in Russia in order to avoid mistakes. An interpreter should never be seated at the head of a table—or between you and your Russian associate. Talk to your associate, not to the interpreter.

DECISION MAKING

Be prepared for a long wait before your Russian associates come to a decision. Decisions in Russia still prove highly centralized and are most commonly made by slow-moving committees; the committee must deliberate carefully on each issue and consensus will be vigorously sought. Russians insist on building a personal relationship with foreign visitors before any agreements are reached. A distrust of their own business laws and courts prompts Russians to weigh strong personal relationships heavier than contracts. Russians dislike what they consider a Western attitude about business: expecting success and a check after only a few hours of work. Keep in mind that many Russians may prefer to keep business deals and wealth secret.

WOMEN

Communism, if nothing else, helped to break down many of the barriers between Russian men and women. However, Russian society has traditionally been divided in terms of sex and class and this tradition dies hard. Many Russian men will not accept women in positions of power, although younger Russian men seem more willing. Women now hold nearly all positions in Russian business, such as architects, managers, and high-level bureaucrats. Many older women in Russia hold jobs traditionally held by men—a necessity because so many Russian men died in World War II. Women may retire at age 55 in Russia, while men must wait until they are 60 years old. Foreign businesswomen should not experience difficulty in Russia so long as they approach each encounter in a no-nonsense manner.

BUSINESS ATTIRE

Conservative business suits are appropriate for all occasions, including formal evening functions. Russians judge others quickly by what they wear, and the first thing they notice is the type of shoe being worn. Shoes are a status symbol in Russia; good ones should be worn in business situations. Avoid excessive jewelry or flashy clothing. Russians will often notice a high-quality watch; if you have one, wear it. Between October and April, one is advised to carry a warm woolen coat, gloves, and hats to combat the freezing weather.

Business Centers
Moscow

CITY VIEW

Moscow is a huge city with a population of 9 million. With a long history of czars, political movement, and an aura of steely mystique, Moscow has moved further away from its previous colorless days with an explosion of business and activity.

AIRPORT

Sheremetyevo-2 Airport to City Center

The airport lies 16 miles (26k.m.) northwest of the city. Travelers are urged to have transportation arranged in advance; otherwise, prepare for hordes of people calling for your taxi business. Most likely these drivers will more than "take you for a ride". If you wish to go by taxi, head for the taxi line where you will still have to negotiate. The 40- to 50-minute taxi ride to the city center will cost around US$25 to $35. Be aware that many driers will try and charge much more. Negotiate travel time, price, and destination before departing.

Most top-end hotels offer shuttle buses for their guests at a cost of US$40 to $75. One may also book a car and driver through one's host company or hotel. Expect to pay about US$75 for the convenience and safety of your own car and driver. The Intourist office in the arrivals area can also assist the traveler by arranging for a car and driver or a rental car if one prefers not to deal with the taxi touts.

Airline Numbers

Aeroflot	(95) 156-8019
Transaero	(95) 578-0537
Air France	(95) 237-2325
Alitalia	(95) 923-9840
Austrian Air	(95) 253-8268
British Airways	(95) 253-2492
Delta	(95) 253-2658
Finnair	(95) 292-8788
Japan Airlines	(95) 921-6441
KLM	(95) 253-2150, 578-2963 (res.)
Lufthansa	(95) 975-2501
SAS	(95) 925-4747
Turkish	(95) 292-1667

HOTELS

Top-end

Baltschug Kempinski; 1 Baltschung Ulista; tel: (95) 230-6500; 007-501-230-9500 outside Russia; fax: (95) 230-6502; 007-501-230-9502 outside Russia; city center; rooms with Kremlin view; restaurant; conference facilities (up to 300); business center; secretarial service; fax/photocopy facilities; corporate rates; in-room safe; parking; fitness; sauna; pool; whirlpool.

Marriott Grand Hotel; 26 Tverskaya St.; tel: (95) 935-8500; fax: (95) 935-8501; 4 restaurants; executive floor; 7 meeting rooms; full service business center; secretarial services; in-room dual phone lines, voice mail, data ports, safe; health club; spa; solarium; sauna; pool; whirlpool.

Metropol;1/4 Teatralny Proezd; tel: (95) 927-6000 or 7501-927-1000; outside Russia; fax: (95) 975-2355; 7501-927-1010 outside Russia; city center, opposite Kremlin; restaurant; conference facilities (up to 600); business center; secretarial service; in-room modem/fax connection; parking; health club; pool.

Sheraton Palace; Tverskaya Ul. 19; tel: (95) 931-9700 or [7] (502) 256-3000; fax: (95) 931-9704; fax: [7] (502) 256-30081 from overseas; near city center; 3 restaurants; conference facilities (up to 80); business center; secretarial service; in-room modem/fax connection; fitness; massage; sauna; whirlpool.

Sofitel Iris Moskva; Korovinskoye Chaussee 10; tel: (95) 488-8000; fax: (95) 488-8888; 502/220-8844 from outside Russia; located near airport; restaurant; parking; conference facilities; business center; fitness; pool.

Radisson Slavyanskaya; Berezhkovskaya Nabereznaya 2; tel: (95) 941-8020; fax: (95) 941-8000; 7-502-224-1225 outside Russia; located in suburb; restaurant; conference facilities; secretarial service; fax/photocopy facilities; in-room modem/fax connection; health club; sauna; pool.

Expensive

Aerostar; 37 Leningradsky Prospekt, Korpus 9; tel: (95) 213-9000 or (95) 213-9001; fax:; 7 502 213-9001 from overseas; http://www.aerostar.ru; near city center; conference facilities (up to 300); business center; secretarial service; internet available; in-room modem/fax connection; secure parking; corporate rates; fitness; sauna.

Hotel Tverskaya; Tverskaya Street; tel: (501) 258-3099; in the U.S., 1-800-777-1700; boutique hotel with extended-stay suites; 2 restaurants; business center; fitness; rooms with coffeemaker and microwaves.

Mezhdunarodnaya; 12, Krasnopresnenskaya Emb.; tel: (95) 253-1391 or (95) 253; 1392; fax: (95) 253-2051; 5-star hotel near exhibition grounds; restaurant; casino; conference facilities (up to 2,000); business center; secretarial service; fax/photocopy facilities; corporate rates; parking; fitness; sauna; pool.

Novotel; Airport Sheremetyevo 2; tel: (95) 578-9401 or (95) 578-9110; fax: (95) 578-2797; 7 502 220-6604 from outside Russia; located near airport; restaurant; conference facilities (up to 400); secretarial service; fax/photocopy facilities; in-room modem/fax connection; corporate rates; fitness; sauna; pool; whirlpool.

Marco Polo Presnya; Spiridonjevskij Per.; tel: (95) 244-3631; fax: (95) 956-6306; 7 503 (95) 956-6306 from overseas; near city center; restaurant; conference facilities (up to 120); business center; secretarial service; internet available; corporate rates; parking; fitness; sauna; whirlpool.

Savoy; Ul. Rozhdestvenka 3; tel: (95) 929-8500; fax: (95) 230-2186; near city center; restaurant; casino; meeting facilities; business center; secretarial service; fax/

photocopy facilities; in-room modem/fax connection; corporate rates; in-room safe; parking; fitness.

Ukraina; 2/1 Kutuzovsky Prospekt; tel: (95) 243-2596 or (95) 243-3030 for reservations; fax: (95) 243-3092; near city center; casino; restaurant; meeting facilities (up to 100); business center; secretarial service; fax/photocopy facilities; in-room modem/fax connection, safe; corporate rates; parking; fitness.

Moderate

Kosmos; 150 Mira Proezd; tel: (95) 217-1066 or (95) 234-1384; fax: (95) 215-8880; opposite VVTS conference center; restaurant; conference facilities (up to 1000); business center; in-room modem/fax connection; fitness; sauna; pool.

Moscva; 2 Okhotny Ryad; tel: 292-2040, 960-2020; fax: 928-5938; historical building; restaurant; conference room (up to 150); secretarial service; fax/photocopying facilities; parking; sauna.

Rossiya; 6 Varvarka Ul; tel: (95) 232-5000; fax: (95) 232-6262; top floors with view of Kremlin; restaurant; conference facilities (up to 150); business center; secretarial service; corporate rates; parking; sauna; pool.

Soyvz; Levoberezhnaya Ul. 12; tel: (95) 457-2088; fax: (95) 457-2096; located in suburb; restaurant; conference room (up to 80); parking; corporate rates.

Vega Izmailovo; 71 Izmailovskoe Shosse; tel: (95) 956-0511; fax: (95) 956-0647; located in suburb; restaurant; casino; conference facilities (up to 500); business center; secretarial service; internet available; laptops available; in-room modem/fax connection; corporate rates; secure parking; fitness; sauna.

MEDICAL CARE

American Medical Center; 3 Shmitovsky Proyezd; tel: 256-8212, 256-8378.

Botkin Hospital; 5 2nd Botkinski Proyezed; tel: 255-0015.

Diplomatic Polyclinic; 3 Sverchkov Per.; tel: 221-5992.

Foreign Vistor Clinic; 12 Ul. Herzen; tel: 229-7323 and 229-0382 (includes dental service).

International Healthcare; 3 Gruzinsky Per., Polyclinic #6; tel: 253-0703.

Sana Medical Center; 65 Ul. Nizhnaya Pervomaiskaya; tel: 464-1254 or 464-2563.

HEALTH CLUB

Note: Top-end and expensive hotels often have fitness centers for guests and club members. See hotel listings.

Atlantis; Krasnopresnenskaya nab., 12, 1st floor, in the Mezhdunarodnaya Hotel; tel: 967-0373; 11a.m. to 11p.m.; English spoken; workout room; massage; solarium; sauna; pool; whirlpools.

Gold's Gym; Leningradskiy prosp., 31; tel: 931-9616 or 9625; M - F 7a.m. to 11p.m., weekends 9a.m. to 10p.m.; English spoken.

Grand Hotel Marriott; Tverskaya u., 26; tel: 935-8500; 24 hours; workout room; solariums; massage; Finnish and Russian saunas; pool.

Moskvich; Volgogradskiy prosp., 46; tel: 178-1710; 9a.m. to 9p.m. daily; Metro stop: Tekstilshchiki; 50-meter pool; basketball; volleyball; indoor track and field; judo; water polo; shaping; tennis.

Planet Fitness; Korolenko ul., 8; tel: 964-2405; workout room, solarium, cardio-vascular training, aerobics, cycle, bar, beauty salon, massage, sauna, whirlpool, Turkish steam baths.

AUTO RENTAL

Avis; Sheremetyevo airport; tel: 578-5646; Goncharnaya ul., 24; tel/fax: 915-1389; email: avismosc@online.ru; http://www.avis.com.

Budget; Verkh. Radishchevskaya ul., 16; tel: 915-0870, 915-5237; http://www.budtgetrentacar.com; M - F 9a.m. to 6p.m.

Europcar; Moscow Airport, Intl. Airport Sherometevovo-2, Sovincenter; tel: 578-3878; Hotel Mezhdunarodnaya-1, Krasnopresnenskaya Nab 12; tel: 253-1369; chauffeur-driven cars available.

Hertz; head office: Chernyakhovskogo ul., 4, tel: 937-3274; 49/11 Prospekt Mira, tel: 284-43-91; Sheremetevo-2 airport, 1st floor, tel: 578-5646; chauffeur-driven cars available; http://www.hertz.com.

IBS (Intl. Business Services); Prechistenka ul., 27; tel: 201-5954, 201-5773; chauffeur-driven cars and minivans available.

Limousine Service; Bumazhnyy proezd, 19; tel: 257-4000, 257-4400; fax: 257-1596; limousines and luxury cars.

Mosrentservice; tel: 963-87-80; Sheremetyevo airport, tel: 578-0919; Krasnobogatyrskaya ul, 79, tel: 963-9215; chauffeur-driven cars available.

WORLD TRADE CENTER

World Trade Center Moscow
12, Krasnopresnenskaya nab.
123610, Moscow, Russia
tel: (095) 256-6303
fax: (095) 253-2749
Telex: 411486 SOVIN RU

CHAMBER OF COMMERCE

Russian Chamber of Commerce and Industry
ul., Ilyinka 6
Moscow 103684
tel: (095) 929-0286, 929-0260; fax: (095) 929-0356/60.
email: rbcnet@rbcnet.ru
Mon. to Fri. 9a.m. to 6p.m.
Metro: Ploshahad Revolyutsii, Kitay-Gorod

Moscow Chamber of Commerce and Industry
Akademika Pilyugina ul, 22
tel: 132-750, 132-1992
Mon. to Fri. 9a.m. to 6p.m.
Metro: Novye Cheremushki

St. Petersburg

CITY VIEW

Definitely more tourist-friendly than Moscow, St. Petersburg is not only Russia's cultural center but also a growing business center. It is compact and easy to navigate. A few times the capital of the former Russia, St. Petersburg has benefited from royal architecture and wide boulevards not to mention that the city spans over 40 islands prompting it also to be called the Venice of the North.

AIRPORT

Pulkovo II Airport to City Center

The airport lies approximately 17km south of the city. Buses between the airport and downtown St. Petersburg run every 40 minutes during the day and every 90 minutes during the nighttime. Purchase tickets on board. A minibus, also known as a Route Taxi, will take passengers to the Moskovskaya subway station between 7a.m. and 10p.m.

Expect a 10- to 15-minute ride. Regular taxis are also available, however, be sure to negotiate a rate before going anywhere; due to crime, take care not to enter a cab with another rider already inside. Expect a 30-minute ride into town by cab.

From a hotel to the airport, cabs will charge about US$30. However, if hailing a sate-operated taxi from the street, it will cost from US$7 to $10. For international flight enquiries, call: (812) 104-3444 or 104-3495; for domestic enquiries, dial: (812) 104-3822. Domestic flights depart from Pulkova I.

If arriving at Pulkova I, one is advised to be met by a driver since only City Bus N13 offers public transportation. Taxis are run by a mini mafia charging about US$25 to $30 for a few minutes of travel.

Airline Numbers

Aeroflot ....(812) 104-3444
Air France..(812) 325-8252
Austrian Airlines ....(812) 325-3260, 3249
Balkan ....(812) 315-5030, 5019
British Airways...(812) 325-6222
Czech Airlines ....(812) 315-5259
Delta...(812) 311-5819, 5820
El Al Israel Airlines ....(812) 275-1721
Finnair ....(812) 315-9736, 314-3645
KLM ....(812) 325-8989
LOT Polish Airlines....................................(812) 273-5721
Lufthansa...(812) 314-4979, 5917
Malev ....(812) 317-5455, 6886
SAS Scandinavian Air ....(812) 325-3255
Swissair..(812) 325-3250
Transaero ....(812) 279-1974

HOTELS

Top-end

Astoria; B. Morskaya ul., 39; tel: 315-9637, 210-5757; fax: 315-9668; near airport and city center; restaurant; conference facilities (up to 200); business center; secretarial service; translators; health club; sauna; pool.

Grand Hotel Europe (Kempinsky); Mikhailovskaya u., 1/7; tel: 217-8051; fax: 311-4611; www.Grandhotel-europe.com; city center; historical building; 7 restaurants; conference room; business center; secretarial service; interpreters/translators; in-room safe; parking; Planeta Fitness health club; sauna; pool.

Nevskij Palace Hotel; Nevskiy pr., 57; tel: 275-2001; fax: 301-7323; near city center; historical building; restaurant; conference facilities (up to 150); secretarial service; fax/photocopy facilities; in-room modem/fax connection, safe; corporate rates; Planeta Fitness health club; sauna; whirlpool.

Expensive

Belvedere Golf Hotel; Spb, Petrodvoretz, Babigonskiy Hill, place of Belvedere; tel: 326-1725; 326-1728; fax: 326-1750; historical building; restaurant; conference room; room service; in-room safe; parking; sauna.

Pribaltiyskaya; Korablestroiteley ul., 14; tel: 356-0263, 356-3001; fax: 356-0094, 356-4496; near city center; restaurant; conference facilities (up to 900); business center; secretarial service; in-room modem/fax connection, safe; parking; corporate rates; fitness; sauna.

Pulkovskaya; Pl. Pobedy, 1; tel: 264-5137; fax: 264-6396; restaurant; conference facilities (up to 500); business center, office rental; in-room modem/fax connection, safe; parking; sauna; pool.

St. Petersburg; Pirogovskaya nab., 5/2; tel: 542-8149,

542-8000; fax: 542-9042, 248-8002; near city center, exhibition grounds; restaurant; conference facilities (up to 800); business center; parking; corporate rates; sauna.

Moderate

Chaika; Serebristy bulvar, 38; tel: 301-7575; fax: 301-5622; historical building; restaurant; conference room; room service; in-room safe; parking; sauna.

Okhtinskaya Viktoria; Bolsheokhtinskiy pr., 4; tel: 227-4438, 222-8602; fax: 227-2618; near city center; restaurant; conference facilities (up to 90); business center; secretarial service; translators; corporate rates; parking; sauna.

Peterhof; Pier Makarov Embankment; tel: 325-8888; fax: 325-8889; floating hotel; near city center; restaurant; conference facilities; corporate rates; fitness; sauna.

Sovetskaya; Lermontovskiy pr. 43/1; tel: 329-0186; fax: 329-0188; restaurant; conference room (up to 200); business center; room service; in-room safe; parking; sauna.

MEDICAL CARE

American Medical Center; 77 Reki Fontanki nab.; tel: [7] (812) 325-61-01.

Pharmacy; Nevskiy pr., 111, tel: 277-2931; Nevskiy pr., 5, tel: 312-7078; Nevskiy pr., 22, tel: 219-6001; Nevskky pr., 50, tel: 312-4269.

Night Pharmacy; tel: 311-2077 (9a.m. to 8a.m.).

HEALTH CLUB

Grand Hotel Europe; Mikhailovskaya u., 1/7; tel: 217-8051; Planeta Fitness health club.

Hotel Astoria; B. Morskaya ul., 39; tel: 315-9637.

Planeta Fitness; Vyborgskoe shosse, 6; tel: 554-4147; M - F 8:30a.m. to 10p.m.; weekends, 10a.m. to 9p.m; sports center, aerobics, workout, solarium, massage, sauna.

Olimpiya; 6-ya Krasnoarmeyskaya ul., 14; tel: 110-1887; M - Sat. 9a.m. to 9p.m.; aerobics, treadmill, solarium, universal room, massage.

Tonus; Chekistov ul., 19; tel: 144-8793; M - F 9a.m. to 10p.m.; workout room, exercise room; sauna; solarium; pools.

AUTO RENTAL

Note: Dial 001 for mobile car breakdown or for collision assistance.

Avis; Konnogvardeyskiy bul., 4; tel: 312-6312.

Executive Car; V.O. 2ya liniya, 35; tel: 213-1121.

Hertz; Nekrasova ul. 40; tel: 272-5045; Hertz- Interauto, Aleksandra Nevskogo pl, 2, tel: 274-2060, foreign car rental with driver.

Interavto; Ispolkomovskaya ul., 9/11; tel: 277-4032.

Matralen; Lyubotinskiy proezd, 5; tel: 298-364.

WORLD TRADE CENTER

World Trade Center St. Petersburg
Tambowskaya Str. 12A
192007 St. Petersburg; Russia
tel: (812) 112-9272; fax: (812) 112-8631
website: www.wtca.org/wta/st_petersburg.html
email: wtcstp@infopro.spb.su

CHAMBER OF COMMERCE

St. Petersburg Chamber of Commerce and Industry
Chaykovskogo ul., 46
tel: 279-0590 or 272-9150

Note: translations, interpreters, courier delivery, faxing available.

Saudi Arabia

At a Glance

THE PEOPLE

Population ....21,504,613(July 1999 est.)
Growth Rate ....3.39% (1999 est.)
Life Expectancy .... 70.55 years
Infant Mortality ..... 38.8 deaths/1,000 live births (1999 est.)

Ethnic Composition

Arab...90%
Afro-Asian...10%

Religious Composition

Sunni Muslim..85%
Shiite Muslim 15%

Languages Spoken

Arabic.

Education and Literacy

Education is free at all levels, including college and post-graduate work. The literacy rate for males at 71.5 percent is significantly greater than females at 50.2 percent, who nonetheless constitute 43 percent of students. Total literacy is 62.8 percent

Labor Force

Total 7,000,000
By occupation: government 40%, industry, construction and oil 25%, service 30%, agriculture 5%.
(Note: Only 5% of the labor force is female)

THE ECONOMY

Saudi Arabia is both the economic and religious center of the Arab world. The discovery and exploitation of its oil reserves transformed the nation from a middling agricultural base to one of great export wealth and political power. The vast majority of the oil wealth is garnered by the royal families and it accounts for 75 percent of government revenues. While it does have a stable services sector and some potential industrial avenues, an over reliance on oil has wreaked havoc on Saudia Arabia in the late '90s as petroleum prices plunged. Some Saudi businessmen such as the world's second wealthiest man, Prince al-Waleed Bin Talal, have wisely diversified and globalized their portfolios. For the most part, however, Saudi fortunes continue to hang on oil exports.

Exports ....US$59.7 billion (f.o.b, 1997)
Imports ....US$26.2 billion (f.o.b, 1997)
Total Trade .... US$85.9 billion
GDP Per Capita................................ US$9,000 (1998 est.)
Unemployment .... NA%

Inflation Rate-0.2 percent (1998 est.) Top Export Partners

Japan 18%, US 15%, South Korea 11%, Singapore 8%, India 4% (1997 est.).

Top Import Partners

U.S. 23%, U.K. 17%, Japan 8%, Germany 8%, Italy 5% (1997 est.).

Top Exports

Petroleum and petroleum products 90%.

Top Imports

Machinery and equipment, chemicals, foodstuffs, motor vehicles, textiles.

BUSINESS WORKWEEK

Note: During Ramadan, business hours are significantly shorter. Important business usually is not done during this period.

Office

Saturday to Thursday 9a.m. to 1p.m., 4:30p.m. to 8p.m.; during Ramadan, 8p.m. to 1a.m.

Banks

Saturday to Wednesday 8:30a.m. to noon, and 5p.m. to 7p.m.; Thursday 8:30a.m. to noon.

Government

Saturday to Wednesday 7:30a.m. to 2:30p.m.; during Ramadan 8p.m. to 1a.m.

Retail

Saturday to Thursday 9a.m. to 1p.m., and 4:30p.m. to 8p.m.

HOLIDAYS

Id al-Fitr, end of Ramadan....................................January 9
Id al-Adha, Feast of the Sacrifice .... March 17
Muharram, Islamic New Year.................................... April 6
Ashoura .... April 17
Mouloud, Birth of the Prophet..................................June 16
Leilat al-Meiraj, Ascension of the
Prophet..October 28
*Exact dates may vary since dates are dependent on the Islamic lunar calendar.

Note: The annual Hajj pilgrimage in the second week of the 12th month of the lunar year brings 2 million pilgrims to the country en route to the holy cities of Mecca and Medina. In the year 2000, the Hajj will take place in mid-March. Business travelers should consider avoiding travel to the country during this time due to extended waiting times at airports and otherwise crowded conditions.

CLIMATE

Seasons

The climate is varied with great extremes of temperature, harsh sand storms, and heat. Due to the vast desert area, most of the country is arid all year. During the summer, the sun is extremely intense, and high temperatures of over 48°C (120°F) in the shade are not unusual. In the winter, temperatures can drop to below zero in the mountain region, but it never really snows. Winters are generally mild.

Regions

The coastal region has high humidity. Central and northern areas can get the coldest in the winter. Rainfall is higher in the north than in the south.

Money & Banking

Currency

The currency of Saudi Arabia is the Saudi Arabia Riyal (R).

Saudi Arabia

SM Santa Barbara, CA

©2001 Magellan Geographix

Denominations

The Saudi Arabia Riyal (R) comes in coin denominations of 50, 25, 10,d 5 halalah, and 10, 5, 2 and 1 qurush, and banknotes of R1, 5, 10, 50, 100, and 500.

Traveler's checks

Traveler's checks are the most widely form of payment in Saudi Arabia, and can be exchanged at banks, exchange shops, hotels, and international airports at tourist exchange rates. Larger banks may offer the best exchange rates, but avoid black marketers at all cost. Consult you bank about current exchange rates before departure. Keep all receipts for reconversion.

Most major currencies can also be exchanged, but try to take only crisp and new notes, wrinkled and soiled notes are likely to be refused.

Major credit cards, American Express, Visa, Diner's Club, and MasterCard, are easily accepted in up-market places, but smaller shops in more rural districts may ask for cash. Some banks in the capital offer cash advances on credit cards, but make sure you bring your passport.

Travel
VISA AND PASSPORT

A passport is required that is valid for at least six months beyond the estimated stay in Saudi Arabia. Visas acquired in advance are necessary from all nationalities except nationals of Bahrain, Kuwait, Oman, Qatar, and the U.A.E.; business visas require a letter of guarantee, itinerary, and an invitation from your sponsor. Visas that require a sponsor can take several months to process, and must be obtained prior to arrival. Do not attempt to conduct business under a tourist visa.

Holders of re-entry permits and Landing Permits issued by the Saudi Arabian Ministry of Foreign Affairs do not require a visa. Women applying for business visas require special authorization and all women must be met upon arrival by their sponsor or husband. Foreign residents traveling within the Kingdom carry travel letters issued by employers and authenticated by an Immigration official or a Chamber of Commerce officer.

Note: Israeli passport holders, or those holding a passport with an Israeli stamp, will be refused entry into Saudi Arabia. Passengers that do not comply with Saudi Arabian conventions of behavior and dress will also not be allowed entry. Special regulations exist for pilgrims going to Mecca and Medina.

DEPARTURE FORMALITIES

There are no restrictions for bringing or taking out Saudi or foreign currencies other than the Israeli Shekel, which is prohibited. Foreign currency must be declared, however. Gold, silver, and Saudi Arabian banknotes require a permit from the Monetary Agency. Residents in Saudi Arabia may not depart the country without obtaining an exit permit prior to leaving and an exit/reentry permit, if they intend to return to Saudi Arabia. One-time visitors on a single entry visa do not need an exit permit.

CUSTOMS ENTRY (PERSONAL)

Duty-free
- Tobacco: 600 cigarettes, 100 cigars, or 500g tobacco
- Perfume for personal use
- Reasonable amount of cultured pearls for personal use
  Note: Duty is levied on cameras and typewriters, but if these articles are re-exported within 90 days the customs charges may be refunded. It is advisable not to put film in cameras.

Prohibited or Restricted
- Alcohol
- Narcotics
- Pornography (may include standard fashion magazines and what customs define as "suggestive" videos)
- Pork and pork products
- Contraceptives
- Firearms
- Natural Pearls
- Non-Islamic religious materials (including Christmas decorations or holiday goods)
- Most live animals, most foods, and items listed as prohibited by the Arab League (copy available from the Embassy)
  Note: Audiovisual media and reading matter are censored.

IMMUNIZATION

Visitors arriving from countries infected with yellow fever need evidence of vaccination. During the Hajj (pilgrimage) period, meningococcal meningitis vaccination is required of arriving visitors. Malaria prophylaxis is recommended and cholera, smallpox, typhoid, and typhus inoculations are recommended but not required.

TIPPING

No tipping is necessary for airport-authorized taxis. Porters should be tipped R5 to 10, waiters and drivers should receive 10 percent. Although tipping is not expected, it is appreciated in other service establishments and is becoming more common.

EMERGENCY INFORMATION

Police and Crime
The Islamic Sharia Law governs the country. As a result, petty crime is literally nonexistent. However, any individual can be arrested for anything that goes against Islamic rule, including the possession of alcohol, wearing clothing inappropriate to Saudi customs, and the association by a female with a non-relative male. Persons in question may be harassed, pursued, or assaulted. Religious police, known as Mutawwa'iin are charged with enforcing Muslim standards. Penalties for the import, manufacture, possession, and consumption of alcohol or illegal drugs are severe. Convicted offenders can

expect jail sentences, fines, public flogging, and/or deportation. The penalty for drug trafficking in Saudi Arabia is death. If arrested, you will be provided with a translator, but you could be detained without trial for some time.

Public observance of any other religion than Islam is forbidden; this includes the public display of non-Islamic religious articles such as crosses and bibles. Travel to the holy cities of Mecca and Medina is prohibited to non-Muslims.

The Saudi Embassy advises women traveling to Saudi Arabia to dress in a conservative fashion, to wear ankle-length dresses with long sleeves, and not to wear trousers in public. In the central part of the Kingdom, including Riyadh, Mutawwa'iin enforce the rule that women wear an abaya (a full-length black covering) as well as a head covering. Some foreign women have been known to dress themselves similarly to avoid harassment. Women who appear to be of Arab or Asian origin, especially those presumed to be Muslim, face a greater risk of harassment.

Some Mutawwai'iin may enforce the rule that men and women may not mingle in public, unless they are family or close relatives. Police may ask to see proof that a couple is married or related. Women who are arrested for socializing with a man who is not a relative may be charged with prostitution. Women who are not accompanied by a close male relative have been denied service at some restaurants and shops. These restrictions are not always posted, and in some cases women violating this policy have been arrested.

Homosexual activity is considered a criminal offense and those convicted may be subject to lashing, a prison sentence, or death.

Emergency Numbers
Accidents 993
Ambulance 997
Fire 998
Police 999

Embassies
Australia ....(1) 488-7788
Canada..(1) 488-2288
Denmark..(1) 488-0101
Finland..(1) 488-1515
France...(1) 488-1255
Germany..(1) 488-0700
Ireland ....(1) 488-2300
Italy......................... (1) 488-1212, Jeddah (2) 642-1451/2
Japan...(1) 488-1100
New Zealand ....(1) 488 7988, Jeddah (2) 651-6504
Spain ....(1) 488-0606
Sweden ....(1) 488-3100
Switzerland..(1) 488-1291
Russia ....(1) 481-1875
United Kingdom...(1) 488-0077
United States............. (1) 488-3800, Jeddah (2) 667-0080

Health
Trachoma, malaria, bilharzia, gastrointestinal troubles, Hepatitis A and Hepatitis B, rabies, typhoid, typhus, yellow fever and tuberculosis exist here, but foreign travelers are more prone to dysentery and colds. Hepatitis A vaccinations are recommended. Visitors to Saudi Arabia generally obtain a meningitis vaccination prior to arrival. Malaria is endemic to the coastal plains of southwest Saudi Arabia, primarily in the Jizan region extending up the coast to the rural area surrounding Jeddah.

Take care of the intense sun and heat. Avoid drinking tap water; bottled water is widely available. Wash all vegetables, peel fruits, and avoid uncooked food. Drink only pasteurized milk. Bring along necessary toiletries, as they may be hard to procure in the country.

Private hospitals are of high standard. Most hospitals are state run, with an abundance of European-trained and U.S.-trained doctors attached to foreign firms. Treatment is expensive, so carry insurance including evacuation costs.

Note: Sleeping pills brought into the country without a doctor's prescription are considered narcotics.

For more information on medical centers, including phone numbers, please see the "Business Centers" section at the end of this chapter.

TAXI

Taxis are very expensive. Government fares are metered. If, however, the cab you have hailed does not have a metered fare, be sure to negotiate before departing.

TRAIN

Rail service is limited in the country, but new rails are being built. A daily (except Thursdays) train service operates between Riyadh and Dammam and offers first-class carriages and a dining car.

BUS

Inter- and intra-city bus service is available. Sections are segregated for men and women as are entry points. Women will usually board at the rear of the bus.

RENTAL CAR

Car rental can be expensive but it is often the only means available to reach smaller towns. Cars usually come with drivers that must be tipped if you expect to make the return trip. It is not recommended that you drive yourself unless you are fluent in local languages and customs.

Essential Terms

English	Arabic
Yes	*Na-a'am*
No	*La; mish*
Good morning	*Al sa-lahm*
Hello (daytime)	*Al sa-lahm*
Hello (evening)	*Ma-sa'el khair*
Hello (telephone)	*Marhaban*
Good-bye	*Be-kha-trahk*
Please	*Min-fahd-lak (M)*
	Min-fahd-lik (F)
Thank you	*Shook-rahn*
Pleased to meet you	*Sorirart biro'aitak*
Excuse me; I'm sorry	*Is-ma-leh*
My name is _____	*'ismii____*
I don't understand	*An-na mish fahem*
Do you speak English?	*Hal tatakallumu l-inkliziyya?*

Communications

DIALING CODES IN SAUDI ARABIA

International country code: [966]
Selected city codes: Jeddah (2), Mecca (2), Riyadh (1)

Dialing Saudi Arabia from Overseas

To dial Saudi Arabia from overseas, dial your country's international dialing code, then 966 (the country code for Saudi Arabia), then the city code, and finally the number. If you were dialing Jeddah, from the United States, for example, you would begin with 011, then 966, then 2 (the city code for Jeddah), and finally the number of the person or office you were trying to reach.

Assistance Numbers

International Operator 901
International Directory 900
Operator/Directory Assistance (English) 905

CALLING WITHIN SAUDI ARABIA

Local Calls

Yet another quality phone service in this Arab region allows ease in placing a local call by dialing direct.

Long Distance Calls

Dial 0 + area code + number to make a long-distance call within Saudi Arabia. This can also be achieved from a pay phone, in which case it is advised to bring along a sack of change if you haven't yet purchased a phone card.

International Calls

To call overseas direct, dial 00 + country code + area code + number. Saudi Telecom runs the telephone show in Saudi Arabia and provides telephone offices in most towns from which one can place a call. Some international call booths are also scattered around Riyadh. Hotels charge a three-minute minimum along with any other surcharges they feel make it worth plugging you into the system. Inquire about fees in advance to avoid falling off the shock wagon. To reach a U.S. operator direct, dial:
AT&T USA Direct 1-800-10

PAY PHONES

Public Telephones

Coin operated phones use R1 coins. If you find yourself lacking coins, money changers are everywhere, although they charge a slight commission.

Calling Cards

Card phones have become more readily available around town; however, the cards to operate them have yet to appear with the same consistency in the shops that supposedly sell them.

CELLULAR PHONES

Several cellular service providers exist in Saudi Arabia. Saudi Telecom is a major service provider, offering NMT-450 for analogue users and GSM for digital. There are other companies that offer GSM, including Royal Palace Network.

Note: Your home country cell phone may not work in this country. If not, we recommend that you rent an international cell phone *before* you leave home. A major US-based cell phone rental provider is **IMC WorldCell**. For information see "International Cell Phone Rentals" on page 14.

CALL BACK

You can (potentially) save significant sums when calling in Saudi Arabia by using one of the call back services listed below. Fees for call back services vary widely, depending on the

Saudi Arabia

company and the type of service required. Be sure to check with these companies before leaving to compare rates.

For a list of callback services, please refer to the "Communications" section in the *Global Road Warrior* Introduction.

PHONE JACKS

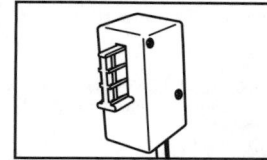

Plug adaptors are available through **iGo Corporation.** (See "Electrical and Telephone Adaptors" on page 19.)

FAX

Fax machines are becoming more widespread, particularly in the cities. Most hotels now have them.

Hours of service
Monday to Friday 7a.m. to 10p.m.

TELEGRAMS
Telegrams can be sent from all post offices.

Business Services
BUSINESS CENTER

Jeddah
Albilad Mövenpick; Al-Corniche Highway; tel: (2) 654-4777; fax: (2) 654-7098.

Jeddah Inter-Continental; Corniche Road; tel: (2) 661-1800; fax: (2) 661-1145.

Jeddah Marriott; Palestine Rd./KIng Fahd Rd.; tel: (2) 671-4000; fax: (2) 671-5990.

Riyadh
Al Khozama Riyadh; Oleya Road; tel: (1) 465-4650; fax: (1) 464-8576; http://www.al-khozana.com.

Riyadh Marriott; Al Maazar St.; tel: (1) 477-9300; fax: (1) 477-9089.

Sheraton Riyadh Hotel & Towers; Olaya and Mecca Road; tel: (1) 454-3300; fax: (1) 454-1889.

COURIER SERVICE

Jeddah
DHL; tel: (3) 882-7777; SNAS Worldwide Express; Al Ghatani Building Al Khobar - Dammam Highway P.O. Box 897 Dhahran 31952 ; Opening hours, Sat-Th 8a.m. to 7p.m.

Federal Express; tel: (2) 682 7243; 6 days 7a.m. to 9:30p.m.; Friday closed.

TNT; SAB Express Worldwide, P.O. Box 25911, Jeddah 21573; tel: (2) 674-4444; fax: (2) 674-4141.

UPS; Jeddah Express Centre; Corner Sari St. and Medina Rd., PO Box 23576, Jeddah 21436; tel: 02-639-2393.

Riyadh
DHL; tel: (3) 857-3333.

Federal Express; tel: (1) 465-4220; 6 days 7a.m. to 9:30p.m.; Friday closed.

TNT; SAB Express Worldwide, P.O. Box 56119, Riyadh 1154; tel: (1) 461-1444; fax: (1) 461-4141.

UPS; Riyadh Express Centre

King Fahd Highway, UPS/Eirad Building, PO Box 63682, Riyadh 11526; tel: 01-462-6655

PRINTING/COPYING

Jeddah
Okaz Printing; tel: (2) 631-4149.

Nasr Printers; tel: (2) 642-0239.

Riyadh
Saudi Arabian Printing Co.; tel: (1) 476-4520.

Jazirah Publishing and Printing; tel: (1) 402-1022.

TRANSLATION SERVICES
Al Madini Translation Office; tel: (1) 478-5962.

Electrical

Current
125/215 volts AC, 50/60Hz

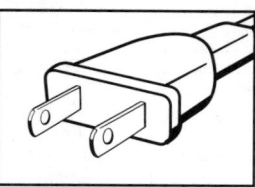

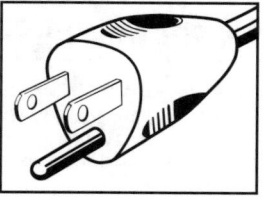

Saudi Arabia

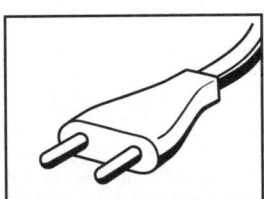

Plug adaptors are available through **iGo Corporation.** (See "Electrical and Telephone Adaptors" on page 19.)

Technical Support

HARDWARE/SOFTWARE VENDOR SUPPORT

Apple/Claris; (in the U.A.E.) tel: [971] 4-513-888; fax: [971] 4-527-444; (in Germany) tel: [49] (1) 803-5018; (in Switzerland) tel: [41] (800) 833-310; (in the U.K.) tel: [44] (990) 127-753; (in the U.S.) tel: [1] (800) 500-7078; http://www.apple.com/.

Compaq/Digital; (U.AE. Office) tel: [971] 4-818-100; fax: [971] 4-818-313; (in Switzerland) tel: [41] (22) 709-5330; fax: [41] (22) 709-5391 (Geneva); tel: [41] (1) 801-2507; fax: [41] (1) 801-2172 (Zurich); (General U.S.) tel: (281) 518-2000; http://www.compaq.com/.

Corel; (in the U.A.E.) tel: [971] 4-523-526 (All Applications); (in Germany) tel: [49] (180) 425-8210 (TS Word Perfect-32 bit); (in the U.S.) tel: [1] (716) 871-2325 (Ask to be Forwarded to Appropriate Program); http://www.corel.com/.

Dell; (in Egypt) tel: [20] 2-360-2234 (Electronics House in Cairo/Mr. Jamal El Bidweihy); fax: [20] 2-361-4576; (in Germany) tel: [49] (61) 039-710; (Dell- Europe) tel: [44] (134) 474-8000; (in the U.S.) tel: [1] (512) 338-4400; fax: [1] (512) 728-3330; http://www.dell.com/.

IBM; tel: (2) 660-0007; fax: (2) 665-1163; (Egypt Office) tel: [20] 2-349-2533; fax: [20] 2-360-1227; (in Switzerland) tel: [41] (22) 310-0418 (in French); (in the U.S.) tel: [1] (919) 517-2800; http://www.ibm.com/.

Microsoft; tel: (1) 218-0808; fax: (1) 218-0809; (in Switzerland) tel: [41] (848) 858-868; fax [41] (1) 831-0869; (in the U.S.) [1] (425) 635-7222; http://www.microsoft.com/.

Novell; (in Germany) tel: [49] (211) 563-2777 (System support); tel: [49] (6196) 904-477; fax: [49] (211) 563-2772; (in Switzerland) tel: [41] (1) 308-4747; fax: [41] (1) 302-0401; (in the U.S.) tel: [1] (408) 434-2300; fax: [1] (408) 577-5775 (Worldwide Sales Headquarters); http://www.novell.com/.

Toshiba; (in Germany) tel: [49] (2131) 158-319; fax: [49] (2131) 158-558; (in Switzerland) tel: [41] (1) 946-0777; fax: [41] (1) 946-0807; (in Ireland) tel: [44] (193) 282-8828; (in the U.S.) [1] (949) 583-3000 (Corporate Headquarters); http://www.toshiba.com/.

Internet Connection

HOW TO CONNECT

Connecting to AOL and Compuserve in Saudi Arabia is similar to using it when traveling outside your own area code. See the introductory section for detailed information on connecting to your account through a different phone number.

America Online

Numbers are available at keyword *international.* Be sure to get several local numbers before leaving. AOL has a new GlobalNet service, available at keyword *access* (a free area).

At press time, America Online had no local access numbers in Saudi Arabia. Check the list of current access numbers at http://intlaccess.web.aol.com/ to see if any numbers have been activated or to locate numbers in neighboring countries.

Compuserve

Numbers are available at Go International. If you are using CompuServe 2000, use GO PHONES within CompuServe 2000 to search for access numbers. The Compuserve Web-site also has a great deal of information for travelers at http://www.compuserve.com/.

At press time, Compuserve had no local access numbers. Check their list of current access numbers to see if any numbers have been activated or to locate numbers in neighboring countries.

Independent Service Providers

Many independent service providers offer discounts if you are only in town for a couple of days.

AwalNet; tel: (1) 460-0111 ext:5; fax: (1) 460-1110; e-mail: info@awalnet.net.sa; http://www.awalnet.net.sa/.

Premier Information Technology; tel: (1) 462-9648; fax: (1) 462-9602; info@premier-it.com; http://www.premier-it.com/.

Sahara Network; tel: (3) 833-2133; tel: 833-2299; fax: (3) 834-5652; email: sales@sahara.com/.sa; http://www.sahara.com/.

Business Culture

GREETINGS AND COURTESIES

Greetings are effusive, eloquent, and elaborate. Saudis pride themselves on their way with words; they will lavish praise and compliments upon greeting one another. There is also a great deal of touching and hand holding, sometimes even a quick kiss on the cheek (even between men). They love to visit and talk with one another, so greetings are rarely curt; be prepared to stop and visit for a while. If the Saudi is accompanied by a female, do not greet or offer your hand unless she should extend her hand first; you will probably not even be introduced to her. One should not inquire of a man's wife if she is not present, nor should one present her with any gifts if invited to a Saudi home. Unless otherwise stated, do not expect that your wife is invited. If she is, she will most likely eat with the women in separate quarters. Keep in mind that it is also forbidden to photograph women.

Saudis are very status conscious; if a Saudi has a title, he expects it to be used. Foreigners meeting titled Saudis are at a distinct disadvantage unless they hold equivalent titles or rank.

Although complementing one's host in generalities is acceptable, take care with complementing specific items that you see or your Saudi host may feel an obligation to present it to you. If a Saudi does give you a gift, do not refuse it or you may offend. Also note that one should use the right hand when presenting a gift.

When dining, refrain from drinking alcohol if it is even offered since it is illegal and may furthermore offend a devout Muslim. Avoid sitting with crossed legs or so that the soles of your feet are pointed toward anyone. If entertaining, always offer your guests tea or coffee, even if in a hotel.

RELIGIOUS NOTES

Saudi Arabia is a country decidedly ruled by Islam. As

such, consider that certain actions or conversations may provoke unnecessary tension or offense. Expect that five times a day Muslims are given to prayer and that all business may cease during those times. One should take care to respect religious rituals and to refrain from proclaiming your own since proselytizing is illegal. Mosques are off limits to non-Muslims unless otherwise specified. Economics, politics, and law should only be discussed if necessary and broached with caution since these subjects are based on the principles of the Koran, the Islamic book of Allah. Never walk in front of a praying individual; and, in case it isn't obvious, never walk on a prayer mat.

BUSINESS ETHIC AND FRAMEWORK

The influence of Islam is everywhere and is felt continuously. Men quote the Koran in business discussions, and the government letterhead carries the Islamic creed. Yet Saudi Arabia has made a tremendous effort to keep pace with the twentieth century; and it has had the resources to do so. The result is a combination of ultramodern high-tech and ancient tradition. Family loyalties remain the most powerful force; family cohesion and solidarity are the sources of a Saudi man's all-important courage and honor. It is honorable to display loyalty to the family, and to do work that does not dirty the hands. But loss of honor means loss of all status; so anything—even lying or killing—is sometimes justified in order to save a man's honor. Job security and advancement are generally based on loyalty and family or friendship ties rather than technical competence or managerial performance.

DECISION MAKING

Decision making by Saudis is highly personalized and is based on the principles of the Bedouin *majlis*. The Saudi manager will consult with several people to gain a consensus; and he will give the greatest credence to those he trusts most as friends, and will consider their opinions over those of experts. In family-controlled businesses, positions of responsibility are built around individuals with whom the senior executive feels comfortable. Delegated authority is frequently reassigned to reward individuals who happen to be in favor at the moment. There is very little teamwork, group cohesion, or company loyalty; and decisions once made are frequently overturned seemingly on a whim.

In the event of any contract dispute, the Saudi authorities will refer to the written Arabic contract. Be advised that verbal assurances or side letters are not binding under Saudi law. Those wishing to break a business contract may have to pay substantial penalties before being allowed to leave the country.

WOMEN

Generally, a woman has only half the legal rights of a man. A Saudi woman's place is still in the home, and Saudi women are segregated from all men except those in her family. Women are not allowed to drive cars, ride bicycles, and cannot even take taxis alone. Women are separated from men at all formal gatherings, and they are not allowed to work without the consent of their male guardians, and, in any event, cannot work in places where they might come into contact with men. This is changing, however slowly. Several women have started women's banks; and women control over a third of the kingdom's wealth. Foreign businesswomen will get very little accomplished in Saudi Arabia; it is best simply to acknowledge this and send a man instead.

MEETINGS

It is difficult for a foreign businessman to obtain access to se-

nior Saudi business and government managers without the help of another influential Saudi; after he does gain access, he must court the Saudi aggressively. Only after several visits to the Saudi's office, and innumerable cups of coffee will the Saudi discuss business, and then only if he trusts the foreigner. Junior level managers should never be sent to business meetings with senior Saudi businesspeople who may look upon this as a slight. A business meeting with Saudi executives is a test of patience. Meetings are generally delayed by the late arrival of the Saudis, who profusely greet each other prior to getting down to business. Coffee is brought in and there is a long period of discussion devoted to non-work related subjects. Rushing into business does not appeal to a Saudi. Even after the meeting starts, it is likely to be constantly interrupted as the Saudis take telephone calls and greet others who enter the room to talk about different subjects.

BUSINESS ATTIRE

Saudis are officially discouraged from wearing Western attire in the kingdom and usually wear their traditional dress. The men wear loose fitting robes and head pieces. Women face far more regulation. Foreign women should wear ankle-length dresses with long sleeves and avoid wearing trousers in public. Loose-fitting clothing is urged. Covering one's entire body is essential, particularly in Riyadh and the central part of the Kingdom where women wear full-length black cloaks (abayas) as well as head coverings. Foreigners do not have to try to imitate this dress (except perhaps in inner Saudi Arabia to avoid harassment), but should dress in very conservative clothing, taking care to make sure most all skin remains unrevealed, and any signs of body form are mitigated.

Business Centers
Jeddah
CITY VIEW

Lying on the waters at the edge of a vast desert nation, Jeddah holds many degrees of fascination along with many titles: "Gateway to Mecca," "Paris of Arabia," "Bride of the Red Sea," and Jeddah's translated meaning of "grandmother," stemming from a legend that Eve, the mother of creation, was buried here. Needless to say, Jeddah has a large reputation to uphold, but has done so with great flair in the feel, air, and color of its inhabitants, location, design, historical, and political prominence. Up until the recent emergence of Riyadh, Jeddah housed the foreign embassies and the seat of the Saudi government.

AIRPORT

King Abdul Aziz Airport to City Center

The airport lies 19 miles (30km.) from the airport. Buses run 24 hours a day and leave every 30 minutes. There are also buses from Mecca. Unmetered taxis prove plentiful. Expect to pay about US$28 to the city center; but check with a dispatcher to confirm a ballpark figure. Then negotiate the fare with the cab driver before departing.

Airline Numbers

Air France	(2) 6515232
Air India	(2) 6512000
Air New Zealand	(2) 661-1222
American Airlines	(2) 6658484
Austrian Airlines	(2) 6652111
British Airways	(2) 6693464
Cyprus Airways	(2) 6513541
CSA	(2) 6857338
EgyptAir	(2) 6441515

Saudi Arabia

Emirates .... (2) 6659405
Ethiopian Airlines.. (2) 6512365
Garuda Indonesia... (2) 6695388
Gulf Air .... (2) 6517756
KLM... (2) 667088
Korean Air .... (2) 6657107
Kuwait Airways... (2) 6694111
Lufthansa.. (2) 6650000
Libyan Arab Airways..................................... (2) 6441200
Olympic .... (2) 6511280
PIA.. (2) 6422642
Royal Jordanian .... (2) 6514949
Swissair .... (2) 6514000
Tunis Air .... (2) 6530881
Turkish Airlines... (2) 6600127

HOTELS

Top-end
Hyatt Regency Jeddah; Medina Road; tel: (2) 652-1234; fax: 651-6260; city center, business district location; restaurants; conference facilities; secretarial service; fax/photocopy facilities; corporate rates; fitness; sauna; pool.

Jeddah Inter-Continental; Corniche Road; tel: (2) 661-1800; fax: (2) 661-1145; email: jeddah@interconti.com; near city center; rooms with sea view; restaurants; conference facilities (up to 1000); business center; secretarial service; in-room safe; Club Inter-Continental rooms; corporate rates; shopping arcade; parking; health club, fitness; sauna; pool; whirlpool; squash.

Jeddah Marriott; Palestine Rd./King Fahd Rd.; tel: (2) 671-4000; fax: (2) 671-5990; near city center; restaurant; 7 meeting rooms; 24-hour business center; secretarial, translation services; voicemail, dataports; parking; hair salon, barber; full spa, health club; sauna; pool.

Sheraton Jeddah; North Corniche; tel: (2) 699-2212; fax: (2) 699-2660; near city and watersports; restaurants; secretarial service; fax/photocopy facilities; sauna; pool.

Sofitel Jeddah Alhamra; Palestine Road; tel: (2) 660-2000; fax: (2) 660-4145; near city; restaurant; conference facilities; secretarial service; fax/photocopy facilities; corporate rates; sauna; pool.

Expensive
Al Fau Holiday Inn; Al Maadi Road, Al Hamra; tel: (2) 661-1000; fax: (2) 660-6326; restaurant; conference facilities (up to 1000); secretarial service; fax/photocopy facilities; in-room modem/fax connection; corporate rates; parking; fitness; sauna; pool.

Jeddah Kaki; Old Airport Road; tel: (2) 631-2201; fax: (2) 631-1350; near city center; restaurant; conference facilities (up to 1000); secretarial service; fax/photocopy facilities; in-room safe; corporate rates; parking; fitness; sauna; pool.

Kandara Palace; tel: (2) 631-2177; fax: (2) 631-4275; near city center; restaurant; parking; pool.

King Abdul Aziz Airport; tel: (2) 685-7725; fax: (2) 685-7730; restaurant; conference facilities (up to 350); in-room safe; corporate rates; parking.

Red Sea Palace; King Abdul Aziz Street; tel: (2) 642-8555; fax: (2) 642-2395; near city center; restaurant; conference facilities (up to 400): pool.

Moderate
Casablanca; Madina Road, Saqr Quraish St.; tel: (2) 682-7771; fax: (2) 682-2656; between airport and city center; restaurant; conference facilities; parking; fitness; pool.

Sahari; tel: (2) 647-7744; fax: (2) 648-5202; near city center; restaurant; secretarial service; fax/photocopy facilities; corporate rates.

MEDICAL CARE
Jeddah King Fahad Hospital; tel: (2) 660-6111; Emergency: (2) 665-9585, ex. 1055; Dentistry: (2) 669-7045, ex. 1843.

HEALTH CLUB
Jeddah Inter-Continental; Corniche Road; tel: (2) 661-1800.

Jeddah Marriott; Palestine Rd./King Fahd Rd.; tel: (2) 671-4000.

AUTO RENTAL
Note: Women may not drive (or ride bicycles) in Saudi Arabia; restrictions also apply to traveling in a car with men who are not blood related. Non-Muslims are not allowed entry into the holy cities of Mecca and Medina. Police checkpoints exist. around the holy cities. Use extreme caution when driving, as driving offences may carry a prison sentence and much hassle. Accidents may require that all persons involved to be taken to the local police station. In many cases, all drivers are held in custody, regardless of fault. Contact your sponsor and your embassy immediately if involved in an accident.

Avis; Airport, tel: (2) 685-3060, Code: JED; North Terminal, intl.: tel: (2) 685-3004, Code: SAO; Sands Hotel, tel: (2) 669-2020, Code: S4B; Main Station, tel: (2) 672-8697, Code: VH6; Palestine Road Station, tel: (2) 672-8697, Code: SQ8.

Europcar; Aliblad Mövenpick Hotel, Corniche Road, tel: (2) 654-4777; Code: JEDR01.

WORLD TRADE CENTER
World Trade Center Jeddah
Palestine St., PO Box 2618
Jeddah 21461
tel: (2) 671-0000
fax: (2) 671-7056

CHAMBER OF COMMERCE
Jeddah Chamber of Commerce and Industry
PO Box 9549
Jeddah 21423
tel: (2) 651-5111
fax: (2) 651-0996

Riyadh
CITY VIEW
A modern blast constructed upon an ancient landscape, Riyadh maintains one similarity with its natural predecessor, stark cleanliness. Now the official headquarters of Saudi Arabia, plenty of activity prevails in the city's core through a maze of high-tech flyovers, skyscrapers, and 2.5 million people. However, if standing at the edge of the surrounding vastness contemplating the scope of this manmade oasis, one may come to the stark conclusion that any waves of human sound eventually disappear into the roaring mouth of the shimmering silent sands.

AIRPORT
King Khalid International Airport to City Center
The airport lies 22 miles (35 km.) from the city center. There are bus services and taxis available.

Airline Numbers
Air France.. (1) 476-9666
American Airlines .... (1) 465-5885
Biman Bangladesh Airlines .... (1) 462-3376

British Airways...(1) 464-5550
EgyptAir..(1) 478-4004
Emirates..(1) 465-5485
Ethiopian Airlines...(1) 478-2140
Garuda ....(1) 465-5898
Kuwait Airways...(1) 463-1218
Lufthansa...(1) 463-2004
MEA...(1) 465-6600
Olympic ....(1) 464-4596
PIA...(1) 465-9600
Royal Jordanian ....(1) 462-5697
Saudia .... (1) 472-222
Swissair...(1) 476-6444
Syrian Arab Airlines..(1) 463-2610
Turkish Airlines...(1) 463-1600

HOTELS

Top-end

Hyatt Regency Riyadh; KIng Abdul Aziz Street; tel: (1) 479-1234; fax: (1) 477-2819; near city center, in business district; restaurant; secretarial service; fax/photocopy facilities; corporate rates; sauna; pool.

Riyadh Inter-Continental; Mather Street; tel: (1) 465-5000; fax: (1) 465-7833; email: riyadh@interconti.com; VIP villas available; restaurant; conference facilities (up to 1500); secretarial service; fax/photocopy facilities; Club Inter-Continental wing; shopping arcade; corporate rates; health club; fitness, 2 gyms; 2 saunas; pools; tennis; squash; bowling.

Expensive

Al Khozama Riyadh; Oleya Road; tel: (1) 465-4650; fax: (1) 464-8576; http://www.al-khozana.com; located in suburb; restaurant; conference facilities (up to 700); business center; secretarial service; fax/photocopy facilities; in-room modem/fax connection; barber/beauty shop; parking; micro-fitness, Nautilus weights; sauna/steamroom; indoor/outdoor pools; squash; bowling.

Atallah Villas Complex; Dabab Street; tel: (1) 401-0100; fax: (1) 401-2070; near city center; restaurant; conference facilities; secretarial service; fax/photocopy facilities; in-room safe; corporate rates; parking; fitness; sauna; pool.

Riyadh Palace; Prince Abdul Rahman Bin, Abdul Aziz Street; tel: (1) 405-4444; fax: (1) 405-3725; near city center; restaurant; conference facilities (up to 700); secretarial service; fax/photocopy facilities; corporate rates; parking; fitness; sauna; pool; whirlpool.

Sahara Riyadh Airport; tel: (1) 220-4500; fax: (1) 220-4505; near airport; restaurant; conference facilities (up to 500); secretarial service; fax/photocopy facilities; corporate rates; parking; fitness; sauna; pool; whirlpool.

Sheraton Riyadh Hotel & Towers; Olaya and Mecca Road; tel: (1) 454-3300; fax: (1) 454-1889; near exhibition grounds; restaurant; conference facilities (up to 350); business center; secretarial service; barber; corporate rates; health club, fitness; steamroom; indoor pool; bowling; tennis.

Moderate

Al Seteen Palace; Seteen Road; tel: (1) 477-3006; fax: (1) 477-3113; near city center; restaurant; conference facilities (up to 200); secretarial service; fax/photocopy facilities; in-room modem/fax connection; corporate rates; parking; pool.

New Assamer; tel: (1) 465-0189; fax: (1) 465-9642; near city center; restaurant; corporate rates; parking; fitness; sauna; pool.

MEDICAL CARE

Al Mubarak; Wazir & Washm Sts.; tel: 401-5282.

King Faisal Specialist Hospital and Research Centre; tel: (1) 464-7272; Emergency, 464-7272 ex. 31436; Ambulatory care, 464-7272, ex. 32060; dentistry, 464-7272, ex. 27651.

Shumaisi Hospital; Shumaisi St.; tel: 435-1900.

Transad Medical Service; Subymaniyah District; tel: 465-0840.

HEALTH CLUB

Riyadh Inter-Continental; Mather Street; tel: (1) 465-5000

Riyadh Marriott; Al Maazar St.; tel: (1) 477-9300.

Sheraton Riyadh Hotel & Towers; Olaya and Mecca Road; tel: (1) 454-3300.

AUTO RENTAL

Note: Women may not drive (or ride bicycles) in Saudi Arabia; restrictions also apply to traveling in a car with men who are not blood related. Non-Muslims are not allowed entry into the holy cities of Mecca and Medina. Police checkpoints exist. around the holy cities. Use extreme caution when driving, as driving offences may carry a prison sentence and much hassle. Accidents may require that all persons involved to be taken to the local police station. In many cases, all drivers are held in custody, regardless of fault. Contact your sponsor and your embassy immediately if involved in an accident.

Avis; King Kahled Intl. Airport, tel: (1) 220-2639, 24 hrs., Code RUH; Main Station: Old Airport Road, tel: (1) 476-1300, tel: (1) 476-1300, Code RU2; Sheraton Hotel, tel: (1) 454-3300, Code R1Y.

WORLD TRADE CENTER

Olaya Street, Opposit Olaya Akariya
P.O. Box 57714
Riyadh, Saudi Arabia 11584
tel: (1) 465-7030; fax: (1) 462-5543
email: worldtr@khaleej.net.bh

CHAMBER OF COMMERCE

Council of Saudi Chambers of Commerce and Industry
PO Box 16683
Riyadh 11471
tel: (1) 405-3200 / 405-7502; fax: (1) 402-4747

Riyadh Chamber of Commerce and Industry
PO Box 596
Riyadh 11421
tel: (1) 404-0044 / 404-0300 / 402-2700
fax: (1) 402-1103

CONVENTION BUREAU

Riyadh Exhibitions Committee
PO Box 56010
Riyadh 11554
tel: (1) 454-1448; fax: (1) 454-4846
email: recsa@midleast.net

Saudi Arabia

Senegal

At a Glance

THE PEOPLE

Population ....10,051,930 (July 1999 est.)
Growth Rate ....3.32% (1999 est.)
Life Expectancy............................ 57.83 years (1999 est.)
Infant Mortality.. 59.81 deaths/1,000 live births (1999 est.)

Ethnic Composition

Wolof 43.3%
Pular 23.8%
Serer..14.7%
Diola 3.7%
Mandingo...3%
Soninke 1.1%
European and Lebanese 1%
Other 9.4%

Religious Composition

Islam..92%
African traditional religions 6%
Christianity...2%

Languages Spoken

French (official language), Wolof, Poular, Diola, Mandingo

Education and Literacy

Education is compulsory at the primary level between ages of 6 and 12. Because of a lack of facilities, however, just over half the children attend school. Literacy rates are low, estimated at 43 percent for men and 23.2 percent for women.

Labor Force

Labor Force .... NA
By sector: Agriculture, 60%.

THE ECONOMY

Senegal entered a period of self-imposed economic reform in 1994 after a sharp GDP decline in 1993. It devalued it currency (CFA franc) by 50% while slashing government subsidies and price controls. Senegal experienced GPD growth in '97 and '98 along with a marked increase in foreign investment. The private sector accounts for over 80% of GDP and inflation has been kept in the low single digits despite regional difficulties. While generally strong, the Senegalese economy has had increasing problems with urban unemployment, crime, and drug abuse.

Exports .... US$925 million (f.o.b., 1998)
Imports .... US$1.2 billion (f.o.b., 1999)
Total Trade .... US$2.125 billion (1999)
GDP Per Capita................................US$1,600 (1998 est.)
Unemployment .... N/A (urban youth 40% - 1998)
Inflation Rate 1.8% (1998)

Top Export Partners

France, other European Community countries, Côte d'Ivoire, Mali.

Top Import Partners

France, other European Community countries, Nigeria, Cameroon, Côte d'Ivoire, Algeria, U.S., China, Japan.

Top Exports

Fish, ground nuts (peanuts), petroleum products, phosphates, cotton.

Top Imports

Foods and beverages, consumer goods, capital goods, petroleum.

BUSINESS WORKWEEK

Offices

Saturday to Thursday 8a.m. to 4p.m.

Banks

Saturday to Wednesday 9a.m. to noon, 2p.m. to 6p.m.

Governments

Saturday to Wednesday 9a.m. to 3p.m.

Retail

Saturday to Thursday 9a.m. to 5p.m.

HOLIDAYS

New Year's Day...January 1
Korité, End of Ramadan.....................................January 10
Tabaski, Feast of the Sacrifice .... March 18
National Day.. April 4
Ashoura .... April 17
Good Friday .... April 22
Easter Monday .... April 24
Labor Day..May 1
Ascension Day ....June 1
Whit Monday ....June 12
Mouloud, Birth of the Prophet................................June 16
Day of Association...July 14
Assumption...August 15
All Saints' Day ....November 1
Christmas ....December 25

*Exact dates may vary with some based on the Islamic calendar.

CLIMATE

Seasons

Senegal has two distinct seasons: the sunny dry season from December to April moderate temperatures with a prevalence of "harmattan" winds. May to November is the rainy season characterized by high humidity and strong southeast winds.

Regions

Temperatures are lowest along the coast and hottest in the inland region. It rains most in the south and least in the north of the country. The highest temperatures are in the northeast. The average summer temperature (between May to November) in Dakar is 30°C to 20°C (86-68°F). In the winter, from December to April, temperatures range from 26°C to 17°C (79 to 63°F). Coastal Dakar is generally much cooler than the rest of the country.

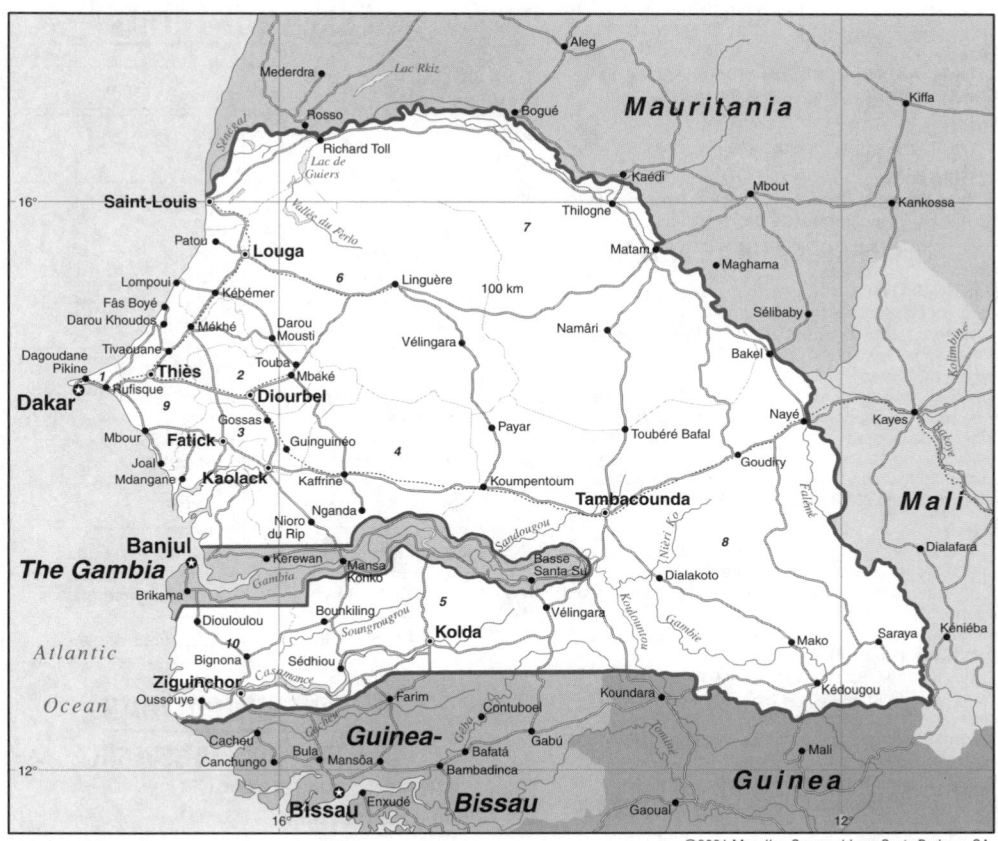

©2001 Magellan Geographix ℠ Santa Barbara, CA

Money & Banking

Currency
The currency of Senegal is the CFA Franc (CFAF).

Denominations
The CFA Franc (CFAF) comes in coin denominations of CFAF500, 100, 50, 25, 10, 5, and 1; and banknotes of CFAF500, 1,000, 5,000, and 10,000.

Traveler's Checks and Credit Cards
Traveler's checks can be exchanged at banks, exchange shops, hotels, and international airports at tourist exchange rates. Larger banks may offer the best exchange rates but avoid black marketers at all cost. Consult your bank about current exchange rates before departure. Keep all receipts for reconversion.

Most currencies can also be exchanged, but try to take only crisp and new notes, wrinkled and soiled notes are likely to be refused.

American Express, Visa, Diner's Club, and MasterCard are easily accepted in up-marketl places, but smaller restaurants, and shops in more rural areas may ask for cash. Transactions made via credit and bank cards receive the optimal exchange rate. Some banks in the capital offer cash advances on credit cards, but make sure you bring your passport. ATM machines are not available on a widescale.

Travel

VISA AND PASSPORT
Visitors must have a valid passport and an onward or return ticket; a visa is not required for stays less than 90 days.

DEPARTURE FORMALITIES
Foreign currency may not be exported from Senegal without an express authority from the Office des Changes of the Banque Centrale des Etats de l'Afrique de l'Ouest. Foreign currency must be declared upon arrival to be exported upon departure. Visitors who work in Senegal must have an income tax clearance certificate to leave the country.

CUSTOMS ENTRY (PERSONAL)

Duty-free
- Tobacco: 200 cigarettes, 50 cigars, or 250g tobacco
- Other: a reasonable quantity of perfume for personal use; gifts up to the value of CFAF5000
  Note: There is no free import of alcoholic beverages.

IMMUNIZATION
Evidence of a vaccination for yellow fever within the past 10 years is mandatory at the port of entry. Malaria and Hepatitis A prophylaxis is also recommended.

Senegal

TIPPING

Taxi
Taxis are all metered, and no additional tip is given above the amount indicated on the meter.

Hotels
Hotel bills usually include a service charge.

Restaurants
In restaurants and bars, tip no more than 10 percent of the bill. Service charges are often included.

EMERGENCY INFORMATION

Police and Crime
Street crime poses the most threat in Senegal. International meetings and conferences cause the frequency of petty crime to rise. Take basic precautions: avoid flashy displays of wealth, and dress and behave conservatively. Leave most of your cash, traveler's checks, jewelry, and your camera in your hotel safe. Carry photocopies of your passport instead of the original. Carry cash in a money belt, and use credit cards or traveler's checks for most transactions. Walk with your bag away from the street to avoid having it snatched away by motorcycle thieves. Never carry a stranger's baggage.

Health
Malaria is endemic, as is bilharzia (caused by water snails), so take medication before departure. Do not swim in nontreated water. Iron all clothing to prevent mango fly worms from surviving. Use screens and insecticides to eliminate insects and snakes. AIDS, especially among prostitutes, is a major problem.

Do not drink tap water or use ice cubes; bottled water is available. Wash all vegetables in a chlorine solution, peel fruits, and avoid uncooked food.

Health care is poor, and most hospitals are operated by the state. Outside of Dakar, health facilities are very limited. Some European- and U.S.-trained doctors exist in Dakar, but for major illnesses, one is advised to leave the country. Evacuation insurance is suggested.

TAXI
Most taxis in the cities are metered. It is cheaper to hail a taxi from the street than call one at a hotel or airport.

TRAIN
Rail services reach most of the country. The tracks are old and service can be slow, but there is a national upgrade service currently underway.

BUS
Buses are dilapidated and uncomfortable. Use them as a last resort or as a source of future travel adventure stories.

TRAVEL ASSISTANCE

Senegal Tourist Office
Tel: 286-0977; Fax: 286-0172

Essential Terms

English	French
Yes	*Oui*
No	*Non*
Good morning	*Bonjour*
Hello (daytime)	*Bonjour*
Hello (evening)	*Bonsoir*
Hello (telephone)	*Allo?*
Good-bye	*Au revoir*
Please	*S'il vous plaît*
Thank you	*Merci*
Pleased to meet you	*Enchanté*
Excuse me; I'm sorry	*Pardon*
My name is _____	*Je m'appelle _____*
I don't understand	*Je ne comprends pas*
Do you speak English?	Parlez-vous anglais?

Communications

DIALING CODES IN SENEGAL
International country code: [221]

Dialing Senegal from Overseas
To dial Senegal from overseas, dial your international dialing code, then 221 (the country code for Senegal), and finally the number. There are no city codes.

CALLING WITHIN SENEGAL

Local Calls
Calling is quite straightforward with six digits for all telephone numbers.

Long Distance Calls
There are no city codes to contend with in Senegal.

International Calls
SONATEL runs the telephone game in this country. You can place calls and pay later at SONATEL offices in Dakar. The direct dial method entails dialing 00 + country code + area code + number. Private telephone centers (centres téléphoniques) allow you to call from a metered booth and pay when your call has been completed. The term for a collect call is "PCV", pronounced with a French accent.
AT&T Direct Access 3072

PAY PHONES

Public Telephones
Phones are located around the country in large cities, but are often undependable or out of order.
1. Deposit coin
2. Dial
Private telecenters (centres téléphoniques), or SONATEL offices provide handier phone access.

Calling Cards

Pre-paid phone cards can be purchased at SONATEL offices.

CELLULAR PHONES

Note: Your home country cell phone may not work in this country. If not, we recommend that you rent an international cell phone *before* you leave home. A major US-based cell phone rental provider is **IMC WorldCell**. For information see "International Cell Phone Rentals" on page 14.

CALL BACK

You can (potentially) save significant sums when calling in Senegal by using one of the call back services listed below. Fees for call back services vary widely, depending on the company and the type of service required. Be sure to check with these companies before leaving to compare rates.

American International Telephone, Inc. (U.S.); tel: [1] (310) 471-6673; fax: [1] (310) 471-0162; email: signal@worldnet.att.ne.

Global Force Ltd. (U.S.); tel: [1] (609) 953-7573; fax: [1] (609) 953-7233; email: sales@global-force.com.

Kallback Africa (South Africa); tel: [27] (11) 646-3670; fax: [27] (11) 646-5477; email: africa@kallback.co.za.

OWC One World Comm. (U.K.); tel: [44] (117) 9077880; fax: [44] (117) 9077880; email: 106144.2740@compuserve.com.

Rhebs Design Agency (Germany); tel: (3695) 60 15 23; fax: (3695) 60 55 48; email: rhebs@compuserve.com.

TeleComInternational; tel: (5221) 57330; fax: (5221) 108187; email: tcint@pobox.com.

World Telenet Communications, Inc. (U.S.); tel: [1] (817) 354-5193; fax: [1] (817) 354-5195; email: wtc@flash.net.

PHONE JACKS

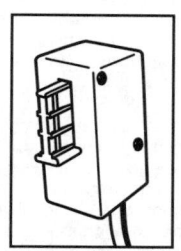

Plug adaptors are available through **iGo Corporation**. (See "Electrical and Telephone Adaptors" on page 19.)

FAX

Some hotels have fax services.

POSTAL SERVICES

Airmail to Europe can take up to 10 days, and airmail to North America usually takes about two weeks. Surface mail can take four months.

Business Services

BUSINESS CENTER

Savana Dakar Hotel; Petite Corniche, Pointe Bernard; tel: 823-6023.

Sofitel Teranga Hotel; Rue Colbert; tel: 823-1044; fax: 823-5001.

COURIER

DHL; tel: 231-394; 2, Avenue Albert Sarraut, BP 3554Dakar.

TNT Express Worldwide; E.M.S. Senegal; O.P.C.E. 6 Rue Abdoulaye SECK M. PARSINE, Dakar; tel: 4864-5972; fax: 4864-5961; fax: 4862-0680.

UPS (Trans Africa Express); 60A Ruell, Amitiell, BP 1800, Dakar; tel: 332-329 or 321-736; fax: 236-378.

Electrical

Current

220 volts AC, 50Hz.

ELECTRICAL PLUG

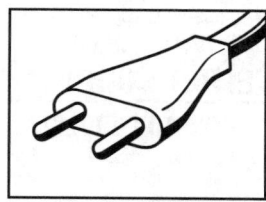

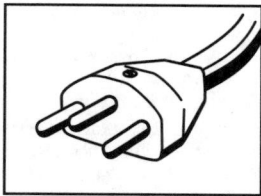

Plug adaptors are available through **iGo Corporation**. (See "Electrical and Telephone Adaptors" on page 19.)

Technical Support

HARDWARE/SOFTWARE VENDOR SUPPORT

Compaq/Digital; (in Switzerland) tel: [41] (22) 709-5330; fax: [41] (22) 709-5391 (Geneva); tel: [41] (1) 801-2507; fax: [41] (1) 801-2172 (Zurich); (General U.S.) tel: (281) 518-2000; http://www.compaq.com/.

Corel; (in Germany) tel: [49] (180) 425-8210 (TS Word Perfect-32 bit); (in the U.S.) tel: [1] (716) 871-2325 (Ask to be Forwarded to Appropriate Program); http://www.corel.com/.

Dell; (Dell- Europe) tel: [44] (134) 474-8000; (in the U.S.) tel: [1] (512) 338-4400; fax: [1] (512) 728-3330; http://www.dell.com/.

Hewlett Packard; (in Switzerland) tel: [41] (22) 780-8111; (in the U.S.) tel: [1] (408) 246-4300; http://www.hp.com/.

IBM; tel: 823-3773; fax: 823-3772; (in Switzerland) tel: [41] (22) 310-0418 (in French); (in the U.S.) tel: [1] (919) 517-2800; (U.S. Main Office) tel: [1] 914-765-1900; http://www.ibm.com/.

Microsoft; (in South Africa) tel: [27] (11) 445-0145; fax: [27] (11) 445-0045/6 (customer service); (in Egypt) tel: [20] (2) 338-8724; tel: [20] (2) 338-9794; (in Switzerland) tel: [41] (848) 858-868; fax [41] (1) 831-0869; (in the U.S.) [1] (425) 635-7222; http://www.microsoft.com/.

NEC; (in Germany) tel: [49] (18) 0524- 1212; tel:[49] (89) 3160-1233; fax: [49] (89) 3160- 1613 (Floppy Disk and Hard Drive); tel: [49] (89) 9627-4233; fax: [49] (89) 9627-4613 (All Other Products); (in the U.S.) [1] (916) 388-0101 (Main Switchboard); http://www.nec.com/.

Toshiba; (in Germany) tel: [49] (2131) 158-319; fax: [49] (2131) 158-558; (in Switzerland) tel: [41] (1) 946-0777; fax: [41] (1) 946-0807; (in Ireland) tel: [44] (193) 282-8828; (in the U.S.) [1] (949) 583-3000 (Corporate Headquarters); http://www.toshiba.com/.

Internet Connection
HOW TO CONNECT
Connecting to AOL and Compuserve in Senegal is similar to using it when traveling outside your own area code. See the introductory section for detailed information on connecting to your account through a different phone number.
America Online
Numbers are available at keyword *international*. Be sure to get several local numbers before leaving. Go to keyword *access* (a free area) and download the software.

There are no direct access numbers for America Online in Senegal. Users will have to pay international rates to use the service.
Compuserve
Numbers are available at *Go International*. The Compuserve Web-site also has a great deal of information, at http://www.compuserve.com.

At the time of publication there were no access numbers for Compuserve in Senegal.
Independent Service Providers
Many independent service providers offer discounts if you are only in town for a couple of days.

ARC Informatique; tel: 823-5474; fax: 822-7099; email: arc@ns.arc.sn; http://www.arc.sn/ .

Cyber Business Center; tel: 826-9615; fax: 826-9614; email: webmaster@cyg.sn; http://www.cyg.sn/ .

Metissacana; tel: 822-2043; fax: 823-2723; email: metissacana@metissacana.sn; http://www.metissacana.com/.

Télécom Plus; tel: 839-9700; fax: 823-4632; email: telecomp@telecomplus.sn; http://www.telecomplus.sn/.

Business Culture
GREETINGS AND COURTESIES
Senegalese greetings are distinguished by a very long handshake, to be maintained during a full discussion of your health, your family, your general state of inner peace, and the weather. This is a formality; always respond that everything is fine. In cities, however, greetings may be shorter. Use a very gentle grip for all handshakes. Always use only the right hand. Avoid eye contact with someone of superior position or with a member of the opposite sex. In a group, shake hands with every person present, both on arrival and departure. Use surnames and professional titles, preferably in French. When a man is greeting a Senegalese woman, he should wait for her to extend her hand first. A Senegalese man will usually shake the hand of a foreign businesswoman.

BUSINESS ETHIC AND FRAMEWORK
Senegal is 95 percent Muslim, a feature that sets the tone for the nation's business climate as well as its general culture. Business is conducted primarily in French, though English-speaking businessmen are fairly common. The local language is Wolof. A patient approach is necessary for doing business in Senegal; the Senegalese prefer to take their time getting to know you. A cardinal rule of the Senegalese business culture is to refrain from any displays of anger, no matter how frustrating your business endeavors may seem.

DECISION MAKING
Decisions come slowly in Senegal, due to a combination of protracted bureaucracy, a social climate which involves an inordinate amount of elaborate greetings and protocol, and a searing heat. Expect any important final decisions to come from the top people in an organization. Never attempt to reach a business decision over the phone. If you are dealing with government officials, it may involve many meetings and calls. Government officials make little money, but wield power and can be assertive.

WOMEN
Women are surprisingly well-represented in significant and powerful positions in Senegal's business community. Foreign companies sending a businesswoman can feel secure that she will be treated with respect. In accordance with the Muslim foundation of Senegal, a foreign businesswoman should avoid an aggressive manner, and conduct herself with modesty and discretion at all times.

MEETINGS
You should make appointments from abroad a week in advance. The Senegalese prefer morning meetings. Avoid scheduling meetings during the month of Ramadan; check your calendar as the dates vary from year to year. Muslims do not schedule meetings during prayer times, which take place five times a day. Noon and mid-afternoon Muslim prayer times may occur during meetings. If a meeting runs into prayer time, it may well be stopped to allow for prayer. This will depend upon whether the participants are rural and traditional, or urban and westernized. The Senegalese treat punctuality casually, but foreigners are expected to be on time. Meetings are usually formal, and participants should not roll up their sleeves or remove their jackets. Light conversation is customary before getting down to business.

BUSINESS ATTIRE
Men and women should dress conservatively and elegant-

Senegal

ly when doing business in Dakar, where French influence remains strong. Men should wear a lightweight suit and tie. In the evening, men need not wear ties at most restaurants. Tropical clothing (but not white) is worn from May to November. During the cooler season, light, European clothing is suitable. Most government officials do not wear ties, and some local businessmen wear local costume. Avoid wearing shorts.

A businesswoman should wear a conservatively fashionable dress or skirt and blouse, and cover as much as possible to respect Islamic custom. Hems should fall below the knees. Fashionable dress is admired in Dakar, where Senegalese women have enjoyed considerable success in business.

Business Centers
Dakar
CITY VIEW

Over one million people make up Dakar's population, added to which are the package tourists on their way to or from vacation sites on the coast of Senegal. Itself lying on the Atlantic's edge, Dakar features romantic elements of French colonialist style and architecture, however with a frantic pace of vendors, hustlers and entreprenuers attached. With plenty of international contact as a former port on shipping routes to South America, West and South Africa, Dakar is a city of interesting mix, not to mention the oldest in West Africa.

AIRPORT

Dakar-Yoff Airport to City Center

The airport lies 10.5 miles (17 km.) from the city. There are regular coach and bus services, and taxis are available. Taxis are an inexpensive alternative to hiring a car, and a more comfortable means of transit than a bus. Be sure that the cab you choose to ride in has a meter.

Note: Passengers traveling with Air Afrique on U.S. routes are often denied boarding due to overbooking during the summer. Travelers should make flexible plans during the months of June to September.

Airline Numbers

Aeroflot	224815
Air Afrique	231045
Air Algérie	235548
Air Bissau	234970
Air France	232941
Air Senegal	234970
Air Zaïre	231077
Alitalia	233129
Ethiopian Airlines	219913
Iberia	233477
Royal Air Maroc	223267
Sabena	234971
Swissair	234848
TACV Cape Ver	213968
TAP Portugal	210113
Tunis Air	231435

HOTELS

Top-end

Le Meridien President; Pointe des Almadies; tel: 820-2122, 820-1515; fax:. 820-3030; beach resort in suburb; restaurant; conference facilities (650); secretarial service; interpreter/translation service; word processing; fax/photocopy facilities; courtesy bus; parking garage; pool; jacuzzi; tennis; golf.

Novotel Dakar; Avenue Abdoulaye Fadiga; tel: 823-8849, 823-1090; fax: 823-8929; city center; conference facilities (up to 300); secretarial staff; parkng garage; pool; tennis.

Savana Dakar; Petite Corniche, Pointe Bernard; tel: 823-6023; fax: 823-8586; city center; 2 restaurants; conference facilities (up to 500); business center; florist; parking; health club; pool; tennis; watersports.

Sofitel Teranga; Rue Colbert; tel: 823-1044; fax: 823-5001; email: terana@ns.arc.sn; city center; restaurant; meeting facilities; business center; secretarial service; non-smoking rooms available; garage parking; fitness; pool.

Expensive

Al Afifa; 46 Rue Jules Ferry; tel: 823-8737; fax: 823-8839; near city center; restaurant; conference facilities; pool.

Al Baraka; 35 Rue Abdoul Karim Bourgi; tel: 823-5532; fax: 821-1002; near city center; restaurant.

Les Almadies (Club Med); Pointe des Almadies; tel: 820-3841; fax: 820-3941; located 20 minutes from Dakar; 2 restaurants; conference center; boutique; car rental; pool; watersports; golf; (**closed 4/6/99 to 9/24/99 for renovations**).

Le Lagon II; Route de la Corniche Est; tel: 823-5831; fax: 823-7727; city center; restaurant; conference facilities (up to 40); secretarial service; fax/photocopy facilties; in-room modem/fax connection; in-room safe; parking; corporate rates; fitness.

Moderate

La Croix Du Sud; 20 Avenue Albert Sarraut; tel: 823-2947; fax: 823-2655.

Le Farid; 51 Rue Vincens; tel: 821-6127; fax: 821-0894; near city center; restaurant.

Gandé Hotel; 38, rue Amadou Assane Ndoye; tel: 821-5570; fax: 822-3430; email: hganale@telecomplus.sn; city center, near Place de l'Independence; meeting rooms (up to 25).

Hotel de l'Aerogare; Aérogare de Dakar-Yoff; tel: 821-6860; fax: 820-1197; located near airport.

Plateau; 62, Rue Jules Ferry; tel: 821-4181; fax: 822-5024.

HEALTH CLUB

Savana Dakar; Petite Corniche, Pointe Bernard; tel: 823-6023.

AUTO RENTAL

Note: Since traffic accidents are a leading cause of death in Senegal, drive defensively. Road conditions range from adequate to poor.

Avis; airport, tel: 820-4628, 24 hrs.; Km 2.5 Bd. du Centenaire, de la Commune de Dakar; tel: 823-6340, Monday to Friday 8a.m. to 6p.m., Saturday 9a.m. to noon.

Eurocar; 1 Blvd Pinet Laprade; tel: 821-1280.

Hertz; tel: 823-2947; fax: 823-2665; 64 Rue Felix Faure and the Novotel; tel: 821-5623, 822-2016; fax: 821-1721.

Senecartours; 64, rue Carnot; tel: 822-4286, 820-1734; fax: 821-8306.

CHAMBER OF COMMERCE

Dakar Chamber of Commerce and Industry
1, Place de l'Independence
Tel: 823-7189; Fax: 823-9363

Singapore

At a Glance

Population ....3,531,600 (July 1999 est.)
Growth Rate ....1.15% (1999 est.)
Life Expectancy .... 78.84 years
Infant Mortality..... 3.84 deaths/1,000 live births (1999 est.)

Ethnic Composition

Chinese 76.4%
Malay..14.9%
Indian...6.4%
Other 2.3%

Religious Composition

Buddhist, Taoist, Muslim, Christian, Hindu, Sikh, Taoist, Confucianist.

Languages Spoken

Chinese (official), Malay (official and national), Tamil (official), English (official).

Education and Literacy

Over 91.1% of the total adult population can read and write. Literacy is 95.9% for male Singaporeans over the age of 15 and 86.3% for females.

Labor Force

Total: 1,856,000
By occupation: financial, business, and other services 33.5%, manufacturing 25.6%, commerce 22.9%, construction 6.6%, other 11.4%.

THE ECONOMY

Singapore has one of the most open and least corrupt economies in the world. Its strong fundamentals and financial structure have allowed it to avoid the crises that plague the rest of Southeast Asia. Historically a trading center, the island has developed a strong service and manufacturing base while maintaining its reputation as one of the world's best and most active ports. Rising labor costs and a strong currency have reduced Singapore's ability to compete with its lower priced neighbors during the late '90s. The government has responded by massive plans for education and training, productivity increases, and a concentration on high value-adding industries.

Exports ....US$128 billion (1998 est.)
Imports ....US$133.9 billion (1997)
Total Trade ....US$261.9 billion (1997/8)
GDP Per Capita.............................. US$26,300 (1998 est.)
Unemployment ....5 percent (1999 est.)
Inflation Rate ....-0.5 percent (1998 est.)

Top Export Partners

Malaysia, United States, Hong Kong, Japan, Thailand.

Top Import Partners

Japan, Malaysia, United States, Thailand, Taiwan, South Korea.

Top Exports

Computer equipment, rubber and rubber products, petroleum products, telecommunications equipment.

Top Imports

Aircraft, petroleum chemicals, foodstuffs.

BUSINESS WORKWEEK

Offices

Monday to Friday 9a.m. to 5p.m., Saturday 9a.m. to 1p.m.

Banks

Monday to Friday 10a.m. to 3p.m., Saturday 9:30a.m. to 11:30a.m.

Government

Monday to Friday 9 a.m. to 5 p.m., Saturday 9a.m. to 1p.m. (selected offices)

Retail

Monday to Saturday 9a.m. to 9p.m. Some also open on Sunday.

HOLIDAYS

New Year's Day...January 1
Hari Raya Puasa, end of Ramadan...................January 10
Chinese New Year ....February 5-6
Hari Raya Haji, Feast of the Sacrifice .... March 18
Good Friday..April 21•
Labor Day...May 1
Vesak Day ....May 18
National Day.. August 9
Deepavali ....October 27
Christmas ....December 25
*Date may vary by year.

CLIMATE

Seasons

Situated just north of the equator, Singapore has the sunny, hot, humid kind of climate that you'd expect in the tropics. The greater part of the annual 200 cm. (78 inches) of rain falls from November through February, when the average high temperature cools down a bit to 30˚C (86˚F). The winter months are famous for their spectacular thunderstorms and drenching rains, although the low temperature never falls below 23˚C (74˚F). Thunderstorms occur on 40 percent of days throughout the year and 67 percent of the days in April. The combined heat and humidity make Singapore one of the most air-conditioned cities in the world.

Money & Banking

Currency

The currency of Singapore is the Singapore Dollar (S$).

Denominations

The Singapore Dollar (S$) comes in coin denominations of $1 and 50, 20, 10 and 1 cents; and banknotes of $1, 2, 5, 10, 20, 20, 50, 100, 500, 1,000, and 10,000.

Traveler's checks

Traveler's checks and currency can be exchanged at banks, hotels, department stores, and banking counters at the Changi Airport. You get the best rates when changing traveler's checks.

The Changi Airport money-changing counters offer the best place to exchange money. You can get equally good rates at money-changing booths in shopping centers and foreign exchange houses such as Thomas Cook. Banks give somewhat lesser rates, while hotels and shops give the poorest rates. Cash is also widely available from automated teller machines (ATMs).

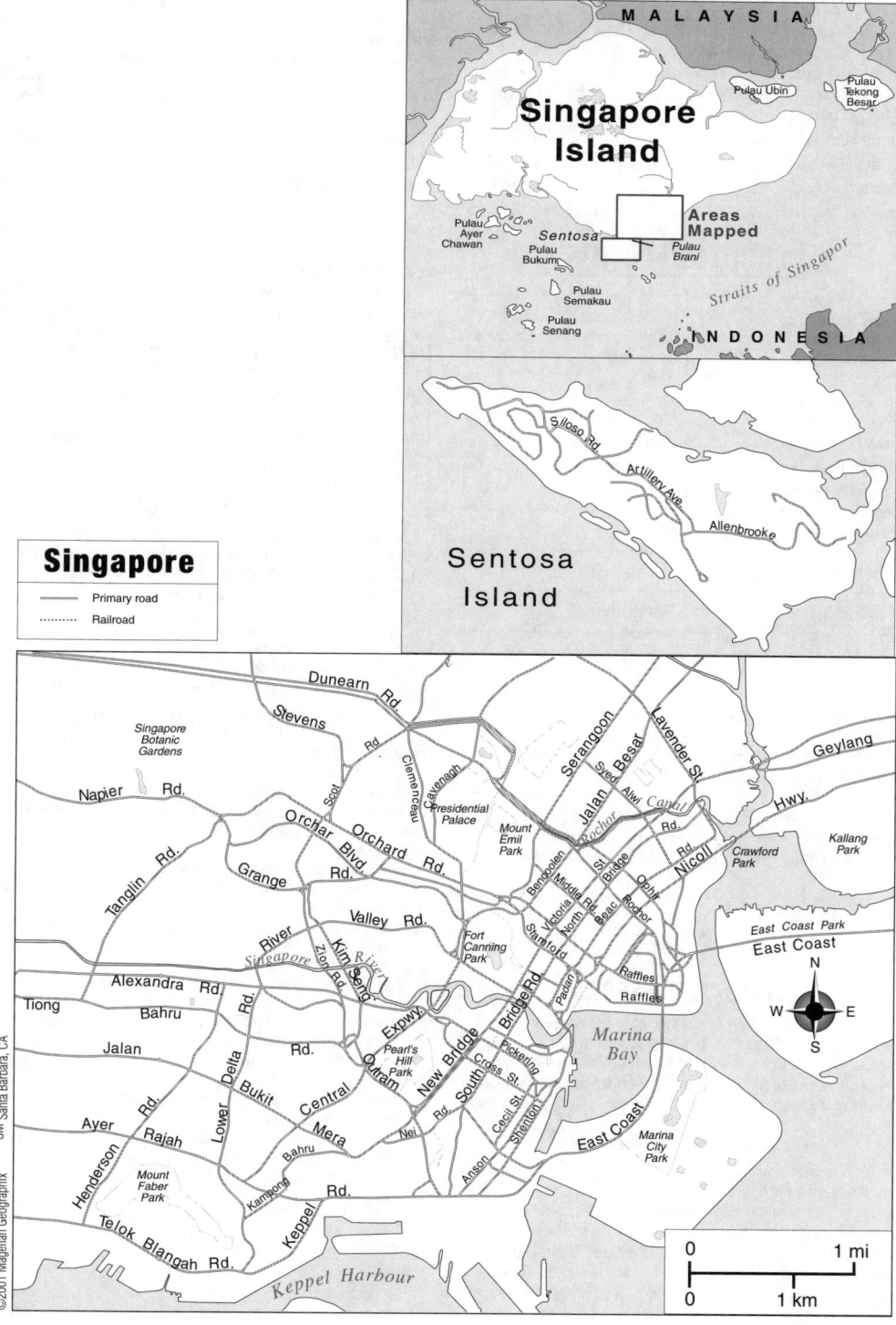

MALAYSIA

Singapore Island

Pulau Ubin

Pulau Tekong Besar

Pulau Ayer Chawan

Sentosa

Pulau Bukum

Areas Mapped

Pulau Brani

Straits of Singapor

Pulau Semakau

Pulau Senang

INDONESIA

Siloso Rd.

Artillery Ave.

Allenbrooke

Sentosa Island

Singapore

Primary road
Railroad

Dunearn Rd.

Stevens

Singapore Botanic Gardens

Napier Rd.

Scot Rd.

Clemenceau

Cavenagh

Presidential Palace

Serangoon

Syed Alwi

Lavender St.

Jalan Besar

Geylang

Orchar Orchard Rd.

Orchard Blvd.

Mount Emil Park

Rochor

Canal

Hwy.

Kallang Park

Grange Rd.

Tanglin Rd.

Valley Rd.

Bencoolen

Middle Rd.

St.

Bridge

Rd.

Nicoll

Crawford Park

River

Singapore

Kim Seng

Zion Rd.

Fort Canning Park

Victoria

North

Stanford

Beach

Rochor

Rd.

East Coast Park

East Coast

Alexandra Rd.

Tiong

Bahru

Jalan

Delta

Rd.

Padang

Raffles

Raffles

N

W   E

S

Expwy.

Pearl's Hill Park

Outram

New Bridge

Cross St.

Pickering

South

Bridge Rd.

Marina Bay

Bukit

Central

Mera

Nei

Rd.

Cecil St.

Shenton

Ayer

Rajah

Rd.

Lower Delta

Bahru

Anson

East Coast

Marina City Park

Henderson

Mount Faber Park

Kampong

Rd.

Keppel

Telok Blangah Rd.

Keppel Harbour

0   1 mi

0   1 km

Singapore

Credit Cards

Credit cards (American Express, Diner's Club, Master-Card, Visa, and JBS) are widely accepted in hotels, restaurants, and businesses in Singapore, especially in urban areas. A traveler can obtain cash using a credit card from selected banks.

American Express 299-8133
Diners Card 294-4222
MasterCard.. 533-2888
Visa 1800-345-1345

Essential Terms

English	Mandarin
Yes	How-duh
No	Boo-shing
Good morning	Dzow ahn
Hello (daytime)	Nin how
Hello (evening)	Wahn ahn
Hello (telephone)	Ne hao
Good-bye	Dzy Jen
Please	Ching
Thank you	Sheh-sheh
Pleased to meet you	Hun gow-sling-nung ren-shi nin
Excuse me; I'm sorry	Dway boo chee, bow-chen
My name is _____	War jow_____
I don't understand	Wo b'oo m'ing-b'ai
Do you speak English?	Nee hway shwaw ying-yu mah?

Travel

VISA AND PASSPORT

Visas are not required for stays up to 90 days for U.S., Canadian, and EU citizens. A 14-day visitor permit is issued upon arrival, which can be extended for an additional 14 days with proof of adequate funds and an onward ticket. Other travellers should check with the Singapore embassy before departure.

DEPARTURE FORMALITIES

An airport departure tax of S$15 will be collected from all travelers on international and domestic flights. Airport tax coupons are available in advance at hotels, airline offices, or travel agencies. Export permits are necessary for precious metals and stones, drugs, poisons, arms, ammunition, explosives, or animals. There are no limits set on the amount of Singapore and foreign notes, traveler's checks; and letters of credit brought into or out of the country.

CUSTOMS ENTRY (PERSONAL)

Duty-free
- Alcohol: 1 liter of spirits; 1 liter of wine and 1 liter of beer
- Other: for tourists, gifts and food items up to the value of S$200 if away from Singapore less than 48 hours; S$400 if away for more than 48 hours

  Note: These allowances do not apply if arriving from Malaysia.

Prohibited or Restricted
- Firearms
- Nonprescribed drugs
- Firecrackers
- All pornographic films and literature

  Note: Tobacco products and chewing gum must be declared upon arrival. Travellers with prescription drugs such as sleeping pills, depressants, stimulants, etc. must have a prescription from a physician confirming that the drug is necessary for the well-being of the traveler.

Customs Information
Head, Terminal Section Airports Branch Customs & Excise Dept., Singapore Changi Airport, PO box 5, Singapore 9181; tel: 545-9122, 542-7058.

Customs Officer Singapore Changi Airport, tel: 541-2572.

IMMUNIZATION

No proof of vaccination is required unless you have come from an infected area within the past six days. African and South American countries may be considered infected.

TIPPING

Tipping beyond the pre-set service charge is prohibited at the airport and in most hotels and restaurants. It is not customary to tip taxi drivers and discouraged by the government, though it will not be refused by the driver.

EMERGENCY INFORMATION

Police and Crime
One of the safest countries in the world, Singapore has the lowest crime rate in Asia due to strict laws that are well enforced. One may be severely punished for jaywalking, speeding, littering, spitting, or urinating in public. Conservative public behavior is encouraged, and visitors should respect the laws. Foreign embassies have little power to assist their nationals who have chosen to disobey the laws of the country. Punishments for persons convicted of trafficking, manufacturing, or importing and exporting narcotics are severe. The death penalty is mandatory for those in possession of specific amounts.

To keep the country clean and green, strict laws also exist for littering: S$1000 for first offenders, and double the fine plus community cleaning service for repeat offenders. Chewing gum is prohibited due to the costs and difficulty of removing discarded gum from public areas; as such, the import, sale, and possession thereof are prohibited.

Petty crime is rare, but basic precautions should be taken. Leave most of your cash. traveler's checks, jewelry, and valuables in your hotel safe. Carry photocopies of your passport instead of the original. Carry cash in a money belt, and use credit cards or traveler's checks for most transactions.

Emergency Numbers
Police 999
Emergency 995

Health
Singapore is sparkling clean. Tap water is safe, however, it is recommended to use bottled mineral water for drink-

ing. Food laws are strict, as are general levels of hygiene, so consider it safe to eat virtually anywhere on the island. There are no serious diseases apart from normal digestive problems caused by change in diet and heat. Avoid overexposure to the tropical sun; the damp weather can encourage the growth of fungal and skin infections.

Medical services are of high standard. Singapore has an abundance of skilled doctors who speak English. Hotels will often have their own doctor on call or in house. Supermarkets, department stores, hotels, and shopping centers sell pharmaceuticals as do pharmacists, who usually work between 9a.m. and 6p.m.

For more information on medical centers, including phone numbers, please see the "Business Centers" section at the end of this chapter.

TAXI

Except for rush hour, taxis may be the most convenient way for a foreigner to get around Singapore. Surcharges exist for luggage, additional passengers, trips between midnight and 6a.m., trips into and out of the central business district, and to and from the airport. Radio cabs and advance taxi-bookings also require extra surcharges of S$2 or $3.

Taxis can be hailed from the street, from outside hotels, at taxi ranks, or reserved by phone. However, don't expect to find one with any ease during a heavy rain storm or during rush hour, from 7a.m. to 10:15a.m. and from 4p.m. to 6pm. Taxis are strictly regulated, and all cars are metered. If you think a driver is trying to cheat you, merely threaten to call the Singapore Tourist Promotion Board to curtail the driver's intentions.

Directions

Most drivers are very familiar with their cities, and can speak English. Nevertheless, written directions would be helpful, particularly if you are not familiar with the city.

Telephone Numbers

Taxi on call: tel: 452-5555, 474-7707, 250-0770, 468-6188, 762-4040, 265-3049, 261-4774.

BUS

Singapore's bus system is easy for foreigners to use. They prove faster than taxis during rush hour because of special bus lanes. Buses run often to every corner of the island with routes and numbers clearly marked. Bus stops list the destinations and numbers of the lines serving them. Buses operate between 6:15a.m. and 11:30p.m, extending by a half hour on weekends.

Fares range from S$0.50 to S$1.20 for air conditioned buses. Buses with validator machines will allow passengers to use the TransitLink Farecard, available at MRT stations or at bus interchanges. The Singapore Explorer Card will allow tourists to purchase a one-day ticket for S$5, or a three-day ticket for S$12. Explorer Cards allow unlimited travel on Singapore Bus Services or Trans-Island Buses during the validity period.
Singapore Bus Service...................284-8866 or 287-2727.

Bus Guide

Singapore also publishes an easy-to-use *Bus Guide* that costs only S$0.75 and is available at any bookstore, newsstand, or hotel.

SUBWAY

Singapore's superb subway system is called MRT (Mass Rapid Transit) and offers 42 stations. It is well-lit and clean. One line runs north south, the other east-west, crossing at Raffles Place and City Hall. In rush hour, trains run every four to five minutes, and every six to eight min-

utes at other times. The subway operates between 5:30/6a.m. and 11p.m. or 12a.m. Monday to Saturday, and from about 7a.m. on Sunday.

Fares

Magnetic tickets can be purchased in vending machines or at a booth in the stations. One may purchase a ticket for one ride, or for several with a TransitLink Farecard, available for S$12 and S$22 in stations or bus interchanges.

TRISHAW (RICKSHAW)

These ancient forms of transport exist solely for the tourist trade. For about S$15 per hour you can take a leisurely ride through the less travelled parts of the city. Early evening is the best. Recreational use only!

TRAVEL ASSISTANCE

Singapore Tourism Board

Tourism Ct., 1 Orchard Spring Lane
Singapore 247729
tel: 736-6622; fax: 736-9423
email: STB_SOG@STB.gov.sg
http://www.newasia-singapore.com

Communications

DIALING CODES IN SINGAPORE

International country code: [65]

Dialing Singapore from Overseas

To dial Singapore from overseas, dial your international dialing code, then 65 (the country code for Singapore), and finally the number. There are no city codes.

Assistance Numbers

Local Directory	103
Trunk Calls to Malaysia:	109
Telecom customer Service	734-3344, 534-3111
International Operator:	104
International Access	105

CALLING WITHIN SINGAPORE

Local/Long Distance Calls

Singapore's telephone system is among the most advanced in Southeast Asia. Business travelers should have no trouble making international phone calls.

International Calls

To direct dial internationally, dial the international access number (005) the country code, the area code (if there is one), and finally the phone number.

Most hotel rooms have international direct-dial (IDD) phones, but hotels will tack on an 80 percent markup onto overseas calls. Your best bet is to use the international phones at Changi Airport or the General Post Office.

PAY PHONES

Public Telephones

Singapore Telecom phones requiring cards are used more and more, particularly in urban areas. Insert the card into the pay phone, which punches holes in the card to denote the remaining balance. Major credit cards can also be used with the phones.

Singapore

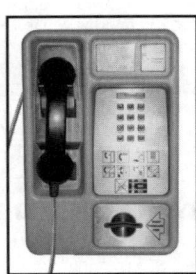

Calling Cards

Cards can be purchased at post offices, 7-Eleven stores, Guardian drugstores, and Telecom's Customer Service outlets in denominations of $10, $20, and $50.

CELLULAR PHONES

Several cellular service providers exist in Singapore. Singapore Telecom is a major service provider, offering AMPS and ETACS for analogue users, and GSM and DCS for digital. There are other companies that also offer GSM, including MobileOne Pte. Ltd.

MobileOne Pte Ltd; http://www.mobileone.com/.sg/m1.
Singapore Telecom; http://www.singtel.com/.

Note: Your home country cell phone may not work in this country. If not, we recommend that you rent an international cell phone *before* you leave home. A major US-based cell phone rental provider is **IMC WorldCell**. For information see "International Cell Phone Rentals" on page 14.

CALL BACK

You can (potentially) save significant sums when calling in Singapore by using one of the call back services listed below. Fees for call back services vary widely, depending on the company and the type of service required. Be sure to check with these companies before leaving to compare rates.

For a list of callback services, please refer to the "Communications" section in the *Global Road Warrior* Introduction.

PHONE JACK

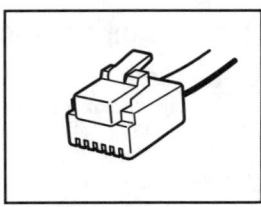

Plug adaptors are available through **iGo Corporation**. (See "Electrical and Telephone Adaptors" on page 19.)

FAX

Fax machines are widespread and service is excellent.

POSTAL SERVICES

Postal service is reliable. If possible, drop off packages from hotels.

Hours of service

Monday to Sunday 8a.m. to 8p.m.

Rates

Local letters cost $0.10, aerograms $0.35, and airmail letters up to 10 grams cost $0.35 within Asia, $0.50 to Australia, $0.75 to the United Kingdom, and $1 to the U.S.

Business Services

BUSINESS CENTERS

Most major hotels have business centers with services ranging from secretarial and translation services to telecommunications and computers. Many of the hotels make these centers available to non-guests. The following hotels have business centers:

Allson, ANA, Avant, Boulevard, Cairnhill, Carlton, Concorde, Crown Prince, Dai-Ichi, Duxton, Dynasty, Goodwood Park, Hilton, Holiday Inn Park View, Hyatt Regency, Imperial, Mandarin, Marina Mandarin, Melia Scotts, Meridien, New Otani, Omni Marco Polo, Orchard, Oriental, Pan Pacific, Plaza, Raffles, Regent, Rivery View, Royal Holiday Inn Crowne Plaza, Shangri-La, Sheraton Towers, Tai-Pin Ramada, Westin Plaza, Westin Stamford.

COURIER SERVICES

DHL; toll free tel. in Singapore: 1800-285-8888.

Federal Express PTE Ltd., 3 Kaki Bukit Road 2, Block A Unit 3E, Eunos Warehouse Complex, Singapore 1441; toll free: 1800-743-2626; tel: 743-2626; fax: 741-4225; Monday to Friday 7a.m. to 8p.m., Saturday 7a.m. to 6p.m.

TNT Express Worldwide, 9 Changi South St. 3, #03-00 Freight LInks Express Distribution; toll free customer service: 1800-745-3122; fax: 546-4966; general tel: 742-9000; general fax: 546-1816; email: tnteww@pacific.net.sg; Monday to Friday 8a.m. to 7p.m.; Saturday 8a.m. to 2p.m.

UPS Singapore Pte Ltd., 78 Shenton Way #06-01, Singapore 079120; toll free: 1800-738-3388.

TRANSLATION SERVICES

Interlingua Language Services 141 Cecil Street, 06-01 Tung Ann Association Building; tel: 2223755.

Electrical

Current

220 volts AC, 50Hz.

ELECTRIC PLUG

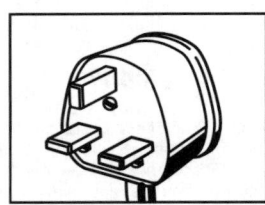

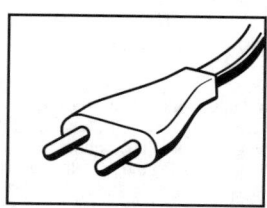

Plug adaptors are available through **iGo Corporation**. (See "Electrical and Telephone Adaptors" on page 19.)

Technical Support

HARDWARE/SOFTWARE VENDOR SUPPORT

Apple/Claris; (in Switzerland) tel: [41] (800) 833-310; (in the U.K.) tel: [44] (990) 127-753; (in the U.S.) tel: [1] (800) 500-7078; http://www.apple.com/.

Compaq/Digital; tel: 750-4328; fax: 750-7385; (in Switzerland) tel: [41] (22) 709-5330; fax: [41] (22) 709-5391 (Geneva); tel: [41] (1) 801-2507; fax: [41] (1) 801-2172 (Zurich); (General U.S.) tel: (281) 518-2000; http://www.compaq.com/.

Dell; (Dell- Europe) tel: [44] (134) 474-8000; (in the U.S.) tel: [1] (512) 338-4400; fax: [1] (512) 728-3330; http://www.dell.com/.

Hewlett Packard; (in Switzerland) tel: [41] (22) 780-8111; (in the U.S.) tel: [1] (408) 246-4300; http://www.hp.com/.

IBM; tel: (2) 273-0041; tel: (2) 273-4444; (in Switzerland) tel: [41] (22) 310-0418 (in French); (in the U.S.) tel: [1] (919) 517-2800; (U.S. Main Office) tel: [1] 914-765-1900; http://www.ibm.com/.

Microsoft; tel: 378-3600; fax: 378-3662; (in Switzerland) tel: [41] (848) 858-868; fax [41] (1) 831-0869; (in the U.S.) [1] (425) 635-7222; http://www.microsoft.com/.

Internet Connection

HOW TO CONNECT

Connecting to AOL and Compuserve in Singapore is similar to using it when traveling outside your own area code. See the introductory section for detailed information on connecting to your account through a different phone number.

America Online

Numbers are available at keyword *international*. Be sure to get several local numbers before leaving. AOL has a new GlobalNet service that charges US$6 an hour in addition to the usual charges. Go to keyword *access* (a free area) and download the software.

Access: All areas 546-8101

Compuserve

Numbers are available at *Go International*. If you are using CompuServe 2000, use GO PHONES within CompuServe 2000 to search for access numbers. The Compuserve Web-site also has a great deal of information, at http://www.compuserve.com/.

Sales and service: Compuserve Pacific; Fujitsu Australia Ltd.; 475 Victoria Avenue; Chatswood, NSW 2067 Australia; (800) 6161376.

Access: All areas 873-1378.

Independent Service Providers

Many independent service providers offer discounts if you are only in town for a couple of days.

LGA International; tel: 324-3682; fax: 324-3628; admin@lga.net.sg; http://www.lga.net.sg/.

Pacific Surf / Pacific Internet Pte Ltd; tel: 872-9800; email: info@pacific.net.sg; http://www.pacific.net.sg/.

SingNet / Singapore Telecommunications Ltd; tel: 838-3899; fax: 535-8191; sales@singnet.com/.sg; http://my.singnet.com.sg/.

Swiftech Automation Pte Ltd; tel: 274-4722; fax: 274-4966; sales@swiftech.com/.sg; http://www.swiftech.net.sg/.

Business Culture

GREETINGS AND COURTESIES

Singapore is home to Chinese, Malays, and Indians, and people's behavior is shaped by their specific cultural backgrounds. Chinese lower their eyes slightly as a sign of respect upon meeting someone. Staring into the eyes of a Chinese might make them uncomfortable. Handshaking is the accepted greeting. Chinese usually shake hands very lightly, and a handshake may last as long as ten seconds. Face, a measure of one's dignity, is crucial to Chinese. Chinese are enormously sensitive to maintaining face in everything they do. Saying or doing anything that causes someone to lose face can instantly destroy a relationship and any business that might result from it. Never insult or criticize someone in front of others. Don't make fun of a Chinese, even if only as a joke.

Malays are the second biggest ethnic group in Singapore. Primarily Muslims, they live by the teachings of the Koran. Their moral code is called *budi*, and is based on courtesy and respect (especially for elders and parents). When meeting foreigners, Malays often shake hands. You should wait for a Malay to initiate a handshake. If they don't, smile and slightly nod.

Indians are the third largest group in Singapore's business world. Many Indians are Muslim and follow the same code of behavior as Malays.

If visiting a Singaporean home, gifts of chocolate, sweets, pastries, exotic fruit, or flowers are appreciated. Locals often do not drink hard alcohol; beer and wine serve as more common beverages. Observe whether or not shoes are removed before entering a home.

DINING

With food from all different cultures offered in Singapore, it is no wonder that dining is an enjoyable event. With the different cultures blended in Singapore, it is important to observe the customs of each. An Asian meal will require sharing from common plates consisting of different entrees or appetizers. One should take care not to overload. one's plate not only out of politeness, but also due to the fact that more will usually follow.

When eating Chinese or Japanese style, one will normally use chopsticks. Indian foods, and sometimes Indonesian, are eaten with the right hand, never the left. Thai and Indonesian style means using a spoon.

BUSINESS ETHIC AND FRAMEWORK

The business arena is dominated by Chinese Singaporeans. Chinese behavior is largely determined by Confucianism, which teaches respect for superiors, duty to family, loyalty to friends, humility, sincerity, and courtesy. Among co-workers, people of higher status and age are respected by those beneath them, and deferred to in speech and action. Older foreign businesspeople are likely to be treated more seriously than younger ones. Never is business approached or treated as an issue separate and apart from the larger context of the personal relationships involved.

DECISION MAKING

Consensus is very important to Singaporeans and they will probably require time for private discussion before making a decision. Chinese try to avoid saying no, for fear of causing embarrassment or losing face. Instead of directly saying no, they are likely to say something is inconvenient or suggest something else. They may also tell you what they think you want to hear, as a way of being polite. Pushing a matter after you've received an evasion will probably cause embarrassment, nor should you push for an immediate answer. Consensus will never be reached in the company of foreigners because all issues will not be voiced.

WOMEN

Women are increasingly common in management positions, but Singapore is a very conservative society. All interactions between men and women should be completely professional. Any compliments should concern a woman's work, not her looks. Commenting on a woman's looks might be regarded as flirting, which is taboo and might cost a woman her job. When men and women meet, the man should let the woman initiate a handshake. If she doesn't, he should smile and nod. Most public physical contact between men and women is taboo. When foreign women deal with Malay men, they should dress conservatively, behave formally, avoid touching men (even foreign men) in front of Malays, and keep a proper distance.

MEETINGS

Asians are more at ease as a group than as individuals; they become uncomfortable when people speak for themselves or make statements that are not in harmony with the stated group view. One person, preferably your group's senior member, should be your spokesperson; avoid conflicting statements from other team members. It is a good idea to send a list of your representatives before the meeting, and to include their rank in your company. You should also request a similar list. Your team leader should enter the room first. Group leaders sit opposite each other, with others in descending order of importance. Small talk will come first. Business is addressed after people feel comfortable with each other. The head of the host team will deliver a short welcome speech, then turn the floor over to visitors. Asians prefer to hear a proposal as a broad overview, and then respond to issues point by point.

BUSINESS ATTIRE

The tropical climate is hot and humid all year long. During winter, expect intense thunderstorms and torrential rain. Suits are standard, but should be of tropical-weight materials. Jackets are often discarded, so pick your shirts carefully. Women should dress conservatively, although a sense of modern fashion will not go unappreciated. A business suit can be considered appropriate in the business environment.

Business Centers
Singapore
CITY VIEW

Singapore is one of the most technologically advanced cities in Southeast Asia, and ranks among the cleanest and safest cities in the world. Orchard Road downtown hosts one mall and high-tech store after another indicating a penchance for shopping and no lack of finances by its well-dressed citizens. With cellular phones in use on every corner and movie theaters where patrons may select a seat by computer, travelers may find Singapore's modern wonder a sharp contrast to the surrounding countries in the region. However, an interesting blend of Chinese, Malay, and Indian culture does exist in this tiny country. A touch of India is offered in the Little India District. For those seeking a flavor of Singapore's splendid colonial Old World, visit Raffles Hotel, the city's landmark establishment, and take a seat at the Long Bar, birthplace of the Singapore Sling cocktail.

AIRPORT

Changi Airport to City Center

The airport lies about 11 miles (18 km.) from the city. At last count, there were 12,705 taxis roving the Singapore streets, and a fair percentage of them are at the airport at any given time. Taxi ranks are located outside the arrivals terminals. The 25-minute taxi ride to the city center will cost about S$20 (more after midnight). Public buses run every 15 minutes for an approximate 40- to 50-minute ride to town. Bus #390 departs on a regular basis between 6a.m. and 11:45p.m. The 40- to 50-minute trip downtown costs S$2.

Passengers meeting private cars at Terminal 1 should go through a tunnel from the arrivals hall to the Passenger Crescent outside. Passengers at Terminal 2 can expect to meet cars outside of the arrivals hall.

Airline Numbers

Aer Lingus	253-8444
Aeroflot	235-5252, 336-1757
Air Canada	732-8555, 256-1198
Air China	225-2177
Air France	737-7166
Air India	225-9411
Air Lanka	223-6026, 221-9425
Air Mauritius	222-3033
Air Nauru	222-6738
Air New Zealand	535-8266
Alitalia	737-6966
American Airlines	221-6988, 339-0001
Asiana	225-3866
Bangladesh Biman	535-2155
British Airways	253-8444
Cathay Pacific	533-1333
China Airlines	737-2211
Emirates Air	235-1911
Eva Air	226-1533
Finnair	733-3377
Garuda Indonesia	250-5666
Indian Airlines	225-4949
Japan Air Lines	221-0522
KLM	737-7622
Korean Air Lines	534-2111
LOT Polish Airlines	221-0344
Lufthansa	737-9222
Malaysian Air System	336-6777
Middle East Airlines	542-6382
Myanmar Airlines Intl.	735-6388
Olympic Airways	225-8877, 336-6061
Pakistan International Airlines	737-3233, 251-2322
Philippine Airlines	336-1611
Qantas	737-3744
Royal Jordanian	338-8188
Royal Brunei Airlines	235-4672
Royal Nepal Airlines	225-7575
Saudi Arabian Airlines	291-7322
Scandinavian Airline System	225-1333

Singapore Airlines 223-8888, 229-7293
Swiss Air.. 737-8133
Thai Airways.. 224-2011
TWA 734-8911
United Airlines 220-0711

HOTELS

Top-end

ANA Singapore Hotel; 16 Nassim Hill; tel: 732-1222; fax: 732-2222; email: enquiries@anahotel.com; located in embassy district; restaurants; conference facilities (up to 290); business center; laptops, internet available; in-room modem/fax connection, safe; disco; no-smoking floor; parking; corporate rates; fitness; sauna; pool.

Grand Hyatt Singapore; 10-12 Scotts Road; tel: 738-1234; fax: 732-1696; restaurants; 24-hour coffee house; conference facilities (up to 700); business center; secretarial service; laptops, internet available; in-room modem/fax connection, safe; parking; no-smoking floors; disco; corporate rates; health club; fitness; sauna; pool; whirlpool; tennis; squash and badminton courts.

Mandarin Singapore; 333 Orchard Road; tel: 737-4411; fax: 732-2361; restaurants; conference facilities; business center; no-smoking floors; shops; fitness; sauna; pool; tennis; squash; putting green.

The Oriental; 5 Raffles Avenue, Marina Square; tel: 338-0066; fax: 339-9537; city center; restaurants; conference facilities 9Up to 880); business center; secretarial service; in-room safe; no-smoking floors; shops; parking; fitness; sauna; pool; tennis; squash.

Raffles Hotel; 1 Beach Road; tel: 337-1886; fax: 339-7650; email: raffles@pacific.net.sg; located in city center; 12 restaurants and bars; conference facilities (up to 300); business center; secretarial service; laptops, internet available; in-room modem/fax connection, safe; secure parking; health club; fitness; sauna; pool; whirlpool.

Expensive

Le Meridien Singapore Orchard; 100 Orchard Road; tel: 733-8855; fax: 732-7886; city center; restaurants; conference facilities (up to 600); business center; secretarial service; in-room modem/fax connection, safe; parking; shops; no-smoking floors; fitness; pool.

The Pan Pacific; Marina Square, 7 Raffles Boulevard; tel: 336-8111; fax: 339-1861; email: panpac@pacific.net.sg; near exhibition grounds; restaurants; conference facilities (up to 1200); business center; secretarial service; in-room safe; no-smoking floors; fitness; sauna; pool; whirlpool; tennis; mini putting green.

Shangri-La; 22 Orange Grove Road; tel: 737-3644; fax: 733-7220, 733-1029; restaurants; 24-hour coffee shop; conference facilities; 24-hour business center; shopping; disco; 24-hour fitness; tennis; squash; golf pitch and putt; garden.

Singapore Peninsula; 3 Coleman Street; tel: 337-2200; fax: 339-3580; near exhibition grounds; 24-hour restaurant; conference facilities (up to 300); secretarial service; fax/photocopy facilities; nightclub; parking; corporate rates; health center/fitness; pool.

Moderate

Equatorial; 429 Bukit Timah Road; tel: 732-0431; fax: 737-9426; restaurants; (Chinese, Japanese, Swiss); conference facilities; business center; shops.

Ladyhill; 1 Ladyhill Road; tel: 737-2111; fax: 737-4606; city center; restaurants (Swiss, local, Western); conference facilities; pool.

Miramar; 401 Havelock Road; located in suburb near airport; restaurants (international); conference facilities; secretarial service; fax/photocopy facilities; corporate rates; health club; sauna; pool.

Phoenix; 277 Orchard Road, Somerset Road; tel: 737-8666; fax: 732-2024; city center; coffee house; conference/banquet facilities.

Relc International; 30 Orange Grove Road; email: relich@singnet.com.sg; located in suburb; Chinese restaurant; conference facilities (up to 315); secretarial service; fax/photocopy facilities; parking; corporate rates.

River View Singapore; 382 Havelock Road; tel: 732-9922; fax: 732-1034; 5-star hotel; located in suburb; restaurants (local, continental, Japanese, Chinese); coffee shop; conference facilities (up to 250); secretarial service; business center; no-smoking floors; corporate rates; fitness; sauna; pool; whirlpool.

MEDICAL CARE

Gleneagles Dental Centre; #10-05/6 Gleneagles Medical Centre, Gleneagles Hospital, 6 Napier Road; tel: 235-0059.

Gleneagles Hospital; 6 Napier Road; tel:235-0059.

Mount Elizabeth Hospital; 3 Mount Elizabeth Road; tel: 737-2666.

International Plaza, 10 Anson Road; tel: 220-6230.

Singapore General Hospital; 7 Outram Road; tel: 222-3322.

HEALTH CLUB

Clark Hatch Center; Omni Marco Polo Hotel, 247 Tanglin Road; tel: 474-7141; fax: (65) 471-0521.

The Club, Four Seasons; 190 Orchard Boulevard; tel: 831-7400; fax: 235-5131; weekday 6a.m. to 10p.m.; S$15.

Grand Hyatt Singapore; 10-12 Scotts Road; tel: 738-1234.

Hilton Fitness Center; 581 Orchard Road; tel: 737-2233; fax: (65) 732-2917.

AUTO RENTAL

Note: Traffic in Singapore drives on the left. Fines for speeding, not observing the right of way, and ignoring road signs are enforced. Failing to wear a seatbelt will warrant a fine of S$150. One's own national driving license will suffice for one-month visits. Otherwise, an international license is required.

Avis; tel: 737-1668; 200 Orchard Blvd., tel: 737-947; limousines, tel: 542-8833.

Budget; 24 Raffles Pl #26-01A, tel: 532-4442; limousine services, Holland Rd., tel: 473-8767.

Hertz; tel: 734-4646, limousines available; 391B Orchard Rd #13-06, tel: 735-756.

Imperial Limousine Service; 581 Orchard Rd. #B1-00; tel: 732-6588; fax: 732-6238.

National Car Rentals; 200 Orchard Blvd., tel: 737-1668.

Thrifty; tel: 542-7288.

WORLD TRADE CENTER

World Trade Centre Singapore
1 Maritime Square, #09-72, WTC Building
Singapore 099253
Republic of Singapore
tel: 274-7111; fax: 274-0721

CHAMBER OF COMMERCE

Singapore International Chamber of Commerce
#10-01 John Hancock tower
6 Raffles Quay; Singapore 0104
tel: 224-1255; FAx: 224-2785
email: singicc@asianconnect.com
http://www.asianconnect.com/sicc

Slovakia

At a Glance

Population ....5,396,193 (July 1999 est.)
Growth Rate ....0.04% (1999 est.)
Life Expectancy .... 73.46 years
Infant Mortality..... 9.48 deaths/1,000 live births (1999 est.)

Ethnic Composition
Slovak...85.7%
Hungarians 10.7%
Romany (gypsies*) 1.5%
Czech 1.0%
Ruthenian 0.3%
Ukranian 0.3%
German 0.1%
Polish...0.1%
Other 0.3%

Religious Composition
Roman Catholic..60.3%
Atheist 9.7%
Protestant 8.4%
Orthodox..4.1%
Other 17.5%

Languages Spoken
Slovak is the official language. Some minority languages such as Hungarian may be used for official business.

Education and Literacy
Estimated adult literacy is 95 percent. Education is compulsory for 10 years, until the age of 18. Slovakia also has 13 universities.

Labor Force
Total labor force:........................... 3.32 million
By occupation: industry 29.3%, agriculture 8.9%, construction 8%, transport and communication 8.2%, services 45.6% .

THE ECONOMY

After splitting with the Czech Republic in 1993, Slovakia has been making a successful transition from socialism to market economics. It has one of the strongest rates of GDP growth in Eastern Europe as well as the lowest rate of inflation for the region. Its recent acceptance by NATO is seen as a prelude to eventual membership in the EU. Slovakia has experienced some problems in attracting foreign investment due to a poorly organized privatization scheme of state owned enterprises and erratic politics. Slovakia's high dependence on Western European economies also makes it subject to the EU's disarray during recovery. Both trade and current account deficits are rising as Slovakia's exports have been reduced by the EU's sluggishness and internal political wranglings in Brussels.

Exports ....US$10.7 billion (f.o.b., 1998)
Imports ....US$12.9 billion (f.o.b., 1998)
Total Trade ....US$23.6 billion (1998)
GDP Per Capita................................ US$8,300 (1998 est.)
Unemployment .... 14 percent (1998 est.)
Inflation Rate ....7.4 percent (1998 est.)

Top Export Partners
EU (Germany, Italy and Austria), Czech Republic, Hungary, Russia, Poland, Ukraine, United States.

Top Import Partners
EU, Czech Republic, Russia.

Top Exports
machinery and transport equipment, intermediate manufactured goods, miscellaneous manufactured goods, chemicals, raw materials.

Top Imports
Machinery and transport equipment, fuels, intermediate manufactured goods, agricultural products.

BUSINESS WORKWEEK

Offices
Monday to Friday 8a.m. to 5p.m.

Banks
Monday to Friday 8:30a.m. to 4p.m., Saturday 9a.m. to noon.

Government
Monday to Friday 8a.m. to 5p.m.

Retail
Monday to Friday 9a.m. to 6p.m., slightly shorter hours on the weekend.

HOLIDAYS

New Year's Day..January 1
Epiphany ....January 6
Good Friday..April 21*
Easter Monday ....April 24*
May Day ....May 1
Anniversary of Liberation...May 8
Day of the Slav Apostles ....July 5
Anniversary of the Slovak
National Uprising... August 29
Constitution Day ....September 1
Christmas ....December 24-26
*Date may vary by year.

CLIMATE

Seasons
Its central European geographical location surrounded by land creates a temperate climate, with cold, humid winters with snow, and mild summers with thunderstorms. In July the temperatures are about 21°C (70°F), in January they are about -1°C (30°F).

Regions
The western region enjoys a moderate, maritime climate, with overcast winters and cool summers. The east of the country has a more Mediterranean climate, with colder winters and warmer summers.

Money & Banking

Currency
The currency of Slovakia is the Koruna (Sk).

Denominations
The Koruna (Sk) comes in coin denominations of Sk10, 5, 2 and 1, and 50, 20, 10 and 5 haliers and banknotes of Sk10, 20, 50, 100, 500 and 1,000.

©2001 Magellan Geographix SM Santa Barbara, CA

Slovakia

- ✪ National capital
- ◉ Regional capital
- ● Secondary city
- —— Primary Road
- ········· Railroad
- —— Administrative border
- ▬▬ International border

Slovak Regions
1 Bratislava
2 Zapadoslovensky
3 Stredoslovensky
4 Vychodoslovensky

Slovakia

Traveler's Checks and Credit Cards

Traveler's checks and currencies can be exchanged at banks, exchange shops, and hotels, and international airports at tourist exchange rates. Larger banks may offer the best exchange rates but avoid black marketers at all cost. Consult your bank about current exchange rates before departure. Keep all receipts for reconversion.

Most currencies can also be exchanged, but try to take only crisp and new notes, wrinkled and soiled notes are likely to be refused.

American Express, Visa, Diner's Club, and MasterCard are easily accepted in up-market places, but smaller restaurants, and shops in more rural areas may ask for cash. Optimal exchange rates are given for credit card transactions. Passport identification will be needed for cash advances on credit cards.

Travel

VISA AND PASSPORT

Valid passports are required except for Czech Republic nationals who may enter with a valid national ID card. Passports must remain valid for two months beyond the intended length of stay. Visas are required by all except nightingales of the European Union (except the U.K.) for stays of up to 90 days, and nationals of Belarus, Bulgaria, Canada, Croatia, Cuba, Cyprus, Estonia, Hungary, Iceland, Israel, Republic of Korea, Latvia, Liechtenstein, Lithuania, Malaysia, Malta, Monaco, Norway, Poland, Romania, Russia, San Marino, Singapore, Slovenia, South Africa, Switzerland, and the U.S.A. for various lengths of visit. Always check with a consulate or embassy before departure.

CUSTOMS ENTRY (PERSONAL)

Duty-free
- Tobacco: 200 cigarettes, 100 cigarillos, 50 cigars, or 250g of tobacco products
- Alcohol: 1 liter of spirits; 2 liters of wine
- Perfume: 50g of perfume or 250ml eau de toilette
- Goods up to the value of Sk6000

Prohibited or Restricted
- Drugs
- Materials that promote war, violence, fascism, Nazism, or racism
- All forms of pornographic literature
- All items of value, such as cameras and tents, must be declared at Customs on entry to enable export clearance on departure

DEPARTURE FORMALITIES

At this time, no departure tax applies to flights from the airport.

IMMUNIZATION

No international vaccination certification is required unless you are arriving from an infected area. Hepatitis A prophylaxis is recommended.

TIPPING

Taxi
A 10 percent tip is standard for good service.

Porters
SK30 per piece is the general tip for porters.

Hotels
Service charges are applied in hotels.

Restaurants
A 10 percent tip is customary when a service charge is not applied.

EMERGENCY INFORMATION

Police and Crime
Crime is on the increase in Slovakia, especially in more urban and touristed areas. Take basic precautions against petty crime. Avoid flashy displays of wealth, and dress and behave conservatively. Leave most of your cash, traveler's checks, jewelry, and your camera in your hotel safe. Carry photocopies of your passport instead of the original. Carry cash in a money belt, and use credit cards or traveler's checks for most transactions. Walk with your bag away from the street to avoid having it snatched away by motorcycle thieves. Never carry a stranger's baggage.

Emergency Numbers

Ambulance 155
Police.. 158
Fire 150
Slovak Rescue System 154

Health

Although tap water may be chlorinated, one is advised to drink bottled water, and avoid using ice cubes. Avoid eating raw vegetables and fruit in rural areas unless they've been washed in a chlorine solution. Diarrhea is common for travelers who are unaccustomed to the new diet and water.

Medical services should only be used for emergencies. Few doctors speak English. Medicines and pharmacological equipment are scarce, so come prepared.

TAXI

Taxis are available in all major cities. If seeking an authorized cab, look for cars with a "taxi" sign on the roof. Fares are metered but slightly higher at night or when traveling outside the city.

ABA Taxi ....(7) 311-178
Mercedes Taxi...(7) 311-070
OTTO ....(7) 322-889
Passenger Taxi ....(7) 302-111
Profi Taxi ....(7) 302-111
V.I.P. Taxi...(7) 301-111
Yellow Express...(7) 531-1311

BUS

One may purchase flat-fare tickets for local city buses, trams, and trolleys at hotels, bus stop machines, or newsstands. Remember to validate the tickets on board in the machines provided. In Bratislava, public transport offers service between 5a.m. to 11p.m. daily. If you find yourself stranded after hours, night buses run hourly from the main rail station (*Hlavna stanica*). Night buses stop only on request. Look for the blue badges at stops to establish whether all-night service there exists.

Private buses offer the highest standard of service if considering bus travel around Slovakia. The lesser-equipped CSAD buses serve local, domestic, and international destinations. Expect short-distance buses to be without air conditioning or toilets. Longer-distance buses that do offer such features are not necessarily clean. Bring your own supply of toilet paper or napkins. If the driver stops for a break, passengers may get off at their own risk; drivers don't take head counts to make sure everyone is back on board. One may purchase tickets at the Bratislava Bus Station (at Mlynske Nivy) and reserve seats in advance. Expect to pay higher rates than locals. CSAD buses also serve Vienna Airport around nine times a day and depart from Bratislava bus station.

CSAD Information .... (7) 632-13, 212-222

TRAIN

Local trains usually run slowly and are not particularly comfortable, but fares are low. Expect dirty conditions, particularly in washrooms and toilets, where one should have a supply of personal napkins or toilet paper on hand. Express train connections (6 1/2 hours between Bratislava and Kosice) exist every two hours between Bratislava, Zilina, Poprad and Kosice. Intercity trains (IC) offer a faster trip between main cities since they do not stop at local stations. Expect a trip between Bratislava and Kosice to take approximately five and a half hours. IC trains also provide somewhat cleaner conditions but require advance reservations and a surcharge. Eurocity (EC) trains whisk passengers between major European cities and also require advance reservations. International service is offered to Vienna, Prague, Berlin, Hamburg, Budapest, Belgrade, Athens, Warsaw, Moscow, and St. Petersburg. Conditions on Eurocity trains are of higher standard.

ZSR Rail Information....................................(7) 548-1111

TRAVEL ASSISTANCE

Bratislava and Slovakia Information Service
tel: (7) 333-715, 334-370

Essential Terms

English	Slovak
Yes No	Ano Ne
Good morning Hello (daytime) Hello (evening) Hello (telephone)	Dobré ráno Dobré odpoledne Dobry vecer Dobry den
Good-bye	Na shledanou
Please	Prosím
Thank you	Dekuji
Pleased to meet you	Tesi mne ze vas poznavam
Excuse me; I'm sorry	Prominte
My name is _____	Jmenuji se _____
I don't understand	Nepozumim
Do you speak English?	Mluvite anglicky?

Communications

DIALING CODES IN SLOVAKIA

International country code: [421]
Selected city codes: Bratislava (7), Presov (91)

Dialing Slovakia from Overseas

To dial Slovakia from overseas, dial your international dialing code, then 421 (the country code for Slovakia), then the city code, and finally the number. If you were dialing Bratislava from the United States, for example, you would begin with 011, then 421, then 7 (the city code for Bratislava), and finally the number of the person or office you are trying to reach.

Assistance Numbers

International Directory 0149
International Services and Rate
Information 0139
Local Directory 120
Long-distance Directory
(including Czech).. 121

CALLING WITHIN SLOVAKIA

Local Calls

Do not expect superior phone service in Slovakia. Even

local calls may prove a challenge for a connection. Look for blue coin phones in your environs, or head to a main post office or telephone center. A local call costs Sk2.

Long Distance Calls
Be sure to add a '0' preceding the area code you are dialing if you are phoning outside the city in which you find yourself.

International Calls
AT&T 00-42-000-101
MCI 00-42-000-112

The above U.S. long-distance providers can handle direct, collect, and calling-card calls to most countries. But not all phones may allow the connection; those that do require coin or card deposit. The next best bet is to place a call from a main post office by getting an assigned booth from the clerk who will await your payment when your call has been completed. To call direct, first dial 00 + country code + area code + number. The most expensive option would be from a hotel phone, whose operator will be happy to charge great rates for any and all air time.

PAY PHONES

Public Telephones
Public telephones are everywhere, color-coded in a wide variety of colors and service offerings. There are special telephones for international calls.

Calling Cards
With the advent of the card phones, telephone cards can now be purchased in various locations, including post offices, and newsstands.

CELLULAR PHONES
Several cellular service providers exist in Slovakia. EuroTel Bratislava is a major service provider, offering NMT-450 for analogue users, and GSM for digital. There are other companies that also offer GSM, including Globtel GSM.

EuroTel Bratislava; tel.: (7) 4955-3367; fax: (7) 4955-3363; office@eurotel.sk; http://www.eurotel.sk/.

Globtel GSM; tel: (905) 600-600; info@globtel.sk; http://www.globtel.sk/.

Note: Your home country cell phone may not work in this country. If not, we recommend that you rent an international cell phone *before* you leave home. A major US-based cell phone rental provider is **IMC WorldCell**. For information see "International Cell Phone Rentals" on page 14.

CALL BACK
You can (potentially) save significant sums when calling in Slovakia by using one of the call back services listed below. Fees for callback services vary widely, depending on the company and the type of service required.

For a list of callback services, please refer to the "Communications" section in the *Global Road Warrior* Introduction.

PHONE JACK

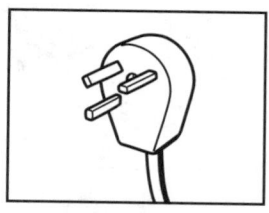

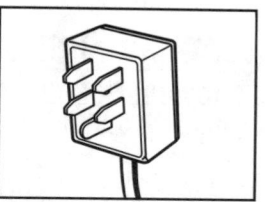

Plug adaptors are available through **iGo Corporation.** (See "Electrical and Telephone Adaptors" on page 19.)

POSTAL SERVICES
Postal services take up to 10 days to reach Western Europe and up to two weeks to reach North America. Valuables should not be sent through the mail.

Hours: Monday to Friday 8a.m. to 6p.m.

Business Services
BUSINESS CENTERS

Danube Hotel; Rybne Namesti 1; tel: (7) 340-000.

Forum Bratislava Hotel; Hodzovo Namestie; tel: (7) 534-8111.

World Trade Center Bratislava; Viedenska cesta 7, 852 51 Bratislava; tel: (7) 6727-2026; fax: (7) 6741-1665; website: www.incheba.sk; email: skurla@incheba.sk.

COURIER SERVICE

DHL Slovakia; Letisko M.R. Stefanika 65 Bratislava 82001; tel: (7) 522-6543; Mon-Fri 08:00-18:00; closed Sat-Sun, holidays.

Federal Express; Inspekta Slovakia, tel: (7) 5556- 8485, 5556- 8486.

UPS Slovakia; M.R. Stefánik Airport, 820 01 Bratislava; Bookings and Inquiries, tel./fax: (7) 16- 877.

Electrical
Current
220 volts AC, 50Hz.

ELECTRIC PLUGS

Slovakia

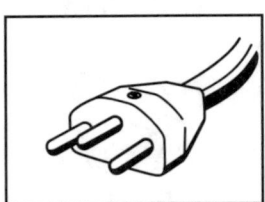

Plug adaptors are available through **iGo Corporation.** (See "Electrical and Telephone Adaptors" on page 19.)

Technical Support

HARDWARE/SOFTWARE VENDOR SUPPORT

Compaq; (in Switzerland) tel: [41] (22) 709-5330; fax: [41] (22) 709-5391 (Geneva); tel: [41] (1) 801-2507; fax: [41] (1) 801-2172 (Zurich); (General U.S.) tel: (281) 518-2000; http://www.compaq.com/.

Dell; (in Germany) tel: [49] (61) 039-710; (Dell- Europe) tel: [44] (134) 474-8000; (in the U.S.) tel: [1] (512) 338-4400; fax: [1] (512) 728-3330; http://www.dell.com/.

IBM; tel: (7) 6925-7111; fax: (7) 6328-6728; (in Switzerland) tel: [41] (22) 310-0418 (in French); (in the U.S.) tel: [1] (919) 517-2800; (U.S. Main Office) tel: [1] 914-765-1900; http://www.ibm.com/.

Microsoft; tel: (7) 5341-9841; fax: (7) 5341-9840; (in Switzerland) tel: [41] (848) 858-868; fax [41] (1) 831-0869; (in the U.S.) [1] (425) 635-7222; http://www.microsoft.com/.

Internet Connection

HOW TO CONNECT

Connecting to AOL and Compuserve in Slovakia is similar to using it when traveling outside your own area code. See the introductory section for detailed information on connecting to your account through a different phone number.

America Online

Numbers are available at keyword *international.* Be sure to get several local numbers before leaving. AOL has a new GlobalNet service that charges US$6 an hour in addition to the usual charges. Go to keyword *access* (a free area) and download the software.

Access: Bratislavia (7) 5556-5773; Kosice (95) 623-0440; Zilina (89) 643-306.

Compuserve

Numbers are available at *Go International.* If you are using CompuServe 2000, use GO PHONES within CompuServe 2000 to search for access numbers. The Compuserve Web-site also has a great deal of information, at http://www.compuserve.com/.

Access: Bratislavia (7) 5556-5773; Kosice (95) 623-0440.

Independent Service Providers

Many independent service providers offer discounts if you are only in town for a couple of days.

Eunet Slovakia, Ltd.; tel: (7) 4445-0044; fax: (7) 4445-0070; info@Slovakia.EU.net; http://www.eunet.sk/.

Gratex International Ltd.; tel: (7) 531-1111; fax: (7) 572-1243; asc@Gratex.sk; http://www.gratex.sk/.

Vadium; tel: (091) 721-160; fax: (091) 721-160; vadium@vadium.sk; http://www.vadium.sk/.

Business Culture

GREETINGS AND COURTESIES

Slovaks will greet foreign visitors warmly. It is customary to shake hands with everyone at an initial meeting. Any other touching is not customary. Men normally wait for women and older people to extend their hands first. Shake hands both upon meeting and departure. Courtesy requires that you use a proper title and surnames when addressing Slovaks. Customarily Slovaks will give you a business card with their title, and you should have one available to give them in return. Slovaks prefer to be addressed by their titles, which is a mark of respect.

BUSINESS ETHIC AND FRAMEWORK

The citizens of Slovakia are committed to democracy and freedom, and proud of their cultural heritage. Their pace of life is slow, which is reflected in their way of doing business. Slovaks are punctual, and expect the same of you. Some English is spoken, but German is commonly the second language; so plan on using an interpreter if you don't speak German or Slovak. In Slovakia, success in business relies heavily on establishing a good personal relationship and mutual trust. Be prepared to re-invest first profits. Slovak business people are wary of Westerners wanting to turn a quick profit and leave. If you are establishing a business presence in Slovakia, you should seek the services of a Slovak lawyer to lead you through the maze of constantly changing regulations. Negotiating can be difficult, as Slovaks expect their proposals to be fully met. A sense of urgency will work to your disadvantage, as Slovaks have no such constraints. Being patient and reasonable brings the best results.

DECISION MAKING

Decision making in a company is usually restricted to a few people, if not just one. Even minor decisions can require the approval of a high- level individual. A decision in your favor will depend upon the mutual trust you have established. You will need to exhibit flexibility and patience, as Slovaks make business decisions in their own good time. Your need for urgency will be counter-productive to eliciting a favorable decision. Your Slovak business associate's personal feelings about you will play a big part of their decision-making process.

WOMEN

Visiting foreign businesswomen are unusual in Slovakia; as such, they can capitalize on their novelty to achieve success. For the best results, a woman should conduct herself in a feminine and non-aggressive manner. On a business trip, spouses are welcomed on social occasions. Many Slovak women hold full-time jobs and have full responsibility for their homes. There is a significant disparity in wages favoring men over women. Slovak women receive paid maternity leave for three years.

MEETINGS

Avoid July and August for scheduling meetings, as many people go on vacation. Make your appointments well in advance (at least 10 days), and reconfirm periodically. This can be difficult, as communications are poor and faxes and letters may not arrive in a timely way. Upon arrival, it is not unusual to receive a message that your meeting is delayed. Be flexible and patient, as your Slovak host may feel dismayed by your sense of urgency. To avoid misunderstandings, it is advisable to hire an English-speaking lawyer who can act as an interpreter.

At the meeting, punctuality is important. Accept drinks or coffee offered to you at the beginning of a meeting. If a toast is offered, offer one in return. Slovak proposals may be unrealistic. Your Slovak hosts may feign agreement to avoid a confrontation as such, an agreement reached at a meeting may not represent the last word on the subject. After the meeting, written summaries, goals, and agreements are advisable to prevent misunderstandings between business partners.

BUSINESS ATTIRE

Although Slovak businessmen are less formal than their counterparts in the West, a dark suit still remains the normal business attire. For informal entertaining or in the evening, slacks, an open-neck shirt and a sweater or jacket will serve appropriate. For women, a skirt and sweater or blouse, or a dress (but not a suit) prove appropriate attire for all occasions.

Business Centers
Bratislava

CITY VIEW

Once the capital of Hungary, Bratislava now reigns as the capital of a recently formed country. If compared to some of the other gems of Eastern Europe, Bratislava may appear a bit drab and functional, still a remnant of the communist era. Concerned with stepping out of the shadow of Prague, however, the country has tried to revive its Old Town. In the meantime, Bratislava is being kept plenty busy in the role of taking full control over its own political destiny.

AIRPORT

M.R. Stefanik Airport to City Center

The airport lies 7.5 miles (12 km.) from the city. Most airlines serving Slovakia are commuter flights to or from major hubs such as Vienna, which only lies about 50km. from Bratislava. Flights also originate from Prague and Zurich. Air Slovakia flies to Tel Aviv during the summer. Taxis service the airport and the 15-minute taxi trip to town will cost about US$6. There are regular bus services, which take about 30 minutes into town; Bus #24 travels to and from Bajkalska Str. in intervals of 15 to 20 minutes. Buses also travel regularly from Vienna Airport to Bratislava. Austrian Airlines shuttle buses operate on weekdays between the Hotel Danube in Bratislava and Vienna Schwechat Airport. CSAD/OBB Buses travel between the Bratislava Bus Station, Vienna Airport, and Vienna's city center.

Bratislava Airport Information ....(7) 236-608
Vienna Airport Information................. [43] (1) 711-10-2231

Airline Numbers

Aeroflot ....(7) 533-5192
Air Slovakia ....(7) 522-2742
Austrian Air/Swissair ....(7) 531-1642
Balkan ....(7) 330-002
British Airways...(7) 499-802
Cassovia Air ....(7) 522-2111
Czech Airlines (CSA)........................ (7) 361-042, 361-045
Delta Airlines ....(7) 533-4718
KLM/Northwest Airlines .... (7) 366-669, (7) 325-002
LOT Polish Airlines...(7) 364-007
Lufthansa/Lauda Air .... (7) 367-814, 367-815
Tatra Air............................... (7) 366-758; airport, 292-306

HOTELS

Expensive

Danube; Rybne Namesti 1; tel: (7) 340-000; fax: (7) 340-833; http://www.hoteldanumbe.com; city center; restaurant; conference facilities (up to 210); business center; secretarial service; computer rental; Executive Floor; car rental; hairdresser; florist; indoor/outdoor parking; shop; fitness; sauna; massage; solarium; pool.

Devin; Riecna 4; tel: (7) 533-0851; fax: (7) 533-0682; email: devin@computel.sk; city center; restaurant; conference facilities (up to 130); secretarial services; fax/photocopy facilities; in-room modem/fax connection, safe; secure parking available; corporate rates.

Forum Bratislava; Hodzovo Namestie; tel: (7) 534-8111; fax: (7) 531-4645; in city center; restaurants; casino; conference facilities (up to 150); business center; secretarial service; Hertz car rental; hairdresser; parking; corporate rates; fitness; sauna; indoor pool.

Moderate

Botel Gracia; Razusovo Nabrezie; tel: (7) 332-430; fax: (7) 332-132; near city center; restaurant; corporate rates.

Bratislava; Seberiniho 9; tel: (7) 332-430; fax: (7) 332-132; located in suburb, near airport; restaurant; conference facilities (up to 250); banquet facilities (up to 600); parking.

Hotel Miva; 5 Bzovicka 38; tel: 822-554; fax: (7) 822-556; 4-star; restaurant; meet facility (up to 25); secretarial service; parking; in-room bath; fitness; sauna.

Incheba; Viedenska Cesta 7; tel: (7) 802-000; fax: (7) 802-542; 3-star hotel; city center, located in premises of Convention Center; restaurant; conference facilities; parking; corporate rates; fitness; sauna.

Kyjev; Rajska 2; tel: (7) 322-041; fax: (7) 326-820; near city center; restaurant; meeting facilities; parking; fitness.

Perugia; Zelena 5; tel: (7) 330-719; fax: (7) 330-719; restaurant; fitness; parking; secretarial service; fax machine; post office; minibar; massage; garden.

Tatra; Namesti 1 Maja 5; tel: (7) 321-464; fax: (7) 323-587; restaurant; fax machine; near city center; corporate rates.

AUTO RENTAL

Note: Seatbelts are mandatory, and a driver's blood-alcohol level may be no higher than zero. Renting a car is expensive and is best done only if the car comes with a local driver.

Avis; Hviezdoslavovo nam. 14; tel: (7) 333-201, 333-233.

Europcar/National; Bratislava airport; tel: (7) 522-0285, M - F 9a.m. to 5:30p.m.; Hotel Danube, tel: 340-841, daily 8a.m. to 8p.m.

Hertz; Bratislava airport; tel: (7) 348-155, Hotel Forum, tel: (7) 226-770.

Recar; Stefanikova 1; tel: (7) 333-420, 333-913.

WORLD TRADE CENTER

World Trade Center Bratislava
Viedenska cesta 7
852 51 Bratislava
Slovak Republic
tel: (7) 6727-2026; fax: (7) 6741-1665
website: www.incheba.sk
email: skurla@incheba.sk
Office rental, exhibition and convention center, business services, restaurant, hotel.

South Africa

At a Glance

THE PEOPLE

Population ....43,426,386 (July 1999 est.)
Growth Rate ....1.32% (1999 est.)
Life Expectancy ....54.76 years (1999 est.)
Infant Mortality... 51.99 deaths/1,000 live births (1999 est.)

Ethnic Composition

Black...75.2%
White 13.6%
Mixed Race(Colored) 8.6%
Asian (Indian) 2.6%

Religious Composition

Christian 68%
African Traditional 28.5%
Muslim 2%
Hindu 1.5%

Languages Spoken

Eleven official languages are recognized including Afrikaans, English, Ndebele, Pedi, Sotho, Swazi, Tsonga, Tswana, Venda, Xhosa, and Zulu.

Education and Literacy

Seven years of education are compulsory for all children, but this is not currently enforced; an estimated two million school-age children do not attend school. Currently 81.8% percent of the population is considered literate.

Labor Force

Total: 15,000,000
By occupation: services 35%, agriculture 30%, industry 20%, mining 9%, other 6%.

THE ECONOMY

South Africa is the leading economy of an impoverished continent. The nation has an abundance of natural resources, a strong legal system, an active financial sector, a credible stock exchange and first rate infrastructure. After being released from the apartheid-era embargo, much was expected of the new black government led by Mandela. Although the economy has experienced some growth during the recent years, it has been insufficient to offset rural poverty and massive unemployment. Although the Mandela government showed a strong embrace of free market economics, his successors have chosen a more socialist path towards the redistribution of wealth. Foreign investment has been drastically reduced as a result. Violent crime and corruption have risen in both city and countryside to add to the problem. A major involuntary currency devaluation in 1998 has also left this promising economy with another hurdle to clear before it reaches long-awaited prosperity.

Exports ....US$28.7 billion (f.o.b., 1998)
Imports ....US$27.2 billion (f.o.b., 1998)
Total Trade ....US$55.9 billion (f.o.b. 1998)
GDP Per Capita................................ US$6,800 (1998 est.)
Unemployment .... 30 percent (1998 est.)
Inflation Rate .... 9 percent (1998 est.)

Top Export Partners

U.K., Italy, Japan, US, Germany .

Top Import Partners

Germany, U.S., U.K., Japan.

Top Exports

Gold, minerals, strategic metals, food, chemicals.

Top Imports

Machinery, transport equipment, chemicals, petroleum products, textiles, scientific instruments.

BUSINESS WORKWEEK

Offices

Monday to Friday 8a.m. to 1p.m. and 2p.m. to 5p.m.

Banks

Monday to Friday 9a.m. to 3:30p.m., Saturday 8:30a.m. to 11a.m.

Government

Monday to Friday 9a.m. to 4p.m.

Retail

8a.m. to 1p.m. and 2p.m. to 5p.m., Monday to Friday
*Shops are generally open from 8:30p.m. to 1p.m. on Saturdays. Legal restrictions on trading hours have been recently been rescinded to increase employment. Consequently, an increasing number of shops in the major cities are now open Saturday afternoons and Sunday mornings.

HOLIDAYS

New Year's Day...January 1
Human Right's Day .... March 21
Good Friday...April 21*
Family Day .... April 5
Freedom Day... April 27
Worker's Day ....May 1
Youth Day...June 16
National Women's Day .... August 9
Heritage Day ....September 24
Day of Reconciliation.....................................December 16
Christmas ....December 25
*Date may vary by year.

CLIMATE

Seasons

Winter temperatures are around 18°C, and summers are as hot as 33°C, with humidity of sometimes 100 percent. Rainy season is from May to September although the country is given to prolonged droughts. Winters are cloudy and overcast. Seasons are the reverse of those in the northern hemisphere.

Regions

Cape Town has warm and dry summers, from December to March, but strong winds tend to cool the air a little. Nights are cooler. In Johannesburg, the winter months have cold and hot days, with varied daily temperatures. Summers are generally hot and sunny with occasional torrential thunderstorms.

Money & Banking

Currency

The currency of South Africa is the Rand (R).

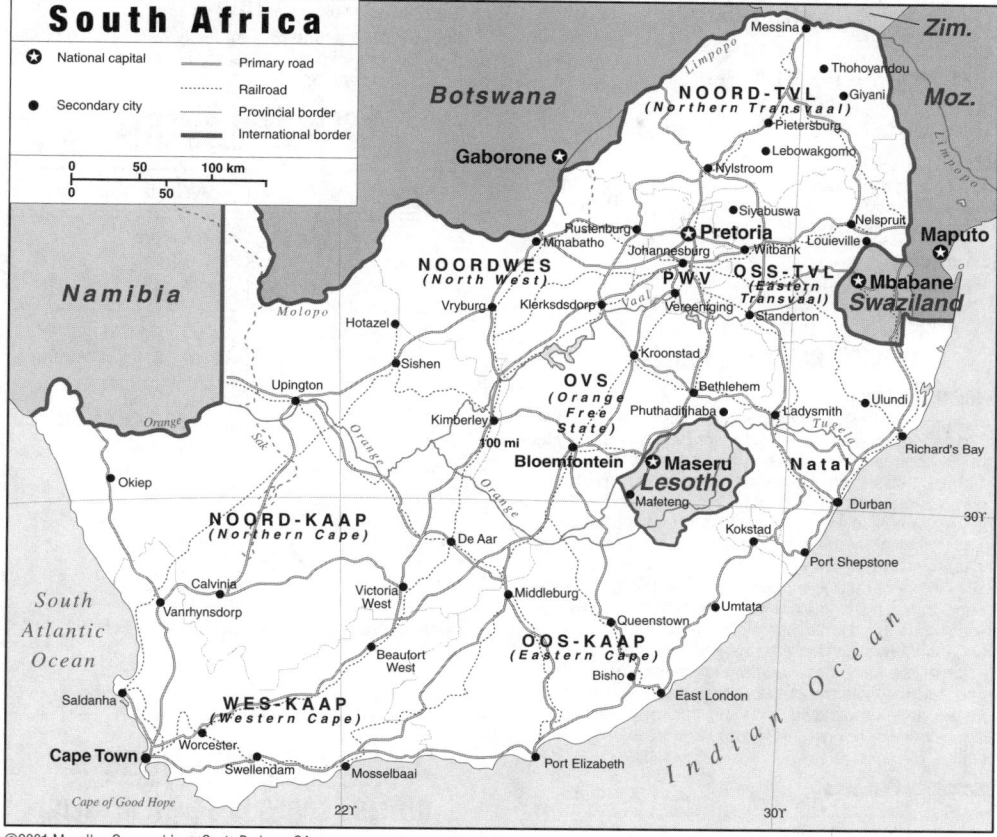

Denominations

The Rand (R) comes in coin denominations of R5, 2 and 1, and 50, 20, 10, 5, 2 and 1cents; and bank notes of R10, 20, 50, 100 and 200.

Traveler's Checks and Credit Cards

Traveler's checks and foreign currency can be easily and efficiently exchanged at banks, foreign exchange bureaus located in the major cities, hotels, and foreign exchange kiosks at the airports. Banks offer the most variable exchange rates. Traveler's checks and credit cards receive a better exchange rate than cash. You can also purchase South African currency traveler's checks in your home market before departure, which can be exchanged almost everywhere.

American Express, Visa, MasterCard, and Diners Club are widely accepted in South Africa. You can get cash advances from your credit card on many of the automated teller machines (ATM). Long-term visitors should set up a checking account in South Africa, and get an ATM card. Robbery of tourists is a major problem in the cities so travel check registers and credit card recovery numbers should be kept in a safe place.

Travel

VISA AND PASSPORT

All visitors to South Africa require valid passports. Foreigners except U.K. citizens need visas, which should be obtained prior to departure.

DEPARTURE FORMALITIES

Export of foreign currency is limited to the amount declared upon arrival. South African currency can be exported up to R200 per person. Gold and diamonds are highly regulated.

CUSTOMS ENTRY (PERSONAL)

Duty-free
- Tobacco: 400 cigarettes, 50 cigars, and 250g of tobacco
- Alcohol: 1 liter of spirits and 2 liters of wine
- Other: 50ml of perfume and 250ml eau de toilette; gifts up to a value of R500 per person

IMMUNIZATION

An international health certificate is required and yellow fever vaccinations are required of visitors from infected areas. Anti-malaria premedication is recommended and should be taken. Hepatitis A prophylaxis is recommended for those intent on travel into the bush and countryside.

South Africa

TIPPING

Taxi
Taxi drivers customarily get 10 percent.

Porters
Porters get about R2 per piece of luggage.

Hotels
No tipping is necessary (unless for exceptional service) at hotels that add a 10 percent service charge. If no service charge was added, tip 10 to 15 percent.

Restaurants
No tipping is necessary (unless for exceptional service) at restaurants that add a service charge. Otherwise, tip 10 to 15 percent.

EMERGENCY INFORMATION

Police and Crime
Crime is epidemic in recent years—muggings, burglaries, car theft and assaults occur both after dark and during daylight. Pickpockets are prevalent, so use basic precautions. Avoid flashy displays of wealth, and dress and behave conservatively. Leave most of your cash, traveler's checks, jewelry and your camera in your hotel safe. Carry photocopies of your passport instead of the original. Carry cash in a money belt, and use credit cards or traveler's checks for most transactions.

Be extra careful on public transportation, in underground car parks and in airports, and do not leave valuables in cars or on tables in cafes. Avoid dimly lit streets at night and know your destination before departure.

The police force has been overwhelmed by the rise in crime and the government is reluctant to return to apartheid-era style crackdowns. Visiting business people may wish to consider bringing their own security teams or hiring locally.

Emergency Numbers
Police... 10111
Hospital (in Johannesburg) 488-4911
Ambulance 999
Fire brigade 624-2800

Health
Sanitation levels vary within the country. Malaria exists. Watch out for the intense sun and heat.

Avoid drinking tap water; bottled water is widely available. Wash all vegetables, peel fruits, and try to avoid uncooked food. Milk is generally pasteurized and safe.

Health care is both private and public, and its quality is possibly the best on the continent. Most doctors are trained overseas; they have up-to-date equipment and medicines are available.

For more information on medical centers, including phone numbers, please see the "Business Centers" section at the end of this chapter.

TAXI AND RENTAL CARS
Taxis are primarily available in the cities. They may not be metered, and a price should be agreed upon beforehand. Violent wars among rival taxi companies happen regularly. Long-term business visitors should hire a car a driver for the duration. Often the South African contact company will provide this service.

BUS
Bus service is the cheapest way to get around town. They are usually efficient and comfortable but they are not suitable for business travel.

TRAIN
South Africa has the best intra-city train service on the continent. If possible, reserve an upper class seat, it is not much more expensive.

Essential Terms

English	Afrikans
Good morning Good-bye How are you/things	Goeie More Tot siens Oe lyk dit?
I don't understand	Ed wird nie (slang) Ek verstaan nie (formal)
OK/fine	Goed
Company/firm	Maatskappy
Money	Kleingeld
Airport	Lughawe
Thank you	Dankie
Where do you come from?	Van waaraf kom jy?
What's your name?	Wat is jou naam?

Communications

DIALING CODES IN SOUTH AFRICA
International country code: [27]
Selected city codes: Cape Town (21), Durban (31), Johannesburg (11), Pretoria (12)

Dialing South Africa from Overseas
To dial South Africa from overseas, dial your country's international dialing code, then 27 (the country code for South Africa), then the city code, and finally the number. If you were dialing Cape Town, for example, you would begin with 011, then 27, then 21 (the city code for Cape Town), and finally the number of the person or office you were trying to reach.

Assistance Numbers
National Directory... 1025
Local Directory 1023

CALLING WITHIN SOUTH AFRICA

Local Calls
Twenty cents will buy three minutes of talk time.

Long Distance Calls
Area codes take effect when dialing long distance within South Africa.

International Calls
Direct dial is available to most countries. To place a call, dial 09 + country code + area code + number. Post offices will charge a three-minute minimum, but still at far reduced rates than calling from a hotel, which may charge two to three times more! Telekom cards or major phone company

cards are also available for direct overseas calls. Connecting to an overseas operator for home-country rates offers another alternative to massive rate pillaging; AT&T's service in South Africa allows connections to virtually any location in the world.

AT&T 0-800-99-0123

PAY PHONES

Public Telephones

Two kinds of phones exist in South Africa: coin and card. However, they seem to be located few and far between. Post offices offer both local and international call capability. And public telephone businesses have sprung up offering better service. Phones on the street are usually blue; those outside the post office are orange, but expect long lines if intending to call around lunchtime or at the end of the working day.

1. Insert coin
2. Dial

Calling Cards

Prepaid phone cards come in R10, 20, 50 and 100 denominations. They are available at news shops, Telekom offices, airports and shopping centers.

CELLULAR PHONES

Several cellular service providers exist in South Africa. Vodacom is a major service provider, offering C-Netz for analogue users, and GSM for digital. There are other companies that also offer GSM, including Mobile Telephone Networks.

Mobile Telephone Networks; tel: (11) 301-6000; fax: (11) 301-6111; cs@mtn.co.za; http://www.mtn.co.za/.

Vodacom; http://www.vodacom.co.za/.

Note: Your home country cell phone may not work in this country. If not, we recommend that you rent an international cell phone *before* you leave home. A major US-based cell phone rental provider is **IMC WorldCell**. For information see "International Cell Phone Rentals" on page 14.

CALL BACK

You can (potentially) save significant sums when calling in South Africa by using one of the call back services listed below. Fees for call back services vary widely, depending on the company and the type of service required. Be sure to check with these companies before leaving to compare rates.

For a list of callback services, please refer to the "Communications" section in the Global Road Warrior Introduction.

PHONE JACKS

Plug adaptors are available through **iGo Corporation.** (See "Electrical and Telephone Adaptors" on page 19.)

FAX

Fax machines have become increasingly common and now most business and hotels have them.

POSTAL SERVICES

International mail is generally good. Airmail takes five to 12 days to reach the U.S., and surface mail takes four to eight weeks.

TELEGRAMS

Telegrams can be sent from most hotels.

Business Services

BUSINESS CENTER

Cape Town

Inter-Continental Cape Sun; Strand Street; tel: (21) 488-5100.

Table Bay Hotel; Quay 6, Victoria and Albert Waterfront; Monday to Sunday 8a.m. to 8p.m.; translation/interpreting; laptops; printers; cell phones; projectors; dictaphones.

Johannesburg

Hilton Sandton; 138 Rivonia Road; tel: (11) 322-1888.

Park Hyatt Johannesburg; 191 Oxford Road, Rosebank; tel: (11) 280-1234; open 24 hours.

Rosebank Hotel; Tyrwhitt & Sturdee Avenue; tel: (11) 447-2700

Samsung Business Center; Michelangelo Hotel, West St., Sandton Square; tel: (11) 784-4103; (11) 784-4140, ex. 7084; email: buscentm@iafrica.com; Monday to Friday 7a.m. to 7p.m., Saturday 8a.m. to noon; typing; printing, fax, flight confirmation, photocopying, courier service, cell phone rental, video machines, boardroom, videoconferencing, meeting rooms, private offices.

COMPUTER RENTAL

Cape Town

Rent A Micro; 185 Buitenkant St., Gardens; tel: (21) 462-1265; fax: (21) 272-1461; email: rent@iafrica.com; conference, seminar rental.

COURIER SERVICE

Cape Town

DHL; Oude Molen Street, Maitland, Capetown 7401; tel: 27-21-508 1990 - International; Mon-Thu 24 hours; Fri 07:30 to 5:30p.m. Sat 8a.m. to noon; Sun 10a.m. to noon; Holidays 08a.m. to 2p.m.

TNT Express Worldwide; Maitland Industrial Park, Unit D4 705-733 Voortrekker Road; Maitland 7405, Cape Town; P.O.Box 39800 Woltemade 7445, South Africa; tel:(21)

593-1280, toll Free 800 122 441.

UPS; Unit 11 Airport Business Park Cnr. Borcherds Quarry & Michigan Road Cape Town International Airport; tel: (21) 386-6677

Johannesburg
DHL International (PTY) Ltd.; Old Mutual Business Park South; Gewel Street, Isando, Johannesburg 1600; Opening hours Mon-Fri 8a.m. to 5:30p.m.; Sat-Sun Closed, Holidays Closed.

Federal Express; (11) 923-8000.

TNT Express Worldwide; Old Mutual Business Park, Gewel Street, Isando, P.O. Box 2185 Johannesburg 2000; tel: (11) 392-2929, toll free: 800 122 441.

UPS; Unit 5 Jan Smuts Park Jones Road, Jet Park; tel: (11) 397-1489; fax: (11) 397-1919.

Electrical

Current
Pretoria: 250 volts AC, 50Hz.
Everywhere else: 220/230 volts AC, 50Hz.

ELECTRIC PLUG

Plug adaptors are available through **iGo Corporation**. (See "Electrical and Telephone Adaptors" on page 19.)

Technical Support
HARDWARE/SOFTWARE VENDOR SUPPORT

Compaq/Digital; (in Switzerland) tel: [41] (22) 709-5330; fax: [41] (22) 709-5391 (Geneva); tel: [41] (1) 801-2507; fax: [41] (1) 801-2172 (Zurich); (General U.S.) tel: (281) 518-2000; http://www.compaq.com/.

Dell; (Dell- Europe) tel: [44] (134) 474-8000; (in the U.S.) tel: [1] (512) 338-4400; fax: [1] (512) 728-3330; http://www.dell.com/.

Filemaker/Claris; (in Germany) tel: [49] (180) 525-8166 (Info-line); fax: [49] (180) 567-2233; tel: [49] (180) 523-6423; (in the U.S.) tel: [1] (800) 965-9090; http://www.claris.com/.

Hewlett Packard; (in Switzerland) tel: [41] (22) 780-8111; (in the U.S.) tel: [1] (408) 246-4300; http://www.hp.com/.

IBM; (in Switzerland) tel: [41] (22) 310-0418 (in French); (in the U.S.) tel: [1] (919) 517-2800; (U.S. Main Office) tel: [1] 914-765-1900; http://www.ibm.com/.

Microsoft; tel: (11) 257-0000; fax: (11) 257-0257; tel: (11) 445-0145; fax: (11) 445-0045/6 (customer service); (in Germany) tel: [49] (89) 31-760; fax: [49] (89) 3176-1000; tel: [49] (89) 3176-1199; (in Switzerland) tel: [41] (848) 858-868; fax [41] (1) 831-0869; (in the U.S.) [1] (425) 635-7222; http://www.microsoft.com/.

Internet Connection
HOW TO CONNECT
Connecting to AOL and Compuserve in South Africa is similar to using it when traveling outside your own area code. See the introductory section for detailed information on connecting to your account through a different phone number.

America Online
Numbers are available at keyword *international*. Be sure to get several local numbers before leaving. AOL has a new GlobalNet service that charges US$6 an hour in addition to the usual charges. Go to keyword *access* (a free area) and download the software.

Access: Cape Town (21) 461-6928; Durban (31) 307-2203; Johannesburg (11) 833-2145.

CompuServe
Numbers are available at *Go International*. If you are using CompuServe 2000, use GO PHONES within CompuServe 2000 to search for access numbers. The Compuserve Web-site also has a great deal of information, at http://www.compuserve.com/.

Access: Cape Town (21) 419-9739, (21) 461-6928, (21) 419-9665; Durban (31) 307-2203; Johannesburg (11) 454-2878, (11) 833-2145.

Independent Service Providers
Many independent service providers offer discounts if you are only in town for a couple of days.

Binary Surgeons / Dream Host; tel: (11) 609-6741; info@dreamhost.net, email: sales@dreamhost.net; http://www.surgeons.co.za/.

BizSA; tel: (11) 675-2608; fax: (11) 675-2549; email: info@bizsa.co.za; http://www.bizsa.co.za/.

Global Internet Access; tel: (11) 803-4024; sales@global.co.za; http://www.global.co.za/home.html/.

InformSA; tel: (12) 362-1462; fax: (012) 362-1482; marketing@informsa.co.za; http://www.informsa.co.za/.

Kingsley Technologies (Pty) Ltd; tel: (21) 762-0276; fax: (21) 761-9930; info@kinglsley.co.za; http://www.kingsley.co.za/.

M-Web; (12) 483-7000; sales@mweb.co.za; http://www.mweb.co.za/.

The Internet Solution; tel: (11) 283-5000; fax: (11) 283-5001; info@is.co.za; http://www.is.co.za/

UUNet Internet Africa; tel: (21) 6588-8700, (800) 020-003; sales@iafrica.com; http://iafrica.com/iafrica/.

Business Culture
GREETINGS AND COURTESIES
The handshake is the standard greeting in South Africa. When a black and a white person shake hands, as well as two blacks, the "African" handshake is used: start with a standard handshake, then slip your hand up around the other person's thumb, then return to the standard grip. Two white people

shaking hands will exchange only the standard handshake; do not attempt the African style. Among good friends, men will often hug, women will exchange kisses on the cheek. Titles, such as Doctor, Professor, or Judge, as well as Mister, Mrs., and Advocate (for a lawyer) should always be used when applicable. Use first names only after the South African uses yours. In initial conversation, do not ask about an Afrikaaner's marital status or family, as they tend to be reserved about discussing such matters.

BUSINESS ETHIC AND FRAMEWORK

While South Africa remains a high-powered industrial juggernaut, the richest and most productive nation in the history of Africa, the recent abolition of its apartheid policies has brought significant changes to every aspect of its society, with more on the way. The business framework, however, remains for the most part a direct reflection of the conservative, austere, and highly motivated character of the Afrikaaner himself. Standards of punctuality, efficiency, and reliability in South African business rival those of Germany or Japan. Further, despite the recent, and continual, expansion of the business community to include more blacks, Indians, and Asians, the defiant isolation of the ruling Afrikaaners during South Africa's apartheid years has produced a marked insularity, an "us and them" character within their business world that precludes easy access by foreigners. Patience and dignified deportment, however, will allow you to demonstrate your integrity and so gain their trust.

DECISION MAKING

Once a bond of trust is established, business will proceed quickly and without interruptions. Tough, protracted bargaining is not a feature of the South African culture. Decisions come from the top people in a South African company, and thus, it is recommended that you send a high-ranking member of your company to the initial meetings. When a South African businessperson does make a decision, he will want a ready response. Patience is more than a virtue in South Africa, it is a must; the phrase "just now" means "in a short while," not "immediately."

WOMEN

The attitude of South Africa's business community towards women remains decidedly chauvinistic and male oriented. There are very few women in senior management positions, and women are generally excluded from decision-making processes. In meetings, women of equal or even superior rank are often expected to make tea. A foreign businesswoman, however, can expect to be treated with respect, providing she is not overly aggressive or indiscreet. South Africans have become accustomed to dealing with Western businesswomen in positions of authority.

MEETINGS

Meetings start on time, are scheduled for any part of the day, and are preceded by a brief but important period of personal conversation. Foreign businesspeople should be thoroughly prepared in advance, with graphics and visual aids, if possible. Business lunches and dinners are common, but they are for the most part social events. The real business takes place in meetings. Don't be surprised if blacks don't rise when introduced, although this is changing as blacks gain more stature in this society. This gesture does not apply when women are being greeted. At an initial meeting, send someone fairly senior in your company's hierarchy; this will make negotiations a little smoother.

BUSINESS ATTIRE

Standard Western business attire is the norm in South Africa. For meetings, businessmen wear a suit and tie; women a suit or conservative dress. In summer (December through March), the acceptable business "uniform" is a khaki shirt and Bermuda shorts. For casual dress in cities, both women and men may wear shorts or jeans. Keep in mind the Boer farmers in rural communities are very conservative. In those areas, women should not wear low-cut tops or short shorts. In other areas, people are used to seeing women in halter tops and sleeveless dresses. Proper attire when visiting someone's home can vary widely, so be sure to ask what you should wear; sometimes people sit around the pool and eat outdoors.

Business Centers
Cape Town

CITY VIEW

Cape Town is a combination of Europe and Africa, first and third world coming together. Probably the safest city in South Africa, Cape Town offers a dry climate in a picturesque setting. Low-lying mountains peppered with vineyards stand as a backdrop to the small, quiet city by the sea.

AIRPORT

D.F. Malan Airport to City Center

The airport lies 14 miles (22 km.) from the city center. Look for *Inter-Cape* buses, which meet all incoming planes. Shuttle buses going to major hotels, the central rail station, and South African Airways City Terminal depart in 30-minute intervals for a fare of R15. Taxis are also available outside of the arrivals hall. Expect to pay about R50 to R70 for the 20 to 30-minute trip into town.

Cape Town International Airport......................... 937-1200
Flight Information.. 934-0407/8/9

Airline Numbers

Air France.................................... (21) 418-8180, 934-8818
Air India .... (21) 418-3558
Air Mauritius .... (21) 216-294
Air Namibia...................................(21) 216-685, 934-0757
Air Zimbabwe 011-331-1541
American Airlines .... (21) 683-2838
Austrian Airlines ....(21) 934-4444
British Airways.. (21) 934-0292
British Airways Intl. ....(21) 683-4203, 934-0292
Egypt Air......................................(21) 461-8065, 936-2425
KLM .... (21) 21-1870, 934-3495
LTU...(21) 936-1190
Lufthansa...................................... (21) 25-1490, 934-8534
Malaysian Airlines .... (21) 419-8010, 934-8794
Namib Air...................................... (21) 21-6692, 934-0757
National Airlines ....(21) 934-0350
Qantas.. (21) 419-9382
SAA .... (21) 936-2021, 936-2664
S.A. Airlink..(21) 936-2204
Sabena Nationwide Air................................(21) 936-2056
Singapore Airlines .... (21) 419-0495, 934-5941
Sunair...(21) 934-9131
Swissair .... (21) 21-4938, 934-8755
Turkish Airlines...(21) 410-8702

South Africa

HOTELS

Top-end

Inter-Continental Cape Sun; Strand Street; tel: (21) 488-5100; fax: (21) 238-875; located in central business district; views of Table Mountain and harbor; restaurant; conference facilities (up to 500); business center; health club; fitness; sauna; pool.

Mount Nelson; 76 Orange St.; tel: (21) 483-1000; fax: (21) 424-7472; email: nellress@iafrica.com; set in seven acres of parkland on lower slopes of Table Mountain; 10-minute walk from city centre; 3 restaurants; conference/banquet facilities (up to 400); executive and business services; airport transfers; parking; beauty salon; fitness; pools; tennis; squash.

Ellerman House; 180 Kloof Road; tel: (21) 439-9182; fax: (21) 434-7257; near mountains; restaurant; secretarial service; fax/photocopy facilities; in-room modem/fax connection, safe; parking; fitness; sauna; pool.

Table Bay - Sun International; Victoria and Albert Waterfront; tel: (11) 780-7800; fax: (11) 783-9308; in U.S. [1] (954) 713-2638; located in heart of Waterfront development; rooms with views of Table Mountain and sea; 2 restaurants; conference facilities; business center; secretarial service; internet; in-room phones with voicemail; beauty parlor; health club; pool.

The Cellars-Hohenort; 15 Hohenort Avenue, Constantia, Cape Peninsula; located in suburb; forest setting with scenic views; restaurants; meeting facilities; (up to 20); secretarial service; fax/photocopy facilities; in-room safe; pool.

Expensive

Commodore, Victoria & Alfred Waterfront; tel: (21) 419-6677; fax: (21) 419-8955; all rooms with view; restaurant; fitness; sauna; steamroom; pool.

Karos Arthur's Seat; Arthur's Road, Sea Point; tel; (21) 434-3344; fax: (21) 434-9768; located in suburb; restaurant; conference facilities (up to 600); secretarial service; fax/photocopy facilities; parking; corporate rates; fitness; sauna; pool.

Mijlof Manor Hotel; 5 Military Road;, Tamboerskloof; tel: (21) 26-1476; fax: (21) 22-2046; city center; restaurant; parking; pool.

Place on the Bay; The Fairway and Victoria Road; tel: (21) 438-7060; fax: (21) 438-2692; near beach; suites; in-room safe; parking; pool.

The Vineyard; Colinton Road; tel: (21) 683-3044; fax: (21) 683-3365; located in suburb; restaurant; conference facilities (up to 100); secretarial service; fax/photocopy facilities; in-room modem/fax connection, safe; parking; fitness; pool.

Moderate

The Capetonian; Herengracht, Pier Place, Roggebaai; tel: (21) 21-1150; fax: (21) 25-2215; restaurant; conference facilities (up to 80); parking.

Cape Manor; 1 Marais Road, Sea Point; tel: (21) 434-9531; fax: (21) 439-6896; located near beach; restaurant; conference facilities (up to 200); secretarial service; fax/photocopy facilities; corporate rates; parking.

Holiday Inn Garden Court; Mill Street, Gardens; tel: (21) 23-2040; fax: (21) 23-8875; near city center; restaurant; conference facilities; secretarial service; fax/photocopy facilities; pool.

Peninsula All-Suite Hotel; tel: (21) 439-8888; fax: (21) 439-8886; suites; near beach; restaurant; conference facilities; secretarial service; fax/photocopy facilities; in-room safe; parking; fitness; sauna; pool.

Town House Hotel; 60 Corporation Street; tel: (21) 45-7050; fax: (21) 45-3891; near city center; restaurant; meeting facilities (up to 30); secretarial service; fax/photocopy facilities; in-room modem/fax connection, safe; parking; fitness; sauna; pool.

HEALTH CLUB

Inter-Continental Cape Sun; Strand Street; tel: (21) 488-5100.

AUTO RENTAL

Budget Rent A Car; regional office, tel: 934-0340/1; fax: 934-0151; airport, tel: (21) 934-0216; fax; (21) 934-8640.

Comet; tel: (21) 386-2411; fax: (21) 386-2430; email: comet@iafrica.com.

Eco Rent-A-Car; tel: (21) 434-5792; fax: (21) 434-3520; email: irs@global.co.za.

Hertz; tel: (21) 386-1560; fax; (21) 386-1570; email: hertzsa@iafrica.com.

Imperial Car Hire; tel: (21) 21-5190; fax: 25-2382; airport, (21) 934-0354 or 0800-226-400.

Levitt's Car Hire; airport, tel: (21) 936-2277.

CHAMBER OF COMMERCE

Cape Town Chamber of Commerce
Chamber House; 19 Louis Gradner St.
Cape Town 8001
tel: (21) 418-4300; Telefax: (21) 418-1800
email: info@capechamber.co.za

Johannesburg

CITY VIEW

Johannesburg, or Jo'Burg as the natives call it, is an industrial center. Tent cities and squatters ring the city, marking it as a target for crime. Robberies and carjackings occur with frequency. Those conducting business in the city should take security precautions.

AIRPORT

Jan Smuts Airport to City Center

The airport lies 15 miles (24 km.) from the city. Major hotels usually offer shuttle buses; however, one should reserve in advance. Tickets for private bus services to the city center are available at the bus counters in the arrivals hall. A 35-minute bus trip will cost about R25. Passengers can also find taxi and minibus taxis outside of the arrivals hall. A regular cab will cost about R100 for the 35-minute trip to the city center. Minibuses that pick up other passengers cost about R10, but will likely prove less efficient and speedy.

Airline Numbers

Air Afrique	(11) 880-8537
Air Botswana	(11) 447-6078/81
Air Canada	(11) 880-8931
Air France	(11) 880-8040
Air Gabon	(11) 289-8114
Air India	(11) 442-4421
Air Madagascar	(11) 289-8222
Air Malawi	(11) 622-0466
Air Mauritius	(11) 444-4600
Air Namibia	(11) 390-2876
Air Seychelles	(11) 453-0655
Air Zimbabwe	(11) 615-7017
American Airlines	(11) 880-6370
Balkan Bulgaria	(11) 883-0957
British Airways	(11) 331-0011
British Airways/Comair	(11) 921-0222

Ghana Airways ....(11) 622-4005
Kenya Airways..(11) 881-9747
Linhas Aereas De Mozambique ....(11) 331-6081
Nationwide Air/Sabena................................(11) 390-1660
KLM ....(11) 881-9600
Luxavia ....(11) 331-3034
MAS...(11) 880-9614
Qantas Airways ....(11) 884-5300
Royal Air Maroc...(11) 884-6732
Royal Swazi Airlines....................................(11) 616-7323
SAA ....(11) 978-2036
South African Airlink....................................(11) 978-1111
South African Express Airways ....(11) 978-5577
Sun Air..(11) 923 6400
Thai Airways..(11) 883-9068
Uganda Airlines ....(11) 616-4672
Varig ....(11) 331-2471
Zambian Express ....(11) 289-8114
Zimbabwe Express.......................................(11) 390-1228/9

HOTELS

Top-end
The Carlton; Main Street; tel: (11) 331-8911; fax: (11) 331-3555; email: Carltonh@iafrica.com; near city center; restaurant; conference facilities (up to 800); in-room safe; parking; fitness; sauna; pool.

Hilton Sandton; 138 Rivonia Road; tel: (11) 322-1888; fax: (11) 322-1818; 1 km from the city centre; restaurants; conference facilities (up to 750); business center; executive level; in-room modem/fax connection, safe, voicemail, dataports; secure parking; gift shop; fitness; saunas, pool, tennis; jogging track.

Michelangelo; West St., Sandton Square; tel: (11) 784-4103; two restaurants, valet services, hairdresser, bank, beauty salon, book shop, chemist; telex and telefax facilities, hospitality lounge with shower facility for early arrivals and late departures; Express check-out, doctor & dentist on call, in-house nurse; health and fitness center; steam bath; pool.

Park Hyatt Johannesburg; 191 Oxford Road, Rosebank; tel: (11) 280-1234; fax: (11) 280-1238; email: parkhyatt@hyatt.co.za; located in northern suburbs; restaurants; conference facilities (up to 280); 24-hour business center; Regency Club floors; non-smoking rooms available; voicemail; fax/modem lines; electronic door locks; medical staff; airport greeting service; limousine service on request; health club; gym; pool; jacuzzis.

Sandton Sun & Towers; tel: (11) 780-5000; fax: (11) 780-5002; heart of exclusive residential suburb of Sandton; direct access to Sandton City, restaurants.

The Westcliff; 67 Jan Smuts Avenue, Westcliff; tel: (11) 646-2400; fax: (11) 646-3500; email: wstcliff@iafrica.com; located in northern suburb; villas; restaurants; meeting rooms (up to 80); business services; secretarial service; in-room digital safe; beauty salon; health club; fitness; pools; tennis; access to Houghton Golf Club.

Expensive
Balalaika Hotel & Crown Court; 20 Maud Street, Sandton; tel: (11) 322-5000; fax: (11) 322-5021; located in suburb; restaurant; conference facilities (up to 400); secretarial service; fax/photocopy facilities; in-room safe; parking; pool.

Parktonian; 120 De Koret Street, Braamfontein; tel: (11) 403-5740; fax: (11) 403-2401; located in suburb; restaurant; conference facilities (up to 280); secretarial service; fax/photocopy facilities; parking; fitness; pool.

Protea Gardens; 35 O'Reilly Road, Berea; tel: (11) 643-6610; fax: (11) 484-2622; email: gphotel@global.co.za; near city center; restaurant; conference facilities (up to 750); secretarial service; fax/photocopy facilities; parking; fitness; sauna; pool.

Rosebank Hotel; Tyrwhitt & Sturdee Avenue; tel: (11) 447-2700; fax: (11) 447-3276; email: rosebank@rosebankhotel.co.za; 5 minutes from Sandton; 3 restaurants; 7 conference rooms; business center; secretarial service; secure parking underground; car hire; gift shop; beauty salon; gym; steambath; pool.

Moderate
The Deveonshire; Melle & Jorissen Streets;, Braamfontein; tel: (11) 403-5740; fax: (11) 339-7440; located in suburb; restaurant; conference facilities (up to 100); secretarial service; fax/photocopy facilities; corporate rates; parking; sauna.

Holiday Inn Johannesburg International; Kempton Park; tel: (11) 975-1121; fax: (11) 975-5846.

Sunnyside Park Hotel; 2 York Road, Parktown; tel: (11) 643-7226; fax: (11) 642-0019; city center; restaurant; conference facilities; pool.

HEALTH CLUB

Michelangelo; West St., Sandton Square.

Park Hyatt Johannesburg; 191 Oxford Road, Rosebank; tel: (11) 280-1234.

The Westcliff; 67 Jan Smuts Avenue, Westcliff; tel: (11) 646-2400.

AUTO RENTAL

Budget; tel: 394-2905; fax: 975-3376; Pretoria, tel: 341-4650/4/7; fax: 341-1688.

Comet; tel: (11) 974-7010; email: comet@iafrica.com.

Elite Chauffeur Services; (Budget's chauffeur and coach division); tel: (11) 447-2051; fax: (11) 788-8597; email: slitecha@iafrica.com; http://users.iafrica.com/e/el/elitecha.

Hertz; Head Office, tel: (21) 386-1560; fax; (21) 386-1570; email: hertzsa@iafrica.com.

Imperial Car Hire; Johannesburg Central Reservations, tel: (11) 453-0005; fax: (11) 453-6278; Sandton Sun Hotel, tel: (11) 883-4352; fax: 883-1449; Airport, tel: (11) 394-4020; fax: (11) 394-4063.

Levitt's Car Hire; 8 Jubilee St., Kempton Park; tel: (11) 394-3580; fax: (11) 975-3521; email: levitts@intelcom.co.za; airport, tel: (11) 390-2342.

WORLD TRADE CENTER

World Trade Center Johannesburg
4 Pybus Rd., Sandton, P.O. Box 500
Kempton Park 1620 South Africa
tel: (11) 884-8467; fax: (11) 783-2697
email: wtc.sales@wtc.co.za
website: http://www.wtcclub.co.za

CHAMBER OF COMMERCE

Johannesburg Chamber of Commerce and Industry
Private Bag 34, Auckland Park
2006 Johannesburg
tel: (11) 726-5300; fax: (11) 482-2000
email: info@jcci.co.za
website: http://www.jcci.co.za/

South Korea

At a Glance

THE PEOPLE

Population ....46,884,800 (July 1999 est.)
Growth Rate ....1% (1999 est.)
Life Expectancy .... 74.3 years (1999 est.)
Infant Mortality ..... 7.57 deaths/1,000 live births (1999 est.)

Ethnic Composition

Ethnic Koreans 99.96%
Ethnic Chinese...................................... 0.04%

Religious Composition

Christian 49%
Buddhist 47%
Folk Religions... 4%
    Buddhism is not technically a religion but, like Taoism and Confucianism, a philosophy.

Languages Spoken

    Spoken Korean is the official language, although English is a mandatory second language taught in schools.

Education and Literacy

    Six years are compulsory and free to the public, while 87% of qualified students attend through secondary school. Currently, 98% of the population over the age of 15 is considered literate.

Labor Force

Total: 20,000,000
    By occupation: services and other 52%, mining and manufacturing 27%, agriculture, aquaculture, forestry 21%.

THE ECONOMY

    As one of the original "four dragons" of Asia, South Korea exemplified the explosive economic growth of the 1970s and '80s. Once grossly impoverished, its GDP per capita now rivals EU standards. Largely set on a Japanese model, Korean industry is highly controlled and reliant on "chaebol" conglomerates with diverse subsidiaries. The financial crisis of 1997 to 1998 sent the Korean economy into a downward spiral as cronyism and erratic lending revealed their weaknesses to the pressures of the global economy. South Korea's disciplined response and deft handling of IMF loans gave the nation the quickest recovery of any of the affected Asian economies. No longer a source of cheap labor (relative to other parts of Asia) Korea has sought out higher value adding industries and productivity increases to position itself globally. Financial reform has exceeded predicted levels and South Korea will enter the 21st century on relatively stable footing and GDP growth. Much, however, still depends on the economic leadership of Japan and the political attitudes of China.

Exports ....US$133 billion (f.o.b., 1998)
Imports .... US$94 billion (c.i.f., 1998)
Total Trade ....US$227 billion (1998)
GDP Per Capita..............................US$12,600 (1998 est.)
Unemployment ....7.9 percent (1998)
Inflation Rate ....7.5 percent (1998)

Top Export Partners

U.S., E.U., Japan.

Top Import Partners

U.S., E.U., Japan.

Top Exports

    Electronic and electrical equipment, machinery, steel, automobiles, ships, textiles, clothing, footwear, fish.

Top Imports

    Machinery, electronic equipment, oil, steel, transport equipment, textiles, organic chemicals, grains.

BUSINESS WORKWEEK

Offices

    Monday to Friday 9a.m. to 6p.m., Saturday 9a.m. to 1p.m.

Banks

    Monday to Friday 9:30a.m. to 4:30p.m.

Government

    Monday to Friday 9a.m. to 6p.m., Saturday 9a.m. to 1p.m.

Retail

    Monday to Saturday 10a.m. to 7p.m. Many stores also are open on Sundays.

HOLIDAYS

New Year... January 1-2
Lunar New Year ....February 3-5
Independence Movement Day .... March 1
Arbor Day .... April 5
Buddha's Birthday ....May 18
Memorial Day ....June 6
Constitution Day ....July 17
Liberation Day ....August 15
Choo-Suk (Thanksgiving)........................September 20-22
National Foundation Day.....................................October 3
Christmas Day...December 25
    Some dates may vary by year.

CLIMATE

Seasons

    South Korea has a temperate climate with distinct four seasons. Summers are humid, rainy, and warm throughout the country. The typical July high temperature hits 31°C (88°F) and but can reach 35°C (95°F). Spring and fall are justifiably celebrated for beautiful weather—warm days, cool nights, fresh breezes.

Regions

    South Korea's climate is generally temperate, but there are slight regional variations. The further south you go the warmer each season is.

Money & Banking

Currency

    The currency of South Korea is the Won (W).

Denominations

    The Won (W) comes in coin denominations of W500, 100, 50, 10, 5 and 1; and banknotes of W1,000, 5,000 and 10,000. A larger denomination, the Chon (jeon), valued at W1,000, is also in use.

South Korea

☆	National capital
•	Administrative capital
●	Secondary city
──	International boundary
──	Administrative boundary
──	Primary road
──	Secondary road
····	Railroad
──	Demarcation line
──	Demilitarized zone
↓	Primary ports
☒	Airfields

0 25 50 75 km
0   25   50 mi

Administrative Notes
*The South Korean Province of Kyonggi is administered from Seoul.
*The South Korean Province of Kyongsang-bukto is administered from Taegu.
*The South Korean Province of Kyongsang-namdo is administered from Pusan.
*The South Korean City of Kwangju is an individual Province, and the administrative Capital of Cholla-namdo Province.

SM Santa Barbara, CA

©2001 Magellan Geographix

Traveler's Checks and Credit Cards

Traveler's checks can be exchanged at banks, exchange shops, hotels, and international airports at tourist exchange rates. Larger banks may offer the best exchange rates, but avoid black marketers at all cost. Consult your bank about current exchange rates before departure. Keep all receipts for reconversion.

Major credit cards, American Express, Visa, Diner's Club, and MasterCard, are easily accepted in good hotels, shops, and car rental places, but smaller restaurants, and markets may ask for cash. Some banks in the larger cities offer cash advances on credit cards, but will require passport identification and possible service fees. Transactions made with credit cards receive the optimal exchange rate.

Travel

VISA AND PASSPORT

A valid passport is required for visits of up to 90 days. Nationals from Western Europe (except Ireland) and several African, American (except U.S.), South and Asian countries do not require visas. Most others can enter the country for 14 days with a confirmed return ticket. Visas for longer stays must be obtained from a consulate prior to entry. Business visas require an invitation from a South Korean business or government agency.

South Korea

DEPARTURE FORMALITIES

Foreign currency exceeding the equivalent of W6 million (US$5,000) will be confiscated upon exit unless pre-registered. Duties will have to be paid on items such as jewelry and camera equipment unless a full declaration is made upon entry to Korea. Receipts are necessary to reconvert Won back to your local currency in amounts exceeding US$500.

CUSTOMS ENTRY (PERSONAL)

Duty-free

- Tobacco: 200 cigarettes, 50 cigars, or 250g pipe tobacco (total quantity not exceeding 500g)
- Alcohol: 1 liter bottle of alcohol
- Perfume: 2oz of perfume; gifts up to W300,000

Prohibited or Restricted

- Any printed material, films, tapes or phonograph records considered by the authorities to be subversive or harmful to national security or public interests
- Any firearms, explosives or other weapons
- Radio equipment and any animals or plants prohibited by the relevant regulations

IMMUNIZATION

Vaccinations are not required for entry unless a traveler is arriving from an area infected with yellow fever or cholera.

TIPPING

Tipping is not common in Korea. Restaurants and hotels add service charges to their bills, but small tips are appropriate for porters, taxi drivers who help with baggage, and guides who are especially helpful. Otherwise, a sincere thank you will do.

EMERGENCY INFORMATION

Police and Crime

Crime is low in South Korea, but petty crime exists. Avoid flashy displays of wealth, and dress and behave conservatively. Leave most of your cash, traveler's checks, jewelry, and other valuables in your hotel safe. Carry photocopies of your passport instead of the original. Carry cash in a money belt, and use credit cards or traveler's checks for most transactions.

Women can walk around in relative safety, but they should be aware of their surroundings at all times. There are police stations literally on every street, and the police are extremely helpful but language skills are limited.

Emergency Numbers

Police 112
Fire 119
Tourist Information (Seoul) 735-0101

Health

Typhoid, diphtheria, typhus, cholera, tuberculosis, internal parasites, hepatitis A, hepatitis B, and leprosy (to a low degree) are present. Seoul has high sanitation standards but high pollution; avoid drinking tap water or eating raw food in more rural areas. Stay away from food sold at roadside stands, and generally stick to milder dishes. Some stomach and digestion problems may occur from spicy food.

Medical services are government controlled and good; doctors are well trained, and many of the staff speak English. Costs are reasonable, pharmacies are plentiful, and all necessary drugs can be found at a low cost.

For more information on medical centers, including phone numbers, please see the "Business Centers" section at the end of this chapter.

TAXI & RENTAL CARS

Taxis are inexpensive and efficient. They are one of the best ways to get around town. Rental cars are available but not recommended for the inexperienced visitor.

BUS

Buses are inexpensive, but drivers often speak no English and help for those who don't speak Korean is sporadic. If boarding a bus, hold on tight as the ride resembles that of an amusement park with fast stops and accelerations. The colorful experience is further excited with loud, blaring music often played on board. Express buses that connect towns cities also exist and compete with trains for passengers.

TRAIN

Rail services connect much of the country. Some higher class cars have air conditioning and dining services. Many station signs are in English as well as Korean.

Essential Terms

English	Korean
Yes No	*Ne* *A ni yo*
Good morning Hello (daytime) Hello (evening) Hello (telephone)	*An nyeong ha se yo?* *An nyeong ha se yo?* *An nyeong ha se yo?* *yeo bo se yo*
Good-bye	*An nyeong hie gye se yo*
Please	*Eo seo jom*
Thank you	*Gam sa ham ni da*
Pleased to meet you	*Man na seo bang gap seum ni da*
Excuse me; I'm sorry	*Jam-kan-man-yo / mi-an ham-ni-da*
My name is _____	*Je i reum-eun im-ni-da*
I don't understand	*Jway-song-ham-ni-da-man*
Do you speak English?	*Yeong-eo-reul ha-shim-ni-ka?*

Communications

DIALING CODES IN SOUTH KOREA

International country code: [82]

Selected city codes: Kyonggi (31), Kangwon (33), Cheju (64), Chonbuk (63), Chonnam (61), Chungbuk (43), Chungnam (41), Daejon (42), Kwangju (62), Kyongbuk (54), Kyongnam (55), Inchon (32), Pusan (51), Seoul (2), Taegu (53), Ulsan (52)

Dialing South Korea from Overseas

To dial South Korea from overseas, dial your country's international dialing code, then 82 (the country code for

South Korea), then the city code and finally the number. If you were dialing Pusan from the United States, for example, you would begin with 011, then 82, then 51 (the city code for Pusan), and finally the number of the person or office you were trying to reach.

Assistance Numbers

Operator (English speaking).. 0077
International Information.. 0074

CALLING WITHIN SOUTH KOREA

Local Calls

A three-minute local call will cost about W40.

Long Distance Calls

Include the correct city area code when dialing long distance within Korea.

International Calls

South Korea's two telephone competitors, Korea Telecom (001) and Dacom (002) both offer international direct dial, although Dacom is the less expensive option. If surmising what the catch is, Dacom may only be reached from a private telephone, and Korea Telecom will not connect you to them. Thirty percent discounts apply between 9p.m. and 8a.m. Monday to Saturday and all day Sundays and holidays. Bear in mind that discounts will be more than amply reassigned if calling from a hotel phone. In this case, it's good to know that Korea also offers Home Country Direct access numbers to reach a home operator:

Australia 0090-610
Canada.. 0090-015
France 0090-330
Germany.. 0090-049
Netherlands 0090-310
New Zealand 0090-640

PAY PHONES

Public Telephones

Public phones are run by Korea Telecom and take 10-won, 50-won, and 100-won coins. Little beeps during a call indicate the box is hungry for more coins. No change will be forthcoming for 50- or 100-won coins, but if the phone isn't hung up, other calls may be made on the leftover credit by pressing the green button and hoping it works. If you spot an off-the-hook telephone receiver, most likely it was left so by the previous user for the next caller's benefit—and if not to provide a random act of kindness, than probably for the universal "we're-all-in-this-together" satisfaction of stiffing the telephone conglomerate by even just a few pennies.

Calling Cards

Cards can be purchased at values of W3,000, W5,000, and W10,000.

CELLULAR PHONES

Several cellular service providers exist in South Korea. Users should note that South Korea has switched over to a digital system and analogue phones will no longer work. Korea Mobile Telecom is a major service provider.

Note: Your home country cell phone may not work in this country. If not, we recommend that you rent an international cell phone *before* you leave home. A major US-based cell phone rental provider is **IMC WorldCell**. For information see "International Cell Phone Rentals" on page 14.

CALL BACK

You can (potentially) save significant sums when calling in South Korea by using one of the call back services listed below. Fees for call back services vary widely, depending on the company and the type of service required. Be sure to check with these companies before leaving to compare rates.

For a list of callback services, please refer to the "Communications" section in the *Global Road Warrior* Introduction.

PHONE JACKS

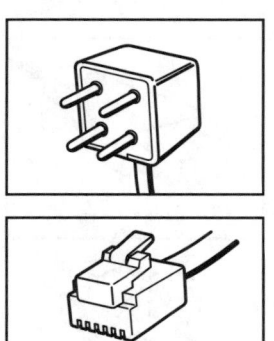

Plug adaptors are available through **iGo Corporation.** (See "Electrical and Telephone Adaptors" on page 19.)

POSTAL SERVICES

Postal service is adequate at best. Authorities often censor mail.

Hours of service

Monday to Friday 9a.m. to 5p.m., Saturday 9a.m. to 1p.m.

Business Services

BUSINESS CENTERS

Seoul Capital, Garden, InterContinental, Koreana, Lotte, Lotte World, New Seoul, Palace, President, Prince, Ramada Renaissance, Riviera, Sunshine, Swiss Grand
    Inchon New Star
    Kyongju Chosun
    Pusan Sorabol
    Taegu Kumho, Prince, Taegu

COURIER SERVICES

DHL; tel: (2) 716-0001; Ilyang Bldg.164-6 Yeomri-dong Mapo-ku, Seoul 121-090.

FedEx; PRI-EX, Inc., 158-11, Dongkyodong, Mapo-gu, Seoul (at Hapchong Subway Station; tel: (2) 333-8000.

UPS; Korea Express Co., Ltd., Dong Ah Training Center 282-19, YeomChang-Dong KangSeo-Gu, Seoul; 157-040; tel: (2) 3665-0016; fax: (2) 3664 0360/3.

South Korea

TRANSLATION SERVICES

International Translation Company, Ltd.; tel: (2) 779-2222, 752-2244, 778-3344; fax: (2) 755-2757.
Korea Translation-Interpretation Service; tel: (2) 555-5373; fax: (2) 557-5533.

Electrical

Current
110 and 220 volts AC, 60Hz.

ELECTRIC PLUGS

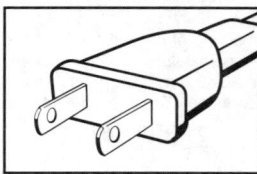

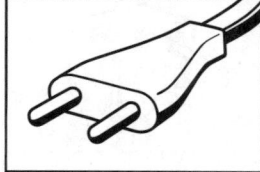

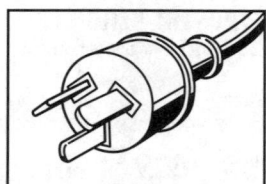

Plug adaptors are available through **iGo Corporation**. (See "Electrical and Telephone Adaptors" on page 19.)

Technical Support

HARDWARE/SOFTWARE VENDOR SUPPORT

Dell; (in Japan) tel: [81] (604) 810-4977 (for Dell listings in Japan); fax: [81] (604) 810- 4273; (in the U.S.) tel: [1] (512) 338-4400; fax: [1] (512) 728-3330; http://www.dell.com/.
Hewlett Packard; (in Japan) tel: [81] (3) 3335 8333; (in Switzerland) tel: [41] (22) 780-8111; (in the U.S.) tel: [1] (408) 246-4300; http://www.hp.com/.
IBM; tel: 3779-5300; tel: 080-023-5050; (in Japan) tel: [81] 3-3586-1111; tel: [81] 0120-04-1992; fax: [81] 44-200-8600; (in Switzerland) tel: [41] (22) 310-0418 (in French);

(in the U.S.) tel: [1] (919) 517-2800; (U.S. Main Office) tel: [1] 914-765-1900; http://www.ibm.com/.
Microsoft; tel: (2) 508-0040; tel: (2) 531-4500; fax: (2) 531-1724; (in Japan) tel: [81] (424) 41-8700 (Technical Support); fax: [81] (3) 5454- 8100; tel: [81] 0120-37-0196 (Microsoft Support Network Sales/toll free); [81] (48) 226-5500 (Customer Service); [81] (48) 226-5514 (Customer Service Fax); (in the U.S.) [1] (425) 635-7222; http://www.microsoft.com/.

Internet Connection

HOW TO CONNECT

Connecting to AOL and Compuserve in South Korea is similar to using it when traveling outside your own area code. See the introductory section for detailed information on connecting to your account through a different phone number.

Korea's Data Communications Corporation (DACOM) has developed a computer data packet network connecting 52 countries with 3,000 domestic end users and provides email, databases, videotex, and value added networks. The number of local area networks (LANs) has been doubling every year since 1980. DACOM's Customer Support Center numbers are (2) 220-0220 or 080-023-0220 (toll free).

America Online

Numbers are available at keyword *international*. Be sure to get several local numbers before leaving. AOL has a new GlobalNet service that charges US$6 an hour in addition to the usual charges. Go to keyword *access* (a free area) and download the software.

Access: Pusan (51) 462-5408; Seoul (2) 775-6647.

Compuserve

Numbers are available at *Go International*. If you are using CompuServe 2000, use GO PHONES within CompuServe 2000 to search for access numbers. The Compuserve Web-site also has a great deal of information, at http://www.compuserve.com/.

Access: Pusan (51) 462-5408; Seoul (02) 775-6647, (02) 725-1003.

Independent Service Providers

Many independent service providers offer discounts if you are only in town for a couple of days.

Chollian / BORANet; tel: (2) 709-3700; fax: (2) 2220-7218; center@chollian.net;
http://www.chollian.net/eng/.
Korea International Trade Association; tel: (2) 551-5111; http://www.kotis.net/.
Korea pc telecom; tel: (2) 513-2200; http://www.kol.net/.
Shinbiro; tel: (2) 720-1140, 725-4286(english), (080) 725-4357(toll-free);
help-eng@shinbiro.com; http://www.shinbiro.com/.

Business Culture

GREETINGS AND COURTESIES

Koreans are extremely polite, friendly, and formal in business dealings. Face, a measure of one's dignity, is crucial to Koreans. They are enormously sensitive to maintaining face in everything they do. Saying or doing anything that causes someone to lose face can instantly destroy a relationship and any business that might result from it. Never insult or openly criticize someone in front of others, no matter how subtle you think the criticism may be. Koreans generally bow to each other, but with foreigners handshaking is now the accepted greeting. In very formal situations, and if dealing with an older person, bowing is appropriate. If you are not sure whether to bow or shake hands, allow the Koreans to take the lead. Business cards are important. At the first meeting, handshakes or bows are followed by a formal exchange of cards, with text in Korean on one side. When receiving a card, do not just put it in your pocket. Take a few moments to study the card, and respond to it with the proper respect.

BUSINESS ETHIC AND FRAMEWORK

Koreans are generally highly disciplined and hard-working, but they can also be distrustful of outsiders and extremely nationalistic. Korean behavior is largely determined by Confucianism, which teaches respect for superiors, duty to family, loyalty to friends, humility, sincerity, and courtesy. Workers generally respect the companies they work for and are driven to help their business succeed. Among co-workers, people of higher status and age are respected by those beneath them, and are deferred to in speech and action. Business friends trust and respect each other, and help each other succeed. Employees work hard and are generally efficient and productive. Management styles are a combination of Confucianism and Western behavior, depending on an individual's background. Generally, business is conducted formally, with great value placed on punctuality, efficiency, and thriftiness.

DECISION MAKING

Koreans make it a point never to act as individuals but to have group cohesion. Before any action is taken or a decision made, there must be consensus from everyone involved. This is reached by circulating written memos that must receive everyone's approval. Koreans try not to say no or deliver bad news. If a project or negotiation develops problems, no one will want to admit there are difficulties and it may be necessary to look for subtle signs that something has gone wrong.

WOMEN

Women are regarded as second-class citizens. Korean women are generally employed only as secretaries, no matter how much education they have or what kind of abilities they demonstrate. However, foreign businesswomen should experience few problems. Nevertheless, they are expected to be highly professional, appropriate, and neither aggressive nor confrontational. Women may generally go on the streets and dine alone, but may feel more comfortable if escorted.

MEETINGS

Business meetings are very formal. Arrange the time and place well in advance, and be sure to be punctual. Before a meeting, mail or fax the subjects and issues under discussion and include as much detail as possible. Koreans generally are not sure how to behave at a first meeting until everyone's status is determined. Questions about one's education, parents, place of birth, or age all help to determine status. Koreans are more at ease as a group than as individuals, and become uncomfortable when people speak as individuals instead of as a group, or when they make statements that are not in harmony with the stated group view. The group's senior member should be designated as your group's spokesman. Koreans will judge the seriousness of your dealings by the status of your representatives in your company. It is a good idea to send them a list of these representatives before the meeting, and to include their rank in your company. You should also request a similar list.

BUSINESS ATTIRE

Koreans dress formally and usually wear three-piece suits for business. You will probably be judged by the quality of your attire, so your best clothes are most appropriate. Accessories and jewelry such as rings and watches will also be taken into account and admired by your Korean business counterparts, but avoid excessively expensive or showy jewelry or ornaments.

Business Centers
Seoul
CITY VIEW

Seoul stands as the gateway to South Korea and houses much of the country's population, not to mention its industry. Warehouse bazaars packed to capacity and modern buildings constantly under construction point to an acumen for trade and industrious flair. With an efficient infrastructure, one can call Seoul a modern city; however, many parts of the city still exhibit second-world status. Notwithstanding, Seoul's citizens exhibit a penchant for modern style and change.

AIRPORT

Kimpo Airport to City Center

The airport lies 16 miles (26 k.m) from the city. With an efficient infrastructure in place, Kimpo Airport is well served by economical modes of transport. Airport express bus line #600 takes travelers between the airport and Chamsil in 7-minute intervals from 5a.m. to 10p.m. Bus #601 transports passengers between the airport and Tondgdaemun (East Gate) every 10 minutes. The KAL Limousine Bus services the airport and the following downtown locations in 15-minute intervals at a cost of W5,000:

Line 1 (6:45a.m. to 10p.m.): Koreana, Seoul Plaza, Lotte, Westin Chosun, KAL Building.

Line 2: (7:09a.m. to 9:39p.m.) Holiday Inn Seoul, Seoul Train Station, Seoul Hilton, Grand Hyatt, Seoul Tower, Hotel Shilla, and the Sofitel Ambassador.

Line 3: (6:35a.m. to 9:50p.m.)Palace Hotel, Ritz Carlton, Novotel, Inter-Continental, and Seoul Renaissance.

Line 4: (6:42a.m. to 10:20p.m.) Lotte World, Dong Seoul Express Bus Terminal, and Sheraton Walker Hill.

Taxis into town are also available; however, expect to pay far more than a bus for the 45 to 60-minute trip into town.

Airline Numbers

Aer Lingus	(2) 756-2000
Aeroflot Soviet Airlines	(2) 551-0321/4
Air Canada	(2) 779-5654/5
Air China	(2) 774-6886
Air France	(2) 3788-0400
Air New Zealand	(2) 723-1114, 779-1671/2/3
Alaska Airlines	(2) 734-7100
Alitalia Airlines	(2) 779-1676
All Nippon Airways	(2) 752-5500
America West	(2) 775-1500
Asiana Airlines	(2) 661-4000
British Airways	(2) 774-5511
Cathay Pacific Airways	(2) 773-0321
China Eastern Airlines	(2) 518-0330
Continental Airlines	(2) 773-0100
Delta Airlines	(2) 754-1921/3
El Al Israel Airlines	(2) 778-3351
Finnair	(2) 734-7107
Garuda Indonesia Airways	(2) 773-2092/3

Japan Airlines .... (2) 757-1711, 664-2871
Japan Air System .... (2) 752-9090, 664-1564
KLM Royal Dutch Airlines .... (2) 753-1093, 664-1850
Korean Air .... (2) 756-2000, 656-7114, 662-2111
Lufthansa.. (2) 538-8141
Malaysia Airlines .... (2) 777-7761/2
Northwest Airlines .... (2) 666-8700
Philippine Airlines.. (2) 501-3581
Qantas Airways .... (2) 777-6871/3, 666-3282
Scandinavian Air System ....(2) 752-5123
Singapore Airlines .... (2) 755-1226, 665-1711
Swiss Air.. (2) 757-8901/8
Thai Airways International .... (2) 3707-0011
United Airlines .... (2) 757-1691, 662-0041
Uzbekistan Airways .... (2) 722-6856, 664-7365
VASP Brazilian Airlines .... (2) 755-4305
Vietnam Airlines .... (2) 775-7666

HOTELS

Top-end

Grand Hyatt Seoul; 747-7 Hannam dong, Yongsan-gu; tel: (2) 797-1234; fax: (2) 798-6953; restaurants; conference facilities; secretarial service; fax/photocopy facilities; in-room safe; parking; corporate rates; fitness; sauna; pool; whirlpool.

Inter-Continental Seoul; 159-8 Samsung-dong, Kangman-ku; tel: (2) 555-5656; fax: 559-7535; near exhibition grounds; restaurants; conference facilities; secretarial service; fax/photocopy facilities; in-room safe; parking; corporate rates; fitness; sauna.

Lotte; 1 Sogong-dong, Chung-ku; tel: (2) 771-1000; fax: (2) 752-3758; email: hotelprd@hotel.lotte.co.kr; city center; restaurants; conference facilities (up to 1500); business center (laptops, internet); secretarial service; in-room safe; secure parking; corporate rates; fitness; sauna; pool; whirlpool.

Expensive

Amiga; 248-7 Non Hyn-dong, Kang Nam-gu; tel: (2) 511-4000; fax: (2) 545-9353; city center; restaurant; conference facilities (up to 400); secretarial service; fax/photocopy facilities; parking; corporate rates; sauna.

King Sejong; 6-13 Chungmu-Ro, 2-ga, Chung-gu; tel: (2) 776-1811; fax: (2) 755-4906.

Seoul Royal; 6, 1-Ga, Myong-dong, Chung-gu; tel: (2) 756-1112; fax: (2) 756-1119; city center; restaurant; conference facilities; corporate rates; sauna.

Sofitel Ambassador; 186-54, 2 Ka-Changchung-dong, Chung-ku; tel: (2) 270-3111; fax: (2) 272-0773; city center; restaurants; conference facilities (up to 1500); parking; sauna.

Novotel Seoul Ambassador; 603, Yoksam-dong, Kangnam-gu; tel: (2) 567-1101; fax: (2) 564-4573; city center; restaurant; conference facilities (up to 600); parking; fitness; pool.

Ramada Olympia Hotel; 103-2 Pyongchang-dong, Chongno-gu; tel: (2) 2287-6000; fax: (2) 369-6633.

Seoul Palace; 63-1 Banpo-dong, Socho-gu; tel: (2) 532-5000; fax; (2) 532-0399.

Tower Hotel; 5-5, San 2-ga, Jangchoong-dong, Chung-gu; tel: (2) 2236-2121; fax: (2) 2235-0276; near city center; restaurant; conference facilities (up to 600); secretarial service; fax/photocopy facilities; in-room safe; parking; corporate rates; fitness; sauna; pool.

Moderate

Bukak Park; 113-1 Pyongchang-dong, Chongno-gu; tel: (2) 352-7101; fax: (2) 356-5559; located near airport; restaurant; conference facilities; parking.

Holiday Inn Seoul; 169-1 Dohwa-dong, Mapo-gu; tel: (2) 717-9441; fax; (2) 715-9441.

Holiday Itaewon Hotel; 737-32 Hannam-dopng, Yongsan-gu; tel: (2) 792-3111.

New Kukje; 29-2, Taepyongno 1-ga, Choong-gu; tel: (2) 732-0161; fax: (2) 732-1774.

Hotel Manhattan; 13-3 Youido-dong, Yongdeungpo-gu; tel: (2) 780-8001; fax: (2) 784-2332; near airport; restaurant; parking; sauna.

Hotel Poongiun; 73-1 Inhyon-dong 2-ga, Chung-gu; tel: (2) 266-2141; fax: (2) 274-5732.

Hotel Seokyo; 354-5 Seokyo-dong, Mapo-gu; tel: (2) 333-7771; fax; (2) 333-3388.

New Seoul Hotel; 29-1 Taep'yongno 1-ga, Chung-gu; tel: (2) 735-9071; fax: (2) 735-6212.

MEDICAL CARE

Cha General Hospital Foreign Clinic; 650-9, Yoksam-dong, Kangnam-gu; tel: (2) 3468-3113; fax: (2) 2224-5004.

Koryo General Hospital; 108 Pyongdong, Chongrogu; tel: (2) 739-3211.

Pharmacy; Itaewon; tel: (2) 797-0478; fax: (2) 797-0478.

Seoul Adventist Hospital; 29-1 Hwaegi 2-dong, Dongdaemoon-gu; tel: (2) 2210-0200; fax: (2) 3410-0229.

Severance International Health Care Center; 134 Shin-chon-dong, Seodaemun-gu; tel: (2) 361-6540; 392-3404; fax: (2) 362-6835.

St. Mary's Hospital; 62 Yoidodong, Youngdongpogu; tel: (2) 789-1114.

HEALTH CLUB

Health clubs in Seoul are very exclusive social institutions run on expensive life-membership payment systems; therefore, it is almost impossible to go for a casual workout. Your best bet is to go with a club member willing to sign you in as a guest. Most deluxe hotels, including the Hyatt, the Hilton, the Shilla and the InterContinental, have their own clubs catering to hotel guests.

AUTO RENTAL

Avis; Airport, tel: (2) 666-1121, 6a.m. to 11p.m.; Hilton Hotel, (2) 319-1121, 8:30a.m. to 6p.m.; Kang Nam, 199-4 Nonhyun-dong, Kangnam-gu, tel: (2) 512-8144, 8a.m. to 6p.m.; Kuro Branch, 689-20 Kuro-dong; tel: (2) 854-0018; Mon. to Sat. 8a.m. to 6p.m.

Daehan Rent-A-Car; 1609-7 Seochodong, Kangnamgu; tel: 585-0801 or 585-0805; 664-7684 at the airport.

WORLD TRADE CENTER

Korea World Trade Center, Seoul
47th Floor, Main Trade Tower
Kangnam-Gu, Seoul, 135-729
Korea
tel: (2) 551-5163; fax: (2) 551-5181
website: http://www.kita.or.kr
email: kwtcsl@kita.or.kr

CHAMBER OF COMMERCE

Korea Chamber of Commerce and Industry
45, Namdaemunno 4-ga, Chung-gu
Seoul 100-3114
tel: (2) 316-3114; fax: (2) 757-9475
email: trade@www.kcci.or.kr

Spain

At a Glance

THE PEOPLE

Population ....39,167,744 (July 1999 est.)
Growth Rate ....0.1% (1999 est.)
Life Expectancy .... 77.71 years (1999 est.)
Infant Mortality..... 6.41 deaths/1,000 live births (1999 est.)

Ethnic Composition
Mediterranean and Nordic composite.

Religious Composition
Roman Catholic.. 99%
Other 1%

Languages Spoken
Castilian Spanish 74%, Catalan 17%, Galician 7%, Basque 2%.

Education and Literacy
Spanish society has a high literacy rate with 96 percent of the population 15 years of age and older considered literate. Education is compulsory until 16 years of age.

Labor Force
Total: 16,200,000
By occupation: services 64%, industry 28%, agriculture 8%.

THE ECONOMY

Spain is one of the poorer EU economies and it has benefited greatly by its membership by securing subsidies otherwise unattainable. It has a "mixed" economy that has elements of capitalism with government control of major industries. Having made the leap to the Euro currency in 1999, Spain hopes to continue to exploit its EU membership although Germany is seeking to reduce the subsidy program. With one of the highest unemployment rates in Europe, Spain has not made significant reforms to its labor laws and pension schemes to keep it competitive. Its government has taken steps towards privatization of state-owned enterprises and deregulation, but the effect on foreign direct investment has yet to materialize.

Exports ....US$111.1 billion (f.o.b., 1998 est.)
Imports ....US$132.3 billion (f.o.b., 1998 est.)
Total Trade ....US$243.4 billion (f.o.b., 1998 est.)
GDP Per Capita.............................. US$16,500 (1998 est.)
Unemployment .... 20 percent (1998 est.)
Inflation Rate .... 2 percent (1998 est.)

Top Export Partners
EU, U.S.

Top Import Partners
EU, U.S., Japan.

Top Exports
Cars and trucks, semifinished manufactured goods, foodstuffs, machinery.

Top Imports
Machinery, fuels, transport equipment, semifinished goods, foodstuffs, consumer goods, chemicals.

BUSINESS WORKWEEK

Offices
Winter: Monday to Friday 9a.m. to 6p.m.
Summer: Monday to Friday 8a.m. to 3p.m.

Banks
Monday to Friday 9a.m. to 2p.m., Saturday 9a.m. to 1p.m.

Government
Monday to Friday 9a.m. to 2p.m. (office hours)

Retail
Monday to Saturday 10a.m. to 6p.m., (hours can vary for peak tourist season and pre-holiday)

HOLIDAYS

New Year's Day...January 1
Epiphany ....January 6
St. Joseph the Workman .... March 19
Maundy Thursday... April 20
Good Friday...April 21*
Easter Celebration..April 24*
Labor Day...May 1
St. Isidro (Madrid only) ....May 15
Corpus Christi...June 22
King Juan Carlos' Saint's Day ....June 24
St. James of Compostela ....July 25
Assumption.. August 15
National Day..October 12
All Saints' Day ....November 1
Constitution Day ....December 6
Immaculate Conception....................................December 8
Christmas ....December 25
Boxing Day (Barcelona) ....December 26
*Date may vary by year.

CLIMATE

Seasons
The overall climate in Spain is considered temperate although the flat plains will differ significantly from mountainous and coastal areas.

Regions
The mainland has extremes of climate, particularly true of central Spain where there are cold, sharp winters and very hot summers. Climate in mainland Spain is varied; the eastern and southern coastal area is Mediterranean, with long hot summers and short winters. The north and west are temperate, with much colder winters. It is dry in the northwest.

Money & Banking

Currency
The currency of Spain is the Peseta (P).

Denominations
The Peseta (P) comes in coin denominations of P500, 200, 100, 50, 25, 10, 5, 2 and 1; and bank notes of P1,000, 2,000, 5,000 and 10,000.

Traveler's Checks and Credit Cards
Traveler's checks and foreign currency can be easily and efficiently exchanged at banks, foreign exchange bureaus located in the major cities, hotels, and foreign exchange kiosks at the

Spain

SM Santa Barbara, CA

©2001 Magellan Geographix

Spain

⊛	National capital
◉	Provincial capital
●	Secondary city
——	Primary road
········	Railroad
——	Administrative border
▬▬	International border

0 50 100km
0 50 100

---

airports. Banks offer the most accessible exchange rates. Traveler's checks receive a better exchange rate than cash, or you can purchase Spanish currency traveler's check before departure, which can be exchanged almost everywhere.

American Express, Visa, MasterCard, and Diners Club, are widely accepted in Spain. Credit card transactions receive the optimal exchange rate. You can get cash advances from your credit card on many of the automated teller machines (ATM). Long-term visitors should set up a checking account in Spain, and get an ATM card.

Travel

VISA AND PASSPORT

Foreigners must have a valid passport, but a visa is not required for tourist stays of up to 90 days. Citizens of E.U. countries need a valid National Identify card from their home state to enter. U.S., Australia, and New Zealand citizens need a valid passport and are given an authorized three-month stay, which can be renewed for three additional months.

DEPARTURE FORMALITIES

The rules for the export of currency from Spain are in a state of flux during the transition to the Euro. Business travellers should check with their consulate or embassy prior to major transactions and currency transfers.

CUSTOMS ENTRY (PERSONAL)

Duty-free

The following items may be imported into Spain by passengers of non-EU countries:

- Tobacco: 200 cigarettes, 100 cigarillos, 50 cigars, or 250g tobacco
- Alcohol: 1 liter of spirits if exceeding 22 percent volume or 2 liters of alcoholic beverage not exceeding 22 percent volume; 2 liters of wine

Other: 250ml eau de toilette and 50g of perfume; gifts to the value of P5000 (P2000 for children under 15 years of age)

Visitors over 17 years of age arriving from EU countries with duty-paid goods:

- Tobacco: 800 cigarettes, 400 cigarillos, 200 cigars, and 1kg of tobacco

Spain

- Alcohol: 90 liters of wine (including up to 60 liters of sparkling wine); 10 liters of spirits; 20 liters of intermediate products (such as fortified wine); 110 liters of beer

IMMUNIZATION

No immunization is required except for travelers entering from infected areas. Typhoid, paratyphoid, polio, and tetanus is recommended for visitors who expect to travel outside of the major cities.

TIPPING

Taxi

Taxi drivers in cities get 5 to 10 percent. In metered taxis from the airport, tip a driver to Madrid 10 percent of the fare and a driver to Barcelona 5 to 10 percent of the fare.

Hotels

Hotel desk clerks and doormen get P100, porters P50 per bag, and maids P200 per week.

Restaurants

Tip 5 to 10 percent in the absence of a restaurant service charge.

EMERGENCY INFORMATION

Police and Crime

Spain is a relatively safe country, but theft is common in larger cities. Madrid and Barcelona suffer increasing crime rates, especially in tourist areas. Pickpockets are prevalent, so use basic precautions. Avoid flashy displays of wealth, and dress conservatively. Leave most of your cash, traveler's checks, jewelry, and other valuables in your hotel safe. Carry photocopies of your passport instead of the original. Carry cash in a money belt, and use credit cards or traveler's checks for most transactions.

Foreign visitors are often the target of thieves; so, purses, laptops and briefcases require additional security. Do not leave valuables in cars or on tables in cafés.

Women are advised to travel in groups after dark or to take taxis after midnight. The police are efficient and courteous with multiple language skills.

Emergency Numbers

Police 36-6141
Ambulance 61-7777
Emergency 115
Information in English 36-9540

Health

Tap water is safe to drink, but most people prefer bottled mineral water. Community health standards are high, and there are no extraordinary diseases here.

Digestive problems may occur for people unaccustomed to the cuisine and dining hours. Wash all vegetables in a chlorine solution, peel fruits, and avoid uncooked food. Drink only pasteurized milk.

The Spanish medical service is adequate, however for more serious medical care, try the private hospitals. Pharmacies in urban Spain have all the necessary drugs, but if traveling to more rural regions, come prepared.

For more information on medical centers, including phone numbers, please see the "City Center" section at the end of this chapter.

TAXIS & RENTAL CARS

Taxis are plentiful in the cities. All should be metered. Rental cars can be found in urban areas but visitors should purchase ample insurance. Hired cars with drivers are recommended for first-time visitors.

BUS

Most areas will have a bus link to major cities. Most buses can only be entered from stations, rarely do they stop at corners and pick up passengers.

TRAIN

Almost all trains are air conditioned and efficient. There is also an intercity express train requiring a reservation.

TRAVEL ASSISTANCE

Hotel Accommodations

Federación Española de Hoteles 91-556 7112

Essential Terms

English	Spanish
Yes No	Sí No
Good morning Hello (daytime) Hello (evening) Hello (telephone)	Buenos días Buenas tardes Buenas noches ¿Hola?
Good-bye	Adiós
Please	Por favor
Thank you	Gracias
Pleased to meet you	Mucho gusto
Excuse me; I'm sorry	Pardón
My name is _____	Me llamo _____
I don't understand	No comprendo
Do you speak English?	¿Habla inglés?

Communications

DIALING CODES IN SPAIN

International country code: [34]

Selected city codes: Alicante (96), Barcelona (93), Bilbao (94), Cadiz (956), Cordoba (957), Granada (958), Las Palmas (928), Madrid (91), Malaga (95), Palma de Mallorca (971), Santa Cruz de Tenerife (922), Sevilla (95), Tarragona (977), Tenerife (922), Gibraltar (350), Andorra (376)

Dialing Spain from Overseas

To dial Spain from overseas, dial your country's international dialing code, then 34 (the country code for Spain), then the number. In April of 1998, all telephone numbers in Spain started using a 9-digit system, which means the city codes were all incorporated into the numbers and no longer exist separately from the number. If you have numbers for Spain that do not have 9 digits, you will need to determine what the city code of their residence was before you can dial the number. If you were dialing Barcelona from the United States, for example, you would begin with 011, then 34, and finally the number of the person or office you were trying to reach.

Spain

Assistance Numbers

International Operator 005
International Information.. 0025
European Long-Distance Operator 008
Local Operator.. 009
Information 003

CALLING WITHIN SPAIN

Local Calls

Spain's telephone service is improving. In April of 1998, all telephone numbers in Spain started using a 9-digit system, which means the city codes were all incorporated into the numbers and must be dialed even when within that city. Most calls can be made easily and will now be free from a private phone.

Long Distance Calls

In April of 1998, all telephone numbers in Spain started using a 9-digit system, which means the city codes were all incorporated into the numbers and must be dialed at all times, regardless of your location in Spain. As such, Madrid's "city code" prefix is 91 and Barcelona's is 93. These prefixes must be dialed even if within the cities themselves. Private telephone carriers have descended upon the scene and offer various rates for calling. Telefonica (Telecom Spain) still provides the most expensive service.

International Calls

Direct dialing is most economical, unless you are doing so from a hotel, which will certainly charge you handsomely for the privilege. Simply dial 07 + country code + area code + number. You can also reach an overseas operator by dialing the appropriate access number from the blue public phones, private phones, or the phone center.
British Telecom Direct 900-99-00-44
Canada Direct 900-99-00-15
U.S. AT&T Direct..900-99-00-11
U.S. MCI World 900-99-00-14
U.S. Sprint..900-99-00-13

PAY PHONES

Public Telephones

There are three types of pay phones in Spain, all colored green. The main kind requires coins, and has a digital readout to show the amount of money remaining during a call. Older models of this phone require lining coins in a groove on top of the dial and dropping them as needed. For newer models, simply insert the coins and wait for a dial tone.

Card phones are also available (and becoming more popular).

Calling Cards

Cards can be purchased at tobacco shops for P1,000 or 2,000.

CELLULAR PHONES

Several cellular service providers exist in Spain. Telefonica Servicios Moviles is a major service provider offering NMT-450 and TACS for analogue users, and GSM for digital. There are other companies that also offer GSM, including Airtel and Amena.
Airtel; http://www.airtel.es/.
Amena; http://www.amena.com/.
Telefonica Servicios Moviles; http://www.telefonica.es/.

Cell phones require a certain prefix before dialing their numbers:
Airtel GSM 607, 670
MoviLine 608
MoviStar GSM 609, 629, 639

Note: Your home country cell phone may not work in this country. If not, we recommend that you rent an international cell phone *before* you leave home. A major US-based cell phone rental provider is **IMC WorldCell**. For information see "International Cell Phone Rentals" on page 14.

CALL BACK

You can (potentially) save significant sums when calling in Spain by using one of the call back services listed below. Fees for call back services vary widely, depending on the company and the type of service required.

For a list of callback services, please refer to the "Communications" section in the *Global Road Warrior* Introduction.

PHONE JACKS

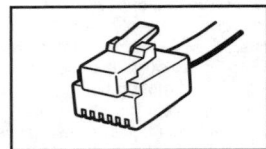

Plug adaptors are available through **iGo Corporation.** (See "Electrical and Telephone Adaptors" on page 19.)

FAX

Fax machines are readily available, and service is generally excellent.

POSTAL SERVICES

Postal services in Spain are generally poor. Mail can be censored (although these days it often is not). Do no send valuables. Unless mail is clearly marked for airmail, it will be sent by sea.

Hours of service

Monday to Friday 9a.m. to 9p.m., usually with a long break (siesta) in the middle.

Business Services

COURIER SERVICES

Madrid

DHL International Espana S.A.; Edificio DHL; Centro De Carga Aerea; Aeropuerto De Barajas; tel: 902 12 24 24; outside Spain: [34] 91-747-3400; web site: http://www.dhl.es; open Mon. to Fri. 9a.m. to 6p.m., closed Sat. Sun. and holidays; Fernan Caballero 18; Mon. to Fri. 9a.m. to 7p.m., closed Sat., Sun., and holidays, tel: 93-321-7316.

Federal Express; toll free: 900-100- 871; or tel: 91- 748-1701; Mon. to Fri. 8a.m. to 7p.m.; Customer Invoicing Services; Invoice enquiries: 91-748-1732; Customer Automation Help Desk; For enquires on any FedEx Customer Automation products: 900/993273.

TNT Express Worldwide; Torres Quevado 1, 28820 Coslada, Madrid; tel: 91 660-5900; fax: 91 660-5928.

UPS Espana, Ltd.; Ctra Villaverde a Vallecas KM 3,500, Floors 3-6 and 9, Centro de Transportes de Madrid; tel; 91-507-1800, 91-507-0888; fax: 91-507-0504, 91-507-0607.

Barcelona
DHL; Hospitalet De Llobregat; Pol Ind Gran Via Sur C/ Botanica; 145-147 Esquina A C/1 De Mayo; Barcelona 08908; tel: 93-263 4500; open Monday to Friday 6a.m. to 7p.m., closed Saturday, Sunday, and holidays.

ESABE-Suresa; tel: 93-232-5013.

UPS Espana Ltd.; Calle Miguel Hernandez 79-99, Poligono Gran Via, Hospitalet De Llobregat; tel: 93-263-4005; fax: 93-263-3909.

SECRETARIAL SERVICES
Madrid
Servicio y Organización de Secretarriado; Hotel Eurobuilding, Calle Juan Ramón Jiménez 8-1; tel: 91-458-8522.

Barcelona
AZAI; Calle Calaf 24; tel: 93-202-2444.

Lexington International Business Center; Av. Diagonal 605; tel: 93-410-7760.

TEASA; Av. Diagonal 539-541; tel: 93-410-8361.

TRANSLATION SERVICES
Madrid
Centro de Traducciones y Congresos; Eurobuilding Hotel, Calle Juan Ramón Jiménez 8-1; tel: 91-458-8522.

Fexco Iberica SRL; C/Medinaceli 5, P4; 28660 Boadilla del Monte - Madrid; tel: 91 632-2538; fax: 91 633-4025; email: fexco@teleline.es fexcoib@teleline.es; fexcoib@jazzfree.com; web: http://www.fexco.purespace.de.

Barcelona
Rosario Tauler de Canals; Passeig de Sant Joan 50; tel: 93-301-7181.

Electrical
Current
220 volts AC, 50Hz.

ELECTRIC PLUGS

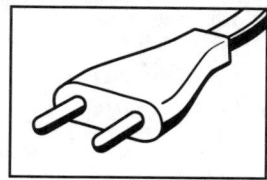

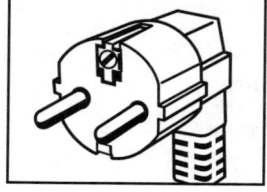

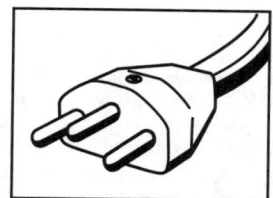

Plug adaptors are available through **iGo Corporation**. (See "Electrical and Telephone Adaptors" on page 19.)

Technical Support
HARDWARE/SOFTWARE VENDOR SUPPORT
Compaq/Digital; (in Switzerland) tel: [41] (22) 709-5330; fax: [41] (22) 709-5391 (Geneva); tel: [41] (1) 801-2507; fax: [41] (1) 801-2172 (Zurich); (General U.S.) tel: (281) 518-2000; http://www.compaq.com/.

Dell; (in Germany) tel: [49] (61) 039-710; (Dell- Europe) tel: [44] (134) 474-8000; (in the U.S.) tel: [1] (512) 338-4400; fax: [1] (512) 728-3330; http://www.dell.com/.

Filemaker/Claris; (in Germany) tel: [49] (180) 525-8166 (Info-line); fax: [49] (180) 567-2233; tel: [49] (180) 523-6423; (in the U.S.) tel: [1] (800) 965-9090; http://www.claris.com/.

Hewlett Packard; (in Switzerland) tel: [41] (22) 780-8111; (in the U.S.) tel: [1] (408) 246-4300; http://www.hp.com/.

IBM; tel: 901 300-000; (in Switzerland) tel: [41] (22) 310-0418 (in French); (in the U.S.) tel: [1] (919) 517-2800; (U.S. Main Office) tel: [1] 914-765-1900; http://www.ibm.com/.

Microsoft; tel: 902 197 198; fax: 91 803 8310; (in Switzerland) tel: [41] (848) 858-868; fax [41] (1) 831-0869; (in the U.S.) [1] (425) 635-7222; http://www.microsoft.com/.

Internet Connection
HOW TO CONNECT
Connecting to AOL and Compuserve in Spain is similar to using it when traveling outside your own area code. See the introductory section for detailed information on connecting to your account through a different phone number.

America Online
Numbers are available at keyword international. Be sure to get several local numbers before leaving. AOL has a new GlobalNet service that charges US$6 an hour in addition to the usual charges. Go to keyword access (a free area) and download the software.

Access: Alicante 9669-19464; Barcelona 9348-78644; Bilbao 9441-59933; Las Palmas de Gran Canaria 9283-85154; Madrid 9153-49345; Malaga 9520-48589; Palma de Mallorca 9717-19568; San Sebastian 9432-12700; Seville 9544-25311; Tenerife 9227-59025; Valencia 9635-20926; Zaragoza 9765-65142.

Compuserve
Numbers are available at *Go International*. If you are using CompuServe 2000, use GO PHONES within CompuServe 2000 to search for access numbers. The Compuserve Website also has a great deal of information, at http://www.compuserve.com/.

Access: Alicante 9669-19464; Barcelona 9348-73888; Bilbao 9441-59933; Las Palmas 9283-85154; Madrid 9139-56500; Malaga 9520-48589; Palma 9717-19568;

San Sebastian 9432-12700; Seville 9544-25311; Tenerife 9227-59025; Valencia 9635-10133; Zaragoza 9765-65142.

Independent Service Providers

Many independent service providers offer discounts if you are only in town for a couple of days.

Adam Internet (Ogic Informatica S.L.); tel: 3446-5000; tel: 9344-65005; http://www.adam.es/.

ATLAS IAP, S.L.; tel: 97173-8871; fax: 9717-38871; info@atlas-iap.es; http://www.atlas-iap.es/(Spanish and English).

Centro Español de Servicios Telemáticos, S.A. / Cesatel; tel: 1871-2095; fax: 1870-2818; info@cestel.es; http://www.cestel.es/ (Spanish and English).

EUnet-Goya; tel: 9175-48000; fax: 9175-48008; email: info@eunet.es; http://www.eunet.es/.

Nova Internet; tel: 9130-86763; fax: 9130-86747; email: admin@nova.es; http://www.nova.es/.

Business Culture

GREETINGS AND COURTESIES

Public display of affection, such as a kiss on the cheek, is for family and friends only; visitors should not initiate such contact. Close male friends exchange an *abrazo*, or hug. Female friends greet and part with a slight embrace. For the first meeting and departure, shake hands with everyone present, even children. Spaniards stand and sit closely, using frequent hand and arm gestures, and often interrupt each other. Address people by their titles, such as *Señor*, *Señorita*, or *Señora*; *Don* and *Doña* show greater respect. First names are used between close friends and young people; in business circles you will probably not be asked to call someone by their first name.

BUSINESS ETHIC AND FRAMEWORK

When dealing with Spaniards, agreements usually start with an oral understanding, followed by a handshake and a contract. The letter of the contract will be strictly fulfilled, and Spaniards expect the same in return. Spanish people are usually very direct; they will tell you exactly what is on their mind. Manners are important, but the Spanish make it a point not to be too stiff or formal. Collaboration is more often an opportunity to voice opinions rather than a path to decisions. Spaniards trust friends and family the most, and nepotism is common.

DECISION MAKING

Family ownership has been common in Spain for decades, centuries in some cases. Ownership structures have become complicated; you may think you are dealing with a decision maker but you probably are not. Spanish businesspeople will present their own views often, but will rarely be convinced with other arguments. Confrontation should be avoided at all costs; admitting an error is one of the worst mistakes you can make. Decisions are slow; they come from a central authority figure less impressed by facts than by intuition. Sharing the burden of decision making is seen as a sign of weakness. The best leader is an autocrat who cares for his people—the patron—but who stands essentially alone. Spaniards are generally conservative, and will resist any risky decisions. Many younger managers are trying to implement Western methods, but it is still not always possible to get access to the decision maker. In that case, help the person with whom you can build a relationship to persuade the decision maker.

WOMEN

Many women in Spain, especially in the larger cities of Madrid and Barcelona, are career oriented and proud of their business success in middle management or above. Social and educational status often determines the role women play in business. Female professionals include lawyers, doctors, scientists, professors, and executives. The macho attitude is a fast-fading cliche, so women executives may not appreciate doors being held open for them. Foreign businesswomen should encounter very little difficulty in accomplishing their business in Spain.

MEETINGS

Punctuality is important only if attending a bullfight. Many businesspersons do not arrive at the office until 11am and take lunch at 5p.m.; yet they will stay at their desks until 8 or 9p.m. Frequent interruption of meetings by phone calls or a personal aside are entirely normal. Prior appointments are absolutely necessary, but do not schedule meetings between 12:30 and 4:30p.m. The predominant air at meetings is informality; meetings are extremely casual. Small talk will occupy at least the first half hour of a meeting; do not begin to discuss business until your host extends the invitation. Spaniards tend to be friendly, individualistic, and stoic. They tend to rely on both verbal and nonverbal communication; sometimes what you say isn't as important as what you don't say. Their advice is meant to correct a visitor's errors. The focus of most meetings is the present; though the *mañana* attitude is no longer dominant, Spaniards prefer to live for the moment and let the future take care of itself.

BUSINESS ATTIRE

Spaniards are usually modest, but take pride in social position and personal appearance; affluence and standing are reflected in the quality of one's clothes. Men usually avoid bright or contrasting colors; women strive to be stylish and children are dressed as well as possible. Business dress is essentially conservative, but becomes more informal the further west you go; European styles predominate.

Business Centers
Madrid

CITY VIEW

The cultural capital of Spain, Madrid is known to locals as the "gateway to heaven". Probably the most active city in Europe, projects to revamp the city are well underway, including well-needed infrastructure development. With a well-established nighttime lifestyle, one might think of Madrid as the European city that never sleeps.

AIRPORT

Barajas Airport to City Center

The airport lies 10 miles (16 km.) from the city. Buses service the airport every 15 minutes and take passengers to the Plaza de Colón, from where one may hail a cab to get to a hotel. Taxis are available with costs ranging from P2,000 to P4,000. Expect to pay P350 extra if traffic is congested. A subway line to the airport has opened. It is an affordable and reliable means of getting to and from Barajas Airport.

Airline Numbers

Aerolíneas Argentinas	91-547-4700
Aer Lingus Reservations	91-541-4216
Air Canada	91-547-9304
Air France	91-330-0400

American Airlines 91-597-2068
　　toll free .... (1) 10-0001
British Airways 91-431-7575
CSA 91-542-6166, 542-6628
Delta 91-577-0650
Iberia 91-587-8109, 587-8787
Lufthansa 91-383-1764
Qantas 91-541-9736
Singapore 91-563-8001
Thai Airways 91-411-6411

HOTELS

Top-end

Castellana Inter-Continental; Paseo de la Castellana 49; tel: 91-310-0200; fax: 91-319-5853; in the U.S. 1-800-327-0200; 3 restaurants; business center; in-room data ports; health club.

Palace Hotel (Sheraton); Plaza de las Cortes 7; tel: 91-360-8000; fax: 91-360-8100; in the U.S. 1-800-325-3535; recently renovated; city center; 2 restaurants; conference facilities (up to 800); secretarial service; 24-hour business center; data ports, voice mail; safe; soundproof windows; corporate rates; 24-hour fitness.

Hotel Ritz (Leading Hotels of the World); Plaza de la Lealtad 5; tel: 91-521-2857; fax: 91-532-8776; 1-800-223-6800 in the U.S.; Old World charm; individually designed rooms; city center; restaurant; conference facilities (up to 450); secretarial service; business center; in-room modem/fax connection; parking; fitness.

Santo Mauro (Relais and Chateaux); tel: 91-319-6900; fax: 91-308-5477; [1] 212-856-0115 in the U.S; small hotel; gourmet restaurant; garden; exercise equipment; indoor pool.

Hotel Villa Magna (Park Hyatt); Paseo de la Castellana 22; tel: 91-576-7500; fax: 91-575-9504; in the U.S. 1-800-233-1234; located in financial district; 2 restaurants; conference facilities (up to 500); business center; secretarial service; internet connection; room fax upon request; 3 digital phones/fax connection; soundproof windows; in-room safe; secure parking; corporate rates; fitness; sauna; steam bath.

Expensive

Conde Duque; Plaza Conde Valle de Suchil 5; tel: 91-447-7000; fax: 91-448-3569; in the U.S. 1-800-223-5652; small hotel located near Colon Square; restaurant; conference facilities; business services (fax and computer rental); in-room data ports, fax connection, dual phones; corporate rates; fitness.

Hotel Emperatriz; Lopez de Hoyos 4-6; tel: 91-563-8088; fax: 91-563-9804; located in Salamanca Quarter; restaurant; in-room safe.

Hotel Wellington; Velazquez 8; tel: 91-574-4400; fax: 91-576-4164; city center; recently renovated; breakfast buffet; secretarial service; fax/photocopy facilities; soundproof windows; in-room safe; parking; pool. (204/262)

Husa Princesa; Princesa 40; tel: 91-542-2100; fax: 91-542-2100; near university; 2 restaurants; conference facilities (up to 825); secretarial service; business center; in-room safe, three phones, modem/fax connection; parking; fitness; pool (196/245).

Suecia; Marques de Casa Riera 4; tel: 91-531-6900; fax: 91-521-7141; city center; restaurant; conference facilities (up to 250); secretarial service; fax/photocopy facilities; in-room safe; parking; corporate rates. (141/181)

Tryp Fenix; Hermosilla 2; tel: 91-431-6700; fax: 91-576-0661; near city center; restaurant; conference facilities; in-room modem/fax connection, safe; parking; corporate rates. (172/215)

Moderate

Atlantico; Gran Via 38; tel: 91-522-6480; fax: 91-531-0210; city center; in-room safe; corporate rates.

Carlos V; Maestro Vitoria 5; tel: 91-531-4100; fax: 91-531-3761; city center; secretarial service; fax/photocopy facilities; in-room safe.

Hotel Santo Domingo; Plaza de Santo Domingo 13; tel: 91-547-9800; fax: 91-547-5995; in the Royal Palace Quarter; restaurant; conference facilities (up to 90); secretarial service; fax/photocopy facilities; internet connection; parking; corporate rates.

Prìncipe Pìo; Cuesta de San Vicente; tel: 91-547-0800; fax: 91-541-1117; near railway; restaurant; conference facilities (up to 200); corporate rates.

Regente; Calle Mesoneros Romanos 12; tel: 91-521-2941; fax: 91-532-3014; near city center.

Señorial; Leganitos 41; tel: 91-52-7870; fax; 91-547-0933; city center; restaurant; conference facilities 9up to 40); in-room safe; parking; corporate rates.

HEALTH CLUB

Instituto Municipal de Deportes (Municipal Sports Centers); Palacete de la Casa de Campa, Puente del Rey; tel: 91-463-55-63

Tablas (women only); 45 General Pardinas Barrio de Salamanca; Metro: Nunez de Balboa; tel: 91-575-85-55.

AUTO RENTAL

Alamo; Aeropuerto de Barajas; tel: 91-349-1393-7232/85; Mon. to Sun. 8a.m. to 11:30p.m.

Avis; Barajas Airport, tel: 91-393-7222 ; Sun. to Sat. 7a.m. to 3a.m.; Hotel Holiday Inn, Plaza Trias Beltran,4 (local), Acceso Gral Peron 32-34, tel: 91-556-7492, Sunday closed, Mon. to Fri. 8a.m. to 7p.m., Sat. 9a.m. to 10p.m.; Plaza De Colon, Bus Terminal, tel: 91-576-2862, Sun. closed, Mon. to Fri. 8a.m. to 1p.m., 4p.m. to 7p.m., Sat. 9a.m. to 12a.m.

Europcar; Barajas Airport, tel: 91-393-7235; fax: 91-393-7240; Mon. to Sun. 7a.m. to midnight; Madrid Orense - IKC, tel: 91- 555-9930, fax: 91- 555-9886, Mon. to Fri. 8a.m. to 2p.m., 4p.m. to 8p.m., closed Sunday.

Thrifty; tel: 91-359-9097, C/Alberto Alcocer No. 12.

WORLD TRADE CENTER

World Trade Center Madrid, S.A.
Paseo de la Habana, 26
3rd Floor, Suite #4
28036 Madrid, Spain
tel: 91-562-4004; fax: 91-562-4004
email: wtcmadrid@mad.servicom.es

Barcelona

CITY VIEW

　　Barcelona is the second largest city in Spain, with a population of about 1.5 million. Thanks to a massive US$2billion development plan for the 1992 Summer Olympics, along with intelligent marketing, it is now a heavily touristed city. With architects called in to mastermind even the street lamps, one could say that Barcelona has a well-designed charm. Development of an efficient infrastructure, enhancing its already favorable location as a transportation hub, puts Barcelona on the business map as well.

AIRPORT

Del Prat Airport to City Center

　　The airport lies 6 miles (10 km.) from the city. The Aerobus operates every 15 minutes to the Plaça Catalunya for P450. Expect a 30-minute ride. Bus service runs until 11:30p.m. Taxis are also available at a cost of about P2,200. Although a train runs to the city every 30 minutes from 6a.m. to 10p.m., the station proves a bit far away.

Airline Numbers

Air Canada	93-41-77-932
Air Europa	93-412-77-33
Air France	93-87-25-26
Alitalia	93-41-60-424
Aviaco and Iberia	93-412-56-67
British Airways	93-487-21-12
CSA	93-41-56-046
KLM	93-379-54-58
Lufthansa	93-487-03-00
Spanair	93-478-66-91
TWA	93-215-84-86

HOTELS

Top-end

Hotel Arts (Ritz-Carlton); Carrer de la Marina 19-21; tel: 93-93-221-1000; fax: 93-221-1070; located on beachfront; 2 restaurants; conference facilities (1100); business center; secretarial service; translation; office equipment rental; Club floors with 5 buffets daily; twin telephone lines, voicemail; modem/fax connection; parking; fitness; pool.

Hotel Claris; Pau Claris 150; tel: 93-487-6262; fax: 93-215-7970; in the U.S. 1-800-525-4800; small, luxury hotel with contemporary rooms; restaurants; conference facilities; parking; fitness; sauna; pool.

Hotel Rey Juan Carlos I; Avenida Diagonal 661-671; tel: 93-448-0808; fax: 93-448-0607; located in suburb; restaurant; conference facilities (up to 1500); secretarial service; fax/photocopy facilities; parking; pool.

Princesa Sofía Inter-Continental; Plaza Rio XII, 4; tel: 93-330-7111; fax: 93-330-7621; renovated; Club rooms available; convention facilities.

Expensive

Calderón; Rambla Catalunya 26; tel: 93-301-0000; fax: 93-317-3157; located near airport; restaurant; fitness; sauna; pool.

Colón; Avenida Catedral 7; tel: 93-301-1404; fax: 93-317-2915; email: colon@nexus.es; http://www.nexus.es/colon; near city center; restaurant; conference facilities (up to 200); parking; corporate rates. (94/141)

Fira Palace; Avenida Rius I Taulet 1-3; tel: 93-426-2223; fax: 93-425-5047; city center; restaurant; conference facilities (up to 2100); secretarial service; fax/photocopy facilities; in-room safe; fitness; sauna; pool.

Gallery; Rosellon 249; tel: 93-415-9911; fax: 93-415-9184; email: gallery@super.medusa.es; city center; restaurant; conference facilities (up to 200); in-room safe; parking; fitness; sauna.

Majestic; Passeig de Gracia 68; tel: 93-488-1717; fax: 93-488-1880; city center; restaurant; conference facilities (up to 600); secretarial service; fax/photocopy facilities; in-room modem/fax connection, safe; parking; corporate rates; pool.

Novotel Barcelona/San Cugat; Plaza Xavier Cugat, S/N, Cugat; tel: 93-589-4141; fax: 93-589-3031; near railway; restaurant; conference facilities (up to 400); secretarial service; fax/photocopy facilities; parking; corporate rates; pool.

The Palace; Gran Via Cortes Catanes 668; tel: 93-318-5200; fax: 93-318-0148; city center; restaurant; conference facilities (up too500); in-room safe; parking; corporate rates.

Moderate

Continental; Rambla 138; tel: 93-301-2508; fax: 93-302-7360; near airport; restaurant.

Duques de Bergara; Bergara 11; tel: 93-301-5151; fax: 93-317-3442; near airport; restaurant; conference facilities.

Gran Derby; Loreto 28; tel: 93-322-2062; fax: 93-419-6820; email: info@derbyhotels.es; restaurant; conference facilities (up to 150); in-room modem/fax connection, safe; parking; pool.

Llicorella; Camino San Antonio, 101, Cubelles; tel: 93-895-0044; fax: 93-895-2417; located near railway; restaurant; conference facilities (up to 40); secretarial service; fax/photocopy facilities; in-room safe; parking; corporate rates; pool.

Mercure (Montecarlo); La Rambla 124; tel: 93-3412-0404; fax: 93-3318-7323; near exhibition grounds; conference facilities (up to 80); in-room safe; parking.

Nouvel; Santa Anna 18-20; tel: 93-301-8274; fax: 93-301-8370; city center; in-room safe; corporate rates.

Rialto; Calle Fernando 41; tel: 93-318-5212; fax: 93-310-4081; located near airport; conference facilities.

San Just; Frederic Mompou 1, Sant Just Desvern; tel: 93-473-2517; fax: 93-473-2450; located in suburb; restaurant; conference facilities (up to 600); secretarial service; fax/photocopy facilities; in-room safe; parking; corporate rates; fitness; sauna; whirlpool.

Suizo; Plaza de l'Angel 12; tel: 93-315-0461; fax: 93-310-4081; located near airport; restaurant; conference facilities.

MEDICAL CARE

Centro Medico; Passeig de Gracia 30; tel: 93-401-3123, 93-403-3124.

Tres Torres; Calle Dr. Roux 76; tel: 93-204-1300.

HEALTH CLUB

Club Natacio Montjuic; tel: 93-325-9281 (pool).

Esportiu Can Carelleu; tel: 93-203-7874.

Gimnas Municipal Montjuic; tel: 93-223-0266.

Tenis Pompeia; tel: 93-325-1348.

AUTO RENTAL

Alamo; airport, tel: 93-298-3433/34, Mon. to Sun. 8a.m. to 11:30p.m; Cal Alaio, 6 Barcelona South

tel: 93-478-5802, Mon. to Fri. 9a.m. to 1:30p.m., 4:30p.m. to 7p.m., Sat. 9:30a.m. to 1:30p.m., closed Sunday. Barcelona Transmediterranea, Muelle San Beltran, tel: 93-442-96/90, Mon. to Sun. 8a.m. to 2p.m. 7p.m. to 11p.m.

Avis; airport, tel: 93-379-4026, Mon. to Sun. 7a.m. to midnight; Hotel Barcelona Plaza, tel: 93-423-3455.

Europcar; Barcelona airport, tel: 93-298-3300; fax: 93-298-3304, Sunday to Monday 7a.m. to midnight; Consejo de Ciento 363, tel: 93-488-1953; fax: 91-488-2192..

Hertz; 10 Tuset; tel: 93-217-32-48.

Thrifty; C/Brasil 40 Bajos, tel: 93-330-9911.

WORLD TRADE CENTER

World Trade Center Barcelona
Moll de Barcelona s/n - Edifici Est. 2c planta
08039 Barcelona
tel: 93-508-8000; fax: 93-508-8010
email: lrovira@wtcbarcelona.es
website: www.wtcbarcelona.com

Sri Lanka

At a Glance

THE PEOPLE

Population ....19,144,875 (July 1999 est.)
Growth Rate ....1.1% (1999 est.)
Life Expectancy .... 72.67 years (1999 est.)
Infant Mortality... 16.12 deaths/1,000 live births (1999 est.)

Ethnic Composition

Sinhalese...74%
Tamil..18%
Moor 7%
Malays and other minorities 1%

Religious Composition

Buddhism..69%
Hindu 15%
Christian..8%
Islamic..8%

Languages Spoken

Sinhala (official) 74%
Tamil (national) 18%
Other...8%

Education and Literacy

More than 90 percent of the population over the age of 15 is considered literate. Education is compulsory for 10 years. All schools, including universities, are free. The educational system has been separated into Sinhala and Tamil.

Labor Force

Total 6,200,000
By occupation: services 46%, agriculture 37%, industry and commerce 17%.

THE ECONOMY

Sri Lanka has transformed itself from a poverty stricken agriculture-based economy into a middle-income service and industry culture in just twenty years. Textiles and garments have become the mainstay exports of a nation where once exports were 93 percent agricultural. Telecommunications and financial services have also made Sri Lanka a leading service vendor in the region. Once a "statist" economy, the nation now looks to the free market as a model for growth. While the government moves ahead with privatization and GDP expansion plans, Sri Lanka has been hampered in attracting foreign investment by the continued civil war among the Tamils and the Sinhalese.

Exports ....US$4.5 billion (f.o.b., 1998)
Imports ....US$5.3 billion (f.o.b., 1998)
Total Trade ....US$9.8 billion (f.o.b., 1998)
GDP Per Capita............................... US$2,500 (1998 est.)
Unemployment ....11 percent (1997)
Inflation Rate ....9.3 percent (1998)

Top Export Partners

U.S., EU, Japan.

Top Import Partners

India, Japan, South Korea, Hong Kong, Taiwan.

Top Exports

Garments and textiles, tea, diamonds, other gems, petroleum products, rubber products.

Top Imports

Textiles and textiles materials, machinery and equipment, transport equipment, petroleum, building materials.

BUSINESS WORKWEEK

Offices

Monday to Friday 9a.m. to 5p.m.

Banks

Tuesday to Friday 9a.m. to 5p.m., Monday and Saturday 9a.m. to noon.

Government

Monday to Friday 9a.m. to 3p.m.

Retail

Monday to Friday 9a.m. to 7p.m., slightly shorter hours at weekend.

HOLIDAYS

New Year's Day...January 1
Id al-Fitr, Ramazan Festival Day ....January 9
Independence Commemoration Day................February 4
Id al-Adha, Hadji Festival Day .... March 18
Good Friday..April 21*
Easter Monday ....April 24*
May Day ....May 1
National Heroes' Day ....May 22
Milad un-Nabi, Birth of the Prophet ....June 15
Special Bank Holiday ....June 30
Christmas ....December 25
Boxing Day ....December 26
Special Bank Holiday ....December 31
*Date may vary by year.

CLIMATE

Seasons

Sri Lanka's climate is tropical, with little seasonal variation. Humidity is relatively high. The island is in path of two monsoons and they give it most of the rainfall. The northeastern monsoons occur from December to March, while the southeast has monsoons from June to October.

Regions

In Colombo, the monthly mean temperature is around 28˚C (82˚F). In the higher altitude of Nuwara Eliya it is at 17˚C (62˚F), and at Kandy at 26˚C (79˚F). The hottest time in Colombo is from March to May, and the coldest is from November to late February.

The southwest has the most rainfall; rain diminishes towards the northwest, and in the southeast.

Money & Banking

Currency

The currency of Sri Lanka is the Sri Lanka Rupee (SLRe, singular; SLRes, plural).

Denominations

The Sri Lanka Rupee (SLR) comes in coin denominations of SLR5, 2 and 1 and 50, 25, 10, 5, 2 and 1 cents; and banknotes of SLR5, 10, 20, 50, 100, 500 and 1,000.

Sri Lanka

Traveler's Checks and Credit Cards

Traveler's checks can be exchanged at banks, exchange shops, hotels, and international airports at varying exchange rates. Larger banks may offer the best exchange rates. Avoid black marketers at all cost for both legal and cost reasons. Consult your bank about current exchange rates before departure. Keep all receipts for reconversion. Most major currencies can be exchanged, but try to take only crisp and new notes, wrinkled and soiled notes are likely to be refused.

Major credit cards, American Express, Visa, Diner's Club, and MasterCard, are easily accepted in up-market places but rural areas may ask for cash. Optimal exchange rates are given for credit card transactions. Some banks offer cash advances on credit cards, with passport identification. ATM facilities are few and far between.

Travel

VISA AND PASSPORT

Foreigners must have a valid passport, onward ticket, and sufficient daily funds. A tourist visa for stays up to 90 days or a business visa for up to 30 days may be obtained upon entry. Foreigners entering Sri Lanka on a tourist visa cannot change the status of their visa. Do not conduct business on a tourist visa.

DEPARTURE FORMALITIES

Amounts exceeding the equivalent of US$5000 that have been declared on arrival but not spent in Sri Lanka may be exported on departure.

CUSTOMS ENTRY (PERSONAL)

Duty-free
- Tobacco: 200 cigarettes, 50 cigars, or 375g of tobacco or a combination of these not exceeding 340g
- Alcohol: 2 bottles of wine and 1.5 liters of spirits.

Note: Precious metals, including gold, platinum and silver (and including jewelry), must be declared upon arrival in Sri Lanka. There is no gift allowance. Non-compliance may result in confiscation.

IMMUNIZATION

Yellow fever and cholera immunizations are recommended for all visitors and are required (with records) for travelers arriving from infected areas. Anti-malaria medication and Hepatitis A prophylaxis are strongly advised.

TIPPING

Hotels
A tip on top of the 10 percent service charge is customary, though not obligatory in hotels.

Restaurants
A 15 percent tip is customary in restaurants and nightspots in the absence of service charges.

EMERGENCY INFORMATION

Police and Crime
Sri Lanka is generally a safe country for visitors, although there has been much social unrest in the region. It is generally safe for travelers if they stick to more authorized routes. Take basic precautions against petty crime. Avoid flashy displays of wealth, dress conservatively. Leave most of your cash, traveler's checks, jewelry and other valuables in your hotel safe. Carry photocopies of your passport instead of the original. Carry cash in a money belt, and use credit cards or traveler's checks for most transactions. Foreign business visitors are often the target of thieves so purses, laptops and briefcases require additional security. Do not leave valuables in cars or on tables in cafés.

Women should dress modestly to avoid harassment. On public transportation, they should try to sit in the family sections; they should not travel alone.

Bring along a supply of toiletries, especially when traveling to more rural areas. Do not give money to beggars, as this will only attract more beggars.

Emergency Numbers
Police... 43-3333
Fire/ambulance....................................... 42-2222
Emergency hospital................................ 69-1111
Tourist police.. 43-2635

Health
Avoid tap water—over 80 percent of diseases in Sri Lanka are related to contaminated water. Use bottled water only, even for brushing teeth, or boil water for 20 minutes if bottled water is unavailable. Wash all vegetables and fruit before eating.

Malaria is endemic. There are high incidents of hepatitis and typhoid, and yellow and dengue fever also exist here. Dust causes allergies, and the sun and heat can literally kill. Take medication and shots before departure.

Hospitals are inexpensive but good for emergencies only, even though most doctors have been trained in Western countries. In case of serious illness or operation, you are advised to leave the country. Evacuation insurance is recommended. Hotels have access to English-speaking physicians.

For more information on medical centers, including phone numbers, please see the "Business Center" section at the end of this chapter.

TAXI & RENTAL CARS

Taxis are available in the cities. Agree on a fare before leaving. Rental cars are few and far between. They should only be used by experienced visitors.

BUS

There is an extensive bus service. Most buses are comfortable and efficient, except during peak hours when they are packed and may run somewhat late.

TRAIN

Trains connect Colombo and tourist towns, but air conditioned cars are a rarity. Be sure to reserve cars in advance. Watch your luggage and be prepared for very basic bathroom facilities. Also, bring your own food unless first-class preparations can be reserved.

Essential Terms

English	Sinhalese
Yes	*Owu*
No	*Naa*
Good morning	*Ayubowan*
Hello (daytime)	*Ayubowan*
Hello (evening)	*Ayubowan*
Good-bye	*Ayubowan geh illa ennam*
Please	*Karunakara*
Thank you	*Istutiy*
Pleased to meet you	*Mata obawa hamba wenna santosai*
Excuse me; I'm sorry	*Samawanna kanagatui*
My name is _____	*Mage nama*
I don't understand	*Mata terenne naa*

Communications

DIALING CODES IN SRI LANKA

International country code: [94]

Selected city codes: Colombo Central (1), Galle (9), Kotte (1)

Dialing Sri Lanka from Overseas
To dial Sri Lanka from overseas, dial your country's international dialing code, then 94 (the country code for Sri Lanka), then the city code and finally the number. If you were dialing Colombo Central, for example, you would begin with 011, then 94, then 1 (the city code for Colombo Central), and finally the number of the person or office you are trying to reach.

Assistance Numbers
International Operator (Colombo)................................. 100
International Directory (Colombo) 134
Domestic Directory (outside Colombo)........................ 161

Sri Lanka

CALLING WITHIN SRI LANKA

Long Distance Calls
You must dial an area code when calling long distance within Sri Lanka.

International Calls
An international call can be placed from a private line, the post office, communication centers, and hotels. To place a direct call overseas, dial 00 + country code + area code + number. It is also possible to book a call with an operator or at the post office. The minimum charge applies to three minutes. Discount rates take place between 10p.m. and 6a.m.

To reach an operator in the U.S., try the AT&T access number:

AT&T 430-430

PAY PHONES

Public Telephones
Private post offices are the fastest and simplest way to go in terms of public telephoning.

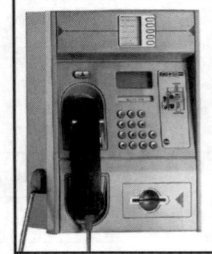

Calling Cards
Sri Lanka Telecom cards may be purchased from the post office or shops near the telephone booths that use the cards. Three other phone card companies operate in Sri Lanka as well: Lanka Pay, Metrocard and Supercard. Each owns separate phones, which use their own cards.

CELLULAR PHONES
Several cellular service providers exist in Sri Lanka. Celltel Lanka and Lanka Cellular Service offer ETACS for analogue users. Mobiltel offers AMPS for analogue users. MTN Network offers GSM for digital users.

Note: Your home country cell phone may not work in this country. If not, we recommend that you rent an international cell phone *before* you leave home. A major US-based cell phone rental provider is **IMC WorldCell**. For information see "International Cell Phone Rentals" on page 14.

A special prefix should precede calls to mobile phones.

CellTel ....72 + 5 digits
CallLink..78 + 5 digits
GSM Dialog ....77 + 5 digits
Mobitel..71 + 5 digits
Bell ....75 + 6 digits
SLT...70 + 6 digits
Suntel ....74 + 6 digits
Air Lanka Ltd. 94-73-5555

CALL BACK
You can (potentially) save significant sums when calling in Sri Lanka by using one of the call back services listed below. Fees for call back services vary widely, depending on the company and the type of service required. Be sure to check with these companies before leaving to compare rates.

For a list of callback services, please refer to the "Communications" section in the *Global Road Warrior* Introduction.

PHONE JACKS

Plug adaptors are available through **iGo Corporation**. (See "Electrical and Telephone Adaptors" on page 19.)

POSTAL SERVICES
Airmail to Europe and North America can take up to 10 days. Mail coming in to Sri Lanka can take much longer.

Business Services

BUSINESS CENTERS

The Ceylon Intercontinental; 48 Janadhipathi Mawatha; tel: (1) 421-221**.**

Galadari Hotel; 64 Lotus Road; tel: (1) 544-544.

Lanka Oberoi; 77 Steuart Place; tel: (1) 437-437

Taj Samudra Hotel; 25 Galle Face Centre Road; tel: (1) 446-622.

COURIER SERVICE

DHL Keells (Pvt) Ltd.; tel: (1) 338-060; International; 130 Glennie St., Colombo 2; Mon. to Fri. 7:30a.m. to 6:30p.m., Sat. 7:30a.m. to 7p.m., Sun. 8a.m. to 5p.m., and holidays 8a.m. to 5p.m.

Federal Express (Mountain Hawk Express); tel: (1) 577-055.

TNT Express Worldwide; Ace Cargo (PVT) Ltd., 315 Vauxhall Street, Colombo 2, SHRIO LA KA; tel: (1) 445-331 / 7644.

Electrical

Current
230/240 volts AC, 50Hz.

ELECTRIC PLUGS

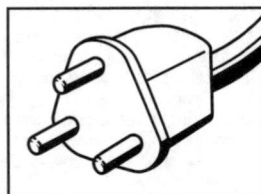

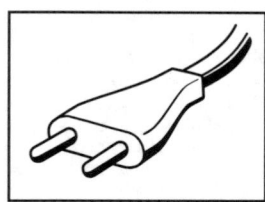

Plug adaptors are available through **iGo Corporation.** (See "Electrical and Telephone Adaptors" on page 19.)

Technical Support

HARDWARE/SOFTWARE VENDOR SUPPORT

Dell; (in India) tel: [91] (80) 5545126; fax: [91] (80) 5545738 (Bangalore); (22) 4973336 (Mumbai); (Dell- Europe) tel: [44] (134) 474-8000; (in the U.S.) tel: [1] (512) 338-4400; fax: [1] (512) 728-3330; http://www.dell.com/.

Hewlett Packard; (in Switzerland) tel: [41] (22) 780-8111; (in the U.S.) tel: [1] (408) 246-4300; http://www.hp.com/.

IBM; tel: (1) 440-810; fax: (1) 434-594; (in India) tel: [91] (80) 526-7117; fax: [91] (80) 527-7991; (in Switzerland) tel: [41] (22) 310-0418 (in French); (in the U.S.) tel: [1] (919) 517-2800; (U.S. Main Office) tel: [1] 914-765-1900; http://www.ibm.com/.

Microsoft; (in India) tel: [91] (80) 559-5733; fax: [91] (80) 559-7133; tel: [91] (11) 646-0694; tel: [91] (11) 646-0767; fax: (11) 647-4714; (in Switzerland) tel: [41] (848) 858-868; fax [41] (1) 831-0869; (in the U.S.) [1] (425) 635-7222; http://www.microsoft.com/.

Internet Connection

HOW TO CONNECT

Connecting to AOL and Compuserve in Sri Lanka is similar to using it when traveling outside your own area code. See the introductory section for detailed information on connecting to your account through a different phone number.

America Online

Numbers are available at keyword *international*. Be sure to get several local numbers before leaving. AOL has a new GlobalNet service that charges US$12 an hour in addition to the usual charges. Go to keyword *access* (a free area) and download the software.

Access: Colombo (1) 343-731.

Compuserve

Numbers are available at *Go International*. If you are using CompuServe 2000, use GO PHONES within CompuServe 2000 to search for access numbers. The Compuserve Web-site also has a great deal of information, at http://www.compuserve.com/.

Access: Colombo (1) 347-420, (1) 343-731.

Independent Service Providers

Many independent service providers offer discounts if you are only in town for a couple days.

Infoscope / Information Laboratories (Pvt) Ltd; tel: (1) 611-061; email: info@infolabs.is.lk; http://www.is.lk/is/infolabs/index.html/.

ITMIN Internet Services Limited; tel: (1) 683-948; fax: (1) 683-948; email: support@itmin.net; http://www.itmin.net/.

Lanka Communication Services (Pvt) Ltd; tel: (1) 437-

545/6; fax: (1) 437-547; support@lankacom.net; http://www.lankacom.net/.

Lanka Internet Services Ltd.; tel: (1) 565-071; tel: (1) 565-077; email: webcare@sri.lanka.net; http://www.lanka.net/.

Business Culture

GREETINGS AND COURTESIES

The traditional greeting among Sri Lankans is the *namaste*, formed by placing the palms together, fingers up, under the chin and bowing the head slightly. When meeting foreigners, the accepted greeting is the handshake. Sri Lankan women will shake hands with foreign men, but do not embrace or kiss a woman. Titles are very important to Sri Lankan businesspeople; Mr., Mrs., or Miss will usually suffice, but if a person has an additional title, be sure to use it. Do not use first names until you know someone fairly well.

BUSINESS ETHIC AND FRAMEWORK

Sri Lanka is a leftist democratic republic. Tamil rebels in the north have been engaged in a sporadic fifteen year armed conflict against the government of Sri Lanka. Due to recent terrorist activity, foreign citizens are strongly encouraged to register with their Embassy upon arrival in Sri Lanka.

Sri Lankans value loyalty to one's group, respect for others, and their ethnic and religious identity. Education is held in high esteem. The ruling Sinhalese majority is Buddhist, while the Hindu Tamils in the north represent the dominant minority. Personal relationships, influenced by tradition and the situation of the moment, prove more important than abstract facts. Courtesy is highly valued. Sri Lankans believe in fate – that outcomes are in the hands of God.

Although Sinhalese and Tamil are the official languages, English is widely spoken and generally used for business; as such, English speakers will normally not require an interpreter.

MEETINGS

Make appointments in advance and reconfirm meetings upon arrival. Sri Lankans value your punctuality, but may exhibit more relaxed attitudes about their own arrival times. Bring plenty of business cards and distribute them to all present. Visitors are usually offered tea prior to a meeting. Accept and compliment the quality of the tea, which is the national drink. In keeping with the relaxed pace of life in Sri Lanka, conversation may prove slow in turning to business. Be patient and adapt to their pace.

DECISION MAKING

Decisions are made slowly. Sri Lankans like to know people before doing business with them and will look upon impatience as rude. In making important business decisions, Sinhalese Sri Lankans are concerned with interpersonal relationships, while Tamil Sri Lankans consider the individual's responsibility to the group. All Sri Lankans tend to place importance on the group and on the individual's position and rank within the group. One should take all of these factors into account when processing or awaiting a decision.

WOMEN

Although one will rarely find women in top business positions in Sri Lanka, the country was the first to have a woman prime minister. Women can expect to be taken seriously and will be treated with respect. Sri Lankans often smile as a way of saying thank you, but may perceive smiling too freely in public as flirting. Sri Lankan businesspeople, both men and women, prove comfortable in dealing with women in management or decision-making positions.

BUSINESS ENTERTAINING

It is common for initial meetings to be held during meals, usually at a restaurant. If you have arranged the meeting, by custom you are responsible for the bill. Signal a waiter by holding up your hand, palm out, and waving your fingers all together.

If invited to the home of your host for lunch or dinner, a small gift is appreciated, although not expected. You will be expected to eat Sri Lankan style, with the right hand only. Pass with the right hand, but give a gift with both hands. Never touch anyone's head, or point with your foot or index finger. You may be asked to remove your shoes before entering, and several hours of conversation may ensue before the meal. If invited to a Sri Lankan home, it is polite to reciprocate by inviting your business associate for a meal at the restaurant in your hotel. Sri Lankan sensitivities remain high due to the ongoing, sporadic civil war. In conversation, avoid any mention of politics, religion, or the caste system.

BUSINESS ATTIRE

The climate in Sri Lanka is tropical. Stay with conservative and lightweight clothing. Businessmen usually do not wear jackets and ties. Businesswomen simply wear a dress or a light blouse and skirt. Modesty is important for women in Sri Lanka. Women should not wear sleeveless dresses, or shorts. Clothing revealing any kind of skin is reserved for the beach.

Business Centers
Colombo

CITY VIEW

The traffic jams and pollution would be serious problems in Colombo if it wasn't for the easy-going attitude of its inhabitants. A colorful city, Colombo resides as Sri Lanka's largest town, not to mention the center for industry, finance, and commercial activity. Sri Lanka's principal port for trade, Colombo also offers modern shipping and warehouse facilities.

AIRPORT

Katunayake Airport to City Center

The airport is 21 miles (32 km.) from the city center. There are bus services that run from 4:30a.m. to 11p.m., just about every thirty minutes or so. These buses stop near the car park, just outside the airport terminal. The bus will take you to the main bus station in Colombo where you can negotiate the city on foot or take a cab to your hotel. The travel time is approximately 1.5 hours.

Airline Numbers

Air India	(1) 25832, 422249
Air Lanka	(1) 27564, 28331-4
Air New Zealand	(1) 430707/8
Aeroflot	(1) 25580, 433062
Gulf Air	(1) 26633, 434662
Indian Airlines	(1) 23136, 29838, 23987
Lufthansa	(1) 574227
Saudi Arabian Airlines	(1) 436725, 27506, 27911

HOTELS

Top End

Colombo Hilton; Echelon Square, Lotus Rd.; tel: (1) 544-644; fax: (1) 544-6571; adjacent to World Trade Center; restaurants; 10 meeting rooms (up to 1000); executive floor; business services; computers/printers available; secure parking; sauna; steam bath; pool; tennis; disco.

Galadari; 64 Lotus Road; tel: (1) 544-544; fax: (1) 449-875; email: galadari@sri.lanka.net; near exhibition grounds; restaurant; conference facilities (up to 500); secretarial service; business services; in-room modem/fax connection; parking; corporate rates; fitness; sauna; pool.

Taj Samudra Hotel; 25 Galle Face Centre Road; tel: (1) 446-622; fax: (1) 446-348; email: taj@sri.lanka.net; city center; restaurant; conference facilities (up to 500); business center; secretarial service; internet connection; secure parking; corporate rates; fitness; sauna; pool; whirlpool; tennis; squash; disco.

Expensive

The Ceylon Intercontinental; 48 Janadhipathi Mawatha; tel: (1) 421-221; fax: (1) 447-326; city center; all rooms with ocean view; restaurant; conference facilities (up to 800); business center; secretarial service; parking; corporate rates; fitness; sauna; pool.

Lanka Oberoi; 77 Steuart Place; tel: (1) 437-437; fax: (1) 449-280; email: lankaobe1@eureka.lk; near airport; restaurant; conference facilities (up to 850); business center; secretarial service; corporate rates; fitness; sauna; pool.

Moderate

Golden Tulip Galle Face; 2 Kollupitiya Road; tel: (1) 541-010; fax: (1) 541-072; email: slcbhq@lanka.ccom.lk; city center; restaurant; conference facilities (up to 400); secretarial service; fax/photocopy facilities; parking; corporate rates; pool.

Holiday Inn Colombo; 30 Sir Mohamed Macan Markar Mawatha; tel: (1) 422-001; fax: (1) 447-977; near city center; restaurant; conference facilities (up to 1200); fitness; pool.

LTI Pegasus Reef; Santa Maria Mawatha, Hendala, Wattala; tel: (1) 930-205; fax: (1) 930-254; email: serenlti@sri.lanka.net; located in suburb; near beach; restaurant; conference facilities (up to 300); parking; corporate rates; fitness; sauna; pool.

Renuka; 328 Galle Road; tel: (1) 573-598; fax; (1) 574-137; email: slcbhq@lanka.ccom.lk; conference facilities (up to 70); business support; pool.

MEDICAL CARE

Nawaloka Hospital; 23 Sri Saugathodaya Mawatha, Colombo; tel: (1) 544444, 546258.

Durdans Hospital; 3 Alfred Place, Colombo 3; tel: (1) 575205/6.

Colombo General; Regent St., Colombo 8; tel: (1) 691111.

AUTO RENTAL

Avis; Mackinnons Travels Ltd.; 4, Leyden Bastian Rd., PO Box 945, Colombo; (1) 329-887; Monday to Friday 8:30a.m. to 4:30p.m., Sat. 9a.m. to noon.

Casons Car Rental; 583/1 2nd Lane, Nawala Rd., Rajagiriya; tel: 071-31084, 071-23808; fax: (1) 864-929.

Dollar/Europcar; airport, tel: (1) 452-388, open 24 hours daily; Colombo Hotel Galadari, tel: (1) 445-860, Sun. to Mon. 7a.m. to 7p.m.

WORLD TRADE CENTER

World Trade Center Colombo
Hospitality International (PVT) Limited
#37-00, West Tower
World Trade Center, Echelon Sq.
Colombo 1, Sri Lanka
tel: (1) 346-777; fax: (1) 346-779
email: wtclo@lankacom.net

Sweden

At a Glance
THE PEOPLE

Population ....8,911,296 (July 1999 est.)
Growth Rate ....0.29% (1999 est.)
Life Expectancy .... 79.29 years (1999 est.)
Infant Mortality..... 3.91 deaths/1,000 live births (1999 est.)

Ethnic Composition
The main population group is composed of Swedish-born Caucasians. Lapps (Sami), and foreign born or first-generation immigrants (Finns, Yugoslavs, Danes, Norwegians, Greeks, and Turks) make up the balance.

Religious Composition
Evangelical Lutheran...94%
Roman Catholic..1.5%
Pentecostal..1%
Other 3.5%

Languages Spoken
Swedish is the official language, although there are also small Lapp- and Finnish-speaking minorities.

Education and Literacy
Sweden has an excellent education system with 99% of the population over the age of 15 considered literate.

Labor Force
Total 4,522,000
(over 80% of labor is unionized)
By occupation: services 68.6%, mining and manufacturing 21.2%, construction 7%, and agriculture, fishing, and forestry 3.2%.

THE ECONOMY
Sweden was long considered an ideal democratic state with a socialist-welfare economy supported by extremely high taxation. Welfare and social benefits have been at the heart of economic planning by the state. The nation has an excellent infrastructure and high-tech capabilities. Heavy taxation and generous social benefits have made foreign investment difficult to attract. Many of Sweden's corporations and entrepreneurs have fled to set up headquarters elsewhere. Lack of competitiveness and a ballooning budget deficit have forced the Swedish government to move away from former socialist policies. Though now a member of the EU, Sweden has opted to not be part of the initial launch of the Euro fearing a too-sudden revamping of its social structure and taxation system by Brussels.

Exports ....US$85.5 billion (f.o.b., 1998)
Imports .... US$66.6 billion
Total Trade .... US$152.1 billion
GDP Per Capita.............................. US$19,700 (1998 est.)
Unemployment .... 6.3 percent (1998 est.)

Inflation Rate 2 percent (1998) Top Export Partners
EU, Norway, U.S.

Top Import Partners
EU, Norway, U.S.

Top Exports
Machinery, motor vehicles, paper products, pulp and wood, iron and steel products, chemicals.

Top Imports
Machinery, petroleum and petroleum products, chemicals, motor vehicles, foodstuffs, iron and steel, clothing.

BUSINESS WORKWEEK
Offices
Monday to Friday 9a.m. to 5p.m. (4:30p.m.)
Banks
Monday to Friday 9:30a.m. to 4p.m.
Government
Monday to Friday 9a.m. to 4p.m.
Retail
Monday to Friday 9a.m. to 6p.m., Saturday 9a.m. to 4p.m.; some open Sundays.

HOLIDAYS
New Year's Day..January 1
Epiphany ....January 6
Good Friday..April 21*
Easter Monday...April 24*
May Day, Labor Day...May 1
Ascension Day ....June 1
Whit Monday ....June 12
Midsummer Holiday...June 24
All Saints' Day ....November 1
Christmas Day...December 25
*Date may vary by year.

CLIMATE
Seasons
The winters are long and are the most severe from January to April. Summers are short but generally warm, but the "midnight sun" makes the days long with average temperatures of 16˚C (61˚F), and sometimes reaching 25˚C. Most of the country, although geographically northern, has a mostly temperate climate.

Regions
The temperatures vary a lot between the north and south of the country. Generally it is colder and dryer in the north, and milder and wetter in the south. In Stockholm, winters last from November to April, and temperatures can fall to as low as -3˚C (27˚F), spring is cold and rainy, and July temperatures are at 17˚C (62˚F) and can rise up to 25˚C (77˚F). The northern-most region is located within the Arctic Circle and can be fatally cold.

Money & Banking
Currency
The currency of Sweden is the Swedish Krona (SKr).
Denominations
The Swedish Krona (SKr) comes in coin denominations of SKr10, 5 and 1, and 50 oere; and bank notes of SKr20, 100, 500 and 1,000.
Traveler's Checks and Credit Cards
Traveler's checks and foreign currency can be easily and efficiently exchanged at banks, foreign exchange bureaus located in the major cities, hotels, and foreign exchange kiosks at the airports. Banks offer the most variable exchange rates.

Sweden

Sweden

National capital
Region capital
Secondary city
Primary road
Railroad
Administrative border
International border

0 50 100 km
0 50

Länners of Sweden

1 Malmöhus Län
2 Kristianstads Län
3 Blekinge Län
4 Hallands Län
5 Kronobergs Län
6 Kalmar Län
7 Gotlands Län
8 Jönköpings Län
9 Alvs Borgs Län
10 Skara Borgs Län
11 Östergötlands Län
12 Göteborgs Och Bohus Län
13 Värmlands Län
14 Örebro Län
15 Södermanlands Län
16 Stockholms Län
17 Uppsala Län
18 Västmanland Län
19 Kopparbergs Län
20 Gälveborgs Län
21 Jämtlands Län
22 Västernorrlands Län
23 Västerbottens Läns
24 Norrbottens Län

Russia
Finland
Norway
Estonia
Latvia
Lithuania
Denmark

©2001 Magellan Geographix · SM Santa Barbara, CA

Traveler's check's receive a better exchange rate than cash, or you can purchase traveler's checks before departure, which can be exchanged almost everywhere.

American Express, Visa, MasterCard, and Diners Club are widely accepted in Sweden. You can get cash advances from your credit card on many of the automated teller machines (ATM). Long- term visitors should set up a checking account in Sweden, and get an ATM card. Optimal exchange rates are given for credit card purchases and some ATM transactions.

Essential Terms

English	Swedish
Yes No	*Ja* *Nej*
Good morning Hello (daytime) Hello (evening) Hello (telephone)	*God morgon* *God dag* *God kaväll / natt* *Hej*
Good-bye	*Adjö*
Please	*Var så god*
Thank you	*Tack*
Pleased to meet you	*Angenämt att träffa dig*
Excuse me; I'm sorry	*Ursäkta mig*
My name is _____	*Jag heter _____*
I don't understand	*Jag förstår inte*
Do you speak English?	*Talar du engelska?*

Travel

VISA AND PASSPORT

Foreigners must have a valid passport. A tourist or business visa is not required for stays up to 90 days, beginning upon entry to the Nordic area: Sweden, Norway, Denmark, Iceland, and Finland.

DEPARTURE FORMALITIES

No more than SKr6,000 may be taken out. of the country. SKr1,000 notes should not be exported because they are not exchangeable at foreign banks.

CUSTOMS ENTRY (PERSONAL)

Duty-free

Non-E.U. residents:
- Tobacco: 200 cigarettes, 100 cigarillos, 50 cigars, or 250g of tobacco (17 years of age or over)
- Alcohol: One liter wine (2 liters if no spirits are imported); One liter spirits (over 20 years of age); 15 liters of beer (over 20 years of age)
- 500g coffee and 100g tea
- Other: 50g perfume; goods up to the value of SKr1700 or ECU 175.
  EU residents:

- Alcohol: One liter spirits or three liters fortified wine; Five liters wine; 15 liters beer
- Tobacco: 300 cigarettes or 150 cigarillos or 75 cigars or 400g of tobacco

Prohibited or Restricted
- Narcotics
- Firearms, ammunition, and weapons
- Most meat and dairy products, eggs, plants and endangered species

IMMUNIZATION

There are no immunization requirements except for travelers coming from infected areas. In such cases records must be presented.

TIPPING

Swedes are in most cases are sparing tippers; as in other parts of Europe, round up the tab for a tip.

Taxi
Tip taxi drivers 10 percent.

Hotels
A service charge of 12 percent for hotel rooms will be added to your bill in most situations.

Restaurants
A service charge of 13 percent in restaurants will be added to your bill in most situations. In addition, the small change may be left for the waiter or bartender.

Other
Tip cloakroom attendants SKr3, porters SKr3 per bag. Barbers are not tipped; however, in most cases hairdressers are. Nightclubs may attach service charges to bills.

EMERGENCY INFORMATION

Police and Crime
Sweden is one of the safest countries in the world. The people are honest and law abiding, but basic precautions must be taken in the larger cities against petty crime. Leave most of your cash, traveler's checks, jewelry, and valuables in your hotel safe. Carry photocopies of your passport instead of the original. Carry cash in a money belt, and use credit cards or traveler's checks for most transactions. Foreign business visitors are often the target of thieves so purses, laptops and briefcases require additional security. Do not leave valuables in cars or on tables in cafés.

Women can walk around with little fear of assault or harassment. The police are extremely efficient and courteous with good language skills.

Emergency Numbers
Ambulance	90 000
Fire	90 000
Police	90 000
Breakdown service	(020) 910040

Health
Sweden poses no serious health risks; the only problematic illnesses are the common flu, bronchitis, sinus problems, and rheumatism caused by the cold, damp weather. Lack of sunlight in the winter months requires extra vitamin supplements. Food laws are extremely strict, and tap water is safe.

The socialized medical establishment is of a very high standard but is not free to foreign travelers. Pharmacies are sometimes open 24 hours a day, but most medicines require prescriptions, so bring along necessities.

Sweden

Sweden

TAXI & RENTAL CARS

Taxis are available at hotels and airports. Long-range taxis are also available. Cab drivers will also accept most credit cards as payment. Rental cars are plentiful and road rules quite orderly. Visitors should be warned that Sweden has very strict drunk-driving laws that include jail sentences.

BUS

Specific information on bus routes is available from Swedish tourist offices. Most services are comfortable and efficient. Order and courtesy rule the day.

TRAIN

The rail system is government run and efficient. The routes are more concentrated in the south, but trains do run to the sparsely populated north also.

TRAVEL ASSISTANCE

Hotel Accommodations
Hotell and Restaurant
Förbund.. (8) 231 290

Communications

DIALING CODES IN SWEDEN

International country code: [46]
Selected city codes: Goteborg (31), Malmö (40), Stockholm (8)

Dialing Sweden from Overseas
To dial Sweden from overseas, dial your international dialing code, then 46 (the country code for Sweden), then the city code and finally the number. If you were dialing Gotebürg from the United States, for example, you would begin with 011, then 46, then 31 (the city code for Goteborg), and finally the number of the person or office you were trying to reach.

Assistance Numbers
International Operator ....0018 (or) 0019
International Directory 07977
Domestic Operator 90130
Domestic Directory 07975

CALLING WITHIN SWEDEN

Local Calls
Calling locally is quite straightforward. Dial the number and get connected.

Long Distance Calls
Within Sweden be sure to include the city code for the place you are dialing, which can be found in any telephone directory.

International Calls
You can call international direct from any phone. Dial 00 + country code + area code + number. If you decide to call direct from your hotel, you can await a blaring surcharge from the normally quiet Swedes. Americans can try and circumvent the raucous charges by connecting to AT&T or MCI for collect and calling card calls by dialing their access codes:
AT&T USA Direct 020-795-611
MCI Call USA 020-795-922

PAY PHONES

Public Telephones
Three kinds of phones still exist in Sweden. Some only take coins, others only credit cards, and the rest prepaid phone cards. Coin phones take two SK1 coins to get started. Fortunately, the Swedes have taken the liberty of post-

ing English instructions inside many phone booths for those not fluent in Swedish telephonic operations.

Calling Cards
Phone cards are available at news outlets and kiosks.

CELLULAR PHONES

Several cellular service providers exist in Sweden. Telia Mobitel is a major service provider offering NMT-450 and NMT-900 for analogue users, and GSM for digital. There are other companies that also offer GSM, including Comvik, Europolitan, and NordicTel.

Comvik; tel: (8) 56-222-040; kundtjanst@comviq.se; http://www.comviq.se/.
Europolitan; info@europolitan.se; http://www.europolitan.se/.
Telia Mobitel; infomaster@mobitel.telia.se; http://mobitel.telia.com/.

Note: Your home country cell phone may not work in this country. If not, we recommend that you rent an international cell phone *before* you leave home. A major US-based cell phone rental provider is **IMC WorldCell**. For information see "International Cell Phone Rentals" on page 14.

CALL BACK

You can (potentially) save significant sums when calling in Sweden by using one of the call back services listed below. Fees for call back services vary widely, depending on the company and the type of service required. Be sure to check with these companies before leaving to compare rates.

For a list of callback services, please refer to the "Communications" section in the *Global Road Warrior* Introduction.

PHONE JACKS

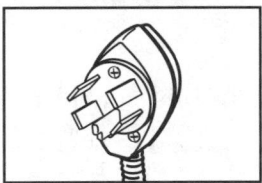

Plug adaptors are available through **iGo Corporation**. (See "Electrical and Telephone Adaptors" on page 19.)

FAX

Fax machines are widely available and service is excellent.

POSTAL SERVICES

Mail service is generally very good. Boxes are yellow and can be found throughout the country.

Hours of service
Monday-Friday 8a.m. to 10p.m.
Saturday 9a.m. to 3p.m.

Rates

Airmail for a five gram letter is Sh3.50; airmail postcards to U.S. and Canada are Sh2.50

TELEGRAMS

Telegrams can be sent from most hotels and post offices.

Business Services

BUSINESS CENTER

Scandic Hotel Slussen; Guldgränd 8; tel: (8) 5173-5300.

COURIER SERVICE

DHL International AB; tel. within Sweden: 020-345 345; outside Sweden tel.: 46-651-19290; web site: http://www.dhl.se; Wenner Gren Center; Sveavagen 170; P.O. Box 23260; Stockholm 10435; Mon. to Fri. 8a.m. to 5p.m., closed Sat., Sun., and holidays; Bldg 079, Sodra Fraktvagen; PO Box 95; Stockholm - Arlanda 19045; Mon. to Fri. 5:30a.m. to 10p.m., closed Sat.,Sun. and holidays.

Federal Express (Universal FDX AB); tel: (8) 797-9960.

TNT Express Worldwide; Kuskvägen 2C, 191 22 Sollentuna Box 93, Stockholm; tel: (8) 625-5800; toll-free number: 020 961 961; fax: (8) 625-5940.

UPS; United Parcel Service Sweden AB Tappvägen 10-22, 168 65 Bromma; tel: (020) 788-799.

Electrical

Current

220 volts AC, 50Hz

ELECTRIC PLUGS

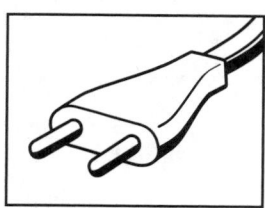

Plug adaptors are available through **iGo Corporation.** (See "Electrical and Telephone Adaptors" on page 19.)

Technical Support

HARDWARE/SOFTWARE VENDOR SUPPORT

Acer/Texas Instruments; (in Germany) tel: [49] (4102) 488-469; fax; [49] (4102) 488-169; (in the U.S.) [1] (408) 432-6200; http://www.acer.com/.

Adobe; (in Austria) tel: [44] (131) 451-6882; (in Germany) tel: [49] (1) 803-5018; (in Switzerland) tel: [41] (800) 833-

310; (in the U.S.) tel: [1] (800) 500-7078; (in the U.S.) tel: [1] (716) 633-3600; http://www.adobe.com/.

Apple/Claris; (in Germany) tel: [49] (1) 803-5018; (in Switzerland) tel: [41] (800) 833-310; (in the U.K.) tel: [44] (990) 127-753; (in the U.S.) tel: [1] (800) 500-7078; http://www.apple.com/.

AST; (in the U.S.) tel: [1] (817) 232-9824 (International Technical Support); (in Ireland) tel: [353] (61) 492-222; (in the U.S.) tel: [1] (949) 727-4141; http://www.ast.com/.

Compaq; (in Switzerland) tel: [41] (22) 709-5330; fax: [41] (22) 709-5391 (Geneva); tel: [41] (1) 801-2507; fax: [41] (1) 801-2172 (Zurich); (General U.S.) tel: (281) 518-2000; http://www.compaq.com/.

Dell; (in Germany) tel: [49] (61) 039-710; (Dell- Europe) tel: [44] (134) 474-8000; (in the U.S.) tel: [1] (512) 338-4400; fax: [1] (512) 728-3330; http://www.dell.com/.

Gateway 2000; (in the U.S.) tel: [1] (605) 232-2191; fax: [1] (605) 232-2023; (in Ireland) tel: [353] (1) 797-2000; http://www.g2k.com/.

Filemaker/Claris; (in Germany) tel: [49] (180) 525-8166 (Info-line); fax: [49] (180) 567-2233; tel: [49] (180) 523-6423; (in the U.S.) tel: [1] (800) 965-9090; http://www.claris.com/.

Hewlett Packard; (in Switzerland) tel: [41] (22) 780-8111; (in the U.S.) tel: [1] (408) 246-4300; http://www.hp.com/.

IBM; tel: (8) 793-1900; fax: (8) 793-2448; (in Switzerland) tel: [41] (22) 310-0418 (in French); (in the U.S.) tel: [1] (919) 517-2800; (U.S. Main Office) tel: [1] 914-765-1900; http://www.ibm.com/.

Microsoft; tel: (8) 752-0929; tel: (8) 752-5600; fax: (8) 750-5158; (in Switzerland) tel: [41] (848) 858-868; fax [41] (1) 831-0869; (in the U.S.) [1] (425) 635-7222; http://www.microsoft.com/.

Quark; (in Switzerland) tel: [41] (1) 808-7722; fax: [41] (1) 808-7799; (in the U.S.) tel: [1] (303) 894-8899; fax: [1] (303) 894-3398 (For Products Registered in the Americas); http://www.quark.com/.

Toshiba; (in Germany) tel: [49] (2131) 158-319; fax: [49] (2131) 158-558; (in Switzerland) tel: [41] (1) 946-0777; fax: [41] (1) 946-0807; (in Ireland) tel: [44] (193) 282-8828; (in the U.S.) [1] (949) 583-3000 (Corporate Headquarters); http://www.toshiba.com/.

Internet Connection

HOW TO CONNECT

Connecting to AOL and Compuserve in Sweden is similar to using it when traveling outside your own area code. See the introductory section for detailed information on connecting to your account through a different phone number.

America Online

Numbers are available at keyword *international*. Be sure to get several local numbers before leaving. AOL's GlobalNet service charges US$6 an hour in addition to the usual charges. Go to keyword *access* (a free area) and download the software.

Numbers

AOL has many numbers in Sweden. Please go to their website at http://intlaccess.web.aol.com/ for further access numbers in other cities.

Access: Alfta - Edsbyn (0271) 729-522; Alingsas (0322) 601-500; Boras (033) 700-9522; Eskilstuna (016) 540-6500; Falun (023) 660-9522; Gamleby (0493) 746-500; Gavle-Sandviken (026) 400-9522; Göteborg (Gothenburg) (031) 758-8996; Halmstad (035) 280-9522; Harnosand (0611) 339-522; Helsingborg (042) 490-9522; Jonkoping

Sweden

(036) 570-6500; Karlskrona (0455) 322-832; Karlstad (054) 775-6500; Kristianstad (044) 780-9522; Linkoping (013) 460-6500; Lulea (0920) 273-500; Lund (046) 286-9522; Malmo (040) 698-8996; Mariestad (0501) 379-522; Norrkoping (011) 440-9522; Nykoping (0155) 449-523; Orebro-Kumla (019) 766-6500; Ostersund (063) 670-9522; Stockholm (North) (08) 5062-8996; Stockholm (South) (08) 5663-8996; Sundsvall-Timra (060) 700-9522; Trelleborg (0410) 731-922; Umea (090) 203-6500; Uppsala (018) 480-8512; Vanersborg (521) 702-832; Vasteras (021) 360-9521; Vaxjo (0470) 731-922.

Compuserve

Numbers are available at *Go International.* If you are using CompuServe 2000, use GO PHONES within CompuServe 2000 to search for access numbers. The Compuserve Web-site also has a great deal of information, at http://www.compuserve.com/.

Access: Göteborg (Gothenburg) (31) 946-475; Malmo (40) 303-068; N. Stockholm (8) 5661-2000; S. Stockholm (8) 5061-2000.

Independent Service Providers

Many independent service providers offer discounts if you are only in town for a couple of days.

ABC-Klubben; tel: (8) 801-725; fax: (8) 801-522; webmaster@abc.se; http://www.abc.se/.

Algonet; tel: (8) 5875-8700; fax: 5875-8733; http://start.telenordia.se/.

ArosNet; tel: (21) 413-360; http://www.arosnet.se/.

Dataphone Communication Networks; tel: Stockholm (8) 5661-0600, Göteborg (Gothenburg) (31) 758-0600, Malmö (40) 698-0600; fax: Stockholm (8) 5661-0601, Göteborg (Gothenburg) (31) 758-0601, Malmö (40) 698-0601; sales@dataphone.net; http://www.dataphone.net/.

GTE Internet; tel: [1] (888) GTE-SURF; slsreq@gte.net; http://www.gte.net/.

Infoscandic; tel: 953-20300; fax: 953-20187; info@infoscandic.se; http://www.infoscandic.se/.

pi.se AB, Professional Internet; tel: (8) 783-2040; fax: (8) 783-2046; adm@pi.se; http://www.pi.se/ (in Swedish and English).

SPRYNET / Mindspring; tel: [1] (800) 777-9638; tel: [1] (404) 815-0082; http://www.sprynet.com/

WinEasy AB; tel: (8) 5060-0000; fax: (8) 5060-0010; info@wineasy.com; http://www.wineasy.com/.

Business Culture

GREETINGS AND COURTESIES

The Swedish are reserved but friendly. They adhere to formality in addressing others; first names are rarely used. Correct forms of address are Herr (Mr.), Fru (Mrs.), and Froken (Miss), followed by the last name. Always use the formal address followed by the last name unless you are invited to do otherwise. The common greeting is a firm handshake, and be sure to shake hands when parting as well. When answering their phones, the Swedish use last names only, often concluding the call without a "good-bye." While their mannerisms seem abrupt to some foreigners, don't take offense, for truly, no offense is intended. In business, the Swedish are always driven to be as efficient as possible. Punctuality in both business and social occasions is a concept that is beyond courtesy; it's an essential practice. In Sweden, being early is often considered as rude as being late and one should never arrive more than five minutes before or after the scheduled time. While the exchange of business gifts is not a Swedish custom,

a bottle of wine or champagne to celebrate a special occasion is a thoughtful gesture (there's a high tax on alcohol and perfume in Sweden; you may wish to bring in your quota if you anticipate occasions of celebration are in the offing). Tasteful gifts representative of your company will always be received with appreciation.

BUSINESS ETHIC AND FRAMEWORK

Sweden's business environment is formal and highly reserved. Third-party introductions are your best method of entry into the community. It is wise to have appointments scheduled before arriving in Sweden as cold calls and drop-ins are not welcome and meet with little success. Trade show attendance and the local Chambers of Commerce may facilitate appropriate introductions for you. If you do attempt self-introduction by way of a letter, be certain to provide substantial amounts of background information regarding yourself, your firm, and your purpose of a business alliance. Time is a valued commodity in Sweden's corporate ranks, where there is much business to transact and few executives to carry out the work. You will be expected to be efficiently prepared, succinct, and to the point during each phase toward concluding a successful relationship. Swedish, English, and German are the business languages of choice.

DECISION MAKING

Swedish bureaucracy leaves little room for individualism and decision making is usually an executive team effort. The entire process takes time, given the constraints of bureaucracy in place. Be patient. Executives rarely take responsibility for a final decision without the consent of their associates. You are more likely to meet with success if you maintain this protocol: prepare your offering well in advance and provide plenty of details; state precisely what it is you want in the beginning and do not quibble or try to alter your proposition along the way; do not plan to engage in a bout of bargaining. Your Swedish associates like to get things right the first time and are not amenable to last-minute revisions.

WOMEN

While women are found in every kind of occupation in Sweden's work force, they have yet to make a remarkable appearance in high levels of management. The nature of the Swedish economy encourages dual wage-earning families. Working mothers are given flexible work hours so they can maintain both career and family, and the *hemmaman* (house husband) is now an acceptable role for men.

MEETINGS

The importance a Swedish corporation places on your meeting will determine the number and level of rank of the executives they send to attend. On your part, advise your Swedish counterparts in advance of who will be attending from your firm and do not bring anyone unannounced. You will have to send your agenda and any pertinent materials in advance. Your Swedish associates do not like surprises; they prefer to work from a fixed agenda and once the agenda is set it will be difficult to change it in any way during the meeting. Advance preparedness on your part is essential.

BUSINESS ATTIRE

Dress is generally conservative; however, there is variance from industry to industry and company to company. Subdued colors are recommended and ties are normally worn with sport jackets. Women's attire is generally conservative as well. Skirts and blouses are considered appropriate.

Business Centers
Stockholm

CITY VIEW

Much of Stockholm seems to be on the waterfront. Boats crowd the harbor town. The rest of the city is small, and looks much the same as it did years ago.

AIRPORT

Arlanda Airport to City Center

The airport lies 25 miles (41 km.) from the city. The SAS Airport Bus transports passengers to the city terminal in the central rail station downtown. Buses depart from the front of the terminal in 10- to 20-minute intervals between 6:30a.m. and 10:30p.m. at a cost of SEK50. Expect a 45-minute ride into town. Taxis will cost at least six times more and take about the same amount of time to the city center. Expect to pay about SEK350, but be sure to clarify with the driver before departing. A high-speed rail service opened in September of 1999 and whisks passengers to the main train station downtown (T-Centralen) in 20 minutes.

Airline Numbers

Air New Zealand .... (8) 79-29-39
American Airlines .... (8) 24-61-45
Czech Airlines .... (8) 30-04-90
SAS .... (8) 020-91-01-50
Finnair .... (8) 679-93-30
British Airways .... (8) 679-78-00
KLM .... (8) 676-08-80
Lufthansa .... (8) 611-22-88
Domestic Airlines
SAS .... (8) 751-59-50
Linjeflyg .... (8) 797-50-80

HOTELS

Top-end

Grand; Södra Blasieholmshamnen 8; tel: (8) 679-3500 or 3560; fax: (8) 611-8686; email: Reserv@grandhotel.se; near city center; restaurant; conference facilities (up too1000); secretarial service; fax/photocopy facilities; parking; sauna. (258/300)

Reso Sergel Plaza; Brunkebergstorg 9; tel: (8) 226-600; fax: (8) 215-070; email: Plaza.sergel@postbox.postnet.se; near city center; restaurant; conference facilities (up to 200); parking; sauna.

Radisson SAS Royal Viking; Vasagatan 1; tel: (8) 141-000 or 800/448-8355; fax: (8) 108-180; http://www.radisson.com; email: gm@stozs.rdsas.com; near city center adjacent central rail station and World Trade Center; restaurant; conference facilities (up to 140); business center (8a.m. to 4p.m.); secretarial service; in-room hairdryer; room service; valet laundry service; parking; sauna; massage; solarium; poo; whrlpool.

Radisson SAS Strand; Nybrokajen 9; tel: (8) 678-7800; fax: (8) 611-2436; http://www.radisson.com; email: sales@stozh.rdsas.com; city center in financial area, restaurant; conference facilities; non-smoking rooms; electronic key cards; in-room a/c, minibar, valet laundry; airline check in; parking; rooftop sauna with views.

Scandic Continental; Klara Vattugränd 4; tel: (8) 244-020; fax: (8) 411-3695; city center; restaurant; conference facilities (up too70); parking; corporate rates; sauna.

Scandic Hotel Slussen; Guldgränd 8; tel: (8) 5173-5300;

fax: (8) 517-3-5311; http://www.scandic.hotels.com; city center; restaurant; conference facilities (up to 500); business center; internet connection; secure parking; hotel safe; fitness; sauna; pool.

Sheraton Stockholm Hotel and Towers; Tagelbacken 6; tel: (8) 142-600, 412-3400; fax: (8) 217-026, 412-3409; http://www.sweden.sheraton.com/stockholm; near Old Town; standard Sheraton amenities.

Victory; Lilla Nygatan 5; tel: (8) 143-090; fax: (8) 202-177; city center; restaurant; conference facilities (up to 90); in-room modem/fax connection, safe; parking; corporate rates; sauna; whirlpool.

Expensive

Amaranten; Kungsholmsgatan 31; tel: (8) 654-1060; fax: (8) 652-6248; http://www.firsthotels.se; city center; restaurant; conference facilities (up to 84); business center; internet connection; hotel safe; secure parking; corporate rates; fitness; sauna; pool.

Berns; Näckströmsgatan 8; tel: (8) 614-0700; fax: (8) 611-5175; near city center; restaurant.

Diplomat; Strandvägen 7 C; tel: (8) 663-5800; fax: (8) 783-6634; http://www.diplomat-hotel.se; near city center, sea views; ; restaurant; secretarial service; fax/photocopy facilities; in-room modem/fax connection, shower, bath, minibar; parking; corporate rates; sauna.

First Reisen; Skeppsbron 12-14; tel: (8) 223-260; fax: (8) 201-559; http://www.firsthotels.se; near city center; restaurant; in-room modem/fax connection; parking; sauna; pool.

Lady Hamilton; Storkyrkobrinken 5; tel: (8) 234-680; fax: (8) 411-1148; near city center; meeting facilities (up to 20); parking; corporate rates.

Lord Nelson; Västerlanggatan 22; tel: (8) 232-390; fax: (8) 101-089; confrence room; sauna; bar.

Stockholm Plaza; Birger Jarlsgatan 29; tel: (8) 145-120; fax: (8) 103-492; near city center; restaurant; conference facilities 9up to 50); parking; corporate rates; sauna.

Wellington; Storgatan 6; tel: (8) 667-0910; fax: (8) 667-1254; near city center; sauna.

Moderate

Bema; Upplandsgatan 13; tel: (8) 232-675; fax: (8) 205-338; near city center.

Oden; Karlbergsvägen 24; tel: (8) 457-9700; fax: (8) 457-9710; http://www.hoteloden.se; near city center; conference facilities (up to 40); fax facilities; in-room modem/fax connection, safe; secure parking; fitness; sauna.

Reso Palace; S.T. Eriksgatan 115; tel: (8) 241-220; fax: (8) 302-329.

Stockholm; Norrmalmstorg 1; tel: (8) 678-1320; fax: (8) 611-2103; near city center; restaurant; conference facilities (up to 40); secretarial service; fax/photocopy facilities; in-room safe; corporate rates.

HEALTH CLUB

World Class Halsostudion; 68 Luntmakargatan T-bana: Radmansgatan; tel: [46] (8) 673-54-10.

Centralbadet; 88 Drottninggatan; T-bana: Hotorget; tel: [46] (8) 24-24-02.

Friskis & Svettis; 54 St. Eriksgatan; tel: [46] (8) 652-04-70.

AUTO RENTAL

Avis; 61 Sveavagen; tel: 34-99-10 or toll-free (020) 78-82-00; Central Station, Vasagatan 10B, tel: (46) 08-202060, Sun. 9a.m. to 2p.m., Mon. to Fri. 7:30a.m. to 6p.m., Sat.

Sweden

Sweden

9a.m. to 2p.m.; Stockholm Arlanda Airport , nxt Radisson SAS Arlandia Htl, tel: (46) 08-797-9970, Sun. to Sat. 7a.m. to 12p.m.

Budget; 153-155 Sveavagen; tel: 33-43-83 or (020) 78-77-87.

Europcar; Arlanda Airport, tel: 5936-0940, fax: (8) 5936-1455, Mon. to Fri. 6a.m. to midnight, Sat. and Sun. from 7a.m.; Bromma domestic airport, tel: 800-807; fax: (8) 751-4960, closed Sunday; Hotel Sheraton, Tegelbacken; tel: 21-06-50 or (020) 78-11-80; Stockholm Sheraton, tel: 210-650; fax: (8) 796-8449.

Hertz; airport, tel: (8) 797-9900; 22-24 Vasagatan; tel: 24-07-20 or 18-13-15.

WORLD TRADE CENTER

World Trade Center Stockholm
Klarabergsviadukten 70
Box 70354
107 24 Stockholm
tel: (8) 700-4500; fax: (8) 210-681
website: www.sto.wtc.se
email: info@wtc.se

CHAMBER OF COMMERCE

Stockholm Chamber of Commerce
Västra Trädgardsgatan 9, Box 16050

S-103 21 Stockholm
tel: (8) 5551-0000; fax: (8) 5663-1600

CONVENTION BUREAU

Stockholmsmässan
Mässvägen 1, Älvsjö

S-125 80 Stockholm
tel: (8) 749-4100; fax: (8) 992-044

Notes

Switzerland

At a Glance

THE PEOPLE

Population ....7,275,467 (July 1999 est.)
Growth Rate ....0.2% (1999 est.)
Life Expectancy .... 78.99 years (1999 est.)
Infant Mortality..... 4.87 deaths/1,000 live births (1999 est.)

Ethnic Composition

German 65%
French 18%
Italian... 10%
Romansch 1%
Other 6%

Religious Composition

Roman Catholic.. 46.1%
Protestant.. 40%
Other 5%
No Affiliation 8.9%

Languages Spoken

German 63.7%
French 19.2%
Italian.. 7.6%
Other 9.5%

Education and Literacy

Primary education is free. There are 26 educational systems, based on cultural and language needs. Switzerland has 99% adult literacy.

Labor Force

Total 3,800,000
(includes 850,000 foreign workers)
By occupation: services 67%, industrial sector 29%, agriculture 4%.

THE ECONOMY

The Swiss have enjoyed one of the highest income levels in the Western world. Specializing in financial services, biotechnology, and high value machinery, Switzerland has carved itself a special niche in modern Europe. Traditionally a great banking center for Europe, this landlocked nation has decided for the time being to remain outside of the EU. Switzerland is, however, very reliant on the EU export market and has experienced very little GDP growth in recent years as it has been tied to regional sluggishness. As it loses more and more of its financial services market share to American and British rivals, the Swiss economy's fate depends more and more on the success of the EU. It is in the process of considering joining the EU although it finds the level of contribution it must make to the general fund quite daunting (SFr3 billion per year). This nation of cantons is also reluctant to abandon the world's highest level of agricultural subsidization and its tradition of bank secrecy.

Exports ....US$94.4 billion (f.o.b., 1998)
Imports ....US$95.5 billion (f.o.b., 1998)
Total Trade ....US$189.9 billion (f.o.b., 1998)
GDP Per Capita.............................. US$26,400 (1998 est.)
Unemployment .... 3.6 percent (1998 est.)
Inflation Rate ....0 percent (1998)

Top Export Partners

E.U., United States, Japan.

Top Import Partners

E.U., U.S., Japan.

Top Exports

Machinery and equipment, chemicals, precision instruments, metal products, agricultural products.

Top Imports

machinery, chemicals, vehicles, metals, agricultural products, textiles.

BUSINESS WORKWEEK

Offices

Monday to Friday 8a.m. to 5p.m. or 5:30p.m.

Banks

Monday to Friday 8:15a.m. to 12:00p.m. and from 1:30p.m. to 4:30p.m.

Government

Monday to Friday 8a.m. to 12:00p.m. and from 2p.m. to 5p.m.

Retail

Monday to Friday 8a.m. to 6:30p.m., Saturday 8a.m. to 4p.m.

HOLIDAYS

New Year's Day..January 1
Epiphany ....January 6
Good Friday...April 21*
Easter Monday ....April 24*
May Day ....May 1
Ascension Day ....June 1
Whit Monday .... June 12
National Day.. August 1
All Saints' Day ....November 1
Christmas Day..December 25
*Date may vary by year.

CLIMATE

Seasons

The climate is temperate, with mild but humid summers of around 30˚C(85˚F). The winters are generally cold, wet and damp, with high precipitation.

Regions

The south is generally warmer, with more Mediterranean-like summers, and moderate temperatures. Winters are harsh in the mountain areas, with plenty of snow fall. The central plateau has rolling hills, large lakes and seasonal humidity.

Money & Banking

Currency

The currency of Switzerland is the Swiss Franc (SFr).

Denominations

The Swiss Franc (SFr) comes in coin denominations of SFr5, 2 and 1 and 50, 20, 10 and 5 centimes and banknotes of SFr10, 20, 50, 100, 500 and 1,000.

Switzerland

Traveler's Checks and Credit Cards

Traveler's checks and foreign currency can be easily and efficiently exchanged at banks, foreign exchange bureaus located in the major cities, hotels, and foreign exchange kiosks at the airports. Banks offer the most variable exchange rates. Traveler's checks receive a better exchange rate than cash and can be exchanged almost everywhere.

Major credit cards are widely accepted in Switzerland. You can get cash advances from your credit card on many of the automated teller machines (ATM). Long term visitors should set up a checking account in Switzerland, and get an ATM card. Optimal exchange rates are given for credit card purchases and some ATM transactions.

American Express Office - Amtrade Holdings, Bahnhofstrasse 20; Zürich 8022, Switzerland; tel: 12115520.

*Note: Although German is the predominate business language, French and Italian are used extensively as well.

Travel

VISA AND PASSPORT

A valid passport is required; a visa is generally not required for tourist or business stays up to 90 days for EU and North American visitors. However, it is advised to check with your consulate first as there are many exceptions. Passports must be good for six months beyond the intended stay. All travelers must hold onward tickets, valid travel documents, and sufficient funds for their stay.

DEPARTURE FORMALITIES

No restrictions apply to the export of Swiss currency and there are no other departure formalities.

CUSTOMS ENTRY (PERSONAL)

Duty-free

- Visitors from European countries:
- Tobacco: 200 cigarettes, 50 cigars, or 250g of tobacco
- Alcohol: two liters of alcohol (up to 15 percent); One liter of alcohol (over 15 percent)

- Other: gifts up to a value of SFr100 (SFr50 for passengers under 17)
  Visitors from non-European countries:
- Tobacco: 400 cigarettes or 100 cigars or 500g of tobacco
- Alcohol: two liters of alcohol (up to 15 percent); I liter of alcohol (over 15 percent)
- Other: gifts up to a value of SFr100 (SFr50 for passengers under 17)

Prohibited or Restricted
- Most meat and processed meat
- Unprocessed agricultural products
- Narcotics
- There are also strict regulations on importing animals and firearms

IMMUNIZATION & HEALTH
No vaccinations or immunizations are required unless the traveler has passed through an infected area before entering Switzerland. The air is thin in much of Switzerland; so, visitors with cardiovascular problems should take precautions. Bring along any medications you may need as local pharmaceuticals can be expensive. Business visitors bent on weekend ski trips should take special care in the mountains - helicopter rescues are very expensive.

TIPPING

Taxi
Taxi rates usually include the tip; if not, 10 to 15 percent is expected.

Restaurants
All Swiss restaurants include tips and service fees in the bills, and no additional tip is expected. Washroom attendants do not generally get a tip.

Other
Doormen and small services are generally tipped in the range of SFr1.

EMERGENCY INFORMATION

Police and Crime
Switzerland has the reputation of being one of the safest countries in the world; however, crime in Zurich has risen increasingly in recent years, and narcotics are prevalent. The people are honest and law abiding. Petty crime is rare, but take basic precautions. Avoid flashy displays of wealth, and dress and behave conservatively. Leave most of your cash, traveler's checks, jewelry, and other valuables in your hotel safe. Carry photocopies of your passport instead of the original. Carry cash in a money belt, and use credit cards or traveler's checks for most transactions.

Foreign business visitors are often the target of thieves; so, purses, laptops and briefcases require additional security. Do not leave valuables in cars or on tables in cafés. Women walking alone will rarely be accosted, although caution should be taken at night in more urban settings. The Swiss police are extremely efficient and courteous.

Health
The only problematic illnesses are the common flu, bronchitis, sinus problems, and rheumatism caused associated with cold, damp winter weather. Tap water is safe, and food laws are extremely strict.

The Swiss medical establishment is of a very high standard but expensive, so carry adequate insurance. Some pharmacies remain open 24 hours a day.

For more information on medical centers, including phone numbers, please see the "Business Centers" section at the end of this chapter.

TAXI & RENTAL CARS
All taxis are metered for short trips. For long journeys, agree on a fare before leaving. Rental cars can be found in urban areas but visitors should purchase ample insurance. Hired cars with drivers are recommended for first-time visitors. Do not head into mountainous areas without a thorough understanding of the region.

BUS
There are few long-distance inter-city buses, but those in the cities are efficient and inexpensive.

TRAIN
The mainline rail service is geared toward the business traveler, with efficient trips between cities. Most trains have dining cars. These lines also serve the main European rail routes. Expect extremely punctual and efficient service. Trains leave exactly on the Swiss minute.

TRAVEL ASSISTANCE

Hotel Accommodations
Schweizer Hotelier Verein .... (31) 370 4444

Essential Terms

English	German
Yes No	Ja Nein
Good morning Hello (daytime) Hello (evening) Hello (telephone)	Guten Morgen Guten Tag Guten Abend Guten Tag
Good-bye	Auf Wiedersehen
Please	Bitte
Thank you	Danke
Pleased to meet you	Angenehm
Excuse me; I'm sorry	Entschuldigung/ Verzeihung
My name is _____	Ich heiße _____
I don't understand	Ich verstehe nicht
Do you speak English?	Sprechen Sie Englisch?

Communications

DIALING CODES IN SWITZERLAND
International country code: [41]
Selected city codes: Berne (31), Geneva (22), Zürich (1)

Dialing Switzerland from Overseas
To dial Switzerland from overseas, dial your country's international dialing code, then 41 (the country code for Switzerland), then the city code, and finally the number. If

you were dialing Berne from the United States, for example, you would begin with 011, then 41, then 31 (the city code for Berne), and finally the number of the person or office you were trying to reach.

Assistance Numbers
International Information and Operator 114
International Directory 191
Domestic Directory 111
24-hour Anglo-Phone 157-5014

CALLING WITHIN SWITZERLAND

Local Calls
A local call may cost you SFr.50 a minute.

Long Distance Calls
The 3-figure code in brackets found next to a number indicates an area or city code. Use it only if located outside of that region.

International Calls
Calling from a train station or post office telephone center is the most economical way to place an international call. Off-peak rates start between 5p.m. and 7p.m. and get better after 9p.m. and also on weekends.

Post office calling is a cultural experience all of its own in Europe. Tell the clerk where you are calling and wait to be assigned a booth where you may or may not be able to dial on your own. The main thing to remember is to pay after leaving your booth. Credit cards are now also accepted as payment.

Public phones require a card or coin deposit if you wish to connect directly to a U.S. operator.
AT&T Direct.........................155-00-11 (or) 0-800-890-001
MCI 155-02-22

PAY PHONES

Public Telephones
Phones exist everywhere in high-tech Switzerland, even in the *hinterlands*.
1. Pick up receiver
2. Deposit coins
3. Dial number
If for some reason this does not work, consult the English instructions posted inside the booth.

Calling Cards
Available at post offices, newsstands, and train stations, telephone cards come in SFr10 or 20 denominations.

CELLULAR PHONES
Several cellular service providers exist in Switzerland. PTT Switzerland / Swisscom is a major service provider offering NMT-900 for analogue users, and GSM for digital. Swisscom offices are located all over Switzerland. Contact an international operator for assistance in locating one, or visit the Swisscom webpage at http://www.telecom.ch/.

If trying to reach a mobile phone, one must first dial a prefix:

Diax 76
Orange 78
Swisscom 79
Note: Your home country cell phone may not work in this country. If not, we recommend that you rent an international cell phone *before* you leave home. A major US-based cell phone rental provider is **IMC WorldCell**. For information see "International Cell Phone Rentals" on page 14.

Other Cellular Service Providers/Rental
diAx Telecommunications; Thurgauerstrasse 60, 8050 Zurich; tel: (800) 333-666; fax: (800) 333-555; email: info@diax.ch; service provider, GSM 1800; English spoken.

Orange Communications SA; World Trade Center, Av. Gratta-Paille 2, Case postale 455, 1000 Lausanne 30 Grey; tel: (800) 800-078; fax: (21) 641-1770; service provider, GSM 1800; English spoken.

CALL BACK
You can (potentially) save significant sums when calling in Switzerland by using one of the call back services listed below. Fees for call back services vary widely, depending on the company and the type of service required. Be sure to check with these companies before leaving to compare rates.

For a list of callback services, please refer to the "Communications" section in the *Global Road Warrior* Introduction.

PHONE JACKS

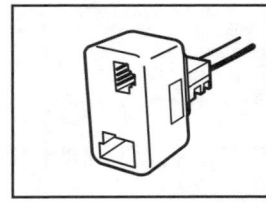

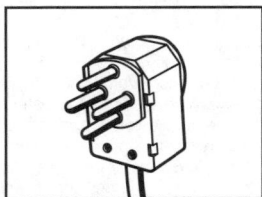

Plug adaptors are available through **iGo Corporation**. (See "Electrical and Telephone Adaptors" on page 19.)

FAX
Fax machines are generally available in offices and hotels, and are very efficient.

POSTAL SERVICES
The mail system is excellent.

Hours of service
Monday to Friday 7:30a.m. to 6:30p.m.

TELEGRAMS
Telegrams can be sent from post offices and most hotels.

Business Services

AUDIOVISUAL RENTAL

Geneva
Action & Light; 9 rue Boissonas; tel: (22) 742-5474.

Audio/Visuel; 4 rue du Beulet; tel: (22) 744-4540.

Zurich
Hausmann; Bahnhofstr. B91; tel: (1) 221-3783.

COMPUTER RENTAL

Geneva
Cefti; 3 ch. Verseuse, Aire; tel: (22) 799-1297.

CMI Cie de Micro-Informatique; 13 ch. Riantbosson; Meyrin; tel: (22) 782-5352.

Zurich
Computerzentrum Fisch; Stampfenbachplatz 4; tel: (1) 363-6767.

COURIER SERVICE

DHL International S.A.; Within: 0800 557777-Toll Free; Avenue d'Aire 40; Geneva 1203; Mon. to Fri. 8a.m. to 5:30p.m., closed Sat., Sun., and holidays; Avenue d'Aire 56, Geneva 1203, tel: (22) 344-4400, Mon. to Fri. 8a.m. to 7p.m., Sat. 8:30a.m. to 12:30p.m., closed Sunday and holidays.

Federal Express; toll free: 0800 55 3757; If you can't access the toll free number call: German-speaking: (1) 874-4 222; French-speaking: (1) 874-4233; Mon. to Fri. 8a.m. to 6p.m.; Customer Invoicing Services, invoice enquiries 022-741-5850; Customer Automation Help Desk, for enquires on any FedEx Customer Automation products. 0800-554-390.

TNT Express Worlwide; Aerogare Fret, C.P. 1144, 1215 Geneva 15; tel: (22) 717-0700; fax: (22) 717-0718.

UPS; United Parcel Service Switzerland; P.O. Box 155,CH-4030; tel: 0800 558-833.

SECRETARIAL SERVICES

Geneva
ABC Executive Services; 20 cours de Rive; tel: (22) 786-5146.

Business Advisory Services; 7 rue Muzy; tel: (22) 736-0540.

Genesis; 4 rue du Mont-Blanc; tel: (22) 732-5174.

Zurich
Friedel Interim Skript; Rislingstr. 4; tel: (1) 221-1515.

International Office Services; Rennweg 32; tel: (1) 214-6111.

TRANSLATION SERVICES

Geneva
California Group; tel: (22) 738-2424.

Intrasco; 61 ave. de Champel; tel: (22) 746-8483.

Transpose; 60 ch. du Vieus Vésenaz; tel: (22) 752-4883.

Zurich
Berlitz; Limmatquai 72; tel: (1) 251-0363.

Interlingua; Limmatstr. 23; tel: (1) 271-5566.

International Office Services; Rennweg 32; tel: (1) 214-6111.

Electrical

Current
220 volts AC, 50Hz

ELECTRICAL SOCKETS

In addition to the typicaly two-prong socket, Switzerland and some Scandinavian Countries use a socket of three round prongs.

ELECTRIC PLUGS

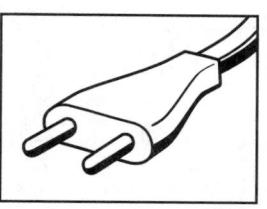

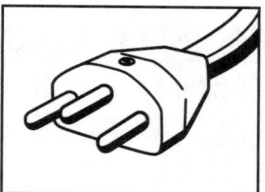

Plug adaptors are available through **iGo Corporation**. (See "Electrical and Telephone Adaptors" on page 19.)

Technical Support

HARDWARE/SOFTWARE VENDOR SUPPORT

Apple/Claris;tel: [41] (800) 833-310; (in Germany) tel: [49] (1) 803-5018; (in the U.K.) tel: [44] (990) 127-753; (in the U.S.) tel: [1] (800) 500-7078; http://www.apple.com/.

AST; (in Ireland) tel: [353] (61) 492-222; (in the U.S.) tel: [1] (817) 232-9824 (International Technical Support); (in the U.S.) tel: [1] (949) 727-4141; http://www.ast.com/.

Compaq/Digital; tel: (22) 709-5330; fax: (22) 709-5391 (Geneva); tel: [41] (1) 801-2507; fax: [41] (1) 801-2172 (Zurich); (in Germay) tel: [49] (89) 9933-0; fax: [49] (89) 933-1158; tel: [49] (130) 6868 (CompaqCare Center/ Information); [49] (0180) 521-2111 (Technical Support) tel: [49] (89) 9933-1380 (QuickLine); (General U.S.) tel: (281) 518-2000; http://www.compaq.com/.

Corel; (in Germany) tel: [49] (180) 425-8210 (TS Word Perfect-32 bit); (in the U.S.) tel: [1] (716) 871-2325 (Ask to be Forwarded to Appropriate Program); http:// www.corel.com/.

Switzerland

Switzerland

Dell; (Dell- Europe) tel: [44] (134) 474-8000; (in Germany) tel: [49] (61) 039-710; (in the U.S.) tel: [1] (512) 338-4400; fax: [1] (512) 728-3330; http://www.dell.com/.

FHewlett Packard; tel: [41] (22) 780-8111; (in Germany) tel: [[49] (0180) 5258-143; (in the U.S.) tel: [1] (408) 246-4300; http://www.hp.com/.

IBM; tel: (22) 310-0418 (in French); tel: (711) 78-50; fax: (711) 785-3511; (in the U.S.) tel: [1] (919) 517-2800; (U.S. Main Office) tel: [1] 914-765-1900; http://www.ibm.com/.

Microsoft; tel: 0848-80-2330; tel: 0848-80-2255 (in German); tel: 022-738-9688 (in French); (in Germany) tel: [49] (848) 858-868; fax: [49] (1) 831-0869; (in the U.S.) [1] (425) 635-7222; http://www.microsoft.com/.

NEC; (in Germany) tel: [49] (18) 0524- 1212; tel: [49] (89) 3160-1233; fax: [49] (89) 3160- 1613 (Floppy Disk and Hard Drive); tel: [49] (89) 9627-4233; fax:[49] (89) 9627-4613 (All Other Products); (in the U.S.) [1] (916) 388-0101 (Main Switchboard); http://www.nec.com/.

Toshiba; tel: [41] (1) 946-0777; fax: [41] (1) 946-0807; (in Ireland) tel: [44] (193) 282-8828; (in the U.S.) [1] (949) 583-3000 (Corporate Headquarters); http://www.toshiba.com/.

Internet Connection

HOW TO CONNECT

Connecting to AOL and Compuserve in Switzerland is similar to using it when traveling outside your own area code. See the introductory section for detailed information on connecting to your account through a different phone number.

America Online

Numbers are available at keyword *international*. Be sure to get several local numbers before leaving. AOL has a new GlobalNet service that charges US$6 an hour in addition to the usual charges. Go to keyword *access* (a free area) and download the software.

Access: Basel (61) 272-5700; Bern (31) 381-0400; Basel (31) 382-9966; Geneva (22) 788-6166; Lausanne (21) 320-2828; Lucerne (41) 360-4151; Lugano (91) 968-1804; St. Gallen (71) 220-9161; Zurich (1) 212-5800.

Compuserve

Numbers are available at *Go International*. If you are using CompuServe 2000, use GO PHONES within CompuServe 2000 to search for access numbers.The Compuserve Web-site also has a great deal of information, at http://www.compuserve.com/.

Access: all areas 0842-111-092.

Independent Service Providers

Many independent service providers offer discounts if you are only in town for a couple of days.

BAR Informatik AG; tel: (27) 924-2600; fax: (27) 924-2919; email: barinformatik@rhone.ch; http://www.bar.ch/.

Deckpoint S.A.; tel: (022) 840-1515; info@deckpoint.ch; http://www.deckpoint.ch/.

Nacamar Data Communications Swiss; tel: [41] 2281-91861; fax: [41] 2281-91951; http://www.nacamar.net/.

SPRYNET; tel: [1] (800) 777-9638; tel: [1] (404) 815-0082; http://www.sprynet.com/.

SwissOnline AG; tel: (1) 846-5801; fax: (1) 846-5861; email: info@swissonline.ch; http://www.swissonline.ch/. [no eng. webpages]

Worldcom; tel: (21) 804-5353; fax: (21) 803-2266; info@worldcom.ch; http://www.worldcom.ch/.

Business Culture

GREETINGS AND COURTESIES

Switzerland is a multilingual, multicultural country, distinct for its regional differences, and greetings there vary accordingly. While English is a predominant language of business, the national languages of German, French, and Italian are also widely spoken. A handshake followed by a polite greeting ("Pleased to meet you") is correct form. In the German region, the address includes *Herr* (Mr.), *Frau* (Mrs.) and *Fraulein* (Miss) followed by the last name only. If the male individual bears a degree or professional title it is appropriate to say "*Herr Doktor*" or "*Herr Professor*" and exclude the last name. However, when addressing professional women you do use the last name; e.g., "*Frau Doktor Schmidt.*" In the French speaking region, use the terms *Monsieur* (Mr.), *Madame* (Mrs. or Ms.), or *Mademoiselle* (Miss) followed by the last name. In the Italian speaking region, use the terms *Signor* (Mr.), *Signora* (Mrs.), or *Signorina* (Miss) followed by the last name. Do not use first names unless invited to do so. Exchanges of gifts upon first meeting is not a custom. As a relationship grows, a gift of fine cognac is always appreciated. Likewise, a box of fine chocolates to be shared by the staff is a thoughtful gesture.

BUSINESS ETHIC AND FRAMEWORK

The Swiss are hard working and extremely formal in business. Third party introductions are very important. Banking and accounting firms can be helpful resources for introductions to people and opportunities in Switzerland. Scheduled appointments are necessary as the Swiss are not receptive to cold calls or to seeing anyone without an appointment. However, it is important to investigate regional differences in order to know specific business practices throughout Switzerland. Quality products and services are essential, more important than price, and the highest standards and quality will be expected from any venture that approaches the Swiss business community. Hard sell techniques are counterproductive and aggressive sales tactics should be avoided. The rank and status of the visiting representatives is not important to the conducting of business, provided the representative is technically competent and has the authority to conclude an agreement.

DECISION MAKING

In larger corporations, decision by consensus among top management is the norm. In smaller firms, a single top manager may render a decision. In either case, and regardless of regional differences, the key to effecting a decision swiftly will depend how well you've presented your program for introducing a high-quality product/service into the Swiss marketplace. Additionally, your Swiss colleagues will place some amount of weight on the longevity of your firm as well as the history of its market performance.

WOMEN

Until recently, women have not had an interest in pursuing corporate management—or so it is said. Having achieved the right to vote as late as 1971, women's roles are rapidly changing. Many women are found at mid-level management positions in banking, insurance, public relations, and advertising. Some have more recently moved into engineering positions. Many Swiss firms have instituted equal opportunity programs to see that women have a chance to advance. Women with families are also increasingly joining the workforce, taking part-time jobs or job-sharing. Many companies are receptive to such arrangements and continue to treat the women professionally.

MEETINGS

The Swiss do not like to mix business with pleasure and they prefer to have meetings take place in the office. Business lunches are few and usually celebrate the success of a completed business transaction. Keeping in mind there are regional differences, generally speaking, the Swiss prefer to get to the point of a purpose and they try to avoid preliminary small talk. Introductions will be made and business cards exchanged. In Switzerland, the host determines when to conclude a presentation, and it is their prerogative to schedule subsequent meetings. You will not be thought aggressive to ask your host for a follow-up meeting or to inquire about the decision-making process. Eye contact during meetings conveys interest and respect.

BUSINESS ATTIRE

Business suits should be conservative. Dark blue or pin stripes are acceptable, and double breasted or three piece suits are preferred over sport jackets and slacks. Ties of sober color and design are appropriate. Women in business should avoid low necklines, costume jewelry, and bright colors. Skirts and blazers or suits and dresses are appropriate.

Business Centers
Geneva
CITY VIEW

With over 250 international companies headquartered in Geneva, it is a truly international city. Swiss watches and jewels gleaming in shop windows contribute to Geneva's cosmopolitan glamour. However, the city's international status belies its small-city feel. Geneva remains so clean and safe that many have complained it does not offer enough excitement.

AIRPORTS

Geneva International Airport to City Center

The airport lies 3 miles (5 km.) from the city. The extremely efficient Swiss Rail System offers an excellent way to get into the city. Merely board a waiting train below the airport for the 7-minute connection into town. Trains depart in 10- to 15-minute intervals between 5:30a.m. and 12:20a.m. for a fare of Sfr4.50. Those going to further destinations should know that direct connections also exist to Basel, Bern, Lucerne, and Zurich as well as destinations in France and Italy.

Taxis depart from outside the arrivals area for a cost of approximately Sfr35 into town. Expect a 10- to 15-minute ride to the city center.

HOTELS

Top-end

Des Bergues; tel: (22) 33 Quai des Bergues; tel: (22) 731-5050; fax: (22) 732-1989; near airport; restaurant; conference facilities (up to 30); in-room modem/fax connection; corporate rates.

Forum Geneva; 19 Rue de Zurich; tel: (22) 731-0241; fax: (22) 738-7514; near city center; restaurant; conference facilities (up to 120); secretarial service; fax/photocopy facilities; in-room modem/fax connection; parking; corporate rates

Inter-Continental; 7-9 Petit Saconnex; tel: (22) 919-3939; fax: (22) 919-3838; near airport, exhibition grounds; restaurant; conference facilities (up to 750); secretarial service; fax/photocopy facilities; in-room modem/fax connection; corporate rates; sauna.

Le Richemond; 8-10 Rue Adhemar Fabri; tel: (22) 731-1400; fax: (22) 731-6709; city center; restaurant; conference facilities (up to 200); secretarial service; fax/photocopy facilities; parking; corporate rates.

Westin Demeure D'Angleterre; 17 Quai du Mont-Blanc; tel: (22) 906-5555; fax: (22) 906-5556; located near lake, city center; restaurant; conference facilities (up to 50); in-room safe; parking; fitness; sauna.

Expensive

Cornavin; 33 Boulevard James-Fazy, Place de la Gare Cornavin; tel: (22) 732-2100; fax: (22) 732-8843; renovated hotel; conference facilities (up to 100); business center; internet connection; in-room modem/fax connection, safe; parking; whirlpool.

De La Paix; 11 Quai du Mont-Blanc; tel: (22) 732-6150 fax: (22) 738-8794; near railway, city center; restaurant; conference facilities (up to 80); parking; corporate rates.

Du-Midi Rive Droite; Quai Des Bergues-Place Chevelu; tel: (22) 731-7800; fax: (22) 731-0020; near railway, airport; restaurant; conference facilities (up to 20).

Mövenpick Geneva; 15 Route de Pre Bois; tel: (22) 798-7575; fax: (22) 791-0284; http://www.movenpick-geneva.ch; near exhibition grounds; 4 restaurants; conference facilities (up to 550); business corner; secretarial service; laptops available; internet connection; in-room modem/fax connection, safe; secure parking; fitness; sauna; disco.

Penta Geneve; 75-77 Avenue Louis Casai; in suburb, near exhibition grounds; restaurant; conference facilities (up to 1700); secretarial service; fax/photocopy facilities; in-room modem/fax connection; parking; corporate rates; fitness; sauna; pool.

Moderate

Cristal; 4 Rue Pradier; tel: (22) 731-3400; fax: (22) 731-7078; located in suburb, near airport; restaurant; conference facilities (up to 80); fax/photocopy facilities; in-room modem/fax connection, safe; parking.

International et Terminus; 20 Rue des Alpes; tel: (22) 732-8095; fax: (22) 774-2571; near city center; railway; restaurant; in-room safe; parking; corporate rates.

Moderne; 1 Rue de Berne; tel: (22) 732-8100; fax: (22) 738-2658; near lake, city; direct dial phone; minibar; t.v./cable.

Montana; 23 Rue des Alpes; tel: (22) 732-0840; fax: (22) 728-2511.

Windsor; 31 Rue de Berne; tel: (222) 731-7130; fax: (22) 731-9325; bar; fax service; laundry service; near airport.

MEDICAL CARE

Hóspital de la Tour; 3 ave. J-D Maillard; tel; 780-0111.
IAMAT Center; 6 rue Bonivard; tel: 314-756.

HEALTH CLUB

Club Migros; 4 Rue Thalberg, Centre des Alpes; tel: 732-77-40.

Gymnase des Eaux-Vives; 15 Rue des Eaux-Vives; tel: 736-51-53.

Nautilus Fitness Center; 12 Rue Gustave-**Revilliod, Acacias**; tel: 343-53-54.

AUTO RENTAL

Alamo, Avis, Budget and **Hertz** are all located at the Geneva airport. They also have downtown offices at the following numbers:

Alamo; Geneva Airport, tel: (22) 717-8430; Monday to Sunday: 7a.m. to 11p.m.

Avis; Airport, tel: (22) 929-0330, Sun. to Sat. 6:30a.m. to 11:15p.m.; Rue de Lausanne 44; tel:(22) 731-9000; Mon. to Sat. 7:30a.m. to 6:45p.m.; Sun. 9a.m. to 1p.m.

Budget; tel: (22) 732-5252.

Hertz; tel: (22) 731-1200; or toll free 155-1234.

WORLD TRADE CENTER

World Trade Center Geneva
WTC II
29, Route de Pre-Bois
1215 Geneva 15 Switzerland
tel: (22) 929 56 56; fax: (22) 791 08 85
email: wtcgv@gluewin.ch
website: http://www.wtc-geneva.ch

Zurich

CITY VIEW

The city is more renowned for its museums than its business, but like other Swiss cities, Zurich is, for the most part, clean and safe and has a great deal to offer to businesspeople.

AIRPORT

Zurich International Airport to City Center

The airport lies 8 miles (13 km.) from the city. Swiss trains run in 10- to 15-minute intervals between the airport and city from 6a.m. to midnight. The ride takes about 10 minutes. Passengers board below the arrivals hall and can depend on plenty of luggage space. Trains also depart for other cities in Switzerland including: Geneva, Bern, Lucerne, and Interlaken. An Airport-City Bus services may hotels in Zurich and operate every 30-minutes during peak hours (morning and evening) and every hour otherwise. Passengers may purchase tickets at the airport welcome desk outside of baggage claim or at information desks. Expect to pay between Sfr14 and Sfr30, depending on the location of your hotel. Those preferring private transportation may catch a taxi outside of the arrivals hall; naturally, it will cost a bit more – about Sfr50 for the 20 to 40-minute ride into town.

HOTELS

Top-end

Eden au Lac; Utoquai 45; tel: (1) 266-2525; fax: (1) 266-2500; http://www.edenaulac.ch; city center, near lake; restaurant; conference facilities (up to 60); fax/photocopy facilities; in-room modem/fax connection, safe; secure parking; corporate rates; sauna.

Widder; Rennweg 7; tel: (1) 224-25-26; fax: (1) 224-24-24; city center, near railway; restaurant; conference facilities (up to 150); secretarial service; fax/photocopy facilities; in-room modem/fax connection, safe; parking; corporate rates; whirlpool.

Expensive

Central Plaza Hotel; Central 1; tel: (1) 251-5555; fax: (1) 251-8535; http://www.astanet.com/get/centralhotel; located in Old Town, Central Square; 4 restaurants; conference facilities; business center; secretarial service; internet connection; in-room modem/fax connection; secure parking; corporate rates.

Mövenpick Zürich-Regensdorf; Im Zentrum, Regensdorf; tel: (1) 871-5111; fax: (1) 871-5011; http://www.moevinpick.ch; located in suburb, near railway; restaurant; conference facilities (up to 1200); secretarial service; fax/photocopy facilities; parking; corporate rates; fitness; sauna; pool; whirlpool.

Sheraton Atlantis; Döltschiweg 234; tel: (1) 463-0000; fax: (1) 463-0388; located in suburb; restaurant; conference

facilities (up to 200); parking; corporate rates; fitness; sauna; pool.

Swissotel Zürich; Am Marktplatz Oerlikon; tel: (1) 311-4341; fax: (1) 312-4468; located in suburb; restaurant; secretarial service; fax/photocopy facilities; corporate rates; fitness; sauna; pool.

Schweizerhof Zürich; Bahnhofplatz 7; tel: (1) 218-8888; fax: (1) 218-8181; city center, near railway; conference facilities (up to 40); in-room modem/fax connection; sauna.

Teifenau; Steinwiesstrasse 8-10; tel: (1) 251-2409; fax: (1) 251-2476; near exhibition grounds, railway; restaurant; conference facilities (up to 250); secretarial service; fax/photocopy facilities; in-room modem/fax connection, safe; parking; corporate rates.

Wellenberg; Niederdorfstrasse 10, Am Hirschenplatz; tel: (1) 262-4300; fax: (1) 251-3130; http://www.hotel-wellenberg.ch; located in Old Town; conference facilities; business facilities; secretarial service; internet connection; in-room modem/fax connection, safe; corporate rates.

Moderate

Basilea; Zäringerstrasse 25; tel: (1) 261-4250; fax: (1) 251-7411; near city center, exhibition grounds; parking; corporate rates.

City; Löwenstrasse 34; tel: (1) 211-2055; fax: (1) 212-0036.

Coronado; Schaffhauserstrasse 137; tel: (1) 363-0650; fax: (1) 363-0656; near airport; restaurant; conference facilities.

Glockenhof; Sihlstrasse 31; tel: (1) 211-5650; fax: (1) 211-5660; restaurant; in-room safe; parking; corporate rates.

Regina; Hohlstrasse 18; tel: (1) 298-5555; fax: (1) 298-5600.

MEDICAL CARE

IAMAT Center; Tafstr. 55; tel: 211-4444.

IAMAT Center; Badenerstr. 41; tel: 241-8081.

Zurich University Hospital; Schmelzbergstr. 8; tel: 255-1111.

HEALTH CLUB

Atmos Fitness Club; Hotel Zurich, 42 Neumuehlequai; tel: 363-40-40.

Town Squash Luxor Fitness Centre; 35 Glaernischstrasse; tel: 202-38-38.

AUTO RENTAL

Alamo; airport, tel: (1) 816-3290, Mon. to Sun. 6:30a.m. to 11p.m., Hoenggerstrasse 40, tel: (1) 271-2646; Mon. to Fri. 7:30a.m. to 7p.m., Sat. 8a.m. to 4p.m.

Avis; airport, tel: (1) 800-7733; Sun. to Sat. 6:30a.m. to 11:30p.m.; 17 Gartenhofstrasse; tel: (1) 296-8787, Mon. to Fri. 7:30a.m. to 6:30p.m., Satu. 8a.m. to noon, 1p.m. to 4:30p.m., Sun. 9a.m. to 1p.m.

Europcar; Zurich Airport, tel: (1) 813-2044; fax: (1) 803-0033, Monday to Sunday 6:30a.m. to 11:30p.m.; Josefstrasse - IKC, tel: (1) 271-5656, fax: (1) 272-0587, Mon. to Fri. 7a.m. to 6:30p.m., Satu. 7:30a.m. to 6:30p.m.; Sunday 8a.m. to noon.

Hertz; 5 Morgartenstrasse; tel: (1) 242-8484.

WORLD TRADE CENTER

World Trade Center Zurich
Leutschenbachstrasse 95
CH-8050 Zurich, Switzerland
tel: (1) 309 11 11; fax: (1) 309 11 22
email: trade@wtc-zurich.ch
website: http://www.wtc-zurich.ch

Switzerland

Taiwan

Taiwan

At a Glance

THE PEOPLE

Population ....22,113,250 (July 1999 est.)
Growth Rate ....0.93% (1999 est.)
Life Expectancy .... 77.49 years (1999 est.)
Infant Mortality..... 6.01 deaths/1,000 live births (1999 est.)

Ethnic Composition

Taiwanese 84%
Mainland Chinese.. 14%
Aboriginal 2%

Religious Composition

Buddhist /Confucian /Taoist Philosophy..................... 93%
Christian 4.5%
Other 2.5%

Languages Spoken

Mandarin (Kuo-yu) Chinese (official), Taiwanese (Min), Hakka, English, Japanese.

Education and Literacy

All children receive nine years of free and compulsory education. Currently 94% of the total population is considered literate.

Labor Force

Total: 9,400,000
By occupation: services 52%, industry 38%, agriculture 10%.

THE ECONOMY

Taiwan was one of the "four dragons" that were at the heart of the so called Asian-miracle of the 1970s and '80s. Originally cast after WWII as a foil to mainland China's centrally planned economy, Taiwan moved away from agriculture to become a productive industrial economy before moving heavily into technology. The financial crisis that swept Asia in the mid-'90s left Taiwan relatively unscathed as its currency held against speculation; this happened despite the heavy investment in its Asian neighbors. Taiwan is currently experiencing GDP growth but not on the scale of a decade ago. Political conflicts with its mainland cousins still keep foreign investment low and domestic expansion cautious. Taiwan has positioned itself for high value-adding technology products, financial services, and as a potential replacement for Hong Kong as a free port.

Exports ....US$122.1 billion (1997)
Imports ....US$114.4 billion (1997)
Total Trade ....US$136.5 billion (1997)
GDP Per Capita....................................US$16,500 (1998)
Unemployment ....2.7 percent (1998)

Inflation Rate2.1 percent (1998) Top Export Partners

United States, Hong Kong, E.U., Japan.

Top Import Partners

Japan, United States, E.U., Hong Kong.

Top Exports

Electrical machinery, electronic products, information/communications , textiles, footwear, foodstuffs, plywood and wood products.

Top Imports

Machinery and equipment, electronic products, chemicals, precision instruments.

BUSINESS WORKWEEK

Offices

Monday to Friday 9:00a.m. to 5:30p.m.

Banks

Monday to Friday 9a.m. to 3:30p.m. without a lunch break, Saturday 9a.m. to noon.

Government

Monday to Friday 8:30a.m. to 5:30p.m, Saturday 8:30a.m. to noon.

Retail

Monday to Friday 9a.m. to 6p.m. Saturday and Sunday 10:00a.m. to 10p.m.

HOLIDAYS

New Years, Founding Day ....January 1
Chinese New Year ....February 5-8
Youth Day... March 29
Children's and Women's Day ....April 4
Tomb-Sweeping Day, Anniversary of Chiang Kai-shek's death ....April 4
Dragon Boat Festival..June 6
Mid-Autumn Festival....................................September 12
National Day (Double Ten)...............................October 10
Chian Kai Shek's Birthday...............................October 31
Constitution Day...December 25
* Date may vary by year.

CLIMATE

Seasons

Taiwanese climate is sub-tropical in the island's northern half and tropical in the southern, giving the island only two seasons—a warm summer and a cool winter—both of them wet. Summers bring the southwest monsoon. Typhoons (hurricanes) are also prevalent on the Pacific coast. You'll find the best weather in October and November.

Regions

Taipei's temperature in the winter ranges from 12˚ to 19˚C (54˚ to 66˚F), with occasional dips to freezing in mountain areas. The summers range from 25˚ to 34˚C (74˚ to 92˚F). Kaohsiung's temperatures are slightly milder in the winter, but just as warm in the summer.

Money & Banking

Currency

The currency of Taiwan is the New Taiwan dollar (NT$).

Denominations

The New Taiwan dollar (NT$) comes in coin denominations of NT$10, 5 and 1, and 50 cents; and banknotes of NT$50, 100, 500 and 1,000.

Traveler's Checks and Credit Cards

Traveler's checks and currency can be exchanged at banks, hotels, department stores, and the banking counter. You get better rates when changing traveler's checks than currency.

Taiwan

A good place to exchange money is at the two international airports, Taipei and Kaohsiung, or at the International Commercial Bank of China, which has numerous branches and takes every kind of traveler's check. Most banks readily accept U.S. dollars and Japanese yen. Cashing checks in more rural areas may prove a little difficult, if not impossible. You can change currency at money-changing booths in shopping centers, and foreign exchange houses such as Thomas Cook. Shun black market dealers. Make sure to always keep your receipts for reconvert of currency. Cash is also widely available from automated teller machines (ATMs).

Credit cards (American Express, Diner's Club, Master-Card, Visa, and JBS) are widely accepted in good hotels, restaurants, and businesses in urban Taiwan. A traveler can obtain cash using a credit card from selected banks. The best exchange rates will be given for credit cards transactions.

Taiwan

Essential Terms

English	Mandarin
Yes No	How-duh boo-shing
Good morning Hello (daytime) Hello (evening) Hello (telephone)	Dzow ahn Nin how Wahn ahn Ne hao
Good-bye	Dzy Jen
Please	Ching
Thank you	Sheh-sheh
Pleased to meet you	Hun gow-sling-nung ren-shi nin
Excuse me; I'm sorry	Dway boo chee, bow-chen
My name is _____	War jow____
I don't understand	Wo b'oo m'ing-b'ai
Do you speak English?	Nee hway shwaw ying-yu mah?

Travel

VISA AND PASSPORT

A passport is required for all visitors. Visas are not required for citizens of the U.S., Canada, EU, Australia, New Zealand and Japan for stays up to 14 days, provided that the traveler is in possession of a passport valid for at least six months and a return or onward ticket. All other visitors must obtain a visa prior to arrival in Taiwan. Business visas for stays of up to 60 days must be obtained prior to entry and are renewable.

DEPARTURE FORMALITIES

Only the equivalent of NT$165,000 worth of foreign currency may be taken out of Taiwan unless it was declared upon arrival, and no more than NT$8,000 can be imported or exported. Visitors leaving from Chiang Kai-Shek International Airport at Taoyaun are subject to a US$12 departure tax.

CUSTOMS ENTRY (PERSONAL)

Duty-free
- Tobacco: 200 cigarettes, 25 cigars, or 454g of tobacco
- Alcohol: one liter of alcoholic beverage
- Other: other goods for personal use up to the value of NT$20,000 (NT$10,000 for passengers under 20 years of age)

Prohibited or Restricted
- Narcotics
- Gambling paraphernalia
- Anti-government materials
- Non-canned meat products

IMMUNIZATION

No international certificates of vaccination are required unless you are arriving from an infected area. Recommended vaccinations include hepatitis A, influenza, polio, tetanus, and typhoid (for non-urban areas).

TIPPING

Tipping is officially discouraged and can be considered an insult, use discretion. Tipping during the Lunar New Year celebration is very common, however.

EMERGENCY INFORMATION

Police and Crime

Taiwan is a fairly safe place, especially compared to some Western cities; street muggings are rare. However, the Taiwanese are aggressive drivers, so don't expect cars to stop for you merely because you're crossing the street.

Take basic precautions against petty crime. Avoid flashy displays of wealth, and dress conservatively. Leave most of your cash, traveler's checks, jewelry, and non-essential valuables in your hotel safe. Carry photocopies of your passport instead of the original. Carry cash in a money belt, and use credit cards or traveler's checks for most transactions.

Foreign business visitors are often the target of thieves for both standard crimes and industrial espionage. Purses, laptops, presentation materials, and briefcases require additional security. Do not leave valuables in cars or on tables in restaurants.

Emergency Numbers

Medical, Fire	119
Police	110
Foreign Affairs Dept., Natl. Police	(2) 396-9781

Health

Taiwan is an advanced society with high standards of health, hygiene, and public safety. However, traffic is a health hazard and a leading cause of death in urban settings. (Bronchitis from pollution, Taiwan's number one disabling illness, is traffic related.)

Hepatitis A and B are rare but do exist here. Travelers' diarrhea is common to first-time visitors, brought on by the change in diet, weather, and water quality. Don't drink tap water or use it to brush your teeth, and avoid ice cubes except in the finest hotels and restaurants. Don't eat raw fruits and vegetables unless they've been washed in a chlorine solution or peeled. Stick to cooked and hot food.

Taiwanese doctors are first rate, and if you need a doctor, your hotel may be able to refer you to one. Hospitals in Taiwan expect to be paid a deposit before treatment. Travel insurance is recommended.

For more information on medical centers, including phone numbers, please see the "Business Centers" section at the end of this chapter.

TAXI & RENTAL CARS

Taxis are the best way to get around in cities, although it can be a hair-raising experience. Many drivers apparently like to imagine they are racers. Taxi drivers rarely speak anything but Chinese, so travel with a friend who speaks the language or have all directions written down for you.

Rental cars are available but not advisable since traffic is heavy and local city drivers are manic. Cars with professional drivers can be leased for extended stays.

BUS

First-class buses come with bathrooms and a smoother ride, but all buses run about the same speed. For a more exciting "after business" ride, hop on board a "wild chicken" bus, with video movies, lower prices, and sometimes faulty brakes and engine (although the horn always seems to work).

TRAIN

Trains are usually crowded, particularly on the weekends and holidays. Reserve seats far in advance. Always keep your ticket as you are expected to present it at the end of the trip as well as the beginning. The rail system is extensive and well used.

Taiwan trains have a first-class service available with air conditioning. A first-class ticket from Taipei to Kaohsiung will cost about NT$600.

TRAVEL ASSISTANCE

Hotel Accommodations

For any questions about Taiwan hotels, consult the Taiwan Hotel and Restaurant Guide. It is available at the Taipei airport and major transport centers.

Taiwan Visitor's Association ....(2) 2594-3261
Tourism Bureau ....(2) 2721-8541
Tourist Information Hotline ....(2) 2717-3737

Communications

DIALING CODES IN TAIWAN

International country code: [886]
Selected city codes: Kaohsiun (7),Taipei (2)

Dialing Taiwan from Overseas

To dial Taiwan from overseas, dial your country's international dialing code, then 886 (the country code for Taiwan), then the city code and finally the number. If you were dialing Kaohsiun from the United States, for example, you would begin with 011, then 886, then 7 (the city code for Kaohsiung), and finally the number of the person or office you were trying to reach.

Assistance Numbers

Directory Assistance (English) ....(02) 311-6796
International Operator 100

CALLING WITHIN TAIWAN

Local Calls

Three minutes cost NT$1 for a local call, thereafter you will be automatically cut off, meaning you must deposit more coins and dial again. All telephone numbers received a preceding '2'.

Long Distance Calls

You may place long distance calls from both public and private phones. Area codes are in effect for different counties in Taiwan and all start with "0." Domestic discounts apply between 7p.m. and 7a.m.

International Calls

Public phones with the ISD label indicate direct international dialing capability. These phones can usually be found around bus and rail stations or the telephone company. Also try the International Telecommunications Administration (ITA) offices for faxes, cables, and telexes. The ITA main office, open 24 hours, is located at 28 Hangchow South Road, Section 1 in Taipei. Discounts for international calls take place between midnight and 7a.m. Don't be fooled, however; discount rates will be more than heftily doubled if calling from a hotel phone. To reach an overseas operator for collect or calling card calls, contact your long-distance carrier at home for your home country access numbers

AT&T USA Direct 0080-10288-0
MCI..0080-13-4567

PAY PHONES

Public Telephones

Pay phones are everywhere, but it's best to use the digital-display models, which are newer and more reliable.

Calling Cards

Cards cost NT$100, and can be found at most shops where you see phones. Ask for a *dianhua ka*.

CELLULAR PHONES

Several cellular service providers exist in Taiwan. Directorate General of Telecommunications - LDTA is a major service provider, offering AMPS for analogue users, and GSM for digital. There are other companies that also offer GSM, including Transasia, MobiTai, and FarEasTone. There are also companies that offer PCS, including FarEasTone, Pacific Comm, KG Telecom, and SmartLink. Contact an international operator for assistance in locating their offices and telephone numbers, or use their internet information listed below.

FarEasTone; tel: (2)2950-5000; http://www.fareastone.com/.tw/.

Note: Your home country cell phone may not work in this country. If not, we recommend that you rent an international cell phone *before* you leave home. A major US-based cell phone rental provider is **IMC WorldCell**. For information see "International Cell Phone Rentals" on page 14.

CALL BACK

You can (potentially) save significant sums when calling in Taiwan by using one of the call back services listed below. Fees for call back services vary widely, depending on the company and the type of service required. Be sure to check with these companies before leaving to compare rates.

For a list of callback services, please refer to the "Communications" section in the *Global Road Warrior* Introduction.

PHONE JACK

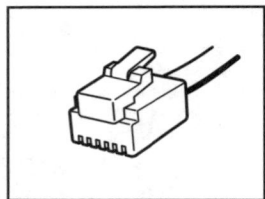

Plug adaptors are available through **iGo Corporation**. (See "Electrical and Telephone Adaptors" on page 19.)

FAX

Fax machines are extremely popular. Virtually all hotels have fax capabilities.

POSTAL SERVICES

The postal service is excellent. Airmail to Europe and North America usually takes five to seven days. It is illegal to send cash through the mail.

Hours of service

Monday to Saturday 8a.m. to 5p.m.

TELEGRAMS

Telegrams can be sent from any hotel and most post offices.

Taiwan

Business Services
COURIER SERVICE

DHL Taiwan Corp.; 1/F, No. 82, Chien Kuo N. Rd.; Sec. 2 ; Taipei; tel: (2) 2503-6858; web site: http://www.tw.dhl.com; Mon. to Sat. 8:30a.m. to 10p.m., Sun. 9a.m. to 6p.m., closed holidays;

Taipei; 10/F No. 82 Chien Kuo N. Rd.; Sec. 2; Taipei; tel: (2) 2503 6858 - International; Mon. to Fri. 8:30a.m. to 5:30p.m.; Sat. 8:30a.m. to 12:30p.m.; closed Sunday and holidays

Federal Express; toll free: 080-075-075;or tel: (2) 2536-9300; Mon. to Fri. from 8a.m. to 7p.m., Sat. from 8a.m. to 5p.m., closed Sunday,

Public Holidays other than Sunday from9 am to 5p.m.

TNT Express Worldwide; No.3, Lane 174,Hsin Min Road, Taipei Nei Hu District 114; tel: (2) 2791-8277 (Switchboard); fax: (2) 2794-8322.

UPS; UPS Taiwan Office 2F. No. 361, Ta Nan Road Shih Lin, Taipei 111; (2) 2883-3868.

Electrical

Current
110 volts AC, 60Hz

ELECTRIC PLUGS

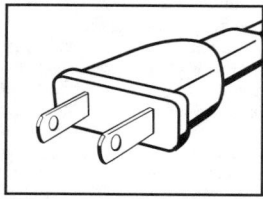

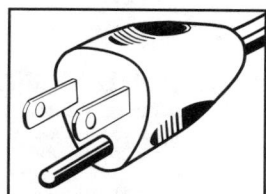

Plug adaptors are available through **iGo Corporation.** (See "Electrical and Telephone Adaptors" on page 19.)

Technical Support
HARDWARE/SOFTWARE

VENDOR SUPPORT

Acer/Texas Instruments; (in Germany) tel: [49] (4102) 488-469; fax; [49] (4102) 488-169; (in the U.S.) [1] (408) 432-6200; http://www.acer.com/.

Adobe; tel: (3) 758-7878; fax: (3) 758-6888 (CSA Malaysia Sdn. Bhd); tel: (3) 293-6000; fax: [60] (3) 293-5500 (Micro Express Sales Sdn. Bhd); (3) 703-9276; (in Switzerland) tel: [41] (800) 833-310; (in the U.S.) tel: [1] (800) 500-7078; http://www.adobe.com/.

Compaq/Digital; (in Switzerland) tel: [41] (22) 709-5330; fax: [41] (22) 709-5391 (Geneva); tel: [41] (1) 801-2507; fax: [41] (1) 801-2172 (Zurich); (General U.S.) tel: (281) 518-2000; http://www.compaq.com/.

Corel; tel: [1] (800) 800-1090 (All Applications); (in Germany) tel: [49] (180) 425-8210 (TS Word Perfect-32 bit); (in the U.S.) tel: [1] (716) 871-2325 (Ask to be Forwarded to Appropriate Program); http://www.corel.com/.**Dell**; tel: (3) 201-8481; fax: (3) 201-8482; (Dell- Europe) tel: [44] (134) 474-8000; (in the U.S.) tel: [1] (512) 338-4400; fax: [1] (512) 728-3330; http://www.dell.com/.

Filemaker/Claris; (in Germany) tel: [49] (180) 525-8166 (Info-line); fax: [49] (180) 567-2233; tel: [49] (180) 523-6423; (in the U.S.) tel: [1] (800) 965-9090; http://www.claris.com/.

Gateway 2000; (in the U.S.) tel: [1] (605) 232-2191; fax: [1] (605) 232-2023; (in Ireland) tel: [353] (1) 797-2000; http://www.g2k.com/.

Hewlett Packard; tel: 03 295 2566; (in Switzerland) tel: [41] (22) 780-8111; (in the U.S.) tel: [1] (408) 246-4300; http://www.hp.com/.

Microsoft; tel: (2) 2508-9501; fax: (2) 2508-9575; tel: (2) 2504-3122; fax: (2) 2504-3121; (in Switzerland) tel: [41] (848) 858-868; fax [41] (1) 831-0869; (in the U.S.) [1] (425) 635-7222; http://www.microsoft.com/.

NEC; tel: (3) 758-7788; fax: (3) 757-7566 (NEC Sales, Head office in Malaysia); tel: (3) 238-7788; fax: (3) 232-3322; (in the U.S.) [1] (916) 388-0101 (Main Switchboard); http://www.nec.com/.

Toshiba; (in Germany) tel: [49] (2131) 158-319; fax: [49] (2131) 158-558; (in Switzerland) tel: [41] (1) 946-0777; fax: [41] (1) 946-0807; (in Ireland) tel: [44] (193) 282-8828; (in the U.S.) [1] (949) 583-3000 (Corporate Headquarters); http://www.toshiba.com/.

Internet Connection
HOW TO CONNECT

Connecting to AOL and Compuserve in Taiwan is similar to using it when traveling outside your own area code. See the introductory section for detailed information on connecting to your account through a different phone number.

America Online

Numbers are available at keyword *international*. Be sure to get several local numbers before leaving. AOL has a new GlobalNet service that charges US$6 an hour in addition to the usual charges. Go to keyword *access* (a free area) and download the software.

Access: Hsinchun (3) 535-8146; Kaohsiung (7) 323-4977; Taichung (4) 328-4257; Tainan (6) 220-3523; Taipei (2) 2356-0786; Taipei Airport (3) 393-1211.

Compuserve

Numbers are available at *Go International*. If you are using CompuServe 2000, use GO PHONES within CompuServe 2000 to search for access numbers. The Compuserve Web-site also has a great deal of information,

Taiwan

at http://www.compuserve.com/.

Access: Kaohsiung (7) 323-4977; Taichung (4) 328-4290; Tainan (6) 220-3523; Taipei (2) 2356-0786.

Independent Service Providers

Many independent service providers offer discounts if you are only in town for a couple of days.

A - 1 Internet; tel: [1] (800) 321-0221; http://www.a1-internet.net/ .

Mackay Telecomm Inc.; tel: 2696-3999; fax: (2) 2696-3396; services@mky.com; email: services@mky.com; http://www.mky.com/ (in Chinese and English).

SEEDNet, Digital United Inc.; tel: (2) 2696-3001, 2733-6454; service@tpts1.seed.net.tw; http://www.seed.net.tw/.

VPM Internet Services; tel: [1] (800) 321-0221 / [1] (916) 983-9876; fax: [1] (916) 983-4375; email: sales@vpm.com; http://www.vpm.com/.

Business Culture

GREETINGS AND COURTESIES

Upon meeting someone, Chinese lower their eyes slightly as a sign of respect. In Taiwan, a smile signifies more than happiness or amusement; it can also signify embarrassment, annoyance, or lack of agreement. Since it is inappropriate to show negative or strong emotions, a smile is used to conceal any such feelings. Staring into the eyes of a Chinese might make them uncomfortable. Face (*mianzi*), a measure of one's dignity, is crucial in Taiwan. Taiwanese are enormously sensitive to maintaining face in everything they do. Saying or doing anything that causes someone to lose face can instantly destroy a relationship and any business that might result from it. Never insult or openly criticize someone in front of others. Do not treat someone as a person of lowly rank if their position in their company is high. A person's face is also their company's face. The relationship you develop with a person represents your relationship with his entire company.

BUSINESS ETHIC AND FRAMEWORK

Dwarfed by and staunchly opposing the People's Republic of China, Taiwan regards business with the rest of the world as crucial to its survival, economically and politically. Taiwanese businessmen are generally practical and shrewd. Work is one of their most prized virtues, and they are willing to work ten or more hours each day. Taiwanese prefer to have their own business rather than be employed by a large corporation. This has resulted in thousands of small-scale, family-owned companies, and potential partners are plentiful. But it also means that business rivalries can be intensely personal and sometimes vicious. Taiwanese behavior is largely determined by Confucianism, which teaches respect for superiors, duty to family, loyalty to friends, humility, sincerity, and courtesy. Among co-workers, people of higher status and age are respected by those beneath them, and deferred to in speech and action. Older businesspeople are likely to be treated more seriously than younger ones. Mandarin Chinese is the official language of Taiwan, but English is spoken widely by members of the business community. Business cards should be printed in both Mandarin and English, and presented with the Mandarin side up and facing the recipient, to the senior member of the group.

DECISION MAKING

Consensus is very important to Taiwanese and they will probably require time for a private discussion before they make a decision. Taiwanese try to avoid saying no, for fear of causing embarrassment or losing face. Instead of directly saying no, they are likely to say something is inconvenient or they might suggest something as an alternative. This is a way of being polite, and pushing a matter after you've received an evasive response will probably cause embarrassment and will probably not close a deal.

WOMEN

Taiwanese are used to doing business with women, and women visiting Taiwan can expect to be treated fairly and respectfully. However, except for the fashion and cosmetic industries, it is not usual for a woman to be the senior member of a business group. If your senior representative is a woman, you might consider including a man to "balance" your group. Women should not be overly aggressive or feel they have to "assert" themselves to be respected by Taiwanese businessmen; they do not. In fact, aggressiveness will be looked on with distaste.

MEETINGS

Taiwanese are more comfortable as a group than as individuals. They become uncomfortable when people speak as individuals, or make statements that are not in harmony with the stated group view. One person, preferably your group's senior member, should be designated as your spokesman. Taiwanese will assume all major communications come from him, and accept what he says as the position of your company. It is a good idea to send a list of your representatives before the meeting, and to include their rank in your company. You should also request a similar list from the Taiwanese. Your team will be led into a room in which the Taiwanese team is already present. The team leader should enter first. Teams sit across a table, leaders opposite each other and others seated in descending order of importance. Small talk will come first. Business is addressed after people feel comfortable with each other. The head of the host team will deliver a short welcome speech, then turn the floor over to the visitors. Your senior team member should speak for your company; avoid conflicting statements from other team members. When talking, your spokesman should address the Taiwanese senior representative. Taiwanese prefer to hear a proposal as a broad overview, and then respond to specific issues or questions point by point.

BUSINESS ENTERTAINING

Taiwanese businessmen like to entertain in Chinese restaurants, and will not expect you to reciprocate. If you do choose to reciprocate, have your hotel arrange a banquet, at which you will be expected to serve your guests. Ask your hotel about banquet etiquette. Wait until business has been concluded, or the night before you depart, to entertain. Although unusual to be invited to a Taiwanese home, if invited, remove your shoes upon entering even though your host may insist that you do not. Business is not usually discussed at meals. Bring a small but tasteful gift that has been wrapped for your Taiwanese business associate. Appropriate gifts include pens, a book from your country, or desk accessories. It is usual for the gift to be refused, although your host may try. Smile and keep insisting until it is accepted. For a hostess gift, bring flowers (never white), foreign liquor or chocolates, toys, perfume for your host's wife, or a memento from your country. Avoid sets of four, considered unlucky, or the color white, associated with death.

When dining out in a restaurant with your Taiwanese hosts, you may find yourself the guest of honor at a formal dinner, at which you should observe certain rules of behavior. Always sit facing the door. Use chop sticks, placing them straight across the bowl or on the table; never cross them. Raise your rice bowl to eat from it. Drink beverages from the container. Watch your hosts, and do as they do. They will disparage the food and service as a way of saying that nothing is good enough for you, their guest. Offer to pay the bill. Smile and continue to insist until it is clear they wish to pay for you.

If you are single, it is a good idea not to reveal if you are divorced, still taboo in Taiwan. Avoid topics of conversation about religion, politics, or mainland China. Refer to Taiwan only as the Republic of China.

BUSINESS ATTIRE

Except for formal situations, Taiwanese do not put much emphasis on dress style, unlike other East Asians. They will, however, expect you to wear a conservative, dark business suit for business occasions. Lightweight suits can be worn year around. One may require a lightweight coat for winters, but summers are especially hot and humid.

Women should wear a lightweight, conservative suit or dress for business occasions, with a light coat or jacket for the winter months.

Business Centers
Taipei

CITY VIEW

Far and away Taiwan's largest city, Taipei is the political, financial, and industrial center of the country.

AIRPORT

Chiang Kai-Shek Airport to City Center

The airport lies 25 miles (40 km.) from the city center. Major hotels often provide shuttle service, which one should order at the time of the hotel reservation. Otherwise, it may take the shuttle up to an hour to arrive at the airport. A special airport shuttle also services two routes into downtown Taipei (one going to the Sungshan Domestic Airport), costing approximately NT$80 and stopping at a variety of hotels. Passengers should make sure to board the correct bus to ensure taking the proper route to their hotel. Should your hotel not be listed at the bus stop in front of the terminal, choose the route going to the central rail station and then take a taxi from there.

C.K.S. Intl. Airport Tourist Service Center
tel: (3) 2398-2194

Airline Numbers

Aer Lingus	(2) 2541-8080
Air Canada	(2) 2507-8133
Air New Zealand	(2) 2531-3980
Air France	(2) 2542-7345
Air India	(4) 2741-0163
Air Lanka	(2) 2594-3911
Alitalia	(2) 2741-5161
Asiana	(2) 2508-1114
Australia Asia	(2) 2522-1001
British Airways	(2) 2541-8080
British Caledonian	(2) 2521-0322
Canadian International	(2) 2503-4111
Cathay Pacific	(2) 2715-2333
China Airlines	(2) 2715-1212
Continental	(2) 2715-2766
CSA	(2) 2577-5752
Delta Airlines	(2) 2551-3656
EVA Airways	(2) 2501-1999
Garuda Indonesia	(2) 2561-2311

Japan Asia	(2) 2776-5151
KLM	(2) 2717-1000
Korean Air	(2) 2521-4242
Lauda Air	(2) 2543-5083
Malaysian Airlines	(2) 2716-8384
Mandarin	(2) 2717-1230, 2717-1188
Northwest	(2) 2716-1555
Philippine Airlines	(2) 2505-1255
Royal Brune	(2) 2531-2884
Sempat	(2) 2396-6934, 2396-6910
Singapore Airlines	(2) 2551-6655
South African Airways	(2) 2713-6363
Thai Airways	(2) 2717-5299, 2717-5200
United Airlines	(2) 2325-8868
Domestic Airlines	
China Airlines	(2) 2715-1122
Far Eastern Airlines	(2) 2361-5431
Formosa Ailrines	(2) 2514-9636
Great China Airlines	(2) 2356-8000
Makung Airlines	(2) 2514-8188
Taiwan Airlines	(2) 2514-8188
Trans-Asia Airways	(2) 2557-9000

HOTELS

Top-end

Asiaworld Plaza Taipei; 100 Tun Hwa North Road; tel: (2) 2715-0077; fax: (2) 2713-4148; city center; restaurant; conference facilities; secretarial service; fax/photocopy facilities; corporate rates; fitness; sauna; pool.

Grand Hyatt; 2 Sung Shou Road; tel: (2) 2720-1234; fax: (2) 2720-1111; http://www.hyatt.com; situated in World Trade Center; restaurant; conference facilities (up to 1300); business center; internet connection; in-room modem/fax connection, safe; secure parking; corporate rates; fitness; sauna; pool; whirlpool; disco.

Grand Formosa Regent; 41 Chung Shan North road, Section 2; tel: (2) 2523-8000; fax: (2) 2523-2828; city center; restaurant; secretarial service; fax/photocopy facilities; dual phones; in-room safe; pool.

The Ritz; 41 Min Chuan East Road, Section 2; tel: (2) 2597-1234; fax: (2) 2596-9222; city center; restaurant; conference facilities; secretarial service; fax/photocopy facilities; sauna.

Expensive

Golden Tulip Howard Plaza; 160 Jen Airoad, Section 3; tel: (2) 2700-2323; fax: (2) 2700-0729; located in business district, near World Trade Center; restaurant; conference facilities (up to 1000)l secretarial service; fax/photocopy facilities; in-room modem/fax connection, double telephone lines, conference call, voicemail; parking; fitness; sauna; pool.

Royal Taipei; No. 37-1, Section 2, Chung Shan North Road; tel: (2) 2542-3266; fax: (2) 2543-4897; city center; restaurant; conference facilities (up to 20); secretarial service; fax/photocopy facilities; in-room modem/fax connection, safe; parking; corporate rates; fitness; sauna; pool.

Taipei Fortuna; 122 Chung Shan Road, Section 2; tel: (2) 2563-1111; fax: (2) 2561-9777; near airport; restaurant; conference facilities; secretarial service; fax/photocopy facilities; fitness; sauna.

Taipei Miramar; 2 Min Chuan East Road, Section 3; tel: (2) 2511-1241; fax: (2) 2541-5571; tel: (2) 2505-3456; fax: (2) 2507-2001; near golf course; parking; corporate rates; sauna; pool.

Taiwan

Moderate

China Hotel Taipei; 14 Kuan Chien Road; tel: (2) 2331-9521; fax: (2) 2381-2349; city center; restaurant.

Cosmos; 43 Chung-Hsiao west Road, Section 1; tel: (2) 2361-7856; fax: (2) 2311-8921; city center; restaurant; conference facilities (up to 60); secretarial service; fax/photocopy facilities; parking; corporate rates.

Golden China Hotel; 306 Sung Chiang Road; tel: (2) 2521-5151; fax: (2) 2531-2914; city center; restaurant; conference facilities 9Up to 200); secretarial service; fax/photocopy facilities; in-room safe; parking; corporate rates.

Leofoo Inn; 168 Chang Chun Road; tel: (2) 2507-3211; fax: (2) 2508-2070; city center; restaurant; conference facilities (up t o 150); secretarial service; fax/photocopy facilities; parking; corporate rates.

Paradise Hotel; 26 Hsi Ning South Road; tel: (2) 2314-1181; fax: (2) 2314-7873; city center; restaurant; conference facilities (up to 200); parking.

Taipei Y.M.C.A.; 19 Hsu Chang Street; tel: (2) 2311-3201; fax: (2) 2311-3209; city center; restaurant; parking.

MEDICAL CARE

Adventist Hospital; 424 Pateh Road, Sec. 2; tel: 771-8151; fax: (2) 2777-5623.

Mackay Memorial Hospital (main); 92 Chungshan N. Road, Sec. 2; tel: (2) 2543-3535.

National Taiwan University Hospital; 7 Chungshan S. Road; tel: (2) 2397-0800.

V.I.P. Clinic; Chang Gung Memorial Hospital, 3/F, 199 Tun Hua N. Rd.; tel; (2) 2713-5211, ext. 606.

HEALTH CLUBS

ARTS Fitness World; 163 Keelung Road, Sec. 1 Sungshan; tel: (2) 2762-3866.

Clark Hatch Physical Fitness Center; 86 Tunhua S. Road, Sec. 1; tel: (2) 2741-6670.

Avance Health Spa; B3, 14, Alley 39, Chung Shan N. Rd., Sec. 2; tel: (2) 2563-3250.

Clark Hatch Exective Fitness Club; 86 Tun Hua s. Rd., Sec. 4; tel: (2) 2741-6670.

Super Shape Health Club; 5/F, 15 Fu Hsing Rd.; tel: (2) 2771-0960.

AUTO RENTAL

Note: Due to traffic conditions, renting a car is not recommended for business travelers. Taxis are readily available.

Avis; tel: 2500-6633; toll free (800) 331-1212; Avis cars can also be reserved at the Car Rental Association at CKS Airport; tel: (03) 2383-4531.

Central Auto Rental; tel: 2882-1000, 2881-9545.

Taipei Budget Rent-A-Car; tel: 2831-2906/7.

WORLD TRADE CENTER

Taipei World Trade Center Co., Ltd.
3-8th Floor, CETRA Tower
333 Keelung Road, Section 1
Taipei 110, Taiwan
tel: (2) 2725-5200

fax: (2) 2757-6042
email: cetra@cetra.org.tw
website: http://twtc.org.tw

Notes

Thailand

Thailand

At a Glance

THE PEOPLE

Population ....60,609,046 (July 1999 est.)
Growth Rate ....0.93% (1999 est.)
Life Expectancy .... 69.21 years (1999 est.)
Infant Mortality.. 29.54 deaths /1,000 live births (1999 est.)

Ethnic Composition
Thai 75%
Chinese 14%
Other 11%

Religious Composition
Buddhist 95%
Muslim 3.8%
Christian, Hindu, Other... 1.2%

Languages Spoken
Thai (official), English, regional and ethnic dialects.

Education and Literacy
Education accounts for 16% of total government expenditures. Six years of education are compulsory beginning at age seven. Currently, 93.8% of the population is considered literate.

Labor Force
Total: 32,600,000
By occupation: agriculture 54%, government and services 31%, industry 15%.

THE ECONOMY

Thailand was the first country in Asia to have its economy "meltdown" in spring of 1997. This process triggered the financial crisis that swept over its Asian neighbors. The sudden devaluation of the Thai currency (baht) resulted in a foreign debt default as Bangkok's major companies withered. Speculators and foreign lenders began to reassess the soundness of all Asian investments. As similar defaults and devaluations washed over the rest of Southeast Asia, Thailand responded to its own crisis with a disciplined adherence to IMF loan requirements. By early 1998, Thailand had stabilized its economy but far below its former prosperity. Currently, it is restoring its export growth and revamping its lax banking system which had been long blamed for the original crisis. Thailand is making steady progress and may soon return to its status as a "mini-dragon" of the Asian economic sphere. The title, unfortunately, will be relative to similarly devastated neighbors.

Exports ....US$51.6 billion (1997)
Imports ....US$73.5 billion (1997)
Total Trade ....US$125.1 billion (1997)
GDP Per Capita................................. US$6,100 (1998 est.)
Unemployment .... 4.5 percent
Inflation Rate .... 4.3 percent (1998 est.)

Top Export Partners
United States, Japan, Singapore, Hong Kong, Malaysia, United Kingdom.

Top Import Partners
Japan, United States, Singapore, Germany, Taiwan, Malaysia.

Top Exports
Manufactures, agricultural products and seafood.

Top Imports
Capital goods, consumer goods, raw materials, fuel.

BUSINESS WORKWEEK

Offices
Monday to Friday 8a.m. to 6p.m. A few offices will have shortened weekend hours.

Banks
Monday to Friday 9a.m. to 5p.m., Saturday 9a.m. to noon.

Government
Monday to Friday 8:30a.m. to 5p.m.

Retail
Monday to Saturday 9a.m. to 9p.m. Only a very few retail outlets are open on Sunday.

HOLIDAYS

New Year's Day..January 1
Makhabuja.. Februay 19
Chakri Day.. April 6
Songkran Festival...April 13-15
Coronation Day,
Royal Ploughing Ceremony Day ....May 5
Visakhabuja..May 18
Asalhabuja..July 17
Beginning of Buddhist Lent ....July
Queen's Birthday.. August 12
Chulalongkorn Day..October 23
King's Birthday ....December 5
Constitution Day ....December 10
New Year's Eve...December 31
Some dates may vary by year.

CLIMATE

Seasons
Thailand has decidedly tropical weather, so it is warm and humid all year round. There are distinct seasonal changes also; March to May are the hottest months with minimal rain. June to October are rainy months, but it is also very hot. The November to February period is cooler with lower humidity and limited rainfall.

Regions
In the north, temperatures range from 16°C (60°F) in the winter to 30°C (85°F) in the summer. Rain storms are sudden and torrential. The dry northwest monsoon appears from November through the end of March, and soaking southwest monsoon sweeps in from mid-May through early October.

In the southern isthmus, the temperatures are fairly constant year-round at 25° to 30°C (76° to 85°F).

Money & Banking

Currency
The currency of Thailand is the Baht (B).

Denominations
The Baht (B) comes in coin denominations of 10, 5, 2 and 1, and 50 and 25 satangs; banknotes come in B1, 5,

Thailand

Provinces of

1	Ang Thong
2	Buriram
3	Chachoengsao
4	Chai Nat
5	Chaiyaphum
6	Chanthaburi
7	Chiang Mai
8	Chaing Rai
9	Chon Buri
10	Chumphon
11	Kalasin
12	Kamphaeng Phet
13	Kanchanaburi
14	Khon Kaen
15	Krabi
16	Krung Thep Mahanakhon
17	Lampang
18	Lamphun
19	Loei
20	Lop Buri
21	Mae Hong Son
22	Maha Sarakham
23	Nakhon Nayok
24	Nakhon Pathom
25	Nakhon Phanom
26	Nakhon Ratchasima
27	Nakhon Sawan
28	Nakhon Si Thammarat
29	Nan
30	Narathiwat
31	Nong Khai
32	Nonthaburi
33	Pathum Thani
34	Pattani
35	Phangnga
36	Phatthalung
37	Phayao
38	Phetchabun
39	Phetchaburi
40	Phichit
41	Phitsanulok
42	Phra Nakhon Si Ayutthaya
43	Phrae
44	Phuket
45	Prachin Buri
46	Prachuap Khiri Khan
47	Ranong
48	Ratchaburi
49	Rayong
50	Roi Et
51	Sakon Nakhon
52	Samut Prakan
53	Samut Sakhon
54	Samut Songkhram
55	Saraburi
56	Satun
57	Sing Buri
58	Sisaket
59	Songkhla
60	Sukhothai
61	Suphan Buri
62	Surat Thani
63	Surin
64	Tak
65	Trang
66	Trat
67	Ubon Ratchathani
68	Udon Thani
69	Uthai Thani
70	Uttaradit
71	Yala
72	Yasothon

Thailand

- ◎ National capital
- • Provincial capital
- • Secondary city
- Railroad
- Primary road
- International boundary
- Province boundary

0   50   100   150   200 km
0   50   100   150 mi

SM Santa Barbara, CA

©2001 Magellan Geographix

10, 20, 50, 100, 500 and 1,000 denominations. The three smallest of these denominations are no longer issued, but are still legal tender.

Traveler's Checks and Credit Cards

Traveler's checks can be exchanged at banks, exchange shops, hotels, and international airports at variable exchange rates. Larger banks will offer the fairest exchange rates, but avoid black marketers at all cost. Consult your bank about current exchange rates before travel.

Most major currencies can be exchanged at hotels and banks, but try to take only crisp and new notes, wrinkled and soiled notes are likely to be refused. All U.S. banknotes above $5 will be inspected for counterfeit control, so don't be offended.

Major credit cards are accepted in good hotels, large shops, and car rental places, but smaller restaurants and markets may ask for cash. Some banks in the capital offer cash advances on credit cards, but make sure you bring your passport. Credit card transactions receive the best exchange rates.

The American Express office in Thailand is located at 388 Phaholyolthin Rd, 9-10th floor, S P Building, Samsennai, Krung Thep Mahanakhon 10400 tel: 6622730033.

Essential Terms

English	Thai
Yes	Krap (M) Ka(F)
No	Mai
Good morning	Sa wat dee
Hello (daytime)	Sa wat dee
Hello (evening)	Sa wat dee
Hello (telephone)	Sa wat dee
Good-bye	Sawasdee krap (M)
	Sawasdee ka (F)
Please	Dai prod
Thank you	Kawkhun krap (M)
	Kawkhunka (F)
Pleased to meet you	Yin dee tee roo jak
Excuse me; I'm sorry	Khor tawt
My name is _____	Pom (di chan) cheur
I don't understand	Pom mai kao jai
Do you speak English?	Khun poot pasa angrit dai mai krap(M) Ka(F)?

Travel

VISA AND PASSPORT

Only a valid passport is required for a 15-day visit if you arrive at an international airport. You may be asked to show an onward ticket or equivalent cash. For longer stays or overland entry, obtain a visa in advance. Multiple-entry and 90-day business visas are available to those visitors than can demonstrate a valid commercial purpose or an invitation. Costs are minimal by Asian standards for these extra visas.

DEPARTURE FORMALITIES

To export large, expensive Buddha images or antiques of archaeological value, you will need a license from the Bangkok National Museum. It is not an easy process and should be initiated well in advance of departure. The sale of "rare" items to foreigners and confiscation by customs officials (for eventual resale) is somewhat of a racket at rural border areas. Handle all such transactions through proper channels and don't hand over your cash to the seller until the paperwork is complete.

Travellers may not take out more than the equivalent of US$10,000 in undeclared foreign money or B500 in Thai currency.

CUSTOMS ENTRY (PERSONAL)

Duty-free
• Tobacco: 200 cigarettes or 250g of tobacco or equal weight of cigars
• Alcohol: One liter of wine or spirits
• Other: goods up to a value of Bt3000

IMMUNIZATION

Vaccination certificates are required of travelers from areas infected with cholera or yellow fever. Visitors should take proper malaria and hepatitis A precautions even in urban areas. Countryside travel will warrant yellow and dengue fever prophylaxis.

TIPPING

Taxi
Taxi drivers do not expect but will not refuse tips.

Porters
Tip porters B50 per bag.

Hotels & Restaurants
Most restaurants and hotels add a 10 percent service charge, so further tipping is optional.

EMERGENCY INFORMATION

Crime
Thailand may seem like a safe haven, but beware. Muggings, burglaries, pickpocket, and bag snatchers riding on mopeds are endemic.

Take basic precautions. Avoid flashy displays of wealth, dress conservatively. Leave most of your cash, traveler's checks, jewelry, and non-essential valuables in your hotel safe. Carry photocopies of your passport instead of the original. Carry cash in a money belt, and use credit cards or traveler's checks for most transactions. Walk with your bag away from the street to avoid having it snatched away by motorcycle thieves.

Drug trafficking is severely punished so do not handle packages or luggage for strangers. Claiming "it isn't mine" is futile.

Foreign business visitors are often the special targets of thieves; as such, purses, laptops and briefcases require additional security. Do not leave valuables in cars or on tables in cafés.

Emergency Numbers
Police, Ambulance, and Fire 191
Tourist Police 195
Immigration Division 287-3101

Health
Although sanitation is adequate in Bangkok, do not drink tap water or eat raw food in more rural areas. Avoid street vendor food in Bangkok if you have a sensitive stomach. Stay away from food sold at roadside stands, and generally stick to milder dishes. Some stomach and digestion problems may be caused my the spicy food, heat, and the basic change of diet.

Malaria is a problem only in the countryside, but AIDS is widespread and growing, as is hepatitis A and hepatitis B which may be sexually transmitted. Rabies is not a rarity in the countryside. Other diseases include gastrointestinal disorders, colds and other respiratory ailments, and fungal infections caused by the damp, hot climate.

Medical services are above average for Southeast Asia and hotels have access to good doctors, many of whom speak English. Costs are inexpensive. Pharmacies are scarce, but hospitals carry necessary drugs.

For more information on medical centers, including phone numbers, please see the "Business Centers" section at the end of this chapter.

TAXI & RENTAL CARS

Taxis from hotels are metered. Other taxis hailed from the streets or at the airport will probably have their meters off; negotiate a price before leaving. Travel at night should be arranged for you by the hotel or a business contact.

Rental cars can be found in urban areas but visitors should purchase ample insurance. Hired cars with drivers are recommended for first-time visitors. Traffic in Bangkok is snail-like but the rural areas are quite navigable even by tourists.

TRAIN

Thailand Railways Corporation (TRC) provides the principal rail services. All trains are efficient but, other than first class, they are not air conditioned and may not prove comfortable. Travel by rail in Thailand is quite relaxing and romantic but is not recommended for business travel unless no alternative exists for reaching remote towns.

Communications

DIALING CODES IN THAILAND

International country code: [66]
Selected city codes: Bangkok (2), Chanthaburi (39), Chiang Mai (53)

Dialing Thailand from Overseas

To dial Thailand from overseas, dial your country's international dialing code, then 66 (the country code for Thailand), then the city code and finally the number. If you were dialing Bangkok from the United States, for example, you would begin with 011, then 66, then 2 (the city code for Bangkok), and finally the number of the person or office you were trying to reach.

Assistance Numbers

Directory Assistance... 13
Long Distance 100
International Assistance 100

CALLING WITHIN THAILAND

Local Calls

A local call costs Bt2 for three minutes.

Long Distance Calls

Private, long-distance telephone offices exist specially for inter-Thailand calls. Another option is the post office. Area codes are in effect, including the initial zero when dialing outside of the zone in which you find yourself. Drop the zero if phoning from outside Thailand.

International Calls

Hotels usually charge an additional fee (sometimes up to 30 percent) for international calls made from rooms. The cheapest way is to call international is from a Communications Authority of Thailand (CAT) office, found in most major cities and open 24 hours. Most CAT offices only accept cash or international phone credit cards.

PAY PHONES

Public Telephones

Red phones are for local calls and blue phones are for long distance calls (within Thailand). Local calls cost Bt2. Although there are three Bt2 coins in circulation, only the mid-sized fits in the phone. Many phones in airports and hotels require phone cards.

The latest phone booth service in Thailand is called Fonepoint. It is a system using a one-way mobile phone network from TOT. These mobile phones can be used to communicate with other mobile phones and pagers. Inquire at a TOT office for Fonepoint services.

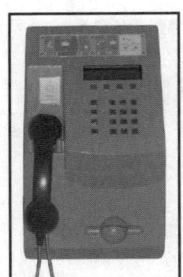

Calling Cards

Calling cards can be purchased in 25Bt, 50Bt, 100Bt, or 240Bt denominations.

CELLULAR PHONES

Several cellular service providers exist in Thailand. Advanced Information Services is a major service provider, offering NMT-900 for analogue users, and GSM for digital. NMT-450 is offered by Telephone Organization of Thailand, NAMPS and DCS by Total Access Communication Co. Ltd., and AMPS by Communications Authority of Thailand.

Note: Your home country cell phone may not work in this country. If not, we recommend that you rent an international cell phone *before* you leave home. A major US-based cell phone rental provider is **IMC WorldCell**. For information see "International Cell Phone Rentals" on page 14..

CALL BACK

You can (potentially) save significant sums when calling in Thailand by using one of the call back services listed below. Fees for call back services vary widely, depending on the company and the type of service required. Be sure to check with these companies before leaving to compare rates.

For a list of callback services, please refer to the "Communications" section in the *Global Road Warrior* Introduction.

PHONE JACK

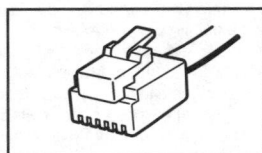

Plug adaptors are available through **iGo Corporation**. (See "Electrical and Telephone Adaptors" on page 19.)

FAX

Fax services are generally available in hotels. The service can be slow.

POSTAL SERVICES

Service is excellent. Airmail takes 3 to 10 days to reach U.S.

Hours of service

Monday-Friday 8a.m. to 10p.m., Saturday 9a.m. to 1p.m.

TELEGRAMS

Telegrams can be sent from hotels, airports, and CAT offices.

Business Services

COURIER SERVICE

DHL International (Thailand) Ltd.; tel: (2) 207-0600; Grand Amarin Tower, Floor 22; 1550 New Petchburi Rd.; Makasan Rachatevee; Bangkok 10310; Open 24 hours, 7 days;

Airport Location: 403/1 Ground Floor, 403 Bldg.; Bangkok International Airport; Donmuang; Bangkok 10210; open seven days, 24 hours

Federal Express (Traffic Express Co, Ltd.); tel: (2) 367-3222; fax:: (2) 367-3221.

Electrical

Current
    220 volts AC, 50Hz.

ELECTRIC PLUGS

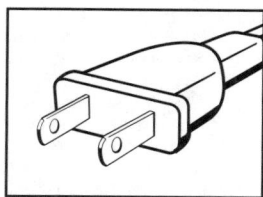

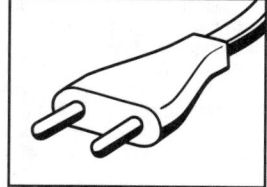

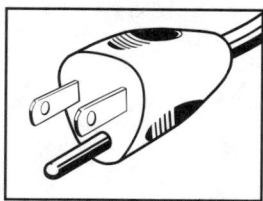

Plug adaptors are available through **iGo Corporation.** (See "Electrical and Telephone Adaptors" on page 19.)

Technical Support

HARDWARE/SOFTWARE VENDOR SUPPORT

Acer/Texas Instruments; (in Germany) tel: [49] (4102) 488-469; fax; [49] (4102) 488-169; (in the U.S.) [1] (408) 432-6200; http://www.acer.com/.

Adobe; tel: (3) 758-7878; fax: (3) 758-6888 (CSA Malaysia Sdn. Bhd); tel: (3) 293-6000; fax: [60] (3) 293-5500 (Micro Express Sales Sdn. Bhd); (3) 703-9276; (in Switzerland) tel: [41] (800) 833-310; (in the U.S.) tel: [1] (800) 500-7078; http://www.adobe.com/.

Apple/Claris; tel: 3-291-8000; (in Switzerland) tel: [41]

(800) 833-310; (in the U.K.) tel: [44] (990) 127-753; (in the U.S.) tel: [1] (800) 500-7078; http://www.apple.com/.

AST; (in the U.S.) tel: [1] (817) 232-9824 (International Technical Support); (in Ireland) tel: [353] (61) 492-222; (in the U.S.) tel: [1] (949) 727-4141; http://www.ast.com/.

Compaq/Digital; (in Switzerland) tel: [41] (22) 709-5330; fax: [41] (22) 709-5391 (Geneva); tel: [41] (1) 801-2507; fax: [41] (1) 801-2172 (Zurich); (General U.S.) tel: (281) 518-2000; http://www.compaq.com/.

Corel; tel: [1] (800) 800-1090 (All Applications); (in Germany) tel: [49] (180) 425-8210 (TS Word Perfect-32 bit); (in the U.S.) tel: [1] (716) 871-2325 (Ask to be Forwarded to Appropriate Program); http://www.corel.com/.

Dell; tel: (3) 201-8481; fax: (3) 201-8482; (Dell- Europe) tel: [44] (134) 474-8000; (in the U.S.) tel: [1] (512) 338-4400; fax: [1] (512) 728-3330; http://www.dell.com/.

Filemaker/Claris; (in Germany) tel: [49] (180) 525-8166 (Info-line); fax: [49] (180) 567-2233; tel: [49] (180) 523-6423; (in the U.S.) tel: [1] (800) 965-9090; http://www.claris.com/.

Gateway 2000; (in the U.S.) tel: [1] (605) 232-2191; fax: [1] (605) 232-2023; (in Ireland) tel: [353] (1) 797-2000; http://www.g2k.com/.

Hewlett Packard; tel: 03 295 2566; (in Switzerland) tel: [41] (22) 780-8111; (in the U.S.) tel: [1] (408) 246-4300; http://www.hp.com/.

IBM; tel: (2) 273-4000; fax: (2) 273-0434; fax: (3) 717-2188; tel: (2) 273-0041; (in Switzerland) tel: [41] (22) 310-0418 (in French); (in the U.S.) tel: [1] (919) 517-2800; http://www.ibm.com/.

Microsoft; tel: (2) 613-7208/9/10/11 ; fax: (2) 613-7198; tel: (2) 266-3300; fax: (2) 266-3310; (in Switzerland) tel: [41] (848) 858-868; fax [41] (1) 831-0869; (in the U.S.) [1] (425) 635-7222; http://www.microsoft.com/.

NEC; tel: (3) 758-7788; fax: (3) 757-7566 (NEC Sales, Head office in Malaysia); tel: (3) 238-7788; fax: (3) 232-3322; (in the U.S.) [1] (916) 388-0101 (Main Switchboard); http://www.nec.com/.

Novell; (in Australia) tel: [61] 2-925-3000 (Asia Pacific Support Center); (in Switzerland) tel: [41] (1) 308-4747; fax: [41] (1) 302-0401; (in the U.S.) tel: [1] (408) 434-2300; fax: [1] (408) 577-5775 (Worldwide Sales Headquarters); http://www.novell.com/.

Quark; (Singapore Office) tel: [65] 467-6675; (in the U.S.) tel: [1] (303) 894-8899; fax: [1] (303) 894-3398 (For Products Registered in the Americas); http://www.quark.com/.

Toshiba; (in Germany) tel: [49] (2131) 158-319; fax: [49] (2131) 158-558; (in Switzerland) tel: [41] (1) 946-0777; fax: [41] (1) 946-0807; (in Ireland) tel: [44] (193) 282-8828; (in the U.S.) [1] (949) 583-3000 (Corporate Headquarters); http://www.toshiba.com/.

Internet Connection

HOW TO CONNECT

Connecting to AOL and Compuserve in Thailand is similar to using it when traveling outside your own area code. See the introductory section for detailed information on connecting to your account through a different phone number.

America Online

Numbers are available at keyword *international*. Be sure to get several local numbers before leaving. Go to keyword *access* (a free area) and download the software.

At press time, America Online had no local access numbers in Thailand. Check their list of current access numbers at http://intlaccess.web.aol.com/ to see if any numbers have been activated or to locate numbers in neighboring countries.

Compuserve

Numbers are available at *Go International*. If you are using CompuServe 2000, use GO PHONES within CompuServe 2000 to search for access numbers. The Compuserve Web-site also has a great deal of information for travelers at http://www.compuserve.com/.

Access: At press time, Compuserve had no local access numbers. Check their list of current access numbers to see if any numbers have been activated or to locate numbers in neighboring countries.

Independent Service Providers

Many independent service providers offer discounts if you are only in town for a couple of days.

A-Net Company Ltd; tel: (2) 861-1533; fax: (2) 861-1544; info@a-net.net.th; http://www.a-net.net.th/. [**note: A-Net** is a subsidiary of **Anew Corporation Ltd**; (2) 861-1555; fax: (2) 861-1544; info@anew.co.th; http://www.anew.co.th/.]

Internet Thailand Co Ltd; tel: (2) 6427-0656; fax: (2) 640-0456; email: info@inet.co.th; http://www.inet.co.th/.

Siam Global Access Co., Ltd; tel: (2) 950-2020; fax: (2) 950-2036; webmaster@sga.net.th; http://www.sga.net.th/.

VIANET; tel: [43] (1) 404-020; fax: (1) 404-0240; sales@vianet.at; http://www.vianet.at/.

Business Culture

GREETINGS AND COURTESIES

The traditional greeting among Thais is the *wai,* which signifies "Hello," "Thank you," and "I'm sorry." One places the palms together, fingers extended at chest level, and bows slightly. The higher the hands are placed, the greater the respect, but the fingers are not placed above eye level. When meeting foreigners, the accepted greeting is the handshake. This applies to both men and women. Thais address each other by using the first name preceded by *Khun.* Surnames are used in formal situations. On formal occasions, foreigners can address Thais by using their last name, preceded by Mr., Mrs., or Miss. Titles are important, and if someone has a title use it when greeting them. Thais are extremely courteous and respectful of others. Thailand is often called the "Land of Smiles." Thais tend to be reserved, and feel it is improper to criticize others. They value a sense of humor, laughter, and a genial attitude.

BUSINESS ETHIC AND FRAMEWORK

The Thai expression, *Mai Pen Rai* (never mind) sums up their attitude toward almost everything. They are by no means lazy or uncaring, but life is to be enjoyed. Problems and reversals are not to be taken too seriously, and they are generally happy with who they are and what they have. Respect is extremely important in Thai culture. Speaking loudly or publicly expressing anger is considered improper behavior and can result in a loss of respect. Showing proper respect is especially important when dealing with older people.

DECISION MAKING

Decisions are made slowly. Thai respect for rank and authority demands that all documents, requests, and proposals must travel up the entire chain of command before they reach the actual decision maker. Thais generally look for some sort of compromise before coming to a decision, even in situations where it may seem no compromise is necessary. They will go to great lengths to avoid giving an outright "no," and believe it is not possible to be too polite. Decisions are made at the top, and subordinates shield high-level executives so they do not have to deal with situations they are not prepared for.

WOMEN

Thai women have long been active and highly visible at all levels of business, and are treated the same as men. Foreign women can expect to be treated with respect and taken seriously, but will find they are more easily accepted if they speak softly. Women should never touch a Buddhist monk, offer to shake his hand, or hand anything directly to him. If a woman must hand something to a monk, she should give it to a man. If no man is around, she should place it on a table or on the ground, and the monk will pick it up. Women should be very careful about their handbags on the street (pursesnatchers often use motorcycles), avoid wearing jewelry in the street, and not go to nightclubs alone. At night, always take taxis (these should be hotel taxis, never unofficial taxis), and if a driver engages you in conversation, tell him you are married and have children.

MEETINGS

Punctuality is not a high priority, but arriving on time for a meeting will earn you respect. However, do not be surprised if your Thai associate is late. The pace is relaxed. Thais often make personal phone calls or run errands during the business meeting. Your first meeting could be a business lunch, at which business might not be discussed at all. Thais like to take time to get to know their potential business partners. When talking business, don't ask questions that require a direct response or a judgment such as, "What do you think of this product?" Such bluntness, and its potential for confrontation, will make a Thai uncomfortable and could be considered impolite. If Thais laugh for seemingly no reason, they are embarrassed and it is best to change the subject.

BUSINESS ATTIRE

Thais are extremely neat, and consider appearance to be very important. Dress formally. For men, a dark suit, tie, and polished shoes are recommended. Thailand is hot and humid, so natural fibers that breathe (cotton, linen) will be more comfortable. Women should wear tasteful, conservative dresses (never sleeveless). Stockings are not necessary because of the intense heat. If you wear makeup, full eye makeup is suggested. During the rainy season (June through November), men should bring extra pants because your clothes will be splashed at the ankles.

Business Centers
Bangkok

CITY VIEW

Six million people call Bangkok home, and it shows. It offers a plethora of traffic, noise, heat (in the hot season), and floods (during the flood season). With shantytowns lining the rail tracks into Bangkok, one might be struck by the squalor of third-world living conditions. However, once swept into the frantic pace of Bangkok, one can easily be consumed in the madness of the upwardly mobile traversing between second- and first-world status. The official name for the city is *Krung Thep* (City of Angels).

AIRPORT

Bangkok International Airport to City Center

The airport lies 19 miles (30 km.) from the city center. Thai Airways operates a limousine service, which may be prepaid at the counter outside of customs. Breathe a sigh of relief in the air-conditioned limousine for B300, or in a shared minivan for B150. If your hotel stands on the Chao Phraya River, consider taking the Airport River Express, a marvelous way to avoid the Bangkok traffic. Boats leave every hour and take about 40 minutes for a fare of B700. River Express staff will take you to the dock and assist with luggage. Reserve a seat on the boat when you book your hotel; seats are often not available if booking at the River Express counter upon arrival at the airport.

The major hotels also provide hotel cars for a fee of B300, which will be added to your hotel bill. Notify them in advance, if possible, so that they may meet you upon arrival.

Taxis are also available; however, be sure to settle on a fare before departing the terminal since meters do not exist. Fares should not run higher than B250.

For those on a budget, consider taking the train for B100, which also includes the shuttle bus going from the airport to the station. The train trip into town takes about 35 minutes, and from the main station one can easily catch a cab to a hotel.

Airline Numbers

Aeroflot .... (2) 233-6956/7
Air Canada .... (2) 233-5900
Air France ....(2) 234-1330/9
Air India .... (2) 256-9614/8
Air New Zealand.................................... (2) 237-1560/1/2
Alitalia.. (2) 233-4000/4
American Airlines .... (2) 251-1393
Bangkok Airways .... (2) 253-4014
Bangladesh Biman .... (2) 235-7643/4, 234-0300/9
British Airways... (2) 236-8655/8
Burma Airways .... (2) 234- 9692, 233-3052
CAAC Airlines........................... (2) 235-6510/1, 235-8159
Canadian Airlines
International................................ (2) 251-4521, 254-8376
Cathay Pacific Airways................................... (2) 235-4330
China Airlines .... (2) 253-5733
CSA .... (2) 308-2106
Delta Air Lines ....(2) 233-8530/2
Egyptair .... (2) 233-7601/3
Finnair .... (2) 251-5445
Garuda Indonesia...................................... (2) 233-0981/2
Gulf Air .... (2) 254-7931/40
Iraqi Airways.. (2) 235-5950/5
Japan Airlines.............................. (2) 234-9111. 233-2420
KLM Royal Dutch
Airlines................................. (2) 235-5150/4, 235-5155/9
Korean Air .... (2) 234-9283/9
Kuwait Airways .... (2) 523-6993
Lao Aviation... (2) 233-7950
Lufthansa... (2) 234-1350
Malaysian Airlines System .... (2) 236-5871
Northwest
Airlines......................... (2) 253-4822, 253-4822/4423
Pakistan International Airlines .... (2) 234-2961
Pan American World Airways.................. (2) 252-2128/30
Philippine Airlines .... (2) 233-2350/2
Qantas .... (2) 236-9193/6
Royal Brunei Airlines .... (2) 234-3100/9
Royal Jordanian Airlines............................... (2) 236-0030
Royal Nepal Airlines .... (2) 233-3921/4

SAS .... (2) 252-4181
Sabena.. (2) 233-2020
Saudi Arabian Airlines .... (2) 236-9400/3
Singapore Airlines .... (2) 236-0303
Swissair .... (2) 233-2935/8
Taron Romanian Air Transport................... (2) 235-2668/9
Thai Airways International ...... (2) 513-0121, 234-3100/19, 288-0090, 280-0070/80, 215-2020/4
United Airlines .... (2) 253-0559

HOTELS

Top-End

Dusit Thani; 946 Rama IV Road, tel: (2) 236-0450; fax: (2) 236-6400; restaurant; bar; business center; tennis; squash.

Grand Hyatt Erewan Bangkok; 494 Rajdamri Road; tel: 254-1234; fax: 253-5856; near city center; restaurant; conference facilities (1500) secretarial services; fax/ photocopy facilities; in-room safe; parking; corporate rates; fitness; sauna; pool.

Mansion Kempinski Bangkok; 75/23 Sukhumvit Soi 11, Prakanong; tel: 255-7200; fax: 253-2329.

The Oriental; 48 Oriental Avenue; tel: 236-0400; fax: 236-1937; 7 restaurants; business center; personal butler service; 24-hour medical service; 24-hour news; airport helicopter service; airport arrival and departure service; limo service; private boat landing; river cruises; fitness; sauna; 2 pools; oriental spa; sports center; massage; tennis; squash; jogging track.

Regent Bangkok; 155 Rajdamri Road; tel: 251-6127; fax: 254-5390; near city center; restaurant; conference facilities (800); secretarial services; fax/photocopy facilities; in-room modem/fax connection; in-room safe; parking; corporate rates; fitness; sauna; pool; whirlpool.

Sukhothai Bangkok; 13/3 South Sathorn Road; tel: 287-0222; fax: 287-4980; near city center; restaurant; conference facilities (200) secretarial services; fax/ photocopy facilities; in-room safe; parking; corporate rates; fitness; sauna; pool; whirlpool.

Expensive

Amari Airport; 33 Chert Wudthakas Road, Don Muang; tel: 566-1020; fax: 566-1941; near airport; restaurant; conference facilities (1000) secretarial services; fax/ photocopy facilities; in-room safe; parking; fitness; sauna; pool.

Emerald; 99/1 Rachadapisek Road; tel: 276-4567; fax: 276-4555; near city center; restaurant; conference facilities (1600); secretarial services; fax/photocopy facilities; in-room modem/fax connection; in-room safe; parking; corporate rates; fitness; sauna; pool.

Holiday Inn Crowne Plaza; 981 Silom Road; tel: 238-4300; fax: 238-5289; http://www.crowneplaza.com/hotels/ bnkth/; near city center; 4 restaurants; conference facilities (600); business center; secretarial services; internet; in-room modem/fax connection; in-room safe; secure parking; corporate rates; fitness; sauna; pool; whirlpool.

Imperial Queen's Park; Sukhumvit Road; tel: 261-9000; fax: 261-9530-5; http://www.imperialhotels.com/; near exhibition grounds; restaurant; conference facilities (2000); business center; secretarial services; fax/photocopy facilities; internet; in-room safe; secure parking; corporate rates; fitness; sauna; pool.

Indra Regent; 120-126 Rajprarob Road; tel: 208-0022; fax: 208-0388; near railway and exhibition grounds; restaurant; conference facilities (1500); secretarial services; fax/ photocopy facilities; parking; corporate rates; fitness; sauna; pool.

Thailand

Mandarin; 662 Rama IV Road; tel: 238-0230; fax: 237-1620; near city center; restaurant; conference facilities (2000) secretarial services; fax/photocopy facilities; parking; corporate rates; pool.

Novotel Bangkok on Siam Square; Rama 1 Road; tel: 255-6888; fax: 255-1824; near city center; restaurant; conference facilities (300) secretarial services; fax/photocopy facilities; in-room safe; parking; corporate rates; fitness; sauna; pool.

Royal Orchid Sheraton Hotel and Towers; 2 Captain Bush Lane, Siphya Road; tel: 266-0123; fax: 236-8320; near city center; restaurant; conference facilities (1250); secretarial services; fax/photocopy facilities; in-room modem/fax connection; in-room safe; parking; corporate rates; fitness; sauna; pool; whirlpool.

Shangri-La; 89 Sol Wat Suan Plu, Bangrak; tel: 236-7777; fax: 236-8579; near city center; restaurant; conference facilities (2000); secretarial services; fax/photocopy facilities; in-room safe; parking; corporate rates; fitness; sauna; pool; whirlpool.

Sol Twin Towers Bangkok; 88 New Rama 6 Road, Rongmuang Patumwan; tel: 216-9500; fax: 216-9544; near city center; restaurant; conference facilities (1000); secretarial services; fax/photocopy facilities; in-room modem/fax connection; parking; corporate rates; fitness.

Moderate

Delta Grand Pacific; 259 Sukumvit Road 17-19; tel: 651-1000; fax: 255-2441; http://www.deltahotel.co.th/; city center; restaurant; business center; fax/photocopy facilities; internet; in-room safe; parking; corporate rates; fitness; sauna; pool.

Jade Pavilion Travelodge; 30 Sukhumvit Soi; tel: 259-4675; fax: 258-2328; near city center; conference facilities; secretarial services; fax/photocopy facilities; pool.

Swiss Lodge; 3 Convent Road; Silom; tel: 233-5345; fax: 236-9425; http://www.swisslodge.com/; boutique hotel in business district; restaurant; conference facilities (20); business center; secretarial services; fax/photocopy facilities; internet; in-room modem/fax connection; in-room safe; secure parking; corporate rates; pool.

Y.M.C.A. Collins International House; 27 South Sathorn Road; tel: 287-2727; fax: 287-1996; near exhibition grounds; restaurant; conference facilities; secretarial services; fax/photocopy facilities; in-room safe; parking; corporate rates; pool.

MEDICAL CARE

Hospitals offering 24-hour emergency care and ambulance service:

Bumrungrad Medical Center and Hospital; 33 Sukhumvit Road, Soi 3; tel: (2) 253-0250 or (2) 253-0250.

Bangkok General Hospital; 2 Soi Soonvichai 7, off New Phetchabori Road; tel: (2) 318-0066.

Samitivej Hospital; 133 Sukhumvit Road, Soi 49; tel: (2) 392-0011 or (2) 281-6807.

Dental Polyclinic; 211/3 New Phetchaburi Road; tel: (2) 314-5070.

Bumrungrad Hospital; 33 Sukhumvit Road, Soi 33; tel: (2) 253-0250.

HEALTH CLUB

Ambassador Hotel Fitness Center; Ambassador Hotel, 171 Sukhumvit Road, Soi 11; tel: (2) 254-0444.

Asoke Sports Club; 302/81-81 Asoke-Din Daeng Road; tel: (2) 246-2260.

Fitness Clinic Health Club; 16/15 Soi Somkit, Ploenchit;

tel: (2) 251-0392.

Landmark Hotel; 138 Sukhumvit Road; tel: (2) 254-0404.

Soi Klang Racquet Club; 8 Sukhumvit Road, Soi 49; tel: (2) 391-0963, 392-8442 or 392-8443.

Sports Center; Oriental Hotel, 48 Oriental Ave; tel: (2) 236-0400 ext. 2018.

Swim & Slim Family Club; 918 Soi 101/1, Sukhumvit Road; tel: (2) 393-0889.

AUTO RENTAL

Note: Due to the horrendous traffic conditions in Bangkok, renting a car is not highly recommended.

Avis; 2/12 Wireless Road; tel: (2) 255-5300 (to 04); Avis also has branches at the Royal Princess, Dusit Thani, Sukhothai and Grand Hyatt Erawan hotels.

Hertz; 1620 New Petchburi Road; tel: (2) 251-7575; 420 Sukhumvit Road, Soi 71; tel: (2) 390-0341.

WORLD TRADE CENTER

World Trade Center Bangkok
World Trade Center Complex, 7th Floor
4 Rajdamri Road
Bangkok 10330, Thailand
tel: (2) 255-9500; fax: (2) 253-4488
website: http://www.infonews.co.th/WTCB/WTCB.html
email: wtcbkk@infonews.co.th

Tunisia

At a Glance

THE PEOPLE

Population ....9,513,603 (July 1999 est.)
Growth Rate ....1.39% (1999 est.)
Life Expectancy .... 73.35 years (1999 est.)
Infant Mortality... 31.88 deaths/1,000 live births (1999 est.)

Ethnic Composition

Arab-Berber...98%
European...1%
Other...1%

Religious Composition

Muslim...98%
Christian...1%
Judaism and other..1%

Languages Spoken

Arabic (official) and French (trade).

Education and Literacy

Tunisia has nine years of compulsory education with Arabic the language of instruction in early grades but replaced by French in higher grades. Tunisia's literacy rate is 66.7 percent.

Labor Force

Total: 3,300,000
By occupation: services 55%, industry 23%, agriculture 22%.

THE ECONOMY

Tunisia's location between problematic Libya and chaotic Algeria in North Africa has had minimal effect on this outward-looking economy. Its GDP growth is fired by its cordial relations with the EU, privatization schemes, and realistic approach to foreign investment. Its manufacturing, mining and agricultural sectors are complemented by one of the few attractive tourism industries on the North African-Mediterranean coast. While it has some Islamic fundamentalist components, politics in Tunisia are decidedly constitutional-republic in method. Tunisia's approach to economics is an efficient, if guarded, market-style bent on increasing GDP per capita for its growing population.

Exports ....US$5.4 billion (f.o.b., 1997 est.)
Imports .... US$7.9 billion (c.i.f., 1997 est.)
Total Trade ....US$13.3 billion (1997)
GDP Per Capita................................ US$5,200 (1998 est.)
Unemployment ....15.6% (1998 est.)
Inflation Rate ....3.3% (1998 est.)

Top Export Partners

E.U., North African countries, Asia , U.S.

Top Import Partners

E.U. countries, North African countries, Asia , U.S .

Top Exports

Hydrocarbons, textiles, agricultural products, chemicals.

Top Imports

Industrial goods and equipment, hydrocarbons, food, consumer goods.

BUSINESS WORKWEEK

Offices

Monday to Friday 8a.m. to 12:30p.m. and 2:30p.m. to 6p.m.

Banks

Summer: 8a.m. to 11a.m. and 2p.m. to 4p.m.
Winter: 8a.m. to 11:30a.m. and 1p.m. to 3:30p.m.

Government

Monday to Friday 9a.m. to 11:30a.m. and 2p.m. to 5p.m.

Retail

Monday to Friday 9a.m. to 7p.m. Slightly shorter hours on weekends and during the summer.

(Note: Islamic nations make allowances for prayer throughout the business day and some offices may be closed briefly.)

HOLIDAYS

New Year's Day..January 1
Independence Day .... March 20
Youth Day... March 21
Aid El Kebir, Feast of the Sacrifice..................... March 18
Martyrs' Day .... April 9
Labor Day..May 1
Republic Day...July 25
Women's Day ....August 13
Evacuation of Bizerta ....October 15
Accession of President Ben Ali ....November 7
Aid el-Seghir (End of Ramadan) ....December 31
Some dates may vary by year.

CLIMATE

Seasons

The northern area of Tunisia has a Mediterranean climate, hot dry summers and cool rainy winters. Average temperatures from May to October are 19˚C to 26˚C. August is the hottest month. April and May weather is unpredictable. In the winter rain is frequent, temperatures averaging 10˚C to 13˚C.

Regions

The northern region features both mountains and coastline with a moderate climate. The southern areas is near the Sahara Desert and is hot and semi-arid. The daytime temperatures in the inland in summer time reach 45˚C, falling to 10˚C at night.

Money & Banking

Currency

The currency of Tunisia is the Tunisian Dinar (TD).

Denominations

The Tunisian Dinar (TD) comes in coin denominations of TD5 and 1, and 500, 100, 50, 20 and 10 millimes and banknotes of TD5, 10 and 20.

Traveler's Checks and Credit Cards

Traveler's checks can be exchanged at banks, exchange shops, hotels, and international airports at tourist exchange rates. Larger banks may offer the best exchange rates. Avoid black marketers at all cost. Consult your bank about current exchange rates before departure. Keep all receipts for reconversion.

Tunisia

Major credit cards are easily accepted in up-market places in the cities, but in more rural areas they may ask for cash. The most favorable exchange rates are used for credit card transactions. ATM facilities are rare but some banks in the capital offer cash advances on credit cards. You will need passport identification.

Travel
VISA AND PASSPORT

All visitors need a valid passport, but visas are generally not required for most European and North American visitors for stays up to three or four months. Tunisia requires visas for a vast number of nations and the list changes regularly so check with a consulate before departure. Business visas and multiple entry visas require special arrangement with immigration officials.

DEPARTURE FORMALITIES

Local currency may not be exported. With proper documentation, only up to TD100 may be reconverted back into hard currency upon departure. Make sure you exchange your money in small increments.

CUSTOMS ENTRY (PERSONAL)

Duty-free

• Tobacco: 400 cigarettes, 100 cigars, or 500g of loose tobacco
• Alcohol: 1 liter of spirits; 2 liters of wine or beer
• Other: 250ml of perfume; 1 liter of eau de toilette; gifts up to a value of TD100; 2 cameras (not identical); 20 rolls of film; 1 video camera with 3 tapes; 1 radio cassette/CD player

Prohibited or Restricted

The export of antiquities is subject to a permit from the Ministry of Cultural Affairs.

IMMUNIZATION

An international vaccination certificate is required of travelers coming from cholera or yellow fever infected areas. Recommended immunizations include polio, diphtheria, tetanus, and hepatitis A.

TIPPING

Taxi

In taxis, tip 10 percent unless the fare was negotiated and includes the tip.

Porters

Porters M500 (TD0.5) per suitcase.

Hotels

Moderate tipping is expected in hotels on top of the service charge.

Restaurants

Restaurant bills include service charges; extra gratuities are not necessary.

Other

Small tips are offered everywhere.Car parkers wearing official badges get M100-200; unofficial parkers get less. Maids get TD1 per day,

EMERGENCY INFORMATION

Police and Crime

Crime in Tunisia is relatively high, and it is not very safe to walk the streets alone. Be careful of purse snatchers and pickpockets, especially in tourist areas and markets.

Avoid flashy displays of wealth, and dress conservatively. Leave most of your cash, traveler's checks, jewelry, and non-essential valuables in your hotel safe.Carry cash in a money belt, and use credit cards or traveler's checks for most transactions. Walk with your bag/purse/briefcase away from the street to avoid having it snatched away by passing thieves on motorbikes.

Foreign business visitors are often the target of thieves; so, purses, laptops and briefcases require additional security. Do not leave valuables in cars or on tables at cafés.

Emergency Numbers

Ambulance (Tunis) 341-250
Fire/Police (Tunis) 197

Health

Malaria and rabies are present in more remote areas. Hepatitis A, intestinal parasites, schistosomiasis, venereal diseases and AIDS also exist here.

Do not drink tap water or use ice cubes unless assured by hotel staff of purity; bottled water is available or use purification tablets. Wash all vegetables in a chlorine solution, peel fruits, and avoid uncooked food. Try to eat simply until your digestive system adjusts to the spicy food.

For more information on medical centers, including phone numbers, please see the "Business Centers" section at the end of this chapter.

TAXI & RENTAL CARS

Long distance taxis (called *louages*) can carry up to five passengers. Louage stations can be found all over the city (most are situated near hotels), and this is the easiest way to get around the cities. Rental cars can be found but should be used only by experienced visitors. Insurance is a must.

TRAIN

Trains connect all the major cities in Tunisia. Tickets purchased at the train cost double than those bought in advance. Two classes of seating are available but the trains are packed and the seating is cramped.

Essential Terms

English	Arabic
Yes No	Na-a'am La; mish
Good morning Hello (daytime) Hello (evening) Hello (telephone)	Al sa-lahm Al sa-lahm Ma-sa'el khair Marhaban
Good-bye	Be-kha-trahk
Please	Min-fahd-lak (M) Min-fahd-lik (F)
Thank you	Shook-rahn
Pleased to meet you	Sorirart biro'aitak
Excuse me; I'm sorry	Is-ma-leh
My name is _____	'Ismii____
I don't understand	An-na mish fahem
Do you speak English?	Hal tatakallumu l-inkliziyya?

Communications

DIALING CODES IN TUNISIA

International country code: [216]

Selected city codes: Bizerte (2), Kairouan (7), Menzel Bourguiba (2), Tunis (1)

Dialing Tunisia from Overseas

To dial Tunisia from overseas, dial your country's international dialing code, then 216 (the country code for Tunisia), then the city code and finally the number. If you were dialing Bizerte from the United States, for example, you

Tunisia

would begin with 011, then 216, then 2 (the city code for Bizerte), and finally the number of the person or office you were trying to reach.

Assistance Numbers

International Operator 17
Directory 1818

CALLING WITHIN TUNISIA

Local Calls

A local call will cost 100 millimes at a phone booth and about 300 millimes from a hotel room.

Long Distance Calls

All numbers in Tunisia have six digits in eight major area codes.

International Calls

A direct call overseas means dialing 00 + country code + area code + number. You can, in theory, dial direct from a coin phone. But given the unreliability thereof, calls from the international telephone office in Tunis, or PTT offices outside Tunis, may prove to be better alternatives. Taxiphone offices also allow international calls. In any telephone, PTT or taxiphone office, payment is made after the call has been completed. International public phones take 500 millimes and D1 coins.

PAY PHONES

Look for the sign 'taxiphone' when attempting to find a public phone; or head to a PTT office. The 100 millimes coin phones may be used for local calls only.

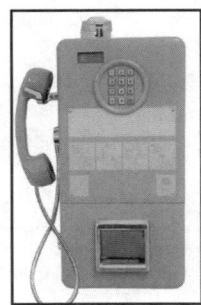

CELLULAR PHONES

Cellular service providers are limited in Tunisia. The Ministry of Communications is a major service provider, offering NMT-450 for analogue users, and GSM for digital.

Note: Your home country cell phone may not work in this country. If not, we recommend that you rent an international cell phone *before* you leave home. A major US-based cell phone rental provider is **IMC WorldCell**. For information see "International Cell Phone Rentals" on page 14.

CALL BACK

You can (potentially) save significant sums when calling in Tunisia by using one of the call back services listed below. Fees for call back services vary widely, depending on the company and the type of service required.

For a list of callback services, please refer to the "Communications" section in the *Global Road Warrior* Introduction.

PHONE JACKS

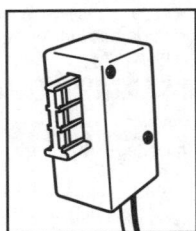

Plug adaptors are available through **iGo Corporation.** (See "Electrical and Telephone Adaptors" on page 19.)

FAX

Fax services are available in hotels and post offices.

POSTAL SERVICES

Postal service is generally efficient and inexpensive. There is an express mail service that can get packages to Europe in under four days.

TELEGRAMS

Telegrams are widely used in Tunisia. They can be sent from most hotels.

Business Services

COURIER SERVICE

DHL; 1 rue Malaga, 2092 El Manar 1, Tunis.

Federal Express (Rapid Poste); tel: (1) 88-599.

TNT Express Worldwide; Aeroport De Tunis - CarthageTunis; tel: 4864-5972; fax: 4864-5961.

Electrical

CURRENT

127/220 volts AC, 50Hz.

ELECTRIC PLUGS

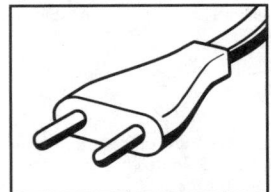

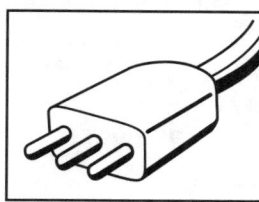

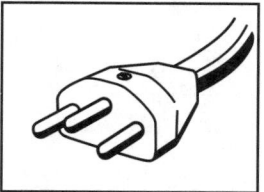

Plug adaptors are available through **iGo Corporation.** (See "Electrical and Telephone Adaptors" on page 19.)

Technical Support

HARDWARE/SOFTWARE VENDOR SUPPORT

Hewlett Packard; (in Switzerland) tel: [41] (22) 780-8111; (in the U.S.) tel: [1] (408) 246-4300; http://www.hp.com/.

IBM; tel: (1) 800-090; fax: (1) 784-538; (Egypt Office) tel: [20] 2-349-2533; fax: [20] 2-360-1227; (in Switzerland) tel: [41] (22) 310-0418 (in French); (in the U.S.) tel: [1] (919) 517-2800; http://www.ibm.com/.

Microsoft; (in Egypt) tel: [20] (2) 338-8724; tel: [20] (2) 338-9794; (U.A.E. Office) tel: [971] 4-513-888; fax: [971] 4-527-444(in Switzerland) tel: [41] (848) 858-868; fax [41] (1) 831-0869; (in the U.S.) [1] (425) 635-7222; http://www.microsoft.com/.

Internet Connection

HOW TO CONNECT

Connecting to AOL and Compuserve in Tunisia is similar to using it when traveling outside your own area code. See the introductory section for detailed information on connecting to your account through a different phone number.

America Online

Numbers are available at keyword *international*. Be sure to get several local numbers before leaving. Go to keyword *access* (a free area) and download the software.

At press time, America Online had no local access numbers in Tunisia. Check their list of current access numbers at http://intlaccess.web.aol.com/ to see if any numbers have been activated or to locate numbers in neighboring countries.

Compuserve

Numbers are available at *Go International*. If you are using CompuServe 2000, use GO PHONES within CompuServe 2000 to search for access numbers. The Compuserve Web-site also has a great deal of information for travelers at http://www.compuserve.com/.

At press time, Compuserve had no local access numbers. Check their list of current access numbers to see if any numbers have been activated or to locate numbers in neighboring countries.

Independent Service Providers

Many independent service providers offer discounts if you are only in town for a couple of days.

Agence Tunisienne Internet (ATI); tel: (1) 846-100; fax: (1) 846-600; email: mhiri@ati.tn; http://www.ati.tn/.

IRSIT/EUnet Tunisia; tel: (1) 800-122; tel: (1) 787-757; fax: (1) 787-827; email: Mondher.Makni@irsit.tn; http: gopher://gopher.rnrt.tn/.

VPM Enterprises; tel: [1] (800) 321-0221 / [1] (916) 983-9876; fax: [1] (916) 983-4375; sales@vpm.com; http://www.vpm.com/.

Business Culture

GREETINGS AND COURTESIES

Frequent handshakes (with the right hand only) are the most common gesture of greeting and departure. Greetings between women may come either in the form of a handshake or a light kiss on both cheeks. When meeting someone for the first time, use surnames and any professional titles, preferably in French. When entering a room, be sure to greet everyone, since not doing so is considered a serious oversight. When addressing someone in Arabic, use Mr. Mrs., or Miss. In introducing yourself, use any professional title you may have, since Tunisians show interest in your background and education. Be aware that the Western 'okay' gesture of forming a circle with thumb and index figure is considered rude, as is pointing with an index finger. To beckon someone, hold your hand with palm downward and fingers waving up and down. Give or receive a gift with both hands.

BUSINESS ETHIC AND FRAMEWORK

Most Tunisians are Islamic, the mores of which shape their attitudes today. But overall, Tunisian culture has survived invasions and conquests from East and West, developing a resiliency which promotes accommodation and economic growth, producing a sound business attitude. Too often those unfamiliar with Tunisia think Islam makes people too unworldly to operate in a pro-Western world; but this is far from correct. The Tunisian businessman combines a conservative attitude with vast patience. His approach to business is even-handed, an attitude not found in some neighboring countries. Pro-Western forces in this culture have opened doors to trade with the West.

Most educated Tunisians speak Arabic and French. Some English is spoken, but you will need an interpreter if you are not fluent in French. To accomplish anything locally other than your own meetings, one is advised to hire a local agent.

DECISION MAKING

Those at the top of an organization make the decisions. Defer to the highest-ranking person in the organization. Don't neglect to give copies of any material to everyone involved in your project, as consensus and egalitarianism within a group is a part of Tunisian business culture. Including everyone involved in your project will promote good will and a favorable outcome. Cultivate patience and flexibility, since Tunisians sometimes treat deadlines casually.

WOMEN

Businessmen will, if necessary, deal with foreign female executives, but it is not their preference. They will prefer to finalize terms with men. Legal equality between the genders is vigorously supported by the government, but less so in practice. A few women serve at various levels of government service, but decisions are made by men. Though most urban Tunisian women wear Western dress, rural women are largely in the same position they have occupied for centuries: keepers of hearth and home. A woman's honor is zealously guarded by her family and by her husband. To avoid being harassed, a Western woman should not go out unescorted.

MEETINGS

Schedule appointments from October through May, avoiding the weeks around Christmas and Easter. Make your appointments from abroad, but reconfirm them upon arrival in Tunisia. Give your business card first to the highest-ranking person at a meeting, then to all others present. Your business cards should be printed in French and Arabic. Tea is likely to be served before the meeting; don't discuss business during tea service. Tunisian businessmen will expect a serious, thorough, but low-key meeting.

Your Tunisian business associates will expect you to be punctual, but may not be themselves; don't be surprised if your 10a.m. meeting doesn't start until after lunch. Accept delays with patience.

BUSINESS ENTERTAINING

Much business is conducted in restaurants, as well as in cafes, which are for men only. Tunisians hold French culture in high esteem, and enjoy being entertained in French restaurants. Except among the urban and well-educated, women stay at home. In extending an invitation to a Tunisian business associate, you could ask, "Would it be proper to invite your wife also?" For a business gift, a coffee table book with pictures of your region would be appreciated. A gift can be given at an initial meeting, but it should not be valuable enough to be construed as a bribe. Avoid giving souvenir-type gifts.

If invited to a Tunisian home, bring a gift, such as a book about your country, fruit, or sweets. Don't compliment or admire anything in your host's home, because by tradition, an Arab will be compelled to give it to you on the spot. If a woman is included in the invitation, avoid all discussion of Western women's issues. If you are invited to a rural or traditional Islamic home, the Western woman should dress with her arms and head covered, and hem well below the knee or longer. You should discern in advance if the wife of your host dresses in Western or traditional style. The Western woman should mirror the dress of the wife of your host. Don't be surprised if men and women are entertained in separate rooms.

BUSINESS ATTIRE

Clothing should be light weight for summer, medium weight for winter. For business, men should wear a conservative suit and tie. A woman should wear a dress or a blouse and skirt. Wear hems below the knee, the longer the better. A woman's sleeves should be long or at least three-quarter length. For casual wear, men can wear slacks and a shirt. A woman should wear a dress or skirt and blouse with long or three-quarter sleeves. A woman's knees, shoulders, and arms should be covered unless at a resort or the beach.

Business Centers
Tunis

CITY VIEW

If expecting a traditional Arabian city, one may be in for a surprise. Tunis is a modern European-blended city complete with glass buildings and wide boulevards. However, a bit of the Arabian flair still remains in the Old Town, or *medina*. If intrigued, escape the noise of the busy streets outside and slip into the small, winding streets of the Old City, blissfully void of vehicles, for a flavor of Mediterranean Arabia.

Carthage International Airport to City Center

The airport lies 5 miles (8 km.) from the city center. Coaches leave the airport every 15 minutes, and buses leave every 30 minutes. Taxis are availabe for transit into the city. There is an extra charge of about 50 percent of the fare for taxi rides at night.

AIRPORT

Airline Numbers

Air Algérie...(1) 34-1590
Air France...(1) 34-1577
Egypt Air...(1) 34-1182
Lufthansa..(1) 34-1049
Royal Air Maroc..................................(1) 24-9016
Tunis Air .... (1) 25-9189, 28-8100

HOTELS

Top-end
L'Africa Meridien; 50 Avenue Habib Bourguiba; tel: (1) 347-477; fax: (1) 347-432; city center; restaurant; conference facilities; parking; fitness; pool.

Oriental Palace; 29 Avenue Jean Jaures; tel: (1) 348-846; fax: (1) 350-327; located near railway; city center; restaurant; conference facilities (up to 600); secretarial service; fax/photocopy facilities; parking; corporate rates; pool.

Expensive
Baal Diplomat; 44 Avenue Hedi Chaker; tel: (1) 785-233; fax: (1) 781-694; near city center

El Mechtel Abou Nawas; boulevard Ouled Haffouz, Belvedere; tel: (1) 350-355; fax: (1) 784-758.

Ez-Zahra Dar Tunis; Route Balneaire Inter communale, Ez-Zahra; tel: (1) 450-788; fax: (1) 452-625; located near beach; restaurant; conference facilities (up t o 40); parking; corporate rates.

Moderate
Golf Royal; 51-53 Rue de Yougoslavie; tel: (1) 344-311; fax: (1) 348-155; near airport; restaurant; secretarial service; fax/photocopy facilities; corporate rates.

IBN Khaldoun; 30 Rue du Koweit, Belvedere; tel: (1) 833-211; fax: (1) 831-689; near exhibition grounds; restaurant; conference facilities (up to 150); secretarial service; fax/photocopy facilities; in-room modem/fax connection; parking; corporate rates.

Les Ambassadeurs; 75 Avenue Taieb M'Hiiri; tel: (1) 288-011; fax: (1) 780-042; restaurant; conference facilities (up to 150); secretarial service; fax/photocopy facilities; parking; corporate rates.

MEDICAL CARE

Habib Thameur Hospital; Rue de Valence, Montfleury; tel: (1) 490-600.

Aziza Othmana Hospital; Place du Gouvernement; tel: (1) 663-655.

AUTO RENTAL

Avis; in the lobby of the Africa Hotel; tel: (1) 34-1249.

Budget; 59 Ave de Carthage; tel: (1) 25-6806.

Hertz; 29 Ave Habab Bourguiba; tel: (1) 24-8559.

WORLD TRADE CENTER

World Trade Center Tunis
6 Avenue Mohamed Ali Akid, 1003
Cite Olympique Tunis, Tunisia
tel: (1) 791-377; fax: (1) 792-373

Turkey

At a Glance

THE PEOPLE

Population ....65,599,206 (July 1999 est.)
Growth Rate ....1.57% (1999 est.)
Life Expectancy ....73.29 years (born 1999 est.)
Infant Mortality ... 35.81 deaths/1,000 live births (1999 est.)

Ethnic Composition

Turkish.. 80%
Kurdish 20%

Religious Composition

Muslim (primarily Sunni).. 99.8%
Other 0.2%

Languages Spoken

Turkish (official), Kurdish, and Arabic.

Education and Literacy

The literacy rate is 82.3 percent. Though education is compulsory and free for children aged 6 to 14. However, only two-thirds of school-aged children to receive an education.

Labor Force

Total: 22,700,000
By occupation: agriculture 42.5%, services 34.5%, industry 23%.
(Note: Almost 1,500,000 Turks work abroad).

THE ECONOMY

Despite its formidable inflation rate and heavy national debt, Turkey is considered to be in decent, if tenuous, economic condition. Government still controls major portions of the financial, telecom and transportation industries. However, the nation's leading export, textiles, is primarily in private sector control. The government is attempting to rework the social welfare and taxation system to help attract foreign investment. Turkey's on-again, off-again relationship with the EU, coupled with internal strife concerning the Kurdish minorities and Islamic fundamentalists, have kept foreign investors wary. Neither thought of as fully Muslim nor fully European, Turkey faces a continual economic identity crisis without sufficient resources or investment to forge its own future. Like its geographic situation, it could go either way—or both.

Exports ....US$31 billion (f.o.b., 1998)
Imports ....US$47 billion (f.o.b., 1998)
Total Trade ....US$78 billion (1998)
GDP Per Capita.......................................US$6,600 (1998)
Unemployment ....10% (1998 est.)

Inflation Rate 70% (1998)6Top Export Partners

E.U., United States, Russia.

Top Import Partners

E.U., United States, C.I.S., Russia.

Top Exports

Textiles and apparel, foodstuffs, iron and steel products.

Top Imports

Machinery and equipment, fuels, minerals, foodstuffs.

BUSINESS WORKWEEK

Offices

Monday to Friday 8:30a.m. to 5:30p.m.

Banks

Monday to Friday 8:30a.m. to 5:30p.m.

Government

Monday to Friday 8:30a.m. to 5:30p.m.
Post Offices in cities are open from 8am to 8pm

Retail

Monday to Saturday 9a.m. to 7p.m.
Note: Offices open and close one to two hours earlier during the hot summer months. Businesses also make allowances for Muslim prayer throughout the day and some may be closed for brief periods.

HOLIDAYS

New Year's Day...January 1
Seker Bayram, End of
Ramadan.. January 7-10
Kurban Bayram, Feast of the
Sacrifice.. March 15-19
National Sovereignty and
Children's Day .... April 23
Commemoration of Atatürk and
Youth and Sports Day ....May 19
Victory Day...August 30
Republic Day ....October 29
Seker Bayram, End of
Ramadan............................December 28-January 1, 2001
Some dates may vary by year.

CLIMATE

Seasons

Winters vary according to regions from moderate to severe in mountainous areas. Summers are hot and dry. Consider the optimum times to visit between April and June and September to December.

Regions

Expect harsh winters in central (plateau) and eastern (mountain) Anatolia with temperatures as low as minus 47˚C. The Black Sea, the Marmara, and the Aegean coastal region can prove wet in winter months. The southern Mediterranean coast is milder in the winter, but more hot and humid in the summer.

Money & Banking

Currency

The currency of Turkey is the Turkish Lira (TL).

Denominations

The Turkish Lira (TL) comes in coin denominations of TL10,000, 5,000, 2,500 and 1,000; and banknotes of TL10,000, 20,000, 50,000, 100,000, 250,000, 500,000 and 1,000,000.
Note: Inflation is rampant so check rates before travel departure.

Traveler's Checks and Credit Cards

Traveler's checks can be exchanged at banks, ex-

Turkey

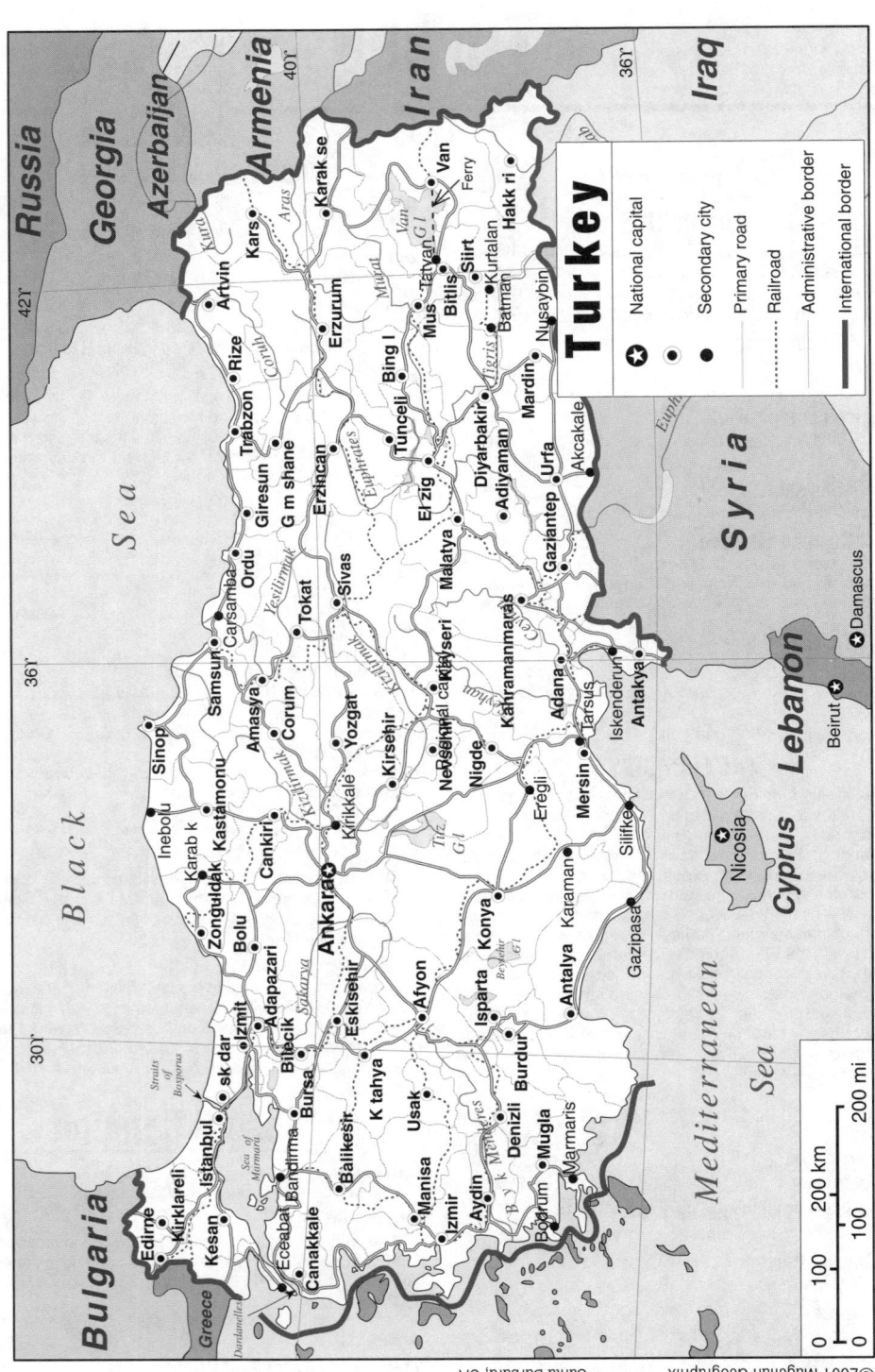

change shops, hotels, and international airports at moderate exchange rates. Larger banks may offer the best exchange rates, but black marketers should be avoided at all cost. Consult your bank about current exchange rates before departure although this will only give you a general range. Keep all receipts for reconversion.

Most major currencies can be exchanged, but try to take only crisp and new notes, wrinkled and soiled notes are likely to be refused.

Major credit cards are easily accepted in up-market places in the main cities, but in more rural areas they may ask for cash. Credit card transactions receive the most favorable exchange rates. ATMs (average exchange rate) are commonplace and some banks in the capital offer cash advances on credit cards if accompanied by passport identification.

Travel

VISA AND PASSPORT

Passports are required for all foreign visitors. Due to continual political turmoil, visa regulations for visiting Turkey are in a constant state of flux. Many visitors are required to obtain visas before entering Turkey. Those with standard passports may obtain visas from any Turkish Consular Office or at the border crossing point. Check with a consulate well in advance of travel and immediately prior to departure. Nations fall in and out of favor quite regularly. Anyone with diplomatic or official passports must also obtain a visa before entering Turkey. Business and multiple entry visas require special processing.

DEPARTURE FORMALITIES

Any unauthorized purchase or removal of antiquities or cultural artifacts is strictly forbidden. Government licensing is required and should be sought well in advance.

CUSTOMS ENTRY (PERSONAL)

Duty-free

- Alcohol: 5 liter bottles or 7 (70cc) bottles of spirits
- Tobacco: 200 cigarettes, 50 cigars, or 200g of tobacco
- Food: 1.5kg of coffee; 500g of tea; 1kg of chocolate; 1kg of sweets
- Perfume: 5 bottles of eau de cologne (120ml), eau de toilette, perfume or lavender water or lotion
- Other: gift value varies and should be checked at entry
  Note: A further 400 cigarettes or 100 cigars or 500g of tobacco may be imported if purchased on arrival at a duty-free shop.

Very specific amounts and categories of personal belongings may be imported duty free, according to a list available from the Consulate General. Most tourists are unlikely to find themselves exceeding these allowances, but should note that the limits imposed on personal belongings include: one camera and five rolls of film; one pocket calculator; one table clock; one manual typewriter (duty must be paid on electric and electronic models); one video camera and five blank cassettes; one 8mm cine-camera and ten blank cassettes; one portable radio or radio/cassette/CD player (speakers should not be detachable); five LPs, cassette tapes or compact discs (no two the same); and one portable computer.

Note: Turkey is in dire need of hard currency, and customs fees provide an easy source. Check with a Turkish consulate just prior to travel to update changes. Value Added Tax (VAT) on large purchases will be reimbursed at departure if records and receipts are kept.

Prohibited or Restricted
- More than two sets of playing cards
- Narcotics
- Firearms and edged weapons

IMMUNIZATION

An international certificate of vaccination is not required unless you are arriving from a cholera- or yellow fever-infected area. It is recommended that business travellers have tetanus and hepatitis A immunizations.

TIPPING

Taxi
For taxi drivers it is not necessary to tip, though it is customary to round up the cab fare.

Hotels & Restaurants
Hotel bellboys should be tipped five percent of your room price. Restaurants usually include service charges on the bill.

EMERGENCY INFORMATION

Police and Crime
Turkey has a low crime rate, but petty crime prevails in more urban settings (mainly Istanbul and Ankara). Drug abuse and prostitution are on the increase, and the law levies harsh punishments for narcotics. Take basic precautions. Avoid flashy displays of wealth, and dress conservatively. Leave most of your cash, traveler's checks, jewelry, and non-essential valuables in your hotel safe. Carry photocopies of your passport instead of the original. Carry cash in a money belt, and use credit cards or traveler's checks for most transactions.

Foreign business visitors are often the target of thieves; so, purses, laptops and briefcases require additional security. Do not leave valuables in cars or on tables in cafés.

Turkey is a male-oriented society; therefore, women should dress modestly. To avoid harassment, women should not travel alone.

Emergency Numbers
Police (Istanbul) 155
Ambulance (Istanbul) 112

Health
Tap water may be safe, but it tastes unpleasant due to excessive minerals; bottled water is widely available. Food quality in Istanbul and Ankara is high; in more rural settings, avoid uncooked meat and seafood. Sanitation is of a reasonable standard, but less so in more rural areas and on the islands.

Air pollution, especially bad in Istanbul, can lead to respiration problems. Otherwise, there are no serious health risks here.

Medical care is adequate in the cities but not in rural areas. Many doctors can speak English and have been trained in Europe. Payments are often expected immediately. For extended stays in rural areas, evacuation insurance may be warranted.

For more information on medical centers, including phone numbers, please see the "Business Centers" section at the end of this chapter.

TAXI & RENTAL CARS

Taxis are quite common in the cities and most have meters. Some drivers will attempt to get foreigners to agree to a flat rate. Unless you are an experienced haggler, demand the meter price.

Rental cars are widely available but expensive. An international driver's license is required. Insurance is also required, and additional insurance should be purchased to cover damage to windshields and windows. Driving in the major cities is frenetic, but, for the most part, the Turks are courteous behind the wheel.

BUS

The most popular form of bus in Turkey is the *dolmus*. It carries several passengers and follows specific routes more akin to a mini-bus. A *dolmus* is recognizable by a yellow band across its side.

Regular bus (inter- and intra-city) service is somewhat cramped though cheap. Many private companies run coach services competing with the state system. They are efficient, although more expensive than the regular bus lines.

TRAIN

Trains are run by the Turkish State Railways (TCDD) for use between cities. Trains are a very popular form of travel and can be crowded. There are express and first-class services available at a premium. Purchase tickets at TCDD offices in train stations. Standard prices are quite reasonable.

Essential Terms

English	Turkish
Yes	Evet
No	Hayir
Good morning	Günaydin
Hello (daytime)	Tünaydn
Hello (evening)	Iyi aksamlar
Hello (telephone)	Merhaba
Good-bye	Allahas marladk
Please	Lutfen
Thank you	Tesekkür ederim
Pleased to meet you	Tanistigimiza memnun oldum
Excuse me; I'm sorry	Affedersiniz
My name is _____	Adim____dir
I don't understand	Anlamiyorum
Do you speak English?	Ingilizce biliyor musunuz

Communications

DIALING CODES IN TURKEY

International country code: [90]

Selected city codes: Ankara (312), Istanbul (European Side) (212), Istanbul (Asian Side) (216)

Dialing Turkey from Overseas

To dial Turkey from overseas, dial your country's international dialing code, then 90 (the code for Turkey), then the city code and finally the number. If you were dialing Ankara from the United States, for example, you would begin with 011, then 90, then 312 (the city code for Ankara), and finally the number of the person or office you were trying to reach.

Assistance Numbers

International Operator 115
Domestic Long Distance Operator 131
Telephone Inquiries.. 118
Wake-up Calls 135

CALLING WITHIN TURKEY

Local Calls

Seven digits make up the local numbers in Turkey. One telephone unit will buy you several minutes of local talk time.

Long Distance Calls

Dial 0 (wait for dial tone) + city code + number. Calls can be made from card or token phones. Discounted rates occur between 6p.m. and 8a.m.

International Calls

It will cost approximately US$3 for a minute-long call to North America. If calling from a phone office, be sure to stay on top of the costs by requesting a receipt since a clerk may try charging more.

PAY PHONES

Public Telephones

Tokens (*jetons*) for public phones can be purchased at post offices, PTT offices, or street booths. Tokens come in three sizes depending on the distance called. However, tokens turn out to be more costly than phone cards or metered phone booths.

1. Deposit token
2. Wait for light at top right of phone to go off
3. Dial

Calling Cards

Card phones can most often be found in tourist spots, normally in the western region of Turkey. Telekarts come in various denominations.

CELLULAR PHONES

Several cellular service providers exist in Turkey. Turkcell is a major service provider, offering NMT-450 and TACS for analogue users and GSM for digital. Other companies that also offer GSM, including Telsim Mobile. Contact an international operator for assistance in locating their offices and telephone numbers, or use their internet information listed below.

Telsim Mobile; http://www.telsim.com/.tr/.

Turkcell; tel: (212) 313-1000; fax: (212) 313-1010; http://www.turkcell.com/.tr/.

Note: Your home country cell phone may not work in this country. If not, we recommend that you rent an international cell phone *before* you leave home. A major US-based cell phone rental provider is **IMC WorldCell**. For information see "International Cell Phone Rentals" on page 14.

CALL BACK

You can (potentially) save significant sums when calling in Turkey by using one of the call back services listed below. Fees for call back services vary widely, depending on the company and the type of service required. Be sure to check with these companies before leaving to compare rates.

For a list of callback services, please refer to the "Communications" section in the *Global Road Warrior* Introduction.

PHONE JACKS

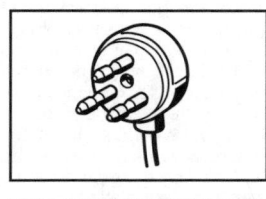

Plug adaptors are available through **iGo Corporation**. (See "Electrical and Telephone Adaptors" on page 19.)

FAX

Fax machines are becoming increasingly popular in business and government offices as well as in hotels.

POSTAL SERVICES

Customs inspections may delay mail.

Hours of service

Monday to Friday 8a.m. to 5p.m.

TELEGRAMS

Telegrams can only be sent from the *Telegraf Gisesi* at Sirkeci in Istanbul.

Business Services

BUSINESS CENTERS

Hotels in Turkey offer many business services, including secretarial and translation services, computer rental and photocopying services.

COURIER SERVICE

DHL Worldwide Express; Yalcin Kores Cad. No. 20 Bagcilar, 34540; tel: 0212-478-1000; Mon. to Fri. 8a.m. to 7p.m., Sat. 8:30a.m. to 5p.m., closed Sundays and holidays.

Federal Express (Coneks A.S.); tel: (212) 549-0404.

Mail Boxes Etc.; Sehit Muhtar Bey Caddesi 2, 1st floor, Taksim; tel: 256-6817.

Sky Net; tel; 253-6348.

TNT; Erturk sok. Uzka Is Merkezi No: 9, Kat:3-4-5 81640 Kavacik - Beykoz, Istanbul; tel: (216) 425-1730; fax: (216) 425-1710.

UPS; United Parcel Service Turkey; Ambarlar Cad., No 6A Blok 34786 Zeytinburnu, Istanbul; tel: (0212) 547-1210/1220 (Bookings and enquiries); tel: (0212) 547-1200 (Reservation); fax: (0212) 547-1205.

TRANSLATION SERVICES

Beyza Diler; tel: 244-0793; fax: 249-8613; Ankara, tel: (312) 434-2357; fax: (312) 432-0649.

Persona; Nispetiye Caddesi, Basa Sokak 13/7, Birinci Levent; tel: 270-7120; fax: 270-7119.

Tercüme 80; Saglik Sokak, Opera Han, Taksim; tel: 243-5364; Turkish/English/French.

Electrical

Current

220 volts AC, 50Hz

ELECTRIC PLUGS

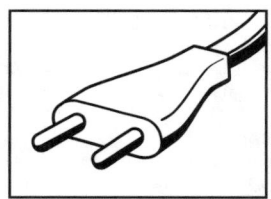

Plug adaptors are available through **iGo Corporation**. (See "Electrical and Telephone Adaptors" on page 19.)

Technical Support

HARDWARE/SOFTWARE VENDOR SUPPORT

Apple/Claris; (in the U.A.E.) tel: [971] 4-513-888; fax: [971] 4-527-444; (in Germany) tel: [49] (1) 803-5018; (in Switzerland) tel: [41] (800) 833-310; (in the U.K.) tel: [44] (990) 127-753; (in the U.S.) tel: [1] (800) 500-7078; http://www.apple.com/.

AST; (in the U.S.) tel: [1] (817) 232-9824 (International Technical Support); (in Ireland) tel: [353] (61) 492-222; (in the U.S.) tel: [1] (949) 727-4141; http://www.ast.com/.

Compaq/Digital; (U.AE. Office) tel: [971] 4-818-100; fax: [971] 4-818-313; (in Switzerland) tel: [41] (22) 709-5330; fax: [41] (22) 709-5391 (Geneva); tel: [41] (1) 801-2507; fax: [41] (1) 801-2172 (Zurich); (General U.S.) tel: (281) 518-2000; http://www.compaq.com/.

Corel; (in the U.A.E.) tel: [971] 4-523-526 (All Applications); (in Germany) tel: [49] (180) 425-8210 (TS Word Perfect-32 bit); (in the U.S.) tel: [1] (716) 871-2325 (Ask to be Forwarded to Appropriate Program); http://www.corel.com/.

Dell; (in Egypt) tel: [20] 2-360-2234 (Electronics House in

Turkey

Cairo/Mr. Jamal El Bidweihy); fax: [20] 2-361-4576; (in Germany) tel: [49] (61) 039-710; (Dell- Europe) tel: [44] (134) 474-8000; (in the U.S.) tel: [1] (512) 338-4400; fax: [1] (512) 728-3330; http://www.dell.com/.

IBM; tel: (312) 454-2625; (Egypt Office) tel: [20] 2-349-2533; fax: [20] 2-360-1227; (in Switzerland) tel: [41] (22) 310-0418 (in French); (in the U.S.) tel: [1] (919) 517-2800; http://www.ibm.com/.

Microsoft; tel: (212) 258-5998; (212) 258-5954; (U.A.E. Office) tel: [971] 4-513-888; fax: [971] 4-527-444(in Switzerland) tel: [41] (848) 858-868; fax [41] (1) 831-0869; (in the U.S.) [1] (425) 635-7222; http://www.microsoft.com/.

Toshiba; (in Germany) tel: [49] (2131) 158-319; fax: [49] (2131) 158-558; (in Switzerland) tel: [41] (1) 946-0777; fax: [41] (1) 946-0807; (in Ireland) tel: [44] (193) 282-8828; (in the U.S.) [1] (949) 583-3000 (Corporate Headquarters); http://www.toshiba.com/.

Internet Connection
HOW TO CONNECT

Connecting to AOL and Compuserve in Turkey is similar to using it when traveling outside your own area code. See the introductory section for detailed information on connecting to your account through a different phone number.

America Online

Numbers are available at keyword *international*. Be sure to get several local numbers before leaving. AOL has a new GlobalNet service that charges US$6 an hour in addition to the usual charges. Go to keyword *access* (a free area) and download the software.

Access: Adana (322) 359-9725; Ankara (312) 468-8042; Antalya (242) 330-3540; Bodrum (252) 313-9204; Bursa (224) 224-5830; Gaziantep (342) 230-1529; Istanbul (212) 234-5168, 234-6100; Izmir (232) 446-2034; Kusadasi (256) 613-3748; Mersin (324) 337-3670.

Compuserve

Numbers are available at *Go International*. If you are using CompuServe 2000, use GO PHONES within CompuServe 2000 to search for access numbers. The Compuserve Web-site also has a great deal of information, at http://www.compuserve.com/.

Access: Ankara (312) 468-8042; Antalya (242) 330-3540; Bodrum (252) 313-9204; Bursa (224) 224-5830; Gaziantep (342) 230-1529; Istanbul (212) 234-6100; Izmir (232) 446-2034; Kusadasi (256) 613-3748; Mersin (324) 337-3670.

Independent Service Providers

Many independent service providers offer discounts if you are only in town for a couple of days.

AdaNET Internet Hizmetleri; (312) 467-3728; fax: (312) 467-3332; email: infoada@ada.net.tr; http://www.ada.net.tr/. [no eng. webpages]

birNET Information Systems; tel: (312) 419-6394; fax: (312) 419-6392; http://www.bir.net.tr/

EgeNet; tel: (232) 388-3378; fax: (232) 388-7230; helpdesk@egenet.com/.tr; http://www.egenet.com/.

Prizmanet; tel: (212) 227-9858; fax: (212) 259-6939; email: webmaster@prizma.net.tr; http://www.prizma.net.tr/.

Business Culture
GREETINGS AND COURTESIES

Shake hands with all present, including wives and children, when arriving and departing. Use the title and surname until told otherwise; first names are reserved only for close friends.

The first name followed by *bey* (sir) or *hanim* (madam) shows special respect, as does *Haj* for those who have made the pilgrimage to Mecca (it can be placed either before or after a name). When greeting a close friend of the same sex, and sometimes the opposite sex, Turks clasp hands and kiss both cheeks. Turkish businesspeople tend to be generous and hospitable, even toward strangers. They enjoy lively conversation and socializing, especially in restaurants, but usually remain private in regards to family and family matters.

BUSINESS ETHIC AND FRAMEWORK

Turkey is the only Islamic country which is a secular state. Turkish people consider themselves neither European nor Arab but rather as a distinct ethnic and cultural group. They align themselves more closely to Europe than to the Middle East. When doing business in Turkey, consider personal relationships the key to success. Whom you know can prove more important than what you know.

Turkish business people work long hours. They expect contracts to leave the quality of the product unquestioned, focusing instead on equitable price. Confirmed letters of credit are safest when dealing with new overseas accounts. The center of Turkish culture is the family, and Turkish people are convinced that money helps keep the family together. Companies are often treated as extended families.

DECISION MAKING

In Turkish business and society, power flows from top to bottom. Try to transact business with the most important person in your field, since lower-level personnel may not have the authority to make decisions. This hierarchical structure is very much in evidence in Turkish offices, where junior employees must demonstrate their respect to senior people in a variety of ways, while those at the top may feel more relaxed and secure in their power and authority. Decisions are based as much on personal relationships and subjective feelings as they are on business practicalities. Thus, proposals couched in personal terms, rather than on strictly business principles, may receive more favorable attention. Expect the Turkish habit of haggling and bargaining to exist as an integral part of any business transaction.

WOMEN

Turkish women often find themselves torn between Western ideas of equality and their more traditional Muslim roles. Due to the high rate of literacy, roles are changing rapidly and women are enjoying expanded rights and freedoms. Many women work in the city, some in the same firm as their husbands. Women are teachers and hold editorial posts on Turkey's major newspapers. They make up twenty per cent of the lawyer population and hold some of the highest positions in government.

As a foreign woman seeking to circumvent harassment, avoid traveling alone or going out alone in the evening, and always walk purposefully. If traveling alone, consider wearing a wedding band.

MEETINGS

Avoid scheduling business meetings during the vacation months of June, July, and August. And if possible, avoid scheduling meetings during the month of Ramadan or on other religious holidays as well.

Make appointments well in advance. Punctuality is very important; arrive on time. Turks are more relaxed about being late themselves, however, usually due to traffic. Business meetings always begin with strong Turkish coffee and light conversation. Group orientation is valued above personal assertion or aggressiveness.

In your own scheduling, take into consideration that meetings often run late.

BUSINESS ENTERTAINING

Turkish businessmen prove very hospitable. Expect to be entertained at both lunch and dinner with long, lavish meals. Most business entertaining is done in restaurants. The host will pay if the invitation is his; you pay if you have done the inviting. It is customary to exchange modest business gifts at the successful consummation of a deal, and at the New Year; a fine book, a leather piece, or a desk accessory would be appropriate.

If you receive an invitation to 'drop in', consider it sincere. Visits in homes usually begin about 9p.m., and it is appropriate to include your spouse. Usually your host will offer you something to eat or drink. Always accept a refreshment offer; to refuse is considered impolite. If you are invited to a Turkish home, arrive punctually, and bring a gift. Flowers or candy are appropriate, as are books or tapes in English; avoid giving wine or spirits. Gifts for the children are appreciated. A wrapped gift usually will not be opened in front of you.

Remove your shoes upon entering a home (or a mosque). Since eating habits differ in many countries, watch your host, and eat as he does. Do not leave the table during the meal. If you are called upon to sit with your legs crossed, in the process of doing so never point the soles of your feet toward anyone. Avoid conversation about politics, in particular, Turkey's relations with other countries.

BUSINESS ATTIRE

Turks often judge others by the way they dress. Western styles are common, especially among the young, and urban people are very fashion-conscious. Men should wear a conservative business suit for all business occasions.

Businesswomen should wear a conservative, dark suit, stockings (always) and high heels for business meetings. Hems should fall below the knee, and arms and shoulders should remain covered with high necklines. Even though the urban culture of Turkey appears European and secular, it is a good idea to carry a head scarf in case an occasion calls for it. Avoid revealing clothing at all times.

Business Centers
Istanbul

AIRPORT

Atatürk Airport to City Center

The airport lies 15 miles (24 km.) from the airport. An airport shuttle bus travels between the airport and the Turkish Airlines City Terminal (near Galata Tower) every 30 minutes during peak travel times and mornings, and every hour otherwise. The 30- to 45-minute trip costs about TL150,000.

Those preferring to take a taxi to a major hotel should expect to pay between TL600,000 and 750,000 for the 30- to 45-minute ride. Fares to the Old Town cost between TL525,000 and 650,000.

Airport 663-6400

Airline Numbers

Aeroflot 243-4725
Air China .... 232-7112; airport, 663-0713
Air France .... 256-4356; airport, 663-0600-1
Air Malta 234-2863
Air Maroc 230-6523
Alia (Jordanian) .... 230-4074; airport, 573-6260

Alitalia .... 231-3391; airport, 663-0577
American Airlines 237-2003, 237-2004
Austrian Airlines .... 232-2200; airport, 573-2920
Balkan Bulgarian .... 245-2456; airport, 573-2920
British Airways .... 234-1300; airport, 663-0574
Czech Airlines 230-4832
Delta Airlines .... 231-2339; airport, 663-0752
Egyptair .... 231-1126; airport, 663-3301
El Al .... 246-5303; airport, 663-0810
Emirates .... 232-3216; airport, 663-0827
Finnair 234-5130
Gulf Air .... 231-3450; airport, 663-0825
Iberia .... 255-1968; airport, 663-0826
Iran Air 225-0255
Japan Airlines 241-7366
JAT Yugoslavian 248-2904
KLM (Holland) .... 230-0311; airport, 663-0603
KTHY .... 267-0973; airport, 663-0759
Kuwait Airlines .... 240-4081; airport, 663-0581
Libyan Arab Airlines 232-4976
LOT Polish 240-7927
Lufthansa .... 288-1050; airport, 663-0594
Malev Hungarian .... 241-0909; airport, 663-0589
MAS (Malaysia) .... 230-7130; airport 663-0814
Middle East Airlines .... 248-2241; airport, 663-0550
Olympic Airways .... 246-5081; airport, 663-0820
PIA (Pakistan) .... 233-0571; airport, 663-0521
Qantas Airways 246-5032, 5081
Sabena (Belgium) .... 254-7254; airport, 663-0824
SAS .... 246-6075; airport, 663-0582
Saudi Arabian .... 256-4800; airport, 663-0582
Singapore Airlines .... 232-3706; airport, 663-0710
Swissair .... 231-2850; airport, 663-6778
Syrian Air .... 246-1781; airport, 663-0815
Tarom (Romanian) 230-7309
Thai Airlines 252-6544/45
Tunis Air 241-7096
Turkish Airlines .... 252-1106; airport 663-6363
TWA 234-5327
United Airlines 224-9180

HOTELS

Top-end

Ciragan Palace Kempinski; Ciragan Caddesi 84, Besiktas; tel: (212) 258-3377; fax: (212) 959-6687; city center; restaurant; casino; conference facilities (up to 1200); secretarial service; fax/photocopy facilities; in-room modem/fax connection, safe; parking; health club; fitness; sauna; pool; whirlpool.

Four Seasons Istanbul; Tevfikhane Sokak Sultanahmet/ Eminönü; tel: (212) 638-8200; fax: (212) 638-8210; email: fseasons@istanbul.com.tr; boutique hotel with 65 rooms; restaurant; 3 meeting rooms; 24-hour business services; airline ticketing; in-room fax/modem connection, safe; two-line telephones; executive suites available; non-smoking rooms available; valet parking; health club; fitness; saunas.

Hyatt Regency; Taskisla Caddesi, Taksim; tel: 225-7000; fax: 225-7007; restaurant; Polo Lounge for members only; casino; conference facilities; business center; information library; private offices; Regency Club floor; health club; pool; tennis.

The Marmara; Taksim Square; tel: (212) 251-4696; fax: (212) 244-0509; city center; restaurant; casino; conference facilities (up to 1500); secretarial service; fax/photocopy facilities; in-room safe; parking; corporate rates; fitness; sauna; pool; whirlpool.

Merit Antique Hotel; Ordu Caddesi 226; tel: (212) 513-9300; fax: (212) 512-6390; Old City; restaurant; casino;

conference/business facilities; secretarial service; fax/photocopy facilities; parking; corporate rates; sauna; pool; whirlpool.

Swissotel Istanbul the Bosphorus; Bayildim Caddesi 2, Macka, Besiktas; http://www.focusmm.com.au/swisswww.swissotel.com; near exhibition grounds; 4 restaurants; conference facilities (up to 1600); business center; secretarial service; internet connection; in-room safe; secure parking; fitness; sauna; indoor and outdoor pools; whirlpool; solarium; Turkish bath; jogging track; disco.

Expensive

Ceylan Inter-Continental Istanbul; Asker Ocagi Caddesi 1, Taksim; tel: (212) 231-2121; fax: (212) 231-2180; city center; restaurant; conference facilities (up t9 750); secretarial service; fax/photocopy facilities; in-room safe; parking; corporate rates; sauna; pool; whirlpool.

Divan; Cumhuriyet Cadddesi 2, Elmadag; tel: (212) 231-4100; fax: (212) 248-8527; city center; restaurant; conference facilities 9UP to 200); secretarial service; fax/photocopy facilities; corporate rates; fitness; sauna.

Hilton; Harbiye; tel: 231-4650; fax: 240-4165; executive floors; restaurant; extensive grounds; pool.

Istanbul Polat Renaissance; Sahil Caddesi, Ysilyurrt; tel: 663-1700; fax: 663-1755; near Sea of Marmara, residential area; near airport and World Trade Center; restaurants; executive floors; non-smoking floors; large conference facilities; health center; fitness.

Istanbul Princess; Büyükdere Caddesi 49, Maslak; tel: (212) 285-0900; fax: (212) 285-0951; near exhibition grounds; restaurant; casino; conference facilities 9up to 1000); secretarial service; fax/photocopy facilities; in-room modem/fax connection. safe; parking; corporate rates; fitness; sauna; pool; whirlpool.

Parksa Hilton; Maçka; tel: 258-5674; fax: 258-5695; popular for business travelers.

Olcay; Millet Caddesi 187, Topkapi; tel: (212) 530-9900; fax: (212) 585-6405; city center; restaurant; casino; conference facilities (up to 500); parking; corporate rates; fitness; sauna; pool; whirlpool.

Moderate

Grand Star; Siraselviler Caddesi 79, Beyoglu; tel: (212) 243-4090; fax: (212) 251-7822; city center; restaurant; parking; pool.

Hotel Spectra; Sehit Mehmet Pasa Yokusu No. 2 Sultanahmet; tel: (212) 516-3546; fax; (212) 638-3379; http://www.hotelspectra.com; located on Hippodrome Square; restaurant; meeting facilities (up to 30); fax facility; internet; secure parking.

Kilim; MIllet Caddesi 85/A, Findikzade; tel: (212) 586-0880; fax: (212) 585-0570; city center; restaurant; conference facilities; secretarial service; fax/photocopy facilities.

Monaco; Ordu Caddesi, Sair Fitnat Sokak 26-28, Laleli; tel: (212) 518-7610; fax: (212) 526-4728; near airport; restaurant; parking.

Savoy Istanbul; Siraselyiler Caddesi 29; tel: (212) 293-8585; fax: (212) 243-2010; 4-star hotel near exhibition grounds; restaurant; conference facilities (up to 120); secretarial service; fax/photocopy facilities; in-room modem/fax connection; corporate rates.

Sultan; Genctürk Caddesi 29, Laleli; tel: (212) 513-5890; fax: (212) 513-0305; city center; restaurant; conference facilities; parking.

Topkapi; Oguzhan Caddesi 20, Findiklizade; tel: (212) 535-4240; fax: (212) 523-7350.

MEDICAL CARE

American Hospital; Admiral Bristol Hastanesi, Nisantas, Güzelbahce Sokak; tel: (212) 131-4050; pulmonary/respiratory/heart specialty; dentistry division.

Cosmodent Dental Clinic; Beytem Plaza, 4th floor, Sisli; tel: 296-1862; English spoken.

European Hospital; Ihlamur; tel: (212) 288-2451; general surgery, internology, obstetrics, gynaecology, children's surgery.

Florence Nightingale Hospital; Çaglayan, Sisli; tel: (212) 224-4950.

German Hospital; Siraselviler, Taksim; tel: (212) 293-2150; renovated; full service, emergency.

International Hospital; Yesilyurt, near the airport; tel: (212) 663-3000; ambulance: 230-9638; well-known private hospital with good emergency services.

HEALTH CLUB

Alkent Hillside Club; Alkent, Etiler; tel: 257-7115; popular with upmarket locals.

Four Seasons Istanbul; Tevfikhane Sokak Sultanahmet/Eminönü; tel: (212) 638-8200; fax: (212) 638-8210; email: fseasons@istanbul.com.tr.

Planet Health Club (worldwide chain); Eski Caykur Binasu, Kuruçesme; tel: 263-1067; 80 fitness machines; aerobic; beauty salon; sauna; jacuzzi; solarium; ricochet court; 7a.m. to 11p.m.

Çiragan Hotel Kempinski Fitness Club; Ciragan Caddesi 84, Besiktas; tel: (212) 258-3377; 7a.m. to 10p.m.; fitness machines; aerobics; indoor/outdoor pools (8a.m. to 7p.m.); Turkish bath (women: 9a.m. to 2p.m.; men: 2p.m. to 10p.m.); massage.

AUTO RENTAL

Avis; Taksim, tel: (212) 241-7896; Cihangir, 249-7941; HIlton Hotel, 248-7752; airport, 663-0646.

Budget; Taksim, tel: (212) 253-9200; airport, 663-0646; Kadiköy, 346-1338.

Europcar; tel: (212) 573-7024 or 254-7788.

Inter Limousine Service; Inter Kat Otoparki, Harbiye; tel: (212) 246-0393.

InterRent/Dollar; tel: (212) 255-0690.

Oscar; Mustafa Kemal Paxa Caddesi 37; tel: 588-3057, 588-2936.

Sun Rent a Car; Cumhuriyet Caddesi 26, Elmadag; tel: 246-0815, 246-0555; fax: 240-8351.

WORLD TRADE CENTER

World Trade Center Istanbul
Cobancesme Kavsagi PIC 40
34830 Havalimani
(Opposite the Airport)
tel: (212) 663-0881; fax: (212) 663-0973

Ukraine

At a Glance

THE PEOPLE

Population ....49,811,174 (July 1999 est.)
Growth Rate ....-0.62% (1999 est.)
Life Expectancy .... 65.91 years (1999 est.)
Infant Mortality... 21.73 deaths/1,000 live births (1999 est.)

Ethnic Composition

Ukrainian 73%
Russian 22%
Asian 1%
Other Slavic 4%

Religious Composition

Ukrainian Orthodox, Kiev Patriarchate, Ukrainian Autocephalous Orthodox, Ukrainian Catholic (Uniate), Protestant, Jewish.

Languages Spoken

Ukrainian (official), Russian, Romanian, Polish, Hungarian.

Education and Literacy

The Ukraine has 98% literacy and a high rate of graduation from secondary schools.

Labor Force

Total: 22,800,000
By occupation: industry 32%, agriculture 24%, services 44%.

THE ECONOMY

Having left the Soviet Union in 1992, the Ukraine in 1999 finds itself once again plagued by its Russian neighbors. Largely dependent on its gigantic neighbor for fuel and heavy machinery imports as well as for agricultural and mineral exports, Ukraine has seen its fortunes fall with Russia's. Although the government has been successful in bringing runaway inflation under control, overall output has dropped to half of 1991 levels. It is still showing negative GDP growth. Widespread corruption and institutionalized resistance to opening up the financial markets has kept foreign investors unenthusiastic. While the Ukraine set its sights on a free-market, democratic society in 1992, the recent impoverishment of its citizens and the political rethinking that has hit Belarus and Russia have given Ukrainians reason to pause. Many inside the government are pushing for a reinstitution of socialist-style central planning and a possible reuniting with former Soviet comrades.

Exports ....US$11.3 billion (1998 est.)
Imports ....US$13.1 billion (1998 est.)
Total Trade ....US$24.4 billion (1998)
GDP Per Capita................................ US$2,200 (1998 est.)
Unemployment 3.7% (1998)
Inflation Rate ....20% (1998 est.)

Top Export Partners

Russia, China,, Turkey, Germany, Belarus.

Top Import Partners

Russia, Germany, US, Poland, Italy .

Top Exports

Ferrous and nonferrous metals, chemicals, machinery parts, transport equipment, grain, meat.

Top Imports

Fuel, electricity, machinery and parts, transportation equipment, chemi

BUSINESS WORKWEEK

Offices

Monday to Friday 9a.m. to 6p.m.

Banks

Monday to Friday 9a.m. to 1p.m.

Government

Monday to Friday 10a.m. to 4p.m. (noon on Friday)

Retail

Monday to Friday 9a.m. to 9p.m., slightly shorter hours on weekends.
Note: Once a month usually in the fourth week shops will shut down for an entire "sanitary" day for extensive cleaning.

HOLIDAYS

New Year's Day.. January 1-2
Orthodox Christmas ....January 7
International Women's Day .... March 8
Spring and Labor Day .... May 1-2
Victory Day...May 9
Navy Day..August 1
Ukrainian Independence Day .... August 24
Revolution Day ....November 7-8
Some dates may vary by year.

CLIMATE

Seasons

Ukraine has a full range of seasons but could be described as a moderate climate. There is more rain in the west and north, least in the east and southeast. Summers are generally warm. Mean temperatures are 10°C (66°F) in July, and -6°C (21°F) in January.

Regions

Winters are warmer along the Black Sea and colder inland. Kiev is quite cold from December through February. The southwest has the hottest summers while the northeast attracts some Siberian like winters.

Money & Banking

Currency

The currency of the Ukraine is the Hryvnya (Hr).

Traveler's Checks and Credit Cards

Traveler's checks can be exchanged at specific banks in large cities, exchange kiosks (obmin valyuty), most large hotels, and international airports. Larger banks may offer the best exchange rates but avoid black marketers on street corners. Consult your bank about current exchange rates before departure.

Most major currencies can also be exchanged, but try to take only crisp and new notes, wrinkled and soiled notes are will be refused. reconversion is next to impossible so exchange cash in small usable amounts.

Ukraine

American Express, Visa, and MasterCard are accepted in up-market places in main cities, but in more rural areas and small shops they will only take cash. A few banks in Kiev and Odessa offer cash advances on credit cards with passport identification. ATM machines are scarce and rarely work if found. Bring cash and travel checks but keep them secure.

Travel

VISA AND PASSPORT

Passports and visas are required of all visitors. Visas should be obtained in advance from Ukrainian embassies or consulates and are cheaper than those acquired in upon arrival in the Ukraine. A letter of invitation from a person, company, or organization in Ukraine, or a tour company voucher is currently required to obtain even a tourist visa. The visa's duration will be determined by this letter. Accommodations must be prearranged.

Tourists who arrive without a visa must obtain one either at the border point or within 24 hours of arrival at a local Visas, Permits, and Passport Department office of the Ministry of Internal Affairs (VVIR). In-transit visas (good only for 72-hours) are issued at most major airports and checkpoints. Special (and expensive) accommodations will be arranged for those arriving at borders without visas.

All foreigners visiting Ukraine are required to register their passports with local law enforcement authorities. Registration is automatic when visitors check into a hotel. Private visitors must have their hosts, relatives, or landlords register their passport at the local VVIR office. A US$10 fee is usually charged. Foreigners staying three working days or less need not register. Visitors who do not register may experience delays when leaving Ukraine.

Business visas require a special invitation from a Ukraine company or government ministry. Do not conduct business without a business visa. Multiple-entry visas are granted only to those with legitimate, long-term business interests.

DEPARTURE FORMALITIES

Visitors leaving Ukraine from Kiev or Odessa airports will not pay a departure tax. Misplaced or damaged travel documents will result in fines.

The only restriction on departing with currency is that it must be less than you brought into the country. The Ministry of Culture must grant permission for the removal of all antiquities.

CUSTOMS ENTRY (PERSONAL)

Duty-free

- Tobacco: 100 cigarettes, cigars
- Alcohol: 1.5 liters of spirits, 2.1 liters of wine
- Other: gifts up to the value of US$5,000; goods for personal use (toiletries and personal effects), other gifts less than 200 grams of total weight.
- Travellers must list all money and travel checks being brought into the country.

IMMUNIZATION

International certificate of vaccination is not required unless you are arriving from an infected area. Hepatitis A and tetanus immunizations are recommended.

TIPPING

Taxi

Drivers only expect tips from foreigners and any amount will suffice.

Porters

Airport porters are rare, but if one is found, they should be tipped—but only a small amount per bag.

Hotel and Restaurants

Most hotels and restaurants apply service charges (5 to 10 percent) to bills. Add a tip only if service is extraordinary which is very rare. Do not be surprised if the price you pay is larger than the menu price. Foreign tourists and business people are the main source of hard currency—meaning, they most often fall prey to elevated prices.

EMERGENCY INFORMATION

Police and Crime

Violent and petty crimes are on the increase in Ukraine, especially in urban areas and around railway stations. However, most crimes against foreigners are non-violent ones.

Take basic precautions. Avoid flashy displays of wealth, and dress conservatively. Leave most of your cash, traveler's checks, jewelry and non-essential valuables in your hotel safe. Carry photocopies of your passport and travel documents instead of the originals. Carry cash in a money belt, and use credit cards or traveler's checks for most transactions.

The police force has diminished in efficiency and size in recent years. Women should be especially careful in urban areas at night. Never get into a taxi with more than one person in it.

Foreign business visitors are often the target of thieves; so, purses, laptops and briefcases require additional security. Do not leave valuables in cars or on tables in cafés. Rental car theft and tire theft are not uncommon.

Emergency Numbers

These numbers are functional anywhere in the country:

Fire 01
Police... 02
Ambulance 03

Health

Avoid drinking tap water; bottled water is widely available. Wash all vegetables, peel fruits, and avoid uncooked food. Drink only pasteurized milk, preferably bought from Western stores. Bring along necessary toiletries, they may be hard to come by here.

Air pollution may cause respiratory problems and affect people with allergies. The air in homes is dry in the winter, so bring moisturizers. Flu and common colds are common due to cold winter months. Bring your own cold and sinus medicines as vodka is a standard remedy in the Ukraine.

Medical care is not free to tourists and you will be expected to pay a heavy price on the spot. In hospitals, medical care can be of a low standard with poor hygiene; for better health care, bribery often works. Bring along prescription drugs and other necessities, as medicines are scarce. Evacuation insurance should be considered for business people on extended stays.

TAXI & RENTAL CARS

Taxis are available, primarily in the cities. Most taxis are not metered; negotiate a price before leaving. Rental cars are common in Kiev and Odessa but should only be used by experienced visitors. Travel to smaller villages should be done with a reputable hired car and driver.

TRAIN

Trains are efficient and routes are extensive, but do not expect great comfort. Reserve seats in advance and bring your own food. Service (and sometimes heat) can be spotty even when travelling first-class.

Essential Terms

English	Russian
Yes No	Tahk Nee
Good morning Hello (daytime) Hello (evening) Hello (telephone)	Do-brihy rah-nok Do-brihy dehn' Do-brihy veh-cheer Prih-veet
Good-bye	Do po-bah-chehn-nya
Please	Bood lahs-kah
Thank you	Dya-koo-yu
Pleased to meet you	Prih-yehm-no poz-nah-yo-mih-tihs'
Excuse me; I'm sorry	Peh-reh-pro-shoo-yu
My name is _____	Meh-neh zvah-tih
I don't understand	Ya ro-zoo-mee-yu neh vseh
Do you speak English?	Chih vih ho-vo-rih-teh po ahn-hleeys-kih?

Communications

DIALING CODES IN UKRAINE

International country code: [380]
Selected city codes: Kiev (44), Odessa (482)

Dialing Ukraine from Overseas

To dial Ukraine from overseas, dial your country's international dialing code, then 380 (the country code for Ukraine), then the city code and finally the number. If you were dialing Kiev from the United States, for example, you would begin with 011, then 380, then 44 (the city code for Kiev), and finally the number of the person or office you were trying to reach.

Ukraine

Assistance Numbers
International Operator (private phones) 079, 073
English Operator (in Kiev) 8-192
Local Directory 09

CALLING WITHIN UKRAINE

Local Calls
Red and yellow phones on the streets allow local calls. The post office or kiosks sell tokens.

Long Distance Calls
Use an inter-city phone to make a long distance call within the Ukraine. Dial 017 (wait for the tone) + city code + number.

International Calls
To make a direct call, dial 8 (wait for dial tone) + 10 + country code + number. Otherwise, you can go to the telephone office or a main post office to order a call. Be prepared to wait up to 30 minutes before eventually being directed to a booth. The cost may hover around US$2.50 per minute and more if you go through the hotel, unless you ask to be connected to UTEL, the Ukrainian telephone company, and they in turn will connect you to an English-speaking operator.

Of course, the most financial-friendly calls can be made by dialing a foreign operator for collect or calling card calls, which can be achieved from a private or UTEL phone.
AT&T USA Direct 8-100-11
U.S. MCI..8-100-13
(Wait for a tone after the initial '8')

PAY PHONES

Calling Cards
UTEL cards for long distance calls can be purchased for selected phones.

CELLULAR PHONES
Several cellular service providers exist in the Ukraine. Ukrainian Mobile Communications is a major service provider, offering NMT-450 for analogue users, and GSM for digital. GSM is also offered by Ukraine Radio Systems, and DAMPS is offered by Digital Cellular Communications and Telecel.

Goldentel; GSM 1800; located in Kiev; http://www.goldentele.com:8100/.

Kyivstar; GSM 900; located in Kiev; http://kyivstar.tsx.org/.

Note: Your home country cell phone may not work in this country. If not, we recommend that you rent an international cell phone *before* you leave home. A major US-based cell phone rental provider is **IMC WorldCell**. For information see "International Cell Phone Rentals" on page 14.

CALL BACK
You can (potentially) save significant sums when calling in Ukraine by using one of the call back services listed below. Fees for call back services vary widely, depending on the company and the type of service required. Be sure to check with these companies before leaving to compare rates. For a list of callback services, please refer to the "Communications" section in the Global Road Warrior Introduction.

PHONE JACK

Plug adaptors are available through **iGo Corporation.** (See "Electrical and Telephone Adaptors" on page 19.)

FAX
Faxes are growing in popularity in the Ukraine, and now they can be found in most hotels.

POSTAL SERVICES
Postal services are less than efficient. Incoming mail could take weeks to be delivered, and it is advised to use courier services to send packages.

TELEGRAMS
Telegrams are still widely used in the Ukraine. They can be sent from most hotels.

Business Services

COURIER SERVICES
DHL; 1 Vasylkivska Street, Kiev 252040; tel: (44) 264-7200.

FedEx; 1 Prospekt Gluskova; Kiev; tel: (44) 261-7987.

TNT Express Worldwide; 23, Klimenko, 252110 Kiev 110; tel: (44) 245-8381; tel: (44) 277-6077; fax: (44) 277-9079.

UPS; 20 Mechnikova St., Kiev; tel: (44) 290-000 - 1019.

TRANSLATION SERVICES
Ukrainian Services Corporation; 11A Yanvarskovo Vosstaniya Ulitsa, Hotel Salyut; Kiev; tel: (44) 290-4022.

Electrical

Current
220 volts AC, 50Hz.

ELECTRIC PLUGS

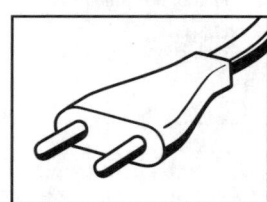

Plug adaptors are available through **iGo Corporation.** (See "Electrical and Telephone Adaptors" on page 19.)

Technical Support

HARDWARE/SOFTWARE VENDOR SUPPORT

Compaq/Digital; tel: (95) 967-3138; fax: (95) 967-1701; (in Poland) [48] (22) 640-0111; fax: [48] (22) 640-0001; (in Switzerland) tel: [41] (22) 709-5330; fax: [41] (22) 709-5391 (Geneva); [41] (1) 801-2507; fax: [41] (1) 801-2172 (Zurich); (General U.S.) tel: (281) 518-2000; http://www.compaq.com/.

Hewlett Packard; (in Switzerland) tel: [41] (22) 780-8111; (in the U.S.) tel: [1] (408) 246-4300; http://www.hp.com/.

IBM; (in Austria) tel: [43] (1) 1706-6172; fax: [43] (1) 1706-6777; (in Germany) tel: [49] (711) 78-50; fax: [49] (711) 785-3511; (in Switzerland) tel: [41] (22) 310-0418 (French); (in the U.S.) tel: [1] (919) 517-2800; (Main Office) tel: [1] 914-765-1900; http://www.ibm.com/.

Microsoft; (in Russia) tel: [7] (095) 916-7171; fax: [7] (095) 916-7112; tel: 7 (095) 745-5445; (in Germany) tel: [49] (89) 31-760; fax: [49] (89) 3176-1000; tel: [49] (89) 3176-1199; (in Switzerland) tel: [41] (848) 858-868; fax [41] (1) 831-0869; (in the U.S.) [1] (425) 635-7222; http://www.microsoft.com/.

Toshiba; (in Germany) tel: [49] (2131) 158-319; fax: [49] (2131) 158-558; (in Switzerland) tel: [41] (1) 946-0777; fax: [41] (1) 946-0807; (in Ireland) tel: [44] (193) 282-8828; (in the U.S.) [1] (949) 583-3000 (Corporate Headquarters); http://www.toshiba.com/.

Internet Connection

HOW TO CONNECT

Connecting to AOL and Compuserve in Ukraine is similar to using it when traveling outside your own area code. See the introductory section for detailed information on connecting to your account through a different phone number.

America Online

Numbers are available at keyword *international*. Be sure to get several local numbers before leaving. AOL has a new GlobalNet service that charges US$6 an hour in addition to the usual charges. Go to keyword *access* (a free area) and download the software.

Access: Donetsk (622) 342-126; Kiev (44) 246-5220; Lvov (322) 699-921; Odessa (48) 731-0421.

Compuserve

Numbers are available at *Go International*. If you are using CompuServe 2000, use GO PHONES within CompuServe 2000 to search for access numbers. The Compuserve Web-site also has a great deal of information, at http://www.compuserve.com/.

Access: Kiev (44) 235-6723 .

Independent Service Providers

Many independent service providers offer discounts if you are only in town for a couple of days.

CS/Monolit / UA.NET; tel: (44) 295-9080, 295-6435; fax: (44) 295-3053; email: info@ua.net.; http://www.ua.net/.

Global Ukraine; tel: (44) 244-9736; tel: (44) 244-9737; email: support@gu.net; http://www.gu.net/.

Telecommunications Resource Centre; tel: (322) 970-143; email: info@lvivnet.com; http://www.link.lviv.ua/.

TriLogiC Group, Ltd.; tel: (552) 226-3746; email: office@3logic.net; http://www.tlc.kherson.ua/.

VinNest; tel: (432) 325-950, fax: (432) 325-833; admin@nest.vinnica.ua; http://www.tlc.kherson.ua/english/.

Business Culture

GREETINGS AND COURTESIES

Ukrainians have a culture of extraordinary hospitality. Although many have scant resources with which to entertain, guests are welcomed warmly.Shake hands both upon arriving and departing. Use surnames and professional titles when addressing people in official situations. Use first names only after establishing a close friendship. Often a Ukrainian man will wait for a woman to extend her hand before shaking it. In an informal setting, Ukrainians wave and give a verbal greeting. Women expect small acts of chivalry, such as doors being opened for them. As friendly and warm as they are, Ukrainians are reserved in their facial expressions, and they do not smile at strangers; to do so would be thought of as strange.

BUSINESS ETHIC AND FRAMEWORK

Even though there is a metal holdover from the old Soviet centrally-planned economy, many Ukrainians have experience in private business operating outside of the official economy. Ukrainians can be shrewd negotiators; beware of pitfalls. The Ukraine's legal infrastructure is in the early stages of development. Some businessmen who have prospered under communism have only a nodding acquaintance with legality. Others, not realizing what is actually necessary to bring a project to completion, may make unrealistic promises. A Ukrainian business associate may insist upon an 'exclusive' clause in a contract, but may not honor it himself. Building a strong personal relationship is important, and is an integral part of a business relationship. It is advisable to back up a business associate's word with trust in a good relationship you have built, and a contract. Trust in a relationship proves all the more important because it may be difficult to enforce the terms of a contract in Ukraine. In spite of the growth of private business, most companies are still government owned, so you may be dealing with bureaucrats, red tape, and waiting. You will need to be patient and flexible. Younger businesspeople are eager to make business alliances with Westerners, but may make exaggerated claims based on their future expectations.

DECISION MAKING

Decisions are made only after a lengthy process of meetings and relationship-building. Ukrainians find it easier to say "no" than to take responsibility for their decisions; so, do not press for a decision until you have formed a relationship and you think your Ukrainian business associate is ready to make a decision. If you are dealing with a government-owned business, a lack of transparency may prevent you from learning who is the real decision-maker.

Ukraine

Ukraine

WOMEN

Women in the Ukraine today are represented in many professions in the workforce, including many jobs usually reserved for men. This tradition stems from so many men having died in World War II. Many women occupy managerial positions, and are high-level bureaucrats. However, chauvinism still exists; many Ukrainian men will not take a woman leader seriously. However, changes are slowly underway with the maturing of the younger generation. Ukrainian women do not tolerate any injustice, and are accustomed to standing up for their rights. The foreign businesswoman will be received and treated with respect.

MEETINGS

Telephone communication in Ukraine is notoriously poor, and could prevent one from scheduling meetings in advance. One may have to make all arrangements face to face upon arrival. In addition, few Ukrainian businessmen have secretaries, so leaving a message may prove unfruitful. Telephone books are not available. Allow time to solve any logistic problems that may arise.

Arrive punctually, and print business cards in English and Ukrainian or Russian. Shake hands during introductions and at the end of a meeting. Defer to the senior Ukrainian official who will lead the meeting, and wait to be given the floor. Negotiations can be lengthy. Do not exhibit impatience or use a hard-sell approach. Most Ukrainians have not traveled to the West, so your interactions may need to take on a teaching role without appearing so. One is advised to have an agenda worked out before the meeting. Meetings usually involve much socializing, with sweets and not just a little drinking; thus, consider it wise to eat something before going to the meeting.

BUSINESS ATTIRE

Ukrainians generally have high expectations of business people from the West. You will be judged by the way you dress. For both men and women, an elegant, dark suit will serve appropriately for all business occasions. Wear lightweight, conservative clothing in the summer months, but dress for very cold weather in the winter. Women may wear pantsuits, dresses, or a blouse and skirt. Fashionable, imported clothing is expensive, so many Ukrainian women make their own clothes.

Business Centers
Kiev

CITY VIEW

Kiev has retained much of its old-world style, but don't be fooled. It is the center of the country, for business as well as the government and education.

AIRPORT

Zhylhany Airport to City Center

The airport lies 3 km. from the city center. Taxis and buses are readily available. Of these two options a taxi is the better choice, ast buses are unreliable. A taxi ride from Zhylhany Airport to Kiev costs in the neighborhood of US$20.

Airline Numbers

Aeroflot	(44) 274-5223
Air Ukraine	(44) 216-7040
Ukraine International	(44) 216-6730
Transaero	(44) 224-8748
Air France	(44) 296-7050
Austrian Airlines	(44) 212-2592, 296-7454
Balkan Bulgarin Airlines	(44) 229-7203
CSA Airlines	(44) 228-0296
Finnair	(44) 296-7240
KLM	(44) 268-9023
LOT Polish Airlines	(44) 228-7150
Lufthansa	(44) 296-7686, 229-6297
Malev	(44) 296-7453

HOTELS

Expensive

Dnipro Hotel; 1/2 Khreshchatik St.; tel: (44) 229-8591; fax: (44) 229-8213; city center; restaurant; conference room; pool.

Impressa; 21 Petra Sagaidachnoho St.; tel: (44) 417-0027; 15 rooms; banquet services.

Moscow; 4 Instytutska St.; tel: (44) 229-0266; city center; restaurant; barber shop; secure parking; sauna.

Kievska Rus Complex; 12 Hospitalna St.; tel: (44) 220-4144; fax: (44) 220-4586; restaurant; conference facilities; supermarket; barber shop; underground parking; pool.

Hotel Khreshchatik Kiev; 14 Khreshchatik St.; tel: (44) 229-7193; fax: (44) 229-8544; city center; restaurant; conference facilities; translation service; airport shuttle service; airline desk; parking.

Salute; 18 Sichnevoho Povstannya St.; tel: (44) 290-6130; fax: (44) 290-7270; restaurant/cafe; conference room; shops; barber shop; post office; parking.

Spartac; 105 Frunze (Spartac Stadium); tel: (44) 435-7078; fax: 435-6316; city center; restaurant; conference room; use of stadium for guests: fitness; sauna; pool; jogging track.

Sport; 55 Chervonoarmiivska St.; tel: (44) 220-0252; restaurants; conference room (up to 150); barber shop.

Ukraina; 5 Blv. T. Shevchenka; tel: (44) 229-2818; fax: (44) 229-8772; 2 restaurants; conference room; shops; fitness; sauna; pool.

Moderate

Andriyivsky Complex; 60 Vozdvizhenska St.; tel: 416-2256, 416-6328; restaurant.

Bratislava; 1 Malishka; tel: 559-6920; near metro station; restaurant; cafe; parking.

Hotel Lybrid; 3 Ploscha Peremohy; tel: (44) 274-0063; near central rail station; 2 restaurants; shops.

Leningradsky; 4 Blv. Tarasa Shevchenko; tel: (44) 225-5101, 229-7364; 19th-century hotel.

Tourist; 2 R. Okipnoi St.; tel: (44) 517-8832; new hotel; restaurant.

Mir; 70 Prospect Sorocorichcha Zhovtnya; tel: (44) 263-7119; fax: (44) 264-9651; adjacent Holoseyevo Park; restaurant; 3 cafes; casino.

Slavutych; 1 Entuziastiv St.; tel: (44) 555-3859; restaurant; cafe; slot machines; theater.

AUTO RENTAL

Cooperative Ton; tel: (44) 221-1454; fax: (44): 556-7446.

Intourist Hotel Rus; tel: (44) 220-4144 or 224-8110.

Ukrintour; tel: (44) 212-5810; fax: (44) 212-4524.

United Arab Emirates

At a Glance

Population ....2,344,402 (July 1999 est.)
Growth Rate ....1.78% (1999 est.)
Life Expectancy .... 75.24 years (1999 est.)
Infant Mortality.......... 14.1 deaths/1,000 births (1999 est.)

Ethnic Composition

South Asian 50%
Arab and Iranian 23%
Emiri 19%
Other 8%

Religious Composition

Sunni Muslim... 80%
Shi'a Muslim 16%
Christian, Hindu, Other... 4%

Languages Spoken

Arabic (official), Farsi, English, Hindi, and Urdu.

Education and Literacy

Education is compulsory from ages six to 12. The national literacy rate stands at 79.2 per cent for those citizens over the age of 15.

Labor Force

Total: 1,300,000
By occupation: services 60%, industry 32%, agriculture 8%. (Note: Over 75 percent of the workforce is comprised of foreign nationals.)

THE ECONOMY

The United Arab Emirate economy is dominated by a single commodity: petroleum. This reliance on gas and oil exports has given this tiny nation one of the highest per capita incomes in the world. Its reserves are expected to last for another century. However, like many of its oil rich neighbors, the UAE has seen its fortunes decline in recent years as oil prices have dropped considerably. Composed of seven individual emirates, each competes for individual wealth with the Abu Dhabi emirate remaining at the top of the heap. While the oil industry dominates the GDP, a sizeable service sector has developed for tourism and cargo re-shipment. The agriculture/aquaculture sectors contribute to exports with dates, vegetables and dried fish although the nation is far from self-sustaining from a food standpoint. Like many nations in the region, the UAE is hampered by a lack of fresh water that raises a number of both political and economic concerns for the 21st century.

Exports .... US$38 billion
Imports .... US$29.7 billion
Total Trade .... US$86.4 billion
GDP Per Capita............................. US$17,400 (1998 est.)
Unemployment .... NA
Inflation Rate ....5% (1997 est.)

Top Export Partners

Japan, South Korea, Singapore, India, Oman.

Top Import Partners

U.S., Japan, U.K., Germany, India.

Top Exports

Crude oil, natural gas, re-exports, dried fish, dates.

Top Imports

Manufactured goods, machinery and transport equipment, food, chemicals.

BUSINESS WORKWEEK

Offices

Saturday to Wednesday 8a.m. to 1p.m., reopen 2:30p.m. to 6:30p.m.

Banks

Saturday to Wednesday 8a.m. to 1p.m., reopen 4p.m. to 7p.m.

Government

Saturday to Wednesday 7a.m. to 1:30p.m.

Retail

Saturday to Wednesday 9a.m. to 7p.m. Large retail centers may be open until 9p.m.

Note: All private and government businesses will have lightly shorter hours during the month of Ramadan and on Thursdays.

HOLIDAYS

New Year's Day...January 1
Id al-Fitr, end of Ramadan...................................January 7
Id al-Adha, Feast of the Sacrifice .... March 18
Muharram, Islamic New Year...............................April 17*
Mouloud, Birth of Muhammad ....June 16
Leilat al-Meiraj, Ascension of
Muhammad ....October 27
First day of Ramadan ....November 28
National Day ....December 2
Christmas Day...December 25
*Date may vary by year.

CLIMATE

Seasons

Summers in the U.A.E. are extremely hot and humid, the winters very mild. From December to March the climate is around 10˚c to 30°C (50°-87°F), but then it gets exceedingly hot with summer temperatures rising to as high as 48°C (118°F), with humidity of 100 percent on the coast. The best time to visit is between October and April.

Regions

There are few regional climate differences in the United Arab Emirates, although it tends to be hotter inland, and in the desert area than in coastal regions. Southern areas tend to be less humid year round.

Money & Banking

Currency

The currency of United Arab Emirates is the U.A.E. Dirham (Dh).

Denominations

The U.A.E. Dirham comes in coin denominations of Dh1, and 50, 25, 10, 5 and 1 fils; and banknotes of Dh1, 5, 10, 50, 100, 200, 500 and 1,000.

Traveler's Checks and Credit Cards

Banks are plentiful in the UAE and are the best choices for

United Arab Emirates

SM Santa Barbara, CA

©2001 Magellan Geographix

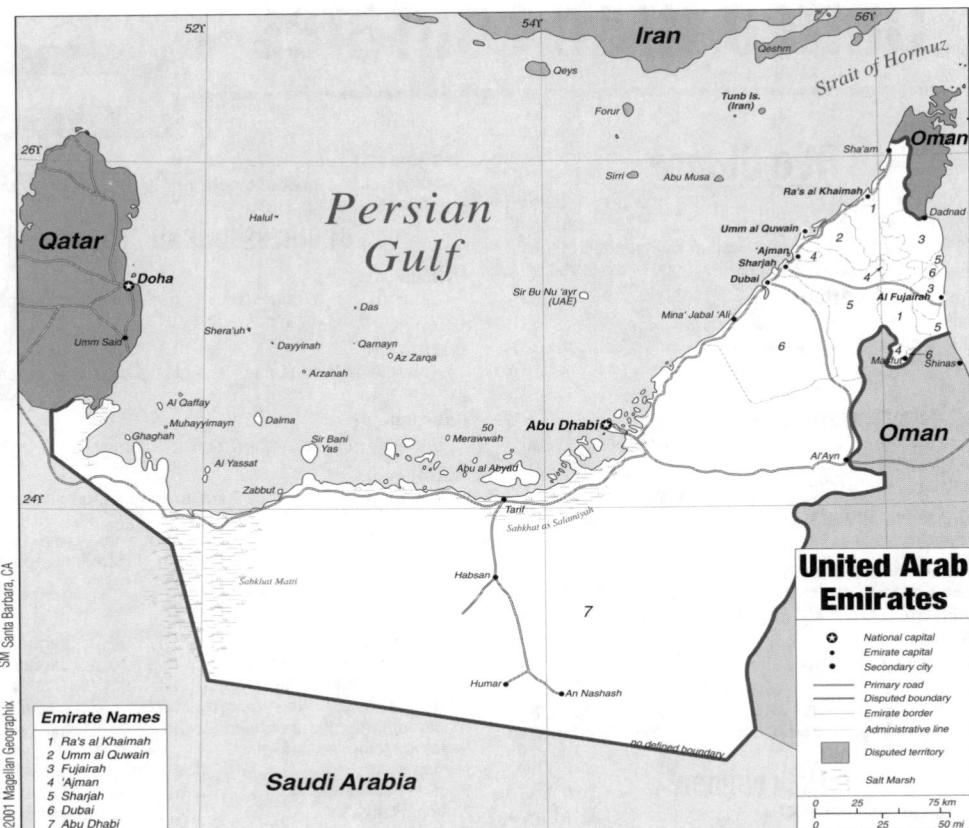

United Arab Emirates

- ⊛ National capital
- ⊙ Emirate capital
- • Secondary city
- ── Primary road
- Disputed boundary
- Emirate border
- Administrative line
- Disputed territory
- Salt Marsh

Emirate Names
1 Ra's al Khaimah
2 Umm al Quwain
3 Fujairah
4 'Ajman
5 Sharjah
6 Dubai
7 Abu Dhabi

0   25   75 km
0   25   50 mi

cash and travel check exchange. Hotels, and international airport kiosks can be used, but the rate is not as favorable. Most major currencies can be exchanged and rates are pretty standard unless large sums are involved.

American Express, Visa, and MasterCard are easily accepted in up-market places in main cities, but in more rural areas they may ask for cash. Some banks in the capital offer cash advances on credit cards, but passport identification will be needed. ATMs are plentiful and provide optimal rates for cash withdraw transactions.

Travel

VISA AND PASSPORT

Members or residents of the Arab Gulf Cooperation Council nations and citizens of the UK do not require visas for UAE travel. Other visitors to the United Arab Emirates need valid passports and visas.

Even tourists must be "invited" by a sponsor in the emirates. Major hotels sponsor tourist and business travelers but business people would be recommended to get an invitation from a local contact. To obtain work or residence permits, an AIDS test is required after arrival.

Visas are often left at the airport for pick-up by travelers upon arrival although this is not suggested if it can be avoided. Transit visas are also available.

Note: If your passport shows any signs of prior travel to

Israel at any time you will most likely be denied entry to the UAE. Business travelers should take special care in this area and make advance arrangements if there is a potential for conflict.

DEPARTURE FORMALITIES

There are no departure formalities for the United Arab Emirates. There is no departure tax from airports, and other exit points have minimal fees. Transit visa carriers must turn in their visa upon departure.

CUSTOMS ENTRY (PERSONAL)

Duty-free
- Tobacco: a generous 2,000 cigarettes or 400 cigars or 2kg of tobacco
- Alcohol: Two liters of spirits or wine (non-Muslims only and never when entering through Sharjah or overland.)

Prohibited or Restricted
- Drugs
- Loose pearls
- Non-Islamic religious books and symbols
- Firearms and ammunition

IMMUNIZATION

International certificate of vaccination not required unless you are arriving from an infected area. An international certificate of vaccine for cholera is required if you are arriving from an infected area within five days of exposure; yellow fever within six days. Prophylaxis for hepatitis A, malaria, polio, tetanus, and typhoid are advised.

TIPPING

Taxi
Taxi drivers are not tipped.

Porters
Porters are generally tipped Dh2 per bag.

Hotels
Most hotel bills include a 10 percent service charge, especially in the northern emirates.

Restaurants
Most restaurant bills include a 10 percent service charge. If a restaurant does not include service charge, tip 10 to 15 percent. Bear in mind that the service charge in the UAE is not distributed to the waitstaff and waiters are usually low-paid foreign nationals.

EMERGENCY INFORMATION

Police and Crime
Islamic Sharia Law governs here, along with a civil criminal system. As a result, petty crime is literally non-existent. However, anyone can be arrested for anything that goes against Islamic rule, including possession of alcohol, blaspheming or indecent behavior.

Take basic precautions against petty crime. Leave most of your cash, traveler's checks, jewelry and non-essential valuables in your hotel safe. Avoid display of any non-Islamic religious medals, jewelry or t-shirts. Carry photocopies of your passport instead of the original. Carry cash in a money belt, and use credit cards or traveler's checks for most transactions.

As with all Islamic nations, women must obey the dress code, behave conservatively, and they are advised not to travel alone. The police force is extremely efficient but impatient with foreigners not willing to abide by local customs.

Foreign business visitors are often the target of thieves so purses, laptops and briefcases require additional security. Do not leave valuables in cars or on tables in cafés.

Emergency Numbers
Police.. 999
Ambulance 998
Fire 997

Health
Upper respiratory ailments, gastrointestinal troubles, amoebic dysentery, stomach cramps and diarrhea, as well as skin irritations brought on by excessive sun and heat, may occur. Malaria is not common.

Avoid drinking tap water for both health and taste reasons; bottled water is widely available. Wash all vegetables, peel fruits, and try to avoid uncooked food. Bring along required medicines, as they may be hard to come by locally.

Health care is adequate and improving. Hospitals are free for all U.A.E. citizens and inexpensive for others. There is an abundance of European- and U.S.-trained doctors. Basic travel health insurance is recommended.

TAXIS & RENTAL CARS
In larger cities, all fares are metered. Taxis are considered the most comfortable way to travel from Abu Dhabi to Dubai.

Rental cars at reasonable rates can be found in urban areas but visitors should purchase ample insurance. Insurance only applies to trips within the UAE. Gasoline is, understand-

ably, cheap. Rental cars are not recommended for first-time visitors. Business travelers may, however, find them to be a necessity so secure ample directions and guidance.

BUS
There is limited service, although many hotels have private services for customers traveling to the airport. There is no service between emirates.

TRAIN
There are no train services into or in the UAE.

Essential Terms

English	Arabic
Yes	Na-a'am
No	La; mish
Good morning	Al sa-lahm
Hello (daytime)	Al sa-lahm
Hello (evening)	Ma-sa'el khair
Hello (telephone)	Marhaban
Good-bye	Be-kha-trahk
Please	Min-fahd-lak (M)
	Min-fahd-lik (F)
Thank you	Shook-rahn
Pleased to meet you	Sorirart biro'aitak
Excuse me; I'm sorry	Is-ma-leh
My name is _____	'Ismii____
I don't understand	An-na mish fahem
Do you speak English?	Hal tatakallumu l-inkliziyya?

Communications

DIALING CODES IN THE UAE
International country code: [971]
Selected city codes: Abu Dhabi (2), Ajman (6), Al Ain (3), Dubai (4), Fujairah (9), Jebel Dhana (52), Khawanij (48), Sharjah (6)

Dialing the United Arab Emirates from Overseas

To dial the United Arab Emirates from overseas, dial your country's international dialing code, then 971 (the country code for the United Arab Emirates), then the city code and finally the number. If you were dialing Abu Dhabi, for example, you would begin with 011, then 971, then 2 (the city code for Abu Dhabi), and finally the number of the person or office you were trying to reach.

Assistance Numbers
International Operator 150
Operator 100
Information .... 180 or 181

United Arab Emirates (vertical, left margin)

CALLING WITHIN THE UAE

International Calls

The U.A.E. offers great telephone service. Telephone offices exist in many towns. The main post office also has a connecting telephone office, and, thankfully, there is also a way to connect to a foreign operator:

France 800-1-9971
U.S. AT&T Direct 800-121
U.S. MCI 800-1-0001

Public phones may require a deposit.

PAY PHONES

Public Telephones

Card Phone:

Common-use telephones take Dh-1, 50, or 25 fils coins.

Calling Cards

Telephone cards are becoming more common in the U.A.E. and are available for purchase.

CELLULAR PHONES

The number of cellular service providers in the United Arab Emirates is limited. Emirates Telecom Corp. is a major service provider offering ETACS for analogue users, and GSM for digital.

Note: Your home country cell phone may not work in this country. If not, we recommend that you rent an international cell phone *before* you leave home. A major US-based cell phone rental provider is **IMC WorldCell**. For information see "International Cell Phone Rentals" on page 14.

CALL BACK

You can (potentially) save significant sums when calling in the United Arab Emirates by using one of the call back services listed below. Fees for call back services vary widely, depending on the company and the type of service required. Be sure to check with these companies before leaving to compare rates. For a list of callback services, please refer to the "Communications" section in the *Global Road Warrior* Introduction.

PHONE JACKS

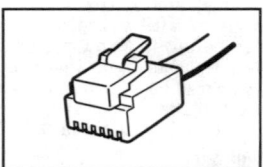

Plug adaptors are available through **iGo Corporation.** (See "Electrical and Telephone Adaptors" on page 19.)

FAX

Most hotels have fax services.

POSTAL SERVICES

Airmail letters and packages take about two weeks to reach Europe and North America.

TELEGRAMS

Most hotels have telegram facilities.

Business Services

COURIER SERVICE

DHL U.A.E.; DHL Air Express Centre; Dubai International Airport; P.O. Box 6252; tel: (4) 299-5333; Open 24 hours a day, seven days.

Federal Express; toll free: 800 40 50; If you can't access the toll free number call: (4) 655-454; Customer Service Hours: 24 hours, 7days; Invoice enquiries: (4) 655-345.

TNT Express; TNT Building, Khalifa Street PO Box 7860, Abu Dhabi; 8002222 (toll-free); tel: 794-448; fax: 795-218.

UPS; United Parcel Service LLC; PO Box 26026, Sheikh Zayed Road, Dubai; tel: (4) 391-939; Toll free within the UAE tel: 800-4774; United Parcel Service LLC, PO Box 30804, Airport Road, Abu Dhabi; tel: (2) 461-961.

Electrical

Current

220 volts AC, 50Hz, in Abu Dhabi 220/240 volts AC, 50Hz.

ELECTRIC PLUGS

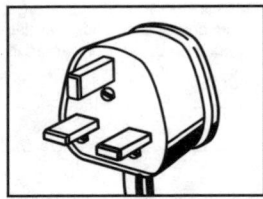

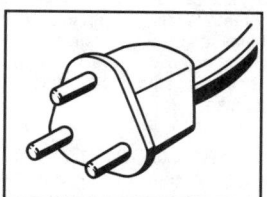

Plug adaptors are available through **iGo Corporation.** (See "Electrical and Telephone Adaptors" on page 19.)

Technical Support

Apple/Claris; (in the U.A.E.) tel: [971] 4-513-888; fax: [971] 4-527-444; (in Germany) tel: [49] (1) 803-5018; (in Switzerland) tel: [41] (800) 833-310; (in the U.K.) tel: [44] (990) 127-753; (in the U.S.) tel: [1] (800) 500-7078; http://www.apple.com/.

Compaq/Digital; (U.AE. Office) tel: [971] 4-818-100; fax: [971] 4-818-313; (in Switzerland) tel: [41] (22) 709-5330; fax: [41] (22) 709-5391 (Geneva); tel: [41] (1) 801-2507; fax: [41] (1) 801-2172 (Zurich); (General U.S.) tel: (281) 518-2000; http://www.compaq.com/.

Dell; (in Egypt) tel: [20] 2-360-2234 (Electronics House in Cairo/Mr. Jamal El Bidweihy); fax: [20] 2-361-4576; (in Germany) tel: [49] (61) 039-710; (Dell- Europe) tel: [44] (134) 474-8000; (in the U.S.) tel: [1] (512) 338-4400; fax: [1] (512) 728-3330; http://www.dell.com/.

Gateway 2000; (in the U.S.) tel: [1] (605) 232-2191; fax: [1] (605) 232-2023; (in Ireland) tel: [353] (1) 797-2000; http://www.g2k.com/.

Hewlett Packard; (in Switzerland) tel: [41] (22) 780-8111; (in the U.S.) tel: [1] (408) 246-4300; http://www.hp.com/.

IBM; tel: (4) 321-321; fax: (4) 321-322; (Egypt Office) tel: [20] 2-349-2533; fax: [20] 2-360-1227; (in Switzerland) tel: [41] (22) 310-0418 (in French); (in the U.S.) tel: [1] (919) 517-2800; http://www.ibm.com/.

Microsoft; tel: (4) 555-443; fax: (4) 523-264; tel: (4) 513-888; fax: [971] 4-527-444(in Switzerland) tel: [41] (848) 858-868; fax [41] (1) 831-0869; (in the U.S.) tel: [1] (425) 635-7222; http://www.microsoft.com/.

NEC; (in Israel) tel: [972] (0)9-59-3300 (Tracker Support); (in the U.S.) [1] (916) 388-0101 (Main Switchboard); http://www.nec.com/.

Toshiba; (in Germany) tel: [49] (2131) 158-319; fax: [49] (2131) 158-558; (in Switzerland) tel: [41] (1) 946-0777; fax: [41] (1) 946-0807; (in Ireland) tel: [44] (193) 282-8828; (in the U.S.) [1] (949) 583-3000 (Corporate Headquarters); http://www.toshiba.com/.

Internet Connection

HOW TO CONNECT

Connecting to AOL and Compuserve in the United Arab Emirates is similar to using it when traveling outside your own area code. See the introductory section for detailed information on connecting to your account through a different phone number.

America Online

Numbers are available at keyword *international*. Be sure to get several local numbers before leaving. Go to keyword *access* (a free area) and download the software.

At press time, America Online had no local access numbers in United Arab Emirates. Check their list of current access numbers at http://intlaccess.web.aol.com/ to see if any numbers have been activated or to locate numbers in neighboring countries.

Compuserve

Numbers are available at *Go International*. If you are using CompuServe 2000, use GO PHONES within CompuServe 2000 to search for access numbers. The Compuserve Web-site also has a great deal of information for travelers at http://www.compuserve.com/.

At press time, Compuserve had no local access numbers. Check their list of current access numbers to see if any numbers have been activated or to locate numbers in neighboring countries.

Independent Service Providers

Many independent service providers offer discounts if you are only in town for a couple days.

Emirates Intenet; tel: (800) 5-244; tel: (2) 208-4563; fax: (4) 226-669; email: help@emirates.net.ae; http://www.emirates.net.ae/.

U.A.E. Net / Universal Enterprises Ltd; tel: (6) 531-3150; fax: (6) 531-3675; info@uaenet.com; http://uaenet.com/.

Business Culture

GREETINGS AND COURTESIES

Businesspeople are generally friendly and open. They embrace or shake hands when meeting and departing, and several times in between. Businesspeople will quickly give much more information about themselves than in the West. Family and social connections are important, more so than personal accomplishments. Expect several invitations to have coffee and meals. Titles are used often, and anyone with an M.D. or Ph.D. must be addressed as "Dr." ("*duktoar*" for a man, "*duktoara*" for a woman).

BUSINESS ETHIC AND FRAMEWORK

U.A.E. culture is somewhat "dualist," with both modernist and traditionalist ways of thinking present at the same time. Businesspeople usually believe that many things in life are controlled by fate, and that the inherent personalities of women and men are vastly different. Honor is often more important than facts; rarely will an Arab admit an error. All beliefs and laws are based on the Islamic creed, even for the minority of people who are not Muslim. Bureaucrats are given a great deal of power; connections with government officials are invaluable.

MEETINGS AND DECISION MAKING

Good personal relationships and contacts are the most important factors in business with Arabs. Faith and friendship are used to decide most issues, sometimes even overriding reasoning. Regulations or decisions can be changed in view of someone's personal situation. Businesspeople have a hard time saying "no," and if your question doesn't get an answer, you should take it as a negative response.

WOMEN

Women can be professionals, but they still acknowledge their place in the family structure and believe in the need to guard their reputation carefully. At social events, if a woman is unmarried or her husband is not present, she should behave in a reserved fashion. Most women veil their faces, at least partially, in public.

United Arab Emirates

Business Centers
Abu Dhabi
CITY VIEW

The capital of this desert nation, Abu Dhabi has risen into a modern metropolis with convenient access to the Persian Gulf. An ecologically-friendly president has brought plenty of greenery to the city in the form of parks and gardens, providing a refreshing solace from the heat.

AIRPORT
Abu Dhabi International Airport to City Center

The airport lies 22 miles (35km.) from Abu Dhabi's center. If looking for comfort, hire a driver from a car rental company to take you into the city for a price of about Dh110. Regular taxis are also available at a cost of about Dh70. Settle the fare before getting into the cab. The trip into town takes about 35 minutes.

Airline Numbers

Aer Lingus	(2) 332-136
Air France	(2) 215-810
Air India	(2) 322-300
Alitalia	(2) 342-053, 321-957
Al-Yemen	(2) 335-028
American Airlines	(2) 333-323
Biman Bangladesh	(2) 325-124
British Airways	(2) 341-328
China Airlines	(2) 345-570
Emirates	(2) 315-888
Egyptair	(2) 344-777
Ethiopian Airlines	(2) 333-153
Garuda Indonesia	(2) 338-700
Gulf Air	(2) 332-600, 757-083
Iran Air	(2) 338-700
KLM	(2) 323-280
Lufthansa	(2) 213-200
Middle East Airlines	(2) 339-000
Pakistan International Airlines	(2) 302-6666
Royal Brunei	(2) 316-100
Royal Jordanian	(2) 321-832
Saudia	(2) 351-400
Singapore Airlines	(2) 221-110
Sirianair	(2) 335-821
Swissair	(2) 343-430
Turkish Airlines	(2) 302-6693
Yemenia	(2) 338-700

HOTELS
Top-end
Hilton International Abu Dhabi; Corniche Avenue; tel: (2) 661-900; fax: (2) 669-696; near city center; restaurant; conference facilities (up to 1000); business center; car rental; parking; fitness; sauna; pool; watersports; tennis & squash.

Inter-Continental Abu Dhabi; Al Khalidya Street; tel: (2) 666-888; fax: (2) 669-153; near city center; restaurant; conference facilities (up to 1600); sauna; pool.

Le Meridien Abu Dhabi; Tourist Club Area; tel: 776-666; fax: 727-221, 729-315; near city center; beach; restaurant; conference facilities (up to 300); secretarial services; fax/photocopy facilities; in-room modem/fax connection; car rental; corporate rates; fitness; sauna; pool; whirlpool; water sports; private beach; squash.

Sheraton Abu Dhabi Resort & Towers; Corniche Road;

tel: (2) 773-333; fax: (2) 725-149; near city center; beach; restaurant; conference facilities (up to 500); business center; secretarial services; fax/photocopy facilities; in-room modem/fax connection, safe; car rental; parking; corporate rates; fitness; sauna; pool; whirlpool; watersports; squash.

Expensive
Alain Palace; Corniche; tel: 794-777; fax: 795-713; near city center; beach; restaurant; conference facilities (up to 15); secretarial services; fax/photocopy facilities; in-room modem/fax connection, safe; parking; corporate rates; fitness; sauna; pool; whirlpool; casino.

Baynunah Hilton Tower; Corniche Road; tel: 327-777; fax: 216-777; near city center; restaurant; conference facilities; business center; free transport to airport; car rental; secure parking; fitness; sauna; pool; water sports.

Gulf Hotel Abu Dhabi; Old Airport Road; tel: 414777; fax: 414537; located in suburb; near to airport; restaurant; secretarial services; fax/photocopy facilities; corporate rates; fitness; sauna; pool.

Holiday Inn Abu Dhabi; Sheikh Zayed II Street; tel: 335-335; fax: 335-766; near city center; restaurant; conference facilities (up to 100); secretarial services; fax/photocopy facilities; parking; corporate rates; fitness; pool.

Moderate
Al Rawda Rotana Suites; Old Airport Road; tel: 457-111; fax: 457-222; near city centre & exhibition centre; restaurant; car rental; parking.

Beach Rotana; Po Box 45200; tel: 743-000; fax: 742-111; restaurant; conference facilities; business center; car rental; parking; fitness; squash courts.

Khalidia Palace; Corniche Street; tel: 650-959; fax: 660-411; located in suburb; restaurant; conference facilities; pool.

Mina; Mina Street; tel: 781-000; fax: 791-000; near city center; restaurant.

Novotel Centre; Sheik Hamdan Street; tel: 333-555; fax: 343-633; near city center; parking; pool.

Zakher; Umm Al Nar Street; tel: 341-940; fax: 326-306; near city center; restaurant; parking.

WORLD TRADE CENTER
World Trade Center Abu-Dhabi
13th Floor, Chamber of Commerce Building
Airport Road
Abu-Dhabi, United Arab Emirates
tel: (2) 339-090; fax: (2) 319-331

United Kingdom

At a Glance

THE PEOPLE

Population ....59,113,439 (July 1999 est.)
Growth Rate ....0.24% (1999 est.)
Life Expectancy .... 77.37 years (1999 est.)
Infant Mortality..... 5.78 deaths/1,000 live births (1999 est.)

Ethnic Composition

English..81.5%
Scottish..9.6%
Irish..2.4%
Welsh...1.9%
Ulster 1.8%
Other 2.8%

Religious Composition

Anglican..45.9%
Roman Catholic...15.3%
Muslim...1.7%
Other Protestant..2.7%
Sikh & Hindu..1.3%
Other 1.0%

(**Note**: Figures are inconclusive because the U.K. does not include a religion question on its census form).

Languages Spoken

English, Welsh, and Scottish Gaelic.

Education and Literacy

Education is compulsory for 12 years and attendance is nearly 100 percent. The literacy rate is 99 percent for citizens over 15 years of age.

Labor Force

Total 28,800,000
By occupation: services 68.9%, industrial 17.5%, government 11.3%, energy 1.2%, agriculture 1.1%.

THE ECONOMY

The United Kingdom has remained an international economic force for centuries. Its deep downward spiral of the 1970s was halted and reversed by the Thatcher government's move toward privatization and away from growing socialization of the economy. It is currently one of the top E.U. economies with a thriving service sector and a highly efficient agricultural component. Its manufacturing and exports are driving GDP growth. As a major banking and insurance center for the globe, London still attracts the bulk of Europe's investment transfers. The U.K. has not fully joined the E.U., and the present Labor government is taking cautious measures towards adopting the Euro. There is continual concern about tampering with the nation's recently revamped social system and healthy employment figures. Other economic growth concerns are based in the political ramifications of Scottish devolution and potential economic separation, as well as Northern Ireland's peace pact.

Exports ....US$271 billion (1998)
Imports ....US$304 billion (1998)
Total Trade ....US$575 billion (1998)
GDP Per Capita............................. US$21,200 (1998 est.)
Unemployment ....7.5% (1998 est.)
Inflation Rate 2.7% (1998)

Top Export Partners

E.U. (Germany, France, Netherlands), United States.

Top Import Partners

E.U. (Germany, France, Netherlands), United States.

Top Exports

Manufactured goods, machinery, fuels, chemicals, foods, beverages, tobacco.

Top Imports

Manufactured goods, machinery, fuels, foodstuffs.

BUSINESS WORKWEEK

Offices

Monday to Friday 9a.m. to 5p.m.

Banks

Monday to Friday 9:30a.m. to 3:30p.m., with Saturday morning hours in some locations.

Government

Monday to Friday 9:30a.m. to 3:30p.m.

Retail

Monday to Friday 9a.m. to 7p.m. Slightly shorter hours on the weekend.

HOLIDAYS

New Year's Day...January 1
Good Friday...April 21*
Easter Monday ....April 24*
Early May Holiday .... May 1*
Spring Bank Holiday..May 29
Summer Bank Holiday (Scotland) .... August 7
Late Summer Bank
Holiday (Everywhere except Scotland) .... August 28
Christmas ....December 25
Boxing day...December 26
*Date may vary by year.

CLIMATE

Seasons

Britain, for the most part, is a damp, often foggy, temperate island in the North Sea. Its weather rarely dips below freezing or rises above 28˚C (80˚F). In recent years, however, the extremes have become more extreme, and the seasons have been more distinct, with a number of extremely hot summers, and daylight lasting past 10p.m. Air-conditioning is often required in the capital. Always pack an umbrella.

Regions

The southern regions can experience more Mediterranean climates; the midlands offer a typical "English" climate of fog and rain. Wales in the west suffers from a profusion of rain, while Scotland experiences harsh winters and moderate, short-lived summers.

Money & Banking

Currency

The currency of United Kingdom is the Pound Sterling (£ Stg).

United Kingdom

Denominations

The Pound (£ Stg.) comes in coin denominations of 1£, and 50, 20, 10, 5, 2 and 1 pence; and banknotes of 5, 10, 20 and 50£s.

Traveler's Checks and Credit Cards

It is quite easy to exchange traveler's checks and major foreign currency at banks, hotels, foreign exchange bureaus, and hotels, as well as foreign exchange kiosks at the airports. Banks offer the most favorable exchange rates. Traveler's checks may receive a better exchange rate than cash.

American Express, Visa, MasterCard, and Diners Club, are widely accepted in the United Kingdom. You can get cash advances from your credit card on many of the automated teller machines (ATM). Long-term business visitors should set up a checking account in the United Kingdom and get an ATM card. One may procure the most favorable exchange rates for credit card and ATM transactions.

Travel

VISA AND PASSPORT

A passport that is valid for at least six months beyond anticipated exit date is required of all visitors, except for citizens of E.U. countries bearing a national ID card, who may visit or work without any immigration controls for up to three months. Once the visitor has gained entry to the U.K., a passport is not required for travel between Great Britain and Ireland, Northern Ireland, the Channel Islands, or the Isle of Man. Passengers who are transiting the U.K. to the Republic of Ireland as their destination should hold return tickets so as to avoid interrogation and delay.

Note: Taiwanese passports are not recognized as valid.

Citizens of the U.S., Canada, Australia, Japan, and New Zealand are usually permitted to remain up to six months with no visa. This six-month stay privilege is also extended to citizens of Iceland, Liechtenstein, Monaco, Norway, and Switzerland for tourist or social visits only, so long as they possess a British Visitor's Card (available through travel agents and obtained prior to arrival in the U.K.).

There is a long list of nationalities for whom a visa is required, mostly in Africa, Asia, the Middle East, and Eastern Europe. If coming from a country in one of these areas, one is advised to check with a British consulate or embassy prior to visiting.

One may procure temporary Visitor and Business visas. Single-entry visas are valid up to six months; multiple-entry visas can be issued in increments of one-half, one, two, or five years. Application fees vary by country of origin.

Transit visas, good for seven days of travel, are necessary for citizens of Afghanistan, China (PR), Dem. Rep. of Congo, Eritrea, Ethiopia, Ghana, Iran, Iraq, Libya, Nigeria, Somalia, Sri Lanka, Turkey and Uganda. For all other nationalities, a transit visa is not required as long as one is continuing the trip within 24 hours to another country on the first available connecting aircraft and one is in possession of confirmed onward travel papers.

Allow for about two to three weeks for visa applications to be processed, depending on the nationality of the applicant. Applications referred to the Home Office can take up to six weeks, or even more. Again, travelers are advised to check directly with an embassy or consulate as early as possible in order to avoid delay.

DEPARTURE FORMALITIES

The following particulars apply to payment of departure taxes:

- Travelers pay £10 if onward travel is within the E.U.
- The departure tax is £20 if onward travel is beyond E.U. boundaries.
- No departure tax is levied if you are leaving by sea or channel tunnel.

CUSTOMS ENTRY (PERSONAL)

Duty Free

The following items may be brought into the U.K. without customs duty being levied; this applies to adult travelers entering from non-EU countries or those who have purchased duty-free items within the E.U.:

- 200 cigarettes or 50 cigars or 100 cigarillos or 250g of tobacco
- One liter of alcoholic beverages more than twenty-two proof, or two liters of fortified or sparkling wine or other liqueurs
- 2 liters of still table wine
- 60g of perfume and 250ml of toilet water

- Other goods (including souvenirs) to the value of £75

For adult travelers arriving from E.U. countries with duty-paid goods, the following duty free limits apply:

- 800 cigarettes and 400 cigarillos and 200 cigars and 1kg of tobacco
- 90 liters of wine, including up to 60 liters of sparkling wine
- 10 liters of distilled spirits
- 20 liters of fortified wine
- 110 liters of beer

The amounts of tobacco and alcohol specified above are only benchmarks for customs officials; if these items are moving from one E.U. country to another; a legal limit no longer exists. However, if a traveler possesses more than the above-listed these quantities, questions at customs may ensue and along with a demand to prove that items are for personal consumption only.

Note: The Channel Islands are considered to be outside of the E.U. for duty-free purposes.

Restricted

There are strictly enforced regulations concerning the import / export of certain items, such as materials deemed likely to ignite racial hatred, and firearms or personal defense weapons like mace or knives.

This is one of the only regions on earth where rabies does not exist; most animals that are brought into the country, including all cats and dogs, are required to undergo quarantine for six months. In order to bring other animals and birds into the U.K., an import license must be obtained, at least six months in advance. Persons who attempt to smuggle animals into the U.K. will be subject to severe penalties; an animal that is illegally imported will likely be destroyed. For more information, contact the Ministry of Agriculture, Fisheries & Food, Government Buildings, Hook Rise South, Kingston Bypass, Tolworth, Surbiton, Surrey KT6 7NF.tel: (020) 8330-4411; fax: (020) 8337 3640

Note: As of this writing, animal import regulations have been eased for certain E.U. countries, eliminating the need for quarantine of domestic animals in favor of inoculation documentation. However, this only applies to a small number of nations at this time. Check in advance if you think this might apply to you.

IMMUNIZATION

Unless a traveler is arriving from a part of the world that is currently impacted by infectious disease, no inoculations are required.

TIPPING

Service charges are customarily added to hotel and restaurant bills, but there is no legal requirement to pay them if the service was unsatisfactory. Visitors should keep in mind, though, that wages for service personnel are set at a low level in anticipation that tips will be forthcoming.

Taxi

A tip in the range of ten to fifteen percent beyond the metered fare is customary.

Porters

Usually, a tip in the range of about fifty pence per bag is sufficient. Conveyance of baggage under difficult circumstances or inordinately long distances calls for a greater amount, of course.

Hotels

Usually, a service charge of ten to twelve percent is added to the bill.

Restaurants

Ten to fifteen percent is customary for most restaurants,

United Kingdom

added to your bill as a service charge. Tipping beyond this amount is not expected.

Other

Hairdressers and bartenders expect a tip in the range of ten to 15 percent. Cloak room attendants, doormen, and other personnel whose service is not connected with a specific tab usually are tipped £1 or so.

EMERGENCY INFORMATION

Police and Crime

PERSONAL SECURITY

Overall, the United Kingdom is a safe place to be, stable and modern. Political rallies are well policed and orderly, except for the situation in Northern Ireland. There is some tiny risk of being caught in the crossfire of terrorist activities growing out of that political situation. In spite of the fact that the primary paramilitary groups in Northern Ireland are currently observing a cease-fire, some acts of violence on the part of dissident groups continue. Citizens of other countries have not been targeted to date, but injuries among those who are accidentally caught up in the commotion have occurred. The summer marching season (April to August) is a time to practice particular caution. At the most, these things may result in delays and disruptions to the visitor's schedule.

CRIMES

Crime rates are generally low in the U.K., and violent crime in particular is rare. However, both petty crimes and incidents of personal assault have increased slightly in large cities such as London, Manchester, and Birmingham.

Occurrences of pickpocketing and the theft of bags left unattended in urban areas are not uncommon. Pickpocketing is widespread at the more popular tourist sites, including restaurants, historic locations, buses, trains, and the Tube (London Underground). Thieves often target rental cars parked at such locations.

For the most part, visitors to the U.K. do not have to produce identity documentation for police authorities. Passports can be left in hotel safes or residences, minimizing the risk of their theft. In Northern Ireland, though, it is wise to carry passports or some other photographic identification at all times.

ATM's are readily accessible throughout the U.K., which means that only those who use traveler's checks need to carry a passport.

English "bobbies," of course, are world-famous and known for their tolerant, bemused demeanor. They are friendly, efficient, and approachable.

Emergency Numbers

Police/fire/ambulance 999
General emergency 112

HEALTH

The U.K. is one of the world's healthiest places. Virtually the only health concerns are minor ailments such as influenza, sinus problems, and occasional rheumatic discomfort stemming from cold, damp weather. Medicines to treat these problems are easily obtainable.

Sanitation laws are strict, so both the food and water are generally safe.

The National Health Service is first-rate and provides free first aid and emergency treatment for all visitors. Further treatment for short-term visitors will be charged at fairly high rates unless their country of origin has a reciprocal medical care agreement with the U.K. It is wise to maintain private medical insurance coverage that specifically provides for this kind of situation. Except under the most extreme of circumstances, though, medical evacuation

coverage is not called for since the level of care here is of the highest order.

The following countries have reciprocal health care agreements with the U.K.: all E.U. countries (excluding Danish residents of the Faroe Islands), Anguilla, Australia, Barbados, British Virgin Islands, Bulgaria, Channel Islands (only applies if visit is under three months), Falkland Islands, Hungary, Iceland, Isle of Man, Liechtenstein, Malta (for stays of thirty days or less), Montserrat, New Zealand, Norway, Poland, Romania, Russia, St. Helena, Slovak Republic, Turks & Caicos Islands, and Yugoslavia (Serbia and Montenegro).

These reciprocal agreements provide for varying amounts of exemption, depending on the visitor's nationality. Compete details of specific agreements can be obtained from the British Department of Health:
DOH website: www.doh.gov.uk/

INTERNAL TRAVEL

Public transportation in the U.K. is of a high quality, overall, but like so much in this country, it can prove pricey. Coaches and local buses are the most economical way to get around, but also the slowest.

An impressive rail network spans the country, including several beautiful routes through sparsely populated areas. Rapid intercity trains render air travel superfluous—unless you happen to be in a big hurry. Auto rental is worth consideration if you wish to explore towns and villages that are remote and at a pace that you control. Taxis are prolific in London, but not so easy to find in many other regional districts.

Channel crossings can be an integral part of the itinerary for any visitor to the U.K.; a special section of this heading follows.

CHANNEL CROSSINGS

THE CHANNEL TUNNEL

Inaugurated in 1994 and known popularly as the Chunnel, this marvel of modern engineering provides a direct land link between London and Paris, or London and Brussels, via rail. It is also a combination road and rail connection between Folkestone (U.K.) and Calais (France). It proves a real boon to both the business traveler and the tourist.

EUROSTAR: The passenger-only rail connection is Eurostar, a high-speed train operated by the railways of the U.K., Belgium, and France. It runs from London (Waterloo station) to Paris (Gare du Nord), with a trip time of three hours; to Brussels (Midi), figure a trip time of two hours and forty minutes. Currently, there are 12 daily departures from London to Paris, and 6 from London to Brussels. A direct service also travels to Lille (Belgium) and departs once daily from London, with a travel time of 2 hours and 10 minutes.

Eurostar trains offer standard-class and first-class passage, a full buffet and bar, and a staff that is both highly trained and multi-lingual.

For details in-country, contact:
Eurotunnel Customer Service .... (020) 7928 5100
or 0990 353 535
European Passenger Services .... (020) 8784 1333

You can also take your own car, truck, motorcycle, or bicycle along for the ride on Le Shuttle, which runs between Folkestone (U.K.) and Calais (France). Vehicles are transported through the tunnel on one- or two-deck shuttles, determined by height. A provision also exists for coaches, minibuses, caravans, and camper vans. Passengers generally ride in their vehicles. Transporters of heavy goods will be conveyed on a special shuttle that offers separate passenger coaches for drivers. The trip takes about 35 minutes between station destinations, or about one hour from roadway to roadway. Trains operate daily all year, two to five per hour, determined by the season and the hour. Book a reservation in advance through Eurotunnel Customer Service (see phone number above), or just show up and take your chances (pretty safe) on getting a slot.

See "Water Travel" for ferry crossing information.

AIR

Many domestic flights are available. But by the time one factors in travel time to and from the airport, check-in, and delays, the train travels to most places just as fast, if not faster. Nevertheless, at times, air travel is appropriate for some travelers. Following are the primary air carriers for domestic routes, along with phone numbers and websites. Advance booking over the internet is generally encouraged.

British Airways...0345-222111
website ....www.britishairways.com
British Midland...0345-554554
website ....www.iflybritishmidland.com
KLM UK 0990-074074
website .... www.klmuk.com
easyJet..0152-445566
website .... easyjet.com
Go..0845 6054321
website ....www.go-fly.com
(Go is British Airways' no-frills carrier)

For free information on domestic air travel:

Air Travel Advisory Bureau
London ....(020) 7636-5000
Manchester...0161 832-2000
Airfares vary tremendously, so shop around.

TAXI

Generally, licensed taxis are metered, including London's famous "black cabs." There may be a small surcharge for weekend service, "bank holidays," late-night travel, or excess baggage. Look for licensed cabs at taxi stands in front of hotels and at train stations, or hail one from the street.

Minicabs offer an alternative, cheaper way to go; one may find them mostly in larger cities. These are usually unlicensed and the drivers will not prove nearly as knowledgeable about destination or efficient navigation; thus, know your stuff if getting around this way. Fares for minicabs are often based loosely on elapsed time or mileage but can also be negotiated before embarking. Maximum capacity is usually four passengers, and fares can be shared. One may only book minicabs by telephone.

Women who are traveling alone are advised to use the black cabs, or:
Lady Cabs ....(020) 7272-3019
For gays and lesbians:
Freedom Cars 0117-734-1313

AUTOMOBILE

Auto rental companies are abundant and can be found at all major airports and hotels. Required documentation includes a national driver's license (from the renter's country) valid for at least one year beyond the then current date. Renters must also purchase third-party insurance.

Traffic stays to the left in the U.K., and driver and front-seat passenger(s) must wear seat belts. If your car possesses rear-seat belts, they must be worn. Service stations are plentiful, clean, and modern.

The roads in Britain are first-rate, but they tend to be congested in urban areas. Primary roads ("A" roads) link all major towns and cities. In rural areas, "B" roads are often slow and winding, and in upland areas these can become impassable during the winter. Highways radiate spoke-like from London with a fine east-west and north-south road system in the northern area as well as in the Midlands.

The automobile associations, AA and the RAC, can provide the traveler with maps, tourist information, and specific routing suggestions to places of special interest. They also offer roadside assistance and other services.

A few cautionary notes:
- Penalties for drunk driving are stiff.
- Pedestrians must remember to look both ways before stepping off curbs; traffic is from the direction opposite of that to which most are accustomed.
- There have been several occurrences of "road rage" in the past year, culminating in the deaths of two motorists. These incidents are uncommon, but those driving rental cars are well advised to be aware of them and to pay attention so as not to be irritating to other motorists.
- Parking in downtown urban areas can be a real nightmare in the U.K.

TRAIN

The U.K. boasts one of the most extensive networks (16,500km / 10,250 mi) of rail service in the world. Quick and efficient inter-city services link London with most major cities in the southeast, Midlands, and Wales, as well as routes between Edinburgh and Glasgow in Scotland.

In some parts of rural Britain, express service is less abundant, but in these cases local rail services cover the territory fairly thoroughly.

The fare structure varies, but one great way to beat the per-trip costs is to purchase a BritRail pass or Flexi Pass, both of which provide for unlimited travel within specified periods of time.

- The BritRail Consecutive Pass provides unlimited rail travel through all of Great Britain, standard or first class, for a duration of 4, 8, 15, 22, or 30 consecutive days.
- The Flexi Pass offers a bit more flexibility, as the name implies, whereby the traveler selects a total of travel days, not necessarily consecutive, to be used within a 2-month period—3, 4, 8, or 15 days of unlimited travel on the railways of Britain.

These are available to North American travelers and to selected Asian-Pacific nationals, including those from the countries of Australia, New Zealand, and South Africa. Passes, provided through travel agents, must be purchased in advance of the trip. They are not available for purchase in-country.

For further information, contact:
National Rail Inquiries 0345-484950
Or, visit the website:
BritRail...www.britrail.com
Inter-Rail cards, which are used for rail travel on the Continent, are also honored, and bearers are eligible for discounts on some ferry rates as well. Travelers who are disabled can also get discounted fares.

British Rail trains make connections to France, Germany, and Belgium with ferries at Dover, Newhaven, Portsmouth, Weymouth, and Folkestone; passengers board at Victoria Station in London. Trains also link up at Harwich with ferries that are headed for The Netherlands, Germany, or Scandinavia; for these connections, board at the Liverpool Street station.

The variety and availability of rail connection options is almost overwhelming in London. Several railway companies operate passenger trains in the city, most of which also link up with the Tube. For more specific and up-to-date information, check locally.

United Kingdom

The urban districts of Glasgow, Cardiff, Manchester, Liverpool, and Birmingham also have extensive local rail services.

URBAN / METRO

There are metro systems in London, Liverpool, Newcastle, and Glasgow. London and Glasgow's are very old, inaugurated in 1863 and 1896, respectively. The metro in Newcastle-upon-Tyne, on the other hand, dates only from 1980.

London's metro is known popularly as the Tube, or the Underground. It is a vast system and can get you just about anywhere you want to go in the city at an economical price. Prepare for narrow, clanking cars, which are not particularly comfortable to use if one has to stand, which may prove more likely than not in the inner-city crush. Certain stations seem endless to traverse depending on your choice of exit. Most exit points are marked by street name or location for easier navigation of the subterranean network. A London Underground map will serve the traveler well. Maps are normally posted in all stations and prove easy to use.

The London Visitor Travelcard is one of the best deals going. It provides for unlimited travel on both underground and buses, as well as connecting surface rail within specified zones. It gives the traveler access to the entire system, including river travel on the Thames, at a fixed price, any time of day. It also means no standing "in queue" for tickets or grappling for exact change. One may procure the Travelcard through London Travel, the parent organization for bus, tube, and river services. For information on maps, fares, and timetables, visit their website:
London Transport .... www.londontransport.co.uk/

BUSES & TRAMS

Virtually all cities and towns in Great Britain have bus services. Efficiency and cost vary. London's fabled red double-decker buses are a wonderful way to get around allowing one to see the sights while in transit.

Express coaches offer service to every part of the country. Many of these have on-board toilets, food, and video displays.

Private coach charters can also be arranged by groups. They can be booked in advance, and stop at most major attractions, many of which now have coach terminals nearby. The primary carrier is National Express.

All major cities have a coach terminus. In London, it is Victoria Coach station, approximately 1km (0.7 miles) away from the train station. British Airways offers a bus shuttle service from both Gatwick and Heathrow airports to Belfast, Edinburgh, Glasgow, and Manchester. For local service, Manchester has also recently inaugurated a modern tram system.

WATER TRAVEL

England is awash in a sea of ferry connections linking it with other countries, as well as having many domestic links carrying the traveler to Scotland, Northern Ireland, Wales, and Ireland. One will do best to contact the ferry companies locally, by contacting U.K. Public Transport Information in advance of travel:
U.K. PTI .... www.pti.org.uk/

This website provides links for all ferry services that have websites as well as links for express coach, rail, and air travel operations.

In terms of channel crossings, the shortest hop is between Dover or Folkestone (U.K.) and Calais or Boulogne (France). P & O Steamline offers service for cars and drivers (£60-130, depending on date and time) or passengers on foot (£24). The company also offers group fares, and special rates for motorcycles.

Hoverspeed offers the fastest water crossing available at 35 minutes port-to-port, utilizing both hovercraft and high-speed catamarans. Cars and drivers £47-90, passengers only £25. Group fares are also available.

Both P&O and Hoverspeed operate every one to two hours, weather permitting.
P&O Steam Line.. 0990-980980
Hoverspeed Fast Ferries........................... 0870-240 8070
.... www.hoverspeed.co.uk
Other connections and services:

To Spain, from Portsmouth:
Brittany Ferries.. 0990-360360
P&O.. 0990-980666

To Scandinavia, from various ports:
P&O... 01244-572615
Color Line (Norwegian) 0191-2961313
Scandinavian Seaways 0990-333000

To Germany, from various ports:
Sally Direct 0845-6002626
Scandinavian Seaways 0990-333000
P&O... 1244-572615

To Ireland:
P&O Stena 01233-647047
A large selection of other ferry transport to Ireland also exists.

Note: This list is not exhaustive, but it will give visitors a start. Travelers are advised to check locally for additional ferry services. Ferry connections are also available to the Channel Islands, the Isle of Wight, the Scilly Isles and the Isle of Man. Further information on these connections can be found at: www.travelbritain.com/UKPassengerFerries.

TRAVEL ASSISTANCE

Association of British Chambers of Commerce
tel: (0171) 565 2000; fax: (0171) 565 2049
website: www.britishchambers.org.uk
British Tourist Authority and English Tourist Board
tel: (0181) 846 9000; fax: (0181) 563 0302
email: 010657.335@compuserve.com
website: www.visitbritain.com
British Travel Centre
12 Lower Regent Street, London SW1
Opening hours:
 9:00a.m.- 6:30p.m. Monday to Friday
 10:00a.m.- 4:00p.m.Saturday and Sunday
 Personal visits only
Scottish Tourist Board (Edinburgh)
tel: (0131) 332 2433; fax: (0131) 343 1513
website: www.holiday.scotland.net
Wales Tourist Board (Cardiff)
tel: (01222) 499 909; fax: (01222) 485 031
website: www.tourism.gov.uk
Northern Ireland Tourist Board (Belfast)
tel: (01232) 231 221; fax: .... (01232) 240 960

Hotel Accommodations
British Hospitality Association .... (020) 7499-6641

Communications

DIALING CODES IN THE UNITED KINGDOM

International country code: [44]

Selected city codes: Belfast (028), Birmingham (0121), Bournemouth (1202), Cardiff (029), Coventry (024), Durham (0191), Edinburgh (0131), Glasgow (0141), Gloucester (1452), Ipswich (1473), Liverpool (0151), London (020), Manchester (0161), Portsmouth (023), Southampton (023).

Dialing the United Kingdom from Overseas

To dial the United Kingdom from overseas, dial your country's international dialing code, then 44 (the country code for the United Kingdom), then the city code and finally the number. If you were dialing Birmingham from the United States, for example, you would begin with 011, then 44, then 121 (the city code for Birmingham), and finally the number of the person or office you were trying to reach.

Assistance Numbers

Britain Directory Assistance	192
International Operator	155
International Directory Assistance	153
London Directory Assistance	142
Telecom Operator	100

CALLING WITHIN THE UNITED KINGDOM

British Telecom (BT) is the major telecommunication service in the country. Making calls is extremely simple. Most BT services are expensive; make directory assistance calls from a public telephone—they're free that way. England will change city codes as of April 2000; areas involved in the changeover include: London, Cardiff, Coventry, Northern Ireland, Portsmouth, and Southhampton. London's previous area codes for inner and outer districts were (171) and (181) respectively. Callers should note that both area codes have changed to (020) and the former middle digit of each area code has been moved to prefix the local numbers. Thus, if you previously dialed (171) 234-5678, you would now dial (020) 7234-5678. The same rings true for a (181) number. Previously (181) 987-6543, the new number would read (020) 8987-6543.

Long Distance Calls

Where local calls are charged by time, national calls are charged by time and distance. For substantial savings, call between 6p.m. and 8a.m., Monday to Friday and midnight Friday to midnight Sunday.

Internal calls outside of a region are cheapest before 8a.m. or after 6p.m. during the week.

International Calls

Direct calling is the most cost-effective way to call out of Great Britain. You can do it with a high-denomination phone card. Dial 00 (then wait for dial tone or announcement) + country code + area code + number. As anywhere else, if you opt to call direct from your hotel, expect exorbitant surcharges.

U.S. AT&T	0800-890-011
U.S. MCI	0800-890-222
U.S. Sprint	0800-890-877

PAY PHONES

Public Telephones

Card Phone:

The famous red booths have nearly disappeared, replaced by glass cubicles of two types: one takes money the other cards. All phones are relatively simple to use.

The public telephones will be marked, telling the user exactly what type of payment the payphone accepts (prepaid calling card or coins).

Calling Cards

Buying a British Telecom (BT) phonecard is far and away the most convenient way to make public phone calls. They can be purchased at just about all convenience stores as well as post offices and hotels. These cards come in increments of £2, £4, and £10. Telephone cards offer the cheapest option for placing long distance calls.

CELLULAR PHONES

Several cellular service providers exist in the United Kingdom. Cellnet and Vodafone are major service providers offering ETACS for analogue users and GSM for digital. Other companies that also offer GSM service include Manx Telecom, Jersey Telecoms, Orange, One2One, and Guernsey Telecoms.

Cellnet; tel: (0990) 214-000; http://www.cellnet.co.uk/.

Orange; tel: (500) 802-080; http://www.uk.orange.net/index.html

Vodafone; tel: 0836-1191; http://www.vodafone.co.uk/.

Note: Your home country cell phone may not work in this country. If not, we recommend that you rent an international cell phone *before* you leave home. A major US-based cell phone rental provider is **IMC WorldCell**. For information see "International Cell Phone Rentals" on page 14.

CALL BACK

You can (potentially) save significant sums when calling in the United Kingdom by using one of the call back services listed in the "Communications" section in the *Global Road Warrior* Introduction. Fees for call back services vary widely, depending on the company and the type of service required. Be sure to check with these companies before leaving to compare rates.

PHONE JACKS

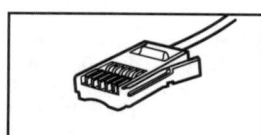

Plug adaptors are available through **iGo Corporation.** (See "Electrical and Telephone Adaptors" on page 19.)

FAX

Fax machines are just about everywhere. Most hotels offer fax services for their guests; top-end hotels may have a fax machine in the guest rooms.

POSTAL SERVICES

All post boxes are red. International postal connections are among the best in the world. One may procure stamps from post offices and shops.

An average letter sent to most parts of Europe costs around 26p. The cost to send a letter most anywhere else is around 43p.

Hours of service

Monday to Friday 9a.m. to 5:30p.m., Saturday 9a.m. to 12:30p.m.

TELEGRAMS

Telegrams can be sent from most hotels and post offices. There is a telemessage system setup in London that can be useful to travelers interested in sending a telegram. Telemessage Service....................................0800-190-190

Business Services

BUSINESS CENTERS

London

Business Centre; Stanbrook House, 2-5 Old Bond Street, Mayfair, W1X 3TB; Tube: Green Park; tel: (020) 7499-9199; fax: (020) 7499-7517; fully serviced offices; secretarial service; fax; telex.

The External Office; 15 Diana Road, London - E17 5LE; tel: 298-6746; fax: 523-5586; email: info@external-office.co.uk; www.external-office.co.uk/about.htm;Word processing, audio, transcription, desk top publishing, translation services, CV service, fax and scanning service, web site design, secretarial, general office duties, collection & delivery; hours: 7days a week, 24 hours.

May Fair Business Centre; May Fair Inter-Continental hotel, Stratton Street, W1A 2AN; tel: (020) 7914-2889; fax: (020) 7629-1459; Tube: Green Park; Monday to Friday 8a.m. to 6p.m.; secretarial service; fax; photocopy; translation; a/v; computer/telephone/dictation machine hire; meeting and conference rooms.

Select Business Centre; Select House, 138 Brompton Road, SW3 1HY; Tube: Knightsbridge; tel: (020) 7581-9510; fax: (020) 7584-9310; Monday to Friday 9:30a.m to 5:30p.m.

COMPUTER RENTAL

London

Business Systems Group; Business Design Center; 52 Upper St.; Islington Green; tel: (020) 7359-7778.

Micro-Rent; Chillingworth Road, Islington N7 8QJ; Tube: Holloway Road; tel: (020) 7700-4848; fax: (020) 7607-5102; Monday to Friday 9a.m. to 5p.m.

Vernon Computer Rentals; Unit 7, 142 Battersea Park Road, SW11 4NB; Tube: Battersea Park; tel: (020 7720-7000; fax: (020) 7720-9656; Monday to Friday 9a.m. to 5p.m.

COPYING/PRINTING SERVICES

Birmingham

Copy+Type+Print; tel: (121) 236-7531.

Prontaprint; tel: (121) 236-2255.

London

Panopus; 1 Baldwin Terrace Islington, London, N17RU; tel: (020) 7354-1568 fax: (020) 7359-2308; email: rayvin@panopus.com; http://www.panopus.com/.

Prorepro; tel: (020) 439-7853; tel: 07000 4 PRO REPRO; 75 Berwick Street, London, W1V 3PF; fax: (020) 734-1083; 22 Dering Street, London, W1R 9AA; fax: (020) 629-6923; http://www.prorepro.com.

Western Printers; 103 Cleveland Street, London W1P 5PN; tel: (020) 631-5225; fax: (020) 323-6512; email: sales@western-printers.co.uk; http://www.western-printers.co.uk/.

COURIER SERVICES

Birmingham

DX Express; tel: (121) 454-2479.

Expressway; tel: (121) 454-0813.

Edinburgh

DHL; Unit 15/4 n 15/5 South Gyle; Crescent; South Gyle Industrial Estate; Edinburgh; EH12-9EB; Open Monday to Friday 8:30am to 7pm, Saturday 9a.m. to 12p.m., Closed Sunday Holidays

London

Airborne Express; Unit 2, Heathrow Intl. Trading Estate, Hounslow, Middlesex TW4 6HB; tel: (020) 8899-9876; fax: (181) 899-9875.

DHL International (UK) Ltd.; Orbital Park; 178-188 Great South West Road; Hounslow; TW4 6JS; toll free: 0345-100300; tel: (020) 8818-9900; web site: http://www.dhl.co.uk; Mon. to Fri. 9a.m. to 5:30p.m., closed Sat., Sun., and holidays;

DHL; Docklands; Unit 24, Mastmaker Court; Mastmaker Road; London; E14 9UB; Mon. to Fri. 8:30a.m. to 6:30p.m., closed Sat. Sun. and holidays

DHL; WTB Express Centre; 3-4 Great Chapel Street; London; W1V 3AG; Mon. to Fri. 8:30a.m. to 8p.m., closed Sat., Sun. and holidays.

Federal Express; toll-free: 0800-123-800; tel: (0)1203 637637; Mon. to Fri. 7:30a.m. to 7:30p.m.; For collections, information or to request a booking call 0800-289-747 Mon. to Fri. 8:30am to 6pm; Invoice enquiries: 0800-123-888.

TNT Express Worldwide; Unit 9 Trident Way International Trading Estate, Southall, Middlesex UB2 5LF; tel: (020) 8574-1414; fax: (20) 8813-9103.

UPS; UPS House, Feltham, Middlesex, TW13 7D4; tel: (020) 8844-1122; fax: (181) 844-2810 or (020) 8384-3363; toll free customer service: 0800-456-789 or 034-587-7877.

SECRETARIAL SERVICES

A & S Consultants; 2 Skelforde Court, 217-219 St. John Street, EC1V 4LY; Tube: Angel; tel: (020) 7490-1528; fax: (020) 7490-1541; Monday to Friday 9a.m. to 5:30p.m.

Angela Pike Associates; Le Meridien Hotel, 21 Piccadilly, W1V 9PF; Tube: Piccadilly; tel: (020) 7434-4425; fax: (020) 7493-7533; Monday to Friday 8a.m. to 5p.m.

London Secretarial Bureau; 267 West Green Road, London, N15 3BH United Kingdom tel: (0208) 802-6646; tel: (07956) 372-686; tel: (0771) 200-1809; fax: (0208) 211-8983; email: d.johnson@cableinet.co.uk.

Outsourced Typing Services; 21 Wigmor Street, London, W1H 9LA; tel: (020) 499-0469; fax: (020) 499-0453; http://www.typing.co.uk.

PRIME Secretarial Services; 483 Green Lanes Palmers Green, London, N13 4BS England; tel: (020) 8882-6719 fax: (020) 8882-8485; email: info@prime-secretarial.co.uk

The External Office; 15 Diana Road - London - E17 5LE tel: (0800) 298-6746; (0181) 523-4343; fax: (0181) 523-5586; email info@external-office.co.uk.

Way With Words; 27b The Market Place, London NW11; tel: 0800-917-4962; fax: (020) 8365-2550; 24 hours, 7 days a week; http://move.to/waywithwords.

TRANSLATION SERVICE

AA MP Translating & Interpreting Ltd.; Southbank House, Black Prince Road, London, SE17SJ; tel: (0800) 137-572; fax: (0800) 413-676; http://www.mptrans.demon.uk/.

Aplomb Translations; 74 Chancery Lane, Holborn, London, WC2A1AA; tel: (020) 831-9444; http://www.aplombarama.com/.

1st Accurate Translations; 162-168 Regent Street, London, W1R 5TB; tel: (020) 734-2955; fax: (020) 287-5744; http://www.accuratetranslations.co.uk.

1st World Language Consultants Ltd.; Panton House, Panton Street, London, SW1Y 4EN; tel: (020) 930-3842; fax: (020) 925-2746; http://www.world-language.com/.

0800 1st Translation Co., International Translation Centre; 24 Holborn Viaduct, London, EC1A 2BN; tel: (020) 329-0108; fax: (020) 329-0035; http://www.1st-translation-co.com.

The Institute of Translation & Interpreting; 377 City Road, EC1V 1NA; tel: (020) 7713-7600; fax: 9020) 7713-7650; Monday to Friday, 9a.m. to 6p.m.; provides list of registered translators/interpreters by language.

Language Line; 18 Victoria Park Square, E2 9PF; ubteroretersL (020) 8981-9911; admin. tel: (020) 8983-4042; fax: (020) 8983-3598; tube: Bethnal Green; open 24 hours; telephone interpreter service.

Saint George International; 4 Duke Street, W1M 5AA; tel: (020) 7486-5481; fax: (020) 7224-1245; Tube: Bond Street; 9a.m. to 5p.m.

Electrical

Current
240 volts AC, 50Hz.

ELECTRICAL SOCKET
Square 3-pin plugs are standard.

ELECTRIC PLUGS

Plug adaptors are available through **iGo Corporation.** (See "Electrical and Telephone Adaptors" on page 19.)

Technical Support
HARDWARE/SOFTWARE VENDOR SUPPORT

Acer/Texas Instruments; tel: (01753) 487-000; (in Germany) tel: [49] (4102) 488-469; fax; [49] (4102) 488-169; (in the U.S.) [1] (408) 432-6200; http://www.acer.com/.

Adobe; tel: 131-451-6888; fax: 458-6972; tel: (161) 374-4000; fax: (161) 374-1000 (All Frame Products); (in Switzerland) tel: [41] (800) 833-310; (in the U.S.) tel: [1] (800) 500-7078; (in the U.S.) tel: [1] (716) 633-3600; http://www.adobe.com/.

Apple/Claris; tel: (990) 127-753; (in Germany) tel: [49] (1) 803-5018; (in Switzerland) tel: [41] (800) 833-310; (in the U.S.) tel: [1] (800) 500-7078; http://www.apple.com/.

AST; (in the U.S.) tel: [1] (817) 232-9824 (International Technical Support); (in Ireland) tel: [353] (61) 492-222; (in the U.S.) tel: [1] (949) 727-4141; http://www.ast.com/.

Compaq/Digital; tel: (181) 332-3000; fax: (181) 332-3409; (181) 332-3888 (CompaqCare Center); tel: (181) 332-9499 (QuickLine); fax: (181) 332-3550 (FaxPaq); (General U.S.) tel: (281) 518-2000; http://www.compaq.com/.

Corel; tel: (0171) 298-8515 (Corel Corporation); (in the U.S.) tel: [1] (716) 871-2325 (Ask to be Forwarded to Appropriate Program); http://www.corel.com/.

Dell; tel: (0870) 908-0800; fax: (1) 286-2020; (Dell-Europe) tel: [44] (134) 474-8000; (in the U.S.) tel: [1] (512) 338-4400; fax: [1] (512) 728-3330; http://www.dell.com/.

Filemaker/Claris; tel: (0845) 603-9100; (in Germany) tel: [49] (180) 525-8166 (Info-line); fax: [49] (180) 567-2233; tel: [49] (180) 523-6423; (in the U.S.) tel: [1] (800) 965-9090; http://www.claris.com/.

Gateway 2000; (in the U.S.) tel: [1] (605) 232-2191; (in the U.S.) tel: [1] (605) 232-2191; fax: [1] (605) 232-2023; http://www.gateway2000.com/.

Hewlett Packard; tel: (0207) 512-5202; (in Switzerland) tel: [41] (22) 780-8111; (in the U.S.) tel: [1] (408) 246-4300; http://www.hp.com/.

IBM; tel: (0990) 426-426; (in the U.S.) tel: [1] (919) 517-2800; (U.S. Main Office) tel: [1] 914-765-1900; http://www.ibm.com/.

Microsoft; tel: (0870) 501-0100; fax: (0870) 602-0100; (in Switzerland) tel: [41] (848) 858-868; fax [41] (1) 831-0869; (in the U.S.) [1] (425) 635-7222; http://www.microsoft.com/.

NEC; tel: 01-838-1216 (Ultracare Support); (in the U.S.) [1] (916) 388-0101 (Main Switchboard); http://www.nec.com/.

Novell; (in Germany) tel: [49] (211) 563-2777 (System support); tel: [49] (6196) 904-477; fax: [49] (211) 563-2772; (in Switzerland) tel: [41] (1) 308-4747; fax: [41] (1) 302-0401; (in the U.S.) tel: [1] (408) 434-2300; fax: [1] (408) 577-5775 (Worldwide Sales Headquarters); http://www.novell.com/.

Quark; tel: (1483) 445-566; fax: (1483) 445-544; (in the U.S.) tel: [1] (303) 894-8899; fax: [1] (303) 894-3398 (For Products Registered in the Americas); http://www.quark.com/.

Toshiba; (U.K. wide enquiries) tel: (01932) 828-828; (in Germany) tel: [49] (2131) 158-319; fax: [49] (2131) 158-558; (in Switzerland) tel: [41] (1) 946-0777; fax: [41] (1) 946-0807; (in Ireland) tel: [44] (193) 282-8828; (in the U.S.) [1] (949) 583-3000 (Corporate Headquarters); http://www.toshiba.com/.

Internet Connection
HOW TO CONNECT

Connecting to AOL and Compuserve in the United Kingdom is similar to using it when traveling outside your own area code. See the introductory section for detailed information on connecting to your account through a different phone number.

America Online

Numbers are available at keyword *international*. Be sure to get several local numbers before leaving. AOL has a new GlobalNet service that charges US$6 an hour in addition to the usual charges. Go to keyword *access* (a free area) and download the software.

Access: all areas 0845-079-8744, 0845-301-0102, 0845-845-7445.

Compuserve

Numbers are available at *Go International*. If you are using CompuServe 2000, use GO PHONES within CompuServe 2000 to search for access numbers. The Compuserve Web-site also has a great deal of information, at http://www.compuserve.com/.

Access: all areas (845) 080-1000.

Independent Service Providers

Many independent service providers offer discounts if you are only in town for a couple of days.

Abel Internet; tel: (131) 445-5555; fax: (131) 447-7131; email: support@abel.co.uk; http://www.abel.co.uk/.

Demon; tel: (845) 272-0666; fax: (845) 8371-1150; email: enquiries@demon.net; http://www.demon.net/.

Easinet Limited; tel: (115) 946-9930; fax: (115) 946-9940; sales@easinet.co.uk; http://www.easinet.co.uk/.

Masterweb / Agnet; tel: (1284) 850-469; fax: (1284) 850-428; email: webmaster@agnet.co.uk; http://www.agnet.co.uk/.

Micronet Communications; tel: (20) 7691-7046; fax: (84) 5333-6481; email: sales@micronet.net; http://www.micronet.net/.

VAS-NET; tel: (0800) 389-0070; fax: (1732) 861-616; email: @vas-net.net; http://www.vas-net.net/.

Zoo Internet; tel: (0870) 750-0966; fax: (0870) 752-1234; email: sales@zoo.net.uk; http://www.zoo.net.uk/.

Business Culture
GREETINGS AND COURTESIES

The U.K. has some of the most polite people on earth. But this is not to say that they are informal. In the business community it is considered bad form to address anyone by a first name unless true familiarity has been established. The correct forms of address include Mr., Mrs., Miss, Dr., Professor, Colonel, etc., followed by the last name. Someone who as been knighted is addressed as, for example, Sir John Ferguson or Sir John but never Sir Ferguson. His wife, however, would be addressed as Lady Ferguson without using the first name.

Shaking hands is the standard form of greeting throughout the U.K. Always wait for a woman to extend her hand first. Business cards are exchanged at meetings but not given the formal treatment seen in Asia. An exchange of gifts might take place (especially with Asian visitors), but, in general, the British do not expect business gifts. If gift-giving is your preferred method of showing appreciation, keep it tasteful and modest.

The British tend to be conservative and suspicious of extremes. They do not appreciate emotional or overtly enthusiastic displays, but prefer calm reserve in both behavior and emotion.

BUSINESS ETHIC AND FRAMEWORK

Corporate offices throughout the United Kingdom are formal and third party introductions are important. Most senior corporate executives comprise a tightly knit network and it can be difficult to penetrate. The British are reluctant to deal with individuals or corporations with whom they are unfamiliar. Gaining access by way of top bank officials, accounting firms, or introductions by members of the diplomatic corps may be helpful. Self-introduction letters, when used, should include appropriate background materials, proper references, and a clear statement of intent. Advance appointments are essential. Unlike the U.S., cold calls and drop-ins are considered impolite.

The British have been global traders for many centuries and they know the value of honest dealings. British contracts are tight and equitable with lots of legal protection for all parties. Though not as litigious as their American cousins, the British are not afraid to turn their lawyers (barristers) loose if they think they have been poorly treated by a foreign partner.

DECISION MAKING

Depending on whether a visitor is dealing with one of the older British firms or one of the new technology or finance groups will determine the decision making process. Older firms tend towards the hierarchical method and often such firms are structured around a family unit. This slow, deliberative method is used throughout continental Europe and it works fine for most industrial units. It does take a lot longer, so patience will be required.

British tech firms, financial groups, and those servicing these fast-paced companies have "flattened" their hierarchies. Authority is dispersed throughout many ranks of management and lower level staff are permitted to make important decisions worth millions of pounds. Sandwiched in between Europe and the United States, decision making processes in the U.K. reflect that positioning. Foreign firms will have to take it on a case-by-case basis.

MEETINGS

Meetings open and close with polite courtesies and informal conversation. Handshakes and cards are exchanged as introductions proceed from upper to lower ranks. Foreign sellers should be prepared to deliver details and facts, presented in a logical format. The British prefer a soft, understated sales presentation as opposed to aggressive hard-sell tactics. Answer questions directly and with as much information or statistics as are available on your topic.

Note: When the British are in a selling mode, counterparts can expect a great deal of Old World charm and socializing as part of business meetings.

Though an advance agenda and other materials should be in place before the scheduled meeting, bring extra copies (if your firm is running the meeting) just in case. Additionally, immediately follow up your meeting with a letter outlining points discussed and how you intend to proceed with your proposal.

Note: English is the recognized language of international business. Though the British do produce many linguists, foreign firms that are selling in the U.K. should have all of their materials translated in advance.

BUSINESS ENTERTAINING

The British are exceptionally charming hosts, and they know how to put visitors at ease. Cocktails or a few pints after business meetings are the prelude to friendly dining. Contrary to popular belief, most U.K. cities have exceptionally good food. Virtually any cuisine is available and special dietary needs of visitors can be accommodated.

Dinner table talk can cover a wide range of topics and the British are very appreciative of a good conversationalist. If it is a large dinner party, seating may be arranged to provoke stimulating repartee.

Note: Business may be discussed at breakfasts or luncheons but rarely at dinner.

Besides dining, weekends at country estates, hunting trips, sightseeing tours, a day at the races, or an evening at the theater may all be part of British business entertaining. It will all exude charm, sophistication, and social grace. Whether buying or selling, the British like to remind foreign counterparts that they have been at this international business game a long time.

Note: When reciprocating, do not attempt to outdo the British on their own turf. If possible, steer them towards your own national cuisine and use venues they may not be familiar with in their own entertaining. Far from offending them, showing them something new will add to the effect.

WOMEN IN BUSINESS

British women now comprise 45 percent of the workforce, and their numbers are growing in both the public and private sector. Women are advancing to management positions in the U.K. and can be found in corporate executive positions. Women are competitive in business and are taken very seriously.

Note: Visitors from societies where women have a secondary role should not assume that all the women at British business meetings are lower level staff. This will not only offend the host company but demonstrate the visitor's lack of knowledge about the modern U.K. marketplace.

BUSINESS ATTIRE

Dark or pinstripe suits of quality fiber are appropriate for men. Make sure the suit is well tailored. Pay special attention to the tie you wear, as striped ties, depending on their colors, may well depict membership in a private club or school. Laced shoes rather than loafers are worn in business. Women should wear suits that are stylish but conservative and tailored to fit. Low necklines, short skirts or slacks are inappropriate forms of attire. Jewelry for both sexes should be simple and elegant.

Note: The above applies primarily to the older corporate atmosphere. High-tech firms in the U.K. have adopted the corporate casual look of America's Silicon Valley. One can even find bedraggled programmers wandering about in cutoffs and t-shirts. It will be some time before such informality reaches the major corporations.

Business Advisory

POLITICS & GRAFT

Occasionally some member of Parliament will get caught taking money for some less than important reason, but the U.K. is not very prone to graft at high or low levels. Foreign firms should have no problems with being approached for bribes. When bribery does occur it is usually because business has approached government and not the other way around.

BUSINESS FRAUD

The U.K.'s lengthy history in international business has taught it that honest dealing is the best for long-term growth. As mentioned earlier, British contracts are detailed but equitable. All signatories are expected to make good faith efforts to fulfill the contract requirements.

Business Centers
London
CITY VIEW

London is the largest city in Europe. At times it is more spectacular than words could describe, at others it is simply dreary, foggy, and expensive. London offers the visitor most anything, except perhaps fresh air. Dark colors will provide the most protection from the black soot and pollution residue that seems to creep onto all surfaces, including one's attire. With the London Underground running most everywhere in the city, getting around does not pose a problem in this massive metropolis. From working class to avant garde, from international to distinctly British, the multitude of districts in the city point to all corners of the earth. Tourism plays a giant role in the city's economy with Heathrow Airport named the busiest in the world. If overwhelmed with the thought of such population masses, take a cup of tea and relax as best as possible in the unperturbed British way. Plenty of parks and greenery surface within the concrete, including the giant Hyde Park in the center of the city. With museums and other cultural sights of interest sprinkled throughout the city, one would be hard-pressed for boredom. As the saying goes, "when one is tired of London, one is tired of life."

AIRPORT
Heathrow Airport to City Center

The airport is linked to London by the underground railway network, otherwise known as "the Tube", allowing quick access to and from the city. The new Heathrow Express bullet train offers far and away the best method to get into town. With a travel time of only 20 minutes from Terminal 4, and 15 minutes from the other terminals, business travelers may rejoice. Passengers are whisked to London's Paddington Station where they can connect to the subway or hail a cab outside. The Express runs between 5:30a.m. and 11:45p.m. in 15-minute intervals. Naturally, one can expect to pay more (about £10 for regular class, and double for first class) for the express service. Other Heathrow rail links running in 15-minute intervals from St. Pancras through West Hampstead and Ealing are also scheduled. Check the following website for further details:
Heathrow Express ....www.heathrowexpress.co.uk

As for regular underground service, many will be happy to know it still services the airport for the most economical prices. The Piccadilly line operates between 6a.m. and midnight and takes passengers to central London where they can transfer or hail a cab. Trains depart about every 10 minutes, except during peak hours, when they run about every 4 minutes. The trip will take about 45 minutes. Follow signs for 'the Tube' in the airport to make your way underground.

Airbuses 1 and 2 offer a doubledecker experience to Victoria Rail Station and the Euston Rail Station respectively with frequent stops at main hotels in downtown London. Have some time on your hands, as the trip takes between an hour and an hour and a half. Buses depart every 30 minutes.

United Kingdom

Other buses also service the airport as do the Black Cabs. For a cost of about £30, a taxi will take you into town and arrive in the time it takes the traffic to move—from 30 minutes to an hour. Private taxi companies may be called if going to parts of greater London.

Gatwick Airport

Gatwick lies 27 miles (43km.) from the city center. The Gatwick Express train offers the best way into town and drops passengers at Victoria Station. Passengers from the north terminal may catch a free shuttle to the train station. Those at the south terminal can walk. Expect a 30-minute ride into town. Trains depart in 15-minute intervals between 6:50a.m. and 8:50p.m. and less frequently during the night. Purchase tickets at the windows in the station.

British Rail also serves Gatwick for a few dollars less and a few minutes more. It also arrives at Victoria Station. For those seeking an alternative station, try the Thameslink or another British Rail train service.

Taxis also service the airport for a much higher fee (£40-45) and take from 40 to 90 minutes for the trip into town. Transfer buses also go to Heathrow Airport. Expect a travel time of an hour. Tourist information booths in the terminal will provide transportation information.

Airline Numbers

Aer Lingus .... (020) 8899 4747; fax: 8745 4848
Aeroflot .... (020) 7355 2233; fax: 8759 0579
Air Canada .... (020) 8759 2636; fax 8897 1331
Air France....................... (020) 8742 6600; fax: 8759 1818
Air India .... (020) 7368 4828; fax: 7745 1000
Air Mauritius ....(020) 7434 4375
.... fax: 7759 1818
Air New Zealand...............................(020) 8846 9595
.... fax: 01426 915500
Air UK .... 0345 666 777; fax: 01279 662 882
Alitalia........................... 0990 074074; fax: 0990 074074
American .... 0345 7897890; fax: 181-572 5555
ANA .... (020) 77355 1155; fax: 7355 1155
British Airways..................... 0345 22211;1fax: 8759 2525
British Midland................................ 0345 554 554
.... fax: (020) 8745 7321
Canadian..................... (020) 8577 7722; fax: 8577 7722
Cathay Pacific ....(020) 7747 8888
.... fax: (020) 8745 7731
Continental .... 01293 776 464; fax: 01293 535 353
Delta AirLines 0800 414 767
.... fax:01293-548774
Emirates .... (020) 7808 0808; fax: 7808 0808
Gulf Air .... (020) 7408 1717; fax: 01426 910 327
Iberia .... (020) 8830 0011; fax: 8897 7941
Japan Airlines 0345 747700
.... fax:87591234
KLM .... 0990 750900; fax: 0990 750900
Kuwait Airways .... (020) 7412 0007; fax: 7745 7772
Lufthansa........................... 0345 737 747; fax: 8750 3300
Malaysia .... (020) 7 341 2020; fax: 8897 4464
Northwest .... 01293 561 000; fax: 01293 535 353
Olympic Airways...............................(020) 7409 3400
.... fax: 7897 3355
Philippine...............(020) 7499 9446; fax: (020) 8759 8636
Qantas........................ 0345 767 767; fax: 01426 910 020
Royal Brunei...(020) 7584 6660
.... fax: 0990-111 666
Royal Jordanian ....(020) 7734 2557
.... fax: 8897 8319
Ryanair........................ 0541 569 569; fax: 0541 569 569
SAS .... (020) 7734 4020; fax: 01426 931 301
Saudia .... (020) 8995 7777; fax: 8745 4373

Singapore .... (020) 8747 0007; fax: 0990 111666
South African...(020) 7312 5000
....fax: 8897 3645
SwissAir......................... (020) 7434 7300; fax: 8745 7163
TAP Air .... (020) 7828 0262; fax: 8745 1818
TWA .... 0990 892892; fax: 01293 567 711
United Airlines 0845 8444747
....fax: 01426 915 500
Virgin Airlines 01293 747 747
....fax: 01293 511 581

Chartered Jets

Air Hanson Chartered Aircraft; Business Aviation Centre, Blackbushe airport, Camberley, Surrey GU17 9LG; tel: (01252-890-089; fax: 01252-860-287; 24 hours.
Gena Aviation Limited; Fairoaks Airport, Chobham, Woking, Surrey GU24 8HX; tel: 01276-856-961; fax: 01276-858-485; 24 hours.

HOTELS

Note: Last-minute London hotel bookings may be secured at a discount through Hotel! Hotel! No restrictions on advance bookings.

Hotel! Hotel! tel: (1372-464-488; fax: 1372-468-844; email: Hotel.Hotel@dial.pipex.com.

Top-end

Brown's Hotel (Raffles Intl.); 30 Albemarle Street; tel: (020) 7493-6020; fax: (020) 7493-9381; http://www.brownshotel.com; 188 rooms; restaurant; 5 meeting rooms (up to 120); business facilities; in-room minibar, modem access, safe, hairdryer, voicemail; 24-hour room service.

Claridge's; Brook St., London W1; tel: (020) 7629 8860; fax: (171) 499-2210; email: info@claridges.co.uk; restored; conference facilities (up to 1000); business services; in-room communications; chauffeur-driven Rolls Royce and Bentley cars available; Olympus health and fitness suite.

The Connaught; 16 Carlos Place, Mayfair; tel: (020) 7499-7070; fax: (020) 7495-3262; near Bond Street; 90 rooms; highly discreet service; restaurant; bar; conference facilities; technical facilities; parking.

The Berkeley; Wilton Place, Knightsbridge, London SW; tel: (020) 7235-6000; fax: (171) 235-4330; email: info@the-berkeley.co.uk; English traditional overlooking Hyde Park; restaurant; 7 private meeting and dining rooms; in-room fax machine, 2-liner telephone, voicemail, U.s. modem and plugs; chauffeur-driven Rolls Royce and Bentley for hire; underground garage; rooftop health club and spa, gym, pool.

Four Seasons London; Hamilton Place, Park Lane; tel: (020) 7499-0888. or 800/223-6800; fax: (171) 493-6629; located near Hyde Park; 2 restaurants; conference facilities (up to 400); business services; in-room 2-line phones, fax machine, computer hookup, voicemail; 24-hour rooms service; garage; fitness club for guests only.

London Hilton on Park Lane; 22 Park Lane (Tube: Hyde Park Corner); tel: (020) 7493-8000; fax: (020) 7208-4142; 446 rooms, 53 suites; Hilton's flagship hotel, renovated; overlooking Hyde Park; restaurants; bars; casino; 12 meeting rooms; ballroom (up to 1250); business center; in-room a/c, minibar; laundry; car rental; beauty parlor; parking; hairdresser; disabled facilities; health club overlooking Hyde Park; disco; golf course; voted best London business hotel by Business Traveler Magazine.

London Marriott County Hall; The County Hall; tel: (020) 7928-5200; fax: (020) 7928-5300; 200 rooms, adjacent Westminster Bridge, opposite Houses of Parliament;

restaurant; 8 meeting rooms; business center; secretarial service; executive floor; in-room work desk, voice mail, data ports, cable tv, all-news channel, newspaper, minibar, in-room coffee, a/c, iron & ironing board, trouser press, hairdryer, safe; 24-hour room service; hair salon/barber; laundry valet; health c0lub; full spa, indoor 25m pool.

The London Ritz; 150 Piccadilly, Mayfair; tel: (020) 7493-8181; fax: (171) 493-2687; email: enquire@theritzhotel.co.uk; 130 individually decorated rooms; restaurant; business center; meeting space; work stations; full office facilities; in-room voice mail, data ports, ISDN lines; barber; full gym.

The Savoy; The Strand; tel: (020) 7836-4343; fax: (171) 240-6040; email: info@the-savoy.co.uk; 207 rooms; overlooking the River Thames in theater district; near business district; personalized service; restaurants; meeting rooms; business services; in-room fax machine, 2-line telephones, voicemail, U.S. modem, ISDN lines; chauffeur driven Bentleys and Rolls Royce available; fitness; saunas; steam rooms; massage; rooftop pool.

Sheraton Park Tower; 101 Knightsbridge; tel: (020) 7235-8050; fax: (020) 7235-8231; 289 rooms; near Hyde Park; restaurants; coffee shop; meeting facilities; translation service; in-room a/c, black-out drapes, cable tv, voice mail, modem/fax connection, minibar, writing desk, sundries, hairdryer; barber shop/beauty salon; shop; massage; complimentary health club/spa/pool passes.

Le Meridien Waldorf; Aldwych; tel: (020) 7836-2400; fax: (171) 836-7244; 292 rooms; suites; Edwardian decor; 2 restaurants; conference facilities; secretarial service; in-room modem/fax connection, a/c, voicemail; 24-hour room service; corporate rates.

Expensive

Abbey Court; 20 Pembridge Gardens; tel: (020) 7221-7518; fax: (020) 7792-0858; 22 rooms; bed and breakfast; breakfast room; business services; in-room bath, tv, minibar; 24-hour room service; fitness.

Durrant's; George St.; tel: (020) 7935-8131; fax: (020) 7487-3510; 92 rooms; Georgian hotel; restaurants; bar; meeting facilities; business services; 24-hour room service; fitness.

Forte Posthouse Kensington; Wrights Lane, Kensington; tel: (020) 7937-8170; fax: (171) 387-2806; near railway station, restaurants/complimentary breakfast; bar; conference facilities (up t o 650); business center; in-room coffeemaker; non-smoking rooms available; parking; fitness; sauna; pool.

Forte Posthouse Regent's Park; Regent's Park, Carburton Street; tel: (020) 7388-2300; reservations, 1-800-543-4300; fax: (171) 387-2806; 326 rooms; renovated; restaurant; 11 soundproof meeting rooms (up to 300) with ISDN lines and data ports; 24-hour business center; parking.

Jarvis Embassy House; 312-33 Queen's Gate; tel: (020) 7584-7222; fax: (171) 589-3910; near city center, restaurant; bar; conference facilities (up to 24); corporate rates.

London Bridge Hotel; 8-18 London Bridge Street; tel: (020) 7855-2200; fax: (020) 7357-6475; 138 rooms; opposite London Bridge; restaurant; pub; in-room modem access, trouser presses, safe.

The London Outpost; 69 Cadogan Gardens; tel: (020) 7589-7333; fax: (020) 7581-4958; 11 rooms; bed and breakfast; 1 suite; all rooms with bath; conference facilities; in-room a/c, tv, minibar; 24-hour room service; health club.

Montague Hotel; 15 Montague Street, Bloomsbury; tel:

(020) 7636-1001; reservations, tel: (800-695-8284; fax: (020) 637-2516; renovated 1997; 104 rooms, some duplex suites; townhouse hotel adjacent British Museum; restaurant; bar/lounge; meeting facilities (up to 150); in-room fax/modem lines, direct dial phones, cable tv, coffee maker, hair dryer; 24-hour room service; spa.

Novotel London Waterloo; 113 Lambeth Road, London SE1; tel: (020) 7793-1010; reservations, 1-800-221-4542; fax: (171) 793-0202; near Waterloo Station, city center; restaurant/pub; 6 meeting rooms; translation services; room service; in-room black-out curtains; 24-hour fitness; sauna; steam room; showers and lockers.

Radisson Edwardian, the Berkshire; Oxford Street; tel: (020) 7629-7474; fax: (020) 7629-8156; reservations, United States: 800-333-3333; UK: 0800 37 4411; http://www.radissonedwardian.com/; restaurant; full English breakfast; conference facilities; non-smoking rooms, tea/coffee maker, direct dial telephone, trouser press, hairdryer, minibar; non-smoking rooms available; concierge.

Note: Radisson has 9 hotels in the London area: Marble Arch, Leicester Square, Covent Garden, Heathrow, Bloomsbury, Tottenham Court Rd., Kensington.

Stakis Islington; 53 Upper Street, Islington, London N1; tel: (020) 7354-7700; fax: (020) 7354-7711; email: reservations@stakis.co.uk; restaurant; bar; 4 boardrooms; hairdresser; adjacent health club with fitness; massage; sauna; solarium.

St. Martin's Lane; 45 St Martin's Lane, Covent Gardent; WC2N 4HX; tel: (20) 7300-5500; fax: (20) 7300-5501; Ian Schrager hotel located in the theater district; 204 rooms; restaurant; rooms with floor to ceiling windows.

Thistle Bloomsbury; Bloomsbury Way; tel: (020) 7242-5881; reservations, 800-847-4358; fax: (020) 7831-0225; 138 rooms; meeting facilities (up to 230); in-room cable tv, coffee maker, iron & ironing board, safe, a/c; non-smoking rooms available; self parking.

Moderate

Anna Hotel; 74 Queensborough Terrace; tel: (020) 7221-6622; reservations: 800-695-8284; fax: (171) 792-9656; near city center; complimentary breakfast; conference facilities; business center; secretarial service; in-room cable tv, hair dryer; car rental.

Beverly House Hotel; 142 Sussex Gardens, W2; tel: (020) 7723-3380; fax: (020) 7262-0324; near Paddington Station; 23 rooms; restaurant; bar; complimentary breakfast; in-room cable tv, hairdryer, safe; valet/laundry.

Comfort Inn Bayswater; 5-7 Princess Square, W2; tel: (020) 7792-1414; reservations, 800-695-8284; fax: (020) 7792-0099; 3 Victorian houses, 65 rooms; bar/lounge; complimentary breakfast; business center; in-room cable tv, coffee maker, hairdryer, iron & ironing board, safe; non-smoking rooms available; self parking; concierge.

Diplomat Hotel; 2, Chesham Street, Westminster SW1 (Tube: Sloane Square/Knightsbridge); Victorian townhouse, near Belgravia; business center; safe; in-room satellite tv, direct dial telephone, hair dryer, trouser press, ironing facilities; laundry/dry cleaning service.

Grand Plaza Hotel; 42 Princes Square, Bayswater; tel: (020) 7229-1292; fax: (171) 221-1172; 301 rooms; near city center; restaurant; bar; conference facilities; fax facilities; in-room direct dial telephone, cable tv, hairdryer; coffee/tea making facilities; porters; shops; currency exchange; newsstand.

Holiday Inn Express Victoria; 106-110 Belgrave Road, London SW1; tel: (020) 7730-8888; reservations, 1-800-465-4329; fax: (171) 828-0441; near Pimlico Station; 19th-

Century building; breakfast room; nearby business center on Buckingham Palace Road;

Ibis Euston; 3 Cardington Street, London NW1; tel: (020) 7388-7777; reservations, 1-800-221-4542; fax: (171) 388-0001; (Tube: Euston); 300 rooms; informal restaurant; bar; 4 meeting rooms (up to 100); secretarial service; in-room direct dial phones, satellite tv; non-smoking rooms available; secure underground parking.

Jury's London Inn; 60 Pentonville Road, Islington, London N1; tel: (020) 7282-5500; reservations, 800-843-3311; fax: (171) 282-5511; 229 rooms; near Business Design Center, Angels and King's Cross subway stations; restaurant/pub; spacious rooms with a/c, modem access, coffee/tea maker; views.

London Putney Bridge Travel Inn Capital; 3 Putney Bridge Approach, SW6; tel: (020) 7471-8300; fax: (020) 7471-8315; 154 rooms; restaurant; in-room coffee/tea maker.

Luna and Simone Hotel; 47-49 Belgrave Rd., Westminster SW1 (Pimlico); tel: (020) 7834-5897; fax: (020) 7828-2478; email: peter.desira@talk21.com; family-run hotel; in-room tv, phones, hair dryer; some rooms with shower and bath; English breakfast included.

New Atlantic Hotel; 1 Queens Gardens; tel: (020) 262-4471; 212 rooms; restaurant; bar; complimentary breakfast; business center; non-smoking rooms; parking.

Quality Hotel Paddington; 10 Talbot Square; tel: (020) 7262-6699; reservations, 800-695-8284; fax: (020) 7402-4848; 75 rooms; restaurant; bar; balconies; in-room cable tv, a/c, minibar, coffee maker, hair dryer, iron/ironing board, safe, data port; concierge; valet/laundry; self parking.

St. Giles Hotel; Bedford Ave., West End; tel: (020) 7300-3030; fax: (020) 7300-3003; 700 rooms; restaurant; bar; in-room coffee maker, hair dryer, safe; non-smoking rooms available; concierge; fitness center; spa; pool.

Swiss House; 171 Old Brompton Rd., SW5; tel: (020) 7373-2769; fax: (020) 7373-4983; email: recop@swiss-hh.demon.co.uk; bed and breakfast; in-room cable tv, telephone; most rooms with fireplaces; continental breakfast included.

HEATHROW AIRPORT HOTELS

Top-End

Hotel Excelsior; Bath road, West Drayton; tel: (0181) 759-6611; fax: (0181) 759-3421; 827 rooms; suites; Crown Club wing; restaurants; bars; conference facilities (up to 700); in-room satellite tv; hair salon; health club with gym, sauna, solarium, spa, pool.

London Heathrow Hilton; Terminal 4, London Heathrow Airport; tel: (020) 7759-7755; fax: (171) 759-7579; conference facilities; business c enter; free transfer to airport; car rental; parking; fitness; pool.

London Sheraton Skyline; Bath Road, Hayes, Middlesex; tel: (020) 7759-2535; fax: (171) 750-9150; near Heathrow Airport; restaurant; conference facilities; business center; car rental; parking; fitness.

Expensive

Forte Posthouse Heathrow Hotel; Heathrow Airport, Bath Road Hayes, Middlesex; tel (020) 7759-2552; fax: (171) 564-9265; located at Heathrow Airport, 186 rooms; restaurant; conference facilities (up to 50); secretarial service; fax/photocopy facilities; in-house pager; express check out; in-room minibar, hairdryer, trouser press; non-smoking rooms avail.; parking.

Novotel London Heathrow; Cherry Lane, West Drayton Midx; tel: (020) 7431-431; fax: (171) 431-221; near airport,

restaurant; conference facilities (up to 180); car rental; parking; pool.

Moderate

Hotel Ibis; 112-113 Bath Road, Hayes, Middlesex; tel: (020) 8759-4888; fax: (020) 8564-7894; 354 rooms; airport shuttle service.

GATWICK AIRPORT HOTELS

Top-End

London Gatwick Airport Hilton; Gatwick Airport, Gatwick; tel: (020) 7518-080; fax: (171) 528-980; restaurant; conference facilities; business center; car rental; parking; fitness; pool.

Expensive

Copthorne Effingham Park; West Park Road; tel: (020) 7714-994; fax; (171) 713-661; near Gatwick Airport; restaurant; conference facilities (up to 600); free transfer to airport; parking; fitness; sauna; pool; golf course.

Moderate

Forte Posthouse Gatwick; Povey Cross Road, Horley Surrey; tel: (020) 7771-621; fax: (171) 771-054; near airport; 210 rooms; 2 restaurants; conference facilities (up to 200); business services; 24-hour rooms service; laundry; babysitting; parking; pool; tennis; golf course.

MEDICAL CARE

Note: Police departments have a comprehensive list of health care providers in their area; your hotel concierge or front desk staff should also have a contact list on hand and the ability to direct you to a nearby establishment.

Charing Cross Hospital; Fulham Palace Road, W6 8RF; tel: (0181) 846-1234.

The Harley Street Clinic; 35 Weymouth Street, London WIN 4BJ; tel: 935-7700; fax: 487-4415.

The Portland Hospital for Women and Children; 209 Great Portland Street, London WIN 6AH; tel: 580-4400; fax: 390-8012.

St. Thomas' Hospital; Lambeth Palace Road SE1 7EH; tel: (0171) 928-9292

The Wellington Private Hospital; 8A Wellington Place, London NW 8 9LE; tel: 586-5959; fax: 586-1960.

University College London Hospitals; 25 Grafton Way, London WC1E 6DB; tel: 380-9964/380-9763; fax: 387-0421.

East London

Barking Hospital; Upney Lane Barking IG11 9LX tel: (0181) 594-3898.

Plaistow Hospital; Samson Street, Plaistow, E13 9EH; tel: (0181) 472-7001.

Greenwich

Brook General; Shooters Hill Road, Greenwich, SE18 4LW; tel: (0181) 856-5555

HEALTH CLUB

Archway Pool and Leisure Centre; MacDonald Road, N9; tel: (020) 7281-41-05.

Cannons Health Club; Endell Street, London WC2H 9SA; Tube: Covent Garden.

The Castle Climbing Centre; Green Lanes, Stoke Newington, London N4 2HA; (climbing wall); Tube: Manor House station; tel: 211-7000. **Paddington Sports Club**; Maida Vale; Tube: Maida Vale or Warwick Avenue; tel:286-8448.

N16 Fitness Centre; 46 Milton Grove, N16; tel: (020) 7249-0631.

Padington Sports Club; Maida Vale; Tube: Maida Vale or Warwick Avenue; tel:286-8448.

Picketts Lock Centre; Picketts Lock Lane; tel: (020) 8345-6666.

Porchester Turkish Baths; Porchester Road; tel: (020) 7792-2919.

The Sanctuary; 11 Floral Street; tel: (020) 7240-96-35 (for women only).

Seymour Leisure Centre; Seymour Place, W1; tel: (020) 7723-80-19.

Waterfront Leisure Centre; High Street, SE18; tel: (020) 8317-50-00.

Westside; 201-207 Kensington High Street; tel: (020) 7937-5386.

AUTO RENTAL

Avis; For central reservations, tel: (020) 8848-87-33; Mayfair branch, tel: 917-6700; reservations and information, 0990-900-500; hours 8:30a.m. to 6p.m. Monday to Friday, 9a.m. to 4p.m. Saturday.

Budget; For central reservations, (0800) 18-11-81; London reservations, 0800-626-063, 24 hours; nationwide reservations and information, (020) 8759-0056; desks at Heathrow, Gatwick, and Stansted Airport terminals.

Eurocar; For central reservations, (0345) 22-25-25; Victoria branch, tel: (020) 7834-8484.

Eurodollar; reservations and information, tel: 0895-233-300; 8a.m to 6p.m., Monday to Friday; 8a.m. to 1p.m., Saturday.

Hertz; For central reservations, tel: (0990) 99-66-99; Marble Arch branch; tel: (020) 7402-60-56.

London Limousine Company; Carriage House, Burrell Street, SE1; tel: (020) 7928-9280; fax: (020) 7928-6150; Monday to Friday 7a.m. to midnight; weekends, 8a.m. to 6p.m.; uniformed chauffeurs, a/c, telephones.

WORLD TRADE CENTER

World Trade Center London
6 Harbour Exchange Square
London E149GE
tel: (020) 7987-3456; fax: (020) 7987-3498

CHAMBER OF COMMERCE

London Chamber of Commerce
33 Queen St., London EC4R1AP
tel: (020) 7248-4444; fax: (020) 7498-0391

Edinburgh

CITY VIEW

Edinburgh is one of the largest cities in Scotland, and probably seems the least-Scottish, because of tourism and its proximity to England. However, its medieval history continues to lure tourists. Expect often foggy conditions, and cool weather.

AIRPORT

Edinburgh Airport to City Center

The travel time to the city is about 25 minutes. Taxis can be hired from stations outside the airport. Taxis are not black and large as is the case in most other parts of Great Britain. They look exactly like your average car. Bus and coach services are also available. Buses run every fifteen to twenty minutes to Edinburgh.

HOTELS

Top-end

The Balmoral; 1 Princess Street; tel: 556-2414; fax: 557-3747; near city center & railway station; restaurant; conference facilities; secretarial services; fax/photocopy facilities; parking; corporate rates; fitness; sauna; pool.

The Caledonian; Princes Street; tel: 459-9988; fax: 225-6632; near city center; restaurant; conference facilities (up to 300); secretarial services; fax/photocopy facilities; in-room modem/fax connection; parking; corporate rates; fitness; sauna.

George Inter-Continental; 19-21 George Street; tel: 225-1251; fax: 226-5644; near city center; restaurant; conference facilities (up to 200); secretarial services; fax/photocopy facilities; in-room modem/fax connection; parking; corporate rates.

Royal Terrace; 18 Royal Terrace; tel: 557-3222; fax: 557-5334; near city center & railway station; restaurant; conference facilities (up to 80); secretarial services; fax/photocopy facilities; corporate rates; fitness; sauna; pool.

Sheraton Grand; 1 Festival Square; tel: 229-9131; fax: 229-6254; 228-4510; near city center & exhibition grounds; restaurant; conference facilities (up to 485); business center; secretarial services; fax/photocopy facilities; in-room modem/fax connection; car rental; parking; corporate rates; fitness; sauna; pool; whirlpool.

Expensive

Dalhousie Castle; Bonnyrigg; tel: 820-153; fax: 821-936; located in city center & train station; restaurant; conference facilities; business center; secretarial services; fax/photocopy facilities; fitness; pool; library.

Gleneagles Hotel; Auchterarder, Perthshire; tel: 662-231; fax: 662-134; near airport; business center; car rental; parking; fitness; pool; golf course; tennis courts.

Golden Tulip Jarvis Ellersly Country House; 4 Ellersly Road, Murrayfield; tel: 337-6888; fax: 313-2643/543; located in suburb; restaurant; conference facilities (up to 75); business center; secretarial services; fax/photocopy facilities; parking; corporate rates.

Holyrood Hotel; Holyrood Road; tel: 550-4500; fax: 550-4545; near city center & railway station; restaurant; conference facilities; business center; free transfer to airport; car rental; parking; fitness.

Marriott Dalmahoy; Kirknewton; tel: 333-1845; fax: 335-3203; located in suburb; near airport & golf course; restaurant; conference facilities (up to 400); secretarial services; fax/photocopy facilities; parking; corporate rates; fitness; sauna; pool; whirlpool.

The Norton House; Ingliston; tel: 333-1275; fax: 333-5303; located in suburb; restaurant; conference facilities (up to 400); secretarial services; fax/photocopy facilities; in-room safe; free transfer to airport; parking; corporate rates. (3-star)

Scandic Crown Edinburgh; 80 High Street; The Royal Mile; tel: 557-9797; fax: 557-9789; near to city center & railway station; restaurant; conference facilities (up to 220); parking; fitness; sauna; pool.

Stakis Edinburgh Airport; Edinburgh International Airport; tel: 519-4400; fax: 519-4422; located in a suburb; near airport; restaurant; conference facilities (up to 260); parking; corporate rates; fitness; sauna.

Stakis Grosvenor; 19 Grosvenor Street; tel: 226-6001; fax: 220-2387; near city center; restaurant; conference facilities (up to 500); secretarial services; fax/photocopy facilities; corporate rates.

Moderate

Commodore; Marine Drive; tel: 336-1700; fax: 336-4934; near to airport; restaurant; corporate rates.

Jury's Edinburgh Inn; Jeffrey Street; tel: 200-3300; fax: 440-9625; near to convention centre; restaurant; conference facilities.

Osbourne; 53-59 York Place; tel: 556-2345; fax: 556-1012; near city center; restaurant.

Royal British; 20 Princes Street; tel: 556-4901; fax: 557-6510; near to city centre; restaurant; conference facilities (up to 50); secretarial services; fax/photocopy facilities; in-room modem/fax connection; corporate rates.

Thistle Inn Jarvis Learmouth; 18-20 Learmouth Terrace; tel: 343-2671; fax: 315-2232; near city center; restaurant; conference facilities (up to 200); parking.

Westbury Hotel; 92-98 St John's Road, Corstorphine Edinburgh; Lothian; tel: 316-4466; fax: 316-4333; near airport; restaurant; conference facilities; parking.

MEDICAL CARE

Royal Infirmary of Edinburgh; 1 Lauriston Place; tel: 229-24-77.

HEALTH CLUB

Meadowbank Sports Centre; 139/141 London Road; Meadowbank, east of city center.; tel: [44] (131) 661-53-51

AUTO RENTAL

Avis; tel: (0645) 12-34-56 (all branches).

Condor Car Hire; 45 Lochrin Place; tel: 229-63-33.

Melville's Self Drive; 9 Clifton Terrace; tel: 337-53-33.

Mitchell's; Torphichen Street; tel; 229-53-84.

Birmingham

AIRPORT

Birmingham International Airport to City Center

The airport lies eight miles (13km.) from the city. A monorail system connects the airport and the New Street Railway Station downtown for a fare of £1.70. The ride takes about 15 minutes. Train service also operates from BIA to London. A public bus travels to the city center in 15-minute intervals. The 30-minute trip costs about £1.20. Taxis wait outside of the arrivals hall and cost about £11 for the 25-minute trip into town.

HOTELS

Top-end

Plough and Harrow; 135 Hagley Road; tel: 454-4111; fax: 454-1868; located in suburb; restaurant; conference facilities (up to 70); secretarial services; fax/photocopy facilities; parking; corporate rates.

Golden Tulip Jarvis International Hotel; The Square; West Midlands; tel: 711-2121; fax: 711-3374; near city center; restaurant; conference facilities; business center; car rental; parking.

Golden Tulip Jarvis Penns Hall Hotel and Country Club; Penns Lane; Wamley Sutton Coldfield; West Midlands; tel: 351-3111; fax: 313-1297; in suburb; conference facilities (up to 600); parking; fitness; pool.

Swallow Hotel; 12 Hagley Road, Five Ways; tel: (121) 452-1144; fax: (121) 456-3442; for conference information email to: info@swallowhotels.com; near city center; 2 restaurants; board rooms (up to 20); library; drawing room; fitness; spa bath; steam room; solarium; indoor pool.

Expensive

The Copthorne Birmingham; Paradise Circus; tel: 200-2727; fax: 200-1197; near city center & train station; restaurant; conference facilities (up to 200); business center; parking; fitness; sauna; pool.

Forte Posthouse Birmingham City (was Forte Crest); Smallbrook, Queensway; tel: 643-8171; fax: 631-2528; http://www.forte-hotels.com/; near city center; restaurant; conference facilities; fitness; pool; golf course.

Forte Posthouse Birmingham; Chapel Lane, Great Barr; tel: 357-7444; fax: 357-7503; http://www.forte-hotels.com/; located in suburb; restaurant; conference facilities (up to 120); parking; fitness; sauna; pool.

Forte Posthouse Birmingham Airport; Coventry Road; tel: 782-8141; fax: 782-2476; http://www.forte-hotels.com/; located in suburb; near to airport; railway station & exhibition center; restaurant; conference facilities (up to 150); parking.

Holiday Inn Crowne Plaza; Central Square, Holiday Street; tel: 631-2000; fax: 643-9018; near city center & railway station; restaurant; conference facilities (up to 150); parking; corporate rates; fitness; pool; whirlpool.

Hyatt Regency Birmingham; 2 Bridge Street; tel: 643-1234; fax: 616-2323; email: hrbirm@hrb.co.uk; near city center & airport; restaurant; conference facilities; secretarial services; fax/photocopy facilities; corporate rates; fitness; sauna; pool.

New Hall Hotel; Walmley Road, Sutton Coldfield; tel: 378-2442; fax: 378-4637; restaurant; conference rooms; car rental; parking; golf course & putting green.

Novotel Birmingham Centre; 70 Broad Street; tel: 643-2000; fax: 643-9796; near city center; restaurant; conference facilities; parking; fitness; sauna; whirlpool.

Strathallan Thistle; 225 Hagley Road; Edgbaston, tel: 455-9777; fax: 454-9432; located in suburb; restaurant; conference facilities (up to 200); parking; corporate rates.

Sutton Court Hotel; 60-66 Lichfield Road; tel: 601-1160; fax: 481-551; restaurant; conference facilities; free transport to airport; railway station; & exhibition center; car rental; parking; fitness; pool; squash; tennis; conservatory.

Moderate

Copperfield House; 60 Upland Road, Selly Park; tel: 472-8344; fax: 472-8344; located in suburb, near airport; restaurant; secretarial services; fax/photocopy facilities; parking.

Great Barr; Pear Tree Drive & Newton Road; Great Barr; tel: 357-1141; fax: 357-7557; located in suburb; restaurant; conference facilities (up to 120); secretarial services; fax/photocopy facilities; parking.

Wheatsheaf; 2225 Coventry Road, tel: 742-6201; fax: 722-2703; restaurant; conference facilities (up to 50); secretarial services; fax/photocopy facilities; parking.

United States

At a Glance

THE PEOPLE

Population ....272,639,608 (July 1999 est.)
Growth Rate ....0.85% (1999 est.)
Life Expectancy .... 76.23 years (1999 est.)
Infant Mortality..... 6.33 deaths/1,000 live births (1999 est.)

Ethnic Composition

White 83.5%
Black..12.4%
Asian 3.3%
Amerindian 0.8%
Other 0.1%

Religious Composition

Protestant 56%
Catholic 28%
Judaic 2%
Other 4%
No Affiliation 10%

Languages Spoken

English is the most common, especially in business and government, followed in popularity by Spanish. A vast number of foreign languages are spoken in various areas throughout the nation. Some local government functions are carried out in non-English formats.

Education and Literacy

Education is compulsory throughout the country through age 16. The college and university system is extensive and open to the general population. Literacy is 97 percent nationwide.

Labor force

Total 137,700,000
By occupation: managerial and professional 29.6%, technical, sales and administrative support 29.3%, services 13.6%, manufacturing, mining, transportation, and crafts 24.8%, farming, forestry, and fishing 2.7%.

THE ECONOMY

The economy of the United States was written off in the 1980s as being in a hopeless state of decline and soon to be outdone by the ascending Asian juggernauts. Instead, the U.S. economy remains atop the global pile with its nearest competitors (EU and Japan) still hampered by disorganization and inflexibility. Driven by a strong technology sector, the United States finishes up the 20th century by accomplishing what was formerly thought impossible: low unemployment coupled with low inflation. Though many of its businesses are global giants, the U.S. was largely shielded from the economic meltdown in Asia and Russia due to its (previously much criticized) lack of investment in those regions. While its stock market continues to soar and its currency remains the dominant force in international trade, the U.S. economy still has its naysayers. Most concerns turn on the huge trade deficit and belief that U.S.-style success cannot be sustainable. Critics predict that a sharp decline (on par with Japan) is in the offing. Counterarguments point to the transparency of the U.S. investment market, the soundness of its governmental financial controls, and the nimbleness of its business sector.

Exports ....US$663 billion(f.o.b., 1998 est.)
Imports .... US$912 billion (c.i.f., 1998 est.)
Total GDP..............................US$8.511 trillion (1998 est.)
GDP Per Capita.............................US$31,500 (1998 est.)
Unemployment 4.5% (1998)
Inflation Rate 1.6% (1998)

Top Export Partners

E.U., Canada, Japan, Mexico.

Top Import Partners

Canada, E.U., Japan, Mexico, China.

Top Exports

Capital goods, automobiles, industrial supplies and raw materials, consumer goods, agricultural products.

Top Imports

Crude oil and refined petroleum products, machinery, automobiles, consumer goods, industrial raw materials, food and beverages.

BUSINESS WORKWEEK

Offices

Monday to Friday 8:30a.m. to 5:30p.m., although these are only general times and businesses hours can vary widely.

Banks

Monday to Friday 8a.m. to 5p.m., Saturday 9a.m. to 1p.m.

Government

Monday to Friday 8:30a.m. to 5p.m.

Retail

Monday to Friday 9a.m. to 6p.m., with extended hours on the weekends.
Note: Many U.S. retail businesses are open 24 hours a day, 7 days a week. This market prides itself on having "everything, all the time".

HOLIDAYS

New Year's Day..January 1
Martin Luther King Day.......................................January 17
Presidents' Day ....February 21
Easter...April 15*
Memorial Day ....May 24
Independence Day ....July 4
Labor Day..September 4
Veterans' Day..November 11
Thanksgiving Day...November 25
Christmas ....December 25
*Date may vary by year.

CLIMATE

Seasons

Although the United States is primarily within a temperate zone, the country encompasses a wide range of topographies and climatic conditions. The extremes of tropical Hawaii and frigid Alaska add to the variety of conditions found in the U.S.

In general, the weather moves from west to east, carried by westerly winds from the Pacific Ocean, which gives the West Coast a moderate climate, while the desert, mountains, Great Plains, Midwest, the Great Lakes region, and the Atlantic Coastal Plain experience much greater extremes in temperature and precipitation.

United States

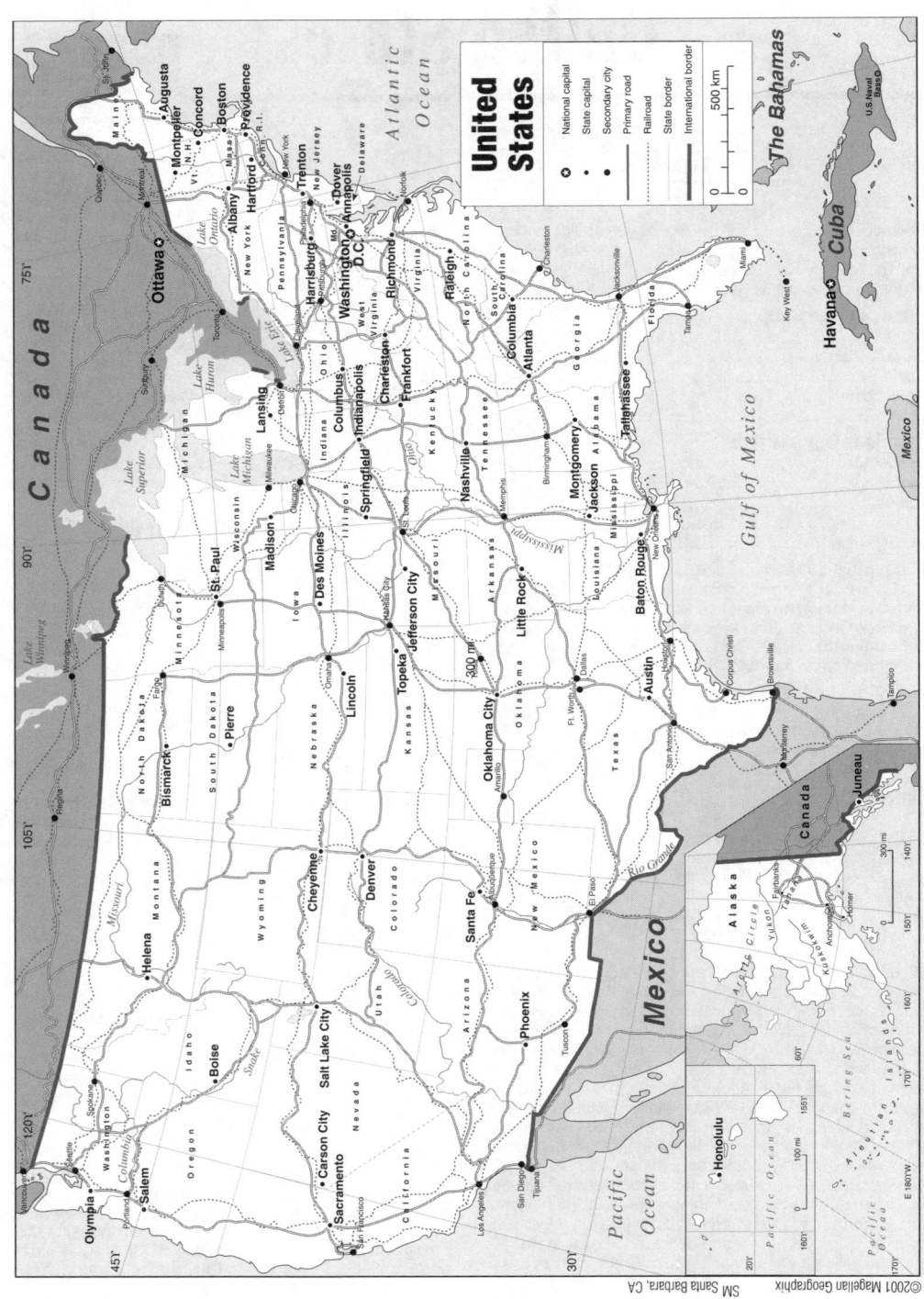

United States

National capital
State capital
Secondary city
Primary road
Railroad
State border
International border

500 km

Canada

St. John
Augusta
Montpelier
Concord
Boston
Providence
R.I.
Maine
N.H.
Vt.
Mass.
Conn.

Ottawa

Atlantic Ocean

Lake Ontario
Lake Erie
Lake Huron
Lake Michigan
Lake Superior

Albany
New York
Hartford
Trenton
Dover
Annapolis
Washington D.C.
Harrisburg
Pennsylvania
New Jersey
Delaware
Richmond
Virginia
West Virginia
Raleigh
North Carolina
Columbia
South Carolina
Charleston
Atlanta
Georgia
Florida
Jacksonville
Miami
Key West
Tampa

The Bahamas

Cuba
Havana
U.S. Naval Base

Lansing
Detroit
Columbus
Ohio
Indianapolis
Indiana
Frankfort
Kentucky
Nashville
Tennessee
Memphis
Montgomery
Jackson
Alabama
Mississippi
Tallahassee
Baton Rouge
New Orleans
Louisiana
Birmingham

Springfield
Illinois
Missouri
St. Louis
Jefferson City
Little Rock
Arkansas
Oklahoma City

St. Paul
Minneapolis
Madison
Wisconsin
Milwaukee
Des Moines
Iowa
Topeka
Kansas
Lincoln
Nebraska

Michigan

Gulf of Mexico

Brownsville
Corpus Christi
Matamoros
Reynosa
Tampico

Mexico

Bismarck
North Dakota
Pierre
South Dakota
Cheyenne
Wyoming
Denver
Colorado
Santa Fe
New Mexico
Amarillo
Albuquerque
El Paso
Austin
San Antonio
Fort Worth
Dallas
Houston
Texas

300 mi

Rio Grande

Helena
Montana
Boise
Idaho
Salt Lake City
Utah
Carson City
Nevada
Sacramento
San Francisco
California
Phoenix
Arizona
Tucson
San Diego
Tijuana
Los Angeles

Olympia
Washington
Salem
Oregon
Portland
Seattle
Spokane

Pacific Ocean

Canada
Juneau

Alaska
Fairbanks
Anchorage
Yukon
Arctic Circle
Bering Sea
Aleutian Islands
Nome
Kodiak

Honolulu

Pacific Ocean

100 mi
300 mi

Winnipeg
Lake Winnipeg
Regina
Quebec
Montreal
Toronto

Columbia
Snake
Missouri
Colorado
Ohio
Mississippi

45°N
30°N
120°W
105°W
90°W
75°W

The Gulf of Mexico roughly influences the southeastern U.S., which is warmer and more humid. Southern Florida has almost tropical conditions. Hurricanes in this region are common.

Regions

New York and Washington D.C. on the Atlantic Coastal Plain have similar climates: below freezing temperatures in the winter, with January temperatures falling to -3°C (27°F). Spring is moderate, with temperatures of around 15°C (59°F) in April, and summer is warm and muggy, with July temperatures reaching 35°C (95°F). Prolonged heat spells at higher temperatures are not rare.

Miami, on the southeast coast, is subtropical in climate and, like Houston on the Gulf of Mexico, is hot and humid. Cities like Chicago and Minneapolis, on the edge of the central Great Plains, have harsh winters with heavy snows offset by blistering hot summers. Los Angeles, on the southern Californian West Coast, has a mediterranean-style climate, with only slight seasonal variation. San Francisco to the north is moderate year-round with moderate to heavy rains in winter and thick fog during the summer months in the city itself. To the north and south of the city, temperatures are mostly sunny and warm, with the occasional hot streak.

Money & Banking

Currency

The currency of United States is the U.S. Dollar (US$).

Denominations

The U.S. Dollar comes in coin denominations of US$1, and 50, 25, 10, 5 and 1 cents; and banknotes of US$1, 2, 5, 10, 20, 50, 100, 500 and 1,000. Larger bills are available but rarely used.

Traveler's Checks and Credit Cards

Traveler's checks in U.S. currency are widely accepted at banks, hotels, department stores, and the banking counter, although smaller establishments may refuse to cash them.

You cannot use any other currency in the U.S., but banks will offer to change other currencies. It is best to buy traveler's checks denominated in U.S. currency before travel. Otherwise, you can change money in airport kiosks, private exchange offices, banks, or at American Express and Thomas Cook offices; none will offer optimal rates.

International bank cards (MasterCard, Visa, and Access) are widely accepted in most businesses, while American Express, Diner's Club, and Discover credit cards are less widely accepted. Hotels accept the full range of bank and credit cards. A traveler can obtain cash using a credit card from selected banks, and there are automated teller machines (ATMs) everywhere. The best exchange rates will be given for credit/bank card and ATM transactions.

Note: Banks will not cash a personal check unless you have an account there. Retail businesses will only accept local (very local) checks. Most major cities have American Express offices.

Lost or Stolen Traveler's Checks

American Express 1-800-221-7282
Citicorp 1-800-645-6556
Thomas Cook/MasterCard 1-800-223-7373
VISA 1-800-227-6811

Lost or Stolen Credit Card

American Express 1-800-528-4800
MasterCard...1-800-826-2181
VISA 1-800-336-8472

Diners Club/Carte Blanche........................1-800-234-6377
Discover1-800-347-2683

Other Financial Information

Western Union (Telegrams, Cablegrams, Intl. Currency Wiring 1-800-325-6000

Travel
VISA AND PASSPORT

Passports that are valid for at least six months beyond expected entry date are required of all visitors. Visas are needed by all travelers to the United States, except those from Canada, Mexico, and the 22 nations that participate in the Visa Waiver Pilot Program (VWPP). Citizens from countries in the VWPP need only a passport, a return ticket, and proof of solvency for a 90-day stay. Canadian and Mexican visitors do not need return tickets.

Transit exemption: passengers in transit with those airlines permitted to convey foreign nationals without a visa; who do not leave the airport and are continuing their journey within eight hours; and who are holding confirmed tickets and other documents for onward travel, are also exempt from the need for a visa.

Visas are available at U.S. embassies and consulates. Types of visa issued:

- Immigrant - single and multiple entry. This visa is good for up to six months overall, and valid if used within ten years of issuance.

- Non-Immigrant - subdivided into categories including Business, Student, Journalist, Temporary Worker, and Transit. Most of these (except the short term transit) have the same terms and validity as the Immigrant visas.

Extensions can be granted on visas by the U.S. Immigration and Naturalization Service, usually without undue difficulty. Business visitors should append a letter to their application, from the U.S. company they are visiting, stating the nature of the business to be transacted, and confirming the length of stay necessary.

The U.S. is constantly besieged with visitors wishing to stay and work in the world's richest nation. Some nationalities may be required to post sizable bonds and have sponsors guarantee exit dates; this may hold true for both tourist and business travelers. Check with your U.S. consulate well in advance of travel.

Allow about three weeks for visa application processing, not including postal delivery time if not handled in person. This process is perhaps a bit more arduous than that of many countries, but once you are in, you are in. This is the land of the free. The police do not stop you on the street and ask for your passport, and there is no requirement to register with the local constabulary when you move between towns.

Interstate travel in the U.S. is also unhampered by the need to cross national borders, which makes things convenient for the business traveler in particular.

Restricted Entry

The following are denied entry to the U.S. without a 'waiver of ineligibility' having first been obtained from U.S. Immigration:

- people diagnosed with specified serious communicable diseases

- persons with a criminal record

- narcotics users and drug traffickers

- anyone previously denied entry or deported from the U.S. within the past five years

DEPARTURE FORMALITIES

An airport departure tax of US$10 is assessed of every foreign traveler, usually included in the airfare.

Note: Large cash transactions (in excess of US$10,000) can stimulate curiosity on the part of customs and drug control agencies. It is not illegal to move around such amounts, but the prudent traveler will have a good explanation.

CUSTOMS ENTRY (PERSONAL)

Duty-free
- Tobacco: 200 cigarettes, 50 cigars, or 2kg of tobacco or proportionate amounts of each
- Alcohol: 1 liter of alcoholic beverage
- Other: gifts or articles up to a value of US$100 (including 100 cigars in addition to the tobacco allowance above); up to US$300 in gifts for Hawaii.

Note: Items should not be gift-wrapped, since they must be available for customs inspection. Check with customs representatives in the entry and exit points, as some states have specific requirements.

The gift allowance may only be claimed once in every six months and is only available to non-residents who intend to stay in the United States for more than 72 hours.

Prohibited or Restricted
The following are either banned or may only be imported under license:
- Narcotics and dangerous drugs (doctor's certificate required)
- Absinthe, biological materials, most seeds, fruits, and plants (including endangered species of plants and vegetables and their products)
- Firearms and ammunition (with some exceptions for collectors or hunters. Consult Customs)
- Hazardous articles (fireworks, toxic materials)
- Meat and poultry products
- Embargo items
- Pornographic material
- Switchblade knives

IMMUNIZATION

No immunizations are required for entry to the United States unless you are arriving from an infected area. Tetanus vaccination is recommended for travel in rural areas.

TIPPING

Tipping is an important supplement to service industry salaries in the U.S. Indeed, it can be a science in itself. Service charges are customarily NOT included in bills. Fifteen percent is considered the standard rate.

Travelers may find it convenient to carry a cache of small bills. With the exception of staff in restaurants, it is best to tip the recipient directly, rather than adding it to a tab. In any event, tip only after a service has been performed.

'Tip cups' have sprung up next to every fast food and bookstore cash register, spreading like a fungus. These are not service sector jobs traditional tipped in the U.S., so do not feel compelled to tip an ordinary cashier for an ordinary retail transaction.

Following is a general guide to tipping in the U.S.

Hotel Staff
Bellhop $1-2/bag
unless the bags weigh like a ton of bricks—in which case, tip more.
Doorman.. $1-3
$1 for hailing a cab or performing any service; $2 for hailing a cab when it's raining.

Concierge.. $5-10
If the concierge has managed to acquire difficult-to-get theater tickets or restaurant reservations, tip 10 to 20 percent of the ticket/tab price; if he/she has truly put in their time but failed to get you the desired hot-ticket item, tip 5 to 10 percent anyway. It is better to tip immediately rather than later. Money envelopes not required.
Housekeeping.. $1-2/night
....top hotels: $2-$5/night
Cash is best. You can leave tips for the chambermaids daily on the nightstand next to your bed or in another obvious place. Envelopes are not necessary to secure the cash.
Laundry/valet.. 15%
Room Service 15%
Only if no gratuity or service charge has been added to your bill.
Parking attendant... $1 to 2
Tip the attendant upon delivery of your vehicle.

Airport
Baggage handlers/curb-side check in................. $1 to 3
Shuttle drivers $1/person
Tip more if the driver assists with baggage.

Restaurant/Bar/Clubs
Maitre'D .... $5-$10
Only required if you arrive with a companion or business associate at a better restaurant without reservations and the maitre'd finds you a table. If you do the same with a large group, tip triple the amount. In both cases, tip only after you've been shown to your table or following your dinner. Pre-paid "bribes" to get a table are considered insulting.
Waiters/waitress... 15-20%
Figure the tip before tax is added. Twenty percent is usually given for excellent service or if the wait staff has gone the extra mile to accommodate you. If you stay at a table longer than the usual time it takes to eat a dinner at a crowded restaurant, consider tipping extra to compensate the waiter for time lost with another customer. Many restaurants already add a 15 percent tip for larger parties—check the menu or inquire if you are unsure about it. If service is poor, first ask the wait staff to correct the problem, if they do not, leave 10 percent. If service is atrocious, tip 5 percent.
Bartender .... 10 to 15%
Tip in bars or if you are sitting at the bar before a meal at a restaurant. Do not tip extra for drinks you order with dinner.
Valet Parking.. $1-3
Coat check .... $1/per coat

Transportation
Taxi 15-20%
Extra luggage or other additional services should be reflected in a larger tip.
Tour guides............................... $2-3/day/group member
Charter/tour bus drivers ....
....................................$2-3/day/group member, 10-20%

Hair salon/spas
Hair stylist.. 15%
Manicurist 10-15%
Shampooer.. $1-2
Massage therapist.. 10-20%

Other
Golf caddy.. 15-25% of green fees
Private ski instructor..$100/day

Police and Crime
Despite its reputation, the U.S. is generally a very safe place to visit, and criminal activity is in decline. The crime rate in some cities may be high, but if you avoid the more dangerous areas and take basic precautions, your chances of be-

coming a victim are low. Inquire of your hotel staff or car rental staff which areas to avoid.

Leave most of your cash, traveler's checks, jewelry, and your non-essential valuables in your hotel safe. Carry photocopies of your passport instead of the original. Carry cash in a money belt, and use credit cards or traveler's checks for most transactions. Avoid being distracted by "helpful strangers" in crowded areas.

Foreign business visitors and tourists are often the target of thieves; so, purses, laptops, and briefcases require additional security. Do not leave valuables in cars or on tables in cafés. Luggage theft at airports is quite common.

Many rental car agencies avoid designating their vehicles as rentals to avoid having their customers targeted. The police force is friendly, efficient, and generally respectful of an individual's rights, but has few non-English language skills.

Emergency Numbers

Police, Fire, Ambulance 911
["911" operates nationally]]

Health

Public drinking water in the U.S. is safe, and food is generally prepared under safe conditions. Pharmacies and grocery stores are everywhere and can be trusted; however, pharmacies cannot sell certain drugs without a doctor's prescription.

The main health hazard in the U.S. is the high cost of medical care. It is highly advisable to carry at least US$500,000 in medical insurance. With the exception (usually) of emergency services, all medical procedures will be performed only after the potential patient has shown evidence of insurance or has made a substantial cash deposit. The quality of the health care is of the highest level, but paying for it can be unnerving.

For more information on medical centers, including phone numbers, please see the "Business Centers" section.

INTERNAL TRAVEL

AIR

By air, it takes only five hours to cross the American continent east to west, and two hours north to south. All cities in the U.S. are interconnected by air. Only the most remote regions are not served by a domestic U.S. airline.

Strong competition among the airlines has led to wide variances in fares on identical itineraries. Customary categories of fares are first-class, coach (economy), excursion, and discount/stand-by. Night flights (red eyes) are usually cheaper.

Traveling by air in the U.S. is relatively inexpensive when compared with most other parts of the world. Only on the Eastern seaboard, between Washington D.C. in the south and Boston in the north, is it feasible to travel by train (or bus) for business transit. Most of the rest of the country's major cities are too far from each other to consider anything other than air travel. Most airlines have toll-free numbers for reservations and inquiries.

U.S. AIRLINES NUMBERS

Aer Lingus .... (800) 223-6537
Aerolineas Argentinas .... (800) 333-0276
Aeromexico .... (800) 237-6639
Aeroperu... (800) 777-7717
Air Afrique... (800) 456-9192
Air Canada .... (800) 776-3000
Air France... (800) 237-2747
Air India .... (800) 223-2250
Air Jamaica... (800) 523-5585

Air New Zealand.. (800) 262-1234
Alaska Airlines... (800) 426-0333
Alitalia... (800) 223-5730
All Nippon Airways .... (800) 235-9262
ALM Antillean Airlines .... (800) 327-7230
American Airlines .... (800) 433-7300
Asiana Ailrines.................. (South Korea) (800) 227-4262
Austrian Airlines .... (800) 843-0002
Avianca Airlines... (800) 284-2622
Bahamas Air... (800) 222-4262
British Airways .... (800) 247-9297
BWIA International .... (800) 327-7401
Canadian Airlines International .... (800) 426-7000
Cathay Pacific .... (800) 233-2742
China Airlines .... (800) 227-5118
Continental Airlines .... (800) 525-0280
Czech Airlines .... (800) 628-6107
Delta.. (800) 221-1212
Egyptair .... (800) 334-6787
El Al Israel Airlines .... (800) 223-6700
Emirates ....(800) 777-3999
EVA Airways.. (800) 695-1188
Finnair .... (800) 950-5000
Garuda Indonesia...................................... (800) 342-7832
Hawaiian Airlines....................................... (800) 367-5320
Japan Airlines.. (800) 525-3663
KLM .... (800) 777-5553
Korean Air .... (800) 438-5000
Kuwait Airlines .... (800) 458-9248
Lan Chile Airlines .... (800) 735-5526
lloyd Aereo Boliviano................................. (800) 327-7407
LOT Polish Airlines.................................... (800) 223-0593
LTU International Airways .... (800) 888-0200
Lufthansa... (800) 645-3880
Mexicana Airlines .... (800) 531-7921
Northwest Airlines .... (800) 225-2525
Olympic Airways .... (800) 223-1226
PIA... (800) 221-2552
Philippine Airlines...................................... (800) 435-9725
Qantas Airlines .... (800) 227-4500
Royal Air Maroc... (800) 292-0081
Sabena .... (800) 955-2000
SAS .... (800) 221-2350
Saudia Arabian Airlines .... (800) 472-8342
Singapore Airlines .... (800) 742-3333
South African Airways .... (800) 722-9675
Swissair... (800) 221-4750
Taca International Airlines.......................... (800) 535-8780
TAP Air Portugal.. (800) 221-7370
Thai International Airways .... (800) 426-5204
TWA International....................................... (800) 892-4141
United Airlines .... (800) 241-6522
USAir... (800) 428-4322
VARIG Brazilian Airways............................ (800) 468-2744
VASP Brazilian .... (800) 433-0444
Viasa Venezuelan .... (800) 468-4272
Virgin Atlantic .... (800) 862-8621

TAXI

Taxis are easily found in urban areas and can be hailed from the street. Color and model of vehicles vary wildly—yellow sedans seem to be popular in most U.S. cities—but the lighted taxi dome on top of the vehicle is fairly universal. Virtually all cabs are metered, and most drivers are relaxed and honest about the fares. Do pay attention, though, as you would in any country.

In rural and suburban areas, one may reserve taxis by telephone. Do not be surprised if you are separated from

United States

the driver by bullet-proof glass. Rarely is there a set price for extra baggage; the driver figures you will build that into the tip, which is normally 15 percent.

AUTO

Automobile rental is a major industry in the U.S., addressing the needs of foreigners and citizens alike. Only a valid driver's license from the traveler's country of origin, purchase of minimum insurance, and a major credit card are generally required. Excellent discount plans for foreign visitors abound. Some of these can be arranged through an airline or travel agent prior to your visit or directly with the rental company itself.

Driving is the true national pastime; gasoline is cheap and easily available everywhere. The highway system is extensive and well maintained. While urban driving may prove daunting (perhaps terrifying) for the novice visitor, motoring through the wide open spaces of the United States is an exhilarating experience. After all, this is the car culture, to the ultimate degree. The experience of driving a road like Route 66 in a convertible American muscle car will impart an insight on U.S. culture available no other way. A few key points about U.S. roads and regulations:

*   If the police stop you for a driving violation, do not try to pay a fine on the spot because it may easily be interpreted as attempted bribery.
*   There are strict laws about drinking and driving, and they are enforced decisively.
*   Speed limits are clearly posted (in miles per hour only, usually) and are enforced.
*   Insurance is of utmost importance and should provide coverage of all passengers and drivers for accidental injury and death. An insurance card for non-resident, interstate motorists is available on request.
*   Regarding U.S. rental car sizing: 'Economy' or 'Compact' means a car that would be called 'Standard' in Europe. The term 'Standard' means a car the length of the QE2. U.S. parking spaces are larger, though.

The U.S. is also the perfect place to travel in a camper or motor home, called "RV's", which can provide substantial amenities and office space. Excellent overnight parks can be found everywhere, some with hotel-quality infrastructure such as room service, swimming pools, spas, and so forth.

The American Automobile Association (AAA) offers maps, trip-planning services, emergency roadside assistance, and insurance policies (compulsory in most of the U.S.) A foreign visitor is entitled to benefits if holding a current membership in the visitor's own national auto club. Contact:

American Automobile Association (AAA)
tel: (407) 253-9100
fax: (407) 253-9107
website: www.aaa.com

One wonderful thing about Americans and their cars is that they usually tend to be happy to flip you the keys and say, "Here, it's yours for the night/weekend/week." If you are not blessed with such friends, family, or business associates, it is easy to find rental cars in the smallest of U.S. towns. Often, the automobile is the only way to reach smaller towns and remote manufacturing facilities.

There are always local rental operations giving the big chains a run for their money. Inquire locally. Following are some of the major rental agencies' phone numbers:

Alamo ....(800) 327-9633
Avis ....(800) 331-1212
Budget ....(800) 527-0700
Dollar...(800) 800-4000
Hertz..(800) 654-3131
National ....(800) 227-7368
All of these companies maintain websites.

TRAIN

Rail travel is a widely overlooked mode of transportation in much of the country. When Americans want to cover short distances, they use cars. If they need to travel across the country, they will usually fly.

Nevertheless, trains remain a mainstay of travel along the northeast seaboard, connecting Washington D.C., Baltimore, Philadelphia, New York, and Boston. Amtrak, the National Railroad Passenger Corporation, operates nearly all the express and long-distance passenger trains, although local agencies do run some regional and suburban services. Currently, Amtrak is introducing 20 high-speed Express trains, capable of speeds up to 240kph (150mph), reducing the Washington to New York trip to two and one half hours, and the New York to Boston trip to three hours.

The rest of the U.S. is like a different country from the densely populated northeast when it comes to train travel. Generally, trains run once daily over a small number of long-distance routes. Chicago is the central rail hub, with routes fanning out over the rest of the U.S., the primary ones being to:

*   Seattle, Portland, Oakland (San Francisco), and Los Angeles (via Omaha–Denver–Salt Lake City–Las Vegas, or via Kansas City–Albuquerque–Flagstaff)
*   New Orleans and San Antonio (via St. Louis and Dallas/ Ft. Worth)
*   San Antonio and Los Angeles are linked via El Paso, Tucson and Phoenix.
*   There is a train from Los Angeles to New Orleans that usually runs three times a week.

Most trains offer one-class seating (comparable to top-rate second class travel in Europe) and air-conditioning, and a range of sleeping accommodations for payment of an additional fare. Long-distance trains all have dining facilities, and often pass through spectacular scenery, especially along east–west routes.

Discount fares are available. The USA Rail Pass, designed specifically for international travelers, entitles the bearer to unlimited travel for terms of 15 or 30 days, on either a regional or national basis. The passes must be purchased outside the U.S. prior to entry. There has been a recent upsurge in rail travel in the U.S., in both commuter and regional transportation, and this trend is expected to continue with growth and modernization.

Terminals are located downtown, usually closer to your hotel than airports are, so total travel time may be shorter than flying. For further details, contact:

Amtrak
tel: (800) 872-7245 (toll free in the U.S. and Canada only)
website: www.amtrak.com

Note: For those expecting European- or Japanese-style on-time, high-speed performance, brace yourselves for a new experience. Long-distance rail travel in north America is notoriously slow and expensive.

METRO

A number of major U.S. cities have underground train systems, including Atlanta, Boston, Chicago, Cleveland, Los Angeles, San Francisco Bay Area, New York, Philadelphia, and Washington, D.C. Many have the most modern and sophisticated types of ticketing machines, some are old enough that humans are still involved. Generally, U.S. subways are clean, well-lighted, and highly efficient and reliable (some of them can be dangerous during off-peak hours, in terms of personal security). Most metros are operated on an integrated fare system and facilitate easy transfers between other modes of transit.

Following is a partial list of subway system information websites for some U.S. cities:

San Francisco / Oakland
www.bart.org

Washington D.C.
www.wmata.com

New York City
www.nycsubway.org

Boston
www.mbta.com

Philadelphia
www.septa.com

Chicago
www.transitchicago.com

Cleveland
http://little.nhlink.net/~rta/index.html

BUS / TRAM

Urban: Since the oil crisis in the 1970's, U.S. cities have shown a marked increase in the quality of public transit. Most medium-to-large sized cities have efficient, reliable bus fleets. In larger urban areas, many buses have reclining seats, air conditioning, overhead reading lights, and even alternative energy power plants, including electric.

Generally, the fare system is an exact-change system, or will take a ticket pre-purchased, often at a discount. You pay as you board, usually by putting your cash or ticket into a metered box next to the driver. There are overhead lines or buttons for you to use to signal that you wish to get off at the next stop. Get a copy of the local bus line's timetable, and learn how to read it. U.S. bus systems are fairly punctual, but to a much lesser degree than European or Japanese bus systems. Every bus operation has a passenger assistance telephone number you can call for further information. Foreign language skills are not to be found among most bus drivers in the U.S., so having a destination or question written down is often a good idea.

Intercity: There are over 11,000 long-distance coach lines in the U.S., crisscrossing the country with economically priced and dependable services. Toilets, airliner-type seats, and air conditioning are standard on intercity routes.

Once you can pinpoint your destinations in the U.S., then a travel agent can put you in touch with the appropriate long-distance bus company. Greyhound is the dominant national coach carrier covering the states of the South, South Central, South Rockies, and Southwest, and extending into Canada and Mexico. If you find yourself suddenly in need of bus transit, the fastest way to find a company is to call Greyhound; they will tell you if they service the area in question, and who else does along with them, or instead of them.

Most sizable companies such as Greyhound have terminals with facilities to store luggage temporarily. You are not permitted to sleep in most bus stations, such as you might in a train station, between connections.

Note: Keep in mind that Greyhound or other long-distance bus stations are not usually located in the best areas of major cities. Rather, some are quite questionable in nature with odd characters and street urchins lurking about. Proceed directly to a cab or have a destination in mind when you disembark.

The larger coach companies offer discount fares, such as Greyhound's Ameripass, which entitles the traveler to 7, 15, 30 or 60 days of unlimited travel throughout the U.S., with daily extensions available. The Ameripass must be purchased outside the U.S., and may be obtained from Greyhound World Travel.
website: www.greyhound.com

WATER TRAVEL

There is extensive water travel, both along the thousands of rivers and lakes and along the immense coastline. The Ohio River alone, for instance, conveys a greater volume of traffic than any other single inland channel in the world. Most U.S. cities that front on the water have passenger and auto ferries. Passenger and freight lines and tour ships traverse all of the Great Lakes, with ports in Duluth, Sault Sainte Marie, Milwaukee, Chicago, Detroit, Buffalo, Rochester, Cleveland, and Toronto. International cruise ships call at all major ports.

TRAVEL ASSISTANCE

United States Tourism Industries
International Trade Administration
Department of Commerce
Room 1860, Herbert C. Hoover Building
14th and Constitution Avenue, NW
Washington, D.C. 20230
tel: (202) 482 4028
fax: (202) 482 2887
website: <www.tinet.ita.doc.gov>
Travel Industry Association of America
1100 New York Avenue, Suite 450 West, NW
Washington, D.C. 20005
tel: (202) 408 1832
fax: (202) 408 1255
website: www.tia.org
Note: Each major city also has a visitors' convention bureau that will assist with questions and information.

Security Briefing

SOCIAL UNREST

Although many visitors to the United States find it hard to believe any U.S. citizens have anything to complain about, there is a degree of social unrest. Racial minority groups clamor for better treatment, environmentalists raise fears of pollution, anti-capitalists decry globalization, religious fanatics bemoan the decline of morality, the poor demand a bigger piece of the economic pie, and the rich want to be left alone in guarded communities. In spite of the occasional flare up, most social unrest is very subdued in the United States. This calm will remain as long as the economy keeps humming along. Americans are just too busy working to either complain or to pay attention to the complaints of others.

ORGANIZED CRIME

Many organized crime groups operate within the United States. From the old school Cosa Nostra, to Jamaican drug runners, to Russian finance swindlers, to urban street gangs, America has a thriving black market economy operating beneath its bustling legitimate economy. Often crime groups will operate legitimate businesses as a front for more nefarious transactions. Whole industries in some cities have strong Mafia components (e.g., New York City's construction trade) that exert stringent control. Politicians at local, state, and federal level have been convicted of "mob ties" while others have been driven from office by similar accusations. Police in many of America's larger cities have faced allegations of cooperation with crime groups, and major U.S. banking firms have been prosecuted for money laundering.

Although some big crime "bosses" have been jailed in recent years (e.g., John Gotti - the Teflon Don), organized crime is still deeply entrenched within the U.S. economy. Government officials only attack the problem if the criminal activities become too egregious, too public, or too violent.

STREET CRIME

Statistically, street crime has been dropping in the U.S. over the last few years. Much of this drop has been caused by longer prison sentences for repeat offenders and by the thriving economy. The United States now has more people incarcerated than any other developed nation. However, street crime still occurs, and often in broad daylight. Visitors from nations with little crime (e.g., Japan, Germany) are often easy targets because they lack security awareness.

Guns have been a part of the American landscape since its inception, and they are enshrined in the Constitution. Street crime often turns violent and urban gangs often have shootouts over turf disputes. It is not unusual for bystanders to be injured or killed. In spite of this, American cities are still very livable if certain neighborhoods are avoided. Visiting business people should consult their hoteliers about security issues before journeying out onto the streets.

Note: Much of the violence in America has been exaggerated in foreign newspapers in an effort to find a "downside" to America's prosperity. With a modicum of common sense, U.S. cities can be experienced with no more likelihood of danger than most major European or Asian cities.

CULTURAL CONFLICTS

Visitors to the U.S. that come from nations with a single ethnicity (e.g., Scandinavians, Asians, Africans) are often struck by the complex ethnic diversity of American cities. Despite incendiary news reports, these various ethnic groups dwell in relative harmony. Visitors should beware of American stereotypes that they have been indoctrinated with back home. Not all blacks are poor, nor whites rich. Not all Latinos are farm workers nor are all Asians small shop owners. The United States probably has the most complex society on the planet and it requires a great deal of insight to make a proper assessment. Resist quick judgments!

Americans do have their internal disputes, but they are notorious for joining together against outside critics. Even when they are complaining, Americans have a fierce pride in their nation. As they often say, "The great thing about travel is that it makes you appreciate just how good it is to be a U.S. citizen." Rightly or wrongly, many Americans think American culture is the best thing going.

Warning: Contrary to popular belief, U.S. business people are well traveled and well informed about the rest of the world. Criticize the U.S. and you will find their assessment of your culture scathing. Honesty and bluntness are American virtues.

Communications
DIALING CODES IN
THE UNITED STATES

International country code: [1]

Selected city codes: Los Angeles (213, surrounding areas 626, 714, 818), San Francisco (415, surrounding areas 510, 650, 408), Miami (305), Chicago (312, 773, 847, suburbs 708), New York City: (212, 917, surrounding areas 718), Houston (713, surrounding areas 281), Seattle (206), Washington, D.C (202)

Dialing the United States from Overseas

To dial the United States from overseas, dial your international dialing code, then 1 (the country code for the United States), then the city code, and finally the number.

Assistance Numbers

Local Operator.. 0
Long-Distance Operator 00
International Access Code 011
Local Directory Assistance 411
Long Distance Assistance ....1 (area code) 555-1212

CALLING WITHIN
THE UNITED STATES

Local Calls

Local calls are unlimited and inexpensive (usually free), but remember that hotels may charge an additional fee for using their phones. Also, calls may be considered long distance even though the area code is the same. San Francisco, for example, uses the code 415 for the city proper, but also for areas north and south. Calling these areas from inside the city (or vice versa) means an additional charge will be tacked on to your bill.

Long Distance Calls

Dial "1" + the area code + the number you wish to reach. Phone companies offer reduced rates for calling in the evening or on weekends, the best time to place long-distance personal calls.

International Calls

International calls can be made from any phone, including pay phones and hotel phones. Telephone companies offer the most economical rates on weekends and after 11p.m. on weekdays. To place a direct international call from a regular phone, dial 011 + country code + city code + number. Hotel phones may require a preceding digit to dial outside of the hotel, and will, of course, charge you handsomely for the privilege.

PAY PHONES

Public Telephones

Most pay phones on the street require coins, US$0.35 for a local call, an additional charge for long distance. Public telephones are everywhere, often at gas service stations, libraries, and other public buildings. They are color-coded in a wide variety of colors and service offerings. Pay phones requiring cards are most often found in hotels and airports/train stations. If dialing long distance, an operator voice will inform you how much the call will cost after you have dialed the number.

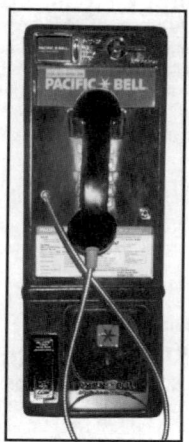

The following pay phone is prevalent in airports:

Calling Cards

Cards can be purchased at airports, hotels, and some convenience stores.

CELLULAR PHONES

There are numerous cellular service providers in the United States, including: GTE, CellularOne, and Sprint.

Cellular One; toll free in the U.S.: 1-800-424-1999; http://www.cellularone.com/.

GTE; toll free in the U.S.: 1-800-424-3636; http://www.gte.com/.

Sprint; toll free in the U.S.: 1-800-480-4727; http://www.sprint.com/.

Note: Your home country cell phone may not work in this country. If not, we recommend that you rent an international cell phone *before* you leave home. A major US-based cell phone rental provider is **IMC WorldCell**. For information see "International Cell Phone Rentals" on page 14.

CALL BACK

You can (potentially) save significant sums when calling in the United States by using one of the call back services listed below. Fees for callback services vary widely, depending on the company and the type of service required. Be sure to check with these companies before leaving to compare rates. For a list of callback services, please refer to the "Communications" section in the *Global Road Warrior* Introduction.

PHONE JACK

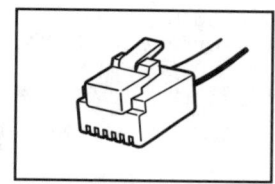

Plug adaptors are available through **iGo Corporation**. (See "Electrical and Telephone Adaptors" on page 19.)

FAX

Fax services are excellent throughout the country. Most copy shops have fax services, although they can be expensive (especially for long distance calls). Almost every office also has a fax machine, as do many homes.

POSTAL SERVICES

Postal services in the country are excellent, although lines at post offices can prove long, with service appearing to move at a snail's pace. Consider it part of the American experience and exhibit patience with the knowledge that service has greatly improved over years past since the post office has privatized. Hours are limited, so plan time to go. Most packages take two to three days to reach other cities, and a week to 10 days to reach other countries.

Hours of service

Monday to Friday 9a.m. to 5p.m.; main post offices are also open Saturday 9a.m. to noon or 1p.m.

TELEGRAMS

Telegrams can be sent from hotels. They are not used much for in-country communications because fax machines are so prevalent. For international messages to countries without an advanced telephone infrastructure, however, telegrams are still the best way to send.
Western Union..(800) 325-6000
AT&T EasyLink...(800) 242-6005

Business Services

BUSINESS CENTERS / ADMINISTRATIVE SUPPORT

Centers catering to business needs are plentiful in the United States, even in suburban areas. Along with popular companies such as Mail Boxes, Etc. and Kinko's (**www.mbe.com** and **www.kinkos.com**) provide links to all locations), many smaller enterprises exist. A few listings are provided below, while others can easily be located in the yellow pages of any local telephone book. The independent companies may prove less expensive but could have less extensive services. Also, U.S. hotels more likely than not will have their own business centers complete with internet connections, fax, and secretarial service. Renting office space with these types of services is also quite feasible in any U.S. city, but astronomical rent fees are difficult to avoid, particularly in San Francisco and New York!

Chicago/Downtown

ABC Secretarial Service; 203 N La Salle St.; tel: (312) 346-2030.

Executive Support, Inc.; 20 N. Wacker Drive, Suite 2262; tel: (312) 630-9660; fax: (312) 630-9882.

H Q Business Center; 70 W Madison St.; tel: (312) 214-3100.

United States *(side margin)*

Michigan Avenue Office Service; 333 N Michigan Ave.; tel: (312) 372-6582.

Chicago/O'Hare Airport Vicinity
A & M Secretarial Service; 800 Busse Hwy, Park Ridge; tel: (847) 698-2613.

Advanced Business Center; 10600 W Higgins Rd., Rosemont; tel: (847) 635-8001.

GSI Systems; 2800 River Rd., Suite 170, Des Plaines; tel: (847) 824-5511.

Houston
Corporate Office Center; 11200 Westheimer Road; tel: (713) 785-2002.

H Q Business Center; 510 Bering Drive; tel: (713) 968-7500.

Richmond Executive Service; 10700 Richmond Avenue; tel: (713) 789-8907.

Los Angeles
Bonaventure Business Center; 404 S. Figueroa Street, Suite 105, Los Angeles; tel: (213) 489-4559; fax: (213) 489-4840.

Los Angeles Convention Center; 1201 South Figueroa Street, Los Angeles; tel: (213) 741-1151

fax: (213) 765-4266.

Miami
Airport Business Center; 3399 NW 72nd Ave. # 207; tel: (305) 592-5424.

H Q Business Center; 801 Brickell Ave. # 900; tel: (305) 372-0220.

T & T Business Center; 13136 W Dixie Hwy; tel: (305) 893-5549.

New York
A Century Business Solutions; 148 Madison Ave.; tel: (212) 779-7171.

Business Center-Rockefeller Center; 630 5th Ave. # 2000; New York, NY; tel: (212) 332-3400.

Copykat Information & Business Center; 1785 Lexington Ave.; tel: (212) 534-1400.

Elite Business Systems Incorporated; 20 W 22nd St. Fl 5; tel: (212) 675-7493.

San Francisco
Alliance Business Center; 1 Embarcadero Center; tel: (415) 433-6363.

Aa Sos Support Office Service; 582 Market St # 218; tel: (415) 391-4578.

Regent Business Center; 225 Bush St # 1600; tel: (415) 439-8300.

Seattle
Adams & Associates, Inc. Adams Temporaries; 701 5th Ave., Suite 3700, Seattle, WA, 98104; tel: (206) 447-9200; fax: (206) 623-2093.

Adecco Employment Services; 220 Blanchard St., Seattle, WA, 98121; tel: (206) 448-2342; fax: (206) 448-8509.

Brown's Office Support Service; 15278 Sunwood Blvd.; tel: (206) 242-6054.

Mailbox & Business Service Center; 2400 NW 80th St.; tel: (206) 789-7007.

Washington DC
Georgetown Business Center; 1101 30th St NW # 500; tel: (202) 625-8300.

H Q Business Center; 1201 Pennsylvania Ave. NW # 300; tel: (202) 661-4600.

COURIER SERVICES
There are literally hundreds of stations for FedEx, UPS, DHL, and TNT. Just walk a few city blocks and you'll see at least one drop box for these services, all with a daily pick-up. There are also offices in all major cities where you can drop off large packages.

Airborne...(800) 247-2676
DHL ....(800) 225-5345
FedEx ....(800) 238-5355
International Bonded Couriers...................(800) 322-3067
National Courier ....(800) 862-7500
TNT Express ....(877) 624-5868
UPS...(800) 742-5877

All major US cities have local package and messenger delivery services. Check the "Yellow Pages" listings for courier services in each city.

PRINTING/COPYING
Copy shops in the U.S. have become elaborate business centers; one example is Kinko's (**www.kinkos.com**), where customers can do just about anything for business, from printing business cards, to making faxes, to extensive graphic design, and all for a hefty price (to print out a report costs US$0.50 a page!). Many hotel business centers also have printing and copying services, and usually for the same or lower prices.

Chicago
Kinko's Inc.; 8535 W Higgins Rd. Chicago; tel: (773) 693-3090.

M Casey & Co; 5841 W Montrose Ave.; tel: (773) 777-1300; http://www.mcaseyco.com.

Mail Boxes Etc.; 47 W Division St.; tel: (312) 943-6260.

Mail Boxes Etc.; 27 N Wacker Dr.; (312) 372-2727.

Kinko's Inc.; 540 N Michigan Ave.; (312) 832-0090.

Sir Speedy Printing Ctr; 311 S Wacker Dr.; (312) 408-1080.

Houston
A&E Products Co., Inc.; 4235 Richmond Ave.; tel: (713) 621-0022; fax: (713) 621-2537; email: info@aeproducts.com.

Above & Beyond Copies; 7502 Harrisburg Blvd.; tel: (713) 926-7887.

Accurate Reproductions; 1430 Yale St.; (713) 659-8369.

Advanced Copies; 9538 Richmond Ave. # B; tel: (713) 549-0900.

Copy.com; 1201 Westheimer; tel: (713) 528-1201.

Copyplus Printing; 3720 S Gessner Rd.; tel: (713) 952-5200.

Sir Speedy Printing Ctr; 3701 W Alabama St. # 380; tel: (713) 622-8823.

Los Angeles
Continental Print Express; 3600 Wilshire Blvd. #100H, Los Angeles; tel: (213) 388-3855; toll-free: (800) 404-0774; fax: (213) 388-3881; e-mail: printex@aol.com.

Kinko's Copies (9 Los Angeles locations); 7630 W Sunset Blvd., Los Angeles; tel: (323) 845-4501.

The Print Network; 3621 Torrance Blvd., Torrance; tel: (310) 543-3544; fax: (310) 316-1902.

Ray's Copy Center, Burbank.

Sir Speedy Printing; 6660 Sunset Blvd. Ste Q, Hollywood; tel: (323) 469-0327; toll-free: (877) 266-7967; fax: (323) 469-9284.

Miami
Copy Center & Office Supply; 9721 S Dixie Hwy; tel: (305) 667-2655.

United States

Copy Depot; 8200 NW 27th St. # 116; tel: (305) 477-9099.

Solo Printing, Inc.; 7860 N.W. 66 St.; tel: (800) 325-0118; fax: (305) 599-5245.

New York
East Side Copy Center; 15 E 13th St.; tel: (212) 807-0465.

Foxy Copy & Typing Center; 211 W 92nd St., New York; tel: (212) 724-1770.

Kopy Kween Incorporated; 25 W 45th St.; tel: (212) 944-7350.

Mail Boxes Etc.(9 locations downtown); 331 W. 57th Street; tel: (212) 489-8004.

San Francisco
Copy Net; 2404 California St.; tel: (415) 567-5888.

International Minute Press; Golden Gateway Center; tel: (415) 956-3395.

Page Street Press; 15 Page Street; tel: (415) 863-0303.

Print Avenue; 1276 Market Street; tel: (415) 551-2222.

Printmasters; 1345 Mission Street; tel: (415) 626-2335.

Seattle
Copy Machine; 562 1st Ave. S # 100; tel: 206-622-3738

Olympic Reprographics; 1016 1st Ave. S; tel: (206) 622-6000.

Kinko's; 1833 Broadway; tel: (206) 329-7445; fax: (206) 329-7554; email: usa5146@kinkos.com.

Kinko's; 735 Pike St Ste 11-13; tel: (206) 467-1767; fax: (206) 467-1321; email: usa5161@kinkos.com.

Professional Copy 'N' Print; 4200 University Way Ne; 206-634-2689

Professional Copy 'N' Print; 706 Ne 45th St.; tel: (206) 634-2689.

Sudden Printing; 11009 1st Ave. S; tel: (206) 243-4444.

Washington DC
Kinko's Inc. (6 locations); 317 Pennsylvania Ave. SE; tel: (202) 547-0421.

Kwik Kopy Printing; 4000 Wisconsin Ave. NW; tel: (202) 362-8399.

P & P Copy Center; 1815 H St NW # 401; tel: (202) 466-2229.

Sir Speedy Printing; 2001 Pennsylvania Ave NW # 175; tel: (202) 785-1818.

TRANSLATION SERVICES
Accredited Language Services...................(800) 755-5775
Ad-Ex...(800) 223-7753
AT&T Language Line Services...................(800) 544-5721
Berlitz Translation Services........................(800) 367-4336
Idem ....(800) 642-4336

Chicago
International Business; 625 N Michigan Ave. # 500; tel: (773) 549-6441.

International Language Ctr.; 79 W Monroe St. # 1310; tel: (312) 236-3366.

Nelles Translations; 6 North Michigan Ave., Ste 1409; tel: (312) 236-2788; fax: (312) 236-0717; e-mail: nelles@concentric.net.

Houston
MasterWord Services, Inc.; 303 Stafford, Suite 204; tel: (281) 589-0810; fax: (281) 589-1104; email: masterword@masterword.com.

Los Angeles
Global Language Solutions; 19800 MacArthur Blvd., Suite. 520, Irvine; tel: (949) 798-1414; fax: (949) 798-1410.

International Conference Systems; 5777 W. Century Blvd., Suite 1000, Los Angeles; tel: (310) 665-4000; fax: (310) 665-4180.

Miami
Haard Translating Service; 201 W Flagler Street; tel: (305) 358-2820; fax: (305) 358-2832; e-mail: info@haardtranslating.com.

International Translation Inc.; 13499 Biscayne Blvd. # 406; (305) 945-6337.

New York
Berlitz Translation Service; 132 W 31st St.; tel: (212) 339-4700.

Interworld Translation Service; 10 W 37th St., Floor 3; tel: (212) 594-8218.

Electrical
Current
11-/120 volts AC, 60Hz.

ELECTRIC PLUGS

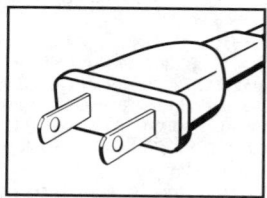

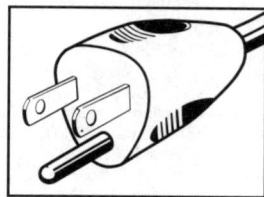

Plug adaptors are available through **iGo Corporation.**
(See "Electrical and Telephone Adaptors" on page 19.)

Technical Support
HARDWARE/SOFTWARE VENDOR SUPPORT

Acer/Texas Instruments; tel: (972) 995-6611; fax: (972) 917-5150; 1- 800-816-2237 (Notebook/Acer Technical Support); [1] (800) 445- 6495 (Acer Hardware Technical Support); http://www.acer.com/.

Adobe; tel: [1] (800) 628-2320 (Customer Service); (Technical Support) tel: (206) 441-5142 (MacIntosh/$25 per incident); (206) 441- 5142 (Windows/$25 per incident); (206) 441-5142 (UNIX/$40 per incident); 1-900-555-3300 (MacIntosh/$2 per minute); 1- 900-555-2200 (Windows/$2 per minute); http://www.adobe.com/

Apple; [1] (800) 776-2333 (Customer Relations); [1] (800) 833-6223 (Customer Relations TDD); [1] (800) 767-2775 (Technical Support); [1] (800) 769-2775 (Software Upgrades); [1] (800) 919-2775 (Service Provider Support); http://www.apple.com/.

AST; tel: [1] (800) 727-1278 (Laptops/Bravo Desktops/Business Computers); tel: [1] (800) 758-0278 (Advantage/Home PC's); (714) 727-4141 (Corporate Office); fax: (817) 232-9824; http://www.ast.com/.

Compaq; tel: [1] (800) 345-1518 (Product Information); [1] (800) 652-6672 (Technical Support, Warranty Service, Software Support); (713) 370-0670 (Main Office); fax: (713) 374-1740; (713) 370-0670 (International Support); fax: (281) 518-1442 (International Fax); http://www.compaq.com/.

Corel; tel: (613) 728-3733 (Customer Service); fax: (613) 761-9176; http://www.corel.com/.

Dell; tel: [1] (800) 624-9897 (Customer Service); [1] (800) 624-9896 (Technical Support); tel: (512) 338-4400 (Main Office); fax: (512) 728-3330; http://www.dell.com/.

Digital; tel: [1] (800) 344-4825 (Sales, Service, General Inquiries, Literature); fax: [1] (800) 676-7517; [1] (800) 722-9332 (PC Orders and Product Information); [1] (800) 354-9000 (For Service/24 hours); [1] (800) DIGITAL (Customer Problem Resolution); fax: (978) 952-4281; http://www.digital.com/.

Gateway 2000; tel: [1] (605) 232-2000; fax: [1] (605) 232-2023; [1] (800) 846-2000 (Customer Service/Technical Support); http://gw2k.com/.

Hewlett Packard; tel: (208) 323-2551 for Printer, Plotter, Fax, Scanner; tel: (208) 344-4131 for HP DeskJet 680C and DeskWriter 680C Printers; tel: (970) 635-1000 for HP Vectra PC, NetServer, Mass Storage; tel: (208) 323-4663 for HP Pavilion; tel: (970) 346-8682 for HP OmniBook Notebook PC; tel: (208) 376-3686 for PhotoSmart PC Photography System; http://www.hp.com/.

IBM; tel: (1) 520-574-4600; [1] (800) IBM-3333 (Toll Free); [1] (800) 426-4968 (Technical Support); http://www.ibm.com/.

Microsoft; tel: [1] (800) 426-9400 (Sales and Technical Support Directory); [1] (800) 936-4100 (Desktop Applications); 1-800-936-4200 (Desktop Systems); [1] (800) 936-4300 (Development Tools); [1] (800) 936-4400 (Business Systems); tel: 1-(206) 882-8080 (Microsoft Operator); fax: 1(206) 883-8101; http://www.microsoft.com/.

NEC; tel: [1] (800) 632-4565 (Power Mates); [1] (800) 632-4525 (Portable PC's); [1] (800) 325-5500 (Servers); [1] (800) 632-4554 (Ready and PowerPlayer); (888) 762-3246 (Ready Office); fax: 978-635- 4100 (Technical Support - Fax); [1] (800) 332-8004/access code 632, 1, 1 (UltraCare New Repairs); [1] (800) 332-8004/access code 632, 1, 2 (UltraCare Repair Status); fax: (603) 894-2849 (UltraCare Depot Fax); (888) 863-2669 (Sales Info Center, Dealer Locations, Product Literature, Factory Store, Order Status); [1] (800) 842-6446 (Versa Laptop Spare Parts); fax: (63) 775-6876; [1] (800) 233-6321 or (972) 406-9593 (PC Spare Parts and Software); http://www.nec.com/.

Novell; tel: [1] (800) 858-4000 or [1] (801) 861-4000; http://www.novell.com/.

Quark; tel: [1] (303) 894-8899; fax: [1] (303) 894-3398; http://www.quark.com/.

Toshiba; tel: [1] (800) 999-4273 (Technical Service and Support), [1] (714) 583-3000 (General Number); http://www.toshiba.com/ and http://pcsupport.toshiba.com/.

Internet Connection
HOW TO CONNECT

Connecting to AOL and Compuserve in the United States is similar to using it when traveling outside your own area code. See the introductory section for detailed information on connecting to your account through a different phone number.

America Online

Hundreds of AOL access numbers (usually several for every area code) are available by selecting "get new number" from the AOL welcome screen. The system then will dial the toll free 800 number and ask for the local area code. Put in the city code and AOL will give you numbers to choose from.

Compuserve

Alternative numbers are available on Compuserve for every area code. If you are using CompuServe 2000, use GO PHONES within CompuServe 2000 to search for access numbers. The Compuserve Web-site also has a great deal of information, at http://www.compuserve.com/.

Sales/service: Compuserve; P.O. Box 20212; 5000 Arlington Centre Blvd.; Columbus, OH 43220; Service: [1](614)529-1340, (800) 848-8199; Service fax: [1](614) 529-1611. Service Hours 8a.m. to midnight (U.S. EST) weekdays, noon to 10 p.m. (U.S. EST) Saturday and Sunday.

Independent Service Providers

There are thousands of I.S.P.'s, most only covering one area code. In the rapidly growing internet market, I.S.P.'s are constantly emerging, being bought and being sold. For current I.S.P.'s in your destination, check out http://www.thelist.com/. It has providers for every area and lists prices and services. You can also look for I.S.P.'s in the Yellow Pages in that area's telephone directory. Below are a few of the larger I.S.P.'s in the United States:

A 1 internetservice; tel: (800) 947-6074; http://www.a1internetservice.com/.

AT&T Network Commerce Services; tel: (800) 467-8467; http://www.ipservices.att.com/wss/.

EarthLink Sprint; tel: (800) 395-8425; email: sales@corp.earthlink.net; http://www.earthlink.net/.

GTE Internet; tel: (888) GTE-SURF; email: slsreq@gte.net; http://www.gte.net/.

MSN Internet Access; tel: (800) FREE-MSN; http://msn.com/.

Prodigy Internet; tel: (914) 448-8000; pibilling@prodigy.net; http://www.prodigy.com/.

Mindspring; tel: (404) 815-9111; tel: (404) 287-6774; http://www.mindspring.com/.

UUNET Technologies; tel: (800) 4UUNET4, (703) 206-5600; http://www.uu.net/.

Verio; tel: (303) 645-1900; fax: (303) 708-2490; email: sales@verio.net; http://www.verio.com/.

VPM Internet Services; tel: (800) 321-0221 / (916) 983-9876; fax: (916) 983-4375; sales@vpm.com; http://www.vpm.com/.

Business Culture
GREETINGS AND COURTESIES

The U.S. is the world's fourth largest country and its society is complex. In addition, many minority groups living throughout the country retain their own cultures. U.S. businesspeople are generally outgoing and pleased with their high standard of living. However, one should be careful not to attach special importance to this geniality. Gestures and invitations that can signal intimacy in other cultures might be nothing more than someone "just being friendly." The accepted greeting is smiling, making eye contact, and shaking hands. Handshakes are generally firm and brief, with a rapid, simple up-and-down motion. Greetings can be followed by general questions about your trip, your health, or the weather. Such questions are a form of politeness. Long, detailed answers are not expected or especially wanted. After this quick, often superficial exchange, the next topic will be business.

BUSINESS ETHIC AND FRAMEWORK

American business people thrive on information. They demand transparency in all dealings and their economic clout allows them to walk away from any deal that "smells fishy." They have no time for counterparts that are evasive or slow in providing answers.

America is awash with lawyers and contracts are held to be sacred. Violate a contract clause and expect to be pummeled with subpoenas and court hearings. Business is never "personal" in the United States, and many people have done business with each other for years yet have never met face-to-face.

Contrary to the stereotype, Americans are very sophisticated negotiators who are skilled at both buying and selling positions. The massiveness of the U.S. national economy has allowed its government to shape the world economy and international laws to suit American firms. The Americans can be the nicest people in the world when dealt with fairly. Attempt to do otherwise and they are more than happy to box the offender's ears. They play for big stakes and they play for keeps.

DECISION MAKING

A common U.S. expression is "time is money." Except for situations involving large corporations, U.S. businesspeople are generally results-oriented, prefer to make quick decisions, and move quickly to put their decisions into action. In smaller businesses, one person could be the sole decision maker for the entire company and might make a decision immediately without even consulting others.

WOMEN

Men hold the vast majority of management positions, but the U.S. has more women in higher-levels jobs than any other country. Women expect to be treated seriously and with the respect to which their position entitles them. Failure to do this will be insulting. A woman may not respond at the moment, but she will probably express her displeasure to her colleagues later. Businesswomen are as open and direct as men. This should not be viewed as anything more than being friendly. Foreign women can expect to be treated the same as men, but exactly how a woman is dealt with will depend on the U.S. person she is encountering. Sexual discrimination is against the law and is not openly practiced, but private biases do exist. If a woman encounters discrimination, it will be more a reflection of the person discriminating than of the company.

MEETINGS

Schedules are busy and work days are full, so meetings start on time. U.S. business culture tends to be informal, with an emphasis on getting things done. Generally, businesspeople are informal and direct, sometimes to the point of being confrontational. They will usually get to business quickly, so as not to waste time. Talk will be open and fast-paced. People might interrupt each other or finish sentences for someone else. They will freely give their own opinions, suggest and debate different ideas or approaches, and contradict senior group members. Control and efficiency are important. U.S. people want to be informed of new developments and changes, good or bad, so they can deal

with them. Holding something back might be viewed as dishonesty. U.S. people value directness about intentions, and what can or can not be done. Evasions, even as a form of politeness, will be seen as irresponsibility or dishonesty.

BUSINESS ENTERTAINING

Americans are a leisurely bunch and they love to show off. Their favorite saying to describe their approach to life is "work hard, play hard" and they abide by the slogan.

Business entertainment can run the gamut from lavish golf outings, to expensive dinners, to parties at country estates, even just a plain old backyard barbecue.

Each region of the United States is as different as a separate country when it comes to entertaining. The east coast has "button down" staid cocktail parties, while the southeast has slow-paced candlelight dinners on balmy porches. Texas is big business mixed with spit-roasted sides of beef and cowboy bravado. California, home of casual dress and microchips, will find business being conducted in hot tubs, at meditation centers, on ranches, or in glass towers. Anything and everything is available anywhere and at anytime in the United States. Visitors should sit back and enjoy the ride. Americans love their fun!

BUSINESS ATTIRE

Standard attire is a business suit, especially when dealing with large companies. However, as in everything else, individuality is accepted. Being neatly dressed and well-groomed is most important. There is generally more latitude when dealing with smaller companies or in rural areas, where ties are not as essential or suits may not be expected. Minimal attire is a jacket and tasteful pants, shirt, and shoes. Women should dress professionally and, for best results, conservatively when conducting business. Avoid extremes in fashion, and excessive jewelry, heavy makeup, or accessories. America is where the concepts of Corporate Casual and Dress Down Friday began. Even vintage brokerage firms, known for their starched-shirt mentality just a few years ago, have given in to golf shirts and khaki pants. (Wear a tie at an American software company and they will assume you are a politician looking for votes.) Though sometimes it is hard to tell the executives from the mailroom delivery staff, comfort is sweeping through American business dress standards.

Business Advisory

POLITICS & GRAFT

Politicians and bureaucrats are well paid in the United States, which greatly limits the temptation for them to ask for bribes. Graft does occur, however, but not that often relative to the number and size of transactions. When discovered, graft draws severe penalties. The U.S. was also the first nation to prosecute its business people for participating in graft when overseas.

BUSINESS FRAUD

American business is ruled by tightly-worded contracts and guarantees. Fraud does occur and is highly publicized. However, considering the billions of transactions that take place in the United States every day, fraud is really an uncommon occurrence.

Note: Americans regularly perform "due diligence" background checks on potential business partners and even on clients. To refuse to participate or to become offended will only cause suspicion. Americans like to know all the facts before they sign contracts. Foreigners should feel free to perform similar checks on American counterparts.

Business Centers
Chicago

CITY VIEW

Chicago is an immense city, but it hasn't lost its midwest charm. Huge skyscrapers lie adjacent to housing developments that look almost the same as they did 50 years ago. Winters in the 'windy city' can be harsh and bitterly cold, while the summers prompt hot and humid conditions. A great deal of business now extends out of downtown along a stretch of the western suburbs surrounding O'Hare Airport. This corridor encompasses towns such as Rosemont and Park Ridge, and many business travelers are likely to stay and conduct most of their affairs in this outlying region. For tourism, it is certainly worth a trip into town, which can be achieved by taxi or an approximately 30-minute train ride. In addition to the many museums the city has to offer, tours are conducted by boat along the Chicago River. Curious travelers may also study Chicago's unique architecture or tour the historic buildings that survived the Fire of 1871.

AIRPORT

O'Hare Airport to City Center

The airport has regular bus and shuttle services, and taxis are readily available. Journey time by taxi to downtown Chicago is about 30 to 45 minutes, depending on traffic. Expect to pay about $30.

Yellow Cab ....(312) 829-4222

The Chicago Transit Authority runs a 24-hour service between downtown and the airport. Blue Line stations downtown include La Salle, Jackson, Monroe, and Washington. The Orange Line from Midway Airport connects with the Blue Line at Clark/Lake station. Expect the ride to take about 45 minutes. Trains run every ten minutes during the day for a fare of $1.50.

The Blue Line train offers an economical and efficient way to the airport from downtown. However, one is advised not to use the train late at night for safety reasons.

Airport Express runs a coach and van service to O'Hare. For information, call: (312) 454-7800.

Airline Numbers

See the "Travel" section earlier in the U.S. chapter for complete airline phone numbers.

TRAVEL ASSISTANCE

Chicago Office of Tourism
78 E. Washington St.
Chicago, IL 60602
tel: (312) 744-2400; Toll Free: 800-226-6632

HOTELS/DOWNTOWN

Top-end

Fairmont; 200 North Columbus Rd.; tel: (312) 565-8000; toll free: (800) 527-4727; fax: (312) 856-1032; 692 rooms; 2 restaurants; conference facilities (up to 1200); business center; in-room data port, cable tv, hair dryer, mini bar; 24 hour room service; airport shuttle; limousine services; corporate rates; health club; sauna; whirlpool; swimming pool.

Four Seasons Chicago; 120 East Delaware Place; tel: (312) 280-8800; toll free: (800) 332-3442; fax: (312) 280-9184; city center; all rooms with view; restaurant; conference facilities (up to 250); banquets (up to 600); full -service business center; secretarial service; in-room computer and fax available; limousine service; valet and self parking; corporate rates; health club; sauna; massage; whirlpool; swimming pool; outdoor jogging track.

Omni Chicago Hotel; 676 N. Michigan Ave.; tel: (312) 944-6664; toll free: (800) 843-6664; fax: (312) 266-3015; 347 suites; city center; restaurant; conference facilities (up to 200); business center; secretarial service; in-room cable tv, mini bar, coffee maker, safe, data line; airport shuttle; corporate rates; fitness center; swimming pool; whirlpool.

Renaissance Chicago Hotel; 1 W. Wacker Dr.; tel: (312) 372-7200; toll free: (800) 468-3571; fax: (312) 372-0093; 513 rooms; city center; 2 restaurants; bar; conference facilities (up to 770); business center; in-room data port, mini bar, cable tv; 24 hour room service; parking; airport transportation; health club/fitness; sauna; indoor swimming pool; whirlpool.

Ritz-Carlton Chicago; 160 E. Pearson St.; tel: (312) 266-1000; toll free: (800) 621-6906; fax: (312) 266-1194; 435 rooms; city center with indoor access to Water Tower Place; near lake; restaurant; meeting facilities; business center; secretarial service; translation; pager; cellular phone; 24-hour business services; airport transportation; parking; Carlton Club and Spa with fitness, steamroom, sauna, massage, indoor swimming pool, whirlpool.

Sheraton Chicago Hotel and Towers; 301 E. North Water Street; tel: (312) 464-1000; toll free: (800) 325-3535; fax: (312) 464-9140; 1204 rooms; 5 restaurants; bar; conference facilities (up to 4600); in-room data port, voice mail, safe, mini bar, cable tv, coffee maker, hair dryer, iron and ironing board; 24 hour room service; airport shuttle; valet and self-parking; corporate rates; health club; indoor swimming pool.

Expensive

Chicago Hilton and Towers; 720 S. MIchigan Ave.; tel: (312) 922-4400; toll free: (800) 445-8667; fax: (312) 922-5240; 1400 rooms; city center; restaurants; conference facilities (up to 3200 one room); business services; luxury-level rooms; in-room data port, cable tv, mini bar, coffee maker, hair dryer, iron and ironing board; 24 hour room service; airport transportation; city transportation; valet parking; corporate rates; athletic club with fitness, massage, indoor pool, whirlpools, running track.

Embassy Suites; 600 N. State St.; tel: (312) 943-3800; toll free: (800) 362-2779; fax: (312) 943-7629; 358 rooms; city center; restaurant; bar; conference facilities (up to 200); fax/photocopy facilities; in-room data port, mini bar, coffee maker, hair dryer, cable tv, videos; room service; corporate rates; sauna; indoor swimming pool; whirlpool.

Holiday Inn Chicago City Center; 300 E. Ohio Street; tel: (312) 787-6100; toll free: (800) 465-4329; fax: (312) 787-6238; 500 rooms; restaurant; conference facilities; fax/photocopy facilities; in-room data port, cable tv; covered parking; corporate rates; connected to McClurg Court sports complex; fitness center; sauna; indoor/outdoor swimming pools; whirlpool; indoor tennis; racquetball.

Hotel Inter-Continental Chicago; 505 North Michigan Avenue; tel: (312) 944-4100; toll free: (800) 327-0200; fax: (312) 944-3050; 844 rooms; city center; 2 restaurants; conference facilities (up to 400); business center; secretarial service; in-room cable tv, mini bar, coffee maker, hair dryer, iron and ironing board; 24 hour room service; Continental Air transport shuttle stop; valet parking; corporate rates; fitness center; massage; sauna; whirlpool; swimming pool.

Hyatt Regency Chicago; 151 E. Wacker Drive; tel: (312) 565-1234; toll free: (800) 233-1234; fax: (312) 565-2966; 2019 rooms; city center; renovated rooms; restaurants; coffee shop; conference facilities (up to 1335); 2 boardrooms; business center; in-room data port, voicemail, cable tv, mini bar, hair dryer; 24 hour room service; airport transportation; parking; corporate rates; nearby health club with sauna, spa, pool.

The Westin Hotel; 909 N. Michigan Ave.; tel: (312) 943-7200; toll free: (800) 228-3000; fax: (312) 943-9347; 739 rooms; renovated hotel opposite Bloomingdale's; restaurants; conference facilities; business services; in-room remote color tv, data ports, desk lamp, work space, fax/photocopier, office supplies; airport transportation; parking; fitness center; saunas.

Moderate

Belden-Stratford; 2300 N. Lincoln Park W.;tel: (312) 281-2900; toll free: (800) 800-8300; fax: (312) 880-2039; 305 rooms; just north of downtown area; restaurant; bar; business center; in-room air conditioning, coffee maker, cable tv; parking; fitness center.

Best Western Inn of Chicago; 162 E. Ohio St. at Michigan Ave.; tel: (312) 787-2100; fax: (312) 573-3140; 358 rooms; restaurant; bar; conference facilities; business services; in-room cable tv, hair dryer, iron and board, data port; airport transportation; valet parking; adjacent health club facilities; swimming pool.

Best Western River North; 125 W. Ohio St.; tel: (312) 467-0800; toll free: (800) 727-0800; fax: (312) 467-1665; 148 rooms; restaurant; bar; conference facilities; business services; in-room air conditioning, cable tv, data port; room service; airport transportation; free parking; fitness center; sauna; indoor swimming pool.

Holiday Inn Mart Plaza; 14th to 23rd floors of Apparel Center, 350 N. Orleans; tel: (312) 836-5000; toll free: (800) 465-4329; fax: (312) 222-9508; restaurant; in-room air conditioning, cable tv; airport transportation; parking; fitness center; indoor swimming pool; retail, entertainment, and commercial complex.

Lenox Suites; 616 North Rush Street; tel: (312) 337-1000; toll free: (800) 445-3669; fax: (312) 337-7217; 324 rooms; near city center; restaurant; bar; business facilities; in-room cable tv, movies, coffee makers, work desk, hair dryers, full kitchens; room service; airport transportation; fitness center.

Quality Inn Downtown; 1 S. Halsted; tel: (312) 829-5000; toll free: (800) 221-2222; fax: (312) 829-8151; 425 rooms; restaurant; business services; conference facilities; in-room air conditioning, cable tv, data port; airport transportation; parking; swimming pool.

HOTELS / O'HARE

Top-end

Hotel Sofitel Chicago; 5550 North River Rd., Rosemont, IL 60018; tel: (847) 678-4488; toll free: (800) 233-5959; fax: (847) 678-9756; 292 rooms; restaurant; bar; business center; in-room air conditioning, mini bar, cable tv; 24 hour room service; valet parking; airport shuttle; laundry; fitness center; sauna; swimming pool.

Westin Hotel O'Hare; 6100 N River Rd., Rosemont, IL 60018; tel: (847) 698-6000; toll free: (800) WESTIN1; fax: (847) 698-5483; 525 rooms; restaurant; bar; conference facilities up to 1200; business center; in-room mini bar, coffee makers, video; 24 hour room service; fitness center; whirlpool; sauna; swimming pool.

Expensive

Hawthorne Hotel and Suites;10233 West Higgins Road, Rosemont, IL 60018; tel: (847) 824-9801; 300 rooms; restaurant; bar; conference facilities; in-room cable tv, video, voice mail, coffee maker, hair dryer, iron and ironing board, data port; parking; fitness center; swimming pool; whirlpool.

O'Hare Hilton; O'Hare Airport; tel: (773) 686-8000; toll free: (800) 445-8667; fax: (773) 601-2873; connected to O'Hare Airport terminals; restaurant; business facilities; in-room air conditioning, hairdryer, coffee maker, data port, mini bar, cable tv, ironing board; 24 hour room service; airport transportation; parking; fitness center; sauna; swimming pool; whirlpool; indoor golf center.

O'Hare Marriott; 8535 W. Higgins Rd.; tel: (773) 693-4444; toll free: (800) 228-9290; fax: (773) 714-4279; 681 rooms; near airport; 3 restaurants; bar; conference facilities; business center; in-room air conditioning, cable tv, hairdryer, iron and ironing board, data port; room service; airport transportation; parking; fitness center; indoor/outdoor swimming pool; whirlpool.

Moderate

Best Western At O'Hare; 10300 W. Higgins Rd.; tel: (847) 296-4471; toll free: (800) 528-1234; 141 rooms; restaurant; bar; conference facilities (up to 40); in-room data port, voice mail, cable tv, iron and ironing board, coffee makers; parking; swimming pool.

Holiday Inn O'Hare; 5440 North River Road; tel: (847) 671-6350;toll free: (800) HOL-IDAY; fax: (847) 671-5406; 507 rooms; located near airport; restaurant; in-room cable tv, mini bar; airport transfer; parking; fitness center; sauna; swimming pool; whirlpool.

MEDICAL CARE

Bethany Hospital; 5550 W North Ave., Chicago; tel: (773) 265-7700.

Cook County Hospital; 1835 W Harrison St., Chicago; tel: (312) 633-6000.

Lutheran General Hospital; 1775 Dempster St., Park Ridge; tel: (847) 723-2210.

Mercy Hospital & Medical Center; 2525 S Michigan Ave., Chicago; tel: (312) 567-2486.

Northwestern Memorial Hospital; 250 E. Superior St., Chicago; tel: (312) 908-2000; emergency: (312) 908-5222; physician referral: (312) 908-8400; psychiatry and crisis intervention hotline: (312) 908-8100; chemical dependence crisis hotline: (312) 908-2255.

University of Chicago Physicians Group and Dental Associates; 222 N. LaSalle St., Chicago; doctor referral and health questions: 1-888-824-0200.

HEALTH CLUB

The Chicago Fitness Center; 3131 N. Lincoln Ave., Chicago, Illinois 60657; tel: (773) 549-8181; fax: (773) 549-4622; email: info@chicagofitnesscenter.com.

New City YMCA; 1515 N. Halsted at Clybourn Avenue, Chicago; tel: (312) 266-1242.

Randolph Athletic Club; Randolph Tower, 188 W. Randolph at Wells, Chicago; tel: (312) 269-5820.

South Side YMCA; 6330 S. Stony Island at 63rd Street, Chicago; tel: (773) 947-0700.

Waves Spa Lakeshore Athletic Club; 211 N Stetson Ave., Chicago, IL 60601; tel: (312) 616-1087; fax: (312) 616-8310.

AUTO RENTAL

Downtown

Alamo Rent A Car; 3800 N Mannheim Rd., Franklin Park, IL 60131; tel: (847) 671-7662; fax: (847) 671-5189.

Avis Rent A Car; North Loop-Downtown, 214 N Clark St., (Clark & Wacker), Chicago IL, 60601; (312) 782-6827.

Budget; 4250 W Diversy, Chicago, IL; tel: (773) 283-1800.

Budget; 1135 West Armitage, Chicago, IL 60614; tel: (773) 686-6800.

United States

Budget; 181 W Washington, Chicago, IL 60601; tel: (773) 686-6800.

Enterprise; 303 W. Lake St., Chicago, IL 60606-1703; tel: (312) 332-7783.

Hertz; 401 North State Street, Chicago; tel: (312) 372-7600; fax: (312) 222-9830.

Hertz; Chicago Bank One, 76 West Monroe Street, Chicago; tel: (312) 726-1476; fax: (312) 726-1481.

O'Hare Airport

Alamo; Chicago O'Hare Intl Airport, 3800 N Mannheim Road, Franklin Park, Chicago, IL 60131; tel: (847) 671-7662; fax: 847-671-5189.

Avis; Chicago O'Hare Intl Airport Chicago IL, 60666; (773) 825-4600.

Budget; O'Hare Airport, Chicago, IL 60666; tel: (773) 686-6800.

Enterprise; O'Hare Airport, 4025 Manheim, Schiller Park, IL 60176-1874; tel:(847) 928-3320.

Hertz; O'Hare Airport, 10000 Bessie Coleman Drive, PO Box 66096; tel: (773) 686-7272; fax: (773) 582-6350.

CHAMBER OF COMMERCE

Chicagoland Chamber of Commerce
330 N. Wabash One IMB Place
Chicago, IL 60611
tel: (312) 494-6400; fax: (312) 494-0196
email: staff@chicagolandchamber.org

WORLD TRADE CENTER

World Trade Center Chicago
Suite 929, the Merchandise Mart
200 World Trade Center, Ste. 2400
Chicago, IL 60654
tel: (312) 467-0550; fax: (312) 467-0615
email: info@wtcc.org
website: http://www.wtcc.org

Houston

CITY VIEW

Although technically one of the largest cities in the country, the city proper actually seems quite small. Don't be fooled. Houston is an international hub and the energy capital of the United States. Houston is the home to the Lyndon Johnson Space Center, where all of the nation's space missions are controlled. Houston was, therefore, a focal point during man's landing on the moon in 1969. The Texas Medical Center, a conglomeration of 20 different medical facilities all in one area, also attracts a lot of national attention. For recreation in Houston, the Astrodome roofs both a domed stadium and amusement park. If a grassy park is more on your mind than roller coasters, Memorial Park extends for over a thousand acres and Houston's zoo is located in Hermann Park. The Port of Houston has the greatest amount of waterborne commerce in the whole United States and stretches for 25 miles along the Houston Ship Channel. Sculpturally, the city of Houston lacks any public zoning, accounting for poverty-stricken shacks pushed up against shining skyscrapers. Avoid the city in the summer, if possible; the heat and humidity can be unbearable.

AIRPORT

Houston Intercontinental Airport to City Center

The airport lies 15 miles north of the city. Buses and taxis are available, and local hotels provide shuttle buses. One can reach Houston by METRO bus for a fare of $1. Board

at Terminal C., between 5:38 a.m. and 12:32 a.m.; buses run every 25 to 40 minutes. A metro bus day pass costs $2 and is good for unlimited rides for 24 hours. Present passes to the operator each time you board a METRO bus during the time the pass is valid.

The Airport Express travels between the airport and downtown hotels in 30-minute intervals between 5:30a.m. and 11:30p.m. Expect a 30- to 60-minute ride into town. The ticket window is located southside of the terminal. Call: (281) 523-8888 for more information.

Downtown	$16
Post Oak/Galleria	$16
Greenway Plaza	$17
Medical Center	$17

The Town & Country Airport Shuttle departs hourly, 5 minutes past the hour, between 6:05a.m. and 11:05p.m. The shuttle serves Adam's Mark, Westchase Hilton, Holiday Inn Houston West, Hilton West, Hyatt Regency, and Sheraton Town & Country for a fare of $17. Call: 230-3100 for more information.

Cabs also ply the route between airport and city center. Fares run about $32 to downtown.

Hobby Airport to City Center

The airport lies nine miles from Houston's city center. If traveling by taxi, expect the trip to take between 20 and 45 minutes for a fare of around $20. An Airport Express bus services downtown and leaves in 30-minute intervals between 5:30a.m. and 11:30p.m. The $12 tickets are available at the ticket counter outside of baggage claims. Expect the travel time to take between 30 and 45 minutes.

Downtown	$11
Uptown/Galleria	$12
Greenway Plaza	$12
Medical Center	$12

Airline Numbers

See the "Travel" section earlier in the U.S. chapter for complete airline phone numbers.

Bush Intercontinental Airport	(281) 230-3000
Hobby Airport	(713) 640-3000

TRAVEL ASSISTANCE

Downtown Houston Association
1221 McKinney, Suite 3434
Houston, TX 77010
tel: (713) 658-8938; fax: (713) 658-0503

Hotel Reservations Network
tel: (800) 964-6835
Web: www.hoteldiscount.com

CHAMBER OF COMMERCE

Cy-Fair Houston Chamber of Commerce
11050 FM 1960 West Suite 100
Houston, Texas 77065-3612
tel: (281) 955-1100; Fax (281) 955-0138

Galleria Chamber of Commerce
5075 Westheimer, Suite 660
Houston, TX 77056-5623
tel: (713) 629-5555; fax: (713) 629-6403
email: info@galleriachamber.com

Greater Houston Partnership Chamber of Commerce
1200 Smith, Suite 700
Houston, Texas 77002-4309
tel: (713) 844-3600; Fax (713) 844-0200

MEETING/CONVENTION BUREAU

Greater Houston Convention & Visitors Bureau
901 Bagby

Houston, TX 77002
tel: (713) 227-3100; Toll-free: (800) 4HOUSTON
email: houstongde@aol.com

WORLD TRADE CENTER

Houston World Trade Association
a Division of the Greater Houston Partnership
1200 Smith St., Suite 700
Houston, TX 77002
tel: (713) 844-3637; fax: (713) 844-0200
email: pfoley@houston.org
website: http://www.houston.org

Los Angeles

CITY VIEW

The 'City of Angels' is thought of as a beach-front para-dise, thanks to Hollywood's images. In reality, Los Angeles is a sprawling metropolis that stretches for miles with packed freeways pointing in every direction. The movie production side of L.A. was introduced to the area in the be-ginning of the twentieth century, and is now joined with many other leading industries such as petroleum, high tech, tourism, and aerospace. Los Angeles is the largest city in California (2nd in nation to New York), but not the capital of the state. It was, however, once capital of Mexi-co's Alta California and an agricultural center. Now, Los Angeles is both a playground for the rich and an urbanized warzone. Beware traveling by yourself if unfamiliar with the city; one can easily go from a nice, middle-class area to a high-crime neighborhood simply by taking the wrong exit. Points of interest are easy to track down, ranging anywhere from a tour of Universal Studios to checking out muscle men on Venice Beach.

AIRPORT

Los Angeles International Airport to City Center

The airport is located 15 miles (24 km.) from the city in Santa Monica Bay. The LAX Shuttle A provides frequent free transfers between all terminals; stops can be found on the lower level of each terminal.

Journey time between downtown L.A. and the airport by taxi takes around 30 minutes but can be much longer de-pending on traffic. Expect to pay between $25 to $30.
Checker Cab 800-300-5007
United Taxi ....(310) 821-1000
Yellow Cab ....(310) 808-1000

By train, the Metro Green Line runs east to west be-tween Norwalk and Redondo Beach. Get off at Aviation Station where a free shuttle bus serves all LAX terminals. Buses arrive at lower levels of the terminals. Trains operate every 8 to 12 minutes between 4:30am and 11:30pm. Con-nections from the Blue Line, which runs north to south, can be made at Imperial Station. The metro fare costs $1.35 one way, and $2.70 round trip. For more metro information, visit the website at http://www.mta.net/metro/metro.htm.

A wide choice of bus and van services also exists: The Metropolitan Transportation Authority provides frequent bus services from downtown LA.; for more information, call: (213) 626-4455.

Many companies provide 24-hour van services from L.A. and surrounding areas to the airport. They cost around $15 from downtown and Pasadena and $25 to $30 from the Valley.
ABC Shuttle... 800-582-1923
Apollo Airport Shuttle.................................... 800-342 9949
Best Shuttle: 800-606-7433
Chequer Shuttle ....(310) 215-9950

Golden Shuttle...(310) 645-7172
Inland Express...(909) 626-6599
LAXpress Shuttle..800-427-7483
Prime Time Shuttle......................................800-733-8267
Quick Trip Shuttle.......................................(310) 838-6440
Roadrunner Shuttle 800-247-7919
Shuttle One 800-400-7488
SuperShuttle..800-554-3146
LAX also offers over 21,000 parking spaces.
Parking Information line............................(310) 646-9070.

Airline Numbers

See the "Travel" section earlier in the U.S. chapter for complete airline phone numbers.

TRAVEL ASSISTANCE

Beverly Hills Visitors Bureau
239 S. Beverly Dr.
Beverly Hills, CA 90212
tel: (310) 248-1015; fax: (310) 248-1020
Long Beach Area Convention & Visitors Bureau
One World Trade Center, STE 300
Long Beach, CA 90831-0300
tel: (562) 436-3645; fax: (562) 435-5653
Los Angeles Business Travel Association
1804 W. Burbank Blvd.
Burbank, CA 91506
tel: (818) 848-5578; fax: (818) 843-7423
email: labta@aol.com
Los Angeles Convention & Visitors Bureau
633 W. Fifth Street, Suite 6000
Los Angeles, CA 90071
tel: (213) 624-7300; fax: (213) 624-9746
Venice Chamber of Commerce & Visitors Bureau
P.O. Box 202
Venice, CA 90294
tel: (310) 396-7016; fax: (310) 392-9868
Ventura Visitors & Convention Bureau
89 S. California St., STE C
Ventura, CA 93001-3799
tel: (805) 648-2075; fax: (805) 648-2150
West Hollywood Convention & Visitors Bureau
8687 Melrose Ave., STE M-25
West Hollywood, CA 90069
tel: (310) 289-2525; fax: (310) 289-2529

HOTELS

Top-end
Beverly Hilton; 9876 Wilshire at Santa Monica Blvd., Beverley Hills; tel: (310) 274-7777; toll free: (800) 445-8667; fax: (310) 285-1313; 591 rooms; 2 restaurants; business services; in-room data port; airport transportation; parking; fitness center; swimming pool; massage.
Century Plaza Hotel and Tower; 2025 Avenue of the Stars, Century City; tel: (310) 277-2000; toll free: (800) 228-3000; fax: (310) 551-3355; 1072 rooms; opposite ABC Entertainment Center; all rooms with balcony and refrigerator; restaurants; business services; in-room data port; parking; fitness center; swimming pool; whirlpool.
Four Seasons Los Angeles; 300 S. Doheny Dr., Los Angeles; tel: (310) 273-2222; toll free: (800) 332-3442; fax: (310) 859-3824; http://www.fourseasons.com; 285 rooms; restaurant; conference facilities; business center; secretarial service; translation service; 24-hour business

services; in-room fax machines, modem connection; computers available; cellular phones; pagers; parking; limousine service available; health/fitness; pool; poolside cabanas with phones, faxes, VCR's; whirlpool.

Meridian at Beverly Hills; 465 S. La Cienega Blvd., Beverly Hills; tel: (310) 247-0400; toll free: (800) 645-5687, or (800) 645-5624; fax: (310) 247-0315; 297 rooms; restaurant; conference facilities; business services; in-room fax machines, data port; airport transportation; parking; fitness center; saunas; swimming pool.

Omni Los Angeles; 930 Wilshire Boulevard, Los Angeles; tel: (213) 688-7777; fax: (213) 612-3987; 935 rooms; city center; restaurant; conference facilities (up to 1200); secretarial service; fax/photocopy facilities; in-room data port; parking; corporate rates; fitness center; swimming pool; whirlpool.

The Peninsula Beverly Hills; 9882 LIttle Santa Monica Blvd., Beverly Hills; tel: (310) 551-2888; toll free: (800) 462-7899; fax: (310) 788-2319; 196 rooms; boutique hotel; personalized service; suites and villas available; restaurant; business services; in-room data port; parking; fitness center; saunas; steamrooms; rooftop swimming pool with cabanas; whirlpool.

Ritz-Carlton Huntington Hotel (Pasadena); 1401 S. Oak Knoll Ave.; tel: (818) 568-3900; toll free: (800) 241-3333; fax: (818) 568-3700; 392 rooms including guest cottages; residential area; landscaped grounds; restaurant; conference facilities; business services; in-room data port; parking; fitness center; swimming pool; tennis; massage; spa with treatment rooms.

Westwood Marquis Hotel and Gardens; 930 Hilgard Ave., Los Angeles; tel: (310) 208-8765; fax: (310) 824-0355;258 rooms; located in suburb; restaurant; conference facilities (up to 40); secretarial service; fax/photocopy facilities; in-room data port, cable tv, voice mail; parking; corporate rates; fitness center; swimming pool.

Expensive

Courtyard Marriott Century City; 10320 W. Olympic Blvd., Los Angeles; tel: (310) 556-2777; toll free: (800) 228-9290; fax: (310) 203-0563; 134 rooms; cafeteria; breakfast buffet; bar; business services; in-room data port, cable tv, air conditioning, mini bar, hair dryer; fitness center; whirlpool.

Holiday Inn L.A. Downtown; 750 Garland Ave., Los Angeles; tel: (213) 628-9900; toll free: (800) 628-5240; fax: (213) 628-1201; 205 rooms; restaurant; business services; in-room data port, cable tv; garage parking; fitness center; whirlpool.

Hyatt Regency Los Angeles; 711 South Hope Street, Los Angeles; tel: (213) 683-12345; toll free: (800) 233-1234; fax: (213) 629-3230; 485 rooms; near airport; restaurant; conference facilities; secretarial service; business center; in-room hairdryer, iron and ironing board; room service; corporate rates; fitness center; whirlpool; spa.

Sheraton Gateway (Airport); 6101 West Century Boulevard, Los Angeles; tel: (310) 642-1111; toll free: (800) 325-3535; fax: (310) 410-1852; 807 rooms; adjacent to airport; restaurant; conference facilities; secretarial service; fax/photocopy facilities; in-room data port, cable tv; airport transportation; parking; corporate rates; fitness center; swimming pool.

Sheraton Universal; 333 Universal Terrace, Universal City; tel: (818) 980-1212; toll free: (800) 325-3535; fax: (818) 985-4980; 442 rooms; located in Universal City; restaurant; business services; in-room data port; transportation to Universal Studios; parking; fitness center; swimming pool; whirlpool.

Westin Los Angeles Airport; 5400 West Century Blvd., Los Angeles; tel: (310) 216-5858; toll free: (800) 695-8284; fax: (310) 670-1948; 723 rooms; restaurant; conference facilities (up to 1700); business center; secretarial service; translations; teleconferencing; non-smoking floors; complimentary airport shuttle; car rental; health club; fitness center.

Moderate

Doubletree Club Hotel LAX; 1985 E. Grand Ave., El Segundo; tel: (310) 322-0999; fax: (310) 322-4758; 215 rooms; restaurant; conference facilities; business services; in-room data port, cable tv, coffee maker, iron and ironing board, hairdryer; airport transportation; fitness center; swimming pool.

Furama; 8601 Lincoln Boulevard; tel: (310) 670-8111; fax: (310) 342-2570; http://www.furama-hotels.com; 760 rooms; restaurant; conference facilities (up to 600); secretarial service; fax/photocopy facilities; in-room data port; airport transportation; parking; corporate rates; fitness center; swimming pool; whirlpool.

Holiday Inn-LAX; 9901 S. La Cienega Blvd., Los Angeles; tel: (310) 649-5151 or (800) 624-0025; fax: (310) 670-3619; 403 rooms; restaurant; business services; in-room data port; airport transportation; parking; fitness center; swimming pool.

New Otani Hotel; 120 S. Los Angeles Street, Los Angeles; tel: (213) 624-5855; toll free: (800) 421-8795; fax: (213) 624-8740; 434 rooms; restaurant; conference facilities; in-room cable tv; parking; fitness center; swimming pool; whirlpool.

Park Plaza; 607 South Park View Street, Los Angeles; tel: (213) 384-5281; fax: (213) 480-1928; 50 rooms; city center/airport; restaurant; conference facilities; corporate rates; fitness center; sauna; swimming pool.

Pasadena Hilton; 150 S. Los Robles Ave., Pasadena; tel: (626) 577-1000; toll free: (800) HILTONS; fax: (626) 584-3148; 296 rooms; conference facilities; business services; in-room data port, mini bar, coffee maker, iron and ironing board; parking; fitness center; swimming pool.

MEDICAL CARE

California Hospital Medical Center; 1401 S. Grand Ave., Los Angeles; tel: (213) 748-2411; fax: (213) 742-5725.

Hospital of the Good Samaritan; 1225 Wilshire Blvd. between Witmer and Sixth Street; tel: (213) 977-2121

Shaw Health Center; 5336 Fountain Ave. at E. Western Avenue; tel: (213) 467-5200.

U.C.L.A. Medical Center; 10833 LeConte Ave.; Patient Business Services: (310) 825-8021; physician referral: 1-800-825-2631; interpreter services: (31) 825-7636.

HEALTH CLUB

Angel City Gym; 8816 Melrose Avenue est Hollywood; tel: (310) 858-6812.

Bally's Fitness Centers; 11500 W. Olympic Blvd. at Colby Street; tel: (310) 479-6310; 888 S. Figueroa at Ninth Street, downtown; tel: (213) 488-0095; 3844 Culver Center St., between Venice and Overland, Culver City; tel: (310) 204-2030.

Beverly Hills Health and Fitness; 8301 Beverly Blvd.; tel: (213) 658-6999.

Biltmore Health Club; 506 S. Grand; tel: (213) 612-1567.

The Los Angeles Athletic Club; 431 West Seventh Street Los Angeles; tel: (213)625-2211. **24-Hour Fitness**; 8612 Santa Monica Blvd., West Hollywood; tel: (310) 652-7440.

24-Hour Fitness; 5711 W. Century Blvd.; tel: (310) 410-9909.

Wilshire Center Health Club; Wilshire Center, tel: (213) 388-4111.

Downtown YMCA; 401 S. Hope St. at Fourth Street; tel: (213) 624-2348.

Downtown Long Beach YMCA; 600 Long Beach Blvd. at Sixth Street, Long Beach; tel: (310) 436-9622.

AUTO RENTAL

Affordable West Hollywood; 1040 N. La Brea Avenue, West Hollywood; tel: (323) 467-7182.

Avis; Los Angeles International Airport; tel: (310) 646-5600.

Avis; Hollywood-Burbank Airport, 2627 Hollywood Way (Between Van Owen & San Fernando), Burbank CA, 91500; tel: (818) 566-3001.

Avon Rent A Car; 7080 Santa Monica Blvd., West Hollywood; tel: (323) 850-0826.

Budget; Los Angeles International Airport; tel: (310) 645-4500.

Budget; Union Station; 800 North Alameda, Los Angeles; tel: (213) 617-2977.

Hertz; Los Angeles International Airport; tel: (310) 646-4861.

Hertz; South Bay Area, 3635 Fashion Way, Los Angeles; tel: (310) 316-3855; fax: (310) 429-2781.

National; Los Angeles International Airport; tel: (310) 670-4950.

Thrifty; Los Angeles International Airport; tel: (310) 645-1880.

Thrifty Car Rental; 9060 Santa Monica Blvd., West Hollywood; tel: (310) 860-9543.

CHAMBER OF COMMERCE

Century City Chamber of Commerce
2049 Century Park E., STE 2600
Los Angeles, CA 90067

tel: (310) 553-2222; fax: (310) 553-4623

Hollywood Chamber of Commerce
7018 Hollywood Blvd.
Hollywood, CA 90028

tel: (323) 469-8311; fax: (323) 469-2805

Los Angeles Area Chamber of Commerce
350 South Bixel Street
Los Angeles, CA 90017

tel: (213) 580-7500; fax: (213) 580-7511

Malibu Chamber of Commerce
23805 Stuart Ranch Rd.
Malibu, CA 90265

tel: (310) 456-9025; fax: (310) 456-0195

WORLD TRADE CENTER

Greater Los Angeles World Trade Center-Long Beach
Greater Los Angeles World Trade Center Associations
One World Trade Center, Suite 295
Long Beach, CA 90831-0295
tel: (310) 495-7070; fax: (310) 495-7071
email: infolb@wtcala-lb.com
website: http://www.wtcala-lb.com

Los Angeles World Trade Center
Greater Los Angeles World Trade Center Association
350 S. Figueroa Street, Suite 172
Los Angeles, California 90071
tel: (213) 680-1888; fax: (213) 680-1878
email: infola@wtcala-lb.com

World Trade Center Irvine
1 Park Plaza, Suite 150
Irvine, California 92614
tel: (714) 724-9822; fax: (714) 752-8723
email: bbuchh@ix.netcom.com
website: http://www.wtca-oc.org

Miami
CITY VIEW

Miami can be beautiful, especially when the humidity and rainfall are at their lowest levels. However, some describe it as a dirty, dangerous city. Whichever your outlook, Miami is a port town that hasn't lost its international flair or its exotic reputation with its proximity to the Caribbean and television shows featuring glamourous drug busting cops in 'Miami Vice' and 'Silk Stalkings', not to mention famous clientele such as Madonna and the late fashion designer Gianni Versace inhabiting walled complexes in this colorful city. Beware wandering or driving around if you are not familiar with the city, some areas can be dangerous. Neighborhoods and attractions that are worth exploring, though, include Little Havana, the Spanish Monastery, and South Beach. Little Havana is the Cuban section, which grew in the 1960s when most Cubans fled to more promising ground. The Spanish Monastery dates back to construction in 1141 in Segovia, Spain. William Randolph Hearst had it dismantled, boxed up, and shipped to Florida. Architecture fans will find South Beach a fascinating enclave of Tropical Art Deco structures and a large array of beautiful people wandering up and down Ocean Drive. Sporting enthusiasts will also find Miami a tropical mecca for diving, sailing, and windsurfing. Afraid of the water? There are plenty of golf courses inside the city and all over the surrounding area.

AIRPORT
Miami International Airport to City Center

The airport lies 6 miles (10 km.) from the city. Shuttles regularly go to city hotels, and buses and taxis are available. Look for taxis on both arrival and departure levels. A taxi ride to Miami takes about 20 minutes. Flat rate fares exist to the following zones:

Port of Miami	$18
Miami Beach (South Beach to 63rd St.)	$24
Miami Beach (63rd St. and 87th Terrace)	$29
Bay Harbor Islands, Bal Harbour	$34
Indian Creek Village, Surfside, Sunny Isles, Golden Beach	$41
Key Biscayne	$31
Zone A Airport Hotels (posted in cabs)	$7
Zone B Airport Hotels (posted in cabs)	$10

The SuperShuttle van service departs from outside of baggage claim on the ground level. Single passenger rates in vans cost $7 to Miami airport area hotels; $14 to Coconut Grove; $17 to Key Biscayne; $9 to downtown hotels; $14 to the North district; and between $14 and $18 to the Miami Beach area. Bus and train service is provided by Tri-Rail. The commuter train runs between the airport and Broward and Palm Beach Counties. Look for the airport station east of the airport, across Le Jeune Road on NW 21st St.

Tri-Rail	(800) TRI-RAIL
SuperShuttle	(800) BLUEVAN
Limousine Service	(800) 872-5460
AAA Atlas Limo & Bus	(800) 854-6687
Elite Transportation Services	(305) 930-8300
Executive Limousine	(800) 833-5594
Network Limousine Services	(800) 638-5466

VIP Limousine Services ....(305) 662-5763
Airport Assistance Center: (305) 876-7862; fax: (305) 876-7398.
Airport website: www.miami-airport.com

Airline Numbers

See the "Travel" section earlier in the U.S. chapter for complete airline phone numbers.

TRAVEL ASSISTANCE

Greater Miami & The Beaches Hotel Association
407 Lincoln Rd., Suite 10G
Miami Beach, FL 33139
tel: (305) 531-3553; fax: (305) 531-8954
Toll-free: (800) SEE-MIAMI
email: info@gmbha.org.

Greater Miami Convention and Visitors Center
701 Brickell Avenue, Suite 2700
Miami, Florida 33131
tel: (305) 539-3000; fax: (305) 539-3113

Immigration and Naturalization
7880 Biscayne Blvd., Room 100, Miami
Toll Free: 1-800-375-5283

Passport Agency
51 SW 1st Ave., Miami
tel: (305) 539-3600

General Information

Post Office Answer Line ....(305) 599-1789
State Operator for Florida..........................(305) 325-2500
Time of Day ....(305) 324-8811
Weather Bureau ....(305) 229-4522

HOTELS

Note: High season rates in Miami last from Oct. or Nov. 1 to April or May 30. If you choose to travel in the summer months, expect higher temperatures instead.

Following are reservation services for Miami:
Accommodations Express............................800-906-4685
Central Reservations..................................800-950-0232
Florida Hotel Network.................................800-538-3616
Hotel Reservation Service...........................305-234-3100
....888-429-4290
Hotel Reservation Network.........................800-964-6835
....800-964-6835

Top-end

Biltmore Hotel Coral Gables; 1200 Anastasia Avenue, Coral Gables; tel: (305) 445-1926, toll free: (800) 727-1926; fax: (305) 448-9976; 315 rooms; located in suburb; 1920's Old World hotel, overlooking golf course; French restaurant and 2 others; business facilities; in-room modem/fax connection; some rooms with fax; airport transportation; valet parking; fitness; massage; pool; tennis; 18-hole golf course.

Fountainbleau Hilton Miami Beach; 4441 Collins Ave.; Miami, FL 33140; tel: (305) 538-2000; toll free: (800) 548-8886; fax: (305)531-9274; 1206 rooms; beachfront property; restaurants; convention facilities; in-room modem/fax connection; tower rooms with elevator keys; continental breakfast; complimentary admission to Club Tropigala; airport transportation; parking; beachside spa; watersports; tennis.

Hotel Sofitel; 5800 Blue Lagoon Dr.; tel: (305) 264-4888; toll free: (800) 695-8284; fax: (305) 262-9049; 281 rooms; near airport overlooking lagoon; conference facilities; in-room data port, cable tv, iron and ironing board, hair dryer; room service; airport transportation; parking; fitness center; swimming pool; tennis court.

Inter-Continental Miami; 100 Chopin Plaza; tel: (305) 577-1000; toll free: (800) 327-3005; fax: (305) 577-0384; http://www.interconti.com; email: miami@interconti.com; 644 rooms; near city center; restaurant; bar; conference facilities (up to 2700); business center; in-room data port, mini bar, cable tv, iron and ironing board, hair dryer; room service; concierge; beauty salon/barber; shops; car rental; valet parking; ($17.71/day); fitness center; spa; pool.

Loews Miami Beach Hotel; 1601 Collins Ave., Miami Beach; tel: (305) 604-1601; fax: (305) 604-3999; http://www.loewshotels.com; email: loewsmiamibeach@loewshotels.com; 800 rooms with ocean views; located on South Beach; 6 restaurants; lounges; conference facilities; business center; in-room 2-line phones, voicemail, computer and data ports, wall safe, honor bar, iron/ironing board, robes, hairdryer; 20-butler served oceanfront cabanas; 24-hour room service; shop; valet parking; spa; fitness with personal trainers; pool; jacuzzi; beach & watersports.

Expensive

The Albion Hotel Miami Beach; 1650 James Ave.; tel: (305) 913-1000; toll free: (888) 665-0008; fax: (305) 674-0507; 93 rooms; 17 suites; restaurant; in-room two line phone with data port, direct dialing, voice mail, minibar;24-hour room service; laundry/dry cleaning; concierge; fitness center with private trainer; outdoor pool with artificial beach; elevated sundeck with Miami Sand.

Hilton Miami Airport & Towers; 5101 Blue Lagoon Dr.; tel: (305) 262-1000; fax: (305) 267-0038; www.hilton.com; 12 acres on private peninsula; 500 rooms, 82 suites; 2 restaurants; 3 bars; conference facilities; business facilities; in-room voicemail, phone, data port, cable tv, a/c, minibar, ironing board, hairdryer, coffeemaker; room service; handicapped access; health club; pool; tennis.

Hyatt Regency City Miami; 400 South-East 2nd Avenue; tel: (305) 358-1234; fax: (305) 358-0529; 615 rooms; near city center on the Miami River; restaurant; conference facilities; secretarial service; business center; money exchange; in-room data port, work desk, cable tv, coffee maker, hair dryer, iron and ironing board; room service; gift shop; parking; corporate rates; fitness center; sauna; swimming pool; spa.

Hyatt Regency Coral Gables; 50 Alhambra Plaza, Coral Gables; tel: (305) 441-1234; fax: (305) 441-0520; 292 rooms; located in fashionable downtown Coral Gables; restaurant; conference facilities; business center; in-room data port, voice mail, coffee maker, cable tv, hair dryer, iron and ironing board; some rooms with fax machine; room service; gift shop; parking; fitness center; sauna; steam room; swimming pool; whirlpool.

Miami International Airport Hotel; Airport Terminal 3; tel: (305) 871-4100; toll free in the U.S. and Canada: 800-327-1276; fax: (305) 871-0800; http://www.miahotel.com; airport; 260 rooms; 3 restaurants; 2 bars; conference facilities (up to 200); business facilities; in-room phone, computer/fax line, cable tv, a/c; room service; health club; spa; pool; $125-199

Radisson Mart Plaza; 711 NW 72nd Ave.; tel: (305) 261-3800, toll free: (800) 333-3333; fax: (305) 261-7665; 334 rooms; access to Merchandise Mart; conference facilities; in-room data port, work desk, cable tv, coffee maker, hair dryer; airport transportation; parking; fitness center; outdoor swimming pool; racquetball; tennis; sun deck.

Westin Resort Miami Beach; 4833 Collins Ave.; tel: (305) 532-3600, toll free: (800) WESTIN-1; fax: (305) 534-7409; 423 rooms; beachfront hotel; restaurant; business center; in-room data port, cable tv; room service; gift shop; parking; fitness center; massage; beach/watersports.

Moderate

Best Western Marina Park; 340 Biscayne Blvd.; tel: (305) 371-4400; toll free: (800) 695-8284; fax: (305) 372-2862; 200 rooms; restaurant; bar; business facilities; in-room data port, cable tv, safe; room service; parking; fitness center; swimming pool.

Cadet Hotel; 1701 James Ave., North of Lincoln Rd., Miami Beach; tel: (305) 672-6688; toll free: 1-800-43-CADET; fax: (305) 532-1676; http://www.cadethotel.com; 44 rooms; bed and breakfast hotel; small, familiar atmosphere; located in Art Deco district; 1 1/2 blocks from Miami Beach Convention Center, Ocean Dr.; in-room bathrooms, a/c, refrigerators, phone, cable tv; free parking; $50+.

Comfort Inn on the Beach; 6261 Collins Ave., Miami Beach; tel: (305) 868-1200; toll free: 800-695-8284; fax: (305) 686-3003; 153 rooms; restaurant; bar; complimentary breakfast; in-room cable tv, coffeemaker, iron/ironing board; room service; valet/laundry; currency exchange; car rental; self parking; airport transportation; fitness.

Crest Hotel; 1670 James Ave., Miami Beach; tel: (305) 531-8180; toll free: 800-531-3880; fax: (305) 531-8180; http://www.cresthotel.com; boutique hotel in South Beach Art Deco district, near Miami Beach Convention Center; cafe; business services, production facilities available; in-room a/c, cable tv, voicemail; suites and studios with kitchenette, refrigerator, coffeemaker, dataport, workspace; laundry/dry cleaning service; daily housekeeping; parking; rooftop solarium, spa, pool; whirlpool; $115+ (low season).

Holiday Inn Coral Gables Business District; 2051 Le Jeune Road; tel: (305) 443-2301; toll free: (800) HOLIDAY; fax: (305) 446-6827; 168 rooms; restaurant; business center; in-room air conditioning, cable tv, data port; airport transportation; parking; fitness center; swimming pool.

Holiday Inn Downtown; 200 SE 2nd Ave.; tel: (305) 374-3000; fax: (305) 374-5897; http://www.basshotels.com/basshotels; 256 rooms; restaurant; bar; meeting facilities; business facilities; secretarial service; in-room tv, electronic door locks, private balconies, voices, coffeemaker, hairdryer, iron/ironing board, a/c; room service; gift shop; corporate rates; fitness; rooftop pool.

Holiday Inn Miami Beach; 6060 Indian Creek Dr., Miami Beach; tel: (305) 865-2565; toll free: 1-800-HOLIDAY; fax: (305) 865-2506; opposite Collins Ave. and beaches; cafe; bar and grill; in-room coffeemaker, iron/ironing board, hairdryer, voicemail, fax, dataport, cable tv, HBO; room service; valet parking; indoor/outdoor pool; whirlpool; sundeck; rooftop garden; boat deck.

Red Sands Hotel; Ocean Dr., Miami Beach.; tel: (305) 672-2020; toll free: 800-695-8284; 43 rooms; complimentary breakfast; in-room phone, computer/fax line, tv, coffeemaker, work desk, kitchen, a/c; non-smoking rooms available; non-smoking rooms available.

Runway Inn Airport; 656 East Dr., Miami; tel: (305) 888-6411; toll free: (800) 446-5508; fax: (305) 887-1194; e-mail: runway@travelbase.com; adjacent to the Miami Airport; free 24 hour airport transportation; in-room air conditioning, cable tv.

MEDICAL CARE

Baptist Hospital of Miami; 8900 N. Kendall Drive; tel: (305) 596-6556, 596-1960.

Butler Chiropractic Health Center; 1948 N.E. 123rd Street, Suite 107, North Miami, Florida 33181; tel: (305) 891-2520; fax: (305) 891-5754; e-mail: butler-chiro@mindspring.com.

Mercy Hospital; 3663 S. Miami Ave.; tel: (305) 285-2171; 854-4400.

Miami Children's Hospital; 3100 S.W. 62nd Ave.; tel: (305) 662-8280, 666-6511.

Mt. Sinai Medical Center; 4300 Alton Road at 43rd Avenue, Miami Beach; tel: (305) 674-2200, 674-2121.

St. Francis Hospital; 250 W. 63rd St., Miami Beach; tel: (305) 672-1111.

University of Miami/Jackson Memorial Medical Center; 1611 N.W. 12th Ave.; tel: (305) 325-7429, 585-1111.

Crisis Hot Lines

Any Emergency 911
Alcoholics Anonymous ....(305) 371-7784
Abuse Hotline 1-800-342-9152
Miami Switchboard ....(305) 358-4357
Miami Teen Line Switchboard ....(305) 377-8336
Miami Mental Health Center ....(305) 774-3300
Attorney ....(305) 931-0100
Dentist Office ....(305) 947-7999
Coast Guard Marine Emerg. ....(305) 535-4368

HEALTH CLUB

Allstar Fitness; 2216 NW 87th Avenue, Miami, FL 33172; tel: (305) 717-0047; fax: (305) 717-0045.

Gateway Fitness Center; Downtown World Trade Center, 90 S.W. Eighth St.; tel: (305) 577-3091.

Club Body Tech; 1253 Washington Ave. at 13th Street, Miami Beach; tel: (305) 674-8222; fax: (305) 674-8352.

XS Fitness; 81 Washington Avenue, Miami Beach; tel: (305) 532-7989; fax: (305) 532-9989; Monday to Friday 6a.m. to 11p.m.; Saturday 8a.m. to 10p.m.; Sunday 9a.m. to 8p.m.; 15000 sq. ft. art-deco styled facility; aerobics, martial arts; gym.

AUTO RENTAL

Miami now offers a parking meter debit card providing a cashless way to use the new electronic parking meters. Purchase the cards at participating hotels and merchants or from:

CMB Parking ....(305) 673-7505
Miami Beach Chamber of Commerce. 672-1270

Alamo; tel: (305) 633-4132; toll free: 800-327-9633.

Avis; Dodge Island Pier 7, 903 S America Way Miami FL, 33132; tel: (305) 377-2531; toll free: (800) 331-1212.

Avis; Miami Intl Airport, 2330 NW 37th Ave., Miami FL, 33142; (305) 341-0936.

Avis; South Miami, 8330 S Dixie Hwy, Dadeland Station Shopping Center, Miami FL, 33143; tel: (305) 661-6414.

Budget; tel: (305) 871-3053; toll free: 800-527-0700.

Esquire Limousine & Bodyguard Service; tel: (305) 358-5599.

Hertz; Miami International Airport, 3795 Northwest 21st Street, Miami; tel: (305) 871-0300; fax: (305) 876-9108; toll-free: (800) 654-3131.

Hertz; Port of Miami, 3795 N.W. 21st Street, Miami; tel: (305) 871-0300; toll-free: (800) 654-3131.

Thrifty; Miami Airport; 2875 N.W. 42nd Ave.; tel: (305) 871-5050; toll free: (800) 367-2277.

WORLD TRADE CENTER

World Trade Center Miami
5600 NW 36th St., Ste. 601
PO Box 590508
Miami, FL 33159-0508
tel: (305) 579-0064; fax: (305) 536-7701
email: info@worldtrade.org
website: http://www.worldtrade.org

CHAMBER OF COMMERCE

Greater Miami Chamber of Commerce
1601 Biscayne Blvd.
Miami, FL 33132
tel: (305) 442-2277

Miami Beach Chamber of Commerce
420 Lincoln Road #2-D
Miami Beach, FL 33139
tel: (305) 672-1270; fax: (305) 538-4336
Web: http://miamibeachchamber.com
email: mbchamber@sobe.com

New York City

CITY VIEW

New York City is one of the most populated cities in the world, and looks just like most may imagine: a huge city with buildings everywhere. Standing on a street corner downtown, one may well feel like a tiny ant caught up in the constant rush of the 'Big Apple'. Looking down from a high-rise hotel room, a sea of yellow taxi roofs ply the city streets. On the ground level, many consider New York to be the only city worth living in the U.S. (although others may heartily argue). The city is divided into five boroughs (Manhattan, Brooklyn, The Bronx, Queens and Staten Island) and takes up 301 square miles (780 sq km) of space on the eastern seaboard. Of course, first-time visitors will need to see the Statue of Liberty, Times Square, Grand Central Station, and Central Park. Rockefeller Center comes alive during the holidays, while the Guggenheim and Natural History Museums are fascinating diversions any time of the year. Those with extra time and interest may want to take note of the gargoyles embedded everywhere in the architecture of city buildings while they make their way around town.

AIRPORT

John F. Kennedy Airport to City Center

The airport lies 15 miles southeast of Manhattan, and occupies almost as much land. Redevelopments since the early 1980's have included a new air traffic control tower, a new parking garage, and a new quadrant roadway system. There are bus and shuttle services available, and taxis are always around for hailing.

JFK provides a regular free bus transfer between terminals. The red, white and blue Airline Connection Bus serves all main terminals including the west and east ends of Terminal 4. Buses stop at the blue 'Bus Connections at JFK' signs outside each terminal. Free buses operate around the clock with departures every 10 to 20 minutes. Expect a journey time of 5 to 20 minutes depending on your destination terminal.

Airline Numbers

See the "Travel" section earlier in the U.S. chapter for complete airline phone numbers.

TRAVEL ASSISTANCE

NYC & Company Visitor Information Center
810 Seventh Avenue (between 52nd and 53rd streets)
New York, NY 10019
tel: (212) 484-1222

HOTELS

Top-end

Four Seasons; 57 East 57th Street; tel: (212) 758-5700; fax: (212) 758-5711; 370 rooms; city center; restaurant; meeting facilities; executive business center; 24-hour business services; secretarial service; translation service; in-room data port, multi-line telephone, voicemail, fax machines; computers available; cellular phones; full-service spa; sauna; steamroom; massage.

The Lowell; 28 E. 63rd St.; tel: (212) 838-1400; toll free: (800) 223-6800; fax: (212) 319-4230; 63 rooms, 44 suites, 21 deluxe rooms; upscale boutique hotel in Manhattan; one suite with private gym; restaurant; bar; afternoon tea room; in-room mini bar, VCR; room service; fitness center.

The Peninsula New York; 700 5th Avenue and 55th Street; tel: (212) 247-2200; toll free: (800) 262-9467; fax: (212) 903-3949; 241 rooms; city center; restaurant; bar; conference facilities (up to 150); business center; in-room data port, safe, cable tv, iron and ironing board, mini bar, hair dryer; fitness center; sauna; spa; swimming pool; whirlpool.

The Pierre (Four Seasons); 5th Avenue and 61st Street; tel: (212) 838-8000; fax: (212) 940-8109; 202 rooms; city center, opposite Central Park; restaurant; meeting facilities; 24-hour business services; cellular telephone; in-room data port, multi-line telephone, voicemail, internet; fitness club; men's and women's salons; massage.

Inter-Continental Central Park; 112 Central Park South; tel: (212) 757-1900; toll free: (800) 241-3333; fax: (212) 757-9620; 208 rooms; city center with views of Central Park; restaurant; conference facilities; secretarial service; fax/photocopy facilities; in-room air conditioning, cable tv, mini bar; room service; corporate rates.

The St. Regis; 5th Avenue and 55th Street, Manhattan; tel: (212) 753-4500; toll free: (800) 759-7550; fax: (212) 787-3447; 321 rooms; traditional Beaux-Arts hotel; city center; restaurant; conference facilities (up to 400); secretarial service; fax/photocopy facilities; 24-hour butler service; in-room safe; valet parking; corporate rates; fitness; saunas; personal trainers; beauty salon.

The Waldorf Astoria (Hilton); 301 Park Avenue, Manhattan; tel: (212) 355-3000; toll free: (800) 925-3673; fax: (212) 758-9209; 1250 rooms; city center; 2 restaurants; bar; conference facilities; business center; in-room cable tv, mini bar; 24 hour room service; parking; fitness center; personal trainers; spa; whirlpool.

W New York—The Tuscany; 120 East 39th Street, Manhattan; tel: (212) 685-1600; toll free: (877) W-HOTELS; fax: (212) 696-2095; 106 deluxe rooms, 16 king and parlor suites; boutique business hotel; cafe; meeting facilities; high-speed internet access, personalized email addresses, dual-line telephones/cordless; fax, printer, scanners on request.; full-service concierge, valet, room service; fitness center; full-service spa.

Expensive

Inter-Continental New York; 111 East 48th Street; tel: (212) 755-5900; toll free: (800) 695-8284; fax: (212) 644-0079; 683 rooms; located in city center; restaurant; bar; business center; conference facilities (up to 320); in-room air conditioning, mini bar, cable tv, voice mail, data port, hair dryer, working desk, safe; fitness center; sauna;.

Loews New York; tel: (212) 752-7000; toll free: (800) 695-8284; fax: (212) 758-6311; 726 rooms; city center; restaurant; conference facilities; business center; business rooms available; in-room cable tv; room service; parking; fitness center.

Marriott World Trade Center; Three World Trade Center, Lower Manhattan; tel: (212) 938-9100; fax: (212) 444-3444; 832 rooms; restaurant; conference facilities; business services; secretarial service; in room work desk, voice mail, data port, cable tv, mini bar, hair dryer, safe; 24

hour room service; beauty salon; parking; health club; indoor swimming pool; jogging track.

Radisson Empire Hotel; 44 West 63rd Street, Manhattan; tel: (212) 265-7400; toll free: (800) 221-6509, or (800) 223-9868; fax: (212) 315-0349; city center; near exhibition grounds; restaurant; conference facilities (up to 160); parking; corporate rates.

Moderate

Best Western Seaport Inn; 33 Peck Slip, Lower Manhattan; tel: (212) 766-6600; toll free: (800) 468-3569; fax: (212) 766-6615; 72 rooms; historic hotel in downtown South Street seaport area; complimentary breakfast; in-room cable tv, mini bar, hair dryer; whirlpool.

The Club Quarters (membership required); 52 Williams Street, between Wall and Pine St.; tel: (212) 575-0006; private hotel chain subsidized by Fortune 500 companies for member guests; located near Wall Street; in-room refrigerator, coffee maker, 2-line speaker phones, data ports, hair dryer; 24-hour shop; garage; fitness.

Cosmopolitan Hotel; 95 West Broadway at Chambers, in Tribeca; tel: (212) 566-1900; toll free: (888) 895-9400; fax: (212) 566-6909; email: info@cosmohotel.com; http://www.cosmohotel.com; 105 rooms; 5 blocks from World Trade Center; refurbished; in room cable tv, air conditioning, private bath.

Herald Square Hotel; 19 West 31st St.; tel: (212) 279-4017; toll free: (800) 643-9208; http://www.heraldsquarehotel.com/130 rooms; central location 2 blocks from the Empire State Building in historic Life Magazine building; in-room voice/ email, safe, air conditioning, color tv.

Hotel Lucerne; 201 W. 79th Street; Manhattan; tel: (212) 875-1000; toll free: (800) 492-8122; fax: (212) 579-2408; http://www.newyorkhotel.com; turn-of-the-century building, 2 blocks from Central Park; business services; dual-line telephones; non-smoking rooms; airport transportation; parking; fitness; rooftop sundeck.

Radio City Apartments; 142 W. 49th St., Manhattan; tel: (212) 730-0728, (212) 921-9321; 75 studio, one and two-bedrooms with full kitchen; in the heart of mid-town Manhattan; restaurant; 24 hour front desk/concierge/ security; laundry facilities; parking.

Ramada Plaza Hotel at J.F.K.; Van Wyck Expressway at junction Belt Parkway, Building 144; tel: (718) 995-9000; fax: (718) 224-8962; restaurant; conference facilities; business services; in room cable tv, hair dryer, data port; room service; airport transportation; city transportation; parking; fitness center.

MEDICAL CARE

Lincoln Medical Practice; 215 Lexington Ave. between 32nd and 33rd; tel: (212) 787-8770.

Colombia-Presbyterian Medical Center; 622 W. 168th St.; tel: (212) 305-2500; physician referral: tel: 1-800-227-2762.

Mt. Sinai Medical Center; One gustave L Levy Place; tel: (212) 241-6500; http://www.mountsinai.org.

New York University Medical Center; 560 First Ave. between 31st and 32nd streets; tel: (212) (212) 263-7300.

New York Hospital; 525 E. 68th St. between York Avenue and FDR Drive; tel: (212) 746-5050.

Roosevelt Hospital Center; 1000 Ninth Ave. between 58th and 59th streets; tel: (212) 523-6800.

HEALTH CLUB

Battery Park Fitness; 375 S. End Ave. at Liberty Street, Battery Park City; tel: (212) 321-1117.

Crunch Fitness; 54 E. 13th St. between Broadway and University; tel: (212) 475-2018.

Equinox; 344 Amsterdam Ave. at 76th Street, Upper West Side; tel: (212) 721-4200.

New York Sports Club; Park Avenue & 59th, 502 Park Avenue; tel: (212) 308-1010.

U.N. Plaza Health Club; U.N. Plaza Hotel, First Avenue at 44th Street, Midtown; tel: (212) 702-5016.

Vanderbilt YMCA; 224 E. 47th St. between Second and Third avenue, Midtown; tel: (212) 756-9600.

AUTO RENTAL

ABC Car Rental; 220 E 9th St., New York; tel: (212) 989-7260.

Autorent Car Rental Corporation; 433 E 76th St., New York; tel: (212) 517-8900.

Budget Rent A Car; 225 E 43rd St., New York; tel: (212) 807-8700.

Budget Rent A Car; 304 W 49th St., New York; tel: (212) 807-8700.

Budget Rent A Car; 207 W 76th St., New York; tel: (212) 807-8700.

Dollar Rent A Car; 329 E 22nd St., New York; tel: (212) 420-0870.

Dollar Rent A Car; 156 W 54th St., New York; tel: (212) 362-1441.

Dollar Rent A Car; 157 E 84th St., New York; tel: (212) 861-2525.

Hertz Rent A Car; 20 Morton St., New York; tel: (212) 989-0807.

Hertz Rent A Car; 152 W 57th St., New York; tel: (212) 373-6400.

WORLD TRADE CENTER

World Trade Center New York
The Port Authority of New York & New Jersey
One World Trade Center, Suite 88 West
New York, New York 10048
tel: (212) 435-7168; fax: (212) 435-2810
email: dmay@panynj.gov

CHAMBER OF COMMERCE

Greater New York Chamber of Commerce
350 Fifth Ave. Suite 3304
New York City, NY 10118
tel: (212) 244-0003
email: info@chamber.com

San Francisco
CITY VIEW

To some, San Francisco is one of the most beautiful cities in the world, with classical architecture and landscapes relatively untouched by civilization. To others, "the city" (as it's called by locals) is a confusing mass of traffic and hills. If renting a car, beware that you may find yourself on some of the steepest paved roads on Earth. A small city with a population of 1,655,454, San Francisco, nevertheless, ranks as one of the top tourist destinations in the world. Its most favored status can be attributed to its clean streets, architectural treasures, first-rate museums, a very international clientele, cultural diversity, a glittering skyline silhouetted by the bay, and the mostly sunny climate and clean skies. Known as the "city by the bay", San Francisco offers relatively fresh air year round. For those imagining sunny, California weather, take heed that the thick, cold fog descending upon the city during the summer months will let locals know who is a tourist and who is not simply by their choice of attire. Spring and Fall offer mostly crisp, sunny skies. Although the city itself may often be shrouded in summer fog, the outlying regions are not. With wine country, spectacular coastal scenery, quaint towns, large universities like Berkeley and Stanford, and Silicon Valley all part of the greater Bay Area, the visitor will have plenty of diversity to meet even the most eclectic tastes. Recreational opportunities abound. Business in the city by the bay is booming with Fortune 500 companies that include Hewlett Packard, Oracle, and Sun Microsystems anchoring the myriad of start-up dot com companies pledging to carve a niche of their own. Those hungering for more may participate in the city's colorful dining scene. San Francisco boasts more restaurants per capita than any other city.

AIRPORT

San Francisco International Airport to City Center

The airport lies 15 miles (25 km.) from the city and is currently under massive construction. Shuttles go all over the Bay Area. Taxi fare costs approximately $30 for the 30-minute ride downtown.

Currently, two train services to San Francisco airport exist - BART and CalTrain. Neither takes you direct to the airport but they both provide shuttle transfer to terminals. The BART system goes to Colma BART station; the nearest CalTrain station is Millbrae. BART extension plans to the airport are currently underway.

Many bus/van operators also serve the city. Frequent services are run by Sam Trans, tel: 800- 660-4287 and S.F.O. Airporter: 800-532-8405. A Sam Trans bus costs $2 to $3, the S.F.O. Airporter will cost $10, and door-to-door van services cost from $10 to $25, depending on pick-up point. San Francisco city guides occasionally provide discount coupons for local transportation; look for them at information desks.

Airline Numbers

See the "Travel" section earlier in the U.S. chapter for complete airline phone numbers.

TRAVEL ASSISTANCE

San Francisco Convention& Visitors Bureau
201 Third Street, Ste. 900,
San Francisco, CA 94103
tel: (415) 391-2000; TDD (415) 392-0328
fax: (415) 974-1992
Web: http://www.sfvisitor.org

HOTELS

Top-end

The Clift; 495 Geary Street; tel: (415) 775-4700; toll free: 800-65-CLIFT; fax: (415) 441-4621; http://www.clifthotel.com; email: res@clifthotel.com; discreet hotel, located near Union Square, city center; restaurant; bar; conference facilities (up to 245); business center; personal computer and cell phone rentals; in-room a/c, cable tv, minibars, 3 telephones with 2-lines, dataports, movies, alarm radio; 24-hour room service; laundry/dry cleaning; pressing service; complimentary weekday downtown limousine; valet parking; fitness.

Mark Hopkins Inter-Continental; 1 Nob Hill; tel: (415) 392-3434 or (800) 327-0200; fax: (415) 421-3302; http://

www.san-francisco.interconti.com; email: SFOHA-RESVN@interconti.com; 390 rooms, 28 suites; French chateau/Spanish Renaissance style hotel; restaurant; business center/services; in-room fax/modem connection; airport transportation; valet parking; fitness; massage.

Renaissance Stanford Court Hotel; 905 California St., Nob Hill; tel: (415) 989-3500; fax: (415) 391-0513; http://www.renaissancehotels.com/SFOSC/; 393 rooms; European boutique hotel; restaurant; conference facilities (up to 750); business center; secretarial service; in-room modem/fax connection; secure parking; airport transportation; corporate rates; fitness.

Sheraton Palace; 2 New Montgomery Street; tel: (415) 512-1111 or (800) 325-3535; fax: (415) 543-0671; http://www.sheraton.com; 519 rooms; 32 suites; renovated historic hotel; near financial district; restaurant; conference facilities; business services; in-room modem/fax connection, alarm clock, a/c, cable tv, voicemail, safe, minibar, hairdryer; laundry/dry cleaning; currency exchange; boutique; airport transportation; valet parking; fitness; pool; jacuzzi.

The Ritz-Carlton; 600 Stockton Street; tel: (415) 296-7465; fax; (415) 291-0288; http://ritzcarlton.com; 336 rooms; city center, near financial district; restaurant; conference facilities; business center; secretarial service; laptops; internet; in-room modem/fax connection, safe; secure parking; airport transportation; corporate rates; fitness; sauna; indoor pool; whirlpool.

W San Francisco; 181 Third Street; tel: (415) 777-5300; toll free: 1-877-W-HOTELS; fax: (415) 817-7800; 423 rooms; opposite Moscone Convention Center, adjacent Museum of Modern Art; restaurant; bar; cafe; meeting facilities; in-room dual-line telephones, high-speed Ethernet laptop access, work desk; printer, fax, scanner on request; 24-hour concierge, valet, room service fitness center; personal training program; steam bath; whirlpool.

Expensive

Galleria Park; 191 Sutter Street; tel: (415) 781-3060 or (800) 792-9639; fax: (415) 433-4409; http://www.galleriapark.com; 177 rooms; city center; restaurant; conference facilities (up to 50); business center; internet; in-room modem/fax connection; in-room stereo; parking; corporate rates; fitness.

Grand Hyatt on Union Square; 345 Stockton St.; tel: (415) 398-1234; fax: (415) 391-1780; http://www.hyatt.com; 655 rooms; located on Union Square, near financial district; restaurant; conference facilities; business services/center; in-room modem/fax connection, voicemail, dataport, electronic door locks, iron/ironing boards, hairdryer, robes, work station, minibar; room service; laundry/dry cleaning; valet parking; airport transportation; parking; fitness.

Hyatt Regency San Francisco Airport; 1333 Bayshore Highway; tel: (650) 347-1234; fax: (650) 347-5948; http://www.hyatt.com; email: reserva@sfobupo.hyatt.com; 767 rooms; restaurant; bar/lounge; conference facilities; business services; in-room modem/fax connection, voicemail, dataport, electronic door locks, iron/ironing board, hairdryer, coffeemaker, 2-phone lines, newspaper; laundry/dry cleaning; currency exchange; valet parking; car rental; airport shuttle service; fitness; sauna; pool; whirlpool.

Hyatt Regency San Francisco; California and Market Streets, 5 Embarcadero Center; tel: (415) 788-1234; fax: (415) 398-2567; tel: (800) 233-1234; http://www.hyatt.com; 760 rooms; convention hotel near financial district, bay; rooftop restaurant; coffee shop; conference facilities; business services/center; in-room modem/fax connection, cable tv, voicemail, 2-line phone with dataport, newspaper, electronic door locks, hairdryer, iron/ironing boards, alarm clock, coffeemaker, safe; some rooms with balcony; room service; concierge; 24-hour on call physician/dentist; car rental; gift shop; parking; fitness; massage.

The Pan Pacific; 500 Post Street; tel: (415) 771-8600; fax: (415) 398-0267; city center; restaurant; conference facilities; secretarial service; fax/photocopy facilities; in-room modem/fax connection; airport transportation; parking; fitness.

Westin St. Francis; 335 Powell Street; tel: (415) 397-7000 or (800) 228-3000; fax: (415) 774-0124; http://www.westin.com; email: stfra@westin.com; 1106 rooms; located on Union Square; 3 restaurants; 2 lounges; conference facilities; business services; in-room modem/fax connection, wireless phones, data ports, voicemail; down comforters, safe, cable tv, movies, coffeemaker; office rooms available; 24-hour room service; dry cleaning/laundry; concierge; parking; fitness.

Moderate

Embassy Suites Airport; 150 Anza Blvd.; Burlingame, CA 94010; tel: (650) 342-4600; tel: (800) EMB-ASSY; fax: (650) 343-8137; near airport; restaurant; business services; in-room modem/fax connection; airport shuttle service; parking; pool.

Handlery Union Square; 351 Geary Street; tel: (415) 781-7800; fax: (415) 781-0269; http://www.handlery.com; 377 rooms; restaurant; conference facilities (up to 70); secretarial service; fax/photocopy facilities; in-room safe; parking; corporate rates; sauna; pool.

Holiday Inn Financial District; 750 Kearny St.; tel: (415) 433-6600; fax: (415) 765-7891; located on the edge of Chinatown in financial district; restaurant; coffee shop; business services; in-room modem/fax connection; fitness; rooftop pool.

Holiday Inn Golden Gateway; 1500 Van Ness Avenue; tel: (415) 441-4000; fax: (415) 776-7155; email: alixhigg@aol.com; 499 rooms; located on main thoroughfare; business services; in-room modem/fax connection; airport transportation; parking; pool.

Kensington Park; 450 Post Street at Powell; tel: (800) 553-1900; 88 rooms; city center, located 1/2 block from Union Square; meeting facilities; business services; in-room modem/fax connection.

Sir Francis Drake Hotel; 450 Powell Street; tel: (415) 392-7755; tel: (800) 795-7129; fax: (415) 677-9341; http://135.145.16.183/sirfrancisdrake.com/; 417 rooms; located on cable car line, near Union Square; restaurant; conference facilities; business services; airport transportation; parking; fitness.

MEDICAL CARE

Dental Referral; tel: (800) 917-6453.

Mental health referral; tel:(415) 981-4700.

California Pacific Medical Center; 2333 Buchanan St.; tel: (415) 923-3333.

S.F. General Hospital; 1001 Potrero Ave. at 22nd Street; tel: (415) 206-8111.

U.C.S.F. Medical Center; 505 Parnassus at Third Avenue; tel: (415) 476-1037.

St. Mary's Medical Center; 450 Stanyon St.; tel: (415) 668-1000.

Stanford University Hospital (San Jose Area); 300 Pasteur Dr.; tel: (650) 723-4000; emergency: (650) 723-7337 (24 hrs.); trauma: (650) 723-7570 weekdays, (650) 723-6661 after hours; physician referral: 1-800-756-5000.

HEALTH CLUB

The Bay Club; Bank of America Center, 555 California St.; tel: (415) 362-7800; 150 Greenwich St., tel: 433-2200.

Club One; 1 Citicorp, Sansome Street, tel: (415) 399-1010; 2 Embarcadero Center, tel: (415) 788-1010, fax: (415) 788-0633; 350 3rd St., tel: 512-1010, fax: (415) 543-2846; 1755 O'Farrell Street, tel: (415) 749-1010, fax: (415) 928-4826.

Kabuki Hot Springs (Only Japanese Spa); 1750 Geary Blvd. at Fillmore Street, Japantown; tel: (415) 922-6000; fax: (415) 922-6005.

Northpoint Health Club; 2310 Powell St. near Bay Street, Fisherman's Wharf; tel: (415) 989-1449.

Pinnacle Fitness; 61 New Montgomery St. at Jessie, Financial District; tel: (415) 543-1110.

24-Hour Fitness; 100 California St. #200; tel: (415) 434-5080, fax: (415) 434-5086; 303 2ndSt, tel: (415) 543-7808, fax: (415) 543-7855; 350 Bay St., tel: 395-9595, fax: (415) 395-9555.

YMCA; 169 Steuart St. between Howard and Mission streets, Embarcadero; tel: (415) 957-9622.

AUTO RENTAL

Alamo; tel: 693-0191 or (800) 327-9633.

Avis; tel: 885-5011 or (800) 331-1212.

Budget; tel: 775-5800 or (800) 527-0700.

Hertz; tel: 771-2200 or (800) 654-3131.

National; tel: 474-5300 or (800) 328-4567.

WORLD TRADE CENTER

World Trade Center of San Francisco, Inc.
250 Montgomery St., 14th Floor
San Francisco, CA 94104
tel: (415) 392-2705; fax: (415) 392-1710
email: leina@bawtc.baytrade.org

CHAMBER OF COMMERCE

San Francisco Chamber of Commerce
235 Montgomery St., 12th Flr.
San Francisco, CA 94104
tel: (415) 392-4520; fax: (415) 392-0485
Web: http://www.sfchamber.com/

SAN JOSE/SILICON VALLEY HOTELS

Top-end

Fairmont Hotel; Fairmont Plaza, 170 S. Market Street; tel: (408) 998-1900; fax: (408) 287-1648; http://www.fairmont.com/Hotels/Index_SJ.html; email: sanjose@fairmont.com; 541 rooms and suites; conference facilities; business center; in-room fax machines, modem connection, dataport, hairdryer, call waiting, voicemail, robes, work area, Sony playstation; concierge; handicapped rooms; laundry service; shops; salon; parking; health club; fitness; personal trainers; saunas; steam rooms; massage; skin care; pool.

Expensive

San Jose Hilton and Towers; 300 Almaden Blvd.; tel: (408) 287-2100; fax: (408) 947-4489; http://www.hilton.com/hotels/SJCSHHF/index. html; connected to San Jose McEnery Convention Center; restaurant; bar; conference facilities; in-room modem/fax connection, robe, a/c, coffee maker, hairdryer, iron/ironing board, newspaper, voicemail, speaker phone, 2-line phone with dataport; premium tv,; business floors include rooms with minibar, fax; airport transportation; parking; fitness; pool.

Hyatt San Jose; 1750 North First Street; tel: (408 993-1234; fax: (408) 453-0261; http://www.hyatt.com; 512 rooms and suites; restaurant; bar; conference facilities; business center; in-room multimedia PC, printer-fax-copier, tv, movies; 14-hour room service; laundry/dry cleaning; currency exchange; gift shop; florist; hair salon; fitness; pool; whirlpool.

Hyatt Sainte Claire - Downtown San Jose; 302 S. Market Street; tel: (408) 885-1234; fax: (408) 977-0403; http://www.hyatt.com; historic hotel, located opposite convention center; restaurant; bakery; bar; conference facilities; in-room modem/fax connection, tv, voicemail, data port; newspaper, iron/ironing board, alarm radio, hairdryer, safe; 24-hour room service; laundry/dry cleaning; valet service; concierge; airport transportation; parking; fitness.

Moderate

Courtyard San Jose Airport; 1727 Technology Drive; tel: (408) 441-6111; fax: (408) 441-8039; http://www.courtyard.com/SJCCA/; 151 rooms. 12 suites; located near airport, near Hewlett-Packard, Novell, Eastman Kodak, GE, AT&T, Ford Aerospace; restaurant; coffee shop; lounge; 2 meeting rooms; fax/photocopy facilities; in-room work desk, voicemail, data ports, cable tv, movies, newspaper, coffee, iron/ironing board; hairdryer; laundry valet; self service laundry; parking.

Crowne Plaza San Jose; tel: (408) 998-0400; toll free: 1-800-HOLIDAY, 1-800-227-6963; fax: (408) 289-9081; http://www.crowneplaza.com/hotels/sjcpc/; 239 rooms; restaurant; in-room modem/fax connection, a/c; airport transportation; parking; fitness; pool.

San Jose Days Inn Convention Center; 4170 Monterey Road; tel: (408) 224-4122; http://www.daysinns.com; 34 rooms; in-room refrigerator, coffee, pastry, microwave; olympic pool; jacuzzi.

Wyndham Hotel; 1350 North First Street; tel: (408) 453-6200; toll free: 1-800-WYNDHAM; fax: (408) 437-9693; 353 rooms, 2 suites; in-room alarm radio, coffee maker; cable tv, weekday newspaper; iron/ironing board, 2-line phone with voicemail; non-smoking/handicapped rooms available; airport transportation; self parking; fitness; pool.

Seattle

CITY VIEW

Once a small port town, Seattle has exploded to become one of the major metropolitan areas in the country. Famed for instituting the underground grunge scene and a penchant for offbeat, Seattle is no slacker in providing some of America's modern-day culture. Spurred on by high-tech companies such as Microsoft (which has its main office in nearby Redmond), and aircraft manufacturer Boeing, Seattle stands as a modern, advanced U.S. city flanked by spectacular scenery and outdoor recreation opportunities in the not-too-far Olympic National Park, North Cascades National Park, and Mt. Ranier National Park. A bit farther afield is Mt. St. Helens Volcanic Monument, a stark reminder of nature's explosive capability. Within the city itself is the Space Needle, built for the 1962 World's Fair, and Pike Place Market, a thriving fish and vegetable market still manned by original characters. Woven within the fabric of the city, is an eclectic mix of people, perhaps brought about by the often gloomy skies. No matter what time of the year you plan a visit, prepare for rain, lots and lots of rain.

AIRPORT

Sea-Tac Airport to City Center

Situated between Seattle and nearby Tacoma, SeaTac

offers a number of bus and shuttle services, as well as a number of taxis. Sea-Tac Airport is located 13 miles south of Seattle and 20 miles north of Tacoma on Interstate 5.

Journey time to Seattle takes around 20 to 30 minutes, and 30 to 40 minutes to Tacoma. The taxi fare to Seattle costs approximately $30 to Seattle and between $35 and $40 to Tacoma.

The Grayline Express airport bus service operates every 30 minutes and services many area hotels. Grayline fares cost $7.50 one way, $13 round trip. For further details, call: (206) 626-6088.

The metro bus offers the most economical way to get to downtown Seattle, with frequent services between the airport and Seattle for a cost of $1.10.

Other companies providing frequent van services to the airport are:

Airporter Shuttle	800 235-5247.
Capital Aeroporter	800 962-3579.
Yellow Express	206 622-3400.

Airline Numbers

See the "Travel" section earlier in the U.S. chapter for complete airline phone numbers.

TRAVEL ASSISTANCE

Seattle-King County Convention & Visitors Bureau

520 Pike Street, Suite 1300
Seattle, WA 98101
tel: (206) 461-5800; fax: (206) 461-5855
TDD telephone: (206) 461-5840
Web: www.seeseattle.org
Monday-Friday, 8:30a.m. to 5 p.m.

WORLD TRADE CENTER

World Trade Center Seattle

2200 Alaskan Way, Ste. 410
Seattle, WA 98121
tel: (206) 441-5144; fax: (206) 374-0410
email: amorgan@wtcseattle.com
website: http://www.wtcseattle.com

CHAMBER OF COMMERCE

Greater Seattle Chamber of Commerce

1301 Fifth Avenue, Suite 2400
Seattle, WA 98101-2603
tel: (206) 389-7200; fax: (206) 389-7288
Web: http://www.seattlechamber.com/

Washington, D.C.

CITY VIEW

The nation's capital is also one of the country's most interesting locations. With the Residence Bill of 1799, President Washington was designated to select a a site for the capitol in the Potamac region "not exceeding 10 miles square". In December of 1800, Congress left a temporary station in Philadelphia and convened permanently in the new seat. Remaining America's political focal point 200 years later, an air of importance stirs the city and one may sense the scent of power emanating from the cracks. In the private sector, the major employers are universities and hospitals - many of which are world famous. Population count for DC in 1999 was at 522,124 with strongest private sector industry contained in business association services. The city offers plenty of sights to see and an efficient subway system. Take care outside downtown as the crime rate is high. Generally, almost all of the NW is safe with the exception of NY Avenue east of 9th Street. Visitors should avoid the three other quadrants (SW, SE, NE) except for Capitol Hill and the Fish Market areas. Washington summers are notoriously hot and muggy, and people spend most of their time either trying to get out of the city or complaining about not being able to leave. Winters, conversely, offer a cold and bitter climate.

AIRPORT

Ronald Reagan Washington National Airport to City Center

The airport lies 3 miles from the city; expect about 20 minutes in travel time. Since District of Colombia taxis operate on a zone basis, be sure to settle on a fare before departing. Virginia and Maryland taxis, however, do offer meters.

The Washington Metro Subway (Metrorail) handily offers two lines to the airport stopping adjacent to terminals B and C. Shuttles arrive in front of the terminal A to take passengers to the subway stop. The Yellow line stops at L'Enfant Plaza, and Gallery Place (7th and G Streets NW). The Blue Line operates to Metro Center Station at 11th and G streets NW where you can transfer or find a taxi to your hotel. Expect about a 20-minute ride between airport and downtown.

Buses also service the airport. The Super Shuttle delivers passengers direct to their destination, while the Washington Flyer bus goes to the 1517 K Street airport terminal downtown for a fare of $8. There is a lso a Metrobus station at the base of the Metrorail station, but it is only wise to use this if it is an area not served by Metrorail. Rental cars are also readily available 24 hours a day.

Dulles International Airport to City Center

Dulles is less convenient but less crowded than National. It lies 26 miles (41 km.) from the city center. A taxi dispatcher stands outside the arrivals hall. Expect to pay around $45 for the hour-long ride into town. The Washington Flyer bus offers a more economical mode of transport ($16) and takes between 45 minutes to an hour to reach the city airport terminal downtown (1517 K St., NW), from which one can catch a cab or take a shuttle bus to the hotel.

Airline Numbers

See the "Travel" section earlier in the U.S. chapter for complete airline phone numbers.

HOTELS

Note: Of the four seasons, Winter and Summer in the capital city offer the lowest hotel rates.

Top-end

Four Seasons Washington D.C.; 2800 Four Seasons Washington D.C.; 2800 Pennsylvania Avenue NW; tel: (202) 342-0444; fax: (202) 944-2076;106 double rooms, 30 suites; adjacent RockCreek Park, city center; restaurant; meeting facilities; 24-hour business services; secretarial service; translation; in-room television, modem/fax connection, multi-line telephone, voicemail, fax available; 24-hour room service; hairdresser; complimentary limousine service; health and fitness club; massage therapy; lap pool; whirlpool; $295-370.

Hay-Adams Hotel; 16th & H Street, NW; tel: (202) 638-6600; fax: (202)638-2716; 113 rooms, 30 suites; city center, near airport; historical hotel; restaurant; bar; conference rooms; in-room television, direct-dial telephone, minibar, safe; fitness room; views of White House; Presidential suite; $265-450.

The Jefferson Hotel; 16th and M Streets, NW; 1200 16th St., NW; tel: (202) 347-2200; fax: (202) 331-7982; http://www.camberleyhotels.com;

100 rooms; intimate hotel; individually decorated rooms/suites; restaurant; bar; business services; in-room refrigerator, coffeemaker, microwave, dataport; 24-hour room service; laundry; valet parking; non-smoking rooms.

The St. Regis; 923 16th St. NW; tel: (202) 638-2626; fax: (202) 638-4231; http://www.luxurycollection.com; 192 rooms; restaurant; bar; conference facilities; business services; in-room safe, minibar, radio, dataport, movies; 24-hour room service; valet parking; laundry; non-smoking rooms; fitness; $345+.

W Washington D.C.; 1 Washington Circle; toll free: 1-877-W-HOTELS; opposite George Washington University; walking distance to Georgetown; meeting facilities; in-room dual-line telephones, television, high-speed Ethernet laptop access, work desk; printer, fax, scanner on request; 24-hour concierge, valet, room service. (opening approximately July 2000).

Willard Inter-Continental; 1401 Pennsylvania Ave., NW; tel: (202) 628-9100; fax: (202) 637-7326; http://www.washington.interconti.com/index.html; 340 rooms; located just east of the White House; restored 1900 atmosphere; restaurant; bar; conference facilities; business services; in-room movies, VCR, radio, coffeemaker, dataports; 24-hour room service; valet parking; laundry; non-smoking rooms; fitness; US$395-480.

Expensive

Carlyle Suites; 1731 New Hampshire Ave., NW; tel: (202) 234-3200; fax:(202) 332-1488; art deco all-suite hotel; restaurant; meeting facilities (up to 100); kitchens; laundry; dry cleaning; valet service available; in-room television, direct-dial telephone, data ports, voicemail; fitness.

Embassy Suites Chevy Chase; 4300 Military Road, NW; tel: (202) 362-9300;toll free: 1-800-362-2779; www.embassy-suites.com; attached to Chevy Chase Pavilion, convenient to airports and attractions; restaurant; conference facilities (up to 120); business center; complimentary, cooked-to-order breakfast; evening cocktails; USA today in-suite daily; 2 in-room televisions, 2 direct-dial telephones with data ports, voicemail, coffee-maker, refrigerator, wet-bar, kitchenettes, iron and ironing board; parking; on site METRO station; atrium; fitness center.

Morrison-Clark Inn; 1015 L St., NW; tel: (202) 898-1200; fax: (202) 289-8576; Victorian mansion; 54 rooms; restaurant; breakfast included; conference facilities (up to 125); in-room cable television, direct-dial multi-line telephone; modem/fax connection, voicemail; fax facilities; fitness; $145-230.

One Washington Circle; 1 Washington Circle NW; tel: (202) 872-1680; fax:(202) 887-4989; boutique hotel located opposite Foggy Bottom Metro stop, near White House; restaurant; business center; fax facilities; suites with kitchenettes; in-room television, direct-dial telephone, modem/fax connection; fitness; pool.

Washington Marriott; 1221 22nd Street, NW; tel: (202) 872-1500; fax: (202)872-1424; http://www.Marriott.com; located in West-End neighborhood; restaurant; conference facilities (up to 600); business center; in-room television, direct-dial telephone, data ports, voicemail; fax facilities; parking; health club; jacuzzi; pool.

Moderate

Best Western Downtown/Capitol Hill; 724 3rd St., NW, D.C. 20001; tel: (202) 842-4466; toll free: 1-800-242-4831; fax: (202) 842-4831; US$79-115; restaurant; complimentary breakfast; complimentary morning newspaper; self parking.

United States

Holiday Inn Central Washington; Rhode Island at 15th Street, N.W.; tel: (202) 483-2000; toll-free in U.S.: 800-248-0016; fax (202) 797-1078; 213 rooms; city center; restaurant; cocktail lounge; meeting facilities (up to 300); fax facilities; in-room tv, coffeemaker, irons/ironing boards, movies, hair dryers, voicemail, dataports; executive rooms with minibars and safe; room service; corporate rates; fitness.

Kalorma Guest House; 1854 Mintwood Place, NW, Washington D.C., 20009; tel: (202) 667-6369; fax: (202) 319-1262; downtown residential neighborhood; turn-of-the-century Victorian townhouses; most bedrooms with fireplaces and period antiques; continental breakfast; garden; US$50-105.

Quality Hotel Downtown; 1315 16th Street, NW; tel: (202) 232-8000; fax: (202) 667-9827; city center; restaurant; conference facilities; in-room television, direct-dial telephone; parking; pool.

Washington Plaza; 10 Thomas Circle; tel: (202) 842-1300; fax; (202) 371-9602; restaurant; conference facilities (up to 500); in-room television, direct-dial telephone, data ports, voicemail; fax facilities; parking; fitness; pool.

Wyndham Bristol; 2430 Pennsylvania Ave., NW; tel: (202) 955-6400; fax: (202)775-8489; 100 single, 100 double, 39 suites; city center; restaurant, bar; parking; corporate rates; in-room television, direct-dial telephone; 24-hour room service; fitness; $89-259.

Budget

Quality Inn Governor; 6650 Arlington Blvd., Falls Church, VA 22042; tel: (703) 532-8900; fax: (703) 532-7121; 121 rooms; US$62-80.

Note: Comfort, Quality, Clarion, Econo, and Rodeway all have other hotels in the Washington area; www.choicehotels.com/.

HEALTH CARE

Alexandria Hospital; 4320 Seminary Road, Alexandria, VA; tel: (703) 379-3000; Interventional Angiography, Oncology, Radiology and Gastroenterology.

Arlington Hospital; 1701 North George Mason Dr., Arlington, VA 22205; tel: (703) 558-5000/6100; Surgery, Pathology, Kidney Care, Pediatric,

Georgetown University Medical Center; 3800 Reservoir Road NW; tel: (202) 687-5055; patient hotline: (202) 784-2273; http://www.dml.georgetown.edu/medctr/; plastic surgery and intensive care specialities

John Hopkins Hospital; 600 North Street, Baltimore, MD 21287; (410) 955-5000; Ophthalmology, Urology, Hematology, Cardiac Surgery, Cardiology, Neurology, and Pediatrics.

HEALTH CLUB

Bally Total Fitness; 2000 L Street, NW #1B; tel: (202) 331-7788.

City Fitness; 1010 Vermont Ave. NW, tel: (202) 638-3539; 3525 Connecticut Ave. NW; tel: 537-0539.

Fitness Company; 1010 Wisconsin Ave., NW#100; tel: (202) 625-9100; Lafayette Center, 1120 20th Ave. NW; tel: (202) 659-6888.

Four Seasons Fitness Club; 2800 Pennsylvania Ave., NW; tel: (202) 944-2022.

Gold's Gym; 408 4th St., SW; tel: (202) 554-4653.

Washington Center Health Club; 1001 G St., NW; tel: (202) 637-4747.

Washington Hilton Sport and Health Center; 1919 Connecticut Ave., NW; tel: (202) 483-4100.

Washington Sports Club; 1835 Connecticut Ave., NW, tel: (202) 332-0100; 20th St. NW, tel: 785-4900; 2233 Wisconsin Ave. NW #214, tel: 337-3500; 2251 Wisconsin Ave. NW, tel: 333-2323; Dupont Circle, tel: 234-4000.

AUTO RENTAL

Avis; tel: (800) 331-1212.

Budget; tel: (800) 527-0700.

Dollar; tel: (800) 800-4000.

Hertz; tel: (800) 654-3131.

National; tel: (800) 328-4567.

Ogilvie Transportation Services; tel: (301) 598-0591; toll free: 1-800406-2227; www. otslimo.com; limousine service.

United Transportation Inc.; tel: 1-888-881-4443; http://www.utilimo.com; limousine service.

CHAMBER OF COMMERCE

District of Columbia Chamber of Commerce
1301 Pennsylvania Avenue, Suite 309
Washington, DC 20004
tel: (202) 347-7201; fax: (202) 347-3538
www.dcchamber.og

WORLD TRADE CENTER

World Trade Center Washington D.C.
1300 Pennsylvania Ave. NW, Ste. M-1100
Washington, D.C. 20004
tel: (202) 418-4224; fax: (202) 4184238
Web: http://www.itcdc.com
email: hosethc@urbanretail.com
Services: translation services, trade education, meeting facilities, temporary offices, display and exhibit, video conferencing, intl. trade library,

World Trade Center Washington Dulles Airport
245 Davis Ave., SW
Leesburg, VA 20175
tel: (703) 779-2014; fax: (703) 779-8611
email: runde@usa.net

Uruguay

At a Glance

THE PEOPLE

Population ....3,308,523 (July 1999 est.)
Growth Rate ....0.73% (1999 est.)
Life Expectancy .... 75.83 years (1999 est.)
Infant Mortality .. 13.49 deaths /1,000 live births (1999 est.)

Ethnic Composition

White 88%
Mestizo 8%
Black.. 4%

Religious Composition

Roman Catholic.. 66%
Protestant 2%
Jewish 2%
Non-Affiliated and Other.. 30%

Languages Spoken

Spanish (official), Portuguese, Brazilero (a Portuguese-Spanish hybrid common along the Brazilian frontier).

Education and Literacy

Elementary education is compulsory for the first six years. Education up through university is tuition free. Adult literacy is 97.3 percent.

Labor Force

Total: 1,380,000
By occupation: government 25%, manufacturing 19%, agriculture 11%, commerce 12%, utilities, construction, transport, and communications 12%, other services 21%.

THE ECONOMY

Uruguay is a tiny country sandwiched between Argentina and Brazil, the two greatest economies in South America. Originally an agricultural export powerhouse, Uruguay has carved itself a sizeable niche in the service sector especially in transportation and communications. Its economy has been plagued by high inflation and what is considered to be overly tight government regulation. Though the rate of inflation is in decline, both factors have made the Uruguayan economy unattractive to foreign investors. Further contributing to the economic plight has been Uruguay's strong dependence on Brazil and Argentina for both imports and exports. As these two giants have faltered, so has their tiny but resilient neighbor. Government attempts to revamp the social security system and advance education have had a minimal effect on a GDP growth rate that remains respectable if stalled.

Exports ....US$2.7 billion (1997)
Imports ....US$3.7 billion (1997)
Total Trade ....US$6.4 billion (1997)
GDP Per Capita................................... US$8,600 (1998 est.)
Unemployment .... 10.5% (1998 est.)
Inflation Rate 8.6% (1998)

Top Export Partners

Brazil, Argentina, United States, EU.

Top Import Partners

Brazil, Argentina, Germany, France, Italy, United States.

Top Exports

Wool and textiles manufactures, beef and other animal products, chemicals, rice, seafood.

Top Imports

Machinery and equipment, oil, vehicles, chemicals, minerals, plastics.

BUSINESS WORKWEEK

Offices

Monday to Friday 8:30 or 9a.m. to 5:30p.m. or 6p.m.

Banks

Monday to Friday 9a.m. to Noon (In Montevideo, 1p.m. to 5p.m.)

Government

Monday through Friday: November to mid-March 7:30 a.m. to 1:30p.m. / Other months - Noon to 7p.m.

Retail

Monday to Friday 9a.m. to 8p.m., Saturday 9a.m. to 1p.m. (some shops have Sunday hours)

Note: Many shops and service offices take an extended break at 1p.m. and reopen at mid-afternoon.

HOLIDAYS

New Year's Day...January 1
Landing of the 33 Patriots .... April 19
Labor Day...May 1
Battle of Las Piedras ....May 18
Birth of General Artigas ....June 19
Constitution Day...July 18
National Independence Day .... August 25
Discovery of America ....October 12
All Souls' Day ....November 2
Christmas Day...December 25
Some dates may vary by year.

CLIMATE

Seasons

The climate is temperate, with opposite season's to the nation's north of the equator. August is the coolest month, January the warmest. The climate is generally pleasant in Uruguay, with similar temperatures all year round. In the summer, from November to March, the average temperatures are 21˚C (70˚F). In the winter, from June to September, the temperatures are below zero, with cold nights and strong wind. Rainfall is equally distributed throughout the year.

Regions

There are few regional differences in Uruguay beyond high coastal versus low inland humidity.

Money & Banking

Currency

The currency of Uruguay is the Urguayan Peso (Ur$).

Denominations

The Peso (Ur$) comes in coin denominations of 500, 200, 100, 50, 10, 5 centesimos and 1 peso; and banknotes of 50, 100, 200, 500, 1,000.

Uruguay

Traveler's Checks and Credit Cards

Traveler's checks can be exchanged at banks, exchange shops (*cambios*), hotels, and international airports at decent exchange rates. Larger banks may offer the best exchange rates for cash and travel checks. Most major currencies can be exchanged, but try to take only crisp and new notes, wrinkled and soiled notes are likely to be refused. Uruguay has no black market exchanges.

American Express, Visa, Diner's Club, and MasterCard are easily accepted in up-market places in main cities, but in more rural areas they will ask for cash. Some banks in the capital offer cash advances on credit cards, but you must bring your passport. Uruguay's ATM machines do not accept cards from banks outside of South America. Credit card transactions will receive the best exchange rates.

Travel

VISA AND PASSPORT

All visitors must have a valid passport for travel to Uruguay. Visitors from Brazil, Argentina, the EU, United States, Japan and Israel do NOT require visas. All other visitors must apply for a 90-day, renewable visa. All visitors on commercial travel must have an invitation to receive a business visa. Do not attempt to transact business on a tourist visa. This proviso does not apply to doing basic business research.

DEPARTURE FORMALITIES

There are no departure formalities for Uruguay. Antiques and works of art for export should be cleared in advance by customs officials prior to departure date.

CUSTOMS ENTRY (PERSONAL)

Duty-free

The following items may be imported into Uruguay without incurring customs duty by residents of Uruguay arriving from Argentina, Bolivia, Brazil, Chile, or Paraguay (maximum four times a year):

- Tobacco: 200 cigarettes, 25 cigars, or 250g of tobacco
- Alcohol: 1 liter of alcohol
- Other: 2kg of foodstuffs
 All other nationals:
- Tobacco: 400 cigarettes, 50 cigars, or 500g of tobacco
- Alcohol: 2 liters of alcohol
- Other: 5kg of foodstuffs

Tourists face vaguer restrictions of "used, personal goods" and other goods "in reasonable quantities" thus remaining open to the discretion and mood of customs officials. Patience and a smile go a long way towards making your processing through customs a pleasant and inexpensive affair.

IMMUNIZATION

International certificate of vaccination is not required unless you are arriving from an infected area. Tetanus, malaria, and hepatitis-A immunizations are recommended. Bring plenty of sunblock if you are prone to sunburn.

TIPPING

Taxi

A 10 percent tip is customary for taxi drivers.

Porters

Porters typically get tipped 50 centesimos per piece.

Hotels and Restaurants

A service charge is included in the bill, but a small additional tip is expected of foreigners and will be much appreciated.

EMERGENCY INFORMATION

Police and Crime

Crime is by no means rampant but take basic precautions. Avoid flashy displays of wealth, and dress conservatively. Leave most of your cash, traveler's checks, jewelry, and your non-essential valuables in your hotel safe. Carry photocopies of your passport instead of the original. Carry cash in a money belt, and use credit cards or traveler's checks for most transactions.

Foreign business visitors are often the target of thieves so purses, laptops and briefcases require additional security. Do not leave valuables in cars or on tables in cafés. Keep briefcases and bags secure while walking to avoid the attention of passing thieves on motorbikes. Possession of illegal drugs by foreigners carries stiff penalties and you will be lucky if you are only deported.

The police in Uruguay have little patience for rich, obnoxious tourists but will treat most visitors with respect and courtesy.

Health

Malaria is endemic, as is bilharzia (caused by water snails), so take medication before departure. Use screens and insecticides to eliminate insects and snakes.

Do not drink tap water or use ice cubes except in top-rated hotels; bottled water is available. Wash all vegetables in a chlorine solution, peel fruits, and avoid uncooked food. Drink only pasteurized milk.

Medical care is relatively poor, but some doctors are European-trained, and the drugs available are French-made. Your hotel will have access to more information. Those on extended business stays should consider evacuation insurance in the event of major medical problems.

For more information on medical centers, including phone numbers, please see the "Business Centers" section at the end of this chapter.

TAXI & RENTAL CARS

All taxis are metered, and drivers should have a list of fares. There is an extra charge for each piece of baggage and for trips taken between midnight and 6a.m.

Rental cars can be found in urban areas but visitors should purchase ample insurance. Driving can be a very "macho" affair and rural police officers are not beyond soliciting bribes from foreign drivers they choose to detain. Hired cars from reputable companies with professional local drivers are recommended for first-time business visitors. your local business contact or hotel can assist in setting up such service.

BUS

Three main bus lines connect all towns and cities. The services are numerous, inexpensive but can be slow.

TRAIN

There is no regular passenger train service in Uruguay.

Essential Terms

English	Spanish
Yes No	Sí No
Good morning Hello (daytime) Hello (evening) Hello (telephone)	Buenos días Buenas tardes Buenas noches ¿Hola?
Good-bye	Adiós
Please	Por favor
Thank you	Gracias
Pleased to meet you	Encantado (a) de conocerle
Excuse me; I'm sorry	¿Perdóneme?
My name is _____	Me llamo _____
I don't understand	No comprendo
Do you speak English?	¿Habla usted inglés?

Communications

DIALING CODES IN URUGUAY

International country code: [598]
 Selected city codes: Canelones (33), Mercedes (532), Montevideo (2)

Dialing Uruguay from Overseas

To dial Uruguay from overseas, dial the international dialing code of the country you are in, then 598 (the country code for Uruguay), then the city code and finally the num-

Uruguay

ber. If you were dialing Canelones, for example, you would begin with 011, then 598, then 332 (the city code for Canelones), and finally the number of the person or office you were trying to reach.

Assistance Numbers

International Operator 218
Operator 12

CALLING WITHIN URUGUAY

Local Calls

One token (ficha) will buy three minutes of time for a local call.

Long Distance Calls

Antel operates long distance offices to place a call more easily.

International Calls

The national telephone company, Antel, operates a system that resembles that of Argentina. An international direct call means dialing 00 + country code + area code + number. Discounted rates occur between 10p.m. and 7a.m. weekdays (even more after midnight), and between 1 p.m. and midnight on Saturday, and all day Sunday.

PAY PHONES

Public Telephones

Phones for common use do not accept tokens (*fichas*) instead of coins. One token equals three minutes.

Calling Cards

Magnetic phone cards are now also available.

CELLULAR PHONES

Cellular service is limited in Uruguay. Antel offers AMPS-TDMA and Abiatar offers AMPS for analogue users. Contact an international operator for assistance in locating their offices and telephone numbers.

Note: Your home country cell phone may not work in this country. If not, we recommend that you rent an international cell phone *before* you leave home. A major US-based cell phone rental provider is **IMC WorldCell**. For information see "International Cell Phone Rentals" on page 14.

CALL BACK

You can (potentially) save significant sums when calling in Uruguay by using one of the call back services listed below. Fees for call back services vary widely, depending on the company and the type of service required. Be sure to check with these companies before leaving to compare rates.

For a list of callback services, please refer to the "Communications" section in the *Global Road Warrior* Introduction.

PHONE JACK

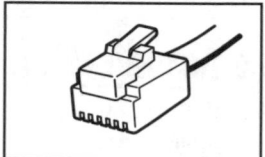

Plug adaptors are available through **iGo Corporation**. (See "Electrical and Telephone Adaptors" on page 19.)

FAX

Most hotels have facilities.

POSTAL SERVICES

Airmail to Europe and North America takes three to five days, although incoming mail takes considerably longer.

Hours of service

Monday to Friday 8a.m. to 6p.m.

TELEGRAMS

Telegrams can be sent from most hotels.

Business Services

COURIER SERVICE

DHL International S.R.L.; Av. de las Americas 7777 Canelones, Montevideo, 11000; tel: (2) 960-217; website: http://www.la-reg.dhl.com/; Monday to Friday 9a.m. to 7p.m., Saturday 9am to 1pm, Closed Sunday Holidays

Federal Express; tel: (2) 916-5544; fax: 598-2-916-4113; Horas de Servicio al Cliente: Lunes a viernes, 9a.m. 6p.m.

TNT Express Worldwide; Cargo Center Washington 236/238; Montevideo; tel: (2) 963-258; fax: (2) 963-257.

UPS; Montevideo Sibel S.A., Treinta y tres 1576, Montevideo; tel: (2) 916-1638; tel: (2) 916-1639; fax: (5982) 916-1635.

Electrical

Current

220 volts AC, 50Hz

ELECTRICAL PLUGS

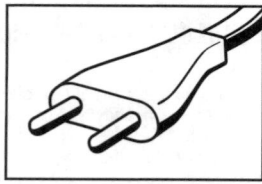

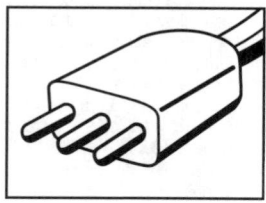

Plug adaptors are available through **iGo Corporation**. (See "Electrical and Telephone Adaptors" on page 19.)

Technical Support
HARDWARE/SOFTWARE VENDOR SUPPORT

Compaq/Digital; (General U.S.) tel: (281) 518-2000; (in Switzerland) tel: [41] (22) 709-5330; fax: [41] (22) 709-5391 (Geneva); tel: [41] (1) 801-2507; fax: [41] (1) 801-2172 (Zurich); http://www.compaq.com/.

Corel; (in the U.S.) tel: [1] (716) 871-2325 (Ask to be Forwarded to Appropriate Program); (in Germany) tel: [49] (180) 425-8210 (TS Word Perfect-32 bit); http://www.corel.com/.

Dell; (in the U.S.) tel: [1] (512) 338-4400; fax: [1] (512) 728-3330; (in Germany) tel: [49] (61) 039-710; (Dell- Europe) tel: [44] (134) 474-8000; http://www.dell.com/.

Hewlett Packard; (in the U.S.) tel: [1] (408) 246-4300; (in Switzerland) tel: [41] (22) 780-8111; http://www.hp.com/.

IBM; (in the U.S.) tel: [1] (919) 517-2800; (in Switzerland) tel: [41] (22) 310-0418 (in French); http://www.ibm.com/.

Microsoft; tel: (2) 774-934; fax: (2) 774-935; (in Switzerland) tel: [41] (848) 858-868; fax [41] (1) 831-0869; (in the U.S.) [1] (425) 635-7222; http://www.microsoft.com/.

NEC; (in Israel) tel: [972] (0)9-59-3300 (Tracker Support); (in the U.S.) [1] (916) 388-0101 (Main Switchboard); http://www.nec.com/.

Toshiba; (in the U.S.) [1] (949) 583-3000 (Corporate Headquarters); (in Germany) tel: [49] (2131) 158-319; fax: [49] (2131) 158-558; (in Switzerland) tel: [41] (1) 946-0777; fax: [41] (1) 946-0807; (in Ireland) tel: [44] (193) 282-8828; http://www.toshiba.com/.

Internet Connection
HOW TO CONNECT

Connecting to AOL and Compuserve in Uruguay is similar to using it when traveling outside your own area code. See the introductory section for detailed information on connecting to your account through a different phone number.

America Online
Numbers are available at keyword *international*. Be sure to get several local numbers before leaving. Go to keyword *access* (a free area) and download the software.

At press time, America Online had no local access numbers in Uruguay. Check their list of current access numbers at http://intlaccess.web.aol.com/ to see if any numbers have been activated or to locate numbers in neighboring countries.

Compuserve
Numbers are available at *Go International*. If you are using CompuServe 2000, use GO PHONES within CompuServe 2000 to search for access numbers. The Compuserve Web-site also has a great deal of information for travelers at http://www.compuserve.com/.

At press time, Compuserve had no local access numbers. Check their list of current access numbers to see if any numbers have been activated or to locate numbers in neighboring countries.

Independent Service Providers
Many independent service providers offer discounts if you are only in town for a couple of days.

InterSys; tel/fax: (2) 915-4816; emal: ventas@intersys.com.uy; http://www.intersys.com.uy/.

Montevideo COMM; tel: (2) 402-2516; fax: (2) 402-2110; info@montevideo.com/.uy; http://www.montevideo.com.uy/.

Netgate; tel: (2) 400-6666; fax: (2) 409-1232; email: dw@netgate.com.uy; http://netgate.com.uy/

Tecnet Consultores / @Internet Uruguay; telefax: (2) 707-4252; info@internet.com/.uy; http://www.internet.com.uy/.

Business Culture
GREETINGS AND COURTESIES

Handshakes are customary for men and women, when arriving and leaving. It is common for women to kiss each other once on the cheek, but it more closely resembles kissing the air and touching cheeks. Uruguayans employ the Latin custom of using both parents' names, with the father's name first. For example, Enrique Munoz Samorano would be formally addressed as *Señor* Munoz, the correct title for a new business associate. You should always use a title, if a person has one. First names are used only between close friends. Present your business card upon introduction. At social events, greet and shake hands with each person individually. When leaving, say farewell to each person you have met.

BUSINESS ETHIC AND FRAMEWORK

The language of the country is Spanish, although many executives speak English. All correspondence, as well as business cards and presentation materials, should be in Spanish. Uruguay is a democratic republic with strong emphasis on the individual. Executives in particular are noted for their strong work ethic. Uruguayan businesspeople are cosmopolitan, sophisticated, and Eurocentric. Initial business encounters are usually quite formal in this otherwise relaxed society. The country adheres faithfully to the general Latin precept that business relationships are based on personal relationships, even to the extent that expertise is considered less important than fitting into the group.

DECISION MAKING

Although Uruguayan business is largely international and sophisticated in style and outlook, authority remains narrowly concentrated, and actual decisions are almost always made at a high level. When negotiating, Uruguayans have a spirit of moderation and compromise.

WOMEN

Women in business are becoming more accepted in Uruguay, although their presence remains rare in the upper levels of management. Although women may walk and dine alone, many will feel more comfortable if escorted, and should take a taxi if venturing out after dark. Women may find it best not to wear shorts, even for casual occasions.

MEETINGS

Arrange business meetings between May and October to avoid the holiday season. If you don't speak Spanish, you can hire an interpreter at most of the better hotels. Although business is conducted at a relaxed pace in Uruguay, meetings tend to run formally even though they rarely start on time. Though Uruguayan punctuality is very relaxed, it is appreciated if you always arrive punctually yourself. Be patient if faced with delays and interruptions. Expect some light conversation before business begins.

BUSINESS ENTERTAINING

Most business entertaining is done in restaurants. If you are invited to an Uruguayan home, consider it appropriate (but not mandatory) to send a gift of flowers or chocolates to your hostess in advance of the occasion. Your visit to an Uruguayan home will be a social occasion, and you should avoid discussing business. Any attention you pay to your host's children will be appreciated.

Uruguayans and most Latin Americans stand very close to each other when conversing, which can prove disconcerting for the first-time visitor. When in conversation, avoid the subject of politics, especially any mention of communism. Don't ask questions about your host's family unless prompted, since family members may have been victims of the military dictatorship that ruled the country for fourteen years. Sport is a favorite topic of conversation. Uruguayans are very proud of their country, and any praise for its beauty will be well-received. They will be pleased at any attempt you make to speak Spanish.

BUSINESS ATTIRE

Fashion in Uruguay is indicative of a person's social status. Uruguayans wear conservative, well-tailored clothes in subdued colors, in the style of Europeans. For men, a conservative suit is appropriate for a business meeting.

Women can consider conservative suits with a white blouse or dresses acceptable for business occasions. Women do not wear much make up or jewelry, but they do wear dresses more often than do American women. In summer, women do not have to wear pantyhose, and men may remove their jacket and loosen their tie. Follow the example of your host.

Business Centers
Montevideo

CITY VIEW

Montevideo is a small city that hasn't grasped commercialism like most Latin American neighbors. The business center is located east of downtown.

AIRPORT

Carrasco Airport to City Center

The airport is 13 miles (22 km.) from the city. Coaches leave every two hours. Average travel time is 35 minutes. Taxis are also available just outside the terminal. Metered cabs are available as well as cabs that carry a list of the flat rates for various trips. Be prepared for an increase in the fare for each piece of luggage and for rides at night.

Airline Numbers

Aerolineas Argentinas	(2) 91-94-66
Aerolineas Uruguayas	(2) 90-18-68
American Airlines	(2) 96-39-29
Ecuatoriana	(2) 91-35-70
Iberia	(2) 98-10-32
LAN-Chile	(2) 98-27-27
Líneas Aéreas Paraguayas	(LAP) (2) 90-79-46
Líneas Aéreas Privadas Argentinas	(2) 90-87-65
Lufthansa	(2) 98-92-65
PLUNA	(2) 98-06-06, 92-14-14

HOTELS

Top-end

Belmont Hotel; Rivera 6512; tel: 600-0430; fax: 600-8609; restaurant; conference facilities; business center; parking; fitness; pool

Victoria Plaza; Plaza Independencia 759; tel: 920-111, 902-0237; fax: 921-628, 902-1628; http://www.victoriaplaza.com/;

near city center; restaurant; conference facilities (up to 1100); secretarial services; fax/photocopy facilities; in-room modem/fax connection, safe; parking; corporate rates; fitness; sauna; pool; whirlpool; casino.

Expensive

Plaza Fuerte Hotel; Bartolome Mitre 1361; tel: 915-9563; fax: 915-9569; near city center; restaurant; conference facilities (up to 30); secretarial services; fax/photocopy facilities; in-room modem/fax connection, safe; car rental; parking; corporate rates; whirlpool.

4 stars - Single Room 110 USD Double Room 195 USD Suite 300 USD

Balmoral Plaza Hotel; Plaza Cagancha 1126; tel: 902-2393; fax: 902-2288; email: balmoral@netgate.com.uy; http://www.balmoral.com.uy/; near city center; restaurant; conference facilities; business center; secure parking.

Holiday Inn Motevideo; Colonia 823; tel: 920-001; fax: 921-242; near to city centre; restaurant; conference facilities (up to 200); secretarial services; fax/photocopy facilities; in-room safe; parking; corporate rates; fitness; pool.

Hosteria Del Lago Hotel; Arizona 9637 Lago De Carrasco; tel: 601-2210; fax: 601-2880; conference facilities; free transport to airport; car rental; parking; watersports; tennis.

Lafayette; Calle Soriano 1170; tel: 924-646, 902-4646; fax: 921-301, 902-1301; near city center; restaurant; conference facilities (up to 300); business center; in-room safe; car rental; secure parking; corporate rates; fitness; sauna; pool; whirlpool.

Moderate

California; San Jose 1237; tel: 920-408; fax: 920-412; near city center & beach; conference facilities; corporate rates.

King's; Andes 1491 Y Avenida Uruguay; tel: 920-927; fax: 920-194; near city center; parking.

Klee International; San Jose 1303, Esquina Yaguaron, tel: 920-606, 902-0606; fax: 987-365, 908-7365; 4-star hotel near city center; conference facilities; business center; secretarial services; fax/photocopy facilities; secure parking; corporate rates.

Lancaster; Plaza Cagancha 1334; tel: 921-054, 902-0029/105; fax: 981-117, 908-1117; near airport & city center; conference facilities; parking.

Oceania; Mar Artico 1227; tel: 600-444; fax: 600-721; restaurant; conference facilities; parking.

Oxford; Paraguay 1286; tel: 920-046; fax: 923-792; 4-star hotel near city center & beach; conference facilities; secretarial services; fax/photocopy facilities.

WORLD TRADE CENTER

World Trade Center Montevideo C.A.
Hidalgos 527 Of. 802
11.300 Montevideo, Uruguay
tel: (2) 710-988; fax: (2) 710-7464
email: wtc@latu.org.uy

Venezuela

At a Glance

THE PEOPLE

Population ....23,203,466 (July 1999 est.)
Growth Rate ....1.71% (1999 est.)
Life Expectancy .... 72.95 years (1999 est.)
Infant Mortality ... 26.51 deaths/1,000 live births (1999 est.)

Ethnic Composition

Mestizo 67%
White 21%
Black 10%
Amerindian 2%

Religious Composition

Roman Catholic 96%
Protestant 2%
Other 2%

Languages Spoken

Spanish and numerous Amerindian dialects.

Education and Literacy

Nine years of schooling is compulsory. Currently, 91.1 percent of the population is literate.

Labor Force

Total: 9,200,000
By occupation: services 64%, industry 23% and agriculture 13%.

THE ECONOMY

Venezuela, one of the two South American members of OPEC, has an economy dominated by petroleum production and export. Weak oil prices in the last few years have caused the Venezuelan government to reassess an industry that once contributed 27 percent of the nation's GDP. The result has been a tightening of currency controls and increased budget cuts. The officials in Caracas have also forged ahead with the privatization of state-owned steel and aluminum industries. While this would normally spark a round of foreign investment inflow, high inflation and a wavering currency have kept offshore money offshore. Like many other South American nations, Venezuela's fate is a function, though somewhat indirectly, of Brazil's and Argentina's economic pattern.

Exports .... US$16.9 billion
Imports .... US$12.4 billion
Total Trade .... US$29.3 billion
GDP Per Capita .... US$8,500 (1998 est.)
Unemployment ....11.5% (1997 est.)

Inflation Rate 29.9% (1998)

Top Export Partners

United States (and Puerto Rico), Colombia, Brazil.

Top Import Partners

United States, EU, Japan, Colombia.

Top Exports

Petroleum, bauxite and aluminum, steel, chemicals, agricultural products, manufactures.

Top Imports

Raw materials, machinery and equipment, transport equipment, construction material

BUSINESS WORKWEEK

Offices

Monday to Friday 8a.m. to noon, 2p.m. to 6p.m.

Banks

Monday to Friday 8:30a.m. to 11:30a.m. and from 2p.m. to 4:30p.m.

Government

Government office hours are staggered, opening Monday to Friday between 7:30a.m. and 9:30a.m., and closing between 3:30p.m. and 5:30p.m. Check with specific agencies.

Retail

Monday to Friday 9a.m. to noon, 2p.m. to 7p.m. Slightly shorter hours on Saturday.

HOLIDAYS

New Year's Day ....January 1
Carnival .... March 6-7
Easter ....April 21-24*
Declaration of Independence .... April 19
Labor Day ....May 1
Battle of Carabobo ....June 24
Independence Day ....July 5
Birth of Simón Bolívar and
Battle of Lago de Maracaibo ....July 24
Civil Servants' Day ....September 4
Discovery of America ....October 12
Christmas ....December 24-25
New Year's Eve ....December 31
*Date may vary by year.

CLIMATE

Seasons

The climate varies from tropical to temperate, depending on elevation. Rainy season is from May to November, and it can be torrential. Temperatures average 23˚C (73˚F) with severe drops in temperatures at night.

Regions

Mountain areas are cool, with snow in the mountains in winter and rain the rest of the year. The Amazon region has rainfall throughout the year (2,000mm/yr) and no discernible dry season. Temperatures in Caracas have a maximum of 32˚C (90˚F) in July and August and a minimum of 9˚C (48˚F) in January and February.

Money & Banking

Currency

The currency of Venezuela is the Bolivar (Bs).

Denominations

The Bolivar (Bs) comes in coin denominations of B5, 2 and 1, and 50, 25, 10 and 5 centimos; and banknotes of B5, 10, 20, 50, 100, 500, 1000, 2000 and 5000.

Traveler's Checks and Credit Cards

Traveler's checks can be exchanged at selected banks, exchange shops (*casa de cambio*), large hotels, and international airports at decent exchange rates. Banks may offer the best exchange rates for foreign cash and travel checks but not all banks will accept them. Most major cur-

Venezuela

○ National capital
⊛ Estado/territorio capital
• Secondary city
━━ International border
┄┄ Estado/territorio border
┄┄┄ Railroad
━━ Primary road

0   100   200
0   100   200 mi

©2001 Magellan Geographix
SM Santa Barbara, CA

rencies can be exchanged, but try to take only crisp and new notes, wrinkled and soiled notes are likely to be refused. Venezuela no longer has black market exchanges.

Visa and MasterCard are the most easily accepted cards in larger cities, but in more rural areas they will ask for cash. Some banks in the capital offer cash advances on credit cards, but you must bring your passport identification. ATM machines are not common and what few are available may not accept cards from banks outside of South America. Credit card transactions at retail stores, hotels, and restaurants will receive the best exchange rates. Note that some retailers charge higher prices for credit and bank card use to offset the processing fees they must pay.

Travel

VISA AND PASSPORT

All visitors must have a valid passport to visit Venezuela. Residents of the EU, the U.S., Japan, Australia, New Zealand and Canada do not need a visa if they enter the country by air. All other nationalities and all people entering by land or sea will need a visa to receive a tourist card. Visa are best received before travel from a consulate in your home country.

To obtain a business visa for up to one year, you must receive prior authorization from the Venezuelan government. This will require a statement of finances and information about your business activity. Visitors with multiple-entry or business visas will be required to pay local income taxes if the stay exceeds 180 days. Carry your passport or a copy at all times.

DEPARTURE FORMALITIES

A departure tax of Bs5,000 (US$10) is required of all visitors when leaving from airports. It can be paid in local currency or U.S. dollars, so be prepared.

CUSTOMS ENTRY (PERSONAL)

Venezuela keeps its custom entry scheme for foreigners rather vague as is the custom in much of South America. The terms "personal use" and "reasonable amounts" give customs officials a lot of discretion—or indiscretion, depending on your point of view. Cameras, laptops, CD-players and videocameras can all be declared contraband if you rile the border guards. Visitors with patience and pleasant demeanors will find their entry and exit from Venezuela a smooth affair. Listed below are basic guidelines that are flexible in either direction:

Duty-free
- Tobacco: 200 cigarettes or 25 cigars
- Alcohol: 2 liters of alcoholic beverages
- Other: 4 small bottles of perfume

Prohibited or Restricted
- Flowers and plants
- Fruit, meat, and meat products
- controlled drugs (severe penalties for violations —visitors crossing at a Colombian border points will be searched thoroughly)

IMMUNIZATION

Smallpox and yellow fever vaccinations are required if the traveler is arriving from an infected area. Tetanus vac-

Venezuela

cinations as well as malaria and hepatitis-A prophylaxis are recommended.

TIPPING

Restaurants have a 10 percent service charge; leave an additional 5 to 10 percent if the service is good. Tips are expected from foreigners by taxi drivers, porters, hairdressers, tour guides, parking and cloakroom attendants, ushers, and maids. Moderation is the best policy.

EMERGENCY INFORMATION

Police and Crime

Violent and petty-crimes are on the increase in Venezuela, especially in Caracas. Terrorism exists, as do armed street robberies and muggings in broad daylight.

Theft of luggage at airports is common. Avoid riding in unauthorized taxis or with a stranger. Stick to well-known tourist routes. Take basic precautions against petty crime. Avoid flashy displays of wealth, behave conservatively. Leave most of your cash, traveler's checks, jewelry, and non-essential valuables in your hotel safe. Carry photocopies of your passport instead of the original. The police may ask for your identification at any time. Carry cash in a money belt, and use credit cards or traveler's checks for most transactions.

Foreign business visitors are often the target of thieves; so, purses, laptops and briefcases require additional security. Do not leave valuables in cars or on tables in cafés.

The police are generally helpful but in rural areas they are prone to soliciting bribes to supplement meager salaries. Even in cities, the police tend to harass backpackers and tourists that seem to be travelling on-the-cheap. As is true in most developing economies, the better you present yourself, the greater the respect accorded to you.

Punishment for "real" crime, especially drug trafficking, is severe. Do not tempt fate or the Venezuelan justice system.

Emergency Numbers

Police (national).. 169
Ambulance (Caracas).. 545-4545
Fire Department (national) 166

Health

Tap water is unsafe to drink except in the grander hotels of Caracas; boil water or use the bottled kind. Wash all vegetables in a chlorine solution, peel fruits, and avoid uncooked food. Avoid curbside restaurants until your digestive system adjusts to the local spices. Drink only pasteurized milk.

Cholera is present in some rural villages so get information before venturing into the countryside. Other diseases include bilharzia, malaria, yellow fever, typhoid, hepatitis (A&B), and respiratory problems (especially in poorer, rural areas). Venezuela can get extremely hot, so drink lots of liquids and use sun block when outdoors.

The medical system is of high standard in Caracas, and medical staff can usually speak English, but laboratories are expensive. Travel-health insurance is a must and business visitors on extended stays should carry evacuation insurance.

For more information on medical centers, including phone numbers, please see the "Business Centers" section at the end of this chapter.

TAXI & RENTAL CARS

Most taxis are not metered so agree on a fare before leaving. Prices are very inexpensive but there may be charges for luggage. Never enter a taxi that is already occupied.

Rental cars can be found in urban areas but visitors should purchase ample insurance. Rental cars are expensive but fuel is very cheap. Hired cars with drivers are recommended for first-time visitors.

BUS

Bus lines are the main form of public transport. Bus service has many levels and many competitors. Inter-city lines travel between main terminals in larger cities (*terminal de pasajeros*) and reservations should be made during holiday seasons. A minibus system (*por puestos*) also exists for short intra-city routes.

TRAIN

The only regular rail service runs between Barquisimeto and Puerto Cabello. Few people travel by train although there are plans to extend the system.

Essential Terms

English	Spanish
Yes	Sí
No	No
Good morning	Buenos días
Hello (daytime)	Buenas tardes
Hello (evening)	Buenas noches
Hello (telephone)	¿Hola?
Good-bye	Adiós
Please	Por favor
Thank you	Gracias
Pleased to meet you	Encantado (a) de conocerle
Excuse me; I'm sorry	¿Perdóneme?
My name is _____	Me llamo _____
I don't understand	No comprendo
Do you speak English?	¿Habla usted inglés?

Communications

DIALING CODES IN VENEZUELA

International country code: [58]

Selected city codes: Barcelona (81), Caracas (2), Ciudad Bolivar (85), Maracay (43), San Cristobal (76), Valencia (41)

Dialing Venezuela from Overseas

To dial Venezuela from overseas, dial your country's international dialing code, then 58 (the country code for Venezuela), then the city code, and finally the number. If you were dialing Barcelona, for example, you would begin with 011, then 58, then 81 (the city code for Barcelona), and finally the number of the person or office you were trying to reach.

Assistance Numbers

International Operator (English-speaking).................... 122
Directory 103

Venezuela

CALLING WITHIN VENEZUELA

Local Calls
Both cards and coins can be used for local calling. Bs3.50 will buy you one minute of local chat time.

Long Distance Calls
Area codes take effect when calling long distance within Venezuela.

International Calls
International direct dial is available to most countries. To make a call, dial 00 + country code + area code + number. But prepare for high rates. A three minute call to the States may cost US$8 and even more when calling outside the Americas. CANTV, the Venezuelan telecommunications service, offers customers offices with full telecommunications services, even allowing credit-card payment. Collect calls are available to certain countries only. Beware of making any calls from the hotel as a 40 percent increase in the rate may knock the wind right out of your stay. For more sane rates, try reaching an operator abroad:

U.K. 800-11-440
U.K. 800-11-441
U.S. AT&T 800-11-120
U.S. MCI...800-11-140
U.S. Sprint...800-11-110

Public phones require a coin or card deposit.

PAY PHONES

Public Telephones
Phones exist everywhere but are sometimes inoperable. CANTV, recently taken over by a U.S. group, is in the process of making modifications to the archaic system in place. CANTV offices should have phones in working condition.

Calling Cards
New card phones have taken the stage with more regularity. Known as "tarjeta CANTV" or 'tarjeta intelligente,' prepaid phone cards come in denominations of Bs250, 500, 1000 and 2000 and are available at pharmacies, metro stations and hotels.

CELLULAR PHONES
Cellular service is limited in Uruguay. *Movilnet* offers AMPS-TDMA and *Telcel* offers NAMPS for analogue users.

Note: Your home country cell phone may not work in this country. If not, we recommend that you rent an international cell phone *before* you leave home. A major US-based cell phone rental provider is **IMC WorldCell**. For information see "International Cell Phone Rentals" on page 14.

CALL BACK
You can (potentially) save significant sums when calling in Venezuela by using one of the call back services listed below. Fees for call back services vary widely, depending on the company and the type of service required. Be sure to check with these companies before leaving to compare rates. For a list of callback services, please refer to the "Communications" section in the *Global Road Warrior* Introduction.

PHONE JACKS

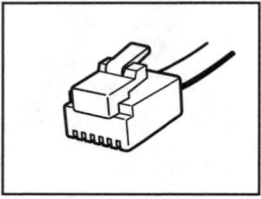

Plug adaptors are available through **iGo Corporation.** (See "Electrical and Telephone Adaptors" on page 19.)

FAX
Most hotels have fax services.

POSTAL SERVICES
International mail is very efficient, with mail to Europe and North America taking three to five days. Internal mail can take longer.

TELEGRAMS
Telegrams can be sent from top-end hotels and public telegram offices in most cities.

Business Services
COURIER SERVICES

DHL; DHL Fletes Aereos, C.A.; Final Av. Principal de los Ruices Edificio DHL Los Ruices, Caracas; tel: (2) 235-9080.

FedEx; Terro Lincoln, Thirteenth floor, Sabana Grande; tel: (2) 781-8520.

TNT Express Worldwide; Aerocav / CCS; Av. Rio de Janerio. Edificio Aerocav, Apdo de Correo 70122, Colinas de los Ruices 1071 - A, Caracas; tel: (2) 205-0585; tel: (2) 205-0583; fax: (2) 256-3553; fax: (2) 256-5345.

UPS; Transvalcar Air Courier, Avenida Principal de la Urbina, Edifico TransvalcarCruce con calle 10 La Urbina, Caracas; tel: 204-1455; tel: 241-8819; tel: 204-1441; tel: 241-6454; fax: 242-6364.

Electrical
Current
110 volts AC, 60Hz

ELECTRIC PLUGS

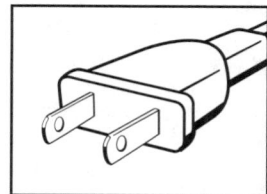

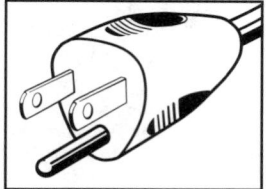

Plug adaptors are available through **iGo Corporation.** (See "Electrical and Telephone Adaptors" on page 19.)

Technical Support
HARDWARE/SOFTWARE VENDOR SUPPORT

Acer/Texas Instruments; (in the U.S.) [1] (408) 432-6200; (in Germany) tel: [49] (4102) 488-469; fax; [49] (4102) 488-169; http://www.acer.com/.

Adobe; tel: (1) 215-0411; fax: (1) 612-5634 (Nexsys All products except FrameMaker); (in the U.S.) tel: [1] (800) 500-7078; (in Germany) tel: [49] (1) 803-5018; (in Switzerland) tel: [41] (800) 833-310 http://www.adobe.com/ .

AST; (in the U.S.) tel: [1] (817) 232-9824 (International Technical Support); (in Ireland) tel: [353] (61) 492-222; (in the U.S.) tel: [1] (949) 727-4141; http://www.ast.com/.

Compaq/Digital; tel: 1-312-0145; fax: 1-312-0164; (General U.S.) tel: (281) 518-2000; http://www.compaq.com/.

Corel; tel: 1-2150-411 (All Applications); (in the U.S.) tel: [1] (716) 871-2325 (Ask to be Forwarded to Appropriate Program); http://www.corel.com/.

Dell; tel: (1) 616-6066 (ComWare Colombia); [57] (1) 616-8488 (Informatica Ltda); (1) 667-7333 (Cali) City code is unknown, but city name is Cali. (Sisa Colombia); (1) 295-9111 (Xerox Colombia); (in the U.S.) tel: [1] (512) 338-4400; fax: [1] (512) 728-3330; http://www.dell.com/.

Gateway 2000; (in the U.S.) tel: [1] (605) 232-2191; fax: [1] (605) 232-2023; (in Ireland) tel: [353] (1) 797-2000; http://www.g2k.com/.

Hewlett Packard; (Brazil Office) tel: (55) 11-7090-1444; (in the U.S.) tel: [1] (408) 246-4300; http://www.hp.com/.

IBM; tel: (2) 908-8111; (U.S. Main Office) tel: [1] 914-765-1900; (in the U.S.) tel: [1] (919) 517-2800; (in Switzerland) tel: [41] (22) 310-0418 (in French); http://www.ibm.com/.

Microsoft; tel: (2) 993-6755; tel: (2) 265-9922; fax: (2) 265-0863; (in the U.S.) [1] (425) 635-7222; http://www.microsoft.com/.

NEC; (in the U.S.) [1] (916) 388-0101 (Main Switchboard); http://www.nec.com/.

Novell; tel: 980-120-962 (Toll Free Technical Support); (in

Switzerland) tel: [41] (1) 308-4747; fax: [41] (1) 302-0401; (in the U.S.) tel: [1] (408) 434-2300; fax: [1] (408) 577-5775 (Worldwide Sales Headquarters); http://www.novell.com/.

Quark; (in the U.S.) tel: [1] (303) 894-8899; fax: [1] (303) 894-3398 (For Products Registered in the Americas); (in Switzerland) tel: [41] (1) 808-7722; fax: [41] (1) 808-7799; http://www.quark.com/.

Toshiba; (in the U.S.) [1] (949) 583-3000 (Corporate Headquarters); (in Switzerland) tel: [41] (1) 946-0777; fax: [41] (1) 946-0807; (in Ireland) tel: [44] (193) 282-8828; http://www.toshiba.com/.

Internet Connection
HOW TO CONNECT
Connecting to AOL and Compuserve in Venezuela is similar to using it when traveling outside your own area code. See the introductory section for detailed information on connecting to your account through a different phone number.

America Online
Numbers are available at keyword *international*. Be sure to get several local numbers before leaving. AOL has a new GlobalNet service that charges US$6 an hour in addition to the usual charges. Go to keyword *access* (a free area) and download the software.

Access: Barquisimeto (51) 549-322; Caracas (2) 237-4633; La Guaira (2) 355-1011; Maracaibo (61) 928-711; Porlamar (95) 624-311; Puerto La Cruz (81) 670-133; Valencia (41) 256-145.

Compuserve
Numbers are available at *Go International*. If you are using CompuServe 2000, use GO PHONES within CompuServe 2000 to search for access numbers. The Compuserve Web-site also has a great deal of information, at http://www.compuserve.com/.

Access: Caracas (2) 237-4633, (2) 794-0544, (2) 709-1000; Cumana (93) 315-321; Maracaibo (61) 590-444, 501-111; Maturin (91) 433-611; Puerto Ordaz (86) 233-022; Valencia (41) 250-011, 202-111.

Independent Service Providers
Many independent service providers offer discounts if you are only in town for a couple of days.

EnlaRed C.A.; tel: (95) 638-495; email: ventas@enlared.net; http://www.enlared.net/.

Internet Comunicaciones; tel: (2) 959-4733; fax: (2) 959-4550; email: info@internet.ve; http://www.internet.ve/.

Netpoint Communications; tel: (305) 891-1955; fax: (305) 891-2110; webmaster@netpoint.net; http://www.netpoint.net/.

Unete; tel: (2) 952-3655; fax: 953-8109; http://www.unete.com.ve/.

Business Culture
GREETINGS AND COURTESIES
Handshakes are customary among both men and women, both when arriving and leaving. Male friends may hug and female friends may kiss each other on the cheek, and even acquaintances may touch (but only men with men and women with women). If you are not introduced by your host, it is acceptable to introduce yourself in both business and social contexts. Always say good-bye to everyone when leaving a social event.

BUSINESS ETHIC AND FRAMEWORK

Venezuelans are considered to be among the most demonstrative South Americans, although Venezuelan business and social culture is based on correct, often strongly hierarchical but personal relationships that recognize personal dignity. To Venezuelans, work is not the most important part of life, but they do adhere strictly to the forms that govern what is nevertheless one of life's more important spheres. Appropriateness is critical, and Venezuelans value tactfulness and sensitivity as much as they dislike overt aggressiveness. However, they can be quite direct and have few cultural inhibitions about saying "no."

DECISION MAKING

Authority remains rather narrowly concentrated and actual decisions are almost always made at a high level. You should approach senior people, but expect that Venezuelans will want to know your standing within the hierarchy and will generally wish to match you with someone of similar rank, despite the fact that only their senior people will actually be able to approve agreements. Cultivate these peer relationships, because the quality of these relationships may strongly influence the actual decision maker even when your immediate counterpart is not the one making the decision.

WOMEN

Although women generally occupy a secondary status in male-dominated Venezuela, many operate businesses and may be accorded considerable freedom. Venezuelan women are becoming more common and more accepted in business in general, although their presence remains rare in the upper levels of business hierarchies. In general, foreign businesswomen should experience few problems. Nevertheless, foreign businesswomen are expected to be highly professional, appropriate, and neither aggressive nor confrontational. Although women may generally go on the streets and dine alone, many will feel more comfortable if escorted, and all should take a taxi if venturing out after dark.

MEETINGS

Introductions and contacts are imperative. If you do not have a mutual business acquaintance to introduce you, consult with your embassy for a referral. Appointments should be made at least two weeks in advance and reconfirmed the day before. Venezuelans may or may not be punctual, but they expect you to be. Because of their international experience, Venezuelans have become accustomed to dealing directly with business issues; however, because business relationships are founded on personal relationships, several meetings and perhaps more than one trip may be required to conclude an agreement. Business entertaining is fairly common, with the business lunch being an institution, but one that is usually initiated by the Venezuelan party. Business is seldom discussed directly at business dinners, which are more social in tone. Invitations to a home are rare, and much entertaining is done at restaurants, hotels, or clubs. Spouses are seldom included; remember that even polite attention to someone else's spouse can be misinterpreted.

BUSINESS ATTIRE

Foreign businessmen are expected to wear rather formal, conservatively fashionable, dark, lightweight suits. Foreign businesswomen should wear elegant suits or dresses, with stockings (although Venezuelan women generally do not) and heels. Formal wear is seldom needed (in case it is, a tuxedo is necessary; and cocktail dresses are worn for both formal and less-formal occasions). A suit and tie or a dress is appropriate for social occasions, such as an invitation to dinner. For less formal social occasions, conservative resort-type wear is suitable; jeans are worn, but often with jackets, which are ubiquitous. Neither men nor women should wear shorts, and women should avoid anything revealing. Flashy accessories or jewelry and excessive makeup should be avoided, but Venezuelans are fashion conscious and tend to judge people by their dress, and particularly by the quality of their accessories.

Business Centers
Caracas

CITY VIEW

Caracas is one of the most "Americanized" Latin American cities. Shopping malls and fast food outlets have appeared everywhere in great contrast to the colonial Caracas of old. Slums and shantytowns also exist in this city of four to five million. Theft, muggings, and hotel break ins occur with frequency. Visitors should avoid quiet streets and avoid navigating the city alone after nightfall. Expensive clothing and jewelry should be left in the hotel safe.

AIRPORT

Simon Bolívar Airport to City Center

The airport lies 14 miles (22 km.) from the city center. There is a 24-hour coach service to the city. The airport bus takes about an hour to get into town and leaves hourly from the airport at a cost of B2000. Taxis are also available for an approximate price of B3500. Pay up front at the taxi booth in the arrivals hall for a pleasant relief from haggling. Expect up to an hour of travel time.

Airport Information .... (2) 282-100

Airline Numbers

Aer Lingus	(2) 718-487
Aeropostal	(2) 576-4511
Avensa	(2) 561-3366
Aerotuy	(2) 571-6231
Aerolineas Argentinas	(2) 781-8044
Air Aruba	(2) 725-042
Air France	(2) 283-5855
Alitalia	(2) 285-2822
ALM	(2) 310-864
American	(2) 209-8111
Avianca	(2) 263-1322
British Airways	(2) 261-8006
BWIA	(2) 718-945
KLM	(2) 285-3333
Laser	(2) 263-4227, 263-4047
LIAT	(2) 327-542
Lufthansa	(2) 951-0044
United	(2) 283-2022
Varig	(2) 238-2111
Viasa	(2) 576-2611
Zuliana	(2) 993-8507

HOTELS

Top-end

Caracas Hilton International; tel: (2) 503-5000 or (800) 221-2424 in the U.S.; fax: (2) 503-5003; http://www.hilton.com/; near city centre & metro station; 3 restaurants; conference facilities (up to 2000); computer facilities; 120V electric sockets (adapters/transformers available); in-room safe; airline desk; car rental desk; secured parking; fitness; sauna; pool; tennis.

Eurobuilding; Final Calle La Guairita, Chuao; tel: (2) 959-1133; fax: (2) 907-2013; near to city centre; 3 restaurants; conference facilities (up to 2500); secretarial services; fax/photocopy facilities; in-room safe; parking; corporate rates; fitness; sauna; pool.

Sheraton Macuto Resort; Caraballeda, La Guaira; tel: (2) 944-300; fax: (2) 944-318; near beach; 3 restaurants; conference facilities (up to 2120); secretarial services; fax/photocopy facilities; parking; corporate rates; fitness; sauna; pool.

Tamanaco Inter-Continental Caracas; Avenida Principal de las Mercedes; P.O Box 467; tel: (2) 909-7111; fax: (2) 909-7116; email: caracas@interconti.com; http://www.interconti.com/; 3 restaurants; conference facilities (up to 1200); business lounge; travel desk; airline desk; car rental desk; parking; health club; fitness; sauna; pool; tennis courts; jog path; massage.

Melia Caracas, Avenida Casanova, Bellomonte; tel: (2) 762-9314; fax: (2) 762-1733; near city center.

Melia Caribe; Urbanizacion Caribe-Caraballenda; tel: (2) 945-555; fax: (2) 941-509; located in suburb, near beach.

Expensive

Aventura Caracas; Avenida Sorocaima, San Bernadin;o; tel: (2) 514-011; fax: (2) 519-186; near city centre; restaurant; conference facilities (up to 300); secretarial services; fax/photocopy facilities; 110/120V electric sockets; in-room safe; parking; corporate rates; fitness; sauna; pool.

Ejecutivo Denu Montalban; 1-2 2DA. Avenida Montalban; tel: (2) 442-0336; fax: (2) 442-4096; near city center; restaurant; conference facilities (up to 45); secretarial services; fax/photocopy facilities; parking; corporate rates.

El Marques; Avenida El Saman; tel: (2) 242-0011; fax: (2) 242-0047; located in suburb; restaurant; conference facilities (up to100); secretarial services; fax/photocopy facilities; in-room safe; parking; corporate rates.

Residencias Anauco Hilton; tel: (2) 573-4111; in U.S. (800) 221-2424; fax: (2) 573-7724; http://www.hilton.com/; near city centre & metro station; 2 restaurants; conference facilities (up to 120); 120V electric sockets (adapters/transformers available); in-room modem/fax connection; parking; fitness; pool.

Savoy; 2DA Transversal, Las Delicias; tel: (2) 762-1971; fax: (2) 762-2792; restaurant; parking; sauna; pool.

Moderate

Best Western CCT; Chuao; tel: (2) 959-0611; fax: (2) 959-6697.

El Condor; 3 Avenida Las Delicias; tel: (2) 762-9911; fax: (2) 762-8621; near; to city centre; restaurant; conference facilities (up to 150); parking.

La Floresta; Altamira; tel:(2) 263-1955; fax: (2)262-1243; near to city centre; restaurant; conference facilities (up to 15); parking; corporate rates.

Las Quince Letras; Avenida La Playa; Machuto; tel: (2) 461-430; fax: (2) 461-432; restaurant; parking.

Luna; Calle El Colegio; tel: (2) 762-5851; fax: (2) 762-5850; near to city centre; restaurant; conference facilities; parking.

Plaza Palace; Las Delicias De Sabana Grande, Avenida Los Mando; tel: (2) 762-4821; fax: (2) 762-6375; near to city centre & airport; restaurant; conference facilities; secretarial services; fax/photocopy facilities.

Plaza Venezuela; Avenida La Salle Los Cabos; tel: (2) 781-7344; fax: (2) 781-9542; restaurant; conference facilities; parking.

MEDICAL CARE

Clinica Caurimare; Avenida Caurimare, Bello Monte; tel: 752-3033.

Policlinica Las Mercedes; Avenida Principal de Las Mercedes; tel: 752-1177.

Policlinica Santiago de Leon; Avenida Libertador; tel: 71-91-51.

AUTO RENTAL

Avis; Final Avenida Libertador, Bello Campo; tel: 261-4532.

Budget Quinta Los Irunes; No. 50, Avenida Luis Roche between Transversales 5 and 6, Altamira; tel: 284-0023.

WORLD TRADE CENTER

World Trade Center Caracas
Torre Seguros Alianza, Piso 5, Oficina 5-B
Calle Guaicaipuro entre Av. Pichincha y Av. Principal de las Mercedes, El Rosal
Caracas, Venezuela 1060-A
tel: (2) 952-2225; fax: (2) 952-0077
email: wtcpatri@telcel.net.ve

Vietnam

Vietnam

At a Glance

THE PEOPLE

Population .... 77,311,210 (July 1999 est.)
Growth Rate .... 1.37% (1999 est.)
Life Expectancy .... 68.1 years (1999 est.)
Infant Mortality ... 34.84 deaths/1,000 live births (1999 est.)

Ethnic Composition

Vietnamese 90%
Chinese 3%
Muong, Tai, Meo, Khmer, Man, Cham 7%

Religious Composition

Mahayana Buddhist, Taoist, Catholic, Hoa Hao, Cao Dai, Protestant, Animist, Islamic.

Languages Spoken

Vietnamese (official), French, English, Chinese, Khmer, and various tribal languages.

Education and Literacy

Vietnam has a strong emphasis on education and a high rate of secondary graduation. The literacy rate of 93.7% is one of the highest in Asia.

Labor Force

Total: 32,700,000
By occupation: agriculture 65%, industrial 17%, services 18%.

THE ECONOMY

Vietnam began its moves away from communist central planning towards a market economy in the late 1980s with its policies of "*doi moi*" (renovation). Using China as its model, it sought to maintain tight political control while loosening up its markets to foreign investment and entrepreneurship. The results, as in China, are far from stellar. The Hanoi government still keeps a wide swathe of the economy under government control while openly protecting its state-owned industries from foreign competition. A lack of codified commercial law and the absence of an independent court system have kept foreign investors to a minimum. Those that have braved Vietnamese waters have drowned in a sea of profitless red tape. While the government is fighting to reduce the rampant corruption that has further stultified the economy, most analysts see it as too little, too late. The financial crisis that swept through the region in '97-'98 has driven Vietnam down to the bottom of the list of potential investment sites in Asia. Vietnam can expect little progress until its neighbors, many of whom invested heavily in Vietnam, are back on their collective feet.

Exports .... US$9.4 billion
Imports .... US$11.4 billion
Total Trade .... US$20.8 billion
GDP Per Capita................................ US$1,770 (1998 est.)
Unemployment 25%
Inflation Rate 5% (1997) 31

Top Export Partners

Japan, Germany, Singapore, Taiwan, Hong Kong, France, South Korea.

Top Import Partners

Singapore, Japan, South Korea, France, Hong Kong, Taiwan.

Top Exports

Crude oil, rice, rubber, tea, seafood, coffee, clothing, shoes.

Top Imports

Refined petroleum products, machinery, steel products, fertilizer, raw cotton, grain, cement, motorbikes.

BUSINESS WORKWEEK

Offices

Monday to Friday 7a.m. to 5p.m.

Banks

Monday to Friday 8:30a.m. to 3p.m., Saturday 9a.m. to noon.

Government

Monday to Friday 9a.m. to 3p.m., Saturday 9a.m. to noon.

Retail

Monday to Friday 9a.m. to 8p.m., slightly shorter hours on Saturday.

Note: Many offices, including government, take an extended break at midday.

HOLIDAYS

New Year's Day..January 1
Tet, Lunar New Year ....February 5-7
Liberation of Saigon .... April 30
May Day ....May 1
National Day...September 2
Some dates may vary by year.

CLIMATE

Seasons

The weather is basically tropical, but considerably cooler in the mountainous interior highland areas. Rain storms in Vietnam are sudden and torrential. Typhoons are fairly common in coastal areas between July and November. The "dry" monsoon season is from November to April, and the "wet" monsoon (rainy) season is May through to October.

Regions

Winter is dry, dusty period in the Hanoi area. In the north, temperatures range from 16°C (60°F) in the winter to 30°C (85°F) in the summer. In the south, temperatures vary from 27°C (80°F) to 36°C (97°F). Unless travelling to mountain areas, visitors can always expect heat. No one should visit southern Vietnam without bringing rain gear.

Money & Banking

Currency

The currency of Vietnam is the Dong (D). It is pronounced as "dom".

Denominations

Notes are in denominations of D100, 200, 500, 1,000, 2,000, 5,000, 10,000, 20,000 and 50,000. Coins are not used.

Traveler's Checks and Credit Cards

Traveler's checks can be exchanged only at specific banks (VietCom), larger hotels, and international airports kiosks. All will apply a service charge and the exchange

Vietnam

rate will moderate. Only exchange in amounts that can be readily used as there is no reconversion for tourists.

Most major currencies can also be exchanged, but try to take only crisp and new notes. Wrinkled and soiled notes will be refused. U.S. dollars are a second currency in Vietnam and are the most readily exchanged. It can even be used for straight transactions although you will find the Vietnamese like to round off the exchange rate in their favor. U.S. currency is widely counterfeited and will be checked for authenticity. Black market exchange operates quite openly but is given to cheating and the issuing of bogus money.

American Express, Visa, and MasterCard are easily accepted in up-market places in main cities, but in more rural areas they will only take cash. ATM machines are not an option. The most favorable exchange rates are given for credit card transactions.

Travel

VISA AND PASSPORT

Visitors to Vietnam need a valid passport and a visa. It is best that the visa be obtained in advance as the expense increases dramatically at the airport. It can take several weeks to secure a visa. Bring two extra visa photographs if you do not secure the document in advance of arrival.

Business travelers need a specific business visa requiring an invitation from a Vietnamese company or government agency. This must be obtained in advance.

All visitors must register with police within 48 hours, but hotels will complete this process. Visitors who do not register can be fined upon departure. All cash and valuables must be declared at arrival in Vietnam. This customs form must be kept with the passport for identification.

Note: People born in Vietnam but now legal residents of another country (Viet Kieu) will find that their visa will be a separate form from the stamped passport of other visitors. The Vietnamese government is highly suspect of its former citizens and such visitors are often harassed at entry points. This can be lessened by entering as part of a larger, non-Viet Kieu group.

DEPARTURE FORMALITIES

The copy of the customs form issued to you when you arrive in Vietnam must be presented upon departure. You cannot take out more cash than you brought into the country. Keep receipts for exchanged money. Loss of the customs form results in heavy fines. Live animals, unregistered antiquities and Vietnamese currency are considered illegal for export. There is a departure tax when leaving from either the Ho Chi Minh City or Hanoi airport.

CUSTOMS ENTRY (PERSONAL)

Duty-free

Duty-free regulations are subject to frequent amendment; check with the Embassy prior to departure. The following could be freely imported to Vietnam by foreign visitors:

- Tobacco: 200 cigarettes, 50 cigars, or 250g of loose tobacco
- Alcohol: 1 bottle of spirits
- Other: a reasonable quantity of perfume.

All videotapes, some software and most books are considered suspect in Vietnam and will be inspected. Fax machines must be registered with the government.

Prohibited or Restricted
- Controlled drugs
- Anti-government material
- Firearms
- Pornography

Note: Customs is handled by military personnel and they have little compunction about rudely handling what they consider to be "disrespectful" tourists. Keep in mind that no matter how beautiful Vietnam may appear, it is still run by a totalitarian, communist government.

IMMUNIZATION

Inoculations are recommended for tetanus, diphtheria, meningitis, and polio, as well as malaria treatments if travel to rural areas is possible. Drink only bottled water. Hepatitis A immunization is recommended for all visitors.

TIPPING

Visitors must be warned that everything in Vietnam is more expensive for foreigners. The "foreigner price" is openly, almost proudly posted. Consequently, tips from foreigners are expected and are certainly appreciated. Vietnam is very poor and the equivalent of US$1 is a fortune in rural areas. However, overtipping should be avoided. Sometimes a single western cigarette can act as a gratuity.

Note: Begging is still widespread, especially in areas frequented by tourists. One gift can unfortunately lead to the sudden appearance of a crowd demanding alms.

EMERGENCY INFORMATION

Police and Crime

Crime is low in Vietnam, but take basic precautions against petty theft. Leave most of your cash, traveler's checks, jewelry, and non-essential valuables in your hotel safe if possible. Carry photocopies of your passport and customs form instead of the original. Carry cash in a money belt, and use credit cards or traveler's checks for most large transactions.

Foreign business visitors are often the target of thieves; so, purses, laptops and briefcases require additional security. Do not leave valuables in cars or on tables in cafés.

Women are safe to walk around, but always be aware of your surrounding. There are police stations literally on every street but have limited language skills. If you are a victim of a crime do not be surprised if the police request a fee for investigating the incident.

Emergency Numbers

Telephones are not very common in Vietnam, so most emergencies are best reported by sending someone to get help. The following numbers may or may not provide assistance:

Police... 113
Fire 114
Ambulance 115

Health

Typhoid, diphtheria, typhus, cholera, tuberculosis, internal parasites, hepatitis A, hepatitis B and leprosy are present. Urban areas have low sanitation standards as the street is often used for toilet facilities. Be even more careful in rural settings.

Do not to drink tap water or eat uncooked food. Stay away from food sold at roadside stands, and generally stick to milder dishes until you acclimate. Some stomach and digestion problems may occur from spicy food. Heat stroke is common as is diarrhea. Simple caution and adequate medication brought from home will divert the disaster of a business trip cut short.

Medical services are adequate. Doctors are well trained, and many of the staff speak English. Costs are reasonable, but medicines are scarce, so come prepared. Evacuation insurance is part of every foreigner's employment package if they are permanently stationed in Vietnam.

TAXI & RENTAL CARS

Taxis are common in the cities and they are metered. Three-wheeled pedicabs (*cyclo*) are also used for short trips but never for use to business meetings. Be sure to agree on a price before leaving.

Rental cars are available in large cities but are not recommended for any but experienced visitors. Cars with local drivers can be had for reasonable daily and weekly rates.

BUS

Buses are inefficient and often overcrowded. They are best avoided for business travel.

TRAIN

Trains are somewhat expensive (different price for foreigners) but are the most comfortable way besides airlines to travel long-distance within the country. Take note that toilet facilities are bleak. On-board food is getting better but it is still best to bring your own or shop at the railside kiosks at various stops. Baggage should be locked in the storage bin in each first-class cabin. Of the three classes available, first class is the only reasonable way for business people to travel. If you have the time, train travel is a great way to see a beautiful country.

Essential Terms

English	Vietnamese
Yes	Vang
No	Khong
Good morning	Buói sang
Hello (daytime)	Buói chieu
Hello (evening)	Buói toi
Hello (telephone)	Tieng chao
Good-bye	Tam biet
Please	Xin
Thank you	Cam on
Pleased to meet you	Han hanh duoc gap
Excuse me; I'm sorry	Xin loi
My name is _____	Toi ten la _____
I don't understand	Toi khong hieu

Communications

DIALING CODES IN VIETNAM

International country code: [84]
Selected city codes: Hanoi (4), Ho Chi Minh City (8)

Dialing Vietnam from Overseas

To dial Vietnam from overseas, dial your country's international dialing code, then 84 (the country code for Vietnam), then the city code and finally the number. If you were dialing Hanoi from the United States, for example, you would begin with 011, then 84, then 4 (the city code for Hanoi), and finally the number of the person or office you were trying to reach.

Assistance Numbers

Central Information.. 108

CALLING WITHIN VIETNAM

Local Calls

Local calls from private phones, hotels and restaurants are free. The post office, however, implements a small fee for the service.

Long Distance Calls

To make a call within Vietnam, dial 01 + area code + number. The discounted rates occur between 10p.m. and 5a.m.

International Calls

Main cities have International Direct Dial (IDD) available from post offices or hotels. Dial 00 + country code + area code + number. The call might cost around US$5.50 per minute. Rumor has it that post office calling is generally less costly than from a hotel. It certainly depends on what the post office clerk feels like charging. The main post offices in Ho Chi Minh and Hanoi are open 24 hours if you want to test the rumors on a free night.

If you prefer not to deal with the vague structure in Vietnam, try to reach a U.S. operator on the ever-expanding AT&T access network:
AT&T USA Direct 1-201-0288

PAY PHONES

Public Telephones

Public phones can be spotted by their yellow or blue color; all are card phones with instructions posted on the phones.

Calling Cards

The yellow phones in main cities take the US$30 phone cards necessary for an overseas call. You can purchase the cards at post offices.

CELLULAR PHONES

Several cellular service providers exist in Vietnam. Saigon Mobile Telephone Co. offers AMPS for analogue users, and Vietnam Telecom Services Co. offers GSM for digital.

Note: Your home country cell phone may not work in this country. If not, we recommend that you rent an international cell phone *before* you leave home. A major US-based cell phone rental provider is **IMC WorldCell**. For information see "International Cell Phone Rentals" on page 14.

CALL BACK

You can (potentially) save significant sums when calling in Vietnam by using one of the call back services listed below. Fees for call back services vary widely, depending on the company and the type of service required. For a list of callback services, please refer to the "Communications" section in the *Global Road Warrior* Introduction.

PHONE JACK

Plug adaptors are available through **iGo Corporation.** (See "Electrical and Telephone Adaptors" on page 19.)

Vietnam

Vietnam

FAX

Most hotels have fax machines.

POSTAL SERVICES

Postal services are extremely slow. Airmail to Europe and North America can take up to a month. Incoming mail can take much longer.

TELEGRAMS

Telegrams are still a popular mode of sending messages in Vietnam. Facilities are available in most major towns.

Business Services

BUSINESS CENTER

Asean International Hotel; 8 Chua Boc Street, Dong Da District; tel: 852-9108, fax: 852-9111.

Hanoi Daewoo Hotel; 360 Kim Ma Street; tel: 831-5000; fax: 831-5010..

Hilton Hanoi Opera Hotel; 1 le Thanh Tong Street, Hoan Kiem; tel: (4) 933-0500; fax: (4) 933-0530.

Hanoi Horison (Swiss-Belhotel); 40 Cat Linh Street; tel: 733-0808; fax: 733-0688.

Sofitel Metropole Hanoi, 15 Ngo Quyen Street; tel: 826-6919; fax: 826-6920.

COURIER SERVICE

Hanoi

DHL; Hanoi; 1 Le Thach St.; Hoan Kiem District; Hanoi; Monday to Saturday 7:30a.m. to 5:30p.m., closed Sunday and holidays.

Federal Express (Hanoi Post and Telecom); tel: (4) 824-9054; fax: (4) 825-2479.

TNT Express Worldwide; NT Vietrans 15 Ly Nam De Street, Hanoi; tel: (8) 434-535; tel: (8) 434-536; fax: (8) 434-550.

Ho Chi Minh

DHL International Ltd.; 4 Huynh Huu Bac St.; Ho Chi Minh City; tel: (8) 844-6203; Monday to Saturday 6:30a.m. to 9:30p.m., Sunday 8a.m. to 4p.m., closed holidays.

Federal Express (Ho Chi Minh Post); tel: (8) 848- 5888; fax: (8) 848-5744.

TNT Express Worldwide; NT Vietrans; 54 Truong Son Street, Tan Binh District, Ho Chi Minh City; tel: (8) 446-460; tel: (8) 446-478; tel: (8) 446-476; fax: (8) 448-909.

Electrical

Current

110/220 volts AC, 50Hz.

ELECTRIC PLUGS

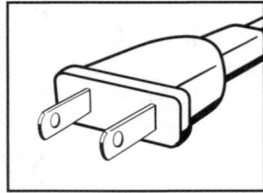

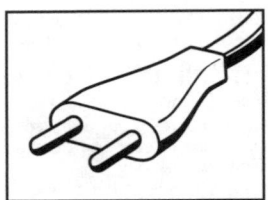

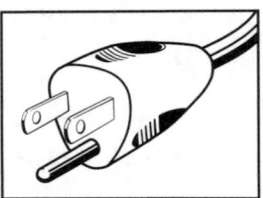

Plug adaptors are available through **iGo Corporation**. (See "Electrical and Telephone Adaptors" on page 19.)

Technical Support

HARDWARE/SOFTWARE VENDOR SUPPORT

Dell; tel: (3) 201-8481; fax: (3) 201-8482; (Dell- Europe) tel: [44] (134) 474-8000; (in the U.S.) tel: [1] (512) 338-4400; fax: [1] (512) 728-3330; http://www.dell.com/.

IBM; (in Singapore) tel: [65] 320-1000; fax: [65] 224-5260; (in Switzerland) tel: [41] (22) 310-0418 (in French); (in the U.S.) tel: [1] (919) 517-2800; http://www.ibm.com/.

Microsoft; (in Thailand) tel: (2) 613-7208/9/10/11; fax: (2) 613-7198; (in Switzerland) tel: [41] (848) 858-868; fax [41] (1) 831-0869; (in the U.S.) [1] (425) 635-7222; http://www.microsoft.com/.

Internet Connection

HOW TO CONNECT

Connecting to AOL and Compuserve in Vietnam is similar to using it when traveling outside your own area code. See the introductory section for detailed information on connecting to your account through a different phone number. The government controls the internet; as such, all connections will be routed through Hanoi and Ho Chi Minh.

America Online

Numbers are available at keyword *international*. Be sure to get several local numbers before leaving. Go to keyword *access* (a free area) and download the software.

At the time of publication there were no access numbers in Vietnam. Check their list of current access numbers at http://intlaccess.web.aol.com/ to see if any numbers have been activated or to locate numbers in neighboring countries.

Compuserve

Numbers are available at *Go International.* If you are using CompuServe 2000, use GO PHONES within CompuServe 2000 to search for access numbers. The Compuserve Web-site also has a great deal of information for travelers at http://www.compuserve.com/.

At press time, Compuserve had no local access numbers. Check their list of current access numbers to see if any numbers have been activated or to locate numbers in neighboring countries.

Independent Service Providers

Many independent service providers offer discounts if you are only in town for a couple of days.

VASC-VDC; tel: (4) 821-7845; tel: 978-0635; fax: (4) 978-0636; P_master@vasc1.vnn.vn; http://www.vnn.vn/.

Business Culture

GREETINGS AND COURTESIES

The accepted greeting is shaking hands (both when saying hello and good-bye).Vietnamese often shake with both hands to show respect for a person. They also bow the head slightly as they shake hands to show respect. If an elderly person does not extend their hand first, the proper greeting is a slight bow. In general, women tend to bow their head rather than shake hands. When meeting a woman, shake hands only if she initiates the gesture. Otherwise smile and nod slightly.

BUSINESS ETHIC AND FRAMEWORK

Vietnamese are hard-working and efficient, but are still recovering from decades of war, coping with the reunification of a nation that is in many ways still two separate countries, and living in a communist economy that is slowly (and often chaotically) introducing free enterprise. Generally speaking, the will to do business is certainly present but the experience and wherewithal may be lacking. Efficient business laws are not yet in place, guidelines and regulations change constantly, and standardized international accounting practices have yet to be instituted. In some instances, agreements have been dissolved after foreign companies believed they had been negotiated and agreed to in good faith; the Vietnamese have no problems with changing agreements at will. Such incidents are caused by inexperience and the turmoil that comes with a society and culture in flux, rather than from any malicious intent. But these problems do exist and anyone engaging in business in Vietnam should be prepared for them.

DECISION MAKING

Politeness and modesty are key elements of Vietnamese behavior. Vietnamese try to avoid direct confrontation and will often talk around a sensitive subject, relying on the other person to understand what they are really saying. Though they are punctual for meetings, Vietnamese also seem to be in no hurry when it comes to decisions or accomplishing things. In addition, the people you meet might not have the authority to make decisions. When negotiating, determine that the person you are dealing with actually has decision-making authority. Also, it is important to speak with everyone who has any power over your efforts, including the appropriate local party and government officials.

WOMEN

Women are prominent in business and government, and foreign women can expect to be treated with respect and taken seriously. The north is more conservative and traditional than the south and women doing business there should make an extra effort to be professional and dress conservatively. Be prepared to deal with women in all capacities and at all levels. Treat them professionally, as business associates rather than as women.

MEETINGS

Be on time—punctuality by visitors is important to the Vietnamese, even so they may arrive late. Meetings are a combination of socializing and formal interaction. First meetings might begin with casual talk over coffee or tea, in a generally informal atmosphere. However, business is not treated lightly and Vietnamese do not welcome jokes or an inappropriately casual attitude. A smile might be a sign of amusement or happiness, but it may also mean embarrassment, frustration, anxiety, or anger. If you are meeting with more than one person, determine who the senior person is, approach them immediately, and give them your card (introducing yourself through an underling is considered insulting). You will probably need an interpreter. Choose one carefully, and be sure they are familiar with the nuances of both Vietnamese and your language. Your Vietnamese associates will probably have their own interpreter, but relying on this person might mean taking a risk, as some interpreters exaggerate their expertise.

BUSINESS ATTIRE

Business dress is casual, but conservative. Suits are worn during the winter, spring and autumn, but during summer both businesspeople and government personnel opt for simply a shirt and tie. The north is more conservative, and women should avoid low necklines or hemlines that rise above the knee. Modest gold jewelry and a quality watch will count in your favor. However, avoid overly expensive jewelry or showy ornaments. In the north, temperatures and weather vary with the seasons; the south is generally hot and humid all year long. April and May are the hottest months, and are also the times when the humidity is highest.

Business Centers
Hanoi

CITY VIEW

Hanoi is smaller than Ho Chi Minh City, and far quieter and serene. This is changing, however, as capitalism continues to move into the country.

AIRPORT

Thu Do International Airport to City Center

The airport is technically at Noi Bai, 28 miles (45 km.) from Hanoi. There are buses and regular taxi services. Expect to pay about US$20 for a taxi. One may also arrange an airport transfer through many hotels, for an approximate price of between US$20 and $30.

Airline Numbers

Aeroflot	(4) 825-6184
Air France	(4) 825-3484
China Southern Airlines	(4) 826-9233, 826-9234
CSA	(4) 845-6512
Pacific Airlines	(4) 826-5350
Vietnam Airlines	(4) 8255284, 8253842, 825-5229

HOTELS

Top-end

Hanoi Daewoo (Leading Hotels of the World); 360 Kim Ma Street; tel: 831-5000; fax: 831-5010; email:

Vietnam

hotel@daewoohn.com.vn; city center, part of Daeha Business Centre Complex; 6 restaurants; conference facilities (up to 800); business center; secretarial service; in-room hairdryer, coffeemaker, safe, work desk, shaver outlet, satellite TV; health club; pool.

Hilton Hanoi Opera; 1 le Thanh Tong Street, Hoan Kiem; tel: (4) 933-0500; fax: (4) 933-0530; near the Hoan Kiem Lake, in business district; 5 restaurants; conference facilities (up to 600); business center; IDD telephone; in-room hairdryer, coffemaker, voicemail, dataport, electronic locks, safe, work desk, non-smoking, internet access; car rental; florist; gift shop; newsstand; secure parking/valet; health cub; fitness; sauna; pool; whirlpool; massage.

Hanoi Horison (Swiss-Belhotel); 40 Cat Linh Street; tel: 733-0808; fax: 733-0688; reservation fax: 733-0888; http://www.prasidha.co.id/hanoi_hor.html; near to exhibition centre, restaurant; complimentary breakfast; conference facilities (up to 500); business center; internet service, IDD telephone; in-room safe, minibar, coffeemaker; 24-hour room service; Horison Club Lounge; shuttle and limousine service; shopping arcade; on-call doctor; parking; health club; pool; tennis.

Expensive

Hanoi Hotel; D8 Giang Vo Street, Ba Dinh District; tel: 845-2270; fax: 845-9209; email: kshanoi@bdvn.vnmail.vnd.net; near city centre & exhibition hall; Chinese restaurant, coffee shop; bar; conference facilities (up to 300), business center; in-room IDD telephone, satellite tv, radio, safe, minibar, a/c; room service; laundry; doctor; foreign exchange; tour desk; limousine; shopping arcade; parking; fitness; sauna, massage, tennis; nigthclub; karaoke, billiard room.

Meritus Westlake Hotel; 1 Thanh Nien Road; tel: 823-8888; fax: 829-3888; 322 rooms; 8 minutes from city center; restaurants; coffee shop; bar; conference facilities, business center; internet service, in-room IDD telephone, a/c, satellite tv and movies, minibar, coffee maker, desk, hair dryer, safe; executive floors with butler service; room service; laundry; foreign exchange; doctor; sauna; indoor/outdoor pool; whirlpool; squash; disco/nightclub.

NIKKO Hotel; 84 Tran Nhan Tong; tel: 822-3535; fax: 844-8223555; city center; restaurants; coffee shop; bar; conference facilities (up to 200); business center; internet service, in-room IDD telephone, modem connection, work desk, safe, satellite tv, fitness machine, a/c, coffee maker, hairdryer, minibar; room service; rooms for disabled; laundry; foreign exchange; tour desk; parking; fitness; sauna; massage; pool; whirlpool; aerobics.

Moderate

Army Guesthouse; 33 Pham Ngu Lao Street, Hai Ba Trung District; tel: 826-5541; conference facilities.

Asean International Hotel; 8 Chua Boc Street, Dong Da District; tel: 852-9108, fax: 852-9111; email: asean@hn.vnn.vn; French colonial house; 66 rooms; city center; restaurants, bar; coffee shop; conference facilities (up to 400), business center; in-room IDD telephone, a/c, cable television, movies, minibar, safe; non-smoking rooms; 24-hour room service; laundry; doctor; courier service, foreign exchange; car rental, parking; fitness, sauna, massage.

Green Park Hotel; 48 Tran Nhan Tong Street; 40 rooms; city center; restaurant; coffee shop; conference facilities; business center; in-room satellite tv, safe, minibar, hairdryer, a/c; sound-proof windows; non-smoking rooms; laundry; foreign exchange; doctor.

HOA BINH Hotel; 27 Ly Thuong Kiet, Hoan Kiem District; tel: 825-4655; fax: 826-9818; conference facilities.

My Lan Hotel; 340 Ba Trieu; tel: 976-1069; conference facilities, in-room safe.

Quoc Hoa; 10 Bat Dan Street; tel: 232-528; fax: 267-424; near to city centre, restaurant, conference facilities (up to 40), secretarial services, fax/photocopy facilities, corporate rates.

Saigon Hotel; 80 Ly Thuong Kiet Street; tel: 826-8499; fax: 826-6631; email: saigonhotel@fpt.vn; restaurant, conference facilities (2 meeting rooms), business center, secretarial services, fax/photocopy facilities, in-room safe, on-call medical staff, currency exchange, sauna, massage.

Thang Loi; Yen Phu Street; tel: 826-8211; fax: 825-2800; near to city centre & lake, restaurant, conference facilities (up to 250), in-room modem.fax connection, in-room safe, parking, corporate rates, sauna, pool.

Ho Chi Minh City

CITY VIEW

Ho Chi Minh City, formerly known as Saigon, is the home of 3.5 million, and seems to have no order. Constant throngs of people and goods ply the streets. Streets jut out from nowhere and head into small alleyways. Stick to the main streets whenever possible; and remember that you are walking at your own risk when crossing the streets.

AIRPORT

Tan Son Nhat International Airport to City Center

The airport lies 4.5 miles (7 km.) from the city center. A throng of taxi touts await your arrival. All taxis are metered in Vietnamese and U.S. dollars. Be sure to take down the registration number of the taxi that your taking for security reasons. The taxi situation is improving, but scams are not uncommon.

Airline Numbers

Aeroflot	(8) 829-3489
Air France	(8) 829-0982
Cathay Pacific	(8) 822-3272
China Southern Airlines	(8) 829-1172
Garuda Indonesia	(8) 844-2696
Lufthansa	(8) 844-0101
Malaysian Airline System	(8) 823-0695
Pacific Airlines	(8) 822-2614
Philippine Airlines	(8) 829-2113
Singapore Airlines	(8) 823-1583
Thai Airways International	(8) 844-6235
Vietnam Airlines	
Domestic	(8) 829-9980
International	(8) 829-2118

HOTELS

Hotel Equatorial; 242 Tran Binh Trong St., District 5; tel: (084) 839-0000; fax: (084) 839-0011; 3 restaurants; coffee shop; bar; convention facilities (up to 800); business center; in-room IDD telephone, magnetic key card access, safe, satellite tv, minibar, a/c; room service; laundry; barber/beauty salon; gift shop; foreign exchange; limousine service; airport shuttle; Equinox fintess and health center; massage; pool; nightclub.

New World Hotel Saigon (Marriott); 76 Le Lai Street, District 1; tel: (8) 822-8888; fax: (8) 823-0710; email: info@nwhs.teltic.com.vn; located in business district; conference facilities (up to 500); business center; currency exchange; in-room IDD telephone, satellite TV, safe, minibar, hair dryer, work desk; 24-hour room service; same-day laundry, valet; florist; shops; Executive floors with data ports, personal concierge, complimentary breakfast, boardrooms; chauferred limousine; airport shuttle service; covered parking; fitness; sauna; massage; pool; tennis; golf driving range, putting green.

Omni Saigon; 251 Nguyen Van Troi Street, Phu Nhuan District; tel: (8) 844-9222; fax: (8) 844-9200;251 Nguyen Van Troi Street, Phu Nhuan District, tel: (8) 844-9222; fax: (8) 844-9200; email: omnires@hcm.fpt.vn; meeting facilities; business center, translation, secretairal service; internet; IDD telephones, mini-bar, refrigerator, coffee/tea maker, satellite tv, safe; non-smoking rooms available; Continental Club floor, with boardroom, fax machines; shuttle to city center; beauty salon; florist; gift shop; newsstand; parking; health club, gym, steam room, pool.

Saigon Floating Hotel; 1 A Me Linh Square, District 1; tel: (8) 829-0783; fax: (8) 829-0784; near city center; restaurant; conference facilities (up to 200); secretarial services; fax/photocopy facilities; in-room safe; parking; corporate rates; fitness; sauna; pool.

Expensive

Delta Caravelle; 19/23 Lam Son Square, 1st District, tel: (8) 829-3704, 823-4999; fax: (8) 829-9902; 335 rooms; near city center; 2 restaurants (including Hard Rock Cafe); coffee shop; conference facilities (up to 140); business center; internet services; fax facilities; in-room IDD telephone, secuirty card door locks, hair dryer, satellite tv, coffe maker, voice mail system, fax machines and computer port on request, minibar, safe; non-smoking rooms; room service; laundry; hairdresser; foreign exchange; doctor; limousine; parking; health club; sauna; steam room; dry sauna; pool; massage; jacuzzi.

Cuu Long (Majestic); 1 Dong Khoi St., Dist. 1; tel: (8) 829-5517: fax: (8) 829-5510; reservations: (8) 822-8750; email: majestic.s.hotel@bdvn.vnd.net; http://www.tlnet.vn.com/ majestic center, overlooking Saigon River; restaurants; meeting facilities; business center; office rental; currency exchange; in-room safe, IDD telephone, minibar, hairdryer, satellite TV; same-day laundry service; florist; gift shop; fitness; massage; sauna; pool.

Rex; 141 Nguyen Hue Blvd. - Dist. 1; tel: (8) 829 2185 , 829-3115; fax: (8) 829-6536; email: REXHOTEL@sgtourist.com.vn; http:// www.vietnamtourism.com/rex; located in commercial center; restaurants; breakfast included; rooftop garden; conference facilities (up to 350); meeting rooms (up to 100); business center; internet facilities; 24-hour rooms service; in-room safe, fax mcahine, hair dryer, mini-bar, satellite TV; car rental; postal service; newsstand; shopping arccade; laundry; beauty salon; health club; fitness; sauna; massage; pool; tennis.

Saigon Prince Hotel; 63 Nguyen Hue Boulevard District 1; tel: (8) 822-2999; fax: (8) 824-1888; email: saigon-princehtl@hcm.vnn.vn; city center, overlooking Saigon River; restaurants; meeting facilities; business center; IDD telephones, mini-bar; currency exchage; laundry service; translation service; 24-hour security; Visa service; limousines available; fitness; massage; steam and dry sauna; indoor pool.

Windsor Saigon Hotel; 193 Tran Hung Dao; tel: (8) 836-7848; fax: (8) 836-7889; boutique hotel near city center; restaurant; coffee shop; bar; conference facilities (up to 200); business center; airport pick-up service; in-room IDD telephone, minibar, electronic safe, hairdryer, coffee maker, a/c, satellite tv; non-smoking rooms; room service; laundry; foreign exchange; parking; fitness.

Moderate

Airport; 108-Hong Ha-Ward 2; tel: (8) 844-5761; fax: (8) 844-0166; near to airport & exhibition grounds; restaurant; in-room safe; parking; corporate rates; sauna.

Bong Sen; 117-119-121-123 Dong Khoi Street, 1st

District; tel: (8) 829-1516; fax: (8) 829-9744; 135 rooms; near airport & city center; 3 restaurants; coffee shop; banquet facilities; busines center; secretarial service; internet service; in-room IDD telephone, a/c, refrigerator, satellite tv, minbar, safe; non-smoking rooms; room service; laundry; tour desk; fitness; sauna; whirlpool; (request room with windows).

Century Saigon; 68A Nguyen Hue Boulevard, 1st District; tel: (8) 823-1818, 829-2959; fax: (8) 829-2732; near city center; restaurant; conference facilities (up to 50); secretarial services; fax/photocopy facilities; internet services; in-room safe; corporate rates; fitness; sauna; pool; massage; karaoke.

The First; 201/3 Hoang Viet Tan Binh; tel: (8) 844-1175; fax: (8) 844-4282; near to airport; restaurant; conference facilities (up to 150); secretarial services; fax/photocopy facilities; parking; corporate rates; sauna; pool.

Lisa Hotel; 353 AnDuongVuong St, District 5; tel:(8) 835-1908; fax:(8) 835-1850; http://www.lisasaigon.com; email: lisa@lisasaigon.com; restaurant; meeting room (up to 100) with city view; internet; laundry service/valet; currency exchange; short/long-term rent; in-room IDD telephone, satellite TV, mini-bar, soundproof windows; fitness; sauna; massage; steambath; jacuzzis.

The Orchid; 29A, Don Dat Street, District 1; tel: (8) 823-1809; fax: (8) 829-2245; near city center; restaurant; conference facilities (up to 12); parking; corporate rates.

Palace Hotel; 56 - 66 Nguyen Hue Blvd; tel: (8) 829-2860, 829-2840; fax: (8) 824-4230, 8244229; email: palace@hcm.vnn.vn; city center; restaurant; in-room IDD telephones, minibar, satellite TV, balcony; daily newspaper; conference room; business center; office rental; laundry, dry cleaning; car rental; massage; steambath; pool; dancing; karaoke.

Pastel Inn Saigon Hotel; 99 Pasteur, 1st District; tel: (8) 822-8222; fax: (8) 822-8242; near city center; restaurant; conference facilities (up to 36); in-room safe; fitness; karaoke.

The Saigon Star; 204 Nguyen Thi Minh Khai Street, 3rd District; tel: (8) 823-0260; fax: (8) 823-0255; near airport, exhibition center & city center; 2 restaurants; conference facilities (up to 100); business center; secretarial services; fax/photocopy facilities; in-room safe; parking; corporate rates; fitness; karaoke.

The Spring Hotel; 44-46 Le Thanh Ton Street, District 1; tel: (8) 829-7362; fax: (8) 822-1383; boutique hotel; near National Theater, city center; rooftop restaurant; meeting room; business center.

AUTO RENTAL

Avis; airport, tel: (8) 829-000; fax: (8) 829-6583 (chauffeur-drive service only).; 42 Dong Du St., District 1, tel: (8) 829-0000; fax: (8) 296-583 (chauffeur drive service only).

WORLD TRADE CENTER

World Trade Center Ho Chi Minh City
6 Hai B Trung Street
Ho Chi Minh City, S.R. Vietnam
tel: (8) 829 63 41; fax: (8) 829 68 56

CHAMBER OF COMMERCE

Foreign Trade and Development Center (FTDC)
Address: 92-96 Nguyen Hue Blvd.,Dist.1, HCMC
tel: (848) 829-0912, (848) 829-090
fax: (848) 822-2983
Telex: 805 811242 EDCE VT
Helps and promotes Vietnam trade

Zimbabwe

At a Glance

THE PEOPLE
Population ....11,163,160 (July 1999 est.)
Growth Rate ....1.02% (1999 est.)
Life Expectancy .... 38.86 years (1999 est.)
Infant Mortality...61.21 deaths/1,000 live births (1999 est.)

Ethnic Composition
Shona...71%
Ndebele 16%
Other tribes..11%
White 1%
Asian and mixed race... 1%

Religious Composition
Syncretic (Animist /Christian) 50%
Christian 25%
Indigenous religions 24%
Muslim and other... 1%

Languages Spoken
English (official), Shona and Sindebele.

Education and Literacy
Adult literacy rate is 85% for those over the age of fifteen. All citizens are educated under the same governmentally regulated system.

Labor Force
Total 5,000,000
By occupation: agriculture 27%, services 46%, industry 27%.

THE ECONOMY
Zimbabwe, formerly Rhodesia, has been shed of its colonial rulers for almost twenty years but has made little progress towards remedying the poverty which plagues the native population. The massive funding once pumped in by the IMF was cut off in 1995 due to governmental mishandling. Meanwhile, private foreign investment has been rebuffed by the corruption and over regulation of domestic business. As a result, the nation has seen its infrastructure crumble and its rich mineral wealth remain unexploited. Once a supplier of labor to South Africa, landlocked Zimbabwe is still unfortunately reliant on its fiscally troubled southern neighbor for both exports and imports. As money begins to trickle back in from the World Bank, government officials have pledged to take a more welcoming approach to foreign investors and budget reform. With an average life expectancy of its citizens under 40 years, this ruling generation may not live to see success.
Exports ....US$1.7 billion (f.o.b, 1998 est.)
Imports ....US$2 billion (f.o.b, 1998 est.)
Total Trade ....US$3.7 billion (f.o.b, 1998 est.)
GDP Per Capita.. US$2,400
Unemployment 45%
Inflation Rate .... 32 percent

Top Export Partners
South Africa, E.U., Japan, U.S.

Top Import Partners
South Africa, U.K., United States, Japan.

Top Exports
Tobacco, gold, ferroalloys, cotton.

Top Imports
Machinery, manufactured goods, chemicals, fuels.

BUSINESS WORKWEEK

Offices
Monday to Friday 8a.m. to 4:30p.m.

Banks
Monday, Tuesday, Thursday, Friday 8:30a.m. to 2p.m., Wednesday 8:30a.m. to noon, Saturday 8:30a.m. to 11a.m.

Government
Monday to Friday 7:45a.m. to 4:45p.m.

Retail
Monday to Friday 8a.m. to 5p.m., Saturday 8a.m. to noon.

HOLIDAYS
New Year's Day...January 1
Easter...April 21-24*
Independence Day .... April 18
Workers' Day...May 1
Africa Day...May 25
Heroes' Day.. August 11
Defence Forces Day..August 12
Christmas ....December 25-26
*Date may vary by year.

CLIMATE

Seasons
Because of its relatively high altitude, Zimbabwe has a mild and pleasant climate by African standards. September to April are the summer season, October and November are the hottest months, then follows the rainy season. From December through to March rainfall is heavy, and no rain falls from April to August, winter months. Days are sunny, nights are cool, both winter and summers are pleasant.

Regions
The average temperature on the plateau region is 22°C (72°F). The Zambezi valley experiences 30°C (85°F) heat in the summer and winters ranging from 13°C (55°F) to 20°C (68°F).

Money & Banking

Currency
The currency of Zimbabwe is the Zimbabwe Dollar (Z$).

Denominations
The Zimbabwe Dollar (Z$) comes in coin denominations of Z$1, and 50, 20, 10, 5 and 1 cents; and banknotes of Z$2, 5, 10, 20, 50 and 100.

Traveler's Checks and Credit Cards
Traveler's checks (denominations of U.S. dollars and British Sterling only) may be exchanged at the Harare airport but not more than the equivalent of US$100. Hotels will cash checks for a commission. Banks will exchange all major currencies but suspicion of counterfeiting causes them to turn away old format US$100 bills. Readers are suggested to avoid contact with black market activity for currency exchange.

Zimbabwe

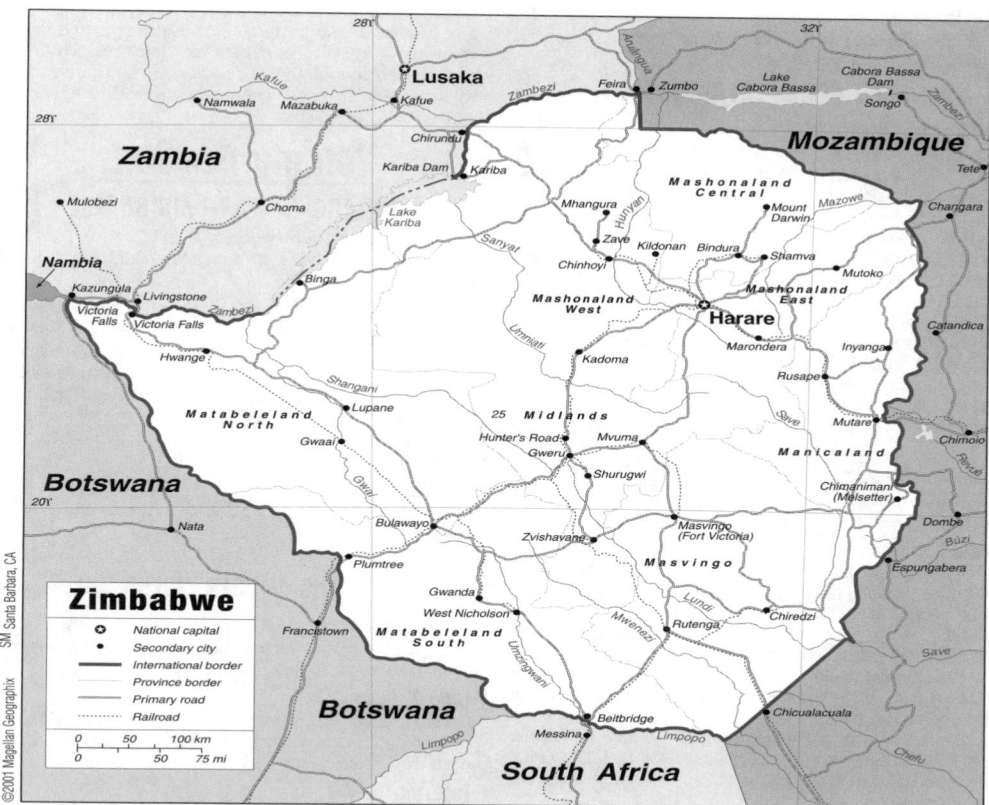

Amex, Visa, Mastercard and Diner's Club are accepted at larger venues. Barclays Bank has ATM facilities in major cities. The best exchange rate is given for credit card and ATM transactions.

Travel

VISA AND PASSPORT

All visitors must have valid passports but visas are not required of those citizen of the British Commonwealth, Japan, EU, United States, Norway or Switzerland. South Africans can receive a visa at the border. All others must secure them in advance from a consulate or embassy. Visas can take at least several weeks to receive. A return ticket must be in the possession of visitors otherwise a US$1,000 deposit must be left with border officials.

DEPARTURE FORMALITIES

An airport departure tax of US$20 will be collected. It must be paid in foreign currency.

CUSTOMS ENTRY (PERSONAL)

Duty-free
- Goods up to a value of Z$2000 inclusive of tobacco, perfume and gifts; Five liters of alcoholic beverages (up to two liters of which may be spirits)

Prohibited or Restricted
- The import of agricultural products including bulbs, cuttings, cycads, eggs, fresh meat, fruit, honey, plants, seeds and vegetables, animals, birds and used beekeeping equipment are prohibited
- Permission for the import of non-prescribed drugs, firearms and replicas, fighting knives, ammunition and explosives, indecent films and publications, and telecommunications equipment must be obtained on arrival.

IMMUNIZATION

Anti-malarial tablets are strongly recommended, particularly if you are traveling to low-lying areas. Drink only bottled water. Foreign travelers from areas infected with yellow fever or cholera must show inoculation certificates to enter the country. Hepatitis A and tetanus immunizations are recommended. Check with health authorities before travel for additional health alerts.

TIPPING

Taxi
Taxi drivers should receive 10 percent of the fare if service is adequate. More if luggage is involved.

Porters
Porters should receive a tip based on the number of bags handled, about Z$0.50 cents per bag.

Hotels
Hotel maids should receive Z$5 when you check out of the hotel.

Restaurants

For restaurants, 10 percent is sufficient if a service charge has not been applied.

EMERGENCY INFORMATION

Police and Crime

Zimbabwe is very poor and crime is increasing. Common crime includes car break-ins, armed robbery and pick-pocketing. Resistance usually results in violence.

Take basic precautions. Avoid flashy displays of wealth, behave conservatively. Leave most of your cash, traveler's checks, jewelry, and non-essential valuables in your hotel safe. Carry photocopies of your passport instead of the original. Carry cash in a money belt, and use credit cards or traveler's checks for most transactions.

Foreign business visitors are often the target of thieves; so, purses, laptops and briefcases require additional security. Do not leave valuables in cars or on tables in cafés. When taking taxis at night, insist that they drop you right at your door, not down the street. Gangs in collusion with drivers will victimize tourists on unlit streets. Hotels will often note the license plate number of taxis servicing their guests.

Emergency Numbers

Emergency, Police, Fire (Harare)99

Health

Avoid tap water in rural areas, and use bottled water even for brushing teeth. Boil water for 20 minutes if bottled water is unavailable. Wash vegetables and fruit in chlorine solution before eating and make sure meat is well cooked, and avoid unpasteurized dairy products.

Malaria exists mainly in the Zambezi valley. Other endemic diseases are AIDS (HIV has currently infected 20 percent of the population), bilharzia, and parasitic diseases.

Zimbabwe can get extremely hot, so take necessary precautions against sun and heat stroke, drink lots of liquids, and use sun block when outdoors. Anti-diarrhea medication is recommended.

Hospitals are passable in Harare, and medical charges are low. Medicines are scarce, so bring along any you believe you might require. Hypodermic needles are in short supply and hospitals in rural areas often reuse them. Visitors requiring regular injections and those on extended stays in the countryside should bring their own as the risk of HIV infection is very high. In case of serious illness and operation, you are best advised to go to South Africa. Travellers on extended business should purchase evacuation insurance.

For more information on medical centers, including phone numbers, please see the "Business Centers" section at the end of this chapter.

TAXI & RENTAL CARS

Taxis are available in major cities only. Very few are metered, so make sure you agree on a price beforehand.

Rental cars can be found in urban areas but visitors should purchase ample insurance. Hired cars with drivers are recommended for first-time visitors. A 4WD (four wheel drive) vehicle is recommended for travel in the countryside. Do not venture in to rural areas without suitable guidance or experience.

BUS

The local services ("African Buses") for both inter- and intra-city travel can be unreliable and are usually crowded. There is a comfortable "express" intercity coach service that is much better to use, especially for business travel.

TRAIN

Rail services are limited to four areas (Harare, Victoria Falls, Bulawayo, Mutare) and travel mainly at night. Sexes are normally separated; so if your business group is mixed, you may wish to reserve a first-class "family compartment" or a smaller "coupe". Dining cars are rare and barely useful when present; so, bring your own supplies. Be prepared for very basic toilet facilities.

Communications

DIALING CODES IN ZIMBABWE

International country code: [263]

Selected city codes: Bulawayo (9), Harare (4), Mutare (20)

Dialing Zimbabwe from Overseas

To dial Zimbabwe from overseas, dial your international dialing code, then 263 (the country code for Zimbabwe), then the city code and finally the number. If you were dialing Bulawayo from the United States, for example, you would begin with 011, then 263, then 9 (the city code for Bulawayo), and finally the number of the person or office you were trying to reach.

Assistance Numbers

Local Operator 967
International Operator 96
Directory 92

CALLING WITHIN ZIMBABWE

Local Calls

Local calling is a bit less hassle free than dialing long distance. Expect some erratic service.

Long Distance Calls

Every telephone exchange in Zimbabwe has a unique code. A dash in the number indicates you should wait for another dialing tone before dialing the main number.

International Calls

Zimbabwe offers IDD or operator connections to dial abroad. There are no telephone offices to contend with, so you're left with private or public phones. Collect calls may be placed from private phones only. The first three minutes may cost Z$14.70 to Australia, North America or Europe. To call direct, dial 110 + country code + area code + number. And remember, Zimbabwe is no different from the rest of the world in that calls placed from a hotel may cost double or more.

To reach an operator from the U.S. for collect or calling card calls, even to other countries, dial:

AT&T 110-899

This access may not be available from every phone.

PAY PHONES

Public Telephones

Public Call Offices (PCO), otherwise known as public phones, exist in most main cities or towns but service is sporadic and lines usually long.

CELLULAR PHONES

Several cellular service providers exist in Zimbabwe. *Retrofit, NetOne, Telecel*, and *Econet* offer GSM for digital users.

Econet; tel: 263-4-486121; fax: 263-4-486120; email: sales@econet.co.zw; http://www.econet.co.zw/.

NetOne; tel: 263-4-775361; fax: 263-4-775363; email: sales@netone.co.zw; http://www.netone.co.zw/.

Note: Your home country cell phone may not work in this country. If not, we recommend that you rent an international cell phone *before* you leave home. A major US-based cell phone rental provider is **IMC WorldCell**. For information see "International Cell Phone Rentals" on page 14.

CALL BACK

You can (potentially) save significant sums when calling in Argentina by using one of the call back services listed below. Fees for callback services vary widely, depending on the company and the type of service required. For a list of callback services, please refer to the "Communications" section in the *Global Road Warrior* Introduction.

PHONE JACKS

Plug adaptors are available through **iGo Corporation**. (See "Electrical and Telephone Adaptors" on page 19.)

FAX

Faxes are very rare in Zimbabwe. Some top-end hotels may have access to a fax, although it is usually expensive.

POSTAL SERVICES

Postal services are usually quite efficient for outgoing mail. Airmail to North America and Europe takes approximately seven days.

TELEGRAMS

The Central Telegraph Office in Lusaka will send telegrams until 4p.m. Monday to Friday. Some top-end hotels also have facilities.

Business Services

COURIER SERVICE

DHL International (Private), Ltd.; Villa Gardens; CNR Central Ave / 4th Stree; P.O. Box CY 338; Causeway; Harare; tel: (4) 700-120; 24 hours, 7 days; Bulawayo;9th Ave/ Main Street; Bulawayo; Monday to Friday 8a.m. to 5:30p.m., Sat. 8a.m. to 12p.m., closed Sundays and holidays.

Federal Express (Rennies); tel: (4) 737-693; fax: (4) 737-694.

TNT Express Worldwide; 113 Samora Machel Avenue, Harare; tel: (4) 708-152; tel: (4) 708-153; tel: (4) 708-290; fax: (4) 705-421.

UPS; 157 Samora Machel Avenue, PO Box 1516, Harare; tel: (4) 726-457; tel: (4) 252-385/6; fax: (4) 252-340.

Electrical

Current

220 volts AC, 50Hz.

ELECTRIC PLUGS

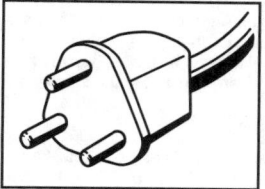

Plug adaptors are available through **iGo Corporation**. (See "Electrical and Telephone Adaptors" on page 19.)

Technical Support

HARDWARE/SOFTWARE VENDOR SUPPORT

Compaq/Digital; (U.AE. Office) tel: [971] 4-818-100; fax: [971] 4-818-313; (in Switzerland) tel: [41] (22) 709-5330; fax: [41] (22) 709-5391 (Geneva); tel: [41] (1) 801-2507; fax: [41] (1) 801-2172 (Zurich); (General U.S.) tel: (281) 518-2000; http://www.compaq.com/.

Corel; (in the U.A.E.) tel: [971] 4-523-526 (All Applications); (in Germany) tel: [49] (180) 425-8210 (TS Word Perfect-32 bit); (in the U.S.) tel: [1] (716) 871-2325 (Ask to be Forwarded to Appropriate Program); http://www.corel.com/.

Dell; (in Egypt) tel: [20] 2-360-2234 (Electronics House in Cairo/Mr. Jamal El Bidweihy); fax: [20] 2-361-4576; (in Germany) tel: [49] (61) 039-710; (Dell- Europe) tel: [44] (134) 474-8000; (in the U.S.) tel: [1] (512) 338-4400; fax: [1] (512) 728-3330; http://www.dell.com/.

Gateway 2000; (in the U.S.) tel: [1] (605) 232-2191; fax: [1] (605) 232-2023; (in Ireland) tel: [353] (1) 797-2000; http://www.g2k.com/.

Hewlett Packard; (in Switzerland) tel: [41] (22) 780-8111; (in the U.S.) tel: [1] (408) 246-4300; http://www.hp.com/.

IBM; tel: (4) 748-700; fax: (4) 78-750; (Egypt Office) tel: [20] 2-349-2533; fax: [20] 2-360-1227; (in Switzerland) tel: [41] (22) 310-0418 (in French); (in the U.S.) tel: [1] (919) 517-2800; http://www.ibm.com/.

Microsoft; (in South Africa) tel: [27] (11) 257-0000; fax: [27] (11) 257-0257; (in Switzerland) tel: [41] (848) 858-868; fax [41] (1) 831-0869; (in the U.S.) [1] (425) 635-7222; http://www.microsoft.com/.

NEC; (in Israel) tel: [972] (0)9-59-3300 (Tracker Support); (in the U.S.) [1] (916) 388-0101 (Main Switchboard); http://www.nec.com/.

Zimbabwe

Toshiba; (in Germany) tel: [49] (2131) 158-319; fax: [49] (2131) 158-558; (in Switzerland) tel: [41] (1) 946-0777; fax: [41] (1) 946-0807; (in Ireland) tel: [44] (193) 282-8828; (in the U.S.) [1] (949) 583-3000 (Corporate Headquarters); http://www.toshiba.com/.

Internet Connection

HOW TO CONNECT

Connecting to AOL and Compuserve in Zimbabwe is similar to using it when traveling outside your own area code. See the introductory section for detailed information on connecting to your account through a different phone number.

America Online

Numbers are available at keyword *international*. Be sure to get several local numbers before leaving. Go to keyword *access* (a free area) and download the software.

At press time, America Online had no local access numbers in Zimbabwe. Check their list of current access numbers at http://intlaccess.web.aol.com/ to see if any numbers have been activated or to locate numbers in neighboring countries.

Compuserve

Numbers are available at *Go International*. If you are using CompuServe 2000, use GO PHONES within CompuServe 2000 to search for access numbers. The Compuserve Web-site also has a great deal of information for travelers at http://www.compuserve.com/.

At press time, Compuserve had no local access numbers. Check their list of current access numbers to see if any numbers have been activated or to locate numbers in neighboring countries.

Independent Service Providers

Many independent service providers offer discounts if you are only in town for a couple of days.

Icon Internet; tel: (4) 705-072; tel: 791-075; help@icon.co.zw; http://www.icon.co.zw/.

Utande Internet Service Pte Ltd; tel: (4) 791-675/6/7/8; fax: (4) 791-674; email: info@utande.co.zw; http://www.utande.co.zw/.

Business Culture

GREETINGS AND COURTESIES

A handshake is the standard greeting. Shake hands with everyone upon entering a room, and distribute business cards freely in a business environment. Only very good friends hug on greeting. Zimbabwean women and girls often curtsy. It is considered rude to look elders in the eye when greeting them. Refrain from using a Zimbabwean's first name until he or she has used yours. Urban adults address each other by first and last name, adding a professional title if one exists.

BUSINESS ETHIC AND FRAMEWORK

After a fifteen-year civil war, Zimbabwe won independence from Great Britain only in 1980, and more recently emerged from ten years of socialism in 1990. By then the country was in such serious debt that it became necessary to open the doors to free trade. The consensus-building of a traditional society as well as one emerging from socialism is carried over into business in Zimbabwe today; as such, it is important to create good personal relationships among your Zimbabwean business associates. A local representa-

tive can prove helpful. Expect red tape and bureaucracy if you are dealing with the government, but patient and persistent companies usually succeed. English is the official language of Zimbabwe, and is spoken by most educated people.

Paved roads and rail links are good. Telephones are readily available in business environments, although one will usually only find them in about half of all residences. Fax, paging, and cellular communications are being upgraded, but still have problems. Office accommodations are excellent.

DECISION MAKING

Progress is slow in arriving at important final decisions, as everyone seems to require the authorization of someone else. Accountability can be lost in the shuffle. Consider persistence and patience as essential tools to success. Decisions can be arbitrary, based on personal rather than objective issues. Decision making in Zimbabwe is a group process, and everybody involved must reach some sort of consensus. For this reason, it is especially important to establish and maintain excellent relationships with business contacts at all levels. Due to the lack of transparency in decision-making, one may never know exactly which factor helped to facilitate a positive outcome.

WOMEN

Zimbabwe remains a traditional, rural-based society, where women still play the traditional roles of caring for children and the household. They sometimes curtsy and in rural settings, sit at levels below men during meals to show respect. Though cities are more cosmopolitan, as a foreign businesswoman, you will have to balance traditional rural customs with a need to be treated as an equal by male Zimbabwean business associates. Few women are in decision-making positions except in the cosmetic and beauty business.

If you are traveling alone you may be regarded with suspicion since people will wonder why you are not at home caring for your family.

MEETINGS

June is the quiet month in Zimbabwe, so avoid scheduling meetings at that time. Zimbabwean business professionals are relaxed about their own punctuality, but they will expect punctuality of you. Official meetings are always preceded by tea and conversations. Always accept the tea that is offered to you at the beginning of a meeting. Since personal relationships are extremely important in Zimbabwe, don't be impatient with prolonged personal conversation before a meeting. Meetings conducted at business lunches are common.

BUSINESS ENTERTAINING

In conversation, stay with subjects like sports, tourist attractions, and family. Avoid discussing politics or economic conditions. Black Zimbabweans are polite and conciliatory toward whites, but can be resentful because of economic inequities. During initial conversations, don't ask about a person's job or marital status.

Much business is done during business lunches. Zimbabweans enjoy being entertained at hotel restaurants, and they appreciate being asked for advice. If you are invited to a private home, bring a small gift. You should give and accept gifts or other items with both hands. It is impolite to refuse refreshments, a meal, or a gift. Avoid direct eye contact in rural areas, as it shows a lack of respect.

Golf is widely played in the business community, especially on Wednesday afternoons.

BUSINESS ATTIRE

One can still feel influences from the British colonial past in Harare. The feeling is formal, and businessmen wear lightweight suits and ties for business appointments. Men may wear dress slacks and a shirt in the evening, but some restaurants require a coat and tie for dinner.

Women should wear a dress or skirt and blouse. Skirt and dress hems should fall below the knee and be worn with pantyhose. Sandals are acceptable footwear. Zimbabweans frown upon slacks for women at work and in restaurants.

Business Centers
Harare

CITY VIEW

Harare is a quiet city compared with other business centers, and offers clean and modern conditions. The compact business district, a cluster of multicolored glass buildings, allows for easy walking access. Gardens sprinkled throughout the city are the only physical reminder of the colonial era that Zimbabwe spent under British rule. Aesthetically, these gardens lend a peaceful feel to Harare, tempering the modernity of the city with small green pockets of vegetation. The entire city offers an attractive manageability that the visitor will appreciate. The only hassle that you may face while walking around Harare is the street vendors. They can be quite persistent, sometimes following after you in an effort to sell their goods. Just keep walking.

AIRPORT

Lusaka Airport to City Center

The airport lies 16 miles (26 km.) from the city. Travel time is approximately 25 minutes. Bus and taxi services are available. Expect to pay about Z$170 for a taxi to the city.

Airline Numbers

Air Botswana	(4) 703132
Air India	(4) 700318
Air Malawi	(4) 706497
Air Mauritius	(4) 735738
Air Tanzania	(4) 706444
Air Zimbabwe	(4) 794481, 737011
Balkan Airlines	(4) 729213
British Airways	(4) 794616
Ethiopian Airlines	(4) 790705
Ghana Airways	(4) 703335
Kenya Airways	(4) 792181
KLM	(4) 705430
Linhas Aereas de Mocambique	(4) 703338
Lufthansa	(4) 707606
Qantas	(4) 794676
Royal Swazi Airlines	(4) 730170
Swissair	(4) 707712
TAP Air Portugal	(4) 706231
UTA	(4) 703868
Zambia Airways	(4) 793235

HOTELS

Top-end

Meikles; Jason Moyo Avenue; tel: (4) 795-655; toll-free in U.S.: 1-800-223-6800; fax: (4) 707-754; city center. opposite African Unity Square; 5 restaurants; conference facilities (up to 500); business center; secretarial services; in-room safe, voice mail, data ports; parking; health club; sauna; pool; massage.

Imba Matombo (Relais and Chateaux); 3 Albert Glen Close, Glen Lorne, Highlands; tel: (4) 499-013; fax: (4) 499-071; 26-rooms; located in suburb; gardens; executive rooms; restaurant; conference room; fitness; pool; tennis.

Sheraton Harare; Pennyfather Avenue; tel: (4) 729-771; 7272-633; fax: (4) 794-308; 774-648; located in suburb; tower rooms available with in-room modem access and butler service; restaurant; casino/nightclub; conference facilities (up to 4500); secretarial services; fax/photocopy services; in-room safe; parking; corporate rates; fitness; sauna; pool; tennis; massage.

Expensive

Cresta Jameson; 21 Samora Machel Avenue; tel: (4) 794-641, (4) 774-106; fax: (4) 794-655; near to city center; restaurant; secretarial services; fax/photocopy facilities; pool.

Crowne Plaza Monomatapa; 54 Park Lane; tel: (4) 734-583; email: crownpla;za@zimsun@gaia.co.zw; 3 restaurants; conference facilities; business center; car rental; in-room fax/modem connection; parking; fitness; pool.

Holiday Inn Harare; Samora Machel Avenue & 5th Street; tel: (4) 795-611; fax: (4) 735-695; email: hreholinn@zimsun.gaia.co.zw; located in suburb; near to railway station; restaurant; conference facilities (up to 300); secretarial services; fax/photocopy facilities; parking; corporate rates; pool.

Moderate

Best Western Oasis; 124 Baker Avenue; tel: (4) 704-217; fax: (4) 790-865; near to city centre; exhibition grounds; and watersports facilities; restaurant; conference facilities (up to 150); secretarial services; fax/photocopy facilities; in-room modem/fax connection; in-room safe; parking; corporate rates; fitness; sauna; pool; whirlpool; casino.

Cresta Oasis; Nelson Mandela Way; tel: (4) 790-861; email: oasgcp@samara.co.2w; near city center; restaurant; conference facilities; business center; secretarial service; parking; pool; massage.

The New Ambassador; 88 Union Avenue; tel: (4) 708-121; near to city center; restaurant; conference facilities; business center.

AUTO RENTAL

Avis; Samora Machel Ave., Harare; tel: (4) 720-351.

Eurocar/ Echo; 19 Samora Machel Ave., PO Box 3430, Harare; tel: (4) 706-486.

Sheraton Hotel; Pennyfather Avenue; tel: (4) 700-080.

Hertz; 4 Park St., Harare; tel: (4) 704-915.

Meikles Hotel, Jason Moyo Avenue; tel: (4) 793-701.

CHAMBER OF COMMERCE

Zimbabwe National Chamber of Commerce
Sixth Floor, Equity House
Rezende Street
Harare
tel: (4) 708-611

Notes / Additions